Contemporary Authors

EDITORS' NOTE

This volume of *Contemporary Authors* introduces two changes in the physical appearance of *Contemporary Authors* original volumes: a new cover design and a new numbering system.

Contemporary Authors, Volumes 97-100, published in 1980, is the last volume with a four-unit volume number.

Contemporary Authors, Volume 101, and subsequent original volumes will carry single volume numbers (e.g., Volume 102, Volume 103, etc.).

The only changes that have been made in *Contemporary Authors* are the cover design and the numbering plan. No change has been made in the amount or type of material included.

Contemporary Authors

A Bio-Bibliographical Guide to
Current Writers in Fiction, General Nonfiction,
Poetry, Journalism, Drama, Motion Pictures,
Television, and Other Fields

FRANCES C. LOCHER
Editor

volume 101

GALE RESEARCH COMPANY • THE BOOK TOWER • DETROIT, MICHIGAN 48226

EDITORIAL STAFF

Christine Nasso, *General Editor, Contemporary Authors*

Frances C. Locher, *Editor, Original Volumes*

Ann F. Ponikvar, David Versical,
and Martha G. Winkel, *Associate Editors*
Marie Evans, Anne M. Guerrini, B. Hal May,
Kathleen Ceton Newman, Nancy M. Rusin, Susan A. Stefani, Les Stone,
Mary K. Sullivan, and Barbara A. Welch, *Assistant Editors*
Denise M. Cloutier, Victoria M. Kurtz, Michaelene F. Pepera, Norma Sawaya,
Shirley Seip, and Laurie M. Serwatowski, *Editorial Assistants*

Alan E. Abrams, Otto Penzler,
and Adele Sarkissian, *Contributing Editors*
Peter Benjaminson, Barbara Braun, C.H. Gervais, Joe Rosenblatt,
Jean W. Ross, and Richard E. Ziegfeld, *Interviewers*
Susette Balogh, Andrea Geffner, Mary F. Glahn,
Linda Metzger, Arlene True, and Benjamin True, *Sketchwriters*
Eunice Bergin, *Copy Editor*

Special recognition is given to the staff of
Young People's Literature Department

Frederick G. Ruffner, *Publisher*   James M. Ethridge, *Editorial Director*

Copyright © 1981 by
GALE RESEARCH COMPANY

Library of Congress Catalog Card Number 62-52046
ISBN 0-8103-1901-2

Preface

EDITORS' NOTE

This volume of *Contemporary Authors* introduces two changes in the physical appearance of *Contemporary Authors* original volumes: a new cover design and a new numbering system. *Contemporary Authors,* Volumes 97-100, published in 1980, is the last volume with a four-unit volume number. *Contemporary Authors,* Volume 101, and subsequent original volumes will carry single volume numbers (e.g., Volume 102, Volume 103, etc.). The only changes that have been made in *Contemporary Authors* are the cover design and the numbering plan. No change has been made in the amount or type of material included.

The nearly 1,300 entries in *Contemporary Authors,* Volume 101, bring to nearly 63,000 the number of authors, either living or deceased since 1960, now represented in the *Contemporary Authors* series. *CA* includes nontechnical writers in all genres—fiction, nonfiction, poetry, drama, etc.—whose books are issued by commercial, risk publishers or by university presses. Authors of books published only by known vanity or author-subsidized firms are ordinarily not included. Since native language and nationality have no bearing on inclusion in *CA*, authors who write in languages other than English are included in *CA* if their works have been published in the United States or translated into English.

Although *CA* focuses primarily on authors of published books, the series also encompasses prominent persons in communications: newspaper and television reporters and correspondents, columnists, newspaper and magazine editors, photojournalists, syndicated cartoonists, screenwriters, television scriptwriters, and other media people.

No charge or obligation is attached to a *CA* listing. Authors are included in the series solely on the basis of the above criteria and their interest to *CA* users.

Compilation Methods

The editors make every effort to secure information directly from the authors through questionnaires and personal correspondence. If authors of special interest to *CA* users are deceased or fail to reply to requests for information, material is gathered from other reliable sources. Biographical dictionaries are checked (a task made easier through the use of Gale's *Biography and Genealogy Master Index* and other volumes in the "Gale Biographical Index Series"), as are bibliographical sources, such as *Cumulative Book Index* and *The National Union Catalog.* Published interviews, feature stories, and book reviews are examined, and often material is supplied by the authors' publishers. All sketches, whether prepared from questionnaires or through extensive research, are sent to the authors for review prior to publication.

New Listings in This Volume

In addition to checking manuscripts of their entries, some authors often work even more closely with *CA*'s editors, both to ensure the completeness of their listings and to provide incisive Sidelights— comments on their lives and writings, personal philosophies, etc. Among the authors in this volume who have amplified their sketches with lengthy Sidelights are Diana Brown, an American librarian and writer, who speaks of her choice of Regency England as the setting for her novel *The Emerald Necklace;* Joel Garreau, a *Washington Post* journalist, who describes how an article he wrote on geographical power centers in the United States became a full-length book, due to overwhelming reader interest; and

L.G. Shreve, a successful American first novelist and biographer, who explains his approach to the writing career he began after his retirement.

Equally extensive efforts go into the compilation of full-length entries on deceased authors of current interest to *CA* readers. This volume contains listings on, among others, David Ben-Gurion, Henri Charriere, R.L. Duffus, Oscar Hammerstein, John K. Jessup, Helen Keller, John H. Knowles, Albert Lamorisse, Gyorgy Lukacs, Fritz Perls, Allan Sherman, Judith Wax, and Walter Winchell.

In addition to the individuals mentioned above, numerous other authors and media people of particular interest are sketched in this volume, such as Michael Bennett, Bill Bradley, Luis Bunuel, Michael Cacoyannis, Bob Hope, Ernst Juenger, Monroe William Karmin, Tadeusz Konwicki, Akira Kurosawa, John Vliet Lindsay, Jeb Magruder, Terrence Malick, Louis Malle, Malcolm Muggeridge, Nigel Nicolson, Liam O'Flaherty, George D. Painter, Mary Ellen Pinkham, Bernard Pomerance, Mario Praz, Eddie Rickenbacker, Anwar Sadat, Mel Shapiro, Mikhail Sholokhov, William C. Westmoreland, Eliot Wigginton, and Alfred M. Worden.

Exclusive Interviews

Generally, authors' remarks to *CA*'s editors are reserved for the Sidelights sections of sketches. While no limitations are placed on the length of such material, the editors believe that readers might want even more comment from some of *CA*'s authors.

Accordingly, *CA* is now providing such additional primary information in the form of exclusive author interviews. Prepared specifically for *CA*, the never-before-published conversations presented in the section of the sketch headed *CA INTERVIEWS THE AUTHOR* give *CA* users the opportunity to learn the authors' thoughts, in depth, about their craft. Subjects chosen for the interviews are, the editors feel, authors who hold special interest for *CA*'s readers.

Authors and journalists in this volume whose sketches include interviews are Thomas Babe, Barry Callaghan, Warren Casey, Barbara Frum, Richard E. Geis, Thomas Hoving, John Milius, Patrick Oliphant, Gail Parent, Henry Regnery, James Marcus Schuyler, Frank Scott, Daniel Taradash, Joan Tewkesbury, Warner Troyer, and Jann Wenner.

Obituary Notices Make *CA* Timely and Comprehensive

To be as timely and comprehensive as possible, *CA* publishes obituary notices on deceased authors within the scope of the series. These notices provide date and place of birth and death, highlight the author's career and writings, and list other sources where additional biographical information and obituaries may be found. To distinguish them from full-length sketches, obituaries are identified with the heading *OBITUARY NOTICE*.

CA includes obituary notices both for authors who already have full-length sketches in earlier *CA* volumes, thus effectively completing the sketches, and for authors not yet sketched in the series. Nearly 50 percent of the obituary notices contained in this volume are for authors with listings already in *CA*. Deceased authors of special interest presently represented in the series only by obituary notices are scheduled for full-length sketch treatment in forthcoming *CA* volumes.

Cumulative Index Should Always Be Consulted

The most recent *CA* cumulative index is the user's guide to the location of an individual author's *CA* listing. The entire *CA* series consists of original volumes, containing entries on authors new to the series, and revision volumes, containing completely updated entries on authors with earlier sketches in the series. The cumulative index, which lists all original and revision volume entries, should always be consulted to locate the specific volume containing an author's original or most recently revised sketch.

For the convenience of *CA* users, the *CA* cumulative index also includes references to all entries in three related Gale series—*Contemporary Literary Criticism* (CLC), which is devoted entirely to current criticism of major novelists, poets, playwrights, and other creative writers, *Something About the Author* (SATA), a series of heavily illustrated sketches on juvenile authors and illustrators, and *Authors in the News* (AITN), a compilation of news stories and feature articles from American newspapers and magazines covering writers and other members of the communications media.

As always, suggestions from users about any aspect of *CA* will be welcomed.

CONTEMPORARY AUTHORS

Indicates that a listing has been compiled from secondary sources believed to be reliable, but has not been personally verified for this edition by the author sketched.

A

ABDUL-RAUF, Muhammad 1917-

PERSONAL: Born December 17, 1917, in Abu Sir, Gharbieh, Egypt; came to United States, 1965; son of Muhammad Abdul-Razik and Hanim B. (Al-Hudary) Abdul-Rauf; married Buthayna E. Ayad, 1946; children: Feisal, Aisha (Mrs. Abdul Sami), Ali, Salwa, Ayman. *Education:* Al-Azhar University, B.A. (with honors), 1942; Cambridge University, B.A. (with honors), 1954, M.A., 1958; University of London, Ph.D., 1963. *Religion:* Islam. *Home:* 2550 Massachusetts Ave. N.W., Washington, D.C. 20008. *Office:* Islamic Center, 2551 Massachusetts Ave. N.W., Washington, D.C. 20008.

CAREER: Al-Azhar University, Cairo, Egypt, associate professor of Islamic studies, 1944-55; Muslim College Malaya, Klang, Malaysia, principal, 1955-58; University of Malaya, Kuala Lumpur, professor and head of department of Islamic studies, 1958-66; Islamic Cultural Center, New York City, director, 1966-71; Islamic Center, Washington, D.C., director, 1971—; Georgetown University, Washington, D.C., adjunct professor, 1975—. *Member:* American Oriental Society. *Awards, honors:* J.M.N. award from King of Malaysia.

WRITINGS: A Brief History of Islam, Oxford University Press, 1964; *The Life and Teaching of the Prophet Muhammad,* Longmans, Green, 1964; *A Manual on Marriage in Islam,* Exposition Press, 1972; *Arabic for English-Speaking Students,* Supreme Council on Islamic Affairs (Cairo, Egypt), 1972; *Al-Qur'an,* Islamic Center, 1974; *Al-Hadith,* Islamic Center, 1974; *Islam Creed and Worship,* Islamic Center, 1974; *Islam: Faith and Devotion,* Islamic Publication Bureau, 1975; *The Islamic View of Women and the Family,* Robert Speller, 1977; *Bilal Ibn Rabah,* American Trust Publications, 1977; *Concept of Islamic Economics and Contemporary Economic Thought,* American Enterprises Institute, 1978; *History of the Islamic Center,* Islamic Center, 1978. Also author of *The Ten Commandments of Islamic Economics: Across the Board,* 1979. Contributor to scholarly journals and popular magazines, including *National Geographic* and *Reader's Digest.*

WORK IN PROGRESS: Shi-ism, as I Understand It; Al-Hadith Al Qudsi.

SIDELIGHTS: Abdul-Rauf commented to *CA:* "Committed to the ideals of my faith, and inspired by the Holy Qur'an and the model of the Prophet Muhammad, I believe in working for the common good of humanity, and in justice for all."

ABERCROMBIE, Nigel J(ames) 1908-

PERSONAL: Born August 5, 1908, in India; son of Alexander William (an officer in British Army) and Ethel Emma (Gordon) Abercrombie; married Elisabeth Brownlees, 1931; children: Alexander, Jane Abercrombie Gardner. *Education:* Oriel College, Oxford, B.A., 1929, D.Phil., 1933, M.A., 1934. *Home:* 32 Springett Ave., Ringmer, Lewes, East Sussex BN8 5HE, England.

CAREER: Oxford University, Oxford, England, lecturer in French at Magdalen College, 1931-36; University of Exeter, Exeter, England, professor of French and head of department of modern languages, 1936-40; British Admiralty, Bath, England, and London, England, in secretary's department, 1940-42, assistant secretary, 1942-56, under-secretary, 1956-62; affiliated with Cabinet Office, 1962-63; Arts Council of Great Britain, London, secretary-general, 1963-68, chief regional officer, 1968-73; writer, 1973—. Vice-president of South-East Arts Association.

WRITINGS: The Origins of Jansenism, Clarendon, 1936; *Saint Augustine and French Classical Thought,* Clarendon, 1938, reprinted, Russsll, 1972; (editor), Moliere, *Le Misanthrope,* Blackie & Son, 1938; (editor) Moliere, *Tartuffe,* Blackie & Son, 1938; (translator) Jean Danielou, *The Lord of History,* Regnery, 1958; *The Life and Work of Edmund Bishop,* Longmans, Green, 1959; *The Arts in the South-East,* South-East Arts Association, 1974; *Artists and Their Public,* Unipub, 1975; (contributor) *Essays on the Religious History of Sussex,* University of Sussex, 1980; (contributor) John Pick, editor, *The State and the Arts,* City University (London, England), 1980.

Work represented in anthologies, including *Times Anthology of Detective Stories,* 1972, and *New Stories I,* 1976. Contributor of articles and reviews to theology, philology, and literary journals. Editor of *Dublin Review,* 1953-55.

WORK IN PROGRESS: Research on the history of Catholicism in England since the Reformation, especially the life and work of Charles Butler, barrister-at-law, 1750-1832.

SIDELIGHTS: Abercrombie told *CA:* "From early schooldays I have been fascinated by language, and increasingly by the use of language to provoke, govern, and determine human action. From my university training onwards, in my three careers—teacher, public servant, and writer—I have found my special bent in reading and writing for and about Catholic action (activity *and* passivity) in England in the period technically known as modern history, that is, post-Renaissance and post-Reformation. I began my writings in the seventeenth century, jumped to the nineteenth century, and am now in the eighteenth century; and I have never separated England from her neighbor, France.

"Particular topics in my writings—Jansenism, Augustinism, liturgiology, and recusant history—have all been suggested by accident. I am better at biographical studies than other historical work, perhaps because I was not trained as an historian in my youth. My 'creative' short stories are a relaxation, but do give scope for my life-long passion for language—I *love* writing."

*   *   *

ABISH, Walter   1931-

PERSONAL: Born December 24, 1931, in Vienna, Austria; son of Adolph and Frieda (Rubin) Abish; married wife, Cecile (a sculptor). *Home:* Five East Third St., New York, N.Y. 10003.

CAREER: Adjunct professor at State University of New York Empire State College, State Springs, N.Y., 1975; Wheaton College, Norton, Mass., writer-in-residence, 1976; visiting Butler Professor of English at State University of New York at Buffalo, 1977; Columbia University, New York, N.Y., lecturer in English, 1979—. *Member:* International P.E.N., Associated Writing Programs. *Awards, honors:* Fellow of New Jersey State Council for the Arts, 1972; grants from Rose Isabel Williams Foundation, 1974-75, and Ingram Merrill Foundation, 1977-78; fellow of National Endowment for the Arts, 1979.

WRITINGS: Duel Site (poems), Tibor de Nagy Editions, 1970; *The Alphabetical Africa,* New Directions, 1974; *Minds Meet,* New Directions, 1975; *In the Future Perfect,* New Directions, 1977; *How German Is It,* New Directions, 1980.

Work represented in anthologies, including *Individuals: Post-Movement Art in America,* Dutton, 1977. Contributor to literary journals, including *New Directions in Prose and Poetry, Partisan Review, Transatlantic, New York Arts Journal,* and *Paris Review.*

WORK IN PROGRESS: Self-Portrait; Poles Apart, a novel set in Tel-Aviv in the 1950's; another collection of fiction.

SIDELIGHTS: Abish told *CA:* "I spent my childhood in China, seeing an incredibly corrupt society slowly disintegrate. It was as if all the life processes were accentuated and crowded into the period of time I lived in Shanghai.

"I have always thought that all the life networks that enable us to proceed wherever we are going, or prevent us from doing so, are predicated on a system we called language. This awareness undoubtedly influenced my approach to writing."

BIOGRAPHICAL/CRITICAL SOURCES: John Updike, *Picked-Up Pieces,* Knopf, 1975; *Fiction International,* Volume IV, number 3, 1976; *New Directions in Prose and Poetry,* autumn, 1977; Jerome Klinkowitz, *The Life of Fiction,* University of Illinois Press, 1977; *Granta,* spring, 1979.

*   *   *

ABLER, Thomas S(truthers)   1941-

PERSONAL: Born August 31, 1941, in Saginaw, Mich.; son of Louis Charles (in bread sales) and Marion (Struthers) Abler; married Trudi E. Bunting (a geographer), July 21, 1976; children: Elizabeth A. B. *Education:* Northwestern University, B.A., 1963; University of Wisconsin, Milwau-

kee, M.S., 1965; University of Toronto, Ph.D., 1969. *Home:* 76 Schneider Ave., Kitchener, Ontario, Canada N2G 1K8. *Office:* Department of Anthropology, University of Waterloo, Waterloo, Ontario, Canada N2L 3G1.

CAREER: University of Waterloo, Waterloo, Ont., assistant professor, 1967-74, associate professor of anthropology, 1974—, chairman of department, 1979—. Conducted field research on Indians of New York, Michigan, and Wisconsin. *Member:* Canadian Ethnology Society, American Anthropological Association (fellow), American Society for Ethnohistory, American Ethnological Society, Royal Anthropological Institute of Great Britain and Ireland, Current Anthropology (associate), Society for Historical Archaeology, Champlain Society, Central States Anthropology Society, Society for Pennsylvania Archaeology. *Awards, honors:* Grant from Canada Council, 1971-72, fellow, 1973-74.

WRITINGS: (With S. M. Weaver and others) *A Canadian Indian Bibliography, 1960-1970,* University of Toronto Press, 1974. Contributor to *Handbook of North American Indians* and *Dictionary of Canadian Biography.* Contributor of more than a dozen articles and reviews to scholarly journals.

WORK IN PROGRESS: Editing the autobiography of an Indian veteran of the American Revolution.

SIDELIGHTS: Abler wrote: "My interest in the native people of this continent was largely fostered by my Scottish grandmother. As I grew intellectually that interest expanded from a curiosity about aboriginal costume and house type to a more scientific interest in the nature of Indian culture, society, and history.

"My research centers on the effects of warfare on native American societies, aspects of Indian war, Iroquois myth, and Seneca politics. In the back of my mind I am considering a general book on aboriginal war as well as a book on native Canadian kinship systems.

"As a hobby I read military history and make model soldiers (toy soldiers some would call them). While I try to keep it a hobby by avoiding Indian subjects for my model soldiers, the insight this avocation gives me of military 'culture' is most useful in pursuit of my professional interests in the military role of Indians in colonial North America."

*   *   *

ABRAHAMSEN, Christine Elizabeth   1916-
(Cristabel, Kathleen Westcott)

PERSONAL: Born September 6, 1916, in Oak Hill, W.Va.; daughter of Charles Earl (an automobile mechanic) and Macie Avis (Booth) Campbell; married Joseph Howard, June 6, 1941 (deceased); married Harry Abrahamsen, October 11, 1943 (divorced, 1945); children: (first marriage) Mary Elizabeth; (second marriage) Cherri Georgette. *Education:* Somerset Hospital, R.N., 1938; Hunter College (now of the City University of New York), B.S., 1954; Columbia University, M.A., 1959, diploma, 1961, further graduate study, 1961-65. *Home:* 213 Washington Ave., Oak Hill, W.Va. 25901. *Agent:* Jay Garon-Brooke Associates, Inc., 415 Central Park W., New York, N.Y. 10025. *Office:* 1710 Harper Rd., Beckley, W.Va. 25801.

CAREER: Somerset Hospital, Somerville, N.J., staff nurse in obstetrics, 1939; Goldwater Memorial Hospital, New York City, staff nurse, 1939-40; research nurse, 1940-41; St. Vincent's Hospital, New York City, staff nurse, 1941-43; American Cyanamid Co., Bound Brook, N.J., laboratory assistant, 1943; Paul Kimball Hospital, Lakewood, N.J., charge nurse, 1943-44; Pinewald Hospital, Bayville, N.J., 1944-46, began as staff nurse, became head nurse; Morrisania City Hospital, Bronx, N.Y., staff nurse, 1946-49, head nurse, 1949-50, clinical instructor in nursing, 1950-54; Department of Hospitals, New York City, institutional inspector, 1950-58; City Hospital, Elmhurst, N.Y., supervisor of education, 1958-60; research assistant for Federation of the Handicapped, 1962-63; Yeshiva University, Lincoln Hospital, New York City, research associate, 1963-64; St. Luke's Hospital, New York City, assistant coordinator of exchange graduate nurse's program, 1964-65, assistant director of nursing service in-service education, 1966-67; National League for Nursing, New York City, consultant to research and hospital nursing service, 1968-70, acting director, 1970, consultant, 1970-71; West Virginia Institute of Technology, Montgomery, associate professor of nursing and head of department, 1971-73; Raleigh General Hospital, Beckley, W.Va., coordinator of patient care, 1975—.

MEMBER: American Nurses Association, National League for Nursing, Science Fiction Writers of America, American Public Health Association, American National Council for Health Education (of Public and International Health Union), American Education Research Association, Aerospace Medical Association, American National Red Cross, New York Academy of Sciences, West Virginia Nurses Association, Public Health Association of New York City, Hunter College Alumni Association, Teachers College Nurses Alumni Association, Pi Lambda Theta, Kappa Delta Pi, American Legion Auxiliary, Daughters of the American Revolution, United Daughters of the Confederacy, Wittenfort Long Rifles, Mountaineer Flintlock Rifles, Rosicrucian Order. *Awards, honors:* U.S. Public Health Service fellow, 1961-63, grant, 1965-66.

WRITINGS—Novels; under pseudonym Cristabel, except as noted: *Manalar of Veltakin,* Curtis Books, 1970; *The Cruachan and the Killane,* Curtis Books, 1970; *The Mortal Immortals,* Walker & Co., 1971; *The Golden Olive,* Curtis Books, 1972. Also author of *The Bride of Kilkerran,* 1972. Author of a gothic novel under pseudonym Kathleen Westcott.*

*   *   *

ABRAHAMSON, Mark J. 1939-

PERSONAL: Born February 8, 1939, in Chicago, Ill.; married in 1960; children: three. *Education:* University of Illinois, B.S., 1960; Washington University, St. Louis, Mo., Ph.D., 1963. *Office:* Department of Sociology, Syracuse University, Room 107, Syracuse, N.Y. 13210.

CAREER: Illinois Institute of Technology, Chicago, assistant professor, 1963-66, associate professor of sociology, 1966-67; Syracuse University, Syracuse, N.Y., associate professor, 1967-71, professor of sociology, 1971—, chairman of department, 1971—. *Member:* American Sociological Association.

WRITINGS: Interpersonal Accommodation, Van Nostrand, 1966; *The Professional in the Organization,* Rand McNally, 1967; *Sociology: An Introduction to Concepts, Methods, and Data,* Van Nostrand, 1969; (editor) *Introductory Readings on Sociological Concepts, Methods, and Data,* Van Nostrand, 1969; *Urban Sociology,* Prentice-Hall, 1976; (with Ephraim H. Mizruchi and Carlton A. Hornung) *Stratification and Mobility,* Macmillan, 1976; *Functionalism,* Prentice-Hall, 1978.*

ACQUAVIVA, Sabino Samele 1927-

PERSONAL: Born April 29, 1927, in Padova, Italy; son of Vito and Francesca (Ricci) Sabino; married Eugenia Gaudenzio, August 30, 1954; children: Francesco, Chiara. *Education:* University of Padova, laurea, 1951. *Home:* 56 Via Altinate, Padova, Italy. *Office:* Faculty of Political Science, University of Padua, 28 Via del Santo, Padua 35100, Italy.

CAREER: University of Padua, Padua, Italy, lecturer, 1959-67, professor of sociology in faculty of political science, 1968—. Visiting fellow at All Souls College, Oxford, 1975-76. *Member:* Societe Europeenne de Culture, Accademia Teatina delle scienze, Accademia Tiberina.

WRITINGS: (With Mario Santuccio) *Social Structure in Italy,* Robertson, 1975; *L'eclissi del sacro nella societa industriale,* Comunita, 1961, translation by Patricia Lipscomb published as *The Decline of the Sacred in Industrial Society,* Harper, 1979.

Other writings: *Sociologia dinamica* (title means "Dynamic Sociology"), Centro Studi Sociali Regionali, 1957; *Automazione e nuova classe* (title means "Automation and the New Class"), Il Mulino, 1958; *Il problema della logica nelle scienze umane* (title means "The Problem of Logics in Human Sciences"), Marsilio, 1964; *Le scelta illusoria* (title means "The Illusory Choice"), Comunita, 1965; *Problemi della civilta contadina nel Veneto* (title means "Problems of the Peasant Civilization in the Venets"), Centro Studi Sociali Regionali, 1965; (with Gottfried Eisermann) *La montagna del sole* (title means "The Mountain of the Sun"), Comunita, 1971; (with Gustavo Guizzardi) *Religione e irreligione nell'eta postindustriale* (title means "Religion and Irreligion in the Post-Industrial Age"), Anonima Veritas Editrice, 1971; (with Guizzardi) *Le secolarizzazione* (title means "Secularization"), Il Mulino, 1973; (with others) *I bambini e la televisione* (title means "Television and Children"), Edizioni Radiotelevisione Italiana, 1973; *Una scommessa sul futuro, sociologia e programmazione globale* (title means "A Bet as to the Future: Sociology and Global Planning"), Istituto Editoriale Internazionale, 1971; *Der Einfluss des Fernsehens auf die Schule in Der Gesellschaft von Heute und Morgen* (title means "The Influence of Television on the School in the Society of Today and Tomorrow"), Enke Verlag, 1974; *La modernizzazione sperata* (title means "The Hoped-for Modernization"), Guida, 1978; *Guerriglia e guerra rivoluzionaria in Italia* (title means "Guerriglia and Revolutionary Warfare in Italy"), Rizzoli, 1979; *Il seme religioso della rivolta* (title means "The Religious Basis of Revolution"), Rusconi, 1979.

WORK IN PROGRESS: A book on the German minority in south Tyrol tentatively titled *Alto Adige: Partition Now;* a book on the effect of theories of sociobiology on sociology, completion expected in 1982-83.

*   *   *

ADAMS, Chuck
See TUBB, E(dwin) C(harles)

*   *   *

AGUOLU, Christian Chukwunedu 1940-

PERSONAL: Born December 22, 1940, in Nimo, Nigeria; son of Samuel A. (a teacher) and Rosaline (Nwabude) Aguolu; married Ify Eunice (a librarian), December 4, 1976 children: *Education:* Attended University of Ibadan, 1961-65; University of London, B.A., 1965; University of Washington, Seattle, M.L.S., 1968; University of California, Berkeley, M.A., 1975, Ph.D., 1977. *Religion:* Anglican.

CAREER: Teacher and head of departments of French and Latin at Anglican grammar school in Nigeria, 1965-66; University of California, Santa Barbara, reference librarian and bibliographer, 1968-72; writer. *Member:* Worldwide Academy of Scholars (fellow), International Platform Association, Intercontinental Biographical Association (fellow), Nigerian Library Association.

WRITINGS: Ghana in the Humanities and Social Sciences, 1900-1971: A Bibliography, Scarecrow, 1973; *Nigerian Civil War, 1967-1970: An Annotated Bibliography,* G. K. Hall, 1973; *Nigeria: A Comprehensive Bibliography in the Humanities and Social Sciences, 1900-1971,* G. K. Hall, 1973. Contributor to African studies and library journals.

SIDELIGHTS: Aguolu commented: "My bibliographical interests are conditioned by the need to order and chart knowledge about Africa, making it readily available to those interested in African subjects." *Avocational interests:* Table tennis, reading, debate.

* * *

AIDOO, (Christina) Ama Ata 1942-

PERSONAL: Born in 1942, in Abeadzi Kyiakor, Ghana. *Education:* University of Ghana, B.A. (with honors), 1964; also attended Stanford University. *Office:* Department of English, University of Ghana, Cape Coast Branch, Cape Coast, Ghana.

CAREER: University of Ghana, Cape Coast, professor of English; writer. *Awards, honors:* Short story prize from Mbari Press competition; prize from *Black Orpheus* for story, "No Sweetness Here."

WRITINGS: Dilemma of a Ghost (play; first produced in Legon, Ghana, at Open Air Theatre, March, 1964), Longmans, Green, 1965, Macmillan, 1971; *Our Sister Killjoy; or, Reflections From a Black-Eyed Squint* (novel), 1966, NOK Publishing, 1976; *Anowa* (play), Humanities, 1970; *No Sweetness Here* (stories), Longmans, Green, 1970, Doubleday, 1971.

Work represented in anthologies, including *New Sum of Poetry From the Negro World,* Presence Africaine, 1966; *African Writing Today,* Penguin, 1967; Joseph Okpaku, editor, *African Literature and the Arts,* Volume I, Crowell, 1970. Contributor of stories and poems to magazines, including *Okyeame, Black Orpheus, Journal of African Literature,* and *New African.*

BIOGRAPHICAL/CRITICAL SOURCES: Cosmo Pieterse and Dennis Duerdon, editors, *African Writers Talking,* Africana Publishing, 1972.*

* * *

AIKEN, John (Kempton) 1913-
(John Paget)

PERSONAL: Born October 10, 1913, in Cambridge, Mass.; son of Conrad Potter (a novelist and poet) and Jessie (McDonald) Aiken; married Paddy Street, May 10, 1970; children: Alison Mary Delano Leacock. *Education:* University of London, Ph.D., 1936. *Agent:* Brandt & Brandt Literary Agents, Inc., 1501 Broadway, New York, N.Y. 10036.

CAREER: Paint Research Station, London, England, research chemist, 1936-45; Geigy Co., Manchester, England, development manager, 1945-64; M. L. Alkan Ltd., London, head of laboratories, 1964-66; Humphreys & Glasgow Ltd., London, patents manager, 1967-70; writer.

WRITINGS: The Lid Off, R. Hale, 1969; (under pseudonym John Paget) *World Well Lost* (novel), R. Hale, 1970, published in the United States under name John Aiken, Doubleday, 1971; *Nightly Deadshade,* Macmillan, 1971. Work represented in anthologies, including *New Worlds, Number Three,* 1946.

AVOCATIONAL INTERESTS: Music, chess, gardening, cats, jokes, booze.*

* * *

AKPABOT, Samuel Ekpe 1932-

PERSONAL: Born October 3, 1932, in Lagos, Nigeria; son of Benjamin (an accountant) and Molly (a schoolteacher; maiden name, Ekere) Akpabot; married Beatrice d'Almeida, 1962 (divorced, 1973); children: Oscar, Samuel, Victor. *Education:* Royal College of Music, London, associate, 1957; University of Chicago, M.A., 1967; Michigan State University, Ph.D., 1975. *Religion:* Protestant. *Address:* University of Ibadan, Ibadan, Nigeria.

CAREER: Nigerian Broadcasting Corp., Lagos, senior music producer, 1959-62; University of Nigeria Nsukka, assistant lecturer, 1962-64, lecturer in music, 1967-70, director of chapel music, 1962-64; University of Ife, Ife, Nigeria, senior fellow in music and director of chapel music, 1970-73; Michigan State University, East Lansing, visiting scholar, 1973-75; College of Education, Uyo, Nigeria, associate professor of music, 1975-79, chairman of division of arts, 1977-79; University of Ibadan, Ibadan, Nigeria, research professor of music, 1979—. Musician, composer, and conductor; exhibitioner at Royal College of Music, London, 1958, fellow, 1967; conductor at Fourth International Choral Festival, Lincoln Center, New York, N.Y., May, 1974. Host of radio program, "In a Lighter Mood," 1976—, and television program, "The Sam Akpabot Show," 1977-80. *Member:* African Studies Association, Society for Ethnomusicology, Performing Rights Society (London), Royal College of Organists (London). *Awards, honors:* First prize at Cannes Music Festival, 1956, for sound track for film on Barclay's Bank; first prize in composition from University of California, Los Angeles, 1972.

WRITINGS: Masters of the Music (poems), Stockwell, 1958; (contributor) Joseph Okpaku, editor, *New African Literature and the Arts,* Third Press, 1972; *Ibibio Music in Nigerian Culture,* Michigan State University Press, 1975; (contributor) *Festac Anthology of Nigerian New Writing,* Ministry of Information (Lagos, Nigeria), 1977; *Introduction to African Music,* Oxford University Press, 1978. Contributor to journals, including *African Arts, African Music, International African Institute Bulletin,* and *Black Perspective in Music.*

Music; published by Oxford University Press: *Overture for a Nigeria Ballet* (small orchestra), 1972; *Scenes From Nigeria* (small orchestra), 1972; *Cynthia's Lament* (wind orchestra, soprano, and eight African instruments), 1972; *Three Nigerian Dances* (string orchestra and percussion), 1978.

Other compositions: "Three Roads to Tomorrow" (sound track for film of same name), 1959; "Ofala Festival" (tone poem; wind orchestra plus five African instruments), commissioned by American Wind Symphony Orchestra, Pittsburgh, Pa., 1963; "Journey Through Africa" (sound track for film of same name), 1965; "Jaja of Opobo" (operetta), 1972; "Nigeria in Conflict" (tone poem; wind orchestra plus eight African instruments), commissioned by American Wind Symphony Orchestra, 1973; "Two Nigerian Folk Tunes" (choir and piano), 1973; "Te Deum Laudamus" (liturgical; choir and organ), 1975; "Verba Christi" (cantata;

three soloists, chorus, narrator, and orchestra), commissioned by Nigerian Broadcasting Corp., 1977.

WORK IN PROGRESS: Research on folk tunes of Nigeria.

SIDELIGHTS: Though born in Nigeria, Samuel Akpabot was introduced to European culture at an early age. He grew up with an English bishop, developing a love for music while singing with a church choir for seven years. His interest in the organ and classical European music followed, and he pursued that interest by studying in London.

It was not until he returned to his native Nigeria that Akpabot came to know the music of his land. As many of the African musical traditions had been destroyed by the "drums-are-the-devil's-tools" attitude of colonialism, Akpabot set out to discover Africa's musical past, learning to play its instruments and to understand the meanings behind its songs. Now as a teacher, composer, and performer, he believes African music "shouldn't be something exotic. It should be part of the world's music literature."

Though he is familiar with both Western and African music, Akpabot considers himself an ambassador on behalf of the latter. His role, he feels, is to bring young people back to the "land." "I am a bit surprised at the young people in Nigeria," he has said. "They know all about modern fashions, James Brown, and current dances, but I feel they are losing their traditional culture."

Akpabot's own performances have attracted a following throughout Nigeria. *West Africa* reports that his television and radio shows are "widely listened to" and are fine examples of his versatility: "He will switch from Chopin to calypso, from Brahms to boogie, interspersed with high life and humor—in fact anything that comes into his head." More praise came from Kenyan professor P. N. Kavyu, who commented on an Akpabot cantata: "In all terms of classical composition, [it] is one of the most brilliant cantatas I have listened to in the modern music and surely among the best contributions to the classical music from Africa."

Akpobot has devoted himself to reviving African music in several other ways. As it had no way of being expressed in written form, Akpabot translated its melodies and rhythms into Western notation. While studying at the University of Chicago and at Michigan State University, he toured parts of the United States and Canada lecturing on and demonstrating his art. And even in his classical music, written for Europeans, he inevitably includes an assortment of African instruments.

Akpabot examined a segment of African life and the role music plays in it in his book *Ibibio Music in Nigerian Culture.* His intent was to show "(a) why the music of the people is shaped the way it is, (b) how it relates to society, (c) what effects it has had on behavioral patterns, (d) what part singing and dancing play in ritual ceremonies, and (e) how musical instruments individually and collectively relate to the daily life of the people." According to K. A. Gourlay, Akpabot "presents Ibibio music as a human activity directed towards social ends—communion with the supernatural, control of the refractory, or simply for entertainment—so that music appears as an inseparable aspect of community life." Gourlay added that "the seeming simplicity of Dr. Akpabot's style disguises his scholarship and demonstrates that such accounts can be both highly informative and extremely readable."

Described by many as an extrovert, Akpabot is by no means shy in making known his plans for the future. "My political ambition is to be the president of this country," the Nigerian told one interviewer. "I have got the education, training and experience, and I think I understand the problems of this country."

BIOGRAPHICAL/CRITICAL SOURCES: Daily Times (Lagos, Nigeria), April 27, 1972, February 11, 1977; *Pittsburgh Courier,* June 30, 1973; *Lansing State Journal,* December 23, 1973; *Michigan State News,* January 25, 1974; *Nigerian Chronicle* (Calabar), March 6, 1976, June 2, 1979; *Sunday Chronicle* (Calabar), March 21, 1976, February 27, 1977, April 15, 1979; *West Africa,* June 28, 1976, April 17, 1978; *Savanna,* December, 1976; *Sunday Punch* (Lagos), March 11, 1979.

*   *   *

ALBERT, Marv 1943-

PERSONAL: Born June 12, 1943, in New York; son of Max and Alida Albert; married Benita Caress, August 15, 1965; children: Ken, Jacqueline, Brian, Denise. *Education:* Attended Syracuse University; received B.S. from New York University. *Agent:* David Cogan, Cogan Management, Empire State Building, New York, N.Y. 10001. *Office:* WNBC-TV, 30 Rockefeller Plaza, New York, N.Y. 10020.

CAREER: WNBC-TV, New York, N.Y., sports commentator for New York Knicks and New York Rangers, and network commentator for boxing, National Football League games, and college basketball games. *Military service:* U.S. Army Reserve. *Awards, honors:* Annually named sportscaster of the year by National Sportscasters and Sportswriters Association, 1969—.

WRITINGS: Krazy About the Knicks, Hawthorn, 1970; *Ranger Fever,* Dell, 1973; *Marv Albert's Sports Quiz Book,* Dell, 1975; *"Yesss!,"* New American Library, 1979.

*   *   *

ALBERTAZZIE, Ralph 1923-

PERSONAL: Born July 16, 1923, in Cassville, W.Va; son of Lorraine Albertazzie; married Carol Jean Wilson, November 22, 1942; children: Lynette Murphy, Sally. *Education:* Attended West Virginia University, 1941-43; Jackson College, B.S., 1955; graduate study at University of Alabama, 1962-63. *Home address:* Route 1, Box 242J, Hedgesville, W.Va. 25427. *Agent:* Bill Adler, 110 East End Ave., New York, N.Y. 10028. *Office address:* Panhandle 76, P.O. Box 993, Martinsburg, W.Va. 25401.

CAREER: U.S. Air Force, 1941-45 and 1951-74; served as commander and pilot of "Air Force One," 1968-74; retired as colonel; West Virginia Department of Commerce, Charleston, commissioner, 1974-77; Panhandle Motor Service Corp., Martinsburg, W.Va., president, 1978—. Director of Aeromech Airlines; trustee of Alderson-Broaddus College; consultant for Lockheed-California Co. *Member:* National Aviation Club (member of board of directors), Air Force Association (West Virginia chapter president, 1977-78), West Virginia Housing Development Fund, West Virginia Industrial Development Fund, Burning Tree Club (Washington, D.C.), Wings Club of New York. *Awards, honors*—Military: Distinguished Flying Cross, Legion of Merit, Air Medal, Bronze Star. Civilian: LL.D. from Alderson-Broaddus College, 1972; Son of the Year citation from West Virginia Society, 1972.

WRITINGS: (With J. F. terHorst) *The Flying White House: The Story of Air Force One,* Coward, 1979.

BIOGRAPHICAL/CRITICAL SOURCES: Detroit News, July 22, 1979.

ALCIBIADE
See PRAZ, Mario

* * *

ALEXANDER, Vincent Arthur 1925-1980

OBITUARY NOTICE: Born November 4, 1925, in Wyckoff, N.J.; died after a long illness, May 22, 1980, in Boston, Mass. Editor best known for his work for Holt, Rinehart & Winston, Inc., on publications involving mathematics and science. In 1969 Alexander was named editor-in-chief of the school department; he became a vice-president in 1972. Obituaries and other sources: *Who's Who in America,* 40th edition, Marquis, 1978; *Publishers Weekly,* June 27, 1980.

* * *

ALFORD, Bernard William Ernest 1937-

PERSONAL: Son of E. E. (a textile worker) and W. D. (Dare) Alford; married Valerie Sandra North, 1962; children: three. *Education:* Received B.Sc. and Ph.D. from London School of Economics and Political Science, London. *Office:* Department of Economic and Social History, University of Bristol, Bristol BS8 1UL, England.

CAREER: University of London, London School of Economics and Political Science, London, England, assistant lecturer in economic history, 1961-62; University of Bristol, Bristol, England, assistant lecturer, 1962-64, lecturer, 1964-73, senior lecturer, 1973-76, reader in economic history, 1976—. *Member:* Economic History Society (member of council).

WRITINGS: (With T. C. Baker) *A History of the Carpenters' Company,* Shoe String, 1968; *Depression and Recovery?: British Economic Growth, 1918-1939,* Humanities, 1972; *W. D. and H. O. Willis and the Development of the United Kingdom Tobacco Industry, 1786-1965,* Methuen, 1973. Also author of *Britain and the World Economy, 1880-1972,* 1981. Contributor of articles and reviews to economic and economic history journals.

WORK IN PROGRESS: Research on business history and the economic history of southern Africa since 1910.

* * *

ALKIRE, Leland George, (Jr.) 1937-

PERSONAL: Born May 11, 1937, in San Diego, Calif.; son of Leland George (a union organizer) and Emma (Green) Alkire; married Maria Belen Bradbury, 1957 (divorced, 1971); children: Kathleen. *Education:* Attended North Idaho College, 1958-60; University of Idaho, B.A., 1962; University of Washington, Seattle, M.L.S., 1966. *Religion:* Unitarian-Universalist. *Home:* 520 Patterson, Cheney, Wash. 99004. *Office:* Library, Eastern Washington State College, Cheney, Wash. 99004.

CAREER: Eastern Washington State College, Cheney, reference librarian, 1966—. *Military service:* U.S. Navy, 1954-58. *Member:* Pacific Northwest Library Association.

WRITINGS: Periodical Title Abbreviations, 2nd edition, Gale, 1977. Contributor to library journals, *Yachting,* and *Golden.*

WORK IN PROGRESS: A survey of authorship publications.

* * *

ALLAN, Elkan 1922-

PERSONAL: Born December 8, 1922, in London, England;

son of Allan Michael and Rose (Praeger) Allan; married Dorotheen Ingham, 1947 (deceased); married Angela Willment, September 5, 1970; children: Andy, Mary, Stephen, Charley, Venice. *Education:* Attended grammar school of London, England. *Home:* Winston Grange, Stowmarket, Suffolk IP14 6LE, England. *Agent:* Hilary Rubinstein, A.P. Watt Ltd., 26/28 Bedford Row, London WC1R 4HL, England. *Office: Now!,* 161 City Rd., London EC1V 1JL, England.

CAREER: Worked for United Press of America, 1939-41; *Daily Express,* London, England, reporter, 1941-43; freelance writer for radio and magazines, 1943-50; Odhams Press, London, staff writer, 1950-55; Rediffusion Television, London, writer, producer, executive, and head of entertainment, 1955-66; *Sunday Times,* London, television preview critic, 1970-79; *Now!,* London, author of column, "Television," and television editor, 1979—. *Member:* National Union of Journalists, Association of Cine Television and Allied Technicians, British Academy of Film and Television Arts (founding member), British Film Institute, Green Street Bridge Club. *Awards, honors:* Three awards from *Melody Maker, Weekend,* and *TV Mirror,* 1963-64, for producing "Ready Steady Go!"; three awards from Berlin Television Festival and Contest, 1965, for writing and producing "Freedom Road."

WRITINGS: (Editor) *Living Opinion,* Hutchinson, 1946; (with D. M. Robinson) *Good Listening: A Survey of Broadcasting,* Hutchinson, 1948; (with wife, Angela Allan) *The Sunday Times Guide to Movies on Television,* Times Books, 1973, revised edition, Hamlyn Books, 1980.

Author of twenty documentary scripts for television, and episodes for "Batman," revue sketches, and television quizzes. Contributor to magazines and newspapers.

WORK IN PROGRESS: Research on outstanding television programs, with a book expected to result.

SIDELIGHTS: Allan commented: "My motivation has always been to entertain while informing and inform while I entertain. This applies to all the television programs, documentary and light entertainment, and to my journalism. I suppose the two contributions I have made, minor as they are, are the 'honesty' of 'Ready Steady Go!,' which presented popular music at its burgeoning period, without mystique, in an honest studio context, and the innovation of the 'TV Preview Page,' in which programs were reviewed ahead of transmission."

* * *

ALLEN, Robert L(ee) 1942-

PERSONAL: Born May 29, 1942, in Atlanta, Ga.; son of Robert Lee and Sadie (Sims) Allen; married Pamela Parker, August 28, 1965 (separated January 1, 1978); children: Casey Douglass. *Education:* Attended University of Vienna, 1961-62; Morehouse College, B.S., 1963; graduate study at Columbia University, 1963-64; New School for Social Research, M.A., 1967; doctoral study at University of California, San Francisco, 1976—. *Home:* 1310 Turk St., No. 603, San Francisco, Calif. 94115. *Agent:* Wendy Weil, Julian Bach Literary Agency, Inc., 747 Third Ave., New York, N.Y. 10017. *Office: Black Scholar,* P.O. Box 908, Sausalito, Calif. 94965.

CAREER: Department of Welfare, New York, N.Y., caseworker, 1964-65; reporter for *National Guardian,* 1967-69; San Jose State College (now University), San Jose, Calif., assistant professor of black studies, 1969-72; Mills College,

Oakland, Calif., lecturer in ethnic studies, 1973—. Active in civil rights and anti-war movements. *Member:* American Sociological Association, African-American Historical and Cultural Society, Bay Area Black Journalists. *Awards, honors:* Merrill grant for Austria, 1961-62; Woodrow Wilson fellowship, 1963-64; Guggenheim fellowship, 1978.

WRITINGS: Black Awakening in Capitalist America, Doubleday, 1969; *Reluctant Reformers,* Howard University Press, 1974. Contributor to magazines. Associate editor of *Black Scholar,* 1972-75, editor, 1975—.

WORK IN PROGRESS: Research on the Port Chicago disaster of 1944.

SIDELIGHTS: Allen told *CA:* "A recurrent theme in my work is a concern with the role of beliefs and ideologies in the process of social change. I consider myself a materialist sociologist, but I also think that human action is shaped by the subjective understandings that people have of their situations; hence, getting inside the heads of actors is as important as measuring the social forces that impinge upon them.

"Following a disastrous explosion at the Port Chicago (California) Naval Ammunition Magazine in July, 1944, fifty black sailors were accused of mutiny when, as part of a larger group, they refused to return to work loading ammunition on ships. (More than three hundred men had been killed in the blast.) The fifty men were court-martialed amid great publicity, convicted, and jailed. A national campaign was organized by the NAACP Legal Defense Fund, under the leadership of Thurgood Marshall, to free the men. Eventually the sentences were set aside and the men released. The Port Chicago explosion was the worst home-front disaster of World War II, and the trial of the fifty men was the largest mass mutiny trial in U.S. Navy history. I am collecting documents and oral histories from survivors with the intent of publishing a book-length account of these events."

*   *   *

ALLEN, William Stannard 1913-

PERSONAL: Born February 23, 1913, in Southampton, England; son of William (a shop assistant) and Mabel (a florist; maiden name, Taylor) Allen; married Hilda Shilston, August 2, 1939 (divorced, 1975); children: Shirley Allen Castle, Jennifer Mary Allen O'Brien. *Education:* University of London, B.A. (with honors), 1936. *Home:* 4 Tollgate, Epsom Rd., Guildford, England.

CAREER: Masaryk University, Brno, Czechoslovakia, lecturer in English, 1937-39; overseas officer for British Council, 1940-60; free-lance writer and lecturer, 1960—. Professional viola player. Member of British Council English-language advisory committee, 1967-72; adviser to British Broadcasting Corp., 1963 and 1966, and Kuwait Ministry of Education, 1966-71. *Member:* Society of Authors, Musicians Union.

WRITINGS—All published by Longman: *Living English Structure,* 1948, 5th edition, 1974; *Living English Speech,* 1954, 3rd edition, 1971; *Living English Structure for Schools,* 1958, revised edition, 1971; (with R. B. Cooke) *Living English for Jordan,* 1962; *Living English for the Arab World,* 1964; *New Living English for the Arab World,* 1966; (with Yusra Salah and Mohammed El-Anani) *New Living English for Jordan,* 1971; *English Secondary Course for the Arab World,* 1972; *Living English Revision Book,* 1973; *Progressive Living English for the Arab World,* 1975; (with L. G. Alexander, R. A. Close, and Robert O'Neill) *English Grammatical Structure,* 1976; (with Alan McLean) *Progressive Living English: For Egyptian Schools,* 1977.

Arranger of "Yugoslav Dances," for recorders and percussion, Schott & Sons, 1957.

Author of "Keep Up Your English," on BBC-Radio. General editor of "Longman Structural Readers," Longman.

WORK IN PROGRESS: A "practical re-presentation of English structural material in notional and situational terms."

SIDELIGHTS: Allen commented: "My plans are triggered by the exaggerated and stereotyped practical material that the fashionable 'notional' approach has tended to bring about. Language-learning seems to be in danger of becoming all play and platitudes."

*   *   *

ALLISON, Ralph B(rewster) 1931-

PERSONAL: Born May 13, 1931, in Manila, Philippines; American citizen born abroad; son of W. Theodore (a minister) and Metta B. Allison; married Mitzi Burden, January 1, 1957; children: Ann, Amy, John, Jill. *Education:* Occidental College, B.A., 1952; University of California, Los Angeles, M.D., 1956. *Politics:* Republican. *Religion:* Presbyterian. *Home:* 620 Hubble St., Davis, Calif. 95616. *Agent:* Dominick Abel Literary Agency, 498 West End Ave., New York, N.Y. 10024. *Office:* Yolo County Mental Health Services, 350 C St., Broderick, Calif. 95605.

CAREER: Highland-Alameda County Hospital, Oakland, Calif., intern, 1956-57; Stanford Medical Center, Stanford, Calif., resident in psychiatry, 1959-62; Santa Clara County Mental Health Services, Palo Alto, Calif., staff psychiatrist, 1962-63; private practice of psychiatry in Santa Cruz, Calif., 1964-78; Yolo County Mental Health Services, Broderick, Calif., staff psychiatrist, 1978—. Guest lecturer at University of Stockholm, University of Gothenburg, and University of Lund. Program chief for Santa Cruz County Mental Health Services, 1964-67; chief of staff at Santa Cruz General Hospital; chief of psychiatry at Domonican Santa Cruz Hospital; founder and chief consultant to Santa Cruz County Suicide Prevention Services, 1968-74. *Military service:* U.S. Air Force, flight surgeon in Medical Corps, 1957-59; became captain.

MEMBER: Union of American Physicians, American Psychiatric Association (fellow), American Society of Clinical Hypnosis, Society for Clinical and Experimental Hypnosis, Swedish Society for Clinical and Experimental Hypnosis, California Medical Association, Central California Psychiatric Society, Yolo County Medical Society.

WRITINGS: (Author of introduction) Henry Hawksworth and Ted Schwarz, *The Five of Me,* Contemporary Books, 1977; (with Schwarz) *Minds in Many Pieces,* Rawson, Wade, 1980; (with Schwarz) *The Hillside Strangler,* Doubleday, 1981. Contributor to psychiatry and therapy journals. Editor of *Memos on Multiplicity,* 1977-78.

SIDELIGHTS: Allison wrote: "I am a full-time practicing psychotherapist who has had a good deal of exposure to patients with multiple personalities. Patients with multiple personalities are extremely hard to treat and go to the hospital often because of their suicide attempts. There they antagonize the nurses and other psychiatrists to no end. These are dramatic, attention-seeking, dependent people, who are also very ill with a severe histrionic character disorder.

"When I began dealing with such patients, I had to figure out what to do with them by myself, since no one else has written about the treatment of people with multiple personalities. When I had dealt with over fifty such patients, I decided that

I had something to offer to other therapists. I started out writing a therapy manual is my spare time at the office and collected a large binder of material. Naturally, I could not find anyone interested in publishing it. Then Ted Schwarz contacted me and we started working together on a popular book on the subject, *Minds in Many Pieces.* The book sought to do three things: 1) tell the story of what a psychiatrist's life is really like, 2) tell the stories of patients with multiple personalities, explaining about their miserable childhoods, their hectic adult lives, and all the strange things that happened to them, and 3) educate the public on some mental health topics, clearing up the common confusions that occur when one talks about multiple personalities.

"While *Minds in Many Pieces* was being written, I was involved in a variety of legal cases that involved a defendant who manifested several personalities. The most infamous of these was Ken Bianchi, the confessed Los Angeles Hillside Strangler. He is the subject of my most recent book."

The Hillside Strangler is scheduled to be presented as a television miniseries by National Broadcasting Co. (NBC-TV).

*   *   *

ALLWORTH, Edward (Alfred)   1920-

PERSONAL: Born December 1, 1920, in Columbia, S.C.; son of Edward Christopher (a college administrator) and Ethel Elaine (Walker) Allworth; married Janet Lovett, December 21, 1952; children: Clark Edward. *Education:* Oregon State University, B.S., 1948; University of Chicago, A.M., 1953; Columbia University, Ph.D., 1959. *Residence:* New York, N.Y. *Office:* Department of Middle East Languages and Culture, Columbia University, 116th & Broadway, New York, N.Y. 10027.

CAREER: Reed College, Portland, Ore., instructor in Russian and humanities, 1957-58; Ford Foundation, New York City, program assistant in international training and research, 1958-59; American Committee, Munich, West Germany, assistant to director of emigrant relations, 1960-61; Columbia University, New York City, assistant professor, 1961-65, associate professor, 1965-69, professor of Turco-Soviet studies, 1970—, director of Program on Soviet Nationality Problems, 1970—. Consultant and advisory editor to publishers. *Military service:* U.S. Army, Airborne, 1942-47; became captain. *Member:* American Research Institute in Turkey (secretary). *Awards, honors:* Fellowship from Social Science Research Council, 1967-68, and American Philosophical Society, 1976.

WRITINGS: Uzbek Literary Politics, Mouton, 1964; *Central Asian Publishing and the Rise of Nationalism,* New York Public Library, 1965; *Nationalities of the Soviet East: Publications and Writing Systems,* Columbia University Press, 1971; *Soviet Asia: Bibliographies . . . and an Essay on the Soviet Asia Controversy,* Praeger, 1975.

Editor and contributor: *Central Asia: A Century of Russian Rule,* Columbia University Press, 1967; *Soviet Nationality Problems,* Columbia University Press, 1971; *The Nationality Question in Soviet Central Asia,* Praeger, 1973; *Nationality Group Survival in Multiethnic States,* Praeger, 1977; *Ethnic Russia in the U.S.S.R.: The Dilemma of Dominance,* Pergamon, 1980.

WORK IN PROGRESS: The Modern Uzbeks, publication by Hoover Institution for War, Revolution, and Peace expected in 1983; research on and translation of Middle Eastern drama; *History of Modern Central Asia.*

SIDELIGHTS: Allworth commented to *CA:* "Nothing in

intellectual life is more exciting than reading a well-written, serious book. I learn constantly from good editors and writers what I would hope to be able to emulate. It's a lifetime process of education and source of stimulation. An academic adviser years ago told me that no book is good if it isn't well-written. I believe it and am still trying to achieve it. A primary aim in my efforts is to bring the civilization and international importance of Central Asia, including Afghanistan and the Soviet and Chinese portions, to the attention of informed people and students everywhere. This involves human rights (free speech in particular) as well as scholarship. Readers in Soviet Central Asia itself respond to foreign writings about their world. This is especially true because the state ideology there has shaped a peculiarly one-dimensional view that sanitizes Kazakh, Tajik, Uzbek, and other history and culture.

"A critic commented negatively (in the officially-sponsored Uzbek-Russian language journal, *Social Sciences in Uzbekistan,* 1980, No. 3, p. 20) upon several of my books: 'Touching on the 1920's and 1930's, he [Allworth] focuses more on the works of complex or contradictory personalities (the reformers Cholpan, Fitrat, and others) and minimizes or vaguely speaks about today's attainments in the cultural life of Central Asia's people. His book, *Uzbek Literary Politics,* for example, testifies to this. . . . Allworth begins to write also [in *The Nationality Question in Soviet Central Asia*] about contemporary phenomena in the cultural life of Central Asia (regarding the younger generation, and about book publishing, for instance).' But a positive insight reached the Uzbek critic when he urged his countrymen to learn foreign languages besides Russian and to acquire disciplinary professionalism in order to win what he calls 'the ideological battle.' With something closer to real exchange of ideas—one cannot speak of free press in the USSR—I have faith in the chances for an informed populace. The more the Central Asians can read for themselves, rather than through selective translation, the better for a true understanding of themselves and of Western democracy with its liberty. My efforts to offer objective analysis are motivated not at all by these Soviet reactions to them, but it is evident that the Central Asian treatment of their own literary and cultural history has broadened as non-Soviet scrutiny has increased in penetrating scholarship, leading Western authors in this field to surmise that we have some impact there as well as among our own readers."

*   *   *

ALMOND, Gabriel Abraham   1911-

PERSONAL: Born January 12, 1911, in Rock Island, Ill.; son of David Moses and Lisa (Elson) Almond; married Maria Dorothea Kaufmann, April 29, 1937; children: Richard J., Peter O., Susan J. *Education:* University of Chicago, Ph.B., 1932, Ph.D., 1938. *Home:* 4135 Old Trace Rd., Palo Alto, Calif. 94306. *Office:* Department of Political Science, Stanford University, Stanford, Calif. 94305.

CAREER: Brooklyn College (now of the City University of New York), Brooklyn, N.Y., instructor in political science, 1939-42; associated with Office of War Information, Washington, D.C., 1942-44, and with U.S. War Department, Washington, D.C., in European theater, 1945; Yale University, New Haven, Conn., research associate at Institute for International Studies, 1947-49, associate professor of political science, 1949-51; Princeton University, Princeton, N.J., associate professor, 1951-54, professor of political science, 1954-59; Yale University, professor of political science, 1959-63; Stanford University, Stanford, Calif., professor of political science, 1963—, head of department, 1964-68. Fellow at Center for Advanced Studies in the Behavioral Sciences, 1956-57; visiting professor at University of Tokyo, 1962; consultant to U.S. Department of State, RAND Corp., and U.S. Air Force.

MEMBER: National Academy of Sciences (fellow), American Academy of Arts and Sciences (fellow), American Philosophical Society, American Political Science Association (president, 1965-66), American Association for Public Opinion Research, Academy of Political Science, Social Science Research Council (member of board of directors; chairman of committee on comparative politics). *Awards, honors:* Social Science Research Council fellow, 1946; Ford Foundation grant, 1962-63; National Endowment for the Humanities senior fellow at Churchill College, Cambridge, 1972-73.

WRITINGS: (Editor) Eugene N. Anderson and others, *The Struggle for Democracy in Germany*, University of North Carolina Press, 1949, reprinted, Russell, 1965; *The American People and Foreign Policy*, Harcourt, 1950, 2nd edition, Greenwood Press, 1977; (with Herbert E. Krugman, Elsbeth Lewin, Howard Wriggins, and others) *The Appeals of Communism*, Princeton University Press, 1954; (editor with James S. Coleman) *The Politics of Developing Areas*, Princeton University Press, 1960; (with Sidney Verba) *The Civic Culture: Political Attitudes and Democracy in Five Nations*, Princeton University Press, 1963; (with G. Bingham Powell, Jr.) *Comparative Politics: A Developmental Approach*, Little, Brown, 1966; *Political Development: Essays in Heuristic Theory*, Little, Brown, 1970; *U.S.: Almond and Verba Five Nation Study*, Dartmouth College, 1971; (editor with Scott C. Flanagan and Robert J. Mundt; and contributor) *Crisis, Choice, and Change: Historical Studies of Political Development,* Little, Brown, 1973; (with Sidney Verba) *The Civic Culture Study: 1959-1960*, Inter-University Consortium for Political Research (Ann Arbor, Mich.), 1974; (editor) *Comparative Politics Today: A World View*, Little, Brown, 1974; (editor with Neil J. Smelser) *Public Higher Education in California*, University of California Press, 1974; (with Powell) *Comparative Politics: System, Process, and Policy*, 2nd edition, Little, Brown, 1978. Also author of *Freedom and Development*.

AVOCATIONAL INTERESTS: Carpentry, swimming, birdwatching.

BIOGRAPHICAL/CRITICAL SOURCES: American Political cal Science Review, March, 1975; *Journal of Higher Education*, July-August, 1975; *American Journal of Sociology*, November, 1975.*

*   *   *

ALTHOUSE, Larry
See ALTHOUSE, Lawrence Wilson

*   *   *

ALTHOUSE, Lawrence Wilson   1930-
(Larry Althouse)

PERSONAL: Born March 21, 1930, in Reading, Pa.; son of Wilson Kauffman and Kathleen Althouse; married Mary Elizabeth Moore, March 31, 1955 (marriage ended, April, 1976); married Valere Fuller (a lecturer), May 29, 1976; children: Kevin Reid, Todd Eric. *Education:* Received B.S. from University of Pennsylvania; received M.Div. from United Theological Seminary, Dayton, Ohio; graduate study at Union Theological Seminary, New York, N.Y. *Politics:* Independent. *Home:* 4412 Shenandoah Ave., Dallas, Tex. 75205. *Agent:* Katherine Kidde, Ann Elmo Agency, Inc., 60

East 42nd St., New York, N.Y. 10017. *Office:* New Dimensions Center, Ross and Harwood Sts., Dallas, Tex. 75201.

CAREER: Ordained United Methodist minister; pastor of United Methodist church in Harrisburg, Pa., 1955-60; associate pastor of United Methodist church in Crestwood, N.Y., 1960-63; senior pastor of United Methodist church in Mohnton, Pa., 1963-75; free-lance writer and group tour organizer for Swissair, 1975-79; New Dimensions Center, Dallas, Tex., co-director, 1979—. *Member:* International Institute of Integral Human Sciences (fellow), American History Society, Spiritual Frontiers Fellowship (national president, 1972-76), Texas Society for Psychical Research (president, 1979-80). *Awards, honors:* D.H.C. from International Order of St. Luke the Physician.

WRITINGS—Under name Larry Althouse: *Youth Guide of Affluence and Poverty*, Friendship, 1966; *Rediscovering the Gift of Healing*, Abingdon, 1977. Also author with wife, Valere Althouse, of *You Don't Have to Lose Your Breast*, 1980. Author of columns "The Bible Speaks," syndicated by Feature Publications, "Travel Talk," in *Park Cities News* and *Roswell Record*, and "Bible Talk," in *Park Cities News*. Educational curriculum writer for United Methodist Church.

WORK IN PROGRESS: Sixty Days With Luke, a study book; *Life Beyond Death: A Christian Perspective*, on the relevance and challenge of thanatology and reincarnation.

SIDELIGHTS: Althouse told *CA:* "As directors of the New Dimensions Center, my wife and I devote most of our time to writing, lecturing, and conducting workshops and tours all over the world. Our areas of concentration are human potential development, stress management, extra-sensory perception, parapsychology, and human relations.

"My forthcoming book, *Life Beyond Death*, is a challenge to organized religions to become conversant and in dialogue with contemporary research into deathbed experiences (a la Moody, Osis), hypnotic regression (Wambaugh and others), and reincarnation (Stevenson). These lines of inquiry need not be regarded as a threat to the truths of religion, but only to the more narrow-minded and arrogant formulations of those truths.

"Reincarnation—for which a persuasive case can be made—if it were to be true would not destroy Christianity any more than Copernicus destroyed Christianity with his insistence that the earth is not the center of the solar system. While we do not embrace reincarnation as an article of faith, we do see it as an interesting possibility. It is the most widely believed expectation on life after death throughout the world today and, contrary to what is often assumed, has Eastern and Western roots as well as some acceptance within early Christianity."

*   *   *

ALYN, Marc [a pseudonym]   1937-

PERSONAL: Born March 18, 1937, in Reims, France; son of a bookseller; married Jacqueline-Claude Argelier (a painter) March 11, 1959. *Religion:* Roman Catholic. *Home:* Mas des Poiriers, Uzes, France 30700.

CAREER: Arts-Spectacles (weekly newspaper), Paris, France, literary critic, 1960-64; poetry critic for *Le Figaro Litteraire* and *Figaro*, 1964—; Editions Flammarion, Paris, director of "Poesie/Flammarion" collection, 1966-70. Lecturer on French poetry. *Military service:* French Army, 1957-59. *Member:* Actuelles-Formes et Langages (president, 1969—), Societe des Gens de Lettres, Club Actuelles (Uzes, France; president), P.E.N., Writers of Champagne. *Awards, honors:* Max Jacob Prize, 1957, for *Le Temps des autres;* Camille Engelmann Prize, 1970, for *Nuit majeure;* Guillaume Apollinaire Prize, 1973, for *Infini au-dela;* Chevalier of the Order of Arts and Letters, 1973.

WRITINGS—Under pseudonym Marc Alyn; in English translation: (With Lawrence Durrell) *Le Grand Supposi-toire: Entretiens avec Marc Alyn,* Belfond, 1972, translation by Francine Barker published as *The Big Supposer: A Dialogue With Marc Alyn,* Abelard-Schuman, 1973, Grove, 1974.

In French; poetry: *Le Chemin de la parole,* Paragraphes, 1953; *Rien que vivre,* Les Cahiers de Rochefort, 1954; *Demain l'amour,* Le Vehicule, 1955; *Liberte de voir,* Terre de feu, 1956 (see below); *Le Temps des autres,* Seghers, 1956 (see below); *Le Temps des autres* [et] *Liberte de voir,* Seghers, 1957; *Cruels Divertissements,* seghers, 1957; (contributor) *Les Poetes francais contre la guerre,* Millas-Martin, 1957; *Bruler le feu,* Seghers, 1959; *Delebiles,* Ides et Calendes, 1962; *Nuit majeure,* Flammarion, 1968; *Infini au-dela,* Flammarion, 1972; *Douze Poemes de l'ete,* Formes et Langages, 1976; *L'Arche enchantee,* Editions Ouvrieres, 1979.

Essays: (And editor) *Francois Mauriac,* Seghers, 1960; (and editor) *Dylan Thomas,* Seghers, 1962; *Les Poetes du XVIe siecle* (title means "Poets of the Sixteenth Century"), J'ai lu, 1962; (and editor) *Gerard de Nerval,* J'ai lu, 1965; (and editor) *Kosovel,* Seghers, 1965; (and editor) *Andre de Richaud,* Seghers, 1966; *Odette Ducarre; ou, Les Murs de la nuit,* Robert Morel, 1967; *La Nouvelle Poesie francaise,* Robert Morel, 1968; *Le Diderot de Bores,* Editions du Salin, 1975.

Other: *Le Secret des pierres,* Terre de feu, 1956; (translator and adapter) Lajos Kassak, *Hommage a Lajos Kassak,* Maison du poete, 1963; *Le Deplacement* (novel), Flammarion, 1964; (author of preface) *Prassinos, Arles, Musee Reattu, juillet-septembre 1970,* Musee Reattu, 1970; *Le Grand Labyrinthe* (opera-verbe), Formes et Langages, 1971; (author of postface) Robert Rovini, *Norge: Une Etude,* Seghers, 1972; (contributor) *Mauriac,* Hachette Realities, 1977. Also author of radio play, *Magie des mots,* 1960.

Contributor to periodicals.

WORK IN PROGRESS: "Short fantastic stories."

SIDELIGHTS: Noted French poet and literary critic Marc Alyn commented to *CA:* "To whom to write today, if not to language? A frozen act, an object that usage (reading) forever restores to a vibrant act, the poem goes from language that creates it to language that divides it, certifies it, or obliterates it. Born of words—existence sometimes becomes symbols—it persists in speaking of something else. If the poem can be the message of a man to his fellow men, the attraction that exerts its origins upon the poet will rather slant the poem to only fully satisfy him with the emotions aroused by its form. At the poem's summit, it is the verb that questions him, dreams, and denies him, the better to preserve from the moment some nuances and some visions which, without it, would be lost without recourse.

"That space, that lasting quality that I call 'poem'—in order to distinguish it, if one can, from poetry, which is often only some of the effects of the poem, the atmosphere that it establishes in the spirit or the senses of the reader—has nothing of the reality of real space and time. It is another world that I compare with this that doesn't satisfy me, an imaginary lasting quality that I hide under the debris of time. I create a place where I become someone else with the help of the quietest form of speech. This mineral murmuring is born of

my silence; this movement is created by my immobility; this relative and menacing absolute aides me to deceive the absence."

* * *

AMES, Lois (Winslow Sisson) 1931-

PERSONAL: Born January 21, 1931, in Boston, Mass.; daughter of Winslow Chase and Lois (Barton) Sisson; married Robert Webb Ames (an architect), December 15, 1956 (divorced August, 1969); children: Elisabeth Harriett Winslow, Adam Barton. *Education:* Smith College, B.A., 1952; University of Chicago, M.A., 1958. *Home:* 285 Marlboro Rd., Sudbury, Mass. 01776. *Agent:* Claire Degener, Sterling Lord Agency, Inc., 660 Madison Ave., New York, N.Y. 10021. *Office:* College of Criminal Justice, Northeastern University, Huntington Ave., Boston, Mass. 02115.

CAREER: Tucson Daily Citizen, Tucson, Ariz., assistant editor of women's page and author of weekly column, "Vocational Leapfrog," 1952-53; Public Welfare Department, Chicago, Ill., caseworker in Children's Division, 1953-56; Institute for Juvenile Research, Chicago, child care caseworker at William Healy Residential Treatment Center, 1957; Lake County Mental Health Clinic, Gary, Ind., psychiatric social worker, 1958-59; Hyde Park Unitarian Cooperative Nursery School, Chicago, counselor, 1959-64, member of board of directors, 1964-68; University of Chicago, Chicago, psychiatric social worker and lower- and middle-school counselor at Laboratory Schools, 1966-69; Northeastern University, Boston, Mass., lecturer, 1969-70, assistant professor of criminal justice and coordinator of social welfare and social work practice curriculum, 1970—, assistant director of Weekend College, 1969-70, director, 1970-72. Private practice of psychiatric social work; member of local Department of Youth Service task force, 1972-74. Public speaker; guest on television programs.

MEMBER: American Association of Suicidology (charter member), American Association of University Professors, National Association of Social Workers, National Organization for Women, National Association for the Advancement of Colored People (member of board of directors, 1963), Women Concerned for Social Justice, Sociologists for Women in Society, Women's Equity Action League, Academy of Criminal Justice Sciences, New England Poetry Society, Eastern Sociological Society, Smith College Alumnae Association. *Awards, honors:* Grants from Ella Lyman Cabot Trust, 1966, and Illinois Arts Council, 1967.

WRITINGS: (Contributor) Charles Newman, editor, *The Art of Sylvia Plath,* Indiana University Press, 1969; (contributor of biographical note) Plath, *The Bell Jar,* Harper, 1971; (editor with Linda Sexton) *Anne Sexton: A Self Portrait in Letters,* Houghton, 1977. Also author of *The Weekend College: A Concept and a Reality, The Biography of Julia Plath,* Harper, and *Memoirs of Sylvia Plath's Friends,* Harper. Contributor of poems, articles, and children's stories to magazines, including *Social Casework,* and newspapers.

* * *

AMIEL, Barbara 1940-

PERSONAL: Born December 4, 1940, in Hertfordshire, England; daughter of Harold Joffre (a lawyer) and Vera Isserles (a nurse; maiden name, Barnett) Amiel; married George Jonas (a producer and writer), October 11, 1974. *Education:* University of Toronto, B.A., 1963. *Religion:* Jewish. *Office: Maclean's,* 481 University Ave., Toronto, Ontario, Canada M5W 1A7.

CAREER: Maclean's, Toronto, Ontario, senior writer and author of column, 1976—. Co-host of "CTV Reports," 1977-78. Awards, honors: Canada Council grant, 1974; award from Media Club of Canada, 1976; Edgar Allan Poe Award from Mystery Writers of America, 1977, for nonfiction book By Persons Unknown; award from Periodical Publishers Association, 1977.

WRITINGS: (With husband, George Jonas) By Persons Unknown: The Strange Death of Christine Demeter, Grove, 1977; Confessions, Macmillan, 1980. Also co-author with Jonas of Time to Kill (nonfiction), 1981. Author of television and radio documentary scripts. Contributor to journals.

SIDELIGHTS: Barbara Amiel is best-known in Canada for her columns and opinions, representing what she calls "a classic liberal (or neo-conservative) position barely evident in Canadian fiction."

Amiel wrote: "My work is motivated by a deep concern for the erosion of individual liberties and the danger to liberal democracy from the growing powers of a statist society."

* * *

AMIEL, Joseph 1937-

PERSONAL: Born June 3, 1937, in New York, N.Y.; son of Jack J. and Ethel (Yanover) Amiel; married Nancy Mirkin (in public relations), June 5, 1960; children: Andrea, Jack Joseph. Education: Amherst College, B.A. (cum laude), 1959; Yale University, J.D., 1962. Agent: Owen Laster, William Morris Agency, Inc., 1350 Avenue of the Americas, New York, N.Y. 10019.

CAREER: Writer.

WRITINGS: Hawks (novel), Putnam, 1979.

BIOGRAPHICAL/CRITICAL SOURCES: Library Journal, June 15, 1979.

* * *

ANDERSEN, Benny (Allan) 1929-

PERSONAL: Born July 11, 1929, in Copenhagen, Denmark; son of Srend Aage and Gudrun (Carlsen) Andersen; married Signe Plesner Boesen, March 30, 1950; children: Lisbet Anja (Mrs. Niels V. Kohl), Kim Plesner. Education: Educated in Denmark. Home: Kastanie Alle 46, 3520 Farum, Denmark.

CAREER: Worked at advertising agency, 1946-49; bar pianist, 1949-62; writer, 1960—. Member: Danish Academy. Awards, honors: Louisianaprisen, 1964; Carol Mollers humoristlegat, 1965; Arbeidernes faellesorganisations kulturpris, 1965; Kritikerprisen, 1966.

WRITINGS—In English translation: Selected Poems, translated from the original Danish by Alexander Taylor, Princeton University Press, 1975.

Other writings: Kamera ned koekkenadgang, Borgen, 1962; Nikke nikke nambo og andre danske boernerim og remser, [Denmark], 1963; Lille Peter Dille, [Denmark], 1964; Den indre bowlerhat, Borgen, 1964; Puderne, Borgen, 1965; (author of text) Lise Roos, Os, Borgen, 1966; Portraetgalleri, Borgen, 1966; Snoevsen og Eigil og katten i saekken, Borgen, 1967; Den musikalske aal, Borgen, 1967; Hov-hov, Andelsbogtrykkeriet i Odense, 1968; Benny Andersen, Gjellerup, 1968; Den haese drage, Borgen, 1969; Det sidste oeh og andre digte, Borgen, 1969.

Snoevsen paa sommerferie, Borgen, 1970; Lejemorderen og andre spil, Borgen, 1970; Man burde burde, Borgen, 1971; Her i reservatet, Borgen, 1971; (with Henning Carlsen) Man sku' vaere noget ved musikken—Oprindelig arbejdstitel:

Den drejer hver sin vej, Borgen, 1972; Snoevsen og Snoevsine, Borgen, 1972; Svantes viser, Borgen, 1972; Barnet der blev aeldre og aeldre: Kronikker og erindringer, Borgen, 1973; Personlige papirer, Borgen, 1974; (with Carlsen) En lykkelig skilsmisse, Borgen, 1975; Nomader med noder, Borgen, 1976; Under begge oejne: Digte, Borgen, 1978; Orfeus i undergrunden, Borgen, 1979.

Scripts: "Snak," first broadcast on radio, 1965; "Leimorderen," first broadcast on radio, 1969; "Glassplinten," first broadcast on television, 1969; "Faders kop," first broadcast on television, 1970.

BIOGRAPHICAL/CRITICAL SOURCES: Times Literary Supplement, October 15, 1976.*

* * *

ANDERSON, Bernice G(oudy) 1894-

PERSONAL: Born November 17, 1894, in Lawrence, Kan.; daughter of Arthur Lincoln (a Congregational minister) and Anita (Melvin) Goudy; married Lyle Anderson, October 24, 1919 (died March 14, 1965); children: Robert Arthur. Education: Attended Academy of Doane College, 1911-12; attended Emporia Normal Teachers College, 1914; Washburn College (now University), diploma, 1917. Religion: Congregationalist. Home: 726 South Chestnut St., Escondido, Calif. 92025.

CAREER: Music teacher at public elementary schools in Norton, Kan., 1914-16, and elementary and high schools in Cedar Vale, Kan., 1917-19, and Partridge, Kan.; private voice teacher, 1919-30. Guest on local television programs. Member: Kansas Authors Club (life member), Poetry Society of Kansas (past president; historian), NONOSO (honorary member), Sigma Alpha Iota. Awards, honors: First prize from Kansas Authors Club, 1930, for poem, "Pageant of the Seasons"; Senator Capper Awards, 1955, for children's operettas, "Purple on the Moon" and "Cabbage Patch Magic."

WRITINGS—Juvenile: Topsy Turvy's Pigtails, Rand McNally, 1930; Topsy Turvy and the Tin Clown, Rand McNally, 1932; Indian Sleep Man Tales, Caxton, 1940; Trickster Tales From Prairie Lodgefires, Abingdon, 1979.

Juvenile operettas: Cabbage Patch Magic (first performed in the elementary school at Partridge, Kan., May 3, 1955, Willis Co., 1955; Purple on the Moon (first performed in Peabody, Kan., March 12, 1955), Raymond A. Hoffman Co., 1955.

Work represented in anthologies, including Kansas Poets, Harrison, 1935. Contributor of stories, articles, and poems to magazines.

SIDELIGHTS: Bernice Anderson told CA: "I had done considerable research among various tribes of American Indians for my two books of authentic legends and have a great accumulation of material yet unused.

"While my husband and I were in Central Africa from early 1962 to the middle of 1964, I collected some material among the Chinyanja- and Tumbuka-speaking tribes for future manuscripts. My husband was sent to Nyasaland (now Malawi) to act as an economic and agricultural adviser. It was a rewarding experience, interesting and challenging.

"On the way home we traveled for two months in Europe and the Scandinavian countries, which provided more material for future writings, if time doesn't run out on me!"

AVOCATIONAL INTERESTS: Photography (color transparencies and color prints), gardening, collecting curios, bells, shells, wall plates, antiques, and autographed books.

ANDERSON, LaVere Francis Shoenfelt 1907-

PERSONAL: Born April 15, 1907, in Muskogee, Okla; daughter of George Burket and Jessie Jonesia (Jordan) Shoenfelt; married French Anderson, June 16, 1928; children: Jessica (Mrs. Lloyd G. Nidiffer), Audrey (Mrs. Thomas C. Thixton), W. French. *Education:* University of Tulsa, B.A., 1928; graduate study, Columbia University, 1928, and University of Oklahoma, 1951. *Religion:* Presbyterian. *Home:* 232 East 27th Pl., Tulsa, Okla. 74114.

CAREER: Tulsa Daily World, Tulsa, Okla., reporter, 1930-42, book editor, 1942-50, 1952-76; University of Tulsa, Tulsa, instructor, in creative writing, 1942-50, 1952-68; Philbrook Art Center, Tulsa, instructor in creative writing, 1953-61. Lecturer, panel member, Regional Writers' Conference, Springfield, Mo. *Member:* National League of American Pen Women, American Association of University Women, Daughters of the American Revolution, Theta Sigma Phi, Delta Delta Delta.

WRITINGS—Juvenile biography; all published by Garrard, except as noted: *Stories About Abraham Lincoln to Read Aloud,* illustrations by Tony Tallarico, Wonder Books, 1965; *Robert Todd Lincoln, President's Boy,* illustrations by Al Fiorentino, Bobbs-Merrill, 1967; *Quanah Parker, Indian Warrior for Peace,* illustrations by Russell Hoover, 1970; *Sitting Bull, Great Sioux Chief,* illustrations by Cary, 1970; *Abe Lincoln and the River Robbers,* illustrations by Cary, 1971; *Frederic Remington, Artist on Horseback,* 1971; *Tad Lincoln, Abe's Son,* illustrations by William Hutchinson, 1971; *Allan Pinkerton: First Private Eye,* illustrations by Frank Vaughn, 1972; *Black Hawk, Indian Patriot,* illustrations by Cary, 1972; *Martha Washington: First Lady of the Land,* illustrations by Cary, 1973; *The Story of Johnny Appleseed,* illustrations by Kelly Oechsli, 1974; *Mary Todd Lincoln: President's Wife,* illustrations by Cary, 1975; *Saddles and Sabers: Black Men in the Old West,* illustrations by Herman Vestal, 1975; *Mary McLeod Bethune, Teacher With a Dream,* illustrations by Hutchinson, 1976.

Juvenile fiction: *Balto, Sled Dog of Alaska,* illustrations by H. B. Vestal, Garrard, 1976; *Svea, the Dancing Moose,* illustrations by Richard Amundsen, Garrard, 1978.*

*   *   *

ANDERSON, Lee Stratton 1925-

PERSONAL: Born December 15, 1925, in Trenton, Ky.; son of Herbert Love and Corinne (Kirkpatrick) Anderson; married Elizabeth McDonald, June 10, 1950; children: Corinne Elizabeth (Mrs. Jeffrey P. Adams); Mary Stewart. *Education:* University of Chattanooga (now University of Tennessee at Chattanooga), A.B., 1948. *Politics:* Independent. *Religion:* Presbyterian. *Home:* 220 North Crest Rd., Chattanooga, Tenn. 37404. *Office: Chattanooga News-Free Press,* 400 11th St., Chattanooga, Tenn. 37401.

CAREER: Chattanooga News-Free Press, Chattanooga, Tenn., reporter, 1942-48, associate editor, 1948-58, editor, 1958—. Notable assignments include coverage of national political conventions, the Soviet Union, Red China, the Middle East, and daily editorials. President of Anderson-Meyers Enterprises Inc., 1957—, Chattanooga Convention and Visitor's Bureau, 1958, and Hamilton Enterprises Inc., 1973—. Chairman of Chattanooga chapter of American Red Cross, 1968-70, and United Fund, 1979. Operator of Confederama, 1957—. *Military service:* U.S. Army Air Forces, 1944-45; became aviation cadet. U.S. Army Reserves, 1943—; became major. *Member:* Rotary Club (president,

1964-65), Sigma Chi. *Awards, honors:* Recipient of numerous Freedoms Foundation awards for editorials and lectures.

WRITINGS: Valley of the Shadow: The Battles of Chickamauga and Chattanooga, 1863, Hudson Printing and Lithographing Co., 1959.

*   *   *

ANDERSON, Maggie
See ANDERSON, Margaret

*   *   *

ANDERSON, Margaret 1948-
(Maggie Anderson)

PERSONAL: Born September 23, 1948, in New York, N.Y.; daughter of Orval James (a teacher of English) and Frances (a teacher of political science; maiden name, Delancy) Anderson. *Education:* Attended West Virginia Wesleyan College, 1966-68; West Virginia University, A.B., 1970, M.A., 1973, M.S.W., 1977. *Home and office address:* Route 1, Box 172-A, Glen Easton, W.Va. 26039.

CAREER: West Virginia Rehabilitation Center, Institute, teacher of adult creative writing classes, 1973-75, rehabilitation counselor for the blind, 1975-77; West Virginia University, Morgantown, research writer for Research and Training Center, 1977; writer, 1977—; poet-in-residence in Marshall County, W.Va., 1977-80. *Member:* National Rehabilitation Association, National Association of Social Workers, Coordinating Council of Literary Magazines, Poets and Writers, Feminist Writers Guild, Phi Beta Kappa. *Awards, honors:* Grant from West Virginia Arts and Humanities Commission, 1980.

WRITINGS: (Editor with Winston Fuller and Irene McKinney) *Trellis One,* Trellis Press Association, 1973; (editor with Fuller and McKinney) *The First Trellis Supplement,* Trellis Press Association, 1974; (editor with Fuller and McKinney) *Trellis Two,* Trellis Press Association, 1976.

Under name Maggie Anderson: (Editor) *Trellis Three,* Trellis Press Association, 1979; *The Great Horned Owl* (poems), Icarus Press, 1979; *Years That Answer* (poems), Harper, 1980.

Work represented in anthologies, including *New Regional Anthology.* Contributor of poems and reviews to magazines, including *Stone, West Virginia Arts News, Thirteenth Moon, Feminary,* and *Laurel Review.* Editor of *Trellis,* 1973—.

WORK IN PROGRESS: A Place for Poetry, essays on teaching poetry; *In Her Fields* (tentative title), poems; translating work of nineteenth- and twentieth-century Austrian women poets.

SIDELIGHTS: Margaret Anderson wrote: "The early circumstances of my life were extremely favorable to writing and to discovering books and art. I grew up in New York City (I moved to West Virginia when I was thirteen), with access to libraries, museums, and theatre and, since my parents were both teachers, there were always books in my home. Since West Virginia is isolated, both culturally and geographically, my discoveries here have become those of the natural world and the plants and animals with which we share it.

"My writing concerns itself with recovery and preservation, and it comes directly out of my early contradictory but enriching city-rural background. I have traveled in the United States and in northern Scandinavia. Travel feeds the writing, as does translating, reading, walking, growing vegetables, making music—anything observed closely and lived intensely and fully. Most important to writing (besides, of course, perseverance), is the time, uninterrupted, in which to do it. In the past two years, I have had that time, and I consider myself very fortunate. I have also worked in circumstances where I did not have that time, and I know what loss and, perhaps irreparable damage, that can cause.

"The writing that interests me most right now is that being done by women (especially my companions in the Appalachian region) and that being done by children. I am working, at present, on a long narrative poem."

* * *

ANDERSON, Walter 1944-

PERSONAL: Born August 31, 1944, in Mount Vernon, N.Y.; son of William Henry and Ethel (Crolly) Anderson; married Loretta Gritz, September 9, 1967; children: Eric Christian, Melinda Christe. *Education:* Westchester Community College, A.A., 1970; Mercy College, Dobbs Ferry, N.Y., B.S. (summa cum laude), 1972. *Home:* 5 Ridgeway, White Plains, N.Y. 10605. *Office:* Parade Publications, Inc., 750 Third Ave., New York, N.Y. 10017.

CAREER/WRITINGS: Reporter Dispatch, White Plains, N.Y., general assignment reporter, 1967-68, night city editor, 1968-69; Westchester Rockland Newspapers, White Plains, police reporter, 1969-70, help editor for action line, 1970-71, investigative reporter, 1971-72, managing editor of news bureau, 1972-73; *Standard Star,* New Rochelle, N.Y., editor and general manager, 1974-75; *Reporter Dispatch,* editor and general manager, 1975-77; *Parade* magazine, New York, N.Y., senior editor, 1977-78, managing editor, 1978-80, executive editor, 1980—. Notable assignments include an expose of the black market in methadone, an eyewitness account of the shooting of Joe Colombo, and a story that uncovered a heroin network, resulting in the arrest of more than fifty dealers. Guest lecturer at Columbia University, New York University, and University of Massachusetts; adjunct professor of psychology and sociology at Westchester Community College, 1972—. Chairman of board of trustees of Mercy College, Dobbs Ferry, N.Y. Director of St. Vincent's Hospital. *Military service:* U.S. Marine Corps, 1961-66, served in Vietnam; became sergeant.

MEMBER: Overseas Press Club, Psi Chi, Sigma Delta Chi. *Awards, honors:* Frank Tripp Memorial Award from Gannett Group, 1971, for report on the shooting of Joe Colombo and for "Inside New York Prisons"; President's Medal for Pre-eminent Scholarship, 1972; *Standard Star* received Frank Tripp Public Service Award and Community Service Award from the Public Relations Society of America, both 1975, while Anderson was editor and general manager; *Reporter Dispatch* received awards for editorial excellence from the New York State Publishers Association and New York State Associated Press, both 1976, while Anderson was editor and general manager; has received individually and shared numerous other journalism awards.

SIDELIGHTS: Anderson told *CA:* "I hope a single driving desire remains with me always, that is to discover and encourage writers of merit. Imagine the sense of achievement, the joy of fulfillment to contribute to the career of a Twain, a Hemingway, or a Mailer. I envy the editors who urged each on before their fame. To share, even in the least of ways, in the growth of a creative talent must be the highest goal of an editor, if his career is to matter at all."

AVOCATIONAL INTERESTS: Jogging, fishing.

ANGEL, J(ohn) Lawrence 1915-

PERSONAL: Born March 21, 1915, in London, England; naturalized citizen; son of John and Elizabeth Day (Seymour) Angel; married Margaret Seymour Richardson (a teacher and poet), July 1, 1937; children: Elizabeth Richardson (Mrs. Joel Hirsh Feigon), Stephen Bearne, Jonathan Seymour. *Education:* Harvard University, A.B. (magna cum laude), 1936, Ph.D., 1942. *Politics:* Democrat. *Religion:* Unitarian-Universalist. *Home:* 5311 Wriley Rd., Bethesda, Md. 20016. *Office:* Department of Anthropology, Smithsonian Institution, Washington, D.C. 20560.

CAREER: University of California, Berkeley, assistant professor of anthropology, 1941-42; University of Minnesota, Minneapolis, assistant professor of anthropology, 1942-43; Jefferson Medical College, Philadelphia, Pa., 1943-62, began as associate professor, became professor of anthropology and anatomy; Smithsonian Institution, Washington, D.C., physical anthropologist, 1962—. Professorial lecturer at George Washington University, 1963—; member of faculty at University of Pennsylvania, 1945-62, U.S. Naval Hospital, 1954-62, Harvard University, 1964-70, and Johns Hopkins University, 1964—.

MEMBER: American Association of Physical Anthropologists (vice-president, 1962-64), American Anthropological Association, American Association of Anatomists, American Society of Human Genetics, American Association for the Advancement of Science, American Association of Forensic Sciences, American Medical Authors, Medical Institute of America, Society for Applied Anthropology. *Awards, honors:* Guggenheim fellow, 1949.

WRITINGS: Troy: The Human Remains, Princeton University Press, 1951; *The People of Lerna: Analysis of a Prehistoric Aegean Population,* Smithsonian Institution Press, 1971. Contributor to anthropology journals. Associate editor of *American Anthropologist, American Journal of Physical Anthropology,* and *Clinical Orthopaedics.*

WORK IN PROGRESS: Health and the Growth of Civilization; research on health, disease, and demography, related to historical change in the eastern Mediterranean and the colonial United States; research on occupation and body structure.

SIDELIGHTS: Angel told *CA:* "There is a positive feedback situation between health and civilization, though all societies carry a load of disease. Skeletons tell us their state of health through length of life, depth of pelvis, growth arrest lines, teeth, and stature (to some extent). Psychological health, as shown in effective blending of diverse peoples, is vital to civilization. Slavery, war, waste, and pollution are obvious enemies of health. Reading occupation from stress of joints is an obvious next step in identifying unknown skeletons for the FBI and the police."

* * *

ANGEL, Marc D(wight) 1945-

PERSONAL: Born July 25, 1945, in Seattle, Wash.; son of Victor B. and Rachel Angel; married Gilda Schuchalter (a free-lance writer), August 23, 1967; children: Jeffrey, Ronda, Elana. *Education:* Yeshiva College, B.A., 1967; Rabbi Isaac Elchanan Theological Seminary, ordination, 1970; Yeshiva University, M.S., 1970, Ph.D., 1975; City College of the City University of New York, M.A., 1970. *Home:* 30 West 70th St., New York, N.Y. 10023. *Agent:* Jean V. Naggar Literary Agency, 420 East 72nd St., New York, N.Y. 10021. *Office:* Shearith Israel, 8 West 70th St., New York, N.Y. 10023.

CAREER: Shearith Israel (Spanish and Portuguese synagogue), New York, N.Y., rabbi, 1969—. Managing editor of *Tradition.* Member of governing boards of National Child Labor Committee, Federation of Jewish Philanthropies of New York, and Union of Sephardic Congregations. *Member:* Rabbinical Council of America.

WRITINGS: The Jews of Rhodes: The History of a Sephardic Community, Sepher-Hermon Press, 1978; (editor) *Studies in Sephardic Culture,* Sephardic House, 1980; (editor) *Rabbi David de Sola Pool,* Amiel Publishers, 1980. Also author of *La America: The Sephardic Experience in the United States,* 1981. Contributor to theology journals.

WORK IN PROGRESS: Voices in Exile, studies of the writings and teachings of Sephardic sages and mystics following the expulsion of Jews from Spain in 1492.

SIDELIGHTS: Angel wrote: "There are very few researchers and writers dealing with the experience of Sephardim—Jews of Spanish origin. My work attempts to fill this void. As rabbi of the oldest Jewish congregation in North America (founded in 1654), I am by birth and professional association deeply involved with Spanish Jews."

BIOGRAPHICAL/CRITICAL SOURCES: Murray Polner, *Rabbi,* Holt, 1977.

*   *   *

ANGELIQUE, Pierre
See BATAILLE, Georges

*   *   *

ANGELL, George 1945-

PERSONAL: Born March 19, 1945, in Norwalk, Conn.; son of Nicholas (a U.S. Treasury Agent) and Margaret Angell. *Education:* New York University, B.A., 1967. *Home:* 22 Crawford Rd., Westport, Conn. 06880. *Office:* 1260 North Dearborn, Chicago, Ill. 60610.

CAREER: Floor broker for MidAmerica Commodity Exchange, Chicago, Ill.

WRITINGS: Winning in the Commodities Market, Doubleday, 1979; *Commodity Spread Trading,* Windsor Books, 1981. Author of "Money," a financial column in *Gentlemen's Quarterly.* Contributor to magazines, including *Money, Moneysworth,* and *California Business.* Contributing editor of *Commodities.*

SIDELIGHTS: Angell wrote: "I am a business and financial writer whose primary interest is the commodity futures market."

BIOGRAPHICAL/CRITICAL SOURCES: Publishers Weekly, March 19, 1979.

*   *   *

ANGELL, Robert Cooley 1899-

PERSONAL: Born April 29, 1899, in Detroit, Mich.; son of Alexis Caswell and Fanny Carey (Cooley) Angell; married Esther Robbins Kennedy, December 23, 1922; children: James Kennedy, Sarah Caswell. *Education:* University of Michigan, A.B., 1921, A.M., 1922, Ph.D., 1924. *Home:* 826 Earhart Rd., Ann Arbor, Mich. 48105.

CAREER: University of Michigan, Ann Arbor, instructor, 1922-26, assistant professor, 1926-30, associate professor, 1930-35, professor of sociology, 1935-69, professor emeritus, 1969—, chairman of department, 1940-52, director of college honors program, 1957-61. Director of tensions project for

UNESCO in Paris, France, 1949-50; member of U.S. national commission for UNESCO, 1950-56, vice-chairman of commission, 1953; member of charter study commission in Ann Arbor, 1953-55; Deiches Lecturer at Johns Hopkins University, 1957; co-director of Center for Research on Conflict Resolution, 1961-65; executive director of Sociological Resources for Secondary Schools, 1966-71. *Military service:* Air Corps Reserve, 1918-19; became second lieutenant. U.S. Army Air Forces, 1942-45; became lieutenant colonel; received decorated Bronze Star.

MEMBER: International Studies Association, International Sociological Association (president, 1953-56), American Sociological Association (president, 1951), American Civil Liberties Union, American Association of University Professors, Michigan Academy of Sciences, Arts, and Letters, Michigan Sociological Society, Sociological Research Association, University of Michigan Research Club, Phi Beta Kappa, Delta Kappa Epsilon, Democrat Club, Ann Arbor Golf and Outing Club. *Awards, honors:* Hum.D. from Western Michigan University, 1967.

WRITINGS: The Campus: A Study of Contemporary Undergraduate Life in the American University, Appleton, 1928; (editor and author of introduction and notes) Charles Horton Cooley, *Sociological Theory and Social Research: Being Selected Papers of Charles Horton Cooley,* Holt, 1930, reprinted, Augusta Kelley, 1969; *A Study in Undergraduate Adjustment,* University of Chicago Press, 1930; *The Family Encounters the Depression,* Scribner's, 1936, reprinted, Peter Smith, 1965; *The Integration of American Society: A Study of Groups and Institutions,* McGraw, 1941, reprinted, Russell, 1974; (compiler) *Readings in American Social Classes,* [Ann Arbor, Mich.], 1945; *The Moral Integration of American Cities,* University of Chicago Press, 1951; *Free Society and Moral Crisis,* University of Michigan Press, 1958; (with Vera S. Dunham and J. David Singer) *A Study in the Values of Soviet and American Elites,* U.S. Naval Ordnance Test Station, 1963; (contributor) Leon Festinger, editor, *Research Methods in the Behavioral Sciences,* Holt, 1966; *Peace on the March: Transnational Participation,* Van Nostrand, 1969; *The Quest for World Order,* University of Michigan Press, 1979. Editor of *American Sociological Review,* 1946-48.

*   *   *

ANGIER, Roswell P. 1940-

PERSONAL: Born December 2, 1940, in New Haven, Conn.; son of Roswell P. and Viola (Buell) Angier; married Elizabeth Commager, 1962 (marriage ended, 1964); married Susan Hawley (a painter), December 20, 1966. *Education:* Harvard University, A.B., 1962; University of California, Berkeley, M.A., 1967. *Home and office:* 65 Pleasant St., Cambridge, Mass. 02139.

CAREER: Boston University, Boston, Mass., instructor in humanities, 1968-72; Art Institute of Boston, Boston, instructor in photography, 1975-80; University of Massachusetts, Boston, lecturer in photography, 1980—. Member of artists' advisory council of Massachusetts Arts and Humanities Foundation, 1977-78, artist-in-residence, 1978.

WRITINGS: (With Norman Hurst) *The Patriot Game,* David R. Godine, 1975; (contributor) *The Photographers' Choice,* Addison House, 1976; *"A Kind of Life": Conversations in the Combat Zone,* Addison House, 1976. Editor of *Fusion,* 1970-73.

WORK IN PROGRESS: Photographing and interviewing native Americans in towns bordering the Navajo reservation in New Mexico and Arizona.

ANNA, Timothy E. 1944-

PERSONAL: Born November 3, 1944, in Lexington, Ky.; son of Anthony E. (a teacher) and Sue (a banker; maiden name, Dickerson) Anna; married Mary Jadwiga Ekiel, September 12, 1970; children: Aaron Bolivar, Elizabeth Eugenia. Education: Duke University, B.A., 1966, M.A., 1968, Ph.D., 1969. Home: 215 Cambridge St., Winnipeg, Manitoba, Canada R3M 3E7. Office: Department of History, University of Manitoba, Winnipeg, Manitoba, Canada R3T 2N2.

CAREER: University of Manitoba, Winnipeg, assistant professor, 1969-74, associate professor, 1974-79, professor of history, 1979—. Member: Canadian Association of Latin American Studies, American Historical Association, Conference on Latin American History, Latin American Studies Association, Midwest Association of Latin American Studies. Awards, honors: Grants and fellowships from Canada Council and Social Science Research Council of Canada.

WRITINGS: The Fall of the Royal Government in Mexico City, University of Nebraska Press, 1978; The Fall of the Royal Government in Peru, University of Nebraska Press, 1979. Contributor to Cambridge History of Latin America. Contributor to history and Latin American studies journals.

WORK IN PROGRESS: Spain and the Loss of America.

SIDELIGHTS: Timothy Anna commented to CA: "The best part about an academic career is that it permits a person with the desire to write the time and support in which to write, while at the same time keeping in touch with students to whom the subject matter still has a touch of mystery and charm. The best thing about history as a subject is that it allows study of human society, politics, and emotions but imposes discipline and critical perspective. You have to be able to 'prove' or substantiate every assertion, yet you know all the time that there is no certainty. All you can do is make a case. This makes it a fascinating 'literary' pursuit."

*   *   *

ANNAND, J(ames) K(ing) 1908-

PERSONAL: Born February 2, 1908, in Edinburgh, Scotland; son of William (a plumber) and Maggie (a dressmaker; maiden name, Gold) Annand; married Beatrice Violet Lindsay, April 1, 1936; children: Rosemary Annand Mutch, Frances Annand Thomson, Pauline Annand Barnet, Lindsay Annand Sharratt. Education: University of Edinburgh, M.A., 1930. Office: Lallans, 174 Craigleith Rd., Edinburgh EH4 2EF, Scotland.

CAREER: High school history teacher in Edinburgh, Scotland, 1932-58; headmaster at school in Wigtownshire, Scotland, 1959-62; principal history teacher at high school in Edinburgh, 1962-71; writer, 1971—. Member of council of Royal Burgh of Whithorn, 1960-62. Military service: Royal Navy, 1941-46. Royal Naval Volunteer Reserve; became lieutenant. Member: International P.E.N., Association for Scottish Literary Studies, Scottish History Society, Scots Language Society, Scottish Mountaineering Club, Scottish Youth Hostels Association (honorary vice-president), Edinburgh Children's Book Group (honorary member). Awards, honors: Burns Chronicle Prize, 1956; special award from Scottish Arts Council, 1979.

WRITINGS—Books of poems: Two Voices, Macdonald Publishers, 1968; Poems and Translations, Akros Publications, 1975; Songs From Carmina Burana, Macdonald Publishers, 1978.

Children's poems: Sing It Aince for Pleisure, Macdonald

Publishers, 1965, 4th edition, 1974; Twice for Joy, Macdonald Publishers, 1973, 3rd edition, 1979; Thrice to Show Ye, Macdonald Publishers, 1980.

Editor: Hugh MacDiarmid: Early Lyrics, Akros Publications, 1968, 2nd edition, 1969; A Scots Handsel, Oliver & Boyd, 1980. Contributor to magazines, including Chapman, Voice of Scotland, Words, English World Wide, and Trapani Nuova. Editor of Broughton, 1925-26, Rebel Student, 1929, Lines Review, 1958-59, and Lallan's, 1973—.

WORK IN PROGRESS: Translating Wilhelm Busch's Max und Moritz into Scots verse.

SIDELIGHTS: Annand commented: "I have been interested in Scottish literature and language since my school days, and most of my creative writing has been in Scots. I had the good fortune to be influenced by the same teacher of English as Hugh MacDiarmid. My knowledge of German, French, and medieval Latin is sufficient to enable me to translate from these languages.

"I have also had a lifelong interest in the open air, in hill walking and mountaineering. I was a founding member of the Scottish Youth Hostels Association, and actively engaged in its development until called up for war service."

AVOCATIONAL INTERESTS: Photographing alpine flowers.

BIOGRAPHICAL/CRITICAL SOURCES: Akros, December, 1974.

*   *   *

APP, Austin Joseph 1902-

PERSONAL: Born May 24, 1902, in Milwaukee, Wis.; son of August Henry and Katherine (Obermaier) App. Education: St. Francis Seminary, Milwaukee, Wis., A.B., 1924; Catholic University of America, M.A., 1926, Ph.D., 1929. Politics: Republican. Religion: Roman Catholic. Home: 8207 Flower St., Takoma Park, Md. 20012.

CAREER: Catholic University of America, Washington, D.C., instructor in English, 1929-35; University of Scranton, Scranton, Pa., professor of English, 1935-42; Jaeger Machine Co., Columbus, Ohio, administrative assistant in personnel, 1943-44; Incarnate Word College, San Antonio, Tex., professor of English, 1944-48; Boniface Press, Takoma Park, Md., director, 1948—. Associate professor at LaSalle College, 1948-68. President of Federation of American Citizens of German Descent, 1960-66, honorary president, 1966—; chairman of Captive Nations Committee of Greater Philadelphia, 1965—. Lecturer in Germany, Austria, and the Netherlands. Military service: U.S. Army, Corps of Engineers, 1942-44.

MEMBER: Modern Language Association of America (life member), Catholic Central Union (life member), Steuben Society of America (president of Pastorius unit, 1949-59). Awards, honors: Award from Deutsches Kulturwerk Europaeischen Geistes, 1970; European Freedom Prize from Deutsche National Zeitung, 1975.

WRITINGS: Lancelot in English Literature, Catholic University of America, 1929; History's Most Terrifying Peace, Mission Press, 1946, reprinted, Boniface Press, 1970; Courtesy, Courtship, and Marriage, Mission Press, 1947; The True Concept of Literature, Mission Press, 1948; Making Good Talk (Catholic Book of the Month Club selection), Bruce, 1950; The Way to Creative Writing, Bruce, 1954; Making the Later Years Count, Bruce, 1960; Morgenthau Era Letters, Boniface Press, 1966; A Straight Look at the

Third Reich, Boniface Press, 1974; *German-American Voice for Truth and Justice,* Boniface Press, 1977; *The Tragedy of the Sudeten Games,* Boniface Press, 1979. Co-founder of *Best Sellers.*

SIDELIGHTS: App wrote: "Until the Potsdam Pact of World War II my interest was centered on English language and literature—teaching and writing it. After 1946 my first interest became revisionism of what converted World War II into 'history's most terrifying peace.' My chief vocational interest remained English literature. What permeated all my teaching and writing was the desire to help make Christian ideals more and more prevalent in the world. I taught that literature was a divine gift for insinuating high ideals and virtue into individuals and the world, that therefore it is an obligation of teachers and publicists to express themselves in the best and most fluent rhetoric they can. For historians and diplomats the top priority ought to be truth and justice: a just peace, not a lasting or enduring peace."

*   *   *

APPELBAUM, Stephen A(rthur) 1926-

PERSONAL: Born December 15, 1926, in New York, N.Y.; married wife, Ann (a psychiatrist), June 13, 1959; children: Eric Nicholas, Anita Carol. *Education:* University of Connecticut, B.A., 1948; graduate study at University of California, Los Angeles, 1952-53; Boston University, M.A., 1954, Ph.D., 1957; postdoctoral study at Topeka Institute for Psychoanalysis, 1962-70. *Office:* Menninger Foundation, P.O. Box 829, Topeka, Kan. 66601.

CAREER: Trainee in clinical psychology at Boston Veterans Administration Hospital, Boston, Mass.; trainee in clinical psychology at Brockton Veterans Administration Hospital, Brockton, Mass.; Children's Hospital, Boston, fellow in clinical psychology, 1956-57; Menninger Foundation, Topeka, Kan., fellow in clinical psychology, 1957-59, senior staff psychologist, 1959—, instructor at School of Psychiatry, 1961-64, member of psychotherapy training committee and teacher of psychotherapy, 1968—, director of psychology at C. F. Menninger Memorial Hospital, 1969—. Diplomate of American Board of Examiners in Professional Psychology; employed by Commonwealth of Massachusetts, Division of Legal Medicine, 1956-57; consultant to Kansas Treatment Center for Children. *Member:* American Psychological Association (fellow), Society for Projective Techniques (fellow), Kansas Psychological Association (fellow), Topeka Society for Psychoanalysis. *Awards, honors:* National Institute of Mental Health fellow, 1957-59.

WRITINGS: (Contributor) Milton Kornrich, editor, *Psychological Test Modifications,* C. C. Thomas, 1965; (contributor) Emanuel Frederick Hammer, editor, *Use of Interpretation in Treatment,* Grune, 1968; (with Richard S. Siegal and Irwin C. Rosen) *The Anatomy of Change: A Menninger Foundation Report on Testing the Effects of Psychotherapy,* Plenum, 1977; *Out in Inner Space: A Psychoanalyst Explores the New Therapies,* Doubleday, 1979. Contributor of articles and reviews to psychology and psychiatry journals.*

*   *   *

APPLETON, William S. 1934-

PERSONAL: Born May 7, 1934, in New York, N.Y.; son of Morris B. and Harriet S. Appleton; married Jane Scovell (a writer and teacher), June 1, 1958; children: Amy Sarah, Lucy Kate, William Scovell. *Education:* Hunter College (now of the City University of New York), B.A. (cum laude), 1955; Columbia University, M.D., 1959. *Home:* 59 Brewster St., Cambridge, Mass. 02138. *Office:* 51 Brattle St., Cambridge, Mass. 02138.

CAREER: Montefiore Hospital, Bronx, N.Y., intern, 1959-60; Massachusetts Mental Health Center, Boston, Mass., resident in psychiatry, 1960-63; private practice of psychiatry in Cambridge, Mass., 1963—. Fellow in child psychiatry at Thom Clinic for Children, Boston, 1963-64; assistant in psychiatry at Harvard University, 1963-66. Assistant clinical professor at Harvard University, 1969—, associate psychiatrist with university Health Services. *Member:* American Psychiatric Association (fellow), American Association for the Advancement of Science, Massachusetts Psychiatric Association, Massachusetts Medical Society, Phi Beta Kappa. *Awards, honors:* Third prize in Harry Solomon Essay Contest from Massachusetts Mental Health Center, 1963, first prize, 1966.

WRITINGS: (With John M. Davis) *Practical Clinical Psychopharmacology,* Medcom, 1973, 2nd edition, Williams & Wilkins, 1980; (with wife, Jane Appleton) *How Not to Split Up,* Doubleday, 1978; *Fathers and Daughters,* Doubleday, 1981; *Layman's Guide to Psychiatric Drugs,* Saunders, 1981. Author of "Analyst's Couch," a monthly column in *Cosmopolitan,* 1975—.

WORK IN PROGRESS: *Pills of the Mind.*

SIDELIGHTS: Appleton commented to *CA:* "I am interested in the responsible presentation of psychiatric knowledge to the public through books, magazines, and television."

In regard to his two most recent books, Appleton said: "*Fathers and Daughters* points out that the father's influence is so pervading that it is often unrecognized until it is too late. This book will aid women in organizing their thoughts about their fathers and their fathers' effect on their lives. I wrote *Layman's Guide to Psychiatric Drugs* because I wish to guide the public between the extremes of excessive medication use and unthinking avoidance of needed help."

*   *   *

ARCHER, John H(all) 1914-

PERSONAL: Born July 11, 1914, in Broadview, Saskatchewan, Canada; son of Charles Hall (a farmer) and Mary (Archer) Archer; married Alice Mary Widdup, August 25, 1939; children: John Widdup, Alice Mary-Lynn Archer Walsh. *Education:* Saskatchewan Normal School, teacher's certificate, 1933; University of Saskatchewan, B.A. (with honors), 1948, M.A., 1949; McGill University, B.L.S., 1949; Queen's University, Kingston, Ontario, Ph.D., 1969. *Religion:* Anglican Church of Canada. *Home:* 1530 MacPherson Ave., Regina, Saskatchewan, Canada S4S 4C9.

CAREER: Public school teacher in Broadview and Kipling, Saskatchewan, 1933-40; Government of Saskatchewan, Regina, administrative assistant to legislative librarian, 1949-51, legislative librarian, 1951-64, provincial archivist, 1957-62; Legislative Assembly of Saskatchewan, Regina, assistant clerk, 1962-64; McGill University, Montreal, Quebec, director of libraries, 1964-67; Queen's University, Kingston, Ontario, associate professor of history and university archivist, 1967-69; University of Saskatchewan, Regina Campus, Regina, principal, 1970-74; University of Regina, Regina, president, 1974-76, professor of western Canadian history, 1976-77, president emeritus, 1976—. President of Saskatchewan Council for Canadian Unity; vice-chairman and director of Saskatchewan 1980 Diamond Jubilee Corp.; member of Saskatchewan Heritage Advisory Board, board of regents of

Notre Dame College (Wilcox, Saskatchewan), prairie committee of National Book Festival, general assembly of Social Science Federation of Canada, Saskatchewan Electoral Boundaries Commission, and Saskatchewan Judicial Commission. Member of Saskatchewan Archives Board, 1951-64, Saskatchewan Research Council, 1970-76, and South Saskatchewan Hospital Board, 1972-76; project officer for Glassco Commission on Federal Government Organization, 1961-62; chairman of Saskatchewan Commission on Continuing Education, 1961-62, Saskatchewan Rural Development Advisory Group, 1975-76, and Celebrate Saskatchewan Citizens Committee, 1978-80; director of Canadian Centenary Council, 1965-67, and Wascana Centre Authority, 1970-79. *Military service:* Canadian Army, Artillery, 1940-45; served in England, Italy, and the Mediterranean; became captain.

MEMBER: Canadian Historical Association, Canadian Citizenship Federation, Canadian Library Association (president, 1967-68), Association of Canadian Archivists, Institute of Public Administration of Canada, Bibliographical Society of Canada, Royal Canadian Legion, Royal Society of Arts, Agriculture, and Commerce (fellow), United Services Institute, Champlain Society, Institute of Professional Librarians of Ontario, Quebec Library Association, Canadian Club, Men's University Club, Assiniboia Club. *Awards, honors:* Coronation Medal from Queen Elizabeth II, 1953, Silver Jubilee Medal, 1978.

WRITINGS: The Story of a Province: A History of Saskatchewan (juvenile), McClelland & Stewart, 1955; (with C. B. Koester) *Footprints in Time,* House of Grant, 1965; (contributor) Richard Simeon, editor, *One Country or Two,* McGill-Queen's University Press, 1969; (contributor) *Canadian Business History,* Macmillan, 1972; (contributor) Simeon, editor, *Must Canada Fail?,* McGill-Queen's University Press, 1978.

Editor: Billy Bock, *The Book of Humbug,* Modern Press, 1958; Charles Schwartz, *Search for Stability,* McClelland & Stewart, 1959; Bock, *Skeletons,* Modern Press, 1960; George Shepherd, *West of Yesterday,* McClelland & Stewart, 1966; (with Robert Peterson) *The Best of Billy Bock,* Modern Press, 1967; John H. Blackburn, *Land of Promise,* Macmillan, 1970; J. G. Diefenbaker, *One Canada,* Macmillan, Volume I, 1975, Volume II, 1976, Volume III, 1977. Canadian advisory editor of *Americana,* 1957-65; member of editorial board of *Saskatchewan History,* 1957-62.

Author of "History of the Canadian West," broadcast by CTV-TV, 1978; "The Saskatchewan Story," a series broadcast by provincial radio stations, 1978-79. Author of historical booklets. Contributor of articles and reviews to history, archival, and library journals.

WORK IN PROGRESS: A history of Saskatchewan, publication by Saskatchewan Archives Board expected in 1980.

SIDELIGHTS: Archer commented to *CA:* "I was farm born, educated in Saskatchewan and in central Canada, was overseas for five years, and came back to Saskatchewan because I find it the most interesting and exciting province in Canada. The arts are experiencing a dramatic upsurge of interest and public participation, and the writing of local histories flourishes. Saskatchewan has made significant contributions to Canadian life in cooperation, public ownership, medicare, and other areas as well, and I respond to the vibrant community thrust for the fuller life.

"My current interests are in promoting the teaching and study of Canadian regional and provincial history in schools. Canada is a federal state but the constitution, as it has devel-

oped, has permitted the growth of strong regional interests and quite distinct provincial societies. This is not to be deplored. Canada is a modern state coping with the facts of geography, economic differences, and multiculturalism. The constitution must change further to accommodate these facts. I believe Saskatchewan will take a leading role in the process of change as this province has come to terms with cultural differences, a harsh environment, and the social measures needed to permit security and stability."

AVOCATIONAL INTERESTS: Bridge, golf, watching football games, curling.

*   *   *

ARCHIBALD, (Rupert) Douglas   1919-

PERSONAL: Born April 25, 1919, in Port of Spain, Trinidad; son of Charles George (an accountant) and Ethel (Gerbig) Archibald; married Maureen Wedderburn Berry, May 23, 1953; children: Jane Harriett, Patrick Douglas. *Education:* McGill University, B.Eng., 1946. *Politics:* None. *Religion:* Roman Catholic. *Home:* 13 Elizabeth St., St. Clair, Port of Spain, Trinidad and Tobago, West Indies.

CAREER: Trinidad Government Railways, student engineer, 1935-41, assistant maintenance engineer, 1946-49; private practice as consulting civil engineer, 1949-63; Trinidad and Tobago Telephone Service, general manager, 1963-68; Trinidad and Tobago Telephone Co. Ltd., managing director, 1968-69; Trinidad Engineering and Research Ltd., Port of Spain, director, 1970—. Riot police officer with Trinidad Special Police, 1937, platoon commander, 1940-41. Head of Trinidad Railway Board, 1963-65, and Trinidad and Tobago Central Water Distribution Authority, 1964-65; vice-chairman of Trinidad and Tobago Public Transport Service Corp., 1965-67. Tutor at University of the West Indies, 1971, 1973, and 1975. *Military service:* Trinidad Army, Light Infantry, 1938-40; became sergeant. Canadian Army Reserve, 1943-45; became second lieutenant.

MEMBER: Readers and Writers Guild of Trinidad and Tobago (founding member; past president), Association of Professional Engineers of Trinidad and Tobago (founding member; past president), Historical Society of Trinidad and Tobago (president, 1967—), Engineering Institute of Canada. *Awards, honors:* Award from Theatre Guild, 1962.

WRITINGS: Isidore and the Turtle (novel), Extra-Mural Studies Unit, University of the West Indies, 1977.

Plays: *Junction Village* (two-act; first produced in Port of Spain, Trinidad, 1954; produced in London, England, 1955), Extra-Mural Studies Unit, University of the West Indies, 1958; *Old Maid's Tale* (one-act; first produced in Port of Spain, Trinidad, 1965), Extra-Mural Studies Unit, University of the West Indies, 1966; *Anne Marie* (three-act; first produced in Port of Spain, Trinidad, 1958; produced in London, England, 1976), Extra-Mural Studies Unit, University of the West Indies, 1967; *The Bamboo Clump* (three-act; first produced in Port of Spain, Trinidad, 1962), Extra-Mural Studies Unit, University of the West Indies, 1967; *The Rose Slip* (three-act; first produced in Port of Spain, Trinidad, 1962), Extra-Mural Studies Unit, University of the West Indies, 1972; *Island Tide* (three-act; first produced in San Fernando, Trinidad), Extra-Mural Studies Unit, University of the West Indies, 1972.

Author of television play, "My Good Friend Justice," 1974. Writer for radio series "That Family Next Door" and "Island Tide." Editor of *Progress,* 1952; member of editorial board of newspaper, *Clarion,* 1954-56.

ARECCO, Vera Lustig
    See LUSTIG-ARECCO, Vera

*   *   *

ARMACOST, Michael Hayden 1937-

PERSONAL: Born April 15, 1937, in Cleveland, Ohio; married, 1959; children: three. *Education:* Carleton College, B.A., 1958; Columbia University, M.A., 1961, Ph.D., 1965. *Home:* 19-5 Sendagi, 5 Chome, Bunkyo-ku, Tokyo, Japan.

CAREER: Pomona College, Claremont, Calif., instructor, 1962-65, assistant professor, 1965-68, associate professor of international relations, 1968-70; U.S. Department of State, Washington, D.C., special assistant to U.S. ambassador to Japan, in Tokyo, 1969—. Visiting associate professor at International Christian University, Tokyo, 1968-69. *Member:* American Political Science Association. *Awards, honors:* White House fellow, 1969-70.

WRITINGS: The Politics of Weapons Innovation: The Thor-Jupiter Controversy, Columbia University Press, 1969; (with Michael M. Stoddard) *The Foreign Relations of the United States,* Dickenson, 1969, 2nd edition, 1974.

BIOGRAPHICAL/CRITICAL SOURCES: Nation, February 16, 1970; *Science,* May 8, 1970; *Choice,* June, 1970; *Annals of the American Academy of Political and Social Science,* July, 1970.*

*   *   *

ARMSTRONG, Joseph Gravitt 1943-

PERSONAL: Born August 23, 1943, in Fort Worth, Tex.; son of Emmett C. and Dorthadele (Greathouse) Gravitt; children: Doyle C.A. (adopted). *Education:* Trinity University, B.A., 1965; University of Texas, J.D., 1968. *Home:* 10 Mitchell Pl., New York, N.Y. 10017. *Office:* New York Magazine Corporation, 755 Second Ave., New York, N.Y. 10017.

CAREER/WRITINGS: Admitted to the Bar of Texas, 1968; Wertheim & Co. (investment bankers), New York City, associate, 1968-72; *Family Week,* New York City, assistant to publisher, 1972-73; *Rolling Stone,* New York City, president and publisher, 1973-77; New York Magazine Corporation, New York City, president, editor in chief and publisher of *New York* and *New West,* 1977—. *Member:* American Bar Association, Texas Bar Association. *Awards, honors:* Named Outstanding Young Man in America by U.S. Junior Chamber of Commerce, 1969.

*   *   *

ARNOLD, R. Douglas 1950-

PERSONAL: Born January 31, 1950, in Plattsburgh, N.Y.; son of Robert D. (a businessman) and Miriam (Hughes) Arnold; married Helen Repas (a policy consultant), August 26, 1972. *Education:* Union College, Schenectady, N.Y., B.A., 1972; Yale University, M.Phil., 1974, Ph.D., 1977. *Home:* 61 Stanworth Lane, Princeton, N.J. 08540. *Office:* Department of Politics, Princeton University, Princeton, N.J. 08544.

CAREER: Brookings Institution, Washington, D.C., research fellow, 1976-77; Princeton University, Princeton, N.J., instructor, 1977-78, assistant professor of politics and public affairs, 1978—. *Member:* American Political Science Association, Phi Beta Kappa.

WRITINGS: Congress and the Bureaucracy: A Theory of Influence, Yale University Press, 1979. Contributor to political science journals.

WORK IN PROGRESS: A book on the politics of policymaking in Congress.

*   *   *

ARROWSMITH, Pat 1930-

PERSONAL: Born March 2, 1930, in Leamington Spa, England; daughter of George Ernest and Margaret Vera (Kingham) Arrowsmith. *Education:* Newham College, Cambridge, B.A., 1951; attended Ohio University, 1951-52; University of Liverpool, certificate in social science, 1955. *Politics:* "Socialist/Pacifist." *Religion:* None. *Home:* 132c Middle Lane, London N.8, England. *Agent:* Bolt & Watson Ltd., 8-12 Old Queen St., Storey's Gate, London SW1H 9HP, England. *Office:* Amnesty International, 10 Southampton St., London, England.

CAREER: Community organizer in Chicago, Ill., 1952-53; Liverpool Family Service Unit, Liverpool, England, social caseworker, 1954; child care officer, 1955; nursing assistant at Deva Psychiatric Hospital, 1956-57; child care officer, 1964; reporter for *Peace News,* 1965; gardener, 1966-68; researcher for Society of Friends Race Relations Committee, 1969-71; caseworker for National Council for Civil Liberties, 1971; Amnesty International, London, England, editorial assistant, 1971—. Artist, with exhibitions of watercolors. Organizer for Direct Action Committee Against Nuclear War, Committee of One Hundred, and Campaign for Nuclear Disarmament, 1958-68; member of Troops Out Movement and Anti-Nazi League. *Member:* War Resisters' International, National Union of Journalists, Transport and General Workers Union, Gateways Club, Sappho.

WRITINGS: Jericho (novel), Cresset, 1965; *Somewhere Like This* (novel), W. H. Allen, 1970; *To Asia in Peace,* Sidgwick & Jackson, 1972; *The Colour of Six Schools,* Society of Friends Race Relations Committee, 1972; *Breakout* (poems and drawings from prison), Student Publications Board, University of Edinburgh, 1975; *On the Brink,* Campaign for Nuclear Disarmament, 1980. Contributor of poems and articles to magazines, including *Guardian* and *New Society.*

WORK IN PROGRESS: Two novels, *The Agency* and *The Prisoner;* two childhood novels; a teenage diary; a book of poems.

*   *   *

ARTMANN, H(ans) C(arl) 1921-

PERSONAL: Born June 12, 1921, in Vienna, Austria. *Residence:* Malmoe, Sweden.

CAREER: Poet, novelist, playwright, and translator.

WRITINGS—In English: The Best of H. C. Artmann, edited by Klaus Reichert, Suhrkamp, 1970; *How Much, Schatzi?,* Suhrkamp, 1971; *Ompuel,* Artemis Verlag, 1974, translation by Olive Jones published as *Angus,* Methuen, 1974.

Other: *Med ana schwoazzn Dintn* (poetry), O. Mueller, 1958; *Von denen Husaren und anderen Seil-Taenzern* (stories), Piper, 1959; *Das Suchen nach dem gestrigen Tag; oder, Schnee auf einem heissen Brotwecken: Eintragungen eines bizarren Liebhabers,* Walter Verlag, 1964; *Verbarium* (poetry), Walter Verlag, 1966; *Gruenverschlossene Botschaft,* Residenz Verlag, 1967; *Allerleirausch: Neue schoene Kinderreime* (poetry), Rainer Verlag, 1967; *Fleiss und Industrie* (also see below), Suhrkamp, 1967; *Persische Quatrainen,* Collispress, 1967; *Toek ph'rong sueleng,* Richard P. Hartmannbibliothek, 1967.

Der handkolorierte Menschenfresser, Collispress, 1968;

(with Friedrich Achleitner and Gerhard Ruehm) *Hossn, Rosn, Baa* (poetry), Frick, 1968; *Die Anfangsbuchstaben der Flagge: Gesichten fuer Kajueten, Kamine, und Kinositze* (stories), Residenz Verlag, 1969; *Frankenstein in Sussex* [and] *Fleiss und Industrie*, Suhrkamp, 1969, *Frankenstein in Sussex* published separately, Lentz, 1974; *Kleinere Taschenkuenste, fast eine Chinoiserie* (play), Universal Edition, 1969; *Ein lilienweisser Brief aus Lincolnshire* (stories), Suhrkamp, 1969; *Ueberall wo Hamlet Hinkam*, Collispress, 1969.

Das im Walde verlorene Totem: Prosadichtungen, 1949-1953, Residenz Verlag, 1970; (contributor) Karlheinz Pilcz, *Grotesken: Zeichnungen, Radierungen*, Weilburg Verlag, 1970; (with Rainer Pichler and Hannes Schneider) *Yeti; oder, John, ich reise*, Willing Verlag, 1970; *Detective Magazine der Dreizehn* (stories), Residenz Verlag, 1971; *Der aeronautische Sindtbart; oder, Seltsame Luftreise von Niedercalifornien nach Crain*, Residenz Verlag, 1972; *Von der Weiner Seite*, Literarisches Colloquium, 1972; *Unter der Bedeckung eines Hutes*, Residenz Verlag, 1974; *Aus meiner Botanisiertrommel: Balladen und Naturgedichten* (stories), Residenz Verlag, 1975; (with Barbara Wehr) *Christopher und Peregrin und was weiter geschah*, Insel Verlag, 1975; *Gedichte ueber die Liebe und ueber die Lasterhaftigkeit*, Suhrkamp, 1975; *Die Jagd nach Dr. U.; oder, Ein einsamer Spiegel, in dem sich der Tag reflektiert*, Residenz Verlag, 1977; *Nachrichten aus Nord und Sued*, Residenz Verlag, 1978.

Translator: (And compiler) *Der Schluessel des Heiligen Patrick* (poetry), O. Mueller, 1959; Edward Lear, *Nonsense Verse*, Insel Verlag, 1964; Ignacy Bernstein, *Je laenger ein Blinder lebt, desto mehr seiht er*, Insel Verlag, 1965; Daisy Ashford, *Liebe und Ehe*, Insel Verlag, 1967; Francois Villon, *Baladn?*, Insel Verlag, 1968; Lars Gustafsson, *Die naechliche Huldigung*, Luchterhand, 1971; Howard Phillips Lovecraft, *Cthulhu: Geistergeschichten*, Suhrkamp, 1972.

Also author of sound recording. "Allerleirausch: Neue schoene Kinderreime [und] Maerchen," released by Preiserrecords, c. 1960.

BIOGRAPHICAL/CRITICAL SOURCES: Forum, November, 1965; *Times Literary Supplement*, March 5, 1970, August 21, 1970, June 11, 1976.*

* * *

ASH, Maurice Anthony 1917-

PERSONAL: Born October 31, 1917; son of Wilfred Cracroft and Beatrice Ash; married Ruth Whitney Elmhirst, 1947; children: one son (deceased), three daughters. *Education:* Received B.Sc. from London School of Economics and Political Science, London. *Home:* Sharpham House, Ashprington, Totnes, Devonshire TQ9 7UT, England.

CAREER: Dartington Hall, trustee, 1964—, chairman of Dartington Hall Trust, 1972—. Member of Southwest Regional Economic Planning Council, 1965-68; founder of Harlow Arts Trust. *Military service:* British Army; served in Italy, Greece, and Africa; mentioned in dispatches. *Member:* Town and Country Planning Association (member of executive committee, 1956—; chairman of executive committee, 1969—), Reform Club.

WRITINGS: (Editor with Kenneth Barnes and others) *Who Are the Progressives Now?: An Account of an Educational Confrontation*, Routledge & Kegan Paul, 1969; *Regions of Tomorrow: Towards the Open City*, Schocken, 1969; *A Guide to the Structure of London*, Adams & Dart, 1972. Contributor to magazines.

BIOGRAPHICAL/CRITICAL SOURCES: New Statesman, March 14, 1969; *Times Literary Supplement*, April 17, 1969; *Encounter*, May, 1969; *Choice*, February, 1970.*

* * *

ATLAS, Helen Vincent 1931-

PERSONAL: Born June 28, 1931, in New York, N.Y.; daughter of Louis and Irene (Papkevich) Vincent; married Kenyon Gillespie, April 2, 1954 (divorced, 1958); married Sheldon M. Atlas, June 2, 1967. *Education:* Mount Holyoke College, A.B., 1953. *Home:* 211 Central Park W., New York, N.Y. 10024. *Office:* Dance News, 119 West 57th St., New York, N.Y. 10019.

CAREER: Columbia University, New York City, administrative assistant at Russian Institute, 1956-61; United Nations, New York City, interpreter of French and Russian into English, 1961-62; Hurok Concerts, Inc., New York City, interpreter for Russian and French concert troupes, 1963-69; *Dance News*, New York City, editor and publisher, 1969—. *Awards, honors:* Distinguished service award from U.S. Information Agency, 1959, for work at American Exhibition in Moscow.

WRITINGS: Natalia Bessmertnova, Dance Horizons, 1975.

Translator of plays: Eugene Ionesco, "Le Pieton de l'air"; Meilhac and Ludovic Halevy, "La Vie parisienne"; "Salut a Moliere"; Georges Feydeau, "Un Fil a la patte"; Henry de Montherlant, "La Reine Morte"; "La Troupe du Roi."

Contributor to *Stagebill* and *Dance News*.

* * *

ATTENBOROUGH, John 1908-

PERSONAL: Surname is pronounced *Att*-en-burr-er; born December 30, 1908, in Bromley, England; son of Ralph Ernest (a solicitor) and Dorothy Frances (Williams) Attenborough; married Edith Barbara Sandle, June 22, 1935; children: Philip John, Michael Francis, Juliet Mary (Mrs. Richard Bourne). *Education:* Trinity College, Oxford, M.A. (with honors), 1930. *Politics:* Liberal. *Religion:* Church of England. *Home:* 7 Roehampton Dr., Chislehurst, Kent BR7 6RS, England.

CAREER: In publishing, 1931-35; Hodder & Stoughton (publisher), Dunton Green, England, 1936-73, held various positions, including director of sales and publicity and chief executive; writer, 1973—. Member of board of directors of Lancet Ltd., 1946-70; chairman of Educational Associates in Hong Kong, 1960-74. Leader of Book Development Council missions to India and Sri Lanka, 1969, and Pakistan and Bangladesh, 1971. *Military service:* British Army, Royal Artillery, 1939-45; served in Europe and Africa; became major; mentioned in dispatches. *Member:* Publishers Association (president, 1965-67), Society of Bookmen, Athenaeum Club. *Awards, honors:* Member of Order of the British Empire, 1944, commander, 1972.

WRITINGS: Faithfully Yours, St. Hugh's Press, 1947; *A Living Memory: Hodder & Stoughton, 1868-1974*, Hodder & Stoughton, 1975; *One Man's Inheritance* (novel), St. Martin's, 1979. Contributor to trade journals.

WORK IN PROGRESS: Novels; short stories.

SIDELIGHTS: Attenborough commented to *CA:* "My motivation in writing comes from a lifetime in book publishing which has included apprenticeship in Germany and worldwide travel, six years of active wartime soldiering, strong Christian convictions, and a happy family.

"My family has been connected with the world of books for over one hundred years. Matthew Hodder, who founded Hodder & Stoughton, was my great grandfather. My uncle, Sir Ernest Hodder-Williams, was a best-selling author as well as a famous publisher. My wife's family controlled a wholesale book business in London's famous pre-war publishing quarter.

"For my part, I have always believed that book publishing is a business for young men. Hence, I decided to retire from Hodder & Stoughton on my sixty-fifth birthday. This decision, extremely rare among heads of London publishing houses, allowed me leisure time to research and write the history of Hodder & Stoughton. Written as a labor of love, this history was so widely reviewed that it came to be read by men and women with no direct book trade or literary connections. It was their letters that led me to write my first novel, *One Man's Inheritance,* a chronicle of one man's life, spanning the last seventy years and centering on a great house in the County of Kent.

"During a life spent in the company of books and bookmen, I have arrived at certain conclusions. First of all, for a publisher, only his authors matter. A publisher who blows his own trumpet is in the wrong job. Secondly, to win success, a publisher has no option but to live his job every hour of the waking day. Lucky is the publisher—and I have been lucky—whose wife and family come to terms with his enthusiasm and obsession. Thirdly, an author is born with an indefinable impulse which forces him to put pen to paper. No man or woman should take up authorship in order to earn a living, although today the successful author, with the help of films and television, rightly makes more money from writing than any publisher makes from publishing. To sum up, publishing and authorship, like war-time soldiering, are high-risk occupations. I am, by nature and inclination, a risk-taker. Thus, my three-sided career as soldier, publisher, and author has brought me much personal satisfaction and a great measure of luck.

"Membership in the Athenaeum Club in London and the Royal St. George's Golf Club in Kent are a fair indication of my ambivalent interests. Apart from an interest in books and a deeply-held Christian faith, I enjoy the frequent company of seven grandchildren and keep reasonably fit by playing golf. I also follow the sporting fortunes of the County of Kent (cricket) and Charlton Athletic (football) with truly English perversity: indeed, with the same fanatical loyalty (win or lose) that I once devoted to my authors on the Hodder & Stoughton list."

*   *   *

ATWATER, James David   1928-

PERSONAL: Born October 25, 1928, in Westfield, Mass.; son of William Henry and Vesta Buffum (Gannett) Atwater; married Patricia Anne Levington, January 15, 1955; children: Mary Elizabeth, Stephen Gannett, Christopher Perry, Andrew, Katharine, Jennifer. *Education:* Yale University, B.A., 1950. *Home:* 40 Mallard Rise, Irvington, N.Y. 10533. *Office: Time,* Time & Life Building, New York, N.Y. 10020.

CAREER: Time, New York City, correspondent, 1953-62; *Saturday Evening Post,* Indianapolis, Ind., contributing editor, 1963-66, senior editor, 1966-69; special assistant to the President of the United States in Washington, D.C., 1969-70; *Reader's Digest,* Pleasantville, N.Y., correspondent in London, 1970-73; *Time,* New York City, associate editor, 1973-77; senior editor, 1978—. *Military service:* U.S. Air Force, 1950-53; became first lieutenant.

WRITINGS: Time Bomb (novel), Viking, 1977. Also author with Ramon E. Ruiz of *Out From Under: Benito Juarez and Mexico's Struggle for Independence,* Doubleday.

WORK IN PROGRESS: Nonfiction on World War I.

*   *   *

AUCHMUTY, James Johnston   1909-

PERSONAL: Born November 29, 1909, in Portadown, Northern Ireland; son of James Wilson (a minister) and Annie Todd (Johnston) Auchmuty; married Margaret Walters, October 20, 1934; children: James Francis Giles, Rosemary Katherine. *Education:* Trinity College, Dublin, B.A., 1931, M.A., 1934, Ph.D., 1935. *Religion:* Anglican. *Home:* 9 Glynn St., Hughes, Australian Capital Territory 2605, Australia.

CAREER: University of Dublin, Dublin, Ireland, lecturer in education, 1936-46; University of Alexandria, Alexandria, Egypt, head of department of modern history, 1946-52; University of New South Wales, Kensington, senior lecturer, 1952-55, professor of history, 1955-64; University of Newcastle, Newcastle, Australia, professor of history, 1965-74, professor emeritus, 1975—, vice-chancellor and principal, 1965-74. Visiting professor at University of Leeds, 1976-77. Member of Australian National Commission for UNESCO, 1962-80, chairman, 1973-76. Chairman of Australian Humanities Research Council, 1962-65, Australian Commonwealth Advisory Committee on the Teaching of Asian Languages and Culture, 1969, Australian Vice-Chancellors Committee, 1969-71, and Australian National Inquiry Into Teacher Education, 1978-80.

MEMBER: Australian Academy of the Humanities (fellow), Royal Historical Society (fellow), Royal Irish Academy. *Awards, honors:* Commander of Order of the British Empire, 1971; LL.D. from University of Dublin, 1974; D.Litt. from University of Sydney and University of Newcastle, both 1974; Symons Award from Association of Commonwealth Universities, 1974.

WRITINGS: Irish Education: A Historical Survey, Harrap, 1937; *The U.S. Government and Latin American Independence, 1810-1830,* P. S. King, 1937; *Sir Thomas Wyse, 1791-1862,* P. S. King, 1939; *The Teaching of History,* Educational Co. of Ireland, 1940; *Lecky,* Longmans, Green, 1945; *John Hunter,* Oxford University Press, 1968; (editor) *The Voyage of Governor Phillip to Botany Bay,* Angus & Robertson, 1970.

Contributor: G. S. Harman and C. Selby Smith, editors, *Australian Higher Education,* Angus & Robertson, 1972; F. K. Crowley, editor, *A New History of Australia,* Heinemann, 1974; *The Australian Encyclopaedia,* Volume VI, Grolier Society of Australia, 1977. Contributor to history and education journals.

WORK IN PROGRESS: The British Empire During and After the American War of Independence.

SIDELIGHTS: Auchmuty commented to *CA:* "My historical work has chiefly been concerned with the expansion of Britain. Having lived in Ireland, Egypt, and Australia, I have found that for the period 1760-1860 the same figures occur again and again in different environments. My interest is in showing these connections. That I have written so much is simply due to my occupation."

AULT, Phil
    See AULT, Phillip H(alliday)

*   *   *

AULT, Phillip H(alliday)   1914-
    (Phil Ault)

PERSONAL: Born April 26, 1914, in Maywood, Ill.; son of Frank W. (a salesman) and Bernda H. (Halliday) Ault; married Karoline Byberg (a nurse), June 5, 1943; children: Frank, Ingrid, Bruce. *Education:* DePauw University, A.B., 1935. *Home and office:* 2614 Terrace Dr., Santa Maria, Calif. 93455.

CAREER: LaGrange Citizen, LaGrange, Ill., reporter, 1935-37; United Press International, correspondent-editor in Chicago, Ill., New York, N.Y., London, England, and in Iceland and North Africa, 1938-48, bureau chief in London, 1944-45; Times-Mirror Co., Los Angeles, Calif., assistant managing editor and director of editorial page of *Mirror-News*, 1948-57; Associated Desert Newspapers, Indio, Calif., executive editor, 1958-68; *South Bend Tribune*, South Bend, Ind., associate editor, 1968-79, consulting editor, 1979—. *Member:* American Society of Newspaper Editors, Western Writers of America, Sigma Nu. *Awards, honors:* Commonwealth Club of California Literature Award, 1959, for *This Is the Desert;* Western Writers of America Spur Award for best western juvenile, 1976, for *"All Aboard!"*

WRITINGS—All published by Dodd, except as noted: (With John Parris, Ned Russell, and Bill Disher) *Springboard to Berlin*, Crowell, 1943; (with Edwin Emery) *Reporting the News*, 1959; *This Is the Desert: The Story of America's Arid Region* (juvenile), 1959; *News Around the Clock* (juvenile), 1960; (with Emery and Warren K. Agee) *Introduction to Mass Communications*, Dodd, 1960, 6th edition, Harper, 1979; *How to Live in California: A Guide to Work, Leisure, and Retirement There and in the Southwest*, 1961; (compiler and editor) *The Home Book of Western Humor*, 1967.

Under name Phil Ault; juveniles: *Wonders of the Mosquito World*, 1970; *These Are the Great Lakes*, 1972; *Wires West: The Story of the Talking Wires*, 1974; *"All Aboard!": The Story of Passenger Trains in America*, 1976; *By the Seat of Their Pants: The Story of Early American Aviation*, 1978.

WORK IN PROGRESS: Perspectives in Mass Communications, publication by Harper expected in 1982; a college textbook on news writing and reporting, publication by Harper expected in 1983; a juvenile travel book on American inland waters, with publication by Dodd.

*   *   *

AUSTIN, Henry Wilfred   1906-

PERSONAL: Born August 26, 1906, in London, England; son of Wilfred (on the stock exchange) and Kate (Cock) Austin; married Phyllis Konstam (an actress and writer), November 14, 1931 (died, 1976); children: Jennifer Austin Bocock, John. *Education:* Cambridge University, B.A., 1928. *Religion:* Church of England. *Home:* 12 Palace St., London S.W.1, England.

CAREER: London Evening News, London, England, lawn tennis feature writer, 1929-39; free-lance writer, 1934—. Professional tennis player, 1926-38. Member of London Stock Exchange, 1929-34. *Military service:* U.S. Army Air Forces, 1943-45. *Member:* Queen's Club. *Awards, honors:* Tennis prizes include British Hard Court Championships, 1929 and 1937, and runner-up in Wimbledon Championships, 1932 and 1938.

WRITINGS: Bits and Pieces, Samson, Low, 1930; (with George Caulfield) *Lawn Tennis Made Easy*, Macmillan, 1935; *Under the Heavens*, Chapman & Hall, 1936; (editor) *Moral Re-Armament: The Battle for Peace*, Heinemann, 1938; (with wife, P. K. Austin) *A Mixed Double*, Chatto & Windus, 1968; *Frank Buchman As I Knew Him*, Grosvenor Books, 1975; *To Phyll With Love*, Grosvenor Books, 1979.

SIDELIGHTS: Austin told CA: "My first book, *Bits and Pieces*, was written at the request of the publishers, as I had recently become prominent as a tennis player. *Under the Heavens* was a nature book, a result of my lifelong interest in and love of nature, particularly birds and butterflies. *Moral Re-Armament: The Battle for Peace* was a collection of letters and statements from prominent men and women calling for the restoration of moral and spiritual values if Britain was to survive the threat of Hitler.

"*A Mixed Double* and *To Phyll With Love* are stories of my wife's and my acceptance of moral and spiritual values and of their effective application in a wide area of life. *To Phyll* is essentially the story of the marriage of two pagans and how the marriage was re-made through the acceptance of Christ, but it is also the story of the growth of a young Jewish girl of no faith into a convinced Christian revolutionary—all her passionate nature, all her gifts of heart and creative talents as an actress and writer used to further God's purposes in the world."

*   *   *

AUTTON, Norman William James   1920-

PERSONAL: Surname is pronounced "Orton"; born October 27, 1920, in Neath, Glamorgan, Wales; married Florence Kate Williams, May 12, 1947; children: Michael James, Mary Autton Cornelius. *Education:* Attended Selwyn College, Cambridge, 1939-1942; St. Michael's Theological College, 1942-1944. *Home:* 77 Rhydhelig Ave., Heath, Cardiff, Wales. *Office:* University Hospital of Wales, Heath Park, Cardiff CF4 4XW, Wales.

CAREER: Ordained minister of Church of England; Deva Hospital, Chester, England, chaplain, 1956-62; St. George's Hospital, London, England, chaplain, 1962-67; Hospital Chaplaincies Council of the General Synod, London, director of training, 1967-72; University Hospital of Wales, Cardiff, chaplain, 1972—. *Awards, honors:* D.Litt., 1970.

WRITINGS:—All published by Society for Promoting Christian Knowledge (S.P.C.K.), except as noted: *The Pastoral Care of the Mentally Ill*, 1963, 2nd editon, 1969; *The Pastoral Care of the Dying*, 1967; *The Pastoral Care of the Bereaved*, 1967; *Pastoral Care in Hospitals*, 1969; (editor) *A Manual of Prayers and Readings With the Sick*, 1970; (editor) *Christianity and Change*, 1971; *From Fear to Faith: Studies of Suffering and Wholeness*, 1971; *When Sickness Comes: A Simple Guide*, Church in Wales Publications, 1973; *Visiting Ours: A Layman's Guide to Hospital Visiting*, Church in Wales Publications, 1975; *Getting Married*, Church in Wales Publications, 1976; *Readings in Sickness*, 1976; *Watch With the Sick*, 1976; (contributor) *Understanding Cancer: A Guide for the Caring Professions*, H.M.S.O., 1977; *Peace at the Last: Talks With the Dying*, CHR Classics, 1978; *Visiting the Sick*, Mowbray, 1980.

WORK IN PROGRESS: A Handbook of Sick Visiting, for Mowbray.

AVOCATIONAL INTERESTS: Music, travel, writing, reading.

B

BABE, Thomas 1941-

PERSONAL: Born March 13, 1941, in Buffalo, N.Y.; son of Thomas (a salesman) and Ruth (Lossie) Babe; married Susan Bramhall, April 1, 1967 (divorced, 1976); children: Charissa Bramhall. *Education:* Harvard University, B.A., 1963, graduate study, 1965-68; St. Catharine's College, Cambridge, B.A., 1965; Yale University, J.D., 1972. *Politics:* "Radical Conservative." *Home:* 103 Hoyt St., Darien, Conn. 06820. *Agent:* Lantz Office, 114 East 55th St., New York, N.Y. 10022.

CAREER: Playwright and director. Co-founder and co-artistic director of Summer Players in Agassiz Theater, Cambridge, Mass., 1966-68. Director of more than twenty plays, including "Trojan Women," "The Bacchae," "In the Jungle of Cities," "Two Small Bodies," and "Justice." *Member:* Writers Guild of America, East, Phi Beta Kappa. *Awards, honors:* Marshall Scholar, 1963-65; CBS fellow in playwrighting at Yale University, 1975-76; Guggenheim fellowship, 1977; Rockefeller grant, 1978; "Rebel Women" was chosen as one of Burns Mantle ten best plays, 1975-76; "A Prayer for My Daughter" was chosen as one of Burns Mantle ten best plays, 1977-78.

*WRITINGS—*Plays: "Kid Champion" (two-act); first produced Off Broadway at Public Theater, January, 1975; "Mojo Candy" (one-act), first produced at Yale Cabaret, July, 1975; "Billy Irish" (three-act), first produced at Manhattan Theater Club, March, 1976; "Rebel Women" (two-act), first produced Off Broadway at Public Theater, June, 1976; "Great Solo Town" (one-act), first produced at Yale Cabaret, July, 1977; "A Prayer for My Daughter" (two-act), first produced Off Broadway at Public Theater, January 17, 1978; "Fathers and Sons" (two-act), first produced Off Broadway at Public Theater, November, 1978; "Taken in Marriage" (two-act) first produced Off Broadway at Public Theater, March, 1979; "Daniel Boone" (for children), first produced in September, 1979; "Salt Lake City Skyline" (two-act), first produced Off Broadway at Public Theater, January 23, 1980; (with Twyla Tharp) "When We Were Very Young," first produced at Wintergarden Theater, March 26, 1980; "Hot Dogs and Soda Pop" (one-act), first broadcast on National Public Radio, April, 1980; "The Volunteer Fireman" (one-act), first broadcast on National Public Radio, spring, 1981.

Screenplays: (With Michael Wadleigh) "The Sun Gods," Warner Bros., 1978; "The Vacancy," Warner Bros., 1979; "Kid Champion" (adapted from the play by Babe), Music Fair, Inc., 1979.

Contributor of scripts to television shows.

WORK IN PROGRESS: Two plays, "Dickers Shows," commissioned by the Los Angeles Ahmanson Theater, and "Kathleen"; a dance piece with Twyla Tharp, "Gat Dickers"; a musical about divorce, for children, "Happy Birthday Beep-Boop"; two film scripts.

SIDELIGHTS: Mel Gussow of the *New York Times* has heralded Babe as "one of the most imaginative and indigenous of young American playwrights." Babe has often been mentioned in the company of such vital young American dramatists as Sam Shepard, David Mamet, and Albert Innaurato. Martin Duberman, writing in *Harper's,* counted Babe "alone among the new playwrights in imaginative daring, in attempting something more than surface renderings." He is, Gussow commented, "intensely aware of our national myths and heroes."

In his first play, "Kid Champion," Babe's subject was a washed-out rock star, an almost mythical character of the 1960's. The *New Yorker's* Edith Oliver wrote that Babe "has presented in melodrama, comedy, drama, soliloquy, projected slides, movie clips, and blaring rock music the anatomy of a rock singer, and in so doing has brought the whole failed, tawdry world of rock onto the stage." Gussow noted that despite problems such as "a slackening of drama in the second act, an interesting but unresolved re-entry into the star's boyhood life, and several characters that are stereotypes without sufficient comment from the author," the play "remains a bruising encounter with a fallen hero—dethroned by a nation's appetite for obsolescence."

On one level, "A Prayer for My Daughter" explores American sexual stereotyping. The play concerns two men being held in a police station for murder and the two policemen who interrogate them. Gussow wrote that the play is "strange and compelling." Although the dialogue is "grounded in gritty reality, . . . there is a feeling of heightened reality. It is as if the characters are in limbo, where, injected with truth serum, they will tell one another more than they would otherwise reveal. The result is a play that sneaks up on us, makes us overlook questionable details, and unsuspectingly, delivers swift body punches."

Duberman was less appreciative of "A Prayer for My

Daughters.'' He commended its ''powerful dialogue'' but complained that the play was ''full of jarring false notes.'' He wrote, ''The theme is bold, hip—and strained. That the play works at all (and a fair amount of the time it does) owes a great deal to the production.''

''Taken in Marriage,'' ''an acerbic comedy of manners,'' according to Richard Eder of the *New York Times*, is set in a church hall where four female family members and an entertainer hired for the nuptials wait for the wedding rehearsal to take place. *Time*'s T. E. Kalem described the action: ''As the afternoon wears on, the clan bitches it up, a diatribe here, a confessional secret there, a bilious distillation from atrabilious people.''

''Nothing remarkable is unloosed in this letting down of four heads of hair,'' Eder wrote. ''Mr. Babe's way with a comb is very deft, however. The characters of the four women are revealed and contrasted with great skill; the author's sense of the rhythm of speech and silence, of revelation and concealment, of attack and retreat, is subtle and fluid.'' Edith Oliver exclaimed that the play ''makes a fascinating and tantalizing show from beginning to end. The writing is witty and precise and it cuts deep.''

Other reviewers criticized ''Taken in Marriage'' and other Babe plays for their unbelievability. Kalem, for example, noted that ''a resistance to close human bonds is characteristic of the people in most of Babe's plays. They are intimate with each other only when they are locked in physical or verbal violence. . . . The plausibility gap in Babe's plays is that almost nothing arouses his characters' passions.'' *Newsweek*'s Jack Kroll similarly wrote: ''Despite their often powerful theatricality, what's hard to believe in Babe's plays is not their 'reality' but their emotional truth. I don't believe his new play, 'Taken in Marriage,' but like some of Liszt's grandiloquent scores, it provides a dazzling vehicle for virtuoso performers.''

Babe's plays have been produced in Canada, England, Holland, and Germany. Two of his plays, ''Taken in Marriage,'' and ''A Prayer for My Daughter,'' have been published in German by Fischer Verlag.

CA INTERVIEWS THE AUTHOR
CA interviewed Thomas Babe by phone March 12, 1980, at his home in Darien, Conn.

CA: Was writing plays an early ambition?

BABE: It wasn't at all. My earliest ambition was to be James Joyce or William Faulkner and write long and wonderful novels. I only came to write plays because I worked in the theater when I went to Harvard, worked with very gifted people. We were all amateurs, all students, but it was very exciting. Then it dawned on me that I wanted to write something for the theater, and that's how it started. Now I would find it impossible to write a megatome about anything, because I'm so used to working with theater, where you have only to deal with voices, and a number of voices are talking to each other contrapuntally. In other kinds of fiction writing, you have to find the narrative voice, whether you're Henry James or William Faulkner or even Peter Benchley. And that narrative voice has been very hard for me to find.

CA: What was the focus of your undergraduate work in college?

BABE: I majored in English. I tried as much as possible to study everything else under the sun, and it was a very liberal liberal arts program. I even sneaked into a course I wasn't supposed to be able to get into—on abnormal personality, in the social relations department. But my main focus was on literature.

CA: Then you went to Cambridge to study literature further?

BABE: Yes. I was a Marshall Scholar. I went there specifically to study Restoration drama, but when I got there I didn't really want to do that. There's no analogy between their system of postgraduate work and ours, so I decided to do what Americans commonly do over there—to get a second B.A. I now have two B.A.'s. Those two B.A.'s and fifty cents will get you a ride on the IRT. But it also allowed me the freedom to live in England and to experience England with people who were roughly my contemporaries, the undergraduates at Cambridge. I had a wonderful time those two years. Saw a lot of good theater, too.

CA: You actually did some work in theater there, didn't you?

BABE: I was in a couple of plays and directed a couple of plays. But I still was not quite sure about the theater as something to write for. At that point I was still writing prose fiction.

CA: Then you went to Yale and got a law degree. Were you planning at some point to practice law?

BABE: I had spent a year working for Mayor Lindsay in New York as a speech writer. It was really the worst year of his tenure. The day I went to work was the day all the teachers went on strike; I couldn't even get near City Hall because there were about five thousand teachers parading. And I left on the day he lost the Republican primary. It was not a good year for him, and not a good year for people writing speeches for him. But I was very concerned about all the issues—I still am—so I wanted to do something, and I figured the way to do that was to have a law degree. I decided to apply to the Yale Law School; I was accepted and I studied there. It was only in the second year that I realized that, even though this was very valuable and something I'd always wanted to do because I'd always had great curiosity about the law, I was probably not going to be happy as a lawyer. I went crazy for a while and hung upside-down in the closet and then decided to write plays.

CA: Has the law education been a help in any way in your work as a writer and director?

BABE: I think the great thing about legal education, which is very strenuous, is that it takes a mental discipline, a discipline in logic, a discipline in *A* leading to *B* leading to *C* leading to *D,* you *hope.* And I face this all the time these days, because not only do I write myself for the theater, but I have a great number of friends and colleagues who are also playwrights. I think the greatest thing one has to acquire is craft—sheer craft. How to make something happen. In an odd way, my sense of craft is tied in to my legal education. I think if I had gone to the Yale Drama School, I would have been about four steps behind. Legal education is great in that regard and great in analyzing a lot of other things that are ancillary.

I was aware when I was there, all the time, that I was forcing myself to think logically; it's not my normal instinct to do so. And doing that for three years made that kind of thinking almost second nature. I analyze problems as opposed to just being puzzled by them, and that's the benefit of Yale Law School. I'm forever in debt.

CA: What playwrights have influenced your work?

BABE: That's hard to say. There are playwrights I admire, playwrights whose work I actually pick up and read because they give me pleasure and also give me some sense of excitement. Shakespeare's one of them. I don't say that in a pious fashion, I just think he's one of the best who ever did this job. And he's also very exciting. I think he and the Greeks—Aeschylus and Sophocles and especially Euripides—have had an enormous influence on my thinking. And I love Chekhov. I could never be him, but on a good day I *think* maybe I could be. Among my own contemporaries, I think the person who has inspired me the most is Sam Shepard. I really have no desire to do his work and never have, but he's inspired me and actually made me feel good about being a playwright. His work is very, very good.

CA: You've said that your directing experience has influenced your writing for theater. Would you elaborate on that?

BABE: It's not my inspiration for writing but my sense of the theater. I've probably in my life directed thirty or forty plays, all the way from the Greeks through Shakespeare to Strindberg—I guess one way or another I've directed one of everybody who's anybody. The great thing about that is that you get to take something apart, especially if you have a good company, and you get down to the nuts and bolts of it all. What's wonderful is you begin to understand the structure and why great plays are great; it's because they're put together as well as they are and not just because they're well-written. The shaping mind behind it is one you get to know through directing, more so than any other way, because you're the one who has to make the representation of it on the stage. So I learned an awful lot long before I even thought I was going to write plays. I directed a large number of them, and when I look back on it, I think this is something that gave me a sort of fingertip sense about the theater.

Lately I've been directing new plays by other people, which is a whole different way to work, because you're working with stuff that's not quite finished. So what I can do is say, "Well, I don't know if that works or not," or "Do this"; but the point is that the author is alive. A lot of people don't like to work with living authors, but I do. Living authors tend to talk back.

CA: Have you ever directed any of your own plays?

BABE: I did one. I directed a revival last summer of "Kid Champion," which was almost five years old since the time it was written and originally produced in public theater. I did that because I felt that I had sufficient distance from it to treat the material as though I were a director coming to it and not trying to protect myself. I looked at the play and I said, "Oh my God, this is awkward—convoluted and weird; but I will do it." And I told the company on the first day of rehearsal, "We're going to treat the author for all intents and purposes as though he were dead and try and do as good as job as possible with this thing." And we did. We had a lot of fun as a result of that production. The play was just published this week, and I got a chance to do it in an entirely different way from the original production. Everything about it was different, and probably much closer to what I intended.

But the point is that I would never direct my own work the first time out. I would miss that valuable collaboration between myself and a director. I think that's the most valuable collaboration that exists for a playwright. I think you have to have enough distance in time; I don't mean in any other way. I just got the published edition of *Kid Champion* a couple of days ago, and in looking at it I realize that I don't really

know the man who wrote that as well as I know myself. That puts me in a good position to work on it. But the thing I write tomorrow I don't think I'd touch; I would need somebody to come back at me.

CA: Have you done any television scripts or screenplays?

BABE: I've done three screenplays so far. One was an adaptation of "Kid Champion" that was commissioned. Another is a movie that's in progress right now for Warner Brothers. The third was a rewrite. It was my first Hollywood experience. I did a little writing for a soap opera once, because I needed the money and also because it was fun. It was like having my own repertory company.

I've always been in love with the movies. Since I was eight years old and saw a double feature on Saturday and a double feature on Sunday, I've been in love with the movies. It would be the dream of a lifetime if one of the scripts I wrote actually became a movie. It's very exciting to me, and also very, very different from playwriting. It's an entirely different discipline—one I've had to try and learn. It's a very visual medium; it's also a director's medium. It's one in which words don't count so much as the shape. That's so different from the theater, where the writer tends, except in odd commercial situations, to be a very important, if not the *most* important, reason for something to be done. In the movies, I guess because of the stakes involved, it's much more across the board. Everybody, even the person who opens the mail, has an idea that might work. It's much more spread out in responsibility, and the vision is much more spread out. The star system really is in many ways like the old-time Hollywood that was fictionalized. There are moguls; there are stars; there are pressures of a very different kind from the theater.

On the other hand, it's real good to do this, because it's fun. And I've read some film scripts that are as elegant as anything I've ever seen written. Like Robert Townes's filmscript for "Chinatown." Just to read it is a treat; it's no wonder the movie turned out so good.

CA: You've also written poetry and had some poetry published in England. Do you still write poetry?

BABE: I do poetry sporadically. I think what's happened is that all the energy that went into poetry has actually gone into playwriting. As far as I'm concerned, the writing of plays is a kind of verbal extension of writing poetry, as well as laying out a plot with all the surprises. The nicest piece of poetry I have written in recent memory is the final speech in "A Prayer for My Daughter," which describes the birth of Jimmy's daughter. It's poetry to me because it's evocative, it's iambic, which is the genius of the English language, and I can go anywhere I want with it—it's like a privileged moment. The drama critic for the *New Yorker,* Edith Oliver, who worked with "A Prayer for My Daughter," at the O'Neill Conference, said, "All of you modern playwrights have this flaw: you want to write these long speeches after you've done the other stuff so well." And I said, "Edith, if I can't do that, I don't want to do it at all."

CA: Do you read much theater criticism?

BABE: I read it more for information about what's going on than I do for evaluation. I think one of the most disappointing things about the profession of being a playwright is that across the board generally the level of criticism is very low. Not that the people are dopes, it's just that they're lazy. If there was criticism of the theater on a par with the energy, vitality, and enthusiasm of the best film criticism, I think we'd all be in better shape. But it tends to be very weary, very exhausted, very jaded kind of writing. So I read it more for information.

I've known the critics long enough now that I can read between the lines and get some idea of what the play really is. Though I'm constantly surprised, because they constantly mislead me. I don't know why they're like that. I know a number of them fairly well, and if you talk to them in private, they do seem to have energy and passion; but when they start writing, it's as though they were conducting an inquest rather than writing about what I consider to be a very vital and lively art form. And also one almost totally unexplored in American history. The theater is really the stepchild of all our arts—theater and dance. We have a great tradition of novels, of poetry; we virtually invented the motion picture; musical comedy is our own special creation. But before O'Neill, we're hard-pressed to find native theater except as a copy of foreign imports, especially British theater. And even O'Neill's not all that hot, when you get right down to it. But he did it: he said, "I'm an American and I'm going to write American plays." And we all stand on his shoulders for that.

CA: What do you think has stayed with us from the very experimental theater of Off-Off Broadway of the 1960's and early 1970's?

BABE: I think what has stayed with us, and I hope it will stay with us forever, is the freedom. In many ways Sam Shepard embodies the literate spirit of this freedom—the spirit that wrote, as opposed to just groaned. When "Kid Champion," was produced in 1975, the raunchiness in the language and what was going on was exactly the same sort of thing that Lenny Bruce got busted for ten years before by D.A. Frank Hogan. I think what that experimental time did was establish a precedent that the theater is up for grabs. And I love that. What I don't like is that it tends to be mindless and self-righteous, but I can live with that. As long as they keep working, I'll keep working. I think they opened all the doors and windows and said the theater can be anything we can make it into, and then we work back from that position, instead of working from the forties position of the well-made play, melodrama, and comedy. That's a very important legacy, and we're all beneficiaries of it.

CA: Has it put a lot of good people to work who wouldn't be working otherwise?

BABE: Yes. And I think it has also helped a lot of people who might have just been good to be better because their imaginations have been freed by the precedents. I know it's true in my case. I thought—and this was quite a revelation when I read my first Sam Shepard play—why, the sky's the limit!

CA: In a 1979 article in the New York Times, *Roger Copeland, comparing the new British playwrights to the new American playwrights, said that the American playwrights are creating plays concerned mainly with private rather than public issues, while their British counterparts are showing in their work more of a sense of public concern. Would you comment on that?*

BABE: I think he could be no further off base. In the first place, I'm very familiar with contemporary British theater. It's narrow in scope; it's unimaginative in conception. It tends to be political, but I don't know what virtue goes along with that. If you want to be political, you might as well do a staged reading of *Das Kapital*. And he missed what I consider to be the real amazing thing about American theater, as

I said in a letter I wrote that was published in the *Times* two or three weeks after the article. That's the pressure and energy of the writing. It's just better written, line for line. Because of that, it's more exciting. There's what I consider to be an unnatural affection in the editorial columns of the *New York Times* for British theater, for things that are British. I think that's because their constituency is by and large people who believe that sophistication is to appreciate that which is British. I don't think they think that consciously. I just think that if something comes over from England, it has that kind of patina on it that gives it an acceptability all the raw and really raunchy stuff that Americans do at their best does not have in their eyes. Any number of British plays that have been very celebrated on Broadway really have nothing to do with anything except the narrow interests of the people who buy theater tickets. They're not very adventurous and they're not very well written.

It goes beyond the question of public consciousness. If you posit public concern as a standard for excellence, then I suppose Ronald Reagan is the ultimate American playwright. He expresses enormous concern for all of our interests and political issues. But I don't think I would like to listen to what he has to say for very long. The problem is, if you set up anything—like moral improvement—as an aesthetic standard, then you forget that the main reason people like theater and like doing theater is because something is exciting and gives them some new vision that they did not have before. And it can come from an amoralist or an atheist, let alone a committed social democrat, which most British playwrights seem to be. But there's nothing any more narcissistic about American play writing than about British play writing. I think the kind of self-righteousness that goes with that political playwriting is in many ways very narcissistic. It's just that it's protected by having a sort of "decent" goal in view.

CA: Are there any great practical differences between the two countries in producing plays?

BABE: Play for play, judging by the productions I have seen in England when I lived there and when I was there recently, there's nothing like it in the English-speaking world. They're real good. The production values, the technical facility of the actors, the shrewdness of all the people involved in the production. They did "A Prayer for My Daughter" over there a year and a half ago, and it was an extraordinary production. It was a completely British company directed by an Englishman. It had such energy, such force, such care. It started out as a workshop, but it was so successful that they moved it upstairs—because of the production, I think. If I died and went to heaven, I'd be an American playwright whose plays are done by Englishmen.

CA: What's your feeling about American theater now generally? Do you think it's healthy?

BABE: As far as the writing and production being done, I think it's in wonderful shape. I'm a little scared about finances at this point, because most of the theaters that do the interesting new work, including most of the American plays that are hits on Broadway, originated in institutional theaters, those theaters that are subsidized in some way by state and federal funds. And this money, in the brave new world we live in, is drying up. Because of that, there are fewer and fewer places that people who want to write for the theater and also want to direct and act can turn to for sustenance.

I think this is verging on a crisis as far as the theater is concerned, at the very moment when the other things are beginning to fall into place—when we actually are beginning to have a healthy back-and-forth in the theater, different styles emerging, people having enormous territorial ambitions for the stage. The people I know, at least the people I've worked with, are about as good as people get in this business—ever—and they need to work. If that platform is taken away from them, then the theater will be poorer. The more stuff that's done, the better.

It's the same as my response to your question about the experimentation of the sixties. If that wasn't there, then we wouldn't be where we are right now. And I'm just afraid it's all going to dry up. That would be very bad. Most of the institutional theaters that have survived—the Public, the Manhattan Theater Club, the Mark Taper, the Arena, the Longwharf—are theaters that have managed somewhere along the line while doing new works to parlay one of those works into a hit. They get a cut, and that's very important. It tends to skew the perspective a bit, but it's important that that money be there. And it's the most capricious kind of money there is, because it depends on the whim of the audience and not on one's own sense of what one ought to be doing.

And it's also a fact of life that it's very hard to make a living as a playwright, period. There's not a lot of money in it. So that's discouraging. It's foundations like the Guggenheim and the Rockefeller that really have made all of us possible, one way or another.

BIOGRAPHICAL/CRITICAL SOURCES: New Yorker, March 3, 1975, June 14, 1976, March 12, 1979; *New York Times,* January 18, 1978, November 17, 1978, February 27, 1979, August 28, 1979, January 24, 1980; *Harper's,* May, 1978; *Newsweek,* March 12, 1979; *Time,* March 19, 1979.

—Interview by Jean W. Ross

*   *   *

BACH, Alice (Hendricks) 1942-

PERSONAL: Born in 1942, in New York, N.Y.; daughter of Henry and Irene (Gibbs) Bach; *Education:* Barnard College, B.A., 1963. *Office:* Dial Press, 750 Third Ave., New York, N.Y. 10017.

CAREER: Associate editor for Harper & Row, New York City; consultant to Bedford-Stuyvesant Writers Workshop; currently senior editor of books for young readers at Dial Books, New York City.

WRITINGS—Juvenile novels; all published by Harper & Row, except as noted: (Translator) Pierre Belves and Francois Mathey, *How Artists Work,* Lion Press, 1968; *They'll Never Make a Movie Starring Me,* 1973; *Mollie Make-Believe,* 1974; *The Day After Christmas,* 1975; *The Meat in the Sandwich,* 1975; *The Smartest Bear and His Brother Oliver,* 1975; *The Most Delicious Camping Trip Ever,* 1976; *A Father Every Few Years,* 1977; *Grouchy Uncle Otto,* 1977; *Millicent the Magnificent,* 1978; *Warren Weasel's Worse Than Measles,* 1980. Contributor of articles to periodicals, including *Publishers Weekly.*

BIOGRAPHICAL/CRITICAL SOURCES: New York Times Book Review, May 19, 1974, July 6, 1975, November 2, 1975; *Best Sellers,* June, 1977.*

*   *   *

BACQUE, James 1929-

PERSONAL: Born in 1929, in Toronto, Ontario, Canada; married Elisabeth Marani, 1955; children: four. *Education:* Attended University of Victoria and Trinity College; University of Toronto, B.A., 1952. *Office:* New Press, 30 Lesmill Rd., Don Mills, Ontario, Canada.

CAREER: Worked as stagehand for Canadian Broadcasting Corp.; assistant editor at *Saturday Night, Canadian Packaging,* and *Canadian Homes;* reporter for *Beacon Herald* in Stratford, Ontario; Macmillan of Canada, Toronto, Ontario, trade editor, 1961-68; New Press, Don Mills, Ontario, founder, 1969—. *Member:* Association of Canadian Publishers (co-founder, 1970).

WRITINGS: The Lonely Ones (novel), McClelland & Stewart, 1969, reprinted as *Big Lonely,* New Press, 1971; *A Man of Talent* (novel), New Press, 1972; *The Queen Comes to Minnicog,* Gage, 1979.

Work represented in anthologies, including *Notes for a Native Land,* edited by A. Wainwright, Oberton Press, 1970; *Creation,* edited by Robert Kroetsch, New Press, 1970; *Marked by the Wild,* edited by Bruce Littlejohn, McClelland & Stewart, 1974. Contributor of articles and poems to literary journals and popular magazines, including *Canadian Forum, Weekend,* and *Canadian Dimension.**

*   *   *

BADCOCK, Christopher Robert 1946-

PERSONAL: Born May 13, 1946; son of Robert Frederick (a lieutenant colonel in the British armed forces) and Phyllis (Wellington) Badcock; married Lenis Gee, June 17, 1967; children: James Christopher, Louis. *Education:* London School of Economics and Political Science, London, B.A. (with first class honors), 1967, Ph.D., 1969. *Home:* 36-A Ross Gardens, Rough Common, Canterbury, Kent, England. *Office:* Department of Sociology, London School of Economics and Political Science, University of London, Houghton St., London WC2A 2AE, England.

CAREER: Polytechnic of the South Bank, London, England, lecturer in sociology, 1969-73; University of London, London School of Economics and Political Science, London, lecturer in sociology, 1974—.

WRITINGS: Levi-Strauss: Structuralism and Sociological Theory, Harper, 1975; *The Psychoanalysis of Culture,* Basil Blackwell, 1980; *Madness and Modernity: A Social Psychopathology of Present-Day Life,* Basil Blackwell, in press. Contributor to sociology journals. Associate editor of British Journal of Sociology.

WORK IN PROGRESS: "A footnote to Freud: Levi-Strauss' Debt to Psychoanalysis," for inclusion in *The Psychoanalytic Study of Society.*

SIDELIGHTS: Badcock commented to *CA:* "Since 1979 I have undergone didactic psychoanalysis with Miss Anna Freud, with funds provided by the Sigmund Freud Archives, Inc. Other interests include the psychoanalysis of art (including a so-far unpublished manuscript on the paintings of Salvador Dali), the significance of psychoanalysis for politics, education, and culture generally. *Madness and Modernity* is a psychoanalytical study of the traumatic impact of modernity, comparing it with the impact of the Neolithic revolution, and drawing conclusions about the psychology of insanity."

*   *   *

BADER, Douglas (Robert Steuart) 1910-

PERSONAL: Born February 21, 1910; son of Frederick Roberts and Jessie (Scott-Mackenzie) Bader; married Olive Thelma Exley Edwards, 1933 (marriage ended, 1971); married Joan Eileen Murray, 1973. *Education:* Attended Royal Air Force College, Cranwell. *Home:* 5 Petersham Mews, Gloucester Rd., London SW7 5NR, England.

CAREER: Worked for Asiatic Petroleum Ltd. and Shell Petroleum Co., 1946-57; managing director of Shell Aircraft Ltd., 1958-69. Member of board of directors of Trafalgar Offshore Ltd. Member of Civil Aviation Authority, 1972-77; chairman of Flight Time Limitations Board, 1974—. *Military service:* Royal Air Force, 1930-33, 1939-45, prisoner of war in Germany, 1941-45; became group captain; received Distinguished Service Order and bar, Distinguished Flying Cross and bar, Legion d'Honneur, and Croix de Guerre; mentioned in dispatches. *Member:* Royal Aeronautical Society (fellow), Buck's Club, Royal Air Force Club. *Awards, honors:* Commander of Order of the British Empire, 1956; knighted, 1976.

WRITINGS: (Editor) *My Favourite Stories of Courage*, Lutterworth, 1963; (editor) *My Favourite Dog Stories*, Lutterworth, 1969; (editor) *Fight for the Sky: The Story of the Spitfire and the Hurricane*, Doubleday, 1973.

SIDELIGHTS: Sir Douglas was first commissioned in 1930, but lost both legs in a flying accident in 1931 and left the Royal Air Force. He returned to service at the beginning of World War II and was involved in the evacuation of Dunkirk in 1940, then commanded the Royal Air Force's first Canadian fighter squadron. He was captured in a collision with enemy aircraft in 1941 and remained a prisoner of war until released by the U.S. Army near Leipzig, Germany, in 1945.

AVOCATIONAL INTERESTS: Golf.

BIOGRAPHICAL/CRITICAL SOURCES: Time, August 2, 1954; Paul Brickhill, *Reach for the Sky: The Story of Douglas Bader, Legless Ace of the Battle of Britain,* Norton, 1954; *Reader's Digest,* September, 1954; *Newsweek,* October 11, 1964; John Canning, editor, *One Hundred Great Modern Lives,* Hawthorn, 1965; Charles Wyndham, *Douglas Bader: A Great Air Ace* (juvenile), Blackie & Son, 1967.*

*   *   *

BADGLEY, Robin F(rancis)   1931-

PERSONAL: Born May 6, 1931, in Montreal, Quebec, Canada; son of Clement Montagu and Joan Gordon (Coles) Badgley; married Jean Winifred Duncan, June 18, 1959; children: Anne Duncan, Mary Elizabeth. *Education:* McGill University, B.A., 1952, M.A., 1954; Yale University, M.A., 1955, Ph.D., 1957, postdoctoral study, 1957-58. *Religion:* Anglican. *Home:* 1104 Balmoral Place, Oakville, Ontario, Canada L6J 2C9. *Office:* Department of Behavioral Science, Faculty of Medicine, University of Toronto, Toronto 2, Ontario, Canada.

CAREER: Sir George Williams College (now Concordia University), Montreal, Quebec, lecturer in sociology, 1953-54; Yale University, New Haven, Conn., instructor in sociology, 1957-58; University of Vermont, Burlington, assistant professor of preventive medicine, 1958-59; University of Saskatchewan, Saskatoon, assistant professor, 1959-62, associate professor of sociology and preventive medicine, 1962-63; Milbank Memorial Fund, New York, N.Y., senior member of technical staff, 1963-68; University of Toronto, Toronto, Ontario, professor of behavioral science, pediatrics, and sociology and chairman of department of behavioral science, 1968—. Visiting lecturer at Yale University, 1963-68; lecturer at Columbia University, 1965—. Representative of Social Security Administration to Welfare Administration, 1966-69; member of health services committee of Ontario Council of Health, 1974—, and health promotion committee of Conference of Federal-Provincial Health Ministers, 1974-76; chairman of committee on operation of the abortion law, of Canadian government's Privy Council,

1975-77; member of Advisory Commission on Medical Research of Pan American Health Organization, 1976—; consultant to World Health Organization.

MEMBER: International Sociological Association, Canadian Public Health Association, Canadian Political Science Association, Canadian Economic Association, Association of Teachers of Preventive Medicine, American Sociological Association (fellow), American Public Health Association (fellow). *Awards, honors:* Russell Sage Foundation fellow, 1957-58; World Health Organization fellow, 1978.

WRITINGS: (Editor) *Readings in Medical Sociology,* Department of Social and Preventive Medicine, University of Saskatchewan, 1962; (editor) *Behavioral Science and Medical Education in Latin America,* Milbank Memorial Fund, 1966; (with Samuel Wolfe) *Doctor's Strike: Medical Care and Conflict in Saskatchewan,* Atherton, 1967, 2nd edition, 1971; (editor) *Social Science and Health Planning: Culture, Disease, and Health Services in Colombia,* Milbank Memorial Fund, 1968; (contributor) Edwin Fuller Torrey, editor, *Ethical Issues in Medicine,* Little, Brown, 1968; (with Wolfe) *The Family Doctor,* Macmillan, 1973.

Contributor of articles and reviews to academic journals. Editor of *Milbank Memorial Fund Quarterly,* 1963-68.*

*   *   *

BAER, Adela S(wenson)   1931-

PERSONAL: Born April 4, 1931, in Blue Island, Ill.; daughter of Eugene Martin (in business) and Golda (Standard) Swenson; children: Susan, Nicoli. *Education:* University of Illinois, B.S., 1953; University of California, Berkeley, Ph.D., 1963. *Office:* Department of Biology, San Diego State University, San Diego, Calif. 92182.

CAREER: San Diego State University, San Diego, Calif., assistant professor, 1962-65, associate professor, 1965-68, professor of biology, 1968—, chairman of department, 1975—. Fulbright professor at University of Malaya, 1967-68; research scientist at University of California's International Center for Medical Research, Kuala Lumpur, Malaysia, 1971-72; visiting professor at University of California, Berkeley, 1975 and 1981. *Member:* Genetic Society of America, American Society of Human Genetics, Society for Social Biology. *Awards, honors:* Fulbright grant, 1971-72; research grants from National Science Foundation and National Institutes of Health.

WRITINGS: (With William Hagen, David Jameson, and William Sloan) *Central Concepts of Biology* (high school textbook), Macmillan, 1971; (editor) *Heredity and Society: Readings in Social Genetics,* Macmillan, 1973, 2nd edition, 1977; *The Genetic Perspective,* Saunders, 1977. Contributor to biology journals.

WORK IN PROGRESS: Biology and Belief: Genetics vs. Eugenics in Pre-1945 Germany; Anthropological Genetics.

SIDELIGHTS: In 1971-72, Adela Baer conducted field work in anthropological genetics with the Temuan tribal group of Malaya.

*   *   *

BAKER WHITE, John   1902-

PERSONAL: Born August 12, 1902, in West Malling, England; son of John Wilfrid and Katherine (Blythe) Baker White; married Sybil Irene Graham, October 21, 1925 (deceased); children: Robin (son), Jennifer Baker White Treherne-Thomas. *Education:* Educated in Malvern, England. *Religion:* Church of England. *Home and office address:* Street End Pl., Street End, near Canterbury, Kent CTU 5NP, England.

CAREER: Worked as laborer and circus hand, 1920-23; journalist; Economic League, London, England, director, 1925-45, publicity director, 1945-60, publicity adviser, 1960-76; writer and farmer, 1976—. Conservative member of Parliament for Canterbury, 1945-53; justice of the peace in Kent, England, 1952—. Chairman of Canterbury Licensing Planning Committee, 1953-78, and Canterbury Archaeological Appeal, 1978-79; committee member of St. Augustine's Recovery Fund; member of board of trustees of Buckminster Estates. *Military service:* British Army, served with Political Intelligence, Raiding Forces, Rifle Brigade, and War Cabinet Offices, 1933-45; served in the Middle East, North Africa, and Italy; became lieutenant colonel; received Territorial Decoration.

MEMBER: Royal United Services Institution, Foreign Affairs Research Institute, National Trust, Society for the Protection of Ancient Buildings, Jacob Sheep Society, Canterbury Society (vice-president; past chairman), East Kent Fruit Society (president), East Kent Ploughing Match Association (vice-president), Stour Valley Society, Central Landowners Association.

WRITINGS: Red Russia Arms, Burrup, 1932; *Dover-Nurnberg Return,* Burrup, 1937; *Gone for Good,* Vacher, 1941; *Nationalisation: Chaos or Cure?,* Falcon, 1946; *The Soviet Spy System,* Falcon, 1947; *The Big Lie,* M. Evans, 1950; *Sabotage Is Suspected,* M. Evans, 1950; *Pattern for Conquest,* R. Hale, 1959; *True Blue: An Autobiography, 1902-1939,* Muller, 1970. Author of "World Spotlight," a weekly column syndicated by Central Press Features. Contributor to magazines and newspapers, including *Soviet Analyst, Signature,* and *Kentish Gazette.*

WORK IN PROGRESS: An anthology of Edwardian humor.

SIDELIGHTS: Baker White told *CA:* "I had become a student of Marxism and communism before I left school in 1920. My mother was a writer and wrote a book, *The Menace of Communism,* in 1921. She was described as a scaremonger. My own knowledge of communism, gained on street corners and working in the mines, enabled me to get the job with the Economic League. Its task was, and still is, to fight subversive forces in industry.

"After World War II I widened my study of Soviet and Chinese communism to cover the economic as well as the political sphere. I took up writing about restaurants and wine as a counter to over-concentration on subversion."

AVOCATIONAL INTERESTS: Archaeology, agriculture, international affairs, gardening.

*   *   *

BALCHIN, W(illiam) G(eorge) V(ictor) 1916-

PERSONAL: Born June 20, 1916, in Aldershot, England; son of Victor and Ellen (Chapple) Balchin; married Lily Kettlewood (a teacher), December 10, 1939; children: Peter, Joan, Anne. *Education:* St. Catharine's College, Cambridge, B.A., 1937, M.A., 1941; King's College, London, Ph.D., 1951. *Religion:* Church of England. *Home and office:* 10 Low Wood Rise, Ben Rhydding, Ilkley, West Yorkshire, England.

CAREER: British Admiralty, London and Bath, England, hydrographic officer, 1939-45; University of London, King's College, London, lecturer in geography, 1945-54; University of Wales, University College of Swansea, Swansea, profes-

sor of geography and head of department, 1954-78, professor emeritus, 1978—, vice-principal, 1964-66 and 1970-73. Treasurer of Second Land Utilization Survey of Britain, 1961—; vice-president of Glamorgan County Naturalists Trust, 1962—; director of Land Decade Educational Council, 1979—. Member of Royal Society's British National Committee for Cartography, 1961-71 and 1975-80, Institution of Civil Engineers hydrology committee, 1962-67, Ministry of Defence meteorological research committee, 1963-69, and Royal Society's British National Committee for Geography, 1964-70 and 1976-80.

MEMBER: British Association (section president, 1972), British Cartographic Society, Royal Geographical Society (vice-president, 1979—), Royal Meteorological Society, Royal Commonwealth Society, Institute of British Geographers, Geographical Association (president, 1971), Geologists Association. *Awards, honors:* Gill Memorial Award from Royal Geographical Society, 1954, for contributions to geomorphology.

WRITINGS: (Editor with A. W. Richards) *Practical and Experimental Geography,* Methuen, 1952; *Cornwall: The Making of Its Landscape,* Hodder & Stoughton, 1954; *Cornwall: The Landscape Through Maps,* Geographical Association, 1967; (editor) *Geography for the Intending Student,* Routledge & Kegan Paul, 1970; (editor) *Swansea and Its Region,* University College of Swansea, University of Wales, 1971. Contributor of more than one hundred articles to scientific journals.

WORK IN PROGRESS: Editing a major historical survey of the British Isles, publication by Midsummer Books expected in 1981; revising *Cornwall: The Making of Its Landscape,* for Hodder & Stoughton.

SIDELIGHTS: Balchin commented to *CA:* "I have been a dedicated geographer for over fifty years. I have traveled alone and with teacher and student groups in Europe, North America, Africa, and Australia, and have been a member of expeditions to Spitzbergen and Arizona."

BIOGRAPHICAL/CRITICAL SOURCES: Concern for Geography, University College of Swansea, University of Wales, 1980.

*   *   *

BALDWIN, John D. 1930-

PERSONAL: Born November 8, 1930, in Omaha, Neb.; son of Dewey M. (a company manager) and Mabel (a teacher) Baldwin; married Teri Shapiro, June 22, 1952 (divorced July 12, 1966); married Linda Shafer (a boutique owner), January 29, 1967; children: (first marriage) Jan, Erica, Lisa, Amy; (second marriage) Alexandra. *Education:* University of Omaha, B.A., 1951; University of Nebraska, M.D., 1955. *Home:* 2130 Woodsdale, Lincoln, Neb. 68502. *Office:* 2221 South 17th St., Lincoln, Neb. 68502.

CAREER: Bishop Clarkson Memorial Hospital, Omaha, Neb., intern, 1955-56; Nebraska Psychiatric Institute, Omaha, resident in psychiatry, 1958-61; private practice of psychiatry in Lincoln, Neb., 1961—. Chairman of department of psychiatry at Bryan Memorial Hospital, 1965-74, member of executive committee, 1965—, chief of staff and member of board of trustees, 1976-78; attending physician at Lincoln General Hospital, 1961—. Associate professor at University of Nebraska, 1975—. Member of board of directors of Community Playhouse. Consultant to Nebraska Center for Children and Youth and Nebraska Department of Vocational Rehabilitation. *Military service:* U.S. Air Force,

Medical Corps, 1956-57; became captain. *Member:* American Psychiatric Association (fellow), Nebraska State Medical Association, Lincoln-Lancaster County Medical Society, Sioux Psychiatric Society (president, 1970-71), University Club (member of board of directors, 1978-80), Lincoln Country Club.

WRITINGS: Marriage Without B.S., Peter H. Wyden, 1979.

*   *   *

BALLANTYNE, Sheila 1936-

PERSONAL: Born July 26, 1936, in Seattle, Wash.; daughter of Edwin and Valery (Ballantyne) Webster; married Philip Spielman (a psychoanalyst), December 22, 1963; children: Anya, Stefan. *Education:* Mills College, B.A., 1958. *Residence:* Berkeley, Calif. *Agent:* Rhoda Weyr, William Morris Agency, 1350 Avenue of the Americas, New York, N.Y. 10019.

CAREER: Worked as a researcher, switchboard operator, and medical secretary, 1958-63; full-time writer, 1971—. *Member:* Amnesty International, Authors Guild, National Wildlife Federation, Sierra Club, Cousteau Society. *Awards, honors:* O. Henry Award, 1977, for short story "Perpetual Care"; MacDowell Colony fellowship, 1978.

WRITINGS: Norma Jean the Termite Queen (novel), Doubleday, 1975. Also author of a second novel, *Missing Persons.* Work represented in anthologies, including *O. Henry Prize Stories,* 1977. Contributor to literary reviews and popular magazines, including *New Yorker, Ms., Feminist Press, American Review, Aphra,* and *Short Story International.*

WORK IN PROGRESS: A novel, *Perfect Binding.*

SIDELIGHTS: "My first novel, *Norma Jean the Termite Queen,* is concerned with the struggle of the modern family to maintain its integrity in the face of modern social disintegration," Ballantyne told *CA.* "Its focus is on the tensions created by the conflict between traditional roles and new visions; the issues of birth, child rearing and family obligations versus personal growth and creative achievement."

BIOGRAPHICAL/CRITICAL SOURCES: Kirkus Reviews, March 15, 1975; *Rolling Stone,* June 3, 1976.

*   *   *

BAMBERGER, Bernard J(acob) 1904-1980

OBITUARY NOTICE—See index for *CA* sketch: Born May 30, 1904, in Baltimore, Md.; died of a heart attack, June 14, 1980, in Manhattan, N.Y. Rabbi, scholar, and author. Bamberger served as president of both the Central Conference of American Rabbis and the Synagogue Council of America. His many works include *The Story of Judaism, The Bible: A Modern Jewish Approach,* and *Proselytism in the Talmudic Period.* Obituaries and other sources: *New York Times,* June 16, 1980; *Chicago Tribune,* June 17, 1980.

*   *   *

BANKS, Laura Stockton Voorhees 1908(?)-1980

OBITUARY NOTICE: Born c. 1908 in Washington, D.C.; died after a stroke, June 18, 1980, in Arlington, Va. Researcher, editor, and author of historical novels for juveniles, including *Washington Adventures.* Banks assisted Allan Nevins on his 1933 biography of Grover Cleveland by doing research on the former president. From 1972 to 1975 she was editor of the *Review of the American Historical Association.* Obituaries and other sources: *Washington Post,* June 27, 1980.

BANNON, Barbara Anne 1928-

PERSONAL: Born August 27, 1928, in Auburn, N.Y.; daughter of Thomas Joseph and Rose Catherine (McCauley) Bannon. *Education:* Manhattanville College, B.A. (with honors), 1949. *Home:* 7 East 14th St., New York, N.Y. 10033. *Office: Publishers Weekly,* 1180 Avenue of the Americas, New York, N.Y. 10036.

CAREER/WRITINGS: Publishers Weekly, New York, N.Y., editorial assistant, 1948-54, assistant editor, 1954-60, associate editor, 1960-67, senior editor, 1971—. Editorial consultant to American Booksellers Association on White House library. Member of awards policy committee of National Book Awards, 1965-73; member of book selection committee of Books Across the Sea program for English Speaking Union, 1965—. Author of column appearing in *Coronet,* 1965. Contributor to *Business of Publishing. Member:* National Book Critics Circle (founder and vice-president), Women's National Book Association (vice-president, 1973-75), English Speaking Union, P.E.N. (member of American management board, 1973—), Publishers Publicity Association (founder and member of board of directors, 1963-68), Publishers' Adclub (member of board of directors, 1958-61).*

*   *   *

BARDON, Jack Irving 1925-

PERSONAL: Born October 24, 1925, in Cleveland, Ohio; son of Isidor (a hat manufacturer) and Rose (Greene) Bardon; married Carla Helene Wininger, September 12, 1948; children: Janet, Ruth. *Education:* Western Reserve University (now Case Western Reserve University), B.A., 1949; University of Pennsylvania, M.A., 1951, Ph.D., 1956. *Home:* 902 Greenwood Dr., Greensboro, N.C. 27410. *Office:* School of Education, University of North Carolina, Curry Bldg., Greensboro, N.C. 27412.

CAREER: School psychologist in Princeton (N.J.) Public Schools, 1952-60; Rutgers University, New Brunswick, N.J., associate professor, 1960-63, professor of education and psychology, 1960-76; University of North Carolina, Greensboro, Excellence Fund Professor of Education, 1976—. Adjunct professor at University of Pennsylvania, 1971-74; visiting professor at Auckland University of New Zealand, 1976, 1979. *Military service:* U.S. Army, 1944-46. *Member:* American Psychological Association (fellow; chairman of board of professional affairs, 1980), American Orthopsychiatric Association (fellow), Sigma Xi. *Awards, honors:* Fulbright-Hays Senior Research Award, 1979.

WRITINGS: School Psychology, Prentice-Hall, 1974. Contributor of more than seventy-five articles to journals in the behavioral sciences. *Journal of School Psychology,* president of board of directors, 1964-70, editor, 1968-71, editorial consultant, 1970—.

WORK IN PROGRESS: Research on application of psychological theory and practice to problems of schooling; development of standards and criteria for training and practice in school psychology and other specialities of professional psychology.

*   *   *

BARLOW, Wilfred 1915-

PERSONAL: Born in 1915, in England; son of Percy (a broker) and Dora (Coop) Barlow; married Marjory Alexander Mechim (a teacher), May 9, 1940; children: Penelope Barlow Oakeley, David. *Education:* Trinity College, Oxford, M.A.,

1938; St. Thomas's Hospital, London, B.M., B.Ch., 1941. *Politics:* Social Democrat. *Religion:* Church of England. *Home and office:* Alexander Institute, 3 Albert Court, Kensington Gore, London S.W.7, England. *Agent:* A.M. Heath & Co. Ltd., 40-42 William IV St., London WC2N 4DD, England.

CAREER: Senior registrar at Middlesex Hospital, 1947-49; Alexander Institute, London, England, medical consultant, 1953—. Medical consultant for Wembley Hospital, 1953—. *Military service:* British Army, Royal Medical Corps, 1942-46; became captain. *Member:* International P.E.N., Royal Society of Medicine, British Association for Rehabilitation and Rheumatology, Philosophy of Science Group.

WRITINGS: The Alexander Technique, Knopf, 1973; *More Talk of Alexander,* Gollancz, 1978; *The Aching Back,* Gollancz, 1980. Editor of *Alexander Journal.*

SIDELIGHTS: Barlow wrote: "I switched from classics (Greek, Latin, philosophy) to medicine and have tried since then to bridge the two worlds. I have encountered much hostility from medical colleagues because of my successful attempts to get the 'Alexander' method of R-education accepted medically. In 1973 my book on Alexander was mentioned in detail at the Nobel Oration in Medicine, in Stockholm, and since then it has been generally accepted."

*   *   *

BARNES, J(ohn) A(rundel) 1918-

PERSONAL: Born September 9, 1918, in Reading, England; son of Thomas D. (in business) and Grace (a manager; maiden name, Nash) Barnes; married Frances Bastable (a medical psychologist), December 16, 1942; children: Keith Rory, Joanna, Ian, Martin. *Education:* St. John's College, Cambridge, B.A., 1939; Balliol College, Oxford, D.Phil., 1951. *Office:* Churchill College, Cambridge CB3 0DS, England.

CAREER: Rhodes-Livingstone Institute, Zambia, research officer, 1946-49; University of London, University College, London, England, lecturer in anthropology, 1949-51; Victoria University of Manchester, Manchester, England, Simon Fellow, 1951-53; University of London, London School of Economics and Political Science, reader in anthropology, 1954-56; University of Sydney, Sydney, Australia, professor of anthropology, 1956-58; Australian National University, Canberra, professor of anthropology, 1958-69; Cambridge University, Cambridge, England, professor of sociology, 1969—. *Military service:* Royal Navy, 1940-46; became lieutenant commander; received Distinguished Service Cross. Royal Naval Volunteer Reserve. *Member:* Academy of the Social Sciences in Australia.

WRITINGS: Inquest on the Murgin, Royal Anthropological Institute, 1967; *Sociology in Cambridge,* Cambridge University Press, 1970; *Three Styles in the Study of Kinship,* University of California Press, 1971; *Social Networks,* Addison-Wesley, 1972; *The Ethics of Inquiry in Social Science,* Oxford University Press, 1977; *Who Should Know What?,* Penguin, 1979.

WORK IN PROGRESS: Island Transformation: A Study of Social Change in Western Norway.

*   *   *

BAROFF, George Stanley 1924-

PERSONAL: Born November 27, 1924, in New York, N.Y.; son of Irving and Ida (Herman) Baroff; married Rose Kislin, June 15, 1952; children: Marina Binet, Roy James. *Educa-*

tion: George Washington University, B.S., 1948, M.A., 1950; New York University, Ph.D., 1955. *Office:* Developmental Disabilities Training Institute, University of North Carolina, Chapel Hill, N.C. 27514.

CAREER: Springfield State Hospital, Sykesville, Md., psychology intern, 1951-52; State Psychiatric Institute, New York, N.Y., senior research scientist in department of medical genetics, 1952-59; Vineland Training School, Vineland, N.J., chief clinical psychologist, 1960-63; University of North Carolina, Chapel Hill, associate professor, 1963-67, professor of psychology and director of Developmental Disabilities Training Institute, 1967—. Research associate at Columbia University, 1952-63; staff psychologist at Lebanon Hospital, Bronx, N.Y., 1957-59. *Military service:* U.S. Army, 1943-45. *Member:* American Psychological Association, American Association on Mental Deficiency, Association for the Severly Handicapped.

WRITINGS: Mental Retardation: Nature, Cause, and Management, Hemisphere Publishing Corp., 1974. Contributor to psychology and psychiatry journals.

WORK IN PROGRESS: Revision of *Mental Retardation;* co-writing a training manual for persons working with mentally retarded individuals.

SIDELIGHTS: Baroff told *CA:* "In my case authorship was made and not born. I envy 'true' authors their compulsion to write; mine is only to finish."

*   *   *

BARR, Densil Neve
See BUTTREY, Douglas N(orton)

*   *   *

BARRACLOUGH, Geoffrey 1908-

PERSONAL: Born May 10, 1908; son of Walter and Edith Barraclough. *Education:* Attended Oriel College, Oxford, University of Munich, Merton College, and British School in Rome.

CAREER: Cambridge University, Cambridge, England, fellow and lecturer at St. John's College, 1936, university lecturer, 1937; University of Liverpool, Liverpool, England, professor of mediaeval history, 1945-56; University of London, London, England, research professor of international history, 1956-62; professor of history at University of California, 1965-68; Brandeis University, Waltham, Mass., professor of history, 1968-70; Oxford University, Oxford, England, Chichele Professor of Modern History, 1970-73, fellow of All Souls College, 1970. *Military service:* Royal Air Force, 1942-45. *Member:* Historical Association (president, 1964-67).

WRITINGS: Public Notaries and the Papal Curia: A Calendar and a Study of a Formularium Notariorum Curie From the Early Years of the Fourteenth Century, Macmillan, 1934; *Papal Provisions: Aspects of Church History, Constitutional, Legal, and Administrative in the Later Middle Ages,* Basil Blackwell, 1935, reprinted, Greenwood Press, 1971; (translator and author of introduction) *Mediaeval Germany, 911-1250* (essays), two volumes, Basil Blackwell, 1938, reprinted, Barnes & Noble, 1967; *Factors in German History,* Basil Blackwell, 1946, reprinted, Greenwood Press, 1979; *The Origins of Modern Germany,* Basil Blackwell, 1946, 2nd edition, 1947, Capricorn Books, 1962.

The Mediaeval Empire: Idea and Reality, George Philip & Son, 1950; *The Earldom and County Palatine of Chester,* Basil Blackwell, 1953; *History in a Changing World,* Basil

Blackwell, 1955, University of Oklahoma Press, 1956; *European Unity in Thought and Action*, Basil Blackwell, 1963; *An Introduction to Contemporary History*, C. A. Watts, 1964, Basic Books, 1965; *History and the Common Man*, Historical Association, 1967; *The Medieval Papacy*, Harcourt, 1968.

(With Robert-Henri Bautier) *The Economic Development of Medieval Europe*, Harcourt, 1971; *The Hamlyn History of the World in Color*, Volume II: *The New Europe* (Barraclough was not associated with other volumes), Hamlyn, 1971; (with A.J.P. Taylor) *Bismark and Germany* (phonotape), Holt Information Systems, 1972; (contributor) *Der Streit um die Gesellschaftsordnung*, Schulthess Polygraphischer Verlag, 1975; *The Crucible of Europe: The Ninth and Tenth Centuries in European History*, University of California Press, 1976; (with Celso Furtado) *La Gran crisis mundial*, Programa de Capacitacion Campesina para la Reforma Agraria, 1976; *Main Trends in History*, Holmes & Meier, 1979; *The Turning Points of World History*, Thames & Hudson, 1979.

Editor: (With H. M. Cam) Gaillard T. Lapsley, *Community and Parliament in the Later Middle Ages*, Basil Blackwell, 1951; *Facsimiles of Early Charters*, Basil Blackwell, 1957; *Social Life in Early England* (essays), Barnes & Noble, 1960; (with Rachel F. Wall) *Survey of International Affairs, 1955-1956*, Oxford University Press, 1960; *Survey of International Affairs, 1956-1958*, Oxford University Press, 1962; *Survey of International Affairs, 1958-1960*, Oxford University Press, 1964; (and author of introduction) F. Graus and others, *Eastern and Western Europe in the Middle Ages*, Harcourt, 1970; W. E. Mosse, *Liberal Europe: The Age of Bourgeois Realism, 1848-1875*, Harcourt, 1974; Sidney Pollard, *European Economic Integration*, Transatlantic, 1974; A. R. Meyers, *Parliaments and Estates in Europe to 1789*, N. Watson, 1975; Frank E. Huggett, *The Land Question and European Society*, N. Watson, 1975; *"The Times" Atlas of World History*, Times Books, 1978. Editor of *Annual Bulletin of Historical Literature*, 1948-49.

BIOGRAPHICAL/CRITICAL SOURCES: Foreign Affairs, July, 1948; *Spectator*, February 17, 1956; *London Times Literary Supplement*, March 2, 1956; *New Statesman and Nation*, March 17, 1956, November 24, 1978; *World Politics*, January, 1957; *Nation*, May 11, 1957, April 13, 1957; *Canadian Forum*, December, 1957; *New York Times Book Review*, May 2, 1965; *Times Literary Supplement*, December 19, 1968; February 29, 1980; *New York Review of Books*, December 7, 1978; *Scientific American*, February, 1979.*

*   *   *

BARRETT, John Henry 1913-

PERSONAL: Born July 21, 1913, in King's Lynn, England; son of John Ambrose (a chemist) and Evelyn Marion (Back) Barrett; married Ruth Mary Byass, June 23, 1940; children: Jane Marion Barrett Higham, Michael John, Richard William, Robert Thomas. *Education:* St. John's College, Cambridge, B.A., 1935, M.A., 1939. *Politics:* "Non-party democratic." *Religion:* Anglican. *Home:* Anchor Cottage, Dale, Haverfordwest, Pembrokeshire, Wales.

CAREER: Dale Fort Field Centre, Haverfordwest, Wales, warden, 1947-68; Pembrokeshire Countryside Unit, Wales, director, 1968-73; writer, 1973—. Vice-chairman of Council for the Protection of Rural Wales and Dyfed Rural Council; member of board of governors of National Museum of Wales and Dyfed College of Art. Member of Dale Parish Council, 1950—. *Military service:* Royal Air Force, 1936-47; became

wing commander. *Member:* British Ecological Society, Institute of Biology (fellow), Ornithologist Union, Geographical Association, National Trust (member of council and executive committee), Nature Conservancy. *Awards, honors:* Member of Order of the British Empire, 1978.

WRITINGS: (With C. M. Yonge) *Pocket Guide to the Seashore*, Collins, 1958; *Life on the Seashore*, Collins, 1974; *The Pembrokeshire Coast Path*, H.M. Stationery Office, 1974. Author of "Countryman," a column in *Western Mail*. Contributor to magazines. Editor of *Field Studies*, 1972-76.

WORK IN PROGRESS: A Handbook to the Natural History of the Coast, for Collins.

SIDELIGHTS: Barrett told *CA:* "I have spent my life trying to conserve the beauty and the complexity of the natural world by teaching, watching, and demonstrating."

*   *   *

BARROLL, John Leeds III 1928-

PERSONAL: Born July 20, 1928, in Lausanne, Switzerland; son of John Leeds and Mary Hargrove (Bellamy) Barroll; married Rayna Sue Klatzkin, March 17, 1951; children: John Leeds IV, James Edmonson, Ellen. *Education:* Harvard University, A.B. (cum laude), 1950; Princeton University, M.A., 1955, Ph.D., 1956. *Religion:* Episcopalian. *Office:* Department of English, University of Pittsburgh, Pittsburgh, Pa. 15213.

CAREER: Teacher of classics at boys' school, 1950-52; English teacher at private school in New York, N.Y., 1952-53; Rutgers University, Douglass College, New Brunswick, N.J., instructor in English, 1955-56; University of Texas, Austin, instructor, 1956-59, assistant professor of English, 1959-60; University of Cincinnati, Cincinnati, Ohio, associate professor, 1960-64, professor of English, 1964-67, assistant dean of Graduate School, 1965-66, associate dean, 1966-67; University of Newcastle upon Tyne, Newcastle upon Tyne, England, visiting professor of English literature, 1967-68; Vanderbilt University, Nashville, Tenn., professor of English, 1968-69; William Paterson College, Wayne, N.J., dean of arts and sciences, 1969-70; University of South Carolina, Columbia, professor of English literature, 1970-74, director of Center for Shakespeare Studies, 1972-74; National Endowment for the Humanities, deputy director of Division of Research Grants, 1974-78; University of Pittsburgh, Pittsburgh, Pa., Andrew W. Mellon Visiting Professor of English Literature, 1978—. Visiting associate professor at Washington University, St. Louis, Mo., 1962. *Military service:* U.S. Army, 1946-48.

MEMBER: International Association of University Professors, Shakespeare Council of America (chairman of board of trustees, 1970—), Shakespeare Association of America, Modern Language Association of America, Malone Society, Modern Humanities Research Association (England), Hasty Pudding Club (Harvard University). *Awards, honors:* Huntington Library fellow, 1957, 1959; Folger Shakespeare Library fellow, 1958; Sachs Award from Cincinnati Institute of Fine Arts, 1966.

WRITINGS: (Contributor) G. R. Smith, editor, *Essays on Shakespeare*, Pennsylvania State University Press, 1965; (editor with Austin M. Wright) *The Art of the Short Story: An Introductory Anthology*, Allyn & Bacon, 1969; (editor) William Shakespeare, *Hamlet*, W. C. Brown, 1970; (editor) Shakespeare, *Othello*, W. C. Brown, 1971; *Artificial Persons: The Formation of Character in the Tragedies of Shakespeare*, University of South Carolina Press, 1974; (with others) *Revels History of Drama in English,* Volume III: *1576-1613,* Methuen, 1975.

General editor of "International Shakespeare," 1971—, and "The South Carolina Shakespeare," 1972; editor of "Shakespeare Studies" (monograph series), 1969—. Contributor to literature journals. Editor of *Shakespeare Studies,* 1965—.*

*   *   *

BARTOLE, Genevieve 1927-

PERSONAL: Born November 8, 1927, in Montmartre, Saskatchewan, Canada; daughter of John (a farmer) and Jennie (Keen) Bartole; married Kenneth McRobbie (a poet; divorced, 1972); children: Lara Helen. *Education:* Attended Columbia University, 1949; University of Manitoba, B.A., 1976. *Home:* Six Cornell Dr., Winnipeg, Manitoba, Canada R3T 3B9.

CAREER: Worked as librarian in Regina, Saskatchewan, Toronto, Ontario, and London, England, 1949—; writer, 1959—. *Member:* Canadian Library Association, Canadian Poets (Manitoba representative, 1977-80), Manitoba Library Association.

WRITINGS: Figure in the Rain (poems), Ryerson, 1950; *Moonwinder* (poems), Mosaic Press, 1981; *A Lesson for All Packrats* (children's stories), Tree Frog Press, 1981.

Work represented in anthologies, including *Made in Canada, Forty Women Poets,* and *Mirrors.* Contributor to magazines, including *Saturday Night, Quarry,* and *Canadian Forum.* Poetry editor of *CV/II.*

WORK IN PROGRESS: A third book of poems, tentatively entitled *House Without Eyebrows.*

SIDELIGHTS: Bartole commented to *CA:* "For a long time I published little poetry, except in magazines, convinced that I could not say in poetry what I really wanted to say. I saw that so much of the poetry being written in Canada and the United States was in the first person *singular,* and not so much in first person *universal.* Then when I read Carl Jung, Doris Lessing, poets like Sylvia Plath, and more recently Margaret Atwood, I realized that what I was missing was the dimensional approach that makes the personal experience a universal one, bridging the gap between inner psyche and outer reality and landscape.

"I like to personify my landscape and my animals as an extension of the personal. My trees might occasionally march and chant, and my people, as in 'Prairie Syndrome,' a poem in *Moonwinder,* can enter the animal world through the influence of landscape, not for the sake of absurdity itself, but to make a point. Like humor, the absurd can often be more effective than the didactic."

*   *   *

BARTUSIS, Mary Ann 1930-

PERSONAL: Born April 16, 1930, in Palmer, Pa.; daughter of Steven (a coal miner) and Anna K. (Polach) Babinsky; married Donald J. Bartusis (a consultant engineer), July 10, 1954; children: Joseph, Deborah, Monica, Michele. *Education:* University of Pittsburgh, B.S., 1952; Woman's Medical College of Pennsylvania, M.D., 1956. *Religion:* Roman Catholic. *Home and office:* 1007 North Pennsylvania Ave., Morrisville, Pa. 19067; (summers) 2100 Wesley Ave., Ocean City, N.J. 08226. *Agent:* Jacqueline Simenauer, 22 Greenview Way, Montclair, N.J. 07043.

CAREER: Philadelphia General Hospital, Philadelphia, Pa., intern, 1956-57; New Jersey State Hospital, Trenton, resi-

dent in psychiatry, 1957-60; Catholic Welfare Bureau, Trenton, associate medical director and administrative assistant at Guidance Clinic, 1960-64, medical director, 1964-67; private practice of psychiatry in Morrisville, Pa., 1967—. Certified by American Board of Psychiatry and Neurology, 1963. Clinical assistant professor at New Jersey College of Medicine, 1964-67, and Medical College of Pennsylvania, 1976—. Member of advisory committee of Young Women's Christian Association's Encore Project on Rehabilitation of Breast Surgery Patients, 1974—; member of board of governors of Greater Trenton Symphony. Past member of professional advisory committees of Mental Health Board of Mercer County and Delaware Valley Rehabilitation Center. Consultant to Mercer County Juvenile Court probation department, 1967-75. Public speaker; guest on more than one hundred television and radio programs in the United States and Canada, including "The Today Show," "Dinah," "The Mike Douglas Show," "Good Morning America," and "The Phil Donahue Show"; appeared regularly on "A.M. Philadelphia."

MEMBER: American Psychiatric Association (fellow; member of board of trustees, 1977-80, member of Commission on Public Affairs, 1980—), American College of Psychiatrists, American Medical Association, National Foundation for Women's Health (member of board of directors, 1978—), American Medical Women's Association, Group for the Advancement of Psychiatry, New Jersey Medical Society, New Jersey Psychiatric Association, New Jersey Medical Women's Association, Mercer County Medical Society, Zonta International. *Awards, honors:* Named "woman par excellence" by Woman's Division of Trenton Trust Co., 1970; achievement award from Church Women United in Greater Trenton, 1976.

WRITINGS: Every Other Man, Dutton, 1978. Contributor of more than thirty articles to professional journals, including *New Jersey Journal of Pharmacy, New Jersey Parent-Teacher,* and *Psychiatric Annals,* and to popular magazines, including *Cosmopolitan, New Woman, Woman's Day, Ladies Home Journal,* and *Self.*

WORK IN PROGRESS: Two books.

SIDELIGHTS: Mary Bartusis wrote: "My primary interest is the treatment of the mentally and emotionally disturbed. I am also thoroughly involved in the education of the lay public to the understanding and the needs of the emotionally and mentally ill and plan to continue my media appearances and my writing."

*   *   *

BATAILLE, Georges 1887-1962
(Lord Auch, Pierre Angelique)

PERSONAL: Born September 10, 1887, in Billom, Puy-de-Dome, France; died July 8, 1962, in Puy-de-Dome, France.

CAREER: Poet, novelist, and philosopher. Bibliotheque Nationale, Paris, France, 1920-42, began as librarian, became deputy keeper and editor of *Documents;* founder and editor of *Critique* (literary review), beginning in 1946.

WRITINGS—In English: (Under pseudonym Lord Auch) *Histoire de l'oeil* (also see below), [France], 1928, published under own name, J. J. Pauvert, 1967, translation by Joachim Neugroschel published as *The Story of the Eye* (also see below), Urizen, 1967; (under pseudonym Pierre Angelique) *Madame Edwarda* (also see below), [France], 1937, published under own name, J. J. Pauvert, 1956, translation by Audiart published as *The Naked Beast at Heaven's Gate* (also see below), Olympia Press, 1956; *A Tale of Satisfied Desire*, translated from the original French by Audiart, Olympia Press, 1953.

Lascaux; ou, La Naissance de l'art, [France], 1955, translation by Austryn Wainhouse published as *Lascaux; or, The Birth of Art: Prehistoric Painting*, Skira, 1955; *Manet*, [France], 1955, translation by Wainhouse and James Emmons published as *Manet: A Biographical and Critical Study*, Skira, 1955; *L'Erotisme; ou, La Mise en question de l'etre*, [France], 1957, translation published as *Death and Sensuality: A Study of Eroticism and the Taboo*, Walker, 1962; *L'Erotisme*, Editions de Minuit, 1957, translation by Mary Dalwood published as *Eroticism*, J. Calder, 1962; *La Litterature et le mal: Emily Bronte, Baudelaire, Michelet, Blake, Sade, Proust, Kafka, Genet*, Gallimard, 1957, translation by Alastair Hamilton published as *Literature and Evil*, Calder & Boyars, 1973; *Ma Mere* (novel), J. J. Pauvert, 1966, translation by Wainhouse published as *My Mother*, J. Cape, 1972; *The Story of the Eye* [and] *The Naked Beast at Heaven's Gate*, Brandon House, 1968; *Blue of Noon*, translated from the original French by Harry Matthews, Urizen, 1978.

In French: *L'Experience interieure* (title means "Inner Experience"), Gallimard, 1943, revised edition, 1967; *L'Archangelique et autres poems*, [France], 1944, Mecure de France, 1967; *Le Coupable* (title means "The Guilty One"), Gallimard, 1944, revised edition, 1961; *Somme atheologique*, [France], 1944, Gallimard, 1961; *L'Orestie* (also see below), Les Editions des Quatre vents, 1945; *Sur Nietzsche: Volonte de chance*, Gallimard, 1945; *Histoire de rats* (also see below), Editions de Minuit, 1947; *La Haine de la poesie* (title means "The Hatred of Poetry"; contains *L'Orestie, Histoire des rats*, and *Dianus*), Editions de Minuit, 1947, 2nd edition published as *L'Impossible, Histoire de rats, suivi de Dianus et de L'Orestie*, 1962; *La Part Maudite: Essai d'economie generale*, Editions de Minuit, 1949.

L'Abbe C., Editions de Minuit, 1950; *Le Bleu de ciel* (novel), J. J. Pauvert, 1957; (author of introduction) Max Ernst, *Max Ernst*, Gonthier-Seghers, 1960; *Les Larmes d'Eros*, J. J. Pauvert, 1961; *Le Petit*, J. J. Pauvert, 1963; *Le Proces de Gilles de Rais: Les Documents*, J. J. Pauvert, 1965; *Le Mort* (also see below), J. J. Pauvert, 1967; *La Pratique de la joie devant la mort*, Mercure de France, 1967; (contributor) Giuseppe Lo Duco, *Eros im Bild: Die Erotik in der europaeischen Kunst*, K. Desch, 1968; *Documents* (art criticism), edited by Bernard Noel, Mercure de France, 1968; *Oeuvres completes*, four volumes, Gallimard, 1970-73; (contributor) *Marcel Proust*, L'Arc, 1971; *Madame Edwarda, Le Mort, Historie de l'oeil*, J. J. Pauvert, 1973; *Theorie de la religion*, Gallimard, 1974; (contributor) *Sade*, Obliques, 1977.*

*   *   *

BATCHELOR, David 1943-

PERSONAL: Born June 19, 1943, in London, England; son of Denzil (a writer) and Eleanor (Pack) Batchelor; married Jane Seymour, June 27, 1964 (divorced, 1976); children: Charlotte, Jessica, Hannah. *Education:* Attended Eton College. *Politics:* "Eternally evolving." *Religion:* Anglo-Catholic. *Home:* 52 Onslow Sq., London S.W.7, England.

CAREER: Worked in advertising and public relations in London, England, 1962; farm laborer in Norfolk, England, 1968-74; writer. *Member:* Society of Authors.

WRITINGS: Brogan and Sons (novel), Secker & Warburg, 1976; *A Dislocated Man* (novel), Secker & Warburg, 1978. Contributor to magazines, including *Punch, St. Mary's An-*

nual, and *Journal of the International Wine and Food Society*.

WORK IN PROGRESS: Night Moves (tentative title).

SIDELIGHTS: Batchelor commented: "I am principally interested in dualism, redemption, and failure. I think it's funny that grave books are frequently written by humourists and hilarious books by grave men. I also like the Midrash: 'If I create the world by mercy alone, sin will abound; if by justice alone, how can the world endure? I will create it by both.'

"Essentially my work is cathartic—for my children's sake. They are most important. That is why children die so often in my work. Of course this is folly. If they survive, they will be as fallible as I am. None are less. I write to purge."

*   *   *

BATES, Lucius Christopher 1901(?)-1980

OBITUARY NOTICE: Born c. 1901; died following intestinal surgery, c. August 22, 1980, in Little Rock, Ark. Civil rights leader and publisher of *Arkansas State Press*. In 1957 Bates and his wife engineered the desegregation of Central High School in Little Rock, despite opposition from the National Guard. They were supported by military troops called into action by President Eisenhower to protect students and thwart intervention by segregationists. Bates's home was subsequently bombed. Obituaries and other sources: *Newsweek*, September 8, 1980; *Time*, September 8, 1980.

*   *   *

BATESON, Gregory 1904-1980

OBITUARY NOTICE—See index for *CA* sketch: Born May 9, 1904, in Cambridge, England; died of respiratory disease, July 4, 1980, in San Francisco, Calif. Anthropologist, social scientist, psychologist, philosopher, and author. Bateson collaborated with his first wife, Margaret Mead, on studies of primitive cultures. Together they founded the science of cybernetics. Bateson later formulated the "double-bind" theory, which describes how children who receive contradictory messages of love and rejection from their parents may develop schizophrenia. In addition to *Balinese Character*, which was written in collaboration with Mead, Bateson wrote *Communication* and *Steps to an Ecology of Mind*. Obituaries and other sources: *New York Times*, July 7, 1980; *Newsweek*, July 21, 1980; *Time*, July 21, 1980; *Publishers Weekly*, July 25, 1980.

*   *   *

BATHERMAN, Muriel
See SHELDON, Muriel

*   *   *

BAUER, Walter 1904-

PERSONAL: Born November 4, 1904, in Merseburg, Germany (now East Germany); came to Canada in 1952.

CAREER: Writer. Worked as elementary school teacher and instructor in universities in Germany. University of Toronto, Toronto, Ontario, lecturer in German, c. 1960.

WRITINGS: Stimme aus dem Leunawerk (verse and prose), Malik Verlag, 1930; *Ein Mann zog in die Stadt* (novel), B. Cassirer, 1931; *Die notwendige Reise*, B. Cassirer, 1932; *Das Herz der Erde: Ein Mutter Roman* (novel), B. Cassirer, 1933; *Die horde Moris* (short stories), B. Cassirer, 1935; *Der Lichtstrahl* (novel), Deutsche Verlags Anstalt, 1936; *Ab-*

schied und Wanderung: Drei Erzaehlungen um Goethe, Propylaeen Verlag, 1939; *Die Armee des don Quijote*, K. Rauch, 1939.

Wanderer im Sueden (travel), Bitter & Co., 1940; *Die zweite Mutter* (fiction), P. Reclam, 1942; *Bis zum Hahnenschrei* (fiction), K. Rauch, 1943; *Degen und Harfe: Sechs Erzaehlungen* (short stories), Propylaeen Verlag, 1943; *Tagebuchblaetter aus Frankreich*, K. Rauch, 1943; *Der Gast* (short stories), C. Bertelsmann, 1943; *Flamme und Asche: Bildnis Georg Forster's*, Staufen Verlag, 1944; *Das letzte Glueck des herrn Giorgione*, Reclamdruck, 1944; *Das Geschenk der Ferne*, C. Bertelsmann, 1947; *Das Gewissen Europas: Bildnis von Nansen*, C. Bertelsmann, 1947; *Das Lied der Freiheit*, K. Desch, 1947; *Die Ueberwindung der Wildnis: Das Leben Livingstones*, C. Bertelsmann, 1947; (editor) Heinrich Heine, *Der junge Heine: Briefe, Berichte, Schriften*, L. Blanvalet, 1948; *Der Gesang vom Sturmvogel: Ueber Antoine de Saint Exupery*, F. Truejen, 1949.

Inga im Wald (juvenile), reprint of 1938 edition, H. Schaffstein, 1950; *Besser zu zweit als allein* (novel), K. Desch, 1950; *Mount Everest: Bericht von Mallory und seinen Freunden*, C. Bertelsmann, 1950; *Die Sonne von Arles: Das Leben von Vincent van Gogh* (biography), Hundt Verlag, 1951, 2nd edition, 1956; *Polflug: Bericht von Andree und dem "Ader,"* C. Bertelsmann, 1952; *Folge dem Pfeil: Traum und Tod des Sieur de la Salle*, K. Desch, 1956; *Die langen Reisen* (biography of Fridtjof Nansen), Kindler, 1956; (editor) Eduard Friedrich Moerike, *Saemtliche Werke*, K. Desch, 1956; *Der Einsame: Bildnis von Caspar David Friedrich*, W. Jess, 1957; *Nachtwachen des Tellerwaeschers*, K. Desch, 1957; (compiler) *Im Banne des Abenteuers: Die spannendsten Geschichten der Welt*, K. Desch, 1958; *Die Traenen eines Mannes* (short stories), Nymphenburger Verlagshandlung, 1958; (editor) Johann Christian Guenther, *Die Harfe der Liebe*, K. Desch, 1958.

Die Familie Fritsche (juvenile), H. Schaffstein, c. 1960; *Griechische Sagen*, Union Verlag, 1960; *Der weisse Indianer, Waescha-kwonnesin: Die Geschichte eines abenteuerlichen Lebens*, Ullstein, 1960; *Die Stimme: Geschichte einer Liebe*, K. Desch, 1961; *Klopfzeichen* (poems), E. Tessloff, 1962; *Maerchen aus tausendundeine Nacht*, Union Verlag, 1962; *Tagebuchblaetter und drei Erzaehlungen*, Matthiesen, c. 1962; *Fremd in Toronto: Erzaehlungen und Prosastuecke* (travel), Hattingen & Humdt, 1963; *Lorbeer fuer Hellas: Grosse Stunden der griechischen Geschichte*, Union Verlag, 1964; *Ein deutscher meiner Generation*, edited by William A. Packer and George A. Kirk, House of Grant, 1965; *Fragment vom Hahnenschrei*, Merlin Verlag, 1966; *Ein Jahr: Tagebuchblaetter aus Kanada*, Merlin Verlag, 1967; (contributor) Friedrich Samuel Rothenberg, editor, *Der helle dunkle Tag*, Brockhaus, 1967; *The Price of Morning: Selected Poems*, translated by Henry Beissel from the original German, Prism International Press, 1968; *Die Kinder und die Armen: Lebensgeschichte Pestalozzis*, Beltz, 1969; *Lebenslauf: Gedichte, 1929-1974*, K. Desch, 1975; *A Different Sun* (poems), translated by Beissel from the original German, Oberon Press, 1976.*

*   *   *

BAUSCH, Richard (Carl) 1945-

PERSONAL: Born April 18, 1945, in Fort Benning, Ga.; son of Robert Carl and Helen (Simmons) Bausch; married Karen Miller (a photographer), May 3, 1969; children: Wesley, Emily, Paul. *Education:* George Mason University, B.A., 1974; University of Iowa, M.F.A., 1975; also attended Northern Virginia Community College. *Politics:* "'. . .only connect. . .' E. M. Forster." *Religion:* Roman Catholic. *Residence:* Fairfax, Va. *Agent:* Harriet Wasserman, Russell & Volkening, Inc., 551 Fifth Ave., New York, N.Y. 10017. *Office:* Department of English, George Mason University, 4400 University Dr., Fairfax, Va. 22030.

CAREER: Worked as singer and comedian. George Mason University, Fairfax, Va., assistant professor of English, 1980—. *Military service:* U.S. Air Force, survival instructor, 1966-69. *Member:* Associated Writing Programs.

WRITINGS: Real Presence (novel), Dial, 1980; *I Don't Care If I Never Get Back* (novel), Dial, 1981. Author of songs.

Work represented in anthologies, including *New Writing From the South*, 1980. Contributor to *Ploughshares*.

WORK IN PROGRESS: The Last Good Time, a novel; *I Hope You Continue to Have a Good Time After I Tell You the News*, stories.

SIDELIGHTS: Bausch wrote: "It seems that ideas for novels come only after many miles in the car, on one journey or another—my first two novels came to me *in* the car midway between home and the destination. I have no idea what this means and I don't intend to fool with a good thing by trying very hard to figure it out. *The Last Good Time* also occurred to me in the car, on a much shorter journey—to my local bank, where a check for almost four thousand dollars proved too complicated for one nervous teller and one recalcitrant loan officer—result: Max Hagood, who, like all of us, hates banks. As a matter of fact I hate all large organizations, mega-bucks, corporations and Incs.—all producers of junk mail and TV ads that demean the human heart. And almost none of this gets into my writing if I can help it, since I'm writing fiction, not essays.

"My vital subjects are family, fear, love, and anything that is irrecoverable and *missed;* but I'll dispense with all of that for a good story. I like to think that in my search for the right events—the story—all the other stuff will take care of itself, assuming I am careful with the words since, finally, it all comes down to that: words. As a boy I was continually astonished by people who disagreed with me if I had put something well in words, and I suppose that's why I write fiction rather than essays. I do not believe that I will ever write a real essay in my life, mostly because that isn't as much fun as writing fiction, but at least partly because of a fundamental distrust, developed over the years of my boyhood, in the power of words to change any *mind*. Still, I remain utterly convinced in the force of words, the possibility in words to transform the heart. At least for a little while.

"As for other interests: I absolutely love jokes, mostly dirty, if told well. I like bourbon, beer, no sweet drinks. I hate literary gatherings, and avoid them as much as possible—at times I would rather talk about changing the carburetor on a Ford than about Ford Madox Ford, and from this perhaps one can surmise I have no literary creed, and belong to no literary school; my only criterion is that fiction make feeling, that it deepen feeling. If it doesn't do that It's not fiction: it's okay to be other than fiction, as long as one knows the difference. We have plenty of elaborate crossword puzzles posing as fiction, and that's okay too, as long as nobody expects me to read them. But a style—a structure—alien to me, alien to the traditions, is just fine if it moves me the way Leonard Michaels moves me, or John Hawkes, or Robbe-Grillet. Bernard Malamud has said that what moves him, moves him to Art. Well, all right: what moves me, moves me to expression.

"As to circumstances: I grew up listening to my father tell stories—he is a great story-teller, and all the Bauschs can do it. There were six children and when we get together the neighbors just listen and laugh. The stories go round the table. My mother is an artist, and early on I knew how to draw, wondered that my classmates could not. I have a twin brother who writes fiction as well as or better than I ever will, and I have a sister who makes wonderful portraits and watercolors for her children. The fact that I am a novelist seems as inevitable to me as the fact that I am past thirty now.

"Finally, I should add that I began as an entertainer—stand-up comedian and songwriter/singer. I still do *shtick* in class—it makes for good teaching, I found—and I can still sing with about anybody, though as a guitarist I'm still looking for the person who plays more poorly than I do—six years, I have been looking for that someone who must be out there who cannot play better than I. My career as a songwriter ended when I got to the end of the possibilities in the key of G. But I still try one occasionally, since I prefer to give a song to my wife on our anniversary, rather than a card. My wife, I think, would probably prefer a card.

"It is on her, finally, that responsibility for my writing rests: I have had the rare luck to find a partner willing to live in the terrible circumstances most writers—particularly unpublished writers—find themselves in these days. For better than two years, before I sold *Real Presence*—before I'd begun to write it—she caught rainwater in pots and pans in the dining room of the shack we lived in. She took angry, threatening phone calls from the bill collectors—phone calls that the Mafia would be proud of—and she persisted with me, humored me, encouraged me. Let no man say that is not the most important thing in any writer's development."

* * *

BAYLEY, Peter Charles 1921-

PERSONAL: Born January 25, 1921, in Gloucester, England; son of William Charles Abell and Irene Evelyn Beatrice (Heath) Bayley; married Patience Clark, June 30, 1951; children: Nicholas William, Rosalind Mary, Clare Sarah. *Education:* Oxford University, M.A., 1947. *Religion:* Church of England. *Office:* Department of English, University of St. Andrews, St. Andrews, Fife KY16 9AL, Scotland.

CAREER: Oxford University, Oxford, England, fellow, 1947-72, paelector, 1949-72, lecturer in English, 1952-72; master of secondary school in Durham, England, 1972-78; University of St. Andrews, St. Andrews, Scotland, Berry Professor of English and head of department, 1978—. Chairman of British Council recorded seminars on Shakespeare, 1976, 1978. *Military service:* British Army, bombardier in Royal Artillery, 1941-44, in Intelligence Corps, 1944-45; served in Far East; became sergeant-major.

WRITINGS: (Editor) Edmund Spenser, *The Faerie Queene,* Oxford University Press, Book II, 1965, Book I, 1966; *Edmund Spenser: Prince of Poets,* Hutchinson, 1971; (editor) *Loves and Deaths: Novelists' Tales of the Nineteenth Century From Scott to Hardy,* Oxford University Press, 1972; (editor) *A Casebook on Spenser's "Faerie Queene,"* Macmillan, 1977; (editor) *Poems by Milton,* Longman, 1981.

Contributor: J. J. Lawlor, editor, *Patterns of Love and Courtesy,* Edward Arnold, 1966; A. E. Dyson, editor, *English Poetry: Select Bibliographical Guides,* Oxford University Press, 1971; J. Como, editor, *C. S. Lewis at the Breakfast Table,* Macmillan, 1979. Oxford University correspondent for *London Times,* 1960-63. Contributor to literature journals and newspapers.

WORK IN PROGRESS: "Investigating the literary relationships between Chaucer, Spenser, and Shakespeare."

SIDELIGHTS: "I always open my Spenser (as my Chaucer and Shakespeare) with confident expectation of pleasure, never unfulfilled," wrote Bayley. "Spenser is the greatest little-read writer in English. I always hope to get more readers for him; he is in danger of 'defoliation' by hard-line professional scholars, and I want to save him for the general reader and encourage more students to read him. I also see him as being in the main line of development—*pace* F. R. Leavis—of English literature, from Chaucer to the novel."

* * *

BAYLIS, John 1946-

PERSONAL: Born March 27, 1946; son of Harold and Sylvia (Williams) Baylis; married Marion Brockhurst (a teacher); children: Emma. *Education:* University College of Swansea, University of Wales, B.A. (with honors), 1968; University College of Wales, Aberystwyth, M.Sc., 1969. *Home:* 1 Glanstew, Penrhyncoch, Aberystwyth, Wales. *Office:* Department of International Politics, University of Wales, University College of Wales, Aberystwyth, Dyfed, Wales.

CAREER: University of Liverpool, Liverpool, England, lecturer in international politics, 1969-71; University of Wales, University College of Wales, Aberystwyth, lecturer in international politics, 1971—. *Member:* International Institute for Strategic Studies, Royal Institute of International Affairs, Royal United Service Institution.

WRITINGS: (With K. Booth, J. Garnett, and P. Williams) *Contemporary Strategy: Theories and Policies,* Croom Helm, 1976; (editor) *British Defence Policy in a Changing World,* Croom Helm, 1977; *Anglo-American Defense Relations, 1939-79,* Macmillan, 1980.

WORK IN PROGRESS: Research on Anglo-American relations and the formation of the North Atlantic Treaty Organization.

SIDELIGHTS: Baylis told *CA* that his motivation for writing is "a crucial concern with understanding the problems of peace and war."

* * *

BECHER, Ulrich 1910-

PERSONAL: Born January 2, 1910, in Berlin, Germany; son of Richard and Elisa Ulrich (von Rickenbach) Becher; married Dana Marie Roda, November 4, 1933; children: Martin Roda. *Education:* Attended University of Geneva, 1928, University of Leipzig, 1929, and University of Berlin, 1930-33. *Religion:* Lutheran. *Home:* Spalenring 95, Basel, Switzerland. *Agent:* Ruth Liepman, Maienburgweg 23, CH-8044, Zurich, Switzerland.

CAREER: Writer. Worked as news correspondent in Paris, France, and Zurich, Switzerland, both 1938, in Brazil, 1941-44, in New York, N.Y., 1945-48, and in Basel, Switzerland, 1949—. *Member:* International P.E.N., Dramatiker Union Berlin. *Awards, honors:* Drama prize from German Stage Club in Cologne, 1955, for "Mademoiselle Loewenzorn"; book-of-the-month award from German Academy of Letters, 1974, for *Williams' Ex-Casino;* Schiller Prize from Swiss Schiller Society, 1976.

WRITINGS: Murmeljagd (novel), Volume I: *Tote Zeit,* Volume II: *Licht im See,* Volume III: *Geisterbahn I,* Volume IV: *Geisterbahn II,* Volume V: *Die Strasse ueber San Gian,*

Rowohlt, 1969, one-volume translation by Henry A. Smith published as *Woodchuck Hunt*, Crown, 1976.

In German: *Maenner machen Fehler: Geschichten der Windrose* (stories; title means "Men Make Mistakes"), Rowohlt, 1932; *Die Eroberer: Geschichten aus Europa*, Oprecht, 1936; *Reise zum blauen Tag* (poems; title means "The Conquerors"), Verlag Bucher Volksstimme, 1946; *Bachtigall will zum Vater fliegen* (novel; title means "The Nightingale Flies to Father"), Universal Editions (Vienna, Austria), 1950; *Brasilianischer Romanzero* (novel; title means "Brazilian Romancero"), W. Classen, 1950; *Der schwarze Hut* (novel; title means "The Black Hat"), Mitteldeutscher Verlag, 1957; *Kurz nach vier* (novel; title means "Shortly Past Four"), Rowohlt, 1957; *Spiele der Zeit* (play; title means "Play of Our Time"), Rowohlt, 1957.

Das Herz des Hais (novel; title means "The Heart of the Shark"), Rowohlt, 1960; *Das Profil* (novel; title means "The Profile"), Rowohlt, 1973; *Williams' Ex-Casino* (novel), Benziger, 1973; *SIFF* (essays; title means "Selective Identification of Friend and Foe"), Benziger, 1978. Also author of *Die nicht so netten Geschichten* (title means "The Not So Nice Stories").

Plays: "Niemand" (title means "Nobody"), first produced in Bern, Switzerland, at Stadttheater, 1934; "Biene gib mir Honig" (title means "Give Me Honey, Honeybee"), first produced at Stadttheater, 1936; "Der Bockerer," first produced in Vienna, Austria, 1948; "Der Pfeiffer von Wien," first produced in Vienna, 1950; "Samba," first produced in Vienna, 1950; "Feuerwasser" (title means "Firewater"), first produced in Goettingen, West Germany, 1951; "Mademoiselle Loewenzorn," 1953; "Die Kleinen und die Grossen" (title means "The Little Ones and the Big Ones"), 1955; "Der Herr kommt aus Bahia" (title means "The Lord Comes From Bahia"), first produced in Goettingen, 1958; "Makumba," 1965; "Das Maerchen vom Raeuber, der Schutzmann wurde" (title means "The Fairy Tale of the Robber Who Became a Policeman"), first produced in Buenos Aires, Argentina.

WORK IN PROGRESS: Adapting plays, "Makumba," for radio, and "Der Bockerer," for the screen.

AVOCATIONAL INTERESTS: Painting, jazz piano.

* * *

BECK, James Murray 1914-

PERSONAL: Born December 2, 1914, in Lunenburg, Nova Scotia, Canada; son of Allan Clyde and Florence Louise (Silver) Beck. *Education:* Acadia University, B.A., 1934, M.A., 1938; University of Toronto, M.A., 1946, Ph.D., 1954. *Religion:* United Church. *Office:* Department of Political Science; Dalhousie University, Halifax, Nova Scotia, Canada B3H 4H6.

CAREER: Teacher at public elementary and high schools in South Brookfield, Lawrencetown, and Guysborough, Nova Scotia, 1934-41; University of Toronto, Toronto, Ontario, instructor in political science, 1948-50; Acadia University, Wolfville, Nova Scotia, assistant professor of political science and history, 1950-52; Royal Military College of Canada, Kingston, Ontario, assistant professor, 1952-54, associate professor, 1954-56, professor of political science, 1956-63; Dalhousie University, Halifax, Nova Scotia, professor of political science, 1963-80, professor emeritus, 1980—. Consultant to Government of Nova Scotia on constitution, 1967-70. *Military service:* Royal Canadian Air Force, radar officer, 1941-45; became flight lieutenant. *Member:* Royal So-

ciety of Canada (fellow), Canadian Political Science Association, Canadian Historical Association.

WRITINGS: Government of Nova Scotia, University of Toronto Press, 1957; *Pendulum of Power: Canada's Federal Elections*, Prentice-Hall, 1968; *The History of Maritime Union: A Study in Frustration*, Maritime Union Study, 1969; (editor) *Joseph Howe: A Voice of Nova Scotia*, McClelland & Stewart, 1964; *The Shaping of Canadian Federalism: Central Authority or Provincial Right?*, Copp-Clark, 1971; *The Evolution of Municipal Government in Nova Scotia, 1749-1973*, Government of Nova Scotia, 1973. Author of booklets. Contributor to history and political science journals.

WORK IN PROGRESS: A biography of Joseph Howe, two volumes; a book on the politics of Nova Scotia, completion expected in 1982.

SIDELIGHTS: Beck commented to *CA:* "Starting with *Government of Nova Scotia* in 1957, I became increasingly interested in the political culture of Nova Scotia. In particular, I have shown that until the Second World War conservatism and traditionalism governed the political behavior of the province's politicians and people, and that although considerable inroads have been made in that conservatism over the past three decades, it is still a basic key to understanding the province's politics. I have also provided a fuller understanding of the most eminent Nova Scotian, Joseph Howe, by demonstrating that in the fight for responsible government, completed in 1848, he was a conservative reformer par excellence. I have examined in detail the stages by which a disillusioned Howe, 'the noblest Briton of all,' was finally content to become a Canadian."

* * *

BEHM, Marc 1925-

PERSONAL: Born January 12, 1925, in Trenton, N.J.; son of Charles A. and Frances Behm; married wife, Francoise Vivien (an English teacher), August 25, 1949; children: Thomas, Julian, Nicholas, Vincent, Antoine, Frederique, Patrick. *Education:* Attended Sorbonne, University of Paris, and Institut des Hautes Etudes. *Religion:* Roman Catholic. *Home:* 10 rue d'Alesia, 75014 Paris, France. *Agent:* Curtis Brown Ltd., 575 Madison Ave., New York, N.Y. 10022.

CAREER: Writer. *Military service:* U.S. Army, 1943-45. *Member:* Authors Guild, Screenwriters Guild. *Awards, honors:* Box office blue ribbon, 1965, for motion picture "Help!"

WRITINGS: The Queen of the Night, Houghton, 1978; *The Eye of the Beholder*, Dial, 1980. Also author with Peter Stone of *The Unsuspecting Wife*.

Films: "Help!," released by United Artists in 1965; "Trunk to Cairo," released by American International in 1967.

WORK IN PROGRESS: The Ice Maiden, a novel about vampires; "Masked Ball," a modern film treatment of the legend of Tristan and Iseult.

SIDELIGHTS: Behm told *CA:* "I began to write after seeing and/or reading the complete works of Shakespeare, Eugene O'Neill, and Thomas Wolfe and listening to the music of Mozart and Beethoven."

* * *

BEHNEY, John Bruce 1905-

PERSONAL: Born October 15, 1905, in Ralston, Pa.; son of John James (an educator) and Margaret Mae (Gottschall)

Behney; married Dorothy Hiester, September 15, 1934; children: Richard John, Susan Behney Joslin. *Education:* Lebanon Valley College, A.B., 1928, D.D., 1941; United Theological Seminary, M.Div., 1932; Yale University, Ph.D., 1941. *Home:* 2059 Ravenwood Ave., Dayton, Ohio 45406.

CAREER: United Theological Seminary, Dayton, Ohio, professor of church history, systematic theology, philosophy of religion, and theology, 1935-73, professor emeritus, 1973—, dean, 1951-63, vice-president, 1963-73. Visiting professor at Union Theological Seminary, Philippines, 1957-58. Member of Sinclair College Citizens Advisory Committee for the Humanities. *Member:* American Society of Church History, Torch International, Young Men's Christian Association.

WRITINGS: History of the Evangelical United Brethren Church to 1890, Cokesbury, 1978.

WORK IN PROGRESS: Further research in denominational history.

SIDELIGHTS: "As an ordained minister in the United Methodist Church and, before church unions in the United Brethren and Evangelical United Brethren Churches, I recognize the influences on me from my family from early years, from church pastors and other leaders, and from college instructors and friends. I am greatly appreciative of the direction received from these sources toward an intellectual and spiritual view of mankind, including humanitarian and social matters. In my educational pursuits I included extensive study in Latin, Greek, and Hebrew. I also gained a working knowledge of French and German. In educational matters I especially stress the importance of the humanities, but regard the current stress on humanism, both religious and 'pragmatic,' as a severe danger to our culture and society."

* * *

BEIGEL, Allan 1940-

PERSONAL: Born April 4, 1940, in Hamilton, Ohio; son of Alfred and Mary (Schachter) Beigel; married Joan Ellen Kaye (a marriage and individual counselor), December 24, 1962; children: Jennifer, Jill. *Education:* Harvard University, B.A. (cum laude), 1961; Albert Einstein College of Medicine, M.D., 1965; postdoctoral study at Western Institute for Family and Group Therapy, 1974-76. *Home:* 30 Camino Espanol, Tucson, Ariz. 85716. *Office:* College of Medicine, University of Arizona, 1501 North Campbell Ave., Tucson, Ariz. 85724.

CAREER: Mount Sinai Hospital, New York, N.Y., research associate at Sleep Laboratory, 1962; Westminster Hospital, London, England, medical and surgical extern, 1964; Mount Sinai Hospital, intern in mixed medicine, 1965-66, assistant resident in psychiatry, 1966-67, chief resident at Day-Night Hospital and assistant instructor in psychiatry, 1967-68; National Institute of Mental Health, Laboratory of Clinical Psychobiology, Bethesda, Md., clinical associate and resident in psychiatry, 1968-69; National Institute of Mental Health, Community Mental Health Centers Support Branch, Chevy Chase, Md., staff psychiatrist in Division of Mental Health Service Programs, 1969-70; University of Arizona, Tucson, assistant professor, 1970-73, associate professor, 1973-79, professor of psychiatry, 1979—.

Clinical associate of National Institute of Mental Health Laboratory of Clinical Science, 1969-70; chief of psychiatry at Pima County Hospital, 1970-76; director of Southern Arizona Mental Health Center, 1970—; private practice of psychiatry, 1970—; senior attending psychiatrist at Kino Com-

munity Hospital, 1976—. Visiting lecturer at Maudsley Hospital Institute of Psychiatry, 1971, Albert Einstein College of Medicine, 1975, Duke University, University of Wisconsin, Milwaukee, and Dartmouth College, all 1976, State University of New York at Stony Brook, Northwestern University, Baylor University, University of Oregon, University of South Florida, University of Cincinnati, Medical College of Wisconsin, University of Texas, Dallas, and Illinois State Psychiatric Institute, all 1978, University of California, Los Angeles, University of North Carolina, Louisiana State University, and State University of New York at Buffalo, all 1979, and Louisiana State University and Baylor University, both 1980; special lecturer at Institute on Hospital and Community Psychiatry, 1978. Coordinator of combined mental health care program of Tucson and Pima County, Ariz., 1970-76; chairman of Arizona Alcoholism Advisory Council, 1973-76, and Tucson Inter-Agency Mental Health Conference. Testified before U.S. Congress; member of President's Commission on Mental Health, 1977-78; consultant to National Center on Alcohol Education. *Military service:* U.S. Public Health Service, surgeon, 1968-70.

MEMBER: International Transactional Analysis Association, American Psychiatric Association (fellow; chairman of scientific program committee, 1977-80), American Medical Association, American College of Psychiatrists (fellow), American Public Health Association, American Academy of Psychiatry and Law, American Orthopsychiatric Association, American Association of Social Psychiatry, National Council of Community Mental Health Centers (member of board of directors, 1975-78; chairman-elect, 1975-76; chairman, 1976-77; president, 1977-78), Pacific Northwest Society of Psychiatry and Neurology (honorary member), Arizona Psychiatric Society, Arizona Medical Association, Pima Medical Society, Pima County Mental Health Association (member of professional advisory committee), Tucson Psychiatric Society, Tucson CODAC (chairman of treatment committee, 1972-76), Group for the Advancement of Psychiatry (chairman of committee on mental health services, 1977-78), El Encanto Neighborhood Association (member of board of directors). *Awards, honors:* Distinguished service award from State of Arizona, 1972; Copper Letter Award from City of Tucson, 1975, 1980; distinguished service award from Pima Alcoholism Consortium, 1975.

WRITINGS: Drug Misuse: A Psychiatric View of a Modern Dilemma, Scribner, 1971; (with Al Levenson) *The Community Mental Health Center: Strategies and Programs,* Basic Books, 1972; *Critical Issues in Alcoholism Service Planning* (monograph), Texas Commission on Alcoholism, 1972; (with H. E. Russell) *Understanding Human Behavior for Effective Police Work,* Basic Books, 1976; (with R. Glasscote and others) *Old Folks at Home,* Joint Information Service, American Psychiatric Association and National Institute of Mental Health, 1976; (with H. Beigel) *Beneath the Badge: A Story of Police Corruption in America,* Harper, 1977. Also author of *The Right to Mental Health Care,* and, with Glasscote and others, of *Primary Prevention in CMHC's* and *Psychiatry in Small General Hospitals.*

Contributor: David B. Wexler and Stanley E. Scoville, editors, *The Administration of Psychiatric Justice: Theory and Practice in Arizona,* College of Law, University of Arizona, 1971; B. L. Danto, editor, *Jail House Blues: Suicidal Behavior in Jail and Prison,* Epic Press, 1973; C. C. Atkisson and other editors, *Resource Materials for Mental Health Program Evaluation,* National Institute of Mental Health, 1974; J. Monahan, editor, *Community Mental Health and the*

Criminal Justice System, Pergamon, 1975; Benjamin Kissin and Henri Begleiter, editors, *The Biology of Alcoholism,* Plenum, 1977; Atkisson, editor, *Evaluation of Human Service Programs,* Academic Press, 1978; Walter E. Barton and C. J. Sanborn, editors, *Law and the Mental Health Profession,* International Universities Press, 1978; Louis E. De-Moll and Sally Jo Andrade, editors, *Mental Health for the People of Texas,* Hogg Foundation for Mental Health, 1978; E. Mansell Pattison, editor, *Selection of Treatment for Alcoholics* (monograph), Rutgers University Press, 1979. Also contributor to *Modern Problems of Pharmacopsychiatry,* edited by P. Pichot, and *Mental Health and Industry.*

Contributor to *International Encyclopedia of Neurology, Psychiatry, Psychoanalysis, and Psychology, Handbook of Alcoholism,* and *Handbook for Community Boards.* Contributor of articles and reviews to medical and mental health journals. Member of editorial board of *Transactional Analysis Journal,* 1978—, and *Community Mental Health Journal,* 1979—.

*   *   *

BELL, James B. 1932-

PERSONAL: Born April 17, 1932, in St. Paul, Minn.; son of John C. (in business) and Mabel (Brugler) Bell; married Miriam Seeger Reay (a university officer), August 3, 1957; children: James, Scott, Elliott, Vanessa. *Education:* University of Minnesota, B.A., 1955; Oxford University, D.Phil., 1964. *Religion:* Episcopalian. *Agent:* R. I. Abrams, 10 East End Ave., New York, N.Y. *Office:* 101 Newbury St., Boston, Mass. 02116.

CAREER: Ohio State University, Columbus, instructor in history, 1964-67; Princeton University, Princeton, N.J., lecturer in history, 1967-69; New England Historic Genealogy Society, Boston, Mass., chief executive officer, 1973—. Chairman of board of trustees of Massachusetts State Archives. *Member:* American Antiquarian Society, Society of Antiquaries, Massachusetts Historical Society, Somerset Club, Union Club, Club of Odd Volumes.

WRITINGS: (Contributor) K. W. Wheeler, editor, *For the Union: Ohio in the Civil War,* Ohio State University Press, 1969; (with Gilbert N. Doane) *Searching for Your Ancestors,* 5th edition (Bell was not associated with earlier editions), University of Minnesota Press, 1980. Contributor to antiquarian and history journals.

*   *   *

BELL, John Patrick 1935-

PERSONAL: Born February 7, 1935, in Murray City, Ohio; married, 1962; children: three. *Education:* Tulane University, B.A., 1953, Ph.D., 1968. *Home:* 1915 Kensington Blvd., Fort Wayne, Ind. 46805. *Office:* Department of History, Indiana University, Fort Wayne, Ind. 46805.

CAREER: College of William and Mary, Williamsburg, Va., assistant professor of history, 1965-68; U.S.-Mexican Commission on Border Development, member of staff in secretariat office, 1968; U.S. Embassy, Buenos Aires, Argentina, second secretary, 1968-70; Indiana University, Fort Wayne, associate professor of history, 1970—. *Military service:* U.S. Coast Guard Reserve, 1957-60; became lieutenant. *Member:* American Historical Association, Latin American Studies Association, Society for Religion in Higher Education, Conference on Latin American History. *Awards, honors:* Cordell Hull fellow at Central University of Venezuela, 1960-61; Danforth fellow, 1968; Social Science Research Council fellow, 1968.

WRITINGS: Crisis in Costa Rica: The 1948 Revolution (monograph), University of Texas Press, 1971.*

*   *   *

BELL, Robert (Ivan) 1942-

PERSONAL: Born October 17, 1942, in Chicago, Ill.; son of Hymen David and Rebecca Ann Bell. *Education:* University of California, Berkeley, B.A., 1964; Brunel University, Ph.D., 1972. *Politics:* Independent. *Religion:* "Unaffiliated." *Home and office:* 130 West 47th St., New York, N.Y. 10036. *Office:* Graduate School of Business, Fordham University, Lincoln Center, N.Y. 10023.

CAREER: Fordham University, Graduate School of Business, Lincoln Center, N.Y., assistant professor of business, 1977—.

WRITINGS: (With John Coplans) *Decisions, Decisions,* Norton, 1976; *Having It Your Way,* Norton, 1977.

BIOGRAPHICAL/CRITICAL SOURCES: Philadelphia Inquirer, December 9, 1977; *Glamour,* May, 1979.

*   *   *

BELLAIRS, George
See BLUNDELL, Harold

*   *   *

BELLAMY, Ralph 1904-

PERSONAL: Born June 17, 1904, in Chicago, Ill.; son of Charles Rexford and Lilla Louise (Smith) Bellamy; married Alice Delbridge, 1922 (divorced, 1930); married Catherine Willard, 1931 (divorced, 1945); married Ethel Smith, 1945 (divorced, 1947); married Alice Murphy, 1949; children (second marriage) Lynn, Willard. *Home:* 8173 Mulholland Ter., Los Angeles, Calif. 90046. *Office:* 116 East 27th St., New York, N.Y. 10016.

CAREER: Actor in plays, including "State of the Union," 1943-47, "Detective Story," 1949-50, and "Sunrise at Campobello," 1958-60; actor in television series, including "Man Against Crime," 1949-54, "The Survivors," 1968-69, and "The Most Deadly Game," 1970; actor in films, including "Sunrise at Campobello," 1960, "The Professionals," 1966, "Rosemary's Baby," 1968, "Cancel My Reservations," 1972, and "Oh God!," 1977. Served on State of California Arts Commission, 1940-60; member of national board of U.S.O., 1958-60; member of board of directors, People to People Project Hope, Theatervision, 1972-73. *Member:* American Arbitration Association (member of board of directors, 1962-64), Actors Equity Association (president, 1952-64), Dutch Treat Club, Lambs Club (member of council, 1952-56). *Awards, honors:* Best actor award from Academy of Radio and Television Arts and Sciences, 1950, for "Man Against Crime"; nomination for Emmy Award for best actor from Academy of Television Arts and Sciences, 1954, for "Fearful Decision," and 1975, for "Missiles of October"; Antoinette Perry, New York Drama Critics, and Delia Austrian awards for "Sunrise at Campobello"; award of merit from State of Israel.

WRITINGS: When the Smoke Hit the Fan (memoirs), Doubleday, 1979.

SIDELIGHTS: In his early career, Bellamy often played the guy who *didn't* get the girl. He also played the title role in the "Ellery Queen" detective series in the 1930's. His most celebrated role is his portrayal of Franklin D. Roosevelt in "Sunrise at Campobello," in both the stage and film productions. Critic Ralph Tyler of *Chicago Tribune Book World* commented on Bellamy's memoirs, *When the Smoke Hit the Fan:* "Well, most writers can't act, and Bellamy proved he was an actor as Franklin Delano Roosevelt in 'Sunrise at Campobello.' He is just not, alas, a Renaissance man."

BIOGRAPHICAL/CRITICAL SOURCES: Chicago Tribune Book World, August 12, 1979.

* * *

BELLERBY, (Mary Eireen) Frances Parker 1899-1975

PERSONAL: Born in 1899 in Bristol, England; died in 1975.

CAREER: Writer.

WRITINGS—Poetry: *Plash Mill,* P. Davies, 1946; *The Brightening Cloud, and Other Poems,* P. Davies, 1949; *The Stone Angel and the Stone Man,* Ted Williams, 1958; *The Stuttering Water, and Other Poems,* edited by A. Ward, ARC Publications, 1970; *Selected Poems,* edited by Charles Causley, Enitharmon Press, 1970; *The First-Known, and Other Poems,* Enitharmon Press, 1974; *Frances Bellerby,* Enitharmon Press, 1975.

Short story collections: *Come to an End, and Other Stories,* Methuen, 1939; *The Acorn and the Cup, With Other Stories,* P. Davies, 1948; *A Breathless Child, and Other Stories,* Collins, 1952.

Novels: *Shadowy Bricks,* Education Services (London, England), 1932; *Hath the Rain a Father?,* P. Davies, 1946.*

* * *

BEN-GURION, David 1886-1973

PERSONAL: Birth-given name, David Green; changed name, c. 1906; born October 16, 1886, in Plonsk, Poland; died of a cerebral hemorrhage, December 1, 1973, in Tel Aviv, Israel; buried in Sde Boker, Negev, Israel; came to Palestine (now Israel), 1906; son of Avigdor (a lawyer) and Sheindel (Friedman) Green; married Paula Munweis, 1917 (died January, 1968); children: Amos, Geulah Ben-Elizer, Renana Leshen. *Education:* Attended University of Constantinople, 1913-14. *Residence:* Sde Boker, Negev, Israel.

CAREER: Organizer of Poale Zion (Workers for Zion) movement in Plonsk, Poland, 1903-06; worked as farm laborer and armed guard in villages in Galilee and Judea, Palestine (now Israel), 1906-c. 1910; organizer of Poale Zion (now Mapei) party, Palestine, c. 1906, editor of its publication, *Achdut* ("Unity"), 1910; founder of Zionist group, Hechalutz, New York, N.Y., c. 1916; organizer and secretary general of Histadrut (General Federation of Labor), Palestine, 1920-35; chairman of Jewish Agency Executive of World Zionist Organization, Palestine, 1935-48; proclaimed independent Jewish state of Israel, May 14, 1948; acting prime minister and minister of defense of provisional government of Israel, 1948-49; member of Knesset (Israeli legislature), 1948-70; prime minister and minister of defense of Israel, 1949-53 and 1955-63; founder and head of Rafi party, 1965-68; founder and head of Independent National List party, 1968-69. Organizer of Haganah (underground military force of Jewish Agency) and Israel Defense Forces. Delegate to World Zionist Congress, 1913-72, London Zionist Conference, 1920, and International Labor Conference, 1930. *Military service:* British Army, 1917-18; organized and served in two Jewish battalions with Royal Fusiliers in Palestine and Egypt; became corporal.

AWARDS, HONORS: Bublick Prize from Hebrew Universi-ty, 1949; Bialik Literature Prize for Judaica, 1952; D.H.L. from Jewish Theological Seminary of America, 1952; Ph.D. from Hebrew University, 1957; Henrietta Szold Award from Hadassah Women's Zionist Organization of America, 1958; LL.D. from Brandeis University, 1960; LL.D. from Rangoon University, 1961; D. Architecture from Israel Institute of Technology, 1962; Stephen S. Wise Award from American Jewish Congress.

WRITINGS—In English; all nonfiction: *Jewish Labour,* translated by Eliahu Werbner and G. Cashman, Hechalutz, 1935; *Rebirth and Destiny of Israel* (essays and addresses), edited and translated by Mordekhai Nurock, Philosophical Library, 1954; *Israel's Security and Her International Position Before and After the Sinai Campaign,* Government Printing Press, 1959; (contributor) *Spoken in Jerusalem,* B'nai B'rith, c. 1959; *Israel: Years of Challenge,* Holt, 1963; (with Moshe Pearlman) *Ben Gurion Looks Back in Talks With Moshe Pearlman,* Simon & Schuster, 1965; (editor) *The Jews in Their Land,* translated by Nurock and Misha Louvish, Doubleday, 1966, revised edition, 1974.

Days of David Ben-Gurion, edited by Ohad Zmora, Grossman, 1967; *Pegishot 'im manhigim 'arviyim,* 1967, edited by Louvish, translation by Aryeh Rubinstein and Louvish published as *My Talks With Arab Leaders,* Keter, 1972; *Mikhtavim el Polah ve-el ha-yeladim,* 1968, translation by Aubrey Hodes published as *Letters to Paula,* Vallentine, Mitchell, 1971, University of Pittsburgh Press, 1972; *Iyunim ba-Tanakh* (addresses and essays), 1969, translation by Jonathan Kolatch published as *Ben-Gurion Looks at the Bible,* Jonathan David, 1972; *Medinat Yisrael ha-mehudeshet,* two volumes, 1969, translation by Nechemia Meyers and Uzy Nystar published as *Israel: A Personal History,* Funk, 1971; *Memoirs: David Ben-Gurion,* edited by Thomas R. Bransten, World Publishing, 1970 (published in England as *Recollections of David Ben-Gurion,* Macdonald & Co., 1970); *Negotiations With Nasser,* Israel Information Center, c. 1973; *David Ben-Gurion,* edited by Ben Moshe, Youval Tal, c. 1974.

In Hebrew: *Ha-Hanhagah ha-'atsmit ba-vilayot,* 1913-14; (with Isaac Ben Zevi) *Erez Israel,* [New York], 1918; *Yidishe arbet,* [Tel Aviv], 1932; *Avodah ivrit,* 1932; *Tenu'at ha-po'alim veha-reviziyonismus,* [Tel Aviv], 1932-33; *Mishmarot,* 1935; *Dos Bukh fun ferat,* [Jerusalem], 1939; *An ent-fer Bevinen,* [Rome], 1946; *Ba-ma'arakhah,* five volumes, [Tel Aviv], 1946-49; *Yihud ve-yi'ud,* [Jerusalem], 1950; *Ba-'avodah uva-haganah,* [Tel Aviv], 1950-51; *Shlihes un eygnartikayt,* [Jerusalem], 1950-51; *Be-hilahem Yisrael* (title means "When Israel Fought in Battle"; speeches), [Tel Aviv], 1950-51, reprinted, 1975; *Hazon ve-derekh,* [Tel Aviv], 1951; *Yhude ha-ruah veha-halutisyut be-Yisrael,* [Jerusalem], 1951; *Yisrael in krig,* [Jerusalem], 1951; *Be-vikuah 'im David Ben-Gurion,* [Tel Aviv], 1953; *Al ha-Komunism veha-Tsiyonut shel ha-Shomer ha-Tsa'ir* (title means "On Communism and Zionism in Hashomer Hatzair"), [Tel Aviv], 1953; *Netsah Yisrael* (title means "The Eternity of Israel"), [Buenos Aires], 1954; *Mediniyut-huts,* [Tel Aviv], 1954-55.

Mi-ma'amad le-'am (title means "From Class to Nation"; addresses, lectures, and essays), [Tel Aviv], 1955; *Tsivuye ha-sha'ah,* [Tel Aviv], c. 1955; *Tsava u-vitahon,* [Tel Aviv], 1955; *ha-Histadrut veha-medinah,* [Tel Aviv], 1956; *Mishnato shel David Ben-Guryon,* edited by Jacob Becker, two volumes, [Tel Aviv], 1958; *Ma'arekhet Sinai* (title means "The Sinai Campaign"), [Tel Aviv], 1959; *Oz le-David* (addresses, lectures, and essays), 1964; *ha-Po'el ha-'ivri ve-histadruto* (articles and addresses), 1964; *Devarim ka-*

havayatam (title means "Things as They Are"), 1965; (contributor) Nathan Alterman, *Ben ha-meshorer la-medinai* (poems), 1971; *Zikhronot* (memoirs), 1971; *Igrot*, 1971; *Ketavim rishonim*, 1971-72; *Tipuse manhigut bi-tekufat ha-Mikra* (title means "Types of Leadership in the Biblical Period"), 1973; *Bet avi*, 1974.

Other: *Le Peuple et l'Etat d'Israel* (in French), Editions de minuit, 1959; *David und Goliath in unserer Zeit* (in German), Ner-Tamid-Verlag, 1961; *El Kibutz: Tres ideas* (in Spanish), Ijud Habonim, 1966.

WORK IN PROGRESS: Memoirs for the year 1937, left unfinished at death.

SIDELIGHTS: David Ben-Gurion was catapulted into world-wide prominence and assured a permanent place in history when on May 14, 1948, he proclaimed the birth of Israel. Coming after years of struggle, the announcement represented the fulfillment of Ben-Gurion's life-long dream of creating an independent Jewish state for his co-religionists scattered around the world. Jews again could claim a homeland more than two thousand years after the diaspora.

The founding father of Israel was born David Green in 1886 in Plonsk, Poland, a Jewish ghetto near Warsaw. During this period of pogroms and burgeoning anti-Semitism, the Green family fell under the influence of the budding Zionist movement. Following the tenets of its founder Austrian writer Theodor Herzl, Ben-Gurion's father shunned traditional Jewish garb in favor of European dress, discussed the new theory of socialism openly, and taught his son Hebrew as a spoken language instead of as the language used exclusively in praying to God. In this environment, the young Ben-Gurion became a committed Zionist envisioning the recreation of a homeland where Hebrew was spoken and Jews could live unmolested. The boy joined the Poale Zion, a workers' organization combining Zionism and socialism, and by the age of fourteen was officiating at meetings. Eventually Ben-Gurion quit school to pursue his cause full-time. Firmly believing, however, that "Zionism is meaningless unless Jews actually go to Israel," he journeyed to Palestine in 1906.

Although arriving in Jaffa against his father's wishes and as an illegal immigrant, Ben-Gurion was deliriously happy. In his first letter home he disclosed: "I did not sleep. I was amid the rich smell of corn. I heard the braying of donkeys and the rustle of leaves in the orchards. Above were massed clusters of stars against the deep blue firmament. My heart overflowed with happiness." He began farming in the small village of Sejera and changed his name in accordance to the custom of the early Zionist settlers. His birth-given name, David Green, became the Hebrew name David Ben-Gurion, meaning "Son of a Young Lion." Significantly, Ben-Gurion was also the name of one of the last champions of Jerusalem against a successful onslaught of Roman armies.

The newly arrived pioneer enjoyed working the land. He explained that farming "was the ideal life I wanted for myself" and added that he "saw in . . . [it] the renewal of the Jewish nation." Ben-Gurion's agricultural career, however, was short-lived. He soon returned to his political activities. Palestine at that time was a nearly forgotten corner of the corrupt Ottoman Empire in which only sixty thousand Jews lived. Ben-Gurion, or "B. G." as his friends often called him, began his political career in Palestine mediating in labor disputes. Quickly he founded the Poale Zion organization and in 1907 his platform, which stated that "the party will strive for an independent state for the Jewish people in this country," was embraced. At this point, though, the Pales-

tinian Zionists still believed they could live in harmony with their Turkish overlords. In an effort to obtain a voice for Jewish Palestine in the Ottoman government, B. G. and other Zionists enrolled at the University of Constantinople in 1913 to study Turkish law. Hoping to "outwit the *pashas* and *effendis,*" they tried to become representatives of Palestine in the government. Their exertions came to nothing, but when World War I broke out, Ben-Gurion proposed creating a Jewish battalion to serve in the Turkish army. Suspicious of B. G.'s advances, the Turks deported him as a subversive in 1915.

The exile and his friend Issac Ben-Zvi then went to the United States. Although forbidden from ever entering Palestine again, Ben-Gurion continued his Zionist work in America. With Ben-Zvi he founded the group Hechalutz, or "The Pioneers," which organized Jewish settlements in Palestine. He also masterminded the creation of two Jewish battalions in Canada and the United States, which ultimately served with the British in the Middle East. Despite his seemingly endless Zionist activities, Ben-Gurion found time to wed in 1917. His wife, Paula Munweis, a nursing student at the time of their marriage, often joked that her husband spent part of their wedding night attending a Zionist meeting.

The Palestinian situation began to change with the defeat of Germany and its ally, Turkey, in World War I. In November, 1917, the Balfour Declaration was issued. The document supported and encouraged the establishment of a Jewish national state in Palestine. Then, four years later in 1922, the British were assigned the mandate for Palestine by the League of Nations. Jewish immigration to the Middle East was allowed. Ben-Gurion returned and organized the Histadrut, or the General Federation of Labor, in 1920, and became chairman of the Jewish Agency Executive of the World Zionist Organization. During these years, B. G. also traveled, wrote books, and lectured to muster support for his Zionist dream.

Tensions, though, began to build up in Palestine. With the rise of Arab nationalism, Ben-Gurion's idea of living in peaceful coexistence with the Arabs began to wither. Soon, the Zionist thought only in terms of establishing a Jewish state instead of a home for both peoples. Palestinian Arabs responded to the ever expanding presence of Jews in their country with a violent uprising in 1936. Claiming that "without a Jewish army, there would never be a Jewish state," Ben-Gurion created an illegal underground army called the Haganah to protect the Jewish settlers. British policy increasingly favored the Arab side of the conflict, and culminated with the issue of the White Paper in 1939. The Paper stated that Jewish immigration to Palestine would be sharply curtailed and on March 31, 1944, totally stopped. Despite this setback to the Zionist cause, Ben-Gurion and the Jews supported Great Britain in its fight against Germany in World War II. They qualified their backing, however, as Ben-Gurion explained: "We shall fight in the war against Hitler as if there were not White Paper, but we shall fight the White Paper as if there were no war."

During the war, as rumors of the Holocaust began to circulate with regularity, Ben-Gurion multiplied his efforts to establish a Jewish state. In 1942 he visited New York City and raised funds to support the Haganah. In 1945 he viewed camps of displaced persons in Germany, and in 1946, promised a group of war victims that "we shall not rest until the last one of you who so desires shall join us in the land of Israel to build the Jewish state together with us." Ben-Gurion put into action a plan to end Britain's mandate over Palestine. He increased the illegal exodus of concentration camp survivors from Europe to Palestine while simultaneously conducting Haganah terrorist raids on British soldiers and bases. Another Zionist group, Irgun Zvai Lemui, or the National Military Organization, also attacked British installations, although they acted in defiance to official Jewish leadership. This militant group claimed responsibility for the bloody bombing of the King David Hotel in Jerusalem that killed ninety people.

On November 29, 1947, the United Nations voted in favor of dividing Palestine into Jewish and Arab states, and B. G. flew into action. He converted the Haganah from its illegal, underground status to the Israel Defense Forces, the official army of the Jews. He accrued surplus World War II weapons from Europe and began to teach his soldiers how to use tanks, planes, and artillery. He prepared for the day the birth of Israel would be announced. That day came on May 14, 1948, when the last British soldier left Palestine. Standing beneath a portrait of Zionist founder Herzl, Ben-Gurion informed the world of the creation of "a Jewish state in the land of Israel." He later described his feelings on that occasion: "At 4 o'clock that afternoon a crowd drunk with joy was dancing in the streets—in all innocence. But I was sad. I knew what was going to happen. It was the most pathetic moment of my entire life."

Israel was at war the next day with its Arab neighbors. Fighting on five fronts, the newborn country contended with Egypt, Syria, Lebanon, Jordan, and Iraq. In addition, B. G. had to deal with the Urgun terrorists, who still shunned his leadership. The matter was settled, though, with one of Ben-Gurion's more controversial actions. When the militant Zionist group attempted to land a ship carrying weapons and soldiers at Tel Aviv, Ben Gurion ordered his troops to fire. Some critics claim B. G.'s actions nearly started a civil war while others speculate his decisive move prevented one. In any case, B. G. achieved his goal that "there shall be one army, one nation, one people."

Israel's War of Independence ended with an uneasy truce in 1949. Under Ben-Gurion's leadership, the Jews won their first battle since the victory of Judas Maccabaeus two thousand years before. Ben-Gurion was regarded by his fellow Israelis as a living legend and was affectionately known throughout the tiny country as "hazaken" or the "old man."

Nevertheless, the old man's political fortunes were choppy. He often became extremely impatient with Israel's coalition government, which interfered with his autonomy. At times the prime minister became so frustrated he would resign and return to his small house at Sde Boker. Frequently, though, the mere threat of B. G.'s resignation won the support the stubborn leader demanded. He did, however, resign and retire for a prolonged period of time in 1953, not returning until 1955.

When Ben-Gurion did come back, he led Israel into its second war with its Arab neighbors. Although the cease-fire agreements officially ended the War of Independence in 1949, border incidents occurred often. Both Jews and Arabs indulged in terrorist attacks and as minister of defense, the old man adopted the policy of immediate retaliation to Arab raids. After seven years of such instability, war broke out in 1956. In complicity with Great Britain and France, Israeli troops took control of Egypt's Gaza Strip and the Sinai. The United States severely censured the actions of the three countries and soon Britain and France withdrew their forces. B. G. then had no choice but move his troops out of the occupied territories also.

Then in 1960, the old man again felt the sting of criticism. He put Nazi war criminal Adolf Eichmann on trial in Jerusalem in a converted theatre. Many were outraged at this presumptuous action, claiming the German could not possibly receive a fair trial in Israel. The ruckus died down, however, and even Eichmann's lawyer admitted the proceedings were extremely fair.

More destructive to Ben-Gurion's career was the break of the "Lavon affair" on the political scene. The scandal involved the discovery of an Israeli espionage ring in Egypt which forced the minister of defense Pinhas Lavon out of office in 1954. The affair was hushed for six years until it emerged again in 1960 when Lavon surfaced to clear his name. He contended that Ben-Gurion helped to besmirch his name and damage his career with forged papers. In a huff, B. G. again resigned, but this time he did not maintain his former support. When he finally returned to his post, Ben-Gurion's power was considerably weakened. Ultimately in 1963, he resigned for the last time and also left his Mapai party. Two years later, B. G. tried to reenter politics by forming his own splinter party, Rafi. The effort was minimally successful and short-lived. After another try with the Independent National List party, Ben-Gurion retired from public life. He resigned from the Knesset in 1970 and resided at the Sde Boker kibbutz in the Negev desert.

Ben-Gurion spoke several languages, including English, Russian, Yiddish, Greek, Turkish, French, and German. He was also proficient in Arabic, Spanish, and Sanskrit.

AVOCATIONAL INTERESTS: Studying the Bible, Buddhism, and Yoga.

BIOGRAPHICAL/CRITICAL SOURCES—Books: Barnet Litvinoff, *Story of David Ben-Gurion,* Oceana, 1959; Robert St. John, *Ben-Gurion: The Biography of an Extraordinary Man,* Doubleday, 1959; Gertrude Samuels, *B-G, Fighter of Goliaths: The Story of David Ben-Gurion,* Crowell, 1961; Amram Ducovny, *David Ben-Gurion in His Own Words,* Fleet Press, 1969; David Ben-Gurion, *Memoirs: David Ben-Gurion,* edited by Thomas R. Bransten, World Publishing, 1970.

Periodicals: *New York Times Magazine,* June 6, 1948, May 6, 1951, March 28, 1954, February 6, 1955, October 14, 1956, July 19, 1959, January 12, 1964, September 24, 1961, October 16, 1966; *Commentary,* December, 1948; *Time,* August 16, 1948, November 16, 1953, January 16, 1956, March 11, 1957, June 28, 1963, October 22, 1965, June 1, 1970, October 18, 1971; *New Statesman and Nation,* November 6, 1954, December 10, 1955; *Newsweek,* February 28, 1955, January 9, 1961, June 12, 1961, December 18, 1961, July 1, 1963, July 12, 1965, October 18, 1971; *New Statesman,* June 21, 1963, October 7, 1966; *New York Times,* October 10, 1971.

OBITUARIES: New York Times, December 2, 1973; *New Statesman,* December 7, 1973; *Newsweek,* December 10, 1973; *Time,* December 10, 1973.*

—*Sketch by Anne M. Guerrini*

*   *   *

BENJAMIN, Burton Richard 1917-

PERSONAL: Born October 9, 1917, in Cleveland, Ohio; son of Sam and Ruth (Bernstein) Benjamin; married Aline L. Wolff, April 5, 1942; children: Ann Norma, Jane Ruth. *Education:* University of Michigan, A.B., 1939. *Home:* Holbrook Rd., Scarborough, N.Y. 10510. *Office:* CBS News, 524 West 57th St., New York, N.Y. 10019.

CAREER/WRITINGS: Reporter with United Press and Newspaper Enterprise Association Service in Cleveland,

Ohio, and New York City, 1939-42; Newspaper Enterprise Association Service, New York City, member of staff, 1945-46; RKO-Pathe, New York City, writer and producer of documentary films, 1946-55; writer of dramatic and documentary scripts for network TV, 1955—; Columbia Broadcasting System (CBS), New York City, executive producer of CBS News series "Twentieth Century," "World War I," 1957, and "The 21st Century," 1967, senior executive producer of CBS News, 1968-75, executive producer of "Evening News," 1975-78, vice president and director of CBS News, 1978—. Lecturer in political science at Manhattanville College; lecturer at Columbia University, 1979. Howard R. Marsh Visiting Professor of Journalism at University of Michigan, 1976. Trustee of Scarborough School. *Military service:* U.S. Coast Guard Reserve, 1942-45; became lieutenant.

MEMBER: National Academy of Television Arts and Sciences, Writers Guild of America. *Awards, honors:* First prize from Fund for Republic, 1955, for "Pepito"; certificate of achievement from Secretary of the Army, 1962; meritorious public service citation from Secretary of the Navy, 1963; meritorious service certificate from Secretary of the Air Force, 1966; Peabody Award, award from Overseas Press Club, Emmy Award from Academy of Television Arts and Sciences, and Ohio State University award, all for "Twentieth Century" series; Emmy Award and Lasker Award, both for "The 21st Century"; Emmy Award, award from American Bar Association, and Ohio State University award for "Justice Black and the Bill of Rights Aftermath," and 1968, for "Martin Luther King Assassination"; Emmy Award, 1972, for "Justice in America," and 1974, for "The Rockefellers" and "Solzhenitsyn."

*   *   *

BENNETT, Michael 1943-

PERSONAL: Original name, Michael Bennett Di Figlia; born April 8, 1943, in Buffalo, N.Y.; son of Salvatore Joseph (a machinist) and Helen (Ternoff) Di Figlia; married Donna McKechnie (a dancer), December 4, 1976 (divorced August, 1978). *Education:* Attended public schools in Buffalo, N.Y. *Office:* 890 Broadway, New York, N.Y. 10003.

CAREER: Dancer, choreographer, writer, producer, and director. Professional dancer in stage plays, including "West Side Story," 1959, "Subways Are for Sleeping," 1961, "Here's Love," 1963, and "Bajour," 1964; choreographer of plays, including "Joyful Noise," 1966, "Henry, Sweet Henry," 1967, "Promises, Promises," 1968, "Coco," 1969, and "Company," 1970; director of plays, including "Twigs," 1971, and "God's Favorite," 1974; co-director and choreographer of "Follies," 1971; director, choreographer, and author of "Seesaw," 1973; co-producer, choreographer, director, and co-author of "A Chorus Line," 1975; director and choreographer of "Ballroom," 1978. Choreographer of film, "What's So Bad About Feeling Good?," 1968, and television programs, including "Hullabaloo," "Dean Martin Show," "Hollywood Palace," and "Ed Sullivan Show."

MEMBER: Society of Stage Directors and Choreographers, League of New York Theatres and Producers. *Awards, honors:* Nominated for sixteen Antoinette Perry (Tony) Awards by League of New York Theatres and Producers; won Tony Awards as best choreographer and best director, 1971, for "Follies," as best choreographer, 1973, for "Seesaw," as best choreographer and best director, 1975, for "A Chorus Line," and as best choreographer, 1979, for "Ballroom";

three New York Drama Critics Circle awards; Outer Critics Circle award; Los Angeles Drama Critics award; Pulitzer Prize for drama, 1975, for "A Chorus Line."

WRITINGS—Plays: "Seesaw" (two-act; adapted from the play by William Gibson, "Two for the Seesaw"), first produced on Broadway at Uris Theatre, March 18, 1973; (with Nicholas Dante and James Kirkwood) "A Chorus Line" (one-act), first produced Off-Broadway at Public Theatre, May 21, 1975, produced on Broadway at Shubert Theatre, July 25, 1975.

SIDELIGHTS: Michael Bennett's "A Chorus Line" has been cheered and praised as one of the best musical plays ever seen on Broadway. Actor Henry Fonda called it "perfection on the stage"; Richard Rodgers, the composer, found himself "in the presence of something great and new"; and actress Ruth Gordon "would like to see it once a week as long as I live." The two-and-a-half-hour show is "an intimate but explosive musical about the theater's dancing proletarians, the sweating, smiling chorus kids who back up the stars in return for peanuts and bruised patellas," wrote Jack Kroll and Constance Guthrie in *Newsweek*. "[It] has aroused one of the most intense emotional responses in the history of American musical theater."

"It all started the summer of the Watergate hearings, 1973," Bennett told Mary Cronin of *Time*. "It was a bad year for Broadway and not so hot for me. I hadn't danced in two years, and I was 25 pounds heavier. That summer I sat out in Bridgehampton, watching the hearings and thinking, 'God, truth! Would I like to see some truth in life. I would like to see some truth on the stage.'" On January 18, 1974, he met with twenty-two dancers, all of them friends he had known as a dancer or choreographer, at a studio in New York City. What happens in "A Chorus Line" is to a large extent a retelling of what happened that night, when they danced for an hour and talked about why they had started dancing.

"What happened was amazing," Bennett said. "It had been years since they had thought about their childhood and how they had become dancers." At a second session Bennett recorded thirty hours of conversation, which became the raw material for "A Chorus Line." "We ended up talking about life," he recalled. "It was like a group session, only everybody was listening and nobody was criticizing or judging. The next morning when I walked out of that studio, I was happy.... I knew I had some kind of a show here."

Bennett's biggest problem was how to condense thirty hours of tape into a two-hour musical. In collaboration with Nicholas Dante, he put together a five-hour show with no music or dancing and decided it was unworkable. Novelist-playwright James Kirkwood was called in to help with the rewriting and composer Marvin Hamlisch and lyricist Edward Kleban worked on the musical numbers. "A Chorus Line" opened one year later at Joseph Papp's Public Theatre in Greenwich Village. The play generated so much praise by word of mouth alone that it was moved to Broadway two months later.

"A Chorus Line" is acclaimed for its energy, intimacy, and emotion, but a simple idea keeps the whole thing moving. Twenty-six dancers audition for a demanding choreographer who asks each one to sing, dance, and explain the life of a dancer. After the first cuts are made, seventeen hopefuls compete for eight roles, and the audience gets to know each one: childhood traumas, personal and professional insecurities, lost and found ambitions, broken families, and the bargains made with love and loneliness for the sake of a short-lived career in the theatre become part of the show's overall portrait of the dancer. A writer for *Time* remarked, "As each character speaks, the ambitions and frustrations of a lowly chorus dancer become synonymous with everyone's battle for a place in the sun."

Kroll and Guthrie made a similar observation in their *Newsweek* article, asserting that "Michael Bennett has created a new kind of Everyperson, someone both special and common, someone with whom audiences sharply identify." But the show works "because it turns life into dazzling theater," they concluded. "Bennett, Dante and Kirkwood have distributed elements of the real source material among the performers like master collagists. Composer Marvin Hamlisch and lyricist Edward Kleban have written songs that sacrifice any attempt to be hit tunes in the service of expressing the nuances of character. Hamlisch has also written an extraordinary underscore that sheathes the entire show in an almost operatic skin of sound and responds to every detail of character, action and mood."

Much of "A Chorus Line" is based on Bennett's own career and ambitions. He made his professional debut in the chorus of "West Side Story" at age sixteen and choreographed his first musical when he was twenty-two. His dance routines for "Promises, Promises," "Coco," "Company," "Follies," and "Seesaw" made him one of the best choreographers on Broadway, but he confides that his success came at the expense of his personal life. "I was the American dream," he remarked. "But I was not a very successful human being in my own eyes when I began work on ['A Chorus Line']. I'm someone who works 24 hours a day, and I've had relations screwed up because work came first, because of wanting to win the Tony Award, wanting to be the No. 1 director and choreographer. It was a sickness."

Bennett has received numerous awards over the years, including two Tony Awards and the Pulitzer Prize for "A Chorus Line," but he has tempered his preoccupation with dance and what he calls "the success syndrome." "I don't really need to dance any more," he told *Time*. "Dancing is only part of what I do. I want to do a movie musical about New York in the '40s. I am very much into words, and maybe I will write something, possibly an autobiography. I can always dance around my living room."

BIOGRAPHICAL/CRITICAL SOURCES: Dance, February, 1970, June, 1975; *Newsweek,* December 13, 1971, December 1, 1975, June 9, 1975; *Time,* July 28, 1975; *New York Times Magazine,* May 2, 1976; *New York Times,* February 22, 1979.

—*Sketch by B. Hal May*

*   *   *

BENSON, Frederick William 1948-
(Ted Benson)

PERSONAL: Born September 26, 1948, in Los Angeles, Calif.; son of Fred S. and Bessie (Vaughn) Benson; married Elizabeth Carolyn Jones, October 23, 1970; children: Jessica Carolyn. *Education:* Modesto Junior College, A.A., 1968; San Jose State College, B.A., 1970. *Residence:* Modesto, Calif. *Office address:* P.O. Box 1164, Modesto, Calif. 95353.

CAREER: Modesto Bee, Modesto, Calif., staff photographer, 1970—. *Member:* National Press Photographers Association, California Press Photographers Association. *Awards, honors:* Grand prize in black and white category from American Freedom Train Photograph Contest, 1977.

WRITINGS—Under name Ted Benson; all with own photographs: *Mother Lode Shortline: A Sierra Railroad Pictorial,*

Chatham, 1970; *Sierra Railroad Film-Making: A Production Handbook,* privately printed, 1976; (with Bruce MacGregor) *Portrait of a Silver Lady,* Pruett, 1977, 2nd edition, 1979; (with Dave Styffe) *Wheels Rolling—West,* Westrail, 1979; *Sierra Railroad Steam in the 1970's,* Westrail, 1981.

Photographer: Harold Edmonson, *Journey to Amtrak,* Kalmbach, 1972; Robert L. Hogan, *Mallet to Mogul,* Chatham, 1973; William D. Middleton, *When the Steam Railroads Electrified,* Kalmbach, 1974; Joe McMillan, *Santa Fe's Diesel Fleet,* Chatham, 1975; Oliver Jensen, *Railroads in America,* American Heritage Books, 1975; Bruce MacGregor, *Narrow Gauge Portrait: South Pacific Coast,* Glenwood, 1975; Joseph A. Strapac, *Diesels of the Southern Pacific,* Chatham, 1975; Strapac, *Cotton Belt Locomotives,* Shade Tree Books, 1977; McMillan, *Route of the Warbonnets,* McMillan Publications, 1977; Richard Steinheimer, *The Electric Way Across the Mountains,* Carbarn Press, 1980. Photographer for *Southern Pacific Motive Power,* 1968-73, *Passenger Train Annual,* 1977 and 1979, and *Southern Pacific Review,* 1978-79.

Contributor of numerous articles and more than one thousand photographs to magazines, including *Trains.*

WORK IN PROGRESS: The Western Pacific Railroad: A Folk History, with Bruce MacGregor, completion expected in 1985.

SIDELIGHTS: Benson told *CA:* "I consider myself very fortunate that I've been able to convert a lifelong interest in railroading into both an avocation and a profession. It was the desire to improve my fledgling snapshot approach to railroad photography that led to my involvement in high school journalism classes, and from this came the decision to major in photojournalism in college and my subsequent employment as a news photographer.

"As a rail photojournalist, my initial magazine and book contributions reflected the traditional approach to railroading, mainly the railroad as tracks and trains with heavy emphasis on mechanics. It has been my intention to expand on this rather narrow approach and deal with railroading on a broader scale and appeal to a larger audience. The railroad as a lifestyle has occupied my work with a growing frequency, beginning in earnest with *Portrait of a Silver Lady.* It was my intention to deal with the *California Zephyr* as a human experience as much as a mechanical one, and in doing so we hoped to break some new ground in rail documentation. *Portrait* met with acclaim beyond my imagination.

"Beyond *Portrait* has come an increased interest in publishing as a complete package where design and production of the publication contributes as much to the total effect as the subject matter itself. The first book to reflect this new direction, *Wheels Rolling—West,* was produced in collaboration with graphic artist and photographer Dave Styffe, and has been greeted warmly by the railfan press.

"Granted, not every railroad enthusiast prefers to have his consciousness hammered at with railroad photography that goes beyond the traditional. Obviously, it is impossible to please everyone and follow my own lead at the same time, but being in the position of doing the railroad work for pleasure, as opposed to its being everyday work, I find it easier to follow my own direction and strive to do things that go beyond the accepted norm. Where this interest will take my work remains to be seen. Growth beyond the traditional railfan markets and publications has begun and I trust the expansion to a more general readership will continue. Not everyone is an avid 'rivet counter,' but a growing majority of people are kindly disposed toward railroading and it's my intention to continue exploring the attraction of the lonely whistles in the night that awaken the vagabond in the soul.''

BIOGRAPHICAL/CRITICAL SOURCES: Trains, April, 1975, January, 1978; *Railfan,* October, 1977.

* * *

BENSON, Ted
See BENSON, Frederick Williams

* * *

BENTLEY, Beth (Rita) 1928-

PERSONAL: Born October 7, 1928; daughter of Arthur G. and Helen (Blumenfeld) Singer; married Nelson Bentley (a professor of English), October 26, 1952; children: Sean, Julian (daughter). *Education:* Received B.A. from University of Minnesota and M.A. from University of Michigan. *Home:* 8762 25th Place N.E., Seattle, Wash. 98115.

CAREER: Bellevue Community College, Bellevue, Wash., instructor, 1969-74; Tacoma Schools, Tacoma, Wash., instructor in "gifted in the humanities" program, 1974-77; writer, 1977—. Participant in writing workshops. *Member:* Academy of American Poets. *Awards, honors:* Awards from Pacific Northwest Booksellers and governor of the state of Washington, both 1971, both for *Phone Calls From the Dead;* National Endowment for the Arts grant, 1976-77.

WRITINGS: Phone Calls From the Dead, Ohio University Press, 1971; *Country of Resemblances,* Ohio University Press, 1976; *Philosophical Investigations* (poem), Sea Pen Press, 1977; *The Purely Visible,* Sea Pen Press, 1980; (editor) *The Selected Poems of Hazel Hall,* Ahsahta Press, 1980. Also author of *Field of Snow,* 1973. Contributor to magazines, including *Sewanee Review, New Yorker, Atlantic, Nation, Saturday Review, Paris Review,* and *Choice.*

WORK IN PROGRESS: Translating work of contemporary French women poets.

AVOCATIONAL INTERESTS: Travel (France).

* * *

BENZONI, Juliette (Andree Marguerite) 1920-

PERSONAL: Born October 30, 1920, in Paris, France; daughter of Hubert-Charles (a manufacturer) and Marie-Suzanne (Arnold) Mangin; married Maurice Gallois (a doctor), March 11, 1941 (marriage ended, June 4, 1950); married Andre Benzoni (a colonel), March 28, 1953; children: (first marriage) Jean-Francois, Anne. *Education:* Attended College d'Hulst; received licence en lettres from Institut Catholique de Paris. *Religion:* Roman Catholic. *Home:* 53 bis avenue Alphand, Saint Mande 94160, France. *Agent:* Opera Mundi, Avenue R. Poincare 100, Paris 16, France.

CAREER: Writer. *Member:* Vieilles Maisons francaises, Amis d'Alexandre Dumas, Association Ars Maudez. *Awards, honors:* Prix Alexandre Dumas, 1973.

WRITINGS—All published by Editions du Trevise; "Catherine" series: *Il suffit d'un amour,* part one, 1963, translation by Jocasta Goodwin published as *One Love Is Enough,* Heinemann, 1964; *Il suffit d'un amour,* part two, translation by Goodwin published as *Catherine,* Pan, 1965; *La Belle Catherine,* 1966, translation by Goodwin published as *Belle Catherine,* Heinemann, 1966, Avon, 1978; *Catherine des grands chemins,* 1967; *Catherine ma mie,* 1967, translation by Goodwin published as *Catherine and Arnaud,* Heinemann, 1967, Avon, 1978; *Catherine et le temps d'aimer,*

1968, translation by Goodwin published as *Catherine and a Time for Love,* Heinemann, 1968, published as *Catherine's Time for Love,* Avon, 1978; *Piege pour Catherine,* 1973, translation by Anne Carter published as *A Snare for Catherine,* Heinemann, 1974, Avon, 1978; *Catherine: Royal Mistress,* translated from original French, Avon, 1978; *Catherine's Quest,* translated from original French, Avon, 1978. Also author of *Catherine: La Dame de Montsalvy.*

"Marianne" series: *Marianne: Une Etoile pour Napoleon,* 1969, translation by Carter published as *Marianne,* Heinemann, 1969, Putnam, 1970; *Marianne et l'inconnu de Toscane* 1971, translation by Carter published as *Marianne and the Masked Prince,* Putnam, 1971; *Marianne: Jason des quatre mers,* 1971, translation by Carter published as *Marianne and the Privateer,* Putnam, 1972; *Toi, Marianne,* 1972, translation by Carter published as *Marianne and the Rebels,* Heinemann, 1973, Putnam, 1974; *Marianne: Les Lauriers de flammes,* two volumes, 1974, translations by Carter published respectively as *Marianne and the Lords of the East,* Putnam, 1975, and *Marianne and the Crown of Fire,* Putnam, 1976.

"Le Gerfaut des brumes" series: *Le Gerfaut des brumes,* 1976, translation by Carter published as *The Lure of the Falcon,* Putnam, 1978; *Un Collier pour le diable,* 1978.

Other: *Les Reines tragiques: Confidences de l'histoire,* 1962; *Adventuriers de passe: Confidences de l'histoire,* 1963; *Par le fer ou le poison: Recits historique,* 1973; *Le Sang, la gloire, et l'amour: Les Maris de l'histoire,* 1974; *Trois Seigneurs de la nuit,* 1978; *Grandes Dames, petite vertus,* 1978.

Contributor of articles to *Journal du Dimanche, Confidences, Histoire Pour Tous,* and *Historia.*

WORK IN PROGRESS: A third volume of the "Le Gerfaut des brumes" series, entitled *Le Masque du Gerfaut,* about Thomas Jefferson when he was ambassador to Paris in 1786.

SIDELIGHTS: Benzoni's series of "Marianne" novels are "swashbuckling adventures" set in Napoleonic France. In *Marianne,* the heroine, then living in England, kills her husband on their wedding night and flees to France. A *Best Sellers* critic reviewing the second "Marianne" book commented that "only in a French tale, with Mrs. Benzoni as its weaver, could one encounter so fascinating an account of the intrigues and activities of the Napoleonic era."

The heroine of the "Catherine" series "might best be described as a female, historical version of James Bond, considering the tight corners she gets herself into and out of with remarkably little difficulty," wrote Anne Britton. In *Catherine and a Time for Love,* the main character searches for a former love who is believed dead. Along the way she encounters a man held captive in an iron cage and "about to be skinned alive whom she personally rescues." She then escapes a fire, confinement in a harem, and other tortures "too horrible to contemplate." Britton admitted that "however ridiculous it all is, Juliette Benzoni is a wow of a story teller, with the gift of transporting the reader into the world of her own imagination."

Benzoni told *CA* that her principal motivation to write is history, and that all her historical novels are based on solid documentation.

Her book *Il suffit d'un amour* was adapted as a motion picture by Lira Films in 1969 under the title "Catherine, il suffit d'un amour."

AVOCATIONAL INTERESTS: Boating, tapestry, painting, cooking.

BIOGRAPHICAL/CRITICAL SOURCES: Books and Book-men, October, 1968; *Variety,* June 4, 1969; *Best Sellers,* February 1, 1970, December 1, 1971; *Library Journal,* March 15, 1970.

* * *

BERG, Leila Rita 1917-

PERSONAL: Born November 12, 1917, in Salford, Lancashire, England; married in 1940; children: one son, one daughter. *Education:* Attended University of London. *Home:* 25 Streatham Common South, London S.W. 16, England.

CAREER: Author and editor. Methuen & Co., Ltd., London, England, children's book editor, 1958-60; Thomas Nelson & Sons Ltd., London, general editor of Salamander Books, 1965; free-lance editor, 1966—. *Awards, honors:* Eleanor Farjeon Award from Children's Book Circle, 1974.

WRITINGS—Juvenile: Fourteen What-Do-You-Know Stories, Epworth, 1948, Roy, 1959; *The Adventures of Chunky,* Oxford University Press, 1950, published as *Chunky,* 1958; *The Nightingale, and Other Stories,* Oxford University Press, 1951; *Little Pete Stories,* Methuen, 1952, revised edition, 1970; *The Tired Train, and Other Stories,* Parrish, 1952; *Trust Chunky,* Brockhampton Press, 1954, reprinted, 1974; *The Story of the Little Car,* Epworth, 1955, revised edition published as *The Little Car Has a Day Out,* Brockhampton Press, 1970, later published as *The Little Car,* Methuen, 1972; *Fire Engine by Mistake,* Brockhampton Press, 1955; *Lollipops: Stories and Poems,* Brockhampton Press, 1957, reprinted, 1980; *Andy's Pit Pony,* Brockhampton Press, 1958, reprinted, 1973; *The Hidden Road,* Hamish Hamilton, 1958; *A Box for Benny,* Brockhampton Press, 1958, Bobbs-Merrill, 1961, reprinted, Hodder & Stoughton, 1979; *Folk Tales,* Brockhampton, 1966; *My Dog Sunday,* Hamish Hamilton, 1968.

Nonfiction: *Risinghill: Death of a Comprehensive School,* Penguin, 1968; (with John Walmsley) *Neill and Summerhill: A Man and His Work,* Penguin, 1969; (with Paul Adams, Nan Berger, Michael Duane, and Robert Ollendorff) *Children's Rights,* Praeger, 1971; *Look at Kids,* Penguin, 1972; (with Pat Chapman) *The Train Back,* Allen Lane, 1972; *Reading and Loving,* Routledge & Kegan Paul, 1977.

Other: (Translator and editor; with Ruth Baer) Irmgard Keun, *The Bad Example,* Harcourt, 1955 (published in England as *Grown-Ups Don't Understand,* Parrish, 1955); (editor) *Four Feet and Two, and Some With None: An Anthology of Verse,* Penguin, 1960; (editor) "Nipper" series, fifteen books, Macmillan, 1968-76; (editor) "Little Nipper" series, nine books, Macmillan, 1972-75; (editor) "Snaps" series, Macmillan, four books, 1977. Also author of a play, "Raising Hell" (adapted from the book, *Risinghill*), produced in Salisbury, England, 1972, and in London, England, 1973.

SIDELIGHTS: Leila Berg's "Nipper" books have been well-received in England, although they have been criticized by some educators for their picture of working-class life. While some critics argued that the portrayal of the working class, complete with the "work-shy dad," was too realistic for children, others described the books as stereotypical and patronizing. The majority of responses, however, were positive, and Berg was praised for her innovations in the field of children's literature.

Among Berg's nonfiction books on education is *Risinghill: Death of a Comprehensive School,* her account of the closing of a progressive school located in a working-class district. Opened in 1960, Risinghill was closed down after only five years of operation. Numerous reasons for the decision were given, including the London authorities assertions that they could not justify keeping a school open that was only two-thirds full. Other people, including parents, students, and Leila Berg, felt that the school's policies and methods of instruction were the primary causes of the closing.

Risinghill's headmaster was a liberal educator who had instituted sculpture classes for those students on probation. He had abandoned corporal punishment and successfully communicated with parents of numerous nationalities. In spite of the opposition to his programs from both staff and school board, Duane's results were startling: when the school opened, 98 children were on probation; in 1964 there were only four.

Blishen praised Berg for her work, and noted that "her analysis of the deep cancer of authoritarianism within the teaching profession is utterly accurate."

Berg's other children's books have also been successful and she continues to champion the rights of children. In a review of her book, *Reading and Loving,* Nicholas Tucker wrote, "As a children's author, Leila Berg has been creative and successful . . . she has . . . provided us with the most lively reading material to be found in primary schools today."

Leila Berg commented: " 'Nippers' was a state school series for children of six to eight who were just learning to read, and I was aiming at making up to such children as needed it for those five years before school in which books had *not* been part of their family or part of their own individual growth and lovedness. So in 'Nippers' I reflected these non-book children—their parents, streets, conversations, happenings—back to themselves. The stories and the pictures recognized, accepted, and welcomed them. Unless books did this, it seemed to me, children would never love them and would probably never read one at all once they left school."

BIOGRAPHICAL/CRITICAL SOURCES: Listener, April 25, 1968; *Observer Review,* April 28, 1968; *Times Literary Supplement,* May 9, 1968, March 25, 1977.

* * *

BERGER, Marilyn 1935-

PERSONAL: Born August 23, 1935, in New York, N.Y.; daughter of William and Celia (Hinderstein) Berger; married Don Hewitt (a television producer), April 14, 1979. *Education:* Cornell University, B.A., 1956; Columbia University, M.S., 1965. *Home:* 220 Central Park S., New York, N.Y. 10019. *Office:* 356 West 58th St., New York, N.Y. 10019.

CAREER/WRITINGS: Newsday, Garden City, N.Y., diplomatic and United Nations correspondent, 1965-70; *Washington Post,* Washington, D.C., diplomatic correspondent, 1970-76; National Broadcasting Co. (NBC-TV), New York City, chief White House correspondent, 1976-77; Council on Foreign Relations, New York City, director of programs, 1977-78; Public Broadcasting Service (PBS-TV), correspondent for WNET in New York City, 1978—. Contributor to magazines, including *New Yorker* and *New York Times Magazine.*

* * *

BERGERON, Paul H. 1938-

PERSONAL: Born February 8, 1938, in Alexandria, La.; married, 1968; children: three. *Education:* Louisiana College, B.A., 1960; Vanderbilt University, M.A., 1962, Ph.D., 1965. *Office:* Department of History, University of Tennessee, Cumberland Ave. S.W., Knoxville, Tenn. 37916.

CAREER: Vanderbilt University, Nashville, Tenn., began as instructor, became assistant professor, then associate professor of history, 1965-72; University of Tennessee, Knoxville, associate professor of history, 1972—. *Member:* American Historical Association, Organization of American Historians, Southern Historical Association.

WRITINGS: (Editor with Herbert Weaver) *The Correspondence of James K. Polk,* Vanderbilt University Press, Volume I, 1969, Volume II, 1972; *Paths of the Past: Tennessee, 1770-1970,* University of Tennessee Press, 1979. Contributor to scholarly journals.*

*   *   *

BERGMANN, Frithjof H.   1930-

PERSONAL: Born December 24, 1930, in Weikelsdorf, Germany; naturalized U.S. citizen; married, 1959; children: one. *Education:* Princeton University, Ph.D., 1958. *Office:* Department of Philosophy, University of Michigan, Ann Arbor, Mich. 48104.

CAREER: University of Michigan, Ann Arbor, 1958—, professor of philosophy, 1965—.

WRITINGS: On Being Free, University of Notre Dame Press, 1977.*

*   *   *

BERLIN, Ira   1941-

PERSONAL: Born May 27, 1941, in New York, N.Y.; son of Louis and Sylvia Toby (Lebwohl) Berlin; married Martha L. Chait, August 31, 1963; children: Lisa Jill, Richard Aaron. *Education:* University of Wisconsin, Madison, Ph.D., 1970. *Office:* Department of History, University of Maryland, College Park, Md. 20242.

CAREER: I. B. Alan, Inc., New York, N.Y., vice-president, 1967-69; *Wisconsin Magazine of History,* Madison, Wis., book review editor, 1969; University of Illinois at Chicago Circle, Chicago, instructor in history, 1970-72; Federal City College, Washington, D.C., assistant professor of history, 1972-74; Princeton University, Princeton, N.J., fellow at Davis Center for Historical Studies, 1975; University of Maryland, College Park, associate professor of history, 1976—. Project editor for National Archives. *Member:* International Sociological Association, American Historical Association, Organization of American Historians, Southern Historical Association, Columbia University Economic Seminars. *Awards, honors:* National Endowment for the Humanities younger humanist fellow, 1971; book prize from National Historical Society, 1975, for *Slaves Without Masters.*

WRITINGS: Slaves Without Masters: Free Negroes in the Antebellum South, Pantheon, 1975; *Studies of Post-Civil War Emancipation,* Cambridge University Press, in press. Contributor to journals.

WORK IN PROGRESS: Social Structure of Nineteenth-Century Southern Cities.

*   *   *

BERNS, Walter Fred   1919-

PERSONAL: Born May 3, 1919, in Chicago, Ill.; son of Walter Fred and Agnes (Westergard) Berns; married Irene Sibley Lyons, June 16, 1951; children: Elizabeth, Emily, Chris-

topher. *Education:* University of Iowa, B.Sc., 1941; graduate study at Reed College, 1948-49, and at London School of Economics and Political Science, 1949-50; University of Chicago, M.A., 1951, Ph.D., 1953. *Home:* 4986 Sentinel Dr., No. 402, Bethesda, Md. 20016. *Office:* Department of Government, Georgetown University, 1400 37th St. N.W., Washington, D.C. 20057; and American Enterprise Institute, 1150 17th St. N.W., Washington, D.C. 20036.

CAREER: Louisiana State University, Baton Rouge, assistant professor of political science, 1953-56; Yale University, New Haven, Conn., assistant professor of political science, 1956-59; Cornell University, Ithaca, N.Y., associate professor, 1959-62, professor of government and chairman of department, 1963-68; University of Toronto, Toronto, Ontario, visiting professor, 1969, professor of political science, 1970-79; Georgetown University, Washington, D.C., professorial lecturer in government, 1979—. Resident scholar at American Enterprise Institute in Washington, D.C. Lecturer at Salzburg Seminar in American Studies, 1959; Charles Evans Hughes Visiting Professor of Political Science at Colgate University, 1970. Member of advisory board of National Institute of Law Enforcement and Criminal Justice, 1974-76. *Member:* American Political Science Association. *Awards, honors:* Carnegie teaching fellow, 1952-53; Rockefeller fellow, 1965-66; Fulbright fellow, 1965-66; Clark Distinguished Teaching Award from Cornell University, 1969; grants from Earhart Foundation, 1969 and 1972; grant from U.S. Department of Justice, 1975-76; Guggenheim fellowship, 1978-79.

WRITINGS: Freedom, Virtue, and the First Amendment, Louisiana State University Press, 1957; (co-author) *Essays on the Scientific Study of Politics,* edited by Herbert J. Storing, Holt, 1962; (editor) *Constitutional Cases in American Government,* Crowell, 1963; *The First Amendment and the Future of American Democracy,* Basic Books, 1976; *For Capital Punishment: Crime and the Morality of the Death Penalty,* Basic Books, 1979.

Contributor: Robert A. Goldwin, editor, *Readings in World Politics,* Oxford University Press, 1962; Leo Strauss and Joseph Cropsey, editors, *History of Political Philosophy,* Rand McNally, 1963; Goldwin, editor, *A Nation of States: Essays on the American Federal System,* Rand McNally, 1963; Hans W. Baade, editor, *Law and Contemporary Problems,* Basic Books, 1963; Goldwin, editor, *Political Parties,* Rand McNally, 1964; Goldwin, editor, *One Hundred Years of Emancipation,* Rand McNally, 1964; Goldwin, editor, *How Democratic Is America?,* Rand McNally, 1971; Harry Clor, editor, *Censorship and Freedom of Expression,* Rand McNally, 1971; Morton J. Frisch and Richard G. Stevens, editors, *American Political Thought,* Scribner, 1971; Clor, editor, *The Mass Media and Modern Democracy,* Rand McNally, 1974; Robert Horwitz, editor, *The Moral Foundations of the American Republic,* University of Virginia Press, 1977; Leonard J. Theberge, editor, *The Judiciary in a Democratic Society,* Lexington Books, 1979.

Contributor of numerous articles to scholarly journals, including *Western Political Quarterly, Journal of Politics, American Political Science Review, Yale Law Journal,* and *Political Science Reviewer.*

SIDELIGHTS: When Walter Berns wrote *For Capital Punishment: Crime and the Morality of Punishment,* he took up a debate that has been raging for centuries. The penal system of today, he maintains, puts its emphasis on rehabilitation or deterrence instead of where it rightfully belongs: on punishment. Francis Canavan of the *National Review* explained that "both rehabilitation and deterrence shift the focus of attention from the crime to the criminal: he is to be either reformed, or prevented by fear from committing crimes in the first place. But he is not to be punished. To inflict a penalty on him because the intrinsic character of his crime *merits* punishment reveals a barbaric desire for revenge unworthy of this enlightened age." Berns, however, argues that society must have the moral dignity to "demand that criminals be paid back, and that the worst of them be made to pay back with their lives."

In his book Berns discusses the popular arguments against the death penalty—biblical, moral, constitutional—and determines them all to be lacking in significant areas. He then goes on to point out the need for the basic principle that the death penalty stands for: punishment of the criminal to fit the crime in order to retain the dignity and responsibility of the rest of society. According to Graham Hughes, such thinking can be likened to "going back to rubbing two sticks together because we are unhappy about nuclear power." He went on to claim that "reading Berns's book powerfully evokes righteous anger and moral indignation. His retributivist theory turns out on inspection to consist of either disguised and unconvincing utilitarian propositions or mystical calls for death that deserve psychoanalytic rather than philosophical refutation." *New York Times* writer Christopher Lehmann-Haupt, however, declared that *For Capital Punishment* "should be attended to by anyone who takes its subject seriously." Canavan, moreover, commended the book, noting that Berns "offers a calm and reasoned case for inflicting the death penalty for certain crimes." Like the author himself, Canavan concluded that "we must come to believe again that punishment, regularly and predictably inflicted, will in fact deter, and, moreover, that crime deserves to be punished."

BIOGRAPHICAL/CRITICAL SOURCES: New York Review of Books, June 28, 1979; *New York Times,* July 16, 1979; *Commentary,* August, 1979; *National Review,* August 17, 1979; *New York Times Book Review,* August 19, 1979; *Nation,* November 24, 1979.

*   *   *

BESCHLOSS, Michael R(ichard) 1955-

PERSONAL: Born November 30, 1955, in Chicago, Ill. *Education:* Williams College (with highest honors), B.A., 1977; Harvard University, M.B.A., 1980. *Politics:* Democrat. *Home:* 180 East Pearson St., Chicago, Ill. 60611.

WRITINGS: Kennedy and Roosevelt: The Uneasy Alliance, Norton, 1980. Contributor of book reviews and articles to periodicals.

SIDELIGHTS: Beschloss's first book, *Kennedy and Roosevelt,* was described by Steve Neal as "a fascinating study" of the unlikely political alliance between Franklin D. Roosevelt and Joseph P. Kennedy. Although the first encounter between the two men was a stormy one, Kennedy later became a staunch Roosevelt supporter during the 1932 election, his personal and financial backing helping F.D.R. to win the Democratic nomination. In turn Kennedy expected, and received, prestigious political appointments: he was named the first chairman of the Securities and Exchange Commission and later ambassador to London. By the 1940 presidential election, however, Kennedy's public opposition to some of Roosevelt's war policies caused a permanent rift in their alliance.

Kennedy and Roosevelt grew out of a senior thesis Beschloss wrote at Williams College. "A form of faint damning is to say that a book began as a thesis in pursuit of an academic

degree," wrote Leonard Silk in the *New York Times.* "But this book is a real credit, not only to the author and his teacher, but also to the academic discipline. . . . Beschloss's thesis is that Franklin D. Roosevelt and Joseph P. Kennedy, the father of an assassinated President and a political dynasty that has not yet ended, were bound together in a love-hate relationship whose twists and turns and ultimate collapse reflected their powerful but opposing visions of the public good and how to achieve it. . . . Beschloss has performed a notable service in disclosing the weakness and dangers of an excessively private approach to public life."

BIOGRAPHICAL/CRITICAL SOURCES: New York Times Book Review, August 12, 1979; *New York Times,* April 7, 1980; *Chicago Tribune,* May 4, 1980; *Washington Post,* May 22, 1980; *Washington Star,* May 24, 1980; *Newsday,* June 8, 1980.

*   *   *

BETTI, Liliana 1939-

PERSONAL: Born March 10, 1939; daughter of Giovanni (a businessman) and Maria (Canotti) Betti. *Education:* Attended Maturita Classica Instituta. *Politics:* "Democratic leftist." *Religion:* Catholic. *Home:* Via Dei Foraggi 91B, Rome, Italy 00186.

CAREER: Writer. Assistant director to Federico Fellini on motion pictures, including "Juliet of the Spirits," 1965, "Fellini Satyricon," 1969, "Roma," 1972, "Amarcord," 1973, and "Casanova," 1976. *Member:* Sindacato Nazionale Scrittori.

WRITINGS—In English: *Fellini: An Intimate Portrait,* translated by Joachim Neugroschel, Little, Brown, 1979.

In Italian: *Tre Passi nel Delirio,* Cappelli, 1968; (co-editor with Eschilo Tarquini) Federico Fellini and others, *Il Primo Fellini* (screenplays; contains "Lo Sceicco Bianco," "I Vitelloni," "La Strada," and "Il Bidone"), Cappelli, 1969; *Federico A. C.* (nonfiction), Milano Libri, 1970; (with Orestedel Buono) *Federcord* (nonfiction), Milano Libri, 1974; (with G. Angelucci) *Amarcord,* Cappelli, 1974; *Rendez-vous con Federico Fellini,* Bompiani, 1975; *Il Casanova di Fellini,* Cappilli, 1976; (with Angelucci) *La Citta Delle Donne,* Garzanti, 1980.

Author of television specials, including "Diario di Amarcord" and "E il Casanova di Fellini?" Author of "Desiderio," a screenplay for Vogue Cinematografia. Contributor to periodicals, including *Gente, Vie Nuove,* and *Il Resto del Carlino.*

WORK IN PROGRESS: Pensione Haeslin, an autobiographical novel.

*   *   *

BETTS, Charles L(ancaster), Jr. 1908-

PERSONAL: Born December 17, 1908, in Philadelphia, Pa.; son of Charles L. (in sales) and Ella (Lucas) Betts; married Victoria Bedford (a writer), January 26, 1952. *Education:* Rensselaer Polytechnic Institute, M.E., 1933. *Home:* 2105 Stackhouse Dr., Yardley, Pa. 19067.

CAREER: Roller Bearing Company of America, Trenton, N.J., cost accountant, 1933-34; Westchester Lighting Co., Mt. Vernon, N.Y., clerk and engineering assistant, 1934-42; Sperry Gyroscope Co., Brooklyn, N.Y., and Lake Success, N.Y., senior technical correspondent and product engineer, 1942-46; Long Island Lighting Co., Mineola, N.Y., engineer, 1946-50; Allstates Engineering Co., Trenton, designer, 1950-

54; Ewing Technical Design Inc., Philadelphia, Pa., chief engineer, 1954-57; United Engineers and Constructors Inc., Philadelphia, project designer, 1957-58; Ewing Technical Design Inc., Philadelphia, designer, 1958-59; Allstates Design and Development Co., Trenton, design specialist, 1959-61; United Engineers and Constructors Inc., Philadelphia, project designer, 1961-73; writer, 1973—. *Member:* Antique Automobile Club of America, Society of Automotive Historians (secretary, 1975—). *Awards, honors:* Byllesby Prize, 1936, and McGraw Prize, 1940, 1942, all from Edison Electric Institute; Thomas McKean Memorial Trophy, 1955, editorial award, 1962, for article "Maxwell Racing History," M. J. Duryea Memorial Cup, 1974, for article "Run Steady: The Story of Ralph K. Mulford," and editorial award for book reviews, 1976, all from Antique Automobile Club of America; editor's certificate from *Antique Automobile* magazine, 1959.

WRITINGS: Auto Racing Winners 1895-1947: An Historical Reference Manual of American Automobile Racing, privately printed, 1948; *American Vintage Cars,* Sports Car Press, 1963; (with Albert R. Bochroch) *American Automobile Racing,* Viking, 1974. Contributor to *Antique Automobile.* Associate editor for Antique Automobile Club of America, 1952—.

*   *   *

BEUTEL, William Charles 1930-

PERSONAL: Born December 12, 1930, in Cleveland, Ohio; son of William Charles and Stella Eileen (Forster) Beutel; divorced; children: Peter, Robin, Colby, Heather. *Education:* Dartmouth College, A.B., 1953; graduate study at University of Michigan Law School, 1953-54. *Religion:* Presbyterian. *Office:* American Broadcasting Co., 1330 Avenue of the Americas, New York, N.Y. 10019.

CAREER/WRITINGS: WGAR-Radio, Cleveland, Ohio, newsman, 1957-59; WEWS-TV, Cleveland, newsman, 1959-60; Columbia Broadcasting System (CBS-Radio), New York City, newsman, 1960-62; American Broadcasting Co. (ABC-TV), New York City, newsman, 1962—, London bureau chief, 1968-70, anchorman for WABC-TV, 1970-77, host of "AM America," 1975. *Military service:* U.S. Army, 1954-56. *Member:* National Academy of Television Arts and Sciences (member of board of governors of New York chapter, 1964), Association of Radio and Television News Analysts, Sigma Delta Chi, Phi Delta Theta. *Awards, honors:* Emmy Award from National Academy of Television Arts and Sciences, 1964, 1965, 1966, and 1967; George Foster Peabody Award, 1970, for "Eye of the Storm."

*   *   *

BHATIA, Jamunadevi 1919-
(June Bhatia, June Edwards, Helen Forrester, J. Rana)

PERSONAL: Born June 6, 1919, in Hoylake, Cheshire, England; married Avadh Behari Bhatia (a professor), May 25, 1950; children: Robert. *Education:* Privately educated in England; attended Liverpool Evening Institutes, 1933-40. *Home:* 8734 117th St., Edmonton, Alberta, Canada T6G 1R5.

CAREER: Writer, 1953—. *Member:* Canadian Authors' Association, Writers' Union of Canada. *Awards, honors:* Beaver Awards, 1970, for *Liverpool Daisy,* and 1977, for unpublished book, *The Moneylenders of Shahpur;* literary excellence citation from city of Edmonton, 1977; Government of Alberta achievement award, 1979.

WRITINGS: (Under psuedonym J. Rana) *Alien There Is None,* Hodder & Stoughton, 1959; (under pseudonym June Bhatia) *The Latchkey Kid,* Longmans, 1970; (under pseudonym June Edwards) *Most Precious Employee,* Robert Hale, 1974; (under pseudonym Helen Forrester) *Twopence to Cross the Mersey,* J. Cape, 1974; (under Helen Forrester) *Minerva's Stepchild* (sequel to *Twopence to Cross the Mersey*), Bodley Head, 1979, new edition (also contains *Twopence to Cross the Mersey*), Beafort Books, 1980; (under June Bhatia) *Liverpool Daisy,* R. Hale, 1979; (fiction editor) *The Alberta Diamond Jubilee Anthology,* Hurtig, 1980. Contributor to *Heritage Magazine;* contributor of book reviews to *Edmonton Journal* and *Canadian Authors.* Fiction editor of *The Alberta Diamond Jubilee Anthology,* Hurtig, 1979.

WORK IN PROGRESS: By the Waters of Liverpool, a sequel to *Minerva's Stepchild,* under Forrester pseudonym, completion expected in 1981; *Everything But the Kitchen Sink,* a novel under own name.

SIDELIGHTS: At the conclusion of *Twopence to Cross the Mersey,* the family of Helen Forrester (Jamunadevi Bhatia) arrives in Liverpool to begin a new life. *Minerva's Stepchild* continues that story, one that began when Helen's father had lost his job and his family's upper-middle-class status in England's depression of the 1930's. After fleeing his debtors he brought his family to Liverpool with hopes of finding work. His job-hunting efforts proved futile, however, and he, his wife, and his children were forced to live in a Liverpool slum.

Helen, the eldest of the seven children, shouldered much of the family burden. Living and caring for her brothers and sisters in the cold and filth of an upstairs room, she struggled against both poverty and her parents' neglect. The income of the little work her father could find was generally spent on liquor and cigarettes instead of food, soap, or fuel for the stove. Helen's mother, outraged by her ignominious fall from society's heights, added to her family's problems by trying to prevent Helen from getting a job. Helen eventually found work, however, and was able to bring hope to the family by enrolling in night school.

Response to *Minerva's Stepchild* has centered upon the author's "indomitable spirit" in the face of continual hardship. "Even writing about those adolescent years," commented Lotta Dempsey, "when Helen once attempted suicide in total despair, she has a great writer's ability to paint the larger canvas—to see herself and her family as victims of the pre-welfare state's degrading poverty which can dehumanize its victims." Dempsey added that Bhatia's presentation of her story is particularly captivating: "I can't remember reading as avidly for so many hours since my teenage discovery of Charles Dickens."

Though now living comfortably as a writer in Edmonton, Bhatia is still reminded daily of her impoverished past. "To this day, I can't bear to throw things away," she says, "and my store cupboards are always full. I just love starting a new bar of soap, and knowing I'll be able to use it all."

BIOGRAPHICAL/CRITICAL SOURCES: Helen Forrester, *Twopence to Cross the Mersey,* J. Cape, 1974; Forrester, *Minerva's Stepchild,* Bodley Head, 1979; *Toronto Daily Star,* October 3, 1979; *Calgary Herald,* November 24, 1979; *Edmonton Journal,* August 25, 1979.

BHATIA, June
See BHATIA, Jamunadevi

*   *   *

BIETENHOLZ, Peter G(erard)   1933-

PERSONAL: Born January 7, 1933, in Basel, Switzerland; son of Alfred and Mary (Gerhard) Bietenholz; married Doris S. Huber, August 29, 1958; children: Michael F., I. Balthasar, Samuel A. *Education:* University of Basel, D.Phil., 1958. *Home:* 117 Albert Ave., Saskatoon, Saskatchewan, Canada S7N 1E6. *Office:* Department of History, University of Saskatchewan, Saskatoon, Saskatchewan, Canada S7N 0W0.

CAREER: University of London, Warburg Institute, London, England, research fellow in history, 1958-59; University of Khartoum, Khartoum, Sudan, lecturer in history, 1959-63; University of Saskatchewan, Saskatoon, 1963—, began as assistant professor, professor of history, 1970—, head of department, 1974-77. Research fellow at Harvard University's Institute for Italian Renaissance Studies in Florence, Italy, 1969-70. *Member:* Canadian Historical Association, Renaissance Society of America, Society for Reformation Research, Swiss-American Historical Association (member of board of directors). *Awards, honors:* Grants from Swiss National Fund for Scientific Research and Canada Council.

WRITINGS: History and Biography in the Work of Erasmus of Rotterdam, Droz, 1966; *Basle and France in the Sixteenth Century: The Basle Humanists and Printers in Their Contacts With Francophone Culture,* University of Toronto Press, 1971.

Other works: *Der italienische Humanismus und die Bluetezeit des Buchdrucks in Basel: Die Basler Drucke italienischer Autoren von 1530 bis zum Ende des Jahrhunderts,* Helbing & Lichtenhahn, 1959; *Pietro della Valle, 1586-1652: Studien zur Geschichte der Orientkenntnis und des Orientbildes im Abendlande,* Helbing & Lichtenhahn, 1962; (contributor) *Colloquia Erasmuana Turonesia,* University of Toronto Press, 1972.

Editor of "Collected Works of Erasmus," University of Toronto Press, 1968-74. Contributor to history journals. Editor of *Canadian Journal of History/Annales Canadiennes d'Histoire,* 1967.*

*   *   *

BILLINGTON, Elizabeth T(hain)

PERSONAL: Born in New York, N.Y.; daughter of Henry Alden and Alice (Fisk) Thain; married Richard Billington (a publisher); children: Richard Alden. *Address:* c/o Frederick Warne & Co., Inc., 101 Fifth Ave., New York, N.Y. 10003.

CAREER: Writer, 1966—.

WRITINGS: Adventure With Flowers, Warne, 1966; *Understanding Ecology,* Warne, 1968, revised edition, 1971; *Randolph Caldecott Treasury,* Warne, 1978; *Part-Time Boy* (juvenile), Warne, 1980.

WORK IN PROGRESS: Fiction for children.

*   *   *

BIRCH, Daniel R(ichard)   1937-

PERSONAL: Born September 1, 1937, in Ganges, British Columbia, Canada; son of George Alfred and Grace Lilian (Poland) Birch; married Rose Arlene McDonald, 1962; children: Carol Leah. *Education:* Northwest Baptist Theological College, diploma, 1958, B.R.E., 1960; University of British Columbia, B.A., 1963, M.A., 1968; University of California, Berkeley, Ph.D., 1969. *Home:* 4185 Rockridge Rd., West Vancouver, British Columbia, Canada V5A 1S6. *Office:* Faculty of Education, Simon Fraser University, Burnaby, British Columbia, Canada.

CAREER: High school history teacher in Maple Ridge, British Columbia, 1959-61, counselor, 1961-63, head of social studies department and vice-principal, 1964-65; Simon Fraser University, Burnaby, British Columbia, research associate at Educational Foundations Centre, 1966-67; University of California, Berkeley, visiting associate professor of education, 1968-69; Simon Fraser University, assistant professor, 1969-71, associate professor, 1971-75, professor of education and associate academic vice-president, 1975—, chairman of Professional Development Centre, 1966-67, dean of faculty of education, 1971-75. Visiting associate professor at University of California, Berkeley, summer, 1971. Liaison with Canadian International Development Agency. *Member:* Canadian Society for the Study of Education, National Council of Social Studies, American Educational Research Association.

WRITINGS—Juveniles: Asia, 1969, revised edition, Addison-Wesley, 1979; *Life in Communist China,* Field Enterprises Educational Corp., 1969; (with D. Ian Allen) *Gandhi,* Field Enterprises Educational Corp., 1969; (with R. L. Carlson and wife, Arlene Birch) *Early Indian Cultures of North America,* with teacher's manual, Fitzhenry & Whiteside, 1974; (with A. Birch and Rosemary Neering) *Growth of a Nation,* with teacher's manual, Fitzhenry & Whiteside, 1971; (with A. Birch and Neering) *Life in Early North America,* with teacher's manual, Fitzhenry & Whiteside, 1974; (with A. Birch and Harry F. Stephens) *Voyages of Discovery,* with teacher's manual, Fitzhenry & Whiteside, 1974; (with A. Birch, Allen B. Cunningham, and A. Stanley Garrod) *Culture Realms of the World,* with teacher's manual, Fitzhenry & Whiteside, 1974; *Sciences humaines,* with teacher's manual, Fitzhenry & Whiteside, 1978. Contributor to education journals.*

*   *   *

BIRMINGHAM, Maisie   1914-

PERSONAL: Born September 28, 1914, in Darjeeling, India; daughter of Andrew Monro (a physician) and Gertrude Elizabeth (a science teacher; maiden name, King) Jukes; married Walter Birmingham (a professor of economics), December 17, 1948; children: Duncan, Richard, Karen. *Education:* St. Hilda's College, Oxford, B.A. (with honors), 1935, M.A., 1937. *Politics:* "Non-Marxist egalitarian socialist member of Labour party." *Religion:* Society of Friends (Quakers). *Home:* 7 Gold Hill, Shaftesbury, Dorset SP7 8JW, England.

CAREER: John Lewis Partnership (retail stores), London, England, personnel assistant, 1936-38; Rowntree & Co. Ltd. (wholesale manufacturers), York, England, personnel manager, 1938-41; British Government, Stoke-on-Trent, England, inspector of factories, 1941-43; Anglo-Iranian Oil Co., Nottingham, England, in personnel, 1943-45; University of Wales, Cardiff, lecturer in social science, 1945-49; University of Ghana, Legon, lecturer in social science, 1958-60; marriage guidance counselor, 1964-70. Member of Cwmbran New Town Development Corp., 1949-51. Secretary of Shaftesbury Christian Council, 1979.

WRITINGS—Crime novels: You Can Help Me, Collins, 1974; *The Heat of the Sun,* Collins, 1976; *Sleep in a Ditch,* Collins, 1978, Scribner, 1979. Author of "Resurrection," on BBC-Radio, 1972.

WORK IN PROGRESS: A crime novel.

SIDELIGHTS: Maisie Birmingham wrote: "Since our marriage, which took place during one of our three working visits to the United States, we have spent twelve years in Ghana, three years in Lesotho, and nine years in the heart of London's multi-racial East End, where my husband was warden of Toynbee Hall, the first of the university settlements (model of Chicago's Hull House). I have thus become very conscious of the inequality and deprivation, greed and cruelty in the world, of the tensions to which these give rise, as well as to the courage, good humor, and kindness with which these are often met.

"In 1972, when we felt our three children were old enough to be left, we returned to Africa, and I found myself with spare time as never before. I decided to try to repay some of the pleasure I have had from crime novels, particularly as I can find too few satisfying themes, characters, settings, and plausible plots in today's crime novels.

"My novels have been designed as entertainment with unusual settings—one in Ghana, two in London's East End, and a fourth (probably) in Lesotho—but inevitably my own interests, questions of social and personal justice, and of faith and compassion, color my characters and add, I believe, to the readability of the books."

*   *   *

BISSELL, Claude T(homas) 1916-

PERSONAL: Born February 10, 1916, in Meaford, Ontario, Canada; son of George Thomas and Maggie Editha (Bowen) Bissell; married Christina Flora Gray, September 12, 1945; children: Deirdre Bissell Macdonald. *Education:* University of Toronto, B.A., 1936, M.A., 1937; Cornell University, Ph.D., 1940. *Religion:* United Church of Canada. *Home:* 229 Erskine Ave., Toronto, Ontario, Canada M4P 1Z5. *Office:* Massey College, University of Toronto, 4 Devonshire Place, Toronto, Ontario, Canada M5S 2E1.

CAREER: Cornell University, Ithaca, N.Y., instructor in English, 1938-41; University of Toronto, Toronto, Ontario, lecturer, 1941-47, assistant professor, 1947-51, associate professor, 1951-56, professor of English, 1956-62, dean in residence, 1946-56, vice-president of university, 1952-56; Carleton University, Ottawa, Ontario, president, 1956-58; University of Toronto, president, 1958-71, professor of English, 1962—, university professor, 1971—, senior fellow at Massey College, 1962—. Chairman of Canada Council, 1960-62, Canadian Universities Foundation, 1962-63, Committee of Presidents of Universities of Ontario, 1962-66, and Carnegie Foundation for the Advancement of Teaching, 1966; president of National Conference of Canadian Universities and Colleges, 1962-63, and World University Service of Canada, 1962-63; member of Ontario Council of the Arts, 1972-75. William Lyon MacKenzie King Professor at Harvard University, 1967-68; Commonwealth fellow at University of Leeds, 1967-68; Aggrey-Fraser-Guggisberg lecturer at University of Ghana, 1976. *Military service:* Canadian Army, Infantry, 1944-45; served in Europe; became captain.

MEMBER: Royal Society of Canada (fellow), American Academy of Arts and Sciences (honorary member). *Awards, honors:* D.Litt. from University of Manitoba, 1958, University of Western Ontario, 1971, University of Lethbridge, 1972, University of Leeds, 1975, and University of Toronto, 1977; LL.D. from McGill University, 1958, Queen's University, Kingston, Ontario, and University of New Brunswick, 1959, Carleton University and University of Montreal, 1970, St. Lawrence University and University of British Colum-

bia, 1962, University of Michigan, 1963, Columbia University, 1965, York University and Prince of Wales College, 1967, University of Windsor, 1968, and University of St. Andrews, 1972; award of merit from city of Toronto, Ontario, 1962; D. es L. from Laval University, 1966; companion of Order of Canada, 1969.

WRITINGS: (Editor) *University College: A Portrait, 1853-1953,* University of Toronto Press, 1953; (editor) *Canada's Crisis in Higher Education,* University of Toronto Press, 1957; (editor) *Our Living Tradition: Seven Canadians,* University of Toronto Press, 1957; (editor) *Great Canadian Writing: A Century of Imagination,* Canadian Centennial Publishing, 1966; *The Strength of the University: A Selection From the Addresses of Claude T. Bissell,* University of Toronto Press, 1968; *Halfway Up Parnassus: A Personal Account of the University of Toronto, 1932-71,* University of Toronto Press, 1974; *The Humanities in the University,* University of Ghana, 1977. Contributor to Canadian and American literary journals.

WORK IN PROGRESS: A biography of Vincent Massey, first governor-general of Canada, publication by University of Toronto Press expected in 1983.

SIDELIGHTS: Bissell commented on his biography of Massey: "Although Massey is a major figure in Canadian diplomatic history, he is no less important for his service to education and the arts. He was an active member of the governing board of the University of Toronto during the early years of my presidency, and I often discussed general university problems with him. My own interests lead naturally into the problems posed by the Massey biography. I can think of no public figure in recent time who has more completely fused politics and the arts. His influence in Canada was far greater than that of the politicians who have been the traditional subjects for Canadian biographers."

BIOGRAPHICAL/CRITICAL SOURCES: Saturday Night, September 12, 1957; *Time,* December 30, 1957; *Toronto Life,* June, 1965; *Canadian,* February 18, 1967; *Canadian Forum,* September, 1968; *Canadian Journal of Higher Education,* Volume IV, number 2, 1974.

*   *   *

BLACK, Earl 1942-

PERSONAL: Born February 1, 1942, in Madill, Okla.; married, 1970. *Education:* University of Texas, B.A., 1964; Harvard University, Ph.D., 1968. *Office:* Department of Government, University of South Carolina, Columbia, S.C. 29208.

CAREER: University of South Florida, Tampa, assistant professor of political science, beginning 1968; affiliated with University of South Carolina, Columbia. *Member:* American Political Science Association.

WRITINGS: Southern Governors and Civil Rights: Racial Desegregation as a Campaign Issue in the Second Reconstruction, Harvard University Press, 1976. Contributor to political science and social science journals.

BIOGRAPHICAL/CRITICAL SOURCES: Annals of the American Academy of Political and Social Science, January, 1977; *American Historical Review,* February, 1977; *Journal of American History,* June, 1977; *Political Science Quarterly,* spring, 1977.*

*   *   *

BLAKESLEE, Thomas R(obert) 1937-

PERSONAL: Born December 30, 1937, in Oak Park, Ill.; son

of Gale Robert (an executive) and Virginia (Cothrin) Blakes-lee; married Maureen Yuen (a consultant), November 20, 1977; children: Steven Robert, Robert Laurence. *Education:* California Institute of Technology, B.S., 1962. *Politics:* Independent. *Religion:* None. *Home:* 172 Otis Ave., Woodside, Calif. 94062. *Office:* Logisticon, Inc., 350 Potrero, Sunnyvale, Calif. 94086.

CAREER: Scantlin Electronics, Los Angeles, Calif., electronic engineer, 1962-64; Scientific Data Systems, Los Angeles, member of technical staff, 1964-69; International Telephone & Telegraph, Bell Telephone, Antwerp, Belgium, senior engineer, 1971-73; Logisticon, Inc., Sunnyvale, Calif., vice-president, 1974—. *Military service:* U.S. Navy, 1955-58. *Member:* Institute of Electrical and Electronic Engineers.

WRITINGS: Digital Design With Standard M.S.I., Wiley, 1975, 2nd edition, 1980; *The Right Brain*, Doubleday, 1980. Contributor to electronics journals.

WORK IN PROGRESS: A Layman's Guide to the New Technology.

SIDELIGHTS: Blakeslee wrote: "When I get involved with an idea, I am sometimes delighted to find that someone has already expressed it perfectly in a book. My own books are an outgrowth of the frustration of finding insights which seem to have been missed. I take great joy in filling the gap, by pursuing the idea until it crystallizes into a book. My greatest satisfaction comes from knowing that at least some of my readers have shared the excitement of my discovery and have incorporated it into their understanding of the world.

"My current interest is in the secrets of life as revealed by microbiology and in an expanded concept of 'self' which considers the fact that we are indeed a colony of independent cells living together symbiotically."

*   *   *

BLANCHARD, Nina

PERSONAL: Daughter of Mildred Bang. *Education:* Attended El Camino College and Columbia University. *Residence:* Los Angeles, Calif. *Agent:* Ben Conway, 999 North Doheney Dr., No. 403, Los Angeles, Calif. 90069. *Office:* Nina Blanchard Agency, 1717 North Highland Ave., Los Angeles, Calif. 90028.

CAREER: Nina Blanchard Agency, Los Angeles, Calif., owner and talent agent, 1961—.

WRITINGS: How to Break Into Motion Pictures, Television, Commercials, and Modeling, Doubleday, 1979.

WORK IN PROGRESS: A novel.

*   *   *

BLOCK, Michael 1942-

PERSONAL: Born February 16, 1942, in New York, N.Y.; son of Jack L. (in manufacturing) and Dorothy Frances (an actress, dancer, and model; maiden name, Sachs) Block; *Education:* New York University, B.A. 1965; studied drama at American Theatre Wing, 1959; studying at Warren Robertson Theatre Workshop. *Home and office:* East River Tower, 1725 York Ave., New York, N.Y. 10028. *Agent:* Harold Matson Co., Inc., 22 E. 40th St., New York, N.Y. 10016.

CAREER: Harvard Lampoon, Cambridge, Mass., advertising executive for parodies of *Time* and *Life* magazines, 1968-70; *National Lampoon*, New York City, advertising execu-

tive, 1969-70; *Playboy*, Chicago, Ill., advertising executive, 1970-71; Transportation Displays, Inc. (TDI), New York City, advertising sales executive, 1975-77; writer, 1977—. Associated with Advertising News of New York, 1966-67, 1975-76. *Member:* Tau Epsilon Phi.

WRITINGS: Letters to Michael, Coward, 1979.

WORK IN PROGRESS: Men: How They Feel About Dating, Relating, and Marriage, publication expected in 1981; research on love relations; "Dear Michael," "a nationally syndicated column on single men and women who want a relationship leading to marriage."

SIDELIGHTS: Letters to Michael is a collection of responses Block received after advertising for a wife. Block posted billboards with his picture and a post office box number in subway stations in New York City. He explained to Anna Quindlen of the *New York Times* that he was tired of the emptiness of the singles-bar scene and longed for monogamy and security. Block received over eight thousand letters and dated about forty of the the women who responded.

Block told *CA:* "I'm still not married. The reason is chemistry. The chemistry hasn't been quite right yet. And that was far more important than just 'getting married.' The two times in my life that I've been in love, there was chemistry. I'm sure there will be a third time, and that thing no one can explain, which just happens between two people will happen again.

"In this liberated day and age, men and women still want close companionship, marriage, children, and stable homes. And it's okay to want these things, to be romantic and to be vunerable.

"In my next book I hope to show that men feel deeply about dating, relationships, and marriage. I think that we'll discover that there isn't a lot that's different between men and women when it comes to needs, desires, and wants concerning dating relationships and marriage, once you put our physicalness aside.

"I'm also excited that my first book is being made into a motion picture by Lorimar Pictures. I'm looking forward to working on the film and acting in it in a small cameo role."

BIOGRAPHICAL/CRITICAL SOURCES: New York Times, July 18, 1977; *Good Housekeeping*, February, 1978; *Washington Post*, November, 1979; *Chicago Tribune*, November 27, 1979; *Cosmopolitan*, June, 1980.

*   *   *

BLOCK, Thomas H(arris) 1945-

PERSONAL: Born February 11, 1945, in New York; son of Benjamin (a foreman of a milk company) and Helen (Zwirko) Block; married Eileen Ferro (a teacher), November 20, 1976; children: Kimberley, Steven, Ryan. *Education:* Attended Morehead State College (now University), 1963. *Politics:* Republican. *Residence:* Sewickley, Pa. *Agent:* Joseph Elder Agency, 150 West 87th St., New York, N.Y. 10024.

CAREER: US Air, Pittsburgh, Pa., airline captain, 1964—. *Member:* Soaring Society of America, Aviation and Space Writers Association, Aircraft Owners and Pilots Association, Air Line Pilots Association.

WRITINGS: Mayday (novel; Literary Guild Book Club selection), Richard Marek, 1980. Author of "Pro's Nest," a monthly column in *Flying*, 1970—. Contributor to magazines and newspapers. Contributing editor of *Flying*, 1970—.

WORK IN PROGRESS: An untitled novel, publication by Richard Marek expected in 1981.

SIDELIGHTS: Block wrote: "A professional pilot for seventeen years, I have also had a successful second career as a writer for the past twelve. I have written on a wide array of subjects, ranging from interviews with top government officials to test and evaluation reports on most everything that flies. I have piloted gliders, single engine lightplanes, seaplanes, the Goodyear Blimp, and large transport jets, to name a few.

"My first novel was, naturally, an airplane adventure and suspense story. My second novel, currently underway, is also an airplane adventure. My wife Eileen works closely with me on the writing."

*   *   *

BLONDEL, Jean Fernand Pierre 1929-

PERSONAL: Born October 26, 1929, in Toulon, France; son of Fernand and Marie (Santelli) Blondel; married Michele Hadet, October 4, 1954; children: Dominique, Natalie. *Education:* Attended Institut d'Etudes Politiques; University of Paris, diploma, 1953; St. Antony's College, Oxford, Litt.B., 1955. *Home:* 13 Beverley Rd., Colchester, Essex, England; and 9 rue General de Partouneaux, Mourillon, Toulon, France. *Office:* School of Comparative Studies, University of Essex, Wivenhoe Park, Colchester, Essex CO4 3SQ, England.

CAREER: University of Keele, Keele, England, 1958-63, began as assistant lecturer, became lecturer in government; University of Essex, Colchester, England, professor of government, 1963—, dean of School of Comparative Studies, 1967-69. Visiting fellow at Yale University, 1963-64; visiting professor at Institut d'Etudes Politiques, 1969—, and Carleton University, 1969-70. Executive director of European Consortium for Political Research, 1970—. *Military service:* French Army, 1955-57; became lieutenant. *Member:* Political Studies Association (England), French Political Science Association. *Awards, honors:* American Council of Learned Societies fellow, 1963-64.

WRITINGS: Voters, Parties, and Leaders: The Social Fabric of British Politics, Penguin, 1963, revised edition, 1967; (with Frederick F. Ridley) *Public Administration in France,* Routledge & Kegan Paul, 1964, Barnes & Noble, 1965, 2nd edition, 1969; (with Frank Bealey and W. P. McCann) *Constituency Politics,* Free Press, 1965; (with E. Drexel Godfrey, Jr.) *Government of France,* Harper, 3rd edition (Blondel was not associated with earlier editions), 1968, 4th edition, Crowell, 1974; *An Introduction to Comparative Government,* Praeger, 1969; (editor) *Comparative Government: A Reader,* Anchor Books, 1969.

Democracy in Crisis: New Challenges to Constitutional Democracy in the Atlantic Area, University of Notre Dame Press, 1971; *Comparing Political Systems,* Praeger, 1972; (with Valentine Herman) *Review Exercises for Comparative Government,* Praeger, 1972 (published in England as *Workbook for Comparative Government,* Weidenfeld & Nicolson, 1972); *Comparative Legislatures,* Prentice-Hall, 1973; *Contemporary France: Politics, Society, and Institutions,* Methuen, 1974; *Thinking Politically,* Westview, 1976; *Political Parties,* State Mutual Book, 1977; *Political Parties: A Genuine Case for Discontent?,* Wildwood House, 1978; (with G. Gordon and J. Gombeaud) *Verites: Est-ce a dire?* (in French), A. Bonne, 1978; *World Leaders: A Study of Heads of Government in the Postwar Period,* Sage Publications, 1979; *Political Leadership,* Sage Publications, 1979; (editor with Carol Walker) *Directory of European Political Scientists,* 3rd edition, Holmes & Meier, 1979.*

BLOOM, Freddy 1914-

PERSONAL: Born in 1914 in New York, N.Y.; married Philip M. Bloom (a physician); children: Virginia, William. *Education:* Attended Columbia University, 1931-34; Trinity College, Dublin, B.A. (with honors), 1936. *Home:* 2 Montagu Sq., London W.1, England.

CAREER: Free-lance writer. Affiliated with Malaya Tribune Group in Singapore, 1939-41; managing director of Youth Book Club, 1947-48. Member of board of governors of Post Graduate Teaching Hospitals and Special School. *Member:* National Deaf Children's Society (founding chairman, 1956-64), Health Visitors Association (vice-president). *Awards, honors:* Malaya campaign medal, 1947; Member of Order of the British Empire, 1964.

WRITINGS: Our Deaf Children, Heinemann, 1963; *The Little Boy Who Could Not Hear* (juvenile), Bodley Head, 1979; *Our Deaf Children: Into the Eighties,* Gresham, 1979; *Dear Philip,* Bodley Head, 1980; *Care to Help?,* John Clare, 1980. Editor of National Deaf Children's Society publication, *Talk,* 1955—.

WORK IN PROGRESS: Face It!, advice for young disabled people from the ages of sixteen through thirty.

SIDELIGHTS: Freddy Bloom commented to *CA:* "For no rational reason, I like people and think they should be nicer to each other even if they look or sound different. Since nobody else has ever thought of saying it before, I keep repeating that greed, intolerance, and materialism do not pay satisfying dividends. As usual, nobody listens. Shame."

BIOGRAPHICAL/CRITICAL SOURCES: Leslie Bell, *Destined Meeting,* Odhams, 1959; Noel Barber, *Sinister Twilight,* Collins, 1968.

*   *   *

BLOOMBERG, Marty
See BLOOMBERG, Max Arthur
*   *   *

BLOOMBERG, Max Arthur 1938-
(Marty Bloomberg)

PERSONAL: Born October 7, 1938, in Fort Worth, Tex.; son of Alexander Jacob (a bookseller) and Sarah (Shosid) Bloomberg; married Leila Ann Manson (a school administrator), August 25, 1963; children: Mark, Stacey. *Education:* Texas Christian University, B.A., 1960; University of Denver, M.A., 1961; University of the Redlands, M.A.T., 1968. *Politics:* Democrat. *Religion:* Jewish. *Home:* 16285 Whispering Spur, Riverside, Calif. 92504. *Office:* Library, California State College, San Bernardino, Calif. 92407.

CAREER: Central Intelligence Agency (CIA), Langley, Va., cataloger, 1961-62; California State University, Hayward, head of education library, 1963-64; Denver Public Library, Denver, Colo., cataloger, 1964-65; California State University, Hayward, cataloger and documents librarian, 1965-66; California State College, San Bernardino, assistant director of library, 1966—. *Member:* Southern California Technical Processes Group.

WRITINGS—Under name Marty Bloomberg: (With G. Edward Evans) *An Introduction to Technical Services for Library Technicians,* Libraries Unlimited, 1971, 4th edition, 1981; *An Introduction to Public Services for Library Technicians,* Libraries Unlimited, 1972, 3rd edition, 1981; (with Hans Weber) *World War Two and Its Origins: A Select Annotated Bibliography,* Libraries Unlimited, 1975; (with

Weber) *An Introduction to Classification and Number Building in Dewey*, Libraries Unlimited, 1976; *The Jewish Holocaust: An Annotated Bibliography*, Borgo Press, 1981.

*   *   *

BLOS, Joan W(insor) 1928-

PERSONAL: Born December 9, 1928, in New York, N.Y.; daughter of Max (a psychiatrist) and Charlotte (a teacher; maiden name, Biber) Winsor; married Peter Blos, Jr. (a psychoanalyst), June 7, 1953; children: one son, one daughter. *Education:* Vassar College, B.A., 1949; City College (now of the City University of New York), M.A., 1956. *Residence:* Ann Arbor, Mich. *Agent:* Curtis Brown Ltd., 575 Madison Ave., New York, N.Y. 10022.

CAREER: Bank Street College of Education, New York, N.Y., associate in publications division and member of faculty, 1958-70; University of Michigan, Ann Arbor, lecturer at School of Education, 1972-80. *Awards, honors:* John Newbery Medal from American Library Association, and American Book Award, both 1980, both for *A Gathering of Days: A New England Girl's Journal, 1830-32*.

WRITINGS—Children's books: (With Betty Miles) *Joe Finds a Way*, L. W. Singer, 1967; *"It's Spring!" She Said*, Knopf, 1968; (with Miles) *Just Think!*, Knopf, 1971; *A Gathering of Days: A New England Girl's Journal, 1830-32*, Scribner, 1979. Contributor of articles and reviews to periodicals, including *School Library Journal, New Outlook*, and *Merrill-Palmer Quarterly*. U.S. editor of *Children's Literature in Education*, 1976—.

WORK IN PROGRESS: Several books for preschool children; a novel (historical fiction) for older children; a book about children's literature.

SIDELIGHTS: Joan Blos received the highest honor in the field of children's literature for her first children's novel, *A Gathering of Days*. The American Library Association awarded Blos the John Newbery Medal in 1979 for the year's most distinguished contribution to American children's literature. *Kirkus Reviews* called the book "carefully researched and convincingly delivered." The *St. Louis Post-Dispatch* noted: "It is [the] careful tuning of psychological nuances to historic elements that gives the story its powerful immediacy. *A Gathering of Days* not only gives the reader a close look at the early 1800's, it offers him a deeply moving human experience."

Set in the early nineteenth century, *A Gathering of Days* is presented as a young girl's journal of her life on a New England farm. The Newbery-Caldecott awards committee observed that the "journal is comprised of skillfully woven threads, each a select detail of her everyday life that develop characters and interweave historic information without interrupting the flow of this well-crafted story. This [novel] . . . reveals the significance of an individual's life and a culture's history."

Blos wrote her novel over a period of twelve years. "It was a case in which a historic interest was converted into a story that says something socially," she said. Fascinated by her husband's family's summer home in New England, she made a study of its past owners and thought that the "history of an actual place" could work well as a background for some "things that needed to be said." Noting that the novel's heroine "meets both the cruel, long and dark winter days and the all-too-short sunny summer days with sturdy endurance and quiet joy," Lavinia Russ of the *Washington Post Book World* commented further that "Blos offers a valuable supplement to students of early American history."

In an interview with Andrea Wojack of the *Detroit News*, Blos talked about the course of children's literature in the "post-Me Decade." "I'm encouraged, because in children's literature, as in all literature, we're seeing . . . a sense of esteem for the self in what you can do and what you can become. Literature is again purposeful and reflective."

Blos told *CA:* "Writing for children and teaching children's literature are closely related activities for me. Both are ways of transmitting to others things as I have come to understand them, and which I hope others can use. Truth is something that interests me a lot. When you write a story you find that you have to deal with three kinds of truthfulness. There is the psychological truthfulness of your characters, the social truthfulness of their situation, and the literary truthfulness of the manner of telling. The story is what results."

BIOGRAPHICAL/CRITICAL SOURCES: Kirkus Reviews, January 15, 1980; *Detroit News*, January 26, 1980, February 3, 1980; *St. Louis Post-Dispatch*, January 27, 1980; *Washington Post Book World*, March 9, 1980.

*   *   *

BLUM, Carol Kathlyn 1934-

PERSONAL: Born May 22, 1934, in St. Louis, Mo.; married, 1964; children: two. *Education:* Washington University, St. Louis, Mo., B.A., 1956; Columbia University, M.A., 1960, Ph.D., 1966. *Office:* Department of French and Italian, State University of New York at Stony Brook, Stony Brook, N.Y. 11790.

CAREER: Columbia University, New York, N.Y., lecturer in French, 1961-62; State University of New York at Stony Brook, 1962—, began as instructor, became assistant professor and associate professor of French. *Member:* American Society for Eighteenth Century Studies, Modern Language Association of America. *Awards, honors:* National Endowment for the Humanities fellow, 1973; Guggenheim fellow, 1975-76.

WRITINGS: Diderot: The Virtue of a Philosopher, Viking, 1974. Contributor to literature journals.*

*   *   *

BLUM, Lucille Hollander 1904-

PERSONAL: Born August 29, 1904, in New York, N.Y.; married, 1925; children: two. *Education:* Columbia University, B.S., 1940, M.A., 1942, Ph.D., 1949; Postgraduate Center for Mental Health, certificate, 1953. *Home:* 3 East 67th St., New York, N.Y. 10021.

CAREER: Psychological consultant to Cerebral Palsy Pre-School Clinic at Lenox Hill Hospital in New York, 1948-53; supervisor and training analyst at Postgraduate Center for Mental Health, 1953—. Research associate at Institute for Psychological Research, Columbia University, 1950-51; special lecturer at Columbia-Presbyterian Medical Center, 1950-58. *Member:* American Psychological Association (fellow), Society for Research in Child Development (fellow).

WRITINGS: Some Psychological and Educational Aspects of Pediatric Practice: A Study of Well-Baby Clinics, Journal Press, 1950; (with Helen H. Davidson and Nina D. Fieldsteel) *A Rorschach Workbook*, International Universities Press, 1954, 2nd edition, 1975; *Reading Between the Lines: Doctor-Patient Communication*, International Universities Press, 1972. Contributor to psychology and medical journals.*

BLUMBERG, Leonard U. 1920-

PERSONAL: Born August 19, 1920, in Philadelphia, Pa.; son of Louis and Jennie (Sherman) Blumberg; married Marjorie Stowell Fox, 1943 (divorced, 1977); married Grace Hummers Dessurreau, 1977; children: (first marriage) Eric, Judith, Martha, James; stepchildren: Katherine, Elisa. *Education:* Wayne State University, B.A., 1947, M.A., 1949; University of Michigan, Ph.D., 1955. *Politics:* Democrat. *Religion:* Quaker. *Office:* Department of Sociology, Temple University, Philadelphia, Pa. 19122.

CAREER: Temple University, Philadelphia, Pa., instructor, 1955-56, assistant professor, 1956-59, associate professor, 1959-65, professor of sociology, 1965—, chairman of department, 1958-62. Research director for Urban League, Philadelphia, 1956-60; co-director of research for Philadelphia Diagnostic and Relocation Center, 1961—. *Member:* American Association for the Advancement of Science, American Sociological Association (fellow), Society for the Study of Social Problems, Eastern Sociological Association.

WRITINGS: (With Thomas E. Shipley, Jr., and Irving W. Shandler) *Skid Row and Its Alternatives: Research and Recommendations From Philadelphia,* Temple University Press, 1973; *Alternatives to Skid Row,* Temple University Press, 1973; (with Shipley and Stephen F. Barsky) *Liquor and Poverty: Skid Row as a Human Condition,* Publications Division, Center of Alcohol Studies, Rutgers University, 1978. Contributor to *Men on Skid Row.* Contributor to journals in the behavioral sciences.

WORK IN PROGRESS: The Washington Temperance Movement; The Washington Institutions for Alcoholics; research on social movements as an aspect of political sociology.

SIDELIGHTS: Blumberg told *CA:* "My continuing interests professionally are divided in two directions—alcoholism (and skid row) and political sociology (with special emphasis on social movements, at the present time). My current work is an effort to bridge the two interests. There are also some other aspects of political sociology that I hope to get to when the current set of projects is completed: a work on utopias and a work on art and society."

AVOCATIONAL INTERESTS: Hiking.

*   *   *

BLUMBERG, Phillip I(rvin) 1919-

PERSONAL: Born September 6, 1919, in Baltimore, Md.; son of Hyman (a labor union leader) and Bessie (Simons) Blumberg; married Janet Helen Mitchell, November 17, 1945 (died April 24, 1976); married Ellen Ash Peters (a state supreme court justice), September 16, 1979; children: (first marriage) William Allen, Peter, Lisa Mitchell Booth, Bruce. *Education:* Harvard University, A.B., 1939, J.D., 1942. *Politics:* Democrat. *Home:* 71 Sycamore Rd., West Hartford, Conn. 06117. *Office:* School of Law, University of Connecticut, West Hartford, Conn.

CAREER: Admitted to the Bar of the State of New York, 1942, and the State of Massachusetts, 1970. Lawyer with firms of Willkie, Owen, Otis, Farr & Gallagher, 1942-43, Szolc & Brandwen, 1946-49, and partner with Szolc, Brandwen, Meyers & Blumberg, 1949-66; Boston University, Boston, Mass., professor of law, 1968-74; University of Connecticut, West Hartford, professor of law and business, and dean of School of Law, 1974—. President and chief executive officer in business, 1962-73. Member of U.S. State Department advisory committee on international investment

and technology transfer; chairman of bankruptcy judge merit screening committee; member of governor's committee to review judicial nominations; member of board of directors of Verde Exploration Ltd. and Mitchell Rand Manufacturing Corp.; member of board of trustees of Connecticut Bar Foundation. President of Edward A. Filene Good Will Fund. *Military service:* U.S. Army Air Forces, 1942-46; received Bronze Star. U.S. Air Force Reserve, Judge Advocate General's Department, 1946-55; became major. *Member:* American Law Institute, American Bar Association, Connecticut Bar Association, Phi Beta Kappa, Harvard Club (New York City and Boston), University Club.

WRITINGS: Corporate Responsibility in a Changing Society, Boston University Press, 1972; *The Megacorporation in American Society: The Scope of Corporate Power,* Prentice-Hall, 1975. Contributor to law journals.

WORK IN PROGRESS: A treatise on the law of parent and subsidiary corporations, completion expected in 1985.

SIDELIGHTS: Blumberg commented to *CA:* "Happiness is the opportunity to work very hard on something you enjoy. Lucky indeed is the man or woman faced with such a challenge."

*   *   *

BLUNDELL, Harold 1902-
(George Bellairs)

PERSONAL: Born April 19, 1902, in Heywood, Lancashire, England. *Education:* Received B.Sc. from London University and M.A. from Manchester University. *Home:* Gat-y-Whing, Colby, Isle of Man, United Kingdom.

CAREER: Free-lance writer, 1930—. Manager of chief Manchester office of Martins Bank, 1953-62. *Member:* Society of Authors, Isle of Man Arts Council, Manchester Club.

WRITINGS—All under pseudonym George Bellairs; all published by Gifford, except as noted; all crime novels: *Littlejohn on Leave,* 1941; *The Four Unfaithful Servants,* 1942; *Death of a Busybody,* 1942, Macmillan, 1943; *Murder Will Speak,* Macmillan, 1943 (published in England as *The Dead Shall Be Raised,* 1943); *Calamity at Harwood,* 1943, Macmillan, 1945; *Turmoil in Zion,* 1943, published as *Death Stops the Frolic,* Macmillan, 1944; *The Murder of a Quack,* 1943, Macmillan, 1944; *He'd Rather Be Dead,* 1945; *Death in the Night Watches,* 1945, Macmillan, 1946; *The Case of the Scared Rabbits,* 1946; *The Crime at Halfpenny Bridge,* 1946; *Death on the Last Train,* 1948, Macmillan, 1949; *The Case of the Seven Whistlers,* Macmillan, 1948; *The Case of the Famished Parson,* Macmillan, 1949; *The Case of the Demented Spiv,* 1949, Macmillan, 1950; *Outrage on Gallows Hill,* 1949.

The Case of the Headless Jesuit, 1950, published as *Death Brings in the New Year,* Macmillan, 1951; *Dead March for Penelope Blow,* Macmillan, 1951; *Death in Dark Glasses,* Macmillan, 1952; *Crime in Leper's Hollow,* 1952; *Half-Mast for the Deemster,* 1953; *Corpses in Enderby,* 1954; *The Cursing Stones Murder,* 1954; *Death in Room Five,* 1955; *Death Treads Softly,* 1956; *Death Drops the Pilot,* 1956; *Death in High Provence,* 1957, Penguin, 1963; *Death Sends for the Doctor,* 1957; *Death in Desolation,* Gifford, 1957; *Corpse at the Carnival,* 1958; *Murder Makes Mistakes,* 1958; *Bones in the Wilderness,* 1959; *Toll the Bell for Murder,* 1959.

Death in the Fearful Night, 1960; *Death of a Tin God,* 1961; *The Body in the Dumb River,* 1961; *Death Before Breakfast,* British Book Centre, 1962; *The Tormentors,* 1962; *Death in the Wasteland,* 1963, London House & Maxwell, 1964; *Sur-*

feit of Suspects, 1964; *Death of a Shadow*, 1964; *Death Spins the Wheel*, 1965; *Strangers Among the Dead*, 1966; *Single Ticket to Death*, 1967; *The Night They Killed Joss Varran*, 1970; *Pomeroy, Deceased*, 1971; *Tycoon's Death-Bed*, F. A. Thorpe, 1971; *Murder Adrift*, 1972; *Devious Murder*, 1973; *Fear Round About*, 1975; *Close All Roads to Sospel*, 1977.

Also author of *A Knife for Harry Dodd*, 1953, *Death in Despair*, 1960, *Intruder in the Dark*, 1966, and *Fatal Alibi*, 1968. Contributor to periodicals, including *Guardian*, *Wine and Food*, *Cheshire Life*, and *Manz Life*.

*   *   *

BOARDMAN, John 1927-

PERSONAL: Born August 20, 1927, in Ilford, England; son of Frederick Archibald and Clara (Wells) Boardman; married Sheila Joan Lyndon Stanford, October 26, 1952; children: Julia, Mark. *Education:* Magdalene College, Cambridge, B.A., 1948, M.A., 1951. *Home:* House of Winds, Harcourt Hill, North Hinksey, Oxford, England.

CAREER: British School at Athens, Athens, Greece, assistant director, 1952-55; Oxford University, Oxford, England, assistant keeper at Ashmolean Museum, 1955-59, reader, 1959-78, Lincoln Professor of Classical Archaeology and Art and fellow of Lincoln College, 1978—, fellow of Merton College, 1963-78. Geddes-Harrower Professor at University of Aberdeen, 1974. Conducted excavations at Chios, 1953-55, and Tocra, Libya, 1964-65. *Military service:* British Army, Intelligence Corps, 1950-52; became second lieutenant. *Member:* Society of Antiquaries (fellow), British Academy (fellow), Hellenic Society, Libya Exploration Society.

WRITINGS: (Editor) Thomas James Dunbabin, *The Greeks and Their Eastern Neighbours: Studies in the Relations Between Greece and the Countries of the Near East in the Eighth and Seventh Centuries B.C.*, Society for the Promotion of Hellenic Studies, 1957, reprinted, Greenwood Press, 1979; (translator from Greek) Spyridon N. Marinatos, *Crete and Mycenae*, Thames & Hudson, 1960; *The Cretan Collection in Oxford: The Dictaean Cave and Iron Age Crete*, Clarendon Press, 1961; *Island Gems: A Study of Greek Seals in the Geometric and Early Archaic Periods*, Society for the Promotion of Hellenic Studies, 1963; (with Leonard Robert Palmer) *On the Knossos Tablets*, Clarendon Press, 1963; *Greek Art*, Praeger, 1964, revised edition, 1973; *The Greeks Overseas: The Archaeology of Their Early Colonies and Trade*, Penguin, 1964, 2nd edition, 1973; (with Jose Doerig, Werner Fuchs, and Max Hirmer) *Die griechische Kunst*, Hirmer Verlag, 1966, translation published as *Greek Art and Architecture*, Abrams, 1967 (published in England as *The Art and Architecture of Ancient Greece*, Thames & Hudson, 1967); (with John Hayes) *Excavations at Tocra, 1963-1965*, Thames & Hudson, Volume I: *The Archaic Deposits*, 1966, Volume II: *Archaic Deposits II and Later Deposits*, 1973; *Excavations in Chios, 1952-1955: Greek Emporio*, Thames & Hudson, 1967; *Pre-Classical: From Crete to Archaic Greece*, Penguin, 1967; *Archaic Greek Gems: Schools and Artists in the Sixth and Early Fifth Centuries B.C.*, Northwestern University Press, 1968; *Engraved Gems: The Ionides Collection*, Northwestern University Press, 1968; *Greek Painted Vases: Catalogue of an Exhibition in the Mappin Art Gallery*, Mappin Art Gallery, 1968.

Greek Gems and Finger Rings: Early Bronze Age to Late Classical, Abrams, 1970; (editor with M. A. Brown and T.G.E. Powell) *The European Community in Later Prehistory: Studies in Honour of C.F.C. Hawkes*, Rowman & Lit-

tlefield, 1971; (with Donna C. Kurtz) *Greek Burial Customs*, Cornell University Press, 1971; *Athenian Black Figure Vases*, Oxford University Press, 1974 (published in England as *Athenian Black Figure Vases: A Handbook*, Thames & Hudson, 1974); *Intaglios and Rings: Greek, Etruscan, and Eastern, From a Private Collection*, Thames & Hudson, 1975; *Oxford, Ashmolean Museum*, Oxford University Press, 1975; *Athenian Red Figure Vases: The Archaic Period, a Handbook*, Thames & Hudson, 1975, Oxford University Press, 1979; (with Diana Scarisbrick) *The Ralph Harari Collection of Finger Rings*, Thames & Hudson, 1977; (with Marie-Louise Vollenweider) *Catalogue of the Engraved Gems and Finger Rings: Ashmolean Museum, Oxford*, Volume I: *Greek and Etruscan*, Oxford University Press, 1978; (with Eugenio La Rocca) *Eros in Greece*, J. Murray, 1978; *Greek Sculpture: The Archaic Period, a Handbook*, Oxford University Press, 1978; (with Martin Robertson) *Corpus vasorum antiquorum: Great Britain, Castle Ashby, Northampton*, Oxford University Press, 1979. Contributor to scholarly journals. Editor of *Journal of Hellenic Studies*, 1958-65.

WORK IN PROGRESS: Early Classical Sculpture: A Handbook; Greco-Phoenician Scarabs.

BIOGRAPHICAL/CRITICAL SOURCES: Classical World, September, 1979.

*   *   *

BOCKLE, Franz
See BOECKLE, Franz

*   *   *

BODDY, William Charles 1913-

PERSONAL: Born in 1913, in London, England; children: three daughters. *Education:* Attended Belmont College. *Home:* Llwyn-barriel Hall, Montmel, Llandrindod Wells, Radnorshire, Wales.

CAREER: Writer. Editorial assistant and advertising manager with *Sports Car*; assistant editor of *Brooklands Track and Air*; editor of *Motor Sport*. *Member:* Vintage Sports Car Club, British Ornithologists' Club, Guild of Motoring Writers, Vintage Sports Car Club of Australia.

WRITINGS: *The Two Hundred Mile Race of the Junior Car Club, 1921-1938*, Grenville Publishing, 1947; (editor) *The Story of Brooklands, the World's First Motor Course: Compiled From the Official Records of the Brooklands Automobile Racing Club*, three volumes, Grenville Publishing, 1948-50; *Continental Sports Cars*, G. T. Foulis, 1951, revised edition, 1952; *The World's Land Speed Record*, Motor Racing Publications, 1951, revised edition, Phoenix House, 1964; (contributor) Charles Gardner, editor, *Fifty Years of Brooklands*, Heinemann, 1956; *The History of Brooklands Motor Course: Compiled From the Official Records of the Brooklands Automobile Racing Club*, Grenville Publishing, 1957.

The Bugatti Story, Sports Car Press, 1960; *The Sports Car Pocketbook*, Batsford, 1961; *Montlhery: The Story of the Paris Autodrome, 1924-1960*, Cassell, 1961; *The Vintage Years of the Morgan Three-Wheeler*, Grenville Publishing, 1972; (editor) *"Motor Sport" Book of the Austin Seven*, Grenville Publishing, 1972; (editor) *"Motor Sport" Book of Donington*, Grenville Publishing, 1973; *The History of Motor Racing*, Putnam, 1977. General editor of "Macdonald Automobile Histories," Macdonald & Co., 1965—. Contributor to magazines, including *Autocar*, *Motor*, *Flight*, and *Safe Driver*.*

BODET, Jaime Torres
See TORRES BODET, Jaime

* * *

BODGER, Joan
See MERCER, Joan Bodger

* * *

BOECKLE, Franz 1921-

PERSONAL: Born April 18, 1921, in Glarus, Switzerland; son of Fridolin (a box maker) and Klara (Lampe) Boeckle. *Education:* Educated in Zurich, Rome, and Munich. *Home:* Am kottenforst 46, 53 Bonn 1, West Germany. *Office:* University of Bonn, Am Hof 1, 53 Bonn 1, West Germany.

CAREER: Ordained Roman Catholic priest, 1945; professor of moral theology and philosophy in Chur, Switzerland, 1953-63; University of Bonn, Bonn, West Germany, professor of moral theology, 1963—. Chairman of Scientific Commission on Evolution and Peace. *Member:* Rotary International.

WRITINGS: Gesetz und Gewissen: Grundfragen theologischer Ethik in oekumenischer Sicht, Raeber Verlag, 1965, translation by M. James Donnelly published as *Law and Conscience,* Sheed, 1966; (editor with Johannes Feiner) *Theology Today,* Bruce, 1965; (editor) *Moral Problems and Christian Personalism,* Paulist, 1965; (editor) *Understanding the Signs of the Times,* Paulist Press, 1967; *Grundbegriffe der Moral: Gewissen und Gewissen bildung,* Paul Pattloch, 1966, translation by William Jerman published as *Fundamental Concepts of Moral Theology,* Paulist Press, 1968; (editor) *The Social Message of the Gospels,* Paulist Press, 1968; (editor) *Dilemmas of Tomorrow's World,* Paulist/Newman, 1969; (editor) *The Future of Marriage as an Institution,* Herder & Herder, 1970; (editor) *The Manipulated Man,* Herder & Herder, 1971 (published in England as *The Manipulation of Man,* Burns & Oates, 1971); *Man in a New Society,* Herder & Herder, 1972; (editor with Jacques-Marie Pohier) *Power and the Word of God,* Herder & Herder, 1973; (editor with Pohier) *Sexuality in Contemporary Catholicism,* Seabury, 1976; (editor with Pohier) *Moral Formation and Christianity,* Seabury, 1978; (editor with Pohier) *The Death Penalty and Torture,* Seabury, 1979. Also author of *War, Poverty, Freedom: The Christian Response,* Paulist/Newman.

Not in English: *Die Idee der Fruchtbarkeit in der Pauluslriefers* [Freiburg], 1953; *Das Wachstum der Weltbevoelkerung,* Polygraphischer Verlag, 1965; (with Josef Koehne) *Geschlechtliche Beziehungen von der Ehe: Die Lage bei der studentischen Jugend,* Matthias-Gruenewald-Verlag, 1967; *Das Problem der bekenntnisverschiedenen Ehe in theologischer Sicht: Als Manuskript gedruckt,* Seelsorge-Verlag, 1967; *Freiheit und Bindung,* Butzon & Bercker, 1968; (with Ingo Hermann) *Die Probe aufs Humane,* Patmos-Verlag, 1970; (with Norbert Greinacher and Felicitas Betz) *Ehe in der Diskussion: Was hat die Kirche zur Ehe zu sagen?,* Herder & Herder, 1970; *Kirche im Umbruch der Gesellschaft,* Paulusverlag, 1970; (with Matthias Kaiser and Wolfgang Beinert) *Beitraege zue Theologie der Ehe,* Butzon & Bercker, 1971; (with Wilhelm Knevels) *Euthanasie,* H. Reich, 1975; *Fundamentalmoral,* [Munich], 1977; *Einheit der Kirche: Einheit der Menschheit,* Herder & Herder, 1978; *Menschenwuerdig sterben,* [Zurich], 1979. Also author of *Die Mischehe in oekumenischer Sicht,* with J. Dupont, X. Oray, and R. Beaupere.

Editor: (With Feiner) *Panorama de la teologia actual,* Ediciones Guadarrama, 1961; *Moral zwischen Anspruch und Verantwortung,* Patmos-Verlag, 1964; *Das Natturecht im Disput,* Patmos-Verlag, 1966; (with Carl Holenstein) *Die Enzyklika in der Diskussion: Eine orientierende Dokumentation zu "Humanae vitae",* Benziger, 1968; *Der Zoelibat: Erfahrungen, Meinungen, Vorschlaege,* Matthias-Gruenewald-Verlag, 1968; *Dibattito sul diritto naturale,* Queriniana, 1970; (with Ernst-Wolfgang Boeckenfoerde) *Naturrecht in der Kritik,* Matthias-Gruenewald-Verlag, 1973; *Menschliche Sexualitaet und kirchliche Sexualmoral: Ein Dauer konflikt?,* Patmos Verlag, 1977; (with Franz Josef Stegmann) *Kirsche und Gesellschaft heute,* Schoeningh, 1979.

Contributor: Joseph Anton Hardegger, editor, *Handbuch der Elternbildung,* two volumes, Benziger, 1966; Heinrich Stirnimann, editor, *Kirche im Umbruch der Gesellschaft: Studien zur Pastoralkonstitution "Kirche in der Welt von heute" und zur Weltkonferenz "Kirche und Gesellschaft,"* Paulusverlag, 1970; Ludger Oeing-Hanhoff, editor, *Naturgesetz und christliche Ethik: Zur wissenschaftlichen Diskussion nach Humanae vitae,* Koesel-Verlag, 1970; Willi Oelmueller, editor, *Fortschritt wohin?: Zum Problem der Normenfindung in der pluralen Gesellschaft,* Patmos-Verlag, 1972; Gerhardt Nissen and Hermann Schmitz, editors, *Strafmuendigkeit,* Luchterhand, 1973.

WORK IN PROGRESS: Probleme der Normbegruendung Menschenrechte konkrete moral, completion expected in 1980.

* * *

BOGGAN, E(lton) Carrington 1943-

PERSONAL: Born October 21, 1943, in New York, N.Y.; son of Elton L. and Dorothy (Wellman) Boggan. *Education:* Eckerd College, B.A., 1965; University of North Carolina, M.A., 1967; Wake Forest University, J.D., 1969. *Office:* Boggan, Patton & Thom, 5 East 57th St., New York, N.Y. 10022.

CAREER: Admitted to the Bar of New York State, 1970, and the Bar of the U.S. Supreme Court, 1974; Rogers, Hoge & Hills, New York City, associate, 1970-75; American Home Products Corp., New York City, division counsel, 1975; private practice of law in New York City, 1975-76; Boggan & Thom, New York City, partner, 1976-78; Boggan, Patton & Thom, New York City, partner, 1978—. Member of board of trustees of Eckerd College, 1969-72. *Member:* American Bar Association (chairman of committee on equal protection of law, 1972-75; chairman-elect of individual rights and responsibilities section, 1978-79), New York State Bar Association, Association of the Bar of the City of New York.

WRITINGS: (With others) *The Rights of Gay People,* Avon, 1975. Editor-in-chief of *Wake Forest Law Review,* 1968-69; member of board of editors of *Human Rights,* 1978—.

WORK IN PROGRESS: Revising *The Rights of Gay People,* with others.

* * *

BOISSONNEAU, Alice

PERSONAL: Born in Walkerton, Ontario, Canada. *Education:* Attended University of Toronto. *Agent:* c/o Simon & Pierre Publishing Co., Ltd., Box 280, Adelaide Street Post Office, Toronto, Ontario, Canada M5C 2J4.

CAREER: Writer. Worked at Vancouver General Hospital in Vancouver, British Columbia, and at Provincial Mental Hospital.

WRITINGS: Eileen McCullough (novel), Simon & Pierre, 1976.

Work represented in anthologies, including *Stories From Ontario,* edited by Germaine Warkentin, Macmillan, 1974. Writer for "Anthology," a series, Canadian Broadcasting Corp. (CBC). Contributor of stories to magazines, including *Canadian Forum* and *Alphabet.*

WORK IN PROGRESS: The Sun at Noon (tentative title), a novel about a woman ready to leave a mental hospital.*

* * *

BOLAND, Bridget 1913-

PERSONAL: Born March 13, 1913, in London, England. *Education:* Oxford University, B.A. (with honors), 1935. *Home:* Bolands, Hewshott Lane, Liphook, Hampshire, England. *Agent:* London Management, 235 Regent St., London W1A 2JT, England.

CAREER: Writer, 1937—. *Military service:* Auxiliary Territorial Force, 1941-46; became senior commander. *Awards, honors:* Co-nominee for award from Writers Guild and Academy Award for best screenplay, both 1969, both for "Anne of the Thousand Days."

WRITINGS—Published plays: *The Return* (three-act; first produced as "Journey to Earth" in Liverpool, England, 1952; produced as "The Return" in London, 1953), Samuel French, 1954; *The Prisoner* (three-act; first produced in London, 1954; released as a film by Columbia, 1955), Dramatists Play Service, 1956; *Temple Folly* (three-act comedy; first produced in London, 1951), Evans Brothers, 1958; *The Zodiac in the Establishment* (first produced in Nottingham, England, 1963), M. Evans, 1963.

Novels: *The Wild Geese,* Heinemann, 1938; *Portrait of a Lady in Love,* Heinemann, 1942; *Caterina,* Souvenir Press, 1975, St. Martin's, 1976.

Nonfiction: (With Maureen Boland) *Old Wives' Lore for Gardeners,* Bodley Head, 1976, Farrar, Straus, 1977; *Gardener's Magic and Other Old Wives Lore,* Farrar, Straus, 1977; *At My Mother's Knee,* Bodley Head, 1978.

Work represented in anthologies, including *Plays of the Year One,* Elek, 1949; *Plays of the Year Ten,* Elek, 1954; *Plays of the Year Twenty-Five,* Elek, 1962.

Unpublished plays: "The Arabian Nights," first produced in Nottingham, England, 1948; "Cockpit," first produced in London, England, 1948; "The Damascus Blade," first produced in Edinburgh, Scotland, 1950; "Gordon," first produced in Derby, England, 1961; "A Juan by Degrees" (adapted from the play by Pierre Humblot), first produced in London, 1965.

Screenplays: (With A. R. Rawlinson) "Gaslight," Anglo-American Films, 1940, re-released as "Angel Street," Commercial Pictures, 1953; (with Rawlinson) "This England," World, 1941; (with Robert Westerby, King Vidor, Mario Camerini, Ennio De Coneini, and Ivo Perilli) "War and Peace" (adapted from the novel by Leo Tolstoy), Paramount, 1956; (with Barry Oringer) "Damon and Pythias," released by Metro-Goldwyn-Mayer, 1962; (with John Hale) "Anne of the Thousand Days" (adapted from the play by Maxwell Anderson), Universal, 1969.

Also author of "Sheba" (radio play), 1954, and "Beautiful Forever" (teleplay), 1965.*

* * *

BOLT, Carol 1941-

PERSONAL: Born August 25, 1941, in Winnipeg, Manitoba,

Canada; daughter of William Victor (a carpenter) and Marjorie (a teacher; maiden name, Small) Johnson; married David Bolt (an actor), June 19, 1969; children: Alexander. *Education:* University of British Columbia, B.A., 1961. *Agent:* Great North Agency, 345 Adelaide St. W., Toronto, Ontario, Canada M5V 1R5.

CAREER: Worked in Canada as statistical researcher for Dominion Board of Statistics, London School of Economics, Market Facts of Canada Ltd., and Seccombe House, 1961-72; Playwrights Cooperative (now Playwrights Canada), Toronto, Ontario, dramaturge, 1972-73, head of management committee, 1973-74; playwright. Dramaturge at Toronto Free Theatre, 1973; writer in residence at University of Toronto, 1977-78. Member of Advisory Arts Panel of Toronto, 1974-75. *Awards, honors:* Grants from Canada Council, 1967, 1972, and Ontario Arts Council, 1972, 1973, 1974, and 1975.

WRITINGS—Plays: "Maurice" (first produced in Toronto, Ontario, 1974), published in *Performing Arts in Canada,* winter, 1974; *Shelter* (first produced in Toronto, 1974), Playwrights Press, 1975; "Cyclone Jack" (first produced in Toronto, 1972), published in *A Collection of Canadian Plays,* Volume IV, Simon & Pierre, 1975; Constance Brissenden, editor, *Playwrights in Profile: Carol Bolt* (contains "Buffalo Jump," first produced as "Next Year Country" in Regina, Saskatchewan, 1971, produced as "Buffalo Jump" in Toronto, 1972; "Gabe," first produced in Toronto, 1973; "Tangleflags," first produced in Toronto, 1973; and "Red Emma: Queen of the Anarchists," first produced in Toronto, 1974), Playwrights Press, 1976; *One Night Stand* (first produced in 1977), Playwrights Press, 1977; *My Best Friend Is Twelve Feet High* (first produced in 1972), Dreadnaught Press, 1978, published in *Kids' Plays,* Playwrights Press, 1980; *Star Quality* (first produced in 1980), Britain-America Repertory Company, 1981.

Unpublished plays: "Daganawida," first produced in Toronto, 1970; "The Bluebird," first produced in Toronto, 1973; "Pauline," first produced in Toronto, 1973; "Finding Bumble," first produced in Toronto, 1975; "Bethune," first produced in Gravenhurst, Ontario, 1976; "Okey Doke," first produced in 1976; "Norman Bethune: On Board the Empress of Asia," first produced in 1976; "Desperados," first produced in 1976; "T.V. Lounge," first produced in 1977; "Deadline," first produced in workshop in 1979.

Teleplays: "A Nice Girl Like You," 1974; "Talk Him Down," 1975.

BIOGRAPHICAL/CRITICAL SOURCES: Constance Brissenden, editor, *Playwrights in Profile: Carol Bolt,* Playwrights Press, 1976.

* * *

BOND, Christopher Godfrey 1945-

PERSONAL: Born in 1945, in Sussex, England. *Education:* Attended Central School of Speech and Drama, and Drama Centre, London, England. *Home:* 17 Waverly Rd., Liverpool 17, England. *Agent:* Blanche Marvin, 21a St. John's Wood High St., London N.W.8, England.

CAREER: Actor and writer. Victoria Theatre, Stoke-on-Trent, England, actor, 1968-70, resident dramatist, 1970-71; Everyman Theatre, Liverpool, England, artistic director, 1976—. *Awards, honors:* Arts Council grant, 1970; West End Managers award for best musical, 1980; eight Antoinette Perry (Tony) Awards, all for "Sweeney Todd."

WRITINGS: The Food of Love: The Sweetest Canticle

(three-act play), Baker's Plays, 1955; *A Policeman's Lot* (comedy), Baker's Plays, 1957; *You Want Drink Something Cold?* (novel), M. Joseph, 1969; *Sweeney Todd: The Demon Barber of Fleet Street* (first produced in Stoke-on-Trent, England, 1970; produced in London, England, at Stratford East, 1973; produced on Broadway at Uris Theatre, 1979), Samuel French, 1974.

Work represented in anthologies, including *Prompt One,* edited by Alan Durband, Hutchinson, 1976.

Unpublished plays: "Mutiny," first produced in Stoke-on-Trent, England, at Victoria Theatre, 1970; "Downright Hooligan," first produced in Stoke-on-Trent at Victoria Theatre, 1972; "Tarzan's Last Stand," first produced in Liverpool, England, at Everyman Theatre, 1973; "Judge Jeffreys," first produced in Exeter, England, at Northcatt Theatre, 1973; produced in London, 1976; "The Country Wife" (adaptation of play by William Wycherley), first produced in Liverpool, 1974; "Under New Management," first produced in Liverpool at Everyman Theatre, 1975; (co-author) "The Cantril Tales," first produced in Liverpool at Everyman Theatre, 1975; (co-author) "Scum: Death, Destruction, and Dirty Washing," first produced in London, 1976. Also author of "George." Author of numerous children's plays.

*   *   *

BONO, Philip 1921-

PERSONAL: Born January 13, 1921, in Brooklyn, N.Y.; son of Julius (a baker) and Marianna (Culcasi) Bono; married Gertrude Camille King, December 15, 1950; children: Richard Philip, Patricia Marianna, Kathryn Camille. *Education:* University of Southern California, B.E., 1947, graduate study, 1948-49. *Home:* 1951 Sanderling Circle, Costa Mesa, Calif. 92626. *Office:* Douglas Aircraft Co., 3855 Lakewood Blvd., Long Beach, Calif. 90801.

CAREER: North American Aviation, Inglewood, Calif., research and systems analyst, 1947; Douglas Aircraft Co., Long Beach, Calif., engineering design specialist, 1948-49; Boeing Airplane Co., Seattle, Wash., preliminary design engineer, 1950-59; Douglas Aircraft Co., Santa Monica, Calif., deputy program manager, 1960-62, technical assistant to director of advanced launch vehicles and space stations in Huntington Beach, Calif., 1963-65; McDonnell Douglas Astronautics Co., Huntington Beach, branch manager in advanced studies and senior staff engineer in advanced technology, 1966-73; Douglas Aircraft Co., Long Beach, senior engineer-scientist, 1974—. President of Cal-Pro Photo Accessories, 1975—. Lecturer at universities, including Soviet Academy of Sciences, and at international seminars all over the world. Inventor, with patent for recoverable single-stage space shuttle. *Military service:* U.S. Naval Reserve, active duty, 1943-46.

MEMBER: International Academy of Astronautics, American Association for the Advancement of Science (fellow), American Institute of Aeronautics and Astronautics (associate), American Astronomical Society (senior member), American Society of Mechanical Engineers, Society of Automotive Engineers (chairman of space vehicle committee), Royal Aeronautical Society (fellow), British Interplanetary Society (fellow), New York Academy of Sciences. *Awards, honors:* Golden Eagle Award from Council on International Nontheatrical Events, 1964, for film script, "The Role of the Reusable Single-Space Shuttle"; A. T. Colwell Merit Award from Society of Automotive Engineers, 1968; M. N. Golovine Space Award from British Interplanetary Society, 1969; named engineer of distinction by Engineers Joint Council, 1971.

WRITINGS: (With Kenneth Gatland) *Frontiers of Space: Pocket Encyclopedia of Space in Color,* Macmillan, 1969, revised edition, 1976. Contributor to scientific journals.

SIDELIGHTS: Bono's books have been translated into Dutch, German, Danish, Swedish, and Russian.

*   *   *

BONY, Jean (Victor) 1908-

PERSONAL: Born November 1, 1908, in Le Mans, France; son of Henri and Marie (Normand) Bony; married Clotilde Roure, June 2, 1936 (died September 2, 1942); married Mary England, July 1, 1953; children: Claire. *Education:* University of Paris, Agregation d'histoire et de geographie, 1933. *Office:* Department of History of Art, University of California, Berkeley, Calif. 94720.

CAREER: University of Paris, Paris, France, research scholar in London, England, 1935-37; assistant master at private school in Windsor, England, 1937-39; Centre National de la Recherche Scientifique, Paris, research scholar, 1944-45; assistant master at private school in Windsor, 1945-46; French Institute, London, lecturer in history of art, 1946-61; University of California, Berkeley, professor of art history, 1962—. Focillon Fellow and visiting lecturer at Yale University, 1949; Slade Professor of Fine Art and fellow of St. John's College, Cambridge, 1958-61; Mathews Lecturer at Columbia University, 1961; lecturer at University of Lille, 1961-62; Wrightsman Lecturer at New York University, 1969. *Military service:* French Army, Infantry, 1939-44; prisoner of war in Germany, 1940-43; became first lieutenant.

MEMBER: International Center of Medieval Art, British Archaeological Association, British Academy (corresponding fellow), Societe nationale des Antiquaires de France, Societe francaise d'Archeologie, College Art Association of America, Royal Archaeological Institute (honorary vice-president), Society of Antiquaries (fellow), Society of Architectural Historians. *Awards, honors:* M.A. from Cambridge University, 1958.

WRITINGS: (With Martin Huerlimann and P. Meyer) *French Cathedrals,* Thames & Hudson, 1951, revised edition, 1967; (editor) H. Focillon, *The Art of the West in the Middle Ages,* two volumes, Phaidon, 1963; *The English Decorated Style: Gothic Architecture Transformed, 1250-1350,* Cornell University Press, 1979; *French Gothic Architecture of the Twelfth and Thirteenth Centuries,* University of California Press, 1980. Also author of *Notre-Dame de Mantes,* 1946. Contributor to art and architecture journals.

*   *   *

BOOKBINDER, David J(oel) 1951-

PERSONAL: Born March 14, 1951, in Buffalo, N.Y.; son of Albert J. (a furniture dealer) and Pearl (Gordon) Bookbinder. *Education:* Attended Cornell University, 1969-70; State University of New York at Buffalo, B.A. (summa cum laude), 1973; graduate study at Boston University, 1980. *Home:* 18 Alberta Dr., Buffalo, N.Y. 14226. *Agent:* Harvey Klinger, Inc., 250 West 57th St., New York, N.Y. 10019.

CAREER: Writer. Also worked in home construction and renovation, photographic research, and photography. Teacher of art and woodworking to children. *Member:* Authors Guild, Associated Writing Programs. *Awards, honors:* Fellowships from Millay Colony on the Arts, 1979, and Virginia Center for the Creative Arts, 1979-80.

WRITINGS: What Folk Music Is All About, Messner, 1979. Contributor to newspapers.

WORK IN PROGRESS: Birthdays (tentative title), a novel about growing up; a book of short stories about street people, illustrated with his own photographs.

SIDELIGHTS: Bookbinder wrote: "I'm obsessed with finding out how people work. I eavesdrop in restaurants and laundromats. I snoop around in living rooms. I bother people with questions all the time, and, I suppose because they can sense I'm actually interested in what they say, people reveal things about themselves to me they wouldn't ordinarily talk about."

* * *

BOWERING, Marilyn R(uthe) 1949-

PERSONAL: Born April 13, 1949, in Winnipeg, Manitoba, Canada; daughter of Herbert James (a carpenter) and Elnora (a purchasing agent; maiden name, Grist) Bowering. *Education:* Attended University of British Columbia, 1968-69; University of Victoria, B.A., 1971, M.A., 1973; also attended University of New Brunswick, 1975. *Home:* 3777 Jennifer Rd., Victoria, British Columbia, Canada V8P 3X1.

CAREER: Teacher at public schools in Masset, British Columbia, 1974-75; free-lance writer and book reviewer, 1975-77; University of British Columbia, Vancouver, extension lecturer in poetry writing, 1977; gregson/graham (marketing and communications firm), Victoria, British Columbia, editor and writer, 1978—. Visiting lecturer at University of Victoria, 1978—. *Member:* Writers Union of Canada, League of Canadian Poets. *Awards, honors:* Du Maurier Award for Poetry from Canada's National Magazine Awards, 1978, for "Rose Harbour Whaling Station"; recipient of various Canada Council Awards for poetry.

WRITINGS: The Liberation of Newfoundland (poems), Fiddlehead Press, 1973; *One Who Became Lost* (poems), Fiddlehead Press, 1976; *The Killing Room* (poems), Sono Nis Press, 1977; (editor with David A. Day) *Many Voices: An Anthology of Contemporary Canadian Indian Poetry,* J. J. Douglas, 1977; *The Visitors Have All Returned* (novel), Press Porcepic, 1979; *Sleeping With Lambs* (poems), Press Porcepic, 1980; (editor) *Guide to the Labour Code of British Columbia,* Government of British Columbia, 1980; *The Red Rain* (novella), Press Porcepic, 1981. Contributor to *Third/Child Zian,* Sceptre Press, 1978, and *The Book of Glass,* Sceptre Press, 1978.

Work represented in anthologies, including *Whale Sound, North American Women Poets,* and *New: West Coast.* Contributor to literary journals, including *Event, Toronto Life, Prism International, Malahat Review, Canadian Forum, New Poetry,* and *Signal Hill Broadsides.*

WORK IN PROGRESS: An anthology of Canadian poetry for children, publication by Oolichan Press expected in 1981; *Oran's Eye,* a novel, publication expected in 1982.

SIDELIGHTS: Doug Beardsly of the *Victoria Times* commented on Bowering's *The Visitors Have All Returned:* "As there are few stylists in our country, either in poetry or fiction, it's a real delight to come across Marilyn Bowering's first book of prose.... The author of several books of poems offers us a poetic prose, stripped bare, exposed, held up to the clear, white light of the page.... Each paragraph seems chiselled, every important word chosen for its resonant qualities. What is left out is as significant as what's left in, and Michael Elcock's fine black-and-white photographs deepen the sense of mystery."

M. Travis Lane offered this criticism of an earlier book by Bowering, *One Who Became Lost:* "I don't like all of Bowerings poems; in particular I think she does not write well in the ballad form.... But the substantial majority of the poems in this book are powerful, original, magnificently formed. I recommend this book most heartily to a serious reader's attention."

Bowering told *CA:* "One of the current major themes in my work is healing and disease—causes and cures. This isn't so much physical as it is an attempt through characters, plot, and imagery to make things whole, to resolve (an impossible task) the moral paradox at the heart of things. I am very interested in dualism.

"I leave Canada, usually every few years, to live in Europe or the United Kingdom, and this affects what I write. Some of my fiction is set in Greece, Turkey, and Scotland, but most of my early work has grown out of (often a reaction against) the powerful landscape and mythology of the British Columbia west coast."

BIOGRAPHICAL/CRITICAL SOURCES: Windsor Star, November 12, 1977; *Fiddlehead,* winter, 1977; *Victoria Times,* July 13, 1979; *Waves,* Volume VIII, number 2, 1980.

* * *

BOYER, Bruce Hatton 1946-
(B. H. Tate)

PERSONAL: Born October 5, 1946, in Evanston, Ill.; son of Paul F. (a lawyer) and Betty (Hatton) Boyer. *Education:* Amherst College, B.A. (cum laude), 1968; University of California, Los Angeles, M.A., 1969, Ph.D., 1973. *Home and office:* 1330 Birchwood Ave., Chicago, Ill. 60626. *Agent:* William Morris Agency, 1350 Avenue of the Americas, New York, N.Y. 10019.

CAREER: Amherst College, Amherst, Mass., assistant professor of dramatic arts, 1972-74; Illinois Bicentennial Commission, Chicago, Ill., program director, 1975-76; Illinois Arts Council, Chicago, ethnic and folk arts program director, 1977; J. Walter Thompson, Chicago, writer, 1978-79. Consulting creative director to One World Film Productions, Los Angeles, Calif., 1980—. *Member:* Mystery Writers of America. *Awards, honors:* Citation for playwriting from *Story* magazine, 1971; Edward Poole lay fellow of Amherst College; National Defense Education Act (NDEA) Title IV fellow; research grants from National Endowment for the Humanities and National Endowment for the Arts.

WRITINGS: The Solstice Cipher, Lippincott, 1979. Also author of numerous short stories under pseudonym B. H. Tate published in *Sir, Gent,* and *Cavalier.*

WORK IN PROGRESS: A novel, *The Rhoikus Bronze;* another novel.

SIDELIGHTS: Boyer told *CA:* "I got into writing because it was the only thing left. I'd tried everything else, it seemed, from advertising to teaching, and this field didn't ask me to specialize in one little area for the rest of my life.

"I had first wanted to be an actor, and indulged that whimsy for years. I did two whole seasons with the Utah Shakespeare Festival, where I played my favorite role, Aguecheek in 'Twelfth Night,' and turned in a non-ending string of villains for three years at the Weston Playhouse in Vermont, if you call the title role in 'Dracula' a villain, that is. All told, I've played over seventy roles, I think, and directed a fair number of stage productions. I even got my Ph.D. in theatre history.

"But eventually I got sick of putting on make-up in sweaty dressing rooms night after night, the 'history' half won out, and I turned to teaching and other pursuits while I completed my first novel. Writing combines the scholar and the madman inside me, which suits me just fine.

"It's a quiet life, and it gives me time, which is precious. I've got the time to cook, eat, drink (a most underrated hobby), stroll the beach outside my North Side apartment, read, and travel. I'm just starting out in this business, but I know already that it agrees with me.

"Spy novels? I rate them seriously as literature, the best ones, the ones by Eric Ambler and Graham Greene, for instance. The bad ones I loath and don't rate at all. Spy novels are a curious blend of the pornographic and the religious—pornographic because they cater to our fantasies about sex, death, violence, and the dark underbelly of life; and religious because they're always about great moral struggles. Their ancestry is most distinguished, to wit, the Elizabethan stage—read *Cymbeline* or *Romeo and Juliet* lately?

"I write spy novels because that's how my mind works. I just love the grotesque, the tacky, the faded, the scary, the perverse, and the ironic. Even better, I like all those things together in the same story. Is it any wonder, after all this, that I ended up doing what I do?"

*   *   *

BOYLE, Hal
    See BOYLE, Harold V(incent)

*   *   *

BOYLE, Harold V(incent)   1911-1974
    (Hal Boyle)

PERSONAL: Born February 21, 1911, in Kansas City, Mo.; died of a heart attack, April 1, 1974, in New York, N.Y.; son of Peter Edward and Margaret (Gavaghan) Boyle; married Mary Frances Young, November 6, 1937. *Education:* Attended Kansas City Junior College, Kansas City, Mo., 1928-30; University of Missouri, B.A. and B.J., 1932. *Home:* 541 East 20th St., New York, N.Y. 10009. *Office:* Associated Press, 50 Rockefeller Plaza, New York, N.Y. 10020.

CAREER: Associated Press, 1928-73; copy boy in Kansas City, Mo., 1928; correspondent in Columbia, Mo., 1933-35; night editor in St. Louis, Mo., 1935; feature editor in Kansas City, 1936; reporter and editor in New York City, 1937-41, night city editor, 1942; war correspondent, covering European and Mediterranean fronts, and author of daily column "Leaves From a War Correspondent's Notebook," beginning 1942; author of "Boyle's Column." *Member:* Overseas Press Club, American Newspaper Guild, Sigma Phi Epsilon, Kappa Tau Alpha. *Awards, honors:* Sigma Delta Chi honorable mention for reporting and Pulitzer Prize for distinguished correspondence, both 1945.

WRITINGS: (Under name Hal Boyle) *Help, Help! Another Day! The World of Hal Boyle* (selections from newspaper columns), Associated Press, 1969. Contributor of articles on journalism and military topics to magazines.

SIDELIGHTS: Boyle gained nationwide attention during World War II as an Associated Press correspondent. He wrote innumerable "on the spot" war stories, and his column, "Leaves From a War Correspondent's Notebook," appeared in more than four hundred U.S. newspapers. His "human side of the war" approach was made possible by his own involvement in it: he interviewed soldiers in trenches, toured European and Mediterranean fronts, and once hitchhiked four hundred miles to cover a battle. Boyle's work

appealed especially to parents of soldiers, many of whom read the words of their sons in his column. For his war coverage, Boyle received a Pulitzer Prize in 1945.

Boyle discontinued writing in 1973, when he disclosed that he was suffering from amyotrophic lateral sclerosis, "Lou Gehrig's disease." A few months before his death he reflected: "I am somewhat abashed that my wordage output is four times that of William Shakespeare. But I savor the fact that it enables me to have more bylined stories on the main wires of The Associated Press than any other writer in its 126 years.

"I guess this is the place to express my deeply felt thanks to all the readers who through the years made the journey with me and shored up my spirits with kind letters of cheer, suggestion and criticism. See you later."

"These," reported the *New York Times,* "were the last words he wrote."

BIOGRAPHICAL/CRITICAL SOURCES: Newsweek, December 25, 1944, November 18, 1957; *New York Times,* May 8, 1945; *Editor & Publisher,* September 14, 1968, September 21, 1968; *New Yorker,* April 15, 1974; *Reader's Digest,* October, 1974.

OBITUARIES: New York Times, April 2, 1974, April 4, 1974; *Time,* April 15, 1974; *Newsweek,* April 15, 1974.*

*   *   *

BRACEGIRDLE, Brian   1933-

PERSONAL: Born May 31, 1933, in Macclesfield, England; son of Alfred Bracegirdle; married Margaret Lucy Merrett, 1958 (marriage dissolved, 1974); married Patricia Helen Miles, 1975; children: (first marriage) one daughter. *Education:* University of London, B.Sc., 1957, Ph.D., 1975. *Home:* 67 Limerston St., London SW10 0BL, England. *Office:* Wellcome Museum of the History of Medicine, Science Museum, London, England.

CAREER: ICI, technician in research department, 1950-57; Erith Grammar School, Erith, England, biology master, 1958-61; University of London, London, England, senior lecturer in biology at St. Katherine's College, 1961-64, principal lecturer in science and learning resources and head of departments of national science and learning resources at College of All Saints, 1964-77; Wellcome Museum of the History of Medicine, London, keeper of museum, 1977—. *Member:* Royal Photographic Society (fellow; past chairman of fellowship and associateship panel), Royal Medical Society (member of council), British Society for the History of Science (member of council), Institute of Biology, Zoological Society (fellow), Institute of Medical and Biological Illustration (past chairman).

WRITINGS: (With William Harvey Freeman) *An Atlas of Embryology,* Heinemann, 1963, 2nd edition, 1967; *Engineering in Chester: Two Hundred Years of Progress,* College of Further Education (Chester, England), 1966; (with Freeman) *An Atlas of Histology,* Dover, 1966, 2nd edition, 1967.

Photography for Books and Reports, David & Charles, 1970, published as *Photography as Illustration: The Use of the Camera for Books and Reports,* A. S. Barnes, 1972; (with Patricia H. Miles) *An Atlas of Plant Structure,* Volume I, Heinemann, 1971, Volume II, Dover, 1973; (with William Harvey Freeman) *An Atlas of Invertebrate Structure,* Heinemann, 1971; (with Donald Gordon Mackean) *Experimental Work in Biology,* Volume I: *Food Tests,* Volume II: *Enzymes,* Volume III: *Soils,* J. Murray, 1972; (with Miles) *Thomas Telford,* David & Charles, 1973; (with Brian Bowers and others) *The Archaeology of the Industrial Revolution*, Fairleigh Dickinson University Press, 1973, new edition, Heinemann, 1980; (with Miles) *The Darbys and the Ironbridge Gorge*, David & Charles, 1974; (with Freeman) *An Advanced Atlas of Histology*, Heinemann, 1976; *A History of Micro Technique: The Evolution of the Microtome and the Development of Tissue Preparation*, Cornell University Press, 1978; (with Miles) *An Atlas of Chordate Structure*, Heinemann, 1978. Contributor to scientific journals.

WORK IN PROGRESS: An Illustrated History of the Microscope, with S.C.F. Turner, publication expected in 1982.

AVOCATIONAL INTERESTS: Industrial archaeology, walking, music, travel.

BIOGRAPHICAL/CRITICAL SOURCES: Science, May 18, 1979.

*   *   *

BRACKENRIDGE, R(obert) Douglas   1932-

PERSONAL: Born August 6, 1932, in Youngstown, Ohio; son of John (a bricklayer) and Azile (Townson) Brackenridge; married Lois Rice, 1954; children: John, Liz, Julie, Laurel, Stuart. *Education:* Muskingum College, B.A., 1954; Pittsburgh Theological Seminary, B.D., 1957, Th.M., 1959; University of Glasgow, Ph.D., 1962. *Office:* Department of Religion, Trinity University, 715 Stadium Dr., San Antonio, Tex. 78212.

CAREER: Ordained Presbyterian minister, 1957; pastor of United Presbyterian church in Washington, Pa., 1958-60; Trinity University, San Antonio, Tex., assistant professor, 1962-65, associate professor, 1966-72, professor of religion, 1972—. Piper Professor, Minnie Stevens Piper Foundation, 1973. *Member:* American Society of Church History, American Academy of Religion, Presbyterian Historical Society (president, 1976-79), Scottish Church History Society. *Awards, honors:* Thornwell Award from Presbyterian Historical Foundation, 1968, for article on Southern Presbyterian history; outstanding professor award from Trinity University, 1971 and 1978; associate of Danforth Foundation, 1972—.

WRITINGS: Voice in the Wilderness: A History of the Cumberland Presbyterian Church in Texas, Trinity University Press, 1968; (with Francisco O. Garcia-Treto) *Iglesia Presbiteriana: A History of Presbyterians and Mexican Americans in the Southwest*, Trinity University Press, 1974; *Beckoning Frontiers: A Biography of James Woodin Laurie*, Trinity University Press, 1976; *Eugene Carson Blake: Prophet With Portfolio*, Seabury, 1978. Contributor to history journals.

WORK IN PROGRESS: Women in the Presbyterian Church, with Lois Boyd, publication expected in 1981 or 1982.

SIDELIGHTS: Brackenridge told *CA:* "Classroom teaching is my greatest delight, followed by jogging and racquetball. Above all, however, being with my family is the most satisfying experience in my life."

BIOGRAPHICAL/CRITICAL SOURCES: Christian Century, October 25, 1978.

*   *   *

BRADDY, Haldeen   1908-1980

OBITUARY NOTICE—See index for *CA* sketch: Born January 22, 1908, in Fairlie, Tex.; died August 16, 1980, in El Paso, Tex. Writer and educator. A professor of English for more than thirty years at the University of Texas at El Paso,

Braddy was highly regarded as an authority on Chaucer. His other main fields of study included Edgar Allan Poe, William Shakespeare, and the history of the American Southwest. Numbered among his books are *Chaucer and the French Poet Graunson, Three Dimensional Poe, Hamlet's Wounded Name*, and *Mexico and the Old Southwest*. Obituaries and other sources: *Publishers Weekly*, September 5, 1980.

*   *   *

BRADFORD, Ernle (Dusgate Selby)   1922-

PERSONAL: Born January 11, 1922, in Cole Green, Norfolk, England; son of Jocelyn Ernle and Ada Louise (Dusgate) Bradford; married Janet Rushbury (a painter), 1948 (marriage ended, 1956); married Marie Blanche Thompson (a painter), 1957; children: (second marriage) Hugh Ernle. *Education:* Educated in England. *Politics:* Monarchist. *Religion:* Church of England. *Residence:* New Forest, England. *Agent:* A. M. Heath & Co. Ltd., 40-42 William IV St., London WC2N 4DD, England.

CAREER: Writer. *Military service:* Royal Navy, 1940-46; became first lieutenant; mentioned in dispatches. *Member:* Royal Naval Sailing Association, Ocean Cruising Club.

WRITINGS—History: *The Mighty "Hood,"* Hodder & Stoughton, 1959, World Publishing, 1960; (translator) Francisco Balbi de Correggio, *The Great Seige: Malta, 1565*, Hodder & Stoughton, 1961, Harcourt, 1962; *Wall of England: The Channel's Two Thousand Years of History*, Country Life, 1966, published as *Wall of Empire: The Channel's Two Thousand Years of History*, A. S. Barnes, 1967; *The Great Betrayal: Constantinople, 1204*, Hodder & Stoughton, 1967; *The Sundered Cross: The Story of the Fourth Crusade*, Prentice-Hall, 1967; *Gibraltar: The History of a Fortress*, Hart-Davis, 1971, Harcourt, 1972; *Mediterranean: Portrait of a Sea*, Harcourt, 1971; *The Shield and the Sword: The Knights of St. John*, Hodder & Stoughton, 1972, Dutton, 1973, also published as *The Shield and the Sword: The Knights of Malta*, Collins, 1974; *The Sword and the Scimitar: The Saga of the Crusades*, Putnam, 1974; *The Year of Thermopylae*, Macmillan, 1980, published as *The Battle for the West: Thermopylae*, McGraw, 1980.

Biography: *A Wind From the North: The Life of Henry the Navigator*, Harcourt, 1960 (published in England as *Southward the Caravels: The Story of Henry the Navigator*, Hutchinson, 1961); *The Wind Commands Me: A Life of Sir Francis Drake*, Harcourt, 1965 (published in England as *Drake*, Hodder & Stoughton, 1965); *The Sultan's Admiral: The Life of Barbarossa*, Harcourt, 1968; *Cleopatra*, Hodder & Stoughton, 1971, Harcourt, 1972; *Christopher Columbus*, Viking, 1973; *Paul the Traveller*, Allen Lane, 1974, Macmillan, 1976; *Nelson: The Essential Hero*, Harcourt, 1977.

Other writings: *Contemporary Jewellery and Silver Design*, John Heywood, 1950, Pitman, 1951; *Four Centuries of European Jewellery*, Philosophical Library, 1953; *The Journeying Moon* (personal account), Jarrolds, 1958; *English Victorian Jewellery*, McBride, 1959; *The Wind Off the Island* (travel), Hutchinson, 1960, Harcourt, 1961; *The Touchstone*, Cassell, 1962; *Antique Collecting*, English Universities Press, 1963; *The Companion Guide to the Greek Islands* (travel), Harper, 1963, 3rd edition, Collins, 1975, also published as *The Greek Islands: A Travel Guide*, Harper, 1966; *Dictionary of Antiques*, English Universities Press, 1963; *Ulysses Found*, Hodder & Stoughton, 1963, Harcourt, 1964; *The America's Cup*, Country Life, 1964; *Three Centuries of Sailing*, Country Life, 1964; *Antique Furniture*, English Universities Press, 1970.

Founder and editor of *Antique Dealer and Collectors' Guide,* and editor of *Watchmaker, Jeweller, and Silversmith.*

WORK IN PROGRESS: A biography, *Hannibal,* for publication by McGraw; *Aspects of a Sea* (tentative title).

SIDELIGHTS: Bradford told *CA* that his work in progress, *Hannibal,* is "a biography of the great Carthaginian who challenged, and nearly defeated, Rome, an event that could have changed the history of the western world. A unique and dedicated character, perhaps the greatest general on record, he has always fascinated me, particularly since I have been to nearly all the places where he lived and fought: from Carthage to Spain, the Rhine valley, and the length and breadth of Italy.

"My other work in progress, *Aspects of a Sea,* views the Mediterranean during three different periods in my life: my three-and-one-half years on Royal Navy destroyers from 1941 to 1944, four years sailing the sea in my three-and-one-half-ton Dutch barge from 1950 to 1954, and ten years living on the island of Malta from 1967 to 1977 when the loss of a leg compelled me to return to England. Thus, the book shows the sea from the three angles of war, peaceful sailing and exploration, and the home of a married man with a small son on a one-time Phoenician island."

Bradford added: "I have never wanted to do anything in my life but write. Although I had my first book accepted by Longman's when I was seventeen years old, unfortunately (or not), the Headmaster of my school persuaded both my father and the publisher that publication at so early an age would harm me. Hence I learned my trade on post-war Fleet Street editing two specialist magazines. Journalism is great training, but if you want to be a writer, it's essential to know when to get out.

"Having spent so many years in Italy, Sicily, Spain, Greece, and the island of Malta, I think I have a more European than English mind. My books have been translated into most European languages from Swedish to Hungarian, and seem to sell best in Germany. This is explained by the fact that Germans are addicts of history and, particularly, Mediterranean subjects. It is curious to me that east European countries seem to like my writing since I am a Romantic, Imperialist, Royalist, and arch-Conservative.

"From my own experience with many people in many countries, a vast number would like to write. My advice is that unless you are driven by such a compulsion that you *have* to—forget it. As an old Greek saying has it: 'There are more bones around the altars of the Muses than around those of any other gods or goddesses.'"

BIOGRAPHICAL/CRITICAL SOURCES: New York Times Book Review, October 28, 1968; *Observer Review,* January 19, 1969; *Christian Science Monitor,* February 3, 1975; *Times Literary Supplement,* April 4, 1980.

*　　　*　　　*

BRADLEY, Bill
   See BRADLEY, William Warren

*　　　*　　　*

BRADLEY, William Warren   1943-
   (Bill Bradley)

PERSONAL: Born July 28, 1943, in Crystal City, Mo.; son of Warren W. (a banker) and Susan (Crowe) Bradley; married Ernestine Schlant, January 14, 1974; children: Theresa Anne. *Education:* Princeton University, B.A., 1965; Oxford University, M.A. (cum laude), 1968. *Politics:* Democrat.

Residence: Denville, N.J. *Agent:* Paul Gitlin, 7 West 51st St., New York, N.Y. 10009. *Office:* U.S. Senate, Washington, D.C. 20510.

CAREER: New York Knickerbockers (basketball team), New York, N.Y., player, 1967-77; U.S. Senate, senator from New Jersey, 1979—. *Military service:* U.S. Air Force Reserve, 1967-78. *Awards, honors:* Rhodes Scholar, Oxford University, 1965-68.

WRITINGS: (Under name Bill Bradley) *Life on the Run* (autobiographical), Quadrangle, 1976.

SIDELIGHTS: "Among basketball players . . . Bill Bradley excites our curiosity the most. He's the square peg; he doesn't belong. And he's the most private and enigmatic figure in a public and straightforward occupation." This statement from *New York Times Book Review* writer Hubert Saal pinpoints the mystique that extends beyond Bradley's athletic career. An all-American at Princeton, a Rhodes Scholar at Oxford, one of three players voted unanimously to be on the twelve-man team in 1964, and the youngest member of that team, a forward for the New York Knickerbockers, and an author, Bradley abandoned professional basketball in 1979 for a political career.

Writer John McPhee, himself a former player on Princeton's freshman basketball team, witnessed Bradley's finesse on the court for the first time in 1962: "Every motion developed in its simplest form," McPhee wrote. "Every motion repeated itself precisely when he used it again. He was remarkably fast, but he ran easily. His passes were so good they were difficult to follow. Every so often, and not often enough, I thought, he stopped and went high into the air with the ball . . . and a long jump shot would go into the net."

McPhee's interest in and admiration for Bradley developed into a book-length narrative and a lasting friendship. In the narrative, McPhee described Bradley as opposite of the stereotypical athlete. Bradley is modest: "He dislikes flamboyance, and, unlike some of basketball's greatest stars, he apparently never made a move to attract attention." He is humble: "Bradley calls practically all men 'Mister' whose age exceeds his own by more than a couple of years. This includes any NBA players he happens to meet."

Bradley, McPhee claimed, is rare because he played "basketball according to the foundation of the game," meaning that Bradley would pass the ball to the teammate who is closest to the net, even if that player was more likely to miss the shot. Bradley was not known to monopolize play unless the team began to lose.

At Princeton and as a New York Knick, Bradley was known for his analytical precision and rigorous self-discipline. McPhee recounted how Bradley would spend "hundreds of hours merely rehearsing the choreography of the game." Systematically practicing shots from every conceivable angle of the court, and shooting with either hand, Bradley would not quit until he had made ten out of thirteen shots from each location. "The average player only likes to play basketball," Princeton coach William Hendrik van Breda Kolff told McPhee. "Bradley practices techniques, making himself learn and improve instead of merely having fun."

Another quality that separated Bradley from the norm was his ability to get along with referees. McPhee quoted van Breda Kolff on the subject: "The refs watch Bradley like a hawk, but, because he never complains, they feel terrible if they make an error against him. They just love him because he is a gentleman."

In 1976, the year before he retired from pro basketball, Bradley wrote a book describing his experience with the team. The book, entitled *Life on the Run*, was warmly received for its honesty and depth of feeling, if not for its literary style. Hubert Saal's review stated: "Bradley is a born observer, insatiably curious, compulsively reflective. He's not a born writer, but his awkwardness with words and sincerity ring true."

Newsweek's Paul D. Zimmerman emphasized that *Life on the Run* should not be overlooked by readers not particularly enthusiastic about basketball. Those readers who expect merely an account of the Knick's standings in the NBA, or a study of the team's strategy and techniques, will be surprised to find that Bradley does not focus on these areas. "Bradley," Zimmerman observed, "has a restless appetite for understanding the particular world in which he has made his fortune." Zimmerman further explained that through *Life on the Run*, "Bradley debunks many prize cliches. He speculates that a father who holds up athletes as models for his son is short-cutting his own responsibility to provide a sturdy example. His warm feelings for his traveling companions . . . does not seduce him into buying the notion of the championship Knicks as a model of social cooperation. 'Groups in the real world cannot be like a championship team', he concludes, 'and ultimately the model of sport is dissatisfying for everyone but the participants.' "

Although Roger Sale, in *New York Review of Books*, felt *Life on the Run* had "little art stylistically," he praised Bradley for being "thoughtful and engaging about many aspects of basketball that others have written about badly or not at all." One of the aspects of the sport that Bradley deals with in his book is the subject of aging: "When the playing is over," he wrote, "one can sense that one's youth has been spent playing a game and now both the game and the youth are gone, along with the innocence that characterizes all games which are at root pure and promote a prolonged adolescence in those who play."

Sale commented that "no one with any kind of success when young can fail to shiver at the sober accuracy of Bradley's reflections" concerning the end of an athletic career, made all the more painful by the degree of achievement and the amount of work that went into it. Bradley wrote: "What is left is the other side of the Faustian bargain: To live all one's days never able to recapture the feeling of those years of intensified youth. . . . The athlete rarely recuperates. He approaches the end of his playing days the way old people approach death. He puts his finances in order. He reminisces easily. He offers advice to the young. But the athlete differs from the old person in that he must continue living. Behind all the years of practice and all the hours of glory waits that inexorable terror of living without the game."

Another problem of the professional athlete, discussed in Bradley's book, is that of becoming insulated and isolated from the non-athletic world because of the demands of rigorous schedules and extensive travel: "The daily worries and pressures of workers concerned about how to pay for food, housing, or medical care never penetrate the glass of our bus window. To do our job, we have to remain healthly and follow orders. In any airline terminal even the sad scene of a soldier's farewell or the joy of a family reunion often by-pass us making no impression. In the airports that have become our commuter stations we see so many dramatic personal moments that we are calloused. To some, [professional athletes] live romatic lives. To me, every day is a struggle to stay in touch with life's subtleties."

It has often been suggested that it was this very struggle that

prompted Bradley to enter and win the 1978 New Jersey senatorial race against Republican Jeffrey Bell. A prediction given by former coach van Breda Kolff in 1963 as to what he thought Bradley would be doing in the next twenty years proved not too far wrong. He remarked, "I don't know. I guess he'll be the governor of Missouri."

To answer the question posed to him by detractors at a campaign dinner as to whether a former professional basketball player was qualified for the position of U.S. senator, Bradley discarded his prepared speech on energy and instead spoke to the audience about his qualifications: "The question is not whether a professional basketball player can be a good United States senator, but whether he can work with people. Does he have the qualities of character is the question—and they are as likely to be found among electricians, lawyers, doctors, businessmen."

BIOGRAPHICAL/CRITICAL SOURCES: John McPhee, *A Sense of Where You Are*, Farrar, Straus, 1965; *New York Times Book Review*, May 2, 1976; *Newsweek*, May 10, 1976, October 16, 1978; *New York Review of Books*, May 27, 1976; *New York*, February 20, 1968; *New Times*, March 6, 1978; *New Republic*, June 3, 1978; *National Review*, October 13, 1978, November 10, 1978.

—*Sketch by Susan A. Stefani*

*   *   *

BRADY, James Winston 1928-

PERSONAL: Born November 15, 1928, in Brooklyn, N.Y.; son of James Thomas and Marguerite (Winston) Brady; married Florence Kelly, April 12, 1958; children: Fiona, Susan. *Education:* Manhattan College, A.B., 1950; attended New York University, 1953-54. *Politics:* Democrat. *Religion:* Roman Catholic. *Home:* 249 East 48th St., New York, N.Y. 10017. *Agent:* Roberta Pryor, International Creative Management, 40 West 57th St., New York, N.Y. 10019. *Office:* World News Corp., 730 Third Ave., New York, N.Y. 10017.

CAREER: Fairchild Publications, Inc., New York City, Washington correspondent, 1956-58, bureau chief in London, England, 1958-59, and Paris, France, 1960-64, publisher of *Women's Wear Daily*, 1964-71, senior vice-president, 1967-71, editorial director, 1968-71; *Harper's Bazaar*, New York City, editor and publisher, 1971-72; *New York*, New York City, contributing editor and author of column, 1973-74; World News Corp., New York City, editor of *National Star*, 1974-75, vice-chairman, 1975—. Vice-president of Capital Cities Broadcasting Corp., 1969-71, and Hearst Corp., 1971-72; editor-in-chief for MBA Communications, Inc., 1976-77. Talk-show host, 1973-74. *Military service:* U.S. Marine Corps Reserve, active duty, 1951-52; became first lieutenant. *Member:* National Press Club, University Club. *Awards, honors:* New York Emmy Award, 1975.

WRITINGS: *Superchic*, Little, Brown, 1974; *Paris One*, Delacorte, 1976; *Nielsen's Children*, Putnam, 1978. Author of columns in *New York Post*, *Los Angeles Times*, and *Advertising Age*. Editor of *New York*, 1977.

WORK IN PROGRESS: A novel.

*   *   *

BRANDEN, Victoria (Fremlin)
(Joanne Stylla)

PERSONAL: Born in Clinton, Ontario, Canada. *Education:* Universitysuof Alberta, B.A. (with honors), 1951; University of Toronto, M.A., 1963. *Politics:* New Democrat. *Religion:* Agnostic. *Home:* 65 Wellington St., Box 581, Waterdown, Ontario, Canada L0R 2H0. *Agent:* Peter L. Ginsberg, James Brown Associates, Inc., 25 West 43rd St., New York, N.Y. 10036. *Office:* Sheridan College, Trafalgar Rd., Oakville, Ontario, Canada.

CAREER: W. J. Gage (publishers), Toronto, Ontario, in editorial department, 1951-52; William Weld Publishing, London, Ontario, women's editor and columnist, 1952-57; teacher of English at high schools in Deep River, Hamilton, and Burlington, Ontario, 1966-70; Sheridan College, Oakville, Ontario, teacher of English, 1970—. *Member:* Society for Psychical Research. *Awards, honors:* Student essay award from *Atlantic Monthly,* 1950; first prize from Simpson Sears/Ontario Department of Education, 1967, for play, "A Number of Things"; award from *Writer's Digest,* 1967, for short story, "If Winter Comes"; award for comic writing from Canadian Press Club, 1968, for radio series, "Peachum's Corners"; award from Canadian Club of Hamilton, 1980, for *Mrs. Job.*

WRITINGS: Mrs. Job (novel), Harper, 1979; *Understanding Ghosts* (nonfiction), Gollancz, 1980.

Plays: "A Number of Things" (one-act), first produced in Hamilton at Ontario Drama Festival, 1967; "The Last Protest" (one-act), first produced in Burlington, Ontario, at M. M. Robinson High School, 1970. Author of about fifty radio and television scripts for Canadian Broadcasting Corp. (CBC).

Work represented in adult and juvenile anthologies, including: "Rubaboo" series, W. J. Gage, 1963-65; *A Century of Canadian Literature,* Ryerson, 1967; *Open Highways,* Scott, Foresman, 1968; *This Book Is About Communication,* Ryerson, 1970; and *Canadian Children's Annual,* 1977. Contributor to Canadian magazines, including *Saturday Night* (once under pseudonym Joanne Stylla), *Chatelaine, Monday Morning, Canadian Boy, This Magazine,* and *New Horizons.*

WORK IN PROGRESS—Novels: *A Fatal Brew,* a study of women with suicidal tendencies; *Family Fortunes,* a comedy novel about snobbery; *The Wild Hunt,* a "modern intellectual Gothic."

SIDELIGHTS: "Writing is a bad habit with me," Victoria Branden commented, "with something like the effects alcoholism has on its addicts. It has kept me poor and solitary and prevented me from living a nice normal life. If any child of mine had ambitions to be a writer I would fetch him a swift clout on the ear. Luckily they are all practically illiterate.

"Subjects I consider vital include pollution of the landscape, and of the English language. I am concerned about the destruction of the environment and the erosion of language into jargon and gutter talk. I get along with animals better than with people. I'm interested in sound ecological practices, and would like to build a solar-heated house, with a greenhouse."

AVOCATIONAL INTERESTS: "I ride and swim and skate and loathe the Canadian winter and having to work at a job. If I were rich I would go and live in Corsica."

*   *   *

BRECKLER, Rosemary   1920-
(Rosemary Winters)

PERSONAL: Born June 5, 1920, in Columbus, Ohio; daughter of Ignatius Benjamin (a builder, tavern keeper, and grocer) and Marie C. (Smith) Breckler; married Joseph Asher, February 29, 1952 (divorced, 1963); children: Melinda (Mrs. Dan Lasater), Brady. *Education:* Ohio State University,

B.A., 1946; attended Valley Community College, 1968-72, and University of California, Los Angeles, 1975. *Residence:* Van Nuys, Calif. *Agent:* Arthur P. Schwartz, 435 Riverside Dr., New York, N.Y. 10025.

CAREER: Columbus Citizen, Columbus, Ohio, feature writer, 1938; *Columbus Dispatch,* Columbus, stringer, 1939-40; *Cheyenne Eagle,* Cheyenne, Wyo., author of column, 1943; *Visalia Times-Delta,* Visalia, Calif., editor of women's page, 1946-47; *Junior Statesman,* San Francisco, Calif., editor, 1951-52; *Valley News,* Van Nuys, Calif., staff writer, 1963-75; private investigator in Los Angeles, Calif., 1975-79; free-lance writer, 1979—. Teacher of creative writing. Owner of public relations consulting firm, 1975-79. *Military service:* U.S. Army, Women's Auxiliary Army Corps, publicity writer and reporter, 1942-43.

MEMBER: American Film Institute, American Rose Society, Women's National Book Association, Society of Children's Book Writers, Society for Psychical Research, Public Relations Round Table of the San Fernando Valley. *Awards, honors:* Two awards from Beta Phi Gamma; award from Association of Junior Publications, 1969.

WRITINGS: Where are the Twins?, Westminster, 1979; (co-author) *Leisure Alternatives,* Delacorte, 1979.

Author of plays, including "Winter Quarters," "Once Upon an Apple-Pated Newton," and "Tie Your Cares to a Big Balloon." Also author of television scripts, including "Fire In The House," "Benicio," and "To Read a BACKword Line." Staff writer for *Sceptre,* 1969-72. Contributor, under pseudonym Rosemary Winters, of stories, articles, and poems to religious journals; contributor to newspapers and children's magazines, including *Child Life* and *Highlights for Children.*

WORK IN PROGRESS: Redwoods; a book on dyslexia; *The Bargain; I Gotta Be Somebody; The Ruby.*

SIDELIGHTS: Rosemary Breckler told *CA:* "I can't remember a day when I didn't want to write a book, but unfortunately, I was dealt a life that consistently demanded all my energy elsewhere. I sold my first short story when I was sixteen years old. The next year I interviewed Judy Garland and it was published in the *Columbus Dispatch.*

"Instead of staying home and writing, I joined the Women's Auxiliary Army Corps at the start of World War II and served as a publicity writer and reporter. I specialized in haunting the hospital at Fort Warren, Wyoming, and writing stories about the injured soldiers returned from overseas, making them look like heroes and sending the stories to their hometown papers.

"When the war was over I lived and wrote in Havana, Cuba, for a short time, and knew Ernest Hemingway and his wife, Mary, while I was there.

"Upon my return I came to Visalia, California, to be women's page editor. I also had a Saturday feature column in which I did the same thing as at Fort Warren—I made ordinary people exotic. The paper sold out every Saturday night—everyone sending copies 'back home.'

"It wasn't until my children had left the house, and I was unable to work away from home, that I finally had time to write full-time. I am, at sixty years old, very content with my life. I am hoping, very soon, for more and more days for writing.

"For excitement and mind-stretching, I belong to the Society for Psychical Research. My idea of a real 'night on the town' is to baby-sit, along with other members, an alleged 'haunted house' and record the sounds. My favorite haunted house is one where Bette Davis once lived.

"I have always been interested in antiquities, Indians, Maoris, and the Indians of Central America. I once lived on an Indian reservation to learn more about them. I have explored and photographed many ruins in New Mexico, Mexico, Yucatan, and Belize. One of my books, *The Ruby*, is about the Maoris in the 1880's."

AVOCATIONAL INTERESTS: Swimming, bicycling, growing award-winning roses.

*   *   *

BREEN, T(imothy) H(all)   1942-

PERSONAL: Born September 5, 1942, in Cincinnati, Ohio; son of G. E. (a writer) and Mary B. Breen; married Susan Carlson, April 5, 1963; children: Sarah Hall, Timothy Bant. *Education:* Yale University, B.A. (cum laude), 1964, M.A., 1966, Ph.D. (with distinction), 1968. *Residence:* Evanston, Ill. *Office:* Department of History, Northwestern University, Evanston, Ill. 60201.

CAREER: Yale University, New Haven, Conn., assistant professor of history, 1968-70; Northwestern University, Evanston, Ill., associate professor, 1970-75, professor of history and American culture, 1975—, director of American culture program, 1976-79, chairman of council of residential college masters and master of Shepard Residential College, 1977-79, member of executive board of university library. Member of Institute for Advanced Study, Princeton, N.J., 1979-80. Lecturer at Marquette University, 1972, University of Virginia, 1978, University of Delaware and University of Pennsylvania, 1980, and University of North Carolina; Otis Memorial Lecturer at Wheaton College, Norton, Mass., 1976; Phi Alpha Theta Lecturer at College of William and Mary, 1978. Public speaker; seminar director for National Endowment for the Humanities.

MEMBER: American Historical Association, Organization of American Historians, Institute of Early American History and Culture (associate). *Awards, honors:* American Philosophical Society travel grant, 1970; American Council of Learned Societies grant, 1971-72; Kellogg Foundation grant, 1973; shared award from Institute of Early American History and Culture, 1973, for article, "Moving to the New World"; Guggenheim fellowship, 1975-76; award from Institute of Early American History and Culture, 1975, for article, "Persistent Localism"; fellowship from Andrew W. Mellon Foundation and Aspen Institute for Humanistic Studies, 1980-81.

WRITINGS: The Character of the Good Ruler: A Study of Puritan Political Ideas in New England, 1630-1730, Yale University Press, 1970; (editor) *Shaping Southern Society: The Colonial Experience*, Oxford University Press, 1976; (with Stephen Innes) *"Myne Owne Ground": Race and Freedom on Virginia's Eastern Shore*, Oxford University Press, 1980; *Puritans and Adventurers: Change and Persistence in Early America*, Oxford University Press, 1980. Contributor to *Encyclopedia of the American West* and *New England Historical and Genealogical Register*. Contributor of articles and reviews to history and regional studies journals.

WORK IN PROGRESS: The Oxford History of the United States, Volume I: *The United States: Colonial America*, publication by Oxford University Press expected in 1986; research on the culture of agriculture in pre-revolutionary Virginia.

SIDELIGHTS: "My writing and teaching reflect a continuing interest as an historian in cultural and social anthropology," remarked T. H. Breen to *CA*. "This interdisciplinary perspective is most apparent in *Puritans and Adventurers* and *"Myne Owne Ground,"* books that attempt to recreate for the contemporary reader the fabric of everyday life in early America. I find this approach both fruitful and exciting, and in my future writings I plan to relate the work culture of colonial American farmers to the acceptance of a radical political ideology in the mid-eighteenth century.

"I have also developed courses that analyze modern American culture, demonstrating that despite our emphasis on change, many traditional values persist. The complex interplay between change and persistence is central to my understanding of American life."

*   *   *

BRENDON, Piers (George Rundle)   1940-

PERSONAL: Born December 21, 1940, in Cornwall, England; son of George (a writer) and Frances (a journalist; maiden name, Cook) Brendon; married Vyvyen Davis (a teacher), 1968; children: George, Oliver. *Education:* Magdalene College, Cambridge, M.A., 1965, Ph.D., 1970. *Politics:* Labour. *Home:* 4B Millington Rd., Cambridge England. *Agent:* Curtis Brown Ltd., One Craven Hill, London W2 3EP, England.

CAREER: Cambridgeshire College of Arts and Technology, Cambridge, England, lecturer in history, 1966-79, head of history department, 1977-79; writer, 1979—.

WRITINGS: (Editor with William Shaw) *Reading They've Liked*, Macmillan, 1967; (editor with Shaw) *Reading Matters*, Macmillan, 1969; (editor with Shaw) *By What Authority?* Macmillan, 1972; *Hurrell Froude and the Oxford Movement*, Merrimack Book Service, 1974; *Hawker of Morwenstow: Portrait of a Victorian Eccentric*, J. Cape, 1975; *Eminent Edwardians*, Secker & Warburg, 1979, Houghton, 1980. Contributor of reviews to numerous periodicals and newspapers, including the *London Times*, *Observer*, and *Evening Standard*.

WORK IN PROGRESS: A book on the development of the popular press in England and the United States.

SIDELIGHTS: Piers Brendon told *CA*: "Were I to fill in this section properly, it would consist of a paean of nihilistic hatred and Swiftian vituperation directed at almost every aspect of public life that I can think of, from Mrs. Thatcher to dumping nuclear waste in the seas, from racialism to killing whales, from sports and sportspersons to the drivel excreted by the media. In short, the only optimistic features on my horizon are private ones—family, friends, and work."

BIOGRAPHICAL/CRITICAL SOURCES: New York Times Book Review, April 20, 1980.

*   *   *

BRENNER, Isabel
See SCHUCHMAN, Joan

*   *   *

BRENT-DYER, Elinor Mary   1895-1969

PERSONAL: Born in 1895, in South Shields, County Durham, England; died September, 1969. *Education:* Attended Leeds University.

CAREER: Author. Teacher and headmistress at Margaret Roper School, Hereford, England.

WRITINGS—All for children, except as noted; all published by W. & R. Chambers, except as noted: *Gerry Goes to School*, illustrations by Gordon Browne, 1922; *A Head Girl's Difficulties*, illustrations by Nina K. Brisley, 1923; *The Maids of La Rochelle*, illustrations by Brisley, 1924; *The School at the Chalet*, illustrations by Brisley, 1925; *Jo of the Chalet School*, illustrations by Brisley, 1926; *The Princess of the Chalet School*, 1927, reprinted, May Fair Books, 1968; *Seven Scamps Who Are Not at All Boys*, illustrations by Percy Tarrant, 1927, reprinted, 1952; *A Thrilling Term at Janeways'*, illustrations by F. M. Anderson, Thomas Nelson, 1927, reprinted, 1951; *The Head Girl of the Chalet School*, illustrations by Brisley, 1928, reprinted, Dymock, 1952; *Judy, the Guide*, illustrations by L. A. Govey, Thomas Nelson, 1928; *The New House Mistress*, Thomas Nelson, 1928, reprinted, 1956; *Heather Leaves School*, illustrations by Tarrant, 1929; *The Rivals of the Chalet School*, illustrations by Brisley, 1929.

Eustacia Goes to the Chalet School, 1930, reprinted, May Fair Books, 1969; *The School by the River*, Burns & Oates, 1930; *The Chalet School and Jo*, illustrations by Brisley, 1931; *A Feud in the Fifth Remove*, Lutterworth, 1931; *The Chalet Girls in Camp*, 1932, reprinted, Armada, 1969; *Janie of La Rochelle*, 1932; *The Little Marie-Jose*, Burn & Oates, 1932; *The Exploits of the Chalet Girls*, illustrations by Brisley, 1933; *Carnation of the Upper Fourth*, Lutterworth, 1934, reprinted, 1958; *The Chalet School and the Lintons*, illustrations by Brisley, 1934; *Elizabeth the Gallant* (adult novel), Butterworth & Co., 1935; *The New House at the Chalet School*, 1935; *Jo Returns to the Chalet School*, illustrations by Brisley, 1936; *Monica Turns Up Trumps*, Lutterworth, 1936; *Caroline the Second*, Lutterworth, 1937; *The New Chalet School*, illustrations by Brisley, 1938; *They Both Liked Dogs*, Lutterworth, 1938.

The Chalet School in Exile, 1940, reprinted, Collins, 1978; *The Chalet School Goes To It*, illustrations by Brisley, 1941; *The Highland Twins at the Chalet School*, 1942; *The Little Missus*, 1942; *Lavender Laughs in the Chalet School*, 1943; *Gay From China at the Chalet School*, 1944; *Jo to the Rescue*, 1944; *The Lost Staircase*, 1946; (editor) *The Chalet Book for Girls*, 1947; *Lorna at Wynyards*, Lutterworth, 1947; (editor) *The Second Chalet Book for Girls*, 1948; *Stepsisters for Lorna*, illustrations by John Bruce, C. & J. Temple, 1948; (editor) *The Third Chalet Book for Girls*, 1949; *Three Go to the Chalet School*, 1949, reprinted, Armada, 1979.

The Chalet School and the Island, 1950, reprinted, May Fair Books, 1967; *Fardingdales*, Latimer House, 1950; *Peggy of the Chalet School*, 1950, reprinted, May Fair Books, 1967; *Bess on Her Own in Canada*, 1951; *Carola Storms the Chalet School*, 1951, reprinted, Collins, 1977; *The Chalet School and Rosalie*, 1951; *A Quintette in Queensland*, 1951; *Sharlie's Kenya Diary*, 1951; *The Chalet School in the Oberland*, 1952; *Shocks for the Chalet School*, 1952; *The Wrong Chalet School*, 1952; *Bride Leads the Chalet School*, 1953; *The Chalet Girls' Cook Book*, 1953; *Changes for the Chalet School*, 1953; *Janie Steps In*, 1953; *The 'Susannah' Adventure*, 1953; *The Chalet School and Barbara*, 1954; *Chudleigh Hold*, 1954; *The Condor Crags Adventure*, 1954; *Joey Goes to the Oberland*, 1954; *Kennelmaid Nan*, Lutterworth, 1954; *Nesta Steps Out*, Oliphants, 1954; *Beechy of the Harbour School*, Oliphants, 1955; *A Chalet Girl From Kenya*, 1955; *The Chalet School Does It Again*, 1955; *Tom Tackles the Chalet School*, 1955; *Top Secret*, 1955; *A Genius at the Chalet School*, 1956, reprinted, Collins, 1977; *Leader in Spite of Herself*, Oliphants, 1956; *Mary-Lou of the Chalet School*, 1956; *A Problem for the Chalet School*, 1956; *Excitements at*

the Chalet School, 1957; *The New Mistress at the Chalet School*, 1957; *The Chalet School and Richenda*, 1958; *The Coming-of-Age of the Chalet School*, 1958; *Theodora and the Chalet School*, 1959; *Trials for the Chalet School*, 1959.

Joey and Company in Tirol, 1960; *Ruey Richardson: Chaletian*, 1960; *The Chalet School Wins the Trick*, 1961; *A Leader in the Chalet School*, 1961; *The Feud in the Chalet School*, 1962; *A Future Chalet School Girl*, 1962; *The School at Skelton Hall*, Parrish, 1962; *The Chalet School Reunion*, 1963; *The Chalet School Triplets*, 1963; *Trouble at Skelton Hall*, Parrish, 1963; *Jane at the Chalet School*, 1964; *Redheads at the Chalet School*, 1964; *Adrienne and the Chalet School*, 1965; *Summer Term at the Chalet School*, 1965; *Two Sams at the Chalet School*, 1967; *Althea Joins the Chalet School*, 1969; *Prefects of the Chalet School*, 1970.

SIDELIGHTS: Elinor Mary Brent-Dyer wrote nearly one hundred books for young girls. Most were part of her "Chalet School" series, the first book of which was published in 1925. Brent-Dyer's famous fictional Chalet School was originally located in the Austrian Tirol. It was later moved to the Channel Islands, then to Wales, and finally to the Oberland. Whether beside a lake or near a mountain, the tri-lingual, non-denominational school was cozily situated.

The adventure stories, which critics appraised as having vitality and dash, appealed to the tastes of young girls. A girls' school headmistress herself, Brent-Dyer possessed a sensitivity to the concerns of students. The situations of the "Chalet School" stories vary from peer rivalry to accepting foreign friends and coping with authority.

The "Chalet School" series became so popular that a Chalet School Club was formed. Members hailed from many parts of the world.

Brent-Dyer died in 1969. The last of the "Chalet School" series was published posthumously.*

                    *   *   *

BRIGGS, Kenneth Arthur 1941-

PERSONAL: Born April 8, 1941, in Gardner, Mass.; son of Clayton Walter and Dora Adele (Havumaki) Briggs; married Kathryn Louise Kent, December 29, 1966; children: Matthew Thomas. *Education:* Bowdoin College, A.B., 1963; Yale University, B.D., 1967. *Office:* New York Times, 229 West 43rd St., New York, N.Y. 11203.

CAREER: Ordained Methodist minister, 1967; assistant pastor of United Methodist church in Hempstead, N.Y., 1967-69; *Newsday*, Garden City, N.Y., religion writer, 1970-74; *New York Times*, New York, N.Y., religion writer, 1974—. *Member:* Religion Newswriters Association, Alpha Delta Phi. *Awards, honors:* Supple Memorial Award from Religion Newswriters Association, 1972.

WRITINGS: (With Arthur Dobrin) *Getting Married the Way You Want*, Prentice-Hall, 1973; (with Janet Briggs) *Yin and Yang Come Home: A Picture Book of Being There*, Branden Press, 1976.*

                    *   *   *

BRILEY, John (Richard) 1925-

PERSONAL: Born June 25, 1925, in Kalamazoo, Mich.; son of William Treve (a salesman) and Stella (a saleswoman; maiden name, Daly) Briley; married Dorothy Louise Reichart, August 23, 1950; children: Dennis Patrick, Paul Christian, Mary Sydney, Shaun William. *Education:* Attended Western Michigan University, 1943; University of Michigan,

B.A., 1951, M.A., 1952; University of Birmingham Shakespeare Institute, Ph.D., 1960. *Home and office:* 24 Highland Rd., Amersham, Buckinghamshire, England. *Agent:* Michael Levy, 9169 Sunset Blvd., Los Angeles, Calif. 90069; and Douglas Rae, 28 Charing Cross Rd., London WC 2, England. *Office:* Suite 505, 5150 Wilshire Blvd., Los Angeles, Calif. 90069.

CAREER: General Motors Corp., Detroit, Mich., in public relations department, 1947-50; U.S. Air Force, South Ruislip, England, director of orientation activities, 1955-60; Metro-Goldwyn-Mayer (MGM), Elstree, England, staff writer, 1960-64; Trevone Productions, Inc., Los Angeles, Calif., and Amersham, Buckinghamshire, England, freelance writer, 1964—. Visiting lecturer at University of Michigan, 1969. President of Chesham Theatre Club. *Military service:* U.S. Air Force, 1943-46; became captain. *Member:* Writers Guild of America, West, Authors Guild, Writers Guild of Great Britain (member of executive council and film committee), Phi Beta Kappa, Phi Kappa Phi, Amersham Swimming Club.

WRITINGS—Novels: *The Traitors,* Putnam, 1968 (published in England as *How Sleep the Brave,* Transworld, 1971); *The Last Dance,* Secker & Warburg, 1978.

Screenplays: (With Jack Trevor Story) "Invasion Quartet" (based on the novel by Norman Collins), Metro-Goldwyn-Mayer (MGM), 1961; (with Story) "Postman's Knock" (based on a story by Story), MGM, 1962; "Children of the Damned," MGM, 1964; "Pope Joan," Columbia, 1972; "That Lucky Touch," United Artists, 1975; "The Medusa Touch" (based on the novel by Peter Van Greenaway), Warner Bros., 1978; "Eagle's Wing" (based on a story by Michael Syson), Rank, 1979.

Plays: "Seven Bob a Buck," first produced at Hampstead Theatre Club, June, 1964, produced on West End at Comedy Theatre, August, 1964; "So Who Needs Men!," produced in Northampton, England, at Northampton Repertory Theatre, May, 1976, produced on West End at New London Theatre, September, 1976. Also author of two series for the British Broadcasting Corp. (BBC-TV), "Hits & Misses," 1962, and "The Airbase," 1965.

Contributor of articles to *Shakespeare Survey* and *Shakespeare Quarterly.*

WORK IN PROGRESS: Three screenplays, "Gandhi," "Enigma," for The Ladd Co., and "Korczek," for Film Polski and the International Film Investors.

SIDELIGHTS: Briley told CA: "I became a screenwriter by accident. I began writing for the stage, but felt I would someday sit in a university lecturing to pretty girls and write the great American novel. When the chance came, however, I realized that like most people of my generation, I had really been more influenced by the screen than by what I had read. Both are important, but the dreams and the ambitions—the secret ones that counted—were formed up there on that silver oblong.

"When I received the chance to write screenplays, I had just come from doing some stage work and could have directed or written. Being raised in the literary tradition I took the writing assignment. It was only later that I learned that the writer of films has almost to be secretly creative. It is the producer and the director who dictate most of what actually happens. Sometimes they can be a productive filter. But they are always the ones who determine the use of your creation—and often (for good and bad) its quality. Hence, your powers of persuasion may be more critical than any 'gift' you may have.

"I think it is beginning to change, but for the writers interested in writing films, I warn them, it is no solo route. Your 'creativity' must be exercised within boundaries set by a budget, by other peoples' imaginations, by the vagaries of agents and someone else's judgment of public taste.

"But films are still written. They begin with the word—be it descriptive or verbal. And films are still the dream-makers of this century. I think it is the place to be—but the road is stony, and I think especially so for the kind of tenderfoot who tends to make the best writer anyway."

Briley considers his "most important work" to be his novel on the Vietnam war, *The Traitors.* It is the story of an American helicopter pilot, Janowitz, who is captured by the Vietcong with the help of a traitorous U.S. private. The Vietcong plan to use Janowitz in an effort to free a North Vietnamese general from a South Vietnamese prison camp. They attempt to convince Janowitz and other captured Americans that this general, if freed, will be able to negotiate an end to the war.

Saturday Review critic Gerald Walker praised Briley for deciding to "take on nothing less that the moral—or rather, immoral—underpinnings of our involvement in that Southeast Asian country. It is a tall order, and in the end the narrative fails to do the job. But it's an honorable failure." Walker added that Briley's "explosive accounts of jungle warfare and . . . his moral passion" are the qualities that make up for the book's "lack of nuances." Martin Russ of *Chicago Sun-Times Book Week* commented that "the story is solid and compelling. . . . For anyone concerned with the problems and puzzles of patriotism in today's world, 'The Traitors' will be a stimulating, sobering, thoroughly shaking-up experience."

BIOGRAPHICAL/CRITICAL SOURCES: Chicago Sun-Times Book Week, August 17, 1969; *New York Times Book Review,* September 7, 1969; *Saturday Review,* September, 13, 1969; *Best Sellers,* October 1, 1969.

*   *   *

BRITSCH, Ralph A(dam)   1912-

PERSONAL: Born January 30, 1912, in Ephraim, Utah; son of Edwin Adam and Clara (Breinholt) Britsch; married Florence Todd, December 18, 1936; children: Todd Adam, R. Lanier, Charlotte (Mrs. David Hamblin), Merlene (Mrs. Timothy Roberts), Royden E. *Education:* Brigham Young University, A.B. (magna cum laude), 1933, M.A., 1951; attended University of Wisconsin—Madison, 1938, University of Washington, 1941, University of Oklahoma, 1950-51, and University of Southern California, 1961. *Politics:* Democrat. *Home address:* P.O. Box 266, Midway, Utah 84049.

CAREER: High school teacher in Gunnison, Utah, 1933-35, and Provo, Utah, 1936-38; Brigham Young University, Provo, instructor, 1938-44, assistant professor, 1944-52, associate professor, 1952-63, professor of English and humanities, 1963-77, professor emeritus, 1977—, chairman of department of English, 1957-60, and department of humanities and comparative literature, 1967-73. Bishop of Church of Jesus Christ of Latter-day Saints (Mormons), 1952-60. *Member:* National Council of Teachers of English, American Society for Aesthetics, American Comparative Literature Association, National Trust for Historic Preservation, Rocky Mountain Modern Language Association. *Awards, honors:* Maeser Award, 1971 and 1978.

WRITINGS: (Editor) *A Humanities Review,* Brigham Young University Press, 1965; (editor with Gail W. Bell and son, Todd A. Britsch) *Literature as Art: A Reader,* Brigham

Young University Press, 1972. Also co-author of *The Arts in Western Culture,* 1978.*

*   *   *

BRITSCH, Todd A(dam) 1937-

PERSONAL: Born September 23, 1937, in Provo, Utah; son of Ralph Adam (a professor) and Florence (Todd) Britsch; married, 1963; children: two. *Education:* Brigham Young University, B.A., 1962; Florida State University, M.A., 1965, Ph.D., 1966. *Office:* Department of Humanities and Comparative Literature, Brigham Young University, A-113 JKB, Provo, Utah 84602.

CAREER: Brigham Young University, Provo, Utah, 1966—, began as assistant professor, professor of humanities, 1977—, chairman of department of humanities and comparative literature, 1973—. *Member:* World Future Society, American Society for Aesthetics, National Association for Humanities Education. *Awards, honors:* National Endowment for the Humanities fellowship, 1972-73.

WRITINGS: (Editor with Gail W. Bell and father, Ralph A. Britsch) *Literature as Art: A Reader,* Brigham Young University Press, 1972; (contributor) *The Next Twenty-Five Years,* World Future Society, 1975. Contributor to scholarly journals.*

*   *   *

BROAD, C(harlie) D(unbar) 1887-1971

PERSONAL: Born December 30, 1887, in Harlesden, Middlesex, England; died March 11, 1971; son of Charles Stephen (a vintner) and Emily (Gomme) Broad. *Education:* Trinity College, Cambridge, degree in philosophy (with first class honors), 1910. *Home:* Cambridge, England.

CAREER: Assistant to professor of logic at St. Andrews University in St. Andrews, Scotland; lecturer at University College in Dundee, Scotland; Bristol University, Bristol, England, professor of philosophy, 1920-c. 1922; Trinity College, Cambridge, England, fellow and lecturer in moral science, c. 1922-33, Knightbridge Professor of Moral Philosophy, 1933-53. Visiting lecturer at Trinity College, Dublin, Ireland, 1929, University of Michigan, 1953-54, University of California, Los Angeles, 1954, and Columbia University, 1960. *Member:* American Academy of Arts and Sciences (fellow), British Academy (fellow), Society for Psychical Research (president, 1935-36, 1959-60), Aristotelian Society (president, 1927-28, 1954-55). *Awards, honors:* Several honorary degrees, including Litt.D. from Cambridge University.

WRITINGS: Perception, Physics, and Reality: An Inquiry Into the Information That Physical Science Can Supply About the Real, Cambridge University Press, 1914, reprinted, Russell, 1972; *Scientific Thought,* Harcourt, 1923, reprinted, Humanities, 1969; *The Mind and Its Place in Nature,* Harcourt, 1925, Routledge & Kegan Paul, 1962; *The Philosophy of Francis Bacon: An Address Delivered at Cambridge on the Occasion of the Bacon Tercentenary, 5 October 1926,* Cambridge University Press, 1926, Octagon, 1976; *Five Types of Ethical Theory,* Harcourt, 1930, Littlefield, 1959; *Examination of McTaggart's Philosophy,* two volumes, Cambridge University Press, 1933-38, reprinted, Octagon, 1976.

Ethics and the History of Philosophy: Selected Essays, Routledge & Kegan Paul, 1952, reprinted, Hyperion Press, 1979; *Religion, Philosophy, and Psychical Research: Selected Essays,* Harcourt, 1953; *Lectures on Psychical Research, Incorporating the Perrott Lectures Given in Cam-*

bridge University in 1959 and 1960, Humanities, 1962; *Induction, Probability, and Causation: Selected Papers,* D. Reidel, 1968; *Broad's Critical Essays in Moral Philosophy,* edited by David R. Cheney, Humanities, 1971; *Leibniz: An Introduction,* edited by C. Lewy, Cambridge University Press, 1975; *Kant: An Introduction,* edited by Lewy, Cambridge University Press, 1978.

Contributor to *Mind* and *Hibbert Journal,* and proceedings of British Academy, Society for Psychical Research, and Aristotelian Society.

SIDELIGHTS: Broad summed up his function as a philosopher in his book, *Scientific Thought.* "If I have any kind of philosophical merit," he wrote, "it is neither the constructive fertility of an Alexander, nor the penetrating critical acumen of a Moore; still less is it that extraordinary combination of both with technical mathematical skill which characterises Whitehead and Russell. I can at most claim the humbler (yet useful) power of stating things clearly and not too superficially."

Broad's first volume of philosophy, *Perception, Physics, and Reality,* is a revision of his Trinity College, Cambridge, fellowship thesis. The book met with glowing reviews. An *Athenaeum* critic proclaimed: "One would almost wish to term Mr. Broad's volume 'palatable philosophy,' it is written in so easy and attractive a style, and shows such excellent common sense.... He may be congratulated upon the success with which he brushes down some ancient cobwebs." Similarly, A. Wolf commented in the *Hibbert Journal* that "there can be no doubt that we are indebted to Mr. Broad for a very searching investigation into some of the most important problems of philosophy, and no serious student of philosophy can afford to overlook this treatise."

Scientific Thought, Broad's next endeavor, also met with an enthusiastic reception. A reviewer for the *Times Literary Supplement* praised the work as a "closely-reasoned and particularly lucid book" and added that it "is certain to take a chief place in the discussions of the philosophical problem which at the present time is of central interest—that of the nature and import of the new concepts of the physical universe which are being adopted in science as the result of recent experimental work devised by mathematicians and physicists." C. J. Keyser of the *Literary Review of the New York Evening Post* asserted that the "book is an exceedingly valuable contribution to Critical Philosophy."

The following book published by the author, *Mind and Its Place in Nature,* caused a commotion in philosophical circles because Broad included evidence of psychic phenomena, which indicated the possibility of human life after death. The book received generally favorable reviews, although critics were skeptical of Broad's conclusions regarding psychic phenomena. Durant Drake remarked in the *Journal of Philosophy* that "the reader needs a good wind to follow the argument through its intricate windings to its rather abrupt and baffling end. But ... he makes his definitions so precise, and so refines his distinctions, that no one can fail to understand exactly what he means or to follow even his most intricate arguments." Bertrand Russell agreed: "It may be doubted whether his results are definitive. Nevertheless, his book is full of accurate thought and useful distinctions to a degree which is surpassed by very few philosophers."

For a later volume, *Five Types of Ethical Theory,* the philosopher was again applauded for his clear, analytical thinking and writing. Henry Hazlitt declared in *Nation* that "Broad has many of the more important merits of a fine philosophical writer.... He is a rigorous and acute logician, quick to smell and pounce upon a fallacy or an ambiguity.'' C.E.M. Joad concurred: ''Broad's may be described as the surgical method. He is for ever dividing thought and cutting it up, introducing distinctions which are usually ignored, and pointing out ambiguities which others have failed to detect.''

In *Religion, Philosophy, and Psychical Research,* Broad expanded on the subject he introduced in *Mind and Its Place in Nature* with favorable results. Huston Smith of *Christian Century* contended that ''if I could name three topics on which I would like to hear one of the best trained and clearest minds of our generation discourse, I think they would be religion, politics, and psychical research.''

Broad followed this volume with the more comprehensive work, *Lectures on Psychical Research.* G.A. Miller of *Scientific American* was doubtful of Broad's belief in psychic phenomena. ''It is uncomfortable to find oneself in disagreement with so gifted and persuasive an author. The most any skeptic must grant when he closes this book is not that paranormal phenomena exist but merely that we cannot prove they do not exist.'' On the other hand, a *Times Literary Supplement* reviewer felt the book was ''admirable'' and its ''clarity of thought, its detailed precision of treatment, and its exact and impartial examination of all that is meant, involved and implied by psychical research could hardly be bettered.''

BIOGRAPHICAL/CRITICAL SOURCES: Athenaeum, July 18, 1914; *Science,* November 20, 1914; *Nation,* December 24, 1914, April 9, 1930; *Hibbert Journal,* January, 1915; *Times Literary Supplement,* March 15, 1923, October 1, 1925, May 15, 1930, February 20, 1953, January 11, 1963; *New Statesman,* May 26, 1923, October 17, 1925; *Boston Transcript,* June 2, 1923; *Nature,* June 30, 1923; *Journal of Philosophy,* December 6, 1923, October 14, 1926, January 29, 1970; *Literary Review of the New York Evening Post,* January 5, 1924; *Nation and Athenaeum,* November 28, 1925, April 12, 1930; *Saturday Review of Literature,* March 6, 1926; *Springfield Republican,* June 6, 1926; *New York Herald Tribune Books,* July 18, 1926; *Christian Century,* June 3, 1953; *Scientific American,* November, 1963.*

* * *

BROCKMAN, Harold 1902-1980

OBITUARY NOTICE: Born in December, 1902; died July 18, 1980. Architect expert and author of works in his field. Brockman worked as an adviser to architects and was known for his constructive assessments. He was architectural correspondent for the *Financial Times* and wrote *The Caliph of Fonthill Abbey* and *The Architect in British Industry.* Obituaries and other sources: *London Times,* August 2, 1980.

* * *

BRODERICK, Francis L(yons) 1922-

PERSONAL: Born September 13, 1922, in New York, N.Y.; son of Joseph Aloysius (a banker) and Mary (Lyons) Broderick; married Barbara Baldridge, June 12, 1950; children: Thomas, Joseph, James, Ann. *Education:* Princeton University, A.B. (with high honors), 1943; Harvard University, M.A., 1947, Ph.D., 1955. *Politics:* Democrat. *Religion:* Catholic. *Home:* 84 Bunker Hill Rd., Stratham, N.H. 03885. *Office:* University of Massachusetts, Boston, Mass. 02125.

CAREER: Princeton University, Princeton, N.J., instructor in history, 1945-46; State University of Iowa (also University of Iowa), Iowa City, instructor in history, 1948-50; Phillips

Exetor Academy, Exeter N.H.; history teacher, 1951-63; U.S. Peace Corps, Washington, D.C., director in Ghana, 1964-66; Lawrence University, Appleton, Wis., Gordon R. Clapp Professor of American Studies and dean of Lawrence and Downer Colleges, 1966-68; University of Massachusetts, Boston, chancellor, 1968-72, Commonwealth Professor, 1972—. Member of national board of consultants of National Endowment for the Humanities. *Military service:* U.S. Army Air Forces, 1943-45; became first lieutenant.

MEMBER: American Catholic Historical Association (president, 1968), American Association for the Advancement of the Humanities. *Awards, honors:* Woodrow Wilson fellowship, 1945-46; National Catholic Book Award, 1964, for *The Life of James Cardinal Gibbons;* LL.D. from Merrimack College, 1969.

WRITINGS: W.E.B. DuBois: Negro Leader in a Time of Crisis, Stanford University Press, 1959; *Right Reverend New Dealer: John A. Ryan,* Macmillan, 1963; (editor) John Tracy Ellis, *The Life of James Cardinal Gibbons,* Bruce, 1963; *The Origins of the Constitution, 1776-1789,* Macmillan, 1964; (editor with August Meier) *Negro Protest Thought in the Twentieth Century,* Bobbs-Merrill, 1965, 2nd edition (with Meier and Elliott Rudwick) published as *Black Protest Thought in the Twentieth Century,* 1971; *Reconstruction and the American Negro, 1865-1900,* Macmillan, 1969.

WORK IN PROGRESS: ''A narrative political history of the election of 1912 (Wilson, Roosevelt, Taft).''

* * *

BRONSON, Lynn
See LAMPMAN, Evelyn Sibley

* * *

BROWN, Anne Ensign 1937-

PERSONAL: Born March 9, 1937, in Phoenix, Ariz.; daughter of Ormsby Herbert (an engineer) and Josephine Marie Ensign; married Joseph Edward Brown (a writer), April 30, 1976. *Education:* Colorado College, B.A., 1960; graduate study at Sorbonne, University of Paris, 1961-62. *Politics:* Republican. *Religion:* Episcopalian. *Home address:* Shelter Cove Marina, 2240 Shelter Island Dr., San Diego, Calif. 92106. *Office:* 4551 Newport Ave., San Diego, Calif. 92107.

CAREER: Scripps Clinic and Research Foundation, La Jolla, Calif., assistant director of development (in public relations and publications) for Friends of Research, 1963-67; Oceanic Research Institute (now Pollution Abstracts, Inc.), La Jolla, writer, editor, and translator, 1968-71; project director and editor under contract to U.S. Department of Commerce, Washington, D.C., 1971-73; free-lance writer, editor, and illustrator, 1973—. *Awards, honors:* Grant from Environmental Protection Agency, 1971-73.

WRITINGS: (Editor) *Bibliography on Subsurface Ocean Currents,* U.S. Department of Commerce, 1973; (with husband, Joseph E. Brown) *Harness the Wind* (juvenile), Dodd, 1977; *Wonders of Sea Horses* (self-illustrated juvenile), Dodd, 1979.

Illustrator: J. Brown, *Wonders of Seals and Sea Lions,* Dodd, 1975; J. Brown, *The Seas Harvest,* Dodd, 1975. Contributor to research journals.

WORK IN PROGRESS: Pelican Island, a self-illustrated children's book, publication expected in 1981; editing and translating a book of Turkish fairy tales, a self-illustrated children's book, publication expected in 1981; ''Gracie'' *Round the World* (tentative title), a sailing book for adults, with husband, Joseph E. Brown.

SIDELIGHTS: In 1980 the Browns began sailing around the world on their home, a thirty-six-foot yawl named *Gracie*. Anne Brown told *CA* that her main writing interests, in addition to sailing, are nature and wildlife (especially dealing with the ocean), and myths and legends from foreign lands.

AVOCATIONAL INTERESTS: Travel, learning languages.

* * *

BROWN, Diana 1928-

PERSONAL: Born August 8, 1928, in Twickenham, Middlesex, England; came to the United States in 1949, naturalized citizen, 1957; daughter of Antranik and Muriel (Maynard) Magarian; married Ralph Herman Brown, December 31, 1964; children: Pamela Hope, Clarissa Faith. *Education:* Attended Sacramento City College, 1972-73; San Jose City College, A.A., 1974; San Jose State University, B.A., 1976, M.A. (librarianship), 1976, M.A. (instructional technology), 1977. *Religion:* Church of England. *Home:* 1612 Knollwood Ave., San Jose, Calif. 95125. *Agent:* Rhoda A. Weyr, William Morris Agency, 1350 Avenue of the Americas, New York, N.Y. 10019.

CAREER: British Embassy, Washington, D.C., secretary to telecommunications attache, 1951-53; Pakistan Consulate General, San Francisco, Calif., librarian, 1953-57; U.S. Army, civilian secretary for intelligence agency in Japan and for medical section in Korea, both 1957-59, for European Military Communications Coordinating Committee and North Atlantic Treaty Association (NATO) in France, 1960-62, and for Armed Forces Network in Korea, 1965-66; television production assistant in San Francisco, 1962-65; U.S. Navy Electronics Laboratory, San Diego, Calif., film editor, 1967-68; Signetics Corp., Sunnyvale, Calif., librarian, 1978-79; National Aeronautics and Space Agency (NASA), Ames Research Center, Moffett Field, Calif., librarian, 1979-80; free-lance library consultant in planning and design, 1980—. *Member:* Special Libraries Association, Authors Guild, Jane Austen Society, Phi Kappa Phi.

WRITINGS: The Emerald Necklace, St. Martin's, 1980, condensed edition published as "Edge of Heaven" in *Good Housekeeping,* April, 1980. Also author of *A Debt of Honor,* 1981.

WORK IN PROGRESS: Research for two books, one set in Regency England and the other set in contemporary times.

SIDELIGHTS: Diana Brown's first novel, *The Emerald Necklace,* follows the life of a young Regency Englishwoman, Leonora, as she accepts a marriage proposal from Etienne Lambert, a nouveau-rich industrialist, in order to save her family from bankruptcy and ruin. Determined to be married "in name only," she shuns her husband but soon discovers him to be a tender, intelligent, and caring man, quite unlike the men she had known in the past. Her newfound insight is to no avail, however, as she has alienated him with her coldness.

"In Leonora Fordyce I set forth a passive, pristine beauty on the burgeoning path of florescence and maturation," explained the author in an article for the *Library Journal.* "She becomes a thinking, acting woman through her own endeavor yet also because her husband allows room for that growth into womanhood. That, to me, is the juxtaposition of romanticism and liberation, for women to be allowed to grow without fear on the part of men that their growth will be either intimidating or diminishing."

In a review of the novel for the *Spokane Daily Chronicle,* Frances Huessy declared that it "is a clean romance, but it isn't romantic fiction in today's gothic-novel sense. Ms. Brown is a writer whose perception of reality comes out of the 18th century—at least in this book. In this way she differs from the other [authors of gothic romance novels] whose characters come from the present and are arbitrarily cast into the past." Eleanor Hodgson of the *San Francisco Examiner & Chronicle* also praised *The Emerald Necklace,* proclaiming it to be "a good old-fashioned love story" and a "sort of British 'Gone With the Wind.'" Hodgson concluded that "the novel will be irresistible to romantics and escapists."

Brown commented to *CA:* "For a long time I had wanted to write but had been inhibited by not having a message—I thought everyone who was serious about writing must have a message. It was only when I sat down to amuse myself that *The Emerald Necklace* was born. It has been termed 'a jolly good read,' a comment that gives me more delight than any of the more ponderous praise.

"While my subject is romantic love—something Bertrand Russell has termed 'that most intense source of human delight'—my writing is far from frivolous. I suspect I sweat and struggle for the right word equally as hard as any writer of more momentous matter. Nor do I apologize for setting my novel in Regency England, a period many consider to be overused.

"To me the Regency was an exciting age, a transitional age, a time when England was moving from an agricultural into an industrial economy just as we today are moving from that very economy into an age of high technology. We have many of the same fears as they: fears that the computer may take our jobs just as the Luddites feared the new weaving machine would take the bread from their mouths. It was a time of paradox, when the trivial and the practical—the tying of a cravat or the construction of a magnificent dwelling—were accounted of equal merit; when outrageous wit could provide an easier entree into society than limitless wealth. It was an age at once ludicrous and tasteful. It was, accordingly, very, very English."

Brown added: "Someday I hope to move my sights to my Armenian heritage, but at the moment I find too much intensity there, too much sadness. For now, I am having fun."

AVOCATIONAL INTERESTS: Writing, photography, Victorian restoration, "watching my daughters grow."

BIOGRAPHICAL/CRITICAL SOURCES: Library Journal, February 1, 1980; *Los Angeles Herald Examiner,* July 13, 1980; *San Francisco Examiner & Chronicle,* July 27, 1980; *Spokane Daily Chronicle,* September 5, 1980.

* * *

BROWN, Frank E(dward) 1908-

PERSONAL: Born May 24, 1908, in La Grange, Ill.; son of Philip Sidney and Rose Louise (Swain) Brown; married Jaquelin Goddard, July 21, 1935. *Education:* Carleton College, A.B., 1929; graduate study at American Academy in Rome, 1931-33; Yale University, Ph.D., 1938. *Home:* Via Giacomo Medici 11, Rome 00153, Italy. *Office:* American Academy in Rome, Via Angelo Masina 5, Rome 00153, Italy.

CAREER: Yale University, New Haven, Conn., assistant director of Dura-Europas excavations, 1932-35, director, 1935-37, assistant professor of classics, 1938-42; Office of War Information, Washington, D.C., general representative to Syria and Lebanon, 1942-45; Republic of Syria, director general of antiquities, 1945-47; American Academy in Rome, Rome, Italy, Mellon Professor of Classics in charge and director of excavations, 1947-52; Yale University, professor of classics, 1952-63, master of Jonathan Edwards College, 1953-56; American Academy in Rome, Mellon Professor of Classics in charge and director of excavations, 1963—, director of academy, 1963-69, 1973. Lecturer at Columbia University, 1963.

MEMBER: International Federation of Societies of Classical Studies (vice-president), International Association of Classical Archaeology (vice-president), Archaeological Institute of America (member of executive committee), American Schools of Oriental Research, American Philological Association, American Oriental Society, American Academy of Arts and Sciences, Instituto di Studi Etruschi ed Italici, German Archaeological Institute, Pontifical Academy of Archaeology, Century Club. Awards, honors: Guggenheim fellowship, 1960-61; Litt.D. from Carleton College, 1968.

WRITINGS: (Co-author) Memoirs: American Academy in Rome, American Academy in Rome, Volume XII, 1935, Volume XX, 1951, Volume XXVI, 1960; The House in Block E4, Block F3, the Roman Baths: Discoveries in the Temple of Artemis-Manaia, Arms and Armor, New and Revised Material From the Temple of Azzanathkona, Elliot's Books, 1936; (editor and contributor) Excavations at Dura-Europas, Volumes VI-IX, Yale University Press, 1936-52; (with Emeline Hill Richardson and L. Richardson, Jr.) Cosa II: The Temples of the Arx, American Academy in Rome, 1960; Roman Architecture, Braziller, 1961; COSA: The Making of a Roman Town, University of Michigan Press, 1979. Also editor of and contributor to Fasti Archeologici, Volumes I-V, 1946-52. Contributor to scholarly journals.*

* * *

BROWN, Harcourt 1900-

PERSONAL: Born May 30, 1900, in Toronto, Ontario, Canada; son of Newton Harcourt and Grace Amanda (Young) Brown; married Dorothy Elizabeth Stacey, April 27, 1927; children: Jennifer. Education: University of Toronto, B.A., 1925, M.A., 1926; Columbia University, Ph.D., 1934. Home: 14 Avenue Rd., Parry Sound, Ontario, Canada P2A 2A7.

CAREER: Dominion Bank, held junior positions in Toronto, and Ottawa, Ontario, 1917-20; Queen's University, Kingston, Ontario, lecturer in French language and literature, 1926-29; Brooklyn College (now of City University of New York), Brooklyn, N.Y., tutor in French, 1930-31; University of Rochester, Rochester, N.Y., instructor in French, 1931-32; Washington University, St. Louis, Mo., professor of French, 1935-37; Brown University, Providence, R.I., professor of French language and literature, 1937-69, professor emeritus, 1969—.

MEMBER: Canadian Historical Association, Modern Language Association of America, Society for French Studies (England), History of Science Society (vice-president, 1949; president, 1950-52), Modern Humanities Research Association (England), Academie des Sciences, Arts et Belles-Lettres (France; corresponding member). Awards, honors: American Council of Learned Societies fellowship, 1934-35.

WRITINGS: Scientific Organizations in Seventeenth-Century France, 1620-1680, Williams & Wilkins, 1934, reprinted, Russell, 1967; (editor) Science and the Creative Spirit: Essays on Humanistic Aspects of Science, University of Toronto Press, 1958; (contributor) W. H. Barber, J. H. Brumfitt, R. A. Leigh, R. Shackleton, and S.S.B. Taylor, editors, The Age of Enlightenment: Studies Presented to Theodore Besterman, Oliver & Boyd, 1967; Science and the Human Comedy: Natural Philosophy From Rabelais to

Maupertuis, University of Toronto Press, 1976; (contributor) Frans C. Amelinckx and Joyce M. Megay, editors, Travel, Quest, and Pilgrimage as a Literary Theme: Studies in Honor of Reino Virtanen, University of Nebraska Press, 1978. Contributor to scholarly journals. Co-founder and associate editor of Annals of Science, 1935-74; member of board of editors of Journal of the History of Ideas, 1944-74.

SIDELIGHTS: Brown told CA: "Science, as a way of understanding events in nature, from Halley's Comet of 1910 and again in 1985, to acorns from different kinds of oaks, has been a matter of much interest. As I developed a sense of history and literary differences, though, the particularities of men who studied and advanced science have intrigued me quite as much as the more humble differences set down in novels, plays, and verse. There may be a kind of comedy in society for Balzac; there is equally a comedy of manners, characters, situations, in many episodes of the history of the sciences. It may not rollick or set off gales of laughter, but it does have conflict and its climaxes. This was evident when half a dozen Frenchmen went to Lapland in the 1730's to clarify the problem of the shape of the earth. Voltaire made a comic tale about it without paying any attention to the essential human aspects of the affair, and this I would have hoped to do if life were easier to control and time did not flee so fast. This episode in the wilderness of Lapland showed as clearly as contemporary doings in Canada did that scientists were human beings with needs and ways of solving their problems. The chasm between literature as a career and the life of the scientist has to be bridged by imagination and searching from either side."

* * *

BROWN, Jamie 1945-

PERSONAL: Born November 3, 1945, in Brantford, Ontario, Canada; son of James E. (a politician) and Elizabeth (Eedy) Brown; married Lorna Ingrid Strom (a film producer), February 28, 1972; children: Jean-Pierre Edwin, Graham-Alexandre. Education: University of Waterloo, B.A., 1969. Residence: Montreal, Quebec, Canada. Agent: Jo Stewart, 201 East 66th St., Suite 18-N, New York, N.Y. 10021.

CAREER: Writer. National Film Board of Canada, consultant, 1974-77; Concordia University, Montreal, Quebec, lecturer in creative writing, 1979—. Member: Writers Union of Canada (officer of Quebec region), Association of Canadian Television and Radio Artists. Awards, honors: Canadian Film Award nomination from Canadian Film Academy, 1978, for screenplay, "The War Is Over."

WRITINGS: The Lively Spirits of Provence (nonfiction), Clarke, Irwin, 1974; Stepping Stones (fiction), Clarke, Irwin, 1975; So Free We Seem (fiction), Clarke, Irwin, 1976; Shrewsbury (fiction), Clarke, Irwin, 1977; Superbike (juvenile), Clarke, Irwin, 1980.

Films: "The War Is Over," National Film Board of Canada, 1979; "Night Letter," Corporation Image, in production; "If You Knew Suzie," Marlow Pictures, in production.

WORK IN PROGRESS: "The Boxty Chronicle," a feature film set in Ireland.

SIDELIGHTS: Brown commented to CA: "Some people feel it takes great courage to be a writer in these days when the publishing business is so shaky; I say it takes great courage to be anything else.

"In all my books, I have tried to write simply, clearly, and directly to ensure first and foremost that they are read. Recently, I have tried to apply what I am learning in writing for film to the novel. I feel it is important for a writer to live what he writes about. In *Superbike,* the background is based on motorcycle racing. To set this down accurately (I once was a racer) I recently rode a grand prix racing bike on a circuit at speeds close to one hundred fifty miles per hour.''

AVOCATIONAL INTERESTS: History, politics, travel, architecture, geography, photography, racing cars and motorcycles.

BIOGRAPHICAL/CRITICAL SOURCES: Toronto Globe & Mail, May 11, 1974; *Ottawa Citizen,* September 9, 1976; *Toronto Star,* September 14, 1976, December 10, 1977; *Toronto Sun,* September 19, 1976.

*   *   *

BROWN, Nathaniel Hapgood 1929-

PERSONAL: Born April 23, 1929, in New York, N.Y.; son of Ralph Wolcott (an attorney) and Esther Fisher (Davis) Brown; married Derval Mackenzie Cohalan (a teacher), July 25, 1959; children: Curry, Gates, Whitney. *Education:* Princeton University, A.B., 1951; Syracuse University, M.A., 1954; Columbia University, Ph.D, 1962. *Home:* 12 Fairfax Circle, Fredericksburg, Va. 22401. *Office:* Department of English, Mary Washington College, Fredericksburg, Va. 22401.

CAREER: Mary Washington College, Fredericksburg, instructor, 1961-64, assistant professor, 1964-68, associate professor, 1968-72, professor of English, 1972—. *Military service:* U.S. Army, 1951-53. *Member:* Modern Language Association of America, Keats-Shelley Association, Byron Society.

WRITINGS: Sexuality and Feminism in Shelley, Harvard University Press, 1979.

WORK IN PROGRESS: A study of women in literature, including Virginia Woolf, Sylvia Plath, and Pauline Reage.

SIDELIGHTS: Brown wrote: "I consider feminist androgyny an idea whose time has come, as I point out in the conclusion of my study of Shelley. Sympathetic cross-gender identification between the sexes can only come about if men and women are encouraged to think of themselves as like each other. The traditional polarization or complementarity of the sexes must give place to an ideal of monosexuality or personhood. This is the only way lasting harmony between the sexes will ever be achieved. I am interested in applying these ideas to literature, highlighting those writers who have maintained the essential identity of the sexes as a social or psychological ideal.''

*   *   *

BROWN, Robert Craig 1935-

PERSONAL: Born October 14, 1935, in Rochester, N.Y.; son of Ralph Nelson Jennings and Marion F. (Black) Brown; married Gail Detgen, May 21, 1960; children: Bradley Bower, Brenda Berkeley, Brian Blair. *Education:* University of Rochester, B.A., 1957; University of Toronto, M.A., 1958, Ph.D., 1962. *Religion:* United Church. *Home:* 175 Glenview Ave., Toronto, Ontario, Canada M4R 1R4. *Office:* Department of History, University of Toronto, Toronto, Ontario, Canada M5S 1A1.

CAREER: University of Calgary, Calgary, Alberta, assistant professor of history, 1961-64; University of Toronto, Toronto, Ontario, assistant professor, 1964-66, associate professor, 1966-70, professor of history, 1970—, director of

graduate studies, 1972-73, associate chairman of department, 1974-77. *Member:* American Historical Association, Canadian Historical Association (member of council, 1964-67; vice-president, 1978-79; president, 1979-80). *Awards, honors:* Canada Council fellowships, 1962, 1963, 1965, and 1973; Izaak Walton Killam senior research scholarship from Canada Council, 1977-78; Social Sciences and Humanities Research Council leave fellowship, 1979-80.

WRITINGS: Canada's National Policy, 1883-1900: A Study in Canadian-American Relations, Princeton University Press, 1964; (editor with M. F. Prang) *The Confederation to 1949,* Prentice-Hall, 1966; (with James Maurice Stockford Careless) *The Canadians, 1867-1967,* St. Martin's, 1967; (with S. F. Wise) *Canada Views the United States: Nineteenth-Century Political Attitudes,* University of Washington Press, 1967; (contributor) John Braeman, Robert H. Bremner, and David Brody, editors, *The Twentieth Century: American Foreign Policy,* Ohio State University Press, 1971; (contributor) J. L. Granatstein and R. D. Cuff, editors, *War and Society in North America,* Thomas Nelson, 1971; (with Ramsay Cook) *Canada, 1896-1921: A Nation Transformed,* McClelland & Stewart, 1974; *Robert Laird Borden: A Biography,* Macmillan, Volume I, 1975, Volume II, 1980. Contributor of articles and reviews to history journals. Editor of *Canadian Historical Review,* 1968-73.

BIOGRAPHICAL/CRITICAL SOURCES: Canadian Forum, March, 1976; *Canadian Historical Review,* June, 1976, September, 1977; *Journal of American History,* December, 1976; *American Historical Review,* June, 1977.

*   *   *

BROWN, Wayne 1944-

PERSONAL: Born July 18, 1944, in Trinidad; married Megan Hopkyn-Rees, 1968. *Education:* University of the West Indies, B.A. (with honors), 1968. *Home:* Whitehill End, Green Lane, Ockham, Woking, Surrey, England.

CAREER: Trinidad Guardian, staff writer, 1964-65; teacher in Jamaica, 1969; *Trinidad Guardian,* art critic, 1970-71; writer, 1971—. School teacher in Trinidad, 1970-71. *Awards, honors:* Poetry prize from Jamaican Independence Festival, 1968; Commonwealth Poetry Prize, 1972, for *On the Coast.*

WRITINGS: On the Coast (poems), Deutsch, 1972; *Edna Manley: The Private Years, 1900-1938,* Deutsch, 1976; (editor with Tom Wharton) *Twenty-One Years of "Poetry and Audience",* Aquila, 1976.

BIOGRAPHICAL/CRITICAL SOURCES: Trinidad Sunday Guardian, February 25, 1973; *Times Literary Supplement,* May 4, 1973; *London,* June, 1973; *Sunday Gleaner,* Kingston, Jamaica, September 16, 1973.*

*   *   *

BROWNE, Gary Lawson 1939-

PERSONAL: Born September 21, 1939, in Lansing, Mich.; son of Lawson Delmer and Helen (Ward) Browne; married Valerie Gerrard, August 24, 1963 (divorced August 24, 1977). *Education:* University of Michigan, B.A., 1961; Wayne State University, M.A., 1965, Ph.D., 1973. *Religion:* Episcopalian. *Home:* 6120 Edmondson Ave., Baltimore, Md. 21228. *Office:* Department of History, University of Maryland, Baltimore Campus, 5401 Wilkens Ave., Baltimore, Md. 21228.

CAREER: Wayne State University, Detroit, Mich., instructor, 1971-73, assistant professor of history, 1973-76; University of Maryland, Baltimore, assistant professor of history,

1976—. Consultant to National Endowment for the Humanities and Baltimore Industrial Museum. *Military service:* U.S. Army, 1961-63; became second lieutenant. *Member:* American Historical Association, Organization of American Historians, Southern Historical Association, Maryland Historical Society.

WRITINGS: Baltimore in the Nation, 1789-1861, University of North Carolina Press, 1980. Contributor to history journals. Editor of *Maryland Historical Magazine* and *Maryland Magazine of Genealogy,* 1978—.

WORK IN PROGRESS: Research on the history of the American tariff and the rise of the United States as a business civilization.

SIDELIGHTS: Browne told *CA:* "I have always been fascinated by what we are and how we came to our present condition. Writing history is an act of philosophy. While researching *Baltimore in the Nation* I discovered that social development has always been a process, and that the Marxian analysis of historical development is wrong. Like any other finite theory, economic determinism cannot explain our infinite world. What I discovered is that modernization and the evolution of America as a business civilization was a highly complex process, one in which social changes frequently set the stage for economic development. Further study may or may not support this contention, but any investigation is valuable if it contributes to our understanding of ourselves."

*   *   *

BRUEGMANN, Robert   1948-

PERSONAL: Born May 21, 1948, in Chicago, Ill.; son of Karl (an engineer) and Margaret (Cartright) Bruegmann. *Education:* Principia College, B.A. (with highest honors), 1970; University of Pennsylvania, Ph.D., 1976. *Home:* 55 West Chestnut St., No. 1102, Chicago, Ill. 60610. *Office:* Department of Architecture and Art History, University of Illinois at Chicago Circle, Chicago, Ill. 60680.

CAREER: Member of faculty at University of Pennsylvania, Philadelphia, 1972-74, Philadelphia College of Art, Philadelphia, 1974-75, and Philadelphia Community College, Philadelphia, 1975-76; University of Illinois at Chicago Circle, Chicago, assistant professor of architecture and art history, 1976—. Affiliated with Historical American Buildings Survey, 1974-78. *Awards, honors:* Founders' Award from Society of Architectural Historians, 1978, for article, "Early Central Heating and Forced Ventilation and Architectural Design."

WRITINGS: (Contributor) Donald Watson, editor, *Energy Conservation Through Building Design,* McGraw, 1978; (contributor) John C. Zukowsky, editor, *The Plan of Chicago, 1909-1979,* Art Institute of Chicago, 1979; *Benicia: Portrait of an Early California Town, an Architectural History, 1846 to the Present,* 101 Productions, 1980. Contributor to *International Handbook of Contemporary Architecture.* Contributor of articles and reviews to architecture and planning journals and newspapers.

WORK IN PROGRESS: Research on architecture of the 1920's and criticism of contemporary architecture.

*   *   *

BRUNDAGE, John Herbert   1926-
(John Herbert)

PERSONAL: Born October 13, 1926, in Toronto, Ontario, Canada. *Education:* Attended Art College of Ontario, 1947-

49, New Play Society School of Drama, 1955-58, and National Ballet of Canada School, 1958-60. *Home:* 101 Roxborough St., Rosedale, Ontario, Canada. *Agent:* Ellen Neuwald, Inc., 905 West End Ave., New York, N.Y. 10025.

CAREER: Writer. Actor, 1939—; director, 1957—. Actor, set and costume designer, and stage and house manager with New Play Society, Toronto, Ontario; dancer with Garbut Roberts's Dance Drama Company; Adventure Theatre, Toronto, artistic director, 1960-62; New Venture Players, Toronto, artistic director, 1962-65; Garret Theatre Company, Toronto, artistic director and producer, 1965-70. Lecturer at Ryerson Polytechnical School, summers, 1969-70, York University, summer, 1972, University of Toronto, summers, 1973-76, and Three Schools of Art, 1975-76.

WRITINGS—All under name John Herbert; plays: *Fortune and Men's Eyes* (first produced in New York, N.Y., 1967), Grove, 1967; *Some Angry Summer Songs* (includes "The Pearl Divers," first produced in Toronto, Ontario, 1974; "Beer Room," first produced in Toronto, 1974; "Close Friends," first produced in Toronto; "The Dinosaurs," first produced in Toronto, 1974), Talonbooks, 1976.

Books: *Christie's Review of the Season, 1974,* Abrams, 1975; *Christie's Review of the Season, 1975,* Abrams, 1976; *Christie's Review of the Season, 1976,* Abrams, 1977.

Unpublished plays: "A Marshmallow Drama," first produced in Canoe Lake, Ontario, 1942; "Private Club," first produced in Toronto, Ontario, 1962; "A Household God," first produced in Toronto, Ontario, 1962; "A Lady of Camellias" (adaptation of play by Alexandre Dumas), first produced in Toronto, Ontario, 1964; "Closer to Cleveland," first produced in Toronto, Ontario, 1967; "World of Woyzeck" (adaptation of play by Buechner), first produced in Toronto, Ontario, 1969; "Close Friends," first produced in Toronto, Ontario, 1970; "Born of Medusa's Blood," first produced in Toronto, Ontario, 1972.

Work represented in anthologies, including "Fortune and Men's eyes" in *Open Space Plays,* edited by Charles Marowitz, Penguin, 1974; "Omphale and the Hero" (first produced in Toronto, Ontario), in *Canadian Theatre Review Three,* 1974. Associate editor of *Onion,* 1975-76.

BIOGRAPHICAL/CRITICAL SOURCES: Nathan Cohen, *Canadian Writing Today,* Penguin, 1970; *Twentieth Century Literature,* July, 1972; Ann P. Messenger, *Dramatists in Canada,* University of British Columbia Press, 1972; Geraldine Anthony, *Stage Voices,* Doubleday, 1978.*

*   *   *

BRUNDAGE, Percival F(lack)   1892-1979

PERSONAL: Born April 2, 1892, in Amsterdam, N.Y.; died July 16, 1979, in Ridgewood, N.J.; son of William M. (a minister) and Charlotte Hannah (Flack) Brundage; married Amittai Ostrander, June 1, 1918 (died, 1977); children: Robert Percival (deceased), Lois Amittai Brundage Baker. *Education:* Harvard University, A.B. (cum laude), 1914. *Religion:* Unitarian. *Home:* 2601 Woodley Pl. N.W., Washington, D.C. 20008; and 969 Hillsboro Mile, Pompano Beach, Fla. 33362.

CAREER: Price Waterhouse & Co., New York, N.Y., staff member, 1916-30, partner, 1930-44, head of Boston office in early 1930's, senior partner and head of firm, 1944-54; U.S. Bureau of the Budget (now U.S. Office of Management and Budget), Washington, D.C., deputy director, 1954-56, director, 1956-58; consultant to numerous national companies and organizations and to governmental agencies, 1958-79. National Bureau of Economic Research, director, 1942-67, president, 1954, honorary director, 1967-79; former director and treasurer of Atlantic Council of the United States; former director, and chairman, 1951-54, of Federal Union, Inc.; former treasurer of International Movement for Atlantic Union. Director of American Christian Committee for Refugees, 1946, and American Relief for Austria; former director and treasurer of People to People Health Foundation; former director and board member of Project Hope. Director of Unitarian Service Committee and Unitarian Development Fund; chairman of Unitarian Development Fund Campaign, 1959-62. Director of Montclair Community Chest, 1950-54; chairman of executive committee of New York Chamber of Commerce, 1952-54. Honorary president of American Youth Hostels. *Wartime service:* Member of accounting section of New York Depot Quartermaster Corps during World War I.

MEMBER: American Institute of Certified Public Accountants (president, 1948-49), National Conference of Lawyers and Certified Public Accountants (former co-chairman), International Association for Religious Freedom (former president), Council on Foreign Relations, Foreign Policy Association, United Nations Association, New York State Society of Accountants (former vice-president), Century Club, Harvard Club (New York), Montclair Club (New Jersey), Chevy Chase Club (Maryland), Cosmos Club (Washington, D.C.). *Awards, honors:* Elected to Accounting Hall of Fame; D.Sc. from New York University, 1950.

WRITINGS: (With others) *Changing Concepts of Business Income,* Macmillan, 1952, reprinted, Scholars Book Co., 1975; *The Bureau of the Budget,* foreword by Robert P. Mayo, Praeger, 1970. Also author of two reports, *The Federal Budget,* 1957, and *U.S. Budget and Fiscal Problems,* 1964. Contributor of articles to newspapers and magazines.

OBITUARIES: Washington Post, July 18, 1979*

* * *

BRUNT, P(eter) A(stbury) 1917-

PERSONAL: Born June 23, 1917; son of Samuel (a Methodist minister) and Gladys Eileen Brunt. *Education:* Received degrees (with first class honors) from Oriel College, Oxford, 1937, 1939. *Home:* 34 Manor Rd., South Hinksey, Oxford, England.

CAREER: Ministry of Shipping, England, 1940-45, began as temporary assistant principal, became temporary principal; Oxford University, Oxford, England, associated with Magdalen College, 1946; University of St. Andrews, St. Andrews, Scotland, lecturer in ancient history, 1947-51; Oxford University, fellow and tutor at Oriel College, 1951-67, dean of Oriel College, 1959-64; Cambridge University, Cambridge, England, fellow and senior bursar at Gonville and Caius College, 1968-70; Oxford University, Camden Professor of ancient history and fellow of Brasenose College, 1970—, fellow, 1973. Member of council of British School at Rome, 1972—. *Member:* British Academy (fellow).

WRITINGS: (Editor of revision and author of introduction) Thucydides, *The Peloponnesian Wars* (translated by Benjamin Jowett), Twayne, 1963; (contributor) John Percy Vyvian Dacre Balsdon, editor, *The Romans,* C. A. Watts, 1965; (editor and author of introduction, with John Michael Moore) *Res Gestae Divi Augusti: The Achievements of the Divine Augustus,* Oxford University Press, 1967; *Italian Manpower, 225 B.C.-A.D. 14,* Oxford University Press, 1971; *Social Conflicts in the Roman Republic,* Chatto & Windus, 1971; Norton, 1972; (editor) Arnold Hugh Martin Jones, *The Ro-*

man Economy: Studies in Ancient Economic and Administrative History, Rowman & Littlefield, 1974; (editor of revision and translation) Flavius Arrianus, *Arrian,* Volume I: *Anabasis Alexandri, Books I-IV,* Harvard University Press, 1976. Contributor to history and classical studies journals. Editor of *Oxford,* 1963-64.

BIOGRAPHICAL/CRITICAL SOURCES: Economist, September 14, 1974; *Times Literary Supplement,* September 17, 1976.*

* * *

BRYFONSKI, Dedria (Anne) 1947-

PERSONAL: Born August 21, 1947, in Utica, N.Y.; daughter of Lewis Francis (a co-owner of a sporting goods store) and Catherine Marie (a co-owner of a sporting goods store; maiden name, Stevens) Bryfonski; married Alexander Burgess Cruden (a newspaper editor), May 24, 1975. *Education:* Nazareth College of Rochester, B.A., 1969; Fordham University, M.A., 1970. *Politics:* Democrat. *Religion:* Roman Catholic. *Home:* 18237 Saxon Dr., Birmingham, Mich. 48009. *Office:* Gale Research Co., Book Tower, Detroit, Mich. 48226.

CAREER: Dial Press, New York City, editorial assistant, 1970-71; Walker & Co., New York City, editor, 1971-73; Gale Research Co., Detroit, Mich., editor, 1974-79, senior editor, 1979, vice-president and associate editorial director, 1979—. Member of board of directors of Friends of Detroit Public Library, 1980—. *Member:* American Management Association, New Girls' Network.

WRITINGS: The New England Beach Book, Walker & Co., 1974; (editor) *Contemporary Literary Criticism,* Gale, Volume 7 (with Phyllis Carmel Mendelson), 1977, Volume 8 (with Mendelson), 1978, Volume 9, 1978, Volume 10, 1979, Volume 11, 1979, Volume 12, 1980, Volume 13, 1980, Volume 14 (with Laurie Lanzen Harris), 1980; (editor) *Twentieth-Century Literary Criticism,* Gale, Volume 1 (with Mendelson), 1978, Volume 2 (with Sharon K. Hall), 1979; (contributor) Elizabeth Geiser, editor, *The Business of Book Publishing,* Praeger, 1981.

WORK IN PROGRESS: A novel.

* * *

BRYSON, Reid Allen 1920-

PERSONAL: Born June 7, 1920, in Detroit, Mich.; son of William Riley and Elma (Turner) Bryson; married Frances Edith Williamson (a handweaver), June 13, 1942; children: Anne (Mrs. J. L. King), William R., Robert U., Thomas T. *Education:* Denison University, B.A., 1941; graduate study at University of Wisconsin—Madison, 1941-46; University of Chicago, Ph.D., 1948. *Home:* 11 Rosewood Circle, Madison, Wis. 53711. *Office:* Institute for Environmental Studies, University of Wisconsin, 1225 West Dayton St., Madison, Wis. 53706.

CAREER: University of Wisconsin—Madison, assistant professor, 1946-50, associate professor of meteorology, 1950-56, head of department, 1948-50 and 1952-54; University of Arizona, Tucson, professor of meteorology, 1956-57; University of Wisconsin, professor of meteorology and geography, 1957—, director of Institute for Environmental Studies, 1970—. Member of National Academy of Sciences National Research Council committees and Smithsonian Council, 1976—; member of board of trustees of University Corp. for Atmospheric Research. Member of Wisconsin Air Pollution Control Council, 1971-73, and Wisconsin Department of Natural Resources citizens' advisory committee on environmental matters, 1976; consultant to United Nations, National Science Foundation, and Environment Canada. *Military service:* U.S. Army Air Forces, 1942-45; became major.

MEMBER: American Meteorological Society (fellow), American Society of Limnology and Oceanography, Association of American Geographers, Society for American Archaeology, Arid Zone Research Association of India, Wisconsin Phenological Society (past president), Wisconsin Academy of Sciences, Arts and Letters, Phi Beta Kappa, Sigma Xi, Phi Kappa Phi, Explorers Club. *Awards, honors:* D.Sc. from Denison University, 1971; Banta Medal for literary achievement from Wisconsin Library Association, 1978, for *Climates of Hunger.*

WRITINGS: (With J. F. Lahey and others) *Atlas of 500 mb Wind Characteristics for the North Hemisphere,* University of Wisconsin Press, 1958; (with Lahey and Eberhard Wahl) *Atlas of Five-Day Normal Sea-Level Pressure Charts for the Northern Hemisphere,* University of Wisconsin Press, 1958; (with Lahey and others) *Atlas of 300 mb Wind Characteristics,* University of Wisconsin Press, 1960; (editor with F. K. Hare) *World Survey of Climatology,* Volume II: *Climates of North America,* Elsevier Scientific Publishing, 1974; (with T. J. Murray) *Climates of Hunger,* University of Wisconsin Press, 1977.

Contributor: W. J. Mayer-Oakes, editor, *Life, Land, and Water,* University of Manitoba Press, 1967; W. L. Garrison and D. F. Marble, editors, *Quantitative Geography,* Volume II: *Physical and Cartographic Topics,* Northwestern University Press, 1968; G. J. Demko, H. M. Ross, and G. A. Schnell, editors, *Population Geography: A Reader,* McGraw, 1970; D. R. Coates, editor, *Environmental Geomorphology and Landscape Conservation,* Volume I: *Prior to 1900,* Dowden, 1972; Nicholas Polunin, editor, *Environmental Future,* Macmillan, 1972; (with John E. Ross) Thomas R. Detwyler, Melvin G. Marcus, and other editors, *Urbanization and Environment,* Wadsworth, 1972; Richard J. Kopec, editor, *Atmospheric Quality and Climate Change,* Department of Geography, University of North Carolina, 1975; *World Development,* Pergamon, 1977; A. B. Pittock, L. A. Frakes, and other editors, *Climate Change and Variability: A Southern Perspective,* Cambridge University Press, 1978; Kaichiro Takahashi and Masatoshi M. Yoshino, editors, *Climatic Change and Food Production,* University of Tokyo Press, 1978.

Contributor of numerous articles to scientific journals, popular magazines, and newspapers, including *Saturday Review, Natural History,* and *Nature.* Advisory editor of *Environmental Conservation.*

WORK IN PROGRESS: The Flute in the Canyon, "a book of intellectual adventures, *cum* poetry," publication expected in 1982; research on climatic forecasting.

SIDELIGHTS: Bryson told *CA:* "My work has led me to believe that nature is understandable and that much about the future may be anticipated if we learn from the past. Climate, for example, is deterministic, not random, and someday soon we will be able to forecast it. A lesson of climatic history is that since variations are significant to society, climate forecasting is socially useful. This and other problems facing mankind today transcend the expertise of single academic disciplines. This fact has directed my work ever more toward interdisciplinary study of the environment of man."

BUCHANAN, Betty (Joan) 1923-
(Joan Shepherd)

PERSONAL: Born September 30, 1923, in California; daughter of Harry W. (a musician) and Nell (a music hall performer; maiden name, Shepherd) Hammer; married Thomas S. Buchanan (a director of motion pictures), 1945 (divorced); children: Denis. *Education:* Attended L'Academie de la Grande Chaumiere, 1951. *Religion:* Protestant. *Home:* 360 11th St., Santa Monica, Calif. 90402. *Agent:* Robert Mills Ltd., 156 East 52nd St., New York, N.Y. 10022.

CAREER: Writer. Walt Disney Studios, Hollywood, Calif., cartoonist, 1939-40; Metro-Goldwyn-Mayer (MGM), Hollywood, cartoonist, 1941-42; RKO Studios, Hollywood, in publicity, 1943-44; *TV-Radio Life* (magazine), Hollywood, assistant editor and writer, 1945-50; Paris correspondent to *Billboard,* 1951; *Daytime TV,* Hollywood, editor, 1973-78. *Member:* Mystery Writers of America, Hollywood Women's Press Club, Santa Monica Historical Society.

WRITINGS—Under pseudonym Joan Shepherd; novels: *The Girl on the Left Bank,* Washburn-McKay, 1954; *Tender Is the Knife,* Washburn-McKay, 1958.

Short stories: "The Fan," published in *Alfred Hitchcock's Mystery Magazine,* January, 1978; "Gee Whiz, My Lovely," published in *Ellery Queen's Mystery Magazine,* June, 1978. "Hollywood Footprints," anthologized in *Tricks and Treats,* 1977.

Contributor to periodicals, including *Billboard* and *Village Voice.*

WORK IN PROGRESS: A novel, *Iris Out on a Small Distant Figure;* researching P. G. Wodehouse.

SIDELIGHTS: Buchanan told *CA:* "I went to work at an early age in order to finance dance lessons. I found myself in writing jobs—what would have been my academic years were spent in the film studios, which I do not regret. In 1951 I went to Paris, feeling that some education was necessary. I became a stringer for *Billboard* and English magazines. Between 1959 and 1973 I was a housewife and a mother.

"I became aware of mystery writing when I discovered the Sherlock Holmes, Edgar Wallace, and S. S. Van Dine novels on my mother's bookshelves. My hero, of course, is Raymond Chandler. He wrote me a short fan letter when I was employed on the *TV-Radio Life* magazine in Hollywood. I'm still stunned."

* * *

BUCKHOLDT, David R. 1942-

PERSONAL: Born April 11, 1942, in Salem, Ohio; son of Robert E. (an engineer) and Florence (Iler) Buckholdt; married Rochelle Handler, June 7, 1970; children: Michael, Mark. *Education:* College of Wooster, B.A., 1964; Washington University, St. Louis, Mo., Ph.D., 1969. *Home:* 1101 East Fairmount, Whitefish Bay, Wis. 53217. *Office:* Department of Sociology, Marquette University, Milwaukee, Wis. 53233.

CAREER: LEMREL, Inc., St. Louis, Mo., director of instructional systems program, 1968-74; Marquette University, Milwaukee, Wis., associate professor of sociology, 1974—, chairman of department. *Member:* American Sociological Association, American Educational Research Association, Association for Humanistic Sociology, Midwest Sociological Association.

WRITINGS: (With R. Hamblin and others) *The Humaniza-*

tion Process, Wiley, 1971; (with J. Gubrium) *Toward Maturity,* Jossey-Bass, 1977; (with Gubrium) *Caretakers: Treating Emotionally Disturbed Children,* Sage Publications, 1979; (with H. Sloane and others) *Structured Teaching,* Research Press, 1979.

WORK IN PROGRESS: A study of the social aspects of physical rehabilitation.

* * *

BUCKLEY, Vincent (Thomas) 1925-

PERSONAL: Born July 8, 1925, in Romsey, Victoria, Australia; son of Patrick and Frances Buckley; married second wife, Penelope Curtis, 1976; children: four. *Education:* University of Melbourne, B.A., 1950, M.A., 1954; attended Cambridge University, 1955-57. *Religion:* Roman Catholic. *Office:* Department of English, University of Melbourne, Parkville, Melbourne 3052, Australia.

CAREER: University of Melbourne, Melbourne, Australia, Lockie fellow, 1958-60, reader, 1960-67, professor of English, 1967—. *Military service:* Australian Air Force. *Awards, honors:* Gold medal from Australian Literature Society, 1959, for *Masters in Israel;* Myer Award, 1967, for *Arcady and Other Places.*

WRITINGS: The World's Flesh (poems), F. W. Cheshire, 1954; *Essays in Poetry: Mainly Australian,* Arno, 1957; *Poetry and Morality: Studies in the Criticism of Matthew Arnold, T. S. Eliot, and F. R. Leavis,* Chatto & Windus, 1959; *Masters in Israel: Poems,* Angus & Robertson, 1961; *Henry Handel Richardson,* Lansdowne Press, 1971, 2nd edition, Oxford University Press, 1970; *Arcady and Other Places: Poems,* Cambridge University Press, 1966; *Poetry and the Sacred,* Barnes & Noble, 1968; *Golden Builders and Other Poems,* Angus & Robertson, 1976; *Late Winter Child,* Humanities, 1979; *The Pattern,* Humanities, 1979.

Editor: *The Incarnation in the University: Studies in the University Apostolate,* University Catholic Federation of Australia, 1955, Young Christian Students, 1957; *Australian Poetry, 1958,* Angus & Robertson, 1958; Leonard French, *The Campion Paintings,* Gayflower Press, 1962; *Eight by Eight* (poems), Jacaranda Press, 1963. Contributor to periodicals. Past member of editorial board of *Prospect.*

WORK IN PROGRESS: A memoir; Irish-Australian essays.

* * *

BUDD, Elaine 1925-

PERSONAL: Born June 27, 1925, in Newton, Mass.; daughter of Charles A. (an electrical engineer) and Elsie (a dancer; maiden name, Stewart) Rounds; married John F. Budd (a public relations executive), December 5, 1953; children: Jonathan, Tracy. *Education:* Attended Rollins College, 1947-49; studied writing at Bread Loaf Writers' Conference, Middlebury, Conn., 1975. *Politics:* Republican. *Religion:* Episcopalian. *Home address:* Newberry Rd., East Haddam, Conn. 06423. *Agent:* Lyle Engel, Schillings Crossing Rd., Canaan, N.Y. 12029.

CAREER: Seventeen magazine, New York City, beauty editor, 1955-60; free-lance editor of several beauty magazines, 1960-66; *Co-ed* magazine, New York City, beauty editor, 1966-79; free-lance writer, 1979—. Member of Bicentennial Commission of Oyster Bay, N.Y. *Member:* Mystery Writers of America, Fashion Group, Baker Street Irregulars. *Awards, honors:* Fifi award from the Fragrance Foundation, 1977, for the best article on perfume in a consumer magazine.

WRITINGS: Beauty Today, Pyramid, 1960; *Your Hairdo,* Scholastic, 1966, revised edition published as *You and Your Hair,* 1978; *Young Beauty,* Scholastic, 1967; *How to Look Like Yourself, Only Better,* Doubleday, 1981. Contributor of articles and stories to newspapers and periodicals, including *New York Sunday News, Women's Day, Skullduggery Magazine, House Beautiful, Harper's Bazaar,* and *New York Times* (Connecticut section).

SIDELIGHTS: Budd told *CA:* "I have always wanted to write a perfect mystery, to give back something to a genre that has given me so much pleasure. *Rebecca* and all the novels of Josephine Tey are my inspiration for this yet-to-be attained goal. And if all this delicious deviltry I contemplate can be written with the grace of a Jane Austen—ah! *Pride and Prejudice* is re-read each year.

"Someone (not I, unfortunately) once said, 'Anybody can write, but writers can't do anything else.' Too true. It's important that a writer face that fact early on. I am not a housewife who writes. I am a writer who lives in a house—and as such, I write, period. I pay someone else to vacuum, to dust and polish, and wax the floors—and if I can't find the 'someone' the housework doesn't get done. My family understands this and I do not apologize for a less-than-perfect house. On the other hand, I would apologize all over the place to an editor for a missed deadline."

* * *

BUEHRIG, Gordon M. 1904-

PERSONAL: Born June 18, 1904, in Mason City, Ill.; son of Fred (a banker) and Louise (Miller) Buehrig; married Elizabeth Whitten, December 22, 1934 (died, 1970); married Kathryn Lundell, January 9, 1971; children: (first marriage) Barbara Buehrig Orlando. *Education:* Attended Bradley University, 1922-23. *Home:* 762 Lochmoor, Grosse Pointe, Mich. 48236.

CAREER: Automobile designer and engineer, 1924-65; began as apprentice body builder for Gotfredson Body Co.; engineer for Dietrich, Inc. and Packard Motor Co.; automobile designer for General Motors, Stutz, Duesenberg, Auburn Auto, Budd Co., and Raymond Lowey Studio; Ford Motor Co., automobile designer, 1954-70. Art Center College of Design, Los Angeles, Calif., teacher of plastics, 1965-70. *Member:* Society of Automotive Engineers (national vice-president, 1954).

WRITINGS: (With William Jackson) *Rolling Sculpture,* Haessner, 1975.

BIOGRAPHICAL/CRITICAL SOURCES: Village Voice, December 15, 1975.

* * *

BUFKIN, Ernest Claude, Jr. 1929-

PERSONAL: Born April 27, 1929, in Monticello, Miss.; son of Ernest Claude Bufkin. *Education:* Tulane University, B.A., 1950, M.A., 1952; attended Harvard University, 1958-59; Vanderbilt University, Ph.D., 1964. *Office:* Department of English, University of Georgia, Athens, Ga. 30601.

CAREER: University of Georgia, Athens, instructor, 1963-65, assistant professor, 1965-69, associate professor of English, 1969—. *Member:* Modern Language Association of America.

WRITINGS: The Twentieth-Century Novel in English: A Checklist, University of Georgia Press, 1967; *P. H. Newby,* Twayne, 1975; (editor) *Foreign Literary Prizes: Romance* *and Germanic Languages,* Bowker, 1980. Contributor to language and literature journals.*

*   *   *

BUHITE, Russell D(evere) 1938-

PERSONAL: Born July 19, 1938, in Reynoldsville, Pa.; married, 1959; children: three. *Education:* Clarion State College, B.A., 1961; Ohio University, M.A., 1962; Michigan State University, Ph.D., 1965. *Home:* 2759 Meadowbrook Dr., Norman, Okla. 73069. *Office:* Department of History, University of Oklahoma, Norman, Okla. 73069.

CAREER: University of Oklahoma, Norman, 1965—, began as assistant professor, professor of history, 1974—. *Member:* American Historical Association, Organization of American Historians. *Awards, honors:* American Philosophical Society grant, 1970.

WRITINGS: Nelson T. Johnson and United States China Policy, 1925-1941, Michigan State University Press, 1968; (editor) A. M. Schlesinger, *The Dynamics of World Power: A Documentary History of United States Foreign Policy, 1945-1974—The Far East,* Chelsea House, 1973; *Patrick J. Hurley and American Foreign Policy,* Cornell University Press, 1973. Contributor to history journals.*

*   *   *

BULLOUGH, William A(lfred) 1933-

PERSONAL: Born January 3, 1933, in Oxnard, Calif.; son of William H. (an oilfield worker) and Mary (Hamill) Bullough; married Patricia J. Pomada, June, 1957; children: Gregory William. *Education:* University of California, Santa Barbara, B.A., 1955, M.A., 1967, Ph.D., 1970. *Office:* Department of History, California State University, 25800 Hillary St., Hayward, Calif. 94542.

CAREER: Public school teacher in Calif., 1957-65; California State University, Hayward, assistant professor, 1970-74, associate professor, 1974-79, professor of history, 1979—. *Member:* American Historical Association, Organization of American Historians.

WRITINGS: Cities and Schools in the Gilded Age: The Evolution of an Urban Institution, Kennikat, 1974; *The Blind Boss and His City: Christopher Augustine Buckley and Nineteenth-Century San Francisco,* University of California Press, 1979. Contributor to history journals.

WORK IN PROGRESS: A history of California, with Richard Orsi and Richard Rice, for Wiley; research on the phenomenon of urbanism on the California mining frontier.

SIDELIGHTS: Bullough told *CA:* "My career as a professional historian began rather late—after a decade as a teacher in public schools. As a somewhat overage graduate student in history, I became interested in the history of American cities and, perhaps as a consequence of prior experience, in the way urban public schools as we know them came into being. This led to curiosity about other urban institutions, especially city politics and bossism in the later nineteenth century.

"Specific interest in San Francisco and its Blind Boss, Christopher Augustine Buckley, resulted from several circumstances. My mentor at the University of California, Santa Barbara, Alexander B. Callow, Jr., had investigated Buckley when he was a graduate student. Next I accepted a teaching position in the San Francisco Bay area. Then luck led me to an acquaintance with Buckley's son and daughter-in-law, who encouraged my work. And finally the work itself

led to two conclusions: one, that the boss was a fascinating individual whose life would make a helluva book; two, the history of his city had much to tell us about urban politics and its implications in general.

"Although I have wanted to write (with nothing to write about) since undergraduate days, I do not consider myself principally a writer. I am first a historian and teacher. Still, writing and the research that accompanies it are important (perhaps inseparable) aspects of the business of teaching, an extension of teaching to a different and wider audience beyond the classroom. And there is something highly exciting (and not a little scary) about seeing one's own work committed irretrievably to print."

BIOGRAPHICAL/CRITICAL SOURCES: Annals of the American Academy of Political and Social Science, November, 1975; *American Historical Review,* April, 1976.

*   *   *

BUNUEL, Luis 1900-

PERSONAL: Born February 22, 1900, in Calanda, Spain; son of Leonardo (a landowner) and Maria (Portoles) Bunuel; married Jeanne Rucar, 1934; children: Rafael, Juan Luis. *Education:* Attended University of Madrid, 1920-23, and Academie du Cinema, 1925. *Office:* c/o Greenwich Film Production, 72 Avenue des Champs-Elysees 75008, Paris, France.

CAREER: Writer, producer, and director of motion pictures. Director of motion pictures in Mexico, including "Las hurdes" (documentary; released in the U.S. as "Land Without Bread"), 1932, "Gran casino," 1947, "El gran calavera" (released in the U.S. as "The Gread Madcap"), 1949, "Susana" (also released in the U.S. as "The Devil and the Flesh"), 1951, "La hija del engano" (released in the U.S. as "Daughter of Deceit"), 1951, "Una mujer sin amor," 1951, "La illusion viaja en tranvia" (released in the U.S. as "Illusion Travels by Streetcar"), 1953. Worked as actor and assistant to Jean Epstein on "Mauprat," 1926, "La sirene du tropiques," 1927, and "The Fall of the House of Usher," 1928; language dubber for Warner Bros., in Paris, France, 1932-34, and Spain, 1935; executive producer in Spain, 1935-36; technical adviser for Metro-Goldwyn-Mayer in Hollywood, Calif., on uncompleted motion picture, "Cargo of Innocence," 1938; assistant on anti-Nazi film projects for Museum of Modern Art in New York, N.Y., 1940; filmmaker for U.S. Army, 1940-43; language dubber for Warner Bros., in Hollywood, 1944-46.

AWARDS, HONORS: Best director award from Cannes Film Festival and International Critics' Prize, both 1951, both for "Los Olvidados"; best avant-garde film award from Cannes Film Festival, 1952, for "Subida al cielo"; special international jury prize from Cannes Film Festival, 1958, for "Nazarin"; *hors concours* recognition from Cannes Film Festival, 1960, for "The Young One"; Golden Palm from Cannes Film Festival, 1961, for "Viridiana"; Golden Lion of St. Mark from Venice Film Festival, 1967, for "Belle de jour"; Order of the Yugoslav Flag, 1971; Academy Award for best foreign language film from Academy of Motion Picture Arts and Sciences, 1972, for "Le Charm discret de la bourgeoisie"; and other film awards.

*WRITINGS—*Screenplays published in English; also director: (With Julio Alejandro) *Viridiana* (produced in Spain by Gustavo Alatriste and Uninci Films 59, 1961; also see below), Interspectacles, 1962; (with Alejandro) *El angel exterminador* (title means "The Exterminating Angel"; produced in Mexico by Uninci Films 59, 1962; also see below), Ayma,

1964; (with Alejandro) *Nazarin* (produced in Mexico by Manuel Barbachano Ponce, 1958; adapted from the novel by Benito Perez Galdos; also see below), Belgium Ministre de l'Education National et de la Culture, Service Cinematographique, 1967; (with Salvador Dali) *L'Age d'or* [and] *Un Chien andalou* (title of former means "The Golden Age," produced in France by Vicomte de Noailles, 1930; title of latter means "An Andalusian Dog," co-produced in France with Dali, 1928), translated by Marianne Alexandre from unpublished French manuscripts, Simon & Schuster, 1968.

(With Alejandro) *Three Screenplays: Viridiana, The Exterminating Angel, Simon of the Desert* (latter by Bunuel only, produced in Mexico as "Simon del desierto" by Gustavo Alatriste, 1965; also see above), Orion Press, 1970; (with Jean-Claude Carriere) *Belle de jour* (produced in France by Paris Film Production, 1966; adapted from the novel by Joseph Kessel), translated by Robert Adkinson from the unpublished French manuscript, Simon & Schuster, 1971; (with Alejandro) *Tristana* (produced in Spain by Epoch Film, Talia Film, Selentia Cinematografica, and Les Films Corona, 1970; adapted from the novel by Galdos), translated by Nicholas Fry from the unpublished French manuscript, Simon & Schuster, 1971; (with Alejandro and Luis Alcoriza) *The Exterminating Angel, Nazarin, and Los Olvidados* (latter co-written with Alcoriza, produced in Mexico by Ultramar Films, 1950; also see above), translated by Fry from the unpublished French translations of the Spanish manuscripts, Simon & Schuster, 1972.

Untranslated works; also director of screenplays: *Un Chien andalou* (poems and stories), [Spain], c. 1927; (with Alcoriza) *Los naugragos de la calle de la providencia*, [Mexico], 1958; (with Carriere) *Le Journal d'une femme de chambre* (screenplay; produced in France by Speva-Filmalliance-Filmsonor-Dear, 1964; released in U.S. as "The Diary of a Chambermaid"; adapted from the novel by Octave Mirbeau), Seuil, 1971; (with Carriere) *El discreto encanto de la burguesia* (screenplay; produced in France as "Le Charme discret de la bourgeoisie" by Greenwich Productions, 1972; released in U.S. as "The Discreet Charm of the Bourgeoisie"), Ayme, 1973; (with Carriere) *El fantasma de la liberte* (screenplay; produced in France as "Le Fantome de la liberte" by Greenwich Productions, 1974; released in U.S. as "The Phantom of Liberty"), Ayma, 1975.

Unpublished screenplays; in English; also director: (With Philip Roll) "Robinson Crusoe" (adapted from the novel by Daniel Defoe), Ultramar Films, 1954; (with H. B. Addis) "The Young One" (adapted from the novel by Peter Matthiesen, *Travellin' Man*), Producciones Olmeca, 1960.

Unpublished screenplays; in Spanish; also director: (With Alcoriza) "El Bruto," International Cinematografica, 1952; (with Alcoriza) "El" (also released in U.S. as "This Strange Passion"; adapted from a novel by Mercedes Pinto), Nacional Film, 1952; "Cumbres borrascosas" (also released as "Abismos de pasion"; adapted from the novel, *Wuthering Heights*, by Emily Bronte), Tepeyac, 1953; (with Alcoriza) "El rio y la muerte" (adapted from the novel by Miguel Alvarez Acosta), Clasa Films Mundiales, 1954; (with Eduardo Ugarte) "Ensayo de un crimen" (released in U.S. as "The Criminal Life of Archibaldo de la Cruz"; adapted from a story by Rodolfo Usigli), Alianza Cinematografica, 1955; (with Alcoriza, Louis Sapin, and Charles Dorat) "La Fievre monte a El Pao" (title means "Fever Mounts in El Paso"; adapted from the novel by Henri Castillou), C.I.C.C., Cite Films, Indus Films, Terra Films, Cormoran Films, and Cinematografica Filmex, 1959.

Unpublished screenplays; in French; also director: (With Jean Ferry) "Cela s'appelle l'aurore" (title means "It's Called the Dawn"; adapted from the novel by Emmanuel Robles), Les Films Marceau and Laetitia Film, 1955; (with Alcoriza, Raymond Queneau, and Gabriel Arout) "La Mort en ce jardin" (title means "Death in This Garden"), Dismage and Teperac, 1956; (with Carriere) "La Voie lactee" (released in U.S. as "The Milky Way"), Greenwich Film Productions and Medusa, 1969; (with Carriere) "Cet obscur objet du desir" (released in U.S. as "That Obscure Object of Desire"; suggested from the novel, *La Femme et le pantin*, by Pierre Louys), Serge Silberman, 1977.

SIDELIGHTS: Bunuel once told an interviewer, "I'm still an atheist, thank God." The comment is an apt example of both Bunuel's obsession and disdain for religion as well as his desire to elicit doubletakes from his audience. In his films, Bunuel welds his love/hate attitude towards religion with an ability to jar audiences, especially those from the upper class, into realizing that the world is not entirely safe or predictable. His first film, "An Andalusian Dog," shocked audiences with its opening depiction of a woman's eye being sliced with a straight razor. Bunuel called it "a desperate appeal to violence and crime." But in a career that spans more than fifty years, he has tempered his disposition to violence by directing his talents towards indictments of the bourgeoisie and the Church. He has persisted in his efforts to eliminate complacency and expose the corruption inherent in social convention. "The final sense of my films is this: to repeat, over and over again, in case anyone forgets it or believes the contrary, that we do not live in the best of all possible worlds," he contends.

Bunuel first became interested in art as a student of entomology in Madrid where he met such artists as Jose Ortega y Gasset, Garcia Lorca, and Salvador Dali. Bunuel and Dali became close friends and began attending films together. After the two established Spain's first film club, however, Bunuel moved to Paris and enrolled in the Academie du Cinema. He subsequently obtained an apprenticeship with filmmaker Jean Epstein on two motion pictures, "Mauprat" and "The Fall of the House of Usher." Through Epstein, Bunuel befriended several artists involved in surrealism, including spokesman Andre Breton and painters such as Pablo Picasso, Max Ernst, Giorgio de Chirico, and Joan Miro. The group met informally in cafes throughout Paris, and their discussions helped Bunuel develop his own philosophy of art.

Inspired by the surrealists, Bunuel rushed back to Spain to fetch Dali. Together they returned to Paris and began work on a film scenario. The two agreed early in the venture to avoid conventional narrative techniques. Instead, they decided to use symbols and images from dreams to create a "poetic" effect similar to that being achieved on canvas by Breton, Ernst, and other surrealists. Their efforts resulted in "An Andalusian Dog," a silent, twenty-five-minute film that defied interpretation. It alternately shocked, humored, and confused the audience with a barrage of bizarre images: a character with ants emerging from a hole in his hand; another man hauling a piano weighted by the bodies of two dead horses; and an androgynous bicyclist who, upon toppling over on a curb, leaves only a single, severed hand at the site of his accident. Bunuel, expecting a violent reaction from the opening-night audience, had smuggled rocks into the theatre for his own protection. To his surprise, though, the crowd errupted into applause following the showing.

Throughout the following weeks, Bunuel and Dali were confronted with numerous interpretations of their film, all of which they denied. "The plot is the result of CONSCIOUS *psychic automatism,*" Bunuel insisted, "and, to that extent, it does not attempt to recount a dream, although it profits by a mechanism analogous to that of dreams." He explained that he and Dali selected the images at random, deliberately discarding anything that could be construed as relevant to a logical storyline. "The motivation of the images was ... purely irrational," claimed Bunuel. "They are mysterious and inexplicable to the two collaborators as to the spectator. NOTHING, in the film, SYMBOLIZES ANYTHING."

Embarrassed by the enthusiastic reception accorded "An Andalusian Dog" by the bourgeoisie they had sought to offend, Bunuel and Dali began work on a second film, "The Golden Age," to rectify the situation. Their collaboration was short-lived, however, for Bunuel, upon discovering that Dali had fallen in love with their producer's wife, accused her of disrupting the filmmakers' relationship and tried to strangle her on the first day of shooting. Outraged, Dali stormed from the set and never returned.

"The Golden Age," as completed by Bunuel, proved quite different from its predecessor. Bunuel abandoned the random imagery of "An Andalusian Dog" in favor of a fairly coherent, though extremely disturbing, narrative. The film chronicles the efforts of two lovers to reunite despite the bourgeoisie's attempts to keep them apart. In the first scene, Bunuel compares the bourgeoisie to the scorpion and cuts from a glimpse of the latter to the lovers coupling in the sand. They are suddenly separated by celebrants attending an inaugural address who claim that the couple's moans are annoying the speaker. The film then proceeds to follow the protagonist in his quest for his lover. He encounters characters who reveal the hypocrisy and ennui that symbolize, for Bunuel, the decadence of bourgeois life. When the lovers are finally reunited, the film accelerates into a series of surrealist images depicting age and death. The film ends with Christ escorting fellow revelers from the Marquis de Sade's castle, where they've just participated in an orgy.

Despite the overt and deliberately offensive depiction of social values as practiced by hypocritical bourgeoisie, "The Golden Age" was shown without incident at its premier. On the second night, however, fights broke out in the audience and viewers hurled inkwells at the screen. After the showing, audience members vented their anger by destroying paintings by Dali, Ernst, and Miro on display in the theatre lobby. For Bunuel, who had considered himself an outsider among his surrealist contemporaries after the bourgeoisie's approval of "An Andalusian Dog," "The Golden Age" was an immense triumph.

"The Golden Age" was shown for two months before French censors yielded to public pressure and banned it. Bunuel became the target of right-wing critics eager to preserve the social status quo. Richard-Pierre Bodin wrote: "A film called *L'Age d'Or*—in which I defy any qualified authority to detect the slightest artistic merit—multiplies (in public showings!) its crop of utterly obscene, repugnant, and tawdry episodes. Country, family, religion are dragged through the mire. All those who saved the grandeur of France, all those who have faith in the future of a race which has enlightened the whole world, all those Frenchmen who have been chosen to protect you against the poison of rotten entertainment, now ask what you think of the job our censorship is doing."

In the wake of this violent reaction, numerous other writers rose to Bunuel's defense. His most celebrated supporter, Henry Miller, wrote: "They have called Bunuel every-

thing—traitor, anarchist, pervert, defamer, iconoclast. But lunatic they have not called him. True, it is lunacy he portrays in his film, but it is not of his making. This stinking chaos which for a brief hour or so is amalgamated under his magic wand, this is the lunacy of man's achievements after ten thousand years of civilization."

Although it elicited dramatic responses from viewers, "The Golden Age" was relatively ignored by film scholars until the 1960's, when Bunuel's rejuvenated career sparked a renewed interest in his early works. Its stature then rose to that of classics such as "Potemkin" and "Citizen Kane," and Carlos Fuentes hailed it as "the greatest of the surrealist films and one of the most personal and original works in the history of the cinema."

While the controversy over "The Golden Age" raged in Paris, Bunuel was in Hollywood studying sequences from American films. He was drawn to the film capital by Metro-Goldwyn-Mayer (MGM) with the understanding that he would be permitted to make a film for the studio. The opportunity, however, never arose, and Bunuel returned to Spain in 1932.

His next film, "Land Without Bread," revealed few of the surrealist elements that characterized his previous films. In detailing the plight of an impoverished Spanish village, he replaced surrealism with realism. Bunuel called it "a simple documentary" and declared: "I didn't invent anything. Pierre Unik wrote a scientific, statistical text. We merely wished to show the most abject region of Spain."

"Land Without Bread" was Bunuel's only film during the next fifteen years. After the political uprising in Spain, he obtained work dubbing dialogue for Warner Brothers in Paris and then returned to Hollywood to work for MGM on a project that was eventually abandoned. In 1940, he was hired by the Museum of Modern Art. One of his tasks there was to re-edit footage from the pro-Nazi films of Leni Riefenstahl for use as American propaganda. But as Bunuel recalled: "Riefenstahl's images were so damned good and impressive ... that the effect would be the contrary of what we were aiming at.... Audiences would be overpowered and come out feeling that German might was irresistible." The project was terminated at President Roosevelt's request.

He left the museum soon afterwards when Dali, in *The Secret Life of Salvador Dali*, revealed that Bunuel was both anti-Catholic and a member of the French Communist party. Bunuel later told Carlos Fuentes that he "resigned ... to avoid embarrassing my good friends [at the museum]." He also recalled his final meeting with Dali. "I had decided to give him a good beating," he claimed. "But when I saw him walk down the lobby, I felt a surge of sympathy for the man, too many fond memories came back, our youth.... So I just called him a son of a bitch and told him our friendship was over. He looked nonplused and said, 'Luis, you understand that my remarks were not intended to hurt you, but to publicize myself.' I've never seen him since."

During the mid-1940's Bunuel resumed his work with Warner Brothers. He developed a number of film projects, including one with Man Ray, but was unable to finance them. In 1947 he moved from California to Mexico to begin work on an adaptation of Garcia Lorca's "The House of Bernard Alba." That project also failed to develop into a film, but that same year Bunuel was hired by a Mexican producer to work in that country as a director.

He directed several films that were essentially showcases for popular actors. In the midst of these mediocre ventures, however, Bunuel made "Los Olvidados," an intense and graphic depiction of slum life in Mexico City. The film is often gruesome in its action, for in proposing that life is essentially a struggle, Bunuel unflinchingly presented torture, rape, and incest. Many critics, including Andre Bazin, defended Bunuel's grim portrayal as part of his surrealist heritage. "It is not possible to avoid touching on the surrealism in Bunuel's films," wrote Bazin in a review of "Los Olvidados." "He is . . . one of the rare valuable representatives of this mode. . . . His surrealism is a part of the rich and fortunate influence of a totally Spanish tradition. . . . It reflects a tragic sense of life, which these painters expressed through the ultimate human degradations. . . . But their cruelty, too, served only as a measure of their trust in mankind itself, and in their art."

Bunuel followed "Los Olvidados" with several more entertaining films, including "The Devil and the Flesh" and "The Daughter of Deceit." When an interviewer remarked to Bunuel during the 1960's that many of his early films in Mexico were rather mediocre, Bunuel responded that even his less-ambitious works reflected his philosophy. "I have made several frankly bad pictures," he confessed, 'but not once did I compromise my moral code. . . . My bad films were always decent. I am against conventional morality."

Throughout the 1950's Bunuel was saddled with minuscule budgets and often untrained actors. He nevertheless produced several films that rank among his finest works. In 1952 he made "El," the story of an obsessively jealous bourgeois poet. The following year he directed "Illusion Travels by Streetcar." This film begins with two trolley operators refusing to scrap their dilapidated car. They take the car on an unscheduled run but are unable to convince passengers that they are taking a "joy ride." Soon the car is overrun with characters, each of whom insists on paying fare. The conductor refuses to accept their money, however, for fear that he will be accused of robbery. This conflict results in a parody of freedom as the right to pay for that which is free. As Jean Delmas noted: "All the riders insist on paying, each for his own personal reason, and each resents the fact that in the society they live in, nothing can be free without being suspect. At this level, comedy becomes philosophy."

Bunuel's next film was an adaptation of Emily Bronte's *Wuthering Heights,* a novel that was particularly prized by his surrealist clan during the 1920's. Unfortunately, the small budget and inconsistent casting undermined the eerie romanticism Bunuel was attempting to evoke. He later dismissed it as "a bad film."

Bunuel fared much better with his next effort, an adaptation of Daniel Defoe's *Robinson Crusoe.* Supplied with American actors and financial backing, he managed to sustain a sense of isolation throughout Crusoe's solitary life on the island while at the same time delving into his subconscious and his past. A particularly memorable scene occurs when the exasperated Crusoe shouts God's name from the mountain top, but hears only his own voice echoing in response. Emilio Garcia Riera called this film "a great triumph" for Bunuel. "One could say . . . that the character of Robinson has been created especially for Bunuel," he observed. "For . . . it is precisely through exceptional characters, alienated by circumstance from the elemental norms of common sense and customary morality, that Bunuel often penetrates into the mysterious, and therefore poetical, regions of the human being."

In 1955, Bunuel explored the relationship between sex and death in "The Criminal Life of Archibaldo Cruz." Cruz possesses a magic box that, when touched, causes the death of anyone he wishes. As a child, his first target is his wet-nurse. Later, he instigates the deaths of a number of people who are subjects in his sexual fantasies. He becomes guilt ridden and confesses to the police, but is released when it becomes impossible to prove that his victims perished through his actions. When he finally attempts to actually murder a woman, he is foiled by a bizarre mishap. He then falls in love with the woman and marries her. "The one point which makes it outstanding is the portrait of the central figure Bunuel offers us," contended Riera. "This central character is really an assassin who wishes and enjoys the death of his fellow beings and who, nevertheless, is quite innocent before the eyes of society; innocent to such a point that when the film ends, he is moving toward the enjoyment of a happy and peaceful future."

Three years later Bunuel made "Nazarin," which many critics consider one of his finest achievements. It details a priest's struggle to live a Christ-like existence. After suffering excommunication for sheltering a whore, Nazarin wanders about the Mexican countryside and unintentionally causes many catastrophes. As Louis Seguin explained, Bunuel "gives rein fully to his unfrocked priest in the certainty that, rejected by the Church, but always inhabited by a desperate love of God and men, he can only do what he does: sow fire and murder in his wake." Despite constant failure, though, Nazarin persists in his efforts to lead a Christian life. "What counts for Bunuel is that Nazarin applies to his own life the perception enunciated by Jesus," wrote Joan Mellen, "and like Jesus he is a man willing to stand up to the repressive ruling order." Bunuel contended: "If Christ were to return, they'd crucify him again. It is possible to be *relatively* Christian, but the *absolutely* pure, the absolutely innocent man—he's bound to fail. . . . I am sure that if Christ came back, the Church, the powerful churchmen, would condemn Him again."

By film's end, Nazarin has rejected the Church and turned against it. Disillusioned, he is offered a pineapple by a sympathetic woman, and the look on his face reveals that he has found a new faith: in humanity. Penelope Gilliatt wrote, "When Nazarin, the failed Christ figure, is on the road and is offered a pineapple, symbol of help and charity, one feels a flash of hope for loosening of human bondage." By putting his faith in humanity, according to Gavin Lambert, Nazarin "finds a reality with which to replace an illusion, and the film itself goes beyond protest to reach affirmation." Ado Kyrou came to a similar conclusion, finding "Nazarin" not merely a renunciation of Christianity but also a celebration of humanity. "This film places love and its Christian caricature in confrontation," wrote Kyrou. "Bunuel contrasts those who love with a man who adores a non-existent being. . . . 'Love your neighbor,' says the man of the Christian myth. 'Love women and your companions,' says Bunuel. The first precept leads to ideological wails, to resignation; the second, to love and rebellion." Kyrou concluded by calling the film one "charged with dynamite, hope, love and certainty—a film addressed to mankind."

Bunuel returned to Spain in 1961 to direct "Viridiana," his first film in that country since "Las hurdes." Ranked by many critics as one of his finest films, "Viridiana" is a variation on the faith-in-humanity theme of "Nazarin." A devout woman, Viridiana is duped by her bizarre uncle into believing that she has lost her virginity on the eve of her entry into the convent. Though she plans to leave her uncle's estate immediately, she suddenly becomes its owner when her uncle commits suicide. She decides to accept her new role and converts the home into a haven for beggars and cripples.

But the vagrants simply exploit Viridiana's Christian charity without embracing Christian tenets. While Viridiana is away one evening, the ingrates stage a raucous banquet and orgy. When she returns to find the house in shambles and the beggars either drunk, sleeping, or fighting, several of them overpower her and rape her. The film ends with Viridiana joining a card game as her belongings, including a cross, nails, and a crown of thorns, burn outside.

Because Bunuel submitted "Viridiana" to Spanish censors in sections, they never perceived the anti-Christian emphasis. When it was shown in Cannes at the film festival, it was a huge success and was awarded the Golden Palm. But Spanish officials responded with outrage to the film's content. The film was banned and its censors fired from their positions. Even the pope condemned it. Bunuel, however, was baffled by the criticism. "It was not my intention to blaspheme," he responded, "but of course Pope John XXIII knows more than I do about these things." He also addressed charges that he had seemed to make a film that justified maliciousness. "I am also reproached for my cruelty," he said. "Where is it in the film? The novice proves her humanity. The old man, a complicated human being, is capable of kindness towards human beings and towards a lowly bee whose life he doesn't hesitate to rescue." Regarding Viridiana's transformation, he added: "I don't see why people complain. My heroine is more of a virgin at the denouement than she was at the start." Perhaps David Robinson summed up Bunuel's attitude best when he wrote, "The film's total effect is invigorating rather than depressing because Bunuel values them all alike as men, and likes them all because they are funny and human."

Despite critical acclaim, "Virdiana" was also banned in France, and Bunuel once again found himself amid controversy. His reaction was to return to Mexico to make another film, "The Exterminating Angel." It concerns a group of bourgeois Mexicans who meet together after attending an opera and find themselves unable to leave the premises. The doors of the home are open; the guests simply cannot leave. No explanation is given. What results, however, is a complete breakdown in the social order cherished by the bourgeois. Hunger and thirst become the primary motivation for the characters' actions, and tension becomes violence. "Coarseness, violence and filth have become our inseparable companions," Bunuel commented. "Death is better than this abject promiscuity." But the trapped figures in "The Exterminating Angel" do not die. They finally escape from the house and flee to a church. But as Bunuel exposes the restrictions imposed by class society as affectations and mannerisms, which conceal the animal-like will to survive that makes all people equal, he similarly indicts organized religion. At film's end, the bourgeois characters discover themselves unable to leave the church. "The implication," declared Randall Conrad, "is that to be free they will now have to kill their host, God."

Bunuel traveled to France for his next film, "The Diary of a Chambermaid." The film details the encounters of Celestine, a chambermaid, with a variety of characters, including Monteil, her employer, who enjoys seducing the chambermaids and firing his rifle; Madame Monteil, a compulsive hygienic who abstains from sex because of the pain it causes her; Captain Mauger, a soldier living with his common-law wife, Rose, whom he eventually evicts in order to pursue Celestine; and Joseph, the coachman whom Celestine loves but whom she nonetheless turns in to the police for having murdered a young girl. Throughout the film, Celestine uses her charms to the best advantage, encouraging Monteil, Cap-

tain Mauger, and Joseph with their romantic notions. Ultimately, as Peter Harcourt noted, she makes the wrong decision. "She sits on her bed, impatient with Mauger's unctuousness," he wrote, "biting her little finger as she recognizes her fate." He added that "there is no sense of divine retribution. The dice have simply rolled the wrong way." The film concludes with Joseph in a cafe watching a Fascist rally. Having been found not guilty by the court, he is now a supporter of the Fascists in Paris. Tom Milne called the last scene "a brilliantly ominous evocation, not only of the imminent rise of Hitler, but of the reverberations which still smolder under the surface today." Similarly, Conrad summarized "The Diary of a Chambermaid" as "Bunuel's strongest politically," and acknowledged it as "a global expression of the pessimism which is after all inherent in Bunuel's vision."

Bunuel returned to Mexico for "Simon of the Desert." The film is based loosely on the life of St. Simon Stylites, a preacher who spoke from a small platform overlooking the desert. More brutally funny than his previous efforts, "Simon of the Desert" reveals the uselessness of Christianity in a world that prizes love over abstract faith, action over prayer. In one scene, Simon performs a miracle, restoring an amputee's hands. The onlookers judge Simon's deed as unimpressive. The former amputee immediately uses his restored limbs to strike his child. Eventually, Simon accompanies Satan, who, as an alluring woman, had previously tempted him, to a bar filled with frenzied teenage dancers. Simon is confronted with the failure of his own actions and preachings to deter humanity from sin.

When Bunuel finally settled in France in 1966, he focused his attentions on the destructiveness of social conventions. In "Belle de jour," he depicts Severin, a woman whose Catholic beliefs were so deeply ingrained that she was incapable of consummating her marriage. She resorts instead to fantasies in which she is degraded by her husband and coachmen. Finally, she decides to overcome her guilt-produced fears by working during the day as a prostitute for an affluent madam. She soon learns, however, that the sex her clients desire involves the enactment of their fantasies. When she does enjoy what appears to be a sexually satisfying relationship, it is with a gangster who follows her home. Fearing that her husband will discover everything, she urges the visitor to leave. The film ends with the gangster shooting her husband before being killed by the police. The husband survives, though blinded and paralyzed. He has learned of his wife's actions from a friend who discovered her at the brothel. Severin assures him that she no longer has any sexual fantasies, at which point he rises from his wheelchair and suggests they take a vacation. Severin then gazes out the window and hears the coachmen's bells that signify a resumption of the fantasies.

With the enormous critical acclaim that was accorded "Belle de jour," Bunuel finally began to receive recognition as one of the world's greatest filmmakers. He began a series of collaborations with producer Serge Silberman and fellow screenwriter Jean-Claude Carriere. In 1969, Bunuel directed "The Milky Way," in which he traced the history of Christianity through the adventures of two travelers. Throughout the film, Bunuel tests the validity of Christian dogma. Oswaldo Capriles called the film "a single-minded, coherent compendium of the devastating reasons for opposing religion as an historical phenomenon, as rational thought, and as providing transcendence."

Bunuel's next film, "Tristana," is a reworking of the sexual repression theme of "Belle de jour." Tristana is a woman totally deprived of freedom by her guardian, Don Lope. An aristocratic lecher, Don Lope adheres to a double standard that permits him the sexual license he paranoically denies Tristana. "The only way to keep a woman honest," Don Lope insists, "is to break her leg and keep her home." Tristana rebels against her mentor by eloping with a young artist. She returns within two years, however, unmarried and disease-stricken. Because of her affliction, her leg is amputated. She takes to teasing a mute lad. As Joan Mellen noted, "Tristana is a woman whose sexuality has been perverted by a fear of seduction by an older, forbidding father figure, and who can now respond only to the brutal and the perverse. In the end, Tristana finally rids herself of Don Lope by opening the bedroom window for the now sickly guardian and allowing the cold air to cause a fatal heart attack.

There is little sense of victory in Don Lope's death. As Bunuel implies in film after film, the parasitic Christian customs and social conventions he exposes are too deeply engrained in society to become vulnerable to his cinematic assaults. Mellen wrote that "Bunuel has relentlessly and brilliantly exposed the destruction of the individual by a corrupt, hypocritical moral code which makes no pretense of improving a society in which class animosities are deepening and brutality is growing." For Bunuel, true freedom involves the choice of the individual to separate from society. This is a choice society guarantees, but, by its parasitic nature, cannot grant. "Group solidarity was a tremendous thing among the surrealists," Bunuel related. "Breton would call us in to sit in judgment if we deviated from the group morality. I learned then that being free is not doing whatever you want, but acting in solidarity with friends you love and respect. But then, by choosing a certain morality, you are not really free at all. Only crypto-Fascists pretend they are ideologically free. Surrealism taught me that man is never free yet fights for what he can never be. That is tragic."

The notion of freedom as a destructive and deceiving element in society is embellished in Bunuel's next two films, "The Discreet Charm of the Bourgeoisie" and "The Phantom of Liberty." In the former, several bourgeois characters find themselves unable to finish their extravagant meals. Bunuel's contention seems to be that the bourgeoisie's wealth affords them no greater escape from a repressive society. Raymond Durgnat declared that "Bunuel has selected only those meals whose bill of fare—or circumstances, or relationships with dream, love, or business—illustrates how a round of dinner parties can do as little to preserve their participants from the emptiness which society has sowed within their hearts as communing with nature could do to redeem the Victorian middle class from its materialism."

In "The Phantom of Liberty," Bunuel begins with a reenactment of the action depicted in Francisco Goya's painting, "The Third of May," as a firing squad executes a group of enemy soldiers. But whereas Goya's work is a passionate plea for peace, Bunuel's film exposes the absurdness of that plea. "Down with freedom!" shout the executioners' targets. "Long live the chains!" Throughout the remainder of the film, Bunuel reveals how society's faith in Christianity and social conventions perpetuates an order that often spawns absurd and criminal actions. In the final sequence, police charge a group of protesters who shout the same epithets as the victims in the initial sequence. For Bunuel, history's lessons are useless: by denying the past and perpetuating a social order that promotes destruction, humanity imprisons itself.

Bunuel's last film during the 1970's, "That Obscure Object of Desire," is a variation on the theme previously explored in both "The Executing Angel" and "The Discreet Charm of the Bourgeoisie." In this film, the object of desire is the virginity of Conchita, a young Spanish woman being pursued by Mathieu, a French businessman. For Mathieu, Conchita's sexual cooperation is always on the verge of acquisition. He tries to use his powers as her employer for seductive purposes, but she quits her job. When Mathieu tries to bribe Conchita's mother into delivering her to him, Conchita becomes incensed and leaves the city. Eventually, Mathieu and Conchita live together, but she continues to withhold herself from him. She then convinces him to give her a home of her own. After doing so, she insults him be feigning sexual intercourse with another man while Mathieu watches through an iron gate. Conchita returns to Mathieu's home the next day, though, and reveals that what he witnessed the previous night was only a simulation. Mathieu then beats her. The film ends with Mathieu and Conchita apparently reconciled, strolling arm-in-arm through a shopping district when a bomb planted by terrorists detonates and kills them.

"That Obscure Object of Desire" is one of Bunuel's many subtle exposes of the bourgeois mentality. Mathieu is not concerned with Conchita, except as a vehicle through which he can prove his power over women. Neither is Mathieu interested in the terrorists whose actions serve as a background to the film. Conchita, however, is as much to blame for her predicament as Mathieu. She teases Mathieu and manipulates his desire in order to further her own material worth. For her, the terrorists are simply another instrument she can use in her relationship with Mathieu. Ultimately, both Mathieu and Conchita fall victim to the terrorists who refuse to accept the parasitic social order maintained by the couple.

Since the mid-1960's, Bunuel has refused to acknowlege any long-range filmmaking projects. He seems content simply listening to classical music and studying insects. "I like idleness," he told an interviewer. "I enjoy my days without doing anything. I am never bored." But he also laments the silence that has existed between Dali and himself since 1930. "I do hope I can invite him to drink a glass of champagne before we both die." In 1975 he finally convinced himself to hang a portrait Dali had painted during the 1920's. "Thirty-five years is too long for a fight."

Bunuel's feelings towards the cinema have also changed during his fifty years as a filmmaker. In 1953 he contended that "in the hands of a free spirit, the cinema is a magnificent and dangerous weapon." But in 1974, with the release of "The Phantom of Liberty," he reiterated Breton's last words to him and acknowledged that "it is no longer possible to scandalize people as we did in 1930." Bunuel also mentioned that he hopes the cinema will "give us the ease of a quest for pleasure and inquiry which isn't followed by the pounding hooves of guilt." He told Gilliatt: "I'm not a Christian, but I'm not an atheist, either. I'm weary of hearing that accidental old aphorism of mine 'I'm not an atheist, thank God.' It's outworn. Dead leaves. In 1951, I made a small film called 'Mexican Bus Ride,' about a village too poor to support a church and a priest. The place was serene, because no one suffered from guilt. It's guilt we must escape from, not God."

AVOCATIONAL INTERESTS: Classical music, entomology.

BIOGRAPHICAL/CRITICAL SOURCES—Books: Henry Miller, *The Cosmological Eye,* New Directions, 1939; Ado Kyrou, *Bunuel: An Introduction,* Simon & Schuster, 1963; Carlos Rebolledo, *Luis Bunuel,* Editions Universitaires,

1964; Raymond Durgnat, *Luis Bunuel*, University of California Press, 1967, revised edition, 1978; Frank Stauffacher, *Art in Cinema*, Arno, 1968; J. H. Matthews, *Surrealism in Film*, University of Michigan Press, 1971; Peter Harcourt, *Six European Directors*, Viking, 1972; Michael Gould, *Surrealism in Cinema*, A. S. Barnes, 1976; J. Francisco Aranda, *Luis Bunuel: A Critical Biography*, translated by David Robinson, Da Capo Press, 1976; Joan Mellen, editor, *The World of Luis Bunuel*, Oxford University Press, 1978.

Periodicals: *Le Figaro*, December 7, 1930; *Sight and Sound*, January-March, 1954, summer, 1962, autumn, 1964; *Yale French Studies*, summer, 1956; *Film Quarterly*, spring, 1960, spring, 1967, winter, 1970-71, summer, 1975; *Film Culture*, summer, 1960, spring, 1962, summer, 1966; *Positif*, March, 1961, July, 1962; *Etudes Cinematographiques*, spring, 1963; *Jeune Cinema*, February, 1966; *Village Voice*, May 2, 1968, May 9, 1968, May 5, 1980; *Show*, April, 1970; *Cine Cubano*, 1970-71; *New York Times*, November 3, 1972, February 25, 1973, October 16, 1977, June 10, 1979; *New York Times Magazine*, March 11, 1973; *American Scholar*, summer, 1973; *Society*, July-August, 1973; *Film Comment*, May-June, 1975; *Cineaste*, Volume VII, no. 3, 1976; *New Yorker*, December 5, 1977.*

—Sketch by Les Stone

* * *

BURCH, Claire R. 1925-

PERSONAL: Born February 19, 1925, in New York, N.Y. *Education:* New York University, B.A., 1947. *Home:* 463 West St., New York, N.Y. 10014.

CAREER: Painter, with group and solo shows in the United States and France, including Brooklyn Museum and Ruth White Gallery. Poet, playwright, and author. *Member:* Schizophrenics Anonymous International, New York Playwrights Cooperative. *Awards, honors:* Art awards include first prize for representational painting from Guild Hall, 1965; first prize for watercolor from North Shore Community Art Center, 1965.

WRITINGS: Winter Bargains (poems), Roko Gallery, 1964; (editor) *Careers in Psychiatry*, Macmillan, 1969; *Stranger in the Family: A Guide to Living With the Emotionally Disturbed*, Bobbs-Merrill, 1972; *Notes of a Survivor* (self-illustrated), Westbeth's Poet's Press, 1972; *The Secret Songs of Claire Burch: A Blues to Be Called Crazy When Crazy's All There Is* (includes musical play "A Blues to Be Called Crazy When Crazy's All There Is"), Westbeth's Poet's Press, 1972. Also author of play "Ten Cents a Dance."*

* * *

BURGESS, Eric (Alexander) 1912-

PERSONAL: Born September 28, 1912, in London, England; son of Oliver (a civil servant) and Lucy (Alexander) Burgess; married Ena May Morley (died, 1966); children: Oliver Mark. *Education:* Attended grammar school in Norwood, England. *Home:* 215 Redland Rd., Bristol, Gloucestershire, England. *Agent:* Elspeth Gordon, Manor House, Popes Ave., Strawberry Hill, Middlesex, England.

CAREER: Officer of customs and excise in England, 1932-62; writer. *Military service:* Served with Fleet Air Arm in Ceylon and India.

WRITINGS—Suspense novels: A Knife for Celeste, M. Joseph, 1948; *The Malice of Monday*, M. Joseph, 1950; *Accident to Adeline*, M. Joseph, 1952; *Divided We Fall*, Collins, 1959; *A Killing Frost*, Collins, 1961; *Closely Confined*,

R. Hale, 1962; *Deadly Deceit*, R. Hale, 1963; *Exit Pretty Poll*, R. Hale, 1968.

Nonfiction: (With Dick Fagan) *Men of the Tideway* (biography), R. Hale, 1966.

Science fiction novels: (With Arthur Friggens) *Mortorio*, R. Hale, 1973; (with Friggens) *Anti-Zota*, R. Hale, 1973; (with Friggens) *Mortorio II*, R. Hale, 1975; *The Mants of Myrmedon*, R. Hale, 1977; (with Friggens) *Hounds of Heaven*, R. Hale, 1979. Contributor to magazines, including *Authors'* and *Crime Writers'*. Editor of *Flip*, 1945-46.

WORK IN PROGRESS: The Hounds of Hell, a science fiction novel, with Arthur Friggens; *Gullible's Travels*, a satire, with Friggens.*

* * *

BURKE, Stanley 1923-

PERSONAL: Born in 1923; children: four. *Education:* Attended University of British Columbia. *Residence:* Vancouver, British Columbia, Canada.

CAREER: Canadian Broadcasting Corp., worked as foreign correspondent and host and interviewer on series, "Air of Death"; writer. President of United Nations press corps, 1960. *Awards, honors:* Award from Resource Ministers' Council and Wilderness Award, both for series, "Air of Death."

WRITINGS—Satire: Frog Fables and Beaver Tales, James Lorimer, 1973; *The Day of the Glorious Revolution*, James Lorimer, 1974; *Blood, Sweat and Bears*, J. J. Douglas, 1976; (with Roy Peterson) *Swamp Song*, Douglas & McIntyre, 1978.

WORK IN PROGRESS: A nonfiction book on Canada and cultural conflict.*

* * *

BURKETT, Jack 1914-

PERSONAL: Born July 19, 1914, in London, England; married Rose Searson (a physiotherapist), May, 1937; children: Colin Ronald. *Education:* University of London, M.A., 1969. *Home:* 3 Whitehouse Close, Chalfont St. Peter, Buckinghamshire, England.

CAREER: Worked variously in charge of information services for Hawker Siddeley Nuclear Power Co., in charge of information services for Rolls Royce Ltd., and in charge of information services for Associated Octel Ltd.; *Nuclear Power*, London, England, assistant editor, 1960-62; Polytechnic of North London, London, lecturer, 1962-65; Ealing Technical College, London, principal lecturer, 1965-76; writer and consultant, 1976—. *Military service:* Royal Air Force, pilot and specialist navigation instructor, 1944. *Member:* Library Association (fellow).

WRITINGS: Microrecording in Libraries, Library Association, 1957; *Special Libraries and Information Services in the United Kingdom*, Library Association, 1961, 2nd edition, 1965; *Special Materials in the Library*, Library Association, 1964; *Concise Guide to the Literature of Geography*, Ealing Technical College, 1967; *How to Find Out in Electrical Engineering*, Pergamon, 1967; *Trends in Special Librarianship*, Bingley, 1968; *Special Libraries and Documentation Services in the Netherlands*, Pergamon, 1968.

Industrial and Related Libraries and Information Services in the United Kingdom, Library Association, 1972; *Government and Related Library and Information Services in the United Kingdom*, Library Association, 1974; (with P. L.

Ward) *Introductory Guide to Research in Library and Information Studies in the United Kingdom,* Library Association, 1975; (contributor) *Textbook on Library Practice,* Library and Information Network, 1977, Aslib, 1978. Also author of *Literature Searching in Science and Technology,* 1978. Contributor to *Agricultural Research Index* and *Medical Research Index.*

SIDELIGHTS: Burkett told *CA:* "I have enjoyed practicing and teaching library and information science through the years but it is really satisfying, having retired, to do all the things I have planned: writing without undue pressures and putting down the pen when the sun shines. I was supposed to take up oil painting and improve my piano playing, but somehow with retirement there is still not enough time in a day. I love visiting Europe whenever I can, especially if offered a consultancy."

*   *   *

BURNHAM, Walter Dean 1930-

PERSONAL: Born June 15, 1930, in Columbus, Ohio; son of Alfred Huntington, Jr., and Gertrude (Hamburger) Burnham; married Patricia Mullan (an art historian), June 7, 1958; children: John Patrick, Anne More. *Education:* Johns Hopkins University, A.B., 1951; Harvard University, A.M., 1958, Ph.D., 1962. *Religion:* Roman Catholic. *Home:* 15 Acacia Ave., Newton, Mass. 02167. *Office:* Department of Political Science, Massachusetts Institute of Technology, Cambridge, Mass. 02139.

CAREER: Kenyon College, Gambier, Ohio, assistant professor of political science, 1961-64; Haverford College, Haverford, Pa., assistant professor of political science, 1964-66; Washington University, St. Louis, Mo., associate professor, 1966-70, professor of political science, 1970-71; Massachusetts Institute of Technology, Cambridge, professor of political science, 1971—. Fellow of Center for Advanced Study in the Behavioral Sciences, 1979-80. *Military service:* U.S. Army, 1953-56. *Member:* American Political Science Association, American Academy of Arts and Sciences, Social Science History Association. *Awards, honors:* Social Science Research Council fellowship, 1963-64; grants from National Science Foundation, 1968-73; Guggenheim fellowship, 1974-75.

WRITINGS: Presidential Ballots, 1836-1892, Johns Hopkins Press, 1955; (editor and contributor) *The American Party Systems,* Oxford University Press, 1967, revised edition, 1975; *Critical Elections and the Mainsprings of American Politics,* Norton, 1970; (editor with Martha W. Weinberg, and contributor) *American Politics and Public Policy,* M.I.T. Press, 1978. Contributor to political science journals.

WORK IN PROGRESS: Dynamics of American Politics; research on historical dynamics of American politics and on recent crises in American politics.

SIDELIGHTS: Burnham commented to *CA:* "For many years I have been primarily concerned with the causes, symptoms, and consequences of the decay of democracy in the United States, and more recently with the manifest crisis of regime (political institutions, structures, and legitimacy) which currently grips the United States. I have lived in Britain for a year and have visited most of Western Europe, Israel, and the Republic of South Africa."

*   *   *

BURNS, Jim 1936-

PERSONAL: Born February 19, 1936, in Preston, Lanca-shire, England; son of James (a seaman and laborer) and Janet (a mill worker; maiden name, Barry) Burns; married, 1958 (divorced, 1973); children: Christopher, Allen. *Education:* Bolton Institute of Technology, B.A. (with honors), 1980. *Home:* 7 Ryelands Crescent, Larches Estate, Preston, Lancashire, England.

CAREER: Poet. Worked in mills, offices, and factories in England, 1952-64; writer and editor, 1964—. *Military service:* British Army, 1954-57.

WRITINGS: Some Poems, Crank Books, 1965; *Some More Poems,* R Books, 1966; *My Sad Story and Other Poems,* New Voice, 1967; *Cells: Prose Pieces,* Grossteste Press, 1967; *Saloon Bar: Three Jim Burns Stories,* Ferry Press, 1967; *The Store of Things* (poems), Phoenix Pamphlet Poets Press, 1969; *Types: Prose Pieces and Poems,* Second Aeon Publications, 1970; *A Single Flower* (poems), Andium Press, 1972; *Leben in Preston* (poems), Palmenpresse, 1973; *The Goldfish Speaks From Beyond the Grave* (poems), Salamander Imprint, 1976; *Fred Engels bei Woolworth* (poems), Rotbuch (Berlin), 1977; *Catullus in Preston* (poems), Cameo Club Alley Press, 1979; *Aristotle's Grill* (poems), Platform Poets, 1979; *Notes From a Greasy Spoon* (poems), Lettera Press, 1980.

Work represented in anthologies, including *Young Commonwealth Poets '65,* Heinemann, 1965; *New British Poetry,* Screeches Publications, 1965; *Tunes on a Tin Whistle,* Pergamon Press, 1966; *An Anthology of Revolutionary Poetry,* Smyrna Press, 1968; *Children of Albion,* Penguin, 1969; *Doves for the Seventies,* Corgi Books, 1969. Contributor to newspapers and magazines, including *Guardian, Ambit, Phoenix, New Society, Tribune, Jazz Journal,* and *Jazz Monthly.* Editor of *Move* (magazine), 1964-68, and *Palantir* (magazine), 1976—.

WORK IN PROGRESS: Poems, articles, reviews, and short stories.

SIDELIGHTS: Jim Burns told *CA:* "I try to write poetry which uses my everyday experiences. It's personal in that sense, but not, I hope, in the sense of being obscure. I like clarity and humor, and I think it's possible to be direct and still be lyrical. However, as an editor, I also try to present a fairly broad spectrum of contemporary work, and I try not to let my own leanings insofar as my writing is concerned blind me to qualities in other people's work. I'm also keen to place poetry in a context where it is part of a general approach involving music, art, politics, and other matters. This is the policy I follow when editing *Palantir,* and the result is that the magazine offers a mixture of poetry and prose.

"When I edited *Move* in the 1960's, I saw the situation as being slightly different in that it was then more necessary to provide a platform for poets who weren't being given the attention they deserved. The situation then was that I thought it necessary to make *Move* such a platform and tie it in with other similar poetry magazines, which were providing what was, in a sense, a notion of community for what might be called the 'nonestablishment' poets in Britain. And I wanted to get them into print alongside similar writers from the United States and Canada. I see *Palantir* as offering something different. Poetry is strongly featured, but the magazine is not just a poetry publication. I think it's necessary at this stage to keep poetry in the mainstream of activity rather than isolating it.

"As for critical opinions of my own work, perhaps I can quote John Freeman who said in his review of *A Single Flower,* 'It is an achievement both of personality and of style. Indeed, stylishness pervades the book despite its apparent simplicity.' Harold Massingham said of *The Goldfish Speaks From Beyond the Grave,* 'He's off-beat rather than offhand; and much in the poetry is off the cuff, his situations directly evoked, and all done as if he were at your elbow.' Bel Mooney said, 'Some of the poems are very slight—little more than hastily jotted diary notes. Others seem exercises in 'wit' and 'imagination'—with, certainly, no profundity. But in some, the frame of reference is complex and erudite—less spontaneous than you might think. And in others the tension creates poems of real value and insight.' Perhaps I also ought to quote Russell Davies who said, 'he writes, in fact, prose broken up.'''

BIOGRAPHICAL/CRITICAL SOURCES: New Society, December 7, 1967; *Guardian,* August 10, 1972; *Daily Telegraph Magazine,* March 2, 1973; *Cambridge Quarterly,* Volume VI, number 3, 1975; *New Statesman,* December 3, 1976; *Times Educational Supplement,* December 3, 1976; *North West Arts News,* March/April, 1977; *Artful Reporter,* May, 1980.

* * *

BURROWS, John 1945-

PERSONAL: Born November 19, 1945, in London, England. *Education:* Received B.A. from Victoria University of Manchester. *Agent:* Michael Imison, Jan Van Loewen Ltd., 81-83 Shaftesbury Ave., London W1V 8BX, England.

CAREER: Actor and director.

WRITINGS: (With John Harding) *The Golden Pathway Annual* (two-act play; first produced in Sheffield, England, 1973; produced in London, England, 1974), Heinemann, 1975.

Co-author of unpublished plays: "For Sylvia," first produced in London, England, 1972; "Loud Reports," first produced in London, 1975; "Dirty Giant" (musical), first produced in Coventry, England, 1975; "The Manly Bit," first produced in London, 1976; "Do You Dig It?" (television play), first broadcast in 1976.*

* * *

BUSTANOBY, Andre S(teven) 1930-

PERSONAL: Surname is pronounced Bus-*tan*-o-bee; born December 29, 1930, in Englewood, N.J.; son of Raymond Andre and Marian (Boyce) Bustanoby; married Faydean Gregg, December 1, 1952; children: Stephen Gregg, David Paul, Peter John, Jonathan Lee. *Education:* Nyack College, B.S., 1957; Dallas Theological Seminary, Th.M., 1961; Azusa Pacific College, M.A., 1973. *Home and office:* 12018 Long Ridge Lane, Bowie, Md. 20715.

CAREER: Ordained Baptist minister, 1959; pastor of Baptist churches in Arlington, Va., 1961-68, and Fullerton, Calif., 1968-73; private practice of marriage and family therapy in Bowie, Md., 1973—. *Military service:* U.S. Air Force, 1948-52; served in Korea; became staff sergeant. *Member:* National Association of Social Workers (associate), American Association for Marriage and Family Therapy (clinical member; president-elect of Middle Atlantic Division, 1982-84), Evangelical Theological Society.

WRITINGS: You Can Change Your Personality, Zondervan, 1976; *But I Didn't Want a Divorce,* Zondervan, 1978; (with wife, Fay Bustanoby) *Just Talk to Me,* Zondervan, 1981. Author of "Heart and Mind," a column in *Today's Christian Woman.*

WORK IN PROGRESS: It's Okay to Be Human (tentative title); *Infidelity: Why It Happens and What to Do About It* (tentative title); research on the biblical doctrine of man.

SIDELIGHTS: Bustanoby commented to *CA:* "My motivation for writing comes from problems I see in the lives of my clients in marriage and family therapy.

"I began writing magazine articles for religious periodicals and have gained a great deal from the guidance of editors. While in the pastoral ministry, I wrote all my sermons, which helped develop a discipline for writing."

* * *

BUTLER, (Frederick) Guy 1918-

PERSONAL: Born January 21, 1918, in Cradock, Cape Province, South Africa; son of Ernest Collett and Alice E. (Stringer) Butler; married Jean Murray Satchwell, 1942; children: three sons, one daughter. *Education:* Rhodes University, M.A., 1939; Brasenose College, Oxford, M.A., 1947. *Home:* "High Corner," Somerset St., Grahamstown 6140, South Africa. *Office:* Department of English, Rhodes University, Grahamstown, Cape Province, South Africa.

CAREER: University of the Witwatersrand, Johannesburg, South Africa, lecturer in English, 1948-50; Rhodes University, Grahamstown, Cape Province, South Africa, professor of English, 1952—. *Military service:* South African Army, 1940-45; served in Egypt, Lebanon, Italy, and England. *Member:* P.E.N., English Academy of Southern Africa, 1820 Settler Monument Foundation, Shakespeare Birthplace Trust. *Awards, honors:* D.Litt. from University of Natal, 1970; C.N.A. award for literature, 1975.

WRITINGS: An Aspect of Tragedy (literary criticism), Rhodes University, 1953; (editor) *A Book of South African Verse,* Oxford University Press, 1959; *Stranger to Europe* (poems), Balkema, 1952, enlarged edition, 1960; *The Republic and the Arts,* Witwatersrand University Press, 1964; *South of the Zambesi: Poems From South Africa,* Abelard, 1966; *On First Seeing Florence* (poem), Rhodes University, 1968; (editor) *When Boys Were Men,* Oxford University Press, 1969; *Selected Poems,* Donker, 1975; *Songs and Ballads,* David Philip, 1978; *Karoo Morning: An Autobiography, 1918-35,* Volume I, David Philip, 1978; (editor, with Chris Mann) *A New Book of South African Verse in English,* Oxford University Press, 1979.

Plays: *The Dam* (three-act; first produced in Cape Town, South Africa, at Little Theatre, 1953), Balkema, 1953; *The Dove Returns* (three-act; first produced in Pretoria, South Africa, at National Theatre, 1954), Fortune Press, 1956; *Cape Charade* (three-act; first produced in Cape Town at Labia Theatre, 1967), Balkema, 1968; *Take Root or Die* (first produced in Grahamstown, South Africa, at University Theatre, 1966), Balkema, 1970.

Editor of *New Coin,* English editor of *Standpunte,* and advisory editor of *Contrast.*

WORK IN PROGRESS: Volume II of autobiography, publication expected in 1981; a volume of poems, publication expected in 1982; a critical work on Shakespeare's mature tragedies, publication expected in 1983.

SIDELIGHTS: Butler told *CA:* "I have spent much thought and time on the promotion of English literature in southern Africa, and have attempted to encourage the use of English as a creative medium for South African writers whatever their racial origins. I have also tried to get works by South African authors into schools and universities. Although English is now an African language, it remains our world-contact language, and South African literature is influenced by and contributes to English world literature. I believe profoundly in the greatness of certain authors (Shakespeare, for example) and their importance to all writers, wherever they may be.''

AVOCATIONAL INTERESTS: Producing plays, restoring old houses.

BIOGRAPHICAL/CRITICAL SOURCES: Saturday Review, February 11, 1967; Guy Butler, *Karoo Morning: An Autobiography, 1918-35,* Volume I, David Philip, 1978.

*   *   *

BUTTREY, Douglas N(orton)
(Densil Neve Barr)

PERSONAL: Born in Harrogate, England. *Education:* Received M.Sc. from University of London. *Home:* 15 Churchfields, Broxbourne, Hertfordshire, England.

CAREER: Scientific/technical consultant with BX Plastics, United Kingdom, Catalin Corp., United Kingdom and United States, and Imperial Chemical Industries, United Kingdom, through 1977; writer, 1977—. *Member:* International P.E.N., Player-Playwrights.

WRITINGS: (Under pseudonym Densil Neve Barr) *The Man With Only One Head* (novel), Rich & Cowan, 1955.

Radio plays: "The Clapham Lamp-Post Saga," first broadcast by Radio Telefis Eireann (RTE), 1967; "Gladys on the Wardrobe," first broadcast by New Zealand Broadcasting Co. (NZBC), 1970; "But Petrovsky Goes on Forever," first broadcast by RTE, 1971; "The Last Tramp," first broadcast by British Broadcasting Corp. (BBC), 1972; "The Square at Bastogne," first broadcast by RTE, 1973; "The Battle of Brighton Beach," first broadcast by RTE, 1974; "To a Green World Far Away," first broadcast by BBC, 1975; "With Puffins for Pawns," first broadcast by Radio New Zealand (RNZ), 1976; "Anatomy of an Alibi," first broadcast by RNZ, 1978; "The Speech," first broadcast by South African Broadcasting Corp. (SABC), 1979; "Two Gaps in the Curtain," first broadcast by Radio Stortford, 1979; "Klemp's Diary," first broadcast by SABC, 1980.

WORK IN PROGRESS: Radio and stage plays.

SIDELIGHTS: Barr's radio plays have been broadcast in Europe, Africa, Asia, and North America.

Buttrey told *CA:* "After a satisfying technical career involving many facets of research, development, consultancy, lecturing, and travel, as well as writing three technical books and editing another on plastics, and contributing over one hundred papers and articles to international journals, I decided to write full time in 1977 using my pseudonym Densil Barr for fiction. Although my novels and short stories were successful and achieved international recognition, I became attracted to play writing as an approach towards greater reality than in narrative fiction.

"I like writing radio plays particularly because of the freedom of imagination they allow to both the writer and the listener, and the technical challenge they provide. I write intensively for the period of time necessary to write the play, with relaxing periods in between. I do not write methodically each day all the year round because I find I have to absorb myself completely in the work in progress until it is completed, then I need a mind-clearing period to mull over new ideas. I am attracted to fantasy or the theater of the absurd as a means of conveying reality through ideas rather than realistic sermonizing.

"A wide traveling experience in my earlier career has devel-

oped a more international rather than national outlook towards man and politics, and this reflects in my writing, making my plays more acceptable in various parts of the world. I translate my own material into other forms. For example, I have used a number of my earlier short stories and novels as a basis for plays. I do not search for ideas but wait until some idea or theme has persistently gone round in my mind for long enough to convince me it has to be written about, and I reject ideas which are not insistent in their demand to be written up.

"Playwrights that have most impressed me, and probably influenced me, have been Pirandello, Brecht, and Beckett, each in his own way using myth or unreality to pinpoint the real. My plays tend to reflect a concern for the individual in an ordered world and a basic belief in the preservation of individuality. There is also a strong sense of the ridiculousness of institutionalism in many facets of life, irrespective of politics. Finally, I write only what I want to write; and while presenting it in a form I hope most acceptable for publication in its broadest sense, I do not 'formula' write merely for the market.''

*   *   *

BUZZLE, Buck
See RUBIN, Charles J.

*   *   *

BYNUM, Terrell Ward   1941-

PERSONAL: Born February 6, 1941, in Chester, Pa.; son of Terrell Waltham and Elizabeth (Warren) Bynum; married Aline Willen (a publisher and free-lance writer), June 22, 1965; children: Timothy Hans, Andrew Jackson. *Education:* University of Delaware, B.A. (with honors) and B.S. (with honors), both 1963; Princeton University, M.A., 1966, further graduate study, 1966-67. *Office:* National Information and Resource Center for the Teaching of Philosophy, P.O. Box 32, Hyde Park, N.Y. 12538.

CAREER: American University, Washington, D.C., assistant professor of philosophy, 1967-68; State University of New York at Albany, assistant professor of philosophy, 1968-74; Ramapo College of New Jersey, Mahwah, visiting assistant professor of philosophy, 1974-75; Dutchess Community College, Poughkeepsie, N.Y., assistant professor, 1975-78, associate professor of philosophy, 1978—. Member of board of directors of Metaphilosophy Foundation, 1969—, president, 1973—; director of National Information and Resource Center for the Teaching of Philosophy, 1976—. Adjunct assistant professor at Union College, Schenectady, N.Y., and Drew University.

MEMBER: American Association of Philosophy Teachers (chairman of steering committee, 1979-80; chairman of board of directors, 1980—), American Philosophical Association, American Association for the Advancement of the Humanities, Association for Symbolic Logic, Mind Association, Philosophy of Science Association, Association of Philosophy Journal Editors, Phi Beta Kappa, Phi Kappa Phi, Omicron Delta Kappa. *Awards, honors:* Fulbright scholar at University of Bristol, 1963-64; Danforth fellow and Woodrow Wilson fellow, both 1964-67; Kellogg Foundation grant, 1973.

WRITINGS: (Editor, translator, and author of introduction) Gottlob Frege, *Conceptual Notation and Related Articles,* Oxford University Press, 1972; (contributor) William Claus, editor, *The Objectives of Project SEARCH,* New York State Education Department, 1975; (editor with Matthew Lipman) *Philosophy for Children* (monograph), Basil Blackwell, 1976;

(editor with Sidney Reisberg) *Teaching Philosophy Today: Criticism and Response,* National Information and Resource Center for the Teaching of Philosophy, 1976; (editor) *The Humanities in Education and Society,* Dutchess Community College, 1979; (editor) *The Philosophy Teacher's Handbook,* Helvetia Press, 1979. Contributor of articles and reviews to philosophy and psychology journals. Editor of *Metaphilosophy,* 1970—; member of editorial board of *Teaching Philosophy,* 1975—.

WORK IN PROGRESS: The Abortion Arguments: A Guide for the Perplexed (tentative title), an attempt to analyze logically the major arguments for and against liberalized abortion laws, publication expected in 1982; with wife, Aline Bynum, *The Life and Work of Gottlob Frege.*

SIDELIGHTS: Bynum commented: "As a high school student I had the foolish dream of discovering 'the fundamental nature of things,' and I believed, of all things, that chemistry would yield the prize. A year of college chemistry soon disabused me of such nonsense. As a sophomore at the University of Delaware I attended the first of the now famous Delaware Seminars in Philosophy of Science. Suddenly, I knew that philosophy had always been my calling.

"I think that philosophers (and indeed all scholars) have a responsibility to help society solve pressing human problems. I see this as an important goal of my teaching, writing, and editing in philosophy and related fields. I would like, in particular, to promote skills in critical thinking and moral analysis to help the world cope with growing problems from technology, population, and world politics.

"My book on abortion is intended, in part at least, to deal with the problem of poor reasoning on both sides of the issue. Unhappily, sincere and well-meaning people, in their zeal to defend an emotionally held position, often use very bad logic. If we can clear away the rhetoric and fallacious thinking, our disagreements can at least be informed and based on rational grounds—and I think they will be diminished.

"When I first joined the philosophical profession, I was disappointed to find most of my colleagues living in ivory towers, withdrawn from practical human problems, failing to use their considerable analytical talents for social good. I'm delighted that this has changed markedly during the past decade, which has witnessed rapid growth in 'applied philosophy' areas, like medical ethics, business ethics, computer ethics, and critical thinking. I was also disappointed to find that most teachers of philosophy were so caught up in the 'publish or perish syndrome' that they had no time or concern for quality teaching. This disappointment explains much of my efforts and publications in recent years in the area of philosophy teaching."

C

CACOYANNIS, Michael 1922-

PERSONAL: Born June 11, 1922, in Limassol, Cyprus; son of Panayotis Loizou (an attorney) and Angeliki (Efthyvoulos) Cacoyannis. *Education:* Gray's Inn, London, LL.B., 1943; attended Central School of Dramatic Arts and Old Vic School. *Home:* 15 Mouson St., Athens 401, Greece.

CAREER: Called to the Bar, Gray's Inn, London, England, 1943. British Broadcasting Corp. (BBC), London, England, producer for Overseas Service, 1941-50; actor in plays, including "Salome," 1947, "Captain Brassbound's Conversion," 1948, "Caligula," 1949, "Two Dozen Red Roses," 1949, and "The Fig Tree," 1956; director of plays, including "A Woman of No Importance," 1954, "The Rainmaker," 1956, "The Trojan Women," 1963-65, "And Things That Go Bump in the Night," 1965, "The Devils," 1965, "Iphigenia in Aulis," 1967, "Romeo and Juliet," 1968, "Beckett—Billetdoux Evening," 1968, "Lysistrata," 1972, "King Oedipus," 1973, "Miss Margarita," 1975, "The Bacchae," 1977, "The Glass Menagerie," 1978, and "Antony and Cleopatra," 1979; director of operas, including "Mourning Becomes Electra," 1967, and "La Boheme," 1972; writer, director, and producer of motion pictures and teleplays. *Member:* Dramatists Guild. *Awards, honors:* Premiere performance of the Edinburgh Film Festival, 1954, for "Windfall in Athens"; Golden Globe Award from Hollywood's Foreign Correspondent's Association, 1957, for "Stella" and "A Girl in Black"; English critics award, 1958, for "A Matter of Dignity"; best film and best director awards from the Greek National Festival, 1960, for "Our Last Spring"; Cannes jury prize, 1962, for "Electra"; Prix Femina for "Electra," 1963, and "Iphigenia," 1978; New York Drama Critics Circle Award and Lola d'Annunzio Award, 1964, for "The Trojan Women"; three Academy Awards and seven nominations from the Academy of Motion Picture Arts and Sciences, 1964, for "Zorba the Greek"; Order of the Phoenix from Greece, 1965; Officior des Arts et des Lettres (France), 1979.

WRITINGS—Screenplays; all as director: "Kyriakatiko Xypnima" (released in U.S. as "Windfall in Athens"), Millas Films, 1953; "Stella" (adapted from the play by J. Campbanelis), Millas Films, 1955; "To Koritsi Me Ta Mavra" (released in U.S. as "A Girl in Black"), Lambiris Films, 1955; "To Telefteo Psemma" (released in U.S. as "A Matter of Dignity"), Finos Films, 1957; "Eroica" (released in U.S. as "Our Last Spring"), Cacoyannis Production, 1960; "Elec-

tra," Cacoyannis Production for United Artists, 1961; "Zorba the Greek," Cacoyannis Production for Twentieth Century-Fox, 1964; "The Day the Fish Came Out," Cacoyannis Production for Twentieth Century-Fox, 1969; "The Trojan Women," Cinerama, 1971; "The Story of Jacob and Joseph," American Broadcasting Co. (ABC), 1974; "Attila," Cacoyannis Production, 1974-75; "Iphigenia," Cacoyannis Production for Greek Film Center, 1977.

WORK IN PROGRESS: Two scripts on contemporary themes.

SIDELIGHTS: Although Michael Cacoyannis spent nearly half of his young adulthood studying and working in England, it was only when he returned to his native Greece that he was able to begin his career as a writer, director, and producer of motion pictures. "I lived in England for thirteen years, but couldn't get a chance to do a film there," Cacoyannis told a *New York Times* interviewer. "When I wanted to do a film I had to go to Greece." His success in Greece has elevated its motion picture industry into international prominence. His films most often deal with Greek subjects. Cacoyannis has successfully produced a number of classic Greek tragedies, including the plays of Euripides: "The Trojan Women," "Iphigenia at Aulis," "Bacchae," and "Electra"; and the play of Sophocles, "Oedipus Rex." He also directed Aristophanes' bawdy comedy, "Lysistrata," for the stage. "The Trojan Women" ran for two years, from 1963 to 1965, a record modern engagement for an ancient Greek tragedy.

Cacoyannis carefully selects his motion pictures because he thinks the impact of films on today's society is great. "It takes a long time to look for a film. Unless one has something to say, one should keep silent. I believe the cinema is the most potent art form today. I feel I am dealing with material that is the basic essence of life." As a result of this conviction, Cacoyannis endeavors to avoid artificiality. In his theatre productions, working under the limited confines of the stage's setting, he uses artificial or fabricated sets, but not in his movies. "Film is a realistic medium, and I try to [film mostly on location]. Real soil, real rock, real sun. In the theatre, you have to build up and project the essential dramatic truth. In cinema, acting has to be the truth itself."

Cacoyannis's films have featured many well-known actors and actresses. In his movie "Stella," Cacoyannis introduced Melina Mercouri, and Anthony Quinn's performance in "Zorba the Greek" was highly acclaimed. One critic said of the movie and Quinn that there "are incidents that Mr. Cacoyannis has staged with such intense reality—as he had the whole of the picture—that they fairly paralyze the senses for brief spells. . . . But out of the whole accumulation of colorfulness and vitality towers the singular, monumental portrait of Zorba, as evolved by Mr. Quinn." "The Trojan Women" similarly featured an impressive cast of actresses, including Katharine Hepburn, Vanessa Redgrave, Irene Papas, and Genevieve Bujold.

AVOCATIONAL INTERESTS: Walking, swimming, painting, composing lyrics.

BIOGRAPHICAL/CRITICAL SOURCES: New York Post, June 11, 1957; *Variety,* May 30, 1962, October 4, 1967; *Saturday Review,* December 15, 1962; *New York Times,* December 18, 1962, December 22, 1963, December 18, 1964, January 24, 1965, November 17, 1965, October 3, 1967; *New Republic,* January 19, 1963; *New York Herald Tribune,* November 5, 1963, December 24, 1963, December 18, 1964, December 20, 1964, November 17, 1965; *Hudson Review,* summer, 1963; *Newsday,* December 24, 1963; *Cue,* January 4, 1964; *Vogue,* May, 1965; *Christian Science Monitor,* February 17, 1965; *New Yorker,* May 8, 1965, October 16, 1971, March 4, 1972; *Time,* October 13, 1967; *Educational Broadcasting International,* September, 1978.

*   *   *

CADDEN, Joseph E. 1911(?)-1980

OBITUARY NOTICE: Born c. 1911; died of lung cancer, June 16, 1980, in New York, N.Y. Public figure and editor. While editing the *National Student Mirror* during the early 1930's, Cadden also helped German citizens escape from their Nazi-ruled country. In 1935 he founded the American Youth Congress and was a member of the U.S. delegation during the World Youth Congress the following year. He also fought in the Spanish civil war. Upon his return to the United States, Cadden worked with the International Youth Brigade and joined the Young Communist League. In 1948 he campaigned for presidential candidate Henry A. Wallace. Obituaries and other sources: *New York Times,* June 17, 1980.

*   *   *

CALLAGHAN, Barry 1937-

PERSONAL: Born July 5, 1937, in Toronto, Ontario, Canada; son of Morley E. (a novelist) and Loretto (Dee) Callaghan; married Nina Ann Rabchuck (an associate producer), July 20, 1965 (separated); lives with Claire Weissman Wilks (an artist); children: Michael. *Education:* Attended University of Windsor, 1957-58; University of Toronto, B.A., 1962, M.A., 1964, further graduate study, 1968. *Politics:* "Bemused disdain." *Religion:* "Born Catholic; now given to Celtic dreams and laughter." *Home and office:* 20 Dale Ave., Toronto, Ontario, Canada M4W 1K4. *Agent:* Nancy Colbert, 303 Davenport Rd., Toronto, Ontario, Canada M5R 1K5.

CAREER: University of Toronto, Toronto, Ontario, teaching fellow, 1960-64; York University, Toronto, assistant professor, 1968-72, associate professor of English, 1972—, chairman of department, 1968. Literary editor of *Toronto Telegram,* 1966-71; publisher of *Exile,* a literary quarterly, 1972—; publisher of Exile Editions, 1977—. Literary commentator for Canadian Broadcasting Corp. (CBC-Radio), 1964-72, literary critic on "Umbrella" program, 1964-66, cohost of "The Public Eye," 1966-68; senior producer for CBC current affairs, 1967-71, war correspondent, 1969-71; host of

series of dramatized novels on OECA-TV, 1977; critic of contemporary affairs on CTV network, 1976—. Co-owner of Villon Films (documentary film company), 1972—. Painter, with exhibition at Isaacs Gallery, Toronto, 1978. *Awards, honors:* Prix Italia, 1977; foreign correspondents selection of Outstanding Achievements of First Twenty-Five Years of CBC; National Magazine Award, 1977, 1978, 1979 (gold medal); best magazine article award and President's Medal, both 1979.

WRITINGS: (Self-illustrated) *The Hogg Poems and Drawings,* General Publishing, 1978; (translator) Robert Marteau, *Atlante,* Exile Editions, 1979; (translator) Marteau, *Treatise on White and Tincture,* Exile Editions, 1980; *Walkie-Talkie* (novel), General Publications, 1980; *The Road to Compostela* (essays on poetics), Exile Editions, 1981; *The Seven Last Words* (poems), Exile Editions, 1981.

Work represented in anthology, *Best Short Stories of Punch,* 1980. Contributor of fiction to magazines; contributor of articles and book reviews to numerous magazines and periodicals, including *Weekend, Maclean's, Saturday Night,* and *Toronto Life.*

WORK IN PROGRESS: The Hogg Journals (1965-80), three volumes, publication by Exile Editions expected in 1981-83.

SIDELIGHTS: The son of distinguished Canadian novelist Morley Callaghan, Barry Callaghan has made his own imprint in Canadian letters with his international quarterly, *Exile.* The journal has featured contributions from Joyce Carol Oates, Margaret Atwood, Jerzy Kosinski, Thomas Kinsella, and Ted Hughes, while Irish poet John Montague and Israeli Yehuda Amichai appear on its editorial masthead.

Callaghan's work in the arts extends far beyond *Exile.* He has done work in journalism, television, and film-making, in addition to his writing. His 1978 volume, *The Hogg Poems and Drawings,* was well received in Canadian literary journals, and seven of his short stories appeared in *Punch* in 1979. While on sabbatical leave from Toronto's York University in 1980, Callaghan translated two books by the French poet Robert Marteau, who had previously translated *The Hogg Poems* into French.

Co-owner of Villon Films and its chief documentarist, Callaghan has done in-depth reporting and filming of the conflicts in South Africa and Lebanon, and in Jordan, where he covered the civil war in 1970. He has also traveled in the Soviet bloc countries as a feature journalist for a number of Canadian publications.

Because of his internationalist perspective on Canadian literature, Callaghan has often been at odds with literary nationalists in Canada. In the 1960's he critically reviewed Al Purdy's *The New Romans,* a collection of nationalistic opinions by poets, politicians, and novelists. The ensuing controversy was carried on, among Callaghan, Purdy, Earle Birney, and others, on the pages of the *Toronto Telegram.* Poet and satirist Irving Layton has also criticized Callaghan. The editor of *Exile* has stuck to his internationalist stance, however, and has attempted to make his magazine a world-class literary publication.

Callaghan admits that Canada "is a peculiar country to be an artist in." Much of that peculiarity stems from Canada's sensitivity concerning its own literature. As the *Toronto Globe and Mail* reported, *Exile* "was labelled 'internationalist' and 'continentalist' as though curiosity about the big wide world was a form of treason." But Callaghan maintains that the range of his publication's influence transcends national boundaries: "The whole principle of *Exile* is that there must be some refuge for the person who says: 'This is my mind. Here it is. Nothing should stand between us. If it can't happen, too bad.'" *Exile*, then, as reported in *Saturday Night*, is "a phenomenon among such magazines in Canada."

AVOCATIONAL INTERESTS: Gambling, muse women, basketball, the African jungle, political power brokers, hucksters and hustlers, priests.

CA INTERVIEWS THE AUTHOR

Barry Callaghan was interviewed by Joe Rosenblatt on March 21, 1980, in Toronto, Ontario. Rosenblatt is a poet whose sketch appears in *CA* 89-92.

CA: As both poet and journalist, you seem to move easily between two distinctly different approaches to the language, while at the same time I suspect that your poetic informs your journalistic approach. For example, in the course of your travels to Rhodesia and the Middle East, and when you were trapped during the shelling of a civil war, you must have seen cadavers and death. Did that make you a religious person?

CALLAGHAN: I am a religious person in the ancient meaning of the word. I am not interested much in religion, and certainly not religiosity. I have too large a sense of laughter for that. I am interested in man's attempt to transcend death. I see life as a pilgrimage. In fact, all great poetry is pilgrimage, and it is pilgrimage in pursuit of love and death.

CA: You have seen death?

CALLAGHAN: I have seen death and I have looked into the barrel of a gun. Fine. I have thought that men were going to kill me. Fine. I've been put in the worst kind of prisons where I thought the rats would get me. I was swallowed for a moment in the institutional prison swamp of South Africa. I've been up against that kind of thing. I have seen fear and I have learned calm in the core of my fear. And this had led, as a state of being, to a discovery of laughter.

CA: You once said that you were possessed by the muse, or had "the very disease of the muse." This sounds poetic, artistic, rather than strictly logical. Are you a very logical person?

CALLAGHAN: No, I'm not, not as most people use the phrase. I'm a gambler. I can't live without risks. I bet on basketball games, football games, whatever is going on: Which cockroach will get across the floor first? Will Jerry Ford and Joe Clark meet in androgynous heaven? I wager two hundred bucks a day, at least. I love it, out on the edge like that. The hand of God touches you, or more perplexing, you get suckered by your own best judgment. For all your wisdom, you lose. Your vain ambitions become laughable, yet, in the midst of your laughter, a dark laughter, you leap again. A tension, like love and death; you see? I like to live in there, in the core. I wrote a letter to my old friend John Montague in which I said, "On the edge is best." I like to be on the edge. I am calm on the edge. This I discovered in the civil war in Amman. Trapped for ten days with the whole city blowing up around me. I was calm. It's a kind of manic calm, but boy, you have lucid insights into the reality of the surreal when you're in the midst of that calm.

CA: So you have magnified reality in your art? You're not an escapist?

CALLAGHAN: Of course. This is what poetry is all about. Look at it as an image. I appear on this show, "Canada A.M." (on CTV, the private television network). It is a great theatrical challenge, setting one million five hundred thousand people laughing in their pajamas while they're sipping freeze-dried coffee. There are few things I'd rather do than laugh at the ludicrous in our politicians. In this country, politics is a substitute for culture. So I laugh at our gods without gonads. I sit there in the dead eye of television, profound and preposterous in pop-land, and then I come home and stare sternly at the snow.

CA: You're one of the few poets who's dealt with hyper-reality, the media. But, you somehow seem to retain your idealism, an integrity, as a humanistic person. It's a contradiction. As the saying goes, one who deals with garbage must be tainted.

CALLAGHAN: Ah well, there is a truth in that, and the truth is this: If you spend too much time arguing with second-rate people, you will end up thinking second-rate thoughts. It's what happens to high school teachers. They become juvenile just like their students, but dangerous because they're the bosses.

Though I operate in the journalistic world, the world of television, I do not engage that world on its own terms. I have adhered to my positions; I have paid certain prices.

CA: But surely you had to play the game.

CALLAGHAN: No. I didn't play the game. For example, I made a film about Quebec in 1969. I did not, as was then the fashion, go to Hugh MacLennan and the doyens of White Rhodesia, Westmount. I didn't go to the "spokesmen" whose role after all is to tell people what they want to hear, to pass received opinion back and forth, mediocrity, as Mencken defined it. No, artists and honest men always see for themselves, always stand apart from the tribe. It's the nature of the beast.

I have an operating principle as a journalist. If you want to know what is really going on in a country, whether it's Czechoslovakia or Israel, find out what the accepted conventional view is and then, as a betting man, take the chance that exactly the reverse is true. Then read—and I'm afraid you have to have a certain trained judgment—read the best contemporary writers. I believe Ezra Pound was right: the artist is the antenna of his race. Put yourself in touch with the best imaginative minds and you'll get closer to the facts. That's another contradiction, another paradox, that all "information" mad people don't understand. That doesn't matter. It's the way to see deeply, to make a quick entry into the realities of any given society. It's how I made my way into Israel and brought the wrath of the local Zionist freedom fighters sitting around their swimming pools down on my head. I saw that Israeli poetry and prose were riddled with melancholy, moral confusion, exactly the reverse of the Moshe Dayan macho image. So I got generals, poets, politicians, farmers to talk about this. I couldn't shut them up. One military guy broke into tears, moaning how he didn't want to be a killer. I was incredulous. It was startling television. It was the beginning of my reputation among the temple-set as a so-called anti-Semite. I'll tell you how such things get started.

CA: Reputations?

CALLAGHAN: Yes, sneering empty-headed animosity, tribal defamation. You see, the intellectual must not curry favor. The truly imaginative person cannot curry favor.

CA: How do you feed your muse in such a system?

CALLAGHAN: This contradiction is a modern thing. The ancient Celtic poets were all close to power. Sometimes they were the right arm of power. They uttered the turbine truths of their time. I want none of the current retreat into the closet that some think is the mark of the sensitive flower poet. It is a mouldering hangover from a romanticism misrepresented; Byron and Shelley were up to their necks in the world. Axel's Castle is a disease, and sometimes I think Canadian literature is a castle constructed of snow, an artificial igloo in the subway system. I am not a cynic because I am not a failed idealist. They are two sides of the same coin. When I went into the world of newspaper journalism, I did not believe I could successfully last forever by pursuing my own ideals. I was more than happy to last five years. The final two years of the five were engaged in outsmarting those who wanted to be rid of me. I didn't blame them. This is the point I want to make. I didn't blame them for wanting to be rid of me because, in reality, I did not fit into their newspaper [*Toronto Telegram*]. Their wonder at my being there was legitimate. It was a fluke moment in our history, those book pages. They were unlike anything before, and you'll never see their like again in a Canadian newspaper.

CA: At one point, a poet with a national reputation referred to you meanly and disparagingly as a son of Morley Callaghan. Was that a slap in the face?

CALLAGHAN: If you want me to talk about the peculiarity of that problem, I can do that. I was lucky. Whatever my temperament is, I was lucky. I remember my first published poem in a college magazine. It caused quite a sensation. It was a long poem, very much in the manner of the Beats, though I didn't know who the Beats were at that stage. And my professor of literature approached me in the halls and said: "That was a remarkable piece of work, but how much of that did your father write?" That was wounding and insulting. He assumed I was a cheat, that my father was a cheat. My response could have gone two ways. I could have been totally humiliated and said, "Ah ha, if this is what I'm going to be up against for the rest of my life, I'd rather be a plumber." Or I could have done what I did: shower the professor with verbal abuse. What I finally realized out of such experiences was that the world is filled with disappointed men who are prepared to engage in gratuitous malice.

CA: You identify very much with victims.

CALLAGHAN: As I found out when I was arrested by the secret police in the middle of the night in South Africa, you go quietly. Naked and alone in the night, you can't believe it, and you go quietly. However, having said that, and having found my own strengths within a cell, I identify with victims only as a man who is never willingly going to be one.

I'm not a victim. I believe I can make it. When I went off into the leper camps in Africa, went down the rivers in dugout canoes, the rivers filled with electric fish—I can't swim much, but I believed I could make it. I'm not a victim, but I do carry in my bloodlines a savage reality. I don't have to look at the Jews or the Armenians as a metaphor. I have the Irish.

There is an island out in the St. Lawrence River which is called Gros Isle. Gros Isle was a graveyard for the Irish. My great-great-grandfather, on my mother's side, got out of Ireland in one of the few ways he could. He joined the English Army and he fought in the War of 1812. And then he was released and was given a land grant and built a log house which is still some kind of historical site down around Kingston. On my father's side, they came out in the famine boats. The famine boats were floating hells, filled with naked, disease-ridden, starving people who were treated like pigs by the English. Those famine ships all docked at Gros Isle. If you had the fur on your tongue, the cholera, you were quarantined to die there.

I carry that within me. Those are my bloodlines. I believe in blood memories. I do not sympathize with the rabid Zionist, or the rabid IRA gunner, or the rabid Afrikaner. I don't sympathize with anybody who's rabid about anything, and by rabid I mean close-minded and tribal. It's true there are memories, and if you negate them you end up rootless. But if you exploit them sentimentally, you will repeat the crimes of the oppressor, not suffer the sores of the victim. Too often we are shaped by what we hate.

CA: Are you an Irish Nationalist?

CALLAGHAN: Absolutely not. I carry within me blood memories of pain. In those terms I don't think of myself as Irish. I have the blood memory of lyricism; I have the blood memory of magic; I have the blood memory of the sardonic. But I am not Irish; I am a Canadian. I am of my ravines, cold black water, stone hills, pine trees, the winter. I'm closer to the steppes than the bog. I am of my place, Hogg's Hollow, just up the hill. I am a Canadian, but I have my blood memory, not just coffins, but lyricism, magic wonder, visions, men running through the tops of trees. I live in a real country where people live in cellars and holes in the ground. Perhaps the tension in my life is that I want to run through the tops of trees with all my people, my roots, trying to lasso me, haul me down into their cellars. This produces good work, this tension. I don't want to be at ease. It is that tension that draws me: the kiss of death, love and death; betrayal as the beginning of the beautiful; the leper's kiss, the white wound of blackness.

CA: Does this same sense of tension inform your poems? Your central guiding spirit in The Hogg Poems *is a kind of Canadian Benedict Arnold, a Mr. Hogg who betrays a democratic revolution in York, or Toronto, of the 1840's. Why do you identify with Hogg, the Tory, the Reactionary?*

CALLAGHAN: I do and I don't. The theme that runs all through *The Hogg Poems* is betrayal, elucidated in a poem called "Judas Priest." He is a contemporary prophet, a street preacher who delivers his sermon, the Gospel of Judas. The concluding point to that sermon is that whether we like it or not, Judas, who hung himself in imitation of the only begotten son and out of his profound love and understanding of the mission of Christ, demonstrated that not only Judas is in us, but Jesus too. They are one.

CA: Whether we like it or not?

CALLAGHAN: The mystery of Jesus and Judas is that though John and Luke were the beloved, God picked Judas for a role—that is unless you want to believe God is an all-knowing monster who knew into all eternity that Judas was to be damned. Unless you want to believe in a monster there is the other possibility: Judas and Jesus struck a love bargain. Someone had to initiate the sacrifice and suffer calumny and hatred. What love! The other guy who betrayed him was Peter; yet he made Peter his founding rock. I happen to believe, as the street preacher says, that it's in betrayal that the beautiful is begun.

CA: You seem to co-exist on at least two levels of perceiving things. How would you define yourself? A visual individual?

A poet? A printmaker? A painter? An editor? A critic? A filmmaker?

CALLAGHAN: I would define myself as at the beginning.

BIOGRAPHICAL/CRITICAL SOURCES: Toronto Globe and Mail, March 29, 1980; *Saturday Night,* April, 1980.

—*Interview by Joe Rosenblatt*

* * *

CALLWOOD, June
See FRAYNE, June

* * *

CAMERON, Ann 1943-

PERSONAL: Born October 21, 1943, in Rice Lake, Wis.; daughter of William Angus (a lawyer) and Lolita (a teacher; maiden name, Lofgren) Cameron. *Education:* Radcliffe College, B.A. (with honors), 1965; University of Iowa, M.F.A., 1972. *Home:* 1683 Third Ave., New York, N.Y. 10028. *Agent:* Ellen Levine, Curtis Brown Ltd., 575 Madison Ave., New York, N.Y. 10022.

CAREER: Writer. *Awards, honors:* MacDowell Colony fellowship, 1968; guest at Yaddo Colony, 1968; National Endowment for the Humanities grant, 1974.

WRITINGS—For children: *The Seed,* Pantheon, 1975; (author of introduction) *The Angel Book,* Balance House, 1978; *Harry, the Monster,* Pantheon, 1980; *Julian's Stories,* Pantheon, 1981. Contributor of stories to *Iowa Review* and *Northwest Review.*

WORK IN PROGRESS: Dig, an account of a Mayan dig in Belize, for children, publication by Pantheon expected in 1983; a novel about Manhattan life, completion expected in 1985.

SIDELIGHTS: Ann Cameron writes: "I started writing children's books after putting aside a couple of adult manuscripts—thinking, 'Children's books are short. I might finish one!' Having started writing for children, aesthetic and psychological concerns became dominant, fortunately. I would like to write children's (and adult) books that convey human richness and possibility, and the individual's ability to affect and improve his destiny. Currently I am influenced by Bruno Bettelheim and what he has to say about developing independent thinking and humane values in children."

* * *

CAMERON, Betsy 1949-

PERSONAL: Born October 5, 1949, in New Jersey; daughter of Robert F. (a builder) and Helen (a teacher; maiden name, Bachmann) Cameron; married Gary Greenip, September 12, 1969 (divorced). *Home:* 15 Birch Ave., Bergenfield, N.J. 07621. *Agent:* Connie Clausen Associates, 250 East 87th St., New York, N.Y. 10028. *Office:* 141 East 56th St., No. 2-A, New York, N.Y. 10022.

CAREER: Photographic model in New York, N.Y., 1969-79; writer, 1979—. Talent consultant to Ford Agency. *Member:* Forest Hills Tennis Club.

WRITINGS: (With Diana Jewell) *Lisanne: A Young Model* (juvenile), Crown, 1979.

WORK IN PROGRESS: A Boy and His Dog; a book on friendship; "A Young Model," a television script.

SIDELIGHTS: Betsy Cameron told *CA:* "I wrote *Lisanne: A Young Model* to inform teenagers about a lucrative career with which they could pay for college. I intend to work on children's projects, ideas that will bring about growth and

education in the family unit, and love and friendship. I have also worked recently with Cambodian refugees for the United Nations."

* * *

CAMUTI, Louis J(oseph) 1893-

PERSONAL: Born August 30, 1893, in Parma, Italy; came to the United States in 1902, naturalized citizen, 1918; son of Count Gaspare (in business) and Corinna (Pomarelli) Camuti; married Alexandra Landi, April 4, 1920; children: Nina Camuti Danielsen, Louis J., Jr. (deceased). *Education:* Cornell University, B.S., 1916; New York University, D.V.S., 1920. *Politics:* Republican. *Religion:* Roman Catholic. *Home:* 249 East Devonia Ave., Mount Vernon, N.Y. 10552. *Agent:* Carl Brandt, Brandt & Brandt Literary Agents, Inc., 1501 Broadway, New York, N.Y. 10036.

CAREER: Private practice of veterinary medicine in New York City, 1920—. Inspector in charge of New York City Department of Health, 1923. President of Dexter Poultry Co., 1927-32; founding president of Research Consultants (federal food and drug regulations experts), 1939-67. Member of staff of U.S. Senator Copeland, 1932-38. Guest on more than twenty radio and television programs. *Military service:* New York National Guard, Cavalry, 1916-19, Medical Regiment, 1921-39, 112th Regiment, 1939-46; became lieutenant colonel. *Member:* International Platform Association, American Veterinary Medical Association (life member; honorary member), New York Society of Military and Naval Officers of the World Wars.

WRITINGS: (With Lloyd Alexander) *Park Avenue Vet* (memoirs), Holt, 1962; (with Haskell Frankel) *All My Patients Are Under the Bed: Memoirs of a Cat Doctor,* Simon & Schuster, 1980. Author of "Camuti's Column," in *Feline Practice.* Contributor to magazines.

SIDELIGHTS: Camuti traces his devotion to cats back to an incident from his childhood, when a family pet saved him from death in a house fire. A veterinary doctor since 1920, when cats were not widely recognized as respectable pets, he limited his medical practice to felines in 1933, and in 1963 confined himself to making house calls. House calls, which have taken him as far from New York as Canada and Florida, seem to Camuti to be worth the effort, in terms of benefit to the pet being treated. His clients have covered a wide range of social classes, from wealthy socialites and well-known entertainers to lonely single people confined to basement apartments.

"My main objective has been to put the cat on a pedestal as a pet and as a companion," Camuti told *CA.* "Only in America could I have done the things that I did and I thank America for having made it possible. I also wish to say that age should not be a handicap to continue one's vocation as long as one's health permits. I am still working a full schedule at eighty-seven."

BIOGRAPHICAL/CRITICAL SOURCES: New York Daily Mirror, April 21, 1953; *Chicago Tribune,* February 24, 1977; *New York Times,* May 4, 1980.

* * *

CANNON, Helen 1921-
(Lincoln Prosper)

PERSONAL: Born April 20, 1921, in Michigan; daughter of George (a U.S. customs official) and Pearl (Emans) Lackey; married James Blacksten, December 26, 1941 (divorced, 1945); married George Cannon (a business manager of a social service agency), December 2, 1947; children: Jack, Georganne Yarger Kamyeb, Mike, Katie Howard. *Education:* Weber State College, B.A., 1965; attended Stanislaus College, 1965. *Politics:* "Rabid Democrat." *Religion:* "None at all." *Home and office:* 4090 39th Ave., Oakland, Calif. 94619. *Agent:* Scott Meredith Literary Agency, Inc., 845 Third Ave., New York, N.Y. 10022.

CAREER: Worked as employment office interviewer, secretary, fruit picker, copywriter, painter, and illustrator, 1942-60; high school teacher in Stockton, Calif., 1965-66; Internal Revenue Service, Washington, D.C., job analyst in Ogden, Utah, Fresno, Calif., and San Francisco, Calif., 1966-78; writer, 1978—. Television script consultant. *Member:* Authors Guild.

WRITINGS: A Better Place I Know (novel), Avon, 1979; *Seasons Change* (novel), Avon, 1980; *Where the Truth Lies* (novel), Avon, 1980. Also author of *The Straight-Eight Nash Convertible* (humorous novel), under pseudonym Lincoln Prosper, 1981.

WORK IN PROGRESS: Out of the Running, a novel based on liquor smuggling on the St. Clair River during Prohibition.

SIDELIGHTS: Helen Cannon wrote: "All of my novels (except for the humorous one under the pseudonym Lincoln Prosper) are based on the ability of ordinary humans to do a good job of living in the face of the natural odds against them.

"Probably this admiration for people is an outgrowth of numerous involvements with youth hot-lines, youth assistance centers, and the like. Contacts in these endeavors have shown that all men are not created equal, but something enables human beings to surmount their unlucky beginnings. So I write hymns to doggedness."

*   *   *

CAPRIO, Frank S(amuel) 1906-

PERSONAL: Born April 22, 1906, in Newark, N.J.; son of Raffaele (a tailor) and Filomena (Vitale) Caprio; married Louise Pfister (a writer), August 28, 1942; children: Frank, Ralph. *Education:* University of Pennsylvania, A.B., 1927; George Washington University, M.D., 1931. *Politics:* Democrat. *Religion:* Agnostic. *Home:* 3100 Northeast 49th St., Apt. 804, Fort Lauderdale, Fla. 33308. *Office:* 2425 East Commercial Blvd., Suite 205, Fort Lauderdale, Fla. 33308.

CAREER: In private practice of psychiatry in Washington, D.C., 1942-72; private practice of hypnosis and marriage counseling in Fort Lauderdale, Fla., 1972—. Lecturer at colleges and universities, including University of Maryland, George Washington University, and American University; guest on more than one hundred fifty television and radio programs. Founder and director of Florida Association for Self-Improvement. *Military service:* U.S. Army, Medical Corps; became captain. *Member:* Medical Authors of America (fellow), Retired Physicians and Dentists.

WRITINGS: (With Owsley Grant) *Why Grow Old?: A Guide-Book for the Man Who Seeks to Remain Physically and Mentally Young,* M. Droke, 1937; *Medical Items of Interest,* Pfister Publishing, 1938.

(With Louis Samuel London) *Sexual Deviations,* Linacre Press, 1950; *Living in Balance,* Arundel Press, 1951 (published in England as *Guide to Living in Balance,* Wilshire); *The Power of Sex,* Citadel, 1952; *The Sexually Adequate Male,* Citadel, 1952, 2nd edition, Wilco, 1962, also published as *The Adequate Male,* Medical Research Press, 1961; *The Sexually Adequate Female,* Citadel, 1953, 16th edition,

1967; *Marital Infidelity,* Citadel, 1953, also published as *Unfaithful,* Fawcett, 1961; *Female Homosexuality: A Psychodynamic Study of Lesbianism,* Citadel, 1954; *Variations in Sexual Behavior: A Psychodynamic Study of Deviations in Various Expressions of Sexual Behavior,* Citadel, 1955; *Sex and Love: A Guide to Sex Health and Love Happiness,* Parker Publishing, 1959; *The Modern Woman's Guide to Sexual Maturity,* Citadel, 1959.

(With Donald R. Brenner) *Sexual Behavior: Psycho-Legal Aspects,* Citadel, 1961; *A Psychiatrist Talks About Sex,* Belmont-Tower, 1962; *Only in Psychiatry,* Citadel, 1962; (with Joseph R. Berger) *Helping Yourself With Self-Hypnosis: A Modern Guide to Self-Improvement and Successful Living,* Prentice-Hall, 1963; *How to Solve Your Sex Problems With Self-Hypnosis,* Citadel, 1964; *Facts and Fallacies About Sex,* Citadel, 1966; *Your Right to Sex Happiness,* Citadel, 1966; *Helping Yourself With Psychiatry: A Practical Guide to Wiser and Healthier Living,* Prentice-Hall, 1967; *The Art of Sexual Lovemaking: A Guide to Happier Sex-Love Life for Married Couples,* Fairview Book Co., 1967; *Variations in Lovemaking: A Modern Guide to What Is Normal and Abnormal in Sex—Advanced Techniques for Achieving Maximum Gratification Through Sexual Experimentation, With Case Histories,* Richlee Publishers, 1968; (with Frank B. Caprio) *Parent and Teenagers,* Citadel, 1968; (with Frances Spatz Leighton) *How to Avoid a Nervous Breakdown,* Meredith Corp., 1969.

(With Sidney Petrie) *How to Heighten Your Sexual Pleasure Through Simple Mental Stimulation,* Galahad Books, 1971; *Add Life to Your Years,* Citadel, 1975. Also co-author of *Sexual Satisfaction,* Health Publications. Author of prologue for film, "Third Sex." Contributor to magazines, including *Hypnosis Quarterly.*

WORK IN PROGRESS: Total Success, with Maxine Rose; *Champagne at My Funeral,* an autobiography.

SIDELIGHTS: As a psychiatrist, Caprio was an early proponent of sex education in the schools, and later a pioneer in the movement for death education. *Add Life to Your Years* is a look at retirement, including senior citizens' problems with depression, death, sex, physical fitness, and "the challenge of life without a mate," and Caprio's solutions. The book also deals with using autosuggestion for self-improvement. Caprio has used self-hypnosis to quit smoking and feels that his ability to use hypnosis for himself contributed to nearly twenty years of excellent health, despite a heart problem.

His twenty or more years of research on the subject have left him opposed to capital punishment. As he told *CA:* "It is definitely not a deterrent."

BIOGRAPHICAL/CRITICAL SOURCES: Western News, October 27, 1977.

*   *   *

CAPUTO, Robert 1949-

PERSONAL: Born January 15, 1949, in Camp Lejeune, N.C.; son of Anthony and Mary (Bowen) Caputo. *Education:* Attended Trinity College, Hartford, Conn., 1967-70; New York University, B.F.A., 1976. *Home and office address:* P.O. Box 486, Burgaw, N.C. 28425.

CAREER: Cameraman in Tanzania for television series, "Jane Goodall and the World of Animal Behavior," 1973; American Museum of Natural History, New York, N.Y., teacher, 1974-76; free-lance photographer and writer in Nairobi, Kenya, 1976—. *Member:* Foreign Correspondents Association of East Africa. *Awards, honors:* Honorable mention for children's science book award from New York Academy of Sciences, 1979, for *Hyena Day*.

WRITINGS—Juveniles: (With Miriam Hsia) *Hyena Day*, Coward, 1978; *More Than Just Pets*, Coward, 1980. Contributor to magazines, including *Life*, *Geo*, and *National Geographic*.

WORK IN PROGRESS: Cheetahs of the Serengeti, a children's book, completion expected in 1980; *Last Look*, a large format photographic book about wildlife and traditional African peoples.

SIDELIGHTS: Caputo commented: "I first went to Africa in 1972 to have a look at a different part of the world. I did not realize it would be *so* different. I was hired by Hugo van Lawick and Jane Goodall to work as a cameraman for their television series, 'Jane Goodall and the World of Animal Behavior.' I became convinced then of the necessity to communicate, especially to children, the majesty of the natural world lest we destroy it. Hopefully, my stories for *Life* magazine, along with my books, will help us learn. Just back from four years in Africa, I am working toward that end."

* * *

CARDWELL, D(onald) S(tephen) L(owell) 1919-

PERSONAL: Born August 4, 1919, in Gibraltar; son of Herbert Joseph (a civil servant) and Norah Agnes (Mason) Cardwell; married Olive Grace Pumphrey, November 5, 1953; children: Michael Richard (deceased), Adrian Stephen, Diana Elaine. *Education:* King's College, London, B.Sc. (with honors), 1939, B.Sc. (physics; with honors), 1940, Ph.D., 1949. *Politics:* "Unenthusiastic." *Religion:* Church of England. *Home:* 54 Stamford Rd., Bowdon, Altrincham, Cheshire WA14 2JW, England. *Office:* Department of History of Science and Technology, Institute of Science and Technology, Victoria University of Manchester, Sackville St., Manchester M60 1QD, England.

CAREER: Admiralty Signals and Radar Establishment, Portsmouth, England, worked in radar and high frequency direction finding, 1941-46; worked on research projects in electronics and industrial economics, 1950-58; University of Leeds, Leeds, England, lecturer in history and philosophy of science, 1958-63; Victoria University of Manchester, Institute of Science and Technology, Manchester, England, reader, 1963-74, head of department, 1963—, professor of history of science and technology, 1963—. Deputy chairman of governors at North Western Museum of Science and Industry in Manchester. *Member:* British Society for the History of Science, Newcomen Society for the Study of the History of Engineering and Technology, Manchester Literary and Philosophical Society. *Awards, honors:* Dexter Prize from Society for the History of Technology (United States), 1973, for *From Watt to Clausius*; Dickinson Medal from Newcomen Society for the Study of the History of Engineering and Technology, 1978.

WRITINGS: Organisation of Science in England, Heinemann, 1957, 2nd edition, 1972; *Steam Power in the Eighteenth Century*, Sheed, 1963; (editor) *John Dalton and the Progress of Science*, Manchester University Press, 1968; *From Watt to Clausius*, Cornell University Press, 1971; *Turning Points in Western Technology*, Neale Watson, 1972 (published in England as *Technology, Science, and History*, Heinemann, 1972); (editor) *Artisan to Graduate*, Manchester University Press, 1974. Contributor to journals in his field. Editor of *Memoirs and Proceedings of the Manchester Literary and Philosophical Society*.

WORK IN PROGRESS: "The definitive biography of James Prescott Joule (1818-1889)."

SIDELIGHTS: Cardwell told *CA:* "As a sedentary academic, I find great pleasure and relaxation in restoring, maintaining, and developing our country cottage and in trying to cope with its rambling garden. This accords well with the (not unfashionable) feeling that my wife and I have, that civilized Western societies have become too dependent on highly centralized and therefore vulnerable industries and technologies. It is therefore desirable, we feel, to be rather more independent of the services such industries/technologies provide. Our Arab friends have recently underlined this point."

* * *

CARLISLE, Thomas John 1913-

PERSONAL: Born October 11, 1913, in Plattsburgh, N.Y.; son of Thomas Houston (a florist) and Ruby Grace (a florist; maiden name, Mann) Carlisle; married Dorothy Mae Davis, August 20, 1936; children: Thomas Dwight, Christopher Davis, David Livingstone Harold and Jonathan Tristram (twins). *Education:* Williams College, B.A. (cum laude), 1934; Union Theological Seminary, New York, N.Y., M.Div., 1937. *Home:* 437 Lachenauer Dr., Watertown, N.Y. 13601.

CAREER: Ordained United Presbyterian minister, 1937; pastor of Presbyterian churches in Tupper Lake, N.Y., 1937-42, and Delhi, N.Y., 1942-49; Stone Street Presbyterian Church, Watertown, N.Y., pastor, 1949-78, pastor emeritus, 1978—. Reader of poetry; poet-in-residence and visiting scholar at colleges and universities. Tutor at State University of New York Empire State College; member of seminar faculty at Princeton Theological Seminary, 1977-79 and 1980. Founding member and past member of board of directors of local Family Counseling Service and Mental Health Association and Clinic. Co-founder of Watertown Urban Mission. *Member:* New York Poetry Forum, Poetry Society of Georgia, Poetry Society of Virginia, Phi Beta Kappa, Delta Sigma Rho, Watertown Rotary Club (president, 1960-61). *Awards, honors:* Phillips-Rice Award from Jefferson County Association for Mental Health, 1960; Paul Harris Award from Watertown Rotary Club, 1977.

WRITINGS—Poetry: *My Names Are Different*, American Weave Press, 1957; *I Need a Century*, Richard R. Smith Co., 1963; *You! Jonah!*, Eerdmans, 1968; *Celebration!*, Eerdmans, 1970; *Mistaken Identity*, Eerdmans, 1973; *Journey With Job*, Eerdmans, 1976. Contributor of more than a thousand articles and poems to religious and literary journals, popular magazines, including *Saturday Review, Ladies' Home Journal, Saturday Evening Post, Good Housekeeping, Enquiry*, and *Christian Century*, and newspapers. Past member of editorial board of *Sketch*.

WORK IN PROGRESS: Demure as Dynamite, poems about women of the Old Testament, publication expected in 1980 or 1981; *On Time for Christmas*, poems; *Two Little Engines*, a children's story in verse; *America Dawn*, poems on American history; another collection of poems.

SIDELIGHTS: Carlisle commented to *CA:* "Life has been kind to me in that I have been able to earn a modest living doing the things I most love to do. I have enjoyed every aspect of being a minister—the preaching, the teaching, the administration, and especially the sharing in people's lives through counseling and the interpersonal dynamics of church life, helping people grow in their abilities and viewpoints.

"I believe that in Jesus Christ (who may be described as Poet and Troubador as well as Savior) we have the power to believe that 'nothing can separate us from the love of God,' despite all the hard things that can and do happen and the mysteries and unanswered questions of life. Love and compassion and concern—these make life worthwhile."

AVOCATIONAL INTERESTS: Nova Scotia, European travel, geneology, history, social justice, philately.

* * *

CARLSON, Paul Robins 1928-

PERSONAL: Born December 10, 1928, in Brooklyn, N.Y.; son of Rudolph F. (a commercial artist) and Betty (a nurse; maiden name, Robins) Carlson; married Myrtle Warner (a hospital administrator), August 5, 1950; children: Paul R., Timothy Eric. *Education:* Barrington College, A.B., 1954; Pittsburgh Theological Seminary, M.Div., 1960; State University of New York at Albany, M.P.A., 1970; New York Theological Seminary, S.T.M., 1973; New York University, Ed.D., 1979. *Politics:* Republican. *Home:* 803 Woodlawn St., Scranton, Pa. 18509.

CAREER: Ordained Presbyterian minister, 1960; World Council of Churches, Geneva, Switzerland, English editor, 1960-61; Presbyterian Office of Information, New York City, associate director, 1962-64; pastor of Presbyterian church in Pine Plains, N.Y., 1964-68; United Church of Christ, New York City, associate director of information, 1968-70; pastor of Presbyterian church in Ozone Park, N.Y., 1970-78; First Presbyterian Church, Edenton, N.C., pastor, 1978-80; Northeastern Pennsylvania Congregations in Christian Mission, Scranton, Pa., executive director, 1980—. Information director at Union Theological Seminary, New York City, 1977-78. Member of executive committee and board of directors of Dutchess County Office of Economic Opportunity, 1964-68; member of Chowan County Youth Task Force, board of directors of Queens division of National Conference of Christians and Jews, and president of Interfaith Council of Southwest Queens, 1976-78.

MEMBER: Religious Public Relations Council, Christians Concerned for Israel, Phi Delta Kappa. *Awards, honors:* Two awards from Pennsylvania Newspaper Publishers Association, 1956, for spot news and human interest stories; educational award from National Conference of Christians and Jews, 1978.

WRITINGS: God's Church—Not Ours, Forward Movement, 1965; *Our Presbyterian Heritage,* new edition, David Cook, 1973; *The Thirteenth American,* David Cook, 1973; *O Christian! O Jew!,* David Cook, 1974; *Before I Wake,* David Cook, 1975. Author of "The Religion Beat," a column in the *Daily Advance* and the *Gleaner.*

SIDELIGHTS: Carlson wrote: "My major professional interest is in the area of Jewish-Christian relations. I am a member of the executive committee of the National Christian Leadership Conference for Israel, an organization of Catholic and Protestant professionals concerned with the religious and cultural integrity of Judaism and with the territorial integrity of the State of Israel. At a professional level, I actively support efforts to expurgate all anti-Semitic references in Christian educational and liturgical materials. I also oppose Christian missionary endeavors among Jews and believe in Judaism's right to self-definition. I reject Christendom's triumphalism and long-standing belief that the so-called 'old' covenant has been superseded by the New Covenant. I am among a growing list of Christian scholars who seek to stand with Israel—People, Land, Torah."

CARLTON, Wendy 1949-

PERSONAL: Born March 2, 1949; married Mark Needleman; children: Joshua N. *Education:* Oberlin College, B.A., 1970; University of Pennsylvania, M.A., 1972, Ph.D., 1976. *Home:* 326 West Navarre St., South Bend, Ind. 46616. *Office:* Department of Sociology and Anthropology, University of Notre Dame, O'Shaughnessy Building, Notre Dame, Ind. 46556.

CAREER: Teacher at public schools in Philadelphia, Pa., 1970-73; University of Pennsylvania, Philadelphia, lecturer in general studies, 1973-74; University of Notre Dame, Notre Dame, Ind., instructor, 1976-77, assistant professor of sociology, 1977—. Guest on television programs. *Member:* American Sociological Association, Sociologists for Women in Society, Society for the Psychological Study of Social Issues, American Public Health Association, National Women's Health Network, American Association of University Professors, North Central Sociological Association.

WRITINGS: "In Our Professional Opinion . . .": The Primacy of Clinical Judgment Over Moral Choice, University of Notre Dame Press, 1978; (contributor) *Age X Gender,* Women's Studies Program, University of Pennsylvania, 1979. Also author of *Between Consenting Parties,* 1981.

* * *

CARO, Robert A.

EDUCATION: Graduated from Princeton University. *Home:* 2500 Johnson Ave., Riverdale, N.Y. 10463. *Agent:* Lynn Nesbit, International Creative Management, 40 West 57th St., New York, N.Y. 10019. *Office:* 18 East 41st St., New York, N.Y. 10017.

CAREER: Writer. *Newsday,* Garden City, N.Y., investigative reporter, 1960-66. Notable assignments include a series on interstate real estate frauds that resulted in the indictment and conviction of thirty-six persons and the passage of both state and federal legislation to curb abuses in the field. *Member:* Authors Guild (president). *Awards, honors:* Recipient of numerous awards and prizes for investigative journalism, 1963-66; Nieman fellow at Harvard University, 1965-66; Pulitzer Prize for biography and Francis Parkman Prize, both 1975, both for *The Power Broker.*

WRITINGS: The Power Broker: Robert Moses and the Fall of New York, Knopf, 1974.

WORK IN PROGRESS: A three-volume biography of Lyndon Baines Johnson, to be published by Knopf.

SIDELIGHTS: Caro's *The Power Broker: Robert Moses and the Fall of New York* is an epic biography of the man who controlled public works developments in New York for more than forty years. In his quasi-public capacity as president of the Long Island State Park Commission and superintendent of New York City construction, as well as other posts, Moses built almost all of the parks, highways, and bridges in the New York City area. Caro has chronicled his career with consummate detail in 1,246 pages. The book took seven years to write, and Caro interviewed 522 persons and poured over numerous documents and blueprints.

Newsweek's Peter S. Prescott wrote that Caro's book is "fascinating, every oversize page of it. Caro combines the research of a historian with the florid prose of an investigative journalist; in his descriptions of New York subways or the Long Island Rail Road at rush hour he reaches an almost Dickensian state of excitement. So skillful is he at narrative that he can make the passage of a bill through the state legislature seem engrossing. His is an argumentative and emotional book, but it is also uniquely thorough and perceptive in its examination of how power works.''

Indeed, Anthony Wolff of *Saturday Review* identified power as the "new all-American aphrodisiac" and placed *The Power Broker* in a series of "hard-core civics" books, saying that it "is certainly the biggest and arguably the best yet, a feast to satisfy even the most prurient interest." Philip Herrera of *Time* suggested that the book's weakness is that while Caro examines the theme of power, he never gets to the heart of Moses's abuse. Partly, Herrera blames this on the fact that Moses was only available for seven interviews with Caro. Caro recalled his meetings with Moses for Herrera: "They weren't interviews. They were monologues. He was absolutely charming. The world's greatest storyteller, a fantastic memory for names and facts. But when I started asking questions about some of those facts that I knew were disproved, Moses pounded the table." The interviews were subsequently ended.

Caro, wrote Richard C. Wade in the *New York Times Book Review*, "questions almost everything about Moses—his strategy and tactics, his methods and ends, his vision and ideology, his honesty and integrity, his character and decency. Everything but his intelligence and self-discipline. These qualities Moses had in lavish amounts, and more than anything else they account for his spectacular success. Yet Caro sees this genius applied to destructive purposes, warped to undermine democratic process and turned unfairly, even viciously, on his adversaries."

Atlantic Monthly's Benjamin DeMott concluded: "Few readers, whatever their distractibility, are likely to find fault with this biography as a work of popular history. Conflict is its center, and the agonists are figures of charisma and wit—FDR, LaGuardia, Ickes, Al Smith—whose wars of will, viewed at a distance, clang with consequence. *The Power Broker* also qualifies as a source book about political power, its creation and nurture. . . . Mr. Caro's examination of the methods by which Robert Moses simultaneously accumulated enormous political power and built an array of parks, bridges, and highways without historical precedent answers these questions, and in the process, teaches a shrewd course in 'public sector' relationship of money, power, and imagination."

BIOGRAPHICAL/CRITICAL SOURCES: New Republic, September 7, 1974; *New York Times Book Review,* September 15, 1974; *Time,* September 16, 1974; *Newsweek,* September 16, 1974; *Nation,* September 28, 1974; *Saturday Review/World,* October 19, 1974; *Atlantic,* December, 1974; *National Review,* December 6, 1974.

*   *   *

CARPENTER, Francis Ross 1925-

PERSONAL: Born January 12, 1925, in Claysville, Ohio; son of John Ross and Mary C. (Foulk) Carpenter; married Josephine F. Forbes (an actress), November 29, 1952; children: Katharine S. Carpenter Holland. *Education:* Muskingum College, B.A., 1947; Stanford University, M.A., 1951; attended London School of Oriental and African Studies, London, 1956-57. *Politics:* Independent. *Home:* 216 St. Paul St., No. 303, Brookline, Mass. 02146. *Office:* Division of University Relations, Boston College, More Hall, Chestnut Hill, Mass. 02167.

CAREER: U.S. Government, Washington, D.C., affiliated with Department of State, 1951-52, and National Security Agency, 1952-65; Springfield College, Springfield, Mass., assistant professor of history, 1965-71; Museum of the

American China Trade, Milton, Mass., associate director, 1971-78; Boston College, Chestnut Hill, Mass., currently manager of research. Vice-chairman of Brookline Arts Council; member of advisory committee of Museum of the American China Trade and of advisory board of Lyric Stage of Boston; development research consultant. *Military service:* U.S. Naval Reserve, active duty, 1941-45. *Member:* New England Historical Association, New England Historic Genealogical Society.

WRITINGS: The Classic of Tea, Little, Brown, 1974; *The Old China Trade,* Coward, 1977.

WORK IN PROGRESS: Research on the life and poetry of Li Po.

*   *   *

CARRIER, Jean-Guy 1945-

PERSONAL: Born September 23, 1945, in Welland, Ontario, Canada; son of Roland and Laurette (Goupil) Carrier; married Linda Suzanne Walker (a photographer), November 19, 1979; children: Gabriel Leopold. *Education:* Attended University of Ottawa, 1964-66. *Politics:* Socialist. *Home:* 304 Royal Ave., Ottawa, Ontario, Canada K2A 1T5.

CAREER: Canadian Broadcasting Corp. (CBC), Fort Churchill, Manitoba, announcer-operator and news director, 1966-68; reporter and photographer for *Dunnville Chronicle* and *Brantford Expositor,* 1968-70; *Ottawa Citizen,* Ottawa, Ontario, Quebec correspondent, feature writer, and political writer, 1970-72; *Canadian Press,* Ottawa, Parliament Hill writer, 1972-73; CTV, Toronto, Ontario, associate producer, 1973-74; press secretary for New Democratic Party Leaders David Lewis and Ed Broadbent, 1974-76; writer, restaurant operator, and farmer, 1976-78; director of communication and editor in chief of *Perception* magazine for Canadian Council on Social Development, 1978—. *Member:* Writers' Union of Canada.

*WRITINGS—*All published by Oberon: *My Father's House* (novel), 1974; *Family* (novel), 1977; *A Cage of Bone* (novel), 1978; *The Trudeau Decade* (nonfiction), 1979. Contributor to newspapers.

WORK IN PROGRESS: A novel, part of a series including *A Cage of Bone,* publication by Oberon expected in 1982; another novel, publication expected in 1982 or 1983.

SIDELIGHTS: Carrier told *CA:* "My work as a journalist was concentrated on political reporting and national affairs. My works of fiction have attempted to show the slow evolution of Quebec from a rural to an urban society. I am currently working on two books that form the beginning and the end of the story contained in my previous three works of fiction. One book takes place at the end of the nineteenth century and the other is situated in the 1970's. All my fiction is rooted in my family and draws on my upbringing and subsequent life in the county of Bellechasse, Quebec.

"*The Trudeau Decade* is a presentation and analysis of editorial comment on major events and issues that arose between 1968 and 1978. The book was meant to be a compendium of some of the best editorial writing of that period and to indicate trends in the journalistic analysis of events."

*   *   *

CARROLL, Carroll 1902-

PERSONAL: Born April 11, 1902, in New York, N.Y.; son of Lucius (a lawyer) and Bertha (Strauss) Weinschenk; married Norma Tobias; children: Leda Carroll Goldsmith,

Bruce, Adam. *Education:* Attended high school in Chicago, Ill. *Residence:* Los Angeles, Calif. *Agent:* Arthur Pine Associates, Inc., 1780 Broadway, New York, N.Y. 10019. *Office:* 1778 Broadway, New York, N.Y. 10019.

CAREER: Professional free-lance humorist, 1925-32; J. Walter Thompson (advertising agency), worked in radio department, 1932-46; Ward Wheelock Co., vice-president, 1947-54; Columbia Broadcasting System (CBS), staff writer, 1954-56; J. Walter Thompson, editor, producer, and supervisor, 1957-67; National Broadcasting Co. (NBC), staff writer, 1957-67; free-lance writer, 1967—. *Member:* American Society of Composers, Authors, and Publishers, American Guild of Authors and Composers, Academy of Motion Picture Arts and Sciences, Players Club.

WRITINGS: None of Your Business, Cowles, 1970, reprinted as *My Life With . . . ,* Major Books, 1977; (with Henny Youngman) *Take My Wife . . . Please,* Putnam, 1973; (with Ed McMahon) *Here's Ed,* Putnam, 1976. Author of a radio column in *New York Sunday World,* 1931-32, and a weekly column "And Now a Word From . . ." in *Weekly Variety,* 1967—. Film critic for *Judge,* 1925-27, *Canada Goblin,* 1926-28, and *New York Evening Sun,* 1928-29.

*   *   *

CARROUGES, Michel
See COUTURIER, Louis (Joseph)

*   *   *

CARTER, Randolph 1914-

PERSONAL: Born October 6, 1914, in Lexington, Neb.; son of Randolph (a lawyer) and Estelle (an actress; maiden name, Vodrie) Carter. *Education:* Attended Sorbonne, University of Paris, 1932, and University of Berlin, 1933; Pomona College, B.A., 1934. *Home:* 324 East 91st St., New York, N.Y. 10028. *Agent:* Diana Hunt, Royalton Hotel, 44 West 44th St., New York, N.Y. 10036.

CAREER: Playwright, 1936—; Theatre of Eleven, New Haven, Conn., stage manager, 1937, director, 1938; production assistant for J. J. Shubert, 1939-41; drama critic for WOR-TV, 1966-69. *Military service:* U.S. Navy, 1941-45. *Member:* Dramatists Guild. *Awards, honors:* Grant from Creative Artists Public Service Program, 1976; grant from National Endowment for the Arts, 1980.

WRITINGS: Fish Cure (one-act play; first produced in Cambridge, Mass., at Radcliff College, May, 1934), Walter H. Baker, 1935; *Wuthering Heights* (three-act play based on the novel by Emily Bronte; first produced in New York at Longacre Theatre, April 27, 1939), Samuel French, 1939; *A Texas Steer* (three-act play; first produced in Litchfield, Conn., at Litchfield Summer Theatre, August, 1938), Samuel French, 1940; *The World of Flo Ziegfeld* (biography), Praeger, 1974.

Unpublished plays: "Arms for Venus" (three-act), first produced in New Haven, Conn., at Theatre of Eleven, May 6, 1937; (co-author) "Gabrielle" (three-act), first produced in New York City at Maxine Elliott Theatre, March 8, 1941; "Florence Nightingale," first broadcast by Little Theatre on the Air, June, 1951; "Eugenia" (three-act; based on novel by Henry James), first produced in New York City at Ambassador Theatre, January 30, 1957; (co-author) "The World's Fair Enough" (two-act musical), first produced in New York City at La Mama, February 16, 1964; "Triple Play" (one-act plays; includes "I Saw a Monkey," "The Late Late Show," and "Save It for Your Death Bed"), first produced in New

York City at Cherry Lane Theatre, November 3, 1968; "Museum Piece" (one-act), first produced in New York City at 44th Street Studio, April 26, 1969; "Battle for Heaven" (three-act), first produced in Yonkers, N.Y., at Elizabeth Seaton College, January 17, 1972.

WORK IN PROGRESS: A critical biography of designer and architect, Joseph Urban, publication by Abrams expected in 1980 or 1981; "The Green Stick," a play; "Come to My Party," a film.

AVOCATIONAL INTERESTS: Music, animals, travel abroad.

*   *   *

CARVER, Jeffrey A(llan) 1949-

PERSONAL: Born August 25, 1949, in Cleveland, Ohio; son of Robert D. (an accountant) and Mildred (Sherrick) Carver. *Education:* Brown University, B.A., 1971; University of Rhode Island, M.Marine Affairs, 1974. *Home and office:* 10 Hancock Place, #3, Cambridge, Mass. 02139. *Agent:* Richard Curtis Literary Agency, 156 East 52nd St., New York, N.Y. 10022.

CAREER: Substitute teacher in Norwood, Mass., 1971-73; teacher of adults in Cambridge, Mass., 1972; diver in Narragansett Bay, R.I., 1974; scuba diving instructor in Norwood and East Greenwich, R.I., 1972-74; United Parcel Service, Watertown, Mass., sorter, 1975-77; full-time writer, 1977—. *Member:* World SF, Science Fiction Writers of America, Authors Guild, Authors League of America, L-5 Society.

WRITINGS—Science fiction novels: *Seas of Ernathe,* Laser Books, 1976; *Star Rigger's Way* (Science Fiction Book Club selection), Dell, 1978; *Panglor,* Dell, 1980.

Work represented in anthologies, including *Futurelove* (Science Fiction Book Club selection), Bobbs-Merrill, 1977; *Dragons of Light, Dragons of Darkness,* edited by Orson Scott Card, 1980; *The Infinity Link,* Dial, in press. Contributor to science fiction magazines, including *Galaxy, Fiction, Galileo,* and *Magazine of Fantasy and Science Fiction.*

WORK IN PROGRESS: Ghost Rigger.

SIDELIGHTS: Carver writes: "My stories deal with personal growth and discovery, with emotions, with the responses of my characters to the technological worlds in which they live. I often write of the far future, of star travel and alien environments, and of nonearthly life and intelligence. Throughout, my primary concern is, 'How do my people feel, and how do they adapt and cope with the situations my stories carry them into? How will humanity change in the future, and how will it remain the same?'

"It is my personal conviction that mankind's future lies in space, among the stars—if only we have the will to reach out, to seek the challenge rather than cringing in the midst of our earthly problems. To this end, I write of characters who are no supermen, but are merely humans with their own share of frailties, anxieties, and insecurities. Setting them into difficult and sometimes bizarre situations, I watch to see if they will grow (even if unwillingly) and if they will learn and give up their illusions, but not their wonder, and accept the challenges put before them.

"A thread of fantasy runs through much of my work to date, even through my 'technological' stories. Fantasy becomes linked with reality in my star rigger stories, in which starship pilots (riggers) guide their vessels across the 'subjective sea' of space—a non-Einsteinian continuum in which tides and currents flow between the stars, taking understandable form only through the perceptions, intuitions, and fantasies of the rigger's mind. Focused through an electrical sensory net, the rigger's daydreams serve as an instrument of navigation, detailing the 'landscape' outside the ship. Technology powers the ship and serves the rigger, human intuition acts as its control.''

AVOCATIONAL INTERESTS: "I enjoy sailing and scuba diving. The undersea world is the nearest thing to an alien environment available to us on earth.''

* * *

CARY, Jud
See TUBB, E(dwin) C(harles)

* * *

CASDORPH, Herman Richard 1928-

PERSONAL: Born November 8, 1928, in Charleston, W.Va.; son of Herman Russell and Dorothy May (Meadows) Casdorph; children: Keith, Kimberly, Kathy, Lisa, Christin, Susan. *Education:* West Virginia University, A.B. (with high honors), 1949; Indiana University, M.D., 1953; University of Minnesota, Ph.D., 1961. *Religion:* Christian. *Agent:* Julian Portman Agency, 1680 North Vine St., Hollywood, Calif. 90028. *Office:* 1729 Termino Ave., Suite A, Long Beach, Calif. 90804.

CAREER: Currently in private practice of internal medicine and cardiology. *Military service:* U.S. Air Force, flight surgeon in Medical Corps, 1955-57; became captain. *Member:* Phi Beta Kappa, Alpha Omega Alpha.

WRITINGS: (Editor) *Treatment of the Hyperlipidemic States,* C. C Thomas, 1971; *The Miracles,* Logos International, 1976; *Dream Journey,* Sword Publishing, 1978. Contributor of about fifty articles to medical journals.

WORK IN PROGRESS: Turn Back the Clock, on chelation therapy.

* * *

CASEY, Warren 1935-

PERSONAL: Born April 20, 1935, in New York, N.Y.; son of Peter L. (a steamfitter) and Signe (a nurse; maiden name, Ginman) Casey. *Education:* Syracuse University, B.F.A., 1957; attended New York State Teachers College, Buffalo, 1958-61. *Residence:* Chicago, Ill. *Agent:* Bridget Aschenberg, International Creative Management, 40 West 57th St., New York, N.Y. 10019.

CAREER: Playwright, actor, lyricist, and composer. Worked as teacher of art in Ellenberg, N.Y., 1958-59, Fort Plain, N.Y., 1959-61, and Herkimer, N.Y., 1961-62; Rose Records, Chicago, Ill., sales clerk, 1962-68; Mary Del (chain store), Chicago, assistant manager, 1968-70. Actor in numerous stage productions, including "Sexual Perversity in Chicago," 1974. *Member:* American Society of Composers, Authors, and Publishers, Dramatists Guild. *Awards, honors:* Nominations for numerous Antoinette Perry (Tony) Awards, 1972, all for "Grease"; nomination for Grammy Award for best score from an original cast show album from National Academy of Recording Arts and Sciences, 1972, for "Grease"; award from American Society of Composers, Authors, and Publishers for longest-running show in Broadway history, 1979, for "Grease."

WRITINGS: (With Jim Jacobs) *Grease: A New Fifties Rock 'n' Roll Musical* (two-act; first produced in Chicago, Ill., at Kingston Mines Theatre, 1971, produced Off-Broadway at

Eden Theatre, 1972, produced on Broadway at Broadhurst Theatre, May, 1972), Pocket Books, 1972. Also author of "Mudgett," 1976, and, with Jacobs, "Island of Lost Coeds," a two-act musical. Contributor of incidental music to "Twelfth Night," 1976, music and new lyrics to "June Moon," 1977, and music to Chicago Joseph Jefferson Awards ceremony, 1980.

WORK IN PROGRESS: A musical production entitled "The Toast of Newark."

SIDELIGHTS: In April, 1979, "Grease" became the longest-running musical in Broadway history. Casey's nostalgic celebration of the 1950's, co-written with Jim Jacobs, was praised by Henry Hewes as a musical that "entertains from start to finish."

CA INTERVIEWS THE AUTHOR
CA interviewed Warren Casey by phone, February 12, 1980, at his home in Chicago.

CA: How do you feel about the unexpected success of "Grease?"

CASEY: Well, *unexpected* implies an abruptness that we didn't experience with the show, because we've been living with this for nine years now. If I knew nine years ago that the show today would be the longest running on Broadway, of course that would have been unexpected. But over the years it's just been a change from day to day, so it's been a very slow process of realizing first that the show was a success and then just how much of a success it was turning out to be. Of course when we wrote the show we had no idea. We figured it would run a few weeks in Chicago, and that was the most we expected from it at the time. Neither [co-author] Jim Jacobs nor I had written a show before that. We figured this would just be a nice experience for us and we'd find out if we had any talent for the theatre, for writing.

CA: How did "Grease" actually start; how did the idea come about?

CASEY: The actual idea itself came about very suddenly one day when we were talking to June Pyskacek, who ran the Kingston Mines Theatre. She was just talking in general terms about what shows she might be doing the following year, and Jim, out of nowhere, said, "We're writing a musical." And she said, "Oh, wonderful. When you get it done, we'll put it on at the Kingston Mines." And that was it. It was just about that simple.

CA: Then you had to start writing it.

CASEY: Then we had to starting writing it. We hadn't even discussed this. I was sitting there and I thought, "We are? We're writing a musical?"

CA: Had you and Jim Jacobs been friends for a long time?

CASEY: We'd been friends ever since I'd come to Chicago, which was in 1963. Before that I was an art teacher in public schools in upstate New York. I decided to leave teaching; I had been teaching for four years and wasn't really prepared to do anything else. I had gotten involved in an amateur theatre group while I was teaching, and theatre was the thing I was most interested in, but I didn't think I could make a living right away as an actor. I thought maybe broadcasting was something close that offered more opportunities for employment, so I came to Chicago intitially to go to broadcasting school and never did get a job in broadcasting but ended up staying here.

CA: When you actually sat down to write the promised music, how much of an idea did you have for it?

CASEY: All we had when we started was the idea that it was going to be a musical about the 1950's written in rock-and-roll style. I'd already written some songs—two of the songs are in the show still. I had written "Beauty School Dropout" and "It's Raining on Prom Night" as parodies of the 1950's rock-and-roll kind of song. We started with the assumption that we'd use those two songs and write some others. We had no idea what the story was going to be like when we started. We thought of making the thing a film parody of the kind of movies they made in the 1950's. But at bottom we weren't really interested in just doing that. Anyway, it evolved into writing about high-school kids who were more or less real and more or less the way they actually were in the 1950's.

And we started more with characters and scenes than we did with any idea of where the story was going to go. What we did was write, either individually or together, little things, just ordinary, everyday things—the kids at school, the kids hanging around on the street corner. Some of these scenes ended up in the show. Eventually we took these scenes to see if any of them led from one to another. As we began to get an idea of who the characters were and what problems they might have, we started adding more scenes.

CA: Do you have formal training in music?

CASEY: I had no formal training, but I was always interested in music, even though I couldn't play any instrument until I got my first guitar when I was about twenty-five. But I could read music, just from what little they taught us in public school, and I began teaching myself. And I'd been writing songs in other styles than 1950's rock and roll before we started writing the show—mostly fairly simple things. I just happened to have these two songs that were light fifties rock-and-roll parodies. The other songs I'd written were mostly parodies, comic songs. The music of the 1950's was very simple, and much of it was probably written by people who didn't know any more than we did when we started. It was all very simple chord structures and very square construction. It doesn't take much to pick up.

CA: Were you terribly sensitive about the negative criticism of "Grease?"

CASEY: I guess you're always sensitive about negative criticism, but there wasn't as much of it as people seem to think. A myth has developed that the show was panned by the critics when it opened, which isn't true. We had generally favorable reviews. One or two very bad reviews—one from the *New York Post,* from the critic who is no longer with them, and bad reviews in the Boston papers. I think Boston is the only city that has always given the show bad reviews. And the show is always immensely popular in Boston in spite of the reviews. Conversely, in Los Angeles the critics have always loved the show, but it's never done that well with the audiences there.

CA: Jim Jacobs has spoken about the difficulties of foreign productions of "Grease" because of cultural and linguistic differences. He cited especially the London production.

CASEY: The London production was the only foreign production we were actually involved in. I imagine it was probably easier for them in Mexico and Japan; we don't know the language or the culture that well, so they could just go ahead and do whatever, and how would we know what was wrong? We understood that in Mexico they couldn't do a lot of the things that they do on Broadway, first of all because they wouldn't understand them and secondly because there is very heavy censorship. But it was very popular in Mexico.

CA: Has "Grease" changed your life in ways you hadn't anticipated?

CASEY: Oh, of course. It's given me freedom to do a lot of things that I wouldn't have been able to do before. Financially we are both much better off. It gave me a chance to do a lot of traveling that I'd always wanted to do, to see places that I never really thought I'd be able to see—Japan and England, and France, where they haven't done the show, but I like to go there. I also started learning to play the piano. I had always wanted to, and when the show became a success, I went and bought a piano and started learning. I'll never be a performer on the piano, never be able to play publicly, but being able to play helps me to do things when I'm writing a song that you can't do on a guitar. When you play a guitar, especially the way I play it, all you can communicate of a song you're writing is the melody and the chords and maybe the beat or a time signature. But I hear all kinds of things in a song that I couldn't communicate before, and I didn't even know before I played the piano whether some of the things I heard in a song were technically possible.

CA: Did your acting experience help in writing the play?

CASEY: It helped us an awful lot, not just in giving us a sense of what would be comfortable for an actor to do on stage. Jim and I both had been acting in a lot of small theatres around Chicago, including a couple of places that specialized in original scripts, most of which, of course, were bad. I think we learned as much from doing bad plays as we did from doing good ones, because we learned a lot of the things you just don't do when you're writing a play.

CA: Have you remained in close touch with any of the original cast?

CASEY: Two of the people from the original show did the show on Broadway and have gone on to quite a bit of success. Marilu Henner was in the show when it first opened at the Kingston Mines; now she's in "Taxi" on television. And Jim Canning was in the show at the Kingston Mines; he's done a couple of movies—he was in "The Boys in Company C." Those two people we still see a lot of, and they've been with the show from the very beginning. There are not too many of the others that we see often unless we run into them around town. Of course a lot of them are still here in Chicago.

CA: How did you feel at the recent invitational performance and celebration marking the record-breaking run on Broadway?

CASEY: The most exciting part for me was the performance itself, when we saw the original people from the Broadway cast and the original people from the first touring company. Most of these were people I hadn't seen in at least five or six years. To see them right back on the stage doing the show almost the way it was done when it first opened on Broadway was tremendously exciting. It didn't even seem that they had aged that much. If anything they were better, because most of them had acquired proficiency since the show opened; it was marvelous—everybody in the show was a star.

When we were first rehearsing the show in New York, we used to talk about how we wanted to keep the rough edge. This was not just us, but the director and the choreographer felt that one of the charms of the show was a roughness, its lack of polish, and the randomness of some of the scenes—that this was all very charming, and if the show were too slicked up it would lose something. But over the years it has become a little more polished, a little slicker, especially that celebration night when we saw these real pros doing the show. I didn't miss the rough edges at all.

CA: Do you want to talk about the new play you're working on, "Island of Lost Coeds?"

CASEY: We've got the script in a pretty finished form. We're looking right now for a place to do it around Chicago. We'd like to do the same thing again—do the show here in one of the Chicago theatres and see if the pattern would repeat itself. That would be wonderful, but we'd be happy if people just liked it, if it had enough success to get an audience here, whether it went on or not.

CA: Are you working full time in theatre now?

CASEY: Yes. We're both full-time writers.

CA: What have you done between writing "Grease" and working on "Island of Lost Coeds?"

CASEY: When a show is as successful as "Grease," you write the show about three or four times. Since "Grease" opened, we've spent another three or four years writing "Grease." I'm sure Jim told you about going to London and trying to make changes that would be understandable to the British but still keep the American flavor. That was one experience. I must say that I was not very happy with that; the English never did take to the show in the way that people in other countries did. I don't know if it's the difference in the English; I think it's maybe an attitude toward the 1950's. We had Eisenhower in the 1950s, and they had the queen and Winston Churchill, and there is a difference in the way you look back.

We also had to clean up the Broadway version when they started the touring companies because a lot of the tours would hit small, Bible Belt towns. I didn't mind that; I found that many of the lines were funnier when we took the dirty words out. We prepared one laundered version that they could do in any city where they were afraid the censors or whoever would object. A strange thing has happened over the years. They had touring companies that played mostly these small towns and midwestern engagements, so those companies just learned the cleaned up version. But when openings came up in the national touring company or on Broadway, they would take people who had gained experience in the roles from the bus-and-truck tours and put them on Broadway. And what's happened over the years is that there's been an amalgam of cleaned-up lines and the original raunchy lines, and you never know what line is going to come out of whom.

CA: What else have you done in those interim years?

CASEY: When the movie came up, we thought for a while we would get to write the screenplay, or work on it. So we wrote "Grease" again when we tried writing a treatment for the film to give them an idea what the movie would be. It turned out that we didn't get to work on the movie, so that was for naught. In addition to that, I've written a few shows, I've written a couple of scripts that haven't been produced, I wrote a score that is yet to be produced. It was written specifically for a theatre here in Chicago with the idea that this theatre group was going to get a new space to perform in. They haven't gotten the space yet, so the show is still sitting

there. That was three years ago. It's a musical about a mass murderer who lived in Chicago at the turn of the century. It's too bad for us that "Sweeney Todd" got to be such a hit.

I have also written songs and incidental music for a couple of local productions in Chicago, as well as doing some more acting. I think outside of "Grease," the most exciting experience I've had in the theatre was playing the role of Bernie Litko in the very first production of David Mamet's "Sexual Perversity in Chicago." A windfall success like "Grease" creates some peculiar problems (which I still wouldn't trade for anyone else's problems). We hadn't prepared for careers as writers, and we found ourselves with a success on our hands unknown to many writers who have spent years learning their craft. So I've had to reverse the usual procedure: I started out a success, then spent the following years learning and paying dues.

BIOGRAPHICAL/CRITICAL SOURCES: New York Times, February 2, 1972, June 4, 1972; *New Yorker,* February 26, 1972, June 26, 1978; *Newsweek,* February 28, 1972, June 12, 1978; *Time,* May 29, 1972, June 19, 1978; *Saturday Review,* July 15, 1972; *Melody Maker,* July 7, 1973; *Dance Magazine,* April, 1975; *New York,* June 26, 1978; *Film Comment,* July, 1978; *Nation,* July 1, 1978; *New Republic,* July 1, 1978; *Encore,* July 10, 1978; *MacLean's,* July 19, 1978; *New Times,* July 10, 1978; *New Leader,* July 17, 1978; *National Review,* July 21, 1978; *Atlantic Monthly,* August, 1978; *Christian Century,* August 30, 1978; *Commonweal,* September 1, 1978; *Contemporary Literary Criticism,* Volume 12, Gale, 1980.

—*Interview by Jean W. Ross*

*   *   *

CASS, James (Michael) 1915-

PERSONAL: Born November 19, 1915, in Saranac Lake, N.Y.; son of James Michael (a minister) and Julia (Monnett) Cass; married Barbara Hillman, June 4, 1946; children: James Michael, Frederick, Williams, Julia. *Education:* Ohio Wesleyan University, B.A., 1937; Columbia University, M.A., 1949. *Politics:* Independent Democrat. *Home:* 100 Plains Rd., New Paltz, N.Y. 12561. *Office:* 342 Madison Ave., New York, N.Y. 10017.

CAREER: National Citizens Commission for Public Schools, New York City, research director, 1951-56; National Citizens Council for Better Schools, New York City, research director, 1956-59; *Saturday Review,* New York City, associate education editor, 1960-66, education editor, 1966-77; writer, 1977—. Member of board of trustees of Citizens Scholarship Foundation of America and Ohio Wesleyan University; consultant to educational institutions, businesses, and government agencies. *Military service:* U.S. Naval Reserve, active duty in Hospital Corps, 1942-45; became chief pharmacist's mate. *Member:* Education Writers Association. *Awards, honors:* LL.D. from MacMurray College, 1966; D.H.L. from Ohio Wesleyan University, 1968; D.Litt from Widner College, 1970; has also received numerous awards for education reporting and editorial commentaries.

WRITINGS: (With Max Birnbaum) *Comparative Guide to American Colleges,* Harper, 1964, 9th edition, 1979; (with Birnbaum) *Comparative Guide to Science and Engineering Programs,* Harper, 1971; (with Careth Ellington) *Directory of Facilities for the Learning Disabled and Handicapped,* Harper, 1972; (editor) *Education U.S.A.: The Great Contemporary Issues,* Arno, 1973; (with Birnbaum) *Counselors Comparative Guide to American Colleges,* Harper, 1974; (with Birnbaum) *Comparative Guide to Two-Year Colleges and Career Programs,* Harper, 1976.

WORK IN PROGRESS: A biography of Hans Maeder and the Stockbridge School.

SIDELIGHTS: Cass commented: "I became a writer by chance and remain one by necessity. I am not sure whether I am a writer who likes to garden on the side, or a gardener who likes to write on the side. Both activities are rewarding."

* * *

CASSOLA, Carlo 1917-

PERSONAL: Born March 17, 1917, in Rome, Italy; married Guiseppina Rabage; children: one daughter. *Education:* Received degree from University of Rome. *Home:* Via Michelangelo 12, Grosseto, Italy.

CAREER: Writer. Teacher in secondary schools in Italy, 1942-61; currently a professor of history and philosophy. *Awards, honors:* Strega literary prize, 1960, for *La ragazza di Bube.*

WRITINGS—In English translation: *Fausto e Anna* (novel), Einaudi, 1952, translation by Isabel Quigly published as *Fausto and Anna*, Pantheon, 1960, 2nd edition of original Italian, Einaudi, 1964; *La ragazza di Bube* (novel), Einaudi, 1960, translation by Marguerite Waldman published as *Bebo's Girl*, Pantheon, 1962; *Un cuore arido* (novel), Einaudi, 1961, translation by William Weaver published as *An Arid Heart*, Pantheon, 1964; *Monte Mario*, Rizzoli, 1973, translation by Sebastian Roberts published as *Portrait of Helena*, Chatto & Windus, 1975.

Other writings: *La visita* (short stories), [Italy], 1942, 2nd edition, Einaudi, 1962; *Alla periferia* (short stories), [Italy], 1942; *I vecchi compagni* (novel), [Italy], 1953; *Il taglio del bosco* (short stories; title means "Timber Cutting"), Nistri-Lischi, 1955, 2nd edition, Mondadori, 1970; (with Luciano Bianciardi) *I minatori della Maremma*, Laterza, 1956; *Viaggio in Cina*, Feltrinelli, 1956; *La casa di via Valadier* (novel), Einaudi, 1956; *Un matrimonio del dopoguerra* (novel), Einaudi, 1957; *Il soldato*, Feltrinelli, 1958.

Il cacciatore (novel), Einaudi, 1964; *Tempi memorabili* (novel), Einaudi, 1966; *Storia di Ada* (title means "Ada's Story"), Einaudi, 1967; *Ferrovia locale* (novel), Einaudi, 1968; *Una relazione*, Einaudi, 1969.

Paura e tristezza, Einaudi, 1970; (with Mario Luzi) *Poesia e romanzo*, Rizzoli, 1973; *Fogli di diario*, Rizzoli, 1974; *Gisella*, Rizzoli, 1974, 2nd edition, 1978; *Troppo tardi*, Rizzoli, 1975; *L'Antagonista*, Rizzoli, 1976; *Il gigante cieco*, Rizzoli, 1976; *Ultima frontiera*, Rizzoli, 1976; *La disavventura*, Rizzoli, 1977; *L'Uomo e il cane*, Rizzoli, 1977; *La lezione della storia*, Rizzoli, 1978; *Un uomo solo*, Rizzoli, 1978; *Il superstite*, Rizzoli, 1978.

Contributor of articles to periodicals, including *Il mondo, Contemporaneo,* and *Corriere della sera.*

SIDELIGHTS: Carlo Cassola's first novel released for English-speaking audiences was *Fausto and Anna.* Based in part on his own experiences as a partisan, the novel follows Fausto as he becomes disillusioned with his middle-class existence, breaks off his relationship with his girlfriend Anna, and joins the communist resistance fighters in Italy. His youthful enthusiasm for the adventure and glory of battle palls, however, when he finally realizes the utter brutality and senseless destruction that is the reality of war. He returns home and seeks out Anna, wishing to renew their love, but finds he is too late, as she is already married.

"Cassola roots his works in understatement," noted Helene

Cantarella of the *New York Times Book Review.* "He writes a terse, dry prose, geared to sparse action conveyed through the medium of an astringent, almost 'hermetic' dialogue." *San Francisco Chronicle* reviewer Douglas Hammond, however, contended that *Fausto and Anna* falls short of "the magnificent force one has come to associate with the neo-realistic Italian novel." T. G. Bergin agreed that "the reader will find variation of emphasis, inconsistency of characterization and some ambiguity about what the story signifies," but added that "at the same time the novel must be conceded a certain vitality, the narrative line holds our attention, the [dialogue] is in the main good, and there is in the telling of the tale a freshness and exuberance."

Bebo's Girl, Cassola's next book in English translation, is the bittersweet love story of Mara and Bebo. Once lauded for killing several fascists during his time as a partisan, Bebo has since been punished for what are now called his crimes. He feels betrayed and deserted by his former comrades who had previously praised his actions. Only Mara does not leave him and promises to wait for him during the fourteen long years of his imprisonment.

Termed "a love story told with realistic directness and poetic delicacy" by Marc Slonim of the *New York Times Book Review,* the novel won critical acclaim both in Italy and the United States for what many believed to be an accurate depiction of the events in Italy following World War II. A reviewer for *Time,* however, found it "a little hard to see why everyone in the novel—and apparently the author too—considers Bebo a fine young man who is down on his luck rather than a nasty young fanatic who has blown the skull off a completely innocent boy." Despite this type of assessment, the *Times Literary Supplement* summarized that the novel "achieves real distinction in its portrayal of the growth and change of character in the face of adversity." Likewise, Olga Ragusa of *Books Abroad* declared *Bebo's Girl* to be "a somber and yet hopeful novel. . . . Cassola strikes a note of faith, if not in the perfectability of man, at least in his possibility to learn from experience, to become more human."

BIOGRAPHICAL/CRITICAL SOURCES: New York Times Book Review, June 26, 1960, June 10, 1962; *New York Herald Tribune Book Review,* July 17, 1960; *Springfield Republican,* July 17, 1960; *San Francisco Chronicle,* August 7, 1960; *Times Literary Supplement,* August 19, 1960, January 26, 1962; *Books Abroad,* spring, 1961, summer, 1963; *Time,* June 22, 1962.*

* * *

CASTILLO, Richard Griswold del
See GRISWOLD del CASTILLO, Richard

* * *

CATHCART, Robert S(tephen) 1923-

PERSONAL: Born January 30, 1923, in Los Angeles, Calif.; son of Stephen P. (a laborer) and Martha L. (a laborer; maiden name, Morley) Cathcart; married Dolores J. Hawley (a writer), July 1, 1944; children: Linda, Stephen. *Education:* University of Redlands, A.B., 1944, M.A., 1947; Northwestern University, Ph.D., 1953; also attended University of Southern California and Purdue University. *Home:* 1 Oakpoint Dr. N., Bayville, N.Y. 11709. *Office:* Department of Communication Arts and Sciences, Queens College of the City University of New York, Flushing, N.Y. 11367.

CAREER: Young Men's Christian Association, Los Angeles, Calif., part-time director of community activities, 1941-

43; Purdue University, West Lafayette, Ind., instructor in public speaking and director of forensics, 1947-49; University of Maryland, College Park, instructor in public speaking and coordinator of public address area, 1953-55; California State College, Los Angeles, assistant professor, 1955-58, associate professor, 1958-61, professor of rhetoric and public address, 1961-68, co-director of Communication Research Center, 1957-62; Queens College of the City University of New York, Flushing, N.Y., professor of communication arts and sciences, 1968—, head of department, 1968-71. Visiting professor at Pennsylvania State University, summer, 1963, and University of Texas, summer, 1964; senior visitor at Magdalen College, Oxford, 1966; visiting lecturer at Christ Church College of Education, 1966, and Sophia University, 1974-75. *Military service:* U.S. Naval Reserve, active duty as communications officer, 1943-46, and executive officer, 1951-53; served in Pacific theater; became lieutenant junior grade. *Member:* Speech Communication Association (member of council, 1970-71), Oxford Philosophical Society, Phi Kappa Phi, Tau Kappa Alpha. *Awards, honors:* Danforth fellow, 1967—.

WRITINGS: (With Marvin Laser and Fred Marcus) *Ideas and Issues: Readings for Analysis and Evaluation,* Ronald, 1963; (with Laser, Marcus, and John Dahl) *Student, School, and Society: Crosscurrents in Secondary Education,* Chandler Publishing, 1964; *Post Communication: Critical Analysis and Evaluation,* Bobbs-Merrill, 1966; (with Larry Samovar) *Small Group Communication,* W. C. Brown, 1970, 3rd edition, 1978; (with Gary Gumpert) *Inter/Media: Interpersonal Communication in a Media World,* Oxford University Press, 1979. Senior editor of "Bicentennial Monographs on the Continuing American Revolution," Speech Communication Association, 1977. Contributor of about twenty-five articles to scholarly journals. Book editor of *Western Speech,* 1961-64.

WORK IN PROGRESS: A Rhetorical/Symbolic Theory of Radical Movements; An Introduction to the Role of Media in Human Communication.

SIDELIGHTS: Cathcart told *CA:* "My concern has always been with how human beings influence and are influenced through the use of communication. I believe we humans are totally involved with our language symbols and that we must continually work to understand what these symbols are and how to use them. Furthermore, I feel that in an electronic-technological age our symbols and our uses of communication are rapidly changing and we must work more diligently to understand these changes."

*   *   *

CAULEY, Lorinda Bryan 1951-

PERSONAL: Born July 2, 1951, in Washington, D.C.; daughter of Robert S. and Lucille E. Bryan; married Patrick Dennis Cauley (an artist), June 15, 1974. *Education:* Montgomery Junior College, associate degree, 1971; Rhode Island School of Design, B.F.A., 1974. *Home and office:* 17 Leonard St., New York, N.Y. 10013. *Agent:* Florence Alexander, 80 Park Ave., New York, N.Y. 10016.

CAREER: Illustrator and writer, 1976—.

WRITINGS—All self-illustrated; all children's books: *Please Porridge Hot,* Putnam, 1977; *The Bake Off,* Putnam, 1978; *Animal Kids,* Putnam, 1979; *The Ugly Duckling,* Harcourt, 1979; *The Story of "The Three Pigs,"* Putnam, 1980; *The Goose and the Golden Coins,* Harcourt, 1981; *The Story of "The Three Bears,"* Putnam, 1981.

SIDELIGHTS: Cauley told *CA:* "Having been an illustrator of children's books first, I like to write stories in which I can visualize each particular scene and how I will portray each character. I think about interesting settings, action, colorful images, and special details—all those things that work together to make a book for children unique and fun to read."

*   *   *

CENTO

See COBBING, Bob

*   *   *

CERVERI, Doris 1914-

PERSONAL: Born May 17, 1914, in Goldfield, Nev.; daughter of Ray L. (a mechanic) and Viola (a waitress; maiden name, Griggs) Rockwood; married Louis F. Pastrell, June 9, 1934 (divorced, 1954); married John Cerveri, December 17, 1955; children: (first marriage) Darrell, Karen Pastrell Wesley, Dana Lee. *Politics:* Democrat. *Religion:* Baptist. *Home:* 1264 Patrick Ave., Reno, Nev. 89509.

CAREER: State of Nevada, secretary, 1947-74, with Department of Health, Department of Agriculture, and University of Nevada, Reno; free-lance writer. *Member:* Western Writers of America, Treasure Hunters of America (member of board of directors), Nevada Press Women (president, 1976), Nevada Pen Women (vice-president, 1979), Washoe Historical Society (member of board of directors). *Awards, honors:* Prizes from national and local associations for work, including two second place awards from National League of American Pen Women, 1976; award from *Real West,* 1977, for story, "Women's Lib Began in the West."

WRITINGS: Nevada: A Colorful Past, Dave's Printing & Publishing, 1975; (editor) *Nevada Historical Miscellany,* Western Printing & Publishing, 1976; *Pyramid Lake Legends and Reality,* Western Printing & Publishing, 1977; *With Curry's Compliments,* Great Basin Press, 1981. Author of "Nevada, A Colorful Past," a weekly column in *Reno Evening Gazette,* 1972—, and a monthly column in *Carson City Appeal.* Contributor of articles and reviews to newspapers and magazines, including *Desert, Sparks Tribune,* and *Nevada State Journal.*

AVOCATIONAL INTERESTS: Collecting music boxes, Indian artifacts, seashells, and paperweights, visiting ghost towns, fishing and hunting, treasure hunting.

*   *   *

CHAMBERLAIN, Jonathan Mack 1928-

PERSONAL: Born August 26, 1928, near Alton, Utah; son of Guy and Vera (Heaton) Chamberlain; married Beverly Christensen, January 16, 1953; children: Charles Jonathan, Lori (Mrs. Darrel R. Judd), Lisa (Mrs. Charles Palmer), Mark Thomas, David Guy. *Education:* Brigham Young University, B.A., 1958; attended University of Nevada, 1961; University of Wyoming, M.Ed., 1964, Ph.D., 1967. *Politics:* Republican. *Religion:* Church of Jesus Christ of Latter-day Saints (Mormons). *Home:* 280 West 1700 S., Orem, Utah 84057. *Office:* Counseling Center, Brigham Young University, C273 ASB, Provo, Utah 84602.

CAREER: Worked as dairy farmer, rancher, and journeyman carpenter in Utah, 1942-48; served as a missionary for LDS church in Minnesota and Manitoba, 1948-50; teacher of English and French in Panaca, Nev., 1958-63; University of Wyoming, Laramie, psychologist at Counseling Center, 1964-67; school psychologist and director of regional child study services in Price, Utah, 1967-70; Brigham Young University, Provo, Utah, assistant professor, 1970-72, associate professor of educational psychology, 1972—, counseling psychologist at Counseling Center, 1970—. Licensed and private practicing psychologist and marriage and family counselor, 1970—. Gives workshops; public speaker; broadcaster on "Crisis Line" on KEYY-Radio, 1979—. *Military service:* U.S. Air Force, career guidance specialist, 1951-53; served in England; became master sergeant.

MEMBER: American Personnel and Guidance Association, American School Counselor Association, Association of Mormon Counselors and Psychotherapists, Rocky Mountain Association of Counselors, Educators, and Supervisors, Utah Personnel and Guidance Association (president, 1977-78; past member of board of governors), Utah Psychologists Association, Utah School Counselor Association, Utah Association of Psychologists in Private Practice, Utah School Psychologists Association, Kiwanis International (member of board of directors, 1977-78; public relations chairman, 1978—; president of local chapter, 1980-81).

WRITINGS: (Editor with J. K. Donaldson) *Understanding Child Behavior: A Teacher Inservice Training Program,* Educational Resources Information Center/Clearinghouse on Rural Education and Small Schools, 1968; (editor with Donaldson) *Behavioral Problems in the Classroom: A Teacher Inservice Training Program,* Educational Resources Information Center/Clearinghouse on Rural Education and Small Schools, 1969; (with Wayne L. Owen) *A Comparison of the Effects of Three Treatment Methods on the Aggressive and Non-Aggressive Elementary School Children,* Educational Resources Information Center/Clearinghouse on Rural Education and Small Schools, 1970; *Behavior Modification Techniques for Teachers of Exceptional Children,* Brigham Young University Home Study, 1972; *Eliminating a Self-Defeating Behavior,* Brigham Young University Press, 1974, 5th edition, 1980; *Eliminate Your SDB's*—*Self-Defeating Behaviors,* Brigham Young University Press, 1978; *Turn Yourselves and Live,* Brigham Young University Press, 1979; *Student Handbook for Eliminating SDB's,* Brigham Young University Press, 1980.

Contributor: Anita M. Mitchell and C. D. Johnson, editors, *Therapeutic Techniques: Working Models for Helping Professionals,* California Personnel and Guidance Association, 1973; Gloria G. Harris, editor, *The Group Treatment of Human Problems: A Social Learning Approach,* Grune, 1977.

Author of "Eliminating Self-Defeating Behaviors," a video tape series, Brigham Young University, 1977. Author of audio tapes. Contributor of about twenty-five articles to scholarly journals.

WORK IN PROGRESS: ESDB Casebook: Treatment of Common and Unusual Cases, publication expected in 1981; *ESDB for Pastoral Counselors,* with Stephen Younkers, publication expected in 1982; research on effects of "ESDB" method on such symptoms as depression; comparing effects of "ESDB" through books, home study courses, live workshops, and ongoing individual counseling; research on characteristics of home study participants in the "ESBD" method.

SIDELIGHTS: Chamberlain commented: "My major motivation has come from seeing the changes that come into the lives of individuals in trouble as they apply simple and tested principles for living. Whether in my live workshops, in individual counseling with me, or in independent study by correspondence, the results are the same.

"Since learning about the Eliminating Self-Defeating Behavior concepts in 1970 and applying them in my life and practice, I have discovered little or nothing written about this therapeutic method. This lack of information motivated me to write and publish about the subject. The ESDB method comes from the work of Dr. Milton R. Cudney of Kalamazoo, Michigan. Simply outlined, it is an individual or group method to aid the individual in overcoming any self-defeating behavior, such as feelings of inferiority, unwanted habits, negative thinking, procrastination, eating disorders, etc., by following this seven-step process: 1. How do I do my SDB? 2. How do I disown doing my SDB? 3. What prices do I pay for doing my SDB? 4. What choices do I make to do my SDB? 5. What techniques do I use to help make my SDB choices? 6. What fears do I need to face to be without my SDB? 7. By facing my fears and discovering my inner best self through guided imagery, I can improve my life.

"This method has been found, through numerous research projects, to produce changes in the participant that raise self-esteem while giving the individual a concrete way to attack an unwanted personal problem. The principles involved with each of these steps are applicable to almost anyone's life. Children from third grade on up can apply them to good advantage. However, most material on the subject has been written for the adult level.

"My hope is always that I can bring hope and change for the better into the life of my reader, that I can in some way help to reveal to the reader the truly great potential that lies within, to get the reader to use the gifts and talents he may have without fear, and to interact in his own personal life with greater love and understanding of self and others.

"*Eliminating a Self-Defeating Behavior* was written in 1974 as a way to reach out to others in the world through the Brigham Young University Home Study program. This program gave the student in his or her own home a way to experience my ESDB workshops by mail. It has proven very effective. *Eliminate Your SDB's* was then written for those who do not wish or who do not have the opportunity to experience personal contact with workshops, groups, individual counseling, or home study, but who want to learn about the method and apply it to themselves as best they can. It is a do-it-yourself book with many examples of how to take each step in the process of ridding the self of unwanted thoughts, feelings, or actions. The feedback from these two books has been most rewarding. *Turn Yourselves and Live* came about because of the many scriptures that I discovered to fit the ESDB method. They deepen the whole process and enliven the concepts that are presented in each step.

"Because the ESDB method, in the way that I do it, requires that I write on the individual participant's diary and return it quickly, I have learned to type my thoughts and feelings rapidly as I respond to what the individual's experience in their efforts to overcome the self-defeating behavior. This is like having a private conference with me in writing. I have found it has many advantages over the usual form of therapy.

"Most of my writings have come from my own experience rather than from influences felt from other writers. Some works I have purposely not read so that I could get my own ideas down first. Even so I find that several writers have similar ideas at about the same time."

*   *   *

CHANT, Donald (Alfred) 1928-

PERSONAL: Born September 30, 1928, in Toronto, Ontario, Canada; son of Sperrin Noah Fulton (a professor) and

Nellie Irene (Cooper) Chant; married C. M. Rutherford (died, 1969); married Karen Merle Hanes, October, 1975; children: Patrick, Jeffery, Timothy. *Education:* University of British Columbia, B.A., 1950, M.A., 1952; University of London, Ph.D., 1956. *Home:* 9 Beaumont Rd., Toronto, Ontario, Canada M4W 1V4. *Office:* Simcoe Hall, University of Toronto, Toronto, Ontario, Canada M5S 1A1.

CAREER: Canadian Department of Agriculture, research officer at entomology laboratory in Vancouver, British Columbia, 1951-56, at Research Institute in Bellevue, Ontario, 1956-60, and director of research laboratory at Vineland, Ontario, 1960-64; University of California, Riverside, chairman of department of biological control, 1964-67; University of Toronto, Toronto, Ontario, professor of zoology, 1967—, chairman of department, 1967-75, vice-president of university and provost, 1975-80, director of Joint Guelph/Toronto Centre for Toxicology, 1980—. Chairman of Canadian Environmental Advisory Committee, Pollution Probe Foundation, and Canadian Commission of University Biology Chairmen; member of board of directors of Institute of Ecology, Washington, D.C.; member of scientific advisory committee of Canadian World Wildlife Fund.

MEMBER: Canadian Society of Zoologists (president), Canadian Entomological Society, British Ecological Society, Ontario Environmental Assessment Board. *Awards, honors:* LL.D. from Dalhousie University; White Owl Conservation award from Imperial Tobacco Co., Ltd., 1972; distinguished public service award from Federation of Ontario Naturalists, 1975.

WRITINGS: (Editor) *Pollution Probe,* New Press, 1st edition, 1970, 2nd edition, 1971, 3rd edition, 1972; (with Ralph Owen Brinkhurst) *This Good, Good Earth: Our Fight for Survival,* Macmillan, 1971; (with F. DeMarco and R. Robertson) *Effect on Human Health of Lead From the Environment,* Ontario Ministry of Health, 1974; (contributor) D. Estrin and J. Swaigen, *Environment on Trial,* New Press, 1974; (contributor) Robert Logan, editor, *The Way Ahead for Canada: A Paperback Referendum,* Lester & Orpen Ltd., 1976. Contributor of about sixty scholarly articles to journals.

AVOCATIONAL INTERESTS: Fishing, camping.

*   *   *

CHAPMAN, Guy (Patterson)   1889-1972

PERSONAL: Born September 11, 1889, in Cookham Dean, Berkshire, England; died June 30, 1972; son of George (a government official) Chapman; married Margaret Storm Jameson (a writer), 1926. *Education:* Received M.A. from Christ Church, Oxford; received B.Sc. from London School of Economics. *Residence:* London, England.

CAREER: Writer. Worked for publishers, including Jonathan Cape and Eyre & Spottiswoode, 1914-40; University of Leeds, Leeds, England, professor of modern history, 1945-53. Member of Institute of Advanced Study in Princeton, N.J., 1957. *Military service:* British Army, 1914-20; served with Royal Fusiliers in France and Germany; became major; received Military Cross and Order of the British Empire; mentioned in dispatches. British Army, 1941-45; served with Army Educational Corps; became lieutenant colonel.

WRITINGS: (Editor) *Travel Diaries of William Beckford of Fonthill,* Houghton, 1928, reprinted, Kraus Reprint, 1972; (with John Hodgkin) *A Bibliography of William Beckford of Fonthill,* Constable, 1930, reprinted, R. West, 1977; *A Painted Cloth* (novel), Cassell, 1930; *A Passionate Prodigal-*

ity: Fragments of Autobiography, Nicholson & Watson, 1933, 2nd edition, MacGibbon & Kee, 1965, Holt, 1966; *Beckford* (biography), Scribner, 1937, reprinted, Norwood Editions, 1976; (editor and author of introduction) *Vain Glory: A Miscellany of the Great War, 1914-1918, Written By Those Who Fought in It on Each Side and on All Fronts,* Cassell, 1937, 2nd edition, 1968; *Culture and Survival,* J. Cape, 1940; *The Dreyfus Case: A Reassessment,* Reynal, 1955, reprinted, Greenwood Press, 1979; *The Third Republic of France: The First Phase, 1871-1894,* St. Martin's, 1962; *Why France Collapsed,* Cassell, 1968, published as *Why France Fell: The Defeat of the French Army in 1940,* Holt, 1969; *The Dreyfus Trials,* Stein & Day, 1972; *A Kind of Survivor: The Autobiography of Guy Chapman,* Gollancz, 1975.

SIDELIGHTS: While still a young man, Guy Chapman became interested in William Beckford of Fonthill—actor, builder, gentleman, and author of the controversial novel, *Vathek.* After editing a volume of Beckford's travel diaries and a bibliography of his works, Chapman wrote what many believe to be the definitive biography of the man. Deemed a "meticulously accurate biographical chronicle" by Alexander Cowie of the *Saturday Review of Literature,* Chapman spent a full ten years in extensive research to produce the work. Edgar Johnson of the *New Republic,* however, noted that "the facts are there, more complete, and more acutely analyzed, than in any previous biography. . . . [The] portrayal lacks only life." But *Spectator* reviewer John Haywood lauded the book as "learned and yet human, sensitive and intelligent in its interpretation of fact, imaginative but never wild in its surmises, and written with just that degree of elegance and formality which its subject requires."

The Dreyfus Case: A Reassessment is widely held to be Chapman's finest work. In it he tells of the famous trial of Alfred Dreyfus, the French-Jewish army officer convicted in the 1890's as a spy, though later acquitted and released from prison. While the case was complex and confusing to many, reviewers agreed that Chapman's narrative was both clear and comprehensive. J. M. Duffy of *Commonweal,* for instance, suggested that "perhaps our greatest indebtedness to Mr. Chapman is for the estimable manner in which he disposes of the shibboleths and the cant which attached themselves to the case and which have remained there to spoil our view of the truth." A reviewer for the *Manchester Guardian,* moreover, observed that "drama and excitement are present in full measure in Professor Chapman's account. But in addition his scholarship and fineness of judgment and perception make this into a work of first-rate importance."

BIOGRAPHICAL/CRITICAL SOURCES: Spectator, April 21, 1928, March 12, 1937; *New York Times,* November 25, 1928; *Books,* May 9, 1937; *Saturday Review of Literature,* May 29, 1937; *New Republic,* August 18, 1937; *Manchester Guardian,* May 10, 1955; *Commonweal,* March 16, 1956, August 22, 1969; *Times Literary Supplement,* March 13, 1969; *New Statesman,* May 2, 1969; *New York Times Book Review,* July 20, 1969; Guy Chapman, *A Kind of Survivor: The Autobiography of Guy Chapman,* Gollancz, 1975.*

*   *   *

CHARGAFF, Erwin   1905-

PERSONAL: Born August 11, 1905, in Austria; came to the United States in 1928, naturalized citizen, 1940; son of Hermann and Rosa Chargaff; married Vera Broido; children: Thomas. *Education:* University of Vienna, D.Phil. (summa cum laude), 1928. *Home:* 350 Central Park W., New York, N.Y. 10025.

CAREER: Yale University, New Haven, Conn., Milton Campbell Research Fellow in Organic Chemistry, 1928-30; University of Berlin, Berlin, Germany, assistant in charge of chemistry in department of bacteriology and public health, 1930-33; Institut Pasteur, Paris, France, research associate, 1933-34; Columbia University, New York, N.Y., research associate, 1935-38, assistant professor, 1938-46, associate professor, 1946-52, professor of biochemistry, 1952-74, Jesup Lecturer, 1959, profesor emeritus, 1974—, chairman of department, 1970-74. Researcher for Office of Scientific Research and Development, 1942-44; member of National Research Council committee on growth, 1952-54; member of advisory council on biology, Oak Ridge National Laboratory, 1958-67. Visiting professor at University of Stockholm, 1949, University of Rio de Janeiro, University of Sao Paulo, and University of Recife, all 1959, and College de France, 1965; Harvey Lecturer, 1956; visiting lecturer at University of Tokyo, University of Sendai, and University of Kyoto, all 1958; K. A. Forster Lecturer, 1968; Miescher Memorial Lecturer, 1969.

MEMBER: National Academy of Sciences, American Academy of Arts and Sciences (fellow), American Philosophical Society, Royal Swedish Physiographic Society (foreign member), German Academy of Science. Awards, honors: Pasteur Medal from Society of Biological Chemistry (Paris), 1949; Guggenheim fellowships, 1949, 1957-58; Carl Neuberg Medal from American Society of European Chemists, 1958; medal from Societe Chimique de Belgique, 1961; Charles Leopold Mayer Prize from French Academie des Sciences, 1963; H. P. Heineken Prize from Royal Netherlands Academy of Sciences, 1964; award from Bertner Foundation, 1965; Gregor Mendel Medal from German Academy of Sciences, 1973; National Medal of Science, 1975; Sc.D. from Columbia University, 1976; D.Phil. from University of Basel, 1976; medal from New York Academy of Medicine, 1980.

WRITINGS: (Editor with J. N. Davidson) The Nucleic Acids: Chemistry and Biology, Academic Press, Volumes I and II, 1955, Volume III, 1960; Voices in the Labyrinth: Nature, Man, and Science, edited by Ruth N. Anshen, Seabury, 1978; Heraclitean Fire: Sketches From a Life Before Nature, Rockefeller University Press, 1978. Also author of Essays on Nucleic Acids. Contributor of more than three hundred articles to scientific journals.

* * *

CHARRIERE, Henri   1906-1973

PERSONAL: Born in 1906; died of cancer, July 29, 1973, in Madrid, Spain; married.

CAREER: Safecracker in Paris, France; convicted of murdering a Montmartre gangster and sentenced to life imprisonment, 1931; escaped from penal colony in Cayenne, French Guiana, c. 1934; later captured and served in solitary confinement at penal colony in Devil's Island, French Guiana; escaped from prison after seven unsuccessful attempts and worked in Venezuela as a gold digger, oil prospector, and pearl merchant; settled in Caracas, Venezuela, and opened a restaurant business; began writing, c. 1968.

WRITINGS: Papillon, Laffont, 1969, translation by June P. Wilson and Walter B. Michaels published under same title (Book-of-the-Month Club selection), Morrow, 1970; Banco, Laffont, 1972, translation by Patrick O'Brian published as Banco: The Further Adventures of Papillon, Morrow, 1973. Author of screenplay, "Popsy Pop."

SIDELIGHTS: Charriere's novel Papillon tells the story of the author's imprisonment and escape from the penal colonies in French Guiana. The adventures take place in prison as well as in the jungles and on the sea outside—which Charriere once escaped on by paddling a raft of dried coconuts over shark-filled waters.

Charriere began recording his story at age sixty-two after reading the novels of Albertine Sarrazin. Altogether he filled thirteen copybooks with his adventures, covering the time from his 1931 murder conviction—for which he always claimed his innocence—to 1945. His second novel, Banco, highlights the events of his life after those told in Papillon.

Commenting on Papillon, James R. Frakes said that the hero "'Papillon,' so-called because of his butterfly tattoo, endures from one cavale [escape] to the next, clawing hope from the intricacy and promise of his newest scheme.... The details are horrendous—murder, suicide, cannibalism, the atrocity of solitary confinement, . . . death by quicksand. Set against these defilements is Papillon's unqualified emphasis on the 'decency' of the convicts, their manners, adherence to a code, integrity, desperate humanity, as opposed to the almost unrelieved swinishness of the police, guards, and the entire French judicial system."

Despite some critics' doubts about the truth of Papillon, Charriere's depiction of life in the penal colonies is considered a highlight. Said Marc Slonim: "As a social commentary it reveals all the cruelties and iniquities of the antiquated French penal system." Though the French did abandon their Guianan penal colonies in 1944, Charriere continued to speak out against the fundamental inadequacies of prisons everywhere. "The best school of crime is jail," he maintained. "The biggest defect of the American system is bail. The ones who have the money can pay the bail. The man with no money must stay in jail."

Papillon enjoyed tremendous success, selling more than five million copies in sixteen languages. In 1974 the book was adapted for the screen in the popular Columbia film of the same title.

BIOGRAPHICAL/CRITICAL SOURCES: Book World, September 6, 1970; New York Times Book Review, September 6, 1970; Newsweek, September 7, 1970; Time, September 14, 1970; Best Sellers, September 15, 1970; Atlantic, October, 1970; New Republic, October 3, 1970; New York Review of Books, October 8, 1970; Saturday Review, October 24, 1970.

OBITUARIES: New York Times, July 30, 1973; Time, August 13, 1973; Newsweek, August 13, 1973.*

* * *

CHENEY, Margaret   1921-

PERSONAL: Born April 5, 1921, in Eugene, Ore.; daughter of George L. (a horse trainer) and Josie (a teacher; maiden name, Goughnour) Swisher; married Michael S. Cheney (a writer), May 29, 1952 (deceased); children: Victoria Leigh. Education: Attended Cornish School of Fine Arts. Residence: California.

CAREER: Associated Press, Seattle, Wash., editor, 1943-46; University of California, Berkeley, writer, 1960-67; Carnegie Commission on Higher Education, Berkeley, Calif., editor, 1970-71; free-lance writer, 1971—. Member: National Audubon Society (president of Gabilan chapter, 1980), Feminist Writers Guild. Awards, honors: Award from Columbus Film Festival, 1963, for "Which Campus?."

WRITINGS: A Brief History of the University of California, University of California Press, 1965; Meanwhile Farm (nonfiction), Celestial Arts, 1975; *Coed Killer* (nonfiction), Walker & Co., 1976; *Tesla: Man Out of Time,* Prentice-Hall, 1981.

Co-author, with Carol Levene, of "Which Campus?," a documentary film released by University of California, 1963.

Work represented in anthologies, including *Audubon Anthology.* Editor of books published in the series, "Carnegie Commission on Higher Education." Reporter for *Aberdeen Daily World.* Contributor to *Encyclopedia Americana.* Contributor to magazines, including *Gourmet.*

WORK IN PROGRESS: A book on animal behaviorism, publication expected in 1982.

SIDELIGHTS: Margaret Cheney wrote: "I am an avid foreign traveler, having lived with my family in the Middle East and in England for several years. Most of my education has occurred outside of classrooms, where the study list is endless. A favorite interest is animal behavior.

"My writing career began at age eight with publishing of newspapers, and continued with reporting for school papers. The choice of career was never a conscious decision although it conflicted with my desire to be a painter.

"The biography of Mikola Tesla is the first comprehensive work on him since John J. O'Neill's *Prodigal Genius,* published in the 1940's, and there appears to be interest in it both in America and abroad. Tesla is a great favorite in Canada as well as the leading folk hero of modern Yugoslavia. A prodigiously gifted scientist—a naturalized American—he may well have been, as Hugo Gernsback thought, 'the greatest inventor in history.' He was a contemporary of Edison's, a friend of Mark Twain's, Anne Morgan's, and J. Pierpont Morgan's; and his alternating current patents helped launch the Westinghouse Electric Co. The idea of writing on Tesla attracted me because of the mystery surrounding his remarkable life and the patent injustices done to his memory, which I hope may be to some degree remedied by this biography. Lee Anderson, the Tesla authority, says he hopes it will at least enable people to learn to spell Tesla's name (i.e. *not* Nicola) correctly!

"With Einstein and Edison, I believe that formal education tends to have a constricting effect upon intellectual growth. Each of my books has been about a radically different subject, a reflection of my pleasure in learning. Like Tesla I find the idea of specializing abhorrent. As i grow older I find it particularly important to tackle mind-stretching subjects. A point I hope to convey with this biography is not only that the ordinary woman *can* understand science but—in view of the ubiquitous, bewildering experts to be found on both sides of every issue—must do so to survive. My use of the word wo*man* subsumes the male gender."

AVOCATIONAL INTERESTS: Naturalist, farmer, vintner.

*   *   *

CHENEY-COKER, Syl   1945-

PERSONAL: Birthgiven name, Syl Cheney Coker; name legally changed in 1970; born June 28, 1945, in Freetown, Sierra Leone; son of Samuel B. and Lizzie (a trader; maiden name, Dundas) Coker. *Education:* Attended University of Oregon, 1967-70, University of California, Los Angeles, 1970, and University of Wisconsin—Madison, 1971-72. *Politics:* "Decidedly Left." *Religion:* None. *Office:* Department of English, University of Maiduguri, Borno, Nigeria.

CAREER: Eugene Register Guard, Eugene, Ore., journalist, 1968-69; Radio Sierra Leone, Freetown, Sierra Leone, head

of cultural affairs, 1972-73; free-lance writer, 1973-75; University of the Philippines, Quezon City, visiting professor of English, 1975-77; University of Maiduguri, Borno, Nigeria, lecturer, 1977-79, senior lecturer, 1979—. Also worked as drummer, radio producer, and factory and dock worker. *Awards, honors:* Ford Foundation grant, 1970.

WRITINGS: Concerto for an Exile: Poems, Africana Publishing, 1973; *The Graveyard Also Has Teeth* (poems), New Beacon Press, 1974, revised edition, Heinemann, 1979. Contributor to *Presence Africaine* and *Solidarity.* Editor of *Ba: Shiru.*

WORK IN PROGRESS: The Blood in the Desert's Eye, poems, completion expected in 1982.

SIDELIGHTS: Cheney-Coker commented: "My being a poet was largely dictated by a nagging desire to understand the contradictions of the elements of my people, as in *Concerto for an Exile.* In the other books I am trying to raise the debased pillars of man's humanity.

"Somehow my poetry begins to make sense, when you really think about it, only from the observation that it is a poetry that owes very little to the English or American masters of the recent past. To express myself in verse, I have had to see poetry as a return to the primordial beginning of the word, when the word was free of associated meaning, of a metric clarity or purity. Neruda speaks of an 'impure poetry,' meaning a poetry without pretences to the right sound of a word, the punctuation, the form. If I understand him, I think he is trying to say that poetry from the nations where the word has been recently freed of its encrustations should be the irrationality of the impulse within the rationality of form. Which is neither here nor there. Yevtushenko says a poet should be the conscience at the border post of his country. Am I at the border post of a country? Maybe, but I wish to make clear that my poetry comes from the wellspring of a country, a world continually brutalized, and from the depths of my own suffering I am trying to reach that man, brother of grief, and his mother, who chews a thousand pieces of cocaine to fill her stomach's void."

BIOGRAPHICAL/CRITICAL SOURCES: Eustace Palmer, *A Celebration of Black and African Writing,* Oxford University Press, 1975.

*   *   *

CHING, Julia (Chia-yi)   1934-

PERSONAL: Born October 15, 1934, in Shanghai, China; came to the United States in 1951, naturalized citizen, 1974; daughter of William L. K. and Christina C. (Tsao) Ching. *Education:* College of New Rochelle, B.A., 1958; Catholic University of America, M.A., 1960; Australian National University, Ph.D., 1971. *Politics:* Democrat. *Religion:* Roman Catholic. *Home:* 66 Helena Ave., Toronto, Ontario, Canada. *Office:* Department of Religious Studies, Victoria College, University of Toronto, Toronto, Ontario, Canada.

CAREER: Australian National University, Canberra, lecturer in Asian studies, 1969-74; Columbia University, New York, N.Y., associate professor of East Asian Philosophy, 1974-75; Yale University, New Haven, Conn., associate professor of East Asian philosophy, 1975-78; University of Toronto, Victoria College, Toronto, Ontario, associate professor of East Asian philosophy and religion, 1978—. Member of board of trustees of United Board for Christian Higher Education in Asia; consultant to National Endowment for the Humanities. *Member:* Association of Asian Studies, Phi Tau Phi. *Awards, honors: Choice* named *Confucianism and Christianity* outstanding academic book of 1977.

WRITINGS: (Translator) Blaise Pascal, Shen-ssu lu (translation of Pensees), Kuangchi Press, 1968; Philosophical Letters of Wang Yang-ming, Australian National University Press, 1972; To Acquire Wisdom, Columbia University Press, 1976; Confucianism and Christianity, Kodansha, 1977. Editor of Journal of the History of Ideas, 1976—.

WORK IN PROGRESS: A critical translation of a seventeenth-century work by Huang Tsung-hsi, publication by Columbia University Press expected in 1982.

SIDELIGHTS: Julia Ching's languages include Chinese (Mandarin, Cantonese, Shanghai), French, German, and Japanese.

*   *   *

CHRISTIAN, A. B.
See YABES, Leopoldo Y(abes)

*   *   *

CHRISTIE, Jean 1912-

PERSONAL: Born February 8, 1912, in Manila, Philippines; naturalized U.S. citizen; daughter of Emerson Brewer (a U.S. State Department official) and Clara Cecilia (Pray) Christie; married Robert Claus (an archivist), June 27, 1938; children: Richard Alan, Peter. Education: George Washington University, B.A., 1934; Fletcher School of Law and Diplomacy, M.A., 1935; Columbia University, Ph.D., 1963. Home: 34 Bellingham Lane, Great Neck, N.Y. 11023. Office: Department of History, Fairleigh Dickinson University, River Rd., Teaneck, N.J. 07666.

CAREER: Brooklyn College (now of the City University of New York), Brooklyn, N.Y., part-time lecturer in history, 1955-60; Hunter College of the City University of New York, New York, N.Y., lecturer, 1960-62; Bronx Community College, Bronx, N.Y., lecturer, 1962-63; Fairleigh Dickinson University, Teaneck, N.J., instructor, 1963-64, assistant professor, 1964-71, associate professor, 1971-75, professor of history, 1975—. Member: American Historical Association, Organization of American Historians, Society for the History of American Foreign Relations, Society for the History of Technology, Institute for Research in History, Conference for Peace Research in History, Berkshire Conference of Women Historians.

WRITINGS: (Editor with Leonard Dinnerstein, and contributor) Decisions and Revisions: Interpretations of Twentieth-Century America, Praeger, 1975; (editor with Dinnerstein) America Since World War II: Historical Interpretations, Praeger, 1976. Contributor to history journals.

SIDELIGHTS: Jean Christie wrote: "I am a lifelong feminist, have welcomed the rise of a new women's movement, and, as a historian, am delighted to see the current interest in the history of women. Peace, including nuclear disarmament and the achievement of a more just and rational social order, are urgent needs, complex and linked together."

AVOCATIONAL INTERESTS: Sports, piano, travel.

*   *   *

CLANCY, Joseph P(atrick) 1928-

PERSONAL: Born March 8, 1928, in New York, N.Y.; son of Joseph A. and Maude H. (Cordier) Clancy; married Gertrude Wiegand, July 31, 1948; children: Katherine Clancy Shales, David, Paul, Margaret, Elizabeth Clancy Palisoc, Patricia, Robert, Thomas. Education: Fordham University, B.A., 1947, M.A., 1949, Ph.D., 1957. Religion: Roman Catholic. Home: 1549 Benson St., New York, N.Y. 10461. Office: Department of English, Marymount Manhattan College, 221 East 71st St., New York, N.Y. 10021.

CAREER: Marymount Manhattan College, New York, N.Y., instructor, 1948, assistant professor, 1952-57, associate professor, 1957-61, professor of English, 1961—. Member: Modern Language Association of America, Yr Academi Gymreig. Awards, honors: Literature award from Welsh Arts Council, 1971, for The Earliest Welsh Poetry.

WRITINGS: (Translator and editor) The Odes and Epodes of Horace, University of Chicago Press, 1960; (translator and editor) Medieval Welsh Lyrics, St. Martin's, 1965; (translator and editor) The Earliest Welsh Poetry, St. Martin's, 1970; Pendragon: Arthur and His Britain, Praeger, 1971; The Significance of Flesh: Poems, 1950-1980, Wiegand & Kennedy, 1980; (translator and editor) Modern Welsh Poems, Gomer, 1980.

WORK IN PROGRESS: Translating modern Welsh plays, completion expected in 1983.

SIDELIGHTS: Clancy commented: "I translate as a means of writing poetry. In my original poems, for better or worse, I am probably the most Welsh-influenced American poet, in subjects and techniques, who has ever written. In general, I write poems that reflect a belief in the need for external as well as internal structures—a rational, analytical attempt to achieve at least a temporary control of experience."

BIOGRAPHICAL/CRITICAL SOURCES: Times Literary Supplement, September 2, 1965, July 31, 1970, October 22, 1971; Poetry, August, 1966; New York Times Book Review, August 29, 1971.

*   *   *

CLARK, John R(alph) K(ukeakalani) 1946-

PERSONAL: Born September 13, 1946, in Honolulu, Hawaii; son of George Victor (a civil engineer) and Alice Lee (a teacher; maiden name, Heywood) Clark; married Linda Fernandez, September 28, 1968 (divorced, 1970); married Camille Stonebraker Smiley, December 26, 1971 (divorced, 1980); children: (second marriage) Jason K. Education: Honolulu Community College, A.S., 1975; University of Hawaii, B.A., 1976. Residence: Kailua, Oahu, Hawaii. Office: Honolulu Fire Department, 1455 South Beretania St., Honolulu, Hawaii 96814.

CAREER: City and County of Honolulu, Parks and Recreation Department, Honolulu, Hawaii, lifeguard, 1970-72; Honolulu Fire Department, Honolulu, firefighter and alarm bureau operator, 1972—. Military service: U.S. Army, 1968-70. Member: Honolulu Fire Department Athletic Association, University of Hawaii Alumni Association, Halona Point Bodysurfing Association (founder and director), Punahou Alumni Association, Hui Makahonu Canoe Club, Tiare Malia Diving Association.

WRITINGS: The Beaches of Oahu, University Press of Hawaii, 1977; The Beaches of Maui County, University Press of Hawaii, 1980.

WORK IN PROGRESS: The Beaches of the Big Island of Hawaii, publication by University Press of Hawaii expected in 1982; research on the beaches of Kauai, Niihau, and the northwestern Hawaiian islands, and on Hawaiian seafood, including its traditional and contemporary preparation.

SIDELIGHTS: Clark told CA: "Hawaii's beaches comprise some of her greatest natural assets, attracting literally thousands of visitors and local residents every year. My reasons for identifying and writing about every beach in the Hawaiian Islands are two-fold. First, I want to provide simple, easy-to-read, but comprehensive water safety guides for all water enthusiasts, especially those who are totally unfamiliar with the power and dangers of the Pacific Ocean surrounding the islands. Every year there are many drownings and near-drownings in Hawaii. Hopefully my books will help to prevent these incidents in the future by alerting people to hazardous areas and to potentially fatal water conditions before these dangers are actually encountered.

"My second reason for writing the books is to provide an accurate ethno-geographical description of every beach in Hawaii. This information makes not only for more interesting reading and serves as an excellent circle island guide, but hopefully will also give both visitors and local residents an in-depth feeling for the areas they are frequenting. I believe it is important for people to be aware of the cultural and historical significance of the place that they are visiting primarily for aesthetic and recreational reasons. I think this type of conscientiousness is vital in helping to protect and preserve Hawaii's shorelines, and it may assist in managing coastal development and in improving governmental decision-making toward natural coastal resources."

*   *   *

CLARK, Mabel Margaret (Cowie) 1903-1975 (Lesley Storm)

PERSONAL: Born in December, 1903, in Maud, Aberdeenshire, England; daughter of William (a minister) and Christian (Ewen) Cowie; married James Doran Clark (a director; died, 1955); children: two sons, two daughters. *Education:* Earned M.A. from Aberdeen University. *Home:* 3 St. Simon's Ave., London S.W. 15, England.

CAREER: Dramatist, screenwriter, and novelist. *Member:* Dramatists Guild.

WRITINGS—All under pseudonym Lesley Storm: *Lady, What of Life?* (novel), Harper, 1927; *Head in the Wind*, Harper, 1928; *Small Rain*, Cassell, 1929, published as *They Loved Too Young*, Harper, 1930; *Robin and Robins: A Light Tale of a Modern Young Man and His Female Counterpart*, Cassell, 1931; *Seven Daughters*, Farrar & Rinehart, 1931 (published in England as *Dragon*, Cassell, 1931); *Strange Man's Home*, Hutchinson, 1935.

Plays: *Tony Draws a Horse* (three-act comedy; produced on the West End at Comedy Theatre, January 26, 1939; produced on Broadway at The Playhouse, December 31, 1939), Samuel French, 1939; *Heart of a City* (three-act; first produced on Broadway at Henry Miller's Theatre, February 12, 1942), Dramatists Play Service, 1942; *Great Day* (three-act; first produced on Broadway at The Playhouse, March 14, 1945), English Theatre Guild, 1946; *Black Chiffon* (three-act; first produced on the West End at Westminster Theatre, May 3, 1949; produced on Broadway at Forty-Eighth Street Theatre, September 27, 1950), English Theatre Guild, 1950, Samuel French, 1951.

The Day's Mischief (two-act; first produced on the West End at Duke of York's Theatre, December 11, 1951), Samuel French, 1952; *The Long Echo* (three-act; first produced on Broadway at St. James Theatre, December 11, 1956), Samuel French, 1957; *Roar Like a Dove* (three-act comedy; first produced on the West End at Phoenix Theatre, September 26, 1957; produced on Broadway at Booth Theatre, May 21, 1964), Samuel French, 1957; *Favonia* (two-act; produced in England), Samuel French, 1958.

"Time and Yellow Roses," first produced in March, 1961; *The Paper Hat*, Samuel French, 1966; "They Ride on Broomsticks" (three-act comedy), produced in Glasgow, Scotland, at Alhambra Theatre, February 24, 1969; *Look, No Hands* (two-act comedy; first produced in Windsor, England, at Theatre Royal, November, 1970; produced on the West End at Fortune Theatre, July 19, 1971), Samuel French, 1972.

Other plays: "Dark Horizon," 1934; "Follow Your Saint," 1937; "A Night in Venice" (for operetta by Johann Strauss), 1944; "Three Goose Quills and a Knife," 1967.

Screenplays: (With James Seymour) "Meet Me at Dawn," Twentieth Century-Fox, 1948; (co-author) "The Fallen Idol," Selznick, 1949; "The Golden Salamander," Elstree, 1951; "The Heart of the Matter," Assoc., 1954; "Personal Affair" (based on own play, "The Day's Mischief"), United Artists, 1954; (with John Bryan) "The Spanish Garden" (based on the novel by A. J. Cronin), Rank, 1958.

SIDELIGHTS: Among Storm's most popular plays are "Black Chiffon" and "Roar Like a Dove," each of which ran for more than one thousand performances. The West End production of "Black Chiffon," said the *London Times*, starred Flora Robson "in one of her most affecting studies: a mother so 'emotionally locked' with her son that, when he is on the verge of marriage, her psychological strain forces her to shoplifting." The *Times* also reported that Storm's "special gift was for crisp and authoritative dialogue."

AVOCATIONAL INTERESTS: Travel.

OBITUARIES: London Times, October 20, 1975.*

*   *   *

CLARK, Robert Alfred 1908-

PERSONAL: Born October 28, 1908, in Boston, Mass.; son of Alfred Pugh and Anna (Gibson) Clark; married Braxton Magruder Guilbeau (a high school counselor), June 3, 1937; children: Allen Magruder, Mary Honore (Mrs. Joseph Gustav Mayo), John Rosslyn. *Education:* Harvard University, A.B., 1930, M.D., 1934. *Politics:* Democrat. *Religion:* Society of Friends (Quakers). *Home:* 8301 Forest Ave., Elkins Park, Pa. 19117.

CAREER: Boston City Hospital, Boston, Mass., resident in neurology, 1934-35; University Hospitals of Cleveland, Cleveland, Ohio, intern in medicine, 1935-37; Boston Psychopathic Hospital, Boston, resident in psychiatry, 1937-39; Harvard University Medical School, Cambridge, Mass., assistant in psychiatry, 1938-39; Rhode Island State Hospital, senior psychiatrist, 1939-42; Western Psychiatric Institute, Pittsburgh, Pa., senior psychiatrist, 1942-44, clinical director, 1944-55; University of Pittsburgh, School of Medicine, Pittsburgh, assistant professor, 1945-54, associate professor of psychiatry, 1954-55; Friends Hospital, Philadelphia, Pa., clinical director, 1955-58, director of medical student education, 1965-73; Northeast Community Center for Mental Health, Philadelphia, medical director, 1958-70, director of outpatient department, 1970-73, psychiatrist, 1973-78; Friends Hospital, member of board of managers, 1973—; Hahnemann Medical College, clinical professor, 1973—. Chairman of Philadelphia Friends Peace Committee, 1961-65; member of board of directors of Philadelphia SANE, 1965-68. *Member:* World Federation for Mental Health, American Psychiatric Association (life fellow), Pennsylvania Psychiatric Society (fellow), C. G. Jung Foundation, Friends Conference on Religion and Psychology. *Awards, honors:* Ford Foundation fellowship, 1948-49, and Bollingen Foundation fellowship, 1954, both for C. G. Jung Institute, Zurich, Switzerland; Isaac Bonsall Award from Friends Hospital, 1978.

WRITINGS: Six Talks on Jung's Psychology, Boxwood Press, 1953; *Mental Illness in Perspective,* Boxwood Press, 1973; (with J. Russell Elkinton) *The Quaker Heritage in Medicine,* Boxwood Press, 1978. Contributor to psychiatry journals.

WORK IN PROGRESS: Studying religious delusions in psychotics, including the relationship to cults.

SIDELIGHTS: Clark wrote: "At Harvard I first read C. G. Jung, eventually studying in Zurich and finishing a Jungian analysis in New York City. I joined the Quakers in 1941, out of my interest in mystical experience and world peace." *Avocational interests:* Travel (including England and South Africa).

*   *   *

CLARKSON, J. F.
See TUBB, E(dwin) C(harles)

*   *   *

CLINE, Edward 1946-

PERSONAL: Born October 22, 1946, in Pittsburgh, Pa. *Education:* Attended South Texas Junior College, 1966-67. *Politics:* "Limited Government." *Religion:* Atheist. *Residence:* New York, N.Y. *Agent:* Peter Lampack Agency, Inc., 551 Fifth Ave., Suite 2015, New York, N.Y. 10017. *Office:* P.O. Box 132, Forest Hills, N.Y. 11375.

CAREER: Writer, 1972—. Also worked in construction and factories, in airline communications and computer operations, and as a bank teller and editor. *Military service:* U.S. Air Force, Air Police, 1964-65.

WRITINGS: A Layman's Guide to Understanding OPEC and the Fuel Crisis, Lion Enterprises, 1979. Author of "Over There," a column in *Gryphon.* Contributor to *Ego.*

WORK IN PROGRESS: We Three Kings, a thriller featuring an American "entrepreneur-hero," publication expected in 1981.

SIDELIGHTS: Cline wrote: "Any journalism I might indulge in will be a result of research for my novels; I like to understand the subjects I use. Essays such as *The Layman's Guide* are valuable to me only as a means of addressing issues.

"I date my intellectual 'birth' to 1956, when I was ten years old. I first paid attention to newspaper headlines then, and these concerned the Hungarian uprising; I wondered why it failed.

"I regard myself as primarily a novelist, of the school Ayn Rand has defined as 'romantic realism.' My interest in drama and conflict was aroused when I saw 'The Time Machine' in 1960. While not strictly a romantic film, it presented value conflicts and imagination as I'd never seen them before, but its chief value to me was its scope and presentation of a comprehensive view of man and history. 'North by Northwest,' which I saw the same year, is a film I enjoyed enormously and still enjoy almost without qualification. A little romanticism will go a long way.

"That brings me to the present. It is still too early to comment on my writing career. I've always had confidence both in my novels and in the possibility that they will be published, but it has been hard to communicate that confidence to editors and publishers in today's literary environment. I think in terms of the long range, and this is at variance with the modern practice of looking ahead only three or four months. There's an economic as well as cultural reason for today's attitudes toward literature and art in general; Ayn Rand discusses it best in her essay, 'Moral Inflation,' and the principles of pragmatism in politics she covers in that piece are also applicable to literature and art. Whether or not my work will be as successful as Miss Rand's, however, remains to be seen.

"Needless to say by now, Ayn Rand is my favorite author. Her novels—in fact, her entire body of work—have had an influence on me that no other author's work has. Suppose you lived at the time of Aristotle: would you recognize the value and importance of his work? This is my approach to Miss Rand's work; it promises to exert an influence on our culture for a long time to come. No other contemporary writer—myself included—can match her depth, scope, insight, and range. I have other favorite writers and novels I like for different reasons, but Miss Rand's works are the only ones I return to for consolation or for the vision that it *is* possible."

*   *   *

CLOVER, Frank Metlar III 1940-

PERSONAL: Born May 5, 1940, in Denver, Colo.; married June 19, 1965; children: two. *Education:* University of Wisconsin—Madison, B.A., 1962; University of Chicago, M.A., 1964, Ph.D., 1966. *Office:* Department of History, University of Wisconsin—Madison, Wis. 53706.

CAREER: University of Wisconsin—Madison, assistant professor, 1966-71, associate professor, 1971-78, professor of history and classics, 1978—. *Member:* Association of Ancient Historians, Society for the Promotion of Roman Studies. *Awards, honors:* Herodotus fellow at Institute for Advanced Study, Princeton, N.J., 1973-74; American Council of Learned Societies fellowship, 1973-74.

WRITINGS: Flavius Merobaudes: A Translation and Historical Commentary, American Philosophical Society, 1971.

WORK IN PROGRESS: The Vandals and Mediterranean Politics in the Age of Geiseric, completion expected c. 1983.

*   *   *

CLURMAN, Harold 1901-1980

OBITUARY NOTICE—See index for *CA* sketch: Born September 18, 1901, in New York, N.Y.; died of cancer, September 9, 1980, in New York, N.Y. Director, drama critic, educator, and author. In 1931 Clurman helped found the innovative Group Theatre, which served as an arena for such playwrights as Clifford Odets and William Saroyan. He also introduced the Stanislavsky method of acting to the American stage. Clurman directed such productions as "Golden Boy," "A Member of the Wedding," "Incident at Vichy," and "Awake and Sing." He served for many years as drama critic for *Nation.* In addition to his autobiography, *All People Are Famous,* he wrote several books, including *The Fervent Years, Lies Like Truth,* and *The Divine Pastime.* Obituaries and other sources: *New York Times,* September 10, 1980; *Washington Post,* September 11, 1980; *Time,* September 22, 1980; *Publishers Weekly,* September 26, 1980; *AB Bookman's Weekly,* October 6, 1980.

*   *   *

CLYNE, Patricia (Edwards)

PERSONAL: Born in New York, N.Y.; daughter of Ray

Augustus and Neta Helen (Bohnsack) Edwards; married Francis Gabriel Clyne; children: Stephen Paul, Christopher Jason, Francis Joseph, Ray Augustus. *Education:* Hunter College (now of the City University of New York), B.A., 1958. *Address:* c/o Library Research Associates, Dunderberg Rd., Monroe, N.Y. 10950.

CAREER: Has worked as newspaper reporter and editor of books and magazines; currently free-lance writer. Member of board of trustees of Chester Public Library.

WRITINGS: The Corduroy Road, Dodd, 1973; *Tunnels of Terror,* Dodd, 1975; *Patriots in Petticoats,* Dodd, 1976; *Ghostly Animals of America,* Dodd, 1977; *Strange and Supernatural Animals,* Dodd, 1979; *Caves of Kids in Historic New York,* Library Research Associates, 1980. Contributor of articles and stories to adult and children's magazines.

*   *   *

COBBING, Bob 1920-
(Cento)

PERSONAL: Born July 30, 1920, in Enfield, Middlesex, England; son of Robert Walter (a signwriter) and Cissie (Barnard) Cobbing; married second wife, Jennifer Pike (an artist and jeweler), June 4, 1963; children; all from first marriage: Julian, Graham, Sheila, Patrick, Barbara. *Education:* Bognor Training College, teaching certificate, 1949. *Home:* 262 Randolph Ave., London W.9, England.

CAREER: Writer and performer. Worked as civil servant, 1937-41; farmer, 1942-43; teacher of art, literature, and music in Swindon, England, 1944-48, and London, England, 1949-64; Better Books Poetry Bookshop, London, manager, 1964-67. Performer in solo readings and with AbAra and Konkrete Canticle; publisher with Writers Forum, 1963—; visual poems exhibited in universities and museums throughout the world. *Member:* Association of Little Presses (vice-president, 1966—, chairman, 1972—), London Musicians Collective.

WRITINGS—Poetry; published by Writers Forum, except as noted: (With John Rowan) *The Massacre of the Innocents,* 1963; *Sound Poems (An ABC of Sound),* 1965; *Kurrirrurriri,* 1967; *Whississippi,* 1969; *Etcetera,* Vertigo Publications, 1970; *Kris Kringles Kesmes Korals,* Writers Forum and Vertigo Publication, 1970; *Konkrete Canticle,* Convent Garden Press, 1971; *Spearhead,* 1971; *Fifteen Shakespeare-Kaku,* 1972; *Circa 73-74,* 1973; *A Winter Poem,* 1974; *Hydrangea: The Verbal Score,* 1975; *Tokyo Kyoto (Kyoto to Tokyo: A Journey),* Good Elf, 1975.

A Round Dance, 1976; *Poems for the North West Territories,* 1976; (and compiler with Sean O'Huigin) *Bill Jubobe: Selected Texts of Bob Cobbing, 1942-75,* Coach House Press, 1976; *Jade-Sound Poems,* 1976; (with Lawrence Upbing) *Furst Fruts Uv 1977,* Writers Forum and Good Elf, 1977; *Title: Of the Work,* 1977; *Tu To Ratu/Earth Best,* 1977; *Number Structures,* 1977; *And Avocado,* 1977; (with Jeremy Adler) *Towards the City,* 1977; *Anan and Nan,* 1977; *Cygnet Ring: Collected Poems Volume I,* Tapocketa Press, 1977; *Windwound,* 1977; *Voice Prints,* 1977; *Janus,* 1977; *Fingrams,* 1977; *Fracted,* 1977; *Cuba,* 1977.

A Movie Book, 1978; *Hats: A Standing Poem,* 1978; *Two Leaf Book,* 1978; *Principles of Movement,* 1978; *ABC/Wan Do Tree: Collected Poems Volume II,* El Uel Uel U, 1978; *Meet Bournemouth,* 1978; *Fugitive Poem No. X,* 1978; *Game and Set,* 1978; *A Peal in Air: Collected Poems Volume III,* anonbeyondgrOnkontaktewild presses, 1978; *Sensations of the Retina,* 1978; *Fiveways,* 1978; *NiagarA,* 1978; (with

Bill Griffiths and Paula Claire) *Gin Chap,* 1978; *Concretion From Within,* 1978; *Grin,* 1979; (with Adler) *A Short History of London,* 1979; *The Kollekted Kris Kringle Volume IV: Collected Poems Volume IV,* Anarcho Press, 1979; *Bob Cobbing's Girlie Book: Collected Poems Volume V,* Good Elf, 1979.

Other; all published by Writers Forum, except as noted: (Editor) *Pamphlet One,* 1968; (editor) *A Typographical Problem,* 1969; (editor) *Free Form Poetry I,* 1970; (editor) *Samples of Concrete Poetry,* 1970; *Three Manifestos,* 1970; (editor) *British Modernism: Fact or Fiction?,* 1971; (editor) *Free Form Poetry II,* 1971; (editor with Peter Mayer) *International Concrete Poetry,* 1971; *Concrete Sound Poetry,* 1974; (editor) *Concrete Poetry: Gloup and Woup,* Arc Publications, 1974; (with Mayer) *Some Myths of Concrete Poetry* (also see below), 1976; *Some Statements on Concrete Sound Poetry* (also see below), 1978; (with Mayer) *Concerning Concrete Poetry* (contains *Some Myths of Concrete Poetry* and *Some Statements on Concrete Poetry;* also see above), 1978.

Recordings of poetry readings: (With Ernst Jandl) "An ABC in Sound" (also see below), 1965; "Chamber Music," 1968; "Marvo Movies Natter and Spontaneous Appealinair Contemprate Apollinaire," 1968; "Whississippi," 1969; "As Easy," 1970; (editor) "Variations on a Theme of Tan," 1970; "Three Poems From An ABC of Sound" (also see above), edited by Franz Mon, 1971; "Four Poems From An ABC of Sound" (also see above), performed by Lily Greenham, 1971; "E Colony," edited by Robert Caldwell, 1973; "Extract From Khrajrej," edited by Francois Dufrene, 1973; "Hymn to the Sacred Mushroom," edited by Maurizio Nannucci, 1975; "Portrait of Robin Crozier," edited by Sten Hanson, 1977; "Fifteen Shakespeare-kaku," edited by Arrigo Lora-Totino, 1978.

Also author of poems published on cards, folders, and triptychs, and recorded on tape. Co-editor with John Rowan of *And;* co-executive editor with Peter Mayer of *Kroklok,* 1971—. Contributor to more than one hundred periodicals, under pseudonym Cento.

WORK IN PROGRESS: Editing more volumes of collected poems; organizing poetry festivals, writing poetry; publishing.

SIDELIGHTS: Cobbing told *CA:* "My life consists of writing, publishing, and printing. I work for the Association of Little Presses and travel, often abroad, giving performances of my sound poems with AbAra and Konkrete Canticle, solo, or with colleague Bill Griffiths. I make my living mainly from these readings and performances. But, as everyone knows, there's not much money to be made by way of poetry!"

*   *   *

COCHRAN, Jacqueline 1910(?)-1980

OBITUARY NOTICE: Born c. 1910 (listed in some sources as born c. 1906); died of heart failure, 1980, near Palm Springs, Calif. Aviator and journalist. Cochran was one-time holder of numerous flight records for speed, distance, and altitude. As a correspondent, she covered Japan's World War II surrender and the Nazi trials at Nuremberg. Obituaries and other sources: *Time,* August 18, 1980.

COCKRELL, Amanda
See CROWE, Amanda Cockrell

* * *

CODY, John 1925-

PERSONAL: Born May 6, 1925, in Brooklyn, N.Y.; son of Joseph Edward and Ellen Margaret (Langstaff) Cody; married Dorothy Casto (a physician), March 19, 1955; children: Loren (Mrs. Mark Shaiken), Andrea, Graham. *Education:* St. John's University, Jamaica, N.Y., B.S., 1947; graduate study at Johns Hopkins University, 1947-50; University of Arkansas, M.D., 1960; postdoctoral study at Menninger School of Psychiatry, 1961-64. *Home:* 2704 Woodrow Court, Hays, Kan. 67601. *Office:* High Plains Mental Health Center, Hays, Kan. 67601.

CAREER: New York Zoological Society, New York, N.Y., staff artist in department of tropical research, 1952; University of Arkansas, Little Rock, medical illustrator, 1953-56; High Plains Mental Health Center, Hays, Kan., director, 1964—. Clinical professor at University of Kansas, 1968—; medical and scientific illustrator. *Military service:* U.S. Public Health Service, assistant surgeon, 1960-61. *Member:* American Psychiatric Association (fellow).

WRITINGS: After Great Pain: The Inner Life of Emily Dickinson, Harvard University Press, 1971. Contributor to medical journals.

WORK IN PROGRESS: A biography of Richard Wagner.

SIDELIGHTS: Cody commented: "I have spent my life struggling to be both scientist and artist, and for the past two decades have been practicing psychiatry, the most 'aesthetic' branch of medicine. I have written a psychological study of a poet and a musician, both informed by my experience as a therapist. A future project is the preparation of large watercolor paintings of the life cycles of the lepidoptera of New Guinea to be published as a book a la Audubon."

* * *

COHANE, John Philip 1911-

PERSONAL: Born October 10, 1911, in New Haven, Conn.; son of Jeremiah J. and Mary (Creegan) Cohane; married Heather Winder Fausset, May 13, 1961; children: Deirdre (Mrs. David Mead), Alexander, Candida, Ondine. *Education:* Yale University, A.B., 1934. *Politics:* Liberal. *Religion:* Christian. *Home and office:* 416 Fulman Rd., Cottage C, London S.W.6, England. *Agent:* Ed Victor, 27 Soho Sq., London W.1V., England.

CAREER: Worked for advertising agencies in New York City, 1934-46; Sullivan, Stauffer, Colwell & Bayles, Inc. (advertising agency), New York City, founding partner, secretary, and director, 1946-59; writer. *Member:* Zeta Psi. *Awards, honors:* Edgar Award for best television mystery of the year, 1965, for "The End of the World, Baby"; *White Papers of an Outraged Conservative* was named among five best books of the year by *Boston Globe*, 1973.

WRITINGS: The Key (selection of Macmillan Natural Science Book Club and Literary Guild Ancient History Book Club), Crown, 1969; *The Indestructible Irish,* Hawthorn, 1969; *White Papers of an Outraged Conservative,* Bobbs-Merrill, 1973; *Paradox: The Case for the Extraterrestrial Origin of Man,* Crown, 1977. Also author of two novels, *The Waking and the Dream* and *Revenge,* and a novelette, *The End of the World, Baby.* Contributor of stories and articles (some syndicated by New York Times Syndicate) to magazines and newspapers.

WORK IN PROGRESS: Three novels.

SIDELIGHTS: Cohane told *CA:* "From 1959 to 1965 I had considerable fiction published in magazines and adapted for television. Notable among these was *The End of the World, Baby,* a novelette adapted by Luther Davis which won an Edgar Award as the best television mystery of 1965. Now, after four nonfiction books, I am concentrating 100 percent on fiction again."

* * *

COHEN, Benjamin J(erry) 1937-

PERSONAL: Born June 5, 1937, in Ossining, N.Y.; son of Abraham (a butcher) and Rachel (Grossman) Cohen; divorced. *Education:* Columbia University, A.B. (magna cum laude), 1959, Ph.D., 1963. *Religion:* Jewish. *Office:* Fletcher School of Law and Diplomacy, Tufts University, Medford, Mass. 02155.

CAREER: Federal Reserve Bank of New York, New York, N.Y., economist, 1962-64; Princeton University, Princeton, N.J., assistant professor of economics, 1964-71; Tufts University, Fletcher School of Law and Diplomacy, Medford, Mass., associate professor, 1971-78, William L. Clayton Professor of International Economic Affairs, 1978—, director of William L. Clayton Center for International Economic Affairs. Lecturer at International School of America, 1965-66; visiting research professor at University of London, 1968-69; visiting research associate and member of research advisory council at Atlantic Institute for International Affairs, 1975-76; visiting professor at Harvard University, 1979. Volunteer speaker for International Communication Agency in Japan, Ethiopia, Liberia, South Africa, Tanzania, Zambia, Germany, Poland, Belgium, Afghanistan, India, Iran, Pakistan, Sweden, Mauritius, Italy, Spain, England, and Ireland, 1975—; consultant to U.S. Treasury, Organization for Economic Cooperation and Development, and U.S. Department of State. *Member:* American Economic Association, Royal Economic Society, Phi Beta Kappa. *Awards, honors:* Fellow of Council on Foreign Relations, 1968-69, and Rockefeller Foundation, 1975-76; Ford Foundation grant, 1978-80.

WRITINGS: Adjustment Costs and the Distribution of New Reserves (monograph), International Finance Section, Princeton University, 1966; (editor and contributor) *American Foreign Economic Policy: Essays and Comments,* Harper, 1969; *Balance-of-Payments Policy,* Penguin, 1969; *The Reform of Sterling* (monograph), International Finance Section, Princeton University, 1969; *The Future of Sterling as an International Currency,* Macmillan, 1971; *The Question of Imperialism: The Political Economy of Dominance and Dependence,* Basic Books, 1973; *Commercial Policy* (monograph), General Learning Corp., 1974; *Organizing the World's Money: The Political Economy of International Monetary Relations,* Basic Books, 1977; *Bank Financing of Balance-of-Payments Deficits,* Allanheld, Osman & Co., 1981.

Contributor: Emil Claassen and Pascal Salin, editors, *Stabilization Policies in Interdependent Economies,* North-Holland Publishing, 1972; Fritz Machlup, Walter S. Salant, and Lorie Tarshis, editors, *International Mobility and Movement of Capital,* National Bureau of Economic Research, 1972; James H. Weaver, editor, *Modern Political Economy: Radical and Orthodox Views on Crucial Issues,* Allyn & Bacon, 1973; Salant and Lawrence B. Krause, editors, *European Monetary Unification and Its Meaning for the United States,* Brookings Institution, 1974; W. F. Hanreider, editor, *The United States and Western Europe: Political, Eco-*

nomic, and Strategic Perspectives, Winthrop Publishing, 1974; Peter B. Kenen, editor, *International Trade and Finance: Frontiers for Research,* Cambridge University Press, 1975; *Critical Choices for Americans,* Volume V: *Trade, Inflation, and Ethics,* Heath, 1976; J. C. Hurewitz, editor, *Oil, the Arab-Israel Dispute, and the Industrial World: Horizons of Crisis,* Westview Press, 1976; Fabio Basagni, editor, *International Monetary Relations After Jamaica,* Atlantic Institute for International Affairs, 1976; Wilfrid F. Kohl, editor, *Economic Foreign Policies of Industrial States,* Heath, 1977.

Editor of series, "The Political Economy of International Relations," Basic Books. Contributor to *Funk & Wagnalls New Encyclopedia.* Contributor of nearly fifty articles and reviews to economic and banking journals and newspapers. Member of editorial board of *International Organization.*

*   *   *

COHEN, Keith 1945-

PERSONAL: Born April 10, 1945, in Quantico, Va.; son of Maxwell Lewis (a dentist) and Dolores (a nurse; maiden name, Keith) Cohen; married Paula Bassoff, August 20, 1967; children: Alex, Marc. *Education:* Columbia University, B.A., 1967; Princeton University, Ph.D., 1970. *Home:* 1711 Regent St., Madison, Wis. 53705.

CAREER: University of Paris VIII-Vincennes, Paris, France, instructor, 1970-74; University of Wisconsin—Madison, assistant professor, 1974-79, associate professor, 1979—. Member of board of directors of Child Development, Inc. (day care center). *Member:* Modern Language Association of America, Poets and Writers, Madison Writers Workshop. *Awards, honors:* Woodrow Wilson fellowship, 1967-68; National Endowment for the Arts grant, 1978.

WRITINGS: Film and Fiction: The Dynamics of Change, Yale University Press, 1979; *Natural Settings* (novel), Full Court, 1980.

Work represented in anthologies, including *A First Reader of Contemporary American Short Fiction,* edited by P. Gleeson, 1979. Contributor to journals, including *Paris Review, Art and Literature, Iowa Review,* and *October.*

WORK IN PROGRESS: Domestic Tranquillity, a novel; research for a book on the 1960's, with an international perspective, completion expected in 1982.

SIDELIGHTS: Cohen wrote: "The experience of living in France and traveling throughout Europe has been invaluable to my writing. I'm very much influenced by French culture and literature in general, especially writers like Proust, Robbe-Grillet, and Roussel. Cinema has also been enormously influential, so pervasive as to defy specification."

*   *   *

COKER, Syl Cheney
See CHENEY-COKER, Syl

*   *   *

COLE, Bill
See COLE, William Shadrack

*   *   *

COLE, William Shadrack 1937-
(Bill Cole)

PERSONAL: Born October 11, 1937, in Pittsburgh, Pa.; son of William Lucius and Gladys (Seel) Cole; married Linda

Punchatz, July 15, 1967; children: Atticus, Zena. *Education:* University of Pittsburgh, A.B., 1967, M.A., 1970; Wesleyan University, Middletown, Conn., Ph.D. (with highest honors), 1974. *Home:* 21 Woodmore Dr., Hanover, N.H. 03755. *Office:* Department of Music, Dartmouth College, 42 Hopkins Center, Hanover, N.H. 03755.

CAREER: Western Psychiatric Institute and Clinic, Pittsburgh, Pa., recreational therapist, 1955-60; Duquesne University, Pittsburgh, pharmacy stock manager for School of Pharmacy, 1960-65; Action Housing, Inc., Pittsburgh, supervisor for Neighborhood Youth Corps and project director, 1965-66; Brashear Association, Pittsburgh, assistant coordinator of Southwest Pittsburgh Community Action Program, 1966-68; University of Pittsburgh, Pittsburgh, lecturer in elementary education, 1969-70; New Haven University, New Haven, Conn., part-time lecturer in music, 1971; Whitman College, Walla Walla, Wash., Eric and Ina Johnson Visiting Professor of Humanities, 1972; Amherst College, Amherst, Mass., assistant professor of black studies, 1973-74; Dartmouth College, Hanover, N.H., associate professor of music, 1974—, chairman of department, 1980—, director of John Coltrane Memorial World Music Lecture/Demonstration Series. Producer and director of "Jazz With Bill Cole," on Vermont public radio; participant in dozens of concerts (plays nagaswarm, shenai, Chinese sona, and Ghanian flute). Guest lecturer at University of Oregon, 1971; lecturer at colleges and universities. Active in Pittsburgh's civil rights programs. *Member:* Society for Ethnomusicology. *Awards, honors:* National Endowment for the Arts grant, 1980.

WRITINGS—Under name Bill Cole: *Miles Davis: A Musical Biography,* Morrow, 1974; *John Coltrane,* Schirmer Books, 1976. Contributor to *Down Beat* and *Coda.* Music editor of *Massachusetts Review,* 1973.

WORK IN PROGRESS: Jazz: To Scrutinize . . . to Find News, publication expected in 1984.

SIDELIGHTS: Cole told *CA:* "My intention in writing books is to try to establish the artist whose creative efforts have made jazz the energetic music that it is. I also wish to focus on the degree of influence that Africa has had on the different forms of music that have emerged out of the black experience. Since I consider myself to be a musician and an educator, my writing has tended to be more in the philosophical vein in terms of black creative music."

*   *   *

COLLINS, Meghan 1926-

PERSONAL: Born June 7, 1926, in New Orleans, La.; daughter of Willard and Maude (Gamble) Roberts; married Sterrett A. Burges, March 24, 1945 (divorced January, 1974); married John S. Collins (a food corporation executive), January 27, 1974; children: (first marriage) Peter C., Laura Burges Ray, Elisabeth R. *Education:* Attended Barnard College, 1944-45; California State College (now University), Hayward, B.A., 1971. *Residence:* Walnut Creek, Calif. *Agent:* Richard Curtis, Richard Curtis Associates, Inc., 156 East 52nd St., New York, N.Y. 10022.

CAREER: Teacher of ballet in Pleasant Hill, Calif., 1960-67; *Contra Costa Times,* Walnut Creek, Calif., author of weekly column, "Meeting People," 1967-68; worked as teacher of dance and recreation director; free-lance writer, 1971—. Volunteer teacher of English as a second language, 1969-71.

WRITINGS: Maiden Crown (young adult historical novel), Houghton, 1979. Contributor to magazines, including *Ms., Saturday Review, Friends' Journal,* and *California Living.*

WORK IN PROGRESS: A historical book on the California Delta region, tentatively entitled *Winding Levee Road,* completion expected in 1982.

SIDELIGHTS: Collins told *CA:* "I write because I like to learn. I am not the kind of writer who develops themes for work from current daily life. A day spent in research on some factual or historical subject is for me a day spent roaming in fields of clover. It seems to set my imagination to forming stories about why humans behaved as they did in those particular circumstances. And since I believe that our present attitudes and customs have their roots in the past, the study seems to me most relevant to our current lives.

"I am interested in the relationships between men and women. The theme of *Maiden Crown,* beneath its fictional narrative, is that the chief problem between the sexes is that historically, even good-hearted men have developed their soldier, hunter, leader qualities while remaining nearly numb to the emotional nuances of life. From antiquity, women have adapted in various ways to men's disregard.

"The resolution of the problem, obviously, is that men must learn to be more concerned with and aware of women as human beings. But I also feel that the great over-reaction of the women's movement so far has been resentful self-pity. Women cannot demand of men to make them happy, but must build their own self-respecting lives within the framework of being female. Women must relinquish their enormous historical grudge and start from now with their men to build new patterns of marriage, in mutual good humor and kindliness."

AVOCATIONAL INTERESTS: Gardens and flowers, art, Japanese brush painting.

*   *   *

COLLINS, Myrtle T(elleen)   1915-

PERSONAL: Born May 23, 1915, in Gowrie, Iowa; daughter of Edwin L. (a farmer) and Maude (Carlson) Telleen; married Dwane R. Collins (an educator), June 18, 1938; children: Beth Allen Collins Lee, Anne Telleen Collins Greer. *Education:* University of Northern Iowa, B.A., 1937; Colorado College, M.A., 1960. *Politics:* Republican. *Religion:* Lutheran. *Home and office:* 1411 East Platte Ave., Colorado Springs, Colo. 80909.

CAREER: Teacher of English and speech at public school in Fontanelle, Iowa, 1937-38; Columbia University, Teachers College, New York, N.Y., secretary at Guidance Laboratory and executive secretary of Student Organizations Office, 1940-42; Sheppard Field, Wichita Falls, Tex., training coordinator for civilian personnel, 1943; National Advisory Committee for Aeronautics, Langley Field, Va., training specialist, 1944-45; Instituto Tecnologico de Aeronautica, Sao Jose dos Campos, Brazil, lecturer in English, 1954-55; teacher of English and remedial reading at public schools in Snyder, Tex., 1955-57, and Colorado Springs, Colo., 1957-58; dean of girls at public schools in Colorado Springs, Colo., 1958-62; University of Hawaii, Honolulu, instructor, 1962-65, assistant professor of education, 1966-67; American School of Vientiane, Vientiane, Laos, principal and counselor, 1967-71; University of Hawaii, assistant professor of education, 1971-73; American School of Vientiane, principal of elementary school and counselor, 1973-75; University of Hawaii, coordinator of federally funded program on mainstreaming the mildly handicapped, 1975-77; writer, 1977—. Past director of Ashford Playhouse. Established Telleen Literary Agency. *Member:* Delta Kappa Gamma (second vice-president, 1978-80).

WRITINGS: Teaching English to Brazilian Children, Yazigi Institute of Languages, 1955; (with husband, Dwane R. Collins) *Survival Kit for Teachers (and Parents),* Goodyear Publishing, 1975; (contributor) Charlie Shedd, editor, *You Are Somebody Special* (juvenile), McGraw, 1978. Contributor to education journals and *These Times.*

WORK IN PROGRESS: Survival Kit for Students; Not Yet, St. Pete!, nonfiction; a book on friendship; a book about grandmothers, with daughter, Anne Greer.

SIDELIGHTS: Myrtle Collins commented to *CA:* "I was born on a farm in Iowa, and attended the same school from grades one through twelve. After my marriage in 1938 the merry-go-round began, with moves to South Dakota, New York City, and eventually through every state in the Union, then on to South America, Asia, and Europe, and eventually back to Colorado for retirement.

"The travels of our family were always tied to the teaching profession. Our first big move came in 1952 when we went to Brazil for a year and stayed three. Then we went to Hawaii for a summer school session and stayed fifteen years.

"During that fifteen-year period we represented the University of Hawaii in Vientiane, Laos, for five and a half years. I was administrator and counselor in the American School of Vientiane, with five-hundred-fifty students of about twenty nationalities, but mostly Americans. This experience was one of the highlights of my professional career.

"My writing affords me the luxury of maintaining communication with teachers, parents, and youth, in whom I have unflagging faith."

AVOCATIONAL INTERESTS: Church activities, reading, writing, drama, antiques, art, cooking, good conversation.

BIOGRAPHICAL/CRITICAL SOURCES: Colorado Springs Sun, February 9, 1978.

*   *   *

COLSON, Frederick
See GEIS, Richard E(rwin)

*   *   *

COMBS, James E(verett)   1941-

PERSONAL: Born May 9, 1941, in Lebanon, Va.; son of Cecil Grayson (in sales) and Jacqueline (a nurse; maiden name, Hobson) Combs; married Deborah Skopek (a historian), June 22, 1976. *Education:* East Tennessee State University, B.A., 1967; University of Houston, M.A., 1969; University of Missouri, Ph.D., 1972. *Home:* 606 Freeman, Valparaiso, Ind. 46393. *Office:* Department of Political Science, Valparaiso University, Valparaiso, Ind. 46383.

CAREER: Valparaiso University, Valparaiso, Ind., assistant professor, 1972-79, associate professor of political science, 1979—, university research professor, 1979-80. Consultant to Civic Services, Inc. *Military service:* U.S. Air Force, 1961-65; served in Vietnam. *Member:* International Communication Association, American Political Science Association, Popular Culture Association.

WRITINGS: (Editor with Michael Mansfield) *Drama in Life: The Uses of Communication,* Hastings House, 1976; *Dimensions of Political Drama,* Goodyear Publishing, 1979; (with Dan Nimmo) *Political Myth and Mythmaking,* Prentice-Hall, 1980. Contributor to *Journal of American Culture.*

WORK IN PROGRESS: Polpop: Contemporary Politics and Popular Culture.

SIDELIGHTS: Combs told *CA:* "In academia, one writes books. Wordworlds are what we are supposed to build, mythical though they may be. If one is a political scientist, one escapes the dreariness of that profession (both in terms of its subject matter and tribal norms) by seeking word-worlds worth building. My motivation is that of every other author: idiocy.

"Perhaps it was this self-definition as a contemporary being that led me to study drama, myth, and its manifestation in popular culture. Politics, like life, is drama. Man is a myth-making animal, and our age is the most myth-ridden since Homer. Popular culture increasingly defines our lives, our dramas, and our myths. The twenty-seventh century will study our popular culture with the same interest and perplexity that archaeologists now study Sumerian potsherds and cuneiform."

*   *   *

CONNOLLY, Ray   1940-

PERSONAL: Born December 4, 1940, in St. Helens, England; son of John (an engineer) and Anne (a shop owner) Connolly; married Elaine Balmforth, April 16, 1966; children: Louise, Dominic, Kieron. *Education:* London School of Economics and Political Science, London, B.Sc., 1963. *Politics:* "Wishy-washy lefty." *Religion:* "Lapsed Roman Catholic." *Residence:* London, England. *Agent:* A. D. Peters & Co., 10 Buckingham St., London W.C.2, England. *Office:* William Collins Sons & Co. Ltd., 14 St. James's Place, London SW1A 1PS, England.

CAREER: Evening Standard, London, England, journalist, 1967-73; free-lance writer, 1974—. *Awards, honors:* Award from Writers Guild of Great Britain, 1974, for screenplay, "Stardust."

WRITINGS: A Girl Who Came to Stay (novel), W. H. Allen, 1973; *That'll Be the Day* (screenplay; released by EMI Films Ltd., 1973), Fontana, 1973; *Stardust* (screenplay; released by EMI Films Ltd., 1974), Fontana, 1974; *Trick or Treat* (novel), W. H. Allen, 1975; *Newsdeath* (novel), Collins, 1978; *A Sunday Kind of Woman* (novel), Collins, 1980.

Author and director of "James Dean: First American Teenager" (documentary film), released by V.P.S. Ltd. in 1975. Author of television plays.

WORK IN PROGRESS: A film script based on *Newsdeath;* four television plays to be broadcast in 1980; *Vacation,* publication expected by Avon.

SIDELIGHTS: Connolly told *CA:* "I am a storyteller. I have no cosmic thoughts, no flashes of illuminating insight into the human psyche. I tell stories for a living, in books, on videotape for television, or on film. I am a craftsman who works to keep house and home happily together. I also enjoy it."

*   *   *

COOKE, Robert (Gordon)   1930-

PERSONAL: Born May 29, 1930, in Llandaff, Wales; son of Robert Victor and Elizabeth Mary Cooke; married Jenifer Patricia Evelyn King, July 30, 1966; children: Robert Patrick Gordon, Elizabeth Jane Louise. *Education:* Christ Church, Oxford, M.A. *Religion:* Church of England. *Home:* Athelhampton, Dorchester, Dorsetshire, England.

CAREER: Oxford Tory, Oxford, England, editor, 1952-53; City and County of Bristol, England, member of council, 1954-57; British Parliament, London, Conservative member of Parliament for Bristol West, 1957-79, Parliamentary pri-

vate secretary to ministers of state, 1958-59, health, 1959-60, and works, 1960-62, member of services committee of House of Commons, 1967-79, Parliamentary delegate to Brazil, 1975; writer, 1979—. U.S. State Department foreign leader visitor, 1961. Vice-chairman of arts and amenities committee of Conservative party, 1959-62, 1964-70, chairman, 1970—, chairman of administration committee, 1974—; chairman of Conservative broadcasting and communications committee, 1962-64, 1973—; chairman of heritage committee and board of directors of British Tourist Authority. Member of Historic Buildings Council for England, 1969-79, board of directors of Westward Television, 1970—, and board of trustees of National Heritage Memorial Fund; special government adviser to Palace of Westminster. *Member:* Royal Society of Arts (fellow), Carlton Club, Pratt's Club, Farmer's Club, Clifton Club. *Awards, honors:* Knighted by Queen Elizabeth II, 1959.

WRITINGS: Government and the Quality of Life, Conservative Political Centre, 1974. Also author of *West Country Houses.*

SIDELIGHTS: Sir Robert is the owner of one of England's historic homes, and his interests include architecture and building. *Avocational interests:* Gardening.

*   *   *

COPELAND, Bonnie Chapman   1919-

PERSONAL: Born March 31, 1919, in Evansville, Ind.; daughter of Roy Kenneth and Evelyn (Merrille) Chapman; married Otis Lee Copeland, Jr., July 25, 1944 (divorced July, 1963); children: Otis Lee III, John Royale. *Education:* Weber State College, B.S., 1964. *Home:* 480 West 1550 North, Harrisville, Utah 84404. *Agent:* Gross Associates, 63 Grand St., Croton-on-Hudson, N.Y. 10520.

CAREER: Affiliated with Martz & Associates (public relations firm), Denver, Colo., 1966-71; writer, 1972—. Member of board of governors of Stage Door Theatre, Boulder, Colo., 1976-78. *Military service:* U.S. Army, Women's Army Corps, 1942-46; became first lieutenant; received Army Commendation Medal. *Member:* National Writers Club.

WRITINGS: Lady of Moray (novel), Atheneum, 1979.

WORK IN PROGRESS: Gruoch, Queen of Scotland, a sequel to *Lady of Moray; Game of Jackals and Hounds,* about an Egyptian princess of the eighteenth dynasty; *The Wizard Earl,* about Francis Stewart Bothwell and King James VI.

SIDELIGHTS: Copeland told *CA:* "My first creative writing began when I was in fourth grade. I composed a murder mystery of such gore and horror that I was afraid to go to sleep in the dark. My mother quickly discovered who turned the lights back on after she had tucked her children into bed and, of course, put an end to that nonsense.

"So the drive to write lay dormant, but each new experience, each new vista, and each new reading finally spilled over into creations of my own. My design in writing is to bring to others the pleasure of knowing another place, another time, and of walking side-by-side with the people who made those times important in the history of the world.

"Thorough research on historical characters is an important tool in the fashioning of a fictional biography—research is also my delight. Seven books may speak of an earl's favorite horse, but only the eighth will give its name. Ah! the thrill of discovery. I spend a year and more in research, insinuating myself into the times and lives of my subjects, but often a single fact will, in a moment, establish itself into a scene which must be captured at once. Then I may put down the bare bones of the idea or, if the impact is compelling, I may flesh out the entire scene. I am enamoured of villainy though I promise never to practice it. And if my interest lies mostly with characters of evil intent and savage purpose, I stand in good company. . . surely Milton's Satan is the most intriguing of all literary portraits.

"I write everyday—at least two hours (discipline is the third necessary ingredient in writing)—and often when it is going well, I lose all track of time and suddenly find the hour is three o'clock in the morning.

"I plan to concentrate on Scottish history. The glens and tarns are alive with the ghosts of the Sons of the MacAlpine, and I want to know them all."

BIOGRAPHICAL/CRITICAL SOURCES: Library Journal, October 1, 1979.

*   *   *

COPPERMAN, Paul   1947-

PERSONAL: Born June 28, 1947, in New York, N.Y.; son of Abraham (a city planner) and Ann Lynn (Sterne) Copperman. *Education:* University of California, Berkeley, B.A., 1969; Lone Mountain College, M.A., 1975. *Home and office:* 426 Castenada, San Francisco, Calif. 94116. *Agent:* John Brockman, 200 West 57th St., New York, N.Y. 10019.

CAREER: Institute of Reading Development, San Francisco, Calif., founder and president, 1971—. Appeared on hundreds of television and radio talk shows, including "CBS Evening News," and "Phil Donahue Show." Testified as expert witness on reading development for several court trials and government committees. Speaker at conventions and numerous other organizations. *Member:* International Reading Association, Phi Beta Kappa.

WRITINGS: Teacher's Training Manual for the Institute of Reading Development College Level Speed Reading and Comprehension Training Program, two volumes, National Institute of Reading Development, 1975, revised edition, 1979; *Teacher's Training Manual for the Institute of Reading Development Secondary Level Developmental Reading Program,* National Institute of Reading Development, 1975, revised edition, 1979; *The Literacy Hoax: The Decline of Reading, Writing, and Learning in the Public Schools and What We Can Do About It,* Morrow, 1978.

SIDELIGHTS: In *The Literacy Hoax,* which James J. Kilpatrick called "one of the most important books of recent years," Paul Copperman discusses the terrible condition of America's educational system, what caused its deterioration, and provides suggestions for its improvement. He points out the lack of discipline, increased vandalism, lenient requirements for basic courses such as math, geography, history, science, and foreign languages, and easier classes with few homework assignments, including English classes with practically no theme writing or memorization required. The average student today, writes Copperman, uses textbooks that "have been rewritten with a reading level two years lower than the grade he is in."

In order to reverse this trend, Copperman urges the courts to refrain from meddling in school policies and calls for "the reinstatement of parental and educational authority and the reaffirmation of traditional social goals," noted Robert Hassenger. An *Atlantic Monthly* reviewer asserted that Copperman's "proposals will be horrifying to many educators because they all have one point in common: they will require both school administrators and classroom teachers to think."

BIOGRAPHICAL/CRITICAL SOURCES: New Republic, December 16, 1978; *Atlantic Monthly,* November, 1978; *National Review,* December 21, 1979, February 8, 1980.

*   *   *

COSTAS, Orlando E(nrique)   1942-

PERSONAL: Born June 15, 1942, in Ponce, P.R.; came to the United States in 1954; son of Ventura Enrique and Rosalina (a seamstress; maiden name, Rivera) Costas; married Rosa Lidia Feliciano, December 28, 1962; children: Annette Michelle, Dannette Gisele. *Education:* Attended Nyack Missionary College, 1962-63; Inter American University of Puerto Rico, B.A. (cum laude), 1966; graduate study at Trinity Evangelical Divinity School, Deerfield, Ill., 1966-67; Winona Lake School of Theology, M.A., 1967; Garrett Theological Seminary, M.Div. (with distinction), 1969; Free (Reformed) University, Amsterdam, Netherlands, D.Th., 1976. *Politics:* Puerto Rican Independent Party. *Home:* 209 James Rd., Broomall, Pa. 19143. *Office:* Eastern Baptist Theological Seminary, Lancaster Ave. and City Ave., Philadelphia, Pa. 19151.

CAREER: Ordained Baptist minister, 1965; interim pastor at Christian church in Bridgeport, Conn., 1961; student pastor in New York City, 1962; pastor of Baptist churches in Yauco, P.R., 1963-66, and Milwaukee, Wis., 1966-69; Latin America Mission, San Jose, Costa Rica, professor of communication and missiology at Latin American Biblical Seminary, 1970-73, director of New York regional center, 1971, coordinator of studies and academic dean, and chairperson of board of directors of seminary, all 1971-72, head of department of religious communication, 1973, secretary of studies and publications of Institute of In-Depth Evangelization and director of Latin American Evangelical Center for Pastoral Studies, both 1973-76; director of Latin American Evangelical Center for Pastoral Studies, 1976—; United Church Board for World Ministries, San Jose, Costa Rica, president of executive committee of International Institute of In-Depth Evangelization, 1977-78. Thormley B. Woods Professor of Missiology and director of Hispanic studies at Eastern Baptist Theological Seminary, 1979—.

Visiting professor at University of Wisconsin—Milwaukee, 1968, Gordon-Conwell Theological Seminary, 1973, Eastern Baptist Theological Seminary, 1978, and Union Theological Seminary, Richmond, Va., 1979; adjunct professor at Fuller Theological Seminary, 1977—. Associate of Partnership in Mission, 1976—; member of Lausanne Theology and Education Working Group, Committee on World Evangelization, and Evangelical-Roman Catholic Dialogue on Mission, 1976—; conducts missions and lecture tours in Latin America, Asia, Europe, and the United States. Founder of Milwaukee's Universidad del Barrio, 1969. Director of special services at Milwaukee Christian Center, 1968-69; member of County of Milwaukee Social Development Commission, 1967; member of Wisconsin governor's Commission on Human Relations, 1969.

MEMBER: World Association of Christian Communication, International Association of Mission Studies (member of executive committee, 1974-76), Missions Commission of the World Evangelical Fellowship, Inter American Society for the Study of Religion, American Society of Missiology, Society for Pentecostal Studies (associate member), Latin American Theological Fraternity (member of executive committee, 1977-80), Latin American Council of Churches (second vice-president, 1978—). *Awards, honors:* William Paton fellowship for Selly Oak Colleges, Birmingham, England, 1975-76.

WRITINGS: The Church and Its Mission: A Shattering Critique From the Third World, Tyndale, 1974; (contributor) J. D. Douglas, editor, *Let the Earth Hear His Voice,* World Wide Publications, 1975; *Theology of the Crossroads in Contemporary Latin America,* Editions Rodopi, 1976; (contributor) C. Rene Padilla, editor, *The New Face of Evangelicalism: A Symposium on the Lausanne Covenant,* Hodder & Stoughton, 1976; *The Integrity of Mission: The Inner Life and Outreach of the Church,* Harper, 1979; *The Upper and the Under Side of Mission,* Harper, 1980; *Out of the Depth: A Contextual Theology of Evangelism,* Harper, 1981.

In Spanish: *La iglesia y su mision evangelizadora* (title means "The Church and Its Evangelizing Mission"), La Aurora, 1971; *Comunicacion por medio de la predicacion* (title means "Communication Through Preaching"), Editorial Caribe, 1973; *Que significa evangelizar hoy?* (title means "What Does it Mean to Evangelize Today?"), Publicaciones INDEF, 1973; (editor) *Hacia una teologia de la evangelizacion* (title means "Toward a Theology of Evangelization"), La Aurora, 1973; *El protestantismo en America Latina hoy* (title means "Protestantism in Latin America Today"), Publicaciones INDEF, 1975; *Mision y compromiso* (title means "Mission and Commitment"), Editorial Caribe, 1979; *Crecer en todo* (title means "Growing in All Things"), Editorial Caribe, 1981.

Contributor to *Diccionario de la Iglesia Cristiana.* Contributor of more than thirty articles and reviews to religious journals in the United States, Latin America, and Europe. Editor of *Occasional Essays* and *Pastoralia,* 1977-79; co-founder of *La Guardia* (newspaper), 1968; associate of *Other Side,* 1973-79.

SIDELIGHTS: Costas writes: "I am from a labor family that migrated to the United States when I was twelve years old. Congruent with my roots, I am deeply sensitive to the situation of the poor and disenfranchised of the world and committed to the social, cultural, economic, and political liberation of my country, Latin America, and the peoples of the Third World.

"I am an ecumenical church person who, though conscious of the chiaroscuro history of the Christian church, believes nevertheless that it is a fundamental instrument of God's mission on earth. Hence I am dedicated to the unity-in-mission of the Christian church around the world, participate in interdenominational and ecumenical bodies and activities, and hold ministerial standing in both the American Baptist church and the United Church of Christ.

"I am dedicated to the promotion of the pastoral ministry throughout Latin America and to the sharing of the gospel with women and men everywhere. Consequently, I am not only engaged in personal evangelism, but hold occasional evangelistic meetings throughout Latin America and the Caribbean. I believe that the theological task is inseparably bound to the obedience of faith, that Christians can *think* their faith only as they *practice* it, and I see theology as a contextual and practical discipline rather than the exclusive franchise of the world of academics."

*   *   *

COSTINESCU, Tristan
    See GROSS, Terence

COUNTRYMAN, The
    See WHITLOCK, Ralph

*   *   *

COUSSE, Raymond 1942-

PERSONAL: Born April 20, 1942, in St. Germain en Laye, France; son of Auguste and Marie Louise (Quemener) Cousse; married Marie-Claude Joly (a professor), December 16, 1971; children: Cecile, Clara, Sophie, Christine. *Politics:* "Nothing, I hope." *Religion:* "Nothing, I hope." *Home:* 7 rue de le Mairie, 28130 Chartainvilliers, Maintenon, France.

CAREER: Firefighter in Paris, France, 1961-68; writer, 1968—; professional actor, 1974—.

WRITINGS—In English translation: *Strategie pour deux jambons* (novel), Flammarion, 1978, translation by Richard Miller published as *Death Sty: A Pig's Tale,* Grove, 1979.

Other writings: *Enfantillages* (novel), Flammarion, 1979; *Theatre 1* (contains seven plays; all one-act, except as noted: "Peripeties" [pantomime], first produced in Puteaux, France, 1971; "Refus d'obtemperer," first produced in Zurich, Switzerland, October, 1970; "La Terrine du chef," first produced in Zurich, October, 1970, produced in Paris, France, October, 1974; "Strategie pour deux jambons" [based on own novel], first produced in Paris, October, 1979; "L'Edifice," first produced in Paris, October, 1980; "Rencontres" [pantomime]; "Lever de raison" [two-act pantomime]), Flammarion, 1980.

WORK IN PROGRESS: Novels and plays.

SIDELIGHTS: Cousse's intent in writing, he says, "is to come to be more in accord with myself. But this is a lost cause in advance. I sustain myself very badly. My self-disgust is limitless. I therefore long to write books that do not systematically drive me to hate myself. It is, alas, a nearly impossible task.

"For the reader, I nevertheless hope there is some pleasure. But the pleasure that I eventually procure comes only through the desperate eagerness that I put towards confronting myself.

"I have no objectives outside of writing. A writing conscious of itself, endlessly questioning itself, ought to contain all possible and conceivable objectives.

"I have one constant preoccupation, however: to remain legible for a reader of good will. I don't believe in the avantgarde writers who follow, in my mind, a totalitarian idea of history. But I believe still less in fossilized writing—the good old traditional novel—that composes nearly all literary production. As far as I'm concerned, it's a question, then, of finding the new small routes outside of the beaten paths."

Cousse also commented on his novel, *Death Sty: A Pig's Tale:* "*Death Sty* recounts the life and death of an ordinary pig. More exactly, the meditations of a pig on his existence after eight days at the slaughterhouse. I was at once struck by the similarity between my own destiny and that of this scorned animal, even though he is the most exploited animal of all creation."

*   *   *

COUTURIER, Louis (Joseph) 1910-
    (Michel Carrouges)

PERSONAL: Born February 22, 1910, in Poitiers, France; son of Henri (a barrister) and Marie (Thomas) Couturier; married Henriette de Ruffray, September 13, 1933; children: Jacqueline, Francois, Therese, Agnes, Jean-Louis, Martine.

Education: Received bachelor of law, 1931. *Politics:* Syndicalist. *Religion:* Roman Catholic. *Home:* 61 Avenue de la Motte-Picquet, Paris XVe, France 75015.

CAREER: Writer. Contentieux d'Assurances, Paris, France, jurist, 1933-46; worked as journalist in Paris, 1946-62. *Military service:* French Army, Infantry, 1932-33. *Awards, honors:* Chevalier of the Legion of Honor.

WRITINGS—All under pseudonym Michel Carrouges; essays: *Eluard et Claudel,* Seuil, 1945; *La Mystique du Surhomme,* Gallimard, 1948; *Kafka,* Labergerie, 1948; *Andre Breton et les donnees fondamentales du surrealisme,* Gallimard, 1950, translation published as *Andre Breton and the Basic Concepts of Surrealism,* University of Alabama Press, 1974; *Les Machines celibataires,* Arcanes, 1954, revised edition, Editions du Chene, 1976; *Foucauld devant l'Afrique du Nord,* Editions du Cerf, 1961; *Kafka contra Kafka,* Plon, 1962, translation published as *Kafka Versus Kafka,* University of Alabama Press, 1968; *Les Apparitions de Martiens,* Fayard, 1963; *Le Laicat mythe et realite,* Centurian, 1965; *Un Patronat de droit divin,* Anthropos, 1971.

Biographies: *Charles de Foucauld explorateur mystique,* Editions du Cerf, 1954, translation published as *Soldier of the Spirit,* Putnam, 1956; *Le Pere Jacques,* Seuil, 1958, translation published as *Pere Jacques,* Macmillan, 1961; *Le Pere de Foucauld et les fraternites aujourd'hui,* Centurian, 1963.

Science fiction: *Les Portes Dauphines,* Gallimard, 1954; *Les Grands-peres prodiges,* Plon, 1957.

Literary critic and contributor of articles to various magazines.

WORK IN PROGRESS: Analyse critique des recontres extraterrestres; Les Tremblements de temps, a science-fiction novel; *Histoire des mondes extraordinaires terrestres; Humanoides automatiques.*

SIDELIGHTS: Couturier told *CA* that he was greatly influenced by surrealism, which he discovered at the age of twenty. "For me, surrealism has never been reducible to one literary or artistic school. It is the most revealing adventure of human life, near and far. Surrealism is the critical and passionate quest for 'surrealite' in its real or unreal appearances.

"Precisely for that reason, after a time the atheism of the surrealist group appeared to me an insufficient boundary. Through a long mental voyage among the great thinkers of India, Japan, the Islamic countries, and Dostoevsky's Russia, as one can see in *La Mystique de Surhomme,* I admitted that the resurrection of Christ was the sun of surrealism.

"At the same time I was confronted with the opposing friendships of Maritain and of de Van der Meer, those of Breton and other surrealists and of George Bataille. In my opinion the most determinant internal difference is that of different levels of research and method."

Couturier added that his works attempt to explore the nature and significance of modern myths in poetry, narratives, social criticism, and art.

*   *   *

COVINA, Gina 1952-

PERSONAL: Born May 13, 1952, in Janesville, Wis.; daughter of Charles Albert (in sales) and Olga (a dance teacher; maiden name, Kowal) Roberson. *Education:* Attended University of Southern California, 1969-70; California College of Arts and Crafts, B.F.A., 1973. *Residence:* Berkeley, Calif.

Agent: Joan Daves, 59 East 54th St., New York, N.Y. 10022.

CAREER: Amazon Press, Oakland, Calif., editor and publisher of *Amazon Quarterly,* 1972-76; Bluestocking Books, Guerneville, Calif., publisher, 1978. Writer, 1976—.

WRITINGS: (Editor with Laurel Galana) *The Lesbian Reader,* Amazon Press, 1975; (with Galana) *The New Lesbians,* Moon Books, 1977; *The Ouija Book,* Simon & Schuster, 1979.

WORK IN PROGRESS: The City of Hermits, a novel, publication expected in 1981.

SIDELIGHTS: Covina told *CA:* "I remember as a child of nine or ten feeling a thrill of terror and wonder at the awareness that I would be living through a period of global transformation the likes of which we have not seen in thousands of years. At that age, attending a fundamentalist church, I thought of the transformation in terms of Christian mythology—the end of the world, the Second Coming—and also in terms of nuclear holocaust, for which I was prepared by elementary school drills in which we hid under our desks with our hands clasped behind our necks. The awareness remains, and the time has come: the twenty years from 1980 to 2000 will see changes we cannot imagine.

"I write to reach forward into those coming changes, to reclaim the full extent of my power and learn to use it, to get comfortable in advance with the reality of cataclysmic change, to find or create a positive, joyful context for the coming years—and I write in such a way that I can hope to bring willing readers along through the journey I take. *The Ouija Book* is a pragmatic, direct, how-to approach to expanding the range of our personal power and awareness of interconnection. *The City of Hermits* has the same purpose but takes the left-handed approach, through the deeper waters of the unconscious, through the telling of a story."

*   *   *

COWLES, Lois Thornburg 1909-1980

OBITUARY NOTICE: Born May 15, 1909, in Des Moines, Iowa; died of a heart attack, March 31, 1980, in New York, N.Y. Philanthropist and journalist. Cowles was associated with numerous organizations, including Planned Parenthood, the National Association for the Advancement of Colored People, and the Northside Center for Child Development in New York City. She worked as a reporter for the *Des Moines Tribune* during the early 1930's. After marrying the executive editor of the *Des Moines Register,* she also contributed a series of travel articles to that paper. Obituaries and other sources: *New York Times,* April 1, 1980.

*   *   *

COX, Joan (Irene) 1942-

PERSONAL: Born March 20, 1942, in San Pedro, Calif.; daughter of Calvin George and Agnes Ella Rasmussen; married James Noel Cox (a rancher and carpenter), October 20, 1957; children: Robyn Lynn, Cheryl Ann, James Edwin. *Education:* Attended high school in Paradise, Calif. *Home:* 960 Northeast Mason Lane, Corvallis, Mont. 59828.

CAREER: Justice court clerk in Hamilton, Mont., 1976, bailiff, 1977—. Rancher and astrologer.

WRITINGS: Mindsong (science fiction), Avon, 1979; *Starweb* (science fiction), Avon, 1980.

WORK IN PROGRESS: A basic astrology text for nonastrologers; *HaShy Va,* a science-fiction novel; a science-fantasy novel.

SIDELIGHTS: Cox told *CA:* "Writing is something I've always done and probably will always do, published or not. I have always had a love for fantasy and science fiction because these fields ignore the impossibilities of the real world and let people believe, if only for a little while, that anything is possible. And when people believe a thing, it usually becomes part of their reality.

"I don't pretend to have any serious justification for writing fiction. It fulfills something in me to write it, and I can only hope it brings pleasure and perhaps a new thought or two to those who read it."

* * *

CRAIG, Elizabeth (Josephine) 1883(?)-1980

OBITUARY NOTICE—See index for *CA* sketch: Born c. 1883 in Addiewell, West Lothian, Scotland; died June 7, 1980, in Farnham Common, Buckinghamshire, England. Editor, columnist, feature writer, and author of books on cooking, gardening, and housekeeping. Throughout World War II Craig served as lecturer for the British Ministry of Agriculture and Ministry of Food. She traveled extensively to gather material for articles on food, wine, and travel. She wrote forty books, including *Cooking With Elizabeth Craig, The Scottish Cookery Book, The Business Woman's Cookbook,* and *Penguin Salad Book.* Obituaries and other sources: *New York Times,* June 12, 1980.

* * *

CRAIG, John Ernest 1921-

PERSONAL: Born July 29, 1921, in Peterborough, Ontario, Canada; son of Fred D. and Dorothy Mae (Fenwick) Craig; married Frances Patten Morrison, June 1, 1945; children: David, Catherine, John and Paul (twins). *Education:* University of Manitoba, B.A., 1951; University of Toronto, M.A. *Home:* 12 Ternhill Crescent, Don Mills, Ontario, Canada M3C 2E5.

CAREER: Canadian Facts Co., Ltd., Toronto, Ontario, market researcher, 1952-69; ORC International, Ltd., Toronto, market researcher, 1969-71; full-time writer, 1972—. *Military service:* Royal Canadian Naval Volunteer Reserve, 1941-45.

WRITINGS—Juvenile; all fiction, except as noted: *Wagons West,* Dent, 1955, Dodd, Mead, 1956; *The Long Return,* Bobbs-Merrill, 1959; *No Word for Good-bye,* Peter Martin Associates, 1969, Coward, 1971; *Who Wants to Be Alone?,* Scholastic, 1975; *Wormburners,* Scholastic, 1976; *By the Sound of Her Whistle* (nonfiction; illustrations by Fred Craig), Peter Martin Associates, 1966; (with wife, Frances Craig) *Track and Field* (nonfiction), F. Watts, 1979.

Fiction: *The Pro,* Peter Martin Associates, 1968, published as *Power Play,* Dodd, Mead, 1973; *If You Want to See Your Wife Again,* Putnam, 1971; *In Council Rooms Apart,* Putnam, 1971; *Superdude,* Warner Paperback, 1974; *All G.O.D.'s Children,* Morrow, 1975; *The Clearing,* Longman, 1975; *Close Doesn't Count,* Macmillan, 1975; *Chappie and Me* (autobiographical novel), Dodd, Mead, 1979.

Nonfiction: *How Far Back Can You Get?,* Doubleday, 1974; (with David Steen) *Canada's Olympic Chances,* Simon & Schuster, 1976; *The Noronic Is Burning,* General Publishing, 1976; *Some of My Best Friends Are Fishermen,* McClelland & Stewart, 1976; *Simcoe County: The Recent Past,* Corporation of the County of Simcoe (Midhurst, Ont.), 1977; *The Years of Agony, 1910-1920,* Natural Science of Canada, 1977.

Also author of scripts for television series "Adventure in Rainbow County," 1970-71, and "Starlost," 1973.

* * *

CRAIG, (Elizabeth) May 1889(?)-1975

PERSONAL: Born c. 1889 in Coosaw Island, S.C.; died July 15, 1975, in Silver Springs, Md.; daughter of Alexander and Elizabeth Anne (Essery) Adams; married Donald Alexander Craig (a journalist), 1908 (died, 1935); children: Donald Alexander, Betty Clagett. *Education:* Attended high school in Washington, D.C. *Residence:* Washington, D.C.

CAREER/WRITINGS: Washington, D.C., correspondent for New York, North Carolina, and Montana newspapers; Washington, D.C., correspondent and author of column "Inside Washington" for Gannett newspapers in Maine, including *Portland Press-Herald, Evening Express, Sunday Telegram, Waterville Sentinel,* and *Kennebee Journal;* Washington, D.C., correspondent for Maine radio and television stations; regular guest on National Broadcasting Co. (NBC-TV) television show "Meet the Press"; notable assignments include coverage of Normandy invasion and liberation of Paris in World War II, Berlin air-lift, and 1948 presidential campaign. Member of standing committee of Press Galleries of Congress, 1945-46. *Member:* National Academy of Television Arts and Sciences, Women's National Press Club (member of board of governors; president, 1943-44), American Women in Radio and Television, American Newspaperwomen's Club, Overseas Press Club of America, Berlin Press Club, Washington Newspaper Guild (director), Theta Sigma Phi. *Awards, honors:* Doctor of Humane Letters from University of Maine, 1946; theater ribbon from U.S. War Department for service as war correspondent, 1946.

SIDELIGHTS: May Craig covered the Washington, D.C., scene during the terms of five presidents, ranging from Franklin D. Roosevelt to Lyndon B. Johnson. Known for her unusual hats and keen questions, Craig was portrayed by a fellow journalist as "the Washington press gallery nemesis of all evasive politicians." Craig was a persistent, delving interviewer who once elicited a plea to "please be merciful" from a scorched Adlai E. Stevenson when he discovered he would be questioned by the reporter a second time. Franklin D. Roosevelt also felt the sting of Craig's tart queries. After being asked a particularly difficult one, Roosevelt quipped, "May, you must have stayed awake all night thinking up that question." Undisturbed, she replied, "as a matter of fact, I did."

Craig broke into the newspaper business in 1923 when she began helping her husband, the chief of the Washington bureau of the *New York Herald,* with a column he wrote for the *Portland Press-Herald.* By the following year she penned the column alone. It was after the death of her husband in 1935, though, when Craig turned to journalism full-time. Working for the Gannett chain, she became the only full-time Washington correspondent for Maine newspapers for more than twenty-five years. Consequently, she was sometimes referred to as the "most influential individual in that State."

The reporter was also a dedicated feminist. She marched in a suffragette parade during the presidential inauguration of Woodrow Wilson and participated in a number of groundbreaking firsts for women. In 1945, Craig became the first woman ever elected to the standing committee of the Press Galleries of Congress. Her most publicized battle for women's rights occured in 1947, however, when Craig was the only female correspondent to accompany President Harry S Truman to the Inter-American Defense Conference in Brazil. On the return trip, the president and news corps were to sail on the ship *Missouri*. Craig, though, was informed that she would have to fly home, as the battleship had no accommodations for women. Despite her vociferous protests, Craig was forced to take the aerial route.

Nevertheless, Craig won her battle two years later when she shattered naval tradition by becoming the first woman reporter to embark on a battleship in order to cover the practice maneuvers of the carrier *Midway*. Craig is also attributed with being the first woman to fly over the North Pole, and the first female correspondent to fly the Berlin air-lift and report on the Korean peace talks.

BIOGRAPHICAL/CRITICAL SOURCES: Ishbel Ross, *Ladies of the Press*, Arno, 1974.

OBITUARIES: New York Times, July 16, 1975; *Newsweek*, July 28, 1975; *Time*, July 28, 1975.*

*　*　*

CRANE, Catherine C(owle)　1940-

PERSONAL: Born July 28, 1940, in Wilkes Barre, Pa.; daughter of William Burdette, Jr. (in steel sales) and Margaret (Cramer) Crane. *Education:* Smith College, B.A., 1961; New York School of Interior Design, certificate, 1970. *Residence:* New York, N.Y. *Agent:* Owen Laster, William Morris Agency, 1350 Avenue of the Americas, New York, N.Y. 10019.

CAREER: World Peace Foundation, Boston, Mass., administrative assistant, 1961-62; International Business Machines, London, England, member of convention staff, 1963-64; Organization for Economic Cooperation and Development, Paris, France, administrative and editorial assistant, 1964; Holt, Rinehart & Winston, Inc., New York City, editorial assistant, 1965-66; *Holiday* (magazine), New York City, editorial office manager, 1966-67; Communicaid, Inc., New York City, assistant in communications consulting, 1967-68; Conso Products Co., New York City, in public relations, 1968-69; *Interiors* (magazine), New York City, editor, 1969-74; interior designer, writer, and consultant, 1974—. Conducts consumer decorating clinics. Volunteer worker at Early Childhood Development Center.

WRITINGS: (Editor) *Residential Interiors Today* (Designers Book Club selection), Watson-Guptill, 1977; *What Do You Say to a Naked Room?* (selection of Book-of-the-Month Club and Better Homes and Gardens Book Club), Dial, 1979. Contributor to magazines and newspapers, including *Newsday, Architectural Forum, American Art and Antiques, New York Times*, and *New York Daily News*.

WORK IN PROGRESS: Setting up seminars at local retail stores; doing decorating shows on radio and television.

SIDELIGHTS: Catherine Crane told *CA:* "The idea for *What Do You Say to a Naked Room?* came from frustration. I think that people are more interested in solving their decorating problems than they are in learning a lot of theory. I organized my book so that people can look up their problems and find what options will work for them."

In a review of *What Do You Say to a Naked Room?* for the *Detroit News*, Linda La Marre noted that the book "is informal without being overly cute, informative without being pedantic. It assumes the reader knows nearly nothing about projecting self into things and seeks to fill the void without being condescending."

AVOCATIONAL INTERESTS: Gourmet cooking, sailing, theatre, travel.

BIOGRAPHICAL/CRITICAL SOURCES: Detroit News, July 10, 1979.

*　*　*

CRAWFORD, Alan　1953-

PERSONAL: Born January 24, 1953, in Evansville, Ind.; son of Charles Eugene (a radio newscaster) and Kathryn (a teacher; maiden name, Pell) Crawford. *Education:* Attended Purdue University, 1971-72; Indiana University, B.A., 1975. *Politics:* "Disraeli conservative/Tory libertarian/skeptic." *Residence:* Washington, D.C. *Office:* 1501½ Church St. N.W., Washington, D.C. 20005.

CAREER: Human Events, Washington, D.C., summer intern, 1973; *Washington Post,* Washington, D.C., summer reporter, 1974; *New Guard,* Sterling, Va., editor, 1975; *Conservative Digest,* Washington, D.C., assistant editor, 1975; speechwriter for U.S. Senator James L. Buckley in Washington, D.C., 1976; *Morgantown Dominion-Post,* Morgantown, W.Va., editor, 1976-78; special assistant to U.S. Representative Dan Quayle in Washington, D.C., 1979—.

WRITINGS: Thunder on the Right: The New Right and the Politics of Resentment, Pantheon, 1980. Contributor of articles and reviews to magazines, including *Inquiry, National Review, Nation, Libertarian Review, Social Policy,* and *Alternative.*

SIDELIGHTS: Crawford wrote: "My limitless interests have resulted in ridiculously diverse files, each of which I hope to write about. These include film and theatre, television, comic strips (popular culture in general), economic history—specifically, the destructive role of the federal government in it—decline of the political parties, criticism of art and photography. I'd also like to write a biography of Randolph of Roanoke.

"The politics that informed *Thunder on the Right* are those, I believe, of a conservative—Burkean variety—plagued with a social conscience. That has not endeared me to some of my colleagues on the Right, the poverty of whose political program I hope my book has successfully demonstrated. If this makes me a renegade, those are the breaks. I am, after all, a journalist first, more interested in chronicling this society's decline than sitting on committees or whatever it is that reformers do. My influences are the obvious ones—Bierce, Twain, Mencken, Beerbohm, Swift and Pope, Petronius, Suetonius. As such, my writings will probably become increasingly satiric, which strikes me as the tone most appropriate to our times."

*　*　*

CREIGHTON, Donald Grant　1902-1979

PERSONAL: Born July 15, 1902, in Toronto, Ontario, Canada; died December 19, 1979, near Toronto, Ontario, Canada; son of William Black (an editor) and Laura (Harvie) Creighton; married Luella Sanders Browning Bruce, June 23, 1926; children: Philip, Cynthia. *Education:* University of Toronto, B.A., 1925; Balliol College, Oxford, B.A., 1927, M.A., 1929. *Home:* 15 Princeton St., Brooklin, Ontario, Canada LOB 1CO. *Office:* Department of History, University of Toronto, Toronto, Ontario, Canada M5S 1A1.

CAREER: University of Toronto, Toronto, Ontario, lecturer, 1927-32, assistant professor, 1932-39, associate professor, 1939-45, professor, 1945-65, Sir John A. Macdonald Professor of History, 1965-68, university professor, 1968-71, professor emeritus, 1971-79, chairman of Department of History, 1955-59. Research assistant for Royal Commission on Dominion-Provincial Relations, 1938-39. Member of Historic Sites and Monuments Board of Canada, 1958-71; Commonwealth member of Monckton advisory commission on Central Africa, 1959, and on Rhodesia and Nyasaland, 1960; member of Ontario advisory committee on Confederation, 1965-70.

MEMBER: Canadian Historical Association (president, 1956-57), Canadian Political Science Association, British Academy (fellow), Royal Society of Canada (fellow), Royal Historical Society (fellow). *Awards, honors:* Guggenheim fellowship, 1940-41; Rockefeller fellowship, 1944-45; LL.D. from University of New Brunswick, 1949, Queen's University (Ontario), 1956, University of Saskatchewan, 1957, University of British Columbia, 1959, St. Francis Xavier University, 1967, University of Victoria (British Columbia), 1967, Dalhousie University, 1970, and University of Toronto, 1974; Nuffield fellowship, 1951-52; Tyrell Medal for History from Royal Society of Canada, 1951; Governor General's Medal for academic nonfiction, 1952 and 1955; medal for popular biography from University of British Columbia, 1955; National Award in Letters from University of Alberta, 1957; D.Litt. from University of Manitoba, 1957, McGill University, 1959, Laurentian University, 1970, and Memorial University (Newfoundland), 1974; Molson Prize from Canada Council, 1964; Companion of the Order of Canada, 1967.

WRITINGS—History, unless otherwise noted: *The Commercial Empire of the St. Lawrence, 1760-1850,* Yale University Press, 1937, published as *The Empire of the St. Lawrence,* Macmillan, 1956; *Dominion of the North: A History of Canada,* Houghton, 1944, revised edition published as *A History of Canada: Dominion of the North,* 1958; *John A. Macdonald* (biography), Macmillan, Volume I: *The Young Politician,* 1953, Volume II: *The Old Chieftain,* 1956; *Harold Adams Innis: Portrait of a Scholar* (biography), University of Toronto Press, 1957; *The Story of Canada,* Macmillan (Toronto, Ontario), 1959, Houghton, 1960, revised edition, Macmillan, 1971.

British North America at Confederation, [Ottawa, Ontario], 1963; *The Road to Confederation: The Emergence of Canada, 1863-1867,* Macmillan (Toronto), 1964, Houghton, 1965; (with others) *Confederation* (essays), Toronto University Press, 1967; *Minorities, Schools, and Politics* (essays), University of Toronto Press, 1969; *Canada's First Century, 1867-1967,* St. Martin's, 1970; *Towards the Discovery of Canada: Selected Essays,* Macmillan, 1972; *Canada: The Heroic Beginnings,* Macmillan, 1974; *The Forked Road: Canada, 1939-1957,* McClelland, 1976; *Takeover* (novel), McClelland, 1978.

Contributor with Ramsay Cook and others to sound recording, "The Craft of History," Canadian Broadcasting Corp. (CBC), 1970.

Chairman of Canadian board of editors for *Encyclopaedia Americana,* 1956-63; advisory editor of "Canadian Centenary Series," 1963.

SIDELIGHTS: Donald Grant Creighton's first book, *The Commercial Empire of the St. Lawrence,* is considered one of the finest works on Canadian history produced to date. In it, the author discusses the seaway and its effects on the political and economic development of Canada. "Mr. Creighton has written a brilliant and attractive essay, which, by its bold use of a dramatic concept and its eloquent language, succeeds throughout in maintaining interest," remarked

A.R.M. Lower. The reviewer concluded that the author's "nice blend of economics and politics helps us to see that the only good history is that which is aware, not of one or two aspects of society, but of all aspects."

Another of Creighton's works to receive high critical acclaim is the two-volume biography of John A. Macdonald, the first prime minister of Canada. A. B. Corey of the *American Historical Review* hailed the first volume, *The Young Politician,* as "the best biography of any major Canadian political figure of the period since the Confederation.... The style is fluent, flamboyant, always lucid." Stuart Keate of the *New York Times,* moreover, felt that "it is remarkable that Canadians had to wait sixty years for the definitive biography of the country's first great statesman; but it proves a book worth waiting for."

In a review of the second volume, *The Old Chieftain,* a writer for the *Times Literary Supplement* noted that "at times the author exercises an over-generous poetic licence in dealing with natural scenery. But such momentary descents into the florid cannot detract from the power and scholarship of this absorbing narrative." L.L.L. Golden of the *Saturday Review* also praised the book, calling it a "brilliant, readable, and carefully documented biography," and placed Creighton in "the first rank of Canadian historians."

BIOGRAPHICAL/CRITICAL SOURCES: Canadian Forum, May, 1938, June 26, 1978; *Canadian Historical Review,* June, 1938, March, 1953; *Times Literary Supplement,* February 20, 1953, May 4, 1956, April 16, 1971; *American Historical Review,* October, 1953; *New York Times,* November 15, 1953; *Political Science Quarterly,* December, 1953; *Saturday Review,* March 24, 1956.

OBITUARIES: AB Bookman's Weekly, February 11, 1980.*

*   *   *

**CRISP, Anthony Thomas   1937-
(Tony Crisp; Mark Western, a pseudonym)**

PERSONAL: Born May 10, 1937, in Amersham, England; son of Alfred (a musician) and Betty (Banning) Crisp; married Brenda Gornall, December 18, 1959 (divorced May 11, 1977); married Hyone King (a renovator and decorator), October 15, 1977; children: Mark, Helen, Neal, Leon, Quentin. *Education:* Attended high school in London, England. *Politics:* "I am still trying to define." *Religion:* "I have sympathy with most major religions." *Home address:* Ashram, King St., Combe Martin, Devonshire EX34 0AG, England.

CAREER: Photographic Enterprise, London, England, photographic trainee, 1952; free-lance photographer, 1953-54, 1956-66; yoga teacher in Buckinghamshire, England, 1966-69, and Combe Martin, England, 1969-79; operator of Ashram (yoga and training center), 1980—. *Military service:* Royal Air Force, 1954-56.

WRITINGS—Under name Tony Crisp: *Relax With Yoga,* Collins, 1970; *Do You Dream?: How to Gain Insight Into Your Dreams,* Neville Spearman, 1971, Dutton, 1972; *Yield,* Turnstone, 1973; *Yoga and Childbirth,* Thorsons, 1975. Contributor to commercial journals under pseudonym Mark Western.

WORK IN PROGRESS: A book on some of the yoga or spiritual practices suggested in the New Testament, entitled *The Yoke of Christ;* an autobiography; a book about the conscious control of the dream process, entitled *Transformation;* a book about the release of the dream process into conscious activity, presented as a personal, semi-fictional account, tentatively entitled *Rabbonai.*

SIDELIGHTS: Crisp wrote: "I was thrown out of school at fifteen for truancy. At sixteen, while studying self-hypnosis and meditation, I found I could radically alter my state of consciousness. Thus began my search to understand the possibilities and geography of consciousness. At eighteen, while serving in Germany with the Royal Air Force, I experienced an extension of consciousness that gave me vivid awareness of events at my home in London. From that time on I have engaged in extensive study of psychic research, hypnosis, yoga, dream analysis, and world religions. I also began writing; at first on the subjects I was studying.

"At twenty-eight I entered another phase of my life and began teaching adult yoga classes. It presented me with the problem of making practical use of my earlier studies and research. During the next seven years I gradually formulated a technique which enabled those using it to allow the spontaneous movements, emotions, and activities of dreaming to break through into consciousness. It allows the practitioner to work consciously with the therapeutic, creative, and self-regulatory activities of the dream process. *Relax With Yoga* and *Do You Dream?* were written during these years, and show signs of the emerging emphasis on a living experience of one's own inner life.

"Working as a lay therapist, and teaching the technique of self-regulation to groups and individuals, I was struck again and again by the enormous impact symbols have on the unconscious, and how much they are employed to express deeply important feelings of human joy, pain, and even wisdom. This led me to write *Yield*, which was an attempt to see the events described in the New Testament as a dream. The book failed miserably as an attempt to communicate to a wide public the impact the New Testament has on the human unconscious. It is still a book I would like to write in a different way, to show Christ as a symbol of mankind's evolutionary life energy, struggling to realise itself amidst the premises and rules of socialised existence, and the maze of human conflicts and values.

"Using the technique of self-regulation, I am engaged in exploring and writing about the inner world of man, its part in history, its heritage, its potential. I feel rather like an explorer who wishes to share his experiences of another country, and to show what the culture of the other country, and its science, has of practical value. Just as the human animal developed the ability to reason, which was a potential existing in the inner world, so I find there are other faculties, or places in consciousness, we can develop to our advantage. It is these further possibilities I am working to define."

*   *   *

CRISP, Tony
See CRISP, Anthony Thomas

*   *   *

CRIST, Steven G(ordon) 1956-

PERSONAL: Born October 29, 1956, in New York, N.Y.; son of William B. (an educational publicist) and Judith (a film critic; maiden name, Klein) Crist. *Education:* Harvard University, A.B., 1978. *Home:* 127 West 96th St., New York, N.Y. 10025. *Office:* New York Times, 229 West 43rd St., New York, N.Y. 10036.

CAREER: New York Times, New York, N.Y., articles editor and staff writer, 1978—. Has also worked as a jazz pianist.

WRITINGS: (Editor and author, with George Meyer) *The Harvard Lampoon Big Book of College Life,* Doubleday,

1978; *The Muppet Movie Book,* Bantam, 1979; (with Tony Hendra and others) *The 80's: A Look Back at the Tumultuous Decade, 1980-1989,* Workman, 1979; *Off Track: Bets and Pieces,* Doubleday, 1980; *The Racetrack Book,* Workman, 1981. Contributor of articles to periodicals, including the *New York Times, Boston Globe, Christian Science Monitor, Esquire, Boston, American Way,* and *Youth.*

WORK IN PROGRESS: An untitled novel.

SIDELIGHTS: Crist told *CA:* "Combining a journalistic career and a private life of writing, moving between the worlds of nonfiction and fiction, is exhausting but the only way I know how to work. If one takes on more work than he can possibly handle, at least something gets completed in the process. I would go batty trying to write in a secluded farmhouse or having nothing to do all day but face the typewriter."

*   *   *

CRISTABEL
See ABRAHAMSEN, Christine Elizabeth

*   *   *

CRONIN, George 1933-

PERSONAL: Born March 17, 1933, in Newark, N.J.; son of George Aloysius (a salesman) and Anne (a nurse; maiden name, Kelly) Cronin; married Gloria Bills (a social worker), 1970; children: Melanie. *Education:* St. Peter's College, B.S., 1960; attended Columbia University, 1970-71; Bernard M. Baruch College of the City University of New York, M.P.A., 1973. *Home and office:* 2602 Routes 5 and 20, Stanley, N.Y. 14561. *Agent:* R & R Associates, 364 Mauro Rd., Englewood Cliffs, N.J. 07632.

CAREER: Equitable Life, New York City, underwriter, 1960-61; B. Gertz Department Store, New York City, buyer, 1961-65; New York City Department of Social Services, New York City, social worker, 1965-74; New York State Department of Audit and Control, New York City, investigator, 1974-79; writer. *Military service:* U.S. Air Force, 1952-55. *Member:* Mystery Writers of America.

WRITINGS: Answer From a Dead Man (mystery novel), Condor, 1978; *Death of a Delegate* (mystery novel), Condor, 1978.

WORK IN PROGRESS: Short stories and a terror novel.

SIDELIGHTS: Cronin told *CA:* "At this point in my life, the only work that interests me is writing. Why? That's a mystery. I'm most interested in telling stories that will entertain."

*   *   *

CROWCROFT, Jane
See CROWCROFT, Peter

*   *   *

CROWCROFT, Peter 1923-
(Jane Crowcroft, James Muntz, Max Orloff)

PERSONAL: Born November 25, 1923, in Watford, Hertfordshire, England; came to United States in 1963; naturalized citizen, 1980; son of H. E. (an engineer) and Zenaida (a princess; maiden name, Katchorovskia) Crowcroft; married Kate Bond, March, 1958; children: Alexandra Maria, Anna Kera. *Education:* Attended University of London, 1946-50. *Politics:* "Radical Pantheist." *Religion:* "Pantheism." *Home:* 1320 North Laurel Ave., West Hollywood, Calif.

90046. *Agent:* Jane Jordan Browne, 410 South Michigan Ave., Chicago, Ill. 60605. *Office address:* P.O. Box 1747, Beverly Hills, Calif. 90213.

CAREER: Actor and writer, 1952—. Has worked in both Hollywood and British repertory companies, and has appeared in such films as "On a Clear Day," "Doctor Doolittle," and in the television series "Daniel Boone." Speaker. *Military service:* British Army, Commandos, 1943-46; served in Europe and Burma; became sergeant. *Awards, honors:* Frank C. Betts Fleet Street Prize from King Features, 1955, for *The Fallen Sky.*

WRITINGS: Remember Me, Jarrolds, 1952; *The Fallen Sky,* Peter Nevil, 1954; *Blue, Blue Sky,* Peter Nevil, 1955; *Hunting Rommel,* Fleetway Press, 1956; *Aeolian Wraith,* Columbia Press, 1973; *That Man Bolt,* Simon & Schuster, 1974; *Blown Up,* Venice Publishing, 1975; (under pseudonym Jane Crowcroft) *Of Love Incarnate,* Simon & Schuster, 1976; (under pseudonym Jane Crowcroft) *Witch Love,* Simon & Schuster, 1976; *Monster,* American Fine Arts Publishing, 1980; (under pseudonym Max Orloff) *Didi in Paris,* Hustler Publishing, 1980. Also author of more than a hundred other novels, some under pseudonyms James Muntz and Max Orloff, and film scripts.

WORK IN PROGRESS: The Goldening Saga, nine volumes, an epic saga based on H. E. Crowcroft, 1899-1949, completion expected in 1982; *Unicorn in Hollywood,* three volumes, an autobiography.

*   *   *

CROWE, Amanda Cockrell   1948-
(Amanda Cockrell)

PERSONAL: Born May 17, 1948, in Los Angeles, Calif.; daughter of Francis Marion (a writer) and Marian (a writer; maiden name, Brown) Cockrell; married John D. Crowe (a reporter), June 13, 1970; children: Jefferson. *Education:* Hollins College, B.A. (with honors), 1969. *Politics:* Democrat. *Religion:* Episcopal. *Home:* 1225 North Roosevelt, Fresno, Calif. 93728. *Agent:* Oliver G. Swan, Collier Associates, 280 Madison Ave., New York, N.Y. 10016.

CAREER: Oxnard Press-Courier, Oxnard, Calif., reporter, 1969-71; KYNO-Radio, Fresno, Calif., copywriter, 1975-77; Clif Furgurson Advertising, Fresno, copywriter, 1977-78; KYNO-Radio, continuity manager, 1978-80; full-time writer, 1980—.

*WRITINGS—*Under name Amanda Cockrell: *The Legions of the Mist* (novel), Atheneum, 1979.

*WORK IN PROGRESS—*Under name Amanda Cockrell: A sequel to *The Legions of the Mist,* tentatively entitled *The Wall at the Edge of the World;* a paperback series for Book Creations.

SIDELIGHTS: Crowe told *CA:* "I am the child of two writer parents, and as a result, any other method of making a living never really occurred to me. I put in a lot of years doing it by writing newspaper articles and radio and television commercials, however, and it is only this year that I have been in a position to write fiction full time. I recommend this background to anyone interested in the field. It brings in a steady check for one thing. And it teaches a number of valuable lessons—meeting deadlines, living with the man who wields the blue pencil, and how to write anyway when you damn well don't feel like it. Writing for me is mostly pure pleasure. I am leery of definitions, but I suppose if I had to define fiction it would be as entertainment, with a subliminal message. Great thoughts should not jump out and hit you on the head. Fic-

tion should be a window onto another world, a journey through a different landscape . . . particularly historical fiction, which is my main interest. The past fascinates me, because it produced our present, and the people in it, if they can be brought to life, are mostly as me and thee.

"My advice to aspiring writers would be: Write. Write anything that anybody will pay you to write. Travel articles, radio commercials, news, editorials, billboards—*anything.* It's all grist for the mill. Every single thing you write teaches you something about some aspect of the craft."

*   *   *

CROZETTI, R(uth G.) Warner
See WARNER-CROZETTI, R(uth G.)

*   *   *

CULEX
See STANIER, Maida Euphemia Kerr

*   *   *

CUMMINGS, D(onald) W(ayne)   1935-

PERSONAL: Born May 21, 1935, in Seattle, Wash.; son of Oliver Warren (a waiter) and Mildred (in food service; maiden name, Thayer) Cummings; married Carol Feuling (a dance teacher), August 10, 1956; children: Daniel Dean, Lon Allen, Jody Inez. *Education:* University of Washington, Seattle, B.A., 1958, M.A., 1964, Ph.D., 1965. *Home address:* Route 4, Box 106, Ellensburg, Wash. 98926. *Office:* Academic Skills Center, Central Washington University, Ellensburg, Wash. 98926.

CAREER: Central Washington University, Ellensburg, began as instructor, 1960, became professor of English, 1971—, director of composition, 1966-71, and academic skills, 1976—. Visiting teacher at high school in Bellevue, Wash., 1971-72. *Member:* Washington State Council of Teachers of English.

WRITINGS: (With John Herum) *Writing: Plans, Drafts, and Revisions,* Random House, 1971; (with Herum) *Tempo: On Life, Work, and Leisure,* Houghton, 1973; (with Nancy Howard) *The Eidos Spelling Program,* Books 1 and 2, Eidos Press, 1978; *The Cummings Basic Speller,* Books 1-3, Eidos Press, 1979. Contributor to language journals.

WORK IN PROGRESS: Field testing Books 4-9 of *The Cummings Basic Speller; The System of American-English Spelling* (tentative title), a study and description of the elements, processes, and patterns of American-English orthography.

SIDELIGHTS: Cummings writes: "Over the years the ideas of Cassirer, Langer, and B. Croce have come to impress me more and more with the importance of symbolic expression, especially linguistic, to the human condition. Thus my increased concern for language arts at the elementary and secondary levels and for remedial language skills at the adult level, as at my university's Academic Skills Center. The job seems too important to continue screwing it up so."

*   *   *

CUNNINGHAM, Richard   1939-

PERSONAL: Born July 30, 1939, in Junction City, Kan.; son of David (a stonemason) and Charlotte (Riley) Cunningham; married Lucia Guerra (a professor), 1968. *Education:* University of Kansas, B.A., 1970, M.A., 1972. *Office:* c/o Sheed, Andrews & McMeel, 6700 Squibb Rd., Mission, Kan. 66202.

CAREER: Bricklayer, 1959—; teacher of brick masonry in Santa Ana, Calif., 1979—; writer. *Military service:* U.S. Air Force, 1960-64; became airman first class. *Member:* Mystery Writers of America. *Awards, honors:* Translation award from Translation Center at Columbia University, 1979, for *New Islands.*

WRITINGS: The Place Where the World Ends (novel), Sheed, Andrews & McMeel, 1973; *A Ceremony in the Lincoln Tunnel* (novel), Sheed, Andrews & McMeel, 1978; (translator) Maria Luisa Bombal, *New Islands,* Farrar, Straus, 1980. Also author of *The Year of the Tiger* (novel), 1981.

SIDELIGHTS: Cunningham told *CA:* "I am going down John Steinbeck's yellow brick road—trying to deal with the disposed, the ruined, and abused but enduring human beings who, by reason of mainly bad luck but at times as part of a political plan, are victims and also, in the truest sense of the word, heroes."

*   *   *

CURRAN, Jan Goldberg 1937-
(Jan Goldberg)

PERSONAL: Born May 2, 1937, in Walla Walla, Wash.; daughter of David (a merchant) and Dora (Copeland) Barer; married Alan Goldberg, June 16, 1957 (divorced); married Donald Curran, December 27, 1976 (divorced); children: (first marriage) Lee, Karen, Linda, Tod. *Education:* Attended University of Washington, Seattle, 1955-58. *Home:* 928 Cochise Court, Walnut Creek, Calif. 94598. *Agent:* Pat Loud, 200 West 58th St., New York, N.Y. 10017. *Office:* East Bay Newspapers, *Contra Costa Times,* 2640 Shadelands, Walnut Creek, Calif. 94598.

CAREER: Al-Wen Productions, San Francisco, Calif., television production assistant, 1969-73; associated with Unlimited Ltd. (public relations), 1974-75; in real estate sales in Contra Costa County, Calif., 1975-76; free-lance writer, 1976—. Chairperson of Birch Branch of Children's Hospital Medical Center of Northern California. Delegate to Northern California Council of City Panhellenics.

MEMBER: Authors Guild, Authors League of America, East Bay Cities Panhellenic (president, 1974), San Francisco City Panhellenic (member of executive board, 1964-74), Contra Costa Press Club, Alpha Epsilon Phi, B'nai B'rith Women. *Awards, honors:* Named outstanding woman of the year by San Francisco and East Bay Cities Panhellenic, 1974, 1976; volunteer of the year award, 1976, and women of achievement award, 1977, both from East Bay Alumnae Panhellenic; outstanding achievement award from Santa Barbara Writers Conference, 1977, for *The Statue of Liberty Is Cracking Up;* merit award from Santa Barbara Writers Conference, 1978, "for body of her work."

WRITINGS: (With Marcy Bachmann Wetton) *The Statue of Liberty Is Cracking Up,* Harcourt, 1979. Author of "Jan Goldberg," a column (under name Jan Goldberg) in *Contra Costa Times.* Contributor to newspapers. Editor of "People Section" of *Contra Costa Times.*

WORK IN PROGRESS: Domestic Blitz, with Marcy Bachmann Wetton; *Once Upon the Times,* with Wetton; "Heavy on the Sugar," a screenplay.

SIDELIGHTS: Jan Curran told *CA:* "In 1975 I was stricken with S.L.E., a rare chronic disease of the connective tissues. I began working in public relations, working in my free time on a book. We sold the book one day, and I was hired as a feature columnist on the next. *Statue* is based on my life and

that of my partner—raising children alone after divorce. All the books I saw at the time were depressing or clinical. This is the book I wish had been on the stands when I was divorced—a humorous look at a serious subject. Nothing is so harsh when you can find humor in it. When life starts to crumble, it's best to laugh."

*   *   *

CURTIS, Anthony 1926-

PERSONAL: Born in 1926 in London, England; son of Emanuel and Eileen Curtis; married Sarah Myers (a journalist), October 3, 1960; children: Job, Charles, Quentin. *Education:* Merton College, Oxford, B.A., 1950. *Home:* 9 Essex Villas, London W.8, England. *Office: Financial Times,* Bracken House, London EC4P 4BY, England.

CAREER: British Institute of the Sorbonne, Paris, France, lecturer, 1951; *Times Literary Supplement,* London, England, staff member, 1955; *Sunday Telegraph,* London, literary editor, 1961-69; *Financial Times,* London, literary editor and radio and theatre reviewer, 1970—. Committee member of Royal Literary Fund. *Military service:* Royal Air Force, 1944-48. *Member:* International P.E.N., Society of Authors, Critics' Circle, Garrick Club, Traveller's Club, Hurlingham Club. *Awards, honors:* Chancellor's Essay Prize, 1949; Harkness fellowship for study at Yale University and Huntington Library, 1959-60.

WRITINGS: New Developments in the French Theatre: Sartre, Camus, de Beauvoir, and Anouilh, Curtain Press, 1949; *The Pattern of Maugham: A Critical Portrait,* Taplinger, 1974; (editor and contributor) *The Rise and Fall of the Matinee Idol,* St. Martin's Press, 1974; *Somerset Maugham,* Macmillan, 1977. Writer for British Broadcasting Corp. (BBC-Radio). Contributor to magazines, including *Critics' Forum, Kaleidoscope, Drama,* and *Plays and Players.*

WORK IN PROGRESS: A biography of Sir Terence Rattigan; *Spillington Slips Up,* a children's book, completion expected in 1981.

SIDELIGHTS: Curtis wrote: "My main job is that of literary editor and book critic on a newspaper, but I try to combine it with occasional books of my own and longer critical projects. My output between stiff covers reveals how difficult in practice I find it to do this double act and where my priorities lie.

"For relaxation I enjoy playing chess by correspondence but I am not a strong player and still have difficulty in beating my chess computer. Chess has similarities to the old-style, well-made play, something that interests me professionally."

*   *   *

CURTIS, Jared Ralph 1936-

PERSONAL: Born March 25, 1936, in Oneonta, N.Y.; son of Ralph E. and Ann (Champlin) Curtis; married Ida Louks, December 29, 1956; children: J. Randall, Idamay. *Education:* Yale University, B.A., 1957; University of Michigan, M.A., 1961; Cornell University, Ph.D., 1966. *Home:* 5365 Kensington Cr., West Vancouver, British Columbia, Canada V7W 1M6. *Office:* Department of English, Simon Fraser University, Burnaby, British Columbia, Canada V5A 1S6.

CAREER: Susquehanna University, Selinsgrove, Pa., instructor in English, 1961-64; Indiana University, Bloomington, assistant professor of English, 1966-70; University of Arizona, Tucson, visiting associate professor of English, 1970-71; Simon Fraser University, Burnaby, British Columbia, associate professor, 1971-79, professor of English,

1979—. *Member:* Association of Canadian University Teachers of English, Modern Language Association of America, Philological Association of the Pacific Coast.

WRITINGS: Wordsworth's Experiments With Tradition, Cornell University Press, 1971; *Poems, in Two Volumes, 1807, and Other Poems, 1800-1807, by William Wordsworth,* Cornell University Press, 1981.

SIDELIGHTS: Regarding his forthcoming book, Curtis told *CA:* "The edition, a volume in *The Cornel Wordsworth,* will present the modern reader not with Wordsworth's much revised 1850 text, the usual basis for current editions, but with a clear sight of the 1807 poems as the poet first offered them to his audience, and a full view of their transformations leading toward and proceeding from their appearance in 1807."

D

DAMON, S(amuel) Foster 1893-1971

PERSONAL: Born February 22, 1893, in Newton, Mass.; died December 26, 1971, in Smithfield, R.I.; son of Joseph Neal and Sarah Wolf (Pastorius) Damon; married Louise Wheelwright, February 4, 1928. *Education:* Harvard University, A.B. (cum laude), 1914, A.M., 1927. *Residence:* Providence, R.I.

CAREER: Harvard University, Cambridge, Mass., instructor in Reserve Officers' Training Corps (ROTC), 1917; teacher of French to soldiers in Boston, Mass., 1918; worked in airplane factory and as an actor, 1918-20; Harvard University and Radcliffe College, Cambridge, assistant in English, 1921-27; Brown University, Providence, R.I., assistant professor, 1927-30, associate professor, 1930-36, professor, 1936-71. Curator of Harris Collection of Poetry and Plays at Brown University, 1929-71. Odist at Beethoven Centenary Festival, 1927. *Member:* Modern Language Association of America, American Antiquarian Society, New England Historic Genealogical Society, New England Poetry Club (honorary president), Rhode Island Historical Society, Providence Art Club, Cambridge Historical Society, St. Botolph's Club, Annisquam Yacht Club. *Awards, honors:* American Scandinavian Foundation traveling fellowship, 1920-21; Golden Rose from New England Poetry Society, 1932; A.M. from Brown University, 1943; Russell Crouse Award, 1954, for "Witch of Dogtown."

WRITINGS: (Editor with Robert Hillyer) *Eight More Harvard Poets,* Brentano's, 1923; *William Blake: His Philosophy and Symbols,* Houghton, 1924, reprinted, Brown University Press, 1973; *One Line of the Pastorious Family of Germantown, Pennsylvania, and Its Intermarriages,* privately printed, 1926; *Astrolabe: Infinitudes and Hypocrisies* (poems), Harper, 1927; *Tilted Moons* (poems), Harper, 1929; *Thomas Holley Chivers, Friend of Poe, With Selections From His Poems: A Strange Chapter in American Literary History* (biography), Harper, 1930, reprinted, Russell, 1973; *The Day After Christmas* (juvenile), Boni, 1930; *Amy Lowell: A Chronicle With Extracts From Her Correspondence* (biography), Houghton, 1935, reprinted, Shoe String, 1966; (contributor) *Job, Invented and Engraved,* United Book Guild, 1947.

The History of Square-Dancing, American Antiquarian Society, 1952; (author of introduction and bibliography) *Punch and Judy: As Presented Annually at the Annisquam Village*

Fair, Barre Gazette, 1957; (author of commentary) *Blake's Grave: A Prophetic Book,* Brown University Press, 1963; *A Blake Dictionary: The Ideas and Symbols of William Blake,* Brown University Press, 1965; (author of introduction and commentary) *Blake's Job: William Blake's Illustrations of the Book of Job,* Brown University Press, 1966; *The Moulton Tragedy: A Heroic Poem With Lyrics,* Gambit, 1970.

Plays: "Witch of Dogtown," 1954.

Editor of *Eight Harvard Poets,* 1917, and *Series of American Songs,* 1936. Translator of *A Book of Danish Verse,* 1922. Also composer of music, including "Crazy Theatre Music," 1938, and "Seven Songs," 1951. Contributor to magazines, including *Bookman, Century, Dial, Atlantic,* and *Harper's.*

SIDELIGHTS: Damon's first work as author, *William Blake: His Philosophy and Symbols,* established him as an expert on Blake. *A New Statesman* critic proclaimed the "volume, with its full and excellent commentary on each of Blake's works, is, so far as we know, the clearest, most convincing and most systematic attempt yet made to unravel the complexities of Blake's mythology." Robert Hillyer agreed: "It is clear that Mr. Damon has written a book which must serve as a foundation to all future study of William Blake." L. W. Griffin elaborated on these praises when reviewing Damon's *A Blake Dictionary.* Griffin exclaimed that "Damon, of Brown University, a Blake scholar of international reputation, has put all specialists, repeat, *specialists,* in his debt with this handsome volume."

Reviewers applauded Damon for his thorough research in his biography of Thomas Holley Chivers, a friend of Edgar Allan Poe. "Whether or not one thinks Chivers worth rescuing from obscurity on his own account, his story (under Professor Damon's competent hands) proves to be fascinating. Professor Damon has combined scholarship and human interest in a rare degree," a *Catholic World* critic asserted. More reserved, Louis Kronenberger of *Bookman* stated that "all in all Mr. Damon's scholarship is more to be commended than his literary judgment; and Chivers had better make the most of the present, for the future, like the past, is apt to prove unkind."

For his next comprehensive biography, *Amy Lowell,* Damon was again heralded for his meticulous research, although he was accused by critics of overkill. Several reviewers commented that the book was so well researched and documented, its length (nearly eight hundred pages) and content

133

became prohibitive. M. L. Becker declared the book "is likely to cripple an editorial hand, and in Mr. Damon's case the one holding the sheers seems often practically paralyzed." E. L. Walton reflected that "Damon works over his material as a scholar would work, dating every item that can be dated, . . . with much more exactness perhaps even than Miss Lowell could have done." Walton also added, though, that the book "is the best record in existence of those lively years in poetry between 1912 and 1925." A *Christian Science Monitor* critic noted that "what Amy Lowell did for John Keats, a younger poet, S. Foster Damon has attempted to do for her. By and large he has succeeded very well."

Though Damon was not well known for his poetry, his books of verse, *Astrolabe: Infinitudes and Hypocrisies* and *Tilted Moons,* were generally well received by critics. A reviewer for the *Literary Review of the New York Evening Post* found *Astrolabe* "a curious jumble of weakness and strength," while M. S. Mansfield of *Bookman* contended that the volume showed an "imaginative preoccupation with science, philosophy, theology" and also had "a sense of satire, and compassion." Similarly, a *Bookman* critic, in referring to *Tilted Moons,* claimed Damon "has a rich humor, a gorgeous palette for descriptive coloring and a trenchant hand at the satiric portrait."

AVOCATIONAL INTERESTS: Alchemy, spiritualism.

BIOGRAPHICAL/CRITICAL SOURCES: New York Times, January 28, 1923, August 3, 1924, August 10, 1930, December 1, 1935; *New York Tribune,* January 28, 1923; *Literary Review of the New York Evening Post,* March 10, 1923, July 26, 1924, April 23, 1927; *Freeman,* May 2, 1923; *New Republic,* October 3, 1923, August 20, 1924, July 23, 1930, January 8, 1936, June 5, 1965; *Nation and Athenaeum,* May 31, 1924; *New Statesman,* June 7, 1924; *Spectator,* June 7, 1924; *Times Literary Supplement,* June 26, 1924, October 23, 1930, September 13, 1963; *Boston Transcript,* July 12, 1924, May 31, 1930, November 12, 1930, November 9, 1935; *Dial,* September, 1924; *Saturday Review of Literature,* October 4, 1924, November 16, 1935; *New York Herald Tribune Book Review,* May 15, 1927; *Bookman,* July, 1927, January, 1930, July, 1930; *New York Evening Post,* November 16, 1929, May 10, 1930; *Outlook and Independent,* May 7, 1930; *New York Herald Tribune,* May 18, 1930, December 21, 1930, November 10, 1935, November 21, 1935; *Nation,* June 4, 1930, December 11, 1935; *New York World,* June 29, 1930; *Catholic World,* October, 1930; *Springfield Republican,* November 3, 1935; *Chicago Daily Tribune,* December 7, 1935; *Christian Science Monitor,* December 18, 1935; *Poetry,* January, 1936; *Library Journal,* June 15, 1965; *New York Review of Books,* October 28, 1965; *Best Sellers,* November 15, 1970.

OBITUARIES: New York Times, December 28, 1971; *AB Bookman's Weekly,* January 17, 1972.*

*   *   *

DANIELS, Pamela 1937-

PERSONAL: Born July 22, 1937, in Mineola, N.Y.; daughter of Milford (a military officer and high school physics teacher) and Ruth (a high school English teacher) Koehler; married Belden Daniels (in economic development finance), July 11, 1959; children: Andrew, Jonathan. *Education:* Wellesley College, B.A., 1959; Harvard University, M.A., 1963. *Office:* Wellesley College Center for Research on Women, 828 Washington St., Wellesley, Mass. 02181.

CAREER: Teaching and research assistant to Erik H. Erikson, Harvard University, 1963-70; free-lance editor and re-

searcher, 1970-75; Wellesley College Center for Research on Women, Wellesley, Mass., research associate, 1975—. Consultant to U.S. Peace Corps. *Member:* Phi Beta Kappa. *Awards, honors:* Woodrow Wilson fellow, 1960-62.

WRITINGS: (Editor with Sara Ruddick) *Working It Out: Twenty-Three Women Writers, Artists, Scientists, and Scholars Talk About Their Lives and Work,* Pantheon, 1977; (contributor) Barbara Forisha and Barbara Goldman, editors, *Outsiders on the Inside: Women in Organizations,* Prentice-Hall, 1980; (with Kathy Weingarten) *Sooner or Later: The Timing of Parenthood in Adult Lives,* Norton, 1981. Contributor to *Collier's Encyclopedia* and *Annals of the American Academy of Political and Social Science.*

*   *   *

DANTZIC, Cynthia Maris 1933-

PERSONAL: Born January 4, 1933, in Brooklyn, N.Y.; daughter of Howard Arthur (an engineer and lawyer) and Sylvia (an educator; maiden name, Wiener) Gross; married Jerry Dantzic (a photojournalist), June 15, 1958; children: Grayson Ross. *Education:* Attended Brooklyn Museum Art School, 1947-50, and Bard College, 1950-52; Yale University, B.F.A., 1955; Pratt Institute, M.F.A., 1963. *Home:* 910 President St., Brooklyn, N.Y. 11215. *Office:* Department of Art, Long Island University, Brooklyn, N.Y. 11215.

CAREER: Art teacher at private schools in Bryn Mawr, Pa., 1955-58, and New York City (also department head), 1958-63; City University of New York, New York City, instructor in art, 1963; Long Island University, Brooklyn, N.Y., lecturer, 1964-65, assistant professor, 1965-69, associate professor, 1969-75, professor of art, 1975—, head of department, 1977—. Work (which includes commissioned work) has been exhibited in solo and group shows, in collection at Brooklyn Museum, and in private collections. Art coordinator of North Shore Community Arts Center, 1963-64; co-chairman of Brooklyn Museum Art Festival for N.A.A.C.P., 1963, member of advisory committee of the museum's Community Gallery, 1973—; consultant to Brooklyn Children's Museum. *Member:* College Art Association of America, American Association of University Professors, United Federation of College Teachers, Long Island University Faculty Federation (member of executive committee, 1979-80).

WRITINGS—Self-illustrated children's books: *Stop Dropping breAd crumBs on my yaCht: A Silent ABC,* Prentice-Hall, 1974; *Sounds of Silents,* Prentice-Hall, 1976.

WORK IN PROGRESS: 1derful 2sday: A Story Wor3ding, a book in rubber stamps, completion expected in 1981; three journals of her travels across the United States and Australia.

SIDELIGHTS: Cynthia Dantzic told *CA:* "As a teacher I saw the need for a book to introduce, as a supplement to the phonics system, the silent letters of the alphabet, surprisingly, all twenty-six letters! As an artist I wanted the book to be handsomely but graphically illustrated, using calligraphy instead of type. And as a game player and puzzle solver I wanted it to be witty and cleverly worded. The result is *Stop Dropping breAd crumBs on my yaCht.*

"Although I've always considered myself first an artist and only more recently an educator, I wouldn't feel complete without creating books—not simply writing them, but creating the art work, even the lettering. I am among those for whom the written document holds almost a ceremonially special place among the civilizing achievements of humankind, so no matter what I may do, I will always do books!"

AVOCATIONAL INTERESTS: Studying the piano, collecting graphic Americana.

BIOGRAPHICAL/CRITICAL SOURCES: New Yorker, May 28, 1966; *Pratt Reports,* spring, 1979.

*   *   *

DAS, Kamala 1934-

PERSONAL: Born March 31, 1934, in Malabar, India; daughter of V. M. (an editor) and Balamani Amma (a poet; maiden name, Nalapat) Nair; married K. Madhava Das (a banker), February 4, 1949; children: Monu Nalapat, Chinnen, Jaisurya. *Education:* Educated privately. *Politics:* "Once upon a time believed in the Indian National Congress." *Religion:* Hindu. *Home:* Nalapat House, Nalapat Rd., Punnayurkulam, Kerala, India. *Office:* Book Point, Ballard Estate, Bombay, India.

CAREER: Writer. Worked as poetry editor of *Illustrated Weekly of India,* Bombay, as president of Jyotsha Art and Education Academy, Bombay, and as director of Book Point, Bombay. Founding president of Bahutantrika Group for poets, playwrights, singers, and dancers. *Member:* International P.E.N., India Pakistan Friendship Association. *Awards, honors:* Prize from International P.E.N., 1964; award from Kerala Sahitya Academy, 1969, for *Thanuppu.*

WRITINGS—In English: Summer in Calcutta: Fifty Poems, Everest Press, 1965, InterCulture, 1975; *The Descendants* (poems), Writers Workshop (Calcutta, India), 1967, InterCulture, 1975; *The Old Playhouse and Other Poems,* Longman, 1973; *Alphabet of Lust* (novel), Orient Paperbacks, 1976; *A Doll for the Child Prostitute* (stories), India Paperbacks, 1977; *My Story* (autobiography), Sterling, 1977.

Other writings; published by Current Books except as noted: *Draksakshi* (juvenile; title means "Eyewitness"), Longman, 1973; *Pathu Kathakal* (title means "Ten Stories"); *Tharisunilam* (stories; title means "Fallow Fields"); *Narachirukal Parakkumbol* (stories; title means "When the Bats Fly"); *Ente Snehita Aruna* (stories; title means "My Friend Aruna"); *Chuvanna Pavada* (stories; title means "The Red Skirt"); *Thanuppu* (stories; title means "Cold"); *Rajavinte Premabajanam* (stories; title means "The King's Beloved"); *Premathinte Vilapa Kavyam* (stories; title means "Requiem for a Love"); *Mathilukal* (stories; title means "Walls").

Editor of *Pamparam.*

WORK IN PROGRESS: A book on herbs and medicinal plants used as cures in ancient India; research on witchcraft for a book on sorcery in Malabar; a book of poems.

SIDELIGHTS: Kamala Das wrote: "Of all the books I have written, my autobiography has been the most successful; it has been translated into eleven languages. The people who have given me encouragement in my career are my mother, the poetess, and my cousin, Aubrey Menen, the novelist." *Avocational interests:* "Travel, but only with my youngest son."

*   *   *

DAVIDSON, Avram 1923-

PERSONAL: Born April 23, 1923, in Yonkers, N.Y.; son of Harry Jonas and Lillian (Adler) Davidson; married Grania Kaiman (a writer; divorced); children: Ethan Michael Anders. *Education:* Attended New York University, 1940-42, Yeshiva University, 1947-48, and Pierce College, 1950-51. *Politics:* Democrat. *Religion:* Jewish.

CAREER: Free-lance writer. *Magazine of Fantasy and Sci-*

ence Fiction, executive editor, 1961-64. *Military service:* U.S. Navy, 1942-46; served with Hospital Corps in Okinawa and China. *Member:* Serendipitous Order of Beavers, Order of Ailing Cockroaches, Berkeley Circle. *Awards, honors:* Ellery Queen Award, 1958, for "The Necessity of His Condition"; Hugo Award for best short story from World Science Fiction Convention, 1958, for "Or All the Seas With Oysters"; Hugo Award for best professional magazine, 1962, for *Magazine of Fantasy and Science Fiction;* Edgar Award from Mystery Writers of America, 1962, for "The Affair at the Lahore Cantonment"; World Fantasy Award for best collection, 1975, for *The Enquiries of Dr. Esterhazy.*

WRITINGS: Or All the Seas With Oysters (short stories), Berkley, 1962; *Crimes and Chaos* (articles), Regency, 1962; (with Ward Moore) *Joyleg* (novel), Pyramid, 1962; (editor) *The Best From Fantasy and Science Fiction,* Doubleday, twelfth series, 1963, thirteenth series, 1964, fourteenth series, 1964; *Mutiny in Space* (novel), Pyramid, 1964; *Masters of the Maze* (novel), Pyramid, 1965; *Rogue Dragon,* Ace, 1965; *Rork!,* Berkley, 1965; *What Strange Skies* (short stories), Ace, 1965; *Clash of Star-Kings,* Ace, 1966; *The Enemy of My Enemy,* Berkley, 1966; *The Kar-chee Reign,* Ace, 1966; *The Island Under the Earth,* Ace, 1969; *The Phoenix and the Mirror* (novel), Doubleday, 1969; *Peregrine: Primus,* Walker, 1971; *Strange Seas and Shores: A Collection of Short Stories,* Doubleday, 1971; *Ursus of Ultima Thule,* Avon, 1973; *The Enquiries of Doctor Eszterhazy,* Warner Books, 1975; *The Redward Edward Papers,* Doubleday, 1978; *The Best of Avram Davidson,* edited by Michael Kurland, Doubleday, 1979. Author of stories for television: "The Ikon of Elijah," and "Thou Still Unravished Bride" for "Alfred Hitchcock Presents" program.

BIOGRAPHICAL/CRITICAL SOURCES: New York Times Book Review, July 25, 1971; *Magazine of Fantasy and Science Fiction,* December, 1971, July, 1972, September, 1976, March, 1979.*

*   *   *

DAVIDSON, John
See REID, Charles (Stuart)

*   *   *

DAVIES, Bettilu D(onna) 1942-

PERSONAL: Born March 30, 1942, in Pontiac, Mich.; daughter of Charles Kenneth (an automobile worker) and Winnie (a secretary; maiden name, Griffin) Maxwell; married Paul F. Davies (a machinist), June 20, 1964; children: Thomas, Christopher, Anita and Annette (twins), Jason. *Education:* Pontiac Business Institute, diploma, 1961; attended Moody Bible Institute; Institute of Children's Literature, diploma, 1978. *Politics:* Independent. *Religion:* Baptist. *Home:* 1911 Burton St., Beloit, Wis. 53511.

CAREER: Michigan Employment Security Commission, Royal Oak, clerk typist, 1961-62; Moody Press, Chicago, Ill., secretary, 1963-64; Fairbanks Morse, Inc., Beloit, Wis., secretary, 1966-67; Pen, Palette & Keyboard, Beloit, writer, artist, and piano teacher, 1968—. Monitor for Faith Christian Academy, 1976—.

WRITINGS: The Secret of the Hidden Cave (juvenile), Zondervan, 1980.

Author of scripts for puppet plays. Contributor to church school periodicals.

WORK IN PROGRESS: Wendy (tentative title), a novel for teenagers; two juveniles in the "Marty" series, *Wear a Big*

Smile (tentative title) and a sequel, publication by Moody expected in 1981; *Step by Awkward Step,* devotions for adults; a school play.

SIDELIGHTS: Bettilu Davies told *CA:* "I am a born-again Christian, not because it is the popular 'in' thing to be, but because I accepted Jesus Christ as my personal savior when I was six years old. From the time I could understand much of anything at all, pleasing God has been the main motivation of my life.

"As a child, I thought I would grow up to be a medical missionary in Africa, and I had ample opportunity to learn about missionaries because they seemed to be at our home for a large portion of their visits to our church, and my own sister eventually became one. However, I always wanted to write, and finally realized as a young adult that missionary work would be mine only through writing.

"I began to read the best books our libraries had to offer for children, and I was shocked a good part of the time. Evidently, these days books aren't good unless they deal with sex, sex, or sex. I decided there was a real need for good, interesting, wholesome books for young people that would not necessarily avoid this important matter, but that would at least place it in its proper perspective. Right there is my main motivation for writing.

"My main position in life is to be wife and mother to my family. Not even writing is more important than my husband and children. However, they supply me with many good story ideas. I work as a monitor in our local Christian school, and I teach music and art and am in charge of reading. I love these young people, whether they are the tiny little kindergartners or whether they are the six-foot seniors.

"Last year I went as a chaperone to a national convention in Pocatello, Idaho. I saw beautiful mountain scenery on that trip, and a month later went on a family vacation to Florida. On a deep-sea fishing expedition, I saw four water spouts that looked just like tornados. I was overwhelmed with awe at God's creation. I also got two good story ideas on that trip.

"The editor of Moody Press has asked me to write a series of books featuring the main character of *Wear a Big Smile* and dealing with real teenage problems. I am at the 'feeling out' stage now, to decide in which direction I want to go. I rather think I will want to do something in the area of teenage runaways or teenage diseases, such as diabetes.

"*Wendy* deals with a teen's acceptance of others, including a troublesome brother and a mentally retarded child.

"One other idea I have worked on a little bit is *Step by Awkward Step,* an adult devotional book. However, I don't know if I'm grown up enough to deal with adult subject matter. It will probably end up appealing to adults with young minds. I don't really feel like I have arrived myself yet, so how can I tell other adults how to live?"

AVOCATIONAL INTERESTS: Knitting, crocheting, quiltmaking, canning her own produce, sewing, painting, singing, calligraphy.

*   *   *

DAVIS, Berrie 1922-

PERSONAL: Born July 19, 1922, in London, England; came to the United States in 1969; daughter of Herbert Almond (an accountant) and Florence (a teacher; maiden name, KingParks) Postlethwaite; married twice (marriages ended); children: Kevin, Joanna. *Education:* Attended high school in Edgbaston, England. *Home and office address:* 4246 Denny Ave., Studio City, Calif. 91602. *Agent:* Harold Ober Associates, Inc., 40 East 49th St., New York, N.Y. 10017.

CAREER: British Ministry of Information, London, England, executive assistant, 1940-45; Angus McDonald & Partners (architects), Bristol, England, executive assistant, 1948-52; writer, 1962—. Public relations officer for British Red Cross, 1959-66.

WRITINGS: The Fourth Day of Fear (novel), Putnam, 1973; *Trevena's Daughter* (novel), Dell, 1976; *Dark Paradise* (novel), Dell, 1980.

Musical plays: "Puss in Boots," 1962; "Rabbit Stew," 1963; "For the Love of Mike," 1964; "Picture of Joy," 1965; "Between One and Two," 1966.

Also author of radio plays. Contributor of stories and articles to magazines.

WORK IN PROGRESS: Two novels, *The Eagle and the Rose* and *A Pair of Ragged Claws.*

SIDELIGHTS: Berrie Davis told *CA:* "I began writing almost twenty years ago for the section of the British Red Cross in charge of the southwestern counties of England. The job was two-fold: to alert the public to the many Red Cross services available in peace as well as war, and to raise funds. When I suggested writing a full-length pantomime, converted to demonstrate with humor the facilities provided, fellow officers reacted with some skepticism—it might be amusing, they said, but it would make no money. But it made a lot of money. On more than one occasion the press likened the style to that of Noel Coward. They were also fascinated to discover during interviews in person and on the British Broadcasting Corp. that I neither wrote music nor played the piano; I hummed the songs to my pianist. A further five musicals were written in this way before I switched to radio plays.

"My next venture was a series of articles describing America through the eyes of an Englishwoman. Then followed many short stories which have appeared in eight countries. The setting for these has become increasingly American.

"Presently I am working on a romance set in England during World War II after the arrival there of the American forces. I was particularly well qualified to write of those times since my wartime job was handling Anglo-American relations for the British Ministry of Information."

AVOCATIONAL INTERESTS: European travel, including Corsica, Sardinia, and France.

*   *   *

DAVIS, Joseph S(tancliffe) 1885-1975

PERSONAL: Born November 5, 1885, in Chester County, Pa.; died April 23, 1975, in Los Altos, Calif.; son of William Harmar (a contractor) and Mary Charles (Siddall) Davis; married Florence Harris Danielson, August 31, 1916; children: Christine, Amy Barbara (deceased), Robert Danielson, Joseph Stancliffe, Jr. *Education:* Harvard University, B.A. (summa cum laude), 1908, Ph.D., 1913. *Religion:* Congregationalist. *Residence:* Stanford, Calif.

CAREER: Harvard University, Cambridge, Mass., instructor, 1913-17, tutor, 1915-20, assistant professor of economics, 1917-21; Stanford University, Stanford, Calif., director of Food Research Institute, 1921-52, professor of economic research, 1938-52, professor emeritus, 1952-75. Assistant statistician, American Shipping Mission to London, England, and Allied Maritime Transport Council, 1918-19; economic assistant to American members of Dawes Commission on German Reparations, 1924; board member of Social Research Council, 1924, 1946; chief economist, Federal Farm Board, 1929-31; member of President's Council of Economic Advisers, 1955-58. Consultant to Brookings Institution, 1933-36, and to Department of Agriculture. Former trustee of American Institute of Pacific Relations. *Member:* American Economic Association (president, 1944), American Farm Economic Association (president, 1936), American Statistical Association (president, 1936; member of census advisory committee, 1959-63), Inter American Statistical Institute, International Statistical Institute, Economic History Association, Royal Economic Society, Agricultural Historical Society, Business Historical Society, Phi Beta Kappa, Delta Upsilon, Delta Sigma Rho, Pi Gamma Mu, Cosmos Club (Washington, D.C.).

WRITINGS: Essays in the Earlier History of American Corporations, two volumes, Harvard University Press, 1917, reprinted, Russell, 1965; (with Wilfred Eldred) *Stale Bread Loss as a Problem of the Baking Industry,* Stanford University, 1923; *The Farm Export Debenture Plan,* Food Research Institute, Stanford University, 1929; *Wheat and the A.A.A.,* Brookings Institution, 1935, reprinted, Da Capo Press, 1973; (with Edwin G. Nourse and John D. Black) *Three Years of the Agricultural Adjustment Administration,* 1937, reprinted, Da Capo Press, 1971; *On Agricultural Policy, 1926-1938,* Food Research Institute, Stanford University, 1939; *International Commodity Agreements: Hope, Illusion, or Menace?,* Committee on International Economic Policy, 1947; (editor) Carl Alsberg, *Scientist at Large,* Stanford University Press, 1948; *The Population Upsurge in the United States,* Food Research Institute, Stanford University, 1949; *The World Between the Wars, 1919-39: An Economist's View,* Johns Hopkins Press, 1975. Also author of *The American Baking Industry, 1849-1923,* Stanford University Press, and numerous economic reports for local, state, and federal agencies. Contributor of articles to *Journal of American Statistical Association, Review of Economic Statistics, Journal of Farm Economics, Quarterly Journal of Economics, Virginia Quarterly Review,* and *Harvard Business Review.* Editor of *Review of Economic Statistics,* 1919-25, and *Wheat Studies,* 1924-44.

AVOCATIONAL INTERESTS: Gardening, camping, reading.

OBITUARIES: New York Times, April 24, 1975.*

*   *   *

DAWSON, Jan   1939(?)-1980

OBITUARY NOTICE: Born c. 1939; died July 29, 1980, in London, England. Film critic. Dawson contributed to numerous film periodicals, including *Take One, Cinema Papers,* and *Sight and Sound.* She was especially renowned for her expertise in German films. From 1976 to 1980 Dawson worked for the Berlin Film Festival in a number of promotional and critical capacities. Obituaries and other sources: *London Times,* August 4, 1980.

*   *   *

DEAN, (Alfreda) Joan   1925-

PERSONAL: Born January 21, 1925, in Twickenham, England; daughter of Alfred Gordon (a company director) and Bessie Winifred Esther (Simpson) Furlong; married David Brian Dean (a company director), March 28, 1953. *Education:* Bishop Otter College, teaching certificate, 1945; Harrow School of Art, N.D.D., 1952; University of Sheffield,

art teacher's diploma, 1957; University of Reading, M.Ed., 1967. *Politics:* "Slightly left of center." *Religion:* Anglican. *Home:* Lakeside House, 70-A Waterloo Rd., Wokingham, Berkshire RG11 2JL, England. *Office:* County Hall, Kingston-on-Thames, Surrey, England.

CAREER: Assistant teacher in secondary schools in Harrow, Middlesex, England, 1945-48; Technical College, Harrow, part-time lecturer in general education, 1948-52; Cheshire College of Education, Crewe, Cheshire, England, lecturer in art and craft, 1952-57; headmistress of primary schools in Froyle, Hampshire, England, 1957-59, and Wareham, Dorsetshire, England, 1959-61; senior adviser for primary education for Berkshire, England, 1961-72; chief inspector for Surrey, England, 1972—. Guest on television and radio programs; chairman of British Broadcasting Corp. (BBC) program committee, 1969-79. Member of Soulbury Committee, 1970-78, chairman of officers' panel, 1972-74. *Member:* School Broadcasting Council, National Association of Inspectors of Schools and Educational Advisers (member of executive committee, 1968-79; president, 1971-72), Schools Council (member of professional committee, 1978-79). *Awards, honors:* Created member of Order of British Empire, 1979.

WRITINGS: Art and Craft in the Primary School, A. & C. Black, 1961; *Reading, Writing, and Talking,* A. & C. Black, 1968; *Religious Education for Children,* Ward, Lock, 1972; *Recording Children's Progress,* Macmillan, 1972; (self-illustrated) *Clay in School,* M. Evans, 1972; (self-illustrated) *Working Space,* M. Evans, 1972; (self-illustrated) *A Place to Paint,* M. Evans, 1972; (self-illustrated) *Language Areas,* M. Evans, 1972; (self-illustrated) *Display,* M. Evans, 1974; (self-illustrated) *Room Outside,* M. Evans, 1974; (with Betty Root and Elizabeth Goodacre) *Teaching Young Readers,* BBC Publications, 1976; *The Literacy Schedule,* Centre for the Teaching of Reading, University of Reading, 1979. Also author with Ruth Nichols of *Framework for Reading,* 1974.

Self-illustrated children's books: *The First Book of Wild Flowers,* A. & C. Black, 1964; *The Second Book of Wild Flowers,* A. & C. Black, 1964; (with David Price) *Understanding Feelings,* Holmes McDougall, 1973. Also author of *You and Others.* Editor of series, "Exploring Your World," Holmes McDougall. Contributor to education journals.

WORK IN PROGRESS: Spelling Programmes; books on school management.

SIDELIGHTS: Joan Dean told *CA:* "I suppose if I had been asked at the age of twenty-five or so about appearing in print, I should have replied that I hoped to illustrate books. I have used these skills almost entirely to illustrate my work, and having the ability to draw has enabled me to use drawing and writing in a combined way which must be much more difficult for those who practice one or the other skill only.

"I didn't set out to be a writer, unlike my sister, Monica Furlong, who never wanted to be anything else. I am first and foremost a teacher, and everything I have written has grown out of my continuing interest in learning and teaching and the way people tick. A good many of my books are how-to-do-it books, because they developed from my own teaching and my observation of good teachers at work.

"I have written four children's books. I find the task of choosing the right language for children's books an interesting activity which makes me think very deeply about what I wish to say, a useful and salutory experience for any writer with some unexpected pitfalls.

"The frustrating thing is that there are so many things I want to write about. I have spent a good deal of time in the last three or four years producing papers for head teachers in their management role for use in connection with a course I have developed with my colleagues in Surrey. I'd like to get these into a form which could have a wider readership. *The Literacy Schedule* is a list of literacy skills which I believe we should be helping children to acquire. I'd like to write the book needed to support the list. I'd also like to write something on pastoral care and discipline in schools and I could think of many more possibilities.

"I write mainly to sort out my own thinking. I enjoy analyzing things and get satisfaction from trying to find useful patterns and structures. Once I am on the way to having thought out a structure, it is very tempting to work out how it could be used. *Religious Education for Children* was very much of this model. I worked with groups of teachers and then began to see a possible framework, and the desire to work this out led me to studying and reading in order to clothe the framework."

AVOCATIONAL INTERESTS: Gardening.

* * *

de BARY, Brett
    See NEE, Brett de Bary

* * *

de GRAFFE, Richard
    See ST. CLAIR, Leonard

* * *

del CASTILLO, Richard Griswold
    See GRISWOLD del CASTILLO, Richard

* * *

de LONE, Richard H.   1940-

PERSONAL: Born January 27, 1940, in Philadelphia, Pa.; son of H. Francis (a lawyer) and Madeline (Heckscher) de Lone; married Talia Trachtenberg (a dancer). *Education:* Harvard University, B.A., 1962; University of California, Berkeley, M.A., 1969. *Residence:* Philadelphia, Pa. *Office:* Public/Private Ventures, 1726 Cherry St., Philadelphia, Pa. 19103.

CAREER: Public/Private Ventures, Philadelphia, Pa., president, 1978—.

WRITINGS: Small Futures: Children, Inequality, and the Limits of Liberal Reform, Harcourt, 1979. Contributor to magazines.

* * *

DEMOREST, Stephen   1949-

PERSONAL: Born May 1, 1949, in Newton, Mass.; son of William J. and Constance G. Demorest. *Education:* Williams College, B.A., 1971. *Home:* 107 West 86th St., New York, N.Y. 10024. *Agent:* Perry Knowlton, Curtis Brown, Ltd., 575 Madison Ave., New York, N.Y. 10022.

CAREER: Circus, New York City, managing editor, 1974-76; *New York Daily News,* New York City, reviewer, 1977; free-lance writer and editor, 1977-80; *Melody Maker,* London, England, author of column, "New York," 1980—.

WRITINGS: Alice Cooper, Popular Library, 1974. Also author of "Lucky's Strike," a screenplay, 1977.

WORK IN PROGRESS: A mystery novel, publication expected in 1981.

DEMPSEY, Lotta

PERSONAL: Born in Edmonton, Alberta, Canada; daughter of Alexander Christopher (a fruit store owner) and Evelyn Louise (Hering) Dempsey; married Richard A. Fisher (an architect; deceased); children: Alson, John, Donald. *Education:* Attended Edmonton Normal School. *Office: Toronto Star,* 1 Yonge St., Toronto, Ontario, Canada M5E 1E6.

CAREER: Worked for *Toronto Globe and Mail,* Toronto, Ontario, and *Edmonton Journal* and *Edmonton Bulletin,* Edmonton, Alberta; editor of *Chatelaine,* 1952, feature editor, 1969—. Co-host of a daily program on CBLT-TV. *Awards, honors:* Memorial awards from Canadian Women's Press Club, 1948, 1967, and 1976; named to Canadian News Hall of Fame, 1975.

WRITINGS: No Life for a Lady, Musson, 1976. Author of "Inside Story" and "Age of Reason," columns in *Toronto Star.*

SIDELIGHTS: Lotta Dempsey wrote: "I was fortunate to learn the newspaper business from tough city editors since I was eighteen. I have been privileged to receive many assignments abroad and in the United States, but especially to have the opportunity to visit my own country from Newfoundland to the tip of Vancouver Island, from the high arctic to the forty-ninth parallel. I can't think of a happier trade than the print press."

* * *

DENHARDT, Robert Moorman   1912-

PERSONAL: Born June 14, 1912, in Colusa, Calif.; son of Thorton T. (a minister) and Grace Lucile (a teacher; maiden name, Moorman) Denhardt; married Sarah Carolyn Brim (a teacher), August 10, 1940; children: Robert Brim, Carol Lynn Denhardt Arens. *Education:* University of California, Berkeley, A.B., 1936, M.A., 1937. *Politics:* Republican. *Religion:* Episcopalian. *Home:* 912 Pendleton Ave., Arbuckle, Calif. 95912.

CAREER: Texas A & M University, College Station, assistant professor of agriculture and economics, 1938-41; United States Department of Agriculture, Porto Alegre, Brazil, agricultural analyst, 1941-45; Southern Methodist University, Dallas, Tex., assistant professor of history, 1945-46; *Western Horseman,* Colorado Springs, Colo., editor, 1947-51; writer, 1951—.

WRITINGS: The Horse of the Americas, University of Oklahoma Press, 1947, revised edition, 1975; (editor) *The Horse of the Conquest,* University of Oklahoma Press, 1949; *Quarter Horses: A Story of Two Centuries,* University of Oklahoma Press, 1967; *King Ranch Quarter Horses,* University of Oklahoma Press, 1970; *Foundation Sires of the American Quarter Horse,* University of Oklahoma Press, 1976; *The Quarter Running Horse,* University of Oklahoma Press, 1979.

WORK IN PROGRESS: Foundation Dams of the American Quarter Horse, publication expected by University of Oklahoma Press; *Foundation Mares of the American Quarter Horse,* publication expected by University of Oklahoma Press.

* * *

DENNIS, Robert C.   1920-

PERSONAL: Born November 17, 1920, in Courtright, Ontario, Canada; came to the United States in 1936, naturalized citizen, 1945; son of Earl (an engineer) and Clara (Huff)

Dennis; married Norma Blanche Wilson, 1954 (deceased). *Education:* Educated in Sarnia, Ontario, Canada. *Home and office:* 8082 Mulholland Dr., Hollywood, Calif. 90046. *Agent:* Molin-Bartok Personal Management, 7029 Trolley Way, Playa del Rey, Calif. 90291.

CAREER: Writer, 1941—. California State University, Northridge, Los Angeles, assistant professor, 1978-79, currently a lecturer. *Member:* Mystery Writers of America (founding member of Los Angeles chapter), Writers Guild of America (West), Authors League of America. *Awards, honors:* Nominated for television drama script award from Writers Guild of America (West), 1959, for "Mail Order Prophet."

WRITINGS—Mystery novels: *The Sweat of Fear,* Bobbs-Merrill, 1973; *Conversations With a Corpse,* Bobbs-Merrill, 1974.

Work represented in anthologies, including *Best Detective Stories.*

Films: "Crime Against Joe," United Artists, 1956; "The Man Is Armed," Republic, 1957; "Revolt at Fort Laramie," United Artists, 1957; "My World Dies Screaming," independently released, 1958, re-released as "Terror in the Haunted House," 1961; "A Date With Death," Favorite Films, 1960; "Danger Has Two Faces."

Author of more than forty plays for radio and more than five hundred plays for television. Creator of television series "Passport to Danger" and "Affairs of China Smith." Contributor of more than one hundred fifty stories to magazines.

WORK IN PROGRESS: Two motion picture screenplays, a contemporary thriller and a baseball comedy.

SIDELIGHTS: Author of more than five hundred plays for television, Dennis is distinguished by the fact that all of his plays have been sold. His is probably the only early writer for television who still works primarily in that medium. Dennis also invented the "teaser," the brief, exciting "hook" at the start of a television play designed to keep the audience tuned past the first commercial break.

Dennis told *CA:* "I began writing because I was under the delusion that I had some talent. My dreams of being a professional baseball pitcher died at the age of nineteen when I broke my ankle. I contracted acute arthritis as a result of continuing to work that day and the following days. In 1936 I got out of the hospital and my doctor told me I might become permanently crippled. I came to California that fall to stay alive.

"As a boy I used to get pulp magazines from my Uncle Art. He worked at the same salt plant in Ontario where my dad did. He sat up in a high room where he took care of the salt pans. He had lots of free time, and had a cupboard full of pulp magazines. I would go there every week and bring home a load. I read Westerns, adventure stories, detective dramas, and of course, novels by the hundreds. The nearest library was twelve miles away—a distance in those days—so I borrowed all the books I could. *Over the Top,* by Arthur Guy Empey, a man I met years later as a writer, and *Treasure Island* were my favorites. *Treasure Island,* in fact, is the most memorable from my childhood.

"I went to adult evening school in Los Angeles in the 1930's and took a test to find out what course I was best suited for and it turned out I was definitely slanted for something literary—creative writing, journalism, or advertising. The high school had all three courses, so I registered in all three. But the night I walked into creative writing I said 'this is it' and I never went back to the others. I never questioned my ability

for years because of that test. By the time I found out the tests weren't trustworthy, I was making so much money I couldn't quit."

"Television was a natural progression from radio. I had been a writer for ten years and as any idiot could see, television was going to be a great medium: movies in your own home; entertainment at the turn of a switch and before your very eyes. I was eleven or twelve when *Popular Mechanics* carried a story along with a sketch of a television set. It was the coming invention, the article explained, though not quite perfected. I thought, gee, what a great thing when it comes along. I always remembered that story. One day when television came along, I was ready for it.

"I've written so many scripts because television was and is a hungry market. It's not as big a market now—every show went a full season in the old days, and they made thirty-nine episodes. Now, nobody makes more than twenty-one or twenty-two. Half hour shows used to be twenty-six and a half minutes long, with three and a half minutes for billboards, commercials, and station identifications. Today, I doubt if they're more than twenty-two minutes long.

"I had hoped for some degree of excellence in television; I thought television could've been an art form like any other. But it didn't turn out that way. Today, artistry and creativity are the last considerations in television."

AVOCATIONAL INTERESTS: Travel (Hawaii and Europe), softball, spectator sports (football and baseball).

*   *   *

DENNISON, George (Harris) 1925-

PERSONAL: Born September 10, 1925, in Ashburn, Ga.; son of George Harris and Gladys Pearl (Bass) Dennison; married Mabel Halliwell Chrystie; children: Susan, Rebecca, Michael. *Education:* Attended Columbia University, 1944-45; New School for Social Research, B.A., 1952; graduate study at New York University. *Home address:* P.O. Box 538, Temple, Maine 04984. *Agent:* Georges Borchardt, Inc., 136 East 57th St., New York, N.Y. 10022.

CAREER: Writer. *Military service:* U.S. Navy, 1943-46. *Member:* International P.E.N.

WRITINGS: The Lives of Children, Random House, 1969; *And Then a Harvest Feast,* Random House, 1972; *Oilers and Sweepers,* Random House, 1979. Also author of four one-act plays. Work represented in anthologies, including *Collected Poems,* edited by Paul Goodman. Contributor of articles and reviews to literary magazines. Associate editor of *Arts* (magazine), 1954-56.

WORK IN PROGRESS: A novel about rural-urban relationships.

*   *   *

DEPP, Roberta J. 1947-

PERSONAL: Born January 13, 1947. *Education:* State University of New York College at Geneseo, B.S., 1969; graduate study at State University of New York College at Brockport, 1972-73; University of Denver, M.A., 1975. *Home address:* P.O. Box 626, Eagle, Colo. 81631. *Office:* Eagle County Public Library, P.O. Box 240, Eagle, Colo. 81631.

CAREER: Worked as school librarian for public schools in Rochester, N.Y.; currently director of Eagle County Public Library, Eagle, Colo. *Member:* American Library Association, Mountain Plains Library Association, Colorado Library Association.

WRITINGS: (Co-editor with Bohdan S. Wynar) *Colorado Bibliography,* Libraries Unlimited, 1979. Assistant editor of *American Reference Books Annual.*

* * *

DePREE, Gladis (Lenore) 1933-

PERSONAL: Born August 1, 1933, in Chicago, Ill.; daughter of John (a minister) and Marguerite (a social worker; maiden name, Kingma) Vogel; married Gordon DePree (an educator), August 26, 1955; children: Marita, Michael, Deidra, Christopher. *Education:* Attended Wheaton College, Wheaton, Ill. *Politics:* Independent. *Religion:* Christian. *Home:* 143 South Centennial St., Zeeland, Mich. 49464.

CAREER: Writer, 1953—. Clothing designer; public speaker. *Awards, honors:* Poetry prize from Radio Hong Kong and *South China Morning Post,* 1971, for "The Shared Shop."

WRITINGS: Line Tree: King's Valley (novel), Zondervan, 1957; *The Spring Wind,* Harper, 1970; *The Self-Anointed* (biography), Harper, 1978.

With husband, Gordon DePree: *A Blade of Grass* (poems), Zondervan, 1967; *Faces of God* (poems), Harper, 1974; *The Gift* (poems), Zondervan, 1976; *Soft Showers* (readings), Zondervan, 1980; *Catch a Red Leaf* (readings), Zondervan, 1980; *The Heat of the Sun* (readings), Zondervan, 1981; *Stars and Firelight* (readings), Zondervan, 1981.

Author of television script, "The Self-Anointed."

WORK IN PROGRESS: Summershell, an intercultural adventure of an American family living on a Chinese junk in a Hong Kong typhoon shelter for a summer, publication expected in 1982; *Festival,* a story of self-discovery about a year spent in a fishing village on the South China Sea, celebrating local festivals with the fishing community.

SIDELIGHTS: Gladis DePree commented: "My writing has grown out of a varied picture of life, ranging from growing up in the Southern mountains of the United States, to raising children of our own while moving around Southeast Asia and learning to speak Chinese. I feel at home everywhere, and a little like a stranger everywhere. I look for the deep underlying threads in all human existence, and do not feel totally contained by any one frame of reference. Although I have been writing for almost twenty years, I am only now beginning to feel that I *understand.* I believe my best work is still ahead."

AVOCATIONAL INTERESTS: East-West intercultural studies.

* * *

DePREE, Gordon 1930-

PERSONAL: Born September 26, 1930, in Zeeland, Mich.; son of Adrian (in business) and Edith (Kroeze) DePree; married Gladis Lenore Vogel (a writer), August 26, 1955; children: Marita, Michael, Deidra, Christopher. *Education:* Hope College, B.A.; Western Theological Seminary, M.Div., 1955; Columbia University, M.A., 1969, M.Ed., 1981. *Politics:* Independent. *Religion:* Christian. *Home:* 143 South Centennial St., Zeeland, Mich. 49464.

CAREER: Ordained minister of Reformed Church in America; worked in service, mission, army, educational, and intercultural projects; United Service Organizations, Hong Kong, director, 1959-62; college chaplain in Orange City, Iowa, c. 1963; youth worker in Hong Kong, 1964-67; high school principal in Hong Kong, 1967-72; Norman Vincent

Peale Foundation, Pawling, N.Y., director of ministries, 1972-76; Guideposts Associates, New York, N.Y., Asian representative in Hong Kong, 1976-79; returned to United States, 1979. *Military service:* U.S. Army, chaplain, 1955-57; became first lieutenant.

WRITINGS—All with wife, Gladis DePree: *A Blade of Grass* (poems), Zondervan, 1967; *Faces of God* (poems), Harper, 1974; *The Gift* (poems), Zondervan, 1976; *Soft Showers* (readings), Zondervan, 1980; *Catch a Red Leaf* (readings), Zondervan, 1980; *The Heat of the Sun* (readings), Zondervan, 1981; *Stars and Firelight* (readings), Zondervan, 1981.

SIDELIGHTS: DePree commented: "The writing of *Soft Showers,* like all our writing, has grown out of our own lives. We are drawn from one place to another, spurred on by ideas and concepts. We live them out, then find we want to write them down, not only as a record of the way we have come, but to remind ourselves of what life is all about. It is gratifying when other people find themselves reflected in our recorded search, but we do not write these books so much to change other people as to crystallize the challenges we faced, to take the puzzles in life and make a design of them."

* * *

DEUTSCH, Arnold R. 1919-

PERSONAL: Born October 9, 1919, in Budapest, Hungary; came to the United States in 1923, naturalized citizen, 1926; son of Louis G. (a cabinetmaker) and Sadie (a singer; maiden name, Kaufman) Deutsch; married Roslyn Mandel, December 26, 1959 (deceased). *Education:* Columbia University, B.A., 1940. *Home:* 35 Park Ave., New York, N.Y. 10016. *Office:* 49 East 53rd St., New York, N.Y. 10022.

CAREER: New York Sun, New York City, staff writer, 1934-36; *New York Journal,* New York City, staff writer, 1936-39; Deutsch, Shea, and Evans (communications firm), New York City, partner and chairman of one board, 1939—. Member of business council of City Centre State Theater. Human resources communications consultant. *Military service:* U.S. Navy, 1942-45. *Member:* American Association of Advertising Agencies (member of board of governors), Morality in Media (member of board of directors), Audubon Society, Friends of Mozart (member of board of directors).

WRITINGS: The Human Resources Revolution: Communicate or Litigate, McGraw, 1979; *Everything You Need to Know About Finding and Holding a Job,* Simon & Schuster, 1980. Author of syndicated column, "The Employment World." Contributor to business journals.

SIDELIGHTS: Deutsch wrote that his second book grew out of the observation "that there was an erosion of the work ethic—a leaning towards a hedonistic society." He was concerned about the factors which contribute to this relaxation, and stated that "the government, the educational system, the unions, and businesses themselves share the responsibility for this 'me first' society." *Avocational interests:* Track, football, music.

* * *

DIAZ-GUERRERO, Rogelio 1918-

PERSONAL: Born August 3, 1918, in Guadalajara, Mexico; son of Antonio (an accountant) and Eva (Guerrero) Diaz-Calderon; married Ethel V. Loving, November 1, 1946 (died June 6, 1966); married Rosario Ahumada Vasconcelos (an educator), May 10, 1969; children: (first marriage) Rolando, Cristina; (second marriage) Rosario. *Education:* University of Guadalajara, B.S., 1937; National University of Mexico, M.D., 1943; Iowa State University, M.A., 1944, Ph.D., 1947. *Home:* Apartado Postal 73-B, Cuernavaca, Morelos, Mexico. *Office:* Faculty of Psychology, National University of Mexico, Retorno Cerro Acasulco 18, Mexico City 21, Mexico.

CAREER: Iowa State Psychopathic Hospital, resident in clinical psychiatry, 1944-45; Iowa University Hospital, Iowa City, resident in clinical neurology, 1945-46; Mexico City College, Mexico City, Mexico, head of department of psychology, 1946-52; National University of Mexico, Mexico City, member of faculty, 1948-58; University of Miami, Coral Gables, Fla., senior resident at Psychiatric and Neurological Institute, 1954-55; National University of Mexico, professor, 1958-73, research professor of psychology, 1974—, academic head of department, 1969-73, director of behavioral research at Center for the Study of Behavioral Sciences, 1964—. Consultant to Hogg Foundation for Mental Health.

MEMBER: International Union of Psychological Science (vice-president, 1976—), International Society of General Semantics, Interamerican Society of Psychology (president, 1967-69), Mexican Society of Neurology and Psychiatry, Mexican Psychological Society (president, 1965—), Instituto Nacional de Ciencias del Comportamiento y de la Actitud Publica (president, 1973—), American Psychological Association, American Association for the Advancement of Science. *Awards, honors:* U.S. Office of Education grant, 1965-69; award from Interamerican Society of Psychology, 1976, for contributions to the science and profession of psychology in the Americas.

WRITINGS: (Contributor) M. Sherif and C. Sherif, editors, *Problems of Youth,* Aldine, 1965; (contributor) W. H. Holtzman, Jon D. Swartz, and Lara Tapia, editors, *Minnesota Symposia on Child Psychology,* University of Minnesota Press, 1968; *Psychology of the Mexican: Culture and Personality,* University of Texas Press, 1975; (with Holtzman and Swartz) *Personality Development in Two Cultures,* University of Texas Press, 1975.

Not in English: *Estudios de psicologia del Mexicano,* F. Trillas, 1970; *Hacia una teoria historico: Bio-psico-socio-cultural del comportamiento humano* (title means "Towards a Historic and Bio-socio-cultural Theory of Human Behavior"), F. Trillas, 1972; (with Raul Bianchi and Rosario Ahumada de Diaz) *La investigacion formativa de Plaza Sesamo* (title means "The Formative Research for Plaza Sesamo"), F. Trillas, 1974; (with Miguel Salas) *El diferencial semantico del idioma espanol* (title means "The Semantic Differential Scale, Its Development and Uses in the Spanish Language"), F. Trillas, 1975. Also author with Philip Emmite of *Innovaciones en la educacion: Un analisis de sistemas de las habilidades basicas en la educacion* (title means "A General Systems Analysis of Basic Abilities in Education"), 1980. Director of technical series in psychology, published by F. Trillas, 1967—. Contributor of more than a hundred articles and poems to journals in the behavioral sciences and literary magazines.

WORK IN PROGRESS: An introduction to psychology, "to make adolescents aware of the multi-level complexity of human life and of their potential to live it realistically and joyfully," publication by F. Trillas expected in 1981; books of poems; a study of mother-child interaction and its effects upon the personality and cognitive development of Mexican children of two social classes; a study of the moral support systems of Mexican families and their effects upon emotional, social, and personality development.

SIDELIGHTS: Diaz-Guerrero told *CA:* "I consider it vital for the human being finally to pass from his present stage of usually thinking of no more than one or two of the consequences of his behavior, to that of an enlightened human being aware of the many consequences of his behavior, both immediate and remote. This type of human being will not make decisions lightly but will enumerate to himself at least three or four consequences on the different levels of his life, such as economic, personal, interpersonal, and environmental. Such a person will be particularly sensitive to other human beings and their reactions to his behavior. This consideration will be reciprocal, for every other human being will also be considerate. This approach to life will have to start very early, and there must be well-trained parents and well-trained teachers to make the child aware of the many consequences of his behavior. Such a life will result in a much greater knowledge of the complexity of nature and human behavior. On the basis of this greater knowledge, the number of errors committed by people will decrease. This will lead to a much higher sense of accomplishment and to a better society. But such a society will not be a utopia, for it will be the result of a greater individual effort to utilize the vast potential the human brain has had from the very beginning. It will not be something given, but something earned through the efforts of everyone and all.

"I have many vocations besides that of research psychologist. Almost anything and everything that surrounds me interests me. I write poetry. Almost all of my poems are unpublished, but two were published recently and I do hope in the future to publish one or two books of my verse."

AVOCATIONAL INTERESTS: Playing tennis, swimming, ping pong, manual activities (particularly electronic kits), collecting stamps, watching sports on television (especially soccer).

*   *   *

di DONATO, Pietro   1911-

PERSONAL: Born April 3, 1911, in West Hoboken, N.J.; son of Geremio (a bricklayer) and Annunziata (Cinquina) di Donato; married Helen Dean, February 24, 1943; children: Peter, Richard. *Home:* 2 Ivy Lane, Setauket, Long Island, N.Y. 11733. *Agent:* Scott Meredith Literary Agency, 845 Third Ave., New York, N.Y. 10022.

CAREER: Bricklayer. Novelist, playwright, biographer, and author of short stories, 1937—. *Awards, honors:* Overseas Press Club Award, 1978, for Aldo Moro story in *Penthouse.*

WRITINGS: Christ in Concrete (autobiographical novel; Book-of-the-Month Club selection), Bobbs-Merrill, 1939, reprinted, 1975; *This Woman* (play), Ballantine, 1958; *Three Circles of Light* (autobiographical novel), Messner, 1960; *Immigrant Saint: The Life of Mother Cabrini* (biography), McGraw, 1960; *The Penitent* (biography), Hawthorn, 1962; *Naked Author* (short stories), Phaedra, 1970. Also author of plays "Christ in Concrete" and "Moro."

Work represented in anthologies, including *Best American Short Stories,* 1938, and *Best One-Act Plays,* 1941. Contributor of short stories to *Esquire* and *American Mercury.*

SIDELIGHTS: Pietro di Donato's autobiographical novel, *Christ in Concrete,* is the story of Italian laborers in America. Like the author, the twelve-year-old Paolino is the son of a bricklayer. After his father is killed by a collapsing building, Paolino takes on the responsibility of supporting his mother and seven younger brothers and sisters. A reviewer for *Books* noted that "there is abundant power [in *Christ in*

Concrete]. So, too, are there plenty of warmth, sympathy, pity, indignation, and the savors of full-blooded life.'' The critic added, however, that ''the turbulent rush of the staccato prose, so choppy, adjective-crammed, and muddled with mixed metaphor, points of suspension, and unscrupulous epithet, will be hard reading for many readers.''

K. M. Chworowsky of *Christian Century* commended the author for his ability to write ''about his people with the deep human understanding of a prophet, with the psychological insight of a learned soul-analyst, and with the literary skill of a seasoned professional at the ancient and honorable art of story-telling.'' L. B. Salomon also praised di Donato: ''His own terse style, made telegraphic by personification and frequent omission of the article, throbs with reality, with the feel of brick and mortar, the smells of labor, the tang of sour wine and olive oil and red peppers. Only a man whose muscles and stomach have felt the fatigue and the hunger of hard manual labor can paint [characters] with such blunt, convincing strokes.''

Although *Three Circles of Light*, di Donato's second novel, is a sequel to his first, it portrays the life of Paolino and his family up to the time of his father's death, chronicled in the first chapter of *Christ in Concrete*. Chad Walsh of the *New York Herald Tribune Book Review* noted that *Three Circles of Light* is ''certainly not a masterpiece of novel construction—but individual parts of it have power to move the reader and lead him into the lives of people who live with a passionate fulness of being.'' *Commonweal* reviewer Philip Deasy, however, was not as kind in his assessment: ''[The book is] a loose collection of episodes rather than a sustained narrative.... The novel's descent into sentimentality, bathos, and just plain scurrility is rapid.'' Deasy went on to deem the work ''a cliche-ridden, overdone piece of hokum.'' *Time* remarked that di Donato ''has written a piece of immigrant Americana that has no more narrative line than an *antipasto*,'' but added that it ''glints with passion and pathos, cruelty and laughter.'' And L. H. Gorn observed that ''di Donato's immigrants are fierce, tender, cruel, loving, petty, proud, generous, kind, bigoted, sensual—in a word, human.''

BIOGRAPHICAL/CRITICAL SOURCES: Time, April 10, 1939, June 6, 1960; *New York Times*, August 20, 1939; *Books*, August 20, 1939; *Nation*, August 26, 1939; *Saturday Review of Literature*, August 26, 1939, March 4, 1961; *New Republic*, August 30, 1939; *Atlantic Monthly*, September, 1939; *Christian Century*, October 4, 1939; *Manchester Guardian*, October 17, 1939; *New Statesman and Nation*, October 21, 1939; *Times Literary Supplement*, October 21, 1939; *Canadian Forum*, December, 1939; *New York Herald Tribune Book Review*, June 5, 1960; *San Francisco Chronicle*, August 7, 1960, May 20, 1962; *Commonweal*, August 19, 1960, February 10, 1961, July 13, 1962; *New York Times Book Review*, April 22, 1962.

*   *   *

DIEHL, William (Francis, Jr.) 1924-

PERSONAL: Born December 4, 1924, in Jamaica, N.Y.; son of William Francis and Catherine Marie Diehl; married Catherine Clifford (divorced, 1980); children: Cathy (Mrs. John Lovern), William Francis III, Stanford Arnold, Melissa, Temple. *Education:* University of Missouri, B.A., 1949. *Politics:* Democrat. *Home and office:* 1310 Old Johnson Ferry Rd. N.E., Atlanta, Ga. 30319. *Agent:* Owen Laster, William Morris Agency, 1350 Avenue of the Americas, New York, N.Y. 10019.

CAREER: Atlanta Constitution, Atlanta, Ga., reporter and author of column ''Around Atlanta,'' 1949-55; free-lance writer and photographer, 1955-60; *Atlanta*, Atlanta, staff writer and managing editor, 1960-66; *New Orleans*, New Orleans, La., consulting and senior editor, 1966-67; *Cincinnati*, Cincinnati, Ohio, consulting and senior editor, 1968-69; free-lance writer, 1969—. Free-lance photographer, 1958-75, with Black Star Agency. *Military service:* U.S. Army Air Forces, ball turret gunner, 1942-45; served in Europe; became master sergeant; received Distinguished Flying Cross, Purple Heart, Air Medal with three Oak Leaf Clusters, and two Presidential Citations. *Member:* Sigma Delta Chi. *Awards, honors:* Distinguished reporting award from Sigma Delta Chi, 1953; spot news award of the year from Associated Press, 1953; annual fiction award from Dixie Council of Writers, 1979, for *Sharky's Machine*.

WRITINGS: A City in Transition, U.S. Department of Housing & Urban Development, 1968; *Sharky's Machine* (novel), Delacorte, 1978; *Chameleon* (novel), Random House, 1981. Contributor of articles and photographs to magazines, including *Esquire, Life, Look*, and *New York*.

WORK IN PROGRESS: A screenplay.

SIDELIGHTS: Diehl's novel, *Sharky's Machine*, has been published in twelve countries, including Mexico, Italy, Turkey, Spain, Japan, Israel, and France.

Diehl wrote: ''During World War II, I worked briefly behind the lines with Yugoslavian guerillas after being shot down during a bombing raid over Munich, Germany, in spring, 1945. Part of the background for *Sharky's Machine* came from this experience.

''I have written magazine articles on a variety of subjects, including five days as an 'inmate' in the Atlanta Federal Penitentiary, a month with a bomber crew in the Strategic Air Command, flying in B-52's, and a month as a steeplejack working on what was then Atlanta's tallest building. Writing is my first love and I enjoy the eight to ten hours a day of solitude necessary to write.

''From 1960 to 1963 I worked closely with Martin Luther King and was, for a short period, his official photographer. I also acted on the local stage from 1958 through about 1963.

''My professional interests—the themes which will always underpin most of my writing—usually deal with the conflict between honor and integrity and corruption. I am, and always have been, an avid anti-establishmentarianist.

''I am avidly interested in psychism and the occult from a research standpoint, as well as Oriental philosophy, early Egyptian history (with a reading knowledge of hieroglyphics), and politics. I am particularly interested in subjects related to honor in both Eastern and Western cultures, and recently completed a course in mercenary and espionage training as research.''

AVOCATIONAL INTERESTS: Films, snow skiing, swimming, travel (especially in the Orient), raising African chameleons, reading.

*   *   *

di GUISA, Giano
See PRAZ, Mario

*   *   *

DINELEY, David Lawrence 1927-

PERSONAL: Born August 24, 1927, in Birmingham, England; son of Leonard Wilfrid and Nellie Dineley; married

Nancy Moore, July 23, 1953; children: Frances, Rachel. *Education:* University of Birmingham, B.Sc., 1948, Ph.D., 1951. *Home:* 12 Hyland Grove, Bristol BS9 3NR, England. *Agent:* Curtis Brown Academic Ltd., 1 Craven Hill, London W2 3EP, England. *Office:* Department of Geology, University of Bristol, Bristol BS8 1TR, England.

CAREER: University of Exeter, Exeter, England, lecturer in geology, 1950-59; University of Ottawa, Ottawa, Ontario, professor of geology, 1960-68; University of Bristol, Bristol, England, Chaning Wills Professor of Geology, 1968—, head of department. Consultant to Canadian petroleum companies. *Member:* Geological Society, Paleontological Society, Paleontological Association, Geologists' Association, Association of Teachers of Geology, Society of Vertebrate Paleontology, Institute of Geologists (corporate member), Conservation Society (local chairman, 1972-75).

WRITINGS: Earth's Voyage Through Time, Knopf, 1973; *Earth Resources: A Dictionary of Terms and Concepts,* Arrow Books, 1976; *Rocks,* Collins, 1977; *Fossils,* Collins, 1979. Television and radio writer for British Broadcasting Corp. (BBC) and Canadian Broadcasting Corp. (CBC). Contributor of about eighty articles to scientific journals.

WORK IN PROGRESS: A book on historical geology, for Macmillan; a book on paleontology, for Collins; research on science in present-day China and on environmental geology of the west of England.

SIDELIGHTS: Dineley wrote: "I am principally interested in research on earth history and early vertebrates, and in teaching, scientific journalism, and educational television. I led several expeditions to the Canadian arctic from 1962 to 1974. My regional interests are North America, Western Europe (especially Spain), and China, which I visited twice at the invitation of Academia Sinica."

AVOCATIONAL INTERESTS: Music, gardening, travel, Chinese art.

*   *   *

DINGES, John (Charles)   1941-
(Ramon Marsano)

PERSONAL: Born December 8, 1941, in Spencer, Iowa; son of C.A. (in small business) and Leta (an English teacher; maiden name, Thompson) Dinges; married Carolina Kenrick (a medical secretary), June 25, 1975; children: Thomas. *Education:* Loras College, B.A., 1964; attended University of Innsbruck, 1964-67; Stanford University, M.A., 1972. *Home:* 3435 Mount Pleasant St. N.W., Washington, D.C. 20010. *Office: Washington Post,* 1150 15th St. N.W., Washington, D.C. 20005.

CAREER: Loras College, Dubuque, Iowa, instructor in theology, 1967-69; *Des Moines Tribune,* Des Moines, Iowa, 1969-71, began as copy editor, became reporter; *Washington Post,* Washington, D.C., correspondent in Chile under pseudonym Ramon Marsano, 1976-78, foreign desk copy editor, 1978—. Co-founder and editor of ACTUALIDAD INTERNACIONAL, Santiago, Chile, 1976-78. *Awards, honors:* Grant from Inter-American Press Association, 1972-73.

WRITINGS: (Editor with Michael Mooney, Michael Scheible, and Joseph Koschler) *Toward a Theology of Christian Faith,* Kenedy, 1968; (translator) Alejandro Foxley, editor, *Income Distribution in Latin America,* Cambridge University Press, 1976; (with Saul Landau) *Assassination on Embassy Row,* Pantheon, 1980. Contributor to magazines, including *Nation* and *Inquiry.*

WORK IN PROGRESS: The Nicaraguan Revolution.

SIDELIGHTS: Dinges commented: "I write because I believe writing can change the world—perhaps that is a holdover from my theological training. My topics, therefore, are people, groups, or nations of people struggling to empower themselves to overcome the control imposed on their lives by aristocratic, propertied, or political elites. I tell the stories, often gruesome, of the men and women who are the instruments of those oppressive systems in so much of the underdeveloped Third World, and of those who fight against them, winning or becoming victims. That is the story of *Assassination on Embassy Row.* It is about a country, Chile, its dictator, the head of its secret police, and the man they killed, Orlando Letelier, because he took the fight against the dictatorship to the corridors of Washington politics and international organizations."

*   *   *

DODDS, E(ric) R(obertson)   1893-1979

PERSONAL: Born July 26, 1893, in Banbridge, Northern Ireland; died April 8, 1979; son of Robert (a headmaster) Dodds; married Annie Edwards Powell, 1923. *Education:* Attended Campbell College, Belfast; University College, Oxford, M.A., 1916. *Home:* Cromwell's House, Old Marston, Oxford, England.

CAREER: University College (now University of Reading), Reading, England, lecturer in classics, 1919-24; University of Birmingham, Birmingham, England, professor of Greek, 1924-36; Oxford University, Oxford, England, Regius Professor of Greek, 1936-60. Sather Visiting Professor at University of California, 1949-50. *Military service:* Served as paramedic in Serbia. *Member:* British Academy (fellow), Society for Psychical Research (president), Hellenic Society (president), Classical Association (president), American Academy of Arts and Sciences (corresponding member), l'Institut de France, Academia Sinica (corresponding member), Bavarian Academy (corresponding member). *Awards, honors:* Hon. D.Litt. from Victoria University of Manchester, University of Dublin, University of Edinburgh, University of Birmingham, and University of Belfast; honorary fellow of University College, Oxford; honorary student of Christ Church, Oxford; Kenyon medal, 1971, for *The Greeks and the Irrational;* Duff Cooper Memorial Prize, 1977, for *Missing Persons: An Autobiography.*

WRITINGS: (Translator from the Greek, editor, and author of introduction) *Select Passages Illustrating Neoplatonism,* Macmillan, Volume I, 1923, Volume II, 1924; *Thirty-two Poems, With a Note on Unprofessional Poetry,* Constable, 1929; (translator from the Greek, and author of introduction and commentary) Proclus, *Stoicheiosis Theologike: The Elements of Theology,* Clarendon Press, 1933, 2nd edition, 1963; (editor and author of memoir) *Journal and Letters of Stephen MacKenna,* Constable, 1936; (editor and author of introduction and commentary) Euripides, *Bacchae,* Clarendon Press, 1944, 2nd edition, 1960.

The Greeks and the Irrational, University of California Press, 1951; (editor) Plato, *Gorgias,* Clarendon Press, 1959; (with others) *Les Sources de Plotin,* Fondation Hardt (Geneva), 1960; *Pagan and Christian in an Age of Anxiety: Some Aspects of Religious Experience From Marcus Aurelius to Constantine,* Cambridge University Press, 1965, Norton, 1970; (editor) Louis MacNeice, *The Strings Are False: An Unfinished Autobiography,* Faber, 1965, Oxford University Press, 1966; (editor) Louis MacNeice, *Collected Poems,* Faber, 1966, Oxford University Press, 1967; *Gilbert Murray's Last Experiments,* Society for Psychical Research,

1972; *The Ancient Concept of Progress and Other Essays on Greek Literature and Belief,* Clarendon Press, 1973; *Missing Persons: An Autobiography,* Clarendon Press, 1977.

SIDELIGHTS: E. R. Dodds had a lifelong interest in the Greek classics, in literature, and in psychic research. Born in Ulster, the young Dodds originally harbored an ambition to be a poet. While still an undergraduate, he became part of a Dublin literary circle that included A. E., James Stephens, and Stephen MacKenna. He was also acquainted with W. B. Yeats. Dodds's friendship with MacKenna was especially influential, for the two men had a common interest in the Roman Neoplatonic philosopher, Plotinus. Later Dodds assisted MacKenna with the translation of Plotinus' *Enneads,* and he himself edited MacKenna's journals and letters.

While Dodds was a student, he developed an interest in psychoanalysis and psychic research. For a time he even considered becoming a psychoanalyst. Dodds practiced telepathy and hypnotism and experimented with such things as Ouija boards and crystal balls. His fascination with the occult was related to his interest in the workings of the imagination and the unconscious mind, and was to serve him well when he later wrote about Greek culture and civilization.

Despite his ties with the Irish literary establishment, Dodds pursued his academic career in England. After serving as a professor of Greek at the University of Birmingham for several years, in 1936 he was named to the prestigious post of Regius Professor of Greek at Oxford University. His work as a Greek scholar earned him an international reputation. One of his books, *The Greeks and the Irrational,* is now acknowledged as a classic. His other scholarly works have also elicited praise. In a review of *Pagan and Christian in an Age of Anxiety,* a critic for the *Times Literary Supplement* summed up Dodds's outstanding characteristics: "A rather rare union of detachment and sympathy, a combination of precise scholarship and a degree of acquaintance with contemporary psychological theories unusual in a classical scholar, and last but not least, an ability to write very well."

While Dodds was in England he continued to move in literary circles. He came to know many of the outstanding literary figures of the day. After the death of his intimate friend, Louis MacNeice, Dodds edited the poet's unfinished autobiography and his collected poems. Another of his close friends was W. H. Auden, who once described the classicist as "that rare creature, a very learned scholar who wishes to share his thoughts not with his fellow scholars only but also with intelligent readers who are not specialists in his field."

In 1977 Dodds's autobiography, *Missing Persons,* was published. After reading the book, F.S.L. Lyons depicted the figure that emerged: "Dodds appears as a man of great toughness and vitality, whose first act, on arriving in any new place, is to climb the nearest mountain. He is also, it is evident, a man of vigorous and combative intelligence, with a wide range of interests and an insatiable desire for conversation, the sharper the better. He has no obvious bump of reverence, either for institutions or for persons, and has generally taken an anti-establishment stance." Other reviewers also commended *Missing Persons.* A critic for *New Yorker* felt that the strength of this "stirring memoir" lies in the author's "ability to communicate the feeling of a real life being lived." Terming the book a "very well written, carefully composed, and entertaining autobiography," Stuart Hampshire noted that Dodds's "dry style, and his habit of detachment, enable him to look at his past, or at the more interesting bits of it, without either egotism or self-concealment."

BIOGRAPHICAL/CRITICAL SOURCES: Yale Review,

spring, 1952; *New Statesman and Nation,* April 19, 1952; *Times Literary Supplement,* September 5, 1952, October 28, 1965, June 15, 1973, November 11, 1977; *New York Review of Books,* February 17, 1966, June 28, 1973, April 6, 1978; *Spectator,* September 8, 1973; E. R. Dodds, *Missing Persons: An Autobiography,* Clarendon Press, 1977; *New Yorker,* March 13, 1978.

[Sketch verified by executor, N. G. Heatley]

*   *   *

DOUGLAS, Helen Gahagan   1900-1980
(Helen Gahagan)

OBITUARY NOTICE: Born November 25, 1900, in Boonton, N.J.; died of cancer, June 28, 1980, in New York, N.Y. Politician, actress, and author. Douglas served three terms in the House of Representatives before running for senator in 1950. During the campaign, opponent Richard Nixon implied that the liberal Douglas held Communist convictions; she subsequently lost the election. Prior to her political career, Douglas appeared in numerous Broadway productions as Helen Gahagan. In 1931 she married actor Melvyn Douglas. She wrote *The Eleanor Roosevelt We Remember.* Obituaries and other sources: *Who's Who in American Politics,* 5th edition, Bowker, 1975; *Who's Who in American Women,* 9th edition, Marquis, 1975; *New York Times,* June 29, 1980; *Newsweek,* July 7, 1980; *Time,* July 7, 1980.

*   *   *

DOUGLAS-HOME, Henry   1907-1980

OBITUARY NOTICE: Born November 21, 1907; died July 19, 1980. Ornithologist and author of works in his field. Douglas-Home broadcast bird sounds for the British Broadcasting Corp. during World War II and was a favorite of British soldiers. He also determined that the swift, a little-researched bird that flies constantly, actually logs more than three million miles in its lifetime. Douglas-Home wrote an autobiography, *The Birdman.* Obituaries and other sources: *London Times,* July 21, 1980.

*   *   *

DOWLEY, Timothy Edward   1946-

PERSONAL: Born June 12, 1946, in London, England; son of Roger and Florence Lydia Dowley. *Education:* Victoria University of Manchester, B.A. (with honors), 1969, Ph.D., 1976. *Home:* 101 Gloucester Ave., Primrose Hill, London N.W.1, England. *Office:* 12 Flitcroft St., London W.C.2, England.

CAREER: Partner of Three's Company; editor with Lion Publishing; project editor with Chris Micsome, Ltd.; scripture distribution consultant for British and Foreign Bible Society. *Member:* Society of Authors.

WRITINGS: The Eerdmans Handbook to the History of Christianity, Eerdmans, 1977; (editor) *The Book of the Cinema,* Crown, 1979; *The Life and Times of J. S. Bach,* Midas Books, 1980; *The Story of Christianity,* Lion Publishing, 1981; *East End: Illustrated History of East London,* Faber, in press.

WORK IN PROGRESS: Taking Off: A Parody Anthology.

AVOCATIONAL INTERESTS: Music, theatre, painting, travel, cinema.

DOWNES, Mollie Patricia Panter
   See PANTER-DOWNES, Mollie Patricia

*   *   *

DOWNEY, James   1939-

PERSONAL: Born April 20, 1939, in Winterton, Newfoundland, Canada; son of Ernest Fletcher and Mimy Ann (Andrews) Downey; married Laura Ann Parsons, July 25, 1964; children: Sarah Elizabeth, Geoffrey James. *Education:* Memorial University of Newfoundland, B.A., 1962, M.Ed., 1963, M.A., 1964; University of London, Ph.D., 1966. *Religion:* United Church. *Home:* 58 Waterloo Row, Fredericton, New Brunswick, Canada E3B 5A3. *Office:* University of New Brunswick, P.O. Box 4400, Fredericton, New Brunswick, Canada E3B 5A3.

CAREER: Carleton University, Ottawa, Ontario, assistant professor, 1966-69, associate professor, 1969-75, professor of English, 1975—, chairman of department, 1972-75, dean of faculty of arts, 1976-78, academic vice-president, 1978-80, president *pro tempore*, 1979; University of New Brunswick, Fredericton, president, 1980—. *Member:* Association of Canadian University Teachers of English (executive), Association of Chairmen of English (Ontario; president).

WRITINGS: Eighteenth-Century Pulpit: A Study of the Sermons of Butler, Berkeley, Secker, Sterne, Whitefield, and Wesley, Oxford University Press, 1979; (editor with Ben Jones) *Fearful Joy: Papers From the Thomas Gray Bicentenary Conference at Carleton University,* McGill-Queen's University Press, 1974. Contributor of articles and reviews to scholarly journals.

WORK IN PROGRESS: Editing *The Sermons of Laurence Sterne,* two volumes, for University of Florida Press.

SIDELIGHTS: Downey told *CA:* "To be born in outport Newfoundland before 1950 was in many respects like being born in eighteenth-century rural England or Ireland. The sociology, the technology, the folklore, the idiom of language and life were all closer to the West Country of Thomas Hardy than to twentieth-century Canada or America. In such a society, religion was not just another aspect of life; it was the essential ingredient of culture: the impetus and principle of social organization. Sunday hymns and sermons subsumed many of the functions and outlets now provided by more specialized agencies—by newscasts, paperbacks, schools of continuing education, and rock concerts, to name only a few.

"Having, as a student minister, tried my hand at preaching, I was anxious to make a serious study of eighteenth-century English preachers. *The Eighteenth-Century Pulpit* is that study. More recently I have been at work on a scholarly edition of Laurence Sterne's *Sermons of Mr. Yorick.* Of all eighteenth-century preachers Sterne is the most eccentrically engaging and it is my hope that a new edition of his sermons will stimulate an interest in the homiletic tradition to which he belongs."

AVOCATIONAL INTERESTS: Tennis, theatre.

*   *   *

DUBLIN, Thomas Louis   1946-

PERSONAL: Born December 1, 1946, in Norwalk, Conn.; son of Amos and Louise (Goldschmidt) Dublin; married Dorcas S. Houston (a social worker), June 22, 1968; children: Sasha, Sonya. *Education:* Harvard University, A.B., 1968; Columbia University, M.A., 1971, Ph.D., 1975. *Home:* 13434 Calais Dr., Del Mar, Calif. 92014. *Office:* Department

of History, C-004, University of California, San Diego, La Jolla, Calif. 92093.

CAREER: Wellesley College, Wellesley, Mass., assistant professor of history, 1975-76; University of California, San Diego, La Jolla, assistant professor of American history, 1976—. *Member:* American Historical Association, Organization of American Historians, Study Group on Labor Working Class History. *Awards, honors:* American Council of Learned Societies grant, 1977; Merle Curti Award from Organization of American Historians and Bancroft Prize from Columbia University, both 1980, both for *Women at Work*; National Endowment for the Humanities grant, 1980-81.

WRITINGS: (Contributor) Milton Cantor and Bruce Laurie, editors, *Class Sex and the Woman Worker,* Greenwood Press, 1977; *Women at Work,* Columbia University Press, 1980; (editor) *Farm and Factory,* Columbia University Press, 1981. Contributor to history and women's studies journals.

WORK IN PROGRESS: A study of economic and social links joining the city and the countryside in New England in the nineteenth century.

SIDELIGHTS: Dublin wrote that *Farm and Factory* is a collection of letters written or received by women who were working in New England textile mills between 1830 and 1860.

*   *   *

DUFFUS, R(obert) L(uther)   1888-1972

PERSONAL: Born July 10, 1888, in Waterbury, Vt.; died of congestive heart failure, November 28, 1972, in Palo Alto, Calif.; son of John McGlashan (a stonecutter) and Helen (Graves) Duffus; married Leah-Louise Deane, February, 1914; children: Mrs. Nairne Louise Wilcox, Mrs. Marjorie Rose Mackay. *Education:* Stanford University, B.A., 1910, M.A., 1911. *Residence:* Palo Alto, Calif.

CAREER: San Francisco Bulletin, San Francisco, Calif., reporter, 1911-13, editorial writer, 1913-18; *San Francisco Call,* San Francisco, editorial writer, 1918-19; *New York Globe,* New York City, journalist, 1919-23; free-lance writer and reporter, 1923-30; *New York Times,* New York City, feature writer and book reviewer on Sunday staff, 1930-37, member of editorial board, 1937-62. *Member:* P.E.N., Phi Beta Kappa, Century Club. *Awards, honors:* LL.B. from Middlebury College, 1938; made Chevalier of the Legion of Honor, 1957.

WRITINGS: Roads Going South (novel), Macmillan, 1921; *The Coast of Eden* (novel), Macmillan, 1923; *The American Renaissance* (nonfiction), Knopf, 1928, reprinted, AMS Press, 1970; *Tomorrow Never Comes* (novel), Houghton, 1929; *The Santa Fe Trail* (history), Longmans, Green, 1930, reprinted, McKay, 1975; *Mastering a Metropolis: Planning the Future of the New York Region* (nonfiction), Harper, 1930; *Books: Their Place in a Democracy* (nonfiction), Houghton, 1930; *Our Starving Libraries: Studies in Ten American Communities During the Depression Years,* Houghton, 1933; (with Frederick P. Keppel) *The Arts in American Life* (nonfiction), McGraw, 1933; *Jornada* (novel), Covici, Friede, 1935; *Democracy Enters College: A Study of the Rise and Decline of the Academic Lockstep* (nonfiction), Scribner, 1936; *The Sky But Not the Heart* (novel), Macmillan, 1936; *Night Between the Rivers,* Macmillan, 1937; *Lillian Wald, Neighbor and Crusader* (biography), Macmillan, 1938.

(With L. Emmett Holt, Jr.) *L. Emmett Holt, Pioneer of a Children's Century* (biography), Appleton-Century, 1940, reprinted, Arno, 1974; *That Was Alderbury* (novel), Macmillan, 1941; *Victory on West Hill* (novel), Macmillan, 1942; *The Valley and Its People: A Portrait of TVA* (nonfiction), Knopf, 1944; *The Innocents at Cedro: A Memoir of Thorstein Veblen and Some Others* (autobiographical), Macmillan, 1944, reprinted, Augustus Kelley, 1972; *Non-Scheduled Flight* (novel), Macmillan, 1950.

All published by Norton: *Williamstown Branch: Impersonal Memories of a Vermont Boyhood*, 1958; *The Waterbury Record: More Vermont Memories*, 1959; *The Tower of Jewels: Memories of San Francisco*, 1960; *Nostalgia, U.S.A.; or, If You Don't Like the 1960's, Why Don't You Go Back Where You Came From?*, 1963; *Adventure in Retirement* (travel), 1964; *Queen Calafia's Island* (history), 1965; *Jimmy's Place: A California Story*, 1966; *Tomorrow's News: A Primer for Prophets*, 1967; *The Cats Pajamas and Related Episodes*, 1967; *West of the Date Line: A Further Adventure in Retirement* (travel), 1968; *The Polar Route to Time Gone By* (travel), 1969; *Jason Goose* (novel), 1969; *Jason Potter's Space Walk* (novel), 1970.

SIDELIGHTS: Duffus worked for thirty-two years with the *New York Times* and when he retired the paper honored him in a special edition. Page one of the *New York Times* limited edition on October 2, 1962, contained only stories by Duffus, written throughout his years of service. His work included Sunday magazine articles, news stories, editorials in verse and prose, book reviews, and travel stories.

A dedicated journalist, Duffus's vacations often turned into on-the-spot reporting when a story broke. Once, while on holiday in Corsica in 1958, a military dictatorship took over the island. Duffus obtained a firsthand account of the affair, supplying the *Times* with information many countries suppressed.

Duffus was also a prolific writer of books. His first volume, *Roads Going South*, a fictionalized account of his own boyhood in Vermont, received favorable reviews. A *New York Times* critic raved: "Severely true in its realism, the story yet holds to the higher levels of the spirit, and it is written with such surety of touch and such insight into the heart of man as to indicate that its author ... possesses gifts that make it worth while to watch for his future performances." Marion Ponsonby of the *Literary Review of the New York Evening Post*, similarly complementary, asserted that "the quiet and capable writing is punctuated interestingly by lyrical paragraphs, which have the effect of a Greek chorus chanting the processional of the Seasons of Time, behind a Vermont village."

Coast of Eden, Duffus's following volume, also met with an enthusiastic reception. Ponsonby claimed that "there isn't one bit of claptrap between the covers of this book," while a *Boston Transcript* critic explained that "the attraction of Mr. Duffus's work lies in his choice of material. His problems are not of today alone, but the universal problems.... He mirrors an unrest which is intensely human. It is the human quality which makes his work so satisfying."

Duffus's next effort, *American Renaissance*, hopefully explores the early signs of an artistic revival in American museums, art schools, universities, and theatres. T. Craven of *Bookman* scoffed that the book "as a true indication of the state of the arts in America today is superficial, misleading and untrustworthy at best." A *New York Times* reviewer more optimistically noted that Duffus "has the gift of dramatizing his subject and his style is always clear and well knit."

A later nonfiction volume, *Books: Their Place in a Democracy*, was highly praised by critics. An "admirable volume," applauded Leon Whipple. "The most complete and organic picture of how books get to people we have ever had." Henry Hazlitt concurred: "Duffus's book is informative, it is attractively written and well put together, and within its chosen field rather thorough."

Duffus's book, *Lillian Wald, Neighbor and Crusader*, met with similar success. "An excellent biography" hailed R. C. Feld of the *New York Times*. "Duffus is to be congratulated upon a triumphant achievement," *Atlantic*'s Florence Converse agreed. "Daring, from an enthusiasm that never falters, to write of Lillian Wald with unshadowed admiration, he yet carries the reader along with him ... in a mounting conviction of the truth and soundness of this sympathetic interpretation of a great American woman."

In his first autobiographical work, *Innocents at Cedro*, Duffus relates his experiences during a year at Stanford University while living with social scientist Thorstein Veblen. The book received a warm welcome. "It is a completely charming book, humorous, thoughtful and wise, in many ways a spiritual partner of the delightful, rambling books of the great Hans Zinsser," commented a *Springfield Republican* reviewer. A *Weekly Book Review* critic concurred in glowing terms: "Like Faust, Mr. Duffus seems to have said to the moment, 'Stay, for thou art so beautiful,' and for him it stayed, and here it is between the covers of this book, a fragment of autobiography and a miniature masterpiece in the literature of memory."

In his later years Duffus continued to write memoirs and autobiographies in addition to his other projects. He explained in the foreword of *Innocents at Cedro:* "I long ago resolved that I would never write anything in the autobiographical line if I could help it. I haven't been able to help it." Hence, *Innocents at Cedro* was followed by *Williamstown Branch*, *The Waterbury Record*, and *The Tower of Jewels*. All typically received favorable reviews. Stewart Holbrook of the *New York Herald Tribune Book Review* labelled *Williamstown Branch* "a delightful book of memories ... refreshing not only for its gentle, quiet prose, but also because Mr. Duffus is not of the total-recall school." Regarding *The Waterbury Record*, Holbrook observed that "in this gentle, unhurried book the past is recaptured and illuminated with insights not often come upon in the memoirs of a village boy." Margaret Parton similarly judged *The Tower of Jewels*, about Duffus's years on the *San Francisco Bulletin*, as "a gentle delight which will arouse almost unbearable nostalgic echoes in the heart of anyone who has ever worked on a beloved paper, or read a newspaper with loyalty and affection."

BIOGRAPHICAL/CRITICAL SOURCES: New York World, February 18, 1923, July 21, 1930; *Boston Transcript*, March 7, 1923, August 18, 1928, August 16, 1930, August 15, 1936; *New York Times*, November 20, 1921, March 11, 1923, September 9, 1928, April 21, 1929, August 3, 1930, January 21, 1934, March 3, 1935, August 16, 1936, July 4, 1937, October 16, 1938, July 19, 1942, November 19, 1944, January 22, 1950, August 31, 1958; *Literary Review of the New York Evening Post*, November 5, 1921, April 7, 1923; *Nation*, October 17, 1928, September 3, 1930, November 26, 1938; *New Republic*, November 28, 1928, December 25, 1944; *Bookman*, November, 1928; *Saturday Review of Literature*, March 16, 1929, August 16, 1930; *New York Herald Tribune*, April 21, 1929, July 20, 1930, April 8, 1934, February 24, 1935, August 16, 1936, July 4, 1937, October 16, 1938; *New Statesman*, August 24, 1929.

Springfield Republican, July 12, 1930, January 17, 1934, July 4, 1937, November 4, 1938, February 6, 1944, November 26, 1944; *Survey,* September 1, 1930; *Review of Reviews and World's Work,* October, 1930; *Times Literary Supplement,* October 30, 1937; *Atlantic,* December, 1938; *American Journal of Public Health and the Nation's Health,* March, 1941; *Christian Science Monitor,* August 22, 1942, January 10, 1963, November 20, 1965; R. L. Duffus, *The Innocents at Cedro: A Memoir of Thorstein Veblen and Some Others,* Macmillan, 1944; *Weekly Book Review,* February 13, 1944; *San Francisco Chronicle,* January 18, 1950; *New York Herald Tribune Book Review,* January 22, 1950, August 31, 1958, September 27, 1959; *Saturday Review,* September 13, 1958, March 2, 1963, May 20, 1967; *New York Herald Tribune Lively Arts,* January 15, 1961; *New York Times Book Review,* January 15, 1961, November 21, 1965.

OBITUARIES: New York Times, November 30, 1972.*

—Sketch by Anne M. Guerrini

*   *   *

DUMERY, Henry 1920-

PERSONAL: Born February 29, 1920, in Aubusson, France. *Education:* Sorbonne, University of Paris, Docteur es lettres, 1957; University of Paris, Docteur de l'Universite, 1968. *Home:* 173 boulevard Saint Germain, Paris 6e, France.

CAREER: Worked as professor at University of Caen, Caen, France, and University of Rouen, Rouen, France; currently professor at University of Paris, Paris, France. *Military service:* Cadre des Commissaires de l'Air; became reserve officer. *Member:* Institut International de Philosophie (secretary), Federation International des Societes de Philosophie (member of board), Societe Francaise de Philosophie. *Awards, honors:* Prix Victor-Delbos, 1950.

WRITINGS: La Philosophie de l'action: Essai sur l'intellectualisme blondelien, Aubier, 1948; *Foi et interrogation,* Editions Tequi, 1953; *Blondel et la religion: Essai critique sur la "lettre" de 1896,* Presses Universitaires de France, 1954; *Regards sur la philosophie contemporaine,* Casterman, 1956; *La Tentation de faire du bien,* Editions du Seuil, 1957; *Le Probleme de Dieu en philosophie de la religion: Examen critique de la categorie d'absolu et du scheme de transcendance,* Desclee de Brouwer, 1957, translation by Charles Courtney published as *The Problem of God in Philosophy of Religion: A Critical Examination of the Category of the Absolute and the Scheme of Transcendence,* Northwestern University Press, 1964; *Critique et religion: Problemes de methode en philosophie de la religion,* Societe d'Edition d'Enseignement Superieur, 1957.

Philosophie de la religion: Essai sur la signification du Christianisme, Presses Universitaires de France, 1957; *Phenomenologie et religion: Structures de l'institution chretienne,* Presses Universitaires de France, 1958, translation by Paul Barrett published as *Phenomenology and Religion: Structures of the Christian Institution,* University of California Press, 1975; *La Foi n'est pas un cri: Suivi de foi de institution,* Editions du Seuil, 1959; *Raison et religion dans la philosophie de l'action,* Editions du Seuil, 1963; *Faith and Reflection,* edited by Louis Dupre, translated by Stephen McNierney and M. Benedict Murphy, Herder, 1968.

WORK IN PROGRESS: Continuing research on the philosophy of religion and the sociology of the conscience.

SIDELIGHTS: Henry Dumery, although considered one of France's leading religious philosophers, is not widely known in English-speaking countries. Only three of his many volumes on Christian philosophy have been translated into English. The ones that have appeared in translation, however, have sparked positive reactions. W. H. Capps of the *Journal of Religion* was impressed with Dumery's thoughts as they were expressed in *The Problem of God in Philosophy of Religion.* "There is no question but that our author has utilized a vast range of new materials in approaching perennial problems in strikingly creative ways," he explained. Capps qualified his statement, however, claiming that "materials of extreme suggestiveness and erudition will perhaps pass unrecognized because of the overcomplicated context in which they occur."

Faith and Reflection, which appeared in 1968, contains selections of Dumery's previously published works. The volume met with W. Richard Comstock's approval. He asserted in *Christian Century* that Dumery's work is indeed important, for "apart from its intrinsic merit as the product of a keen analytic mind, it has special relevance to the current theological concern with the phenomenon of the modern secular consciousness." He added that "many of Dumery's positions are open to doubt. . . . However, the technical skill with which [he] . . . advances his arguments . . . render[s] his work worthy of careful study and deliberation."

BIOGRAPHICAL/CRITICAL SOURCES: Henk van Luijk, *Philosophie du fait chretien: L'Analyse critique du christianisme de Henry Dumery,* Desclee de Brouwer, 1966; *Journal of Religion,* April, 1966; *America,* August 30, 1969; *Christian Century,* July 29, 1970.

*   *   *

DUNLOP, Derrick Melville 1902-1980

OBITUARY NOTICE: Born April 3, 1902; died June 19, 1980. Surgeon, pharmacologist, pathologist, educator, and co-author of *Clinical Chemistry in Practical Medicine* and *Textbook of Medical Treatment.* Dunlop was best known for his efforts to ensure drug quality and safety as chairman of the Safety of Drugs Committee in England. He encouraged cooperation between the medical and pharmaceutical professions to see that drugs were marketed in the safest possible manner. Dunlop taught at the University of Edinburgh from 1936 to 1962. Obituaries and other sources: *London Times,* June 20, 1980.

*   *   *

DUNN, Walter Scott, Jr. 1928-

PERSONAL: Born April 5, 1928, in Detroit, Mich.; son of Walter Scott (an automobile worker) and Minnie M. Dunn; married Jean Wendeberg, July 11, 1959. *Education:* University of Durham, B.A., 1951; Wayne State University, M.A., 1952; University of Wisconsin—Madison, Ph.D., 1971. *Home:* 510 Northeast Eighth, Ankeny, Iowa 50021. *Office:* Des Moines Center of Science and Industry, 4500 Grand, Des Moines, Iowa 50312.

CAREER: Detroit Historical Museum, Detroit, Mich., curator, 1953-56; State Historical Society of Wisconsin, Madison, chief curator, 1956-63; Buffalo and Erie County Historical Society, Buffalo, N.Y., director, 1963-79; Des Moines Center of Science and Industry, Des Moines, Iowa, director, 1979—. President of African Cultural Center, Buffalo, 1964-66; member of Erie County Historical Federation and Puerto Rican Cultural Center. *Military service:* U.S. Army, 1946-47. *Member:* American Association of Museums, Association of Military Historians, Civil War Roundtable, Midwest Museum Conference.

WRITINGS: (Editor) *History of Erie County,* Buffalo and Erie County Historical Society, 1971; *Second Front Now: 1943,* University of Alabama Press, 1980. Contributing editor of *Niagara Frontier,* 1963-78, and *Museologist,* 1975-78.

WORK IN PROGRESS: Administration of Small Historical Agencies; Economics and the Military on the First Frontier, 1760-1783; research on the role of German air defenses in World War II.

SIDELIGHTS: Dunn wrote: "Despite the fact that military expenditures take as much as fifty percent of our national budget in peacetime, and during frequent wars take our entire national effort, the study of recent military history has been left mostly to the military and to participants who seldom have a broad view. My work has been directed at relating the economic and administrative elements to military events. My experience in historical agencies and my concern for adequate evidence results in my work being generally heavily documented. Future revisionists will probably find my work more interesting than will the general reader."

* * *

DURSLAG, Melvin 1921-

PERSONAL: Born April 29, 1921, in Chicago, Ill.; son of William and Frieda (Berliner) Durslag; married Lorayne Jane Sweet, November 21, 1948; children: Ivy, William, James. *Education:* University of Southern California, B.A., 1943. *Home:* 523 Dalehurst Ave., Los Angeles, Calif. 90024. *Office:* 1111 South Broadway, Los Angeles, Calif. 90054.

CAREER/WRITINGS: Los Angeles Examiner, Los Angeles, Calif., reporter and feature writer, 1938-43, reporter, 1946-53; free-lance writer, 1950—; *Los Angeles Examiner* and *Herald Examiner,* columnist, 1953—; syndicated columnist with King Features Syndicate and Hearst News Service, 1956—; contributing editor to *TV Guide,* 1960—. Contributor to periodicals, including *Collier's, Saturday Evening Post, Sports Illustrated, Esquire, Look, Playboy, Sport,* and *Sporting News.* Member of Journalism Board of Directors, University of Southern California; member of board of directors of Los Angeles Press Club Welfare Foundation. *Military service:* U.S. Army Air Forces, 1943-46; received Bronze Star with five oak-leaf clusters. *Member:* Sigma Delta Chi, Kappa Tau Alpha. *Awards, honors:* National Headliner Award, 1960.

* * *

DUVOISIN, Roger Antoine 1904-1980

OBITUARY NOTICE—See index for *CA* sketch: Born August 28, 1904, in Geneva, Switzerland; died of a heart attack, June 30, 1980, in Morristown, N.J. Author and illustrator of children's books. Duvoisin was best known for his illustrations in "The Happy Lion" series, written by his wife,

Louise Fatio. He created such popular animal personalities as Petunia the goose, Hector-Penguin, and Donkey-Donkey. Duvoisin illustrated more than one hundred forty children's books. Of these, he was the author of more than forty, including *Petunia, The Crocodile in the Tree,* and *Chanticleer, the Real Story of the Famous Rooster.* Obituaries and other sources: *Publishers Weekly,* July 25, 1980.

* * *

DYER, Elinor Mary Brent
See BRENT-DYER, Elinor Mary

* * *

DYER, T(homas) A(llan) 1947-

PERSONAL: Born August 19, 1947, in Newberg, Ore.; son of Frederick Calvin (in public administration) and Eldoris (Morter) Dyer; married Elizabeth Ann Easley (a teacher), December 22, 1968. *Education:* Portland State University, B.A. (English), 1970, M.A. (English), 1972; Eastern Oregon State College, B.A. (education), 1975; University of Arizona, M.A. (linguistics), 1978. *Residence:* Klamath Falls, Ore. *Agent:* Frances Golden, 305 East 11th St., New York, N.Y. 10003.

CAREER: Head teacher at school on Warm Springs Indian Reservation, Ore., 1975-77; Klamath County Schools, Klamath Falls, Ore., teacher of third grade, 1978—. *Member:* National Education Association, Authors Guild, Phi Delta Kappa. *Awards, honors:* Children's book award from Child Study Association, 1979, for *The Whipman Is Watching.*

WRITINGS: The Whipman Is Watching (juvenile), Houghton, 1979; *A Way of His Own* (juvenile), Houghton, 1981.

WORK IN PROGRESS: Summit Tournament, an adventure story for young adults, publication expected in 1981; two novels, *Never to the Moon,* publication expected in 1982, and *The Ordination.*

SIDELIGHTS: Dyer told *CA:* "I am a writer of juvenile fiction because I enjoy teaching by parable. And, as I assume is true of many others, I write because it helps me to formalize or give direction to some personal interest or enthusiasm. *The Whipman Is Watching* was written while I lived and taught on an Indian reservation, and it helped me come to terms with some rather explosive emotions in a therapeutic way. *A Way of His Own* followed a remark made in passing by a third grade student that cavemen were stupid. I happened to be studying Clovis Man at the time, and the coincidence was fortuitous. *Summit Tournament* was generated out of twelve years of mountaineering. Climbing is more than a mere sport. It is a way of life, and this book looks at a character coming to understand an enlarging inability and unwillingness to climb competitively. But the story is a true parable in the sense that the larger issues are self-realization and identity dilemmas symptomatic of life in contemporary America."

E

EBERLE, Paul 1928-

PERSONAL: Born August 21, 1928, in New York, N.Y.; son of Chester T. (an author) and Irmengarde (an author; maiden name, Eberle) Crowell; married Shirley M. Johnson (an editor), December 4, 1950. *Education:* University of Washington, B.A., 1954. *Residence:* Woodland Hills, Calif. *Office:* 6381 Hollywood Blvd., No. 207, Los Angeles, Calif. 90028.

CAREER: Worked at several radio stations as an announcer and executive in Seattle, Wash., and Los Angeles, Calif., 1955-67; *Los Angeles Free Press,* Los Angeles, Calif., advertising manager, 1967-69, managing editor, 1969-71; *Los Angeles Star,* Los Angeles, founder and editor, 1971—.

WRITINGS: (With wife, Shirley Eberle) *The Adventures of Mrs. Pussycat* (juvenile), Prentice-Hall, 1972; *The Thraladiddle,* Stanford-Wolfe, 1975; (with Maximilian Leblovic) *Playing to Win: How to Deal With Bill Collectors so You Come Out on Top and They Come Out on the Bottom* (nonfiction), Stanford-Wolfe, 1977; *The Poems of Swan Egan DeButz,* Price, Stern, 1978. Also author of songs and composer of music.

WORK IN PROGRESS: Several fiction and nonfiction books.

SIDELIGHTS: Eberle told *CA:* "When I went to the *Los Angeles Free Press,* it was just beginning to catch on. Arthur Glick Kunkin founded it. He was like a forty-year-old beatnik, except that he'd always worked as a tool and dye maker and was a Trotskyite. His vision of the *Free Press* was that it was just going to be a little paper for the artsy craftsy intelligentsia of Los Angeles. But then came the big wave. The peace movement started along with the drug culture and sexual liberation. All these things just built up into one big tidal wave and he got caught up in it. Kubin had no money, so he hired hippies, some of whom were really brilliant people who came in off the streets. The *Free Press* became the nerve, or information, center for this conglomeration of movements. We felt it was our job to tell people what was happening. The *Free Press* was the first paper that actually dared to cover police brutality.

"We knew the paper was going to collapse eventually, because there were just too many people in it who really didn't understand it. All they knew was that they didn't want to get a haircut and go to work for IBM. And so, it did fall apart. I don't think any of us really believed that Timothy Leary was going to be president.

"I left the *Free Press* and went on with my wife Shirley to start the *Los Angeles Star.* We felt the *Free Press* had stagnated. It was talking to the same people about the same things over and over again. We wanted to break out in some new directions. We opened the *Star* to all the readers and let them write about themselves, write letters, and run ads. We have a much looser policy about censorship than the *Free Press* had. It's been a really interesting nine years since we've been in that.

"The *Star* has given me a way to make a living and work on my writing at my own leisure and not have to feel that I've got to knock out a book by next month, because otherwise I'm not going to have enough money to pay the rent."

*   *   *

EDMONDS, Margaret Hammett
(Margot Edmonds)

PERSONAL: Born in Leipsic, Ohio; daughter of Edward Earle (an accountant) and Anna May (Archer) Hammett; married Albert Sidney Edmonds, Jr. (an engineer), February 27, 1942 (died, 1967); children: Spencer Wadsworth. *Education:* Boston University, diploma, 1927; attended University of Southern California, 1931-32, and San Diego Community College, 1976-80. *Home and office:* 939 Coast Blvd., Apt. 5-J, La Jolla, Calif. 92037.

CAREER: Young Women's Christian Association, program and publicity director in Los Angeles, Calif., Pasadena, Calif., Tacoma, Wash., and Wilkes-Barre, Pa.; writer. *Member:* National League of American Pen Women (president, 1980).

WRITINGS—Under name Margot Edmonds: (With Ella E. Clark) *Sacagawea of the Lewis and Clark Expedition,* University of California Press, 1980.

Work represented in anthologies, including *Tidesong,* San Diego Community College, 1979; *Tidesong II,* San Diego Community College, 1980. Guest editor of *La Jolla Light,* 1979.

WORK IN PROGRESS—Under name Margot Edmonds: *Indian Legends From Coast to Coast,* with Ella E. Clark; *Born to Fly,* a biography of Charles Lindbergh for young adults.*

EDMONDS, Margot
   See EDMONDS, Margaret Hammett

*   *   *

EDWARDS, June
   See BHATIA, Jamunadevi

*   *   *

EIDSVIK, Charles Vernon 1943-

PERSONAL: Born November 25, 1943, in Crookston, Minn.; son of Vernon Charles and Edna Celeste Eidsvik; married Anna-Marie Schumacher (an academic adviser), June 13, 1964; children: Erik, Kara. *Education:* University of South Dakota, B.A., M.A.; University of Illinois, Ph.D. *Home:* 270 Pineforest Dr., Athens, Ga. 30606. *Agent:* Richard Balkin, Balkin Agency, 403 West 115th St., New York, N.Y. 10025. *Office:* Department of Drama, University of Georgia, Athens, Ga. 30602.

CAREER: University of Massachusetts, Amherst, assistant professor of drama, 1970-77; University of Georgia, Athens, associate professor of drama, 1977—. Film director.

WRITINGS: Cine Literacy: Film Among the Arts, Random House, 1978. Contributor to film journals.

WORK IN PROGRESS: Two books; a screenplay.

*   *   *

EISENBERG, Howard 1946-

PERSONAL: Born August 5, 1946, in Montreal, Quebec, Canada; son of Harold (an accountant) and Elsie (Goldbloom) Eisenberg; married Nancy Jeffries (a teacher), January 10, 1976; children: Taryn. *Education:* McGill University, B.Sc. (with honors), 1967, M.Sc., 1971, M.D., 1972. *Office:* Rosedale Medical Center, 600 Sherbourne, Suite 609, Toronto, Ontario, Canada M4X 1W4.

CAREER: University of Toronto, Toronto, Ontario, intern in psychiatry at Sunnybrook Medical Centre, 1973, fellow of clinical investigation unit at Clarke Institute of Psychiatry, 1973; private practice of psychotherapy in Toronto, Ontario, 1973—. Instructor at York University, 1973-78, director of education and growth opportunities program, 1976-78; instructor at Sheridan College, 1974-76; lecturer at University of Toronto, 1975—, coordinator of multi-disciplinary parapsychology course, 1976, special conferences coordinator, 1977-79; instructor at McMaster University, 1980—. Host of "Odyssey," on CBC-Radio, 1977-78. Speaker at schools, clinical institutions, parapsychological organizations, holistic health centers, and human potential movement growth centers; stress management consultant.

MEMBER: International Association for Psychotronic Research, Canadian Medical Association, Canadian Psychiatric Association, Writers' Union of Canada, American Society of Clinical Hypnosis, American Society for Psychical Research, Association for Humanistic Psychology, Association for Transpersonal Psychology, Parapsychological Association, Ontario Medical Association, Ontario Psychological Association, Ontario Society of Clinical Hypnosis.

WRITINGS: Inner Spaces: Parapsychological Explorations of the Mind, Musson, 1977. Contributor to medical and psychology journals. Member of editorial board of *Journal of Research in Psi Phenomena,* 1976-78, and *Communication Therapy,* 1981—.

WORK IN PROGRESS: A science fiction film script; research on the relevance of altered states of consciousness in psychology and on the development of non-drug technologies for inducing altered states of consciousness.

SIDELIGHTS: Eisenberg wrote that he recognized his own psychic ability as a child. As a psychotherapist, he has used that ability, mental telepathy, to reach patients who had been untreatable by more conventional methods. His treatment programs emphasize use of the patient's own mind to control distress, even such physical problems as warts and headaches. Although he does not eschew traditional treatment methods altogether, he believes strongly in replacing drugs with meditation and self-hypnosis to reduce stress, biofeedback, and autogenic training to help control such problems as high blood pressure.

Eisenberg told *CA:* "I am primarily engaged in a search for the 'who,' 'what,' and 'why' of our existence. My motivation is intense curiosity, altruism, and a desire to live a very full life."

BIOGRAPHICAL/CRITICAL SOURCES: Weekend, April 5, 1975; *Toronto Star Magazine,* February 5, 1978; *Toronto Globe and Mail,* February 9, 1979.

*   *   *

ELLIOTT, Malissa Childs 1929(?)-1979
   (Malissa Redfield)

PERSONAL: Born c. 1929 in St. Louis, Mo.; died March 20, 1979, in Hanover, N.H.; daughter of Marquis (a syndicated columnist) and Lue (Prentiss) Childs; married H. J. Redfield (a U.S. Marine colonel; divorced); married Robert Irwin Elliott, 1968. *Education:* Attended Yale University School of Drama; received degree from Stanford University. *Residence:* Springfield, Vt.

CAREER: U.S. State Department, Washington, D.C., specialist on Soviet affairs, 1950-53; editorial assistant at Library of Congress, Washington, D.C.; *Fortune* Magazine, New York City, research assistant, 1959-61; *New York Times,* New York City, member of editorial staff of *Sunday Magazine,* 1961-62; U.S. Information Agency (now International Communication Agency), deputy editor of Arabic language publication, 1962-66, editor of *Amerika* (Russian language publication), 1966-68; writer. *Member:* Phi Beta Kappa.

WRITINGS—All under name Malissa Redfield: *The Country of Love* (novel), Doubleday, 1966; *Games of Chance With Strangers* (novel), Doubleday, 1971; *Scenes From Country Life* (nonfiction), Prentice-Hall, 1979.*

*   *   *

ELLISON, Katherine (White) 1941-

PERSONAL: Born January 17, 1941, in West Virginia; daughter of Christian Streit (an ironmonger) and Katherine (a musician; maiden name, Hughey) White. *Education:* Agnes Scott College, B.A., 1962; Graduate Center of the City University of New York, Ph.D., 1976. *Residence:* Hasbrouck Heights, N.J. *Office:* Montclair State College, Upper Montclair, N.J. 07043.

CAREER: Center for Responsive Psychology, Brooklyn, N.Y., associate director, 1975—. Member of faculty at Montclair State College, 1977—. Consultant and lecturer on psychology and the law. *Member:* American Psychological Association, American Psychology-Law Association, Eastern Psychological Association, Phi Beta Kappa.

WRITINGS: (With Robert Buckhout) *Psychology and Criminal Justice: Common Ground,* Harper, 1980. Contributor of about twenty-five articles to psychology journals. Editor of *Educational Foundations of Human Sexuality and Interpersonal Relations;* associate editor of *Social Action and the Law.*

WORK IN PROGRESS: Police Stress.

SIDELIGHTS: Katherine Ellison told *CA:* "I believe in the convenient fictions of a life of the mind, and of free will. In the best of all possible worlds I should have studied Latin and been a Chaucer scholar. I have a secret passion for Donne, Yeats, Dorothy Sayers, and Eliot. My current life is devoted to raping intellectual virgins. I can spell, my grammar is acceptable, I write double dactyls, I am a workaholic and an inveterate elitist. Rene Dubois's term about a despairing optimist suits me. I plan to include a line from *Just So Stories* on my tombstone."

*   *   *

EMERY, Pierre-Yves 1929-

PERSONAL: Born April 15, 1929, in Utrecht, Netherlands; son of Georges and Helene (Loetscher) Emery. *Education:* University of Lausanne, lic. en theologie, 1952. *Home:* F 71250 Taize Community, near Cluny, Saone-et-Loire, France.

CAREER: Clergyman; pastor of the Taize Community.

WRITINGS: L'Unite des croyants au ciel et sur la terre: La Communion des saints et son expression dans la priere de l'eglise, Presses de Taize, 1962, translation by D. J. Watson and M. Watson published as *The Communion of Saints,* Morehouse, 1966; *La Priere au coeur de la vie,* Presses de Taize, 1971, translation by William J. Nottingham published as *Prayer at the Heart of Life,* Orbis, 1971.

In French: *Le Sacrifice eucharistique selon les theologiens reformes francais du dix-septieme siecle,* Delachaux & Niestle, 1959; *Le Christ notre recompense: Grace de Dieu et responsabilite de l'homme,* Delachaux & Niestle, 1962; *Habiter en freres tous ensemble: Les Psaumes et l'unite de l'eglise selon Saint Augustin,* Presses de Taize, 1965; *Le Meditation de l'ecriture: Les Psaumes, priere pour l'eglise,* 4th edition, Presses de Taize, 1967; (with Rene Beaupere) *Des foyers catholiques-protestants s'experiment: Mariages mixtes, temoignages de foyers, de pasteurs et de pretres, rassembles et presentes,* Mame, 1969.

*   *   *

ENGELMANN, Larry 1941-

PERSONAL: Born April 21, 1941, in Austin, Minn.; son of Stanley Daniel (a laborer) and Delores (a laborer; maiden name, Sherwood) Engelmann; married Margo Morris, June 13, 1965 (divorced October 21, 1979); children: Marya, Erika Anne. *Education:* University of Minnesota, B.A., 1963, M.A., 1965; University of Michigan, Ph.D., 1969. *Home:* 5637 Strawflower Lane, San Jose, Calif. 95118. *Agent:* Emilie Jacobson, Curtis Brown Ltd., 575 Madison Ave., New York, N.Y. 10022. *Office:* Department of History, San Jose State University, 125 South Seventh, San Jose, Calif. 95192.

CAREER: San Jose State University, San Jose, Calif., assistant professor, 1969-76, associate professor of history, 1976—. *Member:* American Historical Association, American Film Institute, Society of American Historians.

WRITINGS: Intemperance: The Lost War Against Liquor, Free Press, 1979. Contributor of more than fifteen articles to history journals and popular magazines, including *Smithsonian.* Film critic for Meredith/Sun Newspapers, Inc.

WORK IN PROGRESS: The Goddess and the American Girl, about the tennis stars Suzanne Lenglen and Helen Wills; *The Murder City,* dealing with organized crime in the Midwest in the 1920's and 1930's.

SIDELIGHTS: Engelmann commented to *CA:* "My primary interest is nonfiction. I try to combine what I learned about research in graduate school with what I learned about good dramatic and precise prose from writers like Joyce Carol Oates, Truman Capote, Sinclair Lewis, and William Styron. I am constantly on the lookout for ideas or information that might be developed in stories or articles. Consequently, I have written about subjects as diverse as the women's fencing champion of the United States, a blimp accident in 1942, a rock and roll riot in 1956, and a tennis player of the 1920's. As in fiction, the possibilities for subject matter are unlimited, and I enjoy the research and discovery as much as I do writing a final narrative."

*   *   *

ENGS, Robert Francis 1943-

PERSONAL: Born November 10, 1943; son of Robert Nathaniel (an army officer) and Myrtle (a teacher; maiden name, Coger) Engs; married Jean Elizabeth Oliver (a teacher), December 20, 1969; children: Robert Nathaniel II. *Education:* Princeton University, A.B. (cum laude), 1965; Yale University, Ph.D., 1972. *Home:* 523 South 46th St., Philadelphia, Pa. 19143. *Office:* Department of History, University of Pennsylvania, Philadelphia, Pa. 19104.

CAREER: Agency for International Development, Washington, D.C., foreign affairs intern, 1964; New Jersey Institute for the Study of Society and Black History, Trenton, N.J., director, 1969-72; University of Pennsylvania, Philadelphia, assistant professor, 1972-79, associate professor of history, 1980—. Field professor at New Jersey Education Consortium, 1969-72; lecturer at Princeton University, 1970-72; guest lecturer at colleges and universities; consultant to U.S. Department of State. *Member:* American Historical Association, Association for the Study of Afro-American Life and History, Organization of American Historians. *Awards, honors:* Grant from U.S. Department of State for study in Africa and Europe, 1971; fellow of Robert Russa Morton Center for Independent Studies, 1977-78; National Endowment for the Humanities summer fellow, 1980.

WRITINGS: Freedom's First Generation: Black Hampton, Virginia, 1861-1890 (monograph), University of Pennsylvania Press, 1979. Contributor to education journals and *Nation.*

WORK IN PROGRESS: Black Frankford, 1760 to 1976; Samuel Chapman Armstrong: A Biography, completion expected in 1985.

SIDELIGHTS: Engs told *CA:* "*Freedom's First Generation* traces the lives of freed blacks in one Southern community. It is a tale of what might have been had the nation lived up to even its most minimal obligations and promises to emancipated slaves. The study demonstrates that myths of black incompetence and unpreparedness for freedom are precisely that—*myths.* The story of Black Hampton, Virginia, proves blacks were more than capable of achievement as free people when given a fair chance to exercise their abilities."

*   *   *

ENO, Susan

PERSONAL: Born in Lincoln, Neb.; daughter of Del G. and Maxine (Shilling) Eno. *Education:* Attended University of

Nebraska, 1964-66; University of Kansas, B.A., 1969. *Residence:* New York, N.Y. *Agent:* Richard Curtis Associates, Inc., 156 East 52nd St., New York, N.Y. 10022. *Office:* Harcourt Brace Jovanovich, Inc., 757 Third Ave., New York, N.Y. 10017.

CAREER: Harcourt Brace Jovanovich, Inc., New York City, editor of college textbooks, 1969-71; American Management Association, New York City, editor in book publishing division, 1972-75; McKinsey & Co. (management consultants), New York City, editor, 1975-77; Harcourt Brace Jovanovich, Inc., editor of college textbooks, 1977—.

WRITINGS: The Truth About What Women Want in Men, Morrow, 1980. Author of "Susan's View," a weekly advice column in *Fire Island News,* 1979.

SIDELIGHTS: Susan Eno told *CA:* "I believe the importance of writers exchanging information, advice, and criticism can't be overemphasized, though many aspiring writers seem determined to go it alone. Being primarily an editor by profession, and now having experienced the writer's end of it, I'm interested in the interaction between the writing and editorial processes, and how one can nourish the other."

AVOCATIONAL INTERESTS: Film, literature, theatre.

*   *   *

ENSIGN, Thomas 1940-
(Tod Ensign)

PERSONAL: Born November 15, 1940, in Battle Creek, Mich.; son of Winfield Scott (a printer and state representative) and Gretchen Louise (a Veterans Administration music and recreation therapist; maiden name, McKinstry) Ensign. *Education:* Michigan State University, B.A., 1963; Wayne State University, J.D., 1966; New York University, LL.M., 1967. *Agent:* Richard Curtis Associates, Inc., 156 East 52nd St., New York, N.Y. 10022. *Office:* 175 Fifth Ave., New York, N.Y. 10010.

CAREER: Admitted to the Bar of the State of Michigan and the State of New York; Citizen Soldier, New York, N.Y., coordinator and counsel, 1970—. *Member:* National Lawyers Guild.

WRITINGS—Under name Tod Ensign: (Editor with Michael Uhl and Jeremy Rifkin) *Dellums Committee Hearings on U.S. War Crimes in Vietnam,* Vintage, 1971; (with Uhl) *G.I. Guinea Pigs,* Playboy Press, 1980. Contributor to magazines, including *Progressive, In These Times, Guardian, High Times,* and *Radical America.*

SIDELIGHTS: Tod Ensign and Michael Uhl, the co-author of *G.I. Guinea Pigs,* are both active in Citizen Soldier, a group concerned with the effects of nuclear and herbicidal warfare on veterans. According to Murray Polner of the *Washington Post, G.I. Guinea Pigs* reminds us that "soldiers have always been the chief victims of stay-at-home warriors and far-from-the-field-of-battle commanders who often use them casually for political and military purposes too arcane for the young to comprehend." Ensign and Uhl give an "emotional and personal" account of the ordeals of "enlisted men who later succumbed to life-threatening diseases." The authors conclude that these victims—soldiers who patrolled the bombed streets of Hiroshima and Nagasaki, those who witnessed the atomic testing in Nevada in the 1950's, those who were showered with Agent Orange in Vietnam—"have been treated like so many no-deposit, no-return soda bottles; once the contents are consumed, the empties are thrown on the junk heap."

Ensign told *CA:* "I primarily consider myself to be an orga-

nizer and activist rather than attorney or writer/author. I am only interested in working on, or writing about, issues which I consider involved in the preparation and research for the plaintiff's case against various herbicide manufacturers for injury and deaths caused by their production of dangerous and inherently unsafe products."

BIOGRAPHICAL/CRITICAL SOURCES: Washington Post Book World, August 17, 1980.

*   *   *

ENSIGN, Tod
See ENSIGN, Thomas

*   *   *

ERICKSON, John 1929-

PERSONAL: Born April 17, 1929; son of Henry and Jessie (Heys) Erickson; married Ljubica Petrovic, 1957; children: one son, one daughter. *Education:* St. John's College, Cambridge, B.A., M.A., *Home:* 13 Ravelston House Rd., Edinburgh EH4 3LP, Scotland. *Office:* Department of Defense Studies, University of Edinburgh, 31 Buccleuch Place, Edinburgh EH8 9JT, Scotland.

CAREER: St. Andrews University, St. Andrews, Scotland, lecturer in history, 1958-62; University of Manchester, Manchester, England, lecturer, senior lecturer, and reader in government, 1962-67; University of Edinburgh, Edinburgh, Scotland, reader and lecturer in high defense studies, 1967-69, professor of politics, 1969—. Research fellow at St. Anthony's College, Oxford, 1956-58; visiting professor at Russian Research Center, University of Indiana, 1967. *Military service:* British Army; became sergeant.

WRITINGS: The Soviet High Command: A Military-Political History, 1918-1941, St. Martin's, 1962; (editor) *The Military-Technical Revolution: Its Impact on Strategy and Foreign Policy,* Praeger, 1966; (editor with J. N. Wolfe) *The Armed Services and Society: An International Conference on Alienation, Management, and Integration,* Edinburgh University Press, 1970; *Soviet Military Power,* Royal United Services Institute, 1971, United States Strategic Institute, 1973; *Stalin's War With Germany,* Harper, Volume I: *The Road to Stalingrad,* 1975; *Soviet-Warsaw Pact Force Levels,* United States Strategic Institute, 1976; (editor with E. J. Feuchtwanger) *Soviet Military Power and Performance,* Archon Books, 1979.

WORK IN PROGRESS: A military history of modern Russia, 1700-1979; a history of the Imperial Russian/Soviet General Staff, 1862-1979; a handbook on Soviet military capabilities.

SIDELIGHTS: Erickson told *CA:* "One morning more than thirty years ago, when serving as a sergeant with the British Army in Austria, I virtually blundered onto a Soviet armored column, replete with T-34/85 tanks and riflemen. Both the men and the machines made an indelible impression on me, combining as they did stark contrast between crudity and sophistication. The inadvertent meeting passed off with good humor, but left me with impressions, images, and a persistent curiosity which could not be stifled. That much I owed to the 44th Rifle Division of the Soviet Army, which then accompanied me—subconsciously, at least—when I returned to St. John's College, Cambridge, to take up the Open scholarship in history which I had previously won.

"Though I intended to pursue a career as a Slav historian, devoting my undergraduate and postgraduate days to the requisite historical and linguistic studies, I did also privately burrow about in Russian and Soviet military matters, finding only mountains of myths and accumulations of grotesque rumors. I did, however, devote my Russian—prior knowledge of which had assuredly extricated me from my encounter with the Soviet tank column—to developing a study of the Red Army and, in particular, the theory and practice of Soviet armored warfare. This took on some bare academic shape, and in the mid-1950's I submitted this preliminary work as a fellowship application to St. Anthony's College, Oxford. Here I began the serious assembling of an academic history of the Soviet military.

"Publishers scoffed at the idea. All material was 'secret,' there was no material (there was a contradiction here, somewhere), there was no market. . . . *The Soviet High Command* finally lumbered to life, all 900 pages of it, and demonstrated that not only was there material, but material in profusion. *The Soviet High Command* has long been out of print, but its early existence prompted an invitation from a very high level of the Soviet leadership in 1963 to work in Moscow with the late Cornelius Ryan and to make use of *every* facility which could be afforded by the Soviet military command. Once again, predictions of doom and despair: there would be no real access, everything would be 'propaganda,' the whole enterprise would be totally abortive. Those days in Moscow proved to be perhaps the most hectic, hard-working of my life, crammed with frequent and extensive access to the most senior Soviet commanders; lengthy and very professional exchanges with Soviet military experts; and latterly recourse to Soviet military archives on my own academic terms, namely, requesting papers and records in *my own* sequences and contexts.

"One day I should like to publish all my bulging notebooks, complete records of those extraordinary and vibrant sessions, ranging all the way from marshals of the Soviet Union to infantry sergeants, from the brutal to the bizarre, from the horrendous to the humorous. Since then I have enjoyed and benefited from further association with Soviet military historians and specialists, much to my advantage. When preparing *The Road to Stalingrad* (Volume I of *Stalin's War With Germany*) I was, after much laborious work, still baffled about what really happened that catastrophic night of June 22, 1941, when the Wehrmacht fell on the Soviet Union. After one seminar, I found myself in the company of several Soviet marshals, and I was given an extraordinary first-hand account of 'that night' by Marshal Voronov, a formidably impressive soldier who (it should be added) probably saved the Red Army in 1941.

"That very first eruption into what had been a world hermetically sealed (from Russians, too) left the most powerful impression. It was not merely the technicalities of military history, but the insights into style, manners, and preoccupations—the ethos—of this military system which counted for so much. I could not understand the prevalent denigration by Western specialists of the Soviet military mind, the extraordinary assumptions before and during SALT I (the first Strategic Arms Limitation Treaty) that *we* would 'teach' them about the sophistications and mysteries of nuclear war. Yet while we prated about 'management,' the Russians spoke of 'leadership'; while we comforted ourselves with notions of 'conflict resolution' and other verbiage, the Russians stared steadily at the implications of *'war';* and while we prided ourselves on the niceties of 'cost effectiveness,' the Soviet command concentrated on *effectiveness.* In short, they had little to learn from our nuclear metaphysicians. One needed only to have some contact with officers of the Soviet General Staff—a unique and powerful organization—to recognize

that here was intellect and intelligence at work, as opposed to the fancies, fads, and vagaries of 'defense intellectuals.' There has long been a Soviet *science of war,* and we would do well to understand it more closely.

"Academic though all my own work will seem, perhaps the academic impress comes quite near to reality. At least it is intended to represent *Soviet* reality (and also to comprehend the impressive legacy inherited from Czarist Russia). The Russians throw nothing away, least of all the lessons of history bought with so much blood. But we still know too little about Soviet military institutions. We have even now, after thirty years or more, a glaring lack of good bibliographies and source compilations. Yet it is precisely in understanding Soviet military performance that we should be most 'academic,' in the rigorous and accepted sense of that word.

"I salute the nuclear metaphysicians, though I can manage only the most perfunctory nod in the direction of *la jeunesse doree* which supposes that the Soviet Army was invented only a decade or so ago. I still incline to the view that we need to know just how a Soviet regiment or battalion actually works, what it is intended to do, and just how well or how badly it might perform. So mayhap it all comes back to the 44th Rifle Division."

AVOCATIONAL INTERESTS: Military models, music.

* * *

ESHLEMAN, J. Ross 1936-

PERSONAL: Born April 11, 1936, in Mount Joy, Pa.; son of John E. and Ruth (Forney) Eshleman; married Janet W. Hershberger, 1958; children: Jill Renee, Sidney Ross. *Education:* Attended Elizabethtown College, 1954-56; Manchester College, B.A., 1958; Ohio State University, M.A., 1960, Ph.D., 1963. *Office:* Department of Sociology, Wayne State University, Detroit, Mich. 48202.

CAREER: Western Michigan University, Kalamazoo, assistant professor, 1963-66, associate professor, 1966-70, professor of sociology, 1970-73; Wayne State University, Detroit, Mich., professor of sociology and head of department, 1973—. Fulbright-Hays lecturer at University of Santo Tomas and DeLaSalle College, 1968-69. Member of International Scientific Commission on the Family, Michigan Commission on Family Life, Social Science Education Consortium, and panels of National Science Foundation. Director of institutes for high school teachers of sociology. Past member of board of directors, vice-president, and president of Kalamazoo Family Service Center.

MEMBER: American Sociological Association (member of board of directors of family section, 1975-78), American Association of University Professors, National Council on Family Relations, Philippine Sociological Society, Michigan Sociological Association, Michigan Council on Family Relations (member of board of directors; member of regional executive committee), North Central Sociological Association (president-elect, 1975-76), Society for the Study of Social Problems, Association for Asian Studies, Manchester College Alumni Association (member of board of directors; vice-president, 1977-78; president, 1978-79), Alpha Kappa Delta.

WRITINGS: (With C. L. Hunt) *Social Class Factors in the College Adjustment of Married Students,* Western Michigan University Press, 1965; *Perspectives in Marriage and the Family,* Allyn & Bacon, 1969; (contributor) Fuad Baali and Clifton D. Bryant, editors, *Introductory Sociology: Selected Readings for the College Scene,* Rand McNally, 1970; (contributor) Ruth Albrecht and E. Wilbur Bock, editors, *Encounter: Love, Marriage, and Family,* Holbrook, 1972; *The Family: An Introduction,* Allyn & Bacon, 1974, 2nd edition, 1978; (with James N. Clarke) *Intimacy, Commitments, and Marriage: The Development of Relationships,* Allyn & Bacon, 1978. Contributor of about a dozen articles and reviews to sociology journals.

*   *   *

ETHELL, Jeffrey L(ance) 1947-

PERSONAL: Surname is accented on first syllable; born September 29, 1947, in Riverside, Calif.; son of Ervin C. (a U.S. Air Force pilot) and T. Jean (Ross) Ethell; married Bettie Taylor, December 19, 1968; children: Jennifer Brooke, David William, Julie Christine. *Education:* King College, Bristol, Tenn., B.A., 1969; graduate study at Union Theological Seminary, Richmond, Va. *Home and office:* 2403 Sunnybrook Rd., Richmond, Va. 23229. *Agent:* John McLaughlin, Campbell Thomson & McLaughlin Ltd., 31 Newington Green, London N16 9PU, England.

CAREER: Ordained Baptist minister, 1970; Richmond Youth Challenge, Inc., Richmond, Va., director of Troubled Youth Ministry, 1970-76; free-lance writer, 1976—. Certified scuba diver and flight instructor; commercial pilot with instrument and multi-engine ratings. *Member:* American Aviation Historical Society. *Awards, honors:* Grants from Smithsonian Institution, 1967, 1968.

WRITINGS: Komet: The Messerschmitt 163, Sky Books Press, 1978; (with Joe Christy) *P-38 Lightning at War,* Scribner, 1978; *Cowboys and Indians,* Graphically Speaking, 1978; *Moving Up to Twin Engine Airplanes,* Tab Books, 1978; (with Keith Ferris) *The Aviation Art of Keith Ferris,* Bantam, 1978; *Used Aircraft Guide,* Scribner, 1979; (with Alfred Price) *The German Jets in Combat,* Jane's, 1979; (with Christy) *P-40 Hawks at War,* Scribner, 1979; (with Garry L. Fry) *Escort to Berlin,* Arco, 1980; *F-15 Eagle,* Ian Allan, 1980; (with Christy) *B-52 Stratofortress,* Ian Allan, 1980; *Mustang: A Documentary History of the P-51,* Jane's, 1981; (with Price) *Target Berlin,* Jane's, 1981; *Fox Two,* Aero, in press. Contributor of more than two hundred articles to magazines, including *Air International, Business and Commercial Aviation, Air Classics,* and *Plane and Pilot.* Military editor of *Air Progress.*

WORK IN PROGRESS: A book on World War II AT-6 training aircraft, with Walter E. Ohlrich, Jr., publication by Specialty Press expected in 1981; a book on the 78th FG in World War II, publication by Battery Press expected in 1983; research on the Panama Canal for a World War II novel, completion expected in 1984; research on fighter aviation since World War I.

SIDELIGHTS: Ethell commented: "My flying experience began at age eight when my father put me behind the controls of a Piper Tri-Pacer. By age thirteen I was regularly flying the Beech T-34 and Ryan Navion out of Quantico Marine Corps Air Station and soloed at age eighteen. In 1972 I was cleared to fly with military services as a writer and since then have logged several hundred hours, both as passenger and pilot, in modern military aircraft of the U.S. Air Force, U.S. Navy, and U.S. Marine Corps.

"I find my faith in Jesus Christ to be sustaining through all my work. I am still an ordained Baptist minister and serve as a counseling elder in my church. I continue to fly as a commercial pilot, which often leads to more books, and I fly antique aircraft as often as I can to get the flavor of the aircraft I write about.

"My opinion is that good research is the heart of a book—there is no excuse for getting things wrong if one is willing to dig for the facts. I believe this is what sets my work apart."

*   *   *

EULENSPIEGEL, Alexander
See SHEA, Robert (Joseph)

*   *   *

EUSTIS, Laurette
See MURDOCK, Laurette P.

*   *   *

EVELAND, Bill
See EVELAND, Wilbur Crane

*   *   *

EVELAND, Wilbur Crane 1918-
(Bill Eveland)

PERSONAL: Born July 1, 1918, in Spokane, Wash.; son of Wilbur Crane (an accountant and merchant) and Minnie (a teacher; maiden name, Doust) Eveland; married Marjorie Prunty, 1943 (divorced, 1958); married Mimosa Giordano, 1959 (divorced, 1967); children: (first marriage) Wilbur Crane. *Politics:* Republican. *Religion:* Episcopalian. *Home and office address:* P.O. Box 990, Cupertino, Calif. 95015. *Agent:* Curtis Brown Ltd., 575 Madison Ave., New York, N.Y. 10022.

CAREER: Served in Marine Corps Reserve, 1936-40. U.S. Army, 1941-54; special agent for Counter Intelligence Corps, 1941-48; attache at American embassy in Baghdad, Iraq, 1949-52; member of general staff, 1952-53; head of Office of the Assistant Secretary of Defense in the Middle East, in Washington, D.C., 1953-54; leaving service as lieutenant-colonel, 1954; member of Military Intelligence Reserve, 1945-67. Affiliated with Executive Office of the President, 1955; Central Intelligence Agency (CIA), Washington, D.C., covert associate in the Middle East and Africa, 1955-60; vice-president of Vinnell Corp. in Rome, Italy, Washington, D.C., and Beirut, Lebanon, 1960-66; free-lance consultant in Beirut to oil companies, petroleum engineering firms, and offshore drilling contractors, 1966-67; head of petroleum industry support companies in the Middle East, the North Sea, and Southeast Asia, 1967-74; vice-president of Fluor Arabia Ltd. in the Middle East, 1974-75; writer, 1975—. *Member:* Federal City Club, Wig & Pen Club. *Awards, honors*—Military: Bronze Star and Army Commendation Medal.

WRITINGS: Ropes of Sand: America's Failure in the Middle East, Norton, 1980. Contributor of articles to newspapers and periodicals, including *Middle East, Foreign Policy, Arab Perspectives, San Francisco Chronicle,* and *Christian Science Monitor.*

WORK IN PROGRESS: A book "examining whether U.S. presidents have instigated, or always been aware of, the Central Intelligence Agency's covert political action operations in the Middle East and Africa"; a book about "the evolution of the power of the shah of Iran from 1941 through his exile in 1979"; *Britannia Waives the Rules,* a personal account; a suspense thriller, "written in a humorous way, about the self-defeating and often conflicting activities of intelligence services in the Middle East."

SIDELIGHTS: Wilbur Crane Eveland, who was sixty-one

years old when he published *Ropes of Sand,* told *CA* that the book had not only "provided an outlet for a lifetime interest in history and creative expression, but had also opened up an exciting new career at an age when most of my generation was contemplating retirement.

"My purpose in writing the book was to remind two generations of Americans of our country's sixty-year history in the Middle East and reveal some of our failures that, although well known to the peoples affected and also to the Russians, have been kept from the American public. In particular, I wanted most to reach young adults with the book because too many of them know only what they read in today's headlines and hear on the electronic media about the Middle East and its problems. Tomorrow they will be the ones making the U.S. policies that can solve our dilemma in that area of the world. That the Hoover Institute on War, Revolution, and Peace has requested my manuscript and research material for its archives and has invited me to contribute additional writings, leads me to hope that scholars may derive benefits from my recollections of history."

In *Ropes of Sand* Eveland relates his experiences during nearly thirty years in the Middle East, six of which as a covert associate for the Central Intelligence Agency (CIA). "Sent to Damascus in 1955 to help 'stem the leftist drift' in Syria and eventually attempt an abortive coup there," explained George Lardner, Jr., of the *Washington Post,* Eveland met with staunch resistance when he informed the CIA of his plans to publish a book about his activities.

Although Eveland was an associate and never an actual member of the CIA, he spent four years in an unsuccessful attempt to determine whether he was obligated to secrecy in any way to that organization. Requests for copies of documents signed by Eveland were ignored; instead, the CIA supplied him only with a list of dates of employment agreements. At one point he received a letter from Assistant General Counsel John F. Peyton, quoted by Lardner as reading: "Writings of this nature must be reviewed by the CIA's Publication Review Board in accordance with the secrecy agreements (sic) which you signed. Because the secrecy agreement (sic) is contained in a document which is currently properly classified, I am not at liberty at this time to forward it to you." Eveland explained to *CA* that "the CIA claimed a right to censor the book, but said that its authority to do so was too secret to show even me."

By the time the CIA demanded a prepublication review of *Ropes of Sand,* galley copies had been sent to major newspapers and magazines, and several reviews were already in print. The CIA then relinquished all right of censorship and the book was released to the public.

Ropes of Sand was greeted favorably by critics and the general public alike. David Schoenbaum of the *Chicago Tribune Book World* praised the work and remarked that "Eveland should be required reading for Congressional committees charged with energy, defense, foreign policy, and—eloquent ambiguity—'Intelligence oversight,' as well as for anybody nostalgic for the Eisenhower era." *Washington Post* writer William Branigin, moreover, claimed that *Ropes of Sand* "makes absorbing and lively reading. From the unique vantage point of his special assignments, Eveland is able to offer some of the best and richest detail yet to appear on American dealings with the Middle East during the period he describes."

BIOGRAPHICAL/CRITICAL SOURCES: Washington Post, April 3, 1980, June 15, 1980, July 29, 1980; *Chicago Tribune Book World,* July 13, 1980; *Christian Science Monitor,* July 16, 1980; *Los Angeles Town Crier,* July 23, 1980; *New York Times Book Review,* August 3, 1980.

F

FAHEY, Frank M(ichael) 1917-

PERSONAL: Born November 21, 1917, in Seattle, Wash.; son of Frank A. (a purchasing agent) and Lilian (Newsome) Fahey; married Marie Lazenby (a writer), July 1, 1951; children: Jim, Sherry, ·Cindy. *Education:* University of Washington, Seattle, B.A., 1939; Stanford University, M.A., 1948, Ph.D., 1957. *Home:* 188 South Palomar Dr., Redwood City, Calif. 94062. *Office:* Department of History, Canada College, 4200 Farmhill Blvd., Redwood City, Calif. 94061.

CAREER: Boise Junior College, Boise, Idaho, instructor in history and political science, 1948-50; Stanford University, Stanford, Calif., instructor in western civilization, 1951-53; Boise Junior College, instructor in history and political science, 1954-55; Stanford University, instructor in western civilization, 1955-56; College of San Mateo, San Mateo, Calif., instructor in American history, 1956-68; Canada College, Redwood City, Calif., instructor in American history, 1968—. *Military service:* U.S. Army, 1941-45; served in Asia and the Pacific; received Bronze Star. *Member:* Phi Alpha Theta.

WRITINGS: (Editor with wife, Marie L. Fahey) *Chapters From the American Experience,* two volumes, Prentice-Hall, 1971.

WORK IN PROGRESS: A Profile of the American Experience, an introductory American history textbook with narrative and biographical approaches, with M. Fahey, publication by Prentice-Hall expected in 1982.

SIDELIGHTS: Frank Fahey writes: "My special research interest is the role of Arthur M. Schlesinger, Jr., in American historiography."

*　　*　　*

FARNUM, K. T.
See RIPS, Ervine M(ilton)

*　　*　　*

FARRAR, Susan Clement 1917-

PERSONAL: Born November 10, 1917, in Billerica, Mass.; daughter of Joseph A. (a shoemaker) and Emily (Potsavich) Clement; married Charles A. Farrar (a postal clerk and restaurant owner), 1946; children: Michelle Farrar Keyes, Douglas, Lisa Farrar Fox, Paul. *Education:* Attended City College (now of the City University of New York); studied dance privately. *Politics:* Democrat. *Religion:* Christian. *Home address:* Spring St., Bethel, Maine 04217.

CAREER: Ballerina and dance teacher in Rumford, Maine, 1935-77; writer, 1977—. Choreographer in Boston, Mass., 1940-42; director of children's dance theaters in Phoenix, Ariz., 1950-60, and Bethel, Maine, 1960-78. *Member:* Maine Dance Teachers Association, Boston Dance Association. *Awards, honors:* Henry Hastings Citizenship Award from Bethel Chamber of Commerce, 1975.

WRITINGS: Samantha on Stage (juvenile), Dial, 1979; *Bravo, Samantha* (juvenile), Dial, 1980; *Clowns in the Kitchen* (novel), Dial, 1980.

WORK IN PROGRESS: A juvenile book, *Folktales of Eastern Europe;* a children's book, *The St. Bernard Who Thought He Was a Kitten;* more "Samantha" novels, for Dial.

SIDELIGHTS: Susan Farrar told *CA:* "I wrote *Samantha on Stage* the year before I retired, after forty years of dance involvement. I felt a strong need to write down the thoughts and feelings that expressed my deep love of ballet. The rest was like a fairy tale, and I embarked on a second career.

"Since my novels deal with the world of dance and young people, I attend classes, dance meets, and dance conventions, observing and keeping my ideas fresh and alive. I've worked with hundreds of children of all ages over the years and relate to them comfortably, I think, because deep inside I'm child-like myself. I know today's young people have the same dreams and fantasies I had as a child, with a slightly different facade.

"I'm hoping that my writing will afford me the opportunity to travel around the world—my biggest dream of all. I've driven through every state in my little camper, and traveled through Mexico, Central America, and Canada as well.

"I also visited the Soviet Union observing classes at the Bolshoi. I toured Moscow, Leningrad, Estonia, Latvia, and Lithuania. The latter was the birthplace of my parents, and for the first time I heard their native tongue spoken all around me, and I understood and answered, though haltingly.

"I have a strong desire to try to preserve the heritage of these brave people. I hope the folktales, as told to me by my mother, will someday be published with very special, authentic illustrations. The little countries are being 'Russianized' and the language, ethnic dances, and songs will soon be wiped out. I find this very sad."

AVOCATIONAL INTERESTS: Painting, carpentry, swimming, jogging, hiking in the woods, walking on rocks in the river, mountain climbing, reading Shakespeare, listening to classical music.

BIOGRAPHICAL/CRITICAL SOURCES: Bittersweet, December, 1977, May, 1979.

* * *

FARRIS, John

CAREER: Novelist, playwright, and screenwriter.

WRITINGS—Novels: *Harrison High,* Rinehart, 1959; *The Long Night of Dawn,* Putnam, 1962; *King Windom,* Trident, 1967; *When Michael Calls,* Trident, 1967; *The Captors,* Trident, 1969; *Shadow on Harrison High,* Pocket Books, 1972; *Sharp Practice,* Simon & Schuster, 1974; *The Fury,* Playboy Press, 1976; *All Heads Turn When the Hunt Goes By,* Playboy Press, 1978. Contributor of articles to magazines.

Other works: "The Death of the Well-Loved Boy" (two-act play), first produced Off-Broadway at St. Mark's Playhouse, May 15, 1967; "The Fury" (screenplay; adapted from own novel), Twentieth Century-Fox, 1978.

SIDELIGHTS: King Windom, Farris's novel about a southern fundamentalist preacher, met with praise from critic Victor Yanitelli: "The complexities of the novel are expertly handled. The entire tale moves logically through each incident and each one is believable. . . . In fact, the preaching is so well researched that at times it threatens to overwhelm the characters."

Two other early Farris novels, *The Captors* and *When Michael Calls,* have been the focus of diverse critical reaction. The latter is the story of a ten-year-old boy who begins to make threatening calls to people in the village where he had died fifteen years earlier. Death after mysterious death occurs until, as Daniel Lawler noted, "the final conclusion is dramatically and masterfully plotted and carried out." Anthony Boucher, meanwhile, thought differently: "The natural solution is so obvious that it seems foolish to read 80,000 words while waiting for detective Doremus Brightlaw to reach the answer."

Another critic impressed by *When Michael Calls* objected to *The Captors:* "[This] is a tremendous disappointment after the great promise [Farris] showed in *When Michael Calls.* . . . One is almost three quarters through the book before it begins to make sense. . . . If you read this one, I hope you won't find it as much of a struggle as I did." Apparently, Allen Hubin found it easier. He wrote, "Few kidnapping stories have been as good as this one—since few mystery-writers have Mr. Farris's talent for masterfully devious plotting, the shatteringly effective use of violence, indepth characterizations, and scenes of gibbering horror guaranteed to turn one's blood to gelatin."

Although Farris's skillfully constructed suspense is a highlight of his work, he has consistently offered more than the "standard shocker." In *Sharp Practice* he wrote about a "Jack the Ripper type character" and included "a socko climax with an unexpected twist." Especially notable in this "very nice piece of work," wrote the *New York Times Book Review,* "is its sophistication," as exemplified by a very literate dialogue, intelligent discussion of music, and the complexities surrounding an "incestuous brother-sister relationship." Similarly, *All Heads Turn When the Hunt Goes By* "is an engaging fantasy of elegance, depravity, and blood."

Not only does it mirror "the current fascination with the horrible, the violent, and the sinister," wrote O. A. Robinson III, it shows "Farris has done his homework. The settings are accurate, the descriptions are vivid, and he knows the ins and outs of pagan religion, cults, and voodoo."

Farris's screenplay, "The Fury," "is about two teenagers, spiritual twins who have met only telepathically," observed Pauline Kael. "They are superior beings; in a primitive tribe, we are told, they would have become the prophets, the magicians, the healers. In modern civilization, they become prisoners of a corrupt government (ours), which seeks to use them for espionage, and treats them impersonally, as secret weapons." Kael continued by praising the screenplay and director Brian De Palma: "No Hitchcock thriller was ever so intense, went so far, or had so many 'classic' sequences. . . . [The finale] is the greatest finish for any villain ever. One can imagine Welles, Peckinpah, Scorcese, and Spielberg still stunned, bowing to the ground, choking with laughter."

BIOGRAPHICAL/CRITICAL SOURCES: Best Sellers, May, 1967, November, 1967, October 1, 1969, July, 1978; *New York Times Book Review,* December 17, 1967, November 9, 1969, December 29, 1974; *Washington Post Book World,* October 12, 1969; *Kirkus Reviews,* August 1, 1974, April 15, 1976; *Psychology Today,* October, 1974; *New Yorker,* March 20, 1978.*

* * *

FARROW, James S.
See TUBB, E(dwin) C(harles)

* * *

FAUCHER, Real 1940-

PERSONAL: Born July 28, 1940, in New York, N.Y.; son of Joseph (an electrical engineer) and Mariette (Gagnon) Faucher; married Ginette Bureau (a writer); children: Glenn, Mona, Kevin. *Education:* University of Sherbrooke, B.A., 1976; graduate study at Concordia University, Montreal, Quebec. *Home:* 82 Main St. N., Windsor, Quebec, Canada J1S 2C6.

CAREER: General Motors Acceptance Corp., New York, N.Y., accountant in computer study group, 1959-65; Eastern Townships School Commission, Windsor, Quebec, teacher, 1965—. Poet; gives poetry readings. *Military service:* U.S. Army, Infantry, 1957-65; became first lieutenant.

WRITINGS: Fires and Crucifixions (poetry chapbook), Samisdat Press, 1979. Contributor of more than two hundred poems to magazines in Canada and the United States.

WORK IN PROGRESS: Stone Totems and Other Poems.

SIDELIGHTS: Faucher comments: "I enjoy getting my feelings on paper. I like teaching and travel. I want my poetry to shock people—whether they agree with me or not—and feel that poets should try to reach the common man, and not just an elite."

* * *

FAY, Stanley
See STANLEY, Fay Grissom (Shulman)

* * *

FAZAKAS, Ray 1932-

PERSONAL: Surname is pronounced Fa-*zay*-kas; born January 23, 1932, in Saskatchewan, Canada; son of Andras (a homesteader) and Elizabeth (Daradics) Fazakas; married

Beverley Greene (a music teacher), July 25, 1958; children: David, Sandra, Derek. *Education:* McMaster University, B.A., 1954; attended Osgoode Hall Law School, 1954-58. *Home:* 60 Marion Ave. S., Hamilton, Ontario, Canada L8S 1T6. *Office:* 942 King St. W., Hamilton, Ontario, Canada L8S 1K8.

CAREER: Fazakas & Nash, Hamilton, Ontario, barrister and solicitor, 1958—. *Member:* Canadian Bar Association, Writers Union of Canada, Law Society of Upper Canada, Genealogical Society of Ontario, Ontario Historical Society, Hamilton Law Association.

WRITINGS: The Donnelly Album, Macmillan, 1977.

WORK IN PROGRESS: Novelistic treatments, television scripts, and screenplays, all based on the Donnelly story.

SIDELIGHTS: Fazakas told *CA:* "*The Donnelly Album* was born of a hobby. Years ago I set out to document the story of the Donnellys and lay to rest much of the controversy surrounding them. It is a true story. Beginning with the hacking out of forest clearings in the Queen's Bush of Upper Canada in pioneer days, it culminates in the massacre of most of the family one wintry February night in 1880 at the height of the reign of Queen Victoria, and ends when the last of the Donnellys dies with the coming of the automobile.

"In the story is mirrored a microcosm of everyday life in Ontario from pioneer times to the modern age. Thus the book is not just the strange account of an Irish faction feud transplanted to Canada, nor just the tale of the sensational murders of almost all the members of a family by a vigilante mob composed of the fellow parishioners of the victims, nor an officially unsolved murder case around which controversy swirls to this day.

"From fatal duels at logging bees the story passes through the American Civil War period in Canada, the coming of the railway age, the brawling stagecoach era in the straggling towns and villages of that part of the country, to the dignified assize trials and court hearings in the city of Toronto. In it is caught the flavor of the make-up of Canadian society, so akin to the American and yet so different, focused into an exciting story about a brash father, a scheming mother, and their seven unruly sons.

"The book is illustrated with photographs, drawings, and sketches collected over many years of ongoing research. Most Canadians are familiar with the Donnelly story and many become intensely fascinated with it."

*   *   *

FEIFEL, Herman   1915-

PERSONAL: Born November 4, 1915, in New York, N.Y.; son of Jacob (a business merchant) and Rebecca (Katz) Feifel. *Education:* City College (now of the City University of New York), B.A., 1935; Columbia University, M.A., 1939, Ph.D., 1948. *Home:* 360 South Burnside Ave., Los Angeles, Calif. 90036. *Office:* 425 South Hill St., Los Angeles, Calif. 90013.

CAREER: Winter Veterans Administration Hospital, Topeka, Kan., supervisory clinical psychologist, 1950-54; Veterans Administration Mental Hygiene Clinic, Los Angeles, Calif., research and clinical psychologist, 1954-59; New York University Research Center for Mental Health, New York, N.Y., visiting senior research scientist, 1960-61; Veterans Administration Outpatient Clinic, Los Angeles, chief psychologist, 1961—; University of Southern California, Los Angeles, clinical professor of psychiatry and the behavioral sciences, 1965—. Diplomate in clinical psychology of Ameri-

can Board of Professional Psychology. Visiting professor of psychology at University of Southern California, 1966-67; Sigma Xi national lecturer, 1975-77. Member of board of governors, academic affairs, of University of Judaism, 1968—; member of board of directors of International Work Group on Death, Dying, and Bereavement, 1979—. *Military service:* U.S. Army Air Forces, 1942-44. U.S. Army, 1944-46; became captain.

MEMBER: American Psychological Association (fellow; president of division of adult development and aging, 1974-75, and board of professional affairs, 1975-77), American Association for the Advancement of Science, Los Angeles County Psychological Association (president, 1964-65). *Awards, honors:* Distinguished scientific achievement award from California Psychological Association, 1974; book of the year award from *American Journal of Nursing,* 1977, for *New Meanings of Death;* Harold M. Hildreth Award from American Psychological Association, 1978; distinguished human service award from Yeshiva University, 1979.

WRITINGS: (Editor) *The Meaning of Death,* McGraw, 1959; (contributor) Albert Deutsch and Helen Fishman, editors, *Encyclopedia of Mental Health,* F. Watts, 1963; *New Meanings of Death,* McGraw, 1977. Consulting editor to *Hospital and Community Psychiatry,* 1979—; advisory editor of *Journal of Clinical and Consulting Psychology,* 1964-74, 1979—.

WORK IN PROGRESS: Research on coping styles and strategies in dealing with illness, old age, and death.

SIDELIGHTS: Herman Feifel is a leading figure in the modern death psychology movement. When Feifel was looking for a publisher for his first book, *The Meaning of Death,* he had trouble interesting anyone in the manuscript because in the 1950's death was still regarded as a taboo subject. The book, which was published in 1959, is now considered a classic in thanatology. According to V. R. Pine, "most authorities agree that it was the most important single work that familiarized the scholarly community with the issues and concerns of dying and death. Moreover, it provided a landmark of legitimacy for the newly emerging field."

The study of death is more acceptable now than it was twenty years ago, but there are still those who wonder why this morbid topic must be dwelt on. In an article in *Death Education,* Feifel sought to answer the question: Why should we be interested in death? "The first answer is personal," he explained. "Death is the greatest democracy of all, and we shall all be observer-participants in it. The second is that we live in an era dominated by a climax of mathematical physics, creation of the H-bomb, bringing along with it a general pessimism concerning the future of humanity. Third, to fully understand ourselves as humans, we must examine the talent that distinguishes us from all other species—our ability to conceptualize a future."

BIOGRAPHICAL/CRITICAL SOURCES: Time, January 11, 1960; *Christian Century,* September 21, 1960; *Death Education,* Number 1, 1977.

*   *   *

FENNELL, William Oscar   1916-

PERSONAL: Born January 10, 1916, in Brantford, Ontario, Canada; son of Harry Stark (a grocer) and Wilto Claire (Charters) Fennell; married Jean Louise Birkenshaw (an office manager), September 1, 1948; children: Paul William, Catherine Louise Fennell Arbour, Stephen Harry. *Education:* University of Toronto, B.A. (with honors), 1939;

Emmanuel College, Victoria University, diploma in theology, 1942; Union Theological Seminary, New York, N.Y., S.T.M., 1950; attended University of Strasbourg, 1950-51, University of Freiburg, 1961, and University of London, 1970-71. *Home:* 50 Wendover Rd., Toronto, Ontario, Canada M8X 2L3. *Office:* Emmanuel College, University of Toronto, 75 Queen's Park Cres., Toronto, Ontario, Canada M5S 1K7.

CAREER: Ordained minister of United Church of Canada, 1942; pastor of United Church of Canada in Levack, Ontario, 1942-44; University of Toronto, Emmanuel College, Toronto, Ontario, lecturer in Christian doctrine and senior tutor at men's residence, 1946, professor of systematic theology, 1957—, college registrar, 1956-60, director of graduate studies, 1962-70, principal, 1972—. Warfield Lecturer at Princeton Theological Seminary, 1974. Staff member at International Students' Service Seminar in Pontigny, France, 1950; chairman of national executive of Student Christian Movement of Canada, 1951-54; chairman of Church and University Commission of Canadian Council of Churches, 1957-59, and Faith and Order Commission, 1964-67; leader of Canadian delegation to International Assembly of World University Service in Nigeria, 1959; chairman of Committee on Cooperation in Theological Education in Toronto, 1967-70; member of board of directors of Fund for Theological Education, 1972-75. *Military service:* Royal Canadian Naval Volunteer Reserve, chaplain, 1953-57.

MEMBER: American Association of Theological Schools (fellow), Canadian Theological Society (president, 1962-63), Karl Barth Society. *Awards, honors:* D.D. from United College, Winnipeg, Manitoba, 1963, and University of Trinity College, Toronto, 1976.

WRITINGS: God's Intention for Man: Essays in Christian Anthropology, Wilfrid Laurier University Press, 1977.

Contributor: W. S. Morris, editor, *The Unity We Seek,* Ryerson, 1962; M. E. Marty and D. G. Peerman, editors, *The Theology of True Secularity in New Theology,* Volume II, Macmillan, 1965; P. C. Empie and J. I. McCord, editors, *A Re-Examination of Lutheran and Reformed Traditions,* Augsburg, 1966; Bernard Murchland, editor, *The Meaning of the Death of God,* Random House, 1967; George Johnston and Wolfgang Ruth, editors, *The Church in the Modern World: Essays in Honour of J. S. Thomson,* Ryerson, 1967; D. S. Schuller, M. P. Strohman, and M. L. Brekke, editors, *Ministry in America,* Harper, 1980. Contributor of articles and reviews to theology journals and *Canadian Forum.* Associate editor of *Canadian Journal of Theology,* 1961-68.

WORK IN PROGRESS: Contribution to *Reflections on the Life and Work of Richard Watson (1781-1833).*

SIDELIGHTS: Fennell told *CA:* "An invitation to deliver the Warfield Lectures at Princeton Theological Seminary in 1974 gave me an opportunity to develop more systematically and comprehensively than before my interest in Christian anthropology. In my book *God's Intention for Man,* which contains the Princeton lectures, I attempt to develop the thesis that a proper Christian understanding of man is to think of his vocation and destiny not in terms of 'deification' but of 'homonization.' God is, so to speak, the Supreme humanist, intent not to absorb man within Himself, or to use him as a stage for fulfilling His divine life, but rather, to serve man in the realization of his whole human potential as a creature.

"Of course, to acknowledge God as God, in worship and service, is the first and necessary step in the achievement of such a destiny. It is indeed the source of man's freedom to be creative in the world.

"In some such fashion, I seek to develop the theme first adumbrated in the published essay 'The Theological Foundation of True Secularity.' Christian theology demands no forsaking the world or human history in favor of some transcendent existence in 'another world beyond.' Rather, it speaks about the enduring intention of God to redeem the world as a realm having meaning and purpose of its own. The implications of such views for an understanding of the relations of Church and culture and of Church and society are large and of fundamental importance."

AVOCATIONAL INTERESTS: Gardening.

*   *   *

FENNER, James R.
   See TUBB, E(dwin) C(harles)

*   *   *

FERGUSON, Pamela   1943-

PERSONAL: Born December 10, 1943, in Chihuahua, Mexico; came to the United States in 1978; daughter of Louis Wright (a geologist) and Pansy (Coombe) Ferguson. *Education:* Attended University of Cape Town, 1961-63, and Shiatsu Education Center of America, 1978-80. *Religion:* Yoga. *Residence:* New York, N.Y. *Agent:* John Hawkins, Paul R. Reynolds, Inc., 12 East 41st St., New York, N.Y. 10017.

CAREER: London Times, London, England, industrial writer, 1967; *Marketing,* London, associate editor, 1968; free-lance writer in the Middle East, 1968-72 and 1975-77; Paul Wimvex Marketing Communications, London, account director, 1972-73; *Adweek,* London, staff writer, 1974-75; full-time writer, 1978—. *Member:* Institute of Public Relations (England; associate member).

WRITINGS—All fiction: The Palestine Problem, Martin Brian & O'Keefe, 1973; *The Pipe Dream,* Everest Books, 1974; *The Olympic Mission,* Everest Books, 1976; *Dominion,* Atheneum, 1978; *The Sacrifice,* Atheneum, 1981. Contributor to journals in the United States and England.

WORK IN PROGRESS: Two books; a play.

SIDELIGHTS: Pamela Ferguson told *CA:* "I started studying the healing art of zen shiatsu to balance my writing, and will write books on healing in the future. I am fanatic about personal fitness; I run and practice hatha yoga daily."

*   *   *

FIELD, George B(rooks)   1929-

PERSONAL: Born October 25, 1929, in Providence, R.I.; son of Winthrop Brooks (an estate manager) and Pauline (Woodworth) Field; married Sylvia Farrior Smith, June 23, 1956 (divorced October, 1979); children: Christopher, Natasha. *Education:* Massachusetts Institute of Technology, B.S., 1951; Princeton University, Ph.D., 1955. *Home:* One Louisburg Sq., Boston, Mass. 02108. *Office:* Harvard-Smithsonian, Center for Astrophysics, 60 Garden St., Cambridge, Mass. 02138.

CAREER: Princeton University, Princeton, N.J., assistant professor, 1957-62, associate professor of astronomy, 1962-65; University of California, Berkeley, professor of astronomy, 1965-72, head of department, 1970-71; Harvard University, Cambridge, Mass., professor of astronomy, 1972—, director of Center for Astrophysics, 1973—. *Member:* International Astronomical Union, American Astronomical Society, American Physical Society (fellow), American Association for the Advancement of Science, Astronomical Society of the Pacific, Sigma Xi. *Awards, honors:* Guggenheim fellow, 1960-61; public service medal from National Aeronautics & Space Administration, 1977; certificate from Smithsonian Institution, 1977.

WRITINGS: (With Halton Arp and John Bahcall) *The Redshift Controversy,* W. A. Benjamin, 1973; (contributor and editor with A. G. W. Cameron) *The Dusty Universe,* Neale Watson, 1975; (with Gerrit L. Verschuur and Cyril Ponnamperuma) *Cosmic Evolution: An Introduction to Astronomy,* Houghton, 1978.

Contributor: Lodewijk Woltjer, editor, *The Distribution and Motion of Interstellar Matter in Galaxies,* W. A. Benjamin, 1962; P. J. Brancazio and A. G. W. Cameron, editors, *The Origin of Atmosphere and Oceans,* Wiley, 1964; Brancazio and Cameron, editors, *Infrared Astronomy,* Gordon & Breach, 1968; Allan R. Sandage and Mary Sandage, editors, *Stars and Stellar Systems,* Volume IX, University of Chicago Press, 1968; Max Chretien, Stanley Deser, and Jack S. Goldstein, editors, *Astrophysics and General Relativity,* Gordon & Breach, 1968; Giuliano Toraldo di Francia, editor, *The Growth Points of Physics,* European Physical Society, 1969.

H. J. Habing, editor, *Interstellar Gas Dynamics,* Springer Verlag, 1970; B. T. Lynds, editor, *Dark Nebulae, Globules, and Protostars,* University of Arizona Press, 1971; W. C. Saslaw and K. C. Jacobs, editors, *The Emerging Universe,* University Press of Virginia, 1972; M. A. Gordon and L. E. Snyder, editors, *Molecules in the Galactic Environment,* Wiley, 1973; Geoffrey Iverson, Arnold Perlmutter, and Stephen Mintz, editors, *Studies in the Natural Sciences,* Volume III: *Fundamental Interactions in Physics and Astrophysics,* Plenum, 1973; M. S. Longair, editor, *Confrontation of Cosmological Theories With Observational Data,* D. Reidel, 1974; George Contopoulos, editor, *Highlights of Astronomy,* Volume III, D. Reidel, 1974; Roger Balian, Pierre Encrenaz, and James Lequeux, editors, *Les Houches Session XXVL: Atomic and Molecular Physics and the Interstellar Medium,* American Elsevier, 1975; E. H. Avrett, editor, *Frontiers of Astrophysics,* Harvard University Press, 1976. Contributor of nearly one hundred articles and reviews to scientific journals, including *American Scientist* and *Nature.*

SIDELIGHTS: Field told *CA:* "My interests have focused on the evolution of the universe. As spelled out in my text, *Cosmic Evolution,* it is now possible to discuss in terms of physical theory the systematic evolution of the universe from its origins in a big bang explosion some ten or twenty billion years ago, through the formation of galaxies like the Milky Way, to the origin of the sun and planets about five billion years ago. The origin of life on earth more than three billion years ago can be discussed within our present understanding of molecular biology. It is still unknown whether the sun is the only star out of the billions believed to be present within the observable universe which has a planet like the earth capable of sustaining life and whether, if there are other such planets in the universe, the earth is unique in actually harboring life.

"The hypothesis that the universe, galaxies, stars, planets, and life all evolve is not unique, in that there are other ways to explain what we observe in astronomy, geology, and biology. Nevertheless, the hypothesis of cosmic evolution is proving to be extremely fruitful in all of these areas. It brings order to a tremendous range of phenomena from quasars to fruit flies. Working within its general framework, scientists in various fields are led to frame research problems which,

when solved, usually provide further support to the evolutionary hypothesis. Thus, a comprehensive scientific view of the cosmos is available even to lay persons who are willing to read some not-so-trivial literature.

"What I have said does not imply that evolutionary theory is complete. There are several key questions which continue to trouble thoughtful scientists, and which ultimately, if not answered convincingly, could force a radical revision of our thinking. There are, in addition, other questions which are interesting and perhaps more important, which may not be answerable in scientific terms. I would phrase one such question: 'Why is there something rather than nothing?'"

*   *   *

FINLETTER, Thomas K(night)   1893-1980

OBITUARY NOTICE: Born November 11, 1893, in Philadelphia, Pa.; died April 24, 1980, in New York, N.Y. Lawyer, public servant, and author. In 1945 Finletter encouraged President Truman to strengthen America's air power. After directing the Marshall Plan in England, Finletter returned to the United States, whereupon President Truman appointed him secretary of the Air Force. He served in that capacity throughout the Korean War. Finletter was also internationally recognized for his pro-disarmament stance regarding nuclear weapons. Although his background in the military seemed to contradict his pacifist position, Finletter stressed that he believed in military defense and not the use of strength and power to threaten other nations. His many writings include *Survival in the Air Age.* Obituaries and other sources: *Who's Who in America,* 39th edition, Marquis, 1976; *The International Who's Who,* 41st edition, Europa, 1977; *New York Times,* April 25, 1980.

*   *   *

FOOT, Philippa Ruth   1920-

PERSONAL: Born October 3, 1920; daughter of William Sydney Bence and Esther (Cleveland) Bosanquet; married M. R. D. Foot, June 21, 1945 (marriage ended, 1960). *Education:* Somerville College, Oxford, B.A., 1942, M.A., 1946. *Home:* 612 Midvale Ave., Los Angeles, Calif. 90024.

CAREER: Oxford University, Somerville College, Oxford, England, lecturer in philosophy, 1947-49, tutor and fellow, 1949-69, vice-principal, 1967-69, senior research fellow, 1969—. Professor at University of California, Los Angeles, 1977—; lecturer in England, Mexico, Yugoslavia, Iceland, and Ireland. *Member:* British Academy (fellow).

WRITINGS: (Editor) *Theories of Ethics,* Oxford University Press, 1967; *Virtues and Vices,* University of California Press, 1978. Contributor of articles and reviews to philosophy journals.

WORK IN PROGRESS: Research on moral philosophy and Wittgenstein's later philosophy.

*   *   *

FORBIS, Judith   1934-

PERSONAL: Born October 29, 1934, in Bayshore, N.Y.; daughter of William L. (a contractor) and Audrey (a secretary; maiden name, Scott) Freni; married Donald L. Forbis (a rancher), March 15, 1958. *Education:* Attended Syracuse University. *Office address:* Ansata Arabian Stud, R.R. 4, Box 902, Lufkin, Tex. 75901; and Ansata Arabian Stud, R.F.D., Mena, Ark. 71953.

CAREER: U.S. Agency for International Development,

Washington, D.C., secretary in Ankara, Turkey, 1957-58; Ansata Arabian Stud, Lufkin, Tex., and Mena, Ark., co-owner, 1958—. Trustee of Arabian Horse Trust. *Member:* Pyramid Society.

WRITINGS: Hoofbeats Along the Tigris, J. A. Allen, 1970; (with Walter Schimanski) *The Royal Arabians of Egypt and the Stud of Henry B. Babson,* Thoth, 1976; *The Classic Arabian Horse,* Liveright, 1976; *Selective Breeding of Arabian Horses,* Norton, 1981; (editor) *Abbas Pasha Manuscript,* Thoth, 1981. Contributor to *Encyclopedia of the Horse* and *Reference Handbook of Straight Egyptian Horses.* Contributor to horse journals, including *Arabian Horse World* and *Horse and Rider.* American editor of *Arabian.*

SIDELIGHTS: Judith Forbis told *CA:* "My life has always centered around horses. While living in Turkey I obtained my first Arabian mare, met my husband, and embarked on a lifelong career of riding, racing, breeding, and owning Arabian horses. Living from 1957 until 1973 in the Arab world provided the background of understanding this particular kind of horse from the viewpoint and in the surroundings of those who originally developed it. This led to the establishment of an Arabian horse ranch in America and to the perpetuation of bloodlines known as 'Egyptian' from stock derived from the Egyptian Agricultural Organization in Cairo. The Ansata Arabian Stud evolved from 1959 to the present day and is known throughout the world for its highly selective breeding program and Arabians of the foremost distinction.

"In writing about Arabian horses, I have always chosen to portray their dignity and grace, and to present these noble creatures in the proper perspective. They are a unique breed, and my life has been dedicated to achieving new heights in the art of Arabian horse breeding.

"Life with the Arabian horse has led me into many foreign countries, and allowed me to develop an artistic talent for painting and sculpting, as well as photography—all horse related, of course. In addition, the companionship and love provided by this particular breed of horse have taught me much about life itself. The Prophet Mohammed taught his followers: 'There is no beast on earth, nor bird which flieth with its wings, but the same is a people like you.' I have realized that our animal friends are individual entities having their own purpose in life and rights of their own. They too are struggling along the difficult road to perfection.

"In the days when 'the whole earth was of one language and speech . . . and all was one grand concord,' humans and animals moved in full accord with one another. One of my lifelong goals is eventually to produce a book which can convincingly convey to everyone the necessity that we learn to move in genuine fellowship with our animal friends."

*   *   *

FORRESTER, Helen
See BHATIA, Jamunadevi

*   *   *

FRAYNE, June   1924-
(June Callwood)

PERSONAL: Born June 2, 1924, in Chatham, Ontario, Canada; daughter of Harold (a manufacturer) and Gladys (an office manager; maiden name, LaVoie) Callwood; married Trent Gardiner Frayne, May 13, 1944; children: Jill Callwood, Brant Homer, Jennifer Ann, Casey Robert. *Education:* Educated in Canada. *Home and office:* 21 Hillcroft Dr., Islington, Ontario, Canada M9B 4X4.

CAREER: Brantford Expositor, Brantford, Ontario, reporter, 1941-43; *Toronto Globe and Mail,* Toronto, Ontario, reporter, 1943-45; free-lance writer, 1945—. Hostess of "In Touch," a television program of Canadian Broadcasting Corp. (CBC-TV), 1975-78. Founder of Yorkville Digger House, 1967; founder and past president of Nellie's (a shelter for women), 1974; founding member of Justice for Children (president, 1979-80). Past president of Learnxs Foundation; member of board of directors of Writers' Development Trusts, 1977-80. Executive of Canadian Council of Christians and Jews, 1979-81. Director of Canadian Society for the Abolition of the Death Penalty, 1980.

MEMBER: Writers Union of Canada (founding member; second vice-chairman, 1978; first vice-chairman, 1979; chairman, 1980), Canadian Civil Liberties Union (vice-president, 1965-80), Periodical Writers Association of Canada (vice-president, 1976), Council Amnesty. *Awards, honors:* Named woman of the year by B'nai B'rith, 1969; award of merit from city of Toronto, Ontario, 1974; member of Order of Canada, 1978; humanitarian award from Canadian Council of Christians and Jews, 1978.

WRITINGS—All as June Callwood: (With Marian Hillard) *A Woman Doctor Looks at Life and Love,* Doubleday, 1957; *Love, Hate, Fear, and Anger,* Doubleday, 1964; (with Charles W. Mayo) *Mayo: The Story of My Family and Career,* Doubleday, 1968; (with Marvin Zuker) *Canadian Woman and the Law,* Copp Clark, 1971; (with Barbara Walters) *How to Talk to Practically Anybody About Practically Anything,* Doubleday, 1973; (with Judianne Densen-Gerber) *We Mainline Dreams,* Doubleday, 1974; (with Zuker) *The Law Is Not for Women,* Pitman, 1976; (with Otto Preminger) *Otto Preminger Remembers,* Doubleday, 1977; *The Naughty Nineties: Canada's Illustrated Heritage,* McClelland & Stewart, 1978; *The Canadas,* Doubleday, 1980. Author of television and radio scripts. Author of "The Informal . . . ," a column in *Toronto Globe and Mail,* 1973-78. Contributor to magazines.

SIDELIGHTS: Callwood commented to *CA:* "My current project is to finish a history book that I've been writing intermittently for ten years. I also hope to reissue *Love, Hate, Fear, and Anger,* updated with a new title. Also, I'm involved in two projects growing out of Nellie's: one, a protected boarding house for women, and the other, a 'mothering house and baby house,' which will serve adolescents younger than sixteen who keep their babies.

"I have given up the following: yearning to become a glider pilot or downhill skier, and attempting a chocolate souffle."

*   *   *

FRAZIER, Kendrick (Crosby)   1942-

PERSONAL: Born March 19, 1942, in Windsor, Colo.; son of Francis Elliott (a pharmacist) and Sidney Lenore (Crosby) Frazier; married Ruth Toelle (an executive of a non-profit Indian child sponsorship program), September 10, 1964; children: Christopher Kendrick, Michele Lenore. *Education:* University of Colorado, B.A., 1964; Columbia University, M.S., 1966. *Home and office:* 3025 Palo Alto Dr. N.E., Albuquerque, N.M. 87111. *Agent:* Harold Matson Co., Inc., 22 East 40th St., New York, N.Y. 10016.

CAREER: Greeley Daily Tribune, Greeley, Colo., reporter, 1962; *Colorado Transcript,* Golden, news editor, 1963, 1964; United Press International (UPI), Denver, Colo., news reporter, 1964-65; National Academy of Sciences, Washington, D.C., editor of *News Report,* 1966-69; *Science News,* Washington, D.C., earth sciences editor, 1969-70, managing editor, 1970-71, editor, 1971-77, contributing editor, 1977—. Guest lecturer at George Washington University, 1974-77; adjunct instructor for University of Missouri, 1975-77; gives seminars. Member of editorial advisory board of Prometheus Books.

MEMBER: National Association of Science Writers, American Polar Society, Society of Professional Journalists, Society of the South Pole, Committee for Scientific Investigation of Claims of the Paranormal (fellow; member of executive council, 1977—; member of board of directors, 1978—), Sigma Delta Chi. *Awards, honors:* Pulitzer traveling fellowship, 1966; Robert E. Sherwood scholarship, 1966.

WRITINGS: (Contributor) James Christian, editor, *Extra-Terrestrial Intelligence: The First Encounter,* Prometheus Books, 1976; *The Violent Face of Nature: Severe Phenomena and Natural Disasters,* Morrow, 1979; *The Changing Sun,* Prentice-Hall, 1981.

Author of "Looking Out," a weekly astronomy column syndicated by Newspaper Enterprise Association, 1969-70. Contributor to *Encyclopaedia Britannica Yearbook of Science and the Future.* Contributor of several dozen articles to scientific journals, popular magazines, and newspapers, including *Mosaic, Smithsonian, Reader's Digest, Rocky Mountain, Science 80,* and *Science News.* Editor of *Skeptical Inquirer,* 1977—.

WORK IN PROGRESS: A book on paleo-Indian culture in the area of Chaco Canyon, N.M., A.D. 900-1250, for Norton; editing "a book of articles of skeptical inquiries into the paranormal and fringe-sciences," publication by Prometheus Books expected in 1981.

SIDELIGHTS: Frazier wrote: "Over the years I have covered dozens of developments in science, including the geological revolution brought about by sea-floor spreading and plate tectonics, unmanned missions to the planets, climate change, weather prediction and modification, forecasting of severe storms, the search for superheavy elements, earthquake prediction, tree ring research, icebergs for fresh water, and the philosophical implications of a future discovery of extra-terrestrial intelligence.

"I have covered scientific activities in such places as Israel and Mexico. In 1973 I traveled to Antarctica and the South Pole, covering the U.S. research program there.

"I am especially interested in science as an exciting and very human intellectual quest, especially in the earth and geophysical sciences. In recent years I have also become interested in public perceptions and misperceptions of science, in public acceptance of claims of paranormal phenomena and fringe-science (UFOs, astrology, psychics) despite the absence of any convincing scientific evidence for their existence, and in the related issues of the psychology of belief and the prevalence of anti-science, anti-intellectual attitudes. I am also interested in the history of science and ideas, in natural history, and in New World archaeology and archaeoastronomy."

AVOCATIONAL INTERESTS: Hiking, camping.

BIOGRAPHICAL/CRITICAL SOURCES: Science News, August 27, 1977; *Albuquerque Journal,* August 2, 1978; *Village Voice,* September 4, 1978; *New Mexico Independent,* December 14, 1979; *Denver Rocky Mountain News,* April 20, 1980; *Los Alamos Monitor,* May 8, 1980; *Technology Review,* June/July, 1980.

*   *   *

FREDERIKSEN, Martin W.   1930-1980

OBITUARY NOTICE: Born September 15, 1930, in Suma-

tra; died in a street accident, July 14, 1980. Historian, educator, and editor. Frederiksen was a Roman historian whose specialty was Campania. He taught at Oxford University's Worcester College, where he had also served as dean and tutor for admissions, and was a frequent visitor to the British School at Rome. From 1968 to 1974 he was the editor of the *Journal of Roman Studies* and chairman of the editorial board since 1976. At the time of his death he was editing and contributing to the *Cambridge Ancient History* and writing a book about Campania. Obituaries and other sources: *London Times,* July 23, 1980.

*   *   *

FREEMAN, Paul   1929(?)-1980

OBITUARY NOTICE: Born c. 1929 in Brooklyn, N.Y.; died August 10, 1980, in New York, N.Y. Artist. Freeman was a painter and sculptor whose works were exhibited at galleries in New York, Paris, and Jerusalem. A designer of textiles, book jackets, and ceramics, he was the author and illustrator of *An Introduction to Sigmund Freud, M.D., and Psychoanalysis.* He also illustrated an anthology of international folk songs, *Songs of Man.* Obituaries and other sources: *New York Times,* August 12, 1980.

*   *   *

FREGAULT, Guy   1918-1977

PERSONAL: Born June 16, 1918, in Montreal, Quebec, Canada; died December 13, 1977; son of Alfred and Lydia (Ouellette) Fregault; married Lilianne Rinfret, November 20, 1943; children: Michel-Guy. *Education:* University of Montreal, B.A., 1938, L. es L., 1940; Loyola University, Chicago, Ill., Ph.D., 1942. *Religion:* Roman Catholic. *Residence:* Sillery, Quebec, Canada.

CAREER: University of Montreal, Montreal, Quebec, professor of history, 1943-59, head of department and vice-dean of faculty of letters; University of Ottawa, Ottawa, Ontario, professor of history and head of department, 1959-61; Province of Quebec, Quebec City, deputy minister of cultural affairs, 1961-68, deputy minister of cultural affairs, 1970-75; Office of the Prime Minister, Quebec City, special adviser on linguistic policy and commissioner-general for cooperaiton with outside governments, 1969-70, special adviser on culture, 1975-77.

AWARDS, HONORS: Prix Duvernay from Societe Saint-Jean-Baptiste de Montreal, 1944, for *Iberville le conquerant;* prize from Academie francaise, 1969, for *Pierre le Moyne d'Iberville;* Prix Montcalm, 1969; Prix France-Quebec from Association des Ecrivains de Lang de Francaise and Province of Quebec, 1969, for *Le Dix-Huitieme Siecle canadien;* D.H.C. from University of Ottawa, University of Sainte-Anne, and University of Waterloo; medal from Societe Historique de Montreal; Prix David from Province of Quebec; Medialle Leo-Parizeau from Association Canadienne-Francaise pour l'Advancement des Sciences; prize from Foundation Therouanne.

WRITINGS—In English: *Canadian Society in the French Regime,* translated from the original *La Societe canadienne sous le regime francais,* Canadian Historical Association, 1954; *La Guerre de la conquete,* Fides, 1955, translation by Margaret M. Cameron published as *Canada: The War of the Conquest,* Oxford University Press, 1969.

In French: *Iberville le conquerant* (title means "Iberville the Conqueror"), Societe des Editions Pascal, 1944, 2nd edition published as *Pierre le Moyne d'Iberville,* Fides, 1968; *La*

Civilisation de la nouvelle-france (title means "The New France Civilization"), Societe des Editions Pascal, 1944; (with Michel Brunet and Marcel Trudel) *Histoire de Canada par les textes* (title means "Canadian History From the Texts"), Fides, 1952; *Le Grand Marquis: Pierre de Rigaud de Vaudreuil et la louisiane* (title means "The Great Marquis: Pierre de Rigaud de Vaudreuil and Louisianna"), Fides, 1952; (with wife, Lilianne Fregault) *Frontenac*, Fides, 1956; *Le Dix-Huitieme Siecle canadien* (title means "The Eighteenth Canadian Century"), Editions H.M.H., 1968; *Chronique des annees perdues* (title means "A Chronicle of Years"), Editions Lemeac, 1976; *Lionel Groulx tel qu'en lui-meme* (title means "Lionel Groulx From the Inside"), Editions Lemeac, 1978. Also editor of *Francois Bigot: Administrateur francais* (title means "Francois Bigot: French Administrator"), two volumes, 1948. Contributor to history and literary journals.

SIDELIGHTS: Fregault's wife, Lilianne, commented to *CA:* "At Montreal University, Professor Fregault introduced historical method and the practice of the seminar. After organizing the studies in history he gathered all the professors into a department and was nominated its director in 1946. He left in 1959 to reorganize the same department at Ottawa University.

"All of my husband's books are described as masterpieces of scholarship, but he was also one of the most gifted French-Canadian writers. The beauty of his prose, his elegance and power with the words, the plan, the order of his writings, his conciseness, and all the qualities you can find in the best French masters in Paris, you can likewise find in Fregault, without imitation. He was a born writer. On the day of his death, he was reading Barres and Sainte-Beuve.

"For background on his books, we depended mostly on the Library of Congress, the Goughton Library on the campus of Harvard University, the public library of Boston, Huntington Library, and the Cabildo, New York Library. They were the sanctuaries where we could find abundant material, so much comfort and facilities that even those years of tense work and near poverty remained for us beautiful memories."

[Sketch verified by wife, Lilianne Fregault]

*   *   *

FRENCH, David 1939-

PERSONAL: Born January 18, 1939, in Coley's Point, Newfoundland, Canada; son of Edgar Garfield (a carpenter) and Edith (Benson) French; married Leslie Gray (a dance teacher), January 5, 1978. *Education:* Studied acting under Al Saxe in Toronto, 1958, at Pasadena Playhouse, 1959, and at Roy Lawler Acting School, Toronto, 1960. *Home:* 254 Brunswick Ave., Toronto, Ontario, Canada M5S 2M7.

CAREER: Canadian Broadcasting Corp. (CBC-TV and -Radio), Toronto, Ontario, actor in plays, 1960-65, writer of radio and television scripts, 1962-72; writer, 1972—. *Awards, honors:* Chalmers Award for best Canadian play from Ontario Arts Council, 1973, for "Of the Fields, Lately"; Lieutenant Governor's Award, 1974, for "Of the Fields, Lately"; Canada Council grants, 1974 and 1975.

WRITINGS—Plays: *Leaving Home* (two-act; first produced in Toronto, Ontario, at Tarragon Theatre, May 16, 1972; produced in New York, N.Y., at Theatre of Riverside Church, November 12, 1974), New Press, 1972, S. French, 1976; *Of the Fields, Lately* (two-act; first produced in Toronto, Ontario, at Tarragon Theatre, September 29, 1973; produced on Broadway at Century Theatre, May 27, 1980),

New Press, 1975, S. French, 1977; *One Crack Out* (three-act; first produced in Toronto, Ontario, at Tarragon Theatre, May 24, 1975; produced Off-Broadway at Phoenix Theatre, January 16, 1978), New Press, 1976; (translator) Anton Chekov, *The Seagull* (four-act; translation first produced in Toronto, Ontario, at Tarragon Theatre, June 4, 1977), General Publishing, 1977; *Jitters* (three-act; first produced in Toronto, Ontario, at Tarragon Theatre, February 16, 1979; produced on Broadway, 1981), Talon, 1980.

Television plays; all produced by Canadian Broadcasting Corp. (CBC-TV), unless otherwise noted: "Beckons the Dark River," 1962; "The Willow Harp," 1963; "A Ring for Florie," 1964; "After Hours," 1964; "Sparrow on a Monday Morning," Westinghouse Broadcasting Corp., 1967; "A Token Gesture," 1970; "A Tender Branch," 1972; "The Happiest Man in the World" (adaptation of the short story by Hugh Garner), 1972.

Radio plays; all broadcast by Canadian Broadcasting Corp. (CBC-Radio): "Angeline," 1967; "Invitation to a Zoo," 1967; "Winter of Timothy," 1968.

Author of *A Company of Strangers* (novel), 1968. Work represented in *In First Flowering,* edited by Anthony Frisch, Kingswood House, 1956. Contributor of short stories to magazines, including *Montrealer* and *Canadian Boy.*

WORK IN PROGRESS: "Me and T. S. Eliot," a comedy, completion expected in 1981.

SIDELIGHTS: "Leaving Home," French's first stage play, concerns a family's frustration with moving from their home in Newfoundland to Toronto. Their sense of displacement aggravates normal family tensions, and bitter arguments result. The play deals mainly with a father and son relationship fraught with conflict. Finally, the son leaves home and the father remains behind hopeless and anguished.

French's next play, "Of the Fields, Lately," continues the exploration of the relationship between the father and son after the elder's death. "This lyrical play is actually an extended flashback that meticulously traces the incidents that day by day, year by year have built up a wall between the two men," explained Michiko Kakutani in the *New York Times.* The play also shows what familial relations might have been if the father and son had reconciled their differences. Such a glimpse makes the son's concluding monologue all the more poignant.

"One Crack Out," the author's following endeavor for the stage, was dubbed by Richard Eder as "a dab of melodrama spread upon a slice of life." The play chronicles how Charlie, a has-been pool hustler, regains enough courage and confidence to meet Bulldog, a cruel, vindictive debt collecter, in a pool-game showdown. Charlie's devoted wife and a reluctantly sympathetic pimp support him in his struggle against his tormentor.

"Jitters" is a backstage comedy, a play within a play, which records the story of a group of actors who have the "jitters" four days before their play is to open. Excitement is also high as a big Broadway producer is expected to be in the audience. With both humor and sentimentality, French explores the personal aspirations and problems of each actor as the fateful day approaches. "Jitters" provoked Mel Gussow to claim that it "is an almost perfect comedy of its kind."

BIOGRAPHICAL/CRITICAL SOURCES: New York Times, January 18, 1978, November 6, 1979, March 12, 1980, April 15, 1980.

FRIEDE, Eleanor Kask 1920-

PERSONAL: Surname is pronounced *Free*-da; born November 12, 1920, in Rochester, N.Y.; daughter of John and Claire (Kassick) Kask; married William H. Pearsall, February 6, 1943 (divorced March 13, 1946); married Joachim Probst, September 4, 1950 (divorced January 27, 1951); married Donald Friede (deceased). *Education:* Hofstra University, B.A. (cum laude), 1942. *Home:* 45 West 12th St., New York, N.Y. 10011; and Dune Rd., Bridgehampton, N.Y. 11932. *Office:* Delacorte Press, 1 Dag Hammarskjold Plaza, New York, N.Y. 10017.

CAREER: McGraw-Hill Book Co., New York City, copywriter, 1942-46; Funk & Wagnalls Co., New York City, assistant to president, 1946-51; Pellegrini & Cudahy, New York City, advertising and publicity manager, 1951-52; World Publishing Co., New York City, in charge of advertising, publicity, and promotion, 1952-61; Macmillan Publishing Co., New York City, marketing director, 1966-68, editor, 1968-71, senior editor, 1971-72; Eleanor Friede, Inc., New York City, independent publisher associated with Macmillan Publishing Co. and Delacorte Press, 1973—. Associate of Creative Enterprises, Inc., 1973-78. *Member:* International P.E.N., National Organization for Women, Wings Club, Ninety Nines.

WRITINGS: (Editor with husband, Donald Friede) *La Bonne Table*, Simon & Schuster, 1963.

AVOCATIONAL INTERESTS: Flying her own plane, travel (Europe, especially France), gardening, cooking, reading.

*   *   *

FRIEDMAN, Michael H(enry) 1945-

PERSONAL: Born February 5, 1945, in Jersey City, N.J.; son of Meyer (a lawyer) and Rose (Siegel) Friedman; married Mary Lusky (a professor of Spanish). *Education:* Columbia University, A.B., 1966, M.A., 1968, Ph.D. (with distinction), 1978. *Home:* 611 Park St., Ripon, Wis. 54971. *Office:* Department of English, Ripon College, Ripon, Wis. 54971.

CAREER: Teacher of English at Columbia University, summer, 1970, Bronx Community College, 1970, Stevens Institute of Technology, 1971-73, Nassau Community College, 1976, and Tufts University, 1977-78; Ripon College, Ripon, Wis., assistant professor of English, 1980—. *Member:* Modern Language Association of America.

WRITINGS: The Making of a Tory Humanist: William Wordsworth and the Idea of Community, Columbia University Press, 1979. Contributor to journals, including *Polit, Wordsworth Circle,* and *Science and Society*.

WORK IN PROGRESS: A Death of Tragedy: William Wordsworth's Conception of the Poet's Vocation; research on the political vision of William Blake.

SIDELIGHTS: Friedman wrote: "I am interested in the inter-relationships between history, society, the poet's psyche, and the finished work of literature. Lionel Trilling taught me to be aware of the moral significance of the literary work. He taught me too of Freud's greatness and literary significance.

"American scholars have neglected the social significance of great works of literature. I hope to help redress this neglect. My major interest is in the first generation of English Romantic poets—Blake, Wordsworth, and Coleridge."

FRIEDMAN, Rose D(irector)

PERSONAL: Born in Poland; married Milton Friedman (an economist), June 25, 1938; children: Janet, David. *Education:* Attended Reed College; University of Chicago, Ph.B., 1932, graduate studies, 1932-36. *Agent:* c/o Laura Schneider, Harcourt Brace Jovanovich, Inc., 757 Third Ave., New York, N.Y. 10017.

CAREER: Writer.

WRITINGS: (Contributor) *Studies in Income and Wealth,* National Bureau of Economic Research, 1947; (with husband, Milton Friedman) *Capitalism and Freedom,* University of Chicago Press, 1963; *Poverty: Definition and Perspective,* American Enterprise Institute for Public Research, 1965; (with M. Friedman) *Free to Choose,* Harcourt, 1979. Contributor to magazines, including *Oriental Economist.*

SIDELIGHTS: Rose Friedman has collaborated with her husband, economist Milton Friedman, on two books. *Capitalism and Freedom* and *Free to Choose* advance her and Friedman's theories about capitalism and the free market. The couple believes the capitalist system should be permitted to operate through its own devices without government interference. Citing that governmental tampering with the economy caused the Great Depression, the Friedmans claim that the best government is the least government. They maintain that the social welfare system actually holds minorities back, instead of letting capitalism work in its own way to supply opportunities to those who will grasp them.

Capitalism and Freedom was widely reviewed. Many critics praised the volume for its clear presentation of important theories, but took umbrage at the Friedmans' "antigovernment extravagances," as A. P. Lerner of *American Economic Review* dubbed them. L. H. Keyserling strongly disagreed with the authors' postulates. In response to the economists' belief that government and not the free market caused the Depression, Keyserling quipped that "if a great fire catches us with an inadequate fire department, the remedy is to do away with fire engines, instead of preventing people from throwing lighted matches around in a paper factory." On the other hand, an *Economist* reviewer described the book as "stimulating" and remarked that it made "ideal reading . . . because it challenges the reader to sort out his own ideas more fundamentally."

The Friedmans' next joint effort, *Free to Choose,* received favorable reviews. *Business Week*'s William Wolman assessed the work as "highly worthwhile," adding that "indeed the very plainness of the language may end up as the book's principal virtue. It makes it possible to apprehend Friedmans' views more easily than ever before." The critic qualified his praise, however, stating that the book "does not provide the 'shock of recognition' about the weakness of the Keynesian welfare state that made the Friedmans' earlier book, *Capitalism and Freedom,* the success that it was."

BIOGRAPHICAL/CRITICAL SOURCES: Economist, February 16, 1963; *American Economic Review,* June, 1963; *American Sociological Review,* June, 1963; *Annals of the American Academy of Political and Social Science,* November, 1963; *Journal of Political Economy,* December, 1963; *Business Week,* January 21, 1980.*

*   *   *

FRIENDLY, Alfred 1911-

PERSONAL: Born December 30, 1911, in Salt Lake City, Utah; son of Edward and Harriet Friendly Rosenbaum; married Jean Ulman, July 23, 1937; children: Alfred, Jonathan, Lucinda, Nicholas, Victoria. *Education:* Amherst College, A.B., 1933. *Home:* 1645 31st St. N.W., Washington, D.C. 20007; and 47 Chenye Pl., London S.W.3, England.

CAREER: Washington Daily News, Washington, D.C., reporter, 1936-39; *Washington Post,* Washington, D.C., reporter, 1939-52, assistant managing editor, 1952-55, managing editor, 1955-66, vice-president and director, 1963-66, associate editor, 1966-71, correspondent, 1966-72. Washington correspondent for *London Financial Times,* 1949-52. Assistant to trustee for reorganization of Associated Gas and Electric Corp., 1940; director of overseas information for Economic Cooperation Administration (ECA), 1948-49; trustee of Amherst College, 1961-67. *Military service:* U.S. Army Air Forces, 1942-45; became major; received Legion of Merit. *Member:* American Society of Newspaper Editors (director, 1961-65), Phi Beta Kappa, Garrick Club, Gridiron Club. *Awards, honors:* L.H.D. from Amherst College, 1958; Pulitzer Prize for international reporting, 1968, for coverage of Arab-Israeli War; Sidney Hillman Foundation Award, 1971.

WRITINGS—Nonfiction: *The Guys on the Ground,* Duell, Sloane, 1944; (with Ronald Goldfarb) *Crime and Publicity: The Impact of News on the Administration of Justice,* Twentieth Century Fund, 1967; *Beaufort of the Admiralty: The Life of Sir Francis Beaufort, 1774-1857,* Random House, 1977; *The Dreadful Day: The Battle of Manzikert,* Hutchinson, 1981. Contributor to magazines, including *Economist, Smithsonian, Harper's,* and *Atlantic Monthly.*

SIDELIGHTS: Friendly commented: "A career as a newspaperman tends to teach you a little about everything, not a great deal about anything, but the technique of learning about something if you set your mind to it—a technique that helps if you decide to write a book."

*   *   *

FRINGS, Ketti 1915-

PERSONAL: Original given name, Katherine; born in 1915 in Columbus, Ohio; daughter of Guy Herbert (a salesman) and Pauline (Sparks) Hartley; married Kurt Frings (an agent), March 18, 1938; children: Kathie, Peter. *Education:* Attended Principia College, St. Louis, Mo.

CAREER: Writer. Advertising copywriter for L. Bamberger & Company (department store) in Newark, N.J.; worked for several advertising agencies in New York, N.Y., and as columnist, script writer, and ghost writer; feature writer for United Press International (UPI), 1950. *Member:* Dramatists Guild, Screen Writers Guild, League of New York Theatres. *Awards, honors:* Pulitzer Prize for drama and New York Drama Critics Circle Award, both 1958, both for "Look Homeward, Angel"; Martha Kinney Cooper Ohiana Award from Library Association, and named woman of the year by *Los Angeles Times,* both 1958; distinguished achievement award from Theta Sigma Phi.

WRITINGS: Hold Back the Dawn (novel), Duell, Sloan & Pearce, 1940; *God's Front Porch* (novel), Morrow, 1944; *Look Homeward, Angel* (three-act comedy-drama; adapted from the novel by Thomas Wolfe; first produced on Broadway at Ethel Barrymore Theatre, November 28, 1957; first broadcast by Columbia Broadcasting System, Inc. [CBS-TV], February 25, 1972), Samuel French, 1958. Also author of *To Paris With Love, Let the Devil Catch You, The Red Sash,* and *The Man Who Waited.*

Plays: "Mr. Sycamore," first produced in New York, N.Y.,

at Guild Theatre, November 13, 1942, released as screenplay by Film Ventures International, 1974; "The Long Dream," first produced on Broadway at Ambassador Theatre, February 17, 1960; (with Roger Hirshon) "Walking Happy," first produced on Broadway at Lunt-Fontanne Theatre, November 26, 1966; "Judgment at Nuremberg" (based on the motion picture by Stanley Kramer and Abby Mann), first produced on Broadway, 1970.

Screenplays: "Guest in the House," United Artists, 1944; "The Accursed," Paramount, 1949; "File on Thelma Jordan," Paramount, 1949; "The Country She Keeps," RKO, 1951; "Because of You," Paramount, 1952; "Come Back, Little Sheba," Paramount, 1952; "About Mrs. Leslie," Paramount, 1954; "Foxfire," Universal, 1955; "The Shrike," Universal, 1955. Also author of "Bernie," "Dark City," and "Lady of Burlesque."

Work represented in *Contemporary Drama: Fifteen Plays,* edited by E. Bradlee Watson and Benfield Pressey, Scribner, 1959.

Contributor of short stories and articles to periodicals, including *Saturday Evening Post, Good Housekeeping, Collier's,* and *McCall's.**

*   *   *

FROBISH, Nestle J(ohn) 1930-

PERSONAL: Born January 9, 1930, in Hawkins Gore, Vt.; son of John and Carnation (Colby) Frobish; married Alice Hawkes, April 13, 1965; children: Anna Rose, Susan. *Education:* Educated in Hawkins Gore, Vt. *Politics:* "Bipartisan." *Religion:* "Eclectic." *Agent:* Barry Vogel, P.O. Box 7, Ukiah, Calif. 95482. *Office address:* P.O. Box 94, Lyndonville, Vt. 05851.

CAREER: Worldwide Fair Play for Frogs Committee, Lyndonville, Vt., chairman, 1961—. *Member:* Newt Protection Society, Save the Efts League, Friends of Toads.

WRITINGS: (With Jerome R. Waldie) *Fair Play for Frogs,* Harcourt, 1977. Also author of *Frogdom Through the Ages,* 1981.

SIDELIGHTS: Frobish commented to *CA:* "My career has been devoted to getting a fair shake for the humble frog, and it began when I chanced to espy a bill introduced in the 1961 California general assembly permitting the taking of frogs by slingshot. Through my efforts, the author of that bill was eventually retired to private life, where he remains today, mired in iniquity and neglect."

The listing in Gale's *Encyclopedia of Associations* for Frobish's Worldwide Fair Play for Frogs Committee describes the organization as a group of "frog lovers united 'to protect the humble frog against undue harassment and extermination and to promote goodwill for the frog.'" The organization "maintains [a] Frog Lovers Hall of Shame 'for particularly obnoxious anti-frog people' [and] publishes [an] occasional newsletter."

BIOGRAPHICAL/CRITICAL SOURCES: Encyclopedia of Associations, 14th edition, Gale, 1980.

*   *   *

FRUM, Barbara 1937-

PERSONAL: Born September 8, 1937, in Niagara Falls, N.Y.; daughter of Harold and Florence (Hirschowitz) Rosberg; married Murray Frum (an executive), September 3, 1957; children: David, Linda, Matthew. *Education:* University of Toronto, B.A. (with honors), 1959. *Office address:*

Canadian Broadcasting Corp., Box 500, Terminal A, Toronto, Ontario, Canada M5W 1E6.

CAREER: Canadian Broadcasting Corp. (CBC), Toronto, Ontario, co-host and interviewer on television series, "The Way It Is" (later "Weekday"), beginning in 1967, host and interviewer on radio series, "As It Happens," 1971—. Host of television series, "The Barbara Frum Journal," 1971-72, "Barbara Frum," 1974, "2 North Series," and "Quarterly Report," 1978—. *Member:* Canadian Civil Liberties Association. *Awards, honors:* Memorial Award top prize for article writing from Media Club of Canada, 1971, for "One Hundred and Five Potential Women M.P.s"; awards from Association of Television and Radio Artists, 1974, 1975, 1979, and 1980, all for "As It Happens."

WRITINGS: As It Happened (interviews), McClelland & Stewart, 1976. Contributor of articles to newspapers and periodicals, including *Saturday Night, Macleans, Toronto Star,* and *Chatelaine.*

CA INTERVIEWS THE AUTHOR

Barbara Frum was interviewed by *CA* on April 30, 1980, in Toronto, Ontario, Canada.

CA: How did you get started in broadcasting?

FRUM: It's hard to answer that question, because there was no real plan. I started to submit articles, radio tapes, and magazine pieces all at the same time with the idea that I'd work as a free-lance writer. I found myself becoming rapidly organized by commitments and other people's schedules. So it was rather accidental.

There was a certain whimsical mentality behind the start, because I've never been trained as a journalist. I've had to learn on my feet, learn how to wing it. When I began in the middle 1960's it was still relatively easy to come in off the street and say, "I've got a story. Would you like to buy it?" And people bought it. That's how I started. I was young at the time and had the willingness to make the effort and see what happened.

CA: Weren't you in television before you came to radio?

FRUM: My first work was for the *Toronto Star.* At the same time that they bought a few pieces from me, I had submitted some tapes to the Canadian Broadcasting Corp. They called and asked if I would do mini-documentaries. So I did that at the same time that I was writing for the *Toronto Star.* I really got into television because of the radio, because of the combination, maybe. Somebody called me for a new television program and they hired me. I worked full time for television for two and one half years, and then went back to my free-lance writing. It was then in 1971 that I was asked to audition for "As It Happens."

CA: And you've been doing that ever since. Did you anticipate it would be so successful?

FRUM: The program had an underground reputation at the start. It was so much of a secret that people used to brag that they listened to the program and then be shocked that someone else did too, and be thrilled that someone they really liked had also discovered the program. So for the first three years it was fun because they had this little secret—they all listened to "As It Happens." We'd get letters from all across the United States saying, "This is incredible! We don't have anything like this here. How long have you been doing this?" It was like discovering something that's been there for thirty years, except that we had just started.

We could chart the evolution of our audience somewhat by the ratings. From the beginning the audience was young and underground in that it wasn't something that anybody ever wrote or talked about; it was just there. Then we went a little more mainstream and our audience became more established, a little older, and we started to get written about. Then we became, as I like to see it, a national institution. I think now that we're part of the Canadian map; we're just there. It took seven years, but now we're a fixture.

CA: Do you regard yourself as Canada's answer to Barbara Walters?

FRUM: When I do some public speaking, as I occasionally do, I always say that Barbara Walters is the Barbara Frum of the United States. I like her, and I've met her, but I don't think I'm anything like her, and I don't think she's anything like me. We do quite different things. I think the success of her interviews is based on her personality and the fascination of her interacting with the person she's interviewing. She's very visible in an interview and has much presence whereas I try to get in and out as quickly as possible in a question. I'm not trying to establish any persona of my own. I don't think most listeners would be able to sketch in who I am and what I'm like.

CA: But you do have a kind of presence. You seem a little more human than she.

FRUM: It could be that she is also affected by the kind of person she interviews. It's hard to have a lot of sympathy for Berjinsky if that's the caliber of people you're talking to. So perhaps it's because I get a chance to talk to more ordinary people, people of the earth. Also, I do more interviews than she does. I doubt if she does one a day, so I experience many more emotions over the course of a day.

CA: In your book, As It Happened, *you wrote that the radio program was successful because it had the essence of a wire-tap. Could such a show be done on television?*

FRUM: There are plans to put "As It Happens" on television, but I don't think it can have the same tone because of the intimacy of the radio and telephone combination. When I'm talking to a person on the air, I'm not aware of any paraphernalia. It's just my personality and my mentality trying to reach out across the ether through some wire, that I don't see, to reach them. So it's different when there is a camera in the way, when there are people watching, and when you're speaking into a camera that is right in front of you. On radio you can put your head down and let your mind fill in all the pieces. So although I think it can be technically accomplished, it won't have that wiretap tone of listening in because on the radio I just talk to them as if no one else were listening at all. I don't think about how the audience will react. I just fly by the seat of my pants and hope that my instincts are still working.

CA: How soon will they be creating such a program on television?

FRUM: I think there are plans to do a nightly affairs program on the CBC. They'll probably bring the person into the studio so that the interviewer will be able to see him or her. But sometimes that's a terrific disadvantage. It's very nice if the guy can break away from a busy day and interrupt what he's doing to talk to you for five minutes, if he doesn't have to make a big deal of packing up his life and coming down to a television studio.

CA: So it's much more immediate and has a certain amount of spontaneity on the radio.

FRUM: Right. It's immediate and it slides into the little chinks and cracks of an ordinary day.

CA: What will happen to "As It Happens" on radio?

FRUM: It will continue. It's not a question of one replacing the other. It will be a whole new show.

CA: What ingredients are necessary to become, as you say in your book, "a catalyst, a watchdog, an editor, a straight-person"?

FRUM: I always joke that the number one ingredient or number one priority in my job is the ability to sit on a chair for eight running hours. I joke with people that the reason I have this job is that they couldn't find anybody else to do it. And I'm sure a lot of people who find themselves in rather demanding spots feel the same way. It's not that I'm so terrific, it's just that nobody else wanted to do this. But there's something to stamina, after all, to possess enough determination and patience to do it. That's part of it. You have to really listen to what people say. And I don't have to tell you just how few interviewers really listen.

CA: You also describe yourself as a kind of "terrier," which gives me the impression of someone who is unrelentless, but not formidable, and still sympathetic.

FRUM: I think it's that I can't stand it when someone's trying to put something over on me. I can't buy it and I can't bear it; and not just on my own, but for the audience. It's almost an ombudsman feeling. My mother tells me I used to argue about everything; maybe it's as simple as that. My mother's teasing me a bit, but she says I never stopped asking questions as a child, and my father claimed I never stuck around for the answers.

CA: Phoning out on the program, you stated in your book, is a breakthrough in radio in North America. Can you explain that?

FRUM: Before I did the radio show and before I did television, I wrote about both media. I wrote about television in *Saturday Night* magazine once a month, and I wrote about radio once a week in the *Toronto Star*. That was during the heyday of the phone-in shows: the loudmouth talk show hosts who took poor defenseless people and their problems out of a bored and miserable day and turned their needs and loneliness back on to the people themselves. They used it against the caller to entertain the audience. It was cheap radio. It was also brilliant because all you needed was a phone and a board that the telephone company gave you anyway, and you could very cheaply entertain people by abusing a few callers. People loved it, and obviously didn't mind the abuse because they kept calling. And I felt, when I was writing about it, that the format was just about exhausted. That was the middle 1960's. And of course it still survives. It goes on, but it's limiting because in the end you only get the people who call. If you do sex shows, for example, you're going to get a lot of hung-up people calling, and if you do an argumentative show, you're going to get people with grudges and grievances. When you phone out, however, you get your pick. You decide who gets air time.

The actual idea of phoning out came from a West German program that was done over their public network station. Someone from the CBC heard it and brought the idea to Canada. It wasn't an evening show and it wasn't a big news show; it was really an afternoon show intended, I believe, to amuse housewives. But it was, nevertheless, a phone-out

show. We modified the West German approach, though. They used a lot of music in their format, and we did in the beginning too, but gradually it became an all talk, all news show.

CA: This isn't being done in the United States, however.

FRUM: National Public Radio has copied much of our format, but they've changed it. They don't do as many interviews as we do, and they do a lot more production pieces where a producer has an idea and puts some script and tape together to make a show.

CA: So Canadians were the first on this scale?

FRUM: Yes, and we've had a lot of imitators.

CA: Is the program still the "iconoclastic, zippy" program that you described in your book or has it gone stale?

FRUM: I think what has happened is that it is no longer an underground program, nor is it a break-ground program. It's established now. It has tons of imitators. At this point I think it's a service program: it's for kids who have a project tomorrow in current affairs, it's for high-school kids who have to be informed, it's for people who would rather listen to the radio and get their own sense of what's happening today instead of getting it third-hand from a wire service. I think it's mainstream. I don't mean to suggest that it's boring or tiresome, because it's still zippy and tough and it's got energy. But it's a more mature show at this point.

CA: What about the funny sidelights, the crazies, the UFO nuts?

FRUM: No, we don't get the kooks anymore. We look just as hard, but we don't know quite what it is. Maybe the world went a little sour and a little bit serious. The UFO craze burned itself out, and so did all those people who claimed they saw the Loch Ness monster. People always asked me about the kooks and whether I was exploiting them. I argued that those people were in fact promoting themselves; they wanted some attention and wanted the world to notice them so that they could feel they had some reality. Maybe we're not finding those kooks anymore because the climate has changed and we're not attuned to what's out there.

CA: What about the idea of writing another book? You've done well with this one.

FRUM: When I first did the book, everybody immediately asked when I was going to do another. But it was so difficult. I'd like to think it was easy when it was all done, but it just wasn't so.

CA: How do you mean?

FRUM: First of all, how do you translate sound into print? How do you put it down on paper so that people who heard the interview originally can hear it again? And how do you make it come out like sound for people who've never heard it at all? How do you convey the pace, the frenetic pace of our day, the pressure of our job? How do you convey that in print, so you can read it slowly and make it sound leisurely? I had to get that kind of staccato effect in my writing.

CA: So how did you do it? How long did it take?

FRUM: It took about four months altogether: about eight weeks to actually do it, and then the other two months to write it. I transcribed maybe two thousand interviews. I did an initial pull of the ones I thought would work. Some did, but a lot of them didn't. So I'd leave the ones that didn't, and

I'd do another pull. I had to find something that I remembered liking enough to want to talk about, but also something that would come through on the page. The Yevtushenko interview that I referred to in the book is a case in point. That was one of the most marvelous days of my life. This man was a giant; he was a bear. He came to the interview in his muskrat otter coat and hat with the son of a friend of his who was wearing an identical muskrat fur coat and hat. The kid couldn't have been more than three years old, and this guy was six-foot-five, blonde, and aggressive. He came into the building for the interview at noon, took one look at two girls in the lobby, and liked them so much that he grabbed one by each hand and took them across the street for lunch. He didn't come back until two thirty for the interview. He was so amusing the way he talked, but I couldn't get the story across on paper, it didn't come through. So it was a difficult process.

CA: Did you suspend time at the CBC to work on the book?

FRUM: No, I don't even mention that. I worked on it at night till two in the morning—I can't work well in the morning. One thing I remember being difficult about the book was that Jack McClelland, my publisher, and his editor, Anna Porter, kept saying: "I can't believe you haven't anything to say about man-woman relations! I can't believe you haven't anything to say about Third World politics. I can't believe you haven't anything to say about Soviet-American who knows what!" But I didn't want to be pedantic and make a speech about all of those things. It was an effort to find some light way of doing it without the book coming off as "After seven years on 'As It Happens' let me tell you how Barbara Frum sees the world!" I thought that would be pretentious.

CA: You don't really think of yourself as an author then. But do you think you'll ever write another book?

FRUM: I just might!

CA: The same kind of thing?

FRUM: No, different I think. I don't know what it would be about. Obviously I'm very interested in journalism: how it works, its sins of omission and commission. I was thinking about doing a book about journalism and Canadian politics. Maybe it was the last federal election in February, 1980, that got me all steamed up. Maybe I feel differently now.

CA: Are you happy with As It Happened *as a book? Would you say you made the leap from craft or journalism to art?*

FRUM: I'm happy with it, though I'd never call it art.

CA: Journalism then?

FRUM: Books like that are put together by authors at the bequest of publishers. I don't think I ever would have done it if I hadn't been ordered to. McClelland just wouldn't take "No" for an answer. He told me that people were interested in my show, that they wanted to know something about who I was and what I'm all about, and he told me to just do it. So I did it for that reason, because he was pushing. When Warner Troyer does a book about divorce, he's got something on the line, he has some emotion, he has some guilt. When he did a book about Joe Clark's two hundred days, he had another motive. There is always a reason for a book. There are ten thousand books and twenty thousand reasons.

CA: Would you like to do any other kind of writing? Newspapers again, perhaps?

FRUM: I think I'm like a lot of journalists who did magazine work in the 1960's. We're nervous and we're worried. We aren't sure people have the staying power to read articles anymore. There's a great move out of journalism and into books. A lot of my friends who write want to do books, and as a result an awful lot of books are just journalism. They're just long magazine articles. I don't care if they call them art, and I don't care if they put them between two hard covers. That's what they are—just long magazine articles. It's just not worth it to put all that effort into a magazine piece. You don't get paid enough for it and the response isn't good.

Where do you see good magazine journalism today? You don't. Tom Wolfe doesn't want to write articles anymore; Gay Talese doesn't want to write them anymore. Magazines all over are suffering from this same problem. People are reading newspapers and listening to broadcasting, and are interested in reading books only when they are serious readers. All my friends who are magazine editors will kill me for this, but I'm sure they're laboring under it. That is why you see all these service magazines now, all these pictorial articles, and all these gimmicky things.

I've had two requests in the last month that typify this trend. One woman came up to me and asked that I show her the contents of my purse because she wanted to take a picture of it and write about it. Another woman asked about my first sexual experience. I declined, explaining, "First of all it's boring, and second of all, I don't want to." But that's what has happened to magazine journalism. In order to titilate and get people's attention, you have to do something like that. There's a real problem with magazines today, but I still love them. And I think we'll soon see a renaissance in that media.

—Interview by C. H. Gervais

*   *   *

FULLER, Dorothy Mason 1898-
(Sterling Thorne)

PERSONAL: Born July 25, 1898, in Boston, Mass.; daughter of Frank Stillman and Bertha (Kent) Mason; married Carlton Perry Fuller (a banker and business executive), October 1, 1921; children: Elsbeth (Mrs. Carlyle Swope), Joyce (Mrs. Robert Baldwin, Jr.), Kent Mason (deceased). *Education:* Radcliffe College, B.A., 1920. *Home:* 12 Fletcher Rd., Belmont, Mass. 02178.

CAREER: Writer, 1938—.

WRITINGS: African Bush Adventures, privately printed, 1965; (editor) *Light in Hours of Darkness,* Abingdon, 1971; (editor and contributor) *Strength for the Soul,* Fortress, 1975. Also author of memoirs, *Of Love and Growing,* 1980. Contributor to magazines (sometimes under pseudonym Sterling Thorne), including *Forum, Pilgrim Scrip, Christian Science Monitor,* and *Appalachia,* and newspapers.

SIDELIGHTS: Dorothy Fuller told *CA:* "Writing has always been my favorite occupation, but for considerable periods administrative duties have had to take priority. The detailed travel records I write after every trip, articles on travel for newspapers, and essays on assorted subjects for Saturday Morning Club keep me in practice.

"*Light in Hours of Darkness* grew out of the death of our only son at age twenty-nine. It is a collection of passages by people of different cultures and eras who had suffered loss. *Strength for the Soul* (originally titled *Journey Toward the Light*) grew from my own search for spiritual succor in crisis, and from my awareness of the plight of young people in the 1960's, of old people who've lost a sense of direction or motivation, and of people afflicted with a terminal illness.

"Dr. William Glasser, a psychologist, states in *Reality Therapy* his belief that to lead a satisfying life a person must have four basic needs fulfilled: to love, to be loved, to do something he considers worthwhile, and to feel useful to others. Judged by those standards, I've been exceptionally blessed. I'd add one thing more to his list, however: man needs to sense that his life and inheritance are not merely human, but from God, that he is not isolated but linked to a high purpose for which he was created and which it is his task to discover and carry out if he is to reach his full spiritual stature, and become, as he longs in his best moments to be, wise, loving, and truly useful to others.

"Not one of these things is taught at college. Scholarship is only a fraction of the worth of a human being. Character is what life's hardships build. At every stage of life we are challenged to grow. For more power to love and for more wisdom and steadfastness the striving is lifelong and costly, but brings fulfillment greater than any ego satisfaction. These things life has taught me and I am grateful."

G

GABEL, Joseph 1912-
(Kalman Geroely, Zoltan Gombossy, Lucien Martin)

PERSONAL: Born July 12, 1912, in Budapest, Hungary; son of William (a professor and journalist) and Therese (Wiegner) Gabel. *Education:* University of Paris, M.D., 1951, Ph.D., 1962. *Politics:* "Free Mason." *Religion:* Jewish. *Home:* 9 rue Emile Dubois, 75014 Paris, France. *Office:* Department of Sociology, University of Picardy, Amiens, France.

CAREER: Centre National de la Recherche Scientifique, Paris, France, research assistant, 1947-61; Universite Mohammed V, Rabat, Morocco, professor of sociology, 1965-71; University of Picardy, Amiens, France, professor of sociology and chairman of department, 1971—.

WRITINGS—In English translation: *Le Fausse Conscience: Essai sur la reification,* Editions de Minuit, 1962, 3rd edition, 1969, translation by Margaret A. Thompson published as *False Consciousness: An Essay on Reification,* Harper, 1975.

Other writings: *Formen der Entfremdung: Aufsaetze zum falschen Bewusstsein* (magazine articles; translated into German by Juliane Stiege and Gernot Gather; title means "Aspects of Alienation: Articles on the Problem of False Consciousness"), S. Fischer, 1964; *Sociologie de l'alienation* (title means "Sociology of Alienation"), Presses universitaires de France, 1970; *Ideologies,* Editions Anthropos, 1974; (editor with Bernard Rousset and Trinh Van Thao) *L'Alienation aujourd'hui* (title means "The Problem of Alienation Today"), Editions Anthropos, 1974; *Ideologies II,* Editions Anthropos, 1978. Also author with Rousset and Van Thao of *Actualite de la dialectique* (title means "Actuality and the Problem of Dialectics"), 1980.

Contributor of numerous articles, sometimes under pseudonyms Kalman Geroely, Zoltan Gombossy, and Lucien Martin, to French, German, Spanish, Hungarian, and English-language medical and political science journals.

WORK IN PROGRESS: A book on the Jewish future and Marxism, completion expected in 1982.

SIDELIGHTS: Gabel told *CA:* "I am particularly interested in questions of ideology, utopia, false consciousness, and reification, and have tried to personalize the school of Hungarian Marxism. According to the general framework of my own scientific career, I consider myself as belonging to this school in spite of being a French citizen.

"This 'desalinating' trend of the Hungarian school is in my opinion due to the crossroad situation in Hungary. The country is in an equilibrium position between German and occidental influences, and between Catholic, Protestant, and Jewish cultural impacts. Additional factors are the isolation of a very modern and occidental capital (Budapest) amidst a country of more or less feudal structures, and the divorce between the official intellectual life (the right-oriented university) and the progressive intellectual life largely independent from the university and to some extent similar to that of Weimar Germany.

"Such a crossroad situation in this country facilitated the mutual compensation of alienating influences. It is almost the same mechanism of sociology of knowledge as that shown on an individual level by Karl Mannheim. This situation makes possible the correct (that is, nonideological) position of problems as alienation, reification, and false consciousness. This, in my view, is the essential trend of the Hungarian school of Marxism."

Gabel added: "In my work I have tried to show that some forms of schizophrenia are tantamount to a process of reification of consciousness. Optics schizophrenia thus appears as an individual form of false consciousness, that is, of the totalitarian mind. At the present moment this theory of the totalitarian mind is current in the French intellectual life."

BIOGRAPHICAL/CRITICAL SOURCES: Telos: A Quarterly Journal of Radical Thought, fall, 1976.

*   *   *

GABRE-MEDHIN, Tsegaye (Kawessa) 1936-

PERSONAL: Born August 17, 1936, in Ambo, Shewa, Ethiopia; son of Roba Kawessa Dabal and Feleketch Dagne Haile Amara; married Laketch Bitew (a secretary), 1961; children: (daughters) Yodit Tsegaye, Mahlet Tsegaye, Adaye Tsegaye. *Education:* Blackstone School of Law, LL.B., 1959; also studied experimental theatre at Royal Court Theatre, London, England, and Comedie Francaise, Paris, France, 1959-60. *Home address:* P.O. Box 6249, Addis Ababa, Ethiopia. *Agent:* Tesfaye Daba, Ethiopia Book Centre, P.O. Box 2400, Addis Ababa, Ethiopia. *Office:* Addis Ababa University, P.O. Box 1176, Addis Ababa, Ethiopia.

CAREER: Ethiopian National Theatre, Addis Ababa, director, 1961-71; Oxford University Press, Addis Ababa, editor, 1971; Ethiopian National Theatre, general manager, 1974-76; Addis Ababa University, Addis Ababa, assistant professor of theatre arts, 1976—. Ethiopian vice-president of Black Arts Festival, 1973-76. Permanent secretary of culture, sports, and youth affairs, 1975-76. Research fellow at University of Dakar. Art adviser to Haile Selassie I National Theatre, Fine Arts Department of Ministry of Education, and Creative Arts Centre at Haile Selassie I University. Secretary general of Ethiopian Peace, Solidarity, and Friendship House, 1978. Delegate to First World Negro Arts Festival, 1964, Afro-Scandinavian Cultural Conference, 1967, International Poets Night, 1968, First Pan-African Cultural Festival, 1969, Afro-European Dialogue, 1969, and African Studies Association Meeting, 1971.

MEMBER: Afro-Asian Writers Union, African Writers Union, African Researchers Union, Ethiopian Writers Union, Society of African Cultures, Association of Africanists. *Awards, honors:* UNESCO fellowship, 1959; Haile Selassie I National Prize from Addis Ababa International Prize Trust, 1965, for Ethiopian literature; made Commander of the Senegal National Order, 1972, in recognition of literary merit.

WRITINGS—Plays; all in Amharic and all first produced in Addis Ababa at Ethiopian National Theatre, unless otherwise noted: *Belg* (title means "Autumn"; three-act; first produced in 1957), Berhanena Selam, 1962; *Yeshoh Aklil* (title means "Crown of Thorns"; two-act; first produced in 1958), Berhanena Selam, 1959; "Askeyami Lijagered" (title means "The Ugly Girl"; one-act), first produced in 1959; "Jorodegif" (title means "Mumps"; one-act), first produced in 1959; "Listro" (title means "Shoeshine Boy"; one-act), first produced in Addis Ababa at Commercial School Theatre, 1960; "Igni Biye Metahu" (title means "Back With a Grin"; one-act), first produced in 1961; "Kosho Cigara" (title means "Cheap Cigarettes"; one-act), first produced in Addis Ababa at Old City Hall Theatre, 1961; "Yemana Zetegn Melk" (title means "Mother's Nine Faces"; three-act), first produced in 1961.

"Tewodros" (in English; title means "Theodore"; two-act; first produced in Addis Ababa at Creative Arts Center, Haile Selassie I University, May 5, 1963), published in *Ethiopian Observer,* 1965; *Othello* (five-act; translation and adaptation of the play by Shakespeare; first produced in Addis Ababa at Addis Ababa University Theatre, 1963), Oxford University Press, 1963; "Tartuffe" (three-act; translation and adaptation of the play by Moliere), first produced in 1963; "The Doctor in Spite of Himself" (five-act; translation and adaptation of the play by Moliere), first produced in 1963; *Oda Oak Oracle: A Legend of Black Peoples, Told of Gods and God, Of Hope and Love, Of Fears and Sacrifices* (in English; two-act; first produced in Addis Ababa at Addis Ababa University Theatre, 1964), Oxford University Press, 1964; "Azmari" (in English; title means "The Minstrel"; two-act; first produced in Addis Ababa at Addis Ababa University Theatre, 1964), published in *Ethiopian Observer,* 1966; *Yekermo Sew* (title means "The Seasoned"; four-act; first produced in 1966), Berhanena Selam, 1967.

"King Lear" (five-act; translation and adaptation of the play by Shakespeare), first produced in 1968; "Kirar Siker" (title means "Kirar Tight-Tuned"; two-act), first produced in 1969; "The Cry of Petros at the Hour" (in English; two-act), first produced in 1969; *Macbeth* (five-act; translation and adaptation of the play by Shakespeare), Oxford University Press, 1972; *Hamlet* (six-act; translation and adaptation of

the play of Shakespeare), Oxford University Press, 1972; *Ha Hu Besdist Wer* (title means "A-B-C in Six Months"; five-act; first produced in 1974), Berhanena Selam, 1975; *Enat Alem Tenu* (five-act; translation and adaptation of "Mother Courage" by Bertolt Brecht; first produced in 1974), Berhanena Selam, 1975; "Atsim Beyegetsu" (title means "Skeleton in Pages"; six-act), first produced in 1975; "Abugida Transform" (five-act), first produced in 1976; *Collision of Altars* (in English; three-act), Rex Collings, 1978; "Melikte Proletarian" (three-act), first produced in Addis Ababa at New City Hall Theatre, 1979; "Mekdem" (title means "Preface"; three-act), first produced in Addis Ababa at New City Hall Theatre, 1980.

Contributor of poems and articles to *Ethiopian Observer, Transition, Presence Africaine,* and *Lotus.*

WORK IN PROGRESS: Rising Ka, a novel on Africa's ancient cultures; a play in Amharic entitled "Gamo" (title means "Warrior"), on the Ethiopian Revolution.

SIDELIGHTS: Tsegaye Gabre-Medhin's play, *Oda Oak Oracle,* is perhaps his most readily available work in English. It is a tragic story in which the village oracle dominates the lives of the southern Ethiopian characters. The play begins as the oracle decrees a marriage between Shanka and Ukutee, with their first-born child pledged as a sacrifice to the ancestral gods. The two wed but the husband, Shanka, refuses to consummate the marriage in defiance of the oracle. Ukutee despairs and finally beds Goaa, a friend of Shanka who has converted to the Christian faith. Ukutee conceives and near the end of the play begins her labor while the sky darkens ominously. Because Shanka and Goaa have attempted to thwart the oracle, tribal law demands that they engage in mortal combat. The battle ends when Shanka slays his opponent. Ukutee subsequently dies while giving birth not to a son, as has been prophesied, but to a daughter. The play ends with the dismal scene of Shanka holding Ukutee's newborn child while an angry mob advances to stone them.

Tsegay Gabre-Medhin told *CA:* "Art and literature are commitments to the life that formed our personalities and our humanity: to the people whose dreams, aspirations, and exploits we interpret. Art is as simple as truth and as clear as good and evil. The artist mirrors and exposes these things for the people to judge. He mirrors the innocent, the weak, the ignorant, and exposes the greedy, the cunning, and the exploiting. And the people shall judge for they shall know. Through knowledge alone shall we all be transformed."

BIOGRAPHICAL/CRITICAL SOURCES: A. S. Gerard, *Four African Literatures,* University of California Press, 1971.

*   *   *

GAHAGAN, Helen
See DOUGLAS, Helen Gahagan

*   *   *

GAINES, Jack
See GAINES, Jacob

*   *   *

GAINES, Jacob   1918-
(Jack Gaines)

PERSONAL: Born September 10, 1918, in New York, N.Y.; son of Harry (a picture framer) and Dora (Schachner) Gaines. *Education:* Attended New York University, 1942, New School for Social Research, 1945-48, and Esalen Institute, 1971-73. *Politics:* Democrat. *Religion:* Jewish. *Home and office:* 526 Comstock Dr., Tiburon, Calif. 94920.

CAREER: Gwines-American Moulding Corp., New York, N.Y., president, 1940-70. Founder and president of Fathers at Large, Inc., 1972-80; presents seminars and workshops at Esalen Institute. *Military service:* U.S. Coast Guard, 1942-45; served in Pacific theater; received nine battle stars. *Member:* Association of Humanistic Psychology.

WRITINGS—Under name Jack Gaines: *Fritz Perls: Here and Now,* Celestial Arts, 1979. Contributor to *Psychology Today.*

WORK IN PROGRESS: A novel, publication expected in 1981; "The Fertile Void," a screenplay.

SIDELIGHTS: Gaines commented: "My teaching is directed at changing courses, an area in which—through which—many people pass with difficulty. I teach resurrection in this lifetime.

"The book, *Fritz Perls,* pioneers a new form of biography in that it is presented through the views of many different people (each arranged in a sequential, evolutionary way that follows the protagonist from birth towards death) and effectively demonstrates how each of us have more options than we are usually aware of in viewing our own lives. Often the difference in the way we see things has a profound effect on the quality of our lives."

BIOGRAPHICAL/CRITICAL SOURCES: New York Times, December 25, 1963; *San Francisco Review of Books,* December, 1979, January, 1980; *Pacific Sun,* April 25, 1980.

*　　*　　*

GALANTAY, Ervin Yvan 1930-

PERSONAL: Surname is pronounced Ga-lan-ta-y; born October 14, 1930, in Budapest, Hungary; son of Eugene (a musician) and Margit (an educator; maiden name, de Toth) Galantay; married Karla Jay Noel (an officer of World Wildlife Fund), October, 1959; children: Roy, Richard. *Education:* Swiss Federal Institute of Technology, B.A., 1955; Miami University, Oxford, Ohio, M.C.D., 1958. *Politics:* "Law and order." *Religion:* "Christian (vaguely)." *Home address:* Le Banneret, Cossonay-Ville, Vaud, Switzerland. *Office:* Graduate Program on Developing Countries, Swiss Federal Institute of Technology, 1001 Lausanne, Switzerland.

CAREER: Philadelphia City Planning Commission, Philadelphia, Pa., planning fellow, 1957; Office of I. M. Pei (architect), New York City, urban designer, 1958-61; Harvard University, Cambridge, Mass., assistant professor of design, 1961-64; Columbia University, New York City, associate professor of architecture, 1964-70; Swiss Federal Institute of Technology, Lausanne, professor of architecture and planning, 1970—, director of graduate program on developing countries. Planning expert for governments of developing countries. Swiss representative to World Health Organization conference on planning of health facilities, in Stuttgart, 1972, and United Nations conferences on human settlements, in Vancouver, 1976, and desertification, in Nairobi, 1977; consultant to United Nations Center for Human Settlements and U.S. Agency for International Development. *Military service:* Royal Hungarian Army, 1941-45; received German Iron Cross, second class.

MEMBER: International Federation on Housing and Planning, World Society for Ekistics, American Institute of Planners (associate member), Institute of Swiss Architects. *Awards, honors:* Architecture and planning awards from in-

ternational competition in Toronto, Ontario, 1958, and national competitions in Boston, Mass., 1961 and 1964.

WRITINGS: New Towns: From Antiquity to the Present, Braziller, 1975. Also author of *Population, Density, and Behavior,* 1981. Author of columns in *Nation,* 1966-70, *Town Planning Review,* 1977—, *Third World Planning Review,* 1979—, and *Progressive Architecture.*

WORK IN PROGRESS: The Third World Metropolis, publication by Praeger expected in 1982; *Urban Planning in Developing Countries,* publication by Massachusetts Institute of Technology Press expected in 1982; a novel, "an ironic tale of a right-wing European professor parachuted into soft-nosed New York liberal society," publication expected in 1982.

SIDELIGHTS: Galantay told *CA:* "As an expert to international organizations, I spend much time traveling on all continents. I speak six languages fluently and can read and understand six more. I consider myself a truly 'global' citizen, which does not mean that I feel the same affection for all countries (let alone political systems). My interest in urban design was awakened during the siege and destruction of Budapest in 1945. Later I contributed to the creation of the new towns of Ciudad Guayana, Venezuela, and Owerri, Nigeria. Chased out of my native Hungary by Soviet occupation, I had to adapt to different lifestyles and hence became fascinated with cultural diversity. I learned that loyalty to one's own past is essential to the understanding of other traditions and other people's aspirations."

*　　*　　*

GALASSI, Jonathan (White) 1949-

PERSONAL: Born November 4, 1949, in Seattle, Wash.; son of Gerard Goodwin (a lawyer) and Dorothea (a volunteer worker; maiden name, White) Galassi; married Susan Grace (an art historian), June 21, 1975. *Education:* Harvard University, B.A. (magna cum laude), 1971; Cambridge University, A.B. (with first class honors), 1973, M.A., 1977. *Office:* Houghton Mifflin Co., 666 Third Ave., New York, N.Y. 10017.

CAREER: Houghton Mifflin Co., Boston, Mass., and New York, N.Y., editor, 1973—. *Member:* International P.E.N. *Awards, honors:* Marshall scholarship for study at Cambridge University, 1971-73; translation award from Columbia University translation center, 1978, for *The Second Life of Art;* grant from Ingram Merrill Foundation, 1979.

WRITINGS: (Editor) *Understand the Weapon, Understand the Wound: Selected Writings of John Comford,* Carcanet Press, 1976; (editor and translator) *The Second Life of Art: Selected Essays of Eugenio Montale,* Ecco Press, 1981.

Work represented in anthologies, including *Ten American Poets,* edited by James Atlas, Carcanet Press, 1973. Contributor of poems, articles, and translations to magazines, including *Poetry, Ploughshares, Canto,* and *Antaeus,* and to the *New York Times Book Review.* Editor of special Eugenio Montale issue of *Pequod,* 1977. Poetry editor of *Paris Review,* 1978—, and of *Pushcart Prize Anthology,* 1980.

WORK IN PROGRESS: Poetry and translations.

*　　*　　*

GALLMAN, Waldemar J(ohn) 1899-1980

OBITUARY NOTICE—See index for *CA* sketch: Born April 27, 1899, in Wellsville, N.Y.; died of a heart attack, June 28, 1980, in Washington, D.C. Foreign Service officer and author. Gallman served as ambassador to Poland, South Africa, and Iraq. In 1958 he became director general of the Foreign Service with the rank of assistant secretary of state. He later served as consultant to South Korea and South Vietnam, where he worked to help establish diplomatic training programs. Gallman was the author of *Iraq Under General Nuri: My Recollections of Nuri Al-Said, 1954-1958.* Obituaries and other sources: *New York Times,* June 30, 1980; *Washington Post,* July 1, 1980.

*   *   *

GAMBINO, Thomas D(ominic)   1942-

PERSONAL: Born July 15, 1942, in Trenton, N.J.; son of Alfonso Michael (a mechanic) and Dora (Berlute) Gambino; married Loretta Krebs (a general manager of a record distribution company), August 24, 1963; children: Marc, Michael, Kim. *Education:* Glassboro State College, B.A., 1964. *Politics:* "World Governmentalist." *Religion:* None. *Home and office:* 64-24 Grand Ave., Maspeth, N.Y. 11378. *Agent:* John Gaeta, 21 Old Wood Rd., Port Washington, N.Y. 11050.

CAREER: Director of instrumental music at high schools in Trenton, N.J., 1964-65, and Hopewell Township, N.J., 1965-66; musician in New York, N.Y., 1966-72; Sunrise Artistries, Inc. (publisher), Maspeth, N.Y., founder and president, 1972—. Co-founder of Umano Foundation and leader of Umano Orchestra; composer and musical arranger, musician, and teacher. Participated in U.S. State Department tours of Europe (including the Soviet Union), 1971 and 1974; guest on Canadian and American television and radio programs. *Member:* Amnesty International, American Federation of Musicians, American Civil Liberties Union, Environmental Defense Fund, Phi Kappa Lambda.

WRITINGS: My Gentle Pearl (poems), Sunrise Artistries, 1973; *Jazz Patterns for the Instrumentalist,* Sunrise Artistries, 1973; *NYET: An American Rock Musician Encounters the Soviet Union,* Prentice-Hall, 1976. Also author of recording, "Sunrise," Agon, 1973. Contributor of articles and reviews to magazines, including *Models Circle* and *Allegro.*

WORK IN PROGRESS: A novel based on two years' research on the concept of world government; a collection of short stories based on musicians' travels.

SIDELIGHTS: In New York City, Gambino performed with such musicians as Tito Puente, Bob Crosby, and Mel Torme. In 1970 he joined the Lionel Hampton Orchestra, and after that worked with jazz musicians Woody Herman, Buddy Rich, B.B. King, and Gene Krupa. He toured the Soviet Union in 1974 with the Joffrey Ballet's rock music group, the Vegetables, the first American rock group to visit that country. *NYET* received publicity when Gambino defeated the State Department's attempt to censor his manuscript.

In 1978 he formed the Umano Orchestra, a twenty-five-piece rock/jazz ensemble influenced by the music of many cultures. Named for turn-of-the-century jurist Gaetano Meale, who assumed the name Umano (meaning humane), the group plays concerts and international tours to promote understanding among peoples. The orchestra is intended to help support the Umano Foundation, which will study international law and cross-cultural barriers, and promote an end to warfare by the establishment of a world federal government and a world center of communication.

Gambino told *CA:* "Beginning with the post-World War II generations, there have been remarkable changes in attitudes concerning war and peace. Many young people feel cheated by their forebears, because they have been unable to live any part of their lives without the threat of nuclear weapons. Others have completely tuned out, either because they feel alienated from a technological society that diminishes their sense of individuality, or because the specter of facing the reality of that destructive nightmare we live under is too much to bear. But the common bond they share with the more concerned members of the older generation is a genuine desire to find a lasting solution to the problem lying at the heart of all human dilemmas—violence and the ultimate violence, war.

"We have gone beyond nations fighting nations. We now live on a planet where worldwide alliances fight each other. This must come to an end. We must bow to history and take those steps which acknowledge our planet's fragile ability to sustain nuclear war.

"There are those who think it is wrong to mix art and political action. I cannot disagree more. This is a wonderful time to be alive. For the first time we are able to communicate instantly with almost anyone anywhere on the planet. For the first time we can view history as it happens. We have begun to plan for the post-military-industrial age. We have already left this planet and begun to explore the solar system. I ask the peoples of the world to join hands and begin a new age, more peaceful and stable than any that has gone before. For, as Umano once said, 'Every day, on this earth, a human being, struggling with some great idea, is slowly dying because of others' neglect, arrogance, or selfishness. And his idea, for lack of help, dies with him to humanity's great loss.'"

*   *   *

GARDNER, Hy   1908-

PERSONAL: Born December 2, 1908, in New York, N.Y.; son of John Jacob and Sarah (Guilden) Gardner; married third wife, Marilyn Boshnick (a writer), April, 1958; children: (previous marriage) Ralph Richard; (third marriage) Jeffrey Scott. *Education:* Attended Columbia University. *Home:* 5601 North Bayshore Dr., Miami, Fla. 33137. *Office:* 1111 Brickell Ave., Miami, Fla. 33131.

CAREER: Worked in advertising and retail promotion; *New York Herald Tribune,* New York, N.Y., author of Broadway column and editor of *Trib TV;* Field Newspaper Syndicate, Chicago, Ill., co-author of column, "Glad You Asked That." Host of "Hy Gardner TV Show"; host of radio and television programs; filmmaker and actor. *Military service:* U.S. Army, 1942-45; became major. *Awards, honors:* Journalism award from Freedoms Foundation.

WRITINGS: Champagne Before Breakfast, Holt, 1954; *So What Else Is New?,* Prentice-Hall, 1959; *Hy Gardner's Off-Beat Guide to New York,* Grosset, 1964. Also author of *Tales Out of Night School.* Author of a column in *Parade.* Contributor to magazines, including *Look, Reader's Digest,* and *TV Guide.*

BIOGRAPHICAL/CRITICAL SOURCES: Editor and Publisher, October 16, 1954.

*   *   *

GARDNER, Marilyn

PERSONAL: Born on September 6th in Brooklyn, N.Y.; daughter of Benjamin and Rebecca (Katz) Boshnick; married Hy Gardner (a columnist and reporter), April, 1958; children: Jeffrey Scott. *Education:* Studied acting with Alfred Dixon in New York, N.Y. *Residence:* Miami, Fla. *Office address:* c/o Field Newspaper Syndicate, 1703 Kaiser Ave., P.O. Box 19620, Irvine, Calif. 92714.

CAREER/WRITINGS: Journalist. Secretary in press information with Columbia Broadcasting System (CBS) in New York City; secretary with William Morris Agency in New York City; columnist with *New York Herald Tribune* in New York City; worked with National Broadcasting Corp. (NBC) in New York City; writer, with husband, Hy Gardner, of celebrity column, "Glad You Asked That," for Field Newspaper Syndicate.

SIDELIGHTS: In their celebrity column, "Glad You Asked That," Marilyn Gardner and her husband, Hy, answer questions sent in by some three thousand readers. Their source of information is the library of public personalities Marilyn has created over the years, which includes cross index files of newspaper, magazine, and personal interview clips, biographies, autobiographies, video and audio tapes, correspondence, photographs, and reference books. The library has become one of the largest and most valuable individual collections of its kind.

Marilyn Gardner told *CA:* "We have a collection of letters from V.I.P.'s in show business, politics, sports, and from presidents through the years. They range from Humphrey Bogart to Harry S Truman, from Ernest Hemingway to Maurice Chevalier to Richard Nixon. We'll probably do a book on them one day."

AVOCATIONAL INTERESTS: Tennis, needlepoint, antiques.

*　　*　　*

GARREAU, Joel 1948-

PERSONAL: Surname rhymes with "arrow"; born September 21, 1948, in Pawtucket, R.I.; son of Roland Joseph (a furniture store owner) and Gloria (a furniture store owner; maiden name, Nadeau) Garreau; married Adrienne Cook (a magazine writer and livestock breeder), May 21, 1976. *Education:* Attended University of Notre Dame, 1965-69. *Residence:* Gainesville, Va. *Agent:* Richard Kahlenberg, Writers and Artists Agency, 450 North Roxbury Dr., Suite 200, Beverly Hills, Calif. 90210. *Office: Washington Post,* 1150 15th St. N.W., Washington, D.C. 20071.

CAREER: Pawtucket Times, Pawtucket, R.I., special assignment reporter and photographer, 1962-65, general assignment reporter, summers, 1966-67; *Scholastic,* Notre Dame, Ind., executive editor, 1965-69; *Focus/Michiana,* South Bend, Ind., founding and assistant editor, 1968-69; *A.D.* (magazine), South Bend, associate editor, 1969-70; managing editor for *Ave Maria; Washington Post,* Washington, D.C., copy editor of "Style" section, 1970-72, graphics coordinator of "Style," 1972-74; *Trenton Times,* Trenton, N.J., assistant managing editor, 1974-76; *Washington Post,* chief of correspondents at national desk, 1976-79; writer, 1979-80; *Washington Post,* assistant editor of "Outlook" section, 1980—.

WRITINGS: The Nine Nations of North America, Houghton, 1981.

SIDELIGHTS: Garreau told *CA:* "What *The Nine Nations of North America* is about is the way North America really works today. When I was chief of correspondents at the *Washington Post,* I ended up talking to reporters all over the United States and we ended up seeing patterns in the news. We started our own internal, private shorthand, trying to describe the new realities of people and power we saw developing in this maturing continent. Our key observation was that there were new power centers emerging, and distinct and characteristic values, views, and cultures growing up

around them. MexAmerica, for example, was how we saw the hot, dry, and increasingly Hispanic Southwest from Los Angeles to Houston. The wet, mild Pacific Coast strip from Pt. Conception, California, to Homer, Alaska, became Ecotopia. The energy-rich, pristine, unpopulated, dry Intermountain West became the Empty Quarter, named after the Saudi Arabian region with similar characteristics. We noted that Miami was becoming the capital of Latin America, and so south Florida and the Caribbean became the Islands.

"An editor at the *Post,* Bill Greider, urged me to put this down in article form, and I did. With those four nations intact, it wasn't hard to add New England, Dixie, the Breadbasket, and the industrial nation of the Foundry, which is basically Washington to Cincinnati to Chicago to New York, which still thinks it is the center of power in the United States, although it is the only region in decline.

"So I started writing an article called 'The Eight Nations of the United States,' and then I started thinking, well, wait a minute. This redefinition ignores almost all existing state political lines. Why am I showing such reverence for national lines? Appropriate portions of Canada and Mexico work just like they do on the other side of our arbitrary borders. Canada is really six nations, with appropriate portions of Ecotopia, the Empty Quarter, the Breadbasket, the Foundry, and New England, not to mention Quebec. Northern Mexico is simply an extension of MexAmerica, being heavily influenced by the U.S. Anglo culture. So I added Quebec as the ninth nation, and suddenly I had the nine nations thereof.

"The article ran, and I prepared to go back about my business, but then, much to my surprise, considering how long the article was in final form, the Los Angeles Times-Washington Post News Service picked it up. They distributed it to our three hundred plus clients worldwide, and son of a gun, dozens and dozens of other papers picked it up, some printing it on the front page. The *Manchester Guardian* in England serialized it. What the hell, I said. What have I done?

"Then the letters started pouring in, from all over the place, saying right on, you've articulated something important here. Then an agent called. He said do you want to write a book. I said no. It sounded like a lot of work, and who needs that? Besides, I said, the only way I'd do it is if they gave me tons of money to travel 100,000 miles all over the continent, and get out from behind this telephone where I have to listen to roving reporters having all the fun. How much? he said. Hell, I didn't know. I pulled a figure out of the air that I thought was astronomical, and surely not what a major publishing house would risk on a first-time nonfiction work. (As it turns out, it was only two-thirds of what I ended up spending. Wow, am I in hock right now.) Anyway, three houses showed interest. At that point, there was really no decision to make. It was either take the money, or spend the rest of my life wondering what it would have been like if I had, and so only ten weeks after the first article was published, I was on the road, wondering what I'd done.

"I traveled for two weeks, wrote for two weeks, traveled for two weeks, wrote for two weeks, for fourteen months. And the amazing thing I discovered was that North America really does work along these lines that we first scribbled on the back of cocktail napkins. I spent many a dark night wondering why. It seems obvious in hindsight, but at the time it was a great revelation. What we'd done is create a news map. This is the way the news breaks down. And to whatever extent news reflects human realities, this is the way the continent operates. More important, somebody has said that news is the first rough draft of history. So what we were doing in anticipating the news was anticipating history. It would be wrong to call this a book of futurology, in the sense that (1) things are happening along the lines I describe right now, and (2) I am not saying that the United States or North America is breaking up or should break up. I have no credentials to say things like that.

"But what I am saying is that those people who think the McDonald's stands and the interstates have made this continent homogenous are out of their minds. As the continent matures, new geographical power and culture structures are being formed and being strengthened. And anybody who ignores that is going to lose elections or money."

*　　*　　*

GAST, Kelly P. [a pseudonym]

PERSONAL—Agent: Robert P. Mills Ltd., 156 East 52nd St., New York, N.Y. 10022.

CAREER: Writer.

WRITINGS—All westerns; all published by Doubleday: Dil Dies Hard, 1975; Murphy's Trail, 1976; The Long Trail North, 1976; The Murder at Magpie Flats, 1978; Last Stage From Opal, 1978; Paddy, 1979.

SIDELIGHTS: Gast told CA: "I write for money."

*　　*　　*

GATER, Hubert   1913(?)-1980

OBITUARY NOTICE: Born c. 1913 in Muskogee, Okla.; died June 10, 1980, in Hillsboro, N.H. Shipper and author. Gater worked in the shipping department of a New Hampshire paper mill. His book, Bataan Diary, is a personal account of the death march imposed on American and Filipino soldiers by their Japanese captors. Two motion pictures were based on Gater's book: "Bataan," starring Robert Taylor, and "Back to Bataan," starring John Wayne. Obituaries and other sources: Washington Post, June 12, 1980.

*　　*　　*

GATLEY, Richard Harry   1936-

PERSONAL: Born June 26, 1936, in Montreal, Quebec, Canada; son of John H. and Ruth (Allard) Gatley; divorced; children: Robert Bruce, Samantha Maria. Education: University of California, Berkeley, B.A., 1962; Michigan State University; M.A., 1965, Ph.D., 1969. Office: Psychological Service Centre, University of Manitoba, Winnipeg, Manitoba, Canada R3T 2N2.

CAREER: Michigan State University, East Lansing, instructor in psychology at counseling center, 1968-69; University of Manitoba, Winnipeg, assistant professor, 1969-75, associate professor of psychology, 1975—. Consultant to Wilbur Hot Springs Health Sanctuary. Military service: U.S. Air Force, 1954-60. Member: National Council on Family Relations, American Psychological Association, Psychological Association of Manitoba, Manitoba Psychological Society, Social Planning Council of Winnipeg, Phi Beta Kappa, Psi Chi.

WRITINGS: (With David Koulack) Single Father's Handbook, Doubleday, 1979. Contributor to magazines and newspapers, including Voices.

WORK IN PROGRESS: The Battle of the Sexists: Chronicle and Guide for Feminist Relationships Between Women and Men, with Patricia A. Wrighton; research on single fathers, the divorce process, marital and conciliation counseling, the need for father involvement and legal reform, and feminist alternatives and therapy for men and women.

SIDELIGHTS: Gatley told CA: "As a single father myself and as an experienced therapist, I advocate more equitable and satisfying solutions for families of divorce than they can presently obtain: mediation rather than adversarial battles; co-parenting and joint custody rather than single and disposable parents. I have presented these views on U.S. and Canadian radio and television."

*　　*　　*

GATLIN, Lila L(ee)   1928-

PERSONAL: Born August 23, 1928, in Hutchinson, Kan.; daughter of Henry (a farm implement manufacturer) and Anna (Schoenhoff) Krause; married Carl Gatlin, September 3, 1947 (died January 22, 1977); children: Amy, Jeff, Laura, Jennifer. Education: University of Tulsa, B.S. (with honors), 1957; Pennsylvania State University, M.S. (with honors), 1959; University of Texas, Ph.D., 1963. Office: Department of Statistics, University of California, Berkeley, Calif. 94720.

CAREER: University of Texas, Austin, fellow at Genetics Foundation, 1964-65; Drexel University, Philadelphia, Pa., assistant professor of chemistry, 1965-66; Bryn Mawr College, Bryn Mawr, Pa., visiting lecturer in molecular biology, 1967-68; University of California, Berkeley, assistant research biophysicist at Space Sciences Laboratory, 1970-73; University of California, Davis, lecturer in genetics and associate research geneticist, 1974-77; Stanford University, Stanford, Calif., Thomas Welton Stanford Psychical Research Fellow in psychology, 1977-78; University of California, Berkeley, research associate at Statistical Laboratory, 1978—. Member: American Association for the Advancement of Science. Awards, honors: Fellow of National Institutes of Health, 1963-64.

WRITINGS: (Contributor) J. N. Davidson and W. E. Cohn, editors, Progress in Nucleic Acid Research and Molecular Biology, Volume II, Academic Press, 1971; Information Theory and the Living System, Columbia University Press, 1972; (contributor) M. Goodman and R. E. Tashian, editors, Molecular Anthropology, Plenum Press, 1976. Contributor of about twenty articles to scientific journals. Member of editorial board of Journal of Molecular Evolution, 1974-79.

WORK IN PROGRESS: A Healing Model, publication expected in 1981.

SIDELIGHTS: Gatlin told CA: "To me, writing is the ultimate form of physical communication because if one is not understood by one's contemporary peer group, i.e., you are 'years ahead of your time,' writing is communication with the future. I find immense satisfaction in the fact that my first book, although respectfully received by my associates at that time, six years later inspired the review by Eric Nygren in Co-Evolution Quarterly which read: 'References to her work are beginning to crop up in the literature of the field, but I doubt this can go far before some controversy erupts. Gatlin's paradigm not only challenges many assumptions of current biological thought, but contributes to a revolutionary scientific view of our evolving selves.'

"When communicating with the future, you experience this expansive feeling that your audience is unlimited, that you are unlimited, and that humanity is unlimited in its capacity to move on to a future of health and peace."

BIOGRAPHICAL/CRITICAL SOURCES: Co-Evolution Quarterly, March 20, 1978.

GDANSKI, Marek
See THEE, Marek

* * *

GEHERIN, David J(ohn) 1943-

PERSONAL: Born June 5, 1943, in Auburn, N.Y.; son of Alfred G. (a vocational instructor) and Margaret A. (Taylor) Geherin; married Diane A. Barresi (an educator), August 29, 1964; children: Christopher, Peter, Daniel. *Education:* University of Toronto, B.A., 1964; Purdue University, M.A., 1967, Ph.D., 1970. *Home:* 1453 Witmire, Ypsilanti, Mich. 48197. *Office:* Department of English, Eastern Michigan University, Ypsilanti, Mich. 48197.

CAREER: Eastern Michigan University, Ypsilanti, assistant professor, 1969-74, associate professor, 1974-79, professor of English, 1979—. Producer of "The Automobile in American Life," a series on WTVS-TV, 1976. *Member:* American Popular Culture Association. *Awards, honors:* Grant from Michigan Council for the Humanities, 1976.

WRITINGS: Sons of Sam Spade, Ungar, 1980. Contributor to magazines, including *Armchair Detective* and *Critique.* Associate editor of *Journal of Narrative Technique,* 1971-77.

WORK IN PROGRESS: Critical work on novels of John D. MacDonald for Ungar.

SIDELIGHTS: Sons of Sam Spade is Geherin's assessment of the modern private eye, focusing on the characters created by Robert B. Parker, Roger L. Simon, and Andrew Bergman. "Geherin's thesis is that detective heroes are neither a dying breed nor watered-down versions of the tough guys of the 1930s and '40s," noted a *Booklist* reviewer, who found the book a "fascinating" and "thoughtful analysis."

BIOGRAPHICAL/CRITICAL SOURCES: Booklist, February 15, 1980.

* * *

GEHRELS, Franz 1922-

PERSONAL: Born March 20, 1922, in Eckernforde, Germany; came to the United States; naturalized citizen, 1931; son of Franz (a physician) and Marie (Barsoe) Gehrels; married Katharine Fechner, November 13, 1950; children: Franziska, Barbara. *Education:* Attended San Mateo Junior College, 1938-40; Stanford University, B.A., 1942, M.B.A., 1947, Ph.D., 1953; postdoctoral study at Johns Hopkins University, 1954-55. *Home address:* Meadowbrook Rd., Bloomington, Ind. *Office:* Department of Economics, Indiana University, 811 Ballantine Hall, Bloomington, Ind. 47401.

CAREER: Mutual Security Agency, economic analyst in Frankfurt, West Germany, 1950-51, and Paris, France, 1952-53; University of Minnesota, Minneapolis, acting assistant professor of economics, 1953-54; Indiana University, Bloomington, assistant professor, 1955-58, associate professor, 1958-62, professor of economics, 1962—. Fulbright lecturer at University of Mainz, 1957-58, and Free University of Berlin, 1962-63; visiting professor at University of Frankfurt, summer, 1958; visiting lecturer at University of Stockholm, 1970. *Military service:* U.S. Army, 1943-46. *Awards, honors:* Social Science Research Council fellowship for Cambridge University and London School of Economics and Political Science, London, 1949-50, grant, 1961; fellow of Institute of International Economic Studies, Stockholm, Sweden, 1969-70.

WRITINGS: (Contributor) T. Bagiotte, editor, *Essays in*

Honor of Marco Fanno, Padova, 1966; (editor with H. Oliver and G. Wilson, and contributor) *Essays in Economic Analysis and Policy,* Indiana University Press, 1970; (contributor) Wilson, editor, *Technological Development and Economic Growth,* School of Business, Indiana University, 1971; *Optimal Growth of an Open Economy,* Vandenhoeck & Ruprecht, 1975. Contributor to *Encyclopedia of the Social Sciences.* Contributor of about twenty-five articles to economic and business journals.

* * *

GEIS, Richard E(rwin) 1927-
(Frederick Colson, Albina Jackson, Sheela Kunzur, Bob Owen, Robert N. Owen, Ann Radway, Peggy Swann, Peggy Swenson)

PERSONAL: Born July 19, 1927, in Portland, Ore.; son of Erwin Walter (a truck driver) and Delores (Petke) Geis. *Education:* Attended Vanport College (now Portland State University), 1942-43. *Agent:* Virginia Kidd, Box 278, Milford, Pa. 18337. *Office address:* P.O. Box 11408, Portland, Ore. 97211.

CAREER: Psychotic (fan magazine), Portland, Ore., publisher and editor, 1954-56, 1967-69; *Science Fiction Review* (fan magazine), Santa Monica, Calif., publisher and editor, 1969-71; *Alien Critic* (fan magazine), Portland, publisher and editor, 1972-75; *Science Fiction Review,* Portland, publisher and editor, 1975—; writer, 1959—. Also worked as a stockman, dishwasher, television repairman, apartment house manager, and auto painter. *Member:* Science Fiction Writers of America, Los Angeles Science Fantasy Society, Fantasy Amateur Press Association. *Awards, honors:* Hugo Award from World Science Fiction Convention, 1968, 1969, 1973, 1974, 1976, and 1978, for best fan magazine, 1970, 1974, 1975, 1976, and 1977, for best fan writer; Locus award, 1973 and 1975, for best critic.

WRITINGS—Novels: Like Crazy, Man, Newsstand Library, 1960, reprinted as "The Beatniks" in *Dollar Double, Dollar Book,* 1962; *Sex Kitten,* Newsstand Library, 1960; *Honeymoon Motel,* International Publications, 1962; *Girlsville,* International Publications, 1963; *The Saturday Night Party,* Beacon Books, 1963; *Slum Virgin,* Saber Books, 1963; *Whistle Them Willing,* Neva, 1964; (under pseudonym Peggy Swann) *Campus Lust,* Neva, 1964; *Sensual Family,* Novel Books, 1964; (under pseudonym Albina Jackson) *Dusky Dyke,* Neva, 1964; *Male Mistress,* Brandon House, 1964.

Twilight Beauty, Novel Books, 1965; *Young Tiger,* Softcover Library, 1965; (under pseudonym Frederick Colson) *The Three Way Set,* Brandon House, 1965; (under pseudonym Frederick Colson) *The Devil Is Gay,* Brandon House, 1965; *Bedroom Blacklist,* Brandon House, 1966; (under pseudonym Ann Radway) *Discotheque Doll,* Brandon House, 1966; (under pseudonym Frederick Colson) *The Passion Thing,* Brandon House, 1966; *Bongo Bum,* Brandon House, 1966; *The Punishment,* Softcover Library, 1967; *In Bed We Lie,* Brandon House, 1967; *Eye at the Window,* Brandon House, 1967; (under pseudonym Frederick Colson) *Roller Derby Girl,* Brandon House, 1967; *Sex Turned On,* Softcover Library, 1967; (under pseudonym Bob Owen) *The Soldier,* All Star, 1967; *Ravished,* Essex, 1968; *The Endless Orgy,* Brandon House, 1968; *The Sex Machine,* Brandon House, 1968; *Raw Meat,* Essex House, 1969; *The Arena Women,* Brandon Books, 1972; (under pseudonym Sheela Kunzur) *Daddy's Harlot,* Beeline, 1976; (under pseudonym Sheela Kunzur) *Honor Thy Parent,* Orpheus, 1976; *Canned*

Meat, privately printed, 1978; *Star Whores,* privately printed, 1979.

Under pseudonym Robert N. Owen; all published by Brandon House: *Man For Hire,* 1965; *The Carnal Trap,* 1966; *Sailor on the Town,* 1966; *Drifter in Town,* 1966; *A Dame in His Corner,* 1966; *Off-Broadway Casanova,* 1966.

Under pseudonym Peggy Swenson: *The Blondie,* Midwood, 1960; *The Unloved,* Midwood, 1961; *Call Me Nympho,* International Publications, 1962; *Easy,* Midwood, 1962; *Pleasure Lodge,* Midwood, 1962; *Pajama Party,* Midwood, 1963; *Sea Nymph,* Midwood, 1963; *Virgin No More,* International Publications, 1963; *Lesbian Lure,* Neva, 1964; *The Gay Partners,* Brandon House, 1964; *Lesbian Gym,* Brandon House, 1964; *Queer Beach,* Brandon House, 1964; *The Three Way Apartment,* Brandon House, 1964; *Suzy and Vera,* Brandon House, 1964; *Beat Nymph,* Brandon House, 1965; *Pamela's Sweet Agony,* Brandon House, 1965; *Amateur Night,* Brandon House, 1965; *Rita and Marian,* Brandon House, 1967; *Teen Hippie,* Midwood, 1968; *The Love Tribe,* Brandon House, 1968; *Odd Couple,* Midwood, 1968; *Time For One More,* Midwood, 1969; *Running Wild,* Midwood, 1969; *Devil on Her Tail,* Brandon House, 1969; *The Mouth Lover,* Brandon House, 1970; *The Mouth Girl,* Volume I, Brandon House, 1969; *The Mouth Girl,* Volume 2, Cameo Books, 1970; *Captive of the Lust Master,* Brandon House, 1971; *Please—Force Me!,* Brandon House, 1971; *Blow Hot, Blow Cold,* Barclay, 1972; *Naked Prisoner,* Brandon House, 1972; *The Twins Have Mother,* Barclay, 1972; *A Girl Possessed,* Brandon Books, 1973; *Mother-Twin Incest,* Brighton, 1973.

Case histories: *Orality '69,* Brandon House, 1969; *Orality '70,* Barclay, 1970; *Nurses Who Seduce the Young,* Barclay, 1970; *Three Way Swap,* Barclay, 1970; *Young Girls Who Seduce Older Men,* Barclay, 1971; *Swap Orgies,* Barclay, 1971; (under pseudonym Peggy Swenson) *The Hot Kids and Their Older Lovers,* Brandon House, 1971; *Anal Husbands and Their Deviant Wives,* Barclay, 1971; *Women and Bestiality,* Barclay, 1971; *Nurses and Young Men,* Brighton, 1973; *Orgy Lovers,* Brighton, 1973.

Author of novel *One Immortal Man,* serialized in *Science Fiction Review,* 1978-79. Author of column "The Alien Viewpoint," in *IF* and *Galaxy,* 1973-79. Contributor of approximately ninety-five stories to magazines, including *Adam* and *Sir Knight.*

SIDELIGHTS: A number of Geis's books have been published in Belgium. *Avocational interests:* Collecting pornography films, studying conspiracy theories.

CA INTERVIEWS THE AUTHOR
Richard Geis was interviewed by telephone on March 18, 1980, while at his home in Portland, Oregon.

CA: In addition to writing a great many books and publishing Science Fiction Review, *you've done assorted jobs ranging from dishwasher to apartment manager. How did these other jobs fit into your writing?*

GEIS: I was a dishwasher and what you might call a menial before I started writing. Then being an apartment house manager was a way of getting free rent while I wrote, because it provided a lot of free time.

CA: But once you started writing, you just wrote?

GEIS: Oh, yeah. I've been a free-lance writer and fan publisher full time since 1969.

CA: When did you know for sure that you wanted to be a writer?

GEIS: When I was about thirteen years old, I guess.

CA: What led you to that ambition?

GEIS: I don't know exactly. I just liked to read a lot, and being a writer was very romantic at the time. I suppose it still is. It appealed to me, and I didn't want to work too hard. Little did I know.

CA: What attracted you to fantasy and science fiction in particular?

GEIS: That's unknowable, really. I don't think you can find that many people who can pinpoint why they like science fiction and fantasy. I suppose either it goes back to my very early childhood or it goes beyond that into the womb. Who knows? I was reading it when I was about nine or ten years old.

CA: Do you feel you've been instrumental in the fan movement in science fiction?

GEIS: I don't think I've been very instrumental at all. I've always been a fringe force, if you want to call it that, in fandom. And fandom itself, as I understand it, is a very small phenomenon, at least *publishing* fandom. There haven't been more than, I'd say, fifty or sixty fanzines published at any one time that one would consider science-fiction fanzines. It's really a fringe, marginal thing. Convention-going fans are much more numerous, and I've never been into that.

CA: Have fanzines figured largely in the growth and acceptance of science fiction and fantasy as a genre?

GEIS: I don't think fanzines have promoted the genre very much at all. I think they've just been going on in a steady state. They appeal to a few people, publishing in the field appeals to a few people, and it's almost a closed world. You get a few dropouts every year and you get a few people coming in, but it stays the same. I suppose it always will, as long as there are mimeographs around. I think fandom overall may expand a little bit as photo-offset fandom, if you want to call it that, expands. Because as fanzines get too ambitious and start going to very expensive ways of reproduction, they require more of a paying audience. They expand; they advertise, as I did and as a few others have done. They get into a different audience mix, so that they lose their real fannish aura and become semipro or small press magazines. I don't see any real changes taking place in publishing fandom at the lowest level. There are three or four semipro magazines that have arisen and are getting a wider audience, but not that much of a wider audience.

CA: How did Science Fiction Review *get started?*

GEIS: Out of sheer greed and a desire to live off of it. It started as *Psychotic* back in the mid-1950's, then for one issue I changed it to *Science Fiction Review,* and then I quit publication for eleven or twelve years as I became a full-time professional writer. I picked it up again as *Psychotic* in the late 1960s and moved to Portland and changed it to *Alien Critic.* Then I found that I was going to get sued if I continued to use the word "critic" by a magazine called the *Critic* in Chicago, which had a patent on the name. So then I went back to *Science Fiction Review.* Really I suppose that's a much more accurate title and a more commercial title.

CA: Could you explain what a fan writer does or should do?

GEIS: It's a very individual thing. I could tell you what *I* do.

I just read books and write what I think of them, and I watch the field as well as I can and write what I think of that. Other fan writers write different things, such as little stories or vignettes about their experiences at conventions, and they create characters. It's sort of a play area for them. It's a unique situation for everyone. And anyone can get published, because if they have to, they can publish themselves.

CA: Do you find a special kind of camaraderie among science-fiction and fantasy writers?

GEIS: Yes. The point has been made before that science-fiction and fantasy professionals are very close to their fans, to their audience, and I would say that at least half of them have come up through the fan ranks. There are at least a dozen new ones who were fans for a long time and are just now beginning to be published writers in the sense of professional publication. It's been going on like that since the 1930's, and I expect it will continue. It's a rather unique phenomenon, I think, in the publishing world. The getting together is the big factor in this closeness. There are writers here in Portland and other places in Oregon who will meet and discuss science ficiton. They don't even have to go to a convention.

CA: There are a number of science-fiction writers in California also. Are there more on the West Coast than anywhere else in the country?

GEIS: I don't know. You'd have to look at a map that the Science Fiction Writers of America puts out to pinpoint who lives where.

CA: Who are your favorite writers?

GEIS: I really don't have favorites anymore among what you might call the mundane writers. I haven't read a modern novel in years, because my time is just devoted to science fiction and fantasy. It's very difficult to find time to read anything else, although I do read the financial press.

CA: What about science-fiction and fantasy writers?

GEIS: It's easier to say the ones I *don't* like. But favorites? Phil Dick—at least the *old* Phil Dick—was one of my very favorites. Poul Anderson. Robert Heinlein has disappointed me of late, in the last five or six years. His latest book is terrible. Fritz Leiber. There's a new young writer, Diane Duane, who is beginning to write very good fiction. Harlan Ellison is dynamic, of course; in fact, he's always been a phenomenon.

CA: Do you see any new trends developing in the genre?

GEIS: Not really. I think you'd have to go to a leading New York editor to ask that question. I think there was a flirtation with fantasy; I don't know if that's working out too well or not. It may be that we're going into hard space adventure, like "Star Wars," for a while. It's hard to say. I think the editors try various types of stories to see what sells, then there's a trend in that area for a while until it peters out, then they go into something else.

CA: You have now published at least ninety books. You must write all the time.

GEIS: I haven't written hard since I moved up to Portland in 1972. I've written a lot of books since then, but not really at the rate I was writing before that. You know, you don't have to write much to publish a lot of novels if you can sell them. Over the period from 1959 till the present day—for a lot of years—I was doing about six or seven books a year. But that's only a couple of thousand words a day. To a writer,

that's not a lot. Especially to some of those old pros who whacked out five to ten thousand words a day. Some people can write a book in a week.

CA: It must take a lot of discipline just to sit there and keep writing.

GEIS: Well, of course, you have to want to do it. And it does take a lot of self-discipline to choose writing and to keep at it. To me it seems normal. I know other people think it's incredible, but I don't understand that.

CA: You've won eleven Hugos. How do you feel about these awards?

GEIS: Very well. I like them very much, and I want more if I can get them. I would really like to set the all-time record for Hugos won. Maybe I have already, I don't know. I'd like to make the history books—in this respect, anyway.

CA: Is there any genre you haven't worked in that you'd like to try?

GEIS: Not really. I think if I had wanted to do something else, I would have done it by now. I think my talent really is in sex writing, very secondarily in science fiction.

CA: Is there still a good market for sex novels?

GEIS: No. That's probably why I've cut out writing it for so long, because the markets have gone away—disappeared and melted and everything else.

CA: Why do you think that's happened?

GEIS: Basically because the films came along and drove the books away. There's more work to reading and visualizing than there is to just looking. Of course they've used up the whole potential. They started very timidly in sex, then became more and more bold, and they've used up every area of sex imaginable in greater and greater detail in graphic illustration and words until they've overkilled it. Now there are one or two small publishers who publish sex novels, but it's just wall-to-wall sex. They have formulas they want you to follow, and they pay at most one thousand dollars, which is actually five hundred dollars in purchasing power nowadays, so it isn't worth doing.

CA: Would you tell me more about Science Fiction Review?

GEIS: It's mainly a subscription magazine; it has about nineteen hundred subscribers now, and I'm selling around five hundred copies to book stores, but it never was really a big seller in book stores. I haven't made a big effort to get into the university libraries. Perhaps I should.

I think the value of the magazine is its material by and about the professional writers, the well-known writers. Over the years, almost everybody has written for *Science Fiction Review,* and they reveal some of the most remarkable things about themselves and their writing. I think the magazine really is a gold mine for researchers, and it's also very interesting. John Brunner, for instance, has a column every few months. He sends installments in which he discusses his writing and his life in England. I should think for someone who's doing research on John Brunner that would be a must to read. The column has run for about ten years. And other known writers have contributed. I have a news section and extensive reviews of magazines and books and just commentary on books and personalities. There's also a letter column, in which we argue back and forth about the future, writers, writing, trends, books—everything.

CA: How can one subscribe?

GEIS: Anyone who wants to subscribe can write to me at my post office box number; I'm interested in increasing subscriptions. I'm beginning to advertise a little bit lately—perhaps too little and too late, given the financial situation of the country.

BIOGRAPHICAL/CRITICAL SOURCES: Contemporary Literary Criticism, Volume 12, Gale, 1980.

—*Interview by Jean W. Ross*

* * *

GEISSMAN, Erwin William 1920-1980

OBITUARY NOTICE: Born September 21, 1920, in New York, N.Y.; died July 30, 1980, in Queens, N.Y. Educator. A specialist in Renaissance literature, Geissman was a professor of English at Fordham University and a founding editor of *Cross Currents.* The journal, started in 1950, features contemporary religious writing from Europe. Obituaries and other sources: *Directory of American Scholars,* Volume II: *English, Speech, and Drama,* 7th edition, Bowker, 1978; *New York Times,* August 4, 1980.

* * *

GENNARO, Joseph F(rancis), Jr. 1924-

PERSONAL: Born April 9, 1924, in Brooklyn, N.Y.; son of Joseph F. (a surgeon) and Elizabeth (Klemper) Gennaro; married Doris E. Margolin (an electron microscopist), November 10, 1943; children: Joanne Gennaro Selin, Tina, Lucia Gennaro Tranel, Joseph F. III, Justin. *Education:* Fordham University, B.S., 1946; University of Pittsburgh, M.S., 1949, Ph.D., 1951. *Home:* 100 Bleecker St., New York, N.Y. 10012. *Office:* Department of Biology, New York University, 952 Brown Building, Washington Square, New York, N.Y. 10003.

CAREER: New York University, New York, N.Y., professor of biology, 1969—. Biological photographer for Photo-Researchers, 1978—; scientific director of American Institute for Toxin Research. *Military service:* U.S. Army, 1943-46. *Member:* American Society for Cell Biology, American Physiological Society, American Association of Anatomists, Meteor Research Society, Royal Microscopical Society. *Awards, honors:* Research fellow at Brookhaven National Laboratory, 1952-56, and Harvard University, 1964-65; American Medical Association service award, 1967, for consultation to the medical faculty of University of Saigon; Gustav Ohaus Award from National Science Teachers Association, 1976, for innovative approaches to science teaching; *Small Worlds Close Up* was named one of the best books of the year by *School Library Journal,* 1978.

WRITINGS: (With Lisa Grillone) *Small World's Close Up,* Crown, 1978.

WORK IN PROGRESS: A photographic view of the body as seen through the eyes of a five-year-old child, with Lisa Grillone, publication by Crown expected in 1982; *Small Worlds of the Sea,* with Grillone, publication by Crown expected in 1982; a photographic view of the body of an adolescent as seen by the subject, with Grillone, publication by Crown expected in 1983.

SIDELIGHTS: Gennaro commented: "Much of contemporary research, especially in the area of cell biology, is lost to the public for want of interpreters. This occurs at a time when our need to understand the physical (and physiological) consequences of environmental conditions could not be greater. Our efforts, however, are directed not to populariza-

tion of conservation data, as has been done by many others, but toward the spread of basic information so that it can easily be comprehended, usually through the use of photographic material. It is our intention to deliver, especially to the youth of today, a simple and useful understanding of the complex scientific information which deals with the structure and function of the units of life."

BIOGRAPHICAL/CRITICAL SOURCES: Times Literary Supplement, March 28, 1980.

* * *

GEORGIOU, Steven Demetre 1948-
(Cat Stevens)

PERSONAL: Professional name, Cat Stevens; born July, 1948, in London, England; son of restauranteurs. *Education:* Attended Hammersmith College, 1966. *Religion:* Islam. *Residence:* London, England.

CAREER: Singer, songwriter, composer, and recording artist, beginning 1966. Performer in concert tours in Europe and the United States. Star of educational television show, KCET-TV, June, 1971. *Awards, honors:* Has received several Gold Albums.

WRITINGS—Under name Cat Stevens: *Teaser and the Firecat* (juvenile), self-illustrated, Scholastic Book Service, 1974.

Recordings: "Matthew and Son," Deram, c. 1967; "New Masters," Deram, c. 1967; "Mona Bone Jakon," A & M/Island, 1970; "Tea for the Tillerman," A & M/Island, 1971; "Teaser and the Firecat," A & M/Island, 1972; "Catch Bull at Four," A & M/Island, 1972; "Very Young and Very Early Songs," Deram, 1972; "Foreigner," A & M/Island, 1973; "Buddha and the Chocolate Box," A & M/Island, 1974; "Numbers," A & M/Island, 1975; "Greatest Hits," A & M/Island, 1975; "View From the Top," Deram, c. 1976; "Izitso," A & M, 1977.

Lyricist and composer of songs, including "I Love My Dog," "Matthew and Son," "I'm Gonna Get Me a Gun," "Here Comes My Baby," "First Cut Is the Deepest," "Mona Bone Jakon," "I Think I See the Light," "Lady D'Arbaville," "Katmandu," "Time," "Fill My Eyes," "Lilywhite," "Where Do the Children Play," "Hard Headed Woman," "Wild World," "Sad Lisa," "Miles From Nowhere," "But I Might Die Tonight," "Longer Boats," "Into White," "On the Road to Find Out," "Father and Son," "Tea for the Tillerman," "Music," "Oh Very Young," "Ghost Town," "Jesus," "Ready," "King of Trees," "Bad Penny," "Home in the Sky," "Moonshadow," "Morning Has Broken," "Peace Train," "Sitting," "The Hurt," "Foreigner Suite," "Bad Breaks," "Days at the Old Schoolyard," "Child for a Day," "I Never Wanted to Be a Star," and "Was Dog a Doughnut?"

SIDELIGHTS: Cat Stevens's first recording, "I Love My Dog," hit Britain's top-thirty charts in 1966. This song, along with "Matthew and Son," which reached number two on the charts, soon established Stevens as a pop star. Touring England and Europe during the next year, he attracted a large following of enthusiastic teenage fans. He also recorded two albums and wrote several songs that were successfully recorded by other performers.

By 1968 Stevens had become dissatisfied with the "bubblegum" image of his songs, but his record company, Deram, opposed his attempts at innovation. Then, in September of that year, Stevens developed tuberculosis and was confined to a sanitorium for three months. During his convalescence,

Stevens completely revamped his style. "His songs, which had been strident, were now hushed—understated, wistful or whimsical. Most of them were mournful, all of them thought out and, if there was still a recurrent glibness, there was also a definite musical personality, a new and distinct flavor," said Nik Cohn.

Nearly forgotten by his early fans, Stevens waited until 1970 to record his new songs on the album "Mona Bone Jakon." Accompanied only by guitar, percussion, and flute, he produced a simpler sound with sensitive lyrics that reestablished his popularity, but this time with a much wider audience. As Bart Mills noted, "the balding can listen to him without earmuffs and the hairy can groove without grass."

The gold albums "Tea for the Tillerman" and "Teaser and the Firecat" contained some of Stevens's biggest hits, including "Father and Son," "Wild World," "Miles From Nowhere," "Moonshadow," "Morning Has Broken," and "Peace Train." Stevens told one reporter that "the song that really did it for me was 'Father and Son.'" It is written as a dialogue in which a father advises his son to marry and settle down, and the son rebels: "It's always been the same old story. / From the moment I could talk I was ordered to listen . . . / If they were right I'd agree but it's them they know not me / now there's a way and I know that I have to go away." Stevens told the reporter that the song took eight months to write because "I had something I wanted to express here, about two generations, and I couldn't get it right. I didn't want anything crappy, it had to be from both sides and different levels. . . . When it was over, though, I felt really marvelous—at last I could express what I wanted and what I needed."

Many of Stevens's followers became disenchanted with his later albums "Foreigner" and "Numbers." In these compositions he abandoned the simple style that had made him popular and delved into increasingly more complex themes and orchestrations. His 1977 "Izitso" album contained the pop singles "I Never Wanted to Be a Star," "Child for a Day," and "Old Schoolyard," but none of these reached the heights of his earlier hits.

In 1977 Stevens embraced the Islamic religion and adopted the name Yusuf. He retired from concert tours and has since lived as a recluse in London.

BIOGRAPHICAL/CRITICAL SOURCES: New York Times, October 24, 1971; *Toledo Blade,* January 6, 1974; *Biography News,* Gale, Volume 1, number 2, 1974; *Crawdaddy,* July, 1977; *People,* August 20, 1979.*

*   *   *

GERLACH, John 1941-

PERSONAL: Born August 1, 1941, in Baltimore, Md.; son of Charles A. (a lawyer) and Doris (a secretary; maiden name, Heintz) Gerlach; married Lana Kutsick (a librarian), December 19, 1970. *Education:* Kenyon College, B.A., 1963; Columbia University, M.F.A., 1965; Arizona State University, Ph.D., 1968. *Home:* 3061 Coleridge Rd., Cleveland Heights, Ohio 44118. *Office:* Department of English, Cleveland State University, Cleveland, Ohio 44115.

CAREER: Maysles Brothers (documentary filmmakers), New York City, apprentice editor, 1964; Columbia University, New York City, equipment supervisor in film department, 1964-65; Cleveland State University, Cleveland, Ohio, assistant professor, 1968-74, associate professor of English, 1974—.

WRITINGS: (With wife, Lana Gerlach) *The Critical Index:*

A Film Bibliography, Teachers College Press, 1974. Contributor to academic journals and film and literary magazines.

WORK IN PROGRESS: The Glass House, a novel.

SIDELIGHTS: Gerlach wrote: "There are two areas I like to work in: film—I want to bring as much to bear as I can on individual films, trying to discover the implications of significant films for film theory; and fiction—my inclination is toward the comic and fantastic."

*   *   *

GEROELY, Kalman
See GABEL, Joseph

*   *   *

GEROLY, Kalman
See GABEL, Joseph

*   *   *

GETZ, Malcolm 1945-

PERSONAL: Born November 1, 1945, in Somerville, N.J.; son of Harold Edward (a farmer) and Catherine (a teacher; maiden name, Minnick) Getz; married Ruthann Lorenzo; children: Wystan, Kiesa. *Education:* Williams College, B.A. (cum laude), 1967; Yale University, Ph.D., 1973. *Home:* 717 Richfield Dr., Nashville, Tenn. 37205. *Office:* Department of Economics and Business, Vanderbilt University, Nashville, Tenn. 37240.

CAREER: Spelman College, Atlanta, Ga., instructor in economics, 1969-71; Vanderbilt University, Nashville, Tenn., assistant professor, 1973-79, associate professor of economics, 1979—. Member of research staff of National Bureau of Economic Research, 1977 and 1978. *Member:* American Economic Association, Southern Economic Association, Western Economic Association, Phi Beta Kappa. *Awards, honors:* Woodrow Wilson fellowship, 1967; National Science Foundation grant, 1974-76, fellowship, 1977; grants from Tennessee State Planning Department, 1975, and U.S. Department of Labor, 1978.

WRITINGS: (Contributor) John Quigley and John Meyer, editors, *Local Public Finance and the Fiscal Squeeze: A Case Study,* Ballinger, 1977; *The Economics of the Urban Fire Department,* Johns Hopkins Press, 1979; *Public Libraries: An Economic View,* Johns Hopkins Press, 1980. Contributor of more than a dozen articles and reviews to magazines, including *Stanford Law Review.*

*   *   *

GIFF, Patricia Reilly 1935-

PERSONAL: Born April 26, 1935, in Brooklyn, N.Y.; daughter of William J. and Alice Tiernan (Moeller) Reilly; married James A. Giff (a detective), January 31, 1959; children: James, William, Alice. *Education:* Marymount College, B.A., 1956; St. John's University, Jamaica, N.Y., M.A., 1958; Hofstra University, diploma, 1975. *Religion:* Roman Catholic. *Home:* 6 Ann Court, Elmont, N.Y. 11003. *Agent:* Marilyn Marlow, Curtis Brown Ltd., 575 Madison Ave., New York, N.Y. 10022. *Office:* Carlson School, Elmont Public Schools, Elmont, N.Y. 11003.

CAREER: Public school teacher in New York, N.Y., 1956-60; Elmont Public Schools, Elmont, N.Y., elementary teacher, 1964-71, reading consultant, 1971—. *Member:* Society of Children's Book Writers.

WRITINGS—Juveniles: Fourth Grade Celebrity, Delacorte,

1979; *The Girl Who Knew It All*, Delacorte, 1979; *Today Was a Terrible Day*, Viking, 1980; *Next Year I'll Be Special*, Dutton, 1980; *Left Handed Shortstop*, Delacorte, 1980; *Have You Seen Hyacinth Macaw?*, Delacorte, 1981.

WORK IN PROGRESS: The Great T L & M Worm Business (tentative title), a juvenile.

*   *   *

GIFFORD, Denis 1927-

PERSONAL: Born December 26, 1927, in London, England; son of William Thomas (a printer) and Amelia (Hutchings) Gifford; married Angela Kalagias (divorced); children: Pandora Jane. *Education:* Attended Dulwich College, London, England. *Politics:* Liberal. *Religion:* Protestant. *Home:* 80 Silverdale, Sydenham, London SE26 4SJ, England.

CAREER: Reynolds News, London, England, staff cartoonist, 1944-45; free-lance cartoonist and writer, 1945—. Producer for compilation film unit of Associated British-Pathe, 1963; program editor for cinemagazines film unit of Central Office of Information, 1965; guest on radio and television programs; lecturer on history of British comics and cartoons. *Military service:* Royal Air Force, 1946-48.

MEMBER: British Film Institute, British Academy of Film and Television Arts, British Music Hall Society, Society of Strip Illustration (founder), Association of Comic Enthusiasts (founder; president), Cartoonists Club, Film Funsters (founder), Ephemera Society, Edgar Wallace Society, Children's Books History Society, Sons of the Desert. *Awards, honors:* Diplomas from International Festival of Comics, 1975, 1976, and 1978, for lectures on British comics history.

WRITINGS: Space Patrol Handbook, Gifford, 1952; *Cinema Britanico*, British Council, 1963; *British Cinema*, Tantivy-Zwemmer, 1968; *Movie Monsters*, Studio Vista, 1969.

Science Fiction Film, Studio Vista, 1971; *Discovering Comics*, Shire, 1971; *Stap Me!: The British Newspaper Strip*, Shire, 1971; *Test Your N.Q.*, New English Library, 1972; *Fifty Years of Radio Comedy*, New English Library, 1972; *A Pictorial History of Horror Movies*, Hamlyn, 1973; *The British Film Catalogue, 1895-1970*, David & Charles, 1973; *Karloff: The Man, the Monster, the Movies*, Curtis, 1973; *Movie Makers: Chaplin*, Macmillan, 1974; *Victorian Comics*, Allen & Unwin, 1974; *The Armchair Odeon: Collector's Guide to the Movies*, Fountain, 1974; *Happy Days: One Hundred Years of Comics*, Jupiter, 1975; *The British Comic Catalogue, 1874-1974*, Mansell, 1975; *Run Adolf Run: The World War Two Fun Book*, Corgi, 1975; *The Morecambe and Wise Comic Book* (juvenile), Carousel, 1977; *Monsters of the Movies*, Carousel, 1977; *Stewpot's Fun Book* (juvenile), Independent Television, 1977; *The Two Ronnies Comic Book* (juvenile), Carousel, 1978; *Eric and Ernie's T.V. Fun Book* (juvenile), Independent Television, 1978; *Quick on the Draw*, Independent Television, 1978; *The Illustrated Who's Who in British Films*, Batsford, 1979; *The Great Cartoon Stars: A Who's Who*, Jupiter, 1979.

Editor: *Six Comics of World War I*, Peter Way, 1972; *Film Pictorial: 1933 Souvenir Edition*, Peter Way, 1973; *Penny Comics of the Thirties*, New English Library, 1974; *Comics 101: Souvenir Book*, Gifford, 1976; *The Best of Eagle*, M. Joseph, 1977.

Scripts: "Morning Melody," released by I.T.V. in 1956; "Highlight: The Singing Cinema," released by Associated British in 1962; "The Sporting Year," released by Pathe in 1963; "Laughter in the Air," first broadcast by British Broadcasting Corp. (BBC), 1979. Author of scripts for commercial advertisements. Creator and compiler of "Sounds Familiar," on BBC-Radio, 1967-75, "Looks Familiar," on Thames Television, 1971—, and "Quick on the Draw," on Thames Television, 1974—. Game creator for "Bruce Forsyth's Generation Game," BBC-TV, 1972. Scriptwriter for Yorkshire Television children's series, "Witch's Brew," "Junior Showtime," and "The Laughing Policeman," 1973.

Cartoonist, writer, and editor for children's comic books and newspaper comic strips, including "Steadfast McStaunch," in *Knockout Comic*, 1950-51, "Flip and Flop," in *Marvelman*, 1955-59, "Telestrip," in *Evening News*, 1956—, "Adventures of Baron Munchausen," in *Classics Illustrated*, 1958, "Koo Koo Klub," in *Whizzer & Chips*, 1969-71, "Tellytoons," in *Rex Magazine*, 1971-72; producer of comic supplement in *Reveille*, 1976, and "Potty Time," in *Daily Star*, 1979.

Contributor to *The World Encyclopedia of Comics*, Chelsea House, 1976, and *The World Encyclopedia of Cartoons*, Chelsea House, 1979. Contributor of articles to magazines and newspapers, including *The Guardian*. Editor and publisher of *Comic Cuts* newsletter and *British Comics Encyclopedia;* co-publisher and editor of *Ally Sloper*, 1976-77.

WORK IN PROGRESS: The Golden Age of Horror Films; Out of the Inkwell: A History of the Silent Animated Cartoon Film; The Great American Comic Books; Entertainers on Film; American Serial Films: A Complete Catalog; The Looks Familiar Nostalgia File; Science Fiction in Comics.

SIDELIGHTS: Gifford told *CA:* "Starting out as a cartoonist and comic strip artist/writer, my career switched in midstream so that my hobby, which had been collecting and researching cinema history, became my livelihood, and my cartooning and collecting of comics became my hobby. All my books reflect my twin interests, and my main aim is to rescue and restore past achievements in both fields, and record for today and posterity the work of forgotten artists in popular entertainment. This is also the motive behind my long-running television series, 'Looks Familiar,' my radio series, 'Sounds Familiar,' and the formation of the largest known private collection of comics."

BIOGRAPHICAL/CRITICAL SOURCES: Stage, March 26, 1964; *Observer*, September 3, 1972; *Reveille*, December 30, 1972; *Newsagent Bookshop*, December 20, 1974; *Guardian*, November 15, 1975; *Times*, March 20, 1976; *Evening News*, July 14, 1978.

*   *   *

GIFFORD, Prosser 1929-

PERSONAL: Born May 16, 1929, in New York, N.Y.; son of John Archer and Barbara (Prosser) Gifford; married Shirley Mireille O'Sullivan (an independent researcher), June 26, 1954; children: Barbara, Paula, Heidi. *Education:* Yale University, B.A., 1951, Ph.D., 1964; Oxford University, B.A., 1953; Harvard University, LL.B., 1956. *Politics:* Democrat. *Religion:* Episcopal. *Home:* 429 N St. S.W., Apt. S608, Washington, D.C. 20024; and Penzance Point, Woods Hole, Mass. 02543. *Office:* Wilson Center, Smithsonian Bldg., 1000 Jefferson Dr. S.W., Washington, D.C. 20560.

CAREER: Yale University, New Haven, Conn., assistant professor, 1964-66, director of five year B.A. program, 1965-66; Amherst College, Amherst, Mass., associate professor, 1967-69, professor of history, 1969-79, dean of the faculty, 1967-79. Wilson Center, Washington, D.C., deputy director, 1975-76 and 1980—. Member of board of trustees of Hotchkiss School, 1970-80, and Concord Academy, 1972-78; chairman of board of trustees of Marine Biological Laboratory, 1978—. *Member:* Century Association, Cosmos Club. *Awards, honors:* Rhodes scholarship, 1951; foreign area fellowship, 1963-64; LL.D. from Doshisha University, 1979; L.H.D. from Amherst College, 1980.

WRITINGS: (Editor and contributor) *Britain and Germany in Africa,* Yale University Press, 1967; (editor and contributor) *France and Britain in Africa,* Yale University Press, 1971; (editor and contributor) *Transfer of Power in Africa,* Yale University Press, 1981.

*   *   *

GILBERT, S(tuart) R(eid)   1948-

PERSONAL: Born March 16, 1948, in Kamloops, British Columbia, Canada; son of John Stuart and Ellen Molly (Reid) Gilbert. *Education:* University of Victoria, B.A., 1969; University of British Columbia, M.A., 1972. *Office:* Department of English, Capilano College, North Vancouver, British Columbia, Canada V7J 3K9.

CAREER: Capilano College, North Vancouver, British Columbia, instructor in English, 1971—, lecturer in cinema, 1972-73, head of Division of Humanities, 1973-75, associate dean of academic studies and educational support services, 1975-79. Instructor at University of British Columbia, summer, 1971. Member of Vancouver Art Gallery, Victoria Art Gallery, and Vancouver Community Arts Council. *Member:* Canadian Theatre History Association, Association of Canadian Community Colleges, Humanities Association of Canada, Pacific Northwest Conference of Teachers of English, Vancouver Symphony Society, Capilano College Faculty Association.

WRITINGS: "A Glass Darkly" (one-act play), first produced in Vancouver, British Columbia, at Counterpoint Theatre, 1972. Also author of other plays, "Grandma's a Little Hard of Hearing" (three-act farce), and "Pomp and Circumstance" (one-act).

Work represented in anthologies, including *Dialogue and Dialectic: An Anthology of Short Canadian Plays,* Alive Press, 1973, and *Transitions I: Short Plays,* Commcept Publishing, 1978.

Contributor to *Contemporary Poets, Contemporary Dramatists,* and *Communique.* Assistant editor of *The Capilano Review,* 1972.

WORK IN PROGRESS: A Reader's/Student's Guide to Canadian Drama.

SIDELIGHTS: Gilbert wrote: "I consider the creation of handy reference material on Canadian literature an essential part of the job of a Canadian scholar, particularly in drama, where little reference material is available." *Avocational interests:* Food; world travel; the language, culture, food, and customs of France and Quebec.

*   *   *

GILDAY, Robert M.   1925(?)-1980

OBITUARY NOTICE: Born c. 1925; died June 18, 1980, in New York, N.Y. Editor. A managing editor of Morehouse-Barlow Co. since 1978, Gilday had worked for such publishers as Crowell Collier Macmillan, McGraw-Hill, and Seabury Press. Obituaries and other sources: *Publishers Weekly,* July 25, 1980.

GILLIAN, Kay
See SMITH, Kay Nolte

*   *   *

GILMORE, Christopher Cook   1940-
(C. C. Pary)

PERSONAL: Born August 3, 1940, in Washington, D.C.; son of Edwin Lanier King Gilmore (a writer) and Margot (an artist; maiden name, Cook) Dawson. *Education:* Attended George Washington University, 1959-61; University of Miami, Coral Gables, Fla., B.A., 1964; attended Stanford University, 1965. *Home:* 8801 Atlantic Ave., Margate, N.J. 08402. *Agent:* Peter Miller Agency, 1021 Avenue of the Americas, Suite 403, New York, N.Y. 10018. *Office:* 161 rue du Faubourg St. Antoine, 75011 Paris, France.

CAREER: Associated Press, bureau news staffer in Richmond, Va., and Denver, Colo., 1965-66; elementary school teacher in Absecon, N.J., 1966-68; writer, 1968—. Beachmaster of Catamaran Racers, Margate, N.J. Member of Margate Beach Patrol, 1957-67. *Military service:* U.S. Marine Corps Reserve, 1964. *Member:* Mensa (life member).

WRITINGS: Atlantic City Proof (novel), Simon & Schuster, 1979; (under pseudonym C. C. Pary) *Slavers* (novelization of a screenplay), Charter, 1980. Contributor of about forty short stories to magazines, including *Gallery, Swank, Chic, Genesis,* and *Surfer.*

WORK IN PROGRESS: A suspense novel about insanity.

SIDELIGHTS: Gilmore told *CA:* "I write in the morning every day but Sunday, working three to four hours, no more. By noon I'm finished and free to spend the day as I like, sailing in the summer, walking in the winter.

"In the fall I need the city, New York, Paris, London, or Rome, and I stay three or four months depending on the action. Then, when change becomes necessary, I get in my van and go camping in Spain, Morocco, Greece, anywhere that's warm. In the spring I head for home, Margate, and the beautiful beaches there.

"I know how to survive and writing is my only source of income. I have no wife, house, or children, but I do have a van, a Hobiecat, the love of a beautiful woman, and plenty of time to enjoy them. I would trade my life for none other, but I would recommend my lifestyle to very few: artists and madmen only, people with few material needs and plenty of imagination.

"Fame and wealth may be in the future, but if they're not I won't mind, just as long as I can keep writing, keep drifting, loving my lady and all the fascinating people and places there are to see. If there is any one thing I'm searching for, I guess it's a good story."

*   *   *

GIOVACCHINI, Peter L(ouis)   1922-

PERSONAL: Born April 12, 1922, in New York, N.Y.; son of Alex (a sculptor) and Therese (Chicca) Giovacchini; married Louise Post, September 29, 1945; children: Philip, Sandra, Daniel. *Education:* Attended Columbia University, 1939; University of Chicago, B.S., 1941, M.D., 1944; postdoctoral study at Chicago Institute of Psychoanalysis, 1949-54. *Politics:* Liberal. *Religion:* None. *Home:* 270 Locust Rd., Winnetka, Ill. 60093. *Agent:* Maria Caravainis, 235 West End Ave., New York, N.Y. 10023. *Office:* 505 North Lake Shore Dr., Chicago, Ill. 60611.

CAREER: Fordham Hospital, New York, N.Y., intern,

1944-45; University of Chicago, Chicago, Ill., resident, 1945-46 and 1948-50, research fellow, 1948-50; private practice of psychoanalysis in Chicago, Ill., 1950—. Clinical associate at Chicago Institute of Psychoanalysis, 1957—; clinical professor at University of Illinois, 1961—; consultant to family service bureaus. *Military service:* U.S. Army, Medical Corps, 1946-48; became captain. *Member:* American Psychiatric Association (fellow), American Orthopsychiatric Association (fellow), American Psychoanalytical Association, Chicago Psychoanalytic Society, Chicago Society for Adolescent Psychiatry (president, 1966-67), Society for Adolescent Psychiatry.

WRITINGS: (With L. B. Boyer) *Psychoanalysis of Characterological and Schizophrenic Disorders,* Jason Aronson, 1967, revised edition, 1980; (editor) *Tactics and Techniques in Psychoanalytic Treatment,* Jason Aronson, Volume I, 1970, Volume II, 1972, revised two-volume edition, 1981; *Psychoanalysis of Character Disorders,* Jason Aronson, 1972, revised edition, 1981; *Treatment of Primitive Mental States,* Jason Aronson, 1979; *The Urge to Die: Suicide and Modern Youth,* Macmillan, 1980. Contributor to medical journals. Co-editor of *Adolescent Psychiatry: Annals of the American Society for Adolescent Psychiatry.*

WORK IN PROGRESS: Regressed States, seminars on the writings of Sigmund Freud.

SIDELIGHTS: Giovacchini commented to *CA:* "As a clinician, I turn to writing to help me organize my thinking. The very act of writing is creative. When I sit down with an empty page in front of me, I do not know how I will fill it. The ideas come as I take the pen in my hand. This capacity can be developed if one feels intensely in the outside world and accumulates experiences. To write, one first has to live."

*   *   *

GIRARD, Robert C(olby) 1932-

PERSONAL: Born January 22, 1932, in Aberdeen, S.D.; son of Colby E. (a grocer) and Viola (Korhonen) Girard; married Audrey Inez Gisselbeck (an elementary school teacher), August 5, 1952; children: Christine Diann Girard Poehls, Robert Colby II, Charity Joy. *Education:* Miltonvale Wesleyan College, B. Rel., 1955; also attended Augsburg College, Minneapolis, Minn., 1956-57. *Home and office:* 13237 North 38th St., Phoenix, Ariz. 85032.

CAREER: Ordained Wesleyan Methodist minister; pastor of Methodist churches in Rice, Kan., 1953-55, Minneapolis, Minn., 1955-57, and Hayward, Wis., 1957-59; Miltonvale Wesleyan College, Miltonvale, Kan., director of development, 1959-64; Billy Graham Evangelistic Association, Minneapolis, Minn., field representative, 1964-65; pastor of Methodist church in Scottsdale, Ariz., 1965-78; team member of Dynamic Church Ministries in Phoenix, Ariz., 1979—. Justice of the peace of Rice, Kan., 1954. *Member:* National Association of Evangelicals.

WRITINGS: Brethren, Hang Loose, Zondervan, 1972; *Brethren, Hang Together,* Zondervan, 1979; *My Weakness: His Strength,* Zondervan, 1981. Contributor to *Action, Wesleyan Advocate,* and *Faith at Work.*

WORK IN PROGRESS: The Protagonist of the Lord, church history, 150-250 A. D., publication expected in 1982.

SIDELIGHTS: Girard wrote: "Most of my motivation for writing grew out of a shaking process of renaissance and renewal which began in Our Heritage Church in Scottsdale, Arizona, during the early days of my pastorate there. This renewal was touching everything in church life, and radical change was taking place. At the urging of author Lawrence O. Richards, I wrote *Brethren, Hang Loose* to describe these changes and the biblical ecclesiology behind them. The book was so well received, and sparked such significant specific change in so many other churches, that it seemed necessary to produce a sequel that would refine and update the message of the first. I write out of deep, personal faith in Jesus Christ, and the belief that He, living His resurrection life through His body, the living church, is the only answer to the persisting dilemma of man."

BIOGRAPHICAL/CRITICAL SOURCES: Lawrence O. Richards, *A New Face for the Church,* Zondervan, 1971; Richards, *Three Churches in Renewal,* Zondervan, 1975.

*   *   *

GIRONELLA, Jose Maria 1917-

PERSONAL: Born December 31, 1917, in Darnius, Gerona, Spain.

CAREER: Writer. *Awards, honors:* Nadal Prize, 1946, for *Un hombre.*

WRITINGS: Un hombre (title means "A Man"), [Spain], 1946, translation by Anthony Kerrigan published as *Where the Soil Was Shallow,* Regnery, 1957; *Los cipreses creen en Dios* (historical novel), [Spain], 1953, translation by Harriet de Onis published as *The Cypresses Believe in God,* Knopf, 1957; *Los fantasmas de mi cerebo* (historical novel), Editorial Planeta, 1959, translation by Terry Broch Fontsere published with *Todos somos fugitivos* as *Phantoms and Fugitives: Journeys to the Improbable,* Sheed & Ward, 1964 (also see below); *Un million de muertos* (historical novel), Editorial Planowa, 1961, translation by Joan Maclean published as *One Million Dead,* Doubleday, 1963; *Todos somos fugitivos* (historical novel), Editorial Planeta, 1961, translation by Fontsere published with *Los fantasmas de mi cerebo* as *Phantoms and Fugitives: Journeys to the Improbable* (see above); *On China and Cuba* (nonfiction), translated from the original Spanish by John F. Byrne, Fides, 1963; *Ha estallado la paz* (historical novel; title means "Peace Has Broken Out"), Editorial Planeta, 1966, translation by Maclean published as *Peace After War,* Knopf, 1969.

In Spanish: *Ha llegada el invierno y tu no estas aqui,* [Spain], 1946; *La marea* (novel; title means "The Tide"), Revista de Occidente, 1949; *El novelista ante el mundo* (nonfiction), Ateneo, 1954; *Mujer, levantate y anda* (novel; title means "Women, Rise and Walk"), Editorial Planeta, 1962; *Personas, ideas, mares* (travel), Editorial Planeta, 1963; *El Japon y su duende* (travel), Editorial Planeta, 1964; *China, lagrima innumerable* (history), Editorial Planeta, 1965; *Gritos del mar,* Editorial Planeta, 1967; *Conversaciones con don Juan de Borbon* (nonfiction), A. Aguado, 1968; *En Asia se muere bajo las estrellas* (travel), Plaza y Janes, 1968; *Cien* (religion; title means "One Hundred"), Ediciones Nauta, 1969; *Gritos de la tierra* (collection), Editorial Planeta, 1970; *Condenados a vivir* (novel), two volumes, Editorial Planeta, 1971; *El Mediterraneo es un hombre disfrazado de mar* (travel), Plaza y Janes, 1974; *El escandola de Tierra Santa* (travel), Plaza y Janes, 1977.

SIDELIGHTS: According to Robert Payne of the *Saturday Review,* Jose Maria Gironella "was the most intelligent and sensitive apologist for Franco, the one man who could describe the Spanish Civil War from the Nationalist side with a sympathetic understanding of all the forces at work." His best-known works in English translation—*The Cypresses Believe in God, One Million Dead,* and *Peace After*

War—chronicle events in Spain from the period of the republic through the civil war to the post-war era. In these three novels, Gironella portrays his country in microcosm, through the medium of the Alvear family and their home in the city of Gerona. With the publication of each novel, heated debates arose over whether Gironella's position was as a pro-Franco propagandist or an objective literary artist.

This controversy is apparent, for example, in the words of Anthony West in the *New Yorker:* "Senor Gironella has, unhappily, given us not Spain . . . but a Spanish novel capably expressing the ideologies of the regime in power." On the other hand, Stephen Klaidman, in a review of *Peace After War* for the *Washington Post,* maintained that "because Gironella lives in Spain, because he wants to be published and read there, he has devised an ingenious method for expressing views inconsistent with those of the Franco regime. He has created a world of mirrors, a universe and a cast of ideological opposites, drawn with such subtlety that one's own ideology necessarily colors the reading." David Gallagher of the *New York Times Book Review,* however, suggested that the foundation of Gironella's work is "a comfortably unshakable belief that, whatever the shortcomings of the brave new republic, unspeakable disaster would have followed its defeat." From this respectable vantage point, Gallagher continued, the author was free to engage in harmless "efforts at impartiality," although his "liberal titillations," such as the idea that "Reds" are "human beings and indeed Spaniards too," are overdone.

J. G. Harrison of *Commonweal* labeled *The Cypresses Believe in God* the "Great Catholic Novel" and described it as "a work of such power, compassion and significance for our century that its publication in the United States is a major literary event." And Thomas Curley of the *New York Times Book Review* praised the excellence of Gironella's ability "to treat a great and widely distorted subject with an impartiality that refuses to hate only one kind of evil, or to love only one aspect of good."

BIOGRAPHICAL/CRITICAL SOURCES: New York Times, April 10, 1955, November 17, 1957; *New York Herald Tribune Book Review,* April 10, 1955; *Commonweal,* April 15, 1955, December 20, 1963; *Atlantic,* May, 1955; *New Yorker,* May 28, 1955; *Christian Science Monitor,* July 8, 1955; *Saturday Review,* October 12, 1957, November 30, 1963, December 10, 1966, May 17, 1969; *New York Times Book Review,* October 20, 1963, May 1, 1964, June 1, 1969; *Newsweek,* October 21, 1963; *Critic,* April, 1964; *Times Literary Supplement,* August 22, 1968; *Best Sellers,* May 1, 1969; *Washington Post,* May 30, 1969; Ronald Schwartz, *Jose Maria Gironella,* Twayne, 1972; *Papers on Language and Literature,* winter, 1974; *Contemporary Literary Criticism,* Volume 11, Gale, 1979.*

*   *   *

GLADILIN, Anatoly (Tikhonovich) 1935-

PERSONAL: Born August 21, 1935, in Moscow, U.S.S.R.; son of Tihon (a lawyer) and Polina (a doctor; maiden name, Taradeyko) Gladilin; married Mary Taitch (a technical editor), April 10, 1955; children: Alla. *Education:* Received certificate from school N73 of Moscow, 1953; attended Institute of Literature, 1958. *Home:* 57 B-d Poniatowski, Paris, France 75012. *Agent:* L. Schroeter, 540 Central Building, Seattle, Wash. 98104. *Office:* Radio "Liberty," 20 Ave. Rapp, Paris, France 75007.

CAREER: Moskovsky Komsomoletz (newspaper), Moscow, U.S.S.R., chief of literature department, 1958-59; *Komso-*

molskaya Pravda (newspaper), Moscow, editor, 1960-61; Cinema Company of M. Gorky, Moscow, motion picture editor, 1962-63; *Fitil* (cinema journal), Moscow, motion picture editor, 1967-69; full-time writer, 1969-76; Radio "Liberty," Paris, France, journalist and correspondent, 1976—.

WRITINGS: Khronika vremen Viktora Podgurskogo (title means "Diary of Victor Podgursky"), Sovetskii pisatel', 1958; *Brigantina podnimaet parusa* (title means "Brigantina Is Raising Sails"), Sovetskii pisatel', 1959; *Vechnaia komandirovka* (title means "Eternal Mission"), Sovetskii pisatel', 1962; *Idushchii vperedi* (title means "Leader"), Molodaia gvardiia, 1962; *Pervyi den' novogo goda* (title means "The First Day of New Year"), Sovetskii pisatel', 1965; *Evangelie ot Robesp'era* (title means "Evangelie of Robespierre"), [Moscow], 1970; *Prognoz na zavtra* (title means "Forecast for Tomorrow"), [Frankfurt], 1972; *Sny Shlissel'burgskol kreposti* (title means "Dreams of Schlisselburg Tower"), [Moscow], 1974; *Dwa goda do wesny* (title means "Two Years Before Spring"), [Moscow], 1975; *Repetisia v piatnicu* (title means "Repetition on Friday"), [Paris], 1978; *The Making and Unmaking of a Soviet Writer,* translated by David Lapeza, Ardis, 1979; *Parigskaya yazmarka* (title means "Fair in Paris"), Effect Publishers (Tel-Aviv), 1980.

WORK IN PROGRESS: A novel, *The Big Derby.*

SIDELIGHTS: Gladilin told *CA:* "I lived in the Soviet Union for the first forty years of my life, and I wrote a considerable number of works on contemporary subjects, but the material on Russia and its problems is far from being exhausted and can furnish topics for many books to come. I shall go on writing here, in immigration, provided I find the time I need for my work."

*   *   *

GLASHEEN, Adaline 1920-

PERSONAL: Born January 16, 1920, in Evansville, Ind.; daughter of Frederick and Irene (Jenner) Erlbacher; married Francis Glasheen (an English professor), April 5, 1958; children: Alison Osborne. *Education:* Attended Indiana University; University of Mississippi, B.A., 1939; Washington University, St. Louis, Mo., M.A., 1940. *Home and office address:* Carrington Lane, Farmington, Conn. 06032.

CAREER: Wheaton College, Norton, Mass., instructor in English, 1943-46. Visiting lecturer at State University of New York at Buffalo, summers, 1967 and 1970.

WRITINGS: A Census of "Finnegans Wake": An Index of the Characters and Their Roles, Northwestern University Press, 1956; *Second Census of "Finnegans Wake,"* Northwestern University Press, 1967; (contributor) Clive Hart and David Hayman, editors, *James Joyce's "Ulysses": Critical Essays,* University of California Press, 1974; *Third Census of "Finnegans Wake,"* University of California Press, 1976. Contributor to literary magazines, including *Hudson Review* and *James Joyce Quarterly.*

WORK IN PROGRESS: Additions to *Third Census of "Finnegans Wake"; research on the narrative in *Finnegans Wake.*

SIDELIGHTS: In the introduction to *A Census of "Finnegans Wake,"* Glasheen wrote: "In 1950 I started, hit or miss, to draw up an alphabetical list of such proper names as I could discern in *Finnegans Wake.* I did it for the diversion of the thing and because I never could find given passages or people. I also had a vague idea that listing all the 'caricatures' of *Finnegans Wake* would solve the riddle of the book. Now I know that the riddle is not solved, nor all the people listed. I stop in mere exhaustion, confident that the *Census* as it now stands is a very fair index to *Finnegans Wake,* that its identifications light up some murky passages, and that it brings together most of the running verbal themes of the book.''

After receiving encouragement from Joycean scholars, Glasheen has continued to expand the census, and considers that to be ''full-time work.''

AVOCATIONAL INTERESTS: Jogging, travel (Ireland, Italy, France, Switzerland, England).

* * *

GLASS, Sandra
See SHEA, Robert (Joseph)

* * *

GLICK, Virginia Kirkus   1893-1980
(Virginia Kirkus)

OBITUARY NOTICE—See index for *CA* sketch: Born December 7, 1893, in Meadville, Pa.; died September 10, 1980, in Danbury, Conn. Editor, critic, businesswoman, and author. Virginia Kirkus headed the children's department at Harper & Brothers publishing company from 1926 to 1932. She later established a prepublication book reporting service, *Kirkus Reviews,* to fill the void that she felt existed between publishers and bookshops. The immensely successful service aided booksellers in deciding which books to order. Her writings include *A House for the Weekends* and *The First Book of Gardening.* Obituaries and other sources: *New York Times,* September 11, 1980; *Newsweek,* September 22, 1980; *Publishers Weekly,* September 26, 1980.

* * *

GLOVER, Denis (James Matthews)   1912-1980
(Peter Kettle)

OBITUARY NOTICE—See index for *CA* sketch: Born December 10, 1912, in Dunedin, New Zealand; died August 9, 1980, in Wellington, New Zealand. Author, poet, and typographer. Glover founded the Caxton Press publishing company in New Zealand and created the literary journal *Landfall.* His works include *Hot Water Sailor, Enter Without Knocking,* and *Wellington Harbour.* Obituaries and other sources: *London Times,* September 12, 1980.

* * *

GODINE, David R(ichard)   1944-

PERSONAL: Born September 4, 1944, in Cambridge, Mass.; son of Morton Robert and Bernice (Beckwith) Godine. *Education:* Dartmouth College, B.A., 1966; Harvard University, Ed.M., 1968. *Office:* David R. Godine, 306 Dartmouth St., Boston, Mass. 02116.

CAREER: Godine Press, Inc., Boston, Mass., founder and president, 1969—. Publication editor for David R. Godine (publisher), 1969—. *Military service:* U.S. Army, 1967. *Member:* American Antiquarian Society (fellow), Society of Printers, Massachusetts Historical Society (fellow), Grolier Club, Players Club, St. Botolph Club. *Awards, honors:* Fellow of Pierpont Morgan Library.

WRITINGS: (Compiler) *Lyric Verse: A Printer's Choice,* [Lunenburg, Vt.], 1966; (compiler with Owen Gingerich) *Renaissance Books of Science: From the Collection of Albert E. Lownes,* Dartmouth College, 1970. Author of *Charleston and Other Stories,* 1978, and *Stories, Fables, and Other Diversions.*

GOLAN, Matti   1936-

PERSONAL: Surname legally changed in 1955; born December 6, 1936, in Tel-Aviv, Israel; son of Shmuel and Shoshana (an artist; maiden name, Braun) Goldwasser; married Tik Nitza (a librarian), September 16, 1961; children: Lee, Tamar. *Education:* Attended University of Tel-Aviv, 1957-59; Hebrew University of Jerusalem, LL.B., 1964. *Religion:* Jewish. *Agent:* Scott Meredith Literary Agency, Inc., 845 Third Ave., New York, N.Y. 10022. *Office:* Ha'aretz, 2 Chavatzelet St., Jerusalem, Israel; and Israel Information Centre for Canada, 102 Bloor St. W., Suite 780, Toronto, Ontario, Canada M5S 1M8.

CAREER: The Jewish Agency, Montreal, Quebec, immigration emissary, 1966-69; *Ha'aretz,* Jerusalem, Israel, columnist, 1969-78; Israeli Embassy, Toronto, Ontario, minister of information for Canada, 1978-80; *Ha'aretz,* Jerusalem bureau chief and author of column ''In the Knesset,'' 1980—. *Military service:* Israeli Army, 1954-56; became lieutenant.

WRITINGS: The Secret Conversations of Henry Kissinger, Quadrangle, 1976; *The Geneva Crisis* (novel), A. & W. Publishers, 1981.

Co-author of ''City'' (three-act play), first produced in Jerusalem, Israel, at Khan Theatre, July, 1973. Also author of motion picture script, ''Son.''

WORK IN PROGRESS: A novel based on the banning of his first book, *The Secret Conversations of Henry Kissinger,* tentatively titled *The Ban;* a script, tentatively titled ''The Third Second World War.''

SIDELIGHTS: Golan told *CA:* ''My book on Kissinger was first banned and confiscated in Israel in March of 1975. The decision to ban the book was received by the Israeli Cabinet at a special meeting. The reason that was given by the prime minister was that the book was full of top secret documents. The revised book was released for publication in June, 1975, after a bitter public campaign. My lawyer in Israel is now engaged in an effort to release the original manuscript of the Kissinger book. If this effort is unsuccessful, we plan to file a petition with the Supreme Court.

''In 1977 the government of Israel offered me the chance to represent it for two years as minister of information in Canada. I decided to accept the offer in part in order to experience the work on the other side of the fence.''

* * *

GOLD, Aaron   1937-

PERSONAL: Born August 4, 1937, in Chicago, Ill.; son of Ben and Anne (a salesperson; maiden name, Silver) Gold; married Judith Ann Schwade (a secretary), August 11, 1957; children: Tracy, Sharon, Andrea. *Education:* Attended Northwestern University, 1955-56. *Politics:* Independent. *Religion:* ''Peripheral.'' *Home:* 1301 North Astor, Chicago, Ill. 60610. *Office:* 435 North Michigan, Chicago, Ill. 60611.

CAREER/WRITINGS: WBBM-TV (CBS affiliate), Chicago, Ill., production supervisor of news department, assistant promotion manager, public service director, and press representative, 1956-64; owner of public relations firm in Chicago, 1964-73; *Chicago Tribune,* Chicago, author of column ''Tower Ticket,'' 1973—. Author of syndicated column, ''Celebrity Ticker,'' for fifty newspapers, including *Chicago Tribune* and *New York Daily News.* Notable assignments include an exclusive interview with Barbra Streisand. Co-producer of ''Status Quo Vadis,'' New York, and associate producer of Ivanhoe Theatre, Chicago. Member of public relations committee for Chicago Red Cross and Chicago Heart Association.

GOLDBERG, Jan
See CURRAN, Jan Goldberg

* * *

GOLDING, Martin Philip 1930-

PERSONAL: Born March 30, 1930, in New York, N.Y.; son of Sidney Israel and Mildred (Lewis) Golding; married Naomi Holtzman, April 8, 1951; children: Shulamith, Belinda, Joshua. *Education:* University of California, Los Angeles, B.A., 1949, M.A., 1952; Columbia University, Ph.D., 1959. *Religion:* Jewish. *Home:* 25 Claremont Ave., New York, N.Y. 10027. *Office:* Department of Philosophy, Duke University, Durham, N.C. 27708.

CAREER: Columbia University, New York City, instructor, 1957-59, assistant professor, 1959-64, associate professor of philosophy, 1964-70; John Jay College of Criminal Justice of the City University of New York, New York City, professor of philosophy, 1970-76; Duke University, Durham, N.C., professor of philosophy and chairman of department, 1976—. Visiting professor at Bar-Ilan University, 1971-72; adjunct professor at Columbia University, 1971—. *Member:* International Society of Legal and Social Philosophy, American Philosophical Association, American Society of Political and Legal Philosophy.

WRITINGS: The Nature of Law, Random House, 1966; *Philosophy of Law,* Prentice-Hall, 1975. Contributor to philosophy and law journals.

WORK IN PROGRESS: A history of the concept of rights, publication by Rowman & Littlefield expected in 1982.

SIDELIGHTS: Golding wrote: "My most interesting writing projects have been three articles my wife and I wrote on population policy and landmarks preservation."

* * *

GOLDMAN, Carl A(lexander) 1942-

PERSONAL: Born September 16, 1942, in Brooklyn, N.Y.; son of Myron (a speech therapist) and Sybil (an executive secretary; maiden name, Lemberg) Goldman. *Education:* San Diego State University, B.B.A., 1965, M.S.B.A., 1968; attended University of California, Berkeley, 1968-71. *Home and office address:* 557 Wellington Dr., San Carlos, Calif. 94070. *Agent:* Michael Larsen, 1029 Jones St., San Francisco, Calif. 94109.

CAREER: Worked in several financial management positions with industrial corporations, 1965-75; Financial Systems Consultants, San Francisco, Calif., owner and president, 1975-79; California Microwave, Inc., Sunnyvale, Calif., supervisor of computer systems, 1979—. Accounting and computer programming instructor at University of California, Berkeley, 1968-71.

WRITINGS: Help!—There's a Computer in the Office!, Rising Star, 1979; *Grey Flannel Haiku,* Rising Star, 1981.

SIDELIGHTS: Goldman told *CA:* "*Help!—There's a Computer in the Office!* was motivated by my perception of the need to explain computers simply, easily, and clearly to people whose lives are being affected by them daily. It is one of very few books to deal with the real-world organizational impact of new computer-based systems." *Avocational interests:* Playing the guitar and handball, "philosphizing about male-female relationships in today's climate."

GOLDSMITH, Howard 1943-
(Ward Smith)

PERSONAL: Born August 24, 1943, in New York, N.Y.; son of Philip (a motion picture engineer) and Sophie (Feldman) Goldsmith. *Education:* City University of New York, B.A. (with honors), 1965; University of Michigan, M.A. (with honors), 1966. *Politics:* "Orwellian." *Religion:* "Humanism." *Home:* 41-07 Bowne St., Flushing, N.Y. 11355.

CAREER: Mental Hygiene Clinic, Detroit, Mich., psychologist, 1966-70; writer and editorial consultant, 1970—. Audiovisual writer for Encyclopaedia Britannica Educational Corp., 1970—. *Member:* Science Fiction Writers of America.

WRITINGS—Juvenile: *Turvy, the Backward Horse* (picture book), Xerox Education Publications, 1973; *The Whispering Sea* (novel), Bobbs-Merrill, 1976; *What Makes a Grumble Smile?* (picture book), Garrard, 1977; *The Shadow and Other Strange Tales,* Xerox Paperback Book Clubs, 1977; *Terror by Night and Other Strange Tales,* Xerox Paperback Book Clubs, 1977; (editor with Roger Elwood) *Spine-Chillers,* Doubleday, 1978; (with Wallace Eyre) *Sooner Round the Corner* (novel), Hodder & Stoughton, 1979; *The Plastic Age,* Educational Progress, 1979; *Invasion: 2200 A.D.* (novel), Doubleday, 1979; *Toto the Timid Turtle* (picture book), Human Sciences Press, 1980.

Work represented in anthologies, including *Crisis,* edited by Roger Elwood, Thomas Nelson, 1974; *Starstream: Adventures in Science Fiction,* Western Publishing, 1976; *Future Corruption,* edited by Elwood, Warner Paperback, 1976. Contributor to numerous adult and children's magazines, including *Saturday Evening Post, Scholastic, Weekly Reader, Highlights for Children, Outlook,* and *Opinion.* Also author of short fiction, sometimes under pseudonym Ward Smith.

WORK IN PROGRESS: A science fiction novel exploring "what might be termed n-dimensional time"; another collection of supernatural stories.

SIDELIGHTS: Goldsmith wrote: "I have a horror of boring the reader. We can all recall plodding through acres of murky narrative and sunless prose. My dread of tedium has, to a large extent, shaped my style and guided my choice of subject matter. I write with sometimes jolting force, not to assault the reader's senses, but to rouse him to a keener awareness. My plots emphasize suspense and mystery that, I hope, compel attention and intrigue the imagination. The challenge is greatest in writing for kids, especially the growing numbers of print-starved, picture-oriented non-readers and reluctant readers.

"Nowhere is storytelling in its purest form more evident than in literature for young people—often underrated, deprecated, or ignored. Yet it is a craft, a discipline, and an art form in every way as sophisticated and demanding as adult fiction. And there is an intimacy of relationship between reader and writer that is seldom equalled."

* * *

GOLDSTEIN, Jerome 1931-

PERSONAL: Born May 8, 1931, in Jersey City, N.J.; son of David (a builder) and Lillian (Greenfield) Goldstein; married Ina Pincus (an editor), August 23, 1952; children: Rill Ann, Nora, Alison. *Education:* Rutgers University, B.A., 1952. *Home:* 812 North Second, Emmaus, Pa. 18049. *Office:* JG Press, P.O. Box 351, Emmaus, Pa. 18049.

CAREER: Roger & Roger, Columbus, Ohio, technical editor, 1952-53; Rodale Press, Emmaus, Pa., executive editor, 1954-78; JG Press, Emmaus, editor and publisher, 1978—. Director of Institute on Man and Science; president of board of directors of Emmaus Public Library, 1966-69, treasurer, 1969-75.

WRITINGS: Garbage as You Like It, Rodale Press, 1970; *How to Manage Your Company Ecologically,* Rodale Press, 1972; *The New Food Chain,* Rodale Press, 1974; *Sensibile Sludge,* Rodale Press, 1976; *The Least Is Best Pesticide Strategy,* JG Press, 1979; *Recycling,* Schocken, 1980; *The New American (Business) Dream,* Scribner, 1981. Contributor to magazines, including *Organic Gardening and Farming, Compost Science,* and *In Business.*

SIDELIGHTS: Goldstein told *CA* that his interests are the relationship of small business to social improvement, waste recycling as energy policy, and turning wastes into resources. He commented: "Many of the same themes keep popping up in these three areas, as personal actions provide the clues to public policies and hopeful economics."

*   *   *

GOLOGOR, Ethan   1940-

PERSONAL: Born December 25, 1940, in New York, N.Y.; son of Harold and Esther (Shapiro) Gologor; married Masha Tumarkin, March 22, 1968; children: Matthew, Benjamin. *Education:* City College of the City University of New York, B.S., 1961; New York University, M.A., 1967; New School for Social Research, Ph.D., 1973. *Home:* 789 West End Ave., New York, N.Y. 10025.

CAREER: State University of New York, New York City, assistant professor of psychology, 1974-78; City University of New York, Medgar Evers College, New York City, associate professor of psychology, 1978—. Peace Corps volunteer in Somali Republic, 1962-64. *Member:* American Psychological Association, Authors Guild, Institute of Rational Psychotherapy.

WRITINGS: Psychodynamic Tennis, Morrow, 1979. Contributor to psychological journals, including *American Psychologist, Journal of Cross-Cultural Psychology, Child Study Journal,* and *Change.*

WORK IN PROGRESS: "I am currently working on a few projects, some of which embrace, some of which flirt with, and some of which painstakingly avoid psychological traditions."

SIDELIGHTS: In *Psychodynamic Tennis* Gologor attempts to provide tennis players with psychological strategies that will improve many aspects of their game. Jeff Greenfield said in *New York Times Book Review* that although Gologor "writes well . . . the problem is that there simply isn't that much to be said about playing tennis better by thinking better. In an effort to separate the front and back covers, Dr. Gologor is compelled to discuss everything: how to practice, how to rally, how to avoid being distracted by balls on the court," and so on. A *Time* reviewer commended the book, noting that Gologor's "courtside manner is casual and unintimidating, his prose free of psychojargon."

Gologor told *CA:* "I think writers are understandably defensive about psychologists, and psychologists are unforgivably arrogant about everyone, including writers, and that more of a *rapprochement* should be attempted, if only to show it's impossible."

BIOGRAPHICAL/CRITICAL SOURCES: New York Times Book Review, April 29, 1979; *Time,* July 2, 1979.

GOMBOSSY, Zoltan
See GABEL, Joseph

*   *   *

GOOCH, Steve   1945-

PERSONAL: Born July 22, 1945, in Surrey, England. *Education:* Trinity College, Cambridge, B.A. (with honors), 1967; graduate study at St. John's College, Cambridge, 1967-68, and University of Birmingham, 1968-69. *Residence:* London, England. *Agent:* Margaret Ramsay Ltd., 14-A Goodwin's Court, London WC2N 4LL, England.

CAREER: Free-lance writer and theatrical director, 1969-72; *Plays and Players,* London, England, assistant editor, 1972-73; Half Moon Theatre, London, resident dramatist, 1973-74; Greenwich Theatre, London, resident dramatist, 1974-75; director, lecturer, and writer, 1975—. Also worked as teacher. *Member:* Theatre Writers Union (member of negotiating team). *Awards, honors:* Arts Council scholarship, 1973; award from Thames Television, 1974, for "The Women-Pirates Ann Bonney and Mary Read."

*WRITINGS—*Plays: *Big Wolf* (two-act; translation and adaptation of play by Harald Mueller; first produced on the West End at Royal Court Theatre, April, 1972), Davis Poynter, 1972; *Will Wat: If Not, What Will?* (two-act; first produced in London at Half Moon Theatre, May, 1972), Pluto Press, 1975; *Female Transport* (two-act; first produced in London at Half Moon Theatre, November, 1973; produced in New York City, 1976), Pluto Press, 1975; (with Paul Thompson) *The Motor Show* (two-act; first produced in Dagenham, England, March, 1974; produced in London at Half Moon Theatre, March, 1974), Pluto Press, 1975; *The Mother* (two-act; translation and adaptation of play by Bertolt Brecht; first produced in London at Half Moon Theatre, May, 1972), Eyre Methuen, 1978; *The Women-Pirates Ann Bonney and Mary Read* (two-act; first produced on the West End at Aldwych Theatre, August, 1978), Pluto Press, 1978.

Translator: Wolf Biermann, *Poems and Ballads,* Pluto Press, 1977; Guenther Wallraff, *Wallraff, the Undesirable Journalist,* Pluto Press, 1978.

Unpublished plays: "Great Expectations" (two-act; adaptation of novel by Charles Dickens), first produced in Liverpool, England, at Liverpool Playhouse, December, 1970; "Man Is Man" (two-act; translation and adaptation of play by Brecht), first produced on the West End at Royal Court Theatre, March, 1971; "It's All for the Best" (two-act; adaptation of Voltaire's *Candide*), first produced in Stoke-on-Trent, England, at Victoria Theatre, May, 1972; "Nick" (one-act), first produced in Exeter, England, at Northcott Theatre, November, 1972; "Dick" (two-act), first produced in London at Half Moon Theatre, December, 1973; "Cock-Artist" (one-act; translation and adaptation of play by R. W. Fassbinder), first produced in London at Almost Free Theatre, November, 1974.

(Co-author) "Strike '26" (two-act), first produced on tour by Popular Theatre, May, 1975; (co-author) "Made in Britain" (two-act), first produced in Oxford, England, at Oxford Playhouse, May, 1976; "Our Land Our Lives" (two-act), first produced on tour by 7:84 Touring Theatre Company, October, 1976; "Back Street Romeo" (two-act), first produced in London at Half Moon Theatre, February, 1977; "Rosie" (one-act; translation of play by Harald Mueller), first produced in London at Half Moon Theatre, June, 1977.

Translator of radio plays: Askenazy, "The Kiosk," 1970; Harald Mueller, "Delinquent," 1978; Martin Walser, "Santis," 1980.

Unproduced plays: "How the Peace Was Lost"; "Passed On"; "What Brothers Are For" (based on Terence, *The Brothers*); "Home Work" (translation of play by Franz X. Kroetz); "Trumpets and Drums" (translation of play by Brecht); "In the Club."

WORK IN PROGRESS: "Public Relations," a play about white-collar workers; "Future Perfect" (tentative title), a play about problematic utopia, written with Paul Thompson and Michelene Wandor.

SIDELIGHTS: Gooch has won aclaim in England for his scholarly translations from French and German, as well as his original plays, and for his ability to represent working-class people realistically on stage.

*　　*　　*

GORDON, Bertram M(artin) 1943-

PERSONAL: Born April 19, 1943, in Brooklyn, N.Y.; married wife, Sherry L. (a professor), June 10, 1965; children: Karen, Andrew. *Education:* Brooklyn College of the City University of New York, B.A., 1963; Rutgers University, M.A., 1964, Ph.D., 1969. *Home address:* P.O. Box 9962, Mills College, Oakland, Calif. 94613. *Office:* Department of Social Science, Mills College, Oakland, Calif. 94613.

CAREER: Brooklyn College of the City University of New York, Brooklyn, N.Y., lecturer in history, 1967-69; Mills College, Oakland, Calif., assistant professor, 1969-76, associate professor of history, 1976—. *Member:* American Historical Association, Society for French Historical Studies, Western Society for French History (president, 1974-75). *Awards, honors:* American Philosophical Society grant, 1974.

WRITINGS: Collaborationism in France During the Second World War, Cornell University Press, 1980. Contributor to history journals.

WORK IN PROGRESS: A study of Germanic influences on the development of American cuisine.

SIDELIGHTS: Gordon told *CA:* "There is much to be learned about people's attitudes toward themselves and others by the way in which they eat and the food they choose. The cultural orientation of a society may be seen in the directions taken by its international cuisine: French, Italian, and Chinese, in the case of contemporary America. Historians of cuisine really study the way in which people think and express themselves in the language of food."

*　　*　　*

GORNICK, Vivian 1935-

PERSONAL: Born June 14, 1935, in New York, N.Y.; daughter of Louis and Bess (an office worker) Gornick. *Education:* City College of the City University of New York, B.A., 1957; New York University, M.A., 1960. *Home and office:* 175 West 12th St., New York, N.Y. 10011.

CAREER: State University of New York at Stony Brook, instructor in English, 1966-67; Hunter College of the City University of New York, New York City, instructor in English, 1967-68; *Village Voice,* New York City, staff writer, 1969-77; free-lance writer. *Member:* Authors Guild, P.E.N.

WRITINGS: (Editor with Barbara K. Moran) *Woman in Sexist Society: Studies in Power and Powerlessness,* Basic Books, 1972; *In Search of Ali Mahmoud: An American Woman in Egypt,* Saturday Review Press, 1973; *The Romance of American Communism,* Basic Books, 1978; *Essays in Feminism,* Harper, 1979.

WORK IN PROGRESS: A book of stories based on her experiences during a six-month trip to Israel in 1977.

SIDELIGHTS: Vivian Gornick's first book, *Woman in Sexist Society,* is a collection of thirty essays by professional writers and scholars. Edited in collaboration with Barbara K. Moran, the book delves into the issue of women in contemporary society and the sex role patterns that have been forced on them since childhood. Margaret Lichtenberg of *Nation* commended the book as a "particularly impressive addition to the writings from the women's liberation movement," and noted that the format of essays by various contributors was "a most appropriate vehicle to present the feminist point of view, since the women's movement is a collective action representing a variety of individuals." A. R. Schiller, moreover, hailed *Woman in Sexist Society* as a "lively, challenging book . . . which raises controversial questions and documents many of the answers."

Gornick's next book, *In Search of Ali Mahmoud,* began as an attempt to learn more about the society that had produced a close Arab friend of hers. She flew to Cairo in 1971 and was welcomed by her friend's family, not as a stranger, but more as a distant relative. While living with this family, she was struck by the warmth and affection surrounding her. Sara Blackburn of *Ms.* observed that "a great deal of the experience that Gornick transmits here about the people of Cairo is unique, a commodity to be cherished because she communicates it with such openness, vigor, and depth of feeling."

The society that Gornick portrays in her book is one in which family relationships and personal friendships take precedence over the acquisition of material goods, success, and the abundance of leisure activities that some other cultures find so appealing. "Tenderness is what you feel in the streets, in the offices, in the conversations, . . . in the way men embrace on the streets, in the way people run to help if someone stumbles, in the way a woman smooths back her servant's hair," reflected Gornick.

During her stay in Cairo Gornick encountered doctors, secretaries, editors, artists, and other professionals of the Egyptian middle class—the class that is changing the face of life and politics in that country. She also witnessed the sexism that locks Egyptian women into a definition of themselves only in relation to their male counterparts. Gornick is sympathetic to the state of these women, but as Blackburn pointed out, "her real interest is in the male society into which she, as an American woman journalist, a safe outsider, could be and was so eagerly accepted." Blackburn further asserted that "the narrative of [Gornick's] journey is . . . a diary of her relationships with Egyptian men [whom she] manages to portray . . . with a dimension, power, and an understanding that I missed in her depiction of the book's women, who are far more fleeting and remote within the society and to her." Elizabeth Janeway, however, defended Gornick as "one of the least obsessed or dogmatic feminists one can imagine," and praised the "glimpse of the chiaroscuro of Egyptian life, and an ineradicable sense of what it must mean to be a woman in this tense, chaotic society."

Although both critics found *In Search of Ali Mahmoud* to be valuable and enjoyable, Blackburn felt somewhat overwhelmed with its length: "I ended up feeling that I'd been exposed to too much of a good thing, surfeited instead of wanting." Janeway disagreed, declaring that "above all, this is a rich book, full of felt life, but structured by a strong and reasoning mind. . . . What keeps the vivid material from getting out of hand is what makes this a truly important book: Miss Gornick's ability to see below the surface and to pull out the meaning of an encounter. She can give us the shocking, moving reality of an event or a scene and then, like a descent in a speeding elevator, fall to the heart of the affair."

BIOGRAPHICAL/CRITICAL SOURCES: Library Journal, July, 1971; *Nation,* November 8, 1971; *New York Times Book Review,* October 21, 1973, December 2, 1973, February 12, 1978, April 2, 1978, February 4, 1979; *New Republic,* November 24, 1973, March 18, 1978, February 24, 1979; *Christian Science Monitor,* December 12, 1973; *Village Voice,* December 20, 1973, February 13, 1978; *Ms.,* February, 1974, March, 1979; *Commentary,* February, 1978; *New Leader,* March 13, 1978; *New Yorker,* March 13, 1978; *Saturday Review,* March 18, 1978; *New York Review of Books,* April 6, 1978; *Commonweal,* August 4, 1978; *West Coast Review of Books,* March, 1979.*

*   *   *

GOTTLIEB, William P(aul)   1917-

PERSONAL: Born January 28, 1917, in New York, N.Y.; son of Samuel (a businessman) and Lena (Barnet) Gottlieb; married Delia Potofsky (a library film programmer), July 2, 1939; children: Barbara, Steven, Richard, Edward. *Education:* Lehigh University, B.S., 1938; graduate study at University of Maryland, 1941-42. *Home and office:* 11 Market Lane, Great Neck, N.Y. 11020.

CAREER: Washington Post, Washington, D.C., advertising solicitor, 1938-40, music columnist, 1939-42; University of Maryland, College Park, instructor in economics, 1940-41; U.S. Government, Office of Price Administration, economist, 1941-42; *Down Beat,* New York City, writer and editor, 1946-47; William Gottlieb Co., New York City, president of University Films, 1949-68; McGraw-Hill Book Co., New York City, president of University Films, 1968-78; writer, 1978—. Photographs exhibited at Aberdeen Art Museum, Nassau Fine Arts Museum, and Israel Art Museum. *Military service:* U.S. Army Air Forces, photographer, 1942-46; became first lieutenant. *Awards, honors:* Thirteen first prizes from Educational Film Librarians Association's American Film Festival, for filmstrips; award from Boys' Clubs of America, 1959, for *Jets and Rockets and How They Work.*

WRITINGS—With own photographs: *Photography, With Basic Cameras: A Family Activity Book,* Knopf, 1953; *Table Tennis: A Sports Activity Book,* Knopf, 1954; *This Is the N.M.U.: A Picture History of the National Maritime Union of America C.I.O.,* William Gottlieb Co., 1956; *The Golden Age of Jazz: On-Location Portraits, in Words and Pictures, of More Than Two Hundred Outstanding Musicians From the Late Thirties Through the Forties,* Simon & Schuster, 1979.

Juvenile; with own photographs; all published by Simon & Schuster except as noted: *Laddie and the Little Rabbit,* 1952; *Laddie, the Superdog,* 1954; *Tiger's Adventure,* 1954; *Pal and Peter,* 1956; *Farmyard Friends,* 1956; *The New Kittens,* 1957; *The Four Seasons,* 1957; *Jets and Rockets and How They Work,* Garden City Books, 1959; *Aircraft and How They Work,* Garden City Books, 1960; *Space Flight and How It Works,* Doubleday, 1963.

Other juvenile: *A Pony for Tony,* Simon & Schuster, 1955; *The Real Book About Photography,* Garden City Books, 1957.

Author of more than four hundred filmstrips.

WORK IN PROGRESS: A science book for young readers, publication by Franklin-Watts expected in 1981; filmstrips for labor unions.

SIDELIGHTS: Gottlieb told *CA:* "I consider myself primarily an explainer. To this end, I try always to put myself in the position of a typical reader, which in turn calls for presentations that are simple and clear. I am especially careful not to assume that members of my audience know more facts than should be expected of them. I even tend to avoid slang words and idioms, since these are not universally understood. And rather than use a puzzling or specialized word, followed by a definition, I prefer to first describe the thing and *then* give the specialized word for it, carrying the reader from the familiar to the unfamiliar, not the other way around.

"In an effort to make myself as clear as possible, I usually combine photos or drawings with my text. I do not simply spot the illustrations here and there. Instead, I try to integrate words and pictures so that one cannot exist without the other; they become completely interdependent. This technique is particularly useful in expository works but I also use it in fiction for children.

"I have been particularly pleased by the reception given my latest effort, *The Golden Age of Jazz,* in which I tried, with words and photographs, to tell about the remarkable musicians who played jazz during the 1930's and 1940's. Reviews have come in from all over the United States and Canada, and from as far away as Scotland, Italy, and Japan. To one extent or another, the reviews say that the book does seem to have captured the qualities of these artists."

Whitney Balliett of the *New Yorker* praised the quality of Gottlieb's photographs in *The Golden Age of Jazz:* "Gottlieb was not taking pictures; he was photographing a music. Again and again, he catches the precise moment when the musician's face is suffused with effort and emotion and beauty: the music is *there.* . . . Gottlieb stopped photographing jazz musicians in 1948. No one has surpassed him yet."

AVOCATIONAL INTERESTS: Father-son team tennis.

BIOGRAPHICAL/CRITICAL SOURCES: New Yorker, October 29, 1979.

*   *   *

GOULDEN, Mark   1896(?)-1980

OBITUARY NOTICE: Born c. 1896 in Bristol, England; died May 3, 1980. Journalist and publisher. At one time the youngest editor of a daily newspaper in England, Goulden was chairman of the W. H. Allen publishing company in England for thirty-six years. Among the writers he introduced to readers were Dylan Thomas and Alan Sillitoe. He was a pioneer of British civil aviation, the inventor of the Gouldris Matrix Machine, and the author of an autobiography, *Mark My Words.* Obituaries and other sources: *The Author's and Writer's Who's Who,* Burke's Peerage, 1971; *Who's Who,* 126th edition, St. Martin's, 1974; *Who's Who in the World,* 4th edition, Marquis, 1978; *The International Who's Who,* Europa, 1979; *Publishers Weekly,* June 20, 1980.

*   *   *

GOULYASHKI, (Stoianov) Andrei   1914-

PERSONAL: Born June 17, 1914, in Rakovitza, Bulgaria; son of Stoian Tzekov (a clerk) and Teodora Petrova (Velkova) Goulyashki; married Emilia Petrova, February 1, 1936; children: Liubomir Andreev, Svetla Andreeva (Mrs. Dimitar Nenkov Balkanski). *Education:* Attended Sofia University, 1936-38. *Politics:* Communist. *Religion:* "No." *Home:* 59 General Biurozov Bldg., Sofia, Bulgaria 1504. *Agent:* Bulgarian Copywrite Agency, 11 Slaveikov Sq., Sofia, Bulgaria 1000. *Office:* Union of Bulgarian Writers, 5 A. Kunchev St., Sofia, Bulgaria 1000.

CAREER: Writer. Worked as director of National Theatre in Sofia, Bulgaria, 1963-66. People's representative in National Assembly of Bulgaria. *Member:* P.E.N. *Awards, honors:* Laureat of Dimitrov's Prize; named Hero of Socialist Labour.

WRITINGS—In English: *Seven Days of Our Lives,* translated from the Bulgarian by Zdravko Stankov, Foreign Languages Press [Bulgaria], 1966; *Prikhucheniiata na Avakum Zakhov* [Bulgaria], translation by Maurice Michael published as *The Zakhov Mission,* Doubleday, 1969; *Prikhuchenie v polunosht* [Bulgaria], translation by Georgina Moudrova published as *Adventure at Midnight,* Sofia Press [Bulgaria], 1976; *Sluchaiat v Momchilovo* [Bulgaria], translation by Moudrova published as *The Momchilovo Affair,* Sofia Press, 1976.

In Bulgarian; English translations of titles: "Don Quixote From Silvezia," Nov Sviat, 1936; "Swamp," Nov Sviat, 1937; "Women," Nov Sviat, 1938; "Death Sentence," Nov Sviat, 1940; "New Moon," Narizdat, 1944; "Steps in the Snow," Narizdat, 1946; "A Machine and Tractor Station," Profizdat, 1950; "Love," Profizdat, 1955; "A Precious Stone," Narodna Mladej, 1956; "The Golden Fleece," Bulgarski Pisatel, 1958; "Vedrovo: A Chronicle of a Village," Profizdat, 1959; "Counterespionage," Bulgarski Pisatel, 1959.

Other Bulgarian titles in English translation; all published by Bulgarski Pisatel, except as noted: "The Sleeping Beauty," 1961; "The Adventures of Avakum Zakhov," 1962; "In a Rainy Autumn," 1963; "A Little Night Music," 1965; "Against 07," 1966; "A Novelette for the Cavalier," 1966; "Himerius: His Life in Pliska and Among the Slavs," 1969; "One Day and One Night," 1969; "The Golden Sleeve," 1969.

"The Golden Century," 1970; "A Romantic Story," Narodna Mladej, 1970; "The Home With the Mahogany Staircase," 1970; "The Three Lives of Iossif Dimov," 1977; "The Last Adventure of Avakum Zakhov and the Gold of Danaia," 1978; "A Department for Reanimation," 1979; "The Fruits of the Seasons," Bulgarian Writer Publishing, 1980.

Editor-in-chief of *Literaturen Front,* 1944, *Plamak,* 1955-66, *Obzor,* 1970, and *Savremennik,* 1970-72.

SIDELIGHTS: Goulyashki told *CA:* "The appearance of fascism and my attitude towards it was one of the circumstances that determined my literary career. Literature became a means of expressing this attitude to the world. My formation as a writer was also connected with looking for happiness, joy, and personal satisfaction, as well as the man/technology revolution and the ecological problem."

Goulyashki also speaks French and Russian.

AVOCATIONAL INTERESTS: Collecting pipes.

*   *   *

GOVIER, Katherine   1948-

PERSONAL: Surname is pronounced Go-*vee*-ay; born July 4, 1948, in Edmonton, Alberta, Canada; daughter of George Wheeler (an engineer) and Doris (a teacher; maiden name, Kemp) Govier. *Education:* University of Alberta, B.A. (with honors), 1970; York University, M.A., 1972. *Agent:* Elaine Markson Literary Agency, Inc., 44 Greenwich Ave., New York, N.Y. 10011.

CAREER: Ryerson Polytechnic Institute, Toronto, Ontario, instructor in English, 1974-75; free-lance writer, 1975—. *Member:* Writers' Union of Canada, Periodical Writers Association of Canada. *Awards, honors:* Authors' award from Foundation for the Advancement of Canadian Letters, 1979, for article, "Radical Sheik"; honorable mention in first novel competition from *Books in Canada,* 1979.

WRITINGS: Random Descent (novel), Macmillan, 1979, New American Library, 1980. Writer for Canadian Broadcasting Corp. (CBC-Radio). Author of "Relationships," a monthly column in *Toronto Life,* 1975-77. Contributor to magazines and newspapers. Associate editor of *Weekend,* 1977.

WORK IN PROGRESS: A novel about a dancer, publication expected in 1981; collecting short stories for a book.

SIDELIGHTS: Govier wrote: "I am an Alberta-born writer living in the east of Canada, still exploring what makes me neither a part of my home province nor my chosen one. I have moved frequently in my life so far, having lived in Alberta, Ontario, and England, and I plan to move again to Washington, D.C. I think I have tried to understand the differences in people and places in my writing. More recently I have turned from writing about place and how it forms people to writing about how the 'artistic' inclination survives today. I love journalism because it keeps me in touch with new things."

*   *   *

GRAHAM, Charles S.
See TUBB, E(dwin) C(harles)

*   *   *

GRANT, James Russell   1924-

PERSONAL: Born December 14, 1924, in Bellshill, Scotland; son of William Martyn (a metallurgist) and Margaret (a company secretary; maiden name, Lawson) Grant; married Olga Zarb (an occupational therapist), March 26, 1955; children: Christopher Russell. *Education:* University of Glasgow, degree, 1945, M.B.Ch.B., 1951. *Politics:* Socialist. *Religion:* Buddhist. *Home:* 255 Creighton Ave., London N.2, England. *Office:* Clinic, Gatesden, Cromer St., London W.C.1, England.

CAREER: Assistant general practitioner of medicine in London, England, 1952-53; Maudsley Hospital, London, registrar at Institute of Psychiatry, 1954-55; Provincial Guidance Clinic, Red Deer, Alberta, psychiatrist, 1955-57; medical practitioner in London, 1958—. Medical adviser to Thomas Coram Foundation (adoption agency); medical officer at King's Cross Hostel for the Homeless, of London's Department of Health and Social Security, 1970—. *Military service:* British Army, Scottish Rifles, 1945-47. *Member:* British Medical Association, Cruising Association.

WRITINGS: Hyphens (poems), Putnam, 1958; *Poems,* Botteghe Oscure, 1959; (translator) Guillaume Apollinaire, *Zone,* Library, Harvard University, 1961; *The Excitement of Being Sam,* Outposts Publications, 1977; *The Cracked Weather Set,* Ambit, 1980. Writer for British Broadcasting Corp. and Canadian Broadcasting Corp. Contributor to psychiatry journals.

WORK IN PROGRESS: The Feeling of One, poems on inner-city life; *The Silent Scream,* cartoon stories; *Self and Social Realism,* essays on positive aspects of anxiety; *State of Emergency,* autobiographical sketches.

SIDELIGHTS: Grant wrote that his motivation is to "understand anxiety as a means to personal, social, and political progress. We must *be* more than we *are*. Social realism is the active presence of personality emerging in the body politic. H. Marcuse said 'It demands the political synthesis of experience as a constitutive act.' Poetry is the written science of this so-far latent power: an awareness of universality in individuality.

"I have lived in post-war Paris, with its existentialism, gloomy tartan bars, jazz and the Bhagavad-Gita, and its other writers. I have lived in the Glasgow slums during the depression of the thirties. In recent years I have lived in Sicily and Brittany."

AVOCATIONAL INTERESTS: Ocean cruising.

*   *   *

GRANT, Venzo
See STANSBERGER, Richard

*   *   *

GRANTON, Ester Fannie   1914(?)-1980

OBITUARY NOTICE: Born c. 1914 in Newport News, Va.; died of a heart attack, June 16, 1980, in Washington, D.C. Journalist. Granton was a reporter and deputy bureau chief in Washington, D.C., for Johnson Publications, publishers of *Ebony* and *Jet* magazines. She had covered the political scene in Washington since 1956, including the White House, Congress, and the Supreme Court, and had served as an unofficial adviser for White House functions. Obituaries and other sources: *New York Times*, June 20, 1980.

*   *   *

GRATTAN, C(linton) Hartley   1902-1980

OBITUARY NOTICE—See index for *CA* sketch: Born October 19, 1902, in Wakefield, Mass.; died June 25, 1980, in Austin, Tex. Educator, expert on Australia and the Southwest Pacific, and author. Gratton taught at the University of Texas and wrote several books, including *Why We Fought, Introducing Australia, The United States and the Southwest Pacific,* and *The Three Jameses*. Obituaries and other sources: *New York Times*, June 30, 1980.

*   *   *

GREEN, Maureen Patricia   1933-

PERSONAL: Born November 23, 1933, in London, England; daughter of Thomas and Edith Florence Snowball; married Timothy Seton Green (a writer), October, 1959; children: Miranda. *Education:* University of London, B.A. (with honors), 1955. *Religion:* None. *Home:* 140 Rosendale Rd., Dulwich, London SE21 8LG, England. *Agent:* A. D. Peters & Co. Ltd., 10 Buckingham St., London WC2N 6BU, England.

CAREER: Time-Life, International, London, England, correspondent, 1956-63; *London Observer,* London, feature editor of color magazine, 1965-70; writer, 1970—.

WRITINGS: Fathering, McGraw, 1976 (published in England as *Goodby Father,* Routledge & Kegan Paul, 1976); *Giving a Party,* Architectural Press, 1980. Contributor to magazines, including *Reader's Digest* and *Smithsonian.*

WORK IN PROGRESS: A book on the current state of marriage in Europe, publication by Collins expected in 1981.

SIDELIGHTS: Maureen Green wrote: "I divide my time between books on the modern family and magazine work in the arts, especially painting and the theatre.

"What mainly interests me in writing books on the role of the father in the modern family and now on contemporary marriage, is the extent to which individuals are influenced in their personal lives by changes in the world of ideas. A decline in respect for masculine authority affects us all, but how exactly? The refusal to put the institution of marriage and its social obligations before our own wishes for personal happiness and growth is based on current changes in moral ideas. By reporting on how those ideas work out in individual lives we will gain the evidence to decide whether the ideas themselves need revision."

BIOGRAPHICAL/CRITICAL SOURCES: People, June 14, 1976.

*   *   *

GREY, Charles
See TUBB, E(dwin) C(harles)

*   *   *

GRIDBAN, Bolsted
See TUBB, E(dwin) C(harles)

*   *   *

GRIFFIN, John Howard   1920-1980

OBITUARY NOTICE—See index for *CA* sketch: Born June 16, 1920, in Dallas, Tex.; died of diabetes, September 9, 1980, in Fort Worth, Tex. Author best known for his book *Black Like Me.* Griffin darkened his skin with chemicals and ultraviolet light and traveled through the South as a black man in 1959. He chronicled his experiences in *Black Like Me* and wrote: "Nothing can describe the withering horror of this. You feel lost, sick at heart before such unmasked hatred." After the book's publication and despite repeated threats against his life, Griffin traveled to racially troubled cities across the United States in an effort to bridge the widening communication gap between the black and white communities. Griffin won several honors for *Black Like Me* and his other works, including the National Council of Negro Women Award, the Anisfield-Wolf Award, the Christian Culture Gold Medal, and the Pan African Association Kunda Humanitarian Award. Although he earned certificates in France for piano and musical composition, the author worked during his career as a photographer, lecturer, and journalist. He wrote syndicated columns for the International News Service and King Features and was also associate editor of *Ramparts.* Griffin's other books include *The Devil Rides Outside, Nuni, A Time to Be Human, Land of the High Sky, Scattered Shadows, Twelve Photographic Portraits, Jacques Maritain: Homage in Words and Pictures,* and *Hermitage Diaries.* Obituaries and other sources: Maxwell Geismar, *American Moderns: From Rebellion to Conformity,* Hill & Wang, 1958; Ann Freemantle, *Pilgrimage to People,* McKay, 1968; W. H. Auden, *A Certain World,* Viking, 1970; *Authors in the News,* Volume 1, Gale, 1976; *Washington Post,* September 10, 1980; *Newsweek,* September 22, 1980; *Time,* September 22, 1980; *AB Bookman's Weekly,* October 6, 1980.

*   *   *

GRIFFITHS, Bryn(lyn) David   1933-

PERSONAL: Born in 1933 in Swansea, Glamorganshire, Wales; son of Gwynrhydd (a docker) and Alice Griffiths; married; children: two. *Education:* Attended Swansea Technical College, 1960-61, and Coleg Harlech, 1961-62. *Religion:* None. *Home:* 182 Westview St., Perth, Western Australia, Australia 6019; and 65 Gwili Terrace, Swansea, Wales. *Office:* T.L.C., Trades Hall, Beafort St., Perth, Western Australia, Australia.

CAREER: Seaman in British Merchant Navy, 1951-58; worked as carpenter, salesman, and building worker, 1958-62; full-time writer, 1962-76; Trades and Labor Council of Western Australia, Perth, Australia, cultural adviser and arts coordinator for industry, 1976—.

WRITINGS—Poetry: *The Mask of Pity,* Christopher Davies, 1966; *The Stones Remember,* Dent, 1967; (editor) *Welsh Voices: An Anthology of New Poetry From Wales,* Dent, 1967; *Scars,* Dent, 1969; *At the Airport,* Sceptre Press, 1971; *The Survivors,* Dent, 1971; *Beasthoods: Poems,* Turret Books, 1972; *Starboard Green,* Imble Publications, 1973; *Dark Convoy: Sea Poems,* Aquila, 1974; *Love Poems,* Artlook Press, 1980; *The Shadow Beasts,* Artlook Press, 1981.

Radio plays: "The Sailor," broadcast on BBC-Radio, 1967; "The Dream of Arthur," broadcast on BBC-Radio, 1968.

Recordings: (With Bryan Walters) "The Stones Remember," Argo, 1973.

Also author of scripts for television programs, including "This Week," "Today," and "Aberfan."

SIDELIGHTS: Bryn Griffiths commented: "I am a writer from Wales currently living in Australia. I am very interested in the past and present of both countries, and I travel frequently between the two. My main areas of interest include community arts, theatre, modern poetry, history (particularly Celtic), the future of mankind, and raising hell."

*   *   *

GRIFFITHS, Naomi 1934-

PERSONAL: Born April 20, 1934, in Hove, England; daughter of Robert Lewis and Agnes Mary (Saunders) Griffiths. *Education:* Bedford College, London, B.A., 1956, Ph.D., 1969; University of New Brunswick, M.A., 1957. *Politics:* New Democrat. *Religion:* Roman Catholic. *Home:* 84 Sunnyside Ave., Ottawa, Ontario, Canada K1S 0R1. *Office:* Faculty of Arts, Carleton University, Ottawa, Ontario, Canada.

CAREER: College Maillet, lecturer in history, 1957-58; Carleton University, Ottawa, Ontario, instructor, 1961-62, lecturer, 1962-64, became assistant professor, 1964, professor of history, 1978—, dean of faculty of arts, 1979—. *Member:* Canadian Association of University Teachers (chairwoman of committee on the status of academic women in Canada, 1973), Canadian Research Institute for the Advancement of Women (member of board of directors), Canadian Historical Association. *Awards, honors:* Goldsmith traveling fellow, 1956; Lord Beaverbrook overseas fellow, 1958-60; Canada Council grants, 1971, 1972, 1973.

WRITINGS: The Acadian Deportation: Deliberate Perfidy or Cruel Necessity, Copp, 1969; *The Acadians: Creation of a People,* McGraw, 1973; *Penelope's Web: Some Perceptions of Women in European and Canadian Society,* Oxford University Press, 1976. Author of pamphlets and educational television scripts. Contributor of articles and reviews to magazines.

WORK IN PROGRESS: Writing on Acadian history and women.

AVOCATIONAL INTERESTS: Music, science fiction, cooking, cross-country skiing.

*   *   *

GRIMM, Cherry Barbara 1930-
(Cherry Wilder)

PERSONAL: Born September 3, 1930, in Auckland, New Zealand; daughter of Alan Hugh (a teacher) and Mamari (a teacher; maiden name, Taylor) Lockett; married Horst Grimm (a compositor), 1963; children: Catherine, Louisa. *Education:* University of Canterbury, B.A., 1952. *Politics:* "Labor voter in Australia; Social Democrat supporter in West Germany." *Religion:* None. *Home:* 16-B Egelsbacherstrasse, Langen 6070, Hessen, West Germany. *Agent:* Virginia Kidd, 538 East Harford St., Milford, Pa. 18337.

CAREER: Writer, 1941—. Worked variously in Australia as director of Theatre Arts Guild, 1954-61, as high school teacher of English and ancient history, 1958-61, and as editorial assistant and film librarian. *Member:* Science Fiction Writers of America, Women Writers of Australia, British Science Fiction Association. *Awards, honors:* Australia Council grant, 1973 and 1975; Australian Science Fiction Achievement Award from Australian National Science Fiction Convention, 1978, for *The Luck of Brin's Five.*

WRITINGS—Under pseudonym Cherry Wilder; science fiction novels: *The Luck of Brin's Five,* Atheneum, 1977; *The Nearest Fire,* Atheneum, 1980; *Second Nature,* Pocket Books, 1981; *The Tapestry Warriors,* Atheneum, in press.

Work represented in anthologies, including *The Ides of Tomorrow,* edited by Terry Carr, Little, Brown, 1976; *Rooms of Paradise,* edited by Lee Harding, Quartet Books, 1977; *Millenial Women,* edited by Virginia Kidd, Dell, 1978.

Contributor of articles, stories, and reviews to magazines, including *Meanjin* and *Prism International.*

SIDELIGHTS: Cherry Grimm told *CA:* "I was born and educated in New Zealand and have lived for many years in New South Wales, Australia. This gives me an unusual world view: I often write from the viewpoint of an alien or a colonial. I wrote short stories, reviews, and articles, and might have followed up with a regional Aussie novel, but I saw the light and turned to science fiction, following the friendly reception of my first science fiction story, 'The Ark of James Carlyle,' in 1974.

"In 1976 my husband and I moved to West Germany. My husband is German, but lived in Australia for twenty years. This is my first time in Europe, and I enjoy traveling in Germany and making visits to England. My German is coming along fairly well, but learning another language is playing hell with my French, which used to be fairly good. Some of my stories and my first novel will be appearing in German, and in August, 1980, I went to the BaerCon Science Fiction Convention in Berlin, where I was an honor member."

AVOCATIONAL INTERESTS: History, criminology, the occult, castles, cats, the women's movement.

*   *   *

GRIMSHAW, Nigel (Gilroy) 1925-

PERSONAL: Born November 5, 1925, in Manchester, England; son of Harold C. (a scientist) and Gladys Jeanne Grimshaw; married Margarete Apell, February 25, 1950; children: Rosemary, Mark, Peter, John. *Education:* Victoria University of Manchester, B.A. (with honors), 1950; University of Nottingham, M.A., 1976. *Home and office:* 3 Plane Trees, Rosedale E., Pickering, North Yorkshire, England. *Agent:* Bolt & Watson Ltd., 8-12 Old Queen St., Storey's Gate, London SW1H 9HP, England.

CAREER: Teachers Training College, Bangkok, Thailand, lecturer in English, 1958-62; grammar school teacher of English and department head, 1962-65; Kesteven College of Education, England, senior lecturer in English, 1965-79; writer, 1979—. *Military service:* Royal Navy, 1943-47. *Member:* International P.E.N., Society of Authors.

WRITINGS: Tiger Gold, Longmans, Green, 1964; *The Painted Jungle*, Longmans, Green, 1965; *David Copperfield, by Charles Dickens*, Longmans, Green, 1968; *The Sign of Indra*, edited by G. C. Thornley, Longmans, Green, 1968; *The Angry Valley*, Longmans, Green, 1970; *Bluntstone and the Wildkeepers* (juvenile), Faber, 1974; *The Wildkeepers' Guest* (juvenile), Faber, 1976.

All with Paul Groves; all for children; all published by Edward Arnold: *Up Our Way*, 1972; *Living Our Way*, 1973; *Thirteen Ghosts: A Collection of Original Ghost Stories With Suggestions for Varied Work in English*, 1976; *The Goodbodys*, 1976; *Thirteen Weird Tales: A Collection of Original Strange Stories With Suggestions for Varied Work in English*, 1977; *Action Stations: Seven Plays to Read or Record*, 1977; *Monsters of Myth and Legend*, 1977; *Smudge and Chewpen: A Book of Exercises for Correction of the Common Errors Made in Writing*, 1977; *Smudge and Chewpen Tests: A Book of Short Tests on the Common Errors Made in Writing*, 1977; *Call to Action: Seven Plays to Read or Record*, 1978; *Thirteen Horror Stories*, 1979; *Thirteen Sci-Fi Stories*, 1979; *Into Action*, 1979.

WORK IN PROGRESS: Another novel for children; textbooks.

SIDELIGHTS: Grimshaw commented: "My first children's novel began as a story I told my own children during a rather wet holiday in Wales. Since that was intentionally comic, I wrote *The Wildkeepers' Guest* in a more serious mode as a companion piece."

*   *   *

GRISE, Jeannette
See THOMAS, Jeannette Grise

*   *   *

GRISWOLD del CASTILLO, Richard 1942-

PERSONAL: Born October 26, 1942, in Los Angeles, Calif.; son of Stanley A. (a contractor) and Rose Marie (in business; maiden name, del Castillo) Griswold; married Maryann Girard, February 1, 1968; children: Charles Franklyn, Ariel Marie. *Education:* Attended University of California, Berkeley, 1960-62, and University of Dijon, 1962-63; University of California, Los Angeles, B.A., 1968, M.A., 1970, Ph.D., 1974. *Home:* 4620 Alice St., San Diego, Calif. 92115. *Office:* Department of Mexican-American Studies, San Diego State University, San Diego, Calif. 92182.

CAREER: Los Angeles Trade Technical College, Los Angeles, Calif., instructor, 1970-71; California Polytechnic State University, San Luis Obispo, assistant professor, 1972-74; San Diego State University, San Diego, Calif., associate professor of Mexican-American studies, 1974—.

WRITINGS: The Los Angeles Barrio, 1850-1890: A Social History, University of California Press, 1980.

WORK IN PROGRESS: A Social History of the Mexican-American Family in the Southwest.

SIDELIGHTS: Griswold del Castillo told *CA:* "I am interested in the history of the American Southwest in relation to its indigenous peoples. I have traveled throughout Arizona and New Mexico with brief excursions into Mexico. I am also committed to quantitative history in conjunction with traditional sources.

"Being a native of Southern California and Los Angeles I feel that the Mexican-American's history is especially important. *The Los Angeles Barrio* was an attempt to tell a ne-glected story of the fate of the thousands of working-class Mexicanos who had to confront a changed political and economic reality. My research in family history is an attempt to expand upon this subject by studying the changing family in four Southwestern towns: Tucson, Los Angeles, Santa Fe, and San Antonio. My work is part of a body of history being written by younger scholars who graduated from the University of California at Los Angeles in the 1970's."

*   *   *

GROPMAN, Donald S(heldon) 1936-

PERSONAL: Born January 26, 1936, in Boston, Mass.; son of Max W. (a bookkeeper) and Ida (Baker) Gropman; married Gabrielle Rossmer (a sculptor), June 21, 1959; children: Sonya, Adam. *Education:* Brandeis University, B.A., 1956; graduate study at Iowa State University, 1959-60; San Francisco State College, M.A., 1962. *Religion:* Jewish. *Home address:* RFD No. 1, West Stockbridge, Mass. 01266. *Agent:* John Brockman Associates, Inc., 200 West 57th St., New York, N.Y. 10019.

CAREER: Worked as a college teacher, social worker, educational and editorial consultant, anti-poverty program administrator, curriculum developer, private investigator, cab driver, and carpenter. *Awards, honors:* Named "Knight of Mark Twain" by *Mark Twain Journal*, for contribution to American biography.

WRITINGS: Say It Ain't So, Joe: The Story of Shoeless Joe Jackson, Little, Brown, 1979; (with Ralph A. DiOrio) *The Man Beneath the Gift: The Story of My Life*, Morrow, 1980. Work represented in anthologies, including *The Best American Short Stories of 1968*, Houghton.

Author of educational scripts. Contributor of about sixty-five articles, stories, and reviews to magazines and newspapers, including *Sport, Boston, Epoch. Literary Review, Yankee*, and *Boston After Dark*.

WORK IN PROGRESS: A murder mystery set in a Boston Jewish neighborhood during World War II; an autobiography; a collection of stories; a screenplay based on *Say It Ain't So, Joe*.

SIDELIGHTS: Gropman told *CA:* "I first heard about Shoeless Joe Jackson from my father when I was a small boy. When my father was young, he'd seen Jackson play baseball and never forgot the way he looked, particularly his gracefulness. My father told me many stories, but Shoeless Joe was one of the characters who stuck in my imagination. Many years later, when I came across a photo article about Joe in an old baseball magazine, my imagination was aroused. I wanted to know more about this shadowy figure and ended up writing a biography. I began my research with the assumption that Jackson was indeed guilty of the act for which he's best remembered—throwing the 1919 World Series. But when my research was concluded, I was convinced of his innocence. My greatest satisfaction from this book was being made a 'Knight of Mark Twain' by *Mark Twain Journal* for my 'contribution to American biography.'

"*The Man Beneath the Gift* grew out of a magazine assignment to do an article about Fr. DiOrio, whom I'd never met before. Fifteen minutes into the interview I suddenly suggested we write a book together. There was a moment of eye contact followed by a handshake. Details were worked out later.

"My plans for the immediate future call for a return to fiction writing, perhaps a play in which two legendary sports figures, Shoeless Joe Jackson and Ty Cobb, confront each other on stage, and an illustrated children's story, 'The Great Three Horned Chocolate Cake Eater.'"

BIOGRAPHICAL/CRITICAL SOURCES: Chicago Tribune, September 2, 1979; New York, October 8, 1979; St. Louis Globe Democrat, October 13-14, 1979; Brookline Chronicle Citizen, December 13, 1979.

* * *

GROSS, Terence 1947-
(Tristan Costinescu)

PERSONAL: Born August 22, 1947, in Buffalo, N.Y.; son of Ernest (a journalist) and Helen (Kniffen) Gross. Education: State University of New York at New Paltz, B.S., 1973. Home: 327 C St. S.E., Washington, D.C. 20003.

CAREER: Cornwall Local, Cornwall, N.Y., editor, 1976-77; Times Herald-Record, Middletown, N.Y., copy desk chief, 1977-79; Washington Star, Washington, D.C., national desk editor, 1979—; writer. Military service: U.S. Air Force, 1968-69. Member: Mystery Writers of America, American Film Institute.

WRITINGS: Tessie the Bitch (novella), Centergram Press, 1978. Also author of Fowler (novel), 1980. Translator of Chinese poetry under pseudonym Tristan Costinescu.

WORK IN PROGRESS: Movies of Themselves, a novel.

* * *

GROTH, John 1908-

PERSONAL: Surname is pronounced "Growth"; born February 26, 1908, in Chicago, Ill.; son of John (a store owner) and Ethel (a saleswoman; maiden name, Bragg) Groth; divorced; children: Tamar Collins. Education: Attended Chicago Art Institute, 1927-28, and Art Students League of New York, 1936-37. Politics: Liberal. Religion: Presbyterian. Agent: Robert Lescher, 155 East 71st St., New York, N.Y. 10021. Office: 61 East 57th St., New York, N.Y. 10022.

CAREER: Artist, illustrator, and journalist. Chicago Tribune, Chicago, Ill., artist, 1927 and 1929-30; Esquire (magazine), Chicago and New York City, art director, 1933-36; Parade (magazine), New York City, art director, 1941-45; Chicago Sun Syndicate, war correspondent in Europe, 1944-45; Art Students League of New York, instructor, 1946—; Pratt Institute, Brooklyn, N.Y., art instructor, 1952-55; Parsons School of Design, art instructor, 1954-55; National Academy of Design, art instructor, 1962-63; University of Texas, Austin, artist-in-residence, 1970. War correspondent in French Indo-China for Metropolitan Group Syndicate, 1951, in Asia for Sports Illustrated, 1954, in Congo-Central Africa for U.S. Air Force, 1960, in Dominican Republic, 1965, and in Vietnam for U.S. Marine Corps, 1967. Art works represented in collections at Museum of Modern Art, Library of Congress, Metropolitan Museum of Art, University of Texas, and University of Georgia.

MEMBER: American Watercolor Society, Overseas Press Club of America, National Academy of Design, Society of Illustrators, Lotus Club, Explorers Club. Awards, honors: D.Arts from Eastern Michigan University, 1976.

WRITINGS—Self illustrated: Studio: Europe, Vanguard, 1945; Studio: Asia, World Publishing, 1952.

Illustrator: (And author of introduction) Ernest Hemingway, Men Without Women, World Publishing, 1946; John Steinbeck, Grapes of Wrath, World Publishing, 1947; Harford Willing Hare Powel, Good Jobs for Good Girls, Vanguard, 1949; Lev Nikolaevich Tolstoi, War and Peace, Heinemann,

1961; Leon Uris, Exodus, Doubleday, 1962; Anna Sewell, Black Beauty, Macmillan, 1962; Charles Dickens, A Christmas Carol, Macmillan, 1963; O. Henry, The Stories of O. Henry, Heritage, 1966; Margaret Mitchell, Gone With the Wind, Heritage, 1968; Mark Twain, War Prayer, Harper, 1968; Erich Maria Remarque, All Quiet on the Western Front, Limited Editions Club, 1969; John Groth's World of Sport, text by Pat Smith, Winchester Press, 1970; Maia Wojciechowska, Life and Death of a Brave Bull, Harcourt, 1972; Giles Tippette, The Brave Men, Macmillan, 1972; Twain, Pudd'nhead Wilson, Limited Editions Club, 1974; John Graves, The Last Running, Encino Press, 1974; Arnold Gingrich, The Fishing in Print, Winchester Press, 1974; Kurth Sprague, The Promise Kept, Encino Press, 1975; Alice Hopf, Biography of an American Reindeer, Putnam, 1976. Sole illustrator of Short Story International, 1964-66 and 1977-80. Contributor of illustrations to periodicals, including Collier's, Esquire, Vogue, Saturday Evening Post, New Yorker, Fortune, Sports Illustrated, and Holiday Magazine.

SIDELIGHTS: Groth told CA: "What writing I've done is truly supplementary to my drawings and paintings. As a World War II artist, I found that if I sent pictures back to the United States without blocks of copy, they just weren't used, so, my sketchbook began to be filled with information (names, dates, places, and written descriptions of the things I saw) as well as drawings. So, with no intent of being an author, I was commissioned to do a book, Studio: Europe, in 1945, and in 1952, commissioned to do another, Studio: Asia, based on my experiences in the Korean War and my tour of duty with the French in the endless Indo-China war against the Viet Mink (later the Viet Cong).

"In the past thirty-five years since the war, I have applied the same technique of sketching and 'noting' in my sketch books, covering several minor wars and, between assignments, sports all over the world. I haven't been asked to write any books and have been too busy illustrating books to conceive of any writing I might do on my own.

"Luckily for me, as an artist, I've been able to do my assignments as portfolios and as I wished to do them. I have been fortunate also in being recognized as a painter as well as an illustrator. The pictures I have in museums are mainly in watercolor, and of sport scenes.

"Usually, when I illustrate a book, I read it two or three times, making notes while reading, then put the book away and proceed on my own, hoping to create a work of art that will complement the author's text."

* * *

GRUBB, Davis Alexander 1919-1980

OBITUARY NOTICE—See index for CA sketch: Born July 23, 1919, in Moundsville, W.Va.; died July 24, 1980, in Manhattan, N.Y. Novelist and short story writer. Grubb chronicled the lives of the West Virginia mountain dwellers in his work. The Night of the Hunter, Grubb's first and most successful novel, was followed by several other books, including Shadow of My Brother, The Golden Sickle, and Fool's Parade. Obituaries and other sources: New York Times, July 25, 1980.

* * *

GRUBB, Frederick (Crichton-Stuart) 1930-

PERSONAL: Born June 18, 1930, near Salisbury, Wiltshire, England. Education: Trinity College, Cambridge, M.A.,

1960; received Ph.D. from London University. *Politics:* Socialist.

CAREER: Writer. *Awards, honors:* Received Arts Council bursary, 1966.

WRITINGS: The Imperfect Day (poetry), Cambridge Express Printing Co., 1953; *Title Deeds and Other Poems,* Longmans, Green, 1961; *A Vision of Reality: A Study of Liberalism in Twentieth-Century Verse,* Barnes & Noble, 1965; *September Sun* (poetry; pamphlet), Sceptre Press, 1969; *Frog* (poetry), Sceptre Press, 1972. Contributor to periodicals, including *World Marxist Review, New Left Review, Le Provencal, La Marseillaise, Listener, Pravda, Phoenix,* and *Wave.*

BIOGRAPHICAL/CRITICAL SOURCES: New Statesman, September 24, 1965.*

*   *   *

GRUNLAN, Stephen Arthur   1942-

PERSONAL: Born February 9, 1942, in New York, N.Y.; son of Magnus Arthur and Esther (Lenea) Grunlan; married Sandra Jean Smits (a nurse), October 7, 1964; children: Stephen Arthur, Jr., Jaime, Rebecca. *Education:* Moody Bible Institute, diploma, 1968; Nyack College, B.S., 1970; Wheaton College, Wheaton, Ill., M.A., 1972; University of Illinois, M.A., 1976; Luther Theological Seminary, D.Min., 1981. *Home address:* P.O. Box 104, Mound, Minn. 55364. *Office:* Department of Social Science, St. Paul Bible College, Bible College, Minn. 55364.

CAREER: Ordained Christian and Missionary Alliance minister, 1977; Moody Bible Institute, Chicago, Ill., instructor in missions, 1972-77; St. Paul Bible College, Bible College, Minn., assistant professor of ministry and social science, 1977—. *Military service:* U.S. Army, 1960-65; served in signal corps. *Member:* American Sociological Association, Society for Applied Anthropology, Society for Psychological Anthropology, Christian Sociological Society.

WRITINGS: (With Marvin K. Mayers) *Cultural Anthropology: A Christian Perspective,* Zondervan, 1979; (editor with Milton Reimer, and contributor) *Christian Perspectives on Sociology,* Zondervan, 1981.

WORK IN PROGRESS: A book for training lay counselors in the church, with Daniel Lambrides, publication by Zondervan expected in 1981.

SIDELIGHTS: Grunlan told *CA:* "I am both a minister and a social scientist. I believe the social sciences have much to contribute to the ministry of the church, and my interest is in that application. I believe all truth is God's truth. The church must minister to society. To engage in that ministry it must understand society and its needs. To make the gospel of Jesus Christ relevant to society the church needs to utilize the findings and methodologies of the social sciences."

*   *   *

GUERRERO, Rogelio Diaz
See DIAZ-GUERRERO, Rogelio

*   *   *

GUTKIN, Harry   1915-

PERSONAL: Born August 10, 1915, in Winnipeg, Manitoba; son of Louis (a tailor) and Etta (Guravich) Gutkin; married Mildred Shanas (a professor), June 9, 1946; children: Diana Ruth Pollock, Risa Ellen Kahanovitch, Ralph Lawrence. *Education:* Attended Winnipeg School of Art, 1932, and Musgrove School of Art, 1933; studied under William Earl Singer, 1937. *Religion:* Jewish. *Home:* 503-301 Mandalay Dr., Winnipeg, Manitoba, Canada R2P 1C5. *Office:* Great Western Graphics Corp., 1328 Clifton St., Winnipeg, Manitoba, Canada R3E 2V2.

CAREER: Writer and illustrator. Publisher and editor for Contemporary Publishers, 1940-45; vice-president and managing director of Phillips-Gutkin & Associates Ltd., 1947-67; president of P.G.A. Films, 1949-67, and Producers Syndicate Ltd., 1957-67; creative director and director of sales of Brigdens of Winnipeg Ltd. Consultant to corporations in advertising, graphics, and design. *Member:* Canadian Jewish Congress, Prairie Region (chairman of the standing committee on research and archives), Jewish Historical Society of Western Canada (vice-president and chairman of exhibits, 1972-77; president, 1977-81). *Awards, honors:* Art Director's Awards for animated films, 1959 and 1960.

WRITINGS: (With Howard Fast) *Tito and His People,* Canadian edition, Contemporary Publishers, 1943; *A Treasury of Left Wing Humour,* Contemporary Publishers, 1945; *Journey Into Our Heritage: The Story of the Jewish People of the Canadian West,* Lester & Orpen Dennys, 1980; *The Jewish Canadians,* Van Nostrand, 1981. Also author of scripts for documentary and animated shorts. Director of *Journal of the Jewish Historical Society of Canada.* Contributor of political cartoons to *Winnipeg Free Press;* syndicated cartoonist for Canadian Weekly Newspapers' Association. Contributor of illustrations to periodicals, including *Toronto Star Weekly, Macleans,* and *Country Guide.*

SIDELIGHTS: Al Abrams, writing in the *Windsor Star,* called Gutkin's *Journey Into Heritage* "a beautiful book about the settlement of the Jews in Western Canada." He added that it is "both a memorial to those hardy pioneers who trekked across a continent, and a visually stunning presentation of living Canadian history." Gutkin himself labeled it "a labor of love." He told the *Toronto Star,* "I labored like a workaholic detective, seven days a week, sleuthing down the material."

Gutkin told *CA:* "If history is when the known past meets the unknown future, then I believe that it is important to know that past, so that we may better know and understand where we are going. Then, and only then, can we face that unknown future."

BIOGRAPHICAL/CRITICAL SOURCES: Windsor Star, June 28, 1980; *Toronto Star,* July 16, 1980.

*   *   *

GUTMAN, Richard J(ay) S(tephen)   1949-

PERSONAL: Born June 24, 1949, in Philadelphia, Pa.; son of I. Cyrus (in transportation) and Mildred (Largman) Gutman; married Kellie O'Connor (a teacher of the deaf), August 18, 1974. *Education:* Cornell University, B.Arch., 1972. *Home and office:* Slide Factor, 75 Gardner St., West Roxbury, Mass. 02132.

CAREER: Poor Willie Productions, Boston, Mass., designer, 1972-75; Pokanoket Club, Dover, Mass., caretaker, 1975-79; Slide Factor (slide show producers), West Roxbury, Mass., owner, 1979—. Instructor at Boston Architectural Center; wrestling coach in Dover, 1977-80. *Member:* Association for Multi-Image, Society for Commercial Archaeology, Lincoln Group of Boston.

WRITINGS: (With David Prendergast and others) *Lo Tech Air Domes,* privately printed, 1973; (with wife, Kellie O. Gutman) *John Wilkes Booth Himself,* Hired Hand Press,

1979; (with Elliott Kaufman and David Slovic) *American Diner,* Harper, 1979. Contributor to magazines and newspapers, including *Perspecta, Canadian Architect,* and *American Heritage.*

SIDELIGHTS: Gutman told *CA:* "I am a very visually oriented person. My writings to date have been heavily illustrated, and they have also tied in very closely with my work with Slide Factor, a multi-image production house. Five slide shows about diners, for example, preceded the publication of *American Diner.* 'Objects for Preparing Food' prompted a piece by George Irow in the *New Yorker*'s 'Talk of the Town'. That in turn led to a nationwide lecture tour of architecture schools with my next show, 'Grab It and Growl!: The Architecture and History of the Diner.'

"Two four-screen slide shows about Abraham Lincoln preceded the publication of *John Wilkes Booth Himself.* These were 'The Assassin's Act' and 'The Lincoln Nobody Knows,' which is permanently installed as the introduction to the Louis A. Warren Lincoln Library and Museum in Fort Wayne, Indiana.

"I like to write about subjects which hold a great deal of interest for me. The story of the diner was unknown before I researched it through oral history. I am proud that through my endeavors there has been an awakening in the mind of the public with regard to such mundane vernacular architecture as the diner. When I was asked in 1975 to make a presentation about diners before the annual meeting of the National Trust for Historic Preservation, I felt a turning point had been reached."

BIOGRAPHICAL/CRITICAL SOURCES: New Yorker, September 30, 1972; *Smithsonian,* March, 1980.

H

HAAS, Robert Lewis 1936-

PERSONAL: Born August 10, 1936, in Galion, Ohio; son of Joseph Michael and Lucille Esther (Ruth) Haas. *Education:* Atheneum of Ohio, B.A., 1958; Xavier University, Cincinnati, Ohio, M.Ed., 1962; Fordham University, M.S.W., 1969. *Home:* 914 Colburn St., Toledo, Ohio 43609. *Office:* Catholic Social Services, 1933 Spielbusch Ave., Toledo, Ohio 43624.

CAREER: Ordained Roman Catholic priest, 1962; assistant pastor of Roman Catholic churches in Defiance, Ohio, 1962-63, and Bowling Green, Ohio, 1963-67; Catholic Social Services, Toledo, Ohio, chaplain of Child Study Institute, 1969—, assistant director, 1969-73, diocesan director of family life, 1969-75, and resettlement, 1975—, diocesan pro-life director, 1972—, co-chairman of campaign for human development, 1974—. Member of Wood County Migratory Farm Labor Commission, 1964-67, Toledo Metropolitan Mission Board, 1970-78, and Economic Planning Opportunities Commission, 1970-73. *Member:* National Conference of Catholic Charities (member of standing committee, 1978—), Toledo Area Clergy Fellowship (president, 1974).

WRITINGS: Max, the Market Mouse (juvenile), Our Sunday Visitor, 1975; (editor with others) *Cantemos al Senor* (hymnal; title means "Let Us Sing to the Lord"), Our Sunday Visitor, 1975.

WORK IN PROGRESS: A book for juveniles, *Max and the House of INRI.*

SIDELIGHTS: Haas commented: "I am concerned about pro-life activities, Indochinese refugees, social work, prison reform and chaplaincy, and religious art. I feel we need to appeal to the higher nature of man, rather than emphasize the base instincts that we see often portrayed in today's mass media. Also, the family should be emphasized in its role of raising children with good moral values."

AVOCATIONAL INTERESTS: Travel (Spain, Mexico, South America).

* * *

HACKER, Shyrle 1910-

PERSONAL: Born March 15, 1910, in San Francisco, Calif.; daughter of Elmer N. (a tax collector) and Mary Theresa (McDonald) Pedlar; married Elmer Michael Hacker, 1934 (died, 1979); children: Gary Michael, Diane Hacker Stevens.

Education: Graduated from high school; received teacher's certificate for adult education from University of California Extension Division, 1975. *Politics:* Independent. *Religion:* "Free-lance." *Home:* 847 Trotter Court, Walnut Creek, Calif. 94596.

CAREER: Toured United States as dancer with Fanchon and Marco Theatrical circuit, 1929-34; Shyrle Dance Studio, Oakland, Calif., teacher and manager, 1934-45; Pleasant Hill Adult School, Pleasant Hill, Calif., teacher of craft of writing, 1975 and 1980. Volunteer teacher at Oakland Public School, 1971; volunteer, Career Incorporated, Fairmont Hotel, 1960. *Member:* Mystery Writers of America, National Association of American Pen Women (past president), California Writer's Club (member of local board, 1964-66), Authors League. *Awards, honors:* Award for best mystery novel from Franklin Watts, Inc., 1965, for juvenile mystery, *The Mystery of the Swan Ballet.*

WRITINGS: The Mystery of the Swan Ballet, F. Watts, 1965; *Whispers in the Dark,* Major Books, 1976. Contributor of articles and short stories to magazines, including *Our Navy, Paradise of the Pacific, Dance, Science of Mind,* and *Writer.*

WORK IN PROGRESS: A juvenile mystery, *Stowaway Mouse;* a California historical novel set in 1850, titled *The Opposite Shore.*

SIDELIGHTS: Hacker told *CA:* "I enjoy creative writing and sharing by teaching craft. My interests, other than books, include music, dance, art, gardening, and travel. I have five grandchildren and have a vital interest in the world they will grow up in. I also enjoy gardening, poetry, and last, but never least, people."

* * *

HADLEY, Lee 1934-
(Hadley Irwin, a joint pseudonym)

PERSONAL: Born October 10, 1934, in Earlham, Iowa; daughter of Oren B. (a farmer) and Pearle Hadley. *Education:* Drake University, B.A., 1956; University of Wisconsin—Madison, M.A., 1961. *Home address:* R.R. 1, Madrid, Iowa 50156. *Office:* Department of English, Iowa State University, 307 Ross Hall, Ames, Iowa 50011.

CAREER: Younkers of Des Moines (department store), Des Moines, Iowa, copywriter, 1955-58; high school English teacher in De Soto, Iowa, 1959-60, and Monmouth, N.J.,

1962-65; Ocean County Community College, Toms River, N.J., instructor in English, 1965-68; Iowa State University, Ames, assistant professor of English, 1969—.

WRITINGS—With Ann Irwin, under joint pseudonym Hadley Irwin; fiction: *The Lilith Summer*, Feminist Press, 1979; *We Are Mesquakie, We Are One*, Feminist Press, 1980; *Bring to Boil and Separate*, Atheneum, 1980; *Moon and Me*, Atheneum, 1981.

WORK IN PROGRESS—With Ann Irwin, under joint pseudonym Hadley Irwin: *What About Grandma?*

SIDELIGHTS: Hadley and Irwin wrote: "The value of writing, whether it is for adults or for children, lies in trying to create beauty and truth through printed words. The best one can hope for is an approximation of those abstractions, but the attempt is worth the work and the risk. Even in failure there is much to be learned.

"Writing means putting words on paper in the most careful way one can and hoping that the reader will receive them with the same awareness. Faulkner said it best and most finally when he said one must forget all '. . . but the old verities and truths of the heart.'"

*   *   *

HAERTLING, Peter   1933-

PERSONAL: Born November 13, 1933, in Chemnitz (now Karl-Marx-Stadt), East Germany; son of Rudolf (a lawyer) and Erika (Haentzschel) Haertling; married Mechthild Maier, July 3, 1959; children: Fabian, Friederike, Clemens, Sophie. *Education:* Educated in Germany. *Home:* Finkenweg 1, 6082 Moerfelden-Walldorf, West Germany.

CAREER: Writer. *Deutsche Zeitung und Wirtschaftzeitung* (newspaper), Stuttgart and Cologne, West Germany, literary editor, 1955-62; *Der Monat* (magazine), West Berlin, West Germany, editor and co-publisher, 1962-70; S. Fischer Verlag (publisher), Franfurt am Main, West Germany, editor and managing director, 1967-74. *Member:* P.E.N., Akademie der Kuenste, Akademie der Wissenschaften und der Literatur. *Awards, honors:* Literaturpreis des deutschen Kritikerverbandes, 1964, for *Niembsch; oder, Der Stillstand;* Literaturpreis des Kulturkreises der deutschen Industrie, 1965; Literarischer Foerderungspreis des landes Niedersachen, 1965; Prix du meilleur livre etranger, 1966, for *Niembsch; oder, Der Stillstand;* Gerhart Hauptmann Preis, 1971; Deutscher Jugendbuchpreis, 1976; Stadtschreiber von Bergen-Enkheim, 1978-79.

WRITINGS—In English translation: *Oma: Die Geschichte von Kalle, der seine Eltern verliert und von seiner Grossmutter aufgenommen wird* (juvenile), Beltz & Gelbert, 1975, translation by Anthea Bell published as *Oma*, Harper, 1977 (published in England as *Granny: The Story of Karl, Who Loses His Parents and Dogs to Live With His Grandmother*, Hutchinson, 1977); *Theo haut ab* (juvenile novel) Beltz & Gelbert, 1977, translation by Bell published as *Theo Runs Away*, Andersen Press, 1978.

In German; novels: *Im Schein des Kometen* (title means "The Shine of a Comet"), H. Goverts, 1959; *Niembsch; oder, Der Stillstand* (title means "Niembsch; or, The Standstill"), H. Goverts, 1964; *Janek: Portraet einer Erinnerung* (title means "Janek: A Portrait of Remembrance"), H. Goverts, 1966; *Das Familienfest; oder, Das Ende der Geschichte* (title means "The Family Festival; or, The End of the Story"), H. Goverts, 1969; *Ein Abend, eine Nacht, ein Morgen* (title means "An Evening, a Night, a Morning"), Luchterhand, 1971; *Zwettl: Nachpruefung einer Erinnerung* (title

means "Zwettl: Checking the Remembrance"), Luchterhand, 1973; *Eine Frau* (title means "A Woman"), Luchterhand, 1974; *Hoelderlin*, Luchterhand, 1976; *Hubert; oder, Die Rueckkehr nach Casablanca* (title means "Hubert; or, The Return to Casablanca"), Luchterhand, 1978; *Nachgetragene Liebe* (title means "A Supplement of Love"), Luchterhand, 1980.

Poetry: *Poems and Songs*, Bechtle, 1953; *Unter den Brunnen: Neue Gedichte* (title means "Below the Wells: New Poems"), Bechtle, 1958; *Spielgeist, Spiegelgeist: Gedichte, 1959-1961* (title means "The Spirit of Play, the Spirit of Mirrors: Poems, 1959-1961"), H. Goverts, 1962; *Yamins Stationen* (title means "Yamin's Way"), H. Goverts, 1965; *Neue Gedichte* (title means "New Poems"), J. G. Blaeschke, c. 1972; *Zum laut und leise Lesen* (juvenile; title means "To Read for Oneself and for All"), Luchterhand, 1975; *Anreden: Gedichten aus die Jahren 1972-1977* (title means "Addresses: Poems From 1972 to 1977"), Luchterhand, 1977; *Ausgewaehlte Gedichte, 1953-1979* (title means "Collected Poems, 1953-1979"), Luchterhand, 1979.

Other writings: *In Zeilen zuhaus* (essays; title means "To Be at Home in Sentences"), Neske, 1957; *Palmstroem gruesst Anna Blume: Essay und Anthologie der Geister aus Poetia* (essays; title means "Palmstoem Greets Anna Blume"), H. Goverts, 1961; *Vergessene Buecher: Hinweise und Beispiele* (essays; title means "Forgotten Books"), H. Goverts, 1966; (editor) Christian Friedrich Damiel Schubart, *Gedichte* (title means "Poems"), Fischer Buecherei, 1968; (editor) Nicolaus Lenau, *Briefe an Sophie von Loewenthal, 1834-1845* (title means "Lenau's Letters to Sophie von Loewenthal"), Koesel Verlag, 1968; (compiler) *Die Vaeter: Berichte und Geschichten* (title means "The Fathers: Reports and Stories"), S. Fischer, 1968; *. . . und das ist die ganze Familie: Tageslaeufe mit Kindern* (title means "This Is The Whole Family: Everyday with Children"), G. Bitter, 1970; *Gilles: Ein Kostuemstuck aus der Revolution* (twenty-two-act play; title means "Gilles: A Play on the French Revolution"; first produced in Hamburg, West Germany, at Ernst-Deutsch-Theatre, September 26, 1973), H. Goverts, 1970; (compiler) *Leporello faellt aus der Rolle: Zeitgenoessische Autoren erzaehlen das Leben von Figuren der Weltliteratur weiter* (title means "Leporello Forgets Himself: The Life of Famous Figures of Literature"), S. Fischer, 1971; *Das war der Hirbel: Wie Hirbel ins Heim kam, warum er anders ist als andere und ob ihm zu helfen ist* (title means "This Was a Poor Boy Called Hirbel: A Novel for Children"), Beltz & Gelberg, 1973; (contributor) Willy Michel, *Die Aktaulitaet des Interpretierens* (title means "The Acute Problem of Interpretation"), Quelle & Meyer, 1978; (author of introduction) *Die Kopfkissen-Gans und andere Geschichten von grossen Dichtern fuer kleine Leute* (title means "The Goose Under the Coverlet: Stories for Children"), Hueber, 1978; *Ben liebt Anna* (juvenile: title means "Ben Loves Anna"), Beltz & Gelberg, 1979; *Sophie macht Geschichten* (juvenile; title means "Stories on Sophie"), Beltz & Gelberg, 1980; *Der wiederholte Unfall* (stories; title means "The Repeated Accident"), Reclam, 1980.

WORK IN PROGRESS: The Old Moerike, a biographical novel.

SIDELIGHTS: In 1966 Peter Haertling's book, *Niembsch; oder, Der Stillstand*, was chosen in France as the best foreign novel of the year. It's main rival was Saul Bellow's *Herzog*. Deemed "a subtle and fascinating work" by Mark Slonim in the *New York Times Book Review*, Haertling's book is the story of Nikolaus Franz Niembsch von Strehlenau, an Austrian poet who wrote under the pseudonym

Lenau in the early nineteenth century and became associated with the German romantics in the 1830's. Slonim explained that the work is not a biography but rather "a fictional narrative, based on some factual material, and revolving around two major themes: the metaphysical concept of time, and erotic experience as a way toward individual fulfillment."

BIOGRAPHICAL/CRITICAL SOURCES: New York Times Book Review, March 12, 1967; Books Abroad, autumn, 1967, spring, 1970.

*   *   *

HAGER, Jean   1932-
(Marlaine Kyle, Amanda McAllister, Sara North, Jeanne Stephens)

PERSONAL: Born June 2, 1932, in Maywood, Ill.; daughter of John Henry (a medical lab technician) and Cleo (Stephens) Luna; married Kenneth C. Hager (a hospital administrator), 1950; children: Kenneth Mark, Elaine Anne Hager Clark, Kyle John. Education: Attended Oklahoma State University, 1950-53, and University of Tulsa, 1964-66; Central State University, Edmond, Okla., B.A., 1969; graduate study at University of Oklahoma, 1969-70. Home address: Route 3, Pawnee, Okla. 74058. Agent: Amy Berkower, Writers House, Inc., 21 West 26th St., New York, N.Y. 10010.

CAREER: University of Oklahoma, Norman, Okla., teacher of English, 1969; Cleveland, Okla., public schools, junior high and high school teacher of English, 1970-74. Secretary of Triangle Heritage Historical Society, 1978. Member: Mystery Writers of America, Oklahoma Writers Federation (vice-president, 1980-81), Tuesday Writers (Tulsa, Okla.). Awards, honors: Teepee Trophy award for best novel of 1977 from Oklahoma Writers Federation, 1978, for Terror in the Sunlight, and for best novel of 1979 for Shadow of the Tamaracks, 1980.

WRITINGS: The Secret of Riverside Farm, Steck-Vaughn, 1970; The Whispering House, Steck-Vaughn, 1970; (under pseudonym Amanda McAllister) Terror in the Sunlight, Playboy Press, 1977; (under pseudonym Sara North) Evil Side of Eden, Playboy Press, 1978; (under pseudonym Sara North) Shadow of the Tamaracks, Playboy Press, 1979; (under pseudonym Jeanne Stephens) Mexican Nights, Silhouette Romances, 1980; Portrait of Love, Dell, 1980; (under pseudonym Jeanne Stephens) Wonder and Wild Desire, Silhouette Romances, 1981; Captured by Love, Dell, 1981; (under pseudonym Marlaine Kyle) A Suitable Marriage, Dell, 1982.

WORK IN PROGRESS: Yellow-Flower Moon, publication by Doubleday expected in 1981 or 1982; research on Choctaw Indians for a novel; research on early history of Florida for a series of novels.

SIDELIGHTS: Hager told CA: "My motivations were a few good teachers in early years who turned me on to books and parents who indulged my desire for books. Although many frightening, sometimes tragic things happen in my books, they always have a 'happy ending.' I try to celebrate life and the human spirit in my novels—I am not a doom-and-gloom writer, nor am I an ivory-tower writer. I write about ordinary people who want what everyone wants—love, achievement, personal fulfillment. Since I am one-eighth Cherokee, I am interested in American Indians, and have written about Cherokees, Osages, and Choctaws.

"I have no grandiose purpose for writing, such as a zeal to change the world. I simply try to tell a good story and, in the process, explore some of the reasons why people behave as they do. I write because I can't not write—not and feel complete. If I go for a very long period without writing I begin to be short-tempered and bored (and, no doubt, boring as well!)."

*   *   *

HAIRE, Wilson John   1932-

PERSONAL: Born April 6, 1932, in Belfast, Northern Ireland; son of a carpenter; married Rita Lenson, 1955 (divorced); married Sheila Fitz-Jones, 1974; children: seven. Education: Attended elementary school at Carryduff, County Down, Ireland. Home: 28 Fellows Rd., London N.W.3, England. Agent: Margaret Ramsay Ltd., 14a Goodwin's Court, London WC2N 4LL, England.

CAREER: Worked as a carpenter; Unity Theatre, London, England, actor, 1962-67; Camden Group Theatre, London, co-director, 1967-71, resident dramatist, 1974—; Lyric Theatre, Belfast, Northern Ireland, resident dramatist, 1976. Awards, honors: George Devine Award, 1972; most promising playwright award from London Evening Standard, 1972, for "Within Two Shadows"; Thames Television Award, 1974; Leverhulme fellowship, 1976.

WRITINGS—Plays: Within Two Shadows (first produced on the West End at Theatre Upstairs of the Royal Court Theatre, 1972; produced in New York, 1974), Davis-Poynter, 1973; Lost Worlds, Heinemann, 1978; Bloom of the Diamond Stone (first produced in Dublin, Ireland, 1973), Pluto Press, 1979.

Unpublished plays: "Clockin Hen," first produced in London, 1968; "The Diamond Bone and Hammer, and Along the Sloughs of Ulster," first produced in London, 1969; "Echoes From a Concrete Canyon," first produced in London, 1975. Also author of "The Latchicoes of Fort Camden."

Also author of television plays "Letter From a Soldier," 1975, "The Dandelion Clock," 1975, and "The Pact," 1976.

SIDELIGHTS: Few contemporary playwrights have delineated the tragedy of Ulster more forcefully than Wilson John Haire. Haire's knowledge of that strife-torn section of Northern Ireland stems from first-hand experience: he grew up on the notorious Shankhill Road in Belfast. The son of a Protestant father and a Catholic mother, Haire often witnessed his parents engaged in bitter fights over religion. He and his sisters were raised as Catholics, but some of his sisters later converted to Protestantism, which created deep rifts between the family members. The family was also buffeted by outside forces. Local Protestant gangs persecuted them, stoning their house and poisoning their well water.

Fleeing the violence, Haire moved to London at the age of twenty-five. Even in that city he was still tormented by his memories and underwent bouts of severe depression. He earned his living as a carpenter while in his spare time he wrote plays. His first play to be produced professionally was the largely autobiographical "Within Two Shadows." This drama shows how religious conflict leads to the destruction of a Belfast working-class family.

Haire explained to an interviewer for the New York Times what he was trying to convey in "Within Two Shadows": "I'm trying basically to show what the two communities are suffering. Both sides have such furies. The Protestants seem incoherent about the past. The Catholics seem to be living off myths and unrealities, too. The myths have got to be destroyed to save Northern Ireland. The people have got to realize that the other side has a different view of the past and different fears in the present. Both sides must understand this.''

Among the other dramas that Haire has written about Northern Ireland are ''Clockin Hen,'' ''Bloom of the Diamond Stone,'' and ''The Dandelion Clock.'' In his most recent plays, however, Haire has tried to break away from his preoccupation with Ulster.

BIOGRAPHICAL/CRITICAL SOURCES: New York Times, April 28, 1972.*

*   *   *

HAKUTANI, Yoshinobu   1935-

PERSONAL: Born March 27, 1935, in Osaka, Japan; came to the United States in 1956; married wife, Michiko, February, 1967; children: Yoshiki, Naoki. *Education:* Hiroshima University, B.A., 1957; University of Minnesota, M.A., 1959; Pennsylvania State University, Ph.D., 1965. *Home:* 503 Sunrise Dr., Kent, Ohio 44240. *Office:* Department of English, Kent State University, Kent, Ohio 44242.

CAREER: South Dakota State University, Brookings, instructor in English, 1959-61; California State University, Northridge, assistant professor of English, 1965-68; Kent State University, Kent, Ohio, assistant professor, 1968-71, associate professor, 1971-78, professor of English, 1978—. *Member:* Modern Language Association of America, Linguistic Society of America, English Literature Association of Japan, Kent Research Group.

WRITINGS: (Editor with Arthur O. Lewis) *The World of Japanese Fiction,* Dutton, 1973; (editor with Lewis Fried) *American Literary Naturalism,* Carl Winter, 1975; *Young Dreiser: A Critical Study,* Associated University Presses, 1980; (editor) *Critical Essays on Richard Wright,* G. K. Hall, 1981. Contributor to literature journals.

*   *   *

HALDANE, J(ohn) B(urdon) S(anderson)   1892-1964

PERSONAL: Born November 5, 1892, in Oxford, England; immigrated to India, 1957; naturalized Indian citizen, 1960; died December 1, 1964, in Bhubaneswar, Orissa, India; son of John Scott (a professor and physiologist) and Louisa Kathleen (Trotter) Haldane; married Charlotte Franken Burghes (a journalist), 1926 (divorced, 1945); married Helen Spurway (a scientist), 1945. *Education:* New College, Oxford, M.A.

CAREER: Oxford University, Oxford, England, fellow of New College, 1919-22; Cambridge University, Cambridge, England, reader in biochemistry, 1922-32; Royal Institution, London, England, Fullerian Professor of Physiology, 1930-32; University College, London, professor of genetics, 1933-37, professor of biometry, 1937-57; research professor at Indian Statistical Institute, 1957-61; Government of Orissa, India, head of genetics and biometry laboratory, beginning 1962. Visiting professor at University of California, 1932; chairman of editorial board of *London Daily Worker,* 1940-49. *Military service:* British Infantry Battalion, Black Watch (France and Iraq), 1914-19; became captain. *Member:* Royal Society of London (fellow), Genetical Society (president, 1932-36), Societe de Biologie (corresponding member), Royal Danish Academy of Sciences, Moscow Academy of Sciences (honorary member), Deutsche Akademie der Wissenschaften zu Berlin (corresponding member), National Institute of Sciences of India. *Awards, honors:* Created chevalier of French Legion of Honor, 1937; D.Sc. from

Groeningen, 1946, and Oxford University, 1961; honorary doctorate from University of Paris, 1949; Darwin Medal from Royal Society of London, 1953; LL.D. from University of Edinburgh, 1956; Darwin-Wallace Commemorative Medal from Linnean Society, 1958; Kimber Medal from National Academy of Sciences (Washington, D.C.), Feltrinelli Prize from Accademia dei Lincei, and honorary fellow of New College, Oxford, all 1961.

*WRITINGS—*All nonfiction, except as noted: *Daedalus; or, Science and the Future,* Dutton, 1924; *Callinicus: A Defense of Chemical Warfare,* Dutton, 1925, reprinted, Garland Publishing, 1972; (with Julian Sorell Huxley) *Animal Biology,* Clarendon Press, 1927; *The Last Judgment: A Scientist's Vision of the Future of Man,* Harper, 1927; *Possible Worlds, and Other Essays,* Chatto & Windus, 1927, published as *Possible Worlds, and Other Papers,* Harper, 1928, reprinted, Books for Libraries, 1971; *Science and Ethics,* C. A. Watts, 1928.

Enzymes, Longmans, Green, 1930, reprinted, M.I.T. Press, 1965; (author of foreword) Johannes Lange, *Crime and Destiny,* Bonibooks, 1930, published as *Crime as Destiny: A Study of Criminal Twins,* G. Allen, 1931; *The Causes of Evolution,* Harper, 1932, reprinted, Cornell University Press, 1966; *The Inequality of Man and Other Essays,* Chatto & Windus, 1932, published as *Science and Human Life,* Harper, 1933, reprinted, Books for Libraries, 1971; (contributor) John Randall Baker, *Biology in Everyday Life,* G. Allen, 1933; *Fact and Faith,* C. A. Watts, 1934; *Human Biology and Politics,* British Science Guild, 1934.

The Outlook of Science, Kegan Paul, 1935; (contributor) Arnold Henry Moore Lunn, *Science and the Supernatural: A Correspondence Between Arnold Lunn and J.B.S. Haldane,* Sheed, 1935; *Science and Well-Being,* Kegan Paul, 1935; *My Friend, Mr. Leakey* (for children), Cresset, 1937, Harper, 1938, reprinted, Penguin, 1971; *A.R.P.* (Air Raid Precautions), Gollancz, 1938; *The Chemistry of the Individual,* Oxford University Press, 1938; *Heredity and Politics,* Norton, 1938; *How to Be Safe From Air Raids,* Gollancz, 1938; *The Marxist Philosophy and the Sciences,* Allen & Unwin, 1938; Random House, 1939, reprinted, Books for Libraries, 1969; (editor) Amram Scheinfeld, *You and Heredity,* Chatto & Windus, 1939; *Science and Everyday Life,* Lawrence & Wishart, 1939, Macmillan, 1940, reprinted, Arno, 1975; *Science and You,* Fore Publications, 1939.

Adventures of a Biologist, Harper, 1940 (published in England as *Keeping Cool and Other Essays,* Chatto & Windus, 1941); (author of preface and notes) Friedrich Engels, *Dialectics of Nature,* International Publications, 1940; *Science in Peace and War,* Lawrence & Wishart, 1940; *New Paths in Genetics,* Allen & Unwin, 1941, Harper, 1942; *A Banned Broadcast, and Other Essays,* Chatto & Windus, 1946; *Science Advances,* Macmillan, 1947; *What Is Life?,* Boni & Gaer, 1947; (with Douglas Dewar and L. Merson Davies) *Is Evolution a Myth?,* C. A. Watts, 1949.

Everything Has a History, Allen & Unwin, 1951; *The Biochemistry of Genetics,* Allen & Unwin, 1954, Macmillan, 1956; *The Unity and Diversity of Life,* Government of India, 1958; *Physiological Variation and Evolution,* Maharaja Sayajirao University of Baroda, 1960; *Science and Indian Culture,* New Age Publications, 1965; *Science and Life: Essays of a Rationalist,* Pemberton Publishing Co., 1968; *The Man With Two Memories* (fiction), Merlin, 1976.

Also author of *Mechanism, Life, and Personality,* 1923, *Dialectical Materialism and Modern Science,* 1942, *Why Professional Workers Should Be Communists,* 1945, *The Philoso-*

phy of a Biologist, 1955, and *The Implications of Genetics for Human Society.*

Contributor to newspapers and periodicals, including the *London Daily Herald, London Daily Worker, New Republic, Century, Science, Forum, Nation, Reader's Digest,* and *Journal of the Royal Anthropological Institute of Great Britain and Ireland.*

SIDELIGHTS: J.B.S. Haldane made numerous contributions to the fields of biology, physiology, and genetics during his lifetime, but he is nearly as well known for his eccentric methods of experimentation and his burly demeanor as for his impact on science.

Haldane was a precocious youngster who could read by age three. When he was four he accompanied his father down into coal mines to experience the addling effects of breathing methane gas. For a study on deep diving and decompression, young Haldane was submerged forty feet below water in a diving suit. In another project, the front yard of the family home housed three hundred guinea pigs with which Haldane conducted genetics experiments.

By the time Haldane entered New College, Oxford, on a scholarship, he was comfortable in several languages, learned in the sciences, and distinguished in mathematics. After Oxford he entered the Black Watch, a British battalion. As reported in Ronald W. Clark's biography, Haldane later referred to the years spent at war as some of the best of his life. He seemingly had no fear on the line, but instead relished the acute awareness of life brought about by the incessant threat of death.

According to a *Newsweek* reviewer and a writer for *Time,* Haldane said he enjoyed killing men. Part of his explanation for taking pleasure from such a morbid practice was, according to Clark, because "we take the higher animals seriously." Haldane regarded the killing of animals as cowardly, while he respected the killing of humans as a vestige of primeval times. War, to Haldane, was the ultimate game, with life or death as the stakes.

From his wartime experiences Haldane became very interested in the study of gas masks and their effectiveness. Though his experiments involved irritating his own lungs, Haldane believed he was his own best guinea pig: after all, a guinea pig or mouse cannot relate whether a gas alters its sense of hearing or smell. Haldane became an expert on poison gases, and his work is estimated to have saved thousands of lives.

After the sinking of a British submarine in which all but four of the crew were killed, Haldane sought to discover how the four survived. He breathed pure oxygen and, with the assistance of a pressure chamber, dove to a depth of seven atmospheric pressures. Although he nearly killed himself in the process, Haldane proved that oxygen becomes poisonous under pressure. He also learned that oxygen under such pressure develops a taste.

Haldane insisted on chewing betel nuts and drinking unboiled water in India to conduct experiments on typhoid. Although he did not succeed in contracting typhoid, he was able to study the effectiveness of the typhoid innoculation.

During World War II, Haldane designed air raid shelters and became an expert on air raid precautions. He promoted the idea that London should dig a tunnel in which the entire metropolitan population could be sheltered. His idea was not carried out, partly because at that time such a tunnel would have cost close to $4 billion. He did, however, design a sufficient shelter, all the while insisting "the best way to avoid an air raid is to avoid war."

Haldane was as unorthodox in his private life as he was in his professional practices. In 1925, the thirty-two-year-old bachelor became involved with a married woman. Realizing that adultery was the only acceptable ground for divorce at that time, Haldane and his mistress did not attempt to hide their relationship from the detective hired to follow them. Cambridge University asked him to resign his post as a reader in biochemistry because of his connection in the divorce case. Haldane refused, appealing to a higher court. In the end Haldane won the case, married Charlotte Franken, and was reinstated to his post.

Haldane's wife, a journalist, helped him publish several books during their years together. But their marriage began to dissolve, Clark reported, because of their inability to have children. In addition, their political views increasingly differed. Charlotte had convinced her husband of the worth of a Communistic ideology. She then became disillusioned and unsuccessfully attempted to change her husband's beliefs again. In 1945 the marriage was dissolved in an uncontested case.

Haldane contributed some of his most important work to the field of genetics. He became one of the world's best-known authorities on heredity and inherited diseases. He also formulated the mathematical theory of natural selection. Haldane was one of the first to estimate the rate of mutation of human genes, and the first to map a human chromosome. He discovered effective treatments for tetanus and convulsions.

Being strong opponents of war, Haldane and his second wife became distressed with the persistent presence of American troops based in Britain. They sought a free environment by immigrating to India in 1957. Haldane adopted Indian customs and dress and became a citizen in 1960.

Three years after attaining Indian citizenship, Haldane discovered he had cancer. Ten months before his death, Haldane pre-recorded his own obituary for the British Broadcasting Co. True to the philosophy held during his lifetime, Haldane arranged to have his remains donated for medical research.

In an article written for *Nation* in 1930, Haldane wrote: "Naturally I regard health as extremely important, far more so than wealth, and I shall regard my life as well spent if I can do a little by research and education to make my fellow-creatures healthier." Haldane, it seems, surpassed his life's goal.

AVOCATIONAL INTERESTS: Swimming, mountain walking.

BIOGRAPHICAL/CRITICAL SOURCES: Times Literary Supplement, February 7, 1924, February 19, 1925, December 8, 1932, June 28, 1947; *New York Times,* April 6, 1924, April 29, 1928, September 25, 1932, April 16, 1933, March 27, 1938, April 16, 1939, June 16, 1940, August 10, 1947, December 28, 1947; *New York Herald and Tribune,* May 11, 1924; *Spectator,* December 24, 1927; *Literary Digest,* June 2, 1928, October 1, 1932; *New York Herald Tribune Books,* June 3, 1928, June 16, 1940; *Saturday Review of Literature,* June 30, 1928, December 24, 1932; *Nation,* July 23, 1930, May 14, 1938, April 15, 1939; *Time,* October 3, 1938, March 13, 1939, July 30, 1945, June 30, 1947, September 27, 1948, August 15, 1949, March 7, 1969; *Newsweek,* January 22, 1940, January 13, 1947, January 13, 1969; *Life,* October 25, 1943; *New Republic,* September 29, 1947; *Atlantic,* November, 1947; *U.S. News & World Report,* August 2, 1957; Ronald William Clark, *The Life and Work of J.B.S. Haldane,* Coward, 1968.

OBITUARIES: *New York Times,* December 2, 1964; *Time,* December 11, 1964; *Newsweek,* December 14, 1964.*

—*Sketch by Susette Balogh*

*   *   *

HALE, J. Russell 1918-

PERSONAL: Born December 14, 1918, in Philadelphia, Pa.; son of Robert Gifford (in real estate) and Dorothy (Graham) Hale; married Marjorie Elinor Hoerman (a school personnel assistant), June 10, 1944; children: Douglas Graham, Dean Edward. *Education:* Muhlenberg College, A.B., 1940; Lutheran Theological Seminary, B.D., 1944, S.T.M., 1950; attended Johns Hopkins University, 1948; attended Columbia University and Union Theological Seminary, received Ed.D., 1970. *Politics:* Democrat. *Home:* 153 South Hay St., Gettysburg, Pa. 17325. *Office:* Department of Church and Community, Lutheran Theological Seminary, Gettysburg, Pa. 17325.

CAREER: Ordained minister of Lutheran Church in America, 1944; pastor of Lutheran churches in Keyport, N.J., and Long Branch, N.J., both 1944-46, Baltimore, Md., 1946-50, and Ramsey, N.J., 1950-59; St. Paul's Lutheran Church, Collingswood, N.J., pastor, 1959-62; Lutheran Theological Seminary, Department of Church and Community, Gettysburg, Pa., instructor, 1962-63, assistant professor, 1963-69, associate professor, 1969-70, professor of church and community, 1970—, chairman of admissions and scholarships program, 1970-72, Division on Studies in Ministry, 1971-73, and graduate degree program, 1972-73, director of advanced studies program, 1975—. Visiting instructor at Lutheran Deaconess Training School, Baltimore, Md., 1948-50, Protestant Episcopal Seminary and Dominican House, both Virginia, both 1972-75, and at Oblate College, Washington, D.C., 1978, 1980; theologian-in-residence at Hothorpe Hall, Theddingworth, England, 1980-81.

Lutheran Church in America, New Jersey Synod, member of stewardship committee, 1951-56, and chairman, 1955-56, secretary, vice-president, and president of Northern Conference, 1955-59, member of examining committee, 1957-58, and chairman, 1958, member of synod executive board, 1959, secretary of Committee on American Missions, 1962-63, chairman of Committee on College and University Work, 1963, Central Pennsylvania Synod, chairman of task force on parish staff needs, 1965-67, board member of Tressler Lutheran Service Associates, 1969-77, and vice-chairman, 1973-77, board member of Lutheran Social Services, 1970-71. Member of board of New Jersey Council of Churches 1957-58, Camden County Council of Churches, 1960-63, and Adams County Council of Churches. 1970-72. Chairman of Adams County Committee for Family Food, 1971-72; member of board of directors of Admas-York Mental Health Clinic, 1975-77. Consultant to various urban church study committees and theological education task forces, including comprehensive study committee of Lutheran Theological Seminary, 1964-66, research task force of Protestant Episcopal Seminary, 1972-73, and Readiness for Ministry Project of Assocation of Theological Schools, 1973.

MEMBER: American Association of University Professors, American Sociological Association, Religious Research Association, Society for the Scientific Study of Religion, Society for Sociology of Religion. *Awards, honors:* Danforth Foundation campus ministry study grant, 1963-65; Lutheran Brotherhood faculty research grant, 1963-64; doctoral study award from Lutheran Board of Theological Education, 1969-70; research grants from Glenmary Research Center and Aid Association for Lutherans, 1976, 1980, and from Lutheran Church in America, 1980-81; grants from Omicron Delta Kappa and Alpha Kappa Alpha.

WRITINGS: *Is It Christian?,* two volumes, Lutheran Church Press, 1964; (with Robert A. Dentler and Alan McFarlane) *The Protestant Campus Ministry in a Northern Metropolitan Area,* Center for Urban Education, 1966; (with John Kerr) *Luv,* two volumes, Lutheran Church Press, 1969; (contributor) Kenneth Underwood, editor, *The Church, the University, and Social Policy,* Wesleyan University Press, 1969; *To Have and to Hold,* two volumes, Lutheran Church Press, 1972; *Case Studies in Evangelism,* [Gettysburg, Pa.], 1972; (contributor) Herman Stuempfle, editor, *Preaching in the Witnessing Community,* Fortress Press, 1973; *Who Are the Unchurched?: An Exploratory Study,* Glenmary Research Center, 1977; *The Unchurched: Who They Are and Why They Stay Away,* Harper, 1980. Contributor of articles to journals and newspapers, including *Baltimore Sun, Dialog,* and *Lutheran Quarterly.* Editor of *Seminary Bulletin,* 1964-69; member of editorial board of *Lutheran Quarterly,* 1966-69.

WORK IN PROGRESS: *Lutheranism in Great Britain: A Case Study in Marginality and Community, 1945-80.*

SIDELIGHTS: Hale commented: "I have, since my entrance into academic work in 1963, been a rather pedestrian sociologist of religion, engaged in the normal academic regimen of teaching, writing, and researching. I was frankly unprepared for the attention given findings from my sabbatical research of 1976, which involved extensive interviews with a sample of the unchurched in America, and the international notoriety that my 1977 monograph received. My work has had coverage in the ecclesiastical and secular press, radio, and TV, both here and abroad. Apparently, I struck a raw nerve in the churches, gained my promoters among the unchurched themselves, and convinced some of my sociological colleagues that here was a phenomenon worth studying."

BIOGRAPHICAL/CRITICAL SOURCES: *Time,* October 3, 1977.

*   *   *

HALL, J(ohn) C(live) 1920-

PERSONAL: Born September 12, 1920, in Ealing, Middlesex, England; son of H. S. (a senior government solicitor) and Alice Martha (Robinson) Hall; married twice (divorced twice); children: (first marriage) Rosamund Cara, Joanna Madeline. *Education:* Attended Oriel College, Oxford, 1938-39. *Home:* 198 Blythe Rd., Hammersmith, London W14 0HH, England. *Office:* Encounter, 59 St. Martin's Lane, London WC2N 4JS, England.

CAREER: John Lehmann Ltd. (publisher), London, England, general manager, 1946-52; Michael Joseph Ltd. (publisher), London, publicity manager, 1953-55; *Encounter,* London, business and advertising manager and reader, 1955—. Poet and editor. Member of poetry panel of Arts Council. *Member:* International PEN (member of executive committee).

WRITINGS: (With Keith Douglas and Norman Nicholson) *Selected Poems,* Staples Press, 1943; *The Summer Dance and Other Poems,* Lehmann, 1951; *Edwin Muir,* Longmans, Green, 1956; *The Burning Hare* (poems), Chatto & Windus, 1966; *A House of Voices* (poems), Chatto & Windus, 1973.

Editor: *Collected Poems of Edwin Muir,* Faber, 1952, revised edition, edited with Willa Muir, published as *Collected Poems of Edwin Muir, 1921-1958,* Faber, 1960; (with Patric

Dickinson and Erica Marx) *New Poems 1955,* M. Joseph, 1955; (with G. S. Fraser and John Waller) *The Collected Poems of Keith Douglas,* revised edition, Faber, 1966.

SIDELIGHTS: Hall has been called a conservative poet who owes his greatest literary debt to Edwin Muir. Early in his career Hall admitted to having difficulty in finding his own voice as a poet; but a more recent work, *A House of Voices,* reveals a new maturity. A "quiet forcefulness" marks these "personal poems," said Alan Brownjohn.

A *Times Literary Supplement* reviewer also commented on *A House of Voices:* "[This] compilation of terse, wry poems in adroitly handled traditional forms directly concerned with the guilts, griefs and ironies of personal experience, could have appeared at almost any time since the war. And there is nothing the matter with that. Mr. Hall has chosen to ignore Pound's injunction to make it new preferring to make it real."

BIOGRAPHICAL/CRITICAL SOURCES: Times Literary Supplement, August 17, 1973; *New Statesman,* November 9, 1973.

* * *

HALL, Kermit L(ance) 1944-

PERSONAL: Born August 31, 1944, in Akron, Ohio; son of Kermit (a tire builder) and Katherine (a bookkeeper; maiden name, Galbraith) Hall; married Phyllis Anne Moke (a librarian), January 1, 1968. *Education:* University of Akron, B.A., 1966; Syracuse University, M.A., 1967; University of Minnesota, Ph.D., 1972; Yale University, M.S.L., 1980. *Home:* 3844 Bishop Rd., Detroit, Mich. 48224. *Office:* Department of History, Wayne State University, Detroit, Mich. 48202.

CAREER: Metropolitan State Junior College, Minneapolis, Minn., instructor in history, 1971-72; Vanderbilt University, Nashville, Tenn., assistant professor of history, 1972-76; Wayne State University, Detroit, Mich., assistant professor, 1976-78, associate professor of history, 1978—. *Military service:* U.S. Army, 1968-70; served in Vietnam; became first lieutenant; received Air Medal. *Member:* American Historical Association, American Society of Legal History, American Judicature Society, Organization of American Historians, Detroit Council on Foreign Relations. *Awards, honors:* Earhart Foundation fellowship, 1979-80; American Bar Foundation fellowship, 1980-81.

WRITINGS: (Editor with Herbert Weaver) *The Correspondence of James K. Polk,* Volume III, Vanderbilt University Press, 1974; *The Politics of Justice: Lower Federal Judicial Selection and the Second Party, 1829-1861,* University of Nebraska Press, 1979; (editor with Harold M. Hyman) *The Constitutional Convention as an Amending Device,* Praeger, 1982. Contributor to history, political science, and law journals. Editor of *Detroit in Perspective: A Journal of Regional History.*

WORK IN PROGRESS: A bibliography of U.S. constitutional and legal history, publication by K.T.O. Press expected in 1982; a history of the American territorial judiciary, publication expected in 1983; research on state constitutional reform in the nineteenth century.

SIDELIGHTS: Hall told *CA:* "The study of American constitutional and legal history has emphasized in recent years the interconnection between the Constitution, the law, society, and economic development. This has provided a healthy and needed antidote to the traditional scholarship that stressed politics. Yet, if there is to be a larger synthesis of American constitutional and legal history, it will only

come about when scholars return to the task of understanding the ways in which the American political culture promoted or discouraged constitutional and legal development.

"To bring about this synthesis, students of American constitutionalism and the law will have to cast a much broader methodological net than they have to date. Historians tend to be long on data (the 'facts'), but frequently short on ways of conceptualizing that data into generalizations. Of course, before any kind of useful synthesis can take place, there will have to be a good bit more digging into the historical record, especially with regard to some of the little-studied provisions of the federal Constitution (the second and eighth amendments, for example), the development of state constitutions since 1787, and substantive areas of American law and legal institutions (inferior state and local courts)."

AVOCATIONAL INTERESTS: Fishing.

* * *

HALL, Willis 1929-

PERSONAL: Born April 6, 1929, in Leeds, England; son of Walter (a fitter) and Gladys (Gomersal) Hall; married wife, Valerie; children: Peter, Macer, Daniel, James. *Education:* Educated in Leeds, England. *Home:* 64 Clarence Rd., St. Albans, Hertfordshire, England. *Agent:* London Management, 235-241 Regent St., London W.1, England.

CAREER: Writer. *Military service:* British Regular Army, 1947-52; served as radio playwright for Chinese Schools Department of Radio Malaya. *Member:* Garrick Club. *Awards, honors:* Drama award for play of the year from *Evening Standard,* 1959, for "The Long and the Short and the Tall."

WRITINGS: (With I. O. Evans) *They Found the World* (juvenile), Warne, 1959; *A Glimpse of the Sea: Three Short Plays* (contains "A Glimpse of the Sea," one-act, first produced in London, England, 1959; "The Last Day in Dreamland," one-act, first produced in London, 1959; "Return to the Sea," television play, first broadcast in 1959), M. Evans, 1960; *The Royal Astrologers: Adventures of Father Mole-Cricket; or, the Malayan Legends* (juvenile), Heinemann, 1960, Coward, 1962; (with Michael Parkinson) *The A to Z of Soccer,* Pelham, 1970; (with Bob Monkhouse) *The A to Z of Television,* Pelham, 1971; *My Sporting Life,* Luscombe, 1975; *Incredible Kidnapping* (juvenile), Heinemann, 1975.

Published plays: *Final at Furnell* (radio play; first broadcast in 1954), M. Evans, 1956; *The Long and the Short and the Tall* (first produced in Edinburgh, Scotland, 1958; produced in London, England, 1959; produced in New York, N.Y., 1962; also see below), Heinemann, 1959, Theatre Arts, 1961; (with Lewis Jones) *Poet and Pheasant* (radio play; first broadcast in 1955), Deane, 1959; *The Play of the Royal Astrologers* (first produced in Birmingham, England, 1958; produced in London, 1968), Heinemann, 1960; *The Day's Beginning: An Easter Play,* Heinemann, 1963; *The Gentle Knight* (radio play; first broadcast in 1964), Blackie, 1966; *The Railwayman's New Clothes* (television play; first broadcast in 1971), S. French, 1974; *Kidnapped at Christmas* (first produced in London, 1975), Heinemann, 1975; *Walk On, Walk On* (first produced in Liverpool, England, 1975), S. French, 1976.

With Peter Waterhouse: *Billy Liar* (adaptation of novel by Waterhouse; first produced in London, 1960; produced in New York, 1963; also see below), Norton, 1960; *Celebration: The Wedding and the Funeral* (first produced in Nottingham, England, 1961; produced in London, 1961),

M. Joseph, 1961; *England, Our England* (musical; first produced in London, 1962), M. Evans, 1964; *The Sponge Room* [and] *Squat Betty* (the former: one-act, first produced in Nottingham, 1962, produced in New York, 1964; the latter: one-act, first produced in London, 1962, produced in New York, 1964), M. Evans, 1963; *All Things Bright and Beautiful* (first produced in Bristol, England, 1962; produced in London, 1962), M. Joseph, 1963; *Come Laughing Home* (first produced as "They Called the Bastard Stephen" in Bristol, 1964; produced as "Come Laughing Home" in Wimbledon, England, 1965), M. Evans, 1965; *Say Who You Are* (first produced in London, 1965), M. Evans, 1967, also published as *Help Stamp Out Marriage* (first produced in New York, 1966), S. French, 1966; (also translators) *Saturday, Sunday, Monday* (adaptation of a play by Eduardo de Filippo; first produced in London, 1973; produced in New York), Heinemann, 1974; *Who's Who* (first produced in Coventry, England, 1971; produced in London, 1973), S. French, 1974; *Children's Day* (first produced in Edinburgh, 1969; produced in London, 1969), S. French, 1975.

Unpublished plays: "Chin-Chin" (adaptation of play, "Tchin-Tchin," by Francois Billetdoux), first produced in London, 1960; (with Robin Maugham) "Azouk" (adaptation of play by Alexandre Rivemale), first produced in Newcastle-Upon-Tyne, England, 1962; (co-author) "Yer What?" (revue), first produced in Nottingham, 1962; "The Love Game" (adaptation of play by Marcel Archard), first produced in London, 1964; (with Waterhouse) "Joey, Joey" (musical), first produced in London, 1966; (with Waterhouse) "Whoops-a-Daisy," first produced in Nottingham, 1968; (with Waterhouse) "The Card" (musical; adaptation of novel by Arnold Bennett), first produced in Bristol, 1973, produced in London, 1973; "Christmas Crackers," first produced in London, 1976; "Stag-Night," first produced in London, 1976; "Filumena" (adaptation of work by de Filippo), first produced in 1977; "A Right Christmas Caper," first produced in 1977.

Author of screenplays, including: "The Long and the Short and the Tall," 1961; (with Waterhouse) "Whistle Down the Wind," 1961; (with Waterhouse) "A Kind of Loving," 1961; "The Valiant," 1962; (with Waterhouse) "Billy Liar" (adapted from novel by Waterhouse), 1963; "West Eleven," 1963; (with Waterhouse) "Man in the Middle," 1964; (with Waterhouse) "Pretty Polly," 1968; "Lock Up Your Daughters," 1969.

Author of television plays, including: "Air Mail From Cyprus," 1958; "On the Night of the Murder," 1962; "By Endeavour Alone," 1963; (with Waterhouse) "Happy Moorings," 1963; "How Many Angels," 1964; "The Ticket," 1969; "They Don't All Open Men's Boutiques," 1972; "The Villa Maroc," 1972; "Song at Twilight," 1973; "Friendly Encounter," 1974; "The Piano-Smashers of the Golden Sun," 1974; "Illegal Approach," 1974; "Midgley," 1975; "Match-Fit," 1976.

Author of radio plays, including: "The Nightingale," 1954; "Furore at Furnell," 1955; "Frenzy at Furnell," 1955; "Friendly at Furnell," 1955; "Fluster at Furnell," 1955; "One Man Absent," 1955; "A Run for the Money," 1956; "Afternoon for Antigone," 1956; "The Long Years," 1956; "Any Dark Morning," 1956; "Feodor's Bride," 1956; "One Man Returns," 1956; "A Ride on the Donkeys," 1957; "The Calverdon Road Job," 1957; "Harvest the Sea," 1957; "Monday at Seven," 1957; "Annual Outing," 1958; "The Larford Lad," 1958; (with Leslie Halward) "The Case of Walter Grimshaw," 1958.

Editor: (With Waterhouse) *Writers' Theatre*, Heinemann, 1967; (with Parkinson) *Football Report: An Anthology of Soccer*, Pelham, 1973; *Football Classified: An Anthology of Soccer*, Luscombe, 1975; *Football Final*, Pelham, 1975.

Work represented in anthologies, including: Michael Barry, editor, *The Television Playwright: Ten Plays for BBC Television*, Hill & Wang, 1960; Stanley Richards, editor, *Modern Short Plays From Broadway and London*, Random House, 1969; John Foster, editor, *Drama Study Units*, Heinemann, 1975; Alan Durband, editor, *Prompt Three*, Hutchinson, 1976.

Writer for television shows, including "Inside George Webley," 1968, "Queenie's Castle," 1970, "Budgie," 1971-72, "The Upper Crusts," 1973, "Three's Company," 1973, "Billy Liar," 1973-74.

*   *   *

HALLMAN, G(eorge) Victor III   1930-

PERSONAL: Born October 17, 1930, in Chicago, Ill.; son of George Victor, Jr. and Blake B. Hallman; married wife, Melitta (a systems engineer), February 9, 1957; children: Susan, George Victor IV. *Education:* University of Pennsylvania, B.S., 1952, M.A., 1954, Ph.D., 1964. *Politics:* Republican. *Religion:* Protestant. *Home:* 824 Pine Tree Rd., Lafayette Hill, Pa. 19444. *Office:* American Institute for Property and Liability Underwriters and Insurance Institute of America, Providence Rd., Malvern, Pa. 19355.

CAREER: Accident and health underwriter for Continental Casualty Co., 1952-53; Upsala College, East Orange, N.J., assistant professor of business administration, 1956-59; Rider College, Trenton, N.J., assistant professor of business administration, 1959-60; American College of Life Underwriters, 1960-69, began as director of educational publications, became assistant dean, associate dean, and dean of Curriculum and Examinations Division; American Institute for Property and Liability Underwriters and Insurance Institute of America, Malvern, Pa., director of examinations, 1970-77, dean of examinations and member of executive council, 1977—. Member of faculty at University of Pennsylvania and Villanova University, 1960-70; professor at Georgia State University, 1969-70; adjunct professor at Temple University, 1971—. Past chairman of Chartered Life Underwriters revision task forces; member of Pennsylvania Worker's Compensation Insurance Advisory Commission, 1978; guest on radio programs throughout the United States; consultant to Merrill Lynch, Pierce, Fenner & Smith and U.S. Savings and Loan League.

MEMBER: American Risk and Insurance Association (chairman of health insurance section, 1971), American Finance Association, American Society of Chartered Life Underwriters, Society of Chartered Property and Casualty Underwriters, Delta Sigma Pi, Beta Gamma Sigma, Alpha Pi Omega.

WRITINGS: Unsatisfied Judgment Funds, Irwin, 1968; (contributor) Leroy E. Varner, editor, *Engineering and Building Structures*, Building Owners and Managers Institute, 1972; (contributor) *Readings in Underwriting for CPCU II*, American Institute for Property and Liability Underwriters, 1973; *Fundamentals of Life Insurance* (monograph), American Institute for Property and Liability Underwriters, 1973; (with Jerry S. Rosenbloom) *Personal Financial Planning* (Fortune Book Club selection), McGraw, 1975, 2nd edition, 1978; (with Rosenbloom) *Employee Benefit Planning*, Prentice-Hall, 1978. Contributor of articles and reviews to professional journals.

WORK IN PROGRESS: Business Uses of Life and Health Insurance, for publication by Ronald; *Principles of Personal Financial Planning,* with Jerry S. Rosenbloom, for Prentice-Hall.

*   *   *

HALLUS, Tak
    See ROBINETT, Stephen (Allen)

*   *   *

HAMILTON, (Charles) Nigel   1944-

PERSONAL: Born February 16, 1944, in Alnmouth, England; son of Denis (a journalist) and Olive (a writer; maiden name, Wanless) Hamilton; married Hannelore Pfeifer, 1966 (died, 1973); married Outi Palovesi, July 31, 1976; children: Alexander, Sebastian, Nicholas. *Education:* Trinity College, Cambridge, B.A. (with honors), 1965, M.A., 1976. *Home:* Heveningham House, Heveningham, Suffolk 1P19 0EA, England. *Agent:* Bruce Hunter, David Higham Associates, 5-8 Lower John St., London WIR 4HA, England.

CAREER: Employed by Andre Deutsch (publishers), London, England, 1965; secondary schoolteacher in London, 1966; Greenwich Bookshop, Greenwich, England, founder and proprietor, 1966-1979; writer, 1979—.

WRITINGS: (With Olive Hamilton) *Royal Greenwich,* privately printed, 1969; *Greenwich in Colour,* Greenwich Bookshop, 1970; *Guide to Greenwich,* Greenwich Bookshop, 1971; *America Began at Greenwich,* Poseidon, 1976; *The Brothers Mann: The Lives of Heinrich and Thomas Mann, 1871-1950 and 1875-1955,* Secker & Warburg, 1978, Yale University Press, 1979. Also author of books under pseudonyms.

WORK IN PROGRESS: Monty: The Life of Field Marshal Montgomery of Alamein, 1887-1976, an authorized biography, completion expected in 1981.

SIDELIGHTS: Hamilton's dual biography of the brothers Thomas and Heinrich Mann "shows a conception imaginative enough and an execution absorbing enough to make one wonder why it has all taken so long," exclaimed Jack Dierks of the *Chicago Tribune Book World.* Thomas, the younger brother, was the Nobel Prize-winning author of such works as *Buddenbrooks, The Magic Mountain,* and *Death in Venice.* Although Heinrich, also a writer, is well known in Europe, most of his writings remain untranslated into English, and today he is known principally as the author of the novel on which the film "The Blue Angel" was based.

If the younger brother eclipsed the elder in terms of their writing, the elder was more involved in the political and social upheaval of twentieth-century Europe. Reviewers have found the strength of *The Brothers Mann* to be in its portrayal of the Manns' life against this backdrop of conflict. Dierks commented that "the story of the Manns' productive life is the story of the capsizing of the cultural, intellectual, and social traditions into which they were born and attained maturity; and of their struggle to keep artistic heads above the undertow.... Hamilton plays on the right dramatic chord here as world conflict, economic and domestic chaos are used as backdrops to the literary growth and evolving political convictions of the brothers."

Peter Gay of the *New York Times Book Review* wrote that Hamilton has "an irresistible subject: the maturation of two immensely gifted brothers, their quarrel about World War I which, in miniature, reflected quarrels between cultures, and their moving reconciliation in the face of personal illness and

the growing public threat of Nazism. In general, Mr. Hamilton deals with his complex subject with effective and sober impartiality; he flags only toward the end—without significantly marring his book as a whole—in his inability to take distance from the Manns' embittered anti-American statements."

The *New Yorker*'s George Steiner also concluded that Hamilton's treatment of the Manns in the United States was the book's weakest section. He claimed that Hamilton "ludicrously exaggerates what he takes to be the 'Facist' forces at work on the American political and social scene at the time."

Critics disagreed whether the unusual structure of the book was successful. Although Christopher Lehmann-Haupt of the *New York Times* found Hamilton's "hopscotching" between the brothers' stories to be "an awkward way to have to tell their lives," Henry Hatfield of the *Washington Post Book World* judged that Hamilton's "shifts from one brother to the other are adroit."

Hamilton told *CA* that he detests "vapid journalism" and has the "usual inferiority complexes," but finds "moral stature/greatness/ achievement" to be of interest.

BIOGRAPHICAL/CRITICAL SOURCES: Chicago Tribune Book World, April 8, 1979; *Washington Post Book World,* April 15, 1979; *New York Times,* May 3, 1979; *New Yorker,* July 9, 1979; *New York Times Book Review,* August 5, 1979.

*   *   *

**HAMMERSTEIN, Oscar (Greeley Glendenning) II
1895-1960**

PERSONAL: Born July 12, 1895, in New York, N.Y.; died August 23, 1960, in Doylestown, Pa.; son of William (a theatrical manager) and Alica Vivian (Nimmo) Hammerstein; married second wife, Dorothy Blanchard (an interior decorator), May 14, 1929; children: (first marriage) William, Alice Hammerstein Byrne; (second marriage) James. *Education:* Columbia University, A.B., 1916, received law degree, 1918.

CAREER: Worked in law office; employed as stage manager, 1918-19; composer, 1919-60. Co-founder and partner of Williamson Music, Inc., 1945. Producer of own plays; co-producer of "I Remember Mama," 1944, "Annie Get Your Gun," 1946, "Happy Birthday," 1946, "John Loves Mary," 1947, "Happy Time," and television production of "Cinderella," 1957. Member of War Music Committee, 1943; sponsor of American Youth Orchestra.

AWARDS, HONORS: Honorary degrees include LL.D. from Drury College, 1949, and D.H.L. from Dartmouth College, 1952, Boston University, Columbia University, University of Massachusetts, and Knox College; Pulitzer Prizes, 1944, for "Oklahoma" and 1949, for "South Pacific"; Donaldson Awards, 1944, for "Oklahoma," 1945, for "Carousel," and 1946, for "Show Boat"; New York Drama Critics Circle Awards, 1945, for "Carousel," and 1949, for "South Pacific"; Academy Awards from Academy of Motion Picture Arts and Sciences, 1945, for "The Last Time I Saw Paris," 1946, for "It Might as Well Be Spring"; medal of excellence from Columbia University, 1949; Alexander Hamilton Award; Antoinette Perry (Tony) Awards, 1950, for "South Pacific," 1952, for "The King and I," and 1960, for "The Sound of Music"; Grammy Award, 1960, for "The Sound of Music."

WRITINGS: Lyrics, Simon & Schuster, 1949; (author of foreword) Richard Rodgers, editor, *The Rodgers and Hart Song Book: The Words and Music of Forty-Seven of Their*

Songs From Twenty-Two Shows and Two Movies, Simon & Schuster, 1951; *Six Plays by Rodgers and Hammerstein* (contains ''Oklahoma!,'' ''Carousel,'' ''Allegro,'' ''South Pacific,'' ''The King and I,'' and ''Me and Juliet''), Random House, 1955; *The Tale of Rodgers and Hammerstein's South Pacific,* edited by Thana Skouras, Lehmann Books, 1958; *Songs of Oscar Hammerstein II,* Schirmer Books, 1975.

Musical plays; all also as lyricist: ''Home, James,'' first produced in New York, N.Y., at Columbia University, 1918; ''The Light,'' 1919; ''Always You,'' first produced in 1920; (with Otto Harbach and Frank Mandel) ''Jimmie,'' first produced in 1920; (with Harbach and Mandel) ''Tickle Me,'' first produced in 1920; ''Daffy Dill,'' first produced in 1922; (with Mandel) ''Queen o' Hearts,'' first produced in 1922; (co-author) ''Wildflower,'' first produced in 1923; ''Mary Jane McKane,'' first produced in 1924; (with Harbach) *Rose Marie* (first produced in 1924; released as a feature film in 1936), Samuel French, 1931; (co-author) ''Sunny,'' first produced in 1925, released as a feature film in 1931; ''Song of the Flame,'' first produced in 1926, released as a feature film in 1930; ''The Wild Rose,'' first produced in 1926; (with Harbach and Mandel) *The Desert Song* (two-act; first produced in 1926; released as a feature film in 1944), Samuel French, 1932; (with Milton Herbert Gropper) *Gypsy Jim* (three-act), Samuel French, 1927; *Show Boat* (first produced in 1927; released as a feature film in 1936), Harms, 1962; ''Golden Dawn,'' first produced in 1927, released as a feature film in 1930; (with Frank Mandel and Lawrence Schwab) ''New Moon,'' first produced in 1927, released as a feature film in 1940; ''Good Boy,'' first produced in 1928; ''Rainbow,'' first produced in 1928; (co-author) ''Sweet Adeline,'' first produced in 1929, released as a feature film in 1935.

''The Gang's All Here,'' first produced in 1931; ''East Wind,'' first produced in 1931; ''Free for All,'' first produced in 1931; (co-author) ''Music in the Air,'' first produced in 1932, released as a feature film in 1935; ''Gentlemen Unafraid,'' first produced in 1938; ''Very Warm for May,'' first produced in 1939.

''Sunny River,'' first produced in 1941; *Oklahoma!* (first produced in March, 1943; released as a feature film in 1955), Random House, 1943; ''Carmen Jones,'' first produced in December, 1943, released as a feature film in 1954; *Carousel* (first produced in 1945; released as a feature film in 1956), vocal score (with Richard Rodgers; edited by Albert Sirmay), Williamson Music, 1956; *Allegro* (first produced in 1947), Knopf, 1948, piano-vocal score (with Rodgers; edited by Sirmay), Williamson Music, 1948; (with Joshua Logan) *South Pacific* (first produced in 1949; released as a feature film in 1958), Random House, 1949, piano-vocal score (with Logan and Rodgers; edited by Sirmay), Williamson Music, 1949.

The King and I (first produced in 1951; released as a feature film in 1956), Random House, 1951; *Me and Juliet* (first produced in 1953), Random House, 1953; *Pipe Dream* (first produced in 1956), Viking, 1956; (with Joseph Fields) *Flower Drum Song* (first produced in 1958; released as a feature film in 1961), Farrar, Straus, 1959.

Author of lyrics for musical plays: ''Ballyhoo,'' first produced in 1931; ''May Wine,'' first produced in 1935; ''American Jubilee'' (revue), first produced in 1940; Howard Lindsay and Russsl Crouse, *The Sound of Music* (first produced in 1959; released as a feature film in 1965), Random House, 1960.

Author of scripts and lyrics for screenplays: ''Swing High,

''Swing Low''; ''The Story of Vernon and Irene Caste''; ''Viennese Nights,'' released in 1930; ''The Night Is Young,'' released in 1935; ''Give Us This Night,'' released in 1936; ''I'll Take Romance,'' released in 1937; ''High Wide and Handsome,'' released in 1937.

Author of lyrics for films: ''Reckless,'' released in 1935; ''The Lady Objects,'' released in 1938; ''The Great Waltz,'' released in 1938; ''Lady Be Good,'' released in 1941; ''State Fair,'' released in 1945; ''Centennial Summer,'' released in 1946; ''The Strip,'' released in 1951; ''Main Street to Broadway,'' released in 1953.

Author or co-author of more than one thousand song lyrics, including ''Ol' Man River,'' ''Lover Come Back to Me,'' ''When I Grow Too Old to Dream,'' ''All the Things You Are,'' ''The Last Time I Saw Paris,'' ''Oh, What a Beautiful Mornin','' ''People Will Say We're in Love,'' ''The Surrey With the Fringe on Top,'' ''If I Loved You,'' ''June Is Bustin' Out All Over,'' ''Stout Hearted Men,'' ''Only Make Believe,'' ''Some Enchanted Evening,'' ''Bali Hai,'' ''Younger Than Springtime,'' ''I'm in Love With a Wonderful Guy,'' ''Indian Love Call,'' ''Who,'' ''One Alone,'' ''I Whistle a Happy Tune,'' ''Hello Young Lovers,'' ''Puzzlement,'' ''We Kiss in a Shadow,'' ''Getting to Know You,'' ''Shall We Dance?,'' ''Can't Help Lovin' Dat Man,'' ''Bill,'' ''Why Was I Born?,'' ''Don't Ever Leave Me,'' ''The Song Is You,'' ''I've Told Ev'ry Little Star,'' ''The Folks Who Live on the Hill,'' ''I'll Take Romance,'' ''It Might as Well Be Spring,'' ''No Other Love,'' ''I Enjoy Being a Girl,'' ''The Sound of Music,'' ''My Favorite Things,'' and ''Climb Every Mountain.''

SIDELIGHTS: Hammerstein was one of the world's best-loved and most prolific lyricists. His collaborations with Jerome Kern, George Gershwin, and Richard Rodgers resulted in such popular musicals as ''Oklahoma!,'' ''Show Boat,'' ''Carousel,'' ''South Pacific,'' and ''The Sound of Music.''

Although he came from a famous theatrical family—his grandfather Oscar Hammerstein was the owner of the Manhattan Opera House—Hammerstein did not become involved in theatre until he was a law student at Columbia University. After writing several student shows he approached his uncle, an impressario, and asked him for a job. The uncle told Hammerstein that before he even wrote a line, he must study technical aspects of the theatre for a year. Hammerstein complied and later said that he had learned a great deal by listening to actors during rehearsals and by working as a stage manager for his uncle's road companies.

After this apprenticeship, Hammerstein wrote a few plays that went relatively unnoticed. ''Wildflower,'' produced in 1923, was the first of a long series of hits. From then on Hammerstein produced an average of one major work each year. He was a quick and proficient writer, often completing a libretto and lyrics in six or seven months. One of his best-known songs, ''Oh, What a Beautiful Mornin','' was completed in only an hour.

Perhaps Hammerstein's most lasting contribution to the American musical will be that he was instrumental in introducing real-life dialogue and genuine plots into the musical theatre. Previously, musicals had been marred by stilted narrative and almost non-existent plots. But Hammerstein transcended this limitation of the genre, and in ''Oklahoma!'' his folksy dialogue and believable story helped earn the play a special Pulitzer Prize.

BIOGRAPHICAL/CRITICAL SOURCES: New York Times Magazine, April 8, 1962; Stanley Green, *The Rodgers and*

Hammerstein Story, Day, 1963; *Opera News*, March 18, 1967; Deems Taylor, *Some Enchanted Evenings*, Greenwood, 1972; *Best Sellers*, October, 1975; Hugh Fordin, *Getting to Know Him: A Biography of Oscar Hammerstein II*, Random House, 1977.*

* * *

HANAGAN, Eva (Helen) 1923-

PERSONAL: Born November 10, 1923, in Inverness, Scotland; daughter of James Macdonald (in business) and Janet Alice (Fraser) Ross; married John Thomas Frederick Hanagan (a British Army officer), June 24, 1947; children: Patrick Sean, Alistair Brian. *Education:* Attended Inverness Royal Academy and Inverness College. *Home:* 4 Hillside, Horsham, Sussex, England. *Agent:* David Higham Associates Ltd., 5-8 Lower John St., Golden Square, London W1R 4HA, England.

CAREER: Inverness Board of Trade, Inverness, Scotland, secretary, 1942-45; executive officer in legal division of Foreign Office of Vienna, Austria, 1945-50; writer.

WRITINGS: In Thrall (novel), Duckworth, 1977; *Playmates* (novel), Duckworth, 1978; *The Upas Tree* (novel), Constable, 1979, St. Martin's, 1980; *Holding On* (novel), Constable, 1980. Contributor of stories to magazines.

WORK IN PROGRESS: A novel.

SIDELIGHTS: Eva Hanagan told *CA:* "My motivation for writing *may* be that on the page the writer is in control of events, whereas in real life one is subject to random disaster. But analysis of motivation and method can be fraught with danger, as Mrs. Craster's 1874 poem warns: 'The centipede was happy quite / Until the toad in fun / Said "Pray which leg goes after which?" / And worked her mind to such a pitch / She lay distracted in the ditch / Considering how to run!'"

* * *

HANAWALT, Barbara A(nn) 1941-

PERSONAL: Born March 4, 1941, in New Brunswick, N.J.; daughter of Nelson G. (a professor) and Pearl (a teacher; maiden name, Bassett) Hanawalt; married Robert S. Westman (marriage ended). *Education:* Rutgers University, Douglass College, B.A. (with highest honors), 1963; University of Michigan, M.A., 1964, Ph.D., 1970. *Home:* 512 East Eighth St., Bloomington, Ind. 47401. *Office:* Department of History, Indiana University, Bloomington, Ind. 47405.

CAREER: San Fernando Valley State College (now California State University at Northridge), Northridge, Calif., instructor in history, 1970-72; University of Oregon, Eugene, visiting assistant professor of history, 1972-73; Indiana University, Bloomington, assistant professor, 1974-78, associate professor of history, 1978—. Member of faculty at University of California, Los Angeles, 1971-72, 1974; visiting assistant professor at University of Southern California, 1972.

MEMBER: American Historical Association, Medieval Academy of America, Social Science History Association, Social History Society, Past and Present Society, Royal Historical Society, Phi Beta Kappa. *Awards, honors:* Woodrow Wilson fellow, 1963-64, 1966-67; American Philosophical Society grant, 1971, 1978; scholar at Center for Medieval and Renaissance Studies, University of California, Los Angeles, 1973-74; fellow of Southeastern Medieval and Renaissance Institute, summer, 1974; Canada Council grant, summer, 1975; American Council of Learned Societies fellow, 1975-76; fellow at Summer Institute for Quantification and Demographic History, 1978; National Endowment for the Humanities grant, 1979, Newberry Library fellow, 1979-80.

WRITINGS: Crime and East Anglia in the Fourteenth Century: Norfolk Goal Delivery Rolls, 1307-1316, Norfolk Record Society, 1976; (contributor) S. M. Stuard, editor, *Women in Medieval Society*, University of Pennsylvania Press, 1976; *Crime and Conflict in English Communities, 1300-1348*, Harvard University Press, 1979; (contributor) Richard Schlatter, editor, *Changing Views on British History*, Harvard University Press, 1980. Contributor to scholarly and popular journals. Associate editor of *American Historical Review*, 1976-77.

WORK IN PROGRESS: A History of Deviance in England, with Martha Francois, for Indiana University Press; *Kith and Kin*, a study of the late medieval family and community in late medieval England, completion expected in 1984.

SIDELIGHTS: Barbara Hanawalt wrote: "I am interested in medieval English social history. My work has concentrated on the peasantry, but I have written on the other social classes as well. I am interested in furthering our knowledge of how these people lived and coped with diseases, economic setback, economic prosperity, political impositions, wars, taxation, family relationships, community ties, religion, and so on. In my writing I have been particularly interested in communicating my information on these matters in a style which both specialists and the general public could read and enjoy."

* * *

HANCOCK, Geoffrey 1946-

PERSONAL: Born April 14, 1946, in New Westminster, British Columbia, Canada; son of Jonas (a scholar) and Margaret (Ramsbottom) Hancock; married Theodora de Vos, June 30, 1974 (separated June, 1978). *Education:* University of British Columbia, B.F.A., 1973, M.F.A., 1975. *Residence:* Toronto, Ontario, Canada. *Office address:* P.O. Box 946, Station F, Toronto, Ontario, Canada M4Y 2N9.

CAREER: Worked as waiter, postman, and writing instructor, 1967-74; *Canadian Fiction Magazine,* Toronto, Ontario, editor-in-chief, 1974—. Lecturer at University of British Columbia, 1974-76, and Simon Fraser University, 1976-77. Treasurer of National Magazine Awards Foundation; consultant to Multiculturalism Directorate and to Canadian Broadcasting Corp. (CBC-Radio) program, "Anthology." *Member:* Canadian Periodical Publishers Association (member of board of directors; president, 1976-78), Periodical Writers Association of Canada. *Awards, honors:* Grant Redford Prize, 1973, for play, "House of Whale, Rising"; eight Canada Council grants, 1974-81; Russel A. Bankson Award from University of British Columbia, 1975, for "The Japanese Claw Hold"; Fiona Mee Award for outstanding literary journalism from *Quill and Quire*, 1979.

WRITINGS: The Dramatic Necessity: Possibilities in the Canadian Short Story, Highway Book Shop, 1980; (editor) *Magic Realism*, Aya Press, Volume I, 1980, Volume II, 1981; (editor) *Fiction in Translation From the Unofficial Languages of Canada*, CFM, 1980. Contributor to magazines and newspapers, including *Lifeline, Books in Canada, Canadian Author and Bookman, Malahat Review, Descant,* and *Quill and Quire*. Book critic for *Toronto Star*, 1979—; member of editorial board of University of British Columbia alumni *Chronicle*.

WORK IN PROGRESS: A book on the art of literary editing, publication by Aya Press expected in 1981; a history of the Canadian literary magazine, for Aya Press, 1981; *One, Two, Three, Testing*, a novel; editing an anthology of French-Canadian short stories.

SIDELIGHTS: Hancock commented to *CA:* "'The island of our knowledge increases the shoreline of our wonder,' says Shelley in *Prometheus Unbound.* So I travel widely in life and also in literature, especially among those writers who evoke the extraordinary. I believe there is progress in the arts and have devoted my literary career to cracking open the possibilities for contemporary creative writing."

BIOGRAPHICAL/CRITICAL SOURCES: Pacific Northwest Review of Books, June, 1978; *Vancouver Sun,* July 16, 1978; *Quill and Quire,* May, 1979; *Saturday Night,* May, 1980.

* * *

HAPPOLD, F(rederick) C(rossfield) 1893-

PERSONAL: Born in 1893 in Lancaster, England; married Dorothy Vectis Halbach; children: one son. *Education:* Received M.A. from Peterhouse, Cambridge. *Home:* High Elms, Redlynch near Salisbury, Wiltshire, England.

CAREER: Assistant master at private school in Cambridge, England; Bishop Wordsworth's School, Salisbury, England, headmaster, 1928-60; writer, 1960—. Lecturer at Cambridge University. *Military service:* British Army, Loyal Regiment, 1914-18; became captain. *Awards, honors:* Distinguished Service Order; LL.D. from University of Melbourne.

WRITINGS: The Adventure of Man: A Brief History of the World, Harcourt, 1926; *The Approach to History,* Christophers, 1928; *Citizens in the Making,* Christophers, 1935; *This Modern Age: An Introduction to the Understanding of Our Own Times,* Christophers, 1938, 6th edition, 1960; *Towards a New Aristocracy: A Contribution to Educational Planning,* Faber, 1943; *Vision and Craftsmanship: Studies in Ends and Means in Education,* Faber, 1949; *Everyone's Book About the English Church,* Faber, 1953; *Adventure in Search of a Creed,* Faber, 1957; *Mysticism: A Study and an Anthology,* Penguin, 1963, revised edition, 1970; *Religious Faith and Twentieth-Century Man,* Penguin, 1966; *The Journey Inwards: A Simple Introduction to the Practice of Contemplative Meditation by Normal People,* Darton, Longman & Todd, 1968, John Knox Press, 1975; *Prayer and Meditation: Their Nature and Practice,* Penguin, 1971. Also author of *The Finding of the King,* Oxford University Press. Author of pamphlets. Contributor to *Encyclopaedia Britannica.* Contributor to magazines and newspapers, including *Spectator.*

* * *

HARALDSSON, Erlendur 1931-

PERSONAL: Born November 3, 1931, in Reykjavik, Iceland; son of Haraldur and Anna (Elinmundardottir) Erlendsson. *Education:* University of Freiburg, diploma, 1969, Ph.D., 1972. *Religion:* Lutheran. *Office:* Department of Psychology, University of Iceland, Reykjavik, Iceland.

CAREER: Free-lance journalist in Reykjavik, Iceland, Berlin, West Germany, and India, 1959-64; University of Iceland, Reykjavik, assistant professor, 1974-78, associate professor of psychology, 1978—. Research fellow at Institute for Parapsychology, 1969-70; research associate for American Society for Psychical Research, 1972-74.

WRITINGS: Med uppreisnarmoennum i Kurdistan (title means "With Rebels in Kurdistan"), Skuggsja, 1964; *Land im Aufstand Kurdistan* (title means "Kurdistan: Land in Revolt"), Matari Verlag, 1966; (with Karlis Osis) *At the Hour of Death,* Avon, 1977; *Thessa heims og annars* (title means "Survey of Psychical Experiences in Iceland"), Bokaforlagid Saga, 1978.

WORK IN PROGRESS: "A work on the famed and controversial Indian religious leader and 'miracle-man', Sri Sathya Sai Baba. It describes an objective investigation into a number of reports of various allegedly miraculous phenomena (materializations, healing, bi-location, telepathy) associated with Sathya Sai Baba as well as direct observations by the author of phenomena occurring in his presence."

SIDELIGHTS: Haraldsson told *CA:* "*At the Hour of Death* describes an extensive transcultural survey among physicians and nurses in the United States and India on near-death experiences (mostly deathbed visions) in a large sample of patients, mostly terminally sick. A vast amount of data was analyzed for possible indications for life after death. Osis and I concluded that some of the data are difficult to explain without assuming some kind of life after death."

At the Hour of Death has been translated into German, Japanese, Icelandic, Dutch, Italian, Spanish, and French.

* * *

HARBESON, Georgiana Brown 1894(?)-1980

OBITUARY NOTICE: Born c. 1894 in New Haven, Conn.; died July 29, 1980, in Philadelphia, Pa. Artist and author. Harbeson specialized in embroidery and needlepoint, and many of her creations, some of which became collectors' items, were exhibited in museums. Among the museums that display her work are the Metropolitan Museum of Art, the Smithsonian-Cooper Hewitt Museum, and the Academy of Fine Arts in Honolulu. She was the author of a book in 1938, *American Needlework.* Obituaries and other sources: *New York Times,* August 2, 1980.

* * *

HARE, Bill
See HARE, William Moorman

* * *

HARE, Norma Q(uarles) 1924-

PERSONAL: Born July 10, 1924, in Dadeville, Mo.; daughter of J. Norman (an educator) and Mary D. (Blakemore) Quarles; married John D. Hare II (in data processing), June 27, 1944; children: J. Daniel III, Thomas Christopher. *Education:* Attended Southwest Missouri State University; California State University, Fresno, B.A., 1958, M.A., 1963. *Religion:* Presbyterian. *Home address:* P.O. Box 161, Millbrae, Calif. 94030.

CAREER: Teacher at schools in Parlier, Calif., 1956-57, in Sanger, Calif., 1958-66, and in South San Francisco, Calif., 1966-67; Hillside Elementary School, South San Francisco, principal, 1967—. *Member:* National Association of Elementary School Principals, Society of Children's Book Writers, Association of California School Administrators, California Historical Society, Society of Mayflower Descendants, Parent-Teachers Association.

WRITINGS—Juvenile: Who Is Root Beer?, Garrard, 1977; *Wish Upon a Birthday,* Garrard, 1979; *Mystery at Mouse House,* Garrard, 1980. Contributor to *National Elementary Principal.*

SIDELIGHTS: Norma Hare told *CA:* "For many children, learning to read is hard work. As an elementary school principal and former classroom teacher, I'll vouch for this. I recently started writing for very young readers because I wanted to give them books that are really fun to spend time with, ones they can clearly understand on their own, and most of all, books that lead to imagining, dreaming, and perhaps, wisdom. Then, I hope my young readers will go to the bookshelf and reach for another book, and another, and another.''

* * *

HARE, William Moorman 1934-
(Bill Hare)

PERSONAL: Born June 9, 1934, in Ann Arbor, Mich.; son of Weldon Parsons and Millicent (Moorman) Hare; married Elaine Pendexter (in production management), September 7, 1955; children: Kimberly, Steven, John, Leigh. *Education:* Northwestern University, B.S., 1956. *Residence:* Calabasas Park, Calif. *Agent:* Warren Bayless, Curtis Brown Ltd., 575 Madison Ave., New York, N.Y. 10022.

CAREER: Writer and producer for educational television and advertising agencies, 1957-67; free-lance writer, director, and producer in Chicago, Ill., 1967-78; affiliated with Calabasas Productions, Inc., 1978—. *Member:* Dramatists Guild, Writers Guild. *Awards, honors:* Numerous international film festival prizes for two feature documentaries and three shorts; recipient of several Clio Awards for commercials; Serr Award, 1970, for feature film, ''Finney.''

WRITINGS—Under name Bill Hare; films: ''The Artist as a Reporter'' (documentary), released by Contemporary Films, 1966; ''The World of Vatican II'' (documentary), released by Contemporary Films, 1967; ''Finney'' (feature), released by Gold Coast Pictures, 1970.

Plays: *God Says There Is No Peter Ott* (two-act; first produced in New York, N.Y., at McAlpin Rooftop Theatre, April 17, 1972), Dramatists Play Service, 1972; ''Opper'' (two-act), first produced in Los Angeles at Callboard Theatre, 1979.

WORK IN PROGRESS: *Robber Baron Bliss,* as both a novel and a screenplay; ''The Wine Country,'' a television series pilot; three screenplays: ''Wish I May,'' ''Coverage,'' and ''The Pit.''

SIDELIGHTS: Hare told *CA:* ''My first free-lance project (1967-70) was a feature film produced out of Chicago. I wrote it, directed it, edited it, and raised the money necessary for those indulgences. It was a critical success and financial disaster. Although I was hooked and have attempted to 'control' my projects since then (which means, among other things, raising a lot of money), I don't recommend this procedure. Better to work up through the 'system'—mindful that there isn't really a system at all. Still, your odds are better and your energy and talent are better utilized if you concentrate on *one* of the disciplines—say, screenwriting. Write well, and worry about the sharks later.''

* * *

HARMAN, Nicholas 1933-

PERSONAL: Born May 10, 1933, in London, England; son of a Lord Justice and Helen Sarah (LeRoy Lewis) Harman; married Constance Freeman, July, 1963; children: Edward, Sam, Rebecca. *Education:* King's College, Cambridge, M.A., 1956. *Religion:* None. *Home:* 68 Stockwell Park Rd., London S.W.9, England. *Agent:* Felicity Bryan, Curtis Brown Ltd., 1 Craven Hill, London W.9, England.

CAREER: *Economist,* London, England, staff writer, 1956-57; *Realities,* Paris, France, writer, editor, and translator, 1957-60; *Economist,* writer and assistant editor, 1960-69; *Sunday Times,* London, writer, 1970-73; British Broadcasting Corp., London, television reporter and presenter, 1972-

75; Commonwealth Secretariat, London, director of information, 1975-77; free-lance writer, 1977—. *Military service:* British Army, Royal Regiment of Fusiliers, 1950-52; became second lieutenant.

WRITINGS: *Dunkirk: The Patriotic Myth,* Simon & Schuster, 1980. Author of television and radio scripts. Contributor of several hundred articles to magazines and newspapers, including *New Statesman, Listener,* and *Daily Telegraph Magazine.*

WORK IN PROGRESS: Research on problems of world economic development.

SIDELIGHTS: Nicholas Harmon told *CA:* ''Ever since I became a professional writer—and I have never done anything else but write—I have focused on politics and economics. But my first full-length book was about war. War is what happens when the politicians and economists finally fail to do their jobs properly. The rise of Hitler, and the failure of the democracies to rally together against him, show humanity at the extreme point ot disintegration. That is what fascinated me about the story. There are plenty of other such stories to tell.''

* * *

HARMSTON, Olivia
See WEBER, Nancy

* * *

HARPER, Joan (Marie) 1932-

PERSONAL: Born January 3, 1932, in Omaha, Neb.; daughter of Lawrence Dean (in sale and breeding of chinchillas) and Genevieve (Lucas) Hurley; married Harold Harper (a physician), March 1, 1969 (divorced, 1975); children: Lisa Harper Nielsen. *Education:* Studied opera privately. *Religion:* Pentecostal Christian. *Residence:* Agoura, Calif. *Office:* 1250 La Venta Dr., No. 202, Westlake Village, Calif. 91361.

CAREER: Office manager for physician in North Hollywood, Calif., 1968-72; church secretary in Van Nuys, Calif., 1973-76; Plastic Surgery Association, Westlake, Calif., surgery scheduler, 1977—. *Member:* American Cancer Society.

WRITINGS: *I'm Still Me* (nonfiction), Logos International, 1979.

SIDELIGHTS: Joan Harper told *CA:* ''*I'm Still Me* is the true story of one woman's triumph over breast cancer. But it is also the odyssey of a girl from Omaha who passed through a series of disadvantageous marriages to social and financial prominence. It was at the pinnacle of that prominence that I discovered I had one of the deadliest varieties of cancer—at that time in its development so early that no known medical procedure could have revealed it.

''Faith had long had a place in my life, but the success of beauty and natural talent had long blunted any impact it might have had. Now, however—with the discovery of cancer—there was nowhere else to turn. My own husband was a physician and I was accorded the best medical science had to offer. But the prospect of a double mastectomy held no comfort for me. So I turned to God. In an experience that defies explanation, I encountered God and his love. I knew that all would be well.

''What followed was an ordeal of nightmarish proportion. I nearly died after surgery, but the grace of God intervened and I emerged alive, only, however, to be struck even harder by the departure of my husband.

"For the next few weeks I did little except listen to tape recorded readings from the Book of Psalms. Slowly, imperceptibly, a change began to come, until the day I was ready to venture out again into a whole new future—bright with promise at last."

AVOCATIONAL INTERESTS: Travel (Eastern and Western Europe, Scandinavia, Greece, Mexico), collecting limited-edition plates, rose gardening.

*   *   *

HARRIS, Hyde
   See HARRIS, Timothy Hyde

*   *   *

HARRIS, Timothy Hyde   1946-
   (Hyde Harris)

PERSONAL: Born July 21, 1946, in Los Angeles, Calif.; son of Donald and Mary Helen (an artist; maiden name, McDermott) Harris; married Mary Bess Walker (a film director), March 21, 1980. *Education:* Peterhouse College, Cambridge, B.A. (with honors), 1969, M.A., 1974. *Politics:* Independent. *Religion:* "Pagan." *Home:* 1053½ South Genesee Ave., Los Angeles, Calif. 90019. *Agent:* Stuart Miller, Stuart Miller Agency, 4444 Riverside Dr., Burbank, Calif. 91505.

CAREER: Sailor, carpenter, and house painter, 1964—. *Member:* Writers Guild of America (West).

WRITINGS—Novels: *Kronski/McSmash,* M. Joseph, 1969, Doubleday, 1970; *Kyd for Hire,* Dell, 1978 (published in England under name Hyde Harris, Gollancz, 1978); *Goodnight and Goodbye,* Delacorte, 1979.

Screenplays: "Cheaper to Keep Her," released by Regal Productions, 1980; "French Kiss," released by Universal, 1980.

WORK IN PROGRESS: A novel set in Mexico; screenplays, including "The Fugitive Pigeon" (adapted from novel by Donald Westlake), for Universal; research on prisons.

AVOCATIONAL INTERESTS: Travel (Europe and Africa), competitive saber fencing, spearfishing, skin diving, tennis (junior champion of Portugal, 1963).

BIOGRAPHICAL/CRITICAL SOURCES: Los Angeles Times, February 27, 1980.

*   *   *

HARRISON, John R(aymond)   1933-

PERSONAL: Born June 8, 1933, in Des Moines, Iowa; son of Raymond and Dorothy (Stout) Harrison; married Lois Cowles, June 24, 1955; children: Gardner Mark, Kent Alfred, John Patrick, Lois Eleanor. *Education:* Harvard University, A.B., 1955, graduate study, 1955-56. *Office address:* P.O. Box 408, Lakeland, Fla. 33802.

CAREER/WRITINGS: Worked as printer with *Ft. Pierce News-Tribune,* Ft. Pierce, Fla.; New York Times Co., New York, N.Y., vice-president and president of New York Times Affiliated Newspaper Group, including ten newspapers in Florida and three in North Carolina. Director of *International Herald Tribune,* Paris, France. Editorial writer. Director of Ft. Pierce-St. Louis County Industrial Development Council, 1959-62; member of board of directors of Ft. Pierce Memorial Hospital, 1959-62, Lincoln Park Child Care Center (Ft. Pierce), 1959-62, Gainesville United Fund, 1965, Gainesville Boys Club, 1965, University of Florida Foundation, 1967—, Greater Lakeland YMCA, 1967-69, Lakeland Human Relations Council, 1967-69, and Lakeland Boys Club; member of Wellesley College President's Resources Council, Florida Southern College board of counselors, 1974, and Greater Lakeland Chamber of Commerce; director of University of Florida Foundation; trustee of Robert H. Anderson Foundation, Ridge School, Barrow, Fla.

MEMBER: Hasty Pudding Institute 1770, Spee Club, Tampa University Club, Lakeland Yacht and Country Club, Lone Palm Country Club (Lakeland). *Awards, honors:* Pulitzer Prize in editorial writing, 1965; Sigma Delta Chi bronze medallion, 1970 and 1973, for editorial writing; National Headliners Award, 1972, for public service editorial writing; Scripps-Howard Foundation/Walker Stone Award, 1974, for editorial writing.

SIDELIGHTS: As president of the New York Times Affiliated Newspaper Group, Harrison has sought to broaden the *Times*'s influence while upgrading the quality of smaller newspapers. Many of the papers in the group receive the *Times*'s "Week in Review" section or its "Sunday Magazine"—features not normally available to smaller communities. By supplementing local papers with such pieces, Harrison feels the educational level of these communities can be raised.

Harrison's goal is to improve the quality of papers in the Affiliated Newspaper Group while strengthening the group's role in the parent company. He told *Editor and Publisher:* "I've been spending a lot of time with editors on product upkeep: I ask that within the newshole they have, can they find ways to satisfy readers without them relying on a second newspaper? . . . I say: give them a strong editorial page, many small items, several thoroughly-done major stories and there is no way you can miss."

Harrison has also distinguished himself as an activist in editorial writing. In 1965 his call for an urban renewal minimum-housing code in Gainesville, Florida, led to the creation of eight thousand minimum-housing units. A series of his 1972 editorials helped enact a state law on competitive bidding for engineering services; and his editorial work in 1974 played significantly in the passing of Florida child care legislation. Later Harrison campaigned for juvenile justice reform, saying "I think our papers will become quite active in studying the use of juvenile-based homes rather than hard-core incarceration for youths." Harrison's editorial work has brought him a number of awards, including a Pulitzer Prize in 1965.

BIOGRAPHICAL/CRITICAL SOURCES: Editor and Publisher, February 28, 1976; *Authors in the News,* Volume 2, Gale, 1976.

*   *   *

HARROWER, Elizabeth   1928-

PERSONAL: Born February 8, 1928, in Sydney, Australia.

CAREER: Writer. Australian Broadcasting Commission, Sydney, member of staff, 1959-60; *Sydney Morning Herald,* Sydney, reviewer, 1960; Macmillan & Co. Ltd., Sydney, member of staff, 1961-67. *Awards, honors:* Fellowships from Commonwealth Literary Fund, 1968, and Australian Council for the Arts, 1974.

WRITINGS: Down in the City, Cassell, 1957; *The Long Prospect,* Cassell, 1958; *The Catherine Wheel,* Cassell, 1960; *The Watch Tower,* Macmillan, 1966. Work represented in anthologies, including *Summer's Tales I,* Macmillan, 1964, *Modern Australian Writing,* Fontana, 1966, and *Australian Writing Today,* Penguin, 1968. Contributor to periodicals, including *Australian Letters.*

BIOGRAPHICAL/CRITICAL SOURCES: Australian Letters, December, 1961; John Hetherington, *Forty-Two Faces,* Cheshire, 1962; *Observer,* October 16, 1966; *Times Literary Supplement,* November 10, 1966; *Books and Bookmen,* December, 1966; *Southerly,* number 2, 1970; R. G. Geering, *Recent Fiction,* Oxford University Press, 1974.*

* * *

HART, Douglas C. 1950-

PERSONAL: Born February 18, 1950, in New York, N.Y.; son of Robert E. and Jean P. (Leaman) Hart; children: Bryan Michael. *Education:* Attended School of Visual Arts, 1968-71 and 1980—. *Home:* 39-51 44th St., Sunnyside, N.Y. 11104.

CAREER: Motion picture cameraman. *Member:* International Alliance of Theatrical Stage Employees, American Film Institute, National Academy of Television Arts and Sciences, National Film Society, Society of Motion Picture and Television Engineers, Association of Independent Video and Filmmakers.

WRITINGS: (With Robert W. Pohle, Jr.) *Sherlock Holmes on the Screen: The Motion Picture Adventures of the World's Most Popular Detective,* A. S. Barnes, 1976. Also author of *The Films of Christopher Lee,* A. S. Barnes. Contributor to *Filmmakers Newsletter.*

WORK IN PROGRESS: Kinetoscope: A History of Edison's Motion Picture System.

* * *

HARTLING, Peter
See HAERTLING, Peter

* * *

HEACOX, Cecil E. 1903-

PERSONAL: Born May 26, 1903, in Farmington, Conn.; son of Frank L. (a doctor) and Isabel (Francis) Heacox; married Dorothy Chatterton (a writer), June 12, 1939. *Education:* Dartmouth College, A.B., 1926; graduate study at Cornell University, 1937. *Politics:* Republican. *Religion:* Protestant. *Home:* Tower Hill, Wassaic, N.Y. 12592.

CAREER: Conservationist, sportsman, and writer. Held several business positions, 1926-36; New York State Conservation Department, Albany, N.Y., fish hatchery assistant, 1937-40, junior aquatic biologist, 1940-43, senior aquatic biologist, 1944-46, district fisheries manager in Rochester and Poughkeepsie, N.Y., 1946-58, secretary of Conservation Department, 1959-66, deputy conservation commissioner, 1966-67. Governor's representative on Interstate Oil Compact Commission, 1959-63. Lecturer on water conservation at New York City high schools and at general conservation seminars for college science teachers. *Member:* American Fisheries Society, Trout Unlimited, Theodore Gordon Fly Fishers, Salmon and Trout Association (London).

WRITINGS: The Compleat Brown Trout (Field and Stream Book Club and Outdoor Life Book Club selection), Winchester Press, 1974; *The Education of an Outdoorsman,* Winchester Press, 1976; (with wife, Dorothy Heacox) *The Gallant Grouse: All About the Hunting and Natural History of Old Ruff,* McKay, 1980.

Author of scripts for motion pictures: "The Story of Fishing in New York," 1946; "Olympic Bobsled Run," 1960; "The Snowshoe Hare," 1960. Author of newspaper column in *Ithaca Journal,* 1939-48. Contributor of stories and articles to magazines, including *New York State Conservationist, Sports Illustrated, Field and Stream, Outdoors, National Sportsman, Travel,* and *Outdoor Life,* and to newspapers, including *New York Times.*

SIDELIGHTS: Heacox told *CA:* "After ten years of dismal failures in the business world, I packed up my books and returned to school (Cornell University). This paid off far beyond my most optimistic dreams." With his graduate courses in conservation, Heacox landed a job with the New York State Conservation Department, where he rose from day laborer to the rank of deputy conservation commissioner before retiring thirty years later. During his tenure, Heacox pioneered many conservation projects, including electrofishing, and helped bring about important legislative changes in the conservation field.

An avid fisherman since his youth, Heacox began his writing career with a book on the subject of brown trout. *The Compleat Brown Trout* tells the history of the fish and its introduction into North American waters, as well as tips for fishermen. Heacox told reporter Tom Duncan that "this is the first time all scientific and sporting aspects of the brown trout have been combined." Reviewer Henry Clepper said the book "is soundly based both on technical knowledge and fishing experience, and moreover, is written with attention to good English usage," and ranks as "one of the year's most delightful and informative books on trouting."

Heacox's second book, *The Education of an Outdoorsman,* is an account of his hunting, fishing, and conservation experiences, including the biopolitical aspects of his career. One point he makes in the book is that during the 1930's "hunting and fishing were synonymous with conservation," whereas today these sports, especially hunting, are frowned upon by conservation groups. Everett Wood commented: "In his closing pages Heacox reflects on . . . the paradox involved in his premise that true sportsmen-conservationists have done more to foster wildlife than all their detractors combined. . . . The pity is how few of those who take to our woods and streams each year share even a fraction of Heacox's love and sense of responsibility for the game they pursue." Heacox told *CA:* "In 1937, when I started working in the field professionally, conservation was generally equated with hunting and fishing. Although still in the growing-pains stage, conservation is gradually coming of age.

"Today, more and more people are becoming aware that all natural resources—air, water, soil, minerals, fish, wildlife, plant life, and human life—are interrelated and the ecological approach is the most meaningful way to solve resource problems caused by an expanding population and a contracting environment.

"In my own writing, I strive for a strong, narrative flow, helped along with anecdotes and dialogue. But, alas, like so many other writers, I get trapped into trite, pedestrian exposition."

BIOGRAPHICAL/CRITICAL SOURCES: Poughkeepsie Journal, April 21, 1974, December 5, 1976; *Newsletter of the American Fisheries Society,* May-June, 1974; *Millbrook Round Table,* March 5, 1975; *Dartmouth Alumni Magazine,* February, 1977; *Outdoor News Bulletin,* April 22, 1977; *Conservationist,* September-October, 1977.

* * *

HEALEY, Larry 1927-

PERSONAL: Born November 10, 1927, in Boston, Mass.; son of William J. (an attorney) and Katherine (Sullivan)

Healey; married Rose Million (a writer), 1958. *Education:* Harvard College, B.A., 1949. *Politics:* Democrat. *Home:* 68 Fifth Ave., New York, N.Y. 10011. *Agent:* McIntosh and Otis, Inc., 475 Fifth Ave., New York, N.Y. 10017.

CAREER: L'Aigon Apparel, Inc., Philadelphia, Pa., salesman, 1952-63; Nelly Don, Inc., Kansas City, Mo., sales manager, 1963-66; Hahne and Co., Newark, N.J., buyer, 1966-71; Hearn's Department Store, New York City, buyer, 1972-77. *Member:* Mystery Writers of America.

WRITINGS: The Claw of the Bear, F. Watts, 1978; *The Town Is on Fire,* F. Watts, 1979; *The Hoard of the Himalayas,* Dodd, 1980.

WORK IN PROGRESS: The Marble Pawn, a mystery on counterfeit classic sculpture, publication expected in 1980.

* * *

HEIDISH, Marcy Moran 1947-

PERSONAL: Born April 22, 1947, in New York, N.Y. *Education:* Vassar College, B.A., 1969; Catholic University of America, M.A., 1972; also attended American University, 1970-72. *Agent:* Jacques de Spoelberch, 1 Wilson Point, South Norwalk, Conn.

CAREER: Writer. *Member:* Washington Independent Writers, Washington Women's Network. *Awards, honors:* National Endowment for the Arts creative writing fellowship, 1980.

WRITINGS: A Woman Called Moses (novel), Houghton, 1976; *Witnesses* (novel), Houghton, 1980. Contributor to Washington newspapers.

WORK IN PROGRESS: A historical novel about Annie Oakley, publication expected in 1982.

SIDELIGHTS: Marcy Heidish's *A Woman Called Moses* is a fictional account of the life and work of Harriet Tubman, the indomitable black woman who directed a secret exodus of slaves from the South to their freedom via the Underground Railroad. After Tubman herself escaped to the North she succeeded in smuggling 300 men, women, and children out of the South. A reviewer for *Time* commented: "In this evocative first novel, the rescuer emerges as an invincibly courageous woman, guided by a deep, mystical religious faith and a tenacious vision. Harriet Tubman used her great intelligence in the service of a passionate love for her people."

A Woman Called Moses was adapted for television in 1978.

BIOGRAPHICAL/CRITICAL SOURCES: Time, February 23, 1976; *New York Times Book Review,* June 20, 1976.

* * *

HEINZELMAN, Kurt 1947-

PERSONAL: Born October 26, 1947, in Monroe, Wis.; son of Frank William and Katherine (Kundert) Heinzelman; married Gillian Adams. *Education:* Middlebury College, B.A., 1969, M.A., 1972; further graduate study at University of Edinburgh, 1977-78; University of Massachusetts, Ph.D., 1978. *Home:* 6805 Citadel Cove, Austin, Tex. 78723. *Office:* Department of English, University of Texas, Austin, Tex. 78701.

CAREER: English teacher and director of creative writing program at private school in Williamstown, Mass., 1969-75; assistant editor of *English Literary Renaissance,* 1975-77; University of Texas, Austin, assistant professor of English, 1978—. *Member:* Phi Beta Kappa. *Awards, honors:* Danforth Foundation fellowship, 1969-78; Fulbright fellowship, 1977-78.

WRITINGS: The Economics of Imagination, University of Massachusetts Press, 1980.

Work represented in anthologies, including *Borestone Mountain Poetry Awards Anthology: Best Poems of 1976.* Contributor of articles and poems to literature journals and literary magazines, including *Arion, Georgia Review, Poetry Northwest, Poetry,* and *Paintbrush.* Founding editor of *Poetry Miscellany,* 1971-77.

* * *

HELLBERG, Hans-Eric 1927-

PERSONAL: Born May 11, 1927, in Borlaenge, Sweden; son of Eric (in business) and Hanna (in business) Hellberg; children: Asa Erica. *Home:* Vasagatan 12 a, S-781 50 Borlaenge, Sweden.

CAREER: Journalist, 1957—; art editor, 1957—; publisher, 1979—. *Member:* Swedish Union of Authors. *Awards, honors:* Nils Holgersson Plaquette, 1971; certificate of honor from International Board on Books for Young People, 1971; diploma of honor from Swedish Academy of Detection, 1976.

WRITINGS—In English translation: Morfars Maria (juvenile), Bonnier, 1969, translation by Patricia Crampton published as *Grandpa's Maria,* Morrow, 1974.

In Swedish: *Jan faar en vaen,* Bonnier, 1958; *Jan och Ann-Charlotte faar en ide,* Bonnier, 1959; *Aelvpirater,* Bonnier, 1960; *Hemligheten,* Bonnier, 1961; *Joakim, kallad jocke,* Bonnier, 1962; *Ung man med kamera,* Prisma, 1962; *Miks fiende,* Bonnier, 1963; *Soeren och silverskrinet,* Bonnier, 1964; *Bjoern med trollhatten* (juvenile), Bonnier, 1965; *Kalle Karolina,* Bonnier, 1965, revised edition, 1978; *Annika paa en soendag,* Bonnier, 1966; *Jonas haemnd,* Bonnier, 1967; *Men mars aer kall och blaasig: En thriller paa skoj,* Bonnier, 1968.

Martins Maria, Bonnier, 1970; *Bogserbaaten,* Raben & Sjoegren, 1970; *Jag aer Maria Jag,* Bonnier, 1971; *Da enoegda banditerna,* Raben & Sjoegren, 1972; *J & J,* Bonnier, 1972; *Kram,* Bonnier, 1973; *Upp genom luften,* Raben & Sjoegren, 1973; *Aelskade Maria,* Bonnier, 1974; *Skuggan som foell,* Raben & Sjoegren, 1974; (with Elvira Birgitta Holm) *Foerbjudet,* Foerfattarfoerlaget, 1974; (with Holm) *Tillaatet,* Foerfattarfoerlaget, 1975; *Raedda paradiset,* Raben & Sjoegren, 1975; *Puss,* Bonnier, 1975; *Som vaenner,* Bonnier, 1976; *Paeivi dyker ned,* Raben & Sjoegren, 1976; *Baklaenges,* Raben & Sjoegren, 1977; *Love Love Love,* Bonnier, 1977; *Behaall dej,* Bonnier, 1977; *Framlaenges,* Raben & Sjoegren, 1978; *Nedbrottslingarna,* Raben & Sjoegren, 1979; *Aelskar, aelskar inte,* Bonnier, 1979; *BUSungen,* Tvaa Skrivare, 1979; *BUSligan,* Tvaa Skrivare, 1979; *BUSfroeet,* Tvaa Skrivare, 1980; *BUSvisslaren,* Tvaa Skrivare, 1980.

Also author of "Skuggornas klubb" (television play), 1959, "Bogserbaaten" (television serial), 1973, "Vaennerna," 1974, and "Jag aer Maria" (film).

SIDELIGHTS: Hellberg told *CA:* "In general, writers don't change society; politicians do. What a writer can hope for is that his books can maybe be of some consolation, a help to understand life's complexities."

* * *

HEMPHILL, Charles F., Jr. 1917-

PERSONAL: Born December 30, 1917, in Gainesville, Tex.; son of Charles F. and Mable Leota (Hugon) Hemphill; married Phyllis Davis (a teacher and writer), February, 1945; children: Thomas, Robert D., Anita. *Education:* Received B.A., 1938, and J.D. from University of Texas; received M.S. from University of Utah. *Religion:* Presbyterian. *Home:* 2601 East Ocean, No. 205, Long Beach, Calif. 90803.

CAREER: Federal Bureau of Investigation, Washington, D.C., agent and supervisor of bank robbery matters at national headquarters, 1941-64; Office of the Attorney General of Utah, Salt Lake City, chief of investigative staff, 1965; Wackenhut Corp., Los Angeles, Calif., senior consultant, 1965-76; writer, 1976—. *Member:* American Society of Industrial Security.

WRITINGS: Security for Business and Industry, Dow Jones-Irwin, 1971; *Security Procedures for Computer Systems,* Dow Jones-Irwin, 1973; (with Allen Z. Gammage) *Basic Criminal Law* (college textbook), McGraw, 1974; *Preventing Loss in Handling Merchandise,* American Management Association, 1974; (with son, Thomas Hemphill) *The Secure Company,* Dow Jones-Irwin, 1975; *Management's Role in Loss Prevention,* American Management Association, 1975; *Criminal Procedure: The Administration of Justice,* with instructor's manual, Goodyear Publishing, 1978; (with wife, Phyllis Hemphill) *Dictionary of Practical Law,* Prentice-Hall, 1979; (with son, Robert D. Hemphill) *Security Safeguards in Computer Operations,* American Management Association, 1979.

*   *   *

HENKIN, Harmon   1940(?)-1980

OBITUARY NOTICE: Born c. 1940; died in a car accident, August 18, 1980, in Dixon, Mont. Screenwriter and author. Henkin wrote a novel, *Criss Cross,* and two books about fishing, *Flytackle: The Tools of the Trade* and *The Complete Fisherman's Catalog.* He was working on another novel at the time of his death. Obituaries and other sources: *Publishers Weekly,* September 5, 1980.

*   *   *

HENSHAW, James Ene   1924-

PERSONAL: Born August 29, 1924, in Calabar, Nigeria; son of Richard (a political agent) and Susana (Antigha Cobham Ene) Henshaw; married Caroline Nchelem Amadi (a dress designer), February 15, 1958; children: James Ewa, Caroline Iyi-Afo, Emmanuel Ekeng, Susan Ene, Joseph Antigha Ene, Helen Bassey, Paul Itiaba, John Peter Etebong. *Education:* National University of Ireland, M.D., 1949; University of Wales, T.D.D., 1954. *Religion:* Roman Catholic. *Home:* Itiaba House, Calabar Rd., Calabar, Nigeria. *Office:* c/o University of London Press, Warwick Lane, London EC4, England.

CAREER: Writer and physician. Worked as medical consultant to Government of Eastern Nigeria, 1955-78. Controller of medical services in South Eastern State of Nigeria (now Cross River State of Nigeria), 1968-72; senior consultant on tuberculosis control to Rivers State of Nigeria, 1973-78. Member of National Council on Health, 1968-72, and Nigerian Medical Council, 1970-72. Chairman of South Eastern State branch of St. John's Ambulance Association of Nigeria, 1973, and Cultural Center Board of Arts Council of the Cross River State of Nigeria, 1976—. *Member:* Nigerian Medical Association, African Club, Port Harcourt Sports Club. *Awards, honors:* Henry Carr Memorial Cup from All Nigerian Festival of the Arts, 1953, for "The Jewel of the Shrine"; named Knight of the Order of St. Gregory the Great by Pope Paul VI, 1965; named Officer of the Order of the Niger, 1977.

WRITINGS—Plays: *This Is Our Chance: Plays From West Africa* (includes "The Jewels of the Shrine," "A Man of Character," and "This Is Our Chance"), University of London Press, 1957; *Children of the Goddess and Other Plays* (includes "Companion for a Chief," "Magic in the Blood," and "Children of the Goddess"), University of London Press, 1964; *Medicine for Love,* University of London Press, 1964; *Dinner for Promotion,* University of London Press, 1967; *Enough Is Enough: A Play of the Nigerian Civil War* (first produced in Benin City, Nigeria, 1975), Ethiope Publishing House, 1976.

"The Jewels of the Shrine" anthologized in *Plays From Black Africa,* edited by Frederic M. Litto, Hill & Wang, 1968.

Contributor of the short story "Matron's Darling" to *Eastern Nigerian Medical Journal.* Also contributor of articles to medical journals in Africa and England.

WORK IN PROGRESS: Three novels, *War of Three Drums, A Tree Falls in Damotu,* and *The River's Eye.*

SIDELIGHTS: Henshaw told *CA:* "Writing plays has been a long-time hobby and comes as a welcome intrusion whenever opportunity occurs in the course of medical practice. It is a great relaxation for which I am always grateful. I do not know how it happened, but I am sure I just strayed into it. The profession itself gives one a lot of opportunity to observe and to interpret all kinds of human behavior and attitudes.

"My books are almost exclusively directed to the young African audience. The matters treated are common and not so common situations of contradictions, conflicts, and agreements. The themes are varied and the introductory essays cover my views on many areas of interest to the African reader in particular. The young African should carry with him his praiseworthy traditions in the course of rapid social progress. These good traditions, such as the respect for the older person (even of the same 'age group') and the obligatory sharing of the other person's burdens, should not merely make the young African distinct, but should continue to be the 'earth he walks on, and the air he breathes' (from 'This Is Our Chance').

"Nigerian theatre is very lively. The plays range from Greek-style tragedies and African folklore to something like what may be called 'realism.' I run away from 'realism' that preaches defeat and pessimism. I prefer a blending of the natural and the ideal, which are beautifully represented in the ordinary lives and traditions of the people of Nigeria.

"Perhaps if I have to state the one single factor which urges me to write, I shall come back to say simply that it is the need to influence younger people through the dramatic medium, which is natural to their environment, and which delights as well as informs them. To the young African, especially the young Nigerian, I try in my books to remain basic, communicative, personal; and by different methods, to keep a dialogue of understanding between them and me. My criterion for a suitable play for the young African is that in which anybody in the audience should be able to feel that he or she could easily have written that play, and that what is being shown on the stage or the television screen is what happened or could have happened to him or her 'just that day.'"

*   *   *

HENSHAW, Richard   1945-

PERSONAL: Born October 6, 1945, in Waltham, Mass.; son of Richard Aurel (a clergyman, linguist, and ancient Near

East scholar) and Marjorie (a teacher; maiden name, Robb) Henshaw. *Education:* Universita Per Stranieri, Perugia, Italy, diploma, 1967; Antioch College, Yellow Springs, Ohio, B.A., 1969. *Home:* 1410 26th St. N.W., Washington, D.C. 20007. *Agent:* Sagalyn & Welton, 1225 19th St. N.W., Washington, D.C. 20036.

CAREER: Film director and camera operator in London, England, 1967-68; Antioch College, Yellow Springs, Ohio, lecturer in film history, 1969; Harrison & Abramovitz (architects), New York City, designer, 1969-70; free-lance writer and filmmaker in New York City, 1970-72; New York University, New York City, guest lecturer in film history, 1972; American Film Institute, Washington, D.C., historian and staff writer, 1973-74; free-lance writer in Washington, D.C., 1975—. Director of film program for "Art Now 74: A Celebration of the American Arts," John F. Kennedy Center for the Performing Arts, 1974; staff volunteer and tour guide at Washington Cathedral; consultant to Washington Sports Authority.

WRITINGS: (Contributor) *The American Film Institute Catalog, 1961-70,* Bowker, 1976; *The Encyclopedia of World Soccer,* New Republic, 1979. Contributor to journals in the United States, England, Germany, and Italy.

WORK IN PROGRESS: World Soccer: A History of the Game, beginning with ancient football games of 2500 B.C., publication expected in 1981; a compilation film on history of soccer; research for a work on cathedral architecture and history.

SIDELIGHTS: Henshaw wrote: "To ascribe a common denominator to my work is perhaps difficult in the context of present-day nomenclature. If anything, I am an encyclopedist and cultural historian. I assume that art and sport are fundamental human expressions. They are inextricably linked. Many ancient cultures, both Eastern and Western, appear to have understood this link. Meanwhile, the proper chronicling of sports history is still in its infancy.

"Living as I do in an era of myopic specialization, I sometimes feel lonely in my admiration for people who gather large amounts of information, organize it in a useful reference format, and write good prose based on it. At the same time, it is sobering to think that Diderot mastered the art of the encyclopedist without benefit of professional typists, copying machines, and international clearinghouses with idyllic Swiss addresses. So, I have recently decided to stop complaining about my loneliness."

* * *

HERBERT, John
See BRUNDAGE, John Herbert

* * *

HERRICK, Joy Field 1930-

PERSONAL: Born July 12, 1930, in Buffalo, N.Y.; daughter of Maurice Goddard (a broker) and Gretchen (Wettlaufer) Field; married Sherlock A. Herrick, Jr. (an engineer), September 12, 1953; children: Thompson, Louisa, Richard. *Education:* Attended Briarcliff Junior College, 1951-52, and State University of New York at Buffalo. *Religion:* Episcopalian. *Home:* 395 Girdle Rd., East Aurora, N.Y. 14052.

CAREER: Writer. Yoga teacher. Member of Himalayan International Institute.

WRITINGS: (With Nancy Schraffenberger) *Something's Got to Help—And Yoga Can,* M. Evans, 1974.

HERTZ, Grete Janus 1915-
(Grete Janus)

PERSONAL: Born November 21, 1915, in Copenhagen, Denmark; daughter of Nielsen (a schoolmaster) and Karla (Pedersen) Janus; married Mogens Hertz (an artist), August 8, 1944; children: Ole, Birgitte. *Education:* University of Copenhagen, M.A. (psychology), 1945. *Residence:* 3760 Gudhjem, Denmark.

CAREER: Translator, journalist, and free-lance writer. Teacher in Copenhagen, Denmark, 1937-46; school psychologist in Copenhagen, 1939-46. *Awards, honors:* Critici in Erba, from Bologna Children's Book Fair, 1975, for *Das Gelbe Haus.*

WRITINGS—All juvenile, except as noted: *Bamse,* Hirschsprung & Carlsen, 1946, translation published as *Teddy,* Lothrop, 1964; *Tit-tit lille far,* Gads Forlag, 1962, translation by Margaret Young Gacza published as *Hi, Daddy, Here I Am,* Lerner, 1964; *Farters Halmhatt,* [Copenhagen], 1962, translation by Marianne Helueg published as *Grandfather's Straw Hat,* McGraw, 1964; *Da Lena og Wise havde rede hunde,* Hirschsprung & Carlsen, 1964, translation by Kay Ware and Lucille Sutherland published as *When Lena and Lisa Had Measles,* McGraw, 1964; (under name Grete Janus) *Da Ole gik til bageren* (title means "When Ole Went to the Bakers"), Gyldendal, 1966; *Dig og mig og vi to: Boernerim og sange* (title means "Mother Goose Rhymes From Denmark"), Illustrationsforlaget, 1971; *Das Gelbe Haus,* Carlsen Verlag, 1975, published as *The Yellow House,* 1977; *Idebog to rare voksne* (title means "Handbook for Adults Who Wish to Entertain Small Children"), Woldike, 1980; *Strik dur og ting at bar ret* (a knitting book for beginners), Borgen, 1980; *Kasper og hans venner* (title means "Kasper's Friends"), Delta, 1980. Contributor of several hundred articles about psychology to magazines and newspapers.

SIDELIGHTS: Grete Hertz commented: "I like to write and have been doing so since I was sixteen years old. My husband and I work best on Bornholm, a small island in the Baltic Sea near Sweden, but we also have a flat in Copenhagen. From my daughter, who is a kindergarten teacher, and my son's two children, I still get a lot of inspiration for books and articles."

* * *

HERZ, Stephanie M(argarette) 1900-

PERSONAL: Born October 8, 1900, in Cologne, Germany; came to the United States in 1929, naturalized citizen, 1938; daughter of Jakob (a factory owner) and Agnes (Kraus) Herz. *Education:* Attended University of Cologne; University of Berlin, Ph.D., 1929; postdoctoral study at Catholic University of America, 1929-31. *Home and office:* 4 Summitcrest Dr., Kansas City, Kan. 66101.

CAREER: Social worker and educator. Georgian Court College, Lakewood, N.J., instructor of German and French, 1933; Mount St. Scholastica College, Atchison, Kan., professor of sociology, 1933-34; Villanova College (now University), Villanova, Pa., professor of sociology, summer, 1934; Manhattanville College, Purchase, N.Y., professor of sociology, 1934-36; Catholic Committee for Refugees, executive secretary, 1937-41; Office of War Information, researcher and specialist on persecution in Germany, 1941-42; Catholic Archdiocese of Portland, Ore., researcher and supervisor of children's bureau, 1943-44; Catholic Social Service, Reno, Nev., supervisor, 1944-45; Dominican College, San Rafael, Calif., professor of sociology, 1945-48; Riverdale Children's

Bureau, social worker, 1949-51; International Institute, Philadelphia, Pa., worked with immigrants, 1951-52; Catholic Charities, Kansas City, Kan., worked in public relations and counseling, 1952-62; Rockhurst College, Kansas City, Mo., professor of sociology, 1953-61; Catholic Social Service, Tucson, Ariz., executive secretary, supervisor, and counselor, 1963-65; free-lance writer, 1965. *Member:* National Association of Social Workers, Secular Order of Carmel (past president; past master of formation; novice mistress).

WRITINGS: My Words Are Spirit and Life (meditations), Doubleday, 1979. Contributor to Roman Catholic periodicals.

WORK IN PROGRESS: A sequel to *My Words Are Spirit and Life*.

SIDELIGHTS: Stephanie Herz commented: *"My Words Are Spirit and Life* is a book of meditations on the Sunday liturgy of Vatican II. Its sequel is a book of meditation and prayer on the weekdays' liturgy of Vatican II.

"While many persons want to write a book, I never was anxious to do so. It was only through my painting that my book came into existence: when I donated to Rockhurst College a geometrical abstract that I had painted, a priest who saw it asked good humoredly, 'What else do you do besides painting?' I told him that I meditated by a special method. He wanted to learn more about it, and had his confreres test my method and my meditations. Three weeks later he recommended that I put my meditations into book form, since they were, in his words, 'the prayer for our times.'

"The method of meditation used in *My Words Are Spirit and Life* varies from what is usually meant by meditation. It is word-prayer that uses repetition as a way of deepening and engraving the word of God into our hearts and souls. The meditations contain five phrases from scripture, and as they are repeated His words become truly 'Spirit and Life' for those who use this way of praying. Christ becomes truly the center of our life, and becomes alive in us."

AVOCATIONAL INTERESTS: Painting.

*   *   *

HERZBERG, Donald Gabriel   1925-1980

OBITUARY NOTICE: Born May 6, 1925, in Orange, N.J.; died of a heart attack, August 11, 1980, in New York, N.Y. Educator and author. Dean of Georgetown University's graduate school, Herzberg was a professor of government since 1963. He was a political consultant for both NBC- and ABC-TV, and had for a number of years appeared on his own television program in New York City. Appointed to several public service positions during his career, Herzberg served as staff director of the President's Commission on Registration and Voting Participation in 1963 and 1964. His books include *A Student Guide to Campaign Politics, Essays on the Legislative Process, American Party Politics: Readings and Essays,* and *Politics Is Your Business.* Obituaries and other sources: *American Men and Women of Science: The Social and Behavioral Sciences,* 12th edition, Bowker, 1973; *Leaders in Education,* 5th edition, Bowker, 1974; *Who's Who in the World,* 3rd edition, Marquis, 1976; *New York Times,* August 13, 1980.

*   *   *

HESTON, Leonard L(ancaster)   1930-

PERSONAL: Born December 16, 1930, in Burns, Ore.; son of Alexander W. (an office worker) and Florence (an office worker; maiden name, Woodhouse) Heston; married Renate

Paetzold, July 27, 1966; children: William, Steven, Diane, Gwendolen, Barbara, Ardis. *Education:* University of Oregon, B.S., 1955, M.D., 1961. *Residence:* New Brighton, Minn. *Office:* Department of Psychiatry, University of Minnesota, Minneapolis, Minn. 55455.

CAREER: Bernalillo County Indian Hospital, Albuquerque, N.M., intern, 1961-62; University of Oregon Medical School hospitals and clinics, Portland, resident, 1962-65; Psychiatric Generics Research Unit, London, England, guest worker, 1965-66; University of Iowa, Iowa City, assistant professor, 1966-70; University of Minnesota, Minneapolis, associate professor, 1970-73, professor of psychiatry and member of graduate faculty in psychiatry, genetics, and psychology, 1973—. *Military service:* U.S. Army, 1949-51. *Member:* Psychiatric Research Society, Behavior Genetics Association, American Society of Human Genetics, American Psychopathological Association, American Psychiatric Association, Minnesota Medical Society.

WRITINGS: (Editor with R. W. Pickens) *Psychiatric Factors in Drug Abuse,* Grune, 1979; *The Medical Casebook of Adolf Hitler,* William Kimber, 1979, Stein & Day, 1980.

Contributor of about fifty articles to scientific and medical journals.

WORK IN PROGRESS: Research on genetics of psychiatric disorders and brain diseases, on drugs and drug abuse, and on histories of individuals with psychiatric and drug abuse problems (such as Adolf Hitler and Howard Hughes) and diseases (such as syphilis).

SIDELIGHTS: Heston wrote: "I am motivated mainly by the opportunity to do scientific research in the biological and medical sciences. Research with social and historical import and ramifications is especially attractive. I like medical practice and try hard to be a good doctor and a good teacher of young doctors."

*   *   *

HEUTERMAN, Thomas H(enry)   1934-

PERSONAL: Born August 13, 1934, in Yakima, Wash.; son of Karel G. F. (an automobile dealer) and Mabel (a teacher; maiden name, Brown) Heuterman; married Gretchen Dow (a microbiologist), June 22, 1957; children: Thomas W., Karl Dow. *Education:* Washington State University, B.A., 1956, Ph.D., 1973; University of Washington, Seattle, M.A., 1961. *Politics:* Independent. *Religion:* Presbyterian. *Home:* 500 Polaris St. N.W., Pullman, Wash. 99163. *Office:* Department of Communications, Washington State University, Pullman, Wash. 99164.

CAREER: Yakima Herald-Republic, Yakima, Wash., staff writer, 1957-65; Washington State University, Pullman, 1965—, began as member of Department of Communications faculty, became associate professor, chairman of department, 1977—. *Member:* Society of Professional Journalists, Association for Education in Journalism.

WRITINGS: Movable Type: Biography of Legh R. Freeman, Iowa State University Press, 1979.

*   *   *

HIGBEE, Kenneth Leo   1941-

PERSONAL: Born June 18, 1941, in Spokane, Wash.; son of Leo Carlyle and Gretta (Woolf) Higbee; married Patricia Verlee Whittaker, January 28, 1965; children: Dawn, Janelle, Loren. *Education:* Brigham Young University, B.S., 1965, M.S., 1966; Purdue University, Ph.D., 1970. *Religion:*

Church of Jesus Christ of Latter-day Saints (Mormons). *Home:* 590 East Stadium Ave., Provo, Utah 84601. *Office:* Department of Psychology, Brigham Young University, Provo, Utah 84602.

CAREER: Purdue University, Indianapolis, Ind., instructor in social psychology, 1969; Brigham Young University, Provo, Utah, assistant professor, 1970-74, associate professor, 1974-79, professor of psychology, 1979—. *Member:* Psychonomic Society, Western Psychological Association, Sigma Xi, Phi Kappa Phi.

WRITINGS: Your Memory: How It Works and How to Improve It, Prentice-Hall, 1977; *Influence: What It Is and How to Use It,* Brigham Young University Press, 1978. Contributor to psychology journals.

WORK IN PROGRESS: Research on memory aids.

*   *   *

HILDESHEIMER, Wolfgang 1916-

PERSONAL: Born December 9, 1916, in Hamburg, West Germany; son of Arnold and Hanna (Goldschmidt) Hildesheimer; married Silvia Dillman, October 19, 1953. *Education:* Attended Central School of Arts and Crafts, London, England, 1937-39. *Home:* 7742 Poschiavo, Switzerland.

CAREER: Writer and artist. British Institute, Tel-Aviv, Palestine (now Israel), lecturer, 1945-46; interpreter at war crimes trial in Nuremberg, West Germany, 1946-49; guest lecturer in poetry at University of Frankfurt, 1967. *Military service:* Served British government as information officer in Palestine, 1943-45. *Member:* Deutsche Akademie fuer Sprache und Dichtung (corresponding member), Akademie der Kuenste. *Awards, honors:* Prize for radio play to aid those blinded in the war, 1955; Literaturpreis der Freien Hansestadt Bremen, 1966; Georg Buechner Prize from Deutsche Akademie fuer Sprache und Dichtung, 1966.

WRITINGS: Lieblose Legenden (short stories), Deutsche Verlags Anstalt, 1952, revised and enlarged edition, Suhrkamp, 1963; (author of libretto) Hans Werner Henze, *Das Ende einer Welt* (opera), Frankfurter Verlagsanstalt, 1953; *Parodies der falschen Voegel* (novel), K. Desch, 1953; *Ich trage eine Eule nach Athen,* Diogenes Verlag, 1956; *Nocturno im Grand Hotel,* Gleerups, 1961; *Betrachtungen ueber Mozart,* Neske, 1963; (translator) Edward St. John Gorey, *Die Draisine von Untermattenwaag,* Diogenes Verlag, 1963; (translator) Gorey, *Eine Harfe ohne Saiten; oder, Wieman einen Roman schreibt,* Diogenes Verlag, 1963; *Tynset* (novel), Suhrkamp, 1965; *Begegnung im Balkanexpress: An den Ufern der Plotinitza,* Reclam, 1968; (translator) Gorey, *La chauve-souris doree,* Diogenes Verlag, 1969; *Interpretationen: James Joyce, Georg Buechner* (criticism), Suhrkamp, 1969.

Zeiten in Cornwall, Suhrkamp, 1971; (translator) Gorey, *Das Geheimnis der Ottomane,* Diogenes Verlag, 1971; (translator) George Bernard Shaw, *Die heilige Johanna,* Suhrkamp, 1971; *Masante* (novel), Suhrkamp, 1973; *Hauskauf,* Suhrkamp, 1974; (compiler and author of introduction) *Mozart Briefe,* Suhrkamp, 1975; *Hoerspiele,* Suhrkamp, 1976; *Theaterstuecke: Ueber das absurde Theater,* Suhrkamp, 1976; *Biosphaerenklaenge,* Suhrkamp, 1977; *Mozart* (biography), Suhrkamp, 1977, translation published as *Mozart,* Farrar, Strauss, 1980. Also author of *Marbot* (fictitious biography), 1981, and of essay collections, *Erlanger Rede ueber das absurde Theater* (title means "Lecture on the Theatre of the Absurd"), and *Die Realitaet selbst ist absurd* (title means "Reality Itself Is Absurd").

Plays: "Der Drachenthron" (title means "The Dragon's Throne"; based on work by Carlo Gozzi), 1955, revised edition published as *Die Eroberung der Prinzessin Turandot* (two-act; title means "The Conquest of Princess Turandot"; also see below), [Germany], 1955; *Spiele, in denen es dunkel wird* (collection; title means "Plays in Which it Gets Dark"; contains "Pastorale," "Landschaft mit Figuren," and "Die Uher"; also see below), Neske, 1958; *Die Verspaetung* (two-act; title means "The Delay"), Suhrkamp, 1961; *Vergebliche Aufzeichnungen: Nachtstueck* (one-act), Suhrkamp, 1963; *Herrn Walsers Raben* [and] *Unter der Erde,* Suhrkamp, 1964; *Das Opfer Helena* (two-act; also see below), Suhrkamp, 1965, translation by Jacques-Leon Rose published as *The Sacrifice of Helen,* University of Pennsylvania Press, 1968; *Die Eroberung der Prinzessin Turandot* [and] *Das Opfer Helena* (also see above), Fischer-Buecherei, 1969; *Mary Stewart: Eine historische Szene,* Suhrkamp, 1970.

Also author of numerous other plays, including "Pastorale" (title means "The Pastoral"; also see above), 1958; "Landschaft mit Figuren" (title means "Landscape With Figures"; also see above), 1959; "Der Schiefe Turm von Pisa" (one-act; title means "The Leaning Tower of Pisa"), 1959; "Die Uhren" (title means "The Clocks"; also see above), 1959; "Die Laesterschule" (title means "School of Vice"; based on the work by Sheridan), 1960; "Die Schwiegervaeter" (title means "The Fathers-In-Law"; based on work by Goldini), 1961; "Rivalen" (adapted from *The Rivals* by Sheridan), 1965.

BIOGRAPHICAL/CRITICAL SOURCES: Times Literary Supplement, May 18, 1973, May 26, 1978.

*   *   *

HILL, Marnesba D. 1913-

PERSONAL: Born March 30, 1913, in La Crosse, Wis.; daughter of Joseph C. (a dining car steward) and Mamie (Edwards) Davis; married Mozell C. Hill (a professor of sociology), May 5, 1935 (deceased); children: Suzenne Hill Slocum, Marnesba M., Alyce P. H. Hill Wright, Stephanie. *Education:* Langston University, B.S., 1940; Atlanta University, B.L.S., 1947; Columbia University, M.A., 1964. *Politics:* Democrat. *Religion:* Protestant. *Home:* 70 La Salle St., New York, N.Y. 10027. *Office:* Library, Herbert H. Lehman College of the City University of New York, Bedford Park Blvd. W., Bronx, N.Y. 10468.

CAREER: Langston University, Langston, Okla., elementary teacher, 1940-41; Atlanta University, Atlanta, Ga., special collections librarian, 1947-58; University of Nigeria, Nsukka, education librarian, 1958-62, library consultant, 1961-62; Hunter College of the City University of New York, New York, N.Y., associate librarian, 1962-68; Herbert H. Lehman College of the City University of New York, Bronx, N.Y., associate librarian, 1968-77, chief librarian, 1977—. *Member:* American Library Association, Seminar for the Acquisitions of Latin American Library Materials, Association of Caribbean University and Research Libraries, Library Association of the City University of New York (vice-president, 1966-68), Council of Chief Librarians of the City University of New York, Kappa Delta Pi (vice-president, 1974-75).

WRITINGS: (With Harold B. Schleifer) *Puerto Rican Authors: A Biobibliographic Handbook* (in English and Spanish; translated into Spanish by Daniel Maratos), Scarecrow, 1974; (with Schleifer) *Cuban Authors: A Biobibliographic Study of Writers, 1959-Present* (in English and Spanish; translated into Spanish by Maratos), Scarecrow, 1978.

SIDELIGHTS: Marnesba Hill commented: "My interest in Puerto Rican writers developed when Lehman College became the first college in the United States to offer a degree in Puerto Rican studies."

* * *

HILL, Weldon
See SCOTT, William R(alph)

* * *

HILLS, Lee 1906-

PERSONAL: Born May 28, 1906, in Granville, N.D.; son of Lewis Amos and Lulu Mae (Loomis) Hills; married Leona Haas, December 25, 1933 (deceased); married Eileen Whitman, June 4, 1948 (died, 1961); married Argentina S. Ramos (a newspaper publisher), October 31, 1963; children: Ronald Lee. Education: Attended Brigham Young University, 1924-25, and University of Missouri, 1927-29; Oklahoma City University, LL.B., 1934. Home: 4450 Banyan Lane, Miami, Fla. 33137. Office: Miami Herald, One Herald Plaza, Miami, Fla. 33101; and Detroit Free Press, 321 West Lafayette Blvd., Detroit, Mich. 48231.

CAREER: Price News-Advocate, Price, Utah, reporter, 1924-25, editor, 1926; Oklahoma City Times, Oklahoma City, Oklahoma, reporter, 1929-32; Oklahoma News, Oklahoma City, political writer, 1932-35, editor, 1938-39; Cleveland Press, Cleveland, Ohio, reporter and copyreader, 1935-36, editor, 1940-42; Indianapolis Times, Indianapolis, Ind., chief editorial writer and associate editor, 1936-37; Memphis Press-Scimitar, Memphis, Tenn., associate editor, 1939-40; Miami Herald, Miami, Fla., managing editor, 1942-51, executive editor, 1951-66, associate publisher, 1966-69, publisher, 1970-79; Detroit Free Press, Detroit, Mich., executive editor, 1951-69, publisher, 1963-79; Knight Newspapers, Inc. (now Knight-Ridder Newspapers, Inc.), chairman of the board, 1973-79, chief executive officer, 1973-76, editorial chairman, 1979—. Admitted to Bar of Oklahoma State, 1935. President of Detroit Arts Commission, 1966—; trustee of Founders Society of Detroit Institute of Arts.

MEMBER: International Press Institute, American Society of Newspaper Editors (president, 1962-63), American Newspaper Publishers Association, National Press Club, Inter American Press Association (director and president, 1967-68), Associated Press Managing Editors Association (past president), Florida Associated Press Association (past president), United Foundation (director), Overseas Press Club, Washington Press Club, Detroit Athletic Club, Bankers, Sigma Delta Chi (past president). Awards, honors: Maria Moors Cabot Gold Medal from Columbia University, 1946, for distinguished contribution to inter-American relations; Pulitzer Prize in journalism, 1956; Sc.D. from Cleary College, 1958; elected to University of Missouri School of Journalism Hall of Honor, 1959; L.H.D. from University of Utah, 1969; L.L.D. from Eastern Michigan University, 1969.

WRITINGS: (With Timothy J. Sullivan) Facsimile, McGraw, 1949.

SIDELIGHTS: In 1967 Hills became the first person outside the immediate family of John Shively Knight to preside over the well-known and influential Knight Newspapers. In an interview with Carla Marie Rupp of Editor & Publisher, Hills reflected on his success: "I always prepare for what I have to do. I believe preparation and hard work have a lot to do with what chances you get and how well you do."

BIOGRAPHICAL/CRITICAL SOURCES: Authors in the News, Volume 2, Gale, 1976; Editor & Publisher, March 13, 1976.

* * *

HIMMELFARB, Milton 1918-

PERSONAL: Born October 21, 1918, in Brooklyn, N.Y.; son of Max and Bertha (Lerner) Himmelfarb; married Judith Siskind, November 26, 1950; children: Martha, Edward, Miriam, Anne, Sarah, Naomi, Dan. Education: City College (now of the City University of New York), B.A., 1938, M.S., 1939; Jewish Theological Seminary of America, B. Hebrew Lit., 1939; University of Paris, diploma, 1939; graduate study at Columbia University, 1942-47. Office: 165 East 56th St., New York, N.Y. 10022.

CAREER: American Jewish Committee, New York, N.Y., director of information and research, 1955—; writer. Visiting professor at Jewish Theological Seminary of America, 1967-68 and 1971-72, and at Reconstructionist Rabbinical College, 1972-73; visiting lecturer at Yale University, 1971.

WRITINGS: The Jews of Modernity, Basic Books, 1973; (editor with Victor Baras) Zero Population—Growth for Whom?: Differential Fertility and Minority Group Survival, Greenwood Press, 1978. Editor of American Jewish Year Book, 1959—. Contributing editor to Commentary, 1960—.

* * *

HIRSCH, William Randolph
See KITMAN, Marvin

* * *

HOAGLAND, Jimmie Lee 1940-

PERSONAL: Born January 22, 1940, in Rock Hill, S.C.; son of Lee Roy and Edith Irene (Sullivan) Hoagland; married Elizabeth Hue Becker (a journalist), 1979; children: Laura Lee, Lily Hue. Education: University of South Carolina, A.B., 1961; attended University of Aix-en-Provence, 1961-62, and Columbia University, 1968-69. Home: 2025 N St. N.W., Washington, D.C. 20036. Office: Washington Post, 1150 15th St. N.W., Washington, D.C. 20005.

CAREER: Rock Hill Evening Herald, Rock Hill, S.C., reporter, 1960; New York Times, Paris, France, copy editor of international edition, 1964-66; Washington Post, Washington, D.C., reporter, 1966-69, Africa correspondent, 1969-72, Middle East correspondent, 1972-75, Paris correspondent, 1975-77, foreign editor, 1979—. Military service: U.S. Air Force, 1962-64; became first lieutenant. Member: American Newspaper Guild, Council on Foreign Relations, Phi Beta Kappa, Pi Kappa Alpha. Awards, honors: Ford Foundation fellowship, 1968-69; Pulitzer Prize for international journalism, 1970, for Washington Post series on South Africa; Overseas Press Club award for international reporting, 1977.

WRITINGS: South Africa: Civilizations in Conflict, Houghton, 1972.

* * *

HOBGOOD, Burnet M. 1922-

PERSONAL: Born June 23, 1922, in Lotumbe, Zaire; son of Henry Clay (a missionary) and Tabitha (a missionary; maiden name, Alderson) Hobgood; married Jane Bishop, June 1, 1957; children: Laurence Bishop, Cathleen Stuart, Brent McLean. Education: Transylvania College (now University), B.A., 1947; Western Reserve University (now Case

Western Reserve University), M.A., 1950, M.F.A., 1950; Cornell University, Ph.D., 1964. *Home:* 3 Illini Circle, Urbana, Ill. 61801. *Office:* Department of Theater, University of Illinois, 4-122 Krannert Center, Urbana, Ill. 61801.

CAREER: Lexington Herald-Leader, Lexington, Ky., reporter, 1947-49; Catawba College, Salisbury, N.C., assistant professor and acting chairman of department, 1950-54, associate professor, 1954-58, professor, 1958-61, director of theater, 1950-61, chairman of department of drama and speech, 1954-61; Southern Methodist University, Dallas, Tex., professor of theater, 1964-75, became chairman of department; University of Illinois, Urbana-Champaign, professor of theater, 1975—, head of department. Summer theater director, 1950; consultant to U.S. Departments of Theater and Drama. *Member:* American Theatre Association (administrative vice-president, 1960-61; chairman of committee on standards in educational theater, 1965-67; president, 1970; chairman of College of Fellows, 1977-80), American Association of University Professors, American Society for Aesthetics, Southwest Theatre Conference (executive secretary, 1956-58; president, 1965-66), Pi Kappa Phi.

WRITINGS: Discovering the Theatre, Allyn & Bacon, 1980. Editor of theatrical adaptation of Homer's *The Iliad* (translated by W.H.D. Rouse), 1960, and co-editor of acting version of Sophocles' *Oedipus the King,* with A. Graham-White, 1971. General editor of *Directory of American College Theatre,* American Theatre Association, 1960. Editor of "Books in Review," a column in *Educational Theatre Journal,* 1966-68. Contributor to theater journals.

SIDELIGHTS: Hobgood commented: "My most important mentor was the late dramatic critic Stark Young, who became a good friend. He felt, as I do, that theater is a humanistic discipline whose work is to embody the beauty of mortal experience through the efforts of actors, designers, and directors. My second major teacher was Stanislavski, whose works I studied in the Russian texts and found that he was a more profound thinker than he is commonly considered to be."

* * *

HOBZEK, Mildred J(ane)   1919-

PERSONAL: Born December 14, 1919, in Cleveland, Ohio; daughter of Mark and Anne S. (Leibitzer) Cukrov; married Norman F. Hobzek (an air conditioning engineer), June 27, 1944; children: Mark L., Bruce N. *Education:* Kent State University, B.S., 1941; attended Cleveland Institute of Music. *Religion:* Methodist. *Home:* 23651 Chardon Rd., Euclid, Ohio 44117.

CAREER: Vocal music teacher and supervisor at elementary and high school in Newton Falls, Ohio, 1941-43; junior high school vocal music teacher in Cleveland, Ohio, 1943-44; choral director for churches in Cleveland, 1945-60; Cleveland Public Library, Cleveland, children's librarian, 1964-76. Soprano soloist; taught voice privately. Director of Euclid Mothersingers, 1954-61; lecturer for schools and organizations. *Member:* National League of American Pen Women, Three Arts Club of Euclid (president, 1963-64).

WRITINGS: We Came A-Marching, One, Two, Three (juvenile; selection of Children's Reading Round Table of Chicago and Book of the Month Club), Parents' Magazine Press, 1978.

WORK IN PROGRESS—Children's books: A German tale about birds; an old Christmas song, arranged for voice, counter voice, and flute; a Fourth of July story, featuring the history of the holiday's celebration through the years.

SIDELIGHTS: Mildred Hobzek wrote: "Presenting the arts to pre-school and early elementary school children and involving them in active participation has held great interest for me. When I was required to create an original work in my field for the Three Arts Club, I had an opportunity to adapt a portion of a humorous old German story my mother had told me when I was a very young child. Knowing how children like to count in foreign languages, I wrote original verses to tell the tale, incorporating the numbers in a different language for each verse, and set it to the tune of an old Slavic folk song in a brisk march tempo. The children responded warmly to the song.

"I have always enjoyed introducing thoughts and ideas to youngsters with an approach spiced with humor. The process of learning should be a joyful experience for young children and to see their faces alight with eager anticipation is truly rewarding."

AVOCATIONAL INTERESTS: Teaching enrichment courses for sixth-grade students, writing plays for children, composing for piano and voice, enameling on copper.

BIOGRAPHICAL/CRITICAL SOURCES: Wickliffe News Herald, April 12, 1978; *Euclid Sun Journal,* October 19, 1978.

* * *

HOCKING, Mary (Eunice)   1921-

PERSONAL: Born April 8, 1921, in Acton, London, England; daughter of Charles (a librarian) and Eunice (Hewett) Hocking. *Education:* Educated in England. *Residence:* Lewes, Sussex, England. *Agent:* Bolt & Watson, 8/12 Old Queen St., London S.W.1, England.

CAREER: Writer. Worked as local government officer, 1946-70. *Wartime service:* Served with meteorology branch of Fleet Air Arm during World War II. *Member:* Royal Society of Literature (fellow), Writers Guild, Society of Authors.

WRITINGS—Novels; all published by Chatto & Windus, unless otherwise noted: *The Winter City,* 1961; *Visitors to the Crescent,* 1962; *The Sparrow,* 1964; *The Young Spaniard,* 1965; *Ask No Question,* Morrow, 1967; *A Time of War,* 1968; *Checkmate,* 1969; *The Hopeful Travellor* (sequel to *A Time of War*), 1970; *The Climbing Frame,* 1971; *Family Circle,* 1972; *Daniel Come to Judgement,* 1974; *The Bright Day,* 1975; *The Mind Has Mountains,* 1976; *Look, Stranger!,* 1978; *He Who Plays the King* (novel), 1980.

WORK IN PROGRESS: A modern novel tentatively entitled *A Good Year for Lunatics.*

SIDELIGHTS: "Mary Hocking writes brilliantly on many levels at once," claims Nick Totton of *Spectator,* "because she knows that the everyday contains another, stranger reality: it only takes attention, an at first casual intensification of vision, to open the crack between the worlds."

Mary Hocking told *CA:* "I find it hard to analyze my own work, and I am grateful to perceptive critics who do the job for me. Looking back over my novels, it is a surprise to find all those people trying to struggle free of the things which hamper and prevent them in their society. So, I suppose, I am concerned with the individual searching for something that will always be beyond his grasp because there is a mystery at the center of life. I try not to be solemn about it, though, because I find I am more effective when I treat characters and events with humor.

"My advice to young writers is to write about something you

believe in; take all the good criticism that comes your way, but don't let anyone try to turn you into another kind of writer because you aren't producing books that sell in vast numbers. Don't look down on your reader; write for someone as intelligent, interesting, perceptive, witty, amusing, caring, compassionate, and iconoclastic—as yourself!''

BIOGRAPHICAL/CRITICAL SOURCES: New Statesman, September 17, 1971, November 3, 1972; *Times Literary Supplement,* December 8, 1972, July 4, 1975, December 17, 1976; *Listener,* July 3, 1975, October 14, 1976; *Observer,* July 27, 1975, October 10, 1976, January 21, 1979; *Contemporary Literary Criticism,* Volume 13, Gale, 1980.

*   *   *

HODGETTS, A(lfred) Birnie   1911-

PERSONAL: Born May 20, 1911, in Omemee, Ontario, Canada; son of Alfred Clark (a banker) and Mary Elsie (Birnie) Hodgetts; married Helen Nicholl Ross, August 12, 1939 (deceased); children: Ross, David, Pauline Hodgetts Marston. *Education:* University of Toronto, B.A., 1933. *Religion:* Anglican. *Home:* 1 Rose Glen Rd., Port Hope, Ontario, Canada L1A 3V9. *Office:* 252 Bloor St. W., Toronto, Ontario, Canada M5S 1V5.

CAREER: History teacher and department head at collegiate schools in Lakefield, Ontario, 1939-42, and Port Hope, Ontario, 1942-66; director of Canadian History project, 1966-68; Canadian Studies Foundation, Toronto, Canada, co-founder and director, 1968-75, chairman and member of board of trustees, 1975—. Founder and director of Camp Hurontario (boys' summer camp), 1947. *Member:* Georgian Bay Association (president, 1955-60). *Awards, honors:* LL.D. from Queen's University, Kingston, Ontario, 1974; Member of Order of Canada, 1976; Lamp of Learning Award from Ontario Secondary School Teachers Federation, 1976, for general work in Canadian studies.

WRITINGS: Decisive Decades, Thomas Nelson, 1960; *What Culture? What Heritage?,* Ontario Institute for Studies in Education, 1968; (with Paul Gallagher) *Teaching Canada in the 1980's,* Ontario Institute for Studies in Education, 1978.

SIDELIGHTS: Hodgetts wrote: ''I believe that education can play a more significant role in fostering a better understanding between the diverse ethnic and regional groups in Canada. Present high levels of social tension in Canada might be lowered to more tolerable levels through improved civic education. I have a longtime interest in experimental efforts toward these interrelated goals.''

*   *   *

HOFFMAN, Edwin D.

PERSONAL: Born in New York, N.Y.; son of Joseph and Sadye (Loewenthal) Hoffman; married Jo Ann Hoff (an industrial manager), December 5, 1969; children: William Elliot. *Education:* City College (now of the City University of New York), B.S., 1940; Columbia University, M.A., 1947, Ed.D., 1952. *Home:* 5320 Virginia Ave. S.E., Charleston, W.Va. 25304. *Office:* Department of History, West Virginia State College, Institute, W.Va. 25112.

CAREER: Allen University, Columbia, S.C., professor of history and chairman of Division of Teacher Education, 1954-58; West Virginia State College, Institute, professor of history, 1960—, provost and dean of instruction, 1966-75. *Military service:* U.S. Army, 1942-46; became first lieutenant. *Member:* American Historical Association, American Association of University Professors.

WRITINGS: Pathways to Freedom, Houghton, 1964; *Fighting Mountaineers: The Struggle for Justice in the Appalachians,* Houghton, 1979. Contributor to history journals.

SIDELIGHTS: Hoffman commented: ''I have sought in my writings to inform on the role that the common people have played in the development of the American democratic tradition. I have researched and narrated dramatic episodes in which groups of ordinary Americans have struggled for justice and a better life in the face of the greed and prejudice that has too often prevailed in our nation's history. I consider myself one of the nontraditional historians who would have student and citizen focus on working people, on women, on Blacks, on Appalachians, Latinos, and Indians, rather than on those who have usually wielded power in American political and economic life.''

*   *   *

HOLDEN, Anthony (Ivan)   1947-

PERSONAL: Born May 22, 1947, in Southport, England; son of John (a company director) and Margaret Lois (Sharpe) Holden; married Amanda Juliet Warren (a musician), May 1, 1971; children: Sam, Joe, Ben. *Education:* Merton College, Oxford, M.A. (with honors), 1970. *Agent:* Curtis Brown Ltd., 575 Madison Ave., New York, N.Y. 10022. *Office: Observer,* 915 National Press Building, Washington, D.C. 20045.

CAREER: London Sunday Times, London, England, staff writer and author of column, ''Atticus,'' 1973-78; *Observer,* London, chief U.S. correspondent, 1979—. *Member:* National Union of Journalists. *Awards, honors:* Named young journalist of the year by National Council for Training of Journalists, 1973, for local newspaper work; named news reporter of the year by British Press, 1977, for work in Ulster, and columnist of the year, 1978, for ''Atticus.''

WRITINGS: (Translator) *Aeschylus' Agememnon,* Cambridge University Press, 1969; (editor and translator) *Greek Pastoral Poetry,* Penguin, 1974; *The St. Albans Poisoner,* Hodder & Stoughton, 1974; *Prince Charles: A Biography,* Atheneum, 1979 (published in England as *Charles, Prince of Wales,* Weidenfeld & Nicolson, 1979). Contributor to magazines in the United States and England, including *Punch, New Statesman, Spectator,* and *National Geographic.*

WORK IN PROGRESS: Nonfiction work on the United States; a novel.

*   *   *

HOLDEN, Ursula   1921-

PERSONAL: Born August 8, 1921, in Dorset, England; daughter of Andrew (a civil servant) and Una (Montgomery) Holden; divorced; children: Deirdre Smith, Kathy, Maureen. *Education:* Attended girls' school in Sussex, England. *Politics:* None. *Religion:* None. *Residence:* London, England. *Agent:* John Johnson, Clerkenwell House, 45-47 Clerkenwell Green, London EC1R 0HT, England.

CAREER: Full-time writer, 1975—. *Military service:* Women's Royal Naval Service, 1941-46. *Member:* Society of Authors, Chiswick Memorial Club. *Awards, honors:* Award from Arts Council, 1975, for *Endless Race.*

WRITINGS—Novels: Endless Race, London Magazine Editions, 1975; *String Horses,* London Magazine Editions, 1976; *Turnstiles,* London Magazine Editions, 1977; *The Cloud Catchers,* Methuen, 1979; *Penny Links,* Methuen, 1981. Contributor of stories to *Over Twenty-One* and *Irish Independent.*

WORK IN PROGRESS: Another novel, completion expected in 1981.

SIDELIGHTS: Ursula Holden commented: "I live to write. It comes first, regardless of success or failure. I have been influenced by Samuel Beckett, Anais Nin, Henry Miller, Carson McCullers, and Jean Rhys.

"Of middle-class origin, I was a loner early, a passionate reader, fond of dancing, music, but drawn towards the 'dark side.' I have had a varied and colorful life, much unhappiness—all grist for a writer. I started late, aged forty-three, attending a 'craft of writing' class. Until that time, I didn't realize I had any aptitude. I am driven to write; it never comes easily. I like to think that one day I might contribute to literature. I write every day, four to five hours, longer if possible. My purpose has always been to tell a tale, to grab the reader's attention. I try to link my stories to some universal theme, reflecting man's predicament. I would advise any would-be writer to stick at it. Talent is cheap, persistance is rare. I waited twelve years for publication; my first book went unpublished. I had scant encouragement from family or friends, but was lucky in finding an agent who had faith in me. I think there is a dearth of quality among contemporary writers, and too much commercially geared fiction. It is a lonely craft, with fleeting rewards, but if you are serious nothing will stop you."

A *Guardian* critic observed: "Ursula Holden is one of the most seriously radiant new English writers, and her second novel, *String Horses,* now takes her without reservations to the top. Her stamina is classical; she has a singular succinctness that is clear as well as allusive, and a fresh sense of fun and wit where they sharpen into calamity."

BIOGRAPHICAL/CRITICAL SOURCES: Guardian, March 18, 1976; *New York Times Book Review,* February 17, 1980.

* * *

HOLL, Adolf 1930-

PERSONAL: Born May 13, 1930, in Vienna, Austria; son of Karl and Josephine Holl. *Education:* University of Vienna, Dr.Theol., 1955, Dr.Phil., 1961, Universitaetsdozent fuer Religionswissenschaft, 1963. *Home:* Hardtgasse 34/2/2, Vienna 1190, Austria.

CAREER: Ordained Roman Catholic priest, 1954; parish priest in Vienna, Austria, 1954-72; Austrian Radio and Television, free contributor, 1960—; University of Vienna, Vienna, lecturer and assistant professor of religious studies, 1963-66. *Member:* International Sociological Association, Austrian Sociological Association. *Awards, honors:* Theodor Kardinal Innitzer Preis from Innitzer Foundation, 1962, for *Die Welt der Zeichen bei Augustin.*

WRITINGS: All originally published by Deutsche Verlags-Anstalt, unless otherwise noted: *Die Welt der Zeichen bei Augustin* (title means "Augustine's World of Signs"), Herder, 1963; *Jesus in schlechter Gesellshaft,* 1971, translation by Simon King published as *Jesus in Bad Company,* Holt, 1973; *Tod und Teufel,* 1973, translation by Matthew J. O'Connell published as *Death and the Devil,* Seabury, 1976; *Wo Gott wohnt* (title means "Where God Dwells"), 1976; *Mystik fuer Anfaenger* (title means "Mysticism for Beginners"), 1977; *Der letzte Christ,* 1979, translation published as *The Last Christian: A Biography of St. Francis of Assisi,* Doubleday, 1980. Also author of *Religionen* (title means "Religions"), 1981.

SIDELIGHTS: Holl told *CA* that because of his book, *Jesus in Bad Company,* the archbishop of Vienna withdrew the

missio canonica from him in 1973, and in 1976 forbade him to carry out his priestly functions.

He commented: "Religion, as I see it now, is a strange bed fellow, and one cannot be divorced from it. In my dreams I am still haunted by popes and cardinals and sometimes I see myself in purple robes. I consider the Roman Catholic church, as it is now administered by its clergy, as fully reactionary; thick layers of gold and dust cover the sweet Lord Jesus. My book, *Jesus in Bad Company,* deals with this subject. Searching for God means freedom from the institutional web of ecclesiastical hierarchies. All my books since 1971 are written in the tradition of Christian dissent, with its noble tradition of a thousand years, since the days of the Cathars in southern France. Renewal does not come from up high—thrones and chairs—but from the poor and humble underground, which is still very much in existence, and has a power of its own."

* * *

HOLZMAN, Red
See HOLZMAN, William

* * *

HOLZMAN, William 1920-
(Red Holzman)

PERSONAL: Born August 10, 1920. *Education:* Attended City College (now of the City University of New York). *Office:* New York Knickerbockers, Madison Square Garden, 4 Pennsylvania Plaza, New York, N.Y. 10001.

CAREER: Professional basketball player, 1945-54; St. Louis Hawks, St. Louis, Mo., coach, 1954-57; New York Knickerbockers, New York, N.Y., scout, 1958-67, coach, 1967-77, general manager, 1970-75, consultant, 1977—. Vice-president of Winner World championship, 1970 and 1973; coach of National Basketball Association (NBA) East All-Star Team, 1970-71. *Awards, honors:* Named coach of the year by National Basketball Association, 1970.

WRITINGS: (Under name Red Holzman; with Leonard Lewin) *Holzman's Basketball: Winning Strategy and Tactics,* Macmillan, 1973.

* * *

HOME, Henry Douglas
See DOUGLAS-HOME, Henry

* * *

HOOPER, Paul F(ranklin) 1938-

PERSONAL: Born July 31, 1938, in Walla Walla, Wash.; son of Dallas Albert (a farmer) and Charlotte (Brewer) Hooper; married Gloria Zitterkopf (a teacher), June 17, 1960; children: Anthony Owen. *Education:* Eastern Washington University, B.A., 1961; University of Hawaii, M.A., 1965, Ph.D., 1972. *Politics:* Independent Republican. *Home:* 700 Richards St., No. 2406, Honolulu, Hawaii 96813. *Office:* Department of American Studies, University of Hawaii, Honolulu, Hawaii 96822.

CAREER: University of Hawaii, Honolulu, instructor in history, 1966-67, chief of resource department at Asia Training Center, 1967-68, chief of center's research branch, 1968-69; Hawaii House of Representatives, Honolulu, director of research division in office of the minority leader, 1969-72; University of Hawaii, assistant professor of American studies, 1972—, executive secretary of advisory council on the international relations of the university, 1976-77. Member of national steering committee of George Bush for U.S. President campaign, 1979-80. Member of board of directors of Hawaii International Forum, 1979—; member of board of governors of Pacific and Asian Affairs Council, 1976-79; consultant on international programs to Young Men's Christian Association (YMCA) of Honolulu.

MEMBER: American Studies Association, American Association of University Professors, Common Cause (founding coordinator of Hawaii chapter, 1973-74), Hawaiian Historical Society. *Awards, honors:* Grants from Juliette and F. C. Atherton Trusts, 1972-73, Chinn Ho Foundation, 1974-75, and East-West Center, 1979-80.

WRITINGS: Elusive Destiny: The Internationalist Movement in Modern Hawaii, University Press of Hawaii, 1980; (editor) *Building the Pacific Community: Regional Perspectives and Problems,* University Press of Hawaii, 1981. Contributor to history, Asian studies, and popular journals.

SIDELIGHTS: Hooper wrote: "Although essentially an academic historian with a special concern for Hawaii and the Pacific Basin, I attempt, for better or worse, to meld the scholarly and 'real' worlds in my undertakings. Hence, my writing ranges from historical texts to commentaries on contemporary politics, I teach courses dealing with current issues as well as the past, and I am involved with political and international affairs in addition to university activities."

*   *   *

HOPE, Bob 1903-

PERSONAL: Birth-given name, Leslie Townes Hope; born May 29, 1903, in Eltham, England; came to United States in 1907, naturalized citizen, 1920; son of William Henry (a stonemason) and Avis (a concert singer; maiden name, Townes) Hope; married Dolores Reade (a singer and president of Eisenhower Medical Center), February 19, 1934; children: Linda Hope Lande, Anthony Reade, William Kelly Francis, Honorah Hope McCullagh. *Education:* Attended primary and secondary schools in Cleveland, Ohio. *Office:* 10000 Riverside Dr., Suite 3, North Hollywood, Calif. 91602.

CAREER: Comedian and actor. Former dance instructor, amateur boxer, and newspaper reporter. Made show business debut in Fatty Arbuckle revue as partner of vaudeville dancing act; made Broadway debut in "Sidewalks of New York," 1922, and subsequently appeared in "Ballyhoo," 1932, "Roberta," 1933, "Say When," 1934, "Ziegfeld's Follies," 1935, and "Red, Hot and Blue," 1936. As motion picture actor, appeared in more than fifty films, including: "The Big Broadcast of 1938," Paramount, 1938; "Road to Singapore," Paramount, 1940; "Road to Morocco," Paramount, 1942; "The Paleface," Paramount, 1948; "Fancy Pants," Paramount, 1950; "The Seven Little Foys," Paramount, 1955; "Call Me Bwana," United Artists, 1963; and "Cancel My Reservation," Warner Brothers, 1972. Host of radio program, "Pepsodent Show," National Broadcasting Co., beginning 1938; made television debut in "Star Spangled Revue," 1950, has appeared in and hosted more than three hundred television specials. Entertainer for United Service Organizations (USO) shows throughout the world, 1941—. Producer of "Paris Holiday," United Artists, 1958, and "Alias Jesse James," United Artists, 1959. *Member:* American Guild of Variety Artists (former president), Friars Club.

AWARDS, HONORS: Received more than one thousand awards and citations for professional and humanitarian endeavors, including: Congressional Gold Medal from President John F. Kennedy; Medal of Freedom from President Lyndon B. Johnson; Peabody Award in recognition of three decades in broadcasting, 1968; Variety Clubs International Humanitarian Award, 1968; Public Service Award from the Department of the Navy, 1971; Emmy Award from the National Academy of Television Arts and Sciences; special Academy Award from Academy of Motion Picture Arts and Sciences; USO Silver Medal of Merit; named to the Entertainment Hall of Fame, 1975; named honorary Commander of the Order of the British Empire.

Received more than forty honorary degrees, including: D.H.L. from Georgetown University, Southern Methodist University, Ohio State University, and Indiana University; D.L. from University of Wyoming, Northwestern University, and University of Scranton; D.F.A. from Brown University and Jacksonville University; D.H. from Bowling Green University and Norwich University; Doctor of Humane Humor from Benedictine College.

WRITINGS: I Never Left Home, Simon & Schuster, 1944; *So This Is Peace,* Simon & Schuster, 1946; (with Pete Martin) *Have Tux, Will Travel: Bob Hope's Own Story,* Simon & Schuster, 1954; *I Owe Russia $1,200,* Doubleday, 1963; *Five Women I Love,* Doubleday, 1966; (with Martin) *The Last Christmas Show,* Doubleday, 1974; (with Bob Thomas) *The Road To Hollywood: My Forty-Year Love Affair With the Movies,* Doubleday, 1977. Also author of *They've Got Me Covered,* 1941.

SIDELIGHTS: Bob Hope's world-wide popularity as a comedic entertainer has lasted for several decades, and he has been hailed as the "King of Comedy" by millions. When presenting him with the Congressional Gold Medal in 1963, President John F. Kennedy called Hope "America's most prized ambassador of goodwill throughout the world."

Hope has also received acclaim from his colleagues and fellow performers. The *New Times* reported that both Dick Cavett and filmmaker Woody Allen confessed to being his fans. In an interview with Cavett, Allen stated: "I found him a very, very gifted comedian. There are films he did, if you watched with a full audience, you'd find quite hilarious, like *Monsieur Beaucaire ... Fancy Pants.... I* mean really funny ... not funny that you have to compromise yourself ... I think if someone put together a compendium of his pictures ... it would become apparent how talented he is."

Nonetheless, critics are not unanimous in their assessment of Hope's talent. While many praise his rapid-fire technique and his encyclopedic memory for jokes, others maintain that his reliance on prepared verbal gags indicates his limitations as a comedian. In addition, Hope has suffered criticism for his fervent support of the U.S. war effort in Vietnam.

Hope's energy and stamina are legendary, however, and his pace would easily leave other performers winded. In 1978, for instance, he did 131 stage shows, appeared on 30 television programs, and played golf for charity 25 times. With regard to his hectic schedule, Hope told *People* interviewer Martha Smilgis: "I just can't sit back and play golf. I want to keep going. There were seven boys in my family and we were poor.... There was a time when I couldn't get a job. I was $400 in debt just for coffee and doughnuts." But he went on to say, "I've never met a comedian who didn't get therapy out of a good audience. I love it. I don't consider it work."

BIOGRAPHICAL/CRITICAL SOURCES: Morella, Epstein, and Clark, *The Amazing Careers of Bob Hope,* Arlington House, 1973; *Library Journal,* July, 1977; *New York Times Book Review,* July 17, 1977; *New York Times,* September 12, 1977; *New Times,* August 7, 1978; *People,* January 15, 1979.

HOPKINS, A. T.
See TURNGREN, Annette

*   *   *

HOPKINS, Antony 1921-

PERSONAL: Born March 21, 1921, in London, England. *Education:* Royal College of Music, L.R.A.M., 1942. *Home:* Woodyard, Ashridge, Berkhamsted, Hertfordshire, England.

CAREER: Composer, pianist, and conductor, 1944—, working with orchestras in England, Ireland, Japan, and Yugoslavia. Professor at Royal College of Music, 1955-70; formerly Gresham Professor of Music at City University, London. Director of Intimate Opera Company, 1952-64. Fellow of Robinson College, Cambridge, 1980. Presented "Talking About Music," a weekly series for British Broadcasting Corp. (distributed to forty-four foreign countries), 1953—. *Member:* Royal College of Music (fellow), Royal Academy of Music (honorary member). *Awards, honors:* Medal of honor from City of Tokyo, 1974; Commander of Order of the British Empire, 1976; honorary doctorate from University of Stirling, 1980.

WRITINGS: Talking About Symphonies, Heinemann, 1961; *Talking About Concertos,* Heinemann, 1964; *Music All Around Me* (anthology), Frewin, 1967; *Lucy and Peterkin* (juvenile), Frewin, 1968; (with Andre Previn) *Music Face to Face* (dialogues), Hamish Hamilton, 1971; *Talking About Sonatas,* Heinemann, 1971; *The Downbeat Guide to Music,* Oxford University Press, 1977; *Understanding Music,* Dent, 1979; *The Nine Symphonies of Beethoven,* Heinemann, 1980.

Composer of operas, including "Three's Company" (one-act), first produced in 1953; "A Time for Growing" (three-act for children), first produced in Norwich, England, at St. Andrew's Hall, 1967, produced in London, England, at Royal Albert Hall, 1968; "Rich Man, Poor Man, Beggar Man, Saint" (two-act for children), first produced at Stroud Festival of Religious Drama, 1969; "Dr. Musikus" (one-act for children), first produced in London at Arts Theatre, 1971.

Composer of numerous musical compositions for orchestration in motion pictures and concerts, including "Riding to Canonbie," "John and the Magic Music Man," and "Early One Morning."

WORK IN PROGRESS: The Sound of Music (tentative title), for Dent.

SIDELIGHTS: Hopkins told *CA:* "My tendency to compose for the young or for amateur music makers indicates a marked preference for tuneful and approachable music that audiences can enjoy at first hearing. It is a gift for communication, whether through music or words, that is perhaps my greatest asset; yet although my writings and broadcasts might be thought too populist in some academic circles, the fact remains that I am much admired by fellow professional musicians for my musical insights and originality of approach in analysis."

AVOCATIONAL INTERESTS: Motor sport.

*   *   *

HORGAN, Denis E. 1941-

PERSONAL: Born November 27, 1941, in Boston, Mass.; son of Cornelius Horgan (an engineer); married Patricia Alerding, November 26, 1967; children: Denis, Timothy. *Edu-*

cation: Northeastern University, B.A., 1964; graduate study at University of Texas, 1964-65. *Home:* 3764 Gunston Rd., Alexandria, Va. 22302. *Office: Washington Star,* 225 Virginia Ave., Washington, D.C. 20061.

CAREER/WRITINGS: Boston Globe, Boston, Mass., editorial assistant and reporter, 1960-64; *Bangkok World,* Bangkok, Thailand, managing editor, 1968, editor and publisher, 1969-71; *Washington Star,* Washington, D.C., assistant national editor, 1971-73, foreign editor, 1973-74, projects editor, 1974—. *Military service:* U.S. Army, 1966-68; became captain.

SIDELIGHTS: Horgan told *CA:* "My current position involves developing the non-breaking aspects of the *Washington Star*'s national, international, and local coverage (analysis, interpretive efforts, features, and so on) for front page display. This is part of an effort to revitalize the *Washington Star* and recast its efforts in the evening market."

*   *   *

HORN, Linda L(ouise) 1947-

PERSONAL: Born January 27, 1947, in St. Paul, Minn. *Education:* Miller Hospital School of Practical Nursing, diploma in practical nursing, 1966; Anoka-Ramsey Community College, A.A., 1969; Marycrest College, B.S.N., 1974; University of Pennsylvania, M.S.N., 1978. *Home:* 6342 Greene St., Philadelphia, Pa. 19144. *Office:* Philadelphia Psychiatric Center, Philadelphia, Pa.

CAREER: United Hospitals, St. Paul, Minn., licensed practical nurse in intensive care unit, 1966-69, general duty staff nurse, 1969-72, senior staff nurse and assistant head nurse, 1972-73; Marycrest College, Davenport, Iowa, resident director and counselor, 1973-74; Zestran Institute, Inc., Philadelphia, Pa., program coordinator and administrative assistant, 1975-76; Albert Einstein Community Mental Health Center, Philadelphia, nurse psychotherapist, 1977-78; Philadelphia Psychiatric Center, Philadelphia, special projects coordinator, 1978—. Private practice as trainer and consultant, 1976-77, and nurse psychotherapist, 1977—. State investigator for Iowa Student Public Interest Research Group, 1973-74; co-coordinator of Davenport mayor's advisory committee, 1973-74; co-project director for national Gray Panther long-term care action project, 1974-76; group psychotherapist at Walnut Park Retirement Plaza, 1978. *Member:* Association for Humanistic Gerontology, Women's Health Concerns, Medical Committee for Human Rights, Delaware Valley Group Psychotherapy/Drama Association, Sigma Theta Tau.

WRITINGS: (With E. Griesel) *Citizens' Action Guide,* Gray Panthers, 1975; (with Griesel) *Nursing Homes: A Citizens' Action Guide,* Beacon Press, 1977. Contributor to nursing journals.

*   *   *

HOSKING, Eric John 1909-

PERSONAL: Born October 2, 1909, in London, England; son of Albert (an accountant) and Margaret Helen (Steggall) Hosking; married Dorothy Sleigh, April 15, 1939; children: Margaret Hosking Woodward, Robin, David. *Education:* Attended trade school, 1919-25. *Religion:* Baptist. *Home:* 20 Crouch Hall Rd., London N8 8XH, England.

CAREER: Photographer, 1929—. Ornithologist; broadcaster. Member of Laboratory of Ornithology at Cornell University, 1961—. Director and leader of expeditions to Spain, Bulgaria, Hungary, Jordan, Pakistan, the Galapagos,

Bangladesh, Antarctica, the Seychelles, and Africa. Work exhibited by Royal Photographic Society and throughout the world.

MEMBER: Royal Photographic Society (fellow; member of council, 1950-56), Royal Society for the Protection of Birds (vice-president), British Trust for Ornithology, British Naturalists Association (vice-president), British Ornithologists Union (vice-president), Nature Photographic Society (vice-president), Nature Conservancy (chairman of photographic advisory committee), Zoological Society (scientific fellow), Institute of Incorporated Photographers (fellow), London Natural History Society (honorary vice-president). *Awards, honors:* Cherry Kearton Award from Royal Geographic Society, 1968; gold medal from Royal Society for the Protection of Birds, 1974; silver medal from Zoological Society, 1975; member of Order of the British Empire, 1977.

WRITINGS—Self-illustrated: (With Cyril W. Newberry) *Intimate Sketches From Bird Life* (introduction by Julian Huxley), Country Life, 1940; (with Newberry) *The Art of Bird Photography,* Country Life, 1944, revised edition, Transatlantic, 1948; (with Newberry) *Birds of the Day,* Collins, 1944; (with Newberry) *Birds of the Night,* Collins, 1945; (with Newberry) *More Birds of the Day,* Collins, 1946; (with Newberry) *The Swallow,* Collins, 1946; (editor with Harold Lowes) *Masterpieces of Bird Photography,* Collins, 1947; (with Newberry) *Birds in Action,* Collins, 1949; (with Stuart Grayston Smith) *Birds Fighting: Experimental Studies of the Aggressive Displays of Some Birds,* Faber, 1955; *Summer Migrants* (stamps based on his photographs), Educational Productions, 1956.

(With Cyril W. Newberry) *Bird Photography as a Hobby,* Stanley Paul, 1961, McBride Books, 1962; (with Winwood Reade) *Nesting Birds: Eggs and Fledglings,* Blandford, 1967, 3rd edition, 1971; (with Frank W. Lane) *An Eye for a Bird: The Autobiography of a Bird Photographer* (foreword by Prince Philip), Hutchinson, 1970, Paul Eriksson, 1973; (with John Gooders) *Wildlife Photography: A Field Guide,* Hutchinson, 1973, Praeger, 1974; (with H. E. Axell) *Minsmere: Portrait of a Bird Reserve,* Hutchinson, 1977; *A Passion for Birds: Fifty Years of Photographing Wildlife,* Coward, 1979. Also author of *Birds of Britain,* 1978.

Illustrator of more than eight hundred books, including: Norman Ellison, *Our British Birds and Beasts,* Open Air Publications, 1947; Garth Christian, editor, *Wings of Light: An Anthology,* George Newnes, 1965: Guy Mountfort, *The Vanishing Jungle: The Story of the World Wildlife Fund Expeditions to Pakistan,* Collins, 1969. Photographic editor of "New Naturalist," a book series, Collins, 1942—. Photographic editor of *British Birds,* 1960-76.

* * *

HOTZ, Robert B(ergmann) 1914-

PERSONAL: Born May 29, 1914, in Milwaukee, Wis.; son of Harry Phillip and Emma (Bergmann) Hotz; married Joan Willison, November 18, 1944; children: George, Michael, Robert Lee, Harry Phillip II. *Education:* Northwestern University, B.S., 1936. *Home:* 9702 Mount Tabor Rd., Middletown, Md. 21769. *Office: Aviation Week & Space Technology,* 425 National Press Building, Washington, D.C. 20045.

CAREER: New York Herald Tribune, New York City, reporter and editor of Paris edition in Paris, France, 1936-37; *Milwaukee Journal,* Milwaukee, Wis., reporter and editor, 1938-41; McGraw-Hill, Washington, D.C., news editor, 1946-49; United Aircraft Corp., Pratt & Whitney Aircraft Division, East Hartford, Conn., public relations manager,

1950-52; *Aviation Week & Space Technology,* Washington, D.C., editor-in-chief, 1952-76, publisher-editor, 1976-79; McGraw-Hill, New York City, editorial consultant, 1979—. Assistant producer of official U.S. Air Force documentary film, "China Crisis." Co-founder of *Air Force Magazine,* 1942. Visiting lecturer at Air University and Air Force Academy. *Military service:* U.S. Air Force, 1942-46; became major; received Air Medal with Oak Leaf Cluster. *Member:* American Institute of Aeronautics and Astronautics, White House Correspondent's Association, National Press Club, Royal Aeronautical Society (companion member), Royal Aero Club of London, International Club of Washington, Caterpillar Club. *Awards, honors:* Paul Tissandier Diploma from Federation Aeronautique Internationale, 1958; Air Power Award from New York wing of U.S. Air Force Association, 1958; National Space Club press award, 1965; Strebig and Ball trophies, 1972, Lyman memorial trophy, 1974, and writing award, 1976, all from Aviation Writers Association; American Astronautical Society Achievement Award, 1974; award from American Business Papers Association.

WRITINGS: (With George L. Paxton, Robert H. Neale, and Parker S. Dupouy) *With General Chennault: The Story of the Flying Tigers,* Coward, 1943; (editor) Claire Lee Chennault, *Way of a Fighter* (memoirs), Putnam, 1949; (with Paul W. Fisher) *The Pratt and Whitney Story,* privately printed, 1950. Contributor of articles to military magazines and to popular periodicals.

SIDELIGHTS: Hotz wrote that he covered every major air show for the past twenty years, including those at Paris, Farnborough, England, and at Tushino, Russia. In 1975, he was the only journalist invited by both Israeli and Egyptian defense ministries to visit their air forces and discuss "airpower lessons of the October War." Hotz also noted that he participated in the first transatlantic test flight of the Concorde and was a guest of the Soviet Ministry of Aircraft Production to tour the supersonic transport production line in Voronezh and the cosmonaut training center at Star City.

* * *

HOUSE, Robert J. 1932-

PERSONAL: Born June 16, 1932, in Toledo, Ohio; son of Lewis H. and Mary M. (Kinn) House; married Patricia Ann Petron, October 22, 1955; children: Daniel, Timothy, Mary Kathleen. *Education:* University of Detroit, B.A., 1955, M.B.A., 1958; Ohio State University, Ph.D., 1960. *Home:* 44 Charles St. W., Toronto, Ontario, Canada. *Office:* Faculty of Management Studies, University of Toronto, 246 Bloor St. W., Toronto, Ontario, Canada M5S 1A1.

CAREER: Chrysler Corp., Detroit, Mich., management trainee, 1955-56, management development research analyst for corporate staff, 1956-57; North American Aviation, Inc., Columbus, Ohio, senior management training specialist, 1958-59; Ohio State University, Columbus, 1959-63, began as instructor, became assistant professor of business organization; University of Michigan, Ann Arbor, research associate at Bureau of Industrial Relations, 1963-65; Bernard M. Baruch College of the City University of New York, New York, N.Y., associate professor, 1965-70, professor of management, 1970-72; University of Toronto, Toronto, Ontario, Shell Professor of Organization Behavior, 1972—. Executive director of McKinsey Foundation for Management Research, 1965-68. Guest lecturer at McMaster University, 1973; conducts seminars; member of board of governors of Eastern Academy of Management, 1973-74; consultant to North American-Rockwell, Eli Lilly International, and Canadian Post Office. *Member:* American Psychological Association (fellow), Academy of Management (fellow; member of board of governors, 1972-74; chairman of Division of Organization Behavior, 1973-74). *Awards, honors:* Canada Council grants, 1974-75, 1975-76.

WRITINGS: Management Development: Design, Implementation, and Evaluation, Bureau of Industrial Relations, University of Michigan, 1967; (with Alan C. Filley) *Managerial Process and Organizational Behavior,* Scott, Foresman, 1969; (with Marvin D. Dunnette and Henry L. Tosi, Jr.) *Managerial Compensation and Motivation,* Bureau of Business Research, Michigan State University, 1972; (with Filley and John Turner) *Readings in Managerial Process and Organizational Behavior,* Scott, Foresman, 1973.

Contributor: *Management Education and Development,* Educational Testing Service, 1968; H. Koontz and C. O'Donnell, editors, *Management: A Book of Readings,* McGraw, 1968; B. E. Fox and M. Elanore, editors, *Corporate Acquisitions and Mergers,* Volume II, Matthew Bender, 1969; Robert Golumbiewski and Arthur Blumberg, editors, *T-Groups and the Laboratory Approach: Readings About Concept and Applications,* F. E. Peacock, 1970; Peter Wiesenberger, editor, *Introduction to Organizational Behavior,* Intext Publishing Co., 1971; William K. Graham and Karlene Roberts, editors, *Organizational Behavior and Human Performance,* Holt, 1972; L. L. Cummings and W. Scott, editors, *Organization Behavior and Human Performance,* Irwin, 1973; Henry L. Tosi, Jr., and H. C. Hamner, editors, *Management and Organization Behavior,* St. Clair, 1974; R. M. Steers and L. W. Porter, editors, *Motivation and Work Behavior,* McGraw, 1975; J. L. Gibson, J. M. Ivancevich, and J. H. Donnelly, Jr., editors, *Readings in Organizations,* Business Publications, revised edition (House was not included in 1st edition), 1976; Theodore T. Herbert, editor, *Organizational Behavior: Readings and Cases,* Macmillan, 1976; F. Starke and J. L. Gray, editors, *Readings in Organization Behavior,* C. E. Merrill, 1976; Cummings, editor, *Introduction to Organizational Behavior,* Irwin, 1977; Richard P. Mowdray, editor, *Behavioral Research in Organizations,* Goodyear Publishing, 1978; S. Maital and N. M. Meltz, editors, *Declining Productivity Growth: Causes and Remedies,* Ballinger, 1979; Thomas H. Patten, Jr., editor, *Classics in Personnel Management,* Moore Publishing, 1979. Also contributor to numerous other volumes.

Contributor of articles and reviews to scholarly journals. Member of editorial review board of *Administrative Science Quarterly,* 1971-78, *Journal of the Academy of Management,* 1973-78, and *Canadian Journal of Behavioral Science,* 1974-78.

SIDELIGHTS: House commented that his research interests include motivation, leadership, and conflict resolution.

*   *   *

HOVEYDA, Fereydoun   1924-

PERSONAL: Born September 21, 1924, in Damascus, Syria; son of Habibollah (a diplomat) and Fatmeh (Sardari) Hoveyda; married Gisela Muller, 1968; children: Mandana, Roxana. *Education:* University of Paris, diploma, 1944, LL.D., 1948. *Home:* 755 Park Ave., New York, N.Y. 10021.

CAREER: United Nations, New York City, permanent representative from Iran, 1971-78; Foreign Friends of New York, New York City, adviser, 1978—. Adviser to Aspen Institute for Humanistic Studies, 1973—. Art work exhibited at shows in New York City and in museum collections, including Chrysler Museum and John F. Kennedy Center.

Awards, honors: Leopold Senghor Literary Prize from French Language Cultural and Technical Society, 1973, for *Les Neiges du Sinai;* named Planetary Citizen by United Nations for work on disarmament.

WRITINGS: Les Quarantaines (novel; title means "The Quarantine"), Gallimard, 1962; *L'Aerogare* (novel; title means "The Airport"), Gallimard, 1965; *Histoire du roman policier* (title means "History of the Detective Novel"), Les Editions du Pavillon, 1965; *Dans une Terre Etrange* (novel; title means "In a Strange World"), Gallimard, 1968; *Le Losange* (stories; title means "Diamond-Shaped"), Losfeld, 1969; *Les Neiges du Sinai* (novel; title means "Snows of the Sinai"), Gallimard, 1973; *The Fall of the Shah,* Simon & Schuster, 1980. Contributor to magazines, including *Positif, Fiction, Cahiers du Cinema,* and *Baker Street Journal.*

WORK IN PROGRESS: A novel on religious people in the Middle Ages; several essays on Iran.

BIOGRAPHICAL/CRITICAL SOURCES: Washington Post Book World, April 13, 1980.

*   *   *

HOVING, Thomas   1931-

PERSONAL: Born January 15, 1931, in New York, N.Y.; son of Walter (in business) and Mary Osgood (Field) Hoving; married Nancy Melissa Bell (a management consultant), October 3, 1953; children: Petrea Bell. *Education:* Princeton University, B.A. (summa cum laude), 1953, M.F.A., 1958, Ph.D., 1959. *Home:* 150 East 73rd St., New York, N.Y. 10021.

CAREER: Metropolitan Museum of Art, Department of Medieval Art and the Cloisters, New York City, curatorial assistant, 1959-60, assistant curator, 1960-63, associate curator, 1963-65, curator, 1965-66; New York City, commissioner of parks, 1966-67, administrator of recreation and cultural affairs, 1967; Metropolitan Museum of Art, director, 1967-77; management consultant, 1977—. Correspondent and interviewer for American Broadcasting Co. (ABC-TV) feature news program "20/20." Director of International Business Machines (IBM) Americas, H. S. Stuttman Co., and Manhattan Industries. *Military service:* U.S. Marine Corps, 1953-55; became first lieutenant. *Member:* American Institute of Architects (honorary member). *Awards, honors:* National Council of the Humanities fellowship, 1955; Kienbusch and Haring fellowship, 1957; distinguished citizen award from Citizens Budget Committee, 1966; award from *Cue* magazine, 1966; LL.D. from Pratt Institute, 1967; distinguished achievement award from Advertising Club of America, 1968; LL.D. from Princeton University, 1968; D.F.A. from New York University, 1968; Litt.D. from Middlebury College, 1968.

WRITINGS: The Sources of the Ivories of the Ada School (Ph.D. thesis), Princeton University Press. 1960; (editor) *The Chase, the Capture: Collecting at the Metropolitan,* Metropolitan Museum of Art, 1975; *Two Worlds of Andrew Wyeth: Kuerners and Olsons,* Metropolitan Museum of Art, 1976; *Tutankhamun: The Untold Story,* Simon & Schuster, 1978. Author of Metropolitan Museum of Art guidebooks and art calendars. Consultant to *Museums, New York* and author of its column "Happenings." Contributor of articles to *Apollo* (magazine) and *Metropolitan Museum of Art Bulletin.*

WORK IN PROGRESS: King of the Confessors, about "the extraordinary story of the acquisition of one of the Metropolitan's most important works of art, the Bury St. Edmunds Cross," publication expected in 1981.

SIDELIGHTS: Hoving joined the Metropolitan Museum of Art in 1959 after James J. Rorimer, the museum director at that time, heard Hoving lecture at New York's Frick Collection on the Annibale Carracci frescoes of the Farnese Gallery in Rome. Hoving started as a curatorial assistant in the Cloisters, the Metropolitan's collection of medieval art, which includes a number of intact medieval cloisters brought over from Europe. Hoving quickly moved up to more responsible positions, propelled in part by his discovery of the Bury St. Edmunds Cross.

In 1962, Hoving learned of the existence of an ivory cross of dubious authenticity. The ivory was kept in a bank vault in Zurich, Switzerland, and its owner refused to permit dealers and museum curators to photograph it. Despite the general notion that the cross was a fake, Hoving's curiosity was piqued. He traveled to Zurich to see for himself.

Hoving once explained his policy on judging a work of art for authenticity and value. "Trust your first impression. . . . Always trust your immediate kinetic reaction. . . . The process is basically intuitive, but it is good to have a guideline. Write down that absolutely immediate first impression, that split second. Write anything. 'Warm.' 'Cool.' 'Scared.' 'Strong.' In six years of studying hundreds of items for the Museum, I never ended up feeling warm about something I had written 'Cool' about, or the reverse."

When Hoving saw the ivory cross in the Zurich bank vault, he wrote his first impression down on a handy pad of paper: "No doubt." Later he further described his thoughts on seeing the cross. "It was staggering. A truly great, great thing. Just exactly where it fitted into history I didn't know, and at that point I didn't give a damn. It didn't seem to have the nervous, fluttering quality of the eleventh century, so I guessed the twelfth."

The Metropolitan bought the cross in 1963 while Hoving continued to search through countless books and sources for a clue to its history. Eventually he discovered that the ivory had apparently been crafted in a monastery near the village of Bury St. Edmunds, in Suffolk, England. Dating from 1148 to 1156, the cross was created by Master Hugo, one of the most renowned artists of the Middle Ages in England. The Cross of Bury St. Edmunds is regarded as a preeminent acquistion of the Metropolitan Museum of Art.

After this achievement, Hoving went on to become curator of the Department of Medieval Art and the Cloisters, but in 1966, was lured from the art world into the realm of public service. Always a supporter of New York Congressman John V. Lindsay, Hoving also helped Lindsay in his bid for mayor of New York. The campaign was successful and Lindsay offered Hoving the position of commissioner of parks. As commissioner, Hoving generated much publicity. During his first year in office, his staff filled more than fifty scrapbooks with stories about New York's recreational areas.

Hoving devised a number of "Happenings"—often called "Hoving's Happenings"—that changed the face of the city's parks. He held kite days, set up one hundred five feet of canvas for citizens to paint on, scheduled concerts in Central Park, and staged a project for building castles out of plastic foam. Under his tutelage, cars were banned from Central Park on Sundays to allow pedestrians and cyclists more freedom of movement. Hoving employed an architect as deputy commissioner to improve the parks and enlisted the services of several internationally-known architects. He surmised that "after all, parks are works of art just as a painting or sculpture is and they need to be cared for as an artistic en-

tity." Hoving also created small parks on vacant lots and parks on temporarily unused land. Such innovations induced cities in Europe and all over the United States to consult Hoving on how to better their areas of recreation. Hoving quit his job as commissioner when he became director of the Metropolitan Museum of Art in 1967, after the death of Rorimer.

In writing his books, Hoving has been equally successful. Riding on the crest of the Tutankhamun craze created by the exhibit touring the United States in 1977, *Tutankhamun: The Untold Story* was a best-seller. Although some reviewers criticized the book because its "untold story" was only the revelation of a few not-too-surprising secrets, they generally agreed that the volume added another interesting dimension to an already fascinating tale.

Hoving contends in *Tutankhamun* that Howard Carter, the discoverer of the tomb in 1922, was not entirely devoted to the selfless pursuit of uncovering archaeological treasures for posterity. He was also interested in attaining personal profit and to that end, without listing them in his personal inventory, he spirited out of Egypt choice pieces from the tomb. Furthermore, Hoving reports that Carter, along with his patrons Lord Carnarvon and Lady Evelyn Herbert, entered the tomb secretly on the night before its public and supposedly first opening.

These revelations prompted British Egyptologist T.G.H. James to assert that "the soiled linen does not amount to much. I am surprised that Mr. Hoving could think so, and be so easily shocked." Critics David M. Walsten and Barbara G. Mertz, however, were of the mind that the book somewhat clarified the real picture of archaeology and Egyptology. Walsten reflected that "the entire realm of Egyptology now seems a little less elegant history, somewhat more a commercial enterprise," while Mertz commented that *Tutankhamun* "gives considerable insight into the sometimes sordid, sometimes amusing complications that affect all human activities, even archaeology."

CA INTERVIEWS THE AUTHOR

Thomas Hoving was interviewed by *CA* at his residence in New York City on May 7, 1980.

Having made a very rapid rise to extraordinary eminence in the museum and art worlds by becoming director of New York's Metropolitan Museum of Art at the unusually young age of thirty-six, Hoving claims that his life was changed by his acquisition of a medieval relic. He was associate curator of the Cloisters, a separate wing of the Metropolitan, when he tracked down and acquired the Bury St. Edmunds Cross in 1963. "That fabulous twelfth-century cross, which I consider to be one of the greatest works of art ever created, and the way in which I managed to acquire it for six hundred thousand dollars for the museum, changed my life," he explained. "It was owing to that cross that I became director of the Metropolitan."

Hoving's ten-year directorship at the Metropolitan, from 1967 to 1977, witnessed an upsurge in the number of big, dramatic visiting exhibitions and the completion of an extensive building program involving five new wings that added an additional five hundred thousand square feet to the museum. He also became embroiled in a controversy over the museum's acquisition of what became known as the Euphronios krater—a notable Greek vase—that led to the publication of his first nonacademic book. *The Chase, the Capture: Collecting at the Metropolitan* was published in 1975. Why did he write it?

"It was written in conjunction with a show on ten years of acquisitions at the museum. But I may have also been trying to propagandize and fight back against the *New York Times* and their art critic John Canaday's coverage of the Euphronios krater acquisition." (The *Times* accused Hoving and the Metropolitan of having paid over one million dollars for a recently looted Greek vase, allegedly taken from an Etruscan tomb.) "There was a great deal of intrigue and confusion about this co-called 'hot pot.' Actually, the whole thing was a case of mistaken identity. Pieces of another calyx krater in the possession of the Louvre since 1859 were confused with this Euphronios vase." Hoving plans to write a book "setting the record straight about this affair, as well as all matters of controversy that took place during my tenure at the Metropolitan Museum. It will be based on the tapes I kept of all my conversations, as well as my daily diary."

Hoving helped make the Metropolitan an overwhelmingly popular place for New Yorkers and tourists with his series of spectacular shows, climaxing with the arrival of the Tutankhamun exhibition, held after his departure from the museum. Other popular shows presented under his directorship included the unveiling of the new Islamic galleries, the French tapestry display, and the Scythian exhibit. "Most people think of the big blockbusters rather than of these quieter shows," he notes resignedly.

It was research for the immensely successful Tutankhamun show, however, which led to Hoving's big best-seller, *Tutankhamun: The Untold Story.* "I found this dynamite material on a shelf in the Egyptian department of the museum that revealed the real truth of what happened during Howard Carter's excavation of the tomb, and it was a good yarn. The book was on the best-seller list for fifteen straight weeks and is now out in paperback. It has appeared in eight languages. I'm not aware of any adverse criticism of the book, except of course by an English Egyptologist at the British Museum who was anxious to defend Carter's reputation. Besides, adverse criticism helps sell books."

How does he write? "In this case, very fast. The whole thing took two steady months. I write in longhand—anywhere, on planes, in cars. Then a secretary types it up. *Tutankhamun* took just two drafts, whereas letters can sometimes take up to twelve drafts."

Another, less widely known Hoving book is *Two Worlds of Andrew Wyeth: Kuerners and Olsons.* Although he feels it "did not sell all that well—only about seventy-five to eighty-five hundred copies," Hoving is proud of the book. "I'm an admirer of Wyeth's work. I felt he had been packaged and dismissed as a conservative; his work is not conservative, but rather as cruel as a surgeon's scalpel. I also felt that some balance had to be put back into the relationship between contemporary art and realism. I prepared for the book, which is a long interview of the artist conducted over five days' time, by looking at all the work he had done, all of his preparatory drawings, private material, and so on, about four thousand pieces. I formulated the questions I wanted to ask him with a view to the layout of the book and memorized them. I used a tape recorder. The artist was very cooperative. The book marks the first time an art historian ever interviewed Wyeth."

What art writers does Hoving particularly admire? His reply is decisive. "Longhi, Max Friedlaender, Krautheimer, and Panofsky. I also admire Kenneth Clark's *Civilisation,* but with reservations, because he left out Germany almost entirely." He does not miss being director of the Metropolitan—"once I got the buildings built, I was bored

there"—and has only gone back "three or four times" since he left in 1977. "One of those occasions was the opening of the Temple of Dendur, because I valued having gotten that prize for the museum."

Hoving leads a busy and varied life, keeping in close touch with the art and museum worlds, though he concedes that "art is behind me now." He works as a management consultant, in partnership with his wife Nancy, for various cultural institutions. "I let them know how to break even on their operations." He is also a consultant to a new publication, *Museums, New York,* in which he holds some equity and for which he writes a column called "Happenings," focusing on artists and individual works of art in New York. His most visible current occupation is working as a correspondent and interviewer for the American Broadcasting Co. (ABC-TV) feature news program "20/20," for which he chooses stories and researches and writes them. His subjects have ranged from the Italian fisherman who found the Getty bronze to a study of television soap operas. "I thoroughly enjoy it, but all these activities go to support my writing, which I like better than anything."

His next writing project is a book to be called *King of the Confessors,* which Hoving remarks "will be a true-to-life story of the uncovering, history, and acquisition of the Bury St. Edmunds Cross. "It will reveal the underworld of high-class art—the corruption, ambition, mystery, and intrigue behind the scenes. The sensational story will include details of how the cross, made at the Bury St. Edmunds monastery in England, was used to foster a political campaign of the abbot of the monastery through the addition of anti-Semitic Latin inscriptions; how its first discoverer in modern times deliberately falsified its date to make it seem earlier than it actually was; how I acquired it from a Yugoslav who was head of espionage for Tito in 1948; how I played down the inscriptions in order to make the cross acceptable to Jewish trustees of the Metropolitan; how additional parts of the cross are still at large—in fact I have my eyes on one now, so that it can be acquired and added to the cross; and how it has operated as a force for good and evil, benevolence and destruction, in the past and present."

BIOGRAPHICAL/CRITICAL SOURCES: The John McPhee Reader, edited by William L. Howarth, Vintage Books, 1977; *Chicago Tribune Book World,* October 22, 1978; *New York Times Book Review,* November 12, 1978; *Washington Post Book World,* November 26, 1978; *New York Times,* December 26, 1978.

—*Sketch by Anne M. Guerrini*
—*Interview by Barbara Braun*

*   *   *

HOWARD, Blanche 1923-

PERSONAL: Born November 7, 1923, in Daysland, Alberta, Canada; daughter of Douglas M. (in business) and Alice (Heald) Machon; married Bruce Howard (a judge), April 3, 1945; children: Allison Howard Zweng, Stephen, Leslie. *Education:* University of Alberta, B.Sc., 1944, C.A., 1962. *Politics:* Liberal. *Religion:* Unitarian-Universalist. *Home:* 3866 Regent Ave., North Vancouver, British Columbia, Canada V7N 2C4.

CAREER: Chemistry instructor, 1945-47; Desbrisay, Hack, and Co. and Peat, Marwick, Mitchell, and Co. (both chartered accountants), Penticton, British Columbia, supervisor, 1958-68; writer, 1968—. Director of Okanagan Summer School of the Arts, 1966-67. Prime Minister's appointee to board of directors of Vanier Institute of the Family, 1978—.

Member: Canadian Institute of Chartered Accountants, Writers Union of Canada, Riding Liberal Association (vice-president, 1977-78). *Awards, honors:* Award from Canadian Publishers Association, 1973, for *The Manipulator;* Canada Council grant, 1978.

WRITINGS: The Manipulator (novel), McClelland & Stewart, 1972; *Pretty Lady* (novel), General Publishing, 1976; *The Immortal Soul of Edwin Carlysle* (novel), McClelland & Stewart, 1977. Contributor of stories to *Chatelaine.*

WORK IN PROGRESS: Life for the Asking, "a novel with a Faustian theme, set against the debate over the use of recombinant DNA in Boston during the early 1970's."

SIDELIGHTS: Blanche Howard wrote: "My university studies in chemistry, physics, and mathematics have left me with an abiding interest in the world of science—or more probably the interest was there and I developed it—but science, in fiction, is usually confined to the science fiction genre. This dichotomy of interests between literature and science has left an ambivalence in me that flows into my writing.

"In human relationships, I'm always fascinated by the way one person will try to dominate another, and my first two novels were built around that theme and attracted a sizeable Canadian readership. However, in *The Immortal Soul of Edwin Carlysle,* I lost them. The novel was too close to science fiction for the non-addict. Can I achieve an amalgamation? I hope so. In *Life for the Asking* I think I've set my character development in readable counterpart to the background of the world of recombinant DNA technology. We'll see."

*   *   *

HOWARD, James T(homas)   1934-

PERSONAL: Born January 3, 1934, in Philadelphia, Pa.; son of James T. (a sheet metal worker) and Alice (Reilly) Howard; married Constance Smith; children: Kimberly Graham, James T. III, Robert Cameron, Peter Carson. *Education:* Gettysburg College, A.B. (magna cum laude), 1955; Jefferson Medical College, M.D., 1959. *Religion:* Protestant. *Residence:* Rye, N.Y. *Agent:* Julian Bach Literary Agency, Inc., 747 Third Ave., New York, N.Y. 10017. *Office:* 170 Maple Ave., White Plains, N.Y. 10601.

CAREER: Pennsylvania Hospital, Philadelphia, intern, 1959-60, resident in obstetrics and gynecology, 1960-63; Westchester Gynecologist-Obstetrics, White Plains, N.Y., obstetrician, 1963—. Assistant clincial professor at Albert Einstein Medical College, 1965-78. Member of board of directors of Planned Parenthood of Westchester County, 1970-74; medical adviser for Westchester Child Services; consulting gynecologist at New York Hospital and Cornell Medical School, Westchester division. *Military service:* U.S. Naval Reserve, Medical Corps, 1965-67; became lieutenant commander.

MEMBER: American Medical Association, American College of Obstetricians and Gynecologists, American Fertility Society, American Society of Clinical Laparoscopists, New York State Medical Society, Westchester County Medical Society, Phi Beta Kappa.

WRITINGS: (With Dodi Schultz) *We Want to Have a Baby,* Dutton, 1979.

WORK IN PROGRESS: An evaluation of infertility diagnosis and treatment.

SIDELIGHTS: Howard told *CA:* "*We Want to Have a Baby* is designed to educate the reader to understand infertility. It attempts to cover all aspects of an infertility examination, so the reader may judge if he or she has had a proper evaluation. It should stimulate questions by the reader to his or her physician to assume all appropriate testing has been done."

*   *   *

HOWE, G(eorge) Melvyn   1920-

PERSONAL: Born April 7, 1920, in Abercymon, Wales; son of Reuben and Edith (Evans) Howe; married Patricia Graham Fennell (a teacher), July 7, 1947; children: Gillian Howe Craig, Lise Howe Moore, Clare. *Education:* University of Wales, B.Sc., 1947, M.Sc., 1949, Ph.D., 1957; University of Strathclyde, D.Sc., 1974. *Religion:* Church of England. *Home:* 24 Birnam Cres., Glasgow G61 2AU, Scotland. *Office:* Department of Geography, University of Strathclyde, Livingstone Tower, 26 Richmond St., Glasgow G1 1XH, Scotland.

CAREER: University of Wales, Aberystwyth, senior lecturer and reader in geography, 1948-67; University of Strathclyde, Glasgow, Scotland, professor of geography, 1967—. *Military service:* Royal Air Force, 1940-46; became squadron leader. *Member:* Royal Geographical Society, Royal Meteorological Society, Royal Scottish Geographical Society, Royal Society of Edinburgh (fellow). *Awards, honors:* Gill Memorial Award from Royal Geographical Society, 1964, for studies in medical geography.

WRITINGS: Wales From the Air, University of Wales Press, 1957, 2nd revised edition, 1966; (with Peter Thomas) *Welsh Land Forms and Scenery,* Macmillan, 1963; *National Atlas of Disease Mortality,* Thomas Nelson, 1963, 2nd revised and enlarged edition, 1970; *The Soviet Union,* Macdonald & Evans, 1968; *The U.S.S.R.,* Hulton, 1971; *Man, Environment, and Disease,* David & Charles, 1972; (with John Loraine) *Environmental Medicine,* Heinemann, 1973, 2nd revised and enlarged edition, 1980; *A World Geography of Human Diseases,* Academic Press, 1977.

WORK IN PROGRESS: Geographical studies of the incidence of disease mortality in the United Kingdom.

SIDELIGHTS: Howe wrote: "I am motivated to help in the unraveling of the causes of cardiovascular disease and cancer by the examination of spatial patterns of these diseases and their environmental associations. I consider the spatial and environmental approach to disease aetiology a valuable counterpoint to the essentially anthropocentric view of most medical scientists. I am also interested in the geography of the U.S.S.R."

*   *   *

HUGHES, Margaret Kelly   1894(?)-1980

OBITUARY NOTICE: Born c. 1894; died July 22, 1980, in New York, N.Y. Author. Before the United States entered World War II, Hughes worked with the American Friends of France in Paris, a war relief organization that assisted French prisoners of war. She wrote a book about her experiences in 1941, *Les Lauriers sont coupes.* Obituaries and other sources: *New York Times,* July 23, 1980.

*   *   *

HUME, Arthur W. J. G. Ord
See ORD-HUME, Arthur W. J. G.

HUNT, Gill
See TUBB, E(dwin) C(harles)

* * *

HUNTLEY, James L(ewis) 1914-

PERSONAL: Born January 23, 1914, in Nampa, Idaho; son of Edmond Arlington and Flossie Ethel (Wolf) Huntley; married Doris A. Parker (divorced, 1939); children: James L., Jr., Lois Ann Huntley Brashear. *Education:* Jan Hus University, B.A., 1972, M.A., 1974, Ph.D., 1979. *Home address:* P.O. Box 484, Marsing, Idaho 83639.

CAREER: Professional musician in Idaho, Oregon, and California, 1935-50; accountant and administrator in construction industry in Alaska, 1951-57; Douthit Boatworks, Santa Rosa, Calif., boatbuilder, 1960-62; Fred Post Woodworking, Tempe, Ariz., sparbuilder, 1964-68; Anchors Way Marine, Ventura, Calif., boatbuilder, 1968-72; archaeologist in Idaho, 1979—. *Military service:* U.S. Army, 1943-45; became staff sergeant. *Member:* Idaho Archaeological Society, Owyhee Historical Society (museum director), Owyhee Gem and Mineral Society (past president).

WRITINGS: Ferryboats in Idaho, Caxton, 1979. Contributor to *Outpost* and *Idaho Archaeologist.*

WORK IN PROGRESS: Research on the history of Owyhee County, Idaho, on the archaeological background of the western Snake River Plain, and on the Snake River Shoshone and Paiute Indians.

SIDELIGHTS: Huntley commented: "My first love was archaeology, but circumstances did not permit me to follow it until later. I did do some survey work for the University of Alaska during my years in the Arctic, and some other work in Mexico during the 1960's. My book about ferryboats was written as a historical archaeology thesis, as this form of water transportation in Idaho was being lost to posterity. I will continue to work and write on the archaeology of my home country, Idaho.

"The past two years I have been working with area archaeologists on salvage projects and digs in the western Snake River plain. Owyhee County, Idaho, where I live, has been called 'the West's forgotten corner' and still retains much of the Old West flavor. The mountains and deserts are sparsely populated. It was the home of many native people in the past and has been little studied and observed archaeologically."

* * *

HURST, Richard Maurice 1938-

PERSONAL: Born September 17, 1938, in Janesville, Wis.; son of Maurice A. (an insurance executive) and Lois (an insurance secretary; maiden name, Donovan) Hurst; married Jolene Nyberg (a medical records administrator), July 20, 1968; children: Ruthann Marie, Richard Michael. *Education:* Indiana University, A.B. (with distinction), 1960, M.A. (folklore), 1962, further graduate study, 1964; State University of New York at Buffalo, M.A. (history), 1976, Ph.D., 1978. *Home:* 5624 Washington Blvd., Indianapolis, Ind. 46220. *Office:* Department of Natural Resources, Indiana State Museum, 202 North Alabama St., Indianapolis, Ind. 46204.

CAREER: Illinois State Historical Society and Historical Library, Springfield, historical markers supervisor, 1964-67; Buffalo and Erie County Historical Society, Buffalo, N.Y., chief of resources, 1967-79; State University of New York at Buffalo, Division of Continuing Education, instructor of history and popular culture, 1970-78; State University of New

York College at Buffalo, adjunct professor of museology, 1978-79; Indiana State Museum, Indianapolis, assistant director, 1979—. *Member:* American Association for State and Local History, American Association of Museums, Popular Culture Association, Midwest Museums Association, New York Folklore Society (member of board of directors, 1968-79), Western New York Popular Culture Society (founder), Phi Beta Kappa, Phi Alpha Theta, Phi Eta Sigma.

WRITINGS: Republic Pictures: Between Poverty Row and the Majors; Its Influence on American Society, Scarecrow, 1979; (contributor) Fred E. H. Schroeder, editor, *Twentieth-Century Popular Culture in Museums, Archives, and Libraries,* Bowling Green State University Popular Press, 1980. Contributor to folklore, history, and museum journals. Associate editor of *Abstracts of Folklore Studies,* 1963-74.

WORK IN PROGRESS: Grassroots History: Coordinated Efforts Between Folklore, Popular Culture, American Studies, and the History of the Common Man as They Pertain to Museology.

SIDELIGHTS: Hurst wrote: "As a child I was interested in B action movies, specifically westerns and serials. As an adult I returned to these interests and began to examine the academic aspects of the cultural importance of Hollywood's 'filler' output to the American scene in the thirties and forties. I am also interested in how such phenomena can be utilized in museum programs since this is the area of my vocational commitment, which is not to say that I take the subject too seriously. I also write about serials for *Serial World* and other fun publications, and sometimes speak on popular culture on interview shows.

"In addition, and to safeguard my professional credentials, I occasionally publish in the more traditional aspects of American history or museology. As a museum administrator, though, much of my 'creative' writing, such as project reports, long range plans, and institutional historical research, rarely sees publication and, given the nature of such material, it's just as well. My main enthusiasm and emphasis remains the influence of the mass media on American culture and mores."

Republic Pictures: Between Poverty Row and the Majors was originally a doctoral thesis about the influence of B motion pictures on a generation of young Americans who grew up watching John Wayne, Roy Rogers, and Gene Autry. According to Hurst, the B westerns and action films of the thirties and forties "reinforced what kids heard in the school system, the church and in family patterns—that if you played the game fairly and you had a just cause, if you were honest and above-board in your approach to your problem, ultimately your side will win." In this book Hurst studies the history and economics of Republic Pictures, examines the films and stars of that time, and shows how the idealism such pictures once inspired gave way to the realism and disillusionment of modern films and anti-heroes.

BIOGRAPHICAL/CRITICAL SOURCES: Indianapolis News, April 11, 1980; *Los Angeles Times,* April 20, 1980.

* * *

HYATT, Richard Herschel 1944-

PERSONAL: Born May 11, 1944, in Atlanta, Ga.; son of Raymond W. (a bookkeeper) and Lois (Ballew) Hyatt; married Linda Davis, March 15, 1969 (divorced, 1972); married Peggy Kaneaster (a teacher), November 23, 1974; children: Heather Delise. *Education:* Attended Georgia State University, 1962-72. *Religion:* Baptist. *Home:* 6251 Rockefeller

Dr., Columbus, Ga. 31904. *Office: Columbus Enquirer,* P.O. Box 711, Columbus, Ga. 31902.

CAREER: Atlanta Times, Atlanta, Ga., sportswriter, 1964-65; Georgia Tech Athletic Association, Atlanta, assistant director of public relations, 1965-68; Atlanta Hawks, Atlanta, director of public relations, 1968; *Atlanta Constitution,* Atlanta, sportswriter, 1969-72; *Columbus Enquirer,* Columbus, Ga., associate editor, 1972—, author of column "Richard Hyatt," 1978—. Member of Columbus Human Relations Committee and board of directors of Columbus Jaycees, 1975-76. *Member:* Columbus Press Club (president, 1976), Metropolitan Sertoma Club (member of board of directors, 1979). *Awards, honors:* Newswriting awards from Georgia Associated Press, 1973, for sportswriting, and 1975 and 1978, both for public service; newswriting awards from United Press International, 1974, for sportswriting; newswriting awards from Georgia Press Association, 1976, for religious heritage editorial, and 1978, for public service; nominated for Pulitzer Prize in journalism, 1976, for coverage of Jimmy Carter's presidential campaign.

WRITINGS: The Carters of Plains, Strode, 1977. Correspondent for *Newsweek* and *New York Times.*

WORK IN PROGRESS: A history of Callaway Gardens, for Peachtree Publications; collected columns and feature articles.

SIDELIGHTS: Hyatt commented: "I see sportswriting as great training for learning the discipline of writing and the enjoyment of the freedom to create. Many great writers began this way and I can see why. The sports page is a place to experiment and grow as an interviewer and writer. It's a great place to start but few are staying there. Writing a column for a newspaper, especially a daily, is also great training because it teaches one creative discipline. The writer is given the freedom to create, but that creativity has a definite deadline. For me, sportswriting and writing a column naturally led to writing books and I have tried to treat each chapter of my books as a 'column.' This has prevented me from being overwhelmed by the length of a book, which can overpower a newspaperman used to turning out stories of a few thousand words."

I

IBARRA, Crisostomo
See YABES, Leopoldo Y(abes)

*   *   *

INGRAO, Charles W(illiam)   1948-

PERSONAL: Surname is pronounced In-*gray*-o; born March 15, 1948, in New York, N.Y.; son of Michael Anthony and Lillian (Palermo) Ingrao; married Kathleen Deborah Beloin (a writer), August 28, 1971; children: Kathleen Deborah, Christopher Jeffrey. *Education:* Wesleyan University, Middletown, Conn., B.A., 1969; Brown University, M.A., 1971, Ph.D., 1974. *Home:* 128 Magnolia Court, West Lafayette, Ind. 47906. *Office:* Department of History, Purdue University, West Lafayette, Ind. 47907.

CAREER: Brown University, Providence, R.I., instructor in history, 1974-76; Purdue University, West Lafayette, Ind., assistant professor of history, 1976—. *Member:* American Historical Association, Fulbright Alumni Association, Phi Beta Kappa. *Awards, honors:* Fulbright fellowship, 1972-73; International Research and Exchanges Board fellowship, 1973; fellowships from Humboldt Foundation and Institut fuer europaeische Geschichte, 1980.

WRITINGS: In Quest and Crisis: Emperor Joseph I and the Habsburg Monarchy, Purdue University Press, 1979. Contributor to history and literary journals.

WORK IN PROGRESS: A book on Frederick II of Hesse-Cassel, publication expected in 1984.

SIDELIGHTS: Ingrao wrote that his book on Frederick II, "the German prince responsible for sending seventeen thousand 'Hessian' mercenaries to fight in the American Revolution, will outline Frederick's numerous social reforms and challenge the accepted U.S. views stemming from his role in the Revolution. It is particularly noteworthy that Frederick used the considerable subsidies paid him by the British for the improvement of the economy and living conditions in his small country, thus earning acclaim within Germany as an 'enlightened despot' even while he was being attacked in the American press as an example of the worst form of tyranny."

*   *   *

INKIOW, (Janakiev) Dimiter   1932-
(Velko Verin)

PERSONAL: Surname is pronounced Inkioff; born October 10, 1932, in Haskowo, Bulgaria; son of Janaki Dimitroff (an administrator) and Nedialka Dimova (a nurse; maiden name, Paneva) Inkiow; divorced; children: Janaki Dimitrioff. *Education:* Sofia Academy of Drama, M.A., 1958. *Politics:* "Democratic." *Religion:* Eastern Orthodox. *Home and office:* Wilhelm-Diess-Weg 13, 8000 Munich 81, West Germany. *Agent:* Madeline E. Unger Ltd., 15 East 26th St., New York, N.Y. 10010.

CAREER: Mariza Mine, Mariza, Bulgaria, mining engineer, 1951; *Science and Technology for the Youth,* Sofia, Bulgaria, science fiction editor, 1952-60; Gabrovo State Theatre, Gabrovo, Bulgaria, director, 1961-62; *Automobile and Sport,* Sofia, editor, 1963-65; Radio Free Europe, Munich, West Germany, senior editor, 1966—. *Military service:* Bulgarian Army, 1954 and 1956; became lieutenant.

WRITINGS—Juvenile; in English translation: *Ich und meine Schwester Klara,* Klopp Verlag, 1977, translation by Paula McGuire published as *Me and My Sister Clara,* Pantheon, 1979; *Ich und Klara und der Kater Kasimir,* Klopp Verlag, 1978, translation by McGuire published as *Me and Clara and Casimir the Cat,* Pantheon, 1979; *Ich und Klara und der Dackel Schnuffi,* Klopp Verlag, 1978, translation by McGuire published as *Me and Clara and Snuffy the Dog,* Pantheon, 1980; *Ich und Klara und der Pony Balduin,* Klopp Verlag, 1979, translation by McGuire published as *Me and Clara and Balduin the Pony,* Pantheon, 1980.

Other writings: *Miria und Raeuber Karabum* (title means "Miria and Karabum the Robber"), Klopp Verlag, 1974; *Die Puppe, die ein Baby haben wollte* (title means "The Doll Who Wanted a Baby"), Jugend & Volk, 1974; *Transi Schraubenzieher* (title means "Transi Screwdriver"), Bertelsmann Verlag, 1975; *Der kleine Jaeger* (title means "The Little Hunter"), Klopp Verlag, 1976; *Reise nach Peperonien* (title means "Journey to Peperonia"), Hoch Verlag, 1977; *Kunterbunte Traumgeschichten* (title means "Topsey-Turvey Multi-Colored Fairy-Tales"), Franz Schneider Verlag, 1978; *Planet der kleinen Menschen* (title means "Planet of the Little People"), Franz Schneider Verlag, 1978; *Der Club der Tausendjaehrigen* (title means "Club of the Millenarians"), Franz Schneider Verlag, 1978; *Der gruenzende Koenig* (title means "The King Who Grunted"), Franz Schneider Verlag, 1979; *Der fliegende Kamel* (title means "The Flying Camel"), Franz Schneider Verlag, 1979; *Der versteckte Sonnenstrahl* (title means "The Hidden Sunbeam"), Franz Schneider Verlag, 1980; *Fuenf fuerchterliche*

Raeubergeschichten (title means "Five Frightening Robber Stories"), Franz Schneider Verlag, 1981; *Ich, der reise Gari-Bari* (title means "I, the Giant Gari-Bari"), Franz Schneider Verlag, 1981; *Leo, der Lachloewe* (title means "Leo, the Laughing Lion"), Loewes Verlag, 1981; *Ich und Klara und der Papagei Pippo* (title means "Me and Klara and the Parrot Pipo"), Klopp Verlag, 1981.

Science-fiction novels: *Helikopter MN3* (title means "Helicopter MN3"), Izdatelstvo Narodna mladezh, 1959; *Sprung ueber die Jahrhunderte* (title means "Leap Across the Centuries"), Verlag Sport und Technik, 1969.

Plays: "Izgrevut" (five-act; title means "The Rise"), first produced in Haskovo, Bulgaria, at State Theatre, September 21, 1960; "Dushteriata zavurshva" (five-act; title means "The Daughter's Graduation"), first produced in Russe, Bulgaria, at State Theatre, January 3, 1961. Author of five-act play, "Legenda za Aidenlarskata gora" (title means "A Legend About the Aidenlar Woods").

Also author of short stories, under pseudonym Velko Verin, for Radio Free Europe.

SIDELIGHTS: Inkiow told *CA:* "As far as I am concerned there is no such thing as a pure 'children's book.' Anyone who knows my books will have become aware that the stories I write are stories for adults and children alike. In *Me and My Sister Clara* every adult can relive his or her own childhood: the delight at the sight of the first 'proper' tooth, or how to get rid of one's baby teeth in the quickest possible way, and 'how can I raid the refrigerator without being caught?'

"My own First Commandment in writing is that a story must not be boring. Children should enjoy reading and have fun in always being able to discover something new as they go, even when, thirty years later, they read it aloud to their own children. The young readers of *Journey to Peperonia* laugh at the stupidity of the Peperonians, who have the shortest working week in the world with only three working days from Monday to Wednesday, but then carry on working from Thursday to Sunday because they are so happy that they have the shortest working week in the world.

"In *Gulliver's Travels* Jonathan Swift presented his own perspective of our world. For me, the old-style fairytale for children is dead. We live in a new age, an age in which an author has something to say or nothing at all. If nothing, then a work of seven hundred pages cannot conceal it. The reader's time is restricted."

BIOGRAPHICAL/CRITICAL SOURCES: Christian Science Monitor, October 15, 1979.

* * *

INNERHOFER, Franz 1944-

PERSONAL: Born May 2, 1944, in Krimml, Salzburg, Austria; son of Rupert (a farmer) and Elise (Bernhard) Brugger; children: Maria, Daria, Mascha. *Education:* Attended University of Salzburg. *Religion:* Roman Catholic. *Home:* Idlhofgasse 86/7/22 Graz, Austria, 8010.

CAREER: Farm worker in Uttendorf, Salzburg, Austria, 1958-61; blacksmith in Uttendorf and Salzburg, 1961-68; writer. *Awards, honors:* Bremer Literaturpreis, 1974, Rauriser Literaturpreis, 1975, and Sandoz Preis, 1975, all for *Schoene Tage.*

WRITINGS—In English: Schoene Tage (novel), Residenz Verlag, 1974, translation by Anselm Hollo published as *Beautiful Days,* Urizen Books, 1976.

Other: *Schattseite* (novel), Residenz Verlag, 1975; *Innenansichten eines beginnenden Arbeitsages,* Pfaffenweiler Presse, 1976; *Die grossen Woerter* (novel), Residenz Verlag, 1977.

WORK IN PROGRESS: A novel "about the different mentality in Germany and Italy."

BIOGRAPHICAL/CRITICAL SOURCES: New York Times Book Review, January 23, 1977.

* * *

IREMONGER, Valentin 1918-

PERSONAL: Born February 14, 1918, in Dublin, Ireland; married Sheila Manning, 1948; children: one son, four daughters. *Education:* Attended Abbey Theatre School of Acting. *Office:* Department of Foreign Affairs, Iveagh House, Dublin 2, Ireland.

CAREER: Poet, playwright, and translator, 1939-46; Irish Foreign Service, Dublin, third secretary, 1946-48, private secretary to foreign minister, 1948-50, first secretary in Political Division, Consular Division, and Economic Division, 1950-55, first secretary, 1956-59, counselor, 1959-64, ambassador to Sweden, Norway, and Finland, 1964-68, ambassador to India, 1968-73, ambassador to Luxembourg, 1973—. Affiliated with Abbey Theatre Company, 1939-40, and Gate Theatre, 1942-44. *Awards, honors:* AE Memorial Award, 1945.

WRITINGS: (With Robert Greacen and Bruce Williamson) *On the Barricades* (poems), New Frontiers Press, 1944; (editor with Greacen) *Contemporary Irish Poetry,* Faber, 1949; *Reservations* (poems), Envoy, 1950; (editor) *Irish Short Stories,* Faber, 1960; (translator) Michael MacGowan, *The Hard Road to Klondike,* Routledge & Kegan Paul, 1962; (translator) Donall MacAmlaigh, *An Irish Navvy: The Diary of an Exile,* Routledge & Kegan Paul, 1966; *Horan's Field and Other Reservations* (poems), Humanities, 1972.

Work represented in anthologies, including "Wrap Up My Green Jacket" (play; first broadcast, 1947) in *The Bell.* Poetry editor of *Envoy,* 1949-51.

* * *

IRWIN, Ann(abelle Bowen) 1915-
(Hadley Irwin, a joint pseudonym)

PERSONAL: Born October 8, 1915, in Peterson, Iowa; daughter of Benjamin (a farmer) and Mary (a teacher; maiden name, Rees) Bowen; married Keith C. Irwin (in business), May 29, 1943; children: Jane Irwin Croll, Ann Irwin Bauer, Rees, Sara. *Education:* Morningside College, B.A., 1937; University of Iowa, M.A., 1967. *Residence:* Lake View, Iowa. *Office:* Department of English, Iowa State University, 347 Ross Hall, Ames, Iowa 50011.

CAREER: High school English teacher in Iowa, 1937-67; Buena Vista College, Storm Lake, Iowa, instructor in English, 1967-68; Midwestern College, Denison, Iowa, instructor in English, 1968-70; Iowa State University, Ames, associate professor of English, 1970—.

WRITINGS—Juveniles: (With Bernice Reida) *Hawkeye Adventure,* Graphic Publishing, 1966; (with Reida) *Hawkeye Lore,* Graphic Publishing, 1968; *One Bite at a Time,* F. Watts, 1973; (with Reida) *Moon of the Red Strawberry,* Aurora, 1977; (with Reida) *Until We Reach the Valley,* Avon, 1979.

With Lee Hadley, under joint pseudonym Hadley Irwin; fiction: *The Lilith Summer,* Feminist Press, 1979; *We Are Mes-*

quakie, We Are One, Feminist Press, 1980; *Bring to Boil and Separate,* Atheneum, 1980; *Moon and Me,* Atheneum, 1981.

Author of one-act plays, *And the Fullness Thereof,* Pioneer, and *Pieces of Silver,* Eldridge Publishing.

WORK IN PROGRESS—With Lee Hadley, under joint pseudonym Hadley Irwin: *What About Grandma?*

SIDELIGHTS: Irwin and Hadley wrote: "The value of writing, whether it is for adults or for children, lies in trying to create beauty and truth through printed words. The best one can hope for is an approximation of those abstractions, but the attempt is worth the work and the risk. Even in failure there is much to be learned.

"Writings means putting words on paper in the most careful way one can and hoping that the reader will receive them with the same awareness. Faulkner said it best and most finally when he said one must forget all '. . . but the old verities and truths of the heart.'"

*　　*　　*

IRWIN, Hadley
  See HADLEY, Lee
  and IRWIN, Ann(abelle Bowen)

J

JACKMAN, Stuart 1922-

PERSONAL: Born July 29, 1922, in Manchester, England; son of Sydney (a builder) and Mary (Tringham) Jackman; married Sheena Grierson (a nurse), July 2, 1948; children: Nicholas, Morag, Maxwell, Andrew. *Education:* Attended University of Edinburgh, 1939-41, and Yorkshire Independent College, 1945-48. *Home:* 36 Chichele Rd., Oxted, Surrey, England. *Agent:* Curtis Brown Ltd., One Craven Hill, London W2 3EP, England.

CAREER: Pastor of Congregational churches in Barnstaple, England, 1948-52, Pretoria, South Africa, 1952-55, Caterham, England, 1955-61, and Auckland, New Zealand, 1961-65; editor with Congregational Council for World Mission, 1965-71; pastor in Oxted, England, 1969—. Television and radio broadcaster. *Military service:* Royal Air Force, 1941-45; became sergeant.

WRITINGS—Novels: *Portrait in Two Colours,* Faber, 1948, Scribner, 1949; *The Daybreak Boys,* Faber, 1961; *The Davidson Affair* (first volume of trilogy; also see below), Faber, 1967; *The Golden Orphans,* Macmillan, 1969; *Guns Covered With Flowers,* Faber, 1970; *Slingshot* (second volume of trilogy; also see below), Faber, 1972; *The Burning Men* (third volume of trilogy), Faber, 1974; *Sandcatcher,* Atheneum, 1980 (published in England as *Operation Catcher,* Hamish Hamilton, 1980).

Nonfiction: *The Numbered Days* (essays on South Africa), S.C.M. Press, 1954; *One Finger for God,* Independent Press, 1957; *This Desirable Property,* Edinburgh House Press, 1968.

Plays: *But They Won't Lie Down,* S.C.M. Press; *Angels Unawares,* S.C.M. Press; "Giving and Receiving," first broadcast by British Broadcasting Corp. (BBC-Radio); "Post Mortem," first broadcast by BBC-Radio.

Contributor of articles and stories to magazines.

WORK IN PROGRESS: A novel.

SIDELIGHTS: Jackman, whose books have been published in German, French, Dutch, Danish, and Norwegian, commented to *CA:* "Basically I think of myself as a teller of stories—both in my vocation as a Christian minister and in my writing. I wrote my 'Davidson' trilogy because I felt the biblical events from Palm Sunday through Holy Week to Easter and on to Whitsuntide ought to translate into twentieth-century terms without losing any of their magnificent impact.

The reception of these three novels has borne out this theory. I am primarily interested in people and how they behave under the pressure of events. Hence, in novels like *Guns Covered With Flowers* and *Catcher,* I have been concerned to examine people caught up in events beyond their control.

"I have lived and worked in various countries and have traveled throughout the Middle East and in eastern Europe. I am currently broadcasting on BBC-Radio a weekly program in which I slot into a program of pop music requests a short piece which takes some biblical theme and gives it a contemporary, relevant treatment in the form of fiction or drama. What I am trying to do in this field is to accept the new translations of the Bible and take the stories a step further.

"In my novels I am now exploring a slightly nostalgic vein, writing about the wartime Royal Air Force—not the usual flying stories, but novels about the men who served on the ground, using the exceptional circumstances in which they found themselves to say something through them about the central themes of life, suffering, courage, and death.

"In my experience the writer of fiction and the minister of truth have much common territory to explore together. In a way, the novelist is now the prophet of our time."

*   *   *

JACKSON, Alan 1938-

PERSONAL: Born September 6, 1938, in Liverpool, England; married Margaret Dickson, 1963; children: Kevin, Yorick. *Education:* Attended University of Edinburgh, 1956-59 and 1964-65.

CAREER: Poet. Worked as laborer and as a psychiatric nursing trainee; secretary for Scottish Committee of 100, 1961-62; Kevin Press, Edinburgh, Scotland, founding director, 1965—. Director of Live Readings, 1967—. *Awards, honors:* Grant from Scottish Arts Council, 1967.

WRITINGS—Poetry: *Under Water Wedding: Poems,* privately printed, 1961; *Sixpenny Poems,* privately printed, 1962; *Well Ye Ken Noo,* privately printed, 1963; *All Fall Down: Poems,* Kevin Press, 1965; *The Worstest Beast,* Kevin Press, 1967; *The Grim Wayfarer,* Fulcrum Press, 1969; *Idiots Are Freelance,* Rainbow Books, 1973. Work represented in anthologies, including *Penguin Modern Poets 12,* Penguin, 1968.

SIDELIGHTS: Jerome Cushman wrote in the *Library Journal* that Jackson's work "has a dark folkloristic quality; it celebrates man the male, using short, familiar terms describing woman's glory and man's pride. His voice is Protestant Scottish and it has a satiric bite that makes us aware that he understands these our times." Another reviewer, Alan Brownjohn of *New Statesman*, observed that the poet "deals in queer, arresting, self-mocking imagery which only effectively makes its point after several re-readings and sometimes remains merely baffling for all its liveliness. But he rings the changes happily on the old theme of poetry as a dance against nothingness."

BIOGRAPHICAL/CRITICAL SOURCES: Times Literary Supplement, August 14, 1969; *Listener,* December 11, 1969; *New Statesman,* January 2, 1970; *Library Journal,* July, 1970; *Poet,* May, 1971*

* * *

JACKSON, Albina
See GEIS, Richard E(rwin)

* * *

JACKSON, Charles (Reginald) 1903-1968

PERSONAL: Born April 6, 1903, in Summit, N.J.; committed suicide, September 21, 1968, in New York, N.Y.; son of Frederick George and Sarah (Williams) Jackson; married Rhoda Booth (an editorial writer), March 4, 1938; children: Sarah Piper, Kate Winthrop. *Education:* Attended Syracuse University. *Residence:* New York, N.Y. *Agent:* Carl Brandt, Brandt & Brandt Literary Agents, Inc., 1501 Broadway, New York, N.Y. 10036.

CAREER: Writer. Worked in a bookstore in Chicago, Ill., a jigsaw factory in Boston, Mass., and as a newspaperman; Columbia Broadcasting System (CBS-Radio), New York City, staff writer, 1936-39; free-lance writer for radio, 1939-44; New York University, New York City, teacher in radio writing, c. 1940. Lecturer in writing at Marlboro College, Columbia University, Dartmouth University, and New York University.

WRITINGS: The Lost Weekend (novel), Farrar, 1944, reprinted, Bentley, 1979; *The Fall of Valor* (novel), Rinehart, 1946, reprinted, Manor, 1974; *The Outer Edges* (novel), Rinehart, 1948; *The Sunnier Side: Twelve Arcadian Tales* (short stories; contains "The Sunnier Side," "The Band Concert," "Palm Sunday," "The Sisters," "In the Chair," "Tenting Tonight," "The Benighted Savage," "How War Came to Arcadia, N.Y.," "By the Sea," "A Night Visitor," "Sophistication," and "Rachel's Summer"), Farrar, Straus, 1950; *Earthly Creatures* (short stories; contains "The Boy Who Ran Away," "Romeo," "The Break," "A Sunday Drive," "Money," "Parting at Morning," "The Cheat," "The Sleeper Awakened," "Old Men and Boys," and "The Outlander"), Farrar, Straus, 1953, revised edition published as *The Cheat,* Belmont, 1961; *How to Buy a Used Car* (nonfiction), Chilton, 1967; *A Second-Hand Life* (novel), Macmillan, 1967. Also author of radio plays, "A Letter From Home," 1939, and "Dress Rehearsal," 1941, and of radio adaptations, "The Devil and Daniel Webster," "Outward Bound," "The Giant's Share," and "Jane Eyre."

Contributor of stories, articles, and book reviews to magazines.

WORK IN PROGRESS: A novel, *Farther and Wilder,* left unfinished at time of death.

SIDELIGHTS: Between 1927 and 1930, Charles Jackson suffered from tuberculosis. Although seriously ill, his years of convalescence allowed him time for reading and continuing his aborted education independently by studying the works of such authors as Shakespeare, Tolstoi, and Thomas Mann. During this period, Jackson lived for a time in Davos, Switzerland, the scene of Mann's novel *Magic Mountain,* in an effort to improve his health. While in Switzerland, he began to write. The author penned three novels and numerous short stories, most of which were rejected by magazines and publishers. Jackson then became a writer for the Columbia Broadcasting System (CBS-Radio) until 1939 when he started freelancing. He wrote seven plays for the "Columbia Workshop" program, as well as five scripts a week for the daytime serial "Sweet River." Finally, in 1939, his work was acknowledged when the *Partisan Review* accepted his story "Palm Sunday" for publication.

The appearance of Jackson's novel *The Lost Weekend* brought him instant fame. A psychological study of an alcoholic's five-day binge, the book was described by Philip Wylie in the *New York Times Book Review* as "the most compelling gift to the literature of addiction since DeQuincey." Edmund Wilson, in the *New Yorker,* called it "a tour de force of some merit" providing "some excellent description of alcoholic states which have rarely, I think, been treated with this intimate yet objective precision." Like Mark Schorer, who wrote in the *New Republic* that *The Lost Weekend* "could no doubt earn an M.A. in psychology from an amiable university," a number of critics praised the novel's accuracy and Jackson's ability to convey the wanderings of an alcoholic's mind. Translated into several languages, including French, Italian, Dutch, Danish, and Norwegian, the book became a best-seller, and the Paramount motion picture version, which starred Ray Milland as the drunkard Don Birnam, won an Academy Award as the best film of 1945.

Jackson's subsequent novels were also studies in deviant psychologies. *The Fall of Valor,* for example, is the story of Ethel and John Grandin's marriage and of the latter's latent homosexuality. Wilson observed that, like its predecessor, the novel successfully created "apprehension and suspense" and sustained its author's sincerity of purpose. But while Wilson saw Jackson's contribution as having "made homosexuality middle-class and thereby removed it from the privileged level on which Gide and Proust had set it," Frederic Wertham in the *New Republic* maintained that the hero's "uncertainty in the sexual sphere is only part of a larger social uncertainty. From that point of view *The Fall of Valor* might be seen as a monument to the middle-class man who can't make up his mind. . . . [It] is a novel in the great tradition of realism. It adds a pigment to the picture of truth in the field of human relationships."

Jackson's last novel, *A Second-Hand Life,* is another study of human weakness. Its heroine, Winifred Grainger, has been described as a nymphomaniac, a woman, as Granville Hicks wrote in the *Saturday Review,* who has "what is commonly thought of as the male attitude toward sex." Although a number of critics, including Webster Schott in the *New York Times Book Review* and a *New Yorker* reviewer, found her character underdeveloped, Hicks compared Winifred to Hemingway's Lady Brett and Dreiser's Sister Carrie and concluded: "She may not go down in literary history as one of the great sinners, but she is worth reading about—and thinking about, too."

AVOCATIONAL INTERESTS: Reading, music, particularly Beethoven and Mozart, oil painting.

BIOGRAPHICAL/CRITICAL SOURCES: Saturday Review of Literature, January 29, 1944, October 5, 1946, April 15, 1950; *New York Herald Tribune Weekly Book Review,* January 30, 1944, October 6, 1946; *New York Times,* January 30, 1944, October 6, 1946, May 30, 1948, April 16, 1950, September 13, 1953, August 13, 1967; *New Yorker,* February 5, 1944, October 5, 1946, June 5, 1948, August 26, 1967; *New Republic,* October 7, 1946, June 7, 1948; *Nation,* October 19, 1946, July 3, 1948; *Commonweal,* November 1, 1946; *San Francisco Chronicle,* June 7, 1948, April 20, 1950; *New York Herald Tribune Book Review,* April 16, 1950; *Saturday Review,* August 12, 1967; *Newsweek,* August 14, 1967; *Best Sellers,* August 15, 1967; *National Review,* September 19, 1967.

OBITUARIES: New York Times, September 22, 1968; *Washington Post,* September 23, 1968; *Time,* September 27, 1968; *Newsweek,* September 30, 1968; *Publishers Weekly,* September 30, 1968.*

* * *

JACKSON, E. F.
See TUBB, E(dwin) C(harles)

* * *

JACKSON, John E(dgar)   1942-

PERSONAL: Born September 22, 1942, in Kingsport, Tenn.; son of John Edgar and Annabell (Wade) Jackson; married Gretchen Neal (a musician), August 14, 1965; children: J. Michael, Carrie Neal. *Education:* Carnegie-Mellon University, B.S., 1965, M.S., 1965; Harvard University, M.P.A., 1966, Ph.D., 1969. *Home:* 1007 Lincoln St., Ann Arbor, Mich. 48104.

CAREER: Department of Defense, Washington, D.C., systems analyst, 1968-69; U.S. Air Force Academy, Colorado Springs, Colo., instructor in economics, 1969-70; Harvard University, Cambridge, Mass., assistant professor of government, 1970-80; University of Michigan, Ann Arbor, professor of political science, 1980—. Member of Swarthmore Community Center, Swarthmore, Pa. *Military service:* U.S. Army, 1968-70; became captain. *Member:* American Political Science Association. *Awards, honors:* Guggenheim fellowship.

WRITINGS: Constituencies and Leaders in Congress: Their Effects on Senate Voting Behavior, Harvard University Press, 1974; (editor and contributor) *Public Needs and Private Behavior in Metropolitan Areas,* Ballinger, 1975; (with Eric A. Hanushek) *Statistical Methods for Social Scientists,* Academic Press, 1977; *The Political Economy of Tax Reform* (monograph), American Enterprise Institute for Public Policy Research, 1980.

Contributor: A. S. Goldberger and O. D. Duncan, editors, *Structural Equation Models in the Social Sciences,* Seminar Press, 1973; George Peterson and Hal Hockman, editors, *Redistribution Through Public Choice,* Columbia University Press, 1974; Edwin Mills, editor, *Economic Analysis of Environmental Problems,* National Bureau of Economic Research, 1975; William Abernathy and D. Ginzburg, editors, *Government, Technology, and the Automobile,* McGraw, 1979; Gary Fromm, editor, *Studies in Public Regulation,* MIT Press, 1980. Contributor to *Electoral Studies Yearbook.* Contributor to political science journals. Editor of *Public Policy,* 1971-74.

WORK IN PROGRESS: Political Parties and the American Electorate.

JACOBS, Barry (Douglas)   1932-

PERSONAL: Born September 10, 1932, in Chicago, Ill.; son of Frank Douglas (a physician) and Edith (Dudley) Jacobs. *Education:* Attended University of Uppsala, 1952-53; DePauw University, B.A., 1954; Harvard University, A.M., 1956, Ph.D., 1964; Centre d'Etudes Universitaires Francaises, degre superieur, 1973. *Religion:* Presbyterian. *Home:* 10 Crestmont Rd., Montclair, N.J. 07042. *Office:* Montclair State College, 470 Partridge Hall, Upper Montclair, N.J. 07043.

CAREER: Northeastern University, Boston, Mass., instructor in English, 1955-57; Harvard University, Cambridge, Mass., instructor, 1963-66, assistant professor of Scandinavian studies and comparative literature, 1966-71; Montclair State College, Upper Montclair, N.J., associate professor of English, 1971—. Lecturer on oriental rugs at Montclair Museum, 1975. *Member:* Textile Museum of America, Strindberg Society (life member), Swedish Academy for Literary Research, Hajji Baba Club of New York. *Awards, honors:* Swedish-American Foundation fellowship, 1952-53; Kendall Foundation grant, summer, 1965; Canaday Humanities Fund grant, summer, 1968.

WRITINGS: (Author of introduction) *Strindberg's One-Act Plays,* translated by A. Paulson, Washington Square Press, 1969; (editor, translator, and author of introduction) Gunnar Brandell, *Strindberg's Inferno Crisis,* Harvard University Press, 1974. Contributor to *Encyclopedia of World Literature in the Twentieth Century.* Contributor of articles and reviews to literature journals.

AVOCATIONAL INTERESTS: Collecting oriental rugs.

* * *

JACOBS, James B.   1947-

PERSONAL: Born April 25, 1947, in Mount Vernon, N.Y.; son of Milton D. and Freda H. Jacobs; married Jan Sweeney (a professor), May 25, 1977; children: Thomas H. *Education:* Johns Hopkins University, B.A., 1969; University of Chicago, J.D., 1973, Ph.D., 1975. *Office:* School of Law, Cornell University, Ithaca, N.Y. 14853.

CAREER: Cornell University, Ithaca, N.Y., professor of law, 1975—. *Military service:* U.S. Army Reserve.

WRITINGS: Stateville: The Penitentiary in Mass Society, University of Chicago Press, 1977.

WORK IN PROGRESS: Social Control.

* * *

JADED OBSERVER
See ZOLF, Larry

* * *

JAFFE, Sandra Sohn   1943-

PERSONAL: Born September 3, 1943, in Chicago, Ill.; daughter of Arthur Goodman (a manufacturer) and Annette (Goldberg) Sohn; married Jerry R. Jaffe (an investor), September 4, 1966; children: Raquel Lyn, Aaron Goodman, Alysa Rose. *Education:* Wayne State University, B.A., 1967; American Society for Psycho-Prophylaxis, C.C.E., 1971. *Home:* 1252 South Orange Grove Ave., Los Angeles, Calif. 90019. *Agent:* Cosay, Werner & Associates, 9744 Wilshire Blvd., No. 310, Beverly Hills, Calif. 90212. *Office:* 5514 Wilshire Blvd., No. 400, Los Angeles, Calif. 90036.

CAREER: University of Illinois at Chicago Circle, Chicago, special assistant to head of art department, 1963-66; art teacher at public schools in Detroit, Mich., 1966-67; high school art teacher in Los Angeles, Calif., 1968-69; private practice as certified childbirth educator, 1971—. Parent support group facilitator, 1974-77; certified childbirth educator at Caring Childbirth Center of Los Angeles, 1978; member of faculty at University of California, Los Angeles, 1978—; director of Los Angeles Babies and Moms Program, 1980. *Member:* International Childbirth Education Association, American Society for Psychoprophylaxis in Obstetrics, Los Angeles Society for Psychoprophylaxis in Obstetrics, Wayne State University Alumni Association, Westside Mental Health Group.

WRITINGS: (With Jack Viertel) *Becoming Parents: Preparing for the Emotional Changes of First-Time Parenthood,* Atheneum, 1979.

WORK IN PROGRESS: Research for a book on the emotional changes of pregnancy; research for a book for prospective fathers (or other support people) on "how to be a good labor and delivery coach"; a program for new mothers and babies, and for hospital personnel, on support systems and positive nurturing for first-time parents.

SIDELIGHTS: Sandra Jaffe wrote: "I have structured my classes in childbirth education to encourage consumer awareness and acceptance of responsibility for one's own body and one's actions. Only through education and questioning of the established norms in pregnancy, childbirth, and parenting will people be able to achieve what they feel is right and comfortable for themselves. I am ever encouraging intergenerational contact and support groups as we seem to have forgotten the benefits of experience and common sense."

*　　　*　　　*

JAMES, Robert Vidal Rhodes
See RHODES JAMES, Robert (Vidal)

*　　　*　　　*

JANTA, Alexander　1908-1974

PERSONAL: Born in 1908 in Poland; died August 19, 1974, in Southampton, N.Y.; came to the United States, c. 1949; married Walentyna Stocker. *Education:* Educated in Poland. *Home:* 88-28 43rd Ave., Elmhurst, Queens, N.Y.; and Hampton Bays, N.Y.

CAREER: Journalist, poet, translator, and author. Served as foreign correspondent in the Far East and in the United States for several international publications; Kosciuszko Foundation, New York City, assistant to president, beginning 1955; Paderewski Foundation, New York City, former director; Alexander Hertz & Co. (rare book dealers), Elmhurst, N.Y., partner, 1960-74. President of American Council of Polish Cultural Clubs for three years. Lecturer. *Wartime service:* War correspondent with French and Polish armies, 1940; member of Polish Underground.

WRITINGS: Psalmy z domu niewoli (poems), Ksiaznica Polska (Glasgow, Scotland), 1944, translation by the author and Gladys Anthony White published as *Psalms of Captivity,* Pocahontas Press, 1947; *Sciana milczenia* (poems; title means "The Silent Wall"), British-Continental Syndicate, 1944; *I Lied to Live: A Year as a German Family Slave* (memoirs), foreword by Rex Stout, Roy Publishers, 1944; *Bound With Two Chains* (memoirs), Roy Publishers, 1945; *Widzenie wiary* (poems), privately printed, 1946; *Wracam z Polski 1948: Warszawa, Wroclaw, Krakow, Poznan, Szczecin—zycie, polityka, gospodarka, sztuka, ludzie i zagadnienia* (nonfiction), Paryz, 1949.

Pochwala wlasnych nog, czyli niech nam stoja! (poems), A. Girs Press, 1951; (editor) *Klapa bezpieczenstwa, czyli, humor zakurtynowy: Almanach do wcipow i anegdot opowiadanych w dzisiejazej Polsce* (collection of Polish humor), [Buffalo, N.Y.], 1953; *Bajka o cieniu: Poemat absurdystyczny* (poem), Poets' and Painters' Press (London), 1954; *Pierwszy szkic "Lorda Jima" i polskie listy Conrada w zbiorach amercykanskich* (title means "First Sketch of 'Lord Jim' and Conrad's Polish Notes in American Collection"), B. Swiderski, 1957; *Duch niespokojny* (poems; title means "Restless Spirit"), Gryf (London), 1957; *Znak tozsamosci, wybor z trzydziestolecia* (collection of poetry), Polish Book Importing Co., 1958.

Wielka gafa ksiezny balaganow (poems), Skladnica Ksiazki Polskiej (Buenos Aires, Argentina), 1960; *Losy i ludzie: Spotkania, przygody, studiea, 1931-1960* (essays and correspondence), Polish Institute of Science in America, 1961; *Linia podzialu* (poems; title means "The Dividing Line"), Poets and Painters' Press, 1963; *Fiet i apokalipsa* (nonfiction), Nakladem czytelnikow, 1964; (translator) *Godzina dzikiej kaczki: Mala antologia poezji japonskiej* (anthology of Japanese poetry), Oficyna Stanislawa Gliwy, 1966; *Ksiega podrozy, przygod i przypomnien* (travelogue), Polish Cultural Foundation (London), 1967.

(Compiler and translator from the English) *Robert Frost i inni amerykanscy poeci: Tlumaczenia* (title menas "Robert Frost and Other American Poets: Translations"), Poets' and Painters' Press, 1970; *Pamietnik indyjski* (poems), Poets' and Painters' Press, 1970; *Schron: Epilog w jednej odslonie* (poems; title means "Shelter"), Tematy, 1970; *Przestroga dla wnukow* (poems), Poets' and Painters' Press, 1971; *"Przyjemnie zapoznac"* (collection of essays), Polish Cultural Foundation, 1972; *Przestrogi drugie* (poems; title means "Second Warning"), Sigma Press, 1973; *Nowe odkrycie Ameryki* (nonfiction; title means "The Rediscovery of America"), Libella, 1973; *Nic wlasnego nikomu* (collection of essays, lectures, and addresses), Czytelnik, 1977. Also author of *Odkrycie Ameryki* (title means "The Discovery of America"), c. 1933. Contributor of articles to journals and newspapers.

*WORK IN PROGRESS—*At time of death: A bio-bibliography on early Polish-American sheet music, containing more than one hundred unrecorded pieces.

SIDELIGHTS: During his lifetime Alexander Janta wrote more than fifty books, including some twenty volumes of poetry. He was fluent in numerous languages and had lived on three continents. Two of his books, *I Lied to Live* and *Bound With Chains,* are accounts of his years as a prisoner of war during the Nazi occupation of Europe. Reviewing *I Lied to Live,* H. B. Krana of *Saturday Review of Literature* observed: "[The book,] while unsensational, catches the reader's attention and holds it. It possesses tension, sustained and skillful progress of narrative. It is brilliantly written. But, unfortunately, the story comes to an end very abruptly." Likewise, its sequel, *Bound With Chains,* met with considerable praise. Leon Valiani wrote that the book "is worth reading because of a kind of constructive optimism pervading it and because here and there Janta has the human courage to picture the prisoners not only as people who suffered but also as people who were capable."

BIOGRAPHICAL/CRITICAL SOURCES: Christian Science Monitor, December 1, 1944, December 29, 1945; *New York Times,* December 3, 1944; *Saturday Review of Literature,* December 9, 1944, December 29, 1945; *Weekly Book Review,* December 23, 1945; *Books Abroad,* winter, 1974, winter, 1975.*

JANUS, Grete
See HERTZ, Grete Janus

* * *

JAY, Peter A. 1940-

PERSONAL: Born November 22, 1940, in New York, N.Y.; son of Peter (a farmer) and Gertrude (McFinley) Ray; married Irna Moore (an editor), December 28, 1973; children: William. Education: Harvard University, B.A., 1962. Address: Box 206, Churchville, Md. 21028. Office: Baltimore Sun, 501 North Calvert St., Baltimore, Md. 21203.

CAREER/WRITINGS: U.S. Peace Corps, Washington, D.C., served as volunteer in Peru, 1962-63; Washington Post, Washington, D.C., reporter, editor, and foreign correspondent, 1965-72, Indochina bureau chief, 1970-72; Baltimore Sun, Baltimore, Md., author of tri-weekly editorial column, 1974—. Contributor of articles to magazines. Awards, honors: Award from American Political Science Association, 1969; Nieman fellow, Harvard University, 1972-73.

SIDELIGHTS: Jay, whose writings focus on politics, American social trends, and environmental matters, told CA: "After covering national and foreign news for a number of years, I'm convinced that local and regional coverage is at least as important and much harder to find."

* * *

JEDREY, Christopher M(ichael) 1949-

PERSONAL: Born October 29, 1949, in Ipswich, Mass.; son of Anthony Joseph, Sr., and Helene (Lucey) Jedrey; married Micheline Eden (a librarian), May 27, 1971. Education: University of Massachusetts, A.B., 1971; Harvard University, A.M., 1972, Ph.D., 1977. Home: I-34 Lowell House, Harvard University, Cambridge, Mass. 02138. Office: I-22 Lowell House, Harvard University, Cambridge, Mass. 02138.

CAREER: Barre Press, Barre, Mass., member of editorial staff, 1972-73; Harvard University, Cambridge, Mass., lecturer in history and literature and Allston Burr Senior Tutor at Lowell House, 1977—. Member: Phi Beta Kappa, Phi Kappa Phi.

WRITINGS: The World of John Cleaveland: Family and Community in Eighteenth-Century New England, Norton, 1979.

WORK IN PROGRESS: Research on early American legal history; studying Nathaniel Hawthorne and The House of Seven Gables.

* * *

JEHLEN, Myra 1940-

PERSONAL: Born March 3, 1940, in Paris, France; married in 1962; one child. Education: City College of the City University of New York, B.A., 1961; University of California, Berkeley, Ph.D., 1968. Home: 44 Horatio St., New York, N.Y. 10014. Office: State University of New York College at Purchase, Purchase, N.Y. 10577.

CAREER: New York University, New York City, instructor in English, 1966-69; Columbia University, New York City, assistant professor of English, 1969-74; State University of New York College at Purchase, associate professor of humanities, 1974—. Visiting senior lecturer at Yale University, spring, 1974. Member: Modern Language Association of America, American Studies Association. Awards, honors: Woodrow Wilson fellow, 1961-62, 1964-65; National Endowment for the Humanities junior fellow, 1973-74.

WRITINGS: Class and Character in Faulkner's South, Columbia University Press, 1976. Contributor of articles and reviews to journals, including Signs and Salmagundi.

* * *

JELENSKI, Constantin 1922-

PERSONAL: Surname is pronounced Ye-len-ski; born January 2, 1922, in Warsaw, Poland. Education: University of St. Andrews, M.A., 1943. Home: 8 rue de la Vrilliere, 75001 Paris, France. Office: Institut National de l'Audiovisuel, 23 Blvd. Jules-Ferry, 75011 Paris, France.

CAREER: Preuves, Paris, France, member of editorial committee, 1953-67; Royaumont Center for a Science of Man, Paris, administrative director, 1968-75; affiliated with Institut National de l'Audiovisuel, Paris, 1976—. Military service: Polish Army, 1940-45; served in France and England; became lieutenant; received Cross of Valor, Military Medal (second class), and Silver Cross of Merit with Swords.

WRITINGS: (Editor) History and Hope, Routledge & Kegan Paul, 1963; (editor) Anthologie de la Poesie Polonaise (title means "Anthology of Polish Poetry"), Seuil, 1965; Leonor Fini (monograph), Olympia, 1966; Hans Bellmer (monograph), St. Martin's, 1972; (with Francois Boudy) Witold Gombowicz: Theater, DTV, 1978. Contributor to magazines in France and the United States, including Arts, Partisan Review, and Le Monde.

WORK IN PROGRESS: A book on the life and work of Witold Gombowicz, with Francois Boudy.

BIOGRAPHICAL/CRITICAL SOURCES: Czeslaw Milosz, The History of Polish Literature, P. Collier, 1969.

* * *

JENSEN, Ole Klindt
See KLINDT-JENSEN, Ole

* * *

JENSON, William R(obert) 1946-

PERSONAL: Born August 15, 1946, in Salt Lake City, Utah; son of Rudolf N. (a construction engineer) and Margaret (Krefeld) Jenson; married Kathy N. Nackowski, September 19, 1973; children: Grayson. Education: University of Utah, B.S. (cum laude), 1969, M.S., 1972; Utah State University, Ph.D., 1976. Politics: Democrat. Religion: None. Home: 1171 First Ave., Salt Lake City, Utah 84103. Office: Children's Behavior Therapy Unit, Salt Lake Community Mental Health Center, 668 South 13th E., Salt Lake City, Utah 84103.

CAREER: Psychology intern at school in Logan, Utah, 1973-74; Las Vegas Mental Health Center, Las Vegas, Nev., clinical psychology intern, 1975, director of adolescent inpatient unit, 1975-76; Salt Lake Community Mental Health Center, Salt Lake City, Utah, director of children's behavioral therapy unit, 1976—. Clinical services member of Utah State University's University Affiliated Exceptional Child Center, 1973-74; adjunct assistant professor at University of Utah, 1977—; consultant to Legal Center for the Handicapped for the State of Utah.

MEMBER: American Psychological Association, Association for the Advancement of Behavior Therapy (state president, 1977-78), National Society for Autistic Children. Awards, honors: National Institute of Mental Health grant, 1977; grants from Utah Association for children's Therapy,

1977, 1978, 1979, Utah Division of Family Services, 1978, Bureau of Education for the Handicapped, 1978, and Utah governor's Council on Developmental Disabilities.

WRITINGS: (Editor with Dennis Burns) *Classroom Management and Communication,* University Affiliated Exceptional Child Center, Utah State University, 1974; (with Howard Sloane, David Buckholdt, and Judith Crandall) *Structured Teaching: A Design for Classroom Management and Instruction,* Research Press, 1979; (with Donna Gelfand and Clifford Drew) *Understanding Childhood Behavior Disorders,* Holt, 1981. Contributor of articles and reviews to education and psychology journals.

SIDELIGHTS: Jenson commented: "Basically my writing is done for teaching purposes, with the point in mind of serving handicapped children. Mentally handicapped children frequently experience multiple failures which affect their later adjustment. This is particularly true for autistic children who are frequently institutionalized for life. Much of this failure is preventable with current effective technologies in teaching and treatment. Much of my writing is geared to disseminating these technologies."

*   *   *

JESSUP, John K(nox)   1907-1979

PERSONAL: Born March 5, 1907, in Rochester, N.Y.; died of a heart attack, October 26, 1979, in Wilton, Conn.; son of John Colgate and Louise (Foote) Jessup; married Margaret Tarbox, September 23, 1932 (divorced); married Eunice Clark Rodman, September 11, 1937; children: (first marriage) John; (second marriage) Nathaniel Foote, Amos Huntington, Rebecca Phelps Jessup Goldstein, Maria Forward Jessup Sobol. *Education:* Yale University, A.B., 1928. *Home:* 122 Ridgefield Rd., Wilton, Conn. 06897.

CAREER: Yale University, New Haven, Conn., assistant professor of English, 1928-29, assistant editor of *Yale Alumni Weekly,* 1928-30; copywriter for J. Walter Thompson (advertising), 1930-35; Time Inc., 1935-69, writer for *Fortune,* 1935-36, editor of *Fortune,* beginning in 1936, head of business section of *Time,* 1940-44, joined staff of *Life,* 1944, chief editorial writer for *Life,* 1951-69. Editorial broadcaster for "Spectrum" series for Columbia Broadcasting System, Inc. (CBS-Radio), 1971-76. Member of Council on Foreign Relations. *Member:* Sigma Delta Chi, Yale Club, Century Association (New York, N.Y.).

WRITINGS: (With others) *The National Purpose,* Holt, 1960; (with the editors of *Life*) *Communism, the Nature of Your Enemy,* Time, Inc., 1962; (editor) *The Ideas of Henry Luce,* Atheneum, 1969.

SIDELIGHTS: Known as a political moderate, Jessup spent nearly thirty-five years with Henry Luce's *Fortune, Time,* and *Life* magazines. He was the editorial writer for *Life,* Luce's only forum for editorials, from 1951 to 1969.

Upon retiring, Jessup released a collection of Luce's thoughts, *The Ideas of Henry Luce.* Critic David Bernstein acknowledged that Luce was "one of the 20th century's great journalists. But he was not, for heaven's sake, a philosopher." Bernstein further expressed his discontent with Jessup's collection by saying: "The reason for this unhappy effect is that Luce's ideas are not sufficiently profound to still seem fresh after the passing of the years. He had some ideas that were new in their time. To meet them again is not to be intrigued but to be somehow annoyed."

BIOGRAPHICAL/CRITICAL SOURCES: New Leader, December 8, 1969; *New York Times Book Review,* January 11, 1970.

OBITUARIES: New York Times, October 27, 1979; *Time,* November 5, 1979; *Newsweek,* November 5, 1979.*

*   *   *

JEUNE, Paul   1950-

PERSONAL: Born October 27, 1950, in Victoria, British Columbia, Canada; son of Kenneth Percy (a barber) and Lucy Martha (Edge) Jeune; married Christina Elaine Penny (a dental hygienist), August 6, 1976. *Home and office address:* P.O. Box 24, Malahat, British Columbia, Canada V0R 2L0.

CAREER: Free-lance writer, 1970-72; *Alberni Valley Times,* Alberni, British Columbia, reporter, 1972-73; *Westcoaster,* Ucluelet, British Columbia, editor and publisher, 1973-74; *Victorian Newspaper,* Victoria, British Columbia, 1974-77; Maritime Museum of British Columbia, Victoria, in charge of public relations and member of board of trustees, 1977-78; free-lance writer and public relations consultant, 1978—. *Member:* International Thunderbird Class Association, Writers' Union of Canada, Outdoor Writers of Canada, Canadian Wildlife Federation. *Awards, honors:* Francis H. Kortright Canadian National Outdoor Writing Award from Canadian National Sportsmen's Shows in cooperation with the Outdoor Writers of Canada, 1980, for *Killer Whale.*

WRITINGS: The Whale Who Wouldn't Die: The True Story of "Miracle," Follett, 1979 (published in Canada as *Killer Whale: The Saga of "Miracle,"* McClelland & Stewart, 1979).

WORK IN PROGRESS: "The Penner Files" (tentative title), a mystery, adventure, and suspense series for young adult readers, based on the international adventures of a young journalist.

SIDELIGHTS: Jeune wrote: "I dropped out of high school a week before final exams in grade eleven to join the fishing fleet off the west coast of Vancouver Island. I had a choice to make—stay in school or pursue an education.

"After leaving school I worked for a year as a deckhand aboard commercial fishing trollers on the west coast. Intertwined with an eight-year career as a journalist I undertook such vocations as boat building, sail making, and newspaper publishing.

"To be a writer is good. To be an author is better. To be a continuously producing author is best. For me, writing is the spice that gives life its tang. My only regret is that I have only one lifetime in which to accomplish all the literary tasks that I have planned."

AVOCATIONAL INTERESTS: Sailing, cross-country skiing, camping, target shooting, hiking, canoeing, photography, reading.

*   *   *

JILES, Paulette   1943-

PERSONAL: Born in 1943 in Salem, Mo.; came to Canada, 1968. *Address:* c/o House of Anansi Press Ltd., 35 Britain St., Toronto, Ontario, Canada M5A 1R7.

CAREER: Writer. Associated with Canadian Broadcasting Corp. (CBC-Radio); appeared as actress in documentary film, "Rose's House," of Canadian National Film Board.

WRITINGS: Waterloo Express (poetry), Anansi, 1973. Also author of screenplay, "Rose's House," released by Canadian National Film Board. Work represented in anthologies, including *Canada First,* edited by P. Anson, Anansi, 1970, and *Mindscapes.* Contributor of short stories to *Saturday Night.*

SIDELIGHTS: Jiles's first volume of poetry, *Waterloo Express,* met with an enthusiastic reception. Dennis Lee commented in *Saturday Night* that "the author is often presented in folk outline: she laments a string of busted love affairs, hits the road again and again to forget, and can talk as sardonic and lowdown as any blues momma. Yet the TNT and agony she drags around come crackling out in images of manic brilliance, controlled by a frequently superb ear." Linda Rogers of *Canadian Literature* was similarly impressed with Jiles's use of language. Her "images have a life of their own," she explained, and "in visual terms, the poems are like the paints of Marc Chagall. Gorgeous disconnected figures float by on wisps of cloud and magic carpets of flowers. All the paraphernalia of life's circus is assembled in a giant mobile moving in the wind."

BIOGRAPHICAL/CRITICAL SOURCES: Saturday Night, December, 1973, December, 1977; *Canadian Literature,* summer, 1974; *Canadian Forum,* August, 1974; *Contemporary Literary Criticism,* Volume 13, Gale, 1980.*

* * *

JOAN, Polly 1933-

PERSONAL: Born May 19, 1933, in Columbus, Ohio. *Education:* Oberlin College, B.A., 1955; attended Goethe Institute, 1969; Cornell University, M.A.T., 1976. *Home address:* R.D.3, Newfield, N.Y. 14867.

CAREER: Teacher of language arts and woodworking, 1971-73; substitute junior high school teacher of social studies, 1974-75; New York State Council on the Arts, writer and consultant for public schools and administrative coordinator of four counties, 1975—. Guest lecturer at Cornell University, 1973, 1974; adjunct professor at Tompkins-Cortland Community College, 1977—; conducts workshops and seminars; gives poetry readings. Associate director of East Harlem-Ithaca summer camp program, 1964-66; member of board of directors of Tompkins County Arts Council, 1976-77. *Member:* Poets and Writers.

WRITINGS: No Apologies (poems and photographs), Women Writing Press, 1976; (co-editor) *Directory of Women Writing,* Women Writing Press, 1976; (co-author) *Guide to Women's Publishing,* Dustbooks, 1978, revised edition, 1980. Contributor of stories, poems, and articles to literary and cultural journals.

WORK IN PROGRESS: A novel combining poetry and prose; a historical novel about Martha Carrier, who was hung as a witch in Salem, Mass., in 1692.

* * *

JOHNSEN, Trevor Bernard Meldal
See MELDAL-JOHNSEN, Trevor Bernard

* * *

JOHNSON, Carl G(raves) 1915-

PERSONAL: Born October 4, 1915, in St. Matthews, S.C.; son of Joseph Leon (a miner) and Effie Lou (Graves) Johnson; married Aretta Blaylock, December, 1937 (died, August 4, 1978); children: Ronald C. *Education:* Moody Bible Institute, diploma, 1948; Beckley College, A.A., 1949. *Home:* 324 Neville St., Beckley, W.Va. 25801.

CAREER: Miner in Eccles, W.Va., 1934-43; ordained Baptist minister, 1949; pastor of Baptist churches in Ingram Branch, W.Va., 1949-53, Thurmond, W.Va., 1951-55, and in Piney View, W.Va., 1955-64; evangelist, 1964—. *Military service:* U.S. Army, 1943-46; became sergeant.

WRITINGS: Fifty-Two Story Telling Programs, Baker Book, 1964; *Scriptural Sermon Outlines,* Baker Book, 1965; *More Story Telling Programs,* Baker Book, 1966; *Ready for Anything,* Bethany Fellowship, 1968; *Preaching Helps,* Baker Book, 1969; *Miracles and Melodies,* Baker Book, 1970; *My Favorite Illustration,* Baker Book, 1972; *Prophecy Made Plain for Times Like These,* Moody, 1972; *Hell You Say!,* Hearthstone Publications, 1974; *Preaching Truths for Perilous Times,* Baker Book, 1976; *My Favorite Outline,* Baker Book, 1977.

WORK IN PROGRESS: So the Bible Is Full of Contradictions?

SIDELIGHTS: Johnson wrote: "I travel extensively for my evangelistic meetings. I love my work because I work with people, and see quite a number of them put their trust in Jesus Christ as their personal savior, and see others encouraged and strengthened as the word of God is preached to them.

"I meet people who have read my books and used them in their ministry for the Lord. This brings joy to my heart. I receive letters from others who have been helped by my books. This illustrates the truth given many years ago by Thomas Brooks: 'Books may preach when the author cannot, when the author may not, when the author dares not, yea, and which is more, when the author is not.'"

AVOCATIONAL INTERESTS: Reading, listening to cassette tapes of sermons and songs.

* * *

JOHNSON, Louis 1924-

PERSONAL: Born September 27, 1924, in Wellington, New Zealand; married; children: three. *Education:* Attended Wellington Teachers' Training College. *Address:* c/o Jacaranda Wiley Ltd., P.O. Box 2259, Auckland, New Zealand.

CAREER: Worked as teacher, 1951-54; editor of *New Zealand Parent and Child,* 1955-59; Department of Education, Wellington, New Zealand, assistant editor for School Publications Branch, 1963-68; Department of Information, Port Moresby, Papua New Guinea, officer in charge of Bureau of Literature, 1968-69; free-lance writer, 1970—.

WRITINGS: Stanza and Scene: Poems, Handcraft Press, 1945; *The Sun Among the Ruins* (poems), Pegasus Press, 1951; *Roughshod Among the Lilies* (poems), Pegasus Press, 1952; (with Anton Vogt and James K. Baxter) *Poems Unpleasant,* Pegasus Press, 1952; *Two Poems: News of Molly Brown, The Passionate Man and the Casual Man,* Pegasus Press, 1955; *The Dark Glass* (poems), Handcraft Press, 1955; *New Worlds for Old: Poems,* Capricorn Press, 1957; (with others) *The Night Shift: Poems on Aspects of Love,* Capricorn Press, 1957; *Bread and a Pension: Selected Poems,* Pegasus Press, 1964; (with others) *Ten Tales,* New Zealand Government Printer, 1965; *Land Like a Lizard: New Guinea Poems,* Jacaranda, 1970; *Onion,* Caveman Press, 1972; *Fires and Patterns* (poems), Jacaranda, 1975. Editor of *New Zealand Poetry Yearbook,* Volumes I-XI, 1951-64; editor of *Numbers,* 1954-60.

BIOGRAPHICAL/CRITICAL SOURCES: Kendrick Smithyman, *A Way of Saying,* Collins, 1965; James K. Baxter, *Aspects of Poetry in New Zealand,* Caxton Press, 1967.*

* * *

JOHNSON, Mendal W(illiam) 1928-1976

PERSONAL: Born May 24, 1928, in Tulsa, Okla.; died February 6, 1976; son of Mendal W. (an executive) and Hazel (McAnaly) Johnson; married Joan Betts (divorced); married Ellen Argo (a writer); children: Lynne Betts, Gail. *Education:* Attended University of Miami, Coral Gables, Fla., 1946-49. *Agent:* Barthold Fles Literary Agency, 507 Fifth Ave., New York, N.Y. 10017.

CAREER: Skipper, Annapolis, Md., managing editor, 1953-55; *Brownsville Herald,* Brownsville, Tex., sports editor, 1956; *Laramie Bulletin,* Laramie, Wyo., night city editor, 1957; affiliated with U.S. Merchant Marine; bank consultant.

WRITINGS: Let's Go Play at the Adams' (novel), Crowell, 1974. Contributor to magazines, including *Popular Boating* and *Yachting.*

WORK IN PROGRESS—At time of death: three novels, *Walking Out, Myth,* and *Net Full of Stars.*

[Sketch verified by wife, Ellen Argo]

*   *   *

JOHNSTON, R(onald) J(ohn)   1941-

PERSONAL: Born March 30, 1941, in Swindon, England; son of H. L. and P. J. (Liddiard) Johnston; married Rita Brennan (a researcher), April 16, 1963; children: Christopher, Lucy. *Education:* Victoria University of Manchester, B.A. (with honors), 1962, M.A., 1964; Monash University, Ph.D., 1966. *Home:* 48 School Green Lane, Sheffield S10 4GQ, England. *Office:* Department of Geography, University of Sheffield, Sheffield S10 2TN, England.

CAREER: Monash University, Victoria, Australia, teaching fellow, 1964, senior teaching fellow, 1965, lecturer, 1966; University of Canterbury, Christchurch, New Zealand, lecturer, 1967-68, senior lecturer, 1969-72, reader in geography, 1973-74; University of Sheffield, Sheffield, England, professor of geography, 1974—. Visiting associate professor at University of Toronto, 1972; academic visitor at London School of Economics and Political Science, London, 1973; official overseas guest at University of the Orange Free State and visitng professor at University of the Witwatersrand, 1976.

MEMBER: Institute of British Geographers (member of council, 1977-80), Social Science Research Council (England), New Zealand Geographical Society. *Awards, honors:* Erskine fellowship for United States, United Kingdom, and South America from University of Canterbury, 1969; British Council fellowship, 1973.

WRITINGS: (With P. J. Rimmer) *Retailing in Melbourne,* Department of Human Geography, Australian National University, 1970; *Urban Residential Patterns: An Introductory Review,* G. Bell, 1971; *Spatial Structures: An Introduction to the Study of Spatial Systems in Human Geography,* Methuen, 1973; *The New Zealanders: How They Live and Work,* David & Charles, 1976; *The World Trade System: Some Enquiries Into Its Spatial Structure,* G. Bell, 1976; (with B. E. Coates and P. L. Knox) *Geography and Inequality,* Oxford University Press, 1977; *Multivariate Statistical Analysis in Geography: A Primer on the General Linear Model,* Longman, 1978; *Political, Electoral, and Spatial Systems,* Oxford University Press, 1979; (with P. J. Taylor) *Geography of Elections,* Penguin, 1979; *Geography and Geographers: Anglo-American Human Geography Since 1945,* Edward Arnold, 1979, Halsted, 1980; *City and Society,* Penguin, 1980; *The Geography of Federal Spending in the United States,* Wiley, 1980; *City and Society in the United States,* St. Martin's, 1981.

Editor: Proceedings of the Sixth New Zealand Geography Conference, New Zealand Geographical Society, Volume I (with Jane M. Soons), 1971, Volume II (with June Chapman): *Geography and Education,* 1971; *Urbanization in New Zealand: Geographical Essays,* Reed Education, 1973; *Society and Environment in New Zealand,* Whitcombe & Tombs, 1974; (with D. T. Herbert) *Social Areas in Cities,* Wiley, Volume I: *Spatial Processes and Form,* 1976, Volume II: *Spatial Perspectives on Problems and Policies,* 1976; *People, Places, and Votes: Essays on the Electoral Geography of Australia and New Zealand,* Department of Geography, University of New England, 1977; (with Herbert) *Geography and Urban Environment: Progress in Research and Applications,* Wiley, Volume I, 1978, Volume II, 1979, Volume III, 1980; (with Herbert) *Social Areas in Cities: Processes, Patterns, and Problems,* Wiley, 1978; (with K. R. Cox) *Conflict: Politics and the Urban Scene,* Longman, 1981; (with D. Gregory, P. Haggett, D. M. Smith, and D. R. Stoddart) *Blackwell's Dictionary of Human Geography,* Blackwell, 1981.

WORK IN PROGRESS: Editing volumes four and five of *Geography and Urban Environment* series, with Herbert; editing *The Changing Geography of the United Kingdom,* with J. C. Doornkamp, publication by Methuen expected in 1983; *Geography and the State,* Macmillan, 1982; *The Public Prose,* with R. J. Bernett; research on the electoral geography of the Post-European Parliament elections, the geography of electoral change, and the geography of price.

*   *   *

JOLL, (Dowrish) Evelyn (Louis)   1925-

PERSONAL: Born February 6, 1925, in London, England; son of Cecil Augustus and Laura Merriall (Winsloe) Joll; married Pamela Sybil Kingzett, September 10, 1949; children: Caroline (Mrs. Nigel W. Duck), William, Charlotte, Harriet. *Education:* Magdalen College, Oxford, B.A. (with honors), 1949. *Politics:* "Floating voter." *Religion:* Church of England. *Home:* 7 Pelham Pl., London, England. *Office:* Thomas Agnew & Sons Ltd., 43 Old Bond St., London W1X 4BA, England.

CAREER: Thomas Agnew & Sons Ltd. (art dealers), London, England, salesman, 1949-55, managing director, 1955—. President of Fine Art Provident Institution, 1978—. *Military service:* British Army, King's Royal Rifle Corps, 1943-46; became lieutenant. *Member:* Society of London Art Dealers (vice-chairman, 1980), Royal Solent Yacht Club, Hurlingham Club, Boodles Club. *Awards, honors:* Mitchell Prize for history of art, 1978, for *The Paintings of J.M.W. Turner.*

WRITINGS: (With Martin Butlin) *The Paintings of J.M.W. Turner,* Yale University Press, 1977. Contributor of articles and reviews to magazines and newspapers, including *Apollo, Burlington Magazine,* and *Master Drawings.* Member of editorial board of bi-annual journal, *Turner Studies,* 1980—.

WORK IN PROGRESS: A catalogue raisonne of the works of John Robert Cozens, 1752-97; a study of Victorian collector Henry Vaughan.

SIDELIGHTS: Joll wrote: "I think I am probably a one-book man. I was attracted to Turner out of enormous admiration and the fact that my firm has specialized in his work and has been the leading dealer in Turner since at least 1863. I was born and lived for many years in Turner's home on 64 Harley Street, although the numbers have been changed since his day."

JONES, David Rhodes 1932-

PERSONAL: Born September 13, 1932, in Connellsville, Pa.; son of David Rhodes (a civil engineer) and Ruth Elizabeth (a teacher; maiden name, Dillon) Jones; married Mary Lee Lauffer, October 8, 1955; children: Elizabeth Lee. *Education:* Pennsylvania State University, B.A., 1954; New York University, M.A., 1961. *Religion:* Presbyterian. *Office: New York Times,* 229 West 43rd St., New York, N.Y. 10036.

CAREER: Wall Street Journal, New York City, reporter, 1957-61, chief of Pittsburgh bureau, 1961-63; *New York Times,* New York City, Detroit correspondent, 1963-65, national labor reporter, 1965-68, assistant national editor, 1969-72, national editor, 1972—. *Military service:* U.S. Air Force, 1955-57; became first lieutenant. *Member:* Sigma Delta Chi, Tau Kappa Epsilon.

WRITINGS: (Editor with Gene Roberts) *Assignment America: A Collection of Outstanding Writing From the "New York Times,"* Quadrangle, 1974.

*   *   *

JONES, Leon 1936-

PERSONAL: Born December 26, 1936, in Vincent, Ark.; son of Lander Corbin (a farmer) and Una Bell (an elementary school teacher; maiden name, Lewis) Jones; married Bobbie Jean Washington (a teacher and reading specialist), December 23, 1965; children: Stephanie Ruth, Gloria Jean. *Education:* University of Arkansas, Pine Bluff, B.S., 1963; University of Massachusetts, Ed. D., 1971. *Politics:* Independent. *Religion:* Baha'i Faith. *Home:* 3104 Castleleigh Rd., Silver Spring, Md. 20904. *Office:* School of Education, Howard University, 2400 Sixth St. N.W., Washington, D.C. 20059.

CAREER: U.S. Army Munition Command, Joliet, Ill., civilian mathematical statistician, 1963-64; Southern Illinois University, Carbondale, instructor in mathematics, 1965-66; International Harvester Co., Memphis, Tenn., time study engineer, 1966-68; evaluator of public schools in West Springfield, Mass., 1968-70; University of Massachusetts, Amherst, lecturer in education, 1970-71; Governors State University, Park Forest South, Ill., coordinator of research and evaluation and professor, 1971-72, assistant dean of College of Human Learning and Development, 1972; Howard University, Washington, D.C., associate professor, 1972-78, professor of education, 1978—, assistant to vice-president for academic affairs, 1972-73, director of Center for Educational Research and Development, 1974-76. Summer intern at U.S. Senate, 1977-78, and U.S. House of Representatives, 1978-79. Coordinator of workshops; chairman of symposia. *Military service:* U.S. Navy, aviation storekeeper, 1958-61; became petty officer second class. *Member:* American Association of University Professors. *Awards, honors:* Ford Foundation grant, 1975-76.

WRITINGS: (Contributor) Ralph W. Colvin and Esther Zaffiro, editors, *Preschool Education: A Handbook for the Training of Early Childhood Educators,* Springer Publishing, 1974; *From Brown to Boston: Desegregation in Education, 1954-1974,* Scarecrow, 1979. Contributor to education and sociology journals and *Trend* magazine.

SIDELIGHTS: Jones commented: "I am particularly interested in the ills of desegregated schooling for blacks during the post-Bakke era. I am presently embroiled in a racial discrimination suit against the Columbus School of Law at the Catholic University of America, Washington, D.C.

"In 1977, I enrolled as an evening law student—the class of 1981. Consistent with the ABA requirements, the Columbus School of Law uses an anonymous grading system. My contracts professor knowingly, willingly, and purposely breached my anonymity. By his own admission he knew that as he scored exam number 195, he was scoring Leon Jones's paper. Consequently, he gave me the lowest failing grade possible. Because of my academic experience I knew that I had not failed the exam. In my efforts to discuss this matter with the professor, he was quick to say to me: 'Why, you can't hack it? Why are you going to law school? There are plenty of other things that you can do and make more money than lawyers make. After a brief pause, he said: 'You treated all of the questions but your writing was so disorganized that I couldn't give you many points.'

"As associate dean of the law school, my contracts professor violated the school's policy by excluding me from law school when my cumulative grades (including the five credit hour contracts failure) warranted academic probation, not exclusion. Pursuant to my petition for readmission, my contracts professor and associate dean denied me my 'due process' by not disqualifying himself as chairman of the Readmission Committee and denying me the opportunity to appear before that Committee. Suffice it to say that as chairman he was successful in persuading the Law School faculty to deny me readmission.

"In returning to the failing grade matter, the University Senate determined that my grade should have been *B* as my paper was academically superior to some forty of my fifty-seven classmates. The University Senate changed my contracts grade to 'Pass.'

"I submitted a second admission's petition the next semester. I filed suit in the District Court also. Three days after my suit was filed, I was readmitted to the law school. After having been excluded for a full academic year, I return to law school as a 'marked student.' By the end of my third year I remained the victim of retaliation with respect to my grades. Blacks and other minorities are common recipient's of low and failing grades doled out as a result of professorial subjectivity as racism continues to run rampant throughout the Law School. Following the 1977-78 term, blacks constituted 100 percent of the students excluded as a result of academic deficiency. I was a part of those statistics. Whereas blacks constituted 71 percent of the fourteen students excluded due to academic deficiency following the end of the 1978-79 term, minorities made up 86 percent of the number of students excluded. Blacks constitute merely 11 percent of the law school of eight-hundred students.

"So pervasive is the academic climate here at the Columbus School of Law that in its April 25, 1980, issue, the *National Catholic Reporter* featured a front page story: "Are Law Schools Failing Minorities?" The essence of this article typifies my views about the short term ills of *Bakke.* For example, minority students trying to enter—or remain in—professional schools are fighting battles on two fronts: the aftermath of the still-unresolved *Bakke* decision and the problems that face all minority students in predominantly white institutions. The combined results of these problems have meant that black enrollment has fallen at an embarrassing rate in the nation's professional schools. The most telling result of the second battle—trying to survive in white institutions—is that they don't.

"The National Black American Law Student Association is aware of at least seven suits similar to mine that are in progress against some of the nation's most prestigious law schools. The executive director of the NAACP, Roy Wilkins, in his foreword to my book, states: 'Mr. Jones has performed a remarkable service in bringing writings on the aftermath of the 1954 Supreme Court decision together in one place so that the reader can better grasp how it came about, how the nation reacted, and, after all this time, how far we still have to go.'

"In view of the foregoing, I see ramifications of the Supreme Court's *Bakke* decision as the basis for my next book."

* * *

JONES, Michael Owen 1942-

PERSONAL: Born October 11, 1942, in Wichita, Kan.; son of Woodrow Owen (a farmer and tool designer) and Anne Elizabeth (a teacher; maiden name, Blackford) Jones; married Jane Dicker (in real estate sales), August 1, 1964; children: David Owen. *Education:* University of Kansas, B.A. (history, international relations, and art), 1964; Indiana University, M.A. (folklore), 1966, Ph.D. (folklore and American studies), 1970. *Residence:* Los Angeles, Calif. *Office:* Department of Folklore and Mythology, University of California, 405 Hilgard, Los Angeles, Calif. 90024.

CAREER: University of California, Los Angeles, assistant professor, 1968-75, associate professor of history and folklore, 1975—. Member of board of directors of Liberty Assembly Folk Dance Ensemble. *Member:* American Folklore Society, American Studies Association, Popular Culture Association, California Folklore Society. *Awards, honors:* Woodrow Wilson fellowship, 1967.

WRITINGS: Why Faith Healing?, National Museums of Canada, 1972; *The Handmade Object and Its Maker,* University of California Press, 1975; (with Robert A. Georges) *People Studying People: The Human Element in Fieldwork,* University of California Press, 1980. Contributor to *Whole Earth Catalogue.* Contributor of about sixty articles and reviews to history, folklore, and popular culture journals. Member of editorial board of *Western Folklore.*

WORK IN PROGRESS: Editing a book of essays on foodways in America, publication by California Folklore Society expected in 1980; research on the relationship of folkloristics to management, especially industrial relations, arts, management, and marketing (both advertising and consumer behavior research).

SIDELIGHTS: Jones commented to *CA:* "That I have degrees in five different fields of study should suggest a basic preoccupation of mine: to familiarize myself with the major considerations in several disciplines in order to take an interdisciplinary approach to a topic (whether art, eating behavior, belief, working, or research methods). The goal ultimately is to develop a 'transdisciplinary' orientation. For example, *People Studying People* examines the process involved when the technique of fieldwork is employed, regardless of the disciplinary identity of the researcher. Hence, illustrative material is drawn from the writings of folklorists, anthropologists, sociologists, psychologists, linguists, and social psychologists. The book has been used by people with these identities as well as by historians, geographers, dance ethnologists, art historians, students of organizational behavior, management consultants, and journalists."

* * *

JONES, Miriam
See SCHUCHMAN, Joan

JONES, Roger (Winston) 1939-

PERSONAL: Born in 1939 in Maidenhead, England; married. *Education:* Attended Jesus College, Oxford, 1963-73. *Home:* Bryn Clettwr, Pontshaen, Llandysul, Dyfed, Wales.

CAREER: Teacher of English as a foreign language in London, England, Oxford, England, and in Athens, Greece; furniture restorer; writer. *Member:* Royal Geographic Society (fellow).

WRITINGS: A Hard Day at the Holy Office (novel), W. H. Allen, 1969; *Programmed English,* Stillit Books, 1970; *The Rescue of Emin Pasha* (history), Allison & Busby, 1972. Contributor of stories, poems, and reviews to journals, including science fiction magazines.

WORK IN PROGRESS: A biographical dictionary of travelers and explorers; a historical novel, set in Carinthia in 1241.

* * *

JONES, Zelda
See SCHUCHMAN, Joan

* * *

JOSS, John 1934-

PERSONAL: Born June 4, 1934, in Weybridge, England; came to the United States in 1956, naturalized citizen, 1962; son of John and Angela Margaret Josephine (Cooper) Joss; married Rosa Maria Ruiz Zuniga (a graphic designer), April 23, 1960; children: Diana, Lisa, Alexandra. *Education:* Attended Royal Naval College, 1950-52. *Politics:* Conservative. *Religion:* Roman Catholic. *Home:* 12201 Colina Dr., Los Altos Hills, Calif. 94022. *Office address:* P.O. Box 960, Los Altos, Calif. 94022.

CAREER: Varian Associates, Palo Alto, Calif., field engineer, 1961-63; Microwave Electronics Corp., Palo Alto, in marketing communications, 1963-65; Philco-Ford, Palo Alto, marketing manager, 1965-67; Computer Usage Corp., Palo Alto, marketing manager, 1967-69; writer, 1969—. Creator of "Technology Update," a radio series broadcast by KPEN-FM in San Francisco, Calif., 1979—. *Military service:* Royal Navy, 1950-54. *Member:* Soaring Society of America (life member). *Awards, honors:* Lincoln Award from Soaring Society of America, 1979, for *Sierra Sierra.*

WRITINGS: (Editor) *Advanced Soaring,* Soaring Press, 1977; (editor) *Soarsierra,* Soaring Press, 1977; (editor) *Soaramerica,* Soaring Press, 1978; *Sierra Sierra* (novel), Morrow, 1978. Also author of novels, *Simia,* 1979, *Janus,* 1980, *Harpy,* 1981, and *Immortal,* 1981. Writer for television shows, including "Ironside."

WORK IN PROGRESS: Decca; The Men Who Invented the Twenty-First Century; Brain Versus Body.

SIDELIGHTS: Joss told *CA:* "In *Sierra Sierra,* an ex-marine fighter pilot, who watched his lead being killed in Vietnam, flies a pressurized sailplane to double world records. In *Simia,* a British anthropologist and American special-effects man, both ruined professionally, create an international scientific hoax by training an actress as a missing link simian discovered in Australia. In *Harpy,* a business school student programs a computer to create a list of elite, rich men, hires an investigator to study the backgrounds of three, then recreates herself as the 'ideal woman' for each, to compromise and blackmail them. In *Immortal,* a scientist isolates a blood enzyme that is the basis for a new drug that will retard or reverse aging. His sponsor is a woman, head of a cosmetics firm, who establishes 'health spas' on the United

States-Mexico border and in Africa and southeast Asia to take in thousands of 'faceless-nameless' men and women, use their blood as a source for a profitable new drug-cosmetic line that promises immortality. And in *Janus*, the protagonists from *Sierra Sierra* attempt to reproduce the Lindbergh flight in a powered two-seat airplane: a man and a woman versus the Atlantic Ocean and recalcitrant technology.''

Joss also describes his nonfiction: "*Decca* is the story of the U.S.-invented, U.K.-implemented, electronic navigation system that became the world standard despite technical/political complications. *The Men Who Invented the Twenty-First Century* contains interviews and prognostications of world technology leaders in every key area of human existence. *Brain Versus Body* is a humorous dialogue between intellect and emotions in an adversary relationship, within a man engaged in the full spectrum of living.''

He added: "The decline in reading and the current disdain for quality writing is a severe threat to the written form of communication, despite the uniquely valuable character of reading. The often crass commercialism in books, television, films, and other communications forms militates against quality in writing, in ideas, in human behavior itself. Integrity in human behavior seems to become rarer, exploitation the rule, and expediency convenient. We need inner quality in people and in their writing as never before.

"In writing, as in many of the arts, many are called but few are chosen. I claim to be a writer, and have over seven hundred credits from twenty years of work in fiction and nonfiction, in films and television, in short stories and poetry, in radio broadcasting, in virtually every form of spoken and written communications. Yet, like thousands of my peers, I cannot claim more than marginal success from an artistic standpoint, and much less from the standpoint of making a living. The only solution, for a writer, is to do the best work he or she can, and hope that the lightning of visibility will strike and make his or her work accessible to wide audiences. I remain an optimist, despite evidence that writing is not a realistic profession for a sane person.''

*   *   *

JUENGER, Ernst   1895-

PERSONAL: Born March 29, 1895, in Heidelberg, Germany (now West Germany); son of Ernst (a chemist and pharmacist) and Lily (Lampl) Juenger; married Gretha von Jeinsen, August 3, 1925 (died, 1960); married Liselotte Baeuerle, March 3, 1962; children: Ernestel (died November, 1944), Alexander J. *Education:* Attended University of Leipzig, 1923-25. *Home:* D7945, Langenenslingen/Wilflingen 60, West Germany.

CAREER: Writer. *Military service:* German Army, 1919-23; became captain; wounded fourteen times; received Pour le merite. Also served with German Army, 1939-44. *Awards, honors:* Literary awards from cities of Bremen and Goslar, West Germany, both 1956; Grand Cross of Merit, 1959; Culture Award from Federation of German Industries, 1960; Immermann Award of Dusseldorf, 1965; Freiherr von Stein Gold Medal, 1970; Schiller Gedaechtnispreis, 1974; Star of the Grand Cross of Merit from Federal Republic of Germany, 1977; Golden Eagle from city of Nice, 1978.

WRITINGS—In English: *In Stahlgewittern: Aus dem Tagebuch eines Strosstruppfuehrers* (personal narrative), E. S. Mittler & Sohn, 1922, published as *In Stahlgewittern: Ein Kriegstagbuch*, [Hamburg, Germany], 1934, translation by Basil Creighton published as *Storm of Steel: From the Diary of a German Storm-Troop Officer on the Western Front*, Doubleday, 1929, reprinted, H. Fertig, 1975; *Das Waeldchen 125: Eine Chronik aus den Grabenkaempfen 1918* (personal narrative), E. S. Mittler & Sohn, 1929, translation by Creighton published as *Copse One Hundred Twenty-Five: A Chronicle From the Trench Warfare of 1918*, Chatto & Windus, 1930; *Afrikanische Spiele* (personal narrative), Hanseatische Verlagsanstalt, 1936, reprinted, E. Klett, 1965, translation by Stuart Hood published as *African Diversions*, 1954; *Auf den Marmorklippen* (novel), De lage Landen, 1942, translation by Hood published as *On the Marble Cliffs*, New Directions, 1947, reprinted, Penguin, 1970; *Der Friede: Ein Wort an die Jugend Europas, ein Wort an die Jugend der Welt* (essay), [West Germany], 1945, translation by Hood published as *The Peace*, Regnery, 1948; *Glaeserne Beinen* (novel), E. Klett, 1957, translation by Louise Bogan and Elizabeth Mayer published as *The Glass Bees*, Noonsday Press, 1961.

In German; history: *Der Kampf als inneres Erlebnis*, E. S. Mittler & Sohn, 1936; *Feuer und Blut: Ein kleiner Ausschnitt aus einer grossen Schlacht*, Hanseatische Verlagsanstalt, 1941; *Gaerten und Strassen: Aus den Tagebuechen von 1939 und 1940* (personal narrative), E. S. Mittler & Sohn, 1942; (with Armin Mohler) *Die Schleife: Dokumente zum Weg*, Verlag der Arche, 1955; *Jahre der Okkupation* (personal narrative; title means "Years of Occupation"), E. Klett, 1958.

Travel: *Atlantische Fahrt*, Verlag der Arche, 1948; *Ein Inselfruehling: Ein Tagebuch aus Rhodes*, Verlag der Arche, 1948; *Myrdun: Briefe aus Norwegen*, Verlag der Arche, 1948, reprinted, E. Klett, 1975; *Am Kieselstrand*, V. Klostermann, 1951; *Am Sarazenenturm*, V. Klostermann, 1955, 2nd edition, 1955; *Zwei Inseln: Formosa, Ceylon*, Olten, 1968. Also author of travel books, *Dalmatinischer Aufenthalt*, 1934, *Aus der goldenen Muschel*, 1948, *Serpentara*, 1957, and *San Pietro*, 1957.

Essays: *Der Arbeiter: Herrschaft und Gestalt*, Hanseatische Verlagsanstalt, 1932; *Blaetter und Steine* (title means "Leaves and Stones"), Hanseatische Verlagsanstalt, 1934; *Geheimnisse der Sprache: Zwei Essays*, Hanseatische Verlagsanstalt, 1939, reprinted, V. Klostermann, 1963; *Der Waldgang*, V. Klostermann, 1952; *Der gordische Knoten*, V. Klostermann, 1953; *Das Sanduhrbuch*, V. Klostermann, 1954; *Ueber die Linie* (title means "Across the Line"), V. Klostermann, 1958; *An der Zeitmauer* (title means "At the Time Barrier"), E. Klett, 1959; *Der Weltstaat: Organismus und Organisation*, E. Klett, 1960; *Essays*, E. Klett, 1960; *Sgraffiti*, E. Klett, 1960; *Typus, Name, Gestalt*, E. Klett, 1963; *Grenzgaenge: Essays, Reden, Traeume*, E. Klett, 1966; *Zahlen und Goette, Philemon und Baucis: Zwei Essays*, E. Klett, 1974; (with Wolf Jobst Sieder) *Baeume: Gedichte und Bilder*, Propylaeen Verlag, 1975.

Other: *Das abenteuerliche Herz: Aufzeichnungen bei Tag und Nacht*, Frundsberg Verlag, 1929, published as *Das abenteuerliche Herz: Figuren und Capriccios*, E. Rentsch, 1942; *Luftfahrt ist not!*, W. Andermann, 1930; *Sprache und Koerperbau*, Verlag der Arche, 1947; *Heliopolis: Rueckblick auf eine Stadt* (novel), Heliopolis Verlag, 1949; *Strahlungen* (personal narrative; title means "Radiation"), Heliopolis Verlag, 1949, three-volume edition, Deutscher Taschenbuch Verlag, 1964.

Besuch auf Godenholm (stories; title means "Visit in Godenholm"), V. Klostermann, 1952; *Capriccios: Eine Auswahl*, Reclam Verlag, 1956; (compiler with Klaus Ulrich Leistikow) *Mantrana: Ein Spiel*, E. Klett, c. 1959; *Erzaehlende Schriften*, E. Klett, 1960; *Werke* (title means "Works"), ten volumes, E. Klett, 1960; *Subtile Jagden* (memoirs; title means "Subtle Fighter"), E. Klett, 1967.

Ad hoc, E. Klett, 1970; *Annaeherungen: Drogen und Rausch,* E. Klett, 1970; *Sinn und Bedeutung: Ein Figurenspiel,* E. Klett, 1971; *Die Zwille* (semi-autobiographical; title means "The Slingshot"), E. Klett, 1973; *Ausgewaehlte Erzaehlungen,* E. Klett, 1975; (with Alfred Kubin) *Eine Begegnung* (correspondences), Propylaeen Verlag, 1975. Also author of collected works, *Saemtliche Werke,* eighteen volumes, 1978.

Editor: *Die Unvergessenen,* W. Andermann, 1928; *Das anlitz des Weltkrieges,* Neufeld & Henius, 1930; *Der Kampf und das Reich,* Rhein & Ruhr, c. 1930; Franz Schauwecker, *Der feurige Weg,* Frundsberg Verlag, 1930; *Krieg und Krieger,* Junker & Duennhaupt, 1930; Antoine Rivarol, *Rivarol,* V. Klostermann, 1956.

SIDELIGHTS: As a young man, Ernst Juenger was fascinated by warfare and the military life. His longing to experience battle first-hand asserted itself when, at the age of sixteen, he ran away from home to join the French Foreign Legion. Juenger's father did not share the boy's enthusiasm, however, and with the help of the authorities, located and returned his errant son to his home. But the boy's dreams of glory did not die, for when World War I erupted he immediately enlisted in the German Army. Juenger distinguished himself on the Western Front, receiving Germany's highest military honor, and was wounded fourteen times. From his World War I experiences came his first book, translated into English as *Storm of Steel,* based on the diaries he kept at the time.

In his introduction to Juenger's *Storm of Steel,* R. H. Mottram asserted that the work was all the more profound and meaningful because the author did not shy away from depicting events and feelings exactly as they occurred, censoring nothing. Mottram's description of Juenger reveals much of the tone of the work: "He was no middle-aged civilian, unwillingly taking up arms and finding all his worst preconceptions abundantly fulfilled. He was nearly as good a specimen as ever worshipped Mars [the Roman god of war], and to what did he come? To that unescapable doom that brings to meet violence precisely such resistance as shall cancel and annul it." Mottram concluded that "on this point the strength and finality of the testimony cannot be missed."

Juenger does not apologize in *Storm of Steel* for the bloodshed and violence of warfare, but rather revels in the glories of battle. As he wrote in his book: "War means the destruction of the enemy without scruple and by any means. War is the harshest of all trades, and the masters of it can only entertain humane feelings as long as they do no harm." The book was praised across the United States as a significant and revealing insight into the mind of a German officer. A reviewer for *New Statesman* declared: "Herr Juenger has a remarkable gift for describing certain emotions, complex and hard of analysis, which beset, and still have power to bewilder, the man of even average sensibility who was brought by war into abrupt contact with the most primitive of human experiences."

In addition to recommending it to the general public, several reviewers felt *Storm of Steel* to be an imperative book for pacifists to read and study. As F. Van de Water of the *New York Evening Post* observed, the book "presents a view of battle not generally recognized, yet too logical to be overlooked." A reviewer for *Spectator* also advised pacifists to heed "this fine book": "It is even better propaganda than [Erich M. Remarque's] All Quiet on the Western Front, for there is a certain horrible lure in the completeness of that work of genius, whereas this is a ghastly, gripping story whose truth and whose horror stand out all the plainer for the author's psychic blindness."

After the war Juenger attended the University of Leipzig where he studied both philosophy and zoology, becoming interested particularly in entomology, the study of insects. Numerous reviewers, in fact, attribute his probing and analytical approach in writing to his university training in the sciences. It was at this time that he first became politically active and participated in radical organizations. His political doctrine, described as "militant nihilism" or "aggressive totalitarianism," maintained that a democracy of all the people could never retain order in the world. He looked forward to the rise of the new "Federation" and the coming of the new man, an industrial individual who would take responsibility to restore order to the chaotic world. He expounded these ideas in his 1932 work, *Der Arbeiter,* or "The Worker."

When Hitler came to power, Juenger dropped out of the political scene due to his disillusionment with the Nazi party. Although they too were striving for totalitarianism, he felt that their interpretation was a mockery of the "true system" he advocated. With this in mind, he wrote *On the Marble Cliffs,* an allegorical novel based on Nazi practices, in 1939. A major turning point in his literary career, he first encompassed in this work a more humanistic and, some insist, an almost Christian point of view.

On the Marble Cliffs depicts the annihilation of a peaceful and gentle country by "barbarian hordes." Quickly recognized as anti-Nazi when released to English-speaking audiences, the book miraculously escaped the censor's eye when published in Germany in 1942. By the time the German government realized the novel's true meaning and halted further publication, tens of thousands of copies were already in circulation. Juenger's honor was not seriously questioned, however, for he was loyally serving with the German Army at the time.

"It is an anti-Nazi document," declared Louis Claire, "but it is also one of the most beautiful novels of imagination of modern Germany, an allegory in the grand symbolist manner of the death of a civilization." Alfred Werner of the *New York Times* also praised the work, but complained that "despite its poetical merits and its unmistakable challenge to Hitlerism, [*On the Marble Cliffs*] fails to uplift the reader because of its impotent hopelessness." A reviewer for *New Yorker,* on the other hand, claimed that "Mr. Juenger's allegory, which is full of the same sort of hobgoblinism that the Nazis themselves went in for—skulls, torches, midnight revels, and so on—is so murky that most readers are likely to miss the point."

Continuing in his new trend toward humanism, Juenger wrote *The Peace* during the last years of World War II. Dedicated to the memory of his son, Ernestel, who was killed in action in 1944, the work is an acknowledgement of Germany's guilt and a plea for world peace to end the senseless sacrifice of human life. Although still totalitarian in spirit, Juenger called for a renunciation of nationalism and the affirmation of the individual. Erik von Kuehnelt-Leddihn of *Catholic World* assessed that *The Peace* "is not only a highly prophetic piece of writing in the finest literary style . . . but it is also a blueprint for the sound peace which should have followed this terrible massacre."

Juenger employed a fantastic and dream-like style of writing in his next book, released in English translation as *The Glass Bees.* This allegorical novel tells of a former cavalryman, Captain Richard, who must perform extensive feats of strength and endurance in the magical garden of Zapparoni, a political dictator, in order to secure employment. The garden is filled with thousands of glass bees, tiny mechanized robots able to lay waste to all civilization if summoned. According to E. S. Pisko of the *Christian Science Monitor,* the glass bees symbolize "the destruction Juenger sees modern technology wreaking upon human society." T. W. Woodland, moreover, suggested that "Juenger is concerned here once more with the problems of man in the bleak surroundings of a modern industrial society where, after two world wars, all values have been destroyed and words have lost their former meaning." Woodland summarized that "Juenger's message is anything but hopeful."

Siegfried Mandel of the *New York Times Book Review* commended the novel as "harrowing and thought-disturbing," asserting that it "contributes not only to prophetic and nihilistic literature but also to an understanding of the inner and outer forces that shape many a man's attitude toward tyranny." But F. J. Warnke was unimpressed: "Ultimately it is unsatisfying, even as a novella, for its basic action . . . never receives satisfactory resolution, and the philosophical implications of the fantasy are never worked out with . . . completeness or profundity." On the other hand, Phoebe Adams declared *The Glass Bees* a "fantastic, tightly compressed novel . . . a wonderfully provocative and successful fusion of fiction and philosophy."

BIOGRAPHICAL/CRITICAL SOURCES: Ernst Juenger, *Storm of Steel: From the Diary of a German Storm-Troop Officer on the Western Front,* Doubleday, 1929, reprinted, H. Fertig, 1975; *Spectator,* June 22, 1929; *New Statesman,* August 17, 1929; *New York Evening Post,* September 28, 1929; *German Life and Letters,* 1947-48, 1950-51, 1958-59, 1959-60, 1960-61; *New Yorker,* March 20, 1948; *Nation,* March 27, 1948; *New York Times,* April 4, 1978; *Catholic World,* November, 1948; J. P. Stern, *Ernst Juenger,* Yale University Press, 1953; *Comparative Literature,* 1958; *New York Times Book Review,* February 19, 1961; *Christian Science Monitor,* March 2, 1961; *Atlantic Monthly,* May, 1961; *Yale Review,* June, 1961; *Texas Studies in Literature and Language,* winter, 1965.*

—*Sketch by Kathleen Ceton Newman*

*   *   *

JUNGER, Ernst
  See JUENGER, Ernst

K

KAHM, H(arold) S.
(Henry Sackerman)

PERSONAL: Born on the twenty-fourth of March, in the United States; son of Sigmund H. and Jeannette (Sackerman) Kahm. *Politics:* "Democrat mostly." *Religion:* "Deist." *Home and office:* 2008 Bryant Ave. S., Minneapolis, Minn. 55405.

CAREER: Writer. Instructor in writing at University of Minnesota, Minneapolis. Honorary member of board of directors of Young Adult Centers, Inc. *Member:* Midwest Travel Writers Association.

WRITINGS—All nonfiction: *Your Place in the Post-War World,* B. C. Forbes, 1943; *A Small Business of Your Own With Capital Investment From One Hundred to Two Thousand Dollars,* Knickerbocker, 1945; *Careers for Modern Women,* Knickerbocker, 1946; *You Can Be Successful and Follow the Golden Rule,* Wilcox & Follet, 1947; (with Melvin E. Wagner) *Basic Principles of American Business,* Prentice-Hall, 1950; *One Hundred and One Businesses You Can Start and Run With Less Than One Thousand Dollars,* Parker, 1968.

Under pseudonym Henry Sackerman; novels: *The Crowded Bed,* Sherbourne, 1967; *The Westbank Group,* Sherbourne, 1970; *The Love Bomb,* Bantam, 1972.

WORK IN PROGRESS: A novel.

SIDELIGHTS: Kahm wrote: "I have traveled aboard thirty-six passenger ships—to Europe, South America, Mexico, Alaska, Haiti, Bermuda, Hawaii, the Dutch Antilles, the Bahamas, and Hudson's Bay. I speak French, plus a smattering of Cantonese, German, Greek, and Spanish. I intensely dislike stuffed shirts and academic snobs. I was a friend of Ernest Hemingway, who taught me how to write; we were neighbors in Key West. I knew Gertrude Stein in Paris and many other great people. None of their greatness rubbed off on me, unfortunately."

*   *   *

KAHN, Arnold Dexter   1939-

PERSONAL: Born January 28, 1939, in Salt Lake City, Utah; son of Ralph M. and Adelaide E. Kahn; married Judith Ream (an interior designer), April 28, 1967; children: Jennifer, Julie, Amanda. *Education:* University of California, Los Angeles, B.A., 1961; University of California, Berkeley,

LL.B., 1964. *Home:* 13251 Ponderosa Dr., Los Angeles, Calif. 90049. *Office:* 1901 Avenue of the Stars, Suite 850, Los Angeles, Calif. 90067.

CAREER: Rosenthal & Green (attorneys), Los Angeles, Calif., associate, 1964-66; Mitchell, Silberberg & Knupp (attorneys), Los Angeles, associate, 1966-69; Irell & Manella (attorneys), Los Angeles, associate, 1969-72, partner, 1972—. *Member:* International Academy of Estate and Trust Law, American College of Probate Counsel (fellow).

WRITINGS: Family Security Through Estate Planning, McGraw, 1979.

*   *   *

KAHN, Judd   1940-

PERSONAL: Born June 24, 1940, in New York, N.Y.; son of Abraham (in business) and Miriam (a volunteer worker; maiden name, Diamond) Kahn; married Coppelia Huber (a professor), December 26, 1963; children: Gabriel. *Education:* Harvard University, A.B., 1962; University of California, Berkeley, M.A., 1963, Ph.D., 1971. *Religion:* Jewish. *Office:* School of Organization and Management, Yale University, Box 1-A, New Haven, Conn. 06520.

CAREER: Wesleyan University, Middletown, Conn., assistant professor, 1971-78; City of Hartford, Conn., humanist-in-residence, 1978-79; Yale University, New Haven, Conn., associate director of placement at School of Organization and Management, 1979-80. Member of Middletown Democratic Committee, 1978—.

WRITINGS: Imperial San Francisco: Politics and Planning in an American City, 1897-1906, University of Nebraska Press, 1980.

BIOGRAPHICAL/CRITICAL SOURCES: Hartford Advocate, June 20, 1979.

*   *   *

KAHN, Margaret   1949-

PERSONAL: Born April 9, 1949, in New York, N.Y.; daughter of Michael M. (a chemical engineer) and Eleanor (a library worker; maiden name, Eckles) Kahn; married Jared Bernstein (a psycholinguist), February 23, 1974; children: Jasmin Kahn. *Education:* Barnard College, A.B., 1971; University of Michigan, M.A., 1972, Ph.D., 1976. *Home:* 2450 Agnes Way, Palo Alto, Calif. 94303.

CAREER: Rezaiyeh Agricultural College, Rezaiyeh (now Urmieh), Iran, assistant professor of English, 1974-75; Heidelberg College, Tiffin, Ohio, special lecturer in linguistics, 1976; Boston University, Boston, Mass., lecturer in English as a second language, 1976; Tufts University, Medford, Mass., lecturer in anthropology, 1977; Alexandria University, Alexandria, Egypt, assistant professor of phonetics, 1978; speech processing technician, Tellesensory Systems, Inc., 1978—. *Member:* Authors Guild, Media Alliance of San Francisco.

WRITINGS: Borrowing and Variation in a Phonological Description of Kurdish, University of Michigan Phonetics Lab, Natural Language Series, 1976; *Children of the Jinn: In Search of the Kurds and Their Country,* Seaview Books, 1980. Contributor to *Harvard Encyclopedia of American Ethnic Groups.*

WORK IN PROGRESS: A novel about a twenty-year-old woman, set in New York during the 1960's.

SIDELIGHTS: Margaret Kahn told *CA:* "I had always planned to be a writer, but somehow my fascination with foreign languages and exotic cultures sidetracked me temporarily into an academic career (which nearly destroyed my writing style). I have studied French, Kurdish, Persian, Arabic, Turkish, and American Sign Language, but I write only in English. I wish there were a methodology for learning to write as accessible as ones for learning a foreign language. Universities and writers' conferences are not the answer. I am slowly learning to write, without pay or fellowships, in the solitude of a small room in my house."

* * *

KANDINSKY, Nina   1896(?)-1980

OBITUARY NOTICE: Born c. 1896; died September 3, 1980, in Gstaad, Switzerland. Author. Kandinsky was the widow of the abstract painter Wassily Kandinsky. After his death in 1944, she worked to promote his paintings, aided scholars interested in his work, and wrote a book about her life with the Russian artist, *Kandinsky and I.* She was apparently killed by a burglar who strangled her to death. Obituaries and other sources: *Newsweek,* September 15, 1980.

* * *

KARAPANOU, Margarita   1946-

PERSONAL: Born July 19, 1946, in Athens, Greece; daughter of George (a lawyer) and Margarita (a writer; maiden name, Liberaki) Karapanou. *Education:* Attended Sorbonne, University of Paris. *Politics:* Democrat. *Religion:* Orthodox. *Home:* Stratioticou Syndesmou 2, Athens, Greece T.T.136. *Agent:* Hy Cohen, 111 West 57th St., New York, N.Y. 10019.

CAREER: Writer. Worked as kindergarden teacher in Athens, Greece.

WRITINGS: Kassandra and the Wolf (novel), translated by Nick Germanakos, Harcourt, 1974.

WORK IN PROGRESS: A thriller novel.

SIDELIGHTS: Karapanou's novel, *Kassandra and the Wolf,* is the story of an over-indulged child who identifies with a wolf from fairy tales. Jerome Charyn described the child's environment as "a kind of netherworld where children are locked into sexual hysteria that transforms everything around them into a frightening, grotesque dreamscape." Much of the novel is written in an experimental style that blurs the distinctions between reality and fantasy. But

P. L. Adams rejected Kassandra's imaginings as "too clever." Adams wrote, "What goes on in this short novel must be taken largely as the muddled sexual fantasies of a small girl . . . but even as fantasy, it fails to convince." John Updike compared the novel to Bruno Schulz's story, "Spring": "One wonders if Schulz's example helped embolden . . . Karapanou," he mused. Updike characterized Karapanou's writing as "lyric ferocity."

Karapanou told *CA:* "I started writing bits and pieces with no intention of publishing, but the book sort of bloomed out by itself and became a novel. Nick Germanakos made a superb English translation and I sent it to Hy Cohen, now my literary agent. With his enthusiasm and his belief in the book, he made it all possible.

"Tony Godwin, editor at Harcourt, played a very important part in my career, too. His editing advice was a constant challenge to do better, to go further. And finally, my meeting with John Updike was extremely important. His intense appreciation of my work led me to consider writing as a profession, and to start a new novel. To these people, I owe my being as a writer. If I stress this point, it is because I believe that some people change our destiny, and that in some way we owe them our spiritual life, which is life itself.

"What I consider vital in the act of writing is that it is an act of love—of total fusion with the world. I always write 'for someone out there,' or for a very specific person. Then there is the writing itself: this terrible struggle to put into words the unsaid, and to transcend it into art. Writing, in a way, is an act of exorcism because of this effort to capture the here and now, having in mind this Hindu verse: 'What is here, is everywhere / What is not here, is nowhere.'

"My new novel is a thriller. A sort of 'apocalyptic' horror story, taking place on a Greek island. In it, there is no psychological study of characters and no motives. There is only a description of what people are at a given moment, and what they do. The whole book is a succession of images, of fragments in time, but all linked together through a very tight story. Curiosity made me choose the thriller form. 'What will happen next?' This question is for me the key question in all great novels. 'Once upon a time. . . . Something happened to someone. . . .' What I am trying to do now is to catch all the magic hidden in this apparently naive narrative form by writing as if somebody else was telling a story."

BIOGRAPHICAL/CRITICAL SOURCES: Atlantic Monthly, July, 1976; *New York Times Book Review,* July 25, 1976, September 9, 1979; *New Yorker,* August 2, 1976; *Contemporary Literary Criticism,* Volume 13, Gale, 1980.

* * *

KARMIN, Monroe William   1929-

PERSONAL: Born September 2, 1929, in Mineola, N.Y.; son of Stanley Albert and Phyllis Rae (Applebaum) Karmin; married Mayanne Sherman (a press secretary), October 30, 1955; children: Paul Nance, Betsy Anne. *Education:* University of Illinois, B.A., 1950; Columbia University, M.S., 1953. *Home:* 7011 Beechwood Dr., Chevy Chase, Md. 20015. *Office:* Knight-Ridder Newspapers, 1195 National Press Bldg., Washington, D.C. 20045.

CAREER/WRITINGS: Wall Street Journal, New York City, writer for bureaus in New York City and Washington, D.C., 1953-74; associated with House of Representatives Committee on Banking, Currency, and Housing, Washington, D.C., 1974-76; *Chicago Daily News,* Chicago, Ill., correspondent in Washington, D.C., 1977-78; Knight-Ridder Newspapers,

Washington, D.C., national economics correspondent, 1978—. Notable assignments include coverage of links between organized crime and the ruling class of merchant-politicians in the Bahama, known as "The Bay Street Boys." *Military service:* U.S. Air Force, 1951-52. *Member:* National Press Club, Sigma Delta Chi, Federal City Club. *Awards, honors:* Pulitzer Prize for national reporting, 1967, for exposure of infiltration of the Mafia into the Bahamas; distinguished service award from Sigma Delta Chi, 1967, for Bahama stories.

SIDELIGHTS: Karmin told *CA:* "Too many journalists think there are only three stories to cover: politics, foreign affairs, and scandal. Journalism is an educational process. The public should be educated on many topics, including economics, energy, consumer affairs, and the entire range of public interest topics."

* * *

KARR, Phyllis Ann   1944-

PERSONAL: Born July 25, 1944, in Oakland, Calif.; daughter of Frank Joseph (an educator) and Helena (an educator; maiden name, Beckmann) Karr. *Education:* Colorado State University, A.B., 1966; Indiana University, Bloomington, M.L.S., 1971. *Politics:* Independent. *Religion:* Roman Catholic. *Residence:* Rice Lake, Wis. *Agent:* Barbara Lowenstein, 250 West 57th St., New York, N.Y. 10019.

CAREER: East Chicago Public Library, Roxana Branch, East Chicago, Ind., branch librarian, 1967-70; Hamill & Barker Antiquarian Booksellers, Chicago, Ill., shop assistant, 1971; University of Louisville Library, Louisville, Ky., cataloguer, 1972-77; writer, 1977—. Volunteer reader and monitor for Recording for the Blind, Louisville, Ky.; member of Communiversity Band, Rice Lake, Wis. *Member:* International Wizard of Oz Club, Mystery Writers of America, Early English Text Society, D'Oyly Carte Opera Trust, Friends of the University of Michigan Gilbert and Sullivan Society, Phi Sigma Iota, Beta Phi Mu.

WRITINGS: My Lady Quixote, Fawcett, 1980; *Frostflower and Thorn,* Berkley, 1980; *Lady Susan,* Everest House, 1980; *Meadow Song,* Fawcett, in press. Author of column, "Thoughts From Oakapple Place," appearing in *GASBAG,* 1970—. Assistant editor of *Fantasy and Terror,* 1975-76.

WORK IN PROGRESS: A sequel to *Frostflower and Thorn; An Arthurian Handbook;* a Regency novel, tentatively titled *Friendship's Sacrifice,* for Fawcett.

SIDELIGHTS: Karr told *CA:* "The first goal of fiction is to entertain. True entertainment is difficult unless there is also some philosophic or other thought-provoking content, but the first duty of the fiction crafter is to tell a story on a clear, coherent level, readily comprehensible to the reader. I think fiction took a wrong turn when the 'literary' authors like James Joyce became a separate breed from the 'popular' authors of fiction. Cervantes, Dickens, and others are great because they have both a popular and a critical appeal, even though the popular may have come first and only been followed later by the critical. The best style is the invisible style, though there are exceptions. I, personally, write because it is an inner need to maintain my balance. Fiction satisfies the need better than nonfiction and is also easier to write, as a rule.

"I can translate from non-technical French, Russian, and Middle English (from verse into verse in the latter) and hope someday to add Polish and maybe Latin. But translation seems an even harder field to break into than original composition. My biggest break to date in getting paid for my writing was the good fortune of obtaining an agent."

* * *

KARRASS, Chester L.   1923-

PERSONAL: Born June 14, 1923, in Brooklyn, N.Y.; son of Jack and Minnie (Reiss) Karrass; married Virginia Zappala (a psychotherapist), August 27, 1949; children: Lynn, Gary. *Education:* University of Colorado, B.E.; Columbia University, M.S.; University of Southern California, D.B.A. *Home and office:* 10686 Somma Way, Los Angeles, Calif. 90024.

CAREER: Karrass Negotiating, Management, and Sales, Inc., Los Angeles, Calif., president, 1970—.

WRITINGS: The Negotiating Game, Crowell, 1970; *Give and Take,* Crowell, 1974; *How to Fight a Price Increase,* Karrass International, 1979; (with William Glasser) *Both Win Management,* Harper, 1980.

BIOGRAPHICAL/CRITICAL SOURCES: New York Times, November 18, 1970.

* * *

KARSAVINA, Jean (Faterson)   1908-

PERSONAL: Surname is accented on second syllable; born February 23, 1908, in Warsaw, Poland; daughter of Adam (in business and banking) and Regina (a pianist; maiden name, Segal) Faterson; married Paul L. Karsavina, 1928 (divorced); married Monroe Schere (a writer), May 1, 1966. *Education:* Attended Smith College, 1924-26; Barnard College, B.A., 1927. *Residence:* New York, N.Y. *Agent:* Knox Burger Associates Ltd., 39½ Washington Square S., New York, N.Y. 10012.

CAREER: Free-lance writer, 1935—. Member of faculty at New York University, 1948-49. *Member:* Authors Guild, Writers Guild of America. *Awards, honors:* Fiction awards include award from Child Study Association, 1946, for *Reunion in Poland;* prize from Jewish Book Council, 1974, for *White Eagle, Dark Skies.*

WRITINGS: Reunion in Poland (juvenile), New World Books, 1946; *Tree by the Waters,* New World Books, 1948; *Polish Cookery,* Crown, 1958; *White Eagle, Dark Skies,* Scribner, 1974. Also translator of Leo Tolstoi's *War and Peace,* published by Bantam.

Opera librettos: *Duenna* (adaptation; first performed in New York, N.Y., at Lemonade Opera, 1948), Am-Rus Music Agency, 1948; (with Lukas Foss) *Jumping Frog of Calaveras County* (first performed at After-Dinner Opera Company, 1950), Carl Fischer, 1951; "Pique Dame" (adaptation from Tchaikovsky), first broadcast by NCB-TV, 1952. Ghost writer. Contributor of about two hundred stories to magazines, including *New York, New World Review,* and *Metropolis.* Editor of *Soviet Review* and *Problems of Soviet Literature,* 1958-65, and *Reprints From the Soviet Press,* 1965—.

WORK IN PROGRESS: A novel about Napoleon in Poland, "when for the only time in his life he was genuinely and profoundly in love"; research for a novel set in an obscure part of the Bahamas during the eighteenth century, with husband, Monroe Schere.

SIDELIGHTS: Jean Karsavina told *CA:* "Born in Warsaw and brought up in Lodz, Poland, in Moscow, and then in New York, with summers spent in France, Germany, and England—and with a dragon of a French governess in the bargain—my background, like the four languages in which I continue to be fluent, is a mixture of cultures and antecedents. It has been fun, but with my roots sunk as deeply in Poland as here in the United States I am a foreigner everywhere as much as an *habitue,* and no where is totally home to me. To put it differently, I belong everywhere yet everywhere I am also an alien: clearly not a good climate for a writer to thrive in.

"The problem doesn't really exist so long as one writes for hire, taking on any assignment—what I call literary carpentry—in order to eat (and far be it from me to knock that!). Alienation hits hard, though, when one writes about what one really knows only to discover that what one knows is, in turn, alien to editors and critics—though not necessarily to the reading public, once one does break through.

"All this I began to feel more and more keenly after World War II, during which time my mother, and my whole childhood world with her, seemed to vanish into the maw of the Nazi invasion of Poland. To fight off the lostness, I finally began *White Eagle, Dark Skies,* not caring whether it would find a publisher or not. *White Eagle* is my own family saga, and in it I tried to recreate my parents and their early impassioned involvement with Poland's independence movement at the turn of the century. The drive behind the book was not only to understand those long-gone figures but to reaffirm the very existence of a world no longer there, to reassert the roots I had almost grown to believe I'd invented.

"The ploy worked. I was lucky. The first publisher who saw the manuscript took it. Later, the interest the book evoked in Poland led to an invitation to visit the city of my birth. And so, through a series of hard-to-imagine, dramatic coincidences, I rediscovered half a dozen 'real-life' relatives, childhood friends with whom an old closeness was quickly and joyously reestablished. So—new strength from the old roots. And while it may be rather late in life for me, the experience has brought on a fresh spurt of creativity. I am now trying to make up for lost time."

*　　*　　*

KAUFMANN, Walter 1921-1980

OBITUARY NOTICE—See index for *CA* sketch: Born July 1, 1921, in Freiburg, Germany; died of a ruptured aorta in 1980 in Princeton, N.J. Educator and author. Kaufmann was a professor of philosophy at Princeton University and wrote a number of books in his field, including *Nietzsche, Critique of Religion and Philosophy,* and *Existentialism From Dostoevsky to Sartre.* Obituaries and other sources: *Time,* September 15, 1980.

*　　*　　*

KAYE, Harvey E(arle) 1927-

PERSONAL: Born April 13, 1927, in New York, N.Y.; son of Jack and Peggy Kaye; married Diane Leslee (a fashion consultant), April 19, 1958; children: Stephen, Julie. *Education:* Syracuse University, A.B., 1948; New York Medical College, M.D., 1952. *Office:* 16 East 80th St., New York, N.Y. 10021.

CAREER: Private practice in psychiatry in New York, N.Y., 1956—. Assistant clinical professor and supervising psychoanalyst at New York Medical College, 1962—. *Military service:* U.S. Navy, 1945-46. *Member:* American Psychiatric Association, American Academy of Psychoanalysis, American Medical Association.

WRITINGS: Male Survival, Grosset, 1974; *Die Mannergrage,* Albert Muller Verlag, 1976; *Man en Mythe,* Mens & Maatschij, 1978.

WORK IN PROGRESS: Research on homosexuality and on executive stress.

*　　*　　*

KEASEY, Carol Tomlinson
See TOMLINSON-KEASEY, Carol

*　　*　　*

KEATING, Diane 1940-

PERSONAL: Born July 20, 1940, in Winnipeg, Manitoba, Canada; daughter of Ernest S. (a teacher) and Muriel (a teacher; maiden name, Dudley) Heys; married Christopher Keating (in business), August 13, 1967; children: Stephanie, Justin. *Education:* University of Manitoba, B.A., 1962. *Politics:* None. *Religion:* None. *Home:* 55 Heath St. W., Toronto, Ontario, Canada M4V 1T2. *Office:* P.O. Box 630, Station Q, Toronto, Ontario, Canada.

CAREER: Free-lance travel writer in Rome, Italy, 1962-64; Hudson Bay Co., Montreal, Quebec, fashion writer, 1965-67; Keating Educational Tours, Toronto, Ontario, director, 1968-78. *Member:* League of Canadian Poets.

WRITINGS: (With husband, Chris Keating) *Montreal,* McGraw, 1967; *In Dark Places* (poems), Black Moss Press, 1978; *The Girl Who Killed the Swan* (poems), Black Moss Press, 1980. Contributor of poems to magazines, including *Antigonish Review, Malahat Review, Northern Lights, Quarry,* and *CV/II.* Founding editor of *Anthol.*

WORK IN PROGRESS: Black Moon, a gothic fantasy novel.

SIDELIGHTS: In a review of *In Dark Places,* Louis MacKendrick observed: "Keating's recurrent subjects and sources are dreams, light and dark, figures from childrens' [sic] stories and fairytales, splitting bodies, stars, mysterious visitants, and flights into fantasy. But the fairytale elements, never as innocent as we would hope, turn into psychological parables about possession and surrender, loss and terror. Dark creatures and tempters have strange compulsions, the results of which are only indirectly insinuated."

Keating commented to *CA:* "The underlying motivation of all my writing is to come to terms with the childhood loss of innocence and with the opposing forces of mind and feeling.

"I've always been intrigued with words. As a child, rather than count sheep on nights I couldn't sleep, I made up rhyming couplets. After years of producing the glossy language of fashion and travel, I woke up one morning and found myself on the bottom of a black hole—thankfully I hadn't been metamorphosed into Kafka's beetle. When I finally dug my way out, I had completed twelve poems (the spine of my first poetry volume, *In Dark Places*) and knew the truth of Tolkien's words, 'without darkness there can be no light.'

"As a counterpoise, my second book of poetry, *The Girl Who Killed the Swan,* focuses on light. It describes a child's inner growth and her symbolic killing of the swan. Only its dying song will give her the secrets of individuality and independence."

BIOGRAPHICAL/CRITICAL SOURCES: Windsor Star, June, 1978; *Quill and Quire,* July, 1978.

*　　*　　*

KEITH, Elmer (Merrifield) 1899-

PERSONAL: Born March 8, 1899, in Hardin, Mo.; son of Forest Everett and Linnie Neal (Merrifield) Keith; married Lorraine Raddall, June 16, 1926; children: Druzinnla (deceased), Ted F. *Education:* Attended Helena Business College. *Politics:* Republican. *Home address:* P.O. Box 1072, Salmon, Idaho 83467.

CAREER: Has worked as cowhand, hunting guide, and rancher. Gun editor for *Outdoorsman, Western Sportsman,* and *Guns.* Member of technical staff of *American Rifleman* and executive editor for *Guns and Ammo.* Affiliated with Petersen Publishing Co., Los Angeles, Calif. Member of California State Police. *Military service:* National Guard. *Member:* National Rifle Association, Masons. *Awards, honors:* Outstanding handgunner award.

WRITINGS: Keith's Rifles for Large Game, Standard Publications, 1946; *Big Game Hunting,* Little, Brown, 1948; *Shotguns by Keith,* Stackpole, 1950, 3rd edition, 1967; *Sixguns: The Standard Reference Work,* Stackpole, 1955, 2nd edition, 1961; *Guns and Ammo for Hunting Big Game,* Petersen, 1965; *Keith: An Autobiography,* Winchester Press, 1974. Also author of *Hell, I Was There!,* published by Petersen. Contributor of several hundred articles to magazines and newspapers.

*   *   *

KELLER, Helen (Adams)   1880-1968

PERSONAL: Born June 27, 1880, in Tuscumbia, Ala.; died June 1, 1968, in Westport, Conn.; buried at St. Joseph's Chapel in Washington Cathedral, Washington, D.C.; daughter of Arthur H. (an editor) and Kate (Adams) Keller. *Education:* Privately tutored by Anne Sullivan Macy, 1887-1936; studied Braille at the Perkins Institution, 1888-90; attended Horace Mann School for the Deaf, 1890-94; attended the Wright-Humason School for the Deaf, 1894-96; Cambridge School for Young Ladies, 1896-97; Radcliffe College, B.A. (cum laude), 1904. *Home:* Westport, Conn.

CAREER: Author, lecturer, social reformer. Served on the Massachusetts state commission for the welfare of the blind, c. 1903; pioneered open discussion of blindness in the newborn in newspapers and magazines such as *Ladies' Home Journal* and *Kansas City Star,* c. 1905; began lecturing in public for the welfare of the handicapped, 1913; reporter for United Press International, 1913; embarked upon her first transcontinental speaking tour with Anne Sullivan Macy, 1914; made the autobiographical motion picture, "Deliverance," 1919; toured vaudeville with the Orpheum Circuit, 1922-24; founded the Helen Keller Endowment Fund for the American Foundation for the Blind, c. 1930; worked with the war-blinded during World War II; served as counselor on national and international relations for the American Foundation for the Blind and the American Foundation for the Overseas Blind; remained active in social reform movement to aid the handicapped of all nations, traveling and lecturing throughout the world.

MEMBER: National Institute of Arts and Letters (trustee of the American Hall of Fame), Phi Beta Kappa. *Awards, honors:* Order of St. Sava (Yugoslavia), 1931; Theodore Roosevelt Distinguished Service Medal, 1936; General Federation of Women's Clubs, scroll of honor for pioneer work in the relief of the handicapped, 1941; American Association of Workers for the Blind, distinguished service medal, 1951; National Institute of Social Sciences, gold medal, 1952; Medal of Merit (Lebanon), 1952; Legion of Honor (France), 1952; Southern Cross (Brazil), 1953; Presidential Medal of Freedom, 1964; American Academy of Achievement, golden plate award, 1965; and many other civic, national, and international awards; D.H.L., Temple University, 1931; Litt.D. from University of Delhi and Harvard University, both 1955;

LL.D. from University of Glasgow, 1932, University of Witwatersrand, Johannesburg, 1951; Free University of Berlin, M.D., 1955.

WRITINGS: The Story of My Life, edited by John Albert Macy, Doubleday, Page, 1903, revised and enlarged edition, Hodder & Stoughton, 1966; *Optimism: An Essay,* Crowell, 1903 (published in England as *My Key of Life, Optimism: An Essay,* Ibister, 1904, reprinted, Crowell, 1926), also published as *The Practice of Optimism,* Hodder & Stoughton, 1915; *The World I Live In* (essays and poems collected from *Century* magazine), Century, 1908; *The Song of the Stone Wall* (poetry), Century, 1910; *Out of the Dark: Essays, Letters, and Addresses on Physical and Social Vision,* Doubleday, Page, 1913; *My Religion,* Doubleday, Page, 1927, large print edition, Swedenborg, 1979; *Midstream: My Later Life* (autobiography), Doubleday, Doran, 1929, reprinted, Greenwood Press, 1968; *Helen Keller in Scotland* (autobiography), edited by James Kerr Love, Methuen, 1933; *Helen Keller's Journal, 1936-1937* (autobiography), Doubleday, Doran, 1938, reprinted with foreword by Augustus Muir, C. Chivers, 1973; *Let Us Have Faith,* Doubleday, Doran, 1940; *Teacher, Anne Sullivan Macy: A Tribute by the Foster Child of Her Mind* (biography), introduction by Nella Braddy Henney, Doubleday, 1955; *The Open Door,* Doubleday, 1957; *Helen Keller, Her Socialist Years: Writings and Speeches,* edited by Philip S. Foner, International Publishers, 1967.

Contributor of numerous articles, poems, and essays to various periodicals, including *Ladies' Home Journal, Atlantic Monthly, Youth's Companion, McClure's,* and *Century.*

SIDELIGHTS: In February, 1882, Helen, the nineteen-month-old daughter of Arthur and Kate Keller, was rendered unconscious by a severe fever. Helen Keller describes the incident in her autobiography, *The Story of My Life:* "They called it acute congestion of the stomach and brain. The doctor thought I could not live. Early one morning, however, the fever left me as suddenly and mysteriously as it had come. There was great rejoicing in the family that morning, but no one, not even the doctor, knew that I should never see or hear again."

Despite her loss of sight and hearing, Keller learned to do many small tasks such as folding the laundry and fetching objects for her mother. In fact, she devised an effective though limited system of signs to make her wishes known. Keller knew she was different from other people; understandably, the girl's frustration was uncontrollable at times. "Sometimes I stood between two persons who were conversing and touched their lips. I could not understand, and was vexed. I moved my lips and gesticulated frantically without result. This made me so angry at times that I kicked and screamed until I was exhausted."

The Kellers were unable to provide Helen with the specialized training required by a child with her handicaps. As the years passed, she became more willful and less responsive to the guidance of her protective parents. "I was strong, active, indifferent to consequences. I knew my own mind well enough and always had my own way, even if I had to fight tooth and nail for it." When Helen was about six years old, her father took her to Washington, D.C., to be examined by Dr. Alexander Graham Bell. Dr. Bell urged him to write to the Perkins Institution for the Blind in Boston requesting that a competent teacher be sent to Tuscumbia to undertake Helen's education.

In answer to this request, twenty-year-old Anne Mansfield Sullivan, a recent graduate of the Perkins Institution, arrived at the Keller home on March 3, 1887. Sullivan was the daughter of poor Irish immigrants. At an early age she and her younger brother were sent to the infamous Tewksbury almshouse in Massachusetts. She was nearly blind as a result of an eye disease, and had entered the Perkins Institution in 1880.

Sullivan knew from her own experience that firmness and determination would be required to teach the undisciplined, though intelligent, Helen. Tempering firmness with love, she spent hours each day teaching Helen the manual alphabet, which the child imitated quickly. It took a great deal of time and perseverance, however, for Sullivan to impress upon Keller the significance of the finger symbols. The moving scene of Keller's discovery that everything has a name has been reenacted time and time again in motion pictures, plays, and dramatizations. Her own description of the incident is quite eloquent: "We walked down the path to the well-house, attracted by the fragrance of the honeysuckle with which it was covered. Some one was drawing water and my teacher placed my hand under the spout. As the cool stream gushed over one hand she spelled into the other the word 'water,' first slowly, then rapidly. I stood still, my whole attention fixed upon the motions of her fingers. Suddenly I felt a misty consciousness as of something forgotten—a thrill of returning thought; and somehow the mystery of language was revealed to me. I knew then that 'w-a-t-e-r' meant the wonderful cool something that was flowing over my hand. That living word awakened my soul, gave it light, hope, joy, set it free! There were barriers still, it is true, but barriers that could in time be swept away."

From that time forward, Keller's curiosity was insatiable and Sullivan's patient perseverance unflagging. Little by little, Keller learned to express herself through the manual alphabet and to read Braille. When Keller was ten years old, Mary Swift Lamson, one of Laura Bridgman's teachers, told Keller about Ragnhild Kaata, a deaf and blind Norwegian child who had been taught to speak. Keller immediately resolved to learn to speak. Sullivan took her to Sarah Fuller, principal of the Horace Mann School for the Deaf. Keller made remarkable progress and eventually learned to speak French and German as well as English. While attending the Wright-Humason School for the Deaf and the Cambridge School for Young Ladies, Keller also studied history, mathematics, literature, astronomy, and physics. Her determination to possess as much knowledge as possible took her to Radcliffe College, from which she graduated, cum laude, in 1904.

Keller's triumph over ignorance was followed by her triumph over public indifference to the welfare of the handicapped. She devoted the rest of her life to the promotion of social reforms aimed at bettering the education and treatment of the blind, the deaf, the mute, and, in effect, all handicapped individuals. The recipient of innumerable humanitarian awards and citations, Keller is credited with prompting the organization of many state commissions for the blind. Her efforts were also very influential in putting an end to the practice of committing the deaf and the blind to mental asylums. In addition, she was a pioneer in informing the public in the prevention of blindness of the newborn. Her candid articles in the *Kansas City Star* and *Ladies' Home Journal* were among the very first public discussions of venereal disease and its relationship to newborn blindness. Keller carried her campaign to improve the condition of the handicapped throughout the world, completing several extensive lecture tours in Europe, Asia, North and South America, and Africa. Keller is universally recognized as one of the foremost humanitarians of the century.

Through all the triumphs and trials, Keller's constant companion was her teacher, Anne Sullivan. Even the older woman's marriage to John Albert Macy, the literary critic and editor of Keller's autobiography, did not interrupt the friendship. Sullivan assisted Keller all through her school and college days, manually spelling the lectures and reading assignments into Keller's palm. Later, she accompanied Keller on her lecture tours, giving full support to her pupil and their joint cause of aiding the handicapped. The partnership was ended only at Sullivan's death in 1936.

A play and several films have been based on the story of Keller's life. "The Miracle Worker" by William Gibson was originally written as a play and was later made into a film. The film version starred Anne Bancroft and Patty Duke, who were named best actress and best supporting actress by the Academy of Motion Picture Arts and Sciences in 1962.

BIOGRAPHICAL/CRITICAL SOURCES—Autobiography: *The Story of My Life,* edited by John Albert Macy, Doubleday, Page, 1903, revised and enlarged edition, Hodder & Stoughton, 1966; *The World I Live In,* Century, 1908; *Out of the Dark,* Doubleday, Page, 1913; *My Religion,* Doubleday, Page, 1927; *Midstream: My Later Life,* Doubleday, Doran, 1929, reprinted, Greenwood Press, 1968; *Helen Keller in Scotland,* edited by James Kerr Love, Methuen, 1933; *Helen Keller's Journal, 1936-1937,* Doubleday, Doran, 1938, reprinted, C. Chivers, 1973; *The Open Door,* Doubleday, 1957.

Biography: Ishbel Ross, *Journey Into Light,* Appleton, 1951; *New York Times Magazine,* June 26, 1955, June 26, 1960; Van Wyck Brooks, *Helen Keller: Sketch for a Portrait,* Dutton, 1956; Lorena A. Hickok, *Touch of Magic: The Story of Helen Keller's Great Teacher, Anne Sullivan Macy,* Dodd, 1961; Richard Harrity and Ralph G. Martin, *Three Lives of Helen Keller,* Doubleday, 1962; Walter R. Bowie, *Women of Light,* Harper, 1963; Jack Belck, *The Faith of Helen Keller: The Life of a Great Woman,* Hallmark Editions, 1967; Joseph P. Lash, *Helen and Teacher: The Story of Helen Keller and Anne Sullivan Macy,* Delacorte, 1980.

Juvenile biography: Eileen Bigland, *True Book About Helen Keller,* illustrations by Janet Pullan, Muller, 1957, revised and enlarged edition, S. G. Phillips, 1967; John W. and Anne Tibble, *Helen Keller,* illustrations by Harper Johnson, Putnam, 1958; Lorena A. Hickok, *Story of Helen Keller,* illustrations by Jo Polseno, Grosset, 1958; Catherine O. Peare, *Helen Keller Story,* Crowell, 1959; Helen E. Waite, *Valiant Companions: Helen Keller and Anne Sullivan Macy,* Macrae, 1959; Marion Brown and Ruth Crone, *Silent Storm,* illustrations by Fritz Kredel, Abingdon, 1963; Stewart and Polly A. Graff, *Helen Keller: Toward the Light,* illustrations by Paul Frame, Garrard, 1965; Norman Wymer, *Young Helen Keller,* Roy, 1965; Katharine E. Wilkie, *Helen Keller: Handicapped Girl,* illustrations by Robert Doremus, Bobbs-Merrill, 1969; Margaret Davidson, *Helen Keller,* Hastings House, 1969; Ann Donegan Johnson, *Value of Determination: The Story of Helen Keller,* Value Communications, 1976; Nancy Kelton, *The Finger Game Miracle,* Raintree, 1977.

OBITUARIES: New York Times, June 2, 1968; *Time,* June 7, 1968; *Newsweek,* June 10, 1968; *Publishers Weekly,* June 17, 1968; *Britannica Book of the Year,* 1969; *Current Biography Yearbook,* 1969.*

—*Sketch by Mary F. Glahn*

KELLY, Karen 1935-
(Kay Lee)

PERSONAL: Born April 26, 1935, in Salem, Ore.; daughter of Francis Foster (a management consultant) and Linda (a writer and researcher; maiden name, Clark) Bradshaw; married William A. Kelly (a teacher and therapist), November 30, 1957; children: Christopher, Peter, Rani, David. *Education:* Received B.A. from University of Connecticut; attended Bethany College. *Home:* 52 Holman Rd., Carmel Valley, Calif. 93924. *Office:* Kit Parker Films, Carmel Valley, Calif. 93924.

CAREER: Worked in Madurai and Bangalore, India, 1960-70; school teacher in Carmel, Calif., 1972-76; Kit Parker Films, Carmel Valley, Calif., assistant to president, 1976—.

WRITINGS: (With Joan Hopkins) *Tilda's Treats: A New Way to Eat* (juvenile), Keats Publishing, 1975; (with mother, Linda Clark) *Beauty Questions and Answers,* Pyramid Publications, 1977. Author of a monthly column in *Let's Live,* under pseudonym Kay Lee.

WORK IN PROGRESS: The Singing Garden: A Sequel, for children.

SIDELIGHTS: Karen Kelly commented: "I was brought up in an environment that supported and advocated sound nutrition. After a period of strong resistance, I became an ardent advocate myself. I believe the way we live and what we eat affect us in far-reaching ways that we are only just beginning to understand. The possible ramifications are sobering. It is essential for children to be introduced to principles of good nutrition at an age when they are receptive and interested—thus, *Tilda's Treats. The Singing Garden,* a sequel, encourages an interest in organic gardening."

AVOCATIONAL INTERESTS: Other countries (especially India), languages (including Tamil).

* * *

KELLY, Nora (Hickson) 1910-

PERSONAL: Born March 8, 1910, in Burton-on-Trent, England; daughter of Samuel Charles and Kate Elizabeth (Bagnall) Hickson; married William Henry Kelly (a member of Royal Canadian Mounted Police), July 10, 1940. *Education:* Saskatoon Normal School, teacher's diploma, 1929. *Religion:* "Humanist." *Home:* 2079 Woodcrest Rd., Ottawa, Ontario, Canada K1H 6H9.

CAREER: Teacher at public schools in McLaren, Saskatchewan, 1929-30, Brightsand Lake, Saskatchewan, 1930-32, Lanigan, Saskatchewan, 1933-34, Abbey, Saskatchewan, 1934-35; Provincial Hospital School, North Battleford, Saskatchewan, teacher, 1935-39; writer, 1939—. *Member:* Writers Union of Canada, Rationalist Press Association (England; life member); National Association for the Advancement of Colored People (NAACP; life member), Voluntary Euthanasia Society of Great Britain (life member), Concern for Dying (U.S.).

WRITINGS: Highroads to Singing (children's songs), School Publications Co., 1939; *Men of the Mounted,* J. M. Dent, 1949; (with husband, William Kelly) *The Royal Canadian Mounted Police: A Century of History,* Hurtig, 1973; (with W. Kelly) *Policing in Canada,* Macmillan, 1975.

Author of children's songs, operettas, plays, and other concert materials, as well as workbooks and teachers' manuals. Contributor to *American Encyclopedia Yearbook.* Contributor to *Canadian Geographical Journal.*

WORK IN PROGRESS: Another book, tentatively titled *I Married a Mountie.*

SIDELIGHTS: Nora Kelly told *CA:* "I taught during the Depression and since the schools could not afford concert material, I wrote my own plays, songs, and operettas. From 1937, when I met my future husband, I became especially interested in the Royal Canadian Mounted Police (RCMP). In 1939 *McClean's* magazine published my first article, the story of a German Shepard, 'Dale of Cawsalta,' the first dog used by the RCMP for special police duty. I wrote my first book of RCMP history, *Men of the Mounted,* because most earlier history books were either too dull to hold the reader's attention or laced with fiction. I aimed at writing a highly readable but factual book."

* * *

KENNEDY-MARTIN, Ian 1936-

PERSONAL: Born May 23, 1936, in London, England; son of Frances Joseph (an engineer) and Kathleen Patricia (a Montessori teacher; maiden name, Flanagan) Kennedy-Martin; married Barbara Ohrbach, January 4, 1970; children: Daniel, Lucy. *Education:* Attended Dublin University. *Home:* 19 Marlborough Place, St. John's Place, London N.W.8, England. *Agent:* A. D. Peters & Co. Ltd., 10 Buckingham St., London WC2N 6BU, England.

CAREER: Writer. Drama staff writer for British Broadcasting Corp. (BBC-TV), 1963; story editor for American Broadcasting Co. (ABC-TV), 1965; story editor for Anglia TV, 1966.

WRITINGS—Novels: *Regan,* Holt, 1975; *The Manhattan File,* Holt, 1976; *The Deal of the Century,* Holt, 1977; *Rekill,* Putnam, 1977; *Billions,* Atheneum, 1980.

Author of more than one hundred fifty screenplays for television, including "The Sweeney," "Juliet Bravo," and "The Chinese Detective," all police series; writer for television programs, including "Colditz," "Onedin Line," and "Rivals of Sherlock Holmes."

WORK IN PROGRESS: A trilogy of novels, entitled *The Acteon Trilogy,* publication of first book, by Atheneum, expected in 1981.

SIDELIGHTS: Kennedy-Martin told *CA:* "After being thrown out of Dublin University, I returned to London and started into the usual spiral of cliche'd jobs for the writer manque—waiter, dishwasher, house cleaner, researcher, etc., and started to write television plays, an area of writing which in those days had undoubtedly high rewards. The intention here was that television writing would give me enough money to afford to write novels. Television writing excludes prose, script writing being a form of controlled hysteria. Novel writing requires calm and patience.

"In 1975, on the temporary financial security of having created 'The Sweeney,' the number-one English television drama series (about 'The Flying Squad,' Scotland Yard's top group of detectives), I started writing novels, and testing the new disciplines of this kind of work. Five novels later, I'm still not confident that I've solved the novel form, but perhaps with the upcoming *Acteon Trilogy,* I will have found a new and original approach."

* * *

KENNERLY, David Hume 1947-

PERSONAL: Born March 9, 1947, in Roseburg, Ore.; son of Orlie Alden (a salesman) and Joanne (Hume) Kennerly. *Education:* Attended Portland State College, 1965-66. *Home:* 3332 P St. N.W., Washington, D.C. 20007. *Agent:* Felix Shagin, 1 Rockefeller Plaza, No. 1030, New York,

N.Y. 10020. *Office: Time* Magazine, Picture Department, Time-Life Bldg., Rockefeller Center, New York, N.Y. 10020.

CAREER: Oregon Journal, Portland, photographer, 1966; *Oregonian,* Portland, photographer, 1967; United Press International, photographer in Los Angeles, Calif., 1967-68, New York, N.Y., 1968-69, Washington, D.C., 1969-70, and Saigon, South Vietnam, 1971-72; *Life,* contract photographer in Southeast Asia, 1972; *Time,* photographer in Southeast Asia, 1973, and in Washington, D.C., 1973-74; personal photographer to President Gerald R. Ford in Washington, D.C., 1974-77; *Time,* Washington, D.C., photographer, 1977—; free-lance photographer, 1977—. *Member:* White House Press Photographers. *Awards, honors:* Pulitzer Prize, 1972, for feature photography in Vietnam; 1st place awards from World Press Photo, 1976, for general news and features.

WRITINGS: Shooter, Newsweek Books, 1979.

SIDELIGHTS: Kennerly was twenty-five when he won the 1972 Pulitzer Prize for his photographs of the war in Vietnam. Two years later he was invited by President Gerald R. Ford to serve as his personal photographer. During his three years at the White House, Kennerly enjoyed a freedom of access never before granted to a president's photographer. As *Family Weekly* reported in 1975, the Pulitzer Prize winner accepted the job only on the condition that he have "the freedom to walk in and out of the President's office at will to take whatever pictures he felt were part of history." As a result his pictures of those years have a candidness and immediacy rarely matched by the work of previous official White House photographers.

In his book *Shooter* Kennerly reviews his career and acknowledges the friends and colleagues who have helped him along the way. He talks about his first staff job at the *Oregon Journal,* his world travels for United Press International, and his favorite anecdotes about the Ford White House. A reviewer for the *Library Journal* observed, "Though he is hugely proud of his work and his associations, his writing displays an engaging modesty that does credit to his tender years.... It combines idealistic verve with workaday competence ..., [and] as a review of the recent past, it is an appealing memoir."

BIOGRAPHICAL/CRITICAL SOURCES: Popular Photography, February, 1975, October, 1979; *Family Weekly,* November 16, 1975; *Authors in the News,* Volume 2, Gale, 1976; Gerald R. Ford, *A Time to Heal,* Harper, 1979; David Kennerly, *Shooter,* Newsweek Books, 1979; *Library Journal,* November 15, 1979.

*   *   *

KENNEY, Douglas   1947(?)-1980

OBITUARY NOTICE: Born c. 1947; died in 1980 on Kauai Island, Hawaii. Kenney helped found and at one time edited the humor magazine *National Lampoon.* He also co-wrote the screenplays "Animal House," 1978, and "Caddyshack," 1980. Kenney died after falling from a cliff while vacationing in Hawaii. Obituaries and other sources: *Time,* September 15, 1980.

*   *   *

KENNY, Anthony John Patrick   1931-

PERSONAL: Born March 16, 1931, in Liverpool, England; son of John and Margaret (Jones) Kenny; married Nancy Caroline Gayley, 1966; children: two sons. *Education:* At-

tended Gregorian University and St. Benet's Hall, Oxford. *Office:* Balliol College, Oxford University, Oxford OX1 3BJ, England.

CAREER: Ordained Roman Catholic priest, 1955; curate of Roman Catholic church in Liverpool, England, 1959-63; legally released from the obligations of the priesthood, 1963; Oxford University, Oxford, England, lecturer at Exeter College and Trinity College, 1963-64, tutor at Balliol College, 1964, senior tutor, 1971-72 and 1976-77, master in philosophy, 1978—, Wilde Lecturer in Natural and Comparative Religion, 1969-72, fellow of Balliol College, 1964-78. Assistant lecturer at University of Liverpool, 1961-63; Joint Gifford Lecturer at University of Edinburgh, 1972-73; visiting professor at Stanford University, Rockefeller University, University of Chicago, University of Washington, Seattle, University of Michigan, and Cornell University. *Member:* British Academy (fellow).

WRITINGS: Action, Emotion, and Will, Routledge & Kegan Paul, 1963; (translator and author of notes and introduction) St. Thomas Aquinas, *Summa theologiae,* Volume XXII: *Dispositions for Human Acts* (in Latin and English), edited by Thomas Gilby and others, McGraw, 1964; *The Five Ways: Saint Thomas Aquinas' Proofs of God's Existence,* Routledge & Kegan Paul, 1969; *Wittgenstein,* Allen Lane, 1973; *The Nature of Mind,* Edinburgh University Press, 1973; *The Anatomy of the Soul: Historical Essays in the Philosophy of Mind,* Basil Blackwell, 1974; *The Development of Mind,* Edinburgh University Press, 1974; *Will, Freedom, and Power,* Basil Blackwell, 1976; *The Aristotelian Ethics: A Study of the Relationship Between the "Eudemian" and "Nichomachean Ethics" of Aristotle,* Clarendon Press, 1978; *The God of the Philosophers,* Clarendon Press, 1979; *Aristotle's Theory of the Will,* Duckworth, 1979; *Freewill and Responsibility,* Routledge & Kegan Paul, 1979; *Aquinas,* Oxford University Press, 1980.

Editor: *The Responsa Scholarum of the English College, Rome,* two volumes, Publications of the Catholic Record Society, 1962-63; *Aquinas: A Collection of Critical Essays,* Macmillan, 1970, University of Notre Dame Press, 1977; (also translator) Rene Descartes, *Philosophical Letters,* Clarendon Press, 1970; Arthur Norman Prior, *Objects of Thought,* Clarendon Press, 1971; Ludwig Wittgenstein, *Philosophical Grammar,* Basil Blackwell, 1974; Prior, *The Doctrine of Propositions and Terms,* Duckworth, 1976; Prior, *Papers in Logic and Ethics,* Duckworth, 1976. Editor of *Oxford,* 1972-73.

BIOGRAPHICAL/CRITICAL SOURCES: Times Literary Supplement, January 25, 1980, May 9, 1980.

*   *   *

KEPES, Gyorgy   1906-

PERSONAL: Surname is pronounced *Kay*-pash; born October 4, 1906, in Selyp, Hungary; came to the United States, 1937; son of Ferenc and Ilona (Fai) Kepes; married Juliet Appleby (an author and illustrator), November 3, 1937; children: Juliet (Mrs. Henry Sawyer Stone, Jr.), Imre Peter. *Education:* Royal Academy of Fine Arts (Budapest, Hungary), M.F.A., 1928. *Home:* 90 Larchwood Dr., Cambridge, Mass. 02138. *Office:* Center for Advanced Visual Studies, Massachusetts Institute of Technology, Cambridge, Mass. 02139.

CAREER: Painter, sculptor, designer, architect, typographer, filmmaker, writer, and editor. Worked on films, stage sets, exhibitions, and graphic designs in Berlin, Germany, 1930-34; experimented with design in London, England,

1935-37; New Bauhaus, Chicago, Ill., head of light and color department, 1937-38; Chicago Institute of Design, Chicago, head of light and color department, 1938-43; instructor at North Texas State Teachers College (now North Texas State University), Denton, and Brooklyn College (now of the City University of New York), New York City; Massachusetts Institute of Technology, Cambridge, professor of visual design, 1946-67, director of Center for Advanced Visual Studies, 1967—. Artist, with exhibitions at one-man shows, including Katherine Kuh Gallery, Chicago, 1939, Art Institute of Chicago, 1944 and 1954, Outline Gallery, Pittsburgh, 1945, Royal Academy, Copenhagen, 1950, Margaret Brown Gallery, Boston, 1951 and 1955, San Francisco Museum of Art, 1952 and 1954, and Museum of Fine Arts in Rome, Houston, and Dallas, all 1958; participant in group exhibits, including those at Carnegie Institute, Pittsburgh, National Collection of Fine Arts, Washington, D.C., and Whitney Museum of Modern Art, New York City. Creator of numerous murals, including those at the Harvard University Graduate Center, Cambridge; at the Sheraton Corporation, Dallas, Chicago, and Philadelphia; at the Travelers Insurance Co., Los Angeles; and at the American Housing Exhibit, Paris. Graphic designer for *Fortune* magazine, Container Corporation of America, and Abbot Laboratories, 1938-50.

MEMBER: National Institute of Arts and Letters, American Academy of Arts and Sciences (fellow). *Awards, honors:* Medallist Award from American Institute of Graphic Arts, 1944 and 1949, for distinguished contributions to the graphic arts; Purchase Prize from University of Illinois, 1954; Guggenheim fellow, 1960-61; silver medal from Architectural League of New York, 1961; Chicago Art Directors Club award, 1963; fine arts medal from American Institute of Architects, 1968, for distinguished achievement; Colombian Bienal Coltejer award, 1972, for "Flame Orchard"; recipient of honorary degrees from Philadelphia College of Art, Loyola University, Carnegie Mellon University, and University of New Mexico.

WRITINGS: Language of Vision, Paul Theobald, 1944; (contributor) *Graphic Forms: The Arts as Related to the Book,* Harvard University Press, 1949; *The New Landscape in Art and Science,* Paul Theobald, 1956.

Editor; essays; all published by Braziller, except as noted: *The Visual Arts Today,* Wesleyan University Press, 1960; *Education of Vision,* 1965; *The Nature and Art of Motion,* 1965; *Structure in Art and in Science,* 1965; *The Man-Made Object,* 1966; *Module, Proportion, Symmetry, Rhythm,* 1966; *Sign, Image, Symbol,* 1966; *Arts of the Environment,* 1972.

SIDELIGHTS: Gyorgy Kepes has utilized his numerous and diverse talents in an effort to unify the arts and the sciences. As a young boy growing up in the small town of Selyp, Hungary, Kepes was encouraged to develop his creative ability by two uncles, one a physicist who painted and the other a magistrate who collected art. Kepes developed his talent further at the Royal Academy of Fine Arts in Budapest, where he studied under Istvan Csok.

After receiving a Master of Fine Arts degree, Kepes went to Berlin to work on graphic designs and films. He became well acquainted with the Hungarian designer, painter, and photographer, Laszlo Moholy-Nagy, and they often collaborated. Both were interested in the Bauhaus, a school of design synthesizing artistic principles and utilitarian design.

In 1937 Moholy-Nagy moved to the United States to take a position as director of New Bauhaus in Chicago. He then sent for Kepes to head the light and color department. The school failed about a year later, and Moholy-Nagy opened the Chicago Institute of Design, again putting Kepes at the head of the light and color department.

Kepes painted only intermittently during the first ten or fifteen years he spent in the United States. His first major one-man show in this country was held at the Katherine Kuh Gallery in Chicago in 1939.

Kepes uses a collage technique in his painting, gluing sand in various forms to a canvas covered with layers of color. He then applies bright color with a palette knife and finally adds glazed layers of more color, creating an abstract expression of the conflict between man and nature. Kepes takes many of his subjects from the outdoors, prompting some to label him a romantic nature painter. A writer for *Time* commented on the "quietness, tenderness and lack of pretension" of one of his exhibitions.

In some of his other art forms, Kepes uses metal, ignited gas, and neon lights. He once worked with the inventor of the strobe light, Harold Edgerton, to create a fountain that would flick like a strobe. His "Flame Orchard," for which he won a top award at the Colombian Bienal Coltejer in 1972, is a twenty-foot field of gas flames which responds to music.

BIOGRAPHICAL/CRITICAL SOURCES: Interiors, October, 1948, May, 1949; *New York Times Book Review,* December 18, 1956; *Time,* March 7, 1960; *New York Herald Tribune,* February 5, 1961; *Saturday Review,* March 13, 1965; *Book Week,* April 18, 1965, January 1, 1967; *Christian Science Monitor,* June 22, 1965, May 26, 1972; *Science,* July 30, 1965; *New Statesman,* January 13, 1967; *Architectural Forum,* March, 1967; *National Observer,* December 26, 1968; *Washington Post Herald,* June 8, 1969; *New York Times,* December 26, 1969; *Newsweek,* April 20, 1970; *Art International,* January, 1975; *Art Journal,* spring, 1976.*

*   *   *

KERN, Gregory
    See TUBB, E(dwin) C(harles)

*   *   *

KERN, Mary Margaret   1906-

PERSONAL: Born November 12, 1906, in Lafayette, Ind.; daughter of Charles B. (a physician) and Flora (Work) Kern; married Herbert L. Garrard (an agronomic photographer), December 31, 1932; children: Flora Jane (Mrs. Ronald K. Richard), Bruce Kern, Sara Ann Garrard Grepp. *Education:* Purdue University, B.S. (with distinction), 1927; also attended Northwestern University, 1927-28. *Religion:* Presbyterian. *Home and office:* 19740 Heather Lane, Craig Highlands, Noblesville, Ind. 46060.

CAREER: Mortar Board Quarterly, Lafayette, Ind., editor, 1928-30; *Union League Club Bulletin,* Chicago, Ill., associate editor, 1930-32; Altrusa International, Chicago, editor of *International Altrusan,* 1932-38, executive secretary, 1935-38; free-lance writer, 1938-58; *Kappa Alpha Theta Magazine,* Noblesville, Ind., editor, 1958-73; Indiana University-Purdue University at Indianapolis, teacher of creative writing, 1976-79; free-lance writer, 1979—.

MEMBER: Woman's Press Club of Indiana, National Federation of Press Women, Women in Communications, Noblesville Writers Club. *Awards, honors:* National awards from National Federation of Press Women, 1965, for feature story "How Not to Be Yourself," 1970, for centennial issue of *Kappa Alpha Theta Magazine,* 1977, for interview "Our Children and Divorce," and 1978, for feature story "The Way Things Used to Be."

WRITINGS: Be a Better Parent, Westminster, 1979. Contributor of more than two hundred articles and stories to adult and juvenile magazines and newspapers, including *Better Homes and Gardens, Parents' Magazine, Today's Health,* and religious magazines. Woman's editor of *Purdue Alumnus,* 1929-30.

WORK IN PROGRESS: Various articles and books.

SIDELIGHTS: Mary Margaret Kern wrote: "I try to consult with and encourage beginning writers whenever and wherever I can, both because I sympathize with their problems and want to help, and also, in this way, to partially pay back those friendly and encouraging writers who helped me along the way.

"In my teaching I felt I could relate particularly to young people wanting to write since I have done it all ways: while holding a full-time job, while raising a family, and now that the family is away from home, being able to give full time to free-lancing, though also carrying a quota of community volunteering besides.

"Specifically, I try to help the beginning writer see that often perseverance is more important than talent, that nothing ever sells if it stays in the desk drawer, and that rejection slips should never be regarded as the end of the world. Every writer receives rejections, and the ones who keep on writing and sending out manuscripts are the ones who win publication (and frequently plaudits) in the end."

AVOCATIONAL INTERESTS: "Stargazing," golf, playing pool.

*   *   *

KETTLE, Peter
See GLOVER, Denis (James Matthews)

*   *   *

KHEDOURI, Franklin 1944-

PERSONAL: Born July 10, 1944, in Teheran, Iran; son of Shaoul (an investor) and Suzette (Somekh) Khedouri; married Amy Fraade (a gourmet caterer), June 9, 1974. *Education:* Union College, Schenectady, N.Y., A.B., 1967. *Home and office:* 8461 Springtree Dr., No. 407, Sunrise, Fla. 33321. *Agent:* Peter Miller Agency, 1201 Avenue of the Americas, Suite 403, New York, N.Y. 10018.

CAREER: Macmillan Publishing Co., Inc., New York City, business editor in sales, 1969-74; Random House, Inc., New York City, business and economics editor, 1975-76. President of Soundscapes, Inc. (recording company); associate of Mescon, Inc. (management consultants). *Military service:* U.S. Naval Reserve, active duty, 1967-69; became lieutenant junior grade.

WRITINGS: (Editor) Faye Kinder and Nancy R. Green, *Meal Management,* 5th edition, Macmillan, 1978; (with Michael H. Mescon) *Management,* Harper, 1980. Author of "Saturday Night" (screenplay), released by Buckley Brothers Films, 1975.

WORK IN PROGRESS: A Professor's Guide to College Publishing; Couplegames.

SIDELIGHTS: Khedouri commented: "I have little interest in writing or working in those areas in which, by dint of past experience, I presumably have expertise. There is not much to learn from repeating what one has already done. The only exception is the area of lifestyle and relationships, in which I have never published, but consider myself to be exceptionally good at. My wife and I believe that reality is subjective, that experience is more real than material possessions, and that 1980 is a good year to spend in Bali."

*   *   *

KIERAN, John Francis 1892-

PERSONAL: Surname is pronounced *Keer*-un; born August 2, 1892, in New York, N.Y.; son of James Michael (an educator and administrator) and Kate (a teacher and musician; maiden name, Donahue) Kieran; married Alma Boldtmann, May 14, 1919 (died June, 1944); married Margaret Ford (a journalist), September 5, 1947; children: (first marriage) James Michael, John Francis, Beatrice. *Education:* Attended College of the City of New York (now City College of the City University of New York), 1908-11; Fordham University, B.S. (cum laude), 1912; Clarkson College of Technology, D.Sc., 1941; Wesleyan University, M.A., 1942. *Home:* Rockport, Mass.

CAREER: Held a variety of jobs during his early career, including teaching in a country school in Dutchess County, New York, running a poultry business, and working as a timekeeper for a sewer construction project; *New York Times,* sports writer, 1915-43; *New York Sun,* columnist, 1943-44. Elector, Hall of Fame for Great Americans, beginning 1945; member of the board of experts on radio program, "Information, Please," 1938-48. *Military service:* Served with the 11th Engineers of the American Expeditionary Forces during World War I. *Awards, honors:* Burroughs Medal, John Burroughs Memorial Association, 1960, for recognition of an outstanding book on natural science.

WRITINGS: The American Sporting Scene, illustrations by Joseph W. Golinkin, Macmillan, 1941; *John Kieran's Nature Notes,* illustrations by Fritz Kredel, Doubleday, Doran, 1941, reprinted, Books for Libraries, 1969; (compiler) *Poems I Remember,* Doubleday, Doran, 1942; *Footnotes on Nature,* wood engravings by Nora S. Unwin, Doubleday, 1947, reprinted, 1971; (editor, with Dan Golenpaul) *Information Please Almanac, Atlas and Yearbook,* Simon & Schuster, 1947; *An Introduction to Birds,* illustrations by Don Eckelberry, Garden City Publishing, 1950; *Come Murder Me,* Gold Medal Books, 1951; *An Introduction to Wild Flowers,* illustrations by Tabea Hofmann, Hanover House, 1952; *An Introduction to Trees,* illustrations by Michael H. Bevans, Hanover House, 1954; (with Margaret Kieran) *John James Audubon,* illustrations by Christine Price, Random House, 1954; *An Introduction to Nature: Birds, Wild Flowers, Trees,* illustrations by D. Eckelberry, T. Hofmann, and M. Bevans, Hanover House, 1955; (editor) *Treasure of Great Nature Writing,* Hanover House, 1957; *A Natural History of New York City,* illustrations by Henry Bugbee Kane, Houghton, 1959, revised and abridged edition, Natural History Press, 1971; *Not Under Oath: Recollections and Reflections,* Houghton, 1964; *Books I Love: Being a Selection of 100 Titles for a Home Library,* Doubleday, 1969.

Author of *The Story of the Olympic Games, 776 B.C.-1936 A.D.,* Frederick A. Stokes, 1936, revised editions (with Arthur Daley) published quadrennially, Lippincott, 1948-77.

Contributor of articles to periodicals, including *Saturday Evening Post, Woman's Home Companion, American Magazine, Literary Digest, Collier's, Audubon Magazine.*

SIDELIGHTS: John Kieran, a noted newspaperman and columnist, is known for the mnemonic skills he displayed as a member of the Board of Experts on the weekly radio quiz program, "Information, Please!" A storehouse of general knowledge, Kieran came to be regarded by the public as "a walking encyclopedia."

BIOGRAPHICAL/CRITICAL SOURCES: Readers Digest, June, 1939; *Life,* June 16, 1941; *Time,* January 4, 1943; *Saturday Review of Literature,* July 12, 1947; *New York Times,* July 20, 1947; *Coronet,* March, 1949; *Saturday Evening Post,* June 18, 1949; *New York Times Book Review,* September 27, 1959; *Saturday Review,* October 24, 1964; *Book Week,* November 1, 1964.*

*　　*　　*

KIMENYE, Barbara   1940(?)-

PERSONAL: Born c. 1940 in Uganda. *Education:* Educated in Uganda. *Home:* 38 Florence St., London N.1, England.

CAREER: Writer. Worked as private secretary for government of the Kabaka of Buganda; journalist and columnist with *Uganda Nation* (Kampala); social worker in London, 1974—.

WRITINGS—Short stories: *Kalasanda,* illustrations by N. Kagwa, Oxford University Press, 1965; *Kalasanda Revisited,* Oxford University Press, 1966.

Juvenile fiction: *The Smugglers,* illustrations by Roger Payne, Thomas Nelson, 1966; *Moses,* illustrations by Rena Fennessy, Oxford University Press, 1967; *Moses and Mildred,* illustrations by Fennessy, Oxford University Press, 1967; *Moses and the Kidnappers,* illustrations by Fennessy, Oxford University Press, 1968; *Moses in Trouble,* illustrations by Fennessy, Oxford University Press, 1968; *The Winged Adventure,* illustrations by Terry Hirst, Oxford University Press, 1969.

Moses in a Muddle, illustrations by Fennessy, Oxford University Press, 1970; *Moses and the Ghost,* illustrations by Fennessy, Oxford University Press, 1971; *Paulo's Strange Adventure,* illustrations by Olga J. Heuser, Oxford University Press, 1971; *Moses on the Move,* illustrations by Mara Onditi, Oxford University Press, 1972; *Barah and the Boy,* Oxford University Press, 1973; *Martha the Millipede,* Oxford University Press, 1973; *Moses and the Penpal,* illustrations by Onditi, Oxford University Press, 1973; *Moses, the Camper,* illustrations by Onditi, Oxford University Press, 1973; *The Runaways,* illustrations by Onditi, Oxford University Press, 1973; *The Gemstone Affair,* Thomas Nelson, 1978; *The Scoop,* Thomas Nelson, 1978.

SIDELIGHTS: Barbara Kimenye is well known in Africa because of a column she wrote for the *Uganda Nation,* a newspaper based in the Nairobi area. In addition to her journalistic endeavors, Kimenye has published a number of books for children.

At least ten titles are included in Kimenye's "Moses" series. These are boys' adventure tales, the hero of which is a young boy full of spunk and energy. Moses and his friends attend a school designed to house rejects from more reputable institutions.

Kimenye's characters encounter all sorts of trying situations, mostly concerning clashes with authority. The author attempts to put her characters in a positive light despite their negative environment. She attempts to illustrate the idea that the boys are not necessarily bad, but merely mischievous or the victims of circumstance.

Since 1974 Kimenye has lived in England where she is a social worker.

BIOGRAPHICAL/CRITICAL SOURCES: African Studies Review, September, 1976.*

KING, Vincent
See VINSON, Rex Thomas

*　　*　　*

KINGMAN, Russ   1917-

PERSONAL: Born August 8, 1917, in Ferrisburg, Vt.; son of Ray A. (a milk plant manager) and Lucy (Kimball) Kingman; married Winifred Harris, November 1, 1941. *Education:* Baylor University, B.A., 1952, M.A., 1955; further graduate study at San Francisco State University, 1961-63. *Politics:* "Best qualified—when and if." *Home and office:* 14300 Arnold Dr., Glen Ellen, Calif. 95442.

CAREER: Ordained Southern Baptist minister, 1949; U.S. Navy, 1935-49, acting chaplain at Naval Air Station, Alameda, Calif., 1940, catapult chief at Naval Aircraft Factory, Philadelphia, Pa., 1942-43, chief master at arms at Tacoma Receiving Station, Tacoma, Wash., 1943-44, aviation chief and machinist's mate on U.S.S. *Currituck,* 1945, photographic chief of the Marianas Islands, 1946-47, fire marshal of the Marianas, 1946-48, fire chief on Guam, 1946-48, leaving service as aviation chief and machinist's mate; pastor of Southern Baptist churches in Millview and Pensacola, Fla., and in Cego, Cottonwood, and Waco, Tex., 1949-61; Sears & Roebuck Co., Inc., San Rafael, Calif., in outside sales, 1961-62; Wyckoff & Associates, San Francisco, Calif., account executive, 1963-68; Russ Kingman Advertising, Oakland, Calif., owner, 1968-73; Jack London Bookstore and Museum, Glen Ellen, Calif., owner, 1971—. Executive director of Jack London Educational and Research Foundation. Member of board of directors of Manila Don Corp. Lecturer at schools, churches, and clubs. *Member:* Jack London Square Association (executive director, 1968-73), Masons, Veterans of Foreign Wars, California Writers Club.

WRITINGS: (Editor and author of introduction) Jack London, *The Valley of the Moon,* Peregrine Press, 1976; (editor and author of introduction) *Jack London's Tales of the North,* Book Sales, Inc., 1979; (editor and author of introduction) *Jack London's Stories of Adventure,* Book Sales, Inc., 1980; *A Pictorial Life of Jack London,* Crown, 1980; *Wolf: The Story of Jack London,* Crown, 1981. Northern California reporter for *Air California* (magazine). Contributor to journals, including *Jack London Newsletter, Pacific Historian, Bay and Delta Yachtsman,* and *Pacific Islands Monthly,* and newspapers.

WORK IN PROGRESS: Jack London in the Klondike; The Crowd, on San Francisco writers and artists, 1876-1916; *Jack London, Agnostic Christian Atheist.*

SIDELIGHTS: Kingman wrote: "I lecture all over the United States on Jack London and other Western authors (mainly from the San Francisco area). My literary work stems from the influence of Irving Stone's *Sailor on Horseback* and London's *Martin Eden.*

"In 1969 I led an expedition to the Klondike to bring back the cabin in which Jack London lived during the gold rush. In 1970 I followed his trail in London, England. In 1979 I retraced his 1911 farm horse trip to Oregon, and in 1980 researched London in Australia and Hawaii. My motivation is to give Jack London the place in the world that his life and works deserve.

"From my first reading of *Sailor on Horseback* in 1968 to the present day, I have been constantly researching the life and works of Jack London. During this period I have been utterly amazed that none of the Jack London biographers, and there have been sixteen, were willing to adequately research before sitting down to write. As a result the world has been unable to know the real Jack London. For instance, one leading biography had over two hundred errors, and a recent biography was a vicious caricature of him and so poorly researched that I wondered who the author was talking about. I determined to set the record straight.

"I started writing only after having read everything available by or about Jack London and amassing a cross-indexed, thirty-five-thousand-card file on his life and work. This research will also be used for my books now in progress on Jack London, his times and his friends. It is my firm belief that an author of biographies owes his subject and his descendants an honest portrayal. And this requires a lot of 'dig,' as Jack London put it."

BIOGRAPHICAL/CRITICAL SOURCES: Hobbies, January, 1974; *Baylor Line,* June, 1974; *Saturday Evening Post,* December, 1976; *Antique Trader,* June 14, 1978; *Los Angeles Times,* February 13, 1980; *Vallejo Times Herald,* March 27, 1980; *Sacramento Bee,* March 30, 1980; *Sunday Oregonian,* March 30, 1980; *Buffalo Evening News,* March 31, 1980; *American Collector,* April, 1980; *Milwaukee Journal,* April 1, 1980; *Norfolk Virginian-Pilot,* April 1, 1980; *St. Louis Globe-Democrat,* April 2, 1980; *Vancouver Sun,* April 3, 1980; *Sonoma Index Tribune,* April 30, 1980.

*   *   *

KINNAIRD, William M(cKee) 1928-

PERSONAL: Born July 14, 1928, in Tacoma, Wash.; son of William H. and Louise (McKee) Kinnaird; married Elizabeth Blakemore, December 28, 1960 (divorced June, 1972); children: William M., Jr., Elleanor G., Elizabeth O. *Education:* Washington and Lee University, B.A., 1949; Harvard University, J.D., 1952, P.M.D. certificate, 1965; further graduate study at Fuller Theological Seminary, 1977-79. *Religion:* Presbyterian. *Home and office:* Webb Co., 1704 Noble Creek Dr., Atlanta, Ga. 30327.

CAREER: Glenmore Distilleries Co., Louisville, Ky., president of International Division, 1954-66; Royal Crown Cola Co., Columbus, Ga., director of staff sales, 1966-69; marketing management consultant in Louisville, 1969-73; Webb Co., St. Paul, Minn., southeastern sales manager, 1973—.

WRITINGS: Joy Comes With the Morning, Word, Inc., 1979; *The Promise of Hope: Coping When Life Caves In,* Abingdon, 1981. Contributor to magazines, including *Christianity Today* and *His.*

SIDELIGHTS: Kinnaird told *CA:* "I had a very meaningful encounter with Jesus Christ in the early 1970's which dramatically changed my life and continues to inspire my writing. I do a great deal of teaching and speaking in churches and I hold seminars. I am a great fan of C. S. Lewis and Paul Tournier, and a good bit of my teaching is about their books, principally *The Chronicles of Narnia* by Lewis."

*   *   *

KIRBY, David G. 1942-

PERSONAL: Born June 14, 1942, in Kirton, England; son of Cyril H. (in dairy work) and Annie (Wood) Kirby; married Paula (a teacher), August 22, 1963; children: Peter, Ann. *Education:* London School of Economics and Political Science, London, B.A. (with honors), 1963; University of London, Ph.D., 1971. *Home:* 24 Grassmount, Taymount Rise, London S.E.23, England. *Office:* School of Slavonic Studies, University of London, Senate House, Malet St., London W.C.1, England.

CAREER: Teacher of English at private schools in Finland, 1963-66; Luton College of Technology, Luton, England, lecturer in history, 1966-68; University of London, School of Slavonic Studies, London, England, lecturer in history, 1969—. *Member:* Turku Historical Society. *Awards, honors:* Leverhulme European scholarship, 1968-69.

WRITINGS: Finland and Russia, 1808-1920: From Autonomy to Independence; A Collection of Documents, Macmillan, 1975; *Finland in the Twentieth Century,* University of Minnesota Press, 1979. Contributor to history journals.

WORK IN PROGRESS: A study of international socialism's response to the 1917 Russian revolution and to the problem of peace in 1917-18.

SIDELIGHTS: Kirby wrote: "My main area of competence is the recent history of northern Europe, which of necessity demands knowledge of a range of languages (Finnish, German, Russian, Estonian, and the Scandinavian languages). I travel regularly to Sweden and Finland, and in my ten years as a teacher in London, I have managed to establish a range of contacts which has borne fruit in the form of seminars and visiting lectures, all of which have helped promote the study of Nordic history in Britain."

*   *   *

KIRKUS, Virginia
See GLICK, Virginia Kirkus

*   *   *

KITMAN, Marvin 1929-
(William Randolph Hirsch)

PERSONAL: Born November 24, 1929, in Pittsburgh, Pa.; son of Myer and Rose (Kaufman) Kitman; married Carol Sibushnick, October 28, 1951; children: Jamie Lincoln, Suzy, Andrea Jordana. *Education:* City College (now of the City University of New York), B.A., 1953. *Home:* 147 Crescent Ave., Leonia, N.J. 07605. *Office: Newsday,* Garden City, N.Y. 11530.

CAREER: Armstrong Daily, New York City, columnist, 1956-66; *New Leader,* New York City, television critic, 1967—. News managing editor of *Monocle,* 1963—, member of board of directors of Monocle Periodicals, 1966—, founding partner of Monocle Book Division, 1968. Staff writer for *Saturday Evening Post,* 1965-66; senior copy writer for Carl Ally, Inc. (advertising agency), 1967-68. Critic-at-large for "Harper News," on WPIX-TV, 1973-74; co-creator of "Ball Four," a series on CBS-TV, 1976. Humorist-in-residence for Solow/Wexton, Inc., 1966-67; lecturer at colleges and universities. *Military service:* U.S. Army, 1953-55. *Member:* Spanish Civil War Roundtable of Northern New Jersey (executive director).

WRITINGS: The Number-One Best Seller (autobiography), Dial Press, 1966; (under pseudonym William Randolph Hirsch; with Lingeman and Navasky) *The RCAF (Red Chinese Air Force) Exercise, Diet, and Sex Book,* Stein & Day, 1967; *You Can't Judge a Book by Its Cover* (autobiography), Weybright, 1970; *George Washington's Expense Account,* Ballantine, 1970; *The Marvin Kitman TV Show,* Dutton, 1972; (with Richard Lingeman, Victor Navasky, and others) *The Coward's Almanac,* Ballantine, 1975;

Author of "The Marvin Kitman Show," a column for *Newsday* and Los Angeles Times Syndicate, 1969—. Contributor of articles and reviews to magazines.

WORK IN PROGRESS: The Making of the President, 1789.

KLEIN, A(braham) M(oses)   1909-1972

PERSONAL: Born February 14, 1909, in Montreal, Quebec, Canada; died August 21, 1972, in Montreal, Quebec, Canada; son of Colman and Yetta (Morantz) Klein; married Bessie Kozlov, February 14, 1935; children: Colman, Sandor, Sharon. *Education:* McGill University, B.A., 1930; University of Montreal, law degree, 1933. *Residence:* Montreal, Quebec, Canada.

CAREER: Writer. Called to the Bar of Quebec, 1933; practiced law in Montreal, Quebec, 1933-54; in public relations in Montreal. Visiting lecturer in poetry at McGill University, 1943-46. *Awards, honors:* Governor General's Award, 1948, for *The Rocking Chair and Other Poems;* Lorne Pierce Medal, from Royal Society of Canada, 1957, for outstanding contribution to Canadian literature.

WRITINGS: Hath Not a Jew (poems), Behrman's Jewish Book House, 1940; *The Hitleriad* (poems), New Directions, 1944; *Poems,* Jewish Publication Society of America, 1944, reprinted, Arno Press, 1975; *The Rocking Chair and Other Poems,* Ryerson Press, 1948; *The Second Scroll* (novella), Knopf, 1951; (translator) Israel Rabinovitch, *Of Jewish Music, Ancient and Modern,* Montreal Book Center, 1952; *The Collected Poems of A. M. Klein,* compiled by Miriam Waddington, McGraw, 1974.

Editor of *Canadian Zionist,* 1936-37, and *Canadian Jewish Chronicle,* 1939-55.

Contributor of poetry to periodicals, including *Canadian Forum, Poetry,* and *Nation.*

SIDELIGHTS: A. M. Klein was basically a poet of the Jewish experience. His first volume, *Hath Not a Jew,* for example, consists of poems reflecting the Judaic culture throughout history. Reviewer Earl Birney asserted that "in polished and mordant satire, dancing wit, metrical versatility and originality of metaphor, [*Hath Not a Jew*] is one of the finest volumes of verse ever written by a Canadian of whatever race." Leon Edel of *Poetry,* however, felt that "the collection does Klein a distinct disservice in that it is not sufficiently representative of his remarkable gifts, the gift above all of eloquent rebellion. . . . And yet, despite their flaws, these poems are a poetic key to an ancient, deep-rooted, emotional and intellectual tradition. As such," he concluded, "they can lay claim to vitality and importance."

Klein's only published novel, *The Second Scroll,* is a symbolic tale of a modern-day search for a Messiah who would lead the Jews to the Promised Land. The title of the work is significant in that the Jewish faith is based on the Old Testament of the Bible, also referred to as the First Scroll. In his review of *The Second Scroll,* Thomas Sugrue suggested that it has "a sound basis for a novel, and Mr. Klein has the intellectual and stylistic talents necessary for its proper development, but he seems to have tired of it too soon." Harvey Swados of *Nation,* on the other hand, commended the book as "the most profoundly creative summation of the Jewish condition by a Jewish man of letters since the European catastrophe."

BIOGRAPHICAL/CRITICAL SOURCES: Canadian Forum, February, 1941, January, 1952; *Poetry,* April, 1941; *Nation,* November 3, 1951; *New York Times,* November 25, 1951; *New York Herald Tribune Book Review,* December 2, 1951.

OBITUARIES: Detroit News, August 22, 1972; *New York Times,* August 23, 1972.*

KLEIN, Charlotte   1925-

PERSONAL: Born April 4, 1925, in Berlin, Germany; daughter of Oscar and Marie (Fessel) Klein. *Education:* University College, London, B.A., 1958, M.A., 1961, Ph.D., 1965. *Religion:* Roman Catholic. *Home:* 17 Chepstow Villas, London W11 3D2, England.

CAREER: Headmistress at English school in Jerusalem, Palestine (now Israel), 1946-55; Georgetown University, Washington, D.C., assistant professor, 1968-69; St. Georgen College, Frankfort on the Main, West Germany, lecturer in theology, 1969-71; Open University, London, England, tutor and counselor, 1972—.

WRITINGS: Theologie und Anti-Judaismus, Kaiser, 1975, translation by E. Quinn published as *Anti-Judaism in Christian Theology,* Fortress, 1975. Contributor to theology journals.

WORK IN PROGRESS: The Sisters of Zion and the Jews: From Conversion to Dialogue; Guidelines on Jewish-Christian Relations: A Critical Appreciation.

* * *

KLEJMENT, Anne M.   1950-

PERSONAL: Surname is pronounced *Klem*-ment; born April 27, 1950, in Rochester, N.Y.; daughter of Z. Henry (a coremaker) and Alice (Wegner) Klejment. *Education:* Nazareth College of Rochester, B.A. (cum laude), 1972; State University of New York at Binghamton, M.A., 1974, Ph.D., 1981. *Residence:* Ithaca, N.Y. *Office:* New York Historical Resources Center, Cornell University, 502 Olin Library, Ithaca, N.Y. 14853.

CAREER: State University of New York at Binghamton, lecturer in history, 1975; Vassar College, Poughkeepsie, N.Y., instructor in history, 1978-79; State University of New York College at New Paltz, instructor in innovative studies program, summer, 1979; Cornell University, Ithaca, N.Y., administrator of historians-in-residence program at New York Historical Resources Center, 1979—. Affiliated with Center for the Study of American Catholicism at University of Notre Dame. *Member:* Organization of American Historians, American Studies Association, American Catholic Historical Association, Radical Historians Association, Berkshire Women's History Conference, Upstate New York Women's History Conference.

WRITINGS: The Berrigans: A Bibliography of Published Writings of Daniel, Philip, and Elizabeth McAlister Berrigan, Garland Publishing, 1979. Contributor to journals.

WORK IN PROGRESS: The Social Catholicism of Daniel and Philip Berrigan, completion expected in 1983; *Dorothy Day: Radical, Feminist, Catholic,* completion expected in 1986.

SIDELIGHTS: Anne Klejment's major interests are American social intellectual history, with emphasis on ethnic Catholics, the Catholic Left, womanhood, feminism, and race.

Klejment told *CA:* "In my writing on the Catholic Left, I argue that political implications can be discovered and identified in one's religious belief. This aspect of religious belief, of course, extends beyond the Catholic Left. I feel it is a general principle, although Americans are loathe to admit it."

* * *

KLIEWER, Evelyn   1933-

PERSONAL: Surname is pronounced "cleaver"; born September 5, 1933, in San Francisco, Calif.; daughter of John E. and Frances (a writer; maiden name, Caldwell) Durland; married Kermit Lee Kliewer (a high school teacher), September 1, 1956; children: Wendy, Bonnie, Bruce, Scott. *Education:* University of California, Berkeley, B.A., 1954; graduate study at San Diego State University, Calexico, 1966-68. *Politics:* Republican. *Religion:* Protestant. *Home:* 464 West B St., Brawley, Calif. 92227. *Office address: Brawley News,* P.O. Box 791, Brawley, Calif. 92227.

CAREER: Brawley News, Brawley, Calif., staff writer, 1977—. Teacher of writing classes. Guest on television programs; public speaker. *Member:* California Press Women, Women's Aglow Fellowship (president, 1975-77).

WRITINGS: Freedom From Fat, Revell, 1977; *Please, God, Help Me Get Well in Your Spare Time,* Bethany Fellowship, 1979; *Combat Kit for Dieters,* Celebration House, 1980. Contributor to magazines, including *Exceptional Parent, Pentecostal Evangel, Geothermal Energy News, Christian Life,* and *American Collector.*

WORK IN PROGRESS: The Think Fat Book, a satire; *The How-to Book for Mothers and Others,* a collection of vignettes.

SIDELIGHTS: Evelyn Kliewer told *CA:* "When I was thirty-eight years old, the writing bug bit—hard. I enrolled in a correspondence course on article writing and have been going strong ever since. My books have all been based on personal experiences which I feel compelled to share. I never anticipated three weight books, but I suppose, because I constantly fight fat, these have been natural. *Please, God* grew out of the experiences I had as we groped through my son's crisis. My mother book, I hope, will be a collection both from my own life and from others'.

"My mother, who is eighty-seven, resumed her writing career when I began writing. I hope I can be that prolific at the typewriter forty years from now!"

*   *   *

KLIGMAN, Ruth 1930-

PERSONAL: Born January 25, 1930, in New Jersey; daughter of Morris (a gambler) and Mary (Warmund) Kligman. *Education:* Attended New School for Social Research, New York University, and Yale University; studied painting privately, 1960-64. *Politics:* "Leftist." *Religion:* "Christian from Judaism." *Home and office:* 242 West 14th St., New York, N.Y. 10011.

CAREER: Director of Washington Square Gallery, 1964-68; administrative assistant, Bert Stern Productions, 1969; artist, with work exhibited in permanent collection at Museum of Modern Art, 1969—. Furniture designer; jewelry designer, 1967. Guest on New York City television programs; lecturer in art history; gives poetry readings.

WRITINGS: Love Affair: A Memoir of Jackson Pollock, Morrow, 1973. Author of "Love Affair: A Memoir of Jackson Pollock" (film script), released by Palomar Productions, 1975.

WORK IN PROGRESS: Just Like a Woman; Letters to God.

AVOCATIONAL INTERESTS: Abstract art, poetry, the Christian religion.

KLIMO, Jake
See KLIMO, Vernon

*   *   *

KLIMO, Vernon 1914-
(Jake Klimo)

PERSONAL: Born August 4, 1914, in Mount Vernon, Iowa; son of John and Berenice (Miller) Klimo; married Anne Ingle (a secretary), 1940; children: Jonathon, Mark, Katharine, Peter, Charles. *Education:* Attended Cornell College. *Politics:* Democrat. *Religion:* "No church." *Home:* 82 Main Ave., Sea Cliff, N.Y. 11579.

CAREER: Master mariner.

WRITINGS: (Under name Jake Klimo; with Will Oursler) *Hemingway and Jake,* Popular Library, 1973. Contributor to *Story Parade.*

*   *   *

KLINDT-JENSEN, Ole 1918-1980

OBITUARY NOTICE—See index for *CA* sketch: Born March 31, 1918, in Naestved, Denmark; died in 1980. Educator and author. Klindt-Jensen was a professor of prehistoric archaeology at the University of Aarhus and wrote several books on Scandinavian history. His works include *Foreign Influences in Denmark's Early Iron Age, Denmark Before the Vikings,* and *Viking Art.* Obituaries and other sources: *London Times,* July 18, 1980.

*   *   *

KNIGHT, Franklin Willis 1942-

PERSONAL: Born January 10, 1942, in Manchester, Jamaica; came to the United States in 1964, naturalized citizen, 1979; son of Willis and Irick Knight; married wife, June, 1965; children: Michael, Brian, Nadine. *Education:* University College of the West Indies, B.A., 1964; University of Wisconsin—Madison, M.A., 1965, Ph.D., 1969. *Office:* Department of History, Johns Hopkins University, Charles at 34th St., Baltimore, Md. 21218.

CAREER: State University of New York at Stony Brook, instructor, 1968-69, assistant professor, 1969-73, associate professor of history, 1973; Johns Hopkins University, Baltimore, Md., associate professor, 1973-77, professor of history, 1977—. Member of American Council of Learned Societies-Social Science Research Council joint committee on Latin American studies, 1971-73; fellow of Center for Advanced Studies in the Behavioral Sciences, 1977-78. *Member:* American Historical Association, Latin American Studies Association, Society for Spanish and Portuguese Historical Studies. *Awards, honors:* Humanity Award from Black Academy of Arts and Letters, 1970, for *Slave Society in Cuba;* National Endowment for the Humanities fellowship, 1977-78.

WRITINGS: Slave Society in Cuba During the Nineteenth Century, University of Wisconsin Press, 1970; *African Dimension in Latin American Societies,* Macmillan, 1974; *The Caribbean: The Genesis of a Fragmented Nationalism,* Oxford University Press, 1978; (editor with Margaret E. Crahan) *Africa and the Caribbean: The Legacies of a Link,* Johns Hopkins Press, 1979.

Contributor: Clara E. Lida and Iris Zavala, editors, *La Revolution de 1868* (title means "The Revolution of 1868"), Americas, 1970; David Cohen and Jack P. Greene, editors, *Neither Slave nor Free,* Johns Hopkins Press, 1972. Contributor to *Encyclopaedia Britannica, Encyclopedia Americana,* and UNESCO *History of Africa.*

WORK IN PROGRESS: Research on Spanish-American Creole society, 1750-1840, and on Jamaican migrants and the Cuban sugar industry, 1900-34.

*   *   *

KNOWLES, A(lbert) Sidney, Jr. 1926-

PERSONAL: Born December 11, 1926, in Savannah, Ga.; son of Albert Sidney and Kitty (Crupper) Knowles. *Education:* Attended West Virginia University, 1944; University of Virginia, B.A., 1949, M.A., 1951. *Home:* 2122 Cowper Dr., Raleigh, N.C. 27608. *Office:* Department of English, North Carolina State University, Raleigh, N.C. 27650.

CAREER: Ohio University, Athens, instructor, 1952-55; North Carolina State University, Raleigh, professor of English, 1955—. *Military service:* U.S. Army, 1945-46. *Member:* Modern Language Association, Renaissance Society of America, Society for the Study of Midwestern Literature, South Atlantic Modern Language Association.

WRITINGS—Contributor: W. G. French, editor, *The Forties,* Everett/Edwards, 1969; L. S. Champion, editor, *Quick Springs of Sense,* University of Georgia Press, 1974; W. G. French, editor, *The Twenties,* Everett/Edwards, 1975. Contributor to journals, including *Modern Fiction Studies, Southern Review,* and *Renaissance Papers.* Also associate editor of *Studies in the Novel.*

WORK IN PROGRESS: A biographical and critical essay on John Dos Passos for *Dictionary of Literary Biography,* for Gale.

SIDELIGHTS: Knowles told *CA:* "The best criticism rests on a foundation of good writing: it is a ratification of Goethe's maxim that an improvement in style is an improvement in thought. In our time, such critics as Van Wyck Brooks, Edmund Wilson, Malcolm Cowley, and Alfred Kayin have written with a combination of passion, lucidity, and insight that is all too often lacking in the work of academic critics. Criticism is an art, and we in the universities need to become less satisfied with mere explication and more responsive to the idea that the critic is an essayist as much as an explainer; that the critic, like the artist, must write well if he is to earn our serious attention."

*   *   *

KNOWLES, John H(ilton) 1926-1979

PERSONAL: Born May 23, 1926, in Chicago, Ill.; died of cancer, March 6, 1979, in Boston, Mass.; son of James (a business executive) and Jean Laurence (an artist; maiden name, Turnbull) Knowles; married Edith Morris LaCroix (a medical technician), June 13, 1953; children: Edith LaCroix, John Hilton, Charles Paine, James Turnbull, Jean Laurence, Robert Munro. *Education:* Harvard University, A.B., 1947, Washington University, St. Louis, Mo., M.D. (cum laude), 1951. *Home:* 28 Fernwood Rd., Chestnut Hill, Mass. 02167; and 860 Fifth Ave., New York, N.Y. 10021. *Office:* Rockefeller Foundation, 1133 Avenue of the Americas, New York, N.Y. 10036.

CAREER: Massachusetts General Hospital, Boston, intern, 1951-52, assistant resident, 1952-53, resident, 1955-56, chief resident, 1958-59, chief of pulmonary disease unit, 1959-61, assistant physician, 1962-64, physician, 1964-72, general director, 1962-72, consultant, 1972-79; Rockefeller Foundation, New York City, president and trustee, 1972-79. Harvard University Medical School, Cambridge, Mass., teach-

ing fellow, 1952-53, assistant, 1958-59, instructor, 1959-60, associate, 1960-63, lecturer, 1963-79, professor of medicine, 1969-72; New York University Medical Center, New York City, professor of medicine, 1972-79. Trustee of Washington University, 1973-77, Harvard University, 1973-79, Duke University, 1974-79, Boston University, 1975-79, and Belmont Hill School. Chairman of General Education Board, 1972-79; member of Commission on Critical Choices for America; member of board of directors of Chase Frontier Fund, Boston Bruins, and New England Patriots; limited partner of Paine, Webber, Jackson & Curtis. Director of BCC Industries and General Telephone and Electronics. *Military service:* U.S. Naval Reserve, Medical Corps, 1953-55; became lieutenant.

MEMBER: American Academy of Arts and Sciences (fellow), American Association for the Advancement of Science (fellow), American Board of Internal Medicine (diplomate), American College of Physicians (fellow), American Public Health Association, American Hospital Association, American Medical Association, American Federation for Clinical Research, National Academy of Sciences—Institute of Medicine, National Institute of Medicine, Association of American Medical Colleges, New York Academy of Medicine (fellow), Council on Foreign Relations, Society of Medical Administrators, Boston Library Society, Harvard Alumni Association (former director), Kappa Phi Eta, Alpha Omega Alpha, Commercial Merchants, Tavern, Tennis, and Racquet, Links, Racquet and Tennis, Aesculapian, Myopia Hunt.

AWARDS, HONORS: U.S. Public Health Service fellowship, 1956-57; LL.D. from Northeastern University, 1969, Babson College, 1971, University of Pennsylvania, 1972, Suffolk University, 1975, and Williams College, 1976; John M. Russell Award of Markle Scholars, 1969, for contributions to medical education; Ruth Gray Lecture Award from Evanston (Ill.) Hospital, 1970; Sc.D. from Washington University, 1970, Hahnemann Medical College, 1971, Albany Medical College, 1972, Pratt Institute, 1973, Middlebury College, 1975, and New York Medical College, 1975; D.C.L. from Union College, 1970; D.H.L. from Ithaca College, 1971, Boston University, 1972, Ohio Wesleyan University, 1973, Pace University, 1975, and Rush University, 1975.

WRITINGS: Respiratory Physiology and Its Clinical Application, Harvard University Press, 1959; (editor) *Hospitals, Doctors, and the Public Interest* (collection of lectures), Harvard University Press, 1965; (editor) *The Teaching Hospital: Evolution and Contemporary Issues* (collection of lectures), Harvard University Press, 1966; (editor) *Views of Medical Education and Medical Care* (collection of essays), Harvard University Press, 1968; *China Diary,* Rockefeller Foundation, 1976; (editor) *Doing Better and Feeling Worse: Health in the United States* (collection of essays), Norton, 1977. Also author with Fran P. Hosken of sound recording, "Health Care and the City," Norton, 1974. Contributor of numerous articles to magazines, including *Time* and *Life,* and to medical and scientific journals.

SIDELIGHTS: When John Knowles became director of the prestigious Massachusetts General Hospital in Boston, things began to change. He quickly replaced the long wooden benches in the Emergency waiting room—the "cattle-car concept of medicine," as he referred to it—with comfortable chairs and a more soothing atmosphere. He installed nine specialized-care units, including coronary-care, and initiated both radiation and cancer treatment units. In addition, Knowles set up social services affiliated with the hospital throughout the community, such as a team of psychiatrists to work in schools, courts, and social agencies on the problems of mental health. A medical health station at the busy Logan International Airport in Boston and several clinics located in the poorer sections of the city are but two more of his successful programs.

A long-time advocate of preventive medicine and an untiring foe of unnecessary operations and the exorbitantly high fees charged by some physicians, Knowles accumulated more than a few detractors in the medical field. According to Knowles, many physicians wish not to cooperate with preventive medicine and health education programs because of the "negligible" emotional, financial, and intellectual rewards involved. "It's much more fun to do acute, curative medicine," he explained. "When you have a stomach ache and they take out your appendix, you love them—there's the emotional reward. You pay them a big fee—there's the money part. And, intellectually, it's a lot more exciting than writing a pamphlet."

Knowles received protest from the private sector as well for his preachings of good health via regular exercise, a balanced diet, alcoholic beverages only in moderation, abstinence from tobacco, and a proper weight level. "One newspaper in Virginia called me a 'health fascist' and said that I was going to remove the last joy of life in the United States," he related to Carol Kahn in *Family Health*. "I've also received letters saying that I wanted to legislate away the freedom to have a can of beer when the sun goes down or to smoke a good cigar. My point is: Take your choice, folks. If you want to booze, smoke, be fat and lie around, then stop complaining about getting sick prematurely and the high cost of treatment."

With his impressive qualifications in the medical field, coupled with his staunch campaigning for Richard Nixon in both 1960 and 1968, Knowles was considered the likely choice for the soon-to-be-vacated post of assistant secretary for health and scientific affairs for the U.S. Department of Health, Education and Welfare (HEW) during the Nixon administration in 1969. In fact, designated secretary Robert Finch himself approached Knowles with the position a month prior to the resignation of the current assistant secretary. When Knowles accepted this initial offer, Finch submitted his recommendation to President Nixon, who said he would appoint Knowles if Finch could "sell" him to Congress. "When word spread that Finch had offered the job," reported *Newsweek*, "the American Medical Association went on the attack."

Although the A.M.A. never admitted publicly to nonsupport of Knowles, his name was conspicuously absent from its list of recommended individuals for the position. "I was . . . depicted by the A.M.A. Board of Trustees and [the American Medical Political Action Committee] as a flaming liberal constantly pleading for so-called 'socialized medicine,'" recalled Knowles in an article for *Life*. "Nothing of course could be further from the truth." He added that "it was put out that I was not a physician who understood patient care; that I was a captive of hospital interests; and that I was not broadly enough based to assume this high position effectively."

According to Knowles, had he not been a chief administrator of a major hospital but instead a physician in private practice, the A.M.A. censure could have had irreversibly devastating results: "I couldn't get patients referred to me, I probably wouldn't be on the staff of any hospital, and I wouldn't be able to buy malpractice insurance at a decent rate."

It was to be a grueling six-month period of waiting for Knowles and his family before a final decision was reached. "It was a tough time for somebody with a wife and six children," he later admitted. "The children were very upset during those six months. . . . They wondered why the Government wouldn't take their dad to fill that important position."

Knowles was passed over for the position of assistant secretary. In his place Nixon appointed Knowles's long-time friend and colleague, Dr. Roger Olaf Egeberg. Ironically, both men held similar views concerning preventive medicine, social welfare programs, and a host of other topics calling for reform in the American health care system.

In 1972 Knowles assumed the post of president and trustee of the Rockefeller Foundation, the second largest research institution in the United States. When accused of abandoning medicine by becoming affiliated with an organization whose interests lie often in other fields, Knowles asserted: "The medical profession should be participating in the larger social issues. . . . I think that cleaning up the social and physical environment will do as much to reduce mental illness and vascular disease and some forms of cancer as anything else we're doing directly now."

Despite the seeming lack of interest and cooperation on the part of both the national government and the general public concerning adequate health care systems and education, Knowles was not easily discouraged or deterred from his goal of making America a nation of healthy individuals. "Good health is the birthright of every American citizen," he always maintained. "I'm practical about these things," he told Kahn, "but I think there is a great hope in the world. There are substantial numbers of well-intentioned, well-educated people in this country and around the world. They are working hard on these problems and making substantial gains. I gotta be an optimist," he concluded. "If I wasn't laughing, I'd be crying. I mean, why else am I knocking myself out?"

BIOGRAPHICAL/CRITICAL SOURCES: American Journal of Public Health, August, 1966, March, 1969; *Harvard Educational Review*, spring, 1967; *Modern Hospital*, January, 1969; *Washington Post*, May 25, 1969; *New York Times*, June 25, 1969, June 27, 1969, June 28, 1969, September 14, 1971; *Time*, July 4, 1969, June 12, 1972, July 17, 1972, August 9, 1976; *Newsweek*, June 9, 1969, July 7, 1969; *Life*, July 11, 1969, June 30, 1972; *Scientific American*, September, 1973; *Redbook*, March, 1975; *New York Times Book Review*, July 24, 1977; *Political Science Quarterly*, winter, 1977-78; *Virginia Quarterly Review*, winter, 1978.

OBITUARIES: New York Times, March 7, 1979; *Washington Post*, March 8, 1979; *Newsweek*, March 19, 1979; *Time*, March 19, 1979.

—*Sketch by Kathleen Ceton Newman*

*   *   *

KOENIG, Franz 1905-

PERSONAL: Born August 3, 1905, in Rabenstein, Pielach, Austria; son of Franz and Maria (Fink) Koenig. *Education:* Attended universities of Vienna, Rome, Lille, and Innsbruck. *Office:* Erzbischoefliches Sekretariat, Rotenturmstrasse 2, 1010 Wein, Austria.

CAREER: Ordained Roman Catholic priest, 1933; served as secular priest in Lille, France; cathedral curate in St. Poelten; instructor at secondary schools; University of Vienna, Vienna, Austria, lecturer in theology, 1946—; titular bishop of Livias, 1952; University of Salzburg, Salzburg, Austria, extraordinary professor, 1952; bishop co-adjutor of St. Poelten, 1952; archbishop of Vienna, 1956—; cardinal, 1958—; Secretariat for Non-Believers, Vienna, president, 1965—. *Member:* American Academy of Arts and Sciences, Catholic Academy of Vienna, Kongregation fuer die Bischoefe. *Awards, honors:* Honorary degrees from Notre Dame University, 1959, University of Vienna, 1963, Canisius College, Catholic University of America, Marquette University, and Sacred Heart College, Manhattanville, all 1964, University of Zagreb, 1970, University of Innsbruck, 1970, and University of Salzburg, 1972.

WRITINGS—In English translation: *Die Stunde der Welt,* Styria, 1971, translation by Herbert W. Richardson published as *The Hour Is Now,* Harper, 1975.

In German, except as noted: (Editor) Joseph Eberle, *Die Bibel im Lichte der Weltliteratur und Weltgeschichte,* Herder, 1949; (editor with others) *Christus und die Religionen der Erde: Handbuch der Religionsgeschichte,* Volume I: *Der ur-und vorgeschichtliche Berelch,* Volume II: *Religionen der alten Voelker und Kulturen,* Volume III: *Die lebenden ausserchristlichen Hochreligionen,* Herder, 1951; *Religionswissenschaftliches Woerterbuch: Die Grundbegriffe,* Herder, 1956; (editor) *Ganz in Gottes Hand: Briefe gefallener und hingerichteter Katholiken, 1939-1945,* Herder, 1957.

Zarathustras Jenseitsvorstellungen und das alte Testament, Herder, 1964; *Kirche im Aufbruch,* Katholische Jugend der Erzdioezese, 1966; *Worte zur Zeit* (addressess, essays, and lectures), edited by Richard Barta, Herder, 1968; *Il Christianesimo e le religioni della terra* (in Italian; lecture), Borla, 1968; *Der Aufbruch zum Geist* (addressess, essays, and lectures), Styria, 1972; *Das zeichen Gottes: Die Kirche in unserer Zeit,* Styria, 1973; *Der Mensch ist fuer die Zukunft angelegt: Analysen, Reflexionen, Stellungnahmen* (addresses, essays, and lectures), Herder, 1975; *Kirche und Welt,* [Vienna], 1978. Also contributor to *Die Freiheit der Kirche in einem christlichen Europa,* Naumann, 1977.

*   *   *

KOENNER, Alfred 1921-

PERSONAL: Born December 2, 1921, in Schalkendorf, Germany (now East Germany); married; children: Stephan, Henry. *Education:* Attended University of Berlin. *Religion:* Catholic. *Home:* Valwigerstrasse 32, East Berlin, East Germany.

CAREER: Assistant at institute for practical pedagogy in East Berlin, East Germany, 1946-49; lecturer in German language and literature, 1953; assistant with writers' association in East Berlin, 1954; Altberliner Verlag (publisher), East Berlin, chief reader, 1959—.

WRITINGS—In English translation; juvenile picture books: *Jolli,* Parabel Verlag, c. 1960, translation by Regina Waldman published as *Jolli,* Lerner Publications, 1967; *The Clever Coot,* translated from the original German, Carolrhoda Books, 1971; *Die Hochzeit des Pfaus,* [East Germany], 1972, translation by Marion Koenig published as *The Peacock's Wedding,* Chatto & Windus, 1973.

In German; juvenile; all picture books, except as noted: (With Karl Fischer) *Wenn ich gross bin, lieber Mond,* Buchheim Verlag, 1961; *Das Pony mit dem Federbusch,* [East Germany], 1962; *Mein bunter Zoo* (poems), [East Germany], 1962; *Kiek in die Welt* (stories), [East Germany], 1964; *Tappelpit,* [East Germany], 1964; *Fertig macht sich Nikolaus,* Altberliner Verlag, 1967; *Der Rummelpott* (rhymes), Altberliner Verlag, 1967; *Der Raeuberhase,* [East Germany], 1969.

Wer maeuschenstill am Bache sitzt, [East Germany], 1971;

Auf dem Hofe tut sich was (poems), [East Germany], 1972; *Eine Wolke schwartz und schwer,* [East Germany], 1973; *Pusteblumen,* [East Germany], 1973; *Sildo,* [East Germany], 1975; *Kieselchen,* [East Germany], 1975; *Olrik,* [East Germany], 1976; *Drei kleine Baerren,* [East Germany], 1976; *Der verwandelte Wald,* [East Germany], 1976; *Schnick und Schnack und Schabernack* (rhymes), [East Germany], 1978; *Ein Bagger geht spazieren,* [East Germany], 1978; *Ich reise ins Blaue,* [East Germany], 1979; *Als Robert aus dem Fenster sah* (cantata), [East Germany], 1979.

SIDELIGHTS: Koenner told *CA* that his writings and other literary activities are concerned with the development and furtherance of books for pre- and school-age children. He is interested in this age group because of their spontaneity and sizable attention span. Consequently, he creates picture books with short stories about animals, often with characters taken from popular fables. He added that a major feature of his work is the linking of poetic fantasy with educational theory.

*   *   *

KOGAWA, Joy Nozomi 1935-

PERSONAL: Born June 6, 1935, in Vancouver, British Columbia, Canada; daughter of Gordon Goichi (a minister) and Lois (Yao) Nakayama; married David Kogawa, May 2, 1957 (divorced, 1968); children: Gordon, Deirdre. *Education:* Attended University of Alberta, 1954, Anglican Women's Training College, 1956, Conservatory of Music, 1956, and University of Saskatchewan, 1968. *Home address:* P.O. Box 2950, Station D, Ottawa, Ontario, Canada.

CAREER: Office of the Prime Minister, Ottawa, Ontario, staff writer, 1974-76; free-lance writer, 1976-78; University of Ottawa, Ottawa, writer-in-residence, 1978; free-lance writer, 1978—. *Member:* League of Canadian Poets.

WRITINGS: The Splintered Moon (poems), Fiddlehead Poetry Books, 1967; *A Choice of Dreams* (poems), McClelland & Stewart, 1974; *Jericho Road* (poems), McClelland & Stewart, 1977. Contributor of poems to magazines in the United States and Canada, including *Canadian Forum, West Coast Review, Queen's Quarterly, Quarry, Prism International,* and *Chicago Review.*

WORK IN PROGRESS: A novel about Japanese Canadians, publication by Lester and Orpen Dennys expected in 1981.

*   *   *

KOLON, Nita
See ONADIPE, (Nathaniel) Kola(wole)

*   *   *

KONIG, Franz
See KOENIG, Franz

*   *   *

KONWICKI, Tadeusz 1926-

PERSONAL: Born July 22, 1926, in Nowa Wilejka, Poland; son of Michal (a metal worker) and Jadwiga (Kiezun) Konwicki; married Danuta Lenica, April 25, 1949; children: Maria, Anna. *Education:* Attended University of Warsaw and Jagellonian University of Cracow, 1945-49. *Home:* 1 Gorskiego, 00-033 Warsaw, Poland.

CAREER: Novelist, screenwriter, film director, and journalist. Director of films, including "Ostatni dzien lata," 1960, "Zaduszki," 1962, "Salto," 1964, "Matura," 1965, and

"Jak daleko stad, jak blisko," 1972. *Wartime service:* Member of Polish underground during World War II. *Member:* Polish Writers' Union, Union of Polish Filmmakers. *Awards, honors:* State Prize for Literature, 1950, for *Przy budowie,* and 1954, for *Wladza;* Venice Film Festival Grand Prix, 1958, for "Ostatni dzien lata"; special jury prize from Mannheim Film Festival, 1962, for "Zaduszki"; prize from San Remo Film Festival, 1972, for screenplay, "Jak daleko stad, jak blisko."

WRITINGS—All novels, except as noted; in English: *Sennik wspolczesny,* Iskry (Warsaw), 1963, translation by David Welsh published as *A Dreambook for Our Time,* M.I.T. Press, 1969; *Zwierzoczlekoupior* (juvenile), illustrations by wife, Danuta Konwicki, Czytelnik (Warsaw), 1969, translation by George Korwin-Rodziszewski and Audrey Korwin-Rodziszewski published as *The Anthropos-Specter-Beast,* S. G. Phillips, 1977.

In Polish: *Przy budowie* (short stories; title means "At the Building Site"), Czytelnik, 1950; *Wladza* (title means "The Power"), Czytelnik, 1954; *Godzina smutku* (title means "The Hour of Sadness"), Czytelnik, 1954; *Klucz* (title means "The Key"), Nasza Ksiegarnia (Warsaw), 1955; *Rojsty* (title means "The Marshes"), Czytelnik, 1956; *Z oblezonego miasta* (title means "From the Besieged Town"), Iskry, 1956; *Ostatni dzien lata* (screenplays; also see below; contains "Ostatni dzien lata," "Zaduszki," "Salto," "Matura," "Zimowy zmlerzch," and "Jak daleko stad, jak blisko"), Iskry, 1966, revised edition, 1973; *Dziura w niebie* (title means "A Hole in the Sky"), Iskry, 1959; *Wniebowstapienie* (title means "Ascension"), Iskry, 1967; *NIC ablo NIC* (title means "Nothing or Nothing"), Czytelnik, 1971; *Kronika wypadkow milosnych* (title means "Chronicle of Love Happenings"), Czytelnik, 1974; *Kalendarz i klepsydra* (title means "The Diary and the Sandglass"), Czytelnik, 1976; *Kompleks polski* (title means "The Polish Complex"), published in *Zapis 3,* Index on Censorship (London), 1977; *Mala apokalipsa* (title means "Little Apocalypse"), published in *Zapis 10,* Index on Censorship, 1979.

Screenplays: "Ostatni dzien lata" (title means "The Last Day of Summer"), Film Polski, 1958; "Matka Joanna od Aniolow" (title means "Mother Joan of the Angels"), Film Polski, 1961; "Zaduszki" (title means "Halloway"), Film Polski, 1962; (with Kawalerowicz) "Faraon" (title means "Pharoh"), Film Polski, 1964; "Salto," Film Polski, 1964; "Matura" (title means "Entrance Examination"), 1965; "Zimowy zmlerzch" (title means "Winter's Twilight"), 1956; "Jak daleko stad, jak blisko" (title means "So Far, So Near"), Film Polski, 1972.

SIDELIGHTS: It was not until the 1956 political and cultural "thaw" in Poland that Konwicki and his contemporaries were able to have their major works published. Prior to that time, Konwicki published minor works, including a collection of short stories entitled *Przy budowie* and a novel entitled *Wladza.* Both are winners of the State Prize for Literature and are, in the opinion of Jerzy Krzyzanowski, "cliches of socialist-realist fiction . . . modeled on Soviet novels," the results of severe state-imposed censorship.

The publication of *Rojsty* in 1956 is considered a turning point in Konwicki's literary career. The author had waited eight years to publish the somber and satirical account of a young man's desperate attempts to become a hero. *Rojsty* is based on Konwicki's own bitter experiences as a guerrilla fighter with the Home Army of the Polish underground, when the guerrillas successfully liberated the city of Wilno

from Nazi occupation and were punished with arrest, deportation, and imprisonment by the advancing Soviet troops. Konwicki managed to escape the concentration camp roundup and join another group in fighting the Soviet invaders. The unit disbanded when the men realized that the situation was indeed hopeless, and Konwicki then embarked on an academic and literary career. But as Krzyzanowski observed, "The psychological wounds inflicted by those tragic events were to remain in his memory during the years to come, affecting, and to a great extent shaping, his artistic vision."

A Dreambook for Our Time is Konwicki's first novel to appear in English translation and has been compared to works of Albert Camus and Joseph Conrad. Ruel K. Wilson theorized that the novel's great overnight success was due to its "brutal frankness of subject matter and imagery." With this book Konwicki began a painful exploration into a world of tormented survivors where, in the words of Wilson, "the past holds them all prisoner, for their attitudes toward the present have been conditioned by their experiences before and during the German occupation."

Dreambook's protagonist, Oldster, is a former partisan consumed with guilt and seeking retribution for his wartime actions. As the novel opens, he "awakens after a suicide attempt, surrounded by inquisitive faces in the remote village to which he has drifted," related Neal Ascherson. "We understand," Ascherson continued, "that he is solitary, crushed and bewildered by memories of the war and the postwar years to which, although some fifteen years in the past, he can still give no meaning. But the other inhabitants are in the same pass. Nothing is happening in this somnolent place, malarial with sinister memories of violence and mystery." Oldster has returned to this valley and forest, the scene of his crime, to find forgiveness.

During the war he had been assigned to kill a fellow countryman who had betrayed partisans to the Germans. Carrying out the order, Oldster had fired his shot with his victim's young daughter as witness. But not having shot to kill, Oldster is convinced that the man has survived and is living in the valley. He also suspects that the partisan chief, who gave the execution order, is still hiding in the nearby forest. "Whether this is delusion, obsession, mania, is never made clear," stated critic Abraham Rothberg.

After experiencing much torment and loneliness, Oldster meets a man who can give him some perspective. "During the war too, I kept to the political average," the man tells him. "Most of the nation neither fought at the front, nor hid in the forests, nor suffered in concentration camps. The ordinary majority stayed in their badly heated houses, ate frozen potatoes and dealt a little in the black market. I did the same. Nobody gave me a medal for what I did during the occupation, but nobody reproved me either. I didn't gain anything, but I didn't lose anything." Oldster finally realizes, Rothberg observed, "that the present, however unheroic and boring, must be lived in and endured. After giving up the nightmare of the past, both its horror and heroism, half-willing, half-pushed, half-knowing, half-duped, he is constrained to leave the valley, saying in the very last lines of the book: '. . . I would scramble with the remains of my strength out of these seething depths to the edge of reality, and would get up to an ordinary, commonplace day, with its usual troubles, its everyday toil, its so well-known familiar drudgery.'"

In *Dreambook,* Konwicki achieves a surrealistic quality with what Mark Schechner called "a blurring of perception." Schechner explained: "This is indeed a dreambook for not only does the past inhabit the present with inescapable recollections but present events themselves dissolve in a dream-like haze of uncertainty. Here . . . the terrors of war lead to emotional anesthesia. . . . As in a play by Beckett, the simplest acts are performed with maddening difficulty, and the most routine thoughts and recollections are achieved only through a tedious grasping with the will to forget.''

Wilson found *Dreambook*'s vision of humanity "gloomy and nihilistic." He elaborated: "Konwicki's grim caricatures perturb and sometimes amuse the reader, although they evoke little sympathy. . . . the novel's message is highly symbolic. The dream atmosphere, visual, pungent, yet impressionistic, inclines us to accept the work for what it is: a montage of apocalyptic events seen and relived by an obsessive and guilty imagination.'' V. D. Mihailovich, in *Saturday Review,* drew a comparison of Konwicki's writing style and filmic technique: "The author, who is also a movie director, mixes dramatic episodes, flashbacks, nightmarish reveries, and inner monologues with abandon.'' He praised Konwicki's "wide use of metaphors, symbols, and irony,'' which he felt "enlivens the style.'' Mihailovich further stated: "Though the characters are full-blooded eccentrics, their antics are in harmony with their inner mechanisms. A certain dreamlike quality, a gossamer of things long past yet somehow still clinging to life, pervades Konwicki's facile and poetic narration. As a result the reader is rewarded with illustrations of the consequences of indelible war experiences and with beautiful prose as well.''

Delving further into the nightmarish world of the guilty survivor, Konwicki produced a subsequent novel, *Wniebowstapienie*. Here "the horrors of war memories give way to the torments of life in the corrupted post-war society,'' Krzyzanowski said. *Wniebowstapienie*'s characters are ghost-like creatures for whom the city of Warsaw serves as a purgatory. "Building the plot around a bank robbery, Konwicki leads his characters through the streets, restaurants, parks and jails but most frequently gathers them together in the empty marble halls of the Palast [Warsaw's Palace of Culture], its basements and power stations, juxtaposing their enormous size and deserted spaces with the ugliness and pettiness of everyday life in contemporary Poland. Such an ironic twist,'' Krzyzanowski wrote, "adds a grotesque flavor to that somber and masterfully written novel, in which realistic presentation of characters and scenery achieves another dimension of supernatural and symbolic vision.'' Because of its pessimistic depiction of Polish society, *Wniebowstapienie* was banned in that country. David Welsh recalled: "Gomulka, then First Secretary to the Party, is believed personally to have ordered the withdrawal of all 30,000 copies some months later, and a wall of silence descended on Konwicki, although he since has been allowed to publish a couple of innocuous novels. His 'editor' is said to have been degraded to 'editing' labels for bottles of mineral water, no doubt with a cut in her wages.''

Like many of his earlier writings, Konwicki's unconventional tale *The Anthropos-Specter-Beast* is woven with elements of the dreamworld. In a review of the original Polish edition Welsh called it "even more comic and weird than [Konwicki's] previous work.'' He continued: "Ostensibly written for children . . . it is not meant for 'good children,' as they will not benefit from it (says Konwicki). The book exists on at least three levels: the narrative itself which can be related to *Winnie-the-Pooh* and *Alice in Wonderland;* the 'real world,' bearing in mind always that reality is something peculiarly ambiguous in Konwicki's fiction; and the narra-

tor's dream. Konwicki's handling of these three levels is masterly.''

NIC ablo NIC is considered by some critics to be Konwicki's most ambitious novel. According to Krzyzanowski, it "explores all the passions, obsessions, fears and complexes he has inherited from the violent past and which he sees in the present.'' Konwicki came from that portion of Poland which was lost to the Soviet Union during World War II, and his feelings of sorrow and estrangement from the loss of his homeland are intensely expressed in *NIC ablo NIC*. Although Konwicki made a "sentimental journey'' to the land of his childhood in one of his minor novels, noted Krzyzanowski, only in the author's major works "does he transform it into an everpresent image of major importance.''

When the Polish motion picture industry became liberated from rigid ideological standards in the late 1950's, Konwicki discovered a new mode of expression. His subsequent films, with themes of self-destructive guilt and deep sexual frustration, are closely related to his novels. One such film is "Ostatni dzien lata,'' a melancholy story of two young lovers who meet on the beach. Krzyzanowski described the film's poignant imagery: "In the fast-moving shadows of jet fighters screaming overhead like modern symbols of doom and destruction the lovers are able to enjoy just a brief moment of happiness, since neither their past experiences nor the uncertain future can provide them with any lasting relationship.'' The film ends as the young woman awakens to find only her lover's quickly disappearing footprints in the blowing sand. Krzyzanowski observed that "the image of water as a primordial source and a final grave for all things also appears in Konwicki's subsequent works.'' He also mentioned that "the motifs of impending doom, the impossibility of sharing one's own past, and the futility of seeking lasting happiness—enhanced with images and visual symbols'' found in the film, are forebearers to the themes of *A Dreambook of Our Time*. Konwicki's next film, "Salto,'' is considered to be "a visual postscript'' to *Dreambook*.

In 1972, following the murder by terrorists of nine members of an Israeli Olympic team, Konwicki expressed his grief: "Whoever looks at my writings now knows that the motif of killing committed in the name of higher ideological and moral principals has become my nightmare. . . . I still cannot forget that winter night . . . when we shot a man whom we did not know, and shooting him we cut the thread of an unknown life forever.''

BIOGRAPHICAL/CRITICAL SOURCES: New York Times Book Review, May 17, 1970; *Saturday Review,* June 20, 1970; *Books Abroad,* winter, 1971, summer, 1974; *New Republic,* April 10, 1976; *New York Review of Books,* May 27, 1976; *Nation,* June 19, 1976; *World Literature Today,* summer, 1977; *Contemporary Literary Criticism,* Volume 8, Gale, 1978.

—*Sketch by Susan A. Stefani*

*   *   *

KOOPMAN, LeRoy George 1935-

PERSONAL: Born April 5, 1935, in Willow Lake, S.D.; son of August John (a pastor) and Bertha (Ramaker) Koopman; married Marjorie Ann Hook, June 4, 1957; children: Kendall, Lori. *Education:* Central College (now Central University of Iowa), B.A., 1957; Western Theological Seminary, Holland, Mich., B.D., 1960; Northern Baptist Seminary, Oakbrook, Ill., Th.M., 1968. *Politics:* Republican. *Home:* 8080 Grove Dr., Jenison, Mich. 49428. *Office address:* Reformed Church in America, P.O. Box 247, Grandville, Mich. 49418.

CAREER: Ordained minister of Reformed Church in America, 1960; pastor of Reformed churches in Stickney, Ill., 1960-66, Morrison, Ill., 1966-69, and Pompano Beach, Fla., 1969-75; Church Herald, Grand Rapids, Mich., associate editor, 1975-79; Reformed Church in America, Grandville, Mich., secretary for mission information, 1979—.

WRITINGS: Guide to Ecclesiastical Birdwatching, Regal Books, 1973; Beauty Care for the Tongue, Zondervan, 1974; Beauty Care for the Eyes, Zondervan, 1975; Notebook of Worship Aids, Liturgy Publications, 1976; Beauty Care for the Hands, Zondervan, 1977; Scriptural Worship Aids, Baker Book, 1978; (editor) Henry Schut, Ten Years to Live, Baker Book, 1978; Seasonal Sermon Outlines, Baker Book, 1979; Beauty Care for the Feet, Zondervan, 1979; Twenty-Six Vital Issues, Baker Book, 1979; Beauty Care for the Ears, Zondervan, 1980; Good Morning Lord: Devotions for Active Christians, Baker Book, 1980.

WORK IN PROGRESS: A graduation gift book for Baker Book, publication expected in 1981.

* * *

KOSTRUBALA, Thaddeus 1930-

PERSONAL: Born September 22, 1930, in Chicago, Ill.; son of Joseph G. (a plastic surgeon) and Emily (Herrick) Kostrubala; married wife, Ann, May 8, 1970 (divorced December, 1977); married Teresa Clitsome (a psychologist), April 19, 1978; children: Nathaniel, Emily Clare, Annika, Christine, Alexandra, Giovanna, Tadeusz. Education: Northwestern University, B.S. (honors in anthropology), 1952; University of Virginia School of Medicine, M.D., 1958. Politics: "Uncertain." Religion: Byzantine Anglican. Home and office: 149 10th St., Del Mar, Calif. 92014.

CAREER: Tripler Army Hospital, Honolulu, Hawaii, intern, 1958-59; Northwestern University Medical School, Department of Neurology and Psychiatry, Evanston, Ill., resident in psychiatry, 1959-62, assistant professor, 1962-70, executive secretary of residency training program, 1963-65; Michigan Avenue Hospital, Chicago, Ill., clinical director of Katherine Wright Clinic, 1961-64, chairman of Department of Neurology and psychiatry, 1962-64; Chicago Board of Health, Mental Health Division, director, 1964-66, member of professional advisory council, 1968-69; director of community psychiatry and senior attending physician, Maine Medical Center, 1969-71; Tufts University Medical School, Medford, Mass., assistant professor, 1969-71; served as medical director of Department of Mental Health, chief of department of psychiatry, and director of psychiatric education at Mercy Hospital and Medical Center, professor of rehabilitation counseling at San Diego State University, assistant clinical professor of psychiatry at University of California, San Diego, and clinical professor of psychiatry at United States International University; founder and former psychiatrist and physician at Askelpian Center, Bishop, Calif.; International Association of Running Therapies, Del Mar, Calif., founder, physician, and therapist trainer, 1980—.

Co-founder of Kostrubala Corp. Visiting instructor at Seabury-Western Theological Seminary, 1962-70; delegate, Harvard Inter-University Forum for Educators in Community Psychiatry, 1967-69. Chairman of medical and psychological committee, Citizens United for the Rehabilitation of Addicts, 1963-65, and of the Education for Life Program, Firman House, 1963-68, both Chicago; member of board of directors of Metropolitan Planning Council on Mental Health, 1963-65; founder and member of board of "Call for

Help" Clinic, Suicide Prevention Center, Chicago, 1963-66; member of State of Illinois Mental Health Fund advisory committee, 1968-69; member of board of directors of Illinois Division of American Civil Liberties Union, 1968-69. Chairman of board of directors, Academy of Religion and Mental Health of Greater Chicago, 1962-63; member of standing committee, Episcopal Diocese of Chicago, 1966-69; director of research, Chicago Archdiocesan Health Program, 1967-69; member of board of directors, California Association of Catholic Hospitals. Member of board of directors of St. Leonard's House, 1960-69, Dyslexia Memorial Institute, 1962-70, St. Louis Home, Portland, Me., 1969-71, and Longevity Research Institute.

MILITARY SERVICE: U.S. Marine Corps, 1950-54; became first lieutenant. Member: American Psychiatric Association (fellow; member of special task force on aggression and violence, 1969-73; member of special task force on third party intervention in community crisis, 1973-74), Illinois Medical Society (member of committee on narcotics and hazardous substances, 1967-69, 1967-69), San Diego Psychiatric Society (member of council, 1973-74), San Diego County Medical Society, Alpha Omega Alpha. Awards, honors: Seven awards for civic achievement, all 1966, from Alpha Phi Alpha, Sisters of the Blessed Sacrament, Chicago Housing Authority, and National Association for the Advancement of Colored People (NAACP), among others.

WRITINGS: (Contributor) J. Masserman, editor, Current Psychiatric Therapies, Volume VI, 1966; The Joy of Running, Lippincott, 1976. Contributor of articles to Psychiatric News, Practical Psychology for Physicians, Chicago Medicine, Illinois Medical Journal, Journal of Marriage and Family Living, and Journal of Community Psychiatry.

WORK IN PROGRESS: Writings on the development of running theory and paleoanalytic psychology.

SIDELIGHTS: Kostrubala commented that he is interested in "holistic health, the psychology and symbolism evoked by long distance running and its effects, and the training of running therapists." He also explained that the International Association of Running Therapies, which he founded, "focuses on the physical, psychologic, and spiritual as applied to the care, management, and prevention of mental illness. There is a particular emphasis on running, diet, wilderness mountain hiking, and explorations of the symbolic aspects of body and mind."

BIOGRAPHICAL/CRITICAL SOURCES: Runner's World, January, 1978, February, 1978; New York, May 29, 1978; Forum, July, 1978; Newsweek, May 23, 1979.

* * *

KRAMER, Nancy 1942-

PERSONAL: Born April 1, 1942, in Rye, N.Y.; daughter of A. Stanley (an advertising executive) and Edith (Roey) Kramer; married Ronald Austin Hollander (divorced, 1966). Education: Brandeis University, B.F.A. (magna cum laude), 1963; Columbia University, LL.B. (with honors), 1966. Religion: Jewish. Home: 900 West End Ave., New York, N.Y. 10025. Agent: Patricia Berens, Sterling Lord Agency, Inc., 660 Madison Ave., New York, N.Y. 10019. Office: Committee for Public Justice, Inc., 132 West 43rd St., New York, N.Y. 10036.

CAREER: Admitted to New York State Bar, 1966; also admitted to practice in Eastern, Northern, and Southern District Courts of New York City. Legal Aid Society, New York City, trial attorney, 1966-1968; Manhattan Bowery

Project, New York City, assistant director, 1968-69; Office of Economic Opportunity, Northeast Region, assistant regional counsel, 1969-70; associate at Moore, Berson, Hamburg, and Bernstein, 1970-71; consultant to Office of Economic Opportunity on national research project, 1971; Council on the Environment of New York City, New York City, general counsel, 1972-73; New York Public Interest Research Group (NYPIRG), New York City, senior staff attorney, 1973-79; Committee for Public Justice, New York City, executive director, 1979—. Co-founder and participant in Consumer Law Training Center of New York Law School, 1975-78. Clerk for Justice Jay A. Rabinowitz, Supreme Court of Alaska, 1966. *Member:* Bar Association of the City of New York (chairperson of Special Committee on Consumer Affairs), Phi Beta Kappa.

WRITINGS: (With Stephen A. Newman) *Getting What You Deserve: A Handbook for the Assertive Consumer,* Doubleday, 1979. Contributor of book reviews to law journals, including *Juris Doctor, Brooklyn Law Review,* and *New York Law Journal.* Contributor of articles to magazines, including *Parade, Family Circle,* and *American Way.* Author of legal pamphlets.

WORK IN PROGRESS: An article on consumer contracts.

*   *   *

KRANZ, Stewart D(uane)   1924-

PERSONAL: Born in August, 1924, in Buffalo, N.Y.; son of Frederick (a research chemist) and Lina (an author; maiden name, Longaker) Kranz; married Susan Nassal; children: Joshua, Nicholas. *Education:* Harvard University, B.A. (magna cum laude), 1949; attended Academie Julien, 1949-50, Art Students League, 1951-53, 1954-55, and Escuela del Bellas Artes, Madrid, Spain, 1951; Columbia University, M.A., 1958, Ed.D., 1969. *Politics:* "Resigned independent, follower of Plato." *Religion:* "Existential/Pantheist." *Home:* 87 Hammond St., Acton, Mass. *Office:* Research and Development, Educational Services, BU/E31, Digital Equipment Corp., Bedford, Mass. 01730.

CAREER: On Film, Princeton, N.J., motion picture staff artist, 1956-57; junior high and high school teacher of art, design, and art history in Ardsley, N.Y., 1964-68, and Merrick, N.Y., 1970-73; Syracuse University, Syracuse, N.Y., assistant professor of design and art education, 1963-65; Center for Urban Education, New York City, supervisor, 1966-68; Columbia Broadcasting System (CBS), New York City, manager of research and development at Learning Center and staff supervisor at Laboratories, 1969-70; Videorecord Corp. of America, co-founder and director of research and development, 1970-73; Barwick/Kranz, Inc. (business communications problem solving company), founder, co-owner, and executive producer of Barwick/Kranz Productions, 1973-78; Stewart Kranz Associates, Green Farms, Conn., founder and president, 1979-80; Digital Equipment Corp., Bedford, Mass., in research and development for educational services department, 1980—. Adjunct assistant professor at Columbia University, 1975-80; adjunct professor at Fairfield University, 1978-79, and Fitchburg State University, 1979-80. Film producer, writer, and graphic artist, 1957-68. Presents seminars to executives, training directors, corporate communications managers, production personnel, writers, and curriculum designers; consultant to organizations and corporations, including Digital Equipment Corp., Sony Corp., and American Telephone & Telegraph. *Military service:* U.S. Army, Infantry, 1943-46; received Purple Heart and Combat Infantry Badge. *Member:* American As-

sociation of Training Directors, Saugatuck River Association (vice-president), Phi Beta Kappa. *Awards, honors:* Traveling fellow of *Boston Globe* in Paris, France, 1949-50.

WRITINGS: (With Robert Fisher) *The Design Continuum,* Van Nostrand, 1966; (with Joseph Deley) *The Fourth "R": Art for the Urban School,* Van Nostrand, 1970; (with Faber Birren, Emily Malino, and others) *Advanced Interior Design Course,* Sears, Roebuck & Co., 1973; (with John H. Barwick) *The Compleat Videocassette Users Guide: Principles and Practice of Programming,* Knowledge Industry Publications, 1973; *Science and Technology in the Arts: A Tour Through the Realm of Science/Art,* Van Nostrand, 1974; (with Barwick) *Why Video?,* Sony Corp., 1975; (with Fisher) *Understanding Visual Forms,* Van Nostrand, 1976; (with Barwick) *Profiles in Video: Who's Using Video and How,* Knowledge Industry Publications, 1976; *Learning Systems for Industry: Theory and Practice,* Van Nostrand, 1981.

Illustrator: Joan Fassler, *My Grandpa Died Today* (juvenile), Behavioral Publications, 1973; Fassler, *The Boy With a Problem* (juvenile), Behavioral Publications, 1973; Fassler, *Don't Worry Dear* (juvenile), Behavioral Publications, 1973.

Media series and programs include "Humanities Series on American Art, History, and Music," Metropolitan Museum of Art; (editor) "Multimedia Current Event Curriculum," Learning Center, Columbia Broadcasting System (CBS), 1968; "Using the Micrometer," Laboratories, CBS, 1969; "Competency Based Education," Videorecord, 1970; "The Abacus," Videorecord, 1972; (illustrator) Joan Fassler, "Emotional Problems of Children," Videorecord, 1972-73; "Self-Instructional Videocassette Course," Videorecord, 1972-73; "The Use of Precision Metal Cutting Tools," Videorecord, 1973; "Home Decoration Course for Adults," Barwick/Kranz Productions, 1974-75; "Point of Sale Skill Development Course," Barwick/Kranz Productions, 1976; "Marriage, Separation, and Divorce" (juvenile), Barwick/Kranz Productions, 1977; "Modern Records Management: Introduction to the Work Force," Barwick/Kranz Productions, 1978; "Conversion of Live-Instruction Course to Media," Stewart Kranz Associates, 1979. Contributor to journals, including *Color Photography, Photomethods,* and *Educational and Industrial Television,* and newspapers.

SIDELIGHTS: Kranz told *CA:* "My writing has followed three areas of interest throughout my adult career: art theory, design theory, and the uses of educational technology. I also have written and produced several educational programs which deal with psychologically relevant themes, the most recent being a series of twelve sound filmstrips on the impact of divorce on American schoolchildren.

"My interest in educational technology stems from my major concern that we are entering an elitist phase of social development in high technology countries which will render ninety-eight percent of human work obsolete within the next decade or so. Advances in microcomputers, videorecord and playback systems, videodiscs, and satellite/cable systems to the home will either turn our society into a collective clan of passive viewers, or, hopefully, will diversify the dissemination of information so freely that any motivated learner will be able to train and retrain himself/herself to be useful and productive in a society undergoing almost total technological obsolescence every five or six years.

"At the present time, the control of all information systems to the home is being reserved for our largest corporations, such as AT & T, IBM, Sony, RCA, and General Electric, to mention a few. My goal for the rest of my life is to be involved in creating equalitarian learning systems which can be delivered to the home so that any citizen can achieve viable information to remain productive throughout his or her life span.

"Another trend which bears considerably on my thought is the fact that our traditional liberal arts curriculum is essential to maintain our humanist tradition and sense of continuity with the entire history of the human race, and yet this tradition is being eroded by the 'functional' needs of industry. Almost ninety percent of job-related learning now takes place when the employee enters a particular corporation. Business has taken over the full responsibility for the education of managers, salespersons, and all skill levels. Although this development is a direct result of the proliferating technology alluded to above, it is resulting in an erosion of the importance of generalist education. This is a serious development that may very well destroy the freedom of expression and choice that characterized American life for the past two hundred years.

"My principal avocational interest is my family, my wife and my two sons. They have taught me how woefully unprepared we all are for the responsibility of parenthood. Our eighteen to twenty years of formal education successfully managed to omit such topics as sex education, how to learn to love another human being, the difference between erotic and emotional love relationships, 'the seven stages of man,' the human body and how it functions, environmental vs. inherited character traits, the importance of a vital social life in each phase of life, personal finances and how to manage money, the characteristics of stress, alcoholism, drug abuse, divorce, and on and on. I find this to be very ironic. Family life has brought home to me the importance of knowing these 'unknowns.'

"Travel is the best mirror one can find for the true nature of one's personal value. Each new country challenges our preconceptions. After I completed my undergraduate work, I spent three years in Europe. This period of my life was a fundamental turning point because I was forced to abandon my preconceptions of what life was and is.

"I have found the French to be absolutely brilliant and very cold; they have taken each facet of life and dissected it with a scalpel to probe its fundamental meaning. They are the smartest folks around. The British taught me the value of a conservative tradition. The Italians taught me that every object made by man can be beautiful, from a Moto Guzzi motorcycle to a typewriter.

"The most *foreign* country I ever visited was Mexico. The persistence of the Mexican Indians was monumental and heroic—the Spanish imitators of the middle and upper class seemed hardly to notice the profound dichotomy between their life style and that of the illiterate Indians who represented the survivors from a proud indigenous truly Mexican inheritance. I found the Mexicans to be the most ingenuous people I have ever visited."

AVOCATIONAL INTERESTS: Still photography.

BIOGRAPHICAL/CRITICAL SOURCES: New York Times Book Review, December 1, 1974; *Training,* January, 1975; *Fairpress,* March 24, 1976; *Rolling Stone,* February 22, 1979.

*   *   *

KRAUES, Judith E.

PERSONAL: Born in Rochester, N.Y.; married Sidney A. Kraues, March 11, 1948 (deceased). *Office:* Para-Educator Center for Young Adults, School of Education, Health,

Nursing, and Arts Professions, New York University, 1 Washington Place, New York, N.Y. 10003.

CAREER: New York University, New York, N.Y., currently professor of education and director of Para-Educator Center for Young Adults.

WRITINGS: The Hidden Handicap, Simon & Schuster, 1980. Contributor of about fifty articles to education journals.

WORK IN PROGRESS: A book.

*   *   *

KRESGE, George Joseph, Jr.
See KRESKIN

*   *   *

KRESKIN   1935-

PERSONAL: Birth-given name, George Joseph Kresge, Jr.; name legally changed; born January 12, 1935, in Montclair, N.J.; son of George Joseph Kresge. *Education:* Seton Hall University, A.B., 1963. *Religion:* Roman Catholic. *Residence:* West Caldwell, N.J. *Office:* c/o Reda, 44 North Second St., Easton, Pa. 18042.

CAREER: Mentalist, lecturer, entertainer, and television personality. Also worked as consultant to a psychologist. National entertainment ambassador of Big Brothers of America.

WRITINGS: The Amazing World of Kreskin, Random House, 1973; *Use Your Head to Get Ahead!: With Kreskin's Mind Power Book,* McGraw, 1977.

SIDELIGHTS: Kreskin insisted to Philip Nobile of the *Detroit News* that he has no supernatural abilities. "Everything I do is inherent in everyone. But what I have done is to learn to sensitize myself to the reactions and attitudes of people around me. Under certain conditions I can sense their thought as well as influence their thoughts. However, this is not accomplished by any psychic ability.... I can't foretell the future, conduct seances or cast spells." Although Kreskin admits that he uses telepathy in conjunction with traditional magic, he also claims his methods are purely scientific. "My concept of telepathy reverses ESP to PSE, that is, phenomena scientifically explainable . . . [but] a direct explanation would subtract from the mystery."

BIOGRAPHICAL/CRITICAL SOURCES: Biography News, Volume I, Gale, 1974; *Detroit News Sunday Magazine,* November 3, 1974; *Popular Mechanics,* December, 1975.

*   *   *

KRISHNA, Gopi   1903-

PERSONAL: Born June 3, 1903, in Gairoo, Kashmir, India; son of Ganga (an accountant) and Kulwanti Rama; married Roopwanti (Mughlani Devi), 1926; children: Ragina Kaul, Jagdish Chander Shivpuri, Nirmal Chander Shivpuri. *Education:* Attended secondary school in Srinagar, Kashmir, and Lahore, Punjab. *Home:* 14 Karan Nagar, Srinagar, Kashmir, India. *Office:* Central Institute for Kundalini Research, International Centre, Nishat, Kashmir, India.

CAREER: Government of India, 1923-50, worked as clerk in Irrigation Division in Srinagar, Kashmir, Office of the Chief Engineer, Irrigation Department in Jammu, and Office of the Director of Education, in Jammu and Srinagar; writer, 1950-75; Central Institute for Kundalini Research, Nishat, India, founder and president, 1975—. President of Samaj Sudhar Samiti, 1946—; member of Bharat Sevak Samaj, 1958-70.

WRITINGS: From the Unseen, privately printed, 1952; *The Shape of Events to Come,* privately printed, 1968, revised edition, Kundalini Research & Publication Trust, 1979; *Kundalini,* Ramadhar & Hopman, 1967; *The Biological Basis of Religion and Genius,* Harper, 1972; *The Secret of Yoga,* Harper, 1972; *Higher Consciousness,* Julian Press, 1974; *The Awakening of Kundalini,* Dutton, 1975; *Panchastavi* (in English; title means "The Hymn With Five Cantos"), Central Institute for Kundalini Research, 1975; *The Riddle of Consciousness,* Kundalini Research Foundation, 1976; *The Dawn of a New Science,* Kundalini Research & Publication Trust, 1978; *Secrets of Kundalini in Panchastavi,* Kundalini Research & Publication Trust, 1978; *Yoga: A Vision of Its Future,* Kundalini Research & Publication Trust, 1978; *The Real Nature of Mystical Experience,* New Concepts Publishing, 1978; *Kundalini in Time and Space,* Kundalini Research & Publication Trust, 1979; *Reason and Revelation,* New Age Publishing, 1979; *Biblical Prophecy for the Twentieth Century,* New Age Publishing, 1979.

WORK IN PROGRESS: The Story of My Life, an autobiography; second volumes of *The Shape of Events to Come* and *The Dawn of a New Science; The Magic of Mind; The Paranormal Brain; From Human to Transhuman Consciousness; Evolution and Psychic Phenomena.*

SIDELIGHTS: Krishna's work with Samaj Sudhar Samiti is aimed at abolition of the dowry system, reduction in expenditure on marriages and other social functions, remarriage of widows, rehabilitation of widows, orphans, and destitutes, as well as improvement and beautification of shrines and holy places.

A writer since the early 1950's, his books have been translated into French, German, Spanish, Italian, Dutch, Gujarati, Portuguese, Hindi, Marathi, Malayam, and Japanese.

Krishna's secretary, Paul Beattie, told *CA:* "The main thrust of Gopi Krishna's writings is to prove that there is a dormant center in the human brain and a reserve store of bio-energy in the human body which, when activated, leads to the illuminated state of consciousness peculiar to prophets and mystics, conferring the extraordinary intellectual or artistic talents that characterize genius, or bestowing the miraculous or psychic gifts as exhibited by saints and mediums. In those cases where there is a malfunctioning of these mechanisms, their activity can result in intractable forms of mental or nervous disorder.

"Based on the strength of the ancient tradition relating to the Serpent Power in India and his own experience, Gopi Krishna believes that a still unrecognized psychic activity in the cerebro-spinal system is at the root of many still inexplicable paranormal and abnormal phenomena of the human mind."

BIOGRAPHICAL/CRITICAL SOURCES: Psychic Dimensions, November, 1978.

*   *   *

KRUMGOLD, Joseph (Quincy) 1908-1980

OBITUARY NOTICE—See index for *CA* sketch: Born April 9, 1908, in Jersey City, N.J.; died of a stroke, July 10, 1980, in Hope, N.J. Producer, screenwriter, and author. Krumgold wrote scripts and produced motion pictures for several film companies, including Metro-Goldwyn-Mayer (MGM), Paramount, RKO, Columbia, and Republic. He is best known, however, for his highly acclaimed children's books. Krumgold won Newbery Awards from the American Library Association for his books *And Now Miguel* and *Onion*

John, becoming the first author ever to receive the award twice. His other works include *Thanks to Murder* and *Sweeney's Adventure.* Obituaries and other sources: *New York Times,* July 16, 1980; *Publishers Weekly,* August 1, 1980.

*   *   *

KUNSTLER, James Howard 1948-

PERSONAL: Born October 19, 1948, in New York, N.Y.; son of Henry Kunstler (a diamond merchant) and Muriel (a businesswoman; maiden name, Imbrey) Glaser. *Education:* Brockport State College, B.S., 1971. *Agent:* Scott Meredith Literary Agency, Inc., 845 Third Ave., New York, N.Y. 10022. *Office:* P.O. Box 193, Saratoga Springs, N.Y. 12866.

CAREER: Boston Phoenix, Boston, Mass., feature writer, 1972; *Knickerbocker News,* Albany, N.Y., feature writer, 1973-74; *Rolling Stone,* San Francisco, Calif., staff writer, 1974-75; free-lance writer, 1975—.

WRITINGS: The Wampanaki Tales (novel), Doubleday, 1979; *Brain Damage: A Love Story* (novel), St. Martin's, 1981; *Bagging Bigfoot* (novel), Ballantine, 1981.

WORK IN PROGRESS: A novel about love and crime.

SIDELIGHTS: Kunstler told *CA:* "I aspire to write novels with broad popular appeal and whether I succeed in this vein remains to be seen."

*   *   *

KUNZUR, Sheela
See GEIS, Richard E(rwin)

*   *   *

KUROSAWA, Akira 1910-

PERSONAL: Born March 23, 1910, in Tokyo, Japan; married Yoko Yaguchi; children: one son, one daughter. *Education:* Attended Tokyo Academy of Fine Arts, c. 1928. *Residence:* Tokyo, Japan. *Office:* c/o Omni-Zoetrope, 916 Kearny St., San Francisco, Calif. 94133.

CAREER: Screenwriter, producer, and director of motion pictures. Associated with PCL Studios (now Toho Films), 1937—; assistant director to Kajiro Yamamoto, 1937-43. Founder of Kurosawa Productions, 1960. *Awards, honors:* Named best director in Japan, 1947, for "Subarshiki nichiyobi"; Gran Prix from Venice Film Festival and Academy Award for best foreign language film from Academy of Motion Picture Arts and Sciences, both 1951, both for "Rashomon"; Silver Lion Award from Venice Film Festival, 1954, for "Schichinin no samurai"; Academy Award for best foreign language film, 1976, and Donatello Prize [Italy], 1977, both for "Dersu Uzala"; award for "humanistic contribution to society in film production" from European Film Academy, 1978; co-winner of Golden Palm from Cannes Film Festival, 1980, for "Kagemusha"; and other film awards.

WRITINGS—Screenplays in English; all as director; all produced by Toho Films except as noted: (With Shinobu Hashimoto and Hideo Oguni) *Ikiru* (title means "Living"; released in 1952; also see below), translated from the Japanese by Donald Richie, Simon & Schuster, 1968; (with Hashimoto) *Rashomon* (released by Daiei, 1950; adapted from the short stories by Ryunosuko Akutagawa, "Rashomon" and "In the Grove"), translated from the Japanese by Richie, Grove, 1969; (with Hashimoto and Oguni) *Seven Samurai* (released as "Shichinin no samurai," 1954), translated from the Japanese by Richie, Simon & Schuster, 1970.

The Complete Works of Akira Kurosawa, Kinema Juni-posha, Volume I: (with Hashimoto and Oguni) *Dodesukaden* (released as "Dodes'ka-den," 1970; adapted from the story by Shugoro Yamamato), 1970, Volume II: *Sugato sanshiro* (title means "Judo Saga"; released in two parts, 1943 and 1945), and (with Eijiro Hisaita) *No Regrets for Our Youth* (released as "Waga Seishum nu kuinashi," 1946), 1970, Volume III: (with Keinosuke Uekusa) *One Wonderful Sunday* (released as "Subarshiki nichiyobi," 1947), and (with Uekusa) *Drunken Angel* (released as "Yoidore Tenshi," 1948), 1970, Volume IV: (with Senkichi Taniguchi) *Quiet Duel* (released as "Shizukanaru Ketto," 1949), 1970, Volume VI: (with Hisaka Aijiro) *The Idiot* (released as "Hikuchi," Shochiku, 1951; adapted from the novel by Dostoevski), and (with Hashimoto and Oguni) *Ikiru* (also see above), 1970, Volume IX: (with Kikushima, Hashimoto, and Oguni) *Three Badmen in a Hidden Fortres* [sic], (released as "Kakushi toride no san akunin," 1958; also released in the U.S. as "The Hidden Fortress"), and (with Hashimoto, Oguni, Kikushima, and Hisaita) *The Bad Sleep Well* (released as "Warni yatsu hodo yoko nemuru," 1959), 1970.

Other screenplays; all in Japanese; all as director; all produced by Toho Films except as noted: "Ichiban utsukush-iku" (title means "Most Beautiful"), 1944; "Toro no o o fumo otoko tachi" (title means "The Men Who Tread on the Tiger's Tail"; adapted from the Kabuki play, "Kanjincho"), 1945; "Shuban" (title means "Scandal"), Shochiku, 1950; (with Hasimoto and Oguni) "Ikimono no kiroku" (title means "I Live in Fear"), 1955; (with Hashimoto, Kikushima, and Oguni) "Kumonosu-jo" (title means "Castle of the Spider's Web"; released in the U.S. as "Throne and Blood"; adapted from the play by William Shakespeare, *Macbeth*), 1957; (with Oguni) "Donzoko" (released in the U.S. as "The Lower Depths"; adapted from the play by Maxim Gorki), 1957.

(With Kikushima) "Yojimbo" (title means "Bodyguard"), 1961; (with Kikushima and Oguni) "Sanjuro" (adapted from the novel by Shugoro Yamamato), 1962; (with Kikushima and Oguni) "Tengoku to jigoku" (title means "High and Low"; adapted from the novel by Ed McBain, *King's Ransom*), 1963; (with Kikushima, Oguni, and Masato Ide) "Aka hige" (released in the U.S. as "Red Beard"), 1965; "Dersu Uzala," Soviet MosFilm, 1977; "Kagemusha" (title means "Shadow Warrior"), 1980.

Also author of screenplays directed by others, including "Uma," 1941, and "Shozo," 1948, and unproduced screenplays.

WORK IN PROGRESS: "Ran," an adaptation of William Shakespeare's play *King Lear*.

SIDELIGHTS: Kurosawa's introduction to filmmaking was more a matter of desperation than design. In 1937, after struggling for years as a painter, he responded out of curiosity to a newspaper advertisement calling for assistant directors at PCL Studios. Surprisingly, one of Kurosawa's comments on the application, that "films could always be made better," piqued the studio's interest, and he was offered the position. He accepted, though he intended to work only long enough to finance another stint as a painter.

Kurosawa was trained by Kajiro Yamamoto, one of Japan's premier filmmakers. Yamamoto taught Kurosawa all the technical aspects of filmmaking and, as if a believer in the *auteur* theory before it became popular, he insisted that Kurosawa master screenwriting, too. For five years Kurosawa wrote scripts and assisted Yamamoto with his directing.

In 1943 Kurosawa directed his first film, "Judo Saga." Although the picture was sufficiently successful to warrant a sequel in 1945, it failed to spark much critical or popular enthusiasm for Kurosawa. Also, because of censorship restrictions imposed on the film industry during World War II, Kurosawa made only one other film, "Most Beautifully," before Japan's surrender to Allied forces.

After the war, Kurosawa became overwhelmingly involved in his craft and abandoned his plans to recommence painting. One of his first postwar efforts, "No Regrets for Our Youth," depicted several students' political attitudes during the years preceding World War II. Kurosawa quickly followed it with "One Wonderful Sunday," a simple romantic film about an impoverished couple unable to locate a free concert.

In 1948 Kurosawa produced the film many critics consider his initial masterpiece, "Drunken Angel." It concerns an alcoholic doctor and his struggles in a slum where his patients include a tubercular girl and a mobster. Critics often point to this film as the first of many in which Kurosawa seconds Albert Camus's opinion that, for the twentieth-century protagonist, effort is everything. Joan Mellen noted that the doctor "can cure a little girl of tuberculosis, but he cannot rid the neighborhood of the swamp which breeds the disease infecting the entire population. . . . Neither can he save the young gangster spawned by this milieu and incapable of freeing himself from it." In "Drunken Angel," according to Benito Ortolani, Kurosawa insists "on a dignity for man, freedom from poverty and oppression, and a chance for each to work out his earthly destiny in an atmosphere of peace and justice."

Kurosawa's next film, "Quiet Duel," confounded critics impressed with "Drunken Angel." Jay Leyda called the film, which dealt with venereal disease, a "step backwards" for Kurosawa. The director, though, recouped the critics' respect with "Stray Dog," which chronicled a policeman's efforts to recover his stolen revolver. The policeman's search takes him into both ghettos and mansions, and he slowly develops an understanding for both the criminal and the wealthy. In considering the sociological essence of "Stray Dog," Mellen compared Kurosawa with Bertolt Brecht, claiming they both create "characters who learn a strong class sense from the dilemma of their social alienation." She added, however, that Kurosawa "does not affect fashionable 'Brechtian' detachment from his subject matter but . . . conveys an abiding sympathy with the less fortunate of his characters."

"Stray Dog" was followed by "Scandal," an obscure, semi-autobiographical film about struggling painters in Tokyo. Kurosawa then made "Rashomon," the film for which he is probably best known. "Rashomon" is a multiple-narrative retracing of a deadly encounter between a bandit and a young couple traveling through a forest. Within a courtroom structure, "Rashomon" presents the testimonies of the bandit, the young woman, and the man (speaking through a medium) as each recounts the actions that resulted in the man's death. More importantly, the various testimonies are recollections within a recollection, for the entire courtroom drama is recounted by a woodcutter while waiting out a storm with other peasants and a priest. Finally, the woodcutter, himself a witness to the incident in the woods, tells his version, and the others accept it as the truth. Then he, too, is exposed as dishonest by the others, for they discover that he's stolen a knife that was left at the scene of the crime. As Douglas McVay noted, the priest's "faith in human nature is steadily weakened as he listens, and almost obliterated at the discovery that the woodcutter, too, has not been scrupulously honest in the business.''

Throughout ''Rashomon,'' Kurosawa strips away the viewer's trust in narrative. If the technical result of this is to free the medium from traditional narrative conventions, the thematic result is to expose humanity as weak and dishonest. But Kurosawa does not end the film with the woodcutter's humiliation. McVay wrote that, after the woodcutter is traduced, ''an attempt to reaffirm the goodness of mankind is clearly called for.'' And the film ends not with the woodcutter's exposure but with the discovery of an abandoned baby. When the woodcutter offers to care for the infant, one of the peasants becomes enraged. The priest, however, understands the essentially good nature of the woodcutter and encourages him to raise the baby. As in ''Drunken Angel'' and ''Stray Dog'' before it, ''Rashomon'' celebrates humanity's dignity and accepts its failures and imperfections.

Though Japanese critics were initially disappointed by Kurosawa's ''retreat into the past'' for the setting of ''Rashomon,'' the film slowly won critics over and was eventually selected as Japan's entry in the Venice Film Festival. Before ''Rashomon'' was shown in Venice, though, Kurosawa made ''The Idiot,'' which was a crushing disappointment both personally and critically. After submitting the film with a running time of three hours, Kurosawa watched helplessly as studio editors pruned ''The Idiot'' to what they considered a more reasonable length. He warned them that, ''if butchered, it would really live up to its title, and the audience would be baffled.'' He was right: audiences and critics seemed confused by what was on the screen. Leyda, noting that Kurosawa had tried to pursue his own ambitions with ''The Idiot'' while working under pressure from the studios, contended that Kurosawa ''tried to please himself and his employers alternately, and ended by pleasing nobody.''

After the debacle of ''The Idiot,'' Kurosawa's spirits were considerably bolstered when ''Rashomon'' surprisingly won the Gran Prix in Venice. The honor sparked international interest in Japanese cinema, and previously ignored filmmakers, including Yasujiro Ozu, Kenji Mizoguchi, and Kon Ichikowa, profited from Kurosawa's success. But Kurosawa seemed disinterested in celebrating the honor. Instead, winning the Gran Prix intensified his devotion to filmmaking. ''I soon realized that this honor obliged me to do something to help humanity and peace in the world,'' he said. ''It was clear to me that I must work harder. Every day since, that thought has spurred me, and I will work to make my films better.''

Kurosawa followed his victory in Venice with ''Ikiru,'' the story of a government worker who learns he is dying of cancer. Confronting his own mortality, the bureaucrat decides *to live*—to accomplish something worthwhile in his final days. Abandoning his office role as a paper pusher, the worker is determined to finalize a proposal to build a children's playground. He dies on the eve of his success. Though ''Ikiru'' proved a marked contrast to the complex ''Rashomon'' or the more relentless ''Stray Dog,'' it nevertheless ranks with those two films and ''Drunken Angel'' as one of his greatest achievements.

In his next film, ''The Seven Samurai,'' Kurosawa mastered the epic form. The film details the success of seven samurai hired by farmers to defend their village from raiders. Though successful, the samurai temper their victory with the knowledge that they are a vanishing class. Some critics complained that ''The Seven Samurai'' lacked the compassion and depth of Kurosawa's earlier work. Others, however, contended

that ''The Seven Samurai'' displays a technical mastery unequaled in his previous pictures. ''Visually the film makes a tremendous impression,'' wrote Tony Richardson. ''Kurosawa can combine formal grace with dramatic accuracy, and many scenes create a startling pictorial impact.'' Leyda declared that ''the style of the film reflects this peculiarly Japanese esthetic: its art conceals itself in a manner that increases its power.''

Kurosawa produced another major work, ''Throne of Blood,'' in 1957. Adapted from William Shakespeare's *Macbeth*, ''Throne of Blood'' is regarded by many critics as one of the most successful screen adaptations of Shakespeare's work. Some reviewers charged that Kurosawa's reworking of the play was made easier by his disregard for the text. However, J. Blumenthal contended that ''Throne of Blood'' is an ''autonomous'' film. He also suggested that action more clearly reveals character than dialogue, and that Macbeth was therefore an easier character to bring to the screen than the more verbal Hamlet. ''The verbal experience is typical of those who never wholly enter their experience, those who can only act at acting,'' wrote Blumenthal. ''It is typical of the theatrical role-playing personality, which is *par excellence* Hamlet's. Macbeth . . . always lives his experiences, and thereby provides Kurosawa with the irreducible core of raw, unquestioned reality that is the first premise of most great films.''

Maxim Gorki's *The Lower Depths* was the source for Kurosawa's next film, ''Donzoko.'' Though some critics panned the film's claustrophobic sets and dialogue-dependent action, a critic for *Film Quarterly* called it a ''brave enterprize'' and contended that Gorki's play was uniquely suited to the Japanese cinema. The reviewer concluded by praising Kurosawa's style as a ''meditative, 'poetical' approach to matters that are in reality simply overwhelming and unbearable.''

Francis Ford Coppola called portions of Kurosawa's ''The Bad Sleep Well'' ''better than Shakespeare.'' The film, which Charles Higham related thematically to *Hamlet*, details a bridegroom's efforts to apprehend his father's murderers. Higham was especially impressed with Kurosawa's depiction of corporate ethics in the film and wrote, ''The final shot of an officer calmly reporting to his superior that the hero has been 'taken care of' is a marvelously offhand comment on the power of big business.''

Reviewers were generally displeased with Kurosawa's ''The Hidden Fortress.'' The film details the efforts of a pair of soldiers to smuggle a princess across enemy lines. Gordon Gow praised Kurosawa's ''flair for composition,'' but found the acting both annoying and ''uncinematic.'' He wrote, ''Characters are over-simplified,'' and declared that ''too often Kurosawa allows more hamming than would be tolerable across a barrier of footlights.''

Kurosawa followed ''The Hidden Fortress'' with ''Yojimbo'' and ''Sanjuro,'' a pair of simple but well-made films detailing the hectic life of the mercenary samurai. In ''Yojimbo,'' the samurai enters a village plagued by feuding gangs. The samurai decides to dispense with each group by duping each of them into hiring him to eliminate the other. After accomplishing his task, as Gow noted, the samurai departs ''in the nearest approximation to peace that he is ever likely to know.''

''Sanjuro'' is a comical variation of ''Yojimbo.'' A mercenary samurai helps a small group of men defeat a villanous gang. Gow called it ''visually superb, with exactly the same richly-textured . . . photography that distinguished *Yojimbo;*

and with a beguiling formalism to it, shading and highlight certain areas within the frame and placing figures in their setting with a sureness rarely matched by any other director.''

Although both ''Yojimbo'' and ''Sanjuro'' were successful entertaining ventures, neither film proved to critics that Kurosawa had overcome the flaws that were evident in ''Donzoko'' and ''The Hidden Fortress.'' His reputation suffered further abuse after the release of ''Red Beard.'' More than two years in production, it had been one of the most anticipated films of 1965. Upon its release, however, many critics compared it to the popular medical dramas of television and, as Benito Ortolani observed, it was deemed ''a string of Ben Casey episodes pieced together.'' Many reviewers also found the film's three-hour length both taxing and unrewarding. For Kurosawa, who had invested an overwhelming amount of time into the film about a valiant surgeon, the reception was humiliating.

''Dodes'ka-den'' marked Kurosawa's further decline as a filmmaker. The picture concerns a multitude of characters living in a ghetto. Roger Greenspun wrote: ''The humor is strained, the ironies are easy and mostly unearned, and even the director's celebrated humanism seems artificially produced, to be hauled out as if for demonstration purposes at appropriate intervals. 'Dodes' ka-den' is an immensely long, elaborately trivial movie in which the compassion does not compensate for the smallness of imaginative life.''

After suffering critical abuse for his last few films, Kurosawa attempted suicide in 1971. Though he failed, he did not return to filmmaking until 1976. ''Dersu Uzula'' was celebrated as Kurosawa's comeback when it was shown that year. His story of a wilderness man unable to accept social customs received the Academy Award for best foreign language film in 1976 and was similarly honored in Italy the following year.

His comeback seemed complete in 1980 when ''Kagemusha,'' a film about feudalism in sixteenth-century Japan, was honored at the Cannes Film Festival. Kurosawa told an interviewer that ''Kagemusha'' was set in his ''favorite period.'' ''People were straightforward and unpretentious then,'' he added. ''It was a time of great ambitions and great failures, great heroes and equally great scoundrels.''

Kurosawa once answered critics who insisted that his films contained the same message by confessing that ''every filmmaker says only one thing.'' Similarly, Ortolani declared that Kurosawa ''leaves a distinguishing 'thumbprint' on all that he does.'' He wrote: ''Kurosawa is not a deep philosopher, nor does he call upon the insights of metaphysics or the cogent arguments of ethics for his answers. But he does insist on a dignity for man, freedom from poverty and oppression, and a chance for each to work out his earthly destiny in an atmosphere of peace and justice.''

BIOGRAPHICAL/CRITICAL SOURCES: Sight and Sound, October/December, 1954, spring, 1955, autumn, 1965; *Film Culture,* Volume II, number 4, 1956; *Film Quarterly,* winter, 1959; *Films and Filming,* May, 1961, July, 1961, August, 1961, August, 1970, January, 1971; *Film Comment,* winter, 1964; *America,* October 2, 1965; *Kenyon Review,* autumn, 1965; *Take One,* April, 1971, March, 1979; *New York Times,* October 6, 1971, April 27, 1980.*

—*Sketch by Les Stone*

* * *

KURRIK, Maire Jaanus 1940-

PERSONAL: Born January 22, 1940, in Tartu, Estonia;

came to the United States in 1950, naturalized citizen, 1956; daughter of Richard (an engineer) and Hedda (a clerical worker; maiden name, Klaser) Jaanus; married Edward W. Said, July 7, 1962 (divorced April, 1970); married Juhan Kurrik (an engineer), May 1, 1970; children: Ilomai. *Education:* Vassar College, B.A., 1961; Harvard University, Ph.D., 1968. *Home:* 910 West End Ave., New York, N.Y. 10025. *Office:* Department of English, Barnard College, Columbia University, New York, N.Y. 10027.

CAREER: Columbia University, Barnard College, New York, N.Y., assistant professor, 1968-76, associate professor of English, 1976—. *Member:* American Comparative Literature Association, American Association of University Professors, American Association for Baltic Studies, Modern Language Association of America. *Awards, honors:* National Endowment for the Humanities younger humanist fellow, 1973-74; Mellon Foundation grant, 1980.

WRITINGS: Georg Trakl, Columbia University Press, 1975; *Literature and Negation,* Columbia University Press, 1979. Also author of *The Human Body in Twentieth-Century Literature and Philosophy.* Contributor to academic journals and popular magazines, including *Partisan Review* and *Salmagundi.*

* * *

KYGER, Joanne 1934-

PERSONAL: Born November 19, 1934, in Vallejo, Calif.; daughter of Jacob Holmes and Anne (Lamont) Kyger; married Gary Snyder (a poet), 1960 (divorced, 1964); married John Boyce (died, 1972). *Education:* Attended Santa Barbara City College, 1952-56. *Home:* Box 688, Bolinas, Calif. 94924.

CAREER: Poet. Performer and poet in an experimental television project, 1967-68. *Awards, honors:* Grant from National Endowments for the Arts, 1968.

WRITINGS—Poetry: The Tapestry and the Web, Four Seasons Foundation, 1965; *The Fool in April: A Poem,* Coyote Books, 1966; *Places to Go,* Black Sparrow Press, 1970; *Joanne,* Angel Hair Books, 1970; *Desecheo Notebook,* Arif Press, 1971; *Trip Out and Fall Back,* Arif Press, 1974; *All This Every Day,* Big Sky Books, 1975; *The Wonderful Focus of You,* Z Press, 1980. Contributor of poems to periodicals, including *Poetry, Coyote's Journal, Paris Review, The World, Turkey Buzzard Review,* and *Rockey Ledge.*

SIDELIGHTS: A leading figure in San Francisco poetry circles, Joanne Kyger is a member of the Duncan-Spicer group that fostered such writers as Richard Brautigan, Michael McClure, and George Stanley.

* * *

KYLE, Marlaine
See HAGER, Jean

* * *

KYRLE, Roger (Ernie) Money
See MONEY-KYRLE, Roger (Ernie)

* * *

KYVIG, David E(dward) 1944-

PERSONAL: Born March 8, 1944, in Ames, Iowa; son of Edward H. (a community college teacher) and Wilma (a community college teacher; maiden name, Jessen) Kyvig; married Barbara Burness, 1967; children: Jennifer, Elizabeth. *Education:* Kalamazoo College, B.A. (cum laude), 1966; Northwestern University, Ph.D., 1971. *Office:* Department of History, University of Akron, Akron, Ohio 44325.

CAREER: National Archives, Washington, D.C., archivist in Office of Presidential Libraries, 1970-71; University of Akron, Akron, Ohio, assistant professor, 1971-79, associate professor of history, 1979—, director of American History Research Center, 1971-79. Visiting assistant professor at Kalamazoo College, summer, 1972. Chairman of sessions at national meetings; member of National Archives and Records Service regional advisory council, 1975-77, and Ohio Historical Records Preservation advisory board, 1976—.

MEMBER: Organization of American Historians, Society of American Archivists, Society for Historians of American Foreign Relations, Ohio Academy of History, Society of Ohio Archivists (member of executive council, 1973-75; chairman of joint archives-library committee, with Ohio Academy of History, 1977-78), Phi Beta Kappa. *Awards,*

honors: Eleutherian Mills-Hagley Foundation grant, 1973; Newberry Library fellowship, 1979; American Council of Learned Societies fellowship, 1980-81.

WRITINGS: (Editor) *F.D.R's America,* Forum Press, 1976; (with Myron A. Marty) *Your Family History: A Handbook for Research and Writing,* AHM Publishing, 1978; *Repealing National Prohibition,* University of Chicago Press, 1979; (contributor) Jack S. Blocker, Jr., editor, *Alcohol, Reform, and Society: The Liquor Issue in Social Context,* Greenwood Press, 1979. Contributor of more than twenty articles and reviews to history and archival journals.

WORK IN PROGRESS: A research guide to community history, with Myron A. Marty, publication by AHM Publishing expected in 1981; a book on constitutional amendment in twentieth-century America.

BIOGRAPHICAL/CRITICAL SOURCES: Times Literary Supplement, February 29, 1980.

L

LACOUTURE, Jean Marie Gerard 1921-

PERSONAL: Born June 9, 1921, in Bordeaux, France; son of Antoine and Anne-Marie (Servantie) Lacouture; married Simonne Gresillon (a writer), August 28, 1951. *Education:* Free School of Political Science, diploma, 1941; attended University of Paris, 1942. *Religion:* Roman Catholic. *Home:* 143 rue d'Alesia, 75014 Paris, France.

CAREER: Headquarters of General Leclerc, press attache in Indochina, 1945-47, member of French general staff in Morocco, 1947-49; diplomatic editor of *Combat,* 1950-51; *Le Monde,* diplomatic editor, 1951-53, head of overseas service, beginning in 1957, chief reporter; Egyptian correspondent for *France-Soir,* 1954-56. Professor at Institute of Political Studies, Paris, France, 1964-78.

WRITINGS—In English translation: (With wife, Simonne Lacouture) *L'Egypte en mouvement,* Editions du Seuil, 1956, revised edition, 1962, translation by Francis Scarfe published as *Egypt in Transition,* Criterion, 1958; (with Philippe Devillers) *La Fin d'une guerre: Indochine, 1954,* Editions du Seuil, 1960, revised translation by Alexander Lieven and Adam Roberts published as *End of a War: Indochina, 1954,* Praeger, 1969; *Le Vietnam entre deux paix,* Editions du Seuil, 1965, translation by Konrad Kellen and Joel Carmichael published as *Vietnam: Between Two Truces,* Random House, 1966; *De Gaulle,* Editions du Seuil, 1965, new edition, 1969, translation by Francis K. Price published as *De Gaulle,* New American Library, 1966, revised edition translated by Price and John Skeffington, Hutchinson, 1970; *Ho Chi Minh,* Editions du Seuil, 1967, revised edition, 1977, translation by Peter Wiles published as *Ho Chi Minh: A Political Biography,* edited by Jane Clark Seitz, Random House, 1968; *Quatre Hommes et leurs peuples: Sur-pouvoir et sous-developpement,* Editions du Seuil, 1969, translation by Patricia Wolf published as *The Demigods: Charismatic Leadership in the Third World,* Knopf, 1970; *Nasser,* Editions du Seuil, 1971, translation by Daniel Hofstadter published as *Nasser: A Biography,* Random House, 1973; *Andre Malraux: Une Vie dans le siecle,* Editions du Seuil, 1973, new edition, 1976, translation by Alan Sheridan published as *Andre Malraux,* Pantheon, 1975; (with Mahmoud Hussein and Saul Friedlaender) *Arabes et Israeliens: Un Premier Dialogue,* Editions du Seuil, 1974, translation published as *Arabs and Israelis,* Holmes & Meier, 1975; *Leon Blum,* Editions du Seuil, 1977, translation published as *Leon Blum,*

New Republic, 1980. Also author with S. Lacouture of *Israel and Arabs: The Third Combat,* 1967.

In French: (With S. Lacouture) *Le Maroc a l'epreuve* (title means "Morocco's Ordeal"), Editions du Seuil, 1958; *Cinq Hommes et la France* (title means "Five Men and France"), Editions du Seuil, 1961; (with Jean Baumier) *Le Poids du tiers monde: Un Milliard d'hommes* (title means "The Weight of the Third World"), Arthaud, 1962; (editor) Charles de Gaulle, *Citations du president de Gaulle* (title means "Quotations of President de Gaulle"), Editions du Seuil, 1968; (with Philippe Devillers) *Vietnam,* Editions du Seuil, 1969; *Un Sang d'encre: Conversations avec Claude Glayman,* Stock, 1974; (with Gabriel Dardaud) *Les Emirats mirages,* Editions du Seuil, 1975; (author of introduction) Georges Buis, *Les Fanfares perdues,* Editions du Seuil, 1975; (with S. Lacouture) *Vietnam: Voyage a travers une victoire,* Editions du Seuil, 1976; (author of introduction) Alexandre Minkowski, *Le Mandarin aux pieds nus,* Editions du Seuil, 1975; (co-author of introduction) Haroun Tazieff, *Jouer avec le feu,* Editions du Seuil, 1976; *Survive le peuple cambodgien!,* Editions du Seuil, 1978; *Le Rugby: C'est un monde,* Editions du Seuil, 1979; *Francois Mauriac,* Editions du Seuil, 1980. Also author with Sihanouk of *L'Indochine vue de Pekin,* 1972; General editor of a series for Editions du Seuil, 1961-77. Editor of *Etudes mediterraneennes,* 1957-62.

*   *   *

LAING, Anne C.
See SCHACHTERLE, Nancy (Lange)

*   *   *

LAMB, Harold (Albert) 1892-1962

PERSONAL: Born September 1, 1892, in Alpine, N.J.; died, April 9, 1962; buried at Brookside Cemetery, Englewood, N.J.; son of Frederick Stymetz (a businessman) and Nellie (Albert) Lamb; married Ruth Lemont Barbour, June 14, 1917; children: Cary, Frederick Stymetz II. *Education:* Columbia University, B.A., 1916. *Home:* 10048 Cielo Dr., Beverly Hills, Calif. 90210.

CAREER: Writer of historical articles and stories. Prior to World War I, worked as a make-up man for a motor trade weekly and as a financial writer for the *New York Times;* contributor of articles and stories to magazines such as *National Geographic, Asia, Adventure,* and the *San Francisco*

Chronicle. Military service: U.S. Army, infantryman, World War I. *Member:* P.E.N., Authors' League, California Writers' Club, St. Anthony Club (New York), Berkeley Tennis Club. *Awards, honors:* Guggenheim fellowship, 1929; Silver Medal, Commonwealth Club of California, 1932, for *Nur Mahal;* Second Order of "Elmi," Persian Government, for *The Crusades,* 1933.

WRITINGS: Marching Sands, Appleton, 1920, reprinted with introduction by L. Sprague de Camp, Hyperion Press, 1974; *The House of the Falcon,* Appleton, 1921; *Genghis Kahn, the Emperor of All Men,* McBridge, 1927, published as *Genghis Khan, the Conqueror, the Emperor of All Men,* Bantam, 1963; *Tamerlane, the Earth Shaker,* McBride, 1928, reprinted with *The March of the Barbarians* (see below) under title *The Earth Shakers,* Doubleday, 1956; *The Boy's Genghis Khan* (edited by James Gilman; illustrated by William Siegel), McBride, 1930; *The Crusades,* Doubleday, Volume I: *Iron Men and Saints* (Book-of-the-Month Club selection), 1930, Volume II: *The Flame of Islam,* 1931, Volumes I and II reprinted as *The Crusades: The Whole Story of the Crusades,* Doubleday, 1962; *Durandal: A Crusader in the Horde* (juvenile; illustrated by Allan McNab; Junior Literary Guild selection), Doubleday, 1931; *Nur Mahal,* Doubleday, 1932; *Kirdy: The Road Out of the World* (juvenile; decorations by Boris Artzbasheff; Junior Literary Guild selection), Doubleday, 1933; *Omar Khayyam: A Life,* Doubleday, 1934, reprinted, Pinnacle Books, 1978; *The March of the Barbarians,* Doubleday, 1940 (also see above); *Persian Mosaic: An Imaginative Biography of Omar Khayyam Based Upon Reality, in the Oriental Manner,* Hale, 1943; *Alexander of Macedon: The Journey to World's End,* Doubleday, 1946; *A Garden to the Eastward,* Doubleday, 1947; *The City and the Tsar: Peter the Great and the Move West, 1648-1762,* Doubleday, 1948; *The March of Muscovy: Ivan the Terrible and the Growth of the Russian Empire, 1400-1648,* Doubleday, 1948.

Suleiman the Magnificent, Sultan of the East, Doubleday, 1951, reprinted, Pinnacle Books, 1978; *Theodora and the Emperor: The Drama of Justinian,* Doubleday, 1952, reprinted, Pinnacle Books, 1977; *Charlemagne: The Legend and the Man,* Doubleday, 1954; *Genghis Khan and the Mongol Horde,* illustrations by Elton Fax, Random House, 1954, reprinted, Pinnacle Books, 1976; *New Found World: How North America Was Discovered and Explored,* Doubleday, 1955; *Constantinople: Birth of an Empire,* Knopf, 1957; (with others) *Hannibal: One Man Against Rome,* Doubleday, 1958, reprinted, Pinnacle Books, 1976; *Chief of the Cossacks,* illustrations by Robert Frankenberg, Random House, 1959; *Cyrus the Great,* Doubleday, 1960; *Babur the Tiger, First of the Great Monguls,* Doubleday, 1961; *The Curved Saber: The Adventures of Khlit the Cossack,* Doubleday, 1964; *The Mighty Manslayer,* Doubleday, 1969.

SIDELIGHTS: Harold Lamb, who spent his adult life studying the history and culture of Asia, Russia, and the Near East, rebelled against academic studies during his school years. Lamb preferred to pursue his own course of study—reading voraciously and writing to vent the creative urges his reading inspired.

Lamb left Columbia the first time in 1914 to take jobs as a make-up man for a trade publication and later as a financial writer for the *New York Times.* In his off hours he continued to study and write, and his stories were first published by *Adventure* magazine. Lamb attributed his eventual success to *Adventure*'s editor Arthur Sullivan Hoffman, who allowed him to write on subjects of his own choosing.

Lamb's stories and articles are based on extensive travel and research. He traveled widely in the regions about which he wrote, even attempting to retrace the paths of men like Marco Polo, Genghis Khan, and Alexander the Great. He was thoroughly grounded in the folklore, literature, and customs of these regions and was fluent in Persian and Arabic.

For the most part, Lamb's writings take the form of romantic adventure stories but never stray from cultural and historical accuracy. He wrote for both adults and children and his works have been published in several countries and languages. Movie adaptations of Lamb's work include Paramount's movies, "The Crusades," 1935, "The Plainsmen," 1936, "The Bucaneer," 1958, and Universal's film, "The Golden Horde," 1951.

OBITUARIES: New York Times, April 10, 1962; *Time,* April 20, 1962; *Newsweek,* April 23, 1962; *Publishers Weekly,* April 23, 1962.*

*   *   *

LAMORISSE, Albert (Emmanuel)   1922-1970

PERSONAL: Born January 13, 1922, in Paris, France; died in a helicopter crash while filming a documentary, June 2, 1970, near Teheran, Iran; buried at Chateau de Meaulvuar, France; son of Albert Gusman (a businessman) and Elise (Decaux) Lamorisse; married Claude Jeanne Marie Duparc (a dancer), November 24, 1947; children: Pascal, Sabine, Fanny. *Education:* Attended Institut des Hautes Etudes Cinematographiques. *Religion:* Roman Catholic. *Residence:* Paris, France.

CAREER: Motion picture writer, producer, and director. Began career as technical assistant for feature film, "Kairouan," Tunisia, 1946; camerman for documentary, "Guatemala," 1955; creator of his own award-winning films. Inventor of helevision, a system of aerial photography, and of board game "Risk." *Awards, honors:* Chevalier of the Order of Arts and Letters (France); recipient of numerous awards, including Grand Prix for short films, Cannes Film Festival, 1953, for "Crin blanc"; Prix Jean Vigo; International Prize for Youth; Epi d'Or of Rome; "Le Ballon Rouge" was awarded the Academy Award for best original screenplay, 1956, Grand Prix for short films, Cannes Film Festival, 1956, Grand Prix of the French Cinema, West German film critics prize for best foreign film, and similar awards in Japan, England, Mexico, the United States, and Switzerland; "Le Voyage en Ballon" was awarded the Blue Ribbon of the French Movie and Television Critics Association, 1960, Concours Technique International du Film (Prague), Prix de l'Office Catholique (Venice), prize from Festival International de l'Enfance (La Plata), and San Gregorio Prize, International Festival of Religious Films; *The Red Balloon* was a *New York Times* choice of Best Illustrated Children's Books of the Year, 1957.

WRITINGS—Published screenplays: (With Jacques Prevert) *Bim, le petit ane* (illustrated with photographs from the film), Le Guilde du livre, 1951, translation by Roger Lubbock published as *Bim, the Little Donkey,* Putnam (London), 1957, Doubleday (translation by Bette Swados and Harvey Swados), 1973; (with Denys Colomb de Daunant) *Crin blanc,* Hachette, 1953, translation published as *White Mane,* Dutton, 1954 (published in England as *The Wild White Stallion,* Putnam, 1955); *Le Ballon rouge* (illustrated with photographs from the film), Hachette, 1956, translation published as *The Red Balloon,* Doubleday, 1957; *Le Voyage en ballon* (illustrated with photographs from the film), Hachette, 1960, translation by Malcolm Barnes published as *Trip in a Balloon,* Doubleday, 1960; *Fifi la plume,* Hachette, 1965.

Screenplays; all originally released in France: "Djerba," 1947; "Bim, le petit ane," 1949; "Crin blanc," 1952 (released in U.S. as "White Mane," United Artists, 1953); "Le Ballon rouge," 1956 (released in U.S. as "The Red Balloon," Lopert, 1957); "Le Voyage en ballon," Filmsonor-Films Montsouris, 1960 (released in U.S. as "Stowaway in the Sky," Lopert, 1962); "Fifi la plume," 1965; "Versailles," 1967; "Paris jamais vu" (title means "Paris Rediscovered"), 1968; "Le Vent des amoureux" (title means "The Lovers' Wind"), 1978.

SIDELIGHTS: Albert Lamorisse's films have won numerous awards and are regarded as classics. His most noted works are his shorter films, projects full of dream-like fantasy and wonderment, all done with an eye toward the poetic.

His "White Mane" details the friendship of a boy and a wild horse. In the film, shot in the wet flatlands of the South of France where wild horses roam and the landscape is desolate, a young boy eagerly attempts to possess a beautiful stallion. He gradually gains the animal's confidence and triumphantly rides off astride the horse into the sea. With this film Lamorisse came to the fore of French filmmaking and, indeed, gained world-wide attention. "White Mane" has been shown before the Queen of England and the King of Greece, and in scores of countries outside France.

"The Red Balloon" was seven years in the making—due to deliberate and painstaking work. Lamorisse went through forty-two scenarios before he was pleased with one. And also, as he told Thompson, "I wait simply because I must be inspired." In the film, a little boy adopts a stray red balloon, which faithfully follows him on his ramblings through Paris. He must defend it from tormentors intent on destroying it. Lamorisse's own son, Pascal, played the main role, and his daughter Sabine also played a small part. The unique atmosphere of Paris permeates the film, and the filmmaking has been called triumphant.

While making "Stowaway in the Sky"—a full-length film in which a boy (again played by Pascal) and his grandfather go aloft in a hot air balloon—Lamorisse developed helevision. Helevision minimizes and cushions vibrations that ordinarily shake a camera mounted in a helicopter. The result is as if the camera were mounted on a solid track, all the while seeming to float in the sky. So in "Stowaway in the Sky," the audience follows a seventy-foot orange balloon as it skims the countryside above such spectacles as Notre Dame, the Eiffel Tower, a bullfight, a forest fire, a stag hunt, and a sailboat race, without the interference of vibrations common in the use of a helicopter.

Lamorisse's feature-length films met with less acclaim and success than had his early short and medium-length films, so at the time of his death he was concentrating on documentary shorts. He was killed in a helicopter crash while filming near Teheran. That film, "The Lover's Wind," was later edited from his notes, receiving a nomination for an Oscar as best feature documentary of 1978.

Lamorisse summed up his art for Howard Thompson of the *New York Times,* "To me cinema is a living art, the only one that has so many varied forms of expression. My own is a kind of visual movement."

BIOGRAPHICAL/CRITICAL SOURCES: Time, October 24, 1960; *New York Times,* June 17, 1962.

OBITUARIES: New York Times, June 4, 1970; *Time,* June 15, 1970.*

LAMPMAN, Evelyn Sibley 1907-1980
(Lynn Bronson)

OBITUARY NOTICE—See index for *CA* sketch: Born April 18, 1907, in Dallas, Ore.; died of cancer, June 13, 1980, in Portland, Ore. Author. Lampman wrote radio scripts and children's books for which she won several honors, including two Golden Spur awards and two Jean Hersholt Awards. Her numerous books include *Cayuse Courage, Bargain Bride, Crazy Creek,* and *Coyote Kid.* Obituaries and other sources: *New York Times,* June 14, 1980; *Washington Post,* June 16, 1980.

* * *

LAND, (Reginald) Brian 1927-

PERSONAL: Born July 29, 1927, in Niagara Falls, Ontario, Canada; son of Allan Reginald (a bank manager) and Beatrice Beryl (Boyle) Land; married Edith Wyndham Eddis (a social worker and editorial researcher), August 29, 1953; children: Mary Beatrice, John Robert Eddis. *Education:* University of Toronto, B.A., 1949, B.L.S., 1953, M.L.S., 1956, M.A., 1963. *Religion:* Anglican. *Home:* 18 Kirkton Rd., Downsview, Ontario, Canada M3H 1K7. *Office:* Ontario Legislative Library, Legislative Building, Queen's Park, Toronto, Ontario, Canada M7A 1A2.

CAREER: T. Eaton Co. Ltd., Toronto, Ontario, copy editor in catalog mail order advertising, 1949-50; Toronto Public Library, Toronto, reference librarian, 1953-55; University of Toronto, Toronto, cataloger at library, 1955-56; Windsor Public Library, Windsor, Ontario, head of division of business and industry, 1956-57; *Canadian Business,* Montreal, Quebec, assistant editor, 1957-58, associate editor, 1958-59; University of Toronto, assistant chief librarian, 1959-63, associate librarian, 1963; Government of Canada, Ottawa, Ontario, executive assistant to minister of finance, 1963-64; University of Toronto, professor of library science, 1964-78, dean of faculty, 1964-72, part-time professor, 1978—; Ontario Legislative Library, Toronto, director of research and information services, 1978—. Member of Canadian Library Research and Development Council (vice-president, 1965-67), Canadian Council of Library Schools (chairman, 1971-72), Institute of Professional Librarians of Ontario (president, 1961-62), Ontario Committee of Deans and Directors of Library Schools (chairman, 1967-71), and Ontario Council of Library Schools (chairman, 1968-72); member of Ontario Provincial Library Council, 1967-70, and Canadian Radio-Television Commission, 1973-78.

MEMBER: Canadian Library Association (president, 1975-76), Canadian Association of Library Schools (president, 1966-67), Bibliographical Society of Canada, Canadian Association of University Teachers, Special Libraries Association, American Library Association (chairman of committee on accreditation, 1973-74), Association of American Library Schools (president, 1973-74), Ontario Library Association (first vice-president, 1962-63), Ontario Genealogical Society, Association of Teaching Staff of University of Toronto, Beta Phi Mu. *Awards, honors:* Kenneth R. Wilson Memorial Award from Business Newspapers Association of Canada, 1959, for best annual article in business and finance, "Here's How Canada's Money Market Keeps Idle Cash at Work"; distinguished achievement award from Ontario Library Trustees Association, 1968; Silver Jubilee Medal from Government of Canada, 1977.

WRITINGS: Eglinton: The Election Study of a Federal Constituency, Peter Martin Associates, 1955; (editor) *Directory of Business, Trade, and Professional Associations in Cana-*

da, Canadian Business, 1959, 2nd edition, 1962; *Sources of Information for Canadian Business,* Canadian Chamber of Commerce, 1962, 3rd edition, 1978; (editor) *Directory of Associations in Canada,* University of Toronto Press, 1974, 4th edition, Micromedia Ltd., 1981. Contributor to business and library journals.

SIDELIGHTS: Land told *CA:* "I am interested in developing more reference works for Canadian use, particularly in the field of business and economics."

*   *   *

LANDER, Jack Robert 1921-

PERSONAL: Born February 15, 1921, in Hinckley, England; son of Robert Arthur and Hilda Mary (Goodman) Lander. *Education:* Pembroke College, Cambridge, B.A., 1942, M.A., 1947, M.Litt., 1950. *Politics:* Liberal. *Home:* Whitehall, 1265 Richmond St., Apt. 1701, London, Ontario, Canada N6A 3M1. *Office:* Department of History, Social Science Centre, University of Western Ontario, London 72, Ontario, Canada.

CAREER: University of Ghana, Legon, lecturer, 1950-58, senior lecturer in history, 1958-63; Dalhousie University, Halifax, Nova Scotia, associate professor of history, 1963-65; University of Western Ontario, London, professor of history, 1965-69, J. B. Smallman Professor, 1969—. Assistant secretary and treasurer of Ghana monuments and relics commission, 1952-60; member of Ghana museums board, 1956-63. *Member:* Royal Society of Canada (fellow), American Historical Association, Mediaeval Academy of America, Royal Historical Society (fellow), Historical Association, Reform Club. *Awards, honors:* Leverhulme fellow, 1959-60.

WRITINGS: The Wars of the Roses, Secker & Warburg, 1965, Putnam, 1966; *Conflict and Stability in Fifteenth Century England,* Hutchinson, 1969; *Ancient and Medieval England: Beginnings to 1509,* Harcourt, 1973; *Crown and Nobility, 1450-1509,* McGill-Queen's University Press, 1976; *Crown and Community in England, 1450-1509,* Harvard University Press, 1980. Contributor to learned journals.

WORK IN PROGRESS: The English Justices of the Peace, 1460-1509.

SIDELIGHTS: Lander wrote: "I have been motivated by a strong interest in medieval history since my undergraduate days. I began to write for pleasure, and I hope to interest a wide general public, not merely specialist scholars. To aspiring writers my advice is to practice good style, reread at least three great classics a year for the sake of style, and write steadily every day—don't wait until you feel that you are in the mood."

AVOCATIONAL INTERESTS: Antique furniture, silver and porcelain, modern pictures, travel.

*   *   *

LANG, George 1924-

PERSONAL: Born July 13, 1924, in Szekesfehervar, Hungary; came to the United States in 1946, naturalized citizen, 1950; son of Simon Deutsch and Ilona Lang; children: Andrea, Brian. *Education:* Attended University of Szeged, 1945, Mozarteum, 1945-46, and University of Stranieri, 1950-51. *Office:* George Lang Corp., 33 West 67th St., New York, N.Y. 10023.

CAREER: Concert and symphony orchestra violinist; violinist with Dallas Symphony Orchestra, Dallas, Tex.; Waldorf-Astoria Hotel, New York City, assistant banquet manager,

1953-58; vice-president in sales and marketing for Brass Rail Organization, 1958-60; vice-president of Restaurant Associations Industries, 1960-71; George Lang Corp., New York City, president, 1971—. Operated "Four Seasons" restaurant. Lecturer to professional restaurateurs all over the world. *Awards, honors:* Hotelman Award, 1975.

WRITINGS: The Cuisine of Hungary, Atheneum, 1971; (contributor) *The Great Cooks' Cookbook,* Doubleday, 1974; *Lang's Compendium of Culinary Nonsense and Trivia,* C. N. Potter, 1980. Author of a monthly column in *Travel and Leisure.* Contributor to *Encyclopaedia Britannica.* Contributor to national magazines, including *Esquire* and *Gourmet.* Contributing editor of *Travel and Leisure, Australian Gourmet,* and *Hospitality.*

WORK IN PROGRESS: The Restaurant Book, publication expected in 1982; a novel.

SIDELIGHTS: Lang's published magazine articles cover a wide range of interests, including architecture and design, calligraphy, and Renaissance history, but his concentration remains what he calls "the art of selecting, preparing, serving, and enjoying fine food," and it is as chef and food consultant that he is best known.

The George Lang Corp. has been likened to a "think tank" and his clients range from international hotel and restaurant chains to cruise ships, airlines, and government agencies. He has created or redesigned more than three hundred restaurants in eleven countries, involving himself with every detail from analysis and planning to design of uniforms and table settings. He has arranged state dinners for such guests as Queen Elizabeth II.

*   *   *

LANG, King
See TUBB, E(dwin) C(harles)

*   *   *

LANTRY, Mike
See TUBB, E(dwin) C(harles)

*   *   *

LARAMORE, Darryl 1928-

PERSONAL: Born May 27, 1928, in Kankakee, Ill.; son of Daniel Earl and Violet Rachael Laramore; married Joyce Hutchison (a high school teacher), November 29, 1958; children: Nina, Christopher, Megan. *Education:* Wheaton College, Wheaton, Ill., B.A., 1950; California State University, Los Angeles, M.A., 1958; University of Maryland, Ph.D., 1971. *Home:* 201 Greenspring Lane, Silver Spring, Md. 20904. *Agent:* Albert Zuckerman, Writer's House, Inc., 21 West 26th St., New York, N.Y. 10001. *Office:* Montgomery County Public Schools, 850 Hungerford Dr., Rockville, Md. 20850.

CAREER: Junior high school teacher of general science and biology in Downey, Calif., 1953-58; Nordhoff Union High School District, Ojai, Calif., counselor and director of guidance program, 1958-62; Sonoma County Office of Education, Santa Rosa, Calif., supervisor of guidance, 1962-73; Montgomery County Public Schools, Rockville, Md., supervisor of guidance, 1973—. Professor at Virginia Polytechnic Institute and State University, 1975—. Owner of private consulting agency, 1978—. Member of board of directors of bilingual radio station in Santa Rosa, 1971-74, and Washington School for Secretaries, 1979—. *Military service:* U.S. Army, Quartermaster Corps, 1951-53. *Member:* American

Personnel and Guidance Association, National Vocational Guidance Association.

WRITINGS: (With Ken Hoyt, Garth Magnum, and Nancy Pensan) *Career Education in the Elementary Schools,* Olympus Research, 1973; *Careers: A Guide for Parents and Counselors,* Brigham Young University Press, 1978. Also author of *Objective: Murder* (novel), 1981. Co-author of "For Parents Only," a column syndicated by Suburban Features, Inc., 1974-75. Contributor of about twenty articles to guidance and education journals. Editor of *Inform* (of American Personnel and Guidance Association).

WORK IN PROGRESS: Research and writing on family issues.

SIDELIGHTS: Laramore wrote: "I first became interested in career counseling as a teacher in 1953 in a junior high school, because of my awareness that students who had career goals did better in school than those who did not. Although those goals usually changed, other goals took their places. Those students who had no life goals were less motivated. I began to wonder whether these goals were based on good information or if they were sterotypes that students held of certain careers (law enforcement is exciting; flight attendants are glamorous).

"In 1967 I started, to my knowledge, the first telephone career information center in the country. A career information specialist took calls from students and answered questions from current written information. If questions became too detailed, the technician contacted a person working in the field from hundreds of community volunteers, and put the student and the worker together in a conference call. This operation gained national publicity. Some of the more interesting conference calls were from a roller derby queen, a professional chess player, and several professional athletes. Many students' stereotyped views were exploded during those conferences; other were validated.

"From this project I went on in 1971 to develop the first career education program that I knew of in the United States, training elementary, junior high, and high school teachers to infuse career concepts into their curriculum areas. As a result of this program, I was asked by the California Department of Education to train personnel in the ten original career education sites in California.

"In 1973 I became aware that career information alone is not sufficient, but that students and adults must understand and use a process including self-awareness, career awareness, decision making, and job-seeking skills in order to have satisfying lives.

"At present, I have begun working not only with family groups, but with industries to assist their employers in this career-development process. I also teach career counseling techniques to graduate students in counseling. As I take them through the process, many quit counseling and move into other careers, confirming my opinion that adults, as well as children, make decisions based on inadequate information about themselves and the world of work.

"My wife and I are interested in the family and feel that families should work together as a unit. To help parents and children develop their skills, we have taught parent effectiveness. In my own life, I have applied the career process to help make changes in education. No one needs to be trapped in a career if he has the skills to move out of it."

*   *   *

LAUDERDALE, Pat 1944-

PERSONAL: Born October 19, 1944, in Hobart, Okla.; son of Tommie and Almeta (Cantrell) Lauderdale. *Education:* University of Oklahoma, B.A., 1967; University of Texas, M.A. (social psychology), 1969; Stanford University, M.A. (sociology), 1972, Ph.D., 1975. *Home:* 77 Orlin S.E., Minneapolis, Minn. 55414. *Office:* Department of Sociology/Criminal Justice, University of Minnesota, Minneapolis, Minn. 55455.

CAREER: Stanford University, Stanford, Calif., instructor in sociology, 1973-74; University of California, Santa Cruz, instructor in sociology, 1974; University of Minnesota, Minneapolis, assistant professor, 1974-78, associate professor of sociology, 1978—. Visiting research scholar at Stanford University, 1978; participant in Cuban criminal justice tour, 1980; United Farm Workers organizer; consultant to U.S. Commission on Civil Rights, Office of Economic Opportunity, and Project Sprint. *Member:* Phi Beta Kappa, Omicron Delta Kappa. *Awards, honors:* Woodrow Wilson fellowship, 1967-68; travel grant from University of Melbourne, 1968-69; National Institute of Mental Health grants, 1974-75, 1975-76; grant for comparative legal development from NSMF, 1976-77; grant from Office of International Programs, 1980.

WRITINGS: *Cultural Alternatives to National Development: The Melting Pot Revisited,* Educational Resources Information Center/Clearinghouse on Urban Education, 1977; (contributor) Saul D. Feldman, editor, *Deciphering Deviance,* Little, Brown, 1978; (contributor) Marvin D. Krohn and Ronald Akers, editors, *Theories of Law, Crime, and Sanctions,* Sage Publications, 1978; (contributor) Donald Black, editor, *General Theory of Social Control,* Academic Press, 1980; (editor and contributor) *A Political Analysis of Deviance,* University of Minnesota Press, 1980; (with James Inverarity) *Sociology of Law,* Winthrop, 1981. Also contributor to *Socio-Pharmacology,* edited by Pat Barchas, 1980. Contributor of more than a dozen articles and reviews to sociology journals. Member of editorial board of *Western Sociological Review,* 1978-80.

SIDELIGHTS: Lauderdale told *CA:* "The conventional wisdom of American society and much of the professional knowledge within the academic community suggests that there is a clear and distinct line between political and deviant activity. This distinction has become blurred in recent years by sociological and historical studies that reveal the political nature of deviance. In most of my recent work I have attempted to explore the changes underlying the creation of deviance. In examining the evidence my writing includes subject matter not found in traditional works on crime and deviance. Police/race riots, hockey violence, social movement protest and political trials are focused upon to explain the importance of the political dimensions of deviance."

*   *   *

LAURANCE, Alice [a pseudonym] 1938-

PERSONAL: Born January 7, 1938, in Brooklyn, N.Y.; daughter of William F. (an attorney) and Ernestine (a secretary; maiden name, Vender) Weber; married a business manager, October 24, 1963; children: Johnny. *Education:* Finch College, B.A., 1959. *Politics:* Libertarian. *Religion:* Society of Friends (Quakers). *Residence:* Hopewell, N.J. *Agent:* Virginia Kidd, 538 East Harford St., Milford, Pa. 18337. *Office:* Department of Developmental Communications, Princeton University, Princeton, N.J. 08541.

CAREER: Wallace Witmer Co., New York, N.Y., manager of New York office, 1960-75; director of development at private academy in Brooklyn, N.Y., 1975-78; Jacksonville University, Jacksonville, Fla., public relations director, 1978-79;

Princeton University, Princeton, N.J., assistant director of developmental communication, 1980—. *Member:* Science Fiction Writers of America.

WRITINGS: (Editor) *Cassandra Rising* (science-fiction anthology), Doubleday, 1978; (editor with Isaac Asimov) *Who Done It?* (mystery anthology), Houghton, 1980.

WORK IN PROGRESS: Speculations, a science-fiction anthology edited with Asimov, for Houghton.

*   *   *

LAWRENCE, P.
    See TUBB, E(dwin) C(harles)

*   *   *

LAWSON, Chet
    See TUBB, E(dwin) C(harles)

*   *   *

LAW YONE, Edward Michael   1911(?)-1980

OBITUARY NOTICE: Born c. 1911 in Nyitkyina, Burma; died June 27, 1980, in Kensington, Md. Editor, author, government worker, and political activist. Law Yone founded and edited the English-language newspaper *Nation* after Burma gained its independence in 1948. He edited another newspaper and headed several Burmese government commissions until 1962, when he was imprisoned for six years following a military coup. After his release he attempted to organize a rebellion against the military government, but moved to the United States when that effort failed. Among his books is a translation of former Burmese Prime Minister U Nu's autobiography, *Saturday Son.* Obituaries and other sources: *New York Times,* June 29, 1980; *Washington Post,* June 30, 1980.

*   *   *

LAZARRE, Jane D(eitz)   1943-

PERSONAL: Born November 16, 1943, in New York, N.Y.; daughter of William and Tullah (Deitz) Lazarre; married second husband, Douglas H. White, April 6, 1968; children: Adam, Khary. *Education:* City College of the City University of New York, B.A., 1964; New School for Social Research, M.A., 1972; also attended American Institute for Practicing Psychotherapists. *Politics:* "Socialist-Feminist." *Home and office:* 150 West 96th St., New York, N.Y. 10025. *Agent:* Wendy Weil, Julian Bach Literary Agency, Inc., 747 Third Ave., New York, N.Y. 10017.

CAREER: High school English teacher in New York City, 1966-68; free-lance writer for *Village Voice, Ms.,* and *Viva;* City College of the City University of New York, New York City, lecturer on women's studies and journalism, 1977—. Member of board of directors of Roxann Dance Foundation and Purple Circle Parents Cooperative Day Care Center, 1972—. Member of Women's Institute for Freedom of the Press. Lecturer at schools and meetings; guest on radio programs; gives readings from her work. *Member:* Poets and Writers, Writers' Guild.

WRITINGS: (Contributor) Uta West, editor, *Woman in a Changing World,* McGraw, 1975; *The Mother Knot* (memoir-novel; Woman Today Book Club selection), Dell, 1977; (contributor) A. Roland and B. Harris, editors, *Career and Motherhood: Struggles for a New Identity,* Human Sciences Press, 1978; *On Loving Men* (essays), Dial, 1980; *Some Kind of Innocence* (novella), Dial, 1980. Contributor of about twenty articles and reviews to magazines and newspapers, including *Feminist Studies* and *Harper's Weekly.*

WORK IN PROGRESS: Translations, a novel, publication by Dial expected in 1983.

SIDELIGHTS: Jane Lazarre commented: "I consider any aspect of my experience vital to my work. I am very concerned with political and cultural values and try to explore these by dissection of intimate experience between people. The women's movement and women's studies classes I teach have been very nourishing to my work and clarifying to my life. I have always been involved with painting and drawing, and these too have fed my relationship with words."

*   *   *

Le BRETON, Auguste
    See MONTFORT, Auguste

*   *   *

LEE, Kay
    See KELLY, Karen

*   *   *

LEIGHTON, Ann
    See SMITH, Isadore Leighton Luce

*   *   *

LEITCH, Adelaide   1921-

PERSONAL: Born February 10, 1921, in Toronto, Ontario, Canada; daughter of Alexander G. (a school inspector) and Roberta (Graham) Leitch; married James Lennox (a printer), 1963. *Education:* University of Toronto, B.A., 1942. *Home:* 169 Hanna Rd., Toronto, Ontario, Canada M4G 3N9.

CAREER: Midland Free Press Herald, Midland, Ontario, reporter, 1943-45; *Windsor Daily Star,* Windsor, Ontario, reporter and feature writer, 1945-48; free-lance writer and photographer, 1948-52; *Guardian Press,* St. John's, Newfoundland, managing editor, 1952-53; free-lance writer and photographer, 1953—. *Member:* Canadian Authors' Association, Writers' Union of Canada, Outdoor Photographers' League. *Awards, honors:* Canadian Women's Press Club Award, 1962, for photo-story in *Canadian Geographical Journal;* first prize in Macmillan Company competition to launch a new juvenile series, 1962, for *The Great Canoe.*

WRITINGS: Flightline North, Guardian Press (St. John's, Newfoundland), 1952; *The Visible Past: The Pictorial History of Simcoe County,* Ryerson, 1967; *Into the High Country: The Story of Dufferin, the Last 12,000 Years to 1974,* County of Dufferin (Toronto), 1975; *Floodtides of Fortune: The Story of Stratford,* City of Stratford, 1980.

For children: *The Great Canoe,* Macmillan (Toronto), 1962, St. Martin's, 1963; *Canada, Young Giant of the North,* photographs by the author, Nelson, 1964, revised edition, 1968; *Lukey Paul From Labrador,* illustrated by Joe Rosenthal, St. Martin's, 1964; *Mainstream,* Friendship, 1966; *The Blue Roan,* illustrations by Charles Robinson, Walck, 1971.

SIDELIGHTS: Two of Leitch's best known books, *The Great Canoe* and *Lukey Paul from Labrador,* were selected for Macmillan's "Buckskin" series. These books present Canadian heroes, history, and geography through the perceptions and experiences of fictional young people. Leitch provides children with an insight not only into Canadian history and geography in her books, but into the nation's cultural heritage as well, since her characters represent various cultural and geographic origins.

Leitch's experiences as writer and photographer on various Canadian publications provide the background necessary for her nonfiction accounts of Canada's past and present. Extensive travel throughout the country, as well as to regions as distant as Central America and Lapland, provide her with insight and material for both written and photographic work.

*   *   *

LEITENBERG, Milton 1933-

PERSONAL: Born August 1, 1933, in New York, N.Y.; son of Julius (a dressmaker) and Libby (Ossofsky) Leitenberg. *Education:* City College (now of the City University of New York), B.S., 1955; attended Johns Hopkins University, 1957, and Brandeis University, 1959. *Religion:* Jewish. *Office:* Swedish Institute of International Affairs, Stockholm, Sweden.

CAREER: Affiliated with Swedish Institute of International Affairs, Stockholm.

WRITINGS: (Co-editor) *A Short Research Guide on Arms and Armed Forces,* Croom-Helm, 1978; *Great Power Intervention in the Middle East,* Pergamon, 1979. Contributor of about eighty articles to books and scholarly journals.

WORK IN PROGRESS: A second edition of *A Short Research Guide on Arms and Armed Forces.*

*   *   *

LELIAERT, Richard Maurice 1940-

PERSONAL: Born November 30, 1940, in Mishawaka, Ind.; son of Maurice August (a gas company employee) and Lucy Leona (a cook and caterer; maiden name, Stevens) Leliaert. *Education:* St. Francis College, Fort Wayne, Ind., B.A., 1965; Catholic University of America, S.T.B., 1967; Graduate Theological Union, Berkeley, Calif., Ph.D., 1974. *Politics:* Democrat. *Home and office:* Nazareth College, Nazareth, Mich. 49074.

CAREER: Ordained Roman Catholic priest of Crosier Fathers (O.S.C.), 1967; Crosier Seminary, Onamia, Minn., instructor in Latin and religion, 1968-69; Crosier House of Studies, Fort Wayne, Ind., assistant professor of historical-doctrinal theology, 1972-73; Catholic Theological Union, Chicago, Ill., assistant professor of historical-doctrinal theology, 1974-77; Nazareth College, Nazareth, Mich., assistant professor of religious studies, 1977—. Priest of Roman Catholic parishes in Anoka and St. Paul, Minn., 1967-69, Fremont, Concord, and Oakley, Calif., 1969-73, Fort Wayne, Ind., 1973-74, and Kalamazoo and Bronson, Mich., 1973—; superior of community of Crosier Fathers in Kalamazoo area; team priest in Worldwide Marriage Encounter movement; member of Kalamazoo Diocese committee on women's roles and rights in the Catholic church. Group leader of Business-Academia Dialogue.

MEMBER: American Academy of Religion, American Society of Church History, American Catholic Historical Association, College Theology Society, World Future Society. *Awards, honors:* Annual prize from Center for the Study of American Catholicism at University of Notre Dame, 1979, for *The Brownson-Hecker Correspondence;* Danforth associate, 1980.

WRITINGS: (Editor with Joseph F. Gower) *The Brownson-Hecker Correspondence,* University of Notre Dame Press, 1979. Contributor to politics, history, and theology journals.

WORK IN PROGRESS: A Catholic theology and history of marriage; research on the role of women in the Christian religion, the development of medical ethics, especially as it relates to issues in death and dying, and the development of audio-visual materials for Bible study, especially the Bible lands.

SIDELIGHTS: Leliaert wrote: "I'm a Belgian-American, having some knowledge of Spanish, French, German, Flemish, Latin, biblical Hebrew, and Greek. My experiences as a Catholic ethnic in America interested me in American religious history in general and American Catholicism in particular. So when Joseph Gower suggested to me that we publish the correspondence between Orestes A. Brownson and Isaac Hecker, I was excited. These two men are very important figures for understanding not only the development of American Catholicism, but also American intellectual history in the nineteenth century. Both Brownson and Hecker were familiar with American trancendentalists, literary and journalistic figures, politicians, and churchpersons in America and abroad.

"Currently I'm working closely with many married couples in the Marriage Encounter movement. Somehow marriage and the family will be under great pressure in the 1980's, but without a strong sense of marital fidelity and family ties, each of us will find it hard to realize our potential both as individuals and as related to the whole human family. For this reason I want to do more work and research on a Catholic theology of marriage and family, meaning not just the nuclear family but the role of the nuclear family in the wider church and civil community.

"Since starting to teach here at Nazareth College, I've been taken up in issues regarding medical ethics and death/dying. So I also accepted an invitation to serve on the ethical-moral committee set up by the Michigan Catholic Hospital Association. Advances in medical science have been profound in their ethical implications, and for every surface problem, like 'test-tube' babies, there are a host of hidden questions connected with it. I think our religious heritage, especially the Judaeo-Christian tradition, can respond to the challenge, but dialogue between the religious and the scientific community needs to be carried on.

"Especially since my graduate studies in Berkeley in the early 1970's, the women's movement has challenged me to move away from the male bias in Catholic theology and church life. Then my involvement with Marriage Encounter and my serving on a local committee dealing with women in the life of the Church have sharpened my thinking and activity. Working with Roman Catholic nuns and Catholic laypersons made me do more research into the Bible and Church documents for insight about the ordination of women in the Catholic church, sexist language in worship services, and the gifts of women to the ministry in non-ordained capacities. A source of personal help, theologically and psychologically, has been androgyny—so I've pursued my own research in this area. My teaching responsibilities, especially courses in marriage and family, love and sexuality, and the feminine in religion, have helped me put all of this together in a more coherent way.

"As much as I enjoy research and writing, my work as a teacher has been more important to me. I've sensed the tension many times between 'publish or perish' and my interaction with searching minds in the classroom. Somehow I want to stimulate the potential in those individuals I meet on a day-to-day basis. I want to be an educator, not an imparter of information, whether I'm working as a priest or an academic professional. Somehow the answers to the questions that plague me have to be found together. Donne's dictum about nobody being an island, everybody being part of the main, has shaped my approach to life quite drastically. That's why, I suppose, I favor thinkers like Plato, St. Paul, Alfred North Whitehead, Teilhard de Chardin, and many others in whom the communitarian bias is evident.''

* * *

LEMIRE, Robert A(rthur)   1933-

PERSONAL: Born January 19, 1933, in Lowell, Mass.; son of Joseph Emile (a teacher) and Blanche Rose (Bisaillon) Lemire; married Virginia Mae Bock, November 24, 1960; children: Elise Virginia, Robert Bock. *Education:* Yale University, B.A., 1954; Harvard University, M.B.A., 1958. *Home address:* Codman Rd., Lincoln, Mass. 01773. *Office:* Lemire & Co., Inc., Codman Rd., Lincoln, Mass. 01774.

CAREER: Lemire & Co., Inc. (investment advisers), Lincoln, Mass., president, 1971—. Carolyn B. Haffenreffer Lecturer at Rhode Island School of Design, 1976; public speaker. Member of Lincoln Conservation Commission, 1963—, chairman, 1966—; public member of Massachusetts Agricultural Lands Preservation Committee; land-use planning and disposition consultant. *Military service:* U.S. Naval Reserve; became lieutenant junior grade. *Awards, honors:* Action Award from Massachusetts Audubon Society, 1972; environmental award from Massachusetts Conservation Council, 1979.

WRITINGS: Creative Land Development: Bridge to the Future, Houghton, 1979. Contributor to professional journals.

* * *

LEVENSON, Sam(uel)   1911-1980

OBITUARY NOTICE—See index for *CA* sketch: Born December 28, 1911, in New York, N.Y.; died of a heart attack, August 27, 1980, in New York, N.Y. Educator, humorist, and author. Levenson taught high school in New York City before entering the entertainment business. He began by touring nightclubs, but soon appeared on such radio and television shows as ''Cavalcade of Stars,'' ''The Milton Berle Show,'' ''Toast of the Town,'' and ''To Tell the Truth.'' Levenson also hosted his own television program, ''The Sam Levenson Show.'' His humorous books include *Sex and the Single Child, In One Era and Out the Other,* and *You Can Say That Again, Sam.* Obituaries and other sources: *Newsweek,* September 8, 1980; *Time,* September 8, 1980.

* * *

LEVI, Vicki Gold   1941-

PERSONAL: Born September 16, 1941, in Atlantic City, N.J.; daughter of Albert (a photographer) and Beverly Gold; married second husband Alex H. Levi (a psychologist), May 31, 1970. *Education:* Attended Montclair State College, 1959-60. *Religion:* Jewish. *Residence:* New York, N.Y. *Agent:* A. Watkins, Inc., 77 Park Ave., New York, N.Y. 10010.

CAREER: Cosmopolitan, New York City, sales representative, 1965-67; Misty Harbor Ltd., New York City, advertising and publicity director, 1967-70; writer and researcher, 1980—. Co-founder of Atlantic City Historical Museum; guest on television and radio programs, including ''The Dinah Shore Show,'' ''The Merv Griffin Show'' and ''The Larry King Radio Show''; public speaker; film consultant. *Member:* American Society of Picture Professionals, American Federation of Television and Radio Artists. *Awards,*

honors: Citations from New Jersey Senate and New Jersey Writers Conference, 1980, for *Atlantic City.*

WRITINGS: (With Lee Eisenberg) *Atlantic City: 125 Years of Ocean Madness,* C. N. Potter, 1979; (with Richard Shepard) *Yiddish Culture in America,* Ballantine, 1981. Contributor to magazines, including *Philadelphia* and *Esquire.*

WORK IN PROGRESS: 42nd Street: A History, publication expected in 1982.

SIDELIGHTS: As the daughter of Atlantic City's first official city photographer, Vicki Levi was caught up almost from birth in the city's tourist promotion and publicity activities. She won a beauty contest at age two and participated as a page in the 1945 Miss America Pageant. Keepsakes gathered over the years have grown into a sizeable collection of memorabilia, which have been part of major exhibitions and were used in the film, ''Atlantic City, U.S.A.'' She is planning to use the collection as a beginning for the Atlantic City Historical Museum. She is also working with old newsreel footage for television presentation.

''I love to help preserve things that contributed to our culture,'' Levi commented. ''In the case of Atlantic City, the past would disappear if no one chronicled it. It would be lost in all the new casino glitter.''

AVOCATIONAL INTERESTS: World travel.

BIOGRAPHICAL/CRITICAL SOURCES: New Jersey Monthly, June, 1980.

* * *

LEVINE, Barry B(ernard)   1941-

PERSONAL: Born January 22, 1941, in New York, N.Y.; son of Nathan L. (an attorney) and Miriam (Margolies) Levine. *Education:* University of Pennsylvania, B.A., 1961; New School for Social Research, M.A., 1965, Ph.D., 1973. *Office: Caribbean Review,* Florida International University, Miami, Fla. 33199.

CAREER: University of Caldas, Manizales, Colombia, fellow at Centro Colombo-Americano, 1963-64; Brooklyn College of the City University of New York, Brooklyn, N.Y., lecturer in sociology, 1968; University of Puerto Rico, San Juan, assistant professor of social sciences, 1965-72, codirector of project on the burden of poverty in Puerto Rico, 1969-72; Florida International University, Miami, assistant professor, 1972-75, associate professor of sociology and anthropology, 1975—, chairman of department, 1975-78, cofounder and editor of *Caribbean Review,* 1969—, member of advisory board of Latin American and Caribbean Center. Member of executive committee and board of directors of greater Miami chapter of American Jewish Committee. Guest on television and radio programs. *Member:* American Sociological Association, Caribbean Studies Association (member of executive council, 1980-81), Latin American Caribbean Periodicals Association (president, 1980-81). *Awards, honors:* Fellowship from U.S. Information Agency, 1963-64.

WRITINGS: (Contributor) Deborah Offenbacher and Constance Poster, editors, *Social Problems and Social Policy,* Appleton-Century-Crofts, 1970; (editor with Rafael Ramirez and Carlos Buitrago) *Problemas de desigualdad social en Puerto Rico* (title means ''Problems of Social Inequality in Puerto Rico''), Ediciones Libreria Internacional, 1972; (contributor) Basil Ince, editor, *Essays on Race, Economics, and Politics in the Caribbean,* University of Puerto Rico in Mayaguez, 1973; (contributor) R. F. Tomasson, editor, *Comparative Studies in Sociology: An Annual Compilation of Re-*

search, Jai Press, 1978; *Benjy Lopez: A Picaresque Tale of Emigration and Return,* Basic Books, 1980. Contributor of articles and reviews to newspapers and social science journals. Contributing editor of *Metas.*

WORK IN PROGRESS: Five Cuban Picaros.

SIDELIGHTS: Levine describes his latest book, *Benjy Lopez,* as "a first-person narrative of the life history of a Puerto Rican of middle years, contradicting the myth that the typical experience of the ordinary Puerto Rican is exclusively defined by privation, fear, prejudice, and culture shock."

*   *   *

LEVY, Benn W(olfe) 1900-1973

PERSONAL: Born March 7, 1900, in London, England; died December 7, 1973, in Oxford, England; son of Octave G. and Nannie (Joseph) Levy; married Constance Cummings (an actress), 1933; children: one son, one daughter. *Education:* Attended University College, Oxford, 1919-22. *Residence:* London, England.

CAREER: Playwright. Managing director of Jarrolds Publishers in London, England; Labour Member of Parliament for Eton and Slough division of Buckinghamshire, England, 1945-50. Director of plays, 1929-52, including "Art and Mrs. Bottle," 1929, "Springtime for Henry," 1932, "The Jealous God," 1939, and "Cupid and Psyche," 1952. Chairman of executive committee for League of Dramatists, 1946-52; Arts Council executive, 1953-61. *Military service:* Royal Air Force, 1918. Royal Navy, World War II; became lieutenant. *Member:* Garrick. *Awards, honors:* Member of the Order of the British Empire, 1944.

WRITINGS—Plays: This Woman Business (three-act; first produced in London, England, 1925; produced in New York, N.Y., 1926), E. Benn, 1925; *Art and Mrs. Bottle* (first produced in London, 1929; produced in New York, 1930; also see below), M. Secker, 1928, Samuel French, 1931; *Mrs. Moonlight* (three-act pastiche; first produced in London, 1928; produced in New York, 1930; also see below), Gollancz, 1929, Samuel French, 1931; *The Devil* (first produced in London, 1930), M. Secker, 1930, published as *The Devil Passes* (three-act religious comedy; first produced in New York, 1932), Samuel French, 1932; *Art and Mrs. Bottle* [and] *Mrs. Moonlight,* Samuel French, 1931; (with John van Druten) *Hollywood Holiday: An Extravagant Comedy* (first produced in London, 1931; produced in Pasadena, Calif., 1936), M. Secker, 1931; *Springtime for Henry* (three-act farce; first produced in New York, 1931), Samuel French, 1932; *The Poet's Heart: A Life of Don Juan,* Cresset Press, 1937; (adapter with Hubert Griffith) *Young Madame Conti* (adapted from the play by Bruno Frank; first produced in London, 1936; produced in New York, 1937), Samuel French, 1938; *The Jealous God* (four-act; first produced in London, 1939), M. Secker, 1939.

Clutterbuck: An Artificial Comedy (three-act; first produced in London, 1946; produced in New York, 1949), W. Heinemann, 1947, Dramatists Play Service, 1950; *Return to Tyassi* (three-act; first produced in London, 1950), Gollancz, 1951; *Cupid and Psyche* (first produced in Edinburgh, Scotland, 1952), Gollencz, 1952; *Triple Bill: The Great Healer, The Island of Cipango, The Truth About the Truth* (first televised, 1952), three volumes, Samuel French, 1952; *The Rape of the Belt* (comedy; first produced in London, 1957; produced in New York at Martin Beck Theatre, November 5, 1960), Samuel French, 1957; *The Member for Gaza* (first produced as "Public and Confidential" in Malvern, Worchestershire, England, 1966), Evans Plays, 1968.

Unpublished plays: "A Man With Red Hair" (based on the novel by Hugh Walpole), first produced in New York, 1928; "Mud and Treacle; or, The Course of True Love," first produced in London, 1928; "Ever Green," first produced in London, 1930; "Tapaze" (based on the play by Marcel Pagnol), first produced in New York, 1930; (adapter) "The Church Mouse" (based on the play by Siegfried Geyer and Ladislaus Fodor), first produced in London, 1931; (adapter) "Madame Bovary" (based on the dramatization by Gaston Baty of the novel by Gustave Flaubert), first produced in New York, 1937; (with Paul Harvey Fox) "If I Were You," first produced in New York, 1938; "Anniversary" (radio play), first broadcast in 1941; "The Tumbler," first produced in New York, 1960; "Little Samson," first produced in Malvern, 1966.

Also author of screenplays, including "Blackmail," 1929, "Lord Camber's Ladies," 1932, "The Old Dark House," 1932, "The Devil and the Deep," 1932, and "The Dictator" (also released as "Loves of a Dictator"), 1935.

OBITUARIES: London Times, December 7, 1973; *New York Times,* December 7, 1973.*

*   *   *

LEWIN, Nathan 1936-

PERSONAL: Born January 31, 1936, in Poland; son of Isaac (a professor) and Poppy (Sternheim) Lewin; married Rikki Gordon (a photographer), August 26, 1962; children: Alyza, Naama. *Education:* Yeshiva University, B.A., 1957; Harvard University, J. D., 1960. *Religion:* Jewish. *Home:* 11723 Gainsborough Rd., Potomac, Md. 20854. *Office:* 2555 M St. N.W., Washington, D.C. 20037.

CAREER/WRITINGS: U.S. Supreme Court, Washington, D.C., clerk to Justice John M. Harlan, 1961-62; U.S. Department of Justice, Washington, D.C., special assistant in Criminal Division, 1962-63, assistant to solicitor general, 1963-67; U.S. Department of State, Washington, D.C., deputy assistant secretary of state, 1967-68; U.S. Department of Justice, deputy assistant attorney general, 1968-69. Visiting professor of law at Harvard University, 1974-75; adjunct professor of law at Georgetown University, 1971-74 and 1975-77. Contributing editor of *New Republic,* 1971—. Contributor of articles on law to *New York Times, Los Angeles Times, Saturday Review,* and *Newsday.*

*   *   *

LEWIS, Clay(ton Wilson) 1936-

PERSONAL: Born August 4, 1936, in Washington, D.C.; son of Albert Clayton (a sales executive) and Elizabeth J. (Kennerly) Lewis; married Beverly Hardcastle, December 29, 1958 (divorced, 1977); married Huston Diehl, June 22, 1979; children: (first marriage) Jennifer Hopkins, Daniel Clayton. *Education:* Attended University of the South, 1954-55; Duke University, B.A., 1958; University of Iowa, M.F.A., 1969, M.A., 1970. *Politics:* Democrat. *Religion:* Episcopalian. *Home:* 1130 Robinhood Lane, Norman, Okla. 73069. *Agent:* Ned Leavitt, William Morris Agency, 1150 Avenue of the Americas, New York, N.Y. 10019. *Office:* Department of English, University of Oklahoma, Norman, Okla. 73069.

CAREER: Gardner Advertising Co., St. Louis, Mo., copywriter, 1961-63; Duke University, Durham, N.C., assistant to director of admissions and to director of alumni affairs, 1963-66; State University of New York College at Geneseo, assistant professor, 1970-79; University of Oklahoma, Norman, assistant professor, 1979—. *Military service:* U.S. Marine Corps, 1958-61; became captain. *Awards, honors:* Research fellowships from State University of New York, 1973, 1974, 1978, and 1979; Chancellor's Award for Excellence in Teaching from State University of New York, 1975; National Endowment for the Humanities grant, summer, 1976; finalist in Associated Writing Programs Award Series in Short Fiction, 1979.

WRITINGS—All short stories, except as noted: "After the War," published in *Story: Yearbook of Discovery 1969,* edited by Whit Burnett and Haley Burnett, Four Winds Press, 1969; "The Search for Prester John," published in *Descant,* autumn, 1970; "The Celebration," published in *Woman's Day,* March, 1972; "Hallelujah!," published in *Descant,* winter, 1972; "What Happened Is," published in *Transatlantic,* winter, 1972; "Nina," published in *Carolina Quarterly,* winter, 1973; "In the Fields of Time," published in *Carolina Quarterly,* winter, 1974; "Movie Time," published in *Carolina Quarterly,* winter, 1975; "Sons of Esau," published in *Virginia Quarterly Review,* winter, 1976; "In Battlefields" (autobiography), published in *Texas Quarterly,* winter, 1976; "The Goat," published in *Virginia Quarterly Review,* 1977; "Style in Jefferson's *Notes on the State of Virginia*" (essay), published in *Southern Review,* autumn, 1978; "American Dreams" (autobiography), published in *Southern Review,* winter, 1980; "Memory's End" (autobiography), published in *Southern Review,* in press.

WORK IN PROGRESS: Violations, a novel; *Children of Time,* a short story collection; *Memory's End,* an autobiography.

SIDELIGHTS: Clay Lewis told *CA:* "I started loving literature and fiction writing when I was thirty. All of my writing comes out of the collision of fiction I have read and my own experience. The interrelationship feeds my work, drives it. Like everybody else, I've been taken with the fictional possibilities inherent in Marquez's work. In it there is a way to see self and experience which avoids both repetitions from the nineteenth century and experimental 'anti-fiction' of the twentieth century. I am trying to follow some of these possibilities in my work, including the autobiography. In it I try to combine personal experience, memory, and recovered past with 'design-making' in the foreground; in this way the autobiography becomes a way to make living connections with ongoing historical processes and the lost past."

*   *   *

LEWIS, Finlay 1938-

PERSONAL: Born July 10, 1938, in St. Paul, Minn.; son of Herbert L. (a newspaper editor) and Georgiana (Ingersoll) Lewis; married Wilda Eskew (a high school teacher), May 3, 1969; children: Finlay Ingersoll. *Education:* Harvard University, A.B. (with honors), 1960; attended University of Paris. *Home:* 2727 Chesapeake St. N.W., Washington, D.C. 20008. *Office: Minneapolis Tribune,* 940 National Press Blvd., Washington, D.C. 20045.

CAREER: Duluth News-Tribune, Duluth, Minn., reporter, 1964-66; *Minneapolis Tribune,* Minneapolis, Minn., reporter, 1966-72, correspondent from Washington, D.C., 1972-77, chief of Washington bureau, 1977—. *Military service:* U.S. Army, 1961-64. *Member:* Washington Press Club, Gridiron Club.

WRITINGS: Mondale: Portrait of an American Politician, Harper, 1980. Contributor to magazines, including *New Republic, Nation, Washington Monthly,* and *Columbia Journalism Review.*

SIDELIGHTS: Lewis told *CA:* "My purpose in writing *Mondale: Portrait of an American Politician,* quite simply, was to introduce to a national audience a politician who stands a good chance of assuming the presidency, either by chance or design, at some point during the next decade. There was also a strong competitive reason: I've been in daily journalism too long not to have fairly strong proprietary feelings about stories that I feel are rightfully mine. Such a story is the career of Walter Mondale.

"I first began to cover Mondale in 1972 when he was just another senator and I was a newcomer to the Washington beat. That was too big of an investment, not to mention a headstart, to squander by allowing someone else to produce the first book on Mondale. Not that I was necessarily anxious to be the one who would strike the first booklength blow helping—or hurting—Mondale in pursuit of the ultimate objective in American politics. My dealings with him have always been at arms length—as a reporter, I would have it no other way. But I felt there was an important public interest to be served by providing a full-length, tough-minded, and fair portrait of a public figure so critically situated in a position of power. Then there was the challenge of applying my painfully acquired skills as a reporter to an assignment vastly larger and more complex than anything I had ever attempted before. I know of nothing more demanding—or ultimately more satisfying—than writing. The book turned out to be its own reward."

In a review of *Mondale: Portrait of an American Politician,* Eleanor Randolph commended it as "a sturdy, unpretentious and quite fascinating biography. . . . There are no psychological gimmicks; it is simply a solid, well-written and well-documented book."

BIOGRAPHICAL/CRITICAL SOURCES: Book World, January 13, 1980.

*   *   *

LEWIS, Margie M. 1923-

PERSONAL: Born May 31, 1923, in Laurelville, Ohio; daughter of James O. and Florence (Brigner) Miller; married Ralph L. Lewis (a professor), May 29, 1943; children: Gregg A., Mark, Mack. *Education:* Asbury College, A.B., 1946; Asbury Theological Seminary, M.R.E., 1948. *Religion:* Protestant. *Residence:* Wilmore, Ky.

CAREER: Writer, 1980—. *Member:* Alumni Association of Asbury Theological Seminary (executive secretary, 1963-70).

WRITINGS: (With son, Gregg A. Lewis) *The Hurting Parent,* Zondervan, 1980.

*   *   *

LIBBY, Leona Marshall 1919-

PERSONAL: Born August 9, 1919, in LaGrange, Ill.; daughter of Weightstill and Mary (Holderness) Woods; married John Marshall, July 3, 1943 (marriage ended); married Willard Libby, December, 1966. *Education:* University of Chicago, B.S., 1938, Ph.D., 1943. *Home:* 129 Ocean Way, Santa Monica, Calif. 90402. *Office:* Environmental Science and Engineering, University of California, Los Angeles, Calif. 90024.

CAREER: Hanford Engineering Works, Hanford, Wash., physicist, 1944-46; University of Chicago, Chicago, Ill., research fellow, 1946-48, research associate at Institute for Nuclear Studies, 1948-53, assistant professor of physics, 1953-60; New York University, New York, N.Y., associate professor, 1960-62, professor of physics, 1962-63; University of Colorado, Boulder, professor of physics, 1963; Rand Corp., Santa Monica, Calif., staff member, 1963-70; R & D Associates, Santa Monica, staff member, 1970-76. Visiting scientist at Brookhaven National Laboratory, 1958—. Adjunct professor at University of California, Los Angeles, 1973—. Fellow of Institute for Advanced Study, Princeton, N.J., 1957-58. Consultant to Los Alamos National Laboratory. *Member:* American Physical Society (fellow), Royal Geographical Society (fellow).

WRITINGS: The Uranium People, Crane, Russak, 1979. Associate editor of *Physical Review,* 1960-62.

WORK IN PROGRESS: The Isotope People; Tree Thermometers and Commodities; Historic Climate Indicators.

SIDELIGHTS: Libby told *CA:* "*The Uranium People* details what everyone said and did in the Manhattan District while *The Isotope People* relates what everyone said and did in inventing radio carbon dating and discovering the stable isotopes."

BIOGRAPHICAL/CRITICAL SOURCES: New York Times Book Review, September 30, 1979.

* * *

LICHT, Fred (Stephen)   1928-

PERSONAL: Born June 9, 1928, in Berlin, Germany; came to the United States in 1941, naturalized citizen, 1946; married Meg Meinecke (a professor of architectural history), 1959; children: three. *Education:* University of Wisconsin—Madison, B.A., 1948; University of Basel, Ph.D., 1952. *Home:* 35 University Place, Princeton, N.J. 08540. *Agent:* Curtis Brown Ltd., 575 Madison Ave., New York, N.Y. 10022. *Office:* Department of Art and Archaeology, Princeton University, Princeton, N.J. 08540.

CAREER: Princeton University, Princeton, N.J., instructor in art history, 1953-58; Williams College, Williamstown, Mass., assistant professor of art history, 1958-61; Brown University, Providence, R.I., associate professor of art history, 1965-68, head of department, 1968; Florida State University, Tallahassee, director of study center in Florence, Italy, 1968; Princeton University, professor, 1968—. Vice-president of Council for Religion and International Affairs, 1967—; member of board of trustees of Peggy Guggenheim Foundation, 1968—. *Awards, honors:* Fulbright fellowship for Italy, 1960-61; named Grande Ufficiale of Republic of Italy.

WRITINGS: Die Entwicklung der Landschaft in den Werken von Nicolas Poussin, Birkhauser, 1954; *Sculpture: Nineteenth and Twentieth Centuries,* New York Graphic Society, 1967; *Goya,* L'Oeil, 1970; (compiler and contributor) *Goya in Perspective,* Prentice-Hall, 1973; *Goya: The Origins of the Modern Temper in Art,* Universe Books, 1979. Contributor of articles and stories to art journals, literary journals, and popular magazines, including *New Yorker, Sewanee Review,* and *Virginia Quarterly.*

WORK IN PROGRESS: Seventeenth- and Eighteenth-Century Plaster Sculpture in Italy; Sculptural Monuments of the Risorgimento; History of Spanish Art.

SIDELIGHTS: Times Literary Supplement reviewer Nigel Glendinning commented on Fred Licht's most recent book, *Goya: The Origins of the Modern Temper in Art:* "Licht, like Hetzer before him, seeks to show how Goya's art embodies the time-spirit of his age: reflecting in style and content the substitution of an egocentric, alienated and sceptical world-view, for the God-centered, aesthetic, social and moral con-

ventions he finds in earlier art." John Russell Taylor praised the book: "Such is the wealth of variety and cross-reference, and the liveliness of Mr. Licht's writing . . . that we may at first be tempted to take the book as a display of intellectual pyrotechnics, dazzling rather than illuminating. But as one reads on . . . the more impressive [one finds] the depth as well as the range of Mr. Licht's thought, and the coherence of his argument."

BIOGRAPHICAL/CRITICAL SOURCES: Times Literary Supplement, March 21, 1980; *London Times,* April 21, 1980.

* * *

LICHTY, Ron   1950-

PERSONAL: Born July 19, 1950, in Waterloo, Iowa; son of Quinter D. (a farmer) and Alice (Schroeder) Lichty. *Education:* Attended Iowa State University, 1968-70. *Office:* 800 Heinz Ave., Berkeley, Calif. 94710.

CAREER: Curb, Chicago, Ill., founder, editor, and publisher, 1971-72; Alternative Press Syndicate, New York City, coordinator of branches in New York, London, Buenos Aires, and Hong Kong, writer, and editor of *APS News Service, Alternative Press Revue,* and *APS Directory,* 1972-74; *High Times,* New York City, co-founder, writer, and contributing editor, 1974-75; *Riverton Ranger,* Riverton, Wyo., reporter, feature writer, and photographer for newspaper and *Funtime* (summer supplement), 1975-76; free-lance writer, editor, photographer, and graphic designer, 1976—. General manager of Quick Trading Co., 1978—; member of board of directors of Alternative Press Syndicate, 1980—. Lecturer at New School for Social Research, University of Kansas, Buena Vista College, University of Wyoming, San Francisco Media Alliance, and San Francisco State University. *Member:* San Francisco Media Alliance. *Awards, honors:* Second place in Photofeature Division from Wyoming Press Association's annual competition, 1977, for feature "A Trek Down the Tracks: From Main Street to the End of the Line."

WRITINGS: The Do-It-Yourself Guide to Alternative Publishing, Alternative Press Syndicate, 1976; (with Ed Rosenthal) *One Hundred Thirty-Two Ways to Earn a Living Without Working (For Someone Else),* St. Martin's, 1979; *Berkeley Guidebook,* Hometown Books, 1980. Writer and designer of brochures. Contributor of articles, reviews, and photographs to magazines, including *Rural Gravure, Agrinews,* and *Zoo World,* and newspapers.

SIDELIGHTS: Lichty wrote: "I've always followed my enthusiasms as a writer—and it's what I've recommended to others (whether with writing or, in the case of *One Hundred Thirty-Two Ways to Earn a Living Without Working,* with business).

"One of my strongest enthusiasms is for ideas, for the power of ideas, for the precise communication of exciting and important ideas—and that's been my motivation as a writer, as an editor, as a photographer, and as a graphic designer.

"I began my writing career by starting a magazine—not for profit, although I did ultimately make a profit—but because the magazine, a 1960's peace and social justice journal, was needed and someone was needed to do it. I slowly learned principles of graphic design and the craft of writing, both of which had suddenly become important to me as the means of presenting my own and others' ideas effectively.

"I spent five years researching and writing *One-Hundred-Thirty Two Ways to Earn a Living Without Working (For Someone Else),* with my co-author Ed Rosenthal. I spent hours in libraries, of course. But the most rewarding part of my research was talking with hundreds of people who are boldly living out what once were only their dreams."

BIOGRAPHICAL/CRITICAL SOURCES: Riverton Ranger, June 25, 1975.

*   *   *

LINDSAY, John Vliet   1921-

PERSONAL: Born November 24, 1921, in New York, N.Y.; son of George Nelson (an investment banker) and Eleanor (Vliet) Lindsay; married Mary Anne Harrison, June 18, 1949; children: Katherine (Mrs. Richard Schaeffer), Margaret (Mrs. Robert Zeeb), Anne, John Vliet, Jr. *Education:* Yale University, B.A., 1944, LL.B., 1948. *Religion:* Episcopalian. *Home:* One West 67th St., New York, N.Y. 10023; and Bridgehampton, Suffolk County, N.Y. 11932.

CAREER: Admitted to the Bar of New York State, 1949, the Bar of the District of Columbia, and the Bar of the U.S. Supreme Court, 1957; Webster & Sheffield (law firm), New York City, associate, 1949-53, partner, 1953-60; U.S. House of Representatives, representative from 17th District of New York, serving on House Judiciary Committee, 1958-65; mayor of New York City, 1965-73; Webster & Sheffield, partner, 1974—. Executive assistant to U.S. Attorney General, 1955-56; represented the United States in Vienna, Austria, during the Hungarian uprising, 1956; U.S. delegate to North Atlantic Treaty Organization (NATO) Parliamentarians' Conferences in Paris, France, and was elected chairman of the Conference's Political Committee, 1964. Substitute co-host for ABC-TV's "Good Morning, America"; commentator on Channel 13, New York. Trustee of Yale University, 1964-70. *Military service:* U.S. Navy, 1943-46; became lieutenant; received five battle stars.

MEMBER: American Bar Association, Council on Foreign Relations, New York Bar Association, Bar Association of the City of New York, Citizens' Committee for Children of New York City. *Awards, honors:* Received degrees from University of Oakland, 1964, Pace College, 1966, Manhattanville College, 1969; LL.D. from Williams College, 1968, and from Harvard University, 1969; citation of merit from the Yale Law School Association, 1969.

WRITINGS: Journey Into Politics (nonfiction), Dodd, 1966; *The City* (nonfiction), Norton, 1970; *The Edge* (novel), Norton, 1976. Contributor of articles on congressional and urban affairs to periodicals, including *Harper's, Atlantic Monthly, Saturday Review,* and *New York Times Magazine.*

SIDELIGHTS: In 1965, when Lindsay first ran for mayor of New York City at the age of forty-three, he was hailed as a fresh presence on the political scene. Formerly a Republican U.S. representative from Manhattan's "silk-stocking district," Lindsay was an attractive and affable candidate. Eliot Fremont-Smith, commenting on Lindsay, maintained that he "did successfully tap a longing for a new independent and energetic city administration that would show not only that New York could be governed, but that it could be governed sensibly, humanely, and with some flair."

As soon as Lindsay's first administration began, however, so did New York City's troubles. Transit workers struck five hours after he took office, shutting down the city, and during his first term in office the city's fire fighters, teachers, and garbage collectors followed suit. Lindsay quickly lost popularity as the public perceived him to be giving the city away to labor and to minorities. Despite his reputation as an inept mayor, Lindsay won a second term as a Liberal and an Independent.

Many commentators feel that Lindsay was largely responsible for the fiscal crisis that plagued the city during the term of his successor, Abe Beam. Harry Stein, writing in the *New York Times Magazine,* explained Lindsay's shortcomings as a fiscal manager: "During his second term in office the city's short-term debt grew from $747.3 million to $3.4 billion, and municipal labor contracts reached unprecedented levels, some charge, because Lindsay was pushed around by the unions." Lindsay has maintained that he left the city in sound financial shape. He is proudest of his accomplishments in the areas of management and administration. During his two terms, he reduced city bureaucracy by whittling down sixty agencies into ten super-agencies. He also oversaw a drop in crime and an increased amount of housing for low- and middle-income people.

Lindsay's greatest contribution as mayor was to bring together the city's racial factions, many observers believe. New York City was one of the few major cities to escape racial violence in 1968 after the assassination of Martin Luther King, Jr. Lindsay was out walking the city's streets comforting people within an hour after the murder, and many credit Lindsay with averting violence.

Lindsay wrote two books during his administration. The first, *Journey Into Politics,* deals almost exclusively with his congressional career. His next book, *The City,* concerns his second mayoral campaign and New York City generally. Richard C. Lee particularly admired the portion of the book entitled "The Deeper Struggle." He wrote that Lindsay "makes a very significant contribution to the study of urban America. He analyzes in detail two of the 'pervasive dilemmas' of urban life—poverty and welfare, and the problem of crime—and proposes new approaches and techniques which will undoubtedly serve as a blueprint for mayors across the country in the coming decade."

New York Times writer Christopher Lehmann-Haupt called the book the work of a "pragmatist." He commented: "It's tailored and articulate, without ever confounding one with originality of style. It has the Mayor's sparkling sense of humor, without ever collapsing into spontaneity. Remarkably, it lifts one out of despair's depths and makes one believe—at least until the next bomb goes off—that there's hope for the City, that New York is a rational situation amenable to reasoned solutions. And I'm sure the cabbies and bartenders will hate it for its twinkling eyes and good looks."

The critic from *Time* also reviewed *The City* favorably. "Perhaps unavoidably," he remarked, "most of the material in it is culled from speeches, position papers, office research. Yet to Lindsay's credit the mark of his personal syntax, the idiosyncratic cadences of his editorial style, glottal-stop through its pages. Touch this book and you may not touch a man, but you will certainly hear him talking."

Lindsay, a maverick in the Republican party, changed his political affiliation to the Democratic party in 1971 and the next year made an unsuccessful run for the Democratic presidential nomination. After retiring from city politics in 1973, Lindsay and his family took a year's sabbatical in Europe. When he returned, he again worked as a partner in his old law firm and began a part-time career as a television commentator for ABC-TV's "Good Morning, America."

In 1976 Lindsay's first novel, *The Edge,* was published. The book is set in the near future. During a period of national emergency, a congressman from California fights the imposition of martial law on the country. Lindsay told John F. Baker in a *Publishers Weekly* interview that he got the idea for the novel from his "growing sense of alarm at what was happening in the U.S.'' He recalled: ''I began to write a series of scenes, pushing the Watergate situation one step further, to see what would happen. That, I thought, was the worst thing that could happen, the use of police power for political purposes; but suppose it got even worse and the military were brought in? What happened to American freedoms?''

The Edge received a less than enthusiastic response from critics. L. W. Lindsay of the *Christian Science Monitor,* for example, declared: ''Lindsay's administration of New York was sometimes characterized as one of 'all style and no substance.' His novel *The Edge* is a book with little style or substance.... Lindsay brings to the writing of fiction many of the same qualities he brought to politics—in particular, wooden language and the ability to string together an endless supply of cliches.'' At least one reviewer had encouraging words for Lindsay's effort, finding *The Edge* a ''surprisingly good first novel.'' ''Though he never quite succeeds,'' wrote J. R. Coyne in *National Review,* ''there is an honest, introspective, and even at times intelligent streak apparent.''

Some have doubted the seriousness of a politician who appears on television, has acted in films and on stage, and who has even written a novel. But Lindsay justified his writing a novel to Baker: ''There's this love of pigeonholing people: but I believe in a bit of role reversal once in a while. If Norman Mailer can run for mayor, why can't I write a novel?''

BIOGRAPHICAL/CRITICAL SOURCES: Barbara Carter, *The Road to City Hall: How John V. Lindsay Became Mayor,* Prentice-Hall, 1967; *New York Times,* October 27, 1967, March 20, 1970, April 22, 1977; *Time,* March 23, 1970, January 5, 1976; Nat Hentoff, *The Political Life: The Education of John V. Lindsay,* Knopf, 1969; *New Republic,* March 28, 1970; *Chicago Daily News,* December 24, 1973; *Biography News,* Gale, Volume 1, 1974, Volume 2, 1975; *Denver Post,* May 4, 1975; *Publishers Weekly,* February 2, 1976; *Christian Science Monitor,* February 4, 1976; *National Review,* April 30, 1976; *New York Times Magazine,* January 8, 1978.

—*Sketch by Barbara A. Welch*

*   *   *

LIPEZ, Richard 1938-

PERSONAL: Born November 30, 1938, in Lock Haven, Pa.; son of Harris (a radio station manager) and Helen (Seltzer) Lipez; married Hedy Harris, 1968; children: Sydney, Zachary. *Education:* Lock Haven State College, B.S., 1961. *Home address:* Box 448, Lanesboro, Mass. 01237. *Agent:* Betty Marks, 51 East 42nd St., New York, N.Y. 10017.

CAREER: Peace Corps, volunteer in Addis Ababa, Ethiopia, 1962-64, program evaluator in Washington, D.C., 1964-67; Action for Opportunity, Pittsfield, Mass., executive director, 1968-70; free-lance writer, 1970—. *Member:* Mystery Writers of America.

WRITINGS: (With Peter Stein) *Grand Scam,* Dial Press, 1979. Contributor of articles and stories to magazines, including *Harper's, Atlantic, New Times, Redbook,* and *Newsweek.*

WORK IN PROGRESS: A novel.

*   *   *

LIPKIN, Mack, Jr. 1943-

PERSONAL: Born May 17, 1943, in New York, N.Y.; son of Mack and Carol H. (Fraenkel) Lipkin. *Education:* Harvard University, A.B. (magna cum laude), 1965, M.D., 1970.

Home: 29 Westmoreland Dr., Rochester, N.Y. 14620. *Office:* Department of Medicine, Strong Memorial Hospital, University of Rochester, Rochester, N.Y. 14620.

CAREER: University of North Carolina, Chapel Hill, 1970-72, intern and later resident in internal medicine; University of Rochester, Rochester, N.Y., resident and fellow in medicine and psychology at Strong Memorial Hospital, 1972-74, assistant professor of medicine and psychology, 1974—. Medical director of Threshold, 1973—. *Member:* North American Primary Care Research Group, American Association for the Advancement of Science, American Psychosomatic Society, Society for Research and Education in Primary Care Internal Medicine, Genesee Valley Health Association, Phi Beta Kappa.

WRITINGS: (Editor with Ian Cooke) *Cellular Neurophysiology,* Holt, 1972; (editor) *Genetic Responsibility: On Choosing Our Children's Genes,* Plenum, 1974; *Care of Patients: Concepts and Tactics,* Oxford University Press, 1974; *Straight Talk About Your Health Care,* Harper, 1977.

WORK IN PROGRESS: A book on psychosocial factors affecting health.

*   *   *

LIPKIND, William 1904-1974
(Will)

PERSONAL: Born December 17, 1904, in New York, N.Y.; died October 2, 1974; married Maria Cimino (a librarian), 1937. *Education:* College of the City of New York (now City College of the City University of New York), B.A., 1927; Columbia University, attended School of Law, 1928, Ph.D. (anthropology), 1937.

CAREER: Researcher on Caraja and Javahe Indians in Brazil, 1938-40; Columbia University, New York City, research associate in anthropology, 1940-42; Ohio State University, Columbus, assistant professor of anthropology, 1942-44; New York University, New York City, adjunct assistant professor, 1948-70; writer. *Military service:* Served in England with the Office of War Information during World War II. *Awards, honors:* Caldecott Medal, 1952, for *Finders Keepers.*

WRITINGS—Juvenile; all under name Will, except as noted; all written with and illustrated by Nicolas Mordvinoff as Nicolas, except as noted: *The Two Reds,* Harcourt, 1950; *Finders Keepers,* Harcourt, 1951; (under name William Lipkind; sole author) *Boy With a Harpoon,* illustrations by Nicolas Mordvinoff, Harcourt, 1952; *Even Steven,* Harcourt, 1952; *The Christmas Bunny,* Harcourt, 1953; *Circus Ruckus,* Harcourt, 1954; (under William Lipkind; sole author) *Boy of the Islands,* illustrations by Mordvinoff, Harcourt, 1954; (under William Lipkind; with Georges Schreiber) *Professor Bull's Umbrella,* Viking Press, 1954; *Chaga,* Harcourt, 1955; *Perry the Imp,* Harcourt, 1956; *Sleepyhead,* Harcourt, 1957; *The Magic Feather Duster,* Harcourt, 1958; *Four-Leaf Clover,* Harcourt, 1959; *The Little Tiny Rooster,* Harcourt, 1960; *Billy the Kid,* Harcourt, 1961; *Russet and the Two Reds,* Harcourt, 1964; (under William Lipkind; sole author) *Nubber Bear,* illustrations by Roger Duvoisin, Harcourt, 1966.

Other: *Winnebago Grammar* (nonfiction), Columbia University Press, 1945; *Beginning Charm for the New Year* (poetry), Weekend Press, 1951; *Days to Remember: An Almanac,* Obolensky, 1961.

SIDELIGHTS: William Lipkind was once described by his collaborator and illustrator, Nicolas Mordvinoff, as an anthropologist by profession, but a poet by inclination. The two met through Lipkind's wife and began a successful partnership that lasted for more than a decade.

The Two Reds, their first joint effort, received favorable reviews from some critics. The story of a cat and a boy and their adventures together, the book has been praised by a *Saturday Review of Literature* critic for the "zest and freshness in every word and line of it." L. S. Bechtel noted that the "art work is brilliant; the text equally so, with its concise statements of sheer action." *The Two Reds* was one of the first books to depict life in the slums. It was banned in Boston with the claim that it was subversive, despite its runner-up finish for the Caldecott Medal in 1951.

In 1952 Lipkind and Mordvinoff won the Caldecott Medal for *Finders Keepers.* A *New York Times* critic observed: "[The] story has a good deal of the quality of a traditional fable, yet it is told in crisp modern style. It isn't, to be sure, quite so funny nor so action-filled as their notable picture book, 'The Two Reds.' However, both story and pictures are done with great good humor."

Lipkind's sole efforts have also received kudos from children's book critics. Bechtel called *Boy With a Harpoon,* "a delightfully told factual story," while Elizabeth Hodges wrote of *Boy of the Islands,* "the excellence of the story lies not so much in its action as in its picture of an ancient civilization and in its portrayal of a boy's growing up."

Together, William Lipkind and Nicolas Mordvinoff produced more than ten children's books. H. A. Masten of *Saturday Review* summed up their efforts in this manner: "The artist and the author ... work so closely and harmoniously that they always achieve a unity that is usually only possible when an author is also the illustrator of his book."

BIOGRAPHICAL/CRITICAL SOURCES: New York Herald Tribune Book Review, September 10, 1950, November 16, 1952; *Saturday Review of Literature,* November 11, 1950; *New York Times,* August 26, 1951, February 27, 1955; *Saturday Review,* November 16, 1957; *Book Week,* October 30, 1966.

OBITUARIES: New York Times, October 3, 1974; *Library Journal,* November 15, 1974.*

*   *   *

LIPSITZ, Lou 1938-

PERSONAL: Born October 29, 1938, in Brooklyn, N.Y.; son of Jack (a salesman) and Estelle (a saleswoman; maiden name, Basch) Lipsitz; married Joan Scheff, 1959 (divorced, 1973); children: Anne, Jonathan. *Education:* University of Chicago, B.A., 1957; Yale University, M.A., 1959, Ph.D., 1964. *Home:* 416 Westwood Dr., Chapel Hill, N.C. *Office:* Department of Political Science, University of North Carolina, Chapel Hill, N.C. 27541.

CAREER: Celina Daily Standard, Celina, Ohio, reporter, 1957-58; University of Connecticut, Storrs, instructor in political science, 1961-64; University of North Carolina, Chapel Hill, assistant professor, 1964-67, associate professor, 1967-74, professor of political science, 1974—. *Awards, honors:* National Endowment for the Arts grant, 1967.

WRITINGS: Cold Water (poems), Wesleyan University Press, 1967; (editor) *American Politics: Behavior and Controversy,* Allyn & Bacon, 1967; "The Limits of Dissent" (two-act play), first produced in Greensboro, N.C., at Guilford County Courthouse, February, 1976; *Reflections on Samson* (poems), Kayak, 1977.

WORK IN PROGRESS: Urges, a novel; a book of poems; a textbook on American politics, publication by Random House expected in 1981 or 1982.

SIDELIGHTS: In his review of *Cold Water,* Barry Spacks declared: "*Buy, read, be grateful,* for this is the pure, renewing elixir, 200 proof, coming out of nowhere like children's wisdom. . . . The intersection of truth with surprise equals poetry, and winsome or raging, always as clear and bracing as the cold water of his title poem, Lipsitz continually gives us just this sort of outrageously unpredictable rightness. Social issues alternate with private celebrations and sorrows without any shift of sensibility, for the city gives and takes its breath through the windows of love and solitude. . . . [Lipsitz] offers nothing less than a vision of the good life and a decimation of its enemies, in a sequence of explosions of feeling controlled by an exuberant but disciplined intelligence."

Lou Lipsitz told *CA:* "At first I wrote as a reflex, an outpouring. Whatever I felt strongly about found itself being transformed into a poem. Teaching political science while writing has helped maintain my sanity. Approaching life from two perspectives is more tolerable than having to grind the stones of language all the time. My hope now is to conquer the realms of fiction—perhaps a novel and some short stories. There's a deliberateness about prose writing I have come to like, although some of the same sense of choice has come into my poetry as well. I still find it hard to write poetry that is all that obscure, but I keep trying. And my interest in social and political subjects has never departed."

BIOGRAPHICAL/CRITICAL SOURCES: Poetry, April, 1968.

*   *   *

LIPTON, Lenny 1940-

PERSONAL: Born May 18, 1940, in Brooklyn, N.Y.; son of Sam and Carrie Lipton; married Diane Zelman (a psychologist), September 13, 1965; children: Chloe. *Education:* Cornell University, A.B., 1962. *Home and office address:* 236 Water St., Point Richmond, Calif. 94801.

CAREER: Time, Inc., New York City, researcher, 1962-63; *Popular Photography,* New York City, editor, 1964-65; *Berkeley Barb,* Berkeley, Calif., film reviewer, 1965-69; San Francisco Art Institute, San Francisco, Calif., instructor in filmmaking, 1970-72; *Take One,* Montreal, Quebec, author of column, "The Filmmaker's Column," 1973-75; free-lance writer and independent filmmaker, 1975—. Instructor at Berkeley Film Institute; consultant to United Artists Theater Circuit. *Member:* Society of Motion Picture and Television Engineers, American Society of Composers, Authors, and Publishers, Canyon Cinema Cooperative. *Awards, honors:* Awards from San Francisco International Film Festival, 1966, for "We Shall March Again," and 1968, for "Show and Tell."

WRITINGS: Independent Filmmaking, Simon & Schuster, 1972; *The Super Eight Book,* Simon & Schuster, 1975; *Lipton on Filmmaking,* Simon & Schuster, 1979.

Screenplays—Shorts, all released by Canyon Cinema Cooperative: "Happy Birthday Lenny," 1965; "We Shall March Again," 1965; "Ineluctable Modality of the Visible," 1966; "The Dunes of Truro," 1966; "Memories of an Unborn Baby," 1966; "Powerman," 1966; "Below the Fruited Plain," 1966; "Cornucopia," 1968; "Show and Tell," 1968; "LP," 1969; "Doggie Diner and the Return of Doggie Diner," 1969; "Let a Thousand Parks Bloom," 1969;

"People," 1969; "The Last March," 1970; "My Life, My Times," 1970; "Far Out, Star Route," 1971; "Dogs of the Forest," 1972; "Life on Earth," 1972; "Children of the Golden West," 1975; "Hilltop Nursery," 1975; "Revelation of the Foundation," 1975; "Nadine's Song," 1975; "Adirondack Holiday," 1975; "The Story of a Man (Going Down in Flames)," 1975; "Father's Day," 1975.

Author of lyrics for song, "Puff, the Magic Dragon." Author of "Filmcraft," a column in *Super Eight Filmmaker,* 1974-78. Contributor to photography magazines, including *Popular Photography.*

WORK IN PROGRESS: A Study in Depth: The Foundations of Stereoscopic Cinema; The Whaling Station; Integral Instant Photography.

SIDELIGHTS: Lipton wrote: "I was trained to be a physicist, but by inclination I've been more interested in the humanities. Before I graduated from school I wrote the lyrics of 'Puff the Magic Dragon,' which somehow or other captured the fancy of the public.

"Much of my energy has gone into filmmaking since 1965. In order to support my filmmaking habit, I decided to fill a gap and write a how-to-do-it book. The result, *Independent Filmmaking,* is in its eighth printing. I've continued to write technical books and articles, and my finest effort, I think, is *A Study in Depth,* which is the result of three years of intensive research.

"Although I'm continuing to write about technical subjects, I've started to write fiction. I'm having a very good time working on a novel about a filmmaker who stumbles onto a murder. I seem to spend more and more of my time writing, and I really don't know whether I'm a filmmaker who's a writer, or a writer who's a filmmaker. It could be I'm both."

*   *   *

LISCHER, Richard   1943-

PERSONAL: Born November 12, 1943, in St. Louis, Mo.; son of Herbert F. (an accountant) and Edna (Alsbrook) Lischer; married Tracy Kenyon (an editorial assistant), June 4, 1966; children: Sarah Kenyon, Richard Adam. *Education:* Attended Concordia College, Milwaukee, Wis., 1961-63; Concordia Senior College, Fort Wayne Ind., B.A., 1965; Washington University, St. Louis, Mo., M.A., 1967; Concordia Seminary, St. Louis, M.Div., 1969; University of London, Ph.D., 1971. *Home:* 2212 Thunder Rd., Durham, N.C. 27712. *Office:* Divinity School, Duke University, 0026 New Divinity, Durham, N.C. 27706.

CAREER: Ordained Lutheran minister, 1972; pastor of Lutheran church in Virginia Beach, Va., 1974-79; Duke University, Durham, N.C., assistant professor of homiletics, 1979—. Member of board of Contact Crisis Counseling Service. *Member:* American Academy of Religion, Academy of Homiletics.

WRITINGS: Marx and Teilhard: Two Ways to the New Humanity, Orbis, 1979; *A Theology of Preaching,* Abingdon, 1981. Contributor to journals, including *Christian Century, Religion in Life, Currents in Theology and Mission,* and *Your Church.*

WORK IN PROGRESS: Speaking of Jesus.

*   *   *

LISSNER, Will   1908-

PERSONAL: Born November 11, 1908, in New York, N.Y.; son of Ferdinand (a restaurateur) and Christina (Sayer)

Lissner; married Ellen A. Batters, November 25, 1929 (divorced, 1971); married Dorothy Lois Burnham (a writer), March 30, 1972; children: Don Byrne, Claire, Ellen B. *Education:* Attended Rand School of Social Science, 1925-27, and New School for Social Research, 1927-30; Lloyd Theological Seminary, Brooklyn, N.Y., Ed.D., 1934. *Politics:* Democrat. *Religion:* Humanist. *Home:* 3610 38th Ave. S., Apt. 87, St. Petersburg, Fla. 33711. *Office:* 50 East 69th St., New York, N.Y. 10021.

CAREER: Affiliated with *Yorkville Spirit,* New York City, 1921-23, and *Harlem Press,* New York City, 1923; *New York Times,* New York City, news department clerk, 1923-26, police reporter, 1926-30, general assignment reporter, 1930, rewrite man, 1930-45, economics reporter, 1945-76; New School for Social Research, New York City, 1953-70, began as assistant professor, became associate professor and professor of business economics; *American Journal of Economics and Sociology,* New York City, founder and editor-in-chief, 1941—. Director of Robert Schalkenbach Foundation, 1940—; consultant to National Bureau of Economic Research, 1945-70. *Member:* American Economic Association, American Statistical Association (chairman of public relations committee), American Sociological Association, Population Association of America, Econometric Society, Society of Professional Journalists, New School for Social Research Alumni Association, Sigma Delta Xi.

WRITINGS: Public Education and Social Action, Land and Freedom Publishing Co., 1939; (with Ben Dalgin) *Advertising Production,* McGraw, 1946; (with A. M. Rosenthal, Arthur Gelb, and others) *The Pope's Journey to the U.S.: The Historic Record,* Bantam, 1963. Also author of *Arthur Hays Sulzberger and the Eastland Investigation,* New York Times Co.

Editor; all published by Robert Schalkenbach Foundation, except as noted: Neil MacNeil, *Without Fear or Favor* (journalism textbook), Harcourt, 1940; Franz Oppenheimer, *Wages and Trades Unions,* 1942; Oppenheimer, *Communism and the World Crisis,* 1942; Oppenheimer, *A Post-Mortem on Cambridge Economics,* 1943; Oppenheimer, *Japan and Western Europe,* 1944; (author of introduction) *Essays in Honor of Franz Oppenheimer, 1864-1943,* 1944; Donald A. MacLean, *The Christian Basis of a New World Order,* 1945; Anna George de Mille, *Citizen of the World,* 1945; Francis Neilson, *The Tragedy of Europe,* five volumes, C. C. Nelson Publishing Co., 1945-50; (contributor and author of foreword) *Essays in Honor of Francis Neilson, Litt. D., on the Occasion of His Eightieth Birthday,* 1947; Neilson, *From Ur to Nazareth,* 1959; Lewis Jay Siegal, *Forensic Medicine,* Grune, 1963.

Also author of numerous reports, monographs, and studies. Contributor to newspapers and periodicals, including *New York Times, Nation's Business, Commonweal, Christian Century, Catholic World, Reader's Digest, New Leader, Finance,* and *Antioch Review.* Founder and contributor to *American Journal of Economics and Sociology.* Member of editorial board of *American Statistician,* 1947-53, and *Social Research,* 1954-70.

SIDELIGHTS: Will Lissner can point to numerous notable assignments during his fifty-three-year career at the *New York Times.* He covered the closing of American banks in 1933, the New Deal programs launched by President Franklin Roosevelt, and the downfall of Czechoslovakia and Poland that led to World War II. As a specialist in Soviet affairs, he disclosed Joseph Stalin's plan to establish a closed system in Eastern Europe, and the Soviet Union's adoption of a state capitalist system. He also worked as a special correspondent in Latin America and the Caribbean, and reported on the establishment of world agencies to foster technical assistance and industrialization in Third World countries.

Lissner's extensive work as an economics and finance correspondent included a series of articles in 1948 and 1949 that investigated measurements of productivity and wage incomes. His suggestion that wage increases be commensurate with increases in productivity led to a national symposium on incomes policy, conducted by Thomas K. Hitch of the President's Council of Economic Advisers in 1949. The anti-inflationary formula Lissner developed from his research became the basis for incomes policy worldwide. He also founded the *American Journal of Economics and Sociology,* described by Lissner as "the first scientific journal in the world to promote interdisciplinary research in the social sciences."

Lissner told *CA:* "Early in my life I was impressed by the fact that social life was subject to two movements, one toward ethical and physical progress, the other toward entropy (deterioration). Impressed with humanism, I came to believe that it was only through human intervention that the former can be strengthened and the latter weakened. I have devoted my life to seeking out rational means for doing this."

*   *   *

LITTLE, Lessie Jones   1906-

PERSONAL: Born October 1, 1906, in Parmele, N.C.; daughter of William Robert (a laborer) and Pattie (Ridley) Jones; married Weston W. Little, October 17, 1926; children: Weston, Jr., Eloise Little Greenfield, Gerald, Vedie Little Jones, Vera Little Black. *Education:* Attended North Carolina State Normal School (now Elizabeth City State University), summers, 1924-26. *Religion:* Protestant. *Home and office:* 239 33rd St. N.E., Washington, D.C. 20019. *Agent:* Marilyn Marlow, Curtis Brown Ltd., 575 Madison Ave., New York, N.Y. 10022.

CAREER: Elementary school teacher in rural North Carolina, 1924-29; U.S. Army, Office of the Surgeon General, Washington, D.C., clerk-typist, 1956-64, coding clerk, 1964-70; writer, 1974—.

WRITINGS: (With daughter, Eloise Greenfield) *I Can Do It by Myself* (juvenile), Crowell, 1978; (with Greenfield) *Childtimes: A Three Generation Memoir,* Crowell, 1979.

WORK IN PROGRESS: An adult novel about a girl growing up during the Depression.

SIDELIGHTS: "I began writing at the age of sixty-seven," Lessie Little told *CA,* "when I was a great-grandmother. I was greatly encouraged by my daughter's publications (over a dozen books).

"I hope children enjoy reading my books and I would like for them to learn something important to their lives. I believe the picture book *I Can Do It by Myself* will give young children confidence in themselves; that it will let them know that they can get a job done if they try hard enough.

"*Childtimes: A Three Generation Memoir* is about three children from three generations: my mother, me, and my daughter. We hope this book gives children some historical facts and shows them the difference between things in use during the three generations: modes of transportation, schools, homes, clothing, and duties. We hope the book shows the worth of the black family; that although they had to face hard circumstances and hurdle many obstacles to

keep on living, they had love for each other which held them together.

"I am overjoyed that in my retirement years I have something to do that gives me so much satisfaction: I don't have any hard and fast rules about my working habits. I find the early morning, around five o'clock, a good, quiet time to concentrate, but I may work at midday or late evening or whenever I feel the urge."

*   *   *

LLOYD, Errol   1943-

PERSONAL: Born April 19, 1943, in Lucea, Jamaica; son of W. A. and Joyce Lucille Lloyd; married Joan-ann Maynard (an actress), July 9, 1977; children: Asana Leah. *Education:* Council of Legal Education, Barrister-at-law, 1974. *Home:* 4c Churchmead Rd., London N.W.10, England.

CAREER: Camden Arts Centre, London, England, teacher of painting, 1976-77; Keskidee Arts Centre, London, resident artist, 1978; writer and artist, 1978—. Art works exhibited at Commonwealth Institute Art Gallery, Liverpool Museum, Warehouse Gallery, and numerous colleges and universities. Advisory member of Camden Council arts and leisure committee. *Awards, honors:* Award from minority Rights Group, 1979, for contribution to ethnic minority arts.

WRITINGS—Children's books; all self-illustrated; all published by Bodley Head: *Nini at Carnival,* 1978; *Nini on Time,* 1981; *Nandy's Bedtime,* 1981.

Illustrator; all children's books; all published by Bodley Head: Petronella Brienburg, *My Brother Shawn,* 1973; Brienburg, *Dr. Shawn,* 1975; Brienburg, *Shawn's Red Bike,* 1976.

WORK IN PROGRESS: Illustrating *Anancy's Day of Cricket* by F. Charles.

SIDELIGHTS: Lloyd wrote: "My introduction to children's book illustrating started more by chance than by design. The editor of the children's department of Bodley Head publications was looking around for an illustrator for a story written by Petronella Brienburg of Surinam, which was aimed at the growing population of children in Britain born of West Indian parentage. She came across some prints in a bookshop that were reproductions of painting I had done, some of which had children as the subject matter. I was approached as a possible illustrator for the story. The result was the successful 'Shawn' series, the first of which, *My Brother Shawn,* was highly commended for the Kate Greenaway Medal for illustrators.

"Since the completion of that series I have started to illustrate my own stories as it affords greater flexibility and allows me to select subject matter that complements the kind of pictures I want to create in the first place.

"Because my involvement in book illustrating is to some extent a chance extension of my initial interest in painting, quite naturally I try to incorporate in my illustrations some of the lessons I learned in the fine arts field. Apart from the need to tell a story in pictures, which is the first requisite of the illustrator, I have tried as far as possible to inject 'painterly' qualities in my illustrations so due regard is paid to the structure and balance of the composition, the selection and use of color as well as the finished texture of the work. More recently I have been exploring the use of perspective as a means of creating space so that there is no undue competition between text and image when they have to share the same spread. If then at the end of the day I can create pictures which not only tell a story but which have some intrinsic artistic integrity and can have some independent existence in their own right, then I am more than satisfied.

"The existence of an obvious sociological and educational need for the kinds of picture books I create has forced me to re-evaluate my role as an artist and has drawn me further into the field of book illustrating as a means of making a concrete contribution to the society in which, like many other West Indians, I have made my home.

"One of the rare advantages of belonging to a fairly new immigrant community from the point of view of the storyteller and illustrator is that there is no comfortable resting place or refuge to be found in the nostalgia of the past. It is the contemporary scene which holds relevance for the new generation of children belonging to ethnic minorities, and stories in which they feature must to some extent reflect their present reality because there is no significant 'past' as far as the British experience is concerned. It is not surprising then that authors and illustrators in a similar position as myself tend to create work which has a certain modernity about it.

"My book, *Nini on Time,* explores contemporary London with what I hope are open eyes. Apart from a fairly metropolitan population, the book mentions double-decker buses, quaint corner shops, modern office buildings, traffic signs, street markets, and so on. Thus in creating books primarily for this generation of new Britons I hope to bring a fresh perspective to the wealth of books for children, from a cultural viewpoint as yet unexplored. In doing so it is my wish that, if successful, the books created will have meaning and relevance to all children who, after all, are far less aware of differences, and attach less significance thereto, than we adults do."

BIOGRAPHICAL/CRITICAL SOURCES: Children's Bulletin, summer, 1979; *Dragon's Teeth,* spring, 1980.

*   *   *

LLOYD, Norman 1909-1980

OBITUARY NOTICE—See index for *CA* sketch: Born November 8, 1909, in Pottsville, Pa.; died of leukemia, July 31, 1980, in Greenwich, Conn. Musician, educator, and author. Lloyd began his career in music as a pianist for silent films and then taught at the Juilliard School of Music and the Oberlin College Conservatory of Music. While at Juilliard he devised a new method for teaching music theory to students. Instead of using textbooks, Lloyd relied primarily on discussions with composers and other people active in the field of music. His works include *Fireside Book of Folksongs, Fundamentals of Sight Singing,* and *Keyboard Improvisation.* Obituaries and other sources: *New York Times,* August 1, 1980.

*   *   *

LOCHHEAD, Marion Cleland 1902-

PERSONAL: Born April 19, 1902, in Wishaw, Lanarkshire, Scotland; daughter of Alexander and Helen (Watt) Lochhead. *Education:* University of Glasgow, M.A. (with honors), 1923. *Religion:* Episcopalian. *Home:* 3 Hope Park Cres., Edinburgh EH8 9NA, Scotland.

CAREER: Writer, beginning in the 1920's; free-lance journalist. *Member:* International P.E.N., Royal Society of Literature (fellow), Ladies Caledonian Club, University Women's Club. *Awards, honors:* Member of Order of the British Empire, 1963.

WRITINGS: The Scots Household in the Eighteenth Cen-

tury: *A Century of Scottish Domestic and Social Life,* Moray Press, 1948; *A Lamp Was Lit: The Girls' Guildry Through Fifty Years,* Moray Press, 1949; *John Gibson Lockhart,* Murray, 1954; *Their First Ten Years: Victorian Childhood,* Murray, 1956; (with Henrietta Leith-Hay) *Trustie to the End: The Story of the Leith Hall Family,* Oliver & Boyd, 1957.

Elizabeth Rigby, Lady Eastlake, Murray, 1961; *Victorian Household,* Murray, 1964; *The Episcopal Church in Nineteenth-Century Scotland,* Murray, 1966; *Portrait of the Scott Country,* Hale, 1968, 2nd edition, 1973; *The Renaissance of Wonder in Children's Literature,* Carongate Publishing, 1977, Good News, 1980; (editor) *Scottish Tales of Magic and Mystery,* Johnston & Bacon, 1978; *The Other Country: Legends and Fairy Tales of Scotland,* Hamish Hamilton, 1978; (editor) *Scottish Love Stories,* Johnston & Bacon, 1979. Contributor of articles, poems, and reviews to journals.

WORK IN PROGRESS: Continuing research on nineteenth-century children's books, autobiographies, and reminiscences of childhood, and on fairy tales.

SIDELIGHTS: Marion Lochhead wrote: "I began as a poet, with an increasing interest in biography and social and domestic history. I no longer travel, but have greatly enjoyed visits to France and Italy." *Avocational interests:* Books, music.

*   *   *

LODEN, Barbara (Ann) 1937-1980

OBITUARY NOTICE: Born July 8, 1937, in Marion, N.C.; died of cancer in 1980 in New York, N.Y. Actress and director, best known for her Tony Award-winning portrayal of Maggie in Arthur Miller's "After the Fall," 1964. In addition to her Broadway performances and her work with the Lincoln Center Repertory Theatre, Loden appeared in the films "Wild River," 1960, and "Splendor in the Grass," 1961. She also wrote "Wanda," a 1970 recipient of the International Critics Prize at the Venice Film Festival. Loden married director Elia Kazan in 1967. Obituaries and other sources: *Celebrity Register,* 3rd edition, Simon & Schuster, 1973; *Who's Who of American Women,* 8th edition, Marquis, 1973; *The Oxford Companion to Film,* Oxford University Press, 1976; *International Motion Picture Almanac,* Quigley, 1975; *Time,* September 22, 1980.

*   *   *

LOEWALD, Hans W. 1906-

PERSONAL: Born January 19, 1906, in Colmar, France; son of Arnold and Meta Loewald; married wife, Nadja, 1935 (marriage ended, 1951); married Elizabeth Longshore (a psychiatrist), 1954; children: Richard Francis, Katherine, Caroline. *Education:* Attended University of Marburg, University of Freiburg, University of Tuebingen, and University of Berlin; University of Rome, M.D., 1935. *Home:* 2 Bayberry Rd., Hamden, Conn. 06517. *Office:* 65 Trumbull St., New Haven, Conn. 06510.

CAREER: Private practice of psychoanalysis, 1943—. Clinical professor at Yale University, 1971-74. Training analyst at Western New England Institute for Psychoanalysis, 1955—, president, 1961-63; attending psychiatrist at Yale-New Haven Medical Center. *Member:* International Psychoanalytic Association, American Psychoanalytic Association, American Psychiatric Association, Western New England Psychoanalytic Society.

WRITINGS: Psychoanalysis and the History of the Individual, Yale University Press, 1978; *Papers on Psychoanalysis,* Yale University Press, 1980.

WORK IN PROGRESS: Research on psychoanalytic theory and psychoanalytic process.

*   *   *

LORD AUCH
See BATAILLE, Georges

*   *   *

LORING, J. M.
See WARNER-CROZETTI, R(uth G.)

*   *   *

LORNQUEST, Olaf
See RIPS, Ervine M(ilton)

*   *   *

LOSE, M(argaret) Phyllis 1925-

PERSONAL: Born November 15, 1925, in Philadelphia, Pa.; daughter of Lloyd Levi (in business) and Margaret (Adams) Lose. *Education:* Immaculata College, B.S., 1951; University of Pennsylvania, V.M.D., 1957. *Politics:* Republican. *Religion:* Episcopalian. *Home and office:* Equine Hospital, Berwyn, Pa. 19312. *Agent:* Harold Matson Co., Inc., 22 East 40th St., New York, N.Y. 10016.

CAREER: Owner and trainer of thoroughbred horses in Maryland, New York, and Delaware, 1940-57; veterinary assistant, 1943-45; private veterinary practice, 1957—; Equine Hospital, Berwyn, Pa., founder and owner, 1973—. Official veterinarian for Devon Horse Show, 1960-74; civil service examiner and official veterinarian for mounted police in Philadelphia, Pa., 1962-74; owner and rider of champion open jumping horses. Member of Valley Forge Women's Republic Committee, 1948-74; member of faculty of Harcum College Student Practicum, 1973-74. *Member:* World Veterinary Association, American Veterinary Medical Association, American Association of Equine Practitioners, American Horse Show Association, U.S. Animal Health Association, Pennsylvania Veterinary Medical Association, Horse Breeders Association, University of Pennsylvania Alumnae Club. *Awards, honors:* State and national riding awards, including national high score award for open jumpers, 1954.

WRITINGS: Blessed Are the Broodmares, Macmillan, 1978; (with Daniel Mannix) *No Job for a Lady,* Macmillan, 1979. Contributor to scientific journals.

WORK IN PROGRESS: Equine Pediatrics.

*   *   *

LOVELACE, Richard Franz 1930-

PERSONAL: Born December 3, 1930, in Los Angeles, Calif.; son of Hunter Price (a writer) and Margaret (Franz) Lovelace; married Betty Lee Agar, July 19, 1958; children: David, Margaret Lee, Jonathan. *Education:* Yale University, B.A., 1953; Westminster Theological Seminary, B.D., 1958; Princeton Theological Seminary, Ph.D., 1968. *Politics:* Independent. *Home:* 180 Gardner St., Hamilton, Mass. 01936. *Office:* Gordon-Conwell Theological Seminary, South Hamilton, Mass. 01982.

CAREER: Associate pastor of Presbyterian church in Scotch Plains, N.J., 1959-68; Gordon-Conwell Theological Semi-

nary, South Hamilton, Mass., associate professor, 1968-74, professor of church history, 1974—. *Member:* American Society of Church History.

WRITINGS: Homosexuality and the Church, Revell, 1978; *The American Pietism of Cotton Mather: Origins of American Evangelicalism,* Eerdmans, 1979; *Dynamics of Spiritual Life: An Evangelical Theory of Renewal,* Inter-Varsity Press, 1979. Contributor to theology journals and religious magazines, including *Christian Century, Christianity Today,* and *Theology Today.*

WORK IN PROGRESS: Personal Renewal: An Outline of Spiritual Dynamics; The Revitalization of the Church.

SIDELIGHTS: Lovelace commented to *CA:* "I am a specialist in spiritual theology—the historical theology of the Christian experience, especially the history of renewal movements in the Church. I am active in Presbyterian renewal movements in both the North and the South, and act as consultant and theological adviser for renewal movements in other mainline denominations."

*   *   *

LOWRY, Beverly (Fey) 1938-

PERSONAL: Born August 10, 1938, in Memphis, Tenn.; daughter of David Leonard and Dora (Smith) Fey; married Glenn Lowry, June 3, 1960; children: Colin, Peter. *Education:* Attended University of Mississippi, 1956-58; Memphis State University, B.A., 1960. *Home:* 6445 Rutgers, Houston, Tex. 77005. *Agent:* Maxine Groffsky, 2 Fifth Ave., New York, N.Y. 10011. *Office:* Department of English, University of Houston, Houston, Tex. 77004.

CAREER: University of Houston, Houston, Tex., associate professor of fiction writing, 1976—. Also worked as actress. Member of humanities board of Cultural Arts Council of Houston and board of directors of Houston Festival. *Member:* International P.E.N., Authors Guild, Poets and Writers, Texas Institute of Letters (member of executive board). *Awards, honors:* National Endowment for the Arts fellow, 1979-80.

WRITINGS: Come Back, Lolly Ray (novel), Doubleday, 1977; *Emma Blue* (novel), Doubleday, 1978; *Daddy's Girl* (novel), Viking, 1981. Contributor of stories, articles, and reviews to magazines, including *Falcon, Viva, Playgirl, Redbook,* and *Forum,* and newspapers.

SIDELIGHTS: Beverly Lowry commented: "A lot of my essays are on physical pursuits—swimming, dancing, playing racquet sports, and performing. I do these things myself and they interest me. My major in college was speech and drama, heavy on the latter. I am interested in Colette, but don't know much French."

AVOCATIONAL INTERESTS: Reading, dancing.

*   *   *

LUCAS, Alec 1913-

PERSONAL: Born June 20, 1913, in Toronto, Ontario, Canada; son of Bertie George and Emma (Crick) Lucas; married Angeline Sperdakos, May 1, 1965; children: George Frederick, Suzanne Arbon. *Education:* Attended Peterborough Normal School, 1935-36; Queen's University, Kingston, Ontario, B.A. (with honors), 1943, M.A., 1945; Harvard University, A.M., 1947, Ph.D., 1951. *Office:* Department of English, McGill University, 853 Sherbrooke St. W., Montreal, Quebec, Canada H3A 2T6.

CAREER: Elementary school teacher in Hamilton Township, Northumberland County, Ontario, 1936-42; high school teacher of English and history in South Porcupine, Ontario, 1942-43; public relations officer for Ontario Department of Planning and Development, 1946; Harvard University, Cambridge, Mass., teaching fellow, 1947-50; University of New Brunswick, Fredericton, associate professor of English, 1950-57; McGill University, Montreal, Quebec, assistant professor, 1957-58, associate professor, 1958-64, professor of English, 1964—. Broadcaster. *Member:* Association of Canadian University Teachers of English.

WRITINGS: Hugh MacLennan, McClelland & Stewart, 1970; *Peter McArthur,* Twayne, 1975; *Farley Mowat,* McClelland & Stewart, 1976; *The Otonabee School,* Mansfield Book Mart, 1977.

Editor: (And author of introduction) *The Last Barrier and Other Stories,* McClelland & Stewart, 1958; *The James Halliday Letters,* Queen's Quarterly, 1966; (and author of introduction) *The Best of Peter McArthur,* Clarke, Irwin, 1967; *Great Canadian Short Stories: An Anthology,* Dell, 1971.

Contributor: Foster Russell, editor, *This Is My Concern,* Northumberland, 1962; Paul Wyczynski, Bernard Julien, and Jean Menard, editors, *Archives des lettres canadiennes,* Volume II, Centre de recherches de litterature canadienne-francaise de l'Universite d'Ottawa, 1962; (author of introduction) Hugh MacLennan, *Each Man's Son,* McClelland & Stewart, 1962; Carl Klinck, editor, *Literary History of Canada,* University of Toronto Press, 1965; (author of introduction) Ernest Thompson Seton, *Wild Animals I Have Known,* McClelland & Stewart, 1977.

Contributor to *Encyclopaedia Canadiana* and *Collier's Encyclopedia.* Contributor of articles and reviews to scholarly journals, literary magazines, and newspapers, including *Dalhousie Review, Atlantic Advocate, Curlew,* and *Canadian Children's Literature.* Editor of *Bulletin of the Humanities Association of Canada,* 1958-61; member of editorial board of *English Studies in Canada,* 1976—, and *Journal of Canadian Fiction,* 1977—.

WORK IN PROGRESS: A book on Roderick Haig-Brown, publication by McClelland & Stewart expected in 1982; research on the Canadian short story.

SIDELIGHTS: Lucas wrote: "I grew up in the country and have always been interested in nature. Next to war (and if man is so stupid as to start a war of world extent, he deserves what he gets) I think conservation of wildlife is most important. Yet we go on *hunting* for *pleasure.* My interest in nature has resulted in my buying an area of some eight hundred acres of woods and lakes for the birds and animals and trees.

"At one time I taught history in the university, while working for the Ontario Department of Planning and Development. My interest in history has resulted in my buying and renovating two log houses, in which I have my library of eighteen thousand books.

"As long as I can remember, books have been my central interest, but when I had to move my library I thought of Thoreau and the men who go through life pushing seventy-foot barns in front of them.

"I always wanted to be a teacher, and have been one since 1935. It was Thomas Wolfe, 'The Elder,' who gave me the urge to go to graduate school. When I was at Harvard, the students knew that, as a Canadian, I played hockey, drank beer, and spoke French. I did play hockey as a young man, and I do drink beer, but I cannot speak French with the same facility."

LUCAS, Robert 1904-

PERSONAL: Birth-given name, Robert Ehrenzweig; name legally changed; born May 8, 1904, in Vienna, Austria; came to England, 1934; son of Sigmund (a businessman) and Emma (Robinsohn) Ehrenzweig; married Ida Klamka (an artist), July 15, 1935; children: John Martin, Charles David. *Education:* Attended Vienna Technical College, 1922-23; University of Vienna, Ph.D., 1927. *Religion:* Jewish. *Home:* 14 Gardner Mansions, Church Row, Hampstead, London N.W.3, England. *Agent:* Laurence Pollinger Ltd., 18 Maddox St., London W.1, England.

CAREER: Free-lance writer. Deutsche Racine Gesellschaft, Berlin, Germany, industrial chemist and publicity manager, 1929; Rudolf Bauer & Co., Vienna, Austria, industrial chemist and publicity manager, 1929-30; Vorwaerts (publishing firm), Vienna, editor, 1930-34; *Neue Freie Presse,* Vienna, correspondent in London, England, 1934-38; British Broadcasting Corp., London, translator, 1938-40, chief scriptwriter, 1940-67. *Member:* P.E.N., London Foreign Press Association. *Awards, honors:* Declared Member of the British Empire by order of Queen Elizabeth II of England, 1966.

WRITINGS: Teure Amalia, vielgeliebtes Weib! Briefe des Gefreiten Adolf Hirnschal (radio scripts; title means "Dear Amalia, Much Beloved Wife: The Letters of Lance-Corporal Adolf Hirnschal"), Europa Verlag, 1946; *Frieda von Richthofen* (biography), Kindler Verlag, 1972, translation by Geoffrey Skelton published as *Frieda Lawrence: The Story of Frieda von Richthofen and D. H. Lawrence,* Viking, 1973. Also editor, with John Hirsch, of *Ein Volk klagt an* (title means "A Nation Accuses"), 1932.

Plays: "Das Jahr Achtundvierzig" (two-act; title means "The Year 1848"), first produced in Vienna at Grosser Konzerthaussaal, 1928; "The Great Pageant" (mass play), first produced in Vienna at the Sports Stadium, 1931; (with Ernst Fischer) "Die neue Buechse der Pandora" (three-act; title means "The New Pandora's Box"), first produced in Vienna at Grosser Konzerthaussaal, 1931; "War and Peace" (three-act; adapted from the novel by Leo Tolstoi), first produced in the West End at Phoenix Theatre, 1943. Also author of three-act play, "The Mohocks Are Coming!" (three-act), 1977, as yet neither published nor produced.

Screenplays: "The Diary of Mr. Pim," Kiba, 1932.

Contributor of sketches and songs to stage show, "Politisches Kabarett," 1926-33. Author of more than two hundred radio plays for stations in England, Germany, Austria, and Switzerland. Publisher and editor of *Die politische Buehne,* 1932-33; regular contributor to *Glasgow Herald,* 1937-38, *Die Zeit,* 1959-74, and *Die Welt,* 1979—. Contributor to periodicals, including *Sie und Er* and *Literatur und Kritik.*

WORK IN PROGRESS: Radio features, book reviews, and other writings.

SIDELIGHTS: Lucas received ample critical praise for his staging of Leo Tolstoi's epic *War and Peace.* "All the mechanical resources of the stage are enrolled," declared a *London Times* reviewer, "and they are used with delicate, imaginative expertness." The reviewer added that Lucas's adaptation was "a victory over material as nearly as intractable to the stage as great imaginative writing can be." A critic for the *London Daily Express* called the play "the most ambitious stage production in London for a generation. . . . It has dignity and beauty. . . . It should be greeted as a magnificent venture."

Frieda Lawrence, Lucas's biography of writer D. H. Lawrence's wife, was also enthusiastically received by reviewers. A critic for *Times Literary Supplement* noted that "it is indeed as an introduction to Lawrence himself that Mr. Lucas's book is most valuable." The reviewer also observed that "while Mr. Lucas draws widely on old sources, he makes, and keeps in perspective, contributions of his own. His judgments of the works are sound." Anais Nin called the book "a fair and objective study of the relationship of Frieda to Lawrence and to his work." She added that it was "a valuable biography."

Lucas told *CA:* "When I finished my science (chemistry and physics) studies in Vienna, unemployment in Austria was considerable, not the least among young academics, and I was unable to find a job. I went to Berlin, where I was engaged by the Deutsche Racine Gesellschaft in the unusual double role of industrial chemist and publicity manager. I was soon transferred to Vienna with the task to establish a similar production plant there and, later on, also in Brno, Czechoslovakia.

"In 1930 I turned my back on science and became a full-time journalist and author. Already in my student days I had been politically active on a fairly low level. I was a Social-Democrat. I felt a passionate urge to devote whatever literary abilities I possessed to the service of social justice and progress. I have always been guided by the conviction that the welfare of the community must be the concern of each individual's conscience. While in Berlin I had begun to contribute articles and poems to Austrian and German papers; in Vienna I was the co-founder of the 'Politisches Kabarett,' a satirical cabaret which in its outlook was clearly social-democratic and aggressively opposed to the then right-wing government. The 'Politisches Kabarett' was remarkably successful; it staged hundreds of performances until it was suppressed in the days preceding the Fascist Putsch of February, 1934. One of its other leading spirits was Victor Gruen, who later became well known as an American architect and town planner. I wrote a considerable part of the programs; another author was Jura Soyfer who died in a Nazi concentration camp. Some other members of the team are now professors at American universities.

"In 1931 I wrote 'The Great Pageant' for the opening of the Vienna stadium, which may well have been the most ambitious mass play ever produced (at least outside Russia). The director was Professor Stefan Hock, Max Reinhardt's permanent production assistant; the number of acting participants exceeded four thousand, and its four performances were attended by 260,000 spectators.

"In April, 1934, I immigrated to England in protest against the establishment of a totalitarian regime by Chancellor Dollfuss (who soon afterwards was assassinated by the Nazis). After first having a tough time in England, I was appointed London correspondent of the *Neue Freie Presse* of Vienna, then the leading Central European daily, a position which I held until the *Anschluss*. During the Sudeten crisis of September, 1938, the British Broadcasting Corp. (BBC), asked me to assist them in the preparation of their first broadcast in German, an attempt to speak to the German people above the heads of the Nazi leaders. This was the beginning of the BBC German Service which, during the war, played an outstanding role in the psychological warfare against Hitler's Germany.

"For a short time I worked as a translator and later on—throughout the war and long afterwards—as the chief scriptwriter. Probably my greatest success was a weekly satirical series consisting of fictitious letters written by a Ger-

man soldier—Adolf Hirnschal—to his wife. The series ran practically throughout the war and, as it turned out, had an enormous audience. In the estimate of American market researchers it reached ten million listeners a week during the last year of the war. The Hirnschal letters were published in Zurich in 1946.

"Since the war and after my retirement from the BBC, I have been working free-lance for German, Swiss, and Austrian broadcasting stations. Although this had not been my intention, the writing for radio had become my principal, though certainly not my exclusive, literary occupation. The number of long radio features I have written must go into many hundreds."

BIOGRAPHICAL/CRITICAL SOURCES: Manchester Guardian, July 10, 1943; *London Daily Express,* August 7, 1943; *London Times,* August 7, 1943; *Glasgow Herald,* August 7, 1943; Ernest K. Bramsted, *Goebbels and National Socialist Propaganda,* Michigan State University Press, 1965; Asa Briggs, *The War of Words,* Oxford University Press, 1970; *London Telegraph,* June 3, 1973; *New Statesman,* June 15, 1973; *Los Angeles Times,* July 29, 1973; *Cosmopolitan,* August, 1973.

*   *   *

LUCKMANN, Thomas   1927-

PERSONAL: Born October 14, 1927, in Jesenica, Yugoslavia; son of Karl (a surveyor) and Verena (a teacher; maiden name, Vodusek) Luckmann; married Benita Petkevie (a political scientist), 1950; children: Maya, Mara, Metka. *Education:* Attended University of Vienna, 1945-48, and University of Innsbruck, 1948-50; New School for Social Research, M.A., 1953, Ph.D., 1956. *Home:* Kirchstrasse 31, CH 8274 Gottlieben, Switzerland. *Office:* Department of Psychology and Sociology, University of Constance, D7750 Constance, West Germany.

CAREER: Hobart College, Geneva, N.Y., 1956-60, began as instructor, became assistant professor; New School for Social Research, New York, N.Y., 1960-65, began as assistant professor, became associate professor; University of Frankfurt, Frankfurt, West Germany, professor of sociology, 1965-70; University of Constance, Constance, West Germany, professor of sociology, 1970—. Visiting professor at University of Freiburg, 1962-64, at Harvard University, 1970, and at Wollongong University, 1978. Frequent lecturer in United States and abroad. *Member:* International Sociological Association, Conference Internationale de Sociologie Religieuse, American Sociological Association, German Sociological Association, Sociolinguistic Research Council.

WRITINGS: Zum Problem der Religion in der modernen Gesellschaft (title means "The Problem of Religion in Modern Society"), Rombach, 1963, revised edition published in English as *The Invisible Religion: The Problem of Religion in Modern Society,* Macmillan, 1967; (with Peter Berger) *The Social Construction of Reality: A Treatise in the Sociology of Knowledge,* Doubleday, 1966; (editor with Walter M. Sprondel) *Berufssoziologie* (title means "Sociology of Occupations"), Kiepenheuer & Witsch, 1972; (editor with Guenter Dux) *Sachlichkeit: Festschrift fuer Helmut Plessner* (title means "Objectivity: Festschrift for Helmut Plessner"), Westdeutscher Verlag, 1973; (with Alfred Schuetz) *The Structures of the Life-World,* Northwestern University Press, 1973; *Sociology of Language,* Bobbs-Merrill, 1975; (editor) *Phenomenology and Sociology,* Penguin, 1978; *Lebenswelt und Gesellschaft,* Schoeningh, 1978, translation published as *Life-World and Society,* Heinemann, 1981.

Contributor: D. Goldschmidt, H. Greiner, and H. Schelsky, editors, *Soziologie der Kirchengemeinde* (title means "Parish Sociology"), Enke, 1960; F. Fuerstenberg, editor, *Religionssoziologie* (title means "Sociology of Religion"), Luchterhand, 1964; Paul Edwards, editor, *The Encyclopedia of Philosophy,* Macmillan, 1968; Rene Koenig, editor, *Handbuch der empirischen Sozialforschung* (title means "Handbook of Social Research"), Enke, 1969, 2nd edition, 1979; Roland Robertson, editor, *Sociology of Religion,* Penguin, 1969.

Peter Worsley, editor, *Modern Sociology: Introductory Readings,* Penguin, 1970; Maurice Natanson, editor, *Phenomenology and Social Reality: Essays in Memory of Alfred Schuetz,* Nijhoff, 1970; Rocco Caporale and Antonio Grumelli, editors, *The Culture of Unbelief,* University of California Press, 1971; Oskar Schatz, editor, *Hat die Religion Zukunft?* (title means "Does Religion Have a Future?"), Styria, 1971; Brigitte Berger, editor, *Societies in Change,* Basic Books, 1971; Lester E. Embree, editor, *Life-World and Consciousness: Essays for Aron Gurwitsch,* Northwestern University Press, 1972; Dirk Kaesler, editor, *Max Weber: Sein Werk und seine Wirkung* (title means "Max Weber: His Work and His Influence"), Nymphenburger Verlag, 1972; Hans-Georg Gadamer and Paul Vogler, editors, *Neue Anthropologie* (title means "New Anthropology"), Thieme und Deutscher Taschenbuch Verlag, 1972; Jakobus Woessner, editor, *Religion im Umbruch* (title means "Religion in Transition"), Enke, 1972; J. Faulkner, editor, *Religion's Influence in Contemporary Society,* Merrill, 1972; Bernhard Badura and Klaus Gloy, editors, *Soziologie der Kommunikation* (title means "Sociology of Communication"), Fromann, 1972; Schatz, editor, *Auf dem Weg zur hoerigen Gesellschaft?,* Styria, 1973; Natanson, editor, *Phenomenology and the Social Sciences,* Northwestern University Press, 1973; Wolfgang Bender and Johannes Deninger, editors, *Religionskritik I,* Bayerischer Schulbuch Verlag, 1973; Heinz Steiner, editor, *Symbolische Interaktion* (title means "Symbolic Interaction"), Klett, 1973.

Bruno W. Nikles and Johannes Weiss, editors, *Gesellschaft, Organismus, Totalitaet,* Hoffmann & Campe, 1975; Karl Otto Hondrich, editor, *Menschliche Beduerfnisse und soziale Steuerung,* Rowohlt, 1975; *Reden und reden lassen* (title means "To Talk and to Let Talk"), Anstalt Verlag, 1975; Johannes Schlemmer, editor, *Der Verlust der Intimitaet* (title means "The Loss of Intimacy"), Piper, 1976; Dennis H. Wrong and Harry L. Gracey, editors, *Readings in Introductory Sociology,* Macmillan, 1977; *Lexicon der germanistischen Linguistik* (title means "Lexicon of German Linguistics"), M. Niemeyer, 1978; Joerg Zimmermann, editor, *Sprache und Welterfahrung: Kritische Information* (title means "Language and the Experience of Reality"), W. Fink, 1978; Walter M. Sprondel and Richard Grathoff, editors, *Alfred Schuetz und die Idee des Alltags in den Sozialwissenschaften* (title means "Alfred Schuetz and the Idea of Everyday Life in the Social Sciences"), Enke, 1979; *Human Ethology: Claims and Limits of a New Discipline,* Cambridge University Press, 1980; G. Klingenstein, H. Lutz, and O. Stourzh, editors, *Wiener Beitraege zur Geschichte der Neuzeit* (title means "Vienna Papers in Modern History"), Verlag fuer Geschichte und Politik, 1980; (with Paul M. Zulehner) F. Boeckle and others, editors, *Christlicher Glaube in moderner Gesellschaft: Eine interdisziplinaere Enzyklopaedie* (title means "Christian Faith in Modern Society: An Interdisciplinary Encyclopedia"), Herder, in press; Michael Brenner, editor, *Social Method and Social Life,* Academic Press, in press; Ulrich Knoop, Wolf-gang Putschke, and Herbert Ernst Wiegand, editors, *Dialektologie: Ein Handbuch zur deutschen und allgemeinen Dialektforschung* (title means "Dialectology: A Handbook of German and General Dialect Studies"), Gruyter, in press.

Author of introduction: L. S. Wygotski, *Denken und Sprechen* (title means "Thought and Language"), S. Fischer, 1969; Alfred Schuetz, *Das Problem der Relevanz* (title means "The Problem of Relevance"), Suhrkamp, 1971; Helmut Gipper, *Gibt es ein sprachliches Relativitaetsprinzip?: Untersuchungen zur Sapir-Whorf-Hypothese* (title means "Is There a Linguistic Relativity Principle?: Studies on the Sapir-Whorf-Hypothesis"), S. Fischer, 1972; Anton C. Zijderveld, *Die abstrakte Gesellschaft* (title means "The Abstract Society"), S. Fischer, 1972; Howard S. Becker, *Aussenseiter* (title means "Outsiders"), S. Fischer, 1973; Bronislaw Malinowski, *Magie, Wissenschaft, und Religion* (title means "Magic, Science, and Religion"), S. Fischer, 1973; Ralph Linton, *Gesellschaft, Kultur, und Individuum* (title means "Society, Culture, and the Individual"), S. Fischer, 1974.

Contributor of numerous articles to newspapers, periodicals, and scholarly journals in the United States and abroad, including *American Sociological Review, Journal for the Scientific Study of Religion, Zeitschrift fuer Theologie,* and *European Journal of Sociology.*

WORK IN PROGRESS: Research in face-to-face communication (problems of notation, transcription, coding, analysis); studying the evolution and history of personal identity.

*   *   *

LUESCHER, Max 1923-

PERSONAL: Born September 9, 1923, in Basel, Switzerland; son of August Luescher. *Education:* Received M.A. and Ph.D. from University of Basel, 1944-45. *Home:* Kreuzbuchrain 14, Lucerne CH-6006, Switzerland.

CAREER: Psychoanalist and lecturer at Universities of Basel, Zurich, and Paris, 1949-57; professor in Amsterdam, Netherlands, 1957-60; lecturer in psychology in Linz, Austria, 1978—. Marketing and design consultant.

WRITINGS: Psychologie der Farben: Texband zum Luescher-Test, Test-Verlag, 1949, translation by Ian A. Scott published as *The Luescher Color Test,* Random House, 1969; *Die Farbe in der Persoenlichkeitsdiagnostik: Lehrbuch des Luescher-Testes, fuer Aerzte, Psychologen und Paedagogen,* Test-Verlag, 1953; *Signale der Persoenlichkeit: Rollen-Spiele und ihre Motive,* Deutshe Verlags-Anstalt, 1973; *Luca Patella e il test Luescher dei colori,* L'attico, 1974; *Der Vier-Farben-Mensch; oder, Der weg zum inneren Gleichgewicht,* Mosaik Verlag, 1977, translation by Joachim Neugroschel published as *The Four-Color Person,* Simon & Schuster, 1979.

SIDELIGHTS: Luescher told *CA:* "The basis of all publication is functional psychology."

*   *   *

LUGT, Herbert Vander
See VANDER LUGT, Herbert

*   *   *

LUKACS, Georg
See LUKACS, Gyorgy

LUKACS, George
See LUKACS, Gyorgy

*   *   *

LUKACS, Gyorgy   1885-1971

PERSONAL: Born April 13, 1885, in Budapest, Hungary; died June 4, 1971, in Budapest, Hungary; son of a titled banker. *Education:* University of Budapest, Ph.D., 1906; attended University of Heidelberg and University of Berlin.

CAREER: Philosopher, writer, and critic. Minister of education during Bela Kun communist regime in Hungary, 1919; Marx-Engels Institute, Moscow, U.S.S.R., staff member, 1930; affiliated with Philosophical Institute of Academy of Sciences in U.S.S.R., c. 1933-45; University of Budapest, Budapest, Hungary, professor of philosophy, 1945-56; minister of culture during Imre Nagy regime in Hungary, 1956. *Awards, honors:* Goethe Prize, 1970, for *Goethe and His Age.*

WRITINGS—In English: *Die Seele und die Formen* (essays), E. Fleischel, 1911, translation by Anna Bostock published as *Soul and Form*, M.I.T. Press, 1974; *Die Theorie des Romans: Ein geschichtsphilosophischer Versuch ueber die Formen der grossen Epik*, P. Cassirer, 1920, reprinted, Luchterhand, 1971, translation by Bostock published as *The Theory of the Novel: A Historico-Philosophical Essay on the Forms of Great Epic Literature*, M.I.T. Press, 1971; *Geschichte und Klassenbewusstsein: Studien ueber Marxistische Dialektik*, Malik Verlag, 1923, reprinted, Luchterhand, 1968, translation by Rodney Livingstone published as *History and Class Consciousness: Studies in Marxist Dialectics*, M.I.T. Press, 1971.

Goethe und seine Zeit, A. Francke, 1947, translation by Robert Anchor published as *Goethe and His Age*, Merlin Press, 1968, Grosset & Dunlap, 1969; *Essays ueber Realismus*, Aufbau Verlag, 1948, reprinted, Luchterhand, 1971, translation by Edith Bone published as *Studies in European Realism: A Sociological Survey of the Writings of Balzac, Stendhal, Zola, Tolstoy, Gorki, and Others*, Hillway, 1950, Grosset & Dunlap, 1964; *Der junge Hegel: Ueber die Beziehungen von Dialektik und Oekonomie*, Europa Verlag, 1948, also published as *Der junge Hegel und die Probleme der kapitalistischen Gesellschaft*, Aufbau Verlag, 1954, translation by Livingstone published as *The Young Hegel: Studies in the Relations Between Dialectics and Economics*, Merlin Press, 1975, M.I.T. Press, 1976; *Thomas Mann*, Aufbau Verlag, 1949, translation by Stanley Mitchell published as *Essays on Thomas Mann*, Merlin Press, 1964, Grosset & Dunlap, 1965.

Der historische Roman, Aufbau Verlag, 1955, translation by Hannah Mitchell and Stanley Mitchell published as *The Historical Novel*, Merlin Press, 1962, Humanities Press, 1965; *Wider den missverstandenen Realismus* (2nd edition of original *Die Gegenwartsbedeutung des kritischen Realismus*), Claassen, 1958, translation by John Mander and Necke Mander published as *The Meaning of Contemporary Realism*, Merlin Press, 1963, published as *Realism in Our Time: Literature and the Class Struggle*, Harper, 1964.

Lenin: Studie ueber den Zusammenhang seiner Gedanken, Luchterhand, 1967, translation by Nicholas Jacobs published as *Lenin: A Study on the Unity of His Thought*, N.L.B. (England), 1970, M.I.T. Press, 1971; (contributor) *Gesprache mit Georg Lukacs, Hans Heinz Holz, Leo Kotler, Wolfgang Abendroth*, Rowolt, 1967, translation by David Fernbach published as *Conversations With Lukacs*, Merlin Press, 1974, M.I.T. Press, 1975.

Solschenizyn, Luchterhand, 1970, translation by William David Graf published as *Solzhenitsyn*, Merlin Press, 1970, M.I.T. Press, 1971; *Writer and Critic, and Other Essays*, translation from the original edited by Arthur D. Kahn, Grosset & Dunlap, 1971; *Political Writings, 1919-1929: The Question of Parliamentarianism and Other Essays*, translated by Michael McColgan from the original *Taktika es Ethika*, N.L.B., 1972, published as *Tactics and Ethics: Political Essays, 1919-1929*, Harper, 1975; *Marxism and Human Liberation: Essays on History, Culture, and Revolution*, translation from the original edited by E. San Juan, Jr., Dell, 1973; *Revolution und Gegenrevolution*, Luchterhand, 1976, translation by Victor Zitta published as *Revolution and Revelation*, 1976.

In German; all published by Aufbau Verlag, unless otherwise noted: *Alte und neue Kultur* (title means "Old and New Culture"), Jungarbeiter Verlag, 1921, reprinted, 1970; *Deutsche Literatur im Zeitalter des Imperialismus: Ein Uebersicht ihrer Hauptstroemungen*, 1945; *Gottfried Keller*, 1946; *Fortschritt und Reaktion in der deutschen Literatur*, 1947; *Karl Marx und Friedrich Engels als Literaturhistoriker*, 1947; *Schicksalswende: Beitrage zu einer neuen deutschen Ideologie*, 1948, 2nd edition, 1956; *Der russische Realismus in der Weltliteratur*, 1949, 3rd edition, 1952.

Existentialismus oder Marxismus?, 1951; *Deutsche Realisten des 19. Jahrhunderts*, 1951; *Skizze einer Geschichte der neuen deutschen Literatur* (title means "An Outline of the History of Modern German Literature"), 1953; *Beitrage zur Geschichte der Aesthetik*, 1954; *Die Zerstorung der Vernunft* (title means "The Destruction of Reason"), 1954; (author of introduction) Georg Wilhelm Friedrich Hegel, *Aesthetik*, 1955; (with Franz Mehring) *Friedrich Nietzsche*, 1957; *Tolstoi und die westliche Literatur*, J. Fladung, c. 1959.

Schriften zur Literatursoziologie, Luchterhand, 1961; *Aesthetik*, four volumes, Luchterhand, 1963; *Die Eigenart des Aesthetischen* (title means "The Specific Nature of the Aesthetic"), Luchterhand, 1963; *Deutsche Literatur in zwei Jahrhunderten*, Luchterhand, 1964; *Der junge Marx: Seine philosophische Entwicklung von 1840-1844*, Neske, 1965; *Von Nietzsche bis Hitler; oder, Der Irrationalismus in der deutschen Politik*, Fischer Bucherei, 1966; *Ueber die Besonderheit als Kategorie der Aesthetik*, Luchterhand, 1967; *Schriften zur Ideologie und Politik*, Luchterhand, 1967; *Die Grablegung des alten Deutschland: Essays zur deutschen Literatur des 19. Jahrhunderts*, Rowolt, 1967; *Faust und Faustus: Vom Drama der Menschengattung zur Tragoedie der modernen Kunst*, Rowolt, 1967; *Frueheschriften*, Luchterhand, 1968; *Werke*, fourteen volumes, Luchterhand, 1968-69; *Probleme der Aesthetik*, Luchterhand, 1969; *Russische Literatur, russische Revolution: Puschkin, Tolstoi, Dostojewskij, Fadejew, Makarenko, Scholochow, Solschenizyn*, Luchterhand, 1969.

(Author of afterword) Hegel, *Phaenomenologie des Geistes*, Ullstein, 1970; *Die ontologischen Grundlagen des menschlichen Denkens und Handelns*, [Vienna], 1970; *Marxismus und Stalinismus*, Rowohlt, 1970; *Zur Ontologie des gesellschaftlichen Seins* (title means "The Ontology of Social Existence"; also see below), Luchterhand, 1971; *Die ontologischen Grundprinzipien von Marx* (selection from *Zur Ontologie des gesellschaftlichen Seins*), Luchterhand, 1972; *Die Arbeit* (selection from *Zur Ontologie des gesellschaftlichen Seins*), Luchterhand, 1973; (contributor) Ruediger Bubner, Konrad Cramer, and Reiner Wiehl, editors, *Ist eine philosophische Aesthetik moeglich?*, Vandenhoeck & Ruprecht, 1973; (contributor) Johann Wolfgang von Goethe, *Die Leiden des jungen Werther*, Insel Verlag, 1973; *Fruehe*

Schriften zur Aesthetik, Luchterhand, Volume I: *Heidelberger Philosophie der Kunst, 1912-1914*, 1974, Volume II: *Heidelberger Aesthetik, 1916-1918*, 1975; (with others) *Individuum und Praxis Positionen der budapester Schule*, Suhrkamp, 1975; *Politische Aufsatze, 1918*, Luchterhand, 1975; *Kunst und objektive Warheit: Essays zur Literaturtheorie und Geschichte*, P. Reclam, 1977; (with Arnold Hauser) *Im Gespraech mit Georg Lukacs*, Beck, 1978.

In Hungarian: *A Modern Drama fejlodesenek tortenete: Kiadja a kisfaludy-tarsasag*, two volumes, Franklin Tarsulet, 1911; *Kristorii realizma*, [Hungary], 1939; *Irastudok felelossege*, Idegennyelvii irodalmi kiado, 1944; *Irodalom es demokracia*, Szikra, 1947; *A Polgari filozofia valsaga*, [Hungary], 1947; *A Realizmus problemai: Nemet eredetibol forditotta*, Atheneum (Budapest, Hungary), 1948; *Balzac, Stendhal, Zola*, Hungaria eloszo, 1949; *Nagy orosz realistak*, Szikra, 1949.

Az esz tronfosztasa: Az irracionalista filozofia kritikaja, Akademiai Kiado, 1956; *A Kulonosseg mint esztetika katagoria*, Akademiai Kiado, 1957; *Istoriski roman*, Kultura, 1958; *Prolegomena za marksisticku estetiku: Posebnost kao centralna kategorija estetike*, Nolit, 1960; *Az esztetikum sajatossaga*, Akademiai Kiado, 1965; *Lukacs Gyorgy valogatott muvei*, Gondolat, 1968; *Muveszet es tarsadalom: Valogatott esztetikai tanulmanyok*, Gondolat, 1968; *Vilagirodalom: Valogatott vilagirodalmi tanulmanyok*, two volumes, Gondolat, 1969; *Magyar irodalom—magyar kultura: Valogatott tanulmanyok*, Gondolat, 1970; *Utam Marxhoz: Valogatott filozofiai tanulmanyok*, Magveto Konyvkiado, 1971; *Adalekok az esztetika tortenetenez*, two volumes, Magveto Konyvkiado, 1972; *Ifjukori muvek, 1902-1918*, Magveto Konyvkiado, 1977.

SIDELIGHTS: In *Language and Silence*, George Steiner extrapolated two principal beliefs from Lukacs's works: "First, that literary criticism is not a luxury, that it is not what the subtlest of American critics has called 'a discourse for amateurs.' But that it is, on the contrary, a central and militant force toward shaping men's lives. Secondly, Lukacs affirms that the work of the critic is neither subjective nor uncertain. The truth of judgment can be verified." With such a basis for his writings, Lukacs has been credited with three major contributions to modern philosophical thought, defined by Alden Whitman in the *New York Times*: "A defense of humanism in Communist letters; elaboration of Marx's theory of the alienation of man by industrial society; and formulation of a system of esthetics that repudiated political control of Socialist artists while emphasizing what Mr. Lukacs termed the 'class nature' of beauty."

Although Lukacs is, as Alfred Kazin wrote in the introduction to Lukacs's *Studies in European Realism*, "an individual thinker who is fascinated by and thoroughly committed to Marxism as a philosophy, and who uses it for the intellectual pleasure and moral satisfaction it gives him," he was throughout his life in conflict with the Communist International. From the appearance of *History and Class Consciousness* in 1923, he was forced in and out of political life by charges of "revisionism." Because in his theories he considered the classics and "bourgeois" writers of the eighteenth and nineteenth centuries, he came under frequent attack and was often compelled to publicly recant his own views. Still, he remained an opponent of the party line in literature and disparaged, as Whitman observed, "writers who were Socialists first and writers second."

After his university studies and travels in Italy, Lukacs lived in Heidelberg for a time, where he associated with Max

Weber and his circle. Weber, Lukacs's former teacher, was a sociologist and historian in the tradition of Georg Wilhelm Friedrich Hegel, whose philosophical idealism, dialectical method, and concern with history were an early influence on both Lukacs and Marxism itself; Hegel's conception of the historical development of artistic form provided the basis of much of Lukacs's aesthetic.

In 1918 Lukacs joined the Communist party. With his international reputation as a literary critic already established with the appearance of *Soul and Form* in 1911, he was made Hungarian minister of culture and public education in the Communist regime of Bela Kun. Kun remained in power briefly, from March to August of 1919, and upon his overthrow, Lukacs went into hiding. Lukacs spent the next ten years in exile in Vienna, where he was granted asylum.

From Vienna, Lukacs carried on a struggle with Kun for control of the Hungarian underground movement. Official denunciation of Lukacs's writing settled the issue against him, but following statements of "self-criticism" he was granted refuge in the Soviet Union during Hitler's rise to power. When he returned to Budapest after World War II, ending a twenty-five-year period of exile, he joined the coalition government as a member of the National Assembly of Hungary. In 1949 the Communist party again took control, establishing the People's Republic of Hungary, which was overthrown in October, 1956, by an anti-Soviet revolt. As a leader of the insurrectionist Petofi circle and then minister of culture in Imre Nagy's regime, Lukacs was deported to Romania when Soviet troops returned the Communists to power. Allowed to return to Hungary in 1957, Lukacs retired from political activity and devoted his last years to teaching and writing.

Lukacs's early publications, which he renounced after joining the Communist party, strongly influenced existential thought. The neo-Kantian aesthetic of *Soul and Form* and *The Theory of the Novel* saw literature as an expression of man's inwardness. The former, for example, is concerned with the relationship between human life and absolute values. Lucien Goldmann pointed out in *TriQuarterly* that with *Soul and Form* Lukacs was "the first to pose in all its acuteness and force the problem of the relation between the *individual, authenticity,* and *death,* . . . affirming the absolute nonvalue of the social world." In *The Theory of the Novel,* on the other hand, Lukacs examined the epic genre as "the expression of complex and multiple relationships between the soul and the world."

Often considered his most important work, *History and Class Consciousness* is marked by a neo-Hegelian idealism, what George Lichtheim called a "belief in the possibility of objective insight into reality." To unify philosophical theory with political practice and to unite Marx's interpretation of history with Hegel's concept of totality, Lukacs here asserted, according to Lichtheim, "that the totality of history could be apprehended by adopting a particular 'class standpoint': that of the proletariat." Lukacs was moving away from his earlier, western humanist conception of literature toward his theory of the "great realism," from his portrayal of man as alienated and alone to his anticipation of a mankind freed from alienation by a consciousness of the historical process.

Although Lukacs eventually repudiated *History and Class Consciousness* along with his first two books, the work contains the seeds of his later orthodoxy, mainly in "its identification of 'true consciousness' with a particular doctrine and a particular class, and its faith in the party as the repository of the doctrine and the vanguard of the class," noted Steven Lukes in the *Washington Post*. Tibor Szamuely, moreover, saw *History and Class Consciousness* as "the best, the frankest, the most wide-ranging and powerful exposition of the philosophy of totalitarianism ever written."

Lukacs's subsequent critical work often ran counter to party position, however. His reading of literature took into account sociology, history, and politics, and he advocated realism as the highest mode of fiction while condemning formalism. But he distinguished realism both from psychological novels and from naturalism, which led him to praise Balzac, for example, and disparage Zola, in direct opposition to party line. Moreover, he valued the realism of such writers as Sir Walter Scott and Tolstoy as manifestations of the dialectical relationship between historical reality and literature. He was opposed, however, to "proletarian realism" and party control of the literary process. He contended, as Whitman explained, that in a Communist society, "noble art would emerge from the artist's interaction with his environment; but works of art could not be summoned forth in a predetermined pattern."

Although the occasion of Lukacs's death in 1971 was scarcely acknowledged in the eastern European Communist press, he was buried with customary party honors, having refrained from personal involvement in politics after 1957. It was only after his death that his works began to be widely available to English-speaking audiences. Despite the limited circulation of Lukacs's works, Lucien Goldman, as early as 1967, deemed Lukacs to be "one of the most influential figures in the intellectual life of the 20th century."

BIOGRAPHICAL/CRITICAL SOURCES—Books: George Steiner, *Language and Silence*, Faber, 1967; George Lichtheim, *George Lukacs*, Viking, 1970; G. H. R. Parkinson, editor, *Georg Lukacs: The Man, His Work, and His Ideas*, Random House, 1970; Ehrhard Bahr and Ruth Kunzer, *Georg Lukacs*, Ungar, 1972; Frederick Ungar, editor, *Handbook of Austrian Literature*, Ungar, 1973; *Georg Lukacs*, Boorberg, 1973.

Periodicals: *Encounter*, May, 1963, April, 1965; *New York Times Book Review*, May 10, 1964, July 18, 1971; *Saturday Review*, June 13, 1964, November 6, 1965, December 4, 1971; *TriQuarterly*, spring, 1967, spring, 1968; *New York Times*, June 11, 1968; *Contemporary Literature*, summer, 1968, winter, 1968; *Canadian Forum*, August, 1968; *Listener*, September 5, 1968; *Nation*, July 14, 1969, December 27, 1971; *Books and Bookmen*, September, 1969; *Times Literary Supplement*, September 25, 1969, November 6, 1970, June 11, 1971; *Commonweal*, November 27, 1970; *National Review*, June 1, 1971; *Washington Post*, July 24, 1971; *New Statesman*, December 17, 1971.

OBITUARIES: New York Times, June 5, 1971; *Time*, June 14, 1971; *Antiquarian Bookman*, July 19-26, 1971.*

—*Sketch by Andrea Geffner*

*   *   *

LUKAS, Mary

PERSONAL: Born in Pennsylvania; daughter of Alex J. (a doctor) and Margaret (a teacher; maiden name, McGuire) Lukas. *Education:* Received B.A. from College of New Rochelle; graduate study at Catholic University and Fordham University. *Politics:* Democrat. *Religion:* Catholic. *Home:* 18 East 27 St., New York, N.Y. 10021. *Agent:* Paul E. Reynolds Inc., 12 East 41st St., New York, N.Y. 10017

CAREER: Writer. Worked as entertainment editor for *Look*

in New York City, theatre critic for *Show* in New York City, and reporter and researcher for *Time* in New York City. Consultant to Catholic Film Review Board. *Member:* P.E.N., Authors Guild, Kappa Gamma Pi. *Awards, honors:* Prize for biography from *Religious Media Today*, 1977, for *Teilhard*.

WRITINGS: (With sister, Ellen Lukas) *Teilhard* (biography), Doubleday, 1977; (translator and author of introduction) *Letters From My Friend: Teilhard to Pierre Leroy, 1946-1955*, Paulest/Newman, 1980. Contributor to periodicals, including *Jubilee, Catholic World,* and *America*.

WORK IN PROGRESS: Two historical biographies; a monograph.

SIDELIGHTS: Lukas told *CA:* "I have a special interest in continuing Teilhard's work by applying his philosophy to the new cosmology with an emphasis on its relationship to high energy physics and microbiology." *Avocational interests:* Early American Georgian furniture, porcelain, seventeenth- and eighteenth-century Chinese art.

*   *   *

LUKODIANOV, Isai (Borisovich) 1913-

PERSONAL: Born June 8, 1913, in Baku, Azerbaijan; son of Boris (a bookkeeper) and Vera (a stenographer; maiden name, Rozengauz) Lukodianov; married wife Olga, 1953; children: Vladimir. *Education:* Central Industrial Institute of Leningrad, mechanical engineering degree, 1936. *Politics:* "I support Communism." *Religion:* Atheist. *Home:* 10 B. Sardarova St., Baku 1, Azerbaijan 370001. *Agent:* VAAP, Bol'shaia Bronnaia 6a, K-104, Moscow, Soviet Union 103104.

CAREER: Chief project engineer at Design Institute of Gipromorneft, 1947—. Works on development and installation facilities of off-shore oil fields. *Military service:* Soviet Union Air Force, 1941-45; received six awards. *Member:* Azerbaijan Writers Union (science fiction section). *Awards, honors:* Second national prize from International Science Fiction Competition, 1964, for short story, "Alatyr-Stone."

WRITINGS—All with Evgenii L'vovich Voiskunskii, unless otherwise noted; all science-fiction novels: *Ekipazh "Mekonga,"* [Russia], 1962, translation by Leonard Stoklitsky published as *The Crew of the Mekong: Being an Account of the Latest Fantastic Discoveries, Happenings of the Eighteenth Century, Mysteries of Matter, and Adventures on Land and at Sea*, Mir Publishers, 1974; *Ochen' delekii Tartess* (title means "The Very Distant Tartess"), Gvardia, 1968; *Plesk zvezdnykh morei* (title means "The Gentle Splash of Stellar Seas"), Detskaya litra, 1970; (with E. Woiskunsky) *Forbidden Planet*, Detgiz, 1980. Also author with Voiskunskii of *Na perekrestakh vremeni* (title means "At the Crossroads of Time"), 1964, *The Formula of the Impossible*, 1964, *A Story of the Ocean and King Cook*, 1969, *The Black Pillar*, 1969, and *Uz, Son of Sham*, 1975. Contributor of about eighty articles and stories to popular science journals and science fiction magazines.

WORK IN PROGRESS: A story based on the Indian War Expedition under Paul I in 1801.

SIDELIGHTS: Lukodianov commented: "I like my professional work as an engineer. Literature is my hobby, although I lack the free time for literary activities. I like research on engineering history." Lukodianov's books have been published in German, Romanian, Czech, Spanish, Arabic, Bulgarian, and Japanese. *Avocational interests:* "I spend my holidays on tourist trips abroad (for example to Finland and

Bulgaria), voyages along the great rivers of Russia and Siberia, traveling around Black Sea resorts, and sailing on the Caspian Sea.''

*   *   *

LUNDE, Donald T(heodore)   1937-

PERSONAL: Born March 2, 1937, in Milwaukee, Wis.; son of Alfred and Evelyn Lunde; married Marilynn Krick; children: Montgomery, Christopher, Glenn, Evan, Bret. *Education:* Stanford University, B.A. (with distinction), 1958, M.A., 1964, M.D., 1966. *Residence:* Stanford, Calif. *Office:* School of Law, Stanford University, Room 211, Stanford, Calif. 94305.

CAREER: Palo Alto/Stanford Hospital, Palo Alto, Calif., intern in internal medicine, 1966-67; Stanford University, Stanford, Calif., resident in psychiatry, 1967-69, instructor in psychiatry, 1969-70; Palo Alto Veterans Hospital, Palo Alto, chief resident in psychiatry, 1969-70, associate chief of training and research section, 1970-72, acting chief, 1971-72; Stanford University, director of medical school education in psychiatry, 1971-74, assistant professor of psychiatry, 1971-75, clinical associate professor of psychiatry and behavioral sciences, 1975—, senior research associate at School of Law, 1978—. Staff physician at Atascadero State Hospital, summer, 1968; consultant in forensic psychiatry. *Member:* American Psychiatric Association, American Academy of Psychiatry and the Law, Northern California Psychiatric Society, Phi Beta Kappa, Alpha Omega Alpha. *Awards, honors:* Falk fellowship from American Psychiatric Association.

WRITINGS: (With Herant Katchadourian) *Fundamentals of Human Sexuality*, Holt, 1972, 3rd edition, 1980; (with Katchadourian) *Biological Aspects of Human Sexuality*, Holt, 1975, 2nd edition, 1980; *Murder and Madness*, Stanford University Press, 1975; (with Katchadourian and Robert Trotter) *Human Sexuality: Brief Edition*, Holt, 1979; (with wife, Marilynn K. Lunde) *The Next Generation: A Book on Parenting*, Holt, 1980; (with Jefferson Morgan) *The Die Song: A Journey Into the Mind of a Mass Murderer*, Norton, 1980; *The Hillside Strangler*, Harper, 1981.

Contributor: Eleanor Maccoby, editor, *The Development of Sex Differences*, Stanford University Press, 1966; J. N. Spuhler, editor, *Genetic Diversity and Human Behavior*, Aldine, 1967; Arthur Burton, editor, *Operational Theories of Personality*, Brunner, 1974; Edward T. Adelson, editor, *Sexuality and Psychoanalysis*, Brunner, 1975. Contributor of about a dozen articles to scientific and law journals.

SIDELIGHTS: Lunde's main interests are forensic psychiatry, child rearing, and human sexuality. His practice of psychiatry has brought him in contact with some of California's most notorious murderers, and he has written books about his experiences. He feels that what seems to be an increasing number of violent murders and other crimes is, in large part, due to the closing of most of California's mental institutions by such politicians as Ronald Reagan and Jerry Brown. This trend, Lunde believes, has allowed many violent (and often insane) criminals to remain free or face imprisonment as legally sane people, when in the past they would have been able to receive humane treatment.

More recently he has reduced his case load of violent criminals and devoted a larger portion of his time to less emotionally taxing but equally important concerns such as parenting and child rearing.

BIOGRAPHICAL/CRITICAL SOURCES: San Francisco Examiner, May 12, 1980.

LUSCHER, Max
See LUESCHER, Max

*   *   *

LUSTIG-ARECCO, Vera   1942-

PERSONAL: Born December 17, 1942, in Argentina; daughter of Carlos (a tennis player) and Jana Herrmann (de Sonnenfeld) Lustig; married Carlos Cristoforo Arecco (in agriculture and economics), June 26, 1967; children: Andres. *Education:* University of California, Los Angeles, B.S., 1966, M.A., 1969, Ph.D., 1977. *Home:* QL 9/conjunto 3/ casa 17, Brasilia, Brazil. *Office:* Department of Social Sciences, University of Brasilia, Brasilia, Brazil.

CAREER: University of Alaska, Museum, Fairbanks, principal investigator of traditional and modern material culture of Kutchin Athabaskan Indians, summer, 1970; California State University, Dominguez Hills, visiting professor, 1973-74; Academia Nacional de Policia, Brasilia, Brazil, visiting professor, 1977; University of Brasilia, Brasilia, assistant professor of social sciences and principal investigator of traditional planting practices of Goias farmers, 1977—. *Member:* American Anthropological Association, American Association for the Advancement of Science, American Museum of Natural History, American Ethnological Society, Anthropological Society of Washington. *Awards, honors:* National Endowment for the Humanities grant, 1970; grants from Conselho Nacional de Desenvolvimento Cientifico e Tecnologico, 1977, and 1977-80.

WRITINGS: (Contributor) Wendell H. Oswalt, editor, *Modern Alaskan Native Material Culture*, Museum, University of Alaska, 1972; *Technology: Strategies for Survival*, Holt, 1975. Contributor to anthropology journals.

WORK IN PROGRESS: Research on the cultural perceptions of Goias farmers of their environment, with publication expected to result.

SIDELIGHTS: "In my youth," wrote Vera Lustig-Arecco, "I lusted for knowledge of scientific facts in almost all fields. Then I discovered anthropology, but did not think of making it my career until somebody suggested I might enjoy graduate studies in the subject. The more I studied the more I realized that, in its characteristics, anthropology is a science of synthesis, equivalent to philosophy and mathematics, with the added dimension of including a human component. This seemed to me the epitome of knowledge. As I was more inclined toward the spiritual than the material aspects of man, I decided I needed to study more the technological facts of Indian societies and that involvement led me to ecological readings which offer excellent possibilities of applying the theories to some major problems of our contemporary world.

"As I have had the opportunity to obtain a good academic training, I would eventually like to return some of the knowledge accumulated on the way, by making anthropology easily available and comprehensible to less academically trained individuals. One way would be to write fiction based on facts, another might be to write scientific books for the layman. Other plans for future research and writing include the study of rock paintings. I am highly intrigued by these attempts at communication by early man. And among my more theoretical interests is the desire eventually to try to piece together information from various fields such as astronomy, biology, and linguistics, with the purpose of showing that all in nature is repetitive and that order and pattern are predominant.

"My life experiences are somewhat varied. I have lived so far in three American countries (Argentina, the United States, and Brazil) and traveled through several Western European countries, Canada, and Mexico. From these experiences and my field work I have learned one important lesson: that man is a cultural animal where 'good' and 'evil' are relative terms that obtain their meaning in cultural context. As long as there are multiple cultures the idea of a 'one truth' is a myth. Perhaps such a viewpoint may be irreverent, coming from an anthropologist; however, I do believe that the path to knowledge is not branching, but a single straight line.

"A wholesome life should include a variety of experiences. The single-minded intellectual soon becomes a half-person. Strong human ties (whether family or friends or both) seem to me vital for the continuous development of the individual. I also believe that physical activity of any kind is important."

AVOCATIONAL INTERESTS: Yoga, tennis, bicycling, hiking, swimming, classical music, reading.

* * *

LYNCH, James 1936-

PERSONAL: Born August 25, 1936, in Bradford, England; married Margaret Ann Smith, 1958; children: Mark Andrew, Angela Margaret, Colette Elizabeth. *Education:* University of Hull, B.A. (with honors), 1957, certificate in education, 1958, advanced diploma in education, 1962, M.Ed., 1966; University of Durham, Ph.D., 1974. *Home:* 9 Ghyll Wood, Ilkley, West Yorkshire LS29 9NR, England; and 12 Third Avenue, Lambton, New South Wales, Australia. *Office:* School of Education, Newcastle College of Advanced Education, Newcastle, New South Wales, Australia.

CAREER: High school teacher in Hull, England, 1958-63, head of department, 1960-63; British Ministry of Defence, Higher Education Centre, assistant lecturer in modern languages, 1963-65; Bede College of Education, lecturer, 1965-67, senior lecturer in education, 1967-68; Southampton School of Education, Southampton, England, lecturer in education, 1968-75; University of Frankfurt, Frankfurt, West Germany, visiting professor, 1975; Bradford College, Bradford, England, head of Margaret McMillan School of Education, 1976-79; Newcastle College of Advanced Education, Newcastle, Australia, head of School of Education, 1979—. Teacher at schools for adult education. Consultant to United Nations Educational, Scientific & Cultural Organization and German Institute for International Educational Research.

WRITINGS: (With H. D. Plunkett) *Teacher Education and Cultural Change,* Allen & Unwin, 1973; (with John Pimlott) *Parents and Teachers: An Action Research Approach,* Macmillan, 1976; *Lifelong Education and the Preparation of Educational Personnel,* United Nations Educational, Scientific & Cultural Organization Institute, 1977; *The Reform of Teacher Education in the United Kingdom,* Society for Research Into Higher Education, 1979; *Education for Community,* Macmillan, 1979.

Contributor: T. G. Cook, editor, *The History of Education in Europe,* Methuen, 1974; Manfrid Heinemann, editor, *Die Historische Paedagogik in Europa und den U.S.A.* (title means "History of Education in Europe and the U.S.A."), Klett-Cotta, 1979; Manfrid Jourdan, editor, *Recurrent Education in Western Europe,* N.F.E.R. Publishing, 1980; Andrew Hargreaves, editor, *Middle School Reader,* Harper, 1980. Contributor of more than thirty articles and reviews to education journals in Great Britain, Europe, Canada, United States, and Australia.

WORK IN PROGRESS: The English Comprehensive Community College: A Case Study in Theory and Practice; One Word and Many: International Perspectives on Multi-Cultural Education; research on multi-cultural education in Australia.

SIDELIGHTS: Lynch told *CA:* "Writing is an important contribution to social and educational change. It is an expression of man's wish both to create and to liberate for himself and others. Problems of emancipatory education in the multi-cultural society are a central theme of my contemporary work and aspiration, focused on what I see as a central feature of current educational prevision, namely its implicit prejudice and social inequity."

* * *

LYNN, Roa 1937-

PERSONAL: Born November 8, 1937, in Toledo, Ohio; daughter of Jules Jay (a designer) and Phyllis (a pianist; maiden name, Kasle) Roskin; married Bernard Kripke (a professor), April 10, 1979. *Education:* Attended Bennington College, 1956-58; New York University, B.A., 1961. *Home:* 131 First Ave., Salt Lake City, Utah 84103.

CAREER: Speechwriter and research assistant for U.S. Senator Hubert H. Humphrey in Washington, D.C., 1958; Japanese Mission to the United Nations, New York City, speechwriter for Japanese ambassador, 1962-63; economic writer and analyst for Zinder International Ltd., 1963-64; registered stockbroker representative, 1965-66; research assistant in advertising department for Saturday Review, 1966-67; United Press International, Rio de Janeiro, Brazil, reporter, 1967-68; free-lance writer, 1968-73; *Newsweek International,* New York City, researcher and reporter, 1973; *Time,* New York City, researcher and reporter, 1973-74; Fairchild News Service, New York City, reporter and financial feature writer, 1974-76; free-lance writer and lecturer, 1976—. Member of Utah Council for Handicapped and Developmentally Disabled Persons, 1979—; research analyst for budget office of State of Utah; consultant to President Carter's Commission on Mental Health. *Awards, honors:* Grants from Rockefeller Brothers Fund, 1977 and 1978, and Utah State Board of Education, 1980.

WRITINGS: (With Neil Gluckin and husband, Bernard Kripke) *Learning Disabilities: An Overview of Theories, Approaches, and Politics,* Free Press, 1979. Contributor of poems to *Elima* and *Rolling Stone,* and book reviews to *New York Times Book Review* and *Saturday Review.*

WORK IN PROGRESS: Research on learning disabilities; a screenplay; a stage play.

SIDELIGHTS: Roa Lynn commented to *CA:* "I started my career as a writer laboring over poems and screenplays. Then one of my friends got the bright idea that since I wrote 'lucid poems with a quiet precision' I could be a reporter. I tried and found the going tough. Some years later I discovered why newspapering was difficult for me. By chance, on a television news show I heard about dyslexia (a form of learning disability) and knew instantly that I had it. Doctors confirmed my diagnosis. I promptly gave up the reporting business and through a grant from the Rockefeller Brothers Fund began educating myself about learning disabilities in the hope of solving my own problems since I knew that no one else was going to solve them for me. In this I have partially succeeded, with the help of my husband and other scientists at the University of Utah College of Medicine.

"I now write and lecture in this field and have just lately gone back to writing screenplays as a surreal outlet to militate against the pain and frustration I feel because of my handicap."

*   *   *

LYONS, Ivan   1934-

PERSONAL: Born October 5, 1934, in New York, N.Y.; son of Martin Pleskow (a pharmacist) and Ruth Lyons (a singer); married Nan Bauer (a writer and singer), May 18, 1958; children: Samantha. *Education:* Attended City College (now of the City University of New York), 1950-54; attended Boston University, 1955-56. *Residence:* New York, N.Y. *Agent:* Lynn Nesbit, International Creative Management, 40 West 57th St., New York, N.Y. 10019.

CAREER: Show Business (trade publication), New York City, reporter, 1956-57; Scott Meredith Literary Agency, New York City, reader, 1957; Plenum Publishing Corp., New York City, advertising and sales manager, 1958-65; Science Associates (publishing firm), New York City, president, 1965—. *Member:* Authors Guild, Writers Guild.

WRITINGS—All with wife, Nan Lyons: *Someone Is Killing the Great Chefs of Europe* (novel), Harcourt, 1976; *Champagne Blues* (novel), Simon & Schuster, 1979; "Champagne Blues" (screenplay; based on own novel), Columbia, 1979. Also contributor of articles to *L'Officiel/USA, Travel and Leisure,* and *Panorama.*

WORK IN PROGRESS: The Million Dollar Auction, a novel with Nan Lyons.

SIDELIGHTS: Nan and Ivan Lyons's first novel was begun when they decided they wanted to do something fun for the summer. Nan, a professional singer and an amateur cook, suggested to Ivan that they write a mystery about a detective who liked to cook. Since Ivan was dieting at the time, they decided the murderer would be a dieter who wanted to kill each of his favorite chefs. "We wrote *Someone Is Killing the Great Chefs of Europe* between the Fourth of July and Labor Day," Ivan told *CA.* "*Chefs* was the first thing we wrote professionally and we've been having fun ever since."

The Lyons's book has been translated into nine languages and was made into a film called "Who Is Killing the Great Chefs of Europe?" starring Robert Morley, George Segal, and Jacqueline Bisset.

Their next novel, *Champagne Blues,* is about a group of kidnapped travel writers. This book, Ivan told *CA,* "took two years because we were 'writers.' We developed writer's cramp, writer's block, and broke two typewriters. We knew we had arrived.

"The most difficult part about working together is fighting over which one of us is to make lunch. Although we often disagree while working, no manuscript is ever submitted on which we are not in complete agreement. Because we are married and have established our egos in other areas, we never compete as collaborators. Our subjects (food, travel, auctions) are selected because of the fun we have doing our research: we'll never write a book about an accountant."

*   *   *

LYONS, Nan   1935-

PERSONAL: Born October 29, 1935, in New York, N.Y.; daughter of Aaron (a labor leader) and Yetta (a model; maiden name, Kleinman) Bauer; married Ivan Lyons (a writer and publisher), May 18, 1958; children: Samantha.

Education: Attended Manhattan School of Music, 1954. *Residence:* New York, N.Y. *Agent:* Lynn Nesbit, International Creative Management, 40 West 57th St., New York, N.Y. 10019.

CAREER: Singer and writer. Singer with Robert Shaw Chorale, 1958-59; singer in churches in New York, 1958-75; writer, 1976—. *Member:* Authors Guild, Writers Guild.

WRITINGS—All with husband, Ivan Lyons: *Someone Is Killing the Great Chefs of Europe* (novel), Harcourt, 1976; *Champagne Blues* (novel), Simon & Schuster, 1979; "Champagne Blues" (screenplay; based on own novel), Columbia, 1979. Also contributor of articles to *L'Officiel/USA, Travel and Leisure,* and *Panerama.*

WORK IN PROGRESS: The Million Dollar Auction, a novel with Ivan Lyons.

SIDELIGHTS: Nan and Ivan Lyons's first novel was begun when they decided they wanted to do something fun for the summer. Nan, a professional singer and an amateur cook, suggested to Ivan that they write a mystery about a detective who liked to cook. Since Ivan was dieting at the time, they decided the murderer would be a dieter who wanted to kill each of his favorite chefs. "We wrote *Someone Is Killing the Great Chefs of Europe* between the Fourth of July and Labor Day," Ivan told *CA.* "*Chefs* was the first thing we wrote professionally and we've been having fun ever since."

The Lyons's book has been translated into nine languages and was made into a film called "Who Is Killing the Great Chefs of Europe?" starring Robert Morley, George Segal, and Jacqueline Bisset.

Their next novel, *Champagne Blues,* is about a group of kidnapped travel writers. This book, Ivan told *CA,* "took two years because we were 'writers.' We developed writer's cramp, writer's block, and broke two typewriters. We knew we had arrived."

M

MacAUSLAND, Earle R(utherford) 1893-1980

OBITUARY NOTICE: Born May 15, 1893, in Taunton, Mass.; died June 4, 1980, on Nantucket Island, Mass. Publishing executive. MacAusland served as vice-president of three publishing companies from 1920 to 1935 before becoming publisher of *National Parents-Teachers Magazine*. In 1940 he founded *Gourmet* magazine, remaining active in its publication until the time of his death. MacAusland once explained his interest in food by saying that "good eating is the key to social activity." Obituaries and other sources: *Who's Who in America*, 40th edition, Marquis, 1978; *New York Times*, June 6, 1980.

*   *   *

MacCORQUODALE, Patricia (Lee) 1950-

PERSONAL: Born August 20, 1950, in Denver, Colo.; daughter of Donald W. (a physician and health administrator) and Zoe (a college administrator) MacCorquodale; married Paul D. Guest. *Education:* Carleton College, B.A. (magna cum laude), 1972; University of Wisconsin—Madison, M.S., 1974, Ph.D., 1978. *Residence:* Tucson, Ariz. *Office:* Department of Sociology, University of Arizona, Tucson, Ariz. 85721.

CAREER: University of Wisconsin—Madison, lecturer in sociology, 1976-78; University of Arizona, Tucson, assistant professor of sociology, 1978—. Research associate at Southwest Institute for Research on Women, 1979—. *Member:* American Sociological Association, Sociologists for Women in Society, American Academy of Political and Social Science, Society for the Study of Social Problems, Western Social Science Association, Pacific Sociological Association, Mortar Board. *Awards, honors:* Grant from National Institute of Education, 1979-81.

WRITINGS: (With John DeLamater) *Premarital Sexuality,* University of Wisconsin Press, 1979.

WORK IN PROGRESS: Research on the participation of Mexican-American women in the science field and on gender roles and sexuality.

SIDELIGHTS: Patricia MacCorquodale wrote: "*Premarital Sexuality* is based upon interviews with 1,376 unmarried men and women, ages eighteen to twenty-three. The study systematically compares the responses of men and women and students and nonstudents in order to determine whether these differences in status affect sexuality. A model of the development of sexuality is developed and tested. Several influences on sexist attitudes, including the individual's gender, social class, and religious background, personal beliefs about the acceptability of premarital sex, and attitudes of parents and friends, are included. When focusing on sexual behavior, measures of sociopsychological characteristics (such as body-image, self-image, self-esteem, and sex role orientation) are major variables that were considered but were not significant predictors of behavior. Characteristics of the relationship (such as characteristics of the sexual partner and degree of emotional intensity and commitment) were important factors that influenced the extent of physical intimacy. By combining sociological and social psychological variables into a multivariate model, we tried to go beyond previous work to determine the most important social influences on premarital sexuality.

"My continuing research interests involve the relationship between gender roles and sexuality. I am pursuing this relationship with respect to sexual behavior, the selection of sexual partners, and contraceptive use."

*   *   *

MACHLOWITZ, Marilyn M(arcia) 1952-

PERSONAL: Surname is pronounced *Mack*-lo-witz; born October 22, 1952, in Philadelphia, Pa.; daughter of Roy A. and Eleanore L. Machlowitz. *Education:* Princeton University, A.B., 1974; Yale University, Ph.D., 1978. *Agent:* Aaron M. Priest Literary Agency, Inc., 150 East 35th St., New York, N.Y. 10016. *Office:* New York Life Insurance Co., 51 Madison Ave., New York, N.Y. 10010.

CAREER: New York Life Insurance Co., New York, N.Y., psychologist and manager of human resource development, 1978—. *Member:* American Psychological Association.

WRITINGS: *Workaholics,* Addison-Wesley, 1980. Contributor to magazines and newspapers.

*   *   *

MACKSEY, Richard (Alan) 1930-

PERSONAL: Born July 25, 1930, in Glen Ridge, N.J.; son of Kenneth William (an engineer) and Hazel Mae (Hennie) Macksey; married Catherine Deriseau Chance (a teacher), September 17, 1956; children: Richard Alan, Jr. *Education:* Attended Princeton University, 1948-51, and Oxford University, 1951; Johns Hopkins University, M.A., 1954, Ph.D.,

1957. *Home:* 107 St. Martin's Rd., Baltimore, Md. 21218. *Office:* Humanities Center, Johns Hopkins University, Baltimore, Md. 21218.

CAREER: Johns Hopkins University, Baltimore, Md., instructor, 1953-55; Loyola College, Baltimore, instructor, 1956-57, assistant professor of English and classics, 1957-58; Johns Hopkins University, assistant professor, 1958-64, associate professor, 1964-72, professor of comparative literature and director of Humanities Center, 1973—, chairman of comparative literature program, 1968—. Lecturer at Baltimore Museum of Art, 1964-65, 1977—. Member of editorial board of Johns Hopkins Press. Member of executive board of Baltimore Film Forum, board of governors of Theatre Hopkins, and board of directors of Bollingen Poetry Festivals, Film Workshop, Tantamount Films, Dialogue of the Arts, and Friends of Johns Hopkins Library; member of Baltimore Film Festival Committee, Maryland Film Festival Committee, and Maryland Committee on Adult Education; judge at film festivals; consultant to Rockefeller Foundation. *Military service:* U.S. Army Reserve; became major.

MEMBER: Amnesty International, Modern Language Association of America, American Society for Aesthetics, American Association of University Professors, Mediaeval Academy of America, Renaissance Society of America, Semiotic Society of America, English Institute, Philological Association (president, 1970), College English Association, History of Ideas Club (president, 1972), South Atlantic Modern Language Association, Phi Beta Kappa, Lambda Iota Tau, Grolier Club, Hamilton Street Club, Bibliophiles, Tudor and Stuart Club (member of board of governors).

WRITINGS: La Lanterne magique, Geneve, 1958; *Florilegium anglicum* (poems), Erasmus, 1964; *The Structuralist Controversy,* Johns Hopkins Press, 1972; *Velocities of Change,* Johns Hopkins Press, 1974; *The Pioneer Century* (monograph), Johns Hopkins Press, 1976.

Author of film scripts and writer for radio program "Dialogue of the Arts." Editor of *Modern Language Notes,* 1962—, *Glyph: Johns Hopkins Textual Studies,* 1977—, and *Semiotic Scene.*

WORK IN PROGRESS: A study of *Tristram Shandy* and *Jacques le Fataliste;* a study of genre in film criticism; a guide to the folkways of contemporary criticism.

*　　*　　*

MACLEAN, Arthur
See TUBB, E(dwin) C(harles)

*　　*　　*

MacLEAN, Jane 1935-

PERSONAL: Born June 22, 1935, in Kansas City, Mo.; daughter of Alvin K. (a certified public accountant) and Nettie (Freeman) Heyle; married Harold Orlando MacLean (a high school English teacher), March 25, 1961; children: Ian, Sean, Justine. *Education:* University of Kansas, B.A., 1957; also attended Sorbonne, University of Paris, 1955-56, and University of Missouri. *Home:* 2368 Vallejo St., San Francisco, Calif. 94123. *Agent:* Cantrell-Colas, Inc., 229 East 79th St., New York, N.Y. 10021.

CAREER: Travel agent and fashion model in Kansas City, Mo., 1952-57; United Nations, New York, N.Y., guide, 1958; International Chamber of Commerce, Paris, France, secretary, 1959-60; Burke School for Girls, San Francisco, Calif., teacher of French, 1960-62; writer, 1979—. Member of board of directors of French American Bilingual School of San Francisco and Opera Guild of San Francisco.

WRITINGS: Deadfall (novel), Dutton, 1979. Contributor to *Playgirl.*

WORK IN PROGRESS: Contradiction, "a European-American love story about honesty and true communication of feelings between people."

SIDELIGHTS: MacLean told *CA:* "The motivation for my first novel was simply to use my creative potential in ways other than domestic; I was going slightly crazy, and turned my dissatisfactions and that madness into a book! Now writing for me is compulsive; I struggle with the certainty that I'm creating a masterpiece one day, and visions of total failure the next; the desire to finish off my second novel before I'm sick of it, and to work on it for years a la Flaubert. (Ah, immortality? Fool!) Up and down, down and up; it's a lonely and demanding business, but I know now I'm doing it for myself only, and must. The second novel is too autobiographical; sometimes I yearn to return to my weird imagination and short stories; I find that trying to describe real people and events is much more difficult than inventing. Self-exposure is painful, enlightening. And perhaps I'm barking up the wrong tree, but it seems to me that the greatest challenge in writing is to present your ideas or experiences in an original manner; I therefore find myself spending too much time on difficult technical problems, but oh, my ideas are good! Today. Tomorrow, I think I'll never make it. But, like a performing musician, I keep on perfecting the counterpoint."

*　　*　　*

MACMANN, Elaine
See WILLOUGHBY, Elaine Macmann

*　　*　　*

MADDOX, Carl
See TUBB, E(dwin) C(harles)

*　　*　　*

MADDOX, Conroy 1912-

PERSONAL: Born December 27, 1912, in Ledbury, England; son of Albert George and Eleanor (Ballinger) Maddox; married Nan Ingram (divorced); children: Stefan (deceased), Lee Maddox Saunders. *Education:* Attended Oxford University, 1929. *Politics:* "Absolute doubt." *Religion:* None. *Home:* 17a Lambolle Rd., Hampstead, London NW3 4HS, England.

CAREER: Artist, 1937—. Lecturer at University of Birmingham, 1946-57. Co-organizer of Exeter Surrealist Festival, 1967. Work exhibited at group and solo shows and represented in collections, including Tate Gallery, Victoria and Albert Museum, and Prince Ruspoli Collection.

WRITINGS: Dali, Hamlyn, 1979; *The Surrealist Movement in England,* Hamlyn, 1981. Contributor to journals, including *Arsenal, Arts Review, Arts Monthly, Moment,* and *Flagrant Delit.*

*　　*　　*

MAGRUDER, Jeb Stuart 1934-

PERSONAL: Born November 5, 1934, in Staten Island, N.Y.; son of Donald Dilworth (a printshop owner) and Edith Bolby (Woolverton) Magruder; married Gail Barnes Nicholas (a writer), October 20, 1959; children: Whitney Craig, Justin Scott, Tracy Lynn, Stuart Cameron. *Education:* Williams College, B.A., 1958; University of Chicago, M.B.A., 1963; Princeton University, M.Div., 1981. *Office address:* Star Dental Co., P.O. Box 896, Valley Forge, Pa. 19482.

CAREER: Crown Zellerbach, San Francisco, Calif., sales representative, 1958-60; Booz, Allen, and Hamilton, Chicago, Ill., consultant, 1960-62; Jewel Tea Co., Chicago, advertising and sales program manager, 1962-66; Broadway-Hale Stores, Inc., Los Angeles, Calif., merchandise manager, 1966-68; Cosmetic Industries, Inc., and Consumer Developments, Inc., Los Angeles, president, 1968-69; associated with presidential administration of Richard Nixon as special assistant, 1969-71, deputy director of communications at the White House, 1970-71, deputy director of Committee for the Re-election of the President (CREEP), 1971-72, and executive director of inaugural committee, 1973; consultant to Metropolitan Research Co., 1972-75; vice-president of Young Life, Inc., 1975-78; currently vice-president of marketing for Star Dental Co., Valley Forge, Pa. Co-chairman of Rumsfeld for Congress committee, 1962; district manager in Illinois' 13th congressional district for Goldwater-Miller campaign, 1964; campaign manager of Illinois governor Richard Ogilvie's campaign, 1966; regional coordinator for Nixon-Agnew campaign in Southern California, 1968. *Military service:* U.S. Army, 1954-56. *Member:* Phi Gamma Delta.

WRITINGS: An American Life: One Man's Road to Watergate (autobiography), Atheneum, 1974; *From Power to Peace* (autobiography), Word Books, 1978.

SIDELIGHTS: A businessman during most of the 1960's, Magruder abandoned his career in 1968 to work for Richard Nixon. "I decided not to follow the path of my peers, to stay in business, move up the ladder and become president of the company," he told an interviewer. "I found I had more energy than my business was using up. I got involved in politics and was off and running. I was a Nixon volunteer in '60. He wasn't a great favorite of mine at the time, but he was the better choice. . . . Politics was much more exciting than business. You're working for a man instead of a product." An advertising and marketing expert, Magruder became one of Nixon's public relations men. He organized "the direct mail, the advertising, the telephone campaign, the marshaling of troops." He considered the staff extremely supportive of Nixon. "We felt," he recalled, "only Nixon could save the world."

Magruder's rise to prominence in Nixon's staff was undermined in August, 1973, when he confessed during the Senate Watergate hearings that he had participated in a number of alleged criminal acts. As reported in *U.S. News and World Report:* "Magruder told the Watergate Committee of a $250,000 plan devised by G. Gordon Liddy to gain illegal entry into the headquarters of the Democratic National Committee, photograph documents there and 'bug' telephones. Information thus gained was to be furnished to the Committee for the Re-election of the President. . . . The plan . . . was discussed on three occasions in the presence of former Attorney General John N. Mitchell and former White House counsel John W. Dean III." When the break-in was discovered, Magruder said, he and the co-conspirators effected an elaborate "cover-up" to prevent disclosure of the full story in order to protect President Nixon and ensure his re-election.

During his trial after the hearings, Magruder agreed to testify for the prosecution and was, therefore, allowed to plead guilty to a one-count federal indictment that charged him with conspiracy to obstruct justice, defraud the United States, and eavesdrop on the Democratic Party's national headquarters. While awaiting sentencing, Magruder wrote *An American Life: One Man's Road to Watergate.* It recounts the events of the Watergate break-in and cover-up as

well as his own early political experiences. One of the most interesting aspects of the book, according to a reviewer for *Encounter,* was Magruder's "account of the incredible technical complications involved in the planning and execution of CREEP's campaign to re-elect the President; it should be read by everyone who is interested in the machinery of how American politics actually work."

In *New Republic,* however, Joseph A. Califano, Jr., lamented Magruder's failure to connect with any insight his plethora of facts. *An American Life,* he wrote, "exposes such pervasive insensitivity to the enormous danger these 'young' men represented to our democratic way of life that it qualifies as a major tragedy." Similarly, Magruder's former instructor William Sloan Coffin, Jr., "found few truths of significance" in the book. "I'm saddened by the thought that I and the many readers of Magruder's book will probably gain more in the reading of it than he did in the writing of it," he said.

On May 21, 1974, Magruder was sentenced to ten months to four years in a federal prison. He served less than one year of that sentence. In a minimum security prison, Magruder worked as a desk clerk and spent afternoons giving tennis lessons. However, he contended that "this is no country club." Prisoners lived in military-style dormitories that afforded little privacy. "The psychological deprivation of freedom is the rough thing," Magruder noted.

After his release from prison, Magruder declared that he had decided to lead a Christian life. In *From Power to Peace,* he detailed his acceptance of Christianity. "It is refreshing and salutary to read such words by one like Jeb Magruder," wrote Senator Mark Hatfield in the book's foreword. "More important they stand out as testimony to the spiritual transformation which has occurred in his own life."

BIOGRAPHICAL/CRITICAL SOURCES: New York Times, January 19, 1973, June 15, 1973; *Time,* April 30, 1973, May 14, 1973; *Newsweek,* April 30, 1973, June 25, 1973, July 15, 1974; *Harper's,* October, 1973, August, 1974; *U.S. News and World Report,* June 3, 1974; *New Republic,* June 29, 1974; *Atlantic,* August, 1974; Jeb Stuart Magruder, *An American Life: One Man's Road to Watergate,* Atheneum, 1974; *Encounter,* April, 1975; Gail Magruder, *Gift of Love,* Holman, 1976; *Publisher's Weekly,* March 27, 1978; *Christianity Today,* May 5, 1978; Jeb Stuart Magruder, *From Power to Peace,* Word Books, 1978.

*   *   *

MAHAN, Pat
See WHEAT, Patte

*   *   *

MAHAN, Patte Wheat
See WHEAT, Patte

*   *   *

MAITLAND, Antony Jasper 1935-

PERSONAL: Born June 17, 1935, in Andover, Somerset, England; son of Percy Eric (an Air Force officer) and Alison Mary (Kettlewell) Maitland. *Education:* West of England College of Art, Bristol, National Diploma in Design, 1957. *Home:* 52b Warrington Crescent, London W9, England.

CAREER: Illustrator and designer. *Military service:* British Army, 1956-58. *Awards, honors:* Leverhulme Research Award, 1958-59; Kate Greenaway Award from British Library Association, 1961, for *Mrs. Cockle's Cat,* and commendation, 1973, for *The Ghost Downstairs;* Children's Spring Book Festival Award from *Book World*, 1963.

WRITINGS—All self-illustrated: *The Secret of the Shed*, Constable, 1962, Duell, 1963; *Ben Goes to the City*, Longmans, Green, 1964, Delacorte, 1967; *James and the Roman Silver*, Constable, 1965; (adapter) *Idle Jack*, Farrar, Straus, 1977.

Illustrator: Philippa Pearce, *Mrs. Cockle's Cat*, Constable, 1961, Lippincott, 1962; Pearce, *A Dog So Small*, Constable, 1962, Lippincott, 1963; Emma Smith, *Out of Hand*, Macmillan, 1963; Anne Molloy, *Proper Place for Chip*, Hastings, 1963; Ruth Ainsworth, *The Ten Tales of Shellover*, Deutsch, 1963, Roy, 1968; Leon Garfield, *Jack Holborn*, Longmans, Green, 1964, Pantheon, 1965; Joan Clarke, *Happy Planet*, Lothrop, 1965; Garfield, *Devil-in-the-Fog*, Pantheon, 1966; Ester Wier, *The Loner*, Constable, 1966; Richard Gavin Robinson, *Captain Sintar*, Deutsch, 1967, Dutton, 1969; Hanna Stephan, *The Long Way Home*, Heinemann, 1967, also published as *The Quest*, Little, Brown, 1968; Garfield, *Smith*, Pantheon, 1967; Garfield, *Black Jack*, Longman Young Books, 1968, Pantheon, 1969; Ruth Ainsworth, *More Tales of Shellover*, Roy, 1968; Verne Davis, *Orphan of the Tundra*, Weybright, 1968; Barbara Willard, *To London! To London!*, Weybright, 1968; Garfield, *The Drummer Boy*, Pantheon, 1969; Garfield, *Mr. Corbett's Ghost and Other Stories*, Longman Young Books, 1969, Penguin, 1972.

Peter Olney, *All Around You Assignment Cards*, Blond Educational, 1970; Penelope Lively, *Astercote*, Heinemann, 1970; Susan Dickinson compiler, *The Restless Ghost, and Other Encounters and Experiences*, Collins, 1970, published as *The Usurping Ghost, and Other Encounters and Experiences*, Dutton, 1971; Ainsworth, *The Phantom Cyclist and Other Stories*, Deutsch, 1971, Follett, 1974; Meta Mayne Reid, *Beyond the Wide World's End*, Lutterworth, 1972; Garfield, *Child o' War*, Holt, 1972; Garfield, *The Ghost Downstairs*, Pantheon, 1972; Elizabeth Goudge, *Henrietta's House*, Penguin, 1972; Margery Bianco, *Poor Cecco*, Deutsch, 1973; Aidan Chambers, *Aidan Chambers' Book of Ghosts and Other Hauntings*, Longman Young Books, 1973; Lively, *The Ghost of Thomas Kempe* (Junior Literary Guild selection), Dutton, 1973.

Ainsworth, *The Bear Who Liked Hugging People, and Other Stories*, Heinemann, 1976, C. Russak, 1978; Charles Causley, *Dick Whittington: A Story From England*, Puffin Books, 1976; Garfield, *The Lamplighter's Funeral*, Heinemann, 1976; Garfield, *Mirror, Mirror*, Heinemann, 1976; Richard Arthur Warren Hughes, *The Wonder-Dog* (short stories), Greenwillow Books, 1977; Andrew Lang, compiler, *Green Fairy Book* (short stories), Viking, 1978.

SIDELIGHTS: Early in his career Maitland gained experience by traveling and working throughout Europe and the Middle East. He designed a crest for a bank in Tehran, worked with an architect in Beirut, and did wall paintings for Madame Tussaud's Wax Works in London. He did design work for the Edinburgh Festival, the Shakespeare Exhibition at Stratford-upon-Avon, and the National Portrait Gallery in London. The Shah of Iran commissioned Maitland to do a family portrait.

BIOGRAPHICAL/CRITICAL SOURCES: Bettina Hurlimann, *Picture-Book World*, Oxford University Press, 1968.*

*   *   *

MAJAULT, Joseph 1916-

PERSONAL: Born December 1, 1916, in Niort, France; son of Firmin (an accountant) and Feamande (Coyault) Majault; married Marie-Therese Pinaud, January 9, 1940; children: Anne-Marie, Jean-Pierre, Francois. *Education:* Universite de Poitiers, licence es lettres, 1939. *Religion:* Roman Catholic. *Home:* 5 rue des Beaux-Arts, Paris, France 75006.

CAREER: Centre National de Documentation Pedagogique, Paris, France, assistant director, 1941-79. Associated with UNESCO and the Counsel of Europe. *Military service:* French Army, 1939-40; served in infantry. *Awards, honors:* Prix de l'Academie Francaise, 1948, for *Mauriac et l'art du roman;* Prix de la Critique, 1967, for *Shakespeare;* Prix des Ecrivains de l'Ouest, 1973, for *Virginie;* officer of French Legion of Honor.

WRITINGS—In English: (With Jean Thomas) *Primary and Secondary Education: Modern Trends and Common Problems*, Council of Europe, 1963; *Education Documentation Centers in Western Europe: A Comparative Study*, Unipub, 1963; *James Joyce*, Editions Universitaires, 1963, translation by Jean Stewart published as *James Joyce*, Pendragon House, 1971; *Virginie; ou, Le Premier Matin du monde* (novel), Laffont, 1973, translation by Norman Shapiro published as *Virginie; or, The Dawning of the World*, Crown, 1974.

In French; novels; all published by Laffont, except as noted: *Je plaide coupable* (title means "I Plead Guilty"), 1953; *Entre tes mains* (title means "Between Your Hands"), 1954; *Les Dernieres Amarres* (title means "The Last Links"), 1956; *Un Amour heureux* (title means "A Happy Love"), 1957; *L'Ete trop court* (title means "A Short Summer"), 1958; *Les Enfants du soir* (title means "Children at the End of the Day"), Casterman, 1962; *La Conference de Geneve* (title means "Conference in Geneva"), 1967; *Les Echeances de Dieu* (title means "God's Will"), 1969.

Essays: *Mauriac et l'art du roman* (title means "Mauriac, Novelist"), Laffont, 1947; *Le Jeu dramatique et l'enfant* (title means "Dramatic Play and Children"), Editions d'Ile-de-France, 1953; (with Violette Morin) *Un Mythe moderne: L'Erotisme* (title means "A Modern Myth: Eroticism"), Casterman, 1962; *Mythologie d'un homme moyen* (title means "Mythology of a Middle Man"), Laffont, 1964; *Camus: Revolte et liberte* (title means "Rebellion and Freedom"), Editions du Centurion, 1965; *Shakespeare*, Editions de Sud, 1966; *La Revolution de l'enseignement* (title means "The Revolution of Education"), Laffont, 1967; *L'Evidence et le mystere* (title means "Truth and Mystery"), Editions du Centurion, 1978.

Other writings: (Editor) *Encyclopedie pratique de l'education en France* (title means "Practical Encyclopedia of French Education"), S.E.D.E., 1960; (editor) *Litterature de notre temps* (title means "Literature Today"), Casterman, 1966; *Rives* (poetry; title means "Shores"), Editions du Temps, 1970; *Une Partie de des* (title means "The Dice"), Editions du Centurion, 1976; *Poemes*, Editions Saint Germain des Pres, 1979.

WORK IN PROGRESS: Comptes, Mecomptes, Decomptes, for Casterman.

SIDELIGHTS: Majault told *CA:* "Writing is not my job, it is my pleasure. I am always happy to take my pen in the morning either for a novel or an essay. For me, writing gives freedom and truth to my life. I am concerned with God and the mystery of life, ways of leading children to maturity, and ways to build peace for men throughout the world."

MALICK, Terrence 1943-
(Terry Malick; David Whitney, a pseudonym)

PERSONAL: Born November 30, 1943, in Waco, Tex. *Education:* Harvard University, B.A., 1966; attended American Film Institute, 1969, and Magdalen College, Oxford. *Office:* c/o Evarts Ziegler Associates, Inc., 9255 West Sunset Blvd., Los Angeles, Calif. 90069.

CAREER: Producer, writer, and director of motion pictures. Journalist for *Newsweek, Life,* and *New Yorker;* Massachusetts Institute of Technology, Cambridge, Mass., lecturer in philosophy, 1968; script rewriter. *Awards, honors:* Rhodes scholar.

WRITINGS—All screenplays: "Lanton Mills" (short film), American Film Institute Center for Advanced Studies, 1969; (under name Terry Malick) "Pocket Money" (adapted from the novel, *Jim Kane,* by J.P.S. Brown), First Artists, 1972; (under pseudonym David Whitney, with Bill Kerby) "The Gravy Train," Columbia & Warner Bros., 1974; (and director) "Badlands," Warner Bros., 1974; (and director) "Days of Heaven," Paramount, 1978.

SIDELIGHTS: Malick made an impressive directorial debut at the age of twenty-nine with "Badlands." The film is set in the 1950's and evokes the peculiar numbness characteristic of that decade in America. *Time*'s Jay Cocks commented: "This is a deadeyed, deadpan existential amorality play that has found a metaphor to make the 1950s come alive. At least it spins a superbly ironic fairy tale out of the emotional hibernation of those years in America, the simmering collective detachment that could muffle hysteria and dull death."

Kit, a twenty-five-year-old drifter, and Holly, a fifteen-year-old high school student, are Malick's characters. When the couple decides to run off together and Holly's father tries to stop them, Kit dispassionately kills him as Holly watches. So begins their murderous spree across the Badlands.

Kit and Holly attempt to reconcile the emptiness of their lives by posing as pop culture heroes: Kit as a James Dean rebel and Holly as a heroine in a true romance story. *Newsweek*'s Paul D. Zimmerman argued that Kit "seems less an individual than a representative figure, evoking a whole spawn of pathologically alienated types who have in recent years risen from the dark places of American society to wreak irrational violence." Holly narrates the film in a singsong confessional magazine style, romanticizing their lives together as she relates the story to viewers. Malick was influenced by characters like Nancy Drew and Tom Sawyer in creating Holly—characters who were innocents involved in dramas over their heads, he told a *Sight and Sound* interviewer.

Neither character shows remorse for their actions. "They are young people who have either lost touch with their feelings or have replaced them with fantasy images of themselves," Hollis Alpert wrote in *Saturday Review.* "They can acknowledge neither their own emptiness nor the emptiness of their environment. But out of this, Malick somehow makes chill poetry."

The film's relationship to its two major characters has provoked the most controversy among critics. The tone of the film is reticent and cool. Malick's refusal to make moral judgments of his characters has angered some critics. Pauline Kael was particularly critical of Malick's cold, formal work. "It is an intellectualized movie," she wrote in *New Yorker,* "shrewd and artful, carefully styled to sustain its low-key view of dissociation. Kit and Holly are kept at a distance doing things for no explained purpose; it's as if the

director had taped gauze over their characters, so that we wouldn't be able to take a reading on them." Despite Malick's obvious gifts as a filmmaker, Kael still complained: "'Badlands' is an art thing, all right, but I didn't admire it, I didn't enjoy it, and I don't like it. It's all rhetoric."

In "Badlands," Malick "focuses on what the couple does and their dim perception of it," commented Zimmerman. His interest isn't with crime itself, but with Kit's and Holly's perception of their crimes. Alan Spiegel explained in *Salmagundi:* "The film indeed doesn't romanticize the lovers but shows us instead their efforts to romanticize their lives and their surroundings which, by contrast, are usually presented as violent, waning, numb, and null. The focus of the film, as opposed to the focus of the lovers, pitches itself firmly on the interface between this imposed romance, and the abrasiveness of the world itself, the disparity between what the lovers want and what the world allows them to take. It is the rich interplay within this disparity that makes 'Badlands' one of the very few sustained works of romantic irony in the American cinema."

Jay Cocks was concerned that Malick "leaves himself open to accusations of condescension to his characters," but concluded that "'Badlands,' which can cut sharply, also has a sort of reluctant compassion for Holly and Kit. The poverty of their desensitized lives not only propels them but makes them true." Neither did William Johnson of *Film Quarterly* find the film patronizing, noting that Malick makes "no attempt to either excuse or condemn the characters." He continued: "Nor does the film make any judgment of the world they live in—though it is easy to think so. Since hardly any scenes cue our emotions, we may attach excessive importance to the few that do."

In a *Sight and Sound* interview, Malick addressed criticism that he patronized Kit and Holly: "I grew up around people like Kit and Holly. I see no gulf between them and myself. One of the things the actors and I used to talk about was never stepping outside the characters and winking at the audience, never getting off the hook. If you keep your hands off the characters, you open yourself to charges like that; at least you have no *defence* against them. What I find patronising is people not leaving the characters alone, stacking the deck for them, not respecting their integrity, their difference."

The haunting beauty of the photography in "Badlands" seemed superficial to some critics. But Johnson, for one, disagreed, writing that the beauty is "not irrelevant at all. It presents us with Kit's and Holly's perception of the world—a random succession of surface phenomena which may fascinate them but convey no meaning. . . . The visual immediacy, which might seem to clash with the formal and narrative distancing of the film, in fact extends it. The viewer sees vividly but always at a distance."

Malick's next film, "Days of Heaven," takes place in the nation's days of innocence just before World War I. The story is melodramatic, yet understated, and the sparse dialogue is often obliterated by other sounds. Bill, his sweetheart Abby, and his kid sister Linda escape their factory jobs in Chicago to work as migrant laborers in the lush wheat fields of the Texas panhandle. Bill and Abby pose as brother and sister and spend the season working on the largest wheat farm in the panhandle. The lonely farmer falls in love with Abby and Bill encourages her to marry him after he learns that the farmer is fatally ill. Abby and the farmer marry, but he doesn't die and Abby begins to love him. Bill and Abby are still attracted to each other and the farmer suspects that they are lovers. In an apocalyptic scene in which the farm is destroyed by a locust plague and fire, Bill kills the farmer in self-defense. Bill, Abby, and Linda escape, but Bill is subsequently killed by police. The penultimate scene shows Abby stepping aboard a train filled with doughboys leaving for the war, her destination unknown. Finally, Linda escapes from boarding school and wanders down the railroad tracks with a friend from the farm.

Much of the film is narrated by Linda as she relates the characters' fall from grace. Her narration won acclaim from almost every reviewer. Alan Spiegel wrote, "Linda's monologue is one of Malick's loveliest inspirations: witty and spare, crimped and lilting, wise and punk, it is street talk of an exceptionally fine and pungent grain and manages to do everything that is asked of it—except convert it to outright poetry (and so compete with and detract from the images themselves)."

The loss of innocence, both of the characters and of America, is a major theme in "Days of Heaven." "To Malick," Frank Rich explained, "all these people are victims of their innocent faith in a warped American dream. Their tragedy is that they blame themselves, rather than their false ideals, for the misery of their lives." When the story shifts at the end from the farm to the town where the doughboys are being shipped to war, "'Days of Heaven' effortlessly transcends its own story to prefigure the history of an era. As Malick's characters lost their innocence on a ravaged wheatfield in Texas, so would a nation on the bloody battlefields of the first World War."

The *New Yorker*'s Penelope Gilliatt called Malick's work a "most eloquent and important film about being American." She thought that Malick was specifically addressing aimlessness and she viewed the bindle stiff as the film's central metaphor. "The halted photography, the waits between the use of music and the use of voice-over narration come to us as if they were signals of a past mislaid," Gilliatt wrote. "Any foreigner in America will recognize this aesthetic hint as telling a truth about the condition of Americanism. All the way through, the devices of the film seem to be meant to transmit loneliness and recovery. We are in the presence of a civilization that is being made in front of our eyes and is fevered with memories of oceans crossed."

If Malick explores much the same national terrain in "Days of Heaven" as he did in "Badlands," he also reuses several of the first film's elements. Richard Combs indicated them in *Sight & Sound:* "Hapless youngsters on the run; a picaresque narrative wrapped in a blandly distanced commentary; an 'ecstatic' flow of imagery which begs our sense of wonder." Combs continued: "Even more dangerously, he has increased the distance between the levels of enchantment and the levels of meaning. Visually, 'Days of Heaven' seems to have set out to be more seductive than 'Badlands,' while in terms of theme, character, and even plot, it is more diffuse, dispersed and secretive."

Most critics agree that the film is a technical advancement over "Badlands." Malick uses such cinematic innovations as Dolby sound, a Panaglide camera, special lenses, and natural light. The musical score by Ennio Morricone is used to stunning advantage. The film is especially notable for cinematographer Nestor Almendros's use of natural light. In a *Film Comment* interview with Brooks Riley, Almendros recalled Malick's insistence that the photographers "keep shooting long after the sun had set. I told him he was like Joshua in the Bible, trying to stop the sun. He was very frustrated; I think he hated us for not stopping the sun, as though it were our fault."

As with "Badlands," critics feared that audiences would fail to see beyond the film's visual attractiveness. But most reviewers recognized that Malick's triumph with "Days of Heaven" was the artful synthesis of beauty and meaning. "He has the unfashionable courage to believe in beauty as both form and power," *Newsweek*'s Jack Kroll commented. "It's dangerous to saturate one's vision with such total ravishment, to find beauty in everything—the semi-literate language of an uneducated child, the wrenching labor of itinerant workers in a field of waving wheat, the fatal choreography of murder."

Richard Corliss, writing in *New Times,* termed the picture one of the most beautiful movies ever made "because every gorgeous frame contributes to the film's grand design. The imagery isn't window dressing, it's the central window into Terry Malick's concerns. In a way, it's the subject of 'Days of Heaven.'" Alan Spiegel concluded: "The point about 'Days of Heaven' however is that the film is beautiful not because it is full of gorgeous images but because these images are the exact formal cognates of the most powerful kinds of emotion (exaltation, joy, awe, loss, separation). And these emotions are present in the film precisely because the photography cannot be extricated from the experience of an expressive totality—of word and deed, actor and setting, sight and sound."

BIOGRAPHICAL/CRITICAL SOURCES: New Yorker, March 18, 1974, September 18, 1978; *Time,* April 8, 1974, September 18, 1978; *Newsweek,* April 8, 1974, September 18, 1978; *Nation,* April 13, 1974, October 7, 1978; *New Republic,* April 13, 1974, September 11, 1978; *Film Quarterly,* spring, 1974, summer, 1974; *Saturday Review,* May 18, 1974, January 6, 1979; *Sight and Sound,* spring, 1975, spring, 1979; *Horizon,* September, 1978; *Film Comment,* September-October, 1978; *New Times,* October 2, 1978; *Rolling Stone,* November 16, 1978; *Salmagundi,* winter-spring, 1980.

—*Sketch by Barbara A. Welch*

*   *   *

MALICK, Terry
See MALICK, TERRENCE

*   *   *

MALLE, Louis 1932-

PERSONAL: Born October 30, 1932, in Thumeries, France; son of Pierre (a director of sugar refineries) and Francoise (Beghin) Malle; married second wife, Candice Bergen (an actress), September 27, 1980; children: Manuel, Justine. *Education:* Attended Institute d'Etudes Politiques, 1951-53, and Institute des Hautes Etudes Cinematographiques, 1953-54. *Office:* 92 Champs-Elysees, Paris, France 75008.

CAREER: Writer, producer, and director of motion pictures. Worked as assistant to Jacques-Yves Cousteau, 1954-55; assistant to Robert Bresson during filming of "Un Condamne a mort s'est echappe," 1956; cinematographer for Jacques Tati on the motion picture "Mon Oncle," 1957; French television correspondent in Algeria, 1962, Vietnam, 1963, and Thailand, 1964. *Awards, honors:* Co-winner of Golden Palm from Cannes Film Festival, 1956, and Academy Award from Academy of Motion Picture Arts and Sciences, 1957, both for "Le Monde du silence"; Prix Louis Delluc, 1957, for "Ascenseur pour l'echafaud"; special jury prize from Venice Film Festival, 1958, for "Les Amants"; special jury prize from Venice Film Festival and nomination for Academy Award for best foreign language film, both 1963, and best film of the year award from Italian Critics

Association, 1964, all for "Le Feu follet"; Grand Prix du Cinema Francais, 1965, and best film of the year award in Czechoslovakia, 1966, both for "Viva Maria"; Grand Prix from Melbourne Film Festival, 1970, for "Calcutta"; nomination for award for best British documentary script from Writers Guild, 1971, for "Phantom India"; nomination for Academy Award for best original screenplay, 1971, for "Le Souffle au couer"; British Academy Award for best film from British Academy of Motion Picture Arts and Sciences, best film of the year award from Italian Critics Association, and nomination for Academy Award for best foreign language film, all 1974, all for "Lacombe, Lucien"; recipient of other film awards.

WRITINGS—Published screenplays; also director: (With Jean-Paul Rappeneau and Jean Ferry) *Vie privee* (released in the U.S. as "A Very Private Affair"), B. Grasset, 1962; (with Jacques Prevert) *Deux Films francais: Les Visiteurs du soir* [and] *Le Feu follet* (title means "Two French Films: 'The Devil's Envoy' [and] 'The Fire Within'"; the former by Prevert, the latter by Malle adapted from the novel by Pierre Drieu La Rochelle), edited by Robert M. Hammond and Marguerite Hammond, Harcourt, 1965; (with Jean-Claude Carriere) *Viva Maria*, Laffont, 1965; (with Federico Fellini and Roger Vadim) *Tre passi nel delirio* (released in the U.S. as "Spirits of the Dead"; contains "Toby Dammit" by Fellini, "Metzengerstein" by Vadim, and "William Wilson" by Malle; all adapted from short stories by Edgar Allen Poe), Cappilli, 1968; *Le Souffle au couer* (released in the U.S. as "Murmur of the Heart"), Gallimard, 1971; (with Patrick Modiano) *Lacombe, Lucien*, Gallimard, 1974, translation from the French by Sabine Destree, Viking, 1975.

Unpublished screenplays; also director: (With Roger Nimier) "Ascenseur pour l'echafaud" (released in the U.S. as "Elevator to the Gallows" and as "Frantic"; adapted from the novel by Noel Calef), 1957; (with Louis De Vilmorin) "Les Amants" (released in the U.S. as "The Lovers"; adapted from the novel by Dominique-Vivant, *Pointe de lendemain*), 1958; (with Rappeneau) "Zazie dans le Metro" (released in the U.S. as "Zazie" and as "Zazie in the Underground"; adapted from the novel by Raymond Queneau), 1960; "Viva le tour" (short documentary), 1965; (with Carriere and Daniel Boulanger) "Le Voleur" (released in the U.S. as "The Thief of Paris"; adapted from the novel by George Darien), 1966; "Calcutta" (documentary), 1969; "Phantom India" (documentary; also released as "Louis Malle's India"), broadcast by BBC-TV in seven parts, 1970, released in U.S., 1972; "Humain trop humain" (documentary; title means "Human, Too Human"), 1972; "Place de la Republique" (documentary), 1973; (with Joyce Bunuel and Ghislain Uhry) "Black Moon," 1975.

WORK IN PROGRESS: Directing the motion picture "Atlantic City, U.S.A."

SIDELIGHTS: "Making a film is like a life cycle," Malle once told an interviewer. "It's like being born, taking your first steps, learning how to talk, developing relationships." Malle's likening of filmmaking to a life cycle probably stems from his approach to the craft; he dislikes repetition and constantly addresses new themes with new styles. "I feel very strongly that if I started to make the same film twice I would be mentally in trouble," he admits, "so there's something experimental about my work." Pauline Kael considers Malle's pursuit of change to be the essence of his work. "The only quality common to the films of Louis Malle is the restless intelligence one senses in them," she writes, "and it must be this very quality that has led Malle to try such different subjects and styles."

A moviegoer in his youth, Malle began pursuing a filmmaking career when he enrolled in the Institute des Hautes Etudes Cinematographiques following a brief stint as a seaman. In 1954 he merged his interests in sailing and filmmaking by leaving the institute for a position as cameraman for underwater explorer Jacques Cousteau on expeditions in the Mediterranean Sea and Indian Ocean. Malle's expertise as as underwater cinematographer earned him high praise from Cousteau, who ranked him among the most talented "in the world." Much of his cinematography was featured in Cousteau's documentary "The Silent World," which received the Golden Palm at Cannes in 1956.

The same year, Malle left Cousteau's crew to assist Robert Bresson with the filming of "A Man Escaped." He then obtained a job as cameraman for Jacques Tati on "Mon Oncle." Finally, in 1957, Malle directed his first film, "Elevator to the Gallows."

Slated as a grade-B thriller by its producers, "Elevator to the Gallows" was transformed by Malle into a polished, technically impressive film. It is essentially an account of one woman's futile search for her co-conspiring lover, who becomes trapped in an elevator after murdering the woman's husband. But Malle underscored the story with subtle editing and a surprisingly adept use of music. Malle was awarded the prestigious Prix Louis Delluc for his work on the film, which Kael called "ingenious."

Despite critical raves and honors, Malle was dissatisfied with the film's pacing. He credited composer Miles Davis with much of the film's success. It's a very interesting film," Malle conceded, "but I find some moments almost embarrassing. Miles Davis made it into something better than it actually was. [His music] gave the picture a style, a tempo and a climax that it didn't have."

Music was also an integral part of Malle's second film, "The Lovers," which dealt with a woman's revived sexual appetite after years of dissatisfaction in a bourgeois marriage. In the film, a sextet by Johannes Brahms establishes a romantic mood, especially during a moonlit, lovemaking scene. But though most reviewers have cited the score as a prime reason for the film's success, Malle was less pleased with it. He deemed the soundtrack "beautiful but ... almost manipulative."

Because of the explicit (by 1958 standards) nature of the lovemaking scenes, "The Lovers" proved to be a controversial film. In Cleveland a distributor of the film even served a brief jail sentence. But in Europe, censorship difficulties only served to boost the film's box-office appeal, and audiences flocked to witness the purportedly graphic coupling. In retrospect, Malle felt that the frankness of the scenes undermined the eroticism. He said: "I remember the days when the code in Hollywood was very strict and when you had comedies like *Pillow Talk,* which were the most obscene pictures ever made.... They all revolved around sex, in a very matter-of-fact and obvious kind of way, but of course there wasn't one explicit scene in any of them. If you have to deal with sex, films like *Pillow Talk* are ... more interesting."

Malle followed "The Lovers" with "Zazie," an adaptation of Raymond Queneau's novel about a worldly child who spends a day in Paris with her transvestite uncle. Taking his cue from Tati, Malle used a variety of cinematographic tricks, including slow motion and upside-down shots, to emphasize the chaotic nature of the story. "I even managed to shoot scenes where in the same dolly shot we would change objects," Malle boasted. "A chair was red and the next time the camera passed by it, it was blue. I made it obvious in a very aggressive way that we live in a world which, we pretend, is one, but instead is multiple and changing—and we try to deal with that contradiction." Kael wrote that "'Zazie' owed a debt to Tati but carried Tati's dry, quick style to nightmarish anxiety." She called the film "a fiendishly inventive slapstick comedy."

Some critics felt that Malle faltered in his next film, "A Very Private Affair." Less engaging than his previous efforts, it dwelled almost obsessively on the face and body of actress Brigitte Bardot, and critics complained that it lacked the subtle psychological nuances that characterized Malle's earlier works. But despite critical displeasure, "A Very Private Affair" was an enormous box-office success, for it allowed viewers to draw parallels between Bardot's own life and the character she portrayed.

Malle spent the next two years as a reporter in Algeria. When he returned to France in 1963 he made "The Fire Within," a film many critics consider his finest. It details the last forty-eight hours in the life of a suicidal playboy. Kael wrote: "It is a study of despair with no possible sign of relief; the man has used up his slim resources and knows it. He does not want to live as what he has become; his taste is too good."

As in Malle's first two films, the music in "The Fire Within" was extremely effective in evoking a mood in the film. But unlike the "manipulative" score of "The Lovers," the music in "The Fire Within," piano pieces by Erik Satie, is used in an ironic sense. "The use of Satie in *The Fire Within* was much more discreet, more like counter-point," Malle noted. "These little piano pieces create a very melancholic atmosphere but . . . there's definitely something ironical about it. It was a sort of distancation from what was going on on the screen."

After completing "The Fire Within," Malle devoted his talents to a series of less ambitious projects. He made "Vive le tour," a short documentary about bicyclists. He then made "Viva Maria," a musical comedy that featured Jeanne Moreau, who had previously appeared in "Elevator to the Gallows" and "The Lovers," and Bardot. Though the film had its detractors, it too was a popular success for Malle and eventually received the Grand Prix du Cinema. Malle followed "Viva Maria" with "The Thief of Paris," an adventure-comedy featuring Jean-Paul Belmondo as a thief preying on the bourgeoisie. And in 1967 he contributed "Woodrow Wilson" to an omnibus that also contained films by Roger Vadim and Federico Fellini.

By the end of 1967, the hectic pace Malle had worked at for several years finally took its toll. Insisting that he was "tired of actors, studios, fiction, and Paris," Malle abruptly divorced his wife and moved to India. There he found a serenity that had eluded him in France. He claimed that "what I saw in India, that paradise of the exotic, *that* is what really changed my life." Malle's time in India, however, was not given entirely to introspection. With the aid of a sound technician and a cameraman, Malle randomly filmed more than forty hours of footage of Indian cities and countrysides. He then edited the footage into seven separate segments for British television. The telecasts caused an immediate furor in England, where viewers felt that the films unjustly blamed the British government for India's strife. In the United States, however, where the films were released as a six-hour feature entitled "Phantom India," they were praised as realistic and sympathetic. "The film's supreme merit," wrote Howard Thompson, "whether it shows a peasant making a

fuel patty of cow dung or tunes in on the roar of the Bombay Stock Exchange, is a texture of realistic truth that conveys the wonder of human life."

Malle left India in 1970 to resume his career in France. "Murmur of the Heart," his first effort upon returning, sparked yet another controversy. Essentially the story of a young boy's budding sexuality, the film dealt briefly with the subject of incest. French audiences were shocked, for in "Murmur of the Heart" incest is not portrayed as an emotionally crippling act. Kael contended that the film is "not about how one has been scarred but about how one was formed." And Roger Greenspun, in a less enthusiastic review, called "Murmur of the Heart" "a happy incest movie." Malle was pleased with the public reaction. "When *Murmur of the Heart* opened on the Champs Elysees, people running out of the theatre were under the charm of it," he recalled. "But at the same time they did sort of a double take on it, and they'd stop and say, 'My God, what did I see?' It's like forcing people to think about incest—why do we have to put such an incredible weight on it, why has it become such an incredible taboo?"

After "Murmur of the Heart" Malle made two documentaries, "Human, Too Human" and "Place de la Republique." The former was filmed entirely in an automobile factory and drew jeers from leftist radicals in France. "I remember," said Malle, "an incredible discussion with French radical-left people who were at me saying: 'What are you trying to prove? You go into a factory, you shoot for three weeks and there's not one word of commentary or interview in the picture. Aren't you going to denounce, don't you come to conclusions?' Malle told Cott, "I would have felt like an idiot if I was going to inject political comments." He also defended his own silence in the film by claiming that "to use words would have been absurd in the face of the slow-motion-fashioned fascination of that *repetition,* which is death—these people doing the same five gestures for eight hours a day for thirty years of their lives, which is the most atrocious thing you could do to a human being." Malle followed the wordless "Human, Too Human" with a series of interviews with French citizens, "Place de la Republique."

Malle's next film, "Lacombe, Lucien," infuriated both conservatives and radicals. It concerned a bored, teenage peasant's whimsical decision to collaborate with Nazis during the occupation of France in World War II. Political observers were outraged by Malle's decision to end the film inconclusively; however, Malle believed the ambiguous ending was the essence of the story. He contended: "It was very difficult to have a judgment about this boy who had been committing the worst possible things and at the same time, in a way, had been innocent. And that's the problem of evil, 'the banality of evil.' He added that whether Lucien "dies or doesn't die—is or isn't executed, becomes a successful shopkeeper or doesn't—makes no difference."

Malle followed "Lacombe, Lucien" with "Black Moon," a children's parable in which men and women, children and adults, exchange roles. Though the film was not as well received as its predecessors, "Black Moon" had its supporters. Vincent Canby called it "baffling and beautiful and occasionally very funny." Jack Kroll described it as "an apocalyptic Alice in Wonderland in which innocence and perversity find a common hideout in a world of dull-eyed executioners who have neither." Noting that the film was inspired by "Lacombe, Lucien," Malle said: "Consciously or unconsciously, I'm trying to express this fundamental doubt that I have about people actually being what they pretend to be. I show people always searching for something else and sometimes being very unhappy with what they are—this search of identity which seems to be one of the traumas of this society.''

In 1978 Malle directed another chronicle of adolescence, "Pretty Baby." In the film, a twelve-year-old prostitute matures during a brief marriage with a French photographer. Malle called the picture, set in New Orleans circa 1917, a "totally immoral situation." He added: "I think that in most of my films the central character is someone who stands at the brink of corruption. It's the moment when you realize that in order to become an adult you have to accept corruption and become a part of it. And that's the moment when you're very strong and very disturbing because you're telling the truth.''

Aside from an unpredictability of style, the notion of maturation-as-corruption is perhaps the only consistency in Malle's work. He contends that "in this disordered and decadent period in which we live it's fascinating to watch people who are coming of age having to deal with this world of hypocrisy and preconceived values and having nothing to do with any of it. . . . If there's anything moral in my pictures, you have to find it in the close-ups of those children . . . looking at you. That's where it is, there's nothing else.''

BIOGRAPHICAL/CRITICAL SOURCES: Newsday, March 10, 1960; *New York Times*, October 18, 1971, February 6, 1972, October 8, 1972; *New Yorker*, October 23, 1971, September 30, 1974; *Saturday Review/World*, October 19, 1974; *New York Post*, October 28, 1975; *Ms.*, April, 1978; *Rolling Stone*, April 6, 1978; *Film Comment*, May, 1978; *Film Quarterly*, summer, 1978.

—*Sketch by Les Stone*

* * *

MALLORY, Walter Hampton 1892-1980

OBITUARY NOTICE—See index for *CA* sketch: Born July 27, 1892, in Newburgh, N.Y.; died of a heart attack, June 17, 1980, in Dunkirk, N.Y. Administrator, editor, and author. Mallory, an expert on China and the Far East, served as executive director of the Council on Foreign Relations for more than thirty years. He lived for several years in China and also served with the International Famine Relief Commission there. Mallory wrote an authoritative book on that country entitled *China: Land of Famine*. He also edited the Council on Foreign Relation's publication *Political Handbook of the World*. Obituaries and other sources: *New York Times*, June 18, 1980; *AB Bookman's Weekly*, August 11, 1980.

* * *

MANDELBAUM, Michael 1946-

PERSONAL: Born September 23, 1946, in Oakland, Calif.; son of David G. (a professor) and Ruth W. (an educator) Mandelbaum; married Anne Hebald (a writer), December 19, 1976. *Education:* Yale University, B.A., 1968; King's College, Cambridge, M.A., 1970; Harvard University, Ph.D., 1974. *Religion:* Jewish. *Office:* Department of Government, Harvard University, Cambridge, Mass. 02138.

CAREER: Harvard University, Cambridge, Mass., assistant professor, 1974-78, associate professor of government, 1978—.

WRITINGS: (With David C. Gompert, Richard L. Garwin, and John H. Barton) *Nuclear Weapons and World Politics: Alternatives for the Future*, McGraw, 1977; *The Nuclear Question: The United States and Nuclear Weapons, 1946-*

1976, Cambridge University Press, 1979; *The Nuclear Revolution: International Politics Before and After Hiroshima*, Cambridge University Press, 1981.

WORK IN PROGRESS: The Security Problem: National Experiences in the Twentieth Century.

* * *

MANDELL, Arnold Joseph 1934-

PERSONAL: Born July 21, 1934, in Chicago, Ill.; son of Allen and Rose (Sugarman) Mandell; children: Donnan Avery, Ross Benjamin. *Education:* Stanford University, B.A., 1954; Tulane University, M.D., 1958. *Office:* Department of Psychiatry, University of California, San Diego, La Jolla, Calif. 92093.

CAREER: Tulane University School of Medicine, New Orleans, La., teaching and research assistant in neurophysiology, 1955-59; Ochsner Foundation Hospital, New Orleans, intern, 1958-59; University of California, Los Angeles, resident in psychiatry, 1959-62, chief resident, 1962-63, assistant professor, 1963-66, associate professor of psychiatry, 1966-68; University of California, Irvine, associate professor of psychiatry, 1968-69; University of California, San Diego, professor of psychiatry, 1969—, founding chairman of department, 1969-74, co-chairman, 1975-77, director of neuropsychobiology research training program, 1979—. Member of board of directors of National Training Laboratories, 1969-72. Member of National Society for Autism Scientific Advisory Committee, 1966-71, National Science Policy Committee, 1969-71, Israeli Center for Psychobiology International Advisory Board, 1973—, Jerusalem Mental Health Center Professional Advisory Board, 1973—, and National Research Council Commission on Human Resources, 1974—. Consultant to numerous institutions and organizations, including Peace Corps Training Program, 1961-63, National Institute of Mental Health Laboratory of Clinical Science, 1968, 1970, San Diego Chargers football team, 1971-73, President's Special Action Office for Drug Abuse Prevention, 1970-73, National Commission on Marijuana and Drug Abuse, 1970-73, Veteran's Administration Narcotic Abuse Program, 1972, and Fine Arts Museums of San Francisco, 1977-79.

MEMBER: American Academy of Psychoanalysis (scientific associate), American Association for the Advancement of Science (fellow), American College of Neuropsychopharmacology (fellow), American College of Psychiatrists (fellow), American Psychiatric Association (fellow), American Psychopathological Association, American Psychosomatic Society, Association for Academic Psychiatry, Association of American Professors of Psychiatry, Psychiatric Research Society, Society of Biological Psychiatry (president, 1976-77), Society for the Neurosciences, Society for the Psychophysiological Study of Sleep, Southern California Psychiatric Society, Phi Beta Kappa, Alpha Omega Alpha, Sigma Xi.

AWARDS, HONORS: March of Dimes research fellow, 1956; grants from California Department of Mental Hygiene, 1961-64, 1963-64, 1964-66, National Institute of Mental Health, 1963-65, 1968-76, 1979—, National Aeronautics and Space Administration, 1964-67, and National Institute on Drug Abuse, 1970-76, 1972—; National Institute of Mental Health Career Teacher Award, 1963-65; Pushcart Prize from Pushcart Press, 1976, for "Is Don Juan Alive and Well?''; Johananoff International Fellow, Mario Negri Institute (Milan, Italy), 1976-77; American Psychiatric Association Foundation Fund Prize, 1979, for research in psychiatry.

WRITINGS: (Editor with Mary P. Mandell, and contributor) *Methods and Theory in Psychochemical Research in Man*, Academic Press, 1969; (editor and contributor) *New Concepts in Neurotransmitter Regulation*, Plenum, 1973; (editor and contributor) *Neurobiological Mechanisms of Adaptation and Behavior*, Raven, 1975; *The Nightmare Season*, Random House, 1976; (editor with Earl Usdin) *The Biochemistry of Mental Disorders*, M. Dekker, 1978; *Coming of Middle Age: A Journey*, Simon & Schuster, 1978.

Contributor: C. W. Wahl, editor, *New Dimensions in Psychosomatic Medicine*, Little, Brown, 1964; (with L. J. West) Freedman and Kaplan, editors, *Comprehensive Textbook of Psychiatry*, Williams & Wilkins, 1966; Wahl, editor, *Sexual Problems in Medical Practice*, Free Press, 1967; (with R. T. Rubin) P. Crandall and R. Walter, editors, *Brain Stimulation*, Harvard University Press, 1967; J. Marmor, editor, *Modern Psychoanalysis*, Basic Books, 1968; (with C. E. Spooner) D. Sankar, editor, *Schizophrenia: Current Concepts and Research*, PJD Publications, 1969.

J. Masserman, editor, *Science and Psychoanalysis*, Volume XVII, Grune & Stratton, 1970; *Biochemistry of Brain and Behavior*, Plenum, 1970; (with S. Knapp) E. Ellinwood and S. Cohen, editors, *Current Research on Amphetamine and Behavior*, U.S. Government Printing Office, 1970; P. Blachly, editor, *Progress in Drug Abuse*, Thomas, 1972; (with M. Karno) Masserman, editor, *Science and Psychoanalysis*, Volume XXI: *Research and Relevance*, Grune & Stratton, 1972; (with D. S. Segal) J. Mendels, editor, *Biological Psychiatry*, Wiley, 1973; (with Knapp) J. Barchas and E. Usdin, editors, *Serotonin and Behavior*, Academic Press, 1973; *Drug Use in America: Problem in Perspective*, U.S. Government Printing Office, 1973; (with Knapp) Usdin, editor, *Neuropsychopharmacology of Monoamines and Their Regulatory Enzymes*, Raven, 1974.

(With M. A. Geyer) Freedman, Kaplan, and Sadock, editors, *The Comprehensive Textbook of Psychiatry II*, Williams & Wilkins, 1975; Usdin, editor, *Biological Schizophrenia*, Brunner/Mazel, 1975; S. Ariete, D. Hamburg, and H. Brodie, editors, *The American Handbook of Psychiatry*, Volume VI: *New Psychiatric Frontiers*, 2nd edition, Basic Books, 1975; (with Segal) Anthony and Benedek, editors, *Depression and the Human Existence*, Little, Brown, 1975; (with Geyer) R. Grenell and S. Gabay, editors, *Biological Foundations of Psychiatry*, Raven, 1976; E. Schopler and R. J. Reichler, editors, *Psychopathology and Child Development*, Plenum, 1976; D. Flinn and L. J. West, editors, *Treatment of Schizophrenia: Progress and Prospects*, Grune & Stratton, 1976; E. D. Wittkower and H. Warnes, editors, *Psychosomatic Medicine: Its Clinical Applications*, Harper, 1977; (with Knapp) E. H. Ellinwood, editor, *Cocaine and Other Stimulants*, Plenum, 1977; E. S. Gershon and others, editors, *The Impact of Biology on Modern Psychiatry*, Plenum, 1976; (with Knapp) W. S. Fields, editor, *Neurotransmitter Function: Basic and Clinical Aspects*, Symposia Specialists, 1977.

(With Geyer) R. Willette and R. Stillman, editors, *Psychopharmacology of Hallucinogens*, Pergamon, 1978; (with Knapp) B. Haber and M. Aprison, editors, *Neuropharmacology and Behavior*, Plenum, 1978; (with Knapp) M. Lipton, A. DiMascio, and K. Killam, editors, *Psychopharmacology: A Generation of Progress*, Raven, 1978; K. Berrin, editor, *Art of the Huichol Indians*, Abrams, 1978; (with Knapp) D. K. Goodwin and C. K. Erickson, editors, *Alcoholism and Affective Disorders*, Spectrum, 1979; J. M. Davidson and R. J. Davidson, editors, *The Psychobiology of*

Consciousness, Plenum, 1980; Cohen and S. Krippner, editors, *LSD Revisited*, Unity Press, 1980.

Member of editorial board of *Psychiatric Research Reports*, 1966-68, *Journal of Biological Psychiatry*, 1968—, *Sleep Reviews*, 1971—, *Behavioral Biology*, 1971—, *Pharmacology, Biochemistry, and Behavior*, 1972—, *Addictive Disease: An International Journal*, 1973—, *Clinical Psychiatry News*, 1973—, *Journal of Neuroscience Research*, 1974—, and *Psychopharmacology Communications*, 1974—.

*   *   *

MANDER, Raymond (Josiah Gale)

PERSONAL: Son of Albert Edwin and Edith Christina (Gale) Mander. *Education:* Attended grammar school in London, England. *Home:* Five Venner Rd., Sydenham, London SE26 5EQ, England. *Office:* Raymond Mander and Joe Mitchenson Theatre Collection Ltd., One Duke St., Manchester Sq., London W.1, England.

CAREER: Professional actor in repertory, on tour, and in London, England, 1934-46; Raymond Mander and Joe Mitchenson Theatre Collection Ltd., London, founder and co-chairman, 1946-77, co-director, 1977—. Guest on television programs. Honorary archivist of Sadler's Wells and Old Vic.

WRITINGS—All with Joe Mitchenson, except as noted: *Hamlet Through the Ages*, Rockliff, 1952, 2nd edition, 1955; *Theatrical Companion to Shaw*, Rockliff, 1954; *Theatrical Companion to Maugham*, Rockliff, 1955; *The Artist and the Theatre*, Heinemann, 1955; *Theatrical Companion to Coward*, Rockliff, 1957; *A Picture History of British Theatre*, Hulton, 1957; (with Mitchenson and J. C. Trewin) *The Gay Twenties*, Macdonald, 1958; (with Mitchenson and Philip Hope-Wallace) *A Picture History of Opera*, Hulton, 1959.

(With Mitchenson and J. C. Trewin) *The Turbulent Thirties*, Macdonald, 1960; *Theatres of London*, Hart-Davis, 1961, 3rd edition, New English Library, 1975; *A Picture History of Gilbert and Sullivan*, Vista, 1962; *British Music Hall: A Story in Pictures*, Vista, 1965, revised edition, 1974; *Lost Theatres of London*, Hart-Davis, 1968, 2nd edition, New English Library, 1976; *Musical Comedy: A Story in Pictures*, P. Davies, 1969.

Revue: A Story in Pictures, P. Davies, 1971; *Pantomime: A Story in Pictures*, P. Davies, 1973; *The Wagner Companion*, L. H. Allen, 1977; *Victorian and Edwardian Entertainments From Old Photographs*, Batsford, 1978; *A Guide to the Somerset Maugham Theatrical Paintings at the National Theatre*, Heinemann, 1980. Contributor to *Encyclopaedia Britannica*. Contributor to *Theatre Notebook* and *Books and Bookmen*.

SIDELIGHTS: Raymond Mander and Joe Mitchenson began their partnership in 1939. During World War II they worked together on theatre gramophone programs for British Broadcasting Corp. (BBC), and they went on tour in 1943.

The Raymond Mander and Joe Mitchenson Theatre Collection, which they owned until 1977, has since been made into a trust and registered as a charity. Mander and Mitchenson remain directors of the collection, and also work as theatrical consultants.

In 1977, the collection was the largest comprehensive theatrical collection in private hands. Now housed in the Lewisham borough of London, it consists of printed and sound archives, library, manuscripts, paintings, costumes, and theatrical memorabilia, as well as thousands of plays, both printed and in manuscript form, photographs, programs, and gramophone records.

The collection, covering most branches of live entertainment, is used by writers, researchers, television and radio producers, theatre managers and directors, and film directors and designers. Its educational value has become more apparent with recent increased interest in theatre history in schools and universities. It has provided exhibitions and loans all over the world, including the United States, Australia, and the Soviet Union.

AVOCATIONAL INTERESTS: Attending the theatre, gardening.

BIOGRAPHICAL/CRITICAL SOURCES: Stage, May 25, 1978.

*   *   *

MANG, Karl 1922-

PERSONAL: Born October 5, 1922, in Vienna, Austria; son of Franz and Karoline (Schmekal) Mang; married Eva Frimmel (an architect), June 1, 1957; children: Brigitte, Carolina, Johanna. *Education:* Technical University, Arch. Dipl.-Ing. (cum laude), 1948; graduate study at University of Rome, 1950-51. *Religion:* Roman Catholic. *Home:* Baumannstrasse 9, A-1030 Vienna, Austria.

CAREER: Independent architect in Vienna, Austria, 1955—. Member of faculty at Federal Trade School, Moedling, Austria, 1954-59; lecturer at Academy of Applied Art, 1963-72. *Military service:* German Army, 1941-45. *Member:* Austrian Institute of Design (president, 1972—), Kunstlerhaus Wien. *Awards, honors:* About thirty architecture prizes, including certificate of excellence from Communications Collaborative, 1975, award from Chicago Book Clinic, 1975, and three other awards for exhibition and catalog, "The Shaker."

WRITINGS—In English: *Geschichte des modernen Moebels,* Hatje, 1978, translation by John Gabriel published as *History of Modern Furniture,* Academy Editions, 1979; *Wiener Architektur, 1860-1930, in Zeichnungen,* Hatje, 1979, translation by Patricia Norris published as *Viennese Architecture, 1860-1930, in Drawings,* Rizzoli International, 1979.

Other writings: *Neue Laeden* (title means "New Shops"), Hatje, 1981; *Das Haus Thonet* (title means "Pentwood Furniture by Michael Thonet"), Molden, 1981. Author of exhibition catalogs, including *Die Shaker* (title means "The Shaker"). Contributor to journals.

SIDELIGHTS: Mang commented: "Sometimes it is rather difficult to realize one's ideas merely by planning buildings. The diversity in architecture and urbanism compels opinions and attitudes that need a written expression in addition to drawings or blueprints. The great task of urbanism and architecture in the end of the twentieth century is not to create monuments, but rather the human environment of broad masses."

BIOGRAPHICAL/CRITICAL SOURCES: Bernd Loebach, *Industrial Design,* Verlag Karl Thiemig, 1976.

*   *   *

MANN, Marty 1904-1980

OBITUARY NOTICE: Born October 15, 1904, in Chicago, Ill.; died of a stroke, July 22, 1980, in Bridgeport, Conn. Writer, publicity director, and worker on behalf of alcoholics. Mann recovered from alcoholism in 1939 and five years later founded the National Council on Alcoholism. As part of her work as Council executive director she delivered nearly two hundred lectures per year, appeared before legislative committees, and served as consultant to various organizations, including the National Institute on Alcohol Abuse and Alcoholism. She also wrote *New Primer on Alcoholism* and *Marty Mann Answers Your Questions About Drinking and Alcoholism.* Obituaries and other sources: *Who's Who in America,* 41st edition, Marquis, 1980; *New York Times,* July 24, 1980.

*   *   *

MANN, Zane B. 1924-

PERSONAL: Born January 28, 1924, in St. Paul, Minn.; married Esther Zessman (a registered nurse), March 25, 1945; children: Michael, Eric. *Education:* Attended University of Minnesota. *Home:* 111 East Ramon Rd., No. 65, Palm Springs, Calif. 92262.

CAREER: Piper, Jaffrey & Hopwood (investment bankers), Minneapolis, Minn., vice-president, 1958-72; sailor and writer, 1972—. *Military service:* U.S. Army Air Forces, 1942-45; served in Pacific theater; received Distinguished Flying Cross, Air Medal, Purple Heart, and four battle stars. *Member:* Authors Guild, Writers Guild of America, West.

WRITINGS: Fair Winds and Far Places, Dillon, 1978. Contributor of numerous articles to sailing and travel magazines.

WORK IN PROGRESS: A book and several articles relating to worldwide travels on own yacht.

*   *   *

MANNING, Olivia 1915-1980

OBITUARY NOTICE—See index for *CA* sketch: Born in 1915 in Portsmouth, England; died July 23, 1980, in Isle of Wight, Great Britain. Author. Manning was best known for her "Balkan Trilogy," which reflected her experiences during World War II. She was appointed Commander of the Order of the British Empire in 1976. Manning's numerous works include *The Wind Changes, The Rain Forest, The Danger Tree,* and *The Battle Lost and Won.* Obituaries and other sources: *London Times,* July 24, 1980; *Publishers Weekly,* September 5, 1980; *AB Bookman's Weekly,* October 6, 1980.

*   *   *

MARKOOSIE
See PATSAUQ, Markoosie

*   *   *

MARKS, Margaret L. 1911(?)-1980

OBITUARY NOTICE: Born c. 1911 in London, England; died of cancer, June 30, 1980, in Leesburg, Va. Painter, translator, and teacher. Marks exhibited her art in Virginia and in New York, N.Y., where she held a show at the Ward-Nasse Gallery in 1980. She also translated foreign folk song lyrics into English, many of which were published in children's song books by Time, Inc. Obituaries and other sources: *Washington Post,* July 1, 1980.

*   *   *

MARS, Florence L. 1923-

PERSONAL: Born January 1, 1923, in Philadelphia, Miss.; daughter of Adam L. and Geneva J. Mars. *Education:* Attended Millsaps College, 1940-42, and University of Mississippi, 1942-44. *Religion:* Methodist. *Home:* 518 Poplar Ave., Philadelphia, Miss. 39350.

CAREER: Photographer in Mississippi, 1954-67, and Louisiana, 1959-62; raised cattle in Neshoba County, Miss., 1949-65.

WRITINGS: Witness in Philadelphia (historical documentary), Louisiana State University Press, 1977.

SIDELIGHTS: Mars told *CA* that her first book, *Witness in Philadelphia,* "tells the inside story by a fourth generation native of the murder of three civil rights workers in 1964 by the Ku Klux Klan. It tells what really happened in a small Southern town when the civil rights movement assaulted its treasured traditions."

*   *   *

MARSANO, Ramon
See DINGES, John (Charles)

*   *   *

MARSTON, Hope Irvin   1935-

PERSONAL: Born January 31, 1935, in Fishing Creek (now Mill Hall), Pa.; daughter of Charles James (a farmer) and Orpha (Harber) Irvin; married Arthur Wakefield Marston, Jr. (an artificial inseminator), August 28, 1961. *Education:* Milligan College, B.A., 1956; State University of New York College at Geneseo, M.A., 1972. *Politics:* Republican. *Religion:* Christian and Missionary Alliance. *Home and office address:* R.F.D. 1, Box 362, Black River, N.Y. 13612.

CAREER: Junior and senior high school teacher of science, English, and social studies in Aberdeen, Md., 1956-61; high school teacher of English and Spanish in Buckfield, Maine, 1962-67; Case Junior High School, Watertown, N.Y., teacher of English, 1967-70, librarian, 1970—. *Member:* American Federation of Teachers, American Library Association, New York State United Teachers, New York Library Association, Delta Kappa Gamma.

WRITINGS: Trucks, Trucking, and You (juvenile), Dodd, 1978; *Big Rigs* (juvenile; Junior Literary Guild selection), Dodd, 1980. Contributor to *Yankee, Grit,* and religious journals.

WORK IN PROGRESS: Juvenile nonfiction, publication by Dodd expected in 1981; an adult devotional book for dog lovers, publication expected in 1981.

SIDELIGHTS: Hope Marston commented: "I am positive that God loves me and has a plan for my life. That plan is perfect for me. My personal goal is to find and fit into it. God has given me some writing ability. I want to develop that talent so that it will reflect honor to the Giver. The way my first books were received shows me God is blessing my efforts. It also encourages me to continue writing, but I never write without first taking time to pray for wisdom to say what I want to say in a manner that the Lord will ultimately receive the credit for any talent that my work might demonstrate."

*   *   *

MARTIN, Albert
See MEHAN, Joseph Albert

*   *   *

MARTIN, Don   1931-

PERSONAL: Born May 18, 1931, in Passaic, N.J.; son of W. Laurence (in sales) and Helen (Husselrath) Martin; married Rosemary Troetschel, December 14, 1956 (divorced January, 1976); married Norma Haimes (a librarian, sculptress, and writer), August 23, 1979; children: (first marriage) Max. *Education:* Attended Newark School of Fine and Industrial Art and Pennsylvania Academy of Fine Art. *Politics:* Democrat. *Religion:* "Wasp." *Residence:* Miami, Fla. *Office: Mad,* 485 Madison Ave., New York, N.Y. 10022.

CAREER: Artist at advertising art studios in New York City, 1954-56; *Mad* (magazine), New York City, cartoonist, 1956—.

WRITINGS—Cartoon books: (With E. Solomon Rosenblum) *Don Martin Steps Out,* New American Library, 1962; (with Rosenblum) *Don Martin Bounces Back,* New American Library, 1963; (with Rosenblum) *Don Martin Drops Thirteen Stories,* New American Library, 1965; (with Dick DeBartolo, Phil Hahn, and Jack Hanrahan) *The Mad Adventures of Captain Klutz,* edited by Nick Meglin, New American Library, 1967; (with DeBartolo) *Mad's Don Martin Cooks Up More Tales,* New American Library, 1969.

(With Dick DeBartolo) *Mad's Don Martin Comes on Strong,* edited by Nick Meglin, New American Library, 1971; (with DeBartolo and Frank Jacobs) *Mad's Don Martin Carries On,* edited by Meglin, Warner Paperback, 1973; *The Completely Mad Don Martin* (reprints from *Mad*), Warner Paperback, 1974; (with DeBartolo) *Don Martin Steps Further Out,* edited by Meglin, Warner Paperback, 1975; *Don Martin Forges Ahead,* edited by Meglin, Warner Paperback, 1977; (with DeBartolo, Edwing, Jacobs, and John Gibbons) *Mad's Don Martin Digs Deeper,* edited by Meglin, Warner Paperback, 1979; *Don Martin Grinds Ahead,* Warner Paperback, 1981.

SIDELIGHTS: Don Martin told *CA:* "My style of drawing was born out of the necessity to be comical. I wanted to draw a funny picture. My ideas and gags also stem from this need. If any commentary is noted in my cartoons, it is by accident."

*   *   *

MARTIN, Francis
See REID, Charles (Stuart)

*   *   *

MARTIN, Ian Kennedy
See KENNEDY-MARTIN, Ian

*   *   *

MARTIN, Lucien
See GABEL, Joseph

*   *   *

MARTINEZ, Julio A(ntonio)   1931-

PERSONAL: Born October 4, 1931, in Santiago, Cuba; came to the United States in 1958, naturalized citizen, 1968; son of Julio Martinez and Maria M. (Gandara) Garcia. *Education:* Southern Illinois University, B.A., 1963; University of Michigan, M.A.L.S., 1967; University of Minnesota, M.A., 1970; University of California, Riverside, Ph.D., 1980. *Office:* 324-A Love Library, San Diego State University, San Diego, Calif. 92182.

CAREER: San Diego State University, San Diego, Calif., assistant librarian, 1973-76, senior assistant librarian, 1976-80, adjunct professor of Mexican-American studies, 1979—, associate librarian, 1980—. *Member:* American Library Association (member of executive council), National Librarians Association (member of executive board; chairman of professional welfare committee), Society for Iberian and Latin American Thought, Society of Interdisciplinary Latin American Thought, Reforma, Southern California Consortium for International Studies, Border State University Consortium for Latin America.

WRITINGS: *A Bibliography of Writings on Plato, 1900-1967,* Library, San Diego State University, 1978; (editor) *A Bio-Bibliographical Directory of Chicano Scholars and Writers,* Scarecrow, 1979. Contributor to journals. Associate editor of *Cognition and Brain Theory.*

WORK IN PROGRESS: With Francisco A. Lomeli, *Cyclopedia of Chicano Literature,* for Campanile Press; *Philosophical Humor: An Anthology;* an article, "The Kantian Thing in Itself and the Noumenon Revisited."

SIDELIGHTS: Martinez wrote: "As a professionally-trained philosopher, my interests lie in the philosophy of mind, or what is commonly known in philosophical circles as the mind-body problem. I am also passionately interested in the philosophy of politics, with emphasis on the concepts of justice and right.

"My avocation is Chicano literature, a field to which I have devoted considerable attention, as well as the field of Chicano studies in general. My research, as a subject specialist for my library, has been concentrated on the preparation of research tools that may aid the Chicano college student to know better his culture and traditions."

*   *   *

MARX, Jenifer (Grant) 1940-

PERSONAL: Born May 1, 1940, in Mount Kisco, N.Y.; daughter of George E. and Marjorie D. (Scribner) Grant; married Robert F. Marx (an underwater archaeologist and writer), 1970; children: India, Hilary. *Education:* Mount Holyoke College, B.A., 1961. *Religion:* Episcopalian. *Home and office:* 330 Thyme St., Satellite Beach, Fla. 32937.

CAREER: U.S. Peace Corps, Washington, D.C., volunteer in Philippines, 1961-63; volunteer worker with United Nations in Lesotho, South Africa, 1963, Jamaica, 1966-68, and Indonesia, 1968-70; writer and amateur marine archaeologist, 1970—. Member of Brevard County Community Services Council, board of trustees of Brevard Art Museum, and Brevard Community College Advisory Council on the Humanities; member of Junior League of South Brevard. *Member:* American Association of University Women.

WRITINGS: *The Magic of Gold,* Doubleday, 1978; *Predators and Prey: Pirates, Buccaneers, and Privateers of the Spanish Main,* Van Nostrand, 1981. Contributor to magazines, including *Oceans,* and to *Collier Encyclopaedia Year Book,* 1980.

*   *   *

MAVIN, John
See RICKWORD, (John) Edgell

*   *   *

MAYER, Harry F(rederick) 1912-

PERSONAL: Born January 19, 1912, in Indianapolis, Ind.; son of Frederick William (a physician) and Margaret (Welch) Mayer; married Mary Insley, November 29, 1933; children: Ann M., Frederick (deceased). *Education:* Purdue University, B.S.E.E., 1932, M.S.E.E., 1933. *Politics:* Republican. *Residence:* Skaneateles, N.Y. *Office:* Department of Science, Cayuga Community College, Franklin St., Auburn, N.Y. 13021.

CAREER: General Electric Co., engineer in Schenectady, N.Y., 1933-45, engineering manager and designing engineer in Syracuse, N.Y., 1945-52, advanced engineering manager in Utica, N.Y., 1952-58, manager of advanced electronics

center in Ithaca, N.Y., 1958-64, manager of electronics laboratory in Syracuse, 1964-77; Cayuga Community College, Auburn, N.Y., associate professor of electronics, 1977—. Part-time instructor in mathematics at Tompkins-Cortland Community College, Dryden, N.Y., 1970. Chairman of airborne radar fire control subpanel of National Military Establishment research and development board, 1949-53; consultant to technical advisory panel on electronics and member of committee on AI radar, 1955-58; chairman of Rome-Utica section of Institute of Radio Engineers, 1955; member of executive committee of Radio Technical Commission for Aeronautics, 1955-59. Member of board of directors of First National Bank of Ithaca, 1962-64. Member of board of directors of Tompkins County United Fund, 1958-64 (president, 1961-63), Ithaca Chamber of Commerce, 1963, and Onondaga County Community Chest, 1965-71 (member of Urban Crisis Committee, 1968-73). President of Baldwinsville Theatre Guild, 1949, and Utica Players, 1956. *Member:* Institute of Electrical and Electronic Engineers (fellow), General Electric Engineers Association, Tau Beta Pi, Eta Kappa Nu. *Awards, honors:* Navy citation for technical contributions, 1945.

WRITINGS: (With daughter, Ann M. Mayer) *Who's Out There? UFO Encounters* (juvenile), Messner, 1979. Contributor of articles to publications including *Electrical Engineering, Electronics,* and *General Electric Review.*

SIDELIGHTS: Mayer told *CA:* "*Who's Out There? UFO Encounters* aims to satisfy the fascination that many youngsters feel for outer space and its mysteries, but at the same time it aims to teach them to think critically not to accept everything they see in print or on TV as necessarily true. The book relates eight well-documented incidents, all with witnesses having good credentials. Three of the incidents were well 'debunked' by objective investigators. The balance stand as unexplained—unexplained, in my opinion, only because no one could afford the cost of a real investigation within a reasonable time after the incident.

"The book does not take a position and I think (I hope) it appears unbiased to a naive reader. The anti-UFO bias is evident to a more sophisticated reader.

"The book was suggested by my daughter, Ann, then a librarian in an elementary school. She said there was a demand from the children for such a book, and proposed that we co-author it. We did. It was fun.

"I used to be inclined to believe in UFO's, until my friend Phillip Klass produced the first of his debunking books, converting me to a firm nonbeliever. I also used to be sold on ESP—actually spent many hours on experiments—only to have that faith demolished by C.E.M. Hansel (*ESP: A Scientific Evaluation*).

"One by one my illusions are destroyed."

Among the eighteen Mayer inventions that have been patented, the most important, he says, is the dual channel oscilloscope.

*   *   *

MAYERSON, Evelyn Wilde 1935-

PERSONAL: Born January 12, 1935, in New York, N.Y.; daughter of Arthur C. and Charlotte (Goodman) Wilde; married Don A. Mayerson (an attorney), June 17, 1953; children: Gary, Robert. *Education:* University of Miami, Coral Gables, Fla., B.A., 1963; Goddard College, M.A., 1973; Laurence University of California, Ed.D., 1975. *Home:* One Grove Isle, No. 702, Coconut Grove, Fla. 33133. *Agent:*

Maryanne C. Colas, Cantrell-Colas, Inc., 229 East 79th St., New York, N.Y. 10021. *Office:* Department of English, University of Miami, Coral Gables, Fla. 33124.

CAREER: Temple University, Philadelphia, Pa., assistant professor of psychiatry, 1971-77; University of South Florida, Tampa, assistant professor of psychiatry, 1977-78; University of Miami, Coral Gables, Fla., currently assistant professor of English. Member of board of directors of North Miami Beach Public Library, 1962-63; consultant to U.S. Department of Commerce and U.S. Civil Service Commission.

WRITINGS: Putting the Ill at Ease, Harper, 1976; *Shoptalk,* Saunders, 1979; *Sanjo,* Lippincott, 1979; *If Birds Are Free,* Lippincott, 1980. Author of "Introduction to Psychiatry" (video cassette series), Lippincott, 1975.

*   *   *

MAYNE, Seymour 1944-

PERSONAL: Born May 18, 1944, in Montreal, Quebec, Canada. *Education:* McGill University, B.A. (with honors), 1965; University of British Columbia, M.A., 1966, Ph.D., 1972. *Office:* Department of English, University of Ottawa, Ottawa, Ontario, Canada K1N 6N5.

CAREER: Poet. Jewish Institute, Montreal, Quebec, lecturer in Jewish Canadian literature, 1964; University of British Columbia, Vancouver, lecturer in English, 1972; University of Ottawa, Ottawa, Ontario, assistant professor, 1973-78, associate professor of English, 1978—. *Awards, honors:* Canada Council arts grants, 1969, 1973, 1977, and 1979; Ontario Arts Council grants, 1974 and 1976; J. I. Segal Prize in English-French Literature, 1974, and York Poetry Workshop Award, 1975, both for *Name.*

WRITINGS—Poetry: That Monocycle the Moon, Catapult, 1964; *Tiptoeing on the Mount,* McGill University Press, 1965, 2nd revised edition, Catapult, 1965; *From the Portals of Mouseholes,* Very Stone House, 1966; *Touches,* University of British Columbia, 1966; *I Am Still the Boy* (broadside), Western Press, 1967; *ticklish ticlicorice* (broadside), Very Stone House, 1969; *the gigolo teaspoon* (broadside), Very Stone House, 1969; *earseed* (broadside), Very Stone House, 1969; *Anewd,* Very Stone House, 1969; *Mutetations,* Very Stone House, 1969; *Manimals* (poems and prose), Very Stone House, 1969; *Mouth,* Quarry Press, 1970; *For Stems of Light,* Very Stone House, 1971, revised edition, Mosaic Press Valley Editions, 1974; *Face,* Blackfish, 1971; *Name,* Press Porcepic, 1975, 2nd edition, Mosaic Press/Valley Editions, 1976; *Diasporas,* Mosaic Press/Valley Editions, 1977; *Begging* (broadside), Valley Editions, 1977; *Racoon* (broadside), Valley Editions, 1979; *Abel and Cain* (broadside), Sifrei Haemek, 1980; *The Impossible Promised Land: Poems Selected and New,* Mosaic Press/Valley Editions, 1981.

Editor: (With Patrick Lane) *Collected Poems of Red Lane,* Very Stone House, 1968; (with Dorothy Livesay) *Forty Women Poets of Canada,* Ingluvin Publications, 1971; *Engagements: The Prose of Irving Layton,* McClelland & Stewart, 1972; *Cutting the Keys,* Mosaic Press/Valley Editions, 1974; *The A. M. Klein Symposium,* University of Ottawa Press, 1975; *Splices,* Mosaic Press/Valley Editions, 1975; *Choice Parts,* Mosaic Press/Valley Editions, 1976; *Irving Layton: The Poet and His Critics,* McGraw, 1978.

Translator: (With Catherine Leach) Jerzy Harasymowicz, *The Genealogy of Instruments,* Valley Editions, 1974.

Work represented in anthologies, including: *The Penguin*

Book of Canadian Verse, edited by Ralph Gustafson, Penguin Books, 1975; *Voices Within the Ark: Modern Jewish Poets,* edited by Anthony Rudolf and Howard Schwartz, Avon, 1979; *Aurora: New Canadian Writing 1979,* edited by Morris Wolfe, Doubleday, 1979.

Co-editor of *Cataract,* 1961-62; poetry editor of *Forge,* 1961-62, and *Ingluvin,* 1970-71; editor of *Catapult,* 1964, Ingluvin Publications, 1970-73, *Jewish Dialog,* 1974—, and *Stoney Monday,* 1978—; managing editor of Very Stone House, 1966-69. Contributor of poetry and prose to journals, including *Canadian Forum, Prism International, West Review, Fiddlehead,* and *Jewish Dialog.*

SIDELIGHTS: Seymour Mayne's poetry is chiefly concerned with sex and death. Although his early verse celebrated love and sex, beginning with *From the Portals of Mouseholes* a new tone is present in his writings. In a review of *From the Portals of Mouseholes,* Peter Stevens commented: "Love and sexual enjoyment do not seem as much now; there are still poems dealing with these subjects in the book but generally they appear to be much more knowing than the ones in his [Mayne's] previous volumes. There is a consciousness of more permanent depth and chasms in personal relationships." This new consciousness is also evident in *Mouth.* As Joseph Pivato pointed out, the themes of *Mouth* are "the loss of virginity and love-making. But to these rather hackneyed themes the poet has brought his craftsmanship, the added perspective of painful separations, sickness and death, and has thus saved the book from being simply titillating juvenilia."

Diasporas, Mayne's most recent book of poetry, reveals a keen awareness of separation and death. After reading *Diasporas,* Kenneth Sherman asserted: "Mayne at his best is the poet of lamentations—conjuring up verse to beat back the Angel of Death. . . . [he] has the uncanny ability to capture the essential, singular qualities of the departed and to render that humanness in vivid and sympathetic terms, making the reader forcefully aware of the loss."

Although Mayne is not known as an experimental poet, his style has elicited favorable responses from critics. Sherman wrote admiringly of Mayne's "erudite playfulness with words," while Stevens praised Mayne's "witty tone" and "neat and precise" language. Allen Barry Cameron discerned a "sense of finish and unity" and "verbal power" in Mayne's poetry.

Mayne wrote:

> "Do not concede
> the demonic madman
> posthumous victory
>
> Nor capitulate
> with no progeny
>
> Pass on those eyes
> Others will hold your words
> and know your voice
> reaching always
> for kindred ears."

Mayne's poetry and criticism have been broadcast on such Canadian Broadcasting Corp. (CBC-Radio) programs as "New Canadian Writing," "Anthology," "Critics on Air," and "The Arts in Review."

BIOGRAPHICAL/CRITICAL SOURCES: Canadian Literature, spring, 1964, winter, 1968, spring, 1972, summer, 1975, spring, 1979; *Fiddlehead,* fall, 1964, spring, 1967; *Canadian Forum,* March, 1968, November-December, 1970; *Ottawa Citizen,* July 12, 1975, May 17, 1978, August 19, 1978; *En-*

glish *Quarterly VIII,* winter, 1975-1976; *Quill & Quire,* December, 1978; *Georgian,* February 6, 1979.

* * *

MAYS, Lucinda L(a Bella) 1924-

PERSONAL: Born June 16, 1924, in Latrobe, Pa.; daughter of Nick (a carpenter) and Angela (Palese) LaBella; married William E. Mays (a sales manager), December 14, 1943; children: William M., Richard, Robin. *Education:* Washington University, St. Louis, Mo., B.A., 1962, M.A., 1968. *Politics:* Independent. *Religion:* Protestant. *Home and office:* 940 Beaver Lane, Glenview, Ill. 60025. *Agent:* Dorothy Markinko, McIntosh & Otis, Inc., 475 Fifth Ave., New York, N.Y. 10017.

CAREER: Elementary school teacher in Creve Coeur, Mo., 1962-65; high school English teacher in Normandy, Mo., 1965-69; elementary school teacher in Glenview, Ill., 1969-72; Providence Day School, Charlotte, N.C., head of social studies department, 1973-75; writer, 1975—. Teacher at Columbia College, Chicago, Ill., spring, 1980. Board member of National Endowment for the Humanities, Italian-American oral history project at University of Illinois at Chicago Circle. *Member:* American-Italian Historical Society, League of Women Voters, Off-Campus Writers' Workshop. *Awards, honors:* Award for best juvenile book from Society of Midland Authors, 1980, for *The Other Shore.*

WRITINGS: The Other Shore (young adult), Atheneum, 1979.

WORK IN PROGRESS: The Candle and the Mirror, a companion to *The Other Shore,* on the feminist movement and labor activities at the turn of the century, publication expected in 1981.

SIDELIGHTS: Lucinda Mays wrote: "My interest in the great migration of the turn of the century began with a research project in college. Since the Italian-Americans I knew as a child were not like those depicted on television or in films, I decided another version was in order. *The Other Shore* is neither a whitewash nor an indictment, as many books about this ethnic group have been, but an honest and sincere attempt to explain why Italians coming to this country at the turn of the century acted as they did and are what they are.

"In my book, Gabriella's father is like my own, who—though he immigrated to Pennsylvania along with my grandfather—encountered many of the hardships of Pietro DeLuca in the book. During the first part of this century, at least a dozen labor activists of Italian ancestry devoted their lives to improving the labor and living conditions among the ethnic groups. Today they are unknown to all except labor historians. Several characters in both my books were inspired by these men and their activities.

"I enjoy writing and teaching young adults because I know and understand them and enjoy their curiosity, enthusiasm, energy, and sense of justice. They are the hope of the future."

AVOCATIONAL INTERESTS: Travel.

* * *

McALLISTER, Amanda
See HAGER, Jean

* * *

McCABE, James P(atrick) 1937-

PERSONAL: Born May 24, 1937, in Philadelphia, Pa.; son

of Felix and Josephine (Murtagh) McCabe. *Education:* Niagara University, B.A. (summa cum laude), 1964; University of Michigan, M.A., 1965, M.A.L.S., 1966, Ph.D., 1968. *Office:* Library, Allentown College, Center Valley, Pa. 18034.

CAREER: Entered Oblati Sancti Francisco Salesii (Oblate Fathers of St. Francis of Sales; O.S.F.S.), ordained Roman Catholic priest; high school teacher, 1963-65; Allentown College, Center Valley, Pa., librarian and library director, 1968—. Secretary and treasurer of Greater Lehigh Valley Library Council, 1973-74. *Member:* American Library Association, Catholic Library Association, Pennsylvania Library Association, Beta Phi Mu.

WRITINGS: Critical Guide to Catholic Reference Books, edited by B. S. Wynar, Libraries Unlimited, 1971, 2nd edition, 1979.

* * *

McCARDELL, John (Malcolm, Jr.) 1949-

PERSONAL: Born June 17, 1949, in Frederick, Md.; son of John Malcolm (a utility executive) and Susan (Lane) McCardell; married Bonnie Greenwald (a teacher), December 30, 1976. *Education:* Washington and Lee University, A.B., 1971; attended Johns Hopkins University, 1972-73; Harvard University, Ph.D., 1976. *Religion:* Episcopalian. *Home:* 35 Weybridge St., Middlebury, Vt. 05753. *Office:* Department of History, Middlebury College, Middlebury, Vt. 05753.

CAREER: Middlebury College, Middlebury, Vt., assistant professor of history, 1976—. *Military service:* U.S. Army Reserve, 1971-77. *Member:* American Historical Association, Organization of American Historians, Southern Historical Association, South Carolina Historical Society, Vermont Historical Society, Vermont Academy of Arts and Sciences. *Awards, honors:* Allan Nevins Prize from Society of American Historians, 1977, for *The Idea of a Southern Nation;* National Endowment for the Humanities fellowship, 1979.

WRITINGS: The Idea of a Southern Nation, Norton, 1979. Contributor to history journals.

WORK IN PROGRESS: A biography of William Gilmore Simms, nineteenth-century South Carolina writer, critic, editor, and "man of affairs."

* * *

McCLOSKEY, William B(ertine), Jr. 1928-

PERSONAL: Born November 17, 1928, in Baltimore, Md.; son of William B. (an accountant and corporate executive) and Evelyn (an artist; maiden name, Kamberger) McCloskey; married Ann Lyell (in social services), September 28, 1956; children: Karin, Wynn. *Education:* Attended Carnegie Institute of Technology (now Carnegie-Mellon University), 1945-47; Columbia University, B.S., 1951. *Residence:* Baltimore, Md. *Agent:* Thomas Lowry Associates, Inc., 156 West 86th St., New York, N.Y. 10024. *Office:* Applied Physics Laboratory, Johns Hopkins University, Laurel, Md. 20810.

CAREER: Merchant seaman, 1947-48; *Baltimore Sun,* Baltimore, Md., reporter, 1954-55; Black & Decker Manufacturing Co., Towson, Md., publicity representative, 1955-57; U.S. Information Agency, Washington, D.C., information officer in Washington, D.C., and Madras, India, 1957-58; Martin-Marietta Corp., in public relations, 1958-61; Johns Hopkins University, Applied Physics Laboratory, Laurel, Md., member of senior staff, 1961—. *Military service:* U.S.

Coast Guard, 1951-53; became lieutenant junior grade. *Member:* P.E.N., National Press Club, Authors League of America, Mensa, Charcoal Club of Baltimore.

WRITINGS: The Mallore Affair (novel), Bantam, 1966; *Highliners* (novel), McGraw, 1979. Contributor to magazines and newspapers, including *New York Times Magazine, Smithsonian, Oceans, Alaska, Fish Boat, National Fisherman, Boston Globe,* and *Baltimore Sun.*

WORK IN PROGRESS: "The subject will concern an aspect of seafaring."

SIDELIGHTS: McCloskey's first novel is about Americans in India. The second is about Alaskan fishermen.

McCloskey told *CA:* "My current writing concerns people who live by the sea. I have been sea-struck all my life and have been a seafarer myself whenever possible, but this has never ruled out a ready interest in most other intense forms of human endeavor. When a subject attracts me enough to write about it, I try whenever possible to become a participant as well as an observer. For example, during the three years of preparing for and writing *Highliners* I worked for several periods (vacations and leaves from my regular job) as a commercial fisherman and cannery hand in Alaska.

"My interests—all the subjects on which I have written, and in which I have participated in one way or another—include the sea, commercial fishing, Alaska, Newfoundland, India (at one time political, but now principally Hindu sculpture and classical dance), the Coast Guard, opera, forestry and logging, politics (especially involving the sea and the forests), and space technology."

Regarding *Highliners,* McCloskey wrote: "It is classified as a novel, since publishers must market under no choices more flexible than fiction and nonfiction. However, *Highliners* contains several chapters of straight author's commentary besides, a la *Moby Dick.* It is a form I find congenial to work in—it might be called documentary novel. For the moment, at least, it is my form: the one in which I can explore the emotions of my characters but also speak in my own voice."

BIOGRAPHICAL/CRITICAL SOURCES: Baltimore Sun, February 26, 1979; *Seattle Post Intelligencer,* November 4, 1979; *Seattle Times,* November 11, 1979; *Washington Star,* March 9, 1980; *Anchorage Daily News,* July 10, 1980.

*   *   *

McCOY, Lois Rich
See RICH-McCOY, Lois

*   *   *

McCRAW, James Edward 1943-

PERSONAL: Born January 23, 1943, in Philadelphia, Pa.; son of James Patrick (a U.S. Navy chief petty officer) and Elizabeth Caroline (Bird) McCraw; married Joan Schwarz (in advertising sales), November 8, 1975. *Education:* Temple University, B.S., 1966. *Residence:* Los Angeles, Calif. *Office:* 8490 Sunset Blvd., Los Angeles, Calif. 90069.

CAREER/WRITINGS: Distribution Age Magazine, Philadelphia, Pa., editorial assistant, 1961-62; *Product Design & Development* Magazine, Philadelphia, Pa., editor, 1966; *Super Stock & Drag Illustrated* Magazine, Alexandria, Va., associate editor, 1967-68, managing editor, 1968-69, editor, 1969-73; *Hot Rod* Magazine, Los Angeles, Calif., competition editor, 1973-74, editor, 1974-76, executive editor, 1976-78; *Motor Trend* Magazine, Los Angeles, feature editor, 1978, executive editor, 1979—. *Member:* Sigma Delta Chi.

Awards, honors: National Hot Rod Association media award, 1971, for outstanding coverage of drag racing events.

WORK IN PROGRESS: Researching development of future automotive and transportation trends, including mass transit, production automobiles, research vehicles, competition vehicles, and sports vehicles.

SIDELIGHTS: McCraw told *CA:* "There is a body of opinion in the literary community that indicates a disdain for the writing specialist, or the specialist writer, based on a supposed narrowness of mind or intellectual curiosity. I disagree vehemently, and I would urge any writer who begins to feel himself moving toward a career in a specialized area to first make sure that he has chosen his specialty correctly, and then plunge into that area with all possible energy and diligence. To become an 'expert' in any specialized field of writing is to insure that that special area of man's experience can never be overlooked or ignored by history."

*   *   *

McCRUM, Robert 1953-

PERSONAL: Born July 7, 1953, in Cambridge, England; son of Michael William (a professor) and Christine (a teacher; maiden name, fforde) McCrum; married Olivia Timbs (a journalist), September 8, 1979. *Education:* Cambridge University, degree (with honors), 1975; University of Pennsylvania, M.A., 1976. *Home:* 87 Honeybrook Rd., London S.W.12, England. *Agent:* John Farquharson Ltd., Bell House, 8 Bell Yard, London WC2A 2JU, England. *Office:* Faber & Faber Ltd., 3 Queen Sq., London WC1N 3AU, England.

CAREER: Associated with Chatto & Windus Ltd., London, England, 1976-79; Faber & Faber Ltd., London, commissioning editor, 1979—.

WRITINGS: In the Secret State (novel), Simon & Schuster, 1980.

WORK IN PROGRESS: A novel.

AVOCATIONAL INTERESTS: Travel.

*   *   *

McDONAGH, Enda 1930-

PERSONAL: Born June 27, 1930, in Ireland. *Education:* Received B.Sc. from National University of Ireland; Pontifical University of Maynooth, S.T.D., 1957; Gregorian and Angelicum Universities, Rome, Italy, L.Ph., 1958; University of Munich, D.C.L., 1960. *Politics:* "Irish." *Office:* Pontifical University of Maynooth, Maynooth, Ireland.

CAREER: Ordained Roman Catholic priest; Pontifical University of Maynooth, Maynooth, Ireland, professor of moral theology, 1960—, dean of faculty. Huisking Professor of Theology at University of Notre Dame, 1979-81; lecturer at schools and conferences in England, Europe, Africa, and North America; member of senate of National University of Ireland. Conducted field work in Zimbabwe. *Member:* Institute of Religion and Theology of Great Britain and Ireland (past vice-president), Irish Federation of University Teachers (past president). *Awards, honors:* Leverhulme fellowship for Cambridge University, 1978.

WRITINGS: Freedom or Tolerance: The Declaration on Religious Freedom of Vatican Council Two, Magi Books, 1967; *Doing the Truth,* Gill & Macmillan, 1979, University of Notre Dame Press, 1980; *Social Ethics and the Christian: Towards Freedom in Communion,* Rowman, 1979; *The Demands of Simple Justice: A Study in Church and Politics*

With Special Reference to Zimbabwe, Rhodesia, Gill & Macmillan, 1980. Also author of *Gift and Call*, 1975. Contributor to scholarly journals. Member of editorial board of *Irish Theological Quarterly*, *Concilium (Moral)*, and *Furrow*.

WORK IN PROGRESS: Creative Discipleship: Dimensions of Moral Theology.

SIDELIGHTS: McDonagh told *CA* that *The Demands of Simple Justice* resulted from his research on the relationships between the philosophical and theological bases of morality and between church and politics, particularly in Northern Ireland and Zimbabwe-Rhodesia. His major interests are fundamental moral theology, the history of church politics, and the relationship between church, politics, and morality.

*   *   *

McDONALD, (Mary) Lynn 1940-

PERSONAL: Born July 15, 1940, in New Westminster, British Columbia, Canada; daughter of Robert Stevenson and Mary Alice McDonald. *Education:* University of British Columbia, B.A., 1961; University of London, Ph.D., 1966. *Home and office:* 419 Carlton St., Toronto, Ontario, Canada M5A 2M3.

CAREER: McMaster University, Hamilton, Ontario, assistant professor of sociology, 1965-72; Dalhousie University, Halifax, Nova Scotia, professor of sociology, 1975-77. Research associate with Drug Inquiry Commission, 1971-72. President of National Action Committee on the Status of Women, 1979-80. *Member:* Canadian Sociology and Anthropology Association (member of executive committee, 1970-73), American Sociological Association.

WRITINGS: Social Class and Delinquency, Faber, 1969; *The Sociology of Law and Order*, Westview, 1975. Contributor to anthropology and sociology journals and *Canadian Forum*. Acting editor of *Canadian Review of Sociology and Anthropology*, 1970-71.

WORK IN PROGRESS: Methodology of Social Science.

*   *   *

McDONALD, Roger 1941-

PERSONAL: Born June 23, 1941, in Young, New South Wales, Australia; son of Hugh Fraser (a minister) and Lorna (a historian; maiden name, Bucknall) McDonald; married Rhyll McMaster (a writer), December 11, 1967; children: Elinor, Anna. *Education:* University of Sydney, B.A., 1962. *Home and office:* P.O. Box 338, Dickson, Australian Capital Territory, Australia 2602.

CAREER: High school teacher in Murrumburrah and Wellington, Australia, 1963-64; Educational Radio and Television, producer in Brisbane, Australia, 1964-67, and Hobart, Australia, 1967-69; University of Queensland Press, St. Lucia, Australia, editor, 1969-76; full-time writer, 1977—. Copy editor for Publishing Division, Open University (Bletchley, England), 1972; delegate to Hari Sastra National Literature Conference, Malaysia, 1973. *Awards, honors:* Senior Writers fellowship from Australia Council, 1977-78; *1915: A Novel* was highly commended by Australian National Book Awards, 1979, was named Book of the Year by *The Age*, 1979, and won Biennial Prize for Literature from South Australian Government, 1980.

WRITINGS: Citizens of Mist (poems), University of Queensland Press, 1968; (editor) *The First Paperback Poets Anthology*, University of Queensland Press, 1974; *Airship* (poems), University of Queensland Press, 1975; *1915: A Novel*, University of Queensland Press, 1979, Braziller, 1980.

WORK IN PROGRESS: A novel with a background of aviation in the 1930's.

SIDELIGHTS: 1915 is McDonald's first novel and recalls the year in which Australian soldiers entered World War I. The loss of national innocence is the author's "larger theme," according to Jeffrey Burke of the *New York Times Book Review*, but the story is most intimately concerned with the youth and early adulthood of two friends in New South Wales. Their shared lives proceed in a conventional way, until they volunteer for military service and end up in the trenches at Gallipoli, Turkey. The Allied failure at Gallipoli "was almost as much Australia's Culloden as her coming of age," remarked Chris Wallace-Crabbe of the *Times Literary Supplement*. Wounded then home again, the two friends return to young women who have also been changed by the war that changed everything.

"McDonald has been for a number of years a stylish and accomplished poet," wrote Wallace-Crabbe. He noted that the tone of McDonald's poetry "has always been modestly self-effacing," quietly evocative, and delivered in a voice that is never raised. "Very little in the careful, tight-lipped poetry could have prepared readers for the width or the originality of *1915*, unless we note in retrospect how free his poetic fictions have been from any mere display of self, any show of the dusty iridescent corners of sensibility." In *1915*, McDonald builds a "complicated solidity of characterization," a prose style that is "intrinsic to the book's achievement," and a temporal scheme that illuminates the author's "presentation of energy, purpose and waste in a random world."

In his review, Burke held that *1915* "would be no more than a standard war novel about people muddling through if Mr. McDonald's characters were not so completely realized—enough, in fact, to overshadow the war itself, however catalytic its role. With prose as spare as the blunt speech of an Australian farmer, he piles up convincing period details of both Australia's rural life and its increasingly urban culture." Wallace-Crabbe added: "The prose fabric keeps testifying to the author's knowledge of modernism, its dissolution of the fluent ego, its grasping at epiphanies.... Almost everywhere McDonald's prose is taut and perceptual ..., whether recreating the countryside, an indoor encounter or the hot trenches above Anzac Cove.... McDonald is one of those very few novelists who can, like Hardy, do complicated movements in extended space and make them memorable."

BIOGRAPHICAL/CRITICAL SOURCES: Times Literary Supplement, January 11, 1980; *New York Times Book Review*, May 11, 1980.

*   *   *

McEWEN, Robert (Lindley) 1926-1980

OBITUARY NOTICE: Born June 23, 1926; died in 1980 in Berwickshire, Scotland. Lawyer, illustrator, and author. McEwen contributed to the *Listener*, wrote a column for the *Spectator*, and authored a number of legal textbooks, including *The Law of Monopolies* and *Gatley on Libel and Slander*. He also illustrated Gavin Maxwell's *Ring of Bright Water*. Obituaries and other sources: *Who's Who*, 131st edition, St. Martin's, 1979; *AB Bookman's Weekly*, July 14-21, 1980.

McGAW, William C(ochran) 1914-

PERSONAL: Born May 14, 1914, in Kokomo, Ind.; son of Thomas Russell (an architect) and Fae Geneve (in retail sales; maiden name, Cochran) McGaw; married Mary Helen Turley, 1933 (divorced); married Dorothy Elizabeth Oliver (a registered nurse), November 7, 1945; children: William Michael, Dorothy Patricia McGaw Moffat. *Education:* Attended Indiana University, 1932-33, Benjamin Harrison Law School, 1934, and University of California, Los Angeles. *Politics:* Democrat. *Religion:* Presbyterian. *Home:* 138 Gibbs St., El Paso, Tex. 79917. *Office:* 2400 Texas Ave., El Paso, Tex. 79901.

CAREER: Indianapolis Times, Indianapolis, Ind., staff writer, 1935; *Burlington Mirror,* Burlington, Ind., owner and editor, 1935; *Indianapolis News,* staff writer, 1936; *Noblesville Morning Times,* Noblesville, Ind., editor, 1936-37; *Tampa Times,* Tampa, Fla., staff writer, 1937-39; *Philadelphia Record,* Philadelphia, Pa., staff writer and copy editor, 1939-47; Metro-Goldwyn-Mayer, Culver City, Calif., writer, actor, and stuntman, 1947-50; producer of "Ford Motor Circus" road shows for Ford Motor Co., 1950-58; *Southwesterner,* Columbus, N.M., owner, editor, and publisher, 1958-68; *El Paso Journal,* El Paso, Tex., editor and publisher, 1968—. *Military service:* U.S. Maritime Service, Medical Corps, 1943-45; served in the Atlantic Theater, the Middle East, and Europe. *Member:* Sigma Delta Chi. *Awards, honors:* Scripps-Howard Award, 1960, for "Last Train From Columbus," and 1962, for "Stradivarius Violins Getting Awful Various."

WRITINGS: The Scene Was Savage (biography of James Kirker), Hastings House, 1972.

Work represented in anthologies, including *U.S. Poetry Anthology,* 1933, and *The Mountain Men and Fur Trade of the Far West,* Volume V, edited by LeRoy R. Hafen, 1968. Author of "Out of the West," a column in *El Paso Herald-Post,* 1960-62. Contributor to magazines, including *Collier's, Argosy,* and *Country Life.*

WORK IN PROGRESS: A book on El Paso border problems with Mexico and a book on the life of Edward Rose, Black Mountain man.

SIDELIGHTS: In 1966 McGaw successfully sued a reader of his newspaper, *Southwesterner,* for publicizing his opinion that McGaw's editorial writing was Communist-oriented.

In 1979 McGaw wrote: "Although I have done an infinite amount of historical research—and I love it—I prefer writing for immediate publication, for newspaper or magazines, for the world and our society presently are changing so fast. History gives you a perspective, or should. My writing is both an occupation and a calling.

"I have been in almost every country except China. The most vital subject for me is what this country will do in the next year to save itself from interests, foreign and domestic, that would destroy our political and economic institutions."

BIOGRAPHICAL/CRITICAL SOURCES: Time, February 11, 1966.

*   *   *

McWILLIAMS, Carey 1905-1980

OBITUARY NOTICE—See index for *CA* sketch: Born December 13, 1905, in Steamboat Springs, Colo.; died of cancer, June 27, 1980, in New York, N.Y. Lawyer and author. McWilliams fought tirelessly for the rights of the underprivileged and once served as the head of California's Division of Immigration and Housing. He was also editor of the liberal magazine *Nation* for twenty years. His works include *The Story of Migratory Farm Labor in California, Prejudice: Japanese-American, Symbol of Racial Intolerance,* and *A Mask for Privilege: Anti-Semitism in America.* Obituaries and other sources: *New York Times,* June 28, 1980; *Washington Post,* June 29, 1980; *Time,* July 7, 1980; *Newsweek,* July 7, 1980; *Publishers Weekly,* July 25, 1980.

*   *   *

MEAD, Matthew 1924-

PERSONAL: Born September 12, 1924, in Buckinghamshire, England; married Ruth Adrian (a translator). *Address:* c/o Anvil Press, 69 King George St., London SE10 8PX, England.

CAREER: Poet. Former editor of *Statis* (magazine) in Edinburgh, Scotland. *Military service:* British Army, 1942-47; served in India, Ceylon, and Singapore.

WRITINGS—Poetry: *A Poem in Nine Parts,* Migrant Press, 1960; *Identities,* Migrant Press, 1964; *Kleinigkeiten* (poems in English), Malcolm Rutherford, 1966; *Identities and Other Poems,* Rapp & Carroll, 1967, Transatlantic, 1971; *The Administration of Things,* Anvil Press Poetry, 1970; (with Harry Guest and Jack Beeching) *Penguin Modern Poets Sixteen,* Penguin, 1970; *In the Eyes of the People,* Satis Press, 1973.

Translator of poetry with wife, Ruth Mead: Johannes Bobrowski, *Shadow Land: Selected Poems,* Donald Carroll, 1966, 2nd edition, 1967; Heinz Winfried Sabais, *Generation,* Malcolm Rutherford, 1967; Nelly Sachs, *O the Chimneys,* Farrar, Straus, 1967 (published in England as *Selected Poems of Nelly Sachs,* J. Cape, 1968); Sabais, *Generation and Other Poems,* Anvil Press Poetry, 1968; Max Hoeltzer, *Amfortiade and Other Poems,* Malcolm Rutherford, 1968; Horst Bienek, *Horst Bienek,* Unicorn Press, 1969; Elisabeth Borchers, *Elisabeth Borchers,* Unicorn Press, 1969; (with Michael Hamburger) Sachs, *The Seeker and Other Poems,* Farrar, Straus, 1970; Bobrowski and Bienek, *Selected Poems,* Penguin, 1971; Sabais, *Mitteilunger/Communications,* Eduard Roether Verlag, 1971.*

*   *   *

MEADOWS, Edward 1944-

PERSONAL: Born May 16, 1944, in Birmingham, Ala.; son of E. Martin (a stockbroker) and Mary (Boisclair) Meadows. *Education:* Citadel, B.A., 1966; doctoral study at University of South Carolina, 1975-78. *Politics:* Independent. *Religion:* Episcopal. *Home:* 136 East 55th St., New York, N.Y. 10022. *Office: Fortune,* Time and Life Building, Rockefeller Center, New York, N.Y. 10020.

CAREER: U.S. Peace Corps, Washington, D.C., volunteer worker in Colombia, 1967-69; *White Plains Reporter-Dispatch,* White Plains, N.Y., reporter, 1969-71; Associated Press, Richmond, Va., editor, 1971; *Today* (newspaper), Cape Kennedy, Fla., editor and reviewer, 1972-74; *Fortune,* New York, N.Y., associate editor, 1978—. *Member:* American Economic Association, Sigma Delta Chi, Omicron Delta Epsilon.

WRITINGS: Up the Down Dollar: A Realist's Guide to the Marketplace, Doubleday, 1980. Contributor of about forty articles to national magazines, including *Fortune, National Review,* and *Harper's.*

WORK IN PROGRESS: A novel, publication expected in 1981; a book on investing.

SIDELIGHTS: Meadows told *CA:* "Most of my writing involves economic issues and such, but it wasn't always so and perhaps it won't be in the future. Writing about "important" issues does pay the bills, but the truly important matters of human existence are more likely to be explored in a good novel. Thus while I work on another 'serious' nonfiction book and continue writing articles for *Fortune,* I am also taking a try at a good storytelling novel (I have written two but never submitted them, and they rest, deservedly, in some dusty boxes). It will be set in France, where I spend all my free time. What it will be about is beyond description for the time, but it will not be one of those ponderous, self-conscious Great Novels.

"It is almost odd that I would end up at *Fortune;* my history is eclectic. I was a television director at seventeen, I worked on motion pictures in South America and Hollywood, I marched in anti-Vietnam demonstrations in Washington, and so on. It was not the Eastern Corridor Ivy League career path at all. Yet the eclecticism is useful; it suggests a happily unpredictable future.

"France must enter more prominently in my writing. My family has two chateaux there, and my working definition of heaven is France in general, Paris in particular."

BIOGRAPHICAL/CRITICAL SOURCES: Fortune, July 31, 1978, March 10, 1980.

*   *   *

MEARIAN, Judy Frank 1936-

PERSONAL: Surname is pronounced *Mare*-i-an; born November 26, 1936, in Cincinnati, Ohio; daughter of Norris Clinton (an insurance adjuster) and Laura Jemima (a teacher; maiden name, Stowe) Frank; married Robert Mike Mearian (an actor), May 28, 1970. *Education:* Indiana University, A.B., 1958; Yale University, M.F.A., 1961. *Home:* 185 West End Ave., New York, N.Y. 10023. *Agent:* Connie Clausen Associates, 250 East 87th St., New York, N.Y. 10028.

CAREER: English teacher at high school in Long Island, N.Y., 1958-59; actress on stage, radio, and television in New York, N.Y., 1961-80; script writer for soap operas, 1980—. *Member:* American Federation of Television and Radio Artists (member of national board), Actors' Fund of America, Actors Equity Association, Screen Actors Guild, Episcopal Actors' Guild (recording secretary).

WRITINGS: Two Ways About It (juvenile), Dial, 1979; *Someone Slightly Different* (juvenile), Dial, 1980; *Take Three, Sarah Marshall,* Dial, 1981.

SIDELIGHTS: Judy Mearian commented to *CA:* "Although I look forward to writing for others someday, just now I'm enjoying writing for pre-teens and teens. That seems to be an age when people first become aware of serious adult problems without the advantage of knowing 'this too shall pass.' The letters from young readers have been worth any work involved. I am still, after all, an actress.

"I write on buses as I travel to and from auditions. My work as an actress has taken me to almost every state in the union, including Hawaii. The people I've met and the experiences I've had as a performer have been extremely helpful to me as a writer. I've played on Broadway, Off-Broadway, and Off-Off-Broadway, done television soap operas and commercials, radio, endless narrations and industrials, national companies and bus and truck tours. I've sung in nightclubs and actually worked on a real, traveling showboat. I feel very fortunate to be part of the acting profession, but I also

love to write. As an actress, the perfect role rarely comes along. As a writer, I can create any character I choose."

AVOCATIONAL INTERESTS: Travel.

BIOGRAPHICAL/CRITICAL SOURCES: Theatre World, Volume XXII, 1965-66, Volume XXIV, 1967-68; *Washington Post,* February 10, 1980.

*   *   *

MEARS, Richard Chase 1935-

PERSONAL: Born January 4, 1935, in Baltimore, Md.; son of Chase Kellum (a pharmacist) and Mildred (a medical secretary; maiden name, Richmond) Mears; married Joan Geider (an artist and high school art and English teacher), December 27, 1962; children: Lisa, Lara. *Education:* Pennsylvania State University, B.A., 1961. *Religion:* "All." *Agent:* Michael Larsen/Elizabeth Pomada, 1029 Jones St., San Francisco, Calif. 94109. *Office:* Richard C. Mears, Inc., 505 Sansome St., Suite 1000, San Francisco, Calif. 94111.

CAREER: ABC-TV, New York City, account executive, 1961-62; J. Walter Thompson, New York City, television advertising producer, 1962-63; Tax Research Institute, New York City, account representative, 1963-70; Capital Analysts (investment firm), San Francisco, Calif., account representative, 1970-72; Richard C. Mears, Inc. (investment firm), San Francisco, president and investment adviser, 1972—. *Military service:* U.S. Air Force, Air Intelligence, 1955-58; served in Okinawa. *Member:* World Organization.

WRITINGS: Ebb of the River (novel), Wyndham Books, 1980.

WORK IN PROGRESS: Another novel, "the second in a trilogy of 'fictional memoirs,' about a boy growing into manhood in Korea"; *Remford's House,* third volume of the trilogy, "about a young man beginning a business career in New York City"; *Annabis Rex,* "about the evil of man and the intellectual growth of lower animals."

SIDELIGHTS: Mears's first novel describes a boy's adolescence, growing up near the Patuxent River in Maryland, where Mears spent much of his own youth. He commented: "Social commitment and conscience are very important to my writing. Perfection and individuality are my goals, solid and classic. Writing enables me to confirm and expand my thoughts; to question my existence; to play with the omnipresent, the omniscient, and the immortal; to enjoy and fathom those mysterious recesses of the mind; to love but to write."

*   *   *

MEDHIN, Tsegaye (Kawessa) Gabre
See GABRE-MEDHIN, Tsegaye (Kawessa)

*   *   *

MEHAN, Joseph Albert 1929-
(Albert Martin)

PERSONAL: Born April 29, 1929, in Stamford, Conn.; son of Frank M. and Anna G. Mehan; married Doris Brezhenridge, August 29, 1953 (divorced, 1974); children: Jeffrey, David, Christopher, Michael. *Education:* Columbia University, A.B., 1950, M.S., 1951. *Politics:* Democrat. *Religion:* Roman Catholic. *Home:* 168 Cascade Rd., Stamford, Conn. 06903. *Agent:* Joan Raines, Raines & Raines, 475 Fifth Ave., New York, N.Y. 10017. *Office:* United Nations Educational, Scientific, and Cultural Organization, United Nations, Room 2401, New York, N.Y. 10017.

CAREER: *Dallas Times-Herald,* Dallas, Tex., reporter, 1953-55; *Newark Star-Ledger,* Newark, N.Y., reporter, 1955-57; National Broadcasting Co. (NBC), New York City, news producer and writer, 1957-71; United Negro College Fund, New York City, director of communications, 1971-78; United Nations Educational, Scientific, and Cultural Organization (UNESCO), New York City, director of public information for United States and Canada, 1978—. *Military service:* U.S. Army, 1951-53.

MEMBER: Overseas Press Club of America. *Awards, honors:* George Foster Peabody Award from University of Georgia School of Journalism, 1963, for "Revolution, '63" (NBC-TV), and 1970, for "The Danger Within: A Study of Disunity" (NBC-RADIO); Council on International Nontheatrical Events (CINE) Golden Eagle, 1966, for "The World of the Teenager," 1972, for "A Young Man Named Harvard," and 1974, for "From Father to Son"; Writers Guild of America award and Ohio State award, both 1971, both for "The Danger Within: A Study of Disunity"; bronze medal from the International Film and Television Festival, 1976, for "The Difference We Make."

WRITINGS: (Under pseudonym Albert Martin) *One Man, Hurt* (nonfiction), Macmillan, 1975.

* * *

MEIKLE, Jeffrey L(ee) 1949-

PERSONAL: Surname is pronounced *Mee*-kul; born July 2, 1949, in Columbus, Ohio; son of Wendell A. (a U.S. Army officer) and Arlene (Craner) Meikle; married Alice M. Stone (a dental hygienist), June 14, 1969; children: Jason. *Education:* Brown University, A.B. and M.A., 1971; University of Texas, Ph.D., 1977. *Home:* 2101 Rundell Place, Austin, Tex. 78704. *Office:* American Studies Program, University of Texas, 303 Garrison Hall, Austin, Tex. 78712.

CAREER: University of Texas, Austin, assistant instructor in American studies, 1973-77; Colby-Sawyer College, New London, N.H., instructor in American studies and English, 1977-78; Smithsonian Institution, Charles Willson Peale Papers, Washington, D.C., fellow in historical editing, 1978-79; University of Texas, assistant professor of American studies and art history, 1979—. *Member:* American Historical Association, American Studies Association, Society for the History of Technology, Association for Documentary Editing, Phi Beta Kappa.

WRITINGS: *Twentieth Century Limited: Industrial Design in America, 1925-1939,* Temple University Press, 1979. Contributor to literature journals.

WORK IN PROGRESS: Works on history of the plastics industry, and on post-modernism in contemporary fiction.

SIDELIGHTS: Meikle commented: "In order to maintain an outside perspective, I believe that cultural historians should begin cold on each research project, with no prior knowledge of the subjects involved. Such an approach yields new insights and prevents the predictability of much scholarship."

* * *

MELDAL-JOHNSEN, Trevor Bernard 1944-

PERSONAL: Born June 9, 1944, in Durban, South Africa; came to the United States, 1969; son of Konrad Mentz Thesen and Mavis F. Meldal-Johnsen; married Marcia Kay Smith (an artist), June 22, 1969; children: Justin, Tiffany. *Education:* Educated in South Africa and New Zealand. *Residence:* Los Angeles, Calif. *Agent:* Richard Curtis Associates, Inc., 156 East 52nd St., New York, N.Y. 10022.

CAREER: Free-lance writer. *Dominion,* Wellington, New Zealand, journalist, 1963-64; *Waikato Times,* Hamilton, New Zealand, journalist, 1964; *Morning Telegraph,* Sydney, Australia, journalist, 1964-65; Australian Broadcasting Commission, Melbourne, journalist, 1965; *True,* Los Angeles, Calif., assistant editor, 1975.

WRITINGS: *Always* (novel), Avon, 1979; (with Vaughn Young) *The Interpol Connection* (nonfiction), Dial, 1979; (with Patrick Lusey) *The Truth About Scientology* (nonfiction), Tempo Books, 1980.

WORK IN PROGRESS: A novel, a generational saga set in South Africa, for Avon.

SIDELIGHTS: Meldal-Johnsen commented: "As a writer I feel a responsibility to develop my craft in order to competently entertain and enlighten. I believe that all men are basically good and I wish to contribute in some way so that this is widely recognized and the potential of man is realized. We are all greater than we have been led to believe. That these views are not generally known, let alone understood, is, I am convinced, a major source of man's tragic experiences, both ancient and modern. Today we face an almost overwhelming tide of calculated nihilism and degradation. The artist has a duty to help his fellows overcome these barriers and thus be able to glimpse their true spiritual nature. Although absolutes don't exist, there are degrees of truth and falsehood. The communication of truth is the challenging and almost impossible task of the artist. I tremendously admire those who try."

* * *

MENDELSOHN, Pamela 1944-

PERSONAL: Born November 19, 1944, in New Haven, Conn.; daughter of William (a physician) and Stella (Levine) Mendelsohn; married George Herr (divorced); married Peter Burgess (divorced); children: Rebekah Elizabeth. *Education:* Attended New York University, 1964-65; Connecticut College for Women, B.A., 1966; Humboldt State University, M.A., 1978. *Religion:* Jewish. *Home address:* P.O. Box 4597, Arcata, Calif. 95521. *Office:* Center for Independent Living, 2539 Telegraph Ave., Berkeley, Calif. 94704.

CAREER: United Nations Association, New York City, coordinator of education department, 1968-69; Macmillan Publishing Co., New York City, publicist, 1969-71; Star of the Sea Children's Home, Inchon, Korea, fund raiser and adoption agent, 1971-72; Grand Comedy Festival at Qual-a-wa-loo, Blue Lake, Calif., publicity director, 1973-74; Interface California Corp., Eureka, Calif., publicity director, 1974-78; Humboldt State University, Arcata, Calif., intern at Child and Family Service Center and Career Development Center, 1977-78; Center for Independent Living, Berkeley, Calif., public relations director, 1979—. Public relations director at Redwood Memorial Hospital, 1975-77. Consultant for reentry education at College of the Redwoods, 1980—.

WRITINGS: *Happier by Degrees,* Dutton, 1980. Contributor to *California Living, Country Women,* and *Jogger.*

SIDELIGHTS: Pamela Mendelsohn commented: "When I decided to return to school for a master's degree in psychology, ten years after receiving my bachelor's degree, I was astounded to find that *no* book was available that would speak to the needs of older students. I hope my book can serve as a resource and support book for women thinking about returning to school. The psychological hurdles and the myriad details involved in reentry justify the need for such a book."

BIOGRAPHICAL/CRITICAL SOURCES: Independent Gazette, June 22, 1980.

*   *   *

MERCER, Joan Bodger 1923-
(Joan Bodger)

PERSONAL: Born August 31, 1923, in San Francisco, Calif.; daughter of Frank David (a military officer) and Joan (Corfield) Higbee; married John Charles Bodger, 1947 (marriage ended, 1966); married Alan Nelson Mercer (a photographer and writer), 1970; children: (first marriage) Ian Corfield, Lucy Stanton (deceased). *Education:* Pomona College, B.A. (cum laude), 1949; attended Columbia University and Gestalt Institute of Toronto, 1972-75. *Politics:* "In 1980?" *Religion:* Episcopalian. *Home:* 484 Church St., No. 1116, Toronto, Ontario, Canada M4Y 2C7. *Agent:* Marilyn Marlow, Curtis Brown Ltd., 575 Madison Ave., New York, N.Y. 10022. *Office:* 412-A College St., Toronto, Ontario, Canada M5T 1T3.

CAREER: Nyack Community Nursery School, Nyack, N.Y., director of school and of the state's first "Headstart" program, 1963-65; St. Agatha Home for Children (orphanage), New York City, director of therapeutic nursery school and play therapy, 1965-66; Bank Street College of Education, New York City, instructor in children's literature, language arts, and storytelling, 1967-68; State Library of Missouri, staff consultant to Children's Division, 1968-69; Random House, Inc., New York City, liaison editor of children's books for Pantheon Books and Alfred A. Knopf, Inc., 1970-71; Mini-Skools (day care centers), program director for Ontario and Manitoba, 1971-75; private practice as Gestalt therapist and professional storyteller. Instructor at Brooklyn College of the City University of New York, 1967-68; workshop leader; member of board of directors of Storytellers School of Toronto; member of advisory board of Mythos Foundation. Resident storyteller at Underground Railroad and Toronto Young People's Theatre; artist-in-residence at Art Park, Lewiston, N.Y.; co-coordinator of Toronto's 1979 Storytelling Festival; consultant to Ontario Ministry of Community and Social Welfare. *Military service:* Women's Army Corps, cryptographer in Signal Corps, 1944-46; became staff sergeant. *Member:* Writers Union of Canada, Canadian Society of Composers, Authors, Illustrators, and Performers, National Association for the Preservation and Perpetuation of Storytelling (United States), Feminist Therapists of Toronto.

*WRITINGS—*Under name Joan Bodger: *How the Heather Looks: A Joyous Journey to the British Sources of Children's Books,* Viking, 1965; (contributor) Margaret Meek and others, editors, *The Cool Web: The Pattern of Children's Reading,* Atheneum, 1978; *Clever-Lazy: The Girl Who Invented Herself,* Atheneum, 1979. Also author of *Belinda's Ball,* Atheneum. Contributor of articles and reviews to library journals and popular magazines, including *Chatelaine.* Guest editor of *Wilson Library Bulletin,* 1970.

WORK IN PROGRESS: A picture book based on a Piagetian theory of preservation of object; research on archaeology and mythology of neolithic Britain and on Phoenician sea routes.

SIDELIGHTS: Joan Mercer commented to *CA:* "I started writing when I was eight years old and have considered myself a writer ever since—even in the years when I did not write. I started telling stories at an even younger age; in 1948 I took a storytelling course at Columbia University and decided to become a professional storyteller. Now I tell stories mostly to adults and I use storytelling as a therapeutic tool. Every valid folktale is a complex mystery—and so is every person. I am interested in the cauldron from which the stories come and am exploring the neolithic world to that end. At the age of fifty-six I hitchhiked in Britain, and in 1980 went on a walking tour of the borders of England and Wales to see ley lines, barrows, and standing stones."

BIOGRAPHICAL/CRITICAL SOURCES: Robert Coles and Marie Piers, *Wages of Neglect,* Quadrangle, 1970; *Wall Street Journal,* April 4, 1980.

*   *   *

MEYERS, Bert(ram) 1928-1979

PERSONAL: Born March 20, 1928, in Los Angeles, Calif.; died of lung cancer, April 22, 1979, in Claremont, Calif.; son of Manuel (an insurance salesman) and Gertrude (Bercovitch) Meyers; married Odette Miller (a college teacher), October 25, 1957; children: Arat, Daniel. *Education:* Claremont Graduate School, M.A., 1967. *Address:* c/o Odette Meyers, 2416-A Stuart St., Berkeley, Calif. 94705.

CAREER: Poet. Held a variety of jobs, including ditchdigger, janitor, warehouseman, and house painter; worked for ten years as a picture framer and gilder; Pitzer College, Claremont, Calif., 1967-79, began as instructor, became professor of English. *Awards, honors:* Awards from Ingram Merrill Foundation, 1964 and 1965; National Endowment for the Arts grant, 1967.

*WRITINGS—*Poetry: *Early Rain,* Swallow Press, 1960; *The Dark Birds,* Doubleday, 1968; (translator with wife, Odette Meyers) Francois Dodat, *Lord of the Village,* West Coast Poetry Review, 1973; *Sunlight on the Wall: Selected Poems,* Kayak, 1977; *Windowsills,* Common Table, 1979; *The Wild Olive Tree,* West Coast Poetry Review, 1979. Also author of *The Blue Cafe* and *In a Dybbuk's Raincoat.* Contributor of poems to periodicals, including *Ante, Choice, Literary Review, Burning Deck, Kayak, American Poetry Review, Transpacific,* and *San Francisco Review.*

*WORK IN PROGRESS—*At time of death: Several manuscripts, which his wife, who owns Meyers's copyrights, hopes to publish.

SIDELIGHTS: Bert Meyers was born and grew up in the Los Angeles area. As a young man he became a member of a group of California poets known as the Coastliners. He was largely self-educated, gaining his knowledge about poetry from reading and coffeehouse conversations. Although he spent his days supporting himself and his family with manual labor jobs, he was able to find time at night to write verse. At the age of thirty-six Meyers was forced to give up his job as a picture framer and gilder because of poor health. On the strength of recommendations by such important poets as Marianne Moore and others, he was accepted into the Claremont Graduate School. After earning an M.A. and doing doctoral work, he took on a teaching position at Pitzer College, which he held until his death.

Meyers's poetry is noted for its lyrical quality and vivid imagery. Although his work is not widely known to the general public, his verse has aroused the admiration of critics and of his fellow poets. Not long after Meyers died, Denise Levertov wrote in tribute to him: "Bert Meyers' work seems all to have been lyrical; he was not drawn to the epic, narrative, or dramatic modes and eschewed the hortatory or didactic. For clarity of discourse, I would reserve the term 'major' for poets whose range of genres and quantity of whose work seem equal in breadth to the depth of their poems. But the term 'great' should be applicable to those who produce deep and exquisite work in fewer modes, or in a single one; though here too some sense of abundance seems to form part of what 'great' implies. I feel Meyers can be called *great,* because of the extraordinary intensity and perfection of his poems and the consistency with which he illumined what he experienced, bodying it forth in images that enable readers to share his vision and thereby extend the boundaries of their own lives.''

BIOGRAPHICAL/CRITICAL SOURCES: Hudson Review, summer, 1968; *Harper's,* August, 1968; *Nation,* October 7, 1968; *Follies,* August, 1979; *Bachy,* fall, 1979; *Third Rail,* Number 4, 1980.

[Sketch verified by wife, Odette Meyers]

*   *   *

MEYERS, Edward   1934-

PERSONAL: Born November 2, 1934, in Flushing, N.Y.; son of Gerson George and Hester (Noble) Meyers; married Marcia Rothman (an artist), June 29, 1958; children: Beth, Adam, Rosemarie. *Education:* Rochester Institute of Technology, B.F.A., 1957. *Home:* 61-68 77th St., Middle Village, New York, N.Y. 11379. *Office: Popular Photography,* 1 Park Ave., New York, N.Y. 10016.

CAREER: Modern Photography, New York City, technical editor, 1957-66; photographer and writer in New York City, 1966-70; *Popular Photography,* New York City, executive editor, 1971—. Lecturer at School of Visual Arts, New York City, 1968—. *Military service:* U.S. Army, 1957-58. *Member:* Society of Photographic Scientists and Engineers, Society for Photographic Education, Industrial Photographers of New York. *Awards, honors:* Alumni Achievement Award from Rochester Institute of Technology, 1972.

WRITINGS: (Co-editor) *The Official Depth of Field Tables for 35mm Cameras,* Amphoto, 1972. Editor of *Modern Photography Photo Almanac,* 1967 and 1969. Contributor of articles to magazines.

*   *   *

MILESTONE, Lewis   1895-1980

OBITUARY NOTICE: Born September 30, 1895, in Kishinev, Russia (now U.S.S.R.); died September 25, 1980, in Los Angeles, Calif. Film director. Milestone directed the 1930 Academy Award-winning ''All Quiet on the Western Front'' as well as nearly forty other films, including ''Pork Chop Hill'' and ''Of Mice and Men.'' He also co-wrote the screenplay for ''Arch of Triumph.'' Obituaries and other sources: *International Motion Picture Almanac,* Quigley, 1979; *Time,* October 6, 1980; *Newsweek,* October 6, 1980.

*   *   *

MILIUS, John   1945-

PERSONAL: Born in 1945 in St. Louis, Mo.; married second wife, Celia Kay (an actress), 1978. *Education:* Attended Los Angeles City College, c. 1966, and University of Southern California, c. 1968. *Residence:* Los Angeles, Calif. *Office:* c/o Omni-Zoetrope, 916 Kearney St., San Francisco, Calif. 94133.

CAREER: Screenwriter, producer, and director of motion pictures. Formed A-Team Productions, 1979. Producer of motion pictures, including ''Hard Core'' and ''1941,'' both 1979, and ''Used Cars,'' 1980. *Awards, honors:* National Student Film Festival Award, c. 1968; nomination for award

from Writers Guild, 1975, for ''The Wind and the Lion''; shared nomination with Francis Ford Coppola for Academy Award for best screenplay from Academy of Motion Picture Arts and Sciences and nomination for award from Writers Guild, both 1979, both for ''Apocalypse Now.''

WRITINGS—Screenplays: (With James Gordon White and Willard Huyck) ''The Devil's 8,'' American International, 1969; (with Alan Caillou) ''Evel Knievel,'' Fanfare, 1971; ''The Life and Times of Judge Roy Bean,'' First Artists, 1972; (with Edward Anhalt) ''Jeremiah Johnson'' (adapted from the novel by Vardis Fisher, *Mountain Man,* and the story by Raymond W. Thorp and Robert Bunker, ''Crow Killer''), Warner Bros., 1972; (and director) ''Dillinger,'' Samuel Z. Arkoff/American International/EMI, 1974; (with Michael Cimino) ''Magnum Force,'' Malposa/Columbia/ Warner Bros., 1974; (and director) ''The Wind and the Lion,'' United Artists, 1975; (with Dennis Aarberg; and director) ''Big Wednesday,'' Warner Bros., 1978; (with Francis Ford Coppola) ''Apocalypse Now,'' United Artists, 1979.

WORK IN PROGRESS: Directing ''Conan,'' a motion picture adapted from the fantasy novels and short stories by Robert E. Howard.

SIDELIGHTS: Many of Milius's screenplays celebrate man's instinctual, and frequently violent, reaction to circumstances that defy compromise. In ''The Life and Times of Judge Roy Bean,'' the judge thwarts criminal activities by immediately hanging suspects. Through this drastic measure of upholding justice, Bean brings peace to a town struggling to flourish in a lawless frontier. But as the town prospers, Bean's methods become offensive to well-mannered citizens lured there by the guarantee of Bean's protection. The base evils of the old West are gradually superseded by the subtly unethical practices of businessmen, and these practices demand less reactionary measures than Bean is capable of using. He senses the passing of less sophisticated times and dies brokenhearted. With Bean gone, the businessmen try to swindle his daughter of his profitable saloon. She defies them, however, and is soon confronted by their henchmen. Aided by the late judge's closest friends—the same men that renounced Bean's crude behavior and adapted to the changing times—she combats the henchmen. Her small group seems defeated until Judge Bean returns ''like some hero from a folktale,'' according to Milius, and violently eliminates the enemy.

The protagonist in ''Jeremiah Johnson'' also finds pacifism useless. Dissatisfied with his life in New England, Johnson heads West to become a mountain man. Unfortunately, after adapting to the constantly threatening environment, he accidently desecrates an Indian burial ground. The Indians retaliate by killing Johnson's wife and son and pursuing him across the frontier. Johnson survives each attack, though, and the Indians eventually regard his fortitude as proof of his superiority. Like Bean, Johnson responds to potentially dangerous situations with animal-like ferocity and, Milius suggests, is a better man for it.

In ''Magnum Force,'' police officer ''Dirty'' Harry Calahan is faced with a similar dilemma. He discovers that fellow police are murdering their suspects instead of arresting them. Although Calahan is sympathetic to the vigilantes' contention that their suspects deserve death, he insists that justice be upheld and condemns the killers as no better than their victims. In a violent climax, Calahan is forced to kill the corrupt policemen. Violence, ''Dirty'' Harry contends, is justifiable only in extreme situations. ''A man's got to know his limitations,'' he notes.

Milius's "Apocalypse Now," co-written with Francis Ford Coppola, exposes the absurdity of permitting violence in wartime only within military law. In the film, Captain Benjamin Willard is ordered to kill Colonel Walter E. Kurtz for authorizing the murder of suspected North Vietnamese spies without due process. During his journey to the colonel's compound, Willard witnesses enough atrocities committed by American troops to convince him that Kurtz is beyond reproach. When the two men finally meet, Kurtz is certain that his actions are correct, yet unacceptable by military standards. He permits Willard to kill him. Although Willard renounces his military duty, he murders Kurtz out of compassion. The captain then embarks for home with Kurtz's records which, Kurtz believed, will convince his son of his innocence.

Throughout Milius's works, including the self-directed "Dillinger" and "The Wind and the Lion," the extremity of the situation acts as a catalyst for violent behavior. In "Apocalypse Now," Willard is briefly escorted by Colonel Kilgore, a fanatical soldier who likes the smell of napalm because "it smells like victory." Kilgore laments that "someday this war's going to end." For Kilgore, as for most of Milius's characters, the passing of danger marks the waning of his most dynamic, and frequently violent, instincts.

AVOCATIONAL INTERESTS: History, surfing, collecting guns.

CA INTERVIEWS THE AUTHOR

John Milius was interviewed by telephone on August 27, 1980.

CA: How did you become a filmmaker?

MILIUS: I went to cinema school. I was really interested in being a writer when I was growing up. I was a pretty good writer in high school, when I saw a lot of Akira Kurosawa's films. I saw practically every film he ever made. I was just knocked out by him.

CA: How did you approach directing your first film?

MILIUS: When I directed "Dillinger" I hadn't directed anything since cinema school, and I directed very little there. So my approach was mostly theoretical. It was a matter of seeing how all these ideas work. Often a lot of things in "Dillinger" look experimental.

CA: Are you drawn to experimentation?

MILIUS: Yes. I try and stretch each time. I try to do something more difficult than the one before.

CA: How accomplished are you at transposing your imagination onto the screen?

MILIUS: I think I'm getting better. There's a couple of films that I've done well. I don't know if my audience is the same anymore. I'm not sure whether I'm communicating to as many people directly as I was, but I think I'm communicating better to those people I want to get through to.

CA: Do you have any perception of your audience?

MILIUS: No. I don't think I should concern myself with the size of my audience. You do a piece of work and somebody responds to that. I really responded to certain movies in my lifetime. They really knocked me out. I want to get through that way to other people. If you worry about an audience, you wind up making something pandering and bad. No one can second-guess an audience. The only thing to do is act

like a painter and do the very best work you can and hope somebody likes it.

CA: Are you testing yourself then?

MILIUS: I test myself in all things. I find that's the most interesting thing to me, but not necessarily to all people. It really is probably very silly to most people, but to me it's a theme that keeps coming up in life. We are civilized and we have very primal and savage instincts. The struggle between our civilizing restraints and our savage instincts really seems to make people what they are.

CA: Are some filmmakers reluctant to test themselves because of the enormous pressure to succeed?

MILIUS: I think people are becoming very aware of this word "successful." These days it means blockbuster movies that make a lot of money. People are prizing success—how much money movies make—over quality. When movies played for one week, the directors were judged more on the quality of their work.

CA: What directors influenced you?

MILIUS: There's a lot of filmmakers I was influenced by, including Kurosawa, Sergei Eisenstein, John Ford, and David Lean. I just love David Lean. There's a great deal of intelligence and humanity in "Lawrence of Arabia," "The Bridge on the River Kwai," and "Doctor Zhivago." These are good films—great filmmaking.

CA: How important was John Ford?

MILIUS: Ford was probably the most important because he was the first filmmaker I became aware of. "The Searchers" was my favorite film. I saw it when it came out in 1957 and I had a paper route. Every day at the end of the paper route I went to the movies for the week it played. I saw "The Searchers" seven days in a row. When I grew up I never saw it on television. I was convinced I had dreamed "The Searchers."

CA: Were you influenced by writers?

MILIUS: I'm much more influenced by writers than filmmakers. I like Melville and Tolstoy. I was really influenced by Hemingway when I was young. But I didn't really learn to write anything from Hemingway. Faulkner was more lasting. I also like Conrad and Jack Kerouac.

CA: Do you find some of your work similar to that of Hemingway or Conrad?

MILIUS: I'm interested in the same themes they were. It seems that all of my films have something to do with what is summed up best by Colonel Kurtz in "Apocalypse Now." The most important lines he says are: "Have you ever considered real freedom? Freedom from yourself and thoughts of others?" That's what the movie is all about: a test of morality—when you've taken away all the restraints. This concept is in all my work. Jeremiah Johnson is just a young Kurtz. He's alone in the wilderness with no one to tell him what to do. He makes his own moral choices and pays for them.

CA: Isn't Kurtz insane in "Apocalypse Now"?

MILIUS: No, Kurtz totally has his sanity. He's the only sane person in the movie. He made his choices and found that the choices didn't fit the world; the choices were evil. But they were truthful choices. He looked into his own heart of darkness. The villains of the movie are the officers in the rear area who will never look into their own hearts.

CA: What about Willard, the officer assigned to kill Kurtz in the film?

MILIUS: Willard looked into the pit and survived. Kurtz has allowed him to do it. Willard is a much richer man afterwards. He comes back, not as a burnt-out shell, but as a man who has looked into hell and been enriched by the colors.

CA: Are symbols and references to mythology important to you when writing about themes as timeless as redemption and evil in "Apocalypse Now"?

MILIUS: Symbols are fun to play with. "Apocalypse Now" is many different allegories and such. The Playboy bunny scene is like something out of Dante's *Inferno;* it's the lustful being tormented. Colonel Kilgore was out of Homer's *The Odyssey;* he's the cyclops who must be fooled. But I think of these elements in a light sense. I don't want people to say, "That's the cyclops," because by the time it gets into the work it shouldn't be recognizable. It keeps the author amused.

CA: Don't you think understanding the symbolism enhances the film for the viewer?

MILIUS: I'm not sure that it does. I use my knowledge of literature and images as I like. John Boorman said that people like to have legends and myths and old stories repeated—it's very soothing to them. I think there is something to that. That's why writers can always go back and use symbols.

CA: Do you think of yourself primarily as a writer?

MILIUS: Yes, I'm a writer first and a director second. I only began directing films in self-defense because I didn't like the way my work was coming out. I really loved the script for "Judge Roy Bean," but the movie is so different. I would say "Judge Roy Bean" and "Jeremiah Johnson" weren't "feral" enough.

CA: Would you describe yourself as a "feral" director?

MILIUS: I'm not a screamer yelling all blood and thunder. I try and cajole actors and get them to be enthusiastic. I try and do that more than anything else. I try to have infectious enthusiasm on the set. People work best that way.

CA: Do you allow actors to improvise?

MILIUS: On "Big Wednesday" it was better if I let the actors add a little. Usually, though, when they added anything I cut it out. On "Conan" it is important that the actors leave the lines alone. "Conan" has a certain kind of style to it, like "Jeremiah Johnson." In that film, the dialogue had to be very carefully done so that the characters didn't sound like they were trying to sound like mountain men.

CA: Do you also give a lot of priority to music?

MILIUS: Tremendously. I think it's the most important thing in movies besides writing. It's more important than photography. I really feel that the mood created by image, music, and dialogue is the most important thing. Music and the expression on characters' faces can provide a mood or sense of the moment. Words are not the most important thing. People don't remember great speeches.

CA: Was there a need in "Apocalypse Now" to have Kurtz speak less and act more?

MILIUS: My favorite version of the film was three hours long. It had more of Kurtz in action. But all that remains in the film is Kurtz philosophizing, and I totally understand Coppola's decision to do that. It's a daring and interesting decision. He said, "We had action until now in the movie. We had madness and big things happen. Now we're just going to have big concepts."

CA: Have you been keeping a low profile since the release of "Apocalypse Now"?

MILIUS: Yes, I didn't like my profile so I decided to keep it low. I didn't like anything that was written about me. I didn't like the character. I took things as a joke and said things that, out of context, could be terrible. I have become tired of listening to myself.

CA: Did you like being mentioned along with Nietzsche and Leni Riefenstahl in Brian De Palma's "Home Movies"?

MILIUS: Oh yes, I know I'm referred to with Riefenstahl. That's great. That's just what I'd like to do. I would just love to be a filmmaker like her. I really want viewers of my films to feel like they've seen some strong cinema. I like what you call "industrial strength" cinema. I'm not one of those guys that says "I'm just trying to entertain" or "I'm trying to make people feel good." I try to make movies that will knock me out. I haven't made any movie as good as the movies I consider great, like "The Searchers" or "My Darling Clementine," but that's what I'm trying to do.

BIOGRAPHICAL/CRITICAL SOURCES: New York Times, December 19, 1972, December 22, 1972; *New Republic,* September 3, 1973; *Time,* September 10, 1973; *Los Angeles Times,* May 22, 1975; *Film Information,* June, 1975; *New York Times Magazine,* May 28, 1978; *Crawdaddy,* July, 1978; *Newsweek,* August 14, 1978; *Rolling Stone,* November 1, 1979.

—*Interview by Les Stone*

*   *   *

MILLER, (Harvey) Brown 1943-

PERSONAL: Born October 9, 1943, in Front Royal, Va.; son of Harvey Brown (a business executive) and Margaret Ann (Yost) Miller; married Sharon Long, June 17, 1961 (divorced, 1970); married Sandra Gail Pompi (an editor and publisher), August 4, 1973; children: Virginia Ann, Barbara Elaine, Carolyn Catherine, Molly Elizabeth, Brown. *Education:* Attended University of California, Berkeley, 1961-62, and Merritt College, 1962-63; San Francisco State University, B.A., 1966, M.A., 1967. *Residence:* San Francisco, Calif. *Agent:* RISE, 1716 Ocean Ave., San Francisco, Calif. 94112. *Office:* Department of English, City College of San Francisco, 50 Phelan Ave., San Francisco, Calif. 94112.

CAREER: City College of San Francisco, San Francisco, Calif., instructor in English and creative writing, 1967—. Conducts seminars on creativity, motivation, and stress reduction for businesses and the public. *Member:* American Federation of Teachers. *Awards, honors:* Grant from National Endowment for the Arts, 1968.

WRITINGS—Poetry: Fertilized Brains, Open Skull Press, 1968; *Autopsies and Family Ghosts,* Runcible Spoon, 1969; *Waters and Shadows,* Twowindows Press, 1969; *Hiroshima Flows Through Us,* Cherry Valley Editions, 1977, revised edition, 1980; *In the Wake of Waking,* Black Thumb Press, 1980.

Work represented in anthologies, including *The American*

Literary Anthology No. 2. Contributor to literary journals, including *New York Quarterly, Ohio Review, New Letters, West Coast Poetry Review,* and *Big Moon.*

WORK IN PROGRESS: Mind Jogging: The Vital Necessity of a Strong Imagination; Creative Coping: Making the Bad Times Good; Cancer Visions: Face to Face With the Interior Cannibal.

SIDELIGHTS: Brown Miller told *CA:* "As a boy I was interested in science, fascinated by nuclear power, which was then a new development. At seventeen I found myself working as an orderly in the cancer ward of a hospital, and somehow that experience went off in me like a bomb. Bombs and cancer got unconsciously tangled up in me, and from today's perspective I see the connection has a real relationship—the fearful fact that radiation can cause cancer.

"From 1973 through 1976, I wrote over one hundred poems about Hiroshima and my life—surreal intertwinings. The most successful of them (a little over fifty) make up *Hiroshima Flows Through Us,* which, unlike most books of poetry, is finding a general audience. I was only a year-and-a-half old when the bomb was dropped on Hiroshima, and many older people who have read my book are startled to find out that I was 'too young' to have been aware of the bombing. Yet I keep getting the comment that they feel the book captures what they felt, that it gets to the heart of the tragedy somehow. Why did it take someone of the next generation to write this kind of book about Hiroshima? It is not that John Hersey's book and Robert Jay Lifton's psychohistorical writings aren't masterpieces; they are. But the imaginative treatment, the direct emotional impact, had to wait until the mid-seventies.

"After allowing Hiroshima as a metaphor to live inside me for several years, I broke away from it and from the cancer obsession in order to build positive, renewing metaphors. I began to see that business people, like my father had been, were in great need of imaginative modes of thought, in need of metaphor in their daily psychic lives. So I have launched into seminars in the business community—a totally unexpected thing for me to do since heretofore I have been the 'pure poet,' untouched by crass commerce.

"Asked what I do in my writing and what I try to get people to do all the time in their heads, I reply: The physical senses are wise, much wiser than our intellect alone. In every way possible I try to tutor my intellect with my senses. Surprising myself is essential. I've got to bring my old senses to renewed life, and to do that I must make the familiar into something strange, even startling. So I jump across categories, breaking the partitions, trying to connect the previously unconnected. It doesn't always work, because fusing physical and mental elements is incredibly difficult. It requires no less than the momentary merging of the left and right brain hemispheres, of the conscious and the unconscious. But just the attempt itself is transformative, and I crave it—a physical-spiritual unity that brings about genuine renewal."

BIOGRAPHICAL/CRITICAL SOURCES: Studies in the Twentieth Century, spring, 1970; *Choice,* May, 1978; *Literary Monitor,* Volume IV, number 1, 1980.

*　　　*　　　*

MILLER, Eugene　1925-

PERSONAL: Born October 6, 1925, in Chicago, Ill.; son of Harry and Fannie (Prosterman) Miller; married Edith Sutker, September 23, 1951 (divorced, September, 1965); married Thelma Gottlieb, December 22, 1965; children: (first

marriage) Ross, Scott, June; (second marriage—stepchildren) Paul, Alan. *Education:* Georgia Institute of Technology, B.S., 1945; Bethany College, A.B. (magna cum laude), 1947; Oxford University, diploma, 1947; Columbia University, M.S., 1948; New York University, M.B.A., 1959; further graduate study at Pace University, 1973—. *Home:* 376 Sunrise Circle, Glencoe, Ill. 60022. *Office:* 101 South Wacker Dr., Chicago, Ill. 60606.

CAREER: Greensboro Daily News, Greensboro, N.C., reporter, 1948-50, assistant city editor, 1950-52; *Business Week,* New York City, chief of Southwest Bureau in Houston, Tex., 1952-54, associate managing editor in New York City, 1954-60; McGraw-Hill Book Co., New York City, director of public affairs and communications, 1960-63, vice-president, 1963-68; New York Stock Exchange, New York City, senior vice-president in public relations and investor relations and member of executive committee, 1968-73; CNA Finance Corp., Chicago, Ill., senior vice-president, 1973-77; U.S. Gypsum Co., Chicago, Ill., vice-president, 1977—. Adjunct professor at New York University, 1963-75; professor at Fordham University, 1969-75; professor and department chairman at Northeastern Illinois University, 1975—; lecturer to business and school groups. Member of board of directors of Tabb, Inc., and Technical Advisers, Inc., and board of trustees of Bethany College; consultant to U.S. Secretary of Commerce. *Military service:* U.S. Naval Reserve, 1943-66, active duty, 1943-46; became commander.

MEMBER: American Economic Association, American Finance Association, National Association of Business Economists, Society of American Business Writers (founder), Public Relations Society of America, Newcomen Society, Sigma Delta Chi, Alpha Sigma Phi, Mid-America Club, Green Acres Country Club, New York University Club. *Awards, honors:* Honors award from School of Journalism at Ohio University, 1964; LL.D. from Bethany College, 1969.

WRITINGS: (Editor with Phillip Lesley, and contributor) *Public Relations Handbook,* Prentice-Hall, 1974; *Your Future in Securities* (juvenile), Richards Rosen, 1974; *Barron's Guide to Graduate Business Schools: Eastern Edition,* Barron's, 1978. Author of "Your Pursestrings," a column syndicated by Newsday Specials Syndicate, 1960-68, and "Your Medicare," syndicated by Miller News Service, 1966—.

WORK IN PROGRESS: A book on financial futures.

AVOCATIONAL INTERESTS: Collecting stamps and coins, photography.

*　　　*　　　*

MILLER, Marjorie M.　1922-

PERSONAL: Born May 28, 1922, in La Porte, Ind.; daughter of Warren Theodore (in advertising) and Helen (an artist; maiden name, Modrall) Mithoff; married William E. Miller, Jr. (a genealogist), January 2, 1943; children: Margaret Miller Benedict, Warren Eldridge, David Jameson, Paul Modrall, Stephen Mithoff. *Education:* University of Texas, B.A., 1943; University of Maryland, M.A., 1969; Catholic University of America, M.S.L.S., 1973. *Religion:* Presbyterian. *Home:* 12511 Brewster Lane, Bowie, Md. 20715. *Office:* Prince George's County Documents Library, Upper Marlboro, Md. 20870.

CAREER: Teacher at public schools in Bowie, Md., 1967-68; Prince George's County Memorial Library System, Bowie Branch, Bowie, Md., librarian, 1970-76; currently affiliated with Prince George's County Documents Library in Upper

Marlboro, Md. *Member:* National Genealogical Society, American Library Association, Science Fiction Research Association, Maryland Library Association, Prince George's County Genealogical Society, Phi Beta Kappa, Phi Kappa Phi.

WRITINGS: Isaac Asimov: A Checklist of Works Published in the United States, 1939-May, 1972, Kent State University Press, 1972; (contributor) Joseph D. Olander and Martin M. Greenberg, editors, *Isaac Asimov,* Taplinger, 1976.

WORK IN PROGRESS: Research on setting up a documents library for a county government.

*   *   *

MILNE, Antony 1942-

PERSONAL: Born April 25, 1942, in Tring, England; son of Robertson W. (a liquor store manager) and Jocelyn (Day) Milne; married Tomris Arisoy, May 30, 1970; children: Handan Serena, Richard. *Education:* Polytechnic of Central London, B.Sc., 1974. *Politics:* "Right of center." *Religion:* Atheist. *Home:* 13 Howarth Rd., Abbey Wood, London, England. *Agent:* Peterborough Literary Agency, 135 Fleet St., London EC4P 4BL, England. *Office:* Press Association, 85 Fleet St., London E.C.4, England.

CAREER: Clerk in London, England, 1957-71; Department of Health, London, clerical officer, 1975-76; North Atlantic Treaty Organization, Committee on the Challenges of Modern Society, London, research fellow in London and Southampton, 1976-77; Press Association (news agency), London, journalist, 1978—. *Member:* British Humanist Association.

WRITINGS: Noise Pollution: Impact and Countermeasures, David & Charles, 1979; *The Drowning of London,* Thames Associates/Methuen, 1981. Contributor to *New Humanist* and *Freethinker.*

WORK IN PROGRESS: Eco Politics and the State, a study of ecology groups and their impact on legislation and government, publication expected in 1982-83.

SIDELIGHTS: "After leaving school with no qualifications at the age of fifteen," Milne wrote, "it was hardly surprising that I had a succession of boring clerical jobs. I decided to go to the Polytechnic of Central London to read social science. It was almost a religious conversion. My college days were so enjoyable I wanted to become an academic of some sort, to continue with the marvelous life of pursuing and disseminating knowledge. In a sense I have fulfilled myself by publishing a book, although it was unplanned and unexpected.

"After graduating I enrolled to do part-time research at Birkbeck College, but I won a full-time research fellowship with a NATO sub-committee while working at civil service. So I promptly abandoned the part-time studies, which were already beginning to flag.

"The research (on the impact of noise pollution) completed in 1977, I hawked the thesis to various publishers and rewrote it for a general audience. But the work remained on the up-market and specialized side, since I still had my eye on an academic post. When I later started work in Fleet Street, I learned to broaden my writing technique and was converted to the belief that a writer has an almost didactic duty to reach as wide an audience as possible.

"So I wrote a more popular book on the flooding threat to London. This widens the scope of any future ventures—politics, environment, even history. The task now is to maintain the momentum.

"However, if I am now committed—in a broad sense—to writing about doom and gloom, I don't wish to be associated with the more radical critics of capitalist society, a point I was careful to make in the introduction of my first book. The pluses still outweigh the minuses."

BIOGRAPHICAL/CRITICAL SOURCES: London Evening News, February 6, 1979.

*   *   *

MILWARD, Peter 1925-

PERSONAL: Born October 12, 1925, in London, England; son of Richard and Hannah (Taylor) Milward. *Education:* Heythrop College, Oxford, lic.phil., 1950; Campion Hall, Oxford, B.A., 1954, M.A. (classics, English), 1957; Sophia University, lic.theol., 1961, M.A. (theology), 1961. *Home:* Society of Jesus House, 7 Kioicho, Chiyoda-ku, Tokyo 102, Japan. *Office:* Department of English Literature, Sophia University, Tokyo, Japan.

CAREER: Entered Society of Jesus (Jesuits), 1943, ordained Roman Catholic priest, 1960; Sophia University, Tokyo, Japan, member of literature staff, 1962-67, professor of English literature, 1967—. Visiting lecturer at Tokyo University, 1963-73, and Chiba University, 1975—. *Member:* Japan Thomas More Association, English Literary Society of Japan, Shakespeare Society of Japan, Hopkins Society of Japan (honorary president), Renaissance Institute of Japan (vice-chairperson), Association of Foreign Language Teachers of Japan (president, 1973; vice-president, 1976—), Modern Language Association of America. *Awards, honors:* Religious Book Award from Associated Church Press and Catholic Press Association, 1975, for *Landscape and Inscape.*

WRITINGS: A Poem of the New Creation, Hokuseido, 1970; *Things Wise and Otherwise,* Eichosha, 1970; *Where East Is West,* Eichosha, 1971; *Schooldays in England,* Hokuseido, 1972; *My Two Island Homes,* Eichosha, 1972; *What Is a Man?,* Asahi Press, 1973; *Contradictions in Character,* Asahi Press, 1974; *England in Sketches,* Seibido, 1974; *Insects Anonymous,* Azuma Shobo, 1974; *A Japanese Englishman in Korea,* Azuma Shobo, 1974; *The Changing Face of England,* Yumi Shobo, 1975; *Annual Animals,* Kinseido, 1975; *Fortunate Failures: An Autobiography of Error,* Azuma Shobo, 1975; *Old America and New England,* Seibido, 1975; *Japan in an Instant,* Asahi Press, 1975; *More Insects Anonymous,* Azuma Shobo, 1976; *To and Fro in Japan,* Azuma Shobo, 1976; *Experiments in Haiku,* Azuma Shobo, 1976; *Culture in Words,* Kinseido, 1977; *Peter* (poems), Stanbrook Abbey Press, 1977; *The Wisdom of the West,* Azuma Shobo, 1977; *The Englishman As He Is,* Seibido, 1977; *Why Am I?,* Seibido, 1978; *Education for Life,* Azuma Shobo, 1978; *A Journey Through England,* Kinseido, 1978; *The World and the Word,* Nanundo, 1978; *Living and Learning in Japan,* Yumi Shobo, 1978; *The Silent World of Colour,* Nanundo, 1978; *Journal of a Journey,* Parts I and II, Aratake Shuppan, 1978; *An Englishman Looks at America,* Shinkosha, 1978; *Animals in the Air,* Tsurumi Shoten, 1979; *Seasons in England,* Nanundo, 1979; *Between England and Japan,* Seibido, 1979; *Golden Words,* Hokuseido, 1979; *An English Education,* Hokuseido, 1979; *Happenings and Non-Happenings,* Eichosha, 1979; *A New Utopia,* Aratake Shuppan, 1979; *The English Way of Life,* Azuma Shobo, 1979; *The Heart of Western Culture,* Kinseido, 1979; *The Mystery of Words,* Nanundo, 1979; *Invitation to Intellectual Life: Conversations With Students,* Seibido, 1979.

Textbooks: *An Introduction to Shakespeare's Plays,* Kenkyusha, 1964; *Christian Themes in English Literature,* Kenkyusha, 1967; *A Commentary on G. M. Hopkins' "The Wreck of the Deutschland,"* Hokuseido, 1968; *A Commentary on T. S. Eliot's "Four Quartets,"* Hokuseido, 1968; *An Introduction to Christianity,* Hokuseido, 1968; *A Commentary on the Sonnets of G. M. Hopkins,* Hokuseido, 1969; *The New Testament and English Literature,* Hokuseido, 1969; *A Historical Survey of English Literature,* Kenkyusha, 1969; *England Through the Ages,* Kaibunsha, 1970; *Anthology of English Thinkers,* Kenkyusha, 1971; *English: Right and Wrong,* Kenkyusha, 1972; *Christianity in England,* Kaibunsha, 1972; *Shakespeare's Religious Background,* Indiana University Press, 1973; *The Continuity of English Poetry,* Hokuseido, 1974; *Shakespeare's Tales Retold,* Azuma Shobo, 1974; *The Meaning of English Masterpieces,* Kaibunsha, 1974; *A Miscellany of Mistakes,* Azuma Shobo, 1974; *Landscape and Inscape: Vision and Inspiration in Hopkins' Poetry,* Eerdmans, 1975; *Biblical Themes in Shakespeare: Centring on King Lear* (monograph), Renaissance Institute of Japan, 1975; *More Shakespeare's Tales Retold,* Azuma Shobo, 1975; *The Heart of England,* Hokuseido, 1976; *Fresh English,* Asahi Press, 1976; *Religious Controversies of the Elizabethan Age: A Survey of Printed Sources,* University of Nebraska Press, 1977; *Jesus and His Disciples,* Tsurumi Shoten, 1977; *Introducing English Literature,* Shinkosha, 1977; *English Delight,* Asahi Press, 1977; *Religious Controversies of the Jacobean Age: A Survey of Printed Sources,* University of Nebraska Press, 1978; *Shakespeare's View of English History,* Shinkosha, 1979; *Shakespeare's Soliloquies,* Shinkosha, 1980.

In Japanese: *Eibungaku to Catholicism* (title means "English Literature and Catholicism"), Chuo Shuppansha, 1969; *Shakespeare to shukyo* (title means "Shakespeare and Religion"), Aratake Shuppan, 1977; *Nichi-ei kotowaza-ko* (title means "Japanese and English Proverbs"), Aratake Shuppan, 1977; *Igirisujin no kotoba to chie* (title means "Golden Words From England"), Asahi Evening News, 1978; *Seiyo bunka no genryu wo tazunete* (title means "In Search of the Sources of Western Culture"), Sanseido, 1979.

Editor: *T. S. Eliot: A Tribute From Japan,* Kenkyusha, 1966; (and author of introduction) G. K. Chesterton, *Essays on Shakespeare,* Kenkyusha, 1968; (and author of introduction) Chesterton, *Orthodoxy,* Hokuseido, 1969; *Edmund Blunden: A Tribute From Japan,* Kenkyusha, 1974; *Readings of the Wreck,* Loyola University Press, 1976; *John Donne: Holy Sonnets,* Kenkyusha, 1979 (Japanese edition published as *John Donne no Sei-naru Sonnets;* see below).

Editor—In Japanese: *G. K. Chesterton no sekai* (title means "Chesterton's World"), Kenkyusha, 1970; *G. K. Chesterton chosaku-shu* (title means "Select Works of G. K. Chesterton"), ten volumes, Shunjusha, 1973-79; *Eikoku renaissance to shukyo* (title means "English Renaissance and Religion"), Aratake Shuppan, 1975; *Lear-O ni okeru shizen* (title means "Nature in 'King Lear'"), Aratake Shuppan, 1976; *Keiji-joshi to meishoshi* (title means "Poetry of Metaphysics and Meditation"), Aratake Shuppan, 1976; *Chusei to renaissance* (title means "Medieval and Renaissance"), Aratake Shuppan, 1977; *Renaissance-ki no shinpi shiso* (title means "Renaissance and Mysticism"), Aratake Shuppan, 1978; *Renaissance to gendai* (title means "Renaissance and Modern"), Aratake Shuppan, 1979; *John Donne no sei-naru sonnets,* Aratake Shuppan, 1980 (see above).

Contributor: Joseph Roggendorf, editor, *Studies in Japanese Culture,* Sophia University Press, 1963; *Eigo no shoso II* (title means "Various Approaches to English"), Kenkyusha, 1965; Sheila Sullivan, editor, *Critics on T. S. Eliot,* Allen & Unwin, 1973; John Sullivan, editor, *G. K. Chesterton: A*

Centenary Appraisal, Elek, 1974; Motoshi Karita, editor, *Toshi to eibei-bungaku* (title means "The City and English Literature"), Kenkyusha, 1974; *Eigo kenkyu no 70 nen* (title means "Seventy Years of 'Eigo Kenkyu'"), Kenkyusha, 1975; Masaho Hirai, editor, *Renaissance no bungaku to shiso* (title means "Literature and Thought in the Renaissance"), Chikuma, 1977; *Nihon to watakushi* (title means "Japan and I"), Asahi Shinbun, 1977; Akio Sawada, editor, *Thomas More to sono jidai* (title means "Thomas More and His Age"), Kenkyusha, 1978; Ikuo Koike, editor, *The Teaching of English in Japan,* Eichosha, 1978; Shunichi Takayanagi, editor, *Juyo no kiseki* (title means "Aspects of Cultural Reception"), Kenkyusha, 1979; Taizo Kusayanagi, editor, *Nichiyobi no oshaberi* (title means "Sunday Talks"), T. V. Hoeichu, 1979; *Eigo kyoiku no haikei* (title means "Background to English Education"), Kenkyusha, 1979. Contributor to literature, theology, and language journals in Japan and throughout the English-speaking world.

SIDELIGHTS: Milward writes: "My position as a Jesuit priest-professor teaching English literature to Japanese students is somewhat unique. My approach to English literature, particularly poetry and drama, is deeply influenced by my general interest in the Christian and classical heritage of the West. I have to make this available to Japanese students in a form they can understand easily, not only by explaining it in simple words and sentences, but also by drawing comparisons with what is familiar to them in Japan.

"At first my modest aim was to produce my own textbooks for use in my lectures on Shakespeare, English thinkers, and poets such as Hopkins and Eliot. Then I began to bring out collections of essays for use as readers in class, and these have proved very popular in Japan. At the same time, I like to keep a balance between popular writings and those of an academic nature. For the latter I often have opportunities to go abroad during the summer vacation and work at libraries in England and America, especially the Huntington Library in California, taking as my special field of research the religious background of Shakespeare and the religious controversies of his age.

"I write, not for the royalties, which accrue to the Jesuit Order, but partly for the enjoyment of writing, partly out of a deep desire to share my ideas and insights on literature and life with as many people as possible. If I feel I have something good, I don't like to keep it to myself. I want to tell others about it.

"What is this good I have? Simply, it is the love of God, which I find at the heart of English literature, especially in Shakespeare and Donne, in Hopkins and Eliot, in Chesterton and C. S. Lewis. These are the writers who have most deeply influenced my thought and feeling. I look at them not with a scholar's eyes, but rather with their eyes at the world around me—at the beauty of nature, at the movement of insects and animals, at the life of man; and I find everything pointing upwards, if with somewhat crooked lines, from man to God."

*   *   *

MIRENBURG, Barry (Leonard Steffan) 1952-

PERSONAL: Born February 16, 1952, in New York, N.Y.; son of Fred and Mildred (Solomon) Mirenburg. *Education:* Attended Fordham University, 1972; Cooper Union for the Advancement of Science and Art, B.F.A., 1974; Mercy College, Dobbs Ferry, N.Y., B.S., 1976; Rhode Island School of Design, M.A.E., 1978; New School of Social Research, M.A., 1978; doctoral study, 1978—. *Residence:* New York,

N.Y. *Office:* Barlenmir House, 413 City Island Ave., New York, N.Y. 10064.

CAREER: Barlenmir House, New York, N.Y., president and publisher, 1970—. President of Barlenmir House of Graphics (also director of design), 1970—, Barlenmir Foundation on the Arts, 1972—, Barlenmir House of Music, 1974—, Barlenmir House Theatres (also chief operating officer), 1974—, and City Island Theatre, Inc. (also chief operating officer), 1974—. Graphic designer; work exhibited at a New York gallery and Metropolitan Museum of Art. Member of advisory board of East Coast Writers Organization and Legislative Advisory Committee of New York; consultant to Film Art Fund and Film Art Archives.

MEMBER: International Platform Association, American Institute of Graphic Arts, American Association of Publishers, Copyright Society of the United States of America (member of advisory board), Mensa, Museum of Modern Art. *Awards, honors:* Art and graphics awards include award from *Art and Design,* 1972; award from Metropolitan Museum of Art, 1972, for poster; book design awards from American Institute of Graphic Arts; awards from New York Printers Association for communication graphics; awards from Society of Publications Designers for various magazine designs; Desi Award from *Graphics* for designs in book and communication graphics.

*WRITINGS—*Illustrator; all published by Barlenmir: *Down Came the Sun,* 1972; *Circle of Thaw,* 1972; *Voices/I Hear/Voices,* 1972; *Clockworks,* 1979; *The American Experience,* 1979; *Life Happiness,* 1979; *Busy People,* 1979; *Design Psychology,* 1980; *The Artist's Life,* 1981; *The Creative Lifestyle,* 1981.

Art editor for Catalyst Press. Contributor to magazines and newspapers in the United States and Europe. wart editor for *Croton Review.*

SIDELIGHTS: Mirenburg's view that the designer must develop as an artist and become intimately involved with the project at hand and the people for whom it is intended is illustrated by the painstaking attention to detail that goes into his own work. He becomes particularly engrossed in publishing limited editions which permit experiments with the "truly unique," although he recognizes the need to keep time and money expenditures within feasible limits.

He told *CA:* "My writings deal with the various states of mind, emotion, and expression as an act and breath of life. I believe highly in human potential, and wish for this kind of transformation in others."

AVOCATIONAL INTERESTS: Jogging, weightlifting, gymnastics, reading, international travel, and collecting fine art, fine antiques, classic Jaguars, first editions, and art and nonfiction books.

BIOGRAPHICAL/CRITICAL SOURCES: At Cooper Union, September, 1978.

*   *   *

MITCHELL, Elizabeth P(ryse)   1946-

PERSONAL: Born November 6, 1946, in Quantico, Va.; daughter of Louis D. (a dentist) and Katharine (a teacher; maiden name, Bowen) Mitchell. *Education:* Attended Smith College, 1964-66, 1967-68; Boston University, B.A., 1970; Simmons College, M.S., 1973. *Home:* 333 East Ontario St., Chicago, Ill. 60611. *Office:* The Public Relations Board, 150 East Huron St., Chicago, Ill. 60611.

CAREER/WRITINGS: Harvard University Library, Cambridge, Mass., editorial librarian, 1972-75; American Library Association, Chicago, Ill., assistant editor of *American Libraries* (magazine), 1975-77; CNA Insurance, Chicago, Ill., senior editor, 1977-78; Public Relations Board, Chicago, account executive, 1978—. Book reviewer for "About Books," a column syndicated by Newspaper Enterprise Association, 1976—. Contributor to *What Else You Can Do With a Library Degree,* edited by Betty-Carol Sellen, Neal-Shuman, 1980.

SIDELIGHTS: Elizabeth Mitchell told *CA:* "Like many writers, I dream of the day I'll have the time and financial security to write books. Meanwhile, as I'm building the foundations of my career, I've found 'hack' writing not only introduces me to areas of the real world I'd never have known about otherwise, it also gives me solid training in the art of word-craft. I enjoy reviewing books regularly and feel it too is a valuable part of my apprenticeship."

*   *   *

MITCHENSON, Francis Joseph Blackett
(Joe Mitchenson)

PERSONAL: Son of Francis William and Sarah (Roddam) Mitchenson. *Education:* Attended Fay Compton Studio of Dramatic Art. *Home:* 5 Venner Rd., Sydenham, London SE26 5EQ, England. *Office:* Raymond Mander and Joe Mitchenson Theatre Collection Ltd., 1 Duke St., Manchester Sq., London W.1, England.

CAREER: Professional actor in repertory, on tour, and in London, England, 1934-46; Raymond Mander and Joe Mitchenson Theatre Collection Ltd., London, founder and co-owner, 1946-77, co-director, 1977—. Guest on television programs. Honorary archivist of Sadler's Wells and Old Vic. *Military service:* British Army, Royal Horse Artillery, 1943.

*WRITINGS—*Under name Joe Mitchenson; all with Raymond Mander: *Hamlet Through the Ages,* Rockliff, 1952, 2nd edition, 1955; *Theatrical Companion to Shaw,* Rockliff, 1954; *Theatrical Companion to Maugham,* Rockliff, 1955; *The Artist and the Theatre,* Heinemann, 1955; *Theatrical Companion to Coward,* Rockliff, 1957; *A Picture History of British Theatre,* Hulton, 1957; (with Mander and J. C. Trewin) *The Gay Twenties,* Macdonald, 1958; (with Mander and Philip Hope-Wallace) *A Picture History of Opera,* Hulton, 1959.

(With J. C. Trewin) *The Turbulent Thirties,* Macdonald, 1960; *Theatres of London,* Hart-Davis, 1961, 3rd edition, New English Library, 1975; *A Picture History of Gilbert and Sullivan,* Vista, 1962; *British Music Hall: A Story in Pictures,* Studio Vista, 1965, revised edition, Gentry Books, 1974; *Lost Theatres of London,* Hart-Davis, 1968, 2nd edition, New English Library, 1976; *Musical Comedy: A Story in Pictures,* P. Davies, 1969.

With Raymond Mander: *Revue: A Story in Pictures,* P. Davies, 1971; *Pantomime: A Story in Pictures,* P. Davies, 1973; *The Wagner Companion,* W. H. Allen, 1977; *Victorian and Edwardian Entertainments From Old Photographs,* Batsford, 1978; *A Guide to the Somerset Maugham Theatrical Paintings,* Heinemann, 1980. Contributor to *Encyclopaedia Britannica.* Contributor to *Theatre Notebook* and *Books and Bookmen.*

SIDELIGHTS: Mitchenson and Mander began their partnership in 1939. During World War II they worked together on theatre gramophone programs for the British Broadcasting Corp., and they went on tour in 1943.

The Raymond Mander and Joe Mitchenson Theatre Collection, which they owned until 1977, was made into a trust and registered as a charity. Mander and Mitchenson remain directors of the collection, with Colin Mauberly as curator. They also work as theatrical consultants.

In 1977, the collection was the largest comprehensive theatrical collection in private hands. Now housed in the Lewisham borough of London, it consists of printed and sound archives, a library, manuscripts, paintings, costumes, and theatrical memorabilia, as well as thousands of plays, both printed and in manuscript form, photographs, programs, and gramophone records.

The collection, covering most branches of live entertainment, is used by writers, researchers, television and radio producers, theatre managers and directors, and film directors and designers. Its educational value has become more apparent with recent increased interest in theatre history in schools and universities. It has provided exhibitions all over the world, including the United States, Australia, and the Soviet Union.

AVOCATIONAL INTERESTS: Sunbathing.

BIOGRAPHICAL/CRITICAL SOURCES: "Aquarius," first broadcast by London Weekend Television, March 20, 1971.

*   *   *

MITCHENSON, Joe
See MITCHENSON, Francis Joseph Blackett

*   *   *

MOLE, John 1941-

PERSONAL: Born October 12, 1941, in Taunton, Somerset, England; son of Edgar Douglas (a chartered accountant) and Lilian Joyce (Hook) Mole; married Mary Norman (a freelance artist), August 22, 1968; children: Simon, Benjamin. *Education:* Magdalene College, Cambridge, B.A. (with honors), 1964. *Home:* 11 Hill St., St. Albans, Hertfordshire, England.

CAREER: Haberdashers' Aske's School, Elstree, Hertfordshire, England, teacher of English, 1964-73; Verulam School, St. Albans, England, teacher of English and head of department, 1973—. Exchange teacher in Riverdale, N.Y., 1969-70. Has made guest appearances on BBC-Radio programs, including "Poetry Now," "Forget Tomorrow's Monday," "Time for Verse," and "Pick of the Week." *Member:* National Poetry Society (member of council), Eastern Arts Association, Ver Poets (vice-president, 1979—). *Awards, honors:* Eric Gregory Award from Society of Authors, 1970.

WRITINGS—Poetry: A Feather for Memory, Outposts Publications, 1961; *The Instruments,* Phoenix Pamphlet Poets Press, 1970; *Something About Love,* Sycamore Press, 1972; *The Love Horse,* Peterloo Poets, 1973; *A Partial Light,* Dent, 1975; *Our Ship,* Secker & Warburg, 1977; *The Mortal Room,* Priapus Poets, 1977; *On the Set,* Keepsake Poems, 1978; *From the House Opposite,* Secker & Warburg, 1979; *Feeding the Lake,* Secker & Warburg, 1981.

Other writings: (With Carol Burgess, Tony Burgess, and others) *Understanding Children Writing* (nonfiction), Penguin, 1973; (editor) *Poetry: A Selection,* Dacorum College, 1974; (with wife, Mary Norman) *Once There Were Dragons* (juvenile), Deutsch, 1979; (editor with Anthony Thwaite) *British Poetry Since 1945,* Longman, 1981. Also author of scripts for "Starting From Home," BBC-Radio, 1980.

Co-founder and editor of Mandeville Press, 1974—. Contributor to newspapers and magazines, including *Times Literary Supplement, New Statesman, Listener, London Magazine,* and *Encounter.*

SIDELIGHTS: John Mole told *CA:* "Much of my work has been concerned with the experience of childhood—not, I hope, in any blandly nostalgic sense, but in the attempt to demonstrate, to dramatize the fascination, the bewilderment of being young. I also find myself moved to composition by 'sacred' places—what the painter Paul Nash called 'charged landscapes.' This sense of the sacred is peculiarly personal and can be fully realized only in the making of poems. Like Louis MacNiece, I write poems because I seem to become restless when I don't.

"Although I have come, increasingly, to agree with Valery's statement that a poem is never finished, only abandoned, I could never make this an excuse for muddled thinking, fudged sentiment, or sloppy versification in my (or any other poet's) work. The passionate, precise ambiguity of true poetry is to be found in its firm, inevitable shape."

In a review of *Our Ship* (1977), a critic for *Thames Poetry* commented that Mole "is intelligent, witty, self-deprecating, a lively and delighted observer of the oddities of persons." The particular strengths of his poetic observations include a "fastidious attentiveness" and a wit that "converts the familiar into the grotesque," according to the *Times Literary Supplement.* "His world is the sharply observed one of literate urban and provincial life," added a writer for *Time Out,* "each line its own scene with a light self-mocking which makes the poems easy and pleasant to read." A review in the *Sunday Telegraph* concludes, "*Our Ship* establishes [Mole] as an anti-romantic with a warm, human sympathy and the ability to embody these attributes in an almost primitive clarity. Of his work for children, *Use of English* has written, "John Mole joins Ted Hughes and Charles Causley in that select group of contemporary poets who can write for children with complete directness and sincerity."

BIOGRAPHICAL/CRITICAL SOURCES: Thames Poetry, Volume I, number 4, 1977; *Sunday Telegraph,* May 8, 1977; *Times Literary Supplement,* May 20, 1977; *Time Out,* August 19, 1977; *Use of English,* summer, 1980.

*   *   *

MOMMSEN, Wolfgang J(ustin) 1930-

PERSONAL: Born November 11, 1930, in Marburg/Lahn, Germany; son of Wilhelm (a professor) and Marie (Iken) Mommsen; married Sabine von Schalburg, October 4, 1965; children: Hans, Kai, Kerstin, Johanne. *Education:* Attended University of Marburg, 1951-53; University of Cologne, Ph.D., 1958; postdoctoral study at University of Leeds, 1959. *Religion:* Protestant. *Home:* Troldheim, Coombe Hill Rd., Kingston-upon-Thames, Surrey, England. *Office:* German Historical Institute, 42 Russell Sq., London WC1B 5DA, England.

CAREER: University of Cologne, Cologne, West Germany, research assistant, 1959-67, private docent, 1967; University of Duesseldorf, Duesseldorf, West Germany, professor of modern history, beginning 1968; German Historical Institute, London, England, director, 1978—. *Member:* Verband Deutscher Historiker, Royal Historical Society.

WRITINGS: The Age of Bureaucracy, Oxford University Press, 1974.

In German: *Das Zeitalter des Imperialismus* (title means "The Age of Imperialism"), Fischer, 1969; *Max Weber und die deutsche Politik* (title means "Max Weber and German Policy"), J.C.B. Mohr, 2nd edition, 1974; *Imperialismustheorien* (title means "Theories of Imperialism"), Vandenhoeck & Ruprecht, 1977; *Der Imperialismus* (title means "Imperialism"), Hoffmann & Campe, 1977.

WORK IN PROGRESS: Research on imperialism, Germany during the Bismarck and Wilhelmine era, the inter-war period, and the political and sociological thought of Max Weber.

*　　*　　*

MONEY-KYRLE, Roger (Ernie)   1898-1980

OBITUARY NOTICE: Born in 1898; died July 29, 1980. Psychologist and author. "One of the last Englishmen to be psychoanalysed in Vienna by Freud himself," Money-Kyrle worked as a lay analyst in London from 1950 until his eightieth birthday. His books, including *Psychoanalysis and Politics,* 1951, *Man's Picture of His World,* 1956, and *Collected Papers,* 1979, are respected for explaining difficult subjects in a forthright style. Obituaries and other sources: *London Times,* August 8, 1980.

*　　*　　*

MONK, Lorraine (Althea Constance)

PERSONAL: Born in Montreal, Quebec, Canada; daughter of Edwin and Eileen Marion (Nurse) Spurrell; married John McCaughan Monk (deceased); children: Leslie Ann, Karyn Elizabeth, John Spurrell, David Chapman. *Education:* McGill University, B.A., 1944, M.A., 1946. *Home and office:* 176 Balmoral Ave., Toronto, Ontario, Canada M4V 1J6.

CAREER: National Film Board, Ottawa, Ontario, writer, 1957-59, director of Still Photography Division, 1960—. Produced "Photography '75," an exhibition for International Women's Year, 1975, and "Year of the Child Exhibition," 1979. Honorary chairman of board of directors of Photo Ecology Foundation of America. *Awards, honors:* Award from Federation Internationale de l'Art photographique, 1966; Centennial Medal from Government of Canada, 1967; member of Order of Canada, 1973; award from Look of Books, 1974, and silver medal from International Book Fair, 1975, both for *Canada;* award from International Gallery of Superb Printing, 1976, and gold medal from International Book Fair, 1977, both for *Between Friends;* fellow of Ontario College of Art, 1980; gold medal from National Association of Photographic Art, 1973, for "distinguished contribution to Canadian photography."

WRITINGS: Canada: A Year of the Land—Canada du temps qui passe, Queen's Printer, 1967; *Call Them Canadians: Ces visages qui sont un pays,* Queen's Printer, 1968; *Stones of History: Canada's Houses of Parliament—Temoin d'un siecle: Le Palais du gouvernement canadien,* Queen's Printer, 1969; *Image,* National Film Board, Volume I: *The Many Worlds of Lutz Dille,* 1967, Volume II: *Photography Canada,* 1967, Volume III: *Other Places: Sous d'autres cieux,* 1968, Volume IV: *If This Is the Time,* 1969, Volume V: *Seeds of the Spacefields,* 1969, Volume VI: *Image Six,* 1970, Volume VII: *Polyptque deux,* 1970, Volume VIII: *BC Almanac,* 1970, Volume IX: *Image Nine,* 1971, Volume X: *Les Ouvriers,* 1971; *A Time to Dream: Reveries en couleurs,* McClelland & Stewart, 1971; (with Allan Fleming and Ernie Herzig) *Canada,* Clarke, Irwin, 1973, 3rd edition, 1974; (editor) *The Female Eye: Coup d'oeil feminin,* Clarke, Irwin, 1975; *Between Friends: Entre amis,* McClelland & Stewart, 1976.

WORK IN PROGRESS: Under the Arctic Ice, with J. MacInnis.

SIDELIGHTS: In 1967 Lorraine Monk was responsible for the opening of the first photo gallery in Canada, the National Film Board Photo Gallery in Ottawa. In the same year she started a program of traveling photographic exhibitions that crossed Canada and toured abroad. In 1974 she opened to the public the Canadian Government Conference Centre for major photographic exhibits. In 1977 she moved to Toronto where she is currently working to establish the Canadian Museum of Photography.

*　　*　　*

MONTERO, Darrel Martin   1946-

PERSONAL: Born March 4, 1946, in Sacramento, Calif.; son of Frank A. (in aerospace work) and Ann (Montero) Naake; married Tara Kathleen McLaughlin (a writer), July 6, 1975; children: David Paul. *Education:* California State University, Sacramento, A.B., 1970; University of California, Los Angeles, M.A., 1972, Ph.D., 1975. *Politics:* Democrat. *Religion:* Roman Catholic. *Home:* 1553 West Jacinto, Mesa, Ariz. 85202. *Office:* School of Social Work, Arizona State University, Mill St., Tempe, Ariz. 85281.

CAREER: University of Southern California, Los Angeles, lecturer in sociology, 1971-72; Case Western Reserve University, Cleveland, Ohio, assistant professor of sociology, 1975-76; University of Maryland, College Park, assistant professor of urban studies and research sociologist for public opinion survey, 1976-79, director of urban ethnic research program, 1977-79; Arizona State University, Tempe, associate professor of social work and director of urban ethnic research program, 1979—. Guest on national television and radio programs. Consultant to Arthur Young & Co. *Member:* International Sociological Society, International Association for Prejudice and Peace Research (founding member), American Sociological Association, Sociological Society for Asia and Asian America, Eastern Sociological Association, Pacific Sociological Association, Southern Sociological Society.

WRITINGS: Urban Studies: An Anthology and Workbook, Kendall/Hunt, 1978; *Vietnamese Americans: Patterns of Resettlement and Socioeconomic Adaptation in the United States,* Westview Press, 1979; *Japanese Americans: Changing Patterns of Ethnic Affiliation Over Three Generations,* Westview Press, 1980. Co-editor of *Journal of Social Issues.*

WORK IN PROGRESS: Principles of Sociology, publication by Houghton expected in 1982; *Social Problems,* with Judith McDowell, Wiley, 1982; *Vietnamese Refugees in America,* completion expected in 1983; *The Sociology of the Family,* 1984.

SIDELIGHTS: Montero commented: "I have had a decade-long career involving the integration of basic and applied research. I have studied racial and cultural minorities, notably Japanese, blacks, and most recently Vietnamese regarding refugee immigration policy. In regard to my study of Vietnamese Americans, I have had the opportunity to testify before the President's Commission on Immigration and Refugee Policy.

"My interest in the study of Japanese Americans was first sparked during my years as a graduate student in sociology at the University of California, Los Angeles, when I became a member of the Japanese American Research Project. As director of research on that project, my work made me acutely aware of the discrimination and hardship the Japanese have faced in America, and the socioeconomic advances they have achieved despite the difficulties they faced. The story of the Japanese in America is one of remarkable endurance and pride. There is much to be learned from their struggles and painstaking progress, and I am ever grateful for the opportunity I have had to know them better. The study of their struggles has led me quite naturally to an interest in other Asian immigrant groups, most recently to the resettlement of some three hundred twenty-five thousand Vietnamese refugees in the United States.

"I soon learned that little research had been conducted on these new arrivals. After much digging at the Interagency Task Force for Indochina Refugees and correspondence with the handful of scholars conducting research on the Vietnamese, I have pieced together what I believe is a large and rich source of data. This will be invaluable to scholars conducting research on Vietnamese resettlement in the United States."

* * *

MONTFORT, Auguste 1913-
(Auguste Le Breton)

PERSONAL: Born February 18, 1913, in Lesneven, France; son of Eugene Montfort; married Marguerite Lecacheur; children: Maryvonne Le Breton Lederfajn. *Politics:* None. *Religion:* "Without *Francmacon.*" *Home and office:* 12 rue Pasteur, 78110 Le Vesinet, France.

CAREER: Worked as a construction worker, elevator repairman, and gambler. Writer, 1953—. *Military service:* Forces Francaises Combattantes, served in World War II; received Croix de Guerre.

WRITINGS—All under pseudonym Auguste Le Breton; in English translation: La Loi des rues, Presses de la Cite, 1955, translation by Nigel Ryan published as *The Law of the Streets,* Collins, 1957; *Du Rififi a New York,* Presses de la Cite, 1962, translation by Peter Leslie published as *Rififi in New York,* Stein & Day, 1962.

Other writings: *Du Rififi chez les hommes,* Gallimard, 1953; *Les Hauts Murs* (novel), Denoel, 1954; *Le Rouge est mis,* Gallimard, 1954, reprinted, 1976; *Razzia sur la chnouf,* Gallimard, 1954; *Rafles sur la ville,* Presses de la Cite, 1956; *Du Rififi chez les femmes,* Presses de la Cite, 1957; *Les Tricards,* Presses de la Cite, 1958.

L'Argot chez les vrais de vrais, Presses de la Cite, 1960; *Les Racketters,* Presses de la Cite, 1960; *Langue verte et noirs desseins,* Presses de la Cite, 1960; *Priez pour nous,* Presses de la Cite, 1961; *Du Rififi au Mexique: Chez Cuanthemoc, empereur azteque,* Presses de la Cite, 1963; *Du Rififi au Proche-Orient,* Presses de la Cite, 1963; *Du Rififi a Panama: Face au syndicat du crime,* Plon, 1964; *Du Rififi a Hong-Kong: Societes secretes criminelles,* Plon, 1964; *Du Rififi a Barcelone: Toreros et truands,* Presses de la Cite, 1964; *Brigade anti-gangs: Section de recherche et d'intervention,* Plon, 1965; *Du Rififi au Cambodge: Opium sur Angkor-Vat,* Plon, 1965; *Le Clan des Siciliens,* Plon, 1967; *Les Juenes Voyous: A Chacun son destin,* Plon, 1967; *Du Rififi derriere le rideau de fer: Le Soleil du Prague,* Plon, 1968; *Du vent,* Plon, 1968; *Les Maq's,* Plon, 1968; *Du Rififi au Canada: Le Bouncer,* Plon, 1969.

Le Tueur a la une, Plon, 1971; *Rouges etaient les emeraudes,* Plon, 1971; *Malfrats and Co.* (biography), R. Laffont, 1971; *Les Bourlingueurs,* Plon, 1972; *Les Pegriots,* R. Laffont, 1973; *Du Rififi en Argentine: Ou souffle le Pampero,* Presses Pocket, *1973;* Monsieur Rififi *(biography) title means "Mr. Rififi"),* Table Ronde, 1976.

Also author of: *Rififi en Bresil: Escadron de la mort,* Presses Pocket; *Adventures sous les tropiques,* Editions Pygmalion; *Les Antigangs,* Presses Pocket, Volume I: *L'As des antigangs,* Volume II: *L'As et belles chaussures,* Volume III: *L'As et le casse du siecle,* Volume IV: *L'As et la marquise,* Volume V: *L'As et l'ennemi public,* Volume VI: *L'As et les terroristes,* Volume VII: *L'As au Senegal,* Volume VIII: *L'As et les Malfrats.*

SIDELIGHTS: Le Breton told *CA* that he published his first book after struggling with life for nearly forty years. An orphan, he left a detention center at age eighteen to take a job as a construction worker. Economic conditions forced him out of his work, however, and onto the streets, where for nine months he slept in parks and subways, eating whatever scraps he could find. After surviving a bout with tuberculosis, Le Breton found employment again as an elevator repairman. His hard luck continued, though, when he was fired for helping a fellow worker organize a strike.

A career as a clandestine gambler followed, he commented to *CA.* La Breton ran illegal poker and roulette games and worked as a bookie until called to do undercover work for France during World War II. He returned from service to become a full-time bookmaker.

Le Breton had decided during one of his unemployment periods that if he were ever to have a child, he would want it to know about and understand his past. So when his daughter was born in 1947, he decided to write a book about his own childhood. The result was *Les Hauts Murs,* which was rejected by publisher after publisher until finally being accepted in 1954. The book became a best seller.

Le Breton has continued to write and has also done a great deal of traveling in order to enrich his experiences and better understand mankind.

* * *

MOORE, Tom 1950-

PERSONAL: Born September 5, 1950, in St. John's, Newfoundland, Canada; son of James Thomas (a sailor) and Mary (a teacher; maiden name, Newbury) Moore. *Education:* Received B.A., B.Ed., and M.A. from Memorial University of Newfoundland. *Religion:* Roman Catholic. *Home address:* Station Rd., Avondale C.B., Newfoundland, Canada A0A 1B0. *Office:* Pius X High School, Baie Verte W.B., Newfoundland, Canada A0K 1B0.

CAREER: Jesperson Press, St. John's, Newfoundland, editor-in-chief, 1978-79; Pius X High School, Baie Verte, Newfoundland, English teacher and head of department, 1979—. Liberal candidate for provincial election, 1979. *Member:* Writers Union of Canada. *Awards, honors:* *Good-Bye Momma* was named one of the best children's books in Canada.

WRITINGS: *Good-Bye Momma* (juvenile novel), Breakwater Press, 1976, 3rd edition, 1980; *A Biography of Norman Duncan,* Memorial University of Newfoundland, 1977; *Tom Cod's Kids and Confederation,* Jesperson Press, 1979; *A Biography of Sir Wilfred Grenfell,* Fitzhenry & Whiteside, 1980. Work represented in anthologies. Contributor of poems to magazines.

WORK IN PROGRESS: *Sally Gordon and the Fishes,* a juvenile novel; *Screechey-vous,* a humorous novel.

SIDELIGHTS: Moore told *CA:* "As a school teacher I am fascinated by the world of my students. Invariably I draw on this world in my poetry and fiction. I enjoy reading to them and discussing my own and others' work with them.

"I have done several reading tours of Canadian schools and universities. Newfoundland is a rather isolated corner of our continent and I enjoyed the exposure."

*   *   *

MOOREHEAD, Caroline 1944-

PERSONAL: Born October 28, 1944, in London, England; daughter of Alan McCrae (a writer) and Lucy (Milner) Moorehead; married Jeremy Swift (an economist), May 27, 1967; children: Martha, Daniel. *Education:* University of London, B.A. (with honors), 1965. *Politics:* Labour. *Religion:* Church of England. *Home:* 36 Fitzroy Rd., London N.W.1, England. *Agent:* Felicity Bryan, Curtis Brown Ltd., One Craven Hill, London W2 3EP, England. *Office: London Times,* Grays Inn Rd., London W.C.1, England.

CAREER: Neuropsychiatric Hospital, Rome, Italy, psychologist, 1966-68; *Time,* Rome, reporter, 1968-69; *London Telegraph,* London, England, feature writer, 1969-70; *London Times Educational Supplement,* London, features editor, 1970-73; *London Times,* London, features writer, 1973—.

WRITINGS: (Editor and translator) *Myths and Legends of Britain,* Burke Publishing, 1968; *Helping: A Guide to Voluntary Work,* Macdonald & Jane's, 1975; (with Margaret Trudeau) *Beyond Reason,* Paddington Press, 1979; *Hostages to Fortune,* Atheneum, 1980. Contributor of articles and reviews to magazines and newspapers.

WORK IN PROGRESS: A biography of Lord Bernstein in Granada, publication by J. Cape expected in 1982; editing letters of Dame Freya Stark.

*   *   *

MOOSE, Ruth 1938-

PERSONAL: Born August 24, 1938, in Albemarle, N.C.; daughter of Ardie L. and Vera (Smith) Morris; married Talmadge Moose (an artist), June 17, 1955; children: Lyle, Barry. *Education:* Attended University of North Carolina. *Home and office address:* Route 2, Stony Mountain, Albemarle, N.C. 28001. *Agent:* Marian McNamara, A. Watkins, Inc., 77 Park Ave., New York, N.Y. 10016.

CAREER: Writer. Stanly Technical Institute, Albemarle, N.C., in public relations, 1974-75; free-lance public relations representative, 1975—. Seminar director; chairman of Artists/Writers Dialog; judge for literary contests; gives readings; member of executive committee for North Carolina Cultural Resources. Teacher of creative writing at Montgomery Technical Institute. *Awards, honors:* First place award from Virginia Highlands Festival, 1976, for plays, "Crucible," "Appalachian Harvest," and "Yankee."

WRITINGS: "To Survive" (collection of plays), Bookmark Press, 1980. Also author of "Finding Things in the Dark" (collection), Briarpatch Press. Work represented in anthologies, including *From the Hills Anthology* and *Southern Poetry Review Anthology.* Contributor of more than one hundred stories, poems, and articles to magazines and newspapers, including *Good Housekeeping, Prairie Schooner, New York Times, Canadian Forum, Woman's Day, Mother Earth News,* and *House and Garden.* Editor of *Uwharrie Review.*

WORK IN PROGRESS: A novel about small-town politics, tentatively entitled *A Few Good Funerals.*

SIDELIGHTS: Ruth Moose wrote: "I live in a house my husband and I designed and built on an eight-hundred-acre mountain near Uwharrie National Forest. There are only

two other houses on the mountain. For four years we walked a mile daily for our mail. The area is noted for its abundant population of deer and other wildlife. It's a quiet place to think and work.

"I can't remember when I wasn't in love with words. Sometimes I think I was born with a book in my hand, but writing was something I did only for myself for many years. The idea of publication did not occur to me until I was well into my twenties and I've published regularly in various forms, from poetry to short stories to plays and articles ever since."

*   *   *

MORAES, (Marcus) Vinicius (Cruz) de (Mello) 1913-1980

OBITUARY NOTICE: Born October 19, 1913, in Gavea, Rio de Janiero, Brazil; died of a lung ailment in 1980 in Rio de Janiero, Brazil. Diplomat, poet, dramatist, and lyricist. Vinicius de Moraes served his native Brazil as a government official in various capacities for nearly twenty years. He was also a noted poet and dramatist. Some of his works include *Cinco elegias, Livro de sonetos,* and *Ordeu da conceicao,* which later provided the basis for the film "Black Orpheus." A noted popular composer and lyricist of sambas and bossa novas, Moraes brought the world such well-known favorites as "The Girl From Ipanema." Obituaries and other sources: *The Penguin Companion to American Literature,* McGraw, 1971; *Who's Who in the World,* 2nd edition, Marquis, 1973; *The International Who's Who,* Europa, 1979; *World Authors, 1970-1975,* Wilson, 1980; *Time,* July 21, 1980.

*   *   *

MORAWETZ, Thomas H(ubert) 1942-

PERSONAL: Born July 22, 1942, in Montreal, Quebec, Canada; came to the United States in 1942, naturalized citizen, 1947; son of Frederick and Melanie (Landau) Morawetz. *Education:* Harvard University, A.B., 1963; attended Oxford University, 1963-64; Yale University, LL.B., 1968, Ph.D., 1969. *Home:* 8-G Staunton Court, Farmington, Conn. 06032. *Office:* School of Law, University of Connecticut, West Hartford, Conn. 06117.

CAREER: Yale University, New Haven, Conn., assistant professor, 1969-74, associate professor of philosophy, 1974-77; University of Connecticut, School of Law, West Hartford, professor of law, 1977—. *Member:* American Philosophical Association, American Society for Political and Legal Philosophy, Phi Beta Kappa. *Awards, honors:* Fulbright scholarship, 1963-64; National Endowment for the Humanities fellowship, summer, 1978.

WRITINGS: Wittgenstein and Knowledge, University of Massachusetts Press, 1978; *The Philosophy of Law,* Macmillan, 1980. Contributor to *Encyclopedia of Bioethics.* Contributor of about a dozen articles to law and philosophy journals.

WORK IN PROGRESS: Paternalism and Rights (tentative title), publication expected in 1983; research on the epistemology of moral judgment and its implications for law.

SIDELIGHTS: Morawetz told *CA:* "My primary research interest is the nature of moral reasoning. I am concerned with the epistemology of moral judgment and with the nature of moral justification in the light of the critique of foundationalism in contemporary philosophy. Wittgenstein's response to foundationalism has influenced my approach to these issues heavily. A special area of interest is the nature of moral resources available in judicial decision-making and the appropriate role of such resources. My work over the next year or two will be an attempt to analyze how the claim that persons have rights may be defended and justified and how personal and governmental interference in the lives of persons is justified. I shall also be writing about related issues in the philosophy of mind such as moral choice and self determination, self-awareness, and understanding the wants and needs of others.''

* * *

MORGAN, Gwen

PERSONAL: Born in Chicago, Ill.; daughter of Edgar Rees (a banker, oil producer, and cattle breeder) and Ethel (Yarick) Morgan; married Arthur Veysey (a journalist and writer), February 24, 1946; children: Priscilla (Mrs. David Donald Skinner). *Education:* Smith College, B.A. *Religion:* Protestant. *Home and office:* Cantigny, 1S 151 Winfield Rd., Wheaton, Ill. 60187. *Agent:* Harold Matson Co., 22 East 40th St., New York, N.Y. 10016.

CAREER: Emporia Gazette, Emporia, Kan., reporter, 1939; *Kansas City Kansan,* Kansas City, Kan., reporter and photographer, 1940; KCKN-Radio, Kansas City, reporter, 1940; *Omaha World-Herald,* Omaha, Neb., reporter, 1941; United Press, staff correspondent in Chicago, Ill., 1942, and in Washington, D.C., 1943-46; *Chicago Tribune,* Chicago, foreign correspondent in Europe, Middle East, Africa, and Far East, 1946-72, bureau chief in Paris, France, 1972-75; Cantigny Trust, Wheaton, Ill., director of Robert R. McCormick Museum, 1975—. Trustee of Illinois Benedictine College, 1977—. *Member:* Washington Press Club (Washington, D.C.), Fortnightly Club of Chicago (Chicago, Ill.), Smith College Club of Chicago. *Awards, honors:* Edward Scott Beck Award from *Chicago Tribune,* 1951, for stories on British election, and 1963, for stories on death and funeral of Pope John and election and coronation of Pope Paul VI.

WRITINGS: Cicero and the Silver Drums (nonfiction), Arlington Books, 1972; (with husband, Arthur Veysey, and George Halas) *Halas by Halas* (autobiography), McGraw, 1979.

WORK IN PROGRESS: A thriller; a narrative of experience in post-World War II Europe; two books about animals.

SIDELIGHTS: As a foreign correspondent for the *Chicago Tribune,* Gwen Morgan covered everything from the Vietnam peace talks in Paris to the marriage of Grace Kelly and Prince Rainier of Monaco. She reported on the deaths, accessions, and coronations of popes, kings, and queens; the trial of Adolph Eichmann in Jerusalem; and the Turkish earthquake of 1966. She told *CA:* "I enjoy seeing a piece of history unfold, setting its scene, describing it, dramatizing it for others to read and, in quickened imaginations, to see. I like writing about individuals who try to do their best and are responsible entities. In thinking persons, geared daily to try choosing the better thing, the hope of democracy lies.''

* * *

MORGAN, Henry
See van OST, Henry Lerner

* * *

MORGENTHAU, Hans Joachim 1904-1980

OBITUARY NOTICE—See index for *CA* sketch: Born February 17, 1904, in Coburg, Germany; died July 19, 1980, in New York, N.Y. Educator and author. Morgenthau, a prominent political scientist, helped establish the study of foreign policy as a separate academic pursuit. He advocated a realistic approach to international relations in which a country's national interests take precedence over worldwide opinion. Morgenthau was an early opponent to American involvement in Vietnam and a critic of the Central Intelligence Agency's (CIA) interference in Chile and other small countries. He taught at several educational institutions, serving the longest time at the University of Chicago. Morgenthau wrote numerous books, including *Politics Among Nations, The Decline of Democratic Politics,* and *A New Foreign Policy for the United States.* Obituaries and other sources: *Chicago Tribune,* July 21, 1980; *New York Times,* July 21, 1980; *Washington Post,* July 22, 1980; *Time,* August 4, 1980; *Newsweek,* August 4, 1980.

* * *

MORRILL, Allen C(onrad) 1904-

PERSONAL: Born November 20, 1904, in Shrewsbury, Mass.; son of Walter A. (a teacher) and Ella (a teacher; maiden name, Robbins) Morrill; married Eleanor A. Dunlap (a teacher), June 14, 1933; children: Walter, Gertrude (Mrs. C. Dean Mitchell), Janet (Mrs. R. Terry Hunter). *Education:* Brown University, B.A., 1926; Harvard University, M.A., 1932, Ph.D., 1937. *Religion:* Presbyterian. *Home and office:* 1065 Shenango Rd., Beaver Falls, Pa. 15010.

CAREER: Brown University, Providence, R.I., assistant, 1926-28, instructor in English, 1928-30; Washington and Jefferson College, Washington, Pa., instructor, 1932-37, assistant professor of English, 1937-38; Geneva College, Beaver Falls, Pa., associate professor, 1938-41, professor of English and dean of faculty, 1941-49; Michigan Mining & Technical College (now Michigan Tech University), Houghton, professor of languages and head of department, 1949-53; Monmouth College, Monmouth, Ill., professor of English and chairman of department, 1953-64; Geneva College, professor of English, 1964-69, professor emeritus, 1969—. *Member:* National Council of Teachers of English, Modern Language Association of America, Phi Beta Kappa, Rotary International.

WRITINGS: (With wife, Eleanor D. Morrill) *Out of the Blanket,* University of Idaho Press, 1978. Contributor to *Idaho Yesterdays.* Contributor to periodicals, including *Journal of Presbyterian History.*

WORK IN PROGRESS: Continuing research on the Nez Perce Indians of Idaho, 1870-1915; genealogical research.

SIDELIGHTS: Morrill commented to *CA:* "I've always been interested in history, especially of the early days of Western development. From the circumstances of my wife's early life in Idaho and our annual trips to that little-known region with close observation of the Nez Perce Indians, I have concentrated on that area of history.''

AVOCATIONAL INTERESTS: Travel (the Mediterranean, Israel, Egypt, England).

* * *

MORRILL, Eleanor D(unlap) 1907-

PERSONAL: Born March 6, 1907, in Mohler, Idaho; daughter of Robert E. (a physician) and Gertrude I. (a teacher; maiden name, Wheldon) Dunlap; married Allen Conrad Morrill (a professor), June 14, 1933; children: Walter, Gertrude (Mrs. C. Dean Mitchell), Janet (Mrs. R. Terry Hunter). *Education:* Whitman College, B.A., 1929; Radcliffe College, M.A., 1937. *Religion:* Presbyterian. *Home and office:* 1065 Shenango Rd., Beaver Falls, Pa. 15010.

CAREER: High school English teacher in Moscow, Idaho, 1929-33, and Monmouth, Ill., 1953-54; Monmouth College, Monmouth, librarian, 1954-60. *Member:* American Association of University Women (past president), Federation of Women's Clubs (president), Phi Beta Kappa.

WRITINGS: (With husband, Allen C. Morrill) *Out of the Blanket,* University of Idaho Press, 1978. Contributor to *Idaho Yesterdays* and to *Incredible Idaho.*

WORK IN PROGRESS: Continuing research on the Nez Perce Indians of Idaho, 1870-1915; genealogical research.

SIDELIGHTS: Eleanor Morrill told *CA:* "Growing up on the Nez Perce Indian Reservation in the first two decades of this century, I had intimate knowledge of white-Indian relationships. I have continued to try to preserve this in my writing and research. My objective has been to record for posterity some of those early impressions and experiences."

* * *

MORRIS, Helen 1909-

PERSONAL: Born September 3, 1909, in Dundee, Scotland; daughter of Charles Geddes (an architect) and Mary (Stewart) Soutar; married Christopher Morris (a university lecturer), March 20, 1933; children: Ann Morris Dizikes, Charles Antony. *Education:* Girton College, Cambridge, M.A. (with honors), 1931. *Home:* 5 Merton St., Cambridge, England.

CAREER: Writer. Associated with Foreign Office, Bletchley, England, 1940-43; lecturer in adult education, 1944-60; Homerton College, Cambridge, England, lecturer, 1958-75, principal lecturer in English and head of department, 1975—. *Member:* British Federation of University Women, Women Citizens Association, Townswomen's Guild.

WRITINGS: Portrait of a Chef (biography), Cambridge University Press, 1938, reprinted, University of Chicago Press, 1975; *Elizabethan Literature,* Oxford University Press, 1958; (contributor) Robert Gittings, editor, *Living Shakespeare,* Heinemann, 1960; *Notes on King Lear,* Basil Blackwell, 1965; *Notes on Richard II,* Basil Blackwell, 1966; *Where's That Poem?,* Basil Blackwell, 1967, 2nd edition, 1974; *Notes on Antony and Cleopatra,* Basil Blackwell, 1968; *Notes on Romeo and Juliet,* Basil Blackwell, 1970; (editor) *Love,* J. Murray, 1978; (editor) *Animals,* J. Murray, 1980. Contributor to literature journals and popular magazines, including *Wine and Food,* and newspapers.

WORK IN PROGRESS: Continuing research on Shakespeare.

SIDELIGHTS: Helen Morris commented: "It is clear that chance has contributed to my writings. My collection of early cookery books led to my 1938 biography of Soyer. Lecturing on Shakespeare led to the books on Elizabethan literature, and my work at Homerton showed the need for *Where's That Poem?*—widely used in schools and colleges of education. An academic friend asked for the love and animals anthologies."

AVOCATIONAL INTERESTS: Collecting eighteenth-century English ceramics, environmental conservation, "keeping the village atmosphere of the 'urban village' in which I live."

* * *

MORRIS, Scot 1942-

PERSONAL: Born August 2, 1942, in Kalamazoo, Mich.; son of David and Priscilla Morris; married Bryce Britton (a

writer), August 12, 1978. *Education:* DePauw University, B.A., 1964; Southern Illinois University, M.A., 1966, Ph.D., 1970. *Office: Omni,* 909 Third Ave., New York, N.Y. 10022.

CAREER: Psychology Today, New York City, associate editor, 1969-72; free-lance writer, 1972-78; *Omni,* New York City, senior editor and author of columns "Games" and "Competition," 1979—.

WRITINGS: The Book of Strange Facts and Useless Information, Doubleday, 1979.

WORK IN PROGRESS: A sequel to *The Book of Strange Facts and Useless Information;* a book of games.

SIDELIGHTS: Morris commented: "The magazine business keeps me busy doing two columns as well as writing feature articles, editing other people's writing, and procuring new material.

"My book is a collection of fascinating facts, *not* trivia."

* * *

MOSS, Ralph W(alter) 1943-

PERSONAL: Born May 6, 1943, in Brooklyn, N.Y.; son of Nat (in business) and Irene (an artist; maiden name, Greenfield) Moss; married Martha Bunim (a typesetter), May 24, 1964; children: Melissa, Benjamin. *Education:* New York University, B.A., 1965; Stanford University, M.A., 1973, Ph.D., 1974. *Residence:* Brooklyn, N.Y. *Agent:* Carol Mann Literary Agency, 168 Pacific St., Brooklyn, N.Y. 11201.

CAREER: University of California, Irvine, lecturer in classics, 1969-71; Hunter College of the City University of New York, New York City, assistant professor of classics, 1973-74; Memorial Sloan-Kettering Cancer Center, New York City, assistant director of public affairs, 1974-77; free-lance writer and consultant, 1977—. *Member:* National Association of Science Writers, American Association for the Advancement of Science, Human Ecology Action League, Phi Beta Kappa. *Awards, honors:* Founder's day award from New York University, 1965, for academic excellence; Humanitarian award from American Academy of Medical Preventics, 1978, for "furthering the efforts of science in preventive medicine."

WRITINGS: The Cancer Syndrome, Grove, 1980; (with Theron G. Randolph) *An Alternative Approach to Allergies,* Lippincott, 1980.

WORK IN PROGRESS: A novel with a scientific theme, publication expected in 1981; studies of controversial areas of science, particularly medicine, with a view toward understanding the nature of scientific progress and regression.

SIDELIGHTS: Moss commented: "In 1974 I was hired as a public relations officer at Memorial Sloan-Kettering Cancer Center. I soon became aware of a cover-up of positive animal data with the controversial anti-cancer substance, Laetrile. I was fired in 1977 for speaking out publicly. This provided the original impetus for *The Cancer Syndrome.* I have since broadened my interests to look at other aspects of suppression in the cultural field, especially medicine."

In her review of *The Cancer Syndrome,* Adelaide C. Rackemain wrote: "This is a shocking, disturbing book, a muckraking book in the best sense, which should be widely read. Some doctors who like the status quo will no doubt be outraged and claim that one or another of the author's well-documented allegations is false." She concluded: "In other readers, indignation will be tinged with sadness. They confront a nagging, unanswerable question: did my father, friend, aunt, brother, husband, or son die of cancer needlessly?'' Dr. Frank Combes concurred with that opinion. He said that some readers may disagree with Moss's contention that ''the traditional treatment of cancer by surgery, radiation, and chemotherapy, at best, is at a stalemate, or worse, apparently lost.'' But Combes added that ''everybody interested in his own health, and that of his family, will find this provocative and controversial book of great interest.'' And Margaret D. Sizemore stated in the *Birmingham News:* ''Dr. Moss will surely stir up a hornet's nest with this book, which is detailed and documented with plenteous examples. It took courage for him to write it.''

BIOGRAPHICAL/CRITICAL SOURCES: New York Times, November 24, 1977; *New Scientist,* December, 1977; *Science,* December 23, 1977; *Sciences,* January, 1978; *Science News,* January 7, 1978.

*   *   *

MUGGERIDGE, Malcolm (Thomas)   1903-

PERSONAL: Born March 24, 1903, in Sanderstead, Surrey, England; son of Henry Thomas (a member of Parliament) and Annie (Booler) Muggeridge; married Katherine Dobbs, September, 1927; children: three sons, one daughter. *Education:* Selwyn College, Cambridge, M.A., 1923. *Home:* Park Cottage, Robertsbridge, East Sussex, England.

CAREER: Egyptian University, Cairo, Egypt, lecturer, 1927-30; *Manchester Guardian,* Manchester, England, editorial staff member, 1930-32, correspondent in Moscow, 1932-33; affiliated with International Labor Office, Geneva, Switzerland, 1933-34; *Calcutta Statesman,* Calcutta, India, assistant editor, 1934-35; *Evening Standard,* London, England, editorial staff member, 1935-36; *Daily Telegraph,* London, correspondent in Washington, D.C., 1946-47, deputy editor, 1950-52; television interviewer for ''Panorama,'' 1951; *Punch,* London, editor, 1953-57; University of Edinburgh, Edinburgh, Scotland, rector, 1967-68. *Military service:* British Army, 1939-45, served in Intelligence Corps; became major; received Legion of Honor, Croix de Guerre with Palm, and Medaille de la Reconnaissance Francaise. *Awards, honors:* Christopher Book Award, 1972, for *Something Beautiful for God.*

WRITINGS: Autumnal Faces (novel), Putnam, 1931; *Three Flats* (three-act play), Putnam, 1931; *Winter in Moscow,* Little, Brown, 1934; (translator) Maurice Bedel, *New Arcadia,* J. Cape, 1935; *The Earnest Atheist: A Study of Samuel Butler,* Eyre & Spottiswoode, 1936, published as *A Study of Samuel Butler: The Earnest Atheist,* Putnam, 1937; (with Hugh Kingsmill) *Brave Old World,* Eyre & Spottiswoode, 1936; (author of introduction) Galeazzo Ciano, *Hidden Diary,* 1937, Dutton, 1953; (with Kingsmill) *A Pre-view of Next Year's News,* Eyre & Spottiswoode, 1937; *In a Valley of This Restless Mind,* Routledge & Kegan Paul, 1938.

The Sun Never Sets: The Story of England in the Nineteen Thirties, Random House, 1940, published in England as *The Thirties: 1930-1940 in Great Britain,* Hamish Hamilton, 1940; (editor) Galeazzo Ciano, *Ciano's Diary, 1939-1943,* Heinemann, 1947; (editor) Ciano, *Ciano's Diplomatic Papers: Being a Record of Nearly 200 Conversations Held During the Years 1936-42 With Hitler,* Odhams, 1948; *Affairs of the Heart,* Hamish Hamilton, 1949.

(With Hesketh Pearson) *About Kingsmill,* Methuen, 1951; (author of introduction) Ciano, *Diary, 1937-1938,* Methuen, 1952; (author of introduction) *Esquire's World of Humor,* Arthur Barker, 1965; *The Most of Malcolm Muggeridge,* Simon & Schuster, 1966; *Tread Softly, for You Tread on My Jokes,* Collins, 1966; *London a la Mode,* Hill & Wang, 1966;

Muggeridge Through the Microphone: BBC Radio and Television, British Broadcasting Corp., 1967; *Jesus Rediscovered,* Doubleday, 1969; (with others) *What They Believe,* Hodder & Stoughton, 1969.

Something Beautiful for God: Mother Teresa of Calcutta, Harper, 1971; (with Alec Vidler) *Paul: Envoy Extraordinary,* Harper, 1972; *Malcolm's Choice: A Collection of Cartoons,* Mowbrays, 1972; *Chronicles of Wasted Time* (autobiography), Morrow, Volume I: *The Green Stick,* 1973, Volume II: *The Infernal Grove,* 1974; *Jesus: The Man Who Lives,* Harper, 1975; *A Third Testament,* Little, Brown, 1976; *Christ and the Media,* Eerdmans, 1977; *Things Past,* Collins, 1978, Morrow, 1979; *A Twentieth Century Testimony,* Collins, 1979.

Contributor to magazines and newspapers, including *Ladies' Home Journal, Esquire, Horizon, Christianity Today, Reader's Digest,* and *Observer Review.*

WORK IN PROGRESS: The third volume of author's autobiography, *Chronicles of Wasted Time.*

SIDELIGHTS: Malcolm Muggeridge has long had a reputation as an iconoclast. A socialist in his younger days, Muggeridge at one time was an avowed atheist. Later he was to eschew socialism and to find God, but his conversion to conservative politics and to Christianity did nothing to mitigate his stinging satire. Organized religion, contraception, abortion, heart transplants, pornography, public education, and egalitarianism have all been the objects of his wrath.

The son of a Fabian socialist, Muggeridge developed a desire to become a writer while he was attending Selwyn College, Cambridge. He launched his career in journalism with the *Manchester Guardian,* serving initially as the newspaper's Cairo correspondent. By the time he was appointed as the *Guardian*'s Moscow correspondent in 1932, he had already branched into other areas of writing, having published a novel and a play. Muggeridge's experience in Moscow was a bitter one. He swiftly became disillusioned with Communism and with the Western correspondents based in the Soviet Union, whom he felt were whitewashing the truth.

When his editor refused to run an exclusive story on the Russian famine, Muggeridge angrily resigned his post. He then set about deriding the Soviet Union in his frankly biased book, *Winter in Moscow.* A critic for the *Saturday Review of Literature* found Muggeridge's subjectivity a welcome relief: ''There is such a thing as wholesome indignation, and there has been so much leaning over backward to be fair to Russia's present dictators, so much pussy-footing and 'on-the-other-hand' stuff, let alone downright misrepresentation, that it is refreshing to come across an intelligent observer who is just plain disgusted all through and doesn't give a hoot who knows it.'' Other reviewers termed Muggeridge's collection of ironic sketches ''entertaining,'' ''brilliant,'' ''amusingly malicious,'' and ''incisive.''

After composing this splenetic attack on the Soviet Union, Muggeridge worked for a time on the staffs of the *Calcutta Statesman* and the *London Evening Standard.* He also turned out a steady stream of books, including a study of Samuel Butler and a history of Great Britain in the 1930's. His biography of Butler, *The Earnest Atheist,* provided a new perspective on that author, but many critics were dismayed by Muggeridge's lack of objectivity. '''The Earnest Atheist' is written from a depth of loathing and horror. As a result it is less objective than a study has a right to be. Allowing for the prejudice, however, it must be admitted that Mr. Muggeridge has succeeded in building up a strong case to prove that far from being the Anti-Victorian a future generation believed him to be, Butler was the Ultimate Victorian,'' Frances Winwar noted in the *New York Times*.

Muggeridge's survey of England in the 1930's, *The Sun Never Sets,* makes no attempt at impartiality, either. "The book crackles with wit, it outdoes earlier only-yesterday studies with its cutting, flashing style, its glittering satire. Its epigrams fairly cry for quotations," observed R. H. Phelps. However, R. H. S. Crossman cautioned that "judged . . . as entertainment, [the book] is to be recommended; judged as a serious estimate of our age, it is clever, hysterical and defeatist, sacrificing truth for the sake of an epigram."

When World War II broke out, Muggeridge joined the Intelligence Corps, serving in East Africa, Italy, and France. During this time he became acquainted with Graham Greene and double agent Kim Philby. Although Muggeridge respected some of the British intelligence operations, by and large he felt that spying was a mockery. At one time he was so depressed by his espionage activities that he considered suicide. This period of his life is discussed in volume two of his autobiography, *The Infernal Grove.* In this book Muggeridge aims his lethal wit at the cult of intelligence, concluding that "diplomats and intelligence agents, in my experience, are even bigger liars than journalists."

After the war, Muggeridge joined the staff of the *London Daily Telegraph,* where he served as Washington correspondent and then deputy editor. From 1953-57 he worked as editor of *Punch,* a weekly humor magazine. By encouraging literary writers to contribute to *Punch,* Muggeridge added a new dimension to the magazine. His acerbic editorials and clever parodies were credited with breathing new life into that long-established journal.

In the 1950's Muggeridge also became a familiar figure to the British television audience. He has conducted television interviews of such notables as Billy Graham, Dr. Christian Barnard, and Brendan Behan, as well as appearing on a number of special programs for BBC-TV. Some of his television commentaries have been collected in an anthology, *Muggeridge Through the Microphone.* Muggeridge's frequent appearances on the screen are somewhat puzzling because he has often inveighed against television and the media. In an article for the *Observer Review,* he wrote: "I see the camera, far more than even nuclear weapons, as the great destructive force of our time; the great falsifier. McLuhan is right; it's replaced the written and spoken word, captured the whole field of art and literature." Nonetheless, Muggeridge went on, he appears on television because "I may find an opportunity to say something, or convey something, which is worth while. . . . Supposing one was a pianist in a whorehouse—one might be able to persuade oneself that occasionally including a hymn like 'Abide With Me' in one's repertoire would have a beneficial influence on the inmates."

Like a pianist playing a hymn in a whorehouse, Muggeridge often sandwiches a sermon into his television broadcasts, his books, and his public speeches, in the hopes that it will have a beneficial influence on the inmates of the world. In a famous speech in 1968, Muggeridge resigned from his post as rector of Edinburgh University when students demanded that birth-control pills be dispensed at the university medical center. "How sad, how macabre and funny it is," he said, "that all they put forward should be a demand for pot and pills, the resort of any old slobbering debauchee anywhere." On another occasion he lambasted sex and violence in the theatre and in the arts. At the 1969 Edinburgh International Festival, he declared: "Let a collection of Yahoos but take

off their clothes, cavort about the stage and yell obscenities, and a great breakthrough in dramatic art is announced and applauded. There is no need to be mesmerized by the motley procession of writers, critics, crazed clerics and other miscellaneous intelligentsia prepared at the drop of a hat to announce the latest outpouring of sub-standard smut an essential contribution to contemporary letters."

Although Muggeridge has never been loath to hold forth on his views, he has become even more outspoken since his conversion to Christianity. Two programs that he did for the BBC contributed to his religious enlightenment. In 1967 he filmed a program at a Cistercian abbey in Nunraw, Scotland. Reflecting on the time spent at the monastery, he penned these lines: "No heavenly visitation befell me, there was no Damascus Road grace; and yet, I know, life will never be quite the same after my three weeks with the Cistercians at Nunraw." Not long afterwards Muggeridge traveled to the Holy Land to film a documentary for the BBC, and it was there that a heavenly vision did befall him. Later he discussed his revelation: "I realized, in the first place, that many shrines, and the legends associated with them, were, for the most part, from my point of view, as fraudulent as the bones of St. Peter, the fragments of the True Cross, and other relics revered by the pious. Then, seeing a party of Christian pilgrims at one of these shrines, their faces so bright with faith, their voices, as they sang, so evidently and joyously aware of their Saviour's nearness, I understood that for them the shrine was authentic. Their faith made it so. Similarly, I, too, became aware that there really had been a man, Jesus, who was also God; I was conscious of his presence."

Of course, a long series of events had led up to Muggeridge's conversion to Christianity. These events are recounted in his book, *Jesus Rediscovered.* He first learned about religion from his father, an agnostic whose religion was socialism. When Muggeridge lost faith in socialism in the early 1930's, he also lost any faith that man could make a heaven on earth. For many years he has hated the ways of the world, viewing death as the final release. These attitudes, which have much in common with traditional Christian beliefs, helped pave the way for his conversion. Reading the works of such religious figures as St. Augustine, John Bunyan, Pascal, and Tolstoi also gave him valuable insights into Christianity. In many ways Muggeridge is far from an orthodox Christian. As he explains in *Jesus Rediscovered,* he believes that Christ is a living force, but he does not believe in the Resurrection. He has no interest in dogma and dislikes institutional religion. He also excoriates church leaders who concentrate on social issues rather than the teachings of Jesus.

Critics generally considered *Jesus Rediscovered* to be a significant book on religion. "This will be one of the widely read books of the religious year. . . . You will be satisfied that your time was well spent with some of the major issues that govern the last part of the 20th century," David Poling remarked. Similarly, Michael Novak observed: "This is an important book for Christianity. It sounds a deep, true note that has been missing from the chorus, a note without which everything else is off." Although Jeffrey Hart found Muggeridge's sense of Christ "convincing and moving," Harvey Cox perceived some un-Christian attitudes in the book: "It is lacking in love, short on hope, and almost completely devoid of charity. The Jesus he has rediscovered is not one I want to follow. Yet Muggeridge himself remains an irresistible old codger."

In recent years, Muggeridge has turned his late-found religious perspective on such subjects as Mother Teresa, founder of the Missionaries of Charity, and on the lives of Jesus and St. Paul. He has also written extensively on his own life, because, he told an interviewer, "In the end, if you want to write about life, the only data you have is your own life." Thus far two volumes of his planned three-volume autobiography, *Chronicles of Wasted Time,* have been published. In a critique of the second volume of *Chronicles of Wasted Time,* John Kenneth Galbraith reflected the views of many other commentators when he wrote: "Muggeridge is a man of deplorable views. . . . [But] the redeeming virtue of Malcolm Muggeridge is his writing, including his eye for illuminating detail, his memory, on occasion one suspects his capacity for minor historical invention and, above all, his impeccable instinct for the absurd." Based on the evidence of these recent books, critics would seem to agree that time has not diminished Muggeridge's mordant wit, nor has it destroyed his talent for provocation.

BIOGRAPHICAL/CRITICAL SOURCES: Times Literary Supplement, December 10, 1931, March 15, 1934, September 5, 1936, March 9, 1940, July 24, 1969, March 31, 1972, September 29, 1972, September 28, 1973, September 12, 1975; *New Statesman and Nation,* December 12, 1931, August 29, 1936, March 9, 1940, September 29, 1972, September 21, 1973, October 17, 1975; *Spectator,* December 12, 1931, March 9, 1934, September 11, 1936; *New York Times,* September 11, 1932, March 14, 1937, June 16, 1940; *New York Herald Tribune Books,* October 30, 1932, March 14, 1937; *New York Post,* May 12, 1934; *Saturday Review,* May 24, 1934, August 30, 1969; *Saturday Review of Literature,* June 9, 1934, May 4, 1940; *Christian Science Monitor,* September 26, 1934, April 7, 1937, June 29, 1940, August 2, 1966; *Time,* March 8, 1937, January 6, 1967, January 26, 1968, September 26, 1969, August 5, 1974; *Nation,* April 3, 1937; *New Republic,* May 5, 1937, May 27, 1940, October 27, 1973, August 23, 1974.

Boston Transcript, May 11, 1940; *New York Times Book Review,* March 5, 1961, September 7, 1969, November 14, 1971, May 7, 1972, September 30, 1973, July 14, 1974; *Best Sellers,* July 1, 1966, October 1, 1969, November 1, 1971; *Book Week,* July 3, 1966; *New York Review of Books,* December 29, 1966; *Observer Review,* August 20, 1967, December 15, 1968; *Listener,* December 7, 1967; *Variety,* September 3, 1969; *Newsweek,* September 8, 1969, July 22, 1974; *Washington Post Book World,* October 12, 1969, December 26, 1971; *Christian Century,* October 22, 1969, November 24, 1971; *National Review,* December 2, 1969, December 19, 1975; *Books and Bookmen,* June, 1971; *America,* November 6, 1971, March 4, 1978; Malcolm Muggeridge, *Chronicles of Wasted Time,* Morrow, Volume I: *The Green Stick,* 1973, Volume II: *The Infernal Grove,* 1974; *Economist,* September 22, 1973; *Washington Star-News,* February 18, 1975; *Authors in the News,* Volume 1, Gale, 1976.*

—*Sketch by Ann F. Ponikvar*

* * *

MUNTZ, James
See CROWCROFT, Peter

* * *

MURDOCK, Laurette P. 1900-
(Laurette Eustis)

PERSONAL: Born July 28, 1900, in Dover, N.J.; daughter of George Eustis (an explosives expert) and Sara White (a writer; maiden name, Call) Potts; married Kenneth B. Murdock, June 24, 1922 (divorced, 1941); children: Mary Lau-

rette (Mrs. Cameron Thompson), Sara (Mrs. Daniel Steinberg). *Education:* Educated in Simsbury, Conn. *Religion:* Episcopal. *Home:* 81½ Warren St., Charlestown, Mass. 02129.

CAREER: Writer. Worked in fruit cannery and plastics factory in California during World War II; Houghton Mifflin Co., Boston, Mass., copy editor, 1946-65.

WRITINGS: "Uncle Pluto" (short story), published in *Audience,* January, 1962; *Someone Is Talking About Hortense* (juvenile), published as a volume in *Four Little Troubles,* four volumes, edited by James Marshall, Houghton, 1975; (under name Laurette Eustis) "The Tower Mill" (short story), published in *Ellery Queen's Mystery Magazine,* May, 1978.

WORK IN PROGRESS: A mystery novel set in Greece.

SIDELIGHTS: Murdock told *CA:* "My writing career didn't begin until my mid-fifties, while working as a copy editor. Having been born at the turn of the century and having lived through astonishing changes from gaslights to the marvels of Thomas Edison, from kitchen pumps and woodburning stoves to tiled bathrooms, microwave cooking, and Cuisinart, I write hoping to share with readers both the delights and miseries of life as I know it."

AVOCATIONAL INTERESTS: Travel, foreign languages, art, housing, architecture.

* * *

MURPHY, Thomas (Bernard) 1935-

PERSONAL: Born February 23, 1935, in Tuam, County Galway, Ireland; son of John (a carpenter) and Winifred (Shaughnessy) Murphy; married Mary Hamilton-Hippisley, November 14, 1966; children: Benin, Nell, John. *Education:* Attended Vocational Teachers' Training College, Dublin, 1955-57. *Home and office:* 32 Highfield Rd., Dublin 6, Ireland. *Agent:* B. Aschenberg, International Creative Management, 40 West 57th St., New York, N.Y. 10019.

CAREER: Playwright. Apprentice welder and fitter in Tuam, Ireland, 1953-55; teacher of engineering in vocational school in Mountbellow, County Galway, 1957-62. Performer and director with Irish Drama Movement, 1951-62; member of board of directors of Abbey Theatre (Dublin), 1973—; founding member of Moli Productions. Past member of International Advisory Committee in English in the Liturgy. *Member:* Writers Guild of Great Britain. *Awards, honors:* First prizes in manuscript competitions from all-Ireland amateur drama competition, 1960 and 1961; award for distinction in literature from Irish Academy of Letters, 1972, for body of work.

WRITINGS—Plays: The Fooleen: A Crucial Week in the Life of a Grocer's Assistant (thirteen scenes; first produced in Dublin, Ireland, at Abbey Theatre, 1969; produced in Los Angeles, Calif., 1971), Proscenium, 1968; *A Whistle in the Dark* (three-act; first produced in London, England, at Theatre Royal, 1961; produced Off-Broadway at Mercury Theatre, 1969), Samuel French, 1970; *The Morning After Optimism* (ten scenes; first produced in Dublin at Abbey Theatre, 1971), Mercier Press, 1973; *The Orphans* (three-act; first produced in Dublin, 1968), Proscenium, 1974; (with Noel O'Donoghue) *On the Outside* (one-act; first produced in Cork, Ireland, 1961), Gallery Press, 1976; *On the Inside* (one-act; first produced in Dublin at Project Theatre, 1974), Gallery Press, 1976; *The Sanctuary Lamp* (two-act; first produced in Dublin at Abbey Theatre, 1976), Poolbeg Press, 1976; *Famine* (twelve scenes; also see below; first produced in Dublin at Abbey Theatre, 1968; produced on West End at Royal Court Theatre, 1969), Gallery Press, 1977.

Unpublished plays: "The Fly Sham" (television play), first broadcast in London by British Broadcasting Corporation (BBC), 1963; "Veronica" (television play), first broadcast in London by BBC, 1963; "Snakes and Reptiles" (television play), first broadcast in London by BBC, 1968; "Young Man in Trouble" (television play), first broadcast in London by Thames Television, 1970; "The White House" (two-act), first produced in Dublin at Abbey Theatre, 1972; (adapter) "The Vicar of Wakefield" (four-act), first produced in Dublin at Abbey Theatre, 1974; "The Moral Force" (television play; first play in trilogy based on play by Murphy, "Famine"), first broadcast in Ireland by Radio Telefis Eireann (RTE), 1973; "The Policy" (television play; second play in trilogy), first broadcast in Ireland by RTE, 1973; "Relief" (television play; third play in trilogy), first broadcast in Ireland by RTE, 1973; "The 'J' Arthur McGinnis Story: The First 36, 525 Days" (ten scenes), first produced in Ireland at Pavillion Theatre, 1977; "Conversations on a Homecoming" (television play), first broadcast in Ireland by RTE, 1977; "Speeches of Farewell" (television play), first broadcast in Ireland by RTE, 1977; "Epitaph Under Ether" (one-act), first produced in Dublin at Abbey Theatre, 1979; "The Blue Macushca," first produced in Dublin at Abbey Theatre, 1980.

WORK IN PROGRESS: "The Gigli Concert," a full-length stage play; "The Informer," an adaptation.

SIDELIGHTS: Thomas Murphy is probably best known for his play, "Whistle in the Dark." The main character is Michael Carney, an Irishman who has fled his turbulent homeland in search of a peaceful existence. He ultimately settles in Coventry, England, with his wife, Betty. Life goes on without incident until the arrival of his family shatters their tranquility. The Carney family is a violent one, headed by a cruel and vindictive father whose resentment toward his nonviolent son Michael is a bitter motif that runs throughout the work.

When he sees that his youngest brother, Desmond, is becoming infected with the hatred that consumes the rest of his family, Michael attempts to extricate him. The young man has learned the ways of his family, though, and when he and Michael are taunted to fight by their father, Michael inadvertantly kills his brother.

"A strange, ugly, impressive play," assessed *New York Times* critic Clive Barnes. "I was struck by the unusual vigor and directness of a play that interweaves themes of violence, loyalty and cowardice in a study of one of the most unpleasant families in stage history." David De Port of *Village Voice* however, was less enthusiastic: "'Whistle in the Dark' isn't a great experience in the theatre.... It's a good play though." The reviewer went on to state that the work is "a melodrama, often sloppily conceived, but earnest, unpretentious, and compelling." And *Variety* called the play "legit-in-the-raw, a consistently absorbing, blisteringly powerful theatre piece that leaves a spectator exhausted but exhilarated."

BIOGRAPHICAL/CRITICAL SOURCES: Variety, October 15, 1969, May 19, 1971; *Time,* October 17, 1969; *Cue,* October 18, 1969; *New Yorker,* October 18, 1969; *Show Business,* October 18, 1969; *New York Times,* October 19, 1969, November 9, 1969; *Newsweek,* October 20, 1969; *Village Voice,* October 23, 1969; *Nation,* November 10, 1969; *New Leader,* November 24, 1969.

N

NAPOLEON, Art
See SUDHALTER, Richard M(errill)

* * *

NAZARETH, Peter 1940-
(Mdogo Wako)

PERSONAL: Born April 27, 1940, in Kampala, Uganda; came to the United States, 1973; son of Pedro Custodio and Ana (Gomes) Nazareth; married Mary Raquela Fernandes (an IWP assistant), January 4, 1964; children: Kathleen Eleanor Ime, Pier Ann Monique. *Education:* Makerere University College (now Makerere University), B.A. (with honors), 1962; University of Leeds, diploma, 1965. *Religion:* Roman Catholic. *Home:* 1110 North Dubuque St., Iowa City, Iowa 52240. *Agent:* Bertha Klausner, International Literary Agency, Inc., 71 Park Ave., New York, N.Y. 10016; and Bolt & Watson, 8 Storey's Gate, London S.W.1, England. *Office:* Department of English, University of Iowa, Iowa City, Iowa 52242.

CAREER: Ministry of Finance, Entebbe, Uganda, administrative officer, 1965-67, finance officer, 1967-68, senior finance officer, 1969-73; University of Iowa, Iowa City, visiting fellow, 1973—, instructor, 1973-78, assistant professor, 1978-80, associate professor of English, 1980—. President of Entebbe Institute, 1966, 1969, 1971, member of board of trustees, 1969-73. *Member:* African Studies Association, African Literature Association. *Awards, honors:* Seymour Lustman fellowship for Yale University, 1973.

WRITINGS: Literature and Society in Modern Africa, East African Literature Bureau, 1972; *In a Brown Mantle* (novel), East African Literature Bureau, 1972; *An African View of Literature,* Northwestern University Press, 1974; *Two Radio Plays* (contains "The Hospital," first broadcast by British Broadcasting Corp. [BBC-Radio], 1964, and "X," first broadcast by BBC-Radio, 1965), East African Literature Bureau, 1976; *The Third World Writer: His Social Responsibility,* Kenya Literature Bureau, 1978; *The General Is Up* (novel), Eastern Africa Publications, 1980; *The Footnote Man* (criticism), Eastern Africa Publications, 1980.

Contributor: Chris L. Wanjala, editor, *Standpoints on African Literature,* East African Literature Bureau, 1973; Arnold Kingston and E. A. Markham, editors, *Merely a Matter of Colour,* Q Books, 1973; Robert D. Hamner, editor, *Critical Perspectives on V. S. Naipaul,* Three Continents Press,

1978; C. D. Narasimhaiah, editor, *Awakened Conscience: Studies in Commonwealth Literature,* Sterling Publishers, 1978.

Work represented in anthologies, including *Stories From Africa and Asia,* edited by Theo Luzuka and Chandran Nair, Woodrose Publications, 1976; *Short Fiction From Africa,* Volume III, edited by Satoru Tsuchiya, Toko-Shiba, 1978; *African Theatre,* edited by Abiole Irele and Oyin Ogunba, Ibadan University Press, 1978. Contributor of articles and stories to magazines in Africa, England, India, Israel, Jamaica, Fiji, Singapore, Poland, Canada, and the United States (sometimes under pseudonym Mdogo Wako), including *Africana Journal, New Letters, Short Story International, Iowa Review,* and *World Literature Today.*

WORK IN PROGRESS: Interviews With Third World Writers, publication by Iowa State University Press expected in 1982.

SIDELIGHTS: Nazareth wrote: "I am concerned with literature and society, with particular relevance (but not exclusive reference) to Third World writing. Simultaneously, I like to tell the stories of people whose stories have not been told before."

* * *

NEE, Brett de Bary 1943-
(Brett de Bary)

PERSONAL: Born October 9, 1943, in Brooklyn, N.Y.; daughter of William T. and Fanny (Brett) de Bary; married Victor G. Nee (a professor of sociology), June 6, 1970; children: William. *Education:* Barnard College, B.A., 1965; Harvard University, M.A., 1970, Ph.D., 1978. *Home:* 111 Northway Rd., Ithaca, N.Y. 14850. *Office:* Cornell University, Ithaca, N.Y. 14850.

CAREER: Cornell University, Ithaca, N.Y., assistant professor of Japanese literature, 1976—. *Member:* Association of Teachers of Japanese, Phi Beta Kappa. *Awards, honors:* Woodrow Wilson fellowship, 1966-67.

*WRITINGS—*Under name Brett de Bary: (With husband, Victor Nee) *Longtime Californ'* (nonfiction), Pantheon, 1974; (translator and contributor) *Three Works by Nakano Shigeharn,* Cornell University Press, 1979. Editor of newsletter of Association of Teachers of Japanese, 1978—.

WORK IN PROGRESS: Five Writers and the End of the War, a study of Japanese literature after World War II.

SIDELIGHTS: Brett Nee wrote: "My professional interest is the study of modern Japanese literature and film in its social context. Currently I am focusing on the literary response to the Pacific war experience in Japan. I anticipate comparative work, including comparisons with postwar German, French, and American literature. Other interests are Asian-American literature and feminism in China, Japan, and the United States."

* * *

NEEDHAM, Richard (John) 1912-

PERSONAL: Born in 1912 in England; immigrated to Canada. *Office: Toronto Globe and Mail,* 444 Front St. W., Toronto, Ontario, Canada M5V 2S9.

CAREER: Writer. Author of column in *Toronto Globe and Mail,* Toronto, Ontario.

WRITINGS: The Garden of Needham, Macmillan, 1968; *A Friend in Needham; or, A Writer's Notebook,* Macmillan, 1969; *Needham's Inferno,* Macmillan, 1966, Simon & Schuster, 1973; *The Hypodermic Needham,* Macmillan, 1970, Simon & Schuster, 1975. *The Wit and Wisdom of Richard Needham,* Hurtig, 1977.*

* * *

NEILL, A(lexander) S(utherland) 1883-1973

PERSONAL: Born October 17, 1883, in Forfarshire, Scotland; died of pneumonia, September 23, 1973, in Aldeburgh, England; son of George and Mary Sinclair (Sutherland) Neill; married Ada Lilian Lindesay-Neustatter (died, 1944); married Ena May Wood, 1945; children: Zoe. *Education:* Attended Edinburgh University.

CAREER: Worked as office boy, draper, teacher, and journalist; co-founder and director of International School in Dresden, Germany (later in Austria), beginning in 1921; co-founder and director of Summerhill School in Leiston, Suffolk, England, 1924-73.

WRITINGS: A Dominie's Log (also see below), McBride, 1916; *A Dominie Dismissed* (also see below), McBride, 1917; *A Dominie in Doubt* (also see below), McBride, 1922; *A Dominie Abroad,* H. Jenkins, 1923; *The Problem Child,* McBride, 1927; *The Problem Parent,* H. Jenkins, 1932; *Is Scotland Educated?,* Routledge & Sons, 1936; *That Dreadful School,* H. Jenkins, 1937; *The Problem Teacher,* H. Jenkins, 1939; *Hearts Not Heads in the Schools,* H. Jenkins, 1945; *The Problem Family: An Investigation of Human Relations,* Hermitage Press, 1949.

The Free Child, H. Jenkins, 1953; (contributor) Paul Ritter, editor, *Wilhelm Reich,* Ritter Press, 1958; *Summerhill: A Radical Approach to Child Rearing,* Hart, 1960 (published in England as *Summerhill: A Radical Approach to Education,* Gollancz, 1962); *Freedom—Not License!,* Hart, 1966; *Talking of Summerhill,* Gollancz, 1967; *The Last Man Alive: A Story for Children From the Age of Seven to Seventy,* Hart, 1969; *Summerhill: For and Against,* Hart, 1970; *Neill! Neill! Orange Peel!* (autobiography), Hart, 1972 (published in England as *Neill! Neill! Orange Peel!: A Personal View of Ninety Years,* Weidenfeld, 1973); *The Dominie Books of A. S. Neill* (contains *A Dominie's Log, A Dominie Dismissed,* and *A Dominie in Doubt*), Hart, 1975. Also author of *The Blooming of Bunkie,* 1919, *Carroty Broon,* 1921, and *A Dominie's Five; or, Free School,* 1924.

SIDELIGHTS: Early in the twentieth century several new ideas evolved concerning educational theory. Experimental schools surfaced in the United States and abroad only to dis-

appear when their temporary popularity waned. The exception to this rule was the Summerhill School in England, headed by A. S. Neill. A staunch defender of youth, Neill felt that the traditional educational system with its strict discipline stifled the creativity and emotional growth of the child. He believed that the child is inherently "good" and, if left to his or her own devices without any artificial adult interference, will grow naturally into a responsible and caring individual.

Prior to founding Summerhill, Neill worked as a teacher in Scotland. It was at this time that he began to doubt the merits of traditional education and to generate his own theories. He discussed and expanded these ideas in his four "Dominie," or "schoolmaster," books: *A Dominie's Log, A Dominie Dismissed, A Dominie in Doubt,* and *A Dominie Abroad.* A reviewer for the *New York Times* described the first volume as "full of sound, original ideas, companioned with joy and whimsicality." A *Nation* writer, however, was less impressed with the book: "Mr. Neill appears to be a tenderhearted person who is fond of children, and who doubtless, in spite of his avowed methods, contrives to teach them something; but one who reasons with the emotions, as does the author of this book, is not qualified to put forward a theory of education." In writing for the *Spectator,* another critic commented that "Mr. Neill appears in this book as an exceptionally original, humorous, and attractive person; a delightful teacher, one would suppose, as certainly as he is an attractive writer."

Neill again told of his own teaching experiences as the head of a school for "backward" children in *The Problem Child.* "The discussions are outspoken and provocative, hence stimulating and interesting," declared a writer for the *Journal of Home Economics.* B. B. Barrett of the *Literary Review,* on the other hand, cited the book as "the negation of orthodoxy in morals and educational theory. It supplies clever criticism, but has nothing to offer as a substitute for old methods except chaotic indiscipline." A *Saturday Review of Literature* critic also renounced the book, claiming that Neill's "pedagogical method is based on about five per cent pure science and ninety-five per cent pure guess." Contrary to this assessment, Agnes de Lima of the *New York Herald Tribune Books* speculated, "As one lays down the book one wonders if there would be any problem children at all if all children could be treated within the good sense and humanity here described."

In 1969, after running his school for more than forty years, Neill wrote *Summerhill: A Radical Approach to Child Rearing.* A writer for the *New Yorker* related that "this is a book on the education of the young that many readers will approach with skepticism, only to find, when they have finished it, that its author has convinced them on a good many points." The reviewer added that while "one may not agree with him in everything, . . . there is no doubt about his deep understanding of children or about the benign influence he has had on those entrusted to his care." A *Times Literary Supplement* writer also praised the author: "A. S. Neill stands as a model of the good teacher. He has all the qualities of sound sense, humour, sympathy and patience untinged by any sentimentality."

Following publication of *Summerhill* in the United States, Neill received an influx of letters from American parents requesting more information on his school and educational theories. In an attempt to further explain and to respond to specific questions raised, Neill compiled *Freedom—Not License!* The book is constructed in a question-and-answer format, utilizing portions of actual letters. "Though some of his advice is sound," observed Paul Woodring of the *Saturday Review,* "Neill's educational psychology will not bear close examination. It is true that the child will learn more easily and rapidly if he is interested and wants to learn, but it does not follow that the curriculum must be based entirely on the interests that the child brings to class with him." Neill's basic premise that children are inherently "good" is "no more tenable than the theory that they are innately 'bad,'" added Woodring. "It cannot be justified scientifically, philosophically, or theoretically."

Much of the criticism of Summerhill and the methods Neill advocates stems from the lack of rigid rules and unbending discipline. "In my school," Neill explained in *Freedom— Not License!,* "a child is free to go to lessons, or stay away from lessons because that is his own affair, but he is not free to play a trumpet when others want to study or sleep." Thus, he maintained, Summerhill is based on *freedom* and not *license.* Another tenet that is often confused by misinformed detractors is the absence of traditional etiquette at Summerhill. "We do not teach etiquette," he stated; "if a child licks his plate, no one cares—indeed no one notices. We never groom a child to say 'Thank You' or 'Good Morning.' But when a boy mocked a new lad who was lame, the other children called a special meeting and the offender was told by the community, and in no uncertain terms, that the school did not relish bad manners."

In one of his later books, *Talking of Summerhill,* Neill expressed the essence of his school: "It takes no genius to be a good teacher, one has not to be a superman, only a man without the wish to tell others how to live."

BIOGRAPHICAL/CRITICAL SOURCES: Nation, July 6, 1916; *Spectator,* July 8, 1916; *New York Times,* August 6, 1916; *Literary Review,* March 19, 1927; *Saturday Review of Literature,* April 9, 1927, January 21, 1961, February 18, 1967; *Journal of Home Economics,* July, 1927; *New York Herald Tribune Books,* July 10, 1927; *New Yorker,* April 29, 1961; *Annals of the American Academy,* May, 1961; *New Statesman,* April 20, 1962, March 17, 1967; *Times Literary Supplement,* April 27, 1962; *Book Week,* July 2, 1967.

OBITUARIES: Washington Post, September 26, 1973; *Newsweek,* October 8, 1973; *Time,* October 8, 1973.*

*   *   *

NETO, Antonio Agostinho   1922-1979

PERSONAL: Born in September, 1922, in Icolo e Bengo, Portuguese West Africa; died of cancer, September 10, 1979, in Moscow, U.S.S.R.; son of Agostinho Pedro (a clergyman) and Maria (de Silva) Neto; married Maria Eugenia da Silva, 1958; children: one son, two daughters. *Education:* Attended University of Coimbra; University of Lisbon, M.D., 1958.

CAREER: Worked for Department of Health in Angola, 1944-47; president of Angola, 1975-79. *Member:* Movimento Popular de Libertacao de Angola (president, 1962-79).

WRITINGS: Colectanea de Poemas (poems), Edicao da Casa dos Estudantes du Imperio, 1961; *Sagrada esperanca* (poems), Livraria Sa da Costa Editora, 1974, translation by Marga Holness published as *Sacred Hope,* Tanzania Publishing, 1974; *Poemas de Angola,* Superbancas, 1976. Also author of several unpublished poetry collections. Contributor of poems to literary periodicals.

OBITUARIES: Newsweek, September 24, 1979.*

*   *   *

NEUBAUER, John   1933-

PERSONAL: Born November 2, 1933, in Budapest, Hungary; came to the United States in 1957, naturalized citizen, 1962; son of Laszlo and Eva (Bergl) Neubauer; married Ursula Rau (a printmaker), December 22, 1964; children: Eva Miriam, Nicole. *Education:* Amherst College, B.A. (cum laude), 1960; Northwestern University, M.S. and M.A., both 1962, Ph.D., 1965; attended University of Munich, 1963-64. *Home:* 1318 Malvern Ave., Pittsburgh, Pa. 15217. *Office:* Department of Germanic Languages, University of Pittsburgh, Pittsburgh, Pa. 15260.

CAREER: Princeton University, Princeton, N.J., instructor, 1964-66, assistant professor of German, 1966-69; Case Western Reserve University, Cleveland, Ohio, associate professor of German, 1969-73; University of Pittsburgh, Pittsburgh, Pa., associate professor, 1973-76, professor of German, 1976—. Visiting professor at Universidad del Valle, 1967-68, University of British Columbia, summer, 1973, and Harvard University, autumn, 1979. *Member:* Modern Language Association of America, American Comparative Literature Association, American Society for Eighteenth Century Studies. *Awards, honors:* Fulbright grant, 1972-73; Guggenheim fellow, 1980-81.

WRITINGS: El romanticismo, la ciencia y el siglo XX (title means "Romanticism, Science, and the Twentieth Century"), Universidad del Valle, 1968; *Bifocal Vision: Novalis' Philosophy of Nature and Disease,* University of North Carolina Press, 1971; *Symbolismus und symbolische Logik: Die Idee der ars combinatoria in der Entwicklung der modernen Dichtung* (title means "Symbolism and Symbolic Logic: The Idea of Ars Combinatoria in the Evolution of Modern Literature"), Fink, 1978; *Novalis,* G. K. Hall, 1980. Contributor of about twenty articles to scholarly journals.

WORK IN PROGRESS: Music and Literature in the Eighteenth Century, publication expected in 1982; *Time and the Rise of the Novel,* 1984.

SIDELIGHTS: Neubauer told *CA:* "My writing and research have been in the general area of intellectual history, with emphasis on the interrelations between science, philosophy, and the arts. In writing about these problems I try to answer the question of how aspects of form, style, and structure may be correlated with conceptual structures in philosophy and the sciences. I find writing a never ending struggle for clarification, but I feel rewarded when I find a more economical mode of expression or a phrase with the right rhythmic cadence."

*   *   *

NEWMAN, Gerald   1939-

PERSONAL: Born May 3, 1939, in New York, N.Y.; son of Harry and Lillie (Meyer) Newman; married Eleanor Weintraub, September 28, 1969 (divorced March 20, 1979); children: Aaron Roy. *Education:* Brooklyn College of the City University of New York, B.A., 1962, M.F.A., 1975. *Home:* 300 West 23rd St., New York, N.Y. 10011.

CAREER: New York City Board of Education, New York, N.Y., teacher of art and creative writing, 1962—.

WRITINGS: Elton John, New American Library, 1976; (editor) *Encyclopedia of Health and the Human Body,* F. Watts, 1977; (editor) *Concise Encyclopedia of Sports* (juvenile), F. Watts, 1978; *Lebanon* (juvenile), F. Watts, 1978; *The Changing Eskimos* (juvenile), F. Watts, 1980; *How to Write a Report* (juvenile), F. Watts, 1981; *Equatorial Africa* (juvenile), F. Watts, 1981.

Films: "The Iron Mountain," released by American Film Foundation in 1978; "Bogota: Fragments of a City," American Film Foundation, 1979.

SIDELIGHTS: Newman wrote: "I find it fascinating to be able to translate sophisticated historical concepts into easily understood information for children. The younger the age level of the book, the more difficult it is to write. I use my son as a sounding board. If I see him diligently reading my manuscript, I know all is well. If he loses interest, I'm in trouble."

*   *   *

NEWTON, Ethel (de la Bete) 1921-

PERSONAL: Born October 20, 1921, in Ponce de Leon, France; came to United States, 1938; daughter of Maurice (a cork master) and Marilyn (a painter; maiden name, Brown) de la Bete; married Frank Newton (an astrologer), November 23, 1960; children: Pramode Zoe (Newton) Murray. *Education:* Attended Midiwiwin College. *Politics:* Liberal. *Religion:* Agnostic. *Home:* 221 Lewiston Rd., Grosse Pointe Farms, Mich. 48236.

CAREER: Knopf's Shoes, Toledo, Ohio, salesperson, 1939-41; Mendez Bookstore, Toledo, salesperson and buyer, 1941-48; Francisco's Greenhouses, Maumee, Ohio, landscaper, 1948-50; Metaphysics Ltd., New York, N.Y., salesperson and buyer, 1953-60; free-lance writer, 1960-63; *Up There* (astronomy/astrology magazine), Beverly Hills, Mich., staff member, 1964-68, associate editor, 1969-74, editor, 1975-77, executive editor, 1977—. *Member:* Better Alchemists League (treasurer, 1967), Society of Tawtic Yoga, Amateur Botanists Club. *Awards, honors:* Best Begonias Award from Amateur Botanists Club, 1966; named honorary member of L'Institute de Manifestations Posthumes, 1974; Double Helix Award in writing, 1977, for *Yours, Mine, and Auras;* honorary member of Tapa Kega Bru.

WRITINGS: The Lighter Side of Tarot, Unknown Digest, 1969; (editor) *Andromeda Art,* Galaxy Books, 1972; (with husband, Frank Newton) *Polarity for People,* Galaxy Books, 1973; *Yours, Mine, and Auras* (autobiography), North Star Press, 1976. Contributor to magazines, including *Up There.*

WORK IN PROGRESS: Writing and producing a made-for-television movie; a sequel to *Yours, Mine, and Auras,* tentatively entitled *After the Show,* which includes author's predicted life after death.

SIDELIGHTS: Newton told *CA:* "I lived in France until being orphaned in 1938 after the death of my parents in an automobile accident. It was then that I was sent to live with my maternal aunt in Toledo, Ohio, where I began to learn about American culture. I feel that my exposure to European life-styles in my early years led to my avant-garde study of the stars. Life in Europe is so much more creative, progressive, and yielding to the free thinker . . . not like Toledo.

"After marrying Frank in 1960, my literary career took off. My first book, *The Lighter Side of Tarot,* was conceived from my experiences at Metaphysics Ltd. I felt that the age-old subject needed to be approached in a new, refreshing manner, since tarot is still associated with witches and black magic. Although my initial intentions were for the book to be informative, I did want to try to give tarot an upgraded image. Unfortunately, the book did not sell very well.

"*Andromeda Art* has been my best seller to date. It has a slightly scientific basis with a central theme as a collection of star formations that are not already found in the astronomy books. Working with my husband was a real joy. We spent many months at a planetarium in Arizona doing the photographic work with our Polaroid.

"Although not the biggest money maker yet, my autobiography, *Yours, Mine, and Auras,* has to be my favorite. I am presently working on the screenplay, which one of the larger studios is very interested in purchasing. I have had such a diversified life: living in France, moving to Toledo, and coming to Detroit to do free-lance work. It all just seems to make good copy.

"Working with *Up There* magazine has become such a vitally important part of my life. Frank's nurtured it from its humble beginnings to make it one of the top twenty astrology/astronomy magazines in the United States. It's hard to believe that only a few short years ago I was only a free-lance writer . . . now, executive editor. Time flies."

AVOCATIONAL INTERESTS: Gardening, jogging, tennis, "yachting on the Great Lakes in our thirty-seven foot sloop, *Illusion.*"

*   *   *

NEWTON, James R(obert) 1935-

PERSONAL: Born December 22, 1935, in Yakima, Wash.; son of James Thompson and Daisy (Coffee) Newton; married Kay M. Fredenburg (a teacher), December 28, 1954; children: Cindy Kay, Mark Andrew. *Education:* Pacific Lutheran University, B.A., 1965; also attended Seattle Pacific University, Western Washington State College, and Central Washington State College. *Religion:* Roman Catholic. *Home:* 14917 82nd Ave. N.W., Gig Harbor, Wash. 98335.

CAREER: Franklin Pierce School District, Tacoma, Wash., elementary school teacher, 1965—. *Member:* National Education Association, Washington Education Association, Tacoma Education Association.

WRITINGS: The March of the Lemmings (juvenile nonfiction), Crowell, 1976; *Forest Log* (nonfiction), Crowell, 1980. Contributor to *Ranger Rick.*

WORK IN PROGRESS: Research on "nature's mysteries."

SIDELIGHTS: Newton wrote: "I spend as much time as I can in field and forest. It is there that I feel closest to my creator, and I never cease to be fascinated by the innumerable mysteries of his creation."

*   *   *

NICHOLSON, Gerald W(illiam) L(ingen) 1902-1980

PERSONAL: Born January 6, 1902, in Weston-super-Mare, England; died February 28, 1980; son of Arthur Thomas and Caroline Dora (Middleton) Nicholson; married Edith Ashcroft, August 10, 1936; children: Dora (Mrs. W. J. Broughton), Sylvia Joan (Mrs. G. J. van der Weg). *Education:* Queen's University, Kingston, Ontario, B.A., 1931; University of Toronto, B.Paed., 1935.

CAREER: Public school teacher in Saskatchewan, 1922-25, high school teacher, 1926-27; high school principal in Foam Lake, Saskatchewan, 1927-30, Wynyard, Saskatchewan, 1931-35, Battleford, Saskatchewan, 1935-40, and Biggar, Saskatchewan, 1941-42; Canadian Army, with Battleford Volunteers, 1940-42, and Prince Albert Volunteers, 1940-43, member of historical section of General Staff in Ottawa, Ontario, 1943-46, deputy director, 1946-59, director, 1959-61, retired as colonel; writer, 1961-80.

WRITINGS: Marlborough and the War of the Spanish Succession, Queen's Printer, 1955; *The Canadians in Italy, 1943-45,* Queen's Printer, 1956; *Canadian Expeditionary Force, 1914-1919,* Queen's Printer, 1962; (with H. H. Boyd,

R. J. Rannie, and A. E. Hobbs) *Three Nations: Canada, Great Britain, and the U.S.A. in the Twentieth Century,* McClelland & Stewart, 1962; *The Fighting Newfoundlander: A History of the Royal Newfoundland Regiment,* [Newfoundland], 1964; *The Gunners of Canada: The History of the Royal Regiment of Canadian Artillery,* McClelland & Stewart, Volume I: *1534-1919,* 1967, Volume II: *1919-1967,* 1972; *The White Cross in Canada: A History of St. John Ambulance,* Harvest House, 1967; *More Fighting Newfoundlanders: A History of Newfoundland's Fighting Forces in the Second World War,* [Newfoundland], 1969; *We Will Remember: Overseas Memorials to Canada's War Dead,* Canadian Department of Veteran Affairs, 1973; *Canada's Nursing Sisters,* Samuel Stevens, 1975; *Seventy Years of Service: A History of the Royal Canadian Army Medical Corps,* Borealis, 1977; *Keep Your Forks: Fifty Years at Red Pine Camp,* Red Pine Camp, 1979. Contributor to history journals.

[Sketch verified by wife, Edith Ashcroft Nicholson]

* * *

NICOLSON, Nigel 1917-

PERSONAL: Born January 19, 1917, in London, England; son of Harold George (a politician, diplomat, and writer) and Victoria (a writer; maiden name, Sackville-West) Nicolson; married Philippa Janet d'Eyncourt, 1953 (divorced, 1970); children: one son, two daughters. *Education:* Attended Eron College, 1930-35, and Oxford University, 1936-39. *Politics:* Conservative. *Home:* Sissinghurst Castle, Kent, England. *Office:* Weidenfeld & Nicolson Ltd., 91 Clapham High St., London SW4 7TA, England.

CAREER: Writer. Weidenfeld & Nicolson Ltd. (publisher), London, England, director, 1947—. Conservative member of English Parliament, 1952-59; chairman of United Nations Association, 1960-67. *Military service:* Grenadier Guards, 1939-45; served in Tunisian and Italian campaigns; became captain. *Member:* Royal Society of Literature (fellow), Society of Antiquaries (fellow), Beafsteak. *Awards, honors:* Member of the Order of the British Empire, 1945; Whitbread Award, 1977, for *Mary Curzon.*

WRITINGS: The Grenadier Guards, 1939-1945, Gale & Polden, 1949; *People and Parliament,* Weidenfeld & Nicolson, 1958, Greenwood Press, 1974; *Lord of the Isles: Lord Leverhulme in the Hebrides,* Weidenfeld & Nicolson, 1960; *Great Houses of Britain,* Putnam, 1965; *Great Houses of the Western World,* Putnam, 1968 (published in England as *Great Houses,* Weidenfeld & Nicolson, 1968); *Alex: The Life of Field Marshal Earl Alexander of Tunis,* Atheneum, 1973; *Portrait of a Marriage,* Atheneum, 1973; *The Himalayas,* Time-Life, 1975; *Mary Curzon,* Harper, 1977.

Editor: *Diaries and Letters of Harold Nicolson,* Atheneum, Volume I: *1930-1939,* 1966, Volume II: *The War Years: 1939-1945* (Book-of-the-Month Club selection), 1967, Volume III: *The Later Years: 1945-1962,* 1968; (with Joanne Trautman) *The Letters of Virginia Woolf,* Harcourt, Volume I: *The Flight of the Mind: 1888-1912,* 1975, Volume II: *The Question of Things Happening: 1912-1922,* 1976, Volume III: *A Change of Perspective: 1923-1928,* 1978, Volume IV: *A Reflection of the Other Person: 1929-1931,* 1979, Volume V: *The Sickle Side of the Moon: 1932-1935,* 1979, Volume VI: *Leave the Letters Till We're Dead: 1936-1941,* 1980.

WORK IN PROGRESS: A biography of Napoleon.

SIDELIGHTS: One of Nigel Nicolson's best-known works, *Portrait of a Marriage,* recounts the nearly fifty-year union of his father, Harold Nicolson, and his mother, Victoria Sackville-West, known to friends as Vita. The book is based on the diary/autobiography of Vita undertaken when she was twenty-eight years old, married for eight years, and already the mother of two sons. She began simply: "Of course I have no right whatsoever to write down the truth about my life, involving as it does the lives of so many other people, but I do so urged by a necessity of truth-telling, because there is no other soul who knows the complete truth." Nigel Nicolson explains in his book that his mother's diary was "a confession, an attempt to purge her mind and heart of a love that had possessed her, a love for another woman, Violet Trefusis."

Although Violet was not the only woman Vita became involved with—another was Virginia Woolf—theirs was "a passion that [was] so intense it [was] like the grip of death," related Eliot Fremont-Smith in *New York.* He went on to note that "in her diary, Vita sees herself as two people (and her son does likewise): a rational, safe, well-born, intelligent, *good* person, wanting and needing her husband as 'safe harbor' and wanting to love him and deserve his amazingly steady devotion; and a rebellious, creative, independent, free spirit, supremely sensual, ready to risk all to satisfy the gift-curse craving the gods implanted in her soul, the essence of herself."

A reviewer for the *Times Literary Supplement* praised Nicolson for his handling of the delicate subject matter in *Portrait of a Marriage:* "He demonstrates an enlargement of sympathy without evading painful realities." Carolyn Heilbrun also commended Nicolson as "an absolutely first-rate editor, combining as he does fastidious exactness with the ability to write gracefully." She had, however, one complaint: "I wish that his antagonism toward his mother had been more honorably faced. He has, for example, exploited his mother's homosexuality while giving us no picture of his father's homosexual affairs, so that we are left with the impression of a transvestite married to a man of lesser passions who occasionally—what? We are never told, and she is made to look a freak beside him." Harold Nicolson's sexual preference was, reportedly, a loosely-guarded secret. In fact, Harold and Vita often chided each other for their indulgences: she for her "muddles," and he for his "fun." And the marriage thrived, according to the *Times Literary Supplement,* for "neither of them felt in the least threatened by what, in both cases, was dismissed as idle peccadilloes, for they knew that they were indissolubly linked by a unique bond of affection, which only strengthened with time."

Fremont-Smith concluded that "one comes away from *Portrait of a Marriage* not exactly liking these people . . . but with a sense of having known them in their souls, of having seen the raw insides of the intensity of their passions. It is all exhausting and haunting, not pleasant, perhaps, but an experience that reverberates, of a sort provided by very few books."

Nicolson again revealed the mind of a woman in *The Letters of Virginia Woolf.* This six-volume work includes correspondences from the time Virginia was six years old until her suicide at age fifty-nine. Although the first volume, covering the period from 1888 to 1912, does not portray the famous literary figure of her later years, it nevertheless "provides the undeniable fascination of watching her become that woman," reported Christopher Porterfield in *Time.* Volume II, subtitled *The Question of Things Happening,* chronicles two of her bouts with insanity and an attempted suicide. Woolf's correspondents at this time included her beloved sister Vanessa, one-time lover Violet Dickenson, future brother-in-law Clive Bell, and the writers Lytton Strachey and Roger Fry.

Letters from the three-year love affair of Virginia and Vita Sackville-West constitute the majority of the third volume. "I doubt there can be other love letters in the language quite like the ones printed here," declared Claire Tomalin in the *New Statesman.* "They can be read without a twinge; open, unembarrassed tributes from one woman to another for her beauty and seductiveness, direct appeals to her to come and hold her in her arms."

The next volume is also dominated by a figure of Virginia's affection, Ethel Smyth, a woman described by various writers as "vehement, impetuous, egotistic," and "a loudmouth." "An old woman of 71 has fallen in love with me," Virginia wrote in 1930. "It is like being caught up by a giant crab." Although Smyth did not at first appeal to Woolf, their relationship grew both in openness and intensity as Virginia poured out some of the most emotional letters of her life. She wrote openly of sex, madness, and other topics Virginia would not readily reveal to others. But their affair soured, and whereas Virginia's letters to Vita were described as gentle, passionate, and moving, even when the two had broken off their relationship, her letters to Smyth were coarse and at times cruel. In one letter, for example, she condemned Smyth as "the rough-haired burr-tangled Cornish pig . . . an uncastrated pig . . . a wild boar, or a savage sow," and in another she railed against the older woman, calling her "a damned Harlot—hoary harpy—or an eldritch shriek of egotism—a hail storm of inconsecutive and inconsequent conceit."

The fifth volume, *The Sickle Side of the Moon,* contains letters written when Woolf was in her early fifties. Though distressed by the deaths of several close friends, including Lytton Strachey and Roger Fry, she remained generally in good spirits and continued her literary endeavors. Reviews of this volume and of Nicolson's editing were decidedly more mixed than in previous volumes. A reviewer for *Economist,* for instance, proclaimed that "the editing is as good as ever, which is high praise." On the other hand, Jane Marcus held the work in low esteem: "This is Nigel Nicolson's fifth time around with Virginia Woolf and he still hasn't got the hang of it. He flails and flounders, clutches at anything to prove his previous statements . . . and so muddles the actual facts with his own steadfastly incorrect opinions that the reader can only wonder: Why should anyone edit the letters of anyone he holds in such contempt?" She conceded, however, that "while obviously not a labor of love, [the work] might have been a labor of respect."

In 1973 Nicolson wrote *Alex,* a biography of World War II hero Earl Alexander. Montgomery's commander in chief at Alamein, Alex, as he was referred to, conquered the whole of Italy, toppling Mussolini's regime and taking Rome. Nicolson, according to several reviewers, was the best person to write Alex's biography, having served under him in the Tunisian and Italian campaigns. "This is an important biography," declared Alun Chalfont, "written with sympathy and perception." The reviewer added that the "portrait is strongly drawn and convincing."

BIOGRAPHICAL/CRITICAL SOURCES: New York Review of Books, March 23, 1967, November 15, 1973, July 15, 1976; *New York Times Book Review,* June 11, 1967, November 10, 1974, November 23, 1975, November 14, 1976, January 8, 1978, March 25, 1979, April 22, 1979; *London Magazine,* October, 1967; *New Statesman,* October 13, 1967; *Saturday Night,* October, 1968; Nigel Nicolson, *Portrait of a*

Marriage, Atheneum, 1973; *Economist,* March 31, 1973, September 20, 1975; *New Yorker,* October 29, 1973, July 18, 1977; *New York,* October 8, 1973; *Times Literary Supplement,* November 2, 1973, September 19, 1975, September 24, 1976, November 11, 1977; *Ms.,* February, 1974; *Newsweek,* November 17, 1975, January 9, 1978; *Christian Science Monitor,* December 22, 1975; *Time,* January 19, 1976; *Yale Review,* spring, 1976; *Library Journal,* November 1, 1976; *New York Times,* December 27, 1977; *Los Angeles Times,* March 26, 1979; *Chicago Tribune Book World,* April 22, 1979, November 4, 1979.

—Sketch by Kathleen Ceton Newman

*   *   *

NIESEWAND, Peter 1944-

PERSONAL: Surname is pronounced *Nees*-wand; born in 1944 in South Africa; married Oenone Fogarty (an editor), June 14, 1944; children: Oliver, James. *Religion:* Church of England. *Home:* 82a Honor Oak Rd., Forest Hill, London S.E.23, England. *Agent:* John Farquharson Ltd., Bell House, 8 Bell Yard, London WC2A 2JU, England. *Office:* *Guardian,* 119 Farringdon Rd., London E.C.1, England.

CAREER: Free-lance writer, 1964-73; *Guardian,* London, England, reporter, 1973—. *Awards, honors:* Named international journalist of the year by British Press, 1973 and 1976.

WRITINGS: In Camera: Secret Justice in Rhodesia, Weidenfeld & Nicolson, 1973; *The Underground Connection,* Secker & Warburg, 1978; *A Member of the Club,* Secker & Warburg, 1979, Dutton, 1980; *The Word of a Gentleman,* Secker & Warburg, 1981. Television writer for British Broadcasting Corp. (BBC), Canadian Broadcasting Corp. (CBC), and Australian Broadcasting Commission. Contributor to magazines, including *Maclean's,* and newspapers.

SIDELIGHTS: Niesewand commented to *CA:* "Most of my fiction is based on fact, or on (secret) plans governments have in hand to protect security (*A Member of the Club*), and the plots are projected ahead to a likely outcome."

*   *   *

NIXON, John Erskine 1917-

PERSONAL: Born June 28, 1917, in Pomona, Calif.; son of Eugene White and Edna Maude (Blair) Nixon; married Julia Eveleth Haskell, February 10, 1945; children: Sarah (Mrs. Kris Esslinger), John H. *Education:* Pomona College, A.B., 1939; Claremont College, M.A., 1941; University of Southern California, Ed.D., 1949. *Home:* 732 Alvarado Court, Stanford, Calif. 94305. *Office:* Stanford University, Stanford, Calif. 94305.

CAREER: Stanford University, Stanford, Calif., professor of education and physical education, 1949—, director of professional physical education program, 1949—. Senior Fulbright lecturer in Austria, Finland, and Denmark, 1956, and Norway, England, Scotland, and Wales, 1971; summer lecturer at University of Colorado, University of Hawaii, University of Washington, Seattle, University of Oregon, and Alaska Methodist University. Vice-president of Hamnic Corp., 1964-72. Member of board of directors of Moore School, 1962-64. U.S. State Department consultant to Egypt. *Military service:* U.S. Army, 1941-46; served in China-Burma-India theater. *Member:* American Academy of Physical Education, National Society for the Study of Education, American Educational Research Association, National College Men's Physical Education Association (president, 1963-64), California Association of Health, Physical

Education and Recreation (president, 1960-61), Phi Beta Kappa, Phi Delta Kappa.

WRITINGS: (With Ann E. Jewett) *Physical Education Curriculum,* Wiley, 1963; (with Lynn Vendien) *The World Today in Health, Physical Education and Recreation,* Prentice-Hall, 1968; (with Jewett) *An Introduction to Physical Education,* Saunders, 1974, 9th edition, 1980. Also author, with Celeste Ulrich, of *Tones of Theory,* 1972. Editor of a series, "Foundation of Physical Education," 1969.

*   *   *

NOAKES, Jeremy 1941-

PERSONAL: Born May 31, 1941, in Singapore; son of Douglas S. and Eve (Marsh) Noakes; married Ingrid Krohn, July 18, 1961; children: Oliver, Sonya. *Education:* Oriel College, Oxford, B.A. (with honors), 1963; received M.A. and D.Phil. from St. Antony's College, Oxford. *Home:* 36 Clobells, Southbrent, Devonshire, England. *Office:* University of Exeter, Exeter EX4 4QJ, England.

CAREER: University of Hull, Hull, England, lecturer, 1965-68; University of Exeter, Exeter, England, 1969—, began as lecturer, currently reader. *Member:* Royal Historical Society (fellow), German History Society.

WRITINGS: The Nazi Party in Lower Saxony, 1921-1933, Oxford University Press, 1971; (editor with G. Ridham) *Documents on Nazism,* J. Cape, 1974, Viking, 1975. Contributor of articles and reviews to academic journals.

WORK IN PROGRESS: Research on the political structure of Nazi Germany.

*   *   *

NOBLE, Charles
See PAWLEY, Martin Edward

*   *   *

NOBLE, William P(arker) 1932-

PERSONAL: Born January 25, 1932, in New York, N.Y.; son of William P., Sr. (a journalist) and Ethel (Karsch) Noble; married June Brogger (a writer), September 26, 1969; children: (from previous marriage) William P. III, John Alden. *Education:* Lehigh University, B.A., 1954; University of Pennsylvania, J.D., 1961. *Politics:* Liberal. *Home and office address:* Rogers Rd., Salisbury, Vt. 05769. *Agent:* Jo Stewart, 201 East 66th St., Suite 18-G, New York, N.Y. 10021.

CAREER: Columbia Broadcasting System, New York, N.Y., production assistant, 1957-58; Townsend, Elliott & Munson (law firm), Philadelphia, Pa., attorney, 1961-62; Armstrong Cork Co., Lancaster, Pa., attorney, 1962-68; Model Cities Program, Lancaster, director, 1968-69; writer, 1969—. Chairman of board of directors of Econ, Inc. (minority business entrepreneurs), 1968-69. Chairman of Avalon Zoning Commission, Avalon, N.J., 1973-76. Urban consultant. *Military service:* U.S. Coast Guard, 1954-57; became lieutenant commander. U.S. Coast Guard Reserve, 1957-62. *Member:* Authors Guild of Authors League of America, League of Vermont Writers.

WRITINGS—All with wife, June B. Noble: *The Custody Trap,* Hawthorn, 1975; *How to Live With Other People's Children,* Hawthorn, 1978; *The Private Me,* Delacorte, 1980. Contributor to magazines and newspapers.

WORK IN PROGRESS: Research for a book on American psychiatry, for Delacorte.

SIDELIGHTS: Noble commented: "The writing life for all its uncertainty and seeming elusiveness, the sense of accomplishment can be outsized. No question, there is a mystique—glamor, mystery, riches, independence. But first and foremost writing is a craft, a skill to be learned, practiced, and honed as the carpenter, the mechanic, the accountant learn and do. Creativity has always been weighted heavily with hard work and inspiration is only a sometime spark. The writer who understands this is the real professional.

"Our books seem to fall into the socio-behavioral field, though we certainly have many other interests. But why people do the things they do, and how, and is that good or right or moral or ethical provides infinite possibilities and fascination. It's a cinch we'll never run out of subjects."

BIOGRAPHICAL/CRITICAL SOURCES: Burlington Free Press, December 13, 1979; *Valley Voice,* March 5, 1980; *Philadelphia Sunday Bulletin,* March 16, 1980; *Washington Post,* March 28, 1980.

*   *   *

NOEL, Daniel C(alhoun) 1936-

PERSONAL: Born April 21, 1936, in Jackson, Miss.; son of L. T. and Eleanor (Daniel) Noel; married Joanna Lane, September 5, 1959; children: Christopher, Rebecca, Jennifer, Susannah. *Education:* Ohio Wesleyan University, B.A., 1958; University of Chicago, M.A., 1960; Drew University, Ph.D., 1967; postdoctoral study at Yale University, 1969-70. *Religion:* Methodist. *Residence:* East Calais, Vt. *Office:* Adult Degree Program, Goddard College, Plainfield, Vt. 05667.

CAREER: Lafayette College, Easton, Pa., teaching assistant, 1964-65, instructor, 1965-67, assistant professor of religion, 1967-72; Bucknell University, Lewisburg, Pa., visiting associate professor of religion, 1972-73; Goddard College, Plainfield, Vt., member of adult degree program's core faculty in religion, literature, and mythology, 1973—. Visiting assistant professor at Miami University, Oxford, Ohio, summer, 1969; visiting associate professor of Emory University, 1976-77; visiting professor at Syracuse University, spring, 1980; visiting lecturer at University of Vermont, Wake Forest University, Catawba College, Lyndon State College, University of California, Davis, West Georgia College, Oxford College, C. G. Jung Foundation, Regis College, Montana State University, Williams College, and Hampshire College. *Member:* American Academy of Religion, Melville Society of America, Society for Values in Higher Education (fellow). *Awards, honors:* Ford Foundation grant, 1969-70.

WRITINGS: (Contributor) John C. Cobb, editor, *The Theology of Altizer: Critique and Response,* Westminster, 1970; (contributor) David Griffin, editor, *Philosophy of Religion and Theology: 1973 Proceedings,* American Academy of Religion, 1973; (editor and contributor) *Echoes of the Wordless "Word": Colloquy in Honor of Stanley Romaine Hopper,* Scholars' Press, 1973; *Carlos Castaneda,* Warner Paperback, 1975; (editor) *Seeing Castaneda: Reactions to the "Don Juan" Writings of Carlos Castaneda,* Putnam, 1976. Contributor of about fifty articles and reviews to scholarly journals.

WORK IN PROGRESS: Approaching Earth: In Search of a Space-Age Mythos Through Metaphor and Serendipity (working title), about "earth images" arising in the age of space.

SIDELIGHTS: Noel wrote: "Notions which have motivated me are the evolution of consciousness, the 'death of God,' the metaphoric nature of perception and realities. I've always been fiercely interdisciplinary and fairly 'alternative' as an academic. My current crotchets include understanding the *post*-modern agenda in Western culture and in my psyche, especially as related to crypto- or pseudo-religious phenomena (such as megalithic sites and basketball). I want to write well about all this while not freezing to death during Vermont winters, remembering Castaneda's lessons that all so-called solid facts eventually thaw out and reveal themselves to be more or less persuasive fictions.''

* * *

NOETHER, Emiliana P.

PERSONAL: Born in Naples, Italy; daughter of Guglielmo and Bianca (Dramis) Pasca; married Gottfried E. Noether, August 1, 1942; children: Monica Gail. *Education:* Hunter College (now of the City University of New York), A.B., 1943; Columbia University, M.A., 1944, Ph.D., 1948. *Office:* Wood Hall, University of Connecticut, Storrs, Conn. 06268.

CAREER: Rutgers University, Douglass College, New Brunswick, N.J., instructor, 1947-50, assistant professor of history, 1950-52; Massachusetts Institute of Technology, Cambridge, research associate at Center for International Studies, 1952-54; Regis College, Weston, Mass., lecturer, 1959-63, associate professor, 1963-64, professor of history, 1964-66; Simmons College, Boston, Mass., professor of history, 1966-68; University of Connecticut, Storrs, professor of history, 1968—. *Member:* American Historical Association (chairperson of committee on women historians; member of council, 1976-79), Society for Italian Historical Studies (member of advisory council, 1979—), American Association of University Women, Berkshire Conference on Women Historians (president, 1967-71; member of executive committee, 1979—), Pi Gamma Mu. *Awards, honors:* Fellow of Harvard University's Bunting Institute and Radcliffe Institute, both 1961-62; American Association of University Women fellow, 1962-63; senior Fulbright scholar in Italy, 1965-66; American Philosophical Society grant, 1970.

WRITINGS: Seeds of Italian Nationalism, Columbia University Press, 1951, 2nd edition, 1969; (co-editor and contributor) *Modern Italy: A Topical History Since 1861,* New York University Press, 1974. Author and co-producer of a film, ''Man in the Renaissance,'' 1972. Contributor to history journals. Editor of Italian sections of *American Historical Review,* 1958-75, and *Recently Published Articles,* 1976—.

WORK IN PROGRESS: Between Myth and Reality: The Dilemma of Italian Intellectuals, 1900-1940; The Role of Women in Italian Society Since the Nineteenth Century; research on women and war in the twentieth century and on the charismatic leader and revolution.

SIDELIGHTS: Emiliana Noether commented: ''A major interest has been social and intellectual history of Europe in the last century, with particular emphasis on Italy. Intellectuals, women, revolutionists have lived and live in dialectical tension with the dominant male group that usually controls political and economic power. Having been brought up to believe that women were fully as capable as men, and that only social customs and outdated concepts prevented them from fully participating—to the extent of their abilities and ambitions—in professional and public life, I have carried my personal convictions over into my work and writing. A broadly-based education gave me fluency in languages. Several years of training in music and art sharpened my awareness of the importance of the humanities. Travel and living in Europe have added to an education that will continue all my life.''

NOLAN, Bob 1908(?)-1980

OBITUARY NOTICE: Born c. 1908 in New Brunswick, Canada; died of a heart attack, June 16, 1980, in Costa Mesa, Calif. Performer and composer of more than one thousand country, western, and gospel songs. Nolan formed the Pioneer Trio with Roy Rogers and Tim Spencer in 1931 and later went on to appear in more than one hundred western films with the Sons of the Pioneers. Among his more popular songs are ''Cool Water,'' ''One More Ride,'' and ''A Touch of God's Hand.'' Obituaries and other sources: *Chicago Tribune,* June 18, 1980; *Time,* June 30, 1980.

* * *

NORI, Claude 1949-

PERSONAL: Born February 4, 1949, in Toulouse, France; son of Raphael and Fanny (Martinotto) Nori. *Education:* Universite de Toulouse, B.A.C., 1968. *Home:* 59 Rue Froidevaux, Paris 14, France. *Office:* Contrejour, 19 Rue de L'Ouest, Paris 14, France.

CAREER: Photographer for *Vogue, Playboy,* and *Daily Telegraph Magazine,* and writer-critic for *Progresso Fotografico,* 1968-73; founded Contrejour (a publishing house, magazine, gallery, and photography workshop), in Paris, France, 1974—.

WRITINGS: Les Masques humains (title means ''Human Masks''), Roma Editor, 1971; *Lunettes* (title means ''Glasses''), Contrejour, 1974; *Occitanie Toulousaine,* Technal, 1977; *La Photographie Francaise des origines a nos jours,* Contrejour, 1979, translation by Lydia Davis published as *French Photography: From Its Origin to the Present,* Pantheon, 1979; *Je vous aime* (title means ''I Love You''), Photoeil, 1979. Contributor of articles to photography periodicals.

WORK IN PROGRESS: A novel and film about a photographer, *The Instant Girl,* completion expected in April, 1981; an essay about photography in Europe, ''Contemporary European Photography.''

SIDELIGHTS: Nori told *CA:* ''I have always been interested in photography as the hub of expression and social reality. My second book, *Lunettes,* was a critique of the official artistic photograph. In 1974 I created a journal, a publishing house, and a gallery that disputed photography as technocratic speculation and will quickly become the forum of the young French photographer.

''My books are very often bound to my personal life. My last book was a love poem for a young photographer girl that I loved very much, and at the same time it was a critique of the love shown on television. My next book will be a novel that tells a story of love set in a photographic milieu and will be illustrated by some souvenir photographs.''

* * *

NORTH, Sara
See HAGER, Jean

* * *

NORTH, Wheeler James 1922-

PERSONAL: Born January 2, 1922, in San Francisco, Calif.; son of Wheeler Orrin (an engineer) and Florence (Ross) North; married Nance Fountain, August 15, 1952 (divorced March, 1964); married Barbara Best (a physician), April 25, 1964; children: Hannah Catherine, Wheeler Orrin. *Education:* California Institute of Technology, B.S. (engineering),

1944, B.S. (biology), 1950; University of California, San Diego, Ph.D., 1953; postdoctoral study at Cambridge University, 1953-54. *Politics:* Independent. *Religion:* None. *Office:* W. M. Keck Laboratory, California Institute of Technology, Pasadena, Calif. 91109.

CAREER: U.S. Navy Electronics Laboratory, San Diego, Calif., electronics engineer, 1946-48; University of California, San Diego, La Jolla, assistant research biologist at Institute of Marine Resources, 1954-63, fellow at Scripps Institute of Oceanography, 1955-56; Lockheed California Co., Burbank, Calif., senior research scientist, 1963; California Institute of Technology, Pasadena, associate professor, 1963-68, professor of environmental science, 1968—. Member of California Advisory Commission on Coastal and Marine Resources, California Navigation and Ocean Development Commission, and California Underwater Parks Advisory Board; consultant to government agencies, Pacific Gas & Electric Co., and Los Angeles Department of Water & Power. *Military service:* U.S. Army Signal Corps, 1942-46; became first lieutenant.

MEMBER: American Association for the Advancement of Science, Society for General Physiology, American Society of Zoology, American Malacological Union, American Geophysical Union, Phycological Society of America, American Botanical Society, American Institute of Biological Sciences, Marine Technology Society, Western Society of Naturalists. *Awards, honors:* National Science Foundation fellowship, 1953-54; Rockefeller Foundation fellowship, 1955-56.

WRITINGS: The Golden Guide to Scuba Diving, Ridge Press, 1968; (editor with C. L. Hubbs, and contributor) *Utilization of Kelp Bed Resources in California,* California Department of Fish and Game, 1968; (editor and contributor) *The Biology of Giant Kelp Beds (Macrocystics) in California,* J. Kramer, 1971; *Underwater California,* University of California Press, 1976. Contributor of about one hundred fifty articles to scientific journals and popular magazines.

WORK IN PROGRESS: Research on marine ecology and alternative energy sources.

SIDELIGHTS: North wrote: "My principal interest is advancing scientific knowledge in ocean farming. The surface of our planet is seventy percent ocean, with relatively small usage by humans. If we could learn how to raise crops in this environment, enormous resources might be gleaned from this part of the earth. The resources could include animal and plant foods, fuels, petrochemicals, and other products presently made from fossil fuels."

BIOGRAPHICAL/CRITICAL SOURCES: National Geographic, August, 1972.

* * *

NORTON, Alden H(olmes) 1903-

PERSONAL: Born July 23, 1903, in Lynn, Mass.; son of Charles A. (a musician) and Katherine (White) Norton; married Margaret Acheson, October 12, 1942. *Education:* Brown University, Ph.B., 1925. *Agent:* Lurton Blassingame, Blassingame, McCauley & Wood, 60 East 42nd St., New York, N.Y. 10017.

CAREER: Popular Publications, Inc., New York, N.Y., 1935-73, editor of *Argosy, Super Science Stories,* and *Astonishing Stories,* all 1941-43, became supervisory editor of all magazines and head of sales department and releases; writer, 1973—. *Member:* American Contract Bridge Association (life master).

WRITINGS: The Award Science Fiction Reader, Award, 1966; *Horror Times Ten,* Berkley Publishing, 1967; *Masters of Horror,* Berkley Publishing, 1968; *Hauntings and Horrors: Ten Grisly Tales,* Berkley Publishing, 1969; *Futures Unlimited* (stories), Pyramid Publications, 1969; *Holler Guy,* Norton, 1969.

With Sam Moskowitz: *Great Untold Stories of Fantasy and Horror,* Pyramid Publications, 1969; *Ghostly by Gaslight: Fearful Tales of a Lost Era,* Pyramid Publications, 1971; *The Space Magicians,* Pyramid Publications, 1971; *Horrors in Hiding,* Berkley Publishing, 1973. Contributor to magazines, including *Detective Fiction Weekly.*

* * *

NUGENT, Elliott (John) 1899-1980

OBITUARY NOTICE—See index for *CA* sketch: Born September 20, 1899, in Dover, Ohio; died August 9, 1980, in New York, N.Y. Actor, director, producer, and author. Since the age of four, Nugent worked at a variety of occupations in show business. He acted in the theatre, in motion pictures, and on television, and also directed and produced stage plays. Nugent was best known for his play "The Male Animal," written in collaboration with James Thurber. His other works include *Kempy, Of Cheat and Charmer,* and *Events Leading Up to the Comedy.* Obituaries and other sources: *New York Times,* August 11, 1980; *Chicago Tribune,* August 14, 1980.

* * *

NUMBERS, Ronald L(eslie) 1942-

PERSONAL: Born June 3, 1942, in Boulder, Colo.; son of Raymond Wilfred (a minister) and Lois (Branson) Numbers; married Janet Schulze (a clinical psychologist), December 27, 1975. *Education:* Southern Missionary College, B.A., 1963; Florida State University, M.A., 1965; University of California, Berkeley, Ph.D., 1969. *Home:* 2134 Yahara Pl., Madison, Wis. 53704. *Office:* Department of the History of Medicine, University of Wisconsin, 1305 Linden Dr., Madison, Wis. 53706.

CAREER: Andrews University, Berrien Springs, Mich., assistant professor of history, 1969-70; Loma Linda University, Loma Linda, Calif., assistant professor of humanities, 1970-74; University of Wisconsin—Madison, assistant professor, 1974-76, associate professor, 1976-79, professor of history of medicine and science, 1979—, chairman of department of history of medicine, 1977—. Fellow at Institute of the History of Medicine, Johns Hopkins University, 1973-74. *Member:* American Historical Association, American Association of the History of Medicine, American Society of Church History, Organization of American Historians, History of Science Society.

WRITINGS: Prophetess of Health: A Study of Ellen G. White, Harper, 1976; *Creation by Natural Law: Laplace's Nebular Hypothesis in American Thought,* University of Washington Press, 1977; *Almost Persuaded: American Physicians and Compulsory Health Insurance, 1912-1920,* Johns Hopkins Press, 1978.

Editor: (With G. B. Risse and J. W. Leavitt) *Medicine Without Doctors: Home Health Care in American History,* Science History Publications, 1977; (with Leavitt) *Sickness and Health in America: Readings in the History of Medicine and Public Health,* University of Wisconsin Press, 1978; *The Education of American Physicians: Historical Essays,* University of California Press, 1980; (with Leavitt) *Wisconsin*

Medicine: Historical Perspectives, University of Wisconsin Press, 1981.

WORK IN PROGRESS: An edited history of Christianity and science, with David Lindberg, publication expected in 1982; a history of science in America, publication expected in 1983.

O

OBERHOLTZER, W(alter) Dwight 1939-

PERSONAL: Born September 6, 1939, in Rhinelander, Wis.; son of Walter Dwight (a Lutheran minister) and Verna Pauline (Baker) Oberholtzer; married Ellen Christine Ostern (an administrative consultant), August 12, 1973. *Education:* Wittenberg University, B.A., 1961; Lutheran School of Theology, Chicago, Ill., B.D., 1965, M.Div., 1972; Graduate Theological Union, Berkeley, Calif., Ph.D., 1969; also attended University of California, Berkeley, 1965-69. *Office:* Department of Sociology, Pacific Lutheran University, Tacoma, Wash. 98447.

CAREER: San Francisco Council of Churches, San Francisco, Calif., assistant night minister, 1967-69; Pacific Lutheran University, Tacoma, Wash., assistant professor, 1969-72, associate professor of sociology, 1972—. *Member:* American Sociological Association.

WRITINGS: (Editor) *Is Gay Good?: Ethics, Theology, and Homosexuality,* Westminster, 1971.

WORK IN PROGRESS: Strategies for Self-Transformation, "an experiential workbook which applies the use of altered states of consciousness to personal growth."

SIDELIGHTS: W. Dwight Oberholtzer told *CA:* "I am concerned presently with the way mental habits paint the world we experience and how those often violent and dark colors can be transformed—at our own direction—into healing ones. The mind heals and destroys, and it is in the tenuous balance between conscious and unconscious experience that the vote for personal growth or decay is made."

*   *   *

O'CONNELL, Michael (William) 1943-

PERSONAL: Born November 11, 1943, in Seattle, Wash.; son of Paul C. (an accountant) and A. Geraldine (a secretary; maiden name, Henderson) O'Connell; married Laura Stevenson (a historian and musician), September 27, 1969; children: Katharine, Margaret. *Education:* University of San Francisco, A.B., 1966; Yale University, M.Phil., 1969, Ph.D., 1971. *Politics:* Democrat. *Religion:* Roman Catholic. *Home:* 430 East Valerio St., Santa Barbara, Calif. 93101. *Office:* Department of English, University of California, Santa Barbara, Calif. 93106.

CAREER: University of California, Santa Barbara, assistant professor, 1970-78, associate professor of English, 1978—.

Member: Modern Language Association of America, Renaissance Society of America, Spenser Society. *Awards, honors:* Woodrow Wilson fellowship, 1966; National Endowment for the Humanities fellowship, 1974.

WRITINGS: Mirror and Veil: The Historical Dimension of Spenser's "Faerie Queene," University of North Carolina Press, 1977. Contributor to scholarly journals.

WORK IN PROGRESS: Research on the religious dimension of Shakespeare's plays.

*   *   *

OFEK, Uriel 1926-

PERSONAL: Original name Uriel Popik; name legally changed in 1949; born June 30, 1926, in Tel-Aviv, Israel; son of Arie (a mason) and Bronia (a kindergarten teacher; maiden name, Vogel) Popik; married Bina Dellman (a writer and editor), April 3, 1952; children: Atara, Amira. *Education:* Hebrew University of Jerusalem, M.A., 1951, Ph.D., 1976; attended University of Toronto, 1959-60. *Religion:* Jewish. *Home:* 18 Haeshel St., Nof-Yam, Herzlia, Israel. *Agent:* Carol Mann Literary Agency, 168 Pacific St., Brooklyn, N.Y. 11201.

CAREER: Davar le Yeladim (children's weekly), Tel-Aviv, Israel, co-editor, 1951-70, editor-in-chief, 1970-76; writer, editor, translator, and script writer, 1976—. Lecturer at Toronto Public Library, 1961-62; lecturer on children's literature and reading, including tour of the United States in 1978. Founder and president of Israeli national section of International Board on Books for Young People. *Military service:* Palmach Har'el, 1944-49; became sergeant. Israel Reserve Defense Forces, 1949-70. *Member:* Hebrew Writers Organization (member of council). *Awards, honors:* Lamdan Prize from Ramat Gan Munic, 1965, for *Me-Robinson ad Lobengulu;* Ze'ev Award from Ministry of Culture and Education, 1974, for *En sodot ba-shekhunah;* Hans Christian Andersen Certificate of Honor from International Board on Books for Young People, 1976, for *Smoke Over Golan.*

WRITINGS: Ha-Hatsagah hayevet le-himashekh (juvenile), Massada, 1967, translation by Ruth Rasnic published as *The Show Must Go On,* Massada, 1971; (editor) *The Dog That Flew, and Other Favorite Stories From Israel,* Funk, 1969; (editor) *Ha-Shalom Sheli,* American Israel Publishing, 1974, translation by Dov Vardi published as *My Shalom, My Peace: Paintings and Poems by Jewish and Arab Children,*

McGraw, 1975; *Tom and Laura From Right to Left: American Children's Books Experienced by Young Hebrew Readers,* American Library Association, 1978; *Ashan kissa et ha-Golan* (juvenile), Mizrachi, 1975, translation by Israel Taslitt, published as *Smoke Over Golan,* Harper, 1979.

In Hebrew: *Masa'el aba ha-hayal* (juvenile; title means "A Journey to Daddy, the Soldier"), Chachik, 1958; *Be-ozne ha-ilan* (poems; title means "In the Tree's Ears"), Mahbarot le-Sifrut, 1953; *Be-sod yeladim* (juvenile; title means "Children's Secrets"), Chachik, 1953; *Yeladim ba-ahu* (juvenile; title means "Children in the Pasture"), Chachik, 1954; *Na'ar kisufim: Sipur hayav shel 'Amikam Rhahalin* (biography; title means "A Longing Lad: Life of Amikam Rhahlin"), Chachik, 1956; *Sheva' tahonat ve'od tahannah* (juvenile; title means "Seven Mills and a Station"), Chachik—Yavneh, 1956, 1980; *Me-Robinson 'ad Lobengulu* (title means "From Robinson to Lobengulu: The Story Behind Great Stories"), Massada, 1962; *Tse'adim ba-hol* (juvenile; title means "Footsteps in the Sand"), Massada, 1966; *Mi-Shilgiyah ve-'ad Emil* (title means "From Cinderella to Emil: The Story Behind the Great Stories"), Massada, 1967; *Hei, habitu le-ma'lah* (juvenile; title means "Hey, Look Up!"), Am Oved, 1968; *Mi-Tarzan 'ad Hasambah* (title means "From Tarzan to Hasamba: The Story Behind Great Stories"), Massada, 1969.

Olam tsa'ir (title means "Young World: Encyclopedia of Children's Literature"), Massada, 1970; *Gibor hidah* (biography; title means "Mysterious Hero"), Sreberk, 1970; *Efoh temunot ha-temunoit* (juvenile; title means "To Pick a Picture"), Millo, 1973; *Hamesh dakot pahad* (juvenile; title means "A Five-Minutes' Fear"), Sifriat Po'alim, 1974; *En sodot ba-skekhunah* (juvenile; title means "No Secrets in the Neighborhood"), Sifriat Po'alim, 1976; *Tmunat dam* (autobiographical; title means "Blood Picture"), Reshafim, 1977; *Sifrut ha-yeladim ha-'ivrit- ha-Hathala* (title means "The Beginning of Hebrew Children's Literature"), Tel Aviv University Press, 1979; *Ba-derekh lagimnasia* (juvenile novel; title means "High School Ways"), Sifriat Po'alim, 1980.

Children's plays—In Hebrew: *Ot be-Eretz ha-Pelaot* (two-act; title means "Letters in Wonderland") Habimah, 1968; *Ha-Yir heha-shir* (two-act; title means "The City and the Song"), Yuval, Kefar Shmaryahu, 1968; *Shlomo he-hakham ba-adam* (two-act title means "King Solomon the Wisest"), Godik, 1969; *Afun ha-pele* (two-act; title means "The Magic Bean"), Lilach, 1972.

Editor of books in Hebrew: *Bene Kiryat Hayim be-milhemet ha-shihrur* (memorial volume; title means "Sons of Kiryat Hayim in the War of Independence") Kiryat Hayim Municipality, 1950; *Mivhar ha-sipur ha-Hodi* (anthology; title means "Best Indian Short Stories"), Hada, 1954; *Gan ha-haruzim* (children's poems; title means "Garden of Verse"), Amichai, 1961; *Min ha-milhamah* (anthology; title means "From the War"), Ministry of Defense, 1969.

Translator of more than fifteen children's books from English into Hebrew, including *Tom Sawyer, Huckleberry Finn,* and the *Uncle Remus Tales.*

Author of "The Miracle," a film script released by Noah Films, 1968. Lyricist and author of scripts for Israeli television. Contributor of articles and reviews to magazines, including *Horn Book, School Library Journal,* and *Phaedrus.*

WORK IN PROGRESS: The History of Children's Literature in Hebrew, publication by Tel Aviv University Press expected in 1983.

SIDELIGHTS: Ofek told *CA:* "I believe that good poetry can be a central link which should bring together children from different countries. But the typical child wants to find his or her own realistic world in books, and of course this is found mainly in fiction. Most boys and girls, no matter what their nationality, seek identification in books. When they read a translated story, they subconsciously compare their own problems with those found in the book. Good books translated from foreign languages convince young readers that other places and cultures, although different from their own, are of equal worth; they reveal the values of human ways of life outside the reader's own limits. This is one of the advantages of removing the barriers in our 'One World' and being aware that a good book is a good book regardless of where and in what language it was written."

AVOCATIONAL INTERESTS: Collecting early children's books and magazines.

BIOGRAPHICAL/CRITICAL SOURCES: Top of the News, spring, 1977.

*   *   *

O'FLAHERTY, Liam   1896-

PERSONAL: Born August 28, 1896, in County Galway, Ireland; son of Michael and Margaret (Ganly) O'Flaherty; married Margaret Barrington (a writer), February, 1926; children: Pegeen. *Education:* Attended Rockwell College, 1908-12, Blackrock College, 1912-13, and University College, 1913-14. *Agent:* A. D. Peters Ltd., 10 Buckingham St., London WC2 N6BU, England.

CAREER: Writer. *Military service:* Served in Irish Guards during World War I. *Awards, honors:* James Tait Black Memorial Prize, 1926, for *The Informer;* Allied Irish Bank—Irish Academy of Letters Award for literature, 1979; doctorate in literature from National University of Ireland, 1974.

WRITINGS—Novels: *Thy Neighbor's Wife,* J. Cape, 1923, Boni & Liveright, 1924, Lythway Press, 1972; *The Black Soul,* J. Cape, 1924, Boni & Liveright, 1925; *The Informer,* Knopf, 1925, New American Library, 1961; *Mr. Gilhooley,* J. Cape, 1926, Harcourt, 1927; *The Assassin,* Harcourt, 1928, Landsborough, 1959; *The House of Gold,* Harcourt, 1929; *The Return of the Brute,* Mandrake Press, 1929, Harcourt, 1930; *The Puritan,* J. Cape, 1931, Harcourt, 1932; *Skerrett,* Long & Smith, 1932, Wolfhound Press, 1977; *The Martyr,* Harcourt, 1933; *Hollywood Cemetery,* Gollancz, 1935; *Famine,* Random House, 1937, New English Library, 1966; *Land,* Random House, 1946; *Insurrection,* Gollancz, 1950, Little, Brown, 1951.

Short stories: *Spring Sowing,* J. Cape, 1924, Knopf, 1926, Books for Libraries Press, 1973; *Civil War,* Archer, 1925; *The Child of God,* Archer, 1926; *The Terrorist,* Archer, 1926; *The Tent and Other Stories,* J. Cape, 1926; *The Fairy Goose and Other Stories,* Faber & Gwyer, 1927, Gaige, 1928; *Red Barbara and Other Stories,* Faber & Gwyer, 1928, Gaige, 1928; *The Mountain Tavern and Other Stories,* Harcourt, 1929, Books for Libraries Press, 1971; *The Ecstasy of Angus,* Joiner and Steele, 1931, Wolfhound Press, 1978; *The Wild Swan and Other Stories,* Joiner & Steele, 1932; *The Short Stories of Liam O'Flaherty,* J. Cape, 1937, abridged edition, New American Library, 1970.

Two Lovely Beasts and Other Stories, Gollancz, 1948, Devin-Adair, 1950; *Duil,* Sairseal Agus Dill, 1953; *The Stories of Liam O'Flaherty,* Devin-Adair, 1956; *Selected Stories,* New American Library, 1958; *Short Stories,* Brown,

Watson, 1961; *Irish Portraits: Fourteen Short Stories,* Sphere, 1970; *More Short Stories of Liam O'Flaherty,* New English Library, 1971; *The Wounded Cormorant and Other Stories,* Norton, 1973; *The Pedlar's Revenge and Other Stories,* Wolfhound Press, 1976; *All Things Come of Age: A Rabbit Story,* Wolfhound Press, 1977; *The Wave and Other Stories,* Longman, 1980.

Other: *Darkness* (short story; limited edition), Archer, 1926; *The Life of Tim Healy,* Harcourt, 1927; *A Tourist's Guide to Ireland,* Mandrake Press, 1929; *Joseph Conrad: An Appreciation,* E. Lahr, 1930, Haskell House, 1973; *Two Years* (autobiography), Harcourt, 1930; *I Went to Russia,* Harcourt, 1931; *A Cure for Unemployment,* E. Lahr, 1931; *Shame the Devil* (autobiography), Grayson, 1934; "Devil's Playground" (screenplay), Columbia, 1937; "Last Desire" (screenplay), Lumen Films, 1939; *The Test of Courage,* Wolfhound Press, 1977; *The Wilderness,* Wolfhound Press, 1978.

WORK IN PROGRESS: The Gamblers, a novel.

SIDELIGHTS: Criticism of Liam O'Flaherty's fiction is marked by a number of paradoxes. He has been both praised and condemned for his "Irishness" and his "anti-Irishness," his naturalism and his expressionism, and his existential awareness and his romantic idealism. While the sheer quantity of his writing could account for such differences in interpretation, the fact that they occur in discussions of the same works implies, rather, that O'Flaherty is a writer of greater complexity than is often acknowledged. William C. Frierson suggests that "the author's writings reflect the chaos of his life." And for a writer who has lived as everything from a hotel porter to a revolutionary fighter, wandering to places as far from Ireland as Canada and Rio de Janeiro, the life and the subsequent fiction could be chaotic indeed.

The setting for most of O'Flaherty's novels and short stories is Ireland, and his central characters are often Irish peasants deeply rooted in the land. James H. O'Brien points out that "collectively O'Flaherty's short stories describe two or three generations of life in the Aran Islands and the west of Ireland; perhaps they reach back even further, so little did life change in those areas until the end of the nineteenth century." Moreover, on the basis of a few of his novels (especially *The Informer*), he is thought of as a novelist of the Irish revolution.

On the other hand, as an early reviewer of *The Informer* noted, O'Flaherty "never makes the common error ... of falling into sentiment about Ireland or slipping out of the world of reality into that non-existent world of petulant, half-godlike and utterly fictitious Irishmen that other writers have created out of their false vision and saccharine fancy." Rather, he was part of a second wave of modern Irish writers, along with James Joyce and Sean O'Casey, who rebelled against the Celtic-revivalist ideals of Yeats and Synge. The fact that O'Flaherty was ultimately forced to leave Ireland and take up residence in England further separates him from the Irish literary tradition.

Nevertheless, one aspect of O'Flaherty's fiction grounds him solidly in an Irish tradition, specifically an oral tradition, and this is his ability as a storyteller. O'Brien explains, "In both novels and short stories, a Gaelic influence is manifest in the directness of narrative, the simplicity of language, and an elemental concern with primary emotions." In a review of *The Tent and Other Stories,* Edward Shanks saw this influence at work and remarked that O'Flaherty "sees directly and puts down directly what he sees. His best pieces, such

as 'The Conger Eel,' have the character of pictures, simple and moving because they mean no more than they say."

A number of critics take exception to O'Flaherty's classification as a naturalist. O'Brien believes that "his purpose is not to present a realistic or naturalistic view of the Irish peasant. . . . Instead, O'Flaherty generally uses the simplicity of peasant life to depict elemental reactions and instincts." Frierson similarly writes: "Although naturalistic in his view of human depravity, in his brutality, and in his insistence upon physical reactions, Mr. O'Flaherty is too forceful to be pessimistic, too violent and too melodramatic to present us with a study of humanity. His distortions are those of the expressionist."

The expressionistic representation of violence and emotion is a characteristic other critics note. Frierson explains it further: "Everywhere there is primitive physical violence, reckless impulse, greed, and cruelty; and the full force of the author's dramatic fervor is exerted by riveting our attention upon physical manifestation of the strongest emotions." Sean O'Faolain also recognized the vital effect of "O'Flaherty's usual formula of a single character about whom the story swirls with such centrifugal force that one is swept out of incredulity by the excitement of feeling at the centre of a vortex." H. E. Bates maintains that "O'Flaherty, like Maupassant, saw life in a strong light, dramatically, powerfully. Energy alone is not enough, but the sensuous poetic energy of O'Flaherty was like a flood; the reader was carried away by it and with it, slightly stunned and exalted by the experience."

These different aspects of O'Flaherty's fiction—the Irishman turning away from yet remaining tied to Ireland, the realistic storyteller imbuing his tales with an intense expression of human emotion—are brought together by John Zneimer's interpretation. Comparing O'Flaherty to Dostoevsky, Sartre, and Camus, Zneimer places him in an existentialist, as well as Irish, tradition. Because the Ireland in which O'Flaherty lived was an Ireland in which the old values and dreams were being destroyed by twentieth-century reality, O'Flaherty's Irishness and his existential awareness are inextricably tied. Zneimer writes, "He speaks in his novels about traditions that have failed in a world that is falling apart, about desperate men seeking meaning through violent acts." Thus Zneimer sees O'Flaherty's concern both with naturalistic details and the turbulence of human emotions as products of "his increasing awareness of man's mortality and ultimate annihilation in a universe that has no meaning and offers no consolation."

O'Flaherty turned his art, Zneimer concludes, into a religious quest, making his novels "spiritual battlegrounds whereon his characters ... struggle to find meaning" in a meaningless world. O'Brien perceives this struggle, too, though he expresses it differently: "Beneath O'Flaherty's absorption in the physical, external world lies a belief in the evolutionary process, of men, especially artists, finding fulfillment in the struggle for perfection."

BIOGRAPHICAL/CRITICAL SOURCES: Spectator, October 3, 1925; *London Mercury,* August, 1926; *New Statesman and Nation,* January 21, 1933; H. E. Bates, *The Modern Short Story,* T. Nelson, 1945; William C. Frierson, *The English Novel in Transition, 1885-1940,* Cooper Square, 1965; James H. O'Brien, *Liam O'Flaherty,* Bucknell University Press, 1970; John Zneimer, *The Literary Vision of Liam O'Flaherty,* Syracuse University Press, 1971; *Contemporary Literary Criticism,* Volume 5, Gale, 1976.

—Sketch by Andrea Geffner

OKUN, Lawrence E(ugene)   1929-

PERSONAL: Born August 14, 1929, in Kalamazoo, Mich.; son of Shay and Fae (Kotzer) Okun; married Barbara Rose, November 4, 1956 (marriage ended, January 4, 1973); children: Wendy, David, Kathy. *Education:* Western Michigan University, B.S., 1951; University of Michigan, M.D., 1958. *Politics:* Independent. *Religion:* Jewish. *Home:* 17170 Fawndale Dr., Los Gatos, Calif. 95030. *Office:* 2577 Samaritan Dr., San Jose, Calif. 95124.

CAREER: Harper Hospital, Detroit, Mich., intern, 1958-59; Crittenton General Hospital, Detroit, resident in obstetrics and gynecology, 1959-62; private practice of obstetrics and gynecology in San Jose, Calif., 1962—. Member of staff at Good Samaritan Community Hospital, Los Gatos Saratoga Hospital, and Valley Medical Center. Diplomate of American Board of Obstetrics and Gynecology; assistant clinical instructor at Stanford University. *Military service:* U.S. Air Force, 1951-54; became first lieutenant. *Member:* American College of Obstetrics and Gynecology, Aircraft Owners and Pilots Association, Flying Doctors, Schufelt Society, Pacific Coast Fertility Society, Peninsula Obstetrical and Gynecological Society.

WRITINGS: On the Eighth Day (science fiction), Celestial Arts, 1980. Contributor to obstetrics and gynecology journals.

WORK IN PROGRESS: A sequel to *On the Eighth Day,* publication by Celestial Arts expected in 1981; an original screenplay for Zeitman-Townsend Productions.

SIDELIGHTS: Okun wrote that, as a private pilot, he enjoys flying to Mexico to perform surgery on indigent Mexican citizens. His special interests are endocrinology, infertility, and genetics. *Avocational interests:* Flying, motorcycling, tennis, racquetball, furniture making, gardening, golf, playing piano and tiple (a Colombian guitar), travel.

*   *   *

OLDS, Sharon   1942-

PERSONAL: Born November 19, 1942, in San Francisco, Calif. *Education:* Stanford University, B.A., 1964; Columbia University, Ph.D., 1972. *Home:* 250 Riverside Dr., New York, N.Y. 10025.

CAREER: Poet. Faculty member at Theodor Herzl Institute, 1976—, and at writing workshops; gives readings of her poems at colleges; co-coordinator of poetry readings series in New York, N.Y. *Member:* Poetry Society of America. *Awards, honors:* Grant from Creative Artists Public Service, 1978; Madeline Sadin Award from *New York Quarterly,* 1978, for "The Death of Marilyn Monroe"; younger poets award from *Poetry Miscellany,* 1979, for "Indictment of Senior Officers" and "The Line."

WRITINGS: Satan Says (poems), University of Pittsburgh Press, 1980. Contributor to literary journals and popular magazines, including *New Yorker, Atlantic Monthly, Paris Review, New Republic, Ms., Nation, Poetry Northwest, Massachusetts Review, Kayak, Conditions, Poetry,* and *New England Review.*

WORK IN PROGRESS: Several books of poems.

*   *   *

OLIPHANT, Patrick (Bruce)   1935-

PERSONAL: Born July 24, 1935, in Adelaide, Australia; came to the United States in 1964; son of Donald Knox and Grace Lillian (Price) Oliphant; married Hendrika DeVries, January 11, 1958 (divorced); children: Laura Marie, Grant, Susan. *Education:* Attended high school in Adelaide, Australia. *Office: Washington Star,* 225 Virginia Ave. S.E., Washington, D.C. 20061.

CAREER: Adelaide Advertiser, Adelaide, Australia, copy boy and press artist, 1953-55, editorial cartoonist, 1955-64; *Denver Post,* Denver, Colo., editorial cartoonist, 1964-75; *Washington Star,* Washington, D.C., political cartoonist, 1975—. Chairman of International Salon Cartoons Jury. *Awards, honors:* Second place award from International Federation of Free Journalists in Fleet Street, London, 1958, for funniest cartoonist; second place award from California Newspapers Publishers Association, 1960, for international cartoon competition; professional journalism award from Sigma Delta Chi, 1966; Pulitzer Prize, 1967, for editorial cartooning; distinguished service award for conservation from National Wildlife Foundation, 1969.

WRITINGS: The Oliphant Book, Simon & Schuster, 1969; (illustrator) John Osborne, *The Third Year of the Nixon Watch,* Liveright, 1972; *Four More Years,* Simon & Schuster, 1973; *Oliphant: An Informal Gathering,* Simon & Schuster, 1978; *Oliphant!,* Andrews & McMeel, 1980. Contributor of political cartoons to more than four hundred newspapers and magazines.

SIDELIGHTS: Perhaps the chief characteristic of an Oliphant cartoon is its humor. A cartoon that appeared during Pope John Paul II's visit to the United States, for example, shows a churlish Henry Kissinger, resplendent in papal robes, grumbling, "I don't know why we had to import a Pope when we have me." Although the humor of his cartoons might remind American readers of Bill Mauldin and Herblock, Oliphant confides that his approach was largely influenced by the work of British artists, among them Ronald Searle, David Low, Michael Cummings, and Emmwood (John Musgrave-Wood). According to James Stevenson of the *New Yorker,* "[Oliphant's] caricatures are merciless, his views lack charity, but his work is probably more visible, and more widely copied, admired, and deplored, than that of any other political cartoonist in America."

At his *Washington Star* office, Oliphant keeps a daily routine that always means working under a deadline. "I usually do ideas early in the morning," he told Stevenson. "I watch the CBS News, read the *Times* and the *Wall Street Journal,* and do some roughs.... I work best with a deadline, and the deadline here is to get the cartoon photographed by the end of the day." Once satisfied with a rough drawing, the artist makes a pencil sketch on illustration paper, then retraces the cartoon with a watercolor paintbrush and black ink. After the caption, signature, and half-tones are added, Oliphant turns the finished cartoon over to the art production department and heads out for lunch.

One of Oliphant's trademarks is a small penguin character tucked away in a corner of the cartoon, making its own statement. "I started doing that years ago," Oliphant said. "It was a chance to make two comments at once and, sometimes, a way of putting in an opinion that the publisher wouldn't allow in the cartoon itself." One example features President Richard Nixon in five different facial expressions. The sixth shows a frustrated Nixon angrily pounding his desk and exclaiming, "I just can't get that candor expression!!" The tiny penguin peering over the top of the desk says, "Tricky!"

Oliphant has published more than eight thousand cartoons since 1955, many of which have been collected for book publication, and he was awarded the 1967 Pulitzer Prize for editorial cartooning. He accepts the risk of offending people and even his editors and publishers. "You can reach a nice rapport with editors, but sometimes you've got to educate them," he observed. "They've got to realize you're not going to take crap any more than they are." He describes himself as a political rather than an editorial cartoonist, and asserts that "there are no sacred cows for me, no forbidden areas." There is one risk he won't take, however: "A few years ago, I met Barry Goldwater, and, to my horror, I found I liked him enormously, so I don't do that anymore."

CA INTERVIEWS THE AUTHOR

CA interviewed Patrick Oliphant by phone on January 8, 1980, during his morning's work at the *Washington Star.*

CA: You've been influenced mainly by the British cartoonists. If you were just beginning now, what contemporaries would you study?

OLIPHANT: I think I'd do the same thing. My influences have been oriented that way. All my life I've had the Australian and British cartoonists as models of what is good in cartooning, and some European influences. There weren't any U.S. influences.

CA: Are there contemporaries that you particularly admire?

OLIPHANT: Giles, Searle, Sorel, Jak, and a bunch of English cartoonists that I still have a great deal of regard for. Most of the rest of the younger cartoonists are drawing in the same style these days; there's not enough differentiation. Tony Auth I think of as an excellent cartoonist who's doing his own work, with the *Philadelphia Inquirer.*

CA: Do you think the majority of cartoonists working today are as skilled technically as they should be?

OLIPHANT: Not all of them. Once again because they're not exploring enough on their own. I wish they'd do more experimenting, get off and move in a different direction, get some other influences of their own and see what they can come up with.

CA: Is it irritating to be as widely imitated as you've been?

OLIPHANT: Disappointing is what it is. If they can use me as an influence, fine; but I wish they'd get off and do something else, explore some other avenue.

CA: An anonymous critic once said, "If Pat Oliphant couldn't draw, he'd be an assassin." How do you feel about that kind of criticism?

OLIPHANT: I don't think that was criticism; I like to think that was an accolade. I know the person who said that. He was doing a special piece for the *Washington Post Magazine* when I first arrived here. I think he made it up as a quote.

CA: I read the quote in the New York Times Magazine.

OLIPHANT: It's been widely used. Very successful.

CA: What are the important ingredients for a really top-notch political cartoon?

OLIPHANT: I think you've got to believe what you're doing first of all. You put your name on it, so you have to have a point of view. Then you've got to be sure that it annoys *somebody.* There's no point in being positive in this business. It's a deliberately negative business—toward *somebody*—and so it should be. Then there's the manner of expressing it. It should be drawn in an appealing manner so it

will entertain at the same time it's making a point. It has to be well thought out from many angles. Then you've got to have an editor who gives you the go-ahead.

CA: Does one need an intricate understanding of politics to do good political cartoons?

OLIPHANT: An understanding to a certain extent, but the main thing you have to do is be able to profess a gut feeling, a reaction to situations. What you're doing with a cartoon, probably, is being an articulator for people less fortunate than yourself. It's an honored thing to be able to put in a nutshell what a lot of other people are thinking.

CA: Is there a single cartoon of yours that's provoked the largest response from readers?

OLIPHANT: This last year I suppose the one that provoked the most response was the one I had of a car with Ted Kennedy in the front seat driving and Jimmy Carter in the backseat in scuba gear. Enormously popular with those people who share my antipathy towards that pair. And there are a great many of them.

CA: Do you ever get a negative response from political figures themselves?

OLIPHANT: Not too often. They don't come back unless they see something they like about it. Some of them are good sports, or maybe it's just conceit—they just like to see their picture in the paper. I get a lot of requests for cartoons even when they are derogatory. Strange business. They sometimes request the original drawing. I usually give it, unless it's somebody I intensely dislike.

CA: Do you have a favorite among your own cartoons?

OLIPHANT: Oh, I like that Kennedy thing. That's the sort of thing I like to do. But it's hard to remember what you do from day to day. You've always got to think of tomorrow, put it behind you and go straight on.

CA: What significant changes has cartooning undergone in the past two decades or so?

OLIPHANT: There's been a change in the approach to cartooning, and that's as it should be; it was very heavy-handed up until about fifteen years ago. We got this new wave going. And we use humor to make a point more now, I hope. There's nothing as effective as ridicule, after all. That's the best political weapon there is.

CA: What is the function of the National Cartoonists Society?

OLIPHANT: I don't know, really. I won their awards a few times. I don't think I'm a member. Their function is to give awards, I suppose. Perhaps they do a little lobbying. We need some, God knows. All of us do, as far as getting tax breaks from the government by donating our stuff to universities. That was taken away from us at the time when Nixon was donating all his useless papers for huge tax write-offs. I believe they're lobbying to have that restored. They could also serve some watchdog purpose, in that the Supreme Court we have now, unless we watch it, will get us into the English situation of not being able to cartoon anybody. We'll have so many libel lawyers looking over our work while we're doing it that our function will be undermined and weakened to the point that we just *won't* function.

CA: As the law stands now, would a libel suit be brought

against you or against the Star?

OLIPHANT: Against the *Star*. They've approved the cartoon, and they will stand by it. That's good. But it will crimp our style, certainly, if newspapers become so scared of libel suits. Right now some of us enjoy complete freedom; we police ourselves, really. That will disappear unless we're careful.

CA: You've been highly critical of the way the Pulitzer Prize is awarded since you won it in 1967. Has the method of selecting the recipients improved significantly as a result of your criticism?

OLIPHANT: Oh, heavens no, no. Year before last they gave it to a photographer and then decided it was the wrong photographer, so they took it back. In 1979 they leaked it to a cartoonist in Ohio that he'd won the Pulitzer, so they packed in the ice and champagne for the big day. He for six weeks believed that he'd won the Pulitzer, and then they announced that they'd had a change of heart and Herblock had won it instead. They do this sort of thing all the time. They're trying to clean up their act now, I believe. I hope they do, because it's just a gold-watch award at the moment: when your turn comes up, you get one. In 1973, after the best year for cartooning there had ever been because of Watergate—even the bad cartoonists were doing great stuff—they decided in their wisdom that no one deserved the prize. That year I sent them a telegram of no confidence. I don't think it did any good. I don't suppose I'll ever win the Pulitzer again. Once is enough, anyway.

CA: What awards have meant the most to you?

OLIPHANT: I got a distinguished service award for conservation from the National Wildlife Federation in 1969. That meant a lot to me.

CA: Have there been figures in the news whom you've found hard to caricature?

OLIPHANT: The more regular a face, the more I dread it. The more good-looking—and therefore featureless—a face, the more trouble I have with it. We had a governor in Colorado called John Love some years ago who looked like William Holden, very good-looking but useless as a cartoon subject, which I told him several times.

CA: What do you do with a person who presents that problem?

OLIPHANT: Try to cartoon him as little as possible. Jerry Ford wasn't all that easy. Those things shake down quite slowly. The audience has to come along with you. It takes about six months, say, for a caricature to settle down and your audience to recognize that that's who you mean it to be. That comes from their seeing the character a lot on television and in the papers. After a while you don't have to label it.

CA: Nixon must have been a cartoonist's delight.

OLIPHANT: Those were lovely years. Then we all had to go back to work again.

CA: Having to meet a deadline five days a week, how do you ever manage to take a vacation?

OLIPHANT: I just have to say screw it and go. It doesn't work to do cartoons in advance. They'd have to be very, very broad cartoons, and as sure as you did that some big thing would break and people would wonder what the hell you were doing. It's best not to do anything. It's never happened that I've been away when something big broke, but I'm always worried that it's going to happen. But you have to do it; you've got to get *some* rest.

CA: What is the greatest compliment you've been paid for your work?

OLIPHANT: I like that assassin remark, and I've not heard anything to top it. William Safire called me "the cruelest cartoonist" in an article he did recently. He was citing a cartoon I did on Kennedy. Nixon was sitting, watching him on a TV set and saying to Pat, "so once upon a time he went on TV and lied to the people. So what's wrong with that?"

BIOGRAPHICAL/CRITICAL SOURCES: Time, September 18, 1964, May 10, 1968; *Newsweek,* June 12, 1972; *New Republic,* February 2, 1974; *New York Times Magazine,* November 9, 1975; *New Yorker,* December 31, 1979.

—Interview by Jean W. Ross

*   *   *

OLMSTEAD, Alan H. 1907(?)-1980

OBITUARY NOTICE: Born c. 1907; died June 24, 1980, in Manchester, Conn. Editor, columnist, and author. Olmstead edited the *Manchester Evening Herald* and contributed columns to other Connecticut newspapers. He wrote a book on his experiences as a European war correspondent in the 1930's, *Europe As I Saw It,* as well as two other books, *Threshold: The First Days of Retirement,* 1975, and *In Praise of Seasons,* 1977. Obituaries and other sources: *New York Times,* June 28, 1980.

*   *   *

O'MAHONEY, Rich
See WARNER-CROZETTI, R(uth G.)

*   *   *

O'MALLEY, Brian (Jack Morgan) 1918(?)-1980

OBITUARY NOTICE: Born c. 1918; died July 17, 1980. Pharmacist and journalist. After serving in World War II with Britain's Royal Army Medical Corps, O'Malley joined the staff of *Chemist and Druggist.* He later became editor of *Alchemist* and then publications manager of the Pharmaceutical Society. Obituaries and other sources: *London Times,* July 29, 1980.

*   *   *

OMMANNEY, F(rancis) D(ownes) 1903-1980

OBITUARY NOTICE—See index for *CA* sketch: Born April 22, 1903, in England; died in 1980 in Cobham, England. Zoologist, marine biologist, and author. Ommanney took part in several scientific expeditions around the world, traveling to such places as Zanzibar, Singapore, South Korea, and Hong Kong. His books, many of which are based on his scientific work and travel, include *The Ocean, Fragrant Harbour,* and *Lost Leviathan: Whales and Whaling.* Obituaries and other sources: *AB Bookman's Weekly,* October 6, 1980.

*   *   *

ONADIPE, (Nathaniel) Kola(wole) 1922-
(Nita Kolon)

PERSONAL: Born July 14, 1922, in Nigeria, Africa; son of David (a produce merchant) and Alice (a trader; maiden name, Talabi) Onadipe; married first wife, Victoria, November 1, 1949 (divorced, 1963); married wife, Ronke; children: Bunmi Onadipe Onabolu, Sola, Ikepo, Tomi, Tope, Foluso,

Dotun. *Education:* University of London, B.S., 1949; Council of Legal Education, London, England, B.L., 1961. *Politics:* "No party politics." *Religion:* Baptist. *Home:* 3 Osinbajo Close, Obanikoro, P.O. Box 985, Lagos, Nigeria. *Office:* Natona Press, 32-A Oshinubi/Igbera Rd., Ijebu-Ode, Ogun, Nigeria.

CAREER: Called to the Bar, 1961; high school teacher of English, mathematics, geography, and English; Olu-Iwa College, Ijebu-Ode, Nigeria, principal, 1950-59; British Petroleum Ltd., Lagos, Nigeria, executive, 1961-66; African Universities Press, Lagos, general manager, 1966-69; Amonat Ltd., Lagos, managing director, 1972-79; Natona Press, Ijebu-Ode, chairman and managing director, 1978—. General manager of Pilgrim Books, 1966-71.

WRITINGS—For children; published by African Universities Press, unless otherwise noted: *The Adventures of Souza, the Village Lad,* 1963, revised edition, 1965; *Sugar Girl,* 1964; *Koku Baboni,* 1965; *The Boy Slave,* 1966; *The Magic Land of Shadows,* 1971; (with M. Murphy) *The Forest Is Our Playground,* 1971; *Return of Shettima,* 1972; (editor) *Economics for Beginners,* Natona Press, 1979. Also author of *Builders of Africa,* and books for adults, including *Tears for Babel, Sweet Mother, Footprints on the Niger, A Pot of Gold, Call Me Michael, Queen for a Day,* and *Sunny Boy.* Also author of *Mothers-in-Law,* under pseudonym Nita Kolon.

SIDELIGHTS: Onadipe wrote: "I started my career as a high school teacher. Later I concentrated on teaching English as a second language to Nigerian children. It was then I discovered that the available reading materials were very unsuitable for young people. They were mostly, if not entirely, English literature books written for English boys and girls who had a different background, culture, environment, and a better grasp of the language. The names and geography of places, the names and reactions of the characters, the allusions and humor in these books were totally foreign to the children here. The need for books especially written for African children by Africans cried aloud. Some expatriates had attempted to write books subtitled 'for African students' but the writers did not succeed. They could not enter into the feeling and therefore could not reach the children.

"Happily, at this time a few publishers, particularly the new/young, far-seeing ones like African Universities Press, understood the need and started a series. They encouraged writers. My very first attempt was accepted for publication and has proved a success. Others followed. I have concentrated on writing for children because available materials for older students are not too bad. The most popular of these have also been written by Africans.

"The first attempt I have made at writing for adults is *Tears for Babel.* It is a satire on the political and social development in Nigeria between 1940 and 1966. A bold and daring attempt, it is bitter, but it is true. Another adult book is *Mothers-in-Law,* as seen from the point of view of the African. The book deals with a social and human problem that is widespread in African society. *Builders of Africa* provides a bridge between the juvenile and adult books. The facts and opinions on the personalities involved are simplified, but the conclusions are very adult.

"In writing for children I aim at making them laugh. In writing for and about adults, particularly on the subjects I have chosen, I want to make them cry. Many of them have gotten away with too many things."

O'NEIL, Will(iam Daniel III)   1938-

PERSONAL: Born September 4, 1938, in Chicago, Ill.; son of William Daniel II (in journalism) and Vivian (a real estate broker; maiden name, Peter) O'Neil; married Anne Frances Murphy (a designer), August 9, 1968; children: William Daniel IV. *Education:* University of California, Los Angeles, B.A., 1960, M.S., 1968. *Home:* 6413 Lyric Lane, Falls Church, Va. 22044. *Agent:* Carl D. Brandt, Brandt & Brandt Literary Agents, Inc., 1501 Broadway, New York, N.Y. 10036. *Office:* Office of the Under Secretary of Defense for Research and Engineering/Naval Warfare, Pentagon 3D 1048, Washington, D.C. 20301.

CAREER: Planning Research Corp., Los Angeles, Calif., associate, 1964-66; Bissett-Berman Corp., Santa Monica, Calif., senior scientist, 1966-67; Litton Systems, Inc., Culver City, Calif., manager of operations research section in Advanced Marine Technology Division, 1967-69; Office of the Secretary of the Navy, Washington, D.C., operations research analyst, 1969-73; Office of the Director of Defense Research and Engineering, Washington, D.C., staff specialist, 1973-77; Office of the Under Secretary of Defense for Research and Engineering, Washington, D.C., director of naval warfare, 1977—. *Military service:* U.S. Navy, 1960-64; became lieutenant. Currently with U.S. Naval Reserve; present rank, commander. *Member:* American Institute of Aeronautics and Astronautics, American Society of Naval Engineers, Authors Guild, Mystery Writers of America, Operations Research Society of America, Society of Naval Architects and Marine Engineers.

WRITINGS: The Libyan Kill, Norton, 1980. Contributor to technical journals.

WORK IN PROGRESS: Research for "a novel with a strong Navy theme, involving much exotic hardware."

SIDELIGHTS: O'Neil commented to *CA:* "The writing of fiction serves two purposes for me. First, there is the relaxation of immersing myself totally in an activity in which, in contrast to my work, I need share control with no one. It also provides an opportunity to allude to matters about which, as a government official with inside knowledge, I cannot speak directly."

BIOGRAPHICAL/CRITICAL SOURCES: National Defense, November-December, 1978.

* * *

O'NEILL, Carlota   1918-

PERSONAL: Born March 27, 1918, in Madrid, Spain; daughter of Enrique (a professor and writer) and Regina (a writer and pianist; maiden name, Lamo) O'Neill; married Virgilio Leret Ruiz, February 14, 1933 (died July 17, 1936); children: Gabriela Leret, Carlota Leret. *Education:* Universidad de Barcelona, Lic.Fil. y Let., 1932. *Home:* Bahia Magdalena, 9 Colonia Anzures, Mexico City, Mexico.

CAREER: Journalist, writer, lecturer. Affiliated with *Ahora* and *Estampas* magazines, both Madrid, Spain, 1933-36, with *Liceo, Siluetas,* and *Menage* magazines, all Barcelona, Spain, 1942-48, and with *El Heraldo, El Nacional,* and *Ultimas Noticias* newspapers, all Caracas, Venezuela, 1950-55; publicist for a Caracas radio station, 1955-58; director and producer of "Radio contiente," 1958-62, and of "Entre nosatras" and "Feliz fin de semana," 1961-65, all Caracas; affiliated with *Letras Femeninas* magazine, Boulder, Colo., 1976-80. Speaker at Carnegie-Mellon University, University of Toronto, University of Texas, Wayne State University, and Universidad Nacional Autonoma de Mexico. *Member:*

Union de Periodistas y Escritoras de Mexico (founder; vice-president, 1975-80), Instituto Nacional de Bellas Artes de Mexico, Asociacion de Escritores de Mexico, Association of Aviators of the Spanish Republic (honorary member). *Awards, honors:* D.H.C. from Universidad de Chilpancingo, 1968; diploma from government of Mexico City, 1968.

WRITINGS—In English: *Una Mexicana en la guerra de Espana* (autobiography), Editorial Populibros La Prensa, 1964, translation by Leandro de la Garza published as *Trapped in Spain*, Solidarity Books, 1978.

In Spanish: *Elisabeth Vigee Lebraun: Pintora de reinas* (biography; title means "Queen's Painter"), Editorial Olimpo, 1944; *El amor imposible de Gustavo Adolfo Becquer* (biography; title means "The Impossible Love of Gustavo Adolfo Becquer"), Editorial Hymsa, 1945; *La dulce romanza de amor de Franz Shubert* (biography; title means "The Sweet Song of Love of Franz Shubert"), Editorial Hymsa, 1945; *Rascacielos* (novel; title means "Skyscraper"), Editorial Rocio, 1946; *Esposa fugitiva* (novel; title means "Fugitive Wife"), Editorial Molino, 1964; *No fue vencida* (novel; title means "She Wasn't Defeated"), Editorial Rocio, 1948; *Que sabe usted de Safo?* (biography; title means "What Do You Know About Safo"), Editorial Costa Amic, 1960; *Amor: Diario de una desintoxicacion* (novel; title means "Intoxication of Love"), Editorial Castalia, 1963; *La verdad de Venezuela* (report; title means "Truthful Venezuela"), Editorial Populibros La Prensa, 1968; *Romanzas de las rejas* (poetic prose; title means "Songs of Prison"), Editorial Castalia, 1968, 2nd edition, Editorial Costa Amic, 1978; *Los muertos tambien hablan* (autobiography; title means "The Dead Speak for Themselves"), Editorial Populibros La Prensa, 1973.

Plays: *Circe and the Swine* (two-act), Editorial Costa, 1974; *Trapped in Spain* (based on autobiography), Editorial Costa, 1974. Also author of "The Fourth Dimension," 1976. Contributor to Spanish and Mexican magazines.

WORK IN PROGRESS: *Cinco maneras de morir* (title means "Five Ways to Death"), dialogues and a monologue for the theater.

SIDELIGHTS: Carlota O'Neill commented: "What made me write? The Latin maxim that says 'the writer is born, not made.' I apply this to myself. I was born a writer just as I was born fragile and small. I was born among papers and books . . . many books! When I married I continued my studies. For me the best of life is to write. I travel because of my work, but I also stop to admire the pieces left by men with talent and art, as I do not forget that other Latin maxim that says 'life is short . . . art is long.'"

*   *   *

ORD-HUME, Arthur W. J. G.

PERSONAL: Born in London, England; son of Arthur W. (a writer and musician) and Rose Marie (a literary critic; maiden name, Tickner) Ord-Hume; married Judith Rose Resnick (a professor of English); children: James Edward, John Geoffrey, Elizabeth Anne. *Education:* Received B.Sc. from University of London. *Politics:* "Whichever party preaches peace and humanity." *Religion:* Church of Scotland. *Office:* Ord-Hume Library of Mechanical Music and Horology, 14 Elmwood Rd., Chiswick, London W4 3DY, England.

CAREER: Worked variously as chief of design for Britten-Norman Aircraft Ltd., as design section leader for Handley Page Aircraft Ltd., as head of design for Agricultural Avia-

tion Co. Ltd., as chief designer for Southern Aircraft, as managing director and chief of design for Phoenix Aircraft Ltd., and as managing director and chief of design for Ord-Hume Aviation; currently owner and manager of Ord-Hume Library of Mechanical Music and Horology in London, England. Consultant to museums; lecturer. *Military service:* Royal Air Force; became flight lieutenant. *Member:* Royal College of Music (associate), Musical Box Society of Great Britain (president, 1976-79), SMMIH (fellow), Popular Flying Association (founder). *Awards, honors:* Awards for aircraft design and musical instrument technology.

WRITINGS: *Aircraft Design and Construction for Amateurs*, George Newnes, 1950; *Personal Flying*, George Newnes, 1951; *Build Your Own Light Aircraft*, George Newnes, 1952; *Wooden Aircraft Construction Manual*, Iliffe, 1954; *Collecting Musical Boxes and How to Repair Them*, Allen & Unwin, 1967; *Player Piano: The History of the Self-Playing Piano*, Allen & Unwin, 1970; *Clockwork Music*, Allen & Unwin, 1973; *Mechanical Music*, Allen & Unwin, 1974; *Barrel Organ*, Allen & Unwin, 1977; *Perpetual Motion*, Allen & Unwin, 1977; *The Musical Box*, Allen & Unwin, 1980; *Restoring Musical Boxes*, Allen & Unwin, 1980. Also author of *The Might of Music*, 1980, and *Pianola*, 1980. Editor of *Music Box*, 1962—; past editor of *Flying Review International* and *Aerospace Review*.

WORK IN PROGRESS: A major work on the history of the free-reed in music; research on the early history of mechanical music.

AVOCATIONAL INTERESTS: Private flying (designed and built his own plane), playing music (designed and built his own pipe organ), photography, listening to music.

*   *   *

ORLEN, Steve 1942-

PERSONAL: Born January 13, 1942, in Holyoke, Mass.; son of Milton H. and B. Florence Orlen; married Gail Marcus (a painter), August, 1968. *Education:* University of Massachusetts, B.A., 1964; University of Iowa, M.F.A., 1967. *Home:* 436 South Fifth Ave., Tucson, Ariz. 85701. *Office:* Department of English, University of Arizona, Tucson, Ariz. 85721.

CAREER: University of Arizona, Tucson, associate professor of English, 1967—. Staff assistant at Bread Loaf Writer's Conference, 1979—; instructor at Goddard College, 1980—. *Awards, honors:* National Endowment for the Arts grants, 1974 and 1980; George Dillon Memorial Award from *Poetry*, 1974; fellow at Bread Loaf Writer's Conference, 1978.

WRITINGS—Poetry: *Sleeping on Doors*, Penumbra Press, 1975; *Separate Creatures*, Ironwood Press, 1976; *Permission to Speak*, Wesleyan University Press, 1978.

Work represented in anthologies, including *Ardis Anthology of New American Poetry* and *A Geography of Poets*, Bantam. Contributor of articles and reviews to *Poets Teaching* and *Ironwood*.

WORK IN PROGRESS: All That We Try to Do, poems.

*   *   *

ORLEV, Uri 1931-

PERSONAL: Original given name, Jerzy Henryk, changed to Uri, 1945; original surname, Orlowski, changed to Orlev, 1958; born February 24, 1931, in Warsaw, Poland; son of Maksymilian (a physician) and Zofia (Rozencwaig) Orlowski; married Erella Navin, 1956 (divorced, 1962); married

Yaara Shalev (a dance therapist), November 19, 1964; children: Lee, Daniella, Itamar. *Education:* Attended Hebrew University of Jerusalem. *Home:* Yemin Moshe, 4 Habrecha, Jerusalem, Israel.

CAREER: Member of Kibbutz in Lower Galilee, Israel, 1950-67; writer, 1967—. Prisoner in German concentration camp during World War II. *Military service:* Israeli Army, 1950-52. *Member:* Hebrew Writers Association. *Awards, honors:* Awards from Broadcast Authorities, 1966, for "The Great Game," 1970, for "Dancing Lesson," and 1975, for "The Beast of Darkness"; prize from Youth Alia, 1966, for *The Last Summer Vacation;* literature award from Prime Minister of Israel, 1972; Ze-ev Prize from Ministry of Education and Culture, 1977, for *The Beast of Darkness;* television prize from Broadcast Authorities, 1979, for youth program, "Who Will Ring First?"

WRITINGS—Titles in English translation: *The Lead Soldiers* (novel), Sifriat-Poalim, 1956, translated from the original Hebrew by Hillel Halkin, P. Owen, 1979, Taplinger, 1980; *Until Tomorrow* (novel), Am-Oved, 1958; *The Last Summer Vacation* (stories), Daga, 1966.

Children's books: *The Beast of Darkness,* Am-Oved, 1976; *The Little-Big Girl,* Keter, 1977; *The Driving-Mad Girls,* Keter, 1977; *Noon Thoughts,* Sifriat-Poalim, 1978; *Siamina,* Am-Oved, 1979; *It's Hard to Be a Lion,* Am-Oved, 1979; *The Lion's Shirt,* Masada, 1979; *The Lucky Pacifier,* Am-Oved, 1980; *Grenny-Knit,* Masada, 1980; *The Island on 78 Birds Street* (stories), Keter, 1981.

Translator from Polish: Henryk Sienkiewicz, *In the Desert and Jungle,* Y. Marcus, 1970; *The Stories of Bruno Schulz,* Schocken, 1979; Janusz Korczak, *King Matthew I,* Keter, 1979; Stanislaw Lem, *Eden,* Masada, 1980.

Author of television and radio plays for adults and children.

WORK IN PROGRESS: The Crown of the Dragon, a science-fiction novel for children.

SIDELIGHTS: Uri Orlev's *The Lead Soldiers* has joined a growing body of fiction generally referred to as Holocaust literature. Like Elie Wiesel's *Night* and Jerzy Kosinski's *Painted Bird,* Orlev's novel is "more than half true," a story composed from memory and imagination about his destroyed childhood and the Nazi occupation of Poland. First published in Israel in 1956, it is the only one of Orlev's books that has been translated into English. "Through the eyes of a child," wrote Thomas Sabulis of the *Boston Globe,* "the Holocaust is described both in dreamy sequences and nightmarish reality. It is apolitical, savage and steaming with the fury of unfulfilled childhood."

The two boys featured in *The Lead Soldiers,* Yurik and Kazik, are Polish Jews who at the outset of the story do not yet know their Jewish origins. According to "the fashionable leftism of the times," their parents had sent them to Catholic schools and done their best to conceal their heritage. "Like birds caught in violent winds, the boys are driven along by forces they cannot comprehend," commented Scott Sanders in the *Chicago Sun-Times.* A critic for the *New York Review of Books* added, "They are also exposed to a psychological experience which many European Jews did not share . . . : they suffer anti-Semitism without being aware that they are Jews."

Shortly after the German invasion of Poland, the boys lose their parents and are delivered into the care of their resourceful aunt. For a time she manages by luck and bribery to hide her nephews in the homes, attics, and cellars of the Warsaw ghetto, until the city is razed and the family is shipped to the concentration camp at Bergen-Belsen. Despite the turmoil and loss, the sudden displacements and dangers that overwhelm their lives, the boys respond to events with children's instincts. "Throughout their ordeal the brothers keep escaping into imagination, inventing games, spinning stories, maneuvering their lead soldiers," Sanders noted. As Leslie Epstein of the *New York Times Book Review* observed, "the various games the brothers play . . . form a strategy to master their own inner turmoil as well as that which exists in the wider world."

Although Orlev is concerned with the particular drama of Yurik and Kazik, he does comment on the larger realities of war and mass extermination. Victoria Neumark of the *New Statesman* remarked, "*The Lead Soldiers* touches one of the most poignant stories of the Holocaust, the story of the butterflies children drew on the walls before they went into the gas chambers, keeping faith with their imaginary worlds in the optimism of a Stoic who can't see beyond the moment." Carole Woiwode contended that such scenes "are handled with an authorial restraint that lifts the writing above the sensational or sentimental. Any overt statement about the war is tempered by an objectivity and a humor that keep the work from being a polemic or a journalistic recapitulation of events."

Orlev survived Bergen-Belsen, as do Yurik and Kazik, and settled in Israel after the war. *The Lead Soldiers* was his first book, and as such it contains some of the weaknesses of all first novels. Epstein noted that "the real reason the first third of the book is less satisfactory [than the remaining two thirds] is simply that Mr. Orlev used it to teach himself his craft." However, many reviewers concurred with the conclusion reached by Sabulis: "Orlev's account of his childhood in the Jewish ghetto of Warsaw during the second World War is brilliant, wretched and agonizing. It's a punch in the kidneys. Anyone faintly interested in the Holocaust will want to read it."

BIOGRAPHICAL/CRITICAL SOURCES: New Statesman, June 7, 1979; *Daily Telegraph,* June 21, 1979; *New York Times Book Review,* March 23, 1980; *Chicago Sun-Times,* March 23, 1980; *Boston Globe,* March 30, 1980; *Los Angeles Times Book Review,* May 18, 1980; *Chicago Tribune Book World,* April 27, 1980; *New York Review of Books,* June 12, 1980.

*   *   *

ORLOFF, Max
See CROWCROFT, Peter

*   *   *

ORPAZ, Yitzhak 1923-

PERSONAL: Born in 1923, in Zinkow, Soviet Union; son of Ze'ev and Esther Orpaz; children: Ze'ev, Orna, Talila, Atalia. *Education:* University of Tel Aviv, B.A., 1964. *Home:* 9 Kikar Malkei Israel, Tel Aviv, Israel. *Agent:* C. D. Lieber, 1841 Broadway, New York, N.Y. 10023.

CAREER: Member of Yas'ur kibbutz in Palestine (now Israel), 1938-40; worked as diamond cutter, 1940-42; Israel Army, 1948-62, leaving service as major; news editor of daily newspaper, *Al Hamishmar,* 1962—. *Military service:* British Army, Jewish Brigade, 1942-46. *Member:* International P.E.N., Organization of Writers (member of central committee), Organization of Journalists. *Awards, honors:* Asher Barash Award for Literature, 1964, for novel, *Or be'ad or;* Miriam Talpir Award for Literature, 1968, for novella, *Nemalim;* national prize for creative writing, 1976; Yacov Fichman Award for Literature, 1977, for novel, *Bait le'adam Echad.*

WRITINGS: Mot Lysanda, Sifriat Poalim, 1964, translation by Richard Flint published as *The Death of Lysanda,* J. Cape, 1970.

Not in English: *Esev pere* (title means "Wild Grass"), Mahbarot Lesifrut, 1959; *Or be'ad or* (title means "Skin for Skin"), Masada, 1962; *Zed hazeviyah* (title means "The Hunting of the Gazelle"), Daga, 1966; *Nemalim* (title means "Ants"), Am Oved, 1968; *Masa Daniel* (title means "Daniel's Trials"), Am Oved, 1969; *Shalosh novelot* (title means "Three Novellas"), Sifriat Poalim, 1972; *Ir she'ein bah mistor* (title means "A City With No Shelter"), Hakibutz Hameuhad, 1974; *Bait le'adam Echad* (title means "A House for One"), Hakibutz Hameuhad, 1975; *Rehov hatomozhenna* (title means "Tomozhenna Tales"), Hakibutz Hameuhad, 1979.

Work represented in anthologies of Israeli and general writing. Contributor to magazines, including *Stand.* Editor of *Mivhar Sifruteinu Laham;* member of editorial board of *Al Hamishmar.*

WORK IN PROGRESS: A five-part novel, featuring five characters, a death, a suicide, a ferment, and an "Israeli-Galuth dialectic."

SIDELIGHTS: Orpaz wrote: "'A Pilgrim—says the dictionary—is a person who journeys to a Holy Place. The protagonist of a Secular Pilgrim story—the kind that we are discussing here—is a Pilgrim who has no Holy Place. His pilgrimage is a journey of the spirit, a thirst, an unrest, a rebellion. A pilgrimage that becomes an aim in itself.' These opening lines of my essay, 'The Secular Pilgrim,' are in a way indicative of my motivation as a writer."

BIOGRAPHICAL/CRITICAL SOURCES: Hillel Barzel, *Metarealistic Hebrew Prose,* Masada, 1974; Israel Barama, *The Writings of Yitzhak Orpaz,* Ah'shav, 1979.

*   *   *

OWEN, Bob
   See GEIS, Richard E(rwin)

*   *   *

OWEN, Robert N.
   See GEIS, Richard E(rwin)

P

PADFIELD, Peter 1932-

PERSONAL: Born April 3, 1932, in Calcutta, India; son of William L. N. (a British Army captain) and Annice Edna (Abbott) Padfield; married Dorothy Jean Yarwood, 1960; children: Deborah, Guy, Fiona. *Education:* Attended Thames Nautical Training College, 1948-50. *Religion:* Church of England. *Home:* Westmoreland Cottage, Drybridge Hill, Woodbridge, Suffolk, England. *Agent:* McIntosh & Otis, Inc., 475 Fifth Ave., New York, N.Y. 10017.

CAREER: Shaw Savill & Albion Shipping Line, London, England, cadet, 1950-53; Peninsular and Oriental Steam Navigation Co., London, officer, 1953-58; *Shipbuilding and Shipping Record,* London, editorial assistant, 1960; Angula Engineering Co. Ltd., London, director, 1960-63; writer, 1963—. *Member:* Society for Nautical Research.

WRITINGS—Nonfiction: *The Sea Is a Magic Carpet,* P. Davies, 1960; *The "Titanic" and the "Californian,"* John Day, 1965; *An Agony of Collisions,* Hodder & Stoughton, 1966; *Aim Straight: A Biography of Admiral Sir Percy Scott,* Hodder & Stoughton, 1966; *Broke and the "Shannon": A Biography of Admiral Sir Philip Broke,* Hodder & Stoughton, 1968; *The Battleship Era,* McKay, 1972; *Guns at Sea: A History of Naval Gunnery,* St. Martin's, 1973; *The Great Naval Race: Anglo-German Naval Rivalry, 1900-1914,* McKay, 1974; *Nelson's War,* Hart-Davis, 1976; *Tide of Empires: Decisive Naval Campaigns in the Rise of the West,* Routledge & Kegan Paul, Volume I: *1481-1654,* 1979, Volume II: *1655-1763,* 1981; *The Victorian and Edwardian Navy,* Routledge & Kegan Paul, 1981.

Novels: *The Lion's Claw,* Hutchinson, 1978; *The Unquiet Gods,* Hutchinson, 1980. Contributor to *Oxford Companion to Ships and the Sea* and *Purnell's History of the First World War.*

WORK IN PROGRESS: *Tide of Empires: Decisive Naval Campaigns in the Rise of the West,* Volumes III and IV, publication by Routledge & Kegan Paul expected in 1982; a historical novel set during the Boer War in South Africa, 1899-1900, for Hutchinson, 1981; *Rule Britannia;* a social history of passenger travel by the P & O line, for Hutchinson.

SIDELIGHTS: Padfield wrote: "I was fortunate to gain a berth as a mariner aboard *Mayflower II,* which sailed to Plymouth, Mass., in 1957, and subsequently to travel independently in the United States and the Pacific. The experiences provided material for my first book, which was an account of those travels and, as it were, set me on a writing course.

"Since then I have concentrated on naval history, which has become I fear a rather specialized subject. My concern now is to widen the scope and bring naval history back into the mainstream of general history where it belongs, and where it has for too long been neglected.

"My latest work, *Tide of Empires: Decisive Naval Campaigns in the Rise of the West,* places naval and mercantile struggles at the very center of the development of civilization, and indeed of future developments; the struggle for world markets continues as fiercely as ever, so does the struggle between the great territorial empires, now represented by Russia and China, and the market-acquisitive sea peoples, represented by the United States, Japan, and Western Europe. I believe that the struggle between these two different types of power (at present labeled communist and capitalist, but in reality the old 'centrally-controlled' and 'market-acquisitive' powers) will be decided, as it has been in the past, by trading power and the wealth and sophisticated banking systems that have always followed trading power. In short I believe that economic and mercantile and naval history are inseparably linked, and together these factors add up to the driving force in world history, which if studied in these terms yields much food for thought about the present global struggle."

*   *   *

PAGDEN, Anthony 1945-

PERSONAL: Born May 27, 1945, in Sussex, England; son of John Brian and Joan (Dewchfield) Pagden; married Sylvia Ferino (an art historian), February 24, 1978. *Education:* Attended Universidad de Barcelona, 1964-67; Merton College, Oxford, received B.A. and M.A.; also attended Warburg Institute, London, 1976-79, and Institute for Advanced Study, Princeton, N.J., 1979-80. *Politics:* Socialist. *Religion:* None. *Office:* Girton College, Cambridge University, Cambridge, England.

CAREER: Trianon Press, Paris, France, editor, 1967-68; translator and editor in London, England and Madrid, Spain, 1969-70; currently member of faculty at Girton College, Cambridge University, Cambridge, England. *Member:* Royal Historical Society (fellow), Real Academia de Buenas Letras (fellow).

WRITINGS: Hernan Cortes, Grossman, 1972; *The Maya,* J. Philip O'Hara, 1975; *Beasts, Barbarians, or Men?: A Study of European Views on the American Indian,* Cambridge University Press, in press.

WORK IN PROGRESS: A study of religious syncretism in the Yucatan; a novel.

SIDELIGHTS: Pagden commented: "I have traveled in Europe, Latin America, and the Near East. I fell ill of typhoid in the mountains of Kurdistan, or I would have written an account of Kurdish nomads and rebels. I have a keen interest in contemporary European politics, especially Italian." *Avocational interests:* Flying (especially aerobatics).

*   *   *

PAGET, John
See AIKEN, John (Kempton)

*   *   *

PAINTER, George D(uncan)   1914-

PERSONAL: Born June 5, 1914, in Birmingham, England; son of George Charles (a musician, singer, and schoolteacher) and Minnie Rosendale (Taylor) Painter; married Isabel Joan Britton, 1942; children: Charlotte, Louise. *Education:* Trinity College, Cambridge, M.A., 1945. *Home:* 10 Mansfield Rd., Hove, East Sussex 5NN, England.

CAREER: University of Liverpool, Liverpool, England, assistant lecturer in Latin, 1937; British Museum, Department of Printed Books, London, England, member of staff, 1938-74, assistant keeper in charge of fifteenth-century printed books, 1954-74. *Member:* Royal Society of Literature (fellow, 1965—), Societe Chateaubriand. *Awards, honors:* Second Chancellor's Classical Medalist, 1936; Duff Cooper Memorial Prize for *The Later Years,* Volume II of *Proust;* James Tait Black Memorial Prize for *The Longed-for Tempests,* Volume I of *Chateaubriand: A Biography;* D.Litt. from University of Edinburgh, 1979.

WRITINGS: Andre Gide: A Critical and Biographical Study, A. Barker, 1951, revised edition published as *Andre Gide: A Critical Biography,* Atheneum, 1968; *The Road to Sinodun: A Winter and Summer Monodrama* (poems), Clarke, Irwin, 1951; (translator) Andre Gide, *Marshlands and Prometheus Misbound* (two satirical novels), New Directions, 1953; (editor and translator) Marcel Proust, *Marcel Proust: Letters to His Mother,* Rider, 1956, Greenwood Press, 1973; *Proust,* Little, Brown, Volume I: *The Early Years,* 1959, Volume II: *The Later Years,* 1965 (published in England as *Marcel Proust: A Biography,* Chatto & Windus, Volume I, 1959, Volume II, 1965); (with R. A. Skelton and T. E. Marston) *The Vinland Map and the Tartar Relation,* Yale University Press, 1965; (translator) Andre Maurois, *The Chelsea Way; or, Marcel in England: A Proustian Parody,* Heinemann, 1967; *William Caxton: A Quincentenary Biography of England's First Printer,* Chatto & Windus, 1976, published as *William Caxton: A Biography,* Putnam, 1977; *Chateaubriand: A Biography,* Chatto & Windus, Volume I: *The Longed-for Tempests,* 1977, Knopf, 1978. Also author of articles on fifteenth-century printing.

WORK IN PROGRESS: The Valley of Wolves (Volume II of *Chateaubriand: A Biography*); *The Inexplicable Heart* (Volume III of *Chateaubriand: A Biography*); *Stendhal; or, The Hunt for Happiness* (a biography in two volumes).

SIDELIGHTS: George D. Painter might have been a poet or novelist himself but for the overriding interest he found in writing about the lives and works of other authors. In 1951,

he published a book of poems (*The Road to Sinodun*) he had written during the war years, but he had already decided that the lives of his favorite writers were more engaging than his own. Even more fascinating to him was the way an author's works disclose a symbolic autobiography. After reading a collection of Marcel Proust's letters, for instance, he was struck by the relationship between the author's personal experience and its reappearance in *A la recherche du temps perdu.* In 1947, he set out to write a definitive biography of the French novelist which was completed eighteen years later, and he has ever since believed that literary biography is an essential tool of criticism.

In the preface to *Proust: The Early Years,* Painter summarizes his intentions and approach: "I have endeavored to write ... a complete, exact, and detailed narrative of [Proust's] life ..., based on every known or discoverable primary source.... [It is] my belief that Proust's novel cannot be fully understood without a knowledge of his life.... I shall show that it is possible to identify ... the sources in Proust's real life for all major and many minor characters, events, and places in his novel ... [which] is not, properly speaking, a fiction, but a creative autobiography." When the book appeared in 1959, many critics were compelled to agree with Painter's claim that it was a "definitive biography."

Charles Rolo of *Atlantic Monthly* commented: "Mr. Painter's book is, unquestionably, a master stroke of enterprising and industrious research, a biography of great originality.... [He] has succeeded in conducting his immensely detailed scrutiny without slipping into the dry tone of pedantry; he has pieced together a picture of Proust and his world and the making of his masterpiece that is continuously absorbing.... One of the two or three major texts in the vast literature on Proust." *New Statesman's* P. H. Johnson called *Proust* "the finest literary biography of our time ..., a beautifully-mannered book, the result of intensive scholarship, imaginative sympathy, love and cool-thinking."

Volume II, *Proust: The Later Years,* also won critical praise. Roger Shattuck, writing in the *Washington Post Book World,* observed that more people "will read this magnificent work by George Painter than will penetrate beyond one-fifteenth of the way into Remembrance of Things Past." Another critic, Peter Quennel of the *New York Times Book Review,* commented that Painter "helps us to understand not only the methods by which [Proust] realized his creative gifts, but the origin of those gifts in the special circumstances of his youth and manhood." And Laurent Sage of *Saturday Review* concluded that it "is as a monument of erudition, a *summa* of information about a great novelist and his work that Painter's study takes a place on our shelves."

England's first printer is the subject of another Painter biography, *William Caxton.* A critic for the *Economist* noted that the author "has charted Caxton's life through every dramatic folio and every change of type. For bibliophiles, the book will be compulsory and compelling reading. But it is rather a dull trek for those who like the coloured folk-pictures of Caxton's life.... The truth is that Caxton, for all Mr. Painter's dedication, is not a good subject for large-scale biography." But Curt Buhler of the *Times Literary Supplement* held that "Painter's bio-bibliography of William Caxton is, however viewed, a remarkable and distinguished achievement. It is notable for the wealth of its documentation, the result of tireless research."

A third biography, *Chateaubriand,* is similar in scope to the two-volume *Proust.* The first of three volumes, *Chateaubriand: The Longed-for Tempests,* was published in 1977, and two more volumes are yet to come. In the opening work, Painter follows Chateaubriand from Brittany to Paris at the time of the Revolution, his escape to America and return to France, and his eventual exile in England. Once again, Painter received high critical praise for his large undertaking.

"The author is in full control of his material," wrote Victor Brombert of the *New York Times Book Review.* "[He] shows an archivist's passion for facts and writes with sensitivity and occasional wry humor.... American readers will find particularly rewarding Mr. Painter's lively narrative of Chateaubriand's visit to this continent in 1791." Another critic, Anita Brookner of the *Times Literary Supplement,* commented: "It is amazing, incredible, both as an achievement and a narrative, and there is so much more to come.... [Painter] has now given us the biography that was most astonishingly missing from our shelves."

AVOCATIONAL INTERESTS: Walking, gardening, travel, music, medieval art.

BIOGRAPHICAL/CRITICAL SOURCES: Saturday Review, August 15, 1959, October 23, 1965; *New York Herald Tribune Book Review,* August 16, 1959; *Time,* August 17, 1959, October 22, 1965, May 1, 1978; *New York Times Book Review,* August 30, 1959, November 7, 1965, April 24, 1977, May 7, 1978; *New Statesman,* September 19, 1959, July 9, 1965; *Guardian,* September 25, 1959; *Atlantic Monthly,* October, 1959; *Nation,* October 3, 1959; *Commonweal,* October 16, 1959; *Spectator,* October 16, 1959; *Times Literary Supplement,* November 13, 1959, August 5, 1965, July 29, 1977, October 21, 1977; *Encounter,* October, 1965; *Washington Post Book Week,* November 7, 1965; *New York Review of Books,* November 11, 1965, July 20, 1978; *Virginia Quarterly Review,* winter, 1966; *Newsweek,* January 10, 1966, May 1, 1978; *Economist,* October 16, 1976, November 5, 1977; *Washington Post Book World,* April 17, 1977; *New Republic,* July 2, 1977, April 22, 1978; *New York Times,* May 2, 1978.

—*Sketch by B. Hal May*

*   *   *

PALMER, Edward L.   1938-

PERSONAL: Born August 11, 1938, in Hagerstown, Md.; son of Ralph Leon (a factory foreman) and Eva Irene (Brandenburg) Palmer; married Ruth-Ann Pugh (a public school administrator), June 2, 1962; children: Edward Lee, Jennifer Lynn. *Education:* Gettysburg College, B.A., 1960; Lutheran Theological Seminary, Gettysburg, Pa., B.D., 1964; Ohio University, M.S., 1967, Ph.D., 1970. *Home address:* Route 1, Box 1792, Davidson, N.C. 28036. *Office:* Department of Psychology, Davidson College, Davidson, N.C. 28036.

CAREER: Western Maryland College, Westminster, assistant professor of psychology, 1968-70; Davidson College, Davidson, N.C., assistant professor, 1970-77, associate professor of psychology, 1977—. Guest researcher at Harvard University's Center for Research in Children's Television, 1977. Consultant to Council on Children, Media and Merchandising. *Military service:* U.S. Army Reserve, 1960-66. *Member:* International Communication Association, American Psychological Association, Southeastern Psychological Association, Southern Association for Public Opinion Research, North Mecklenburg Child Development Association (member of board of directors, 1971-73), Phi Beta Kappa. *Awards, honors:* Grant from North Carolina Governor's Committee, 1971.

WRITINGS: Children and the Faces of Television: Teach-

ing, Violence, Selling, Academic Press, 1980. Contributor to professional journals.

WORK IN PROGRESS: "Developing program and commercial separation formats with the goal of testing and identifying one that will enable the young child to make accurate distinction between programs and commercials."

SIDELIGHTS: In 1975 Edward Palmer began studying the effects of television on children. His conclusions to date show that, in addition to making kids junk food addicts, television indirectly undermines the parent-child relationship. Also, commercials induce children to pressure their parents into buying advertised toys and food products. According to Palmer, "a child puts into these commercials the same trust and gullibility that he has for the show itself, and has no notion that that commercial has a selling function."

Palmer also wrote: "I am committed to reaching out to young people, helping them to discover and to shape their talents and skills in service to others and to the society at large."

BIOGRAPHICAL/CRITICAL SOURCES: Chicago Tribune, April 20, 1980.

*   *   *

PANETTA, Leon Edward   1938-

PERSONAL: Born June 28, 1938, in Monterey, Calif.; son of Carmelo Frank and Carmelina Maria (Prochilo) Panetta; married Sylvia Marie Varni (a Congressional district coordinator), July 14, 1962; children: Christopher, Carmelo, James. *Education:* University of Santa Clara, B.A., 1960, LL.B. and J.D., 1963. *Religion:* Roman Catholic. *Home:* 15 Panetta Rd., Carmel Valley, Calif. 93021. *Office:* U.S. House of Representatives, 437 Cannon House Office Building, Washington, D.C. 20515.

CAREER: Legislative assistant to U.S. Senator Thomas Kuchel in Washington, D.C., 1966-69; U.S. Department of Health, Education & Welfare (HEW), Washington, D.C., director of U.S. Office of Civil Rights, 1969-70; executive assistant to the mayor of New York, N.Y., 1970-71; Panetta, Thompson & Panetta, Monterey, Calif., partner, 1971-76; U.S. House of Representatives, Washington, D.C., Democratic representative from the 16th District of California, 1976—. Member of board of trustees of School of Law, University of Santa Clara. *Military service:* U.S. Army, 1964-66. *Awards, honors:* Lincoln Award from National Education Association, 1969; distinguished service award from Bread for the World, 1978.

WRITINGS: Bring Us Together, Lippincott, 1971.

*   *   *

PANTER-DOWNES, Mollie Patricia   1906-

PERSONAL: Born August 25, 1906, in London, England; daughter of Edward (a British Army major) and Kathleen (Cowley) Panter-Downs; married Clare Robinson (a civil servant), July 12, 1927; children: Virginia Downes, Diana Downes. *Home:* Roppelegh's, Haslemere, Surrey, England. *Office:* New Yorker, 25 West 43rd St., New York, N.Y. 10036.

CAREER: New Yorker, New York, N.Y., London correspondent and author of column "Letter From London," 1939—.

WRITINGS: The Shoreless Sea (novel), Murray, 1923, Putnam, 1924; *The Chase,* Putnam, 1925; *Storm Bird,* Putnam, 1930; *My Husband Simon,* Collins, 1931; *Letter From En-*

gland, Little, Brown, 1940; *Watling Green* (juvenile), Scribner, 1943; *Ooty Preserved: A Victorian Hill Station in India*, Farrar, Straus, 1967 (published in England as *Ooty Preserved: A Victorian Hill Station*, Hamilton, 1967); *At the Pines: Swinburne and Watts-Dunton in Putney*, Gambit, 1971; *London War Notes, 1939-1945*, edited by William Shawn, Farrar, Straus, 1971. Also author of *One Fine Day*, 1947.

*   *   *

PAPERT, Emma N.   1926-

PERSONAL: Born June 29, 1926, in Monticello, N.Y.; daughter of Elias (an engineer) and Kate (Kahn) Papert. *Education:* Hunter College (now of the City University of New York), B.A., 1947; attended Columbia University, 1947; New York University, M.A., 1956. *Politics:* Democrat. *Home:* 80-09 35th Ave., Jackson Heights, N.Y. 11372.

CAREER: Metropolitan Museum of Art, New York, N.Y., assistant, 1949-56, library assistant, 1956-57, librarian, 1957-65, senior librarian, 1965-73, assistant museum librarian, 1973-74, associate museum librarian, 1974-78; writer, 1978—. *Member:* International Congress of Museums, American Association of Museums, Victorian Society in America (founding member), Smithsonian Institution (associate), Friends of Cast Iron Architecture, Friends of Attingham Park, England. *Awards, honors:* Corning Museum of Glass fellowship, 1956; Metropolitan Museum of Art European travel grants, 1965, 1977.

WRITINGS: The Illustrated Guide to American Glass, Hawthorn, 1972; (with Ethne K. Marenco) *The Invader* (historical novel), Pyramid Publications, 1973.

Author of "The Byzantine World," a juvenile picture booklet, Metropolitan Museum of Art, 1960. Contributor to *McGraw-Hill Dictionary of Art*, 1969. Contributor to *Early American Life*.

WORK IN PROGRESS: Dictionary of Symbols in Art, Volume I: *The Old World*, Volume II: *The New World*.

SIDELIGHTS: Emma Papert wrote: "I am basically interested in the history of art, especially architecture, archaeology, and the history and technology of glass. I travel as much as possible and have studied buildings and mosaics in Italy, Turkey, France, and England. I also have a strong interest in literatures of various cultures and in comparative linguistics (my languages are French, German, Italian, and Spanish), possibly stemming from the fact that my major in college was anthropology.

"My interest in writing stems from the desire to communicate my discoveries about various subjects to everyone that can possibly be reached by the written word. The world is so full of fascinating areas of history that I have a vast amount of material at my disposal. Humankind is the greatest study of them all, and I would love to be able to bring to the reader's attention all the great happenings which have now been largely forgotten."

*   *   *

PARENT, Gail   1940-

PERSONAL: Born August 12, 1940, in New York, N.Y.; daughter of Theodore (a Wall Street executive) and Ruth (Goldberg) Kostner; married Lair Parent (a television producer), June 24, 1962 (divorced, 1979); children: two sons. *Education:* Attended Syracuse University, 1958-60; New York University, B.S., 1962. *Religion:* Jewish. *Residence:* Los Angeles, Calif. *Agent:* Owen Laster, William Morris

Agency, 1350 Avenue of the Americas, New York, N.Y. 10019.

CAREER: Writer. Worked at Columbia Broadcasting System (CBS-TV), as writer for television series, including "The Carol Burnett Show" and "The Mary Tyler Moore Show," and specials, including "Sills and Burnett at the Met." *Awards, honors:* Co-winner of Emmy Award for television variety writing from Academy of Television Arts and Sciences, 1972, for "The Carol Burnett Show."

WRITINGS—Novels: *Sheila Levine Is Dead and Living in New York*, Putnam, 1972; *David Meyer Is a Mother*, Harper, 1976; *The Best Laid Plans*, Putnam, 1980.

Other writings: (With Kenny Solms) "Call Her Mom" (teleplay), ABC-TV, 1972; (with Solms) "Lorelei" (musical play adapted from the play by Joseph Fields and Anita Loos, "Gentlemen Prefer Blondes"), first produced in 1972; (with Andrew Smith) "The Main Event" (screenplay), Warner Bros., 1979. Contributor to television series "Mary Hartman, Mary Hartman," 1975. Contributor to periodicals, including *Esquire* and *Harper's Bazaar*.

WORK IN PROGRESS: Uneasy Lies the Head, a novel.

SIDELIGHTS: Parent was dubbed a "female pioneer in writing TV comedy" by *Newsweek*. In the late 1960's, her collaboration with Kenny Solms on television series such as "The Carol Burnett Show" and "The Mary Tyler Moore Show" contributed to CBS-TV's top earnings among the networks. Her career in television culminated with the winning of an Emmy Award, the medium's most prestigious honor.

Parent has also distinguished herself as a novelist. Her first effort, *Sheila Levine Is Dead and Living in New York*, was a popular success. The title character is a lonely, thirtyish, overweight woman living in New York City. Parent invested much of her own personality in Sheila Levine. "It's me, it's absolutely my psyche," she told *Newsweek*. "From 0 to 21, getting married was my orientation to life." The marriage-obsessed Levine was later featured in motion picture and television adaptations of the novel.

On stage, Parent was less successful in adapting "Gentlemen Prefer Blondes" as the musical "Lorelei." Betsy Carter and Martin Kasindorf contended that the play's Broadway earnings were largely due to Carol Channing's performance in the title role. Parent also failed to match her early television success with her first screenplay, "The Main Event." But most critics, including Vincent Canby, attributed the film's flaws to the zealousness of its leading actress and co-producer, Barbra Streisand.

CA INTERVIEWS THE AUTHOR

Gail Parent was interviewed by phone during a break from her work on November 30, 1979.

CA: Is it difficult for writers to break into television writing?

PARENT: They can't break into variety television because there is very little variety television. I think the breaking-in factor has stayed the same for quite a while. Most people are full of ideas, but they don't sit down and write, and that's what it takes, sitting down and writing scripts.

CA: You started writing comedy as a student at New York University. When you were younger, did you know you wanted to be a writer?

PARENT: I always communicated by writing. If I was mad at a member of my family, I wrote them a letter—when I was really young. Hiding behind a letter seemed easier. I never knew there was such a job as comedy writing. It's the same thing as my youngest son now wanting to be an artist. He has no idea of the different fields, about commercial art or fabric design. I took a course in journalism in high school one year during the summer; I knew that people wrote for newspapers. But I never did know *really* when I was growing up that you could make a living writing comedy material.

CA: How did that ambition evolve?

PARENT: I was really very influenced in high school, and maybe even junior high, by Mike Nichols and Elaine May. They fascinated me. While other teenagers were listening to music, I was listening to them over and over. Hopefully, I picked up some of their rhythm. In college I met Kenny Solms, my partner, and he had also had the same passion for Nichols and May. So we started by repeating their routines and then evolving into our own. At that time in New York, there was a place called Upstairs at the Downstairs, which did afford new writers a chance to have sketch material performed. We submitted some material that was used in the shows, and it was reviewed by the *New York Times* and the *New Yorker*. That gave us an opportunity. They don't have that type of opportunity anymore.

CA: Does living in Hollywood and being in the entertainment profession make it difficult to spend as much time as you'd like with your family?

PARENT: It is very sporadic. Since last January, I haven't left the house. I was working on a book. There are many days that I don't even go out. So that's great, because I'm here when my kids go to school and when they come home from school. Fortunately, I write in the mornings and late at night, so that I do have time most of the day and I don't feel like running around. Other times, and this is very difficult on a marriage, if I'm working on a show or a film, it really is a seven-day-a-week job, from early in the morning often until very late at night. It can be very taxing for somebody who cannot absorb that. And the stakes are so high. I'm fairly even, but a lot of writers are manic depressives. I don't know whether one *is* a manic depressive and then becomes a writer, or whether being a writer makes one that way. Because the stakes are so high, the mood swings are very strong.

Having children has kept me very normal, because I haven't been able to go off and celebrate joyously over something for a week or take off or do what I feel like, nor have I allowed myself to dwell on unhappiness when something has gone wrong. You can't do that when you have children, and I attribute my sanity to having them.

CA: You've said that you work with the attitude of doing it because you enjoy it, whether things are successful or not. But isn't there an immediate feeling of great disappointment when a show or movie isn't well received?

PARENT: That's an incorrect statement, because the actual work is torture. It's just awful writing. It's lonely; it's like having homework every day of your life, every minute of your life. You can never get away from it and go on vacations, because there's always something you should be doing. The actual process of it is no fun. It's fun for two minutes: the minute you've gotten the job and the minute that somebody likes it. That's all. So I was wrong there. If I were a psychiatrist and knew the film business in Los Angeles, I would think that anybody who was trying to put a film together was a masochist.

CA: Does it happen that something seems very funny while you're writing it, but fails later?

PARENT: That happens, but the opposite also happens. I have to be totally honest: sometimes people make it funnier. Carol Burnett does. It can happen both ways. Although I do admire all those people—those real writers—like J. D. Salinger, who will not allow any of his things to go to theatrical production. It is difficult. It becomes a collaborative process.

CA: In creating sketches for a big television show, does primarily one writer come up with the ideas and bounce them off the others, or is there a lot of brainstorming?

PARENT: On "The Carol Burnett Show" there wasn't much brainstorming. There were several sets of teams; Kenny Solms and I were one of the sets. We knew who was going to be on the show. We'd go to the head writer and he'd look at the schedule to see what they needed. Kenny and I would come up with premises for sketches, go to the head writer, and he would approve or disapprove them; then we'd go back and write them. The times we all got together would be when the show was on its feet, once a week on Wednesday afternoon, to watch the whole thing through and then to discuss it afterwards. Sometimes when there was an emergency situation, when a sketch wasn't working and we needed another idea, we'd all get together. But there were not many general meetings on that show.

I find that all comedy writers are funny people. If they *are* funny, they *write* funny. That image of the dissipated older man who drinks too much and smokes too much and drinks coffee all the time and is very serious but writes funny—I really have not come across that.

CA: When you hire writers to work for you, can you easily get someone you know, or do you often have to take a chance on someone you've never worked with before?

PARENT: We have done both. When you're putting a staff together, as we have done a couple of times, you read a lot of material from new people, looking for at least one new person or one new team of people. You look for a well-rounded staff. You take somebody you know, someone you've worked with many times before and you're confident with; you take somebody someone else recommended; you take somebody brand new whose material you've read. Also, people usually have different specialties. Somebody will be political, somebody will do a very physical type of material; you do need different talents within one show. For "The Carol Burnett Show," Kenny and I did the first twelve soap operas, "As the Stomach Turns." And we'd do a lot of political stuff. But we would not really do some of the physical humor. You find even within a staff that different people have different talents, and when you're putting it together, you look for everybody good, but also for a cross section.

CA: If you hire someone you don't really know, do you base your decision on material that person has written?

PARENT: Yes.

CA: So you're taking a chance on the person's working capabilities. Does it usually work out well?

PARENT: Usually it does. Every once in a while there's a mistake, but usually it works out well. So many people feel they can write because they have ideas, but it's very important to actually get it down on paper.

CA: How do you feel about your success?

PARENT: I'm always surprised that somebody knows me whom I don't know. I'm always surprised that somebody's read something or seen something of mine that I don't know about. "Mary Hartman, Mary Hartman" did a lot of that because it was so successful. Another thing I can say is that the struggle continues. A lot of new and starting writers would think that I had it very easy, and I don't have the same battles that they do. And yet it really does continue. Each project is hard all over again; its starting from scratch each time you start. I have more doors open to me, but that doesn't necessarily mean that there's a better chance of success each time I go to bat.

BIOGRAPHICAL/CRITICAL SOURCES: Variety, February 25, 1970, February 23, 1972; *New York Times Book Review,* July 9, 1972, January 10, 1973, February 29, 1976; *Harper's Bazaar,* January, 1974; *New York Times,* February 2, 1976, June 22, 1979; *Newsweek,* July 23, 1976; *Washington Post,* June 26, 1979.

—*Interview by Jean W. Ross*

*   *   *

PARKER, Edna Jean 1935-

PERSONAL: Born June 26, 1935, in Akron, Ohio; daughter of Murray Stephen (a lawyer) Parker; married Robert J. Crawford, Jr. (a property manager), June 14, 1975. *Education:* Attended Mexico City College, 1954; Ohio State University, B.A., 1955; University of Akron, B.A., 1962; graduate study at Kent State University, 1962; University of Alaska, M.A., 1971. *Politics:* Independent. *Religion:* Presbyterian. *Home:* 74 Maplewood Ave., Akron, Ohio 44313.

CAREER/WRITINGS: Teacher at secondary schools, Summit County, Ohio, 1959-60; *Akron Beacon Journal,* Akron, Ohio, reporter and editor, 1961-69; University of Alaska, Fairbanks, writer for university news service, 1970-71; Sun Newspapers, Cleveland, Ohio, writer and editor, 1972—. Contributor of free-lance articles to newspapers and magazines, including *Cleveland Plain Dealer* and *Grit.* Lecturer at University of Akron, 1972-80; Messenger Newspapers, Norton, Ohio, writer, 1980—. President of Hillcrest Recreation Center, Inc., 1963—. *Member:* American Association of University Professors, National Federation of Press Women (first vice-president, 1979—), Women in Communications (president of Akron chapter, 1972-73), Ohio Newspaper Women's Association, Ohio Press Women (president, 1968-70), Ohio Women's Equity Action League (trustee, 1975-76), Order of Eastern Star, Delta Zeta. *Awards, honors:* Has received more than one hundred fifty writing awards.

WORK IN PROGRESS: A gothic romance.

SIDELIGHTS: Edna Parker told *CA:* "I started writing at thirteen, and I fell into it. I intensely disliked the all-girls school I attended. In hopes of diverting me from my hate of the place, an English teacher suggested I become involved in the National Forensic League. I did. I entered the original oration category, which meant I had to write my own speech. I was on my way. I wish I could remember that teacher's name. If I was able to find any peace and happiness some place other than a typewriter, I would, because this is damn tough."

*   *   *

PARKER, Julia (Louise) 1932-

PERSONAL: Born July 27, 1932, in Plymouth, England; daughter of Lester Francis and Edna Charity (Tapson) Lethbridge; married Derek Parker, July 27, 1957. *Education:* Attended Plymouth College of Art, 1946-52; Faculty of Astrological Studies, D.F.Astrol.S., 1967. *Politics:* Liberal. *Religion:* Agnostic. *Home:* 37 Campden Hill Towers, London W11 3QW, England. *Agent:* David Higham Associates Ltd., 5-8 Lower John St., Golden Square, London W1R 4HA, England.

CAREER: Arts and crafts teacher at Plymouth College Preparatory School, 1953-57; Hammersmith Girls' Comprehensive School, London, England, art and dance teacher, 1959-64; Faculty of Astrological Studies, London, secretary, 1967-72, president, 1973-79. Professional dancer, 1953-57; set designer for TWW-TV, Cardiff, Wales, 1957. *Member:* Society of Authors.

WRITINGS: (With husband, Derek Parker) *The Compleat Astrologer,* McGraw, 1971; (with D. Parker) *The Compleat Lover,* McGraw, 1972; (with D. Parker) *The Natural History of the Chorus Girl,* Bobbs-Merrill, 1975; (with D. Parker) *The Immortals,* McGraw, 1976; (with D. Parker) *The Story and the Song,* Elm Tree, 1979; (with D. Parker) *How Do You Know Who You Are?,* Macmillan, 1980; *The Pocket Guides to Astrology,* Simon & Schuster, 1981.

WORK IN PROGRESS: The Natural Life and How to Live It, with D. Parker, publication by Macmillan expected in 1982; *The Pocket Guides to Astrology,* a new edition, publication expected in 1982.

SIDELIGHTS: Julia Parker wrote: "I am concerned to further a much wider knowledge of astrology, educating the public away from the simplistic Sun-sign columns common in newspapers and magazines. I see astrology as a helpful discipline, furthering man's awareness of himself and his potential, making life generally easier, pointing out how we can best develop our talents, develop positive characteristics, and negate negative traits.

"Astrology apart, my interests center around the arts: I paint and sculpt, and have been involved in classical ballet, teaching, choreographing, and performing for almost all my life. For the past four years I have been studying classical guitar.

"I feel strongly there should be a change in educational methods: with increasing leisure time becoming available, the only possible way to fulfillment is going to be in increased education for leisure, and an early encouragement of skills. Often the approach in art training, in particular, is far too narrow; greater versatility should be encouraged and aimed for, and the more attention that can be given to the development of new techniques in varying media the better for all concerned."

*   *   *

PARRINO, John J(oseph) 1942-

PERSONAL: Born September 9, 1942, in Tampa, Fla.; son of Joseph (in road construction) and Angela (an interior decorator; maiden name, Nuccio) Parrino. *Education:* University of South Florida, B.A., 1964; Louisiana State University, M.A., 1966, Ph.D., 1969. *Home:* 2633-E Oak Shadow Court, Atlanta, Ga. 30345. *Office:* Tarkenton & Co., 3340 Peachtree Rd., Suite 444, Atlanta, Ga. 30326.

CAREER: Georgia Regional Hospital, Atlanta, chief psychologist, 1969-77; Tarkenton & Co., Atlanta, Ga., consultant, 1972—. Private practice of psychology, 1969—. *Member:* American Psychological Association, Association for the Advancement of Behavior Therapy, Society for Psychophysiological Research, Biofeedback Society of America, Phi Kappa Phi.

WRITINGS: Helping Others, EB Press, 1975; *From Panic to Power: The Positive Use of Stress,* Wiley, 1979. Contributor to journals in the behavioral sciences.

WORK IN PROGRESS: Research on the use of personal feedback to increase peripheral blood flow in individuals with chronically cold hands.

SIDELIGHTS: Parrino commented: *"From Panic to Power* was stimulated by my work with thirteen cases of severe stress reactions, cases ranging from neurological problems, to depression and exhibitionism. Stress management is a skill that can be learned (similar to learning any skill like tennis, golf, etc.), but people must put out the effort and time for doing so. What puzzles me is the enormous effort exerted in learning other skills, particularly when the management and control of our emotions is left to caretakers—physicians, psychologists. This caretaker mentality, relinquishing the total responsibility for physical and psychological well-being to 'experts,' must be changed before we make major inroads into the problems of stress."

*   *   *

PARRY, Michael Patrick 1947-

PERSONAL: Born October 7, 1947, in Brussels, Belgium; son of Arthur Glyn and Lucille (Leopoldine) Parry; married Patricia Kinsella (divorced, 1972); children: Kirsten Marianne. *Education:* Attended London School of Film Technique. *Home:* 137 Windmill Rd., Brentford, Middlesex, England. *Agent:* Jon Thurley, 78 New Bond St., London W1Y 9DA, England.

CAREER: American International Films, story editor, 1969-70; Sphere Books Ltd., outside editor, 1970-73; free-lance writer, 1973—. *Member:* Writers Guild of Great Britain, British Fantasy Society, Association of Independent Producers.

WRITINGS: Countess Dracula (adaptation from the film), Sphere, 1971; (with Garry Rusoff) *Chariots of Fire* (novel), Orbit, 1974; *Great Black Magic Stories,* Taplinger, 1977; (with Chris Dempster and Dave Tomkins) *Fire Power* (nonfiction), St. Martin's, 1981.

Screenplays: "The Uncanny," 1977; "Sweeney Todd," 1980.

Editor: *Beware of the Cat: Weird Tales About Cats,* Gollancz, 1972, Taplinger, 1973; *Strange Ecstasies: Stories About Strange and Unearthly Drugs,* Panther, 1973; *The Devil's Children: Tales of Demons and Exorcists,* Orbit, 1974, Taplinger, 1975; *The Hounds of Hell: Weird Tales About Dogs,* Taplinger, 1974; *Dream Trips: Stories of Weird and Unearthly Drugs,* Panther, 1974; *The First Mayflower Book of Black Magic Stories,* Mayflower, 1974; *The Second Mayflower Book of Black Magic Stories,* Mayflower, 1974; *The Roots of Evil,* Taplinger, 1976; *The Supernatural Solution,* Taplinger, 1976; *Savage Heroes,* Taplinger, 1980.

European editor of *Castle of Frankenstein,* 1964—. Contributor to *Encyclopedia of Horror.* Contributor to film magazines.

WORK IN PROGRESS: "Getting Even," a screenplay; research on Jack London's science-fiction and fantasy stories, with a book expected to result.

SIDELIGHTS: Parry commented: *"Fire Power* is an account of the civil war in Angola, 1966 to 1967, written with two men who fought in the war as mercenaries. I am now concentrating on my work as a screenwriter." *Avocational interests:* Cinema, book collecting, martial arts, parapsychology, "all forms of spiritual self-development, such as meditation and yoga."

*   *   *

PARSONS, R(ichard) A(ugustus)

PERSONAL: Born in Bay Roberts, Newfoundland, Canada; son of William and Dorcas Catherine (Mosdell) Parsons; married Bessie Ash Somerton (deceased); children: R. Austin, Helen Parsons Shepherd, Paul, Sheila Parsons Curren. *Education:* McGill University, B.C.L., 1921. *Politics:* Conservative. *Religion:* Anglican. *Home:* 34 Queen's Rd., St. John's, Newfoundland, Canada A1C 5M9. *Office:* Parsons & O'Neill, Board of Trade Building, 115 Water St., St. John's, Newfoundland, Canada A1C 5M9.

CAREER: Called to the Bar in Newfoundland, 1924; schoolteacher in Newfoundland, from 1910 to about 1915; appointed Queen's Counsel; attorney in Newfoundland; partner with Parsons & O'Neill, in St. John's, Newfoundland. Clerk of legislative council. *Military service:* Canadian Army; served with Royal Newfoundland Regiment during World War I. *Awards, honors:* D.Litt. from Memorial University of Newfoundland, 1974; named honorary associate in education by Nova Scotia Teachers College, 1974.

*WRITINGS—*Books of poems: *Reflections,* Ryerson, 1954; *Reflections, Books I and II,* Ryerson, 1958; *The Village Politicians,* Newfoundland Academy of Art, 1960; *Sea Room,* Newfoundland Arts Centre, 1963; *The Rote,* Ontario Publishing, 1965; *The Village and the Wayside,* Ontario Publishing, 1967; *Interludes,* Ryerson, 1970; *The Tale of a Lonesome House,* Ontario Publishing, 1971; *The Legend of the Isle,* Ontario Publishing, 1973; *Salute to Port de Grave,* Ontario Publishing, 1975; *Contemplations,* Ontario Publishing, 1977; *Curtain Call,* privately printed, 1980.

Work represented in anthologies, including *Book of Newfoundland,* edited by Smallwood. Contributor to *London Times.* Member of editorial board of *Chitty's Law Journal.*

SIDELIGHTS: In the foreword to *Curtain Call,* Harry A. Cuff and Daphne Benson wrote: "Dr. Parson's imagery is strong, precise and concrete, never crude. His tone is reverent without being maudlin. His satire does not deteriorate to invective. His diction is refined rather than grandiose, while his use of the Newfoundland dialect is astute and never offensive. Although he has dealt with a wide range of subjects there is the sense of a unity of theme—the indomitable human spirit portrayed against a Newfoundland background. Dr. Parsons' fascination with Newfoundland and the qualities that make her unique is revealed in every line. His devotion and attachment to Newfoundland is displayed in every phrase.

"Dr. Parsons has produced his work at a time when the value and richness of Newfoundland's culture and history is being realized by her people, however, the quality of that work, rather than a public interest in Newfoundland, will be the primary element in its survival. Accurate word pictures of our land, our history and our people have been drawn with sensitivity. We sense his keen awareness and intimate knowledge of our way of life. Though we, his contemporaries, read him with pleasure and affirmation, it will be our children's children who will reap the greatest benefits from his poetry. Dr. Parsons has effectively linked the past with the present and has constructed a bridge to the future. His poetry will enable future generations to participate imaginatively in their Newfoundland heritage."

AVOCATIONAL INTERESTS: Hunting, fishing.

* * *

PARY, C. C.
See GILMORE, Christopher Cook

* * *

PASAMANIK, Luisa 1930-

PERSONAL: Born December 16, 1930, in Buenos Aires, Argentina; daughter of Gregorio (a manufacturer) and Berta Renee (a manufacturer; maiden name, Lew) Pasamanik. *Home:* Carlos Calvo 4198, Buenos Aires 1230, Argentina.

CAREER: Librarian in Buenos Aires, Argentina, 1950-53; journalist for *Amanecer,* 1956-58; Helena Rubinstein (cosmetic company), publicist, 1959-63; editor and translator for Reuters News International Agency, 1963-65; translator, journalist, and teacher of French and English in Argentina and abroad, 1965—. Translator for publishers in Buenos Aires and for United Nations Educational, Scientific & Cultural Organization (UNESCO). Gives poetry readings in Argentina and Mexico. *Awards, honors:* Short story prize from *La Epoca,* 1957, for "El sueno"; short story award from *Gaceta Literario,* 1958, for "Toribio"; band of honor from Argentine Writers Association, 1961, for *Vacio para cuerdas;* Leopoldo Panero Prize from Institute of Hispanic Culture, 1968, for *Tlaloke;* Boscan Prize from Catalan Institute of Hispanic Culture, 1972, for *Sinfonia alucinada;* short story prize from municipal government of Badalona, 1969, for "Boogie"; special mention from city of Martorell, 1979, for unpublished book, *Estaciones de un sueno.*

WRITINGS—In English translation: *El angel desterrado* (poems), Editorial la Mandragora, 1962, translation by Jack Hirschman published as *The Exiled Angel,* Red Hill Press, 1973, translation by Carter Aldridge published as *The Banished Angel,* text in English and Spanish, Green River Press, 1979.

Other writings; poems: *Poemas al hombre del manana* (title means "Poems for the Man of Tomorrow"), Ediciones Botella al Mar, 1953; *Plegaria grave* (title means "Grave Prayer"), Editorial Alpe, 1958; *Vacio para cuerdas* (title means "Voidness for Strings"), Editorial la Mandragora, 1960; *Sinfonia de las esferas* (title means "Spheres Symphony"), Coleccion Lirica Hispana, 1963; *Metal y vidrio* (title means "Metal and Glass"), Coleccion Lirica Hispana, 1967; *Sermon negro* (title means "Black Sermon"), Ediciones Finisterre, 1968; *Tlaloke,* Ediciones Cultura Hispanica, 1970; *Primero el fuego* (title means "Fire, First"), Coleccion Arbol de Fuego, 1972; *Sinfonia alucinada* (title means "Hallucinated Symphony"), Coleccion Juan Boscan, 1973.

Translator of books into Spanish, including: Dorothy W. Smith, *Cuidados de enfermeria para adultos* (title means "Nursing of Adults"), La Prensa Medica Mexicana, 1967; Charles T. Wood, *Felipe "El Hermoso" y Bonifacio VIII* (title means "Philip the Fair and Boniface VIII"), Uteha, 1968; Esther Lucile Brown, *Nuevas dimensiones en el cuidado de los pacientes* (title means "Newer Dimensions of Patient Care"), La Prensa Medica Mexicana, 1971.

Plays: "When Light Will Mount the Hills" (three-act); "My Mother's Watch" (one-act); "The Trunk" (two-act); "The Yellow Horse" (three-act). Contributor of articles, stories, poems, and reviews to magazines in North, Central, and South America, and Spain.

WORK IN PROGRESS: Books of poems; plays; short stories.

SIDELIGHTS: Luisa Pasamanik wrote: "I have traveled through Europe and Latin America, living for several years in Mexico City and Jerusalem. I am competent in English, French, Hebrew, German, Italian, and Portuguese.

"The subject I consider vital and always write about is human beings—their present, future, and past. I never joined any literary group, sustaining an independence of mind as an independent creator in order to firmly safeguard my authenticity as a writer and as a human being."

* * *

PASMANIK, Wolf 1924-

PERSONAL: Born May 3, 1924, in Tarnopol, Poland; came to the United States, 1960, naturalized citizen; son of Isaye and Betty Pasmanik. *Education:* Literary Institute of the Union of Soviet Writers, Moscow, received degree of writer, 1943; Henry George School, certificate in social work, 1976. *Home:* 350 East 67th St., New York, N.Y. 10021.

CAREER: Poet and journalist. Worked as television announcer in Italy; International Center in New York, New York City, director of Poetry Club, teacher of creative writing at Literary Club, 1969-75; free-lance writer, 1974-76; Rutgers University, New Brunswick, N.J., poet-in-residence; United Nations, New York City, Yiddish poet-in-residence; World Union Press, New York City, associate editor, editor, and currently U.N. correspondent. Speaker; gives poetry readings in Yiddish. Guest on television programs, including "Joe Franklin Show." *Member:* P.E.N., Poetry Society of America. *Awards, honors:* Willy and Lisa Shor Prize from World Congress for Jewish Culture, for *Mayne Lieder.*

WRITINGS—Poems; all in Yiddish: *Meine Haime* (title means "My Home"), [Poland], 1947; *Blumen* (title means "Flowers"), Yiddischbuch Publishing House, 1959; *Mayne Lieder* (collection of work previously published in *Meine Haime* and *Blumen;* title means "My Poems"), Cyco Publishing House, 1970. Contributor of poems, both in Yiddish and in English translation, to newspapers and magazines, including *Christian Science Monitor, Courant, Jewish Daily Forward,* and *Unzer Zeit.*

WORK IN PROGRESS: Poems in Yiddish.

SIDELIGHTS: "The Yiddish language," Pasmanik once stated, "cannot be taught just as language. It is the quintessence of a full Jewish experience—the art, history, emotions of a people." In his search for a nurturing and free country in which to pursue his writing, Pasmanik has traveled far from his native Poland. He originally left that country in May 1939, narrowly escaping the Nazi blitzkrieg. He journeyed to the Soviet Union and enrolled in classes at the Literary Institute of the Union of Soviet Writers in Moscow. It was there that Pasmanik met the Russian poet Yevgeny Yevtushenko, of whom he later declared: "I sensed a greatness in this man, even when he was quite young and unknown. I admired the courage of his outspoken statements and was deeply impressed by his obvious creative talents."

After several years in Russia, Pasmanik returned to Poland only to discover that his family had been exterminated during the Holocaust and his birthplace totally destroyed. He then immigrated to Italy where he studied Italian at a university and tried his hand at television broadcasting. Although he made numerous friends in Italy and loved the country deeply—"it is as though everyone is a poet there, the language is so beautiful"—Pasmanik yearned for closer ties to Jewish culture.

In 1961 he arrived in the United States and was, as he now

admits, dismayed at the sparsity of Yiddish theatre and newspapers available in New York City. Since that time, he has worked toward improving the quality of the Yiddish experience for young American Jews. Pasmanik writes in Yiddish and also gives poetry readings before Jewish and non-Jewish groups in Yiddish. He considers it his mission "to nurture the beautiful language of Yiddish, not to let it die. I take it to campuses, to lecture halls, to meeting places. Whether fully understood or not, the sound of Yiddish must be heard."

Since the summer of 1979, Pasmanik has led a one-man campaign to erect a monument in New York City in memory of the six million Jews who perished in the Holocaust. He hopes such a memorial will remind future generations of "the horrors of World War II and its tragic attendant circumstances." His poem "There's No Monument in New York" was written to dramatize the situation.

BIOGRAPHICAL/CRITICAL SOURCES: Jewish News (New Jersey), February 26, 1976.

* * *

PATERSON, Diane (R. Cole) 1946-

PERSONAL: Born July 23, 1946, in Brooklyn, N.Y.; daughter of A. R. and T. E. (Isaacs) Cole; divorced, 1978; children: Elizabeth, Jana. *Education:* Attended Pratt Institute, 1966-68. *Home address:* R.D. 1, Box 123A, High Falls, N.Y. 12440. *Agent:* Frank Crump, Bookmakers, Inc., 305 North Main St., Westport, Conn. 06880.

CAREER: Writer and illustrator. *Member:* Authors Guild.

WRITINGS—Self-illustrated children's books: *The Biggest Snowstorm Ever,* Dial, 1974; *Eat!,* Dial, 1975; *Smile for Auntie,* Dial, 1976; *If I Were a Toad,* Dial, 1977; *Wretched Rachel,* Dial, 1978; *The Bathtub Ocean,* Dial, 1979.

WORK IN PROGRESS: The Diane Paterson Storybook, publication by Dial expected in 1980-81.

SIDELIGHTS: Paterson told *CA:* "Sometimes I draw a character and then another and they carry on their own story which hopefully leads to a humorous situation. I illustrate all of my books and feel a close relationship between image and words. I draw words into the pictures so they are one, trying to get as close to animation as possible. I hope to keep my material humorous and imaginative to appeal to all ages."

AVOCATIONAL INTERESTS: Gardening, swimming, painting.

* * *

PATSAUQ, Markoosie 1942-
(Markoosie)

PERSONAL: Born June 19, 1942, in Port Harrison, Quebec, Canada; son of Alex and Edith Patsauq; married Zipporah Kudluk, November, 1961 (divorced March, 1974); children: Ipelee (son), Susie, Carol, Doreen, Polly. *Education:* Attended public high school in Yellowknife, Northwest Territories, Canada; earned commercial pilot's license and carpentry diploma. *Residence:* Inukjuak, Quebec, Canada J0M 1M0. *Agent:* McGill-Queens University Press, 1020 Pine Avenue W., Montreal, Quebec, Canada H3A 1A2. *Office:* Government of Quebec, Inukjuak, Quebec, Canada J0M 1M0.

CAREER: Atlas Aviation, Resolute, Northwest Territories, Canada, pilot, 1969-75; Northern Quebec Innuit Association, translator in Montreal, Quebec, and Port Harrison, Quebec, 1975-76; Community Council, Inukjuak, Quebec,

manager, 1976—. Government of Quebec administrator of public services, 1978—; secretary of local government, Inukjuak, Quebec, 1976—. Writer.

WRITINGS: (Under name Markoosie) *Harpoon of the Hunter* (juvenile), McGill-Queen's University Press, 1970.

WORK IN PROGRESS: Footprints in the Tundra, "a historical novel from past lives in Inuit, but no publication is expected."

SIDELIGHTS: In *Harpoon of the Hunter,* Markoosie sets down on paper an Eskimo legend about a young boy's initiation into manhood. The story was first serialized in the Eskimo newsletter *Inuttituut;* later Markoosie translated the story for English readers. The publication of *Harpoon of the Hunter* marked the first time in Canadian history that an Eskimo fiction story was published in English.

Markoosie told *CA:* "Although my people, the Inuit, have no written history, the fact of our being the first inhabitants of North America is obvious. Only through the tongues of our ancestors and from the countless stories passed on from generation to generation can we say we have been around North America for the last ten thousand years. I know one old Inuit who remembers the story about his ancestors coming into the great land before it was covered with ice. It is stories of this type, and stories of personal lives such as the boy I wrote about in *Harpoon of the Hunter,* that have fascinated me since my childhood.

"Because the old Inuit people, those who have the stories of our past, are dying, I decided to write the books in my spare time because I felt the legends should not be told only to Inuit but to the people of the south as well. It was the stories written by Farley Mowat about the people of the north that inspired me to write our legends. I only wish that I had more time to write, but I have a family to support."

* * *

PATTON, Frances Gray 1906-

PERSONAL: Born March 19, 1906, in Raleigh, N.C.; daughter of Robert Lilly (an editor) and Mary (a writer; maiden name, MacRae) Gray; married Lewis Patton (a professor emeritus), August 20, 1927; children: Robert Gray, Mary MacRae and Susannah (twins). *Education:* Attended Trinity College (now Duke University), 1922, and University of North Carolina, 1923-25. *Religion:* Christian. *Residence:* Durham, N.C. *Address:* c/o Dodd, Mead & Co., 79 Madison Ave., New York, N.Y. 10016.

CAREER: Short-story writer and novelist. Lecturer in creative writing programs. *Awards, honors:* Christopher Award, 1955, for *Good Morning, Miss Dove;* Sir Walter Raleigh Award for best North Carolina fiction of the year from Historical Book Club of North Carolina, 1955, for *Good Morning, Miss Dove,* and 1956, for *A Piece of Luck;* North Carolina Medal for Literature; Doctor of Literature from University of North Carolina at Greensboro; Doctor of Humanities from North Carolina State University; distinguished alumnus award from University of North Carolina at Charlottesville.

WRITINGS—All published by Dodd, except as noted: *The Finer Things of Life* (short stories), 1951; *Good Morning, Miss Dove* (novel), 1954; *A Piece of Luck* (short stories), 1955 (published in England as *A Piece of Luck and Other Stories,* Gollancz, 1955); *Twenty-Eight Stories,* 1969. Contributor of short stories and articles to magazines, including *New Yorker, McCall's,* and *Ladies' Home Journal.*

SIDELIGHTS: Frances Gray Patton, an author whose work

centers around the life and people of the South, aspired to be a writer from her early childhood. The daughter of writers, Patton began to pursue writing seriously as a student at the University of North Carolina, where she held a playwrighting fellowship. She was active in dramatics, and was a member of the Stuart Walker stock company in Cincinnati, Ohio, when her first play was published by the University of North Carolina's magazine. Following college, Patton turned to short-story writing, earning the title "the Jane Austen of North Carolina" for her sharp observations of Southern manners and attitudes. A clear condemnation of white supremacy is present in her portraits of Southern life.

Patton possesses "the infallible eye and ear, the acute sympathies, of a born storyteller," wrote L. T. Nicholl in the *New York Herald Tribune Book Review*. Agreeing with this assessment, Marge Lyon commented in the *Chicago Sunday Tribune* that the stories collected in *The Finer Things of Life* are "whimsical in spots, faintly poignant in others, but lit with a glowing, humorous aura made up of bright observations, sparkles of wit, and diamond bright philosofy [sic], shot with incandescent characterizations." Reviewing *A Piece of Luck* for the *New York Times*, Charles Lee also found Patton's characters to be memorable. "[The stories] turn around human predicaments rather than plots," Lee assessed. "Miss Patton is much more the observer of emotional climate than the engineer of contrivance. The result is that her stories are weather reports of the mind, its subtle changes in temperature and pressure, its shifts, occlusions and tensions."

Patton's most successful book is her novel for young people, *Good Morning, Miss Dove*, the story of a strict but sensitive school teacher. Comparing *Good Morning, Miss Dove* to James Hilton's *Goodbye, Mr. Chips*, J. H. Jackson of the *San Francisco Chronicle* noted that it is probably "heresy to suggest that a story in this category might be even better than *Goodbye, Mr. Chips*. But I think this can be said of *Good Morning, Miss Dove*." Reviewing the novel in the *Saturday Review*, Martin Levin described the novel as "sentimental without being cloying, and artful without seeming forced." Dan Wickenden disclosed that *Good Morning, Miss Dove* "stand[s] some chance of becoming a minor classic." He further commented in the *New York Herald Tribune Book Review*: "Leavened with wit and sound common sense, written with an unerring rightness of touch, the whole book rings with the truth about human nature in its nicer aspects. . . . *Good Morning, Miss Dove* is just about flawless and completely enchanting."

BIOGRAPHICAL/CRITICAL SOURCES: San Francisco Chronicle, November 8, 1951, November 4, 1954; *Chicago Sunday Tribune*, November 11, 1951, October 31, 1954; *New York Herald Tribune Book Review*, December 9, 1951, October 31, 1954, October 2, 1955; *Christian Science Monitor*, January 3, 1952; *Atlantic Monthly*, October, 1954; *New York Times*, October 31, 1954, October 16, 1955; *Saturday Review*, November 6, 1954.

*   *   *

PAVLETICH, Aida

PERSONAL: Born in Buenos Aires, Argentina; came to the United States; naturalized citizen, 1958. *Education:* Hunter College of the City University of New York, B.A., 1966. *Politics:* "Depends on the issue." *Residence:* Los Angeles, Calif. *Agent:* Julian Bach Literary Agency, Inc., 747 Third Ave., New York, N.Y. 10017.

CAREER: Writer.

WRITINGS: Rock-a-Bye, Baby (nonfiction), Doubleday, 1980.

SIDELIGHTS: Aida Pavletich commented: "I try to perform on the page with the passion of a graffitist tempered by the warmth of an epistolary writer."

*   *   *

PAWELCZYNSKA, Anna 1922-

PERSONAL: Born April 29, 1922, in Pruszkow, Poland; daughter of Henryk and Zofia (Ruszczyc) Pawelczynski. *Education:* University of Warsaw, M.A., 1950, Ph.D., 1960. *Home:* Uniwersytecka 1 m. 16, Warsaw, Poland. *Office:* Institute of Philosophy and Sociology, Polish Academy of Sciences, Nowy Street 72, Warsaw, Poland.

CAREER: Polish Academy of Sciences, Institute of Legal Studies, Warsaw, Poland, researcher, 1953-56; University of Warsaw, Institute of Sociology, Warsaw, assistant professor, 1957-60; Public Opinion Research Center, Warsaw, director, 1957-64; Polish Academy of Sciences, Institute of Philosophy and Sociology, professor of sociology, 1965—. Visiting sociologist at Institute of Demography and Public Opinion Research in France; member of Commission of Experts and planning commission of Ministry of Art and Culture; director of field study projects on the subject of leisure for Commission on Physical Culture and Tourism; scientific consultant for studies on foreign travel in cooperation with the government of the German Democratic Republic. *Member:* Polish Sociological Association. *Awards, honors:* Stanislaw Ossowski Award from Polish Sociological Association and award from *Polityka* (weekly newspaper), both 1974, both for *Wartosci a przemoc.*

WRITINGS: Przestepczosc grup nieletnich (title means "Delinquency of Juvenile Groups"), Wydawnictwo Ksiazka i Wiedza, 1964; *Dynamika przemian kulturowych na wsi* (title means "Dynamics of Cultural Changes in the Country Side"), Panstwowe Wydawnictwo Naukowe, 1966; (with Wanda Tomaszewska) *Urbanizacja Kultury w Polsce* (title means "Urbanization of Culture in Poland"), Panstwowe Wydawnictwo Naukowe, 1972; *Wartosci a przemoc: Zarys socjologicznej problematyki Oswiecimia*, Panstwowe Wydawnictwo Naukowe, 1973, translation from the Polish by Catherine S. Leach published as *Values and Violence in Auschwitz: A Sociological Analysis*, University of California Press, 1979; (with Andrzej Sicinski) *Uczestnictwo w Kulturze a jakosc zycia* (title means "Participation in Culture and Quality of Life"), Polska Akademia Nark, 1974; *Zywa historia: Pamiec i ocena wojny i okupacji* (title means "Living History: Memory and Evaluation of War and Occupation"), Komitet do Spraw Redia i Telewizja, 1977.

WORK IN PROGRESS: Time in Culture and Life Style.

SIDELIGHTS: In August 1942, when she was just twenty years old, Anna Pawelczynska was arrested by the Gestapo, tortured, and sent to the Auschwitz-Birkenau concentration camp in southern Poland. Classified as a political prisoner, Pawelczynska was a member of the underground, and had acted as courier for its press and as liason for a partisan officer in Warsaw. She also helped to set up an army hospital and coordinated aide programs for wounded soldiers in the aftermath of the Nazi blitzkrieg of September 1939. In addition to these already dangerous activities, she had attended clandestine study sessions, when all forms of higher education had been expressly forbidden by the Nazis.

Pawelczynska lived in the Birkenau women's camp for two years before she was transferred to another camp, in Flossenburg, Germany, in October 1944. She worked in a factory there, until she escaped during the evacuation of the camp in April 1945. Once in Poland, as translator Catherine S. Leach observed, Pawelczynska must have been "driven by an urgent desire to participate in the remaking of the 'good society,'" for she immediately enrolled in sociology classes at the University of Warsaw.

It was at the university that she met, and later studied under, the distinguished sociologist Stanislaw Ossowski, whose influence is evident in her work. According to Leach, it is from Ossowki that Pawelczynska learned to "combine a precise conceptual framework and expository style with rigorous inductive analysis [and] to view results from a broad historical and cultural perspective." *Values and Violence in Auschwitz* is a notable example of Pawelczynska's work as a sociologist, as well as a valuable first-hand insight into a terrifying nightmare from man's past.

A short book, just under one hundred fifty pages, *Values and Violence* examines the "structure of terror" in that infamous Nazi death camp and the psychological tools one needed in order to survive in an atmosphere that was designed not only to kill, but also to strip human beings of their humanity and will to live. Among numerous recently-published studies and personal accounts of the death camps, Pawelczynska's book is important because it is a sociological analysis without the use of cumbersome professional jargon. In addition to being understandable, her observations are valuable because she has tried to write objectively of concentration camp existence, and has deliberately withheld those gory details so often present in Holocaust literature. "I have tried," wrote Pawelczynska," to approach the subject with maximum reserve. Its 'horrors' I have purposely avoided because it is my profound conviction that to broadcast naturalistic descriptions of atrocities can be harmful to those fortunate enough not to have met with concentration-camp reality." Thus, without being subjected to passages of explicit camp atrocities, the reader can gain insight into the ways in which conditions designed only for a two-month survival period were altered by the smuggling of extra food into the barracks, and by the transmitting of outside news and messages between loved ones.

Along with Terrence Des Pres, author of *The Survivor,* Pawelczynska takes issue with Bruno Bettelheim's theory that a camp survivor unconsciously identifies with his captor and assumes a childlike role. Rather, she postulates that active and internal resistance brought about survival. Those who lived were those who worked to smuggle in extra food, and who were alert enough to get themselves assigned to an easier work force.

Pawelczynska's most important conclusion, as Leach observed, is "that a deeply internalized value system enabled many prisoners to survive biologically and morally, that is, to resist violence." The values or "moral norms of the civilized world" were reinterpreted in the camp structure so that "Love your neighbor as yourself," for example, became "Do not harm your neighbor and, if at all possible, save him." In spite of the divergence from standardized values of free and civilized societies, prisoner conduct in the camps succeeded in establishing a basic norm and new moral value: "that bond with the wronged which demands the greatest renunciation."

BIOGRAPHICAL/CRITICAL SOURCES: Anna Pawelczynska, *Values and Violence in Auschwitz,* University of California Press, 1979.

PAWLEY, Martin Edward 1938-
(Charles Noble, Rupert Spade)

PERSONAL: Born in 1938, in London, England; son of Edward Albert (a sound engineer) and Dorothy (Ruby) Pawley; married Margaret Tordiff Johnston, September, 1961 (died September 5, 1964); married Margaret Clare Wheldon (a photographer), September 12, 1971; children: Harry Tordiff, Oliver Labarte. *Education:* Attended Ecole Nationale Superieure des Beaux-Arts, 1958-59; Architectural Association, London, A.A., 1968. *Home:* 21 Bramham Gardens, London S.W.5, England. *Agent:* Patrick Seale Books Ltd., 2 Motcomb St., Belgrave Sq., London SW1X 8JU, England.

CAREER: Architects Journal, London, England, news editor, 1967-69; Government of the Republic of Chile, housing consultant, 1972-73; Cornell University, Ithaca, N.Y., visiting professor, 1973; *Ghost Dance Times* (weekly newspaper), editor, 1974-75; Rensselaer Polytechnic Institute, Troy, N.Y., visiting professor, 1975-76; Florida A & M University, Tallahassee, visiting professor, 1977-79; University of California, Los Angeles, visiting professor, 1979-80. Consultant to United Nations.

WRITINGS: Le Corbusier, Simon & Schuster, 1970; *Mies van der Rohe,* Simon & Schuster, 1970; *Architecture Versus Housing,* Praeger, 1971; *Frank Lloyd Wright: Public Buildings,* Simon & Schuster, 1971; *The Private Future,* Random House, 1974; *Garbage Housing,* Wiley, 1975; *Home Ownership,* Architectural Press, 1978; *Waste as Evolutionary Opportunity,* Sierra Books, 1981.

Under pseudonym Charles Noble: *Philip Johnson,* Simon & Schuster, 1972.

Under pseudonym Rupert Spade: *Richard Neutra,* Thames & Hudson, 1971; *Eero Saarinen,* Simon & Schuster, 1971; *Paul Rudolph,* Simon & Schuster, 1971; *Oscar Neimayer,* Simon & Schuster, 1971.

WORK IN PROGRESS: Housing as the Function of Great Historical Events, 1880-1980.

SIDELIGHTS: Pawley commented: "After five years in the United States, teaching at universities and experimenting with building from waste, I returned to England. It is the only place where I can write."

*   *   *

PEACH, Lawrence du Garde 1890-1974

PERSONAL: Born January 14, 1890, in Sheffield, England; died December 30, 1974; son of Charles (a minister) and M. (Jefferies) Peach; married Emily Marianne Leeming (a skin specialist; deceased). *Education:* Victoria University of Manchester, M.A., 1909; University of Sheffield, Ph.D.; also attended University of Goettingen.

CAREER: English teacher at school in Burnley, England; University of Exeter, Exeter, England, lecturer in English; writer until 1974. Founder of theatre in Great Hucklow, England. *Military service:* British Army, 1914-18; became captain. Home Guard, 1939-45; became major. *Awards, honors:* Member of the Order of the British Empire; D.Litt. from University of Sheffield.

WRITINGS—Plays: Sale by Auction (one-act), Baker International Play Bureau, 1926; *Ever Ready Plays,* Samuel French, 1926; *More Ever Ready Plays,* Samuel French, 1926; *Numbered Chickens: A Cockney Intrigue in One Scene,* Samuel French, 1926; *Broadcast Sketches,* Samuel French, 1927; *The Proposals of Peggy,* Samuel French, 1928; *Motoring Without Tears,* Samuel French, 1929;

Radio Plays, G. Newnes, 1931; Crooks' Christmas (one-act), [London], 1931; Meet Mrs. Beeton (one-act), Baker International Play Bureau, 1934; The Path of Glory, Baker International Play Bureau, 1934; Practical Plays for Stage and Classroom, University of London Press, first series, 1935, second series, 1936, second series reprinted, 1960; Plays for Young People, Pitman, 1937; Shells (one-act), Playwrights and Publications, 1937; Five Plays for Boys, Pitman, 1937; Scenario (one-act), Baker International Play Bureau, 1937; The Castles of England, University of London Press, 1938; Mrs. Grundy Comes to Tea (one-act), Baker International Play Bureau, 1938; Famous Men of Britain (contains five plays), Pitman, 1938; Famous Women of Britain (contains five plays), Pitman, 1938; Smuggler Jack (one-act), University of London Press, 1939; Plays of the Family Goodman, 1485-1666, Pitman, 1939; A Dramatic History of England (contains thirty plays), University of London Press, 1939.

Music Makers (contains four plays), Thomas Nelson, 1940; The Story of Sigurd (contains five plays), Pitman, 1940; Knights of the Round Table (contains five plays), Pitman, 1940; Story-Tellers of Britain (contains twelve plays first broadcast on British Broadcasting Corp.-Radio), three volumes, University of London Press, 1941; Biographical Plays, Collins, 1942; According to Plan (three-act), Samuel French, 1943; Co-operative Centenary: A Pageant of the People, Manchester Co-operative Union, 1944; The Story of David, King Over Israel [and] The Last Days of David, University of London Press, 1944; Plays for Youth Groups, Samuel French, 1945; Tomorrow: A Pageant of Youth, Thomas Nelson, 1945; A Criminal Introduction (one-act), Samuel French, 1946; The Tribulations of Wing Lu (one-act), Samuel French, 1946; An Improbable Episode (one-act), Samuel French, 1947; The Queen's Ring (one-act), Samuel French, 1947.

Mate in Three (four-act), Samuel French, 1950; Queen's Pawn (one-act), Samuel French, 1951; Roots Go Deep (one-act), Samuel French, 1951; The Spinsters of Lavender Lane (one-act), Samuel French, 1951; The Town That Would Have a Pageant (two-act), Samuel French, 1952; (with John Hay Beith) The White Sheep of the Family (three-act), Samuel French, 1953; A Horse! A Horse!, Samuel French, 1953; Collected Plays, four volumes, Countrygoer Books, 1955; Six Wives in Favour (one-act), Samuel French, 1956; A Ghost of a Chance (one-act), Samuel French, 1956; Rough Diamond (one-act), Samuel French, 1958; Jam for Mrs. Hooper (one-act), Samuel French, 1958; Landed Gentry (one-act), Samuel French, 1958; Four Queens Wait for Henry, Evans Brothers, 1959.

A Wife for the Captain (one-act), Samuel French, 1960; Welcome Home (one-act), Samuel French, 1960; Just a Princess (one-act), Samuel French, 1961; Christmas and Mrs. Hooper (one-act), Samuel French, 1961; Mrs. Hooper in the Round (one-act), Samuel French, 1961; If You Please, Ladies (one-act), Samuel French, 1963; (adapter) Vassili Gregorovich Smirnov, The Lopotkin Inheritance (two-act), Samuel French, 1963; Droit du Seigneur (one-act), Hub Publications, 1972.

Children's books; all published by Ladybird Books: King Alfred the Great, 1956; William the Conqueror, 1956; Sir Walter Raleigh, 1957; The Story of Nelson, 1957; The First Queen Elizabeth, 1958; The Story of Captain Cook, 1958; Florence Nightingale, 1959; Julius Caesar and Roman Britain, 1959.

Charles II, 1960; David Livingstone, 1960; Christopher Co-lumbus, 1961; Stone Age Man in Britain, 1961; Henry V, 1962; Marco Polo, 1962; Alexander the Great, 1963; Captain Scott, 1963; Oliver Cromwell, 1963; Robert the Bruce, 1964; Charles Dickens, 1965; Richard the Lion Heart, 1965; Cleopatra and Ancient Egypt, 1966; Warwick the Kingmaker, 1966; James I and the Gunpowder Plot, 1967; Kings and Queens of England, two volumes, 1968; Napoleon, 1968; King John and the Magna Carta, 1969.

The Story of the Theatre, 1970; Pirates, 1970; Madame Curie, 1970; Joan of Arc, 1971; Pilgrim Fathers, 1972; Michael Faraday, 1973; Henry VIII, 1973; Elizabeth Fry, 1973; Charles Darwin, 1973; Bonnie Prince Charlie, 1975; Hannibal, 1975.

Other: Unknown Devon, John Lane, 1927; A Dramatic History of England, A.D. 900-1901, University of London Press, 1939. Also author of Twenty-Five Years of Play Producing: 1927-1952 and The Company of Cutlers in Hallamshire in the County of York: 1906-1956. Contributor to magazines, including Punch, and newspapers.*

*   *   *

PEERCE, Jan 1904-

PERSONAL: Birth-given name, Jacob Pincus Perelmuth; born June 3, 1904, in New York, N.Y.; son of Louis and Anita Peerce; married Alice Kaye, May 10, 1929; children: Larry, Joyce, Susan. Education: Attended medical school for two years. Studied voice with Emilio Roxas and Giuseppe Boghetti. Home: 370 Beechmoal Ave., New Rochelle, N.Y. Office: c/o Gene Mack, 527 Madison Ave., New York, N.Y. 10022.

CAREER: Professional singer (tenor). Made debut as tenor with NBC Orchestra under Arturo Toscanini, February 6, 1938; made operatic debut in "Rigoletto" in Baltimore, Md., May 26, 1938; made debut at Metropolitan Opera in "La Traviata," November 29, 1941; made Broadway debut in "Fiddler on the Roof," 1971. Has held concerts in the United States, Canada, Central America, South America, Africa, Australia, Europe, and Israel. Guest on television talk shows with Johnny Carson, Merv Griffin, and Mike Douglas.

WRITINGS: (With Alan Levy) The Bluebird of Happiness: The Memoirs of Jan Peerce, Harper, 1976.

*   *   *

PEFFER, Randall S(cott) 1948-

PERSONAL: Born June 16, 1948, in Natrona Heights, Pa.; son of Chester Robie and Marian (Smith) Peffer; married Marilyn Howell (a teacher), May 3, 1970; children: Noah. Education: Washington and Jefferson College, B.A., 1971; University of New Hampshire, M.A., 1973. Politics: Independent. Home: America House, Phillips Academy, Andover, Mass. 01810. Agent: Theron Raines, Raines & Raines, 475 Fifth Ave., New York, N.Y. 10017. Office: Department of English, Phillips Academy, Andover, Mass. 01810.

CAREER: Teacher of English at private school in Mercersburg, Pa., 1973-78, editor of publications, 1975-78; Phillips Academy, Andover, Mass., instructor in English, 1978—. Awards, honors: Watermen was named Critic's Choice by Baltimore Sun, 1979.

WRITINGS: Watermen (nonfiction), Johns Hopkins Press, 1979. Contributor of nearly fifty articles to magazines, including Reader's Digest, National Geographic, Yankee, Sail, and Finance. Associate editor of WoodenBoat, 1974-78.

WORK IN PROGRESS: The authorized biography of clown Emmett Kelly, publication expected in 1982.

SIDELIGHTS: Peffer commented: "I am particularly interested in writing about vanishing breeds and fringe lifestyles. I find these subjects rich in fresh tall tales and vibrant, hard-times humor. For me these tales and this type of humor form the essence of the American spirit: pure American optimism still exists. I'll write about that wherever I can find it."

* * *

PERLS, Frederick S(alomon)   1893-1970
(Fritz Perls)

PERSONAL: Born in 1893; died of heart failure, March 14, 1970, in Chicago, Ill.; son of Nathan and Amalie (Rund) Perls; married Laura Posner (a psychotherapist), August 23, 1930; children: Renate, Stephen. *Education:* Educated in Berlin and Frankfurt, Germany and Vienna, Austria; attended Berlin Institute of Psychoanalysis. *Home:* Lake Cowichan, Vancouver Island, British Columbia, Canada.

CAREER: Known professionally as Fritz Perls; private practice in Berlin, Germany, Johannesburg, South Africa, and New York, N.Y.; founder of New York Institute for Gestalt Therapy, 1952; Esalen Institute, Big Sur, Calif., resident psychiatrist, 1964-68; founder of training community for therapists at Lake Cowichan, Vancouver Island, British Columbia, Canada, 1968-69.

WRITINGS: Ego, Hunger, and Aggression: A Revision of Freud's Theory and Method, Knox (Durban, South Africa), 1945, revised edition published as *Ego, Hunger, and Aggression: The Beginning of Gestalt Theory,* Vintage, 1969; (with Ralph F. Hefferline and Paul Goodman) *Gestalt Therapy: Excitement and Growth in the Human Personality,* Julian Press, 1951, reprinted, Crown, 1977; John O. Stevens, editor, *Gestalt Therapy Verbatim,* Real People Press, 1969; *In and Out the Garbage Pail,* Real People Press, 1969; *The Gestalt Approach and Eye Witness to Therapy,* Science & Behavior Books, 1973; John O. Stevens, editor, *Gestalt Is: A Collection of Articles About Gestalt Therapy and Living,* Real People Press, 1975; (with Patricia Baumgardner) *Gifts From Lake Cowichan* [and] *Legacy From Fritz* (the former by Baumgardner, the latter by Fritz Perls), Science & Behavior Books, 1975. Author of recordings, including "Gestalt Therapy and How It Works," Big Sur, 1966, and "Dream Theory and Demonstration," Big Sur, 1968. Also author of films.

SIDELIGHTS: Perls is founder of the Gestalt school of psychotherapy with wife Laura, Paul Goodman, and others. Gestalt theory maintains that the whole of a personality is more than the sum of its parts; that the parts of the whole are not combined to create the whole, but, rather, are derived from the whole and obtain their character from it. It integrates psychoanalytical, existential, and phenomenological approaches. Gestalt psychotherapy is concerned mainly with the present and is "designed to make people less alienated and more alive by integrating neurotic symptoms into the total personality.... As a therapy, it stands in contrast to the older Freudian reductive process of tracing symptoms back to their origins," observed Stefanie Halpern.

Perls also experimented with "dream workshops" in which group members would identify with dream elements as parts of the total self.

BIOGRAPHICAL/CRITICAL SOURCES: Library Journal, January 15, 1970; Martin Shepard, *Fritz,* Saturday Review Press, 1975.

OBITUARIES: New York Times, March 17, 1970; *Time,* March 30, 1970; *AB Bookman's Weekly,* April 6, 1970.

[Sketch verified by wife, Laura Perls]

* * *

PERLS, Fritz
See PERLS, Frederick S(alomon)

* * *

PERRIN, Ursula   1935-

PERSONAL: Born June 15, 1935, in Berlin, Germany; came to the United States in 1938, naturalized citizen, 1944; daughter of Max (a physician) and Gretchen (Kemp) Gutmann; married Mark Perrin (a physician), August 25, 1956; children: Thomas, Christopher, Nicholas. *Education:* Smith College, B.A., 1956. *Politics:* Democrat. *Religion:* Protestant. *Home and office:* 175 Springfield Ave., Summit, N.J. 07901. *Agent:* Russell & Volkening, Inc., 551 Fifth Ave., New York, N.Y. 10017.

CAREER: Writer. *Member:* Authors Guild, Authors League of America.

WRITINGS: Ghosts (novel), Knopf, 1967; *Heart Failures* (novel), Doubleday, 1978; *Unheard Music* (novel), Dial, 1981.

WORK IN PROGRESS: A novel tentatively titled *The Last Happy Woman,* publication by Dial expected in 1981.

* * *

PERRY, Anne   1938-

PERSONAL: Born October 28, 1938, in London, England; daughter of Walter A. B. (an industrial engineer) and H. Marion (a teacher of the mentally handicapped; maiden name, Reavley) Perry. *Education:* Educated privately. *Politics:* Liberal. *Religion:* Church of Jesus Christ of Latter-day Saints (Mormons). *Home:* Fox Cottages, Darsham, Saxmundham, Suffolk IP17 3QE, England. *Agent:* Janet Freer, MBA Literary Agents Ltd., 118 Tottenham Court Rd., London, England.

CAREER: Airline stewardess in Northumberland, England, 1962-64; assistant buyer for department store in Newcastle, England, 1964-66; property underwriter for Muldoon & Adams in Los Angeles, Calif.; writer, 1972—. Volunteer driver for hospital automobile service. *Member:* Mystery Writers of America.

WRITINGS—Mystery novels: The Cater Street Hangman, St. Martin's, 1979; *Callander Square,* St. Martin's, 1980.

WORK IN PROGRESS: A three-generation saga of an American pioneer family, 1830-70, completion of Volume I expected in 1981, Volume II, 1982; a mystery, for St. Martin's.

SIDELIGHTS: "My major interest is in conflict of ethics," Anne Perry told *CA,* "especially involving honesty with oneself, which is why the Victorian scene, with its layers of hypocrisy, appeals to me. My other favorite periods are the Spanish Inquisition and the French Revolution, because of the question of free agency and the use of force to make others believe as we do, in what we believe to be their best interest.

"I am not sure what motivates me; a fascination with people, motives, the belief that the written word is the means by which we can give something of ourselves, hopefully the best of our pleasures and beliefs, to everyone else who can read, in any country, and in the present or the future. My own joy in reading, and the wealth gained, has been immeasurable. The world never stops growing, becoming more complex and more marvellous to one who can read.

"My working habits? I am compulsive. I usually work at least some part of every day, except Sunday, frequently all day, if I have an idea burning a hole in my head.

"Other writers who have influenced me are a little old fashioned, I'm afraid. I have always loved G. K. Chesterton, his prose and poetry. *The Man Who Was Thursday* is so far my favorite single book, for its lyricism, humor, and message that we all face the same battles, but to overcome when believing yourself alone, simply because you care so much, is the ultimate victory. I also admire Oscar Wilde for wit, style, observation, and in short stories especially, his compassion. Dostoevsky, too, for his brilliant understanding and, again, compassion, and Josephine Tey for her style."

* * *

PERRY, Michael (Charles) 1933-

PERSONAL: Born June 5, 1933, in Ashby-de-la-Zouch, England; son of Charlie and Kathleen (May) Perry; married Margaret Adshead, July 13, 1963; children: Andrew, David, Gillian. *Education:* Trinity College, Cambridge, B.A. (in natural science), 1955, B.A. (in theology), 1957; Westcott House, Cambridge, M.A., 1959. *Home:* 7 The College, Durham DH1 3EQ, England.

CAREER: Ordained priest of Church of England, 1959; assistant curate of Church of England in Berkswich Stafford, England, 1958-60; Ripon Hall, Oxford, England, chaplain at Theological College, 1961-63; Society for Promoting Christian Knowledge, London, England, chief assistant for home publishing, 1963-70; Durham Cathedral, Durham, England, archdeacon of Durham and canon residentiary of cathedral, 1970—. Selwyn Lecturer at St. John's College, Auckland, New Zealand, 1976; Marshall Memorial Lecturer at Trinity College, Melbourne, 1976; Beard Memorial Lecturer at College of Psychic Studies, London, 1977; lecturer in the United States, New Zealand, Singapore, and on British television programs. Secretary to Archbishop's Commission on Christian Doctrine, 1967-70. *Member:* Studiorum Novi Testamenti Societas, Society for the Study of Theology, United Society for the Propagation of the Gospel (member of council, 1975—), Society for Psychical Research, Churches' Fellowship for Psychical and Spiritual Study.

WRITINGS: The Easter Enigma, Faber, 1959; *The Pattern of Mattins and Evensong,* Hodder & Stoughton, 1961; *Meet the Prayer Book,* Church Information Office, 1963; (with D. W. Cleverley Ford, D. N. Sargent, and Reginald Cant) *The Churchman's Companion,* Hodder & Stoughton, 1964, published in the United States as *Confirmation Crisis,* Seabury Press, 1967; (editor) *Crisis for Confirmation,* S.C.M. Press, 1967; (with Dewi Morgan) *Declaring the Faith: The Printed Word,* S.P.C.K., 1969.

Sharing in One Bread, S.P.C.K., 1973, revised edition, 1980; *The Resurrection of Man,* Mowbray, 1975; *The Paradox of Worship,* S.P.C.K., 1977; *A Handbook of Parish Worship,* Mowbray, 1977; (with Phyllis Carter) *A Handbook of Parish Finance,* Mowbray, 1981.

Editor of "Mowbray's Library of Theology," a series, Mowbray. Contributor of articles and reviews to theology and psychic studies journals, including *Theology, Spiritual Frontiers,* and *Parapsychological Review.* Editor of *Church Quarterly,* 1968-71; co-editor of *Christian Parapsychologist,*

1977-78, editor, 1978—; assistant editor of report of Lambeth Conference of Anglican Bishops, 1968, senior editor, 1978.

SIDELIGHTS: Perry commented: "I am a campaigner for the ordination of women in the Church of England, and write pamphlets and articles on this theme. I have also for many years been interested in psychical research and its relation to the Christian faith. I joined the Society for Psychical Research at the age of seventeen-and-a-half and have been a member for the best part of thirty years."

* * *

PERSKY, Stan 1941-

PERSONAL: Born January 19, 1941, in Chicago, Ill.; son of Morris (a grocer) and Ida (Malis) Persky. *Education:* University of British Columbia, B.A., 1969, M.A., 1972. *Politics:* New Democrat. *Home:* 2504 York, Vancouver, British Columbia, Canada V6K 1E3. *Office:* Northwest College, P.O. Box 726, Terrace, British Columbia, Canada V8G 4C2.

CAREER: Mental Patients Association, Vancouver, British Columbia, sociologist, 1973-75; Northwest College, Terrace, British Columbia, instructor, 1975—. *Military service:* U.S. Navy, 1958-61. *Member:* Writers Union of Canada.

WRITINGS: Wrestling the Angel, Talonbooks, 1977; *Son of Socred,* New Star, 1979; *The House That Jack Built,* New Star, 1980. Contributor to magazines and newspapers, including *Canadian Dimension* and *Columbian.*

AVOCATIONAL INTERESTS: Travel (China and Nicaragua).

* * *

PESNOT, Patrick 1943-

PERSONAL: Born December 30, 1943, in Versailles, France. *Education:* Attended Sorbonne, University of Paris, and a school of journalism in Paris. *Home:* Rue du Four a Chaux, Bonville-Aumeru, France 28730.

CAREER: Writer. Journalist on French radio and television, 1965—.

WRITINGS: (With Philippe Alfonsi) *Satan qui vous aime beaucoup,* Laffont, 1970, translation published as *Satan's Needle: A True Story of Drug Addiction and Cure,* Morrow, 1972; (with Alfonsi) *L'Eglise contestee,* Calmann-Levy, 1971; (with Alfonsi) *L'Oeil du Sorcier,* Laffont, 1973; (with Alfonsi) *Vivre a gauche,* Albin Michel, 1975; *Une Semaine en enfance,* Laffont, 1978; *Le Valeur de memoire,* Mercure de haute, 1979. Also author of several plays for television.

WORK IN PROGRESS: Two reports; two novels.

* * *

PETERS, Edward Murray 1936-

PERSONAL: Born May 21, 1936, in New Haven, Conn.; son of Edward Murray and Marjorie (Corcoran) Peters; married Patricia Ann Knapp, July 8, 1961; children: Nicole, Moira, Edward. *Education:* Yale University, B.A., 1963, M.A., 1965, Ph.D., 1967. *Home:* 4225 Regent Sq., Philadelphia, Pa. 19104. *Office:* Department of History, University of Pennsylvania, Philadelphia, Pa. 19104.

CAREER: Quinnipiac College, Hamden, Conn., instructor in English and history, 1964-67; University of California, San Diego, La Jolla, assistant professor of history, 1967-68; University of Pennsylvania, Philadelphia, Henry Charles Lea Assistant Professor of Medieval History, 1968-70, Henry Charles Lea Associate Professor of Medieval History, 1970—, curator of Henry Charles Lea Library, 1968—. High school French and Spanish instructor, summer, 1964; visiting professor of history, Moore College of Art, 1970-71. *Military service:* U.S. Army, 1956-59. *Member:* American Historical Association, Mediaeval Academy of America, Royal Historical Society (fellow). *Awards, honors:* Woodrow Wilson fellow, 1963-64; Foote fellowship, 1963-64; Woodrow Wilson dissertation fellowship, 1966-67; honorary Sterling fellowship, 1966-67; John Addison Porter dissertation prize, 1967; University of Pennsylvania faculty research grants, 1969 and 1970; American Philosophical Society research grant, 1972; honorary M.A. from University of Pennsylvania, 1973.

WRITINGS: The Shadow King, Yale University Press, 1970; *The First Crusade,* University of Pennsylvania Press, 1971; *Christian Society and the Crusade, 1198-1229,* University of Pennsylvania Press, 1971; (editor with Alan C. Kors) *Witchcraft in Europe, 1100-1750: A Documentary History,* University of Pennsylvania Press, 1972; *Monks, Bishops, and Pagans,* University of Pennsylvania Press, 1975; *Europe: The World of the Middle Ages,* Prentice-Hall, 1977; *The Magician, the Witch, and the Law,* University of Pennsylvania Press, 1978. Author of "The World Around the Revolution," a television series, 1977.

WORK IN PROGRESS: Research on medieval cultural history.

* * *

PFEIFFER, Carl Curt 1908-

PERSONAL: Born May 19, 1908, in Peoria, Ill.; son of Curt Richard and Minnie D. (Meiers) Pfeiffer; married Lillian H. Twenhofel, June 13, 1930; children: Helen Nancy, Edward Carl. *Education:* University of Wisconsin—Madison, A.B., 1931, A.M., 1933, Ph.D., 1935; University of Chicago, M.D., 1937. *Home address:* R.D. 5, 169 Cherry Hill Rd., Princeton, N.J. 08530. *Office:* Brain Bio Center, 1225 State Rd., Princeton, N.J.

CAREER: University of Wisconsin—Madison, assistant instructor in pharmacology, 1930-35; University of Chicago, Chicago, Ill., instructor in pharmacology, 1936-40; Wayne State University, Detroit, Mich., assistant professor of pharmacology, 1940-41; Parke-Davis & Co., Detroit, chief of pharmacology, 1941-42; University of Illinois, Medical School, Chicago, head of pharmacology, 1945-54; Emory University, Atlanta, Ga., professor of pharmacology and head of department, 1954-57; director of Division of Basic Health Sciences, 1956-60; New Jersey Neuropsychiatric Institute, Princeton, head of psychopharmacology section in Bureau of Research, 1960-74; Brain Bio Center, Princeton, director, 1974—. Intern at Wisconsin General Hospital, 1937-38. *Military service:* U.S. Naval Reserve, active duty in charge of pharmacology and toxicology at Naval Medical Research Institute, Bethesda, Md., 1943-45; became lieutenant.

MEMBER: American Medical Association, Brain Research Foundation (member of board of trustees), American Society of Pharmacological and Experimental Therapeutics (president, 1961-62), American Chemical Society, Schizophrenic Association (member of scientific advisory board), New York Academy of Sciences. *Awards, honors:* Certificate of merit from University of Chicago, 1952; Crawford Long Award from Emory University, 1967; award from Academy of Orthomolecular Psychiatry, 1971; Dixie Annette Award from Huxley Institute, 1979.

WRITINGS: (With others) *The Schizophrenias: Yours and Mine,* Pyramid Publications, 1970; *Mental and Elemental*

Nutrients: A Physician's Guide to Nutrition and Health Care, Keats Publishing, 1976; *Zinc and Other Micro-Nutrients,* Keats Publishing, 1978; (with Jane Banks) *Dr. Pfeiffer's Nutritional Guide to Total Health,* Simon & Schuster, 1980. Co-editor of *International Review of Neurobiology,* 1955-76.

* * *

PFEIFFER, John E(dward) 1914-

PERSONAL: Born September 27, 1914, in New York, N.Y.; son of Edward Heymann and Jeannette (Gross) Pfeiffer; married Naomi Ranson (a writer and artist), September 9, 1939; children: Anthony John. *Education:* Yale University, B.A., 1936. *Politics:* Democrat. *Home:* 170 North Main St., New Hope, Pa. 18938. *Office:* 28 West Bridge St., New Hope, Pa. 18938.

CAREER: Newsweek, New York City, science and medicine editor, 1936-42; staff member in weapons research for Naval Ordnance Laboratory, Washington, D.C., 1942-44, and for Army Chief of Ordnance, Philadelphia, Pa., 1944-46; Columbia Broadcasting System, New York City, science director, 1946-48; *Scientific American,* New York City, member of editorial board, 1948-50; free-lance writer, 1950—. Adjunct professor at Rutgers University, 1968—. Member of board of trustees of Solebury School. Consultant to National Science Foundation and Thames Television.

MEMBER: American Association for the Advancement of Science, American Anthropological Association, Society of American Archaeologists, National Association of Science Writers (past president), Prehistoric Society (England). *Awards, honors:* John Simon Guggenheim awards, 1952 and 1954; Fulbright fellow, 1958; writing award from CBS-TV, 1959, for research in astronomy, brain structure, and human evolution; Westinghouse Science Writing Award from American Association for the Advancement of Science, 1961, for an article on DNA; grants from Wenner-Gren Foundation for Anthropological Research, 1961, 1979, and Carnegie Corp., 1964, 1969; Henry Frank Guggenheim awards, 1979 and 1980.

WRITINGS: Science in Your Life, Macmillan, 1939; *The Human Brain,* Harper, 1955; *The Changing Universe: The Story of the New Astronomy,* Random House, 1956; *From Galaxies to Man: A Story of the Beginnings of Things,* Random House, 1959; *The Thinking Machine,* Lippincott, 1962; *The Search for Early Man* (juvenile), American Heritage Publishing, 1963; *The Cell,* Time, Inc., 1964; *The Emergence of Man,* Harper, 1969, 3rd edition, 1978; *The Emergence of Society: A Pre-History of the Establishment,* McGraw, 1977; (with John Friedl) *Anthropology: The Study of People,* with instructor's manual, Harper's College Press, 1977. Contributor of more than two hundred articles to magazines, including *Smithsonian, Natural History,* and *Harper's.* Contributor of book reviews to newspapers, including *New York Times.*

WORK IN PROGRESS: The Cultural Explosion, a study of the origins of art and complex societies, publication by Harper expected in 1982.

SIDELIGHTS: Pfeiffer told *CA:* "My specialty is writing on technical subjects without the jargon. As a result, for example, *The Emergence of Man* has had success both as a trade book and a college text. My writing since then has been increasingly a matter of bringing together discoveries in different social science research fields that bear on prehistory and the future of human evolution. The release of atomic energy marked a high point in the physical sciences. The discovery of DNA, the material out of which genes are made, accelerated the advance of the biological sciences. And today we are on the verge of equally significant developments in the social science, and high time too—since our biggest problems are social problems."

AVOCATIONAL INTERESTS: Playing tennis, rowing on the Delaware River.

* * *

PHELAN, Nancy 1913-

PERSONAL: Born August 2, 1913, in Sydney, Australia; daughter of William John (a solicitor) and Florence Amelia (Mack) Creagh; married Raymond Sydney Phelan, June 21, 1939; children: Vanessa. *Education:* Attended University of Sydney and Sydney Conservatorium of Music. *Home:* 297 Macleay St., Potts Point, Sydney, New South Wales 2011, Australia. *Agent:* Jo Stewart, 201 East 66th St., Suite 18-N, New York, N.Y. 10021.

CAREER: Common Ground Ltd. (educational graphics company), London, England, director of illustration research, 1945-46; South Pacific Commission, assistant organizer for island literature, 1950-52, visual aids officer, 1953-55; Cook Island Administration, Rarotonga, visual aids adviser, 1956; writer, 1956—. Broadcaster for British Broadcasting Corp. and Australian Broadcasting Corp. *Member:* Australian Society of Authors. *Awards, honors:* Australia Council senior fellowships, 1973-76, 1976-77.

WRITINGS: Atoll Holiday (travel book), Angus & Robertson, 1958; *The River and the Brook* (novel), Macmillan, 1962; *Welcome the Wayfarer: A Traveller in Modern Turkey,* St. Martin's, 1964; *Serpents in Paradise* (novel), Macmillan, 1967; *Pillow of Grass* (travel book), British Book Co., 1969; *A Kingdom by the Sea* (autobiography), Angus & Robertson, 1969; *Some Came Early, Some Came Late* (history of Australia), Macmillan, 1970; *The Chilean Way* (travel book), Macmillan, 1973; *A Beginner's Guide to Yoga,* Pelham, 1973. Also author of *Morocco Is a Lion,* a travel book, 1980.

With Michael Volin: *Yoga for Women,* Harper, 1963; *Yoga for Backache,* Pelham, 1964; *Yoga Over Forty,* Harper, 1965; *Yoga Breathing,* Pelham, 1966; *Yoga for Beauty,* Pelham, 1966; *Yoga and Sex,* Harper, 1967; *Growing Up With Yoga,* Harper, 1968. Also co-author of *The Spirit and Practice of Yoga,* Doubleday.

With Nina Nicolaieff: *The Art of Russian Cooking,* Doubleday, 1969; *Cooking With Nina: A Book of Russian Food,* Macmillan, 1971.

Work represented in anthologies, including *Coast to Coast,* Angus & Robertson, and *Summer's Tales,* Macmillan. Contributor of articles and reviews to literary magazines and newspapers.

WORK IN PROGRESS: An autobiography; short stories.

SIDELIGHTS: Much of Nancy Phelan's life has been spent outside her native Australia. She worked in the islands of the South Pacific for six years and made several visits to Turkey, the Soviet Union, India, the United States, and Canada. Her extensive travel in Europe includes an overland trip from London to Katmandu. Shorter trips have taken her to Japan, Morocco, and Israel and, in 1970, she traveled by bus from Tierra del Fuego to New York City.

* * *

PHILLIPS, James Emerson, Jr. 1912-1979

PERSONAL: Born November 11, 1912, in Los Angeles, Calif.; died July 24, 1979; son of James Emerson and Lucy (Batman) Phillips; married Geneva A. Ficker, June 6, 1955. *Education:* University of California, Los Angeles, A.B., 1934, M.A., 1936; Columbia University, Ph.D., 1940.

CAREER: University of California, Los Angeles, instructor, 1939-42, assistant professor, 1946-49, associate professor, 1949-55, professor of English, 1955-79, head of department, 1955-60, dean of Graduate Division, 1974-79. Church organist, 1933-36. *Military service:* U.S. Army, 1942-46. *Awards, honors:* Guggenheim fellowship, 1945; Fulbright scholarship, 1954-55.

WRITINGS: The State in Shakespeare's Greek and Roman Plays, 1940, reprinted, Octagon, 1971; *Images of a Queen: Mary Stuart in Sixteenth-Century Literature,* University of California Press, 1964; *Twentieth-Century Interpretations of Coriolanus,* Prentice-Hall, 1970. Contributor of articles and reviews to academic journals.

* * *

PHILLIPS, Jayne Anne 1952-

PERSONAL: Born July 19, 1952, in Buckhannon, W.Va.; daughter of Russell and Martha Jane (Thornhill) Phillips. *Education:* West Virginia University, B.A., 1974; University of Iowa, M.A., 1978. *Residence:* Cambridge, Mass. *Agent:* Lynn Nesbit, International Creative Management, 40 West 57th St., New York, N.Y. 10019.

CAREER: Writer. *Awards, honors:* Pushcart Prize, 1977, for *Sweethearts,* and 1979, for short stories "Home" and "Lechery"; National Endowment for the Arts fellowship, 1978; St. Lawrence Award for Fiction, 1979, for *Counting;* Sue Kaufman Award for First Fiction from American Academy and Institute of Arts and Letters, 1980, for *Black Tickets;* Bunting Institute fellowship from Radcliffe College, for body of work.

WRITINGS—Short Stories: *Sweethearts,* Truck Press, 1976; *Counting,* Vehicle Editions, 1978; *Black Tickets,* Delacorte, 1979. Contributor of short stories to periodicals, including *Fiction, Redbook, Iowa Review, Fiction International,* and *North American Review.*

WORK IN PROGRESS: A novel.

SIDELIGHTS: "Jayne Anne Phillips is a wonderful young writer," John Irving wrote in the *New York Times Book Review,* "concerned with every sentence and seemingly always operating out of instincts that are visceral and true—perceived and observed originally, not imitated or fashionably learned."

Many of the stories in *Black Tickets* are about love. They are also "inhabited by dope freaks, convicts, pimps, whores, the alienated young, separation, desperate sexual journeys, the lonely, dark side of life," Lowell B. Komie explained in the *Chicago Tribune.* Garrett Epps of the *Washington Post Book World* felt, contrary to the impressions of other critics, that "Phillips' version of this nightmare world is flat, unconvincing and even cliched." He favored the stories that are "fairly conventional views of middle-class life, of young women struggling to understand their parents and their own lives."

Sixteen of the twenty-seven stories in *Black Tickets* are extremely short. Most reviewers preferred Phillips's longer, more complex stories. For example, *Newsweek*'s Peter S. Prescott commented: "The shorter tales are, I think, on the whole less impressive than the longer; too often they seem no more than showcases for their author's surprising imagination and for her experiments in overwrought prose. No matter. One of Phillips's purposes in this book is to endow the inarticulate with a convincing eloquence and in this she often succeeds.''

Irving agreed with this assessment. He found Phillips "at her best when she tells the biggest story she can imagine, and *Black Tickets* tells at least a dozen big ones. When her characters and their stories matter most to us, and to Miss Phillips, she stops writing every sentence with quite such self-conscious verve; she trusts in her own good gift for words and doesn't permit her language to swamp the clarity of the tale she's telling; she doesn't obscure her characters with virtuoso displays of 'voice' and other exercises of the craft.''

Phillips, according to *Newsweek*'s James N. Baker, regards her writing "as almost a metaphysical process.'' She told him: "It's a privilege to have a passion. Real writers serve their material. They allow it to pass through them and have the opportunity to move beyond the daily limitations of being inside themselves. It's like being led by a whisper.''

Phillips has been influenced by Flannery O'Connor, Katherine Anne Porter, Eudora Welty, William Faulkner, Sherwood Anderson, Gabriel Garcia Marquez, and William Burroughs.

BIOGRAPHICAL/CRITICAL SOURCES: New York Times Book Review, September 30, 1979; *Chicago Tribune,* September 30, 1979; *Newsweek,* October 22, 1979; *Washington Post Book World,* December 21, 1979.

* * *

PIAGET, Jean 1896-1980

OBITUARY NOTICE—See index for *CA* sketch: Born August 9, 1896, in Neuchatel, Switzerland; died September, 1980, in Geneva, Switzerland. Psychologist, educator, and author. Piaget was one of the first psychologists to explore the development of intelligence in children. Searching for an "embryology of intelligence,'' he worked with and observed hundreds of children in his more than forty years at the University of Geneva. Piaget's revolutionary theory on the intelligence of children proposes that a child's mind is neither a blank page to be filled with information nor a smaller version of the adult mind; rather it is active from birth and progresses through a number of developmental stages until the approximate age of fifteen, when logical thinking is finally mastered. Piaget wrote numerous books advancing this and his other theories, including *The Language and Thought of the Child, The Origins of Intelligence in Children,* and *The Psychology of the Child.* Obituaries and other sources: *Time,* September 29, 1980; *Newsweek,* September 29, 1980.

* * *

PIECHOCKI, Joachim von Lang
See von LANG-PIECHOCKI, Joachim

* * *

PILLING, Christopher Robert 1936-

PERSONAL: Born April 20, 1936, in Birmingham, Warwickshire, England; married wife, Sylvia, 1960; children: one son, two daughters. *Education:* Attended Institute of French Studies, La Rochelle, France, 1955; University of Leeds, B.A. (with honors), 1957; University of Nottingham, certificate in education, 1959.

CAREER: Ecole Normale, Moulins, France, assistant in English, 1957-58; teacher of French at grammar schools in Wirral, England, 1959-61, in Birmingham, England, 1961-62, and in Pontefract, England, 1962-73; Knottingley High School, England, teacher and head of department of modern

languages, 1973—. *Member:* Whitwood and District Arts Association (member of committee). *Awards, honors:* New poets award from Arts Council, 1970, and grant, 1971.

WRITINGS—Poetry: *Snakes and Girls,* University of Leeds School of English Press, 1970; *Fifteen Poems,* University of Leeds School of English Press, 1970; *In All the Spaces on All the Lines,* edited by Harry Chambers, Phoenix Pamphlet Press, 1971; *Wren and Owl,* University of Leeds School of English Press, 1971; *Andree's Bloom and the Anemones,* Sceptre Press, 1973.*

* * *

PINKHAM, Mary Ellen

PERSONAL: Daughter of Pearl Higginbotham; married Sherman Pinkham; children: one son. *Office:* Mary Ellen Enterprises, Box 444, Minneapolis, Minn. 55440.

CAREER: Owner of Mary Ellen Enterprises, Minneapolis, Minn. Guest on television talk shows.

WRITINGS: (With mother, Pearl Higginbotham) *Mary Ellen's Best of Helpful Hints,* privately printed, 1976, Warner Books, 1979; *Mary Ellen's Best of Helpful Kitchen Hints,* Warner Books, 1980. Author of column in *Family Circle.*

SIDELIGHTS: Mary Ellen Pinkham first suggested printing a collection of helpful household hints as a fund raiser for a local charity, but when they were unable to finance the project she delved into it on her own. Working with her mother, Pearl Higginbotham, Pinkham compiled hundreds of tips on how to run and clean a house using items already on hand instead of commercial cleaning products. "According to *Mary Ellen's Hints,*'' related Susan Dworkin, "you clean copper with catsup; get red wine out with white wine; drive a nail into your potato to make it cook faster; put your leftover birth-control pills (should you still have any in the house) in your violets to make them grow stronger; get white water stains off furniture with toothpaste; clean windows with ammonia, vinegar, cornstarch, and water.''

Pinkham printed fifty thousand copies of *Mary Ellen's Best of Helpful Hints* and sent samples to bookstores and gift shops throughout the country. Her success was phenomenal; she sold nearly one million copies of the original edition before Warner Books took over publication.

As the popularity of the book grew, Pinkham formed her own company, Mary Ellen Enterprises, so christened because Mary Ellen learned from her mother's business experience that you have to "promote your own name.'' Two of the company's projects currently include a wall calendar and a "Hint-a-Day'' desk calendar, both for 1981.

BIOGRAPHICAL/CRITICAL SOURCES: Ms., October, 1979; *Publishers Weekly,* April 18, 1980.*

* * *

PITT-RIVERS, Julian Alfred 1919-

PERSONAL: Born March 16, 1919, in London, England; son of George Henry Lane-Fox and Rachel (an actress under stage name Mary Hinton; maiden name, Forster) Pitt-Rivers; married Francoise Geoffroy (a magazine editor), September 11, 1971. *Education:* Attended University of Grenoble, 1937, and Ecole Libre des Sciences Politiques, 1938-39; Oxford University, license, 1948, M.A., 1949, D.Phil., 1953. *Politics:* "Agnostic.'' *Religion:* "Believer.'' *Home:* 3 rue de l'Universite, 75007 Paris, France. *Agent:* Stephanie Townsend, Campbell, Thomson & McLaughlin Ltd., 31 Newington Green, London N16 9PU, England. *Of-*

fice: Ecole Pratique des Hautes Etudes, 45-47 rue des Ecoles, Paris 5e, France.

CAREER: Teacher and riding master to King Faisal II in Baghdad, Iraq, 1945-47; University of California, Berkeley, visiting assistant professor of anthropology, 1956-57; University of Chicago, Chicago, Ill., visiting professor of anthropology, 1957-64; Ecole Pratique des Hautes Etudes, Paris, France, visiting professor of anthropology and director of studies, 1964-71; University of London, London School of Economics and Political Science, London, England, Malinowski and Raymond Firth Professor of Anthropology, 1972-77, head of department, 1973-76; University of Provence, University of Aix-Marseille I, Marseille, France, visiting professor of sociology and ethnology, 1977-78; University of Paris X, Nanterre, France, visiting professor of ethnology, 1978-79; Ecole Pratique des Hautes Etudes, professor of religious science, 1980—. Visiting professor at University of Chicago, 1964-69. *Military service:* British Army, Cavalry, 1940-45; served in North Africa and Europe; became second lieutenant.

WRITINGS: The People of the Sierra, Criterion, 1954, 2nd edition, University of Chicago Press, 1971; *The History of the Royal Dragoons,* Clowes, 1955; (editor and author of introduction) *Mediterranean Countrymen: Essays in the Social Anthropology of the Mediterranean,* Mouton, 1963; (editor with Norman A. McQuown) *Estudios anthropologicos sobre Chiapas de la Universidad de Chicago,* Instituto Nacional Indigenista, 1969; (with McQuown) *Ensayos de antropologia en la Zona Central de Chiapas,* Instituto National Indigenista, 1970; *Tres ensayos de antropologia estructural,* Editorial Anagrama, 1973; (editor and contributor) *Mexico and Central America,* Danbury Press, 1973; *The Fate of Shechem; or, the Politics of Sex: Essays in the Anthropology of the Mediterranean,* Cambridge University Press, 1977.

Contributor: J. G. Peristiany, editor, *Honor and Shame: The Values of Mediterranean Society,* University of Chicago Press, 1966; John Hope Franklin, editor, *Color and Race,* Houghton, 1968; Peristiany, editor, *Contributions to Mediterranean Sociology,* Mouton, 1968; Mary Douglas, editor, *Witchcraft: Confessions and Accusations,* Tavistock Publications, 1970; Jean Pouillon and Pierre Maranda, editors, *Echanges et Communications: Melanges offerts a Claude Levi-Strauss,* Mouton, 1970; T. O. Beidelman, editor, *The Translation of Culture: Essays to E. E. Evans-Pritchard,* Tavistock Publications, 1971; John Rankine Goody, editor, *The Character of Kinship,* Cambridge University Press, 1973; (author of preface) J. B. Aceves and W. A. Douglass, editors, *The Changing Faces of Rural Spain,* Schenkman, 1976; Peristiany, editor, *Mediterranean Family Structures,* Cambridge University Press, 1976; G. Condominas and S. Dreyfus-Gamelon, editors, *Situation actuelle de l'anthropologie en France,* Editions du CNRS, 1979; *Actes du Colloque: Vetement et Societe,* Musee de l'Homme, 1979; H. Mendras, editor, *La Sagess et le desorde,* Gallimard, 1980. Also contributor to *Homenaje a Julio Caro Baroja,* 1979.

Contributor to *Encyclopaedia Britannica, International Encyclopedia of the Social Sciences,* and *The Anthropologists' Cookbook.* Contributor of articles and reviews to sociology and anthropology journals.

WORK IN PROGRESS: Ethnic Identity in Europe; Ritual in Modern Society; Popular Religion.

SIDELIGHTS: Pitt-Rivers wrote: "My grandfather was General A.C.F. Pitt-Rivers, the founder of modern archaeological excavation and a collector whose first collection became the anthropological museum at Oxford University. Despite a certain reluctance to follow the family tradition I did so—largely as a result of my experiences in Baghdad as the king's tutor. I consider myself an anthropologist and nothing else."

*   *   *

PIZER, Harry F(rancis) 1947-

PERSONAL: Born May 26, 1947, in Brooklyn, N.Y.; son of Harry L. and Estelle (Young) Pizer; married Christine M. Garfink (a writer and researcher); children: Katherine Amy Fallow. *Education:* University of Wisconsin—Madison, B.A. (with honors), 1969; also attended University of California, Berkeley. *Residence:* Cambridge, Mass. *Home:* 4 Pleasant Place, Cambridge, Mass. 02139. *Agent:* Katinka Matson, John Brockman Associates, 200 West 57th St., New York, N.Y. 10019.

CAREER: Roxbury Comprehensive Health Center, Roxbury, Mass., physician assistant, 1977; Jewish Memorial Hospital, Boston, Mass., physician assistant, 1978-79; Pondville Hospital, Walpole, Mass., physician assistant, 1980—. *Member:* American Academy of Physician Assistants, Massachusetts Association of Physician Assistants (president; past chairman of legislative committee), Word Guild.

WRITINGS: The New Birth Control Program, Bolder Books, 1978; *The Post Partum Book,* Grove, 1979; *Coping With a Miscarriage,* Dial, 1980; *Regulatory Change and Cost Effectiveness of the Physician Assistant in Massachusetts,* Massachusetts Association of Physician Assistants, 1980.

WORK IN PROGRESS: Over Fifty-Five, Healthy, and Alive: A Complete Health Manual for the Coming of Age, publication by Van Nostrand expected in 1982.

SIDELIGHTS: Pizer commented: "My overall goal is to provide medical information to the public in a form that can be understood and used in daily life, and to make consumers more able to get complete, appropriate, and reasonable health care from physicians because of their own understanding of their bodies and the health care system."

*   *   *

PLAYER, Gary (Jim) 1935-

PERSONAL: Born November 1, 1935, in Johannesburg, South Africa; son of Francis Harry Audley (a miner) and Muriel (Ferguson) Player; married Vivienne Verwey, January 16, 1957; children: Jennifer, Marc, Wayne, Michele, Theresa, Amanda-Leigh. *Education:* Educated in South Africa. *Home address:* P.O. Box 566 Honeydew, Transvaal, South Africa 2040. *Office:* International Management, 1 Erieview Plaza, Suite 1300, Cleveland, Ohio 44114.

CAREER: Professional golfer, 1953—. Winner of numerous golf tournaments, including South African Open, 1956, 1960, 1965, 1966, 1967, 1968, 1969, 1972, 1975, 1976, 1977, Australian Open, 1958, 1962, 1963, 1965, 1969, 1970, 1974, British Open, 1959, 1968, 1974, U.S. Masters, 1961, 1974, 1978, Professional Golfers Association (PGA) Championship, 1962, 1972, U.S. Open, 1965, and South African Dunlop Masters, 1976. *Awards, honors:* Named sportsman of the year in South Africa, 1956, 1959, 1961, 1963, 1965, 1972, 1974, and 1978; Kennedy Award, 1965; International award from British Broadcasting Corp. (BBC), 1965; Bobby Jones Award, 1966, for distinguished sportsmanship in golf; Charlie Barlett Award, 1972, for unselfish contribution to the betterment of society; inducted into World Golf Hall of Fame, 1974; named sportsman of the decade in South Africa, 1978; award from University of Pretoria, 1978, for achievements in golf; also many other awards.

WRITINGS: *Golf Secrets*, Prentice-Hall, 1962; *Play Golf With Player*, Collins, 1962; *Positive Golf: Understanding and Applying the Fundamentals of the Game*, McGraw, 1967; *Grand Slam Golf*, 3rd edition, Cassell, 1967; *124 Golf Lessons*, Golfer's Digest Association, 1968; *395 Golf Lessons*, Follett, 1972; (with Floyd Thatcher) *Gary Player: World Golfer* (autobiography), Word Books, 1974; *Gary Player's Golf Class: 162 Lessons for the Weekender*, Beaverbrook Newspapers, 1975.

SIDELIGHTS: Gary Player has often said that he wants to become the greatest golfer who ever lived. One of only four players to win the "grand slam" of golf—the U.S. Open, the British Open, the Masters, and the PGA—he is almost unchallenged in his quest. Since turning professional at age seventeen, he has been one of the most consistent winners on the world golf tour, competing in Africa, Australia, Europe, Asia, and the United States.

Player is several times a millionaire, but his first three years as a professional golfer were a financial struggle. "I survived on about $90 a month," he recalled. "I dragged my golf clubs in one hand and my suitcase in the other from one course to another." After two years on the British tour, he became critical of the way prize money was distributed in England, announcing in 1957 that he would boycott most British tournaments in the future. He joined the U.S. tour in 1958, but returned to Britain one year later to win the 1959 British Open. He was the youngest player in almost one hundred years to win that prestigious tournament.

Player's early years of competition in the United States were spent largely in the shadow of Arnold Palmer. In 1961, however, he emerged as one of the most formidable players on the circuit, defeating Palmer twice and winning three tournaments, including the Masters. Since then he has become one of those few on the U.S. tour to win more than one million dollars, and he has twice donated his winnings to charity. His yearly return to the United States has been prompted by more than the lucrative U.S. tour, however. In Player's opinion, "You can never be considered a champion unless you can win in America because this is where the best players are."

Long ago dubbed "the black knight of the fairways," Player usually competes wearing all-black golfing outfits because, he says, black makes him feel stronger. He attributes much of the consistency in his game to a combination of factors; his superior physical strength; a thorough familiarity with the fundamentals of golf; a rigid diet of unprocessed foods; and eight-hour-a-day practice rounds. "Some people think that golfers aren't athletes but I'm an athlete," he once remarked. "The more dedicated you are, the more sacrifices you make, the more you appreciate winning a major championship. No golfer has ever practiced more than I have."

Player, who lives on a ranch of several thousand acres near Johannesburg, South Africa, has often criticized his country's apartheid policies. For years he has struggled for equality for black athletes and disavowed his nation's official policies of discrimination against non-Europeans. In the 1970's he presented a series of exhibition matches between himself and Lee Elder, a black American golfer, and publicly protested his government's refusal to grant tennis star Arthur Ashe a visa. As a tribute to Player's efforts over the years on his behalf, golfer Charlie Sifford once remarked, "You couldn't ask for a finer man than Gary Player. He's helped me so many times I've stopped counting."

BIOGRAPHICAL/CRITICAL SOURCES: *Newsweek*, April 3, 1961, April 29, 1974, May 8, 1978; *Life*, April 21, 1961; *Time*, April 21, 1961, August 3, 1962, May 8, 1978; *Sports Illustrated*, May 8, 1961, March 18, 1963, May 23, 1966, April 17, 1978, May 1, 1978; *Saturday Evening Post*, April 13, 1963; *Look*, June 18, 1963; Ronald Heager, *Kings of Clubs*, Paul, 1968; Michael McDonnel, *Golf: The Great Ones*, Drake, 1971; Gary Player and Floyd Thatcher, *Gary Player: World Golfer* (autobiography), Word Books, 1974; *New York Times*, April 15, 1974, April 10, 1978; *Winston-Salem Journal & Sentinel*, August 6, 1974; *Biography News*, Gale, September, 1974; Frank Litsky, *Superstars*, Derbibooks, 1975.

*   *   *

PLENDER, Richard O(wen) 1945-

PERSONAL: Born October 9, 1945, in Epsom, England; son of George (a chartered secretary) and Louise (Savage) Plender; married Patricia Clare Ward (a secretary), December 16, 1978. *Education:* Queens' College, Cambridge, B.A. (with honors), 1967, LL.B. (with honors), 1968, M.A., 1970; University of Sheffield, Ph.D., 1970; University of Illinois, LL.M. (summa cum laude), 1971, J.S.D., 1972. *Politics:* Conservative. *Religion:* Anglican. *Home:* 28 March Court, Warwick Dr., London S.W.15, England. *Office:* Faculty of Laws, King's College, University of London, Strand, London W.C.2, England; and Goldsmith Buildings, Temple, London E.C. 4, England.

CAREER: Called to the Bar, London, England, 1972; University of Sheffield, Sheffield, England, assistant lecturer in law, 1968-70; University of Exeter, Exeter, England, lecturer in law, 1971-74; University of London, King's College, London, lecturer in law, 1972—; barrister-at-law in London, 1975—. Legal adviser to United Nations high commissioner for refugees, 1976-78. *Member:* International Law Association, British Institute of International and Comparative Law, Royal Institute of International Affairs, United Kingdom Association for European Law, American Society of International Law, Bar European Group, University Association for Contemporary European Studies, Honourable Society of the Inner Temple.

WRITINGS: *International Migration Law*, Sijthoff, 1972; (editor with John Bridge, Dominik Lasok, and David Perrott, and contributor) *Fundamental Rights*, Sweet & Maxwell, 1973; (contributor) F. G. Jacobs, editor, *European Law and the Individual*, North-Holland Publishing, 1976; *The Compulsory Acquisition of Land*, Butterworth & Co., 1976; (contributor) Georges Dogos-Docovitch, editor, *The European Parliament*, Greek Parliament, 1978; (with John Usher) *Cases and Materials on the Law of the European Communities*, Macmillan, 1979; *European Community Law: A Practical Introduction*, Sweet & Maxwell, 1980. Contributor to *Halsbury's Laws of England* and *Encyclopedia of European Community Law*. Contributor of about twenty articles to British, European, and American law journals. Member of editorial board of *New Community*.

WORK IN PROGRESS: A book on the international law of treaties, publication expected in 1983.

SIDELIGHTS: Plender wrote: "I attempt to combine the practice of law with its teaching and to play a part in breaking down the formidable barriers which still stand between the academic and the practical divisions of law. I hope that this ambition is reflected in my writings. *International Migration Law*, although concerned with questions of public international law, hitherto of more interest to the academic than to the practical community, was written with an emphasis on the daily recognition of international principles in domestic legislation and in decisions of national tribunals. Our book of cases and materials, although designed principally for students, concentrates on recent developments of practical significance and is divided equally between general principles, for the beginner, and substantive law. In writing the introductory book for practitioners, I tried to produce a work that was not a mere primer or a synthesis, but rather a publication designed to attract the attention and interest of the practitioner to a subject, which had hitherto been rather the preserve of the academic.''

*   *   *

POINTER, Larry 1940-

PERSONAL: Born May 14, 1940, in Sheridan, Wyo.; son of Leslie O. and Freda (Headley) Pointer; married wife, Patsy K., April 14, 1972; children: Danny, Joli, Rick, Nicci, Jade. *Education:* Sheridan College, A.A., 1960; Iowa State University, B.S., 1962; University of Minnesota, M.S., 1963; University of Denver, M.A., 1975. *Home:* 1021 Dorothy Lane, Billings, Mont. 59101. *Office:* U.S. Bureau of Land Management, P.O. Box 30157, Billings, Mont. 59101.

CAREER: Sheridan College, Sheridan, Wyo., instructor in botany, 1963-66; Oregon State University, Corvallis, instructor in botany, 1966-67; Blue Mountain Community College, Pendleton, Ore., instructor in botany, 1967-68; Central Wyoming College, Riverton, instructor in biology, 1968-74; U.S. Environmental Protection Agency, Denver, Colo., library assistant, 1974-75; U.S. Bureau of Land Management, Billings, Mont., agronomist, 1975—. *Member:* Western Writers of America.

WRITINGS: In Search of Butch Cassidy, University of Oklahoma Press, 1977; *Harry Jackson,* Abrams, 1980; *The Rodeo Epoch,* University of Oklahoma Press, 1980. Contributor to *Western Horseman, Rodeo Sports News,* and *World of Rodeo.*

WORK IN PROGRESS: In Search of Kid Curry, publication by University of Oklahoma Press expected in 1982.

*   *   *

POLAND, Larry 1939-

PERSONAL: Born September 29, 1939, in Mansfield, Ohio; son of Frank J. (in business administration) and Alta (a secretary; maiden name, Dawson) Poland; married Donna Lynn Petersen, August 4, 1962; children: Christian, Desiree, Cherish, Destiny, Chalet. *Education:* Wheaton College, Wheaton, Ill., B.A., 1961; Grace Seminary, M.Div., 1965; Purdue University, M.S., 1966, Ph.D., 1967. *Home:* 3296 North Broadmoor Blvd., San Bernardino, Calif. 92404. *Office:* Arrowhead Springs, San Bernardino, Calif. 92414.

CAREER: Ordained minister in National Fellowship of Brethren Churches, 1973; Grace College, Winona Lake, Ind., professor of sociology and college registrar, 1961-65, director of institutional studies, 1966-67; Miami Christian College, Miami, Fla., college president, 1967-73; Arrowhead Springs, San Bernardino, Calif., director of ''Agape'' movement, 1973—. Founder of WMCU-Radio (Christian radio station); co-founder and chairman of the board of Arrowhead Christian Academy, Inc., 1979—; developer and director of World Thrust; host of Canadian television specials, ''Here's LIFE.'' Member of Kosciusko County Republican steering committee, 1964. *Member:* National Fellowship of Brethren Churches, Brethren Ministerium, Phi Delta Kappa.

WRITINGS: Spirit Power: All You Need When You Need It, Here's Life Publishers, 1978; *Rise to Conquer,* Christian Herald Books, 1979; *Thresholds of Spirit Power,* Here's Life Publishers, 1981. Contributor to *Worldwide Challenge* and *Collegiate Challenge.*

WORK IN PROGRESS: Character Through Contrast (tentative title), ''a topical and practical approach to Biblical proverbs,'' with Patrick K. Skinner, completion expected in fall, 1980; a book about ''effective interpersonal relationships from a spiritual perspective.''

SIDELIGHTS: Poland wrote that his commitment to Christian service began when he was an exchange student in Germany as a teenager. Since then his work with the ''Agape'' movement, which ''seeks to contribute vocational and spiritual impact in the cause of world evangelism,'' has taken him to nearly seventy foreign countries. He also created World Thrust, ''a nation-wide urban conference strategy challenging Christians to involvement in international service.'' His current work includes research on ''human behavior, the spiritual dimension of human life, practical Christian living, and the Christian home and family.''

Poland believes that ''the increased secularization of American culture and the dramatic shift to relative morality threatens the future of the Western world and America in particular. I sense a personal obligation to contribute, through my writing, speaking, and television communication, to a re-emphasis on spiritual values and moral absolutes.''

AVOCATIONAL INTERESTS: Building model ships, collecting toy trains.

*   *   *

POLL, Richard Douglas 1918-

PERSONAL: Surname rhymes with ''doll''; born April 23, 1918, in Salt Lake City, Utah; son of Carl William (an accountant) and Annie (Swenson) Poll; married Emogene Hill, November 22, 1943; children: Marilyn Poll Bell, Nanette Poll Allen, Jennifer Poll Robison. *Education:* Texas Christian University, A.B., 1938, A.M., 1939; University of California, Berkeley, Ph.D., 1948. *Religion:* Church of Jesus Christ of Latter-day Saints (Mormons). *Home:* 712 Briarwood Dr., Macomb, Ill. 61455. *Office:* Department of History, Western Illinois University, 457 Morgan Hall, Macomb, Ill. 61455.

CAREER: Brigham Young University, Provo, Utah, assistant professor, 1948-51, associate professor, 1951-54, professor of history, 1954-69, head of department, 1955-60; Western Illinois University, Macomb, professor of history, 1970—, vice-president for administration, 1970-75. *Member:* Organization of American Historians, American Association of University Professors, Mormon History Association (president, 1969-70), Western History Association, Phi Beta Kappa.

WRITINGS: (With Eugene E. Campbell) *Hugh B. Brown: His Life and Thought,* Book Craft, 1975; (editor and contributor) *Utah's History,* Brigham Young University Press, 1978; *Howard J. Stoddard: Founder, Michigan National Bank,* Michigan State University Press, 1980. Contributor to Mormon and history journals.

WORK IN PROGRESS: A biography of Henry D. Moyle, Utah business and church leader.

*   *   *

POLLOCK, Penny 1935-

PERSONAL: Born May 24, 1935, in Cleveland, Ohio;

daughter of William Caswell (a candy maker) and Eleanor (a teacher; maiden name, Cadman) Morrow; married Stewart Glasson Pollock (a state supreme court justice), June 9, 1956; children: Wendy, Stewart, Jeffrey, Jennifer. *Education:* Mount Holyoke College, B.A., 1957; Kean College, M.A., 1973. *Religion:* Society of Friends (Quakers). *Home address:* Burnett Rd., Mendham, N.J. 07945.

CAREER: Village Nursery School, Brookside, N.J., head teacher, 1973—. Lecturer at Fairleigh Dickinson University, 1980. Member of board of trustees of Mendham Township Public Library. *Member:* Authors Guild of Authors League of America, Society of Children's Book Writers, Patricia Lee Gauch Writers' Workshop.

WRITINGS—Juveniles: Ants Don't Get Sunday Off, Putnam, 1978; *The Slug Who Thought He Was a Snail* (Junior Literary Guild selection), Putnam, 1980; *Garlanda: The Ups and Downs of an Uppity Teapot,* Putnam, 1980; *The Spit Bug Who Couldn't Spit,* Putnam, 1981.

WORK IN PROGRESS: Sand Castle King, a juvenile fantasy; research on stink bugs for an "easy-to-read" book.

SIDELIGHTS: Penny Pollock told *CA:* "I think my writing grows from my father's love of adventure and my mother's love of the natural world. A feeling of kinship with all living things pervades my life. A feeling of faith in the goodness of all people stems from (or reflects) my Quaker beliefs."

*   *   *

POMERANCE, Bernard 1940-

PERSONAL: Born in 1940 in Brooklyn, N.Y. *Residence:* London, England.

CAREER: Playwright. Founder of Foco Novo theatre group. *Awards, honors:* Antoinette Perry (Tony) Award, New York Drama Critics Circle Award, Drama Desk Award, and Obie Award, all 1979, all for "The Elephant Man."

WRITINGS—Plays: "Foco Novo"; "High in Vietnam Hot Damn"; "Someone Else Is Still Someone"; *The Elephant Man* (first produced in England, at Hampstead Theatre; first produced Off Broadway at the Theatre of St. Peter's Church, January 14, 1979; first produced on Broadway at Booth Theatre, April 19, 1979), Grove, 1979.

SIDELIGHTS: When Bernard Pomerance left his native New York City to settle in London in the early 1970's, his ambition was to be a novelist. Before long, however, he realized that drama was his forte. Pomerance became involved with the left-wing fringe theatre groups that were flourishing in London at the time. Teaming up with director Roland Rees, he founded the Foco Novo theatre group, which has subsequently produced all of his plays, including "High in Vietnam Hot Damn" and "Someone Else Is Still Someone." The play that first brought Pomerance to the attention of the general public was "The Elephant Man," which had a long and successful run at the Hampstead Theatre before being brought to New York City in January of 1979, where it met with widespread critical acclaim.

Pomerance's award-winning play is based on the true story of Englishman John Merrick (1863-1890). Merrick was afflicted with a disease (scientists now believe it was neurofibromatosis, a genetic disorder) that grotesquely deformed him. His head was thirty-six inches in circumference, hideous growths covered his body, and his hips were so deformed that he could hardly walk. He earned a living as a sideshow freak before he was befriended by Frederick Treves, a prominent surgeon. In addition to providing Merrick with a home at London Hospital, Treves sought to intro-

duce the young man to Victorian society. Under Treves's guidance, Merrick became a figure in London society, visited by members of the Royal Family and aristocrats. Pomerance first learned of Merrick while he was visiting the medical museum at London Hospital, where Merrick's bones are on display. A book written by Treves, *The Elephant Man and Other Reminiscences,* and a study of Merrick by Ashley Montagu provided the source material for Pomerance's play.

One of the problems in staging "The Elephant Man" is how to convey the sense of Merrick's hideously misshapen body. In a prefatory note to "The Elephant Man," Pomerance wrote: "Any attempt to reproduce his [Merrick's] appearance and his voice naturalistically—if it were possible—would seem to me not only counterproductive, but the more remarkably successful it was, the more distracting it would be." Instead of relying on make-up and padding to suggest Merrick's deformity, Pomerance uses a clever theatrical device. Early in the play, Treves brings Merrick to London Hospital to lecture about him. In the course of the lecture the audience views enlarged photographs of the real Merrick. "The pictures are so horrifying, so explicit in their detail, that we transfer the image to the actor beside the screen, even though he is simply contorting his body," Martin Gottfried observed in the *Saturday Review.* Other critics as well found that they had no difficulty in believing that the actor on the stage was horribly deformed. Many paid tribute to the talent of Philip Angrim, who played the part of Merrick in the New York production. Through his twisted motions and muffled speech, Angrim convinced the audience that the man he was playing was so repulsive that people would shriek and run away from him in terror.

However deformed his body, Merrick is portrayed in the play as an intelligent and sensitive man. His innocence often causes him to challenge the ideas and assumptions presented to him by his more worldly benefactors. According to Richard Eder, Pomerance "has made Merrick not an abstract figure, but a most individual exemplar of Natural Man. His deformities are external; they stand for the deformities, social and moral, that twist the lives of those who crowd about him; but his spirit is clear, vulnerable and acute." As the play progresses, Merrick's pure and questioning spirit is subdued. The drama, Eder explained, is a "haunting parable about natural man trading his frail beauty and innocence for the protection and prison of society."

The two other principal characters in the play are Treves and Madge Kendal. Treves, Edith Oliver pointed out, is portrayed as "a complex man, responsible, encouraging, and sympathetic, but a Victorian whose spontaneous kindness seems to conflict with his squeamishness about sex and his utter trust in rules and standards." The kindly physician teaches Merrick how to conform to society, but he tragically comes to realize that this educational process has had many detrimental effects on both the physical and mental health of his patient.

Initially Treves had difficulty finding anyone who would care for the horribly deformed Merrick. He resorts to hiring an actress, Madge Kendal, to visit Merrick in the hopes that she can use her acting skills to hide her repulsion. Merrick and Kendal become close friends. He is able to express his deepest feelings to her, and in a moving scene she reaches out to this sexually repressed man by undressing to the waist for him. Both characters benefit from their relationship. Carole Shelley, the actress who played Kendal in the New York production, asserted that Kendal is "a woman who has crippled herself by not trusting others. It's through her experience with Merrick that she opens herself to goodness again.

It comes full circle at the end. She has given him the ability to laugh at his pain and she herself comes out richer, having known the elephant man.''

Several critics observed that "The Elephant Man" falls off in the second act. John Simon described the first act as "terse, thoughtful, theatrical in the best sense, and devoid of spurious rhetoric—a lesson from Brecht well learned, with an added touch of humanity often lacking in the master." However, he felt that the second act suffers from "some insufficiently developed marginalia . . . , some less than revelatory speechifying . . . , some top-heavy irony with a few minor characters reduced to overconvenient contrivances. Above all, too many, and conflicting, layers of symbolism." Eder offered an explanation as to why the second act is the weaker half of the play: "In part it is inevitable: the opening up of the Elephant Man is more exciting than his decline. And furthermore many of the themes that are dramatized at the beginning remain to be expounded at the end. They are expounded very well indeed, but some of the play's immediacy flags a bit.''

In viewing "The Elephant Man" as a whole, however, reviewers were generous with their praise. Gottfried commented that its flaws "do not fatally mar the play, for what counts most is its overwhelming humanity; its tragedy and compassion; its soaring poetry; the theatrical beauty it makes of the contrast between innocence, deformity, and the stark Victorian staging." "The Elephant Man," Stanley Kauffmann maintained, "is the best new American play since 1972," while T. E. Kalem declared that the drama is "lofted on poetic wings and nests in the human heart."

Despite the stunning success of "The Elephant Man," Bernard Pomerance remains a mysterious figure. He fled back to England shortly after "The Elephant Man" opened in New York City. In a rare interview, he talked with Michael Owen of the *New York Times* about his conception of drama. "The most important element in theater is the audience's imagination," he remarked. "What is in them, is in me. It goes back to the function of memory. My function is—I don't know the proper word—is to remind them that this too is true, though our consciousness may deny it. I don't mean to tell them something they do not already know. I'm not bringing hot news. My interest in the audience is to remind them of a common thing and, if only temporarily, they do then become a unity, a community."

BIOGRAPHICAL/CRITICAL SOURCES: Drama, winter, 1972, autumn, 1974, winter, 1977-1978; *New York Times,* January 15, 1979, February 4, 1979, April 15, 1979, April 20, 1979, April 21, 1979, May 1, 1979, June 3, 1979, August 14, 1979; *New Yorker,* January 29, 1979, April 30, 1979; *Time,* January 29, 1979; *Newsweek,* February 5, 1979; *New Republic,* February 17, 1979, May 12, 1979; *Saturday Review,* March 17, 1979; *New York Magazine,* May 7, 1979; *Washington Post,* May 20, 1979; *Chicago Tribune,* June 6, 1979; *Contemporary Literary Criticism,* Volume 13, Gale, 1980.*

—*Sketch by Ann F. Ponikvar*

*   *   *

POMMERY, Jean 1932-

PERSONAL: Born January 3, 1932, in Villiers/Marne, France; son of Jean Pommery (a publicity agent); married Catherine Guenault (a professor of dance), November 29, 1976; children: Tristan. *Education:* Toulouse Veterinarian School, D.V.M., 1956. *Religion:* Roman Catholic. *Home:* 4 Ave. du 11 Novembre, 94350 Villiers/Marne, France. *Office:* 35 Blvd. Chanzy, 93100 Montreuil, France.

CAREER: Surgical assistant at Toulouse Veterinarian School, Toulouse, France; veterinarian to the king of Morocco, 1959-62; currently in private practice of veterinary medicine in Montreuil, France. Guest on television and radio programs. *Military service:* French Army, Cavalry, 1958-60; served in Algeria; became lieutenant. *Member:* Conference Nationale des Veterinaires des Animaux de Compagnie, Jeunes Amis des Animaux de Paris (honorary president).

WRITINGS—In English translation: (With Othilie Bailly) *Que faire en attendant le veterinaire,* Laffont, 1973, translation by Glenn E. Weisfeld published as *What to Do Till the Veterinarian Comes,* Chilton, 1976; *Entre betes et hommes,* Calmann-Levy, 1977, translation by Weisfeld published as *How Human the Animals,* Stein & Day, 1979.

Other: (With others) *Encyclopedie des animaux familier,* Denoel, 1966; *Dictionnaire des Animaux,* Nathan, 1980; *Allo Docteur . . . Mon chien,* Revue Chien Zow, 1980; (with others) *Les animaux de la ferme,* Denoel, 1980.

*   *   *

POMROY, Martha 1943-

PERSONAL: Born March 28, 1943, in Detroit, Mich.; daughter of William Homer (a corporate executive) and Tessie (Cooper) Miller. *Education:* Parsons College, B.S., 1964; Northwestern University, J.D., 1967. *Residence:* New York, N.Y. *Agent:* Meredith G. Bernstein, Henry Morrison Agency, Inc., 58 West 10th St., New York, N.Y. 10011.

CAREER: Walgreen's Drug Stores, Chicago, Ill., in corporate planning, 1968-70; professional actress in Chicago and New York City, 1970-75; NBC News, New York City, tax and financial reporter, 1975-76; tax consultant in New York City, 1976—. *Member:* Actors Equity Association, Screen Actors Guild, American Federation of Television and Radio Artists.

WRITINGS: What Every Woman Needs to Know About the Law, Doubleday, 1980.

WORK IN PROGRESS: A novelized treatment of a business fraud case; a spy novel.

SIDELIGHTS: Martha Pomroy told *CA:* "I'm not sure that I'm a person to consult on the subject of writing, but here goes. I sit down at the typewriter, and then I take a good hard look at the machine. Something goes 'bling' in my mind. Out comes a sentence, and then another. Concentration seems to be a key for me. Writing is like anything else; you either do it, or you don't do it."

*   *   *

PONIATOWSKA, Elena 1933-

PERSONAL: Born May 19, 1933, in Paris, France; daughter of John E. and Paula (Amor) Poniatowski; married Guillermo Haro (an astronomer); children: Emmanuel, Felipe, Paula. *Education:* Educated in Philadelphia, Pa. *Religion:* Roman Catholic. *Home:* Cerrada del Pedregal 79, Coyoacan, Z.P. 21, Mexico City, Mexico. *Office:* Novedades, Balderras 87, Mexico City 1, Mexico.

CAREER: Member of staff with *Excelsior,* 1954-55; *Novedades,* Mexico City, Mexico, staff member, 1955—. Founder of Editorial Siglo Veinte Uno, Cineteca Nacional, and Taller Literario; teacher at Injuve; speaker at schools and conferences; guest on radio and television programs. *Member:* International P.E.N. *Awards, honors:* D.H.C. from University of Sinaloa; fellowship from Centro de Escritores, 1957; Premio de Periodismo from Turismo Frances,

1965; Premio Mazatlan, 1970, for *Hasta no verte Jesus mio;* Premio Villaurrutia, 1970, for *La noche de Tlatelolco;* Premio de Periodismo from *Revista Siempre,* 1973; Premio Nacional de Periodismo, 1978.

WRITINGS—In English translation: *La noche de Tlatelolco: Testimonios de historia oral,* Ediciones Era, 1971, translation by Helen R. Lane published as *Massacre in Mexico,* introduction by Octavio Paz, Viking, 1975.

Other: *Lilus Kikus,* Los Presentes, 1954; *Meles y teleo: A puntes para una comedia,* Editorial Panoramas, 1956; *Palabras cruzadas: Cronicas,* Ediciones Era, 1961; *Todo empezo el domingo,* Fondo de Cultura Economica, 1963; *Los cuentos de Lilus Kikus* (title means "The Stories of Lilus Kikus"), Universidad Veracruzana, 1967; *Hasto no verte, Jesus mio,* Ediciones Era, 1969; (contributor) *El Primer Primero de Mayo,* Centro de Estudios Historicos del Movimiento Obrero Mexicano, 1976; *Querido Diego, te abraza,* Ediciones Era, 1978; *Gaby brimmer,* Editorial Grijalbo, 1979; *De noche vienes* (stories), Editorial Grijalbo, 1979; *Fuerte es el silencio,* Eras Cronicas, 1980.

Author of "Hasta no verte, Jesus mio" (film), released by Producciones Barbachano Ponce.

Work represented in anthologies, including *Antologias de Cuentistas Mexicanos,* Emmanuel Carballo, 1956; *Rojo de vida, y negro de muerte,* edited by Carlos Coccoli. Contributor to magazines, including *Revista Mexicana de literature, Siempre!, Estaciones, Abside,* and *Evergreen Review.*

SIDELIGHTS: A recording has been made of "Hasta no verte, Jesus mio," released by Voz Viva de Mexico.

*   *   *

PONNAMPERUMA, Cyril A.   1923-

PERSONAL: Born October 16, 1923, in Galle, Ceylon (now Sri Lanka); came to United States in 1959, naturalized citizen, 1967; son of Andrew (a teacher) and Grace (a teacher; maiden name, Siriwardene) Ponnamperuma; married Valli Pal, March 19, 1955; children: Roshini. *Education:* University of Madras, B.A., 1948; Birkbeck College, London, B.Sc. (with honors), 1959; University of California, Berkeley, Ph.D., 1962. *Home:* 4452 Sedgwick St. N.W., Washington, D.C. 20016. *Office:* Laboratory of Chemical Evolution, University of Maryland, College Park, Md. 20742.

CAREER: National Aeronautics & Space Administration, Ames Research Center, Exobiology Division, Moffett Field, Calif., research associate, 1962-63, research scientist, 1963-65, chief of Chemical Evolution Branch, 1965-71; University of Maryland, College Park, professor of chemistry and director of Laboratory of Chemical Evolution, 1971—, distinguished professor, 1978—. Principal investigator for analysis of organic compound in returned lunar sample, 1967-73. Member of visiting faculty at Stanford University, University of Nijmegen, and Sorbonne, University of Paris; distinguished visiting professor of Indian Atomic Energy Commission, 1967; guest lecturer at the Soviet Union's Academy of Sciences, 1970. President of Sri Lanka Overseas Foundation. Director of United Nations Educational, Scientific & Cultural Organization's program for the development of basic research in Sri Lanka, 1970-71.

MEMBER: International Society for the Study of the Origin of Life (executive council member, 1970-78), American Chemical Society (member of International Affairs Committee, 1976—), Radiation Research Society, American Society of Biological Chemists, American Geophysical Union, American Astronomical Association, Geochemical Society

of America, American Association for the Advancement of Science (member of advisory board of council of international activities), Chemical Society (England; fellow), Royal Institute of Chemistry (England; fellow), Indian National Academy of Sciences (foreign fellow), Cosmos Club. *Awards, honors:* Fellowship from National Academy of Sciences, 1962; awards from National Aeronautics and Space Administration, 1964, 1966; Phi Beta Kappa scholarship, 1976.

WRITINGS: (Editor with R. Buvet) *Molecular Evolution I,* North-Holland Publishing, 1971; (editor) *Exobiology: A Series of Collected Papers,* North-Holland Publishing, 1972; *The Origins of Life,* Dutton, 1972; (editor with J. Oro, S. Miller, and R. S. Young) *Cosmochemical Evolution and the Origins of Life,* Volumes I and II, D. Reidel, 1974; (editor with A.G.W. Cameron) *Interstellar Communication: Scientific Perspectives,* Houghton, 1974; (editor) *Chemical Evolution of the Giant Planets,* Academic Press, 1976; (editor) *Chemical Evolution of the Precambrian,* Academic Press, 1976; (editor) *Chemical Evolution: Comparative Planetology,* Academic Press, 1978; (with G. Field and G. Verschuur) *Cosmic Evolution,* Houghton, 1978. Contributor of more than two hundred articles to scientific journals and popular magazines. Editor-in-chief of *Origins of Life;* editor of *Journal of Molecular Evolution.*

WORK IN PROGRESS: Chemistry in Our Lives; A Book of Origins; The Origins of Life.

*   *   *

PONTE, Pierre Viansson
See VIANSSON-PONTE, Pierre

*   *   *

POPE, Michael James   1940-

PERSONAL: Born August 28, 1940, in Plattsburgh, N.Y.; son of Nicholas and Henrietta (Latourelle) Pope. *Education:* State University of New York at Plattsburgh, B.S., 1963; New York University, M.A., 1964; State University of New York at Albany, M.L.S., 1966; Rutgers University, Ph.D., 1972. *Politics:* Republican. *Home:* 9 Collegeview Ave., Poughkeepsie, N.Y. 12603. *Office:* Library, Dutchess Community College, Pendell Rd., Poughkeepsie, N.Y. 12601.

CAREER: High school English teacher in Plattsburgh, N.Y., 1964-65; Dutchess Community College, Poughkeepsie, N.Y., director of library, 1966-69, 1972—.

WRITINGS: Sex and the Undecided Librarian: A Study of Librarians' Opinions on Sexually-Oriented Literature, Scarecrow, 1974.

WORK IN PROGRESS: An index to film criticism; a compilation of film criticism, including major credits, summary of film, selected film reviews, bibliography of film reviews, and critical summary.

SIDELIGHTS: Pope wrote: "My areas of interest include film history and criticism and censorship. When time allows I hope to start additional research projects in both areas, particularly critical evaluations of several film directors."

*   *   *

PORTER, Katherine Anne   1890-1980

OBITUARY NOTICE—See index for *CA* sketch: Born May 15, 1890, in Indian Creek, Tex.; died September, 1980, in Silver Spring, Md. Author best known for her only full-length novel, *Ship of Fools*. Porter primarily wrote short stories and novellas that were critically acclaimed but not financially successful. She did not become popular until after her novel was published. Porter received several awards for her writing, including the 1966 Pulitzer Prize and the National Book Award. Her other works include *Flowering Judas, Pale Horse, Pale Rider,* and *A Defense of Circe.* Obituaries and other sources: *Time,* September 29, 1980; *Newsweek,* September 29, 1980.

* * *

POSTMA, Lidia 1952-

PERSONAL: Born April 2, 1952, in Hoorn, the Netherlands; daughter of Durk (an administrator) and Hillegonda (Druif) Postma; married Gerrit Hartog (an architect), May 10, 1972; children: Meryn, Jurriaan (both sons). *Education:* Attended Gerrit Rietveld Academie, 1969-74. *Home:* Dr. DeVriesstraat 8, Benningbroek, the Netherlands. *Awards, honors:* Gouden Penseel, 1976, for illustrations for *Sprookjes en Vertellingen van Hans Christiaan Andersen;* Gouden Appel from Biennale d'Illustrations de Bratislava, 1979, for *The Stolen Mirror* and *The Witch's Garden.*

WRITINGS: (Illustrator) *Sprookjes en Vertellingen van Hans Christiaan Andersen,* Van Holkema & Warendorf, 1975; (self-illustrated) *De Gestolen Spiegel* (juvenile), Lemniscaat, 1976, translation published as *The Stolen Mirror,* McGraw, 1976; (self-illustrated) *De Heksentuin* (juvenile), Lemniscaat, 1978, translation published as *The Witch's Garden,* McGraw, 1978; (contributor) *A Tolkien Bestiary,* Mitchell Beazley, 1979.

WORK IN PROGRESS: Illustrations for another picture book.

SIDELIGHTS: Lidia Postma told *CA:* "I have an eager interest in people and nature; my aim is to catch their magic in pictures. A picture book is a splendid way to present my vision to other people (including children, not excluding adults)." Reviewing Postma's first picture book, *The Stolen Mirror,* the *Publisher's Weekly* writer calls it "an eerily compelling story, enhanced by her masterful pictures." Other reviewers found the book's text somewhat lacking, but praised Postma's illustrations. The critic for the *San Diego Union* remarks, "The story is kind of thready, but the colorful drawings gleam like Old World paintings by a sunny window." The writer for the *Bulletin of the Center for Children* criticizes the text's unevenness, its appropriateness in different portions for varying age levels, but adds that despite this, *The Stolen Mirror* "should be treasured for its illustrations: a delicate control of color (and fine color printing), imaginative details, figures as romantic as Rackham's or as comic-grotesque as the trolls of the d'Aulaires, and a superb sense of dramatic composition."

The influence of other painters was noted by several other reviewers also. The *Booklist* writer comments that "the illustrations in Michael's real world have a Brechtian quality, while the fantasy paintings, though original in conception, show the fine strength of Rackham and Dulac." The *New York Times Book Review*'s Karla Kuskin feels that this eclecticism is a fault in *The Stolen Mirror.* Although Kuskin calls Postma "an unusually talented illustrator," she continues: "Ghosts of Arthur Rackham, Rembrandt, Henry Koerner, E. H. Shepard, Brueghel, Renaissance and Oriental painters slip in and out of her work. While there is a consistent fascination with the grotesque that colors the ordinary as well as the extraordinary characters in her story, Postma's approach is so eclectic that she never achieves a strongly unique style."

Like the reviewers of *The Stolen Mirror,* Georgess McHargue finds fault with the text of *The Witch's Garden,* calling it a "simple and not altogether original tale, rather gracelessly told," but she praises the book's illustrations. "Postma's full-color ink drawings are intricately textured and possessed of a charm than can only be described as elfin," McHargue writes in the *New York Times Book Review.* "Each of Postma's pictures is worth at least 10,000 well-chosen words."

BIOGRAPHICAL/CRITICAL SOURCES: Publishers Weekly, April 12, 1976; *St. Louis Post-Dispatch,* May 16, 1976; *Booklist,* June 7, 1976; *Philadelphia Inquirer,* August 22, 1976; *New York Times Book Review,* September 12, 1976, October 7, 1979; *Bulletin of the Center for Children,* Volume XXX, number 2, University of Chicago Press, October, 1976; *San Diego Union,* November 7, 1976.

* * *

POTTER, Stephen 1900-1969

PERSONAL: Born February 1, 1900; died December 2, 1969, in London, England; son of Frank Collard and Elizabeth (Reynolds) Potter; married Mary Attenbourgh (a painter; divorced); married Heather Lyon, 1965; children: three sons. *Education:* Attended Merton College, Oxford.

CAREER: Secretary to playwright Henry Arthur Jones; lecturer in English literature at University of London, London, England, beginning 1925; writer-producer for British Broadcasting Corp. (B.B.C.), London, 1935-45; book and drama critic for various British magazines and newspapers, beginning 1945; editor of *Leader* and *London Magazine,* 1949-51. *Military service:* Coldstream Guards, special reserve, 1919.

WRITINGS: The Young Man (novel), J. Cape, 1929; *D. H. Lawrence: A First Study,* J. Cape, 1930; *Coleridge and S.T.C.,* J. Cape, 1935; *The Muse in Chains: A Study in Education,* J. Cape, 1937, reprinted, Norwood Editions, 1978; *The Theory and Practice of Gamesmanship; or, The Art of Winning Games Without Actually Cheating,* Hart-Davis, 1947, published as *Gamesmanship; or, The Art of Winning Games Without Actually Cheating,* Holt, 1948; *Some Notes on Lifemanship, With a Summary of Recent Research in Gamesmanship,* Hart-Davis, 1950; *One-Upmanship: Being Some Account of the Activities and Teaching of the Lifemanship Correspondence College of One-Upness and Gameslifemastery,* Holt, 1962; *Sense of Humour* (anthology), Holt, 1954; *Christmas-ship; or, The Art of Giving and Receiving,* Hart Press, 1956; *Potter on America,* Hart-Davis, 1956, Random House, 1957; *Supermanship; or, How to Continue to Stay on Top Without Actually Falling Apart,* Hart-Davis, 1958, Random House, 1959; *Steps to Immaturity* (autobiography), Hart-Davis, 1959; *The Magic Number: The Story of "57,"* Max Reinhardt, 1959.

Three-Upmanship: The Theory and Practice of Gamesmanship; Some Notes on Lifemanship and One-Upmanship, Holt, 1962; *Squawky: The Adventures of a Clasperchoice* (juvenile), Lippincott, 1964; *Anti-Woo: The First Lifemanship Guide; The Lifeman's Improved Primer for Non-Lovers, With Special Chapters on Who Not to Love, Falling Out of Love, Avoidance Gambits, and Coad-Sanderson's Scale of Progressive Rifts,* McGraw, 1965; *Golfmanship,* McGraw, 1968 (published in England as *The Complete Golf Gamesmanship,* Heinemann, 1968); *The Complete Upmanship, Including Gamesmanship, Lifemanship, One-Upmanship, Supermanship,* Hart-Davis, 1970. Editor of *Selected Poetry and Prose,* by Samuel Taylor Coleridge, 1933, *Minnow Among Tritons: Mrs. S. T. Coleridge's Let-*

ters to Thomas Poole, 1934, and *Selected Poems of Coleridge,* 1935.

SIDELIGHTS: Stephen Potter was known for his development of and his books on the theory of gamesmanship. He believed that a "courteously clever" person could successfully defeat a talented opponent in any game. Potter was indirectly introduced to this technique by a colleague and tennis partner, Dr. Cyril Joad. During a game with two undergraduate students, Joad politely requested that they clearly state whether the ball landed in or out. This remark caught the students off guard and, as a result, they lost the game. Potter reasoned that their performance was hindered when their etiquette and sportsman-like conduct was questioned.

Potter's first books were scholarly: studies of D. H. Lawrence and Samuel Taylor Coleridge, and a book on education. But when faced with unemployment during a fuel crisis in England in 1947, Potter turned to what he had always used successfully: gamesmanship. *The Theory and Practice of Gamesmanship* was published in 1947 and several other volumes followed during the next twenty years. B. V. Winebaum found *Some Notes on Lifemanship* to be "a mine of practical strategy, a highly mannered exercise in the study of manners." C. E. Vulliamy agreed and also commented, "The fun of Mr. Potter has the extraordinary merits of being subtle yet hilarious, concealed and open, allusive and self-evident; and how delightful it is to find a wit that is neither sick nor soured." In his review of *Golfmanship,* Rex Lardner noted: "[It is] fitting that Mr. Stephen Potter should produce a new text on modern gamesmanship—more subtle, sophisticated and precisely directed than the old.... Here are listed verbal ploys, sartorial ploys, fiduciary ploys.... Difficult situations are faced and questions answered.... This is a splendidly funny book."

Some critics, however, tired of the novelty of gamesmanship after the publication of several books on the subject. A *New Yorker* critic reported: "Admirers of Mr. Potter's [earlier books] may find that his methods and the point of view behind them don't seem as funny or as sharp as they once did, possibly because they are no longer surprising, or possibly because he is getting a little tired of his own joke." But Edmund Wilson defended Potter, noting that "what is so good in these books of Potter's is the brevity and compactness of the presentation. As in any practical manual, the principles are stated and concisely illustrated. Nothing goes on too long."

BIOGRAPHICAL/CRITICAL SOURCES: Spectator, February 9, 1934; *Saturday Review of Literature,* January 8, 1949; *Times Literary Supplement,* November 17, 1950, October 10, 1952; *New Yorker,* November 8, 1952; *Manchester Guardian,* July 2, 1954; *Christian Science Monitor,* May 23, 1957, January 15, 1959; *Nation,* September 26, 1959; *Book World,* January 5, 1969.

OBITUARIES: New York Times, December 3, 1969; *Time,* December 12, 1969; *Antiquarian Bookman,* December 15, 1969; *Publishers Weekly,* December 15, 1969; *Books Abroad,* spring, 1970.*

*   *   *

POWERS, M. L.

See TUBB, E(dwin) C(harles)

*   *   *

PRATSON, Frederick John 1935-

PERSONAL: Born October 4, 1935, in Hartford, Conn.; son of John and Catherine Anne Pratson; married Patricia Gibson O'Neil (a teacher), December 26, 1959; children: Lincoln, Eric, Laura, David, Scott, Andrea. *Education:* Attended Northeastern University; Boston College, B.S., 1959. *Politics:* Democrat. *Religion:* Roman Catholic. *Home and office:* 55 Mann Hill Rd., North Scituate, Mass. 02060.

CAREER: Worked as assistant advertising and sales promotion manager for Corning Glass Works, 1959-64; advertising copywriter, 1964-65; free-lance writer, 1965-71; corporate public relations writer for Gilette Co., 1971-72; executive speechwriter and public affairs consultant, 1972—. *Military service:* U.S. Army Reserve, Infantry, 1959-67; became first lieutenant. *Awards, honors:* Grant from Maine State Commission on the Arts and Humanities, 1972.

WRITINGS: Land of the Four Directions (nonfiction), Chatham Press, 1970; *The Sea in Their Blood* (nonfiction), Houghton, 1972; *A Guide to Atlantic Canada,* Chatham Press, 1973; *The Special World of the Artisan,* Houghton, 1974; *New Hampshire,* Stephen Greene Press, 1974; *Perspectives in Galbraith,* CBI, 1978.

Photographer: Patricia Pratson, *Seedtime: A Celebration of Childhood,* Little, Brown, 1974. Contributor to magazines, including *National Review, Smithsonian, Yankee, Saturday Evening Post,* and *Travel and Leisure,* and newspapers, including *Boston Globe* and *Christian Science Monitor.*

WORK IN PROGRESS: A novel "about a man who attempts to start a second newspaper in a large northeastern city which was up to that time monopolized by one staid paper," completion expected in 1981.

SIDELIGHTS: Pratson commented: "I have worked as a free-lance writer since 1965. For six months in 1972 I had a grant to write, photograph, and produce documentaries on the Indians, fishermen, farmers, and lumber people of Maine. I have also done a great deal of writing on Canada. I have traveled throughout the country and have come to know its various racial and cultural groups.

"My writing has evolved from nonfiction to fiction, which is my current activity. Although I have some talent in art and photography, I feel writing best expresses the range and substance of my ideas and thoughts. Instead of looking at the things I've done in the past, I look forward with excitement to the books and plays I will do in the future. And I feel my powers as a writer increasing. I have a great love for the English language and hope that I can use it well for my own self-expression and for the benefit of those who care to read my work."

*   *   *

PRATT, Robert Cranford 1926-

PERSONAL: Born October 8, 1926, in Montreal, Quebec, Canada; son of Robert Goodwin and Henrietta (Freeman) Pratt; married Renate Hecht, July 15, 1956; children: Gerhard, Marcus, Anne. *Education:* McGill University, B.A., 1947; attended Institut de Science Politique, 1948-49; Balliol College, Oxford, B.Phil., 1952. *Politics:* New Democrat. *Religion:* Anglican. *Home:* 205 Cottingham St., Toronto, Ontario, Canada M4V 1C4. *Office:* Department of Political Economy, University of Toronto, Toronto, Ontario, Canada M5S 1A1.

CAREER: McGill University, Montreal, Quebec, assistant professor of political science, 1952-54; Makerere University College (now Makerere University), Makerere, Uganda, lecturer in politics, 1954-56; McGill University, assistant professor of political science, 1956-58; Oxford University,

Oxford, England, research officer at Institute of Commonwealth Studies, 1958-60; University of Dar-es-Salaam, Dar-es-Salaam, Tanzania, principal of university college, 1961-65; University of Toronto, Toronto, Ontario, professor of political science, 1966—, director of international studies program, 1967-72. Commonwealth visiting professor at University of London, 1980. President of Ecumenical Forum of Canada, 1980-82; consultant to Canadian International Development Agency, Ford Foundation, and president of Tanzania. *Member:* Royal Society of Canada (fellow), Canadian Association for African Studies (president, 1976-77), Canadian Political Science Association. *Awards, honors:* Killam Award from Canada Council, 1969, for research on Tanzanian politics; International Development Research Centre fellowship, 1978-79.

WRITINGS: (With Anthony Low) *Buganda and British Overrule,* Oxford University Press, 1960; (editor with Colin Leys) *A New Deal in Central Africa,* Heinemann, 1960; *Nyerere and the Emergence of a Socialist Strategy,* Cambridge University Press, 1976; *The Critical Phase in Tanzania, 1945-68,* Cambridge University Press, 1976; (editor with Bismark Mwansasu) *Towards Socialism in Tanzania,* University of Toronto Press, 1979. Chairman of editorial board of "Perspectives on Development," a series, Cambridge University Press, 1972-77. Contributor to political science and African studies journals. Chairman of editorial board of Centre for Development Area Studies, McGill University, 1969-75.

WORK IN PROGRESS: Canada: The Common Fund and Commodity Agreements (tentative title), publication expected in 1981; research on Canadian relations with the Third World.

SIDELIGHTS: Pratt told *CA:* "After over two decades of scholarly writing concentrated upon East African politics, I have in the past two years continued my primary involvement in issues related to Africa and the Third World but have changed the focus of my interest to those policies in the developed world which are major obstacles to sustained and balanced economic development in Third World countries."

*   *   *

PRAZ, Mario 1896-
(Alcibiade, Giano di Guisa)

PERSONAL: Born September 6, 1896, in Rome, Italy; son of Luciano (a bank clerk) and Giulia (di Marsciano) Praz; married Vivyan Eyles, March 17, 1934 (divorced October 27, 1947); children: Lucia (Mrs. Mohammed Ali Shakir). *Education:* University of Rome, Dr.Juris, 1918; University of Florence, D.Litt., 1920. *Religion:* Roman Catholic. *Home:* Via Zanardelli 1, Rome 00186, Italy.

CAREER: Writer, 1919—; Liverpool University, Liverpool, England, senior lecturer in Italian, 1924-32; Manchester University, Manchester, England, professor of Italian studies, 1932-34; University of Rome, Rome, Italy, professor of English, 1934-66, professor emeritus, 1966—. *Member:* International P.E.N., Socio Nazionale Accademia dei Lincei, Modern Language Association of America (honorary member), American Academy of Arts and Sciences, Socio dell'Arcadia Accademia Letteraria Italiana, Sezione Artistica e Culturale del Cenacolo Triestino. *Awards, honors:* British Academy Gold Medallist for Anglo-Italian Studies, 1935; Premio Marzotto, 1952, for *La Crisi dell'eroe nel romanzo vittoriano;* Italian Gold Medal for cultural merits, 1958; Knight of the Order of the British Empire, 1962; Grande Ufficiale della Repubblica Italiane, 1972. Litt.D.

from Cambridge University, 1957, Aix-Marseille University, 1964, and Sorbonne, University of Paris, 1967; D.Litt. from University of Uppsala, 1977.

WRITINGS: La fortuna di Byron in Inghilterra, La Voce (Florence), 1925; *Secentismo e marinismo in Inghilterra: John Donne—Richard Crashaw,* La Voce, 1925, revised and expanded version published in two volumes as *La poesia metafisica inglese del seicento, John Donne,* Edizioni Italiane, 1945, and *Richard Crashaw,* Morcelliana, 1946; *Machiavelli and the Elizabethans,* H. Milford, 1928, reprinted, R. West, 1978, original Italian edition published as *Machiavelli e inglesi dell'epoca Elisabettiano,* Vallecchi, 1930; *Penisola pentagonale,* Alpes (Milan), 1928, 2nd edition, Sansoni, 1955, translation by author published as *Unromantic Spain,* Knopf, 1929.

La carne, la morte e il diavolo nella letteratura romantica, La Cultura, 1930, 5th edition, Sansoni, 1976, translation by Angus Davidson published as *The Romantic Agony,* Oxford University Press, 1933, 2nd edition, 1951, reprinted with corrections and a new foreword, 1970; *Studi sul concettismo,* La Cultura, 1934, translation by author of expanded version published in two volumes as *Studies in Seventeenth-Century Imagery,* Warburg Institute, 1939, 2nd edition, Edizioni du Storia e Letteratura, 1964, and *A Bibliography of Emblem Books,* Warburg Institute, 1948; *Storia della letteratura inglese,* Sansoni, 1937, 11th edition, 1979; *Studi e svanghi inglese,* Sansoni, 1937.

Gusto neoclassico, Sansoni, 1940, 3rd edition, Rizzoli, 1974, translation by Angus Davidson published as *On Neoclassicism,* Northwestern University Press, 1969; *Machiavelli in Inghilterra,* Tumminelli, 1943, expanded and revised edition published as *Machiavelli in Inghilterra ed altri saggi sui rapporti letterari anglo-italiane,* Sansoni, 1962; *Viaggio in Grecia, diario del 1931,* Edizione de Lettere d'Oggi, 1943; *Fiori freschi,* Sansoni, 1944; *Ricerche anglo-italiane,* Edizioni di Storia e Letteratura, 1944; *Motive e figure,* Einaudi, 1945; *La filosofia dell'arredamento,* Documento, 1945, revised and expanded edition published as *La filosofia dell'arredamento: I mutamenti nel gusto della decorazione interna attraverso i secoli dall'antica Roma ai nostri tempi,* Longanesi, 1964, translation by William Weaver published as *An Illustrated History of Furnishing, From the Renaissance to the 20th Century,* Braziller, 1964 (published in England as *An Illustrated History of Interior Decoration, From Pompeii to Art Nouveau,* Thames & Hudson, 1964); *Il dramma Elisabettiano: Webster, Ford,* Edizioni Italiane, 1946; *La poesia di Pope e le sue origini,* Edizioni dell'Ateneo, 1948.

Cronache letterarie anglosassoni, four volumes, Edizioni di Storia e Letteratura, 1951-66; *La casa della fama: Saggi di letteratura e d'arte,* Ricciardi, 1952; *Lettrice notturna,* G. Casini, 1952; *La crisi dell'eroe nel romazo vittoriano,* Sansoni 1952, translation by Angus Davidson published as *The Hero in Eclipse in Victorian Fiction,* Oxford University Press, 1956; *Viaggi in Occidente,* Sansoni, 1955; *La casa della vita* (autobiography), Mondadori, 1958, 2nd edition, Adelphi, 1979, translation by Angus Davidson published as *The House of Life,* Oxford University Press, 1964; *The Flaming Heart: Essays on Crashaw, Machiavelli, and Other Studies in the Relations Between Italian and English Literature From Chaucer to T. S. Eliot,* Doubleday, 1958, reprinted, Norton, 1973; *Le bizzarre sculture di Francesco Pianta,* Sodalizio del Libro, 1959.

Bellezza e bizzarria, Il Saggiatore, 1960; *I volti del tempo,* Edizioni Scientifiche Italiane, 1964; *Panopticon romano,*

Ricciardi, Volume I, 1967, Volume II, 1978; *Il libro della poesia inglese,* D'Anna, 1967; *Caleidoscopio Shakespeariano,* Adriatica, 1969.

Scene di conversazione, U. Bozzi, 1970, translation published as *Conversation Pieces: A Survey of the Informal Group Portrait in Europe and America,* Pennsylvania State University Press, 1971; *Mnemosyne: The Parallel Between Literature and the Visual Arts,* Princeton University Press, 1970; (with Folco Quilici) *Toscano,* Dell'Ufficio Pubbliche Relazioni della Esso Italiana, 1971; *Il patto col serpente,* Mondadori, 1972; (with Quilici) *Puglia,* Dell'Ufficio Pubbliche Relazioni della Esso Italiana, 1974; (with Quilici) *Lazio,* Dell'Ufficio Pubbliche Relazioni della Esso Italiana, 1975; *Il giardino dei sensi: Studi sul manierismo e il barocco,* Mondadori, 1975; *Perseo e la Medusa: Dal romanticismo all'avanguardia,* Mondadori, 1979.

Editor: *Antologia della letteratura inglese,* Principato, 1936; Lorenzo Magalotti, *Lettere sopra i buccheri con l'aggiunta di lettere sopra l'ateismo, scientifiche e erudite, e di relazioni varie,* Le Monier, 1945; *Prospettiva della letteratura inglese da Chaucer a V. Woolf,* Bompiani, 1946; *Geoffrey Chaucer e i racconti di Canterbury,* Edizioni Italiane, 1947; (with Ettore Lo Gatto) *Antologia della letteratura straniere,* Sansoni, 1947; *Teatro Elisabettiano,* Sansoni, 1948; *Il libro della poesia inglese presentato e commentato da Mario Praz,* D'Anna, 1951; *William Shakespeare: Teatro,* three volumes, Sansoni, 1957; (and author of introduction) *Tre drammi Elisabettiani,* Elizioni Scientifiche Italiane, 1958; William Shakespeare, *Tutte le opere,* 4th edition, Sansoni, 1965.

Translator into Italian: Charles Lamb, *I saggi di Elia,* Carabba, 1924; *Poeti inglese dell'Ottocento,* Bemporad, 1925; George Moore, *Esther Waters,* Mondadori, 1934; Shakespeare, *Misura per misura,* Sansoni, 1939; Shakespeare, *Troilo e Cressida,* Sansoni, 1939; Joseph Addison, *Lo spettatore,* Einaudi, 1943; Ben Jonson, *Volpone,* Sansoni, 1943; Walter Pater, *Rittratti immaginari,* De Luigi, 1944, 2nd edition, 1980; (and editor and author of introduction) *Pater,* Garzanti, 1944; Pater, *Il rinascimento,* Edizioni Scientifiche Italiane, 1946; Samuel Coleridge, *La ballata del vecchio marinaro,* Fussi, 1947; Bernard Berenson, *Estetica, etica, e storia nelle arti dalla rappresentazione visiva,* Electa, 1948; T. S. Eliot, *La terra desolata, Trammento di un agone, Marcia trionfale,* Fussi, 1949; Frederick S. Oliver, *Elogio dell'uomo politico,* Ricciardi, 1950; John Webster, *La duchessa d'Amalfi,* published in *Teatro Elisabettiano,* edited by A. Obertello, Bompiani, 1951; Jane Austen, *Emma,* Garzanti, 1951. Also translator of works by Rimbaud and Valery.

Author of introduction or preface: Giovanni Battista Piranesi, *Magnificenza di Roma,* Edizione Il Polifilo, 1961, translation by R. M. Boothroyd published as *The Magnificence of Rome From the Views of Giovanni B. Piranesi,* Harcourt, 1962; *Lazio,* Touring Club Italiano (Milan), 1967.

Contributor to *Paese sera* under pseudonym Alcibiade and to *Il Giornale Nuovo* under pseudonym Giano di Guisa; contributor to *La Stampa, Corriere della Sera, La Nazione, Il Tempo, London Mercury, English Studies,* and other philological, art, and literary journals. Co-editor, *La Cultura;* editor, *English Miscellany.*

WORK IN PROGRESS: Editing an anthology of his own writing, for Adelphi.

SIDELIGHTS: "[Mario Praz] will come to be known to posterity—so far as a foreigner can judge—as one of the best Italian writers of his time," Edmund Wilson wrote in the *New Yorker.* "I do not know of anyone else on the continent who is capable of such competent reviewing of current English and American books. . . . Yet to think of Mario Praz as primarily an English expert and a literary critic is largely to misconceive his role. He should be considered as primarily an artist—and I do not even say literary artist, for the results of his activities as a collector of furniture, pictures, and objets d'art are as much a part of his *oeuvre* as his books. He is an artist and a unique personality who expresses himself through his art in connection with any subject he is treating."

Wilson believed that even Praz's earlier books, such as *Unromantic Spain,* contain "some of the most striking features of this highly idiosyncratic writer: his brilliant powers of description, his interludes, which are really prose poems, and his Proustian reflections on life. . . . And we have also his saturnine humor. . . . He loves the grotesque, the incongruous, and his books, among other things, are cabinets of curios. There is nothing that Praz enjoys more than a bit of unexplored monstrosity."

This fascination for the macabre is evident in what is perhaps Praz's best-known book, *The Romantic Agony,* which Piers Brendon called "a classic of literary criticism and interpretation." *The Romantic Agony* traces the influence of the Marquis de Sade and other connoisseurs of the macabre on the Romantic writers. Reviewing the book for the *Saturday Review of Literature,* Arnold Whitridge commented: "He pursues the macabre with unflagging energy in the paintings of Delacroix and Moreau as well as in the novels of Flaubert and Barbey d'Aurevilly. The result of this research is not an indictment of the romantic movement, . . . but a logical explanation of pathological phases of romanticism which scholars have hitherto ignored." Brendon wrote in *Books and Bookmen:* "It has become part of the intellectual texture of a whole generation. It has shaped the awareness of academics, it is plagiarised on a large scale in undergraduate essays and it is plundered to provide the juicier cliches for colour supplement articles celebrating the anniversaries of prominent Romantics. It is a work of the most colossal erudition, supported by a cumbersome apparatus of footnotes, yet its insights into what was probably the most important cultural revolution since the Renaissance remain fresh and exciting."

The critics were not unanimous in their praise of the book, however. The *Spectator*'s I. M. Parson found fault in the "general nature of the subject" and in Praz's "hopelessly unimaginative treatment of it." Although his review was generally laudatory, Brendon also believed that the book had a "major defect—its lack of conclusion or synthesis. . . . Praz's achievement has been to draw up a gigantic inventory of previously obscure and taboo aspects of Romanticism, but he has not appended the deeds, the explanation of their place in and their importance to the whole edifice." Despite this criticism, Wilson wrote that *The Romantic Agony* "cannot be ignored by anybody who is interested in modern literature."

Some critics, Wilson included, believed the autobiographical *House of Life* to be Praz's masterpiece. Wilson found it "a much more complete expression of Mario Praz's sensibility than any of his other books." Frank Kermode wrote in the *New Statesman:* "It can be called a fault in Praz's admirable book that he stands aloof, collecting, assembling, not participating. If so, he would admit that it is a fault of character; and in his autobiography he presents himself as in all things a man of that kind: an obsessed collector, with a deep streak of melancholy and an habitual detachment from persons, even perhaps from ideas.'' *Book Week*'s Wylie Sypher thought that the book must be read as ''a commentary on the art-view of life achieved by the connoisseur, whose cynicism arises from a discovery that 'people disappoint us too often.' ... Unless we feel this bitter and disenchanted tone, his book becomes merely a catalog of furnishings.''

Writing in the *New York Times Book Review,* Aubrey Menen called *The House of Life* ''remarkable [in the] description of the joys, the agonies, and the downright pottiness of a devoted collector. It is brilliantly done.... The description of his collection is only the frame for a series of portraits in words of the people he has met in the course of his life.... Slowly, as one turns the pages of this beautifully produced book, one realizes that it is not a description of a house or an autobiography, but something much more. It is a masterly example of that most difficult of all things to write, the long essay.'' And Robert J. Clements believed the book explains Praz's mastery of numerous scholarly pursuits. ''Praz shows that he has had to combat the great afflictions which have beset lesser men: loneliness, fear of death, betrayal, inarticulateness, misunderstanding. Without preaching, he showed us that there is a solution, his own: develop several absorbing interests and strive to master them.''

BIOGRAPHICAL/CRITICAL SOURCES: Times Literary Supplement, October 17, 1929, July 20, 1933, June 15, 1956, November 23, 1967, May 2, 1980; *New Statesman,* November 2, 1929, July 29, 1933, April 2, 1956, September 25, 1964; *Spectator,* January 4, 1930, December 8, 1933, April 20, 1956; *New York Times,* February 16, 1930, August 5, 1956; *Saturday Review of Literature,* April 19, 1930, August 12, 1933, September 23, 1933, October 24, 1964; *Yale Review,* winter, 1957; A. F. Arocca, editor, *Ritratti su misura di scrittori italiani,* Soldalizio del Libro, 1960; Mario Praz, *The House of Life* (autobiography), Oxford University Press, 1964; *New York Times Book Review,* November 8, 1964; *Book Week,* November 15, 1964; *New York Review of Books,* December 17, 1964, April 9, 1970; Edmund Wilson, *The Bit Between My Teeth,* Farrar, Straus, 1965; *New Yorker,* February 20, 1965; Vittorio Gabrieli, editor, *Friendship's Garland: Essays Presented to Mario Praz on His Seventieth Birthday,* Edizioni di Storia e Letteratura, 1966; *Comparative Literature,* fall, 1968; *Books and Bookmen,* February, 1971, March, 1971.

—*Sketch by Linda Metzger*

*   *   *

PRINCE, F(rank) T(empleton) 1912-

PERSONAL: Born September 13, 1912, in Kimberley, Cape Province, South Africa; son of Henry (a businessman) and Margaret (a teacher; maiden name, Hetherington) Prince; married Pauline Elizabeth Bush, March 10, 1943; children: Rosanna Mary Prince Salbashian, Caryll Elizabeth Prince Barber. *Education:* Balliol College, Oxford, B.A., 1934; attended Princeton University, 1935-36. *Politics:* Conservative. *Religion:* Roman Catholic. *Home:* 32 Brookvale Road, Southampton, Hampshire, England SO2 1QR.

CAREER: Royal Institute of International Affairs, Study Groups Department, London, England, 1936-40; University of Southampton, Southampton, England, lecturer, 1946-55, reader, 1955-56, professor of English, 1957-74, dean of arts faculty, 1962-65; University of the West Indies, Mona, Kingston, Jamaica, professor of English, 1975-78; Brandeis University, Waltham, Mass., Fannie Hurst Visiting Professor, 1978-80; Washington University, St. Louis, Mo., visiting professor, 1980-81. Visiting fellow of All Souls College,

Oxford, 1968-69; Clark Lecturer at Cambridge University, 1973. *Military service:* British Army, Intelligence Corps, 1940-46; became captain.

WRITINGS: Poems, Faber, 1938; *Soldiers Bathing and Other Poems,* Fortune Press, 1954; *The Italian Element in Milton's Verse,* Clarendon Press, 1954; *The Stolen Heart* (poems), Press of the Morning Sun, 1957; *William Shakespeare: The Poems,* Longman, 1963; *The Doors of Stone: Poems, 1938-1962,* Hart-Davis, 1963; *Memoirs in Oxford* (poem), Fulcrum Press, 1970; (with John Heath-Stubbs and Stephen Spender) *Penguin Modern Poets Twenty,* Penguin, 1971; *Drypoints of the Hasidim* (poems), Menard Press, 1975; *Afterword on Rupert Brooke,* Menard Press, 1976; *Collected Poems,* Sheep Meadow Press, 1979.

Editor: John Milton, *Samson Agonistes,* Oxford University Press, 1957; William Shakespeare, *The Poems,* third edition, Harvard University Press, 1960; Milton, *Paradise Lost, Books I and II,* Oxford University Press, 1962; Milton, *Comus and Other Poems,* Oxford University Press, 1968.

Translator: Sergio Baldi, *Sir Thomas Wyatt,* Longman, 1961.

Contributor: B. Dobree, editor, *Shakespeare: The Writer and His Work,* Longman, 1964; W. Buckley, editor, *Milton Encyclopedia,* University of Texas Press, 1979. Contributor of articles and reviews to periodicals, including *Review of English Studies, Essays and Studies, Review of the University of Pietermaritzburg, English,* and *Times Literary Supplement.*

SIDELIGHTS: F. T. Prince is best known for his poem, ''Soldiers Bathing,'' which Donald Davie called ''perhaps the finest poem in English to come out of World War II,'' second only to Eliot's ''Four Quartets.'' Most of Prince's subsequent poetry received little notice until the publication of *Collected Poems,* in which he included only what he considered to be his best verse. Blake Morrison remarked: ''It's clear that no major talent has been overlooked, but this is an attractive collection.'' Richard Lattimore, however, declared that Prince ''is all his own man, he is like no one else, he is a major poet.'' A *Choice* reviewer was also generous: ''Prince's linguistic and technical virtuosity—rhythm, cadence, rhyme, assonance—show how carefully and profitably he has studied Hopkins, Yeats, and Eliot. Above all, as an accomplished scholar, he wears his erudition lightly.''

Prince told *CA:* ''From the beginning it seemed to me that I would have to go my own way. But it takes a long time, and varied experience, to learn what one really thinks and feels—longer if one is a poet, and if one lives in this century. Some of my past work looks strange to me now, but I have kept it because at the very least it can help towards an understanding of the better things.''

BIOGRAPHICAL/CRITICAL SOURCES: Times Literary Supplement, September 12, 1968; *Guardian,* April 4, 1979; *New York Times Book Review,* April 8, 1979; *Hudson Review,* autumn, 1979; *Choice,* September, 1979.

*   *   *

PROSPER, Lincoln
See CANNON, Helen

*   *   *

PULSIPHER, Gerreld L(ewis) 1939-

PERSONAL: Born March 25, 1939, in Las Vegas, Nev.; son of J. L. (in business) and Marian (Lee) Pulsipher; married Nancy Funk, September 11, 1964; children: David, Holly,

Marta, Rebecca, Carrie. *Education:* University of Utah, B.S., 1964. *Office:* 2290 East 4500 S., Suite 120, Salt Lake City, Utah 84117.

CAREER: Millenial Star, London, England, managing editor, 1961-62; Gillham Advertising Agency, Inc., Salt Lake City, Utah, account executive, 1962-65; Utah Travel Council, Salt Lake City, associate director, 1965-66, director, 1966-68; ExhibiGraphics, Inc., Salt Lake City, vice-president, 1968-72; Concept Design Associates, Inc., Salt Lake City, president, 1972—. Director of Golden Spike Centennial Commission, member of Salt Lake County Convention Board, and member of Utah Outdoor Recreation Committee, all 1966-68. *Military service:* Utah Air National Guard, 1958-65; became staff sergeant. *Member:* National Trust for Historic Preservation, Nature Conservancy, National Audubon Society, National Parks and Conservation Association, Association of Interpretive Naturalists, National Parks and Recreation Association, Western Interpreters Association, Sigma Delta Chi. *Awards, honors:* University of Utah alumni achievement award.

WRITINGS: (With Kurt Hanks and Larry Belliston) *Getting Your Message Across,* Information Design, 1978; (with John E. Rosenow) *Tourism: The Good, the Bad, and the Ugly,* Century Three Press, 1980. Author of audio-visual scripts and professional reports.

WORK IN PROGRESS: A history of travel and tourism in the United States, with Rosenow, for Century Three Press.

SIDELIGHTS: Pulsipher wrote: "I have never considered myself as a writer in the artistic sense; rather, as an individual utilizing the written word to communicate ideas. To me, the written word is most effective when used in combination with graphic and visual images. While I appreciate words used well, my major criterion has been not 'Is it well written?' but 'Does it communicate?'

"Writing, to me is a tool utilized largely in an active concern with the interaction between human beings and their natural and cultural environment. *Tourism: The Good, the Bad, and the Ugly* focuses on the impact of tourism and recreation on the quality of the environment and community life. The aim of much of my professional writing is to communicate the sense of different places and to aid in their preservation and appropriate use.

"My personal and professional interests have long been centered in places and what makes them the way they are—both tangibly and intangibly. These interests have spawned intense involvement with geography, environmental science, tourism/recreation, and history. Extensive travel in the United States, Europe and the Middle East has only fueled a passion to learn more about the places of this planet and human interaction with them."

Q

QUIGLEY, Austin E(dmund) 1942-

PERSONAL: Born December 31, 1942, in Newcastle-upon-Tyne, England; came to the United States in 1969; son of Edmund (a headmaster) and Marguerita (a teacher; maiden name, Crilley) Quigley; married Patricia D. Denison (a college lecturer), June 1, 1979; children: Laura, Rebecca. *Education:* University of Nottingham, B.A. (with honors), 1967; University of Birmingham, M.A., 1969; University of California, Santa Cruz, Ph.D., 1971. *Residence:* Charlottesville, Va. *Offfice:* Department of English, University of Virginia, Wilson Hall, Charlottesville, Va. 22903.

CAREER: University of Massachusetts, Amherst, assistant professor of English, 1971-73; University of Virginia, Charlottesville, associate professor of English, 1973—, associate chairman, 1974-81. *Member:* Modern Language Association of America, Linguistics Society of Great Britain. *Awards, honors:* National Endowment for the Humanities fellowship, 1977-78.

WRITINGS: The Pinter Problem, Princeton University Press, 1975. Contributor to drama journals. Member of editorial board of *Modern Drama* and *New Literary History.*

WORK IN PROGRESS: Two books on modern drama, completion expected in 1983; a book on linguistics, philosophy of language, and literary theory.

QUINN, Terry 1945-

PERSONAL: Born July 15, 1945, in New York, N.Y.; son of Hugh V. (a court clerk) and Jean F. (O'Reilly) Quinn; married Jane Magrum (a social worker and writer), June 13, 1970. *Education:* Catholic University of America, B.A. (summa cum laude), 1967; Harvard University, M.A., 1968; University of Chicago, M.A., 1971. *Home:* 116 11th St. N.E., Washington, D.C. 20002. *Agent:* Eugene Winick, Ernst, Cane, Berner, & Gitlin, 7 West 51st St., New York, N.Y. 10019.

CAREER: Speechwriter for U.S. Congressmen Seymour Halpern and Mario Biaggi in Washington, D.C., 1971-73; Office of the President, Washington, D.C., writer at the White House, 1973; National Coordinating Council for Drug Education, Washington, D.C., writer and editor, 1974-76; *The Hill* (newspaper), Washington, D.C., editor-in-chief, 1976; free-lance writer, 1976—. *Member:* Phi Beta Kappa.

Awards, honors: Woodrow Wilson fellowship, 1967; National Institute of Mental Health fellowship, 1969.

WRITINGS: The Great Bridge Conspiracy (novel), St. Martin's, 1979. Contributor of about a dozen articles and reviews to *Games.*

WORK IN PROGRESS: A biography of Katherine Wei; a novel, *Winterrun;* two juvenile novels, *The Breakout* and *The Rainmaker.*

R

RABKIN, Brenda 1945-

PERSONAL: Born August 22, 1945, in Montreal, Quebec, Canada; daughter of Wolfe and Adela (Goldberg) Yablon; married Simon William Rabkin (a physician), June 17, 1969; children: Jessica, Richard. *Education:* Attended Hebrew University of Jerusalem, 1964-65; McGill University, B.A., 1966; University of Montreal, M.A., 1969. *Home:* 336 Dromore Ave., Winnipeg, Manitoba, Canada R3M 0J5.

CAREER: Sir George Williams University, Montreal, Quebec, instructor, 1968-69; University of Cincinnati, Cincinnati, Ohio, instructor, 1969-71; Georgia State University, Atlanta, instructor, 1971-72; free-lance writer and filmmaker. *Awards, honors:* Award from Association of Canadian Television and Radio Artists, 1977, for documentary film on adolescent suicide.

WRITINGS: Growing Up Dead, Abingdon, 1979. Contributor to Canadian magazines, including *Weekend, Canadian, Homemaker, Maclean's,* and *Chatelaine.*

WORK IN PROGRESS: "Growing Up Dead," a film script.

SIDELIGHTS: Brenda Rabkin wrote: "I have a special interest in medical journalism." *Avocational interests:* Racquet sports, jogging, body building.

*   *   *

RADOSH, Ronald 1937-

PERSONAL: Born November 1, 1937, in New York, N.Y.; son of Reuben (a milliner) and Ida (Kreichman) Radosh; married Alice Schweig, 1959 (divorced, 1970); married Allis Wolfe (a consumer's union consultant), October 15, 1975; children: (first marriage) Laura, Daniel; (second marriage) Anna. *Education:* University of Wisconsin—Madison, B.A., 1959, Ph.D., 1967; University of Iowa, M.A., 1960. *Politics:* "Democratic socialist." *Residence:* New York, N.Y. *Agent:* Betty Anne Clarke, 28 East 95th St., New York, N.Y. *Office:* Department of History, Queensborough Community College of the City University of New York, Bayside, N.Y. 11364.

CAREER: Queensborough Community College of the City University of New York, Bayside, N.Y., instructor, 1964-68, assistant professor, 1968-71, associate professor, 1971-78, professor of history, 1978—. Member of graduate faculty at City University of New York Graduate Center. *Member:* P.E.N., American Historical Association, Organization of American Historians, Radical Historians Organization, Columbia University Faculty Seminars in U.S. Civilization.

WRITINGS: (Editor with Louis Menashe) *Teach-Ins U.S.A.,* Praeger, 1967; *American Labor and United States Foreign Policy,* Random House, 1969; (editor) *Eugene V. Debs,* Prentice-Hall, 1972; (editor with Murray N. Rothbard) *A New History of Leviathan,* Dutton, 1973; *Prophets on the Right: Profiles of Conservative Critics of American Globalism,* Simon & Schuster, 1975; (editor) *The New Cuba: Paradoxes and Potentials,* Morrow, 1976. Contributor of articles and reviews to magazines, including *Nation, New Republic, Progressive, In These Times,* and *Dissent,* and newspapers. Member of editorial board of *Marxist Perspectives.*

WORK IN PROGRESS: A book about the Rosenberg case and cold-war America, publication by Holt expected in 1982.

SIDELIGHTS: Radosh wrote: "I agree with the views of my mentor, William Appleman Williams, that the study of history does not allow us to reach back to the past and find ready-made answers for today. Rather, it does allow us to learn how we got to where we are, so that individually and collectively we can formulate relevant alternatives for the present and become actors in making our own history. History can then become both a way of learning and looking at the past, as well as a way of breaking the chains of an earlier era. My own work is written in this spirit."

*   *   *

RADWAY, Ann
See GEIS, Richard E(rwin)

*   *   *

RAEBURN, Antonia 1934-

PERSONAL: Born October 27, 1934, in London, England; daughter of Walter Augustus Leopold (Queen's Counsel) and Dora Adelaide Harvey (an artist; maiden name, Williams) Raeburn; married Alan Jefferson (a writer), 1976; children: Adam Raeburn, Andreas Raeburn. *Education:* Bath Academy of Art, diploma in education and art teacher's diploma, 1955. *Religion:* Church of England. *Home address:* Cair Farm, Downderry, Torpoint, Cornwall PL11 3DN, England. *Agent:* A. D. Peters & Co. Ltd., 10 Buckingham St., London WC2N 6BU, England.

CAREER: Art teacher at rural primary schools in Hertfordshire, England, 1955-59; art director and head of art and craft department at experimental school in Norfolk, England, 1959-62; Bath Academy of Art, Corsham, Wiltshire, England, lecturer, 1962-67; British Broadcasting Corp. (BBC-TV), London, England, art director, 1968; television researcher and art director, 1968-74; writer, 1974—. Art counselor at a camp in Tennessee, 1963; picture researcher for London publishers, 1963-74.

WRITINGS: The Militant Suffragettes (Victorian Book Club selection), M. Joseph, 1968; *The Suffragette View,* David & Charles, 1976. Contributor to journals.

SIDELIGHTS: Antonia Raeburn wrote: "My purpose in writing is educational and I am hoping, in the next few years, to write more children's books of a historical nature." *Avocational interests:* Farming.

* * *

RAFFERTY, Milton 1932-

PERSONAL: Born November 24, 1932, in Jewell County, Kan.; son of Peter John (a farmer) and Mattie (Clemens) Rafferty; married Emma Jean Frink (a mail carrier), July 28, 1956. *Education:* Kansas State University, B.A., 1959, B.S., 1960; University of Utah, M.S., 1965; University of Nebraska, Ph.D., 1970. *Home:* 1351 East Rosebrier, Springfield, Mo. 65804. *Office:* Department of Geography and Geology, Southwest Missouri State University, Springfield, Mo. 65802.

CAREER: High school science teacher in Salina, Kan., 1959-69; Southwest Missouri State University, Springfield, professor of geography, 1966—, head of department of geography and geology, 1972—. Member of Springfield City Planning and Zoning Commission. *Military service:* U.S. Army, 1953-55. *Member:* Association of American Geographers, National Council for Geographic Education, Missouri Council for Geographic Education.

WRITINGS: The Ozarks: Life and Land, University of Oklahoma Press, 1977; (with Scott Harris) *Basic World Place Location,* Kendall/Hunt, 1977; *Historical Atlas of Missouri,* University of Oklahoma Press, 1981; *Ouachita Mountains Guidebook,* University of Oklahoma Press, 1981; *The Ozarks Outdoors: Guidebook for Hunters, Fishermen, and Tourists,* University of Oklahoma Press, 1981; *Missouri: Its Resources and People,* Westview Press, 1981.

WORK IN PROGRESS: World Regional Geography, a textbook; *Historic County Boundary Data File for Arkansas and Missouri.*

SIDELIGHTS: Milton Rafferty told *CA:* "My work on the Ozarks and Missouri extends over a period of fourteen years. The region is much misunderstood in the popular mind. The people readily accept outside assistance and welcome new industries and employment opportunities. While it is true that the region has suffered from isolation and a low level of investment and development, the picture is changing rapidly. The region possesses exceptional amenities for retirement living, including scenic beauty, recreational opportunities, and relatively low cost. Barring unusual national economic crises, the region should show exceptional progress and growth in the next generation."

* * *

RAHNER, Raymond M.
(Ray Rayner)

PERSONAL: Born in New York, N.Y.; son of Michael J. (an industrial foreman) and Sadie (Loughlin) Rahner; married Jeanne D. Lockhart, September 3, 1949; children:

Mark, Christina. *Education:* Fordham University, B.A., 1949; University of Chicago, M.A., 1969. *Office:* WGN-TV, 2501 Bradley Place, Chicago, Ill. 60618.

CAREER: WONE-Radio, Dayton, Ohio, newscaster and news director, 1949-50; WOOD-TV, Grand Rapids, Mich., talk show host, 1950-53; WBBM-TV, Chicago, Ill., performer, 1953-61; WGN-TV, Chicago, Ill., 1961—, host of "The Dick Tracy Show," 1961-66, member of cast of "Bozo's Circus" for nine years, currently host of children's program, "Ray Rayner and His Friends." Actor in a wide variety of stage plays, including "The Odd Couple," "Fiddler on the Roof," "The Only Game in Town," "The Crucible," "The Caine Mutiny," and "The Rainmaker." Director of student productions at Loyola Academy. *Military service:* U.S. Army Air Forces, navigator, 1942-45, prisoner of war in Germany; became first lieutenant; received Distinguished Service Cross, Air Medal with cluster, and Purple Heart.

MEMBER: American Federation of Television and Radio Artists, Screen Actors Guild, Actors' Equity Association, Academy of Television Arts and Sciences. *Awards, honors:* Emmy Awards from Chicago Academy of Television Arts and Sciences, 1961, 1963, and 1964; Daniel Lord Award from Loyola Academy, 1979.

WRITINGS: (Under name Ray Rayner) *The Story of Television: Inside Creative Careers,* Hubbard Press, 1971.

SIDELIGHTS: Rayner's book tells how he produces his morning television program, "Ray Rayner and His Friends," which features cartoons, songs, jokes, and riddles for children, as well as news, sports, and weather information for parents.

* * *

RAILTON, Esther P(auline) 1929-

PERSONAL: Born December 29, 1929, in Reeman, Mich.; daughter of William C. (a farmer) and Adeline (a teacher) Roossinck; married Edward E. Railton (a writer), March 21, 1964. *Education:* Western Michigan University, B.S., 1951; University of Michigan, M.S., 1955; University of Illinois, Ed.D., 1960. *Religion:* Christian. *Office:* Department of Teacher Education, California State University, Hayward, Calif. 94542.

CAREER: Elementary school teacher in Fremont, Mich., 1951-54; Battle Creek Outdoor Education Center, Battle Creek, Mich., resource teacher, 1954-56; University of Illinois, Urbana, instructor, 1956-59; elementary school teacher in Muskegon, Mich., 1959; California State University, Hayward, 1960—, began as assistant professor, currently professor of teacher education. Demonstration teacher at Central Michigan University, 1956, 1957; member of faculty at University of California, Los Angeles, 1961; demonstration teacher at University of California, Berkeley, 1962; member of faculty at Northern Iowa State University, 1963; workshop leader. *Member:* International Reading Association, Conservation Education Association (member of board of directors), American Nature Study Society (past member of board of directors), Association for Outdoor and Environmental Education (past president; past member of board of directors), Pi Lambda Theta (vice-president), Delta Kappa Gamma.

WRITINGS: (With Phyllis Gross) *Teaching Science in an Outdoor Environment,* University of California Press, 1972; *Hawaii: Lava or Leave It,* Educational Resources Information Center, 1979; (contributor) William Hammerman, editor, *Fifty Years of Outdoor Education,* American Camping Association, 1980. Contributor to academic journals.

SIDELIGHTS: Railton told *CA:* "Having a husband who takes writing more seriously than I do keeps me from devoting all of my time to teaching, which is my first vocation. My first article was submitted to *Nature* magazine while I was in high school and returned with the comment 'overwritten.' That editor doesn't know how much he helped me."

AVOCATIONAL INTERESTS: Nature, rural settings, travel, needlework, music.

BIOGRAPHICAL/CRITICAL SOURCES: Environmental Education Reports, July-August, 1979, January, 1980.

*   *   *

RAKSTIS, Ted J(ay) 1932-

PERSONAL: Born December 11, 1932, in Chicago, Ill.; son of Julius P. (a metallurgist) and Ulyssa Alice (a teacher; maiden name, Moskos) Rakstis. *Education:* Benton Harbor Junior College, A.A., 1952; Michigan State University, B.A., 1954; Northwestern University, M.S., 1955. *Politics:* Independent. *Home and office:* 7621 Little Paw Paw Lake Rd., Coloma, Mich. 49038.

CAREER/WRITINGS: Benton Harbor News-Palladium (now *Benton Harbor-St. Joseph Herald-Palladium*), Benton Harbor, Mich., staff writer, 1955-57; free-lance writer, 1958—. Chicago editor of *Playthings* magazine, 1959—. Public relations director of United Community Fund; member of board of directors of Cinema Arts Society, Benton Harbor, and of Barrien chapter of Michigan Society for Mental Health. Contributor of articles to numerous periodicals and newspapers, including *Reader's Digest, Chicago Tribune, Saturday Evening Post, Cosmopolitan, Coronet, Chicago Sun-Times,* and *Writer's Digest. Member:* American Society of Journalists and Authors, Society of Professional Journalists, Sigma Delta Chi. *Awards, honors:* National School Bell Award, 1964, for articles on education in *Kiwanis* magazine; Mort Weisinger Award from American Society of Journalists and Authors, 1980, for article, "The Poisoning of Michigan."

SIDELIGHTS: Rakstis commented to *CA:* "Writing has been my life since I began publishing a grade-school newspaper, and I've been a full-time freelancer for all but a few years since college. Like all freelancers, I have problems: cash flow, dry assignment periods, too many deadlines at one time, and the chronic loneliness and sense of isolation that befall all those who don't have regular office hours and daily contact with people.

"Still, with all its perils and frustrations, I believe that freelancing is the most rewarding of all journalistic endeavors. Unlike many nine-to-fivers, we are free of bureaucratic policies; our work schedule is based on our own wants and needs and those of our families. If we're well enough known—or perhaps just plain lucky—we often can write on whatever subject we choose. Some articles are written through decades of expertise in one field—in my case, business. Others are done for fun—for example, the travel pieces that finance an all-too-infrequent vacation.

"For those of us who have stuck it out during an era when television has transformed the role of the magazine, there are great rewards and challenges. In many ways, television has been an important ally of the serious magazine journalist. The nightly news feeds enormous masses of information into American homes and, as cable television takes hold, we face an overload of electronic dissemination of facts. But television can do little more than recite the basics. Similarly, most newspapers are limited in the space they can devote to

any one subject. That leaves the door open for the magazine journalist to dig in and tell the story at expanded length.

"Some magazines rely on staff writers, but most turn to the freelancer, especially those of us who have displayed investigative reporting skills. Editors depend on us not only to root out the facts but also to present them with viewpoint and conviction. When you see your by-line over a story that can have important national impact, you forget all the pitfalls of free-lance journalism. The glow may last only until you're again driven to the typewriter to find new assignments, but it's the force that keeps you going."

*   *   *

RAMOND, Charles K(night) 1930-

PERSONAL: Born October 9, 1930, in New Orleans, La.; son of Charles Knight and Ethel Chamberlain (Bauer) Ramond; married Ethel Lynn Hock, June, 1950 (divorced, 1953); married Mary Minter Patterson, 1959; children: (second marriage) Nicholas Bauer. *Education:* Tulane University, B.S., 1950; University of Iowa, M.A., 1952, Ph.D., 1953. *Home:* 1170 Fifth Ave., New York, N.Y. 10029. *Office:* Predex Corp., 680 Fifth Ave., New York, N.Y. 10019.

CAREER: Human Resources Research Organization, Washington, D.C., research associate, 1953-54; E.I. du Pont de Nemours & Co., Wilmington, Del., manager of advertising and research, 1956-59; Advertising Research Foundation, New York City, technical director of research, 1959-65; Marketing Control, Inc., New York City, president, 1966-74; Predex Corp., New York City, president, 1974—. Associate professor at Columbia University, 1965-68, adjunct professor, 1968-71. President of Market Research Council, 1973. *Military service:* U.S. Army, 1954-56; served in Japan; became first lieutenant. *Member:* American Psychological Association, American Marketing Association, Operations Research Society of America, Institute of Management Sciences, Academy of International Business. *Awards, honors:* Marcel Dassault Medal for the best paper in media research from Jours de France Foundation, 1970.

WRITINGS: Measurement of Advertising Effectiveness, Stanford Research Institute, 1967; *The Art of Using Science in Marketing,* Harper, 1974; *Advertising Research: The State of the Art,* Association of National Advertisers, 1976. Contributor to business, psychology, and banking journals, including *Euromoney.* Editor of *Journal of Advertising Research,* 1960-80; publisher of *Predex Forecast,* 1974—.

SIDELIGHTS: Ramond writes that his sole interest at present is the work at Predex Corp., a system of economic models that predict exchange rates of the currencies of twenty countries.

*   *   *

RAMOS, Suzanne 1942-

PERSONAL: Surname is pronounced *Ray*-mos; born February 27, 1942, in Poughkeepsie, N.Y.; daughter of Theodore (in real estate) and Hetty (Heermann) Becker; married Joseph E. Ramos, Jr. (a president of a marketing research company), November 21, 1964; children: John, Julie. *Education:* Russell Sage College, B.A., 1964; Columbia University, M.A., 1966. *Residence:* New York, N.Y. *Agent:* Mary Yost Associates, Inc., 75 East 55th St., New York, N.Y. 10003.

CAREER: Elementary school teacher in New York City, 1964-67; Paul Revere School, New York City, teacher, 1967-70; writer, 1971—. *Member:* Manhattan Association of Parents for Gifted Children (president).

WRITINGS: Teaching Your Child to Cope With Crisis, McKay, 1975; *The Complete Book of Child Custody,* Putnam, 1979. Contributor to magazines, including *Redbook, Teacher,* and *Family Circle,* and newspapers.

WORK IN PROGRESS: A novel dealing with a crime of passion, completion expected in 1980.

SIDELIGHTS: Suzanne Ramos commented: "Circumstances were such that I did not begin writing professionally until I took a leave of absence from teaching to be at home with my children. Then I was able to work on a free-lance basis. The family, a growing interest of mine, became a logical choice of subject matter, and coincided with my academic training in sociology and psychology. Out of my first few articles came deeper research into child development and ultimately my two books on family crisis and child custody.

"As a former teacher, I have retained a strong involvement with education. I write on educational subjects and am active in education-related causes."

*   *   *

RAMSEY, Dan(ny Clarence) 1945-

PERSONAL: Born March 11, 1945, in San Fernando, Calif.; son of Clarence Allen and Florence May (Curtis) Ramsey; married Judith Kay Richards (an editor and journalist), November 13, 1970; children: Heather Kay, Byron Hyun Mo, Brendon Yun Mo. *Education:* Attended Clark College, Vancouver, Wash., 1969-70. *Home and office:* 1615 Northeast 129th Ave., Vancouver, Wash. 98664. *Agent:* Richard A. Balkin, Balkin Agency, 403 West 115th St., New York, N.Y. 10025.

CAREER: Disc jockey, program director, and news director for radio stations KGAR, Vancouver, Wash., KAVA, Burney, Calif., KFTM, Ft. Morgan, Colo., KOHI, St. Helens, Ore., KNND, Cottage Grove, Ore., and KLAD/KJSN, Klamath Falls, Ore., 1970-77; *Creswell Chronicle,* Creswell, Ore., publisher, 1974-76; *Coburg Countryman,* Coburg, Ore., publisher, 1974-76; in real estate sales, Vancouver, 1977-78; free-lance writer, 1978—. *Member:* Authors Guild, Aircraft Owners and Pilots Association.

WRITINGS: How to Earn Over $50,000 a Year at Home, Parker Publishing, 1979; *How to Make Your First Quarter Million in Real Estate in Five Years,* Prentice-Hall, 1979; *How to Make $100,000 a Year Selling Residential Real Estate,* Prentice-Hall, 1980; *One Hundred and One Successful Ways to Turn Weekends Into Wealth,* Parker Publishing, 1980; *Budget Flying: How to Earn Your Private Pilot License and Enjoy Flying Economically,* McGraw, 1980. Contributor to national magazines, including *New Woman, Mother Earth News, Camping Journal, Science and Mechanics,* and *Today's Home.*

WORK IN PROGRESS: A book on disc jockeys; a book on fundamental aircraft; a Western novel; "how-to" books and articles on consumer subjects.

SIDELIGHTS: Ramsey wrote: "Life has been a pleasant variety, reaching an apex with writing. Over the past fifteen years I've worked at many jobs, from factory worker to disc jockey, from truck driver to newspaper publisher. Writing fuses this varied background with my inquisitive nature to grant me a comfortable living as a detective of facts. Writing allows me to become a six-month expert on a variety of subjects that fascinate me. I thoroughly enjoy being paid for helping others solve their problems rather than for filling hours on someone else's clock. To me, writing is a business. But it is also a lifestyle."

RANA, J.
See BHATIA, Jamunadevi

*   *   *

RANSOM, Bill 1945-

PERSONAL: Born in 1945 in Puyallup, Wash. *Education:* Attended Washington State University and University of Puget Sound; received degree from University of Washington; graduate studies at University of Nevada at Reno. *Agent:* c/o G. P. Putnam's Sons, 200 Madison Ave., New York, N.Y. 10016.

CAREER: Writer and poet. Worked with Poetry-in-the-Schools; currently writer-in-residence at Centrum Foundation. Poetry reader in tours with Western States Art Foundation. Instructor and poetry reader at colleges and universities. Judge of *Penthouse* (magazine) short fiction contest, 1977. *Awards, honors:* National Defense Education Act (NDEA) Title IV fellowship; *Finding True North and Critter* was nominated for the Pulitzer Prize and National Book Award; National Endowment for the Arts honors fellowship in poetry, 1977.

WRITINGS: Finding True North and Critter (poetry), Copper Canyon Press, 1974; *Waving Arms at the Blind* (poetry), Copper Canyon Press, 1975; *Last Rites* (poetry), Jawbone Press, 1978; (with Frank Herbert) *The Jesus Incident* (novel), Putnam, 1979.

Work represented in anthologies, including *From the Belly of the Shark,* Random House, 1975; *Carriers of the Dream Wheel,* Harper, 1976; *Sense,* Scott, Forsman, 1977; *Iron Country,* Copper Canyon Press, 1979; *Bear Crossings,* New South, 1979.

WORK IN PROGRESS: A novel; a collection of poems.

BIOGRAPHICAL/CRITICAL SOURCES: New York Times, June 1, 1979.

*   *   *

RAPOPORT, Janis 1946-

PERSONAL: Born June 22, 1946, in Toronto, Ontario, Canada; daughter of Maxwell Lewis (a lawyer) and Roslyn (Cohen) Rapoport; married David J. Seager, December 22, 1966 (divorced February 21, 1980); married Douglas F. Donegani (a filmmaker), May 20, 1980; children: (first marriage) Jeremy, Sara, Julia. *Education:* Attended University of Toronto, 1964-67. *Religion:* Jewish. *Home and office:* 112 Brunswick Ave., Toronto, Ontario, Canada M5S 2M2.

CAREER: Which? (magazine), London, England, editorial assistant, 1968-69; Paul Hamlyn Ltd., London, assistant editor, 1969-70; Bellhaven House, Toronto, Ontario, assistant editor, 1971-73; Canadian Broadcasting Corp. (CBC), Toronto, story editor in drama, 1973-74; free-lance editor, 1974—. Hostess at Canadian Pavilion for Canadian government, in Montreal, Quebec, 1967. Playwright-in-residence at Tarragon Theatre, Toronto, 1974-75, and Banff Centre, summer, 1976. Commmittee member of Downtown Jewish Community Centre. *Member:* League of Canadian Poets, Guild of Canadian Playwrights (chairperson of workshop committee, 1979), Association of Canadian Television and Radio Artists, Playwrights Canada (committee member, 1980-81).

WRITINGS: Within the Whirling Moment (poems), House of Anansi Press, 1967; *Jeremy's Dream* (poems), Press Porcepic, 1974; (editor with Gay Allison and Karen Hood) *Landscape* (poems), Women's Writing Collective, 1977;

Winter Flowers (poems), Hounslow Press, 1979; *Dreamgirls* (two-act play; first produced in Toronto, Ontario, at Theatre Pusse-Muraille, January 4, 1979), Playwrights Canada, 1979.

Plays: "And She Could Eat No Lean" (three-act), first produced in Toronto, Ontario, at Tarragon Theatre, June 17, 1975; "Gilgamesh" (one-act), first produced in Toronto, at U. C. Playhouse, May 25, 1976.

Work represented in anthologies, including *Landscape, Tributaries,* and *Whale Sound.*

Contributor to literary journals, including *Malahat Review, Quarry, Canadian Forum, West Coast Review,* and *Black Cat,* and newspapers. Associate editor of *Tamarack Review,* 1970—; regional editor of *CV/II.*

WORK IN PROGRESS: A children's book and musical play; research for a play and film script exploring issues of human liberty and social justice.

SIDELIGHTS: Janis Rapoport told *CA:* "I may not have become a writer were it not for Dave Godfrey, my creative writing instructor at the University of Toronto. I now write because I have to; in the act of writing I am following an inner compulsion. Through my artistic efforts—in whatever medium—I hope to take people, in a metaphoric sense, on new journeys and return them to reality with their sensibilities extended and enriched. I believe in the moral—that is, life affirming—value of art."

*   *   *

RATHBONE, Julian   1935-

PERSONAL: Born February 10, 1935, in London, England. *Education:* Cambridge University, degree, 1958. *Politics:* "Unaffiliated Marxist." *Religion:* Atheist. *Agent:* C. & J. Wolfers, Three Regent Sq., London WC1H 8HZ, England.

CAREER: Teacher at schools in Turkey, 1959-62, and in England, 1962-73; writer, 1973—. *Awards, honors:* Booker Prize nominations, 1976 and 1979.

WRITINGS: King Fisher Lives, St. Martin's, 1976; *Carnival,* St. Martin's, 1976; *Joseph,* St. Martin's, 1979; *The Euro-Killers,* M. Joseph, 1979, Pantheon, 1980; *A Last Resort,* M. Joseph, 1980. Contributor to *Edinburgh Literary Review.*

WORK IN PROGRESS: Research for a novel about English middle-class dissidents in the 1930's and 1940's.

*   *   *

RAUF, Muhammad Abdul
See ABDUL-RAUF, Muhammad

*   *   *

RAYNER, Ray
See RAHNER, Raymond M.

*   *   *

READ, Kenneth E(yre)   1917-

PERSONAL: Born December 29, 1917, in Sydney, Australia; son of Samuel Kenneth (a pastoralist) and Dorothy (Clark) Read; divorced; children: Michael Andrew Eyre. *Education:* University of Sydney, B.A., 1939, M.A., 1946; London School of Economics and Political Science, London, D.Phil., 1948. *Home:* 1104 Grand Ave., Seattle, Wash. 98122. *Office:* Department of Anthropology, University of Washington, Seattle, Wash. 98105.

CAREER: Australian School of Pacific Administration,

Sydney, lecturer in anthropology, 1948-49, senior lecturer in anthropology, 1953-56; Australian National University, Canberra, research fellow, 1950-53; University of Washington, Seattle, visiting associate professor, 1957-58, associate professor, 1958-64, professor of anthropology, 1964—, head of department, 1961-70. *Military service:* Australian Imperial Forces, 1940-45; became sergeant. *Awards, honors:* Bollingen Foundation fellowship, 1958-60; Guggenheim fellowship, 1966-67.

WRITINGS: The High Valley, Scribner, 1965; *The Human Aviary,* photographs by George Holton, Scribner, 1971; *Other Voices,* Chandler & Sharp, 1979. Contributor to anthropology journals and popular magazines, including *Seattle.*

WORK IN PROGRESS: A Shattering of Glass, a novel; research on the subcultures of disadvantaged urban populations in the United States.

SIDELIGHTS: Read has conducted field work in New Guinea and Turkey. He wrote: "Beyond what anthropology may contribute to our understanding of human differences and similarities, I am enamored of the English language. This probably derives from my classical schooling in literature. I am concerned about such matters as balance, clarity, and sound in prose, and I abhor jargon. When I was writing *The High Valley,* I hoped that most of those who might read it would recognize it as a work of art, something quite additional to its anthropological value. Writing is a very difficult task for me, for I am seldom certain that I used *the* right word to convey a particular idea or to produce a particular effect. I like simplicity, and I am easily bored by scholarly authors whose neologisms and latinizations obscure rather than illuminate what they are trying to say."

*   *   *

REDFIELD, Malissa
See ELLIOTT, Malissa Childs
*   *   *

REECE, Jack Eugene   1941-

PERSONAL: Born January 4, 1941, in Kalamazoo, Mich.; son of Paul Eugene and Beulah C. Reece. *Education:* University of Michigan, B.A., 1963; Stanford University, M.A., 1964, Ph.D., 1971. *Politics:* Democrat. *Religion:* Christian. *Home:* 416-C South Hutchinson St., Philadelphia, Pa. 19147. *Office:* Department of History, University of Pennsylvania, Philadelphia, Pa. 19104.

CAREER: University of Pennsylvania, Philadelphia, instructor, 1968-71, assistant professor of history, 1971—. *Member:* American Historical Association, Society for French Historical Studies, Phi Beta Kappa. *Awards, honors:* Woodrow Wilson fellowship, 1963-64; American Council of Learned Societies fellowship, 1974-75; National Endowment for the Humanities fellowship, 1974-75.

WRITINGS: The Bretons Against France, University of North Carolina Press, 1977. Contributor to history journals.

WORK IN PROGRESS: A book on the Mafia in Sicily, publication expected in 1982.

SIDELIGHTS: Jack Reece told *CA:* "My interest in Breton and Sicilian history stems from my longstanding belief that the study of regional cultures in Europe has for too long been neglected in favor of narrow focus on the major centralized nation-states of the continent. In the post-1945 period, when the historical significance of such states as France, Germany, and even the United Kingdom has clearly declined before the growing realities of the new salience of their regional components on the one hand and of the Common Market on the other, scholarly attention to the so-called "little peoples' of Europe is particularly appropriate."

*   *   *

REEDER, John P., Jr. 1937-

PERSONAL: Born July 11, 1937, in Charlotte, N.C.; married Mary Jane Clark, 1965; children: Nicholas Clark, Katherine Whitworth. *Education:* Yale University, A.B., 1960, B.D., 1963, M.A., 1965, Ph.D., 1968. *Home:* 51 Barnes St., Providence, R.I. 02906. *Office:* Department of Religious Studies, Brown University, Providence, R.I. 02912.

CAREER: Princeton University, Princeton, N.J., instructor, 1967-68, assistant professor of religion, 1968-71; Brown University, Providence, R.I., assistant professor, 1971-72, associate professor, 1973-79, professor of religious studies, 1979—. *Member:* American Academy of Religion, American Society of Christian Ethics, American Civil Liberties Union (state vice-chairperson, 1977; member of board of directors, 1979—).

WRITINGS: (Editor with Gene Outka, and contributor) *Religion and Morality*, Doubleday, 1973; *Source, Sanction, and Salvation: An Introduction to Religious Interpretations of Morality*, Prentice-Hall, in press. Co-editor of series, "Studies in Religion," Prentice-Hall. Contributor of articles and reviews to religious studies journals. Ethics editor of *Religious Studies Review*, 1977—.

WORK IN PROGRESS: God and the Moral Law, an analysis and critique of the notion of God as the source of the moral "law" in classic patterns of Jewish and Christian thought; a series of essays on killing.

*   *   *

REES, Margaret A(nn) 1933-

PERSONAL: Born July 3, 1933, in Southport, England; daughter of Benjamin (a school teacher) and Minnie (in business; maiden name, Bate) Williams; married Gwilym O. Rees (a university teacher), April 4, 1961; children: Gareth David, Owen Lewis. *Education:* Westfield College, London, B.A. (with honors), 1954, M.A., 1956, Ph.D., 1959. *Religion:* "Nonconformist." *Home:* 51 Weetwood Lane, Leeds, West Yorkshire LS16 5NP, England. *Office:* Department of Spanish, Trinity and All Saints' Colleges, Brownberrie Lane, Horsforth, Leeds, West Yorkshire LS18 5HD, England.

CAREER: University of Liverpool, Liverpool, England, fellow in Spanish, 1958-60, lecturer in French, 1960-67; teacher of Spanish at schools in Southport, England, 1967-69; Trinity and All Saints' Colleges, Leeds, England, lecturer, 1970-76, senior lecturer in modern languages and European studies, 1976—. *Member:* Modern Language Association of America, Association of Teachers of Spanish and Portuguese, Society for French Studies, Association of Hispanists. *Awards, honors:* Leverhulme fellowship, 1958-60.

WRITINGS: Alfred de Musset, Twayne, 1971; (editor) Alfred de Musset, *Contes d'Espagne et d'Italie* (title means "Stories of Spain and Italy"), Athlone Press, 1973; *French Authors on Spain, 1800-1850*, Grant & Cutler, 1977; *Espronceda's "El Estudiante de Salamanca,"* Grant & Cutler, 1980. Contributor to language and European studies journals.

WORK IN PROGRESS: Research on parallel descriptions in French and Spanish.

REGNERY, Henry 1912-

PERSONAL: Born January 5, 1912, in Hinsdale, Ill.; son of William Henry and Frances Susan (Thrasher) Regnery; married Eleanor Scattergood, November 12, 1938; children: Susan, Alfred S., Henry F., Margaret. *Education:* Massachusetts Institute of Technology, B.S., 1934; graduate study at University of Bonn, Germany, 1934-36; Harvard University, M.A., 1938. *Home:* 70 East Cedar St., Chicago, Ill. 60611. *Office:* 120 West LaSalle, South Bend, Ind. 46624.

CAREER: American Friends Service Commission, Philadelphia, Pa., member of staff, 1938-41; Joanna Western Mills Co., Chicago, Ill., officer, 1941-47, director, 1945—; Henry Regnery Co., Chicago, Ill., founder, 1947, president, 1947-66, chairman of the board, 1967-77; Gateway Editions, Ltd. (company became Regnery/Gateway, Inc., 1979), South Bend, Ind., founder and president, 1977—. *Awards, honors:* LL.D. from Mt. Mary College.

WRITINGS: Wyndham Lewis: A Man Against His Time, Chicago Literary Club, 1969; (editor) *Viva Vivas!*, Liberty Press, 1976; *Memoirs of a Dissident Publisher*, Harcourt, 1979. Contributor of articles to periodicals, including *Modern Age, American Spectator*, and *National Review*.

SIDELIGHTS: In 1947 Henry Regnery founded his own publishing company with a pledge to "publish good books, wherever we find them." His *Memoirs of a Dissident Publisher* is a look back on his years in the industry, with descriptions of Regnery-published works by William F. Buckley, Russell Kirk, James J. Kilpatrick, and other writers who were highly influential in the American conservative movement following World War II. Regnery includes in his discussions both positive and negative reviews of the books and "lucidly" explains the authors' ideas, according to Bill Steigerwald. But Steigerwald added that despite the balanced view, "conservatives will find themselves concurring with the majority of Regnery's conclusions . . . [and] liberals will not."

Doris Grumbach of the *New York Times Book Review* remarked that "so cogent and convincing are Regnery's summaries that I felt the urge to look again at such books as William Henry Chamberlain's 'America's Second Crusade' and Harry Elmer Barnes's 'The Genesis of the World War.'" *Chicago Tribune* reviewer Alan Moores commented that "coming from one so accustomed to the printed word, the author's writing style is rather dry, at times leaden, and there are a number of remarks that seem gratuitous. . . . Still, those interested in the development of the conservative movement during the postwar years will find in this unpretentious account a valuable perspective."

CA INTERVIEWS THE AUTHOR
CA interviewed Henry Regnery by phone April 30, 1980, at his office in South Bend, Indiana.

CA: You describe yourself as a personal publisher. Richard Grossman has characterized a personal publisher as somebody who works from the inside out, a man who works primarily from personal interests and worries later about whether anyone outside is also interested in them.

REGNERY: I think that's pretty much true of my publishing; that is, it reflected my own prejudices and ideas and conceptions—not entirely, but it did largely. Sometimes I published books because someone on my staff thought they should be published; sometimes I published books which I didn't really agree with but I thought were deserving of publication; and I published books sometimes that I didn't think much of but that I thought might sell. But largely I think my publishing reflected my own point of view.

CA: Could you give me a few examples of books you thought reflected your personal tastes?

REGNERY: I think the first book I published to be widely reviewed and to attract attention was called *And Madly Teach* by a man named Mortimer Smith. The book came to me through the then head of the University of Chicago Press, William Couch. He felt the university press couldn't publish it. It very much reflected my own views. It was a book on public education and was very critical of the Dewey idea of the child-centered school. It was by a man who believed that the schools should teach the basic things and that there should be discipline. I was delighted to have the manuscript and publish it. I would say that was an example of personal publishing, although whether another publisher would have brought it out I have no idea.

Another early book of mine which I think very much reflected my own point of view was William Henry Chamberlin's *America's Second Crusade,* a book on American intervention in World War II. Chamberlin had been a correspondent in Russia for ten or twelve years for the *Christian Science Monitor.* He was finally expelled by the Russian government. This book had been turned down by several publishers. He had written a good many books before, including a history of the Russian revolution that was published, I think, by Macmillan. This was at a time—it must have been in the early 1950's —when feelings were still quite strong about intervention in World War II. My father was very active in America First; I was very much opposed to our getting into the war; and I published this book, which was highly critical of Roosevelt and of the whole realm of American policies involving World War II. Very gladly, I must say.

CA: Would you try to summarize some of the values you feel you've represented as a personal publisher?

REGNERY: I would say that I believe in the need for order. I agree with something that my old friend Richard Weaver once said: that there are principles and laws and regulations governing the order of being which are beyond man's control, which are there and which are very real. Their existence is as real as the table in front of you. We have to accept them. I remember Albert J. Nock remarking in quoting Bishop Berkeley, "Things are as they are and their consequences will be as they will be. Why should we delude ourselves to the contrary?"

CA: I'm curious about how your interest in publishing some of the existentialists—or the phenomenologists in particular, like Heidegger—fits in with the philosophical position you've just described. He certainly doesn't believe that things "are as they are."

REGNERY: I'm not a professional philosopher at all, and I really don't get much out of reading Heidegger, much as I try. I got into those books I think largely because of a man who was associated with my firm for the first four or five years, Paul Scheffer, a German. He used to read manuscripts for me. It was he who got me into those first two or three books involving philosophy. Then I published paperback editions of "great books" for the Great Books Foundation. That was quite early in my career. There were a good many philosophical texts in the Great Books series.

CA: You'd say then that the philosophical books were not so

much an example of personal publishing as other demands?

REGNERY: No. They were just books that happened to come my way through Scheffer and then the Great Books arrangement. And I used to read quite a bit of Nietzsche; there were two or three volumes of Nietzsche in the Great Books series, so I arranged to get a better translation. At that time, the only translations of Nietzsche were very inadequate. I arranged to get a new translation of *Beyond Good and Evil* and *Thus Spake Zarathustra* and one or two others done by a woman at Princeton, Marianne Cowan.

CA: So the Nietzsche publications were a reflection of personal interest?

REGNERY: Yes. I got into that, again, through the Great Books arrangement, more through that than an overwhelming interest in philosophy—although I did enjoy Nietzsche, I must say; I particularly enjoy his style.

CA: One of the things that has interested me about your publishing operation is that you've taken the chance to publish some writers who've been unpopular because of their conservative political stance. Could you offer any specific details about problems you found in trying to publish unpopular literary writers such as Pound or Wyndham Lewis?

REGNERY: Yes. I've published at least five books of Wyndham Lewis's. It was rather strange with Lewis. Of course he had a big reputation. He was always accused of being a Fascist. His books were pretty well reviewed—the books I published, that is. I think the first was *Revenge for Love,* which is a novel, and maybe Lewis's best novel. It's certainly *one* of his best novels. I remember *Time* gave it a long review, but they always brought up the "fact" that he'd been a Fascist and pro-Hitler. But he was no more pro-Hitler than, say, Winston Churchill was. Lewis had been in World War I as a soldier at the front; he was an artillery officer. He was very much concerned about the prospect of a repetition of World War I. And I think his apparent partiality for Hitler was much more a reaction against the anti-Hitler feeling which he feared would lead to another war.

I published only one book of Pound's, and that was a book of essays; I remember that *Commonweal,* a Catholic publication, gave it a very bad review. The reviewer added, "Who but Regnery would have published such a book as this?"

CA: Are there any specific classifications or types of problems that you encountered in trying to publish writers of this sort?

REGNERY: I think the big problem is trying to get them fairly reviewed, and the second problem is to get the books into the bookstores. If you can't get a book reviewed it makes it very difficult to sell it.

CA: Did you find that you were having to do more than the other publishers were having to do to promote their books?

REGNERY: Oh, we had to do much more. We had to advertise much more. Sometimes the only way to get a review was to run a big ad and more or less shame a publication into reviewing the book. As I remember, we had quite a hard time with that book of Chamberlin's, which of course was very much contrary to the prevailing attitude at the time. That was just a few years after the war, and Roosevelt was still regarded as a great statesman. It was very difficult to get the book fairly reviewed and in the bookstores, but it sold fairly well.

CA: Do you recall having resorted to techniques other than the ads in order to get reviews that you might not ordinarily have gotten?

REGNERY: One thing I used to do was just go down to New York to see the reviewers and try to convince them that this was a book they had an obligation to review, whether favorably or not. I'd spend a whole week and go around to see the book review people—*Time* and the *New York Times, Harper's, Atlantic,* whatever it was.

CA: Did you get to know them well enough that after a while you were able to rely on phone calls and letters?

REGNERY: I got to know some of them fairly well. Francis Brown at the *Times,* for instance, became quite friendly. He was a very fair man. A personal call was better than letters, because the reviewers are under a great deal of pressure. There are far more books published than can possibly be reviewed, so that you just have to make an effort to get your book into that little crack.

CA: Did you ever sense that there were times when an author ran into some difficulty because Regnery was publishing him, difficulty he might not have run into had somebody else published him?

REGNERY: I just don't know. It could be. I don't think so. After all, I published Buckley's first book, and he went on to have quite a distinguished career, and successful.

CA: Kirkus Review, *in its May 15, 1979, coverage of your memoirs, talked about that "opprobrious object the one-sided publisher's list." Obviously the* Kirkus Review *is biased. What are the advantages in a one-sided list?*

REGNERY: It indicates that a publisher stands for something, and a book that he publishes is automatically put into a certain category. This can also be a disadvantage. Lewis, for instance, in one of his books (I think it was *The Writer and the Absolute*) argues that one of the troubles with French publishing is that French publishers are inclined to be more or less categorical. That is, a publisher is allied with a certain intellectual position, which causes a book to be automatically categorized in the minds of the public.

CA: So people won't read it, but on the other hand you get people who will automatically read it because they know it's allied with that position.

REGNERY: I don't take Virginia Kirkus very seriously. But, on the other hand, one of the real problems in publishing is that you have a very strongly biased service, such as the Kirkus service, which goes to libraries and has a good deal of influence on the sale of a book.

CA: Can you think of any other advantages of the one-sided list?

REGNERY: I suppose it also attracts certain types of manuscripts. We have started up for the second time, and with the kind of reputation I have, we get very high-quality manuscripts by people who feel that we're the right publisher for them. It's also an identity for quality, not only for a certain intellectual or political position. I think we do have, at least to some extent, such an identity—for quality, that is.

CA: What do you consider the most significant contribution you've made (1) to publishing and (2) to serious literature? In other words, what do you like best about what you've done?

REGNERY: I think maybe publishing Russell Kirk's *The Conservative Mind.* And I think getting Wyndham Lewis

back in this country, which is something I did do, at least to some extent, was a real contribution. Another author I published whom I consider to be a major figure is the German economist Wilhelm Roepke. He's not as much recognized as he should be, but an enormously courageous man. I think he's probably a more important economist than Friedman, although I admire Friedman very much, because I think that Roepke saw the whole issue in greater perspective and also saw the moral issues involved in the free market.

CA: What you've mentioned so far are contributions in terms of specific books. How about innovations or elements in publishing?

REGNERY: I don't know about publishing itself, but I think I did have a good deal of influence on the development of the modern Conservative movement, that is through my publishing people like Kirk and Willmoore Kendall and others. That's quite a different thing from something like the Republican party or that organization that was opposed to Roosevelt during the 1930's. I think the modern Conservative movement has a very definite intellectual content; it's more than just opposition to high taxes. It's a much more positive and constructive movement than just simply opposition.

CA: The New York Times Book Review, *August 5, 1979, said that your memoirs reveal very little about your personal life. Is that a kind of deliberate, conscious style, or is it a reflection of your personality?*

REGNERY: It's a reflection of my personality. I've gotten quite friendly with some of the authors I've published; for instance, I consider myself a good friend of Bill Buckley, of Russell Kirk. But I suppose I never established the close personal relationship with an author that some publishers I've read about have.

CA: Do you see advantages in that sort of position?

REGNERY: Oh, yes, sure. There are advantages and, I suppose, disadvantages. I felt that the best thing a publisher can do for an author is to bring his book out in good form, edit it properly, and sell it as best he can. I have made suggestions to authors. I suggested a good many books to Russell Kirk; at least two were written at my definite suggestion. But I don't think my relationship with any author is as close as some publishers' and some publishers' editors.

CA: What disadvantages do you see in the intimate relationship somebody like Max Perkins had with Fitzgerald or Wolfe?

REGNERY: Well, of course it ties him up. It must have taken an awful lot of time, for one thing. I don't think any publisher could permit an editor to spend that much time now on a book, because the costs are so high and the margin of profit so low—that sort of thing isn't as possible as it was then.

CA: You spent several years in Germany studying. How would you characterize the influence of your years in Germany on your publishing career?

REGNERY: Well, for one thing I learned the German language. If I had known French, for instance, as well as I knew German, I probably would have published many more French books than I did. If I had studied in England I probably would have become acquainted then with such people, at least with the work of such people, as Lewis and others. I could have gotten into that sooner than I did.

CA: How influential do you think intimate knowledge of the language is for a publisher in his acquisitions?

REGNERY: Very influential. He is able to read the book and that makes a great difference. And if you know a language you're bound to have more curiosity about what's being written in that language than if you didn't.

CA: Do you get the sense that perhaps you might have been aware of books in German long before another publisher might have been aware, simply because you were keeping up with what was going on in Germany?

REGNERY: I suppose I was, although most of the German books that I did were not particularly successful. One German author I published several books of was Luise Rinser. She was very gifted but she didn't follow through. I thought that a couple of books of hers that I did were quite good, but she didn't come up to her promise. I talked to her German publisher and he said that he felt exactly the same way about it. Romano Guardini, of course, I did publish and quite successfully. I probably would not have done so had I not been able to read German. He was my most successful author, by the way.

CA: Did you see any intellectual influence from Germany?

REGNERY: I don't know. I had a very good German friend, whom I met at Harvard, which was the reason that I went to Germany, actually. He was a very distinguished art historian, a remarkable man, a very cultivated man, and a good musician. We became close friends; he had far more influence on me than any college or university.

CA: So it was a single individual who happened to be German rather than the cultural influence?

REGNERY: It could have been French. He was born right on the border. He had a great deal of influence on me.

CA: Your father said that if you're making money in publishing you are publishing the wrong kind of books. Do you still believe that?

REGNERY: To a certain extent. I think we have to face the fact that *Playboy* makes a lot more money than *Harper's.* And that's just the way our world is. I think that you *can* make money publishing books. I expect to make money in my new firm. Not a lot, but I think we can operate profitably. It has to be done by watching costs awfully carefully and hoping to have an occasional successful book. In my former publishing firm I took over an old firm in Chicago that published mostly children's books. I had hoped that with the children's book list and a few popular books I could put the whole operation on a profitable basis. But you still have to face the fact that serious books are hard to sell and for the most part have a limited sale.

CA: One of the things that fascinated me in your book was a very brief comment: you referred to a publisher's "secondary creativity." Could you expand upon this?

REGNERY: It had occurred to me that when a publisher suggests a book to an author, the publisher is not the creative person, but he has a creative influence. An example of it: Russell Kirk wrote a book called *The American Cause.* I suggested the book to him. You may remember that during or after the Korean War it came out that the American prisoners had behaved very badly. They were easily coerced by the Russians or the Communists into confessing all sorts of things that they couldn't possibly have done, such as engag-

ing in germ warfare and all of that sort of thing. People were simply appalled that American prisoners had behaved so badly, that they had little or no knowledge of American history or of American traditions. I got interested in this subject and then somehow or other—I can't remember how—I met a man who had been a jet pilot and had been captured in Korea. He had signed confessions that he had been involved in germ warfare and all sorts of ridiculous things. I spent a whole day with him. It was very interesting to talk with him, and to see how little he knew. He had come from Ardmore, Pennsylvania, and went to a public school. He had never read a serious book in his life. When he was in this prison camp, the Russians gave him *Grapes of Wrath* and other similar books which dwelled a lot on poverty and that sort of thing in this country. Then they gradually worked things up until they had him convinced that our country was sort of a large concentration camp where the rich were oppressing the poor. Then from that they went on to having him sign all sorts of confessions. He admitted all this very freely.

Well, I talked to Russell Kirk about all of this and suggested that maybe it would be a good idea to get out a book which would set forth clearly and succinctly what the basic American ideal was, what we represented in history. He was interested in the idea. I talked with somebody in the armed forces and they arranged for Russell to go down to someplace in Georgia, where they had all the records of the prisoners. He went over all of that and eventually wrote his book. And it was a very good little book; I think it's still in print. That was what I meant by secondary creativity.

CA: Do you see any differences for the possibilities of secondary creativity in one literary genre over another, such as drama over poetry?

REGNERY: I haven't had enough experience with that sort of thing to know. Did you read the letters of Flannery O'Connor? She didn't take too kindly to suggestions from editors and publishers, did she? She knew exactly where she stood and what she wanted to say and that was that. That's a great book, her volume of letters. I wish I had published it.

CA: How would you describe the ideal author-publisher relationship? That is, what ingredients do you see coming into play?

REGNERY: That the author trust the publisher, his judgment, feel that he is competent. That makes an *enormous* difference. And I think that the publisher should respect the author. Respect him as a person and respect his competence. He's taken his book because he thinks he has something to say, because he *wants* to publish it. But in such matters as advertising, promotion, etc., the author should feel that that's the publisher's job. If he doesn't know how to do it, he ought to go to somebody else. Mutual respect and mutual trust. Of course there can be personality conflicts, but I don't know that that should make so much difference.

CA: What roles do publishers fulfill for authors beyond some of the obvious ones such as editor, confidant, etc.?

REGNERY: One thing a publisher can do for a new author is to introduce him. That is, a man who comes along with a first book usually doesn't know very many people, hasn't been around much. You provide contacts. You also increase his self-confidence. I can think of one author whose name I would not want to mention who was very shy and unsure of himself. I think we helped in that respect, meeting people and taking him around. A publisher can broaden an author's acquaintanceship and in that way help his career.

CA: Do you see publishers using specific techniques in working with authors? Or do you see it as individual reaction to specific personality?

REGNERY: Every situation is so different. I think that you always have to approach every situation very gingerly and very carefully. The light touch and discretion become the key issues. It's very easy to set things off in the wrong direction. You're always walking on a mine field in dealing with an author. This can be very different, of course, depending upon the author, but it's always something to keep in mind. After all, an author's manuscript represents a good deal of work; a serious book is a part of his personality. And if you don't approach it as part of his personality, as something he's very devoted and attached to and as a part of him, you can quickly get into trouble.

There is one thing that you should keep in mind: that the publisher is a victim of his times. He cannot publish better books than are being written in his time. And he also cannot publish books that people are not willing to buy. When I first went into publishing right after World War II, I was under the illusion that we were going to have a great creative period, as followed World War I. Well, it didn't happen. But this was not the fault of the publishers really. No T. S. Eliots came along or Wyndham Lewises or Ezra Pounds. That's why a publisher has to be judged on the basis of how much he was able to do within the limitations of his period.

BIOGRAPHICAL/CRITICAL SOURCES: Virginia Quarterly Review, spring, 1977; *Christian Century,* April 27, 1977; *Los Angeles Times Book Review,* June 24, 1979; *Chicago Tribune,* July 29, 1979; *New York Times Book Review,* August 5, 1979.

—*Interview by Richard E. Ziegfeld*

* * *

REID, Charles (Stuart) 1900-
(Charles Stuart; John Davidson, Francis Martin, pseudonyms)

PERSONAL: Born November 11, 1900, in Bradford, England; son of William James and Annie (Heaps) Reid; married Louise Clapham, March 6, 1943; children: Thomas James Stuart, John Francis Martin (deceased). *Education:* Attended high school in Bradford, England. *Politics:* "Independent Right." *Religion:* Roman Catholic. *Home:* 10/23 Compayne Gardens, London NW6 3DE, England.

CAREER: Yorkshire Observer, Bradford, England, general reporter, art critic, music critic, book critic, special news-writer, and news editor; *Sketch,* London, England, reporter; *Observer,* London, profile writer and chief music critic (under name Charles Stuart); currently free-lance writer. *Member:* National Union of Journalists, London Critics Circle.

WRITINGS: Peter Grimes, Boosey & Hawkes, 1947; *Thomas Beecham: An Independent Biography,* Gollancz, 1961, Dutton, 1962; *Malcolm Sargent: A Biography,* Hamish Hamilton, 1968, Taplinger, 1970; *John Barbirolli: A Biography,* Taplinger, 1971; *Fifty Years of Robert Mayer Concerts,* Colin Smith, 1972. Also author of *Bleeding Hands,* East Anglia University Press. Contributor to magazines in England and the United States, sometimes under pseudonyms John Davidson and Francis Martin. Music critic for *Punch, News Chronicle, Evening Standard, Daily Mail, Spectator,* and *High Fidelity.*

WORK IN PROGRESS: Research for *Davison of the Times: His Crimes,* on England's "first music critic."

SIDELIGHTS: "Writing for print is traceable in my family

on the paternal side to 1840," Reid commented, "and probably predates that period. Each generation has produced a writer or writers. My son is a journalist in Fleet Street.

"I did not come up to Fleet Street myself until I turned forty. On becoming a father for the first time, at age forty-four, I moved to London, quickly became a star reporter for a 'pop' daily, the *Sketch,* and two years later transferred to the *Observer,* during the decades when the *Observer*'s successive music critics were always among the four pre-eminent music critics of London. All my later achievements were based on this appointment. For several journals, including *Punch* under Malcolm Muggeridge's editorship, I also wrote on non-musical topics, using pen-names at discretion."

* * *

REID, Escott (Meredith) 1905-

PERSONAL: Born January 21, 1905, in Campellford, Ontario, Canada; son of A. J. (an Anglican minister) and Morna (Meredith) Reid; married Ruth Herriot, August 30, 1930; children: Patrick, Morna, Timothy. *Education:* University of Toronto, B.A., 1927; Oxford University, M.A., 1930. *Religion:* Anglican. *Home address:* R.R.2, Sainte Cecile de Masham, Quebec, Canada J0X 2W0.

CAREER: Canadian Institute of International Affairs, Toronto, Ontario, national secretary, 1932-38; Department of External Affairs, Ottawa, Ontario, served in Washington, D.C., London, Ontario, and in Ottawa, 1939-47, assistant under-secretary, 1947-48, deputy under-secretary, 1948-52, acting under-secretary, 1948-49, high commissioner in India, 1952-57, ambassador to West Germany, 1958-62; International Bank for Reconstruction and Development, Washington, D.C., director of Southeast Asia and Middle East department, 1962-65; York University, Toronto, professor of political science and principal of Glendon College, 1965-69; Canadian International Development Agency, Ottawa, consultant, 1970-72; Queen's University, Kingston, Ontario, Skelton-Clark fellow, 1972-73; writer, 1973—. Acting professor at Dalhousie University, 1937-38. Member of executive committee of Preparatory Commission of United Nations in London, England, 1945, chairperson of United Nations Assembly committee on procedure and organization, 1947. *Awards, honors:* Rhodes scholar, 1927-30; Rockefeller Foundation fellow, 1930-32; honorary doctorates from Mount Allison University, 1955, York University, 1972, and Carleton University, 1979; Companion of Order of Canada, 1971.

WRITINGS: The Future of the World Bank, World Bank, 1965; *Strengthening the World Bank,* University of Chicago Press, 1973; *Time of Fear and Hope: The Making of the North Atlantic Treaty, 1947-1949,* McClelland & Stewart, 1977; *Envoy to Nehru,* Oxford University Press, 1980.

WORK IN PROGRESS: Nehru and the Hungarian Revolt.

* * *

REIFFEL, Leonard 1927-

PERSONAL: Surname is pronounced "rifle"; born September 30, 1927, in Chicago, Ill.; son of Carl (a silversmith) and Sophie (a school administrator; maiden name, Miller) Reiffel; married Judith Blumenthal, June, 1952 (divorced February, 1961); married Nancy Jeffers, June, 1971; children: Evan Carl, David Lee. *Education:* Illinois Institute of Technology, B.S., 1947, M.S., 1948, Ph.D., 1953. *Home:* 602 West Deming Place, Chicago, Ill. 60614. *Agent:* Robbin Reynolds, Robbin Reynolds Agency, 501 Madison Ave.,

New York, N.Y. 10022. *Office:* Interand Corp., 666 North Lake Shore Dr., Chicago, Ill. 60611.

CAREER: Illinois Institute of Technology Research Institute, Chicago, vice-president, 1944-65; Instructional Dynamics, Inc., Chicago, chairman of board of directors, 1964—. Chairman and president of Interand Corp., 1969—; president of Theodoron Foundation. Physicist at University of Chicago's Institute for Nuclear Studies, 1948-49; past deputy director for sciences of National Aeronautics and Space Administration (NASA) *Apollo* lunar landing program, executive secretary of *Apollo* landing site selection board, and technical director of manned space flight experiments board; science commentator for Columbia Broadcasting System (CBS), presented television series "Backyard Safari," daily radio program "Dimension for Tomorrow's Living," and appeared on "Science for the Seventies"; science editor for WEEI-Radio, WBBM-TV and Radio, and WTTW-TV. Member of board of directors of Student Competitions on Relevant Engineering (SCORE); consultant to National Academy of Sciences, U.S. Department of Defense, Atomic Energy Commission, and Government of Korea.

MEMBER: American Nuclear Society (Chicago chairman, 1960-61; vice-chairman of national Isotopes and Radiation Division, 1960-61), American Physical Society (fellow), Chicago Literary Club, Sigma Xi, Eta Kappa Nu, Tau Beta Pi. *Awards, honors:* Merit award from Chicago Technical Societies Council, 1968; George Foster Peabody Award from University of Georgia's School of Journalism, 1968, for "The World Tomorrow"; Emmy Award nomination from Academy of Television Arts and Sciences, 1973, for "Backyard Safari"; three IR-100 awards from Industrial Research Magazine, 1970, for inventing Telestrator, 1972, for Maritime Communications System, and 1973, for DISCON Audiografix; award from Aviation Writers Association, 1971, for coverage of space events.

WRITINGS: The Contaminant (novel), Harper, 1978. Author of "Science and You," a column distributed by Los Angeles Times Syndicate, 1966-72. Contributor of about seventy articles to scientific journals. Editor of volume on space exploration for American Astronautical Association, 1964.

WORK IN PROGRESS: Two novels.

SIDELIGHTS: Reiffel was a part of the team that conducted the first hydrogen bomb experiments in the Pacific Ocean and atomic bomb experiments at Frenchmen's Flat, Nevada. He has conducted nuclear experiments on cosmic rays in aircraft flights from below the equator almost to the North Pole. He also participated in American high altitude nuclear weapons tests in the Pacific.

He holds patents in several fields, including nuclear physics, optics, electronics, video systems, and space sciences. His Telestrator is a device for creating instant animated notations on television images; the Maritime Communications System and DISCON (Display Conferencing) comprise crisis communications and management systems that permit real-time interactive graphical information exchange and teleconferencing wherever voice communication exists.

Recently he has also been involved with Student Competitions on Relevant Engineering, which organizes such events as National Clean Car Races, Students Against Fires Competition, and Energy Efficient Vehicles Competition.

Reiffel told *CA:* "I wrote *The Contaminant* specifically to warn the public about the real-world danger of the type of undeclared biomedical war the novel describes. It was cer-

tainly also my intention in *The Contaminant* to be entertaining, although I must admit I based the 'entertainment' once again on a real-world message since the suspense in the novel derives from the ebb and flow of presidential decision-making under circumstances where he can neither trust the information he has nor be sure he has all the information he needs. My experience in Command and Control tells me that this is the way things actually happen. At the time I was writing the fictional story, *Contaminant,* I was also creating what have come to be known as 'The Doomsday Tapes,' a set of factual video tapes for the Federal Civil Defense Agency designed to teach people lifesaving actions in the last few days before a nuclear confrontation. Thus, I was continuously moving between the fictional world of the novel and the real world of actual preparations for nuclear war—an eerie experience!

"At this writing, Universal Studios has purchased an option on *The Contaminant* and if it is actually made into a film or television presentation, it will be an interesting opportunity to teach the public about civil defense as an incidental aspect of entertaining and scaring the hell out of them.

"Having tasted the experience of writing fiction, I am now hard at work on two other novels that will again mix in scientific reality and fiction but which will, I think, be less terrifying than *The Contaminant.*"

*   *   *

REIGER, George W. 1939-

PERSONAL: Born April 7, 1939, in Brooklyn, N.Y.; son of Anthony C. (a physician) and Sally Elton (a nurse; maiden name, Dance) Reiger; married Barbara Burton Banks (an editorial assistant), January 16, 1970; children: Christopher Anton Robert. *Education:* Princeton University, A.B. (cum laude), 1960; graduate study at University of Virginia, 1961-62; Columbia University, M.A., 1964. *Home address:* Seaside Rd., Locustville, Va. 23404. *Agent:* John Boswell, 45 East 51st St., Suite 301, New York, N.Y. 10021. *Office: Field and Stream,* 1515 Broadway, New York, N.Y. 10036.

CAREER: Popular Mechanics, New York City, boating and outdoor editor, 1969-71; *Field and Stream,* New York City, associate editor, 1972-74, conservation editor, 1974—. *Military service:* U.S. Navy, 1964-69, instructor at U.S. Naval Academy, 1967-68, interpreter and translator at Paris peace talks, 1969; served in Vietnam; became lieutenant; received Purple Heart and Vietnamese Medal of Honor, first class.

WRITINGS: (Editor) *Zane Grey, Outdoorsman,* Prentice-Hall, 1972; *Profiles in Saltwater Angling,* Prentice-Hall, 1973; (editor) *Fishing With McClane,* Prentice-Hall, 1975; (with wife, Barbara Reiger) *Zane Grey Outdoor Cookbook,* Prentice-Hall, 1976; *The Wings of Dawn,* Stein & Day, 1979; *The National Audubon Society Book of Marine Wildlife,* Chanticleer, 1980.

Contributor to numerous books. Associate and senior editor of *National Wildlife* and *International Wildlife,* 1971-75; Washington and field editor for *Audubon,* 1975-79. Contributor of more than two hundred articles to magazines, including *Fly Fisherman, Foreign Service Journal, New Scientist, Sea Frontiers,* and *True.*

WORK IN PROGRESS: A book on Atlantic coastal resources for publication by Simon & Schuster.

*   *   *

REILL, Peter Hanns 1938-

PERSONAL: Born December 11, 1938, in New York, N.Y.;

son of Albert and Lillian (Kirchner) Reill; married French Prescott (a teacher), July 16, 1968; children: Dominique Kirchner. *Education:* New York University, A.B., 1960; Northwestern University, received M.A. and Ph.D.; also attended University of Goettingen, 1963-65. *Politics:* Democrat. *Religion:* Roman Catholic. *Home:* 156 Muerdago Rd., Topanga, Calif. 90290. *Office:* Department of History, University of California, Los Angeles, Calif. 90024.

CAREER: Northwestern University, Evanston, Ill., instructor in history, 1965-66; University of California, Los Angeles, assistant professor, 1966-74, associate professor of history, 1974—. *Member:* American Historical Association, Lessing Society, Goethe Society, Western Association for German Studies. *Awards, honors:* Fulbright fellow, 1963-65, senior fellow, 1979-80; Guggenheim fellow, 1978-79.

WRITINGS: The German Enlightenment and the Rise of Historicism, University of California Press, 1975. Contributor to history and German studies journals.

WORK IN PROGRESS: A study of the thought of Wilhelm von Humboldt and Barthold Georg Niebuhr, within the context of late eighteenth-century German social, scientific, and political thought.

SIDELIGHTS: Reill commented: "I am interested in the intellectual history of Germany, especially of the eighteenth and early nineteenth centuries."

*   *   *

REILLY, Christopher T(homas) 1924-

PERSONAL: Born September 22, 1924, in Paterson, N.J.; son of Edgar A. (a textiles manufacturer) and Ellen (a secretary; maiden name, Matchett) Reilly; married Elsa Ruth Hoyns, June 21, 1947; children: Stephen Thomas, Paul Christopher, Ruth Ann Reilly Rudd, Philip Edward. *Education:* Attended New York University, 1942-44, and University of Pennsylvania, 1944-45; Long Island College of Medicine (now State University of New York Downstate Medical Center), M.D., 1949. *Religion:* Christian. *Home:* 506 Linwood Ave., Ridgewood, N.J. 07450. *Office:* Ridgewood Gynecology Associates, 65 North Maple Ave., Ridgewood, N.J. 07451.

CAREER: Paterson General Hospital, Paterson, N.J., intern, 1949-50, resident in obstetrics, 1950-51; Cooper Hospital, Camden, N.J., resident in gynecology, 1953-54; private practice of obstetrics and gynecology in Ridgewood, N.J., 1954—. Associate attending physician at Paterson General Hospital, 1954-63, and Bergen Pines Hospital, 1960—, director of department of obstetrics and gynecology, 1974; attending physician at Valley Hospital, 1954—, and Martland Medical Center, 1969—. Clinical assistant professor at New Jersey College of Medicine, 1966—; director of New Jersey Study of Maternity Bed Utilization, 1964-66. Member of Gideons, 1943—, and Word of Life Council; member of board of directors of Medical Assistance Program, Wheaton, Ill., 1965-69, and Eastern Christian Children's Retreat, 1968-74 and 1977—. Member of Christian Business Men's Committee, 1969—, member of county board of directors, 1974-76. *Military service:* U.S. Air Force, obstetrician and gynecologist, 1951-53; became captain.

MEMBER: International College of Surgeons (fellow), American Medical Association, American College of Obstetricians and Gynecologists (fellow; district vice-chairperson, 1971-74), American College of Surgeons (fellow), American Society for Colposcopy and Colpomicroscopy (chairperson of ethics committee, 1976), Christian Medical Society (mem-

ber of board of directors, 1965-72 and 1973-74; president, 1969-71; member of House of Delegates, 1976—), Medical Society of New Jersey, New Jersey Obstetrical and Gynecological Society (member of council, 1963-66; vice-president, 1967; president-elect, 1968; president, 1969), Bergen County Medical Society, New York Metropolitan Area Christian Medical Society (president, 1974).

WRITINGS: (Contributor) W. O. Spitzer and C. L. Saylor, editors, *Birth Control and the Christian,* Tyndale, 1969; (with L. P. Bird) *Learning to Love: A Guide to Sex Education Through the Church,* Word, Inc., 1971. Contributor to *Bakers' Dictionary of Christian Ethics.* Contributor to medical and religious journals.

WORK IN PROGRESS: Research on colposcopy, cryocautery, and laser therapy for treatment of cervical neoplasia.

SIDELIGHTS: Reilly's major concerns are ethics and the relationship between medicine and religion. He told *CA:* "My background is both theological and medical, being raised in conservative Christian milieu and following through with a medical education, specializing in obstetrics and gynecology. It became obvious that a physician must treat the whole person, physically, mentally, and spiritually. I observed that the time-honored traditional standards that society recognizes as ideal, although not lived up to, are in reality best for man's physical and emotional well-being and for the welfare of society, whether one believes that they were revealed by God or discovered by man. In the past, societies which have not adhered to these standards have crumbled. In those countries where they have socialized medicine, it has been discovered that the cost of the program could be reduced fifty percent if you could change the lifestyle of the people.

"Recent statistics have demonstrated that the incidence of neoplastic lesions of the cervix is related to one's marital history and sexual lifestyle. I have become interested in the most modern way of following abnormal Pap smears, namely colposcopy, and the office treatment of neoplasia with cryocautery and laser therapy. I anticipate that the end result of my research in this area will be a scientific paper. I am also contemplating writing a book evaluating how lifestyle has much to do with one's health, not only in sexual morality but all phases of living."

*   *   *

REITER, Seymour 1921-

PERSONAL: Born November 29, 1921, in New York, N.Y.; married, 1949. *Education:* Brooklyn College (now of the City University of New York), B.A., 1943; New York University, M.A., 1947, Ph.D., 1954. *Home:* 215 West 78th St., New York, N.Y. 10024. *Office:* Department of English, Brooklyn College of the City University of New York, Brooklyn, N.Y. 11210.

CAREER: Grace Church School, instructor in English and science, 1944-46; Yale University, New Haven, Conn., instructor in English, 1946-47; Athens College, Athens, Greece, instructor in English, 1947-48; American Book Co., editor, 1949-51; New York University, New York City, instructor in English, 1952-56; Brooklyn College of the City University of New York, New York City, professor of English, 1956—. *Member:* Modern Language Association of America, Modern Humanities Research Association of Drama.

WRITINGS: (With Bernard David Grebanier) *College Writing and Reading,* Holt, 1959, published as *A Practical Guide to Rhetoric,* Weybright, 1969; *Introduction to Imaginative Literature,* Crowell, 1960; *A Study of Shelley's Poetry,* University of New Mexico Press, 1967; *World Theatre,* Horizon Press, 1973.

Plays: (Librettist) "The Cask of Amontillado" (adapted from the short story by Edgar Allan Poe), first produced in New York City at Eastman School of Music, April, 1968; "Adam and Eve," first produced in New York City at Joseph Jefferson Theatre, December, 1974; (and lyricist) *Alice Through the Looking Glass,* Dramatic Publishing, 1976; "The Well," first produced in New York City at Joseph Jefferson Theatre, December, 1976; (and lyricist) "The Gift of the Magi" (adapted from the short story by O. Henry), Dramatic Publishing, 1977; (librettist) "Three Shepherds and a Lamb" (opera; based on the "Second Shepherds Play"), first produced in Brooklyn at Union Church of Brooklyn, December, 1977; (and lyricist) "Joan and the Devil," first produced Off-Off Broadway at 13th Street Theatre, February, 1978. Also librettist of "The Bells."

WORK IN PROGRESS: A libretto for an opera being scored by Peter Mennin.

*   *   *

RENDALL, Ted S.

PERSONAL: Born in Edinburgh, Scotland; son of Jane (Rendall) Rendall; married Norline Norbo; children: Steven, David. *Education:* Attended London Bible College, London, England, Bible Training Institute of Glasgow, and Prairie Bible Institute. *Home address:* P.O. Box 128, Three Hills, Alberta, Canada T0M 2A0. *Office:* Prairie Bible Institute, Three Hills, Alberta, Canada T0M 2A0.

CAREER: Ordained minister; former pastor of Bethel Fellowship Church, Three Hills, Alberta; currently pastor of preaching of the Prairie Tabernacle Congregation and vice-president of ministries and principal of Bible School Division at Prairie Bible Institute, Three Hills.

WRITINGS: Living the Abundant Life, Prairie Press, 1969; *In God's School,* Prairie Press, 1971; *Fire in the Church,* Moody, 1974; *Jeremiah, Prophet of Crisis,* Prairie Press, 1979. Editor of *Prairie Overcomer* and *Young Pilot.*

*   *   *

RENETZKY, Alvin   1940-

PERSONAL: Born August 2, 1940, in Brooklyn, N.Y.; son of Sam and Anna (Preiser) Renetzky; married Phyllis Ann Schroeder (divorced); children: Davida P. *Education:* California State University, Northridge, B.A., 1961; University of Southern California, Ph.D., 1966. *Residence:* Santa Monica, Calif. *Office address:* P.O. Box 5169, Santa Monica, Calif. 90405.

CAREER: Academic Media (publisher), Los Angeles, Calif., publisher and editor-in-chief, 1966-71; writer and researcher, 1971-76; Ready Reference Press, Santa Monica, Calif., publisher and editor-in-chief, 1976—.

WRITINGS: (Editor-in-chief) *NSF Factbook,* Academic Media, 1971; (editor-in-chief) *NASA Factbook,* Academic Media, 1971; (editor-in-chief) *Directory of Scholarly and Research Publishing Opportunities,* Academic Media, 1971; (editor-in-chief) *Directory of Internships, Work Experience Programs, and On-the-Job Training Opportunities,* Ready Reference Press, 1976, 1st supplement, 1978; *Listening to Myself,* Newaves Publishing, 1978; (editor-in-chief) *Mental Health Services Information and Referral Directory,* Ready Reference Press, 1978; (editor-in-chief) *Directory of Career*

Training and Development Programs, Ready Reference Press, 1979; (editor-in-chief) *Directory of Career Resources for Women,* Ready Reference Press, 1979; (editor-in-chief) *Career Employment Opportunities Directory,* Ready Reference Press, 1980. Also editor-in-chief of *Annual Register of Grant Support* and *Standard Education Almanac,* 1967-70, and *Yearbook of Higher Education,* 1968-80.

WORK IN PROGRESS: Career planning publications.

SIDELIGHTS: Renetzky told *CA:* "I am currently going through what can best be described as a transitional period in my publishing and editing positions. I'm looking forward to getting involved in some new and different publishing projects in the near future that I hope will provide a sense of challenge and excitement."

*   *   *

RENNER, K(enneth) Edward   1936-

PERSONAL: Born January 6, 1936, in Altoona, Pa.; son of Kenneth E. (in sales) and Sarah M. (White) Renner; married Charlene Masters (marriage ended); children: Charles, Christopher. *Education:* Pennsylvania State University, B.S., 1957; Northwestern University, M.A., 1959, Ph.D., 1961. *Residence:* Halifax, Nova Scotia, Canada. *Office:* Department of Psychology, Dalhousie University, Halifax, Nova Scotia, Canada.

CAREER: Columbus Psychiatric Institute and Hospital, Columbus, Ohio, intern in clinical psychology, 1959-60; University of Pennsylvania, Philadelphia, instructor, 1961-62, assistant professor of psychology, 1962-65; University of Illinois, Champaign, associate professor, 1965-69, professor of psychology, 1969-76; Dalhousie University, Halifax, Nova Scotia, professor of psychology, 1976—. *Member:* American Psychological Association, American Association for the Advancement of Science, National Council on Crime and Delinquency, Eastern Psychological Association, Midwestern Psychological Association, Psychonomic Society, Society for the Study of Social Problems.

WRITINGS: (Contributor) B.A. Maher, editor, *Progress in Experimental Personality Research,* Volume IV, Academic Press, 1967; (with J. S. Wiggins, Gerald Clore, and Richard Rose) *The Psychology of Personality,* Addison-Wesley, 1971; *What's Wrong With the Mental Health Movement?,* Nelson-Hall, 1975; (contributor) Gordon Bowers, editor, *The Psychology of Learning and Motivation,* Volume X, Academic Press, 1976; (with Wiggins, Clore, and Rose) *Principles of Personality,* Addison-Wesley, 1976. Contributor of about thirty-five articles and reviews to journals in the behavioral sciences. Associate editor of *Learning and Motivation,* 1975-76; member of editorial board of *Journal of Research in Personality* and *Canadian Journal of Behavioral Sciences,* both 1977—.

WORK IN PROGRESS: A book on police-citizen interaction, with Tom Barrett, completion expected in 1981; *Experimental Psychology and Personality,* a monograph; a three-year national demonstration project on diversion from the criminal justice system.

*   *   *

REYNOLDS, John
See WHITLOCK, Ralph

REYNOLDS, Madge
   See WHITLOCK, Ralph

*   *   *

RHODES JAMES, Robert (Vidal) 1933-

PERSONAL: Born April 10, 1933, in Murree, India, son of William (a military officer) and Violet (Swinhoe) Rhodes James; married Angela Margaret Robertson, 1956; children: four daughters. *Education:* Worcester College, Oxford, B.A., 1955, M.A., 1963. *Religion:* Church of England. *Agent:* Anthony Sheil Associates Ltd., 2-3 Morwell St., London WC1B 3AR, England. *Office:* House of Commons, London SW1A OAA, England.

CAREER: House of Commons, London, England, assistant clerk, 1955-61, senior clerk, 1961-64; Oxford University, Oxford, England, fellow of All Souls College, 1965-68; University of Sussex, Brighton, England, director of Institute for the Study of International Organisation, 1968-73, professorial fellow, 1973; United Nations, New York, N.Y., principal officer of executive office of the secretary-general, 1973-76; House of Commons, Conservative member of Parliament, 1976—, Parliamentary private secretary to Foreign and Commonwealth Office, 1979—. Kratter Professor of European History at Stanford University, 1968; consultant to United Nations. *Member:* Royal Society of Literature (fellow), Royal Historical Society (fellow), Travellers Club, Century Association. *Awards, honors:* John Llewelyn Rhys Memorial Prize from the Rhys Memorial Trust, 1961, for *An Introduction to the House of Commons;* award from Royal Society of Literature, 1963, for *Rosebery;* North Atlantic Treaty Organization fellowship, 1965.

WRITINGS: Lord Randolph Churchill: Winston Churchill's Father, Barnes & Noble, 1959; *An Introduction to the House of Commons,* Collins, 1961; *Rosebery: A Biography of Archibald Philip, Fifth Earl of Rosebery,* Weidenfeld & Nicolson, 1963, Macmillan, 1964; *Gallipoli,* Macmillan, 1965; (editor) *"Chips": The Diaries of Sir Henry Channon,* Weidenfeld & Nicolson, 1967; (editor) *The Czechoslovak Crisis, 1968,* Weidenfeld & Nicolson, 1969.

The United Nations, Grossman, 1970; (editor) John Colin Campbell Davidson, *Memoirs of a Conservative,* Macmillan, 1970; *Churchill: A Study in Failure, 1900-1939,* World Publishing, 1970; *Britain's Role in the United Nations,* United Nations Association of Great Britain and Ireland, 1970; *Ambitions and Realities: British Politics, 1964-70,* Harper, 1972; (editor) Winston S. Churchill, *Complete Speeches, 1897-1963,* Bowker, 1974; *Victor Cazalet: A Portrait,* Hamish Hamilton, 1976; *British Revolution: British Politics, 1880-1939,* Hamish Hamilton, Volume I: *From Gladstone to Asquith, 1880-1914,* 1976, Volume II: *From Asquith to Chamberlain,* 1977, reprinted in one volume, Methuen, 1978.

Contributor: *Suez Ten Years After,* B.B.C. Publications, 1967; *Essays From Divers Hands,* Oxford University Press, 1967; *Churchill: Four Faces and the Man,* Penguin, 1969; *International Administration,* Oxford University Press, 1971; Hugh Seton-Watson, editor, *Tomorrows in Europe,* University of South Carolina Press, 1973; *The Prime Ministers,* Volume II, Allen & Unwin, 1975.

WORK IN PROGRESS: A biography of Prince Albert, with publication by Knopf.

SIDELIGHTS: Rhodes James commented: "The task of the historian or the biographer is the pursuit of truth, motivated by a love of learning for its own sake, combined with the ambition—never satisfactorily fulfilled—of conveying that truth to a wider audience."

*   *   *

RICE, David G(ordon) 1938-

PERSONAL: Born January 31, 1938, in Charleston, W.Va.; son of Gordon R. (an accountant) and Garnet (a teacher; maiden name, Stover) Rice; married Joy M. Straka (a clinical psychologist and professor), September 1, 1962; children: Scott Alan, Andrew David. *Education:* College of William and Mary, B.S., 1959; University of Wisconsin—Madison, M.S., 1961, Ph.D., 1964. *Home:* 4230 Waban Hill, Madison, Wis. 53711. *Office:* Department of Psychiatry, University of Wisconsin, 600 Highland Ave., Madison, Wis. 53792.

CAREER: University of Wisconsin—Madison, instructor, 1964-65, assistant professor, 1965-70, associate professor, 1970-78, professor of psychiatry, 1978—, director of outpatient clinic, 1973-76, director of psychology training, 1974—, chief psychologist, 1975—. Consultant to Veterans Administration, Wisconsin Division of Corrections, and Tri-County Human Services Center. *Member:* Association of Psychology Internship Centers (member of executive committee, 1976—), American Psychological Association, American Association of Marriage and Family Therapists (clinical member), Wisconsin Psychological Association.

WRITINGS: (Contributor) Norman S. Greenfield and Richard A. Sternback, editors, *Handbook of Psychophysiology,* Holt, 1972; (editor with A. S. Gurman) *Couples in Conflict: New Directions in Marital Therapy,* Jason Aronson, 1975; *Dual-Career Marriage: Conflict and Treatment,* Free Press, 1979. Contributor of more than thirty articles and reviews to professional journals.

WORK IN PROGRESS: Psychotherapy and Divorce, expected in 1982.

SIDELIGHTS: Rice commented: "I am interested in contemporary marriage and alternative marital life-styles (including dual-career marriage). I am particularly interested in writing for the benefit of other mental health professionals."

*   *   *

RICE, Thomas Jackson 1945-

PERSONAL: Born August 13, 1945, in Troy, N.Y.; son of Edward Francis Taylor (a technical editor) and Greta (a teacher; maiden name, Jackson) Rice; married Diane Marie Billingsley (a teacher), August 11, 1967; children: Andrew David, Jennifer Kelly. *Education:* University of Delaware, B.A., 1967; Princeton University, M.A., 1969, Ph.D., 1971. *Religion:* Roman Catholic. *Home:* 3005 Duncan St., Columbia, S.C. 29205. *Office:* Department of English, University of South Carolina, Columbia, S.C. 29208.

CAREER: University of South Carolina, Columbia, currently teacher of English. *Military service:* U.S. Army Reserve, Military Intelligence, 1967—; present rank, captain. *Member:* Modern Language Association of America, Dickens Society, James Joyce Foundation, D. H. Lawrence Society, South Atlantic Modern Language Association, Princeton Graduate Alumni Association, Friends of Woodrow Wilson National Fellowship Foundation. *Awards, honors:* Woodrow Wilson fellowship, 1967-68.

WRITINGS: British Fiction, 1900-1950, Volume I, Gale, 1978. Contributor to literature journals.

RICH, Russell R(ogers) 1912-

PERSONAL: Born January 5, 1912, in Chicago, Ill.; son of Jesse Pomeroy (a lawyer) and Louise (Rogers) Rich; married Margaret Cardon (a teacher), June 3, 1936; children: Merilynne Smith, Suzanne Sadler, Renee Mounteer, Stephen R. C., David C., Barbara, Charles C. *Education:* Utah State University, B.S., 1936; Brigham Young University, M.A., 1949; University of Wyoming, Ed.D., 1955. *Religion:* Church of Jesus Christ of Latter-day Saints (Mormons). *Home:* 480 South Fourth E., Orem, Utah 84057. *Office:* Department of Religious Instruction, Brigham Young University, Provo, Utah 85602.

CAREER: Director of Latter-day Saints Institute of Religion, 1946-53; Brigham Young University, Provo, Utah, assistant professor, 1953-55, associate professor, 1955-61, professor of history of religion, 1961-77, professor emeritus, 1977—. Director of Foundation for Indian Development; member of Ayuda, Inc.

WRITINGS: Those Who Would Be Leaders, Extension, Brigham Young University, 1958; *Little Known Schisms of the Restoration,* Extension, Brigham Young University, 1961; *Land of the Sky-Blue Waters,* Brigham Young University Press, 1963; *Ensign to the Nations,* Brigham Young University Press, 1972.

* * *

RICHARDS, Stanley 1918-1980

OBITUARY NOTICE—See index for *CA* sketch: Born April 23, 1918, in Brooklyn, N.Y.; died July 26, 1980, in New York, N.Y. Educator, theatre critic, screenwriter, and playwright. Richards wrote more than two dozen plays, many of which have been produced abroad. He also edited numerous anthologies, including *Best Mystery and Suspense Plays of the Modern Theatre, Great Musicals of the American Theatre,* and *America on Stage: Ten Great Plays of American History.* Obituaries and other sources: *Publishers Weekly,* August 15, 1980.

* * *

RICHARDSON, Ivan L(eRoy) 1920-

PERSONAL: Born December 14, 1920, in Donovan, Ill.; son of Arthur (a farmer) and Elsie (Markley) Richardson; married Frances J. Carlson, February 12, 1945; children: Robert Steven, Patricia Ann, John Bruce. *Education:* University of Illinois, B.A., 1943; University of Iowa, M.A., 1948, Ph.D., 1950. *Office:* California State University, Fullerton, Calif. 92634.

CAREER: Fort Hays State College, Hays, Kan., assistant professor, 1950-54, associate professor, 1954-57, professor of political science, 1957-59; University of Southern California, Los Angeles, visiting associate professor of public administration, 1959-64, adviser to Brazilian School of Public Administration, 1961-64; California State University, Fullerton, professor of public administration, 1964-70, director of public administration program, 1964-71, head of department of political science, 1966-70, vice-president for administration and executive director of Urban Research Institute, both 1971—. Administrative analyst for Kansas legislature, 1958; member of California governor's Public Service Training and Education Advisory Council, 1968-71; consultant to Interamerican School of Public Administration and International Development Foundation.

MEMBER: American Political Science Association, American Society for Public Administration (member of executive committee of Los Angeles Metropolitan chapter, 1966-68; Orange County chapter vice-president, 1967-68, president, 1968-69; vice-president of state coordinating council, 1968-69), Pacific Coast Council on Latin American Studies (member of executive committee, 1966-67), California Association for Public Administration Education (member of executive committee, 1967-68; vice-president, 1969-70; president, 1972-73), Southern California Political Science Association. *Awards, honors:* Social Science Research Council grant for study in Brazil, 1968; American Philosophical Society grant, 1970-71.

WRITINGS: Bibliografia Brasileira de Administracao Publica (title means "Brazilian Bibliography of Public Administration"), Fundacao Getulio Vargas, 1964; *Urban Government for Rio de Janeiro,* Praeger, 1973; (with Signey Baldwin) *Public Administration: Government in Action,* C. E. Merrill, 1976. Contributor to *Journal of Comparative Administration.*

* * *

RICH-McCOY, Lois 1941-

PERSONAL: Born July 5, 1941, in Newark, N.J.; daughter of Harry (a merchant) and Ruth (Glassman) Rich; married Floyd W. McCoy, Jr. (an oceanographer); children: Mark, Jill, Brent, Elana. *Education:* Attended University of Miami, Coral Gables, Fla., 1964-66; Goddard College, B.S., 1971, M.S., 1972. *Home and office address:* Sneden's Landing, Palisades, N.Y. 10964; and Old Bottles, School St., Woods Hole, Mass. 02543. *Agent:* Joan Stewart, William Morris Agency, 1350 Avenue of the Americas, New York, N.Y. 10019.

CAREER: Stockbroker with firms in Miami, Fla., 1962-65; Boston University, Boston, Mass., biologist in medical research, 1965-67; Marine Biological Laboratory, Woods Hole, Mass., biologist, 1967-69; Harvard University, School of Medicine, Brookline, Mass., biologist, 1969-72; U.S. Geological Survey, Woods Hole, research coordinator, 1972-73; writer, 1973—. Owner of a business in Miami, 1962-64. Advertising consultant. *Member:* Authors Guild. *Awards, honors: Millionairess* was named among best business books of the year by *Library Journal,* 1978.

WRITINGS: Millionairess: Self-Made Women of America, Harper, 1978; *Late Bloomer: Profiles of Women Who Found Their True Calling,* Harper, 1980. Contributor to popular magazines, including *Sail, Oceans, Scientific American, Harper's Bazaar, Fifty-Plus, Family Weekly,* and *Family Circle.* Founder of *10964* (community newsletter).

WORK IN PROGRESS: Science Under Sail, for children, completion expected in 1980; *Spare Parts,* 1981; *Science Under Siege,* 1982; *The Forming of the First Lady,* 1984; research on "wonder drugs and scientific serendipity."

SIDELIGHTS: Lois Rich-McCoy told *CA:* "After working for years in scientific research laboratories, I began writing magazine articles in the area of science and history of science, then three books as a ghost writer for physicians. *Millionairess* was the first volume under my own name.

"I enjoy the quiet and solitary journalistic profession I practice in my at-home office, working at Andrew Carnegie's old library table, with a view of the Hudson River peeking through a maple forest. Writing allows me to enjoy our little children as they come home from school every day—I feel it is a particularly appropriate discipline for a parent.

"Our summers are spent on Cape Cod—a good deal of my writing takes place on the beach—and we also travel. In the summer of 1979 I joined my sea-going husband on a scientific cruise in the Mediterranean Sea.''

AVOCATIONAL INTERESTS: ''Hate jogging, love murder mysteries.''

BIOGRAPHICAL/CRITICAL SOURCES: Miami Herald, September 10, 1978; *Nyack Journal-News,* October 26, 1978; *Women's Wear Daily,* November 1, 1978, November 30, 1978; *Falmouth Enterprise,* July 10, 1979; *Fort Lauderdale News,* January 23, 1980.

*   *   *

RICHTER, David H.   1945-

PERSONAL: Born October 1, 1945, in Chicago, Ill.; son of William (a marker) and Shirley (a secretary; maiden name, Hirsch) Richter; married Janice Lee, October 11, 1969 (divorced September 24, 1979). *Education:* University of Chicago, A.B., 1965, A.M., 1966, Ph.D., 1971. *Politics:* Liberal. *Religion:* Jewish. *Home:* 201 West 70th St., New York, N.Y. 10023. *Office:* Department of English, Queens College of the City University of New York, 65-30 Kissena Blvd., Flushing, N.Y. 11367.

CAREER: Roosevelt University, Chicago, Ill., instructor in English, 1967-70; Queens College of the City University of New York, Flushing, N.Y., instructor, 1970-71, assistant professor, 1971-75, associate professor of English, 1975—. *Member:* Modern Language Association of America, American Society for Eighteenth Century Studies.

WRITINGS: Fable's End: Completeness and Closure in Rhetorical Fiction, University of Chicago Press, 1975; *Ten Short Novels,* Knopf, 1980. Contributor to literature and language journals. Editor of *Chicago Literary Review,* 1966-68; associate editor of *Language and Style,* 1977-79.

WORK IN PROGRESS: Editing *The Power of Form: Essays on the History and Theory of Fiction,* a collection of Neo-Aristotelian criticism of fiction, with Walter E. Anderson; *Assumptions in Criticism,* on the structure of literary theories and the role of assumptions at the three levels of theory, hypothesis, and interpretation.

SIDELIGHTS: Richter wrote: ''The function of academic criticism at the present time seems to be to obfuscate the obvious, to make mysteries where none exist, all to promote a priesthood of the Word. It seems to me that what critics should do is to make more explicit the intuitions of competent readers, and that the use of literary theory is uncovering the sources of the expertise which good readers bring to bear upon poetic texts. My own work, seen charitably, is a small effort directed at these ends.''

*   *   *

RICHTER, Derek   1907-

PERSONAL: Born January 14, 1907, in Bath, England; son of Charles Augustus (a designer) and Frances (Mann) Richter; married Beryl Ailsa Griffiths, December 27, 1937 (divorced, 1953); married Winifred Molly Hoskin (a community care director), December 18, 1953; children: Sally Richter Festing, John, Polly Richter Ionides. *Education:* Magdalen College, Oxford, B.Sc. (with first class honors), 1930, M.A., 1935; University of Munich, Ph.D., 1932; St. Bartholomew's Hospital, London, M.R.C.S. and L.R.C.P., 1945, M.R.C.P., 1965, F.R.C.P., 1971. *Politics:* Liberal. *Religion:* ''Humanist.'' *Home and office:* Deans Cottage, Walton-on-the-Hill, Tadworth, Surrey KT20 7TT, England.

CAREER: Biochemical Laboratory, Cambridge, England,

assistant demonstrator, 1933-37; Maudsley Hospital, London, England, research fellow at Central Pathology Laboratory, 1938-40; Mill Hill Emergency Hospital, London, director of Biochemical Laboratory, 1941-45; Welsh National School of Medicine, Cardiff, director of Neuropsychiatric Research Centre, 1946-58; Medical Research Council, director of Neuropsychiatry Research Unit in Carshalton, England, 1959-72, and Epsom, England, 1959-72; writer, 1972—. Visiting professor at Menninger Foundation, 1959, and Mount Sinai Hospital Medical School, New York, N.Y., 1969; honorary lecturer at London Institute of Neurology, London, 1963-72; lecturer in Japan, China, Italy, East and West Germany, France, India, and Iran. Managing editor of *Journal of Neurochemistry,* 1957-67. Liaison officer for World Health Organization, 1972—. Member of Mental Health Research Fund, 1949-74; member of board of trustees of Mental Health Foundation.

MEMBER: International Brain Research Organization (secretary-general, 1972-77), International Society of Neurochemistry (chairman, 1969-71), Royal College of Psychiatrists (honorary fellow; chairman of Biological Psychiatry Group, 1979—), South Lodge Housing Association (chairman, 1958—). *Awards, honors:* Fellow of London Institute of Biology, London; Semmelweis Medal from University of Budapest, 1971, for contributions to medical science.

WRITINGS: (Editor and contributor) *Perspectives in Neuropsychiatry,* H. K. Lewis, 1950; (editor and contributor) *Schizophrenia: Somatic Aspects,* Pergamon, 1957; (editor and contributor) *Metabolism of the Nervous System,* Pergamon, 1957; (editor with J. M. Tanner, Lord Taylor, and O. L. Zangwill) *Aspects of Psychiatric Research,* Oxford University Press, 1962; (editor and contributor) *Comparative Neurochemistry,* Pergamon, 1964; (editor and contributor) *Aspects of Learning and Memory,* Heinemann, 1966; (editor and contributor) *The Challenge of Violence,* Ardua Press, 1972; (editor with Dargut Kemali and Giuseppe Bartholini) *Schizophrenia Today,* Pergamon, 1976; (editor and contributor) *The Road to Liberation,* Macmillan, 1980; (editor) *Addiction and Brain Damage,* Croom Helm, 1980. Contributor of nearly two hundred articles to scientific journals.

WORK IN PROGRESS: Research on schizophrenia, drug addiction, and mental health.

SIDELIGHTS: Richter commented: ''This statement would be incomplete without mention of my contributions to science, especially the discovery of the active protein metabolism of the brain. I value greatly the invitations from colleagues to lecture on scientific and medical topics, and have lectured by invitation in many countries.''

*   *   *

RICHTER, Joan   1930-

PERSONAL: Born January 27, 1930, in New York, N.Y.; daughter of Emil (a draftsman) and Eleanor (Jelinek) Skrivanek; married Richard Richter (a television producer), 1951; children: David, Robert. *Education:* Hunter College (now of the City University of New York), B.A., 1951. *Home:* 8 Harvard Lane, Hastings-on-Hudson, N.Y. 10706. *Office: Travel and Leisure,* 1350 Avenue of the Americas, New York, N.Y. 10019.

CAREER: U.S. Peace Corps, Nairobi, Kenya, consultant, 1965-67; *New York Times,* New York City, stringer, 1971-77; *Trib,* New York City, travel editor, 1977-78; *Travel and Leisure,* New York City, director of publisher relations, 1978—. *Member:* Mystery Writers of America, Hastings Creative Arts Council, African Travel Association.

WRITINGS: (With Rita Gelman) *Professor Coconut and the Thief* (novel), Holt, 1977. Work anthologized in *Alfred Hitchcock Presents*, Random House, 1973. Contributing editor of *Westchester*, 1971-79.

WORK IN PROGRESS: A novel and an anthology of short stories, both set in Africa.

SIDELIGHTS: Joan Richter told *CA:* "My family and I spent two years in Kenya when my husband was an administrator with the Peace Corps (1965-67). Many of my recollections and reminiscences found their way into short stories. *Professor Coconut and the Thief* is an amusing story of two small boys, one African and the other American, who become friends in an archaeological camp in East Africa and solve a mystery together.

"I have been back to other parts of Africa many times since. Each time my fascination with its variety of land, cultures, and people is always renewed."

* * *

RICKENBACKER, Eddie
See RICKENBACKER, Edward Vernon

* * *

RICKENBACKER, Edward Vernon 1890-1973
(Eddie Rickenbacker)

PERSONAL: Original name, Edward Richenbacher, name legally changed during World War I; born October 8, 1890, in Columbus, Ohio; died July 23, 1973, in Zurich, Switzerland; buried in Columbus, Ohio; son of William (a building contractor) and Elizabeth (Barcler) Richenbacher; married Adelaide Frost Durant, September 16, 1922; children: David E., William F. *Education:* Attended elementary school in Columbus, Ohio.

CAREER: Worked in a brewery, shoe factory, stonecutter's yard, locomotive shop, and glass factory and as a garage mechanic; Frazer-Miller Cooled Car Co., Columbus, Ohio, in engineering and Sales Division, 1906; Columbus Buggy Co., Columbus, engineer, 1907; professional automobile racer, 1907-17; Rickenbacker Motor Car Co., Detroit, Mich., organizer, sales director, and vice-president, 1921-26; Cadillac Motor Car Co., assistant sales manager in La Salle division, 1927-29; Fokker Aircraft Corp. of America, New York City, vice-president and director of sales, 1929-32; Aviation Corp. of America, vice-president of American Airways, Inc., 1932-33; North American Aviation, Inc., vice-president, 1933-35; Eastern Air Lines, Inc., New York City, general manager and director, 1935-38, president, 1938-53, chairman of board of directors, 1954-63. Civilian inspector of American air bases abroad during World War II. Co-owner of Indianapolis Speedway, 1927-45. President of Army Air Forces Aid Society. Chairman of Will Rogers Memorial Fund and Aeronautic Division of Greater New York Fund, 1943; chairman of sports committee for New York World's Fair; member of board of sponsors of World Council of Christian Education; member of executive board of National Council of Boy Scouts of America; member of board of directors of Foremost Dairies and board of trustees of Ithaca College and Asheville School for Boys. *Military service:* U.S. Army, 1917. U.S. Aviation Service, pilot, chief engineering officer, commander of 94th Aero Pursuit Squadron, 1917-18; served in Europe; became major; received Croix de Guerre with four palms, Legion d'Honneur, Distinguished Service Cross with nine oak leaf clusters, and Congressional Medal of Honor. U.S. Air Force Reserve; became honorary colonel.

AWARDS, HONORS: Honorary degrees include Doctor of Aeronautical Science from Pennsylvania Military College, 1938, John Brown University, 1940, and University of Miami, 1941, D.Sc. from University of Tampa, 1942, and Westminster College, New Wilmington, Pa., 1944, D.H.L. from University Foundations and American Theological Seminary, Wilmington, Del., 1943, LL.D. from Oklahoma City University, 1944, Capital University, 1945, and College of South Jersey, 1948, and D.Eng. from Lehigh University, 1948; winner of national and international automobile races; American Educational award from Associated Exhibitors of National Education Association, 1943; Silver Buffalo award from National Council of Boy Scouts of America, 1944; scroll from World Council of Christian Education, 1948; medal for merit and gold medal from International Benjamin Franklin Society, 1951; named outstanding leader in business by *Forbes* magazine, 1951.

WRITINGS—All autobiographical; some under name Eddie Rickenbacker: *Fighting the Flying Circus*, A. Stokes, 1919, revised edition, Bailey & Swinfen, 1973; *Seven Came Through: Rickenbacker's Full Story*, Doubleday, 1943; *Rickenbacker*, Prentice-Hall, 1967; *From Father to Son: The Letters of Captain Eddie Rickenbacker to His Son William, From Boyhood to Manhood*, edited by William F. Rickenbacker, Walker & Co., 1970. Contributor to magazines, including *Look*.

SIDELIGHTS: Eddie Rickenbacker, the "Ace of Aces" of World War I, began working at the age of fourteen. His father had died and left the large Rickenbacker family without an income. At his first job, young Rickenbacker toiled at a glass factory twelve hours a day, six days a week for three and a half dollars per week. The enterprising boy eventually moved onto a number of better paying occupations, however, while studying combustion engines through an International Correspondence School course on mechanical engineering.

After working for the Frazer-Miller Cooled Car Co. and the Columbus Buggy Co., Rickenbacker began racing automobiles. He drove in the first five-hundred-mile race held at the Indianapolis Speedway in 1911 and finished eleventh. He also set a speed record in Florida, clocking 134 miles per hour. In 1916, the American Automotive Association rated Rickenbacker third among American race car drivers.

The entry of the United States into World War I put an end to Rickenbacker's racing career as he immediately enlisted. He wanted to be a fighter pilot, but instead became a sergeant in General John J. Pershing's motor pool in France. Later, despite his persistent efforts to join an aviation squadron, Rickenbacker was assigned to Issoudun Field as an engineering officer. He continued to request transfers to the front, but was just as often refused on the premise that he was indispensable at Issoudun. Rickenbacker then contrived to get himself sent to the hospital to illustrate that he could be spared. Eventually, he obtained his goal and was sent for active duty to the 94th Aero Pursuit Squadron, the first American aviation unit to fight on the front.

In 1918, Rickenbacker assumed command of this fighting air unit that was also dubbed the "Hat-in-the-Ring Squadron," after its adopted insignia. Both the squadron and its commander distinguished themselves as leaders in combat. The squadron topped all other similar American units by downing sixty-nine enemy planes, while Rickenbacker alone was credited with twenty-six of the victories. "Captain Eddie"'s most notable deed of single-handedly confronting seven German fighter planes and destroying two earned him the

Congressional Medal of Honor. The "Hat-in-the-Ring Squadron" later participated in the occupation of Germany.

Once at home, Rickenbacker recorded his wartime experiences in *Fighting the Flying Circus*. A *New York Times* reviewer lavishly applauded the book: "The most human and most engaging book that has come out of the war.... It is fairly bubbling with the spirit of youth and adventure, of satisfaction in perils braved and survived, of joy in achievement."

Back in civilian life, Rickenbacker returned to his first love—cars. He launched his own automobile company in Detroit, Mich., but it was an unsuccessful venture. Rickenbacker once quipped, "our own four-wheel brakes broke us." In 1927, though, Rickenbacker bought the controlling stock in the Indianapolis Speedway, which he later sold in 1945 at a healthy profit. After briefly working with the Cadillac Motor Car Co., the flying ace entered the growing aviation industry. Rickenbacker headed a number of airline companies, but settled on Eastern Air Lines, Inc. Under his helm, Eastern became the first airline company to make a profit and continue to do so without government subsidies.

During World War II, Rickenbacker again saw service, but as a civilian inspector of American air bases abroad. On one of these missions, the plane on which he flew crashed in the ocean approximately six hundred miles away from Samoa. Rickenbacker and six other men survived the landing and lived on small rafts, sustaining themselves by drinking rain water and catching fish. Over three weeks later they were finally rescued by a Navy helicopter. As before, Rickenbacker's wartime experiences provided fuel for a book. *Seven Came Through: Rickenbacker's Full Story*, published in 1943, favorably impressed critics. Russell Owen of the *New York Times* observed that "this is really the story of the personality of a strong man, strong in disaster, a fighter for what he believes in and what he intensely feels.... He towers over the scene, a Conradian figure." *Weekly Book Review*'s Stanley Walker commented that "his forthrightness and his sincerity are inplicit in every passage, although the last thing Rickenbacker pretends to be is a hero or a superman."

Rickenbacker returned to Eastern Air Lines after the war and wrote another autobiography in 1967. *Rickenbacker* met with a lukewarm reception. Although *New York Times Book Review*'s Richard Witkin found parts of the book "of unusual interest," he regretted that the author "offers only intimations of the emotional and mental process that produced such ... control of fear and impatience with those who did not share his views or virtues." E. K. Gann of *Saturday Review* criticized another aspect of the autobiography, complaining that the plentiful "verbiage on national policies and politics, ... and on aviation financial manipulations, ... belong in the drearist sections of the Wall Street Journal."

BIOGRAPHICAL/CRITICAL SOURCES: New York Times, June 15, 1919, March 21, 1943; *Springfield Republican*, March 21, 1943; *Weekly Book Review*, March 21, 1943; *Saturday Review of Literature*, March 27, 1943; *Commonweal*, April 2, 1943; *New Republic*, April 5, 1943; *Atlantic*, May, 1943; *Newsweek*, October 9, 1967; *Saturday Review*, October 14, 1967; *New York Times Book Review*, November 5, 1967; *Christian Science Monitor*, November 25, 1967; *National Review*, December 26, 1967; *Book World*, December 31, 1967; *Reader's Digest*, May, 1968.

OBITUARIES: New York Times, July 24, 1973; *Washington Post*, July 24, 1973; *Time*, August 6, 1973; *Newsweek*, August 6, 1973; *National Review*, August 17, 1973; *Reader's Digest*, December, 1973.*

—Sketch by Anne M. Guerrini

*   *   *

RICKWORD, (John) Edgell 1898-
(John Mavin, a joint pseudonym)

PERSONAL: Born October 2, 1898, in Colchester, Essex, England; son of George (a librarian) Rickword; married; children: two. *Education:* Attended Pembroke College, Oxford, 1919. *Address:* c/o E. and J. Stevens, 2 Prospect Rd., London N.W.2, England.

CAREER: Writer and editor. *Calendar of Modern Letters*, London, England, editor, 1925-27; *Left Review*, London, associate editor, 1934-38; *Our Time*, London, editor, 1944-47. *Military service:* British Army, 1916-18; became lieutenant. *Awards, honors:* Arts Council Prize, 1966; doctor of literature degree from Essex University, 1978.

WRITINGS: Behind the Eyes (poems), Sidgwick & Jackson, 1921; *Rimbaud: The Boy and the Poet*, Knopf, 1924, revised edition, Daimon Press, 1963, Haskell, 1971; *Invocations to Angels and the Happy New Year* (poems), Wishart, 1928; *Love One Another: Seven Tales*, Mandrake Press, 1929; *Twittingpan and Some Others* (poems), Wishart, 1931; *Milton: The Revolutionary Intellectual* (criticism), 1940; *Collected Poems*, Bodley Head, 1947; *William Wordsworth, 1770-1850*, Bureau of Current Affairs (London), 1950; *Fifty Poems: A Selection*, Enitharmon Press, 1970; (with Michael Katanka) *Gillray and Cruikshank: An Illustrated Life of James Gillray (1756-1815) and of George Cruikshank (1792-1878)*, Shire Publications, 1973; *Behind the Eyes: Selected Poems and Translations*, Carcanet New Press, 1974, Dufour, 1977; *Essays and Opinions, 1921-1931*, Carcanet New Press, 1974; *Literature in Society: Essays and Opinions II, 1931-1978*, Humanities Press, 1978. Also author of *Selected Essays*, Dufour.

Editor: *Scrutinies by Various Writers*, Wishart, 1928, reprinted, Folcroft, 1976; *Scrutinies*, Volume II, Wishart, 1931, reprinted, Folcroft, 1976; (with Jack Lindsay) *A Handbook for Freedom: A Record of English Democracy Through Twelve Centuries*, Lawrence & Wishart, 1939; *Soviet Writers Reply to English Writers' Questions*, Society for Cultural Relations With the U.S.S.R., 1948; Christopher Caudwell, *Further Studies in a Dying Culture*, Bodley Head, 1949; *Radical Squibs and Loyal Ripostes: Satirical Pamphlets of the Regency Period, 1819-1821*, Barnes & Noble, 1971.

Translator: (With Douglas Mavin Garman, under joint pseudonym John Mavin) Francois Porche, *Charles Baudelaire: A Biography*, Wishart, 1928; Marcel Coulon, *Poet Under Saturn: The Tragedy of Verlaine*, 1932; Ronald Firbank, *La Princess aux soleils* [and] *Harmonie*, Enitharmon Press, 1973.

WORK IN PROGRESS: Memoirs, for Carcanet New Press.

BIOGRAPHICAL/CRITICAL SOURCES: Essays in Criticism, July, 1962; *Times Literary Supplement*, July 21, 1966, November 9, 1967, February 19, 1971; C. H. Sisson, *English Poetry, 1900-1950: An Assessment*, Hart Davis, 1971.

*   *   *

RIDGWAY, Whitman H(awley) 1941-

PERSONAL: Born November 13, 1941, in Schenectady, N.Y.; son of Whitman (a manager) and Priscilla H. Ridgway; married June, 1964 (divorced, 1978); children: Sean Lars, Siobhan Linthicum. *Education:* Kenyon College, A.B., 1963; San Francisco State College, M.A., 1967; University of Pennsylvania, Ph.D., 1973. *Office:* Department of History, University of Maryland, College Park, Md. 20742.

CAREER: University of Maryland, College Park, lecturer, 1969-73, assistant professor, 1973-78, associate professor of history, 1978—. Fellow at University of Wisconsin—Madison, 1979-80. *Member:* Organization of American Historians, Social Science History Association. *Awards, honors:* Newberry Library fellowships, 1974, 1977; National Endowment for the Humanities grant, summer, 1976; Social Science Research Council fellowship, 1979-80.

WRITINGS: (Contributor) Aubrey C. Land, E. C. Paperfuse, and L. G. Carr, editors, *Law, Society, and Politics in Early Maryland,* Johns Hopkins Press, 1977; *Community Leadership in Maryland, 1790-1840: A Comparative Analysis of Power in Society,* University of North Carolina Press, 1979. Contributor of articles and reviews to history journals. Contributing editor of *Historical Methods Newsletter,* 1971-73, member of editorial board, 1973-79.

WORK IN PROGRESS: A study of the social and spatial transformation associated with the industrial revolution in urban America, 1780-1840.

* * *

RIESENBERG, Felix, Jr. 1913-1962

PERSONAL: Surname is prounced *Ree*-sen-berg; born August 5, 1913, in New York, N.Y., died March 22, 1962, in Florida; son of Felix (a writer, engineer, and sea captain) and Maud (Conroy) Riesenberg; married Priscilla Frances Alden, June 6, 1936; children: Joan Riesenberg Barrett, Felix III. *Education:* Attended Columbia University, 1932-34. *Politics:* Republican. *Religion:* Catholic.

CAREER: Writer. *San Francisco News,* San Francisco, Calif., reporter, shipping editor, and columnist, 1936-39; Pacific coast correspondent for *Nautical Gazette;* technical adviser for Warner Bros. and Republic studios. *Wartime service:* U.S. Maritime Service (merchant marine), served in World War II; became lieutenant senior grade. Radio news editor for Office of War Information.

WRITINGS—Juvenile: Yankee Skippers to the Rescue: A Record of Gallant Rescues on the North Atlantic by American Seamen, Dodd, 1940, reprinted, Books for Libraries, 1969; *Full Ahead! A Career Story of the American Merchant Marine,* Dodd, 1941; *Salvage: A Modern Sea Story,* Dodd, 1942; *The Phantom Freighter,* Dodd, 1944; *The Man on the Raft,* Dodd, 1945; *Galapagos Bound! Smuggling in the Tuna Fleet,* Dodd, 1947; *The Crimson Anchor: A Sea Mystery,* Dodd, 1948; *The Mysterious Sailor: A Sea Adventure,* Dodd, 1949.

Great Men of the Sea, Putnam, 1955; *Balboa: Swordsman and Conquistador,* Random House, 1956; *The Story of the Naval Academy,* Random House, 1958; *The Vanishing Steamer,* Westminster Press, 1958; *The Undercover Sloop,* Westminster Press, 1962.

Other: *Golden Gate: The Story of San Francisco Harbor,* Knopf, 1940; *Waterfront Reporter,* Rand McNally, 1950; *Sea War: The Story of the U.S. Merchant Marine in World War II,* Rinehart, 1956; *The Golden Road: The Story of California's Spanish Mission Trail,* McGraw, 1962.

SIDELIGHTS: Riesenberg first developed his sea legs as a deck boy when he was ten. Like his father and grandfather who were sea captains, he would eventually sail the world. Riesenberg spent many summer vacations from school on board a ship, traveling to Europe, Africa, South America, and the West Indies. He later sailed the Atlantic and Pacific coasts of the United States.

Riesenberg followed his father's footsteps in another direc-

tion. Like his father he published a number of books, drawing on experiences at sea for subject matter. The majority of Riesenberg's books are tales of high adventure at sea.

AVOCATIONAL INTERESTS: Boxing, swimming, model ship building.

BIOGRAPHICAL/CRITICAL SOURCES: Springfield Republican, December 8, 1940; *Christian Science Monitor,* December 12, 1940, July 8, 1948, June 14, 1956; *New York Times Book Review,* December 22, 1940, October 7, 1962; *New York Herald Tribune Books,* November 15, 1942, November 11, 1945, April 27, 1947, May 9, 1948, October 14, 1962; *Saturday Review,* June 2, 1956; *San Francisco Chronicle,* June 5, 1956; *Chicago Sunday Tribune,* August 12, 1956.

[Sketch verified by wife, Priscilla Riesenberg Place]

* * *

RILEY, Dick 1946-

PERSONAL: Born May 31, 1946, in Youngstown, Ohio; son of Richard Anthony (in newspaper work) and Eleanor (Donnelly) Riley; married Marcia Jo Clendenen (a psychotherapist), August 23, 1975; children: Richard Ian. *Education:* University of Notre Dame, B.A., 1968; Columbia University, M.A., 1969. *Agent:* Gloria Safier, Inc., 667 Madison Ave., New York, N.Y. 10021.

CAREER: Associated Press, New York, N.Y., reporter, 1969-70 and 1971-75; free-lance writer, 1975—. *Military service:* U.S. Army, 1970-71; became first lieutenant. *Member:* Mystery Writers of America.

WRITINGS: (With T. Harris and S. Maull) *Black Sunday,* Putnam, 1975; *Rite of Expiation,* Putnam, 1976; (editor) *Critical Encounters: Writers and Themes in Science Fiction,* Ungar, 1978; *The Bedside, Bathtub, and Armchair Companion to Agatha Christie,* Ungar, 1979.

Author of "Middleman Out" (one-act play), first broadcast by National Public Radio, 1980.

* * *

RILEY, (Hugh) Ridge(ly, Jr.) 1907-1976

PERSONAL: Born September 28, 1907, in Annapolis, Md.; died January 6, 1976, in State College, Pa.; son of Hugh Ridgely (an attorney and sportswriter) and Frances M. (a pianist; maiden name, Basil) Riley; married Margaret Tschan (a library assistant), August 21, 1935; children: Frances Anne, Mary (Mrs. Daniel H. Graves), Hugh Ridgely III. *Education:* Pennsylvania State University, B.A., 1932.

CAREER: Pennsylvania State University, University Park, manager of Student Union and graduate manager of student publications, 1932-34, assistant director of department of public information and director of sports information, 1934-43, founder of "Football Letter," 1938, assistant executive secretary of Alumni Association, 1943-47, executive secretary, 1947-70, member of board of trustees of the university, 1971-76. Past member of board of directors of American Alumni Council. *Awards, honors:* Lion's Paw Medal from Alumni Association of Lion's Paw, 1971.

WRITINGS: Road to Number One: A Personal Chronicle of Penn State Football, Doubleday, 1977. Author of sports column in *Centre Daily Times.* Past editor of *American Alumni Council News.*

SIDELIGHTS: Riley's wife, Margaret, told *CA:* "*Road to Number One* is long because Ridge wanted to project the game as an American intercollegiate tradition through his richly anecdotal story of Penn State and its illustrious opponents from 1881 through 1975. This attention to the ambience of college football in general, noted by few reviewers, applies particularly to the early days in the East, where it all began in the late 1870's. Ridge wrote of campus influences that produced the game, the effect of its growing public popularity, and its close identity with the academic institutions where it continues in one fashion or another. This historical account is 'personal' because he chose to write more about people than about each and every game.

"Since Penn State figures intimately and illustrates the changes in college football, this book should be considered a valuable historical reference, a 'case history' based on official records, printed sources, reminiscences, correspondence, interviews, and since the late 1920's, personal association and observation."

BIOGRAPHICAL/CRITICAL SOURCES: Centre Daily Times, January 7, 1976; *Kirkus Reviews*, August 1, 1977.

[Sketch verified by wife, Margaret T. Riley]

*   *   *

RIPS, Ervine M(ilton)   1921-
(K. T. Farnum, Olaf Lornquest)

PERSONAL: Born March 7, 1921, in Tulsa, Okla.; son of Abraham S. (a watchmaker) and Isabelle (Radman) Rips; married Gladys Nadler, March 20, 1948 (separated June, 1979); children: Ethan, Avram, Darius. *Education:* Massachusetts Institute of Technology, S.B., 1942; Carnegie Institute of Technology (now Carnegie-Mellon University), M.S., 1947. *Politics:* "Socialist with a small 's'." *Religion:* Atheist. *Home:* 25 Clifton Ave., Apt. D-1305, Newark, N.J. 07104. *Office:* New Jersey Institute of Technology, 323 High St., Newark, N.J. 07102.

CAREER: Sloan-Kettering Institute for Cancer Research, assistant in experimental historadiography, 1948-50; Polytechnic Institute of New York, Brooklyn, N.Y., instructor in electrical engineering, 1950-52; Central Transformer Co., Illinois, assistant chief engineer, 1952-56; Hamner Electronics Co., New Jersey, chief engineer, 1956-58; New Jersey Institute of Technology, Newark, assistant professor, 1957-61, associate professor of electrical engineering, 1961—. *Military service:* U.S. Army Air Forces, 1942-46; became captain. *Member:* Institute of Electrical and Electronics Engineers (senior member).

WRITINGS: (Under pseudonym Olaf Lornquest) *The Moon-lovers* (science fiction novel), Pinnacle Books, 1975. Contributor to professional and trade journals and popular magazines, including *Screw* (under pseudonym K. T. Farnum) and *Jewish Digest*.

WORK IN PROGRESS: An engineering textbook; two novels, one a mystery.

SIDELIGHTS: Rips commented: "I've always had a hankering to write. One day, several years ago, on a commuter train, I began scribbling in a big notebook I carried with me. Soon I made it a practice to write every day on that train. Just for the hell of it I decided to write science fiction/pornography. To my amazement, it was accepted and published. Now I've turned away from that and am trying straight writing—not from a prudish point of view, but not from a prurient one, either."

*   *   *

RIST, John M(ichael)   1936-

PERSONAL: Born July 6, 1936, in Romford, England; son

of Robert Ward (an accountant) and Phoebe May (a teacher; maiden name, Mansfield) Rist; married Anna Therese Vogler, July 30, 1960; children: Peter, Alice, Thomas, Rebecca. *Education:* Cambridge University, B.A., 1959, M.A., 1963. *Office:* Department of Classics, University of Aberdeen, Aberdeen AB9 1FX, Scotland.

CAREER: University of Toronto, Toronto, Ontario, lecturer, 1959-63, assistant professor, 1963-65, associate professor, 1965-69, professor of classics and philosophy, 1969-80, chairman of graduate department of classical studies, 1971-75; University of Aberdeen, Aberdeen, Scotland, Regius Professor of Greek, 1980—. Past president of Coalition for Life; past member of board of directors of Oxfam Canada and Canairelief. *Military service:* Royal Air Force, 1954-56. *Member:* Royal Society of Canada (fellow), Classical Association of Canada, American Philological Association.

WRITINGS: Eros and Psyche: Studies in Plato, Plotinus, and Origen, University of Toronto Press, 1964; *Plotinus: The Road to Reality*, Cambridge University Press, 1967; *Stoic Philosophy*, Cambridge University Press, 1969; *Epicurus: An Introduction*, Cambridge University Press, 1972; *On the Independence of Matthew and Mark*, Cambridge University Press, 1978; (editor) *The Stoics*, University of California Press, 1978. Contributor of more than forty articles to classical and philosophy journals.

WORK IN PROGRESS: Human Value: A Study of Ancient Philosophical Ethics, publication by E. J. Brill expected in 1982.

*   *   *

RIVERS, Julian Alfred Pitt
See PITT-RIVERS, Julian Alfred

*   *   *

ROACH, Joyce Gibson   1935-

PERSONAL: Born December 18, 1935, in Jacksboro, Tex.; daughter of Dave (an independent grocer) and Ann (an independent insurance agent; maiden name, Hartman) Gibson; married Claude D. Roach (a supervisor), June 15, 1957; children: Darrell, Delight. *Education:* Texas Christian University, B.F.A., 1958, M.A., 1964. *Address:* Box 143, Keller, Tex. 76248. *Agent:* Nancy Crow, Cordovan Corp., 5314 Bingle R., Houston, Tex. 77092.

CAREER: Currently a teacher of history and English at public schools in Keller, Tex. Guest lecturer at East Texas State University. Member of board of directors of Keller Community Education, 1975-79. *Member:* Western Writers of America, Texas Folklore Society (president, 1976). *Awards, honors:* Spur Award from Western Writers of America, 1977, for *The Cowgirls*.

WRITINGS: C. L. Sonnichsen: Folk Historian, Boise State University Press, 1980; (contributor) *Women Who Made the West*, Doubleday, 1980. Also author of *The Cowgirls*, published by Cordovan Corp. Contributor of articles to periodicals, including *Western Folklore, Publications of Texas Folklore Society, Horseman, Quarter Horse Journal, Western Treasures, Southwest Heritage*, and *Golden West*.

WORK IN PROGRESS: A chapter on ranch women, for publication by American Folklore Society.

SIDELIGHTS: Roach told *CA:* "Writing *The Cowgirls* was a project in which I hoped to show that ranch women were different from other frontier-pioneer types. I have always lived in ranch country among ranch women. My work habits vary, for my two children keep me busy, and writing sometimes takes a backseat to other activities."

ROBERSON, Ricky James 1956-

PERSONAL: Born March 22, 1956, in Anchorage, Alaska; son of James Early (a builder) and F. Eugenia (Stewart) Roberson; married Tomme Marie Trikosko, September 1, 1979. *Education:* University of Tennessee, B.A. (mathematics), 1977, B.A. (physics), 1978; Massachusetts Institute of Technology, M.S. (aeronautics and astronautics) and M.S. (interdisciplinary science), both 1979. *Politics:* "I vote for the best person." *Religion:* Baptist. *Home Address:* Route 2, Box 573-M, Cleveland, Tenn. 37311. *Office:* Teledyne Brown Engineering, Huntsville, Ala. 35807.

CAREER: Teledyne Brown Engineering, Huntsville, Ala., engineer, 1979—.

WRITINGS: (Editor with Sylvia Engdahl) *Universe Ahead,* Atheneum, 1975; (contributor) Engdahl, editor, *Anywhere, Anywhen,* Atheneum, 1976; (with Engdahl) *The Subnuclear Zoo,* Atheneum, 1977; (with Engdahl) *Tool for Tomorrow,* Atheneum, 1979.

SIDELIGHTS: Roberson commented: "I grew up with the ABC's of science fiction: Asimov, Bradbury, and Clarke. Of the three, Bradbury had the greatest influence, particularly with *R Is for Rocket.* I started reading science as well as science fiction, and I've been hooked ever since.

"I would like to write an adult novel set in the mid-1990's, exploring the U.S. space program and its impact in that time frame. It will probably be the 1990's when I find time to write such a book!"

* * *

ROBERT, Paul 1911(?)-1980

OBITUARY NOTICE: Born c. 1911 in Algeria; died August 10, 1980, in Mougins, France. Lexicographer and writer. While still a student of law in Paris, Paul Robert realized the inadequacies of the available French dictionaries and thus compiled the highly acclaimed *Dictionnaire alphabetique et analogique de la langue francaise* ("Alphabetical and Analogical Dictionary of the French Language"). Serving as a thesaurus as well as a dictionary, this seven-volume work has since become known simply as "Le Grand Robert." Another of his works, a four-volume listing of proper names, is similarly referred to as "Le Petit Robert." He has in addition published two books of memoirs. Obituaries and other sources: *Chicago Tribune,* August 13, 1980; *Time,* August 25, 1980.

* * *

ROBERTS, David D(ion) 1943-

PERSONAL: Born August 3, 1943, in Jacksonville, Fla.; son of Merrill J. (a professor) and Janet (Dion) Roberts; married Beth Ellis (an editor), June 19, 1966; children: Ellen, Trina, Anthony. *Education:* Stanford University, A.B., 1965; University of California, Berkeley, Ph.D., 1971. *Home:* 64 Gregory Hill Rd., Rochester, N.Y. 14620. *Office:* Department of Humanities, Eastman School of Music, University of Rochester, Rochester, N.Y. 14604.

CAREER: University of Virginia, Charlottesville, assistant professor of history, 1972-78; University of Rochester, Rochester, N.Y., associate professor of history, 1978—, chairman of department of humanities, 1980—. *Member:* Society for Italian Historical Studies, Phi Beta Kappa. *Awards, honors:* Woodrow Wilson fellow, 1965-66.

WRITINGS: The Syndicalist Tradition and Italian Fascism, University of North Carolina Press, 1979.

WORK IN PROGRESS: Taking History Seriously: The Historical Theme in Modern Culture; research on liberalism, historicism, and the ideas of Benedetto Croce.

* * *

ROBERTS, Geoffrey R(ansford) 1924-

PERSONAL: Born March 20, 1924, in Buckley, England; son of Thomas (a headmaster) and Kate (Aston) Roberts; married Tegwen Jeremy (a teacher), August 5, 1954; children: Sian Eleri, Jonathan Neal. *Education:* University of Wales, University College, Aberystwyth, B.A. (with honors), 1951, teaching diploma, 1952, M.A., 1958. *Politics:* Labour. *Home:* 33-A Hill Top Ave., Cheadle Hulme, Cheshire SK8 7H2, England. *Office:* Department of Education, Victoria University of Manchester, Oxford Rd., Manchester M13 9PL, England.

CAREER: Civil Service, Army Audit Office, Chester, England, clerk, 1941-42; high school teacher of general subjects in Coventry, England, 1952-54; elementary school teacher in Coventry, 1954-57, deputy head teacher, 1957-61; Victoria University of Manchester, Manchester, England, lecturer, 1961-73, senior lecturer in education, 1973—. Visiting professor at Sir George Williams University, 1973, and University of Newcastle, 1977; member of summer faculty at Western Washington State College, 1975, and State University of New York at Albany, 1976; lecturer at colleges and universities; conducts seminars. Committee member of Universities Council for the Education of Teachers. *Military service:* Royal Air Force, Bomber and Transport Command, 1943-47. *Member:* United Kingdom Reading Association.

WRITINGS: Reading in Primary Schools, Routledge & Kegan Paul, 1969; (with Vera Southgate) *Reading: Which Approach?,* University of London Press, 1970; *English in the Primary Schools,* Routledge & Kegan Paul, 1972; *Early Reading,* Open University, 1973; *Student Workshop: Option Two,* Open University, 1973.

Contributor: J. C. Daniels, editor, *Reading: Problems and Perspectives,* Partisan Press, 1967; M. M. Clark and S. M. Maxwell, editors, *Reading Influences on Progress,* United Kingdom Reading Association, 1967-68; E. A. Lunzer and J. F. Morris, editors, *Development in Learning,* Volume II, Staples, 1968; Keith Gardner, editor, *Reading Skills,* Ward, Lock, 1970; J. M. Morris, editor, *The First R,* Ward, Lock, 1972; Vera Southgate, editor, *Literacy at All Levels,* Ward, Lock, 1972; J. F. Reid, editor, *Reading: Problems and Practice,* Ward, Lock, 1972, revised edition, 1977; Elizabeth Hunter-Grundin and H. U. Hunter-Grundin, editors, *Reading: Implementing the Bullock Report,* Ward, Lock, 1978; *Language, Reading, and Learning,* Blackwell, 1979. Contributor of more than one dozen articles to education journals.

WORK IN PROGRESS: Research toward a fundamental change in the methods used to teach young children to read.

SIDELIGHTS: Roberts told *CA:* "My main concern is the improvement of standards of teaching in our schools so that all our children may have equality of opportunity to develop their full potentials and to develop their personalities. I believe that teachers of young children should be as highly qualified as high school teachers, and all teachers should be high quality graduates.

"I enjoy public lecturing, in particular teaching at summer schools for teachers in America. I feel that we have much to learn from each other's methods of teaching and attitudes toward schooling. For example, there seems to be a greater emphasis on the development of written English in British schools, whereas American children develop an easy facility in spoken English; detailed guidance through teacher's manuals finds greater support amongst American teachers; and the freedom granted to British teachers permits the spontaneous integration of all aspects of learning, so that no particular aspect becomes compartmentalized (although there is the danger of dissipating the energies of the teachers and the children).''

*   *   *

ROBERTSON, Brian 1951-

PERSONAL: Born March 19, 1951, in Houston, Tex.; son of Bill and Elizabeth Robertson; married Susan O'Connor (a nurse), 1980; children: Angela. *Education:* University of St. Thomas, B.A., 1975. *Home and office:* 715 South 10th St., Edinberg, Tex. 78539.

CAREER: Inlet Crisis Center, Houston, Tex., director, 1973-75; Helpline Crisis Phone Service, Edinberg, Tex., director, 1975-80; personnel training officer in Edinberg, 1980—; writer. Writer-in-residence at Texas Committee on Arts and Humanities. Member of musical group Whiskers. *Member:* Mystery Writers of America, Royal Knights of the Blue Pen.

WRITINGS: The Poets Are Off Welfare!, Beeper, 1974; *The Appointment,* Blind Alley, 1977; *Siege of Hampton Mall* (novel), Manor, 1979; *Dreamer in the Dirt* (novel), Manor, 1980.

WORK IN PROGRESS: Feeding Time at the Brasa Zoo; a mystery-suspense novel.

SIDELIGHTS: Robertson told *CA:* "My own interests are now limited to the novel, although in the past I have done work with poetry, short stories, and humor. I spent a few years editing and contributing to the small press scene. Although the experience there has limbered up my writing muscles, I can't think of many excuses for cutting down trees to make paper for most small press publications. The few excellent poets and writers, such as Jim Hubert, are swallowed up in the crush of the friends of those persons (editors) who own the mimeo machines.

"I've been fortunate enough to run into several sympathetic editors and agents and have just begun to find outlets for my novels. At the moment, I enjoy moving back and forth between established forms such as suspense/mystery and the broader field of general/humor. I write for the same reason most writers do—because we'd like to be paid for being who we are, and writing seems a deeply rooted part of our nature. Still, there is a feeling with most writers that they are special, and as special people they'd like to be rewarded. It defies logic and skirts reality, of course, but it's a harmless enough lie.

"Outside of writing, my interests lie with my wife, Susan, and my daughter, Angela. In addition, I play pretty acceptable music through a group known as Whiskers. Again, take any writer and chances are they dabble in some secondary creative attempts. All in all, I'm a student of life looking for a way to cheat on the final."

*   *   *

ROBICHON, Jacques 1920-

PERSONAL: Born November 8, 1920, in Sevran, France; son of Edgard (a businessman) and Jane (Ranger) Robichon. *Education:* Educated in France. *Home:* La Maison tranquille, 22 rue des Ecoles, Bandol 83150, France.

CAREER: Member of French delegation of the interallied Control Council, Berlin, Germany, 1945-47; journalist in Germany, 1948-51; Editions Amiot-Dumont, Paris, France, director of the press, 1952-56; writer, 1956—. *Military service:* French Army; received Croix de Guerre and Legion of Honor. *Awards, honors:* Prix Raymond-Poincare, 1962, for *Le Debarquement de Provence.*

WRITINGS—In English translation: *Le Debarquement de Provence,* Robert Laffont, 1962, translation by Barbara Shuey published as *The Second D-Day,* Walker, 1969.

Other writings; novels: *La Mise a mort* (title means "Put the Death"), Julliard, 1951; *Poussiere de l'ete* (title means "Dust of the Summer"), Julliard, 1952; *Les Faubourgs de la ville* (title means "The Town's Outskirts"), Julliard, 1956; *Les Flammes de la nuit* (title means "The Flames of the Night"), Julliard, 1960; *Les Cartes du diable* (title means "The Devil's Cards"), Julliard, 1974; *Le Puzzle* (title means "The Puzzle"), Denoel, 1979.

Historical books: (With J. V. Ziegelmeyer) *L'Affaire de Berlin, 1945-1959* (title means "The Berlin Affair"), Gallimard, 1959; *Jour J en Afrique* (title means "D-Day in Africa"), Robert Laffont, 1964; *Extraordinaires Histoires vraies* (title means "Extraordinary True Stories"), Perrin, 1966; *Les Grands Dossiers du troisieme reich* (title means "Great Dossiers of the Third Reich"), Perrin, 1971; *Les Francais en italie, 1943-1944* (title means "The French in Italy"), Les Presses de la Cite, 1980.

Other: *Francois Mauriac* (essay), Editions Universitaires, 1953, fifth revised edition, 1964; *Le Roman des chefs-d'oeuvre* (title means "The Novel of Masterpieces"), A. Fayard, 1959, enlarged edition, Perrin, 1969; *Le Defi des Goncourt* (title means "The Goncourt's Challenge"), Denoel, 1975; *L'O.M. que j'aime: Radioscopie d'une equipe de football* (title means "Radioscopy of a Soccer Team"), Julliard, 1975. Also author of *La Cote d'Azur* (title means "The French Riviera"), Editions Sun. Contributor to numerous journals, including *Le Figaro Litteraire, Arts, Carrefour, Le Monde, France-Soir,* and *Historia.*

WORK IN PROGRESS: A novel, *Les Palmiers de Bandol;* a television version of *Les Cartes du diable; Les Guerriers,* a novel on the Battle of Monte Cassino; *Nero,* a biography of the Roman emperor.

SIDELIGHTS: French journalist and author Jacques Robichon has written mysteries, novels, and essays, but he is probably best known for his historical works. One of the latter, translated into English as *The Second D-Day,* describes the Allied landing in Provence, France, on August 15, 1944, an invasion often overshadowed in history books by the Normandy invasion that occurred two months earlier. D. C. Goddard of the *New York Times Book Review* wrote that although the book's "choppy, crosscutting style" has limitations, Robichon does succeed in "catching the partly organized chaos of a major air-sea landing with real fidelity." A *Times Literary Supplement* critic commented that *The Second D-Day* provides "a kaleidoscope of interesting anecdotes concerning a great variety of participants. On these M. Robichon has clearly done a great deal of research, and he has succeeded admirably in recapturing the excitement, the tragedies, and the splendid Free French panache."

Robichon's 1975 book, *Le Defi des Goncourt,* tells the history of the Goncourt Prize, one of the most important and best-known French literary awards. This prize for best novel of the year was first awarded in 1903 by the Academie Goncourt. Composed of ten prominent literary figures, the group traditionally meets in the Drouant restaurant each year to announce the winner of the award. In researching for the book, Robichon became the first writer ever to be allowed access to the Academie Goncourt's entire collection of documents.

Robichon commented to *CA:* "I am a novelist turned historian through my experiences in World War II (in Berlin, the Third Reich, the war in Africa and in Europe). I attempt to write history certainly not as the equivalent of a novel but in the most lifelike way possible, at the same time taking into account everything that the records and the evidence can provide in order to reach this goal. In any case, that is my aim.

"I think that, unconsciously, I have always sought to infuse into my contemporary historical accounts that which the novel has taught me, since the novel is the reflection and expression of life. I am surely not the only such author—and neither is it a fluke that the best historical accounts, from 1940 to 1980, have come from the United States. Your authors, who are themselves novelists, journalists, or historians, have taught me a lot on this subject.

"On that account, French editors have a particular tendency to demand that I write historical works. But that never has prevented me from making some 'sauts de puce' and from returning, now and then, to novels.

"One remark, however: My tendency now is to rely upon real life as a basis for my fictional stories. Curious, isn't it?"

BIOGRAPHICAL/CRITICAL SOURCES: New York Times Book Review, June 1, 1969; *Times Literary Supplement,* June 26, 1969.

* * *

ROBINETT, Stephen (Allen) 1941-
(Tak Hallus)

PERSONAL: Born July 13, 1941, in Long Beach, Calif.; son of Melvin Allen (a machinist) and Frances (a plumber and fashion model; maiden name, Vaden) Robinett; married Louise Yeisley (an airline passenger-service supervisor), March 15, 1969. *Education:* California State University, Long Beach, B.A., 1966; Hastings College of the Law, University of California, San Francisco, J.D., 1971. *Home and office:* 718½ Fernleaf Ave., Corona del Mar, Calif. 92625. *Agent:* Hy Cohen Literary Agency Ltd., 111 West 57th St., New York, N.Y. 10019.

CAREER: Attorney in California, 1971-73; writer, 1973—. Member of California State Bar. *Military service:* U.S. Army National Guard, 1963-68, active duty, 1964; became sergeant.

WRITINGS—All science fiction: *Stargate* (novel), St. Martin's, 1976; *The Man Responsible* (novel), Ace Books, 1978; *Projections* (stories), Ace Books, 1979. Contributor to science fiction magazines (sometimes under pseudonym Tak Hallus), including *Analog, Galaxy, Orbit,* and *Omni.*

WORK IN PROGRESS: Three novels, one a mystery.

SIDELIGHTS: Robinett commented: "Having begun my writing career for the most part in the science fiction field, I am currently trying to broaden the nature of my work to include more than paper rocketships and awesome gadgets, namely, to show something of the complexity and folly of human existence."

* * *

ROBINSON, Marileta 1942-

PERSONAL: Born December 26, 1942, in Kansas City,

Kan.; daughter of Thomas B. (employed by U.S. Department of Agriculture) and Rebecca (Hurt) Sawyer; married Patrick Leland Robinson (an attorney), March 26, 1973; children: John Leland, Bennett Nicholas. *Education:* Grinnell College, B.A., 1965; attended Northern Arizona University, 1969-70; University of New Mexico, M.A., 1973. *Home:* 4301 Sussex Dr., Montgomery, Ala. 36116.

CAREER: U.S. Peace Corps, Washington, D.C., volunteer teacher in Togo, 1965-67; Scott, Foresman & Co., Glenview, Ill., assistant editor, 1967-69; Rough Rock Demonstration School, Rough Rock, Ariz., teacher, 1970-72; writer, 1973—. *Member:* Alabama Writers Conclave, Creative Writers of Montgomery. *Awards, honors:* First prize from Alabama Writers Conclave, 1979, for juvenile story, "Bessie, the Christmas Cow."

WRITINGS: Mr. Goat's Bad Good Idea (juvenile), Crowell, 1979.

WORK IN PROGRESS: A juvenile novel set in Togo, publication expected in 1984; juvenile stories.

SIDELIGHTS: Marileta Robinson told *CA:* "Sharing my interest in people of other cultures was one motivation for writing *Mr. Goat,* but the primary motivation was the desire to entertain Navajo children with stories containing situations familiar to them. Raising two children has focused my interests more closely at home lately, but I enjoy exploring the world as much as I can."

AVOCATIONAL INTERESTS: Reading (science fiction, fantasy, natural history, anthropology), language.

* * *

ROBSON, Elizabeth 1942-

PERSONAL: Born November 3, 1942, in Hackensack, N.J.; daughter of John F. (a chemist) and Jane (a teacher; maiden name, Kelly) Robson; married Lee David Goldstein (an attorney), April, 1971; children Jesse John. *Education:* University of Chicago, B.S., 1962; Columbia University, M.S.S.W., 1965; also studied at Moreno Institute of Psychodrama and New England Institute of Psychodrama. *Politics:* "Feminist." *Religion:* Jewish. *Home:* 195 Davis Ave., Brookline, Mass. 02146. *Office:* Associates in Feminist Therapy, 51 Bratttle St., Cambridge, Mass. 02138.

CAREER: Illinois Department of Mental Health, caseworker with parents of retarded children and therapist for retarded young adults at Mental Health Center in Chicago, 1962-63, caseworker and co-founder of crisis intervention unit at Charles Read Zone Center in Chicago, 1965-66, caseworker at Illinois State Psychiatric Institute in Chicago, 1966-68, social worker and training director at Sedgewick Mental Health Center in Chicago, 1969-72; Associates in Feminist Therapy, Cambridge, Mass., private practice of psychotherapy, 1972—. Member of faculty at Goddard College, 1974—, New England Institute of Psychodrama, 1976-78, Newbury Junior College, and Tufts University. Workshop leader. *Member:* Association of Women in Psychology.

WRITINGS: Off the Couch (pamphlet), Women and Therapy Collective, Goddard College, 1975; (with Gwenyth Edwards) *Getting Help: A Woman's Guide to Therapy,* Dutton, 1980.

WORK IN PROGRESS: An article on the non-verbal aspects of feminist therapy, to be included in *Gender and Non-Verbal Behavior,* edited by Nancy Henley and Clara Mayo, publication by Springer expected in 1981; research on daycare and mothering.

SIDELIGHTS: Elizabeth Robson wrote: "Gwenyth Edwards and I have long had a commitment to consumer advocacy for clients buying therapy services and, in addition to our book, we frequently speak on this topic to conferences or other interested groups.

"My involvement with feminism and the feminist movement, starting in 1969, has had important effects on my entire life. I have been committed to making therapy more accessible and less damaging to women, to working in alternate (and feminist) education for women, and in general to making a better world for all of us. Since the birth of my son, I have been more interested in daycare and the possible variations of the kind of care offered for children. This is an area which I believe needs the same demystification as we offered about therapy."

* * *

ROCHE, Douglas J. 1929-

PERSONAL: Born June 14, 1929, in Montreal, Quebec, Canada; son of James J. and Agnes (Douglas) Roche; married Eva Nolan (a university teacher), September 26, 1953; children: Evita, Michaelene, Douglas F., Mary Ann, Patricia. *Education:* St. Patrick's College, B.A. (with honors), 1951; attended New York School of Visual Arts. *Politics:* Progressive Conservative. *Religion:* Roman Catholic. *Residence:* Edmonton, Alberta, Canada. *Office:* House of Commons, Room 402-South, Ottawa, Ontario, Canada K1A 0A6.

CAREER: Ensign, Montreal, Quebec, news editor, 1951-52; *Toronto Telegram,* Toronto, Ontario, political reporter, 1953-55; *Catholic Universe Bulletin,* Cleveland, Ohio, reporter and columnist, 1956-57; *Sign Magazine,* Union City, N.J., associate editor, 1958-65; *Western Catholic Reporter,* Edmonton, Alberta, founder and editor, 1965-72; Canadian Parliament, House of Commons, Ottawa, Ontario, member of parliament, representing Edmonton-Strathcona, 1972-79, and Edmonton South, 1979—, chairman of Progressive Conservative Caucus Committee on External Affairs, parliamentary secretary to Secretary of State for External Affairs, and Canadian delegate to 34th Assembly of United Nations. President of Canadian Church Press, 1972. Member of board of directors of World Conference on Religion and Peace and Canadian Council for International Co-operation. Speaker. *Member:* Writers Union of Canada. *Awards, honors:* Doctor of Divinity from St. Stephen's College, Edmonton, 1977.

WRITINGS: The Catholic Revolution, McKay, 1968; (with Remi DeRoo) *Man to Man; A Frank Talk Between a Layman and a Bishop,* edited and introduced by Gary MacEoin, Bruce Publishing, 1969; *It's a New World,* Western Catholic Reporter, 1970; (contributor) Michael McCauley, editor, *On the Run: Spirituality for the Seventies,* Thomas More Press, 1974; (contributor) Dean Walker, editor, *Canada and The Third World: What Are the Choices?,* Yorkminster Publishing, 1975; *Justice Not Charity: A New Global Ethic for Canada,* McClelland & Stewart, 1976; *The Human Side of Politics:* Clarke, Irwin, 1976; (contributor) *Canada and the United Nations in a Changing World,* United Nations Association in Canada, 1977; *What Development Is All About: China, Indonesia, Bangladesh,* NC Press, 1979. Contributor of articles to newspapers and magazines, including *Toronto Globe and Mail, America, Saturday Night, Canadian Forum, New West Review, Ottawa Journal, Edmonton Journal, Canadian Churchman,* and *Reader's Digest.*

SIDELIGHTS: Roche has traveled around the world as both a participant in and reporter on the Second Vatican Council, 1967, World Conference of Catholic Press, 1968, the World Conference on Religion and Peace, 1976, and the North-South Roundtable and Society for International Development Conference, 1979. He also toured Syria, Jordon, Israel, India, Hong Kong, South Korea, and Japan, in 1978, on behalf of the Progressive Conservative Party, and accompanied Prime Minister Joe Clark to Africa in 1979. He writes that he will be continually involved in "external affairs and international development on behalf of the Canadian government."

* * *

ROCK, David (Peter) 1945-

PERSONAL: Born April 8, 1945, in Blackburn, England; came to the United States in 1977; son of William and Elsie Rock; married Rosalind Louise Farrar, August 3, 1968; children: Edward David. *Education:* St. John's College, Cambridge, 1967, M.A., 1970, Ph.D., 1971. *Home:* 1509 Olive St., Santa Barbara, Calif. 93101. *Office:* Department of History, University of California, Santa Barbara, Calif. 93106.

CAREER: Cambridge University, Cambridge, England, research officer at Centre of Latin American Studies, 1970-74; London Institute of Latin American Studies, London, England, assistant secretary, 1974-77; University of California, Santa Barbara, associate professor of history, 1978—. *Member:* Society of Latin American Studies, Conference on Latin American History. *Awards, honors:* Herbert E. Bolton Prize from Conference on Latin American History, 1976, for monograph, *Politics in Argentina.*

WRITINGS: Politics in Argentina: The Rise and Fall of Radicalism, Cambridge University Press, 1975; (editor) *Argentina in the Twentieth Century,* University of Pittsburgh Press, 1975. Contributor of articles and book reviews to British, American, Dutch, and Latin American journals.

WORK IN PROGRESS: History of Argentina, publication by University of California Press expected in 1983; three articles for *Cambridge History of Latin America,* 1982-85.

SIDELIGHTS: David Rock told CA: "Latin America for me began in childhood dreams of color, romance, and exoticism. The adventure became possible in the late 1960's when the universities were offering student ships to the area; Argentina and Buenos Aires were the destination on the chance suggestion of a tutor at Cambridge. Twelve years have elapsed, four lengthy research visits, and a move with my family from England to California. Amidst the conventional responsibilities of the university professor, I spend much of my time writing and puzzling out one of the great South American enigmas, unable to stop till I have satisfied my curiosity.

"Along with all historians, I seek to rekindle a past reality (or many realities) and also to offer a picture to understand the present. The layman would probably judge Argentina as the embodiment of irrationality; I believe the opposite and feel that I may eventually be able to understand from history some of its rationale. Writing about and researching this country is also an oblique means to understand my own society: my present book forces me to contemplate the history of the past four hundred years. It's sometimes very serious and very heavy, and then I am sustained once more by the dreams of childhood."

* * *

ROCK, Phillip 1927-

PERSONAL: Born in 1927 in Hollywood, Calif.

CAREER: Novelist and screenwriter.

WRITINGS—Novels: *The Extraordinary Seaman*, Meredith Press, 1967 (also see below); *The Dead in Guanajuato*, Meredith Press, 1968; *The Cheyenne Social Club* (adapted from the original screenplay by James Lee Barrett), Popular Library, 1970; *Flickers*, Dodd, 1977; *The Passing Bells* (Book-of-the-Month Club alternate selection), Seaview Books, 1979.

Screenplays: "The Extraordinary Seaman" (adapted from own novel), Metro-Goldwyn-Mayer, 1969.

SIDELIGHTS: The central character in *Flickers* is a con man who wheels and deals his way into the country clubs and boardrooms of Hollywood. Set in the 1920's, when the silent movie was rapidly overtaking vaudeville, the novel presents "a marvelously varied group of players," wrote Jane Larkin Crain in the *New York Times Book Review*, around which "whole worlds spring up." Starting from seedy origins, Earl P. Donovan scrambles to the top of Hollywood's magic mountain, acquiring both eminence and riches as a producer. Imaginary scenes and characters are freely mixed with the historical in a tale that features parties and starlets, politicians and moguls, and the recreation of an American era.

In her review of the book, Crain found that "'Flickers' doesn't focus with any special disdain on the greed and corrupted ambition it documents; the novel's real energy is reserved for the exploration of its characters. Neither cynical nor tendentious, this is nonetheless a backstage tale that reflects everything that is venal and tawdry in the milieu it describes. Still, it is the author's discerning affection and enthusiasm for his subject that finally holds sway in this altogether irresistible and sophisticated production."

Rock's *The Passing Bells*, a Book-of-the-Month Club alternate, has been described by Gene Lyons as "a sort of 'panoramic' history, . . . a combination, if you will, of 'The Thorn Birds,' 'Upstairs Downstairs' and the novels of Anthony Powell." Twelve major characters join a cast of thousands in this World War I story, and "no matter how often the contemporary audience may have contemplated that event, so skillful and engaging a narrative as Mr. Rock has written retains a capacity to shock, to astonish and to engage," Lyons commented in the *New York Times Book Review*.

The larger themes in *The Passing Bells* are "the social and spiritual changes wrought in England" by the war, noted reviewer Linda Osborne in the *Washington Post*. Britain's aristocracy and class system are already in decline as the novel begins, but "it takes the war to give dimension to both the story and the characters," Osborne remarked. John Fludas, writing in the *Chicago Tribune Book World*, held that the book is "more than a skillful evocation of a bygone era, for as the war progresses, [it] resonates with humanistic values and makes demands on the heart and the mind. Rock exposes the stupidity of the Chinese-box bureaucracies that spur the Great War to its mindless devastations." Yet, "while the war is devastating," Osborne observed, "it is, ironically, the vehicle by which the characters mature."

Lyons concluded that the author "seems to have done an enormous amount of homework to put this novel together, all to good effect. . . . Despite its length, 'The Passing Bells' is written throughout with economy and wit, and its hospital and battle scenes achieve a gruesome intensity." Osborne added that the novel "is a readable, often moving account of war's effect on a generation of men and women who entered it idealistically, only to see it claim a million dead."

BIOGRAPHICAL/CRITICAL SOURCES: New York Times Book Review, February 9, 1969, January 15, 1978, March 25, 1979; *New York Times*, February 14, 1969; *Chicago Tribune Book World*, April 1, 1979; *Washington Post*, April 14, 1979.*

*　　*　　*

ROCK, Stanley A(rthur) 1937-

PERSONAL: Born April 22, 1937, in Pontiac, Mich.; son of Stanley Arthur and Helen Cecilia Slaybaugh (DeLongchamp) Rock; married Nancy Rupp, September 8, 1962; children: Lisa Joanne, Amy Lynn, Julie Rebecca. *Education:* University of Michigan, B.A., 1959, M.A., 1960; Western Theological Seminary, B.D., 1966; Drake University, Ed.D., 1975. *Home:* 573 Elmdale Court, Holland, Mich. 49423. *Office:* Department of Christian Ministry, Western Theological Seminary, Holland, Mich. 49423.

CAREER: Ordained minister of Reformed Church in America, 1966; Inter-Varsity Christian Fellowship, Boston, Mass., member of New England field staff, 1960-63, area director for the middle Atlantic in Philadelphia, Pa., 1966; American Bible Society, New York, N.Y., assistant secretary for translations, 1967-68; pastor of Reformed church in Blawenburg, N.J., 1968-70; Drake University, Des Moines, Iowa, campus minister and adjunct member of faculty, 1970-76; Western Theological Seminary, Holland, Mich., assistant professor, 1970-75, associate professor of pastoral counseling, 1976—, director of counseling, 1970—. Vice-president of Christian Counseling Service, Holland. Chaplain at Training School for Boys, Skillman, N.J., 1969-70; member of New Jersey Council of Churches department of college and universities ministries; member of Reformed Church Historical Commission; member of denominational committees and task forces; workshop and retreat leader. *Member:* American Association of Pastoral Counselors, National Campus Ministry Association, Phi Eta Sigma.

WRITINGS: This Time Together: A Guide to Premarital Counseling, Zondervan, 1980. Contributor to religious and counseling journals, including *His, Reformed Review, Moody Monthly*, and *Christian Ministry*.

SIDELIGHTS: In the preface of his book, Rock wrote: "*This Time Together* is presented as a contribution for professionals and lay readers who wish to explore the small-group approach to marriage preparation. There is no substitute for the kind of relationship built between a pastor and an individual couple in premarital counseling. Yet no marriage can be built in a vacuum. The small-group approach carefully developed and illustrated in this book provides the kind of supportive community in which couples may help each other to grow."

*　　*　　*

RODGERS, William Henry 1947-

PERSONAL: Born December 23, 1947, in Hartford, Conn.; son of Charles Andrew (a professor) and Kathryn (a nurse's aide; maiden name, Molloy) Rodgers; married Ellen Lalone (a manufacturer), September 13, 1975. *Education:* Wesleyan University, Middletown, Conn., B.A., 1970; Boston College, M.A., 1975. *Politics:* Democrat. *Home:* 32 Parks Dr., Sherborn, Mass. 01770. *Agent:* Sterling Lord Agency, Inc., 660 Madison Ave., New York, N.Y. 10021. *Office:* B.R. & Co., 372 Chestnut Hill Ave., Boston, Mass. 02146.

CAREER: Currently associated with B.R. & Co. in Boston, Mass.

WRITINGS: Marathoning, Simon & Schuster, 1980. Contributor to magazines, including *Runner*.

RODITI, Edouard Herbert   1910-

PERSONAL: Born June 6, 1910, in Paris, France; son of Oscar and Violet (Waldheim) Roditi. *Education:* Attended Balliol College, Oxford, 1927-28; University of Chicago, B.A., 1939; graduate study at University of California, Berkeley. *Home:* 8 Gregoire de Tours, Paris 6, France. *Agent:* Hope, Leresche & Steele, 11 Jubilee Pl., London S.W.3, England.

CAREER: Writer. Served as interpreter at war crimes trial in Nuremberg, West Germany, following World War II. *Wartime service:* Affiliated with Voice of America in New York. *Awards, honors:* Grant from Gulbenkian Foundation, 1969.

WRITINGS—Poetry: Poems for F, privately printed, 1935; *Prison Within Prison: Three Elegies on Hebrew Themes,* J. A. Decker, 1941; (with Paul Goodman and Meyer Liben) *Pieces of Three,* 5 x 8 Press, 1942; *Poems, 1928-1948,* New Directions, 1949; *New Hieroglyphic Tales: Prose Poems,* Kayak Books, 1968; *Surrealist Poetry and Prose,* Black Sparrow Press, 1973; *Thrice Chosen: Poems on Jewish Themes,* Tree Books, 1974; *Emperor of Midnight,* Black Sparrow Press, 1974.

Other: *Oscar Wilde: A Critical Guidebook,* New Directions, 1947; *Dialogues on Art* (collection of interviews), Secker & Warburg, 1960, Horizon Press, 1961; *Joachim Karsch,* Verlag Gebr. Mann, 1960; *De l'Homosexualite,* Editions Sedimo, 1962; *Magellan of the Pacific* (biography), Faber, 1972, McGraw, 1973; *The Delights of Turkey: Twenty Tales* (short stories), New Directions, 1974; (editor) Hamri, *Tales of Joujouka,* Capra Press, 1975; *The Disorderly Poet* (essays), Capra Press, 1975; *Meetings With Conrad,* Press Pegacycle, 1977.

Translator: Andre Breton, *Young Cherry Trees Secured Against Hares,* View Editions, 1946; Albert Memmi, *The Pillar of Salt,* Elek, 1956; Ernest Namenyi, *The Essence of Jewish Art,* Yoseloff, 1960; Yashar Kemal, *Memed, My Hawk,* Harvill Press, 1961; Pablo Picasso, *Toros y Toreros,* Thames & Hudson, 1961; Robert Schmutzler, *Art Nouveau,* Thames & Hudson, 1964; *Genesis Rejuvenated,* Menard Press, 1973.

Art critic for *L'Arche.* Contributing editor of *Antaeus, European Judaism, Expatriate Review,* and *Shantih.* Co-founder of literary journal, *Das Lot,* 1947.*

*   *   *

ROEBUCK, Julian B(aker)   1920-

PERSONAL: Born July 25, 1920; son of Henry Llewelyn (a farmer) and Elizabeth (Wynn) Roebuck; married Mary Elizabeth Gonzales (a secretary), February 15, 1960; children: Marybeth Louise, Lance Llewelyn, Julian Wynn, Mary Elizabeth. *Education:* Atlantic Christian College, A.B., 1941; Duke University, M.A., 1944; University of Maryland, Ph.D., 1958. *Politics:* Socialist. *Religion:* "Protestant background." *Office:* Department of Sociology, Mississippi State University, Mississippi State, Miss. 39762.

CAREER: District of Columbia Department of Corrections, Washington, D.C., research analyst, 1950-55; San Jose State University, San Jose, Calif., 1956-60, began as assistant professor, became associate professor of sociology; Louisiana State University, Baton Rouge, associate professor of sociology, 1960-63; University of Texas at El Paso, professor of sociology, 1964-70; Mississippi State University, Mississippi State, professor of sociology, 1971—. *Member:* American Criminological Society, American Sociological Association, National Council on Crime and Delinquency, Society for the Study of Symbolic Interaction, Society for the Study of Social Problems, Mid-South Sociological Association (president, 1976), Alpha Kappa Delta.

WRITINGS: Criminal Typology: The Legalistic, Physical-Constitutional-Hereditary, Psychological-Psychiatric and Sociological Approaches, C. C Thomas, 1967; (with Raymond G. Kessler) *The Etiology of Alcoholism: Constitutional, Psychological, and Sociological Approaches,* C. C Thomas, 1972; (with Thomas Barker) *An Empirical Typology of Police Corruption: A Study in Organizational Deviance,* C. C Thomas, 1973; (with James B. Cowie) *An Ethnography of a Chiropractic Clinic: Definitions of a Deviant Situation,* Free Press, 1975; (with Wolfgang Frese) *The Rendezvous: A Case Study of an After-Hours Club,* Free Press, 1976; (with Stanley Weeber) *American Political Crime: Crimes by and Against Government,* Praeger, 1978; (with Paul Friday, Harry Allen, and Edward Sagarin) *Crime and Punishment,* Free Press, in press.

Contributor of articles and reviews to sociology journals. Executive editor of *Mid-South Sociological Review;* associate editor of *Deviant Behavior: An Interdisciplinary Journal and Sociological Forum;* advisory editor of *Symbolic Interaction.*

WORK IN PROGRESS: A study of the Southern white working man.

SIDELIGHTS: Roebuck wrote: "The early part of my career was devoted to prison work. My academic career has been concerned with the study of deviant and criminal behavior. Currently, I am interested in political economy, organizational, political, and corporate crime, and race relations. Practically, I am interested in basic and radical structural changes in the economic and political system in the United States. I write from a populist or socialist perspective and maintain that when the necessary economic and political structural changes are made in this age of advanced socialism, the race problem will no longer exist. Additionally, the crime problem will subside."

*   *   *

ROGERS, Florence K(atherine)   1936-

PERSONAL: Born April 21, 1936, in Pensacola, Fla.; married second husband, Norman Saville (a writer; divorced); children: Gerradette Ann Saville Rogers, David Michael, Benjamin Lee. *Education:* Attended Furman University; University of Pittsburgh, B.A., 1969; also attended California State College, California, Pa. *Home:* 305 South Narberth Ave., Narberth, Pa. 19072.

CAREER: Henderson Advertising Agency, Greenville, S.C., assistant director of market research, 1959-63; freelance writer and editor, 1964-68, 1970-72; Saville et al., Bala Cynwyd, Pa., president and creative director, 1972-75; Roy Larry Schein & Associates, Inc. (consulting engineers), Philadelphia, Pa., vice-president in operations, 1975-77; freelance writer, 1977—. *Member:* American Dairy Goat Association, Philadelphia Club of Advertising Women, City Business Club, Ecology Cooperative. *Awards, honors:* Art directors' award, 1974; silver medal from Neographics, 1974.

WRITINGS: Real Food for Your Baby, Simon & Schuster, 1974; *Another Little Mouth to Feed,* Simon & Schuster, 1978; *Parenting the Difficult Child,* Chilton, 1979.

WORK IN PROGRESS: The Rise and Fall of the Little Red School House in America; Goats, Cats, Kids, and Other Things; The Real Food Cookbook.

SIDELIGHTS: Florence Rogers commented: "I live in a

large disreputable suburban house with my two sons, six cats, a very small dog, numerous fish, a guinea pig, sixty rabbits, and nine registered dairy goats (expecting more momentarily).

"I've probably always been a writer. I just got side-tracked along the way. Hopefully, I won't again."

*   *   *

ROGERS, Millard F(oster), Jr. 1932-

PERSONAL: Born August 27, 1932, in Texarkana, Tex.; son of Millard Foster and Jessie (Hubbell) Foster; married Nina Olds (a teacher), August 3, 1963; children: Seth Olds. *Education:* Michigan State University, B.A., 1954; University of Michigan, M.A., 1958. *Office:* Cincinnati Art Museum, Cincinnati, Ohio 45202.

CAREER: Toledo Museum of Art, Toledo, Ohio, assistant to director, 1959-63, assistant curator, 1963-66, curator of American art, 1966-67; University of Wisconsin—Madison, professor of art history, 1967-74, director of Elvehjem Art Center, 1967-74; Cincinnati Art Museum, Cincinnati, Ohio, director, 1974—. Member of Cincinnati Arts Management Council. *Military service:* U.S. Army, 1954-56; became first lieutenant. *Member:* Association of Art Museum Directors, American Association of Museums, Midwest Art History Society, Ohio Museums Association, Phi Beta Kappa. *Awards, honors:* Gosline fellowship for Victoria and Albert Museum, 1959.

WRITINGS: Randolph Rogers: American Sculptor in Rome, University of Massachusetts Press, 1971; *Spanish Paintings in the Cincinnati Art Museum,* Cincinnati Art Museum, 1978. Contributor to journals, including, *Goya, Apollo, Connoisseur, Art Quarterly,* and *Antiques.*

WORK IN PROGRESS: A monograph and *catalogue raisonne* on American painter, Junius Brutus Stearns.

SIDELIGHTS: Rogers wrote: "My experiences indicate a need for increasing university-level instruction (in all disciplines) in the importance and usefulness of museums, and I hope to participate in this instruction. There is a need, too, for more extensive publication on museum history in the United States."

*   *   *

ROGERS, Peter 1934-

PERSONAL: Born January 24, 1934, in Hattiesburg, Miss. *Education:* University of Southern Mississippi, B.S., 1957. *Home:* 215 East 79th St., Apt. 9F, New York, N.Y. 10021. *Office:* Peter Rogers Associates, 730 Fifth Ave., New York, N.Y. 10019.

CAREER: Worked in production for Warwick & Legler (advertising agency), 1957-60; in traffic department for Doyle, Dane & Bernbach (advertising agency), 1960-62; Trahey Advertising, 1963-74, began as account executive, became executive vice-president; Peter Rogers Associates (advertising agency), New York, N.Y., president and creative director, 1974—. Guest on television and radio programs. *Military service:* U.S. Army, 1957-58; served in Germany. *Awards, honors:* Advertising and communications awards include Andy Awards for Advertising, 1978 and 1979.

WRITINGS: What Becomes a Legend Most?: The Blackglama Story, Simon & Schuster, 1979.

*   *   *

ROGIN, Michael Paul 1937-

PERSONAL: Born June 29, 1937, in Mount Kisco, N.Y.;

son of Lawrence (an educator) and Ethel (a librarian; maiden name, Lurie) Rogin; married Deborah Donohue, November 19, 1959; children: Isabelle Rose, Madeleine Anne. *Education:* Harvard University, B.A. (summa cum laude), 1958; University of Chicago, M.A., 1959, Ph.D., 1962. *Office:* Department of Political Science, University of California, Berkeley, Calif. 94720.

CAREER: University of Chicago, Chicago, Ill., assistant professor of political science at Makerere University College (now University), Kampala, Uganda, 1962-63; University of California, Berkeley, assistant professor, 1963-69, associate professor, 1969-75, professor of political science, 1975—. Fulbright lecturer at University of Sussex, 1967-68. Visiting fellow at Center for the Humanities, Wesleyan University, Middletown, Conn., autumn, 1975. *Member:* Phi Beta Kappa. *Awards, honors:* Albert J. Beveridge Award from American Historical Association, 1968, for *The Intellectuals and McCarthy: The Radical Specter;* Guggenheim fellowship, 1972-73; National Endowment for the Humanities fellowship, 1979; Pi Sigma Alpha Award from Western Political Science Association, 1980.

WRITINGS: (Contributor) Gwendolyn Carter, editor, *National Unity and Regionalism in Eight African States,* Cornell University Press, 1966; *The Intellectuals and McCarthy: The Radical Specter,* M.I.T. Press, 1967; (with John L. Shover) *Political Change in California: Critical Elections and Social Movements, 1890-1966,* Greenwood Press, 1970; (contributor) Philip Green and Sanford Levinson, editors, *Power and Community,* Pantheon, 1970; *Fathers and Children: Andrew Jackson and the Subjugation of the American Indian,* Knopf, 1975; (contributor) J. David Greenstone, editor, *The Transient and the Permanent: Essays in American Politics,* University of Chicago Press, 1980. Contributor of nearly fifty articles and reviews to political science and sociology journals and to popular magazines, including *Transition, Commonweal, Listener,* and *Partisan Review.*

WORK IN PROGRESS: A book on politics and family in Herman Melville.

*   *   *

ROGNESS, Michael 1935-

PERSONAL: Born March 23, 1935, in Duluth, Minn.; son of Alvin N. (a professor) and Nora (Preus) Rogness; married Eva Maria Kirchner, June 2, 1958; children: Maria, Paul, Jonathan. *Education:* Augustana College, Sioux Falls, S.D., B.A., 1956; Luther Theological Seminary, St. Paul, Minn., B.D., 1960; University of Erlangen-Nuernberg, D.Th., 1963. *Home:* 140 Waverly Place, Duluth, Minn. 55803. *Office:* First Lutheran Church, 1100 East Superior, Duluth, Minn. 55802.

CAREER: Ordained Lutheran minister, 1964; pastor of Lutheran church in Howard Lake, Minn., 1964-67; Institute for Ecumenical Studies, Strasbourg, France, associate professor, 1967-70; First Lutheran Church, Duluth, Minn., senior pastor, 1970—. Instructor at St. Olaf College, 1965; assistant professor at Luther Theological Seminary, 1964, 1974. President of Arrowhead Council of Churches (vice-president of northern Minnesota district).

WRITINGS: Melanchthon: Reformer Without Honor, Augsburg, 1965; *The Church Nobody Knows,* Augsburg, 1971; *Follow Me,* Augsburg, 1978. Contributor to magazines.

SIDELIGHTS: Rogness wrote: "My expertise and training is in the field of Reformation history. This background has been followed by extensive training and writing in the field of ecumenical relationships between church groups."

ROHRBAUGH, Joanna Bunker 1943-

PERSONAL: Born September 1, 1943, in Washington, D.C.; daughter of Lewis H. (an educator) and Ruth (a silversmith; maiden name, Bunker) Rohrbaugh. *Education:* Brown University, B.A., 1964; attended San Diego State University, 1970, and Boston University, 1970-71; Harvard University, received M.A., Ph.D., 1976. *Office:* Department of Psychiatry, Massachusetts General Hospital, Fruit St., Boston, Mass. 02114; and 4 Pinckney St., Boston, Mass. 02114.

CAREER: Houghton Mifflin Co., Boston, Mass., copywriter in College Textbook Division, 1964-66; Pine Manor Junior College, Chestnut Hill, Mass., director of publications and public relations, 1966-67; Department of Public Welfare, San Diego, Calif., social worker in children's program, 1967-69; Boston Center for Adult Education, Boston, instructor in psychology of women, 1975-77; Massachusetts General Hospital, Boston, clinical fellow, 1976-78, clinical assistant, 1978-79, clinical associate in psychology, 1980—. Instructor at Boston University, summer, 1976; research fellow at Harvard University, 1976-78, instructor, 1977, 1978—; lecturer at University of Massachusetts, 1979; assistant professor at Wellesley College, 1980-81.

MEMBER: American Psychological Association, Association for the Advancement of Psychology, Association of Women in Psychology, American Association for the Advancement of Science, Massachusetts Psychological Association, Phi Beta Kappa. *Awards, honors:* National Institute of Mental Health grant, 1976-78.

WRITINGS: Women: Psychology's Puzzle, Basic Books, 1979.

*   *   *

ROLO, Charles J(acques) 1916-

PERSONAL: Born October 16, 1916, in Alexandria, Egypt; came to the United States in 1938, naturalized citizen, 1954; son of I. J. (in business) and Linda (Suares) Rolo; married Helen Mendelson, September 27, 1954 (divorced, 1968); married Estella Bugara (in public relations), February 9, 1977; children: Claude Robert. *Education:* Oriel College, Oxford, B.A. (with honors), 1938; Columbia University, M.S., 1939. *Religion:* Church of England. *Home:* 420 East 51st St., New York, N.Y. 10022. *Agent:* Russell & Volkening, Inc., 551 Fifth Ave., New York, N.Y. 10017. *Office: Money,* 1270 Avenue of the Americas, New York, N.Y. 10022.

CAREER: Institute for Advanced Study, Princeton, N.J., report writer and translator from French, German, and Italian at Princeton Listening Center, 1940; British Information Services, New York City, head of section reporting on U.S. press, radio, and public opinion, 1940-44; *Atlantic Monthly,* Boston, Mass., war correspondent from Europe and the Middle East, 1944-45, literary critic and contributing editor, 1948-61; free-lance writer and editor, 1946-48; McDonnell & Co., New York City, securities analyst, 1961-63; H. Hentz & Co., New York City, securities analyst, research and advertising director, and vice-president, 1963-71; Edward A. Viner, New York City, partner, securities analyst, and member of board of directors, 1971-73; Halle & Stieglitz, New York City, research director and vice-president, 1973; Thomson & McKinnon Auchincloss Kohlmeyer, New York City, vice-president in investment research, 1973-76; *Money,* New York City, staff writer, 1976—. Lecturer at Columbia University, 1951-53; lecturer to institutional investors in Europe and with National Concert and Artists Corp. Presented weekly stock market commentary on WOR-Radio, 1967-68;

guest on television and radio programs, including "Walter Cronkite." Member of jury for National Book Award, 1951, 1960, and Carey-Thomas Award, 1954—.

MEMBER: International P.E.N. (member of executive board, 1953-61; vice-president, 1955-56), Publishing and Printing Analysts Association, New York Society of Security Analysts, New York Athletic Club, Shinnecock Hills Golf Club.

WRITINGS: Radio Goes to War (on radio propaganda during World War II), Putnam, 1942; *Wingate's Raiders,* Viking, 1944; (editor) *The World of Aldous Huxley,* Harper, 1947; (author of introduction) Aldous Huxley, *Brave New World,* Harper, 1950; (author of introduction) Alberto Moravia, *Five Novels,* Farrar, Straus, 1955; (author of introduction) A. Huxley, *Antic Hay and The Giaconda Smile,* Harper, 1957; (editor) *The World of Evelyn Waugh,* Little, Brown, 1958; (editor) *Psychiatry in Modern Life,* Little, Brown, 1963; (editor with G. J. Nelson) *The Anatomy of Wall Street,* Lippincott, 1968; *Investing in the Eighties,* Little, Brown, 1980.

Contributor: *This America,* Macmillan, 1942; *Readings for Citizens at War,* Harper, 1943; *The One Hundred Best Stories of World War II,* Wise & Co., 1943; *New World Writing,* New American Library, 1952; A. Klein, editor, *The Empire City: A Treasury of New York,* Rinehart, 1955; B. Rosenberg and D. M. White, editors, *Mass Culture,* Glencoe, 1957; W. V. O'Connor, editor, *Modern Prose: Form and Style,* Crowell, 1959; *S.R.A. Reading Laboratory,* Science Research Associates, 1959; R. A. King and F. R. McLeod, editors, *A Reader for Composition,* American Book Co., 1962; *Essays of the Twentieth Century,* Farrar, Straus, 1966; Alan Paton, editor, *Cry the Beloved Country,* Scribner, 1968.

Author of "Stock Trends," a column in *Forbes,* 1969-71, and "Family Investment Planning," a column in *Better Homes and Gardens,* 1970-71. Contributor of more than one hundred articles to magazines, including *Fortune, Reader's Digest, Saturday Evening Post, Book World, Barron's Financial Weekly,* and *American Journal of Psychoanalysis,* and newspapers. Articles editor for *Harper's Bazaar,* 1958-60.

SIDELIGHTS: Rolo's books have been published in Mexico, Spain, France, Sweden, India, and Israel.

Rolo wrote: "My literary hero at college was Aldous Huxley, who dazzled me with his erudition, which I naively planned to emulate. Although I doubt that I acquired one-tenth of one percent of Huxley's learning, his example is responsible for the fact that I'm moderately well-educated. One of the most gratifying experiences in my life was editing an anthology of Huxley's works and making his acquaintance in the late 1940's.

"Nowadays, my tastes are strictly nostalgic—nineteenth-century biographies and novelists who flourished in the first half of the twentieth century are my favorite reading."

AVOCATIONAL INTERESTS: "On a modest scale, I have collected Chinese porcelain and eighteenth-century flower paintings, and I'm addicted to auction galleries. I have a Philistine passion for golf and a puritanical faith in more strenuous forms of exercise."

*   *   *

ROMANUCCI-ROSS, Lola 1928-

PERSONAL: Born June 13, 1928, in Hershey, Pa.; daughter of Ignazio and Josephine (Giovannozzi) Romanucci; married John Ross, Jr. (a professor of medicine), August 26, 1972;

children: Deborah Lee, Adan Antony. *Education:* Ohio University, A.B., 1948; University of Minnesota, M.A., 1955; Indiana University, Ph.D., 1963. *Home:* 8599 Prestwick Dr., La Jolla, Calif. 92037. *Office:* Department of Community Medicine, University of California, San Diego, La Jolla, Calif. 92093.

CAREER: University of California, San Diego, La Jolla, lecturer, 1969-71, assistant professor, 1971-75, associate professor of community medicine and anthropology, 1975—. *Member:* American Anthropological Association (fellow), Society of Psychological Anthropologists, Society for Medical Anthropology.

WRITINGS: Violence: Conflict and Morality in a Mexican Village, Mayfield, 1973; (with George de Vos) *Ethnic Identity in Cultural Continuities and Change,* Mayfield, 1975.

Contributor: James Short and Marvin Wolfgang, editors, *Collective Violence,* Aldine, 1972; Peter Morley and Roy Wallis, editors, *Culture and Curing,* P. Owens, 1978; Bruce T. Grindal and Dennis Warren, editors, *Essays in Humanistic Anthropology,* University Press of America, 1979. Contributor to anthropology journals.

WORK IN PROGRESS: The Anthropology of Medicine, publication expected in 1981; *And West of the Moon: Reflections on the Logic of Discovery,* publication expected in 1981.

SIDELIGHTS: Lola Romanucci-Ross wrote that the motivation for her work has come from the people with whom she has worked: Margaret Mead, Erich Fromm, and Claude Levi-Strauss.

"My current work in the anthropology of medicine is a step from culture to method, an attempt to go beyond the current theoretical groundings in medical anthropology," Romanucci-Ross told CA. "One can look at medicine and its institutions as a cultural enclave, analyzing culture-bound problems of medical care and scientific research strategies. This might lead to a demonstration of the specifics of a growing recognition that the somatic drama is culturally informed.

"My work on *Reflections on the Logics of Discovery* deals with an analysis of the *process* through which an anthropologist in the field discovers an 'exotic' or 'primitive' culture. This has never been properly discussed among professionals, let alone illuminated for the intelligent person in our society who might be interested."

*   *   *

ROONEY, James 1938-
(Jim Rooney)

PERSONAL: Born January 28, 1938, in Boston, Mass. *Education:* Amherst College, B.A., 1960; Harvard University, M.A., 1962. *Home:* 1906 South St., No. 404, Nashville, Tenn. 37212.

CAREER: Writer. *Awards, honors:* Woodrow Wilson fellow; Fulbright fellow at American School of Classical Studies, 1963-64.

WRITINGS—Under name Jim Rooney: *Bossmen: Bill Monroe and Muddy Waters,* Dial, 1970; (with Eric Von Schmidt) *Baby, Let Me Follow You Down,* Anchor Books, 1979.

*   *   *

ROONEY, Jim
See ROONEY, James

ROONEY, John F(rancis), Jr. 1939-

PERSONAL: Born December 15, 1939, in Detroit, Mich.; son of John Francis (a chemist) and Ade Lynn (a nurse; maiden name, McKoane) Rooney; married Sandra A. Schriner, October 7, 1961; children: Elizabeth, Kathleen, Daniel. *Education:* Attended University of Illinois, 1957-58; Illinois State University, B.S.Ed., 1961, M.S., 1962; Clark University, Ph.D., 1966. *Religion:* Roman Catholic. *Home:* 2624 Black Oak Dr., Stillwater, Okla. 74074. *Office:* Department of Geography, Oklahoma State University, Stillwater, Okla. 74078.

CAREER: University of Wyoming, Laramie, instructor in geography, 1963-65; University of California, Los Angeles, assistant professor of geography, 1965-66; Southern Illinois University, Carbondale, assistant professor of geography, 1966-68; University of Exeter, Exeter, England, visiting lecturer in geography, 1968-69; Oklahoma State University, Stillwater, professor of geography, 1969—, head of department, 1969-78. Research fellow at University of South Carolina, 1976-77; consultant to Cecil & Associates Sports Research Corp. *Member:* Society for the North American Cultural Survey (executive director, 1975—). *Awards, honors:* Grants from U.S. Department of the Interior, 1968-69, 1970-71, 1971-73, 1972-74, 1974-75, and National Science Foundation, 1979-81.

WRITINGS: (With Richard D. Hecock) *An Analysis of Latent Demand for Water-Based Outdoor Recreation Facilities* (monograph), U.S. Office of Water Resources Research, 1972; (with Hecock) *Water-Oriented Regional Recreation Opportunities for Oklahomans* (monograph), U.S. Office of Water Resources Research, 1974; *A Geography of American Sport: From Cabin Creek to Anaheim,* Addison-Wesley, 1974; *Seeing the United States,* Milton Bradley, 1975; (with Hecock) *Land Use Changes and Reservoir Development: An Application of Land Use Information Systems* (monograph), U.S. Office of Water Resources Research, 1976; *A Social and Cultural Atlas of the United States,* Denoyer-Geppert, 1979; *The Recruiting Game: Toward a New System of Intercollegiate Sports,* University of Nebraska Press, 1980; (editor) *This Remarkable Continent: An Atlas of North American Society and Culture,* Texas A & M University, 1981.

Contributor: Richard Chorley, editor, *Water, Earth, and Man,* Methuen, 1969; Robert G. Putnam, Frank J. Taylor, and Phillip G. Kettle, editors, *A Geography of Urban Places,* Methuen, 1970; Lawrence Brant, editor, *Relevant Geography,* Mss Information, 1974; Donald W. Ball and John W. Loy, editors, *Sport and Social Order: Contributions to the Sociology of Sport,* Addison-Wesley, 1975. Contributor to geography journals.

WORK IN PROGRESS: A Geography of American Leisure, with Richard D. Hecock; research on regional changes in American sports preferences, the U.S. soccer revival, sport and the character of place, and regionalism in America.

SIDELIGHTS: In the preface to *The Recruiting Game,* Rooney wrote: "The past few years have witnessed an explosion of criticism concerning big-time collegiate sports. Football and basketball have been the primary targets of the critics' wrath, though no sport has totally escaped their attention. Most of the literature has focused on the excesses involved in the hunting, recruiting, pampering and/or mistreatment of young athletes.

"The cheaters have been exposed. The sordid details of the collegiate sports scene have been hashed and rehashed ... I am greatly concerned that the recent exposes, as well as the criticisms that characterized the 1910-1950 development period of major college athletics, have failed to produce any meaningful change.''

"My training as a geographer," he added, "equips me with unusual insights concerning the origin, development, and support of intercollegiate sport. I believe that the desire of Americans for recognition of the superiority of the place (town, state, and university) with which they are associated explains the workings of our unique intercollegiate athletic system. Place pride and the pressing need for identity, together with more leisure time and more money, have made big-time intercollegiate sport what it is today. Consequently, many of the problems related to it have a geographical cause—and a geographical solution.''

Rooney continued: "I spent the 1968-69 academic year as an exchange professor at the University of Exeter. It was a great escape, but most important, it introduced me to the British system of intercollegiate sport. In Britain, pros are pros, amateurs are amateurs, student athletes are really students, and little, if any, aid is given to collegiate athletes. The entire experience made me wonder why our system, which was originally similar to the one in England, is now so very different.''

In the preface to *A Geography of American Sport,* he commented: "My research has grown out of a persisting love for sport, coupled with a great curiosity about the character of place. It has been my belief for some time that the total feeling which a place transmits is integrally tied to the sports which it embraces. Cricket and soccer are somehow symbolic of England, hurling of Ireland, and football of present day America. This book then endeavors to provide a better understanding of the American scene through the media of sport and geography.''

*   *   *

ROPER, H(ugh) R(edwald) Trevor
See TREVOR-ROPER, H(ugh) R(edwald)

*   *   *

RORABAUGH, William Joseph 1945-

PERSONAL: Born December 11, 1945, in Louisville, Ky.; son of Matthew Irvin (an engineer) and Agnes (Graf) Rorabaugh. *Education:* Stanford University, A.B., 1968; University of California, Berkeley, M.A., 1970, Ph.D., 1976. *Office:* Department of History, DP-20, University of Washington, Seattle, Wash. 98195.

CAREER: San Jose State University, San Jose, Calif., lecturer in history, 1976; University of Washington, Seattle, assistant professor of history, 1976—. *Member:* American Historical Association, Organization of American Historians, Society of Historians of the Early American Republic. *Awards, honors:* Fellow of Newberry Library, 1979, Huntington Library, 1980, and National Endowment for the Humanities, 1981.

WRITINGS: The Alcoholic Republic: An American Tradition, Oxford University Press, 1979.

WORK IN PROGRESS: Research on apprenticeship in the early nineteenth-century United States.

SIDELIGHTS: Rorabaugh told *CA:* "I became interested in the history of drinking when I stumbled across a batch of old temperance pamphlets. What I found was that America's drinking habits before 1830 were highly intoxicating and that all that alcohol was covering up a lot of social problems. And no, I am not a teetotaler.

"While researching for my book, *The Alcoholic Republic,* I found that the typical adult male in the United States in the 1820's was drinking nearly one half pint of whiskey a day—more than three times the present rate. Such a high flow of spirits was made possible by a hearty tradition stressing the value of liquor for health combined with plentiful cheap whiskey (twenty-five cents per gallon) produced in a glut in the Midwestern corn belt. What made so many Americans imbibe so much, however, was the trauma of a society being transformed by steamboats, new factories, mushrooming cities, unprecedented western settlement, and the breakdown of social class lines. Many Americans tried to cope with the change by drinking. The great binge came to an end when the leaders of the temperance movement persuaded a majority to give up the bottle for the Bible.

"One hundred fifty years ago the United States was being transformed by the Industrial Revolution. Both the economy and society changed, and bewildered Americans took to drink. Eventually, they discovered that the new industrial system required work discipline, and they gave up drink. Today the United States is being transformed by a post-industrial revolution. Per capita consumption of alcohol—not to mention other drugs—has been increasing. During the 1980's we will begin to see what the post industrial society will look like, and I would predict declining alcohol and drug use.''

BIOGRAPHICAL/CRITICAL SOURCES: Times Literary Supplement, May 30, 1980.

*   *   *

ROSALDO, Michelle Zimbalist 1944-

PERSONAL: Born May 4, 1944, in New York, N.Y.; daughter of Samuel H. (a lawyer) and Dorothy (a librarian; maiden name, Hirsch) Zimbalist; married Renato I. Rosaldo (a professor), June 11, 1966; children: Samuel Marco. *Education:* Radcliffe College, B.A., 1966; Harvard University, Ph.D., 1972. *Politics:* "Radical." *Religion:* Jewish. *Office:* Department of Anthropology, Stanford University, Stanford, Calif. 94305.

CAREERS: Stanford University, Stanford, Calif., assistant professor of anthropology, 1972—. *Member:* American Anthropological Association.

WRITINGS: (Editor with Louise Lamphere) *Woman, Culture, and Society,* Stanford University Press, 1974. Contributor to anthropology journals.

*   *   *

ROSE, Anthony Lewis 1939-

PERSONAL: Born August 19, 1939, in Los Angeles, Calif.; son of Sydney G. (a business executive) and Lolita (Sloan) Rose; married Lenora Oh Young, December 1, 1976; children: Ava Francesca, Joshua Sloan. *Education:* University of California, Los Angeles, B.A., 1961, M.A., 1963, Ph.D., 1967. *Home address:* P.O. Box 488, Hermosa Beach, Calif. 90254. *Agent:* Jonathan Rose, Tepoztlan, Morelos, Mexico. *Office:* Kaiser-Permanente Medical Care Program of Southern California, 11777 San Vicente, No. 555, Los Angeles, Calif. 90049.

CAREER: Center for Studies of the Person, La Jolla, Calif., founder and director, 1968-75; Behavioral Science Applications, Los Angeles, Calif., president, 1975—. Manager of organization design and research for Kaiser-Permanente Medical Care Program of Southern California, 1978—. Director of Olympian International of San Diego, Calif; vice-president of Western States Development Office of Oxnard; consultant to U.S. Navy, Roman Catholic church, and U.S. Forest Service. *Military service:* U.S. Army Reserve, 1957-60. U.S. Air Force Reserve, 1960-65. *Awards, honors:* Peabody Broadcasting Award from Academy of Television Arts and Sciences, 1971, for documentary, "Because That's My Way."

WRITINGS: (With Andre Auw) *Growing Up Human,* Harper, 1974; (contributor) Margules and Adams, editors, *Organization Development in Health Care Organizations,* Addison-Wesley, 1980.

Films: "Rapping and Tripping," released in Los Angeles, Calif., by Film Fair, 1970; (co-author) "Because That's My Way," released in Pittsburgh, Pa., by WQED-TV, 1971.

Creator of psychological games, "Feel Wheel" and "Body Talk." Contributor to psychology journals, including *Psychology Today.*

WORK IN PROGRESS: Sidewalk Cracks, "one hundred poems from the first half of my life"; *Designing the Future,* "a program for assuring the success of personal, organizational, and cultural planning."

SIDELIGHTS: Rose told *CA* that his first book, *Growing Up Human,* is "intended to help children of all ages to re-examine their lives and get ready for a new adulthood. My next book, *Designing the Future,* takes up where the first left off and presents a new and intuitive approach to human life planning. And yet with all this interest in dreams and schemes, my Taoist nature reminds me that the best stories are never told. The best poems write themselves. The best lives go unnoticed. The best futures *pull* us toward tomorrow. If you've got to try hard to make it work, rest assured that you're on the wrong path. If you seek fame, success will elude you. Life is meant to be easy and simple. Enjoy what it brings you. You won't get a second chance."

*   *   *

ROSE, Jennifer
    See WEBER, Nancy

*   *   *

ROSEN, Mortimer (Gilbert)   1931-

PERSONAL: Born December 31, 1931. *Education:* University of Wisconsin—Madison, B.S., 1951, graduate study, 1951-53; New York University, M.D., 1955. *Home:* 19715 Shelburne Rd., Shaker Heights, Ohio 44118. *Office:* 3395 Scranton Rd., Cleveland, Ohio 44109.

CAREER: Bellevue Hospital, New York, N.Y., intern, 1955-56, assistant resident in obstetrics and gynecology, 1956-57; Genesee Hospital, Rochester, N.Y., assistant resident, 1959-60, associate resident, 1960-61, chief resident in obstetrics and gynecology, 1961-62; University of Rochester, Rochester, N.Y., instructor, 1962-63, senior instructor, 1963-65, assistant professor, 1965-68, associate professor of obstetrics and gynecology and director of research at School of Medicine and Dentistry, 1968-73; Case Western Reserve University, Cleveland, Ohio, professor of reproductive biology and director of perinatal research unit, 1973—, member of advisory board of Design Research Center. Director of department of obstetrics and gynecology (and maternity and infant care project) at Cleveland Metropolitan General Hospital, 1973—. Examiner for American Board of Obstetrics and Gynecology; chairman of National Institute of Child Health and Human Development's mental retardation research committee and consensus panel on Cesarean section.

Military service: U.S. Air Force, 1957-59; served in Japan; became major.

MEMBER: American College of Obstetricians and Gynecologists, American Academy of Pediatrics, Society for Neuroscience, Society for Psychophysiological Research, Perinatal Research Society, Association of Professors of Obstetrics and Gynecology, Association of Program Directors of General Clinical Research Center (director-at-large), Society for Perinatal Obstetricians (member of board of directors), Royal Society of Medicine, Central Association of Obstetricians and Gynecologists, Ohio Perinatal Society, New York Academy of Sciences, Academy of Medicine of Cleveland, Cleveland Society of Obstetricians and Gynecologists (chairman of maternal health committee).

WRITINGS: (With Lynn Rosen) *Your Baby's Brain Before Birth,* Plume Books, 1975.

Contributor: M. B. Sterman, D. J. McGinty, and A. Adinolfi, editors, *Brain Development and Behavior,* Academic Press, 1971; J. J. Rovinsky, editor, *Davis' Gynecology and Obstetrics,* Harper, 1972; C. D. Clemente, D. P. Purpura, and F. E. Mayer, editors, *Sleep and the Maturing Nervous System,* Academic Press, 1972; *Clinics in Obstetrics and Gynecology,* Saunders, 1974; *Fetal Physiology and Medicine,* Saunders, 1976; Peter Mittler, editor, *Research to Practice in Mental Retardation,* Volume III: *Biomedical Aspects,* International Association for the Scientific Study of Mental Deficiency, 1977; Louis Gluck, editor, *Intrauterine Asphyxia and the Developing Fetal Brain,* Year Book Medical Publishers, 1977; *Coping With Pregnancy,* North-Holland Publishing, 1979; *Laboratory Diagnosis of Fetal Disease,* John Wright & Sons, 1979. Contributor of about eighty articles to medical journals and popular magazines, including *Harper's.* Guest editor of *Clinical Obstetrics and Gynecology,* September, 1979.

WORK IN PROGRESS: I, the Fetus, with Lynn Rosen.

*   *   *

ROSENAU, Helen

PERSONAL: Born in Monte-Carlo, Monaco; daughter of Albert (a physician) and Clara (Lion) Rosenau; married Zvi Carmi (deceased); children: Michael. *Education:* University of Hamburg, Ph.D., 1930; University of London, Ph.D., 1940. *Politics:* "Left of center." *Religion:* Liberal Jewish. *Home:* 84-A Ridgmount Gardens, London W.C.1, England. *Agent:* Curtis Brown Ltd., 1 Craven Hill, London W2 3EP, England.

CAREER: Victoria University of Manchester, Manchester, England, reader in art history, 1951-67; University of London, London, England, extra-mural lecturer in art history, 1967-79; Polytechnic of Central London, London, lecturer in history of architecture, 1979—. *Member:* International P.E.N., Association of Art Historians, Royal Commonwealth Society, Jewish Historical Society.

WRITINGS: Design and Medieval Architecture, Batsford, 1934; *Woman in Art,* Isomorph I, 1948; *A Short History of Jewish Art,* James Clark, 1948; *Boullee's Treatise on Architecture,* Tiranti, 1953; *The Ideal City,* Routledge & Kegan Paul, 1959, revised edition, 1974; *Social Purpose in Architecture,* Studio Vista, 1970; *Boullee and Universal Architecture,* Harper, 1975; *Vision of the Temple,* Two Continents, 1979. Contributor of articles to journals.

WORK IN PROGRESS: Moses Montefiore and the Visual Arts; Visual Aspects of the Family; Le Doux As a Town Planner.

SIDELIGHTS: Helen Rosenau commented: "I am interested in the relationship of the visual arts and religion and ethics, as art for art's sake is a rare minority pursuit. Art is intimately wedded to associations, and great art is inconceivable without this element. Therefore the history of art cannot be studied fruitfully from a narrow viewpoint."

*　　*　　*

ROSENZWEIG, Michael L(eo) 1941-

PERSONAL: Born June 25, 1941, in Philadelphia, Pa.; son of Max (a physician) and Phyllis (Fine) Rosenzweig; married Carole Citron (an editorial assistant), June 4, 1961; children: Abby, Juli, Ephron. *Education:* University of Pennsylvania, A.B. (with honors), 1962, Ph.D., 1966. *Religion:* Jewish. *Residence:* Tucson, Ariz. *Office:* Department of Ecology, University of Arizona, Tucson, Ariz. 85721.

CAREER: Bucknell University, Lewisburg, Pa., assistant professor of biology, 1965-69; State University of New York at Albany, assistant professor of biology, 1969-71, visiting assistant professor at Cranberry Lake Biological Station, summer, 1969; University of New Mexico, Albuquerque, associate professor of biology, 1971-75; University of Arizona, Tucson, professor of ecology and evolutionary biology, 1975—. President of board of directors of Tucson Hebrew Academy, 1979—. Consultant to U.S. Congress, National Science Foundation, and Environmental Protection Agency. *Member:* Ecological Society of America, American Society of Mammalogists, American Society of Naturalists, Society for the Study of Evolution, British Ecological Society, Society of Population Ecology (Japan), Phi Beta Kappa, Sigma Xi, Pi Mu Epsilon, Pi Gamma Mu, Alpha Epsilon Delta. *Awards, honors:* Grants from Theodore Roosevelt Memorial Fund of the American Museum of Natural History, 1966, National Science Foundation, 1967—, and United States-Israel Binational Science Foundation, 1980-82.

WRITINGS: And Replenish the Earth: The Evolution, Consequences, and Prevention of Overpopulation, Harper, 1974; (editor with G. P. Patil, and contributor) *Contemporary Quantitative Ecology and Related Ecometrics,* International Cooperative Publishing House, 1979.

Contributor: W. W. White, Jr. and F. J. Little, Jr., editors, *Ecology and Pollution,* North American Publishing, 1972; Martin Cody and Jared Diamond, editors, *The Ecology and Evolution of Communities,* Harvard University Press, 1975; I. Prekash and P. K. Ghosh, editors, *Rodents in Desert Environments,* Monographiae Biologicae, 1975; Bernard Stonehouse and Christopher Perrins, editors, *Evolutionary Ecology,* Macmillan, 1977; R. D. Allen, editor, *The Science of Life,* Harper, 1977. Co-editor of series on population biology, for Chapman & Hall. Contributor of about forty articles and reviews to scientific journals. Editor of *Ecology* and *Ecological Monographs,* both 1977—.

WORK IN PROGRESS: Optimal Foraging Behavior, on how animals select their habitats and resources when faced with variable competitive pressures from other species; *Speciation Dynamics,* on what mechanisms add species to nature ("Are they competitive or is extinction the only competitive process?"); *Community Structure,* comparing desert rodent associations of the Middle East and the United States from a functional, ecological point of view.

SIDELIGHTS: Rosenzweig told *CA:* "The evolutionary ecologist is at once the most ambitious and arrogant of biologists. He wants merely to be able to explain the ultimate biological mechanisms responsible for life's intricacies and variation. If that were not enough, he also seeks the knowledge to predict these things in the future. He is doomed to failure. His only hope is that the failure will be partial.

"Paradoxically, he must go about his work half-blind and mostly deaf in order to achieve even the partial failure. He must search for broad, even crude patterns, sometimes within a place, but more often from continent to continent and eon to eon. His greatest occupational hazard is that he will yield to the temptation to open his eyes wide, to achieve the immediate pleasure and gratification of describing in detail the myriad behaviors and interactions that characterize anybody's backyard.

"Not only is it fun to succumb to that temptation, but it is also diverting. More than any other science, evolutionary ecology can be melancholy in the extreme. It has been said that economics is the dismal science. Not accidentally, many of the tools and questions of economics are quite similar to ours. Not accidentally, we are both often confronted with gnashing of teeth, deprivation, and the competitive struggle to exist. But evolutionary ecology also encounters, time and again, the melancholy conclusion that things have to be the way they are; there is no sense trying to change them much.

"As I read this over, it dawns on me that evolutionary ecology is more an aberration, more a mental disorder than anything else. It is rather like the vision of Ezekial, which if studied, it is said, can drive a human being to insanity or apostasy. And yet, isn't it Ezekial which is the most fascinating of Biblical mysteries? Can anyone fail to be interested in it?"

*　　*　　*

ROSKOLENKO, Harry 1907-1980
(Colin Ross)

OBITUARY NOTICE—See index for *CA* sketch: Born September 21, 1907, in New York, N.Y.; died of cancer, July 17, 1980, in New York, N.Y. Author and poet. Roskolenko spent much of his life traveling about the world, working variously as a seaman on an oil tanker, drawbridge operator, patent researcher, law clerk, and foreign correspondent. He wrote several books of poetry as well as travel books, novels, and autobiographies. His 1965 book, *When I Was Last on Cherry Street,* told of his early life in the lower east side of New York City. Roskolenko was a contributor to the *New York Times Book Review, New Republic, Partisan Review,* and other periodicals. Obituaries and other sources: *New York Times,* July 19, 1980.

*　　*　　*

ROSS, Colin
See ROSKOLENKO, Harry

*　　*　　*

ROSS, Ian
See ROSSMANN, John F(rancis)

*　　*　　*

ROSS, Lola Romanucci
See ROMANUCCI- ROSS, Lola

*　　*　　*

ROSSMAN, Michael Dale 1939-

PERSONAL: Born December 15, 1939, in Denver, Colo.; son of Harold Samuel (a journalist) and Beatrice (a social worker; maiden name, Robbins) Rossman; married Karen McLellan (a therapist), April 25, 1969; children: Lorca. *Education:* Attended University of Chicago, 1956-58; University of California, Berkeley, A.B., 1963. *Office:* 1741 Virginia St., Berkeley, Calif. 94703.

CAREER: Writer. *Awards, honors:* Woodrow Wilson fellow, 1963.

WRITINGS: The Wedding Within the War, Doubleday, 1971; *On Learning and Social Change,* Random House, 1972; *New Age Blues: On the Politics of Consciousness,* Dutton, 1979.

*   *   *

ROSSMANN, John F(rancis)   1942-
(Ian Ross)

PERSONAL: Born September 27, 1942, in St. Louis, Mo.; son of John and Bernice (Graf) Rossmann; married Lois Gayle Giles, October 26, 1968; children: Erik, Kristin. *Education:* St. Louis University, B.S., 1964; Pepperdine University, M.B.A., 1978. *Religion:* Presbyterian. *Home:* 32692 Redwood, Avon Lake, Ohio 44012. *Agent:* James R. Gorman, 4910 Birch, Suite 200, Newport Beach, Calif. 92660. *Office:* Sachs Motor Corp., 909 Crocker Rd., Westlake, Ohio 44145.

CAREER: St. Louis Urban Renewal Authority, St. Louis, Mo., public information officer, 1964-66; California Credit Union League, Pomona, manager of news and publications, 1966-68; The Garret Corp., Los Angeles, Calif., editor, 1968-70; The Fluor Corp., Los Angeles, director of employee communications, 1970-71; The Times Mirror Co., Los Angeles, manager of corporate communications, 1971-74; Hester Communications, Santa Ana, Calif., vice-president of publishing and product development, 1974-78; Sachs Motor Corp., Westlake, Ohio, president of vehicle division, 1978—. *Military service:* Missouri Army National Guard, 1965-67. *Member:* Sales and Marketing Executives (Cleveland, Ohio). *Awards, honors:* Award for best feature article, 1968, for best human interest article, 1969, and for best special format magazine, 1970, all from Southern California Industrial Editors Association (SCIEA); Award for Excellence for magazine editorial, 1971, from Professional Industrial Communicators Association.

WRITINGS—Novels; all published by Signet: *Mind Masters No. 1,* 1974; *Mind Masters No. 2: Shamballa,* 1975; *Mind Masters No. 3: The Door,* 1975; *Mind Masters No. 4: Amazons!,* 1976; (under pseudonym Ian Ross) *Mind Masters No. 5: Recycled Souls,* 1976. Contributor to marketing journals.

WORK IN PROGRESS: Two series of children's books; a Christian meditation series for adults.

SIDELIGHTS: Rossmann writes: "Since I am a marketing man who is accustomed to making long-range forecasts based on demographic data and other socioeconomic and sociocultural data, I purposely constructed the 'Mind Masters' series to take into account conditions which I predicted back in 1973 would be occurring in the future. For that reason, the series is as timely for today's readers as it was in the mid-seventies. The mind control dynamics involved in some of today's headline stories of individual and group mind control tragedies are clearly set forth in the mystery/adventure context of the fact-based 'Mind Master' series.

"Frankly, the series was ahead of its time in dealing with such subject matter as neurochemical mind control, cloning, and military applications of what were formerly thought of as 'psychic' phenomena prior to the discovery in just the past

two or three years of the physical basis for these phenomena.

"The fact-based action/adventure format of the series was successful as a literary vehicle for delivering to readers this information about new mind control technologies.

"Even though the 'Mind Masters' series is viable for continuation, my market research data show conclusively that, due to working women dropping out of the work force at the moment because of economic slowdown and other factors, there will be a 'baby boom' which will result in approximately three and a half million new births per year through the early 1980's.

"Children's books for three- to five-year-olds will be in great demand within two years, and I already have underway two series of children's books for this age group. Both are adventure series; one, however, is pure adventure, the other packages perceptual training in an adventure format.

"The Christian meditation series is targeted for use in the expanding retreat programs which Christian churches in this nation and throughout the world are scheduling to handle the influx of persons, expecially young adults, who have not had their inner needs met by the myriad non-Christian, non-religious meditation fads that have sprung up and faded out in recent years."

BIOGRAPHICAL/CRITICAL SOURCES: Advertising Age, January 17, 1977, November 12, 1979.

*   *   *

ROTH, William   1942-

PERSONAL: Born June 1, 1942, in New Haven, Conn.; son of Oscar (a physician) and Stefanie (a physician; maiden name, Zeimer) Roth; married Judith Hand (an artist), August, 1978; children: Daniel Noah Hand. *Education:* Yale University, B.A. (magna cum laude) 1964; University of California, Berkeley, Ph.D., 1970. *Home:* 144 Lancaster St., Albany, N.Y. 12210. *Office:* Department of Social Welfare, State University of New York at Albany, 1400 Washington Ave., Albany, N.Y. 12222.

CAREER: Carnegie Council on Children, New Haven, Conn., senior research associate, 1972-76; Institute for Research on Poverty, Madison, Wis., research associate, 1976-78; State University of New York at Albany, associate professor of social welfare, 1978—. *Awards, honors:* American Film Institute fellowship, 1968—.

WRITINGS: The Unexpected Minority: Handicapped Children in America, Harcourt, 1980; *The Handicapped Speak,* McFarland Publications, 1981. Contributor to magazines, including *Film Culture, Bennington Review, Art in America, New Republic, Exceptional Parent, Disabled U.S.A.,* and *Social Work.*

SIDELIGHTS: Roth commented: "My education at Yale was in economics, politics, and mathematics. At Berkeley it was in political philosophy and other matters, including art and film. I have always looked on my work as applied political philosophy—my writing on film and art no less than my writing on politics, economics, and the handicapped. I have never been able to settle for either the moral or the esthetic. At its best I like to think my work encompasses both."

*   *   *

ROWBOTHAM, Sheila   1943-
(Sheila Turner)

PERSONAL: Born in 1943, in Leeds, England; daughter of

Lancelot (a salesman) and Jean (a clerical worker; maiden name, Turner) Rowbotham; children: William Sames Atkinson. *Education:* Oxford University, B.A., 1966. *Politics:* "Socialist Feminist." *Residence:* London, England.

CAREER: Teacher with Workers Educational Association at technical colleges and schools in England, 1964-79; *Black Dwarf* (socialist paper), London, England, staff writer, 1968-69; writer for *Red Day* (socialist feminist paper), 1972-73. Involved in women's movement in England since its origins in the late 1960's.

WRITINGS: Women's Liberation and the New Politics, Bertrand Russell Peace Foundation, 1971; *Women, Resistance, and Revolution: A History of Women and Revolution in the Modern World,* Pantheon, 1972; *Hidden From History: Rediscovering Women in History From the 17th Century to the Present,* Vintage Books, 1973 (published in England as *Hidden From History: 300 Years of Women's Oppression and the Fight Against It,* Pluto Press, 1973); *Women's Consciousness, Man's World,* Penguin, 1973; (with Jean McCrindle) *Dutiful Daughters: Women Talk About Their Lives,* Allen Lane, 1977; (with Jeff Week) *Socialism and the New Life: The Personal and Sexual Politics of Edward Carpenter and Havelock Ellis,* Pluto Press, 1977; *A New World for Women: Stella Browne, Socialist Feminist,* Pluto Press, 1978. Also author of political writings under pseudonym Sheila Turner.

WORK IN PROGRESS: Beyond the Fragments: Feminism and the Making of Socialism, with Hilary Wainwright and Lynne Segal.

SIDELIGHTS: "Any historian would admit that his material involves a process of selection, but he would perhaps be less ready to confess that this process can involve gross distortion of the truth. And yet until lately women have been consistently omitted: they have, apparently, no history," observed Eva Figes. Such was the paradox that troubled Sheila Rowbotham. An active member of the women's movement in England, Rowbotham realized the importance of a heritage for the "emerging woman." To this end she wrote *Women, Resistance, and Revolution* and *Hidden From History.*

"Miss Rowbotham has made a tremendous and unstinting effort to create history out of silence. . . . [She] is to be congratulated on at least trying to get women off their backs and into some kind of 'brave, responsible, thinking and diligent, frame of mind," proclaimed Monica Foot. Figes agreed, and asserted: "In an age of phoney specialisation I admire her willingness to admit ignorance. Women should be grateful for a book of this kind, which fills in our inadequate record of the past."

BIOGRAPHICAL/CRITICAL SOURCES: Economist, March 3, 1973; *Times Literary Supplement,* March 23, 1973, November 30, 1973, June 10, 1977; *Books and Bookmen,* August, 1973; *American Scholar,* autumn, 1973; *Observer,* January 20, 1974; *New Statesman,* November 15, 1974; *Newsweek,* January 20, 1975; *New York Times Book Review,* March 16, 1975.

*   *   *

ROWE, Frederick William 1912-

PERSONAL: Born September 28, 1912, in Lewisporte, Newfoundland, Canada; son of Eli and Phoebe Ann (Freake) Rowe; married Edith Laura Butt, December 25, 1936; children: Frederick Butt, Stanley Harold, William Neil, George Edward. *Education:* Memorial University of Newfoundland,

diploma (with first class honors), 1936; Mount Allison University, B.A., 1941; University of Toronto, B.Paed. (with honors), 1949, D.Paed., 1951. *Religion:* United Church of Canada. *Home:* Elizabeth Towers, St. John's, Newfoundland, Canada A1B 1S1. *Office:* Senate, Ottawa, Ontario, Canada K1A 0A4.

CAREER: Principal of schools in Bonne Bay, Newfoundland, 1931-33, Bishop's Falls, Newfoundland, 1934, Lewisporte, Newfoundland, 1934-35, Wesleyville, Newfoundland, 1936-40, and Grand Bank, Newfoundland, 1941-42; supervising inspector of schools, 1942-43; principal of private academy in St. John's, Newfoundland, 1943-48; first deputy minister of public welfare in Newfoundland, 1949-52; Government of Canada, Ottawa, Ontario, minister of mines and resources, 1952-56, public welfare, 1955-56, education, 1956-59, highways, 1959-64, finance, 1964-67, community and social development, 1966-67, Labrador affairs, 1967-68, education, 1967-71, and finance (also president of council), 1971, deputy premier of Newfoundland, 1969-71; Canadian Senate, Ottawa, Liberal senator, 1971—. Broadcaster for Canadian Broadcasting Corp. Member of board of regents of Memorial University of Newfoundland. Vice-chairman of Canadian Commission to United Nations Educational, Scientific & Cultural Organization, 1970; member of Inter-Parliamentary Conferences in Italy, 1962, and Sri Lanka, 1975. *Member:* Canadian Good Roads Association (president, 1963).

WRITINGS: History of Education in Newfoundland, Ryerson, 1951; *Blueprint for Education in Newfoundland,* Department of Education, 1958; *The Development of Education in Newfoundland,* Ryerson, 1964; *Education and Culture in Newfoundland,* McGraw, 1976; *Extinction: The Beothuks of Newfoundland,* McGraw, 1977; *A History of Newfoundland and Labrador,* McGraw, 1980.

AVOCATIONAL INTERESTS: Swimming, bridge, reading, music, tennis, badminton.

*   *   *

ROWES, Barbara Gail

PERSONAL: Born in Brooklyn, N.Y.; daughter of Bernard (a diamond importer) and Emily Rowes. *Education:* Attended Cornell University, 1964-66; New York University, B.A., 1968; Johns Hopkins University, M.A., 1969; State University of New York at Buffalo, Ph.D., 1973. *Home and office:* 415 East 52nd St., New York, N.Y. 10022. *Agent:* Owen Laster, William Morris Agency, 1350 Avenue of the Americas, New York, N.Y. 10019.

CAREER: Toronto Globe & Mail, Toronto, Ontario, dance critic, 1969-72; California State College, Bakersfield, assistant professor of English, 1972-73; writer and critic, 1973—. Feature writer for *Washington Post,* 1969-71; feature writer and dance and music critic for *Los Angeles Times,* 1972-74; contract writer for *People* magazine, 1976—. Volunteer worker at New York Foundling House.

WRITINGS: Rock Talk (juvenile), Scholastic Book Services, 1976; *The Book of Quotes,* Dutton, 1979; *Georgette Klinger's Skin Care,* Morrow, 1979; *Grace Slick: The Biography,* Doubleday, 1980. Contributor to magazines, including *People* and *Apartment Life.*

SIDELIGHTS: Barbara Rowes told *CA:* "The popularization of Western culture is the major thrust of my activities. I have applied knowledge from my doctoral study in Renaissance literature to lend substance to my perspective on contemporary issues. I have been a dance critic since 1968 because I still feel it is the most vital of all the arts. I have competent training in modern dance and have taught dance classes on the college level.

"American dance achieved a popularization in the 1960's that has withdrawn the severe line between classical, modern, and jazz. Today Bob Fosse remains one of the greatest unrecognized serious choreographers in the history of the art. His Broadway show 'Dancin'' is currently the greatest breakthrough on the scene, creating a new vocabulary of popular movement. What remains a serious problem is the development and pay of artists who face deprivation and lack of financial nurturance because of our system of endowments in this country. The recent and first lockout of the American Ballet Theatre documents this struggle which will continue to develop during the next decade.

"The beauty of dance transcends the other arts because it requires not only mental and emotional discipline and control, but also a physical exactness that turns the human body into a musical instrument. It is the highest form man can achieve, because in this art he or she is the instrument. What interests me about dance and dancers is the control and allotment of energy, the stamina combined with grace that is literally a superhuman skill."

*   *   *

ROWLAND, J(ohn) R(ussell) 1925-

PERSONAL: Born February 10, 1925, in Armidale, New South Wales, Australia; son of Louis Claude (a naval officer) and Elsie (Wright) Rowland; married Moira Enid Armstrong (an economist), February 19, 1956; children: Andrew, Katherine, Philippa. *Education:* University of Sydney, B.A., 1945. *Home:* Australian Embassy, 13 rue las Cases, Paris 75007 France. *Office:* Australian Embassy, 4 rue Jean Rey, Paris 75015 France.

CAREER: Member of Australia's Department of Foreign Affairs, in Canberra, Australia, 1944, Moscow, U.S.S.R., 1946-48, London, England, 1948-49, Canberra, 1949-52, Saigon, Vietnam, 1952-55, Washington, D.C., 1955-57, London, 1957-59, Canberra, 1959-65; Australian ambassador to U.S.S.R., 1965-68; high commissioner to Malaysia, 1969-72; ambassador to Austria, Czechoslovakia, and Hungary, in Vienna, Austria, 1973-74; deputy secretary of Department of Foreign Affairs, 1975-78; ambassador to France, 1978—.

WRITINGS—Poetry: *The Feast of Ancestors,* Angus & Robertson, 1965; (translator) Robert Ivanovich Rozhdestvenskii, *A Poem on Various Points of View and Other Poems,* Sun Books, 1968; *Snow,* Angus & Robertson, 1971; *Times and Places,* Bundabella Press, 1975; *The Clock Inside,* Angus & Robertson, 1979. Contributor of translations to *Postwar Russian Poetry,* Penguin, 1975.

SIDELIGHTS: Rowland told *CA:* "I am a spare-time poet, not a professional one, writing verse as the by-product of a peripatetic diplomatic life."

*   *   *

ROYAL, William Robert 1905-

PERSONAL: Born March 16, 1905, in Bay City, Mich.; son of Hiram William and Mary (Blake) Royal; married fifth wife, Shirley Egglefield, December 11, 1970; children: Walter, Ivan, Robert, Kathryn Royal Bowers, Elizabeth Royal Hull, William, Muriel. *Education:* Attended high school in Bay City, Mich. *Politics:* Independent. *Religion:* None. *Home:* 410 Sebastian Rd., Warm Mineral Springs, Fla. 33596; (summers) Star Route, Elizabethtown, N.Y. 12932.

Agent: Paul R. Reynolds, Inc., 12 East 41st St., New York, N.Y. 10017.

CAREER: Worked as plumbing and heating contractor in Michigan, 1926-42; U.S. Air Force, career officer, 1942-65, ferried bombers overseas for Royal Air Force Ferry Command, 1942-43, ferried various aircraft to England, Africa, India, and Persia for U.S. Air Force, 1943-46, served as installation engineer at bases in Colorado, Kansas, Texas, and Johnson Island, 1951-58, directed construction of radar sites for NATO bases, retiring as lieutenant colonel; General Dynamics Astronautics, resident engineer on Atlas missile complexes at Abilene, Tex., and Roswell, N.M.

WRITINGS: (With Robert F. Burgess) *The Man Who Rode Sharks,* Dodd, 1978. Contributor to *American Antiquities.*

WORK IN PROGRESS: Archaeological research in the Gulf of Mexico.

SIDELIGHTS: "For the last twenty-five years," Royal told *CA,* "I have theorized that early man in the Western hemisphere would be found best preserved under water out on the Continental Shelf, where he lived and hunted animals like the bison, mammoth, mastodon, and ground sloth. Sea level was much lower, up to 450 feet lower, during the Ice Ages eighteen thousand years ago.

"I found this to be true in two unique springs in Sarasota County, Florida—Warm Mineral Springs and Little Salt Spring. To date these are the only sites where stalactites, extinct animals, and human bones have been found together in caverns seventeen to thirty meters below present sea level. In 1958, when I first confirmed my theory that Florida had been high and dry with temperatures below zero degrees Fahrenheit in winter, I immediately took this information to the University of Florida in Gainesville. I was ridiculed for even suggesting that man had existed in Florida twelve thousand years ago. How could a retired Air Force officer know something that professional archaeologists did not know? Although archaeologists and anthropologists are divided as to when man first arrived in the Western hemisphere—some say twelve thousand years before the present and some say as long ago as two hundred thousand years—it has been proven beyond doubt that he was here at least twelve thousand years before the present.

"I am convinced that we must search underwater to find this evidence of the earliest possible date. Diving whenever weather permits in the Gulf of Mexico, ever searching for conclusive evidence of early man's occupation in North America, I have found sink holes and caverns where man very likely lived when this land was dry. I have found artifacts forty feet below sea level indicating that man fashioned the teeth of the extinct Carcharodon Megalodon shark into spear points and scrapers.

"For the past twenty-eight years, I have been diving in oceans, rivers, and underwater caverns in search of evidence that man inhabited North America twelve thousand years before the present. Using scuba equipment, I am still searching for clues to push this date back even further."

BIOGRAPHICAL/CRITICAL SOURCES: William M. Stephens, *Our World Underwater,* Lantern Press, 1962; Eugenie Clark, *Lady and the Sharks,* Harper, 1969; Robert F. Marx, *The Underwater Dig,* Henry Z. Walck Publications, 1975; Robert F. Burgess, *The Cave Divers,* Dodd, 1978; Burgess, *Man: Twelve Thousand Years Beneath the Sea,* Dodd, 1980.

ROYCE, Anya Peterson 1940-

PERSONAL: Born April 11, 1940, in Berkeley, Calif.; daughter of Richard Samuel (a pharmacist) and Margery Idele (a poet, maiden name, Nowlin) Peterson; married Ronald R. Royce (an anthropologist), June, 1968. *Education:* Stanford University, A.B. (with distinction), 1968; University of California, Berkeley, M.A., 1971, Ph.D., 1974; studied at School of American Ballet, Ballet Russe de Monte Carlo, and San Francisco Ballet. *Home:* 114 East 19th St., Bloomington, Ind. 47401. *Office:* Department of Anthropology, Indiana University, Bloomington, Ind. 47401.

CAREER: Instructor in classical ballet and ethnic dance in San Francisco, Calif., 1964-68; Oakland Ballet Academy, Oakland, Calif., teacher, 1971; Ballet Arts Academy, Bloomington, Ind., teacher, 1975; Indiana University, Bloomington, visiting lecturer, 1973-74, assistant professor, 1974-78, associate professor of anthropology, 1978—, director of Latin American studies, 1980-83. Dancer with Brooklyn Ballet Company, Deutsche Operetten Theatre, and San Francisco Russian Center Opera and Ballet. Organizer of international dance conference. *Member:* American Anthropological Association (fellow), Society for American Archaeology, Latin American Studies Association, Committee on Research in Dance. *Awards, honors:* Ford Foundation scholarship, 1967; National Institutes of Health grant for Mexico, 1968-73; Guggenheim fellowship, 1980-81.

WRITINGS: Mexican Dance Forms: A Bibliography With Annotations, Institute for the Study of Contemporary Cultures, Stanford University, 1967; *Prestigio y Afiliacion en una Comunidad Urbana: Juchitan, Oaxaca* (title means "Prestige and Affiliation in an Urban Community: Juchitan, Oaxaca"), Instituto Nacional Indigenista, 1974; *The Anthropology of Dance,* Indiana University Press, 1977; *Movement and Meaning: The Silent Languages of Dance and Mime,* Indiana University Press, in press. Contributor to professional journals. Associate editor of *American Ethnologist;* member of editorial board of *International Encyclopedia of Dance,* 1977.

WORK IN PROGRESS: Ethnic Identity: Strategies of Diversity, publication by Indiana University Press expected in 1982; a book on Isthmus Zapotec women and men.

SIDELIGHTS: Anya Royce wrote: "My teaching and research interests include ethnic identity, social organization, Latin America, the anthropology of dance, and the problem of meaning in dance. I have studied classical ballet with Anatole Vilzak, Ludmilla Shollar, Carmelita Maracci, Vladimir Kanstantinov, Anatole Joukovsky, and Sergei Temoff.

"In the summer of 1967, I studied the transition of Mexican dance forms from the village setting to the theatre. I did research on the dance styles of two San Francisco Bay area American Indian powpow groups in 1970.

"My long-standing interests in the Isthmus Zapotec, social class, and ethnic identity and dance as an indicator of identity came together in *Ethnic Identity.* The fundamental view presented in the book is that ethnic identity is one of many identities available to people and that it is developed, displayed, manipulated, or ignored in accordance with the demands of the situation. While this view stresses the adaptive nature of human beings, it does so with the awareness of the many factors that shape or influence behavior.

"From my observations of the exchange of information about identity in social interaction, both among the Isthmus Zapotec and in dance contexts in Mexico and the United States, I have been led to explore the relationship between movement and meaning. *Movement and Meaning* examines such questions as how and through what channels dance and mime convey information; how meaning is transferred in the interaction between performer and spectator; why information is conveyed in these forms rather than or in addition to other means of communication. These questions are explored through an intensive examination of the structure and context of dance and mime in both their theatrical and folk forms."

Royce's languages include French, German, Isthmus Zapotec, Italian, Russian, and Spanish. The research for *Movement and Meaning* took her to Poland, France, China, and Mexico.

*   *   *

ROYSTER, Charles 1944-

PERSONAL: Born November 27, 1944, in Nashville, Tenn.; son of Ferd Neuman and Laura (Smotherman) Royster. *Education:* University of California, Berkeley, A.B., 1966, M.A., 1967, Ph.D., 1977. *Office:* Department of History, University of Texas, P.O. Box 19529, Arlington, Tex. 76019.

CAREER: University of Maryland, Far East Division, Nakhon Phanom, Thailand, instructor in history, 1969; University of California, Berkeley, instructor in history, 1974-76; College of William and Mary, Williamsburg, Va., assistant professor of history, 1977-79; University of Texas, Arlington, assistant professor of history, 1979—. *Military service:* U.S. Air Force, 1967-71; became captain. *Member:* American Historical Association. *Awards, honors:* John D. Rockefeller III Book Award from Bicentennial Council of the Thirteen Original States Fund, 1979, for *A Revolutionary People at War.*

WRITINGS: A Revolutionary People at War: The Continental Army and the American Character, 1775-1783, University of North Carolina Press, 1980; *Light-Horse Harry Lee and the Legacy of American Revolution,* Knopf, 1981. Contributor to *William and Mary Quarterly.*

WORK IN PROGRESS: Research on military conflict and American nationality.

*   *   *

RUBASHOV, Zalman
See SHAZAR, (Schneor) Zalman

*   *   *

RUBIN, Charles J. 1950-
(Buck Buzzle)

PERSONAL: Born May 27, 1950, in New York, N.Y.; son of Issac (a judge) and Lucille (Lyons) Rubin. *Education:* Attended Wellesley College, 1970-71; Williams College, B.A., 1972. *Religion:* Jewish. *Home and office:* 253 East 31st St., No. 1-B, New York, N.Y. 10016. *Agent:* Gail Hochman, Paul R. Reynolds, Inc., 12 East 41st St., New York, N.Y. 10017.

CAREER: Free-lance writer and editor.

WRITINGS: (Editor and contributor) *Junk Food,* Dial, 1980. Also author of stories under pseudonym Buck Buzzle.

WORK IN PROGRESS: I Get Back at the Kids I Went to Summer Camp With, memoirs; research on Jews in sports and on World Fairs.

*   *   *

RUBIN, Dorothy 1932-

PERSONAL: Born February 11, 1932, in New York, N.Y.;

daughter of Harry and Clara (Schweller) Schleimer; married Arthur I. Rubin, August 24, 1950; children: Carol Anne (Mrs. John Holmes Smith IV), Sharon Anne (Mrs. Seth Johnson). *Education:* Rutgers University, B.A., 1959, M.Ed., 1961; Johns Hopkins University, Ph.D., 1968. *Home:* 917 Stuart Rd., Princeton, N.J. 08540. *Office:* Department of Elementary/Early Childhood Education and Reading, Trenton State College, P.O. Box 940, Hillwood Lakes, Trenton, N.J. 08625.

CAREER: Teacher at public schools in New Jersey, 1959-62; Coppin State College, Baltimore, Md., assistant professor of education, 1962-63; Towson State College (now University), Baltimore, assistant professor of education, 1963-66; Rollins College, Winter Park, Fla., adjunct professor of education, 1968-69; Trenton State College, Trenton, N.J., associate professor, 1969-73, professor of education, 1973—. Lecturer and conductor of workshops; has appeared on television and radio. *Member:* International Reading Association, American Educational Research Association, National Council of Teachers of English, Society for Creative Behavior, College Reading Association, New Jersey Reading Association, Kappa Delta Pi, Pi Lambda Theta.

WRITINGS: Teaching Elementary Language Arts, Holt, 1975, 2nd edition, 1980; *Gaining Word Power,* Macmillan, 1978; *The Vital Arts: Reading and Writing,* Macmillan, 1979; *Reading and Learning Power,* Macmillan, 1980; *The Teacher's Handbook of Reading/Thinking Exercises* (Teacher Bookclub selection), Holt, 1980; *The Primary Grade Teacher's Language Arts Handbook* (Teacher Bookclub selection), Holt, 1980; *The Intermediate Grade Teacher's Language Arts Handbook,* Holt, 1980; *Gaining Sentence Power,* Macmillan, 1981; *The Teacher's Handbook of Writing/Thinking Exercises,* Holt, 1981.

Author of sound tapes. Author of "Let's Do It Together," a syndicated column (also appearing as "Fun With Words" and "Word Games"), distributed nationally twice a week by Gannett Wire Service. Contributor of about twenty articles to education and psychology journals. Consultant for Harper & Row language art series, "Language Basic Plus," and for their reading series of the 1980's.

WORK IN PROGRESS: Major reading method books, for Holt; a two-volume revision of *Gaining Word Power,* for Macmillan; preparation for work as executive producer, writer, and host of television program for Renaissance Broadcasting Corp. in New Jersey.

SIDELIGHTS: Dorothy Rubin's books on reading and language arts skills have been highly praised. Her *Teaching Elementary Language Arts,* for example, "provides a balanced view of the elementary language art curriculum and is ... suited for teachers needing specific and carefully planned experential activities," said Idahlynn Karre. Walburga von Raffler-Engel also praised Rubin's book as a "refreshing change . . . solidly grounded in linguistics."

Rubin commented: "What can be more gratifying than to have someone write to tell you how helpful your books are? I try to write substantive textbooks that are readable and enjoyable, and one of my greatest joys is when students say that they can't believe that they are reading a textbook."

BIOGRAPHICAL/CRITICAL SOURCES: Reference Services Review, July/December, 1975; *Communication Education,* March, 1976; *Language Sciences,* December, 1976.

*   *   *

RUBIN, Morris H(arold)   1911-1980

OBITUARY NOTICE: Born August 7, 1911, in New York,

N.Y.; died of heart failure, August 8, 1980, in Madison, Wis. Journalist and writer. Morris Rubin began his career in journalism in 1929 when he joined the *Portland Evening Express* in Maine. He subsequently worked for the *Boston Globe, New York Times, New York Herald Tribune, Time, Milwaukee Journal,* and *Wisconsin State Journal* before becoming editor of *Progressive* magazine in 1940. By the time of his retirement in 1976 Rubin had risen to the position of president and publisher of the monthly periodical. He was also the editor of two books, *McCarthy: The Documented Record,* 1954, and *The Crisis of Survival,* 1970. Obituaries and other sources: *Who's Who in America,* 41st edition, Marquis, 1980; *Newsweek,* August 18, 1980.

*   *   *

RUDY, Ann   1927-

PERSONAL: Born August 28, 1927, in San Mateo, Calif.; daughter of Hector Lui (a civil engineer) and Hazel (a singer; maiden name, McKee) Morisette; married Ralph Rudy, June 23, 1950 (divorced, 1980); children: Robin Rudy Chancellor, Andrew Rudy. *Education:* Attended San Mateo College. *Religion:* Roman Catholic. *Home:* 2201 Pacific Ave., Manhattan Beach, Calif. 90266. *Agent:* Lorrie Helton, 8961 Sunset Blvd., Los Angeles, Calif. 90069.

CAREER: Writer, 1959—. Also worked as sign painter and fashion commentator, fashion model, and salesperson.

WRITINGS: Mom Spelled Backward Is Tired, Bobbs-Merrill, 1980. Author of "Once Over Lightly," a humorous weekly column syndicated by Copley News Service, 1966-74.

WORK IN PROGRESS: Humorous book on mid-life crisis; articles on women's image in media.

SIDELIGHTS: Ann Rudy told *CA:* "To tell a story, to make a statement, to stir the human heart to feel, the mind to think—this the task of the writer. For those of us who are published, it is no less a joy than it is for the so-called nonprofessional who labors with words to create a bond with other men and women."

*   *   *

RUGEL, Miriam   1911-

PERSONAL: Born January 20, 1911, in Philadelphia, Pa.; daughter of Jacob (an insurance broker) and Sarah (in retail business; maiden name, Seigle) Rugel; married Joseph N. Stern (a manufacturer), January 11, 1931; children: Peter Michael, Lillian Ruth, Karen Debra, Daniel Laurence. *Education:* Attended Charles Morris Price School of Advertising, 1929-31, Middlebury College, 1939, New School for Social Research, and Columbia University, 1937, 1954-55. *Home:* 412 Beaver Hill N., Jenkintown, Pa. 19046. *Agent:* Emilie Jacobson, Curtis Brown Ltd., 575 Madison Ave., New York, N.Y. 10022.

CAREER: Philadelphia Evening Bulletin, Philadelphia, Pa., proofreader, 1929-31; free-lance writer, 1931—. Teacher of creative writing classes; worked as advertising copywriter. *Member:* Authors Guild, Authors League of America. *Awards, honors:* First prize from Writer's Digest short story contest, 1950, for "Flowers on the Table."

WRITINGS—Short stories in anthologies: "Do You Believe in Love, My Darlings?," published in *O. Henry Prize Award Stories,* 1954; "The Flower," published in *Prize Stories: The O. Henry Awards,* 1954; *American Accent,* edited by Elizabeth Abell, Ballantine, 1954; *The Chosen,* edited by Harold Ribalow, Abelard, 1959; "Whoever You Are," published in

Ideas in Literature, edited by L. B. Jacobs and S. L. Root, C. E. Merrill, 1966; *Tales of Our People,* edited by Jerry D. Lewis, Geis, 1969; "The Sweet Forever," published in *My Name Aloud,* edited by Harold Ribalow, A. S. Barnes, 1969; "Paper Poppy," published in *Best American Short Stories,* edited by Martha Foley, 1969. Author of "Magic Sentence," released by Columbia Pictures in 1953. Contributor of more than one hundred fifty articles, stories, and reviews to magazines, including *Saturday Evening Post, Chatelaine, Harper's, Epoch, Mademoiselle, Kenyon Review,* and *Family Circle.*

WORK IN PROGRESS: A History of Women's Suffrage in America, a short story collection.

SIDELIGHTS: Miriam Rugel told *CA:* "Writing has been my only vocation and I have pursued it all my life. My avocations have been related: literature, literary criticism, language, even style, structure, and punctuation.

"At eleven I ran a gossip column for a local paper; at seventeen I held copy at a typesetting firm, where I learned to love printing and the smell of hot lead; at eighteen I was reading proof at the *Philadelphia Evening Bulletin,* attending advertising school at night and writing advertising copy during lunch.

"Two years later I was selling features to the metropolitan papers in town, reviewing books, doing articles, and introducing myself into fiction by way of pulp magazines.

"My first married summer was spent in writing classes at Columbia, to which I returned at intervals during the following years. Bread Loaf at Middlebury College was helpful later, as were private critics. I also owe a large debt to friendly editors.

"By thirty I had won an international short story contest and with the help of my first agent had broken into mass magazines. During the day I wrote the mass magazine stories; at night I did 'my own.' My work has been published in Canada and England, dramatized on television, transcribed into Braille, and translated for publication in Italy, Africa, Norway, Sweden, and Denmark."

*　　*　　*

RUPPLI, Michel 1934-

PERSONAL: Born July 3, 1934, in Coulommiers, France; son of Charles (a physician) and Marie-Helene (Sill) Ruppli; married Ariane Lafaurie, May 20, 1960 (died, 1972); married Claudine Benezet, June 22, 1974; children: Philippe, Frederic, Isabelle, Helene. *Education:* University of Paris, lic.-es-sciences, 1955; Ecole Nationale Superieure des Telecommunications, civilian engineer of telecommunications, 1957. *Home:* 325 Route de l'Empereur, 92500 Rueil-Malmaison, France.

CAREER: Electronics engineer in France, 1960—. Discographer, 1955—.

WRITINGS: Prestige Jazz Records, 1949-1971, Karl Emil Knudsen, 1972; *Atlantic Records: A Discography,* four volumes, Greenwood Press, 1979; (with Bob Porter) *The Savoy Label: A Discography,* Greenwood Press, 1980; (with Porter) *The Prestige Label: A Discography,* Greenwood Press, 1980. Contributor to *Jazz Hot.*

WORK IN PROGRESS: A Blue Note discography, publication by Greenwood Press expected in 1981; a Capitol discography; a Verve discography, and other labels of the postwar era.

SIDELIGHTS: Ruppli commented: "My work on discographies is a contribution to a better knowledge of recorded material, particularly in the jazz field. Research has led me to specialize in label discographies, with my main interest in music of the postwar era. It is hoped that all large record companies will open their files to similar discographical research, in order to have, at some time, a fairly complete picture of the field."

*　　*　　*

RUSHFORTH, Peter (Scott) 1945-

PERSONAL: Born February 15, 1945, in Blackhill, County Durham, England; son of Samuel Thomas (an engineer) and Emily (Scott) Rushforth. *Education:* University of Hull, B.A., 1966; University of Nottingham, certificate in education, 1967. *Office:* Friends' School, Great Ayton, Cleveland TS9 6BN, England.

CAREER: Huddersfield New College, Huddersfield, England, teacher of English, 1967-71; Friends' School, Great Ayton, Cleveland, England, head of English department, 1971—. *Member:* Society of Authors. *Awards, honors:* Hawthornden Prize from Society of Authors, 1980, for *Kindergarten.*

WRITINGS: Kindergarten (novel), Hamish Hamilton, 1979, revised edition, Knopf, 1980.

WORK IN PROGRESS: A novel.

SIDELIGHTS: Rushforth's first book, *Kindergarten,* is about a young boy who "is discovering his own Jewish ancestry, and through this the experience of the Jews in the last world war," related Maev Kennedy in the *Irish Times.* Michael Parnell wrote in the *Literary Review* that "this is a novel that bears, indeed requires, re-reading, for though its story is simple enough, it is told with remarkable and individual artisty and has a complexity of reference and form in which all the individual bits do not fall into place until you near the end."

BIOGRAPHICAL/CRITICAL SOURCES: Irish Times, November 10, 1979; *Literary Review,* December 12, 1979; *New York Times,* July 8, 1980.

*　　*　　*

RUSHTON, William Faulkner 1947-

PERSONAL: Born November 4, 1947, in Louisville, Ky.; son of George L. (a chemist) and Evelyn (Rose) Rushton. *Education:* Tulane University, B.Arch., 1970. *Home:* 400 West 43rd St., No. 20-H, New York, N.Y. 10036. *Agent:* Bob Cornfield, 145 West 79th St., New York, N.Y. 10024. *Office:* CNB-TV, Automation House, 49 East 68th St., New York, N.Y. 10021.

CAREER: New Orleans Courier, New Orleans, La., managing editor, 1970-77; CNB-TV, New York, N.Y., director of research, 1978—. Art director for *Manhattan Plaza News.* Member of board of directors of New Orleans Video Access Center, 1975-76. *Member:* National Federation of Local Cable Programmers, Society of Architectural Historians, American Civil Liberties Union (member of board of directors, 1972-73), Sigma Delta Chi. *Awards, honors:* Fellow of Loyola Institute of Politics, 1971; national writing awards from American Society of Planning Officials, 1974, and National Wildlife Federation, 1975; "Cityscape" was named best column in the state by Louisiana Press Association, 1976.

WRITINGS: The Cajuns: From Acadia to Louisiana, Farrar, Straus, 1979; *Project Metro-Link,* Volume I, Tri-State

Regional Planning Commission, 1979. Author of "Cityscape," a column in *New Orleans Courier*, 1969-78. Contributor to architecture and planning journals, popular magazines, and newspapers, including *Rolling Stone, New York Times, Environmental Action,* and *Public Telecommunications Review.*

WORK IN PROGRESS: A public arts television network feasibility study, for New York State Council on the Arts.

SIDELIGHTS: Rushton told *CA:* "'New journalism,' also known as 'faction,' is one of the few literary forms that can compete successfully with television and film. Good writing melts in your mind, not in your hand.

"There is a 'new television' emerging that will abolish the strictures of the 'old TV' and introduce unprecedented opportunities for interactive communications. The fight for its control and use will be the major intellectual issue of the 1980's."

* * *

RUSTOMJI, Nari Kaikhosru 1919-

PERSONAL: Surname is accented on first syllable; born May 16, 1919, in Lahore, India; son of K. J. and Homai (Cooper) Rustomji; married Hilla Master, 1951 (died, 1953); married Avi Dalal, 1963; children: Tusna, Rashne, Shahnaz (daughters). *Education:* Christ's College, Cambridge, M.A., 1942. *Home:* Jony Castle, 96 Wodehouse Rd., Colaba, Bombay 400 005, India.

CAREER: Indian Civil Service, 1941-77; appointed in the United Kingdom, 1941; assistant commissioner in Sylhet, India, 1942; head of South Sylhet subdivision, 1943-44; under-secretary of home and political department in Assam, India, 1945-47; district commissioner for tribal areas and states in Lakhimpur, India, 1947-48; adviser to governor of Assam, 1948-54; prime minister of Sikkim (Indian protectorate; now Indian state), speaker of Sikkim council, and president of Sikkim executive council, 1954-59; adviser to governor of Assam for North East Frontier Agency and Nagaland, 1959-63; adviser to king of Bhutan, 1963-66; development commissioner, chairman of electricity board, and chief secretary to government of Assam, 1966-70; chief secretary to government of Meghalaya, India, 1971-77. Nuffield Fellow at Cambridge University, 1979-80. *Military service:* United Kingdom Home Guard, 1939-42, served in Royal Observer Corps. *Member:* Institute of Tibetology (founding member). *Awards, honors:* Ford Foundation fellowship, 1974.

WRITINGS—All published by Oxford University Press: (Editor) Verrier Elwin, *The Nagas in the Nineteenth Century,* 1969; *Enchanted Frontiers: Sikkim, Bhutan, and India's North-Eastern Borderlands,* 1971; *Bhutan: The Dragon Kingdom in Crisis,* 1978; *Acculturation: Conflict and Reconciliation,* 1981.

SIDELIGHTS: Rustomji told *CA:* "I have been deeply concerned since my earliest years about the underprivileged. My work in the Indian Civil Service was mainly connected with materially backward people. My books are intended to focus attention on our moral obligations to minorities." *Avocational interests:* Music, wildlife, environmental conservation, youth education.

BIOGRAPHICAL/CRITICAL SOURCES: Verrier Elwin, *The Tribal World of Verrier Elwin,* Oxford University Press, 1963.

* * *

RYGA, George 1932-

PERSONAL: Born July 27, 1932, in Deep Creek, Alberta, Canada; son of George (a farmer) and Maria (Kolodka) Ryga; married Norma Lois Campbell; children: Lesley, Tanya, Campbell, Sergei, Jamie. *Education:* "Self-educated." *Politics:* Socialist-humanitarian. *Home and office address:* R.R.2, Summerland, British Columbia, Canada V0H 1Z0. *Agent:* Nina Froud, Harvey Unna & Stephen Durbridge Ltd., 14 Beaumont Mews, Marylebone High St., London W1N 4HE, England; and Sam Adams, Adams, Ray & Rosenberg, 9200 Sunset Blvd., Penthouse 25, Los Angeles, Calif. 90069.

CAREER: Worked in farming, construction, and hotel industry; worked for radio station in Edmonton, Alberta, 1950-54; full-time writer, 1962—. Guest professor at University of British Columbia, Banff School of Fine Arts, and Simon Fraser University. *Member:* Association of Canadian Television and Radio Artists, Writers Guild of America, West, British Columbia Civil Liberties Association (honorary member). *Awards, honors:* Imperial Order Daughters of the Empire Award, 1950, 1951; Canada Council senior arts grant, 1972; Fringe Frist Award, Edinburgh Festival, 1973.

WRITINGS—Novels, except as indicated: *Hungry Hills,* Longmans, Green (Toronto), 1963; *Ballad of a Stone-Picker,* Macmillan (Toronto), 1966, revised edition, Talonbooks, 1976; *Night Desk,* Talonbooks, 1976; *Beyond the Crimson Morning* (travel book), Doubleday, 1979.

Plays: "Nothing But a Man," produced in Vancouver, British Columbia, at New Play Centre, 1966; *The Ecstasy of Rita Joe* (two-act; see below; produced in Vancouver at Playhouse Theatre, 1967; produced in Washington, D.C., 1973), Talonbooks, 1970; "Grass and Wild Strawberries" (also see below), produced in Vancouver, 1969; (author of music and lyrics) *Captives of the Faceless Drummer* (produced in Vancouver at Vancouver Art Gallery, 1971), Talonbooks, 1971; (author of music) *Sunrise on Sarah* (produced in Banff, Alberta, 1972), Talonbooks, 1973; "A Portrait of Angela" (also see below), produced in Banff, 1973; "A Feast of Thunder," music by Morris Surdin, produced in 1973; *Indian* (also see below; produced in Winnipeg, Manitoba, 1974), Book Society, 1967; "Twelve Ravens for the Sun," music by Mikis Theodorakis, 1975; *Ploughmen of the Glacier* (also see below; produced in Vancouver, 1976), Talonbooks, 1977; *Seven Hours to Sundown* (also see below; produced in Edmonton, Alberta, 1976), Talonbooks, 1977.

Play anthologies: *The Ecstasy of Rita Joe and Other Plays* (contains "The Ecstasy of Rita Joe," "Indian," and "Grass and Wild Strawberries"), introduction by Brian Parker, New Press, 1971; *Country and Western* (contains "A Portrait of Angela," "Ploughmen of the Glacier," and "Seven Hours to Sundown"), Talonbooks, 1976. Also author of play, "Paracelsus," published in *Canadian Theatre Review,* fall, 1974.

Radio plays: "A Touch of Cruelty," 1961; "Half-Caste," 1962; "Masks and Shadows," 1963; "Bread Route," 1963; "Departures," 1963; "Ballad for Bill," 1963; "The Stone Angel," 1965; "Seasons of a Summer Day," 1975. Author of scripts for "Miners, Gentlemen, and Other Hard Cases" series, 1974-75, and "Advocates of Danger" series, 1976.

Television plays: "Indian," 1962; "The Storm," 1962; "Bitter Grass," 1963; "For Want of Something Better to Do," 1963; "The Tulip Garden," 1963; "Two Soldiers," 1963; "The Pear Tree," 1963; "Man Alive," 1965; "The Kamloops Incident," 1965; "A Carpenter by Trade" (documentary), 1967; "Ninth Summer," 1972; "The Mountains" (documentary), 1973; "The Ballad of Iwan Lepa" (documentary), 1976. Author of scripts for "The Manipulators" series, 1968, and "The Name of the Game" series, 1969.

SIDELIGHTS: George Ryga's plays and novels usually center around an individual isolated in some manner from society who must choose how to react to societal neglect and his or her own loneliness and isolation. Some critics have mentioned that Ryga's characters all lack a personal base or home. Neil Carson, for example, comments in *Canadian Literature* that "the sense of spiritual homelessness is common in Ryga's work and many of his characters define themselves by their relationship to a country they have lost or one they never find." In "Indian" and "The Ecstasy of Rita Joe" (which Carson believes "establishes Ryga as the most exciting talent writing for the stage in Canada today"), the protagonists are native Americans who are humiliated and alienated by white society's racism. In "Grass and Wild Strawberries," it is an individual from the "hippy" subculture who is isolated by his inability to accept as his own either the values of his drug culture friends or of his "establishment" socialistic uncle. Terrorists are the outsiders and underdogs depicted in "Captives of the Faceless Drummer," and in "Paracelsus," Ryga suggests that even a "genius" or person of outstanding ability will be rejected by society.

Another of the isolated individuals is Romeo Kuchmir of Ryga's novel, *Night Desk*. W. H. Rockett, writing in *Saturday Night*, believes that Kuchmir "has made what Brian Parker has called a Ryga folk ballad. Words trigger other words, responses, new anecdotes, old ideas. Everything weaves back on senseless legs to the same loneliness.... Romeo is his own best audience. He is probably the most interesting Ryga character since Rita Joe. What is amiss is that he is alone: soliloquizing before the night desk. He is a character in need of other characters as strong as he. He has to be seen." Carson elaborates on this in the *Journal of Canadian Fiction,* pointing out that although some critics believe Ryga's works to be socialist tracts, it is his existentialism that is most prominent. "What impresses in his work is not his social criticism, still less his portrayal of the agents of justice and bureaucracy, but his assertion of individual courage and dignity in the face of those most terrible oppressions—loneliness and death."

BIOGRAPHICAL/CRITICAL SOURCES: Spectator, January, 1966; *Books and Bookmen,* February, 1966; *Saturday Night,* May, 1966, January/February, 1977; *Canadian Literature,* summer, 1970; William H. New, editor, *Dramatists in Canada: Selected Essays,* University of British Columbia Press, 1972; Mavor Moore, *Four Canadian Playwrights,* Holt, 1973; *Journal of Canadian Fiction,* Volume IV, number 4, 1979; *Canadian Forum,* January-February, 1979; *Contemporary Literary Criticism,* Volume 14, Gale, 1980.

S

SABBAG, Robert 1946-

PERSONAL: Born June 21, 1946, in Boston, Mass.; son of George (a naval officer) and Evelyn Sabbag. *Education:* Georgetown University, B.A., 1968. *Residence:* South Wellfleet, Mass. *Agent:* Dorothy Pittman, Illington Rd., Ossining, N.Y. 10562.

CAREER: Washington Daily News, Washington, D.C., general assignment reporter, 1968-69; *Boston Record-American,* Boston, Mass., general assignment reporter, 1970; writer.

WRITINGS: Snowblind: A Brief Career in the Cocaine Trade (nonfiction), Bobbs-Merrill, 1977.

WORK IN PROGRESS: A novel, publication by Simon & Schuster expected in 1982.

* * *

SABOURIN, Anne Winifred 1910-
(Justine Sabourin)

PERSONAL: Surname is pronounced *Say*-burn; born October 28, 1910, in Alpena Township, Mich.; daughter of Joseph (a foreman) and Mary Elizabeth (Sheehan) Sabourin. *Education:* Loras College, B.A., 1938; University of Notre Dame, M.A., 1945; University of Michigan, Ph.D., 1964. *Politics:* "Changes with candidates." *Home and office:* 1100 Michigan Ave., Grayling, Mich. 49738.

CAREER: Roman Catholic nun of Religious Sisters of Mercy (R.S.M.), name in religion, Sister Mary Justine; high school teacher of English, Latin, and commercial subjects in Michigan and Iowa, 1930-40; assistant mistress of novices at convent in Dubuque, Iowa, 1940-41; Mercy College of Detroit, Detroit, Mich., academic dean, 1941-45; principal of Roman Catholic high school in Muskegon, Mich., 1945-48; Religious Sisters of Mercy, community supervisor of elementary and secondary schools in Iowa and Michigan, 1948-50; Mercy College of Detroit, head of department of education, 1950-51, academic dean, 1951-61; Religious Sisters of Mercy, Detroit, administrator of Province of Detroit, 1961-67; writer, 1967-73; Mercy Hospital, Grayling, Mich., administrative assistant in charge of special projects, 1973-77. *Member:* Federation of the Sisters of Mercy of the Americas (charter member), Sigma Phi Sigma (founder; national moderator, 1955), Phi Kappa Phi, Pi Lambda Theta.

WRITINGS—Under name Justine Sabourin: *The Amalgamation: A History of the Union of the Religious Sisters of Mercy in the United States of America,* Abbey Press, 1976. Contributor to education and architecture journals.

AVOCATIONAL INTERESTS: Travel (England, Europe, South and Central America).

* * *

SABOURIN, Justine
See SABOURIN, Anne Winifred

* * *

SACK, James J(ohn) 1944-

PERSONAL: Born December 4, 1944, in Monroe, Mich.; son of Walter J. (a merchant) and Janet (a teacher; maiden name, Carroll) Sack. *Education:* University of Notre Dame, B.A., 1967; University of Michigan, M.A., 1968, Ph.D., 1973. *Religion:* Roman Catholic. *Office:* Department of History, University of Illinois at Chicago Circle, Box 4348, Chicago, Ill. 60680.

CAREER: University of Illinois at Chicago Circle, Chicago, assistant professor, 1973-80, associate professor of history, 1980—. *Member:* American Historical Association, American Society for Eighteenth Century Studies, Conference on British Studies.

WRITINGS: The Grenvillites, 1801-1829: Party Politics and Factionalism in the Age of Pitt and Liverpool, University of Illinois Press, 1979. Contributor to history and theology journals.

* * *

SACKERMAN, Henry
See KAHM, H(arold) S.

* * *

(el-)SADAT, Anwar 1918-

PERSONAL: Born December 25, 1918, in Mit Abu el Kom, Egypt; son of Mohammed el-Sadat (an army hospital clerk); married second wife Jihan Raouf, May 29, 1949; children: (second marriage) Gamal, Lubna, Jihan, Noha. *Education:* Royal Military Academy, graduated, 1938. *Religion:* Moslem. *Residence:* Cairo, Egypt. *Office:* Office of the President of the United Republic of Egypt, Cairo, Egypt.

CAREER: Egyptian Army, commissioned officer, 1938; organized and founded Free Officers' Organization (a group committed to British withdrawal from Egypt); arrested for revolutionary activities and subsequently released; during World War II worked with German spies in Cairo to weaken British position in Egypt; arrested and court-martialed for anti-British activities in 1942; imprisoned, 1942-44; escaped from prison in November, 1944, and went into hiding until charges against him and other conspirators were dismissed; during this time worked at a variety of jobs, including driving a cab; returned to army, 1944; arrested for participation in the political assassination of government minister Amin Osman Pasha, 1946; imprisoned, 1946-48; acquitted of charges and released from prison, 1948; worked as a rewriter for Al Hilal (publishing company), 1948; returned to army in January, 1950, with rank of captain; became lieutenant-colonel, then colonel; resumed anti-British activities as a member of the Revolutionary Command Council, and succeeded with Nasser in overthrowing the government of King Farouk, July 22, 1952; founder and editor-in-chief of newspaper *al-Gomhouriya* (title means "The Republic"), director of army public relations; Government of Egypt, Cairo, minister of state, 1954-56, deputy speaker, then speaker of National Assembly; United Arab Republic, speaker of the Federal National Assembly, 1960-69; member of Presidential Council, 1962-64; vice-president, 1964-66, 1969-70; United Republic of Egypt, president, 1970—, prime minister, 1973-74, military governor-general, 1973, member of Higher Council on Nuclear Energy, 1975—. Secretary-general of Islamic Congress, 1955; Arab Socialist Union (political organization; formerly National Union), secretary-general, 1957-61, chairman, 1970—; president of Council Federation of Arab Republics, 1971—. *Awards, honors:* Sinai Medal, 1974; named Man of the Year by *Time* magazine, 1977; Nobel Peace Prize, 1978.

WRITINGS: Revolt on the Nile, foreword by Gamal Abdel Nasser, John Day, 1957; *In Search of Identity: An Autobiography,* Harper, 1977.

SIDELIGHTS: In their January 2, 1978, issue, the editors of *Time* magazine named Anwar Sadat "Man of the Year" for "his willingness to seize upon a fresh approach, for his display of personal and political courage, and for his unshakable resolve to restore a momentum for peace in the Middle East." This momentum for peace was ignited by what Sadat has called his "sacred mission"—his journey to Jerusalem on November 19, 1977. Sadat is the only Arab leader to visit the state of Israel. Henry Kissinger said of Sadat's trip: "By going to Jerusalem, President Sadat cut through the mindset of a generation. He allowed the people of Israel to judge for themselves his commitment to peace."

As a young army officer, Sadat was fiercely anti-British and was imprisoned twice for his revolutionary activities. While in prison for the second time in the now famous Cell Fifty-Four, Sadat found his true self and a deep inner peace. In his autobiography, *In Search of Identity,* Sadat wrote: "Two places in this world make it impossible for a man to escape from himself: a battlefield and a prison cell."

After the revolution of 1952, which ousted both the corrupt Farouk monarchy and the British from Egypt, Sadat continued to work for the benefit of the Egyptian people. He had seen them suffer under the rule of Farouk and had witnessed their humiliation at the occupation of their country by the British. During Nasser's regime, Sadat saw signs of the same kind of fear and anguish. Nasser's dictatorship had brought the confiscation of public property and the frequent use of detention centers. Sadat sees fear as debilitating: "[It is] the most degrading of all emotions for a human being. In fear personality disintegrates, [and] the human will is para-

lyzed." From his observations of the Egyptians during these periods, Sadat wrote in his autobiography: "It would be a mistake . . . to think that the spirit of the Egyptian people could ever be stifled. It is a great spirit, capable of enduring all hardships, and is never subdued by adversity. Our people have withstood the worst types of oppression, both domestic and foreign, and emerged unharmed. It was the great fortitude and self-confidence of that people that enabled them to endure the pain."

During his years under Nasser, Sadat was thought by many other politicians, including Nasser, to be a man without ambitions, "a man who cared more about smart clothes, his home and car, than Cabinet meetings and political responsibility." But Sadat saw the revolution as "the culmination of a life-long struggle" and was satisfied with continuing to work for a better Egypt. He refused to take part in a power struggle that was plaguing many of the officers of the Revolutionary Command Council. His life in Cell Fifty-Four had taught him "to value that inner success which alone maintains one's inward equilibrium and helps a man to be true to himself." He saw power as "a petty thing I felt one needed to rise above." Because he showed no political ambitions, Sadat was trusted implicitly by Nasser and was later named his vice-president. After Nasser's death, he became president of Egypt.

The differences between the two leaders became apparent soon after Sadat took office: he reversed the decree that called for confiscation of public property; in a public ceremony burned the government's collection of taped conversations; and abolished the widespread use of concentration camps. Another difference between Nasser and Sadat was their opposing views of Soviet intervention. During his regime Nasser had courted Soviet backing, relying on Russian military expertise and arms. Sadat, and eventually Nasser, came to see that the weapons deals with the Soviet Union severely limited Egypt's political independence. In a surprise move in 1972, he expelled Soviet military advisers from Egypt.

In his political career, one quality of Anwar Sadat shows clearly—his capacity for change. Time and time again, the Egyptian leader has displayed the ability to be flexible and innovative when the situation called for it. This has caused more than one diplomat to observe that Sadat is "a far more vigorous and visionary statesman than has been generally perceived." Sadat credits his experiences in Cell Fifty-Four with providing him the strength to change. In his autobiography, he wrote: "My contemplation of life and human nature in that secluded place had taught me that he who cannot change the very fabric of his thought will never be able to change reality, and will never, therefore, make any progress."

For all his dramatic flair, flexibility, and imaginative thinking, Sadat still remains personally, according to *Time* correspondent Robert Ajemian, "a withdrawn, introverted man." In a rare glimpse into the daily activities of the Egyptian leader, Ajemian offered this portrait: "A devout Muslim, he never touches liquor or wine. . . . Every evening without fail, Sadat schedules two movies, mostly American westerns; he watches them, usually alone, in his pajamas. . . . Sadat, the imaginative thinker, is a poor administrator who shuns detail. . . . He detests reading reports and prefers to have them delivered orally."

Reviewing *In Search of Identity,* Nadav Safran, a critic for the *New York Times Book Review,* wrote: "Whatever one may think of his self-depiction and of his interpretation of history, there is no doubt that President Sadat's undertaking in itself constitutes a human and political document of first-rate importance." Safran concluded: "The final lesson . . . is that so long as a man like Anwar el-Sadat remains at the helm in Egypt, the world will not be done with surprises from there."

BIOGRAPHICAL/CRITICAL SOURCES: Anwar el-Sadat, *In Search of Identity: An Autobiography,* Harper, 1977; B. K. Narayan, *Anwar el-Sadat: Man With a Mission,* Vikas Publishing House, 1977; *New Statesman,* August 12, 1977; *Time,* November 28, 1977, January 2, 1978, January 9, 1978, January 16, 1978, January 30, 1978, February 13, 1978, February 20, 1978, March 20, 1978, April 10, 1978, May 29, 1978, July 24, 1978, September 11, 1978, September 25, 1978, October 23, 1978; *Newsweek,* November 28, 1977, December 5, 1977, September 18, 1978, September 25, 1978; *National Review,* December 9, 1977; *Commonweal,* December 23, 1977.*

—*Sketch by Nancy M. Rusin*

* * *

SAFRAN, Claire 1930-

PERSONAL: Born March 18, 1930, in New York, N.Y.; daughter of Simon (an entrepreneur) and Flora (in real estate; maiden name, Rand) Safran; married John Milton Williams (a photographer), June 8, 1958; children: Scott Edward. *Education:* Brooklyn College (now of the City University of New York), B.A. (cum laude), 1951. *Home and office:* 53 Evergreen Ave., Westport, Conn. 06880.

CAREER/WRITINGS: Photo Dealer, New York City, news editor, 1951-53; *TV Radio Mirror,* New York City, associate editor, 1954-58; *Photoplay,* New York City, managing editor, 1958-61; *TV Radio Mirror,* editor in chief, 1961-65; *In Magazine,* New York City, editor in chief, 1965-67; *Family Weekly,* New York City, associate editor, 1967-68; *Coronet,* New York City, editor in chief, 1968-71; *Redbook,* New York City, contributing editor, 1974-77, 1978—, executive editor, 1977-78. Contributor to magazines including *Reader's Digest, TV Guide,* and *Today's Health. Member:* American Society of Journalists and Authors, National Organization for Women. *Awards, honors:* American Psychological Foundation media award and Penney-Missouri magazine award finalist, both 1977; award of merit from Religious Public Relations Council, 1978; honorable mention for American Academy of Pediatrics Journalism award and Odyssey Institute Media award for national editorials, both 1979.

WORK IN PROGRESS: Reports on women and the family.

SIDELIGHTS: Safran told *CA:* "All writers have those gray mornings when sentences seem clumsy, and those dark afternoons when words simply fail. The secret is to persist. The comfort is in the way Dorothy Parker summed up the way we all feel: I HATE writing but I LOVE having written."

* * *

ST. CLAIR, Leonard 1916-
(Richard de Graffe)

PERSONAL: Surname legally changed, 1933; born April 5, 1916, in San Francisco, Calif.; son of Charles E. (a realtor) and Cora M. (St. Clair) Cooper; married Catherine Osborn (an interior designer), 1946. *Education:* Attended University of California, Los Angeles. *Politics:* "Republican, nominally." *Home and office:* 7110 Senalda Rd., Los Angeles, Calif. 90068. *Agent:* Harold Ober Associates, 40 East 49th St., New York, N.Y. 10017.

CAREER: St. Clair Estate Co. (investment company), Bakersfield, Calif., vice-president, 1956-59; writer, 1959—. *Member:* Mystery Writers of America, Author's League, P.E.N.

WRITINGS—Novels: *A Fortune in Death,* Fawcett, 1972; *The Emerald Trap,* Putnam, 1974; *The Seadon Fortune,* Simon & Schuster, 1977; *Obsessions,* Simon & Schuster, 1980. Also author of more than two hundred fifty radio and television scripts, including shows for Lux Radio Theatre, Hallmark Playhouse, Hallmark Hall of Fame, and Four Star Playhouse. Contributor of articles to periodicals, including *Esquire,* under pseudonym Richard de Graffe.

WORK IN PROGRESS: A modern day love story, publication expected in 1981.

SIDELIGHTS: St. Clair told *CA:* "My motivation in writing is in response to the age-old request: 'Tell me a story.' It is the same old desire that dates all the way back to Homer. The driving force behind my books is primarily to entertain myself and, hopefully, to entertain others; and, in consequence, to earn a decent living.

"My opinion of the current literary scene is that too many books are being published, resulting in some very good books being smothered in the avalanche of the mediocre. I wish that today there were more outlets for the young writer, places where he could learn his skills by the doing. When I began, there were dramatic radio shows that gave the young writer a chance to experiment, to fail, and, hurrah!, sometimes to succeed. My advice to those just beginning today is: Courage! Never give up. If you have the talent, someone somewhere will recognize it. But note that one all-important word: 'if.'"

* * *

St. JAMES, Bernard
See TREISTER, Bernard W(illiam)

* * *

SALTMAN, Juliet 1923-

PERSONAL: Born April 30, 1923, in Haifa, Israel; American citizen born abroad; daughter of Samuel H. (an accountant) and Bertha (a teacher; maiden name, Eisenberg) Zion; married William Saltman (a physical chemist), February 14, 1943; children: David, Nina, Daniel. *Education:* Rutgers University, B.A., 1943; University of Chicago, M.A., 1948; Case Western Reserve University, Ph.D., 1971. *Politics:* Democrat. *Religion:* Jewish. *Home:* 844 Frederick Blvd., Akron, Ohio 44320. *Office:* Department of Sociology, Kent State University, Kent, Ohio 44242.

CAREER: Los Angeles Civil Service Commission, Los Angeles, Calif., research assistant, 1945-46; University of Akron, Akron, Ohio, lecturer in sociology, 1957-68; Kent State University, Kent, Ohio, associate professor, 1971-77, professor of sociology, 1977—. Member of board of directors of National Committee Against Discrimination in Housing, National Neighbors, and Akron West Side Neighbors; founder and president of Akron Fair Housing Contact Service, 1972-74.

MEMBER: American Sociological Association, Society for the Study of Social Problems, League of Women Voters, American Civil Liberties Union, North Central Sociological Association (public policy chairperson, 1975-77). *Awards, honors:* National Defense Education Act (NDEA) fellow, 1968-71; National volunteer award from National Center for Voluntary Action, 1973; federal women's program award from U.S. Department of Housing and Urban Development, (HUD), 1975; named public citizen of the year by National Association of Social Workers, Northeast Ohio Chapter, 1975.

WRITINGS: Open Housing as a Social Movement, Heath, 1971; *Economic Consequences of Disarmament,* Canadian Peace Research Institute, 1972; *Open Housing: Dynamics of a Social Movement,* Praeger, 1978; (editor) *Integrated Neighborhoods in Action,* National Neighbors, 1978. Contributor to sociology and voluntary action journals, including *Annals of the American Academy of Political and Social Science.*

WORK IN PROGRESS: Action Research on Redlining, publication expected in 1980; *School Desegregation and Housing Desegregation,* publication expected in 1980; *Neighborhood Revitalization,* publication expected by 1981.

SIDELIGHTS: Juliet Saltman wrote: "Sociologist and scholar Louis Wirth taught me long ago that 'housing is a sociological and social concern.' A study of a blighted area of Chicago in 1948 was the beginning of my interest in housing, an interest which has not diminished over the years. The development of my focus has been from blight to equal access."

AVOCATIONAL INTERESTS: Travel (Europe, Latin America, the Orient).

BIOGRAPHICAL/CRITICAL SOURCES: Review of Research in Human Behavior, August, 1975.

* * *

SAMPSON, Fay (Elizabeth) 1935-

PERSONAL: Born June 10, 1935, in Plymouth, England; daughter of Edmar Ismail (a member of Royal Marine Staff Band) and Edith Maud (a hotel waitress; maiden name, Cory) Sampson; married Jack Greaves Priestley (a lecturer in religious education), March 30, 1959; children: Mark Alan, Katharine Fay. *Education:* University College of the Southwest, B.A. (with honors), 1956; University of Exeter, certificate in education, 1957. *Politics:* Radical. *Religion:* Christian. *Home:* Christie Cottage, Tedburn St. Mary, Exeter, Devonshire EX6 6AZ, England.

CAREER: Assistant mathematics teacher at high school in Mytholmroyd, England, 1957-58, bilateral school in Nottingham, England, 1959-60, and technical school in Eastwood, England, 1960-61; Bishop Blackall High School, Exeter, England, part-time assistant mathematics teacher, 1973—, evening class lecturer in writing, 1979—. Volunteer librarian in Zambia, 1962-64; volunteer at work camps in Germany, Greece, France, Jordan, South Africa, and Ireland; organized dramatic readings. Member of international committee of Student Christian Movement, 1956-57; member of national executive of NALSO, 1956-57. *Member:* Exeter UNA.

WRITINGS—For children: *F.67,* Hamish Hamilton, 1975; *Half a Welcome,* Dobson, 1977; *The Watch on Patterick Fell,* Dobson, 1978, Morrow, 1980; *The Empty House,* Dobson, 1979; *Landfall on Innis Michael* (sequel to *The Watch on Patterick Fell*), Dobson, 1980; *The Hungry Snow,* Dobson, 1980; *The Chains of Sleep,* Dobson, 1981.

WORK IN PROGRESS: Pengur Ban, based on a poem about a cat.

SIDELIGHTS: Sampson commented: "I was a solitary child, taking pleasure in reading and long walks with a dog on the hills above the fishing village where I lived. I loved

writing, but no one ever suggested that I might earn a living by it. That had to wait until I had returned from Zambia and my younger child was starting school. Having made a break in my teaching career, I had to face the question, 'What next?' It was my husband and the late Sidney Robbins, an enthusiast for children's literature in education, who encouraged me to take writing seriously.

"I spent five very enjoyable years writing books that almost, but not quite, got published. I finally struck lucky with *F.67.* At first I wrote out of a deep love of my native west-country, its landscape, history, and legends. But success came when I turned to the present and the near future (I regard *F.67* and *The Watch on Patterick Fell* not as science fiction, but as social fantasy—shaking the kaleidoscope of the present and seeing what new patterns might emerge from the chaos). I still have a strong attachment to the west-country, particularly its Celtic past, and this is reflected in my more recent books. But however old the theme, it must still speak to today.

"Every week of the year I come across a news item or a snippet of history that would make a good book. But nineteen times out of twenty I don't want to write it. It is too rounded, complete. For me the essential motivation in writing is curiosity. 'What would it be like if . . . ?' 'What if they had . . . ?' Or just 'Why?' My books are an exploration of these questions. For instance, *F.67* began with the influx of Ugandan Asian refugees when I visited one of their camps and asked 'What would it be like if my own children were put into this situation?' But if I have done my work well, the books themselves will raise more questions than they answer, so that at the end the reader is just beginning his own adventure of the mind."

AVOCATIONAL INTERESTS: Walking, sailing, travel, Celtic history, mythology, attending plays.

* * *

SANDFORD, John 1929-

PERSONAL: Born July 23, 1929, in Joplin, Mo.; son of George O. (in sales) and Zelma (a knitting instructor; maiden name, Potter) Sandford; married Paula Bowman (a writer, lecturer, and counselor), January 12, 1951; children: R. Loren, Amilee K. Sandford Blessinger, Mark S., John P., Timothy J., Andrea M. *Education:* Drury College, B.A., 1951; University of Chicago, M.Div., 1958. *Home:* 3657 Highland Dr., Coeur d'Alene, Idaho 83814. *Office:* Elijah House, Inc., P.O. Box 722, Coeur d'Alene, Idaho 83814.

CAREER: Ordained minister of United Church of Christ (Congregational), 1958; pastor of Congregational churches in Streator, Ill., 1956-61, Council Grove, Kan., 1961-65, and Wallace, Idaho, 1965-74; Elijah House, Inc., Coeur d'Alene, Idaho, co-founder and co-director, 1974—.

WRITINGS: (With wife, Paula Sandford) *The Elijah Task,* Logos International, 1977; (with P. Sandford) *Restoring the Christian Family,* Logos International, 1979; (with P. Sandford) *Transformation of the Inner Man,* Logos International, 1981. Contributor to *Baptist Student Journal.*

SIDELIGHTS: Sandford wrote: "My wife and I are in a full-time team ministry of international scope, which includes writing, lecturing, and counseling. We travel extensively, teaching in all denominations (Protestant and Catholic) and in interdenominational camps and conferences. Our cassette tapes are used all over the world. The main thrust of the teaching has to do with restoration of the family and renewal in the church. At home we provide a Christian counseling service and we often hold seminars for Christian counselors.''

AVOCATIONAL INTERESTS: Racquetball, camping, hiking.

* * *

SANDFORD, Paula 1931-

PERSONAL: Born November 30, 1931, in Dodge City, Kan.; daughter of Paul M. (in sales) and Edna (a teacher; maiden name, Breshears) Bowman; married John Sandford (a minister, writer, lecturer, and counselor), January 12, 1951; children: R. Loren, Amilee K. Sandford Blessinger, Mark S., John P., Timothy J., Andrea M. *Education:* Attended Drury College, 1949-51, University of Chicago, 1953, University of Kansas, University of Idaho, and Northern Idaho College. *Religion:* United Church of Christ (Congregational) and American Baptist. *Home:* 3657 Highland Dr., Coeur d'Alene, Idaho 83814. *Office:* Elijah House, Inc., P.O. Box 722, Coeur d'Alene, Idaho 83814.

CAREER: Southwestern Bell Telephone Co., St. Louis, Mo., accountant, 1949; University of Chicago, Chicago, Ill., research associate, 1953-54; high school teacher of Spanish, English, and history in Mullan, Idaho, 1969-71; substitute teacher at junior and senior high schools in Wallace, Idaho, 1972-74; Elijah House, Inc., Coeur d'Alene, Idaho, co-founder and co-director, 1974—. Art teacher at elementary school in Wallace, summers, 1973-74.

WRITINGS: (With husband, John Sandford) *The Elijah Task,* Logos International, 1977; (with J. Sandford) *Restoring the Christian Family,* Logos International, 1979; (with J. Sandford) *Transformation of the Inner Man,* Logos International, 1981.

SIDELIGHTS: Paula Sandford commented: ''My husband and I are in a full-time international team ministry of writing, lecturing, and counseling. We travel extensively, teaching in all denominations (Protestant and Catholic) and in interdenominational camps and conferences. Our tape cassettes are used all over the world. The main thrust of the teaching has to do with restoration of the family and renewal in the church. At home we provide a Christian counseling service and we often hold seminars for Christian counselors.''

AVOCATIONAL INTERESTS: Camping, hiking.

* * *

SANKHALA, Kailash S. 1925-

PERSONAL: Born January 30, 1925, in Jodhpur, Rajasthan, India; son of K. R. and Satyawati Sankhala; married wife, Suraj, April 27, 1948; children: (sons) Kuldeep, Pradeep. *Education:* Jaswant College (Jodhpur), M.S., 1950; Indian Forest College (Dehra Dun), A.I.F.C., 1953. *Religion:* Hindu. *Home:* 21 Dhuleshwar Garden, Jaipur, Rajasthan, India 302001. *Agent:* Pradeep Sankhala, E5 Nizamuddin, New Delhi, India. *Office address:* Chief Wildlife Warden, Jaipur, Rajasthan, India 302001.

CAREER: Officer in Rajasthan Forest Management and Administration, 1954-62; Watershed Management, Jaipur, Rajasthan, India, soil conservation officer, 1962-65; Delhi Zoological Park, Delhi, India, director, 1965-70, Project Tiger (conservation project), New Delhi, India, director, 1972-77; Management of Wildlife Sanctuaries, Jaipur, Rajasthan, chief wildlife warden, 1978—. Member of International Union of Zoo Directors, 1968-70, and Rajasthan State Wildlife Preservation Board, Jaipur (secretary); founding member and member of executive board of Environmental Trust

of India, 1979—. *Member:* Wildlife Preservation Society of India (executive member). *Awards, honors:* Wildlife conservation merit award from Government of Rajasthan, 1965; Jawaharlal Nehru Memorial Fund fellowship, 1970-72; Dr. A. N. Jha Prize from Wildlife Preservation Society of India, 1972.

WRITINGS: National Parks, Wildlife Preservation Society of India, 1969; *Wild Beauty: A Study of Indian Wildlife,* National Book Trust (India), 1975; *Tigerland,* foreword by Indira Gandhi, Collins, 1975; *Tiger! The Story of the Indian Tiger,* Simon & Schuster, 1978.

WORK IN PROGRESS: A document on wildlife reserves in India; research on the ecological significance of waterholes in arid and semi-arid regions.

SIDELIGHTS: Kailash Sankhala has been called the ''best friend a tiger ever had.'' His love for the unspoiled Indian wilderness and the legendary cat that inhabits it might more accurately be considered an obsession. ''He sits for hours and reads about them and writes about them and looks at their pictures,'' reports his wife. ''He feels for them. He really does. When one dies, he feels it.'' That prospect of the tiger's death—made real by an encroaching civilization and man's rifles—has compelled Sankhala to act. His Project Tiger and his book, *Tiger!,* are two of his most notable efforts on behalf of the animal he loves.

With the aid of a million-dollar grant and the enthusiastic support of Indian Prime Minister Indira Gandhi, Sankhala formed Project Tiger in 1972. He had warned about the world's decreasing tiger population a few years earlier when he estimated there were fewer than twenty-five hundred tigers in India and fifteen hundred elsewhere in the world. Through the establishment of nine wildlife preserves throughout India, Sankhala hoped to not only save the tiger from extinction, but also to increase the population above its critically low level.

The threat of extinction has moved Sankhala to tell the world about the tiger. His book, *Tiger!,* combines a history of the animal along with the author's first-hand observations. ''It fills up a regrettable gap in our knowledge,'' reported Nirad C. Chaudhuri of the *New Statesman.* ''His observations,'' said the *Economist,* ''are impeccably measured and acutely—often humorously—described. To make an obsession understandable, to communicate a love so unworldly, represents a genuine literary achievement.''

Sankhala's love of the tiger and the Indian wilderness is copiously detailed in his writing, as demonstrated in this passage from *Tiger!:* ''When I close my eyes, I see the nests of half a million Flamingoes in the Runn of Kutch, the carpet of a million flowers in the Himalayan meadows, the deciduous forests in the extravagent reds, the lushness of the evergreen rain forests. I see shaded brooks banked with ferns, with frolicking deer coming down to drink or a tiger sleeping half submerged, unaware of my presence. . . . When I look back over the half century, I feel, I have lived one glorious day after another, watching the splash of colour of the setting sun, hearing the alarm call of Chital and Sambar, warning of the presence of the predator prowling in the night.''

This and the rest of Sankhala's work led Jan Morris of the *London Times* to remark: ''To say that he is a tiger addict would be preposterous understatement.'' He is an honorary tiger himself!''

Sankhala told *CA:* ''The population of tigers had reached a stage that could be described as almost a point of no return, and if the massive conservation Project Tiger had not been launched in 1973 with worldwide support, the species would have disappeared from its natural habitat. Guy Mountfort in *Back From the Brink* aptly credits Project Tiger with saving this species from extinction. This state was mainly due to a greedy trade in skins and notions about the species. The ecological fact that the predator being at the apex of the biological triangle acts as an index of environmental quality of the habitat was hardly understood. *Tiger!* has helped in exploding myths and settling controversies about the behavior of the species and has lead to a better understanding of ecological significance of the tiger to ensure its survival in its natural ecosystems.''

BIOGRAPHICAL/CRITICAL SOURCES: Chicago Tribune Magazine, December 18, 1977; Kailash Sankhala, *Tiger! The Story of the Indian Tiger,* Simon & Schuster, 1978; *Economist,* June 3, 1978; *Observer,* July 30, 1978, December 17, 1978; *New Statesman,* September 1, 1978; *London Times,* November 24, 1978.

* * *

SANTOS, Bienvenido N(uqui)   1911-

PERSONAL: Born March 22, 1911, in Manila, Philippines; came to the United States in 1970, naturalized citizen, 1976; son of Tomas and Vicenta (Nuqui) Santos; married Beatriz Nidea, December 23, 1933; children: Arme Santos Tan, Lina Santos Cortes, Lily Santos Anonas, Tomas. *Education:* University of the Philippines, B.S.Ed., 1932; University of Illinois, M.A., 1942; also attended Harvard University, 1945-46, and University of Iowa, 1958-61. *Home:* 1717 North Vassar, No. 208, Wichita, Kan. 67208. *Office:* Department of English, Wichita State University, Wichita, Kan. 67208.

CAREER: Elementary and high school teacher in Philippines, 1932-41; Embassy of the Philippines, Washington, D.C., public relations officer, 1942-45; Legazpi College (now Aquinas University), Legazpi City, Philippines, professor and vice-president, 1946-57, president, 1958; University of Nueva Caceres, Naga City, Philippines, dean of College of Arts and Sciences, 1961-66; University of Iowa, Iowa City, Fulbright professor of English, 1966-69; University of Nueva Caceres, dean of graduate school and vice-president for academic affairs, 1969-70; University of Iowa, Iowa City, lecturer at writer's workshop, 1970-73; Wichita State University, Wichita, Kan., professor of creative writing and distinguished writer-in-residence, 1973—. Office of the President of the Philippines, Manila, member of textbook board, 1962-64, acting chairman of board, 1964-65.

AWARDS, HONORS: First prize in Philippine section from *New York Herald Tribune*'s international short story contest, 1952, for ''The Naked Eye''; Rockefeller Foundation fellow, 1958-59; Guggenheim fellow, 1960; Republic Cultural Heritage Award in Literature, 1965, for body of work; medallion of honor from City of Manila, 1971, for writings and work as educator; fiction award from *New Letters,* 1977, for ''Immigration Blues.''

WRITINGS: You Lovely People (stories), Benipayo Press, 1955; *The Wounded Stag* (poems), Capitol Publishing House, 1956; *Brother My Brother* (stories), Bookmark, 1960; *Villa Magdalena* (novel), Erehwon Publishing House, 1965; *The Volcano* (novel), Phoenix Publishing House, 1965; *The Day the Dancers Came* (essays), Bookmark, 1967; *Scent of Apples* (stories), University of Washington Press, 1979.

Work represented in more than a dozen anthologies, including *Best American Short Stories,* 1978; *New Voices Three,* Ginn, 1978; *The United States in Literature,* Scott, Foresman, 1979. Contributor to journals, including *Short Story*

International, Solidarity, Manila Review, and *Ark River Review.* Editor of *Philippines,* 1942-45. Member of editorial board of *Amerasia Journal,* 1978-81.

WORK IN PROGRESS: What the Hell for You Left Your Heart in San Francisco?, a novel.

SIDELIGHTS: Santos's books have been widely translated into foreign languages, including Chinese, Malay, French, and Russian. One novel, *The Praying Man,* was scheduled for 1973 publication in Manila but after its serialization in *Solidarity* was censored under Philippine martial law and remains unpublished in book form.

Santos commented: ''All my published books deal with the Filipino at home and abroad. The Philippine-American relationship is viewed from various directions. On the whole I find myself writing more and more about the exile, the comic-tragic predicaments in which he finds himself, his nostalgia and his guilt, his doubts and fears about his identity, his coming to terms with himself, finally, not truly at peace, but resigned somehow to a fate he has to accept if he must spend the rest of his life with as much grace as he can summon.''

BIOGRAPHICAL/CRITICAL SOURCES: Miguel A. Bernad, *Bamboo and the Greenwood Tree,* Bookmark, 1961; Leonard Casper, *The Wounded Diamond,* Bookmark, 1964; Casper, *New Writing From the Philippines: A Critique,* Syracuse University Press, 1966; Antonio Manuud, editor, *Brown Heritage,* Ateneo de Manila University Press, 1967; *New Writers,* May, 1976; Soledad S. Reyes, *Essays on Filipino Novel in English,* Ateneo de Manila University Press, 1979.

* * *

SASEK, Miroslav   1916-1980

OBITUARY NOTICE—See index for *CA* sketch: Born November 18, 1916, in Prague, Czechoslovakia; died May, 1980. Illustrator and author. Sasek wrote and illustrated a series of children's books on travel in cities and countries throughout the world, including Paris, London, San Francisco, Israel, and Australia. *This Is London,* 1959, and *This Is New York,* 1960, were chosen best illustrated children's books of the year by the *New York Times.* Obituaries and other sources: *Publishers Weekly,* June 27, 1980.

* * *

SATCHIDANANDA, Sri Swami   1914-

PERSONAL: Born December 22, 1914, in Chettipalayan, India. *Education:* Educated in Coimbatore, South India. *Religion:* Ecumenical. *Home and office address:* Satchidananda Ashram, P.O. Box 108, Pomfret Center, Conn. 06259.

CAREER: Founder and director of Satchidananda Ashrams International, 1967—; founder and director of Integral Yoga Institutes, Pomfret, Conn., 1967—; co-director of Center for Spiritual Studies, New York City, 1968—; founder and president of Light of Truth Universal Shrine, Pomfret, 1978—. Member of board of directors of Integral Health Services, Putnam, Conn., 1976—, and Temple of Understanding, New York City, 1979—. Member of advisory board of World Monastic Council. Patron of International Yoga Teachers Association, Sydney, Australia, 1976—, European Yoga Union Federation, Paris, France, 1977—, and California Yoga Teachers Association, 1979—. *Awards, honors:* Martin Buber Award for Outstanding Service to Humanity, 1966; fellow of College of Human Sciences at Concordia University.

WRITINGS: *Integral Yoga Hatha,* Holt, 1970; *Beyond Words,* Holt, 1977; *Living Yoga,* Gordon & Breach, 1977; *How to Succeed in Yoga and Other Talks,* Integral Yoga Publications, 1978; *To Know Yourself,* Doubleday, 1978; *Integral Yoga: The Yoga Sutras of Patanjali,* Integral Yoga Publications, 1978; *Swami Satchidananda,* Integral Yoga Publications, 1981. Author of booklets. Contributor to *Integral Yoga.*

WORK IN PROGRESS: *The Living Gita,* publication by Integral Yoga Publications expected in 1982.

SIDELIGHTS: Satchidananda commented: "My interest is to retain my health and peace and to share the same with one and all, to live my life as much as possible in observing Nature's way, following Nature, to be always available to people and to put myself in the hands of God through His creation."

*   *   *

SAVAGE, Lee   1928-

PERSONAL: Born December 17, 1928, in Charleston, W.Va.; son of Joseph W. (a writer) and Janet (a writer; maiden name, Kelly) Savage; married Karen Haagensen (a therapist), March 2, 1964; children: Peter, Will, Kate, Kristin, Adam, Miranda. *Education:* Attended West Virginia University, 1946-48, Pratt Institute, 1948-49, Art Students League and New School for Social Research, both 1949-50. *Politics:* "Radical-Reactionary." *Religion:* "Artist." *Home and office:* 25 Millard Ave., North Tarrytown, N.Y. 10591.

CAREER: N.W. Ayer Advertising, art director, 1954-57; J. Walter Thompson, New York City, art director, 1957-59; Electra Film Productions, New York City, owner, creative director, and president, 1960-61; free-lance artist, designer, writer, and painter, 1961-63; Electra Film Productions, owner, creative director, and president, 1963-65; Savage Friedman Productions, New York City, owner and president, 1965-70; Lee Savage, Inc., North Tarrytown, N.Y., painter, animator, writer, and director, 1970—. Teacher of art classes; exhibitor of paintings. Consultant to Bank Street College. *Military service:* U.S. Army, 1951-53. *Awards, honors:* Awards from Silvermine Guild and Metropolitan Young Artists Guild, both 1959, both for painting; Guggenheim fellowship, 1962-63; Childe Hassam Award from American Academy of Arts and Letters, 1976; several animated film festival awards, including first prize from San Francisco, Oberhausen, London, and Tokyo film festivals.

WRITINGS: *Aldo's Doghouse,* Coward, 1978; (self-illustrated) *What Should I Say?,* Coward, 1981.

Other: "Ten, Nine, Eight, Seven, Six, Five, Four, Three, Two, One" (script), 1967; "Brother's Keeper" (film), 1968; "Max the Two-Thousand-Year-Old Mouse" (film), Steve Krantz and Ralph Bakshi Productions, 1968; "Rainbow for President" (script), 1980. Author of "Savage on Film," a column in *Art Direction,* 1964-66. Writer for television series, "Sesame Street" and "Electric Company," 1971-80. Writer, designer, and art director of "Three to Get Ready," Bank Street College and Columbia Broadcasting System (CBS) Publications, 1977-79. Contributor to *New York Times.*

WORK IN PROGRESS: Television film scripts for "Children's Television Workshop" series, 1980-81.

SIDELIGHTS: Lee told *CA:* "I consider myself the one common denominator, the subjective *sine qua non* of all the arts. All the arts are one art put through one subjective: me. I make paintings, film, books, sculpture, and I cook, too.

Sometimes I can't tell one from the other: they are only different external problems for my subjective to solve."

*   *   *

SAVAGE, Michael D(onald)   1946-

PERSONAL: Born May 6, 1946, in New Haven, Conn.; son of Bernard L. and Mildred Savage; married Mirtha Calvo (a designer), March 19, 1975. *Education:* Yale University, B.A., 1968; Georgetown University, J.D., 1973. *Home:* 3107 Hawthorne St., Washington, D.C. 20008. *Agent:* Robbin Reynolds Agency, 1021 Park Ave., New York, N.Y. 10028. *Office:* Hedrick & Lane, 1211 Connecticut Ave., Suite 700, Washington, D.C. 20036.

CAREER: Hedrick & Lane (law firm), Washington, D.C., partner, 1973—. *Military service:* U.S. Army Reserve, 1969-75. *Member:* American Bar Association, Authors Guild, Authors League of America, Supreme Court Bar Association, District of Columbia Bar Association, Georgetown Club.

WRITINGS: (With Don Schollander) *Deep Water,* Crown, 1971, abridged edition, Reader's Digest Press, 1971; *Everything You Always Wanted to Know About Taxes But Didn't Know How to Ask,* Dial, 1979, revised edition, 1980. Contributor to law and tax journals and popular magazines, including *Self* and *Dollars and Sense.*

WORK IN PROGRESS: A book on tax shelters.

SIDELIGHTS: Savage wrote that his books are "motivated by the viewpoint that law should be understandable to people besides lawyers."

*   *   *

SAVILLE, (Leonard) Malcolm   1901-

PERSONAL: Born February 21, 1901, in Hastings, Sussex, England; son of Ernest Vivian (a bookseller) and Fanny Ethel (Hayes) Saville; married Dorothy May McCoy, 1926; children: two sons, two daughters. *Education:* Educated in England. *Home:* Chelsea Cottage, Winchelsea, East Sussex, England. *Agent:* A. P. Watt Ltd., 26-28 Bedford Row, London WC1R 4HL, England.

CAREER: Cassell & Co. (publishers), London, England, in publicity, 1920-22; Amalgamated Press, London, sales promotion manager, 1922-36; George Newnes Co. (publishers), London, sales promotion manager, 1936-40; *My Garden* (magazine), London, associate editor, 1947-52; Kemsley Newspapers, London, writer, 1952-55; George Newnes & C. Arthur Peterson Ltd. (publishers), London, general books editor, 1957-80; full-time writer, 1966—. *Member:* Savage Club (London).

WRITINGS—All juvenile, except as noted: *Mystery at Witchend,* George Newnes, 1943, published as *Spy in the Hills,* Farrar, 1945; *Country Scrap Book for Boys and Girls,* National Magazine Co., 1944, 3rd edition, Gramol, 1946; *Seven White Gates,* George Newnes, 1944; *The Gay Dolphin Adventure,* George Newnes, 1945; *Open-Air Scrap Book for Boys and Girls,* Gramol, 1945; *Trouble at Townsend,* Transatlantic, 1945; *Jane's Country Year,* George Newnes, 1946, 3rd edition, 1953; *The Riddle of the Painted Box,* Transatlantic, 1947; *The Secret of Grey Walls,* George Newnes, 1947, revised edition, Armada, 1975; *Redshank's Warning,* Lutterworth, 1948; *Two Fair Plaits,* Lutterworth, 1948; *Lone Pine Five,* George Newnes, 1949; *Strangers at Snowfell,* Lutterworth, 1949.

The Adventure of the Life-Boat Service, Macdonald & Co.,

1950; *The Flying Fish Adventure*, J. Murray, 1950; *The Master of Maryknoll*, Evans Bros., 1950, revised edition, Collins, 1971; *The Sign of the Alpine Rose*, Lutterworth, 1950; *All Summer Through*, Hodder & Stoughton, 1951; *The Elusive Grasshopper*, George Newnes, 1951; *The Buckinghams at Ravenswyke*, Evans Bros., 1952, revised edition, Collins, 1971; *Coronation Gift Book*, Pitkin, 1952; *The Luck of Sallowby*, Lutterworth, 1952; *The Ambermere Treasure*, Lutterworth, 1953, published as *The Secret of the Ambermere Treasure*, Criterion, 1967; *Christmas at Nettleford*, Hodder & Stoughton, 1953; *The Neglected Mountain*, George Newnes, 1953; *The Secret of the Hidden Pool*, J. Murray, 1953; *The Long Passage*, Evans Bros., 1954; *Spring Comes to Nettleford*, Hodder & Stoughton, 1954; *Saucers Over the Moor*, George Newnes, 1955, revised edition, Collins, 1972; *The Secret of Buzzard Scar*, Hodder & Stoughton, 1955; *Where the Bus Stopped*, Basil Blackwell, 1955.

Young Johnnie Bimbo, J. Murray, 1956; *Wings Over Witchend*, George Newnes, 1956; *The Fouth Key*, J. Murray, 1957; *Lone Pine London*, George Newnes, 1957; *Treasure at the Mill*, George Newnes, 1957; *King of Kings*, Nelson, 1958; *The Secret of the Gorge*, George Newnes, 1958; *Four-and-Twenty Blackbirds*, George Newnes, 1959, reprinted as *The Secret of Galleybird Pit*, Armada, 1968; *Mystery Mine*, George Newnes, 1959; *Small Creatures*, Edmund Ward, 1959; *Sea Witch Comes Home*, George Newnes, 1960; *Malcolm Saville's Country Book*, Cassell, 1961; *Malcolm Saville's Seaside Book*, Cassell, 1962; *Not Scarlet but Gold*, George Newnes, 1962; *A Palace for the Buckinghams*, Evans Bros., 1963; *Three Towers in Tuscany*, Heinemann, 1963; *The Purple Valley*, Heinemann, 1964; *Treasure at Amorys*, George Newnes, 1964.

Dark Danger, Heinemann, 1965; *The Man With Three Fingers*, George Newnes, 1966, revised edition, Collins, 1971; *The Thin Grey Man*, St. Martin's, 1966; *White Fire*, Heinemann, 1966; *Come to London*, Heinemann, 1967; *Strange Story*, Mowbray, 1967; *Power of Three*, Heinemann, 1968; *Come to Cornwall*, Benn, 1969; *Come to Devon*, Benn, 1969; *Come to Somerset*, Benn, 1970; *Dagger and the Flame*, Heinemann, 1970; *Good Dog Dandy*, Collins, 1971; *The Secret of Villa Rosa*, Collins, 1971; *Where's My Girl?*, Collins, 1972; *Diamond in the Sky*, Collins, 1975; *Portrait of Rye* (adult nonfiction), Henry Goulden, 1976; *Countryside Quiz*, Carousel, 1978; *Home to Witchend*, Armada, 1978; *Marston, Master Spy*, Heinemann, 1978; *Wonder Why Book of Exploring a Wood*, Transworld, 1978; *Wonder Why Book of Exploring the Seashore*, Transworld, 1979; *Words For All Seasons* (anthology), Lutterworth, 1979; *Wonder Why Book of Wild Flowers Through the Year*, Transworld, 1980. Also author of *The Roman Treasure Mystery* and *See How It Grows*.

"Susan and Bill" series; published by Thomas Nelson: *Susan and Bill and the Ivy Clad Oak*, 1954; *. . .and the Wolf Dog*, 1954; *. . .and the Golden Clock*, 1955; *. . .and the Vanishing Boy*, 1955; *. . .and the Saucy Kate*, 1956; *. . .and the Bright Star Circus*, 1960; *. . .and the Pirates Bold*, 1961. Also author of *Susan and Bill and the Dark Stranger*.

SIDELIGHTS: Malcolm Saville began writing books for young people in 1942. The son of a bookseller, he was exposed from childhood to books and reading. Consequently, it was no surprise when he pursued a career in publishing, later becoming a full-time writer.

Saville's first book, *Mystery at Witchend*, was written in installments while he was employed by a London publisher. Each installment was sent to his wife and children who were staying in Shropshire for the duration of World War II.

When *Mystery at Witchend* was finally published, it proved to be extremely successful and was serialized by the British Broadcasting Corp. (BBC-Radio). His second book, *Seven White Gates*, included characters from the first book who called themselves "The Lone Pine Club." The adventures of the Lone Pine Club grew to include twenty titles, some of which were also broadcast by BBC-Radio.

The greatest share of Saville's stories are set in England—the locale most familiar to him and his readers—although some tales for older readers are set in such places as Italy, France, Holland, Luxembourg, and Spain. "All fiction is influenced by 'place,'" he told *CA*. "Consequently, I travel as widely as possible." Saville's appreciation for locale has also lead him to write nonfiction accounts of various areas in Britain; most notable are those dealing with his home regions of Sussex and the West Country.

Saville's fiction is designed to appeal to a wide age range. The adventures of secret agent Marston Baines, for example, appeal to adolescents while the Susan and Bill series is aimed at younger readers.

All in all, Saville has written more than eighty books for young readers with the foremost objectives being to entertain and inform. In addition to fiction, he has written books on nature, travel, and gardening.

BIOGRAPHICAL/CRITICAL SOURCES: Sussex Life, September, 1978; *Country Life*, November 19, 1979.

*　　*　　*

SCHACHTERLE, Nancy (Lange) 1925-
(Anne C. Laing)

PERSONAL: Born October 5, 1925, in Sault Ste. Marie, Ontario, Canada; daughter of Albrecht (a mining engineer) and Mary Georgina (a telegrapher; maiden name, McEachern) Hasselbring; married E. George Schachterle (a jeweler), 1964; children: Gary Allen. *Education:* Ontario Ladies College, diploma, 1943. *Religion:* Protestant. *Home:* Star Route 81133, South Fork, Colo. 81154.

CAREER: Ontario Ladies College, Whitby, Ontario, secretary to principal, 1943-49, teacher of commercial course, 1950-51; secretary in Haileybury, Ontario, 1951-57; U.S. Air Force, Colorado Springs, Colo., civil service secretary, 1957-64. Instructor in creative writing for adult education courses; volunteer worker with Ark Valley School for Physically and Mentally Handicapped, in La Junta, Colo., 1967-72. *Member:* Mystery Writers of America.

WRITINGS: (Under pseudonym Anne C. Laing) *How to Get Food Without Paying a Cent*, Laing Publishing, 1980. Also author of column, "Merry-Go-Round," appearing in *Mineral Co. Miner and South Fork Tines*. Contributor of short stories to *Alfred Hitchcock's Mystery Magazine*.

WORK IN PROGRESS: With Menace Toward One, a suspense novel; *Queen of Ice, Queen of Fire* (tentative title), a novel.

SIDELIGHTS: Schachterle told *CA:* "When I was old enough to hold a pencil, I was making up stories and putting them down on paper. Perhaps the fact that my mother wrote, although she never sold, started my own interest. Several cousins on my mother's side of the family are also writers or are working on it, so there's some argument for heredity as having something to do with my vocation.

"My aim is to please the reader, as I want to be pleased by other writers. This has to be done by respecting her or him, and includes a constant striving for excellence. P. D. James, who uses words seldom seen outside her books, writes to satisfy herself, and it is obvious that her excellence satisfies her readers, too. Writing down to the reader, or writing what you think will sell this year, can kill creativity.

"I am voraciously curious about almost everything. In spite of never having enough time, I can spend fifteen minutes on my knees in the dirt watching an earthworm or an ant. Life, in its greatest and most minute forms, fascinates and awes me."

*   *   *

SCHAFFER, Lewis A(dam) 1934-

PERSONAL: Born April 16, 1934, in East Orange, N.J.; son of Nathan and Estelle (Muscatt) Schaffer; married Debra Simon (a sculptress), June 16, 1957; children: Michael, Steven. *Education:* Brown University, A.B., 1956; University of Pennsylvania, M.D., 1960. *Home:* 10 Windmill Place, Armonk, N.Y. 10504. *Office:* Armonk Medical Center, Route 22, Armonk, N.Y. 10504.

CAREER: Philadelphia General Hospital, Philadelphia, Pa., intern, 1960-61; Children's Hospital of Philadelphia, Philadelphia, resident in pediatrics, 1961-62, assistant chief resident, 1962-63; private practice of pediatrics in Armonk, N.Y., 1965—. Diplomate of National Board of Medical Examiners and American Board of Pediatrics. Physician for Westchester County Child Health Clinics, 1965—; member of county maternal-child welfare committee, 1969-74; attending physician at Northern Westchester Hospital, 1965—. Clinical instructor at Albert Einstein School of Medicine, 1966-76. *Military service:* U.S. Army Reserve, Medical Corps, assistant chief of pediatric service at McDonald Army Hospital, 1963-65; became captain. *Member:* International Oceanographic Foundation, American Academy of Pediatrics (fellow), Undersea Medical Society, Oceanic Society, Alpha Omega Alpha, Country Cycle Club, League of American Wheelmen.

WRITINGS: (With Barbara Kaye Greenleaf) *Help: A Handbook for Working Mothers,* Crowell, 1980. Contributor to medical journals.

SIDELIGHTS: Schaffer commented: "I am dealing with larger and larger numbers of families (mothers and kids) with a full-time working mother. My book is an attempt to support these working moms." *Avocational interests:* Bicycling, scuba diving, underwater photography.

*   *   *

SCHARFSTEIN, Ben-Ami 1919-

PERSONAL: Born April 12, 1919, in New York, N.Y.; son of Zevi (a writer, educator, and publisher) and Rose (a publisher; maiden name, Goldfarb) Scharfstein; married Ghela Efros, June 15, 1952; children: Doreet. *Education:*Brooklyn College (now of the City University of New York), B.A., 1939; Harvard University, M.A., 1940; Columbia University, Ph.D., 1942. *Home:* Gluskin St. 1, Tel-Aviv, Israel. *Office:*Department of Philosophy, Tel-Aviv University, Tel-Aviv, Israel.

CAREER: Brooklyn College (now of City University of New York), Brooklyn, N.Y., fellow, 1942-43, tutor, 1944, instructor in philosophy, 1945-49; Columbia University, New York City, lecturer in philosophy, 1949-50; Reali School and Teachers Seminary, Haifa, Israel, teacher of English, history, and education, 1950-51; Hunter College (now of City University of New York), New York City, instructor in philosophy, 1953-54; University of Utah, Salt Lake City, assis-

tant professor of philosophy, 1954-55; Tel-Aviv University, Tel-Aviv, Israel, associate professor, 1955-76, professor of philosophy, 1976—, head of department, 1955-72, vice-rector, 1969-72. Guest lecturer in philosophy of education at Teachers Institute of the Jewish Theological Seminary of America, 1946-47. *Member:* International Society for the Comparative Study of Civilization, American Philosophical Association, Association for Chinese Philosophy.

WRITINGS: Roots of Bergson's Philosophy, Columbia University Press, 1943; (with Mortimer Ostow) *The Need to Believe,* International Universities Press, 1954; *Mystical Experience,* Bobbs-Merrill, 1972; *The Mind of China,* Basic Books, 1974; (editor with Yoav Ariel, Shlomo Biderman, and others, and contributor) *Philosophy East/Philosophy West,* Oxford University Press, 1978; *The Philosophers,* Oxford University Press, 1980.

In Hebrew: *Ha'Oman B'Tarbuyot Ha'Olam* (title means "The Artist in World Art"), Am Oved, 1970. Associate editor of *Keshet.*

WORK IN PROGRESS: Esthetic Universality: A Transcultural Essay on the Nature of Art; Sketch for a World History of Philosophy, completion expected in 1984.

SIDELIGHTS: Scharfstein commented: "I have a passionate interest in art (I paint), in philosophy, in comparative culture, and in learning generally. In writing, I'm apparently attracted to difficult syntheses, the difficulty of which is increased by my attempt to balance the claims of good writing against those of accuracy of scholarship and of some elusive general truth.

"In writing about philosophers and artists, I've come to emphasize an emotion that runs through all expressive behavior and especially through art. It seems to me that the work of art carries the message, 'This is what I am like,' to which it adds, 'I appeal to you to sympathize with me, empathize with me, identify with me, resemble me, join me, or at least pay attention to me, as I really am.' Art (including literature) therefore makes an incessant moral demand, for it is, among other things, the willed antithesis of loneliness. It is an antithesis, however, for which the artist sets all the terms."

*   *   *

SCHARY, Dore 1905-1980

OBITUARY NOTICE—See index for *CA* sketch: Born August 31, 1905, in Newark, N.J.; died of cancer, July 7, 1980, in New York, N.Y. Motion picture producer and director, screenwriter, and playwright best known for his Oscar-winning script for "Boys' Town" and his Broadway hit, "Sunrise at Campobello," which won five Tony Awards. During his years with Metro-Goldwyn-Mayer (MGM) and RKO, Schary wrote more than forty scripts and helped develop the talents of stars, including Judy Garland, Lassie, and Van Johnson. His other screenplays include "Murder in the Clouds," "Young Thomas Edison," and "Lonely Hearts." Obituaries and other sources: *Detroit News,* July 8, 1980; *Time,* July 21, 1980; *Newsweek,* July 21, 1980.

*   *   *

SCHEFLEN, Albert E. 1920-1980

OBITUARY NOTICE—See index for *CA* sketch: Born November 15, 1920; died August 14, 1980, in Chester, Pa. Psychiatrist, psychoanalyst, educator, and author of books in his field. In addition to operating his own psychiatric practice, Scheflen was a professor of psychiatry at Albert Einstein College of Medicine and carried out psychiatric research at the Bronx Psychiatric Center. Among his books are *Direct Analysis, Body Language and Social Order,* and *How Behavior Means.* Obituaries and other sources: *New York Times,* August 14, 1980.

* * *

SCHELLIE, Don 1932-

PERSONAL: Born March 8, 1932, in Chicago, Ill.; son of Leslie D. and Elsie (Osterberg) Schellie; married Coralee Rice (a school librarian), August 15, 1953; children: Leslie Ann, Kendall Sue, Kristina Lee. *Education:* Attended University of Arizona, 1955-56; University of Illinois, B.S., 1957. *Politics:* Independent. *Religion:* Protestant. *Home:* 5641 North Bonita Dr., Tucson, Ariz. 85704. *Agent:* John Cushman, J.C.A. Literary Agency, Inc., 200 West 57th St., New York, N.Y. 10019. *Office:* Tucson Citizen, P.O. Box 26767, Tucson, Ariz. 85726.

CAREER: Champaign News-Gazette, Champaign, Ill., reporter, 1954-55, 1956-57; *Douglas Daily Dispatch,* Douglas, Ariz., reporter, 1957-58; *Tucson Citizen,* Tucson, Ariz., reporter, 1958-60, author of column "Don Schellie," 1960—. *Military service:* U.S. Air Force, 1951-54. *Member:* National Society of Newspaper Columnists, Authors Guild, Western Writers of America, Arizona Historical Society, Arizona Press Club. *Awards, honors:* American Library Association notable children's book citation, 1978, for *Kidnapping Mr. Tubbs.*

WRITINGS: Vast Domain of Blood (nonfiction), Westernlore Press, 1968; *The Citizen: A Century of Arizona Journalism,* Citizen Publishing, 1970; *Me, Cholay & Co.—Apache Warriors* (young adult novel), Scholastic Book Services, 1973; *Kidnapping Mr. Tubbs* (young adult novel), Scholastic Book Services, 1978; *Maybe Next Summer* (young adult novel), Scholastic Book Services, 1980; *Shadow and the Gunner,* (young adult novel), Scholastic Book Services, 1981. Contributor to *Arizona Highways.*

WORK IN PROGRESS: Novels.

SIDELIGHTS: Schellie told *CA:* "All of my working life I have been a full-time newspaperman, and the few books I have written over the years have been the product of evenings, weekends, holidays, and vacations spent at the typewriter. Not surprisingly, my first book, *Vast Domain of Blood,* had its roots in my column, being based upon some historical pieces I wrote for the *Citizen* about the Camp Grant massacre.

"In that 1871 incident some one hundred twenty-five 'peaceful' Apaches were murdered by a party of Tuscon-area residents and Papago Indians. *Vast Domain of Blood* was an adult, nonfiction book, and my wife, a history teacher-turned-school librarian, felt the story should be made available to school-age readers. What developed was *Me, Cholay & Co.—Apache Warriors,* an historical novel for young readers.

"Perhaps because of the influence of three daughters in our family I felt comfortable writing at that level, and have since written a couple of young adult novels dealing with contemporary problems, and a World War II period piece novel for the same age group. A few other novels for teenagers are in the works.

"As a story-teller—in newspaper, longer nonfiction, fiction—I have attempted first to entertain my reader, provide him with some moments of pleasure, some excitement, and perhaps, along the way, impart a bit of knowledge."

SCHER, Les 1946-

PERSONAL: Born May 9, 1946, in Honolulu, Hawaii; son of Meyer (an attorney) and Hannah (Horn) Scher. *Education:* University of California, Los Angeles, B.A. (cum laude), 1968; Hastings School of Law, J.D., 1971. *Home address:* P.O. Box 344, Redway, Calif. 95560. *Office address:* P.O. Box 644, Garberville, Calif. 95440.

CAREER: Attorney in California.

WRITINGS: Finding and Buying Your Place in the Country (selection of fifteen book clubs, including Book-of-the-Month Club and Quality Paperback Club), edited by Carol Wilcox, Macmillan, 1974.

WORK IN PROGRESS: Research for a book on protecting one's property.

SIDELIGHTS: Scher's book has been favorably reviewed by various scholarly and popular magazines and newspapers, from *Business Week* to *Rolling Stone,* and *Harper's* to *Mother Earth News.* It has been described as an extraordinarily complete book on buying rural property. It covers real estate and law in terms for the layman, with suggestions for avoiding the pitfalls many consumers encounter.

* * *

SCHERER, Klaus R(ainer) 1943-

PERSONAL: Born March 18, 1943, in Leverkusen, Germany; son of Willibald Josef (a painter) and Kaethe (Ludwig) Scherer; married Ursula Zuendorf (a research associate), January 3, 1968. *Education:* University of Cologne, diploma, 1967; attended London School of Economics and Political Science, London, 1964-65; Harvard University, Ph.D., 1970. *Home:* Posenerstrasse 5, 6300 Giessen, West Germany. *Office:* Department of Psychology, University of Glessen, FB 06 Behagelstrasse 10 F, 6300 Giessen, West Germany.

CAREER: University of Pennsylvania, Philadelphia, assistant professor of psychology, 1970-72; University of Kiel, Kiel, West Germany, associate professor of psychology, 1972-73; University of Giessen, Giessen, West Germany, professor of psychology, 1973—. *Member:* International Association of Applied Psychology, European Association of Experimental Social Psychology, Deutsche Gesellschaft fuer Psychologie, American Psychological Association, Acoustical Society of America. *Awards, honors:* Charles-Holtzer fellowship from Harvard University, 1967-68.

WRITINGS: (With R. P. Abeles and C. S. Fischer) *Human Aggression and Conflict: Interdisciplinary Perspectives,* Prentice-Hall, 1975; (editor with Howard Giles, and contributor) *Social Markers in Speech,* Cambridge University Press, 1979; (contributor) C. E. Izard, editor, *Emotions in Personality and Psychopathology,* Plenum, 1979; (contributor) Giles and Robert St. Clair, editors, *The Social Psychology of Language,* Basil Blackwell, 1979; (contributor) Giles and St. Clair, editors, *The Social and Psychological Contexts of Language,* Erlbaum, 1979; (contributor) W. I. Singleton, editor, *Social Skills,* Plenum, 1980; (contributor) Giles, Peter Robinson, Philip Smith, editors, *Social Psychology and Language,* Pergamon, 1980; (editor with Paul Ekman, and contributor) *Handbook of Research Methods in Nonverbal Communication,* Cambridge University Press, in press; (contributor) Izard, editor, *Measuring Emotions in Infants and Children,* Cambridge University Press, in press.

In German: *Nonverbale Kommunikation* (title means "Nonverbal Communication"), Buske Verlag, 1970; (contributor) Jan van Koolwijk and Maria Wieken-Mayser, editor, *Techniken der empirischen Sozialforschung* (title means "Methods of Empirical Social Research''), Oldenbourg-Verlag, 1974; (contributor) F. X. Kaufmann, editor, *Buergerhahe Gestaltung der sozialen Umwelt: Probleme und theoretische Perspektiven* (title means ''Citizen Orientation in Public Social Administration''), Hain-Verlag, 1977; Roland Posner and H. P. Reinecke, editors, *Zeichenprozesse—Semiotische Forschung in den Einzelwissenschaften* (title means ''Sign Processes: Semiotic Research''), Athenaion, 1977; (contributor) Dirk Wegner, editor, *Gespraechsanalyse* (title means ''Conversation Analysis''), Buske, 1977; (editor with H. G. Wallbott, and contributor) *Nonverbale Kommunikation: Ausgewaehlte Forschungsberichte zum Interaktionsverhalten* (title means ''Nonverbal Communication: Research Reports on Interactive Behavior''), Beltz, 1979; (contributor) Hildegard Hetzer, editor, *Angewandte Entwicklungspsychologie des Kindes-und Jugendalters* (title means ''Applied Developmental Psychology''), Quelle & Meyer, 1979.

Contributor of about twenty-five articles to professional journals in Germany and the United States.

WORK IN PROGRESS: Research on stress, emotion, nonverbal communication, and social interaction.

*   *   *

SCHLEE, Ann 1934-

PERSONAL: Born May 26, 1934, in Greenwich, Conn.; daughter of Duncan and Nancy (Houghton) Cumming; married D.N.R. Schlee, July 27, 1957; children: Emily, Catherine, Duncan, Hannah. *Education:* Somerville College, Oxford, B.A., 1955. *Residence:* London, England. *Agent:* Deborah Rogers Ltd., 5-11 Mortimer St., London W1N 7RH, England.

CAREER: Tutor and writer.

WRITINGS—All juvenile, except as noted: *The Strangers,* Macmillan, 1971, Atheneum, 1972; *The Consul's Daughter,* Atheneum, 1972; *The Guns of Darkness,* Macmillan, 1973, Atheneum, 1974; *Ask Me No Questions,* Macmillan, 1976; *Desert Drum,* Heinemann, 1977; *The Vandal,* Macmillan, 1979; *Rhine Journey* (adult novel), Holt, 1981.

WORK IN PROGRESS: A second historical novel for adults.

SIDELIGHTS: Ann Schlee's historical novels for children are noted for their clear writing and deft characterization. Typically her stories deal with events in English history as seen through the eyes of a child or adolescent.

BIOGRAPHICAL/CRITICAL SOURCES: Times Literary Supplement, October 22, 1971, April 28, 1972, June 15, 1973, October 1, 1976; *Observer,* July 22, 1973, September 28, 1975, November 28, 1976; *Books and Bookmen,* October, 1973; *Center for Children's Books: Bulletin,* October, 1974; *New Statesman,* November 5, 1976.

*   *   *

SCHLINK, Klara 1904-
(M. Basilea Schlink, Mother Basilea Schlink)

PERSONAL: Listed in some sources as Basilea Schlink; born October 21, 1904, in Darmstadt, Germany; daughter of a college professor. *Education:* University of Hamburg, Ph.D., 1934. *Home:* Evangelical Sisterhood of Mary, P.O. Box 13 01 29, D-6100 Darmstadt 13, West Germany. *Office:* American Branch, Evangelical Sisterhood of Mary, 9849 North 40th St., Phoenix, Ariz. 85028.

CAREER: Evangelical Sisterhood of Mary, Darmstadt,

West Germany, co-founder and leader, name in religion, Mother Basilea, 1947—. Founder of sisterhoods in Frankfurt, West Germany, Phoenix, Ariz., Israel, Greece, England, Italy, and Denmark; founder of worldwide radio ministry, including program ''God Lives and Works Today.'' Former national president of German Student Christian Movement.

WRITINGS—All published by Evangelische Marienschwesternschaft, except as noted; in English translation: *Israel, Mein Volk: Israels Vegangenheit, Gegenwart und Zukunft im Blickpunkt des Wortes Gottes,* 1958, translation by Alfred Wiener and Teresa Mary Wiener published as *Israel, My Chosen People: A German Confession Before God and the Jews,* Faith Press, 1963; *Busse, glueckseliges Leben: Die taegliche Umkehr als befreiende Loesung und Quelle bestaendiger Freude,* 1959, translation by Harriet Corbin and Sigrid Langer published as *Repentance: The Joy-Filled Life,* Zondervan, 1968; *Ich will euch troesten: Trostbuechlien fuer Trauernde,* 1959, translation published as *My Father, I Trust You* (songs); *Geistliche Dienstregel: Ausrichtung fuer den Dienst,* 1960, translation published as *Ruled by the Spirit,* Bethany Fellowship, 1970; *Krankentrost-Buechlein: Umfassende Antworten auf Fragen und Noete des Kranken,* 1960, translation published as *The Blessings of Illness; Das Ende ist nah,* Oekumenische Marienschwesternschaft, 1961, translation by Neville B. Cryer, John Foote, and Mary Foote published as *Lo, He Comes,* Faith Press, 1965; *Realitaeten: Gottes Wirken, heute erlebt,* 1962, translation by Larry Christenson and William Castell published as *Realities: The Miracles of God Experienced Today,* Zondervan, 1966; *Heiliges Land heute,* 1962, translation by Cryer published as *The Holy Land Today,* Faith Press, 1963; *Immer ist Gott groesser,* 1963, translation by Cryer published as *God Is Always Greater,* Faith Press, 1963; *Und Keiner wollte es glauben: Positionslicht in Nebel der Zeit,* 1964, translation by Christenson and M. D. Rogers published as *And None Would Belive It: An Answer to the New Morality,* Zondervan, 1967; *Alles fuer Einen,* 1969, translation published as *My All for Him,* Oliphants, 1971.

Zum ersten Mal, seitdem es Kirche Jesu Christi gibt, 1970, translation published as *Never Before in the History of the Church,* Marshall, Morgan & Scott, 1970; *Sieben mal um Jericho: Dreissig Lieder fuer den Kampf des Glaubens mit vierstimmigen Saetzen,* 1971, translation published as *Seven Times Around Jericho* (songs); *Umveltverschmutzung und dennoch Hoffnung,* 1972, translation published as *Pollution: But There Is An Answer,* Lakeland Paperbacks, 1973; *Sinai: Ein Berg redet,* 1972, translation published as *Sinai: A Mountain Speaks; Kurz vor der Weltkatastrophe: Bedrohung und Bewahrung,* 1973, translation published as *Countdown to World Disaster: Hope and Protection for the Future,* Marshall, Morgan & Scott; *Hoelle, Himmel, Wirklichkeiten,* 1974, translation published as *What Comes After Death?: The Reality of Heaven and Hell,* Lakeland Paperbacks, 1976; *Wie ich Gott erlebte: Sein Weg mit mir durch sieben Jahr-zehnte,* 1975, translation published as *I Found the Key to the Heart of God: My Personal Story,* Bethany Fellowship, 1975 (published in England as *A Foretaste of Heaven*); *Im Sog der Verfuehrung unserer Zeit,* 1975, translation published as *Escaping the Web of Deception,* 2nd edition, Evangelical Sisterhood of Mary, 1976; *Patmos: Da der Himmel offen war,* 1976, translation published as *Patmos: When the Heavens Opened,* Creation House, 1976.

Other writings: *Gewissensspiegel: Die sieghafte Macht des Glaubens,* 1949; *Das Koenigliche Priestertum: Berufung zum Dienst Gottes nach neutestament-lichem Verstaendnis,* 1949; *Dem Urberwinder die Krone: Ein Ratgeber in Sorgen, Leiden, Aufechtungen, und Schwierigkeiten mit Mitmenschen,* 1949.

Macht des Gebets: Eine Hinfuehrung zu Bittes, Dank, Anbetung und immerwaehrundem Gebet, 1950; *Reich des Himmels, Reich der Hoelle: Unser Leben; Eine Entscheidung fuer Licht oder Finsternis,* 1950; *Gebetswaffe,* 1952; *Mitarbeiter Gottes: Ein Wort an solche, die im Dienst Jesu stehen und nach Vollmacht und Frucht in ihrem Dienst verlangen,* 1952; *Glaubenssieg: Die glueckseligmachende Liebe zu Jesus,* 1953; *Ehre, Ehre sei dem Lamm: Ein Aufruf, Jesus als demm Lamm Gottes Liebe und Huldigung zu bringen,* 1954; *Kommt, es ist alles bereit: Das grosse Angebot im Heiligen Mahl,* 1954; *Lammesweg: Der Weg zum Sieg in Alltagsnoeten,* 1954; *Liebesweg: Das Wesen wahrer Bruderliebe,* 1954; *Gebetsleben: Anleitung und Gebete,* 1955; *Lass mein Lieben dich begleiten: Die Passion Jesu, ein Ruf an uns,* 1956; *Jesus mitten unter uns: Sein Lieben und Leiden heute,* 1957; *Trost-Buechlein: Fuer Bekuemmerte,* 1957; *Vater der Liebe: Vaterguete Gottes und doch unverstaendliche Fuehrungen?,* 1957; *Vatergebete: Zur Anregung fuer das persoenliche Gebet,* 1957; *Wege durch die Nacht zur Heiligen Dreieinigkeit: Vom offenbarten Geheimnis der Gemeinschaft mit dem Dreieinigen Gott,* 1957; *Geduld-Buechlein: Fuer Wartezeiten,* 1958; *Sieg durch Geduld,* 1958; *Jesu Weg, Unser Weg: Antwort auf Fragen zur Nachfolge Jesu aus der Wirklichkeit des Lebens,* 1959; *Weihnachts-Buechlein: Gesprache an der Krippe,* 1959.

Geistliche Dienstregel: Ausrichtung fuer den Dienst, 1960; *Marie: Der Weg der Mutter des Herrn; Das Zeugnis der Schrift ueber ihr Leben in der Nachfolge,* 1960; *Morgen und Abendgebete: Fuer jeden Tag der Woche,* 1960; *Himmels-Buechlein: Ausblick auf das Ziel,* 1961; *Die Ihn lieben: Lieben zu Jesus als lebens gestaltende Macht,* 1961; *Wider die Verzagtheit: Glanbenshilfe fuer dunkle Stunden,* 1961; *Heute, Eine Zeit eiw nie,* 1962; *Jesus am See Genezareth: Ein See unter der Bitschaft der Koenigsherrschaft Gottes,* 1963; *Zielklar ist Gott am Werk: Der Weg von zwei frueh heimgegangenen Marienschwestern,* 1963; *Mitmenschlichkeit,* 1965; *Der niemand traurig sehen kann: Ein Wort des Zuspruchs fuer jeden Tag des Jahres,* 1965; *Sinai Heute: Staetten der Gottesoffenbarung zwischen Nil und Moseberg!,* 1966; *Wo der Geist weht: Wesen und Wirken des Heiligen Geistes damals und heute,* 1967; *Er redet noch: Gottes Gebot fuer jeden Tag, Gottes Angebot fuer jeden Tag,* 1968; *Um Jerusalems willen: Prophetie realisiert sich,* 1968; *Mein Beten: Eine Gebetshilfe fuer den Alltag,* 1969; *Welt im Aufruhr,* 1969; *Wir bergen uns in Deine Hand: Trost, Staerkung und Bereitung fuer Notzeiten,* 1969.

So wird man anders: Seelsorgerlich Hilfe fuer den konkreten Fall, 1971; *Wenn einer nicht lieben kann: Schluessel zu versoehntem Leben,* 1971; *Wenn ich nur Jesus liebe: Aus dem Leben unserer Schwester Claudia,* 1971; *Dich will ich besingen: 37 Lieder der Liebe zu Jesus,* 1972; *Im Namen Jesu ist die Macht: Gebete und Lieder fuer den Kampf des Glaubens,* 1972; *Reiche der Engel und Daemonen: Aktuelle Wirklichkeit fuer unsere Zeit,* 1972; *Kurz vor der Christenverfolgung: Liebe will leiden,* 1973; *Wenn Gott liebt: Durch Wuestenwege zur Freude,* 1973; *Werr Er erscheint: Lieder von der Wiederkunft Jesu und von der himmlischen Herrlichkeit,* 1973; *Ich vertraue Dir, mein Vater: Lieder fuer dunkle Tage,* 1974; *Heilige Staetten heute,* 1975; *Ich will hier bei dir stehen: Jesu Lieben und Leiden damals und heute,* 1975.

Other writings in English translation; all published by Bethany Fellowship, except as noted: *Those Who Love Him,* Oliphants, 1969; *Praying Our Way Through Life,* 1970; *Ruled by the Spirit,* 1970; *Father of Comfort,* 1971; *You Will Never Be the Same,* 1972; *Behold His Love,* 1973; *More Precious Than Gold,* 1978.

Also author of *The Eve of Persecution, Well-Spring of Joy* (songs), *Songs and Prayers of Victory, Jesus: A Portrait of Love, Let Me Stand at Your Side, O None Can Be Loved as Is Jesus* (songs), *The King Draws Near, In the Name of Jesus* (songs), and *For Jerusalem's Sake I Will Not Rest,* all published by Evangelical Sisterhood of Mary. Author of film, "God Lives and Works Today," released by Canaan Studio. Composer of more than three thousand religious songs. Author of pamphlets, tracts, and posters.

SIDELIGHTS: Mother Basilea's dream of a religious community, where love for Jesus Christ is a way of life, began after her birthplace, Darmstadt, was leveled by an air raid in 1944. At the time it was an impossible dream, but by 1973 Canaan was completed. Now her teachings have reached around the world, inspiring the clergy and lay people as well. Her books have been published in forty languages (including Twi, Swahili, Amharic, Afrikaans, Thai, and Mandarin Chinese), and her teachings, in almost every printed form, are available nearly everywhere.

Sound recordings of her songs include "Jesus O Joy Eternal," "Glory Beyond Compare," "In Praise of Our Heavenly Father," "Lift Up Your Voices in Joy," and "With Praise and Rejoicing."

BIOGRAPHICAL/CRITICAL SOURCES: Basilea Schlink, *I Found the Key to the Heart of God: My Personal Story,* Bethany Fellowship, 1975; *Christian Life,* April, 1976, August, 1977; *Bookstore Journal,* June, 1976.

*   *   *

SCHLINK, M. Basilea
  See SCHLINK, Klara

*   *   *

SCHLINK, Mother Basilea
  See SCHLINK, Klara

*   *   *

SCHLOSSBERG, Dan   1948-

PERSONAL: Born May 6, 1948, in New York, N.Y.; son of Ezra (a physician) and Miriam (a nurse; maiden name, Serbin) Schlossberg; married Karen Spindel, June 12, 1969 (divorced August 4, 1978); children: Samantha. *Education:* Syracuse University, B.A. (journalism) and B.A. (political science), both 1969. *Politics:* Liberal Democrat. *Religion:* Jewish. *Home and Office:* 77 Brook Ave., Apt. D-13, Passaic, N.J. 07055. *Agent:* Bev Norwood, International Literary Management, Inc., 767 Fifth Ave., Suite 601, New York, N.Y. 10022.

CAREER: Passaic Herald-News, Passaic, N.J., staff writer, summers, 1966-68; Associated Press, Newark, N.J., reporter, broadcast editor, and state sports editor, 1969-71; Motor Club of America Companies, Newark, N.J., director of public relations and editor of *Motor Club News,* 1971-75; M. Silver Associates, New York City, travel writer and public relations account executive, 1976-77; Enterprise Newsfeatures (newspaper syndicate), New York City, sports and travel editor, 1977-78; American Express Co., New York City, travel writer, 1979—. Reporter for United Press International (UPI) Audio, 1977 and 1979, and *Baseball Hotline,*

1980. *Military service:* U.S. Army Reserve, 1971-75; served as announcer, reporter, and interviewer for 340th Public Information Detachment.

MEMBER: Communicators Association of New Jersey (treasurer, 1975; president, 1976), Sigma Delta Chi (president of Syracuse chapter, 1968-69). *Awards, honors:* Communicators Association of New Jersey awards for general excellence, 1972, for best news story, 1973, for best newspaper layout award, 1973, and for newswriting, 1976, all for work as editor of *Motor Club News;* certificate of merit from Highway Users Federation, 1973; Uniroyal Journalism Safety Awards, 1974 and 1975, both naming *Motor Club News* the national runner-up in excellence in trade publications.

WRITINGS: (Contributor) Ray Robinson, editor, *Baseball Stars of 1973,* Pyramid Publications, 1973; (contributor) Robinson, editor, *Baseball Stars of 1974,* Pyramid Publications, 1974; *Hammerin' Hank: The Henry Aaron Story,* Stadia Sports Publishing, 1974; (contributor) Robinson, editor, *Baseball Stars of 1975,* Pyramid Publications, 1975; *Barons of the Bullpen,* Grosset, 1975; *The Baseball Catalog* (alternate selection of Book-of-the-Month Club), Jonathan David, 1980.

Writer of "Race for the Pennant," a Home Box Office (HBO) television series produced by Major League Baseball Productions, 1979; writer-designer of *Rolaids Relief Man Media Guide,* 1979. Author of monthly columns in *Baseball Bulletin,* 1975-80, and weekly sports and travel columns syndicated by Enterprise Newsfeatures, 1977-78. Contributor of articles and photographs to magazines and newspapers, including *New York Post, Carte Blanche, Continental Flightime, Atlanta, Travel, Sporting News,* and *TV Star Parade.* Associate editor of *Baseball;* contributing editor of *Baseball Illustrated.*

WORK IN PROGRESS: "Celebrities Reveal Their World Series Heroes," a feature article for the 1980 World Series program. The article will include "quotes from Gerald Ford, Mel Brooks, Anne Bancroft, Ken Howard, Cheryl Tiegs, Alan King, and others."

SIDELIGHTS: Schlossberg wrote: "Though my original intent in journalism was to be a political commentator, the 1968 Nixon victory and subsequent landslide of the same corrupt administration four years later completely erased that yearning. In the interim, I found immense personal enjoyment in combining my love of writing with my enthusiasm for baseball and travel. I have managed to specialize in these two areas, but have written widely on other subjects as well."

* * *

SCHLUETER, June 1942-

PERSONAL: Born November 4, 1942, in Passaic, N.J.; daughter of Alex and Erna (Schwedler) Mayer; married Paul Schlueter (a professor and writer), November 9, 1974. *Education:* Fairleigh Dickinson University, B.A. (magna cum laude), 1970; Hunter College of the City University of New York, M.A., 1973; Columbia University, Ph.D., 1977. *Home:* 314 McCartney St., Easton, Pa. 18042. *Office:* Department of English, Lafayette College, Easton, Pa. 18042.

CAREER: Hoffmann-La Roche, Nutley, N.J., affiliated with fine chemicals division, 1960-66; Schlanger, Blumenthal & Lynne, New York City, legal assistant, 1967-69; Stamer & Haft, New York City, legal and administrative assistant, 1969-72; Schlanger, Blumenthal & Lynne, legal assistant,

1972-73; Kean College of New Jersey, Union, adjunct professor of English, 1973-76; Kenneth P. Newman, New York City, legal and administrative assistant, 1976-77; Lafayette College, Easton, Pa., assistant professor of English, 1977—. Fulbright professor in Kassel, West Germany, 1978-79. Member of North America Study Program's selection committee for German Academic Exchange Service. *Member:* American Theatre Association, Modern Language Association of America, College English Association, Conference on Christianity and Literature, Fulbright Alumni Association.

WRITINGS: Metafictional Characters in Modern Drama, Columbia University Press, 1979; (contributor) Patricia De La Fuente, editor, *Edward Albee,* Pan American University, 1980; (with husband, Paul Schlueter) *The English Novel: Twentieth Century Criticism,* Volume II, Swallow Press, 1981; (with Ellis Finger) *Peter Handke: An Annotated Bibliography,* Garland Publishing, 1981. Contributor of articles and reviews to literature journals.

WORK IN PROGRESS: A critical study of the plays and novels of Peter Handke; critical essay on the novels of Margaret Atwood; short fiction.

SIDELIGHTS: Schlueter told *CA:* "My book on modern drama, *Metafictional Characters in Modern Drama,* is intended for students and scholars familiar with the plays of significant twentieth-century dramatists such as Pirandello, Genet, Beckett, Albee, Stoppard, Weiss, and Handke. It examines the recurring emphasis on the inherent duality of the dramatic character. Though realistic drama still maintains a foothold on American and European stages, it is those plays that go beyond mimesis that most effectively reflect the changing values of our age and expand the boundaries of this art."

* * *

SCHMELING, Marianne 1930-

PERSONAL: Born in 1930, in Gumbinnen, Germany; came to the United States in 1958; daughter of Fritz and Maria (Urbat) Schmeling; married husband, December 25, 1925; children: six. *Education:* Attended Borough of Manhattan Community College. *Home:* 25-26 33rd St., New York, N.Y. 11102. *Agent:* Richard H. Roffman Associates, 697 West End Ave., New York, N.Y. 10025.

CAREER: Arthur Young & Co., New York, N.Y., staff accountant, 1970—.

WRITINGS: Flee the Wolf: The Story of a Family's Miraculous Journey to Freedom, Donning, 1978.

WORK IN PROGRESS: Two children's books, *Summer in the Country* and *Ogie,* both self-illustrated.

SIDELIGHTS: Marianne Schmeling told *CA:* "To be a successful accountant requires organization and discipline. This fact also holds true for a writer. Having had *Flee the Wolf* as a complete work in the back of my mind, it was just a matter of putting it into words. However, for a foreign born this meant taking courses in English and creative writing. It was my professor's suggestion to begin the work while attending classes. His promise to assist me encouraged me to set out on the work immediately, instead of writing the book during my retirement years as originally planned.

"Sacrificing every spare moment from June, 1975, to October, 1976, including holidays, vacations, and evenings, the work was rewritten and reread at least twenty times. Combing it doggedly for repetition of words and phrases, cutting the weightless narrative, the manuscript was submitted for publication in October, 1976, and accepted.

"*Flee the Wolf* was published in December, 1978. The work received enthusiastic reviews from the news media and encouraging responses from the readership. Many people wrote, stating that they had lived through my own experiences in World War II, suffered the same anguish and anxieties, prayed in the desperate struggle for life, and were grateful to have come through alive. One friend even had nightmares about Russians pursuing him! This was my purpose for the book, not only to write about World War II in Germany, but to let the reader experience it. Having achieved this was a great satisfaction to me. Many readers have expressed the desire to see the story filmed."

*　　　*　　　*

SCHNABEL, Billie H(agen)　1944(?)-1980

OBITUARY NOTICE: Born c. 1944 in Ashville, N.C.; died of cancer, June 8, 1980, in Washington, D.C. Prior to founding, presiding over, and editing the newsletter of the Old Town College Park Preservation Association, Billie Schnabel was involved in numerous community service organizations, including the Maryland Historic Trust and the Maryland National Capital Park and Planning Commission. She was a frequent contributor to the *Washington Post* and *Prince George's Journal*. Obituaries and other sources: *Washington Post*, June 12, 1980.

*　　　*　　　*

SCHOEMAN, Karel　1939-

PERSONAL: Born October 26, 1939, in Trompsburg, South Africa; son of Marcus and Anny (van Rooijen) Schoeman. *Education:* University of the Orange Free State, B.A., 1959, diploma in librarianship, 1965. *Residence:* Bloemfontein, South Africa. *Agent:* David Higham Associates Ltd., 76 Dean St., London W.1, England.

CAREER: Writer. Worked as librarian, translator, and nurse in South Africa, Glasgow, Scotland, and Amsterdam, Holland. *Member:* Free Statia Historical Society. *Awards, honors:* Hertzog Prize from South Africa Academy, 1970; C.N.A. Prize, 1973, for *Na die gelietde land.*

WRITINGS—All published by Human & Rousseau, unless otherwise noted: *Veldstag: Twee novelles,* 1965; *Die hart van die son,* 1965; *By fakkellig* (novel), 1966; *'N Lug vol helder wolke,* 1967; *Son op die land,* Tafelberg, 1967; *Lig in die donker,* 1969; *Uit die Iers,* 1970; *Op 'n eiland* (novel), 1971; *Spiraal,* 1971; *Na die geliefde land* (novel), 1972, translation by Marion V. Friedmann published as *Promised Land,* Summit Books, 1978; *Eroica* (juvenile), 1973; (editor) *Helde van die rooi tak: Die saga van Cucullin en die Veeroof van Culne,* 1973; *Die Noorderlig,* 1975; *Afrika: 'N roman,* 1977; *Koninkryk in die Noorde: 'N boek oor Skotland* (travel), 1977. Author of television scripts.

WORK IN PROGRESS: A history of Bloemfontein, South Africa.

*　　　*　　　*

SCHOEN, Elin　1945-

PERSONAL: Born December 26, 1945, in Lebanon, Pa.; daughter of Irwin D. (an interior designer) and Marva (Gruman) Schoen. *Education:* Sarah Lawrence College, B.A., 1967. *Residence:* New York, N.Y. *Agent:* Wendy Weil, Julian Bach Literary Agency, Inc., 747 Third Ave., New York, N.Y. 10017.

CAREER: Writer.

WRITINGS: Tales of an All-Night Town, Harcourt, 1979. Contributor to popular magazines, including *Mademoiselle, Cosmopolitan, Esquire, Ladies' Home Journal,* and *Redbook,* and newspapers. Past contributing editor of *New York.*

WORK IN PROGRESS: A novel.

SIDELIGHTS: Elin Schoen told *CA:* "I've traveled on assignments throughout Mexico, Europe, the Middle East, the Caribbean, and Ethiopia. Although I have never had a 'specialty,' and have written articles about everything from carrot cake to roller disco to prison journalism, I am now concentrating on crime, the criminal justice system, and prison reform—and I am now doing my own photography."

*　　　*　　　*

SCHOFIELD, Paul
####　　See TUBB, E(dwin) C(harles)

*　　　*　　　*

SCHOLER, David M(ilton)　1938-

PERSONAL: Born July 24, 1938, in Rochester, Minn.; son of Milton N. and Bernice (an antiques dealer; maiden name, Anderson) Scholer; married Jeannette Mudgett (a college teacher), August 16, 1960; children: Emily, Abigail. *Education:* Wheaton College, Wheaton, Ill., B.A., 1960, M.A., 1964; Gordon Divinity School (now Gordon-Conwell Theological Seminary), B.D., 1964; Harvard University, Th.D., 1980. *Religion:* American Baptist. *Home:* 12 Arlington Ave., Beverly, Mass. 01915. *Office:* Gordon-Conwell Theological Seminary, South Hamilton, Mass. 01982.

CAREER: Ordained American Baptist minister, 1966; Gordon-Conwell Theological Seminary, South Hamilton, Mass., assistant professor, 1969-75, associate professor of New Testament, 1975—, director of admissions, 1976-78. *Member:* North American Patristic Society, Catholic Biblical Association of America, Conference on Faith and History, Institute for Biblical Research, Society of Biblical Literature.

WRITINGS: (Assistant editor) *The Encyclopedia of Modern Christian Missions: The Agencies,* Thomas Nelson, 1967; *Nag Hammadi Bibliography, 1948-1969,* E. J. Brill, 1971; *A Basic Bibliographic Guide for New Testament Exegesis,* Eerdmans, 1973. Contributor of articles and reviews to theology journals.

SIDELIGHTS: Scholer wrote: "My Christian commitment and my assessment of my gifts and abilities has led me to be deeply involved in graduate theological education." *Avocational interests:* Travel, collecting antiques and stamps, attending theatre.

*　　　*　　　*

SCHRADER, Constance　1933-

PERSONAL: Born February 9, 1933, in Newark, N.J.; daughter of Jacob J. and Charlotte (Styler) Delbourgo; married Gunard E. Bergman (divorced); married Ernst J. Schrader (an editor). *Education:* Attended State University of New York College at Oswego. *Politics:* None. *Religion:* Jewish. *Home:* 610 West 110th St., New York, N.Y. 10025. *Agent:* Julia Coppersmith Literary Agency, 10 West 15th St., New York, N.Y. 10011. *Office:* E.P. Dutton & Co., Inc., 2 Park Ave., New York, N.Y. 10003.

CAREER: Elementary school teacher, 1954-60; Harcourt Brace Jovanovich, Inc., New York City, editor; Macmillan

Publishing Co., Inc., New York City, editor in textbooks and trade books; E. P. Dutton & Co., Inc., New York City, currently nonfiction director. Also worked as illustrator and model.

WRITINGS: Wrinkles: How to Prevent Them, How to Erase Them, Prentice-Hall, 1978; *Makeovers,* Prentice-Hall, 1979. Also author of *Nine to Five.*

WORK IN PROGRESS: The Horizontal Ladder: A Study of Sex in the Office; House Style, a novel about women in publishing.

*   *   *

SCHRAFF, Francis Nicholas 1937-

PERSONAL: Born August 17, 1937, in Cleveland, Ohio; son of Frank Casimir (a postal inspector) and Helen (a teacher; maiden name, Benninger) Schraff; married Remedios Curato (a school director), December 17, 1974; children: Andrew Curato. *Education:* Los Angeles Pierce College, A.A., 1957; attended Los Angeles State University, 1957-58; San Fernando Valley State University (now California State University, Northridge), B.A., 1959. *Politics:* Republican. *Religion:* Roman Catholic. *Home and office address:* P.O. Box 1346, Spring Valley, Calif. 92077.

CAREER: Teacher in public schools in Los Angeles, Calif., 1960-62, and Roman Catholic schools in Los Angeles, 1962-67, and San Diego, Calif., 1967-68; teacher at ranch school and summer camp in Alpine, Calif., 1967-74; Mount Miguel Learning Center, Spring Valley, Calif., director, 1974—. *Awards, honors:* Named outstanding teacher by Outstanding Elementary Teachers of America, 1973.

WRITINGS: (With sister, Anne E. Schraff) *Jesus, Our Brother,* Liguori Publications, 1968; (with A. E. Schraff) *Adventures of Peter and Paul,* Liguori Publications, 1978.

WORK IN PROGRESS: "An encyclopedic study of selected historical texts as they relate to certain cultural folkways," completion expected in 1983.

SIDELIGHTS: Schraff commented to *CA:* "There must be a deep reverence for nature and all of its life. It is God himself who manifests himself not only in things of the spirit, but in the harmony of the visible world of matter. It is from him that nature has its being. Man can ascend to God by reconciling himself with creation—as Francis of Assisi—or he can destroy, defile, and desecrate and suffer from the consequences."

AVOCATIONAL INTERESTS: Music (piano), astronomy, photography.

*   *   *

SCHUCHMAN, Joan 1934-
(Isabel Brenner, Miriam Jones, Zelda Jones)

PERSONAL: Born October 13, 1934, in Rockway, N.Y.; daughter of Samuel Henry (a dentist) and Irene (a social worker; maiden name, Greenberger) Shapiro; married Hilton Schuchman (a sales manager), November 27, 1954; children: Leonard George, Jim Steven. *Education:* Attended Brooklyn College (now of the City University of New York), 1952-54; University of Minnesota, B.A., 1970. *Home:* 1750 Beechwood Ave., St. Paul, Minn. 55116.

CAREER: Free-lance writer and editor, 1970—. National Forum Foundation for American Education, Circle Pines, Minn., editor of research project on aging, 1979. *Member:* International Association of Business Communicators, American Association of University Women. *Awards, hon-*

ors: Awards from *Writer's Digest* contests, 1976, for article, "Depression: The Living Death Disease," and 1977, for "The Diet That Calms Hyperactive Children."

WRITINGS: (Under pseudonym Miriam Jones) *Astrology: Science or Hoax,* Pamphlet Publications, 1978; (with Michael Appleman) *Help for Your Hyperactive Child,* Pamphlet Publications, 1978; *Two Places to Sleep* (juvenile), Carolrhoda, 1979. Contributor of about twenty-five articles to magazines, sometimes under pseudonym Zelda Jones or Isabel Brenner.

WORK IN PROGRESS: A play, for television or stage.

SIDELIGHTS: Joan Schuchman told *CA:* "My main interests are reading, writing, and research. Special reading interests are eighteenth-century British poetry and prose, twentieth-century British and American drama and fiction, Ibsen's and Shakespeare's plays, and Alexander Solzhenitsyn's writings, especially his fiction. My major writing problem is that I spend too much time reading and not enough time writing."

AVOCATIONAL INTERESTS: Photography, travel.

BIOGRAPHICAL/CRITICAL SOURCES: Publisher's Weekly, November 19, 1979; *School Library Journal,* April, 1980.

*   *   *

SCHUDSON, Michael 1946-

PERSONAL: Born November 3, 1946, in Milwaukee, Wis.; son of Howard M. (a small business proprietor) and Lorraine (Spira) Schudson. *Education:* Swarthmore College, B.A., 1969; Harvard University, M.A., 1970, Ph.D., 1976. *Residence:* Chicago, Ill. *Office:* Department of Sociology, University of California, San Diego, La Jolla, Calif. 92093.

CAREER: University of Chicago, Chicago, Ill., assistant professor of sociology, 1976-80; University of California, San Diego, La Jolla, associate professor of sociology and communication, 1980—. *Member:* American Sociological Association, American Historical Association, American Studies Association.

WRITINGS: Discovering the News: A Social History of American Newspapers, Basic Books, 1978.

WORK IN PROGRESS: A book on the social and cultural consequences of advertising; a book on a theory of American popular culture.

*   *   *

SCHUH, Dwight R(aymond) 1945-

PERSONAL: Born May 21, 1945, in Corvallis, Ore.; son of Joe (an entomologist) and Josephine (a secretary; maiden name, Higgs) Schuh; married Laura Newman, June 20, 1971; children: Emily Ruth. *Education:* University of Idaho, B.A. (English), 1971; University of Oregon, B.A. (journalism), 1977. *Religion:* Society of Friends (Quakers). *Home:* 1425 Worden Ave., Klamath Falls, Ore. 97601. *Office: Outdoor Life,* 380 Madison Ave., New York, N.Y. 10017.

CAREER: Free-lance writer, 1971-79; *Outdoor Life,* New York City, Pacific field editor, 1979—. *Military service:* U.S. Army, 1966-69; became staff sergeant. *Member:* Outdoor Writers Association of America.

WRITINGS: Modern Survival, McKay, 1979.

WORK IN PROGRESS: The Outdoor Photographer's Handbook.

SIDELIGHTS: Schuh commented: "My major motivation is

to make a living for my family. Writing is not fun. It's not for pleasure or release. It's nothing but darned hard work. Deadlines are another motivating force. When an editor or publisher gives me a deadline for a manuscript, I know he's counting on me. I must come through and will work as hard and long as necessary to do it. I'm now strictly an outdoors writer, but plan to branch into Christian and family writing as time allows."

* * *

SCHULMAN, Janet 1933-

PERSONAL: Born September 16, 1933, in Pittsburgh, Pa.; daughter of Albert C. (in insurance) and Edith (Spielman) Schuetz; married L. M. Schulman (a writer and editor), May 19, 1957; children: Nicole. *Education:* Antioch College, B.A., 1956. *Residence:* New York, N.Y. *Office:* Random House, 201 East 50th St., New York, N.Y., 10022.

CAREER: Writer. Macmillan Publishing Co., Inc., New York City, vice-president and juvenile marketing manager, 1961-74; Random House, Inc., New York City, director of library marketing, 1978-79, executive editor of children's books, 1980—. Member of board of directors of Children's Book Council, 1970-73 and 1979; member of publishing industry committees; consultant to juvenile publishers. *Member:* American Library Association.

WRITINGS—Juveniles; all published by Greenwillow, except as noted: *The Big Hello*, 1976; *Jack the Bum and the Halloween Handout*, 1977; *Jack the Bum and the Haunted House*, 1977; *Jenny and the Tennis Hut*, 1978; *Jack the Bum and the UFO*, 1978; *Camp KeeWee's Secret Weapon*, 1979; *The Great Big Dummy*, 1979; (author of adaptation) E.T.A. Hoffmann, *The Nutcracker*, Dutton, 1979. Author of abridgements of literary works, including C. S. Lewis's *Chronicles of Narnia* and nineteenth-century literary classics, for Caedmon Records.

SIDELIGHTS: Schulman told *CA:* "I was the 'baby' of the family and always felt the outsider. During World War II my older brother was in the Air Force, my other brother was in the Navy, my sister was a secretary at U.S. Steel, and I was in elementary school. My role in the war effort was in buying war stamps with my ten-cents-a-week allowance and, as a Junior Commando, collecting scrap iron, tin cans, and newspaper for recycling. At some point I quite sensibly ceased trying to compete with my glamorous brothers and sister and began creating a world of my own, mainly through books, drawing, and making up stories. They thought I was strange, perhaps a bit daft, as I sat huddled under a tent blanket construction in the corner of the livingroom, talking to myself. But what I was really doing was creating little story/plays, in which I played all roles. Many of them were about a child who miraculously saved her family when the father lost his job or had to go to war.

"I was very much a child of the Great Depression, when my mother literally counted pennies to put food on the table for us, and the World War II era, both of which helped me keep a wary eye on reality. I think it shows in the kinds of stories I write for children today. Though none of them are set in those periods, I try to show children operating not in a vacuum but surrounded by circumstances of reality which do affect their lives. In *The Big Hello* a little girl moves to California because her father has gone there to find a new job. In *Camp KeeWee's Secret Weapon* Jill has to go to summer camp because her mother has just gotten a job and Jill is too young to stay home alone during the day. In *Jenny and the Tennis Nut* Jenny's father wants to see Jenny take up tennis enthusiastically because tennis is his game.

"Growing up in a large family also exposes one to a certain amount of teasing, and I think I learned at an early age that a sense of humor and a sharp wit are good defenses against a lot of things. I am always happy when a child says my books are funny because you can't trick children: they know when something is funny and when it isn't.

"Another thing that makes me happy is hearing a reviewer call my books non-sexist. I would hate to set out to write a non-sexist book—it would be awfully dull—but if some of my books just happen to be non-sexist, among other things, it must be because I grew up believing that I did not have to live a certain way because I was a girl, and I have pretty much followed that all my life. Nowadays many girls are doing just that. I wish they had been around when I was growing up!

"My daughter, Nicole, has also helped me as a writer. I doubt if I would have written the kinds of stories I write if I had not started just at the time Nicole was in the first grade. I wanted to write stories for her, stories she could read and would like. None of my stories are based directly on anything that has happened in our family, but all of them have grown or been inspired by my daily life with Nicole. And she is my most severe critic! She is the one who gives me encouragement but also criticism (much of it very sound) before I even take the manuscript to my editor, who helps me make my books even better."

AVOCATIONAL INTERESTS: Tennis.

BIOGRAPHICAL/CRITICAL SOURCES: New York Times Book Review, May 1, 1977.

* * *

SCHUYLER, James Marcus 1923-

PERSONAL: Surname is pronounced *Sky*-ler; born November 9, 1923, in Chicago, Ill.; son of Marcus James (a reporter) and Margaret (Connor) Schuyler. *Education:* Attended Bethany College, Bethany, W.Va., 1941-43, and University of Florence, 1947-48. *Home:* Hotel Chelsea, 222 West 23rd St., No. 625, New York, N.Y. 10011. *Agent:* Maxine Groffsky, 2 Fifth Ave., New York, N.Y. 10011.

CAREER: Poet, novelist, and playwright. Museum of Modern Art, New York, N.Y., member of staff, 1955-61; art critic at *Art News. Awards, honors:* Longview Foundation award, 1961; Frank O'Hara Prize from *Poetry*, 1969, for *Freely Espousing: Poems;* National Endowment for the Arts grant, 1971 and 1972; National Institute of Arts and Letters award, 1976.

WRITINGS—Poetry: *Salute*, Tiber Press, 1960; (with Kenward Elmslie) *The Wednesday Club*, East End Theatre, 1964; *May 24th or So*, Tibor de Nagy, 1966; *Freely Espousing: Poems*, Doubleday, 1969; *The Crystal Lithium*, Random House, 1972; *A Sun Cab*, Adventures in Poetry, 1972; *Hymn to Life: Poems*, Random House, 1974; *Song*, Kermani Press, 1976; *The Home Book: Prose and Poems, 1951-1970*, Z Press, 1977; *The Morning of the Poem*, Farrar, Straus, 1980. Also author of *Wild Oats*. Poetry represented in anthologies, including *Penguin Modern Poets 24*, edited by John Ashbery, Penguin, 1974; *ZZZZ*, Z Press, 1976.

Novels: *Alfred and Guinevere*, Harcourt, 1958; (with John Ashbery) *A Nest of Ninnies*, Dutton, 1969; *What's for Dinner?*, Black Sparrow Press, 1978.

Plays: "Presenting Jane" (one-act), first produced in Cambridge, Mass., at Poets' Theatre, 1952; "Shopping and Waiting" (one-act), first produced in Cambridge at Poets' Theatre, 1953; (with Elmslie) "Unpacking the Black Trunk" (one-act), first produced Off-Broadway, 1965.

Other writings: (With Paul Bowles) "A Picnic Cantata" (recording), Columbia Records, 1955; *The Fireproof Floors of Witley Court: English Songs and Dances,* Janus Press, 1976. Contributor to periodicals, including *Art News, New Yorker, Poetry,* and *Paris Review.*

WORK IN PROGRESS: A Few Days (poetry), publication by Farrer, Straus expected in 1982; *Heck Kelly and the Kellys of Kellyville* (comic novel), Farrer, Straus, 1982; a novel, *Small Crimes,* with Tom Carey; a novel, *In County Wexford,* with Helena Hughes.

SIDELIGHTS: James Schuyler is regularly grouped with John Ashbery, Frank O'Hara, and Kenneth Koch, all poets of the New York School. His poetry, like that of his confreres, celebrates the universe of objects, or the "joy in random surfaces," as David Kalstone noted in the *New York Times Book Review.* Three books of poetry, *Freely Espousing, The Crystal Lithium,* and *Hymn to Life,* reveal a poet who "speaks softly and carries no *shtick* at all," commented Edmund White of the *Village Voice.* "The moments of relaxed awareness, of a serenity achieved in spite of suffering, moments that many other poets would ignore or fail to see as poetic occasions—these moments Schuyler preserves and explores." A novelist as well as a poet, Schuyler's *A Nest of Ninnies* and *What's for Dinner?* are similar in purpose, presenting what Eve Ottenberg called "an easy and humorous middle-class world betwixt shopping center and commuter train."

Freely Espousing, Schuyler's first major collection of poems, introduced critics to the work of a mature poet who had been writing for almost twenty years. John Koethe remarked in his review that "not only is *Freely Espousing* a collection of extremely good poems, but it also embodies the sort of vision that periodically reawakens us to the infinite range of possibilities open to the poet." The "bewildering, breathing" accumulation of objects and perceptions in his poems recalls the poetry of Elizabeth Bishop and Marianne Moore, he observed, although Schuyler's poems are delivered with a personal, "disarmingly open" voice that distinguishes them from the impersonal tone of Moore's poetry. Another critic, Guy Davenport of the *New York Times Book Review,* suggested that Schuyler's is a lyric poetry, one that "channels the world through a single sensibility" and makes it part of "a new Romanticism . . . and a new subjectivity."

David Shapiro's reading of *The Crystal Lithium,* a collection of poems published in 1972, held that Schuyler "always observes vibrantly before any interpretation, and renders all as vividly as possible." The poems address the minutiae of daily life, such as the smell of coffee on a winter morning, and again reveal "a meticulous, Williams-like devotion to the physical world," according to the *Virginia Quarterly Review.* As Stephen Spender observed, "It is as though the poem were a sensitized plate held up to a real landscape, transforming the objects actually there into poetry and creating form which is dictated by the rhythms of the sights and sounds actually present." David Kalstone contended that these are "the best poems [Schuyler] has ever written," and Shapiro concluded that the poet's "uneasy rapports with the personal, his delicate epistles, his reportage, his catalogue raisonne of the perishable, constitute paradoxically a transcendental poetry without the divine term."

In his *Village Voice* review of *Hymn to Life* (1974), Edmund White reflected on the sense of immanence found in Schuyler's work: "Schuyler senses that time and nature are always *about* to surrender their meanings, if we could only decode them, the 'untranslatable glyphs' of raindrops caught on a window screen or the gray April light that 'spells out bare spots' on the lawn. We are surrounded by the stuff of meaning but we don't know how to fashion it into explanations. What we are left with are dark and bright scraps, with sumptuous, ordinary moments."

In 1969 Schuyler co-wrote *A Nest of Ninnies* with his friend John Ashbery. There was a mixed critical response to the novel, depending on the features critics chose to emphasize. Some dismissed its plotless banality as just another attack on the vacuity of middle-class life in America. Others thought its pointlessness was the point worth stressing, finding its unseriousness an especially effective way to highlight the book's genuine concern: language. As Mary Ellmann noted in the *Yale Review,* "The real subject is expression, varieties of expression in English."

Part of the book's charm for some readers is the way two families from Kelton, N.Y., the Bushes and the Bridgewaters, live in such uneventful weightlessness that it defeats the whole idea of a plot. Nothing of any earth-shaking import happens to these people, submerged as they are in the most ordinary activities of suburbia; the commonplace overwhelms their lives. As John Koethe observed, it almost eliminates the purpose, even the possibility of characterization: "Careers of eating, drinking, conversing and marrying are pursued by the characters, who have a way of merging into each other so much that after the grand finale it is a little difficult to remember exactly what was done, and by whom, and who has married whom."

Sara Blackburn of *Nation* found it a "maddening . . . boring" book; Audrey C. Foote of *Book World* complained about its plotlessness, its mockery of suburbanites, and its lunch-counter dialogue. But other reviewers called it "immensely hilarious . . . an extremely funny novel"; "a delight to read"; "a weightless, pointless, and delightful book." Ellmann contended that the playfulness of words and expressions accounts for the book's humor and value; it is crammed full of formal discourse, archaic phrases, colloquialisms, mock-heroic diction, jargon, gratuitous French, and English idioms. She observed that "what the writers share with the readers is a fondness for every fixed form or phrase in English. It is not mockery, but a delight in the basic inanity of these forms. . . . [There is] much *bidding good night* and *bending steps* and *there we must leave them for a while.* . . . The pointless point seems to be: words are multitudinous, ridiculous, and entirely enjoyable."

In his *Poetry* review, Koethe warned against reading the book "as another heavy-handed expose of the emptiness of the middle class. . . . Not only are the people here treated with the fond acceptance that characterizes Schuyler's attitude towards things in *Freely Espousing,* but also the depiction is so realistic that it tends to deflate the myth that there is some more fulfilling way of life lurking somewhere nearby. For the disarming thing about the ninnies is that despite their apparent vacuity they live pretty much like most of us do. . . . [Their lives] suggest that the situation in which we and the other ninnies find ourselves may be either more earth-shakingly banal than we know, or an unrecognized heaven."

Schuyler's 1978 novel, *What's for Dinner?,* returns to the suburban ambience of *A Nest of Ninnies.* Eve Ottenberg, in the *Village Voice,* noted that the pervasive sense of well-being of the earlier book is not as long-lived this time around—nearly a third of the story is set in a hospital alcoholic ward—but that the new novel is still a "tight, comic" estimation of middle-class life. Once again nothing much happens in the novel, the characters are devoid of history, and life consists largely of ordinary, anonymous occasions. As Dean Flower of the *Hudson Review* observed, "Schuyler constructs his novel out of all the little rituals of polite society: having friends for dinner, playing bridge, drinking, making conversation, . . . managing an affair, minding other people's business."

The story concerns an alcoholic housewife, Lottie Taylor, her philandering husband Norris, and their lumbering, conventional neighbors. In short, Lottie undergoes detoxification, Norris has an affair in her absence, and the neighbors constantly gossip. In the end Lottie is returned to health, Norris returns to Lottie, and the neighbors constantly gossip. Almost all of the story is presented as dialogue; there is very little narration. "The characters are mere voices, but ingeniously consistent voices—they have the consistency found in life," Ottenberg remarked. "It is the surface of life that Schuyler is after; the deliberate, yammering silliness of these characters persists through the tragedies of their lives, and in the end it makes them more than ninnies and even helps them endure."

In his review of the novel, Stephen Spender found an underlying pattern to these lives that illustrates something about social neurosis in America: "Perhaps there is irony in the happy ending with which [Schuyler] provides Lottie and Norris Taylor. . . . The deeper irony lies perhaps in the implication that the circle which is the home feeds its unfortunates into the circle which is the hospital, and the hospital feeds the 'cured' back into the home." Each character is enclosed somehow in "this claustrophobic world of material satisfactions," he suggested, and none really has any idea how to break out of it without risking hospitalization or something worse. Flower concluded: "The novel offers no cures, only a skeptical picture of the enclosed self. Although Schuyler celebrates the disruptive impulses, . . . the therapeutic moments of desire or anger, he shows that in the end these amount to little more than shaking the bars of a comfortable cage."

CA INTERVIEWS THE AUTHOR

CA interviewed James Schuyler by phone March 27, 1980, in New York City.

CA: How did you decide to be a poet?

SCHUYLER: I decided to be a writer rather than a poet. One day in my tent in East Aurora, N.Y., when I was about fifteen, I was reading *Unforgotten Years* by Logan Pearsall Smith. He described how Walt Whitman visited his home outside Philadelphia when he was a child, and how one day when he was hearing the poet sing "Jim Crow" in the bathroom, the thought dappled his mind like reeds that he might be a writer someday, too. I looked up from my book, and the whole landscape seemed to shimmer. I realized that, rather than an architect, I wanted to be a writer and *would* be one. But my ambition was to write short stories for the *New Yorker*, like John Cheever and John O'Hara.

CA: So you started out writing short stories?

SCHUYLER: Yes. When I first lived in New York, in the late 1940's, I became a friend of the poet W. H. Auden, and I also lived in his house in Forio d'Ischia in the Bay of Naples for two years. I used to type his manuscripts, and I thought, "If this is what poetry is like, it is something far beyond my powers." So knowing him was both inspiring and, at the same time, as Truman Capote warned me, inhibiting. I didn't

really start writing until I was twenty-five, back in New York.

CA: What took you to Italy?

SCHUYLER: My paternal grandmother had died and left me her farm in Arkansas. I sold that. I both wanted to see Italy and also to have the freedom to write without having to hold down a desk job.

CA: What poets besides Auden influenced you?

SCHUYLER: Marianne Moore and Elizabeth Bishop very much. The Italian poet Leopardi. I wish English were as musical as his Italian, but it isn't. And Walt Whitman's "Song of Myself." Also Wallace Stevens very strongly and Boris Pasternak. But not Mayakovski. I didn't care for him. Most of all, Frank O'Hara and John Ashbery, whom I met in 1951.

CA: You've written a great deal on art. Are you a painter, too?

SCHUYLER: No, I'm not. I've made a few drawings, but I'm not a painter. I was on the staff of *Art News* for ten years as top critic. Mostly I did ephemeral reviews, which I enjoyed writing very much. At the same time I was in the department of circulating exhibitions at the Museum of Modern Art, where I organized a number of shows, only one of which was seen in New York. They were shows that circulated throughout the country and Europe. I was at the museum for five years.

CA: Is there a conscious relationship between painting and your poetry?

SCHUYLER: Yes, there is a conscious relationship. I once showed some poems of mine to my dear friend Fairfield Porter, the painter, who read them and said, "Jimmy, you're much more visual than I am." To me, much of poetry is as concerned with looking at things and trying to transcribe them as painting is. This is not generally true of poetry. As Virgil Thomson said the other day to me, "Poetry and song are about feelings." Personally, I think it's about anything you damn please.

CA: You said in one of your poems, "I don't want to be open, merely to . . . see and say, things as they are." You don't feel that poets should be expected to espouse causes?

SCHUYLER: Not at all. I think it's very rare for good poetry to come out of the espousal of causes. Milton wrote great *prose* in the espousal of causes, and I suppose *Paradise Lost* could be the espousal of Christianity. Of course, Pope espoused a very strong moral stand. But in general I don't think poetry is about that. What you get is newspaper editorials and propaganda.

CA: You're generally considered a poet of the New York School. How do you feel about the grouping of poets into so-called schools?

SCHUYLER: That's really just one way of adumbrating a small number of people who happen to live in a particular place. It could also be called "Harvard Poets and Friends."

CA: Is there any poetry criticism that you feel is valuable reading for information?

SCHUYLER: Precious little. T. S. Eliot, Colerige, the *Biographia Literaria*. William Hazlitt. Matthew Arnold.

CA: No contemporaries?

SCHUYLER: I think both Harold Bloom and David Kalstone are very interesting critics. Harold Bloom has of course written the most thorough study of my friend John Ashbery's poetry. I was quite stunned to be told the other day that he also likes my poetry, since I thought he was a one-poet critic.

CA: Aside from Ashbery, what favorites do you have among contemporary poets?

SCHUYLER: I like Barbara Guest very much, Frank O'Hara, Ron Padgett, Aline Miles, Gary Snyder, and a few others. Not a great many. Much original poetry that I read seems to be written by the same machine.

CA: Your play "Unpacking the Black Trunk" was produced in 1965. Was it part of the Off-Off-Broadway movement?

SCHUYLER: It was Off-Broadway. I guess you could call it a movement.

CA: Was it a very experimental play?

SCHUYLER: No! Not at all. Just people unpacking a trunk and commenting on the things they took out. I wrote that with Kenward Elmslie.

CA: Have any of your other plays been staged?

SCHUYLER: "Shopping and Waiting" and "Presenting Jane." Perhaps another one that I was told might be produced, but I never heard anything further about it.

CA: Were you involved in the production of the plays?

SCHUYLER: No.

CA: I hope you went to see them.

SCHUYLER: I stood by muttering curses. One of them, "Shopping and Waiting," I was very pleased with. But not the others. I also did a collaboration for music with Paul Bowles. It's not commonly known that he is as much a composer as he is a writer. We did "A Picnic Cantata," for two pianos, percussion, and four women's voices. That was recorded by Columbia Records. I did the words; it was mostly collage from newspapers. I've also done another text for music—*The Fireproof Floors of Witley Court*—which is collage out of a 1912 issue of the English magazine *Country Life*. That was done for Paul Bowles, but he hasn't set it; so I think Virgil Thomson or John Cage or George Crumb may set it.

CA: Do you write every day?

SCHUYLER: No. I just this last October came out of a four-year silence, which I think was caused by a traumatic experience: I fell asleep smoking and was nearly killed. I have rather horrible scars. Why that should stop one from writing I don't know, but I'm sure that was the cause. But now I'm writing both a long poem called "A Few Days" and a comic novel called *Heck Kelly and the Kellys of Kellyville,* which should take about a year to write. I'm planning to move to France in June—Provence. My friend, the painter Anne Dunn, and her husband have a very beautiful chateau near Aix-en-Provence. It won't be permanent, necessarily, but I'll just stay until I feel the urge to come back here, which will probably be several years. I should very much like to find a small house in Vermont or on one of the islands off the coast of Maine. The only thing that's difficult about that for me is that I don't drive, so I have to be dependent on someone else.

CA: How do you feel about the city? Do you work better away from it?

SCHUYLER: Well, I'm really happiest in the country or in a small village, but I accept the city and the many things that I find beautiful about it. I think I write more easily in the country—no, I think it's about equal.

CA: Do you revise a lot?

SCHUYLER: Not at all. Punctuation, perhaps, but that's all. I'm mystified why people have to revise. Some people really labor for hours and hours, and I can't see any difference between version one and version one hundred.

CA: Do you then have a very clear idea about what you're going to do when you sit down to start writing?

SCHUYLER: No, on the contrary. Along with Logan Pearsall Smith, I was very inspired by the American French writer Julien Green. His second novel was called *Adrienne Mesurat (The Closed Garden,* in English). He had no idea of what he was going to write; all he had was a postcard on which you could see a painting by Utrillo of a very ugly, empty suburban street. He let that guide him into this incredibly tragic novel, which is not nearly so well known as it should be. Also, I think I was very affected by reading Somerset Maugham's *Summing Up* in my teens. In that book he describes how he really tried to learn by copying out long passages of Dryden's prose. I did the same thing, only I chose Walter de la Mare and Cardinal Newman. I would say Cardinal Newman and Sir Thomas Browne are the finest prose writers.

CA: Have you done any teaching?

SCHUYLER: None. I can't think of anything I would do but read the students some poets and say try to write like them and know other poets. My friends Kenneth Koch and John Ashbery and Ron Padgett all teach their heads off and seem to find plenty to say, but I wouldn't.

CA: How do you feel about poetry readings?

SCHUYLER: I'm going to give my first this May. That took eight years of psychoanalysis. It's going to be at the Poetry Project at St. Mark's in the Bowery. I've always been shy, but somehow I've lost my shyness and my reticence. Also, I'll be reading in duo with Tom Carey, which should make it easier.

CA: When you are writing something, do you show your work to friends for their criticism?

SCHUYLER: No, never. I used to show things, quite frequently, when I'd finished them to Kenneth Koch, who would say, "It's great, but why don't you take off the last line?" And then I'd show it to John Ashbery, who'd say, "One of your loveliest efforts, dear." Mighty constructive.

CA: What do you think is the best thing about your work?

SCHUYLER: My work seems to be especially musical, and, as I said, very visual. I think that I tend to let it all hang out, if that's not too vulgar an expression. That's all I can think of to say about it.

CA: Are you involved with art in any way now?

SCHUYLER: No. I often model for my friends who are painters. I guess I'm involved to that extent. I've been painted quite a number of times. It's fun. I don't know why it should be fun, but it is. I suppose I'm a narcissist.

CA: Do you see any new trends in poetry?

SCHUYLER: I wish I did, but I don't. John Ashbery, of course, is a total innovator. He's as innovative as Gertrude Stein.

CA: In what way?

SCHUYLER: Perhaps in the abstract quality that he's able to bring into apparently logical and straight-forward verse. I'm not sure that there's a possibility of any further innovation. Where do you go beyond Gertrude Stein? And people who present empty pages and say it's poetry. I've gotten rather bored with absolutely minimal writing and painting. If I want to see blue, I can look out the window.

CA: Do you see any trends in art?

SCHUYLER: Yes. The return to realistic painting, which is fostered largely by my friend, the late Fairfield Porter. I lived with Mr. and Mrs. Porter in Southampton for fifteen years, and that was much the happiest period in my life.

BIOGRAPHICAL/CRITICAL SOURCES: Nation, April 14, 1969; *Washington Post Book World,* June 29, 1969, March 2, 1980; *Yale Review,* autumn, 1969; *New York Times Book Review,* December 14, 1969, November 5, 1972; *Poetry,* October, 1970, July, 1973; *Virginia Quarterly Review,* winter, 1973, summer, 1980; *New York Review of Books,* September 20, 1973, October 11, 1979; *Village Voice,* August 29, 1974, July 16, 1977; *Contemporary Literary Criticism,* Volume 5, Gale, 1976; *Times Literary Supplement,* November 18, 1977; *Hudson Review,* summer, 1979; *New York Review of Books,* August 14, 1980.

—Sketch by B. Hal May
—Interview by Jean W. Ross

*   *   *

SCHWENINGER, Loren (Lance) 1941-

PERSONAL: Born January 7, 1941, in Palms, Calif.; son of Ivan Franklin (a teacher) and Wanda Butler (a secretary; maiden name, Wolmuth) Schweninger; married Patricia Jean Eames (a teacher), August 21, 1965; children: John Franklin, Michael Ivan, James Lee. *Education:* University of Colorado, B.A., 1962, M.A., 1966; University of Chicago, Ph.D., 1972. *Home:* 807 Rankin Place, Greensboro, N.C. 27403. *Office:* Department of History, University of North Carolina, Greensboro, N.C. 37412.

CAREER: High school history teacher in Jefferson County, Colo., 1962-65; University of North Carolina, Greensboro, instructor, 1971-73, assistant professor, 1973-78, associate professor of history, 1978—. *Member:* American Historical Association, Organization of American Historians, Association for the Study of Afro-American Life and History, Southern Historical Association. *Awards, honors:* American Philosophical Society grant, 1978; Robert Brown Award from Louisiana State Historical Society, 1979, for article, "A Negro Sojourner in Antebellum New Orleans."

WRITINGS: James T. Rapier and Reconstruction, University of Chicago Press, 1978. Contributor of articles to history journals.

WORK IN PROGRESS: Research on wealthy Negroes in nineteenth-century America.

SIDELIGHTS: Schweninger told *CA* that her first book, *James T. Rapier and the Reconstruction,* "examines the role of Rapier and other blacks during reconstruction. I suggest

that Rapier and his Negro colleagues struggled desperately, though unsuccessfully, to bring meaning to Jefferson's words that 'all men are created equal.' His life and those of other leaders poignantly illustrate the inadequacy of conservative stereotypes in recounting the Negro in American history. Dignified, intelligent, principled, fully aware of their heritage in slavery and freedom, black leaders spent their lives trying to improve the social, political, and economic conditions of blacks in the South.

"For more than a century now observers have shown a keen interest, even fascination, in the most unique and anomalous group in the South—wealthy Negroes—yet there is no general study of this group. In the antebellum era there were rich free Negroes who lived on sprawling plantations and controlled large contingents of slaves, and late in the nineteenth century, there were wealthy black undertakers, bankers, and insurance company owners. Yet, many questions about this group remain unanswered: how they acquired their wealth, how they maintained or failed to maintain their status, and how the relentless passing of time affected them and their children."

*   *   *

SCOTT, F(rancis) R(eginald) 1899-
(Frank Scott)

PERSONAL: Born August 1, 1899, in Quebec City, Quebec, Canada; son of Frederick George (a poet and Anglican priest) and Amy (Brooks) Scott; married Marian Mildred Dale (a painter), February 28, 1928; children: one son. *Education:* Bishop's College, Lennoxville, Quebec, B.A. (with honors), 1919; Magdalen College, Oxford, B.A., 1922, B.Litt., 1923; McGill University, B.C.L., 1927. *Home and office:* 451 Clark Ave., Montreal, Quebec, Canada H3Y 3C5.

CAREER: Called to the Bar of Quebec, 1927. High school teacher in Quebec, 1919-23; Lafleur, MacDougall, Macfarlane & Barclay (law firm), Montreal, Quebec, staff lawyer, 1927-28; McGill University, Montreal, assistant professor, 1928-34, professor of civil law, 1934-54, Macdonald Professor of Law, 1955-67, visiting professor for French Canada studies program, 1967-69, dean of law faculty, 1961-64. Member of national council of Canadian Institute of International Affairs, 1935-50; delegate to Institute of Pacific Relations Conference in Yosemite, 1936; delegate to British Commonwealth Labour parties conferences in London, England, 1944, and in Toronto, Ontario, 1947; adviser to Government of Saskatchewan at constitutional conferences, 1950 and 1960-61; United Nations technical assistant in Burma, 1952; visiting lecturer at University of Toronto, 1953-54, Michigan State University, 1957, and Dalhousie University, 1969-71; chairman of legal research committee for Canadian Bar Association, 1954-56; chairman of Canadian Writers Conference, 1955; civil literaties counsel before Supreme Court of Canada, 1956-64; member of Royal Commission on Bilingualism and Biculturalism, 1963-71; writer-in-residence at Concordia University, 1979-80.

MEMBER: Royal Society of Canada (fellow), American Academy of Arts and Sciences (honorary foreign member), Association of Canadian Law Teachers, Cooperative Commonwealth Federation (chairman of Quebec section, 1942-43; national chairman, 1943-50), League for Social Reconstruction (co-founder; president, 1935-36). *Awards, honors:* Rhodes scholar at Oxford University, 1920-23; Guggenheim fellowship, 1940; guarantor's prize from *Poetry,* 1945; fellowship from Royal Society of Canada, 1947; award from *Northern Review,* 1951, for poem, "Lakeshore"; gold medal from Banff Springs Festival, 1958; LL.D. from Dalhousie University, 1958, University of Manitoba, 1961, Queen's University, 1964, University of Saskatchewan, 1965, University of British Columbia, 1965, University of Montreal, 1966, Osgoode Hall Law School, 1966, McGill University, 1967, University of Laval, 1969, and Simon Fraser University, 1980; Lorne Pierce Medal from Royal Society of Canada, 1962, for distinguished service to Canadian literature; named to Queen's Council, 1962; prize from Government of Quebec, 1964; Molson Prize from Canada Council, 1965, for outstanding achievements in the arts, the humanities, and the social sciences; Companion of the Order of Canada, 1967; D.Litt. from University of Toronto, 1969; D.C.L. from Bishop's College and University of Windsor, both 1970; Governor General's Award, 1978, for *Essays on the Constitution: Aspects of Canadian Law and Politics;* Canada Council prize for translation, 1978, for *Poems of French Canada.*

WRITINGS: Labour Conditions in the Men's Clothing Industry, T. Nelson, 1935; (editor with A.J.M. Smith; and contributor) *New Provinces: Poems of Several Authors,* Macmillan, 1936; *Canada Today: A Study of Her National Interests and National Policy,* Oxford University Press, 1938, 2nd edition, 1939; *Canada and the United States,* World Peace Foundation, 1941; (with David Lewis) *Make This Your Canada: A Review of C.C.F. History and Policy,* Central Canada Publishing, 1943; (with Lewis) *Un Canada nouveau* (in French; title means "A New Canada"), B. Valiquette, 1944; (with Alexander Brady) *Canada After the War: Attitudes of Political, Social, and Economic Policies in Post-War Canada,* Canadian Institute of Internal Affairs, 1944, reprinted, Books for Libraries Press, 1970; *Cooperation For What?: United States' and Britain's Commonwealth,* American Council Institute of Pacific Relations, 1944; *Overture* (poems), Ryerson, 1945.

Events and Signals (poems), Ryerson, 1954; *The World's Civil Service,* Carnegie Endowment for International Peace, 1954; (editor with Smith) *The Blasted Pine: An Anthology of Satire, Invective, and Disrespectful Verse, Chiefly by Canadian Writers,* Macmillan, 1957, revised and enlarged edition, 1967; *The Eye of the Needle: Satire, Sorties, Sundries,* Contact Press, 1957; *Evolving Canadian Federalism,* Duke University Press, 1958; *Civil Liberties and Canadian Federalism,* University of Toronto Press, 1959.

(Translator) *St-Denys Garneau and Anne Hebert* (poems in French and English), Klanak Press, 1962; (editor with Michael Oliver) *Quebec States Her Case: Speeches and Articles From Quebec in the Years of Unrest,* Macmillan, 1964; *Signature* (poems), Klanak Press, 1964; *Selected Poems,* Oxford University Press, 1966; (contributor) Milton T. Wilson, editor, *Poets Between the Wars,* McClelland & Stewart, 1967; *Trouvailles: Poems From Prose,* Delta Canada, 1967; (with Anne Hebert) *Dialogue sur la traduction a propos du "Tombeau des rois"* (in French; title means "A Dialogue on Translation Based on 'The Tomb of the Kings'"), Editions H.M.H., 1970; *The Dance Is One* (poems), McClelland & Stewart, 1973; *Essays on the Constitution: Aspects of Canadian Law and Politics,* University of Toronto Press, 1977; (translator) *Poems of French Canada,* Blackfish Press, 1977.

Also author of radio talks, *The Canadian Constitution and Human Rights,* Canadian Broadcasting Corp. (CBC-Radio), 1959.

Contributor of poems and articles to periodicals in Canada and the United States, including *Poetry, Northern Review, Canadian Forum,* and *American Journal of International Law.*

Work represented in anthologies, including *Ten Canadian Poets,* edited by Desmond Pacey, Ryerson, 1958; *The Oxford Book of Canadian Verse,* edited by A.J.M. Smith, Oxford University Press, 1960; *The Literary History of Canada,* edited by Carl F. Klinck, University of Toronto Press, 1965; *How Do I Love Thee: Sixty Poets of Canada (and Quebec) Select and Introduce Their Favorite Poems From Their Own Work,* edited by John Robert Colombo, M. G. Hurtig, 1970.

Co-founder and editor of *McGill Fortnightly Review,* 1925-26, and *Preview,* 1942-45. Editor of *Canadian Mercury,* 1928-29, *Canadian Forum,* 1936-39, and *Northern Review,* 1945-47.

WORK IN PROGRESS: Collected Poems; a book of essays, tentatively entitled *A Democratic Socialist in Quebec;* assisting in the preparation of a biography.

CA INTERVIEWS THE AUTHOR

F. R. Scott was interviewed by *CA* on May 3, 1980, in Saskatoon, Saskatchewan, Canada.

CA: When did you begin writing?

SCOTT: I was a late starter in the sense that my first hope was to become a pianist. My mother played the piano beautifully and I used to go to sleep at night hearing Beethoven sonatas. I guess I was about seven years old when I wrote my first poem, just a childish scribble in a book. I have no other record of anything I wrote except for a diary that my father taught me to keep since I was twelve, but it only contained the temperature of that morning, whether it rained or not, and nonsense of that sort.

I didn't actually start writing until I had gone to Oxford University. I then began writing in the good Victorian manner, following the established rules of meter, rhyme, and rhythm. I wrote sonnets. You'd think they would be difficult things to write, but I found them easy and wrote plenty of them. I didn't come across any of the modern literature and poetry that was accumulating around me because I didn't read literature, I read history. I came to the writing of more contemporary verse only after my happy meeting with A. J. M. Smith when I was twenty-one.

CA: You have said that your meeting with Smith turned you around, changed your life.

SCOTT: It changed my whole life because I obviously had an increasing interest in poetry. I came back from Oxford armed with the English classics, but had never heard of Eliot, Pound, or Hopkins. I knew D. H. Lawrence somewhat, and a small anthology entitled *The New Poetry.* I was obviously just beginning to be interested in poetry. When I showed him my first offerings from the *McGill Fortnightly Review* he told me to throw it all away; he meant that I had to get into the new groove. At that time there wasn't very much in the *Fortnightly Review* that would be considered very contemporary by today's standards. People were choosing different subjects to write about. But poetry was slowly coming free—that is to say, Canadian poetry and, for that matter, American poetry too.

CA: In those days did they talk about Canadian poetry in a nationalistic manner, as something different from others?

SCOTT: We used to have arguments in the *Fortnightly Review* over what Canadian poetry really was. And we had fiercer arguments some twenty years later over the essence of a Canadian poem when *Preview* was being edited in Montreal by Patrick Anderson, Neville Shaw, P. K. Page, and myself. We all decided quite easily that a poem didn't have to have canoes and moose in it to be considered Canadian. I suggested that if we could write about the "moose-iness" of the moose the essence of Canada might get into the poem, but not if it was just describing a moose or if it was just meant to be a symbol of Canada.

I remember once being asked what symbols first came into my head when I thought of Canada. I couldn't easily answer that. I think to me it would be something about the Laurentian Mountains. I was born in Quebec City—the mountains were only ten miles away—and we spent much time picnicing in the woods during the summers down the St. Lawrence River. My father was a great lover of the woods and of nature. In fact, he earned the title "Poet of the Laurentians" when he was about thirty-five years old. He thought I was writing extremely avant-garde poetry at that time.

CA: But you haven't stopped writing avant-garde poetry. Didn't you recently put together a whole collection of "found" verse?

SCOTT: Yes, "found" poetry is a gimmicky kind of interest. But all these things have grown out of the poetic movement of our day. I must confess that "sound" poetry does not attract me other than in the use of sound as contained in the line of words. The sound of the words is crucial, of course, but I don't think you can make a poem out of mere chanting.

I experimented with concrete poetry too. As a matter of fact, I wrote my first concrete poem when I was a young man around 1940. I thought I had invented a new form of verse; I called it "poetage," like "montage." I used to take a copy of the *New York Times* on Sunday and look for a line in dark type or something in the advertisements, and suddenly see a phrase that could be cut out and put on a white sheet of paper. It would be a phrase that, because of its magnetic power to attract like or repel unlike words, would make me see another phrase. You'd be surprised at how quickly you get excited about an idea emerging. I did six or eight of these before stopping when my ten-year-old son began producing better ones than mine. I still have two or three of them left. One was about women beginning to wear trousers.

I suppose I can be said to have written in the contemporary manner, as it were, but I don't like the notion that there is any break with the previous form of writing. I think the innovation that's likely to last is the one made by someone who knows what has been in the past, what elements are still valid, and which parts must be dropped; someone who builds on what is good and goes forward. Then it has continuity. I don't think there is such a thing as tabula rasa in the arts.

CA: What do you think about this idea of a kind of chasm that exists between the private sector of the poet—the psychic—and his relationship to society? Isn't there a kind of loneliness there?

SCOTT: I don't think so. One of my first solid sonnets, believe it or not, was entitled "To Beauty." We used to joke in the *Fortnightly Review* about the Victorian poets and how when they wrote the word "beauty" they used a capital "B." Well, I had committed that very early in my writing career. We got talking about it and decided that if you could only get to the *source* of beauty, then you would abandon these playmates of distress—that is to say, all forms of art and writing, the proof and feeble prize of unsuccess—because if you came into its presence you'd be silent. It was almost like the Platonic idea of something that you

reach out to, that all art is an effort of getting as close as you can to that which you have never yet wholly found. Maybe there is a profound religious idea, like Nirvana, in that. Although I was brought up in an extremely religious household, I'm no longer a practicing member of any denomination. I understand religion in a much more all-inclusive way. All the great religions ask the right question: "Why are we here?"

CA: Do you think that the belief in God is an incredible poetic idea?

SCOTT: Yes, but it must be something that draws you always into a deeper and more profound appreciation, perception, and questioning. This quality that I describe as "wonder" is based on the ideas of Newton. He said that he had made his great discoveries only because he stood on the shoulders of other people—others helped him to achieve the profundity of his simplicities. Then having found out these great laws, all he did was to open up further questions. Every time you increase the shoreline there is more sea to look at, more questions to ask. So instead of achieving an increasing knowledge, you only achieve an increasing and more profound ignorance.

CA: Does all this questioning make you a cynic?

SCOTT: If I understand it right, a cynic is someone who doesn't believe anything he's told or that there is anything reliable. I must admit that in one of my poems I wrote the phrase "religions build walls around our loves and science is equal of error and truth." I'm not sure that's a statement I can still stand by. What I meant was no matter how man explains an event or something in the universe at any given moment in time, there is going to be a better explanation at a later time. The later explanation will probably subsume the first and totally overcome it.

CA: You sound like a very deliberate writer and that although you may be moved by an experience you have a very deliberate purpose in mind when writing a poem.

SCOTT: I want to correct that impression because if I had been interviewed twenty-five years ago I would have been much more involved in practical affairs. I guess one gets more philosophical as one gets older. I always liked a statement I read of Elizabeth Barrett in one of her letters to Browning before they married; she said that to her, all religions were epic poetry. If you think of them as a form of poetic utterance, then you're much more ready to believe, not in the scientific accuracy, but in the process of trying to explain their position in the universe.

CA: In practical terms, how do you actually get down to the writing of a poem? Do you store up images to use at a later date?

SCOTT: If I had ever developed proper writing habits, I believe I would have written much more poetry. In the days when I used to smoke, if a thought came into my head, an idea that I felt was just the beginning of something, I would open the flap of my pack of cigarettes, write it down, and tear off the flap. I had a great many flaps.

I suppose out of every ten or fifteen things I write down, one or two will grow. I can remember Mavis Gallant saying that she always felt that the poet's brain was like a tree: every now and then a bird will fly in and sit for a moment on a branch. If you don't grab it right off, you'll wake up and find it gone—you'll have forgotten your idea. I always thought that if I had written as many poems as I have written resolutions for the Cooperative Commonwealth Federation party, I'd be far better known today.

CA: That raises an interesting question about you. As someone so involved in politics, how do you make the jump to the poetic world? Is it a contradiction?

SCOTT: Politics to me is one of the most important activities of man. After all, who makes the decision to drop a bomb? A politician. Who decides when there is going to be a war? Another group of politicians. Who decides when there's going to be a coup d'etat? Some miserable little sergeant in a regiment who takes it over, shoots all the cabinet ministers, and so on. That's how it happens. These miserable politicians have the fate of humanity in their hands. We've got to learn how to run politics in a way that it doesn't produce permanent and perpetual warfare. We haven't done it yet, but we've made some great advances and we have to keep right on trying. Actually, there are some countries where a power can change hands without any shooting. We got rid of Joe Clark, after all.

I see law as crystallized politics. In our society laws are made by legislatures. If they're not made by the legislature, they're made by the dictator and his friends and become the laws of the land, the guiding principles nevertheless. As I have said, a good constitution is like a good poem: they're both concerned with the spirit of man. The writing of a law is a creative act. It's an art form.

BIOGRAPHICAL/CRITICAL SOURCES: Poetry, February, 1968; *Saturday Night,* July, 1968; *Canadian Forum,* October, 1978.

—*Interview by C. H. Gervais*

*   *   *

SCOTT, Frank
See SCOTT, F(rancis) R(eginald)

*   *   *

SCOTT, Peter (Markham) 1909-

PERSONAL: Born September 14, 1909; son of R. F. (an Antarctic explorer) and Kathleen (Bruce) Scott; married Jane Howard, 1942 (marriage ended); married Philippa Talbot-Posonby, 1951; children: (first marriage) Nicola (Mrs. S.A.R.M. Asquith); (second marriage) Dafila, Falcon. *Education:* Trinity College, Cambridge, M.A. *Home:* New Grounds, Slimbridge, Gloucester GL2 7BT, England.

CAREER: Painter, 1933—. Writer, 1935—. Rector of University of Aberdeen, 1960-63; chancellor of University of Birmingham, 1974. Paintings exhibited at Royal Academy and in New York, N.Y. Guest on television programs, including regular appearances on "Children's Hour," 1946-66, "Look," 1953-70, and "Survival," 1971—; lecturer all over the world; guest lecturer on M.S. *Lindblad Explorer.* Conducted field studies in the Caspian Sea, 1937, Lapland, 1938 and 1950, arctic Canada, 1949, and Iceland, 1951 and 1953, with later trips all over the world. Founder of Severn Wildfowl Trust (now Wildfowl Trust), 1946; vice-president and chairman of World Wildlife Fund, vice-president and founder of British National Appeal, 1961-77; president of Wildlife Youth Service and Gloucestershire Trust for Nature Conservation; chairman of Survival Service Commission of International Union for Conservation of Nature and Natural Resources; vice-president of Charles Darwin Foundation for the Galapagos Islands and Loch Eil Centre Trust; member of Home Office Advisory Committee on the Protection of Birds

and International Ornithological Congress Committee of One Hundred; member of board of trustees of West Wales Naturalists Trust, Conder Conservation Trust, Baharini Wildlife Sanctuary, Kenya, Mlilwane Game Sanctuary, Botswana, and Ontario Waterfowl Research Foundation. President of Home Counties North Young Conservatives, 1946-47; member of council of Winston Churchill Memorial Trust. Chairman of Olympic Yachting Committee, 1948, and international jury for yachting at Olympic Games, 1946-64. *Military service:* Royal Navy, 1939-45; served in France and Germany; received Distinguished Service Cross and bar; mentioned in dispatches.

MEMBER: International Yacht Racing Union (president, 1955-69; councillor of honor), International "C" Class Catamaran Association (president), International Fourteen Foot Dinghy Association (chairman), Fauna Preservation Society (chairman of council), Society of Wildlife Artists (president), British Butterfly Conservation Society (president), Inland Waterways Association (vice-president), National School Sailing Association (vice-president), Sail Training Association (member of council), British Schools Exploring Society (member of council), Nature Conservancy, New Zealand Antarctic Society (fellow), London Zoological Society (fellow), Gloucestershire Outward Bound Association (member of council), Gloucestershire Association of Youth Clubs (president), Great Ouse Restoration Society (president), Bristol Gliding Club (vice-president), Royal Thames Yacht Club, Reynolds Club, Explorers Club (honorary member), Boone and Crockett Club (honorary member).

AWARDS, HONORS: Prince of Wales Cup for sailing, 1937, 1938, 1946; member of Order of the British Empire, 1942, commander of order, 1953; named honorary director of Wildfowl Trust; set sailing speed record in Cowes, 1954; award from Television Society, 1955; Bernard Tucker Medal from British Ornithologists Union, 1959; medal from Societe Nationale de Protection de la Nature, 1961; named admiral of Manx Herring Fleet, 1962-65; named British national gliding champion, 1963; LL.D. from University of Exeter and University of Aberdeen, 1963, and University of Birmingham and University of Bristol, 1974; medal from Zoological Society of San Diego, 1966; Cherry Kearton Medal from Royal Geographical Society, 1967; Icelandic Order of the Falcon, 1969; Albert Medal from Royal Society of Arts, 1970; Arthur Allen Medal from Laboratory of Ornithology at Cornell University, 1971; created knight bachelor by Queen Elizabeth II, 1973; fellow of Victoria University of Manchester Institute of Science and Technology, 1974; gold medal from New York Zoological Society, 1975; international conservation award from National Wildlife Federation of America, 1975; commander of Dutch Order of the Golden Ark, 1976; Pahlavi Environment Prize from United Nations, 1977; D.Sc. from University of Bath, 1979.

WRITINGS—Self-illustrated: *Morning Flight,* Country Life, 1935, Scribner, 1936; *The Battle of the Narrow Seas: A History of the Light Coastal Forces in the Channel and North Sea, 1939-1945,* Country Life, 1945, Scribner, 1946; *Portrait Drawings,* Country Life, 1949; *Wild Geese and Eskimos,* Scribner, 1951; (with James Fisher) *A Thousand Geese,* Collins, 1953, Houghton, 1954; *A Coloured Key to the Wildfowl of the World,* Wildfowl Trust, 1957, Scribner, 1961, revised edition, International Publications Service, 1972; (with Hugh Boyd) *Wildfowl of the British Isles,* Scribner, 1957; (with wife, Philippa Scott) *Far-Away Look,* Cassell, 1960; *The Eye of the Wind* (autobiography), Houghton, 1961; (with P. Scott) *Animals in Africa,* C. N. Potter, 1962; *My Favorite Stories of Wild Life,* Lutterworth Press, 1965; *Happy the*

Man, Sphere Books, 1967; (with Wildfowl Trust) The Swans, Houghton, 1972. Also author of Wild Chorus, 1938, and Observations of Wildlife, 1980.

Illustrator: Ian Pitman, And Clouds Flying, Faber, 1947; Paul Gallico, The Snow Goose, M. Joseph, 1969; Charles C. G. Chaplin, Fishwatchers' Guide to West Atlantic Coral Reefs, Livingston Publications, 1972; Jean Delacour, Waterfowl of the World, four volumes, Arco, 1973.

Other illustrations: Lord Kennet, A Bird in the Bush; Michael Bratby, Through the Air; Bratby, Grey Goose; Richard Perry, The Turn of the Tide; Countryside Character; Adventures Amongst Birds; Handbook of British Birds, Volume III; Ray Gregorson, Lemuel; Brooke Bond, Wildlife in Danger; Stanley Cramp, The Birds of the Western Palearctic; L. A. Knight, The Morlo; Nicholas Witchell, The Story of Loch Ness.

BIOGRAPHICAL/CRITICAL SOURCES: Peter Scott, The Eye of the Wind (autobiography), Houghton, 1961.

*   *   *

SCOTT, Robin
See WILSON, Robin Scott

*   *   *

SCOTT, William R(alph)   1918-
(Weldon Hill)

PERSONAL: Born May 19, 1918, in Skedee, Okla.; son of Absolem (a railroad worker) and Mary V. (a teacher; maiden name, Anderson) Scott; married wife, Wanita Josephine (a teacher's aide), May 16, 1944; children: Randy, Mike, Susan, Steve, David. Education: Attended University of Oklahoma. Politics: Liberal Republican. Religion: "Backslid Methodist." Home: 616 Jean Marie Dr., Norman, Okla. 73069. Agent: Paul R. Reynolds, Inc., 12 East 41st St., New York, N.Y. 10017.

CAREER: Writer. Also worked as farmer and bookkeeper. Military service: U.S. Coast Guard, cook, 1941-46. Awards, honors: Award from Friends of Writers for Rafe.

WRITINGS: Gunslingers Can't Quit, Gold Medal, 1962.

Novels; under pseudonym Weldon Hill: Hunger Mountain, Dell, 1955; Onionhead, McKay, 1957; The Long Summer of George Adams, McKay, 1961; One of the Casualties, Doubleday, 1964; Rafe, McKay, 1966; A Man Could Get Killed That Way, McKay, 1967; Lonesome Traveler, McKay, 1970; Jefferson McGraw, Morrow, 1972; The Iceman, Morrow, 1976. Also author of screenplays, "Hunger Mountain," "Lonesome Traveler," "Blue Light in a White World." Contributor of about thirty-five stories to popular magazines, including Saturday Evening Post and Collier's.

WORK IN PROGRESS: The Hawkins Overdraft, a novel.

SIDELIGHTS: Scott told CA: "I dropped out of the university (art school) when magazines began buying four out of five of my short stories. Now I regret the lack of a degree; I find the only jobs available are manual and menial. I prefer custodian jobs because I can work nights and write a few hours every day. I would prefer being a full-time novelist, and will be again as soon as a novel sells movie rights. Hope endures."

*   *   *

SEBALD, William J(oseph)   1901-1980

OBITUARY NOTICE—See index for CA sketch: Born November 5, 1901, in Baltimore, Md.; died of emphysema, 1980, in Naples, Fla. U.S. diplomat, translator, and author best known for his role as political adviser to General Douglas MacArthur in Japan after World War II. Sebald served as U.S. ambassador to Burma and to Australia during his years with the Foreign Service. He translated and annotated two books, Civil Code of Japan and Criminal Code of Japan, and wrote several other books on Japan, including With MacArthur in Japan. Obituaries and other sources: Time, September 1, 1980.

*   *   *

SEEGER, Charles Louis   1886-1979

PERSONAL: Born December 14, 1886, in Mexico City, Mexico; died February 7, 1979, in Bridgewater, Conn.; son of Charles Louis and Elsie Simmons (Adams) Seeger; married Constance de Clyver Edson, December 2, 1911 (marriage ended); married Ruth Crawford (a composer), November 14, 1931 (marriage ended); married Margaret Adams Taylor, March 10, 1955 (divorced); children: (first marriage) Charles Louis, John, Peter; (second marriage) Michael, Margaret, Barbara Seeger Singleton, Penelope Seeger Cohen. Education: Harvard University, A.B., 1908. Residence: Bridgewater, Conn. 06752.

CAREER: Composer and musicologist. Cologne Opera, Cologne, Germany (now West Germany), conductor, 1910-11; University of California, Berkeley, professor of music, 1912-19; Institute of Musical Art, New York City, lecturer, 1921-33; New School for Social Research, New York City, lecturer, 1931-35; Resettlement Administration, Washington, D.C., technical adviser in special skills division, 1935-38; Works Progress Administration (WPA), Washington, D.C., assistant to director of Federal Music Project, 1938-40; Pan-American Union, Washington, D.C., chief of music division, 1941-53; University of California, Los Angeles, research associate in Folklore Group, 1957-70. Visiting professor at Yale University, 1949-50; research musicologist at Institute of Ethnomusicology, 1961-71, regent professor, 1961-62; lecturer at Harvard University, 1972.

MEMBER: International Folk Music Council, American Musicological Society (founder), American Folklore Society (fellow), Society for Ethnomusicology (founder; president, 1960-61; honorary president, 1972—), American Society for Comparative Musicology (founder; past president), Gesellschaft fur Vergleichende Musikwissenschaft (chairman, 1935), American Council of Learned Societies (past chairman of committee on musicology), Cosmos Club. Awards, honors: D. Fine Arts, from University of California at Berkeley, 1968; Comendador, Orden al Merito from Chile.

WRITINGS: (With Edward Griffith Stricklen) Harmonic Structure and Elementary Composition; An Outline of a Course in Practical Musical Invention, [Berkeley, Calif.], 1916; (editor and translator) Aleksandr Petrovich Izvol'skii, The Memoirs of Alexander Iswolsky, Formerly Russian Minister of Foreign Affairs and Ambassador to France (published with The Politics and Diplomacy of A. P. Izvolsky by William L. Mathes), 1920, reprinted, Academic International Press, 1974; The Ballad of Hattonchatel (limited edition), Scribner, 1921; Systematic and Historical Orientations in Musicology, [Copenhagen, Denmark], c. 1939; (arranger) Alan Lomax, editor, Folk Song U.S.A.: The 111 Best American Ballads, Duell, Sloan, & Pearce, 1947; Toward a Universal Music Sound-Writing for Musicology, International Folk Music Council, 1957; On the Moods of a Music-Logic, American Musicological Society, 1960; Preface to the Critic of Music, Pan American Union, 1965; (with son, Pete Seeger) *The Foolish Frog,* Macmillan, 1973; *Studies in Musicology, 1935-1975,* University of California Press, 1975.

Contributor of articles on music and musicology to periodicals and encyclopedias. Editor of American Library of Musicology, 1932-38; editor of music section of *Handbook of Latin American Studies,* 1943-50.

WORK IN PROGRESS—At time of death: *Principia Musicologica;* an autobiography.

SIDELIGHTS: Seeger, one of the nation's foremost musicologists, taught the first course in musicology at the University of California at Berkeley from 1912 to 1919. That university held a Charles Seeger celebration in 1977 to honor Seeger's contributions to the field of musicology.

OBITUARIES: New York Times, February 8, 1979; *Time,* February 19, 1979.*

*   *   *

SEGAL, Hanna M(aria)   1918-

PERSONAL: Born August 20, 1918, in Poland; daughter of Czeslaw (a lawyer and journalist) and Isabelle (Weintraub) Poznanski; married Paul Segal (a mathematician), September 16, 1946; children: Daniel, Michael, Gabriel. *Education:* Polish Medical School, Edinburgh, Scotland, M.D. *Politics:* Labour. *Religion:* None. *Home:* 3 Lyndhurst Rd., London N.W.3, England.

CAREER: Private practice in psychoanalysis, 1947—. Freud Professor of Psychoanalysis at University of London, 1977-78. *Member:* International Psychoanalytical Association, Royal Society of Psychiatrists (fellow), British Psychoanalytical Society (president, 1977-80).

WRITINGS: Introduction to the Work of Melanie Klein, Hogarth Press (Honolulu, Hawaii), 1973, enlarged edition, Basic Books, 1974; *Melanie Klein,* Viking, 1980. Contributor to psychiatry and psychoanalytic journals.

WORK IN PROGRESS: Collected papers, publication by Jason Aronson.

SIDELIGHTS: Hanna Segal told *CA:* "My main motivation in writing is to share my psychoanalytic experience with other psychoanalysts and students, and to acquaint the psychoanalytic community with the work of Melanie Klein and her followers, as this is often unknown or misunderstood. I also want to bring psychoanalytic ideas to topics of general interest, such as art, and to inform the general public about psychoanalysis."

*   *   *

SEGAL, Joyce   1940-

PERSONAL: Born December 7, 1940, in Brooklyn, N.Y.; daughter of Irving (a traffic manager) and Birdie Cohen; married Robert Segal (a teacher), 1958; children: Carolyn. *Education:* City College (now of the City University of New York), B.B.A., 1960. *Politics:* Independent. *Religion:* Jewish. *Home address:* P.O. Box 29, Teaneck, N.J. 07666.

CAREER: Free-lance advertising copywriter, 1964—. *Member:* Mystery Writers of America, Author's Guild, Society of Children's Book Writers.

WRITINGS: It's Time to Go to Bed, Doubleday, 1979; (with Mary Freericks) *Creative Puppetry in the Classroom,* New Plays, 1979; *Monster Knock Knocks,* Scholastic Book Services, 1981; *The Scariest Witch in Wellington Towers,* Coward, 1981.

SIDELIGHTS: Joyce Segal told *CA:* "I enjoy writing adver-

tising copy, children's books, and mystery stories. I find switching from one type of writing to another both a change and a challenge."

*   *   *

SENGSTACKE, John H(erman Henry)   1912-

PERSONAL: Born November 25, 1912, in Savannah, Ga.; son of Herman Alexander (a minister) and Rosa Mae (Davis) Sengstacke; married Myrtle Elizabeth Picou, July 9, 1939 (divorced); children: John Herman, Robert Abbott. *Education:* Hampton Institute, B.S., 1934; also attended Northwestern University and Ohio State University. *Religion:* Congregationalist. *Office:* 2400 South Michigan Ave., Chicago, Ill. 60616.

CAREER/WRITINGS: Robert S. Abbott Publishing Co. (newspaper publishers), Chicago, Ill., assistant to president, 1933, vice-president and general manager, 1934-40, president and general manager, 1940—, editor of *Chicago Defender,* 1940—, president of affiliated newspapers, including *Tri-State Defender,* Memphis, Tenn., Michigan Chronicle Publishing Co., Detroit, Florida Courier Publishing Co., Miami, and New Pittsburg Courier Publishing Co., Pittsburgh, Pa., and chairman of the board of Sengstacke Newspapers. President of Amalgamated Publishers, Inc. Appointed member of advisory committee of U.S. Office of War Information, 1941; appointed member and secretary of Committee on Equality of Treatment and Opportunity in the Armed Forces, 1948; appointed member of board of directors of Virgin Island Corp., 1952; appointed member of President John F. Kennedy's New Advisory Committee on Equal Opportunity in the Armed Forces, 1962; appointed member of U.S. Assay Commission, 1964; member of board of governors of United Service Organizations (U.S.O.), 1965-71; appointed member of executive board of National Alliance of Businessmen, 1968. Co-chairman of United Negro College Fund Drive; Boy Scouts of America, vice-president of Chicago Council and member of national advisory board.

Member of Illinois Commission on Human Relations, 1955, Chicago National Political Conventions Committee, 1963, Illinois Sesquicentennial Commission, 1965-69, and Chicago Economic Council. Chairman of the board of Provident Hospital and Training School Association; chairman of selection committee of Health and Hospitals Governing Commission of Cook County; member of South Side Planning Board; vice-chairman and founding member of Illinois Federal Savings and Loan Association. Trustee of Hampton Institute and Bethune-Cookman College.

MEMBER: American Newspaper Publishers Association, American Society of Newspaper Editors (member of board of directors), Negro Newspaper Publishers Association (now National Newspaper Publishers Association; founder, 1940, past director, and past president), Chicago Press Club, Rotary Club, Metropolitan Club, Royal Order of Snakes, Masons, Elks, Original Forty Club of Chicago. *Awards, honors:* Mass media award from American Jewish Committee; doctor of law degree from Elmhurst College, Bethune-Cookman College, and Allen University; Two Friends Award, 1950, and Freedom Fighters Award, both from Chicago Urban League; alumni award from Hampton Institute, 1954; Commander of Star of Africa (Liberia), 1958.

*   *   *

SENKEVITCH, Anatole, Jr.   1942-

PERSONAL: Born August 1, 1942, in Beirut, Lebanon; naturalized U.S. citizen, 1955; son of Anatole V. (an engineer) and Liubov (Stolitsa) Senkevitch; married Judith Anne Jamison (an information scientist), December 4, 1965; children: Anna A., Alexander A. *Education:* University of Texas, B.S., 1967; University of Virginia, M.A.H., 1970; Cornell University, Ph.D., 1974. *Home:* 6005 Rossmore Dr., Bethesda, Md. 20014. *Office:* School of Architecture, University of Maryland, College Park, Md. 20742.

CAREER: Swanson, Hiester, Wilson & Boland, Brownsville, Tex., designer, 1967-68; University of Virginia, Charlottesville, instructor in general studies, 1969; Cornell University, Ithaca, N.Y., instructor in architecture, 1971-72; University of Maryland, College Park, assistant professor, 1972-77, associate professor of architectural history, 1977—. Visiting professor at University of Pennsylvania, 1979; lecturer at universities and art galleries; organizer and director of seminars. Guide for U.S. Information Agency architecture exhibit in the Soviet Union, 1965; member of U.S. historic preservation team in joint U.S./Soviet Union working group on urban environment, 1974; member of senior scholar exchange in humanities at Institute of the History of the Arts, in Moscow, 1977. Consultant to National Park Service.

MEMBER: Society of Architectural Historians (local president, 1968-69), National Trust for Historic Preservation, American Institute of Historic Preservationists, American Association for the Advancement of Slavic Studies, Metropolitan Washington Planning and Housing Association (member of board of directors, 1976-77), Columbia Historical Society, Maryland Historical Society, Alaska Historical Society, Sitka Historical Society, Kodiak Historical Society, Phi Kappa Phi. *Awards, honors:* Special award from local chapter of American Institute of Architects, 1975, for Old Anacostia preservation study; Fulbright fellow in the Soviet Union, 1977; citation from local chapter of American Institute of Planners, 1978, for Rockville preservation planning study.

WRITINGS: Soviet Architecture, 1917-1962: A Bibliographical Guide to Source Material, University Press of Virginia, 1974; (contributor) William Howard Adams, editor, *The Eye of Thomas Jefferson,* National Gallery of Art, 1976. Contributor of articles and reviews to architecture and Slavic studies journals.

WORK IN PROGRESS: Compendium of Original Source Material on Soviet Architecture, 1917-1932; translating and writing introduction to *Style and Epoch,* by Moisei I. Ginzburg; a two-volume history of Russian architecture from the late tenth century to the Soviet period.

*   *   *

SERIG, Beverly J.   1934-

PERSONAL: Born October 29, 1934, in Independence, Mo.; daughter of Bernard C. (an engineer) and Emma C. (a medical receptionist; maiden name, Peek) Wilson; married Joe A. Serig (a Mormon minister), December 27, 1957; children: Deborah Serig La Lone, Marjorie, Craig, Danny. *Education:* Graceland College, A.A., 1955; San Jose State University, B.A., 1957; University of Missouri, Kansas City, M.A., 1977. *Politics:* Republican. *Religion:* Church of Jesus Christ of Latter-day Saints (Mormon). *Residence:* Independence, Mo. *Office:* William South School, 5300 Phelps, Independence, Mo. 64055.

CAREER: Teacher at public schools in San Jose, Calif., 1957-58, 1969-70; Herald House (publisher), Independence, Mo., editor, 1971-73; William South School, Independence, Mo., teacher, 1973—. Member of board of directors of Harry

S Truman Neurological Center. *Member:* National Education Association, Association for Supervision and Curriculum Development, Association for Children With Learning Disabilities, Delta Kappa Gamma.

WRITINGS: (Editor) *Daily Bread,* Herald House, 1971; (with husband, Joe Serig) *Growing Into God's Love,* Herald House, 1978.

WORK IN PROGRESS: Wait, I'm Not There Yet, on learning readiness; *No Time for Tears,* on children's personal problems.

SIDELIGHTS: Serig told *CA:* "I am a teacher. Working with children is challenging, exciting, and exhilarating. I have a great deal I am anxious to share about children—our most valuable natural resource. If only I can find the time to do the writing!"

*   *   *

SEXTON, Linda Gray   1953-

PERSONAL: Born July 21, 1953, in Newton, Mass.; daughter of Alfred M. (a wool broker) and Anne (a poet; maiden name, Harvey) Sexton; married John Freund (a doctor), August 19, 1979. *Education:* Harvard University, B.A., 1975. *Office:* Pat Berens, Sterling Lord Agency, 660 Madison Ave., New York, N.Y.

CAREER: Writer.

WRITINGS: (Editor) Anne Sexton, *Mercy Street,* Houghton, 1977; (editor with Lois Ames) *Anne Sexton: A Self-Portrait in Letters,* Houghton, 1977; (editor) A. Sexton, *Words for Dr. Y,* Houghton, 1978; *Between Two Worlds: Young Women in Crisis,* Morrow, 1979. Member of editorial board, *Radcliffe Quarterly.*

WORK IN PROGRESS: A novel, *Rituals,* completion expected in 1981.

BIOGRAPHICAL/CRITICAL SOURCES: Chicago Tribune Book World, October 28, 1979.

*   *   *

SEYMOUR, (William Herschel Kean) Gerald   1941-

PERSONAL: Born November 25, 1941, in Surrey, England; son of William Kean (a poet) and Rosalind (a novelist; maiden name, Wade) Seymour; married Gillian Nary Roberts, May 3, 1964; children: Nicholas, James. *Education:* University College, London, B.A. (with honors), 1963. *Agent:* A. D. Peters & Co., 10 Buckingham St., London WC2N 6BU, England.

CAREER: Writer. Independent Television News, London, England, staff reporter, 1963-78.

WRITINGS: Harry's Game, Random House, 1976; *The Glory Boys,* Random House, 1976; *Kingfisher,* Summit Books, 1978; *The Harrison Affair,* Summit Books, 1980.

SIDELIGHTS: Termed "one of the best thrillers ever" by *Critic* magazine, Gerald Seymour's first book earned him a reputation as a fine suspense novelist. *Harry's Game* is the story of a political assassination in London and the tracking down of the killer by secret agents. The book exhibited a firsthand knowledge of British bureaucracy that Seymour gained during his years as a reporter for Independent Television News.

Seymour wrote three more suspense novels which reviewers praised for their believable characters. In *Kingfisher,* for example, the protagonists are three young "Soviet Jews who hijack a Russian jet in a fumbling attempt to escape to the

West. Instead of inverting the cliche and creating 'good terrorists,' Mr. Seymour opts for an ambiguity of characterization that is rare in a thriller,'' said Jack Sullivan. Similarly, in *The Harrison Affair* "each member of the cast down to the least spear-carrier is drawn in depth and with a high degree of plausibility,'' noted Stanley Ellin.

The Harrison Affair tells another terrorist attack: the kidnapping of an employee of a multinational corporation in Italy. The abductors demand the release of a terrorist gang leader from jail as the condition of the employee's release. But there seems little hope for the victim's safe return because the Italian government staunchly refuses to yield to kidnappers. Ellin called the book "a compelling and excellent novel which cuts to the heart of both commercial and political terrorism in today's Italy. . . . Most readers will emerge from it as I did, with a headful of troubled thoughts and the sense of having undergone a journey of discovery through strange and alarming territory.''

BIOGRAPHICAL/CRITICAL SOURCES: Critic, winter, 1975, winter, 1976; *New York Times Book Review,* October 5, 1975, October 17, 1976, March 5, 1978; *New York Times,* October 16, 1976, February 9, 1978; *Times Literary Supplement,* December 9, 1977; *Washington Post Book World,* February 17, 1980.

* * *

SHACKLETON, Philip 1923-

PERSONAL: Born November 30, 1923, in Fort Erie, Ontario, Canada; married wife, Doris (a writer). *Education:* Received B.A. from University of Toronto. *Home address:* P.O. Box 280, Manotick, Ontario, Canada KOA 2NO.

CAREER: Writer. Photographer and "merchant of antiquarian materials." *Member:* Writers Union of Canada.

WRITINGS: The Furniture of Old Ontario, Macmillan, 1973; (contributor) D. B. Webster, editor, *The Book of Canadian Antiques,* McGraw, 1974.

WORK IN PROGRESS: Historical writing.

* * *

SHAEVITZ, Marjorie Hansen 1943-

PERSONAL: Born May 22, 1943, in Fresno, Calif.; daughter of Robert Vedsted and Evelyn (Beck) Hansen; married Morton H. Shaevitz (a psychologist and writer), March 11, 1972; children: Geoffrey Hansen, Marejka Hansen. *Education:* Fresno State College, B.A., 1964; Stanford University, M.A., 1967; attended Keio University, 1967. *Residence:* La Jolla, Calif. *Agent:* Julian Bach Literary Agency, Inc., 747 Third Ave., New York, N.Y. 10017. *Office:* Institute for Family and Work Relationships, 1020 Prospect, Suite 400, La Jolla, Calif. 92037.

CAREER: East-West Center, Honolulu, Hawaii, orientation officer, 1967-68; University of California, San Diego, La Jolla, instructor in disadvantaged employee development program, 1970, director of counseling and registration services, 1970-73, coordinator of adult vocational counseling program, 1971-76, and Extension Study Skills Institute, 1976-78, director of Programs for Mental Health Professionals, 1973-78; Institute for Family and Work Relationships, La Jolla, Calif., co-director, 1977—. Director of Women in Transition, 1970-73; private counseling practice; public speaker; guest on local and national radio and television programs.

MEMBER: American Psychological Association (associate member), American Personnel and Guidance Association,

National Council on Family Relations, California State Personnel and Guidance Association, California Association of Marriage and Family Counselors, California State Psychological Association, La Jolla Farms Community Association (co-president, 1977-78), Charter One Hundred.

WRITINGS: (With Eleanor Lenz) *So You Want to Go Back to School: Facing the Realities of Re-Entry,* McGraw, 1977; (with husband, Morton H. Shaevitz) *Making It Together as a Two-Career Couple,* Houghton, 1980. Contributor to professional journals and local magazines.

WORK IN PROGRESS: Research on couple relationships, family systems, and two-career couples in business.

SIDELIGHTS: Marjorie Shaevitz told *CA:* "My practice is focused in three areas of specialization: working with women who want to gain a career direction, change jobs and/or careers, go back to school, and learn job search techniques. I also assist these women in developing better techniques for managing households, choosing child care, and other related matters. I work with adolescents on choosing and gaining acceptance to a college/university, planning for careers, and developing a program for increasing their study skills effectiveness. I work, in association with my husband, assisting couples to deal more effectively with marital issues, dual-career stresses, and other family system problems.

"My husband and I have long been interested in family systems and in using a preventative approach in dealing with mental health issues in the family. Our private practice, our consulting work with public and private institutions, and our writing all reflect these interests.

"We are continuously identifying the predictable problems of normal family systems to help family members know the differences between their own idiosyncratic issues and issues that are common to all families. For example, many working couples are unaware that *all* families in which both spouses work have difficulties over such issues as household management, the lack of time for self and spouse, and the inadequacy of contemporary child-care resources. Our book, *Making It Together,* outlines the many new issues that couples must face today and gives practical methods for coping with these issues.''

* * *

SHA'KED, Ami 1945-

PERSONAL: Born July 21, 1945, in Palestine (now Israel); son of Zuriel (a teacher) and Esther (a teacher; maiden name, Tayar) Sha'Ked; married Drora Slonim (a school psychologist), September, 1968; children: Tallie, Sharon, Eli. *Education:* Received B.A. from Bar-Ilan University; received M.Sc. and Ph.D. from University of Wisconsin—Madison. *Home:* 47 Ben Zakair St., B'nai Berak, Israel. *Office:* Institute for Sex Therapy, Education, and Research, Sheba Medical Center, Tel-Hashomer, Israel.

CAREER: Purdue University, West Lafayette, Ind., assistant professor of psychology, 1975-78; director of Institute for Sex Therapy, Education, and Research, Sheba Medical Center, Tel-Hashomer, Israel. Research associate at University of Wisconsin—Madison, 1976-78; consultant to Levinshtien Rehabilitation Center. *Military service:* Israeli Defense Army, 1963-66; became first sergeant. *Member:* American Psychological Association.

WRITINGS: Human Sexuality in Physical and Mental Disabilities and Illnesses, Indiana University Press, 1978. Editor of *Sexuality and Disability.*

WORK IN PROGRESS: Sexuality in Rehabilitation Medicine for Williams & Wilkins.

SIDELIGHTS: Sha'Ked told *CA:* "It is vital for me to encourage an open-minded discussion of sexuality in the physically disabled person and to encourage medical professionals to attend to their patients' sexual concerns and difficulties."

*   *   *

SHANKS, Bob 1932-

PERSONAL: Born October 8, 1932, in Sullivan, Ill.; son of W. Glenn and Deveta (Benoit) Shanks; married Ann Zane (a film director and producer), September 25, 1959; children: Jennifer, Anthony, John. *Education:* Indiana University, B.S., 1954. *Office:* COMCO Productions, Inc., 4151 Prospect Ave., Hollywood, Calif. 90027.

CAREER: National Broadcasting Co. (NBC-TV), New York City, "Tonight Show," talent coordinator, writer, associate producer, and producer, 1959-62; Columbia Broadcasting System (CBS-TV), New York City, producer and writer for "Candid Camera," 1962-64, producer and writer for "Merv Griffin Show," 1965-70; producer and writer for "Great American Dream Machine," 1970-72; producer and writer for "American Lifestyle," 1971—; American Broadcasting Co. (ABC-TV), New York City, vice-president of production of early morning and late night specials, including "In Concert," "California Jam," "Good Morning America," and "20/20," 1972-78; COMCO Productions, Inc., Hollywood, Calif., owner, 1978—. *Military service:* U.S. Army, 1954-56. *Member:* National Academy of Television Arts and Sciences (past governor). *Awards, honors:* Three Emmy awards from National Academy of Television Arts and Sciences; Cine Golden Eagle certificate from Council on International Nontheatrical Events (CINE).

WRITINGS: (With wife, Ann Zane Shanks) *The Name Game,* Chilton, 1961; *The Cool Fire,* Norton, 1976; *I Can Make It Without You,* Putnam, 1980.

*   *   *

SHAPIRO, Mel 1937-

PERSONAL: Born December 16, 1937, in Brooklyn, N.Y.; son of Benjamin and Lillian Shapiro; married Jeanne Paynter (in advertising), January 26, 1963; children: Joshua, Benjamin. *Education:* Carnegie Institute of Technology, B.F.A., 1961, M.F.A., 1961. *Home:* 100 Bleecker St., New York, N.Y. 10012. *Agent:* Frank Weissberg, 505 Park Ave., New York, N.Y. *Office:* Drama Department, College of Fine Arts, Carnegie-Mellon University, Pittsburgh, Pa. 15213.

CAREER: Director of Broadway and Off-Broadway shows, including "Two Gentlemen of Verona," 1971, "Stop the World," 1978, and "Bosoms and Neglect," 1979; director of plays for New York Shakespeare Festival, including "Richard III," "Rich and Famous," "Marco Polo Sings a Solo," and "Older People"; director of television shows, including "Phyllis," 1977, "Doc," 1977, and "On Our Own," 1978; Carnegie-Mellon University (formerly Carnegie Institute of Technology), Pittsburgh, Pa., head of drama department, 1980—. *Military service:* U.S. Army, 1954-57; served as Korean interpreter. *Member:* Society of Stage Directors and Choreographers (member of executive board). *Awards, honors:* New York Drama Critics Circle Award, 1971, for "House of Blue Leaves," 1972, for "Two Gentlemen of Verona"; Antoinette Perry Award (Tony), 1972, for "Two Gentlemen of Verona"; Obie Award from *Village Voice,* 1972, for direction of "Two Gentlemen of Verona"; Drama Desk Award, 1972, for direction of "Older People" and "Two Gentlemen of Verona."

WRITINGS: (With John Guare; also director) *Two Gentlemen of Verona* (musical libretto; adaptation of the play by Shakespeare; first produced in New York City at Delacorte Theatre, August, 1971; produced on Broadway at St. James Theatre, December 1, 1971), Holt, 1972. Founder of *Journal of Society of Stage Directors and Choreographers,* 1979.

WORK IN PROGRESS: A textbook on directing, with Richard Schechner.

SIDELIGHTS: "Two Gentlemen of Verona" was first produced by Joseph Papp at the Delacorte Theatre for the free New York Shakespeare Festival in Central Park. This version of Shakespeare's first comedy mixes music, humor, and a multi-national cast to produce "a wacky and wonderfully funny pastiche," exclaimed *Cue*'s Marilyn Stasio. The critic went on to note that Shapiro and Guare have aimed for "a true Americanization of Shakespearean comedy by combining our various musical traditions with our motley comic heritage and bouncing it all off the richness of our ethnic pattern." "Two Gentlemen of Verona" was so successful that it was produced on Broadway in the same year, receiving equally enthusiastic reviews. A *Newsweek* critic raved that rarely has Broadway "breathed such an air of joyous skylarking as this show whooshes in." The same critic theorized that Guare and Shapiro's adaptation reintroduced New York City "to its own piebald, polyglot dramatis personae."

Shapiro told *CA:* "I began directing plays while in service in Japan. I was a Korean interpreter and my friend across the hall was a Chinese linguist. He was directing an English language production of 'Blithe Spirit' and needed an assistant. His lead got sick and he had to play the part, so I ended up as director. This was in 1955. The bug bit. I went to Carnegie after the army and then on to the regional theatre: Arena Stage, Tyrone Guthrie, Center Theatre Group, Eugene O'Neil. I am now very interested in the training and development of new American writing for the theatre and hope Carnegie will be a good place for that to happen."

BIOGRAPHICAL/CRITICAL SOURCES: Cue, August 7, 1971; *Variety,* December 8, 1971; *Newsweek,* December 13, 1971.

*   *   *

SHAVE, Gordon A(shton) 1922-

PERSONAL: Born October 11, 1922, in Winnipeg, Manitoba, Canada; son of Harry (an insurance executive) and Edith (Francis) Shave; married Ida May Till, October 11, 1946; children: Lynda C. Shave Mulligan, Dennis, Cathy, Debby Shave Nichol, Cindy Sue. *Education:* Attended Queen's University, Kingston, Ontario. *Home:* Ste. 37, 645 West Victoria Park, North Vancouver, British Columbia, Canada. *Office address:* P.O. Box 86, 142, North Vancouver, British Columbia, Canada.

CAREER: Worked as agent at Monarch Life, credit manager at Industrial Acceptance Corp., owner of Shave Motors, Ltd., regional sales manager at King Merritt & Co., and publisher of *Tuxedo Heights Journal,* 1945-63; *Winnipeg Tribune,* Winnipeg, Manitoba, public relations reporter, 1963-66; management consultant in North Vancouver, British Columbia, 1967—. Owner of Logo Dynamics Ltd. *Military service:* Canadian Army, 1941-45; became lieutenant; received Canada Medal. *Member:* Chamber of Commerce (president).

WRITINGS: Nuts, Bolts, and Gut Level Management, Prentice-Hall, 1974. Author of "The Manager's Corner," a column syndicated by Logo Dynamics Ltd. to a dozen newspapers, 1978—. Contributor to *Financial Post.*

WORK IN PROGRESS: MBO: Gut Level or Gut Ache, publication expected in 1981; continuing research on management by objective.

SIDELIGHTS: Shave commented: "I'm a teacher of management communications and supervisory skills. The longer I stay in it the more I realize how management has centered its knowledge acquisition on technology rather than on people. In the main, managers are technicians who have forgotten the word 'man' in 'manager.'"

*   *   *

SHAW, Brian
See TUBB, E(dwin) C(harles)

*   *   *

SHAW, Luci N(orthcote)   1928-

PERSONAL: Born December 29, 1928, in London, England; came to the United States in 1953; daughter of John Northcote (a surgeon) and Gladys Mary Deck; married Harold F. Shaw (a publisher), August 20, 1953; children: Robin Shaw Schramer, Marian (Mrs. K. Kussro), John, Jeffrey, Kristin. *Education:* Wheaton College, Wheaton, Ill., B.A. (magna cum laude), 1953. *Religion:* "Christian believer." *Home:* 2N734 Wayne Oaks Lane, West Chicago, Ill. 60185. *Office:* Box 567, 388 Gundersen Dr., Wheaton, Ill. 60187.

CAREER: Moody Press, Chicago, Ill., free-lance editor, 1953-56; *Christian Medical Society Journal,* Oak Park, Ill., editor, 1967-69; free-lance editor for Tyndale House, Wheaton, Ill.; Harold Shaw Publishers, Wheaton, editor-in-chief, 1967—. Lecturer at colleges and poetry workshops; conducts study groups. *Member:* Wheaton Scholastic Honor Society (director, 1973-76; president, 1976-79). *Awards, honors:* Book of the year award from *Campus Life,* 1977, for *The Secret Trees.*

WRITINGS: Listen to the Green (poems), Harold Shaw Publishers, 1971; (editor) *Sightseers Into Pilgrims* (anthology), Tyndale, 1973; *The Risk of Birth* (anthology), Harold Shaw Publishers, 1974; *The Secret Trees* (poems), Harold Shaw Publishers, 1976; (editor) *Prayers and Promises for Every Day From the Living Bible,* Harold Shaw Publishers, 1977. Also editor of *My Living Counselor,* 1977. Contributor of poems, articles, and reviews to magazines, including *Campus Life, Moody Monthly, Decision,* and *Christianity Today.* Contributing editor of *For the Time Being* and *Today's Christian Woman.*

WORK IN PROGRESS: Another book of poems, publication by Harold Shaw Publishers expected in 1981.

SIDELIGHTS: Luci Shaw writes: "I was brought up in a family to whom words and their precise meanings were very important. Moreover, I had a British education that made the kind of demands on me which are lacking in most American education systems. Studies in Latin, French, and Greek added to my understanding of language and gave me the insight into word meaning and word play essential to good poetry. With that solid foundation, the expression of an imaginative gift became almost second nature.

"My exposure to different climates and cultures supplied me with a broad backdrop for creative and original expression. But it has been my years in the American Midwest that have given me roots and a foundation in the same way that Andrew Wyeth's art is an outgrowth of his environment in Pennsylvania and Maine. Though I have a British background I identify myself as an American poet.

"I see poets today as having an essential and vital, but often neglected, role to play in an increasingly technological world. They fulfill the function that the biblical prophets had in an earlier age. Where most scientists, politicians, business executives, and technicians in most fields, even most philosophers, are taxed to keep pace with the ever-increasing input of ideas and information, and therefore develop 'tunnel vision', unable to see beyond their own narrow field of expertise, the poet can take the broader view of a universe packed with meaning and value and integrate it, pulling it together by saying, 'Yes, *this* is like *that!*' The poet's vision encompasses the subtle correspondences and connections that link every part of the created universe with the others and with God and ultimate significance.

"As a Christian poet I emphatically reject a relativistic value system. I am convinced that everything means something, that we are all given enough intuitive wisdom to set us squarely on the road that leads to God's truth. I see Christianity not as a legalistic, obscurantist's bondage, but as a structure of archetypal significance that frees us to see clearly much as bones and muscles free us to move. It is up to the Christian poet to interpret the world in terms of these archetypes and symbols in such a way as to involve the reader both cerebrally and emotionally in this structure of significance."

AVOCATIONAL INTERESTS: Entertaining, growing and freezing vegetables.

*   *   *

SHAZAR, (Schneor) Zalman   1889-1974
(Zalman Rubashov)

PERSONAL: Birth-given name, Schneor Zalman Rubashov; hebraicized surname, 1963; born October 6, 1889, in Mir, Russia (now U.S.S.R.); died October 5, 1974, in Tel Aviv, Israel; son of Yehuda Leib and Sarah (Ginzburg) Rubashov; married Rachel Katznelson (a writer), May 2, 1920; children: Rhoda. *Education:* Studied at Academy of Jewish Learning, St. Petersburg (now Leningrad), 1907-11, University of Freiburg and University of Strasbourg, 1912-14, and at University of Berlin, 1917-20. *Religion:* Jewish. *Residence:* Jerusalem, Israel.

CAREER: Israeli statesman, editor, translator, and author. Delegate to secret Zionist labor conference in Minsk, Russia (now U.S.S.R.), 1906; staff member of Zionist labor newspaper in Vilna, Lithuania (now U.S.S.R.); translator in Zionist publishing house in Russia; lecturer in history at Jewish Teachers' Seminary in Russia; founded German Labor Zionist movement in 1916; delegate to World Zionist Congress, beginning 1921; member of World Zionist Actions Committee, 1923-51; immigrated to Palestine (now Israel), 1924; *Davar* (daily newspaper), Tel Aviv, Palestine, co-founder, 1925, member of editorial board, 1925-48, acting editor, 1931-33, editor, 1938-48; Histadrut, member of executive committee, 1925-49, member of fund-raising missions to United States, 1927, 1932, 1934-36, and to Europe, 1929, 1934-36; co-founder of Mapai (Labor party), 1929; Jewish Agency of World Zionist Organization, Jerusalem, Palestine, member of delegation to U.N. General Assembly, 1947; drafter of declaration of independence for the State of Israel, 1948; member of Yishuv Electoral Assembly, 1948, and of Israeli Constituent Assembly, 1949; Israeli Government, Jerusalem, minister of education and culture, 1949-50; Jewish Agency of World Zionist Organization, head of Department of Education and Culture for the Diaspora, 1950-63, member of executive board, 1951-63, member of mission to United States, 1954; Israeli Government, president, 1963-73, made official visits to Uruguay, Chile, Brazil, and Washington, D.C., all 1966, and to Canada, 1967. Delegate to International Socialist Conferences in Vienna, Austria, Hamburg, Germany, and Berlin, Germany. *Awards, honors:* Ussischkin Prize for *Kokhve-voker;* Bialik Prize for *Or ishim.*

WRITINGS—In English: (Translator from the Hebrew; under name Zalman Rubashov) Rachel Bluwstein, *Rachel: Poems,* [Winnipeg], 1932; (under name Rubashov) *Kokhve-voker* (memoirs), [Israel], 1950, translation by Shulamith Schwartz Nardi published as *Morning Stars,* Jewish Publication Society of America, 1967; (under name Rubashov) *Mahazir ha-atarah/Chaim Weizmann, Reviver of Sovereignty* (Hebrew/English edition), translated by Nardi, Weizmann Institute of Science (Rehovot, Israel), 1960; *Zalman Shazar, the President and the Writer* (in Yiddish, English, and Hebrew), edited by Abraham Lis, [Israel], 1969; *Farzikh,* [Isreal], 1972, translation by Joseph Leftwich published as *Poems,* A. S. Barnes, 1974; *The Book of Jonah* (Bible commentary), translated from the original Hebrew by Morrison David Bial, Temple Sinai Foundation Press, 1973.

In Hebrew, except as noted: (Under name Rubashov) *Gehn oder nit gehn tsun Tsiyonistishen kongres?* (in Yiddish), [Vienna], 1921; (under name Rubashov) *Privatwirtschaftliche und genossenschaftliche Kolonisation in Palastina* (in German), F. Ostertag, 1922; (under name Rubashov) *'Al tile bet Frank* (in Yiddish), [Berlin], c. 1922; (under name Rubashov) *Mi-Korban le-lohem,* [Tel Aviv], 1943; (under name Rubashov) *Beth Berl,* [Tel Aviv], 1947; (under name Rubashov) *Shtern fartog* (in Yiddish), [Buenos Aires], 1952; (under name Rubashov) *Or ishim* (correspondence), [Tel Aviv], 1955; (under name Rubashov; editor) *Me'asef Davar,* [Tel Aviv], 1955; (contributor) Shlomo Shunami, *Kitve Yitshak Ben-Tsevi* (title means "The Writings of Ishak Ben-Zvi: A Bibliography, 1904-1958"), Hebrew Union College, 1958.

Likhtike perzenlekhkaytn (in Yiddish), [Israel], 1963; *Mivhar amarot,* [Israel], 1964; *Mi-tuv Teveryah,* [Israel], 1968; *Le'atid ha'hinukh ha'yehudi ba-tefutsot,* [Jerusalem], 1969; *Tsofayikh tsefat* (nonfiction), [Israel], c. 1969; *Navi ba-hatsar ha-melekh,* [Israel], *Yemamah shel yam* (poems), [Israel], 1969; *Sofro shel Mashiah,* [Israel], 1969; *Ha-Tikvah li-shenat ha-tak* (title means "The Messianic Hope for the Year 1740"), [Israel], 1970; *Tsiyon ve-tsedek* (essays, lectures, and addresses), two volumes, [Israel], 1971; *Mivhar ketavim* (correspondence), [Israel], c. 1972; *Zer li-gevurot* (jubilee volume of addresses and essays), compiled and edited by Ben-Zion Lurie, Society for Biblical Research, 1973; *Ba-hatsar ha-matarah* (title means "Bahazar Hammattara: Essays and Speeches Concerning the Jewish People and Its Land, 1911-1948"), [Israel], 1974; *Livyat-niv* (poems), [Israel], 1974. Contributor of articles to newspapers and journals. Editor of *Ahdut Ha-avoda,* 1930-32, and *Davar Yearbook,* 1936-43.

SIDELIGHTS: Known primarily for his fiery orations in defense of Zionism, Zalman Shazar worked for more than sixty years in support of the Jewish national cause. As a teenager in Czarist Russia, he served as a delegate to a secret Zionist labor conference in Minsk and later lent his editorial skills to several Zionist newspapers and publishing houses. In 1907, Shazar was among those staff members of the Zionist newspaper in Vilna who had been arrested and imprisoned for their activities. After his release several months later, he embarked upon an academic career that eventually led him to study history and philosophy in Germany. He founded the German Labor Zionist movement in 1916, and at the outbreak of World War I was declared an enemy alien by the German government.

Shazar first visited Palestine in 1911 when it was still under Turkish domination. After making several successive visits, he finally immigrated there in 1924. A year later he helped found the Zionist newspaper *Davar.* Although most of his energies were devoted to the publication, Shazar managed to take an active role in several Zionist labor organizations.

He was a member of Vaad Leumi, the association that represented Palestinian Jews, and made many trips to Europe and America in support of a Jewish Palestine. Shazar also was a co-founder of Hehalutz, the European movement that trained young Jews for pioneer work in Palestine.

During World War II, the British Government increased their restrictions on Jewish immigration into Palestine. At this same time, more and more Palestinian Jews were fiercely working towards the creation of a separate state, Israel. Shazar participated in the hunger strikes protesting British immigration standards on Jewish refugees of Nazi concentration camps. In 1948, he assisted in the drafting of the declaration of independence for the State of Israel.

Shazar became Israel's first minister of education in 1949 and announced to Parliament that education would be free and compulsory. He was not, however, a good administrator, and Ben-Gurion replaced him a year later. Shazar was later elected to the Jewish Agency of the World Zionist Organization. For thirteen years, he served in its education department and on its executive board.

Shazar was elected president of Israel in 1963 and served for two terms. Although the office was mainly ceremonial, he worked tirelessly to obtain funds for struggling writers and publishers. He also organized a Bible study group in his official residence. During his lifetime, Shazar wrote more than twenty books, including several collections of poetry and essays. He wrote primarily in Hebrew, and once commented that "Zionism without Hebrew or loyalty to Hebrew without Zionism are both expressions of an infantile stage of Jewish consciousness."

BIOGRAPHICAL/CRITICAL SOURCES: Jerusalem Post, May 17, 1963; *New York Herald Tribune,* May 19, 1963; *New York Times,* May 22, 1963.

OBITUARIES: New York Times, October 6, 1974; *Time,* October 14, 1974.*

*   *   *

SHEA, Robert (Joseph) 1933-
(Alexander Eulenspiegel, Sandra Glass)

PERSONAL: Born February 14, 1933, in New York, N.Y.; son of Robert Joseph (a physician) and Ruth Dolores (Kobell) Shea; married Joyce Christine Hurley, April 20, 1963 (divorced, 1965); married Yvonne June Bremseth (an advertising executive), March 7, 1970; children: (second marriage) Michael Erik. *Education:* Manhattan College, B.A., 1954; Rutgers University, M.A., 1958. *Politics:* "Anarchist." *Religion:* None. *Home and office:* 284 Greenwood Ave., Glencoe, Ill. 60022. *Agent:* Albert Zuckerman, Writers House, 21 West 26th St., New York, N.Y. 10010.

CAREER: Ronald Press Co., New York City, advertising copywriter, 1958-59; Magnum Publications, New York City, managing editor, 1959-60; West Park Publishing Co., New York City, editor, 1960-63; *True,* New York City, associate editor, 1963-65; *Cavalier,* New York City, editor, 1965-67; *Playboy,* Chicago, Ill., senior editor, 1967-77; free-lance writer, 1977—. *Military service:* U.S. Army, 1954-56. *Member:* Social Revolutionary Anarchist Federation, Coalition Against Registration and the Draft, Richard III Society, Japanese Sword Society.

WRITINGS: (With Robert Anton Wilson) *Illuminatus!* (novel; produced as a cycle of five three-act plays in England, Germany, the Netherlands, and the United States, 1976-78), Dell, 1975; *Zinja,* Jove, 1981. Contributor, occasionally under pseudonyms Alexander Eulenspiegel and Sandra Glass, to magazines, including *Today's Health, Ampersand, Fantastic Universe,* and *TeenSet,* and newspapers.

SIDELIGHTS: Shea told *CA:* "Science fiction has always been the great love of my life, and my first published novel, *Illuminatus!,* is usually classified as science fiction, although it actually crosses genre boundaries into fantasy, political satire, and pornography. *Zinja* is a historical romance set in thirteenth-century China, Japan, and Mongolia. I am interested in all aspects of the history, martial arts, and daily life of these countries during that period of history but I haven't found this to be a difficult transition from science fiction since both categories place similar demands on the author's ability to imagine a setting different from his own."

* * *

SHEATS, Paul Douglas 1932-

PERSONAL: Born June 17, 1932, in Albany, N.Y.; son of Paul Henry and Dorothea Ruth (Jones) Sheats; married Audrey Hathaway, July 4, 1964 (marriage ended, 1975); children: Alice Elizabeth, Paul William. *Education:* Harvard University, B.A., 1954, M.A., 1963, Ph.D., 1966; Oxford University, B.A., 1957. *Home:* 406½ Landfair Ave., Los Angeles, Calif. 90024. *Office:* Department of English, University of California, Los Angeles, Calif. 90024.

CAREER: Haverford College, Haverford, Pa., instructor in English, 1958-60; Harvard University, Cambridge, Mass., teaching fellow, 1963-66; University of California, Los Angeles, assistant professor, 1966-72, associate professor, 1972-78, professor of English, 1978—, vice-chairman of department, 1976-78, chairman of department, 1978—, chairman of English Council, 1979. Consultant to President's Committee on Scientists and Engineers. *Military service:* U.S. Air Force, 1957. *Member:* Modern Language Association of America, Keats-Shelley Association, Wordsworth-Coleridge Association, American Association of University Professors. *Awards, honors:* Rhodes scholar at Oxford University, 1957.

WRITINGS: The Making of Wordsworth's Poetry, Harvard University Press, 1973; (editor) *The Poetical Works of John Keats,* Houghton, 1975.

* * *

SHEETZ, Ann Kindig 1934-

PERSONAL: Born October 8, 1934, in Kosciusko County, Ind.; daughter of Foster Leon (a farmer) and Margaret Louise (Hammerel) Kindig; married Loren Dean Sheetz (a printer), June 28, 1953; children: Todd Kevin, Douglas Brian. *Education:* Attended Indiana University, 1952-53, and Manchester College. *Religion:* Methodist. *Home address:* R.R.2, Box 101, Akron, Ind. 46910. *Office:* Akron Exchange State Bank, Akron, Ind. 46910.

CAREER: Akron/Mentone News, Akron, Ind., editor and author of column, 1962-77; Akron Exchange State Bank, Akron, marketing director, 1978—. Chairman of local Council on Ministries. *Member:* National Federation of Press Women, Bank Marketing Association, Women's Press Club of Indiana (past second vice-president). *Awards, honors:* Writing awards from Hoosier Press Association, 1968-69, and Woman's Press Club, 1970-74.

WRITINGS: Born Again ... But Still Wet Behind the Ears, Christian Herald, 1979. Author of a monthly column in *Tri State Trader.*

* * *

SHELDON, Muriel 1926-
(Muriel Batherman)

PERSONAL: Born October 16, 1926, in New York, N.Y.; daughter of Samuel (an electrical contractor) and Shirley (Gold) Batherman; married Arthur Sheldon (a chemical engineer), January 4, 1953; children: Peter, Tina. *Education:* Attended Pratt Institute, 1944-47. *Home and office:* 37 Ogden Place, Morristown, N.J. 07960.

CAREER: Helena Rubinstein, New York City, promotional designer, 1947-48; *Charm,* New York City, assistant art editor, 1949-56; illustrator and writer. *Member:* Authors Guild of Authors League of America, Society of Children's Book Writers. *Awards, honors:* Certificates of excellence from American Institute of Graphic Arts, 1954, 1956-57; award of distinctive merit from Art Directors Club of New York, 1956; book award from *New York Herald Tribune,* 1964, for *Alphabet Tale,* which was also named among one hundred best children's books by American Institute of Graphic Arts, 1964; award from Printing Industries of America's graphic arts competition, 1972, for *Hey, Riddle Riddle; Some Things You Should Know About My Dog* was included in Children's Book Showcase of Children's Book Council, 1977; *Animals Live Here* was named one of the outstanding science trade books for children in 1979 by the National Science Teachers Association.

WRITINGS—Self-illustrated children's books; all under name Muriel Batherman: *Big and Small, Short and Tall,* Scholastic Book Services, 1972; *Some Things You Should Know About My Dog,* Prentice-Hall, 1976; *Animals Live Here,* Greenwillow Books, 1979.

Illustrator: Jan Garten, *The Alphabet Tale,* Random House, 1964; "Little Overcoat" (film), Silver Burdett Inc., 1969; "Sheep Shearing" (film), Silver Burdett, Inc., 1969; "One Little Blackbird" (film), Silver Burdett Inc., 1969; Bill Martin, Jr., *Sounds After Dark,* Holt, 1970; Martin, *Welcome Home Henry,* Holt, 1970; Vaclav Ctvrtek, *The Little Chalk Man,* Knopf, 1970; Thomas Rockwell, *Humph!,* Pantheon, 1971; Ann Bishop, *Hey, Riddle Riddle,* Western Publishing, 1972; Elizabeth Levy, *Tips for Traveling in Space,* Holt, 1974; Blanche Dorsky, *Harry: A True Story,* Prentice-Hall, 1977; Deborah Hautzig, *The Handsomest Father,* Greenwillow Books, 1979; Helen V. Griffith, *Mine Will, Said John,* Greenwillow Books, 1980.

WORK IN PROGRESS: The First People of North America (tentative title) publication by Houghton expected in 1981.

SIDELIGHTS: Sheldon told *CA:* "I came to publishing primarily as an illustrator though the total concept of a book was always uppermost in my mind. It wasn't till later that I published as an author. I do wish that my writing career had developed earlier in my life. I would have delighted in exploring and discovering the world of words with my children when they were younger. Now they are grown and I can only try to recall those impressionable years and in doing so think of the many questions they asked.

"I find being an author/illustrator wonderful. Not only do I have the pleasure of visualizing the complete book, I also have the job of sharing my interests with young people as well. I can think of nothing more rewarding."

SHELDON, Roy
See TUBB, E(dwin) C(harles)

* * *

SHEPHERD, Joan
See BUCHANAN, Betty (Joan)

* * *

SHERER, Mary Louise 1901-

PERSONAL: Born November 18, 1901, in Sandon, British Columbia, Canada; daughter of George (a geologist) and Rosina (Mayhaber) Huston; married E. C. Sherer (a mining engineer; deceased). *Education:* University of Idaho, B.S., 1924; attended University of Washington. *Home:* 2222 West Lake Sammamish N.E., Redmond, Wash. 98052.

CAREER: Teacher in Mullan, Idaho, Belt, Mont., and Honolulu, Hawaii, 1926-28; Seattle Housing Authority, Seattle, Wash., in management, 1954-70; writer, 1955—. *Member:* Seattle Free Lance Writers.

WRITINGS—For children: *Ho Fills the Rice Barrel*, Follett, 1957; *Mystery of the Black Friday Mine*, Criterion, 1965; *The Secret of Bruha Mountain*, Harvey House, 1972. Contributor to magazines.

WORK IN PROGRESS—For children: *Prospecting for Gold*, nonfiction, for Atheneum; a tiger story set in Korea.

SIDELIGHTS: Sherer told *CA:* "My father wrote for technical magazines and fostered my interest in writing. My first article was published in the college paper. A deeply felt experience or contact seems to be essential when I do a book. A young Korean friend taught me much of the Korean lifestyle and lore."

Sherer lived for five years in Korea and China.

* * *

SHERMAN, Allan 1924-1973

PERSONAL: Birth-given name, Allan Copelon; born November 30, 1924, in Chicago, Ill; died of respiratory failure, November 20, 1973, in Los Angeles, Calif.; son of Percy (a race car driver and automobile mechanic) and Rose (Sherman) Copelon; married Delores Miriam Chackes, June 15, 1945; children: Robbie, Nancy. *Education:* Attended University of Illinois, 1941-42, 1943-44. *Residence:* Los Angeles, Calif.

CAREER: Entertainer, television producer, singer, comedy writer. Gag writer for radio comedian Lew Parker, New York City, 1945; wrote jokes and songs for television variety shows, including "Cavalcade of Stars," "Broadway Open House," and "The 54th Street Revue," and for comedians Jackie Gleason, Jack E. Leonard, Victor Borge, and Phil Silvers, New York City, 1946-51; co-creator of television game show, "I've Got a Secret," New York City, 1951, associate producer, 1952-53, producer, 1953-58; "Masquerade Party" (television game show), New York City, producer, 1959-60; co-creator of television game show, "Your Surprise Package," 1960, producer in Los Angeles, Calif., 1960-62. Wrote and recorded numerous song parodies, including "Sarah Jackman," "Seltzer Boy," "Harvey and Sheila," "Hello Muddah, Hello Fadduh," "The Twelve Gifts of Christmas," "The Drop-Outs March," "The End of a Symphony," "Variations on 'How Dry I Am,'" "The Drinking Man's Diet," "Crazy Downtown," and "The Mouse That Roared." Starred in television special, "Allan Sherman's Funnyland," National Broadcasting Co. (NBC-TV), Janu-

ary 18, 1965; appeared on television shows, including "The Tonight Show Starring Johnny Carson," 1963. *Military service:* U.S. Army, 1942-43.

AWARDS, HONORS: Gold album for "My Son, the Folksinger" and "My Son, the Celebrity," both 1962; Grammy Award for best comic performance from National Academy of Recording Arts and Sciences, 1963, for song "Hello Muddah, Hello Fadduh."

WRITINGS: (With Arnold Peyser and Lois Peyser) *Allan Sherman's Instant Status; or, Up Your Image*, Putnam, 1964; *Hello Muddah, Hello Fadduh!*, Harper, 1964; *I Can't Dance!*, Harper, 1964; *A Gift of Laughter: The Autobiography of Allan Sherman*, Atheneum, 1965; (author of book and lyrics) "The Fig Leaves Are Falling" (musical play), first produced on Broadway, 1969; *The Rape of the APE (American Puritan Ethic)*, Playboy Press, 1973. Contributor of articles to magazines.

Albums: "My Son, the Folksinger," Warner Bros., 1962; "My Son, the Celebrity," Warner Bros., 1962; "My Son, the Nut," Warner Bros., 1963; "Allan in Wonderland," Warner Bros., 1964; (with the Boston Pops Orchestra) "Peter and the Commissar," RCA Victor, 1964; "For Swingin' Livers Only!," Warner Bros., 1964; "My Name Is Allan," Warner Bros., 1965.

SIDELIGHTS: Allan Sherman's voice was once compared to that of a strangling mynah bird, and he often declared that his own singing was "lousy." Nevertheless, it was his song parodies that earned him a place in American memory. His most popular tune was undoubtedly the Grammy Award-winning "Hello Muddah, Hello Fadduh," which related a young boy's letter home from summer camp. Sung to the music of "Dance of the Hours" from Ponchielli's opera "La Gioconda," the song includes these endearing lyrics: "Hello Muddah! Hello Fadduh! / Here I am at Camp Granada. / Camp is very entertaining, / And they say we'll have some fun / If it stops raining ... / Wait a minute, it's stopped hailing, / Guys are swimming, guys are sailing, / Playing baseball, / Gee, that's better! / Muddah, Fadduh, kindly disregard this letter!"

Sherman's recording debut came on the tail of an already successful entertainment career. He had written jokes and songs for numerous television programs during the 1940's and then enjoyed six years in the top-ten ratings as producer of the game show "I've Got a Secret," which he created with Howard Merrill in 1951. Sherman remained on the game-show circuit until 1962, bailing out several failing programs with his production expertise and also producing another of his co-creations, "Your Surprise Package."

After moving to California to work on "Your Surprise Package," Sherman became a big hit at Hollywood parties by singing parodies of Broadway show tunes. Warner Brothers discovered his talent and signed him to a recording contract. To avoid copyright problems, Sherman recorded only take-offs of folk songs such as "Frere Jacques," "Water Boy," and "Battle Hymn of the Republic." The *New York Times* noted that the entertainer's "antic wit" transformed the "Battle Hymn" "into the saga of a garment cutter who trampled 'through the warehouse where the drapes of Roth are stored.'"

The album, "My Son, the Folksinger," was so popular that Sherman began a concert tour in 1962. On stage his act included some of his parodies of such Broadway tunes as Rodgers and Hammerstein's "There Is Nothing Like A Dame," which he converted to "There Is Nothing Like a Lox": "We got herring sweet and sour / We got pickles old and young / We got corned beef and salami and a lot of tasty tongue / We got Philadelphia cream cheese in a little wooden box / What ain't we got? / We ain't got lox.'' These travesties rankled the original composers and several threatened him with lawsuits. The *New York Times* reported that Sherman once told an interviewer, ''I'm thinking of putting out a new album called 'My Son, the Defendant.'''

With his first two albums each selling over one million copies, Sherman went on to cut five more LPs. In 1965 he also starred in his own television special, ''Allan Sherman's Funnyland.'' But because he had to tone down his usual Jewish ethnic jokes for television, the show was a disappointment to his fans. From this time on Sherman's popularity waned, and he never again achieved the heights of his ''Hello Muddah, Hello Fadduh'' days.

AVOCATIONAL INTERESTS: Golf, model railroading, photography, collecting antiques.

BIOGRAPHICAL/CRITICAL SOURCES: Allan Sherman, *A Gift of Laughter: The Autobiography of Allan Sherman,* Atheneum, 1965.

OBITUARIES: New York Times, November 22, 1973; *Washington Post,* November 22, 1973; *Newsweek,* December 3, 1973; *Time,* December 3, 1973.*

*   *   *

SHIGA, Naoya 1883-1971

PERSONAL: Born February 20, 1883, in Ishinomaki, Miyagi, Japan; died of pneumonia, October 21, 1971, in Tokyo, Japan; married wife, Sada, 1913. *Education:* Attended Tokyo Imperial University, 1906-c. 1908.

CAREER: Writer. Founder of literary magazine, *Shirakaba,* 1910-c. 1920. *Awards, honors:* National cultural award from Japan, 1949, for literature.

WRITINGS—In English: (Editor with Motoi Hashimoto) *Gardens of Japan: A Pictorial Record of the Famous Palaces, Gardens, and Tea-Gardens,* Zauho Press, 1935; *An'ya koro,* [Japan], 1922, reprinted, 1953, translation by Edwin McClellan published as *A Dark Night's Passing,* Kodansha, 1976; *Morning Glories,* translated by Allen Say and David Meltzer, Mackintosh, 1975.

In Japanese; all published in Japan: *Otsu Junkichi* (short stories), 1912, reprinted as volume in ''Shinsen meicho fukkoku zenshu, Kindai Bungakukan'' series, 1970; *Wakai* (title means ''Reconciliation''; autobiographical novel), 1917, reprinted, 1968; *Amagaeru* (short stories), 1925; *Shiga Naoya shu* (fiction; volume from ''Gendai shosetsu zenshu'' series), 1926; *Shiga Naoya shu* (short stories; volume in ''Gendai Nihon bungaku zenshu'' series), 1928; *Shiga Naoya zenshu,* 1937-38; *Shiga Naoya shu* (short stories; volume from ''Shirakaba sosho'' series), 1943; *Mushibamareta Yujo* (title means ''Worm-Eaten Friendship''), 1947; *Yuki no hi,* 1948.

Akikaze (essays and plays), 1950; *Nara,* 1950; *Shiga Naoya sakuhin shu* (short stories and fiction), 1951; *Rojin* (short stories; two volumes from ''Shiga Naoya jisen tampen shu'' series), 1951; *Haiiro no tsuki* (title means ''Gray Moon''; short stories; volume in ''Shiga Naoya jisen tampen shu'' series; see below), 1951; *Wakai: Kozo no kamisama* (short stories), 1952; *Shiga Naoya shu* (short stories), 1952; *Shiga Naoya shu* (short stories; volume from ''Gendai bungo meisaku zenshu'' series), 1953; *Shiga Naoya zenshu,* edited by Kazuo Ozaki, 1955-56.

Shiga Naoya no hitoto sakuhin, edited by Hiroyuki Agawa, 1964; *Abashiri made* (short stories), 1968; *Biwa no hana* (short stories and essays), 1968; *Haiiro no tsuki, Manreki akae* (short stories; see above and below), 1968; *Seibei to hyotan* (title means ''Seibei and Gourds''; short stories), 1968; *Shiga Naoya shu* (short stories; volume in ''Shincho Nihon bungaku'' series), 1969; *Shiga Naoya taiwashu,* 1969; *Yoru no hikari* (short stories; volume in ''Meicho fukkoku zenshu, Kindai Bungakukan'' series), 1969; *Tera no kawara,* 1971; *Kuroto shiroto* (short stories), 1971; *Manreki akae* (short stories; see above), 1972; *Shiga Naoya zenshu,* 1973-74; *Gendai Nihon kiko bungaku zenshu,* twelve volumes, 1976; *Shiga Naoya shu* (fiction; volume from ''Chikuma gendai bungaku taikei'' series), 1976; *Shiga Naoya shu* (fiction; volume from ''Gendai Nihon no bungaku'' series), 1977.

Other: (Editor) *Gendai Nikon bungaku senshu,* 1948; (contributor) Jun Takami, *Taiden gendai bundan shi,* 1957; *Shiga Naoya, Arishima Takeo no bungaku* (addresses, essays, and lectures; volume from ''Shirizu bungaku'' series), 1973; *Shiga Naoya ate shokan* (correspondence), 1974.

SIDELIGHTS: Known as ''Emperor Shiga'' to his Japanese colleagues, Naoya Shiga was a staunch individualist who allied himself to no literary school. As a young man, the author was strongly influenced by his friend and mentor, Saneatsu Mushakaji, an optimistic humanist. Though the two men helped found the magazine *Shirakaba,* or ''White Birch,'' which reflected Mushakaji's idealism, Shiga was of another mind. He observed too clearly the negative aspects of human nature to be anything more than sympathetic to Mushakaji's unwavering faith in the individual.

Instead, Shiga explored variable human psychology and conflict in his short stories and novels. One such short story, ''Kurodiasu no Nikki,'' or ''The Diary of Claudius,'' gives Claudius' version of Hamlet's situation. Another story, ''Han no Hanzai,'' or ''Han's Crime,'' is about a knife thrower who, after years of conflict, kills his unfaithful wife during their stage show. Shiga probes the thoughts and feelings of Han in an effort to determine his guilt or innocence. Even Han does not know if his action was intentional. In these works, Shiga's style is noted for its subtlety and apparent simplicity. His writing is clear, lucid, and realistic while the symbolism he employs seems uncontrived.

Many, though, consider Shiga's autobiographical novel, *An'ya koro,* his greatest work. The author toiled for more than twenty-five years to complete it. The novel loosely chronicles Shiga's quest for independence and maturity. Also covered in the book is a fictionalized account of Shiga's real-life conflict with his father, who never understood his son's desire for a literary career or his renunciation of many old Japanese customs and traditions. With the completion of this work, the author's reputation was secured. He became known as the ''Divine Novelist'' and was honored with the national cultural award in 1949. *An'ya koro* is considered a masterpiece in Japanese literature. The finishing of the volume, however, also marked the end of Shiga's serious literary career. Afterwards, he penned only occasional short sketches and journalistic pieces.

BIOGRAPHICAL/CRITICAL SOURCES: Saturday Review, December 11, 1976; *Choice,* February, 1977; *World Literature Today,* winter, 1978.

OBITUARIES: Time, November 1, 1971.*

*   *   *

SHOLOKHOV, Mikhail (Aleksandrovich) 1905-

PERSONAL: Surname is pronounced *Shaw-loh-khoff;* born

May 24, 1905, in Kruzhlino, Russia (now U.S.S.R.); son of Aleksander Mikhailovich (a farmer, cattle buyer, clerk, and owner of a power mill) and Anastasiya Danilovna (Chernikova) Sholokhov; married Maria Petrovna Gromoslavskaya (a teacher), 1923; children: four. *Education:* Attended public schools in Voronezh; studied under Ossip Brik and Viktor Shklovsky. *Politics:* Communist. *Residence:* Stanitsa Veshenskaya, Rostov Region, U.S.S.R. *Address:* Union of Soviet Writers, Ulitsa Vorovskogo 52, Moscow, U.S.S.R.

CAREER: Writer. Held a variety of jobs, including teacher, laborer, musician, playwright, actor, and journalist; worked as a war correspondent during World War II. Elected Deputy to the Supreme Soviet, 1937; member of Communist Party of Soviet Union Central Committee and of Committee for Defense of Peace. *Military service:* Red Army, c. 1920-22, served in various capacities, including journalist, freight handler, food inspector, mason, and machine gunner. *Member:* Academy of Sciences of the U.S.S.R., Union of Soviet Writers. *Awards, honors:* Stalin Prize, 1941, for *Tikhii Don;* Nobel Prize for literature, 1965; named Hero of Socialist Labor, 1967; has received Order of Lenin eight times.

WRITINGS—In English translation: *Donskie rasskazy* (short stories), [Moscow], 1925, reprinted, 1975, translation by H. C. Stevens published as *Tales From the Don,* Putnam, 1961, published as *Tales of the Don,* Knopf, 1962; *Tikhii Don* (novel; title means "The Quiet Don"), Volumes 1-3 serialized in *Oktiabr,* 1928-32, Volume 4 serialized in *Novyi Mir,* 1937-40, revised Russian edition of Volumes 1-4 published in 1953, translation of Volumes 1-2 by Stephen Garry published as *And Quiet Flows the Don,* Putnam, 1934, reprinted, Knopf, 1973, translation of Volumes 3-4 by Garry published as *The Don Flows Home to the Sea,* Putnam, 1940, Knopf, 1941, translation of Volumes 1-4 published as *The Silent Don,* Knopf, 1941.

Podniataia tselina (novel), Volume 1 published serially in *Novyi Mir,* 1932, revised Russian edition, 1953, Volume 2 published serially in *Pravda, Ogonyok,* and *Oktiabr,* 1955-60, translation of Volume 1 by Garry published as *Seeds of Tomorrow,* Knopf, 1935, reprinted, 1959 (published in England as *Virgin Soil Upturned,* Putnam, 1935), translation of Volume 2 by Stevens published as *Harvest on the Don,* Putnam, 1960, Knopf, 1961; *Nauka nenavisti,* [Moscow], 1942, translation published as *Hate,* Foreign Languages Publishing House, 1942; *Oni srazhalis' za rodinu* (novel), Volume 1, [Moscow], 1943, translation published as *They Fought for Their Country* in *Soviet Literature,* July and August, 1959, excerpts from Volume 2 published in *Pravda,* 1969; *Sud'ba cheloveka,* [Moscow], 1957, reprinted, 1975, translation by Robert Daglish published as *The Fate of a Man,* Foreign Languages Publishing House, 1957, published as *The Fate of Man,* Von Nostrand, 1960, translation by Stevens contained in *One Man's Destiny, and Other Stories, Articles, and Sketches* (also see below), Knopf, 1967.

Slovo o rodine (title means "A Word on Our Country"), [Moscow], 1965, translation by Stevens contained in *One Man's Destiny, and Other Stories, Articles, and Sketches,* Knopf, 1967; *Early Stories* (contains "The Birthmark," "The Herdsman," "The Bastard," "The Azure Steppe," "The Foal," "Alien Blood"), translation by Daglish and Yelena Oltshuler, Progress Publishers, 1966; *Fierce and Gentle Warriors* (short stories; contains "The Colt," "The Rascal," "The Fate of a Man"), translation by Miriam Morton, Doubleday, 1967; *Selected Tales From the Don* (biography in English; stories in Russian), introduction and notes by C. G. Bearne, Pergamon Press, 1967; *Po veleniiu dushi,* [Moscow], 1970, translation by Olga Shartse published as *At*

the Bidding of the Heart, Progress Publishers, 1973; *Stories* (contains "The Birthmark," "The Herdsman," "The Bastard," "The Azure Steppe," "The Foal," "Alien Blood," "The Fate of a Man"), Progress Publishers, 1975.

Other: *Nakhalenok,* 1925, reprinted, [Moscow], 1967; *Lazorevaya Steppe* (short stories; title means "The Azure Steppe"), 1925; *Sobranie sochinenii* (collected works), eight volumes, Goslitzdat [Moscow], 1956-60; *Sbornik statei,* Izdvo Leningradskogo Universiteta, 1956; *Rannie rasskazy,* Sovetskaia Rossia, 1961; *Plesums, romans,* [Riga], 1961; *Put'dorozhen'ka,* Molodaia Gvardiia, 1962; *Izbrannoe,* Molodaia Gvardiia, 1968; *Rossiia v serdtse,* [Moscow], 1975; (with others) *Slovo k molodym* (addresses, essays, and lectures), [Moscow], 1975.

SIDELIGHTS: Few writers have been more revered by Soviet officials and the Russian people than Mikhail Sholokhov. *The Quiet Don,* his epic about life in a Cossack village from 1912 to 1922, and *Virgin Soil Upturned,* his story of the collectivization of agriculture, are part of the curriculum in all Soviet schools. Sholokhov has been showered with honors by the Communist regime, including the Stalin Prize and the Order of Lenin. In 1955 his fiftieth birthday was declared a national celebration. But Sholokhov's fame extends far beyond the borders of the Soviet Union. His works have been translated into more than forty languages and have sold millions of copies. In recognition of "the artistic power and integrity with which, in his epic of the Don, Sholokhov has given expression to the history of the Russian people," the Swedish Academy awarded him the Nobel Prize for literature in 1965.

Despite these laurels, in the 1960's Sholokhov came under increasing attack by liberal Russian intellectuals and Western observers. Some critics have accused him of being nothing more than an apologist for Communism. Others have even gone so far as to suggest that *The Quiet Don* was plagiarized. Although there has been a tendency to portray Sholokhov in black-and-white terms, he is, as Alexander Werth pointed out, "an extremely puzzling man." Sholokhov has ardently defended the concept of socialist realism, which holds that the purpose of art is to glorify socialism, even though his own work has not always been acceptable to government censors. He has repeatedly declared his loyalty to the Soviet regime, but on occasion has criticized authorities.

If this "extremely puzzling man" is ever to be understood, an examination of his background is essential. He was born on a farm not far from the river Don. This region was dominated by the Cossacks, a privileged group of people who were required to serve in the Russian Army and who were often used by the czar to suppress revolutionary movements. Sholokhov's father, Alexander Mikhailovich Sholokhov, was an "outlander" whose family had moved to Veshenskaya from the Ryazan region near Moscow. His mother, Anastasiya Danilovna Chernikova, was half-Turkish and half-Cossack. While working as a maid in the Sholokhov household, she met and fell in love with the young Alexander Mikhailovich. When she discovered she was pregnant, the older Sholokhovs were so dismayed by the prospect of their son wedding a peasant that they quickly married the servant girl off to an elderly Cossack officer. Not one to be thwarted by his parents, Alexander Mikhailovich collected his inheritance, purchased his own house, and hired Anastasiya Danilovna as his servant.

Since her legal husband was a Cossack, when she gave birth to Mikhail in 1905 he inherited all the rights and privileges of the Cossacks. When the old man died in 1912, however,

Anastasiya Danilovna and Alexander Mikhailovich were officially married. This act meant that Mikhail lost his Cossack status. "What problems this may have caused a seven-year-old boy we do not know," D. H. Stewart noted, "though echoes of traumatic discomfiture can be detected in Sholokhov's early stories about children. The crucial fact is that Sholokhov lacked full Cossack status."

Although Sholokhov's father had received little schooling, he was a well-read man. In contrast, his mother was illiterate. It was only after her son was sent away to school that she learned to read and write, for she wanted to keep in contact with him. Sholokhov attended public school in Boguchar, Voronezh Province, but was forced to leave school because of the German invasion. Upon his return home, he devoted much of his time to reading. Despite the fact that the area he was living in was dominated by the Whites, he began to develop a sympathy for the revolutionary movement. At the age of fifteen he went to work for the Revolutionary Committee. He performed a variety of tasks, including writing and acting in plays and establishing a collective youth theatre at Veshenskaya. For a time he served as a machine gunner with a Red Army supply detachment, hunting down kulaks (anti-Bolshevik farmers) and White Guards.

In 1922 Sholokhov went to Moscow to resume his education. While he was in that city he came under the tutelage of writers Ossip Brik and Viktor Shklovsky, and his essays and short stories began to appear in print. He returned to Veshenskaya in 1923 to marry Maria Gromoslavskaya, the daughter of a clerk in a Cossack regiment. After living for a short time in Moscow, the couple settled down in the Don Region, where they have lived ever since. Sholokhov found living on his native turf to be much more conducive to his writing than big-city life. He distrusted the urban intellectuals whom he had met in Moscow; besides, he had already determined that his literary creations would deal with the people of the Don Region. "I wanted," he later recalled, "to write about the people among whom I was born and whom I knew."

This regional interest is reflected in his first two books, *Tales of the Don* and *The Azure Steppe,* both of which were published in 1925. In retrospect, some critics have discerned in these short story collections the same qualities that distinguish Sholokhov's subsequent work. For instance, Marc Slonim remarked: "'Tales of the Don' contains all the elements that later made Sholokhov a master of representational narrative; tense dramatic plots, fresh landscape, catching humor and a racy, uninhibited popular idiom. It is true that they are lacking in depth and character portrayal, but these primitive stories about primitive men are interesting as a document of an unsettled time, and they offer revealing material about the origins of an important Soviet writer." Commenting on the stories in *The Azure Steppe,* Ernest J. Simmons declared that "we see in embryo in these early tales the future powerful psychological realist as he creates characters and bold, dramatic situations."

In October of 1925, when he was only twenty-one, Sholokhov began writing his masterpiece, *The Quiet Don,* a work that took him nearly fourteen years to complete. From 1925 to 1930 he worked on *The Quiet Don* almost constantly. In order to collect material for his book, he examined documents in the archives in Moscow and Rostov, listened to the tales of his Don Cossack neighbors, and read newspapers from the Czarist era. The first two segments of *The Quiet Don* were published serially in *Oktiabr* in 1928 and 1929. Because of objections by Communist officials that the book was not sufficiently proletarian in outlook, publication

ceased in April of 1929. It did not resume until 1932, when Sholokhov gained full membership into the Communist party. At this time the novelist became increasingly involved with public affairs. This new demand on his time, coupled with further censorship problems, delayed the publication of the final installment of *The Quiet Don* until 1940. *The Quiet Don* was published in English in two parts: *And Quiet Flows the Don* and *The Don Flows Home to the Sea.*

Sholokhov's epic portrays the life of the Don Cossacks during World War I and the Bolshevik Revolution. Because of the book's huge cast of characters and panoramic sweep, some critics have termed it "Tolstoian." The central figure in the story is Gregor Melekhov, a young Cossack so beset by conflicting loyalties that he comes to believe that all is meaningless. Most Western critics feel that *The Quiet Don* demonstrates the principle of historical inevitability, in which people must either adapt to or be destroyed by historical forces. Rufus W. Mathewson, for instance, commented that the theme of *The Quiet Don* is that "private moral judgment is sometimes irrelevant to the higher struggles of historical forces, and . . . in this fact there is genuine human tragedy."

Sholokhov's deep feeling for the land and for the people of the Don Region is evident throughout *The Quiet Don.* The book is filled with lyrical descriptions of nature. "Of the Russian authors I have read, Sholokhov is almost the only one with a highly developed sense of locality," Malcolm Cowley asserted in an article for the *New Republic.* He went on: "But besides his sense of locality, he also has a sense of people that is somewhat commoner in Russian fiction, though rare enough in the literature of any country. He writes about them as if he had always known and loved them and wanted the outside world to understand just why they acted as they did." Numerous critics describe Sholokhov's characters as primitive, and many feel that he excels at describing the instinctual urges of people rather than in capturing psychological depth. Helen Muchnic, for example, held that "the primitive, the naive, the elemental are his [Sholokhov's] province: palpable matter, physical actions, simple feelings; the impact of a blow, the reflex of anger, the surging of lust; and also sentiment, gentleness."

One of the most striking characteristics of *The Quiet Don* is its dispassionate objectivity. Sholokhov's allegiance to the Communist party, Slonim pointed out, "did not affect his artistic integrity and his objectivity in description. . . . *The Quiet Don* told a story of nation-wide significance. . . . Sholokhov never subordinated these stories to his political ideas, never used his plot to drive a point home." Simmons also remarked upon the lack of political posturing in *The Quiet Don:* "*The Quiet Don* . . . represents with near perfection that fusion of traditional Russian realism with Soviet socialist realism, and was written by a Communist who, because of his artistic integrity, all but refused to sacrifice either the logic of his design or—in the Tolstoyan sense—the truth of his hero to extraneous demands of Party doctrine. If there is any point in the old cliche that all literature is propaganda, but not all propaganda is literature, then it may be said that propaganda is brilliantly sublimated in *The Quiet Don.*"

Between the publication of the third and fourth volumes of *The Quiet Don,* Sholokhov began work on *Virgin Soil Upturned.* This novel tells the story of the efforts to organize collective farming in the Cossack village of Gremyachy Log. Sholokhov had witnessed both the virtues and the drawbacks of this system in his own village of Veshenskaya. In 1933 he had become so incensed at some of the injustices perpetrated against the Cossack farmers that he wrote a letter of complaint to Stalin. Later, in 1937 and 1938, he displayed a similar courage when he helped reinstate some local Communist officials who had been wrongfully convicted.

In Volume I of *Virgin Soil Upturned,* as in his personal life, Sholokhov had the courage to point out both the pros and cons of collective farming. In this book, a critic for the *Saturday Review* wrote, "the artist in Sholokhov triumphs over the propagandist, for not only are we presented with the wonderfully sympathetic picture of the Cossacks' love for their land and their fierce determination to acquire it for themselves, but the absurdities of the whole Soviet mechanising system and the stupidities of its officials are relentlessly exposed with an audacity that is almost incredible." The explanation for Sholokhov's audacity, Mihajlo Mihajlov observed, "lies in the fact that Sholokhov had been dedicated to the Party heart and soul all his life and was a true believer in Communism, just like the people who crucified Russia, and he could therefore allow himself to depict reality much more truthfully than those who did not share his belief. He described reality honestly because he believed that in spite of all sacrifices the imposed collectivization would benefit Russia in the long run."

In Volume II of *Virgin Soil Upturned* (published in the United States as *Harvest on the Don*), the propaganda is much more overt. More than twenty-five years elapsed between the publication of the first and second volumes, and rumors circulated that the reason for the long delay in publication was that Sholokhov had been fighting with Communist censors about the conclusion of the novel. When the final installment of *Virgin Soil Upturned* appeared in *Pravda* in February of 1960, Sholokhov denied that he had changed the ending to conform with the party line. Many American critics, however, complained about the book's rigid adherence to Communist dogma, and several felt that he had let ideological considerations take precedence over artistic integrity. Anthony West asserted in the *New Yorker* that "it is all too clear in 'Harvest on the Don' that Sholokhov's gifts have been eroded by a lifetime in a literary world ruled by the inevitably second-rate utilitarian aesthetics that fosters this kind of thing. His intuitive grasp of what writing can and should be . . . has deserted him, and he now alternates uneasily between broad vulgarities and parodies of the official style."

Despite *Harvest on the Don*'s bias, commentators did find much of merit in the book. Its warmth, humor, and powerful evocation of the Russian landscape were widely praised. Many critics valued it as a realistic portrayal of an important period in Soviet history. "To Americans its slant may seem rather obvious and its view of good men and bad men ingenuous, but it should still be recognized as the most intimate and vivid record of Russian rural life during the most momentous social change of our time," Milton Rugoff contended. Similarly, George Reavey maintained that "I know of no better account in fiction of this period of 'enforced civil war.'"

In *They Fought for Their Country,* Sholokhov set out to give a fictional account of the Soviet people's valiant struggles during the German invasion of World War II. Sholokhov had ample opportunity to observe the war effort, for he served as a correspondent on the front lines. Volume I of *They Fought for Their Country,* published in 1943, describes the Russian retreat in the Don area. Further installments of the novel were not published until 1969, when excerpts began to appear in *Pravda.* At that time it was announced that Volume II would be published shortly, but it has never appeared. The excerpts in *Pravda* contained an unfavorable depiction of Stalin's capacity as a wartime leader, and some observers believe that the complete book was never published because of this negative portrait.

In his well-known short story, "The Fate of a Man," Sholokhov again dramatizes the heroism of the Russian people during World War II. The protagonist of the story, Andrei Sokolov, is a Soviet soldier who escapes from a Nazi prison camp. He returns home only to discover that his entire family has been killed in the fighting. His sole consolation is the war orphan whom he adopts. Muchnic described "The Fate of a Man" as "a story of physical endurance and spiritual fortitude, and so long as memory lasts, no one is likely to question that Andrei Sokolov is a typical example, not an exception, of that stoic Russian heroism which roused the world's admiration in the great sieges and defenses of World War II." Although some critics complained about the Communist dogma contained in the story, most readers found the tale sentimental but moving. E. J. Czerwinski noted that the story "adheres to all the strictures of Socialist Realism and yet somehow manages to overcome the handicaps that such a narrow artistic policy forces upon a work of art."

Aside from "The Fate of a Man" and Volume II of *Virgin Soil Upturned,* Sholokhov has published very little since the war. Indeed, he has never been able to match his years of great creativity between 1925 and 1930. One reason for his scanty output is the active role he has played in the Communist party. "I am first and foremost a Communist; only thereafter am I a writer," Sholokhov once declared. Sholokhov was elected to the Supreme Soviet in 1937 and in 1939 became a member of the Academy of Sciences. Over the years he has frequently been called upon to make public appearances and to write propaganda pieces for the government, and as a result the time that he has devoted to literary pursuits has been limited.

Another reason for Sholokhov's relative silence in the past four decades has been censorship problems. Despite his avowal that he is "first and foremost a Communist," Sholokhov has often quarreled with censors when they attempted to inject political messages into his literary work. In the 1930's he was compelled by censors to make many revisions in the original text of *The Quiet Don.* In an edition that was published in 1953, the novel was revised extensively to adhere more closely to the Communist party line. It is not clear whether this bowdlerized version was prepared with the approval of Sholokhov, however. In 1956, after Stalin's death, a new edition of *The Quiet Don* came out, similar in nearly every way to the original. As mentioned previously, there are also reports that Sholokhov had difficulties getting *Harvest on the Don* and *They Fought for Their Country* past government censors.

Whatever difficulties Sholokhov may have had with censors in private, publicly he stoutly denies allegations that he has had to alter his work. In 1965, when asked about literary freedom in the Soviet Union, he asserted: "No one is being prevented from writing anything he wants to. The only problem is how to write it and for what purpose. There is a way of writing everything honestly. I stand for those writers who look honestly into the face of Soviet power and publish their works here and not abroad." Although there is evidence that Sholokhov has often chafed under the bonds of socialist realism, he has publicly averred that he is a supporter of that doctrine. In his Nobel Prize acceptance speech, he extolled socialist realism because "it expresses a philosophy of life that accepts neither a turning away from the world nor a flight from reality, a philosophy that enables one to comprehend goals that are dear to the hearts of millions of people and to light up their path in the struggle.''

Those writers who have refused to deal with Soviet authorities or who have eschewed the doctrine of socialist realism have earned Sholokhov's unending scorn. He vilified Boris Pasternak as ''a poet for old maids'' and a ''hermit crab.'' In 1966, after a celebrated trial in which Andrei Sinyavsky and Yuri Daniel were convicted of publishing anti-Soviet propaganda abroad, he delivered an address before the twenty-third congress of the Communist party in which he insinuated that the two writers should have been summarily shot rather than sentenced to prison terms. More recently, he described Aleksandr Solzhenitsyn as a ''Colorado beetle'' who should be exterminated. He has also castigated Andrei Voznesensky and Yevgeny Yevtushenko for criticizing Soviet society in their poetry and for taking trips to the United States to recite their works.

Sholokhov's criticism of his fellow writers has aroused the anger of many literary figures on both sides of the Iron Curtain. After his attack on Sinyavsky and Daniel, Soviet writer Lydia Chukovskaya wrote a scathing open letter to him in which she accused him of literary sterility. In an even more vociferous attack, Solzhenitsyn denounced Sholokhov as a plagiarist. Specifically, he charged that *The Quiet Don* was actually written by Fyodor Kryukov, a Cossack who had served with the Whites during the Civil War. After Kryukov died in 1920, Solzhenitsyn maintained, Sholokhov got his hands on the manuscript, added some sections sympathetic to the Communist cause, and then passed it off as his own.

Solzhenitsyn's charges are nothing new. Rumors began circulating that Sholokhov plagiarized *The Quiet Don* as early as 1928. In 1977 Roy Medvedev wrote a study of the case, *Problems in the Literary Biography of Mikhail Sholokhov.* Among the arguments that Medvedev cites as evidence that Sholokhov was not the sole author of *The Quiet Don* are his young age when he began writing the novel, the low level of his succeeding work, and the humanism displayed in *The Quiet Don* (which Medvedev thinks Sholokhow has never personally demonstrated). Other commentators have suggested that Sholokhov may have used Kryukov's manuscript as source material, but that he reworked it into his own novel. It is unlikely that the issue will ever be resolved. The original manuscript of the book was destroyed during a German bombing raid in World War II, so it can provide no clues for investigators. Sholokhov has always dismissed charges of plagiarism as nonsense.

Assaults on Sholokhov's character tend to depict him as a man who once had the courage to fight for his art, but who in old age has become little more than a bloody-minded party hack. But to dismiss Sholokhov as a toady is too simplistic. Striving to explain the many contradictions in this bewildering man, Stewart pointed out: ''Sholokhov's relationship with Communism was symbiotic—if not altogether healthy for his art. They share the same impulse to glorify 'mankind' just as they share a purely aesthetic disinterestedness about the fate of individuals. This is perhaps why they can be sentimentally humanitarian one moment but adamantly cruel the next. During the time when Sholokhov achieved equilibrium between the two, his artistic impulse balanced his Communist allegiance and he composed his one masterpiece, *The Quiet Don.* . . . The difficulties he overcame no less than the form his art took made Sholokhov the best example of the virtues and limitations of Soviet literature as a whole during its first fifty years—from epic heroism to drudgery.''

The Quiet Don, Virgin Soil Upturned, and ''The Fate of a Man'' have all been produced as motion pictures. Ivan Dzerzhinsky has written operas based on *The Quiet Don* and *Virgin Soil Upturned. Virgin Soil Upturned* has also been dramatized as a four-act play.

AVOCATIONAL INTERESTS: Fishing, hunting, breeding cattle.

BIOGRAPHICAL/CRITICAL SOURCES—Selected periodicals: *Books Abroad,* autumn, 1933, winter, 1967, spring, 1971; *Times Literary Supplement,* April 5, 1934, October 5, 1940, November 4, 1960, December 1, 1961, February 16, 1967; *Spectator,* April 6, 1934, October 11, 1935, October 18, 1940; *Books,* July 1, 1934, August 3, 1941; *New York Herald Tribune,* July 3, 1934; *Saturday Review of Literature,* July 7, 1934, August 9, 1941; *Nation,* July 11, 1934, August 16, 1941; *New Republic,* August 15, 1934, December 25, 1935, August 18, 1941, May 8, 1961; *Saturday Review,* October 26, 1935; *New York Times,* November 10, 1935, August 3, 1941, March 4, 1962, April 2, 1966, October 16, 1965, December 1, 1965, December 10, 1965, December 11, 1965, May 27, 1969, June 25, 1970; *Christian Science Monitor,* November 20, 1935, February 23, 1961; *New Yorker,* August 9, 1941, April 29, 1961; *Yale Review,* autumn, 1941; *Soviet Literature,* August, 1948, September, 1963.

Thought, spring, 1951; *Russian Review,* April, 1957; *New Statesman,* October 29, 1960, May 6, 1977; *Columbia University Forum,* winter, 1961; *Saturday Review,* February 18, 1961, February 24, 1962, June 17, 1967; *New York Times Book Review,* February 19, 1961, March 4, 1962, March 5, 1967, August 20, 1967; *Time,* February 24, 1961, September 16, 1974; *Atlantic Monthly,* March, 1961; *Survey,* April-June, 1961; *Commonweal,* May 11, 1962, October 20, 1967; *Slavic Review,* September, 1964; *Observer Review,* February 5, 1967; *London Magazine,* April, 1967; *Book Week,* May 7, 1967; *New York Review of Books,* June 15, 1967; *Books and Bookmen,* November, 1977; *World Literature Today,* Winter, 1978.

Selected books: Marc Slonim, editor, *Modern Russian Literature: From Chekhov to the Present,* Oxford University Press, 1953; Ernest J. Simmons, *Russian Fiction and Soviet Ideology: Introduction to Fedin, Leonov, and Sholokhov,* Columbia University Press, 1958; Rufus W. Mathewson, Jr., *The Positive Hero in Russian Literature,* Columbia University Press, 1958, 2nd edition, Stanford University Press, 1975; Helen Muchnic, *From Gorky to Pasternak,* Random, 1961; Olga Carlisle, *Voices in the Snow,* Random, 1962; Vera Alexandrova, *A History of Soviet Literature,* translated by Mirra Ginsburg, Doubleday, 1963; Max Hayward and Edward L. Crowley, editors, *Soviet Literature in the Sixties,* Praeger, 1964; Ernest J. Simmons, *Introduction to Russian Realism,* Indiana University Press, 1965; D. H. Stewart, *Mikhail Sholokhov: A Critical Introduction,* University of Michigan Press, 1967; Mihajlo Mihajlov, *Russian Themes,* Farrar, Straus, 1968; Michael Klimenko, *World of Young Sholokhov: Vision of Violence,* Christopher Publishing House, 1972; Roy A. Medvedev, *Problems in the Literary Biography of Mikhail Sholokhov,* Cambridge University Press, 1977; *Contemporary Literary Criticism,* Volume 7, Gale, 1977.*

—*Sketch by Ann F. Ponikvar*

*   *   *

SHREVE, L(evin) G(ale) 1910-

PERSONAL: Born February 17, 1910, in Baltimore, Md.; son of Arthur Lee (a civil engineer) and Harriet Rebekah (Gale) Shreve; married Barbara Harris, June 27, 1935. *Edu-*

cation: Johns Hopkins University, A.B., 1932. *Religion:* Episcopalian. *Home:* 101 Goodale Rd., Baltimore, Md. 21212. *Agent:* Eleanor Merryman Roszel, 1710 Bolton St., Baltimore, Md. 21217.

CAREER: Worked variously as government employee and in banking, 1932-41; Counsel Services, Inc. (public relations agency), Baltimore, Md., president, 1946-50; Central Intelligence Agency, Washington, D.C., intelligence officer, 1950-70; First National Bank of Maryland, Baltimore, officer, 1970-72; writer, 1972—. *Military service:* U.S. Army Reserve, 1932-63; served in South Pacific and China Theaters; worked on U.S. Army publications, *South Pacific Daily News* and *Stars and Stripes;* became lieutenant colonel; received Army Commendation Ribbon with Oak Leaf Cluster, Bronze Star with Oak Leaf Cluster, and Air Medal. *Member:* Maryland Historical Society, Maryland Club (president, 1976-80), Society for the Preservation of Maryland Antiques, Metropolitan Club (Washington, D.C.), Hamilton Street Club, Howard County Hunt, Alpha Delta Phi.

WRITINGS: A National Program of Social Education For the Republic of China (monograph), Ministry of Education, 1946; *The Phoenix With Oil Feathers* (novel), Moore Publishing, 1980. Contributor of reviews to *Baltimore News American* and *Baltimore Evening Sun.*

WORK IN PROGRESS: A biography of Tench Tilghman, aide-de-camp to General George Washington, publication expected in 1981 or 1982; another novel.

SIDELIGHTS: L. G. Shreve told *CA:* "I think I always wanted to write, an ambition accentuated by winning a prize in a short-story contest while in preparatory school. The compelling necessity of making a living after graduating from college in the depths of the Depression, however, led me to other pursuits where the financial rewards were more promising. At age sixty two and financially secure, I finally started down the road to the realization of a life-long goal. I remember the day well. Fifteen minutes after quitting my job, which took place early on a Friday afternoon, I was hard at it, yellow pad and pencil in hand. I've been at it ever since and intend to continue indefinitely. I've got enough material backed up, including parts of three separate novels, to keep me going until the last horn blows.

"By far the most interesting and rewarding period of my life was my long service with the Central Intelligence Agency (CIA). I started working for the agency early on, surviving the lean years when government salaries were not exactly golden. The psychiatric income was very high, however, and more than compensated for the loss of dollars. Moreover, in a sort of 'Catch 22' situation, the experience provided me with a wealth of background material which would have been denied me if I had set out earlier in life to be a full-time writer. In the CIA a lot of reporting must be done by officers in the field. In the course of twenty years or more I must have written the equivalent of ten novels on the whole range of esoteric stuff attributed, rightly or wrongly, to intrigue and espionage.

"After I had recovered from the initial euphoria induced by the publication and surprisingly high sales of my first novel, *The Phoenix With Oily Feathers,* and after a flurry of guest spots on radio and television talk shows featuring me as a late-blooming author, I found myself mouthing a gaggle of self-evident truths. Among these pearls of wisdom were such hackneyed statements as: 'First novels by unknown authors are a drug on the market and harder to get published than getting that first olive out of the bottle'; or 'Novels are not written, they're rewritten.' Writing a novel, or any other

major work, is extremely hard work; the fun comes only when you're finished. Any honest writer will endorse that last statement. In fact, I think both statements are true—a belief reinforced by the pain of five rewrites of my novel. All of these sublime revelations, however, shed little light on the quality with which I hope to infuse my fiction, or on the identity of the master mariners to whose works I look to guide me through troubled waters.

"Although the next book of mine to see the light of day will be a biography, I much prefer to write fiction. It has the marvelous quality of flexibility, and I am constantly amazed at how some characters change in the very process of creation. Nonfiction must be exact. Woe betide the biographer who makes the slightest error in, for example, the date of an important battle or whether or not it was raining on that particular day.

"In researching my upcoming biography of Tench Tilghman, I've covered all the principal repositories of information on the American Revolution on the East Coast from Maine to North Carolina, several in Michigan and California, and have made two trips to England and one to France as well. The subject of the biography, Lieutenant Colonel Tench Tilghman, was General Washington's most devoted aide-de-camp and confidant. Why a definitive account of his life has never been written I'll never know, as he was the aide with the longest service—seven years—and a loyal friend to Washington when others, including Alexander Hamilton, also an aide, and Dr. Benjamin Rush, a signer of the Declaration of Independence and surgeon general of the Continental army, turned against him. After Tilghman's premature death in 1786, Washington spoke about him with true reverence.

"In the same vein, since my novels are of the genre associated with intrigue, espionage, and high-level skulduggery, I consider it essential that they also be considered credible. Happily for me, the critics found *The Phoenix With Oil Feathers* to fit this mold. I would like to say, however, that the historical personages who people the pages of my books do not, in fact, play dominant roles in the unraveling of the plot. Rather, they are the more or less stationary chessmen on the board whereon my imaginary characters move. To have it otherwise would, in my opinion, create the very atmosphere of unreality I seek to avoid. 'Character is plot,' said Scott Fitzgerald. True enough; for me it's the light and the way, although some of my critics don't give me full marks here. Next time out, in a novel that pits the Irish Republican Army against the British, I hope to confound them."

Shreve added: "Count me as a disciple of such storytellers as Frederick Forsyth, Morris West, and Helen MacInnes. For all the aura which surrounds him and his works, I find John LeCarre precious and obscure."

Shreve's first novel, *The Phoenix With Oil Feathers,* was well-received by critics and the general public alike. A reviewer for the *Library Journal,* for example, declared the book to be "credible, well written and surprisingly entertaining." David Atlee Phillips, former director of the Western hemisphere division of the CIA, also commended the book: "Shreve has written, as only an insider could, a chillingly authentic tale of intrigue born in the ashes of the Reich." Scott C. S. Stone, writing for the dust jacket of the novel, agreed with Phillips: "Obviously Shreve knows his way around these murky waters. . . . His first-rate and innovative story is matched only by the authenticity of his locales and the precision of his events." Reviewer Virginia Leache concluded that the book was more than a novel: "*Phoenix* belongs possibly to the new literary genre *faction,* or the docu-novel, in which a work of fiction is seeded with real life characters and events. The technique is exploited with such skill in the *Phoenix* that the narrative assumes a convincing aura of authenticity, leaving the reader trying to recall headlines of the period."

BIOGRAPHICAL/CRITICAL SOURCES: Baltimore Sunday Sun, September 30, 1973; *Library Journal,* July, 1980; *Baltimore News American,* August 10, 1980; *Baltimore Evening Sun,* October 9, 1980.

*   *   *

SHUTE, Nerina

PERSONAL: Born in Northumberland, England; married Howard Marshall (a commentator; separated). *Education:* Attended University of London. *Politics:* Conservative. *Home:* 31 Cadogan Place, London S.W.1, England.

CAREER: Worked as publicity manager for Max Factor; writer. *Member:* Hurlingham Club.

WRITINGS: We Mixed Our Drinks: The Story of a Generation, Jarrolds, 1945; *Victorian Love Story: A Study of the Victorian Romantics Based on the Life of Dante Gabriel Rossetti,* Jarrolds, 1954; *Come Into the Sunlight: The Story of My Edwardian Mother,* Jarrolds, 1958; *The Escapist Generations: My London Story,* R. Hale, 1973; *London Villages,* St. Martin's, 1977; *More London Villages,* St. Martin's, 1980. Also author of *Another Man's Poison* (novel), Grant Richards, *Georgian Lady* (biography of Fanny Burney), Jarrolds, *Poet Pursued* (biography of P. B. Shelley), Jarrolds, *Malady of Love,* Jarrolds, and *Favourite Books for Boys and Girls,* Jarrolds. Contributor to magazines, including *Linguist,* and newspapers.

WORK IN PROGRESS: Another book about London.

*   *   *

SIDDONS, Anne Rivers

PERSONAL: Married; children: four stepsons.

CAREER: Writer. Worked in advertising.

WRITINGS: John Chancellor Makes Me Cry, Doubleday, 1975; *Heartbreak Hotel,* Simon & Schuster, 1976; *The House Next Door,* Simon & Schuster, 1978; *Go Straight on Peachtree,* Dolphin Books, 1978. Contributor to *House Beautiful, Redbook, Reader's Digest, Atlanta,* and *Georgia.*

SIDELIGHTS: Siddon's first book, *John Chancellor Makes Me Cry,* chronicles one year of her life in Atlanta, Ga., humorously reflecting on the frustrations and joys of life—serving jury duty, hosting parties, and taking care of a husband suffering with the flu. The author's style in *John Chancellor Makes Me Cry* has been favorably compared to that of Erma Bombeck, whose own review of the book praised Siddons: "She is unique. She's an original in her essays that combine humor, intimacy and insight into a marriage." Bombeck found the most "poignant and very real" chapter to be the one describing "the month [Siddons's] husband lost his job, her Grandmother died, a Siamese cat they were keeping for a friend was hit by a car, their house was burgled and their Persian cat contracted a $50-a-week disease."

Heartbreak Hotel is a novel about a young Southern woman who must choose between her two suitors and the very different lifestyles they represent. Katha Pollitt asserted: "The author dissects the 1950's, Southern style, with a precision that is anything but nostalgic; and yet somehow the very

wealth of detail she provides makes 'Heartbreak Hotel' a good-natured rather than an angry look backward. . . . This is a marvelously detailed record of a South as gone with the wind as Scarlett O'Hara's."

Jane Larkin Crain was disappointed with the lack of drama in Siddons's third novel, *The House Next Door.* This tale of an affluent young couple whose lives are changed by the mysterious evils occurring in a neighboring house, according to Crain, "is suffused with tacit New Class moralism and snobbery and populated with characters of such smugness and self-satisfaction that it is hard to work up much sympathy or distress when they are forced into the author's idea of extremity. . . . With lives as bland and complacent as those in this novel, one would think that all concerned might welcome a little murder and mayhem in the neighborhood, just to liven things up a bit."

BIOGRAPHICAL/CRITICAL SOURCES: Anne Rivers Siddons, *John Chancellor Makes Me Cry,* Doubleday, 1975; *New York Times Book Review,* April 13, 1975, September 12, 1976, October 23, 1977, December 10, 1978; *Library Journal,* June 15, 1975.*

*   *   *

SIEGEL, Beatrice

PERSONAL: Born in New York, N.Y.; daughter of Samuel and Sophie (Kopp) Jacobson; married Samuel R. Siegel (a dentist); children: Andra Sigerson Patterson. *Education:* Brooklyn College (now of the City University of New York), B.A., 1932; Cornell University, M.A., 1936. *Residence:* New York, N.Y. *Agent:* Frances Schwartz Literary Agency, 60 East 42nd St., New York, N.Y. 10017.

CAREER: Retail Drug Employees Union, Local 1199, 1950-55; Neighborhood Youth Corps, 1966-68; writer, 1971—.

WRITINGS—For children: Indians of the Woodland: Before and After the Pilgrims, Walker & Co., 1972; *Living With Mommy* (story), Feminist Press, 1974; *A New Look at the Pilgrims: Why They Came to America,* Walker & Co., 1977; *Alicia Alonso: The Story of a Ballerina* (American Dance Guild Book Club selection), Warne, 1979; *An Eye on the World: Margaret Bourke-White, Photographer* (Junior Literary Guild selection), Warne, 1980; *Trappers and Traders: The Indians, the Pilgrims, and the Beaver,* Walker & Co., 1980.

WORK IN PROGRESS: A biography of a woman reformer of the late 1800's and early 1900's.

SIDELIGHTS: Siegel told *CA:* "I did my undergraduate college work in French and German. My graduation from college during the years of the Great Depression cancelled my interest in languages and turned me to more immediate interests, such as history and political theory.

"My employment has been with non-profit organizations. In the community I am involved in the struggle against war, the rights of minority peoples, and the efforts toward a safe ecological world."

*   *   *

SIEGEL, Maxwell E(dward) 1933-

PERSONAL: Born November 12, 1933, in Brooklyn, N.Y.; son of Louis and Frances (Goldklang) Siegel; married Georgette Jasen, April 1, 1962. *Education:* Columbia University, B.A., 1954. *Residence:* Sussex County, N.J. *Agent:* Harold Matson Co., Inc., 22 East 40th St., New York, N.Y. 10016.

CAREER: Writer. Director of Huntsville Little Theatre,

Huntsville, Ala., 1957-58; member of board of directors of American Creative Theatre, New York, N.Y., 1960-62. *Military service:* U.S. Army, Missile Command, 1956-58. *Member:* Authors Guild of Authors League of America, Laughing Lion Society.

WRITINGS: Central Park Underground (novel), Walker & Co., 1968; *Vibrations; or, It Seemed Like a Good Idea at the Time* (novel), Morrow, 1979.

Plays: "The World of Donald" (one-act), first produced in New York, N.Y., at Eleanor Gould Theatre, August 11, 1960; "Three on the Aisle" (one-act), first produced in New York, N.Y., at American Creative Theatre, October 31, 1960; "Inside" (one-act), first produced in New York, N.Y., at America Creative Theatre, October 31, 1960.

Author of song lyrics for "Sick," "Bless This School," and "Beyond," for cabaret revues. Contributor to *Travel* and newspapers.

WORK IN PROGRESS: Curse You, San Berdu, a comic novel about the Peace Corps; *The Worth,* a comic novel about the residents of an old Manhattan apartment house.

SIDELIGHTS: Siegel wrote: "I don't remember ever not writing. I have always preferred writing humor because I have always preferred reading humor, and anyone who plans to lock himself up in a room with a typewriter for extended periods of time had better damn well be prepared to keep himself or herself entertained. H. Allen Smith's gloriously quirky anthology, *Desert Island Decameron,* was to me at twelve what Chapman's *Homer* was to Keats at twenty.

"I have always believed that the Royal Road to good writing exists. It is good reading, and I am unhappily convinced that television (whatever its debatable effect on intelligence) is rapidly poisoning (and may ultimately kill) literacy as we have known it."

*　　　*　　　*

SILANGAN, Manuel
See YABES, Leopoldo Y(abes)

*　　　*　　　*

SILMAN, Roberta 1934-

PERSONAL: Born December 29, 1934, in Brooklyn, N.Y.; daughter of Herman (a curtain manufacturer) and Phoebe (Brand) Karpel; married Robert Silman (a structural engineer), June 14, 1956; children: Miriam, Joshua, Ruth. *Education:* Cornell University, B.A., 1956; Sarah Lawrence College, M.F.A., 1975. *Politics:* "Right now—desperate at the choices." *Religion:* Jewish. *Home and office:* 18 Larchmont St., Ardsley, N.Y. 10502. *Agent:* Lois Wallace, Wallace & Sheil Agency, Inc., 177 East 70th St., New York, N.Y. 10021.

CAREER: Saturday Review, New York, N.Y., secretary and science writer, 1957-61; free-lance writer, 1961—. Gives readings and workshops. *Member:* International P.E.N., Authors Guild, Authors League of America, Poets and Writers, Friends of the Ardsley Public Library, Friends of Hoff-Barthelson Music School, Phi Beta Kappa. *Awards, honors:* Award from Child Study Association, 1977, for *Somebody Else's Child;* Hemingway Prize and Janet Kafka Prize honorable mentions, both 1978, both for *Blood Relations;* Guggenheim fellow, 1979.

WRITINGS: Somebody Else's Child (juvenile), Warne, 1976; *Blood Relations* (stories), Little, Brown, 1977; *Boundaries* (novel), Little, Brown, 1979.

WORK IN PROGRESS: The Dream Dredger, a novel.

SIDELIGHTS: Silman commented: "I started to write fiction when my children were still young and began, as many women do, with stories. As the children got older there was more uninterrupted time to write, so I made the longer commitment to the novel. Now I am working on a novel and several stories at once.

"For me, fiction is the history of the world. I think it is my job as a serious fiction writer to tell the truth about what I know or what I have the imagination to invent. The writing itself becomes a way of understanding something I have been unable to fathom or untangle—certain kinds of family relationships in *Blood Relations,* what an adopted child feels in *Somebody Else's Child,* and the modern relationship between Jews and Germans in *Boundaries.*

"I like families. I was brought up in a close Jewish family on Long Island and I care very much about my family now. I also feel very lucky in my husband, who has given me encouragement and emotional and financial support throughout the years. If I had to support a family by writing fiction my life would be much harder than it is."

AVOCATIONAL INTERESTS: Music, playing the piano, gardening, reading, hiking, ice skating, cross-country skiing.

*　　　*　　　*

SILVERMAN, Robert J(ay) 1940-

PERSONAL: Born January 14, 1940, in Paterson, N.J.; son of Louis (a businessman) and Bernadine (a businesswoman; maiden name, Wein) Silverman; married Maxine Mironov (a teacher), August 14, 1963; children: Rachael Ann, H. David, Alana Judith. *Education:* Rutgers University, A.B., 1961; Columbia University, M.A., 1963; Cornell University, Ph.D., 1969. *Home:* 207 Abbot Ave., Worthington, Ohio 43085. *Office:* 1945 North High St., Columbus, Ohio 43210.

CAREER/WRITINGS: Ohio State University, Columbus, assistant professor, 1969-73, associate professor, 1973-78, professor of education, 1978—, editor of *Journal of Higher Education,* 1970—. Member of professional development committee, Association of College Unions, 1964-66; member of editorial advisory board, Association for Institutional Research, 1972—; member of research advisory board, University Council for Educational Administration, 1977—. *Military service:* U.S. Army, 1961-69; became captain. *Member:* American Educational Research Association, American Association for Higher Education (member of program committee, 1972-74), American Sociological Association, American Association for the Advancement of Science, Society for Social Studies of Science, Association for the Study of Higher Education (member of program committee, 1978), Phi Delta Kappa, Phi Kappa Phi. *Awards, honors:* Grants from the U.S. Office of Education, 1968, and National Institute of Education, 1973 and 1979.

Contributor of articles to journals, including *Viewpoints in Teaching and Learning, Research in Higher Education, Focus on Guidance, Journal of College Student Personnel, Journal of Research and Development in Education,* and *American Quarterly.*

WORK IN PROGRESS: Research on the uses of scientific literature.

SIDELIGHTS: Silverman commented to *CA:* "My work as an editor and my professional involvement in the sociology of science speak to my interest in knowledge creation and dissemination from both scholarly and pragmatic perspectives. I am concerned with styles of professional communication and more effective communication among constituencies. This concern is also manifested through my research in inter-organizational relationships.''

* * *

SILVERSTEIN, Mel(vin Jerome) 1940-

PERSONAL: Born April 29, 1940, in New York, N.Y.; son of Louis and Jeannette Silverstein; married Cathie Ragovin (a physician), August 31, 1969 (marriage ended, 1973); married Karen Sperling (a writer), January 31, 1976; children: (second marriage) Max Charles. *Education:* Johns Hopkins University, A.B., 1961; Albany Medical College, M.D., 1965. *Religion:* Jewish. *Home:* 200 Bentley Circle, Los Angeles, Calif. 90049. *Agent:* William Morris Agency, 1350 Avenue of the Americas, New York, N.Y. 10019. *Office:* Breast Center, Valley Medical Center Foundation, 14533 Gault St., Van Nuys, Calif. 91405.

CAREER: Worked in fields of surgery, 1972-75, and cancer control, 1975-76, at University of California, Los Angeles; City of Hope Medical Center, Duarte, Calif., surgical oncologist, 1973-79; Valley Medical Cancer Foundation, Van Nuys, Calif., surgical oncologist, 1979—. *Military service:* U.S. Army, 1970-72; became major. *Member:* American Society of Clinical Oncology, American Association for Cancer Research, American Mastology Association, American Cancer Society (member of Los Angeles board of directors), Association of Academic Surgeons, Society of the Study of Breast Diseases, Alpha Omega Alpha.

WRITINGS: (With wife, Karen Sperling) *Side Effects* (novel), Doubleday, 1978; (with K. Sperling) *Conspiracy of Silence*, Doubleday, 1980. Contributor of numerous articles to scientific journals.

WORK IN PROGRESS: A book on adoption.

SIDELIGHTS: Silverstein commented to *CA:* "I am a cancer doctor and educator. I write novels so that I may educate the lay public painlessly through fiction."

* * *

SIMMS, Eric Arthur 1921-

PERSONAL: Born August 24, 1921, in London, England; son of Levi (a gardener) and Amy Margaret Simms; married Nora Thelma Jackson; children: (adopted) David Barford, Amanda Jane. *Education:* Merton College, Oxford, B.A., 1941, M.A., 1946. *Home:* 85 Brook Rd., Dollis Hill, London N.W.2, England.

CAREER: British Broadcasting Corp., ornithologist, 1951-58, natural history producer, 1958-67; free-lance writer, broadcaster, and lecturer, 1967—. Member of Laboratory of Ornithology at Cornell University, 1957—. Justice of the peace, 1965—. *Military service:* Royal Air Force, Bomber Command, 1941-46; received Distinguished Flying Cross. *Member:* World Wildlife Fund (member of United Kingdom council, 1980—), Royal Society for the Protection of Birds (member of council, 1953-63), British Ornithologists Union.

WRITINGS: Bird Migrants, Cleaver-Hume, 1952; *The Songs and Calls of British Birds,* Royal National Institute for the Blind, 1955; *Voices of the Wild,* Putnam, 1957; *Witherby's Sound-Guide to British Birds,* Witherby, 1958; *Woodland Birds,* Collins, 1971; *Birds of Town and Suburb,* Collins, 1975; *Birds of the Air: An Autobiography,* Hutchinson, 1976; *British Thrushes,* Collins, 1978; *Wild Life Sounds and Their Recordings,* Elek, 1979; *The Public Life of the Street Pigeon,* Hutchinson, 1979; *A Natural History of Britain and Ireland,* Dent, 1979. Contributor to journals, including *British Birds, Bird Notes, John Bull,* and *Tape Recorder.*

WORK IN PROGRESS: The Lazy Wind: A Portrait of Peterhead; A Natural History of Birds for Dent; research for a book on British warblers for Collins.

* * *

SIMON, Bennett 1933-

PERSONAL: Born November 6, 1933, in Brooklyn, N.Y.; son of Walter V. and Mollie E. Simon; married wife, Nancy J., August 19, 1962 (died, 1977); married Roberta J. Apfel (a psychiatrist), January 6, 1979; children: Jonathan Z., Amy R.; (stepchildren) Michael, Molly, Celia. *Education:* Harvard University, A.B. (summa cum laude), 1955; Columbia University, M.D., 1959. *Politics:* Democrat. *Religion:* Jewish. *Home:* 170 Chestnut St., West Newton, Mass. 02165. *Office:* Department of Psychiatry, Cambridge Hospital, Cambridge, Mass. 02139.

CAREER: Albert Einstein College of Medicine, Bronx, N.Y., 1964-71, began as instructor, became assistant professor; Harvard University, Cambridge, Mass., 1971—, began as lecturer, became assistant clinical professor, currently associate clinical professor. Member of faculty at Boston Psychoanalytic Institute, 1971—; director of psychiatric residency at Cambridge Hospital, 1976—. *Member:* American Psychiatric Association, American Psychoanalytic Association, American Philological Association, American Association for the History of Medicine. *Awards, honors:* Guggenheim fellow, 1976.

WRITINGS: Mind and Madness in Ancient Greece: The Classical Roots of Modern Psychiatry, Cornell University Press, 1978. Contributor of more than a dozen articles and reviews to psychiatry journals. Member of editorial board of *Psychoanalytic Quarterly* and *Psychoanalysis and the Social Sciences.*

WORK IN PROGRESS: Psychoanalysis and Mythology; The Clinical Theory of Psychoanalysis; The History of Psychiatry in Late Antiquity.

SIDELIGHTS: Bennett commented to *CA:* "I have tried to achieve in my writing and teaching the mutual interdependence of psychiatry, humanities, psychiatry, and the social sciences."

* * *

SIMON, Sidney B(lair) 1927-

PERSONAL: Born May 27, 1927, in Pittsburgh, Pa.; son of Frank Edward and Bessie (Finkelstein) Simon; children: John, Douglas, Julianna, Matthew. *Education:* Pennsylvania State University, B.A., 1949, M.Ed., 1952; New York University, Ed.D., 1958. *Home:* 25 Montague Rd., Box 846, Leverett, Mass. 01054. *Office:* School of Education, University of Massachusetts, Amherst, Mass. 01002.

CAREER: High school English teacher in Bradford, Pa., 1950-52, and Baldwin, N.Y., 1952-54; teacher of English and social studies at school in New York City, 1954-57; New York University, New York City, part-time instructor in secondary education, 1957-58; Paterson State College, Paterson, N.J., assistant professor of education, 1958-59; Queens College of the City University of New York, New York City, assistant professor of education, 1959-65; Temple University, Philadelphia, Pa., associate professor of education, 1965-69; University of Massachusetts, Amherst, professor of education, 1969—. Member of summer faculty at Rutgers University, Princeton University, University of Rochester, City College of the City University of New York, and New York University; conducts workshops in the

United States, Canada, Mexico, and Europe. Member of executive committee of National Conference of Core Teachers, 1958-61; member of board of directors of Richard Welling Foundation's national self-government committee, 1961-68; chairperson of board of advisers of Sagamore Institute, 1970—; member of board of advisers of New England Center for Personal and Professional Growth, 1973-76. *Military service:* U.S. Navy. *Member:* John Dewey Society (member of board of directors, 1973-75), Association for Student Teaching, Association for Supervision and Curriculum Development.

WRITINGS: (With Louis Raths) *Values and Teaching,* C. E. Merrill, 1966, revised edition, 1978; (with Howard Kirschenbaum) *Wad-ja-Get?: The Grading Game in American Education,* Hart Publishing, 1971; (with others) *Values Clarification: A Handbook of Practical Strategies for Teachers and Students,* Hart Publishing, 1972, revised edition, 1976; (with Merrill Harmin) *Clarifying Values Through Subject Matter,* Winston Press, 1973; *I Am Loveable and Capable,* Argus, 1973; (with Robert C. Hawley) *Composition for Personal Growth,* Hart Publishing, 1974; (with Kirschenbaum) *Readings in Values Clarification,* Winston Press, 1974; *Meeting Yourself Halfway,* Argus, 1974; (with Jay Clark) *Beginning Values Clarification: A Guide for the Use of Values Clarification in the Classroom,* Pennant Press, 1975; (co-author) *Humanistic Education Sourcebook,* Prentice-Hall, 1975; *Caring, Feeling, Touching,* Argus, 1976; (co-author) *Helping Children Learn Right From Wrong,* Simon & Schuster, 1976; (with D. Read) *Health Education: The Search for Values,* Prentice-Hall, 1977; *Vulture: A Modern Allegory to the Art of Putting Oneself Down,* Argus, 1977; *Negative Criticism,* Argus, 1978.

Children's books: *Henry the Uncatchable Mouse,* Grosset, 1964; *The Armadillo Who Had No Shell,* Grosset, 1966. Contributor of more than one hundred articles to education and guidance journals. Co-editor of *Grass Roots* (of New Jersey Conference of Core Teachers), 1959-60.

SIDELIGHTS: Simon has described himself as "a pioneer in the human potential movement, working on linking many professional and personal experiences into a new theory of human growth."

*   *   *

SIMPSON, George E(dward) 1944-

PERSONAL: Born November 10, 1944, in New York, N.Y.; son of Alan R. (in textile sales) and Roslyn (Schenker) Simpson; married Maureen McAndrew (a photographer), February 14, 1976; children: Anna-Claire. *Education:* University of California, Los Angeles, A.B., 1966, M.F.A., 1968. *Residence:* Los Angeles, Calif. *Agent:* Stuart Miller Co., 4444 Riverside Dr., Burbank, Calif. 91505.

CAREER: Universal Pictures, Universal City, Calif., film editor, 1966-74; writer, 1974—. *Member:* Motion Picture Editors Guild, Writers Guild of America (West). *Awards, honors:* Porgie Award in fantasy from *West Coast Review of Books,* 1977, for *Ghostboat.*

WRITINGS—Novels, unless otherwise noted: (Co-author) "The Disappearance of Flight 412" (film), aired by NBC-TV, 1974; (with Neal R. Burger) *Ghostboat,* Dell, 1976; (with Burger) *Thin Air,* Dell, 1978; (with Burger) *Fair Warning,* Delacorte, 1980.

WORK IN PROGRESS: "Up the Garden Path," a comedy screenplay, with Neal R. Burger, for Dick Clark Productions.

SIDELIGHTS: Simpson told *CA:* "I have always felt that aspiring authors ought to be given one good piece of advice. Along the way someone is going to say, 'Write about what you know,' possibly the oldest aphorism in writing, and one that has been sorely misused.

"Imagine telling a student of eighteen tender years to 'write about what you know.' In no time at all, you will be up to your belt buckle in student romance, adolescent rebellion, and the tough life on the affluent side of the tracks. What else does a student know?

"Taken literally, then, it is bad advice. Write about what you don't know—then you may learn something. I believe in research—on things, events, and character. Into that insert what you 'know': the whole range of emotions—love, pity, sorrow, jealousy, rage, and the people around you. Write the queen of England as your mother; let your uncle be Jack the Ripper; your father a scheming banker; your sister a prostitute.

"Use what you know to breathe life into your characters, but do not feel constrained to write only about your humdrum or not so humdrum life. You can be more objective writing about killers, kings, and commandos because you are not tied to events as they happened. You are not obliged to be faithful to reality. Instead, you create your own.

"What you *know* ultimately consists of your awareness of emotion and human reaction, and not much more. Everything else can be learned.

"I enjoy writing stories that mix genres and confound the categorizers of literature. *Ghostboat* was science fiction, horror, war adventure, and detection. I am not interested in being accepted by one group or another as a particular kind of writer. I wish to extend and perfect my craft, but not by writing the same thing over and over again. I have already turned to comedy and expect to try short stories and plays of varying subject matter."

*   *   *

SIMPSON, Leo 1934-

PERSONAL: Born September 26, 1934, in Limerick, Ireland; came to Canada, 1961; naturalized Canadian citizen, 1972; son of Gerald and Anne (Egan) Simpson; married Jacqueline Anne Murphy (a teacher), March, 1964; children: Julie. *Education:* Educated in Ireland. *Politics:* "Politics are complicated." *Religion:* Roman Catholic. *Home and office:* 18 Livingstone Ave., Madoc, Ontario, Canada K0K 2K0. *Agent:* Claire Smith, Harold Ober Associates, Inc., 40 East 49th St., New York, N.Y. 10017.

CAREER: Writer. Publicity manager and editor at Macmillan Publishing Co. in Toronto, Ontario, 1961-66; writer in residence at University of Ottawa, 1973-74, and at University of Western Ontario, 1978-1979. *Member:* Quinte Irish Society, Madoc Rod and Gun, Marmora Procrusteans.

WRITINGS: Arkwright (novel), Macmillan, 1971; *The Peacock Papers* (novel), Macmillan, 1973; (editor) *Selected Stories of D. Spettigue,* University of Ottawa Press, 1975; *The Lady and The Travelling Salesman* (short stories), University of Ottawa Press, 1976; *Kowalski's Last Chance* (novel; adapted from Simpson's own radio play; see below), Clark, Irwin, 1980. Also author of radio plays, including "A Fish in the Sea of Tranquillity," "Kowalski's Last Chance," "The Ferris Wheel" (also a stage play), and "The Lady and the Travelling Salesman."

Contributor: Morris Wolfe and Ivon M. Owen, editors, *Best Modern Canadian Stories,* Hurtig, 1972, 1973, 1975; Joan

Harcourt and David Helwig, editors, *Canadian Stories,* Oberon, 1978.

WORK IN PROGRESS: The True Adventures of Invisible Jack, a novel.

BIOGRAPHICAL/CRITICAL SOURCES: Authors in the News, Volume 2, Gale, 1976; John Moss, *The Ancestral Present: Sex and Violence in the Canadian Novel,* McClelland & Stewart, 1978.

* * *

SINGH, Bawa Satinder 1932-

PERSONAL: Born March 5, 1932, in Bannu, Pakistan; son of Bawa Balwant (an educator) and Sumitra Devi (Talwar) Singh; married Karen Lee Thoreson (a professor), September 9, 1961; children: B. Robin, B. Kevin. *Education:* University of Panjab, B.A., 1951; University of Wisconsin (now University of Wisconsin—Madison), M.A., 1961, Ph.D., 1966. *Home:* 3732 Forsythe Way, Tallahassee, Fla. 32308. *Office:* Department of History, Florida State University, Tallahassee, Fla. 32306.

CAREER: Florida State University, Tallahassee, instructor, 1965-66, assistant professor, 1966-73, associate professor of history, 1973—, director of department of Asian studies, 1966-68. *Member:* Association of Asian Studies, Carolinas Symposium of British Studies. *Awards, honors:* American Council of Learned Societies fellow, 1976-77.

WRITINGS: The Jammu Fox: A Biography of Maharaja Gulab Singh of Kashmir, 1792-1857, Southern Illinois University Press, 1974. Contributor to history and Asian studies journals, including *Modern Asian Studies,* and *Red River Valley Historical Journal.* Also contributor to *Encyclopedia of Sikhism.*

WORK IN PROGRESS: Editing and writing annotations for *The Hardinge Papers,* the private papers of Lord Henry Hardinge, governor-general of India, 1844-48; *Lord Henry Hardinge: A Biography.*

AVOCATIONAL INTERESTS: Travel (England, Germany, Switzerland, Austria, Italy, Sweden, Denmark, Norway, Finland, the Soviet Union, Turkey, Egypt, India, Afghanistan, Thailand, the Philippines, Hong Kong, Japan).

* * *

SITOMER, Harry 1903-

PERSONAL: Born December 31, 1903, in Russia (now U.S.S.R.); son of Benjamin (a butcher) and Rose (Pontach) Sitomer; married Mindel Miller, August 31, 1923; children: Alice Sitomer Ross, Daniel. *Education:* New York University, B.A. (summa cum laude), 1926; Columbia University, M.A., 1927. *Residence:* Huntington, N.Y.

CAREER: High school teacher, 1927-61; Long Island University, C. W. Post College, Brookville, N.Y., associate professor, 1967-73; writer, 1973—. *Member:* American Mathematical Society, Association of Teachers of Mathematics (chairman).

WRITINGS: (Co-author) *The City Junior Mathematics,* C. E. Merrill, 1941, revised edition, 1942; (with Myron Frederick Rosskopf) *Modern Mathematics: Geometry,* Silver Burdett, 1966; (with Rosskopf and others) *Geometry,* Silver Burdett, 1971; (with Allan Gewirtz and others) *Constructive Linear Algebra,* Prentice-Hall, 1974.

Children's books; with wife, Mindel Sitomer: *What Is Symmetry?,* Crowell, 1970; *Circles,* Crowell, 1971; *Lines, Segments, Polygons,* Crowell, 1972; *Spirals,* Crowell, 1974;

How Did Numbers Begin?, Crowell, 1976; *Zero Is Not Nothing,* Crowell, 1978. Contributor to mathematics journals.

SIDELIGHTS: Sitomer told *CA:* "I have been a composer of contest problems for Nassau County for twenty-four years and New York City for about fifteen years. My major interest in my retirement is playing the cello in amateur chamber music groups."

* * *

SITOMER, Mindel 1903-

PERSONAL: Born May 5, 1903, in New York, N.Y.; daughter of Morris (a machinist) and Lena (Gogolick) Miller; married Harry Sitomer (a professor and writer), August 31, 1923; children: Alice Sitomer Ross, Daniel. *Education:* New York University, B.S. (cum laude), 1931. *Residence:* Huntington, N.Y.

CAREER: Department of Welfare, New York, N.Y., investigator, 1939; school clerk in Brooklyn, N.Y., 1947-53; writer, 1970—. *Member:* Phi Beta Kappa.

WRITINGS—Children's books; with husband, Harry Sitomer: *What Is Symmetry?,* Crowell, 1970; *Circles,* Crowell, 1971; *Lines, Segments, Polygons,* Crowell, 1972; *Spirals,* Crowell, 1974; *How Did Numbers Begin?,* Crowell, 1976; *Zero Is Not Nothing,* Crowell, 1978.

* * *

SLATTERY, William J(ames) 1930-

PERSONAL: Born July 21, 1930, in Norfolk, Va.; son of William J. (a naval officer) and Mary (Stout) Slattery; married Martha Taylor, 1951 (divorced, 1972); married Rosemary Enright (a computer analyst), October 20, 1973; children: (first marriage) William, John, Michael, Price. *Education:* Columbia University, B.S., 1957. *Politics:* Radical. *Home:* 27 Clarke St., Jamestown, R.I. 02835. *Agent:* Dominick Abel Literary Agency, 498 West End Ave., New York, N.Y. 10024.

CAREER: Motorship magazine, Stamford, Conn., editor, 1951-55; Sperry and Hutchinson Co., New York City, 1956-57; Hanson, Van Winkle, Munning Co., Matawan, N.J., advertising manager, 1957-61; Burson Marsteller, New York City, publicist, 1961-63; Batten, Barton, Durstine, and Osborn, New York City, publicist, 1963-65; free-lance publicist, 1965-68; free-lance writer and journalist, 1968—. *Military service:* U.S. Army, 1948-51. *Member:* American Society of Journalists and Authors, Authors Guild.

WRITINGS: The Erotic Imagination: Sexual Fantasies of the Adult Male, Regnery, 1975. Contributor to newspapers and periodicals, including *New York Times, New York Daily News, Providence Journal Sunday Magazine, Esquire, TV Guide, True, Writer's Digest, Penthouse, Audience, Good Food,* and *Cosmopolitan.* Contributing editor to *Writer's Digest,* 1980—.

WORK IN PROGRESS: Research on a book about Edward R. Murrow.

SIDELIGHTS: The Erotic Imagination is a collection of fantasies contributed by several hundred men in response to an advertisement that William Slattery had placed in various men's magazines. Grouping the fantasies together under such categories as "heterosexual" and "fetishistic," Slattery added only "a minimum of commentary or other scholarly trappings," said Martha Cornog. A *Publishers Weekly* reviewer complained that "Slattery's research methods seem haphazard at best, and he makes no attempt to assess his findings. In effect the book is a sprawling wallow of raw material that demands a strong stomach and ultimately a high tolerance for tedium.''

Slattery told *CA:* "Owing to pressing financial needs, I wrote *The Erotic Imagination.* It was sloppily researched, pasted together by an unknown editor, sold to Playboy Book Club, sold to Bantam as a paperback, made enough money for me and my family to live well for three years and to buy a house. A concise assessment of the book's literary merit would be 'zilch'; a brief characterization of the book would be 'loathsome.' A number of reviewers actually liked the book, a circumstance I find baffling.

"I have been at work on a novel for almost six years, and have written nearly six hundred pages, not one of which is entirely satisfactory. Many people, including myself, believe I am a much better cook than I am a writer. However, I prefer writing to cooking because cooking is work.''

BIOGRAPHICAL/CRITICAL SOURCES: Library Journal, April 1, 1975; *Publishers Weekly,* April 21, 1975.

*   *   *

SMITH, Anthony D(avid)   1939-

PERSONAL: Born September 23, 1939, in London, England. *Education:* Wadham College, Oxford, B.A., 1962; College d'Europe, certificate, 1963; London School of Economics and Political Science, M.Sc., 1966, Ph.D., 1970, diploma (with distinction), 1975. *Office:* Department of Sociology, London School of Ecomonics and Political Science, University of London, Houghton St., London WC2A 2AE, England.

CAREER: Polytechnic of South Bank, London, England, lecturer in sociology, 1967-68; University of York, York, England, lecturer in sociology, 1968-70; University of Reading, Reading, England, lecturer in sociology, 1970-79; University of London, London School of Economics and Political Science, London, lecturer in sociology, 1980—. *Member:* British Sociological Association, National Trust for Historic Preservation. *Awards, honors:* M.A. from Oxford University, 1965.

WRITINGS: Theories of Nationalism, Duckworth, 1971; *The Concept of Social Change,* Routledge & Kegan Paul, 1973; (editor) *Nationalist Movements,* Macmillan, 1976; *Social Change,* Longman, 1976; *Nationalism in the Twentieth Century,* Martin Robertson, 1979; *The Ethnic Revival: A Theoretical Interpretation,* Cambridge University Press, 1981. Contributor of about a dozen articles to sociology journals in France, England, and Canada.

WORK IN PROGRESS: Research on patriotism in late eighteenth-century England and France.

AVOCATIONAL INTERESTS: Classical music, theater.

*   *   *

SMITH, Carole   1935-

PERSONAL: Born February 2, 1935, in Kalamazoo, Mich.; daughter of R. O. (a salesman) and Florence (a teacher; maiden name, Francis) Crossley; married Walter S. Smith (an engineer), 1960; children: Steven, Laure. *Education:* Kalamazoo College, B.A., 1956. *Religion:* Presbyterian. *Home:* 3520 Hidden Hills S.E., Grand Rapids, Mich. 49508.

CAREER: Encyclopaedia Britannica, Chicago, Ill., in public relations, 1956-61; World Book, Chicago, in sales promotion and advertising, 1961; writer. *Member:* Mystery Writers of America, Children's Reading Round Table, Chicago.

WRITINGS: (With Ruth Hooker) *The Pelican Mystery,* Albert Whitman, 1977; (with Hooker) *The Kidnapping of Anna,* Albert Whitman, 1979. Contributor of short stories and articles to periodicals, including *Michigan History.*

WORK IN PROGRESS: Researching European history, 1940-50, for possible novel.

SIDELIGHTS: Smith told *CA:* "I tend to get excited about the plot of the story I'm working on and rush forward as fast as possible to find out what's going to happen next. That's why I'm grateful to have a co-author with a beautifully developed sense of detail, who can make a house a home and a character a person.''

*   *   *

SMITH, Gary V(incent)   1943-

PERSONAL: Born January 11, 1943, in Torrington, Conn.; son of Aylmer Vincent (a furniture merchant) and Eileen Virginia (Sarkis) Smith; married Elizabeth F. Kucera, September 16, 1966; children: Gretchen E. *Education:* Villanova University, B.S., 1964; New York University, M.A., 1968; Wesleyan University, Middletown, Conn., M.A.L.S., 1974; Lehigh University, D.Arts, 1976. *Home:* 1253-D Bassett Dr., Montgomery, Ala. 36116. *Office:* Department of Political Science, Alabama State University, Montgomery, Ala. 36101.

CAREER: Ricker College, Houlton, Maine, instructor, 1968-70, assistant professor of political science and head of department, 1970-72; Pennsylvania State University, Fogelsville Campus, Fogelsville, part-time instructor in political science, 1973-74; Moravian College, Bethleham, Pa., part-time instructor in political science, 1974-75; Alabama State University, Montgomery, assistant professor, 1975-78, associate professor of political science, 1978—. *Member:* American Political Science Association, Alabama Political Science Association, Alabama Education Association, Caucus for a New Political Science.

WRITINGS: (Editor and author of introduction) *Zionism: The Dream and the Reality,* Barnes & Noble, 1974; (contributor) *Proceedings of the International Forum on Zionism and Racism,* International Organization for the Elimination of All Forms of Racial Discrimination, 1977. Contributor of articles and reviews to academic journals, including *Arab Studies Quarterly.*

WORK IN PROGRESS: Research on American genealogy and Zionist political thought.

SIDELIGHTS: Smith commented: "It has always been my belief that the study of politics must be accompanied by political values. The political scientist must not only strive for more precise quantitative techniques to explain political phenomena, but must be committed to a set of principles which propels him into the political arena, like a contemporary prophet, to challenge, curse, and combat forces destructive of civilization. So much of the literature of our profession is sterile, torn from the reality of everyday events and needs. Normative values are both the backbone and rudder of politics, providing strength, support, and direction.''

*   *   *

SMITH, Isadore Leighton Luce   1901-
(Ann Leighton)

PERSONAL: Born December 20, 1901, in Portsmouth, N.H.; daughter of Thomas W. Luce; married A. W. Smith, December 16, 1926 (died, 1962). *Education:* Smith College,

B.A., 1923. *Home address:* Little Hill, Argilla Rd., Ipswich, Mass. 01938.

CAREER: Free-lance writer. Designer and caretaker of historic garden restorations. *Awards, honors:* Awards from National Council of State Garden Clubs, Massachusetts Horticultural Society, and Sons of Colonial Wars.

WRITINGS—Under pseudonym Ann Leighton: *While We Are Absent,* Little, Brown, 1943; *Early American Gardens: For Meate or Medicine,* Houghton, 1970; *American Gardens in the Eighteenth Century: For Use or for Delight,* Houghton, 1976; *American Gardens in the Nineteenth Century,* Houghton, 1981. Contributor to magazines, including *Atlantic Monthly, Harper's,* and *Harper's Bazaar.*

* * *

SMITH, James R. 1941-

PERSONAL: Born September 20, 1941, in Kansas City, Mo.; son of James F. and Frances R. Smith; married wife, Lynn, August 20, 1966 (divorced). *Education:* University of Missouri, B.A., 1963; University of Hawaii, M.A. (philosophy), 1964, M.A. (political science), 1966; University of California, Berkeley, Ph.D., 1972. *Politics:* Independent. *Home:* 1185 Sterling, Berkeley, Calif. 94708.

CAREER: Director of Self-Actualization Laboratory, 1971-75; Group Against Smoking Pollution, Berkeley, Calif., director of research and educational programs, 1978; Lake of the Ozarks Council of Local Governments, Camdenton, Mo., economic development coordinator, 1978—.

WRITINGS: (Editor with Lynn G. Smith) *Beyond Monogamy: Recent Studies of Sexual Alternatives in Marriage,* Johns Hopkins Press, 1974.

WORK IN PROGRESS: Second-Hand Smoke: The Effects of Smoking and Smoking Pollution on the Non-Smoker; The Great Depression II: The American Economy at the Brink.

SIDELIGHTS: Smith told *CA:* "I am a would-be college teacher of social, political, and economic philosophy. Sex research is a major interest, and sometimes I am a jazz drummer. I have 'dropped out' in the Missouri Ozarks, hopefully to complete books in progress."

* * *

SMITH, Kay Nolte 1932-
(Kay Gillian)

PERSONAL: Born July 4, 1932, in Eveleth, Minn.; daughter of Clifford Paul (in civil service) and Sigrid (a librarian; maiden name, Johnson) Nolte; married Phillip J. Smith (a professor), 1958. *Education:* University of Minnesota, B.A. (summa cum laude), 1952; University of Utah, M.A., 1955. *Politics:* "Advocate of laissez-faire capitalism." *Home:* 73 Hope Rd., Tinton Falls, N.J. 07724. *Agent:* Meredith Bernstein, Henry Morrison, Inc., 58 West 10th St., New York, N.Y. 10011.

CAREER: Stern Brothers, New York City, copywriter, 1957-59; Fletcher, Richards, Calkins, and Holden, New York City, copywriter, 1959-63; free-lance actress under stage name Kay Gillian, 1963-73; Brookdale Community College, Lincroft, N.J., instructor, 1976-79. *Member:* Mystery Writers of America, Actors Equity Association, Phi Beta Kappa.

WRITINGS: The Watcher, Coward, 1980. Work represented in anthologies, including *Every Crime in the Book,* Putnam, 1975; *Best Detective Stories of 1975,* Dutton, 1975; *One Hundred Miniature Mysteries,* Taplinger, 1980. Author of

columns appearing in *Objectivist,* 1968-71, and *TV Show-people,* 1973. Contributor of articles to *Vogue, Opera News,* and *American Baby.*

WORK IN PROGRESS: A novel about unions and the underworld in the theatre; translation of French romantic dramas, particularly those of Edmond Rostand.

SIDELIGHTS: Kay Smith told *CA:* "The two things I greatly admire in other's work, and try for in my own, are a strong plot and the revelation and/or exploration of some aspect of human psychology. It seems sad, if not criminal, that these two elements, which coexisted happily in the great nineteenth-century works, are now split apart. Today the suspenseful, inventive plots of much 'popular' fiction often have paper-thin people and no real themes; and the 'serious' writers, who otherwise can probe deeply, frequently disdain the very concept of plot. For me the ideal is to have both: a real 'page-turner' that also reaches the heart and mind."

AVOCATIONAL INTERESTS: Philosophy, psychology, classical music, nineteenth-century romantic literature.

* * /*

SMITH, Mildred C(atharine) 1891-1973

PERSONAL: Born in 1891 in Smethport, Pa.; died August 30, 1973, in King's Point, Long Island, N.Y.; daughter of Charles A. and Jane (Haskell) Smith. *Education:* Wellesley College, A.B., 1914, M.A., 1922. *Residence:* Long Island, N.Y.

CAREER/WRITINGS: Wellesley College, Wellesley, Mass., instructor in English literature, 1915-16; teacher of English at private schools in the northeastern United States; worked for Woman's Press of Young Woman's Christian Association (YWCA), New York City, became editorial consultant; R. R. Bowker Co., New York City, assistant editor of *Publishers Weekly,* 1920-33, co-editor, 1933-59, editor in chief, 1959-67, director of company, 1934-67, secretary, 1936-67. *Awards, honors:* Constance Lindsay Skinner Award from National Book Association, 1944; Van Doren Award, 1968, for contributions to the book as an instrument of American culture.

SIDELIGHTS: Smith took graduate courses in Shakespeare under Professor George Lyman Kittredge. At *Publishers Weekly* she worked under a tandem editing arrangement with Frederic G. Melcher which lasted nearly fifty years.

OBITUARIES: New York Times, August 31, 1973; *AB Bookman's Weekly,* September 24, 1973.*

* * *

SMITH, Ray 1941-

PERSONAL: Born December 12, 1941, in Cape Breton, Nova Scotia, Canada; son of Fred (a banker) and Jean (MacMillan) Smith; married Anja Mechielsen. *Education:* Dalhousie University, B.A., 1963. *Politics:* "A pox on all their houses." *Religion:* Protestant. *Home:* 2151 Lincoln St., No. 10, Montreal, Quebec, Canada H3H 1J2.

CAREER: Manufacturer's Life, Toronto, Ontario, systems analyst, 1963-64; full-time writer, 1964-70; Loyola College, Montreal, Quebec, instructor in English, 1970; Dawson College, Montreal, instructor in English, 1971—. *Military service:* Royal Canadian Air Force, 1959-64; became flying officer. *Member:* Writers Union of Canada.

WRITINGS: Cape Breton Is the Thought Control Center of Canada (stories), House of Anansi Press, 1969; *Lord Nelson Tavern* (novel), McClelland & Stewart, 1974; (contributor)

Bill Schermbrucker, editor, *Readings for Canadian Writing Students*, Capilano, 1976.

Plays: "Lord Nelson Tavern" (radio play), first broadcast by Canadian Broadcasting Corp., 1975; "Lord Nelson Tavern" (one-act), first produced in Toronto, Ontario, February, 1976.

Work represented in anthologies, including *The Narrative Voice*, edited by John Metcalf, McGraw, 1972; *Breakthrough Fictioneers*, edited by Richard Kostelanetz, Something Else, 1973; *East of Canada*, edited by Ray Fraser, Breakwater, 1976. Contributor of articles and stories to magazines, including *Maclean's, Journal of Canadian Fiction, Prism International*, and *Tamarack Review*.

WORK IN PROGRESS: A novel with an international theme, publication expected in 1981.

SIDELIGHTS: Smith commented: "Excellence is all. From an early age I wanted to write; I consider myself lucky to have been able to do so."

* * *

SMITH, Roger H(askell) 1932-1980

OBITUARY NOTICE—See index for *CA* sketch: Born April 25, 1932, in Detroit, Mich.; died July 12, 1980, in New York, N.Y. Editor and author best known as former executive editor of *Publishers Weekly*. Smith wrote two books, *The American Reading Public* and *Paperback Parnassus: The Birth, the Development, the Pending Crises of the Modern American Paperbound Book*, and was a contributor to newspapers and magazines. Obituaries and other sources: *New York Times*, July 16, 1980; *Publishers Weekly*, July 25, 1980.

* * *

SMITH, Sydney Goodsir 1915-1975

PERSONAL: Born October 26, 1915, in Wellington, New Zealand; died January 5, 1975; son of Sydney Smith (a professor); married Marion Elise Welsh, 1938 (marriage ended); married Hazel Williamson; children: one son, one daughter. *Education:* Attended Edinburgh University; received M.A. from Oxford University. *Residence:* Edinburgh, Scotland.

CAREER: Poet. Worked as journalist, broadcaster, and teacher. *Wartime service:* Teacher of English to Polish Army in Scotland for war office during World War II. *Awards, honors:* Atlantic-Rockefeller Award, 1946; Scots poetry prize from Festival of Britain, 1951; Oscar Blumenthal Prize from *Poetry*, 1956; Thomas Urquhart Award, 1962.

WRITINGS—Poetry, unless otherwise noted: *Skail Wind*, Chalmers Press, 1941; *The Wanderer and Other Poems*, Oliver & Boyd, 1943; *The Deevil's Waltz*, MacLellan, 1946; *Carotid Cornucopius, Caird o the Cannon Gait and Voyeur o the Outluik Touer: A Drammatick, Backside, Bogbide, Bedride or Badside Buik, by Gude Schir Skedderie Smithereens* (novel), Caledonian Press, 1947, published as *Carotid Cornucopius, Caird of the Cannon Gait and Voyeur of the Outlook Touer: His Splores, Cantraips, Wisdoms, Houghmagandies, Peribibulatiouns, and all Kinna Abstrapulous Junketings and Ongoings Abowt the High Toun of Edenberg, Capitule of Boney Scotland*, M. Macdonald, 1964; *Selected Poems*, Oliver & Boyd, 1947.

The Aipple and the Hazel, Caledonian Press, 1951; *A Short Introduction to Scottish Literature* (criticism), Serif, 1951; *So Late Into the Night: Fifty Lyrics, 1944-1948*, P. Russell, 1952; *Cokkils*, M. Macdonald, 1953; *Under the Eildon Tree: A Poem in XXIV Elegies*, Serif, 1954; *Omens: Nine Poems*,

M. Macdonald, 1955; *Orpheus and Eurydice: A Dramatic Poem*, M. Macdonald, 1955; *Figs and Thistles*, Oliver & Boyd, 1959.

The Vision of the Prodigal Son, M. Macdonald, 1960; *The Wallace: A Triumph in Five Acts* (play; first performed in Edinburgh, Scotland, at Edinburgh International Festival of Music and Drama, 1960), Oliver & Boyd, 1960; *Kynd Kittock's Land*, M. Macdonald, 1965; *Girl With Violin*, Oxford University Press, 1968; *Fifteen Poems and a Play*, Southside, 1969; *Gowdspink in Reekie*, M. Macdonald, 1974; *Collected Poems, 1941-1975*, J. Calder, 1975. Also author of *The Merrie Life and Dowie Death of Colicke Meg, the Carlin Wife of Ben Nevis*, 1956.

Editor: *Robert Fergusson, 1750-1774: Essays by Various Hands to Commemorate the Bicentenary of His Birth*, Nelson, 1952; (and author of introduction) *Gavin Douglas: A Selection From His Poetry*, Oliver & Boyd, 1959; (with Robert Barke and J. Delancey Ferguson) Robert Burns, *The Merry Muses of Caledonia*, M. Macdonald, 1959, Putnam, 1964; (with Kulgin Dalby Duval and others) *Hugh MacDiarmid: A Festschrift*, K. D. Duval, 1962; *Bannockburn: The Story of the Battle and Its Place in Scottish History*, Scots Independent, 1965; Robert Burns, *A Choice of Burns's Poems and Songs*, Faber, 1966.

SIDELIGHTS: Sydney Goodsir Smith was considered one of the finest Scottish poets of recent times. A disciple of Hugh MacDiarmid, Smith employed the centuries-old Gaelic language of Lallans in his poems. *Under the Eildon Tree*, regarded as his best work, consists of twenty-four elegies mourning the tragic loves of classical mythology, including Orpheus and Eurydice and Dido and Aeneus.

OBITUARIES: London Times, January 21, 1975; *AB Bookman's Weekly*, February 17, 1975.*

* * *

SMITH, Ward
See GOLDSMITH, Howard

* * *

SMITHYMAN, (William) Kendrick 1922-

PERSONAL: Born October 9, 1922, in Te Kopuru, New Zealand; son of William Kendrick (a sailor) and Annie Lavinia (a nurse; maiden name, Evans) Smithyman; married Mary Isobel Stanley, August 26, 1946; children: Christopher Brian, Stephen, Gerard Bernard. *Education:* Attended Seddon Memorial Technical College, 1935-39, Auckland Teachers College, 1940-41, and Auckland University College, 1940-41, 1946. *Politics:* "Leftish." *Office:* Department of English, University of Auckland, Auckland, New Zealand.

CAREER: Teacher at elementary schools in Auckland, New Zealand, 1946-63; University of Auckland, Auckland, New Zealand, senior tutor in English, 1963—. Visiting lecturer at University of Leeds, 1969. *Military service:* New Zealand Army, 1941-42. Royal New Zealand Air Force, 1942-45. *Member:* New Zealand Linguistic Society. *Awards, honors:* Jessie Mackay Prize, 1968, for poetry, *Flying to Palmerston*.

WRITINGS—Poetry: *Seven Sonnets*, Pelorus Press, 1946; *The Blind Mountain and Other Poems*, Caxton Press, 1950; *The Gay Trapeze*, Arena Press, 1955; (with James K. Baxter, Charles Doyle, and Louis Johnson) *The Night Shift: Poems on Aspects of Love*, Capricorn Press, 1957; *Inheritance: Poems*, Blackwood and Janet Paul, 1962; *Flying to Palmerston: Poems*, Oxford University Press, 1968; *Earthquake Weather*, Auckland University Press, 1972; *The Seal in the*

Dolphin Pool, Auckland University Press, 1974; *Dwarf With a Billiard Cue,* Auckland University Press, 1978.

Other writings: *A Way of Saying: A Study of New Zealand Poetry,* Collins, 1965; (editor) William Satchell, *The Land of the Lost* (novel), Auckland University Press, 1971.

WORK IN PROGRESS: Articles on New Zealand vocabulary; studies relating to European records of settlement in northern New Zealand.

SIDELIGHTS: In one critic's view, "Kendrick Smithyman epitomises the poet-craftsman, the contriver of 'verbal contraptions.'" MacDonald P. Jackson, in an essay for *Thirteen Facets,* observed that Smithyman's "verse is oblique, intricate, allusive, mannered, 'conceited' in the Jacobean sense, peppered with puns, and sometimes unrewardingly obscure.... He has a keen eye for the precise concrete detail which will serve to evoke a scene, but his imagination seldom fails to descry a metaphorical dimension.... He nods towards an older view of poetry as cultivated entertainment, where a game-playing delight in the resources of language and the formation of pattern dominates the creative drive, the play becoming serious when the deeper levels of the personality are engaged.... The poetic personality emerging from Smithyman's volumes is sane, good-humoured, quirky, and in the least histrionic way compassionate. A strong sense of human limitation is accompanied by a strong sense of human worth and dignity."

BIOGRAPHICAL/CRITICAL SOURCES: Ian M. Wards, editor, *Thirteen Facets,* New Zealand Government Printer, 1978.

*   *   *

SMOOHA, Sammy 1941-

PERSONAL: Born July 13, 1941, in Baghdad, Iraq; son of Nathem (an administrator) and Rina (Katab) Smooha; married Tsofiya Natanely (a clinical psychologist), August 10, 1966; children: Shahar, Adi, Gil. *Education:* Bar-Ilan University, B.A., 1965; University of California, Los Angeles, M.A., 1968, Ph.D., 1973. *Office:* Department of Sociology, University of Haifa, Haifa, Israel.

CAREER: University of Washington, Seattle, assistant professor of sociology, 1971-73; University of Haifa, Haifa, Israel, lecturer, 1974-77, senior lecturer in sociology, 1978—. Visiting associate professor of sociology at State University of New York at Binghamton, 1980-81. *Military service:* Israel Defense Forces, officer in Research Division, 1964-66. *Member:* International Sociological Association, Israeli Sociological Association, American Sociological Association.

WRITINGS: Israel: Pluralism and Conflict, University of California Press, 1978; (with Ora Cibulski) *Social Research on Arabs in Israel,* Turtledove Publishing, 1978.

WORK IN PROGRESS: Ruling Without Consensus: The Arab Minority in the Jewish-Zionist State (tentative title).

SIDELIGHTS: Smooha wrote: "My deep concern with issues of ethnic division, cultural pluralism, and social inequality has grown out of personal experience. Most influential is my exposure to three different cultures—the Arab culture of Iraq where I was born and raised, the Jewish culture of Israel where I have spent most of my life, and the western culture of the United States. Not less sensitizing are the internal splits dividing these societies. Being keenly aware of Israel's conflicting images the world over as an exemplary society and as a colonial state, I am seeking more realistic perspectives and answers."

SMYTHE, Ted Curtis 1932-

PERSONAL: Surname is pronounced with long "y"; born May 6, 1932, in Tacoma, Wash.; son of Ted M (a teamster) and Hilda M. (a pianist; maiden name, Mastrude) Smythe; married Barbara Ann Matthews (a teacher), June 1, 1956; children: Timothy Neil, Randall Kent, Kristin Ann. *Education:* Sterling College, B.S., 1954; University of Oregon, M.S., 1962; University of Minnesota, Ph.D., 1967. *Politics:* Democrat. *Religion:* Evangelical Free Church. *Home:* 519 Swanson St., Placentia, Calif. 92670. *Office:* Department of Communications, California State University, Fullerton, Calif. 92634.

CAREER: Sterling College, Sterling, Kan., director of promotion and publicity, 1956-60; California State University, Fullerton, assistant professor, 1963-67, associate professor, 1967-72, professor of communications, 1972—. *Military service:* U.S. Army, 1955-56; served in Europe. *Member:* Association for Education in Journalism, Society of Professional Journalists, Sigma Delta Chi. *Awards, honors:* Frank Luther Mott Award from Kappa Tau Alpha, 1972, for *Readings in Mass Communications.*

WRITINGS: (Editor with Michael Emery) *Readings in Mass Communications: Issues and Concepts in the Mass Media,* W. C. Brown, 1972, 4th edition, 1980; (editor with George A. Mastroianni) *Issues in Broadcasting,* Mayfield, 1975. Past North American editor of *Asian Messenger;* member of editorial board of *Journalism Quarterly;* corresponding editor of *Journalism History.*

WORK IN PROGRESS: Commercialization of the Press, 1875-1915; The Reporter, 1880-1900; Working Conditions and Their Influence on the News; The New World Information Order: A Two-Sided Sword for Developing Nations.

SIDELIGHTS: Smythe wrote: "I am caught between an interest in the history of American mass media and an interest in contemporary American and international communication. The readers I have edited with other colleagues reflect my contemporary interest, but my research interests lie in history and the international fields. Since any one of these fields is quite sufficient in terms of writing demands, I am constantly under a self-imposed pressure to keep up while seeking to perform research at a qualitative depth."

*   *   *

SNOW, C(harles) P(ercy) 1905-1980

OBITUARY NOTICE—See index for *CA* sketch: Born October 15, 1905, in Leicester, England; died of a perforated ulcer, July 1, 1980, in London, England. Physicist, government official, educator, playwright, and author. Noted for his achievements in both scientific and literary worlds, Snow created a controversy in 1959 when he urged man to close the gap between art and technology, an idea that was controversial at the time but which eventually gained wide acceptance. He wrote numerous books, plays, and scientific studies, but is best known for his "Strangers and Brothers" series of eleven novels about the statesmen of England. Obituaries and other sources: *Chicago Tribune,* July 3, 1980; *Time,* July 14, 1980; *Newsweek,* July 14, 1980; *Publishers Weekly,* July 25, 1980; *AB Bookman's Weekly,* August 11, 1980.

*   *   *

SOBOL, Rose 1931-

PERSONAL: Born October 25, 1931, in New York, N.Y.; daughter of Maurice (a manufacturer) and Lillian (Himoff)

Tiplitz; married Donald J. Sobol (a writer), August 14, 1955; children: Diane, Glenn, Eric, John. *Education:* Brandeis University, B.A., 1953. *Home and office:* 12505 Vista Lane, Miami, Fla. 33156.

CAREER: Bendix Aviation, Teterboro, N.J., engineer, 1953-56; Computer Usage, New York, N.Y., programmer, 1956-57; Beth Am Library, Miami, Fla., librarian, 1970—. *Member:* Association of Jewish Libraries (regional president, 1976-77).

WRITINGS: (With husband, Donald J. Sobol) *Stocks and Bonds,* F. Watts, 1963; *Woman Chief* (fictionalized biography), Dial, 1976. Author of pamphlets.

WORK IN PROGRESS: Research on camping.

SIDELIGHTS: Rose Sobol commented: "Writing is terribly painful for me, but research is my joy. I feel I can only indulge in research if I justify any intensive project by writing a book.

"As a librarian, I find gaps in children's literature, yet these areas usually do not motivate me. My own interests are the prime movers in my writing.

"Happily, writing is not a full-time commitment. I am an ardent camper, and at present this holds the number one priority in my life. I have traveled extensively throughout the United States and Europe, and have discovered after three trips to England that I am, indeed, an anglophile."

AVOCATIONAL INTERESTS: "I am a tennis devotee and have played in the women's league for seven years. With the energy crunch, I rather delight in being able to bicycle to tennis, to my library job, and to another part-time job for a plant nursery. The nursery job satisfies my need to dig in the dirt and see nature in action."

*   *   *

SODARO, Craig 1948-

PERSONAL: Born May 25, 1948, in Chicago, Ill.; son of Eugene J. (a physician) and Eleanore (Klasen) Sodaro; married Suzanne Cooper (a teacher), 1972; children: Sally, Amy, Katie. *Education:* Marquette University, B.A., 1970. *Religion:* Roman Catholic. *Home and office:* 3773 Big Horn, Torrington, Wyo. 82240.

CAREER: English, journalism, and art teacher in Glennallen, Alaska, 1970-71; Appel Farm Art and Music Center, Elmer, N.J., art specialist, 1971; English and journalism teacher in Marty, S. D., 1972-73; Torrington Middle School, Torrington, Wyo., English teacher and chairman of department, 1973—. Member of Goshen County Fine Arts Council Board, 1980-82. *Member:* National Educational Association, Mystery Writers of America, Wyoming Writers, Wyoming Educational Association, Goshen County Educational Association, Kappa Tau Alpha. *Awards, honors:* Dretzka Award from Marquette University, 1969, for "The Plants"; Art Core radio drama honorary mention, 1979, for "No Chance of Error"; American Radio Theatre Award, 1980, for "No Chance of Error."

WRITINGS: Tea and Arsenic (mystery), Heuer, 1976; *Joint Return,* Heuer, 1976; *Mummy Sea, Mummy Do* (mystery), Heuer, 1976; *Search Me* (mystery), Performance Publishing, 1977; *Be Our Guest* (mystery), Performance Publishing, 1979. Also author of plays, "The Cracked Pot," "Chutluh Calls," 1974, "No Chance of Error" (radio play; first broadcast by American Radio Theatre, March, 1980), "Forlorn at the Fort," 1980.

WORK IN PROGRESS: A juvenile mystery, *Mystery of the Old Fort;* two plays, "Chatauqua" and "A Ghost Off the Family Tree."

SIDELIGHTS: Sodaro told *CA:* "I work mainly in the theatre as a teacher, a playwright, and at times, an actor. While the publication of one's prose work is indeed exciting, nothing quite matches the satisfaction of immediate response from an audience that's achieved through being involved in any aspect of a staged play. This is especially true when one writes (or is a part of) a mystery play or a comedy, because the screams or the laughs, or a combination of the two, means immediate success and gives one good cause to get back to the typewriter!

"During the summers I have my own production company, and we produce melodramas. I usually play the villain. While this isn't typecasting, it keeps me in touch with the actor's problems as well as the playwright's."

*   *   *

SOHN, Louis B(runo) 1914-

PERSONAL: Born March 1, 1914, in Lvov, Poland; came to the United States in 1939, naturalized citizen, 1943; son of Joseph and Fryderyka (Hescheles) Sohn; married Elizabeth Mayo. *Education:* John Casimir University, LL.M. and Diplomatic Sc.M., both 1935; Harvard University, LL.M., 1940, S.J.D., 1958. *Home:* 780 Boylston St., Boston, Mass. 02199. *Office:* School of Law, Harvard University, Cambridge, Mass. 02138.

CAREER: Harvard University, Cambridge, Mass., lecturer, 1947-51, assistant professor, 1951-53, professor, 1953-61, Bemis Professor of International Law, 1961—, John Harvey Gregory Lecturer in World Organization, 1951—. Legal affairs officer for United Nations, 1950-51; chairman of Commission to Study the Organization of Peace, 1969—; counselor on international law to U.S. Department of State, 1970-71; U.S. deputy delegate to United Nations Conference on the Law of the Sea, 1973-80; chairman of U.S. Commission for UNESCO, 1979—; vice-president of UNESCO World Conference on Disarmament Education, 1980. *Member:* International Law Association (vice-president of American branch, 1959—), World Parliament Association (legal adviser, 1954-64), American Society of International Law (member of executive council, 1954-57; vice-president, 1965-66; honorary vice-president, 1980—), American Law Institute, American Bar Association, Federation of American Scientists (vice-chairman, 1963; member of council, 1964-65, 1968-69), American Academy of Arts and Sciences. *Awards, honors:* World Peace Hero Award from World Federalists of Canada, 1974.

WRITINGS: Cases on World Law, Foundation Press, 1950; *Cases on United Nations Law,* Foundation Press, 1956, 2nd edition, 1967; (with Grenville Clark) *World Peace Through Law,* Harvard University Press, 1958, 3rd edition, 1966; *Basic Documents of African Regional Organizations,* four volumes, Oceana, 1971-72; (with Thomas Buergenthal) *International Protection of Human Rights,* Bobbs-Merrill, 1973. Contributor to law journals. Member of editorial staff of *American Bar Association Journal,* 1947-50; member of board of editors of *American Journal of International Law,* 1958—.

WORK IN PROGRESS: Research on law of the sea.

SIDELIGHTS: Sohn commented: "The greatest challenge to humanity is to prevent a nuclear war, to stop the deterioration of the environment, to strengthen the United Nations so that it would have real power to maintain peace, and to establish a more rational and equitable management of the economic affairs of the world community. For most of my life, I have devoted a large share of my time to these issues, both through my writings and through active participation in world affairs. I have found long ago that one can accomplish a lot more by letting others take the credit than by pushing oneself to the front.''

* * *

SOLOMON, Brad 1945-

PERSONAL: Born January 10, 1945, in Syracuse, N.Y.; son of Irving (an electrical contractor) and Bea (a singer and actress) Solomon. *Education:* Brandeis University, B.A., 1966; University of California, Los Angeles, M.F.A., 1968. *Residence:* Jackson Heights, N.Y. *Agent:* William Morris Agency, 1350 Avenue of the Americas, New York, N.Y. 10019.

CAREER: Writer.

WRITINGS: The Gone Man (novel), Random House, 1978; *The Open Shadow* (novel), Summit Books, 1979; *Jake and Katie* (novel), Dial, 1979.

* * *

SONTHEIMER, Morton

PERSONAL: Born in New York, N.Y.; son of Emanuel W. and Sadie (Alderman) Sontheimer; married Ruth Drewes (divorced); married Alice Hradecky, July 3, 1948; children: Marcia Jean Sontheimer Preciado, Donna Jo Sontheimer Acquavella. *Education:* Attended Temple University. *Residence:* New York, N.Y. *Office:* Sontheimer & Co., Inc., 445 Park Ave., New York, N.Y. 10022.

CAREER: Sportswriter and reporter, *Atlantic City Daily Press,* Atlantic City, N.J.; reporter, *Philadelphia Inquirer,* Philadelphia, Pa.; police reporter, *Newark Star-Eagle,* Newark, N.J.; reporter and feature writer, *New York Telegram,* New York City; worked variously as reporter, assistant city editor, city editor, news editor, and managing editor, *San Francisco News,* San Francisco, Calif.; assistant to the president, American Heritage Foundation, New York City; Sontheimer & Co. (public relations firm), New York City, president, 1957—. Vice chairman of Sex Information and Education Council of the United States; director of Richmond Fellowship. Consultant on industrial and tourism development to U.S. State Department, 1961; consultant to governments of Surinam, Venezuela, Guatemala, Indonesia, Japan, Puerto Rico, Jamaica, Kenya, Netherlands Antilles, and Taiwan. *Military service:* U.S. Army, 1943-45; became captain; received Bronze Star with oak-leaf cluster. *Member:* American Society of Journalists and Authors (vice-president, 1954; president, 1955).

WRITINGS: Newspaperman (nonfiction), Whittlesey House, 1941; *Attention Comrades* (nonfiction), Viking, 1954. Contributor to periodicals, including *Cosmopolitan, Good Housekeeping, Ladies' Home Journal, McCall's, Reader's Digest, Redbook,* and *Saturday Review.*

SIDELIGHTS: Sontheimer told *CA:* "I have had three separate careers, all in communications, only one of them by choice—writing. I drifted into my first career, the newspaper business, without intending to, but I loved it. I fell into public relations rather by accident and I must like it—I'm still in it. The most agonizing and the most satisfying was the one I chose myself, writing."

SOPHER, Sharon Isabel 1945-

PERSONAL: Born October 20, 1945, in Streator, Ill.; daughter of Raymond Otto and Marie Isabel (Connor) Sopher. *Education:* University of Wisconsin—Madison, B.A. (with honors), 1968. *Home:* 315 West 57th St., No. 5-D, New York, N.Y. 10019. *Office:* NBC News, 30 Rockefeller Center, New York, N.Y. 10020.

CAREER: Worked for Columbia Broadcasting System (CBS); currently writer and producer for National Broadcasting Co. (NBC) News in New York, N.Y. *Member:* National Academy of Television Arts and Sciences. *Awards, honors:* Award from Associated Press; Front Page Award, 1977, for television news writing; award from World Institute of Black Communications; Emmy Award from National Academy of Television Arts and Sciences, 1978.

WRITINGS: Up From the Walking Dead, Doubleday, 1978.

WORK IN PROGRESS: A collection of political poems; a "female western" screenplay.

* * *

SOUPCOFF, Murray 1943-

PERSONAL: Born February 15, 1943, in Toronto, Ontario, Canada; son of Louis Edward (a financial analyst) and Rose (Poleen) Soupcoff; married Bonnie Pape (a teacher); children: Marni. *Education:* University of Toronto, B.A., 1964, M.A., 1967, Phil.M., 1969. *Home:* 79 Castle Knock Rd., Toronto, Ontario, Canada M5N 2J8.

CAREER: Canadian Broadcasting Corp. (CBC—Radio), Toronto, Ontario, creator and head writer of "Inside From the Outside," 1969-76, producer, 1975-76, panelist on "Yes, You're Wrong," 1976-78; free-lance writer, 1978—. Associate of Ian Sone & Associates (social research consultants), 1969—.

WRITINGS: (Editor and contributor) *Good Buy, Canada* (satire), Lorimer, 1975; *Canada 1984: The Year in Review* (satire), Lester & Orpen Dennys, 1979. Television and radio writer for Canadian Broadcasting Corp.

WORK IN PROGRESS: America 1990: The Year in Review.

SIDELIGHTS: Soupcoff has been writing satire since his college days; but on the more scholarly side, he also concerns himself with such subjects as the social role of the writer and the media in Canada.

BIOGRAPHICAL/CRITICAL SOURCES: Baltimore Evening Sun, December 9, 1971; *Indianapolis News,* December 13, 1971; *Toronto Star,* October 4, 1974; *Toronto Globe & Mail,* April 5, 1975; *Calgary Albertan,* November 10, 1975; *Vancouver Sun,* November 14, 1975; *Edmonton Journal,* November 22, 1975; *Ottawa Citizen,* November 29, 1975; *Toronto Sun,* November 30, 1979.

* * *

SPADE, Rupert
See PAWLEY, Martin Edward

* * *

SPANIER, David 1932-

PERSONAL: Born April 30, 1932, in London, England. *Education:* Attended Cambridge University. *Office: London Times,* Gray's Inn Rd., London XC1X 8E2, England.

CAREER: London Times, London, England, diplomatic correspondent, 1973—.

WRITINGS: Europe Over Europe, Secker & Warburg, 1972;

Total Poker, Simon & Schuster, 1977; *Gambler's Pocket Book,* Simon & Schuster, 1980.

*   *   *

SPENCER, Ross (Harrison) 1921-

PERSONAL: Born August 21, 1921, in Hughart, W.Va.; son of Ross Clinton (a timekeeper) and Virginia Susan (an office manager) Spencer; married Shirley Rita Alshanski, 1952; children: Alice Virginia, Lani Lucille, Dawn Rita. *Education:* Educated in Ohio. *Politics:* "Staunch conservative (former staunch liberal)." *Agent:* Scott Meredith Agency, 845 Third Ave., New York, N.Y. 10022.

CAREER: Worked as steel mill worker, aircraft worker, truck driver, and railroad worker; owner and operator of landscaping and fencing business; writer. *Military service:* U.S. Army Field Artillery during World War II. U.S. Air Force during Korean War; became communications chief. *Member:* Mystery Writers of America.

WRITINGS—Mysteries: The Dada Caper, Avon, 1978; *The Reggis Arms Caper,* Avon, 1979; *The Stranger City Caper,* Avon, 1980; *The Abu Wahab Caper,* Avon, 1980; *The Radish River Caper,* Avon, 1981; *Echoes of Zero,* St. Martin's Press, 1981. Contributor of more than one hundred poems to *American Turf.*

WORK IN PROGRESS: Franklin Park Caper, Blotters Club Caper, Grizzly Gulch Caper, Soldier Field Caper, Jacob's Paw Caper, The Missing Bishop, and *The Dragon of Foo Foo Forest,* all novels; *Welcome, Losers,* a volume of poetry.

SIDELIGHTS: Spencer told *CA:* "I am most influenced by Ring Lardner, Damon Runyan, Stephen Leacock, and Robert Service. Service wrote: 'Those who have imagination live a land of enchantment which the eyes of others cannot see. Yet if it brings marvelous joy it also brings exquisite pain. Who lives a hundred lives must die a hundred deaths.' He also said, 'Out of this brief, perishable Me I will have made something concrete, something that will preserve my thought within its dusty covers long after I am dead and dust. . . .' Thirty years ago I copied those words and carried them in my billfold."

*   *   *

SPERRY, Kip 1940-

PERSONAL: Born May 25, 1940, in Chardon, Ohio; son of Sherman Alfred and Ann Effie (Morse) Sperry; married Elisabeth Anne Pearson. *Education:* Brigham Young University, A.S., 1970, B.S., 1971, M.L.S., 1974. *Home address:* P.O. Box 11381, Salt Lake City, Utah 84147.

CAREER: Genealogical Society of Utah, Salt Lake City, senior reference consultant and librarian, 1971-76, senior research specialist, 1976—. Genealogist and consultant, 1968—. Instructor at genealogical seminars. *Member:* Association for Genealogical Education (councillor-at-large), National Genealogical Society, New England Genealogical Association, Utah Genealogical Association.

WRITINGS: (Contributor) *Professional Genealogical Handbook,* Utah Genealogical Association, 1976; (compiler) *Index to the Genealogical Journal, Volumes 1-5, 1972-76,* Utah Genealogical Association, 1977; (editor) *A Survey of American Genealogical Periodicals and Periodical Indexes,* Gale, 1978; (editor) *Index to Genealogical Periodical Literature, 1960-1977,* Gale, 1979; (editor) *Connecticut Sources for Family Historians and Genealogists,* Everton, 1980. Contributor of articles and book reviews to magazines. Editor of *Genealogical Journal.*

WORK IN PROGRESS: Two genealogical reference books expected in 1981.

SIDELIGHTS: Sperry told *CA:* "Alex Haley is credited with stimulating an interest in family heritage—of whetting the roots appetite of millions of people all over the world. As a result of Haley's best-seller and the corresponding television series, as well as America's Bicentennial and the continuing interest in genealogical research, researchers have access to dozens of genealogical and family history books, genealogies, historical accounts, biographies, local histories, and other traditional sources of genealogical and historical research. The genealogical literature continues to grow prodigiously. Most genealogical books are well written and are very useful publications, while some contain errors and should be used cautiously.

"Genealogical and family history research is a complex discipline, requiring the researcher to adopt a systematic research strategy and to familiarize himself with the literature. A knowledge of and familiarity with the literature must be an integral part of a genealogist's research methodology.

"Although a prolific amount of general guidebooks written for the beginner is available, there is a need for specialized genealogical reference books. Researchers use indexes, bibliographies, finding aids, books, and articles that discuss a particular aspect of the discipline, and other reference tools.

"My books and articles attempt to meet functional reference needs—to assist the user in his genealogical and family history research. Genealogical and family history writing is a rewarding experience. Self-discipline is an important work habit—compiling specialized genealogical reference books is tedious work. Many hours are spent in gathering and checking facts, rechecking facts, and in writing and rewriting.

"Practical experience combined with academic training provides the background to my research, writing, and teaching. Research into original records in courthouses, archives, libraries, and historical societies is always beneficial to my work. Searching microfilm copies of records—such as those in the Genealogical Society Library in Salt Lake City—is also an effective approach to research and a substitute for using original records.

"In addition to writing and editing, my interests include teaching, American genealogical and family history research, American history, and photography."

BIOGRAPHICAL/CRITICAL SOURCES: Genealogy, January, 1979, May, 1980; *National Genealogical Society Quarterly,* March, 1979.

*   *   *

SPIEGELMAN, Judith 1942-

PERSONAL: Born January 27, 1942, in San Francisco, Calif.; daughter of Henry (a salesman) and Reva Spiegelman; children: Joshua Alan. *Education:* California State College at Los Angeles (now California State University, Los Angeles), B.A., 1965. *Office:* Soul Publications, 6331 Hollywood Blvd., No. 1103, Hollywood, Calif. 90028.

CAREER/WRITINGS: Los Angeles City Schools, Los Angeles, Calif., fifth grade teacher, 1965-68; Soul Publications, Los Angeles, managing editor, 1968-73; Stax Records, Memphis, Tenn., public relations consultant, 1973-75; Soul Publications, special projects editor, 1976—. Notable assignments include first nationally published major feature articles on such record industry giants as Isaac Hayes, The Jacksons, and Al Bell. Contributor to periodicals, including *Jazz Review* and *Live.*

WORK IN PROGRESS: An untitled novel; a picaresque memoir; *Black American Music;* "an unsold film and a TV series that I am continuously revising."

SIDELIGHTS: Spiegelman told *CA:* "Soul Publications, under my editorial direction, has led the quest for equality for blacks in entertainment and the struggle to upgrade black images in the media. During my years at Soul two main themes have run through my experience: being white in a black world and learning the business of entertainment from industry leaders. I have met and developed personal relationships with every major black entertainer over the past fifteen years. I have advised and been advised by industry leaders at every level."

BIOGRAPHICAL/CRITICAL SOURCES: Michael Haralambos, *Right On: From Blues to Soul in Black America,* Eddison Press, 1974, Drake, 1975.

*   *   *

SPIKE, Paul   1947-

PERSONAL: Born in 1947; son of Robert W. (a minister, educator, and religious executive) Spike. *Agent:* c/o Maryann Palumbo, New American Library/Signet, 1301 Avenue of the Americas, New York, N.Y. 10019.

CAREER: Writer. *Awards, honors:* Paris Review Humor Award, 1969.

WRITINGS: Bad News (short stories; contains "Bad News," "Specks Saga," "Box 456," "A. B. Dick," "A Good Revolution," "The Conference Man," "The Diary of Noel Wells," "Multi," "Broadway Joe"), Holt, Rinehart, 1971; *Photographs of My Father* (autobiography), Knopf, 1973; *The Night Letter* (novel), Putnam, 1979.

SIDELIGHTS: Paul Spike's first book, *Bad News,* is a collection of nine stories in which "bits of science-fiction, cinema stencils, erotic reveries are rolled up into one nihilistic ball of wax," wrote Martin Levin in the *New York Times Book Review.* Although one of the stories won the 1969 Paris Review Humor Award, Christopher Ricks remarked, "I don't think much of, or because of, Mr. Spike's jokes," especially his ethnic jokes and other attempts at being "impeccably leftishly zany." Levin noted that "Spike's modus operandi is to juxtapose the trite and the grotesque, leading sometimes to a hollow laugh, and sometimes nowhere at all." Although Donald Gilzinger also questioned the book's merit, he pointed out that at times the author "does manage to convey some of the frustration, emptiness, and psychotic weariness of those who cannot make their way in society."

Following his first book, Spike wrote *Photographs of My Father,* an autobiographical look at his father, Robert W. Spike. A widely-known religious professional who had served as the first director of the National Council of Churches' Commission on Religion and Race, Spike was found murdered in a motel room in 1966. The book relates the author's discovery of his father's bi-sexuality and his suspicions of government involvement in his father's death. *Best Seller* critic W. B. Hill complained that "the book is terribly confessional; it tells all," but added that "the brave championship of rights on the part of the father, and the instillation of a sense of justice in the mind of the son—all of these are quite well recorded."

The Night Letter combines fact and fiction in a thriller about an imaginary plot to create a nationwide scandal by revealing a twenty-year romance between President Franklin D. Roosevelt and his secretary. A *Chicago Tribune* reviewer wrote that the book's "pugnacious fun dwindles into preachy melodrama" and the events portrayed as shocking are already "familiar motifs" from recent political events such as Watergate.

BIOGRAPHICAL/CRITICAL SOURCES: New York Times Book Review, April 4, 1971, July 29, 1973; *Library Journal,* May 1, 1971; *New York Review of Books,* July 22, 1971, September 20, 1973; *New Yorker,* September 25, 1971; *Best Seller,* July 15, 1973; *Chicago Tribune Book World,* April 22, 1979.*

*   *   *

SPIKES, Brian S. J.

OFFICE: Brian S. J. Spikes & Associates, 21 Fintona Ave., West Hill, Ontario, Canada.

CAREER: Affiliated with Brian S. J. Spikes & Associates (management consultants), West Hill, Ontario. Seminar organizer; public speaker; guest on television and radio programs; consultant to business and government.

WRITINGS: Boss Is a Four Letter Word, General Publishing, 1977. Contributor to Toronto newspapers.

SIDELIGHTS: Spikes's motto is "Every organization pays for a training program . . . whether it has one or not."

*   *   *

SPILKE, Francine S.

PERSONAL: Born in New York, N.Y.; daughter of Joseph J. (an oil company executive) and Ruth S. Schwartz; married Michael B. Nitsberg, June 16, 1963 (divorced January, 1972); married David H. Spilke (a textile business executive), May 4, 1976; children: (first marriage) Steven, Gary; (second marriage) Pia Eileen. *Education:* Hofstra University, B.S., 1965; Yeshiva University, M.S., 1977; attended Tufts University. *Home:* 16 Sinclair Dr., Kings Point, N.Y. 11024.

CAREER: Writer and lecturer. Volunteer worker with autistic children, 1960; adviser on youth programs for "Big Joe's Happiness Exchange," on WABC-Radio, 1962-64; organized child care programs for preschool children, 1965-67, and discussion groups for parents and children of single parent families, 1972-73. Established emotional support programs for children in public and private schools; guest on television and radio programs. Associated with Doris Whitney Home for Wayward Girls and Correction Commission's Anne Cross Women's House of Detention.

WRITINGS: What About the Children? (divorce handbook for parents), Crown, 1979; *What About Me?* (divorce guide for teenagers), Crown, 1979; *The Family That Changed* (divorce book for preschool children), Crown, 1979. Also author of *Family Partners* (for teenagers), and *A Family Can Grow* (for children), 1980.

WORK IN PROGRESS: A series of coloring books, with brief text on divorce and remarriage; developing a concept for animated children's films on divorce and remarriage.

SIDELIGHTS: Francine Spilke commented to *CA:* "I am particularly interested in family relationships. I have traveled extensively—to China, India, Europe, Israel, the Orient—and pay close attention to the kind of parent-child interactions and behavioral patterns in different parts of the world and in different cultures. There are major differences in the way children in different parts of the world are raised. One day I plan to do a book on the psychological differences of the value systems in which children are raised."

BIOGRAPHICAL/CRITICAL SOURCES: Los Angeles Times, April 17, 1980; *New York Times,* April 20, 1980.

SPOTTS, Frederic 1930-

PERSONAL: Born February 2, 1930. *Education:* Swarthmore College, B.A., 1952; Fletcher School of Law and Diplomacy, M.A., 1953; Oxford University, D.Phil., 1960. *Politics:* Anarchist. *Religion:* Atheist. *Home:* Via del Quirinale 21, Rome, Italy. *Office:* American Embassy, Rome, Italy.

CAREER: U.S. Foreign Service, Washington, D.C., served in Paris, France, in Bonn, West Germany, and in Rome, Italy. *Military service:* U.S. Army, 1953-56. *Member:* American Civil Liberties Union, Oxford and Cambridge Club.

WRITINGS: The Churches and Politics in Germany, Wesleyan University Press, 1973.

WORK IN PROGRESS: Italy: The Difficult Democracy, with Theodor Wieser.

*   *   *

SPRINGER, Nancy 1948-

PERSONAL: Born July 5, 1948, in Montclair, N.J.; daughter of Harry E. (in business) and Helen (an artist; maiden name, Wheeler) Connor; married Joel Springer (a Lutheran minister), September 13, 1969; children: Jonathan, Nora. *Education:* Gettysburg College, B.A. (cum laude), 1970. *Home address:* Route 2, Box 257, Seven Valleys, Pa. 17360. *Agent:* Virginia Kidd, P.O. Box 278, Milford, Pa. 18337.

CAREER: Delone Catholic High School, McSherrystown, Pa., teacher, 1970-71; writer, 1972—. Guitarist for amateur musical productions. *Member:* Science Fiction Writers of America, Women in Communication, Phi Beta Kappa.

WRITINGS—Fantasy novels: *The Book of Suns,* Pocket Books, 1977; *The White Hart* (Science Fiction Book Club selection), Pocket Books, 1979; *The Silver Sun* (based on *The Book of Suns*), Pocket Books, 1980; *The Sable Moon,* Pocket Books, 1981.

WORK IN PROGRESS: The Black Beast, a fantasy novel; research on Celtic mythology, symbolist art, metallurgy, and the poetry of William Morris.

SIDELIGHTS: Nancy Springer told *CA:* "*The Black Beast,* like all my books so far, is a story of adventure—quest, really—set in an imaginary land. One can read it on that level, or one might be able to discern something about anger in it, or even something about me.

"As a writer of fantasy novels, I must entertain, but my real aim is to communicate. I choose this odd way to go about it because I am basically a shy person; the work provides me with a mask. My thoughts disguise themselves as symbols, take the shape of moving trees, dark mountains, perhaps birds that speak.

"I enrich this 'vocabulary' by reading folklore and mythology, especially Celtic mythology, since my personal heritage is strongly Celtic (Irish and Welsh). Though I am not by nature a traveler, I recently visited Ireland and found the legendary past very lively there. My relatives seemed at a loss to understand my fantasies; they have their own, of which they may be hardly aware.

"Daydreaming, I become a singer with incomparable power to move listeners—but only daydreaming! Since I'm not really much of a singer, I write books, trying to make them sing."

BIOGRAPHICAL/CRITICAL SOURCES: Gettysburg Times, November 2, 1977; *Susquehanna,* May, 1978, April, 1980; *York Daily Record,* January 8, 1980.

SPYKER, John Howland 1918-

PERSONAL: Born February, 1918, in Hudson Falls, N.Y.; children: Alistair. *Education:* Dartmouth College, B.A. (summa cum laude), 1933. *Politics:* "Free thinker." *Religion:* "Free thinker." *Home and office address:* P.O. Box 216, Stony Brook, N.Y. 11790. *Agent:* John Hawkins, Paul R. Reynolds, Inc., 12 East 41st St., New York, N.Y. 10017.

CAREER: President of Spuycker & Son, 1933-75; writer, 1975—. *Military service:* U.S. Army, 1941-45; became sergeant major. *Member:* Poltroon Families Association, Oddfellows (president).

WRITINGS: Little Lives, Grosset, 1978. Contributor of poems to magazines.

WORK IN PROGRESS: My Life and Loves, an autobiography.

SIDELIGHTS: Little Lives is about the residents of Washington County, which is approximately two hundred miles away from New York City. It is said this county produced no notable persons except Grandma Moses. "But the 'little lives' described by Spyker, in a series of witty and wicked vignettes," commented Sandra Salmans in the *Times Literary Supplement,* "evoke not so much the prim canvases of Grandma Moses as the paintings of Bruegel and even, at times, of Hieronymus Bosch." Indeed, the supposedly unremarkable lives of the inhabitants of Washington County were far from boring. While using stock historical documents such as official papers and birth and death notices, Spyker also spices up his stories with gossip, hearsay, and speculation. He details the lives of local personages, including the neighborhood doctor who was so proficient in ministering to his patients that many young Washington County children resembled him; two lesbians who lived together, and when they died, were buried under a single tombstone on which a nude female figure was chiseled; the village prostitute who could twirl her breasts in different directions; and a family that supposedly lived on earth worms. Salmans concluded that "*Little Lives* is great fun."

AVOCATIONAL INTERESTS: Gardening, morel mushrooms, croquet.

BIOGRAPHICAL/CRITICAL SOURCES: Times Literary Supplement, April 25, 1980.

*   *   *

SPYKMAN, E(lizabeth) C(hoate) 1896-1965

PERSONAL: Surname is pronounced Speakman; born July 17, 1896, in Southboro, Mass.; died August 7, 1965; married Nicholas Spykman (an educator), 1931 (died, 1943); children: Angela, Patricia. *Residence:* New Haven, Conn.

CAREER: Writer.

WRITINGS—Juvenile: *A Lemon and a Star,* Harcourt, 1955; *The Wild Angel,* Harcourt, 1957; *Terrible, Horrible Edie,* Harcourt, 1960; *Edie on the Warpath,* Harcourt, 1966. Other: *Westover,* [Middlebury, Conn.], 1959. Contributor of articles to *Atlantic Monthly.*

SIDELIGHTS: Spykman's popular juvenile books all feature the misadventures of four lively children growing up in the early twentieth century. Polly Goodwin of the *Chicago Sunday Tribune* declared: "No one who has met the Cares family . . . can ever forget them, for no more entertaining quartet of children ever stirred up excitement in the pages of a book." A *New York Times* critic commented that the books are "an almost starkly honest portrayal of relationships among passionately individualistic, unrestrained children."

Another *New York Times* reviewer remarked that the books' "lighter moments are done with a fine wit, a keen sense of comic action and dialogue. The Cares are a formidable family, truly, and perhaps not for everybody but they live with an intensity that makes them very real."

BIOGRAPHICAL/CRITICAL SOURCES: New York Times, October 23, 1955, May 19, 1957; *New York Herald Tribune Book Review,* November 13, 1955, May 12, 1957, May 8, 1960; *Chicago Sunday Tribune,* December 18, 1955, May 22, 1960; *New York Times Book Review,* May 22, 1960, May 8, 1966, June 5, 1966; *Times Literary Supplement,* May 25, 1967.*

*   *   *

STACEY, C(harles) P(erry)   1906-

PERSONAL: Born July 30, 1906, in Toronto, Ontario, Canada; son of Charles Edward and Pearl (Perry) Stacey; married Doris Newton Shiell, August 26, 1939 (deceased). *Education:* University of Toronto, B.A., 1927; Corpus Christi College, Oxford, B.A., 1929; Princeton University, A.M., 1931, Ph.D., 1933. *Religion:* Anglican. *Home:* 89 Tranmer Ave., Toronto, Ontario, Canada M5P 1E3.

CAREER: Princeton University, Princeton, N.J., instructor, 1934-39, assistant professor of history, 1939-40; Canadian Army, career officer, 1940-59, historical officer at Canadian military headquarters in London, England, 1940-45, director of historical section at headquarters in Ottawa, Ontario, 1945-59, official historian of World War II, retiring as colonel; University of Toronto, Toronto, Ontario, special lecturer, 1959, professor of history, beginning in 1960, university professor, 1973-75. Director of history at Canadian Forces Headquarters in Ottawa, 1965-66. President of Canadian Writers' Foundation, 1958-59; member of advisory council of Toronto Historical Board; honorary curator of Old Fort York. *Military service:* Canadian Army, Signals Corps, 1924-29, member of Reserve of Officers, 1929-40.

MEMBER: Canadian Historical Association (president, 1952-53), American Historical Association, Royal Society of Canada (fellow), Royal Canadian Military Institute. *Awards, honors:* Award for academic nonfiction from governor-general of Canada, 1948, for *The Canadian Army, 1939-45;* Tyrrell Medal in Canadian History from Royal Society of Canada, 1955; Officer of the Order of Canada, 1969; Canadian Forces Decoration; Member of the Order of the British Empire; received three honorary degrees.

WRITINGS: Canada and the British Army, 1846-1871: A Study in the Practice of Responsible Government, Longmans, 1936, reprinted, University of Toronto Press, 1974; *Canada and the Second World War,* Farrar, 1940; *The Military Problems of Canada: A Survey of Defence Policies and Strategic Conditions Past and Present,* Ryerson Press, 1940; *Canadian Army Overseas, 1941-1942,* Canadian Printing, 1942; *The Canadian Army, 1939-1945: An Official Historical Summary,* King's Printer, 1948; *Introduction to the Study of Military History for Canadian Students,* [Ottawa], 1955, fourth edition, 1955; *Six Years of War: The Army in Canada, Britain, and the Pacific,* Cloutier, 1955; (editor) *Records of the Nile Voyageurs, 1884-1885,* Champlain Society, 1959; *Quebec, 1759: The Siege and the Battle,* St. Martin's, 1959.

The Victory Campaign: The Operations in Northwest Europe, 1944-1945, Queen's Printer, 1960; *The Undefended Border: The Myth and the Reality,* Canadian Historical Association, 6th edition, 1967; *Arms, Men, and Government,* Queen's Printer, 1970; *The Arts of War and Peace, 1914-1945,* Macmillan, 1972; (with Ken Bell) *Not in Vain,* University of Toronto Press, 1973; *A Very Double Life: The Private World of Mackenzie King,* Macmillan, 1976; *Mackenzie King and the Atlantic Triangle,* Macmillan, 1976; *Canada and the Age of Conflict: A History of Canadian External Politics,* Volume I, Macmillan, 1977. Also author of *Canada's Battle in Normandy,* 1948.

BIOGRAPHICAL/CRITICAL SOURCES: Michael Cross and Robert Bothwell, editors, *Policy by Other Means: Essays in Honour of C. P. Stacey,* University of Toronto Press, 1972.

*   *   *

STAEBLER, Edna

PERSONAL: Born in Kitchener, Ontario, Canada; daughter of John G. (a factory owner) and Louise R. (Sattler) Cress; married F. Keith Staebler (divorced, 1962). *Education:* Attended Ontario College of Education; University of Toronto, B.A. *Home address:* R.R.3, Waterloo, Ontario, Canada N2J 3Z4.

CAREER: Writer. Past chairman of Kitchener Public Library Board; member of Midwestern Regional Library Board. *Member:* Writers Union of Canada, Canadian Authors Association, Canadian Federation of University Women (past president), Toronto Heliconian Club. *Awards, honors:* Award from Canadian Women's Press Club, 1950.

WRITINGS: Food That Really Schmecks: Mennonite Country Cooking, McGraw, 1968; *Sauerkraut and Enterprise,* McClelland & Stewart, 1969; *Cape Breton Harbour,* McClelland & Stewart, 1972; *More Food That Really Schmecks,* McClelland & Stewart, 1979. Contributor to magazines and newspapers in both Canada and the United States, including *Maclean's, Chatelaine,* and *Reader's Digest.*

WORK IN PROGRESS: Research on food; a book on ethnic groups.

SIDELIGHTS: Writing assignments have taken Edna Staebler to many remote parts of Canada, including Mennonite, Amish, and Hutterite communities, and an Iroquois Indian reservation. She says her interest in travel and people is unending. *Avocational interests:* Reading, swimming, cooking, European travel.

BIOGRAPHICAL/CRITICAL SOURCES: Homemaker's, March-April, 1973.

*   *   *

STAGNER, Lloyd Ernest   1923-

PERSONAL: Born March 2, 1923, in Newkirk, Okla.; son of Lloyd Everett (an oil pumper) and Della Mae (Thompson) Stagner; married Colleen Doyle, June 3, 1951 (divorced May, 1972); married Marilyn Davis (a railway office worker), October 12, 1972; children: Marla Jane Stagner Schleider, Murray Lloyd, Matthew Ward. *Politics:* Democrat. *Religion:* United Methodist. *Home:* 1402 West Fifth St., Newton, Kan. 67114.

CAREER: Atchison, Topeka & Santa Fe Railway Co., Newton, Kan., supervisory freight agent, 1942-79; writer, 1979—. *Military service:* U.S. Army, 1943-46; became staff sergeant. *Member:* National Railway Historical Society (member of national board of directors, 1980), Railway and Locomotive Historical Society, Lexington Group in Transportation History.

WRITINGS: Steam Locomotives of the Frisco Line, Pruett, 1976; *Rock Island Motive Power, 1933-1955,* Pruett, 1980.

Contributor to magazines, including *Trains* and *Railway Age*.

WORK IN PROGRESS: Research on Santa Fe Railway operations in Kansas, Colorado, and New Mexico.

SIDELIGHTS: Stagner wrote: "My principal interest is railway operation and history, with an emphasis on steam locomotive power, in the United States, Canada, and Mexico. I have no overseas interests. I have traveled extensively by rail in these countries in North America, in excess of two hundred fifty thousand miles since the end of World War II, to further my knowledge and to collect data and information, and I maintain an extensive railroad library."

*   *   *

STALLEY, Roger 1945-

PERSONAL: Born July 12, 1945, in Coventry, England; son of Frank Earnest (a minister) and Margaret (Smith) Stalley; married Petrina Mary Hogg, August 8, 1971; children: Rebecca Jane, Benedict Sebastian, Clare Francesca. *Education:* Worcester College, Oxford, B.A. (with honors), 1967; Courtauld Institute of Art, London, M.A., 1969. *Home:* 24 Sutton Downs, Dublin 13, Ireland. *Office:* Trinity College, University of Dublin, Dublin 2, Ireland.

CAREER: University of Dublin, Trinity College, Dublin, Ireland, lecturer in medieval art, 1969—. Research fellow at Queen's University, Belfast, Northern Ireland, 1976-77. *Member:* Royal Society of Antiquaries of Ireland, Irish Railway Record Society, British Archaeological Association, Royal Archaeological Institute, Societe Francaise d'Archeologie, Society of Antiquaries (fellow).

WRITINGS: Architecture and Sculpture of Ireland, 1150-1350, Barnes & Noble, 1971; (with Brian de Breffny and others) *The Irish World,* Thames & Hudson, 1977; (with G. F. Mitchell and others) *Treasures of Early Irish Art,* Metropolitan Museum of Art, 1977.

WORK IN PROGRESS: The Architectural History of Mellifont Abbey; Art and Architecture of Cistercian Monasteries of Ireland.

SIDELIGHTS: Stalley told *CA:* "I lecture on medieval art, with a special interest in Ireland. I also conduct student study trips to France, where I am a frequent visitor." *Avocational interests:* Railways of the British Isles, cricket, gardening.

*   *   *

STANIER, Maida Euphemia Kerr 1909-
(Culex)

PERSONAL: Born September 1, 1909, in Edinburgh, Scotland; daughter of T. B. (a headmaster) and M. (Yorston) Burnett; married R. S. Stanier, December 12, 1935; children: Robert, Tom. *Education:* University of Edinburgh, M.A. (with first class honors), 1931. *Politics:* Socialist. *Religion:* Church of Scotland. *Home:* 211 Morrell Ave., Oxford, England. *Agent:* Murray Pollinger, 4 Garrick St., London WC2 9BH, England.

CAREER: Free-lance writer and contributor to radio programs, 1950—. Teacher of classics, St. Felix School, 1933-34.

WRITINGS: Light and Shade (poems), Abbey Press Abingdon, 1953; (under pseudonym Culex) *Culex's Guide to Oxford* (poems), Abbey Press Abingdon, 1955; *Free and Easy: A Prospect of Oxford* (poems), Oxford Mail & Times Publications, 1957; *The New Oxford Spy* (poems), Blackwell,

1969; *The Ruins of Time and Other Plays* (contains "The Ruins of Time," first produced on radio, 1966; "Storm Over Otmoor," first produced in Oxford, England, at Magdalen School, 1966; "The Expulsion," first produced on radio in 1970), Methuen, 1969; *More Talking About Oxford: Family Portraits and Other Sketches,* privately printed, 1974; *The Singing Time* (novel), M. Joseph, 1975; *The Adventure of Captain Jason* (for children), Hutchinson, 1980; *The School by the Bridge* (play), privately printed, 1980. Also author of *Talking About Oxford.* Author of radio plays. Contributor to *Oxford Mail, Oxford Times,* and *Guardian.*

WORK IN PROGRESS: "A Distant View," a play.

SIDELIGHTS: Stanier commented: "I can write to order. I am keen on local history and give talks for the British Broadcasting Corp. I enjoy writing for ten-to-fourteen-year-olds because there are not enough good quality plays (discounting Shakespeare) for young schoolchildren."

*   *   *

STANLEY, Fay Grissom (Shulman) 1925-
(Stanley Fay)

PERSONAL: Born December 10, 1925, in Haskell, Tex.; daughter of Ernest and Pearl (Bunkley) Grissom; married Carl Shulman (a professor), 1970; children: Diane Stanley Vennema. *Education:* Attended Stephen's College, Columbia, Mo., Southern Methodist University, Dallas, Tex., and New School for Social Research. *Religion:* Episcopalian. *Home:* 41 Bethune St., New York, N.Y. 10019. *Agent:* Robert P. Mills Ltd., 156 East 52nd St., New York, N.Y. 10022. *Office:* Faberge, 1345 Avenue of the Americas, New York, N.Y. 10019.

CAREER: Affiliated with fashion and cosmetic organizations; currently associated with Faberge in New York, N.Y. *Wartime service:* Women's Air Raid Defense (Hawaii), 1941. *Member:* National Arts Club.

WRITINGS: Murder Leaves a Ring, Rinehart, 1950; *Portrait in Jigsaw,* Popular Library, 1975. Contributor, sometimes under pseudonym Stanley Fay, of short stories and articles on crafts, beauty, and travel to periodicals.

WORK IN PROGRESS: A mystery novel, *Fair Game,* publication expected in 1981.

*   *   *

STANLEY, Robert Henry 1940-

PERSONAL: Born January 28, 1940, in New York, N.Y.; son of Edward and Lillian Stanley; married Eija Ayravainen (a college lecturer), September 2, 1977. *Education:* State University of New York, B.A., 1965; Queens College of the City University of New York, M.A., 1967; Ohio University, Ph.D., 1970. *Home:* 185 East 85th St., New York, N.Y. 10028. *Office:* Department of Communications, Hunter College of the City University of New York, New York, N.Y. 10021.

CAREER: Mount Holyoke College, South Hadley, Mass., professor of communications, 1967-71; Hunter College of the City University of New York, New York, N.Y., professor of media studies, 1971—. Consultant to international council of National Academy of Television Arts and Sciences. *Military service:* U.S. Army, 1959-61. U.S. Army Reserve, 1961-66.

WRITINGS: The Broadcast Industry: An Examination of Major Issues, Hastings House, 1975; (with Charles S. Steinberg) *The Media Environment: Mass Communications in American Society,* Hastings House, 1976; *The Celluloid*

Empire: A History of the American Motion Picture Industry, Hastings House, 1978. Contributor of articles and reviews to communications and television journals.

WORK IN PROGRESS: Television: The Cultural Crucible.

*   *   *

STANLIS, Peter J(ames) 1919-

PERSONAL: Born August 12, 1919, in Newark, N.J.; son of James Ignatius (a machinist) and Annelle (Kliever) Stanlis; married Alma Nielsen (a librarian), August 15, 1945 (divorced February, 1969); married Eleanor Thomas Batjer (a violinist), July 26, 1971; children: (first marriage) Ingrid Alma, Eleanor Marie. *Education:* Middlebury College, B.A., 1942, M.A. (Bread Loaf School of English), 1944; University of Michigan, Ph.D., 1951. *Politics:* "Independent, States' Rights, Strict Constructionist, Constitutional Limited Government Democrat." *Religion:* Augustinian Roman Catholic. *Residence:* Rockford, Ill. *Office:* Department of English, Rockford College, Rockford, Ill. 61101.

CAREER: Ithaca College, Ithaca, N.Y., assistant professor of English, 1945-46; University of Michigan, Ann Arbor, instructor in English, 1946-48; Wayne State University, Detroit, Mich., instructor in English, 1948-52; University of Detroit, Detroit, instructor, 1952-53, assistant professor, 1953-56, associate professor, 1956-60, professor of English, 1960-68; Rockford College, Rockford, Ill., professor of English, 1968-74, distinguished professor of humanities, 1974—, chairman of department of English, 1968-74. Guest professor at Middlebury College Bread Loaf School of English, 1961, 1962; guest lecturer at Salzburg University, Austria, 1963, Heidelberg University, West Germany, 1974, St. Andrews University, Scotland, 1976, and at more than one hundred American colleges and universities. Member of city council of Trenton, Mich., 1955-61, member of city charter commission, 1957; appointed to Michigan Constitutional Revision Commission, 1961-62; researcher and writer for Southeastern Michigan Metropolitan Community Research Corp., 1961-62. Member of Conference on British Studies, 1961-69; member of Edmund Burke Memorial Foundation, 1963-70. *Military service:* U.S. Air Force, 1942-43.

MEMBER: American Society for Eighteenth-Century Studies (member of executive board and national treasurer, 1970-73; president of midwestern branch, 1971-72), Johnson Society of the Great Lakes Region (president, 1964-65), Philadelphia Society, Mont Pelerin Society. *Awards, honors:* Robert Frost fellowship, Bread Loaf School of English, 1940; Horace H. Rackham fellow, University of Michigan, 1944-45; Major Hopwood Writing Award for nonfiction, 1948; postdoctoral writing fellowships, University of Detroit, 1954-55; Newberry Library fellowship, 1955; grants from Relm Foundation and Earhart Foundation, 1955-67, Ford Foundation, 1961, Mellon Foundation, 1964, and American Philosophical Society, 1965, 1966; Huntington Library fellowship, 1969.

WRITINGS: Edmund Burke and the Natural Law, University of Michigan Press, 1958, 2nd edition, Ann Arbor Paperbacks, 1965; *A Methodology for Studying the Services of Local Government,* Southeastern Michigan Metropolitan Community Research Corp., 1961; (editor and author of introduction) *Edmund Burke: Selected Writings and Speeches,* Doubleday, 1963; (editor) *The Relevance of Edmund Burke,* Kenedy, 1964; (editor) *Edmund Burke, the Enlightenment and the Modern World,* University of Detroit Press, 1967; *Robert Frost: The Individual and Society,* Rockford College Press, 1973, abridged edition, Minibooks, 1979; (editor)

Edmund Burke on Conciliation With the Colonies and Other Papers on the American Revolution, Stinehour Press, 1975.

Contributor: *The Law Schools Look Ahead,* University of Michigan Law School, 1959; (author of introduction) Edmund Burke, *The Sublime and Beautiful,* translated by Noritada Nabeshima, Riso-Sha (Tokyo), 1973; Jac Tharpe, editor, *Frost Centennial Essays,* University Press of Mississippi, Volume I, 1974, Volume II, 1976, Volume III, 1978; Henry Regnery, editor, *Viva Vivas,* Liberty Press, 1976; (author of introduction) Burke, *Reflection on the Revolution in France,* translated by Nabeshima, Riso-Sha, 1978; Leonard Gilhooly, editor, *No Divided Allegiance: Essays in Brownson's Thought,* Fordham University Press, 1980; *An Annotated Bibliography on Edmund Burke,* Garland, 1981.

Contributor of numerous articles to journals and periodicals, including *Modern Age, Journal of British Studies,* and *American Journal of International Law.* Editor and contributor of articles and book reviews to *Studies in Burke and His Time* (formerly *The Burke Newsletter*), 1959-73.

WORK IN PROGRESS: Studies in Robert Frost; studies in aesthetic theory and literature.

SIDELIGHTS: As an undergraduate at Middlebury College, Stanlis was awarded a Robert Frost fellowship for its Bread Loaf School of English. The experience, says Stanlis, "proved decisive in determining both my academic and writing careers. The poet Robert Frost helped to shape my conception of literature and poetry, and determined the course of my academic life by directing me to the University of Michigan. The 'New Critics' at Bread Loaf, my teachers John Crowe Ransom and Donald Davidson, provided the practical literary methods and standards for much in my teaching and writing."

The impact of seven summers of conversation with Frost at Bread Loaf remains: "Frost was undoubtedly the greatest single personal influence on me," maintains Stanlis, "both in my academic career and my writing. My aesthetic theory is identical with that of Frost. He pulled me into his orbit, and I found his aesthetic universe very congenial and satisfactory to my character and temperament." In recent years Stanlis has devoted increasing attention to Frost and his works, publishing *Robert Frost: The Individual and Society* in 1973 and contributing to each of the three volumes of *Frost Centennial Essays.* His contribution to the third volume is a record of his conversations with Frost at Bread Loaf during the summers of 1939 to 1941.

Stanlis helped honor Frost when he spoke at the University of Detroit conferment of a doctor of humane letters degree upon the poet in 1962. In his address he outlined his beliefs in the revelatory powers of poetry and the honor poets deserve: "Poetry in the modern world, as in the ancient and medieval era, is largely concerned with revealing God, man, and nature to the human race. A finished poem is capable of revealing the deepest insights into the meaning and value of the universe and ourselves. As revelation, a finished poem is so rooted in objective reality that it becomes a new thing, capable of appealing to our senses, our minds, our imaginations and emotions, in short, to our total nature.

"The revelation is not merely of knowledge, but of love; it involves not recognition only, but response, beginning in ecstatic pleasure and ending in calm wisdom. Between a good poem and a responsive reader there is instant rapport, pure *sympatico.* That is what makes poetry at once undefinable and unmistakable. The value of poetry is like the value of a state of grace—an end in itself. Poetry for its own sake implies that our love of it should be audacious and intrinsic, unmixed by motives of practical utility, or the dilletantish knowledge of the culture vulture.''

Stanlis concluded: ''All honor belongs to those who perfect our forms of revelation—whether theologians, historians, scientists, or poets. The processes of revelation have been with man from the beginning, and seem destined to continue till time has stopped.... And it is because each of us benefits from all that our inheritance has given us, from each past probe and revelation, that we pay homage to poetry, and honor our poets.''

Though Stanlis has been most influenced by Frost, he has concentrated most of his critical efforts on Edmund Burke. Considered one of the world's foremost Burke scholars, Stanlis has written and edited a number of works on the British political philosopher, including the journal *Studies in Burke and His Time.* Praise of Stanlis's scholarship was offered by Russell Kirk, who commented on *Edmund Burke and the Natural Law:* ''Dr. Stanlis's book does more than any other study of this century to define Burke's position as a philosopher, relating the convictions of Burke to the great traditions of Christian and classical civilization.... No one who hopes to understand modern politics will be able to ignore Dr. Stanlis' remarkable study.''

BIOGRAPHICAL/CRITICAL SOURCES: Peter Stanlis, *Edmund Burke and the Natural Law,* foreword by Russell Kirk, University of Michigan Press, 1958, 2nd edition, Ann Arbor Paperbacks, 1965; Stanlis, editor, *Edmund Burke: Selected Writings and Speeches,* Doubleday, 1963; *University Bookman,* winter, 1969; *Rockford Register-Republic,* July 26, 1978.

*   *   *

STANSBERGER, Richard 1950-
(Venzo Grant)

PERSONAL: Born October 19, 1950, in Massillon, Ohio; son of H. D. (a mail carrier) and P. M. (Pydynkowsky) Stansberger. *Education:* University of Cincinnati, B.A., 1973, M.A., 1975; Bowling Green State University, M.F.A., 1977. *Home:* 2805 Stratford, No. 6, Cincinnati, Ohio 45220. *Office:* Department of English, University of Cincinnati, Cincinnati, Ohio 45220.

CAREER: University of Cincinnati, Cincinnati, Ohio, assistant director of Writing Laboratory, 1977-79, instructor in English, 1979—. Founding director of Cincinnati Area Poetry Project; member of editorial board of La Reina Press.

WRITINGS: Don't Forget to Wind Up the Moon (poetry), C.A.P.P. Books, 1978; *Glass Hat* (poetry), Louisiana State University Press, 1979.

Plays: ''Greyhound'' (three-act), first produced in Cincinnati, Ohio, at St. John's Unitarian Church, December 10, 1975; ''But What About Kryptonite?'' (three-act), first produced in Bowling Green, Ohio, at Bowling Green State University, November 8, 1976. Contributor of poems (sometimes under pseudonym Venzo Grant) and articles to magazines, including *Mother Jones, Hanging Loose, Cincinnati Poetry Review,* and *Hiram Poetry Review.* Literary editor of *Creative Arts.*

WORK IN PROGRESS: The Harding Poems (tentative title), publication expected in 1981; *Hell Broke Loose on Lucky Seven,* a science-fiction novel, with Jack Heffron, publication expected in 1982.

SIDELIGHTS: Stansberger told *CA:* ''Over my desk is a quotation from a Sakkudei medicine man: 'We must always behave so that our soul will like to stay with us.' Writing is one of the ways I entertain my soul. The Sakkudei believe that it is possible to forget who you are in living by the rules and roles of daily life. They use their religious rituals, their poetry and dance, as ways of getting back in touch. This matter of the soul should not be underestimated. When I write, I try to have as few preconceptions and ulterior motives as possible. I let myself wander through my own experiences and discover them anew. I am calling my soul back. I am learning more about myself and my world. The self that writes is different from the selves who live and work under the name 'Stansberger'; it is the sum of the parts, and something else, too. I don't think a writer or any other human being can be much use to anybody else if he is not acting from a source close to his center, close to his soul. The soul is where the great cord is that plugs one into the world.''

AVOCATIONAL INTERESTS: Reading (especially science fiction), cooking, backpacking, handwriting analysis, ''various forms of divination and perception.''

*   *   *

STARR, John 1914(?)-1980

OBITUARY NOTICE: Born c. 1914; died June 14, 1980, in Suffern, N.Y. Editor and writer. Starr was a senior story editor for the McGraw-Hill Book Co., working with such authors and celebrities as Geoffrey Bocca, A. B. Guthrie, and Chet Huntley. Starr himself wrote several books, including *Hospital City* and *The Purveyor.* Obituaries and other sources: *Publishers Weekly,* July 11, 1980.

*   *   *

STATHAM, Frances P(atton] 1931-

PERSONAL: Surname is pronounced *Stay*-tum; born January 26, 1931, in Catawba, S.C.; daughter of Ernest Boyd (a civil servant) and Kathleen (a teacher; maiden name, Garrison) Patton; married George Wilkes Statham (a physician), June 28, 1952 (divorced November 17, 1976); children: George Wilkes, Jr., Meredith Statham Outlaw, Timothy Patton. *Education:* Winthrop College, B.S. (magna cum laude), 1951; University of Georgia, M.F.A., 1970; also studied at Royal Conservatory of Canada and Decatur Art Center, and with tenor Ralph Errolle. *Religion:* Presbyterian. *Home and office:* 2248 Marann Dr. N.E., Atlanta, Ga. 30345. *Agent:* William Morris Agency, 1350 Avenue of the Americas, New York, N.Y. 10019.

CAREER: Choral music teacher in Winston-Salem, N.C., 1951-52; Ashford Park School, DeKalb County, Ga., choral music teacher, 1974; writer, 1974—. Past president of DeKalb General Hospital Auxiliary; historian and member of board of management of Georgia Council on Hospital Auxiliaries; member of Junior League of DeKalb County. *Member:* National League of American Pen Women, Dixie Council of Authors and Journalists (member of board of trustees), Atlanta Press Club, Atlanta Writers Club, Village Writers Group, Inc. (vice-president and member of board of directors, 1979-82), Women's Association for the Atlanta Symphony, Rabun Gap-Nacoochee Guild. *Awards, honors:* Awards from National League of American Pen Women include first place in Georgia competition, 1978, for oil painting, ''Versailles''; named author of the year by Dixie Council of Authors and Journalists, 1978, for *Flame of New Orleans;* Frank Stieglitz Memorial Award from Atlanta Writers Club, 1979, for musical composition, ''Song Cycle for Soprano, Flute and Piano''; named fiction writer of the year by Southeastern Writers Association, 1979, for three novels, *Flame of New Orleans, Jasmine Moon,* and *Daughters of the Summer Storm.*

WRITINGS—Romantic novels: *Bright Sun, Dark Moon,* Ace Books, 1975; *Flame of New Orleans,* Fawcett, 1977; *Jasmine Moon,* Fawcett, 1978; *Daughters of the Summer Storm,* Fawcett, 1979; *Phoenix Rising,* Fawcett, 1981.

SIDELIGHTS: Frances Statham wrote: "As a lyric-coloratura soprano with a master's degree in voice, I never suspected I would ever make my living writing romantic fiction. I was perfectly happy singing and painting, rearing three highly individualistic children, and being a professional volunteer in a multitude of organizations. But it was precisely this involvement with a national volunteer organization that sent me to a writing class at Emory University.

"I realized that if I were to keep on doing that sort of thing, I needed a course in writing. I wanted to enroll in a nonfiction class, but it was the same night as my choir rehearsal. Thinking that any course in writing would be helpful, I signed up for the fiction class. The moment I walked in, I knew that was where I had belonged all the time. The wild imagination I had tried to subdue from childhood erupted, and now, five years later, shows no sign of dissipating.

"Weaving fact with fiction is exciting to me, and for the first time in my life I am enjoying history. But it's history with a difference—flavored by stories and old letters handed down from one generation to another in my family. In *Daughters of the Summer Storm* I left the South for Brazil, but my great-grandfather's letters from Rio in 1866 were directly responsible.

"Riding in my publisher's black, elegant limousine in 1978 brought back memories, for I used to be carted regularly in a limo when I was soloist for a funeral home during my college days. Each afternoon I was to sing for a funeral, the limo would pull up in front of the conservatory and, with all the other girls hanging out of their practice room windows, I would climb in and be whisked through the wrought iron gates of Winthrop College. That went on for four years, and I never told anyone where I was going. If I ever write another gothic, you know what the opening scene will be.

"My background in music and art is important in my writing. Understanding how a piece of music is put together, being able to dissect the colors of a sunrise and put them on canvas—all these experiences of awareness can be transferred to my writing and, with luck, make the story a richer experience for the reader."

*   *   *

STEEN, Edwin B.   1901-

PERSONAL: Born July 23, 1901, in Wheeling, Ind.; son of Henry Wylie (a minister) and Lora May (Benzel) Steen; married Harriet Lewis (a piano teacher), July 23, 1927; children: Marjory Alice (Mrs. Dayton D. Dickinson), Philip Lewis. *Education:* Wabash College, A.B., 1923; Columbia University, A.M., 1926; Purdue University, Ph.D., 1938. *Politics:* Republican. *Religion:* Presbyterian. *Home:* 2011 Greenlawn, Kalamazoo, Mich. 49007.

CAREER: Wabash College, Crawfordsville, Ind., instructor in zoology, 1923-25, 1926-27; University of Cincinnati, Cincinnati, Ohio, instructor in zoology, 1927-31; Purdue University, West Lafayette, Ind., instructor in zoology, 1931-37; City College (now of the City University of New York), New York, N.Y., instructor in biology, 1938-40; Western Michigan University, Kalamazoo, assistant professor, 1941-46, associate professor, 1946-52, professor of biology, 1952-72, professor emeritus, 1972—, head of department, 1963-65. Member of Michigan Board of Examiners in Basic Sciences,

1960-63. *Member:* American Association for the Advancement of Science, American Institute of Biological Sciences, Michigan Academy of Arts, Letters, and Science, Sigma Xi.

WRITINGS: (With Ashley Montagu) *Anatomy and Physiology,* with laboratory manual and study guide, Volumes I-II, Barnes & Noble, 1959, 3rd edition, 1976; *Medical Abbreviations,* F. A. Davis, 1968, 4th edition, Balliere Tindall, 1978; *Dictionary of Biology,* Barnes & Noble, 1971; (with James H. Price) *Human Sex and Sexuality, With a Dictionary of Sexual Terms,* Wiley, 1977; (contributor) Ellen Crowley, editor, *Acronyms, Initialisms, and Abbreviations Dictionary,* 6th edition, Gale, 1978. Also contributor to *Taber's Cyclopedic Medical Dictionary,* 12th edition, 1970.

WORK IN PROGRESS: *Dictionary of Human Sex and Sexuality,* with James H. Price; *Dictionary of Zoology; Dictionary of Botany.*

SIDELIGHTS: Steen told *CA:* "My more recent work in lexicography has led me to believe that the use of dictionaries should be encouraged much more than educators presently do. The study of a page in any dictionary provides diverse sources of subject matter and is a broadening experience. The various words, their derivations, pronunciations, meanings, and their relationships to each other are a source of information that is seldom touched upon in formal classes or discussions. A knowledge of words is a gateway to understanding and scholarship."

*   *   *

STEIN, Robert H(arry)   1935-

PERSONAL: Born March 13, 1935, in Jersey City, N.J.; son of William and Ella Freda Stein; married Joan Lila Thatcher (a teacher), June 28, 1958; children: Julie Joan, Keith Robert, Stephen William. *Education:* Rutgers University, A.B., 1956; Fuller Theological Seminary, B.D., 1959; Andover-Newton Theological School, S.T.M., 1966; Princeton Theological Seminary, Ph.D., 1968; postdoctoral study at University of Heidelberg, 1975-76. *Home:* 3872 Effress Rd., White Bear Lake, Minn. 55110. *Office:* Sources Division, Bethel Theological Seminary, 3900 Bethel Dr., St. Paul, Minn. 55112.

CAREER: Ordained Baptist minister, 1960; pastor of Baptist churches in Ellendale, N.D., 1960-64, and Freehold, N.J., 1965-69; Bethel College, Bethel Theological Seminary, St. Paul, Minn., assistant professor, 1969-71, associate professor, 1971-76, professor of New Testament, 1979—. Lecturer at schools, churches, and conferences. *Member:* Society of Biblical Literature, Evangelical Theological Society, Institute for Biblical Research.

WRITINGS: *The Method and Message of Jesus' Teachings,* Westminster, 1978; *An Introduction to the Parables of Jesus,* Westminster, 1981. Contributor to Bible encyclopedias and to theology journals in the United States, Great Britain, the Netherlands, and West Germany.

SIDELIGHTS: Stein told *CA:* "Because of my great interest in understanding the message of Jesus, I was concerned with the investigation of the methodology Jesus used in his teaching. As a result I wrote *The Method and Message of Jesus' Teachings* and another book dealing with the most popular teaching method used by Jesus—the parables." *Avocational interests:* Hunting, fishing, basketball, softball, jogging, weight lifting.

*   *   *

STEM, Thad(deus Garland), Jr.   1916-1980

OBITUARY NOTICE—See index for *CA* sketch: Born January 24, 1916, in Oxford, N.C.; died June 22, 1980, in Oxford, N.C. Poet, essayist, journalist, and author of short stories. Stem contributed a daily editorial to the *Raleigh News and Observer* from 1955 until the time of his death. He was a legendary figure in North Carolina letters: "No contemporary writer so faithfully captured the flavor of small-town North Carolina," eulogized H. G. Jones. Among his books are *Penny Heels and Wild Plums*, 1961, *Entries From Oxford*, 1971, and *Thad Stem's Ark*, 1979. Obituaries and other sources: *Chapel Hill Newspaper*, June 26, 1980; *Washington Daily News*, July 9, 1980.

* * *

STEPHENS, Jeanne
See HAGER, Jean

* * *

STEPTO, Robert B(urns) 1945-

PERSONAL: Born October 28, 1945, in Chicago, Ill.; son of Robert Charles (a professor of medicine) and Ann (a teacher; maiden name, Burns) Stepto; married Michele Leiss (a college teacher), June 21, 1967; children: Gabriel Burns, Rafael Hawkins. *Education:* Trinity College, Hartford, Conn., B.A. (cum laude), 1966; Stanford University, M.A., 1968, Ph.D., 1974. *Office:* Department of English, Yale University, New Haven, Conn. 06520.

CAREER: Williams College, Williamstown, Mass., assistant professor of English, 1971-74; Yale University, New Haven, Conn., assistant professor, 1974-79, associate professor of English and Afro-American studies, 1979—, director of Afro-American graduate studies, 1978—, fellow of Timothy Dwight College, 1975—. Visiting assistant professor at Trinity College, Hartford, Conn., summer, 1969, member of board of fellows, 1980-83; visiting associate professor at Wesleyan University, Middletown, Conn., summer, 1980; lecturer at colleges and universities. Connecticut Humanities Council, board member, 1980-82. Seminar director; guest on radio programs. *Member:* Modern Language Association of America (chairman of Commission on the Literatures and Languages of America, 1977-78), American Studies Association. *Awards, honors:* Woodrow Wilson fellow, 1966-67.

WRITINGS: (Editor with Dexter Fisher, and contributor) *Afro-American Literature: The Reconstruction of Instruction*, Modern Language Association of America, 1978; *From Behind the Veil: A Study of Afro-American Narrative*, University of Illinois Press, 1979; (editor with Michael Harper, and contributor) *Chant of Saints: A Gathering of Afro-American Literature, Art, and Scholarship*, University of Illinois Press, 1979; (contributor) Charles T. Davis, editor, *The Slave's Narrative: Text and Context*, Louisiana State University Press, 1981; (contributor) Robert Hemenway and Donald Ringe, editors, *Toward a New Century: American Literary Study in 1980*, University of Kentucky Press, 1981; (editor with John M. Reilly) *Afro-American Literature: The Reconstruction of a Literary History*, Modern Language Association of America, 1981; (editor with Robert O'Meally) *The Collected Papers of Sterling Brown*, Volume I, Garland, 1981. Contributor to literature journals.

WORK IN PROGRESS: Editing *The Collected Papers of Sterling Brown*, with Robert O'Meally, for Garland; research on narrative and cultural geography.

SIDELIGHTS: Stepto commented: "Despite my work in many areas, I am fundamentally an English teacher dedicated to the ideal of helping college students achieve a certain high level of literacy—regardless of their field or major. So, when I write about the passion for literacy that one sees, for example, among former slaves, I am attempting to pursue scholarly interests and provide my students with models for their educational careers. A student who can write will go far; a student who can read both books and the world surrounding him or her will go even further."

BIOGRAPHICAL/CRITICAL SOURCES: Times Literary Supplement, May 30, 1980; *Washington Post*, June 3, 1980.

* * *

STERN, Geraldine 1907-

PERSONAL: Born July 14, 1907, in Milwaukee, Wis.; daughter of Abraham P. (in business) and Ida (in business; maiden name, Goldstein) Rosenberg; married Herman Stern, January 19, 1929 (divorced, 1948); married Milton Wayne (a sculptor), February 4, 1961; children: (first marriage) Ellen Stern Harris, Alfred Phillip. *Education:* Attended Milwaukee Downer College, 1925-26, and Smith College, 1926-28. *Home:* 2311 Paulsen Rd., Harvard, Ill. 60033.

CAREER: Los Angeles Vocational Counseling Bureau, Los Angeles, Calif., organizer and president, 1939-41; Americans for Progressive Israel, Los Angeles, Calif., executive director, 1948-50; painter, 1955—, with solo shows in Paris, New York, Amsterdam, and Los Angeles. President of Los Angeles Service League, 1939-41; consultant to Woodstock Center. *Member:* Authors Guild of Authors League of America, Artists Equity Association of New York. *Awards, honors:* Outstanding achievement award in painting and literature from National Federation of Jewish Women's Organizations, 1967.

WRITINGS: Daughters From Afar: Profiles of Israeli Women, Abelard, 1958, revised edition, Bloch Publishing, 1963; *Israeli Women Speak Out*, Lippincott, 1979. Contributor to magazines and newspapers, including *Nation, United Nations World, Commentary*, and *Hadassah*.

SIDELIGHTS: Geraldine Stern wrote: "My professional writing started late, after a divorce, and was stimulated by my first trip to Europe and Israel in 1949. The extraordinary events in the lives of the Israeli women I met struck me so forcibly that I couldn't help comparing them to life in America. My life, and the lives of most American women, no matter how difficult, emotionally or materially, seemed relatively benign. How did they cope? How did they overcome Hitler's brutality, ejection from Arab lands of their birth, and war? Thirteen women answered these questions for me.

"A generation later, *Israeli Women Speak Out* reflects the traumas of repeated wars and personal loss. But the emphasis is on the growing awareness of women for a need of change in status. The stereotype of women working side by side with men, as was the case in the pre-state and early years of independence, does not hold today. Women are in traditional service jobs in the kibbutz, in the army, and in the general stream of work. They are particularly restricted by ancient orthodox religious laws which control all matters of marriage and divorce, with the premise that the woman is the property of the man. There is no civil marriage or divorce. Although the women's movement is several years behind that of America, intensive taped interviews with twenty-six women reveal strong feelings for a need for equality with men.

"I had intended to write the second book earlier, but an invitation to join an art class in New York accidentally launched me on a painting career that found me in Paris soon after, where I stayed for two years and started exhibiting. The writing continued occasionally.

"I am now in a writing period, with a new book contemplated, but not defined. My advice to women of all ages who want to write, paint, or do anything else is to banish fear, listen to your own voices, don't be put off by failure, and carry on the search for fulfilling work."

*   *   *

STEVENS, Cat
  See GEORGIOU, Steven Demetre

*   *   *

STEVENS, John
  See TUBB, E(dwin) C(harles)

*   *   *

STEWART, Charles T(odd), Jr.   1922-

PERSONAL: Born May 13, 1922, in New York, N.Y.; son of Charles Todd (an educator) and Leonor (a translator and editor; maiden name, Pereira de Magalhaes) Stewart; married Nancy T. Thayer (a music teacher), January 21, 1953; children: Eileen M., David T., Jocelyn N. *Education:* Attended Georgia Institute of Technology, 1938-39, and University of Georgia, 1939-41; George Washington University, B.A., 1946, M.A., 1948, Ph.D., 1954. *Home:* 5147 Macomb St. N.W., Washington, D.C. 20016. *Office:* Department of Economics, George Washington University, 2201 G St. N.W., Washington, D.C. 20052.

CAREER: Utah State University, Logan, assistant professor of economics, 1947-49; Georgetown University, Washington, D.C., senior research analyst, 1953-58; Chamber of Commerce of the United States, Washington, D.C., research economist, 1958-62, director of economic research, 1962-63; George Washington University, Washington, D.C., research professor of economics, 1963-65, professor of economics, 1965—, chairman of department, 1974-76, 1979—. Consultant to Interamerican Development Bank, National Science Foundation, National Aeronautics and Space Administration, and Organization of American States. *Military service:* U.S. Army, Infantry, 1942-45; received Bronze Star and Purple Heart. *Member:* American Economic Association, American Association for the Advancement of Science, Public Choice Society, Regional Science Association, Southern Economic Association.

WRITINGS: The Promise of Economic Growth (monograph), Chamber of Commerce of the United States, 1960; *The United States Balance of Payments Position* (monograph), Chamber of Commerce of the United States, 1962; *Automation and Unemployment* (monograph), Chamber of Commerce of the United States, 1962; *Criteria for Government Spending* (monograph), Chamber of Commerce of the United States, 1962; (with George Macesich) *Economic Change and Adjustment* (monograph), Chamber of Commerce of the United States, 1962; (with J. M. Peterson) *Employment Effects of Minimum Wages,* American Enterprise Institute for Public Policy Research, 1969.

(With C. M. Siddayao) *Increasing the Supply of Medical Personnel,* American Enterprise Institute for Public Policy Research, 1973; *Low Wage Workers in an Affluent Society,* Nelson-Hall, 1974; *Air Pollution, Human Health, and Public Policy,* Heath, 1979. Contributor to journals in economics, geography, law, and the social sciences.

WORK IN PROGRESS: What Price Health? (tentative title), dealing with issues in the demand for and supply of health care in a period of escalating costs for medical care and growing public commitment to universal access to most medical needs, completion expected in 1981; *The Distribution of Income and Other Desiderata* (tentative title), assessing current states of knowledge about the distribution of opportunities for consumption and production, the extent to which these opportunities are and ought to be mediated by income, and considering the consequences of alternative methods of allocating scarce desiderata, such as prestigious jobs and occupations as well as income, completion expected in 1982.

SIDELIGHTS: Stewart wrote: "I spent most of my childhood in Brazil, with Portuguese my first language. There I was exposed very early to histories of the classical world. Later I became an avid reader of philosophies of history. These experiences and my service in the Pacific during World War II addicted me to travel, to nature, and to the study of diverse cultures. I have traveled extensively in Asia, Latin America, and Europe, and hope to continue traveling. Jungles, deserts, and coral reefs all fascinate me.

"But my enduring interest is in the human beings who live in such varied natural and cultural habitats, in trying to understand the causes of culture and history, insofar as they are subject to any law. This interest has led me to dabble in all the social sciences. It is scarcely reflected in my writing to date, and perhaps it never will be."

AVOCATIONAL INTERESTS: Visual arts, painting and sketching, reading science fiction (good and bad) and books of Lawrence Durrell.

*   *   *

STEWART, Donald Ogden   1894-1980

OBITUARY NOTICE—See index for *CA* sketch: Born November 30, 1894, in Columbus, Ohio; died August 2, 1980, in London, England. Parodist, playwright, and screenwriter. During the 1920's Stewart wrote humorous pieces for *Vanity Fair* while belonging to the famed writers' group, the Algonquin "round table." His first books were mainly parodies and satires on social etiquette and middle-class values. In the 1930's he left New York to begin a Hollywood career, which peaked with the Academy Award-winning "Philadelphia Story" in 1940. Stewart's involvement in labor and civil liberties causes brought him under attack during the Cold War era, however, and he was eventually blacklisted from his screenwriting job. He then headed for England, where, with the exception of his autobiography in 1975, he wrote little in his remaining years. His other writings include the novel *Mr. and Mrs. Haddock Abroad,* the play "Rebound," and the screenplay "Life Without Father." Obituaries and other sources: Donald Ogden Stewart, *By a Stroke of Luck: An Autobiography,* Paddington Press, 1975; *New York Times,* August 3, 1980; *Washington Post,* August 4, 1980; *Chicago Tribune,* August 5, 1980; *Time,* August 18, 1980; *Newsweek,* August 18, 1980.

*   *   *

STEWART, Ella Winter   1898-1980

OBITUARY NOTICE: Born March 17, 1898, in Melbourne, Australia; died August 5, 1980, in London, England. Known as a "radical activist," Ella Winter Stewart fought to relieve the plight of migrant workers and was adamantly opposed to the rise of terrorism and political violence evident in the world. In 1931 she made the first of her two trips to the Soviet Union. She wrote two books based on her experiences there: *Red Virtue,* dealing with the role of women in the U.S.S.R., and *I Saw the Russian People,* depicting life in wartime Russia. Stewart's autobiography, *And Not to Yield,* was published in 1963. Obituaries and other sources: *Washington Post,* August 6, 1980.

* * *

STEWART, George Rippey   1895-1980

OBITUARY NOTICE—See index for *CA* sketch: Born May 31, 1895, in Sewickley, Pa.; died August 22, 1980, in San Francisco, Calif. Educator and writer. Stewart was affiliated with the University of California at Berkeley for nearly forty years when he was named professor emeritus in 1962. His fields of study included history, forestry, meteorology, and onomastics. In addition to his well-known novels, *Storm* and *Fire,* Stewart wrote nonfiction books, including *The Year of the Oath, Committee of Vigilance: Revolution in San Francisco,* and *Pickett's Charge.* Obituaries and other sources: *Time,* September 8, 1980; *Publishers Weekly,* September 12, 1980; *AB Bookman's Weekly,* October 6, 1980.

* * *

STEWART, Kerry
See STEWART, Linda

* * *

STEWART, Linda
(Kerry Stewart, Sam Stewart)

PERSONAL: Born in New York, N.Y.; daughter of a physician; married a screenwriter (divorced). *Education:* Brandeis University, B.A. *Residence:* New York, N.Y. *Agent:* Ziegler, Diskant, Inc., 9255 Sunset Blvd., Suite 1122, Los Angeles, Calif. 90069.

CAREER: Batten, Barton, Durstine & Osborn, New York City, advertising copywriter; Grey Advertising, New York City, copy group head; McCann Erikson, New York City, vice-president and copywriter/producer; free-lance advertising writer for Citizens for Clean Air, New York City Environmental Protection Agency, and Urban League; *Consumer Action Now,* New York City, editor and writer, 1970-73; free-lance writer, 1972—. *Member:* Writers Guild of America.

WRITINGS—Novels; under name Linda Stewart: *The Peking Dossier,* Award, 1973; *The Jerusalem File,* Award, 1975; *Same Time Next Year,* Dell, 1978; *Panic on Page One,* Delacorte, 1979.

Under pseudonym Kerry Stewart: *Ruby,* Berkley Publishing, 1978; *If Ever I See You Again,* Bantam, 1978; *The Concorde: Airport 79,* Dell, 1978.

Under pseudonym Sam Stewart: *McCoy,* Dell, 1976; *Harry and Walter Go to New York,* Dell, 1976; *Jackson County Jail,* Dell, 1977; *Fun With Dick and Jane,* Dell, 1977.

Writer for television science fiction series, "Touch of Evil," 1975, and Time/Life documentary series, "G.I. Diary," 1978. Script rewriter of television film, "City of Fear," 1980. Co-author of television film, "Murder on Ice," CBS-TV, 1980. Author of lyrics and special material for Julius Monk Revues, Tamamint Playhouse, Edie Adams, and Julie Wilson.

WORK IN PROGRESS: A novel (a thriller); a television pilot film.

SIDELIGHTS: Linda Stewart wrote: "My uncle was a Pulitzer Prize-winning writer. As a kid I was not so much impressed by the money or fame, but by the fact that he got to sleep late. Any job that let you sleep late seemed like a good idea. I think I like to write because fantasy is often more interesting than reality; also I like the kind of people I meet there. I love doing the research for books and learning, in as much depth as I can, about different subjects. I also love words; they're wonderful toys. What's my motivation? To pay the rent; not to have to take a nine-to-five job."

Panic on Page One is "a sharp-witted, acid-tongued, engrossing novel," according to the *Los Angeles Times Book Review.* When a psychopathic killer sets out to rid Los Angeles of its "harlots," the publisher of the financially-troubled *Tribune* sees a way to boost circulation. He hires a yellow journalist, gives page-one prominence to the murder stories, and pits police and journalists against each other. "As hard-boiled and cynical as, but without the leavening sentimentality of 'The Front Page,' this is a superbly written book," wrote S. L. Stebel. "The dialogue sounds as if it's snarled around a saliva-drenched cigar; characters are drawn (and sometimes quartered) unsparingly."

BIOGRAPHICAL/CRITICAL SOURCES: Los Angeles Times Book Review, September 16, 1979; *New York Times Book Review,* October 28, 1979.

* * *

STEWART, Sam
See STEWART, Linda

* * *

STOBAUGH, Robert B. (Jr.)   1927-

PERSONAL: Born in 1927, in McGehee, Ark.; son of Robert B. Stobaugh. *Education:* Louisiana State University, B.S., 1947; Harvard University, D.B.A., 1968. *Home:* 4 Ross Rd., Belmont, Mass. 02178. *Office:* Graduate School of Business Administration, Harvard University, Cambridge, Mass. 02138.

CAREER: Harvard University, Cambridge, Mass., began as assistant professor, became associate professor, professor of business administration, 1967—, head of Energy Project, 1972—. *Member:* American Economic Association.

WRITINGS: Petrochemical Manufacturing and Marketing Guide, Gulf Publishing Co., 1966; *The U.S. Oil Import Program and the Petrochemical Industry,* Cabinet Task Force on Oil Import Control, 1969; *The Likely Effects on the U.S. Economy of Eliminating the Deferral of U.S. Income Tax on Foreign Earnings,* Management Analysis Center, 1973; (with Sidney M. Robbins) *Money in the Multinational Enterprise: A Study of Financial Policy,* Basic Books, 1973; (with Joan P. Curhan) *An Exploratory Study Concerning Published Information Available on Channels Used by U.S.-Based Multinational Enterprises to Transfer Technology Internationally,* Harvard Business School, 1974; (with Robbins, William T. Gregor, and John C. Kirby) *How to Use International Capital Markets: A Guide to Europe and the Middle East,* Financial Executives Research Foundation, 1976; (with Dario Iacuelli and others) *U.S. Taxation of United States Manufacturing Abroad: Likely Effects of Taxing Unremitted Profits,* Financial Executives Research Foundation, 1976; (editor with Daniel Yergin) *Energy Future: Report of the Energy Project at the Harvard Business School,* Random House, 1979.

SIDELIGHTS: Energy Future summarizes four years of research by Harvard's Energy Project, an academic program organized by Robert Stobaugh in 1972 to study and evaluate

America's energy needs. Within four months of its release in July, 1979, *Energy Future* had sold more than 100,000 copies and was number eight on the *New York Times* best-seller list. "I don't think anybody *dreamed* that we would have this kind of sale," Stobaugh remarked. "Generally, academic books don't do very well on the broad market. I know, because I've been the author or co-editor of eight of them, and one even sold under 1,000 copies."

According to the publisher, Random House, *Energy Future* provides a historical perspective on the uses and availability of energy resources, describes the current debate about how to best solve the problem of reduced energy supplies, and advocates a course of action. Stobaugh and co-editor Daniel Yergin contend that the United States has two options: it can import more OPEC oil, thus increasing its dependence on the Middle East; or it can pursue a nationwide policy of energy conservation while developing the technology necessary for solar power. The editors "argue convincingly for the second alternative," *Atlantic Monthly* observed, "and their book is a clear, intelligent, and non-polemical analysis of the costs and hazards of the conservation strategies they favor."

Peter Passell of the *New York Times Book Review* called *Energy Future* "the best single examination of America's energy problem in print. What explains this excellence is the competent integration of geopolitics, economics and science.... Much of [the book] consists of concise essays on the prospects for natural gas, coal, nuclear and solar power." John Kenneth Galbraith, writing in the *New York Review of Books,* added that the book "has been praised, and deservedly, as a model of what university research and monograph writing on a major question of policy should be."

BIOGRAPHICAL/CRITICAL SOURCES: New York Times Book Review, July 29, 1979, November 18, 1979; *New Republic,* August 18, 1979; *Atlantic Monthly,* September, 1979; *Saturday Review,* September 1, 1979; *New York Review of Books,* September 27, 1979.*

*　　*　　*

STOCKING, Hobart E(bey)   1906-

PERSONAL: Born November 11, 1906, in Clarendon, Tex.; son of Jerome Daniel (a physician) and Sarah Maria (Ward) Stocking; married Helen Berenice Smith (a geneticist), August 25, 1934 (deceased); children: Sarah A. Stocking Ben-Bouchta, Martha L. Stocking Swanson. *Education:* Attended Clarendon Junior College, 1923-26, and University of Texas, 1927-28; Johns Hopkins University, M.A., 1938; University of Chicago, Ph.D., 1949. *Home:* 108 Berry St., Stillwater, Okla. 74074. *Office:* Department of Geology, Oklahoma State University, Stillwater, Okla. 74078.

CAREER: Companhia de Petroleo de Angola, topographic engineer, 1929-31; U.S. Geological Survey, assistant geologist, 1933-34; Shell Petroleum Co., Midland, Tex., geologist, 1936-38; West Virginia State University, Morgantown, assistant professor of geology, 1940-43; Petroleum Administration, Washington, D.C., chief geologist in District One, 1943-45; U.S. Department of State, Washington, visiting professor at University of Costa Rica, 1945-46; Oklahoma State University, Stillwater, professor of geology, 1946-52; Atomic Energy Commission, Washington, chief geologist in Grand Junction Division, 1952-58, chief of Argentine mission, 1958; Oklahoma State University, professor of geology, 1958—. Honorary professor at University of Costa Rica, 1948; distinguished lecturer for American Association of Petroleum Geologists, 1956; professor at Johns Hopkins University, summers, 1962-73. *Member:* Geological Society

of America (fellow), American Association for the Advancement of Science (fellow), Common Cause (district coordinator, 1973-75).

WRITINGS: The Road to Santa Fe, Hastings House, 1971. Contributor to professional journals and popular magazines, including *Nature* and *Natural History.*

WORK IN PROGRESS: Principles of Optical Mineralogy; The Butterfield Stage Road.

AVOCATIONAL INTERESTS: Travel in Morocco.

*　　*　　*

STONE, Hoyt E(dward)   1935-
(Eddie Vernon)

PERSONAL: Born March 16, 1935, in St. Charles, Va.; son of Herbert A. (a minister) and Eloise (Holmes) Stone; married Blanche Dodson (a teacher), April 9, 1955; children: Hoyt Edward, Jr., Vince Anthony. *Education:* Lee College, B.A. (biblical education), 1957; Roanoke College, B.A. (history), 1966. *Politics:* Democrat. *Home:* 1513 Everhart Dr., Cleveland, Tenn. 37311. *Office:* 922 Montgomery Ave., Cleveland, Tenn. 37311.

CAREER: Ordained minister of Church of God, 1964; Church of God, evangelist, 1957-58, pastor in Bassett, Va., 1958-62, and Tabb, Va., 1962, state director of youth and Christian education in Virginia, 1962-66, and pastor in Danville, Va., 1966-68; Lee College, Cleveland, Tenn., director of alumni affairs, placement, and public relations, 1968-72; Church of God, pastor in Bluefield, Va., 1972-76, director of evangelism in West Virginia, 1976-78, and editor of youth and Christian education literature in Cleveland, Tenn., 1978—.

WRITINGS: Of Course You Can, Pathway Press, 1973; *Yet Will I Serve Him,* Pathway Press, 1976; *Moments,* Beacon Hill, 1975; *The Inner Quest,* Pathway Press, 1980. Contributor of more than one hundred fifty articles and stories (some under pseudonym Eddie Vernon) to magazines. Editor of *Lighted Pathway.*

*　　*　　*

STONE, Merlin   1931-

PERSONAL: Born September 27, 1931, in New York, N.Y.

CAREER: Sculptor, 1958-67; university teacher of art and art history; writer.

WRITINGS: (Editor) *An Enlarged European Community and the Less Developed Countries,* University of Sussex, 1973; *Product Planning: An Integrated Approach,* Wiley, 1976; *When God Was a Woman,* Dial, 1976 (published in England as *The Paradise Papers: The Suppression of Women's Rites,* Quartet Books, 1976). Also author of *Our Goddess and Heroine Heritage,* Volume I of *Ancient Mirrors of Womanhood,* published by New Sibylline Books.

WORK IN PROGRESS: Volume II of *Ancient Mirrors of Womanhood.*

*　　*　　*

STORM, Lesley
See CLARK, Mabel Margaret (Cowie)

*　　*　　*

STOUT, Russell, Jr.   1932-

PERSONAL: Born June 6, 1932, in Bronx, N.Y.; son of Russell Seward and Frances Marie (Sullivan) Stout; divorced; children: Russell James, Karen Lynn Stout Hitchcock. *Education:* University of California, Berkeley, A.B., 1972, M.A., 1973, Ph.D., 1979. *Office:* School of Government and Public Administration, American University, Washington, D.C. 20016.

CAREER: U.S. Air Force, noncommissioned officer in communications, 1951-71, retiring as master sergeant; Indiana University, Bloomington, associate director of International Development Institute and adjunct lecturer, 1975-80; American University, Washington, D.C., associate professor of government and public administration and director of Master's in Public Administration Program, 1980—. *Member:* American Political Science Association, American Society for Public Administration. *Awards, honors:* William E. Mosher Award from American Society for Public Administration, 1979, for article, "To Manage Is Not to Control; or, The Folly of Type II Errors."

WRITINGS: Management or Control?: The Organizational Challenge, Indiana University Press, 1980; *Organizations, Management, and Control,* Indiana University Press, 1980. Contributor to management and public administration journals.

WORK IN PROGRESS: Studying the effect of evaluation and accountability on policy in organizations; a study of the U.S. Agency for International Development, as part of a comparative review of bilateral development assistance agencies.

SIDELIGHTS: Stout commented: "Large scale formal organizations are the instruments by which most things get done in the modern world. Yet ignorance of their operations persists. The popular press and scholars most often portray government and private bureaucracies as malevolent machines with a will of their own, when in fact the best that can be said for these agencies is that they 'muddle through'. My work is aimed at improving our understanding of organizations so that they can better serve us. Right now, I am convinced that our efforts to control (in the literal sense) large organizations further complicates matters, and may even reduce our ability to manage them."

*   *   *

STRAUSS, Leo   1899-1973

PERSONAL: Born September 20, 1899, in Kirchhain, Germany (now West Germany); died of pneumonia, October 18, 1973, in Annapolis, Md.; came to United States, 1938; son of Hugo and Jennie (David) Strauss; married Miriam Bernson, June 20, 1933; children: Jennie, Thomas. *Education:* University of Hamburg, Ph.D., 1921. *Residence:* Annapolis, Md.

CAREER: Academy for Jewish Research, Berlin, Germany, research assistant, 1925-32; New School for Social Research, New York City, professor, 1938-49; University of Chicago, Chicago, Ill., Hutchins Distinguished Service Professor of political science, 1949-68; Claremont Men's College, Claremont, Calif., professor of political science, 1968-69; St. John's College, Annapolis, Md., Scott Buchanan Scholar in residence, 1969-73. *Military service:* German Army, served in World War I. *Member:* American Political Science Association.

WRITINGS—In English: *Die religionskritik Spinozas als grundlage seiner Bibelwissenschaft,* Akademie-Verlag, 1930, translation by Elsa M. Sinclair published as *Spinoza's Critique of Religion,* Schocken Books, 1965; *The Political Philosophy of Hobbes: Its Basis and Its Genesis,* translated from the original German by Sinclair, Clarendon Press, 1936,

reprinted, University of Chicago Press, 1963; *On Tyranny: An Interpretation of Xenophon's Hiero,* Political Science Classics, 1948, revised and enlarged edition, Cornell University Press, 1968; *Natural Right and History,* University of Chicago Press, 1950; *Persecution and the Art of Writing,* Free Press of Glencoe, 1952; *Thoughts on Machiavelli,* Free Press of Glencoe, 1959; *What Is Political Philosophy? and Other Studies,* Free Press of Glencoe, 1959.

(Editor with Joseph Cropsey) *History of Political Philosophy,* Rand McNally, 1963; *The City and Man,* Rand McNally, 1964; (contributor) Keith C. Brown, editor, *Hobbes: Studies,* Harvard University Press, 1965; *Socrates and Aristophanes,* Basic Books, 1966; *Liberalism: Ancient and Modern,* Basic Books, 1968; *Xenonphon's Socratic Discourse: An Interpretation of the Oeconomicus,* Cornell University Press, 1970; *Xenophon's Socrates,* Cornell University Press, 1972; *The Argument and the Action of Plato's Laws,* University of Chicago Press, 1975; *Political Philosophy: Six Essays,* edited by Hilail Gilden, Pegasus, 1975.

In German: (Editor with others) Moses Mendelssohn, *Gesammelte Schriften,* Akademie-Verlag, 1929; *Philosphie und Gesetz,* Schocken, 1935; *Hobbes' politische Wissenschaft,* new edition, Luchterhand, 1965.

SIDELIGHTS: A well-known scholar, Leo Strauss was noted for his lucid and insightful interpretations of classical political theories. The *New York Times* observed that "Strauss is credited with keeping the study of the political classics alive and for showing students that thinkers such as Plato, Machiavelli, and Hobbes were relevant to present-day political dilemmas."

Most of Strauss's books were geared toward scholarly readers, but J. H. Hallowell noted that *History of Political Philosophy* may be of interest to general readers as well. He also believed that Strauss's earlier book, *Natural Right and History,* "deserves a wide audience, not only among political theorists, for whom it is indispensable, but among political scientists generally," because of its "admirable scholarship" and incisiveness.

Reviewers throughout the years have stressed Strauss's role in the study of political philosophy. A *Choice* reviewer said that "Strauss was an eminent and stormy figure in recent American political theory and his comments are important." Rubin Gotesky commented that the author "has an extraordinarily interesting and devious mind, often rich in insights and scholarly subtleties." *Ethics* critic H. M. Lubasz echoed this opinion: "Professor Strauss's arguments are often illuminating and sometimes challenging, so much so that one regrets that he deals almost exclusively with scholarly, historical, textual, interpretative problems rather than with the systematic philosophical problems of contemporary politics."

BIOGRAPHICAL/CRITICAL SOURCES: American Academy of Political and Social Science Annals, May, 1937, January, 1953, May, 1969; *New York Times,* May 1, 1949; *American Political Science Review,* June, 1954; *Ethics,* April, 1960; *Commonweal,* November 4, 1960; *America,* September 7, 1963; *Choice,* February, 1967, January, 1973, November, 1975; *Commentary,* October, 1967, January, 1975; *National Review,* December 7, 1973; *Times Literary Supplement,* April 9, 1976.

OBITUARIES: New York Times, October 21, 1973; *Washington Post,* October 23, 1973; *Social Research,* spring, 1974.*

STREET, Jonathan
  See TINER, John Hudson

*   *   *

STUART, Charles
  See REID, Charles (Stuart)

*   *   *

STUCKEY, Sterling 1932-

PERSONAL: Born March 2, 1932, in Memphis, Tenn.; son of Ples S. (a luggage maker) and Elma (a poet; maiden name, Johnson) Stuckey. *Education:* Northwestern University, B.A., 1955, M.A., 1968, Ph.D., 1972. *Home:* 2075 Yale, Palo Alto, Calif. 94306. *Agent:* Bertha Klausner International Literary Agency, Inc., 71 Park Ave., New York, N.Y. 10016. *Office:* Harris 201-C, Northwestern University, Evanston, Ill. 60201.

CAREER: Chicago (Ill.) Public Schools, teacher of history and geography, 1960-65; University of Illinois, Center for Inner City Studies, Chicago, teacher of history, 1967; University of Minnesota, Minneapolis, Hill Foundation Visiting Professor of Afro-American History, 1971; Northwestern University, Evanston, Ill., associate professor, 1971-77, professor of history, 1977—. Founder and chairman of Emergency Relief Committee for Fayette County (Tenn.), 1960-61; regional director of Congress for Racial Equality, 1960-62. Consultant in American history to Encyclopaedia Britannica Films, Inc., 1964; consultant to Lilly Endowment, 1978-79. *Member:* American Historical Association, Organization of American Historians, Association for the Study of Afro-American Life and History. *Awards, honors:* W.E.B. DuBois research fellowship at Center for Afro-African Studies, University of California, Los Angeles, 1975, and at Center for Advanced Study in the Behavioral Sciences, Stanford University, 1980-81.

WRITINGS: The Ideological Origins of Black Nationalism, Beacon Press, 1972. Also author of *A People Uprooted,* with Benjamin Quarles, 1965, *Chains of Slavery,* 1965, *Separate and Unequal,* 1965, and *Quest for Equality,* 1965. Contributor of articles to newspapers and magazines, including *New York Times Book Review, Negro Digest,* and *Massachusetts Review.*

WORK IN PROGRESS: A critique, with Joshua Leslie, of Melville's *Benito Cereno;* a biography of Paul Robeson; poetry.

SIDELIGHTS: Stuckey commented: "My mother's interest in the pursuit of knowledge and her ability as a poet, as well as reading W.E.B. DuBois in high school and meeting Paul Robeson in my teens, were easily the greatest influences on my life."

*   *   *

STURSBERG, Peter 1913-

PERSONAL: Born August 31, 1913, in Chefoo, China; son of Walter Arthur (a postal commissioner) and Mary Ellen (Shaw) Stursberg; married Jessamy Anderson Robertson, October 5, 1946; children: Richard Barclay, Judith Mary Stursberg Maus. *Education:* Attended McGill University, 1930-32. *Religion:* Anglican. *Home:* 5132 Alderfield Place, West Vancouver, British Columbia, Canada V7W 2W7.

CAREER: Daily Times, Victoria, British Columbia, reporter, 1934-38; Empire Press Union (now Commonwealth Press Union), exchange reporter with *Daily Herald,* Lon-

don, England, 1938-39; *Daily Province,* Vancouver, British Columbia, reporter, 1939-40; Canadian Broadcasting Corp. (C.B.C.), Vancouver, news editor, 1941-43, war correspondent, 1943-45; *Daily Herald,* roving foreign correspondent, 1945-50; Canadian Broadcasting Corp., United Nations correspondent in New York, N.Y., 1950-56, Ottawa correspondent, 1956-79, and co-host of "Looking Through the Papers"; free-lance writer, 1979—. Research officer for prime minister in Ottawa, Ontario, 1957-58. Newscaster for CJOH-TV; editor of "Question Period," on CTV-TV. Has conducted four Canadian Club lecture tours; member of board of governors of United Nations International School, 1952-55. *Member:* Parliamentary Press Gallery (honorary life member), National Press Club of Canada (honorary life member), Canadian War Correspondents Association. *Awards, honors:* Canadian Radio Award, 1950, for reports on the United Nations.

WRITINGS: Journey Into Victory (war correspondence), Harrap, 1944; *Agreement in Principle* (foreign correspondence), Longmans, Green, 1961; *Those Were the Days* (memoirs of the 1930's), Peter Martin Associates, 1969; *Mister Broadcasting: The Ernie Bushell Story,* Peter Martin Associates, 1971; *Diefenbaker Leadership Gained, 1956-62,* University of Toronto Press, 1975; *Diefenbaker Leadership Lost, 1962-67,* University of Toronto Press, 1976; *Lester Pearson and the Dream of Unity,* Doubleday, 1978; *Lester Pearson and the American Dilemma,* Doubleday, 1980. Ottawa correspondent for *Toronto Star,* 1956-57, and *Newsweek;* Ottawa editor of *Saturday Night,* 1960-65, and *Commentator,* 1965-70. Contributor to magazines, including *Maclean's.*

WORK IN PROGRESS: Recording memoirs of Canadian political leaders; a volume for Doubleday's Canadian history series.

SIDELIGHTS: In his review of *Lester Pearson and the American Dilemma* in the *Toronto Globe and Mail,* Robert Bothwell noted: "Over the past few years, Peter Stursberg has made a name for himself as the most eminent Canadian practitioner of a new style of historical research—oral history. Devotees of the art roam the world searching out the once newsworthy, cornering them in their clubs and living rooms and extracting their memories of events past in the service of books future. Stursberg has done a good job of it. Over the past decade he has interviewed hundreds of people for thousands of hours. The results are now on file in the Public Archives of Canada and appealing excerpts are now published in four books of which *Lester Pearson and the American Dilemma* is the last."

Stursberg wrote: "The documentary technique of oral or living history, as I like to call it, is in keeping with the electronic age; people tend to be more frank and forthcoming when they are speaking than when they are writing, even though they know their words are being recorded for use. The autumn 1979 issue of *Canadian Forum* found 'the varied and often rough texture produced by the technique of tape-recorder mosaic' to be more stimulating than 'the characterless blandness of Pearson's own memoirs' and that 'Stursberg's earlier garlands of tape recordings about Diefenbaker were also more interesting than what Diefenbaker had to say about himself.' However, it is not a technique which is much admired by academic historians, and Ramsay Cook, in reviewing *Lester Pearson and the Dream of Unity,* cried out, 'if this be living history then I prefer mine dead.'

"I acquired my expertise in interviewing through broadcasting. I was the first correspondent of the Canadian Broadcasting Corporation to cover the Canadian troops in action in World War II. For the first time, the sound of battle was heard in the living rooms of the nation, and such was the impact of this radio reporting that it made me a nationally known figure.

"I wrote a book about my war experiences, *Journey Into Victory.* The second book, *Agreement in Principle,* was an account of my years as a foreign correspondent. *Those Were the Days* is a memoir of the depression and the thirties in Canada's lotus land, Vancouver Island. *Mister Broadcasting* has been described by an American communications expert as a personalised history of broadcasting in Canada."

AVOCATIONAL INTERESTS: Tennis, reading.

BIOGRAPHICAL/CRITICAL SOURCES: Maclean's, September 3, 1943; A. E. Powley, *Broadcast From the Front,* Hakkert, 1975.

* * *

STYLLA, Joanne
See BRANDEN, Victoria (Fremlin)

* * *

SUDHALTER, Richard M(errill) 1938-
(Art Napoleon)

PERSONAL: Born December 28, 1938, in Boston, Mass.; son of Albert William and Esther Frieda (Stearns) Sudhalter; separated; children: Kimberley Lyle, Adrian Vaile. *Education:* Attended Harvard University, 1958-60; Oberlin College, B.A., 1960.

CAREER: Bavarian State Radio, Munich, West Germany, staff musician, 1964; United Press International, Frankfurt am Main, West Germany, political correspondent from West and East Germany, 1964-66, staff correspondent from the United Kingdom and Northern Ireland, 1966-68, bureau manager for Yugoslavia and the Balkans in Belgrade, Yugoslavia, 1968-70; writer, jazz archivist, and cornetist in London, England, 1972-75; performer, writer, and producer in New York City, 1975-77; *New York Post,* New York City, free-lance critic, 1978—. Music director of Nice Jazz Festival; producer of selected concerts at Newport Jazz Festival; organizer, director, and performer with New Paul Whiteman Orchestra; administrator of New York Jazz Repertory Company; producer and soloist for "Paul Whiteman Evenings" in New York City and Philadelphia, Pa., and "W. C. Handy Commemorative" in Washington, D.C. Guest on television and radio programs; news and feature writer for London Broadcasting Co.; broadcaster for British Broadcasting Corp. (BBC-Radio and Television); consultant to Franklin Mint, Time-Life Records, and Reader's Digest Records.

WRITINGS: Bix: Man and Legend, Arlington House, 1975; (contributor) *Jazz Now,* Quartet Books, 1975. Author of columns and record sleeve essays. Contributor of articles, translations, and reviews to magazines and newspapers (sometimes under pseudonym Art Napoleon), including *Down Beat, Jazz Journal, Jazz Magazine, Storyville, Newsweek,* and *Punch.* Chief editor in London office for Educational Audio Visual, Inc., 1974.

SIDELIGHTS: Sudhalter told *CA:* "Assigned to Belgrade as United Press International manager for eastern Europe and the Balkans, I found a bureau with great potential, not only as a news center for Yugoslavia, Romania, Bulgaria, Albania, and Greece, but as a sensitive listening post for other eastern points and developments in the Third World.

"I had to develop and maintain a wide network of 'sources', official and clandestine, and because of the round-the-clock nature of wire service work, I had to be the best informed of all foreign newsmen in town, aware of potential breaks even before they happened, and able to walk a political tightrope between what I knew and what I wrote.

"During research for *Bix: Man and Legend,* I discovered the entire library of arrangements for the Paul Whiteman Orchestra of the 1920's on file at Williams College—and an idea was born. It came to fruition in 1974, when a hand-picked twenty-nine-piece orchestra of top British musicians under my leadership presented an evening of the finest music of Whiteman's 'Bix years' at a London jazz festival otherwise devoted to contemporary works and performers. With a knowledge based on lifelong study of the scores and style of the period, I both selected and rehearsed the musicians, and appeared as solo cornetist in the role of Bix Beiderbecke.

"This 'New Paul Whiteman Orchestra,' as we called it, recorded its first album immediately, and became a regular feature on BBC-Radio. Other concerts followed, then another record and a BBC-TV documentary. This led, in turn, to concerts in Philadelphia and at Carnegie Hall with an all-star American orchestra.

"Among the events I produced under the auspices of the New York Jazz Repertory Company was a four-concert Duke Ellington retrospective, the first of its kind since the composer's death. It was presented at Carnegie Hall as a highlight of the 1976 Newport New York Jazz Festival. Other Newport events included a 1979 Hoagy Carmichael tribute, with the composer present and participating, and a 1980 Fred Astaire evening.

"At the moment I am enjoying living as public and diversified a life as I can, which means maintaining concurrent careers as a jazz cornetist and bandleader, writer, critic, broadcaster, and sometime concert producer. I am continually delighted to discover how much can be wedged into each day, still leaving room for purely hedonistic pleasures."

AVOCATIONAL INTERESTS: "I nurse a passion for archaeology, in particular the unfolding history of the Minoan kingdom on and around Crete. I retain an abiding interest in Yugoslavia—history and politics, a legacy of the years I worked there. Literary preoccupations include the 'war poets' of World War I, in particular Isaac Rosenberg. I also greatly admire James Agee, whom I consider the last great American prose stylist of this century, and Joseph Conrad, whose preoccupations are my preoccupations, speaking to me clearly and poignantly."

* * *

SUID, Lawrence Howard 1938-

PERSONAL: Born July 13, 1938, in Cleveland, Ohio; son of Ben and Regina Suid; married Patricia Steckler, May 14, 1971 (marriage ended June, 1976). *Education:* Case Western Reserve University, B.A., 1961, Ph.D., 1980; Duke University, M.A., 1962; Brandeis University, M.F.A., 1971. *Politics:* Democrat. *Religion:* Jewish. *Home and office:* 4751 West Braddock Rd., No. 203, Alexandria, Va. 22311.

CAREER: Writer. Windsor Mountain School, Lenox, Mass., high school history teacher, 1964-65; Winona State College, Winona, Minn., assistant professor of history, 1966-67; Newton Public Schools, Newton, Mass., high school and junior college teacher of history, 1968-70; contract historian for Army Corps of Engineers, 1979-80. Visiting assistant professor of communications, University of Vermont, 1978-79; instructor in American studies, Case Western Reserve

University, summer, 1976. *Member:* American Historical Association, American Studies Association. *Awards, honors:* American Council of Learned Societies, research grant, 1975; American Film Institute, research grant, 1975; U.S. Marine Corps, historical research grant, 1977-78.

WRITINGS: Guts and Glory: Great American War Movies, Addison-Wesley, 1978; (contributor) John E. O'Connor and Martin A. Hackson, editors, *American History: American Film,* Ungar, 1979; *Film and Propaganda in America: A Documentary History,* Volume 4 (Suid was not associated with earlier volumes), Greenwood, 1980; *Hollywood and the Marine Corps,* Marine Corps Historical Monograph, 1980; (editor and annotator) *Air Force: A Script,* Wisconsin Press, 1981; *Fred Zinnemann: A Bibliography and Research Guide,* G. K. Hall, 1981; *Fred Zinnemann: A Film Biography,* Twayne, 1981.

Contributor of articles to journals, magazines, and newspapers, including *Film Comment, Journal of Popular Film, New York Times, Los Angeles Times,* and *Washington Post.*

WORK IN PROGRESS: A History of the U.S. Army Facilities Support Agency, publication by the Army Corps of Engineers expected in 1981.

SIDELIGHTS: Suid commented on his work in progress, *A History of the U.S. Army Facilities Support Agency:* "The Army Corps of Engineers nuclear power program, my primary concern for the next several months, is an example of an idea that was ahead of its time. When the program was initiated in 1953, the military wanted to demonstrate the peacetime use of nuclear energy for the generation of power. At the same time, the military had a requirement for small, mobile generators to supply power in remote locations such as Alaska, the DEW line, Greenland, and Antarctica. Unfortunately, after building five small, reliable powerplants, Secretary McNamara decided nuclear power on a small scale was not cost-effective and the program was phased out. Ironically, the first powerplant to go into operation in 1957, the proto-type at Fort Belvoir, was shut down in 1973 just as the oil embargo was beginning. If the production of small, nuclear powerplants had continued beyond the first generation of prototypes, the program might have made a significant contribution to solving the military's current and continuing energy problem in non-tactical (i.e., behind the lines) areas. I am writing a history of the program and its transition to a power program and now also a facilities support program."

*   *   *

SUKNASKI, Andrew   1942-

PERSONAL: Born July 30, 1942, in Wood Mountain, Saskatchewan, Canada; son of Andrew and Julia (Karasinski) Suknaski. *Education:* Attended University of Victoria, 1964-65, Montreal Museum of Fine Arts School of Art and Design, 1965, and Notre Dame University, Nelson, British Columbia, 1966-67; Kootenay School of Art, diploma, 1967; attended University of British Columbia, 1967-68, and Simon Fraser University, 1968-69. *Politics:* "New Left working dreamer." *Religion:* "Pantheist." *Residence:* Wood Mountain, Saskatchewan, Canada S0H 4L0.

CAREER: Elfin Plot, Wood Mountain, Saskatchewan, editor, 1968-74; Deodar Shadow Press, Wood Mountain, editor, 1970-71; Anak Press, Wood Mountain, editor, 1971-76; *Sundog,* Wood Mountain, editor, 1973-76; Sundog Press, Wood Mountain, editor, 1973-78. Writer-in-residence at University of Manitoba, 1977-78; promoter of National Film Board of Canada, 1980. *Member:* League of Canadian Poets. *Awards,*

honors: Canada Council grants, 1971, 1972, 1973, 1976, and 1978; poetry prize from Canadian Authors Association, 1978, for "The Ghosts Call Your Poor."

WRITINGS—Poetry: The Shadow of Eden Once, Deodar Shadow Press, 1970; *Circles,* Deodar Shadow Press, 1970; *In Mind or Xrossroads or Mythologies,* Anak Press, 1971; *Rose Way in the East,* Ganglia Press, 1972; *Old Mill,* Blewointment Press, 1972; *The Nightwatchman,* Anak Press, 1972; *The Zen Pilgrimage,* Anak Press, 1972; *Yth Revolution Into Ruenz,* Anak Press, 1972; (with Earle Birney, Bill Bissett, and Judith Copithorne) *Four Parts Sand: Concrete Poems,* Oberon Press, 1972.

Wood Mountain Poems, Anak Press, 1973, revised edition edited by Al Purdy, Macmillan, 1976; *Suicide Notes, Book One,* Sundog Press, 1973; *Phillip Well,* College of New Caledonia, 1973; *These Fragments I've Gathered for Ezra,* Funch Press, 1973; *Leaving,* Repository Press, 1974; *On First Looking Down From Lion's Gate Bridge,* Anak Press, 1974, revised edition, Black Moss Press, 1976; *Blind Man's House,* Anak Press, 1974; *Leaving Wood Mountain,* Sundog Press, 1975; *Writing on Stone: Poem Drawings, 1966-1976,* Anak Press, 1976; *Octomi,* Thistledown Press, 1976; *Almighty Voice* (broadsheet), Dreadnaught Press, 1977; *Moses Beauchamp,* (broadsheet), Turnstone. Press, 1978. *The Ghosts Call You Poor,* Macmillan, 1978; (with George Morrissette) *Two for Father,* Sundog Press, 1978; *East of Myloona,* Thistledown Press, 1979; *Montage for an Intersellar Cry,* Turnstone Press, 1980; *In the Name of Narid,* Porcupine's Quill, 1980.

Other: (Translator) Andrei Voznesensky, *The Shadow of Sound,* College of New Caledonia, 1975; (co-author) "Don'tcha Know the North Wind and You in My Hair" (two-act play), first produced in Saskatoon, Saskatchewan, at University of Saskatchewan, 1978.

WORK IN PROGRESS: In Search of Parinti: A History of the Romanians of Western Canada, publication by NeWest Press expected in 1983; *Ussuri Line,* a cycle of poems about Chinese railroad workers in the eastern Soviet Union, Australia, California, and British Columbia, publication by NeWest Press expected in 1984.

SIDELIGHTS: Suknaski told *CA:* "My deepest wish is to always retain a sense of place informed by innate duplexity where art emanates from my awareness that the greater possibilities and strength lie in dream time founded on a guilt vacillating between profound respect for the autochthons who first inhabited Turtle Island (or "The Great Island," as North America was first named) and my indigenous ethnicity predestined by a double code: the mythic mainsprings of a Slavic pantheism vis a vis the white Anglo-Saxon/Judeo-Christian cosmology. Believing my mythic origins and dream time to be twofold, I—through birthright—claim the inalienable right to honor both the aboriginal and white ethnic peoples who were mutally victimized by the white supremist. The obvious price of this art, built on the sentient wish to never fully empathize with a single people, is a guilt anchored in a deep sense of betrayal.

"As a Canadian writer, I am mostly concerned with finding a cipher that will decode a fourfold dream: the Anglo Saxon's dream and search for the Northwest Passage to further expand the British Empire (the human toll among many peoples being the price of that dream); the European immigrant's dream of a New Jerusalem in the new life (a second chance) in the New World; the Chinese dream of the 'Golden Mountains' in California, or the 'Gold Mountain in Canada's West' (the only chance for three hundred dollars and passage back home to be reunited with one's family and find another home elsewhere beyond crowded cities and states); and finally the Amerindian dreaming of homeland, *Manitou's abundance* to keep body and spirit where no boundaries are ever drawn—except by the migration of game, and alluring mythical places where the gods impart their secrets.

"What one hopes to achieve through writing is to teach people the value of comparing mythologies and those things that mirror common earth and humanity; to show the sentient reader the value of growing compassion towards others (some who as anomolies mirror one's otherness, as Leslie Fiedler points out in *Freaks: Myths and Images of the Secret Self*), remembering 'it's not the colour of the skin that matters, it's the way you feel when you get there' (as an anonymous metis, ruminating on love, said in the West Hotel pub somewhere on North Main in Winnipeg, Manitoba, the autumn of 1979). It was western Canadian novelist Rudy Wiebe who once said: 'The whole purpose of art, of poetry of storytelling is to make us better.' A writer cannot settle for less.

"My advice to aspiring writers is to *run*, don't walk, to the nearest bookstore and purchase: *The Jerusalem Bible*, the one that Tolkien helped translate; *A Distant Mirror* by Barbara W. Tuchman, and study the knight errant tradition in the face of man and his extensions where the knight's armour and vulcanized dream of B. F. Goodrich carry the Firestone sexual fantasy of America cradled in Bethlehem Steel; *The Icon and the Axe* by James H. Billington, learn the slavic 'memory' and ponder the populist agony of the St. Petersburg populists and face the art casualities of America as witnessed in John Berryman's *Dream Songs*, Saul Bellow's *Humboldt's Gift*, Delmore Schwartz's *In Dreams Begin Responsibilities*, and James Atlas's *Delmore Schwartz: The Life of an American Poet*—and merge that knowledge with Leslie Fiedler's *Freaks* and *Looking Far West: The Search for the American West in History, Myth, and Literature*, edited by Frank Bergon and Zeese Papanikolas—and finally temper those things with Borges's *Dreamtigers* and *One Hundred Years of Solitude* by Gabriel Garcia Marquez.

"Memorize the words of Ursula Iguaran: 'We will not leave,' she said. 'We will stay here, because we have had a son here.' 'We have still not had a death,' he said. 'A person does not belong to a place until there is someone dead under the ground.' Etch those words (and the Greek etymon of autochthonous) in memory forever. Read *Bury My Heart at Wounded Knee* and ask yourself how many bones of loved ones beneath the earth it takes to claim a place. Remembering the true meaning of autochthonous ('[I] . . . of the/this earth'), and ask how many stories it takes to keep us—in this place of lethal myth.

"Ultimately, when the sources are exhausted, do what poet/historian Charles Olson said: '[Go] back to the simpler things'—get to know your own place, with your own feet and body in the true Greek sense of *history (istorin,* 'to know/learn with one's own self [being]'). Become the myth you study; become the story you tell—to keep you, and others."

BIOGRAPHICAL/CRITICAL SOURCES: Canadian Literature, Number 71, 1976; *Canadian Forum,* December, 1976-January, 1977; *Books in Canada,* April, 1977; *Contemporary Verse Two,* spring, 1977; Eli Mandel, *Another Time,* Press Porcepic, 1977; *NeWest Review,* October, 1978; "Wood Mountain Poems," a film released by National Film Board of Canada, 1979.

SUTTON, David 1947-

PERSONAL: Born October 5, 1947, in Birmingham, England; son of James Edward (a toolmaker) and Rose (Hayling) Sutton; married Sandra Carroll (a postal officer), July 11, 1970. *Education:* Attended secondary school in Birmingham, England. *Politics:* "Fortean." *Religion:* "Fortean." *Home:* 194 Station Rd., Kings Heath, Birmingham B14 7TE, England. *Agent:* Edward P. Berglund, 5247 Alabama Ave., Camp Lejeune, N.C. 28542.

CAREER: Employed by British Postal Service, 1970—, currently junior manager in administration department.

WRITINGS: (Editor) *New Writings in Horror and the Supernatural,* Sphere Books, Volume I, 1970, Volume II, 1972; (editor) *The Sayr's Head and Other Tales of Terror,* Corgi Books, 1975. Short stories represented in anthologies and in magazines, including *World of Horror, Gothic,* and *Dark Horizons.* Editor of *Shadow,* 1968-74; associate editor of *Fantasy Tales* and *Fantasy Media.*

WORK IN PROGRESS: Editing *Masters of Terror,* Volume II: *J. Sheridan le Fanu,* with publication by Corgi Books.

SIDELIGHTS: Sutton commented: "You could say I am motivated by the *Illuminati* and Charles Fort. Fort is a prime figure in my thinking, and I wholeheartedly bow to his wisdom. I am very interested in this rather unusual world in which we live—the one that the scientists, politicians, and other freaks don't tell people about. I think we must all begin to merge with different realities very soon, otherwise the planet will be turned to dough by those scientists and politicians and other freaks who seem to want to do that while pretending otherwise. I am highly stimulated by the writings of Fort, Colin Wilson, Stan Gooch, Robert Anton Wilson, Jacques Vallee, and Colin Bord. I am particularly interested in the UFO phenomena and not at all interested in scientists who scoff from the safety of their labs and financial grants, while undertaking no research at all in the matters which we currently term paranormal, occult, or what have you.

"I also love the writings of Fritz Leiber, Ray Bradbury, H. P. Lovecraft, and Stephen King. I am addicted to horror and science fiction films, with particular interest in Polanski, Roeg, Kubrick, and Boorman. Musically, I was motivated by Soft Machine and Pink Floyd, and lately find solace with Tangerine Dream, National Health, Miles Davis, Steve Hillage, Brian Eno, and so on. 23 Skiddoo."

*   *   *

SWAIN, Bruce M(cArthur) 1943-

PERSONAL: Born August 13, 1943, in Augusta, Ga.; son of Bruce (a physician) and Eunice (McArthur) Swain; married Pamela O'Neill, 1966 (marriage ended, 1974); married Alison F. Campbell (an artist), January 22, 1977; children: April Anne. *Education:* Davidson College, A.B., 1965; Harvard University, M.A.T., 1966; Columbia University, Ed.D., 1970. *Religion:* Society of Friends (Quakers). *Home:* 60 Springdale St., Athens, Ga. 30601. *Office:* School of Journalism, University of Georgia, Athens, Ga. 30601.

CAREER: Capital Times, Madison, Wis., reporter, 1971-73; *Louisville Courier-Journal,* Louisville, Ky., copy editor, 1973-74; University of Kentucky, Lexington, assistant professor of journalism, 1974-80; University of Georgia, Athens, assistant professor of journalism, 1980—. *Member:* American Association of University Professors, Association for Education in Journalism, Sigma Delta Chi.

WRITINGS: Reporters' Ethics, Iowa State University Press, 1978. Contributor to magazines and newspapers, including *Newspaper Research Journal.*

WORK IN PROGRESS: Studies on current press performance.

SIDELIGHTS: Swain commented to *CA:* "My major interests are press and media ethical dilemmas, 'fringe' sciences such as parapsychology, religion, and philosophy, and the role played by mass media in determining what is accepted as scientific.

"Visits to the Findhorn community in Scotland and holistic health centers in California and elsewhere have increased my interest in the possibility that a so-called New Age in medicine, psychology, and physics—combining 'spiritual' and 'natural' laws—may well be underway. Those endeavors may yield far more tangible solutions to current problems than traditional sciences and media suggest."

* * *

SWAN, Gladys 1934-

PERSONAL: Born October 15, 1934, in New York, N.Y.; daughter of Robert J. (in business) and Sarah (Taub) Rubenstein; married Richard Borders Swan (a professor), September 9, 1955; children: Andrea, Leah. *Education:* New Mexico Western University, B.A., 1954; Claremont Graduate School, M.A., 1955. *Home:* 450 East Madison, Franklin, Ind. 46131. *Office:* Department of English, Franklin College, 501 East Monroe, Franklin, Ind. 46131.

CAREER: Junior high school English teacher at public schools in Raton, N.M., 1958-59; part-time lecturer and instructor, 1961-66; Franklin College, Franklin, Ind., assistant professor, 1968-78, associate professor of English, 1979—. *Member:* Associated Writing Programs. *Awards, honors:* Lilly Endowment fellowship, 1975-76.

WRITINGS: On the Edge of the Desert (short fiction), University of Illinois Press, 1979.

WORK IN PROGRESS: Shadows on the Eve of the Next Revolution, stories; *The Wanderings of Jason Hummer, Descendent of Wild Bill Hickok: His True Exploits and Erring Ways; Gate of Ivory, Gate of Horn,* a novella; *Gil and the Kid,* a novella; *The Entrepreneur of Darkness,* poems; translating stories of Yuri Rytkeou of Siberia, with Monique Salzmann.

SIDELIGHTS: Gladys Swan wrote: "What I am trying to communicate through my stories is a way of perceiving, a way of knowing and responding to experience that goes beyond the intellect or rational mind. What some people have been ready to call 'mood' in my stories is to my mind that area of sensitivity evoked by image and which is the province of imagination, intuition, and feeling. My efforts in my stories have been to explore what seems to me a largely neglected area of the psyche, particularly in modern America.

"I have also been largely devoted to exploring the West, where I grew up, as the imaginative landscape in which various people existing outside the framework of society have conducted their individual search for meaning. Because the conventional structures no longer answer to their deepest needs and longings, the people I write about have the task of facing the chaos such a situation presents—its inherent threat and promise—and recognizing and responding to their condition. How they make that response or come to that recognition is what my stories deal with.

"The West has long served an important imaginative function in American life. As Paul Horgan says in his book *Great River: The Rio Grande,* Jefferson had, in his concept of democracy, 'opened up political frontiers in the thoughts of men that only the West, in its sheer space, could contain.'

But the implications of the West have been far more than political or economic, though generated by these. For the imagination, the West has been the landscape in which the individual could achieve his fullest potentiality and to which he could venture in search of a new life. Nor, I believe, have these implications been lost under the pressures of modern society, fearful of the loss of individual freedom. What then are the territories to be discovered, the possibilities to be realized? Perhaps they lie within. This is the point at which my fiction begins."

AVOCATIONAL INTERESTS: Ethnic art, cinema, analytical psychology, travel.

* * *

SWANN, Peggy
See GEIS, Richard E(rwin)

* * *

SWARTZ, Marvin 1941-

PERSONAL: Born July 28, 1941, in Boston, Mass.; son of Sidney and Esther May (Boydman) Swartz; married Helen Margaret Wise (an editor), September 23, 1969; children: Reuben, Jonathan. *Education:* Princeton University, A.B., 1963; Yale University, M.A., 1964, Ph.D., 1969; attended St. Antony's College, Oxford, 1966-67. *Home:* 28 Ridgewood Ter., Northampton, Mass. 01060. *Office:* Department of History, University of Massachusetts, Herter Hall, Amherst, Mass. 01003.

CAREER: University of Massachusetts, Boston, instructor in history, 1967-68; University of Massachusetts, Amherst, assistant professor, 1970-74, associate professor of history, 1974—. Tutor at St. Edmund's Hall, Oxford, 1967. *Member:* Audubon Society, Appalachian Mountain Club. *Awards, honors:* Woodrow Wilson fellowships, 1963-64 and 1966-67; Danforth fellowships, 1964-66 and 1968-69; German Thyssen grant from University of Marburg, 1969-70.

WRITINGS: The Union of Democratic Control in British Politics During the First World War, Clarendon Press, 1971; (contributor) A.J.A. Morris, editor, *Edwardian Radicalism, 1900-1914,* Routledge & Kegan Paul, 1974; (editor with wife, H. M. Swartz) *Disraeli's Reminiscences,* Hamish Hamilton, 1975, Stein & Day, 1976. Also author of *Origins of Parliamentary Democracy: British Politics and Foreign Policy, 1865-1885,* 1980. Contributor of articles to *History of the First World War* magazine.

SIDELIGHTS: Swartz told *CA:* "My education at Princeton and Yale shaped my intellectual life and instilled in me the belief that intellectual achievement entails not only individual growth but also social responsibilities. My vocational interest focuses on the study of modern Europe, and particularly on England."

He added: "During the century after 1850 European nations sought answers to the questions raised by political, social, and economic change; at the same time the great powers tried to maintain their vital international interests through competition and cooperation with each other. The problems of domestic politics and foreign policy, and the interactions between them, are of particular concern to me, and perhaps of some general concern to a democratic society."

AVOCATIONAL INTERESTS: Jogging, cycling, hiking.

SWENSON, Peggy
See GEIS, Richard E(rwin)

*   *   *

SYLVESTER, A(lbert) J(ames) 1889-

PERSONAL: Born November 24, 1889, in Harlaston, Staffs, England; son of Albert and Edith Sylvester; married Evelyn Annie Welman, 1917 (deceased); children: Joan Maureen (Mrs. Alun Sylvester-Evans). *Education:* Attended Guild Street School, Burton-on-Trent. *Politics:* "Lloyd George liberal." *Religion:* Church of England. *Home:* Rudloe Cottage, Corsham, Wiltshire, England.

CAREER: Farmer and writer. Worked as private secretary in England to secretary of the Committee of Imperial Defence, 1914-21, secretary of War Cabinet, 1916-21, secretary of Imperial War Cabinet, 1917, British secretary at peace conference, 1919, prime ministers, 1921-23, and Earl Lloyd George, 1923-45. Justice of the Peace for County of Wiltshire. *Awards, honors:* Commander of the Order of the British Empire, 1920; named Commander of the Order of the Crown of Italy, 1920; Sacred Treasure of Japan, 1921; supreme award for ballroom and Latin American dancing from Imperial Society of Teachers of Dancing, 1977; Alex Moore Award for ballroom dancing, 1977.

WRITINGS: Life With Lloyd George (diaries), edited by Colin Cross, Harper, 1975. Also author of *The Real Lloyd George* (biography), 1947.

SIDELIGHTS: Sylvester told *CA:* "I accompanied Mr. Lloyd George and Sir Maurice Hankey to all the Allied conferences abroad during World War I, including the conference in which the terms of Armistice were established. I was present at Versailles when these were presented to the German plenipotentiaries, and was present at the signature of the Treaty of Peace on June 28, 1919. I was, in addition to my other duties, the official shorthand writer to the British delegation, and collaborated with the American staff in producing the public record.

"Meantime, I was in general charge of the office of the secretary of the British delegation under Sir Maurice Hankey. With him I produced the record of the 'Council of Four': President Woodrow Wilson, Lloyd George, Clemenceau, and Orlando.

"I was invited by Prime Minister Lloyd George to join his personal staff in 1921, and accompanied him to all the post-war Allied conferences, including Cannes and Genoa in 1922. I assisted him during the protracted peace negotiations on the Irish Treaty in 1921. When he resigned the premiership in 1922, I continued as secretary to the new prime minister, Mr. Bonar Law. When Bonar Law retired because of ill health, I worked with his successor, Mr. Baldwin.

"Then, at the invitation of Mr. Lloyd George, I resigned from civil service and rejoined him as his principal private secretary. I remained with him and was present with him when he died in 1945. I accompanied him and his family when he toured Canada and the United States. It proved to be a right royal tour: the press claimed that no other foreign visitor had ever been such an outstanding success.

"I was with Lloyd George in all his work. During his writing of his war memoirs, including six volumes, and two of the peace treaties, which took from 1931 to 1938, I did all the interviewing of his old cabinet colleagues and war-time associates, and carried out all the secret research in the Department of State in Whitehall. I was the keeper of his secret archives. I was in an advantageous position for I had a close knowledge of these documents, which came into existence over the years when I was their keeper at the Cabinet Secretariat."

Sylvester is listed in the *Guiness Book of Records,* 1977 edition, as the world's oldest competing ballroom dancer.

AVOCATIONAL INTERESTS: Riding, golf.

T

TALMON, Jacob L(aib)   1916-1980

OBITUARY NOTICE—See index for *CA* sketch: Born June 14, 1916, in Rypin, Poland; died of a heart attack, June 16, 1980, in Jerusalem, Israel. Historian and writer. A highly respected professor at the Hebrew University in Jerusalem, Talmon was an authority on the development of totalitarian ideologies in history since the French Revolution. During his later years he strongly urged Israel to withdraw from the West Bank and called for the resignation of Prime Minister Menachem Begin. Talmon was the author of numerous books, including the trilogy that contains *Origins of Totalitarian Democracy, Political Messianism: The Romantic Phase,* and *The Myth of the Nation and the Vision of Revolution: The Origins of Ideological Polarization in the Twentieth Century,* the latter as yet unpublished. Obituaries and other sources: *London Times,* June 18, 1980; *New York Times,* June 18, 1980; *Newsweek,* June 30, 1980; *Time,* June 30, 1980.

*   *   *

TARADASH, Daniel   1913-

PERSONAL: Born January 29, 1913, in Louisville, Ky.; son of William (a manufacturer) and Elizabeth (Bornstein) Taradash; married Madeleine Forbes, November 20, 1944; children: Jan Elizabeth, Meg, William Brian. *Education:* Harvard University, A.B., 1933, L.L.B., 1936. *Residence:* Beverly Hills, Calif. *Office:* c/o International Creative Management, 8899 Beverly Blvd., Los Angeles, Calif. 90048.

CAREER: Screenwriter, 1938—; director, 1955—. Member of Public Media General Programs Panel of National Endowment for the Arts, 1975; member of board of trustees of Entertainment Hall of Fame Foundation, 1976; chairman and trustee of Producers-Writers Guild Pension Plan, 1960-73; member of executive committee of board of trustees for Humanitas Prize, 1980—. *Military service:* U.S. Army, 1940-45; became officer. *Member:* American Film Institute (member of board of trustees, 1967-69), Writers Guild of America, West (president of screen writers branch, 1955-56, vice-president, 1956-59, president, 1978-80, national chairman, 1979-81), Academy of Motion Picture Arts and Sciences (member of board of governors, 1964-74, vice-president, 1968-70, president, 1970-73). *Awards, honors:* First prize from Bureau of New Plays, 1938, for "Thy Mercy"; *Look* film award, Page One Award from Newspaper Guild of New York, Writers Guild Award, and Academy Award from Academy of Motion Picture Arts and Sciences, all 1953, all for "From Here to Eternity"; Writers Guild nomination, 1955, for "Picnic"; Cannes Film Festival Chevalier de la Barre award for film "which best helps freedom of expression and tolerance," 1957, for "Storm Center"; Valentine Davies award from Writers Guild of America, West, 1971, for bringing dignity and honor to profession.

WRITINGS—Screenplays: (With Lewis Meltzer, Sarah Y. Mason, and Victor Heerman) "Golden Boy" (based on the play by Clifford Odets), Columbia, 1939; "For Love or Money," Universal, 1939; (with Gertrude Purcell and Harold Goldman) "A Little Bit of Heaven," Universal, 1940; (with John Monks, Jr.) "Knock on Any Door" (based on the novel by Willard Motley), Columbia, 1949.

"Rancho Notorious," RKO, 1952; "Don't Bother to Knock" (based on the novel *Mischief,* by Charlotte Armstrong), Twentieth Century-Fox, 1952; "From Here to Eternity" (based on the novel by James Jones), Columbia, 1953; "Desiree" (based on the novel by Annemarie Selinko), Twentieth Century-Fox, 1954; "Picnic" (based on the play by William Inge), Warner Bros., 1955; (with Elick Moll; and director) "Storm Center," Columbia, 1956; "Bell, Book and Candle" (based on the play by John Van Druten), Columbia, 1958.

"Morituri" (based on the novel by Werner Joerg Luedecke), Twentieth Century-Fox, 1965; (with Dalton Trumbo) "Hawaii" (based on the novel by James Michener), United Artists, 1966; (with David Rayfiel) "Castle Keep" (based on the novel by William Eastlake), Columbia, 1969; "Doctor's Wives" (based on the novel by Frank G. Slaughter), Columbia, 1971; (with Herman Raucher) "The Other Side of Midnight" (based on the novel by Sidney Sheldon), Twentieth Century-Fox, 1977.

Plays: "Red Gloves" (based on the play by Jean Paul Sartre), first produced in New York City at Mansfield Theatre, 1948; *There Was a Little Girl* (based on the novel by Christopher Davis; first produced on Broadway at Cort Theatre, February 29, 1960), Myerson, c. 1960. Also author of "Thy Mercy," 1938.

CA INTERVIEWS THE AUTHOR

CA interviewed Daniel Taradash by phone on April 28, 1980, at his home in Beverly Hills, Calif.

CA: Your movie career began with the winning of a playwriting contest in 1938. Would you tell me more about that?

TARADASH: It was called the Bureau of New Plays and financed by the motion-picture companies. They were anxious to find and encourage young playwrights, or people who might be able to write dramatically and therefore be adaptable to screenwriting. It was a nationwide contest and my play, ''Thy Mercy,'' won it. The play was based on a sit-down strike—there were a number of sit-down strikes then; it was a period of labor unrest. They took the twelve most promising young playwrights of the group that submitted plays and formed a playwriting course in New York under the supervision of Theresa Helburn, who was a very famous lady in her time. She was head of the Theatre Guild. The instructors were people like Lee Strasberg, John Gassner, and Terry, as we all called Miss Helburn. Occasionally we had visiting artists like Robert Sherwood and John Mason Brown, who was an eminent theatre critic in his day. Essentially it was a course devoted to writing plays as well as listening to lectures. One of the writers in the course, by the way, was John Crosby, who became at one point America's leading television critic. He has been living in London for some time and has written several well-known novels in the last five or six years. Another was Lewis Meltzer, who had had a play tryout in Boston, but it closed there and didn't get to New York. It starred Ina Claire and was directed by Otto Preminger. It was Meltzer and I who were selected by Rouben Mamoulian to come out to Hollywood and do ''Golden Boy.'' This was after Mamoulian had been handed a screenplay of the project by Columbia Pictures, hated it, and threw it in the wastebasket.

CA: Was it an early ambition of yours to go into movies?

TARADASH: Not really. It had been my ambition since I went to college to be a playwright. I wrote a play the year I got out of law school, and that was the play that won the playwriting course. I also wrote a play while I was *in* law school, but nothing much happened with that except some encouragement from an agent.

CA: Were you planning at some point to practice law?

TARADASH: Not really. It was a fallback position, I think, although it was kind of foolhardy to believe that I could become a writer in one year after law school; but it worked out. I was very, very lucky.

CA: Has the training in law been helpful to you in your career?

TARADASH: The legal training has been helpful not in terms of writing material with legal background, although ''Knock on Any Door'' did have a trial in it, but in terms of the kind of thinking that is taught to you in law school. You learn to think in contingencies, as many contingencies that might occur as possible. I think this can only be helpful to a person who is going in for a dramatic or literary career, particularly in fiction. It also helped me materially, I think, in making deals early in my career. Because at various times I did not have an agent, I made the deals on my own. For example, the deal on ''From Here to Eternity'' I made myself, and I was the first writer ever to get a percentage of a picture which was not an original script. I collected a great deal of money on my percentage of ''From Here to Eternity.'' The creative bookkeeping wasn't as creative as it is now. I honestly believe that in that period, certainly when I was working at Columbia, they were scrupulously fair about their handling of the net profits.

CA: You've been active in the Academy of Motion Picture Arts and Sciences since the mid-1960's and have served as vice-president and president of that organization. What were your major concerns in those positions?

TARADASH: When I became president I had several ambitions, some of which were realized. We had a very old building; we'd been in it twenty-seven years, and it was hopelessly small. The library, where the board of directors met, was all jumbled together. I formed a new building committee and worked like hell to build a new building, which we finally have. The whole project—finding the proper site, construction, furnishing, etc.—took three or four years. I asked Walter Mirisch to be head of the building committee when I was president, and when he became president he asked me to be head of the building committee, so we worked together in putting up the building. It's a beautiful building and has, I would say, perhaps the finest auditorium in the world for hearing and viewing films.

That was one of the things I did. I also felt that there should be younger people on the board of governors, and we added twelve comparatively young board members to the twenty-four members we already had. That continues till now. The student awards began during the years I was president, at least the nucleus of that program. I was very pleased that during my tenure of three years the only person who was awarded the Thalberg Award (by the board of governors), which is the highest award the Academy can give, was Ingmar Bergman. He is still the only foreigner who has ever won it. And of course one of the crowning achievements was my sparking the board's interest in having Charles Chaplin come back to Hollywood to appear on the ''Academy Awards Presentation'' for an honorary award. I got the notion that if we gave no other awards that year—omitted the Thalberg and Hersholt Humanitarian and any other honorary awards and gave but one honorary award, and that to Chaplin, we might get him; and with the help of a few friends of his, we did get him. That was quite an evening.

CA: You've won a number of top awards and honors yourself, among them the Valentine Davies Award of the Writers Guild of America in 1971 for your contribution to the motion-picture community. What do you feel your greatest contribution to the industry has been?

TARADASH: Perhaps the things I just mentioned. And I always worked very hard for the status of the writer in every possible way I could. Certainly being president of the Academy was one, winning the Prix Chevalier de la Barre at the Cannes Festival in 1957 was another. That prize was given for ''this year's film which best helps freedom of expression and tolerance.'' The winning film that year was ''Storm Center,'' which I co-authored and directed. It starred Bette Davis. I had also been president of the screen branch of the Writers Guild, which was at one time divided into two sections—the screen branch and the television branch.

CA: What awards have meant the most to you?

TARADASH: The Chevalier de la Barre was one, and I suppose winning the Oscar for ''From Here to Eternity.'' I was very excited about that, as I suspect even Dustin Hoffman is about his Oscar this year.

CA: A number of your screenplays have been adaptations—

TARADASH: Almost all of them. I look upon myself as an adapter. If I went back to the theatre, I don't know whether I'd be capable of writing original material or not.

CA: What are the inherent difficulties in adapting a literary work for the screen?

TARADASH: Well, assuming that the work is one that you respect and that you feel has something of some importance to say to you and to the public, I think the major problem is a sort of intangible: it's trying to maintain the integrity of the work itself, of the author's point of view, and shift the whole process of prose writing into dramatic writing. Most writers of novels write narratively rather than dramatically; they often don't write in scenes, but in terms of what people are thinking about. Of course, almost all of them do use some dialogue—it would be very difficult to adapt a book with no dialogue. One of the problems, then, is to try and match the dialogue. And in cases like "Eternity," for example, which is an enormously long book, it is a problem to eliminate material and make bold breaks with material when you feel it just can't be done—either for reasons of length, or in those days censorship, or public opinion.

In "From Here to Eternity" the character that Sinatra played, Maggio, did not die in the novel; therefore there was no opportunity for the other character, the bugler Prewitt, to play taps after his death, which was a very moving scene and was actually the climax of the so-called second act if you work in terms of first, second, and third acts, which I try to do. This was an idea I had before I started—that Maggio would not just dwindle off as he did in the novel and get a mental discharge and go back to Brooklyn, but would die as a result of the brutal treatment he received in the stockade; and that Prewitt would play taps after Maggio died and the men would be listening to it in the dark, and that it could be a very touching moment, as it turned out to be. That's the sort of creative adaptation that becomes important, and yet it still does not violate the spirit of the book. There are many other examples in which I had to alter or invent areas of the source material in order to get it on the screen.

CA: What was the most difficult adaptation you ever did?

TARADASH: I think it was one that was never made, but I still think it would make a fantastic picture. It was an adaptation of MacKinlay Kantor's Pulitzer Prize novel *Andersonville* that I wrote for Columbia in 1958. That was the year that Harry Cohn, then president of Columbia, died. I have a feeling that if Cohn hadn't died, the picture would have been made. That was a story about the stockade in the South in which thirty thousand Yankee prisoners were held by the Confederates and around ten thousand of them died of exposure and disease. The studio felt that there was too much horror and shelved the project. Well, compared to what you see on the screen today, that was utter gentleness. The reason I think it would have made a wonderful film is the theme I saw in it. In a strange way, even though many people died and it was an infamous, dreadful moment in American history, various individual stories in the novel culminated in one and, I thought, made the point that man's humanity to man is greater than his inhumanity. If you can do it in an intelligent way, that's a beautiful theme. Particularly if you do it in terms of beauty coming out of evil.

CA: Is there any chance that it will ever be picked up and made into a movie?

TARADASH: I don't know. It's still over at Columbia. It would have been a very expensive picture then and I don't know what interest there has been since, if any. So many changes in leadership over there; so many different people have been around. And I don't even know if the present-day people are aware of it. They probably have literally hundreds and hundreds of scripts on the shelf that they haven't made; and they've long since, I'm sure, written it off their books from a tax point of view.

CA: Have you been deeply involved in the productions of many of the movies you've written screenplays for?

TARADASH: At one point, Julian Blaustein and I formed an independent company, financed by and releasing through Columbia Pictures. Blaustein produced the two pictures we made; I co-wrote and directed one and wrote the other. These were "Storm Center" and "Bell, Book and Candle." And I was intimately connected with all the details of production on those. I was also intimately connected with the production of "From Here to Eternity" and, to a good extent, "Picnic." In later years there have been a number of writers on a group of pictures I have done. In some cases I haven't even met the other writers, and in some cases I don't even know the directors, literally. Never met them.

That's one of the strange aspects of Hollywood today. Fifteen or twenty years ago the producers of pictures under the studio system were thinking primarily in terms of one picture, one writer. Today it's a very splintered system in which the studios really don't produce for themselves very much. They are almost funneling channels for independent producers. They often put up the money and they do the distribution, but the producers, or some of them anyway, are not creatively on secure ground and they feel that four writers are better than one. They get writer A to do a quick first draft, then get writer B to polish it, and then they get, say, Pollock to direct the picture and he almost always brings his favorite writer in, then they might get writer X in for a few weeks to put in a few one-liners. They're thinking in terms of grosses and making Christmas or July dates rather than making first-rate films. There are exceptions, and certainly the five pictures nominated for the Academy Awards this year were awfully good. There were other good pictures too, but there seems to be an emphasis on getting the buck rather than getting the picture. Usually in the old days they ran along together: if you did a good picture you usually made money, which I still have to believe today. Except in rare cases, a good picture will make money. Certainly the whole box-office situation is different.

CA: You've been appointed a member of the executive committee of the board of trustees for the Humanitas Prize. Could you describe that award?

TARADASH: The Humanitas Prize awards $50,000 each year to the writers of television programs which have been shown on the air by the three networks. It has a very interesting and good board of trustees, including Cicely Tyson and Bob Wise and Helen Hayes, as well as distinguished people who are not in the theatre or movies—Norman Cousins, for example. There are about twenty-five people on the board of trustees and seven of us on the executive board, which does most of the work. However, the trustees do read the material as well. The Libby Endowment has been funding it. As the word *humanitas* implies, the prizes are for the best scripts that try to improve human relationships, affirm human dignity, illumine the search for meaning, freedom, and love. It is an effort to improve the level and stature of television. We hope to get people not to be afraid to write in terms of quality and brotherhood.

CA: Is there anything in your field you haven't tried that you would like to try?

TARADASH: I don't know. I've always thought it would be

fun to do a Broadway musical, but I don't know how that's ever going to work out. Obviously everybody these days would like to write a novel, but I don't know how good I am at prose. I've been writing in terms of straight dramatic structure for so long, to break into a different form might be very difficult.

CA: Of the changes in the movie industry over the years, what would you like to see reversed?

TARADASH: What I've talked about. I'm not second-guessing the studios' business ability, because God knows the companies have been making millions of dollars. But I would like to see more creative people in charge of each individual project, and I would like to see the writer have more control over his material, definitely. I would like to see the writer kept on as long as possible, at least until it becomes fairly obvious that he cannot continue and turn out a successful script. I think if the writer turns out a good first draft there's no reason why he shouldn't turn out a good *last* draft, with a little patience and a little thought on the part of the other people connected with the project. A lot of directors are frustrated writers and would like to get their ideas into the material, and as a result, a lot of what we see on the screen has no individual personality. Somehow I think the audience feels it, and it pervades the industry today to a great degree. If "Kramer vs. Kramer" had had four writers, it would probably never have been nominated for the Academy Awards.

CA: What changes are you happy about?

TARADASH: I'll give you a kind of gross answer to your question. That's not a pun, but I'm happy that the Writers Guild has had enough clout to get a percentage of the gross of all films sold to free television and will eventually have a piece of the gross of pictures shown on pay TV. I'm pleased that the writers have gotten themselves into a position of having more clout in financial terms than they used to. And I suppose it's pleasant to know that one's films eventually will be shown to a nationwide audience on tv. I really can't think of anything else that I feel today is vastly improved over the motion-picture industry some years ago. It's very good to know that television has provided many, many jobs for writers. I'm glad there's a public broadcasting system, although I think it ought to be strengthened and should stop using so many English imports and try to use more native work. Somehow there ought to be a way of funding this so that the public really gets a chance to see much more done by American authors.

—*Interview by Jean W. Ross*

*   *   *

TARBERT, Gary C(harles) 1937-

PERSONAL: Born December 3, 1937, in Baltimore, Md.; son of Warren Edward and Louise Cecilia (Watson) Tarbert. *Education:* Loyola College, Baltimore, Md., B.S., 1964; Wayne State University, M.S.L.S., 1975. *Politics:* Independent. *Religion:* Roman Catholic. *Home:* 1511 First St., Apt. 815, Detroit, Mich. 48226. *Office:* Gale Research Co., Book Tower, Detroit, Mich. 48226.

CAREER: Loyola College, Baltimore, Md., acquisitions librarian, 1964-66; Aetna Casualty & Surety, Baltimore, casualty underwriter, 1966-69; Gale Research Co., Detroit, Mich., editorial assistant, 1969-70, editorial associate, 1970-72, associate editor, 1972-74, editor, 1974—. *Military service:* U.S. Army, 1961-63. *Member:* Friends of the Detroit Public Library.

WRITINGS—All published by Gale: (Editor) *Book Review Index*, ... *1969 Cumulation*, 1975, ... *1970 Cumulation*, 1975, ... *1971 Cumulation*, 1974, ... *1972 Cumulation* (associate editor), 1973, ... *1973 Cumulation* (associate editor), 1974, ... *1974 Cumulation*, 1974-75, ... *1975 Cumulation*, 1976, ... *1976 Cumulation*, 1977, ... *1977 Cumulation*, 1978, ... *1978 Cumulation*, 1978-79, ... *1979 Cumulation*, 1979-80; *Library of Congress and National Union Catalog Author Lists, 1942-62: A Master Cumulation*, Volumes 69-88 (editorial assistant), Volumes 89-152 (editorial associate), 1970-71; (editor) *Children's Book Review Index*, Volume 1: *1975 Cumulation*, 1976, Volume 2: *1976 Cumulation*, 1977, Volume 3: *1977 Cumulation*, 1978, Volume 4: *1978 Cumulation*, 1979, Volume 5: *1979 Cumulation*, 1980, Volume 6: *1980 Cumulation*, 1981. "English Language Books by Title" Series, assistant editor, ... *1969-1970 Cumulation*, twenty volumes, 1971, ... *1971 Cumulation*, eight volumes, 1972.

SIDELIGHTS: Tarbert told *CA:* "I enjoy doing reference work and research. Several of my associates outside of Gale are librarians and I keep in touch with them for mutual exchanges of information. Also, I have an opportunity for a greater exchange of ideas through my attendance at the annual conference of the American Library Association.

"During the 1980 Republican convention in Detroit, I participated in working with one hundred other volunteer librarians in offering the media and convention delegates access to more than six million books, periodicals, newspapers, and documents. This was a non-partisan effort called the Detroit Libraries Information Project—the first such offering in the history of the national political convention."

AVOCATIONAL INTERESTS: Swimming, water skiing, sunning, walking, dancing, attending theatre and classical ballet.

*   *   *

TATE, B. H.
See BOYER, Bruce Hatton

*   *   *

TAYLOR, Charles D(oonan) 1938-

PERSONAL: Born October 20, 1938, in Hartford, Conn.; son of Jack D. (a financier) and Ruth (a teacher; maiden name, Hunter) Taylor; married Georgeanne L. Laitala (a teacher), July 24, 1965; children: Jack M. T., Bennett Hunter. *Education:* Middlebury College, B.A., 1960. *Residence:* Manchester, Mass. 01944. *Office:* Books and Production East, Inc., Manchester, Mass. 01944.

CAREER: Addison-Wesley Publishing Co., Reading, Mass., salesman and editor, 1965-71; Book Production Services, Inc., Danvers, Mass., president and treasurer, 1971-78; Books and Production East, Inc., Manchester, Mass., packager and agent, 1979—. *Military service:* U.S. Naval Reserve, 1961-64; became lieutenant junior grade. *Member:* U.S. Naval Institute.

WRITINGS: Show of Force, St. Martin's, 1980.

WORK IN PROGRESS: Research for a novel based on future conflict between the Soviet Union and People's Republic of China, with possible United States involvement.

SIDELIGHTS: Taylor told *CA:* "First-time authors shouldn't say much about themselves at all. Suffice it to say that reviews were a mixed bag with an emphasis on the positive. They ranged from raves comparing *Show of Force* favorably to General Sir John Hackett's best seller, *The Third World War,* and to Herman Wouk's war novels, to the *West*

Coast Review of Books missing the boat totally and calling an anti-war book 'a right wing diatribe.'

"What struck me most about the first-book experience (beyond the diverse interpretations of a simple theme) was the fact that the book will make much more money in Japan than it will in its country of origin, the United States. The message about our defense systems, politics, etc., meant for Americans will unfortunately have more of an impact in another country. My concept of attracting concern by placing many real-life situations in a fictional setting apparently missed, due to a desire to avoid these real situations in the U.S.

"Like most other things in life, writing is also a full-time learning experience that is both fun and frustrating at the same time."

* * *

TAYLOR, Elizabeth Tebbetts
(Elizabeth Tebbets-Taylor)

AGENT: c/o Jane Heller, Dell Publishing & Co., Inc., One Dag Hammerskjold Plaza, New York, N.Y. 10017.

CAREER: Worked as writer for Columbia Pictures Industries, Inc., and RKO General, Inc., and as reporter for *San Bernardino Sun Telegram, Hi-Desert Star,* and *Desert Trail;* writer.

WRITINGS: (Under name Elizabeth Tebbetts-Taylor) *Now I Lay Me Down Down to Die,* Arcadia House, 1955; *Tarifa* (novel), Dell, 1978.

SIDELIGHTS: Tarifa is a historical novel set in the California mission period between 1820 and 1848. It is a family story revolving around a Gypsy who came to America from Seville, Spain. The novel also chronicles the dissolution of the missions after Mexico gained its independence.

BIOGRAPHICAL/CRITICAL SOURCES: San Bernardino Sun, April 8, 1979.*

* * *

TAYLOR, Richard K(night)   1933-

PERSONAL: Born February 25, 1933, in Philadelphia, Pa.; son of Herbert Knight (in business) and Edith M. Taylor; married Phyllis Brody (a nurse), March 24, 1963; children: Deborah Minja, Daniel Randolph. *Education:* Haverford College, B.A., 1954; attended Yale University, 1956-57, and Cornell University, 1957-58; Bryn Mawr College, M.S.W., 1962. *Politics:* Democrat. *Religion:* Society of Friends (Quakers). *Home:* 307 West Mount Pleasant Ave., Philadelphia, Pa. 19119. *Office:* Jubilee Fellowship of Germantown, 312 Logan St., Philadelphia, Pa. 19144.

CAREER: American Friends Service Committee Project, assistant director of community development in El Salvador, 1954-56, and assistant director of housing program, 1958-60; executive director of Fair Housing Council of Delaware Valley, 1960-65; member of research staff of North City Congress, 1967-68; Southern Christian Leadership Conference, Atlanta, Ga., administrator of Philadelphia office, 1968-69; Crozier Theological Seminary, Chester, Pa., instructor in comparative economics, 1970; free-lance writer, 1971-78; Jubilee Fellowship of Germantown Church, Philadelphia, Pa., associated with neighborhood ministries, 1978—. Member of board of directors of American Friends Service Committee. Member of corporation of Haverford College. *Member:* Association of Christian Therapists, American Civil Liberties Union. *Awards, honors:* Christophers Award, 1977, for *Blockade.*

WRITINGS: Economics and the Gospel, United Church Press, 1973; *Moving Toward a New Society,* New Society Press, 1976; *Blockade,* Orbis, 1977. Correspondent for *Sojourners.* Contributor of articles to periodicals, including *Red Book, Christian Century, Progressive, One World, Philadelphia Evening Bulletin,* and *Christian Home.*

WORK IN PROGRESS: Christians in a Nuclear Age (tentative title), with Ronald J. Sider, publication by Intervarsity Press expected in 1982.

SIDELIGHTS: Taylor commented: "I am a Christian who believes that God calls us to work for justice and peace, and especially to try to ameliorate the conditions which crush the faces of the poor. Most of my writing has come from this call. I see myself primarily as an activist, part of whose action is writing. I am especially concerned about the threat to the world and to humanity posed by nuclear weapons. We are prepared to commit a thousand holocausts where many more will die than in Hitler's ovens. There must be a better way."

BIOGRAPHICAL/CRITICAL SOURCES: Marjorie Hope and James Young, *The Struggle for Humanity,* Orbis, 1977.

* * *

TAYLOR, Ruth Mattson   1922-

PERSONAL: Born October 14, 1922, in St. James, Minn.; daughter of Alvin Daniel (a theologian) and Freda Amalie (Anderson) Mattson; married Harold V. Taylor (a radio and television producer, musician, and writer), July 10, 1948; children: Bruce Mattson, Lynne Ingrid. *Education:* Augustana College, Rock Island, Ill., A.B., 1943; attended University of Wisconsin—Madison, 1947-48; Northwestern University, M.S., 1949. *Religion:* Christian. *Residence:* South Portland, Maine. *Agent:* Carol Dechant, 3805 North Fremont St., Apt. N, Chicago, Ill. 60613.

CAREER: Caterpillar Tractor Co., Peoria, Ill., spectrochemist, 1943-46; Hal Taylor Productions, Scarsdale, N.Y., vice-president, 1967-79. Advertising manager of religious journals, 1961—. *Member:* American Association of University Women (local vice-president), Academy of Religion and Psychical Research, Spiritual Frontiers Fellowship, Spiritual Advisory Council, Religion Publishers Group, Publishers Ad Council.

WRITINGS: (Editor) *Witness From Beyond: After-Death Communications From A. D. Mattson, Noted Theologian, Through the Distinguished Clairvoyant Margaret Flavell Tweddell,* Hawthorn, 1975.

WORK IN PROGRESS: A book containing additional communication from Alvin Daniel Mattson, publication expected in 1982.

SIDELIGHTS: Taylor told *CA:* "In life, my father, theologian A. D. Mattson, had probed evidence on the paranormal areas and had told me that he would try to communicate with me after his death. His death in 1970 marked the end of thirty-six years of seminary teaching. He was professor emeritus of the Lutheran School of Theology at Chicago, and had an equally distinguished career as author of books on Christian ethics and social consciousness.

"Not quite five months after my father died, Margaret Flavell, a close friend from London, was visiting us. She is one of the most respected clairvoyants in England, and has a remarkable record of accomplishment in the field of psychic communication. As an example, during World War II at the request of Lord Hugh Dowding, Marshall of the Royal Air Force, she traced many missing fliers, both alive and deceased, with a remarkable degree of accuracy.

"On the morning of March 2, 1971, we decided to see if we could get in touch with my father from the world beyond and to tape record our attempt. We had expected to make contact with him and to get evidence that he does survive, but little did we expect the quantity and quality of the very significant communication and information that we received. From March 1971 through October 1973, we received fifty-five communications amounting to over five hundred legal-sized pages of typed transcripts. *Witness From Beyond* is edited from the material we received.

"The book presents Dr. Mattson's first impressions when he passed over and basic concepts of the realm beyond, as related by him through Margaret Flavell. The down-to-earth concerns with which he deals show the intimate interexistence of God's realms. Far from being 'otherworldly,' the topics he speaks about are 'interworldly.' He once commented: 'We shall attempt to convey everyday revelations that will help take people the next step on their pilgrimage within the Kingdom of God. We want them to know more so that they can live life more fully. Knowledge about life everlasting can make the living of every single day on earth an exciting new adventure.'

"It has been a great privilege for me to edit the material for *Witness From Beyond*. I believe that many new dimensions of reality are being revealed through parapsychological studies. Studies of life after death can add greatly to the spiritual dimensions of life and can help make us realize that life here and now is a very precious gift to be carefully used for one's own spiritual development and in the service of others."

*   *   *

TEBBETTS-TAYLOR, Elizabeth
See TAYLOR, Elizabeth Tebbetts

*   *   *

TEMPLETON, Charles B.   1915-

PERSONAL: Born October 7, 1915, in Toronto, Ontario, Canada; son of William Loftis and Elizabeth Marion (Poyntz) Templeton; divorced; children: Deborah A., Michael D., Bradley S., Tyrone M. *Education:* Attended Princeton Theological Seminary, 1948-51; Lafayette College, D.D., 1952. *Religion:* Agnostic. *Home:* 44 Charles St. W., Toronto, Ontario, Canada M4Y 1R8. *Office:* One Yonge St., Toronto, Ontario, Canada M5E 1E5.

CAREER: Toronto Globe and Mail, Toronto, Ontario, sports cartoonist, 1932-36; Avenue Road Church, Toronto, minister, 1941-48; National Council of the Churches of Christ, New York City, secretary of evangelism, 1952-54; Presbyterian Church of the United States of America, New York City, director of evangelism, 1955-57; *Toronto Star,* Toronto, member of editorial staff, 1957, features editor, then executive managing editor, 1958, executive news editor, 1960-64; CTV Television Network Ltd., Toronto, director of news and public affairs, 1967-69; *Maclean's* magazine, Toronto, editor, 1969; Templex Research Industries Ltd., Toronto, president, 1964-80. Former evangelist, often toured with Billy Graham. Host of numerous radio and television programs, including "Dialogue," 1965-80, and "Issues." Consultant to Canadian Broadcasting Corp. *Member:* Writers Union of Canada, Association of Canadian Television and Radio Artists, Canadian Association of Publishers and Composers. *Awards, honors:* Award for best radio program from Association of Canadian Television and Radio Artists, 1978.

WRITINGS: Life Looks Up, Harper, 1955; *Evangelism for*

Tomorrow, Harper, 1957; *Jesus,* Simon & Schuster, 1973; *The Kidnapping of the President* (novel), McClelland & Stewart, 1974, Simon & Schuster, 1975; *Act of God* (novel), Little, Brown, 1977; *The Third Temptation,* McClelland & Stewart, 1980. Author of screenplays and teleplays for the British Broadcasting Corp., Canadian Broadcasting Corp., and Australian Broadcasting Corp. Contributor of articles to newspapers and magazines.

WORK IN PROGRESS: "The Cozy Tea Room" and "The Random Factor," plays.

SIDELIGHTS: Templeton left his work as a preacher when he "came to a point finally where to go on would have meant preaching things I didn't believe." Now he describes himself as an agnostic; but, he told the *Windsor Star,* "I make a very big distinction between agnostic and atheist. An atheist says there is no God. In my view that is presumptious. How do you know? Have you examined all the evidence that you can flatly say there is no God? I wouldn't dare say that. . . . The man, Jesus Christ, is still the biggest influence in my life. I think he is a spiritual and moral genius. I think his understanding of human beings and the human dilemma is far more profound that anyone else I've ever read . . . but I don't worship him."

Templeton's *The Kidnapping of a President* has been adapted as a motion picture by Sefel Pictures.

BIOGRAPHICAL/CRITICAL SOURCES: Time, October 3, 1960, May 22, 1978; *Toronto Star,* November 2, 1974; *Windsor Star,* September 27, 1980.

*   *   *

TEWKESBURY, Joan   1936-

PERSONAL: Born April 8, 1936, in Redlands, Calif.; daughter of Walter S. (an office machine repairman) and Frances (a registered nurse; maiden name, Stevenson) Tewkesbury; married Robert F. Maguire III, November 29, 1960 (divorced January, 1973); children: Robin Tewkesbury, Peter Harlan. *Education:* Mt. San Antonio Junior College, 1956-58; University of Southern California, 1958-60. *Residence:* Los Angeles, Calif. *Agent:* Jeff Berg, International Creative Management, 8899 Beverly Blvd., Los Angeles, Calif. 90048.

CAREER: Director and choreographer of little theatre productions near Los Angeles, Calif., 1956-64; Mt. San Antonio Junior College, Pomona, Calif., teacher of dance, 1956-58; American School of Dance, Los Angeles, teacher, 1959-69; Immaculate Heart College, Los Angeles, teacher of theatre arts, 1960-64; University of Southern California, Los Angeles, teacher of theatre arts, 1967-69; script supervisor for motion picture "McCabe and Mrs. Miller," 1969-70; motion picture director, 1976—. *Member:* Screen Actors Guild, Actors Equity, Writers Guild, Directors Guild. *Awards, honors:* Los Angeles Critics Award, 1975, for "Nashville"; named Outstanding Junior College Alumni by Mt. San Antonio Junior College, 1979.

WRITINGS—Screenplays, except as noted: "Thieves Like Us," based on novel by Edward Anderson, United Artists, 1974; *Nashville,* Paramount, 1975, published by Bantam, 1976; (and director) "The Hampstead Center" (documentary), 1976; (and director) "Cowboy Jack Street" (two-act play), first produced in New York City at Perry Street Theatre, December, 1977; (and director) "The Tenth Month" (television movie), Columbia Broadcasting System (CBS), 1979; (with Paul Schrader; and director) "Old Boyfriends," Avco-Embassy, 1979; (and director) "The Acorn

People,'' adapted from the book by Ron Jones, National Broadcasting Corp. (NBC), 1980. Also author of "After Ever After," 1972, "Tender Is the Night," 1976, and "Fragile Underground," 1978.

WORK IN PROGRESS: A screenplay, "Living Well Is the Best Revenge," a fictionalized adaptation of the book by Calvin Tompkins; a novel, *Venice/Texas.*

SIDELIGHTS: Screenwriter and director Joan Tewkesbury began her entertainment career at the age of ten, dancing in a motion picture starring Cyd Charrisse. Later she was Mary Martin's flying understudy and played an ostrich in a 1954 Broadway production of "Peter Pan." In addition, Tewkesbury worked her way through college by dancing in night clubs.

Switching to the role of director, Tewkesbury later became involved in theatre productions at Actors Studio West and at University of Southern California. Her work in the theatre led to her first big break into the motion picture industry, as Susan Broudy explained in *Ms.* magazine: "In 1970 when Tewkesbury heard that Bob Altman liked one of the plays she had directed, she wrote to him and then asked if she could observe him shoot 'McCabe and Mrs. Miller' in Vancouver. Altman doesn't like people just watching, so he made her script supervisor—the person who coordinates new scenes, dialogue, and background dialogue into the script while the film is shot. A difficult job since Altman does so much improvisation."

Altman, who was favorably impressed with Tewkesbury's work and with a film script she had written, asked her to write the screenplay for "Thieves Like Us." The success of this film and of "Nashville," which she also wrote, earned Tewkesbury the opportunity of making her film directing debut with the 1976 documentary "The Hampstead Center."

Tewkesbury told *CA:* "Reading a great deal as a child, dancing, and working with Jerome Robbins on the 1954 production of 'Peter Pan' were important influences on me. All of this diverse implosion has served a career in film very well. I travel a great deal because it is important to see the world firsthand if I am trying to unravel human conditions. Also it is imperative for me visually, for I am constantly fed by the impact of certain images."

CA INTERVIEWS THE AUTHOR
CA interviewed Joan Tewkesbury by phone April 16, 1980 at work in Los Angeles.

CA: You've said you learned the craft of structuring a script through working with Robert Altman as script girl on "McCabe and Mrs. Miller." What do you find most difficult about putting a screenplay together?

TEWKESBURY: I'd say that there are two things. As I look back, I learned about screenplay structuring from that experience, but the more I do of it, the more I realize how much I had learned from dance. I was a dancer and a choreographer before I began to do this, and I was involved in theatre. I realize how much that experience has helped with the writing experience, because in dance you set things with a beginning, a high point, and an end. One goes for a certain amount of time based on what the human body can do in that amount of time. Screenplay structuring is much like that. It is a whole piece of material that is made up of a lot of small pieces of material. Each scene has some kind of beginning, middle, and end; but the overview is never quite wrapped up until all of these pieces are orchestrated together. I would say that the most difficult thing about structuring a screen-

play is to constantly keep away from being predictable. In dance, you can always break out of it with a physical movement—you can do a jump or a turn, which affords the viewer an intake of breath, a surprise. Oftentimes in writing, when you are structuring a linear piece, there is only one way to go, and that's straight across the horizon line. I really prefer to work with an audience as if they were an Indian taking a long walk across the desert. He does not walk from point to point; he walks from one thing that interests him back to another thing that interests him—almost in a zigzag. But people feel the viewer, or the filmgoer, can't take that long journey to each zigzag because it takes too much time, so you make shortcuts. "Nashville" was an exercise in how to take that zigzag journey, however.

CA: You've described your scripts as being structured like trains—made of separate cars, each with its own separate entrance and exit for the director to go in and out of. Do you ever see a part of the structure getting away from your original intention for it?

TEWKESBURY: Yes, which is interesting. I sit down with an outline, and those outlines are very important, because they are like the superstructure of a building. But you sit down and begin to write to your own outline, and you'll find that the characters or a location that you have found or what is happening between the characters dictates something entirely different than what is indicated on the outline. So you have to take the journey with them. If it doesn't work you can always take it out. But I think it is important to take that part of the journey with the material. And in the actual production, there is still enough room left for the actor to come in and feel his humanity in the construct.

As a director now, I find it interesting that I am much more tight-reined than I ever thought I would be, but I'm sure that comes from dance training too. That is a discipline I was involved in from the time I was three years old. In dance, there is a feeling that everything is happening spontaneously, yet the movement comes from very carefully planned plots of organization that must occur over and over in rehearsal before you go out on stage.

A lot of the achievement and the success of Altman's films is because there is a carefully laid out atmosphere. While you're shooting on the set it seems that these events are just happening. They are *not* just happening. They have been extremely well organized and preplanned and though actors may feel as though they have stepped onto a set and are improvising like crazy, they are really involved in a process where they are encouraged to use as much of themselves as they want to. It gets publicized in a very peculiar way, as if there is a happy accident every other take. But that isn't quite the way it works. There is a lot of talking and a lot of feedback and a lot of exchange that happens between himself and his actors. Certainly when we did "Nashville" there was an enormous amount of exchange, and an enormous amount of the actors' writing. I would edit and then we would talk and then they would do the work. So it's not like a Cassavetes movie, where people *do* sit at the dinner table and improvise, and you shoot it. There's room for that sometimes, but you have to be very careful because it alters the style of your film. Now if that's the style of your film, that's just fine. But if you are working with satin furniture and suddenly you bring in four bamboo chairs, it's kind of peculiar.

CA: Has Altman been the strongest influence on your own writing style?

TEWKESBURY: No, but certainly the way he works with

people has reinforced the way I've always felt you should work with people. I read from childhood. I was an only child and books and the characters in them became my friends and family. I know that everything I ever read influenced me but I am not certain how because I haven't really thought about myself as a writer much—in terms of writing a literate body of work—because I write screenplays. But certainly the Southern writers with their sharp sense of place and eye for the unusual human being: Capote, Faulkner, and the American writers and poets who were involved in the literary movement in France in the 1920's. I read, and always have, more nonfiction than fiction and more biographies than anything else. Joan Didion's work has influenced a way of looking at the work as a whole—her terseness, the way her stories become the sum total of content and space. Somehow the experience has impact and becomes tactile for me in that I *feel* as much as I process intellectually. I am sure my friend Robert Irwin has had an enormous impact on my work. He is an artist whose sensibility and way of working with a particular kind of committedness and self-discipline allow one to work *in* time rather than against it. Altman, Jerome Robbins, a woman lawyer named Norma Zorkey have been role models: people wheeling and dealing in the entertainment marketplace. So those models plus Irwin, who has worked very intuitively with his own vision, have been instrumental in my shaping my course.

In terms of film work, people inspire characters for me. I write for specific people and usually I have an actor in mind that I'm writing for. Whether he or she does the role is irrelevant. A character can develop from somebody that I've heard talk in a restaurant. I'm a great eavesdropper, and I collect a lot of information traveling. When I'm not working, I travel, because that seems to be where I gather the most information on what people talk about and how they talk. *Theives Like Us* is a gorgeous book. I knew that Keith Carradine and Shelley Duvall and Burt Remsen and John Schuck were going to do it. I had spent six months of my life with all of them on the set of "McCabe and Mrs. Miller," so when I wrote dialogue or had to write additional dialogue, I could hear those actors saying it. So one could say it came from them.

I write for specific people even if they never do the part. I have written a screenplay called "Fragile Underground" for Genevieve Bujold and Julie Christie. It's an interesting tale. It travels from Canada all the way across the United States. It is about two women who have always been attached to active men and for the first time in their lives set out on a journey alone. Because their men are involved in a revolutionary activity, the ladies have to get out of town. So it is their trip, not only of survival and to get from Quebec to Seattle, but it's like this hall of mysteries—everything they go to opens another thing. One of them finally journeys to visit her child whom she hasn't seen in ten years. So as you're taking the exterior journey, you take the internal journey as well. I'd known Julie's work for a long time and I had met Genevieve Bujold. I could hear the sound of those two women. It's like music, like writing a piece of music for two instruments. That's how I write.

CA: Research is a very important part of your writing also, isn't it?

TEWKESBURY: Absolutely.

CA: How much inspiration comes from the process of research?

TEWKESBURY: I have completed a screenplay called "Living Well Is the Best Revenge," a piece that takes place in Europe in the 1920's. It's fictionalized from Calvin Tomkin's book by the same name about Gerald and Sara Murphy. But what was imperative before I could begin to write was that I take the trip, that I see also as a filmmaker what exists and doesn't exist, so I'm not writing for pie in the sky. Some people say that's stupid but I just think it's good sense. I also am able perhaps to touch on what remains. Sometimes certain essences that were really important to those people remain, so it becomes clear why they chose to live in those places at that time. And I do an enormous amount of book and periodical research on a thing like that, because I need to know as much as I can about the day-to-day things so the period will be real and not a cartoon.

I'm doing another piece called *Venice/Texas.* It is the overlap of Venice, Italy, and most of the state of Texas. It's too complex to explain to you, but it is in essence exactly what "Nashville" was, only larger. I am drawing on all the things that are wonderful and magnificent and peculiar about Texas and all the things that are wonderful and magnificent and *very* peculiar about Venice, Italy. It may sound weird, but it's a wonderful thing to do, because, in your own way, without disturbing anybody, you get to come in and play God a little bit. You say, all right, what if you take a piece of sky from Texas and a piece of water from Italy? And what happens if you overlap them in an image? And what if a human being who has always lived in the flatland of Texas goes to a place like Venice, Italy? Then after you overlap a few images or emotions you begin to find that there really are overlaps in the two societies. The minute you start looking for these things you find them. People in Italy are dying to tell you the twelve stories about Aunt Anna who lived in the closet and drank wine, and then you'll find out that, yes, in Texas somebody has an Aunt Winnie who made gin in the basement. What I think I'm trying to do with all this is to show that the world is a very small place, and that though we become more and more at odds with other cultures, human beings function similarly.

CA: You worked summers at the Edinburgh Festival and in London for BBC-TV. What of most value came out of that work?

TEWKESBURY: I was going to the University of Southern California then—well, actually I had finished—and I had two children and my marriage was very dodgy. An old instructor of mine, John Blankenship, asked me if I'd like to join a repertory company he was going to take to the Edinburgh Festival, and I said yes. What I was given was the opportunity to do everything. I acted; I directed; I choreographed; if you wanted scenery you had to go beg, borrow, and steal for it. I had to manage my children and navigate all of that at the same time.

The first year we went was my first trip to Europe, my first awakening to other sensibilities than American. We arrived just a few days after Robert Kennedy had been shot. It was the first time I had been confronted with a microphone and asked questions about my opinions on politics in the United States. I was about thirty-two years old; some of the students who were with the group were very young and I was aware that the students were more in tune with what was going on in that way than I was. It was also the first time that I began to realize you could do more than one thing at the same time, that if you had children, you didn't have to seal yourself off in a cedar chest. So I went back to Edinburgh for two more years, each time taking on more and more responsibility.

We did so well that the BBC, both in Edinburgh and in London, became interested, and I had the opportunity to extend whatever I had done on stage to this other medium. People were very kind. David Cunliffe, the television director, allowed me to come into the control room where he was overviewing the whole show, so I was able to work with my material and him in this new way.

It was very important for me to have that experience. In Europe there is not the movie-star overtone to everything that there is here. If you are a director or an actor, you might as well be a plumber or a dentist or a doctor—it's a profession and you go to work. So being deglamorized, there is no mythological hierarchy, and you get a better range of experience because you can simply go to work. I was very fortunate.

That experience still exists every other year at USC, and I would say that it was one of the most valuable training experiences I ever had. It really paved the way for how I operate on a movie set. It also paved the way for my responding to the way Altman works, because it was the same way I worked in repertory theatre. The difference was that Altman had two cameras and a better sense of humor.

CA: From screenwriting to directing was a seven-year process for you. What were the major obstacles?

TEWKESBURY: Just finding somebody that would let me do it. Altman knew that I wanted to direct. When I came to him I told him that was what I wanted to do, and he gave me the job as script girl because he said it was the best way to learn the medium. I had worked in movies as a kid, but I didn't know much, and I was very afraid of all the machinery. What the opportunity allowed me to understand was that I didn't have to be afraid of the machinery; there were trained professionals who took care of that and I didn't have to. After "McCabe" I wrote something to direct that Altman tried to get financed but he couldn't do it, and that's when I started writing directly for him, as an act, really, of trying to repay him for this swell opportunity he had given me, but also as an exercise—to see what Altman wanted and what he didn't want and what he absolutely didn't need and what he could use a little of. So the first writing experiences were directly for this man that I respect so much.

Then other writing experiences came, and they were very different. I wrote on assignment, I did a screenplay of "Tender Is the Night" that will never be done. I've probably done about ten assignment screenplays that ended like that. They were fine experiences—I learned from each one of them—but they were not the kind of collaborative thing that I was looking to do, and it was extremely frustrating. What I really wanted to do was direct.

Finally, in 1976, my family doctor said, "Would you like to meet Anna Freud?" And I said, "You're kidding!" He said that there was a group of doctors who were trying to help her raise money for her clinic in London, that Sydney Pollack was involved with the project, and would I be interested in interviewing her. Well, I went and talked with Pollack, who is an incredibly gracious man. He was doing "Bobby Deerfield" at the time he was supposed to shoot the documentary. Well of course he didn't have time to do it, so I said, "Look, this is a wonderful thing, an opportunity for me to direct my first film. May I?" And he said yes.

So my first film was a documentary called "The Hampstead Center." It is about Anna Freud and her successful work with children. It afforded me a working experience with Pollack for about six months. He set up an editing room with one of his assistants, Jerry Jackson, and we edited the documentary as Pollack was editing "Bobby Deerfield" next door. What I learned from him was a different kind of expertise. Pollack is extremely meticulous; Altman is a little looser in certain things. Pollack works in many ways much more like I work, in that kind of organized, structured way. So it was nice to have the best of both. The film has been very carefully shown: there are certain restrictions placed on it because it is a fund-raising film. No, it was not shown on television; no, it was not viewed for the Academy; none of those things. But it didn't matter. Paul Schrader was looking for someone to rewrite and direct a script of his. He looked at the film and basically what he saw was that I could put one foot in front of the other, so to speak. So that's how "Old Boyfriends" happened.

There had been several attempts to do other things or seductive offers that would fall through. But after "Old Boyfriends" Carol Burnett and her producers were looking for someone to write and direct "The Tenth Month" for her on television. Talia and David Shire recommended me very highly so I was very fortunate because I went, literally as we were editing "Old Boyfriends," to work for Carol. It was a nice experience, because I had a framework of a book to work with; but what I wrote to was Carol Burnett, the sound of her, what her abilities were, how far she wanted to stretch, what we wanted to discuss. She's one of the most gifted human beings I've ever known. She is quite, quite extraordinary. So it was an opportunity to play with an actress who is deeply talented. And an actor, Keith Michell, who is equally talented. We had a splendid time.

Then all last year was devoted to the release of "Old Boyfriends." It was a lot of travel that was paid for, and that part is fine; but you don't ever get to see enough that way. Then the film went to Cannes for Directors' Fortnight. That was terrific, because it was a very nice category for that film to be in—new directors, their first or second or third film—small films. And it was well received. *That* is nice.

After we finished in Cannes I began work on "Living Well"; I extended the trip and went on to research that. While I gather financing for it, I'm collecting material for *Venice/Texas*. And I have just adapted and will direct a project called "The Acorn People." It's from a book by Ron Jones about severely handicapped kids in a summer camp. It's very irreverent, very funny, and I want to do it like "M*A*S*H." Whatever information you can put out about these kids is important. They possess a lot more than we give them credit for; and as long as people keep their opinions of them locked in sentiment, the kids will never be allowed to break out. Now if you look at them as these really interesting creatures from another planet or from another time dimension, or people who are here to teach us something about communication, the whole thing takes on a different color. So that's the way I'm going to look at it.

CA: You've described your drastic break from what you called the "normal" life. What did you find the hardest part of making that break, of starting out on your own?

TEWKESBURY: Leaving the children. Leaving the construct of our routine, our schedule. I'm forty-four and I grew up believing the most important thing was the family structure even though I hadn't had one as a child. My belief created an "idealic myth" that really didn't exist. But as I look back I see how that construct formed the basis for what I am doing now. I am working in family structures. I am combining personalities. I am budgeting money. I am making sure that people are cared for properly, that they get fed on time, that they are properly clothed, etc., etc. So that family experience—which I never had as a kid because I was an only child and I grew up quite alone—was imperative. But leaving became just as imperative due to the nature of the personalities involved. "Idealic myths" die hard, especially your own.

The most difficult thing was the reaction other people had to my leaving my kids. Though it was a very mutual arrangement between my ex-husband and me based in mutual respect, other people tended to take it personally, as though this act would unhinge their family construct. So the children's father's home has been their permanent home for the last few years, but now they may be spending more time with me again. I probably at some time will do a little writing about it. People love to make judgments about things that they don't know the interior workings of. Basically all of us have gotten on much better, and the children have benefited from the experience of having had both kinds of parents, because we are about as different as night and day.

CA: Would you advise other women to do this?

TEWKESBURY: No, because it is really personal. I don't even think of it as a woman thing, as much as I think of it as somebody who is trapped with a talent inside. It was just as difficult for my ex-husband when he left us to go work on his journey alone for a few years as it was for me. Talent is a human statement; it has nothing to do with being male or female. You respond in different ways because you are a mother or a father—that's secondary. The first issue is the trapped talent. And if you have that, the other ingredient that you have to have to get you out of the house, and that people often don't consider, is ambition. People often classify ambition as an ego trip, as being un-Christian, all those moral judgments. If you do not have a high degree of ambition—not for yourself, not for recognition, but to put something into the world—don't do it. Because it's much too painful. Odds are that you'll die of loneliness in a hotel room somewhere. But if you have that absolutely burning desire, get on with it, because you will drive yourself and everyone around you crazy if you don't.

Everything balances out. You learn to spend time with yourself in a new way and restructure your time. It's really nice. And if you do have children, what you give them is a look at an alternative, an alternative choice, an alternative way to do it. But if you can't do it, it's not something that you should beat yourself with because you can't make that step out the door. That is absurd. There are things that can be done within the structure of your own home that are not just homemaker-related. A lot of people work within the complexity of their homes and they enjoy it. So it is deeply personal. These people are fueled by the interaction at home.

I know a lot of writers, directors, teachers, and artists who really need that kind of construct to work out of. Certainly Altman does and enjoys it. Each film is a huge family that he incorporates with his personal family. In that respect we are very different. I'm there daily for everyone on my set, whatever happens, whatever they need, but when I go home I want a little solitude so I can incorporate the experiences of the day and prepare, as best I can, for whatever tomorrow might bring.

BIOGRAPHICAL/CRITICAL SOURCES: Ms., July, 1975; *Film Quarterly,* winter, 1975-76; *New York Times,* December 13, 1977; *Feature,* March, 1979; *Dialogue in American Film,* March, 1979.

—*Interview by Jean W. Ross*

THE COUNTRYMAN
See WHITLOCK, Ralph

*   *   *

THEE, Marek 1918-
(Marek Gdanski)

PERSONAL: Born November 21, 1918, in Rzeszow, Poland; son of Maurycy (a merchant) and Adela (Zimmermann) Thee; married Erna Zimmermann (a translator), August 20, 1942; children: Maya, Halina. *Education:* University of Warsaw, M.J., 1955. *Home:* Doenskitoppen 12, 1351 Rud, Norway. *Office:* International Peace Research Institute, Raadhusgate 4, Oslo 1, Norway.

CAREER: Press attache, 1946-49; Polish consul in Tel Aviv, Israel, 1949-52; Polish Institute of International Affairs, Warsaw, senior researcher, 1953-68; International Peace Research Institute, Oslo, Norway, senior research fellow, 1968—, research director, 1979—. Council member of Polish delegation to International Commission for Supervision and Control in Vietnam, 1955; Polish representative at International Commission for Supervision and Control in Laos, 1956-57, 1961-63. *Member:* International Peace Research Association.

WRITINGS: Laos and the Second Indochinese War: Notes of a Witness, Random House, 1973; (editor) *Armaments and Disarmament in the Nuclear Age: A Handbook,* International Peace Reasearch Institute (Stockholm, Sweden), 1976; (editor with Asbjoern Eide) *Problems of Contemporary Militarism,* Croom Helm, 1980.

In Polish; under name Marek Gdanski: *Bliski i srodkowy wschod, 1945-1955, rywalizacja mocarstw zachodnich* (title means "The Near and Middle East, 1945-1955: The Rivalry Between the Western Powers"), Ksiazka i Wiedza, 1956; *Arabski wschod: Historia, gospodarka, polityka* (title means "The Arab East: History, Economy, Politics"), Ksiazka i Wiedza, 1963; *Niespokojny Laos: Z dziejow kryzysu, 1954-1964* (title means "Laos in Turmoil"), Polski Instytut Spraw Miedzynarodowych, 1965. Contributor to social science and peace research journals.

WORK IN PROGRESS: Research on armaments and disarmament, military research and development, and development problems in general.

SIDELIGHTS: Thee commented: "I left Poland as a result of the political ferment in 1968. I have been active since then in the peace research movement, endorsing the broad definition of peace as 'absence of violence in both international and intra-national affairs'; that is, the absence of armed conflict and realization of social justice and equity. I have published many articles on the Indochina conflict, armaments and disarmament, and military research and development."

*   *   *

THELWELL, Michael Miles 1939-

PERSONAL: Born July 25, 1939, in Ulster Spring, Jamaica; came to the United States, 1959; son of Morris M. (a member of the House of Representatives) and Violet (McFarlane) Thelwell; married; children: two. *Education:* Howard University, B.A., 1964; University of Massachusetts, Amherst, M.F.A., 1969. *Home:* 5 Gulf Rd., Pelham, Mass. 01002. *Office:* Department of Afro-American Studies, University of Massachusetts, Amherst, Mass. 01002.

CAREER: Jamaica Industrial Development Corp., Kingston, Jamaica, public relations assistant, 1958-59; Student

Nonviolent Coordinating Committee, Washington, D.C., director of Washington office, 1963-64; Mississippi Freedom Democratic Party, Washington, D.C., director of Washington office, 1964-65; University of Massachusetts, Amherst, chairman of W.E.B. Dubois department of Afro-American studies, 1969-75, associate professor of literature, 1975—. *Awards, honors:* First prize in short story contest from *Story* magazine, 1967, for "The Organizer"; National Foundation on the Arts and Humanities award, 1968, for "Notes From the Delta"; fellow of Cornell University's Society for the Humanities, 1969; literary award from Rockefeller Foundation, 1969-70.

WRITINGS: The Harder They Come, Grove, 1980.

Film scripts: "Washington Incident," Intent Films, 1972; (with Paul Carter Harrison) "Girl Beneath the Lion," Grove Films, 1978.

Contributor to anthologies, including: *The Stone Soldier,* Fleet, 1964; *Best Stories by Negro Writers,* edited by Langston Hughes, Little, Brown, 1966; *American Literary Anthology,* Farrar, Straus, 1968; *Theme Book 10: Text for Sophomores,* edited by Irene Wilson, Glenn, 1970; *Modern College Reader,* edited by Diane Millan, Scribner, 1970; *Cosmos Reader,* Harcourt, 1971; *Black Hands on a White Face,* edited by Whit Burnett, Scribner, 1971; *The Fact of Fiction,* edited by Cydril M. Gulassa, Harper, 1973. Contributor to periodicals, including *Negro Digest, Spectrum, Massachusetts Review, Story,* and *Motive.* Member of editorial board, *Massachusetts Review,* 1969—, *Black Scholar,* 1970—, and *Okike,* 1972—.

WORK IN PROGRESS: Two novels on Jamaican society.

SIDELIGHTS: Thelwell's book, *The Harder They Come,* is based on a 1973 Jamaican movie of the same name. Rather than writing a standard novelization, Thelwell built a larger novel around the characters and situations in the movie. This extra effort resulted in "a novel that is virtually an in-depth study of Jamaican culture and folkways," declared Thomas Lask. "It is dense with detail, chronicling the life of the countryside, the culture of the principal city, Kingston, and the effect of each on the other.... 'The Harder They Come' is both local and universal, ... for, although the events could not be more home grown and intimate (the dialect is endlessly fascinating), the themes could apply to striving people everywhere."

Thelwell told *CA:* "My intention is to create a body of fiction which explores the development of modern Jamaican society. These works will utilize the cultural metaphors, the narrative styles and forms of indigenous Afro-Jamaican culture."

BIOGRAPHICAL/CRITICAL SOURCES: Library Journal, October 1, 1979; *New York Times,* February 1, 1980; *Publishers Weekly,* April 4, 1980.

*   *   *

THIRION, Andre   1907-

PERSONAL: Born April 18, 1907, in Baccarat, Lorraine, France; son of Louis (a compositor of symphonic music) and Jeanne (Camet de Sainte-Laudy) Thirion; married Katia Drenovska, September 30, 1930; children: Francoise (Mrs. Yvan Audouard). *Education:* University of Nancy at Sorbonne, baccalaureat, 1925. *Home:* 50 avenue Simon Bolivar, Paris, France 75019.

CAREER: France Mutualiste, Paris, chef du service des retraites, 1931-45; Etablissements Fontvielle, Dunkirk, France, attache de direction, 1949-53; Societe Industrielle de

Recherche Technique, Puteaux, France, manager, 1952-53; Mouvements Jeunes Science, delegue general, 1955-75. Author. Counsellor of city of Paris, 1945-53; vice-president of Paris council, 1951-52; rapporteur general du compte du Departement de la Seine, 1945-53. *Military service:* French Engineering Corps, 1939-40; French Forces of the Interior, 1943-45; received Croix de Guerre. *Awards, honors:* Created chevalier of French Legion of Honor, 1953; Prix Roger Nimier, 1972.

WRITINGS: Le Grand Ordinaire, privately printed, 1943, Losfeld, 1970; *Revolutionnaires sans revolution,* Laffont, 1972, translation by Joachim Neugroschel published as *Revolutionaries Without Revolution,* Macmillan, 1975; *Eloge de l'indocilite,* Laffont, 1973; *Beatrice* (novel), Laffont, 1975; *Defense de,* Sagittaire, 1976. Contributor to *La Revolution surrealiste,* 1928-29, *Le Surrealisme au service de la revolution,* 1930-33, *Volontes de ceux de la resistance,* 1944-45, and *L'Oeil,* 1955-59.

WORK IN PROGRESS: "L'Ange et les homards," a three-act dramatic comedy.

SIDELIGHTS: Thirion told the story of his involvement with the French Surrealists and the Communist cause in his book, *Revolutionaries Without Revolution.* During the 1920's Thirion left his provincial bourgeois family and joined Surrealist leaders Andre Breton and Louis Aragon in Paris. There the spirit of the Russian Revolution had spread, with Thirion and the Surrealists in the center of revolutionary activity.

"*Revolutionaries Without Revolution* is a collage of people, places, gossip, political intrigue and philosophical reflection whose focus is the inter-war years," summarized Shiva Naipaul. "At its heart, however, is the absorbing chronicle of one man's involvement with the Communist faith and his gradual—and painful—alienation from it.... His book tells the story of a thorough-going apostasy."

Thirion told *CA:* "Defense de la Liberte."

BIOGRAPHICAL/CRITICAL SOURCES: Spectator, May 1, 1976; *New Statesman,* July 2, 1976.

*   *   *

THOLLANDER, Earl   1922-

PERSONAL: Born April 13, 1922, in Kingsburg, Calif.; son of Gustave Alfred (a contractor) and Helen Marie (Peterson) Thollander; married Janet Marie Behr, May 31, 1947; children: Kristie, Wesley. *Education:* San Francisco City College, A.A., 1942; University of California, Berkeley, B.A., 1944; also attended Art League of California, Academy of Art, and San Francisco Art Institute. *Politics:* Democrat. *Religion:* Unitarian-Universalist. *Home:* House in the Woods, Murray Hill, Calistoga, Calif. 94515.

CAREER: San Francisco Examiner, San Francisco, Calif., artist, 1949-56; Landphere Associates (commercial artists), San Francisco, illustrator, 1956-58; free-lance artist, designer, and illustrator in San Francisco, 1958-70, and Calistoga, Calif., 1970—. Member of faculty at Napa College, 1972-73. Work exhibited in group and solo shows all over the world. *Military service:* U.S. Navy, 1944-47; served in Pacific theater; became lieutenant junior grade. *Member:* Depot Gallery (member of board of directors). *Awards, honors:* Award of merit from Los Angeles Art Directors Club, 1956; citation of merit from Society of Illustrators National Exhibition, 1959; *Ramon Makes a Trade* was named one of the hundred best children's books of 1959, by American Institute of Graphic Arts, *Sunset Cookbook,* was named one of fifty best books of 1960, and *Delights and Prejudices* was named one of fifty best books of 1965; certificate of excellence from Art Directors Club of Chicago, 1970; award of excellence from San Francisco Society of Communicating Arts, 1975.

WRITINGS—Self-illustrated: *Back Roads of California*, Sunset Books, 1971, revised edition, Lane, 1977; *Back Roads of New England*, C. N. Potter, 1974; *Barns of California*, California Historical Society, 1974; *Back Roads of Arizona*, Northland Press, 1978; *Back Roads of Oregon*, C. N. Potter, 1979; *Back Roads of Texas*, Northland Press, 1980.

Illustrator: *The Sunset Cookbook*, Lane, 1960; James Beard, *Delights and Prejudices*, Atheneum, 1964; Gloria Bey Miller, *The Thousand Recipe Chinese Cookbook*, Atheneum, 1966; T. H. Watkins, *On the Shore of the Sundown Sea*, Sierra Books, 1973.

WORK IN PROGRESS: Back Roads of Washington; Back Roads of New Mexico.

SIDELIGHTS: Thollander began his travels, and the sketching that always accompanies his trips, during World War II, on a landing ship that made its way past New Guinea, through the Philippines, on to Korea and Japan. He has been traveling ever since, adding sketches and paintings to his collection. Much of his work is commissioned before a trip begins, but many drawings are saved for future use.

In the 1950's he worked in Mexico, Hawaii, Scandinavia, the Soviet Union, Italy, and Eastern Europe. The sixties took him to the Orient, Malaya, and Thailand, the Middle East, Africa, and Europe, including Greece. He also participated in a U.S. Air Force art program in Vietnam.

Then he returned to the United States for the extensive research and travel that led to his books on the back roads of America, beginning with twenty thousand miles of travel throughout his native California.

In 1974 Thollander led a group of artists on a sketching tour through the wine country of France. Sponsored by Wine Tours International, the trip was successful enough to warrant additional tours of the European wine country to Italy in 1975, Germany in 1976, and Spain and Portugal in 1978. In 1977 and 1979 he worked as an art instructor on the S.S. *Santa Magdalena,* which sailed around South America, and then returned to his quiet farm in the wine country of Napa Valley, California.

Much of Thollander's work has been commissioned editorial illustrating and advertising art. He now prefers pen-and-ink drawings and watercolors. All his work is done on location, to give it "the special touch that only 'presence' at the time of execution can bring to such work."

AVOCATIONAL INTERESTS: Chinese and Japanese art.

BIOGRAPHICAL/CRITICAL SOURCES: American Artist, April, 1954, March, 1960; *Journal of Commercial Art,* November, 1959, September/October, 1962; *Napa Register,* March, 1975; *Vacaville Reporter,* March 16, 1975.

*   *   *

THOMAS, Helen A.   1920-

PERSONAL: Born August 4, 1920, in Winchester, Ky.; daughter of George and Mary Thomas; married Douglas B. Cornell (a journalist), October 11, 1971. *Education:* Wayne State University, B.A., 1942. *Home:* 2501 Calvert St. N.W., Washington, D.C. 20008. *Office:* National Press Building, Washington, D.C. 20004.

CAREER: Formerly affiliated with United Press Interna-

tional; wire service reporter in Washington, D.C., 1973-74, White House bureau chief, 1974—. *Member:* Women's National Press Club (president, 1959-60), American Newspaper Women's Club (former vice-president), White House Correspondents Association (president, 1976), Sigma Delta Chi, Delta Sigma Phi (honorary member). *Awards, honors:* Named woman of the year in communications by *Ladies' Home Journal,* 1975; L.L.D. from Eastern Michigan State University, 1972, and Ferris State College, 1978; L.H.D. from Wayne State University, 1974, and University of Detroit, 1979.

WRITINGS: Dateline: White House, Macmillan, 1975.

SIDELIGHTS: Helen Thomas is one of the most widely known wire service reporters in the United States. Since 1961 she has covered the White House for United Press International, and in 1974 was named White House bureau chief.

Some of Thomas's biggest scoops were provided by Martha Mitchell. During the Watergate affair, Mitchell would often make revealing telephone calls to Thomas. "Martha loved the press. And any time she spoke out it was usually with a block-buster," Thomas told an interviewer for the *Grand Rapids Press.* "Martha could never give you one, two, three, in sequence, but if you pieced the facts together you found them valid. Listen to the White House tapes and you'll find the proof."

An account of Martha Mitchell, as well as an inside look at the White House during the administrations of Kennedy, Johnson, Nixon, and Ford, is contained in Thomas's *Dateline: White House.* Godfrey Sperling of the *Christian Science Monitor* found the book to be filled with "behind-the-scenes nuggets and acute observations." Richard Reeves was equally admiring. He noted that *Dateline: White House* contains "fascinating material on the Johnsons, a touching portrait of Pat Nixon and an interesting portrait of a very tough and very feminine woman named Helen Thomas succeeding in the male world of journalism. More than that, in total, 'Dateline: White House' is a valuable firsthand report on how reporting itself actually works."

BIOGRAPHICAL/CRITICAL SOURCES: Grand Rapids Press, November 1, 1974; Helen Thomas, *Dateline: White House,* Macmillan, 1975; *Biography News,* Gale, January/February, 1975; *New York Times Book Review,* November 30, 1975; *Christian Science Monitor,* December 30, 1975.

*   *   *

THOMAS, J. W.   1917-

PERSONAL: Born July 31, 1917, in Paden, Okla.; son of Douglas Edward (in business) and Evalena (Glasscock) Thomas; married Martha Jane Vandruff (a vice-president of administration), September 6, 1946; children: Mark Douglas, Thomas Jay. *Education:* Attended Stanford University, 1946, and Southern Methodist University, 1946-47; Oklahoma State University, B.A., 1948, M.S., 1950, Ed.D., 1955. *Home and office address:* 1126 Brandy Station, P.O. Box 1237, Richardson, Tex. 75080.

CAREER: Oklahoma State University, Stillwater, institutional counselor, 1953-55; Rohrer, Hibler & Replogle (psychologists to management), Dallas, Tex., psychologist, 1955-60; private practice as management psychologist in Richardson, Tex., 1960-66; Bi/Polar, Inc. (psychological consulting firm), Richardson, president, 1966—. *Military service:* U.S. Navy, aviator, 1941-46; became commander; received three Air Medals. *Member:* American Psychological Association.

WRITINGS: *Your Personal Growth,* Fell, 1971; *Bi/Polar: A Positive Way of Understanding People,* Bi/Polar, Inc., 1978; *Bi/Polar Pattern Relationships* (workbook), Bi/Polar, Inc., 1979, revised edition, 1980.

SIDELIGHTS: Thomas told *CA:* "I am the originator of the Bi/Polar theory of personality. This is at the center of my life's work, and I expect to continue developing this approach to understanding people for the rest of my life."

In a description of the Bi/Polar concept, Thomas wrote: "People are created with two basic strengths, forming a Bi/Polar pair: the strength to THINK . . . and the strength to RISK . . . Each side of the basic Bi/Polar pair comprises another polar pair. The Thinking Strength is comprised of two kinds of thinking: Practical Thinking . . . and . . . Theoretical Thinking. In turn, the Risking Strength is made up of two kinds of risking: Dependent Risking . . . and . . . Independent Risking. As in the basic pair, the supporting pairs are composed of two strengths—not a strength and a weakness. When you let your strengths interact and cross-feed, you express a more creative blend of strengths. This allows you to achieve truly valuable goals. To purposefully invest your strengths in the creative process is to gain maturity, productivity, and growth."

*   *   *

THOMAS, Jeannette Grise   1935-
(Jeannette Grise)

PERSONAL: Born April 4, 1935, in Brookline, Mass.; daughter of Lucien Alexis and Dorothy (Tabony) Grise; married Richard B. Thomas (a college instructor), June 20, 1959; children: Andrew. *Education:* Simmons College, B.S., 1957; Radcliffe College, A.M., 1959; University of Pennsylvania, Ph.D., 1969. *Politics:* Independent. *Religion:* Roman Catholic. *Home and office:* 105 Grasmere Rd., Bala-Cynwyd, Pa. 19004.

CAREER: Writer.

WRITINGS—Children's books; under name Jeannette Grise: *Robert Benjamin and the Blue Dog Joke,* Westminster, 1978; *Robert Benjamin and the Vanishing Act,* Westminster, 1980.

WORK IN PROGRESS: Another Robert Benjamin book; a story set in Scotland, about a scientific expedition to Loch Ness.

SIDELIGHTS: When *CA* asked Jeannette Grise about her current activities, she responded: "It's this way. Pick any day and I am in the process of either writing a book or reading a book. I live two blocks from a combined elementary school and public library. In 1978 the township closed the school. Now they propose to use that portion of the building for a police station. Lately I have been devoting a great deal of time and carbon typewriter ribbons to trying to defeat this project."

*   *   *

THOMAS, Norman (Mattoon)   1884-1968

PERSONAL: Born November 20, 1884, in Marion, Ohio; died December 19, 1968; son of Welling Evan (a Presbyterian minister) and Emma (Mattoon) Thomas; married Frances Violet Stewart (a social worker), September 1, 1910 (died, 1947); children: Norman Mattoon, Jr. (deceased), William Stewart, Mary Cecil, Frances Beatrice, Rebekah Lovett, Evan Welling. *Education:* Princeton University, B.A., 1905; Union Theological Seminary, B.D., 1911; also attended Bucknell University. *Residence:* Huntington, N.Y.

CAREER: Socialist party leader and writer. Social worker at Spring Street Presbyterian Church and Settlement House, c. 1905; assistant to pastor of Christ Church, New York City, 1907; associate minister of Brick Presbyterian Church, New York City, 1910-11; ordained Presbyterian minister, 1911; pastor of East Harlem Presbyterian Church, c. 1911, and chairman of the American Parish (federation of local Presbyterian churches); Fellowship of Reconciliation, member, beginning 1917, founder of *World Tomorrow,* 1918, and editor, 1918-21; resigned from church responsibilities in 1918, and left the ministry in 1931; joined Socialist Party in 1918; associate editor of *Nation,* 1921-22; co-director of League for Industrial Democracy, 1922-37; editor of *New York Leader,* 1923; consultant to *New Leader,* 1924-35; unsuccessfully ran for political offices as Socialist and Progressive candidate, including governor of the State of New York, 1924, mayor of New York City, 1925, 1929, and president of the United States, 1928-48; assumed leadership of Socialist Party, c. 1926; co-founder of Civil Liberties Bureau (now American Civil Liberties Union); speaker. Member of Workers Defense League, Post War World Council, Institute for International Labor Research, National Committee for a Sane Nuclear Policy, American Committee for Cultural Freedom, American Committee on Africa, Spanish Refugee Aid, Inc., and Keep America Out of War Committee. *Member:* American Newspaper Guild, Phi Beta Kappa. *Awards, honors:* Litt. D. from Princeton University, 1932.

WRITINGS: *The Conscientious Objector in America,* B. W. Huebsch, 1923; *The Challenge of War: An Economic Interpretation,* League for Industrial Democracy, 1923, 3rd edition, 1927 (also see below); *What Is Industrial Democracy?,* League for Industrial Democracy, 1925; *Is Conscience a Crime?,* Vanguard Press, 1927, reprinted, J. S. Ozer, 1972; *America's Way Out: A Program for Democracy,* Macmillan, 1931; (with Paul Blanshard) *What's the Matter With New York: A National Problem,* Macmillan, 1932; *As I See It* (essays), Macmillan, 1932; *The Choice Before Us: Mankind at the Crossroads,* Macmillan, 1934, reprinted, AMS Press, 1970 (published in England as *Facism or Socialism?: The Choice Before Us,* Allen & Unwin, 1934); *Human Exploitation in the United States,* Frederick A. Stokes, 1934; *War: No Glory, No Profit, No Need,* Frederick A. Stokes, 1935 (also see below); *After the New Deal, What?,* Macmillan, 1936; *Socialism on the Defensive,* Harper & Bros., 1938; (with Bertram D. Wolfe) *Keep America Out of War: A Program by Norman Thomas and Bertram D. Wolfe,* Frederick A. Stokes, 1939.

We Have a Future, Princeton University Press, 1941; *World Federation: What Are the Difficulties?,* Post War World Council, 1942; *What Is Our Destiny?,* Doubleday, Doran & Co., 1944; *Appeal to the Nations,* Henry Holt, 1947; *How Can the Socialist Party Best Serve Socialism?,* [Gramercy, N.Y.], 1949; *A Socialist's Faith,* Norton, 1951; *The Test of Freedom,* Norton, 1954; *Mr. Chairman, Ladies and Gentlemen: Reflections on Public Speaking,* Hermitage House, 1955; *The Prerequisites for Peace,* Norton, 1959.

Great Dissenters, Norton, 1961; *Socialism Re-Examined,* Norton, 1963; *The Choices,* I. Washburn, 1969; *What Are the Answers?: Norman Thomas Speaks to Youth* (essays), compiled and edited by Bettina Peterson and Anastasia Toufexis, I. Washburn, 1970; *War: No Glory, No Profit, No Need; and, The Challenge of War: An Economic Interpretation,* Garland Publishing, 1972 (also see above); *Norman Thomas on War: An Anthology,* edited and introduced by Bernard K. Johnpool, Garland Publishing, 1974.

Pamphlets: (With Charles P. Howland) *The League of Na-*

tions and the Imperialist Principle, Foreign Policy Association, 1923; (with Mary Agnes Hamilton and Raymond Leslie Bell) *In the League and Out,* Foreign Policy Association, 1930; *The Socialist Cure for a Sick Society,* John Day Co., 1932; *A Socialist Looks at the New Deal,* League for Industrial Democracy, 1933; *The Plight of the Share-Cropper,* League for Industrial Democracy, 1934; *The New Deal: A Socialist Analysis,* Committee on Education and Research of the Socialist Party of America, 1934; *War as a Socialist Sees It,* League for Industrial Democracy, 1936; *Democracy Versus Dictatorship,* League for Industrial Democracy, 1937; *Russia—Democracy or Dictatorship?,* League for Industrial Democracy, 1939; *Democracy and Japanese Americans,* Post War World Council, 1942; *Conscription: The Test of the Peace,* Post War World Council, 1944; *A Socialist Looks at the United Nations,* Syracuse University Press, 1945; *The One Hope of Peace, Universal Disarmament Under International Control,* Post War World Council, 1947; *Democratic Socialism: A New Appraisal,* League for Industrial Democracy, 1953, new edition, 1963.

Contributor of articles to newspapers and magazines, including *New America.*

SIDELIGHTS: For more than forty years, Norman Thomas championed the causes of pacifism and socialism in the United States. He actively supported the efforts of conscientious objectors during both world wars, and was one of few prominent Americans to be horrified at the bombings of Nagasaki and Hiroshima. Together with Roger N. Baldwin, Thomas founded the Civil Liberties Bureau, which later became the American Civil Liberties Union. He also played an important role in organizing the Agricultural Workers' Union.

The foundation for Thomas's interest in socialism was laid during his years as a social worker in a settlement house in a blighted area of New York City and in his experiences as a traveler in Asia. He became a fierce opponent of colonialism and, at the outset of World War I, an advocate of Christian socialism and pacifism. Although he left the ministry officially in 1931, Thomas had already resigned from his church duties in 1918. He did not want to jeopardize the parish's financial position because of his participation in free speech rallies and picket lines.

Throughout his lifetime support of the Socialist party and its goals, Thomas ran for public office many times, including six campaigns for the presidency of the United States. During the campaign of 1932, he emphasized the need for a public works system and unemployment insurance. That year was his most successful—he won 884,781 votes. Each successive election saw a dwindling of support for Thomas and the Socialist party. By 1944, he was down to eighty thousand votes.

Although he retired from politics in 1948, Thomas continued to speak out on such issues as world peace, nuclear disarmament, and world poverty. He believed that the resources of the United States could be used to alleviate Third World poverty and became very critical of American right-wing parties. Looking back on his life, Thomas once remarked: "I suppose it is an achievement to live to my age and feel that one has kept the faith, or tried to . . . [and] to have had a part . . . in some of the things that have been accomplished in the field of civil liberties, in the field of better race relations, and the rest of it. . . . It is something of an achievement, I think, to keep the idea of socialism before a rather indifferent or even hostile American public."

AVOCATIONAL INTERESTS: Gardening, swimming, music.

BIOGRAPHICAL/CRITICAL SOURCES: James Nelson, editor, *Wisdom for Our Times,* Norton, 1961.

OBITUARIES: London Times, December 20, 1968; *New York Times,* December 20, 1968; *Detroit Free Press,* December 20, 1968; *Time,* December 27, 1968; *Newsweek,* December 30, 1968; *Antiquarian Bookman,* January 6-13, 1969; *National Review,* January 14, 1969.*

*   *   *

THOMAS, Robert C(harles)   1925-

PERSONAL: Born April 3, 1925, in Detroit, Mich.; son of John P. (an accountant and lawyer) and Jane B. (a high school teacher) Thomas. *Education:* University of Michigan, A.B. (Far Eastern languages and literatures), 1955, A.M. (library science), 1956. *Politics:* Independent. *Home:* Leland House, Apt. 1407, 400 Bagley Ave., Detroit, Mich. 48226. *Office:* Gale Research Co., Book Tower, Detroit, Mich. 48226.

CAREER: Cornell University, Ithaca, N.Y., assistant librarian in serials and binding department, 1956-59; Gale Research Co., Detroit, Mich., became senior editor, 1960—. *Military service:* U.S. Army, 1947-53; became sergeant; received Commendation medal. *Member:* American Society of Indexers, Book Club of Detroit (president, 1973—), Creative Arts Alliance of Greater Detroit.

WRITINGS—Editor; all published by Gale: (Senior editor) *Encyclopedia of Associations,* 3rd edition, 1961, 4th edition, 1964, 5th edition, 1968, 6th edition, 1970; *Contemporary Authors,* Volume 1 (research editor), 1962, Volume 2 (senior editor), 1963, Volume 3, 1963, Volume 4, 1963, Volumes 5-6, 1963, Volumes 7-8, 1963, Volumes 9-10, 1964, Volumes 11-12, 1965, Volumes 13-14, 1965, Volumes 15-16, 1966, Volumes 17-18, 1967, Volumes 1-4 revised, 1967, Volumes 19-20, 1968; (with Frederick G. Ruffner) *Code Names Dictionary,* 1963; (with James M. Ethridge and F. G. Ruffner) *Acronyms and Initialisms Dictionary,* 2nd edition, 1965, 3rd edition (with Ellen T. Crowley), 1970, 4th edition, 1973; *Library of Congress and National Union Catalog Author Lists, 1942-62: A Master Cumulation,* Volumes 1-152, 1969-71; (with Crowley) *Reverse Acronyms and Initialisms Dictionary,* 1st edition, 1972; *Book Review Index, . . . 1972 Cumulation,* Volume 8, 1973, *. . . 1973 Cumulation,* Volume 9, 1974; *National Directory of Newsletters and Reporting Services,* 2nd edition, 1978; (with Anthony T. Kruzas) *Business Organizations and Agencies Directory,* 1st edition, 1980; (with James A. Ruffner) *Research Centers Directory,* 7th edition, 1981. Associated with *Biographical Dictionaries Master Index,* 1974-75.

WORK IN PROGRESS: Editing the *Obituary Index* series, publication by Gale expected to begin in 1981.

SIDELIGHTS: Thomas speaks Chinese and French. *Avocational interests:* International travel.

BIOGRAPHICAL/CRITICAL SOURCES: Grosse Pointe News, July 7, 1966.

*   *   *

THOMSON, Edward
See TUBB, E(dwin) C(harles)

*   *   *

THORNE, Sterling
See FULLER, Dorothy Mason

TILLER, Terence (Rogers) 1916-

PERSONAL: Born September 19, 1916, in Truro, Cornwall, England; son of George Henry Rogers (a businessman) and Catherine Mary (Stoot) Tiller; married Doreen Hugh Watson (a welfare officer at time of marriage), January 11, 1945; children: Elizabeth Verity Tiller Marshall, Sarah Valerie. *Education:* Jesus College, Cambridge, B.A. (with honors), 1937, M.A., 1940. *Address:* c/o Chatto & Windus Ltd., 40 William IV St., London WC2N 4DF, England.

CAREER: Cambridge University, Cambridge, England, research scholar and director of studies, 1937-39, lecturer in medieval history, 1939; Fuad I University, Cairo, Egypt, lecturer in English history and literature, 1939-46; British Broadcasting Corp., London, England, radio writer and producer in features department, 1946-65, radio writer and producer in drama department, 1965-76. Former member of the Committee of the English Festival of Spoken Poetry and of the Poetry Panel of the Arts Council of Great Britain. *Member:* BBC Club. *Awards, honors: That Singing Mesh* was a Poetry Book Society choice, spring, 1979; Cholmondeley Award for poetry, 1980.

*WRITINGS—*Poetry: *Poems*, Hogarth Press, 1941; *The Inward Animal*, Hogarth Press, 1943; *Unarm, Eros*, Hogarth Press, 1947; *Reading a Medal and Other Poems*, Hogarth Press, 1957; *Notes for a Myth and Other Poems*, Hogarth Press, 1968; *That Singing Mesh*, Chatto & Windus, 1979.

Editor: (With Anthony Cronin and John Silkin) *New Poems, 1960: A P.E.N. Anthology*, Hutchinson, 1960; (and translator) John Gower, *Confessio Amantis*, Penguin, 1963; (and translator, with others) Dante, *The Inferno* (bilingual edition), BBC Publications, 1966, Schocken, 1967; *Chess Treasury of the Air*, Penguin, 1966; (and translator) William Langland, *Piers Plowman*, BBC Publications, 1981.

Plays: "The Death of Adam" (one-act), first produced in Edinburgh, Scotland, at Gateway Theatre, 1950.

Radio plays; all first broadcast on BBC-Radio: (Adapter and translator) "The Wakefield Shepherd's Play," 1947; (adapter and translator) "The Wakefield Play of Noah," 1948; "The Death of a Friend" (verse play), 1949; (adapter and translator) "The Cornish Cycle of Mystery Plays," 1949-62 (includes "The Passion of Our Lord," "The Harrowing of Hell," "The Death of Pilate," and "The Ascension," all 1962); "Lilith" (verse play), 1950; "The Tower of Hunger" (verse play), 1952; (adapter and translator) "The Parlement of Foules" (based on Chaucer's "The Parlement of Foules"), 1958.

"Final Meeting," 1966; (adapter and translator) "The Carde of Fancie" (based on Robert Greene's romance of the same title), 1966; (adapter) "The Diversions of Hawthornden" (based on William Drummond's *Conversations With Ben Johnson*), 1967; (translator and adapter) "The Assembly of Ladies" 1968; (translator and adapter) "Euphorion" (based on Goethe's *Faust*), 1969; (translator and adapter) "Zeus the Barnstormer" (based on Lucian's *Zeus Rages*), 1969; (adapter) "After Ten Years" (based on C. S. Lewis's story of the same title), 1969.

(Adapter and translator) "The Flower and the Leaf," 1970; (adapter) "The Batchelar's Banquet" (based on Dekker's pamphlet of the same title), 1971; (adapter and translator) "Four of a Kind" (based on Verlaine's *Les Uns et les autres*), 1975; (adapter and translator) "Madame Aubin" (based on Verlaine's one-act play of the same title), 1976; (adapter) "The Defence" (based on Nabokov's novel of the same title), 1979.

Also author of hundreds of radio features, including "The Baker's Daughter," 1950, "The Juniper Tree," 1950, "Lord Randal," 1952, "The Conscience of the King," 1952, "The Symbols at Your Door," 1953, "Verlaine in England," 1958, "The Devil's Bible," 1959, "If the Angel Hadn't Directed Us," 1959, "Caveat Auditor," 1965, "Farewell, Earth's Bliss," 1965, "Philidor and England," 1965, "Richard Parson," 1967, "The Readiest Way to Hell," 1968, "The Story of Kaspar Hauser; or, The Master-Liars of Nuremberg," 1968, "Aphrodite the Luxuriant Pig," 1970, "The Road to Astolat," 1971, and "The Road to Camelot," 1972.

Contributor of poetry, reviews, and essays to periodicals, including *Listener, Times Literary Supplement, New Statesman and Nation, Cambridge Review, Vogue, Horizon,* and *Poetry London.*

WORK IN PROGRESS: Various short story anthologies; translation and adaptation of Chaucer's *Roman de la rose* for radio, 1981; complete edition, in modern English equivalent of Langland's meter, of *Piers Plowman.*

SIDELIGHTS: A modern metaphysical poet who prefers traditional verse forms, Terence Tiller has sometimes been accused of being too obscure. In an article for the *Poetry Book Society Bulletin*, he wrote: "Many [of my poems] have been—as critics wrote both in blame and in praise—mandarinesque, arcane, metallic-surfaced, polymathic, modern-Metaphysical. Most have been in developments of orthodox metres, yet strange; and I have given perhaps excessive attention to *precision* of language and logic. Those are not the paths to the anthology and the Christmas shopping-list! For most readers, the poems have just been *too darn hard.*" Because of the difficulty of his verse, Tiller is regarded as a "poet's poet." However, in his more recent poetry Tiller discerns a new development toward greater accessibility. In *That Singing Mesh*, he has even provided notes to aid the reader.

Tiller told *CA:* "A poet cannot know too much—his business is to relate the entirety of human experience to himself and itself."

AVOCATIONAL INTERESTS: Music, chess, cricket, philately.

BIOGRAPHICAL/CRITICAL SOURCES: New Statesman, April 25, 1969; *Virginia Quarterly Review,* summer, 1969; *Poetry Book Society Bulletin,* spring, 1979.

* * *

TINER, John Hudson 1944-
(Jonathan Street)

PERSONAL: Born October 8, 1944, in Pocahontas, Ark.; son of John A. (a pipeline construction inspector) and Martha (a clerk; maiden name, Hudson) Tiner; married Delma Jeanene Watson (an elementary school teacher), May 5, 1962; children: John Watson, Lambda Jeanene. *Education:* Harding College, B.S., 1965; Duke University, M.A.T., 1968; also attended Arkansas State University, 1965-68. *Politics:* Independent. *Religion:* Church of Christ. *Home:* 6440 Kathy Lane, High Ridge, Mo. 63049. *Office:* Bible Truth, P.O. Box 38, House Springs, Mo. 63051.

CAREER: Pipeline construction worker, 1960-62; high school teacher of mathematics and science in Harrisburg, Ark., 1965-68, head of mathematics department, 1968; junior high school mathematics teacher in High Ridge, Mo., 1968-72; high school teacher of physics, astronomy, and science in House Springs, Mo., 1972-77; Defense Mapping Agency, Aerospace Center, St. Louis, Mo., photogrammetric cartographer, 1977—. Photographer for *Harrisburg Modern News*, 1966-68. Instructor at Jefferson College, Hillsboro, Mo., 1972-77. *Member:* Missouri Association for Creation, Missouri Writers Guild, Jefferson County Writers Guild, Jefferson County Teachers Association (chairman of mathematics chapter, 1969). *Awards, honors:* Plaque from Missouri Writers Guild, 1977, for *Johannes Kepler;* National Science Foundation grants.

WRITINGS: When Science Fails, Baker Book, 1974; *Isaac Newton* (juvenile), Mott Media, 1976; *Johannes Kepler: Giant of Faith and Science* (juvenile), Mott Media, 1977; *How to Earn Extra Income as a Free-Lance Writer*, Pamphlet Publications, 1977; *Evolution Versus Creation*, Pamphlet Publications, 1978; *Space Colonies*, Pamphlet Publications, 1978; *College Physical Science*, Accelerated Christian Education, 1980; *Seven Day Mystery*, Baker Book, 1981.

Contributor of more than four hundred articles, stories, and poems for children (sometimes under pseudonym Jonathan Street) and adults to religious periodicals. Editor of *Castor*, 1965. Editor and publisher of *Bible Truth*, 1978—.

WORK IN PROGRESS: Louis Agassiz, a biography; *Survival Handbook for Planet Earth*, Christian devotions and essays.

SIDELIGHTS: Tiner's writings have covered a wide variety of subjects and styles. He has written mysteries and science fiction, articles on such hobbies as coin collecting, photography, and astronomy, and scientific papers. His religious writing has been published by most Christian denominations.

Tiner told *CA:* "I like to write, especially biographies of historical characters. After the research is finished and the outline complete, a magic moment occurs when the story takes over and the characters come alive. No longer am I a writer, but a time traveler who stands unobserved in the shadows and reports the events as they occur. The time traveling goes forward in time as well as backward. What is committed to paper today will speak to readers who are not yet born.

"Writing gives a person leverage. The relatively simple action of putting words on paper has the potential to produce far-reaching and longlasting results. Because of this potential I believe a writer should feel strongly about his subject and express himself clearly and forcefully. And the writer has the responsibility to state the truth as he understands it.

"My background in science and strong Christian faith has attracted me to write about the interaction of science and religion. In a sense the two activities, science and religion, are closely related because both scientists and Christians have a relentless dedication to truth.'

*　　*　　*

TINGAY, Lance　1915-

PERSONAL: Born July 15, 1915, in Seven Kings, England; son of Charles (a company traveler) and Abigail (Buck) Tingay; married Daphne Gilbert, August 11, 1937; children: Kevin, Gabrielle Tingay Palmer, Michael, Marianne Tingay Eve. *Education:* Attended University of London, 1931. *Religion:* Roman Catholic. *Home:* 10 Hill Court, Wimbledon Hill Rd., London S.W.19, England. *Office: London Daily Telegraph*, Fleet St., London E.C.4, England.

CAREER: Free-lance journalist, 1935-39 and 1946-52; currently staff sports writer for *London Daily Telegraph*, London, England. *Military service:* Royal Air Force, 1940-46; became flight sergeant. *Member:* International Lawn Tennis Club of Great Britain, International Lawn Tennis Club of France, All England Lawn Tennis Club, Lawn Tennis Writers Association of Great Britain (vice-president), Queen's Club. *Awards, honors:* Danzig Writers award from Longwood Tennis Club, 1968, for service to tennis.

WRITINGS: The Bedside Barsetshire, Faber, 1948; *History of Lawn Tennis*, Tom Stacey, 1973; *One Hundred Years of Wimbledon*, Guinness Superlatives, 1977. Editor of *World of Tennis*, 1970-81.

WORK IN PROGRESS: A biography of Anthony Trollope; a bibliography of Trollope; research on the history of lawn tennis.

SIDELIGHTS: Tingay told *CA:* "I wish to further the writing of literature about lawn tennis, as distinct from its reporting."

*　　*　　*

TINKER, Ben (Hill)　1903-

PERSONAL: Born January 29, 1903, in Prescott, Ariz.; son of John George (a newspaper publisher) and Edna Grace (Hill) Tinker; married Violet Marie Martin, April 9, 1972. *Education:* Attended University of Arizona, Tucson, Columbia University, and University of Mexico. *Politics:* Republican. *Religion:* Catholic. *Home:* 1775 North Acacia Ave., Rialto, Calif. 92376.

CAREER: Cattle rancher in Mexico, Arizona, and California; writer. Federal game guardian in northern Mexico, 1922-26. Member of forum lecture advisory board at San Bernadino Valley College, 1975-78. Consultant to Time-Life Books on the Sierra Madre and the American wilderness. Member of Immaculate Conception Church parish council. *Member:* Arizona Game Protective Association (vice-president, 1928).

WRITINGS: (Editor) George H. Tinker, *Arizona: A Land of Sunshine*, revised from original 1887 edition, Arthur H. Clark Co., 1969; *Mexican Wilderness and Wildlife*, University of Texas Press, 1978. Author of column, "Fish and Game," for *Tucson Daily Citizen*, 1927-29. Contributor of articles on northern Mexico to periodicals, including *Arizona Wildlife, Outdoor Life, Los Angeles Times, Arizona Daily Star, Tucson Daily Citizen, Gun World, Western Out of Doors, Outdoors Calling, Turkey World, Colorado Magazine, Westways*, and *Mexico This Month*.

WORK IN PROGRESS: Five books, tentatively titled *The Trail, Baja California, The Assassin, Via Con Dios*, and *The Devil's Backbone*.

SIDELIGHTS: Tinker told *CA* that his motivation to record data on the wildlife and wilderness of Mexico stemmed from his experiences as a federal game guardian and cattle rancher in the Sierra Madres. *Arizona: A Land of Sunshine*, which Tinker edited, was written by his grandfather in 1887. "As a sportsman," Tinker commented, "I believe in promoting a sensible attitude toward the environment and the conservation of wildlife."

Tinker has made hunting expeditions to Africa, Alaska, British Columbia, Mexico, and South America. He speaks Yaqui Indian and Papago Indian, as well as Spanish.

AVOCATIONAL INTERESTS: Music and the arts, hunting, trout fishing, outdoor life.

*　　*　　*

TODD, Malcolm　1939-

PERSONAL: Born November 27, 1939, in Durham, England; son of Wilfrid and Rose (Johnson) Todd; married

Molly Tanner, September 2, 1964; children: Katharine Grace, Malcolm Richard. *Education:* University of Wales, B.A., 1961; Oxford University, diploma in archaeology, 1963. *Office:* Department of Archaeology, University of Exeter, Exeter EX4 4QH, England.

CAREER: University of Nottingham, Nottingham, England, lecturer in archaeology, 1965-77, reader in archaeology, 1977-79; University of Exeter, Exeter, England, professor of archaeology, 1979—. *Member:* Society of Antiquaries (fellow), German Archaeological Institute.

WRITINGS: Everyday Life of the Barbarians, Batsford, 1972; *The Coritani,* Duckworth, 1973; *The Northern Barbarians,* Hutchinson, 1975; *The Walls of Rome,* Elek, 1978; *Studies in the Romano-British Villa,* Leicester University Press, 1978; *Roman Britain,* Collins, 1980. Contributor to *Encyclopaedia Britannica.* Contributor to scholarly journals.

WORK IN PROGRESS: Barbarian Invasions of the Roman Empire; archaeological studies.

SIDELIGHTS: Todd commented: "Most of my writing arises out of my teaching and lecturing, and is thus a by-product of another side of my life. I prefer to have one book in the making at a time, occupying leisure and vacations. Writing full-time seems attractive from a distance, but I am doubtful whether I could live under the tyranny of the empty piece of paper."

* * *

TOLEDANO, Roulhac (Bunkley) 1938-

PERSONAL: Born December 16, 1938, in New Orleans, La.; daughter of Thomas Allen (a physician) and Phylis (a decorator; maiden name, Gewin) Bunkley; married Benjamin Casanas Toledano (an attorney), October 1, 1959; children: Macon Cheek, Gabrielle Beauregard, Roulhac d'Arby, Cleanth Brooks. *Education:* Tulane University, B.F.A. (with honors), 1960; also attended University of Madrid, 1958-59. *Politics:* Republican. *Religion:* Episcopal. *Home:* 5360 Chestnut, New Orleans, La. 70115.

CAREER: Teacher of art history at private school in Chattanooga, Tenn., 1960-61; Tulane University, New Orleans, La., staff member, 1961-62; New Orleans Academy, New Orleans, La., teacher of French, 1962-64; consultant on historic architecture, 1965—. Owner and proprietor of Bozart Book and Print Shop, 1969-78. Lecturer at University of New Orleans, spring, 1977; speaker at Southern museums and schools. Founder of Central Business District Improvement Association, co-founder and member of Little/Big Oaks Islands Museum and Parks Development Committee, 1969-76; co-founder and lecturer for New Orleans Building Watchers, 1973-78; member of board of directors of Friends of the Cabildo, 1963-80; member of regional advisory committee of National Park Service, 1976-78. Associate member of Christian Women's Exchange; charter member of New Orleans Resource Center; past member of board of directors of Council for the Development of French in Louisiana. *Awards, honors:* Beautiful Activist Award from Germaine Monteil, 1971, for community work; Alice Hitchcock Award from Society of Architectural Historians, 1978, for best book on architecture published in North America from 1976-78.

WRITINGS: Audubon in Louisiana, Friends of the Cabildo, 1960; (with husband, Ben C. Toledano) *Charles Hutson, Louisiana Painter,* New Orleans Museum of Art, 1965; (editor) Samuel Wilson, Jr., *Bienville's New Orleans,* Friends of the Cabildo, 1967; *Louisiana Indians: Twelve Thousand*

Years, Friends of the Cabildo, 1965; (contributor and editor with Mary Louise Christovich and Mary Davis) *Two-Hundred-Fifty Years of Life in New Orleans,* Friends of the Cabildo, 1968; (editor with Christovich, Bernard Lemann, Betsy Swanson, and Wilson, and contributor) *New Orleans Architecture,* Volume I: *Lower Garden District,* Pelican 1971; (contributor) *The Plantation Cookbook,* Doubleday, 1972; (with Christovich, Lemann, Swanson, and Pat Holden) *New Orleans Architecture,* Pelican, Volume II: *The American Sector,* 1972, Volume IV: *The Creole Faubourgs,* 1974, (with Christovich and Sally Evans) Volume V: *The Esplanade Ridge,* 1977, (with Christovich) Volume VI: *Faubourg Treme and the Bayou Road,* 1980; (with August Trovaioli) *William Aiken Walker: Southern Genre Painter,* Louisiana State University Press, 1972; *Richard Clague: Southern Landscape Painter,* New Orleans Museum of Art, 1974. Author of column, "House of the Week," in *Figaro,* 1974-79. Contributor to magazines, including *New Orleans* and *Antiques.*

WORK IN PROGRESS: Research on the history of New Orleans during the early French and Spanish periods and on the expansion of the Council for Development of French in Louisiana.

AVOCATIONAL INTERESTS: Creole cooking, designing patchwork quilts.

BIOGRAPHICAL/CRITICAL SOURCES: New Orleans Times-Picayune, January 20, 1974.

* * *

TOMLINSON-KEASEY, Carol 1942-

PERSONAL: Born October 15, 1942, in Washington, D.C.; daughter of Robert Bruce (a U.S. Army officer) and Geraldine (Howe) Tomlinson; married Charles Blake Keasey (a psychologist), June 13, 1964; children: Kai Linson, Amber Lynn. *Education:* Pennsylvania State University, B.A., 1964; Iowa State University, M.S., 1966; University of California, Riverside, Ph.D., 1970. *Home:* 6140 Port au Prince, Riverside, Calif. 92506. *Agent:* John Brockman Associates, Inc., 200 West 57th St., New York, N.Y. 10019. *Office:* Department of Psychology, University of California, Riverside, Calif. 92521.

CAREER: Trenton State College, Trenton, N.J., assistant professor of psychology, 1969-70; Rutgers University, New Brunswick, N.J., assistant professor of psychology, 1970-72; University of Nebraska, Lincoln, assistant professor, 1972-74, associate professor of psychology, 1974-77; University of California, Riverside, professor of psychology, 1980—. *Member:* International Neuropsychological Society, American Psychological Association, Society for Research in Child Development, American Association for the Advancement of Science, Sigma Xi, Psi Chi.

WRITINGS: Patterns of Learning (monograph), Nebraska Television Council for Nursing Education, 1973; (contributor) R. G. Fuller, editor, *ADAPT: A Piagetian Based Program for College Freshmen,* University of Nebraska, 1976; *A Child's Eye View,* St. Martin's, 1980. Contributor of about thirty articles to scientific journals.

WORK IN PROGRESS: Contributing to *The Taming of Piaget,* edited by Sohan Modgil and Celia Modgil; a book on gifted children.

SIDELIGHTS: Carol Tomlinson-Keasey told *CA:* "I wrote *A Child's Eye View* because there was so little information available about *normal* development, and I wanted parents and professionals to see the world through a child's eyes for a change."

TONKIN, Peter (Francis) 1950-

PERSONAL: Born January 28, 1950, in Limavady, Londonderry, Ireland; son of Francis Alexander (a Royal Air Force officer) and Evelyn (Johnston) Tonkin; married Charmaine May (a cordon bleu caterer), March 21, 1980. *Education:* Queen's University, Belfast, Northern Ireland, B.A. (with honors), 1973, M.A., 1974. *Politics:* Conservative. *Religion:* Church of England. *Home:* 94 The High, Streatham High Rd., London SW16 1EZ, England. *Agent:* Harold Ober Associates, Inc., 40 East 49th St., New York, N.Y. 10017; and David Higham Associates, 5-8 Lower John St., Golden Sq., London W1R 4HA, England.

CAREER: Inner London Education Authority, London, England, high school teacher of English, history, and geography, 1975-79; writer, 1979—. *Member:* Crime Writers Association.

WRITINGS: Killer (novel), Coward, 1979; *The Journal of Edward Underhill,* Hodder & Stoughton, 1981.

WORK IN PROGRESS: Action, a thriller; *The Mills of God,* a thriller.

SIDELIGHTS: Tonkin told *CA:* "In spite of the fact that I have traveled widely (in Europe, North Africa, the Middle East), I believe in running counter to the present trend of fictionalized reportage. I believe in imagination as the writer's primary tool, supported by research, of course. If reality gets in the way—it is out of place. One does not have to have suffered an experience in order to be able to communicate that experience. Over and above that, there is the unrelenting hard work, the joy of convincing the experienced that you are among their number and of bringing to people who would never have experienced them, passion, excitement, and adventure far beyond the norm."

*   *   *

TORRES BODET, Jaime 1902-1974

PERSONAL: Born April 17, 1902, in Mexico City, Mexico; died by his own hand, May 14, 1974, in Mexico City, Mexico; son of Alejandro and Emilie (Bodet) Torres; married Josefina Juarez, 1929. *Education:* University of Mexico, graduated, 1917. *Residence:* Mexico City, Mexico.

CAREER: Head of libraries department of Ministry of Education in Mexico, 1922; University of Mexico, Mexico City, professor of French literature, 1924-28; secretary to Mexican legation in Spain, 1929, France, 1931, and Belgium, 1938-40; Mexican charge d'affaires in the Netherlands, 1932; head of diplomatic department of Ministry of Foreign Affairs in Mexico, 1936; under secretary for foreign affairs in Mexico, 1940-43; minister of education, 1943-46 and 1958-64; minister of foreign affairs, 1946-48; director general of UNESCO, 1948-52; Mexican ambassador to Paris, France, 1954-58. *Member:* International P.E.N.

AWARDS, HONORS: Gold medal of Pan American League; member of French Legion of Honor: National Prize for Literature; Doctor honoris causa from University of New Mexico and University of Southern California; received decorations from Order of the Glittering Stars (China), Order of the Cedar (Lebanon), Order of Polonia Restituta (Poland), Order of the Polar Star (Sweden), Order of Leopold and Order of the Crown (both Belgium), Order of Merit Carlos Manuel de Cespedes (Cuba), Order of Juan Pablo Duarte and Order of Christophe Colomb (both Dominican Republic), Order of Vasco Nunez de Balboa (Panama), Order of Morazan (Honduras), Knight Commander of Order of Quetzal (Guatemala), Order of the Liberator (Venezuela), Order of the Sun (Peru), Great Officer of Order of the Andean Condor (Bolivia), Order of "Al Merito" (Ecuador), Order of Boyaca (Colombia), Order of Merit (Chile), Great Cross of the Order of San Martin the Liberator (Argentina).

*WRITINGS—*Poetry: *Fervor,* [Mexico], 1918; *Canciones,* [Mexico], 1922; *Poemas* (title means "Poems"), Herrero, 1924; *Biombo,* Herrero, 1925; *La Casa,* Herrero, 1925; *Los dias,* Herrero, 1928; *Destierro* (title means "Exile"), Espasa-Calpe, 1930; *Cripta* (title means "Crypt"), Loera y Chavez, 1937; *Fronteras,* Tezontle, 1954; *Sin tregua,* Tezontle, 1957; *Selected Poems of Jaime Torres Bodet* (text in English and Spanish), translated from the original by Sonja Karsen, Indiana University Press, 1964.

Other: *Margarita de niebla* (novel; title means "Fog's Margaret"), Editorial Cvltvra, 1927; *Perspectiva de la literatura mexicana,* [Mexico], 1928; *Contemporaneos: Notas de critica* (essays; title means "Contemporaries"), Herrero, 1928; *La educacion sentimental* (novel; title means "The Sentimental Education"), Espasa-Calpe, c. 1929; *Proserpina rescatada* (novel; title means "Proserpina Rescued"), Espasa-Calpe, 1931; *Estrella de dia* (novel), Espana-Calpe, 1933; *Primero de enero,* Ediciones Literatura, 1935; *Sombras* (novel), Cvltvra, 1937.

Nacimiento de Venus y otros relatos (novel; title means "Venus' Birth and Other Stories"), Nueva Cvltvra, 1941; *Mision del escritor,* Impreso al Cuidado de la Compania Editora y Liberra Ars, 1942; *Educacion mexicana: Discursos, entrevistas, mensajes* (essays; title means "Mexican Education"), Secretario de Educacion Publica, 1944; *Uma grande esperanca,* Departamento de Cooperacao Intelectual, Uniao Panamericana, 1946; *Educacion y concordia internacional: Discursos y mensajes, 1941-1947* (essays; title means "Education and International Concord"), El Colegio de Mexico, 1948; *Sonetos,* [Mexico], 1949.

Tiempo de arena (autobiography), Fondo de Cultura Economica, 1955; *Tres inventores de realidad: Stendhal, Dostoyevski, Perez Galdos,* [Mexico], 1955; *Balzac,* Fondo de Cultura Economica, 1959; *Trebol de cuatro hojas,* Universidad Veracruzana, 1960.

All published in Mexico: Leon Tolstoi: Su vida y su obra, 1965; *Tiempo y memoria en la obra de Proust,* 1967; *Anos contra el tiempo* (autobiography), 1969; *La victoria sin alas* (autobiography), 1970; *El desierto internacional* (autobiography), 1971; *La tierra prometida* (autobiography), 1972.

WORK IN PROGRESS: A sixth volume of his autobiography, left unfinished at time of death.

OBITUARIES: New York Times, May 14, 1974, May 15, 1974; *Time,* May 27, 1974.*

*   *   *

TOTH, Emily 1944-

PERSONAL: Surname rhymes with "both"; born March 17, 1944, in New York, N.Y.; daughter of John J. (an executive) and Dorothy (a citator; maiden name, Ginsberg) Fitzgibbons; married Bruce Toth (a professor), July 15, 1967. *Education:* Swarthmore College, B.A., 1965; Johns Hopkins University, M.A.T., 1966, M.A., 1973, Ph.D., 1975. *Residence:* State College, Pa. *Agent:* Elaine Markson Literary Agency, Inc., 44 Greenwich Ave., New York, N.Y. 10011. *Office:* Department of English, Pennsylvania State University, University Park, Pa. 16802.

CAREER: Morgan State University, Baltimore, Md., instructor in English, 1967-72; University of New Orleans, New Orleans, La., instructor in English, 1974-75; University

513

of North Dakota, Grand Forks, assistant professor of English, 1975-77; Pennsylvania State University, University Park, assistant professor of English, 1977—. *Member:* Popular Culture Association (vice-president), Modern Language Association of America, Authors Guild, National Women's Studies Association, Women's Caucus for the Modern Languages.

WRITINGS: (With Janice Delaney and Mary Jane Lupton) *The Curse: A Cultural History of Menstruation*, Dutton, 1976; *Grace Metalious and Peyton Place* (biography), Doubleday, 1981. Editor of *Regionalism and the Female Imagination* (journal).

WORK IN PROGRESS: Female Wits, on women's humor; a historical novel, set in antebellum New Orleans.

SIDELIGHTS: Emily Toth commented: "I am both Irish and Jewish, a weirdly American combination that I like to think accounts for my inability to fit any niche neatly. I'm apt to laugh first, with a Jewish irony and an Irish morbidity that some of my students think is 'sick'. I think it's funny. I've always wanted to be a writer, and I did the biography of Grace Metalious because her *Peyton Place* was the only book in the 1950's that told me a girl could grow up to be a writer. Of course I was sidetracked into becoming an academic, and frequently find myself torn between the need to be academically respectable and an equally strong desire to be flamboyant and eccentric. I am an anti-authoritarian personality, a feminist, a social critic who revels in satire, and a ham."

*   *   *

TOTMAN, Conrad 1934-

PERSONAL: Born January 5, 1934, in Conway, Mass.; son of Raymond S. (a farmer) and Mildred (Kingsbury) Totman; married Michiko Ikegami (a bilingual teacher), February 10, 1958; children: Kathleen, Christopher. *Education:* University of Massachusetts, B.A., 1958; Harvard University, M.A., 1960, Ph.D., 1964. *Residence:* Evanston, Ill. *Office:* Department of History, Northwestern University, Evanston, Ill. 60201.

CAREER: University of California, Santa Barbara, assistant professor of history, 1964-66; Northwestern University, Evanston, Ill., assistant professor, 1966-68, associate professor, 1968-72, professor of history, 1972—, chairman of department, 1977-80. *Military service:* U.S. Army, 1953-56. *Member:* American Historical Association, Association for Asian Studies (chairman of Northeast Asia Council; member of executive committee, 1978-80), Association for Teachers of Japanese. *Awards, honors:* Fulbright grant; National Endowment for the Humanities senior fellow.

WRITINGS: Politics in the Tokugawa Bakufu, 1600-1843, Harvard University Press, 1968; *The Collapse of the Tokugawa Bakufu, 1862-1868*, University Press of Hawaii, 1980; *Japan Before Perry*, University of California Press, 1981. Contributor to Asian studies journals.

WORK IN PROGRESS: A biography of Tokugawa Ieyasu (1542-1616), founder of the Tokugawa regime; a study of forest management during Japan's Tokugawa period.

*   *   *

TOULSON, Shirley 1924-

PERSONAL: Born May 20, 1924, in Henley-on-Thames, England; daughter of Douglas Horsfall Dixon (a writer) and Marjorie Brown; married Alan Brownjohn, February 6, 1960 (divorced, March, 1969); children: Janet Sayers, Ian Toulson, Steven Brownjohn. *Education:* Birbeck College, London, B.A., 1953. *Home:* 16 Priest Row Wells, Somerset, England. *Agent:* Bruce Hunter, David Higham Associates, 5-8 Lower John St., Golden Sq., London WIR 4HA, England.

CAREER: Writer. Features editor of *Teacher* (journal of National Union of Teachers), 1967-70; editor of *Child Education*, 1970-74. Teacher of creative writing for adults. *Member:* Society of Authors.

WRITINGS: Shadows in an Orchard (poems), Scorpion Press, 1960; *Circumcision's Not Such a Bad Thing After All and Other Poems*, Keepsake Press, 1970; *All Right, Auden, I Know You're There: A Quick Thought* (poems), Offcut Press, 1970; *For a Double Time* (poems), Sceptre Press, 1970; *The Fault, Dear Brutus: A Zodiac of Sonnets*, Keepsake Press, 1972; *Education in Britain*, M. Evans, 1974; *Farm Museums and Farm Parks*, Shire, 1977; (with Fay Godwin) *Drovers' Roads of Wales*, Wildwood House, 1977; (with John Loveday) *Bones and Angels* (poems), Mid-Day Publications, 1978; *East Anglia: Walking the Leylines and Ancient Tracks*, Wildwood House, 1979; *The Drovers*, Shire Publications, 1980.

Editor: *The Remind-Me Hat and Other Stories* (juvenile), M. Evans, 1973; *Dickens*, S. Low, 1977; *Kipling*, S. Low, 1977; *Milton*, S. Low, 1977; *Shakespeare*, S. Low, 1977.

Contributor to *Reader's Digest, The Past Around Us*, and *Mysteries of the World*. Regular reviewer for British Council's *British Book News*.

WORK IN PROGRESS: "A companion volume to the East Anglia book, based on Derbyshire," publication expected in 1980; third volume of the trilogy "which concerns the ancient roads of the southwestern moors"; a book of folklore "concerning the traditions connected with the winter solstice," publication by Jill Norman expected in 1981.

SIDELIGHTS: Toulson commented: "Apart from the social history of the British countryside, my main interest is in contemporary English and American verse. I have recently started working on the interpretation of folklore, and am particularly interested in comparing the traditions of the American Indians with what is being discovered about pre-Celtic rituals in Britain."

*   *   *

TOWNSEND, Irving 1920-

PERSONAL: Born November 27, 1920, in Springfield, Mass.; son of Irving J. (a teacher) and Marguerite (Noble) Townsend; divorced; children: Nicole Townsend Gueracague, Jeremy (daughter). *Education:* Princeton University, B.A., 1942. *Home address:* P.O. Box 701, Santa Ynez, Calif. 93460. *Agent:* Fox Chase Agency, Inc., 419 East 57th St., New York, N.Y. 10022.

CAREER: Associated with Columbia Records, Keynote Records, RCA Victor Records, and Donahue & Coe Advertising, 1946-51; Columbia Records, New York, N.Y., vice-president, 1951-75. *Military service:* U.S. Naval Reserve, active duty, 1943-46; became lieutenant. *Member:* National Academy of Recording Arts and Sciences (president, 1970-72).

WRITINGS: The Less Expensive Spread, Dial, 1971; *John Hammond on Record*, Summit Books, 1978; *The Tavern*, Presidio Press, 1979. Contributor to magazines, including *Country Journal, Ladies Home Journal, Atlantic, Reader's Digest*, and *Horizon*.

WORK IN PROGRESS: A novel.

SIDELIGHTS: Irving Townsend told *CA:* "My writing to date has been concerned with nature (biology, ethology, animals) and with music. I am a former jazz musician and producer of jazz records. I majored in music at Princeton and led my own band until the war. As a record producer, I worked principally with Duke Ellington, Mahalia Jackson, Miles Davis, and other jazz artists, but also with many types of music, including that of Percy Faith and Andre Previn. My interests other than jazz and music in general are nature and animals. Most of my nonfiction has been in those areas."

*   *   *

TOZER, Mary (Christine)   1947-

PERSONAL: Born February 18, 1947, in London, England; daughter of Christopher (a civil servant) and Violet (a nursing matron; maiden name, Brown) Jackson; married Gerald Tozer (an artist), December 23, 1966. *Education:* Attended Reigate School of Art and Design, 1963-65. *Home:* 29 St. Marys Rd., Reigate, Surrey RH2 7JH, England.

CAREER: Newmarks Ltd., Reigate, England, illustrator for technical animations, 1965-68; free-lance writer, 1968—.

WRITINGS—Self-illustrated children's books: *Sing a Song of Sixpence,* World's Work, 1976; *Old Mother Hubbard,* World's Work, 1977; *The King's Beard,* Harcourt, 1978; *Peter Pipkin and His Very Best Boots,* World's Work, 1979; *The Grannies Three,* World's Work, 1980. Contributor to local newspapers.

WORK IN PROGRESS: The Queen Who Was Always Changing Her Mind.

SIDELIGHTS: Mary Tozer commented: "The most important thing for me is to enjoy my work. I receive much inspiration from the tales of Hans Christian Andersen, the Brothers Grimm, and the Nordic sagas; all are filled with lands and people of mystery and magic which conjure up ideas for my painting and writing. Having sold every painting I exhibited (in London and New York) I am sure people enjoy fairy-tale escapism. Visual humor is another factor I like to include in my work. I hope eventually to write books which appeal to children and adults alike, uncluttered by morals or social messages."

BIOGRAPHICAL/CRITICAL SOURCES: Arts Review, January 7, 1977, December 22, 1978; *Arts and Artists,* May, 1977.

*   *   *

TRACY, David W.   1939-

PERSONAL: Born January 6, 1939, in Yonkers, N.Y.; son of John Charles and Eileen Marie (Rossell) Tracy. *Education:* Cathedral College, Yonkers, N.Y., B.A., 1960; Pontifical Gregorian University, S.T.B., 1962, S.T.L. (summa cum laude), 1964, Ph.D., 1969. *Office:* Divinity School, University of Chicago, 401-A Swift Hall, Chicago, Ill. 60637.

CAREER: Ordained Roman Catholic priest; assistant pastor of Roman Catholic church in Stamford, Conn., 1964-65; Loyola University, European branch, Rome, Italy, lecturer in metaphysics, 1966; North American College, Rome, lecturer, 1966; English College, Rome, lecturer, 1967; Catholic University of America, Washington, D.C., instructor in theology, 1967-69; University of Chicago, Chicago, Ill., assistant professor, 1969-71, associate professor, 1971-76, professor, 1976—. Dudleian Lecturer at Harvard University, 1972; Thomas More Lecturer at Yale University, 1973; Bellarmine Lecturer at St. Louis University, 1975; guest lecturer at Hebrew Union College, 1975. Visiting professor at University of Notre Dame, summer, 1969, Boston College, summers, 1970-73, St. Joseph's Seminary, summer, 1970, University of San Francisco and Iliff School of Theology, summer, 1971, Princeton Theological Seminary, summers, 1972 and 1975, St. John's University, Collegeville, Minn., summer, 1976, and Pontifical Gregorian University, autumn, 1976; lecturer at colleges and universities throughout the world. Member of National Conference of Catholic Bishops' Committee for Ecumenical and Interreligious Affairs. *Member:* American Academy of Religion, Catholic Theological Society of America (president, 1976-77), American Theological Society, Council on the Study of Religion in Higher Education.

WRITINGS: Bernard Lonergan's Interpretation of the Theological Exigence in St. Thomas Aquinas, Pontifical Gregorian University Press, 1969; *The Achievement of Bernard Lonergan: The New Pluralism in Theology,* Herder & Herder, 1970; *The Analogical Imagination: Christian Theology and the Culture of Pluralism,* Seabury, 1981. Also author of *Vatican II* and *Celebrating the Medieval Heritage.*

Contributor: *God—Jesus—Spirit,* Doubleday, 1969; Philip McShane, editor, *Foundations of Theology: Papers From the International Lonergan Conference,* 1970, Gill & Macmillan, 1971; Andrew Greeley and Gregory Baum, editors, *The Persistence of Religion Concilium,* Herder & Herder, 1973; *Christianity and Marxism,* Orbis, 1976; Robert Evans and Thomas Parker, editors, *The Test-Case Method in Systematic Theology,* Harper, 1976.

Contributor to *Encyclopedia of Bio-Ethics.* Contributor of numerous articles and reviews to theology journals and religious magazines, including *Christian Century* and *Christianity and Crisis.* Co-editor of *Journal of Religion* and *Religious Studies Review;* member of editorial board of *Journal of the American Academy of Religion, Concilium, Cultural Hermeneutics, Journal of Pastoral Psychology,* and *Theology Today,* 1977—.

*   *   *

TRASK, Willard (Ropes)   1900(?)-1980

OBITUARY NOTICE: Born c. 1900 in Berlin, Germany; died August 10, 1980, in New York, N.Y. Translator. Willard Trask came into the public eye following World War II with the publication of his twelve-volume translation of Giacomo Casanova's *The History of My Life.* He received a National Book Award in 1967 in recognition of this work. His other translations include *Joan of Arc: Self Portrait* and Victor Serge's *The Case of Comrade Tulayev.* Obituaries and other sources: *New York Times,* August 12, 1980; *Chicago Tribune,* August 15, 1980.

*   *   *

TREFIL, James   1938-

PERSONAL: Born September 10, 1938, in Chicago, Ill.; son of Stanley (a personnel manager) and Sylvia (a social worker; maiden name, Mestek) Trefil; married Elinor Pletka, September 2, 1960 (divorced, January, 1972); married Jeanne Waples, October 20, 1973; children: James, Stefan, Dominique, Flora. *Education:* University of Illinois, B.A., 1960; Oxford University, B.A., 1962, M.A., 1962; Stanford University, M.S., 1964, Ph.D., 1966. *Agent:* Scott Meredith Literary Agency, Inc., 845 Third Ave., New York, N.Y. 10022. *Office:* Department of Physics, University of Virginia, Charlottesville, Va. 22901.

CAREER: Stanford Linear Accelerator Center, Stanford, Calif., fellow, 1966; European Center for Nuclear Research, Geneva, Switzerland, fellow, 1966-67; Massachusetts Institute of Technology, Cambridge, fellow at Laboratory for Nuclear Science, 1967-68; University of Illinois, Urbana, assistant professor of physics, 1968-70; University of Virginia, Charlottesville, associate professor, 1970-75, professor of physics, 1970—.

WRITINGS: Physics as a Liberal Art, Pergamon, 1978; *From Atoms to Quarks,* Scribner, 1980; (with Robert T. Rood) *Are We Alone?,* Scribner, 1981; *Colonies in Space,* Scribner, 1981.

WORK IN PROGRESS: Research on science books for general audiences.

SIDELIGHTS: Trefil commented: "I regard my writing as an outgrowth of my work as a teacher. Both involve explaining concepts clearly. I write about physical science, which is the area of my research, and about energy, a subject which I teach. I am particularly interested in wood heating, as I have used it myself for a number of years.

"I feel that science has come to play such a large role in our lives that it is absolutely crucial that the general public know what is happening. Unfortunately, very few scientists involve themselves in this sort of work. The situation may be changing, but not fast enough."

* * *

TREISTER, Bernard W(illiam) 1932-
(Bernard St. James)

PERSONAL: Born November 8, 1932, in Berlin, Germany; came to United States, 1938; naturalized U.S. citizen, 1944; son of Max (a furrier) and Rosa (Guth) Treister; married Miriam Carol, 1956 (divorced); married Tiffany Holmes (a writer), 1979. *Education:* City College of New York (now City College of the City University of New York), B.A., 1954; University of California, Los Angeles, M.A., 1959. *Agent:* Wieser & Weiser, 60 East 42nd St., New York, N.Y. 10017.

CAREER: Worked as teacher in New York City, 1960-61; Cosmos Travel, New York City, assistant manager, 1973-76; Jet and Cruise, Ltd., New York City, manager, 1975-78; Union Tours, New York City, manager, 1976-78; writer. *Military service:* U.S. Army, 1954-56. *Member:* Mystery Writers of America, Bruckner Society of Florence, Italy (honorary member).

WRITINGS: (Under pseudonym Bernard St. James) *April Thirtieth* (novel), Harper, 1978; (under St. James pseudonym) *The Witch,* Harper, 1979; (contributor) Dilys Winn, editor, *Murderess Ink,* Workman, 1979. Also author of radio script "Adventures in Judaism," for CBS-Radio.

WORK IN PROGRESS: A novel, *The Seven Dreamers.*

SIDELIGHTS: Treister told *CA:* "My greatest literary influences have been George Orwell, for his command of the English language, and George Simenon, for his psychological insights and mastery of the 'procedural' detective story. My greatest honor has been a letter from Simenon complimenting me on my first novel, *April Thirtieth.*

BIOGRAPHICAL/CRITICAL SOURCES: Avenue, October, 1979.

* * *

TRENTO, Salvatore Michael 1952-

PERSONAL: Born March 12, 1952, in New York, N.Y.; son of Angelo R. and Carmella (Napoli) Trento. *Education:* State University of New York at Buffalo, B.A. (magna cum laude); Linacre College, Oxford, diploma. *Agent:* Nat Sobel Associates, New York, N.Y. *Office:* Middletown Archaeological Research Center, Inc., P.O. Box 761, Middletown, N.Y. 10940.

CAREER: Deya Archaeological Museum and Research Center, Deya, Spain, acting director, 1975-76; Middletown Archaeological Research Center, Inc. (private research center), Middletown, N.Y., founder and executive director, 1976—. Insturctor at Delaware Valley College, 1977-78. Director of Earthwatch Expedition to Mallorca's prehistoric ruins, 1975. Guest on television and radio programs in the United States and Canada; appeared in films. *Member:* Phi Beta Kappa, Phi Eta Sigma. *Awards, honors:* National Science Foundation grant, 1973.

WRITINGS: Clemson Park, Historical Society of Wallkill Precinct, 1975; *The Search for Lost America,* Contemporary Books, 1978; *Weekdays in the Soil,* Mid-Hudson School Study Council, 1980. Contributor to anthropology and archaeology journals.

WORK IN PROGRESS: Examining stone ruins in the United States; analyzing subcutaneous fat saturation levels in archaeological excavators.

SIDELIGHTS: Trento's book on lost America is based on his interest in the ancient inscribed stones, found in Pennsylvania and New York, that suggest Columbus's visits to the Americas may have been preceded by Celt, Phoenician, and Iberian expeditions. He has confined most of his own research to the New England area, and with the help of more than two hundred volunteers, has conducted surveys and field research and compiled a detailed catalog of major North American stone sites.

Trento wrote: "I started writing detailed letters to friends, enemies, and editors while in college. The experience was invaluable. It immediately brought attention to my ability to express complex emotions, situations, and events. It also taught me what editors like and dislike. One must be careful not to confuse scholarship with writing popular pieces."

BIOGRAPHICAL/CRITICAL SOURCES: Village Voice, August 2, 1976; *Etcetera,* October 8, 1978; *Hudson Valley,* October, 1979.

* * *

TRESS, Arthur 1940-

PERSONAL: Born November 24, 1940, in Brooklyn, N.Y.; son of Martin (a surplus dealer) and Yetta (Ner) Tress. *Education:* Bard College, B.F.A., 1962. *Politics:* Liberal Democrat. *Religion:* Jewish. *Home:* 2 Riverside Dr., New York, N.Y. 10023.

CAREER: Stockholm Ethnographical Museum, Stockholm, Sweden, photographer, 1966-68; photographer in New York, N.Y., 1968—. Work exhibited by Smithsonian Institution and Sierra Club and on tour. Photographer for Volunteers in Service to America (VISTA). *Awards, honors:* National Endowment for the Arts grant, 1975.

WRITINGS—All with photographs by the author: Songs of the Blue Ridge Mountains, Oak, 1968; *Open Space and the Inner City,* New York State Council on the Arts, 1970; *The Dream Collector,* Westover Books, 1972; *Shadow,* Avon, 1975; *Theater of the Mind* (monograph), Morgan & Morgan, 1976; *Reves,* Editions Complexe, 1979; *Facing Up,* St. Martin's, 1980.

SIDELIGHTS: Tress commented: "For a period of four years after college, I traveled and studied the arts in Japan, Mexico, and Europe. In 1966 I obtained a position as a photographer in Sweden, where I prepared filmstrips on the folkways of various primitive tribal groups such as the Eskimo, Lapp, Dogon, and other Asian Hill tribes.

"In 1968 I returned to New York where, because of my previous experience as a folklorist, I was commissioned by the Smithsonian Institution to prepare a large exhibit of photographs and crafts, entitled 'Appalachia: People and Places.' I also worked for VISTA, preparing photographic studies of various ethnic poverty groups—the Chinese, Hasidim, and black sharecroppers.

"In 1970 I was commissioned by the Sierra Club to prepare an exhibit for their New York gallery, called 'Open Space in the Inner City,' about places where you could build parks in the confined urban environment. This was such a success that I was given a grant to expand that exhibit into a traveling show.

"In 1972 I worked with poet Richard Lewis, doing 'Dream Workshops' in various New York City schools, getting children to express themselves more creatively through the imagery they discover in their own dreams. These photographs were eventually brought together in *The Dream Collector.*

"Following that I became a student of Jungian psychology and wrote *Shadow,* which combines personal experiences with anthropological data on the shamanistic experiences to reproduce an ecstatic visionary experience. In 1976 I wrote *Theater of the Mind,* dealing with the dream fantasies of adults who journey inward into their own mental worlds."

*   *   *

TREVOR-ROPER, H(ugh) R(edwald) 1914-

PERSONAL: Born January 15, 1914, in Glanton, Northumberland, England; son of Bertie William Edward and Kathleen (Davison) Trevor-Roper; married Alexandra Haig, October 4, 1954. *Education:* Christ Church, Oxford, B.A., 1936, M.A., 1939. *Home:* 8 Aldate's, Oxford, England. *Office:* Department of History, Oriel College, Oxford University, Oxford OX1 2JD, England.

CAREER: Oxford University, Oxford, England, research fellow at Merton College, 1937-39, at Christ Church, 1946-57, Regius Professor of Modern History, 1957—. Director of Times Newspapers Ltd., 1974—. *Military service:* Served as intelligence officer. *Member:* Athenaeum, Savile, Beafsteak. *Awards, honors:* Chevalier in French Legion of Honor, 1975.

WRITINGS: Archbishop Laud, 1573-1645, 1940, 2nd edition, Archon Books, 1962; *The Last Days of Hitler,* Macmillan, 1947, 4th edition, 1971; *Hitler's Secret Conversations, 1941-1944,* 1953, reprinted, Octagon Books, 1972 (published in England as *Hitler's Table Talk, 1941-1944,* 1953, reprinted, Weidenfeld & Nicholson, 1973); *The Gentry, 1540-1640,* Cambridge University Press, 1953; *Men and Events: Historical Essays,* Harper, 1957 (published in England as *Historical Essays,* St. Martin's, 1957); *The Rise of Christian Europe,* Harcourt, 1965; *George Buchanan and the Ancient Scottish Constitution,* Longmans, Green, 1966; *Religion, the Reformation, and Social Change, and Other Essays,* Macmillan, 1967, 2nd edition, 1972, published as *The Crisis of the Seventeenth Century: Religion, the Reformation, and Social Change,* Harper, 1967; *The Philby Affair: Espionage, Treason, and Secret Services,* Kimber, 1968; *The European Witch-Craze of the Sixteenth and Seventeenth Centuries,*

Harper, 1969; *The Plunder of the Arts in the Seventeenth Century,* Thames & Hudson, 1970; *Queen Elizabeth's First Historian: William Camden and the Beginnings of English "Civil History,"* J. Cape, 1971; *A Hidden Life: The Enigma of Sir Edmund Backhouse,* Macmillan, 1976, published as *Hermit of Peking: The Hidden Life of Sir Edmund Backhouse,* Knopf, 1977; *Princes and Artists: Patronage and Ideology at Four Habsburg Courts, 1517-1633,* Thames & Hudson, 1976.

Editor: Martin Bormann, *The Bormann Letters,* 1954, reprinted, AMS Press, 1979; Edward Gibbon, *The Decline and Fall of the Roman Empire,* Twayne, 1963; *Blitzkrieg to Defeat: Hitler's War Directives, 1939-1945,* Holt, 1964; *Essays in British History,* St. Martin's, 1964; Thomas Babington Macaulay, *Critical and Historical Essays,* McGraw, 1965; *The Age of Expansion: Europe and the World, 1559-1660,* McGraw, 1968; Macaulay, *The History of England,* Washington Square Press, 1968; Winston Churchill, *History of the English-Speaking Peoples,* B.P.C. Publishing, 1969; Joseph Goebbels, *Final Entries 1945: The Diaries of Joseph Goebbels,* Putnam, 1978. Also co-editor with J.S.W. Bennett of *The Poems of Richard Corbett,* 1955.

SIDELIGHTS: Regius Professor of Modern History at Oxford University, H. R. Trevor-Roper has written more than fifteen books and edited ten additional works by other authors on periods in history ranging from the Roman Empire to Hitler's Germany. *The Crisis of the Seventeenth Century: Religion, the Reformation, and Social Change,* one of his better-known works, is a collection of nine essays on topics such as Protestantism and capitalism, witch hunts, and the Counter-Reformation. G. R. Elton of the *New York Times Book Review* explained that in this book Trevor-Roper has "chosen to express himself in an art form rarely encountered today, especially among academics: the long essay on some major topic, embodying vast reading rather than detailed research, and concerned to establish interpretative schemes which seize upon the imagination and stimulate thought." *Book World* critic J. M. Levine called the book "lively and provocative" but also expressed a wish that Trevor-Roper, at some future date, expand upon the ideas set forth in the book to "write the major work which his theme demands."

Another of his well-known works, *The Rise of Christian Europe,* based on a series of his own lectures at Oxford University, chronicles events from the Roman Empire through to the Middle Ages. Applauded by numerous reviewers as "colorful," "exciting," "provocative," and "illuminating," the book also had a few detractors. K. B. McFarlane of the *New Statesman,* for instance, declared it a "hasty, shallow, somewhat philistine little book . . . [that] betrays a deplorable absence of the faculty of self-criticism." A reviewer for the *Times Literary Supplement,* on the other hand, praised it as "one of the most brilliant works of historiography to be published in England in this century."

BIOGRAPHICAL/CRITICAL SOURCES: New Statesman, February 18, 1966, October 22, 1976; *Christian Science Monitor,* February 24, 1966; *Times Literary Supplement,* April 7, 1966, October 19, 1967, October 29, 1976; *Critic,* August, 1966; *New York Times Book Review,* March 31, 1968, April 24, 1977; *National Review,* July 2, 1968, June 4, 1977; *Book Week,* July 14, 1968; *Commonweal,* February 7, 1969; *New York Review of Books,* April 14, 1977; *New York Times,* April 15, 1977.*

*   *   *

TRICKETT, Mabel Rachel 1923-

PERSONAL: Born December 20, 1923, in Lathom, England;

daughter of James (a post office superintendent) and Margaret (a post office clerk) Trickett. *Education:* Lady Margaret Hall, Oxford, B.A. (first class honors), 1945, M.A., 1949. *Religion:* Christian. *Home:* 72 Woodstock Rd., Oxford, England. *Office:* St. Hugh's College, Oxford University, Oxford, England.

CAREER: Manchester City Art Galleries, Manchester, England, assistant to curator, 1945-46; University of Hull, Hull, England, lecturer in English, 1946-54; Oxford University, Oxford, England, fellow and tutor in English, 1954-73; St. Hugh's College, Oxford, principal, 1973—. Visiting lecturer at Smith College, 1962-63, visiting Drew Professor, 1971; lecturer at Bread Loaf School of English, Middlebury College, 1967 and 1969. *Awards, honors:* Commonwealth Fund fellowship, 1949, for Yale University; Rhys Memorial Prize, 1953, for *The Return Home.*

WRITINGS—Novels; all published by Constable: *The Return Home,* 1952; *The Course of Love,* 1954; *A Point of Honour,* 1958; *A Changing Place,* 1962; *The Elders,* 1966; *A Visit to Timon,* 1969.

Nonfiction: *The Honest Muse: A Study in Augustan Verse,* Oxford University Press, 1967; *Browning's Lyricism,* British Academy, 1971.

Opera libretti; music by John Joubert: *Antigone* (first broadcast on BBC, 1954), Novello, 1954; *Silas Marner* (first produced in Cape Town, South Africa, 1960) Novello, 1960.

Contributor to *Cornhill.*

WORK IN PROGRESS: "A memoir of my parents and another novel."

SIDELIGHTS: Trickett wrote: "I have enjoyed keeping up the academic and the creative side of my writing, though there is always a danger of the first inhibiting the second. But I like the divided academic year: term time for scholarship, vacation for novels."

*   *   *

TROLLOPE, Joanna 1943-

PERSONAL: Born December 9, 1943, in England; daughter of Arthur George Cecil (a managing director of a building society) and Rosemary (a painter; maiden name, Hodson) Trollope; married David Roger William Potter (a banker), May 14, 1966; children: Louise, Antonia. *Education:* Oxford University, M.A., 1965. *Politics:* Conservative. *Religion:* Church of England. *Residence:* Hampshire, England. *Agent:* Georges Borchardt, Inc., 136 East 57th St., New York, N.Y. 10022.

CAREER: Associated with Foreign Office, London, England, 1965-67; worked as English teacher and in children's clothing business; writer. *Member:* International P.E.N., Royal Society for Asian Affairs. *Awards, honors:* Historical novel of the year award from Romantic Novelists Association, 1979, and Elizabeth Goudge Historical Award, 1980, both for *Parson Harding's Daughter.*

WRITINGS: Eliza Stanhope, Hutchinson, 1978, Dutton, 1979; *Parson Harding's Daughter* (historical novel), Hutchinson, 1979, published in the United States as *Mistaken Virtues,* Dutton, 1980; *Leaves From the Valley* (historical novel), Hutchinson, 1980.

WORK IN PROGRESS: Research on the Far East and the American South.

AVOCATIONAL INTERESTS: Travel, gardens, racing horses, poetry, nineteenth-century fiction.

TROYER, Warner 1932-

PERSONAL: Born January 16, 1932, in Cochrane, Ontario, Canada; son of J. Gordon and Ruth (Warner) Troyer; divorced; children: Peggy, Marc, Scott, Jill, Jennifer, John, Peter, Anne. *Education:* Educated in Canada. *Agent:* Nancy Colbert, 303 Davenport Rd., Toronto, Ontario, Canada M5R 1K5.

CAREER: Worked as radio reporter, stringer for *Canadian Press* and *Toronto Star,* and editor of daily newspaper in Portage la Prairie, Manitoba; *Winnipeg Free Press,* Winnipeg, Manitoba, reporter, 1958-61; Canadian Broadcasting Corp. (CBC-TV), Ottawa, Ontario, writer, director, and producer of "Inquiry," 1961-64, and "This Hour Has Seven Days," 1964-66, executive producer of "Public Eye," 1966-68, "W-5," 1968-70, "Fifth Estate," 1973-76, and "Sunday Morning," 1977-79; organizing national television station for government of Sri Lanka, 1980—. Free-lance journalist, 1961—. *Awards, honors:* Wilderness Award, 1962; two awards from Association of Canadian Television and Radio Artists, both 1976; award from New York International Film Festival.

WRITINGS: No Safe Place, Clarke, Irwin, 1977; *Divorced Kids,* Clarke, Irwin, 1979; *200 Days: Joe Clark in Power,* Personal Library, 1980; *The Sound and the Fury: An Anecdotal History of Canadian Broadcasting,* Wiley, 1980. Contributor of articles to Canadian newspapers and magazines.

WORK IN PROGRESS: Who's Minding the Store, a look at the inner workings of the Canadian government.

CA INTERVIEWS THE AUTHOR

Warner Troyer was interviewed by C. H. Gervais on March 14, 1980, at a Windsor, Ontario, restaurant, The Old Fish Market. Gervais is book and religion editor for the *Windsor Star* and the publisher of Black Moss Press.

CA: You're a professional journalist, known all over Canada. You've worked for newspapers, radio, magazines, and you're also a writer of books. How did it all begin for you?

TROYER: I guess I really began by accident like a lot of people used to, before it became fashionable or almost essential to go to journalism school and study it. I started in private radio, reading news and writing it and then going out and reporting, and that got me itchy and interested. I started attending meetings, like the Manitoba Legislature in Winnipeg when I was there, just out of curiosity. Then I'd phone stories in on my free time, and my boss got interested and said, "I guess I should assign you to that—nobody's ever covered that before for radio." At the same time I started writing trade magazine pieces. I was a stringer for *Canadian Press* when I was living in Fort Frances, Ontario, a small town, and then I became a stringer for the *Toronto Star* when I was in Winnipeg working for radio, and got intensely interested in political journalism.

I covered the 1958 Liberal leadership convention in Ottawa for a string of radio stations when Lester B. Pearson was elected leader, and in the course of that week I met the editor of the *Winnipeg Free Press* and tried to persuade him that I should be writing full time for newspapers instead of radio, because newspapers made news a full-time business—it wasn't five minutes every hour. And I was doing a lot of writing anyway, part time. But you've got to have some experience somewhere. I got back to Winnipeg, and two days later I was offered a job, which he obviously had engineered, as editor of the small daily paper in Portage la Prarie, and worked there for a year as the editor of a daily and a chain of weeklies. I did all the editorials, half the news writing, all the layout, the works. Then I went to the *Winnipeg Free Press.*

CA: How old were you then?

TROYER: When I started in radio, I was twenty. By the time I got out to Portage la Prarie I was twenty-six and had been in radio for about six years. I was twenty-seven when I went to the *Free Press,* and at that point my career just turned around and did a complete flip flop—I was now working in newspapers and doing free-lance work in radio and television.

I did a lot of that for three years at the *Free Press,* chiefly because I had radio experience, and television was so new that anybody who had radio experience was regarded as a "find" to do interviews or commentaries. The first thing I did on television was a series of political commentaries on a woman's program in the afternoon in Winnipeg. Then I hosted a weekly public affairs show for a couple of years and continued doing a lot of free lance writing for *Saturday Night, Star Weekly, Liberty,* publications like that. That was the period between 1958 and 1961. I wanted to go to Ottawa to cover the House of Commons, but I couldn't get the *Free Press* to send me because they had three guys in Ottawa. Why did they need one more? I wanted to be a political reporter, and I figured I had done everything I could do in Manitoba. I wanted to get to where the real action was, so I quit and went free lance, packed the kids in the car and drove to Ottawa.

CA: To cover Ottawa as a reporter on your own?

TROYER: To do it on my own on a free-lance basis. I've been free-lancing ever since. That was in 1961. Then I fell into a lot of television work, and that was the heavy preponderance of what I did for the next ten years.

CA: "This Hour Has Seven Days" in Canada was a kind of forerunner to the kind of shows now being taken up in the United States. You were in on that show from the very beginning, and in a way made a reputation nationally as a journalist there. Tell us about the background, style, and significance of it.

TROYER: "This Hour Has Seven Days" was the program that succeeded two other network public affairs shows on CBC, "Document," and "Inquiry." The producers of those shows, Douglas Leiterman and Pat Watson, got together and wanted to produce an hour-long magazine network show. They had seen shows like "That Was the Week That Was" on BBC-TV and they thought, we all thought, that Canada was ripe for something a lot raunchier, a lot tougher journalistically, a lot more acerbic with satire, with really tough interviews and so on. We had developed—most of us—techniques in the "Inquiry" series and to a great degree in the "Document" series. So it was a marriage of those two groups of people, fewer than a dozen in the beginning, with some help of two or three CBC public affairs supervisors who were very bright. We all got together, got the thing going and on the air in 1964. But it was in planning stages for two years before that.

CA: Why was something like that show happening in Canada and not in the United States where you would expect it to be, because one would think Americans were further ahead with TV news, journalism, and public affairs?

TROYER: I think we were a lot looser in Canada; I think we were a lot freer. I don't know whether we had a good deal more imagination—I don't think so—I think we just didn't have the same constraints, or didn't feel we did. The fact is, for example, in the period between 1960 and 1964, before "Seven Days" came on the air, a number of us were going down and making documentary films in the States on the black revolution, on a number of things, and some of these films were a lot tougher—a helluva lot tougher—than anything they were making there. To put it at its crudest, we didn't have the problem of CBS or NBC or ABC that if they ran a film about blacks in Alabama, say, that thirty of their affiliated stations south of the Mason-Dixon line might say, "Hey, we're not going to run that show." That just couldn't happen here. And so we had fewer constraints, either real or imagined. There obviously is, too, a substantive advantage of being with a public broadcasting agency: there are fewer direct commercial pressures and at that period in the States the sponsors had enormous control over program production and writing.

CA: In No Safe Place, *your first book, you said that Canada is probably the least adventurous of all Western nations in developing specialist journalists. I wonder, in light of that statement, why Canada could have produced such a far advanced and imaginative public affairs show like "Seven Days" and yet lag in the other fields of journalism. Why isn't Canada doing the adventurous journalism of Woodward and Bernstein?*

TROYER: I think you can see that response in Canada in all kinds of fields. Taking the journalistic example "Seven Days" was an attempt to prove that public affairs, that politics, that things of that kind could be made exciting, and interesting, and relevant to anybody . . . no matter what their interests were, whether it was hockey, wrestling, or "I Love Lucy," or something much more scholastic or erudite. I think we succeeded—I know we did—because of the audiences we pulled and the reaction we got across the country for that two years. It was incredible. It was kind of an exciting and noble experiment, I think, but then the show died because of bureaucrats in the head office of the Canadian Broadcasting Corporation who couldn't stand the heat. If you were a vice-president of the CBC, and by that time there were nine of them, everytime you went to a cocktail party a cabinet minister or a senior mandarin, a bureaucrat, would grasp you by the lapels and say, "What the hell are you doing to us on that show? Why do you hate us? Why are you crucifying us?" It would get uncomfortable. They just didn't like it, and that's respectable. It's a normal human response.

What wasn't respectable was the next step—to kill the series. But the fact that that advance was made and then kind of lost, well, look around, look at the fact that Canada had for a long time one of the most advanced aeronautical design and engineering facilities in the world. Canada built and flew the first commercial jet passenger airplane in the world, but we only made two of them. Canada designed, built, and flew a jet interceptor fighter, the Arrow, that was so good that it had all the capabilities of anything we have in the air now, twenty-five years later. That's incredible, but we only built four of them. The jolly jumper for infants was invented in Canada, but they had to go to the States for capital and it's manufactured in the States. There seems often to be in the Canadian character some kind of embarassment about success, some kind of fear that it's vulgar to do well, and that when things start to go really well, it's ostentatious of you, you should back off, you should be more careful. But there is always some spillover; there's some residue. I think Canadian journalism, generally, is a lot tougher than it used to be—more probing and more analytical.

CA: Does Canada have shows now on radio and television that are like "Seven Days," as bold as "Seven Days"?

BOYER: No, I don't think so. Well, we do to a degree on radio. I think that shows on CBC like "As It Happens" and "Sunday Morning" and to a degree "Morningside" are bright and raunchy and tough and imaginative. But in television, I don't think so. I don't think we have it anymore, because eventually the bureaucrats just wore everybody down with the paper war. It was like Chinese water torture with memos. People can be conditioned—don't rock the boat, don't take chances, don't make enough waves to splash the poop deck—and there is a degree to which people are tired and not inspired.

CA: Was No Safe Place *a turning point for you in journalism? You do talk about making that leap from trade to craft, and I wonder if you decided to embark on book writing as a means of reporting?*

TROYER: I think everybody who writes for a living, whether it's in radio, television, magazines, newspapers, or whatever, hankers to write a book, to see it in hard covers. It's an ego trip as much as anything else. All of the craft and dedication that went into *No Safe Place* I had put into documentary films again, again, again, and again . . . over fifteen years, but it was a chance of doing it at more length. In fact, I had made a documentary film about that same topic (mercury contamination among the native peoples in Canada) the year before, and when it was over I was dissatisfied in the sense that I didn't think it had all that much impact. I knew there was a helluva lot more to say than one could say even in a thirty-five-minute film. When I was given a chance to explore it in depth and do a real major job, I took it.

In terms of Canadian numbers and Canadian audiences, I know that when I make a documentary film that works well, I might get to maybe a million and a half people, maybe two million on an extraordinary day. With a book I'm going to get to five or ten thousand in Canada, or fifteen if I have a runaway best seller. So you're not hitting the same number of people, and you're not having the same immediate gut response that film can elicit. But of course with a book you can do it much more thoroughly.

CA: Isn't the impact longer lasting with a book?

TROYER: Certainly that's what you hope for, and certainly there's a different kind of satisfaction, a deeper kind of satisfaction in writing books. In most western societies, maybe in most societies, people tend to take a book much more seriously than a magazine piece, a newspaper piece, a television interview, a film documentary, even a feature film. Somehow books seem to have more weight, be thought of as more serious works and taken more seriously.

CA: Do you approach writing a book like No Safe Place *or even the Joe Clark book* [200 Days: Joe Clark In Power] *with the same fury and style as writing for newspaper deadlines, just sitting down and banging out the story. I'm sure there's more research, but is the process somewhat the same?*

TROYER: I tend to think so. There's that awful old line about anybody who writes has to have a deadline, or he won't write anything. And like most people, I stall when it comes time to sit down at the typewriter: I sharpen pencils, make a pot of coffee, go to the can, rearrange my books, get out nine reference books, do anything to avoid that first tap at the keys. I treat—I guess now that I've done four—book writing the same way I treat a television interview, a film documentary, a newspaper piece, a book review, or any-

thing else, in that I try to get all the research material together.

You start with a basic question or thesis, "What about so and so?" or "Is it true that . . .?" and then you go do your research. And I'm one of those people who tends to try and get it all in his head and then write it all. I don't normally refer back and forth a lot, although with books one has to—there's just so much. In *No Safe Place* it was bone crushing because the research was so massive by the time we finished it. In effect each chapter of that book was treated like a separate project. We'd stack up all the research for one chapter, and I would spend some days reading and absorbing and sorting it, shuffling it, doing a rough outline, and then I'd sit down and write that chapter. With the Joe Clark book, with *Divorced Kids* and with *The Sound and the Fury,* the history of broadcasting, the research wasn't as massive. Although with the Clark book I did it a chapter at a time.

CA: You wrote that book in two weeks. Were you put upon to get the book written when the election was called? You once said you were going to do a report-card kind of book on Clark. What really happened?

TROYER: I started collecting the material for the book on May 24, 1979, the day after the election. I called my agent and said, "Hey, we're going to have the first Conservative government in Canada in sixteen years. It would really be fun to write a book about their first two hundred days. It would sort of take them up to New Year's Eve, do a kind of report card. Find a publisher." So she found a publisher, Personal Library, and we signed a contract in June. The research, collection, collation, sorting, and indexing went on from then until I sat down to write, after Christmas. Whenever I was in Ottawa I would talk to people there and pick up all the gossip I could, all the back-room information I could.

The government was defeated December 13, 1979. At that point I was working on this book on broadcasting and finishing it up, and we had agreed way back in June that we would publish the Clark book late February, early March, which would have been fine. It was going to be a book on the first two hundred days of the Tory government, but when the government self-destructed the whole focus changed. It became terribly important for the publisher in purely commercial terms that the book be in the stores before the election, which was February 18. So the publisher called me December 14, the day after the government was defeated, and said, "I know you can't start writing now, but when can you have it finished?" And I said, "How does January 4 sound?" And he said, "Fine." And so I started writing on Boxing Day [December 26th].

CA: What was your schedule? How much time did you spend on it daily?

TROYER: Once we had sorted all the research, stacked it up and put it into separate file folders by topic, I typed an outline for the book the length of two typewritten sheets of letter-size paper, that's all, and pinned it up on the wall. I put up two big pieces of cardboard, bristol board, and got a big felt pen and began writing dates in chronological order of everything from May 23 to December 14. I was surrounded by clippings stuck up with push pins all over the bookcases in the den, just surrounded by it. Then I sat down, and what I did literally was type on an average of about twelve hours, and I would have sandwiches and coffee and a Scotch. After about twelve hours I would go to bed, collapse for two hours, set the alarm, get up, have a shower, have a cup of coffee, and go back to it and write for another twelve hours.

I worked that way until I finished the manuscript; it was twelve-hour spurts with two-hour breaks. I'd never want to do that again, even if I'd had one more week. I was averaging two hours sleep every twenty-four. It ain't enough.

CA: Was there any need for revisions? Or was there time? Was it a pretty clean manuscript?

TROYER: It was pretty clean. I tend to write quickly anyway, because I spend a lot of preparation time, and it's in my head, and then it comes out fairly fast. There were no major revisions. Certainly, there was a lot of tidying up. The editor, the publisher, and I let two really dumb factual errors, which were obviously the result of late-night Freudian slips at the typewriter, get through. Just stupid things. I typed Tory instead of Liberal in one sentence, so I made a Liberal senator come out a Tory senator. It didn't happen to be especially relevant, but it made me feel like an ass. And I buried former Prime Minister John Diefenbaker in Prince Albert instead of Saskatoon, which was really dumb of me. I knew perfectly well John Diefenbaker was buried in Saskatoon, but I think I was sitting there that night, probably 5:00 A.M. or 6:00 A.M., thinking about Diefenbaker when I was typing. My first interview with him was 1956, and I covered the election campaigns in '57, '58, '62, '63, '65, '68, '72, and '74. I knew him so well and had interviewed him so often that I think I was sort of reminiscing subconsciously about all those meetings in Prince Albert, his home town, and it just came out Prince Albert on the page, and nobody caught it. So there were two dumb factual errors, both of which we'll catch in the second edition.

CA: In the second edition, will you make any reference to Canada's role in getting the Americans out of the Canadian Embassy and Iran [February, 1980] during the hostage-taking incident there? It wasn't known at the time you wrote the Clark book, but will you do some rewriting, since Clark's government was directly involved?

TROYER: No, I don't think so. That's cheating, you know. That's using twenty-twenty hindsight to make yourself look better after the event. This book was written before we knew about that, and I think that would be a case of trying to bail myself out. I wouldn't do it.

CA: Tell us about your fourth book, The Sound and the Fury.

TROYER: The book is an illustrated anecdotal history of Canadian broadcasting, radio and television, very opinionated with, I hope, a lot of color and a lot of fun. It's very subjective, with some gassy old photographs that were great fun, although they were enormously difficult to collect. I guess it's a fairly acerbic critique of the industry and of the politics that have been involved in it from the beginning. It's a light book; but it was meant to be a way of making the sort of politics of this peculiar industry accessible to people who aren't interested in politics. I suppose in a sense it's a between-hard-covers emulation of the "Seven Days" philosophy. Seems to me that there's no point talking into a vacuum or peeing into the wind, you know, if people aren't interested in what's happening; if it's not colorful and interesting, you're wasting your time.

CA: Any other books in the offing?

TROYER: I'm still palpitating from the Joe Clark book. I am contracted to do another book, however, for this year [1980]. It's intended also to be anecdotal, one which will make information available to people who aren't scholars. The working title is *Who's Minding the Store?* It's intended to be a fun

look at our system of government, how the hell does it work, you know, what't the difference between a municipal councillor and a privy councillor. I think that obviously it matters a helluva lot to all of us—how the system works or how it doesn't work, how it malfunctions. And I don't think most people have a good enough fix on it to know even who to get mad at when things don't work out the way they want them to. So it'll be an attempt to redress some of that balance. I suppose in real terms I've started it, because I've got a whole shelf of books that I've been reading away at over the last year. But I haven't started in terms of developing a hard focus or doing any writing, and I won't for, oh, a couple of weeks.*

—*Interview by C. H. Gervais*

*   *   *

TSEGAYE, Gabre-Medhin (Kawessa)
See GABRE-MEDHIN, Tsegaye (Kawessa)

*   *   *

TUBB, E(dwin) C(harles)   1919-
(Chuck Adams, Jud Cary, J. F. Clarkson, James S. Farrow, James R. Fenner, Charles S. Graham, Charles Grey, Volsted Gridban, Gill Hunt, E. F. Jackson, Gregory Kern, King Lang, Mike Lantry, P. Lawrence, Chet Lawson, Arthur Maclean, Carl Maddox, M. L. Powers, Paul Schofield, Brian Shaw, Roy Sheldon, John Stevens, Edward Thomson)

PERSONAL: Born October 15, 1919, in London, England; son of Edwin Margrie (an engineer) and Marie Francois (a dress designer; maiden name, Bonzec) Tubb; married Iris Kathleen Smith, 1944; children: Jennifer Evelyn, Lina Edwina. *Home:* 67 Houston Rd., London SE23 2RL, England. *Agent:* Leslie Flood, E. J. Carnell Literary Agency, The Bungalow, Near Old Hollow, Essex CM20 2EX, England.

CAREER: Writer, 1950—. Worked as welfare officer, catering manager, and advisory consultant. *Awards, honors:* Cytricon literary award for best British science fiction author, 1955; co-guest of honor at twenty-eighth World Science Fiction Convention in Heidelberg, West Germany, 1970; special award for best short story, Eurocon 1, Trieste, 1972, for "Lucifer."

WRITINGS—Science fiction: *Alien Impact,* Hamilton & Co., 1952; *Atom War on Mars,* Panther House, 1952; *The Mutants Rebel,* Panther House, 1953; *Venusian Adventure,* Comyns, 1953; *Alien Life,* Paladin Press, 1954; *City of No Return,* Scion, 1954; *The Hell Planet,* Scion, 1954; *Journey to Mars,* Scion, 1954; *The Resurrected Man,* Scion, 1954; *The Stellar Legion,* Scion, 1954; *World at Bay,* Panther House, 1954; *Alien Dust,* Boardman, 1955; *The Space-Born* [and] *The Man Who Japed* (the latter by Philip K. Dick), Ace Books, 1956.

Target Death, Micron, 1961; *Lucky Strike,* Fleetway Publications, 1961; *Calculated Risk,* Fleetway Publications, 1961; *Too Tough to Handle,* Fleetway Publications, 1961; *The Dead Keep Faith,* Fleetway Publications, 1961; *The Spark of Anger,* Fleetway Publications, 1962; *Full Impact,* Fleetway Publications, 1962; *I Vow Vengeance,* Fleetway Publications, 1962; *Gunflash,* Fleetway Publications, 1962; *Hit Back,* Fleetway Publications, 1962; *One Must Die,* Fleetway Publications, 1962; *Suicide Squad,* Fleetway Publications, 1962; *Airborne Commando,* Fleetway Publications, 1963; *No Higher Stakes,* Fleetway Publications, 1963; *Penalty of*

Fear, Fleetway Publications, 1963; *Moon Base*, Ace Books, 1964.

Ten From Tomorrow, Hart-Davis, 1966; *Death Is a Dream*, Hart-Davis, 1967; *C.O.D. From Mars* [and] *Alien Sea* (the latter by John Rackham), Ace Books, 1968; *Escape Into Space*, Sidgwick & Jackson, 1969; *S.T.A.R. Flight*, Paperback Library, 1969; *Century of the Manikin*, Daw Books, 1972; *Sword in the Snow*, Fantasy Booklets, 1973; *The Primitive*, Futura Publishing, 1977; *Death Wears a White Face*, R. Hale, 1979; *Stellar Assignment*, R. Hale, 1979; *The Luck Machine*, D. Dobson, 1980.

"Dumarest of Terra" science-fiction series: *The Winds of Gath* [and] *Crisis in Cheiron* (the latter by Juanita Coulson), Ace Books, 1967 (published in England as *Gath*, Hart-Davis, 1968); *Derai* [and] *The Singing Stones* (the latter by Coulson), Ace Books, 1968; *Toyman* [and] *Fear That Man* (the latter by Dean R. Koontz), Ace Books, 1969; *Kalin* [and] *Bane of Kanthos* (the latter by Alex Dain), Ace Books, 1969.

The Jester at Scar [and] *To Venus! To Venus!* (the latter by David Grinnell), Ace Books, 1970; *Lallia* [and] *Recoil* (the latter by C. Nunes and R. Nunes), Ace Books, 1971; *Technos* [and] *A Scatter of Stardust*, Ace Books, 1972; *Veruchia*, Ace Books, 1973; *Mayenne*, Daw Books, 1973; *Jondelle*, Daw Books, 1973; *Zenya*, Daw Books, 1974; *Eloise*, Daw Books, 1975; *Eye of the Zodiac*, Daw Books, 1975; *Jack of Swords*, Daw Books, 1976; *Spectrum of a Forgotten Sun*, Daw Books, 1976; *Haven of Darkness*, Daw Books, 1977; *Prison of Night*, Daw Books, 1977; *Incident on Ath*, Daw Books, 1978; *The Quillan Sector*, Daw Books, 1978; *Web of Sand*, Daw Books, 1979; *Iduna's Universe*, Daw Books, 1980; *The Terra Data*, Daw Books, 1980.

"Space 1999" science-fiction series: *Breakaway*, Pocket Books, 1975; *Collision Course*, Amereon, 1975; *Alien Seed*, Pocket Books, 1976; *Rogue Planet*, Pocket Books, 1976; *Earthfall*, Futura Publishing, 1977.

Under pseudonym Charles Grey: *Dynasty of Doom*, Milestone, 1953; *I Fight for Mars*, Milestone, 1953; *Space Hunger*, Milestone, 1953; *The Tormented City*, Milestone, 1953; *The Wall*, Milestone, 1953; *Enterprise 2115*, Merit, 1954, published as *The Mechanical Monarch* [and] *Twice Upon a Time* (the latter by Charles L. Fontenay), Ace Books, 1958; *The Extra Man*, Milestone, 1954; *The Hand of Havoc*, Merit, 1954.

Under house pseudonym Volsted Gridban: *Alien Universe*, Scion, 1952; *Reverse Universe*, Scion, 1952; *DeBracy's Drug*, Scion, 1953; *Fugitive of Time*, Milestone, 1953; *Planetoid Disposals Ltd.*, Milestone, 1953.

Under pseudonym Gregory Kern; "Cap Kennedy" science-fiction series; all published by Daw Books: *Galaxy of the Lost*, 1973; *Slave Ship From Sergan*, 1973; *Monster of Metelaze*, 1973; *Enemy Within the Skull*, 1974; *Jewel of Jarhen*, 1974; *Seetee Alert!*, 1974; *The Gholan Gate*, 1974; *The Eater of Worlds*, 1974; *Earth Enslaved*, 1974; *Planet of Dread*, 1974; *Spawn of Laban*, 1974; *The Genetic Buccaneer*, 1974; *A World Aflame*, 1974; *The Ghosts of Epidoris*, 1975; *Mimics of Dephene*, 1975; *Beyond the Galactic Lens*, 1975.

Under various house pseudonyms: (As King Lang) *Saturn Patrol*, Curtis Warren, 1951; (as Gill Hunt) *Planetfall*, Curtis Warren, 1951; (as Brian Shaw) *Argentis*, Curtis Warren, 1952; (as Roy Sheldon) *House of Entropy*, Hamilton & Co., 1953; (as Sheldon) *The Metal Eater*, Panther House, 1954; (as Carl Maddox) *The Living World*, Pearson, 1954; (as Maddox) *Menace From the Past*, Pearson, 1954.

Under other pseudonyms: (As Arthur Maclean) *Johnny San-*

tee, Hamilton & Co., 1954; (as Maclean) *Three Men From Tucson*, Hamilton & Co., 1954; (as Paul Schofield) *The Fighting Fury*, J. Spencer, 1955; (as Jud Cary) *Sands of Destiny*, J. Spencer, 1955; (as J. F. Clarkson) *Men of the Long Rifle*, J. Spencer, 1955; (as E. F. Jackson) *Comanche Capture*, J. Spencer, 1955; (as Mike Lantry) *Assignment New York*, J. Spencer, 1955; (as Chuck Adams) *Trail Blazers*, J. Spencer, 1956; (as James S. Farrow) *Vengeance Trail*, J. Spencer, 1956; (as P. Lawrence) *Drums of the Prairie*, J. Spencer, 1956; (as Chet Lawson) *Men of the West*, J. Spencer, 1956; (as M. L. Powers) *Scourge of the South*, J. Spencer, 1956; (as John Stevens) *Quest for Quantrell*, J. Spencer, 1956; (as James R. Fenner) *Colt Vengeance*, J. Spencer, 1957; (as Charles S. Graham) *Wagon Trail*, J. Spencer, 1957; (as Maclean) *Touch of Evil*, Fleetway Publications, 1959; (as Edward Thomson) *Atilus the Slave*, Futura Publishing, 1975; (as Thomson) *Atilus the Gladiator*, Futura Publishing, 1975; (as Thomson) *Gladiator*, Futura Publishing, 1978.

Editor of *Authentic Science Fiction*, 1956-57, and *Eye and Vector*, 1958-60.

Contributor of short stories to numerous science-fiction periodicals, reportedly under more than fifty pseudonyms.

* * *

TUCKER, Archibald Norman 1904(?)-1980

OBITUARY NOTICE: Born c. 1904; died in 1980 in England. Writer and linguist. An authority on the languages of Africa, Tucker wrote more than twenty-five books on subjects ranging from the structure of language to the representation of sounds by printed symbols. In addition to this study of orthography, Tucker was also a professor of languages and a member of the executive council of the International African Institute. Obituaries and other sources: *AB Bookman's Weekly*, October 6, 1980.

* * *

TUCKER, David M(ilton) 1937-

PERSONAL: Born November 28, 1937, in Pottsville, Ark.; son of Milton C. (a school administrator) and Hallene (Rentfrow) Tucker; married Cynthia Grant (a professor), 1966; children: Hope, Grant. *Education:* College of the Ozarks, B.A., 1959; Oklahoma State University, M.A., 1961; University of Iowa, Ph.D., 1965. *Office:* Department of History Memphis State University, Memphis, Tenn. 38152.

CAREER: Memphis State University, Memphis, Tenn., assistant professor 1965-70, associate professor, 1970-75, professor of history, 1975—. *Member:* Organization of American Historians.

WRITINGS: Lieutenant Lee Of Beale Street, Vanderbilt University Press, 1971; *Black Pastors and Leaders*, Memphis State University Press, 1975; *Memphis Since Crump*, University of Tennessee Press, 1980. Contributor to history journals.

WORK IN PROGRESS: Arkansas: The Cinderella State, 1985.

SIDELIGHTS: Tucker told *CA:* "My work generally falls into the category of old fashioned social history—the study of groups without using the computer. My impressionistic efforts began with a dissertation on mugwumps and continued with publications on black businessmen, black ministers, and white civic reformers. In the Arkansas study, my interest is not only the hillbillies, the sharecroppers, and the planters, but also the enterprising promoters who three times pushed the 'land of opportunity' into state bankruptcy. Arkansas has remained next to the bottom in most leading indicators except optimism that her day is coming.''

*   *   *

TUCKNER, Howard   1932(?)-1980

OBITUARY NOTICE: Born c. 1932; committed suicide, June 4, 1980, in New York, N.Y. Television and newspaper journalist. During his career as a journalist, Howard Tuckner reported the news from such places as Vietnam, Cambodia, Bangladesh, and Hong Kong. He worked for the *New York Times* and *Newsweek* and was the chief correspondent in Johannesburg, South Africa, for the American Broadcasting Co., Inc. (ABC) News at the time of his death. Obituaries and other sources: *Newsweek,* August 25, 1980.

*   *   *

TURCHIN, Valentin F(yodorovich)   1931-

PERSONAL: Born February 14, 1931, in U.S.S.R.; son of Fyodor (a scientist) and Lyubov (Bagler) Turchin; married Tatiana Novikova; children: Peter, Dimitri. *Education:* Moscow State University, B.S., 1952; Physics and Energy Institute, Ph.D., 1958. *Home:* 75-34, 113 St., Forest Hills, N.Y. 11375. *Office:* City College of the City University of New York, 140th St. and Convent Ave., New York, N.Y. 10031.

CAREER: Physics and Energy Institute, Obninsk, U.S.S.R., scientist, 1953-64; Academy of Science, Institute for Applied Mathematics, Moscow, U.S.S.R., senior scientist, 1964-73; City College of the City University of New York, New York City, professor of computer science, 1979—.

WRITINGS: Slow Neutrons, Davey, 1965; *The Phenomenon of Science,* Columbia University Press, 1977; *The Inertia of Fear and the Scientific World View,* Columbia University Press, 1980.

In Russian: (Editor) *Fiziki Shutiat* (title means ''Physicists Laugh''), MIR, 1966; (editor) *Fiziki Propolzhaiut Shutit* (title means ''Physicists Continue to Laugh''), MIR, 1968; *Inertsiia Strakha* (title means ''The Inertia of Fear''), Khronika Press, 1977. Author of more than sixty scientific papers and pamphlets.

WORK IN PROGRESS: A book and papers about computer science.

SIDELIGHTS: Turchin was one of the leading activists of the human rights movement in the Soviet Union. His work began in 1968 when he signed a petition on behalf of political prisoners and circulated a critical article about the Soviet Union's socio-political conditions. The dissident also wrote ''Open Letter to Party and Government Leaders of the U.S.S.R.'' with the academician Andrei Sakharov and the historian Roy Medvedev, in which the authors argued that ''persistent and profound democratization is essential to Soviet society.'' In 1973 Turchin helped organize a human rights group, Amnesty International, and a year later was dismissed from his job. The activist was interrogated repeatedly and his house searched. When Soviet authorities finally informed Turchin that he would never again obtain professional employment in Russia and would be put on trial, he emigrated with his family to the United States.

Turchin told *CA:* ''I believe that the scientific method and the contemporary scientific philosophy of nature provide a sound basis for an optimistic and life-asserting world view. In my nontechnical books I try to contribute to the creation of this world view, which I believe will eventually replace

traditional religion. Only when this world view, or new religion, is firmly established and taken as seriously as all the great religions are, will the emerging global civilization consolidate and overcome the degrading temptation of totalitarianism.''

*   *   *

TURNER, Sheila
See ROWBOTHAM, Sheila

*   *   *

TURNEY, Catherine   1906-

PERSONAL: Born December 26, 1906, in Chicago, Ill.; daughter of George (a manufacturer) and Elizabeth (Blamer) Turney; married Cyril Armbrister, 1931 (divorced, 1938); married George Reynolds, February 18, 1940 (divorced, 1948). *Education:* Attended Columbia School of Journalism, 1925, and Pasadena Playhouse School of the Theatre, 1930-31. *Politics:* Democrat. *Home:* 156 California Terrace, Pasadena, Calif. 91105. *Agent:* Shirley Burke, 370 East 76th St., New York, N.Y. 10021.

CAREER: Pasadena Community Playhouse, Pasadena, Calif., theatre worker and director of workshops, 1927-30; Raymond R. Morgan Advertising Agency, Hollywood, Calif., writer for radio programs, including ''Strange as It Seems,'' 1934-36; Metro-Goldwyn-Mayer (MGM), Hollywood, contract writer, 1936-37; Warner Bros., Hollywood, contract writer, 1943-48; writing assignments with Universal, Paramount, and MGM, 1948; television writer in Hollywood and New York City, producing scripts for programs, including ''Studio One,'' ''Cavalcade of America,'' ''Fireside Theatre,'' and ''One Step Beyond,'' 1949-69. Playwright, director, and novelist. *Member:* Writers Guild of America, West, Dramatists Guild, Byron Society, The Westerners. *Awards, honors:* Fanny Morrison Award from Pasadena Playhouse, 1947.

WRITINGS: Bitter Harvest (three-act play; first produced in London, England, at Stage Society, 1936, produced on the West End at Arts Theatre, January 29, 1936), Hamish Hamilton, 1936; (with Jerry Horwin) *My Dear Children* (three-act play; first produced in Chicago, Ill., at Selwyn Theatre, 1939, produced on Broadway at Belasco Theatre, January 31, 1940), Random House, 1940; *The Other One* (novel), Holt, 1952, published as *Possessed,* Paperback Library, 1968; *Byron's Daughter: A Biography of Elizabeth Medora Leigh,* Scribner, 1972; *Stronger Than Death* (historical novel), Pocket Books, 1981.

WORK IN PROGRESS: The Beautiful One, a biographical novel set in the early nineteenth century.

SIDELIGHTS: Turney told *CA:* ''Biographies and history, especially told through biographical data, are my main interests. For escape I read good suspense fiction, preferably English which deals more with character and not so much mayhem. I love the theatre but find the newer playwrights hard to relate to. I prefer reading to watching TV, except public TV, and rarely attend movies. Since 1972 I have been writing and doing research at the Huntington Memorial Library, San Marino, Calif. I love working there—the surroundings are so beautiful. New and stimulating scholars come and go from every place in the world.

''In the past two years there have been many authors interviewing me about my years at Warner Bros., especially my work with Bette Davis and scripting 'Mildred Pierce.' A cult for the older pictures is proliferating among younger people.

A number of books have already been published using quotes from me.''

Some of Turney's more recent work has focused on Lord Byron. Her *Byron's Daughter* is about Elizabeth Medora Leigh, believed by some, including Turney, to be the daughter of Byron and his half-sister, Augusta Leigh. F. W. Bateson faulted Turney for the absence of ''crucial'' footnotes, but added: ''Nevertheless I am convinced by her story. There are a few embarrassingly sentimental passages, but on the whole it rings true.''

BIOGRAPHICAL/CRITICAL SOURCES: New York Review of Books, February 22, 1973.

*   *   *

TURNGREN, Annette 1902(?)-1980
(A. T. Hopkins)

OBITUARY NOTICE—See index for *CA* sketch: Born c. 1902 in Montrose, Minn.; died May 14, 1980, in Hopkins, Minn. Editor and author. Turngren held editorial positions at a number of magazines, a book publisher, and the *New York Times.* She wrote several books for children, including *Flaxen Braids, The Mystery of the Hidden Village,* and *Mystery Plays a Golden Flute.* Obituaries and other sources: *AB Bookman's Weekly,* July 14-21, 1980.

*   *   *

TUROW, Rita P(astron) 1919-

PERSONAL: Born December 24, 1919, in Chicago, Ill.; daughter of Sam (a food distributor) and Fannie (Epstein) Pastron; married David D. Turow (a gynecologist and obstetrician), January 31, 1943; children: Scott, Vicki. *Education:* Roosevelt University, B.A., 1941; Chicago Teachers College, M.E., 1943; also attended University of Chicago, 1943-45. *Home:* 920 Pine Tree Lane, Winnetka, Ill. 60093.

CAREER: High school teacher of English and French in Chicago, Ill., 1943; elementary school teacher in Chicago, 1943-49; Skokie School, Winnetka, Ill., teacher of creative writing, 1971-77; writer, 1977—. Member of group counseling program at private medical clinic. *Member:* Authors Guild, Authors League of America, American Society of Journalists and Authors, Society of Midland Authors, Chicago Children's Reading Roundtable.

WRITINGS: Daddy Doesn't Live Here Anymore (adult nonfiction), Great Lakes Living Press, 1977. Contributor to magazines, including *Progressive Women, Health, Healthways,* and *Curriculum Innovations,* and newspapers.

WORK IN PROGRESS: We're Growing a Baby at Our House, a children's book, publication expected in 1981 or 1982.

SIDELIGHTS: Rita Turow commented: ''I have had a lifelong romance with all the arts—theatre, dance, music, painting, sculpture, architecture, and especially the printed word. *Daddy Doesn't Live Here Anymore* grew out of my experience of working with children of divorced parents, and the fact that my brother was divorced three times. Divorce is part of almost everyone's experience; if it hasn't happened to you, it has most likely happened to your relative, friend, or neighbor. The television and radio work I did nationwide in connection with the book, and the response to that work, further cemented my understanding that it is an almost universal experience today.

''*Daddy Doesn't Live Here Anymore* has had portions reproduced in about twenty newspapers to date. It has been re-

viewed very favorably by the *Library Journal* and the *Journal of Divorce* as well as on many radio and television stations. It has been purchased and included in many high school and university libraries.''

AVOCATIONAL INTERESTS: Travel (Europe, Africa, Australia, New Zealand, the Soviet Union.)

*   *   *

TWIN, Stephanie L. 1948-

PERSONAL: Born September 26, 1948, in Kansas City, Mo.; daughter of Edward James (a physician) and Margaret (in business; maiden name, Litwin) Twin; married Richard Charles Smuckler (a project director), September 8, 1968; children: Alexandra, Danielle. *Education:* University of Wisconsin, Madison, B.A., 1970, M.A., 1972; Rutgers University, Ph.D., 1978. *Home:* 170 Prospect Park W., Brooklyn, N.Y. 11215. *Office:* Center for Productive Public Management, 445 West 59th St., New York, N.Y. 10019.

CAREER: New Jersey Office of Equal Access, Edison, writer on sex and race bias and editor, 1978; Center for Productive Public Management, New York, N.Y., deputy project director, 1979—. Member of adjunct faculty at LaGuardia Community College of the City University of New York; consultant to Training Institute for Sex Desegregation of the Public Schools. *Member:* Amnesty International, American Civil Liberties Union, Phi Beta Kappa.

WRITINGS: Out of the Bleachers: Writings on Women and Sport, Feminist Press, 1979. Contributor to magazines, including *In These Times,* and newspapers.

AVOCATIONAL INTERESTS: Fiction, biographies, autobiographies, travel, film, theater, bicycling, walking.

*   *   *

TYLER, J. Allen 1924-

PERSONAL: Born March 10, 1924, in Norfolk, Va.; son of John Goodenow (in sales) and Augustine (Allen) Tyler; married Jane Abbott, August 2, 1968. *Education:* Virginia Polytechnic Institute and State University, B.S., 1949; Middlebury College, M.A., 1956; University of Virginia, Ph.D., 1971. *Home:* 925 Lake Powell Rd., Williamsburg, Va. 23185.

CAREER: French teacher at private school in Norfolk, Va., 1953-65; College of William and Mary, Williamsburg, Va., assistant professor of French, 1969-76; writer. Member of Metropolitan Opera Guild. *Military service:* U.S. Army, 1943-45. *Member:* American Horticultural Society. *Awards, honors:* Smith-Mundt grant for Morocco, 1958-59.

WRITINGS: (Editor) *A Concordance to the Fables and Tales of Jean de la Fontaine,* Cornell University Press, 1974.

*   *   *

TYNAN, Kenneth 1927-1980

OBITUARY NOTICE—See index for *CA* sketch: Born April 2, 1927, in Birmingham, England; died of pulmonary emphysema, July 26, 1980, in Santa Monica, Calif. Critic, playwright, and author. Regarded as ''the greatest theater critic since Shaw,'' Tynan had an enormous influence on the development of theatre in England. His intention to ''raise tempers, goad, lacerate, raise whirlwinds'' as drama critic for the *London Observer* made him an often times precocious, controversial exponent of a new realism in English drama. He promoted the so-called New Drama of writers like John Osborne and Arnold Wesker, contending that ''no theater could sanely flourish until there was an umbilical connection between what was happening on the stage and what was happening in the world." His own play, "Oh! Calcutta!," produced in London and New York, created debate on both sides of the Atlantic about what *Time* called its "simulated sex and unsimulated nudity," involving issues of morality and taste in the theatre. Tynan also worked as drama critic for the *New Yorker* in the early 1960's before joining Britain's National Theatre as its literary manager in 1963. When his emphysema worsened, Tynan moved to California in 1976, describing himself as "a climatic emigre." Many of the profiles he wrote for the *New Yorker* in his last years were collected for *Show People,* his last book. Among Tynan's other writings are *He That Plays the King, Curtains, Tynan Right and Left,* and *Bull Fever.* Obituaries and other sources: *London Times,* July 29, 1980; *New York Times,* July 29, 1980; *Chicago Tribune,* July 30, 1980; *Time,* August 11, 1980; *Newsweek,* August 11, 1980.

*   *   *

TYSSE, Agnes N.   1904-

PERSONAL: Surname is pronounced *Ty*-see; born June 17, 1904, in East Williamson, N.Y.; daughter of Gerrit (a minister) and Eva (Van Oostenbrugge) Tysse. *Education:* Hope College, A.B., 1928; University of Michigan, A.B.L.S., 1936, A.M.L.S., 1942. *Politics:* Republican. *Religion:* Presbyterian. *Home:* 505 Packard, No. 5, Ann Arbor, Mich. 48104.

CAREER: High school English teacher in Cedar Springs, Mich., 1928-29; Hope College, Holland, Mich., librarian, 1929-37; New Mexico A & M University (now New Mexico State University), Las Cruces, cataloger at library, 1937-40, acting librarian, 1940-41; University of Michigan, Ann Arbor, associate reference librarian, 1942-58, reference librarian and head of reference department, 1958-70; writer, 1970—.

WRITINGS: (Editor with Rolland C. Stewart) *Current Russian Science and Technology: Selected Scientific Journals and Bibliographies Available in the University Library of the University of Michigan,* Library, University of Michigan, 1942; (contributor) Robert E. Kingery and Maurice F. Tauber, editors, *Book Catalogs,* Scarecrow, 1963; (editor) *International Education: The American Experience,* Scarecrow, Volume I: *Dissertations and Theses,* 1974, Volume II: *Periodical Articles,* Part I: *General,* Part II: *Area Studies and Indexes,* 1977.

WORK IN PROGRESS: The International Education: The American Experience: Volume III: *Books, Essays, Government Documents.*

AVOCATIONAL INTERESTS: Reading, travel, music.

*   *   *

TZONIS, Alexander   1937-

PERSONAL: Born November 8, 1937, in Athens, Greece; came to the United States in 1965; son of Constantinos (a professor) and Chariclea (a chemist; maiden name, Xanthopoulos) Tzonis; married Liane Lefaivre (a writer), October 27, 1973. *Education:* Technological University of Athens, diploma in architectural engineering, 1961; Yale University, M.Arch., 1963. *Office:* Department of Architecture, Graduate School of Design, Harvard University, Gund Hall, Cambridge, Mass. 02138.

CAREER: Anagnostopoulos, Calogeras, & Tzonis, Athens, Greece, partner, 1963-66; Yale University, New Haven, Conn., instructor in architecture, 1965-67; Harvard University, Cambridge, Mass., assistant professor, 1967-75, associate professor of design, 1975—, associate of Mather House. Visiting professor at University of Montreal, 1970-71 and 1973-79, Institut d'Architecture et d'Urbanisme, Strasbourg, France, 1972-73, Columbia University, 1974-75, and Technische Hogenschool of Eindhoven, 1977-78; lecturer at universities throughout the world. Member of Planning Science Institute. Art director of films and operas, including "Never on Sunday," released by United Artists in 1960. Architecture and paintings exhibited in Greece; organizer of international conferences at University of Eindhoven, 1977-78. *Military service:* Greek Army, 1963-65.

MEMBER: American Society of Architectural Historians, Royal Society of Arts (fellow), Societe Francaise d'Etude Dix-huitieme Siecle. *Awards, honors:* Grants from Twentieth Century Fund, 1965-67, U.S. Bureau of Standards, 1966-67, Milton Fund, 1973, 1974, and 1975, French Centre Nationale de Recherche Scientifique, 1973-75, and University of Montreal, 1978-80; Ford Foundation fellow, 1961-63.

WRITINGS: (With Manfred Ibel) *Kavafi* (lithographs; poems by Constantinos Kavafi translated by Nikos Stangos and Stephen Spender), Yale University Press, 1966; (with Serge Chermayeff) *Toward an Urban Model,* Yale University Press, 1967; (with Chermayeff) *The Shape of Community,* Penguin, 1970; *Toward a Non-Oppressive Environment,* I Press, 1972; (with Ovadia Salama) *Problems of Programmatic Analysis in Architecture,* Graduate School of Design, Harvard University, 1972; *The Study of Development of Architectural Thinking,* Technische Hogenschool Eindhoven, 1979; (editor and author of introduction) *Towards a History of Innovation and Invention in Architecture: The Avant-Garde,* Technische Hogenschool Eindhoven, 1979; (editor and contributor) *An Annotated Bibliography of Publications in French on Architecture, Engineering, Urbanism, Perspective, Decorative Arts, Landscape Architecture, and Military Architecture From 1500 to 1800,* Garland Publishing, 1981.

General editor of "Man Made Environment," a series, Penguin, 1969-75. Contributor of more than twenty articles to art and architecture journals. Member of editorial board of *Habitat, Carre Bleu,* and *Arch.* Consulting editor to Garland Publishing.

WORK IN PROGRESS: Architecture and Society, 1000-1800, with wife, Liane Lefaivre, publication expected in 1982; *Roots of Modern Architecture,* an investigation of the origins, conceptual and institutional, of modern architecture, with L. Lefaivre, publication expected in 1983.

SIDELIGHTS: Tzonis commented to *CA:* "My writings have been devoted to the formation of the artificial environment as a cultural as well as technological phenomenon. My preoccupation is the social context within which this process takes place and the impact it has on society. I believe the quality of the man-made products depends on the way they shape human relations and not only on their intrinsic technical or formal qualities, and that history is the best way to understand it.

"These ideas come from a large number of authors but I should stress two major influences on me as early as my adolescence: Goethe and Lewis Mumford."

U

UNDERWOOD, Barbara 1952-

PERSONAL: Born February 17, 1952, in Eugene, Ore.; daughter of Raymond Preston (a lawyer) and Mary Betty (a writer; maiden name, Anderson) Underwood; married Gary Michael Scharff (a counselor), September 3, 1979. *Education:* University of California, Berkeley, B.A., 1979. *Politics:* Democrat. *Religion:* "Quaker background; currently nondenominational Christian." *Home:* 2604 Regent St., Berkeley, Calif. 94704. *Agent:* Jean V. Naggar Literary Agency, 420 East 72nd St., New York, N.Y. 10021.

CAREER: Unification Church, Berkeley, Calif., fundraiser, counselor, and teacher, 1974-77; Freedom of Thought Foundation, Tucson, Ariz., counselor and public speaker, summer, 1977; *Business Week,* New York City, secretary in public relations, 1978; Random House, Inc., New York City, intern and editor in School Division, 1978; free-lance writer, 1978—. Member of American Family Foundation and Citizens Freedom Foundation Information Service. *Member:* American Association of University Women, Phi Beta Kappa.

WRITINGS: (With mother, Betty Underwood) *Hostage to Heaven,* Crown, 1979. Work represented in anthologies, including *College Poetry Review 1978.* Contributor of articles and poems to magazines, including *California Journal* and *Blue Unicorn Triquarterly.*

WORK IN PROGRESS: Research on deprogramming methods, writer-editor relations, and women's issues, including anorexia nervosa and adolescent female rebellions.

SIDELIGHTS: Hostage to Heaven describes Barbara Underwood's own experiences as a member of the Unification Church (Moonies), the 1977 court hearing in San Francisco at which her parents tried to regain legal custody, and her subsequent deprogramming. Other writing interests include religious communities in general, women's self-discovery, public affairs, mind control, and family relations. She is also interested in public affairs radio interviews and broadcasting.

She told *CA:* "No imaginative fiction could possibly stretch the range of experience contained in the contradictions of reality. People amaze me and intrigue me. People concern, terrify, excite, and mystify me. Observing and recording consensual human relationships is my goal in writing—especially noting how people reconcile (or don't integrate) opposites: the dream versus reality, relativism versus absolutes, sin versus self-acceptance, romance versus friendship.

"There are many explosive secrets in these dualities about the human condition that I want to explore through documentary writing."

AVOCATIONAL INTERESTS: Travel (including Europe and Australia), mountain climbing in the Cascades, caving in Virginia, swimming, jogging, racquetball, backpacking, photography, art appreciation, reading women's literature, the piano.

BIOGRAPHICAL/CRITICAL SOURCES: Oregonian, May, 1977; *Oregon Journal,* November 21, 1979; *Journal-American,* November 24, 1979; *Chicago Sun-Times,* November 29, 1979; *San Jose Mercury News,* November 30, 1979; *People,* January 28, 1980; *In These Times,* February 13-19, 1980.

*   *   *

UNDERWOOD, Benton J. 1915-

PERSONAL: Born February 28, 1915, in Center Point, Iowa; son of Willie B. and Blanche (Campbell) Underwood; married Hazel Louise Olson, June 1, 1939; children: Judith (Mrs. John Maples), Kathleen (Mrs. Thomas F. Olsen). *Education:* Cornell College, Mt. Vernon, Iowa, B.A., 1936; University of Missouri, M.A., 1940; University of Iowa, Ph.D., 1942. *Home:* 1745 Stevens Dr., Glenview, Ill. 60025. *Office:* Department of Psychology, Northwestern University, Evanston, Ill. 60201.

CAREER: Northwestern University, Evanston, Ill., faculty member, 1946-52, professor of psychology, 1952—. *Military service:* U.S. Naval Reserve, active duty in naval aviation psychology, 1943-46. *Member:* American Psychological Association (division president, 1960, 1970), National Academy of Sciences, American Association for the Advancement of Science, Society of Experimental Psychologists, Psychonomic Society, Midwestern Psychological Association (president, 1957). *Awards, honors:* Warren Medal from Society of Experimental Psychologists, 1964; D.Sc. from Cornell College, 1966; distinguished scientific contribution award from American Psychological Association, 1973.

WRITINGS: Psychological Research, Prentice-Hall, 1957; *Meaningfulness and Verbal Learning,* Underwood, 1960; *Experimental Psychology,* Prentice-Hall, revised edition, 1966; *Problems in Experimental Design and Influence* (workbook), Prentice-Hall, 1966; (with John J. Shaughnessy) *Experimentation in Psychology,* Wiley, 1975; *Temporal Codes for Memories: Issues and Problems,* Halsted, 1977. Editor of *American Journal of Psychology,* 1969-76.

*   *   *

UNGER-HAMILTON, Clive (Wolfgang) 1942-

PERSONAL: Born June 2, 1942, in Preston, England; son of Wolfgang (a physician) and Mori (Boursnell) Unger; married Romana Blacher (an archaeologist), December 8, 1968 (divorced); children: Felix, Ferdinand. *Education:* Attended National University of Ireland, 1961-62, and Trinity College of Music, London, 1963-66. *Home:* 8 Wendover Court, Chiltern St., London W.1, England.

CAREER: Fellow of Trinity College of Music, London, England, 1966; concert harpsichordist, 1966-70; free-lance journalist, 1970-73; writer and editor, 1977—.

WRITINGS: (Compiler) *Royal Collection,* Novello, 1977; *The Music Makers,* Abrams, 1979; *Encyclopedia of Theatre: The Entertainers,* Pitman, 1980. Also compiler of the *Victorian Christmas Song Book,* 1980.

WORK IN PROGRESS: English Folk Songs; a music and theatre encyclopedia.

V

VAIL, Priscilla L. 1931-

PERSONAL: Born November 20, 1931, in New York, N.Y.; daughter of David L. (an industrialist) and Priscilla (a psychologist; maiden name, Silver) Luke; married Donald Vail (a lawyer), July 13, 1951; children: Melissa Vail Selby, Mary B., Lucia, Angus. *Education:* Attended Vassar College, 1949-51, New York University, 1954-59, and Sarah Lawrence College, 1963-64; Manhattanville College, B.A., 1973, M.A.T., 1974. *Politics:* Republican. *Religion:* Episcopalian. *Home address:* Guard Hill Rd., Bedford, N.Y. 10506. *Office:* Rippowam-Cisqua School, Bedford, N.Y. 10506.

CAREER: Rippowam-Cisqua School, Bedford, N.Y., director of Reading Center, 1972—. *Member:* Authors Guild of Authors League of America, American Association for Gifted Children, National Orton Society (member of state board of directors), National Association of Independent Schools, Westchester Reading Council. *Awards, honors:* First prize from Independent School, 1976, for article, "The Silent Crippler: Receptive Language Disability."

WRITINGS: (With Sherry Migdail) *A Teacher's Notebook,* National Association of Independent Schools, 1977; *Reading Disability and the Gifted Child,* National Association for Gifted Children (London, England), 1978; *The World of the Gifted Child,* Walker & Co., 1979; *Improving Writing Skills,* Walker & Co., 1980. Contributor to education journals. Member of board of advisers of *Journal of the National Association for Gifted Children.*

SIDELIGHTS: Priscilla Vail told *CA:* "The role of language development (receptive and expressive) in reading comprehension and expository writing has been established in the research laboratories, but needs to be interpreted so the findings will help real live children.

"Because many children who struggle with reading disability are also bright (some gifted) it is vital to expose them to good literature, hard questions, and intriguing concepts in addition to giving them sound mechanical training for decoding and encoding.

"Teaching the gifted and the disabled is similar in many ways. Many of their needs spring from the same source, and many of their bluffs attempt to cover identical fears. With both groups, teachers and parents must see them first as children and then as children with special learning styles."

VALDEZ, Luis 1940-

PERSONAL: Born June 26, 1940; son of Francisco (a farm worker) and Armeda Valdez; married wife, Guadalupe, August 23, 1969; children: Anahuac, Kinan, Lakin. *Education:* San Jose State University, degree, 1964. *Home:* 53 Franklin St., San Juan Bautista, Calif. 95045. *Agent:* Joan Scott, Writers & Artists Agency, 450 North Roxbury, Suite 200, Beverly Hills, Calif. 90210. *Office:* 705 Fourth St., San Juan Bautista, Calif. 95045.

CAREER: Writer, actor, and director. United Farmworkers Organizing Committee, Delano, Calif., union organizer; University of California, Santa Cruz, lecturer in Chicano history and theater; University of California, Berkeley, lecturer in theater arts; El Teatro Campesino, currently artistic director. Member of California Arts Council; member of National Endowment for the Arts congressional committee for the state of the arts; member of board of directors of Theater Communications Group. Appeared in "Which Way Is Up?" a film released by Universal, 1977, and "Visions," a Public Broadcasting Service television series, 1976.

MEMBER: Writers Guild of America, Society of Stage Directors and Choreographers. *Awards, honors:* Obie award from *Village Voice,* 1968, and award from Los Angeles Drama Critics, 1972, both for El Teatro Campesino; special Emmy Award for directing from KNBC-TV, 1973; Rockefeller Foundation grant, 1978.

WRITINGS: *The Shrunken Head of Pancho Villa* (play), El Centro Campesino Cultural, 1967; *Actos* (play), Cucaracha Press, 1971; (editor with Stan Steiner) *Aztlan: An Anthology of Mexican American Literature,* Knopf, 1972; *Pensamiento serpentino: A Chicano Approach to the Theater of Reality,* Cucaracha Publications, 1973.

Unpublished plays: "La Virgen del Tepeyac"; "El Fin del Mundo"; "Zoot Suit," produced in New York, N.Y., at Winter Garden Theater, 1979.

WORK IN PROGRESS: "Tiburcio Vasquez," a play.

SIDELIGHTS: Valdez wrote: "Since 1965 I have actively pursued the creation of Chicano theater in the United States. Though Hispanic drama has been part of the American scene since 1958, it is still largely a folk cultural phenomenon. My intent is to see Chicanos participating in the mainstream of the American theater. I believe that Chicano contributions to American culture in general, coming as they do from the soon-to-be largest minority in the country, are vital and necessary to a true perception of our national reality.

"I view art as a human necessity and as a social right. Participation in any democratic society requires open and free expression, and art is the quintessence of human communication. Through the years I have endeavored in my personal and public life to make the tools of the performing arts accessible to Chicanos. El Teatro Campesino has labored as a group to learn and teach the basic techniques of the theater arts. We have worked with farm workers, students, housewives, street people, and migrant children.

"As the playwright/director of El Teatro I have concentrated on creating theater images rooted in the realities of the Southwest. Ethnic and regional as those images might be, I feel we have nevertheless penetrated through the superficial differences that separate us all into a level of universal significance. Our study of Chicano culture has led us into investigations of the entire history of America, from the mythological origins of the Mayans to the latest statistics of gang warfare in the cities. We feel we are inexorably a part of the evolution of America, and assume the right to participate as artists in the creation of its future.

"As an individual artist I feel the need to explore all the levels of consciousness that our mortal human condition provides. I am determined to use my theater to improve the lot of as many people as I can reach.

"I am fluent in English and Spanish, and believe that Anglo-Hispanic relations have been touch-and-go since the days of Queen Elizabeth I and the Spanish Armada. The entire colonization of America has pivoted on this Anglo-Hispanic crux for nearly five hundred years. History, therefore, is one of my favorite subjects, particularly the history of America. I have been to Mexico many times, as well as to Europe, and have found these travels essential to an understanding of daily life in California.

"The most persistent, undying cause in my life is the struggle of the United Farm Workers of America."

BIOGRAPHICAL/CRITICAL SOURCES: New York Times, May 4, 1978, March 26, 1979.

*   *   *

VALENTINE, Alan (Chester) 1901-1980

OBITUARY NOTICE—See index for *CA* sketch: Born February 23, 1901, in Glen Cove, N.Y.; died July 14, 1980, in Rockland, Me. Educator and author. A Rhodes scholar at Oxford's Balliol College, Valentine became president of the University of Rochester in 1935, making him one of the youngest men in the United States to ever head a major university. He had previously been a professor in the history, arts, and letters department at Yale University. He was also a director of industrial firms, railroads, and banks, and was appointed administrator of the Economic Stability Agency by President Harry S Truman in 1950 after helping to implement Truman's Marshall Plan for Europe. An athlete in his youth, Valentine won a gold medal in rugby at the 1924 Olympics in Paris. His books about American and English history include *The English Novel, The Age of Conformity,* and *Vigilante Justice.* Obituaries and other sources: *New York Times,* July 15, 1980.

*   *   *

VALENZUELA, Arturo A. 1944-

PERSONAL: Born January 23, 1944, in Concepcion, Chile; son of Raymond A. (a minister) and Dorothy B. (a therapist)

Valenzuela; married Marilyn Stoner (a psychiatric social worker), June 12, 1965; children: Jennifer Andrea, Mark Andrew. *Education:* Drew University, B.A. (summa cum laude), 1965; Columbia University, M.A., 1967, Ph.D., 1971. *Religion:* Methodist. *Residence:* Durham, N.C. *Office:* Department of Political Science, Duke University, Durham, N.C. 27706.

CAREER: Duke University, Durham, N.C., instructor, 1970-71, assistant professor, 1971-76, associate professor of political science, 1976—. Senior researcher at University of Chile, 1969; visiting fellow at University of Sussex, 1978. *Member:* American Political Science Association, Latin American Studies Association. *Awards, honors:* Danforth fellowship, 1965; Fulbright-Hays fellowship, 1968; Social Science Research Council fellowship, 1974.

WRITINGS: (Editor with J. Samuel Valenzuela, and contributor) *Chile: Politics and Society,* Transaction Books, 1976; *Political Brokers in Chile,* Duke University Press, 1977; *The Breakdown of Democratic Regimes: Chile,* Johns Hopkins Press, 1978. Contributor to political science and Latin American studies journals. Associate editor of *Latin American Research Review.*

WORK IN PROGRESS: Editing *Six Years of Military Rule in Chile; The Origins, Evolution, and Crisis of Chilean Democracy.*

*   *   *

VALENZUELA, Luisa 1938-

PERSONAL: Born November 26, 1938, in Buenos Aires, Argentina; daughter of Pablo Francisco (a physician) and Luisa Mercedes (a writer; maiden name, Levinson) Valenzuela; divorced; children: Anna-Lisa. *Education:* University of Buenos Aires, B.A. *Home address:* c/o Drenka Willen, 17 Charlton St., New York, N.Y. 10014.

CAREER: La Nacion, Buenos Aires, Argentina, editor, 1961-72; free-lance writer for magazines and newspapers in Buenos Aires, Argentina, 1972-78; Columbia University, New York, N.Y., writer-in-residence, 1979—. *Awards, honors:* Awards from Fondo Nacional de las Artes, 1966 and 1973, and Instituto Nacional de Cinematografia, 1973, for script based on novel, *Hay que sonreir.*

WRITINGS—In English: *Hay que sonreir* (novel), Americalee, 1966, translation by Hortense Carpentier and J. Jorge Castello contained in *Clara: Thirteen Short Stories and a Novel* (also see below), Harcourt, 1976; *Los hereticos* (stories), Paidos, 1967, translation by Carpentier and Castello contained in *Clara: Thirteen Short Stories and a Novel,* Harcourt, 1976; *Strange Things Happen Here: Twenty-Six Short Stories and a Novel,* translation by Helen Lane, Harcourt, 1979.

Other: *El gato eficaz* (novel), Joaquin Mortiz, 1972; *Aqui pasan Cosas raras* (stories), Ediciones de la Flor, 1976; *Como en la guerra?* (novel), Sudamericana, 1977.

WORK IN PROGRESS: Cronica de los diablos, a novel; *El embajador y la Bella,* a novel.

SIDELIGHTS: Luisa Valenzuela is presently living in Manhattan, and spending long periods in Mexico, lecturing on Latin American and Argentine literature and organizing writers' workshops in Spanish.

*   *   *

VALIANI, Leo 1909-

PERSONAL: Born February 9, 1909, in Fiume, Italy (now

part of Yugoslavia); son of Adolfo (in business) and Margherita (Geller) Valiani; married Nidia Pancini, September 29, 1945; children: Rolando. *Politics:* Republican. *Religion:* Jewish. *Office:* Via Brera 3, Milan 20121, Italy.

CAREER: Bank employee, 1924-36; arrested for opposition to fascism, 1928; journalist, 1936—; *Corriere della Sera,* Milan, Italy, editorialist, 1970—. Member of Italian Senate, 1980. *Military service:* Italian Army, 1943-45; became lieutenant colonel. *Awards, honors:* Named honorary citizen of Milan, Italy, 1975; journalism awards include Premio Sala Stampa from Milan, 1979.

WRITINGS: Dall'antifascismo alla resistenza, Feltrinelli, 2nd edition, 1960; *Il partito socialista italiano nel periodo della neutralita, 1914-1915* (title means "The Italian Socialist Party in the Period of Neutrality, 1914-1915"), Feltrinelli, 1963, new edition, 1977; *La dissoluzione dell'Austria-Ungheria,* Il Saggiatore, 1966, translation by Eric Mosbacher published as *The End of Austria-Hungary,* Knopf, 1973; *L'Historiographie de l'Italie contemporaine* (title means "Historiography of Contemporary Italy"), Droz, 1968; *Questioni di storia del socialismo* (title means "Problems of the History of Socialism"), Einaudi, 1975; *La lotta sociale e l'avventto della democrazia in Italia, 1876-1915* (title means "Social Struggle and the Beginning of Democracy in Italy"), Unione Tipografia Editrice Torivese, 1976; *La sinistra democratica in Italia,* Edizioni della Voce, 1977. Author of "La storia," a column in *L'Espresso,* 1956-77. Coeditor of *Rivista storica italiano.*

SIDELIGHTS: Valiani has been active in the anti-fascist movement in Italy and abroad. He speaks six languages and has traveled widely over the world.

* * *

VALIN, Jonathan Louis 1948-

PERSONAL: Born November 23, 1948, in Cincinnati, Ohio; son of Sigmund and Marcella (Fink) Valin; married Katherine Brockhaus (a poet), January 3, 1971. *Education:* University of Chicago, M.A., 1974; doctoral study at Washington University, St. Louis, Mo., 1976-79. *Agent:* Dominick Abel Literary Agency, 498 West End Ave., New York, N.Y. 10024.

CAREER: University of Cincinnati, Cincinnati, Ohio, lecturer in English, 1974-76; Washington University, St. Louis, Mo., lecturer in English, 1976-79; writer, 1979—. *Member:* Mystery Writers of America, Modern Language Association of America. *Awards, honors:* Norma Lowry Memorial Fund Prize, 1978, for "Replay."

WRITINGS—Novels; all published by Dodd: *The Lime Pit,* 1980; *Final Notice,* 1980; *Full Fathom Five,* 1981; *The Celestial Railroad,* 1981; *The Winter's Tale,* 1982.

Work represented in anthologies, including *Subject to Change,* 1978. Contributor to *Writer.*

WORK IN PROGRESS: "The Franchiser," a film script; short stories.

* * *

VANDER LUGT, Herbert 1920-

PERSONAL: Born January 7, 1920, in Ogilvie, Minn.; son of Tunis (a worker) and Henrietta (Droug) Vander Lugt; married Virginia Bosworth, June 16, 1941; children: Daniel Neal, Catherine Jean. *Education:* Attended Moody Bible Institute, Grand Rapids Bible College, and Grand Rapids Theological Seminary. *Politics:* Independent. *Home:* 7240 68th St., Caledonia, Mich. 49316. *Office:* Radio Bible Class, Grand Rapids, Mich. 49555.

CAREER: Pastor of Baptist churches in Carson City, Nev., 1948-50, Zeeland, Mich., 1950-59, and various other cities; associated with Radio Bible Class, Grand Rapids, Mich., 1967—. Holds Bible seminars; guest on television programs. *Military service:* U.S. Army, Medical Corps, 1943-46; became technical sergeant. *Member:* Haiti Baptist Mission Society (past president).

WRITINGS: (With Richard DeHaan) *Satan, Satanism, and Witchcraft,* Zondervan, 1972; (with DeHaan) *Wonderful Difficult Years,* Victor, 1973; (with DeHaan) *The Art of Staying Off Dead-End Street,* Victor, 1974; (with DeHaan) *Good News for Bad Times,* Victor, 1975; (with Carl Smith) *As the Ushers Come Forward,* Radio Bible Class, 1976; (with DeHaan) *Studies in Second Peter,* Victor, 1977; *Light in the Valley,* Radio Bible Class, 1977; *Would a Good Rock Lie?,* Radio Bible Class, 1978; (with DeHaan) *King in Your Castle,* Radio Bible Class, 1978; *God's Plan in All the Ages: The Kingdom and Redemption From Genesis to Revelation,* Zondervan, 1980. Also author of *The Book in Review* and *The Gift of Tongues.* Contributor to *Discovery Digest.* Contributing editor of *Our Daily Bread.*

SIDELIGHTS: Vander Lugt began his ministry at the age of eighteen, preaching in Grand Rapids jails, mission halls, and on street corners. During World War II his evaluation of Scripture interpretation changed his theological viewpoint and led him to Moody Bible Institute.

He writes: "From boyhood I took a keen interest in social conditions and the Christian religion. I wrote articles on democratic socialism while in school and felt a deep sense of concern for the plight of the masses. I had an underlying feeling of a call to the ministry which couldn't be answered because of the financial plight of the family. I was the oldest of eight boys in a poor home during the Depression. My interest in the problems of the poor is still present, but my vocation lies in the spiritual rather than physical-material realm."

* * *

VAN GOETHEM, Larry 1934-

PERSONAL: Surname is pronounced van *Goth*-em; born April 13, 1934, in Goodman, Wis.; son of Victor (a merchant) and Martha (Bauer) Van Goethem; married Bette Mae Gillespie (a clerical worker), July 21, 1956; children: Heidi, Wendy, Laurie. *Education:* Attended Los Angeles State College and El Camino College. *Home and office address:* Star Route, White Lake, Wis. 54491. *Agent:* Julian Bach Literary Agency, Inc., 747 Third Ave., New York, N.Y. 10017.

CAREER: Writer. Worked as reporter and editor at newspapers in Maryland, Delaware, and Wisconsin; currently owns and operates news feature service. *Military service:* U.S. Marine Corps, 1953-57. *Awards, honors:* Award from American Political Science Association, 1971, for reporting.

WRITINGS: The Fifth Horseman Is Riding, Macmillan, 1974. Also author of *Not Long Ago* (nonfiction), 1979. Contributor to magazines, including *Reader's Digest, Travel and Leisure,* and *National Wildlife,* and newspapers.

WORK IN PROGRESS: The Great Escape: So You Want to Get Away, "a look at how Americans perceive and pursue the good life by escaping to simpler lives in rural or wild regions of America."

SIDELIGHTS: Van Goethem wrote: "I consider myself a craftsman like a bricklayer or carpenter, with this difference:

I string words together, and there are an infinite number of ways to do this. My philosophy as a journalist and writer is that most readers are not interested in much information, as such, but in how it's presented. The trouble with many publications is that they become so slick (or smooth) that vital style differences and individual inflections are edited out. Today's writer is faced with a market that is dominated, shaped, and often aimed by editors. What this means is that most writers seldom have much opportunity, unless they're writing books, to write the way they want to write.

"It's my feeling that the article or essay of today is locked in such a seamless structural vise that the best writers may be rewarded less than the merely competent. As a writer I am concerned that most of my best work for magazines is done without sponsor—and generally is the most difficult to sell. I believe the problem is that editors and writers alike must work to avoid making publications so slick that they lose their vitality in committee."

* * *

van HERK, Aritha 1954-

PERSONAL: Born May 26, 1954, in Wetaskiwin, Alberta, Canada; daughter of Willem (a farmer) and Maretje (van Dam) van Herk; married Robert Jay Sharp (a geologist), September 14, 1974. *Education:* University of Alberta, B.A. (with honors), 1976, M.A., 1978. *Residence:* Calgary, Alberta, Canada. *Agent:* Virginia Barber Literary Agency, Inc., 44 Greenwich Ave., New York, N.Y. 10011.

CAREER: Writer.

WRITINGS: Judith (novel), Little, Brown, 1978; (editor with Rudy Wiebe) *More Stories From Western Canada,* Macmillan, 1980. Contributing editor of *Branching Out.*

SIDELIGHTS: Aritha van Herk writes: "I believe that all writers are regionalists, that writers have a definite moral responsibility to recreate a world they know well for their readers. I write unashamedly about my place, my time, and the immediate world of western Canada. I am a feminist, although my writing is not at all feminist propaganda. *Judith* is being translated into Dutch, French, German, Italian, and Finnish."

* * *

Van STEENWYK, Elizabeth Ann 1928-

PERSONAL: Born July 1, 1928, in Galesburg, Ill.; daughter of Wilson Andrew and Edith Viola Harler; married Donald H. Van Steenwyk (an executive), June 12, 1949; children: Kedrin, Matthew, Brett, Gretchen. *Education:* Knox College, B.A., 1950. *Politics:* Republican. *Religion:* Methodist. *Home and office:* 885 Chester Ave., San Marino, Calif. 91108.

CAREER: WGIL-Radio, Galesburg, Ill., producer, 1948-51; KTSM-TV, El Paso, Tex., producer, 1951-52; writer. President of Cardiac League, Guild of Huntington Memorial Hospital. *Member:* International P.E.N., Society of Children's Book Writers, Phi Beta.

WRITINGS—Children's books: Dorothy Hamill, Olympic Champion, Harvey House, 1976; *Women in Sports: Figure Skating,* Harvey House, 1976; *The Best Horse,* Scholastic Book Services, 1977; *Larry Mahan,* Grosset, 1977; *Barrel Horse Racer,* Walker & Co., 1977; *Women in Sports: Rodeo,* Harvey House, 1978; *Mystery at Beach Bay,* Bowmar, 1978; *Ride to Win,* Bowmar, 1978; *Cameo of a Champion,* McGraw, 1978; *Fly Like an Eagle,* Walker & Co., 1978; *Rivals on Ice,* Albert Whitman, 1978; *Illustrated Dictionary of*

Skating, Harvey House, 1979; *Presidents at Home,* Messner, 1980; *Tracy Austin,* Childrens Press, 1980; *Quarter Horse Winner,* Albert Whitman, 1980; *Stars on Ice,* Dodd, 1980; *Illustrated Dictionary on Riding,* Harvey House, 1981. Contributor of more than one hundred articles and stories to magazines.

WORK IN PROGRESS: The Witness Tree, a fictional story of a migrant worker's son trying to find a place to which he can belong; *Amusement Park Science,* a technical approach to theme parks.

SIDELIGHTS: Van Steenwyk told *CA:* "Why do I write for children? I can sum it up in the words of a child who wrote to me after reading one of my books. She said, 'Happiness must be writing children's books.' I wonder how she knew? Simply, I write for young readers because there are so many more possibilities than limitations."

The Best Horse was made into a motion picture by Learning Corporation of America in 1979.

* * *

Van VLECK, David B. 1929-

PERSONAL: Born July 11, 1929, in Montclair, N.J.; son of Joseph (a teacher) and Mary (McLain) Van Vleck; married Eunice Amelia Holt, June 19, 1951; children: Carolyn, David B., Jr., Sarah. *Education:* Princeton University, B.A., 1951; Cornell University, M.S., 1960, Ph.D., 1963. *Home address:* R.D.2, Middlebury, Vt. 05753.

CAREER: Teacher of mathematics and science in Windsor, Conn., 1954-58; University of Miami, Coral Gables, Fla., assistant professor of biology, 1963-68; Middlebury College, Middlebury, Vt., associate professor of biology, 1968-72; Middlebury Union High School, Middlebury, biology teacher, 1973—. Vice-chairman of local Regional Planning Commission. *Military service:* U.S. Navy, aerographer, 1952-54. *Member:* American Association for the Advancement of Science, American Society of Mammalogists, American Forestry Association, Zero Population Growth (member of national board of directors), Sigma Xi.

WRITINGS: How and Why Not to Have That Baby, Paul Eriksson, 1971; *The Crucial Generation,* Optimum Population, 1974.

SIDELIGHTS: Van Vleck wrote: "I have been interested in human population growth and conservation of natural resources for thirty years. William Vogt's *Road to Survival* and *People, People, People* got me started. As a graduate student I did considerable amounts of reading and research on rodent populations. Since then I have written and spoken in public about the need for Zero Population Growth. With a little luck and intense effort, I believe the world's population will reach a minimum of ten billion. What this will mean in terms of military, social, political, and economic changes is anybody's guess, given the obvious impacts on natural resources and effects from pollution. If the world's leaders would recognize population growth and lack of energy as the prime problems and try to solve them instead of solving symptoms of the problems, I would be more optimistic about the future."

* * *

Van ZANTEN, John W(illiam) 1913-

PERSONAL: Born March 12, 1913, in Metuchen, N.J.; son of John W., Sr. (a minister) and Margaret Zabriskie (Pockman) Van Zanten; married Julia Porter Blossom, September 15, 1939; children: John W. III, David T., Julia P. Van Zanten Mansfield, Margo Z. Van Zanten Schuttenberg, Jacqueline L. *Education:* Williams College, A.B., 1935; Union Theological Seminary, New York, N.Y., M.Div., 1939. *Politics:* Independent. *Home:* 201 North Swarthmore Ave., Swarthmore, Pa. 19081.

CAREER: Ordained Presbyterian minister, 1939; professional actor in New York, N.Y., 1934-36; pastor of Congregational churches in Deansboro, N.Y., and Sherburne, N.Y., 1939-45; pastor of Presbyterian churches in Roslyn, N.Y., 1945-58, and Riverdale, N.Y., 1958-62; Board of Christian Education, United Presbyterian Church, U.S.A., Philadelphia, Pa., administrator of continuing education for ministers, 1962-70; First Presbyterian Church, Englewood, N.J., senior pastor, 1970-79; writer 1979—.

WRITINGS: Caught in the Act: Modern Drama as Prelude to the Gospel, Westminster, 1971.

SIDELIGHTS: Van Zanten told *CA:* "I turn to the artists and writers of our time to indicate the nature of the new culture. They are a kind of advance warning system. They suggest the new social structures that are even now being formed as the old structures fade away. Artists and writers, as people of imagination and insight, do not give complete answers, but they provide the most provocative 'hints' of what is in store for Western humanity. It is our task to listen to them, look at their works, and ponder their responses to experience. They tell us what it 'feels like' to be alive today. Our leaders tend to propose solutions that worked in past years but fail today. I feel it is my task to struggle with the images and imaginings of the creative people in order to be somewhat at home in this rapidly changing age. It is only as we become part of a 'critical mass'—sharing in the thoughts and responses of the artists and writers—that our minds and imaginations come alive and we have something of value to reveal."

*   *   *

VARLEY, Gloria   1932-

PERSONAL: Born March 31, 1932, in Toronto, Ontario, Canada; daughter of Harry Clive and Gladys Marion (Sexsmith) Mitchell; married Charles E. Israel (a novelist and screenwriter), September 23, 1979; children: (from previous marriage) Michael. *Education:* Ryerson Polytechnical Institute, diploma, 1953; attended McGill University, 1957; University of Toronto, B.A., 1977. *Home and office:* 31 Walmer Rd., Town House #6, Toronto, Ontario, Canada M5R 2W7.

CAREER: CBC-Radio, Montreal, Quebec, production assistant, 1953-55; *Toronto Telegram,* Toronto, Ontario, in promotion, 1955-56; Montreal General Hospital, Montreal, research secretary in psychiatry, 1957-59; Harris Advertising, Miami, Fla., assistant secretary, 1959-60; Copp Clark (publisher), Toronto, Ontario, promotion supervisor in Educational Division, 1960-65; free-lance writer, editor, and photostylist in Toronto, Ontario, 1965—. Free-lance biographical researcher for National Gallery of Canada project. *Member:* Writers' Union of Canada, Periodical Writers Association of Canada, Canadian Civil Liberties Association, Canadian Association for Repeal of Abortion Laws, Royal Horticultural Society, Art Gallery of Ontario.

WRITINGS: To Be a Dancer, Peter Martin Associates, 1971.

Work represented in anthologies, including *Peter Gzowski's Spring Tonic,* Hurtig, 1979. Monthly contributor to *Canadian,* 1975-79. Contributor to magazines, including *Chatelaine, Toronto Calendar, City, Today Magazine,* and *Canada Green,* and newspapers.

WORK IN PROGRESS: Two books on food and social history.

SIDELIGHTS: Varley told *CA:* "The world presents each of us with an amazing number of things to be curious about. Writing (whether fact or fiction) offers both a means of exploring the territory and of discovering—with enormous luck—a few more questions." *Avocational interests:* Medicine, bioethics, psychology and parapsychology, dream research, travel, wine and food.

*   *   *

VAUGHN, Stephen L.   1947-

PERSONAL: Born January 3, 1947, in Poplar Bluff, Mo.; son of William Jackson (in business) and Flaulein (a teacher; maiden name, Riddle) Vaughn; married Beverly Mullen (a writer), June 15, 1974; children: William Eugene. *Education:* Southeast Missouri State University, B.A., 1968; Indiana University, M.A., 1970, Ph.D., 1977. *Office:* Organization of American Historians, 112 North Bryan, Bloomington, Ind. 47401.

CAREER: Organization of American Historians, Bloomington, Ind., historical assistant to executive secretary and editor of *Newsletter,* 1977—, associate editor of *Journal of American History,* 1979—. Assistant professor at Indiana University, 1977-79. *Military service:* U.S. Army. *Member:* American Historical Association, U.S. Handball Association. *Awards, honors:* International fellowship from University of Toronto, 1974-75.

WRITINGS: Holding Fast the Inner Lines: Democracy, Nationalism, and the Committee on Public Information, University of North Carolina Press, 1980. Also editor of *Diaries of Guy Stanton Ford.*

WORK IN PROGRESS: A History of American Nationalism in the Twentieth Century; The Value of Historical Study; research on Walter Lippmann and the writing of *Public Opinion* and on Guy Stanton Ford and the image of German autocracy.

SIDELIGHTS: Vaughn commented: "*Holding Fast the Inner Lines* grew out of my interest in American nationalsim and how the United States has defined the citizen's responsibility to the state. In terms of personal interests outside history, at one point in my career I had aspirations to become a professional athlete and was, in fact, drafted to play professional baseball by the Chicago White Sox. I currently play handball and have been runner-up in both the state singles and doubles tournaments during the past two years."

*   *   *

VENNEMA, Alje   1932-

PERSONAL: Born August 11, 1932, in Leeuwarden, Netherlands; naturalized Canadian citizen, 1956; came to United States, 1974; son of Sytze and Tryntje (Hiemstra) Vennema. *Education:* Western Reserve University (now Case Western Reserve University), B.A., 1958; McGill University, M.D., C.M., 1962; Medical College of Canada, L.M.C.C., 1964; Tulane University, M.P.H.-T.M., 1969; attended Hammersmith Post-Graduate Medical School, 1969; Welsh National School of Medicine, D.T.C.D., 1970; University of London, M.S., 1973, and graduate study. *Home:* 136 East 36th St., New York, N.Y. 10016. *Office:* New York City Bureau of Tuberculosis, 93 Worth St., New York, N.Y. 10013.

CAREER: Farmhand in Hamilton, Ontario, 1951-52; Royal Victoria Hospital, Montreal, Quebec, intern, 1962-63; Cottage Hospital, Newfoundland, medical officer, 1963-64; Provincial Hospital, Quang Ngai, South Vietnam, team captain of Care-Medico volunteer medical team, 1964-65, technical adviser to government of South Vietnam, 1965-66, director of Canadian medical assistance to South Vietnam, 1966-68; University of Dar-es-Salaam, Dar-es-Salaam, Tanzania, lecturer in community medicine, 1970-72; University of London, London School of Hygiene and Tropical Medicine and London School of Economics and Political Science, London, England, research analyst in department of demography; Charity Hospital, New Orleans, La., resident in pediatrics, 1974-75; New York University, New York City, lecturer in pulmonary pathology, 1975—, resident in pediatrics at Medical Center, 1975-76, chief resident, 1976-77, assistant professor of clinical pediatrics, 1977—. Tuberculosis consultant at Muhimbill General Hospital, 1970-72; honorary lecturer at Tulane University, 1974-75; medical director of Tom Dooley Memorial Hospital, Pua, Thailand, 1975—; director of New York City Bureau of Tuberculosis, 1977—; director of pediatric education at New York Infirmary Hospital, 1978—; attending physician at Bellevue Hospital and New York Infirmary Hospital. Member of board of directors of Tom Dooley Heritage, Inc.

MEMBER: International Union Against Tuberculosis, American Thoracic Society, American Lung Association, Canadian Medical Association, Canadian Tuberculosis and Respiratory Disease Association, Ontario Medical Association, Nutrition Today Society (founding member), Trudeau Society. *Awards, honors:* Order of Merit from Government of South Vietnam, 1965; Order of Distinguished Service to the Vietnamese People, 1968; Order of Canada, 1966; Canadian centenary medal of service, 1967.

WRITINGS: (With J. B. Neilands, Orians, Pfeiffer, and Westing) *Harvest of Death,* Free Press, 1972; *The Viet Cong Massacre at Hue,* Vantage, 1975. Contributor to medical journals.

WORK IN PROGRESS: Research on population growth in seven areas of Tanzania, 1967-71, the prevalence and diagnosis of atypical mycobacterial infections, the risk of tuberculosis infection in the New York City population, resistant cases of tuberculosis in New York City, tuberculosis in New York City children, and nonefficiency of the Tine Test in pediatric health studies in New York City.

SIDELIGHTS: Vennema told *CA:* "My work in Africa concerned itself primarily with delivering better medical care and involvement in updating public health services. My work in tuberculosis led to the development of a national tuberculosis program for Tanzania. The work on population growth concerned itself with the development of better, more reliable statistics concerning fertility and mortality. To develop basic health services these crucial statistics are required.

"My work in Vietnam concerned also the development of medical services as well as the improvement of public health services. My involvement in tuberculosis work led directly to the creation of a provincial tuberculosis program which continues to function to this date in the province of Quang Ngai.

"My book *Harvest of Death* concerns biological and chemical warfare. My work on this, and that of other authors led to the Nixon Administration's passing of anti-chemical warfare legislation. Tragically, the Defense Department continues to work with these substances. Hopefully, the substances we investigated and described will never be used on the human race. The book on Hue deals with the lesser known aspect of the Tet offensive and describes the tragic happenings in the

months of February and March, 1968, around the City of Hue."

*   *   *

VERIN, Velko
    See INKIOW, (Janakiev) Dimiter

*   *   *

VERNON, Eddie
    See STONE, Hoyt E(dward)

*   *   *

VIANSSON-PONTE, Pierre   1920-1979

PERSONAL: Born August 2, 1920, in Clisson, France; died of cancer, May 7, 1979, in Paris, France; son of Henry and Laure (Beneyton) Viansson-Ponte; married Jeanne Coyne, 1942; children: Francoise-Charlotte. *Education:* Attended University of Strasbourg and University of Nancy, received LL.D., 1940; also did graduate work in political science at Institute d'Etudes Politiques. *Home:* 5 Place Paul Painleve, Paris 5e, France. *Office:* Le Monde, 5 rue des Italiens, Paris 9, France.

CAREER: Journalist affiliated with Agence France-Presse, 1945-51; *L'Express,* Paris, France, founder with Jean-Jacques Servan-Schreiber and Francoise Giroud, 1953, editor-in-chief, 1953-58; *Le Monde,* Paris, head of domestic political section, senior analyst and commentator, 1958-69, assistant editor-in-chief, 1969-72, columnist and editorial adviser, 1972-79. Also taught journalism and participated in radio panels. *Wartime service:* French Army, 1940; later joined French Underground. *Awards, honors:* Received War Cross and Medal of Resistance.

WRITINGS: Risques et chance de la veme Republique, Plon, 1959; *Les Gaullistes, rituel et annuaire,* Editions du Seuil, 1963, translation by Elaine P. Halperin published as *The King and His Court,* Houghton, 1965; *Les Politiques,* Calmann-Levy, 1967; *Des Jours entre les jours: Chroniques,* Stock, 1974; *Lettre ouverte aux hommes politiques,* A. Michel, 1976. Also author of a book on cancer, *Changer la Mort* (title means "How to Change Dying"). Contributor of political comment to two Parisian dailies, and of articles to international publications, including *New York Times.*

OBITUARIES: New York Times, May 8, 1979.*

*   *   *

VICKERY, Donald M(ichael)   1944-

PERSONAL: Born August 22, 1944, in Brookhaven, Miss.; son of Raymond Ezekiel and Clarene Helen Vickery; married Shelley Lawrence, June 24, 1966; children: Meredith Reid, Andrew Dickens. *Education:* Harvard University, B.A. (cum laude), 1965, M.D., 1969. *Home:* 11917 Richland Lane, Herndon, Va. 22070. *Office:* Center for Consumer Health Education, 380 West Maple Ave., Vienna, Va. 22180.

CAREER: Georgetown University Community Health Plan, Washington, D.C., special assistant for clinical systems, 1973-74, health services director, 1974-75; Georgetown University School of Medicine, Washington, D.C., instructor, 1974-77; Medical College of Virginia, associate professor, 1975—; Center for Consumer Health Education, Vienna, Va., president and chairman of board, 1976—; Georgetown University, Washington, D.C., assistant professor, 1979—. Member of staff of MITRE Corp., 1975-77. Member of national advisory council of Boys' Clubs of America; consultant to Health Care Delivery Research and Consumer Health

Education, 1973—. *Military service:* U.S. Army, 1971-73; became captain. *Member:* American College of Physicians, American Federation for Clinical Research, American Public Health Association, Group Health Association, Society for Advanced Medical Systems (member of board of directors, 1980), Fairfax County Medical Society. *Awards, honors:* American Medical Writers Association award, 1978, for *Taking Care of Your Child: A Parents Guide to Medical Care.*

WRITINGS: Triage: Problem-Oriented Sorting of Patients, Robert J. Brady, 1975; (with J. F. Fries) *Take Care of Yourself: A Consumer's Guide to Medical Care,* Addison-Wesley, 1976; (with Fries and R. L. Pantel) *Taking Care of Your Child: A Parent's Guide to Medical Care,* Addison-Wesley, 1977; (contributor) A. I. Wertheimer and P. J. Bush, editors, *Perspectives on Medicines in Society,* Drug Intelligence Publications, 1977; *Life Plan for Your Health,* Addison-Wesley, 1978. Contributor to medical journals.

WORK IN PROGRESS: A revision of *Take Care of Yourself* with Fries and Donald M. Vickery.

*   *   *

VINGE, Vernor (Steffen) 1944-

PERSONAL: Surname is pronounced *Vin*-jee; born October 2, 1944, in Waukesha, Wis.; son of Clarence Lloyd (a professor of geography) and Ada Grace (a geographer; maiden name, Rowlands) Vinge. *Education:* Michigan State University, B.S., 1966; University of California, San Diego, M.A., 1968, Ph.D., 1971. *Agent:* Lea Braff, Jarvis, Braff, 133 Seventh Ave., Brooklyn, N.Y. 11215. *Office:* Department of Mathematic Sciences, San Diego State University, San Diego, Calif. 92182.

CAREER: San Diego State University, San Diego, Calif., assistant, professor, 1972-78, associate professor of mathematics, 1978—. *Member:* Science Fiction Writers of America, American Mathematical Society.

WRITINGS—Science fiction novels: *Grimm's World,* Berkley Publishing, 1969; *The Witling,* DAW Books, 1976. Contributor to magazines, including *New Worlds* and *Analog.*

AVOCATIONAL INTERESTS: Astronomy.

*   *   *

VINSON, Rex Thomas 1935-
(Vincent King)

PERSONAL: Born October 22, 1935, in Falmouth, England; son of Ernest Leonard (a builder) and Irene (Verran) Vinson; married Jean Blackler, 1961 (divorced, 1978); children: Mark, Kay. *Education:* Attended Falmouth College of Art, 1952-57, West England College of Art, 1959-60, and University of London, 1960-62. *Politics:* "Contemptuous." *Home:* Rollestone, 94 Albany Rd., Redruth, Cornwall, England. *Agent:* Leslie Flood, E. J. Carnell Literary Agency, Rowneybury Bungalow, Sawbridgeworth, near Old Harlow, Essex CM20 1EX, England.

CAREER: College of Art, Newcastle-upon-Tyne, England, lecturer in drawing, painting, and printmaking, 1963-68; Redruth County Grammar School, Redruth, England, art teacher and department head, 1968—. Lecturer; exhibits paintings and prints. *Member:* Artists International Association, Penwith Society of Artists.

WRITINGS—Science fiction novels; all under pseudonym Vincent King: *Light a Last Candle,* Ballantine, 1969; *Another End,* Ballantine, 1971; *Candy Man,* Ballantine, 1971.

Work represented in anthologies, including *New Writings in Science Fiction No. 9,* Dobson, 1966; *Timesnake and Superclown,* Ballantine.

WORK IN PROGRESS: The Age of Miracles, a novel.

SIDELIGHTS: Vinson commented: "I hope to be paid for what I write—so I suppose does everyone—and that's my basic motivation. But the serious will creep in. I am appalled by how badly (and for the wrong reasons) things are done—politics, organization, education, world affairs—just about everything. It's mostly by default, but 'the bastards on top' will do anything to anyone and then ask you to thank 'em for it! But there *are* good things—things could be better; hence, more motivation. I admire efficiency and skill, lucid prose, and craftsmanship."

Vinson's books have been published in France, Germany, Denmark, Spain, and Italy.

AVOCATIONAL INTERESTS: Etching, painting, gliding, chess, fishing, blues and jazz music, pottery, prints.

*   *   *

VLADECK, Bruce C. 1949-

PERSONAL: Born September 13, 1949, in New York, N.Y.; son of Stephen C. (an attorney) and Judith P. (an attorney) Vladeck; married Fredda Wellin (a social worker), August 5, 1973; children: Elizabeth, Stephen. *Education:* Harvard University, B.A. (magna cum laude), 1970; University of Michigan, M.A., 1972, Ph.D., 1973. *Home:* 3 Timber Rd., East Brunswick, N.J. 08816. *Office:* Division of Health Planning and Resources Development, New Jersey State Department of Health, P.O. Box 1540, Trenton, N.J. 08625.

CAREER: Rand Institute, New York City, associate social scientist, 1973-74; Columbia University, New York City, assistant professor, 1974-78, associate professor of public health and political science, 1978-79; New Jersey State Department of Health, Trenton, assistant commissioner in Division of Health Planning and Resources Development, 1979—. Guest lecturer at New York University, Massachusetts Institute of Technology, University of Pittsburgh, University of Massachusetts, and New School for Social Research; testified before U.S. House of Representatives. Member of New York State Health Advisory Council and research project director for Twentieth Century Fund, 1977-79; member of New York State Council on Health Care Financing, 1978; past member of American Blood Commission and New York State Health Planning Commission; consultant to RAND Corp. and U.S. Department of Health, Education and Welfare.

WRITINGS: (Contributor) Kenneth S. Friedman and Stuart H. Rakoff, editors, *Towards a National Health Policy: Public Policy and the Control of Health Care Costs,* Lexington Books, 1977; (contributor) Curtis J. Tompkins and L. E. Grayson, editors, *Management of Public Sector and Non-Profit Organizations,* Holden-Day, 1978; *Unloving Care: The Nursing Home Tragedy,* Basic Books, 1980. Contributor of about a dozen articles to political science and health care journals and popular magazines, including *Change.*

BIOGRAPHICAL/CRITICAL SOURCES: New York Times Book Review, April 6, 1980; *Washington Post Book World,* June 29, 1980.

*   *   *

VOGEL, Jerry 1896(?)-1980

OBITUARY NOTICE: Born c. 1896; died June 5, 1980, in the

Bronx, N.Y. Music publisher. Jerry Vogel is credited with introducing the listening public to such old favorites as "Melancholy Baby," "Shine on Harvest Moon," "Twelfth Street Rag," and "Take Me Out to the Ball Game." He was also a dedicated humanitarian who regularly visited hospitalized and underprivileged children, distributing comic books and candy to lift their spirits. His reported yearly shipment of several thousand parcels of candy and other assorted delectables to children across the country accordingly earned him the nickname of the "Candy King." Obituaries and other sources: *New York Times*, June 9, 1980.

* * *

VOLIN, Michael 1911-

PERSONAL: Born August 12, 1911, in China; son of Nicolas (a diplomat) and Nina (Firsoff) Volin; married wife, Nina, August 3, 1948 (divorced); married Daphne Elisabeth Hewson, August 3, 1979; children: Irene, Owen, Michael, Jr. *Religion:* Christian. *Home and office address:* Gedney St., Apt. 6-R, Nyack, N.Y. 10960.

CAREER: Journalist, lecturer, and physical culturist.

WRITINGS: (With Nancy Phelan) *Yoga for Beauty*, Pelham, 1966; (with Phelan) *Essence of Yoga*, Digmoer's, 1967; (with Phelan) *Yoga for Women*, Harper, 1968; (with Phelan) *Yoga Over Forty*, Harper, 1969; (with Phelan) *Sex and Yoga*, Harper, 1970; *Challenging the Years: A Book of Ancient Wisdom and Modern Knowledge for Health and Long Life*, Harper, 1979. Also author of *Growing Up with Yoga, Yoga Breathing, The Quiet Hour*, and *Immortality*.

WORK IN PROGRESS: Man From Somewhere Else.

SIDELIGHTS: A former athlete and champion runner, Volin has worked as a physical culturist and lecturer in India, Australia, and New York City. His current interest is gerontology, specifically ancient and modern ideas for delaying the aging process. *Avocational interests:* Travel, surfing, swimming, diving.

BIOGRAPHICAL/CRITICAL SOURCES: Harvey Day, *Yoga Illustrated Dictionary*, Emerson, 1971.

* * *

von FRISCH, Otto 1929-

PERSONAL: Born December 13, 1929, in Munich, Germany; son of Karl and Margarethe (Mohr) von Frisch; married Heide Franke-Stehmann, 1960; children: Barbara, Julian. *Education:* University of Munich, Ph.D., 1957. *Religion:* Lutheran. *Home:* Braunschweigerstrasse 9, 3304 Wendeburg, Niedersachsen, West Germany. *Office:* Naturhistorisches Museum, Pockelsstrasse 10a, 3300 Braunschweig, Niedersachsen, West Germany.

CAREER: Naturhistorisches Museum, Braunschweig, West Germany, assistant, 1959-65, assistant director, 1965-77, director, 1977—. *Member:* German Zoological Society, Society to Protect European Otter (chairman), Rotary International. *Awards, honors:* German Youth Book Prize, 1973.

WRITINGS—In English; juvenile: *Animal Migration*, McGraw, 1969; *Animal Camouflage*, F. Watts, 1973; (with father, Karl von Frisch) *Animal Architecture*, Harcourt, 1974; (with Anne Folsom) *The American Bestiary*, Harcourt, 1976.

In German: *Spaziergang mit Tobby: Tierkinder wachsen auf Gesellschaft der Naturfreunde* (title means "Walk With Tobby"), Franckh, 1963; *Der Grosse Brachvogel (Numenius arquata L.)* (title means "The Great Curlew"), Z. Ziemsen,

1964; *Bei seltenen Voegeln in Moor und Steppe* (title means "Rare Birds in Marshes and Deserts"), Parey, 1965; *Alle Taschen voller Tiere* (title means "All Pockets Filled With Animals"), Parey, 1966; *Tierwelt voller Wunder: Saeugetiere, Voegel, Fische, Amphibien, Reptilien* (title means "Wonder of Animal Life"), J. F. Schreiber, 1967; *Saeugetiere* (title means "Mammals"), J. F. Schreiber, 1967; *Voegel* (title means "Birds"), J. F. Schreiber, 1967; *Fische, Amphibien, Reptilien* (title means "Fishes, Amphibians, and Reptiles"), J. F. Schreiber, 1967; *Findelkinder: Tips fuer Aufzucht und Pflege von Jungsvoegeln* (title means "A Guide for Rearing and Keeping of Young Birds"), Franckh, 1968; *Tarnkappe der Tiere: Insekten, Saeugetiere und Fische, Amphibien, Reptilian*, J. F. Schreiber, 1969; *Die ersten Stunden ihres Lebens: Voegel, Fische, Amphibien, Reptilien, Saeugetiere* (title means "The First Hours of Their Lives"), J. F. Schreiber, 1969.

Das Wasser und seine Tiere (title means "The Water and Its Animals"), Atlantis-Verlag, 1970; *Ueber Leander und Meere: Geheimnis der Tierwanderung* (title means "Over Land and Oceans"), Oesterreichischer Verlag, 1971; *Tausend Tricks der Tarnung: Verborgenes Leben im Tierreich*, Oesterreichischer Bundesverlag, 1973; *Der Hamster und die Eidechse* (title means "The Hamster and the Lizard"), Atlantis Verlag, 1973; *Ein Haus und viele Tiere* (title means "A House and Many Animals"), Rowohlt, 1975; *Voegel in Kaefig: Voliere und Garten* (title means "Birds in Cages, Voliers and Garden"), Graefe und Unzer, 1977; *Kanarienvoegel* (title means "Canaries"), Graefe und Unzer, 1978; *Tiere in unserer Nachbarschaft* (title means "Animals in Our Neighborhood"), Atlantis-Verlag, 1979; *Erklaere mir die Haustiere* (title means "Explain the Domestic Animals"), Piper, 1980.

Contributor of more than sixty articles to scientific journals.

WORK IN PROGRESS: Children's books on animal behavior.

SIDELIGHTS: Von Frisch commented: "I find it necessary to instruct young people about biological facts in a way that is interesting and easy to understand."

* * *

von LANG, Jochen
See von LANG-PIECHOCKI, Joachim

* * *

von LANG-PIECHOCKI, Joachim 1925-
(Jochen von Lang)

PERSONAL: Born May 14, 1925, in Altandsberg, Germany; divorced. *Education:* Educated in Germany. *Religion:* Lutheran. *Home and office:* Strehlowweg 3, 2000 Hamburg 52, West Germany.

CAREER: German Broadcasting Corp., Berlin, apprentice, 1942; war correspondent for radio programs, 1943-45; *Kieler Nachrichten*, Kiel, West Germany, chief reporter, 1946-48; *Der Spiegel*, correspondent from Schleswig Holstein; *Der Stern*, Hamburg, West Germany, free collaborator, 1948-63, editor, 1963—, chief of production, 1967-71. Television film producer, 1972—. *Military service:* German Army, 1943-45.

WRITINGS—All under name Jochen von Lang: *Adolf Hitler: Gesichter Eines Diktators*, Christian Wegner Verlag, 1968, translation published as *Adolf Hitler: Faces of a Dictator*, Harcourt, 1969; *Hitlers Tischgespraeche im Bild*, Stalling-Verlag, 1969, translation published as *Hitler Close-Up*, Macmillan, 1973 (published in England as *The Hitler*

Phenomenon, David & Charles, 1974); *Der Sekretaer Martin Bormann: Der Mann, der Hitler beherrschte,* Deutsche Verlags-Anstalt, 1977, translation published as *The Secretary: Martin Bormann, the Man Who Manipulated Hitler,* Random House, 1979 (published in England as *Bormann: The Man Who Manipulated Hitler,* Weidenfeld & Nicolson, 1979).

Contributor: Baldur von Schirach, editor, *Ich Glaubte an Hitler,* Mosaik-Verlag, 1967; *Margret-Bachler: Warten auf Antwort,* Kindler-Verlag, 1978.

Television films: "Kempner" (on the prosecutor at Nuremberg); "Trepper" (on the chief of Red Chapel, a World War II Communist spy organization); "Bird" (on the American director of Spandau, Berlin's war criminal prison); "Earl of Einsiedel" (on the vice-president of Freies Deutschland, a World War II national committee).

BIOGRAPHICAL/CRITICAL SOURCES: Frankfurter Allgemaine Zeitung, February 1, 1978; *Aufbau,* May 18, 1979; *Washington Post,* May 24, 1979; *Militaergeschichtliche Mitteilungen,* February 1, 1978.

*   *   *

von MOLTKE, Konrad 1941-

PERSONAL: Born September 23, 1941, in Kreisau, Germany; came to United States in 1967; son of Helmuth James and Freya (Deichmann) von Moltke; married Ulrike von Haeften, August 21, 1965; children: Johannes, Dorothea, Daniel. *Education:* Attended University of Munich, 1961-62; Dartmouth College, B.A., 1964; University of Goettingen, Ph.D., 1967. *Religion:* Christian. *Home address:* Four Wells, Norwich, Vt. 05055. *Office:* European Cultural Foundation, Adenauerallee 214, D5300 Bonn, West Germany.

CAREER: State University of New York at Buffalo, assistant professor, 1968-72, associate professor of history, 1972-74, director of collegiate system, 1970-72; Curriculumgruppe Amerikakunde, Hamburg, West Germany, director, 1973-76; European Cultural Foundation, Bonn, West Germany, director of Institute for European Environmental Policy, 1976—. Member of board of directors of Eugen Rosenstock-Huessy Fund. *Member:* International Council of Environmental Law, International Association of Environmental Coordinators, Athenaeum.

WRITINGS: Siegmund von Dretrichstein, Vandenhoeck & Rupprecht, 1970; (editor with Georg Igge) *Leopold von Ranke: The Theory and Practice of History,* Bobbs-Merrill, 1972; *Educational Leaves for Employees,* Jossey-Bass, 1976; *Baustein Curriculum Amerikakunde* (title means "Modular American Studies Course"), Metzler, 1976.

WORK IN PROGRESS: Editing the works of Eugen Rosenstock-Huessy; comparative studies of environmental policy.

SIDELIGHTS: Von Moltke writes: "My principal current interest is the development of non-governmental European institutions, primarily in the field of European cultural policy."

*   *   *

von OST, Henry Lerner 1915-
(Henry Morgan)

PERSONAL: Born March 31, 1915, in New York, N.Y.; son of Henry (a banker) and Eva (Lerner) von Ost; married Isobel Gibbs (an actress), August 17, 1946 (marriage ended); married Karen Sorensen, March 31, 1978. *Education:* Attended Suffolk Law School. *Residence:* Truro, Mass. 02666.

CAREER: Comedian. WMCA-Radio, New York City, page boy, 1931-33, announcer, 1933; WCAU-Radio, Philadelphia, Pa., announcer, 1933; WEBC-Radio, Duluth, Minn., chief announcer, program director, and host of "Strictly Masculine"; WNAC-Radio, Boston, Mass., host of "House Party," until 1940; WOR-Radio, New York City, 1940-42, began as staff announcer, became host of "Meet Mr. Morgan" and host of "Here's Morgan"; American Broadcasting Co. (ABC-Radio), host of "Here's Morgan," beginning in 1945. Panelist on "What's My Line" television show. Made guest appearances on numerous radio and television shows. *Military service:* U.S. Air Force, 1942-45. *Awards, honors:* Named "most promising star of tomorrow" by *Motion Picture Daily,* 1946.

WRITINGS—All under name Henry Morgan: (With Gary Wagner) *And Now a Word From Our Sponsor,* Citadel Press, 1960; *O-Sono and the Magicians Nephew, and the Elephant,* Vanguard, 1964; (with George Booth) *Dogs,* Houghton, 1976. Contributor to *New York Times.*

BIOGRAPHICAL/CRITICAL SOURCES: Newsweek, December 25, 1961.

W

WAKEFIELD, Tom 1935-

PERSONAL: Born December 13, 1935, in Staffordshire, England; son of Richard (a coal miner) and Esther (Bird) Wakefield. *Education:* University of London, B.Ed., 1967. *Politics:* Social Democrat. *Residence:* London, England. *Agent:* Richard Scott Simon, 32 College Cross, London W.1, England.

CAREER: Worked in England as teacher, 1969-77, and head teacher, 1971-79; free-lance writer and lecturer, 1979—. Adviser to BBC-TV. *Member:* International P.E.N., Society of Authors.

WRITINGS—Novels: *Trixie Trash, Star Ascending,* Routledge & Kegan Paul, 1977; *Isobel Quirk in Orbit,* Routledge & Kegan Paul, 1978; *The Love Siege,* Routledge & Kegan Paul, 1979.

Nonfiction: *Special School,* Routledge & Kegan Paul, 1977; *Some Mothers I Know* (biography), Routledge & Kegan Paul, 1978; *Forties Child* (autobiography), Routledge & Kegan Paul, 1980. Contributor to newspapers.

WORK IN PROGRESS: A novel; a dictionary, with Michael Jones.

SIDELIGHTS: Wakefield wrote: "I was brought up in a mining family in the West Midlands. My fiction is often described as bizarre and idiosyncratic, yet it is always ethically concerned."

*　　*　　*

WAKO, Mdogo
See NAZARETH, Peter

*　　*　　*

WALDRON, Eli 1916(?)-1980

OBITUARY NOTICE: Born c. 1916; died in an automobile accident, June 9, 1980, in Culpepper, Va. Writer. Eli Waldron was an assistant editor with *Collier's* magazine at the time of his death. He was also a short-story writer and a frequent contributor of articles and fiction to various periodicals, including *Saturday Evening Post, New Yorker, Kenyon Review, Look,* and his own *Collier's.* Obituaries and other sources: *New York Times,* June 12, 1980.

*　　*　　*

WALDROP, Rosemarie 1935-

PERSONAL: Born August 24, 1935, in Kitzingen/Main, Germany; came to the United States in 1958, naturalized citizen, 1962; daughter of Josef and Friederike (Wolgemuth) Sebald; married Bernard Keith Waldrop (a professor of English and writer), January 20, 1959. *Education:* Attended University of Wuerzburg, University of Freiburgh, and University of Aix-Marseille, 1954-58; University of Michigan, M.A., 1960, Ph.D., 1966. *Home:* 71 Elmgrove Ave., Providence, R.I. 02906.

CAREER: Wesleyan University, Middletown, Conn., assistant professor of German and comparative literature, 1964-70; free-lance poet and translator, 1971-77; Southeastern Massachusetts University, North Dartmouth, Mass., visiting poet, 1977; Brown University, Providence, R.I., visiting lecturer in English, 1977-78; Tufts University, Medford, Mass., visiting lecturer in English, 1979—. *Member:* Modern Language Association of America, John Barton Wolgamot Society. *Awards, honors:* Humboldt fellowship, 1970; Howard Foundation fellowship, 1975; award from Columbia Translation Center, 1978, for *Book of Questions;* National Endowment for the Arts grant, 1980.

WRITINGS: Against Language? (criticism), Mouton, 1971; *The Aggressive Ways of the Casual Stranger* (poems), Random House, 1972; *The Road is Everywhere; or, Stop This Body* (poems), Open Places, 1978; *When They Have Senses* (poems), Burning Deck, 1980.

Translator: Peter Weiss, *Bodies and Shadows,* Delacorte, 1969; Edmond Jabes, *Elya,* Tree Books, 1973; Jabes, *The Book of Questions,* seven volumes, Wesleyan University Press, 1976; Jabes, *The Book of Yukel/Return to the Book,* Wesleyan University Press, 1977. Editor of poetry series published by Burning Deck, 1968—.

WORK IN PROGRESS: The Hanky of Pippin's Daughter, a novel; translating additional volumes of *The Book of Questions,* by Edmond Jabes.

*　　*　　*

WALICKI, Andrzej 1930-

PERSONAL: Born May 15, 1930, in Warsaw, Poland; son of Michael (an art historian) and Anna (a social worker) Walicki; married Janina Derks, 1953 (divorced, 1970); married Maria Wodzynska (a historian of philosophy), June 17, 1971; children: (first marriage) Matgorzata; (second marriage) Adam. *Education:* University of Warsaw, Ph.D., 1958. *Religion:* Roman Catholic. *Home:* Rozlogi 14a, m.43, Warsaw

01-310, Poland. *Agent:* Authors' Agency, Hipoteczna 2, Warsaw 00-950, Poland. *Office:* Institute of Philosophy and Sociology, Polish Academy of Sciences, Nowy Swiat 72, Warsaw 00-330, Poland.

CAREER: Polish Academy of Sciences, Institute of Philosophy and Sociology, Warsaw, adjunct, 1958-64, dozent, 1965-72, professor, 1972—. Visiting fellow of All Souls College, Oxford, 1966-67; visiting Kratter Professor of History at Stanford University, spring, 1976; fellow of Woodrow Wilson International Center for Scholars, 1977-78. *Member:* Polish Philosophical Society. *Awards, honors:* Award from Polish Academy of Sciences, 1970, for *Philosophy and Messianism.*

WRITINGS: W kregu konserwatywnej utopii: Struktura i przemiany rosyjskiego slowianofilstwa, [Poland], 1964, translation published as *The Slavophile Controversy: History of a Conservative Utopia in Nineteenth Century Russian Thought,* Clarendon Press, 1975; *The Controversy Over Capitalism: Studies in the Social Philosophy of the Russian Populists,* Clarendon Press, 1969; *Rosyjska filozofia i mysl spoleczna od Oswiecenia do marksizmu,* [Poland], 1973, translation published as *A History of Russian Thought From the Enlightenment to Marxism,* Stanford University Press, 1979.

In Polish: *Osobowosc a historia: Studia z dziejow literatury i mysli rosyjskiej* (title means "Personality and History: Studies in Russian Philosophy and Literature"), [Poland], 1959; *Filozofia a mesjanizm: Studia z dziejow filozofii i mysli spoleczno-religijnej romantyzmu polskiego* (title means "Philosophy and Messianism: Studies in Polish Philosophical and Religious Thought of the Romantic Epoch"), [Poland], 1970; *Stanislaw Brzozowski: Drogi Mysli* (title means "Stanislaw Brzozowski: An Intellectual Portrait"), [Poland], 1977.

Contributor to journals in England, the United States, Poland, Italy, and France.

WORK IN PROGRESS: Philosophy and Romantic Nationalism: The Case of Poland, 1831-1864, for Oxford University Press.

SIDELIGHTS: Walicki wrote: "I felt that a deeper knowledge of Russian intellectual history is of vital importance for my country, as well as for the West. In my studies of Polish intellectual history I am motivated by a feeling of its importance for the Polish national identity and also for a comparative intellectual history of European (especially Slavic) countries."

*   *   *

WALKER, Claxton   1924-

PERSONAL: Born July 11, 1924, in Washington, D.C.; son of Curtis (an appraiser) and Helen (Claxton) Walker; married Jacqueline Northrup (divorced, 1968); married Nancy Edwards Maury (a company president), June 9, 1969; children: Helen Christine, Curtis Reed, Jonathan Kim, Joseph Claxton, Mark Northrup, Cindy Shane. *Education:* University of Maryland, B.S., 1953. *Politics:* "Republican/Democrat, as the case may be." *Religion:* "Sort of Protestant." *Home:* 9930 Logan Dr., Potomac, Md. 20854. *Office:* 10000 Falls Rd., Potomac, Md. 20854.

CAREER: Teacher of industrial arts and athletic director at high school in Bethesda, Md., 1949-58; president of construction company, 1957-70; home inspector and construction consultant in Potomac, Md., 1970. Instructor for U.S. Power Squadron. Member of board of directors at Longfel-

low School. *Military service:* U.S. Marine Corps, 1943-45; served in Pacific theater. *Member:* American Society of Home Inspectors (member of board of directors), American Arbitration Association (arbitrator), Construction Specifications Institute, Building Officials Code Administrators, Rotary Club (president).

WRITINGS: (With J. C. Davis) *Buying Your House: A Complete Guide to Inspection and Evaluation,* Emerson, 1975; (with Davis) *Wage the Energy War at Home,* Emerson, 1978. Contributor to trade journals and newspapers. Consulting editor for home improvement and repair series, "Roofs and Siding," Time-Life, 1978-80, "The Old House," and "Walls and Ceilings."

SIDELIGHTS: Walker commented: "I was a pioneer in the new profession of home inspection, a service essentially consumer-oriented, offered to prospective home purchasers to investigate and bring into the open the structural and mechanical programs connected with a house under consideration for purchase. The home inspector is the only person with no proprietary interest in consummation of the 'deal' that fully represents the purchaser in the transaction of real estate."

*   *   *

WALKER, Margaret Pope   1901(?)-1980

OBITUARY NOTICE: Born c. 1901 in Chicago, Ill.; died of emphysema, August 8, 1980, in Evanston, Ill. Writer and philanthropist. Walker, a victim of polio, dedicated her life to helping others similarly stricken. The Pope Foundation, established in collaboration with her father, Henry Pope, has provided through the years the funding necessary for research and for agencies for the physically handicapped. Her frequent articles and reports on the problems of the physically handicapped on a day-to-day basis led to many architectural innovations in both public and private circles. Obituaries and other sources: *Washington Post,* August 10, 1980.

*   *   *

WALKER, Martin   1947-

PERSONAL: Born January 23, 1947, in Durham, England; son of Tom and Dorothy (McNeill) Walker; married Julia Watson (a writer), May 6, 1978. *Education:* Balliol College, Oxford, M.A. (with first class honors), 1969; graduate study at Harvard University. *Politics:* "Libertarian anti-fascist." *Religion:* "Vague." *Residence:* London, England. *Agent:* A. P. Watt Ltd., 26/28 Bedford Row, London WC1R 4HL, England.

CAREER: Affiliated with *Johannesburg Star* and *Newscheck,* both in South Africa; speechwriter for U.S. Senator Edmund Muskie, 1970-71; *Guardian,* Manchester, England, reporter and columnist, 1972-79. *Military service:* Royal Air Force, pilot, 1960-65. *Member:* National Union of Journalists. *Awards, honors:* Congressional fellow of American Political Science Association, 1970-71.

WRITINGS: The National Front, Collins, 1977, revised edition, 1979; *Daily Sketches* (history of political cartoons), Muller, 1978; *The Infiltrators* (novel), Dial, 1978; (editor and translator from Arabic) *Poems on the Glass of Windows,* OCPD, 1979; *A Mercenary Calling* (novel), Doubleday, 1980; *The Eastern Question* (novel), Hart-Davis, 1981.

Work represented in anthologies, including *The Young Unicorns,* Sidgwick & Jackson, 1973. Writer for British Broadcasting Corp. World Service. Contributor to *Encyclopaedia Britannica.* Contributor to American newspapers.

WORK IN PROGRESS: The Great Papers, nonfiction, a study of the world's twelve top newspapers, with comparative analysis of their 1979-80 Iranian coverage; *Stechkin,* a novel on modern Russia.

SIDELIGHTS: Walker commented that in the 1960's he "reported on and suffered wars in the Congo, the Spanish Sahara, Iran, and Afghanistan." During the 1970's his work as a journalist included an interview with Idi Amin, then president of Uganda, and an expose which prevented the sale to South Africa (by Jordan) of modern tanks, anti-aircraft missiles, and jet fighter aircraft.

Walker wrote: "*The National Front,* on fascist movements in modern Britain, was in response to an emerging political crisis in Britain. My first novel, *The Infiltrators,* was written while I was covering the Portuguese revolution for the *Guardian,* to tell of the political machinations I knew to be happening, but could not prove adequately for a newspaper. My other novels follow a similar pattern."

He added: "My wife and I spent a year traveling around the world, and were on the last civilian convoy down the Khyber Pass from Afghanistan."

*   *   *

WALLACE, Beverly Dobrin   1921-

PERSONAL: Born March 16, 1921, in Chattanooga, Tenn.; daughter of Harry (an engineer) and Lillian (a secretary; maiden name, Zinn) Dobrin; married Henry Wallace (an ink chemist), February 1, 1948; children: Joshua, David. *Education:* Attended Carnegie Institute of Technology (now Carnegie-Mellon University), Arts Students League of New York, and Pratt Center for Contemporary Printmaking; Hofstra University, B.S., 1964, M.A., 1970. *Politics:* "Liberal and Democratic." *Home address:* RFD 1, Bullet Hole Rd., Mahopac, N.Y. 10541. *Agent:* Toni Mendez, 140 East 56th St., New York, N.Y. 10022. *Office:* Scotland Elementary School, Ridgefield, Conn. 06817.

CAREER: Winnicomac Elementary School, Commack, Long Island, N.Y., art teacher, 1964-68; Somers Middle School, Somers, N.Y., art specialist, 1968-71; Hebrew Hospital for Chronic Sick, Bronx, N.Y.; occupational therapist, 1971-72; Scotland Elementary School, Ridgefield, Conn., art teacher, 1972—. Illustrator and writer. *Member:* International Defenders of Wildlife, National Education Association, Common Cause, Connecticut Education Association, Beekeepers Association of Putnam County, Putnam Arts Council. *Awards, honors:* Emily Lowe Award, 1963, for excellence in painting.

WRITINGS: (Self-illustrated) *Insects: The Seasons in Their Lives,* Bobbs-Merrill, 1975.

Illustrator: Mary Louise Sherer, *The Secret of Bruja Mountain,* Harvey House, 1971; Barbara Williams, *Desert Hunter: The Spider Wasp,* Harvey House, 1975.

WORK IN PROGRESS: Doing research on spiders for illustrating a book; a fictional story for children based on characteristics of the crow; a series of articles for a magazine in the field of art education.

*   *   *

WALLACE, Karl R(ichards)   1906-1973

PERSONAL: Born November 10, 1906, in Hubbardsville, N.Y.; died October 16, 1973; son of Lew (a carpenter) and Rena (Dart) Wallace; married Dorothy M. Peirce, August 27, 1929; children: Margit Melissa Wallace Gerow, Elizabeth Ellen Wallace Empen, Peter Dart. *Education:* Cornell University, B.A., 1927, M.A., 1931, Ph.D., 1933. *Politics:* Democrat. *Religion:* Methodist. *Residence:* Frankfort, Mich.

CAREER: Iowa State College (now University), Ames, began as instructor, became assistant professor of speech, 1927-30; Cornell University, Ithaca, N.Y., instructor in public speaking, 1931-33; University of Missouri, Columbia, assistant professor of English, summers, 1933-34; Iowa State College (now University), assistant professor of speech, 1934-36; Washington University, St. Louis, Mo., assistant professor of English in charge of speech, 1936-37; University of Virginia, Charlottesville, associate professor, 1937-40, professor of speech, 1940-47, chairman of School of Speech, 1937-44, and School of Speech and Drama, 1944-47; University of Illinois, Champaign-Urbana, professor of speech and head of department of speech and theatre, 1947-68; University of Massachusetts, Amherst, professor of speech, 1968-73. Advisory editor for Dodd, Mead & Co. (publisher), 1956-73. Member of summer faculty at University of Michigan, 1954.

MEMBER: American Association of University Professors (president of Illinois chapter, 1957-58), National Council of Teachers of English, Speech Association of America (member of executive council, 1944-60, president, 1954, chairman of board of finance, 1972-73), Renaissance Society of America, Eastern Speech Association, Southern Speech Association, Central States Speech Association, Speech Communication Association, Delta Sigma Phi, Omicron Delta Kappa, Phi Beta Kappa, Phi Kappa Phi, University Club (Illinois; former president and member of board), Rotary Club. *Awards, honors:* James A. Winan Award for Distinguished Scholarship in Rhetoric and Public Address, 1969; book award from Speech Association of America, 1969; posthumous distinguished service award from Speech Communication Association, 1973.

WRITINGS: Francis Bacon on Communication and Rhetoric, University of North Carolina Press, 1943; (editor with D. C. Bryant, B. W. Hewitt, and H. A. Wichelns) *Studies in Speech and Drama in Honor of Alexander M. Drummond,* Cornell University Press, 1944; (with Bryant) *Fundamentals of Public Speaking,* Appleton, 1947, 4th edition, 1969; (with Bryant) *Oral Communication,* Appleton, 1948, 3rd edition, 1960; (editor) *Background Studies in the History of Speech Education in America,* Appleton, 1954; *Francis Bacon on the Nature of Man: The Faculties of Man's Soul,* University of Illinois Press, 1967; (editor with Bryant, C. C. Arnold, F. W. Haberman, and Richard Murphy) *An Historical Anthology of Select British Speeches,* Ronald, 1967; *Understanding Discourse: The Speech Act and Rhetorical Action,* Louisiana State University Press, 1970; (editor with E. Neal Claussen) John Lawson, *Lectures Concerning Oratory,* Southern Illinois University Press, 1972.

Contributor: Bryant, editor, *Papers in Rhetoric,* privately printed, 1940; *Humanistic Studies in Honor of James Calvin Metcalf,* University of Virginia, 1941; Bryant, editor, *The Rhetorical Idiom,* Cornell University Press, 1958; R. F. Howes, editor, *Historical Studies of Rhetoric and Rhetoricians,* Cornell University Press, 1961; Roger E. Nebergall, editor, *Dimensions of Rhetorical Scholarship,* Department of Speech, University of Oklahoma, 1963. Contributor to *History and Criticism of American Public Address,* edited by W. N. Brigance, 1943, and *Studies in Honor of C. M. Wise,* 1970. Contributor of numerous articles and reviews to speech journals. Editor of *Quarterly Journal of Speech,* 1945-47.

SIDELIGHTS: Wallace's wife, Dorothy, told *CA:* "My husband's chief area of interest was rhetoric and public address, his research was on the writings of Francis Bacon, and his teaching area was the rhetoric of Aristotle. His close concern for graduate students and young teachers led to the establishment of an annual award in his name for study and research in classical rhetoric. His travels in the United States and abroad were to further his own research in classical rhetoric and British orators. A symposium dedicated to him was held at University of Michigan after his death."

BIOGRAPHICAL/CRITICAL SOURCES: Speech Teacher, September, 1974.

[Sketch verified by wife, Dorothy M. Wallace]

*   *   *

WALLACE, Marjorie

PERSONAL: Born in Nairobi, Kenya; daughter of William (a civil engineer) and Doris (a pianist; maiden name, Tulloch) Wallace; married Count Andrew Skarbek (a consulting psychiatrist); children: Sacha, Stefan, Maximilian. *Education:* University of London, B.A. (with honors), 1965. *Religion:* Church of England. *Home:* 26 Belsize Sq., London N.W.3, England. *Office: Sunday Times,* 200 Gray's Inn Rd., London W.C.1, England.

CAREER: Independent Television Authority (now Independent Broadcasting Authority), London, England, worked for Rediffusion and London Weekend Television as writer for David Frost programs, researcher, and producer of religious and current affairs programs, 1966-69; British Broadcasting Corp., London, television reporter and film director, 1969-72; *Sunday Times,* London, feature writer and social services correspondent, 1972-80. *Member:* Medical Journalists' Association. *Awards, honors:* International Emmy Award, 1979, for best television drama, "On Giant's Shoulders."

WRITINGS: On Giant's Shoulders: The Story of Torry Wiles, Times Books, 1976; *Suffer the Children,* Viking, 1978; (with Tom Mayerson) *The Superpoison: The Poisoning of Seveso,* Macmillan, 1979. Author of television adaptation, "On Giant's Shoulders," broadcast by British Broadcasting Corp., 1979.

WORK IN PROGRESS: A book and television documentary on "the genius of Christopher Nolan, a fourteen-year-old spastic boy who cannot speak or control his muscles, but who has written poetry acclaimed by university professors, critics, and fellow writers."

SIDELIGHTS: Marjorie Wallace has written and campaigned for brain-damaged people, hemophiliacs, and schizophrenics. She has produced pamphlets on case studies of thalidomide-damaged and brain-damaged children. More recently, she has campaigned for the use of new technology to help the disabled.

The emphasis on misfortune in her writings comes from her belief that suffering can only be tolerated if the victim is given some vision of its pattern and purpose. She hopes to expose the indifference of governments, professionals, and organizations, and to educate and influence uncommitted people.

*   *   *

WALLSTEN, Robert 1912-

PERSONAL: Born March 3, 1912, in New York, N.Y.; son of Leonard M. (an attorney) and Olive (Roe) Wallsten; married Cynthia Rogers, August 21, 1954 (died, 1971). *Education:* Harvard University, B.A., 1932. *Home:* 171 East 62nd St., New York, N.Y. 10021. *Agent:* Audrey Wood, International Creative Management, 40 West 57th St., New York, N.Y. 10019.

CAREER: Actor on Broadway, on tour, in summer stock and films, 1932-42; writer, 1932—. *Military service:* U.S. Naval Reserve, active duty, 1942-46; became lieutenant junior grade. *Awards, honors:* Award from Mystery Writers of America, c. 1958, for story, "The Children of Alda Nuova."

WRITINGS: (With Elaine Steinbeck) *Steinbeck: A Life in Letters,* Viking, 1975.

Plays: "Tom Jones" (three-act), first produced in Cincinnati, Ohio, 1935; "Marriage Royal" (three-act), first produced in Dewnis, Mass., at Cape Playhouse, c. 1937; (with Mignon S. Eberhart) "Eight O'Clock Tuesday" (two-act), first produced in New York, N.Y., at Henry Miller Theatre, 1939. Also translator of two-act play by Daniel Colas, "A Play About Lovers."

Television writer. Contributor to magazines, including *Ellery Queen's Mystery Magazine, Woman's Home Companion, Ladies' Home Journal, Redbook,* and *Collier's.*

SIDELIGHTS: Wallsten commented: "I have lately been extremely interested in the underrated art of translation, and have translated from Italian and French to English."

*   *   *

WALSH, M.M.B.
(Marnie Walsh)

PERSONAL—Education: Pennsylvania State University, B.A. (history), B.A. (English); University of New Mexico, M.A. *Agent:* Joan Daves, 59 East 54th St., New York, N.Y. 10022.

CAREER: Writer.

WRITINGS: Dolly Purdo, Putnam, 1975; *The Four Colored Hoop,* Putnam, 1976; (under name Marnie Walsh) *A Taste of the Knife* (poems), Ahsahta Press, 1976.

*   *   *

WALSH, Marnie
See WALSH, M.M.B.

*   *   *

WARBURTON, Minnie 1949-

PERSONAL: Born July 12, 1949, in Beverly, Mass.; daughter of Barclay H. and Margarett (Vernon) Warburton. *Education:* Attended private preparatory school in Providence, R.I. *Politics:* "Feminist/Humanist." *Religion:* None. *Home:* 1229 North Flores, No. 5, Los Angeles, Calif. 90069. *Agent:* Maggie Field, 554 South San Vicente, Los Angeles, Calif. 90048.

CAREER: Writer, 1968—; National Education Association, Washington, D.C., student club coordinator, 1969; South Street Seaport Museum, New York, N.Y., record producer and public relations worker, 1970; Clear White, Los Angeles, Calif., manager, 1975-80.

WRITINGS: Mykonos (novel), Coward, 1979.

WORK IN PROGRESS: The House of Atreus, a novel set in Mycenae, 1250-1190 B.C., retelling the story of Agamemnon, Klytemnestra, and Elektra from women's point of view; *The Androgynes,* a novel; two young adult novels.

SIDELIGHTS: "I am basically a self-taught person with a

passion for writing," Warburton told *CA*, "especially novels. *The House of Atreus* demanded an exploration of mythology, ancient religion, anthropology, archaeology, and research on location. I lived in Greece, on the island of Mykonos, from 1971 to 1974.

"I grew up in New England among five sisters and brothers, and my books so far seem to be about jealousy—sister/sister, man/woman, parent/child. I have also made a video documentary on incest-as-child-abuse, of which I am the subject.

"Although writing novels is my love, and I am finally becoming good at it, living in Los Angeles makes it almost inevitable that, in some capacity, I will work in film or television."

BIOGRAPHICAL/CRITICAL SOURCES: Primal Institute Newsletter, Volume I, number 11, 1979.

* * *

WAREHAM, John 1940-

PERSONAL: Born January 4, 1940, in New Zealand; son of Albert John and Yvonne Jean (Presling) Wareham; married Margaret Ann Owles (a public relations officer), May, 1961; children: three sons, one daughter. *Education:* Victoria University of Wellington, B.Comm., 1962. *Residence:* New York, N.Y. *Office:* Wareham Associates, 45 Rockefeller Plaza, New York, N.Y. 10011.

CAREER: Worked in New Zealand for Coopers & Lybrand, and Charles Haines Advertising; associated with Wareham Associates, New York, N.Y., 1964—. *Member:* Institute of Directors (fellow), New Zealand Society of Chartered Accountants, Royal Sydney Yacht Squadron.

WRITINGS: How to Climb the Money Tree, A. H. & A. W. Reed, 1971; *Secrets of a Corporate Headhunter,* Atheneum, 1980; *The Mystic Executive Survival Handbook,* Atheneum, 1981. Contributor to magazines and newspapers in the United States, New Zealand, and Australia, including *Across the Board, New Zealand Listener,* and *Wharton.*

WORK IN PROGRESS: Moments in the Private Life of a Corporate Headhunter, stories; *The Emperor of Madison Avenue.*

* * *

WARNER, Philip 1914-

PERSONAL: Born May 19, 1914, in England; son of William T. and Maude A. Warner; widowed; children: three. *Education:* Cambridge University, B.A. and M.A., 1939. *Agent:* Campbell Thompson & McLaughlin Ltd., 31 Newington Green, London N16 9PU, England.

CAREER: Writer and lecturer. *Military service:* British Army, 1939-45.

WRITINGS: Sieges of the Middle Ages, Bell, 1969; *The Medieval Castle,* Arthur Barker, 1971; *Special Air Service, 1941-71,* Kimber, 1971; *The Japanese Army of World War II,* Osprey, 1972, Hippocrene, 1973; *The Battle of Jutland,* Lutterworth, 1972; *The Crimean War: A Reappraisal,* Taplinger, 1973; *Dervish: The Rise and Fall of an African Empire,* Taplinger, 1974; *The Soldier: His Daily Life Through the Ages,* Taplinger, 1975; *Guide to Castles in Britain: Where to Find Them and What to Look For,* New English Library, 1976; *The Best of British Pluck: "Boy's Own Paper" Revisited,* Beekman, 1976; *The Battle of Loos,* Kimber, 1976; *Panzer,* Weidenfeld & Nicolson, 1977; *Zeebrugge Raid,* Kimber, 1978; (editor) Richard Temple Godman, *Fields of War,* Transatlantic, 1978; *Famous Welsh Battles,* Fontana,

1978; (editor) *Best of "Chums,"* Cassell, 1978; *Invasion Road,* Cassell, 1980; *The D Day Landings,* Kimber, 1980. Contributor of articles and reviews to magazines and newspapers, including *Daily Telegraph, Spectator,* and *Times Literary Supplement.*

WORK IN PROGRESS: A biography of Field Marshal Sir Claude Auchintech.

AVOCATIONAL INTERESTS: Military and general history, castles.

* * *

WARNER-CROZETTI, R(uth G.) 1913-
(J. M. Loring, Rich O'Mahoney)

PERSONAL: Born May 18, 1913, in Indianapolis, Ind.; daughter of Harry William (a builder) and Evelyn D. (Morgan) Warner; married Jay Crozetti (a cook), October 16, 1937 (died, 1952); children: Margaret Jeannette. *Education:* Attended high school in Indianapolis, Ind.; studied privately in Australia. *Religion:* Protestant. *Home:* 709 Cone Dr., Prescott, Ariz. 86301. *Agent:* Forrest J. Ackerman, Ackerman Sci-Fi Agency, 2495 Glendower Ave., Hollywood, Calif. 90027.

CAREER: Writer, 1960—. Worked as secretary and bookkeeper, office manager, and costume designer. *Member:* Los Angeles Fantasy Society.

WRITINGS: The Widderburn Horror (novel), Leisure Books, 1971. Also author of *Merry Christmas, You Bastards,* under pseudonym Rich O'Mahoney, 1967. Designer of book covers for Fantasy Publishing. Contributor to *Spaceway* (under pseudonym J. M. Loring) and *Fate.*

WORK IN PROGRESS: Two novels, based on characters from *The Widderburn Horror;* a fourth Widderburn novel; research on pollution, 1973-80, and its effect on humans.

* * *

WARREN, Lucian (Crissey) 1913-

PERSONAL: Born February 12, 1913, in Jamestown, N.Y.; son of Lucian Jason and Bernice (Scofield) Warren; married Katherine Smith, June 17, 1939; children: Sylvia, Lucian James, Katherine Sites, Nancy Stringos. *Education:* Denison University, A.B., 1936. *Politics:* Democrat. *Religion:* Protestant. *Home:* 1600 South Eads St., Apt. 1034-N, Arlington, Va. 22202. *Agent:* Curtis Brown, Ltd., 575 Madison Ave., New York, N.Y. 10022. *Office:* 1296 National Press Bldg., Washington, D.C. 20045.

CAREER/WRITINGS: Buffalo Courier-Express, Buffalo, N.Y., reporter, 1937-43, chief of Washington, D.C., bureau, 1945-68; *Buffalo Evening Press,* Buffalo, chief of Washington, D.C., bureau, 1968-78; free-lance journalist in Washington, D.C., 1979—. Notable assignments include coverage of both Republican and Democratic national political conventions, 1948—, Vietnam War, 1971, and series of articles on the Eastern European Communist countries, 1972, Scandinavia, 1977, and the Middle East, 1978. Public relations director of Colonial Radio Corp., Buffalo, 1945. Lecturer. Editor of *World News Digest,* 1956, and *World Highways,* 1966-71. Contributor of articles to magazines, including *New York Times Magazine, Esquire, Coronet, Parade,* and *New Republic.*

MEMBER: National Press Club (president, 1955), Academy of Political Science, Overseas Writers of Washington, Standing Committee of Correspondents (chairman, 1968), Phi Beta Kappa, Sigma Delta Chi, Phi Gamma Delta (editor, 1961-64),

Omicron Delta Kappa, Gridiron Club (president, 1975). *Awards, honors:* Distinguished alumnus citation from Denison University, 1952; Ernie Pyle Award, for coverage of Vietnam War.

* * *

WATEN, Judah Leon 1911-

PERSONAL: Born July 29, 1911, in Odessa, Russia; son of Solomon (a hawker) and Nehemia (a midwife; maiden name, Press) Waten; married Hyrell McKinnon Ross (a high school principal), 1945; children: Alice Nadya. *Education:* Attended high schools in Perth and Melbourne, Australia. *Politics:* Left-wing socialist. *Religion:* Jewish. *Home:* 1 Byron St., Box Hill, Melbourne, Victoria 3128, Australia.

CAREER: Junior state school teacher in Carlton and Melbourne, Australia, 1927; salesman in Melbourne and Sydney, Australia, 1928-30; novelist and literary critic, 1931-33; journalist on left labor press for *Guardian, Tribune,* and *Workers Voice,* 1935-38; cook and scullion at tourist resort and boarding house in New Zealand, 1939-40; full-time writer, 1940—. Foundation member of literature board of Australia Council, 1973-74. *Member:* International P.E.N. (president of Melbourne center, 1977-78), Fellowship of Australian Writers. *Awards, honors:* Short story prize from *Sydney Morning Herald,* 1947, for "Young Combo's Day"; Commonwealth Literary Fund fellowship, 1952, 1970, 1976; award from Melbourne Moomba Festival, 1965, for *Distant Land;* member of Order of Australia, 1979, for service to literature.

WRITINGS—Novels: *The Unbending,* Australasian Book Society, 1954; *Shares in Murder,* Australasian Book Society, 1957; *Time of Conflict,* Australasian Book Society, 1961; *Distant Land,* Angus & Robertson, 1964; *Season of Youth,* F. W. Cheshire, 1966; *So Far No Further,* Wren, 1971.

Other: (Editor with Victor G. O'Connor) *Twenty Great Australian Stories,* Dolphin, 1946; (translator) Herz Bergner, *Between Sky and Sea,* Dolphin, 1946; *Alien Sun* (short stories), Angus & Robertson, 1952, Anglobooks, 1953; *From Odessa to Odessa: Journey of an Australian Writer* (travel), Cheshire, 1969; *The Depression Years, 1929-1939,* Cheshire, 1972; *Bottle O!* (juvenile), Cassell, 1973; (editor with Stephen Murray-Smith) *Classic Australian Short Stories,* David & Charles, 1975; *Love and Rebellion* (short stories), Macmillan, 1978. Contributor of reviews to *Age* and *Sydney Morning Herald.*

WORK IN PROGRESS: A novel, *Scenes of Revolutionary Life.*

SIDELIGHTS: Waten told *CA:* "My four books, *Alien Son, The Unbending, Distant Land,* and *So Far No Further,* constitute a chronicle of Jewish migrant life in Australia from 1914 to the 1960's. I am the first Australian writer to write extensively of non-English speaking migrants—Jews mainly, but also Italians and Greeks.

"I have had two literary careers. My first began when I was about twenty. I had written a number of short stories and a novel which I took to England in 1931, hoping to get them published there. I was not successful. My stories and my novel were far too immature. I was under the influence of James Joyce and the American left-wing writers like John Dos Passos, who eventually turned against the left, and Michael Gold, who remained a Communist until his death in 1969. One of my stories appeared in an avant-garde, three-language magazine, *Front,* in Paris. In the same issue there

were contributions from William Carlos Williams and Ezra Pound.

"My second literary career began in the 1940's when my story 'To a Country Town' was published in the *Australian Coast to Coast.* This was the first story in *Alien Son,* a collection of stories with the same characters, arranged in rough chronological order. *Alien Son* was one of the first pieces of fiction about foreign migrants written inside a foreign community to appear in Australia."

A number of Waten's works have been translated into other languages. *The Unbending* has appeared in a Chinese edition, and *Shares in Murder* in both Dutch and German. Some of the stories from *Alien Son* have been translated into Hungarian, Hebrew, Yiddish, Russian, and German.

BIOGRAPHICAL/CRITICAL SOURCES: Times Literary Supplement, August 5, 1955, May 21, 1970; David Martin, *On Native Grounds,* Angus & Robertson, 1968; A. D. Hope, *Native Companions,* Angus & Robertson, 1974; D. R. Burns, *The Directions of Australian Fiction, 1920-1974,* Cassell, 1975; Nancy Keesing, *Australian Post-War Novelists,* Jacaranda Press, 1975; Jack Beasley, *Red Letter Days,* Australasian Book Society, 1979.

* * *

WAX, Judith 1932(?)-1979

PERSONAL: Born c. 1932 in Quakerstown, Pa.; died May 25, 1979, in Chicago, Ill.; daughter of Milton and Lilli Weiss; married Sheldon Wax (a magazine editor), 1951; children: Paul, Claudia. *Residence:* Chicago, Ill. *Agent:* Pat Berens, Sterling Lord Agency, Inc., 660 Madison Ave., New York, N.Y. 10021.

CAREER: Writer, 1973-79. Worked in sales at Lord & Taylor and as a catalog copywriter for Montgomery Ward, both in New York City, during the early 1950's. Bunny director for Playboy, Inc., Chicago, Ill.

WRITINGS: Starting in the Middle (nonfiction), Holt, 1979. Contributor of poems and articles to periodicals, including *New York Times Magazine, Harper's, Playboy, New York, Time, Newsweek, Washington Post, New Times, Vogue, Cosmopolitan, New Republic,* and *Seventeen.*

SIDELIGHTS: Wax had been meaning to begin writing long before she actually did: "As I look back, it's clear that I could have stayed home with my children and scribbled away; certainly there was nothing to stop me once they started school," she wrote in *Starting in the Middle.* "I made stirring resolutions, instead, like the one on my twenty-eighth birthday giving myself two more years to alter the course of my life. (That meant begin writing.) And from the moment I committed myself to that resolve—stand back for the inspiring part—it took me only fourteen more years to run out and buy typing paper."

When Wax finally did begin writing, at age forty-two, she said it was perhaps because "I was afraid that my life . . . was turning into another too scantily used." Her first professional effort was "The Waterbury Tales," a long Chaucerian poem satirizing the Watergate hearings. It was an overwhelming, overnight success: *New Republic* bought and printed it; it was syndicated by Reuters and appeared in newspapers around the world; *Time* and *Newsweek* ran it prominently. With characteristic humor, Wax recalled: "There was a Krakatoa of mail—book nibbles from publishing houses, interview invitations for radio and TV, job offers, including one from a newspaper syndicate to do a daily feature for the next five years. It was a nice way to start, particularly since I'd have been pleased with a by-line in *Dry Cleaning World.''*

Wax had not been prepared for such success. Earlier, she had wondered if a certain passage of the poem was a bit too strong. She tossed off the doubt instantly. "Who'd ever read the thing," she laughed. When publishers did read the thing and began to ask for more, Wax was caught off guard: "My nervous system shifted into emotional overdrive. I couldn't sleep or digest; I'd forgotten the techniques for such niceties. Dazed, crazed, and mumbling, I'd careen around the house granting imaginary interviews."

Starting in the Middle, Wax's first full-length work, celebrates the joys and confronts the anguish of mid-life. *Washington Post*'s Lou Cook humorously summarized the book's message: life begins at forty, *providing* one has a sense of humor, candid friends, a supportive husband, and a wildly successful first book. "For those with none of the above," Cook observed, "Wax would be hard to take if she didn't write with warmth and wit tempered by glimpses of her own dark nights of the soul. . . . Judith Wax was at her best when describing the 'guilt-edged insecurities' of our generation."

Humor consistently tempers the pain of realization in Wax's writing. For example: "I had disinterred my [wedding] gown because I was thinking about old marriages, wondering what keeps them going, why some stay happy, what my own was *really* like. It was thorny stuff, and I suppose that staring at the gown was my idea of scholarly investigation. (Besides, I'd finished my research into whether, if you listen closely, you can hear your own arteries hardening, and you can't.)"

An especially poignant chapter describes the agony of watching old friends cope with illness and death: "The best thing about the midyears, at least about mine, is the depth of the friendships. The worst thing can be losing them. It's to be expected that in middle age, mortality is not only intimated, but sometimes delivered, that pain and death are birthday presents nobody asks for. . . . But things have gotten out of hand, the timing's way off, and the present generation of the middle-aged is suffering from an unprecedented epidemic of horror." Wax talks about the guilt she felt for being healthy when so many of her friends were suffering.

Humor once again comes to the rescue in the following chapter. Wax recalls a relatively carefree period, early in her marriage: "I look back on those casual Sunday barbeques as the days of our innocence. Some of us might have chewed our potato chips with less complacency if we'd known that what was ahead was hardly a picnic. . . . Like most people, we expected more considerate trauma or a chance to pick and choose something palatable from the groaning board of griefs—and do it later, of course, always later. (When my dearest old friend Carole and I were young mothers, we took a sacred vow that the first of us to succumb to dimming eyesight could *depend* on the other to shave her legs for her as long as we both should live. Having disposed in advance the worst that far-off middle age might hurl at us, we settled ourselves into deck chairs in our tract-home driveways and spoke of other weighty matters while our children spooned dirt into each other's mouths.)"

On May 25, 1979, Judith Wax and her husband Sheldon, managing editor of *Playboy* magazine, were killed in the crash of a DC-10 jumbo jet en route to an American Booksellers Association convention in Los Angeles. The crash occurred just moments after takeoff from Chicago's O'Hare International airport. Lou Cook commented that the tragic accident, so soon after publication of Judith Wax's first book, "makes her book title, 'Starting in the Middle,' an ironic epitaph to a promising beginning. The gift of laughter is hard to find lately. Judith Wax had a fresh supply and should be remembered for it."

BIOGRAPHICAL/CRITICAL SOURCES: Judith Wax, *Starting in the Middle,* Holt, 1979; *Washington Post Book World,* May 31, 1979; *Washington Post,* June 3, 1979.

OBITUARIES: Chicago Tribune, May 27, 1979.*

—*Sketch by Susan A. Stefani*

*   *   *

WAYMAN, Thomas Ethan   1945-
(Tom Wayman)

PERSONAL: Born August 13, 1945, in Hawkesbury, Ontario, Canada; son of Morris (a chemist) and Sara (a social worker; maiden name, Zadkin) Wayman. *Education:* University of British Columbia, B.A., 1966; University of California, Irvine, M.F.A., 1968. *Home:* R.R. 1, Nelson, British Columbia, Canada V1L 5P4. *Office:* School of Writing, David Thompson University Centre, Nelson, British Columbia, Canada V1L 3C7.

CAREER: Colorado State University, Fort Collins, instructor in English, 1968-69; held various jobs in Vancouver, British Columbia, including construction worker, teacher's aide, and factory assemblyman, 1969-75; University of Windsor, Windsor, Ontario, writer-in-residence, 1975-76; Wayne State University, Detroit, Mich., assistant professor of English, 1976-77; University of Alberta, Edmonton, writer-in-residence, 1978-79; David Thompson University Centre, School of Writing, Nelson, British Columbia, instructor of writing, 1980—. *Awards, honors:* Helen Bullis Prize from *Poetry Northwest,* 1972; Borestone Mountain poetry awards, 1972, 1973, 1974, and 1976; medal for poetry and monetary prize from Canadian Authors' Association, 1974; Canada Council Senior Arts awards, 1975 and 1977; A.J.M. Smith Prize from Michigan State University, 1976, for distinguished achievement in Canadian poetry; first prize from U.S. National Bicentennial Poetry Awards, 1976, for poem "Garrison."

WRITINGS—Under name Tom Wayman; poetry: *Waiting for Wayman,* McClelland & Stewart, 1973; (editor) *Beaton Abbot's Got the Contract: An Anthology of Working Poems,* Newest Press, 1974; *For and Against the Moon: Blues, Yells, and Chuckles,* Macmillan, 1974; (editor) *A Government Job at Last: An Anthology of Working Poems, Mainly Canadian,* MacLeod Books, 1976; *Money and Rain: Tom Wayman Live!,* Macmillan, 1975; *Free Time: Industrial Poems,* Macmillan, 1977; *Living on the Ground: Tom Wayman Country,* McClelland & Stewart, 1980; *Introducing Tom Wayman: Selected Poems, 1973-80,* Ontario Review Press, 1980; (editor) *Going for Coffee,* Harbour Publishing, 1980.

SIDELIGHTS: Tom Wayman told *CA:* "It is my intention to set at the heart of my writing what is the center of my daily existence. Hence my interest in writing about the jobs that I have had; the jobs that occupy most of my waking hours and which so influence all aspects of my life in those hours *off* the job. Thus, too, my interest in collecting the poems others have written about their own daily work, in my anthologies *Beaton Abbot's Got the Contract, A Government Job at Last,* and *Going for Coffee.*"

BIOGRAPHICAL/CRITICAL SOURCES: Saturday Night, July, 1973, December, 1973; *Canadian Forum,* August, 1973, January, 1975, June, 1976; *Little Magazine,* winter, 1975-76; *Minnesota Review,* fall, 1977; *Newest Review,* January, 1979; *Quarry,* autumn, 1979.

WAYMAN, Tom
See WAYMAN, Thomas Ethan

*   *   *

WEBB, Francis Charles   1925-1973

PERSONAL: Born February 8, 1925, in Adelaide, Australia; died November 23, 1973. *Education:* Attended University of Sydney.

CAREER: Poet. Worked for several Canadian publishers. *Military service:* Royal Australian Air Force; served in Canada during World War II. *Awards, honors:* Commonwealth Literary Fund fellowship, 1960.

WRITINGS—Poetry: A Drum for Ben Boyd, Angus & Robertson, 1948; *Leichhardt in Theatre,* Angus & Robertson, 1952; *Birthday,* Advertiser Printing Office (Adelaide, Australia), 1953; *Socrates and Other Poems,* Angus & Robertson, 1961; *The Ghost of the Cock: Poems,* Angus & Robertson, 1964; *Collected Poems,* Angus & Robertson, 1969.*

*   *   *

WEBER, Eric   1942-

PERSONAL: Born August 30, 1942, in New York, N.Y.; son of Alex (a business president) and Doris (a psychiatrist) Weber; married Joanna Sure, 1968; children: Nick, Jessica, Gillian, Sam. *Education:* New York University, B.A., 1965. *Home:* 15 Birchwood Place, Tenafly, N.J. 07670. *Agent:* William Morris Agency, 1350 Avenue of the Americas, New York, N.Y. 10019. *Office:* Symphony Press, Inc., 7 West Clinton Ave., Tenafly, N.J. 07670.

CAREER: Benton & Bowles, New York City, advertising copywriter, 1967-69; Young & Rubicam, New York City, vice-president and creative director, 1969-78; Symphony Press, Inc., Tenafly, N.J., president, 1978—; writer, 1978—. *Awards, honors:* Has won numerous advertising awards, including Gold and Silver Lions from Cannes Film Festival of Commercials and several Clio Awards.

*WRITINGS—*All published by Symphony Press, except as noted: *How to Pick Up Girls,* 1970; (with M. Rob Frazier) *The Complete Guide to America's Best Pick Up Spots: 910 Fantastic Places to Pick Up Girls,* 1974; *Getting Together,* 1977; (with others) *Inner Looks,* 1977; *One Hundred Best Opening Lines,* 1977; *Raise Power,* 1978; *How to Take a Successful Job Interview,* 1978; *The Indispensable Employee,* 1978; *Separate Vacations* (novel), Avon, 1979; (with Judi Miller) *The Shy Person's Guide to Love and Loving,* Times Books, 1979; *How to Pick Up Girls: Summer Edition,* 1979; (with Madeline De Vries) *Body and Beauty Secrets of the Super Beauties,* Putnam, 1980.

Film scripts: "How to Pick Up Girls," first broadcast by ABC-TV, November, 1978; "How to Make Love to a Single Girl," Troma Productions, 1980.

WORK IN PROGRESS: Another novel.

*   *   *

WEBER, Nancy   1942-
(Olivia Harmston, Jennifer Rose, Lindsay West)

PERSONAL: Born January 22, 1942, in Hartford, Conn.; daughter of Saul (a president of a printing corporation) and Caroline (a painter; maiden name, Fox) Weber; married Charles Platt, May 31, 1977 (divorced, December, 1979); children: Rose Weber. *Education:* Attended University of Geneva, 1961-62; Sarah Lawrence College, B.A., 1964. *Residence:* New York, N.Y. *Agent:* Jane Rotrosen Agency, 318 East 51st St., New York, N.Y. 10022.

CAREER: Writer. Assistant managing editor of *Scanlan's,* 1968; managing editor of *Lifestyle,* 1973.

WRITINGS: Star Fever (novel), New American Library, 1970; *The Life Swap* (nonfiction), Dial, 1974; (under pseudonym Olivia Harmston) *The Coeds, Part Two* (novel), Ace Books, 1976; *Five Hundred Dollars* (novel), Ace Books, 1977; (under pseudonym Lindsay West) *Empire of the Ants* (novel based on the film), Ace Books, 1977; *Lily, Where's Your Daddy?* (nonfiction), Richard Marek, 1980; (under pseudonym Jennifer Rose) *Blueprint for Ecstasy* (novel), Berkeley Publishing, in press.

Author of about two hundred scripts for Canadian television series, including "Magistrate's Court" and "Marriage Confidential." Author of columns in *Eye, Gentleman's Quarterly,* and *Manhattan East.* Editorial assistant for *New York Post,* 1964-65.

*   *   *

WECHSLER, James A(rthur)   1915-

PERSONAL: Born October 31, 1915, in New York, N.Y.; son of Samuel (a lawyer) and Anna (Weisberger) Wechsler; married Nancy Fraenkel (a lawyer), October 5, 1934; children: Michael Barnaby (died, 1969), Holly Carol Wechsler Schwartztol. *Education:* Columbia University, B.A., 1935. *Home:* 185 West End Ave., New York, N.Y. 10023. *Office:* New York Post, 210 South St., New York, N.Y. 10002.

CAREER: Editor of *Student Advocate,* 1936-37; *Nation,* New York City, assistant editor, 1938-39; *PM* (newspaper), labor editor, 1940-41, Washington bureau chief, 1942-44; *New York Post,* New York City, Washington correspondent, 1946-49, editor, 1949-61, columnist, 1949—, editor of editorial page, 1961-80, associate editor, 1980—. *Military service:* U.S. Army, 1945. *Member:* American Civil Liberties Union, Americans for Democratic Action (member of executive committee, 1947—). *Awards, honors:* Award from American Veterans Committee, 1948, for journalistic effort in defense of civil liberties; Florence Lasker Civil Liberties Award from New York Civil Liberties Union, 1968; elected to Deadline Club Hall of Fame by Sigma Delta Chi (New York chapter), 1977.

WRITINGS: Revolt on the Campus, Covici, Friede, 1935, reprinted, University of Washington Press, 1973; (with Joseph P. Lash) *War, Our Heritage,* 1936; (with Harold Lavine) *War Propaganda and the United States,* Yale University Press, 1940, reprinted, Garland Publishing, 1972; *Labor Baron: A Portrait of John L. Lewis,* Morrow, 1944, reprinted, Greenwood Press, 1972; *The Age of Suspicion* (autobiographical), Random House, 1953; *Reflections of an Angry Middle-Aged Editor,* Random House, 1961; (with wife, Nancy F. Wechsler, and daughter, Holly Schwartztol) *In a Darkness* (personal account), Norton, 1972.

SIDELIGHTS: James Wechsler had been associated with the *New York Post* for fifteen years when he wrote *Reflections of an Angry Middle-Aged Editor* in 1961. A running commentary on the political state of affairs in the United States since World War II, the book drew cheers from reviewers for its "provocative" diatribe, but also received complaints concerning what was felt to be the author's disregard of tenable proposals to alleviate the problems he saw in society. "Much of what Wechsler writes seems unanswerable, and some of it needed saying," assessed W. E. Leuchtenburg of *Saturday Review.* "Unfortunately, he is much stronger on exortation and recrimination than he is on analysis." *Atlantic Monthly* writer Phoebe Adams, on the other hand, voiced her approval of the work: "Mr. Wechsler is neither a sociologist, a social psychologist, nor a philosopher. He does not probe into dark corners, and the materials of his book are the observations of a practical journalist with a passionate interest in politics and a conviction that, although utopia is unreachable, betterment is always obtainable." E. J. Hughes of the *New York Times Book Review* concurred that the book "is the echo of a lively mind, and a keen conscience, passionately at work."

BIOGRAPHICAL/CRITICAL SOURCES: *New York Times Book Review*, May 22, 1960; *Atlantic Monthly*, June 15, 1960; *Saturday Review of Literature*, July 23, 1960; *New York Review of Books*, May 18, 1972; *National Review*, May 26, 1972.

*   *   *

WEISS, Kenneth M(onrad)   1941-

PERSONAL: Born November 29, 1941, in Cleveland, Ohio; son of Harry (a federal government news officer) and Ella Weiss; children: Richard. *Education:* Oberlin College, B.A., 1963; St. Louis University, certificate in meteorology, 1964; University of Michigan, M.A., 1969, Ph.D., 1972. *Religion:* Unitarian-Universalist. *Home:* 2815 Stanton, Houston, Tex. 77025. *Office:* Center for Population Genetics, University of Texas, P.O. Box 20334, Houston, Tex. 77025.

CAREER: University of Michigan, Ann Arbor, research associate at School of Medicine, 1972-73; University of Texas, Center for Population Genetics, Houston, assistant professor, 1973-78, associate professor of genetics, 1978—. Visiting scholar at Stanford University, 1977. *Military service:* U.S. Air Force, meteorlogist, 1964-68; became captain. *Member:* American Association for the Advancement of Science, American Association of Human Genetics, American Association of Physical Anthropology, Population Association of America, Society for Medical Anthropology, Society for Epidemiological Research, Sigma Xi.

WRITINGS: *Demographic Models for Anthropology,* American Archaeological Association, 1973; (with P. A. Ballonoff) *Demographic Genetics,* Dowden, 1974; (with R. H. Ward) *The Demographic Evolution of Human Populations,* Academic Press, 1975. Cartoonist. Contributor of about thirty-five articles and reviews to scientific journals. Editor of *Historical Population Research.*

WORK IN PROGRESS: *The Tale of Tymzer,* a self-illustrated children's book; research on human genetics, epidemiology of cancer and aging, and human evolutionary demography.

SIDELIGHTS: Weiss wrote: "My professional work has been in the study of family risk to serious degenerative diseases like cancer and heart disease by studying very large genealogies with computers. I am also interested in the reason that so many different diseases strike humans (and other animals) at the same age, relative to their natural lifespan, and how diseases relate to the biology of aging. My light fiction writing was initially done for my son, motivated by his being kidnapped away during a divorce dispute (an American pastime); however, I intend to publish it and to carry on with it in the future."

AVOCATIONAL INTERESTS: Writing humorous verse, running, tennis, opera, walking in California, travel (Europe).

*   *   *

WEISSMAN, Rozanne   1942-

PERSONAL: Born September 14, 1942, in Cleveland, Ohio; daughter of Jack (a businessman) and Gert (Hibshman) Weissman. *Education:* Ohio University, B.S.J., 1964; also attended Georgetown University and American Management Association. *Home:* 1101 New Hampshire Ave. N.W., Washington, D.C. 20037.

CAREER/WRITINGS: Fairchild Publications, Inc., Cleveland, Ohio, reporter, 1964-66; *Cleveland Plain Dealer,* Cleveland, feature writer and promotion specialist, 1966-67; *Consumer News,* Washington, D.C., reporter and columnist, 1968; National Education Association, Washington, D.C., editor, media relations specialist, and head of communications network, 1968—; free-lance writer, 1976—. Contributor to numerous newspapers and magazines, including *Washington Post, Washington Star, Women's Wear Daily, Ladies' Home Journal, Playgirl, MORE, Education Digest, Washington Journalism Review,* and *Family Weekly.* Press worker for Utah Congressman Wayne Owens, 1974; investigative reporter for syndicated columnist Jack Anderson, 1974-75; public relations consultant to Karen Diamond's Figure Factory; instructor in social climbing at Open University, 1977—. *Member:* Education Writers of America, Educational Press Association of America, National Press Club, Washington Independent Writers. *Awards, honors:* Awards for feature writing from Educational Press Association of America, 1974, 1975; placement of articles in National Archives by Mrs. Lyndon B. Johnson.

SIDELIGHTS: Rozanne Weissman has had wide experience in newspaper, magazine, and newsletter writing, as well as all phases of public relations. Her writing assignments at the *Cleveland Plain Dealer* included travel articles, a restaurant column, ads, brochures, and numerous community events. She later helped write a syndicated column at *Consumer News.* As an investigative reporter, she helped columnist Jack Anderson break major stories about the Central Intelligence Agency, Capitol Hill abuses, and international human rights violations in Chile and elsewhere.

She told *CA:* "Though I have had a varied career as a reporter, writer, public relations specialist, and teacher of a zany, well-publicized course, nothing I have ever done compares with the phenomenal highs and lows of free-lance writing. The pay generally doesn't reflect the work and hours involved. Publishing is a revolving door, necessitating constant cultivation of new contacts and following a good editor wherever he or she may go, because really good editors are harder to find than a tankful of gas during an energy crisis!"

BIOGRAPHICAL/CRITICAL SOURCES: *Los Angeles Times,* November 16, 1978, November 30, 1978; *Maclean's,* December 11, 1978; *Washington Post,* February 4, 1979; *People,* February 26, 1979; *Playboy,* June, 1979, March, 1980; *New York Times,* October 20, 1979; *Boston Phoenix,* December 25, 1979; *London Times,* April 21, 1980.

*   *   *

WELLS, M. Gawain   1942-

PERSONAL: Born September 29, 1942, in St. George, Utah; son of George (a dairy farmer) and Hannah (a professor of home economics; maiden name, Hegsted) Wells; married Gayle Jensen, December 7, 1967; children: Matthew, Gregory, Stefanie, Carin, Jed. *Education:* Brigham Young University, B.S., 1967, M.S., 1968; Purdue University, Ph.D., 1972. *Religion:* Church of Jesus Christ of Latter-day Saints (Mormons). *Home:* 1463 West 1150 N., Provo, Utah 84601. *Office:* Comprehensive Clinic, Brigham Young University, Provo, Utah 84601.

CAREER: Brigham Young University, Provo, Utah, assistant professor, 1972-79, associate professor of psychology, 1979—, psychologist at Comprehensive Clinic. Private practice in clinical psychology; member of executive board of local drug abuse agency. *Member:* Utah Psychological Association.

WRITINGS: (With Larry Jensen) *Feelings: Helping Children Understand Emotions,* Brigham Young University Press, 1979. Contributor to psychology and education journals.

WORK IN PROGRESS: Research on adjustment processes for single adults—those divorced, widowed, or never married.

SIDELIGHTS: Wells commented: "Many try to teach children moral behavior by telling children (or others) how they should feel. However, being told to love or be generous does not teach or produce love or generosity; instead, it produces obligation or resentment. Emotional/moral education comes about by creating the emotion through stories or cases. The feeling is refreshed or newly discovered by the teacher. That is the focus of my book."

*   *   *

WELSH, Anne 1922-

PERSONAL: Born September 19, 1922, in Johannesburg, South Africa; married; children: four. *Education:* Attended University of the Witwatersrand and Somerville College, Oxford.

CAREER: University of the Witwatersrand, Johannesburg, South Africa, lecturer in economics.

WRITINGS: (Editor) *Africa South of the Sahara: An Assessment of Human and Material Resources,* Oxford University Press, 1951; *Set in Brightness* (poems), Purnell, 1968.*

*   *   *

WENNER, Jann S(imon) 1946-

PERSONAL: Born December 7, 1946, in New York, N.Y.; son of Edward (a businessman) and Ruth N. (Simmons) Wenner; married Jane Ellen Schindelheim, July 1, 1968; *Education:* Attended University of California, Berkeley, 1964-66. *Residence:* New York, N.Y. *Office:* Rolling Stone, 745 Fifth Ave., New York, N.Y. 10022.

CAREER: Ramparts, San Francisco, Calif., staff writer, 1966-67; *Rolling Stone,* San Francisco, founder and editor-in-chief, 1967—. Publisher of *Earth Times,* 1970-71; editor and publisher of *Outside,* 1976-77, and *Look,* 1979. Producer for Paramount Pictures, 1979—.

WRITINGS: (With John Lennon) *Lennon Remembers,* Straight Arrow Books, 1971; (with Jerry Garcia and Charles A. Reich) *Garcia: The Rolling Stone Interview by Charles Reich and Jann Wenner,* Straight Arrow Books, 1972.

SIDELIGHTS: In 1967 Jann Wenner borrowed $7,500, set up offices in a San Francisco printing plant, and launched the first issue of *Rolling Stone.* He told readers then that the magazine would be more than just another trade paper about artists and the music industry. Although it would feature comprehensive record reviews, inside looks at the recording industry, and exhaustive interviews with rock stars, Wenner explained that *Rolling Stone* was "not just about music, but also about the things and attitudes that the music embraces." In just four years, *Rolling Stone* became the leading rock music paper in the country, and ended its tenth year of publication with ad revenues of $8 million and a circula-

tion of 600,000. As Jay Acton noted in his book *Mugshots,* "There is *Stone* and then there is everything else."

To a large extent, the success of *Rolling Stone* can be attributed to its staff of writers, most of whom Wenner recruited. Jon Landau's music reviews, Joe Eszterhas's reports on modern culture, and Hunter S. Thompson's political writing created much of the magazine's identity in the 1970's. *Rolling Stone* covered aspects of a counter culture "that most national media hadn't yet discovered," observed *Newsweek's* Tony Schwartz. Award-winning articles on Charles Manson and the Altamont rock festival, interviews with John Lennon, Paul McCartney, Bob Dylan, and the Rolling Stones distinguished the magazine from a crowded field of similar publications and made Wenner, in Acton's estimation, "the single most powerful person in the rock press."

As Wenner and the magazine's audience matured, however, *Rolling Stone* underwent a "shift in emphasis from rock stars and political dissidents to show-business and political celebrities," Schwartz commented. Thompson and Eszterhas pursued movie-oriented careers, but equally talented writers like Howard Kohn and Alexander Cockburn took their places. "People leave and Rolling Stone goes on," Wenner mused. The editor disagrees with those who have criticized *Stone's* changing format, claiming that "Music is more broadly defined now—the President can quote Bob Dylan—and Rolling Stone is about modern American culture."

CA INTERVIEWS THE AUTHOR
CA interviewed Jann Wenner on April 25, 1980, at his office in New York City.

CA: What gave you the idea of starting Rolling Stone *in the first place?*

WENNER: I was a rock and roll music fan and there was no publication of any kind with regular coverage about music that reflected the quality, the mood, the attitude of the music.

CA: There were British rock and roll publications at the time, weren't there?

WENNER: I had been in England the summer before (1966) and had seen *Melody Maker* and *New Musical Express.* They were so far and away better than anything that was being published in the United States. *Melody Maker* was a little bit of an inspiration. It wasn't a great paper, but it was run by serious people covering music in a serious way, and you could read about the Beatles in it. I was really taken with it.

CA: There are a lot of differences between Rolling Stone *and* Melody Maker *even now.*

WENNER: Quite a few. But in the early days we used to take a lot of articles out of *Melody Maker.* We would reprint some of their stories and they would reprint some of ours.

CA: Is there some way you can sum up the historical significance of rock music?

WENNER: On the broadest level, I'd advise you to read Nietzsche's essay, called "The Birth of Tragedy," about Dionysian rites and the uses of music. In a political and social sense, in more than any other single way, rock and roll was the expression of young people after the war, the expression of the postwar baby boom, or whatever it was. Starting with Chuck Berry—up in the morning and off to school, ring ring goes the bell, can't wait til three o'clock rolls around to get out of here—Elvis, and the Beatles, it was a physical and spiritual place to escape, a place of communication where people could share ideas.

CA: You were at a convention in Atlanta recently, and at one point you talked about the low quality of television. Does your opinion of low quality extend to other media, and, if so, do you think that's the reason why Rolling Stone *was as successful as it was?*

WENNER: It is. I mean, we walked into a vacuum. Nobody was writing about music or covering it seriously. It was all Beatlemania-type stuff. Nobody realized what was going on there. Nobody was really seriously dealing with what the sixties were about or what they continue to be about.

CA: What do you think the sixties stood for?

WENNER: The sixties, which didn't end until 1974, was a period which affected the attitudes of a new generation toward themselves and their country in a parallel with the way the Depression affected our parents. With the Depression, we had a breakdown of economic systems in the country. Thus our parents all set out on the business of being secure—social security, national reconstruction, etc. In the sixties, we saw a breakdown of the moral systems in the country: Nixon, Vietnam, civil rights, drugs, and so we set out—in one fashion or another, some deliberately, some not so deliberately, some inadvertantly—to make sure that moral systems would never happen again, in a likewise manner.

CA: Do you think it's fair to say that Rolling Stone's *coverage has become more celebrity-oriented over the years?*

WENNER: We don't cover celebrities as such. We don't cover people for their celebrity. I don't like the word. We usually cover people who are well known—at least in terms of who is on the cover. Always have. Our first cover was John Lennon. Call him a celebrity, an artist, a musician, whatever you want. We aren't doing much now that is different than ten years ago. The times have changed as much as we have.

CA: Is Rolling Stone *any less liberal or radical than it used to be?*

WENNER: Probably a little more sober.

CA: Wasn't there a time when you decided that politics would be given equal coverage with rock music in Rolling Stone?

WENNER: We've been writing about politics since day one. If it wasn't the first issue, it was the second issue. We've done special issues on Chicago, Cambodia, Kent State, and the presidential elections every year. I happen to be interested in politics myself. I kept putting it in *Rolling Stone* in spite of every argument to the contrary. And it has paid off, it has worked. Having Hunter Thompson and Timothy Crouse cover the 1972 elections for us was a great coup. Who's done that lately? Not since Huntley-Brinkley anchored the conventions has there been that dramatic and new development in national political coverage. What brilliant political reporting can you remember in the last ten or fifteen years? That's it. And Richard Avedon, the pictures [of prominent Americans, mostly politicians] he took for us? We have distinguished ourselves in this area.

CA: One thing you haven't done from the beginning is inves-

tigative reporting. Why did you decide to go into that?

WENNER: The writers come along, the stories come along.

CA: Is there one of those pieces you're most proud of, most glad you did?

WENNER: We did a great job with Patty Hearst. [A detailed chronology, written by Howard Kohn and David Weir, of Patty Hearst's adventures during the first eight months following her abduction in February, 1974.]

CA: Two of your investigative reporters, Howard Kohn and Joe Eszterhas, had had bad experiences at other jobs before they started working for you. [Kohn was fired by the Detroit Free Press *in 1973 for allegedly fabricating a story about his own alleged kidnapping; Eszterhas had been fired by the* Cleveland Plain Dealer *for allegedly fabricating a story there.] Yet they did some good work for you.*

WENNER: Broken careers are our specialty. We'll mend your broken career.

CA: Weren't you a little worried about taking them on, or printing their material?

WENNER: No. I knew essentially what had happened in each case. It was all quite understandable. I guarantee you those papers wish they had those boys back.

CA: Joe Eszterhas is in Hollywood, now, isn't he?

WENNER: Joe's writing screenplays, though he still lives in northern California. Howard's finishing his book on Karen Silkwood. We did a good job on Karen Silkwood, too. It was Howard's idea.

CA: Did you consider New Times *a competitor of yours?*

WENNER: They went after a lot of the same stories we were going after, but because their standards were lower, in terms of writing, research, and accuracy, they could get it out a lot faster. But they never beat us on anything. And how long have they been dead, five years? They claimed they went out of business because nobody was interested in investigative reporting. Actually, no one's interested in boring reporting.

*CA: In the years much earlier, there were other magazines that were competing more closely—*Cheetah *and* Eye *(circa 1967 and 1968).*

WENNER: I don't know why *Cheetah* didn't make it. It had some interesting things in it. But come on, "Cheetah" was the name of a discotheque and not exactly reflective of the mood of the country. *Eye* never knew what it was doing. They were just trying to cash in on something they didn't really understand.

CA: Earlier, you were talking about putting political material in the magazine despite opposition. From other editors?

WENNER: The only serious flack I got was very early on, in 1970. Some of the political coverage we were then doing was terribly ordinary and undistinguishable. So I just ended it. A long, long time ago in a staff dispute I asked some people to leave, or they quit, and all these people went around saying they had left *Rolling Stone* because I was returning it to a music magazine intended not to cover politics, and they didn't want to be associated with it. "Politics" was basically a disguise for the real reasons they left, why they couldn't stay with me, or whatever. The upshot of it, the silliness of it, I think this was in 1970, was that we got more into politics since then than ever, and the record speaks for itself.

CA: Are you as active in the day-to-day operations of the magazine as you used to be?

WENNER: Not at all.

CA: What's your main activity now? Making movies?

WENNER: I take about three months off a year: recreation, skiing, or at the beach. I have a group of four people who report directly to me. I have nothing to do with getting each issue out. I spend time on movies, but right now the movies are in the process of getting the scripts going.

CA: You edited Look?

WENNER: We ran it for about two issues.

CA: What do you think the problem there was?

WENNER: Difficulty in dealing with the ownership. [French magazine magnate Daniel Filipacchi owned *Look* when Wenner edited its July and August, 1979, issues.]

CA: You were going to bring it out again on your own?

WENNER: We were going to, but we couldn't raise the money.

CA: Why did you want to edit Look *in the first place?*

WENNER: Because it was so much fun. I love doing magazines. The way those two issues turned out was a reflection of plans I'd had in my mind for years.

CA: There were a couple of other magazines you ran which didn't do very well: Earth Times *and* Outside. *Why didn't they do as well as* Rolling Stone?

WENNER: In regards to *Earth Times,* I was only twenty-four years old, thus I can't count that as a serious, adult thing. *Outside* was superb, but we did it at the same time we were moving to New York City. We did it—it survived; it's still being published. We sold it to somebody else. That was a fine magazine. I was very proud of that.

CA: Why did you move Rolling Stone *to New York?*

WENNER: I finally developed substantial offices of the company in both places. I had to fly back and forth all the time to run the business side here and editorial there. It became obnoxious, and I had to consolidate the offices in one place, and New York is where the publishing is.

CA: Isn't there a lot of tension now in the magazine between the literary, political, and investigative material on one side and the rock coverage on the other side? Aren't there really two audiences?

WENNER: We surveyed this for the first time years ago. Twenty percent of the people then read *Rolling Stone* for the music coverage, 20 percent read it for the general reporting, and 60 percent read both and liked both. I suspect that people who like the general interest features also read the music reporting, and people who like the music read the other writing.

CA: What are your plans for Rolling Stone *over the next couple of years?*

WENNER: We're going to study and then execute a plan to move circulation to a million. We've never done widespread, sophisticated marketing before, and I think we're going to start. And I think I'll need another broadening of the edi-

torial content: recreation, travel.

BIOGRAPHICAL/CRITICAL SOURCES: Look, December 15, 1970; Jay Acton, *Mugshots: Who's Who in the New Earth,* World, 1972; *Time,* July 15, 1974; *Newsweek,* October 3, 1977.

—*Interview by Peter Benjaminson*

*　　*　　*

WESLEY, Charles H(arris)   1891-

PERSONAL: Born December 2, 1891, in Louisville, Ky.; son of Charles Snowden and Matilda (Harris) Wesley; married Louise Johnson, November 25, 1915 (died, 1973); married Dorothy B. Porter, November 30, 1978; children: Louise Johnson (deceased), Charlotte Harris Wesley Holloman. *Education:* Fisk University, B.A., 1911; Yale University, M.A., 1913; attended Guilde Internationale, Paris, 1914, and Howard University Law School, 1915-16; Harvard University, Ph.D., 1925. *Politics:* Independent. *Religion:* Methodist. *Home:* 7632 17th St. N.W., Washington, D.C. 20012.

CAREER: Howard University, Washington, D.C., instructor in teaching history, 1913, instructor, 1914-18, assistant professor, 1918-19, associate professor, 1919-20, professor of history and head of history department, 1921-42, director of summer school program, 1937, acting dean of College of Liberal Arts, 1937-38, dean of Graduate School, 1938-42; Wilberforce University, Wilberforce, Ohio, president, 1942-47; Central State University, Wilberforce, president, 1942-65, president emeritus, 1965—; Association for the Study of Negro Life and History, Washington, D.C., president, 1950-65, executive director, 1965-72, director of research, 1972-74. Young Men's Christian Association (Y.M.C.A.), educational secretary, 1919-20, overseas secretary, 1920-21; president of Inter-University Council in Ohio, 1955-56; executive director of Afro-American Bicentennial Historical and Cultural Museum in Philadelphia, Pa., 1975-76.

MEMBER: American Antiquarian Society, American Historical Association, American Association of School Administrators, American Association of University Professors, American Geographical Society (fellow), National Council for Social Studies, National Historical Society, National Education Association, Society for the Advancement of Education, Black Academy of Arts and Letters, Southern Historical Association, Ohio College Association (member of executive committee, 1947-49, 1960-61, and 1964-65; chairman of resolutions committee, 1951-53; president, 1963-64), Association of Ohio College Presidents and Deans (president, 1954-55), Phi Beta Kappa, Alpha Phi Alpha (general president, 1931-64; historian, 1940-80), Masons. *Awards, honors:* Honorary degrees include D.D. from Wilberforce University, 1928, LL.D. from Allen University, 1932, Virginia State College, 1943, Morris Brown University, 1944, Paul Quinn College and Campbell College, both 1946, Morgan State College, 1961, University of Cincinnati, 1964, Tuskegee Institute, 1968, and Howard University, 1970; Ed.D. from Central State College, 1965; L.H.D. from Berea University, 1971. Guggenheim fellowship, 1930-31; Social Science Research Council grant, 1936-37; awards from Kentucky Education Association, Phi Beta Kappa, and Xenia Chamber of Commerce.

WRITINGS: The Collapse of the Confederacy, [Washington, D.C.], 1922, revised edition, Associated Publishers, 1937, reprinted, Russell, 1968; *Negro Labor in the United States, 1850-1925: A Study in American Economic*

History, Vanguard, 1927, reprinted, Russell, 1967; *The History of Alpha Phi Alpha: A Development in Negro College Life,* Howard University Press, 1929, 8th edition published as *The History of Alpha Phi Alpha: A Development in College Life,* Foundation Publishers, 1957, 11th edition, 1969; *Richard Allen: Apostle of Freedom,* Associated Publishers, 1935, reprinted, 1969; (editor) *The Negro in the Americas,* Graduate School, Howard University, 1940; *A Manual of Research and Thesis Writing for Graduate Students,* Graduate School, Howard University, 1941; *History of Sigma Pi Phi, First of the Negro-American Greek-Letter Fraternities,* Association for the Study of Negro Life and History, 1954; *History of the Improved Benevolent and Protective Order of Elks of the World, 1898-1954,* Association for the Study of Negro Life and History, 1955; (with Carter G. Woodson) *Negro Makers of History,* 5th edition (Wesley was not associated with earlier editions), Associated Publishers, 1958, 6th edition, 1968; (with Woodson) *The Story of the Negro Retold,* 4th edition (Wesley was not associated with earlier editions), Associated Publishers, 1959.

The History of the Prince Hall Grand Lodge of Free and Accepted Masons of the State of Ohio, 1849-1960: An Epoch in American Paternalism, Central State College Press, 1961; *Ohio Negroes in the Civil War,* Ohio State University Press, 1962; (with Woodson) *The Negro in Our History,* 10th edition (Wesley was not associated with earlier editions), Associated Publishers, 1962, 12th edition, 1972; *Neglected History: Essays in Negro History by a College President, Charles H. Wesley,* Central State College Press, 1965; (with Patricia W. Romero) *Negro Americans in the Civil War: From Slavery to Citizenship,* Publishers Co., 1967, 2nd edition, 1970; *In Freedom's Footsteps: From the African Background to the Civil War,* Publishers Co., 1968, revised edition, 1970; *Negro Citizenship in the United States: The Fourteenth Amendment and the Negro-American; Its Concepts and Developments, 1868-1968,* Association for the Study of Negro Life and History, 1968; *The Quest for Equality: From Civil War to Civil Rights,* Publishers Co., 1968; (editor and author of introduction) *The Mis-Education of the Negro,* Associated Publishers, 1969; *The Fifteenth Amendment and Black America, 1870-1970,* Associated Publishers, 1970; (reviser with Thelma D. Perry) Sadie Iola Daniel, *Women Builders,* Associated Publishers, 1970; *Prince Hall: Life and Legacy,* Prince Hall Affiliation, 1977; *Henry Arthur Callis: Life and Legacy,* Foundation Publishers, 1977. Editor of *The International Library of Negro Life and History,* eleven volumes, 1966-1967. Contributor of articles to magazines and newspapers.

SIDELIGHTS: Wesley commented to *CA:* "History should be an expanding subject, embracing all peoples and reflecting not only people of one color but all people. It should not be a part story but a whole one, written honestly and objectively. It should include both white and black. It must be devoid of racial or color superiority or inferiority. Historians are now witnessing the passing of the myths and assumptions about black folk. From our colleges have come the Negro scholars whose intellectual integrity and expanding brotherhood have been crossing the barriers made by the segregated school and the segregated life in order to achieve a whole life serviceable to all people."

*   *   *

WESLING, Donald 1939-

PERSONAL: Born May 6, 1939, in Buffalo, N.Y.; son of Truman Albert (a plant guard) and Helene Marguerite (Bullinger) Wesling; married Judith Elaine Dulinawka (a sports

manager), July, 1961; children: Benjamin, Molly, Natasha. *Education:* Harvard University, B.A., 1960, Ph.D., 1965; Trinity Hall, Cambridge, B.A., 1962. *Home:* 5649 Beaumont Ave., La Jolla, Calif. 92037. *Office:* Department of Literature, University of California, San Diego, Box 109, La Jolla, Calif. 92037.

CAREER: University of California, San Diego, La Jolla, assistant professor of literature, 1965-67; University of Essex, Colchester, England, lecturer in literature, 1967-70; University of California, San Diego, associate professor, 1970-78, professor of English, 1979—. *Member:* Modern Language Association of America. *Awards, honors:* National Endowment for the Humanities younger humanist fellowship, 1973-74.

WRITINGS: Wordsworth and the Adequacy of Landscape, Routledge & Kegan Paul, 1970; *The Chances of Rhyme,* University of California Press, 1980; *John Muir: To Yosemite and Beyond,* University of Wisconsin Press, 1980; *American Sentences* (prose poems), Black Mesa Press, 1980. Contributor to literature journals.

WORK IN PROGRESS: A book on modern theories of meter; a book on poetic technique since Wordsworth.

SIDELIGHTS: Wesling commented to *CA:* "To me it seems there is no privileged form of discourse. Mandlesh'tam was right: 'Do not compare; the living are incomparable.'"

*   *   *

WEST, Lindsay
See WEBER, Nancy

*   *   *

WEST, Marion B(ond) 1936-

PERSONAL: Born July 8, 1936, in Elberton, Ga.; daughter of Thomas Marion and Jewette (a bank officer; maiden name, Smith) Bond; married Jerry Michael West (a health service manager), April 9, 1958; children: Julie West Garmon, Jennifer, Jon and Jeremy (twins). *Education:* Attended Lander College, 1956-58. *Religion:* Baptist. *Home:* 1221 Stephens St., Lilburn, Ga. 30247.

CAREER: Southern Bell Telephone & Telegraph Co., Atlanta, Ga., stenographer, 1957-58; stenographer in Gainesville, Ga., 1959-60; writer, 1974—. Member of Mothers on the March (MOMS). *Member:* Scribe Tribe.

WRITINGS—Nonfiction: Out of My Bondage, Broadman, 1976; *No Turning Back,* Broadman, 1978; *Two of Everything But Me,* Broadman, 1979; *Learning to Lean,* Doubleday, 1980. Contributor of more than fifty articles to inspirational magazines, including *Guideposts, Home Life, Marriage and Family, Sunday Digest,* and *Catholic Digest.*

WORK IN PROGRESS: Daily devotionals for *Guideposts.*

SIDELIGHTS: "I can't remember when I didn't want to write," Marion West told *CA.* "I even liked the way paper smelled. For over twenty years I wrote. Everything I submitted was rejected. I still wrote, but almost gave up hope of ever having anything published. After I had four children and motherhood had become almost too much for me (especially after having twin sons), one day I just gave up trying to run my life. In my den alone, I surrendered my life and my will to God. I fully expected to be called to Africa to the mission field the next day. (What else was there for a woman who had committed the rest of her life to God?)

"Miracle of miracles! God didn't want me to go to Africa. That week my first article was accepted, misspelled words and all. *Guideposts* had accepted 'Thank You, Lord, for My Broken Dishwasher.' That was in March of 1974. In 1976 my first book was published, and by 1980 three more had been published.

"Even though writing is important, and I feel the secret was that now I could be fully honest, *not writing* has also become very important. There are times when I must abandon it completely and see about my family. I feel God helps me not to write as much as he helps me to write.

"I always felt our family was unusual, even strange. But now through many confirmations from people who've read what I wrote, I have discovered that we are quite normal. It is a source of encouragement that so many families identify with our struggles and victories. There have been many days when I feel I would gladly have given up writing and even motherhood in order to go to Africa and be that missionary. Surely, it must be easier."

AVOCATIONAL INTERESTS: "Rescuing stray animals and finding homes for them."

BIOGRAPHICAL/CRITICAL SOURCES: Thomasville Times-Enterprise, November, 1979.

*   *   *

WESTCOTT, Kathleen
See ABRAHAMSEN, Christine Elizabeth

*   *   *

WESTELL, Anthony   1926-

PERSONAL: Born January 27, 1926, in Exeter, England; son of John Wescombe (an insurance agent and manager) and Blanche (Smedley) Westell; married Jeanne Margaret Collings (a writer), January 10, 1950; children: Dan, Tracy. *Education:* Educated in Exeter, England. *Office:* Department of Journalism, Carleton University, Ottawa, Canada.

CAREER: Express and Echo, Exeter, England, apprentice reporter, 1942-43, 1945-48; associated with *Evening World,* Bristol, England, 1948-49; Northcliffe Newspaper Group, London, England, political correspondent, 1950-55; *Evening Standard,* London, diplomatic correspondent, 1955-56; *Globe and Mail,* Toronto, Ontario, reporter, 1956-59, member of editorial board, chief editorial writer, and assistant to editor, 1959-64, chief of Ottawa bureau, 1964-69; *Toronto Star,* Toronto, affairs columnist and Ottawa editor, 1969-71, Ottawa editor, 1973-74; Carleton University, Ottawa, Ontario, 1972-73, 1974-75, associate professor, 1975—, visiting fellow at Institute of Canadian Studies, 1974-75. Founding associate director of Carleton Journalism Poll (public opinion research organization); founding editor of *Carlton Journalism Review;* senior associate at Carnegie Endowment for International Peace, 1980. Radio and television commentator. *Military service:* Royal Navy, 1943-46. *Member:* National Press Club, Newspaper Guild, Britannia Yacht Club. *Awards, honors:* National Newspaper Awards, 1963, for spot news reporting, and 1970, for staff correspondence.

WRITINGS: Paradox: Trudeau as Prime Minister, Prentice-Hall, 1972; *The New Society,* McClelland & Stewart, 1977. Contributor to American magazines and newspapers. Founding editor of *Carleton Journalism Review.*

WORK IN PROGRESS: A collection of his Ottawa writings, 1964-70; research on Canadian-U.S. economic relations, with publication expected to result.

SIDELIGHTS: Westell wrote: "I am by profession a political journalist. Both my books have been works of extended journalism: *Paradox* was an account of Prime Minister Trudeau's first four years in office; *The New Society* was an analysis of Canada's constitutional, economic, and social problems, with prescriptions."

*   *   *

WESTERN, Mark
See CRISP, Anthony Thomas

*   *   *

WESTMORELAND, William C(hilds)   1914-

PERSONAL: Born March 26, 1914, in Spartanburg County, S.C.; son of James Ripley (a textile plant manager) and Eugenia (Childs) Westmoreland; married Katherine Stevens Van Deusen, 1947; children: Katherine Stevens, James Ripley, Margaret Childs. *Education:* U.S. Military Academy, West Point, B.S., 1936; attended Advanced Management Program, Harvard University, 1954. *Religion:* Protestant. *Home address:* P.O. Box 1059, Charleston, S.C. 29402.

CAREER: U.S. Army, career officer, 1936-72; retired as general. During World War II was commanding officer of the Thirty-fourth Field Artillery Battalion in North Africa and Sicily; landed in D-Day offensive with Ninth Infantry Division, and became chief of staff of the division in 1944; chief of staff of Eighty-second Airborne Division, 1947-50; instructor at Command and General Staff College, Fort Leavenworth, Kan., 1950, and at Army War College, Fort Leavenworth, 1951-52; commander of 187th Airborne Regimental Combat Team in Korea, 1952-53; secretary of Army General Staff, Washington, D.C., 1955-58; became major general, 1956; commander of 101st Airborne Division "Screaming Eagles," 1958-60; superintendent of U.S. Military Academy, West Point, N.Y., 1960-63; became general, 1964; commander of U.S. Military Assistance Command, Vietnam, 1964-68; Chief of Staff of the U.S. Army, 1968-72. Chairman of Governor's Task Force for Economic Growth for the State of South Carolina, 1972-74. Lecturer; member of board of directors of several corporations and foundations.

AWARDS, HONORS—Military: Received more than thirty national and international awards, including: Legion of Merit with two Oak Leaf Clusters; Bronze Star with Oak Leaf Cluster; Air Medal with nine Oak Leaf Clusters; Order of Military Merit (Brazil); Order of Guerrileros Lanza (Bolivia); Order of the Rising Sun, First Class; Order of Military Merit Taeguk (Korea); Legion of Honor (France); Order of Sikatuna (Philippines); Chuong My Medal, National Order of Vietnam. Civilian: More than twenty awards for service, including: Franklin Award from Printing Industries of Metropolitan New York; gold medal for distinguished achievement from Holland Society of New York; named "Man of the Year" by *Time* magazine, 1965; and Patron of the Year award from University of Notre Dame. Doctor of Law from Temple University, 1963, University of South Carolina, 1967, and Howard Payne College; Doctor of Military Science from the Citadel, 1960, and Norwich University, 1970.

WRITINGS: A Soldier Reports (memoirs), Doubleday, 1976. Contributor to reports on operations in Vietnam, 1969. Also contributor of articles to national newspapers and magazines.

SIDELIGHTS: Although he played a key role in the D-Day offensive of World War II, General William Westmoreland is best known to most Americans as the commander of U.S. forces in Vietnam during the late 1960's. He is also a public figure who very rarely draws impartial response. During the war, hawks saw him as a dedicated military officer whose ethics and judgement needed no defense. But then came My Lai, a tragic incident in which Vietnamese civilians were shot and killed by American soldiers, and liberals and peace groups insinuated that Westmoreland should be held responsible for the actions of Charlie Company, one of approximately one thousand infantry companies in his American command.

Telford Taylor, U.S. prosecutor at the Nuremburg trials, once stated that Westmoreland "could be found guilty of Vietnam war crimes if he were to be tried by the same standard under which the U.S. hanged Japanese General Tomayuki Yamashita." Yamashita, in an unprecedented decision, was held responsible for the atrocities committed by his troops in the Philippines, even though he had never issued orders for such actions. After the decision in the Calley court martial, Westmoreland was asked about his culpability in the My Lai incident and a few lesser instances of American atrocities in Vietnam. He flatly rejected any blame: "No, I feel no guilt, not in the least. It is an absurd allegation. You cannot compare my role and conduct in Vietnam with that of General Yamashita. He failed to follow up on allegations and reports of atrocities and bring the men to justice."

Even though Westmoreland recommended demotions for Major General Samuel Koster and Brigadier General George Young, Jr., the highest ranking American officers during My Lai, he could not totally dispel the suspicions of many Americans that the Calley verdict was a whitewash. Westmoreland noted that while several officers were court-martialed, only Calley was convicted. "Many Americans did not understand," he wrote, "that under the Law of the Land (the Uniform Code of Military Justice) the Chief of Staff [Westmoreland] had no jurisdiction over the Army's court-martial system. That power was vested in the Secretary of the Army, a civilian appointed by the President."

Encouraged by the late president, Dwight D. Eisenhower, Westmoreland kept a journal of his years in Vietnam and has taken much material from it for his book, *A Soldier Reports*. *National Review* critic Norman Hannah called it "an account of a generation of staggering military change as reflected in the life and experiences of one of the leading professionals of the period. . . . a soldier who is competent, devoted, straightforward, possessed of patience, and tolerance for the view of others, a man who modestly did his best for his country."

Westmoreland told *CA:* "History may well pass the judgment that the Vietnam war was a watershed for America. One can make a case for the proposition that we should have never made the political commitment to the people of South Vietnam. But, having made it, we should have made good our pledge. It was in our grasp following the Tet Offensive of 1968. Our default has plagued us and will continue to do so."

BIOGRAPHICAL/CRITICAL SOURCES: Time, May 10, 1968, December 12, 1969, January 18, 1971, January 21, 1974; *Newsweek,* April 21, 1969, January 11, 1971, April 12, 1971; *U.S. News and World Report,* September 29, 1969, June 19, 1972; *Christian Century,* June 9, 1971; *Biography News,* Gale, February, 1974; *New York Times Book Review,* February 1, 1976; *New York Review of Books,* May 13, 1976; *National Review,* June 11, 1976.

*   *   *

WHALE, John (Hilary) 1931-

PERSONAL: Born December 19, 1931, in Oxford, England; son of John Seldon (a theologian) and Mary (Carter) Whale; married Judith Laurie Hackett (an actress and writer), Octo-

ber 22, 1957; children: Toby James. *Education:* Corpus Christi College, Oxford, B.A., 1955, M.A., 1958. *Politics:* None. *Religion:* Church of England. *Home:* 21 Melville Rd., Barnes, London SW13 9RH, England. *Office:* London Sunday Times, 200 Gray's Inn Rd., London WC1X 8EZ, England.

CAREER: University of Minnesota, Minneapolis, teaching assistant, 1957-58; Office de Radiodiffusion Television Francaise, Paris, France, writer, 1958-60; Independent Television News (ITN), reporter in London, England, 1960-67, and in Washington, D.C., 1967-69; *London Sunday Times,* London, editorial writer, 1969—, religious affairs correspondent, 1979—. Director of London reporting program, University of Missouri School of Journalism, 1980—. Church warden of Barnes parish church, 1976—. *Military service:* Royal Army Intelligence Corps, 1950-51; became lieutenant. *Member:* International Institute of Communications, Media Society. *Awards, honors:* Winifred Mary Stanford Prize, 1980, for *One Church, One Lord.*

WRITINGS: The Half-Shut Eye: Television and Politics in Britain and America, St. Martin's, 1969; (with others) *Ulster,* Penguin, 1972; *Journalism and Government: A British View,* University of South Carolina Press, 1972; *Politics of the Media,* Humanities, 1977, revised edition, 1980; *One Church, One Lord,* SCM Press, 1979; (editor) *The Man Who Leads the Church,* Harper, 1980. Contributor of articles to professional journals and reviews to *Times Literary Supplement.*

SIDELIGHTS: According to *New Statesman* reviewer Anthony Howard, Whale's *The Half-Shut Eye* is "in part the story of how one professional reporter gradually grew totally disillusioned with the limitations of a medium in which he had initially chosen to make his career. . . . It is also a shrewd and perceptive study of the whole complex mesh between politics and television both in Britain and America, as observed by someone lucky enough to have a ringside seat for three elections (two in the UK, one in the US) virtually on the trot."

Among the problems of television Whale cities in his first book are its limitations in grasping complex issues and the inability of pictures to adequately report events. The disturbances at the 1968 national Democratic convention in Chicago, for example, were recorded in depth by the cameras; but, as critic Neil Compton pointed out, television "could neither show why it was happening, nor expect the audience to tolerate the kind of long narrative that would explain why: Television is graphic rather than analytic."

In the end, reported Compton, Whale "attacks the view that television is a noble instrument misused by crassly commercial interests: 'Public opinion is not wrongly informed by television, but inadequately informed. People who lean chiefly on television for reports of current events cannot always reach sensible judgments because television's limited capacities only allow it to dispense limited information.'" Both Compton and Howard agreed that *The Half-Shut Eye* was "one of the best books ever written on television."

Whale studied the "role of journalism as the prime distributor of information and opinion concerning world affairs" in his second book, *Journalism and Government. New Republic* praised Whale's "comprehensive and well-balanced" account of the functions of journalism as an "indispensable instrument of government." *Economist* added that Whale "knows his journalists and what is wrong and vain and fallible about them. He can also be very commonsensical: the fashionable remedies for the sicknesses of the press, as an industry, do not persuade him."

Whale told *CA:* "Having had time as a television foreign correspondent in Washington to write a book about television, I realized that I belonged more to the written word than to the spoken word. I have been happy ever since with the *Sunday Times,* the best of English newspapers, and have sought to defend its values in a couple of other books. As a journalist I have written a good deal about Northern Ireland, and now find my writing interests shifting from politics squarely to religion. My latest book is a serial biography of the Church of England, told in the lives of the rectors of a single parish church—my own."

BIOGRAPHICAL/CRITICAL SOURCES: New Statesman, May 23, 1969, June 16, 1972; *Economist,* May 31, 1969, May 13, 1972; *Saturday Review,* August 9, 1969; *Book World,* August 10, 1969; *New Republic,* June 17, 1972.

*   *   *

WHALLEY, George 1915-

PERSONAL: Born July 25, 1915, in Kingston, Ontario, Canada; son of Arthur Francis Cecil and Dorothy (Quirk) Whalley; married Elizabeth Cecilia Muriel Watts, July 25, 1944; children: Katharine Cecilia Whalley Clark, Christopher Gilbert, Emily Elizabeth. *Education:* Bishop's University, B.A., 1935, M.A., 1948; Oriel College, Oxford, B.A., 1939, M.A., 1945; King's College, London, Ph.D., 1950. *Religion:* Anglican. *Home address:* R.R.1, Hartington, Ontario, Canada K0H 1W0. *Office:* Department of English, Queen's University, Kingston, Ontario, Canada K7L 3N6.

CAREER: Rothesay Collegiate School, New Brunswick, teacher, 1935-36, 1939-40; Bishop's University, Lennoxville, Quebec, lecturer, 1945-47, assistant professor of English, 1947-48; Queen's University, Kingston, Ontario, assistant professor, 1950-53, associate professor, 1953-58, professor of English, 1958-80, James Cappon Professor, 1962-67, 1977-80, head of department, 1962-67, 1977-80, professor emeritus, 1980—. Visiting professor at University of Wisconsin—Madison, 1962. Member of Advisory Committee on Canadian Service Colleges and Ontario Rhodes Scholarship Selection Board, 1962-67. *Military service:* Royal Canadian Navy Volunteer Reserve, 1940-56, active duty, 1940-45; served in Atlantic and Mediterranean theaters; became commander; received Canadian Forces Decoration.

MEMBER: Canadian Federation of the Humanities (member of board of directors, 1978-80), Royal Society of Canada (fellow), Association of Canadian University Teachers of English (chairman, 1958-59), Humanities Association of Canada (founding member; life member), Charles Lamb Society, Bibliographical Society, Royal Society of Literature (fellow), Kingston Symphony Association (president, 1963-70). *Awards, honors:* Rhodes scholar at Oxford University, 1936; Bronze Medal from Royal Humane Society, 1941, for saving life at sea; Nuffield fellow, 1956-57; Guggenheim fellow, 1967-68; Killam senior fellow, 1973-75; D.Litt. from Carleton University, 1977, and University of Saskatchewan, 1979; D.C.L. from Bishop's University, 1979.

WRITINGS: Poems, 1939-1944, Ryerson, 1946; *No Man an Island* (poems), Clarke, Irwin, 1948; *Poetic Process,* Routledge & Kegan Paul, 1953, Meridian, 1967; *Coleridge and Sara Hutchinson,* Routledge & Kegan Paul, 1955; *The Legend of John Hornby,* Macmillan, 1962; *Marginalia of S. T. Coleridge,* Volume I, Princeton University Press, 1980.

Editor: *Selected Poems of George Herbert Clarke,* Ryerson, 1954; *Writing in Canada,* Macmillan, 1956; *A Place of Liberty,* Clarke, Irwin, 1964; *Death in the Barren Ground: The Diary of Edgar Christian,* Oberon, 1980; *Christopher Pepys,* privately printed, 1980.

Contributor: George Watson, editor, *Cambridge Bibliography of English Literature,* Volume 5, Cambridge University Press, 1958; Allan Wade, *A Bibliography of the Writings of W. B. Yeats,* second revised edition, Hart-Davis, 1958; John Enck, editor, *Academic Discourse,* Appleton, 1964; John Glassco, editor, *English Poetry in Quebec,* McGill University Press, 1965; Alex Preminger, *Encyclopaedia of Poetry and Poetics,* Princeton University Press, 1965; S. P. Zitner, editor, *The Practice of Modern Literary Scholarship,* Scott, Foresman, 1966; Kathleen Coburn, editor, *Coleridge: A Collection of Critical Essays,* Spectrum, 1967; Andy Wainwright, editor, *Notes for a Native Land,* Oberon, 1969; Griogio Tagliacozzo and Hayden V. White, editors, *Giambattista Vico: An International Symposium,* Johns Hopkins University Press, 1969; George Watson, editor, *New Cambridge Bibliography of English Literature,* Volume III, Cambridge University Press, 1969.

Hans Eichner, editor, *"Romantic" and Its Cognates: The European History of a Word,* University of Toronto Press, 1972; John D. Baird, editor, *Editing Texts of the Romantic Period,* Hakkert, 1972; AJ. M. Smith, editor, *The Canadian Century: English-Canadian Writing Since Confederation,* Gage, 1973; James Downey and Ben Jones, editors, *Fearful Joy: Thomas Gray Bicentenary Conference,* McGill University Press, 1974; John Beer, editor, *Coleridge's Variety: Bicentenary Studies,* Macmillan, 1974; Smith, editor, *The Canadian Experience: A Brief Survey of English Canadian Prose,* Gage, 1974; Joseph Gold, editor, *In the Name of Language!,* Macmillan, 1975; Juliet McMaster, editor, *Jane Austen's Achievement: Jane Austen Bicentennial Conference,* Macmillan, 1976; Heather Robertson, *A Terrible Beauty: The Art of Canada at War,* James Lorimer, 1977.

Author of more than sixty scripts for radio and television, including Canadian Broadcasting Corp. and narrations for National Film Board. Contributor of nearly one hundred articles and reviews to scholarly and critical journals.

WORK IN PROGRESS: Marginalia of S. T. Coleridge, Volumes II-V, publication by Princeton University Press expected in 1981-85; translating and writing commentary for Aristotle's *Poetics,* publication expected in 1981.

AVOCATIONAL INTERESTS: Music, typography, skiing.

*   *   *

WHEAT, Patte 1935-
(Pat Mahan, Patte Wheat Mahan)

PERSONAL: Born October 1, 1935, in Los Angeles, Calif.; daughter of Robert Burdette (a salesman) and Evelyn (Allen) Wheat; married William Allen Mahan (a writer, actor, and producer), April 20, 1955 (divorced April 3, 1973); children: Kerrigan Patrick Mahan, Colleen Shannon Mahan, Erin Kelly Mahan. *Education:* Attended Loyola-Marymount College, Los Angeles, Calif., and El Camino College, 1970-71, 1974-75. *Politics:* "Registered Democrat." *Religion:* None. *Home:* 764 Avenue B, Redondo Beach, Calif. 90277. *Office:* Parents Anonymous, 22330 Hawthorne Blvd., Torrance, Calif. 90505.

CAREER: American International Pictures, Beverly Hills, Calif., story analyst, 1969-70; Register & Tribune Syndicate, writer of column "Potomac Fever," under name Pat Mahan, 1971-73; Parents Anonymous, Torrance, Calif., staff writer and editor of house newsletter, *Frontiers,* 1974—.

WRITINGS: (Under name Patte Wheat Mahan) *Three for a Wedding* (novel), McKay, 1965; *By Sanction of the Victim* (nonfiction), Major Books, 1976; (with Leonard Lieber)

Hope for the Children: A Personal History of Parents Anonymous, Winston Press, 1979; (with Dale Hale) *You're Getting Closer* (cartoons), Price, Stern, 1979.

Other: "The Game" (screenplay; short subject), 1964; "Doctor, You've Got to Be Kidding" (screenplay; adapted from own novel, *Three For a Wedding*), Metro-Goldwyn-Mayer, 1967; (author of narration) "Treasure Trove of the Century" (teleplay), broadcast by American Broadcasting Co. (ABC-TV), 1967. Author, with Dale Hale, of panel cartoons "You're Getting Closer," King Features, 1976—. Contributor of articles to magazines, including *Los Angeles* magazine and *Better Homes and Gardens.*

SIDELIGHTS: Wheat told *CA:* "Parents Anonymous is a self-help organization for parents who abuse their children or feel that they might have the potential for abuse. It is funded by the Department of Health, Education, and Welfare (now the Department of Health and Human Services), and has over one thousand chapters internationally. I began researching child abuse in the late sixties because of one particular case that sparked my interest and resulted in my writing *By Sanction of the Victim.* My research led to the discovery of Mothers Anonymous in 1970, which later became Parents Anonymous. My years with Parents Anonymous culminated in one book, *Hope for the Children,* and a lifelong interest in family relationships."

AVOCATIONAL INTERESTS: Parenting, writing comedy, nutrition.

BIOGRAPHICAL/CRITICAL SOURCES: South Bay Daily Breeze, May 10, 1976.

*   *   *

WHELAN, Gloria (Ann)   1923-

PERSONAL: Born November 23, 1923, in Detroit, Mich.; daughter of William Joseph (a contractor) and Hildegarde (Kilwinski) Rewoldt; married Joseph Leo Whelan (a neurologist), June 12, 1948; children: Joseph William, Jennifer Ann Whelan Smeeton. *Education:* University of Michigan, B.A., 1945, M.S.W., 1948. *Religion:* Roman Catholic. *Home and office address:* Oxbow, R.R.2, Mancelona, Mich. 49659. *Agent:* Mitch Douglas, International Creative Management, 40 West 57th St., New York, N.Y. 10019.

CAREER: Minneapolis Family and Children's Service, Minneapolis, Minn., social worker, 1948-49; Children's Center of Wayne County, Detroit, Mich., supervisor of group services and day care program, 1963-68; Spring Arbor College, Spring Arbor, Mich., instructor in American literature, 1979—. Member of board of directors of Archives of American Art, and Friends of Modern Art of Detroit Institute of Arts; chairman of Detroit Artists Market. *Awards, honors:* Award from Friends of American Writers, 1979, for *A Clearing in the Forest.*

WRITINGS: A Clearing in the Forest (young adult novel), Putnam, 1978; *A Time to Keep Silent* (young adult novel), Putnam, 1979; *The Pathless Woods* (biographical novel), Crowell, 1980. Contributor of stories, poems, and reviews to literary journals and newspapers, including *Kansas Quarterly, Michigan Quarterly, South Shore, Ontario Review,* and *Country Life.*

WORK IN PROGRESS: A young adult novel about the Vietnamese Boat People; a short story for the *Virginia Quarterly.*

SIDELIGHTS: Whelan told *CA:* "We moved from Detroit to the woods of northern Michigan in 1973. Life in a remote setting is always an inward journey. For me, it has meant a certain surprise at discovering how much my own values conflict with those of today's society. I, who began life as something of a radical, am rather appalled at what I wrought. In my short stories, I find myself exploring this theme by inventing situations in which the old and the young confront one another. I am trying to do what Henry James did in setting the American and the European at one another.

"James has been a constant resource for me. I like his preoccupation with small, troublesome moral decisions that have a way of adding up and defining your life. In gratitude to Henry James for all he has given me, some years ago I began collecting James's first editions and sending them to his home in Rye, England, now owned by the British National Trust. So far, I have sent eighty-six first editions. I have six to go. James was prolific.

"My young adult novels reflect the impact a wilderness setting has on my writing. I view nature as a kind of Rorschach test. We see what we are looking for, what our mood dictates—all spring flowers and birdsong one day and a bloated deer carcass and ransacked bird's nest the next. I try to remain objective about nature, to report what I see. But it's the mystery that attracts me.

"On a trip to the Redwoods National Park in California, I came upon a series of signs that carefully set forth all the specific details of the history of the redwoods. The last sign, obviously put there by a naturalist with tongue in cheek, was a quote by Walt Whitman: 'You must not know too much or be too precise or scientific about birds and trees and flowers . . . a certain vagueness, perhaps ignorance, credulity—helps your enjoyment of these things.' I agree. Maybe this is what Henry James meant when he said, 'Thoreau is best read in the city.'"

*   *   *

WHITE, Benjamin V(room)   1908-

PERSONAL: Born February 19, 1908, in Summit, N.J.; son of Benjamin Vroom, Sr. (an architect) and Margaret (Risk) White; married Charlotte Green Conover, September 6, 1933 (died April 6, 1966); married Helen Cobb Solomon, June 14, 1969; children: (first marriage) Thomas Conover, James Boyd, Benjamin Vroom III, Richard Conover, Charlotte Conover; (second marriage) Stanley Cobb, John Cobb. *Education:* Princeton University, A.B., 1930; Harvard University, M.D., 1934, postdoctoral study, 1936-38. *Residence:* West Hartford, Conn. *Office:* 85 Jefferson St., Hartford, Conn. 06106.

CAREER: In private practice of internal medicine (specializing in gastroenterology). Assistant clinical professor at Yale University, 1947-77; member of board of directors of Gaylord Hospital and board of trustees of Wainwright House Center for Human Development. *Member:* American College of Physicians (past member of board of governors), American Gastroenterological Association, American Clinical and Climatological Association, Connecticut Society of Internal Medicine (past president), Hartford County Medical Society (past president), Hartford Medical Society (past president). *Awards, honors:* Named physician of the year by Connecticut Digestive Disease Society, 1974; distinguished service award from Connecticut Society of Internal Medicine, 1974.

WRITINGS: (With Stanley Cobb and C. M. Jones) *Mucous Colitis,* National Research Council, 1939; (with Charles F. Geschickter) *Diagnosis in Daily Practice,* Lippincott, 1947; *Ancestors and Descendants of Jeremiah White and Matilda Howell,* Progress Publishing, 1965; (with wife, Helen C. S. White) *The Excitement of Change,* Seabury, 1975.

WORK IN PROGRESS: A biography of Dr. Stanley Cobb, with wife, Helen C. S. White.

SIDELIGHTS: White wrote: "I have always been interested in mind-body problems. I have had at least one peak religious experience and have been fascinated by the growth process ever since. My wife and I have held 'receptive listening' (Rogerian with a pinch of Jung) at Wainwright House Center for years. We have also been working with Gestalt."

AVOCATIONAL INTERESTS: Art, sailing.

* * *

WHITE, Gordon Eliot 1933-

PERSONAL: Born October 25, 1933, in Glen Ridge, N.J.; son of Maurice B. (an engineer) and Sarah G. (a teacher) White; married Nancy Johnson, 1955 (divorced, 1957); married Mary Joan Briggs (a reporter), August 6, 1960; children: Sarah Elizabeth, Gordon O'Neal Brewster, David McIntyre. *Education:* Cornell University, B.A., 1956; Columbia University, M.S., 1957. *Religion:* Episcopal. *Home:* 1502 Stonewall Rd., Alexandria, Va. 22302. *Office:* P.O. Box 3067, Alexandria, Va. 22302.

CAREER: Nassau Daily Review-Star, Nassau, N.Y., reporter and photographer, 1948-50; *Morris County Citizen,* Mountain Lakes, N.J., reporter and photographer, 1950-51; *Ithaca Journal,* Ithaca, N.Y., reporter and photographer, 1951-55; *Paterson Evening News,* Paterson, N.J., reporter, 1956; *American Banker,* New York, N.Y., copy editor, 1958; *Deseret News,* Salt Lake City, Utah, Washington correspondent, 1958—. Reporter and photographer for *Freeport Leader,* 1948-50; Washington correspondent for *Chicago American, Lincoln Journal, Albuquerque Journal, Jacksonville Times-News,* 1958-61, KLS-TV, 1958-64, WJR-Radio, 1959, and KGMB-Radio, 1961-65; reporter from Europe, 1959, the Antarctic, 1959, and the Caribbean, 1962. *Military service:* U.S. Army, 1957. *Member:* National Press Club, Sigma Delta Chi, Pi Delta Epsilon, National Yacht Club. *Awards, honors:* First prize from Sigma Delta Chi, 1955, for news photograph; Raymond Clapper Award from White House Correspondents' Association, 1978, for "painstaking reporting and good craftsmanship" in Washington correspondence; National Press Club Award, 1978, for outstanding Washington correspondence on the White House and executive agencies; Sigma Delta Chi National Award for Washington correspondence, 1979; Roy W. Howard Award, 1979, for outstanding public service in Washington correspondence; Regional Associated Press Award, 1979, for investigative reporting; Mark E. Peterson Award, 1979, for outstanding journalistic achievement; Investigative Reporters and Editors' Award, 1980, for distinguished Washington reporting.

WRITINGS: A Brief Early History of Christ Church, Alexandria, Virginia, Christ Church Foundation, 1976. Author of "Washington," a column in *Deseret News,* 1958—, and of "Surplus Sidelights," a column in *CQ Magazine,* 1964-75.

WORK IN PROGRESS: The story of radioactive fallout from the 1945-62 U.S. atomic weapons test, tentatively titled "Fallout!"

SIDELIGHTS: White has covered the military, the space program, and general politics in the United States and overseas. His reporting focuses on the Department of Interior, including water and mineral resources and geology. *Avocational interests:* Flying (licensed pilot), sailing small boats, restoring antique automobiles.

WHITE, John Baker
See BAKER WHITE, John

* * *

WHITE, William L(indsay) 1900-1973

PERSONAL: Born June 17, 1900, in Emporia, Kan.; died July 26, 1973, in Emporia, Kan.; son of William Allen (a journalist) and Sallie (Lindsay) White; married Katherine Klinkenberg, April 29, 1931; children: Barbara (Mrs. Paul David Walker). *Education:* Attended Kansas University, 1918-20; Harvard University, A.B., 1924.

CAREER: Emporia Gazette, Emporia, Kan., reporter, 1914, 1924-35; member of Kansas State Legislature, 1931-32; Republican county chairman, Lyon County, Kan., 1933-34; *Washington Post,* Washington, D.C., staff member, 1935; *Fortune* magazine, New York City, staff member, 1937-39; European correspondent for Columbia Broadcasting Systems (CBS) and for forty newspapers, including *New York Post,* 1939-40; *Reader's Digest,* representative in London, England, 1940-41, roving editor, 1942-44; *Emporia Gazette,* editor and publisher, 1944-73. Member of board of overseers at Harvard University, 1950-56. *Member:* International Press Institute, American Society of Newspaper Editors, American Friends of the Middle East, American Committee for Liberation, American Association of Indian Affairs, American Numismatic Society, American Civil Liberties Union, Inter-American Press Institute, National Association of Newspaper Editors, National Press Club (Washington, D.C.), Theodore Roosevelt Memorial Association, Freedom Home, Overseas Press Club, Century Club, Harvard Club, Coffee House (New York City). *Awards, honors:* First prize for best European broadcast from National Headliners Club, 1939, for broadcast from Mannerheim Line in Finland.

WRITINGS—All published by Harcourt, except as noted: *What People Said* (novel), Viking, 1938; (contributor) *Zero Hour: A Summons to Be Free,* Farrar & Rinehart, 1940; *Journey for Margaret,* 1941; *They Were Expendable,* 1942; *Queens Die Proudly,* 1943; *Report on the Russians,* 1945; *Report on the Germans,* 1947; *Lost Boundaries,* 1948; *Land of Milk and Honey,* 1949; *Bernard Baruch: Portrait of a Citizen,* 1950; *Back Down the Ridge,* 1953; *The Captives of Korea,* Scribner, 1957; *The Little Toy Dog,* Dutton, 1962; *Report on the Asians,* Reynal, 1969.

SIDELIGHTS: After holding several positions as a reporter and foreign correspondent for various publications, White succeeded his father, William Allen White, as editor and publisher of the *Emporia Gazette.* White also wrote more than one dozen books during his career, many based on his experiences as a war correspondent. *Journey for Margaret,* for example, is the story of how he adopted a three-year-old war orphan while working in England for *Reader's Digest. They Were Expendable,* written as a book-length interview, plus *Queens Die Proudly* and *Back Down the Ridge* were among his other books dealing with different aspects of World War II combat.

BIOGRAPHICAL/CRITICAL SOURCES: William L. White, *Journey for Margaret,* Harcourt, 1941.

OBITUARIES: New York Times, July 27, 1973; *Washington Post,* July 27, 1973; *Time,* August 6, 1973; *Newsweek,* August 6, 1973.*

* * *

WHITING, Frank M. 1907-

PERSONAL: Born December 6, 1907, in Wallsburg, Utah;

son of John C. (a rancher) and Elizabeth (a teacher; maiden name, McCoard) Whiting; married Jeannette Cook, September 10, 1931; children: Douglas, Gordon, Bruce, John, Wendy (Mrs. Toney Beatley). *Education:* Brigham Young University, B.A., 1930; University of Utah, M.A., 1932; University of Minnesota, Ph.D., 1941. *Home:* 1457 Uintah Circle, Salt Lake City, Utah 84105.

CAREER: Teacher of physics, speech, and dramatics at high school in Kimberly, Idaho, 1932-34; University of Utah, Salt Lake City, instructor in theatre and stage electrician, 1934-37; University of Minnesota, Minneapolis, instructor, 1937-44, assistant professor, 1944-46, associate professor, 1946-50, professor of theatre, 1950-73, director of theatre, 1944-73, director and captain of Showboat Theatre, 1958-74; University of Utah, adjunct professor of drama and theatre director, 1974; writer. Originated overseas touring for American Educational Theatre Association (now American Theatre Association) and United Service Organizations and conducted tours in Europe, South America, and the Far East.

MEMBER: American Theatre Association (vice-president, 1965; president, 1966), American National Theatre and Academy, National Theatre Conference, North Central Theatre Association (president, 1951). *Awards, honors:* Order of the North Star, 1958; Eaves Senior Award, 1961; Good Neighbor Award from WCCO-Radio, 1963; award of merit from American Educational Theatre Association, 1967; distinguished service award from Brigham Young University, 1979.

WRITINGS: "Huckleberry Finn" (three-act play; based on book by Mark Twain), first produced in Minneapolis, Minn., at University of Minnesota Theatre, 1945; *An Introduction to the Theatre,* Harper, 1954, 4th edition, 1978; (editor with Melvin R. White) *Playreader's Repertory: Drama on Stage* (anthology), Scott, Foresman, 1970; *One of Us Amateurs,* Stevensons Geneological Center, 1980. Contributor to journals and newspapers.

SIDELIGHTS: Whiting has directed nearly two hundred full-length plays, ranging from the work of Aeschylus to present-day playwrights. It was he who convinced Sir Tyrone Guthrie to locate the Guthrie Theatre in Minneapolis, and many of Whiting's students have become well-known entertainers and educators.

*   *   *

WHITLOCK, Ralph 1914-
(John Reynolds, Madge Reynolds, The Countryman)

PERSONAL: Born February 7, 1914, in Salisbury, England; son of Edwin (a farmer) and Alice (White) Whitlock; married Hilda Pearce, November 1, 1939; children: Wendy Anne, Rosalie Margaret, Edward Ralph. *Education:* Attended grammar school in Salisbury, England. *Religion:* Christian. *Home:* The Lodge, Limington, near Yeovil, Somerset BA22 8EH, England. *Agent:* Laurence Pollinger Ltd., 18 Maddox St., Mayfair, London W1R 0EU, England.

CAREER: Writer, 1973—. Farmer in Wiltshire, England, 1932-68; agricultural consultant, Methodist Missionary Society, London, England, 1968-73. Presented "Cowleaze Farm," a children's program on British Broadcasting Corp. (BBC)-Radio, 1945-62; panelist on "Slightly Quizzical," on BBC-TV, 1971-74; guest on radio and television programs in England, the United States, Europe, Scandinavia, and Africa; lecturer for National Children's Home; lecturer in the

United States, Europe, Africa, India, and the Caribbean. *Military service:* Home Guard, 1940-45. *Awards, honors:* Junior Information Book Award from *Times Educational Supplement,* 1975, for *Spiders.*

WRITINGS: Round Roundbarrow Farm, Jenkins, 1946; *Peasant's Heritage,* Jenkins, 1947; *Common British Birds,* Elek, 1948; *Wiltshire,* Elek, 1949.

The Other Side of the Fence, Jenkins, 1950; *Rare and Extinct British Birds,* Phoenix House, 1953; *Wild Life on the Farm,* Falcon Press, 1953; *The Land First,* Museum Press, 1954; *Salisbury Plain,* R. Hale, 1955; *Farming as a Career,* R. Hale, 1959.

A Short History of British Farming, John Baker, 1965, revised edition, 1977; *Farming From the Road,* John Baker, 1967; (editor) *Agricultural Records,* John Baker, 1968, revised edition, A. & C. Black, 1978; *The Great Cattle Plague,* John Baker, 1968; *A Family and a Village,* John Baker, 1969.

Squirrels, Priory Press, 1974; *Rats and Mice,* Priory Press, 1974; *Otters,* Priory Press, 1974; *Deer,* Priory Press, 1974; *Rabbits and Hares,* Priory Press, 1974; *Feast or Famine?,* Wayland, 1974; *Somerset,* Batsford, 1975; *Whitlock's Wessex,* Moonraker Press, 1975; *My World of the Past,* Hamlyn, 1975; *Spiders,* Priory Press, 1975; *Wiltshire,* Batsford, 1976; *Exploring Rivers, Lakes, and Canals,* E. P. Publishing, 1976; *The Everyday Life of the Maya,* Batsford, 1976; *Naturalists' Guide to Wessex,* Moonraker Press, 1976; *The Folklore of Wiltshire,* Batsford, 1976; *Bulls Through the Ages,* Lutterworth, 1977; *The Warrior Kings of Saxon England,* Moonraker Press, 1977; *Penguins,* Wayland, 1977; *Chimpanzees,* Wayland, 1977; *A Closer Look at Butterflies and Moths,* Archon, 1977; *The Folklore of Devon,* Batsford, 1977; *Growing Unusual Vegetables,* E. P. Publishing, 1978; *Thinking About Rural Development,* Lutterworth, 1978; *A Calendar of Country Customs,* Batsford, 1978; *Pond Life,* Wayland, 1978; *The Shaping of the Countryside,* R. Hale, 1979; *Historic English Forests,* Moonraker Press, 1979; *In Search of Old Gods,* Phaidon, 1979; *Eels,* Wayland, 1979; *Ducks,* Wayland, 1979; *Wild Cats,* Wayland, 1979.

Royal Farmers, M. Joseph, 1980; *Rare Breeds,* Prism Press, 1980; *Thinking About Food,* Lutterworth, 1980.

Children's books: *Cowleaze Farm,* Jenkins, 1948; *Harvest at Cowleaze Farm,* Jenkins, 1951; *Winter on Cowleaze Farm,* Jenkins, 1952; *A Year on Cowleaze Farm,* R. Hale, 1964.

Under pseudonym John Reynolds: *Bees and Wasps,* Priory Press, 1974; *Birds of Prey,* Priory Press, 1974; *Stoats and Weasels,* Priory Press, 1974.

Under pseudonym Madge Reynolds: *The Farmer's Wife,* John Baker, 1960.

Contributor: *The AA Book of the British Countryside,* Drive Publications, 1973; *Folklore, Myths, and Legends of Britain,* Reader's Digest Association, 1973; William G. Duncalf, editor, *The Guinness Book of Plant Facts and Feats,* Guinness Superlatives, 1976; *Grow Your Own,* Cavendish, 1977.

Author of radio plays, including "The Oldstock Curse," first aired on British Broadcasting Corp. (BBC-Radio), c. 1950.

Author of a column of country notes in *Western Gazette* under pseudonym The Countryman, 1932—; farming correspondent for *Field,* 1945-80. Editor of "Land Books," a series, Hutchinson. Contributor to *Gardening Encyclopaedia.* Contributor to magazines and newspapers, including *Country Fair.* Editor and publisher of *South-Eastern Bird Report,* 1933-44; past editor of *Wiltshire Courier.*

WORK IN PROGRESS: Books on folklore, rural life in England, England's royal family, ornithology, farming, and ancient history; documentary television programs.

SIDELIGHTS: Whitlock told *CA:* "I am regarded, I think, as an authority on agriculture, gardening, many aspects of natural history, certain periods of ancient history, folklore and the topography of the west of England. And yet, I tend to be an increasingly frustrated writer. To supplement my small pension I need to maintain a steady literary output, and what publishers want me to write and what I want to write are two very different things. Publishers offer me plenty of contracts for run-of-the-mill books that fit into their series, but are not interested in my memories of a way of life that is gone forever, nor in my experiences in the tropics. Several novels I have written are sitting on a shelf, with rejection slips from publishers who say that they are 'exquisitely written but do not fit into any category for which we have a market.'"

"In particular, although life in this present time is so comfortable and exciting (for many people though not for all), I feel that, compared to the harder and more restricted life that I once knew and have met again in the Third World, there is something lacking. In the simple community of my boyhood every person had a place and a significance. So it still is in the villages of Africa and India, but not in the huge, ungainly urban complexes into which so many of the human race are now being squeezed. There are also certain spiritual elements to life which are very real to those fortunate enough to live in the country. Most people I meet nowadays seem out of touch with them."

* * *

WHITNEY, David
See MALICK, TERRENCE

* * *

WIENER, Sally Dixon 1926-

PERSONAL: Born September 18, 1926, in Burlington, Iowa; daughter of George Lane (a physician) and Ellen (a nurse; maiden name, Swanson) Dixon; married John Alfred Wiener (an attorney), April 10, 1951; children: John Dixon, Ellen Claire, Ann Lucy. *Education:* Attended Barnard College, 1945-46; University of Arizona, B.A., 1947; also attended New School for Social Research and Musical Theatre Workshop. *Religion:* Episcopalian. *Home:* 40 Tunstall Rd., Scarsdale, N.Y. 10583. *Agent:* Robert A. Freedman, Harold Freedman Brandt & Brandt Dramatic Department, Inc., 1501 Broadway, New York, N.Y. 10036.

CAREER: Tucson Daily Citizen, Tucson, Ariz., reporter, 1943-47; *Salt Lake City Telegram,* Salt Lake City, Utah, reporter, 1947-48; *Tucson Daily Citizen,* foreign correspondent, 1949; *White Plains Reporter Dispatch,* White Plains, N.Y., reporter, 1949-50; *New York Times,* New York, N.Y., part-time reporter, 1951-56; playwright, 1968—. Reporter and feature writer for *Dramatists Quarterly* and *Newsletter,* 1976-79. *Member:* Dramatists Guild (associate member).

WRITINGS—Plays: "Prologue" (juvenile musical, first produced in New York City at Chapel of the Intercession, 1968; "Marjorie Daw" (musical), first produced in New York City at Library and Museum of the Performing Arts, February 2, 1970; *Telemachus, Friend* (musical; first produced in New York City at St. Peter's Gate, April 17, 1972), Samuel French, 1974; "The Blue Magi," first produced in New York City at St. Peter's Gate, December 11, 1972; "The Pimienta Pancakes" (musical), first produced in New York City at Theatre Off Park, March 7, 1976; "Flyin'

Turtles," first produced in Silver City, N.M., at Western University of New Mexico, March 26, 1976; "Show Me a Hero," first produced in Carmel, Calif., at Sunset Center, September, 1979, produced in New York City at St. Malachy's Theatrespace, March 11, 1980.

Author of lyrics and music for "Let's Hear It for Miss America" (musical), first produced in St. Petersburg, Fla., at Country Dinner Playhouse, August, 1976.

WORK IN PROGRESS: A musical play about Calvin Coolidge; a play about an elderly woman's coming to grips with her life and love; a play about St. Paul.

SIDELIGHTS: Sally Wiener wrote: "As a playwright (as well as composer and lyricist), I found my years of newspaper work very good training. Writing headlines is a good way to learn to be a succinct lyricist. I have a long-time interest in older American short stories and regional literature. From this I found material for adaptations for musicals from O. Henry and Thomas Bailey Aldrich. And as for nursing a play or musical through production, motherhood was excellent training."

BIOGRAPHICAL/CRITICAL SOURCES: New York Times, March 29, 1980.

* * *

WIGGINTON, Eliot 1942-

PERSONAL: Born November 9, 1942, in Wheeling, W.Va.; son of Brooks (a landscape architect) and Lucy (a landscape architect; maiden name, Smith) Wigginton. *Education:* Cornell University, A.B., 1965, M.A., 1966; Johns Hopkins University, M.A., 1969. *Residence:* Mountain City, Ga. *Office: Foxfire,* Foxfire Fund, Inc., Rabun Gap, Ga. 30568.

CAREER: High school teacher of English, geography, and journalism at Rabun Gap-Nacoochee School, Rabun Gap, Ga., 1966-76, and at Rabun County High School, 1976—. Founder and president of Foxfire Fund, Inc. Member of boards and advisory councils for National Endowment for the Humanities, National Endowment for the Arts, National Trust for Historic Preservation, Georgia Council for the Arts and Humanities, Highlander Center, RIF, Phi Delta Kappa's Walkabout project, and Teachers and Writers Collaborative. Has appeared on numerous television programs, including the "Today Show." Educational consultant. *Awards, honors:* John D. Rockefeller III Youth Award from the Rockefeller Foundation, 1974; one of fifty people named by *Time* magazine as emerging national leaders, 1979; honorary doctorates from Columbia College, Chicago, Ill., Bethany College, Bethany, W.Va., and Duquesne University.

WRITINGS: Moments: The Foxfire Experience, Ideas, Inc., 1975; (editor) *I Wish I Could Give My Son a Wild Raccoon,* Doubleday-Anchor, 1976.

"Foxfire" series; all published by Doubleday-Anchor; editor and author of introductions: *The Foxfire Book: Hog Dressing, Log Cabin Building, Mountain Crafts and Foods, Planting by the Signs, Snake Lore, Hunting Tales, Faith Healing, Moon Shining, and Other Affairs of Plain Living,* 1972; *Foxfire 2: Ghost Stories, Spring Wild Plant Foods, Spinning and Weaving, Midwifing, Burial Customs, Corn Shuckin's, Wagon Making, and More Affairs of Plain Living,* 1973; *Foxfire 3: Animal Care, Banjos and Dulcimers, Hide Tanning, Summer and Fall Wild Plant Foods, Butter Churns, Ginseng, and Still More Affairs of Plain Living,* 1975; *Foxfire 4: Water Systems, Fiddle Making, Logging, Gardening, Sassafras Tea, Wood Carving, and Further Affairs of Plain Living,* 1977; *Foxfire 5: Ironmaking, Black-*

smithing, *Flintlock Rifles, Bear Hunting, and Other Affairs of Plain Living,* 1979; *Foxfire 6: One Hundred Toys and Games, Gourd Banjos and Song Bows, Wooden Locks, A Waterpowered Sawmill, Shoemaking, and Other Affairs of Just Plain Living,* 1980.

Editor of *Foxfire* magazine, 1966—. Contributor of articles to journals, including *Education Digest, Media and Methods, English Record, Appalachian Journal, Southern Exposure, Quest, PTA,* and *Synergist.* Contributor of poetry to small magazines.

WORK IN PROGRESS: A book on education, publication by Doubleday expected in 1981.

SIDELIGHTS: As a new teacher in the small town of Rabun Gap, Georgia, Eliot Wigginton soon realized that his high school students were bored and restless. When they set fire to his classroom lectern, Wigginton decided that if he wanted to prevent such pranks in the future, he would have to set fire to their imaginations. To capture his pupils' interest and encourage their self-sufficiency, he devised a new program that required them to interview older people in the community about the early days in southern Appalachia. Students then wrote stories recording what they had learned about the traditions, crafts, and folklore of the area. These stories were printed in a magazine produced by the students, which was called *Foxfire,* after a lichen that glows in the dark.

Foxfire magazine in turn spawned a number of extremely popular "Foxfire" books that deal with such subjects as building log cabins, dressing hogs, churning butter, and making flintlock rifles. Proceeds from the books are used to finance programs that will further enhance the education of Rabun Gap students. Royalties have been used to purchase videotape equipment so that pupils can produce programs for local television stations. A publishing company, a record company, and a furniture company have also been founded by the students with funds from the sale of "Foxfire" books. More "Foxfire" books will probably be forthcoming, for Wigginton feels that there is a great deal more to say about southern Appalachian culture.

In a review of *Foxfire 5,* Nicholas Silitch noted that the books have changed somewhat since the first one was published in 1972. "The original purpose of these books seemed to be to educate students, readers and the teacher," he wrote in the *Washington Post.* "The purpose seems to have grown over the years, become more archival, and now records methods and techniques of doing things that are close to being forgotten. As such they are valuable to future generations, while still immensely [sic] enjoyable dream starters for us today." Although the "Foxfire" books do document the culture of the people of Rabun Gap, Wigginton has never lost sight of the original purpose of the Foxfire program. The aim of the program is not to collect folklore, but to motivate students to learn. "Folklore is simply the *vehicle,*" Wigginton told an interviewer for *Publishers Weekly.* "What we're really trying to do is get into the hands of kids the hard skills that are supposed to be taught in school—particularly language arts skills, communication skills; and we follow these on into photography, proof correction, layout."

The Foxfire concept of education has caught on in other parts of the United States. To help teachers who want to establish such programs in their own schools, Wigginton wrote a book about his experiences, *Moments: The Foxfire Experience.* In the book he stresses the importance of student involvement, personal growth, and the techniques of collecting oral history. Wigginton has also traveled across the country in an effort to encourage other educators to experi-

ment with Foxfire programs. Each cultural program, he emphasizes, must be adapted to the community in which the pupils live. Hundreds of urban as well as rural school systems have conducted Foxfire programs, including such diverse cities as New York City, Washington, D.C., and St. Louis, Missouri.

BIOGRAPHICAL/CRITICAL SOURCES: Time, August 14, 1972, July 2, 1973; *Journal of American Folklore,* April, 1973; *Christian Science Monitor,* June 13, 1973; *Washington Post Book World,* August 12, 1973, June 3, 1979; *America,* August 18, 1973, November 17, 1973; *Miami Herald,* April 21, 1974; *Newsweek,* August 25, 1975; *Authors in the News,* Volume 1, Gale, 1976; *Harvard Educational Review,* August, 1976; *Publishers Weekly,* September 6, 1976; *Audubon,* March, 1977; *New York Times,* May 27, 1977.

*　　*　　*

WILDER, Cherry
See GRIMM, Cherry Barbara

*　　*　　*

WILKINSON, James Harvie III　1944-

PERSONAL: Born September 29, 1944, in New York, N.Y.; son of James Harvie, Jr. (a banker) and Letitia (Nelson) Wilkinson; married Lossie Noell, June 30, 1973; children: James Nelson. *Education:* Yale University, B.A., 1967; University of Virginia, J.D., 1972. *Religion:* Episcopal. *Agent:* Sterling Lord Agency, 660 Madison Ave., New York, N.Y. 10016. *Office:* School of Law, University of Virginia, Charlottesville, Va. 22903.

CAREER: Admitted to the Bar of Virginia State, 1972; U.S. Supreme Court, Washington, D.C., law clerk to Justice Lewis Powell, 1972-73; University of Virginia, Charlottesville, assistant professor, 1973-76, associate professor of law, 1976—; *Norfolk Virginian-Pilot,* Norfolk, Va., editor, 1978—.

WRITINGS: Harry Byrd and the Changing Face of Virginia Politics, University Press of Virginia, 1968; *Serving Justice: A Supreme Court Clerk's View,* Charterhouse Books, 1974; *From* Brown *to* Bakke: *The Supreme Court and School Integration, 1954-1978,* Oxford University Press, 1979.

SIDELIGHTS: In the quarter century since the Supreme Court, in the landmark case of *Brown* v. *Board of Education,* unanimously declared unconstitutional state ordered racial segregation in the public schools, racial desegregation in the United States has remained an elusive goal. That early consensus about how the goal was to be reached has eroded, and as the Court has been faced with increasingly complex racial problems, it has often been sharply divided in its desegregation decisions.

By 1978, in *Bakke* v. *Regents of the University of California,* the Court found itself divided down the middle on the question of racial quotas in educational programs. The justices, in a five-to-four decision, struck down the use of strict racial quotas, but allowed race to be considered in admissions procedures. Wilkinson, basically agreeing with the decision, termed it "a Solomonic compromise."

At the end of Wilkinson's chronicle of the Court's role in school desegregation, *From* Brown *to* Bakke, he declared that for him "the goal of racial justice remains as luminous as ever." C. Vann Woodward, reviewing the book in *New Republic,* commented: "For those who believe there is only one way to pursue that goal and only one side to any controversy about the means, this book will be a disappointment.

For those who hold it is not all that simple there is much to learn." Jack Fuller of the *Chicago Tribune* similarly assessed the book's impact: "What will most displease some readers of his book is also its greatest strength as history; its willingness to endow with eloquence all the conflicting claims and aspirations that found their way into federal courtrooms in the desegregation movement."

However, Mary Ellen Gale, writing in the *New York Times Book Review,* criticized Wilkinson for finding "only what he sets out to look for" in suggesting that "the nation can balance on both horns at once—preserving white privileges while accomodating black rights." Gale was saddened by Wilkinson's conclusions, but admitted that he "speaks for a powerful constituency." She continued: "Too many white Americans are still looking for an easy way out of the maze of race relations. Too few have acknowledged that the white majority must unite against its own prejudices and give up some of its comforts in the name of justice."

Fuller, in summing up his impressions of what he called "a magnificent book," wrote: "All in all, however, the book is touched by a kind of melancholy, a yearning for some way simply to achieve the 'luminous' goal of racial justice. If there is anything unsatisfying in Wilkinson's work it is that it avoids telling the court what to do next the better to move toward that goal. If this is a sense of defeat, it can be faulted. But I read it as a sad honesty to a divided conscience. And perhaps of the honesty something can grow."

BIOGRAPHICAL/CRITICAL SOURCES: New York Times Book Review, May 27, 1979; *Chicago Tribune,* June 10, 1979; *New Republic,* June 23, 1979; *Washington Post Book World,* July 8, 1979; *Virginia Quarterly Review,* spring, 1980.

*   *   *

WILL
See LIPKIND, William

*   *   *

WILLIAMS, David Ricardo   1923-

PERSONAL: Born February 28, 1923, in Kamloops, British Columbia, Canada; son of Humphrey David (a banker) and Mary Elizabeth (Cassady) Williams; married Laura Ella-Belle Bapty, May 29, 1948; children: Bruce, Suzanne, Harry, Owen, Jonathan. *Education:* University of British Columbia, B.A., 1948, LL.B., 1949. *Politics:* Conservative. *Religion:* Anglican. *Home:* 3355 Gibbins Rd., Duncan, British Columbia, Canada V9L 1W1. *Office:* 170 Craig St., Duncan, British Columbia, Canada V9L 1W1.

CAREER: Barrister and solicitor in Duncan, British Columbia, 1949—. Writer-in-residence at University of Victoria, 1980-81; member of board of governors of Brentwood College; past member of board of governors of University of British Columbia. Past president of Duncan Chamber of Commerce; past chairman of British Columbia Forest Museum and King's Daughters' Hospital. *Military service:* Canadian Army, 1943-45; became lieutenant. *Member:* Writers Union of Canada, Foundation for Legal Research (fellow), Association for Canadian Studies, Oregon Historical Society. *Awards, honors:* Medal for Canadian biography from University of British Columbia, 1978, for *The Man for a New Country;* grant from Association for Canadian Studies, 1979.

WRITINGS: One Hundred Years at St. Peter's Quamichan, Cowichan Leader, 1966, 2nd edition, 1977; *The Man for a New Country: Sir Matthew Baillie Begbie,* Gray's Publish-

ing, 1977; *Begbie,* Fitzhenry & Whiteside, 1980. Contributor to *Pacific Northwest Quarterly.*

WORK IN PROGRESS: Gun-a-Noot, a biography of the Canadian Indian outlaw; research for a biography of Sir Lyman Poore Duff, former chief justice of Canada.

BIOGRAPHICAL/CRITICAL SOURCES: Canadian Studies, July, 1978; *University of British Columbia Alumni Chronicle,* winter, 1978.

*   *   *

WILLIAMS, Justin, Sr.   1906-

PERSONAL: Born March 2, 1906, in Greenbrier, Ark.; son of Isom G. (in insurance business) and Elizabeth (Clements) Williams; married Ellawitt Brewer, August 13, 1927; children: Justin, Jr., Nicholas B. *Education:* Arkansas State Teachers College, A.B., 1926; University of Iowa, M.A., 1928, Ph.D., 1933. *Home:* 1613 44th St. N.W., Washington, D.C. 20007.

CAREER: Wisconsin State College (now University of Wisconsin), River Falls, assistant professor of social studies, 1928-30, professor of social studies and chairman of department, 1931-42; Headquarters of Supreme Commander of Allied Powers, Tokyo, Japan, division chief, 1945-52; Agency for International Development, Washington, D.C., division chief in Korea, 1953-60; Interregional Technical Cooperation Division, Paris, France, chief, 1960-62; University of Maryland, College Park, assistant to president, 1962-67; U.S. Army Institute of Land Combat, Alexandria, Va., international affairs specialist, 1967-71. Member of advisory board of Japan-United States Friendship Commission. *Military service:* U.S. Army Air Forces, 1942-46; became captain. *Member:* American Historical Association. *Awards, honors:* Meritorious civilian service awards from U.S. Department of the Army, 1952, 1953.

WRITINGS: Japan's Political Revolution Under Mac-Arthur: A Participant's Account, University of Georgia Press, 1979. Contributor to history and political science journals.

WORK IN PROGRESS: An article, "U.S. Occupation Policy for Japan, 1945 to 1948."

SIDELIGHTS: Williams commented: "I had to write the book about Japan's political revolution for two reasons: the story had never been fully told, and a number of myths needed to be set straight. Some American and Japanese scholars are still baffled by the magnitude and complexity of the Allied occupation, 1945-1952. They have not achieved a comprehensive view of this gigantic military and diplomatic undertaking. Precisely how the policy, written in part by idealists in Washington, was altered by General MacArthur, whose broad grant of power from President Truman was also a significant component of U.S. policy, continues to elude them. Refusing to see that a great capitalist country would not deliberately create a socialist state in the Far East, they conjured up the idea of a 'reverse course' in U.S. policy in the Far East in 1948 to explain why Japan's leftwing socialists and Communists never came to power. U.S. policy to establish a parliamentary government was never changed."

*   *   *

WILLIAMS, Richard Lippincott   1910-

PERSONAL: Born November 28, 1910, in Seattle, Wash.; son of Charles Richard and Dolly DeMaris (White) Williams; married Mary McGee (a writer and editor), December 31, 1957; children: Richard J., David M., Robert A., Mary C.,

Virginia A. *Education:* University of Washington, Seattle, B.A., 1933. *Religion:* Roman Catholic. *Home:* 5918 Chesterbrook Rd., McLean, Va. 22101.

CAREER: Writer. Associated with *Seattle Times*, Seattle, Wash., 1933-41; Washington State Defense Council, Olympia, director of public information, 1941-43; Boeing Aircraft Co., Seattle, in production and public relations, 1943-45; Time, Inc., New York City, staff writer for *Time* and *Life*, 1945-53; Dell Publishing Co., Inc., New York City, editor of special projects, 1953-61; Time-Life Books, New York City, editor of food and photography sections, 1961-73; free-lance writer, 1973-75; *Smithsonian*, Washington, D.C., writer and member of board of editors, 1975—. *Member:* Overseas Press Club of America, Deadline Club, Time-Life Alumni Society, Sigma Delta Chi, Alpha Delta Sigma, Tau Kappa Epsilon.

WRITINGS: Family Doctor (novel), Random House, 1953; *The Northwest Coast* (nonfiction), Time-Life, 1974; *The Cascades* (nonfiction), Time-Life, 1976; *The Loggers* (nonfiction), Time-Life, 1977.

* * *

WILLIAMSON, Anthony George   1932-
(Tony Williamson)

PERSONAL: Born December 18, 1932, in Manchester, England; son of Kenneth George (a salesman) and Louise (O'Ryan) Williamson; married Dorothy Hartley, April 15, 1959 (divorced August, 1973); married Penelope Green, August 29, 1980; children: Martin James, Deborah Jane. *Education:* Educated in Manchester, England. *Religion:* Christian. *Home:* Brambles, Weeke Hill, Dartmouth, Devon, England. *Office:* c/o Robin Lowe, M.L. Representation, 194 Old Brompton Rd., London, England.

CAREER: Kemsley/Thomason Newspapers, journalist, 1954-60; Canadian Broadcasting Corp. (CBC-TV), member of staff, 1960-62, news editor, 1962-64; free-lance television and motion picture scriptwriter, 1964-74; writer, 1974—. Drama consultant to British Broadcasting Corp. (BBC), 1968—. *Military service:* Royal Air Force, 1950-54. *Member:* Mystery Writers of America, Writers Guild of Great Britain, Crime Writers. *Awards, honors:* Zita Award from Writers Guild of Great Britain, 1965, for television writing.

WRITINGS—All under name Tony Williamson; all novels, unless otherwise noted: *The Connector*, Collins, 1975, Stein & Day, 1976; *Counterstrike Entebbe* (nonfiction), Collins, 1976; *Doomsday Contract*, Collins, 1977, Simon & Schuster, 1978; *Technicians of Death*, Collins, 1978, Atheneum, 1979; *The Samson Strike*, Collins, 1979, Atheneum, 1980.

Screenplays: "Night Watch," 1974; "Woman Hunter," 1979; "Breakthrough," 1979.

Television plays: "Ask Any Neighbor," produced by American Broadcasting Co. (ABC-TV), 1966; "Cage of Canvas," produced by British Broadcasting Corp. (BBC-TV), 1967; "Victim," produced by Granada Television, 1968. Also writer for television series, including "The Avengers," "The Persuaders," "Jason King," "The Champions," "Department S," "Z Cars," "The Spies," "Randal and Hopkirk Deceased," "The Return of the Saint," "Dr. Finlay's Casebook," and "Mask of Janus."

WORK IN PROGRESS: Screenplay of *Night Without End;* a novel set in the Middle East and Africa.

SIDELIGHTS: Williamson told *CA:* "All my work is thoroughly researched and therefore travel is a major activity for me. For *Technicians of Death,* I went to Thailand and

Burma to research the locations and learn about the drug activity.

"Terrorism is one of my specialties and I have made a close study of it over the years. I have broadened this interest in recent years to include anti-terrorist groups such as Germany's GSG9 unit, but in particular the British SAS."

* * *

WILLIAMSON, Bruce   1930-

PERSONAL: Born December 31, 1930, in Michigan; son of Jasper E. and Hannah L. Williamson; married Phyllis M., February 2, 1957 (separated); children: Stephanie Scott. *Education:* Attended Columbia University School of General Studies, 1948-53, and Stella Alder Theatre School, 1955-57. *Politics:* Independent. *Home:* 135 MacDougal St., Apt. 1B, New York, N.Y. 10012. *Office: Playboy*, 919 North Michigan Ave., Chicago, Ill. 60611.

CAREER/WRITINGS: Free-lance journalist and writer of humor pieces, travel stories, revue songs, and sketches, 1956-63; *Time* (magazine), New York, N.Y., motion picture critic, 1963-66; *Playboy* (magazine), Chicago, Ill., contributing editor and motion picture critic, 1967—; notable assignments include interviews with Frederico Fellini, Robert Altman, Sarah Miles, and George Burns. Instructor of cinema at St. John's University, New York, 1975-80. Contributor to *Film 71/72*, edited by David Denby, Simon & Schuster, 1971, and *Movie Comedy*, edited by Stuart Byron and Elizabeth Weis, Viking, 1977. Also contributor to periodicals, including *New York Times* and *Toronto Star. Member:* National Society of Film Critics, New York Film Critics Circle.

* * *

WILLIAMSON, Tony
See WILLIAMSON, Anthony George
* * *

WILLOUGHBY, Elaine Macmann   1926-
(Elaine Macmann)

PERSONAL: Born March 22, 1926, in Boston, Mass.; daughter of Walter T. and Mabel E. Macmann; married Robert Hugh Willoughby (a professor of flute), August 17, 1957; children: John W. *Education:* Wheelock College, B.S.Ed., 1949; Columbia University, M.A., 1954, Ed.D., 1957. *Politics:* "Middle of the road." *Religion:* Protestant. *Home and office:* 268 Forest St., Oberlin, Ohio 44074. *Agent:* Janet Loranger, P.O. Box 113, West Redding, Conn. 06896.

CAREER: Elementary school teacher in Norwood, Mass., 1949-51, Arlington, Va., 1951-52, Wilmington, Del., 1952-53, and New York, N.Y., 1953-57; substitute teacher in Oberlin, Ohio, 1972; full-time writer, 1977—. Member of extension faculty at Bowling Green State University and Kent State University in the early 1960's; assistant professor at University of New Hampshire, summers, 1960-61, 1963, 1969-71, and Oberlin College, spring, 1974; associate professor at Baldwin-Wallace College, autumn, 1974; teacher of gifted children at Lorain County Community College, 1979. Public speaker; guest on television programs. *Member:* National Book League (England), Royal Oak Foundation.

WRITINGS—Under name Elaine Macmann: *Risky Business* (juvenile), Putnam, 1956; *Ozzie and the Nineteenth of April* (juvenile), Putnam, 1957.

Under name Elaine Macmann Willoughby: *The Story of*

Strawbery Banke in Portsmouth, New Hampshire (pamphlet), privately printed, 1970; *That's How the Ball Bounces* (juvenile), Garrard, 1972; *No, No, No and Yes* (juvenile), Garrard, 1973; *Mystery of the Lobster Thieves* (juvenile; Xerox Book Club selection), Weekly Reader Family Books, 1978; *Boris and the Monsters* (juvenile), Houghton, 1980. Contributor to magazines.

WORK IN PROGRESS: Humorous fiction for children, set in England; a book for children about a former German who was an American prisoner of war in World War II.

SIDELIGHTS: Willoughby told *CA:* "Writers are constantly being asked to explain themselves, their ways of working, their craft, their fantasies, and their views on aesthetics because non-writers hope that somewhere there is a universal recipe for turning out excellent literature. Recipes are comfortable. Writing is not comfortable (at least for most of us) because there is no recipe. In 1957 I wrote my doctoral dissertation on what creative writers say they know about their own process and I found out that although they do write (for various reasons) about their ways of creating, there are no two alike, no common recipe. Of course, there are a few basics, like being human, but this is hardly a recipe for creating on paper.

"It is obvious that writers write from some inner need (and now I talk about children's authors)—some write for the child they once were (or still are), some write for money, some write because they feel they have something to say to children, and some write because they like to tell a good story. I write from a combination of the preceding—I have always loved to tell a story and I feel that I have something to say to children. I feel that children often move in a world of partly deaf giants who are hell-bent upon molding the young into some pre-conceived idea of mental and physical behavior, regardless of whether it is fun or beneficial. I say that these giants are partly deaf, because although they can hear their alarm clocks, their favorite newscaster on television, their friends on the telephone, and their boss at work, they very often do not hear what children are saying from deep down inside. I have not forgotten that precious deepdown part from my own childhood. I listened to it again when my son was young and I hope I hear it with children today as I visit schools, tell stories at library story hour, and entertain the neighborhood children.

"I feel most fortunate in having grown up in Lexington, Mass., where there is so much fascinating history. It was a good feeling to know that I had roots in the past and was part of a process of going towards the future. My family also had a summer home on the coast of Maine, where I developed a great love for the sea. I am fascinated by the life in and around the ocean, especially the toughness needed to exist in the zone between low tide and high tide. Perhaps it is this same kind of toughness that is needed to keep at the business of writing, because it is a lonely and frustrating profession. Only once in a while is it a beautiful experience. But when it is beautiful, when the ideas come just right or when you've just had a manuscript accepted or published, the beauty can indeed be overwhelming."

AVOCATIONAL INTERESTS: Travel (especially England), gardening.

* * *

WILSON, Eric 1940-

PERSONAL: Born November 24, 1940, in Ottawa, Ontario, Canada; son of Robert S.S. (a Royal Canadian Mounted Police superintendent) and Evelyn (a nurse) Wilson. *Educa-*

tion: University of British Columbia, B.A., 1963, graduate study, 1964. *Home:* 610 Third St., Nelson, British Columbia, Canada V1L 2P9. *Agent:* William Reiss, Paul R. Reynolds, Inc., 12 East 41st St., New York, N.Y. 10017.

CAREER: Teacher of English to slow learners at junior high school in White Rock, British Columbia, 1967-71; writer, 1971-73; teacher of English and mathematics to slow learners at junior high school in Campbell River, British Columbia, 1973-74; writer, 1974-75; teacher of English and mathematics to slow learners at junior high school in Nanaimo, British Columbia, 1975-76; writer, 1976-77; teacher of English and mathematics at alternative school in Blubber Bay, British Columbia, 1977-78; writer, 1978-79; Brooks Junior Secondary School, Powell River, British Columbia, teacher, 1979—. *Member:* Crime Writers Association, Mystery Writers of America.

WRITINGS—Juveniles: *Murder on The Canadian*, Bodley Head, 1976, Elsevier/Nelson, 1979; *Vancouver Nightmare*, Bodley Head, 1978; *Susie-Q*, Scholastic Book Services, 1978; *Terror in Winnipeg*, Bodley Head, 1979; *The Lost Treasure of Casa Loma*, Bodley Head, 1980.

SIDELIGHTS: Wilson's books are for all young people to enjoy, but they are aimed especially at holding the interest of the reluctant reader. The action and excitement in each book begins on the first page and continues unabated throughout. His characters are always contemporary Canadians.

Wilson wrote: "I first became aware of the need for contemporary Canadian novels for reluctant readers when I began teaching in White Rock, and was assigned a class of students who had no interest whatsoever in reading. After deciding what I thought would appeal to these students, I set about writing my first book, which was called *Fat Boy Speeding*.

"Although this novel was never published, it attracted enough favorable comment to keep me going. It took five years and five unpublished manuscripts before I produced *Murder on The Canadian*. Subsequent mysteries revolving around boy detective Tom Austen have since been published, and my goal is to make this young Canadian detective the hero of a series of books which will be read by young people both here and in other countries."

BIOGRAPHICAL/CRITICAL SOURCES: Toronto Globe and Mail, December 10, 1976; *Muskoka Free Press*, August 15, 1979; *Winnipeg Tribune*, October 3, 1979.

* * *

WILSON, Margaret Gibbons 1943-

PERSONAL: Born November 14, 1943, in Chicago, Ill.; daughter of Joseph (a union organizer) and Florence (a teacher; maiden name, Greenberg) Gibbons; married David Louis Wilson (a professor), July 8, 1967. *Education:* University of Chicago, A.B., 1965, M.A.T., 1969; University of Southern California, M.A., 1972, Ph.D., 1978. *Residence:* Coral Gables, Fla. *Office:* Center for Labor Research and Studies, Florida International University, Miami, Fla. 33194.

CAREER: High school history teacher in Chicago, Ill., 1966-68; Central Young Men's Christian Association Community College, Chicago, instructor in history and social science, 1968-69; University of Miami, Coral Gables, Fla., instructor in women and politics, 1977; Florida International University, Miami, job development specialist at Occupational Institute for the Handicapped, 1977-78, assistant professor of industrial systems and director of research at Center for Labor Research and Studies, 1978—. *Member:* American

Historical Association, Organization of American Historians, Oral History Association, Coordinating Council of Women Historians, University and College Labor Education Association, League of Women Voters, Southern Labor Studies Association.

WRITINGS: The American Woman in Transition: The Urban Influence, 1870-1920, Greenwood Press, 1979.

WORK IN PROGRESS: Women and the Labor Movement in the South; The Victims of McCarthyism: An Oral History.

SIDELIGHTS: Margaret Wilson told CA: "I consider myself to be a social historian, and as such I am interested in a number of historical questions and sectors often overlooked by more traditional historians. For example, until recently the role and contributions of women in American society have been ignored. Similarly, the impact of the modern-day witch-hunt of McCarthyism upon its victims has not received enough attention. These and similar issues continue to fascinate me and will provide a focus for my research and writing interests in the future."

*   *   *

WILSON, Phoebe Rous   1924(?)-1980

OBITUARY NOTICE: Born c. 1924; died June 9, 1980, in Cambridge, Mass. Editor. During her more than twenty years as an editor with the Harvard University Press, Phoebe Rous Wilson edited numerous works, including a collection of letters of David Garrick, a noted English actor of the eighteenth century. Obituaries and other sources: Publishers Weekly, July 11, 1980.

*   *   *

WILSON, Robin Scott   1928-
(Robin Scott)

PERSONAL: Born September 19, 1928, in Columbus, Ohio; son of J. Harold (a teacher) and Louise (Walker) Wilson; married Patricia Van Kirk (a graphic designer), January 20, 1951; children: Kelpie, Leslie, Kerry, Andrew. Education: Ohio State University, B.A., 1950; University of Illinois, M.A., 1954, Ph.D., 1959. Religion: Episcopalian. Home: 275 West Southington Ave., Worthington, Ohio 43085. Agent: Robert P. Mills Ltd., 156 East 52nd St., New York, N.Y. 10022. Office: 203 Administration Building, Ohio State University, 190 North Oval Mall, Columbus, Ohio 43210.

CAREER: Central Intelligence Agency, Washington, D.C., intelligence officer, 1959-67; Clarion State College, Clarion, Pa., professor of English and founder/director of Clarion Writers' Workshop in Science Fiction, 1967-70; Committee on Institutional Cooperation, Evanston, Ill., associate director, 1970-77; Ohio State University, Columbus, associate provost and part-time instructor, 1977—. Visiting lecturer at Tulane University, 1971, and Michigan State University, 1972-74, 1976-77. Member: Modern Language Association of America, Science Fiction Writers of America, American Association for Higher Education, American Association for the Advancement of Science.

WRITINGS: (Editor) The Clarion Experiment, Signet, 1971; (editor) Clarion: An Anthology of Speculative Fiction and Criticism From the Clarion Writers' Workshop, Signet, 1971; (editor) Clarion II: An Anthology of Speculative Fiction and Criticism, Signet, 1972; (editor) Clarion III: An Anthology of Speculative Fiction and Criticism, Signet, 1973; Those Who Can: A Science Fiction Reader, New American Library, 1973; (with R. W. Shryock) To the Sound of Music, Ace Books, 1974. Contributor to magazines (sometimes under pseudonym Robin Scott), including Analog.

SIDELIGHTS: Wilson told CA: "Clarion, the workshop, continues to flourish at Michigan State University. I continue to teach the first week of the workshop and probably will continue to do so as long as I am invited. Workshop graduates now represent a considerable fraction of working, producing science fiction writers in the country, and, like most teachers, I take inordinate pride in the productions of former students, even though I know they would have done well without my ministrations and those of my colleagues. Science fiction is maturing as a genre, reaching a vastly larger audience today, and science fiction writers are maturing along with it. It is rapidly becoming the literary form of our times. I guess that is a good thing."

AVOCATIONAL INTERESTS: Sailing.

*   *   *

WIMMER, Larry T(urley)   1935-

PERSONAL: Born December 8, 1935, in Snowflake, Ariz.; son of J. Ivan (an oil company wholesale distributor) and Corinne (Turley) Wimmer; married M. Louise Johnson (a teacher), November 26, 1958; children: Brian, Greg, Kendall, Eric, Brett. Education: Brigham Young University, B.S., 1960; University of Chicago, M.A., 1962, Ph.D., 1968. Religion: Church of Jesus Christ of Latter-day Saints (Mormons). Home: 810 East 3950 N., Provo, Utah 84601. Office: Department of Economics, Brigham Young University, Provo, Utah 84601.

CAREER: Brigham Young University, Provo, Utah, assistant professor, 1963-69, associate professor, 1969-77, professor of economics, 1977—, chairman of department, 1969-72, 1980—, member of advisory council of Charles Redd Center for the Study of Western History, 1971-72, 1973—, member of board of editors of Center for Historical Population Studies and member of staff of Family and Demographic Research Institute, 1978—. Visiting professor at National Chengchi University, Soochow University, and Tam Kang College of Arts and Sciences, 1972-73; research associate at National Bureau of Economic Research, 1979—; consultant to Navajo Tribal Council.

MEMBER: American Economic Association, Economic History Association, Organization of American Historians, Economic and Business Historical Society (member of board of trustees, 1976-78), Mormon History Association, Western Economic Association (member of executive committee, 1972-75), Utah Academy of Sciences, Arts and Letters, Phi Kappa Phi, Blue Key. Awards, honors: Fulbright grant for Taiwan, 1972-73; Danforth associate, 1972—; award from Mormon History Association, 1978, for best article of the year by a senior scholar; award from Freedoms Foundation, 1979, for excellence in economic education; Karl G. Maeser Distinguished Teacher Award, 1978, from Brigham Young University.

WRITINGS: Economy, Society, and Public Policy, Morton Publishing, 1974, 3rd edition, 1978; The Kirtland Economy Revisited, Brigham Young University Press, 1978. Contributor to economic and history journals.

WORK IN PROGRESS: Compiling an index of Utah heads of households from censuses of 1850, 1860, and 1870; research in income and wealth for nineteenth-century America, changing economic structure in Utah, 1850-70, and economic demography of North America, 1650-1910.

*   *   *

WINCHELL, Walter   1897-1972

PERSONAL: Original name, Walter Winchel; born April 7,

1897, in New York, N.Y.; died of cancer, February 20, 1972, in Los Angeles, Calif.; son of Jacob and Janette (Bakst) Winchel; married Rita Greene (a vaudeville performer), 1920 (divorced, 1922); married June Magee (a dancer), 1923 (died, 1970); children: Walda, Walter, Jr. (died, 1967). *Education:* Attended public school in New York, N.Y. *Residence:* Los Angeles, Calif.

CAREER: Vaudeville performer, 1909-20; free-lance gossip columnist, 1920-22; *Vaudeville News,* New York City, reporter, advertising manager, and chief photographer, 1922-24; *New York Evening Graphic,* New York City, columnist, theatre critic, drama editor, amusement editor, and advertising solicitor, 1925-29; *New York Daily Mirror,* New York City, columnist, 1929-63; *New York Journal-American,* New York City, columnist, 1963-66. Radio commentator, beginning c. 1932, joined Blue Network (radio), 1943; narrator of television program, "The Untouchables," and commentator on ABC-TV, 1960. Appeared in motion pictures, including "Love and Hisses," 1938. Founder of Damon Runyon Memorial Fund for Cancer Research, 1946. *Military service:* U.S. Naval Reserves, 1917-18, 1934-43; became lieutenant commander.

WRITINGS: Winchell Exclusive: Things That Happened to Me–And Me to Them, Prentice-Hall, 1975. Author of numerous newspaper columns, including "Stage Whispers," in *Vaudeville News;* "Your Broadway," in *New York Evening Graphic;* and "On Broadway," "This Town of Ours," and "Man About Town," in *New York Daily Mirror.* Columns syndicated by King Features in about one thousand newspapers.

SIDELIGHTS: Without stooping to hyperbole, writers have described the breadth of Walter Winchell's readership in grand terms. His friend and legal adviser Ernest Cuneo maintained in the *Saturday Evening Post:* "In the Thirties nine out of ten American adults heard or read Walter Winchell between his 9:00 Sunday night broadcast and his famed Monday Morning Column. His readers per day averaged 50 million, a column-reading total of 300 million per week." Michael Zwerin, in *Esquire,* described him no less modestly as "a very powerful man, syndicated in almost a thousand newspapers. Twenty-one million Americans once listened to 'The Boss' on the radio every Sunday night.... Winchell was the most widely read columnist in the world."

Alden Whitman, writing in the *New York Times,* characterized Winchell's column as "a melange of intimate news about personalities, mostly in show business or politics; 'inside items' about business and finance; bits and pieces about the underworld; denunciations of Italian and German Fascism; diatribes against Communism; puffs for people, stocks and events that pleased him, and a large smattering of innuendoes." Although his content consisted of fleeting gossip, his influence nevertheless transcended the usual Broadway milieu of the gossip column.

On one level, of course, "making Winchell" (that is, being mentioned in his column) was a major concern of celebrities; public relations men flocked to Winchell's regular table at the Stork Club in New York City to try to get their clients' names in print. But politicians and underworld figures also recognized the power of Winchell's words. Men as different as Franklin Delano Roosevelt and Louis Lepke Buchalter used him for their own ends. For example, when Lepke, a New York gangster wanted by the federal government, decided to surrender, he agreed to turn himself in to J. Edgar Hoover (the head of the FBI and also a close friend of Winchell's) only if Winchell were present.

Roosevelt, in contrast, depended on Winchell for the success of his third-term presidential campaign. As Cuneo put it, "Winchell blasted the 'Draft Roosevelt' trumpet from 'Border to border and coast to coast,'" thus helping to remove F.D.R.'s one significant obstacle, the two-term tradition. On the other hand, Winchell could destroy political careers as well as support them. When he took on Senator Burton K. Wheeler of Montana, who accused Winchell of being in the pay first of the British and then of the New Deal, the encounter resulted in Wheeler's being pelted with garbage by an angry mob. Indeed, mention in Winchell's column could mean the success or failure of a book, a film, a public figure, or even a Wall Street stock.

Sometimes, however, Winchell's quick pen got him into trouble. Zwerin related one such incident involving Winchell's underworld connections: "When he printed an item about the imminent murder of mobster Vincent 'Mad Dog' Coll the night before it happened ... some people wanted to know howcum. Winchell split town that time. Dropped his column for six weeks." At other times, though, his gangster friends, including Frank Costello and Dutch Schultz, protected him.

Also among Winchell's friends was Damon Runyon, the Broadway writer who died of cancer in 1946; in his honor, Winchell established the Damon Runyon Memorial Fund for Cancer Research. But over the years Winchell tended to make more enemies than friends. Two of his most notorious and long-standing battles were with Ed Sullivan, the columnist and television personality, and Dorothy Schiff, publisher of the *New York Post.* After Roosevelt's death he even took on President Truman. Ultimately, in the 1950's, he turned politically to the far right, championing Senator Joseph McCarthy and writing strident anti-Communist columns. It was then, reported the *New York Times,* that "communications executives became wary of him" for devoting so much of his time to vendettas and feuds.

Still, at the height of his career from 1930 to 1950, Winchell's impact on journalism was great. He devised a language and style that, as Whitman noted, "imparted a certain urgency and importance to what he wrote and said." On paper, in Zwerin's words, "his three-dot punctuation made the language flow ... a breath rather than a stop." On the radio, accompanied by the sound of a telegraph key, he achieved the flow with a 237-word-per-minute pace that included no more than one pause for breath every twenty seconds. To Cuneo, Winchell's was a distinctly New York style: "Walter created New Yorkese by recording it. The words of New Yorkers are hard and clipped. Like machine gun bullets, they're fired in short, sharp bursts." Even on his television show in the early 1960's, Winchell kept up his rhythmic rat-a-tat.

Winchell, whose familiar voice later narrated television's successful series "The Untouchables," began all his radio broadcasts with the memorable, "Good evening Mr. and Mrs. America—from border to border and coast to coast, and all the ships at sea." "Always looking for a more exciting way to say the trite," as Zwerin observed, he contributed many such catch-phrases to the language. According to H. L. Mencken, Winchell created more neologisms than any other newspaper columnist of his day. In *The American Language,* Supplement One, Mencken said: "He is not only an assiduous inventor and popularizer of new words and phrases, but also no mean student of them." In fact, Winchell's name was among the ten most prolific makers of American slang, a list compiled in 1933 by W. J. Funk of the Funk and Wagnall's Company.

In an obituary notice in the *New York Graphic,* Winchell acknowledged Jack Conway as "my tutor of the slanguage he helped me perfect." Conway, who wrote for the theatrical weekly *Variety,* is credited with coinages as "baloney," "palooka," "belly-laugh," and "pay-off." But Winchell took Conway's knack of borrowing and reshaping the slang of criminals and other sub-cultures even further. On the one hand, he gave vogue to already-exising terms such as "whoopie," "phooie," and "pash" (passion). He also employed phonetic spellings, among them "moom pitcher" (motion picture), "Joosh" (Jewish), and "dotter" (daughter). On the other hand, Winchell coined new phrases, often by merging two or more words into one: "intelligentlemen," "Chicagorilla," and "profanguage."

As suited a gossip columnist, still more of Winchell's vocabulary consisted of improvised synonyms. People who married were "lohengrined," "middleaisled," or "sealed." Those in love were described as "Adam-and-Eveing," "man-and-womaning it," "on the merge," or "that way." In case of separation or divorce, Winchell used words and phrases like "curdled," "in husband trouble," "on the verge," "phfft," "telling it to a judge," and "Reno-vated." In addition, he created his own Broadway jargon, including "Hard-Times-Square" (Times Square) and "The Hardened Artery" (Broadway).

Winchell began his working life as a newsboy on the streets of New York and, at the age of twelve, entered vaudeville, where the seeds of his gossip column were planted. While on tour with a Pantages road show in 1919, he started a one-page bulletin called "The News Sense" (pronounced "nuisance"). Zwerin described the flyer: "It told where meals were cheap in town, what hotels had just fumigated its rooms, where the floating crap games were. Anticipating his future calling, it also included this item: 'Which tumbler in the Morrissey Brothers act has tumbled for a restaurant waitress at Larry's Bar? Is it the single one or the one whose wife slaves over a hot scrubbing board in Scranton?'" Gradually, Winchell began submitting his gossip columns in *Billboard* and the *Vaudeville News,* where he turned to journalism full time.

In the final analysis, Winchell is usually credited with inventing the gossip column, paving the way for such writers as Louella Parsons, Leonard Lyons, Ed Sullivan, and Earl Wilson. Stanley Walker, former editor of the *New York Herald Tribune,* wrote: "Winchell did much for journalism, for which journalism has been slow to thank him. He helped change the dreary, ponderous impersonality which was pervading the whole press." Yet, for the last decade of his life, after the closing of the *New York Daily Mirror* in 1963, his column appeared in fewer than two hundred newspapers. His decline has been variously attributed to the deterioration of Broadway, changing social mores, and the tendency of his enemies to eventually strike back. Summing up Winchell's career, Cuneo said: "For the record, Walter admittedly was not a Great Man. He wasn't a Great Guy, either. But that didn't particularly interest him. What did was that he wanted to be a Great Newsman. That was his driving obsession. He drove himself night and day without mercy to reach that pinnacle, and he did. He became the Greatest of the Great Gossips."

BIOGRAPHICAL/CRITICAL SOURCES—Books: H. L. Mencken, *The American Language,* Knopf, 1936, Supplement One, 1945; St. Clair McKelway, *Gossip: The Life and Times of Walter Winchell,* Viking, 1940; Lyle Stuart, *The Secret Life of Walter Winchell,* Boars Head, 1953; Ed Weiner, *Let's Go to Press: A Biography of Walter Winchell,*

Putnam, 1955; Bob Thomas, *Winchell,* Doubleday, 1971; Herman Klurfeld, *Winchell: His Life and Times,* Praeger, 1976.

Periodicals: *Vanity Fair,* November, 1927; *American Speech,* October, 1931, April, 1932, October, 1937, February, 1939, April, 1942; *American Mercury,* February, 1937; *Collier's,* February 28, 1948, November 23, 1956; *Newsweek,* May 7, 1951, October 10, 1960; *Time,* January 21, 1952, June 9, 1958, May 5, 1958; *Esquire,* August, 1968; *Saturday Evening Post,* September, 1976.

OBITUARIES: New York Times, February 21, 1972; *Time,* March 6, 1972; *Newsweek,* March 6, 1972.*

—*Sketch by Andrea Geffner*

*   *   *

WINSLOW, Pauline Glen

PERSONAL: Born in London, England; daughter of Stanley Glen (a boxer); married Raymond Winslow (a trombonist). *Education:* Attended Hunter College of the City University of New York, New School for Social Research, and Columbia University. *Residence:* New York, N.Y.

CAREER: Free-lance court reporter in New York, N.Y. *Awards, honors:* Fellowships from Yaddo Foundation and Huntington Hartford Foundation.

WRITINGS—Novels: *The Strawberry Marten,* Macmillan, 1973, published in the United States as *Gallows Child,* St. Martin's, 1978; *Death of an Angel,* Macmillan, 1975, St. Martin's, 1975; *The Brandenburg Hotel* (Detective Book Club selection), Macmillan, 1975, St. Martin's, 1976; *The Witch Hill Murder* (selection of Thriller Book Club and Detective Book Club), St. Martin's, 1977; *Coppergold* (Detective Book Club selection), St. Martin's, 1978; (contributor) Dilys Winn, editor, *Murderess Ink,* Workman Publishing, 1979; *The Counsellor Heart,* St. Martin's, 1980; *The Windsor Plot,* Warner Paperback, 1981; *The Rockefeller Gift,* St. Martin's, 1981. Author of two novels under pseudonyms.

WORK IN PROGRESS: A novel under a pseudonym.

*   *   *

WINTERS, Marian   1924-1978

PERSONAL: Born April 19, 1924, in New York, N.Y.; died in 1978 in Warwick, N.Y.; married Jay H. Smolin (an advertising executive) November 18, 1945. *Education:* Attended Brooklyn College (now of the City University of New York). *Home:* West Ridge Corners, Warwick, N.Y. 10990. *Agent:* Flora Roberts, 65 East 55th St., New York, N.Y. 10022.

CAREER: Stage actress, beginning 1940, appearing in productions including "King John," Equity Library Theatre, 1949; "Dream Girl," New York City Center, 1951; "Sing Me No Lullaby," Phoenix Theatre, 1954; "Tall Story," Belasco Theatre, 1959; and "Mating Dance," Eugene O'Neill Theatre, 1965. Television actress, beginning 1949, appearing in more than three hundred roles including appearances on "Love of Life," (CBS), "The Guiding Light" (CBS), "The Defenders" (CBS), "Philco Television Playhouse" (NBC), and "Hawk" (ABC). Director. Playwright, beginning 1966. *Member:* American Federation of Television and Radio Artists, Screen Actors Guild, Actors Equity Association, New Dramatists, Inc. *Awards, honors:* Antoinette Perry (Tony) Award, Donaldson Award, *Theatre World* award, and *Variety* New York Drama Critics Poll award, all c. 1952, all for role as Natalia Landauer in "I Am a Camera"; *Variety* New York Drama Critics Poll nomination, c. 1963, for performance as Marge Weber in "Nobody Loves an Albatross";

Emmy Award, 1967, for "Animal Keepers"; Provincetown Living Arts Award, for "All Saints Day"; Getchel Award from South Theatre Conference, 1970, for "All Is Bright"; first prize from University of Miami, for "Breadwinner."

WRITINGS: (With Wilbur Pippin) *Catwise,* Knopf, 1979.

Plays: *A Is for All* (one-act plays; contains: "Animal Keepers," first produced Off-Off Broadway at 13th Street Theatre, October, 1966, produced on television by CBS; "Assembly Line," first produced at Neighborhood Playhouse School of the Theatre, May 12, 1969; and "All Saint's Day"), Dramatists Play Service, 1968. Also author of "All Is Bright," 1970, "Breadwinner," "The Tour," and "Getting There Soon."

SIDELIGHTS: Winters's award-winning "Animal Keepers" is set in a veterinarian's waiting room, where its lonely occupants share a warm moment of communication. The comedy "Breadwinner" tells about a father's efforts to lift his family from the Great Depression, and "All Is Bright" is about a struggling artist and his writer wife. Winters's favorite role as an actress was that of Constance in "King John." *Avocational interests:* Cooking, gardening.*

*　　　*　　　*

WINTERS, Rosemary
See BRECKLER, Rosemary

*　　　*　　　*

WIRTZ, (William) Willard   1912-

PERSONAL: Born March 14, 1912, in DeKalb, Ill.; son of William Wilbur and Alpha Belle (White) Wirtz; married Mary Jane Quisenberry, September 8, 1936; children: Richard, Philip. *Education:* Beloit College, A.B., 1933; Harvard University, LL.B., 1937. *Home:* 5009 39th St. N.W., Washington, D.C. 20016. *Office:* Wirtz & Lapointe, 1211 Connecticut Ave. N.W., Washington, D.C. 20036.

CAREER: Worked as high school teacher in Kewanee, Ill., 1933-34; University of Iowa, Iowa City, instructor, 1937-39; Northwestern University, Evanston, Ill., assistant professor of law, 1939-42; assistant general counsel of Board of Economic Welfare, 1942-43; associated with War Labor Board, 1943-45; National Wage Stabilization Board, Washington, D.C., chairman, 1946; Northwestern University, Evanston, Ill., professor of law, 1946-54; practiced law, 1956-61; U.S. Department of Labor, Washington, D.C., U.S. Secretary of Labor, 1962-69; Wirtz & Gentry, Washington, D.C., partner, 1970-78; Wirtz & Lapointe, Washington, D.C., partner, 1979—.

WRITINGS: Labor and the Public Interest, Harper, 1964; *The Boundless Resource: A Prospectus for an Education Work Policy,* New Republic Press, 1975. Contributor to *New Republic.*

*　　　*　　　*

WITHERS, Josephine   1938-

PERSONAL: Born July 3, 1938, in Cambridge, Mass.; daughter of Charles Cole (a photographer and businessman) and Fanny (Rolands) Withers. *Education:* Oberlin College, B.A., 1960; Columbia University, M.A., 1965, Ph.D., 1971. *Home:* 2122 Decatur Place N.W., Washington, D.C. 20008. *Office:* Department of Art, University of Maryland, College Park, Md. 20742.

CAREER: Detroit Institute of Arts, Detroit, Mich., junior curator in education, 1960-62; Museum of Modern Art, New

York, N.Y., guest director, 1968; Temple University, Philadelphia, Pa., assistant professor of art, 1968-69; University of Maryland, College Park, associate director of art gallery, 1970-73, instructor, 1970-71, assistant professor, 1971-78, associate professor of art, 1978—, and seminar director. Lecturer at Wayne State University, 1960-62, and Smithsonian Institution, 1975, 1977; member of board of directors of Washington Women's Art Center, 1976-77. *Member:* College Art Association, Women's Caucus for Art (member of board, 1980-83).

WRITINGS: Julio Gonzalez: Sculpture in Iron, New York University Press, 1978; (contributor) L. Sandler and M. Barasch, editors, *Essays in Honor of H. W. Janson,* New York University Press, 1978; *Women Artists in Washington Collections,* University of Maryland Press, 1979. Author of exhibition catalogs. Contributor of articles and reviews to art journals. Art history editor of *Womansphere Journal,* 1975-76; editor of *Newsletter* of Washington Women's Art Center, 1976-77; art editor of *Feminist Studies,* 1978—.

WORK IN PROGRESS: Self-Portraits: The Self-Image of the Modern Artist.

SIDELIGHTS: Josephine Withers told *CA:* "The relationship between an artist's words and artwork is usually problematical, often illuminating, and always in flux. I spend quite a bit of my research time talking with artists and reading what they've written as well as looking at and thinking about their work. I think of my writing as a creative mix of factual information, historical analogy, and intuitive interpretation. I consider a piece successful when the artist comes back to me and says: 'I learned something there. I hadn't thought of that before.'"

*　　　*　　　*

WITTIG, Alice J(osephine)   1929-

PERSONAL: Born February 2, 1929, in Lincoln, Neb.; daughter of Chauncey W. (a professor) and Emma (a teacher; maiden name, Falter) Smith; married Donald R. Wittig (a singer, teacher, and librarian), April 29, 1961; children: Robert Gardner, Amy Judith. *Education:* University of Nebraska, B.S. in Ed., 1951; University of Denver, M.A., 1960. *Home address:* P.O. Box 1048, Mendocino, Calif. 95460. *Office:* Mendocino Unified School District, P.O. Box 226, Mendocino, Calif. 95460.

CAREER: University of Denver, Denver, Colo., government documents librarian, 1960-62, instructor in Graduate School of Librarianship, 1962; Stanford University, Stanford, Calif., assistant reference librarian at Law School Library, 1966-70; Mendocino Unified School District, Mendocino, Calif., elementary school librarian, 1974-79, district librarian, 1979—.

WRITINGS: U.S. Government Publications for the School Media Center (self-illustrated), Libraries Unlimited, 1979. Contributor to library journals.

WORK IN PROGRESS: An illustrated children's book.

SIDELIGHTS: Wittig told *CA:* "School media centers are at a crossroads now where certain decisions are being forced upon us. We can no longer afford to include everything, serve everyone, and fill all roles possible. We have an exciting opportunity to decide what we can do best and to get on about the business of doing it."

*　　　*　　　*

WOITITZ, Janet G.

EDUCATION: Antioch College, B.A., 1960; Montclair State

College, M.A., 1971; Rutgers University, Ed.D., 1976. *Home:* 27 Marquette Rd., Upper Montclair, N.J. 07043.

CAREER: In private practice in human relations counseling. Adjunct professor at Montclair State College; instructor at Rutgers University. Member of New Jersey Task Force on Women and Alcohol. Presents workshops on alcoholism and the family; consultant. *Member:* American Personnel and Guidance Association, National Advocacy Group for Children of Alcoholics (co-founder), New Jersey Association of Alcoholism Counselors, New Jersey Alcohol Association.

WRITINGS: (Contributor) David H. Olson and Nancy S. Dahl, editors, *Inventory of Marriage and Family Literature,* Volume V: *Family Social Science, 1977-1978,* Sage, 1979; *Marriage on the Rocks,* Delacorte, 1979. Contributor to academic journals.

* * *

WOLLHEIM, Richard Arthur 1923-

PERSONAL: Born May 5, 1923, in London, England; son of Eric and Constance (Baker) Wollheim; married Anne Powell, 1950 (divorced, 1967); married Mary Day Lanier (a potter), 1969; children: (first marriage) Rupert Daniel, Bruno Richard. *Education:* Balliol College, Oxford, M.A., 1948. *Home:* 20 Ashchurch Park Villas, London W.12, England.

CAREER: University College, London, England, assistant lecturer, 1949-51, lecturer, 1951-60, reader in philosophy, 1960-63, Grote Professor of Philosophy of Mind and Logic, 1963—. Visiting professor at Columbia University, 1959-60 and 1970, Visva-Bharati University, Santiniketan, India, 1968, University of Minnesota, 1972, City University of New York, 1975, and University of California, Berkeley, 1981; Power Lecturer at University of Sydney, 1972. *Military service:* British Army, 1942-45, served in Northern Europe; became captain. *Member:* British Society of Aesthetics (vice-president, 1969—), Aristotelian Society (president, 1967-68).

WRITINGS: F. H. Bradley, Penguin, 1959, 2nd edition, 1969; *Art and Its Objects: An Introduction to Aesthetics,* Harper, 1968, 2nd edition, Cambridge University Press, 1980; *A Family Romance* (novel), Farrar, Straus, 1969; *Sigmund Freud,* Viking, 1971 (published in England as *Freud,* Fontana, 1971); *On Art and the Mind* (essays and lectures), Allen Lane, 1973, Harvard University Press, 1974; *The Good Self and the Bad Self,* British Academy, 1976; *The Sheep and the Ceremony,* Cambridge University Press, 1979.

Editor: (And author of introduction) Francis Herbert Bradley, *Ethical Studies,* 2nd revised edition, Oxford University Press, 1962; David Hume, *Hume on Religion,* Collins, 1963; (and author of introduction) Bradley, *Appearance and Reality: A Metaphysical Essay,* Oxford University Press, 1969; Adrian Durham Stokes, *The Image in Form: Selected Writings of Adrian Stokes,* Harper, 1972; *Freud: A Collection of Critical Essays,* Doubleday/Anchor, 1974; John Stuart Mill, *Three Essays,* Oxford University Press, 1975.

Contributor of articles to philosophical and literary anthologies and journals.

SIDELIGHTS: Richard Wollheim is interested in the philosophy and psychology of art. His book, *Art and Its Objects,* received enthusiastic reviews. *Art and Its Objects,* Michael Podro declared in the *New Statesman,* "is perhaps the first really important and fertilising book by a modern analytical philosopher on aesthetics, and the sheer inventiveness of its arguments makes most recent discussion from the side of

professional philosophy look mechanical." Anthony Quinto was equally admiring. "To say that it [*Art and Its Objects*] is the best modern book on philosophical aesthetics is fainter praise than it deserves," he wrote in the *Listener.* "In about 50,000 words it covers a wide range of problems with great verve and originality. Professor Wollheim is a highly sophisticated man, as is shown by the vast range of his allusions to works of art of all kinds, by the mannered but engaging elegance of his style and by the authority with which he handles a large number of complex disciplines that overlap marginally in the field of his interest—the kind of authority that consorts with high lucidity and the brisk exclusion of inessentials."

In addition to his scholarly works, Wollheim has written one novel, *A Family Romance.* Written in diary form, the book explores the narrator's relationships with his wife, his mistress, and his father. Although granting that the book is "cleverly conceived and very well written," Sara Blackburn felt that "the tension that sustains our early interest in its wordy, introspective narrator gradually fades away as his total humorlessness neutralizes even its calculated-to-shock ending." A critic for the *New York Times Book Review* had a more positive response: "Peering backward into memory and forward into illusion, the narrator keeps returning to the increasingly unbearable present. The effect is to produce a sequence of Proustian variations, in which the sins of the son are visited on the father. It is old fashioned in a refreshing way—post-Freud, and pre-war."

BIOGRAPHICAL/CRITICAL SOURCES: Listener, November 7, 1968; *New Statesman,* December 6, 1968, May 2, 1969, February 1, 1974; *Times Literary Supplement,* May 22, 1969; *New York Times Book Review,* September 7, 1969; *Nation,* October 13, 1969, February 26, 1973.

* * *

WOODARD, Bronte 1941(?)-1980

OBITUARY NOTICE: Born c. 1941; died of liver failure, August 6, 1980, in Los Angeles, Calif. Writer. Bronte Woodard wrote the screenplays for several popular films, including "Grease" and "Can't Stop the Music." He had just complete the screenplay for his novel, *Meet Me at the Melba,* at the time of his death. Obituaries and other sources: *New York Times,* August 8, 1980.

* * *

WOODRUFF, William 1916-

PERSONAL: Born September 12, 1916, in Blackburn, England; came to the United States in 1953, naturalized citizen, 1973; son of William (a weaver) and Anne (a spinner; maiden name, Kenyon) Woodruff; married Kay Wright, September 20, 1941 (died, 1959); married Helga Gaertner, July 19, 1960; children: David, Roger, Kirsten, Mark, Peter, Andrew, Thomas. *Education:* Oxford University, B.A., 1940, M.A., 1946; University of London, B.Sc., 1949; attended Harvard University, 1951-52; University of Nottingham, D.Phil., 1952. *Home:* 1710 Northwest 66th Ter., Gainesville, Fla. 32605. *Office:* Department of History, University of Florida, 4109 G.P.A., Gainesville, Fla. 32622.

CAREER: University of Nottingham, Nottingham, England, lecturer in economic history, 1946-50; Bank of England, London, Houblon-Norman research fellow, 1950-51; University of Illinois, Urbana, associate professor, 1953-55, professor of economics, 1955-56; University of Melbourne, Melbourne, Australia, professor of economic history, 1956-64, dean of faculty of economics and commerce, 1963-64;

Institute for Advanced Study, Princeton, N.J., visiting member of staff, 1964-65; University of Florida, Gainesville, graduate research professor of economic history, 1966—. *Member:* American Economic Association, American Economic History Association, British Economic Association, British Economic History Society. *Awards, honors:* Fulbright scholarship, 1951-52; honorary degree from University of Melbourne, 1957; senior research award from Japan Society for the Promotion of Science, Tokyo, 1975; teaching award from Florida College Teachers of History, 1980.

WRITINGS: (With Lachlan McGregor) *The Suez Canal and the Australian Economy,* Cambridge University Press, 1957; *The Rise of the British Rubber Industry,* Liverpool University Press, 1958; *Impact of Western Man,* Macmillan (London), 1966, St. Martin's, 1967; (with wife, Helga Woodruff) *Technology and the Changing Trade Patterns of the United States,* Bureau of Economic and Business Research, Florida University, 1968; *Vessel of Sadness,* Kallman, 1969, 3rd edition, University of Southern Illinois Press, 1978; *Emergence of an International Economy,* Collins, 1971; *America's Impact on the World: A Study of the Role of the United States in the World Economy, 1750-1970,* Halsted, 1975; *The Impact of Technology on Western Culture,* Science Museum of Victoria (Melbourne, Australia), 1976; *The Struggle for World Power, 1500-1980,* St. Martin's, 1980.

Contributor: Elizabeth Crittall, editor, *Victoria County History of England,* Volume IV: *Wiltshire,* Oxford University Press, 1959; Tomiju Masuda, editor, *Industrialization and Modernization,* Ichijo Shoten (Tokyo), 1968; Ronald Hilton, editor, *The Movement Toward Latin American Unity,* Praeger, 1969; R. B. Gray, *Essays in Latin American History,* F. E. Peacock, 1971; L. T. Houmanidis, editor, *Economic Growth and Development,* Dept. of International Relations, University of Athens, 1974; V. K. Zimmerman, editor, *The Impact of Inflation on Accounting: A Global View,* Center for International Education and Research in Accounting, University of Illinois, 1979. Contributor to *Encyclopaedia Britannica* and *Dictionary of American History.* Contributor to scientific journals.

WORK IN PROGRESS: A book of economic and social criticism, publication expected in 1981; books on world history and world economic development.

SIDELIGHTS: "Having taught at major universities on four continents," Woodruff wrote, "my aim is to provide a universal (in contrast to an ethnocentric) historical perspective for the world in which we live. My first concern is to cast light, not so much on the past, but on the present. The importance of world history and development for me is *now.* While recognizing the need for specialization in the social sciences, I deplore the present accumulation of disconnected historical minutiae. Specialism to me is not an end in itself but a means to a greater whole. I no more think the present atomization of knowledge is normal and permanent than I think ultimate and universal history is just around the corner. The Balkanization of the social sciences has brought us to a state of ever-growing general ignorance and dehumanized science. Hence, I have stressed the central role, not of methods or theories or systems, but of humanity."

*   *   *

WOODS, Elizabeth 1940-

PERSONAL: Born January 10, 1940, in Prince George, British Columbia, Canada. *Education:* University of British Columbia, B.A., 1961. *Home:* 57 Shaw St., Toronto, Ontario, Canada M6J 2W3.

CAREER: Poet. Worked as civil servant, clerk, and research assistant. Member of Canada's Book and Periodical Development Council (chairman of freedom of expression committee), Writers' Development Trust, and Canadian Copyright Institute; chairman of joint copyright committee of League of Canadian Poets and Writers Union of Canada. Gives readings on Canadian Broadcasting Corp. (CBC-Radio), including "Anthology" and "Tuesday Night." *Member:* League of Canadian Poets (first vice-president, 1977—), Writers Union of Canada.

WRITINGS: The Yellow Volkswagen (novel), Simon & Schuster, 1971; *Gone* (poems), Ladysmith Press, 1972; *Men* (poems), Fiddlehead Poetry Books, 1979; *The Amateur* (novel), Paperjacks, 1980.

Author of "Maya," a verse drama, first broadcast by CBC-Radio, 1974. Contributor to literary journals, including *Event, Canadian Forum, Miss Chatelaine, Prism International,* and *Tamarack Review.*

WORK IN PROGRESS: If the N.D.P. Had Won: A Utopian Novel; The Secular Nun, poems.

*   *   *

WOOSTER, Claire 1942-

PERSONAL: Born June 19, 1942, in Tarrytown, N.Y.; daughter of John B. and Lillian (Muller) Wooster; married J. Robert Meyners; children: Alexis. *Education:* University of Rochester, B.A., 1964; Cornell University, M.Ed., 1965. *Home:* 2304 134th St., Hopkins, Mich. 49328. *Agent:* Jane Rotrosen Agency, 318 East 51st St., New York, N.Y. 10022.

CAREER: Reading and language teacher at public schools in London, England, 1964-73; Chicago Theological Seminary, Chicago, Ill., co-administrator at Logos Institute, 1975-76; writer, sex educator, and workshop participant, 1976—. *Member:* American Association of Sex Educators and Counselors.

WRITINGS: (With husband, Robert Meyners) *Solomon's Sword: Clarifying Values in the Church,* Abingdon, 1977; (with R. Meyners) *Sexual Style: Facing and Making Choices About Sex,* Harcourt, 1979.

WORK IN PROGRESS: Research for a book on the roles and function of friendship in our society.

SIDELIGHTS: Claire Wooster wrote: "Living nearly ten years abroad and teaching in multi-ethnic schools has made me very conscious of the relativity of values and has led to an interest and belief in the necessity of assisting people to discover and develop their own value systems in the face of cultural pluralism. In particular, I've developed an interest in helping people sort out issues and values of vital personal importance in everyday life."

*   *   *

WOOTTEN, Morgan 1931-

PERSONAL: Born April 21, 1931, in Durham, N.C.; son of Charles T. (a lieutenant commander in the U.S. Navy) and Clare Wootten; married Kathryn Bourg, May 16, 1964; children: Kathleen, Carol, Patricia, Brendan, Joey. *Education:* University of Maryland, degree, 1955; graduate study at American University. *Religion:* Roman Catholic. *Home:* 6912 Wells Parkway, University Park, Md. *Office:* De Matha High School, 4313 Madison St., Hyattsville, Md. 29781.

CAREER: High school teacher of world history in Washington, D.C., 1955-56; De Matha High School, Hyattsville, Md., history teacher and basketball coach, 1956—. Member of Maryland governor's council on physical fitness in the state of Maryland. *Military service:* U.S. Naval Reserve, active duty, 1951-52. *Member:* Touchdown Club, Knights of Columbus, Order of Alhambra, Kentucky Colonels, Kappa Alpha, Omicron Delta Kappa (Sigma Circle). *Awards, honors:* Distinguished citizenship award from State of Maryland, 1965; named coach of the year by *Washington Daily News,* 1961, 1965, and 1969, and by National Coaches Association, 1973.

WRITINGS: (With Bill Gilbert) *From Orphans to Champions,* Scribner, 1979. Also author of two privately printed books, *De Matha High School Basketball Notebook* and *De Matha High School Blitz Defense.*

* * *

WORDEN, Alfred M(errill) 1932-

PERSONAL: Born February 7, 1932, in Jackson, Mich.; son of Merrill Bangs and Helen (Crowell) Worden; married Sandra Lee Wilder, 1974 (divorced, January, 1980); children: Merrill Ellen, Alison Pamela. *Education:* U.S. Military Academy, B.S., 1955; University of Michigan, M.S. (astronautical and aeronautical engineering), 1963, M.S. (instrumentation engineering), 1963. *Home:* 334 Australian Ave., Palm Beach, Fla. 33480. *Office:* Alfred M. Worden, Inc., 340 Royal Palm Way, Palm Beach, Fla. 33480.

CAREER: U.S. Air Force, 1955-75, pilot and armament officer at Andrews Air Force Base, Md., 1957-61, flight proficiency officer at Selfridge Air Force Base, Mich., 1961-63, instructor at Aerospace Research Pilot School, 1964-66, director of Systems Studies Division at Ames Research Center, 1972-75, retired as colonel; Alfred M. Worden, Inc. (energy management service company), Palm Beach, Fla., president, 1975—. Director of energy management programs at Northwood Institute, 1975—. Employed by National Aeronautics and Space Administration, 1966-75, member of support crew for *Apollo 9,* back-up pilot of command module for *Apollo 12,* pilot of command module for *Apollo 15,* 1971. President of Boys' Club of America.

MEMBER: American Institute of Aeronautics and Astronautics, Society of Experimental Test Pilots, American Astronautical Society, American Society of Heating, Refrigerating, and Air Conditioning Engineers, National Association of Corporate Real Estate Executives, Association of Energy Engineers, Royal Aeronautical Society, Explorers Club, Circumnavigators Club, Sports Car Club of America. *Awards, honors:* Command Pilot Astronaut Wings; distinguished service medal from National Aeronautics and Space Administration, 1971; peace medal from United Nations, 1971; medal from city of New York, N.Y., and gold medal from city of Chicago, Ill., both 1971; David C. Schilling Trophy from Air Force Association, 1971; Kitty Hawk Memorial Award from Los Angeles Chamber of Commerce, 1971; Doctor of Astronautical Science degree from University of Michigan, 1971; member of Belgiums's Order of Leopold, 1971; Robert J. Collier Trophy from Air Force Association, 1971; Haley Astronautics Award from American Institute of Aeronautics and Astronautics, 1972.

WRITINGS: Hello Earth: Greetings From Endeavour (poems), Nash Publishing, 1974; *I Want to Know About–A Flight to the Moon* (juvenile), Doubleday, 1974.

WORK IN PROGRESS: A "how-to" book on home energy conservation.

SIDELIGHTS: Worden wrote that he was commissioned in the Air Force directly after graduation from West Point in 1955. He received his flight training in Texas and Florida and graduated from Empire Test Pilots School at Farnborough, England. One of nineteen astronauts selected in 1966, he served as command module pilot of *Apollo 15* with spacecraft commander, Dave Scott, and lunar module pilot, Jim Irwin. *Apollo 15* was the fourth manned lunar landing mission, the first to operate a scientific instrument module bay, and the first to launch a sub-satellite in lunar orbit. On the return trip to earth, Worden performed a thirty-eight minute walk in space, the first while not in earth orbit. On that flight he logged nearly three hundred hours and covered a distance of nearly one-and-a-half million miles.

AVOCATIONAL INTERESTS: Bowling, skiing, water skiing, swimming, handball, automobile racing.

* * *

WORTH, C. Brooke 1908-

PERSONAL: Born September 4, 1908, in Coatesville, Pa.; son of George S. and Nora (Stabler) Worth; married Merida Grey, April 18, 1931; children: Valerie (Mrs. George W. Bahlke), Michael, Douglas. *Education:* Received B.A. from Swarthmore College and M.D. from University of Pennsylvania. *Politics:* None. *Religion:* None. *Home address:* Rural Delivery, Delmont, N.J. 08314.

CAREER: Swarthmore College, Swarthmore, Pa., instructor in biology, 1936-46; Philadelphia Zoo, Philadelphia, Pa., assistant pathologist, 1946-47; Rockefeller Foundation, member of field staff, 1947-66; writer. Member of board of trustees of Wetland Institute, Stone Harbor, N.J., 1970—; member of National Academy of Sciences expeditions to Honduras, Panama, and Mexico. *Military service:* U.S. Army, Medical Corps, Department of Tropical Medicine and Parasitology, 1942-46.

WRITINGS: A Manual of Tropical Medicine, Saunders, 1945; *The Nature of Living Things,* New American Library, 1955; *A Naturalist in Trinidad,* Lippincott, 1967; *Mosquito Safari,* Simon & Schuster, 1971; *Of Mosquitos, Moths, and Mice,* Norton, 1972.

WORK IN PROGRESS: Investigating the biology of saturniid moths; continuing studies of bird-banding.

AVOCATIONAL INTERESTS: Playing jazz piano music of the 1930's.

* * *

WRIGHT, Norman Edgar 1927-

PERSONAL: Born January 9, 1927, in Murray, Utah; son of Cleeo Datell (a wool grower) and Mary Hill (Musser) Wright; married Carolyn LaRene Bevan, April 9, 1954 (died April 20, 1977); married Daniele Yvonne Michelle Piquee, September 30, 1977; children: (first marriage) Preston Dean, Craig Jeremy, Joel Kirk, Marie-Agnes, Jerry Bevan, Diane Lucille, Suzanne Marie, Kathryn Ann, Nathan Mark; (stepchildren) Don-Paul Bearnson, Mark Sebastian Bearnson, Soroya Rachelle Bearnson. *Education:* Brigham Young University, B.S., 1956; Utah State University, M.S., 1958. *Politics:* "Varies." *Religion:* Church of Jesus Christ of Latter-day Saints (Mormons). *Home:* 520 East 200 N., Pleasant Grove, Utah 84062. *Office:* Department of History, Brigham Young University, Provo, Utah 84602.

CAREER: Church of Jesus Christ of Latter-day Saints, missionary in New Zealand, 1948-50, researcher for Genealogical Society in Salt Lake City, Utah, 1957-64; Brigham Young University, Provo, Utah, associate professor of family and local history, 1964—. *Military service:* U.S. Merchant Marine, 1945-46; served in Pacific theater. U.S. Army, 1946-47, 1950-56; served in Japan and Korea; became sergeant first class.

WRITINGS: (With David Heber Pratt) *Key to Genealogical Research Essentials,* Birgham Young University Press, 1966; (with Pratt) *Genealogical Research Essentials,* Bookcraft, 1967; (with Pratt) *Migration Sources: Great Britain and North America,* Brigham Young University Press, 1967; (editor) *North American Genealogical Sources,* Volume I: *Mid-Atlantic States and Canada,* Volume II: *Midwestern States,* Volume III: *Southern States,* Volume IV; *Southwestern States,* Brigham Young University Press, 1968; *Genealogy in America,* Volume I: *Genealogical Research Methods and Sources for Massachusetts, Connecticut, and Maine,* Deseret, 1968; (editor) *Genealogical Reader: Northeastern United States and Canada,* Brigham Young University Press, 1973; *Building an American Pedigree,* Brigham Young University Press, 1974.

WORK IN PROGRESS: Revising *Building an American Pedigree,* publication expected in 1980; *Regional Genealogical Sources: The United States and Canada.*

*   *   *

WYATT, Rachel 1929-

PERSONAL: Born October 14, 1929, in Bradford, England; daughter of Kenneth J. R. (a wool merchant's manager) and Rachel (Brumfitt) Arnold; married Alan Wyatt (an engineer); children: Antony, Diana, Timothy, Sally. *Education:* Attended grammar school in Bradford, England. *Home:* 207 Cottingham St., Toronto, Ontario, Canada M4V 1C4. *Agent:* David Higham Associates Ltd., 5-8 Lower John St., London W1R 4HA, England.

CAREER: Writer. *Member:* Canadian Authors Association, Writers' Union of Canada, Association of Canadian Television and Radio Artists.

WRITINGS: The String Box (novel), House of Anansi Press, 1970; *The Rosedale Hoax* (novel), House of Anansi Press, 1977; *The Racists* (novel), House of Anansi Press, 1980.

Work represented in anthologies, including *Anthology,* Canadian Broadcasting Corp. Author of about thirty radio and television scripts for British Broadcasting Corp. and Canadian Broadcasting Corp. Contributor of articles and stories to magazines, including *Chatelaine* and *Punch,* and newspapers.

WORK IN PROGRESS: A novel spanning forty years of a woman's life.

SIDELIGHTS: Rachel Wyatt commented: "It took me a long time to realize that my 'vision' was slightly different from other people's, and that if I wrote down what I saw people would read it or listen to it and be amused, pleased, enlightened, disappointed, or furious. I have usually been led into the different kinds of writing I have done by someone saying to me, 'Why don't you write a . . .?' I am waiting for someone to come along and ask me to write a stage play because I think that immediate contact with the audience must be the most exciting thing in the world for a writer.

"To me the important subject is people. I write in terms of ordinary humans doing their everyday things and along the way I look for some truth, some answer to the great 'Why?' that I might be able to pass on to others."

*   *   *

WYATT, (Alan) Will 1942-

PERSONAL: Born January 7, 1942, in Oxford, England; son

of Basil (a builder) and Hettie (Hooper) Wyatt; married Jane Bagenal (a picture restorer), April 2, 1966; children: Hannah, Rosalind Alison. *Education:* Emmanuel College, Cambridge, history tripos, 1964. *Home:* 4 Ashchurch Ter., London W.12, England. *Agent:* Hilary Rubinstein, A.P. Watt Ltd., 26/28 Bedford Row, London WC1R 4HL, England. *Office:* Television Centre, British Broadcasting Corp., Wood Lane, London W.12, England.

CAREER: Telegraph, Sheffield, England, reporter, 1964-65; British Broadcasting Corp. (BBC), London, England, news sub-editor for Radio News, 1965-68, director and producer at television center, 1968-77, head of presentation programs, 1977—.

WRITINGS: The Secret of the Sierra Madre, Doubleday, 1980 (published in England as *The Man Who Was B. Traven,* J. Cape, 1980). Contributor to *Listener.*

SIDELIGHTS: Wyatt's book, *The Secret of the Sierra Madre,* evolved from "B. Traven: A Mystery Solved," a documentary film that he produced for the British Broadcasting Corp. (BBC-TV). The name B. Traven was one of the numerous aliases used by the author of the *Treasure of the Sierra Madre, The Death Ship,* and other popular novels. Throughout his life he sought anonymity, claiming several contradictory birth dates, places, and names. As Traven's fans sought his true identity, rumors spread that he might really be Jack London, President Lopez Mateos of Mexico, a leper, or even the illegitimate son of Kaiser Wilhelm II of Germany. Even after Traven's death in 1969, no one was sure who he was.

Wyatt took up the search for a solution to the Traven mystery. After making repeated trips to Mexico, Poland, Germany, and the United States, combing through birth registers and FBI records, he finally discovered that Traven had been born Herman Albert Otto Max Feige in Schweibus, Germany (now Poland).

Upon reading Wyatt's book, George Woodcock said he was convinced that Wyatt had "finally solved one of the most tantalising literary mysteries of our age, and has established, as firmly as it ever will be, the identity of the novelist who called himself B. Traven." Brian Masters wrote that though Wyatt "knows the answer to the Traven riddle, with superb control he will give nothing away before it is time, and the result is a thrilling detective story."

BIOGRAPHICAL/CRITICAL SOURCES: London Sunday Times, June 22, 1980; *London Review of Books,* July 3-16, 1980; *London Times,* July 16, 1980; *London Evening Standard,* July 29, 1980.

*   *   *

WYMAN, Mark 1938-

PERSONAL: Born September 8, 1938, in River Falls, Wis.; son of Walker D. (a historian and writer) and Helen (an artist; maiden name, Bryant) Wyman; married Eva M. Goldschmidt (a teacher of Spanish), December 27, 1964; children: Daniel, Ruth and Miriam (twins). *Education:* Attended River Falls State College, 1956-58; University of Wisconsin—Madison, B.S., 1960, M.S., 1966; University of Washington, Seattle, Ph.D., 1971. *Home:* 807 North School St., Normal, Ill. 61761. *Office:* Department of History, Illinois State University, Normal, Ill. 61761.

CAREER: River Falls Journal, River Falls, Wis., general reporter, 1960; *Livingston Enterprise,* Livingston, Mont., general reporter, 1961-62; *Minneapolis Tribune,* Minneapolis, Minn., copy editor, 1962-64, labor reporter, 1966-68; Illinois State University, Normal, assistant professor, 1971-79, associate professor of history, 1980—. *Military service:* U.S. Army Reserve, 1961-66, active duty, 1961.

MEMBER: American Committee for Irish Studies, Organization of American Historians, Western History Association, Labor Historians, Authors Guild, Illinois State Historical Society, Illinois Labor History Society, Idaho Historical Society, McLean County Historical Society, Phi Beta Kappa. *Awards, honors:* Grant from Inter-American Press Association, 1964, for Chile; O. O. Winther Award from Western History Association, 1974, for ''Industrial Revolution in the West: Hard-Rock Miners and the New Technology''; National Endowment for the Humanities grant, 1978-79.

WRITINGS: Hard Rock Epic: Western Miners and the Industrial Revolution, 1860-1910, University of California Press, 1979.

WORK IN PROGRESS: A book on the influx of Irish and German immigrants into the Upper Mississippi Valley, 1830-1860, and their relations with the Yankees, Easterners, Southerners, and other native-born Americans also entering the region, publication expected in 1981.

SIDELIGHTS: Wyman commented: ''My work as labor reporter for the *Minneapolis Tribune* introduced me to the varied world of work as well as the need to seek information from many different sources. That early experience continues to motivate me as I continue writing on historical themes. Also, newspaper writing has helped me develop as a less-stodgy scholarly writer, I hope; at least, my goal is to write about history in a way that will be readable and even fascinating to non-academics. I'm not there, yet, but I'm working on it.''

Y

YABES, Leopoldo Y(abes) 1912-
(A. B. Christian, Crisostomo Ibarra, Manuel Silangan)

PERSONAL: Born November 15, 1912, in Sinait, Philippines; son of Julian Ibus and Catalina (Salcedo) Yabes; married Maria Ines Guerrero, September 5, 1936; children: Leonardo, Manuel, Marina Yabes Quiambao, Jesus. *Education:* University of the Philippines, B.Phil., 1935, M.A., 1950; further graduate study at University of Chicago, 1951-52. *Politics:* "Liberal democrat and nationalist." *Religion:* Christian. *Home:* 36 Maginhawa St., U.P. Village, Quezon City, Metro Manial 3004, Philippines.

CAREER: Commonwealth of the Philippines, Manila, technical assistant and chief clerk at Institute of National Language, 1937-42, feature writer for Department of Instruction, 1945-46; Office of the President of the Philippines, Manila, historical researcher, 1946-48; University of the Philippines, Quezon City, instructor, 1948-49, assistant professor, 1949-55, associate professor, 1955-59, professor of English, humanities, and Philippine institutions, 1959-76, university professor, 1976-77, professor emeritus, 1977—, head of department of humanities and Philippine institutions, 1959-60, executive secretary of Institute of Asian Studies, 1960-61, head of department of Filipino and Philippine literature, 1966-69, dean of graduate school, 1969-77. Assistant managing editor of *Philippine Social Sciences and Humanities Review,* 1948-58, managing editor, 1959-62; managing editor of *Diliman Review,* 1961-62. Member of National Research Council of the Philippines, 1977—; member of board of directors of University of the Philippines Alumni Association Recreation Corp.; member of board of trustees of Bayanikasan Research Foundation; vice-chairman of board of trustees of Ilocano Heritage Foundation.

MEMBER: International P.E.N. (member of board of directors of Philippine Center, 1958-62), International Association of Historians of Asia (charter member), Philippine Society for the Advancement of Learning (founding member; chairman, 1971—), Philippine Fulbright Scholars Association (member of board of directors, 1954-55, 1956-57; president, 1955-56), Philippine Historical Association (member of board of directors, 1957-58), Folklore Society of the Philippines, Bibliographical Society of the Philippines, Filipiniana Research Society (president, 1935-51), American Association for the Advancement of Science, American Society for Aesthetics, American Folklore Society, Modern Language Association of America, University of Chicago Alumni Association, Knights of Rizal (commander, 1959-60; supreme trustee and supreme archivist, 1960-64), Pi Gamma Mu, Phi Kappa Phi (vice-president, 1954-57, 1958-59). *Awards, honors:* Fulbright grant, 1951-52; fellowship from University of the Philippines, 1951-52, for University of Chicago; Rizal Centennial Award from Jose Rizal National Centennial Commission, 1961, for *Jose Rizal: Sage, Teacher, and Benefactor of Humanity;* distinguished service award from Knights of Rizal, 1965; fellow of China Academy, Taipei, Taiwan, 1974, D.Letters, 1975; outstanding educator award from University of the Northern Philippines, 1978.

WRITINGS—All published by University of the Philippines, except as noted: *The Ilocano Epic: A Critical Study of "The Life of Lamang,"* Carmelo & Bauermann, 1935; *A Brief Survey of Iloko Literature,* privately printed, 1936.

The University and the Fear of Ideas, privately printed, 1956; *Philippine Literature in English (1898-1957): A Bibliographical Survey,* 1958; *The Filipino Struggle for Intellectual Freedom and Other Essays on Philippine Life and Thought,* privately printed, 1959.

In Larger Freedom: Studies in Philippine Life, Thought, and Institutions, 1961; (under pseudonym Manuel Silangan) *Jose Rizal: Sage, Teacher, and Benefactor of Humanity,* 1961; *Two Intellectual Traditions: An Introduction,* 1963; *The Filipino Scholar,* 1965; *Rizal and National Greatness,* G. S. Rangol & Sons, 1966.

Toward a Greater University of the Philippines, 1970; *For a Strengthened Graduate Program of the University,* 1971; *The University of the Philippines in Perspective,* 1971; *Let's Study the New Constitution: The Language Provision,* 1973; *Graduate Education at the University of the Philippines,* 1975; *A Philosophy for Human Survival,* University of the Philippines Press, 1976; *Rafael Palma as Liberal Thinker and Man of Letters,* University of the Philippines Press, 1977; *A Common Scientific-Humanistic Culture and the Study of Literature,* University of the Philippines Press, 1977; *English in the Next Twenty Years,* University of the Philippines Press, 1977; *Report on Graduate Education,* University of the Philippines Press, 1977; (contributor) Bonifacio P. Sibayan and Andrew B. Gonzalez, editors, *Language Planning and the Building of a National Language: Essays in Honor of Santiago A. Fonacier on His Ninety-Second Birthday,* Linguistic Society of the Philippines and

Language Study Center, 1977; (contributor) Alejandrino G. Hufana, editor, *Philippine Writings*, Regal Publishing, 1978.

Editor: (With E. G. de los Reyes) *Essays in Freedom by Certain Filipinos*, privately printed, 1948; *Filipino Essays in English, 1910-1937*, 1954; *Rizal as an Internationalist*, United Nations Educational, Scientific, and Cultural Organization, 1961; *Jose Rizal on His Centenary*, 1963; *The Culture of the Philippines: Lectures*, 1965; *The Ordeal of a Man of Academe*, 1967; *The University of the Philippines and Graduate Education Goals*, 1973; *Philippine Short Stories, 1925-1940: An Anthology With Critical Introduction*, University of the Philippines Press, 1975; *Selected Papers of Bienvenida M. Gonzalez*, 1977; *Philippine Short Stories, 1941-1955*, University of the Philippines Press, 1980.

Author of underground writings under pseudonym Crisostomo Ibarra and of other writings under pseudonym A. B. Christian before and during World War II. Contributor of about three hundred articles and stories to magazines and newspapers, including *Solidarity* and *Panama*. Associate editor of *Diliman Review*, 1952-60, editor, 1963-65; editor of *Philippine Social Sciences and Humanities Review*, 1963-77; editor of *Research Digest*, of University of the Philippines, 1966-68; member of editorial board of Folklore Society of the Philippines, 1964—.

WORK IN PROGRESS: A history of Philippine literature, completion expected in 1982.

SIDELIGHTS: Yabes wrote: "For over three decades now I have had a reputation, on and off campus, for independent thought and candid opinion. Unremittingly I have fought for academic freedom. Twenty years ago I published a historical document on the growth of agrarian unrest in Central Luzon, and was taken to court for 'inciting to sedition.' I fought hard, but it was only after four years that I was able to obtain an acquittal.

"Those were 'witch-hunting' days, when the influence of U.S. Senator Joseph McCarthy was still strong in the Philippines. The fight for academic freedom was also strong. A Congressional investigation did not bring out any Communists among the faculty or students. Failing to do that, the reactionary forces seized upon my publication of the historical document as a clear instance of subversion.

"On the day the press published my indictment, two friends were brave enough to visit me at home to offer their help, but once the case was filed in court, there was a change of atmosphere on campus. Friends tried to avoid my company. All throughout my morale was strong, but it was strengthened when the university did not suspend me for the duration, which meant that it was firmly convinced of my innocence.

"Another interesting event in my life was the trip I made in 1976 to the United States, United Kingdom, France, Germany, and Japan, for the purpose of studying higher education and contemporary literature. It enriched my experience, and will be of great use to me."

*   *   *

YANCEY, Philip D(avid)   1949-

PERSONAL: Born November 4, 1949, in Atlanta, Ga.; son of Marshall Watts and Mildred (a teacher; maiden name, Diem) Yancey; married Janet Norwood (a research consultant), June 2, 1970. *Education:* Columbia Bible College, Columbia, S.C., B.A., 1970; Wheaton College, Wheaton, Ill., M.A., 1972. *Religion:* Protestant. *Residence:* Chicago, Ill.

CAREER: *Campus Life*, Wheaton, Ill., editor, 1971-79, executive editor, 1979; free-lance writer, 1980—. *Member:*

Evangelical Press Association (member of board of directors, 1979—). *Awards, honors:* Golden Medallion Award from Evangelical Christian Publishers Association, 1978, for *Where Is God When It Hurts?.*

WRITINGS: After the Wedding, Word, Inc., 1976; *Where Is God When It Hurts?*, Zondervan, 1977; (with Jay Kesler) *Growing Places*, Revell, 1978; (with Tim Stafford) *Unhappy Secrets of the Christian Life*, Zondervan, 1979; (with Paul Brand) *Fearfully and Wonderfully Made*, Zondervan, 1980. Contributor of about three hundred articles to magazines, including *Reader's Digest*, *Saturday Evening Post*, and *Christianity Today*.

SIDELIGHTS: Yancey told *CA:* "Most of my writing, except for occasional *Reader's Digest* articles, is targeted toward an orthodox Christian audience. I have come to that position after a strong reaction against the hyper-fundamentalism in which I was reared. I resigned as editor of *Campus Life* in 1979 to devote most of my time to free-lance writing. I write to stimulate change or reflection in readers, and try to cut through the phony facade common to religious experience.

"I have been greatly influenced by Annie Dillard, Leo Tolstoi, Lewis Thomas, Frederick Buechner, and G. K. Chesterton."

*   *   *

YARMEY, A(lexander) Daniel   1938-

PERSONAL: Born December 17, 1938, in Toronto, Ontario, Canada; son of William Jerry (a physician) and Helen (Keller) Yarmey; married Judith Sutherland (a registered nurse), September 7, 1964; children: Craig, Linda, Meagan. *Education:* Attended Wilfrid Laurier University, 1958-60; University of Western Ontario, B.A., 1962, M.A., 1963, Ph.D., 1965. *Home:* 37 Sherwood Dr., Guelph, Ontario, Canada N1E 6E6. *Office:* Department of Psychology, University of Guelph, Guelph, Ontario, Canada N1G 2W1.

CAREER: Wilfrid Laurier University, Waterloo, Ontario, assistant professor of psychology, 1965-67; University of Guelph, Guelph, Ontario, assistant professor, 1967-70, associate professor, 1970-80, professor of psychology, 1980—. Visiting professor at University of Tennessee, 1975-76. Consultant to Guelph Department of Corrections. *Member:* Canadian Psychological Association (fellow), Psychonomic Society.

WRITINGS: The Psychology of Eyewitness Testimony, Free Press, 1979. Contributor to journals in the behavioral sciences. Member of editorial board of *Journal of Mental Imagery*.

WORK IN PROGRESS: Social Psychology of Law, for police officers, completion expected in 1984; research on the elderly as eyewitnesses.

SIDELIGHTS: Yarmey wrote: "I am one of the fortunate few who likes their work. My motivation gives me a sense of accomplishment. I believe that scientists should be interested in the practical application of their work, and that motivated me to turn from the traditional study of human memory to the psychology of law and social cognition."

BIOGRAPHICAL/CRITICAL SOURCES: Psychology Today, March, 1980; *Victimology*, May, 1980.

*   *   *

YARNELL, Allen   1942-

PERSONAL: Born August 17, 1942, in Brooklyn, N.Y.; son

of Max and Lillian (Ember) Yarnell; married Pat Clancy (divorced); married Denise Andres, August 4, 1979. *Education:* Harpur College of State University of New York, B.A., 1964; State University of New York at Binghamton, M.A., 1966; University of Washington, Seattle, Ph.D., 1969. *Home:* 2200 Brigden Rd., Pasadena, Calif. 91104. *Office:* Office of Academic Programs, University of California, 2221 Murphy Hall, 405 Hilgard Ave., Los Angeles, Calif. 90024.

CAREER: Washington State University, Pullman, assistant professor of history, 1969-70; University of California, Los Angeles, lecturer, 1970-76, instructor in history at U.C.L.A. extension, 1970—, assistant vice-chancellor of student relations, 1980—. Seminar leader; guest on television and radio programs; consultant to Walt Disney Productions and CBS-TV. *Member:* American Historical Association, Organization of American Historians, Center for the Study of the Presidency. *Awards, honors:* Grant from U.S. Steel Foundation, 1967-69; fellow of Harry S Truman Library Institute, 1971, 1975.

WRITINGS: (Editor) *The Postwar Epoch: Perspectives on American History Since 1945,* Harper, 1972; *Democrats and Progressives: The 1948 Presidential Election as a Test of Postwar Liberalism,* University of California Press, 1974. Contributor of articles and reviews to history and regional studies journals.

WORK IN PROGRESS: A study of the relationship between President Dwight D. Eisenhower and Senator Joseph McCarthy, for publication by University of California Press; a study of the United States since 1945, for Harper; a survey textbook of U.S. history, for Harper.

SIDELIGHTS: Yarnell told *CA:* "My current work focuses on demonstrating that Dwight D. Eisenhower was a much stronger and effective president than many have thought. Specifically with regard to Senator Joseph McCarthy, my contention is that Eisenhower worked behind the scenes to help destroy his influence."

*   *   *

YARWOOD, Doreen 1918-

PERSONAL: Born December 12, 1918, in London, England; daughter of Herman (a sculptor) and Lilian Cawthra; married John Yarwood (a professor of physics), December 8, 1948. *Education:* Institute of Education, London, A.T.D., 1940. *Home:* 3 Garden House Lane, East Grinstead, West Sussex RH19 4JT, England.

CAREER: Lecturer in art, 1945-48; free-lance writer and artist, 1949—. *Military service:* Women's Auxiliary Air Force, administrative officer, 1940-45. *Member:* Society of Authors, Association of Art Historians, Society of Architectural Historians, Costume Society, Furniture Society.

*WRITINGS—*Self-illustrated: *English Costume From the Second Century B.C. to 1950,* Batsford, 1952, 4th revised edition published as *English Costume From the Second Century B.C. to 1972,* 1972; *The English Home: A Thousand Years of Furnishing and Decoration,* Scribner, 1956; *The Architecture of England From Prehistoric Times to the Present Day,* Putnam, 1963; *Outline of English Architecture,* Batsford, 1965, new edition, 1977; *English Houses,* Batsford, 1966; *Outline of English Costume,* Batsford, 1967, 4th edition, 1977; *Robert Adam* (biography), Dent, 1970; *The Architecture of Italy,* Chatto & Windus, 1970; *The Architecture of Europe,* Hastings House, 1974; *European Costume: Four Thousand Years of Fashion,* Larousse, 1975; *The Architecture of Britain,* Scribner, 1976; *Encyclopaedia of*

World Costume, Batsford, 1978; *Costume of the Western World: Pictorial Guide and Glossary,* Lutterworth, 1980; *Two Thousand Years of Housewifery and Appliances,* Batsford, 1981. Contributor to *Children's Britannica, World Book Encyclopedia, Teachers World, Childcraft International,* and *Macmillan Educational Yearbook.*

WORK IN PROGRESS: *Encyclopaedia of Architecture,* self-illustrated, publication by Batsford expected in 1983.

AVOCATIONAL INTERESTS: International travel (including the United States).

BIOGRAPHICAL/CRITICAL SOURCES: House and Garden, July-August, 1979.

*   *   *

YEAGER, Allan Edward 1943-

PERSONAL: Born July 21, 1943, in Sebastopol, Calif.; son of C. Ross (an accountant) and Bernice (Oehlman) Yeager. *Education:* Santa Rosa Junior College, A.A., 1963; Abilene Christian College, B.S., 1965. *Home:* 8 Jordan Ave., San Francisco, Calif. 94118. *Office:* La Fiesta School, 8511 Liman Way, Rohnert Park, Calif. 94928.

CAREER: Elementary school teacher in Santa Rosa, Calif., 1965-68, Rohnert Park, Calif., 1968-70, Cotati, Calif., 1970-72, and Rohnert Park, 1972-75; La Fiesta School, Rohnert Park, elementary teacher, 1975—. Laboratory school demonstration teacher at Sonoma State University, summer, 1971, resource instructor, 1972, 1980; workshop leader. *Member:* International Reading Association (member of executive board of Gateway Council, 1967-73), National Education Association, National Council of Teachers of English, American Library Association, Association for Library Service to Children, California Teachers Association, California Reading Association.

WRITINGS: Using Picture Books With Children (Instructors Book Club selection), Holt, 1973. Author of teachers' guides for Viking. Contributor to education journals. Children's book reviewer for *Instructor,* 1979—.

BIOGRAPHICAL/CRITICAL SOURCES: Rohnert Park-Cotati Times, September 15, 1977, December 13, 1979.

*   *   *

YEE, Min S. 1938-

PERSONAL: Born August 5, 1938, in Baltimore, Md.; married Helene Joyce Kantor (died, 1967); married Marcia Hollowell Reed (divorced, 1975); married Candace McCulloch (divorced, 1980); children: Keetja Hollowell (daughter), Tai Reed (son), Min Lorentz (son). *Education:* Denison University, A.B. (with honors), 1960; graduate study at Columbia University, 1961-63. *Politics:* Independent. *Religion:* "Hindu Baptist." *Home:* 48 Cornelia, Mill Valley, Calif. 94941. *Office:* 575 Market St., San Francisco, Calif. 94105.

CAREER: Worked at *Time* and *New York Times,* New York City, 1964-66; *Boston Globe,* Boston, Mass., reporter, 1967-68; *Newsweek,* staff correspondent from Boston, New York City, Los Angeles, Calif., and San Francisco, Calif., 1968-71; *Ramparts,* Berkeley, Calif., managing editor, 1972-73; *San Francisco,* San Francisco, author of column, 1976-77; Ortho Books, San Francisco, editorial director, 1977—. Free-lance correspondent in Vietnam, 1966. Co-chairperson of San Francisco Artists and Writers, 1973-74. *Member:* Association of American Publishers, Western Publishers Association, Bookbuilders West.

WRITINGS: The Melancholy History of Soledad Prison,

Harper, 1973; *The Great Escape*, Bantam, 1974; *The Driver's Handbook*, Bantam, 1975; (with Don K. Wright) *The Sports Book*, Holt, 1976; *The Plant Book*, Holt, 1977; *In My Father's House*, Holt, 1981.

Contributor to magazines and newspapers, including *Saturday Review, Rolling Stone, Life, Sports Illustrated, Look,* and *Fortune.* Editor and publisher of *Great Escape*, 1973—.

SIDELIGHTS: Yee commented: "Writing books is a continuing education. It's a license to learning. Because I believe that life is a never-ending learning process, I try to write about things that I want to learn about. I suppose, however, that while I will continue learning, I'm getting old enough now that I might want to start writing about things that I care about."

In My Father's House is nonfiction, about the People's Temple in Jonestown and the Layton family.

*   *   *

YIM, Kwan Ha   1929-

PERSONAL: Born May 5, 1929, in Korea; son of Choong-jo and Chin Yim; married wife, Elizabeth Ellen (a physical therapist), September 9, 1961; children: Anthony, Richard, Peter, Andrew. *Education:* Dartmouth College, B.A., 1957; Fletcher School of Law and Diplomacy, M.A.L.D., 1959, Ph.D., 1963. *Home:* 549 Westfield Dr., Valley Cottage, N.Y. 10989. *Office:* Department of Political Science, Manhattanville College, Purchase, N.Y. 10577.

CAREER: Bowdoin College, Brunswick, Maine, assistant professor of government, 1961-63; Manhattanville College, Purchase, N.Y., currently professor of political science. Research associate at East Asian Institute, Columbia University, 1968-75. *Military service:* South Korean Army, 1950-54; became captain; received Bronze Star with "V." *Member:* American Political Science Association, Association for Asian Studies, Phi Beta Kappa. *Awards, honors:* Fulbright fellowship; Social Science Research Council fellowships.

WRITINGS: China and the United States, 1955-1972, two volumes, Facts on File, 1975. Contributor to scholarly journals.

WORK IN PROGRESS: Research on U.S.-East Asian relations; re-evaluating East Asian international relations since 1850.

SIDELIGHTS: Yim wrote: "My interest is in interpreting developments in international relations. I maintain my scholarly research as a way of keeping my intellectual life alive."

*   *   *

YONE, Edward Michael Law
See LAW YONE, Edward Michael

*   *   *

YOUNG, Allen   1941-

PERSONAL: Born June 30, 1941, in Liberty, N.Y.; son of Louis (a chicken farmer) and Rachel (Goldfarb) Young. *Education:* Columbia University. A.B., 1962, M.S., 1964; Stanford University, M.A., 1963. *Home address:* RFD No. 2, Orange, Mass. 01364. *Agent:* Berenice Hoffman, 215 West 75th St., New York, N.Y. 10023. *Office:* Athol Daily News, 225 Exchange St., Athol, Mass. 01331.

CAREER: Free-lance writer. *New York Times,* New York City, stringer, 1964-67; English teacher in Rio de Janeiro, 1966-67; *Washington Post,* Washington, D.C., staff writer,

1967; Liberation News Service, New York City, staff member, 1967-70; Butterworth Corp., Westwood, Mass., partner, 1972-73; *Athol Daily News,* Athol, Mass., reporter and feature writer, 1979—. Clerk for board of health in Royalston, Mass., 1978—; member of Royalston Conversation Commission, 1979—. *Member:* American Civil Liberties Union, National Gay Task Force, Environmental Action, Millers River Alliance. *Awards, honors:* Editing prize from Columbia University School of Journalism, 1964; Fulbright scholarship, 1964-65; Inter-American Press Association scholarship, 1965-66.

WRITINGS: (Co-editor with Karla Jay) *Out of the Closets: Voices of Gay Liberation,* Douglas Books, 1972; *Allen Ginsberg: Gay Sunshine* (chapbook), Grey Fox Press, 1974; (co-editor with Jay) *After You're Out: Personal Experiences of Gay Men and Lesbian Women,* Links Books, 1975; (editor with Jay) *Lavender Culture,* Jove, 1979; (with Jay) *The Gay Report,* Summit Books, 1979. Member of features staff of *Gay Community News;* contributing editor of *Gay Sunshine.* Contributor to periodicals, including *Canadian Dimension, Berkeley Barb, Body Politic, Guardian, New Left Review,* and *Christian Science Monitor.*

WORK IN PROGRESS: "Ongoing interest in environmental issues and sexual politics."

SIDELIGHTS: Young told *CA:* "My career evolved from 'straight journalism' to new left activism/journalism to gay liberation activism/journalism. In 1979, I returned to daily newspaper work in rural Massachusetts. I have also been active in the anti-nuclear movement. I traveled to Cuba in 1969 and 1971 representing Liberation News Service (LNS), participated in the World Youth Festival in Sofia, Bulgaria, in 1968, representing LNS, and also traveled to the Soviet Union that summer with the post-festival delegation. I am fluent in Spanish and Portuguese."

AVOCATIONAL INTERESTS: Gardening, alternative energy.

*   *   *

YOUNG, J(ohn) Z(achary)   1907-

PERSONAL: Born March 18, 1907, in Bristol, England; son of Philip (an engineer) and Constance Maria (Lloyd) Young; married Raymonde May Parsons (a painter); children: Kate Frances. *Education:* Magdalen College, Oxford, M.A., 1928. *Politics:* Labour. *Religion:* None. *Home:* 166 Camden Rd., London N.W.1, England. *Office:* Wellcome Institute for the History of Medicine, 183 Euston Rd., London N.W.1, England.

CAREER: Oxford University, Oxford, England, demonstrator in zoology and comparative anatomy and fellow of Magdalen College, 1931-45; University of London, London, England, professor of anatomy, 1945-74, professor emeritus and fellow, 1975—. Fullerton Professor at Royal Institution, 1958-61. Affiliated with Wellcome Institute for the History of Medicine.

MEMBER: Royal Society (fellow), Marine Biological Association (president, 1976—), American Academy of Arts and Sciences (foreign member), American Philosophical Society (foreign member), Accademia dei Lincei (foreign member). *Awards, honors:* D.Sc. from University of Bristol, 1965, McGill University, 1967, University of Durham, 1969, University of Bath, 1973, Duke University, 1978, and Oxford University, 1979; LL.D. from University of Glasgow, 1975, and University of Aberdeen, 1980; Royal Medal from Royal Society, 1967; honorary fellow of University College, University of London, 1976, and Magdalen College, Oxford University, 1978; Jan Swammerdam Medal from Amsterdam Science Society, 1980.

WRITINGS—All published by Oxford University Press: *The Life of Vertebrates*, 1950; *Doubt and Certainty in Science*, 1951; *The Life of Mammals*, 1957; *A Model of the Brain*, 1964; *The Memory System of the Brain*, 1966; *An Introduction to the Study of Man*, 1971; *The Anatomy of the Nervous System of "Octopus vulgaris,"* 1971; *Programs of the Brain*, 1978. Contributor to scientific journals.

* * *

YOUNG, Michael (Dunlop) 1915-

PERSONAL: Born August 9, 1915, in Manchester, England; son of Gibson (a musician) and Edith (a writer; maiden name, Dunlop) Young; married Joan Lawson, 1945 (marriage ended); married Sasha Moorsom, 1960; children: (first marriage) Christopher, David, Emma; (second marriage) Sophie, Toby. *Education:* University of London, received B.Sc., M.A., and Ph.D. *Office:* Institute of Community Studies, 18 Victoria Park Sq., Bethnal Green, London E2 9PF, England.

CAREER: Called to the Bar at Gray's Inn; director of political and economic planning, 1941-45; Labour Party, London, England, secretary in research department, 1945-51; Institute of Community Studies, London, England, director, 1953—. Fellow of Churchill College, Cambridge, 1961-66; visiting professor at Ahmadu Bello University, 1974. Chairman of National Extension College, 1962-71, president, 1971—; chairman of Advisory Centre for Education, 1959-76, president, 1976—; chairman of Social Science Research Council, 1965-68, Dartington Amenity Research Trust, 1967—, International Extension College, 1970—, National Consumer Council, 1975-77, and Mutual Aid Centre, 1977—; director of Mauritius College of the Air, 1972; member of Central Advisory Council for Education, 1963-66, and National Economic Development Council, 1975—. Member of board of trustees of Dartington Hall, 1942—. *Member:* Consumers Association (chairman, 1956-65; president, 1965—), Reform Club. *Awards, honors:* Litt.D. from University of Sheffield, 1965; doctorate from Open University, 1973; D.Litt. from University of Adelaide, 1974.

WRITINGS: *Civil Aviation*, Pilot Press, 1944; (with Theodor Prager) *There's Work for All*, Essential Books, 1945; *Labour's Plan for Plenty*, Gollancz, 1947; (with Peter Willmott) *Family and Kinship in East London*, Free Press, 1957; *The Rise of the Meritocracy, 1870-2033: An Essay on Education and Equality*, Thames and Hudson, 1958, Random House, 1959; (with Willmott) *Family and Class in a London Suburb*, Humanities Press, 1960; (with Michael Armstrong) *New Look at Comprehensive Schools*, Fabian Society, 1964; *Innovation and Research in Education*, Routledge & Kegan Paul, 1965; (with P. J. McGeeney) *Learning Begins at Home: A Study of a Junior School and Its Parents*, Routledge & Kegan Paul, 1968; (editor) *Forecasting and the Social Sciences*, Heinemann, 1968; (with Willmott) *The Symmetrical Family: A Study of Work and Leisure in the London Region*, Routledge & Kegan Paul, 1973, Pantheon, 1974; (editor) *Poverty Report 1974: A Review of Policies and Problems in the Last Year*, Temple Smith, 1974, 1975; (with Hilary Perraton, Janet Jenkins, and Tony Dodds) *Distance Teaching for the Third World*, Routledge & Kegan Paul, 1980.

AVOCATIONAL INTERESTS: Painting.

YOUNG, Robert J(ohn) 1942-

PERSONAL: Born April 27, 1942, in Moose Jaw, Saskatchewan, Canada; son of John Andrew and Helen Patricia (MacDonald) Young; married Kathryn Hird, September 11, 1965; children: Kendal, Kevin, Christopher. *Education:* University of Saskatchewan, B.A. (with honors), 1964, M.A., 1965; London School of Economics and Political Science, London, Ph.D., 1969. *Office:* Department of History, University of Winnipeg, Winnipeg, Manitoba, Canada R3B 2E9.

CAREER: University of Winnipeg, Winnipeg, Manitoba, assistant professor, 1968-74, associate professor of history, 1974—. *Member:* Canadian Historical Association, Society for French History.

WRITINGS: *In Command of France: French Foreign Policy and Military Planning, 1933-1940*, Harvard University Press, 1978; *French Foreign Policy, 1918-1945: A Guide to Research*, Scholarly Resources, 1981. Contributor to history and European studies journals.

WORK IN PROGRESS: Research on French military intelligence, 1938-39.

* * *

YOUNGER, Paul 1935-

PERSONAL: Born November 30, 1935, in Kingston, Pa.; son of James (a minister) and Mary (a teacher; maiden name, Goodman) Younger; married Susanna Oommen (a teacher), April 15, 1961; children: Prakash, Ajit. *Education:* Lafayette College, A.B., 1955; Banaras Hindu University, M.A., 1959; Serampore College, B.D., 1960; Princeton Theological Seminary, M.Th., 1962; Princeton University, Ph.D., 1965. *Home:* 45 Melville, Dundas, Ontario, Canada L9H 1Z7. *Office:* McMaster University, Hamilton, Ontario, Canada.

CAREER: Lafayette College, Easton, Pa., instructor in religion, 1960-64; McMaster University, Hamilton, Ontario, assistant professor, 1964-68, associate professor, 1968-74, professor of religion, 1974—, associate dean of studies, 1968-72. *Member:* Canadian Society for the Study of Religion, American Academy of Religion, Association of Asian Studies.

WRITINGS: *The Indian Religious Tradition*, Bharatiya Varanasi, 1971; *Introduction to Indian Religious Thought*, Westminster, 1972; (with wife, Susanna Oommen Younger) *Hinduism*, Argus Books, 1979.

WORK IN PROGRESS: *The Indian Political Tradition: Roots, Vision, and Order; South Indian Temple Religion.*

SIDELIGHTS: Younger wrote: "I went to India in 1957 with a group of concerned friends called the International Studies Programme. My first book was an attempt to give a chronological arrangement of the major periods in the Indian tradition. The second sought to interpret India to the West. The third allowed my wife and me to present an overview."

* * *

YUZYK, Paul 1913-

PERSONAL: Born June 24, 1913, in Pinto, Saskatchewan, Canada; son of Martin (a miner and laborer) and Katherine (Chaban) Yuzyk; married Mary Bahniuk, July 12, 1941; children: Evangeline Paulette (Mrs. George Duravetz), Victoria Irene (Mrs. Robert Karpiak), Vera Catherine, Theodore Ronald. *Education:* Attended Saskatoon Normal School, 1932-33; University of Saskatchewan, B.A. (mathematics), 1945, B.A. (history; with honors), 1947, M.A., 1948; University of Minnesota, Ph.D., 1958. *Politics:* Progressive Conservative. *Religion:* Ukrainian Catholic. *Home:* 1839 Camborne Cres., Ottawa, Ontario, Canada K1H 7B6. *Office:* Senate of Canada, Room 207, East Block, Ottawa, Ontario, Canada K1A OA4.

CAREER: Public school teacher in Hafford, Saskatchewan, 1933-40; high school teacher at one-room school near Hafford, 1940-42; University of Saskatchewan, Saskatoon, instructor in mathematics, 1944-48; University of Manitoba, Winnipeg, assistant professor, 1951-58, associate professor of history and Slavic studies, 1958-63; University of Ottawa, Ottawa, Ontario, professor of Russian and Soviet history and Canadian-Soviet relations, 1966-78; writer, 1978—. Life member of Canadian Senate, 1963—; Canadian delegate to the United Nations, 1963, 1979, Parliamentary observer, 1975; member of Canadian Parliamentary delegations to Poland, West Germany, England, France, Denmark, Yugoslavia, and Portugal; member of Senate committees on foreign affairs, 1964—, health, welfare, and science, 1967-73, science policy, 1968-76, mass media, 1969-70, national finance, 1973-78, agriculture, 1973—, subcommittee on national defense, 1980—, and joint Parliamentary committees. Founder and first president of Ukrainian National Youth Federation of Canada, 1934-36; founder of Ukrainian Canadian University Students' Union, 1953; president of Ukrainian Cultural and Educational Centre, 1955-71, and Higher Education Scholarship Foundation, 1966-71; vice-president of Ukrainian Free Academy of Sciences, 1953-68, Ukrainian Canadian Foundation of Taras Shevchenko, 1964—, and Canadian World University Committee, 1972—; chairman of Human Rights Commission of World Congress of Free Ukrainians, 1967—, and Canadian Folk Arts Council, 1975-80 (president, 1980—); acting chairman of Canadian Parliamentary Amnesty International Group, 1974—; vice-chairman of Canadian Parliamentary Helsinki Group, 1977—; director of Winnipeg Symphony Orchestra, 1962-68, Canadian Council of Christians and Jews, 1963—, Canadian Scholarship Trust Foundation, 1971—, and Canadian Human Rights Foundation, 1971—; member of board of directors of Canadian Centenary Council, 1965-67, and CHIN-Radio, 1972-78. Organized Thinkers' Conference on Canadian Cultural Rights, 1968; public speaker. *Military service:* Canadian Army, 1942-43.

MEMBER: Canadian Association of Slavists (founder; president, 1962-64), Canadian North Atlantic Treaty Organization Parliamentary Association (vice-chairman, 1975—), Canadian Interparliamentary Union, Canadian Society for Abolition of the Death Penalty (member of board of directors), Commonwealth Parliamentary Association, Ukrainian National Association (vice-president, 1970—), Manitoba Historical Society (fellow; vice-president, 1952-61; president, 1961-63; chairman of ethnic group studies). *Awards, honors:* Canadian Centennial Medal, 1967; Taras Shevchenko Gold Medal from Ukrainian Canadian Congress, 1968; gold medals from city of Sudbury, Ontario, 1968, and Ukrainian Canadian Committee of Toronto, 1973; Canada Council grant, 1970-77; Manitoba Centennial Medal, 1970; Silver Jubilee Medal from Queen Elizabeth II, 1977; LL.D. from University of Saskatchewan, 1977.

WRITINGS: The Ukrainians in Manitoba: A Social History, University of Toronto Press, 1953, 2nd edition, 1977; (with Honore Ewach) *Ukrainian Reader* (elementary and high school textbook), Ukrainian Canadian Committee, 1960; (contributor) *Canadian Slavonic Papers,* Volume VII, University of Toronto Press, 1965; *Ukrainian Canadians: Their Place and Role in Canadian Life,* Ukrainian Professional

and Businessmen's Federation, 1967; (editor) *Concern for Canadian Cultural Rights: A Conference to Study Canada's Multicultural Patterns in the Sixties,* Canadian Cultural Rights Committee, 1968.

(With John B. Aird and others) *Canadian-Caribbean Relations: Report of the Standing Committee on Foreign Affairs of the Senate of Canada* (in English and French), Queen's Printer for Canada, 1970; (with Keith Davey and others) *Mass Media: Report of the Special Senate Committee on Mass Media,* Volume I: *The Uncertain Mirror,* Volume II: *Words, Music , and Dollars,* Volume III: *Good, Bad, or Simply Inevitable: Research Studies* (in English and French) Queen's Printer for Canada, 1970; (with Maurice Lamontagne and others) *A Science Policy for Canada: Report of the Senate Special Committee on Science Policy* (in English and French), Queen's Printer for Canada, Volume I: *A Critical Review: Past and Present,* 1970, Volume II: *Targets and Strategies for the Seventies,* 1972, Volume III: *A Government Organization for the Seventies,* 1973, Volume IV: *Progress and Unfinished Business,* 1977.

(Author of foreword) Victor Peters, *Nestor Makhno: The Life of an Anarchist,* Echo Books, 1970; (with G. L. Molgat, Kark MacGuigan, and others) *The Constitution of Canada* (in English and French), Queen's Printer for Canada, 1972; *For a Better Canada,* Ukrainian National Association, 1973; (with Aird and others) *Canadian Relations With the European Community: Report of the Standing Committee on Foreign Affairs of the Senate of Canada* (in English and French), Queen's Printer for Canada, 1973; (with Douglas D. Everett and others) *Information Canada* (in English and French), Queen's Printer for Canada, 1974; (with Maurice Riel, Martin O'Connell, and others) *Immigration Policy* (in English and French), Queen's Printer for Canada, 1975; (with G. C. van Roggen and others) *Canada-United States Relations* (in English and French), Queen's Printer for Canada, Volume I: *The Institutional Framework for the Relationship,* 1975, Volume II: *Canada's Trade Relations With the United States,* 1978.

(With Everett and others) *Canada Manpower* (in English and French), Queen's Printer for Canada, 1976; (with Hazen Argue and others) *Recognizing the Realities: A Beef Import Policy for Canada* (in English and French), Queen's Printer for Canada, 1977; (contributor) Walter Dushnyck, editor, *Ukraine in a Changing World,* Ukrainian Congress Committee of America, 1977; (with Everett and others) *The Accommodation Program of the Department of Public Works* (in English and French), Queen's Printer for Canada, 1978; (editor with William Darcovich, and contributor) *A Statistical Compendium on the Ukrainians in Canada, 1891-1976,* University of Ottawa Press, 1980; *The Ukrainian Greek-Orthodox Church of Canada, 1917-51,* Canadian Institute of Ukrainian Studies, 1980.

Contributor to *Encyclopedia Canadiana* and *German-Canadian Yearbook.* Contributor to magazines, including *Canada Month,* and newspapers. Editor of *Holos Molodi* (title means "Youth Speaks"), 1948-49; associate editor of *Opinion,* 1948-49; editorial associate of *Ukrainian Directory and Year Book,* 1952-56; editor of *Transactions of the Manitoba Historical Society,* 1953-58; member of editorial board of *Manitoba Pageant* (juvenile), 1956-63, and *Studia Ucrainica,* 1978—; member of editorial advisory board of *Ukrainian Quarterly: A Journal of East European and Asian Affairs,* 1970—.

SIDELIGHTS: Yuzyk wrote: "The research for the publication of *The Ukrainians in Manitoba: A Social History* laid the groundwork for my future scholarly activities and career, which has continued unabated since my appointment for life to the Senate in 1963.

"Published just prior to the celebration of Canada's Centennial, in 1976, the small illustrated book, *Ukrainian Canadians: Their Place and Role in Canadian Life,* was sent to all the Canadian libraries and parliamentarians. The many reviews and numerous letters received in return welcomed this source of useful information about the fourth largest ethnic group in Canada, following the Anglo-Celts, French, and Germans. The achievements of this dynamic people in all walks of life during the past seventy-five years were regarded as impressive and remarkable. The book was also published in French and Ukrainian, gaining a wide circulation.

"The policy of multiculturalism which was pioneered in this book became the basis for a Thinkers' Conference, attended for the first time by delegates of twenty-one ethnic groups in Toronto, in December of 1968, during the first Federal-Provincial Conference on constitutional issues. The proceedings were published in *Concern for Canadian Cultural Rights,* which exerted a strong influence on the Trudeau government. In 1971 the Canadian government, with the unanimous support of all four parties in Parliament, adopted the policy of multiculturalism, after the recognition of French as an official language.

"My active participation in the Joint Parliamentary Committee on the Constitution of Canada, 1971-72, which toured forty-nine larger centers in the vast country, and debates on constitutional issues are reflected in the book *For a Better Canada.* I advocate a new Canadian constitution, which would recognize the Canadian identity as 'an independent, democratic, officially bilingual, multicultural federal state.'

"As a lawmaker and professor of history, I undertook a project of immense proportions. I assembled eight scholars who, in their spare time over a period of seven years, carried out intense, exhaustive researches and produced a large volume called *A Statistical Compendium on the Ukrainians in Canada, 1891-1976.* The first work of its kind on any ethnic group in Canada, this is a full statistical study of all aspects of life and the activities of the eight-hundred-thousand Ukrainian Canadians. For me it is a crowning achievement."

Z

ZAFFUTO, Anthony A(ngelo) 1926-

PERSONAL: Born November 4, 1926, in Rochester, N.Y.; son of John (a laborer) and Providenzia (a seamstress; maiden name, Cordado) Zaffuto; married Mary Quinn (divorced, 1978); married Patricia Kay Ozios (an administrator), July 4, 1979; children: John, Beverly Zaffuto Miester, Daniel. *Education:* Biola College, B.A., 1960; attended California State University, Northridge, 1961-63; St. Andrew Episcopal University, Ph.D., 1967. *Politics:* None. *Religion:* None. *Home and office address:* Santa Barbara Alphagenic Center, P.O. Box 421, Santa Barbara, Calif. 93101.

CAREER: Ordained Baptist minister, 1961; assistant pastor of Baptist church in Canoga Park, Calif., 1960-64; Teen 'N' Trouble Counseling Center, Van Nuys, Calif., director, 1964-67; Sherman Oaks Family Counseling Center, Sherman Oaks, Calif., director, 1967-68; Santa Barbara Alphagenic Center, Santa Barbara, Calif., founder and director, 1969—. Member of faculty at Santa Barbara City College, 1969-77. Consultant to Lompoc Federal Correctional Institution. *Member:* American Association for Social Psychiatry, Academy of Parapsychology and Medicine, Institute of Human Engineering Sciences, Institute of Noetic Sciences, California State Hypnosis Association.

WRITINGS: Alphagenics: How to Use Your Brain Waves to Improve Your Life, Doubleday, 1974. Contributor to *McCall's.*

WORK IN PROGRESS: "Sundown to Sunrise," a video presentation for surgery patients, to help the patient scheduled for surgery to relax and maintain a healthy mental attitude for quick recovery after surgery.

*   *   *

ZELMAN, Aaron S(hepard) 1946-

PERSONAL: Born March 4, 1946, in Winthrop, Mass. *Home and office address:* Box 76, Milwaukee, Wis. 53201.

CAREER: Independent insurance agent and registered representative affiliated with Vanguard Financial Services and Anchor National Financial Services, Milwaukee, Wis., 1975—; University of Wisconsin—Milwaukee, extension instructor, 1978—; writer. *Military service:* U.S. Navy, 1964-65, and U.S. Marine Corps, 1965-66; served as medic. *Member:* Wisconsin Consumer League (member of board of directors).

WRITINGS: (With Peter Spielmann) *Holmes and Watson Solve the Almost Perfect Crime: Life Insurance,* privately printed, 1976, revised edition (with Spielmann and Dean Sharp) published as *The Life Insurance Conspiracy: Made Elementary by Sherlock Holmes,* Simon & Schuster, 1978; *The Credit Conspiracy and You,* Simon & Schuster, in press.

WORK IN PROGRESS: A novel.

SIDELIGHTS: According to independent insurance agent and financial consultant Aaron Zelman, the American consumer is being mislead by the major life insurance companies who regularly push whole-life insurance over term policies. In *The Life Insurance Conspiracy,* written with free-lance writer Peter Spielmann and attorney Dean Sharp, he exposes the practice of offering agents higher commissions for selling whole-life policies and at the same time overcharging and underinsuring the public. As an example, Zelman noted that during his short career with a prominent Midwest life insurance company the philosophy was "What's best for the client is what makes the agent the most money."

Victoria Irwin of the *Christian Science Monitor* described the book as an "easy to understand and practical guide to the world of life insurance. It helps cut through insurance jargon, explaining clearly the difference between types of insurance, how to call bluffs when agents bring out complicated charts, and how to examine the fine print of a policy."

Zelman wrote that "insurance ought to provide a family with financial welfare." He believes that a nation-wide program of public education will aid the consumer in making the best choice of an insurance policy. He also noted that "we should have minimum federal standards and let states regulate the industry."

BIOGRAPHICAL/CRITICAL SOURCES: Milwaukee Journal, May 24, 1979, December 2, 1979; *Chicago Sun Times,* July 15, 1979; *Atlanta Constitution,* August 27, 1979; *St. Paul Dispatch,* August 29, 1979; *Seattle Times,* September 2, 1979; *San Jose Mercury News,* September 2, 1979; *Christian Science Monitor,* September 5, 1979; *Pittsburgh Press,* September 23, 1979; *Windsor Star,* November 10, 1979.

*   *   *

ZELMAN, Anita 1924-

PERSONAL: Born August 27, 1924, in San Francisco, Calif.; daughter of Benjamin (a ship steward and union organizer) and Julia (Lewis) Magdoff; married Julius L. Zelman (an executive contractor), 1944; children: Julia Uslan, David. *Education:* Attended University of California, Berkeley, 1941-43. *Politics:* Democrat. *Religion:* Jewish. *Home:* 1301 Carla Lane, Beverly Hills, Calif. 90210. *Agent:* Ruth Cantor, 156 Fifth Ave., New York, N.Y. 10010.

CAREER: Free-lance writer. *Member:* Authors Guild, Mystery Writers of America, Women's National Book Association. *Awards, honors:* Third place for National Catholic Press award, 1976, for short story "A Fun Paper."

WRITINGS: "Alone at Last" published in *Mike Shayne Mystery Magazine,* September, 1977. Contributor of short stories and poems to periodicals, including *Prairie Schooner, Green's, Jewish Digest, Boys and Girls, San Fernando Valley, Reconstructionist,* and *Scholia Satyrica.*

WORK IN PROGRESS: Two novels, *Move by Move* and *The Goddess Lives.*

SIDELIGHTS: Zelman told *CA:* "I began writing when my two kids were in college. When I was younger, the word wasn't out that you could raise children and write at the same time. Where was the women's movement when I needed it? I've dropped chess, luncheons, community work, department stores, and cleaning house (that one was easy) to focus on writing."

*   *   *

ZEMAN, Jarold Knox 1926-

PERSONAL: Born February 27, 1926, in Semonice, Czechoslovakia; son of Jaroslav (a teacher) and Jaroslava (Potuckova) Zeman; married Lillian M. Koncicky (a teacher), June 18, 1951; children: Miriam, Dagmar Zeman-Carter, Timothy, Janice. *Education:* Charles University, Prague, Czechoslovakia, Grad. Phil., 1948; Hus Theological Faculty, Prague, Th.Cand., 1948; Knox College, B.D., 1952; University of Zurich, Dr.Theol., 1966. *Home address:* P.O. Box 164, Wolfville, Nova Scotia, Canada B0P 1X0. *Office:* Department of Church History, Acadia University, Wolfville, Nova Scotia, Canada B0P 1X0.

CAREER: Ordained Baptist minister, 1950; pastor of Baptist churches in Toronto, Ontario, 1949-55, and Villa Nova, Ontario, 1955-59; Baptist Convention of Ontario and Quebec, Toronto, secretary of Canadian missions, 1959-68; Acadia University, Wolfville, Nova Scotia, associate professor, 1968-72, professor of church history and director of continuing education, 1972—. Visiting lecturer at Baptist Theological Seminary, Ruschlikon-Zurich, 1965, Chicago Theological Seminary and Associated Mennonite Seminaries, 1976-77, and at Regent College, Vancouver, 1979. Chairman of Atlantic Baptist Historical Records Committee; president of Baptist Federation of Canada, 1979-82. Member of religious advisory committee of Canadian Broadcasting Corp. *Member:* Canadian Society of Church History, American Historical Association, American Society of Church History, American Academy of Religion, American Society for Reformation Research, Czechoslovak Society of Arts and Sciences in America.

WRITINGS: God's Mission and Ours, Baptist Federation of Canada, 1963; *The Whole World at Our Door,* Baptist Convention of Ontario and Quebec, 1964; *Historical Topography of Moravian Anabaptism,* Mennonite Press, 1967; *The Anabaptists and the Czech Brethren,* Mouton, 1969; *Baptists in Canada and Co-Operative Christianity,* Baptist Federation of Canada, 1972; (contributor) J. L. Garrett, editor, *Baptist Relations With Other Christians,* Judson, 1974; *The Hussite Movement and the Reformation,* University of Michigan

Press, 1977; *Baptist Roots and Identity,* Baptist Convention of Ontario and Quebec, 1978; (editor with Walter Klaassen) *The Believers' Church in Canada,* Baptist Federation of Canada, 1979; (editor) *Baptists in Canada,* G. R. Welch Co., 1980. Contributor to journals.

WORK IN PROGRESS: The Changing Concept of the Church; The Hussite Movement as a Religious Renewal, publication by Moravian Church Press expected in 1982.

SIDELIGHTS: Zeman wrote that he was raised in a United Presbyterian home in Czechoslovakia, and was "born anew through the reading of the Bible" during the Nazi occupation of his homeland in 1941. He "responded to a call from God into the Christian ministry as a university student in Prague," and moved to Toronto to complete his theological training. Zeman joined the Baptist church and eventually was ordained a minister. He has lectured and preached throughout Canada, and in some cities in the United States, England, Europe, and the Caribbean.

Zeman commented: "My writings are the result of research in two main fields: present trends in the religious life of my adopted country, Canada, particularly as expressed in Baptist churches; and issues in the history and heritage of my native land, Czechoslovakia, during the Hussite era (1400-1620)."

AVOCATIONAL INTERESTS: Music, gardening, hiking.

*   *   *

ZEVI, Bruno 1918-

PERSONAL: Born January 22, 1918, in Rome, Italy; son of Guido (an engineer) and Ada (Bondi) Zevi; married Tullia Calabi (a journalist), December 26, 1940; children: Adachiara, Luca. *Education:* Attended University of Rome, 1937-39, D.Arch., 1945; Harvard University, M.Arch., 1941. *Politics:* Liberal socialist. *Religion:* Jewish. *Home and office:* Via Nomentana 150, Rome 00162, Italy.

CAREER: University of Venice, Venice, Italy, associate professor, 1948-60, professor of architectural history, 1960-63; University of Rome, Rome, Italy, professor of architectural history, 1963-79, director of Institute of Operative Criticism of Architecture, 1968-79. Associate professor at Graduate School of Art History, University of Rome, 1948-55. General secretary of Italian Institute of Town Planning, 1952-68; president of International Technical Cooperation Center, 1967-70.

MEMBER: Comite International des Critiques d'Architecture (president, 1979—), Italian Institute of Architecture (vice-president, 1959-80), Royal Institute of British Architects (honorary corresponding member), American Institute of Architects (fellow). *Awards, honors:* European Prize for Art Criticism from Ulisse-Cortina, 1951, for *Saper vedere l'architettura;* D.H.C. from University of Buenos Aires, 1951; academician of Venice Academy of Fine Arts, 1951, Genoa Academy of Fine Arts, 1959, Accademia Nazionale di San Luca, 1960, and Accademia delle Arti del Disegno, 1963; Tor Margana Prize from Cultural Committee of Rome, 1958, for *L'architettura, cronache e storia;* grand officer of merit of Italian Republic, 1968; named honorary professor of Universidad Nacional de Cuzco and Universidad Nacional Federico Villarreal of Lima, both 1977.

WRITINGS: Verso un'architettura organica, Einaudi, 1945, translation published as *Towards an Organic Architecture,* Faber, 1950; *Saper vedere l'architettura,* Einaudi, 1948, translation by Milton Gendel and J. A. Bazzy published as *Architecture as Space,* Horizon Press, 1957; *Il linguaggio*

moderno dell'architettura, Einaudi, 1973, translation by Roland Stzom and W. A. Packer published as *The Language of Modern Architecture*, University of Washington Press, 1978.

In Italian: *Architectura in nuce* (title means "Architecture in Its Essence,"), Sansoni, 1960; *Michelangiolo Architecto* (title means "Michelangelo As Architect"), Einaudi, 1964; *Erich Mendelsohn: Opera completa* (title means "Erich Mendelsohn: Buildings and Imaginary Sketches,"), Etas Libri, 1970; *Saper vedere l'urbanistica: Ferrara di Biagio Rossetti* (title means "How to Look at a City: Ferrara by Biagio Rossetti"), Einaudi, 1971; *Cronache di architettura* (title means "Architectural Reportages"), Volumes I-XXII, Bari, 1971-79; *Spazi dell'architettura moderna* (title means "Spaces in Modern Architecture"), Einaudi, 1973; *Poetica dell'architettura neoplastica* (title means "Syntax of 'De Stijl' Architecture"), Einaudi, 1974; *Storia dell'architettura moderna* (title means "History of Modern Architecture"), Einaudi, 1975; *Editoriali di architettura* (title means "Editorials on Architecture"), Einaudi, 1979; *Frank Lloyd Wright*, Zanichelli, 1979.

Author of a weekly column in *L'Espresso*, 1955—. Editor of "Universale di architettura," a book series, 1978—. Editor and publisher of *L'architettura, cronache e storia*, 1955—.

WORK IN PROGRESS: A history of architecture, with emphasis on Italian development.

SIDELIGHTS: Zevi commented: "My main purpose is to re-evaluate and re-interpret the history of architecture in such a way that it can be useful to the modern architect. The past is generally used as an instrument to limit and mortify today's creativity. Instead, it should be used for its many heretical aspects in order to encourage contemporary architects to be more inventive."

BIOGRAPHICAL/CRITICAL SOURCES: Nueva Forma, October, 1974.

*   *   *

ZIEGLER, Richard S. 1931-

PERSONAL: Born April 3, 1931, in St. Paul, Minn.; son of Samuel (a dentist) and Renata (a teacher; maiden name, Sanicola) Ziegler; married Karen M. Lindhelm, September 25, 1955; children: Richard C., Ann L., Susan R. *Education:* University of Minnesota, B.B.A., 1953, M.B.A., 1954, J.D., 1959. *Politics:* Republican. *Religion:* Unitarian-Universalist. *Home:* 5211 Humboldt Ave. S., Minneapolis, Minn. 55419. *Office:* Moss, Flaherty, Clarkson & Fletcher, 2350 IDS, Minneapolis, Minn. 55402.

CAREER: Northwestern National Bank, Minneapolis, Minn., trust officer, 1960-65; Moss, Flaherty, Clarkson & Fletcher, Minneapolis, attorney, 1966—. Chairman of Henn City Probate Committee. *Military service:* U.S. Army, 1954-56; became first lieutenant.

WRITINGS: Estate Planning for Everyone, World Publishing, 1972.

SIDELIGHTS: Ziegler commented: "Many decendents' estates are distressed by failure to plan. A simple message was needed to incite action."

*   *   *

ZIMMERMANN, Arnold E. 1909-

PERSONAL: Born August 25, 1909, in Munich, Germany; son of Walther E. (a gallery director) and Maria (Seybold) Zimmermann; married Elizabeth Lloyd-Jones (a designer

and writer), July 27, 1937; children: Thomas S., Caroline L. Zimmermann Schwartz, Margaret G. Zimmermann Swansen. *Education:* Attended high school in Munich, Germany. *Residence:* Babcock, Wis. 54413.

CAREER: Rheingold Breweries, Brooklyn, N.Y., assistant master brewer, 1937-46; Peoples Brewery, Trenton, N.J., master brewer, 1946-49; Joseph Schlitz Brewing Co., Milwaukee, Wis., head maltster, 1949-53, assistant master brewer, 1953-58, master brewer at Milwaukee plant, 1958-61, director of brewing at all plants, 1961-63, vice-president of brewing, 1963-70; writer and illustrator, 1970—.

WRITINGS—Self-illustrated children's books: *Fafnerl, the Ice Dragon,* Crossing Press, 1973; *Troll Island,* Crossing Press, 1977.

WORK IN PROGRESS: Alain: The Adventures of a Seafaring Mouse, a self-illustrated children's book.

SIDELIGHTS: Zimmermann commented: "I wrote quite a few self-illustrated stories for my grandchildren. The editor of Crossing Press saw them, contacted me, and the publication was set in motion." *Avocational interests:* European travel, riding through the Mississippi hills on motorcycle.

*   *   *

ZIMMERMANN, Jon E(mil) 1933-

PERSONAL: Born June 1, 1933, in Rottenburg, Germany; came to the United States in 1955, naturalized citizen, 1960; son of Hans and Klara (Neu) Zimmermann. *Education:* University of Wisconsin—Madison, B.S., 1957; University of Colorado, M.A., 1962, Ph.D., 1967. *Religion:* Roman Catholic. *Home:* 1612 Redcliff St., Los Angeles, Calif. 90026. *Office:* Department of Foreign Languages and Literatures, California State University, Fullerton, Calif. 92634.

CAREER: High school teacher of history, German, and physical education in Racine, Wis., 1959-61; University of Colorado, Boulder, instructor in Conversation and Methodology at National Defense Education Act Academic Year Institute, 1962-63, director of institute, 1963-65; National Defense Education Act Overseas Institute, Munich, West Germany, instructor in methodology, 1966; California State University, Fullerton, assistant professor, 1966-69, associate professor, 1969-74, professor of German linguistics, 1974—. *Military service:* U.S. Army, 1957-59. *Member:* Modern Language Association of America, American Association of Teachers of German (member of executive council; southern California president), California Liaison Committee on Foreign Languages, Delta Phi Alpha.

WRITINGS: (With others) *Fles Guide for German in Grade Three,* Teachers Publishing, 1965; (with others) *Fles Guide for German in Grade Four,* Teachers Publishing, 1965; *Word Frequency in the Modern German Short Story,* U.S. Office of Education, 1966; *Contemporary German Two,* Titan Book Co., 1972; *Contemporary German Life,* McGraw, 1975, teacher's handbook, 1976. Contributor to language journals.

WORK IN PROGRESS: Deutsch im Kontext, Volume I: *Lesebuch,* Volume II: *Stukturen,* publication by Holt expected in 1982.

*   *   *

ZOLF, Larry 1934-
(Jaded Observer)

PERSONAL: Born July 19, 1934, in Winnipeg, Manitoba, Canada; son of Falek Yoshua (a teacher) and Freda Rachel (Pasternak) Zolf; married Patricia Beatrice Legge (a city planner), May 29, 1957; children: David, Rachel. *Education:* University of Manitoba, B.A., 1956; attended Osgoode Hall Law School and University of Toronto. *Politics:* New Democrat. *Religion:* Jewish. *Home:* 62 Balsam St., Toronto, Ontario, Canada. *Office:* Canadian Broadcasting Corp., 790 Bay St., Toronto, Ontario, Canada.

CAREER: Province of Ontario, government archivist, 1958-59; Toronto Labor Council, Toronto, Ontario, publicist, speechwriter, and public relations representative, 1959-61; Canadian Broadcasting Corp., Toronto, writer, reporter of news and current affairs, and producer, 1962—. Lecturer at Carleton University. *Member:* Association of Canadian Radio and Television Artists, Toronto Press Club (member of board of directors, 1975-79), Toronto Producers Association, Caveat Reginam. *Awards, honors:* Wilderness Award, 1961, for television journalism; prize from Brussels International Labor Film Festival, 1966.

WRITINGS: (Contributor) John Keats, editor, *The New Romans,* Hurtig, 1968; (contributor) *The Peaceable Kingdom,* Macmillan, 1969; (under pseudonym Jaded Observer) *Dance of the Dialectic,* J. Lewis & Samuel, 1973. Also contributor to *Watkins to Gordon to You,* edited by Mordecai Richler, Columbo Books. Contributor to magazines and newspapers, including *Saturday Night, MacLean's, City,* and *Weekend.*

WORK IN PROGRESS: A satirical "Who's Who in Canada," with cartoonist, Aislin; a murder comedy television series, for Canadian Broadcasting Corp.; autobiographical sketches.

SIDELIGHTS: Zolf wrote: "My motivation is to teach and influence by engaging television programs, books, and articles that hold the audience's and readers' attention. I was the star of Canada's 'Seven Days,' the best television show of its kind on the continent, better than 'Sixty Minutes.' 'Seven Days' gave me the image that helped me get started."

*   *   *

ZULAUF, Sander W(illiam) 1946-

PERSONAL: Born November 5, 1946, in Paterson, N.J.; son of S. William (in industrial purchasing) and Marion (a secretary; maiden name, Campbell) Zulauf; married Chris-

tianne Beresford, June 15, 1968 (divorced November 7, 1977); married Madeline Slocum Stoddard, May 26, 1979; children: Scott Sander; (stepchildren) Michael, Mary Beth. *Education:* Gettysburg College, B.A., 1968; Indiana University, M.A., 1973. *Home:* 36 Main St., Succasunna, N.J. 07876. *Office:* County College of Morris, Dover, N.J. 07801.

CAREER: Elementary school teacher in Paterson, N.J., 1968-69; high school English teacher in East Hanover, N.J., 1969-71; County College of Morris, Dover, N.J., instructor in English, 1973—. *Member:* Modern Language Association of America, Academy of American Poets, National Education Association, Associated Writing Programs, Poets and Writers, Inc., New Jersey Education Association. *Awards, honors:* National Endowment for the Humanities grant, 1977-78.

WRITINGS: (Editor) *Index of American Periodical Verse,* Scarecrow, 1971 edition (with Irwin H. Weiser), 1973, 1972 edition (with Weiser), 1974, 1973 edition (with Weiser), 1975, 1974 edition (with Weiser), 1976, 1975 edition (with Weiser), 1977, 1976 edition (with Edward M. Cifelli), 1978, 1977 edition (with Cifelli), 1979, 1978 edition (with Cifelli), 1980, 1979 edition (with Jandra Milkowski), 1981, 1980 edition (with Milkowski), 1981.

Work represented in anthologies, including *Yardbird Reader.* Contributor of poems to literary journals, including *Southern Poetry Review, Kansas Quarterly, Madrona, Windless Orchard,* and *English Journal.*

SIDELIGHTS: Zulauf wrote: "The *Index,* a 'reader's guide' to contemporary poetry, and teaching occupy my waking hours pretty completely. While doing both of these, I catch poems as they emerge from the recesses, nooks, and islands of my mind. Poetry led me to the *Index,* and that obsession has led me to some surprising poems. My motivation comes from love, sex, death, and the whole horse race of existence. The beautiful knowledge that Jesus is Lord is undeniably more helpful in combating my daily neuroses than just about anything. And food. Indexing tends to make one hungry. Prime influences on my poetry are Philip Appleman, James Wright, Paul Zimmer, Elizabeth Bishop, Charles Bukowski, and J. Peter Williams. As far as influences on the *Index,* Philip B. Daghlian, Donald J. Gray, Appleman, Anthony Shipps, and Eric Moon have all lent distinction to my harmless drudgery."